THE PENGUIN GUIDE TO COMPACT DISCS AND DVDs YEARBOOK 2004/5

IVAN MARCH,
EDWARD GREENFIELD and
ROBERT LAYTON
Edited by Ivan March
Assistant Editor Paul Czajkowski

D1414999

PENGUIN BOOKS

PENGUIN BOOKS

Published by the Penguin Group
Penguin Books Ltd, 80 Strand, London WC2R 0RL, England
Penguin Group (USA) Inc., 375 Hudson Street, New York, New York 10014, USA
Penguin Books Australia Ltd, 250 Camberwell Road,
Camberwell, Victoria 3124, Australia
Penguin Books Canada Ltd, 10 Alcorn Avenue, Toronto, Ontario, Canada M4V 3B2
Penguin Books India (P) Ltd, 11, Community Centre,
Panchsheel Park, New Delhi – 110 017, India
Penguin Books (NZ), cnr Airborne and Rosedale Roads,
Albany Auckland 1310, New Zealand
Penguin Books (South Africa) (Pty) Ltd, 24 Sturdee Avenue,
Rosebank 2196, South Africa

Penguin Books Ltd, Registered Offices: 80 Strand, London WC2R 0RL, England

www.penguin.com

This edition first published 2004
1

Copyright © Ivan March Publications, 2004
All rights reserved

Set in Minion and ScalaSans
This book was produced using Librios® authoring & content management technology
Typeset by Letterpart Ltd, Reigate, Surrey
Printed in England by Clays Ltd, St Ives plc

THE PENGUIN GUIDE TO COMPACT DISCS & DVDS YEARBOOK 2004/5

EDWARD GREENFIELD, until his retirement in 1993, was for forty years on the staff of the *Guardian*, succeeding Neville Cardus as Music Critic in 1975. He still contributes regularly to the record column, which he founded in 1954. At the end of 1960 he joined the reviewing panel of *Gramophone*, specializing in operatic and orchestral issues. He is a regular broadcaster on music and records for the BBC, not just on Radios 3 and 4 but also on the BBC World Service, latterly with his weekly programme, *The Greenfield Collection*. In 1958 he published a monograph on the operas of Puccini. More recently he has written studies on the recorded work of Joan Sutherland and André Previn. He has been a regular juror on International Record awards and has appeared with such artists as Dame Elisabeth Schwarzkopf, Dame Joan Sutherland and Sir Georg Solti in public interviews. In October 1993 he was given a *Gramophone* Award for Special Achievement and in June 1994 received the OBE for services to music and journalism.

ROBERT LAYTON studied at Oxford with Edmund Rubbra for composition and with Egon Wellesz for the history of music. He spent two years in Sweden at the universities of Uppsala and Stockholm. He joined the BBC Music Division in 1959 and was responsible for Music Talks, including such programmes as *Interpretations on Record*. He contributed 'A Quarterly Retrospect' to *Gramophone* magazine for thirty-four years and writes for the *BBC Music Magazine*, *International Record Review* and other journals. His books include studies of the Swedish composer Berwald and of Sibelius, as well as a monograph on the Dvořák symphonies and concertos for the *BBC Music Guides*, of which he was General Editor for many years. His prize-winning translation of Erik Tawaststjerna's definitive five-volume study of Sibelius was completed in 1998. In 1987 he was awarded the Sibelius Medal and in the following year he was made a Knight of the Order of the White Rose of Finland for his services to Finnish music. His other books include *Grieg: An Illustrated Life*, and he has edited the *Guide to the Symphony* and the *Guide to the Concerto* (OUP). In 2001, at a ceremony to mark the Swedish presidency of the European Union, he was made a Knight of the Royal Order of the Polar Star.

IVAN MARCH is a former professional musician. He studied at Trinity College of Music, London, and at the Royal Manchester College. After service in the Central Band of the RAF, he played the horn professionally for the BBC and travelled with the Carl Rosa and D'Oyly Carte opera companies. He is a well-known lecturer, journalist and personality in the world of recorded music and acts as a consultant to Squires Gate Music Ltd, a UK mail order source for classical CDs (www.lprl.demon.co.uk). As a journalist he has contributed to a number of record-reviewing magazines, but now reviews solely for *Gramophone*.

THE PENGUIN GUIDE:
CD, SACD, DVD AND THE FUTURE

The compact disc remains the basis on which the coverage of classical music firmly rests. The success of SACD, compatible and non-compatible, still remains an unknown quantity. The possibilities of surround sound – even with the seeming drawback of requiring extra speakers and amplification – are enticing, but still conjectural. The treatment of a two-track stereo master in this way may well increase the sense of spectacle or enhance the ambient effect or both, but it cannot be depended upon to produce greater realism without affecting the integrity of the original sound-balance.

Undoubtedly some SACDs are very impressive indeed, but to set up the necessary reproducing equipment to do them full justice needs a good deal of technical expertise, to say nothing of the expense. Meanwhile, as our Foreword makes clear and the content of our *Yearbook* illustrates, the current (still expanding) range of outstanding audio recordings available on CD in the lower price-ranges is remarkable, and one does not need expensive reproducing equipment to enjoy them!

The arrival of DVD is another matter. It is a profound advance. Now at last we can watch and be involved in the performance itself, almost like being in the theatre, concert hall or opera house, as well as listen to the music in enhanced sound; and if we prefer to dispense with the visual image, this can be managed at the touch of a button. And all this is possible with just the purchase of a DVD player (now very inexpensive) and setting up one's stereo speakers on either side of a reasonably large TV screen.

While this advantage is obvious in the world of ballet and opera (where optional surtitles are available), DVD can and does add immediacy to the musical experience in the concert hall. It catches the magnetism between the conductor and the orchestra, between soloist and accompanist, and the intercommunication within a small group of musicians; above all, it can convey to a remarkable degree the projection of tension from the performers to their audience.

The most tangibly inspirational example of this communication is the more extraordinary for being totally unselfconscious. When, on an EMI 'Classic Archive' DVD, we watch Wilhelm Kempff play Schumann or Beethoven, it is obvious that he is hardly aware at all of the presence of an audience. He is totally immersed in the world of the composer and communicates to us directly from there, without any barriers engendered by his own personality.

It is perhaps in Beethoven's '*Moonlight*' Sonata that this absorption is especially remarkable. The performance is photographed in colour, and the camera lets us watch Kempff's every expression, while he plays with total concentration and wonderful spontaneity. Just occasionally, in the Minuet, he allows himself the hint of a smile, but for the most part the face, while mobile, does not convey the inner secrets of his response to Beethoven – that comes from his fingers and through the music itself, with its infinitely varied range of colour and dynamic. And this unforgettable Kempff recital is only a single instance of the treasure the DVD catalogue is uncovering for us.

CONTENTS

EDITOR'S NOTE:
THE KEY RECORDINGS

The huge number of recordings now covered by our main volume, plus the many further additions in this *Yearbook*, demonstrate the significantly expanded repertoire coverage now available on CD. So we have thought it essential to offer our readers a selection of 'Key' recordings, which may be used as the basis for a personal collection. While our list has been compiled to include only the most important works in the standard repertoire, we have spread our net much wider, to embrace CDs that would not automatically be chosen for a small collection, and by so doing we hope to make the list of greater interest to the more experienced reader. We have also sometimes included more than one choice, especially where there are attractive alternative couplings of music available, and also where there are highly recommendable versions on both CD and DVD. In our main volume we have selected about 1,300 CDs and 70 SACDs and DVDs, and now we add to this figure a further 283 recommendations, some of which are reissues of recordings already chosen and which in certain cases are made even more attractive by being less expensive. Of course, we are not suggesting you will want to acquire them all but that you will use our recommendations to expand your own individual collection.

IVAN MARCH

FOREWORD

We are astonished to discover, on a last-minute count, that there are just over 530 composers covered in the 421 pages of the composer index of this volume, to say nothing of the countless further names in the Concerts and Recital sections! The coverage of the present *Yearbook* is unique in that it includes recordings of some minor composers (and also some of the less recommendable recorded versions of major works) for which there was not enough space in our main volume. However, there is also plenty of new main-line repertoire – led by a superb new period-instrument recording of the Four Bach *Orchestral Suites*, from the Boston Baroque under Martin Pearlman on a single Telarc CD, and an outstanding new coupling of the Grieg and Schumann *Piano Concertos* from Leif Ove Andsnes and the BPO under Mariss Jansons – 'a gramophone classic for the present decade'.

The present coverage also sees many important reissues, among which Universal's 'Penguin Rosette Collection' stands out. This gathers together a number of CDs, previously deleted, that now return to the catalogue at medium price with full booklet notes, libretti and translations. On a similar basis is the same company's 'Gramophone Awards Collection', while EMI have their own 'Great Recordings of the Century' and 'Great Artists of the Century', and RCA a 'Classic Library', although these are all less well documented. And, of course, there is also Warner's budget Apex series.

Among the new issues there are many discoveries to be made. The repertoire of little-known symphonies is continually widening, including those of Anton Fils (1733–60), who was part of the Mannheim scene, the delightful works of Josef Mysliveček (1737–81), and the Bohemian Adalbert Gyrowetz (1763–1850). There are also attractive examples by the protégé of Beethoven, Ferdinand Ries (1784–1838), and the American William Henry Fry (1813–64), who wrote an intriguing *Santa-Claus Christmas Symphony*, while those of Kurt Atterberg (1889–1974) and Ludolf Nielsen (1876–1933), eleven years younger than his more famous namesake, are also well worth exploring. Yet none is more fascinating or more rewarding than the quite splendid *First Symphony* of the all-but-forgotten Frederic Cliffe (1857–1931), a contemporary of Elgar, who now even has a website all to himself!

To these unfamiliar names must be added Vernon Handley's distinguished new complete cycle of the symphonies of Arnold Bax on Chandos, which we hope many readers will be tempted to explore.

Outstanding issues in the field of early vocal music include Gesualdo's *Leçons de ténèbres for Maunday Thursday*, gloriously sung by the King's Singers, the hardly less memorable *Verse anthems* of Pelham Humphrey (1647–74), a superb *Magnificat in B flat* by Francesco Durante (1684–1755) and, unexpectedly, a remarkable *Missa Solemnis* and *Te Deum* from Hummel. On Hyperion the King's Consort has begun a complete coverage of Monteverdi's sacred music; and, on Signum, Alistair Dixon and the Chapelle du Roi have reached Volume 7 of their complete Tallis Edition.

Naxos have arrived at the tenth and final disc in their remarkably successful series of English choral music from Christopher Robinson and the St John's College, Cambridge, Choir. The result is a superb Elgar collection, not all of it familiar, but every item rewarding.

Other ongoing non-vocal series include the eight volumes of the Naxos coverage of the complete music of Rodrigo, while on the companion Marco Polo label there are already four volumes of the music of Johann Strauss Sr, and three more volumes have now been added to the music of Josef Strauss, making 26 in all.

BRITISH LIGHT MUSIC

The expansion of recordings in the area of British light orchestral music has been something of a recording industry phenomenon in recent years, and there are single-CD composer collections of the music of Eric Coates (of course), Trevor Duncan, Robert Farnon, Montague Phillips, Roger Quilter, W. H. Reed, Ernest Tomlinson, Percy Whitlock and many others – not forgetting Albert Ketèlbey, who is represented by some fascinating Naxos period recordings from the early 78rpm era. But our Concerts include many highly attractive miscellaneous anthologies, led by a first-class Hyperion series from the New London Orchestra under Ronald Corp, but later capped by the Royal Ballet Sinfonia, conducted by Gavin Sutherland, whose ASV (mid-priced) series has now expanded to twelve CDs. This music occupies a musical world all its own, and a very British one. Unpretentious, well crafted, tuneful ('it's the tune that counts') and engagingly and often seductively orchestrated, this is repertoire that may not ever seek profundity but that does not wear out its welcome either.

The other main feature of our Concerts section is the now remarkably comprehensive coverage of the work of the 'great conductors', always illuminating, and offering younger readers an introduction to the interpretative skills of artists from a past era, as well as those of our own time.

The range of instrumental and vocal recitals is now equally wide. From the fomer we would especially draw readers' attention to the two Decca boxes of the recordings of Clifford Curzon; among the latter, the comprehensive Naxos Caruso Edition is a quite remarkable achievement – as well documented as it is technically impressive.

DVDS

The Concerts Section also includes some fascinating DVDs, notably from the Berlin Philharmonic Orchestra, and the Vienna Philharmonic New Year Concerts, all of which gain much from the visual element. The DVDs featuring individual artists include Rostropovich's recording of Bach's *Unaccompanied Cello Suites*, and performances from Grumiaux, Michelangeli and, of course, Wilhelm Kempff. In the world of opera, Debussy's *Pélleas et Mélisande*, Glinka's *Ruslan und Ludmilla*, Mussorgsky's *Boris Godunov* and *Khovanshchina* stand out, while there are fine documentary portraits of Alfred Brendel, Erich Korngold and, most impressive of all, Hildegard of Bingen, which features a remarkable re-creative performance of her *Ordo virtutum* ('The Play of the Virtues'), in which she supplied the text, the music (which is truly haunting) and the pictorial background.

INTRODUCTION

As in previous editions, the object of *The Penguin Guide to Compact Discs and DVDs Yearbook* is to give the serious collector a continuing survey of the finest recordings of permanent music on CD, irrespective of price, but also evaluating the quality of the compatible and non-compatible SACDs, video and audio DVDs. As most recordings are issued almost simultaneously on both sides of the Atlantic and use identical international catalogue numbers, this *Guide* should be found to be equally useful in the UK and the USA, as it will too in Australia, Canada, India, New Zealand and South Africa. The internationalization of repertoire and numbers now applies to almost all CDs issued by the major international companies and also by the smaller ones. Many European labels are imported in their original formats, both into Britain and the USA. Those CDs that are available only in the UK can be easily obtained by overseas collectors via the internet.

We feel that it is a strength of our basic style to let our own conveyed pleasure and admiration (or otherwise) for the merits of an individual recording come over directly to the reader, even if this produces a certain ambivalence in the matter of such a final choice. Where there is disagreement between us (and this rarely happens), readers will find an indication of our different reactions in the text.

We have considered (and rejected) the use of initials against individual reviews, since this is essentially a team project. The occasions for disagreement generally concern matters of aesthetics – in the manner of recording balance for instance, where a contrived effect may trouble some ears more than others, or in the matter of style, where the difference between robustness and refinement of approach appeals differently to listening sensibilities rather than involving a question of artistic integrity. But over the years our views seem to have grown closer together rather than diverging; perhaps we are getting mellower, but we are seldom ready to offer strong disagreement following the enthusiastic reception of a controversial recording by one of the team, providing the results are creatively stimulating.

As period-instrument playing standards have advanced and mellowed, our perceptions of the advantages and disadvantages of performances of early music on original (as against modern) instruments seem almost irrelevant. It is the quality of the performance itself that counts, and so expert is the performer's control of period instruments today, while modern instrument performances have often been so influenced by period-instrument styles, that sometimes one is hardly aware of the difference, especially in orchestral music.

EVALUATION

Most major recordings issued today are of a high technical standard and offer performances of a quality at least as high as is experienced in the concert hall. In adopting a star system for the evaluation of records, we have decided to make use of from one to three stars. Brackets around one or more of the stars indicate some reservations about a recording's rating, and readers are advised to refer to the text. Brackets around all the stars usually indicate a basic qualification: for instance, a mono recording of a performance of artistic interest, where some allowances may have to be made for the sound quality, even though the recording may have been digitally remastered.

Our evaluation system may be summarized as follows:

⊸ Key recording – suitable as a basis for a collection;

*** An outstanding performance and recording in every way;

** A good performance and recording of today's normal high standard;

* A fair or somewhat routine performance, reasonably well performed or recorded.

Our evaluation is normally applied to the record as a whole, unless there are two main works or groups of works, and by different composers. In this case, each is dealt with separately in its appropriate place.

ROSETTES

To certain special records we have awarded a Rosette: ❀.

Unlike our general evaluations, in which we have tried to be consistent, a Rosette is a quite arbitrary compliment by a member of the reviewing team to a recorded performance that, he finds, shows special illumination, magic, a spiritual quality, or even outstanding production values, that place it in a very special class. Occasionally a Rosette has been awarded for an issue that seems to us to offer extraordinary value for money, but that presupposes that the performance or performances are also outstanding. The choice is essentially a personal one (although often it represents a shared view) and in some cases it is applied to an issue where certain reservations must also be mentioned in the text of the review. The ❂ is placed before the usual evaluation and the record number. It is quite small – we do not mean to imply an 'Academy Award' but a personal token of appreciation for something uniquely valuable. We hope that, once the reader has discovered and perhaps acquired a 'rosetted' CD, its special qualities will soon become apparent. There are, of course, more of them now, for our survey has become a distillation of the excellence of CDs issued and reissued over a considerable span of years.

Readers will note that Universal Classics (which include the Decca, DG and Philips labels) have given the *Penguin Guide* an accolade by reissuing at mid-price some of their finest recordings that have received a Rosette in our pages over the years. They now become part of their 'Penguin ❂ Collection' (with new catalogue numbers), each illustrated with the original LP sleeve or CD leaflet design, and including full booklet notes, libretti and translations. The first two sets of releases are included within these pages, with reviews as appropriate.

DIGITAL RECORDINGS

Nearly all new compact discs are recorded digitally, but an increasingly large number of digitally remastered, reissued analogue recordings are now appearing, and we think it important to include a clear indication of the difference.

All listed CDs are digital *unless* they include (ADD) in the titling, which indicates Analogue-to-Digital remastering, while of course the term 'mono' is self-explanatory.

The indication ADD/DDD or DDD/ADD applies to a compilation where recordings come from mixed sources.

LISTINGS AND PRICE RANGES

Our listing of each recording assumes that it is in the premium-price category, unless it indicates otherwise, as follows:

  (M)   Medium-priced label;
  (B)   Bargain-priced label;
  (BB) Super-bargain label.

See below for differences in price structures in the UK and the USA.

LAYOUT OF TEXT

We have aimed to make our style as simple as possible. So, immediately after the evaluation and before the catalogue number, the record make is given, sometimes in abbreviated form. In the case of a set of two or more CDs, the number of units involved is given in brackets after the catalogue number.

AMERICAN CATALOGUE NUMBERS

The numbers that follow in square brackets are US catalogue numbers if they are different from UK catalogue numbers (and this applies in particular to EMI's 'Great Recordings of the Century', which have a different number on each side of the Atlantic). Some EMI Encore CDs are also differently numbered, so it is always advisable to check. Where a record is available in the USA but *not* in the UK, *it will appear in square brackets only*, and that applies especially to many Mercury CDs. However, we are delighted to learn that the best of these will be reappearing in the UK during the lifetime of this book in new, 'enhanced' SACD format.

EMI and Virgin have now abandoned the use of alphabetical prefixes, and it is no longer possible to determine the price range from the catalogue listing itself, although budget-priced Encore CDs are clearly marked, as are the two-for-the-price-of-one *double forte* Gemini and Virgin reissues.

We have taken care to check catalogue information as far as is possible; but, as all the editorial work has been done in England, there is always the possibility of error. American readers are therefore invited, when ordering records locally, to take the precaution of giving their dealer the fullest information about the music and recordings they want.

The indications (M), (B) and (BB) immediately before the starring of a disc refer primarily to the British CD, as pricing systems are not always identical on both sides of the Atlantic. When CDs are imported by specialist distributors into the USA, this again usually involves a price difference. When mid-priced CDs on the smaller labels are imported into the USA, they often move up to the premium-price range. American readers are advised to consult their local record store.

ABBREVIATIONS

To save space, we have adopted a number of standard abbreviations in listing record companies, orchestras and performing groups (a list is provided below), and the titles of works are often shortened, especially where they are listed several times. Artists' forenames are omitted if they are not absolutely necessary for identification purposes. Also, we have not usually listed the contents of operatic highlights and collections.

We have followed common practice in the use of the original language for titles where it seems sensible. In most cases, English is used for orchestral and instrumental music, and the original language for vocal music and opera. There are exceptions, however: for instance, the Johann Strauss discography uses German in the interests of consistency.

ORDER OF MUSIC

The order of music under each composer's name broadly follows the following system: orchestral music (including concertos and symphonies); chamber music; solo instrumental music (in some cases with keyboard and organ music separated); vocal and choral music; opera; vocal collections; miscellaneous collections. Within each group our listing follows an alphabetical sequence, and couplings within a single composer's output are *usually* discussed together instead of separately with cross-references. Occasionally (and inevitably because of this alphabetical approach), different recordings of a given work can become separated when a record is listed and discussed under the first work of its alphabetical sequence. The editor feels that alphabetical consistency is essential if the reader is to learn to find his or her way about.

CATALOGUE NUMBERS

Enormous care has gone into the checking of CD catalogue numbers and contents to ensure that all details are correct, but the editor and publishers cannot be held responsible for any mistakes that may have crept in despite all our zealous checking. When ordering CDs, readers are urged to provide their record-dealer with full details of the music and performers, as well as the catalogue number.

DELETIONS

Compact discs regularly succumb to the deletions axe, and many are likely to disappear during the lifetime of this book. Sometimes copies may still be found in specialist shops, and there remains the compensatory fact that most really important and desirable recordings are eventually reissued, often costing less!

Universal Classics have an import service for certain CDs that are not carried in their UK inventory, and these CDs are indicated with the abbreviation IMS. A small extra charge is made for these discs, which may have to be obtained from Germany or Holland.

COVERAGE

As the output of major and minor labels continues to expand, it is obviously impossible for us to mention every CD that is available within the covers of a single book; this is recognized as a practical limitation if we are to update our survey regularly. Indeed, we have now to be very selective in choosing the discs to be included, and some good recordings inevitably fall by the wayside. There is generally a reason for omissions, and usually it is connected with the lack of ready availability. However, we do welcome suggestions from readers about such omissions if they seem to be of special interest, although we cannot guarantee to include them in a future survey!

ACKNOWLEDGEMENTS

Our thanks are due as usual to Paul Czajkowski, Assistant Editor, who was responsible for most of the titling, helped with retrieval of earlier reviews (connected with reissues) and also contributed many specialist reviews, particularly in the areas of film and ballet music, light music and operetta. Our Penguin copy-editor, Roger Wells, continued to be indispensable, as were Penguin's in-house editorial staff, Ellie Smith and her colleagues Sarah Chatwin and Daisy Jackson, who were thrown in at the deep end to help during the last few weeks before we went to print.

Alan Livesey and Kathleen March have once again helped with checking the final copy for factual and musical errors, and our team of Penguin proofreaders have also proved themselves invaluable. Grateful thanks also go to all those readers who write to us to point out factual errors and to remind us of important recordings which have escaped our notice.

THE AMERICAN SCENE

CDs are much less expensive in the USA than they are in the UK and, because of this (so we are told), many bargain recordings available in Britain are not brought into the USA by their manufacturers, so that they have to be imported by the major US record stores and mail-order outlets. This means that while almost any recording mentioned in these pages will be available in the USA, sometimes it will cost more than the buyer might reasonably expect.

Duos and Doubles, where available, remain at two discs for the cost of one premium-priced CD in both countries, and here US collectors can have a price advantage. However, many excellent lower-priced discs are not issued in the USA. Where a recording is of extra special interest, American collectors can obtain it readily by mail order from the UK, through various website sources. However, it will inevitably cost more than it would domestically.

PRICE DIFFERENCES IN THE UK AND USA

Retail prices are not fixed in either country, and various stores may offer even better deals at times, so our price structure must be taken as a guide only. This particularly applies to the line drawn between Bargain and Super-bargain CDs. Premium-priced CDs cost on average approximately the same number of dollars in the USA as they do pounds in the UK.

Duos and Doubles are two-for-the-cost-of-one premium-priced disc the world over. Classics for Pleasure, EMI Gemini and the Virgin Classics 2 × 1 Doubles are two-for-the-price-of-one mid-priced CD.

OTHER COMPARABLE PRICES IN THE UK AND USA

Here are comparative details of the other price-ranges (note that sets are multiples of the prices quoted):

MID-PRICED SERIES
(as indicated by (M) in the text)
UK: £10.99; often £9–£10;
USA: Under $13; usually under $12.

BARGAIN-PRICED SERIES
(as indicated by (B) in the text)
UK: £5.50–£7;
USA: Under $7.

SUPER-BARGAIN BUDGET SERIES
(as indicated by (BB) in the text)
UK: CDs: £5–£5.50;
USA: CDs: $5–$6.

THE AUSTRALIAN SCENE

We have been fortunate in obtaining for review a considerable number of recordings from the Australian branch of Universal Classics (responsible for the three key labels, Decca, DG and Philips), who have been making a series of local issues of Decca, DG and Philips repertoire of considerable interest, mostly not otherwise available. These are bargain issues in Australia but, because of import costs, are more expensive in the UK and USA. All these Universal Australian CDs can be purchased via the Australian website: www.buywell.com

A MAIL-ORDER SOURCE FOR RECORDINGS IN THE UK

Readers are urged to support a local dealer if he is prepared and able to give a proper service, and to remember that obtaining many CDs involves expertise and perseverance. However, in recent years many specialist sources have disappeared; for that reason, if any difficulty is experienced in obtaining the CDs you want, we suggest the following mail-order alternative, which offers competitive discounts in the UK. Through this service, advice on choice of recordings from the Editor of *The Penguin Guide to Compact Discs and DVDs Yearbook* is always available to mail-order customers:

Squires Gate Music Centre Ltd (PG Dept)
615 Lytham Road,
Squires Gate, Blackpool,
Lancashire FY4 1RG, UK
Tel. and Fax: (+44) (0) 1253 782588;
Website address: www.lprl.demon.co.uk
E-mail address: sales@lprl.demon.co.uk

This organization can supply any recording available in Britain and patiently extends orders until they finally come to hand. A full guarantee of safe delivery is made on any order undertaken. Please write or fax for further details, or make a trial credit-card order, by fax, e-mail or telephone. This service now operates only in the UK.

● THE ROSETTE SERVICE

Squires Gate also offers a try-before-you-buy weekly loan service (within the UK only) so that customers can try out rosetted recordings at home, plus a hand-picked group of recommended key-repertoire CDs, for a small charge, without any obligation to purchase. A short list of recommended DVDs is also available. If a recording is subsequently purchased, it will be discounted and the trial charge waived. Full details sent on request.

Squires Gate Music Centre also offers a simple bi-monthly mailing, listing a hand-picked selection of current new and reissued CDs, chosen by the Editor of the *Penguin Guide*, Ivan March. Customers of Squires Gate Music Centre Ltd, both domestic and overseas, receive the bulletin as available, and it is sent automatically with their purchases.

ABBREVIATIONS

AAM	Academy of Ancient Music	IMS	Import Music Service (Polygram – UK only)
Ac.	Academy, Academic		
(ADD)	originally an analogue recording	⚷	Key Recordings
Amb. S.	Ambrosian Singers	L.	London
Ara.	Arabesque	LA	Los Angeles
arr.	arranged, arrangement	LCO	London Chamber Orchestra
ASMF	Academy of St Martin-in-the-Fields	LCP	London Classical Players
		LMP	London Mozart Players
(B)	bargain-price CD	LOP	Lamoureux Orchestra of Paris
(BB)	super-bargain-price CD	LPO	London Philharmonic Orchestra
Bar.	Baroque	LSO	London Symphony Orchestra
Bav.	Bavarian	(M)	mid-price CD
BBC	British Broadcasting Corporation	Mer.	Meridian
BPO	Berlin Philharmonic Orchestra	Met.	Metropolitan
BRT	Belgian Radio & Television (Brussels)	min.	minor
		MoC	Ministry of Culture
Cal.	Calliope	movt	movement
Cap.	Cappriccio	N.	North, Northern
CBSO	City of Birmingham Symphony Orchestra	nar.	narrated
		Nat.	National
CfP	Classics for Pleasure	Nim.	Nimbus
Ch.	Choir; Chorale; Chorus	NY	New York
Chan.	Chandos	O	Orchestra, Orchestre
CO	Chamber Orchestra	OAE	Orchestra of the Age of Enlightenment
COE	Chamber Orchestra of Europe		
Col. Mus. Ant.	Musica Antiqua, Cologne	O-L	Oiseau-Lyre
		Op.	Opera (in performance listings); opus (in music titles)
Coll.	Collegium		
Coll. Aur.	Collegium Aureum	orch.	orchestrated
Coll. Voc.	Collegium Vocale	ORR	Orchestre Révolutionnaire et Romantique
Concg. O	Royal Concertgebouw Orchestra of Amsterdam		
		ORTF	L'Orchestre de la radio et télévision française
cond.	conductor, conducted		
Cons.	Consort	Ph.	Philips
DG	Deutsche Grammophon	Phd.	Philadelphia
DHM	Deutsche Harmonia Mundi	Philh.	Philharmonia
E.	England, English	PO	Philharmonic Orchestra
E. Bar. Sol.	English Baroque Soloists	Qt	Quartet
ECCO	European Community Chamber Orchestra	R.	Radio
		Ref.	Références
ECO	English Chamber Orchestra	RLPO	Royal Liverpool Philharmonic Orchestra
ENO	English National Opera Company		
Ens.	Ensemble	ROHCG	Royal Opera House, Covent Garden
ESO	English Symphony Orchestra		
Fr.	French	RPO	Royal Philharmonic Orchestra
GO	Gewandhaus Orchestra	RSNO	Royal Scottish National Orchestra
Häns.	Hänssler	RSO	Radio Symphony Orchestra
HM	Harmonia Mundi	RTE	Radio Television Eireann
Hung.	Hungaroton	S.	South
Hyp.	Hyperion	SCO	Scottish Chamber Orchestra

Sinf.	Sinfonietta	trans.	transcription, transcribed
SIS	Special Import Service (EMI – UK only)	V.	Vienna
		V/D	Video Director
SNO	Scottish National Orchestra	Van.	Vanguard
SO	Symphony Orchestra	VCM	Vienna Concentus Musicus
Soc.	Society	VPO	Vienna Philharmonic Orchestra
Sol. Ven.	I Solisti Veneti	VSO	Vienna Symphony Orchestra
SRO	Suisse Romande Orchestra	W.	West
Sup.	Supraphon	WNO	Welsh National Opera Company

ABEL, Carl Friedrich (1723–87)

6 Symphonies, Op. 7.
**(*) Chan. 8648. Cantilena, Shepherd.

The six *Symphonies* of Op. 7 speak much the same language as J. C. Bach or early Mozart. The performances are not the last word in elegance but they are lively and enjoyable and well recorded.

ADDINSELL, Richard (1904–77)

(i) *Film music: Blithe Spirit (Waltz Theme).* (ii) *The Day Will Dawn (Tea-time Music). Greengage Summer: Suite.* (ii) *Highly Dangerous: Theme. The Lion Has Wings: Cavalry of the Clouds (March). Out of the Clouds: Theme. The Passionate Friends: Lover's Moon. Sea Devils (Prologue). Under Capricorn: Theme. Radio themes: Britain to America: March of the United Nations.* (ii) *Journey into Romance: Invocation for Piano & Orchestra.* (i) *Warsaw Concerto.*
🔾— (M) *** ASV CDWHL 2108. Royal Ballet Sinfonia, Alwyn; with (i) Jones; (ii) Lawson.

Roy Douglas here receives belated recognition for his work in fashioning Addinsell's musical ideas and cleverly scoring them as a Rachmaninov pastiche for the justly famous *Warsaw Concerto.* But there are many other good things here, and Philip Lane's cleverly fashioned suite from the film *The Greengage Summer* brims over with delightful ideas. Douglas Gamley assisted the composer in this instance, and other credits include Leonard Isaac and Ron Goodwin (who scored the *Cavalry of the Clouds* march). When trifles like the *Tea-time Music* from *The Day Will Dawn* and the delicious *Waltz* from *Blithe Spirit* are played with such affection and polish under the understanding Kenneth Alwyn, their gentle spirit is life-enhancing. The *Warsaw Concerto* is treated as a miniature masterpiece and given a performance that is as dramatic as it is heart-warming. Martin Jones is the splendid soloist, and Peter Lawson contributes equally sensitively to the several other concertante numbers. The recording is first class in every way. Not to be missed.

✓ *Film Music: Blithe Spirit: Prelude & Waltz. Encore: Miniature Overture. Fire Over England: Suite. Parisienne – 1885. The Passionate Friends: Suite. Scrooge: Suite. Southern Rhapsody; South Riding: Prelude. Waltz of the Toreadors: March & Waltz. WRNS March (arr. Douglas).*
(M) **(*) ASV CDWHL 2115. Royal Ballet O, Alwyn.

Richard Addinsell's distinct melodic gift is heard at its best here in his early score for *Fire Over England* (1937) and, more especially, in the suite of music from *Scrooge* (the definitive, 1951 version with Alastair Sim). As the *Waltz* for *Blithe Spirit* and the brief *March* for *Waltz of the Toreadors* show, there are some deft inventions elsewhere, but their composer needed help from others to realize them orchestrally. All this music is slight, but it is very well played by the Royal Ballet Orchestra, affectionately and stylishly conducted by Kenneth Alwyn and very well recorded.

Film and theatre music: Fire Over England: Suite. Goodbye Mr Chips: Theme. Journey to Romance: Invocation. The Prince and the Showgirl: selection. Ring round the Moon: Invitation Waltz. (i) *A Tale of Two Cities: Theme.* (ii) *Trespass: Festival (beguine). The Isle of Apples;* (ii) *Smokey Mountain Concerto;* (i) *Tune in G.*
**(*) Marco Polo 8.223732. BBC Concert O, Alwyn, with (i) Elms; (ii) Martin.

Kenneth Alwyn has pieced a good deal of the material together here where original scores are lost, notably in the 'Overture' from the film music for *Tom Brown's Schooldays* and the charming introductory sequence for *Goodbye Mr Chips.* The *Invitation Waltz* for Christopher Fry's translation, *Ring round the Moon*, of Jean Anouilh's *L'Invitation au château* is quite haunting, as is the gentle idyll *The Isle of Apples* and the simple *Tune in G* with its piano embroidery. These pieces, like the *Smokey Mountain Concerto*, were independent compositions. Alwyn and the BBC Concert Orchestra are thoroughly at home in this repertoire, and they present it all freshly, the recording bright but with rather a brash sonority.

Warsaw Concerto (orch. & arr. Roy Douglas).
(B) *** Ph. 411 123-2. Dichter, Philh. O, Marriner (with Concert ***).
(M) *** Decca 430 726-2. Ortiz, RPO, Atzmon –
   GERSHWIN: *Rhapsody* **(*); GOTTSCHALK:
   Grand Fantasia *** (with LISZT: *Hungarian Fantasia*; LITOLFF: *Scherzo* ***).

Richard Addinsell's pastiche miniature concerto, written for the film *Dangerous Moonlight* in 1942, is perfectly crafted; moreover it has a truly memorable main theme. It is beautifully played on Philips, with Marriner revealing the most engaging orchestral detail. The sound is first rate and the Virtuoso reissue has an attractive new livery.

The alternative from Cristina Ortiz is a warmly romantic account, spacious in conception. If the couplings are suitable, this is a rewarding collection, more substantial than Dichter's. The recording is first class.

ADÈS, Thomas (born 1971)

(i; ii; iii) *America (A Prophecy).* (iii; iv) *Brahms.* (v) *Cardiac Arrest; Les Baricades mystérieuses.* (vi) *The Fayrfax Carol;* (vi) *Fool's Rhymes; January Writ* (viii) *O Thou, who did with pitfall and with gin; Life Story* (ix) *The Lover in Winter.*
(M) *** EMI 5 57610-2. (i) Bickley; (ii) CBSO Ch.;

(iii) CBSO, composer; (iv) Maltman; (v) Composer's
Ens., composer; (vi) Poster, Webb, Benjafield;
(vii) Bowers Broadbent (organ); (viii) McFadden,
Polyphony, Layton; (ix) Blaze.

The cantata *America*, for mezzo-soprano, large chorus and orchestra, was one of six pieces commissioned from various composers by Kurt Masur for
the celebration of the millennium in New York.
Inspired by the Spanish conquest of the Mayan civilization 500 years earlier, it involves an extraordinary
kaleidoscope of original sounds and effects, with
Spanish as well as Mayan influences inspiring the
musical material. The piece is brilliantly performed
and recorded here, with Susan Bickley singing a
stylized text drawn from Mayan sources, using a raw,
child-like tone. The other works, all much shorter –
some (like the four *Lover in Winter* songs for
counter-tenor) mere fragments – together make up a
colourful survey of Adès and his work, with highly
inventive and original choral effects in many of
them, superbly presented by Polyphony under its
director, Stephen Layton. One very striking example
is the setting of lines from *Omar Khayyam* for male
voices in 14 parts, using echo effects, *O Thou who
didst with pitfall and with gin.* Comparably memorable are Adès's transcriptions, including *Cardiac
Arrest*, involving a jazz number seen through the
composer's distorting lens, and *Life Story*, with the
singer, Claron McFadden, instructed to sing in the
style of Billie Holliday. The Couperin transcription,
Les Baricades mysterieuses, is improbably dominated
by two clarinets, while the final item, *Brahms*, for
baritone (Christopher Maltman) and orchestra, is a
grand setting of a surreal poem in German by Alfred
Brendel. Least radical but still original is the *Fayrfax
Carol* that Adès wrote for the King's College Carol
Service in 1997. This is an hour of pieces so varied
and inventive that it should attract far more than just
devotees of new music.

ADORNO, Theodor (1903–69)

*String Quartet; 2 Pieces for String Quartet, Op. 2; 6
Studies for String Quartet.*
(BB) ★★★ CPO 999 341-2. Leipzig Qt – EISLER:
Prelude & Fugue on B-A-C-H, etc. ★★★

Adorno's *Six Studies* show an awareness of Schoenberg's musical language. There are many imaginative
touches, both here and in the *String Quartet* of the
following year. Neither is negligible, even if neither
possesses a significantly personal voice. Berg exerted
some influence on the *Two Pieces for String Quartet*,
Op. 2. The performances and recordings qualify for a
three-star rating – though the music itself is another
matter! But at its new budget price this is worth
trying.

AGRICOLA, Alexander
(*c.* 1446–1506)

Songs: Adieu m'amour (3 versions); *A la mignonne
de fortune; Allez, regretz; Ay je rien fet; Cecus non in
dicat de coloribus; De tous bien plaine* (3 versions);
*Et qui la dira; Fortuna desperata; Guarde vostre
visage* (3 versions); *J'ay beau huer; S'il vous plaist;
Soit loing ou pres; Sonnes muses melodieusement.*
(BB) ★★★ Naxos 8.553840. Unicorn Ens., Posch.

Agricola's music is expressive, but its structure and
polyphony are quite complex, his polyphonic style
nearer to Ockeghem than to Josquin, while his musical personality is less individual than either. Nevertheless, these secular love songs (sung in medieval
French) are full of interest, the more so as they are
often presented with a mixed consort of voices and
instruments sharing the polyphony, with close
blending of the whole ensemble. The piece that gives
the disc its title, the sombre *Fortuna desperata*, makes
a powerfully sonorous conclusion. The presentation
is scholarly, direct and appealing, the recording excellent, and the documentation could hardly be bettered, with full translations included.

AHO, Kalevi (born 1949)

(i) *Symphony No. 11 (for 6 percussionists &
orchestra). Symphonic Dances (Hommage à Uuno
Klami).*
★★★ BIS CD 1336. Lahti SO, Vänskä, (i) with Kroumata
Percussion Ens.

Kalevi Aho is the foremost Finnish composer of his
generation and BIS has his cause served well. The
Symphonic Dances derive from a completion Aho
made of the ballet *Whirls* by Uuno Klami (1900–
1961), whose inspiration, like so much Finnish music,
derives from the *Kalevala*, the last act of which the
composer left unfinished. It was this project that
formed the origin of the *Symphonic Dances*, completed in 2001. Like many of its predecessors, the
Eleventh Symphony includes an important role for a
solo instrument or instruments – in this case a
battery of percussion performed expertly by the six
members of the Kroumata Ensemble. This is a vital
work, which will give pleasure to Aho's growing band
of admirers and which is given state-of-the-art
recording by the BIS team and some pretty state-of-
the-art playing by Osmo Vänskä and his Lahti musicians.

CHAMBER MUSIC

(i) *Bassoon Quintet;* (ii) *Quintet for Alto
Saxophone, Bassoon, Viola, Cello & Double Bass.*
★★★ BIS CD 866. (i) Sinfonia Lahti Chamber Ens.

The *Bassoon Quintet* shows great understanding of

the instruments though it has its longueurs. The *Quintet for Alto Saxophone, Bassoon, Viola, Cello and Double Bass* – an unusual combination but one rich in tonal variety – is the more concentrated of the two and leaves no doubt as to Aho's instrumental resourcefulness and imagination in writing for this ensemble. Virtuoso performances and natural, vivid recording.

Oboe Quintet (for flute, oboe, violin, viola and cello); 7 *Inventions & Postlude for Oboe & Cello.*
*** BIS CD 1036. Sinfonia Lahti Chamber Ens.

The *Quintet for Flute, Oboe, Violin, Viola and Cello* was written in 1977, when Aho was 28, and it is far more concentrated than the overlong *Bassoon Quintet* from the same year. It draws the listener into its world from the first bar. There is a strong feeling for nature, and the melodic invention is fresh, even if interest is not sustained consistently over the piece's 30-minute span. Like the more recent *Inventions and Postlude*, this music is well worth investigating and both performances and recording are of a high quality.

ALBÉNIZ, Isaac (1860–1909)

Iberia, Book IV: *Málaga; Jerez; Eritaña; 6 Pequeños valses; Serenata árabe; Sonata No. 3; Suite ancienne No. 1.*
**(*) BIS CD 1243. Baselga.

Thanks to the flood of new issues, we somehow missed earlier records in the Albéniz series of piano music on the ever enterprising BIS label. Born in Luxembourg in 1966, Miguel Baselga studied at the Liège Conservatoire and then with Eduardo del Pueyo, and he is completely at one with the idiom. The last Book of *Iberia*, which Albéniz premièred in Paris three months before his death, is technically the most demanding of the four. He has the necessary virtuosity and rhythmic vitality to do justice to this repertoire, though his dynamic range and command of keyboard colour could at times be wider. It may well be, of course, that the balance (which is a little close) and the lively acoustic of the Palacio de Congresos, Zaragoza, contribute to this impression. All the same, there is some very satisfying playing here.

Merlin (opera; complete).
*** BBC Opus Arte **DVD** OA0888D (2).
Wilson-Johnson, Marton, Skelton, Vaness, Odina, Sierra, Madrid Symphony Ch. and O, José de Eusebio.

This DVD version of Albéniz's Arthurian opera, *Merlin*, recorded at the staging in Madrid in 2003, makes a valuable supplement to the Decca discs of this rare piece. It may be a flawed opera, seriously impeded by the libretto of the eccentric banker, Francis Burdett Money-Coutts, with its clumsy dramatic structure and doggerel verse, but the score finds Albéniz at his most inspired, and having a video version certainly helps to enhance involvement. As stage director, John Dew sets out the story clearly, helped by stylized sets and costumes, designed respectively by Heinz Balthes and José Manuel Vazquez. They are medieval enough to create the right atmosphere, with a touch of space fiction.

Though the cast is not as starry as that on the discs (which had Plácido Domingo as King Arthur), there is obvious benefit in having English speakers in three of the principal parts: David Wilson-Johnson commanding and noble as Merlin, the American tenor Stuart Skelton as Arthur, powerful rather than subtle, and Carol Vaness, also American, as Nivian, the second of the two main female roles. The big snag in the cast is the singer who might have been counted the star, Eva Marton as the evil Morgan le Fay. The unsteadiness of her voice, so extreme that one can hardly tell what pitch she is aiming at, may convey the wickedness of the character, and she acts convincingly, but it is painful on the ear. As her son, Mordred, Angel Odena characterizes well, but he also has bouts of unsteadiness, while Victor Garcia Sierra, taking the role of King Lot of Orkney, is another wobbler.

Happily, the chorus work is first rate and, as in the audio recording, Eusebio draws warmly committed playing from the Madrid Symphony Orchestra. Eusebio also contributes an essay to the booklet about the background to the opera, explaining how the material to complete the score was brought together, rebutting the accusation that the orchestration was by Manuel Ponce. He repeats that rebuttal in the interview (in Spanish) that comes on the second disc, along with interviews (in English) with Eva Marton and David Wilson-Johnson. With so rare an opera it is a pity that the booklet contains no synopsis. Despite the banality of Money-Coutts's verses, what shines out above all is the richness and variety of Albéniz's musical inspiration.

ALBERT, Eugen d' (1864–1932)

Piano Concertos Nos. 1 in B min., Op. 2; 2 in E, Op. 12.
*** Hyp. CDA 66747. Lane, BBC Scottish SO, Francis.

The *Piano Concerto No. 1 in B minor* (1884) is the more ambitious of the two works, written in a style halfway between Liszt and Rachmaninov, with a rather extraordinary fugal outburst towards the end of the work. Piers Lane plays with delicacy and virtuosity and is well supported by the BBC Scottish Symphony Orchestra. The *Piano Concerto No. 2 in E major* is a one-movement piece, though in four sections, following the style of Liszt's concertos. The recording is expertly balanced by Tony Kime.

Overture: Esther, Op. 8.
*** Hyp. CDA 67387. BBC Scottish SO, Brabbins
LAMOND: *Symphony in A etc.* ***

This colourful, generously inventive overture of Eugen d'Albert makes an apt coupling for the orchestral works of Frederic Lamond, when each was born in the Glasgow area of Scotland in the 1860s (d'Albert of a French father and a Scottish mother) and each gravitated to Germany, both becoming famous as piano virtuosos. Like Lamond, d'Albert had an easy mastery of orchestration, with dramatic writing for brass punctuating the piece, beautifully played by the BBC Scottish Symphony Orchestra under Martyn Brabbins and very well recorded by the BBC engineers.

Piano Sonata in F sharp min., Op. 10; 8 Klavierstücke, Op. 5; Klavierstücke, Op. 16/2-3; 5 schliche Klavierstücke (Capriolen), Op. 32; Serenata.
*** Hyp. CDA 66945. Lane.

Eugen d'Albert's solo keyboard music inhabits the worlds of Brahms and Liszt, but there is much that can lay claim to a quiet individuality. Piers Lane plays it with total commitment. No want of virtuosity and dedication here, and very good recorded sound.

Die Abreise.
(M) **(*) CPO/EMI (ADD) CPO 999 558-2. Prey, Moser, Schreier, Philh. Hung. O, Kulka.

Eugen d'Albert wrote this charming one-acter, *Die Abreise* ('The Departure'), in 1898, five years before his most celebrated opera, *Tiefland*. Gilfen, bored with his wife Luise, plans to depart on a journey, but the machinations of his friend Trott alert him to the dangers, and it is Trott who departs. With delicate orchestral writing, it tells the story deftly in 20 brief sections of melodic conversation – though there are no separate tracks after the overture, and their absence makes it harder to follow the synopsis, which is provided instead of a libretto. Nevertheless, this is a first-rate, highly enjoyable performance, recorded in 1978 with three outstanding and characterful soloists. Warm, clear EMI sound.

Die toten Augen (complete).
*** CPO 999 692-2 (2). Schellenberger, Gjevang, Walker, Orth, Chalker, Odinius, Bär, Dresden PO Ch. & O, Weikert.

Die toten Augen ('The Dead Eyes') is a luscious piece set at the time of Christ. The central action is framed by a Prelude and Postlude in which a shepherd (beautifully sung here by the tenor Lothar Odinius), meets another symbolic character, the Reaper (the celebrated Olaf Bär), and goes off in search of a lost sheep. The central action, much more realistic, is then compressed into a single act, telling of a Roman official, Arcesius, whose wife, Myrtocle, is blind. She is cured by the intervention (offstage) of Christ but, as predicted by Christ, the gift of sight proves a curse, bringing the disruption of her marriage and the murder of the handsome Galba, whom she initially mistakes for her husband. In her love for Arcesius she opts to be blind again, with her 'dead eyes'.

The evocative pastoral sweetness of the Prelude and Postlude is set against the ripe German verismo style of the central action. It could easily be a sickly story, but d'Albert with rich orchestration and surging melody carries it off impressively. This live recording of a concert performance, well recorded, offers a persuasive account of the piece, with Dagmar Schellenberger powerful as Myrtocle, well matched by the fine mezzo, Anne Gjevang, as Mary of Magdala. A rarity to recommend to those with a sweet tooth.

ALBINONI, Tomaso (1671–1751)

12 Concerti, Op. 10.
(BB) *** Warner Apex 2564 61136-2 (Nos. 1–6); 2564 61256-2 (Nos. 7–12). Carmignola, Toso, Sol. Ven., Scimone.

Scimone's set of Albinoni's Op. 10 is praised in our main volume. They radiate simple vitality and a love of life, and they are now even more welcome on the budget Apex label.

ALFVÉN, Hugo (1872–1960)

(i) *Revelation Cantata, Op. 31* (ii) *Cantata for the 450th Anniversary of Uppsala University, Op. 45.*
**(*) Sterling CDS 1058-2. (i) Boman, Zetterström; (ii) Larsson, Zetterström; Malmö Op. Ch. & O, Volmer.

Alfvén wrote prolifically for choral forces: there are in all some 60 pieces. The *Revelation Cantata* comes from 1913 for the consecration of the newly erected Church of the Revelation at Saltsjöbaden. It is for two soloists, two choirs, organ, harmonium, celesta, harp and string quartet. More conventional in its scoring, the *Cantata for the 450th Anniversary of Uppsala University* was commissioned in 1927 and is characteristic but not quite top-drawer Alfvén. Both works are certainly worth hearing and get good performances. Charlotta Larsson in the *Uppsala Cantata* is an eloquent artist, and what a fine singer the baritone Fredrik Zetterström is! All the same, at 49 minutes this is short measure for a full-price disc.

ALKAN, Charles-Valentin (1813–88)

25 Préludes, Op. 31.
(M) *** Decca 475 212-2. Mustonen – SHOSTAKOVICH: *24 Preludes.* ***

Alkan's *Préludes* are more poetic than barnstorming and date from 1847. They go through all the major and minor keys, returning to C major in No. 25, and are designed for piano or organ or the pedaler (a piano with pedal-board), the instrument for which the composer had a special affection. Some of the pieces are affecting in their simplicity, and the Finnish pianist Olli Mustonen (whose début this was on the Decca label) plays them supremely well on the piano. He gives us a very well-filled disc, which won the *Gramophone* Instrumental Award in 1992, for the generous Shostakovich coupling is equally successful. The recording is absolutely first class, though the pedal-stamping in the *Tenth Prélude, Dans le style fugué*, should have been curbed. Strongly recommended, nevertheless.

ALONSO-CRESPO, Eduardo
(born 1956)

Juana, la loca (overture and ballet music); *Putzi: Mephisto* (waltz); *Yubarta:* overture.
*** Ocean OR101. Cincinnati CO, composer –
GALBRAITH: *Piano Concerto No. 1.* ***

The Argentinian-born Alonso-Crespo writes colourfully in a style that absorbs Latin-American rhythms and that clearly reflects eclectic lyrical influences from his adopted North American homeland, not least from Aaron Copland. There is no shortage of melody. His operetta *Putzi* mixes Lisztian biography with the Faust legend, and the *Mephisto Waltz* is used as a springboard for a rather charming pastiche. The Cincinnati Chamber Orchestra responds to the composer's direction with considerable aplomb, and the recording is excellent.

ANDERSON, Leroy (1908–75)

Belle of the Ball; Blue Tango; Bugler's Holiday; Fiddle-Faddle; Forgotten Dreams; The Girl in Satin; Jazz Legato; Jazz Pizzicato; March of the Two Left Feet; The Penny Whistle Song; The Phantom Regiment; Plink, Plank, Plunk!; Promenade; Sandpaper Ballet; Saraband; Serenata; Sleigh Ride; The Syncopated Clock; Trumpeter's Lullaby; The Typewriter; The Waltzing Cat.
(BB) ** Naxos 8.559125. O, Hayman.

Belle of the Ball; Blue Tango; Chicken Reel; China Doll; Fiddle-Faddle; The First Day of Spring; The Girl in Satin; Horse and Buggy; Jazz Legato; Jazz Pizzicato; The Phantom Regiment; Plink, Plank, Plunk!; Promenade; Saraband; Scottish Suite: The Bluebells of Scotland. Serenata; Sleigh Ride; Song of the Bells; Summer Skies; The Syncopated Clock; The Typewriter; The Waltzing Cat. Arr. of HANDEL: *Song of Jupiter.*
(M) *** Mercury (ADD) 432 013-2. Eastman-Rochester Pops O, or O, Fennell.

(i) *Carol Suite:* excerpts. *A Christmas Festival. Goldilocks: Pirate Dance.* (ii) *Irish Suite. Bugler's Holiday; Forgotten Dreams; Penny Whistle Song; Sandpaper Ballet; Trumpeter's Lullaby.*
(M) *** Mercury (ADD) [434 376-2]. (i) London Pops O; (ii) Eastman-Rochester Pops O; Fennell (with COATES: *Four ways, etc.* **(*))

The reissue of Frederick Fennell's Mercury performances is most welcome; they have a witty precision that is most attractive. The second disc (available only in the USA) includes the *Irish Suite*, one of Anderson's more ambitious enterprises. Its highlight is a clever arrangement of *The Minstrel Boy* in the form of a haunting little funeral march, advancing and retreating. Fennell also includes some arrangements of notable Christmas carols; and the vintage, rather dry and studio-ish recording suits the bright precision of the playing.

After playing the classic Mercury account with the Eastman-Rochester Pops Orchestra (432 013-2), this 1989 Naxos recording sounds rather anaemic. This is partly due to the recording, which, though more refined, sounds distant next to the exceptionally vivid Mercury sound. Richard Hayman's performances are good, but the Mercury ones have greater character and come over with tingling immediacy. It is definitely worth paying more for the Mercury CD, although the repertoire is slightly different.

ANTHEIL, George (1900–59)

Symphonies Nos. 1 (Zingareska); 6 (after Delacroix); Archipelago.
*** CPO 999 604-2. Frankfurt RSO, Wolff.

This CPO coupling of Antheil's first and last symphonies is very welcome, showing the marked contrast between the style of his time in Paris – when he associated with such fellow artists as Joyce, Hemingway, Pound and Picasso – and his later style, influenced by Soviet composers. The gypsy echoes suggested by the title for No. 1, *Zingareska*, are minimal. Far more important are the echoes of early Stravinsky, occasionally mixed with Gershwin, with the finale bringing direct imitations of passages from both *Petrushka* and *The Rite of Spring*. Though it is an attractive, at times brilliant work, the three-movement *Symphony No. 6* is more consistent, with the central slow movement languorously beautiful in its echoes of Satie's *Gymnopédies*, and with the Soviet-style ostinatos of the outer movements crisply and urgently controlled, helped by brilliant sound, enhanced by sumptuous orchestration. The Rumba, *Archipelago*, dazzlingly scored, makes a delightfully colourful supplement.

Symphony No. 4, '1942'.
(*) Everest (ADD) EVC 9039. LSO, Eugene Goossens – COPLAND: *Statements for Orchestra.* *

(M) (***) ADD Cala mono CACD 0528. NBC SO, Stokowski – BUTTERWORTH: *Shropshire Lad* **; VAUGHAN WILLIAMS: *Symphony No. 4* (***).

Symphonies Nos. 4; 6 (after Delacroix); Concert Overture: McConkey's Ferry.
(BB) **(*) Naxos 8.559033. Ukraine Nat. SO, Kuchar.

There are influences of the composer's East European background in *Symphony No. 4*, which is probably his best. The performance, from a famous advocate of contemporary music, could not be more convincing, and the Everest stereo (from 1959) entirely belies its age. This music is not deep, but it communicates readily, and one's only real complaint is that this excellently remastered reissue has not been offered less expensively – the disc plays for only 49 minutes.

In February 1944 Stokowski – temporarily replacing Toscanini with the NBC Symphony – conducted a radio performance of the *Fourth Symphony*. Dating from 1942, it relies greatly on march rhythms and persistent ostinatos, often in support of Prokofiev-like melodies; though the radio sound is limited in dynamic as well as frequency range, the clarity and weight are more than enough to convey the power, urgency and dramatic incisiveness of Stokowski's performance, with full and rich string-sound very different from that under Toscanini. With the two English works for coupling, it makes an attractive and revealing disc.

The Naxos issue pairs what are probably Antheil's two most colourful symphonies. They are vividly recorded, with the Ukraine orchestra sounding very idiomatic in Antheil's jazzy syncopations even while they relish the many echoes of Prokofiev and Shostakovich. Both these symphonies were written in Antheil's productive period in the 1940s, when for a while he was a war correspondent. Though the playing is not as polished as in rival versions, this is well worth considering, with the *Concert Overture*, *McConkey's Ferry*, dating from the same period, a lively and attractive supplement.

ANTILL, John (1904–86)

Corroboree (ballet suite).

(*) Everest EVC 9007. LSO, Eugene Goossens – GINASTERA: *Estancia*, etc. *; VILLA-LOBOS: *Little Train of the Caipira* **(*).

The ballet score *Corroboree* is based on an Aboriginal dance-ceremony. Its primitivism generates imaginatively exotic invention, very colourfully scored, to include an enticing *Dance to the Evening Star*, a strongly rhythmic *Rain Dance* and a boisterously frantic *Closing Fire Ceremony*. The performance here generates plenty of energy and, if the recording is over-resonant, it is immensely vivid.

ARÁMBARRI, Jesús (1902–60)

Fantasía española; 4 Impromptus; In memoriam (Elegy); Ofrenda; Preludio Gabon-zar sorgiñak (Witches on New Year's Eve); Viento sur (South Wind); (i) *8 Basque Songs.*

(BB) ** Naxos 8.557275. Bilbao SO, Mena; (i) with Itxaro Mntxaka.

Jesús Arámbarri is a Basque composer who studied composition in Paris with Dukas and conducting with Vladimir Golschmann and then with Felix Weingartner. On his return to Bilbao, Arámbarri spent the greater part of his time as a conductor; the majority of the pieces on this disc come from his early years, apart from *Elegía* (1939) and the *Ofrenda*, composed in 1946 on the death of Falla. Don't be put off by the rather crude *Preludio Gabon-zar sorgiñak* ('Witches on New Year's Eve') that begins the CD, as many of the other pieces are scored with great transparency and skill. There are reminders of Ravel and Falla, and some of the quicker, dance-like pieces sound like the work of a Basque Malcolm Arnold. Very slight but often attractive music here, and decent rather than distinguished performances and acceptable sound.

ARENSKY, Anton (1861–1906)

Suites Nos. 1 in G min., Op. 7; 2 (Silhouettes), Op. 23; 3 (Variations in C), Op. 33.

(BB) **(*) Naxos 8.553768. Moscow SO, Yablonsky.

What a good idea to put Arensky's three attractive orchestral *Suites* on a single CD: *Suite No. 1 in G minor* opens with a Russian theme with variations, and the Russian feel continues in the ensuing three dance numbers, with a bright Scherzo at the centre. *Suite No. 2* (*Silhouettes*), the best known, is a group of character studies: *The Scholar*, *The Coquette* and *The Buffoon*, which all have plentiful invention. *The Dreamer* is especially beautiful, and the work finishes with the spirited portrait of *The Dancer*. *Suite No. 3* is another set of variations (mainly dance forms), brightly coloured, the *Andante* theme itself beginning in a romantic chorale style and ending as a spirited polonaise. The performances are good and enthusiastic, if not always refined, and, while it all emerges quite vividly, the 1995 sound feels a bit under-recorded, lacking the richness and depth of the finest recordings. It is an enjoyable disc, nevertheless.

Symphony No. 1 in B min., Op. 4; (i) *Fantasia on Themes by I. T. Ryabinin, Op. 48* (for piano & orchestra); *Variations on a Theme by Tchaikovsky, Op. 35a;* (ii) *Cantata on the 10th Anniversary of the Coronation, Op. 26; 3 Vocal Quartets with Cello accompaniment. Op. 57.*

*** Chan. 10086. Russian State SO, Polyansky; with (i) Tatiana Polyanskaya; (ii) Sharova, Baturkin, Russian State Symphonic Capella.

Symphony No. 2 in A, Op. 22; Intermezzo, Op. 13; Overture: A Dream on the Volga, Op.16; Suite No. 3 (Variations), Op. 33; Nal and Damayanti (opera): Introduction, Op. 47.

*** Chan. 10024. BBC PO, Sinaisky.

Arensky studied with Rimsky-Korsakov but he was

closer in feeling to Tchaikovsky, who became his mentor and whose vein of elegiac lyricism he shared. He belongs to the same generation as Liadov, Grechaninov and Taneyev and he taught at the Moscow Conservatoire (1882–95) before becoming Director of the Imperial Chapel at St Petersburg (1895–1901) and then, in the last years of his life, settling on the Gulf of Finland. The two symphonies and the three suites have previously appeared on an RCA 'Twofer' (now deleted) with Evgeny Svetlanov and the USSR Symphony Orchestra, together with the overtures to *A Dream on the Volga* and *Nal and Damayanti*; but these date from the early 1980s, and the sound, though good, tends to coarsen on climaxes. The fluent and inventive *First Symphony* comes from 1883, when Arensky was in his early twenties, and it is a work of not only astonishing promise but very considerable fulfilment. The *Second Symphony* of 1889 is harmonically the more adventurous of the two as well as being tauter: the four movements are rolled into one. These two Chandos issues are of special interest in that they bring some rarities: the *Fantasia on Themes by Ivan Ryabinin* for piano and orchestra and the first recording of the *Cantata on the 10th Anniversary of the Coronation*, as well as giving us the most popular of Arensky's works, the *Variations on a Theme by Tchaikovsky*. None of the above rarities is of much musical substance, though the *Three Vocal Quartets* with cello, which came late in his creative career, could well be the only music written for four-part choir and cello! All the performances are very persuasive and very well recorded, and they supersede the Svetlanov recordings in most respects. However, those who acquired the old set should hang on to it for the sake of the charming orchestral suites.

ARMSTRONG, Thomas
(1898–1994)

Sinfonietta; Fantasy Quintet; Vocal music: (i, ii) *Friends Departed;* (ii) *Never Weather-beaten Sail; O Mortal Folk;* (ii, iii) *A Passer-by;* (ii) *She Is Not Fair to Outward View; Sweet Day; With Margerain Gentle.*
*** Chan. 9657. LPO, Daniel; with (i) Watson; (ii) LPO Ch.; (iii) Varcoe.

As a distinguished academic Sir Thomas Armstrong was a key figure in British musical life. In their echoes of English choral music from Parry to Vaughan Williams, and Holst by way of Delius, both *A Passer-by* (with baritone soloist) and *Friends Departed* (with soprano) have an immediate impact, passionate, not academic. The *Fantasy Quintet* and the *Sinfonietta* are even more sensuous yet amiable pieces, and the six part-songs are beautifully written too. Paul Daniel is a most persuasive advocate in the big pieces, and the recording is warm and atmospheric.

ARRIAGA, Juan (1806–26)

Symphony in D; Overture: Los esclavos felices.
(BB) *** Naxos 8.557207. Algarve O, Álvaro Cassuto– Concert of music by CARVALHO; MOREIRA; PORTUGAL; SEIXAS. **(*)

The sheer quality of Arriaga's invention and the astonishing maturity of his creative gifts never cease to amaze. The *Overture* is the work of a 13-year-old boy whose opera had been given with great success. The *Symphony in D* was written two years later after he had been sent to the Paris Conservatoire, where his progress astonished his professors. These performances, recorded in Faro, convey the sunny high spirits of the pieces and also bring four other rarities that few readers are likely to know and that are discussed in the Concerts section below. Good playing and recording.

String Quartets Nos. 1 in D min.; 2 in A; 3 in E flat.
⊕╍ *** HM HMI 987028. Cuerteto Casals.

The three miraculous quartets by the 18-year-old Arriaga still continue to astonish. While we retain a warm affection for the mellow, Schubertian accounts by the Voces Quartet on MDG (603 0236-2), these new performances by the youthful Spaniards, recorded in 2003, must now take pride of place. The group was formed in 1997 in Madrid; these young players use modern instruments, yet they show a background understanding of period-instrument practice without creating abrasivness or linear distortion. Their ensemble is impeccable and their group personality striking, while their playing combines expressive freedom with fine control and matching of timbres. They present the *Andante con variazioni* of the *A major Qartet* with much imagination and a wide range of dynamics; and they are at their finest in the gentle *Andantino* of the *E flat major*, which has a simmering underlying depth of feeling that can suddenly burst passionately to the surface. The work's lighthearted, bouncily rhythmic *Presto Agitato* finale is also splendidly characterized. Excellent, truthfully balanced recording.

ATTERBERG, Kurt (1887–1974)

Ballade and Passacaglia, Op. 38; (i) *Piano Concerto in B flat min., Op. 37; Rhapsody for piano & orchestra, Op. 1.*
*** CPO 999 732-2. (i) Derwinger; N. German R. PO, Hanover, Rasilainen.

Atterberg himself made records of his attractive *Ballade and Passacaglia* for Swedish HMV in the dying days of 78rpm records, and the Finnish conductor Ari Rasilainen gives a very good account of it. The *Piano Concerto* is pure kitsch, the Rich Man's 'Warsaw Concerto'. The solo piano writing is unremitting and relentless, with hardly a minute's rest, and the work is overscored. Dan Franklin Smith recorded it for the ever-enterprising Sterling label, but this is the more subtle of the two performances. Even so, not even the artistry of Love Derwinger and the ardour of Rasilainen and the NordDeutscher Rundfunk Orchestra, Hanover, can save the day. Atterberg struggled for eight long years before finishing the *Piano Concerto*, but it remains one of his feeblest efforts. The *Rhapsody*, Op. 1, comes from 1908, the year after he began his studies in electrical engineering, and before he decided to opt for a musical career. It is an accomplished piece, Lisztian in character but very well crafted. The three stars are for the performers and the very acceptable recorded sound – not for the music.

Symphonies Nos. 1 in B min., Op. 3; 4 in G min. (Sinfonia piccola), Op. 14.

*** CPO 999639-2. Frankfurt RSO, Rasilainen.

Atterberg's *First Symphony* is naturally derivative, but none the worse for that. The *Fourth (Sinfonia piccola)* of 1918 is distinctly folksy but enjoyable, particularly in this committed performance. Anyone coming to these symphonies for the first time will find these performances well played and with the advantage of superior recorded sound.

Symphonies Nos. 3 in D, Op. 10 (Västkustsbilder); 6 in C, Op. 31.

*** CPO 999640-2. Hanover RSO, Rasilainen.

The *Third (West Coast Pictures)* and the *Sixth* (the so-called *Dollar* Symphony, since it won the composer $10,000 in the 1928 Schubert Centenary Competition) are representative of the best in Atterberg's symphonic output. Although the Dutton Laboratories transfer of the pioneering recordings made by Sir Thomas Beecham in 1929 sounds astonishingly good, readers will want a more modern version, and this issue fills the bill admirably. It maintains the high artistic and technical standards that Ari Rasilainen set in his earlier CPO recording of Nos. 1 and 4.

Symphony No. 6 in C, Op. 31; Ballad without Words, Op. 56; A Värmland Rhapsody, Op. 36.

** BIS CD 553. Norrköping SO, Hirokami.

Atterberg's *Sixth Symphony* is a colourful and inventive score that deserves wide popularity. *A Värmland Rhapsody* is, appropriately enough, strongly folkloric. The *Ballad without Words* has many imaginative touches. The Norrköping orchestra includes many sensitive players, but the string-tone lacks weight and opulence. The recording is very clean.

Symphonies Nos. 7 (Sinfonia romantica), Op. 45; 8, Op. 48.

*** CPO 999 641-2 SWR SO, Stuttgart, Rasilainen.
** Sterling CDS 1026-2. Malmö SO, Jurowski.

Ari Rasilainen and the Sudwestfunk Orchestra of Stuttgart give a very good account of both symphonies, more persuasive than Jurowski – though there is

not a great deal in it. The CPO recording is excellent. No. 7 is the more impressive of the two. It draws on (or, in this instance, rescues) material from an earlier opera. It is romantic in feeling, a protest against the modernity of the times. The *Eighth* is less successful, even if the slow movement has some characteristically beautiful ideas. The finale is insufferably folksy. Good playing from the Malmö orchestra and well-detailed recording.

(i) Symphony No. 9 (Sinfonia visionaria). Alven (The River), Op. 33.

*** CPO 999 913-2. NDR PO, Rasilainen, with (i) Vihavainen, Suovanen, NDR Ch., Prague Chamber Ch.

The *Ninth Symphony (Sinfonia visionaria)* is scored for two solo singers, chorus and orchestra and is a setting of verses from the *Edda*. First performed in Helsinki in 1957 (Atterberg was very much a back number in 1950s and '60s Sweden), it did not receive a performance in his homeland until 1975, a year after his death, when it was given in Gothenburg. It is undoubtedly derivative (and a bit overblown) with lots of Strauss – and of Wagner too, as perhaps one might expect from a work inspired by Norse mythology. But to be fair it is by no means as inflated as its immediate predecessors and, though there are naive touches (and one would welcome greater rhythmic variety), there are some imaginative – indeed highly imaginative – passages. The level of inspiration is higher than in the *Seventh* and *Eighth Symphonies*, and both soloists and the fine NDR Orchestra under their Finnish conductor give a dedicated performance.

The River is much earlier and was commissioned by the Gothenburg Orchestra just after Atterberg scored such a success with the *Sixth Symphony*. Comparisons have been made with Smetana's *Vltava*, doubtless because of the subject-matter and also perhaps because Smetana had been conductor in Gothenburg in the late 1850s, though they are very much in Smetana's favour. Be that as it may, this is an effective (if distinctly overlong) piece of post-romantic tone-painting – and it is very expertly laid out for the orchestra. Good recording and excellent notes.

AUBER, Daniel (1782–1871)

Le Dieu et la Bayadère: Overture & ballet music; L'Enfant prodigue: Overture; Jenny Bell: Overture; La Muette de Portici: Ballet music; Le Premier Jour de Bonheur: Overture; La Sirène: Overture; Vendôme en Espagne: Boléro & Air pour le second ballet.

**(*) Sterling CDS 1039-2. Gothenburg Op. O, Andersson.

Though not all of this music shows Auber at his best, it is all thoroughly entertaining and almost all of it is unknown. Auber had the knack of writing catchy tunes and, with piquant orchestration, splashes of local colour, bacchanales and waltzes, and wit in plenty, one understands how this composer was such a success during the nineteenth century. The performance and recordings are very good, though they just miss the sheer exhilaration that Paul Paray and his Mercury team brought to this repertoire. This disc will bring much pleasure to those who respond to the repertoire.

Overtures: The Bronze Horse; Fra Diavolo; Masaniello.

⊕ ❂ *** Mercury (ADD) **SACD** 470 638-2. Detroit SO, Paray – SUPPE: *Overtures.* ***

Mercury are bringing out some of their most admired recordings on SACD and, although they are not due to be released until the autumn of this year, we feel sure that listeners will want to be informed of their publication in advance. The new format should go some way to further enhance the already spectacular results afforded by the 'Living Presence' technology.

(i) Le Domino noir (complete); Gustave III ou Le Bal masqué (Overture & ballet music).

❂ *** (M) Decca 476 2173 (2). Jo, Vernet, Ford, Power, Bastin, Olmeda, Cachemaille, L. Voices, ECO, Bonynge.

For *Le Domino noir* Auber was inspired to write a sparkling score, full of delightful invention. The opening number directly anticipates the celebrated duet in Delibes's *Lakmé*, and other numbers bring clear anticipations of Gounod's *Faust* and of Verdi's *Il trovatore*, not to mention Gilbert and Sullivan. Three accompanied recitatives, written by Tchaikovsky for a planned performance in St Petersburg, are used very effectively in Act II. Bonynge makes the ideal advocate, moulding melodies, springing rhythms and aerating textures to make the music sparkle from first to last. The playing of the ECO is outstanding. Sumi Jo takes on a role leading her into dazzling coloratura. Bruce Ford as the hero and Patrick Power as his friend, Juliano, sing stylishly in well-contrasted tenor tones, while Isabelle Vernet is excellent as Brigitte. Martine Olmeda and Jules Bastin are both characterful in servant roles. The recording is among Decca's most vivid. On the second disc, after Act III, the fill-up aptly comes from another colourful but more serious opera of Auber, the one that, translated into Italian, prompted Verdi's *Ballo in maschera*. This has now been reissued by Universal as one of the 'Penguin ❂ Collection' at mid-price with full documentation included.

AUBERT, Jacques (1689–1753)

Concerts de Simphonies for Violins, Flutes & Oboes: Suites: Nos. 2 in D; 5 in F; Concertos for 4 Violins,

Cello & Bass Continuo: in D & G min., Op. 17/1 & 6; in E min. (Le Carillon), Op. 26/4.
*** Chan. 0577. Coll. Mus. 90, Standage.

Aubert was a contemporary of Rameau and Leclair; he possessed much of the former's melodic flair and feeling for orchestral colour and he shared the latter's interest in extending violin technique. The leader (here the inestimable Simon Standage) has most of the bravura; the other violin soloists are subservient, and sometimes the cello joins the solo team. The orchestral concertos are neatly scored and full of attractive ideas. The performances here are polished, refreshingly alive and invigorating, and the recording is first class. Well worth investigating.

AUFSCHNAITER, Benedikt Anton (1665–1742)

Concors Discordia: Serenades Nos. 1–6.
*** CPO 999 457-2. L'Orféo Bar. O, Gaigg.

These six *Serenades* are in essence elegant orchestral suites in the French style. Originally scored for strings alone, the composer commended the use of oboes or shawms, and bassoons, if 'among your musicians a few do a fine job of playing them'. So Michi Gaigg has taken him at his word and also included a recorder, to double up the string parts. They are given vigorous, polished performances. Although the somewhat edgy attack that the Orféo violins bring to allegros seems a shade over-enthusiastic, the ear soon adjusts when the contrasting dance movements are so graceful and amiable, and the wind playing is excellent. The recording too is warm and the acoustic unconfined.

AURIC, Georges (1899–1983)

Film scores: Suites from: Caesar and Cleopatra; Dead of Night; Father Brown; Hue and Cry (Overture); The Innocents; It Always Rains on Sunday; The Lavender Hill Mob; Moulin Rouge; Passport to Pimlico; The Titfield Thunderbolt.
*** Chan. 8774. BBC PO, Gamba.

It is remarkable that a French composer should have provided the film-scores for some of the most famous Ealing comedies, so British in every other respect. But Auric's delicacy of orchestral touch and his feeling for atmosphere (together with his easy melodic gift) made him a perfect choice after his first flamboyant venture with Rank's *Caesar and Cleopatra*. From the witty railway music of *The Titfield Thunderbolt* and the distinct menace of *Dead of Night*, Auric moved easily to the buoyantly spirited *Passport to Pimlico*. But it was *Moulin Rouge* that gave Auric his popular hit, with a charming Parisian waltz song (delicately sung here by Mary Carewe) that was understandably to be a remarkable commercial success. Most of the excerpts are short vignettes but they make enjoyable listening when so well played and recorded.

Film scores: Suite: *Du rififi chez les hommes. Macao, l'enfer du Jeu; Le Salaire de la Peur* (excerpts); *La Symphonie Pastorale:* Suite, with *Valse et Tango.*
*** Marco Polo 8.225136. Slovak RSO, Adriano.

Auric's distinctive language is apparent from the first few seconds on this CD. His style is symphonic, with elements of popular songs (such as the *Valse* and *Tango,* which are heard on a gramophone in *La Symphonie Pastorale*), and all with Gallic flair. *Macao* is largely reconstructed from music that was written for, but not used in, the final edit of the film (including an exotic piece entitled *Chinoiserie*). Auric mixes melodrama and comedy with equal sophistication, and these varied suites stand up remarkably well on their own, which is important as most readers will not have seen the films to which they owe their existence.

Auric's imaginative scoring for a large orchestra is always ear-catching: the use of saxophone, high strings and bass drum at the beginning of *Du rififi chez les hommes,* for example, or the eerie *Etude sombre* of *Macao,* which sounds a little like Rachmaninov's *Isle of the Dead.*

Much background work by Adriano was involved in making this recording possible, not least his fascinating and lucid notes. The orchestra plays very well, the sound is atmospheric, and the CD presentation cannot be faulted.

Film scores (suites): *Orphée; Les Parents terribles; Ruy Blas; Thomas L'Imposteur.*
*** Marco Polo 8.225066. Slovak RSO, Adriano.

Jean Cocteau considered Auric 'his' composer, and the music recorded here was for films that were either directed by Cocteau or for which he was the screenwriter. The elements of fantasy and imagination that marked *Orphée* are reflected in the music: though scored for a large orchestra, it has a classical restraint and is most haunting throughout. Also included is Auric's arrangement of *Eurydice's Lament* from Gluck's opera – a lovely, piquant bonus. For *Les Parents terribles* Auric dispenses with the strings and uses a large wind band, percussion, and piano: a short '*image musicale*' has been assembled for this recording. *Thomas L'Imposteur* starts off in military style and includes a wistful waltz for Clémence and Henriette. For the swashbuckler *Ruy Blas* Auric had to compose straightforward and colourful music, which gave him plenty of scope for his own distinctive brand of orchestration. Adriano has done sterling work in assembling these suites and securing first-class playing from the orchestra, and the recording is good too.

AVALON, Robert (born 1955)

(i) *Piano Concerto, Op. 10;* (ii) *Flute & Harp Concerto, Op. 31.*
**(*) Centaur CRC 2482. (i) composer; (ii)

Meisenbach, Golden; Houston Foundation for Modern Music O, composer.

The *Piano Concerto* of the Texan composer, Robert Avalon, is a large-scale, accessible work with an essentially lyrical core. The first movement is effectively written and scored, but at 20 minutes 26 seconds is a shade too long, although its invention does not really falter. The Scherzo is busy and lighthearted; the delicately atmospheric *Andante* is the work's highlight and is quite haunting; the finale sums up what has gone before and ends positively. The *Concerto for Flute and Harp,* written to be played either with string quartet or with string orchestra as here, is texturally attractive, but less tangible in melodic content. However, both works are very well played, with the composer a confident soloist in the *Piano Concerto.* The recording is first class, but it is a pity that the notes offer a 'press-type' interview with the composer, instead of offering his analysis of the music.

(i) *Flute Sonata, Op. 26;* (ii) *Violin Sonata;* (iii) *Sextet to Julia de Burgos, Op. 21.*
⊕ *** Centaur CRC 2430. (i) Meisenbach; (ii) Lewis; (iii) Lattimore, Ens.; composer.

This is an outstanding CD in every respect, and a more rewarding way to explore the music of Robert Avalon than the concerto pairing above. Both the *Violin* and *Flute Sonatas* are inspired works, profoundly lyrical, showing Avalon writing in a highly communicative and appealingly melodic style, yet with his own individual voice. The Adagio of the *Violin Sonata* has real depth of feeling, and the brief *moto perpetuo* finale ends the piece with infectious brilliance. The *Flute Sonata* is also haunting from the first bar and has a memorably imaginative closing climax to cap the first movement, before the gentle melancholy of the flowing *Adagio.* With the composer at the piano, both performances are outstanding, conveying a natural spontaneity, as at a live performance. The *Sextet,* for soprano, string trio, flute and piano, was inspired by Casals, whom the composer greatly admires. A passionate setting of three extraordinarily intense poems by the Puerto Rican poet Julia de Burgos, it is remarkably colloquial in its Mediterranean style and atmosphere, with the instrumental writing just as ear-catching as the solo line, passionately declaimed here by Jonita Lattimore. The recordings are of great vividness and this collection is highly recommended.

AVISON, Charles (1709–70)

Concerti grossi, Op. 9/1, 4, 6–9.
**(*) Divine Art 2-4108. Georgian Cons.

Charles Avison's set of *Twelve Concertos,* Op. 9, was published in London in 1766. Written in four parts, the composer invites the use of keyboard (notably organ) as a replacement for the violin as the concertino soloist. The music is elegant and easy-going, which is reflected in the pleasingly polished and stylish performances by the Georgian Consort, who play the slightly melancholy slow movements with grace and charm. Their double-dotting, however, could ideally be a shade crisper, and allegros given more bite (although the finale of No. 8 dances agreeably). The recording is natural and the ambience just right and, with the reservations expressed above, this makes enjoyably relaxed listening.

12 Concerti grossi after Scarlatti.
**(*) Hyp. CDA 66891/2. Brandenburg Consort, Goodman.

Those seeking a period-instrument performance of these attractive concertos will find that Roy Goodman's version has plenty of vitality. Fast movements fizz spiritedly, but the linear style of the slower movements, though not lacking expressive feeling, is altogether less smooth, and these performances are essentially for those who are totally converted to the authentic movement. The recording is excellent. However, we still recommend Marriner's pioneering ASMF recording on modern instruments (Ph. Duo 438 806-2).

BABADZHANIAN, Arno
Harutyuni (1921–83)

Heroic Ballade; Nocturne.
*** ASV CDDCA 984. Babakhanian, Armenian PO, Tjeknavorian – TJEKNAVORIAN: *Piano Concerto.* ***

Babadzhanian won a Stalin Prize for the *Heroic Ballade* but, after a flamboyant opening, it turns out to be a rather engaging set of concertante variations. The writing is eclectic (mixing Armenian influences with Rachmaninov and water), returning to populist flamboyance at the close, but not before giving the soloist a chance to be poetically expressive. The performance is excellent, the recording vivid.

(i–iii) Piano Trio in F sharp min.; (ii, iii) Violin Sonata in B flat min. (Piano) (i) Impromptu.
*** Marco Polo 8.225030. (i) Kuyumjian; (ii) Kavafian; (iii) Bagratuni.

Both major works here show a strong lyrical impulse, plenty of ideas, recognizably Armenian in colouring, and an ability to create a cogent whole out of a loosely structured form. The volatile *Violin Sonata* (1959) has plenty of energy, but even the vibrant, syncopated finale gives way to a hauntingly nostalgic closing section – reminiscent of Shostakovich. The *Piano Trio* opens with a grave, sustained *Largo* (whose theme is to dominate the work) and it develops a passionate impetus of a very Russian kind. The catchy, syncopated finale has the energetic rhythmic drive we recognize in Khachaturian's better music, balanced by a warmly flowing secondary theme on the cello. The engaging *Impromptu* for piano acts as a

cantabile encore. The performances here are fierily passionate, but the players relax naturally into tenderness whenever needed. The recording is bright, full and well balanced.

THE BACH FAMILY
before Johann Sebastian

Heinrich Bach (1615–92)
Georg Christoph Bach (1642–97)
Johann Christoph Bach (1642–1703)
Johann Michael Bach (1648–94)

J. C. BACH: Cantatas: *Ach, dass ich Wassers g'nung hätte; Er erhub sich Streit; Die Furcht des Herren; Herr, wende dich und sei mir gnädig; Meine Freundin; Wir bist du denn.* J. M. BACH: Cantatas: *Ach bleib uns, Herr Jesu Christ; Ach, wie sehnlich wart' ich der Zeit; Auf lasst uns den Herren loben; Es ist ein grosser Gewinn; Liebster Jesu, hör mein Flehen.* G. C. BACH: Cantata: *Siehe, wie fein und lieblich.* H. BACH: *Ich danke dir, Gott.*
(M) *** DG Blue 474 552-2 (2) Soloists, Rheinische Kantorei, Col. Mus. Ant., Goebel.

Johann Sebastian not only wrote a short family history, he also made a compilation of the family's music (*Altbachisches Archiv*), which he passed on to Carl Philipp Emanuel. These eventually found their way into the archives of the Berlin Singakademie and were published in 1935; the whole collection was destroyed during the war. These two CDs include all the cantatas and vocal concertos by Bach's forefathers that he preserved, with, in addition, a vocal concerto, *Herr, wende dich*, by Johann Christoph Bach. This survives in an autograph at the Berlin Staatsbibliotek and receives its first publication here in any form.

Johann Michael Bach, who was orgainst and parish clerk at Gehren for the last two decades of his life and died when Johann Sebastian was nine, is represented by his five delightfully fresh and inventive cantatas. He was obviously familiar with such models as Hassler and Praetorius. All are much shorter even than those of Buxtehude and much less ambitious than *Meine Freundin, du bist schön* by his older brother, Johann Christoph, the greatest of Bach's precursors. This is the most substantial of the works on the first disc, and the five other cantatas of his dominate its companion. Bach praised Johann Christoph as profound, and Carl Philipp Emanuel spoke of him as a 'great and expressive composer'. There are certainly many powerful and haunting passages to be found in *Meine Freundin, du bist schön* and the lament *Ach, dass ich Wassers g'nung hätte*. Only one work by his father, Heinrich Bach, survives, the vocal concerto *Ich danke dir, Gott*, a short piece of some six minutes, which calls to mind the Venetian style of Schütz. The last of the four Bachs represented in the set was his nephew Georg Christoph, a cousin of the brothers Johann Michael and Johann Christoph. His charming wedding cantata, *Siehe, wie fein und lie-blich*, records a happy family event. When first issued in 1986, this set broke new ground for the gramophone, and it did so with great distinction. It has more recently been followed by another, equally stimulating set of performances of this repertoire from the Cantus Cölln on Harmonia Mundi, which explores the Bach family tree even more widely (● HMC 901783/84). Even so, this earlier collection (at mid-price) is well worth investigating.

BACH, Carl Philipp Emanuel
(1714–88)

Ton Koopman Edition

Flute Concertos: in D min., Wq.22, H.425; in B flat, Wq.167, H.435; in A, Wq.168, H.428 (with Hünteler; 0630 16183-2).

Flute Concertos: in A min., Wq.166, H.431; in G, Wq.169, H.445 (with Hünteler); *Double Harpsichord Concerto in F, Wq.46, H.408* (with Koopman, Mathot; 0630 16184-2).

Oboe Concertos: in B flat, Wq.164, H.466; in E flat, Wq.165, H.468; Sonata for Oboe & Continuo in G min., Wq.135, H.549 (with Ebbinge; 0630 16182-2).

Double Concerto for Harpsichord & Fortepiano in E flat, Wq.43, H.479 (with Koopman, Mathot); *4 Hamburg Sinfonias, Wq.183/1–4, H.663-6* (0630 16181-2).

Koopman Edition (as above).
(M) ✱✱✱ Erato (ADD) 0630 16180-2 (4). Soloists, Amsterdam Bar. O, Koopman.

If you want all the music in Koopman's collection, these well-recorded performances can certainly be recommended. Konrad Hünteler is a nimble and expressive player and is fully responsive to the *A major Concerto*, Wq.168, while the sprightly *Allegretto* which opens the *B flat major*, Wq.167, is pleasingly vivacious. The spirited and delightful *Concerto for Harpsichord and Fortepiano* and the *F major Double Harpsichord Concerto* are persuasively presented and the recording is deftly balanced. The two *Oboe Concertos* are very appealing in their wide range of mood in Ku Ebbinge's hands. Koopman and his talented Amsterdam players (like their soloists) use period instruments and, while they tend to favour relatively relaxed speeds in the four *Hamburg Sinfonias*, the music-making is very enjoyable in its easy-sounding spontaneity. At present these discs are not available separately.

Flute Concerto in D min., Wq.22.
✱✱✱ HM HMC 901803. Huntgeburth, Berlin Akademie for Alte Musik, Mai – J. C. BACH: *Harpsichord Concerto* etc. ✱✱✱

This highly engaging *Flute Concerto*, written in 1747, is also available in a harpsichord version. But it suits the flute (and indeed the members of the Berlin Akademie) admirably, with its impetuous, brusque outer movements framing an *Andante* that has a melody of great charm. The solo playing from Christoph Huntgeburth is both sensitive and dazzlingly virtuosic, and the recording is excellent.

Keyboard Concertos: in C, Wq.20; in F, Wq.38; Sonatina in D, Wq.102.
✱✱(✱) BIS CD 1127. Miklós Spányi (tangent piano), Concerto Armonico, Szüts.

The most fascinating work here is the concertante *Sonatina* of 1763, which is a series of joined-up and attractively diverse movements, alternating *Allegretto* and *Presto* and winningly scored to include flutes and horns. The two *Concertos* both have quite solemn *Adagios*, with the spirits lifted in the finales, although the opening allegro of the *F major* (1763) is also attractively animated. The first movement of the much earlier *C major* work (1746) opens boldly and vigorously in the orchestra and then maintains a contrasting dialogue, with continuing swift interchanges between the rather gruff tuttis and the lighter keyboard writing. Altogether a rewarding collection, very well played and recorded – the tangent piano has a most pleasing and characterful sound.

Double Concerto for Harpsichord & Fortepiano in E flat, Wq.43.
(BB) ✱✱✱ Warner Apex 2564 61137-2. Uittenbosche, Antonietta, Leonhardt Cons. – J. C. BACH: *Sinfonia concertante in F*; W. F. BACH: *Double Concerto for 2 Harpsichords*; J. S. BACH: *Double Harpsichord Concerto No. 1 in C min. etc.* ✱✱(✱)

The spirited and delightful *E flat Concerto for Harpsichord and Fortepiano*, which comes from Bach's last year, ought to be far better known than it is. The Leonhardt performance is attractive, the fortepiano has a bold, tangible image, and the interplay between the two soloists is felicitous, within a good overall balance. This comes generously coupled with four other *Double Concertos* by members of the Bach family.

Organ Concertos (i): in G, Wq.34; in E flat, Wq.35. Sinfonia for Strings in C, Wq.182/3. (Solo) Organ Sonatas: in F; A min.; G min.; D, Wq.70/3–6.
(M) ✱✱✱ DHM/BMG 82876 51863-2. Oster; (i) Ens. Parlando, Oster or Adorf.

This collection is quite a find. It seems likely that these works (or most of them) were written for Princes Anna Amalia at the Prussian Court; she owned a splendid 22-stop instrument (without pedals). The two *Concertos* are quite different in style. The *G major* of 1754 is written in 'ritornello style' with five orchestral ritornellos alternating with four extended solo episodes. The *E flat major Concerto* (more robustly scored to include horns in the outer movements) has a normal concertante interplay between soloist and orchestra. Both works are attractively inventive, but the *E flat Concerto* has a memorably solemn *Adagio sostenuto*, followed by a robust and busy finale, using the horns most effectively. In between the two concertos comes a *String Sinfonia* in the form of an Italian overture, with a closing *Allegretto*.

The four solo *Sonatas* were written together in the same year. They are fantasia-like, with phrases continually in imitation, using echoing registration, or a chordal sequence, followed by a more florid response. The slow movements are simple and serene, and are registered to bring out the organ colouring, with the *Adagio* of the *G minor*, Wq.70/6, very piquant.

Rainer Oster plays splendidly and uses a highly suitable organ in Saint-Adelphe-in-Albestroff/ Moselle, which has a rich palette and fine sonorities. He is able to create a spatial effect with the answering phrases on different stops, which technique the princess must have relished. Don't be put off by the opening tutti of the *G major Concerto* on the first CD, where the period strings are a bit fierce and biting; the quality soon settles down, and it is generally excellent. The orchestra provides characterful accompaniments, while the organ itself sounds first rate.

4 Hamburg Sinfonias, Wq.183/1–4.
(BB) ** Warner Apex 2564 60369-2. Franz Liszt CO, Rolla.

All six symphonies are accommodated on the Capella Istropolitana's Naxos competitor (8.553285 – see our main volume) and, while Rolla's are expert performances (especially the *B minor*, Wq.182/5, which receives the liveliest advocacy), they are a little dry, as are the recordings, which are bright and clinical. The Naxos disc is the one to have.

KEYBOARD MUSIC

6 Easy Keyboard Sonatas, Nos. 1 in C; 2 in B flat; 3 in A min., Wq. 53/1-3; Sonatas: in B flat & G, Wq.62/16 & 19.
** BIS CD 964. Spányi (clavichord).

6 Easy Keyboard Sonatas, Nos. 4 in B min.; 5 in C; 6 in F, Wq.53/4–6; Keyboard Sonatas: in G min. & C, Wq.62/18 & 20.
** BIS CD 978. Spányi (clavichord).

Miklós Spányi continues his series with two major sonatas and three very simple works written for amateurs. Spányi is recording all the *Sonatas* (previous releases have appeared on BIS 879, 882 and 963) and chooses a clavichord here for his performances (a copy of a German instrument from about 1770). Its sound is comparatively full and robust (take care not to set the volume level too high). His playing is alive and sympathetic, but not everyone will respond to the eccentric little pauses with which he interrupts the melodic flow, especially in slow movements.

Keyboard Sonatas: in F & D, Wq.62/9 & 13; in G & G min., Wq.65/26 & 27; Suite in E min., Wq.62/12.
**(*) BIS CD 1189. Spányi (clavichord).

Keyboard Sonatas in C, G min. & B flat, Wq.65/16, 17 & 20; Fantasia in E flat, W. deest. (H.348).
**(*) BIS CD 1195. Spányi (fortepiano).

The first CD here (BIS 1189) offers four diverse sonatas written in Berlin between 1749 and 1752; they have a *galant* style, although the *E minor* work has more than a little depth. The *Suite* is more strikingly individual and has an attractively expressive *Sarabande* and a lively closing *Gigue*. These works suit the clavichord admirably, and Miklós Spányi uses an appropriate modern copy of a 1785 Dresden instrument, which is recorded most successfully.

The second CD here offers three large-scale *Sonatas* and a *Fantasia*. All three *Sonatas* come from the period 1746–7 and are therefore associated with the new Silbermann fortepiano, which had so captivated Frederick the Great in 1746. Spányi uses a copy of a 1749 Silbermann instrument. The *Sonatas* bear witness to C.P.E. Bach's increasing engagement with the fantasia, for all three have the long, sweeping roulades found in his unmeasured fantasias. Each has some of the rhythmic vagaries that lend them an improvisatory character. As with earlier issues in the series, Spányi plays with scholarly feeling and freshness, although some will not take to his nudging pauses and his *rubato* in slow movements, which sound considered rather than spontaneous. Very truthful recorded sound.

Keyboard Sonatas for Harpsichord: in E min., Wq.62/12, H.66; in E min., Wq.65/5, H.13; in B flat, Wq.65/20, H.51; for Fortepiano: in B flat, Wq.65/44, H.211; in C, Wq.65/47, H.248; in G, Wq.65/48, H.280.
**(*) Metronome MET CD 1032. Cerasi (harpsichord or fortepiano).

In the *Harpsichord Sonatas*, the resonance of the recording does not help Carole Cerasi, but her very free musical line often brings a fussy effect. The opening *Allemande* of the *E minor Sonata*, Wq.62/12, is an obvious example of her very free rubato, and the lively closing *Gigue* too, marvellously articulated as it is, needs a cleaner outline, with the decorations less boldly done.

In the works played on the fortepiano it is the impulsiveness of Cerasi's approach that is daunting, with sudden *forte* accents and forward surges, especially well demonstrated in the finale of the *G major*, Wq.65/48. The preceding *Adagio* is more successful, but even here she seems determined to prove that C. P. E. Bach's music is quixotically temperamental.

BACH, Johann Christian (1735–82)

(i) *Harpsichord Concerto in B, Op. 13/4;*
Symphonies: in E flat; G min., Op. 6/6.
*** HM HMC 901803. Berlin Akademie for Alte
Musik, Mai – C. P. E. BACH: *Flute Concerto.* ***

This collection starts with the *E flat major Symphony*
which, as it opens (unexpectedly) with a delicate
Adagio, may be of questionable authenticity. Here it
is introduced very quietly indeed and, although
there is a slow crescendo, a diminuendo follows and
the listener all but jumps when the *Allegro molto*
begins with an explosive *fortissimo*. As usual with
the Akademie, the string virtuosity is breathtaking,
but *fortissimos* are gruff and accents are strong –
although the pizzicato *Allegretto* brings a brief,
charming interlude.

The *Keyboard Concerto* that follows is one of
Johann Christian's most characterful. It has a bold
opening, but the harpsichord enters elegantly, and
the contrasts between tutti and the gentle keyboard
response are very nicely managed. The *Adagio* brings
more pizzicatos and an amiably *galant* melody, and
the finale produces an equally winning set of variations on the Scottish folksong 'The yellow-hair'd
laddie'.

Bold, staccato accents underline the vigorous,
highly strung opening movement of the *G minor
Symphony*, followed by lurching duplets in the similarly tense *Andante*. The finale is played and accented
with enormous gusto, and again the orchestra is
impressively virtuosic. So, if you like the abrasive
style of this period-instrument ensemble, these
works show the group at their most virile and exciting, and they are very well recorded. Carl Philipp
Emanuel's *Flute Concerto* provides an agreeable light-
hearted contrast.

Sinfonia concertante in F for Oboe, Cello &
Orchestra, T.VIII/6.
(BB) **(*) Warner Apex 2564 61137-2. Schaeftlein,
Bylsma, Leonhardt Cons. – C. P. E. BACH: *Double
Concerto for Harpsichord & Fortepiano* ***; W. F.
BACH: *Double Concerto for 2 Harpsichords*; J. S.
BACH: *Double Harpsichord Concerto No. 1 in C
min. etc.* **(*)

The *Sinfonia concertante in F* is a pleasing but not
distinctive work in two movements, here given a
good rather than a distinctive performance. The key
work of this collection is Carl Philipp Emanuel's
engaging *Concerto for Harpsichord and Fortepiano*.

BACH, Johann Sebastian (1685–1750)

Brandenburg Concertos Nos. 1–6, BWV 1046–51.
(M) *** Warner Elatus 2564 60658-2 (Nos. 1–3); 2564
60803-2 (Nos. 4–6). Il Giardino Armonico, Antonini.
(M) **(*) Astrée ES 9948 (2). Concert des Nations,

Capella Reial de Catalunya, Savall.
**(*) BIS CD 1151/2 (with additional early version of
first movement of No. 5). Bach Coll., Japan, Suzuki.
(M) ** Sony (ADD) 515 305-2 (2). Marlboro Festival O,
Casals (with rehearsal sequences included).

Brandenburg Concertos Nos. 1–6; (i) *Oboe*
Concertos: in A (from BWV 1055); *in D min.* (from
BWV 1059); *in F* (from BWV 1053).
(M) **(*) DG (ADD) 445 578-2 (2). COE, (i) with
Boyd.

Brandenburg Concertos Nos. 1–6; (i) *Violin*
Concertos Nos. 1 in A min.; 2 in E; (i, ii) *Double*
Violin Concerto in D min., BWV 1041–3.
(BB) *** Virgin 2x1 5 61403-2 (2). Scottish Ens., Rees;
with (i) Rees; (ii) Murdoch.

Brandenburg Concertos Nos. 1–6; Brandenburg
Concerto No. 5 (early version), *BWV 1050a; Triple*
Concerto in A min. for Flute, Violin & Harpsichord.
(M) *** Virgin 5 45255-2 (2). La Stravaganza,
Hamburg, Rampe.

These exhilarating performances by Il Giardino
Armonico are highly praised by us in our main *Guide*
as being among the very finest available on period
instruments, and in their mid-priced reissue they
hold their place at the very top of the list, alongside
Pinnock, and they have the advantage of even finer
(1996) recording.

The La Stravaganza *Brandenburgs* are immensely
vigorous and stimulating. Overall, the tempi must be
among the fastest on record (disconcertingly so upon
first hearing) and the throaty hand-horn playing in
the outer movements of No. 1 brings the most
extraordinary virtuosity – while the intonation is
remarkably accurate. The buoyant outer movements
of No. 2 are just as spirited. The strings in No. 3 play
with enormous zest, particularly in the finale. Yet
throughout, slow movements bring the warmest
expressive feeling. No. 5 is offered not only in the 1719
version we know so well but also in an earlier,
chamber version, probably written in Carlsbad a year
earlier, when Bach had only five players at his disposal. It is refreshingly light-textured. The *Triple
Concerto* is played with comparable spirit and
finesse. Outstandingly realistic recording.

The Jonathan Rees modern-instrument Scottish
Brandenburgs are in every way competitive. Directed
with much spirit, they are freshly played, with warm,
clear recording and excellent internal balance. The
tempi seem very apt when the players so convey their
enjoyment and the sound has such a pleasing bloom.
Rees then becomes the principal soloist in equally
warm, buoyant performances of the *Violin Concertos*,
with Jane Murdoch matching his stylishness in the
Double Concerto.

A spirit of fun infects the COE version of the
Brandenburg Concertos. Using modern instruments,
these are among the happiest performances ever,
marked by easily bouncing rhythms and warmly

affectionate – but never sentimental – slow movements. Unfortunately, the first movement of No. 1 – the movement which many will sample first – takes relaxation too far, becoming almost ragged; conversely, the first movement of No. 6 is uncharacteristically rigid. Otherwise these performances, well recorded, give pure joy. The three *Oboe Concertos* are reconstructed from keyboard concertos and cantata movements. The soloist, Douglas Boyd, principal oboe of the COE from its foundation, directs his colleagues in delectable performances. First-rate sound.

Savall's period-instrument set of the *Brandenburgs* is engagingly fresh. Textures are clear and often translucent, allegros are spirited but never rushed, tempi are well judged (No. 3 is just right), and slow movements are warmly expressive yet in perfect style. There is some breathtaking bravura from the hand horns in No. 1, especially in the closing *Polacca and Trio*, but Friedemann Immer's slightly throttled trumpet sounds in No. 2 are less appealing. At other times, ensemble and intonation are not without flaw, but there is no edginess from the strings, and the spontaneous vitality of this playing carries the day. Not a first choice, but an enjoyable one when the sound is so pleasing.

Suzuki's set of the *Brandenburgs* with his Bach Collegium of Japan proves to be a partial disappointment. Of course there is much fine playing from woodwind soloists and the strings (especially in the finale of No. 3), and Suzuki's own harpsichord contribution, notably in Nos. 4 and 5, is pretty dazzling, with the excellent balance ensuring that he does not dominate the texture too much. Tempi are comparatively relaxed and the overall atmosphere is sunny. But unfortunately the brass players let the side down. The horns are clumsy in the first movement of No. 1, and the trumpet playing of Toshio Shimasda in No. 2, using a specially designed coiled trumpet, sounds strained. He uses lip-pressure instead of valves or 'tone-holes' to 'bend' the upper partials to achieve accurate intonation, and some listeners may find the result slightly uncomfortable; others might relish the extra tension.

Casals was 88 in 1964 when he directed these highly individual performances in the Marlborough Festival in Vermont. By the standards of those days, some of the speeds (especially that for the first movement of No. 2) tended to be fast; now they have fallen into place. Against the fast tempi he gives slow, heavy accounts of the two concertos for strings alone, Nos. 3 and 6. Throughout, his approach to phrasing is unashamedly romantic, with a high degree of warm expressiveness in slow movements (sample the *Adagio* of No. 1). Yet the music-making is full of vitality and affection, and the nimble pianoplaying of Rudolf Serkin in the first movement of No. 5 makes a refreshing change from the usual harpsichord. An endearing reminder of a great musician, while the sound is pleasingly full, to suit the warm-hearted nature of the performances.

(i) *Brandenburg Concertos Nos. 1–3*; (ii) *Flute Concerto in E min., BWV 1059 & 35* (reconstructed Radeke).

(BB) ★★★ Warner Apex (DDD/ADD) 2564 61363-2. (i) Amsterdam Bar. O, Koopman; (ii) Rampal, Paillard CO, Paillard.

Brandenburg Concertos Nos. 4–6; (i) *Suite No. 2 in B min., BWV 1067.*

(BB) ★★★ Warner Apex (DDD/ADD) 2564 61364-2. Amsterdam Bar. O, Koopman, (i) with Rampal.

Koopman's account is among the most attractive of those using period instruments, suitable for those who prefer expressive contrasts to be less sharply marked. Like Pinnock, Koopman is not afraid to read *Affettuoso* in the slow movement of No. 5 as genuinely expressive and warm, though without sentimentality. As with Pinnock, the players are one to a part, with excellent British soloists included in the band. In the *Third Concerto*, Koopman effectively interpolates the *Toccata in C*, BWV 916, as a harpsichord link betwen the two movements. The sound is immediate, but not aggressively so. As a bonus on the first disc, Rampal gives a nimble (1972) performance of what is obviously one of his favourite Bach flute concertos, as he has recorded it more than once. Reconstructed by Winfried Radeke, it is based on a harpsichord concerto fragment, BWV 1059 (originally in D minor), and instrumental material from Bach's *Cantata No. 35*. The second disc is even more generous in including Rampal's participation in the *Second B minor Orchestral Suite*.

Brandenburg Concertos Nos. 1–6, BWV 1046–51; Suites Nos. 1–4, BWV 1066–9; (i) *Violin Concertos Nos. 1 in A min.; 2 in E*; (i; ii) *Double Violin Concerto in D min., BWV 1041–3.*

(B) ★★ Ph. Trio (ADD) 470 934-2 (3). ASMF, Marriner; with (i) Szeryng; (ii) Hasson.

The first of the Philips new series of 'Trios' (three CDs in a box, offered for the cost of two mid-priced CDs) is something of a mixed blessing. Like the Duo listed in our main volume, it includes Marriner's outstanding 1980 set of the *Brandenburgs* in which he introduces such distinguished soloists as Szeryng, Rampal and Michaela Petri, and features George Malcolm as an ideal continuo player. But his second Philips recording of the *Orchestral Suites* is no match for his first (1970) ASMF set on Decca, which is still available and sounding pretty good on a single disc (430 378-2). The movements where he has changed his mind – for example, the famous *Air* from the *Suite No. 3*, which is here ponderously slow and mannered – are almost always less convincing, and that reflects an absence of the very qualities of urgency and spontaneity that made the earlier version so enjoyable. Similarly, there are reservations about Szeryng's accounts of the *Violin Concertos*. He had recorded them earlier (also for Philips) with dignity and classical feeling, accompanied by the excellent Winterthur Collegium Musicum, with Peter Rybar a responsive partner in the *Double Concerto*. The slow movements of all three concertos were particularly fine. It is a pity that these performances were not included here, for Szeryng's later record with Marriner, in spite of its fuller, more modern recording with an excellent balance, shows rather less spontaneity (and that in the accompaniments as well as the solo playing). In depth of feeling and understanding, the Winterthur accounts are preferable, although the later versions are by no means to be dismissed.

Brandenburg Concertos Nos. 2–5.
(BB) **(*) DG Entrée 474 560-2 (from above). COE, Boyd.

This music-making would be an almost ideal recommendation as an entrée into Bach's orchestral music if the set on Entrée was complete.

Brandenburg Concertos Nos. 1–6; (i) Triple Concerto for Flute, Violin and Harpsichord; Orchestral Suites Nos. 1–4, BWV 1066–9.
(B) ** DG (ADD) 463 657-2 (3). Munich Bach O, K. Richter; (i) with Nicolet, Hetzel, K. Richter.

In the *Brandenburgs* Karl Richter draws superb playing from his Munich orchestra and the recording is full and clear. His admirers will not be disappointed with this bargain reissue, but in his German way Richter puts the music rather into a rhythmic straitjacket – witness the first movement of No. 6, which needs more persuasive handling. Fortunately, in slow movements he allows a greater degree of expressive relaxation, and this also applies in the *Triple Concerto*, where the effect is warmly romantic, partly because of the rich recorded sound. Aurèle Nicolet's flute playing is delightfully fresh, and in the slow movement Richter provides a neat keyboard embroidery. But in the outer movements the harpsichord is less attractively focused and rhythmically very insistent. Richter's account of the *Orchestral Suites* is more heavy-handed, less spontaneous; moreover he fails to observe the 'double-dotting' convention in the overtures. All in all, this set is primarily of historic interest.

Brandenburg Concertos Nos. 1–6; (i) Violin Concertos Nos. 1–2, BWV 1041/2; in D min., BWV 1052; in G min., BWV 1056; (i; ii) Double Violin Concerto, BWV 1043; (i; iii) Triple Violin Concerto in D, BWV 1064; (i; iv) Concerto for Violin & Oboe, BWV 1060; (i; v) Concerto for Flute, Violin & Harpsichord, BWV 1044.
(BB) *** Virgin 5 62281-2 (4). OAE with (i) Wallfisch; (ii) Bury; (iii) Pavlo Beznosiuk, Mackintosh; (iv) oboist unnamed (v); Lisa Beznosiuk, Nicholson.

With the direction of the *Brandenburgs* shared by four violinists – Monica Huggett, Catherine Mackintosh, Alison Bury and Elizabeth Wallfisch – the Orchestra of the Age of Enlightenment brings all the advantages of light, clear textures and no sense of haste, even when a movement is taken faster than has become traditional. For the *Violin Concertos* Elizabeth Wallfisch takes over as director and principal soloist. Her playing is vigorously stimulating and does not shirk tasteful expressiveness, and her colleagues are equally expert. Their playing has plenty of character, with felicitous, unfussy decoration; the arrangement of the *Triple Harpsichord Concerto* for three violins is particularly convincing. Excellent balance and believable sound make this a highly recommendable budget reissue.

(i) Brandenburg Concerto No. 5 in D, BWV 1050; Triple Concerto in A min. for Flute, Violin & Keyboard, BWV 1044. Italian Concerto, BWV 971.
*** Sony SK 87326. Murray Perahia, (i) with Jaime Martin, Kenneth Sillito, Jacob Lindberg, ASMF.

Murray Perahia's *Fifth Brandenburg* is among the freshest and most enjoyable we have heard since Serkin and the Busch Chamber Players, which of course it surpasses in recording quality, but also, in many respects, artistically. The excellence of Perahia's Bach is well known, and his peerless pianism is perfectly displayed in the *Concerto in the Italian Style* where refinement of keyboard colour and feeling for line are much in evidence. Bach playing on the keyboard (piano or harpsichord) does not come better than this.

Harpsichord Concertos Nos. 1 in D min.; 2 in E; 5 in F min.; 6 in F, BWV 1052–3 & 1056–7.
(M) *(*) Warner Elatus 2564 60329-2. Koopman, Amsterdam. Bar. Ens.

Warner are now reissuing Ton Koopman's complete coverage of the *Harpsichord Concertos* from the late 1980s and early 1990s. He is a fine player who has many fine Bach recordings to his name. However, the present set is disappointing. The harpsichords are made to sound unpleasantly jangly, with mechanical noise intruding, while the orchestra sounds too heavy, lacking the transparency of period performances, with Koopman often failing to lift rhythms. Pinnock is far preferable in this repertoire (DG Trio 471 754-2 – see our main volume).

Harpsichord Concerto No. 3 in D, BWV 1054; Concerto for Violin & Oboe in C min., BWV 1060; Violin Concertos: in D min., BWV 1052; in G min., BWV 1056.
*** Virgin 5 45361-2. Ciomei, Biondi, Bernadini, Europe Galante.

In the hands of such fine players these four works, all familiar and all reconstructed from other concertos, make a rewarding collection, casting new light on the music, when the performances are so freshly and warmly played (on period instruments) and beautifully recorded. The *Double Concerto for Violin and Oboe* is a highlight, for Alfredo Bernadini's baroque oboe has a most appealing timbre and the balance with the violin is felicitous. Fabio Biondi, playing spiritedly and with easy virtuosity, then makes a good case for the two transcribed *Violin Concertos* (arranged from keyboard concertos), and his expressive line in the two slow movements is also memorable.

(i) *Double Harpsichord Concerto No. 1 in C min., BWV 1060;* (ii) *Double Concerto in D min. for Oboe & Violin.*

(BB) **(*) Warner Apex 2564 61137-2. (i) Leonhardt, Miller, VCM, Harnoncourt; (ii) Schaeftlein, Alice Harnoncourt, Leonhardt Cons. – J. C. BACH: *Sinfonia concertante in F* **(*); C. P. E. BACH: *Double Concerto for Harpsichord and Fortepiano* ***; W. F. BACH: *Double Concerto for 2 Harpsichords* **(*).

These are enjoyable performances from two different sources, although the *Andante* of the *Double Harpsichord Concerto* is a little heavy-handed, and in the work for oboe and violin Alice Harnoncourt is balanced rather backwardly, seeming to be placed within the orchestra itself. However, here the *Adagio* is beautifully played and the outer movements have plenty of vitality. The analogue recordings have transferred faithfully to CD. The main interest of this inexpensive reissue is the very winning *Concerto for Harpsichord and Fortepiano* by Carl Philipp Emanuel.

(i) *Violin Concertos Nos. 1–2 in E, BWV 1041–2;* (ii) *Double Concerto in D min., BWV 1043;* (iii) *Double Concerto for Violin and Oboe in C min., BWV 1060.*

(M) **(*) EMI (ADD/DDD) 5 62602-2. Perlman, with (i, ii) ECO, Barenboim; (ii) Zukerman; (iii) with Ray Still, Israel PO.

Perlman's two solo concertos and the *Double Violin Concerto* with Zukerman (recorded in the early 1970s) are in every way recommendable and are available on a budget EMI Encore CD (5 74720-2), praised in our main volume. For the 'Perlman Edition' EMI have added the *Concerto for Violin and Oboe*, recorded in Tel Aviv in 1982 which is not an asset. The sound is dry and close and the performance (directed by Perlman himself) is heavy in the first two movements, with the *Largo* almost coming to a halt!

Violin Concertos Nos. 1–2; (i) *Double Concerto;* (ii) *Triple Concerto for Flute, Violin & Harpsichord, BWV 1044.*

(B) *** DG 463 014-2. Standage, E. Concert, Pinnock; with (i) Wilcock; (ii) Beznosiuk, Pinnock.

This collection of violin concertos, played on original instruments, is welcome back into the catalogue. Rhythms are crisp and lifted at nicely chosen speeds – not too fast for slow movements – and the solo playing is very stylish. The *Triple Concerto* is also very successful. The only snag is the edge on violin timbre, which will not please all ears.

Violin Concerto No. 2 in E, BWV 1042.

**(*) Simax PSC 1159. Tellefsen, Oslo Festival Strings, Berglund – SHOSTAKOVICH: *Violin Concerto No. 1.* **(*)

(M) *(*) BBC (ADD) BBCL 4050-2. Menuhin, ECO, Malcolm – BRAHMS: *Double Concerto.* MENDELSSOHN: *Violin Concerto.* *(*)

Arve Tellefsen has never enjoyed the international exposure to which his gifts entitle him, but he is a fine musician who plays with great spirit, and he is well recorded too. Good, stylish playing that should enjoy wide appeal.

Menuhin's BBC version of the *E major Concerto* was recorded at the Aldeburgh Festival in 1963. It is conducted well by George Malcolm and played decently, although Menuhin is nowhere near his best.

(i) *Double Violin Concerto, BWV 1043.* Suite No. 3, BWV 1068: Air (arr. Wilhelmj). (Unaccompanied) *Violin Sonata No. 1 in G min., BWV 1001: Adagio.*

(M) (***) Biddulph mono LAB 056-7 [id.]. Arnold Rosé, (i) with Alma Rosé, O – BEETHOVEN: *String Quartets Nos. 4, 10 & 14.* (***)

Arnold Rosé's sonata-partner was Bruno Walter and his brother-in-law was Mahler. His daughter, Alma, with whom he is heard in a 1931 recording of the Bach *D minor Double Concerto*, perished in Auschwitz. Interesting though these recordings are, the principal musical rewards in the set come from the three Beethoven quartets with which they are coupled.

(i) *Double Violin Concerto in D min., BWV 1043;* (ii) (Unaccompanied) *Cello Suite No. 1 in C: Bourrée I & II.*

(*) EMI **DVD 490449-9. (i) D. Oistrakh, Y. Menuhin, RTF CO, Capdevielle; (ii) Rostropovich – MOZART: *Sinfonia concertante;* BRAHMS: *Double Concerto.* **(*)

The *Double Concerto in D minor* was recorded at the Salle Pleyel in October 1958 with the French Radio Chamber Orchestra under Pierre Capdevielle. The two great soloists first played this together at the 1947 'Prague Spring', and their Paris account affords an admirable opportunity for contrasting the golden tone of the one with the (on this occasion) seraphic playing of the other. Of course the sound calls for some tolerance, but this film is a rarity and is to be treasured. Rostropovich playing with enormous intensity the *Bourrées* from the *Third Suite for Solo Cello*, recorded in December 1962, is a welcome bonus.

Orchestral Suites Nos. 1–4, BWV 1066–9.

🔚 *** Telarc CD 80619. Boston Bar., Pearlman.

(B) ** DG 463013-2. E. Concert, Pinnock.

A spendid new period-instrument recording of the *Orchestral Suites* from the excellent Boston Baroque under Martin Pearlman. All four fit onto a single CD, yet speeds are well judged and lively but not pressed too hard. Pearlman does not present the *Suites* in the usual way but follows the order of composition as suggested by modern scholarship. Thus No. 4 comes first, followed by Nos. 1, 3 and 2. For continued listening this works very well, with the famous *Badinerie* (with stylish flute-playing from Christopher Krueger) making a sprightly end to the programme. Period-instrument playing has come a long way in the last decade, and it is a joy to hear the famous *Air* from the *Third Suite* sounding warmly expressive again instead of vinegary. But what is especially attractive about these performances, apart from their buoyancy, is the internal clarity of the woodwind interplay within a warm acoustic. Altogether these are most enjoyable performances and they are given first-class Telarc recording.

Pinnock's earlier, analogue recording of the *Suites* (now neatly fitted onto a single CD), dates from 1979, when period-instrument performances were still full of stylistic excesses, and the unprepared listener could find the bright edge on the squeezed vibrato-less string-timbres disconcerting.

(Orchestral) Suites Nos. 1–4, BWV 1066–9 (transcribed for guitar quartet by Amaral or Gloeden).
*** Delos DE 3254. Brazilian Guitar Qt.

The baroque era, and the music of Bach in particular, was a watershed for transcribing music from one set of instruments to another, so there is no absence of precedent for what seems a very audacious modern arrangement of the four *Orchestral Suites* for guitar quartet (made by two members of this Brazilian group). The result is astonishingly successful, with the four instruments perfectly integrated in ensemble, while contrapuntal detail emerges clearly within a pleasingly warm ambience. The playing itself is expert, choice of tempi is relaxed but seems unerringly apt, and these players never sentimentalize: the famous *Air* from the *Third Suite* (placed first on the CD) is most appealing, as is the *Sarabande* of the *Second*. The rhythms of the following *Bourrées* are engagingly crisp, as is the ensuing *Polonaise and Double*. One misses the flute most in the *Badinerie*, but this too remains bright and attractive. More surprisingly, it is the lesser known *First* and *Third Suites* that are given the most refreshing new presentation by the well-lifted rhythms of the playing here. The expert and communicative music-making is very enjoyable throughout, making this more than just a disc for guitar specialists.

Orchestral Suite No. 3 in D, BWV 1068.
**(*) Testament SBT2 1217 (2). BPO, Klemperer –
BEETHOVEN: *Symphony No. 6 (Pastoral)*;
MOZART: *Symphony No. 29.* ****(*)**

In May 1964 Otto Klemperer, then aged 79, returned to Berlin to conduct the Berlin Philharmonic in three works that were favourites with him, and he won a rapturous reception. It was over forty years since his first appearance with the Berlin Philharmonic, and he seemed determined above all to get Karajan's orchestra to produce a distinctive 'Klemperer' sound. The Bach is weightily traditional with the *Air* expansively romantic.

CHAMBER MUSIC

The Art of Fugue, BWV 1080.
**(*) DG 474 495-2. Emerson Qt.
**(*) ECM 1652. Keller Qt.
** MDG 619 0989-2. Calefax Reed Quintet.
** DG 463 027-2. Cologne Musica Antiqua, Goebel.

The Emerson Quartet move through Bach's fugal masterpiece with great concentration, revealing every detail. They are closely balanced and play immaculately with a fine body of tone, yet with a purposeful briskness that some will find unrelenting, although the cello solo in *Contrapunctus III* has a deep underlying expressive feeling. Then, from the *Canon per Augmentationem* onwards, the players' approach suddenly mellows and becomes quite touching (with vibrato bringing warmth), carrying through to the closing chorale, *Von deinen Thron tret ich Hiermat*, which acts as a reverent epilogue.

The Hungarian Keller Quartet gives the impression of using a fair degree of vibrato, and this brings a more expressive style, so that the cello solo that opens *Contrapunctus III* is almost a lament. There is plenty of variety of both mood and tempo. Nevertheless, keyboard versions delineate the part-writing more pointedly. The recording is full and naturally balanced.

The five players of the Calefax Quintet play many more than five instruments, including oboe d'amore, cor anglais, basset horn, bass clarinet, soprano and alto saxophones. The palette of colours they produce often gives an exotic tinge to Bach's contrapuntal exploration, although lively rhythms and sensible tempi prevent the results from being too eccentric. Nevertheless, this version is obviously aimed at the listener for whom variety of colour is essential to approach Bach's polyphony agreeably.

Goebel's Cologne Musica Antiqua performance has genuine vitality, but the bite on the string-tone, and also the expressive bulges, which at times are exaggerated, will pose a listening problem for some listeners. The Delmé Quartet on Hyperion CD 67138 (see our main volume) outclasses other string quartet versions.

(Unaccompanied) Cello Suites Nos. 1–6, BWV 1007–12.
⊕—ᵥ ⊕ *** EMI DVD DVA 5 99159 9. Rostropovich.

Rostropovich was filmed recording the six Bach *Cello Suites* in 1991 in the Basilique Sainte Madeleine, Vézelay, Yonne, France, a venue he chose for the comparative severity of its interior architecture, which, he felt, created the right backcloth for the music. He introduces the whole project by telling us about his own approach to the interpretation of these masterpieces, with which he has lived all his life, and of his visit to Casals, who played Bach especially for him, creating a rhapsodical dialogue that took his presence into account. Rostropovich then verbally characterizes each one of the *Suites* before he performs it, moving through sorrow and intensity, brilliance and majesty, and from darkness into the sunlight of the *Sixth, D major* work, which he describes as a '*Symphony for Solo Cello*'. The analyses he offers on the way are as much connected with emotions and feelings as with the intellect and are easy to follow. Of course, one can choose to hear the music without the commentaries. The performances hardly need recommendation from us: they are totally compelling and truthfully recorded.

(Unaccompanied) *Cello Suites Nos. 1–6, BWV 1007–12.*
(M) (★★★) EMI mono 5 62611-2 562617-2 (2). Pablo Casals.
(BB) ★★(★) Warner Apex (ADD). Harnoncourt.

It was Casals who restored these pieces to the repertory, after long decades of neglect. Some of the playing is far from flawless; passage-work is rushed or articulation uneven, and he is often wayward. But he brought to the *Cello Suites* insights that remain unrivalled, and he brings one closer to the music than most other performers of this extraordinary music. Just sample the *Fourth Suite*, which opens the second disc, to experience the remarkably live and spontaneous character of this Bach-playing. The recordings, dating from 1936 and 1938, have been freshly remastered for this reissue as one of EMI's 'Great Recordings of the Century', and their presence is uncanny.

Nikolaus Harnoncourt's performances, recorded in 1965, remind us that he was a cellist before he became a conductor, and a very good one. They suggest that we are eavesdropping on a solitary musician communing with Bach in private for his own pleasure, rather than projecting the music as at a concert performance. There are moments (for instance, in the *First* and *Fourth Suites*), when the playing could be more positive and rhythmically crisper, yet there are others too where one can feel the cellist's affectionate response to Bach's lyrical phrases. The recording is intimate to match, and this is a fascinating document that should attract all those who admire Harnoncourt's work on the rostrum.

(Unaccompanied) *Cello Suites Nos. 1–6, BWV 1007–12; (i) Viola da gamba Sonatas Nos. 1–2, BWV 1027–8.*
(M) ★★(★) Mercury (IMS) 432 756-2 (2). Starker, (i) with Sebök.

Janos Starker's performances come from 1963 and 1965 and are of great integrity and dedication, with

out having quite the same electric communication of his earlier, mono recording. The two *Viola da gamba Sonatas* are not ideally balanced and favour György Sebök's piano, though there is no question of his artistry.

(Unaccompanied) *Cello Suite No. 1 in G, BWV 1007.*
(M) (★★★) EMI mono 5 67008-2. Casals –
BEETHOVEN: *Cello Sonata No. 3;* BRAHMS: *Cello Sonata No. 2.* (★★★)

The *G major Suite* was recorded in 1938, and nobility shines through every bar. Of course this is available with the other suites, but duplication is worthwhile for the sake of its companions.

(i) *Unaccompanied Cello Suites Nos. 1–6, BWV 1007–12.*

(ii) *Lute Suites* (arr. for guitar) *Nos. 1–4, BWV 995–7 & 1006a; Fugue in G min., BWV 1000; Prelude, Fugue & Allegro in E flat, BWV 998; Prelude in C min., BWV 999.* Guitar Transcriptions:
Arrangements of Cello Suites: Nos. 1 in G, BWV 1007 (trans. in E flat); *2 in D min., BWV 1008* (trans. in G min.); *6 in D, BWV 1012* (trans. in E flat): *Sarabande & Gavotte* (only). *Arrangement of Violin Sonata No. 3 in C, BWV 1005* (trans. in B flat).

(iii) *(Unaccompanied) Violin Sonatas Nos. 1–3, & Partitas Nos. 1–3, BWV 1001–1006.*
(B) ★★(★) DG 474 641-2 (6) (i) Maisky; (ii) Söllscher (guitar); (iii) Mintz.

This compilation in DG's bargain-price Collector's Edition is more of a mixed bag than usual, although all the recordings are digital and come from the 1980s (except the guitar transcriptions, which date from 1981). Mischa Maisky's performances of the *Cello Suites* are beautifully cultured and played at a high emotional temperature. However, he is rather less inclined to let the music speak for itself than some of his rivals. The *Sarabande* of the *D minor Suite* is a little narcissistic, nor is that of No. 5 in *C minor* free from affectation. There are times in the quicker dance movements when one longs for him to move on – the *Allemande* of No. 6 is taken excessively slowly. However, there is no doubt that he makes an absolutely glorious musical sound and commands an unusually wide range of colour and tone.

By contrast, the distinguished guitarist Göran Söllscher is not in the least self-indulgent in his approach to Bach, and his performances of the *Lute Suites* are thoughtful, highly musical and technically impeccable. There is judicious use of light and shade; they also have the semi-improvisational quality of a live recital. He uses an eleven-stringed guitar especially made for Renaissance and Baroque repertoire, which is beautifully recorded here within an agreeably warm acoustic. While the inclusion of his own transcriptions of the works for violin and cello necessitate changes of pitch, there is no reason in principle why they should not work well enough on the guitar. However, although his performances are of the usual high calibre, and he is at his very best in the *Sarabandes*, played very freely but not eccentrically, overall the music just fails to lift off in this format.

Shlomo Mintz takes all the technical difficulties of the solo *Violin Sonatas* in his stride, and again he is excellently recorded in a suitable acoustic. His playing has youthful vitality and power, and generally these recorded accounts give much musical satisfaction. But the famous *Chaconne* from the *D minor Partita* finds him wanting. Intonation is generally secure but goes seriously awry in the middle of the *G minor Fugue*. The sound is bold and clear, but this would not be a first choice among recorded versions.

A Musical Offering, BWV 1079.
(B) **(*) HM (ADD) HMA 1951260. Moroney, Cook, See, Holloway, Ter Linden.

The introductory *Ricercar* and first group of *Canons* are presented clearly but not pedantically on one or two harpsichords, and the sensitively played *Trio Sonata* follows, given added colour by using flute, violin and continuo. The *Canon perpetua* is then heard on the same combination, and for all the remaining *Canons*, except one, Moroney returns to his harpsichord(s). Good recording, truthfully transferred.

Flute Sonatas Nos. 1–6, BWV 1030–35.
⊝⊸ (BB) *** ASV Resonance CD RSN 3008. Bennett, Malcolm (harpsichord), M. Evans.

Flute Sonatas Nos. 1–6, BWV 1030–5; in G min., BWV 1020; Partita in A min. (for solo flute), BWV 1013; Trio Sonata in G, BWV 1039.
** Hyp. CDA 67264/5. Beznosiuk, Nicholson, Tunnicliffe; with Kenny (archlute in BWV 1031); Brown (2nd flute in BWV 1039).

Flute Sonatas Nos. 1–6; Partita, BWV 1013; Trio Sonatas, BWV 1038–9; Suite, BWV 997.
(M) **(*) Häns. CD 92.121 (2). Gérard, Azzaloni, Blumenthal, Forchert, Formisano, Kleiner.

Flute Sonatas Nos. 1, 4, & 6, BWV 1030, 1033 & 1035; Trio Sonata (for 2 flutes & continuo), BWV 1039; (Solo) Flute Partita, BWV 1013.
**(*) MDG 309 0932-2. Kaiser, Musica Alta Ripa.

Flute Sonatas Nos. 2, 3, & 5, BWV 1031–2 & 1034; in C min., BWV 1079 (from Musical Offering); Trio Sonata (for flute, violin & continuo), BWV 1038.
**(*) MDG 309 0931-2. Kaiser, Musica Alta Ripa.

William Bennett uses a modern flute, and in the first three sonatas he and George Malcolm manage without the nicety of using a viola da gamba in the continuo. In *Sonatas Nos. 4–6* the two players are joined by Michael Evans, and the bass is subtly but tangibly reinforced and filled out, though the balance

remains just as impressive. The playing, as might be expected of these artists, has superb character: it is strong in personality yet does not lack finesse. Moreover it is strikingly alive and spontaneous and, since the CD transfer brings the most vivid presence without the sound being in the least overblown, this budget reissue can be enthusiastically recommended to all but those who demand the finer points of authenticity above all else. Bennett himself has made the reconstruction of the first movement of BWV 1032.

Jean-Claude Gérard is a fine player, but it seems curious that all this repertoire should have been recorded (in 1999) with piano instead of harpsichord and using a bassoon continuo. This is all very musical and pleasing enough in its way, but is hardly a first choice.

Karl Kaiser is a thoroughly musical and accomplished soloist, and the members of Musica Alta Ripa all play period instruments very smoothly. Their performances are stylishly pleasing, if at times perhaps a little bland. Twice they use a fortepiano rather than a harpsichord (BWV 1035 and 1039), but to good effect. The set is well balanced and truthfully recorded, but would not be a first choice.

After their success with Handel (CDA 67278 – see our main volume) these performances by the Beznosiuk/Nicholson/Tunnicliffe team are a disappointment. The playing lacks sparkle, but the group are not helped by the too-reverberant acoustic, which puts a resonant halo round the flute timbre in the solo *Partita*, and prevents internal clarity in the *Trio Sonata*. Moreover, the harpsichord is too backwardly placed.

Flute Sonatas Nos. 1; 3; 5; 6, BWV 1030, 1032, 1034–5.
(BB) **(*) HM HCX 3957024. See, Moroney (harpsichord), Springfield.

Flute Sonatas Nos. 1, 4, 5, & 6; (Solo) Partita, BWV 1013.
**(*) Channel CCS 15798. Solomon, Charlston.

The *American Capital Times* describes the See/ Moroney performances as 'wickedly charming'. Janet See's baroque flute has a warm yet watery timbre, which is rather appealing, as is her lyrical phrasing, while she is chipper and lively in the allegros. Moroney's support is impeccable, and Mary Springfield adds the viola da gamba part very neatly in the two last works. The balance is excellent and this is certainly refreshing, but the disc is upstaged by Marc Beaucondray and William Christie, who offer the same music.

Ashley Solomon's solo playing is always flexible and spontaneous in feeling (especially in the solo *Partita*), and Terry Charlston makes up an impressive partnership. They too are well recorded, but the snag here is that the close microphones mean that every time Solomon takes a breath it is all too audible, which could be a problem for some listeners.

Violin sonatas

(Unaccompanied) *Violin Sonatas Nos. 1–3, BWV 1001, 1003 & 1005; Violin Partitas Nos. 1–3, BWV 1002, 1004 & 1006.*

(B) **(*) EMI (ADD) double forte 5 73644-2 (2). Suk.

**(*) Analecta FL 2 3147-8 (2). Ehnes.

**(*) Channel CCS 12198 & 14498. Podger.

(B) ** Teldec Ultima 3984 21035-2 (2). Zehetmair.

Josef Suk is a superb artist – but his playing, although technically immaculate, is curiously self-conscious. There seems a tendency to over-inflate the music with broad tempi, and these are not the searching performances one expects in this repertoire.

James Ehnes, the prize-winning young Canadian violinist, gives traditional readings, which may not be quite as distinctive as some, but they have a concentration that, combined with flawless technique, makes them constantly compelling. Ehnes tends to favour broad speeds in the slower movements, so that the initial impression of the opening Adagio of the *First Sonata* is one of heaviness. In context, on repeated hearings, the Ehnes approach is readily acceptable, with those slow openings consistent with the unforced concentration of the rest. Final movements tend to be taken fast, with exhilarating results, and with slow movements such as the *Sarabande* of the *Partita No. 1* beautifully tender. Not only that; Ehnes in the biggest challenge of all, the great *Chaconne* that concludes the *D minor Partita*, crowns the whole sequence with his finest performance, readily sustaining the massive scale, so the minor-key variations of the first half lead with seeming inevitability to the moment of resolution when, at a hushed *pianissimo*, D minor resolves on D major, with Ehnes at his most dedicated. Excellent recording.

Rachel Podger uses a period instrument, but her technique and intonation are secure, her tone is full and clean without scratchiness or edge. Only in slow movements is there a minor reservation about the linear style, with moments of minor tonal swelling slightly disturbing the phrasing. There is much to praise in this artist's simplicity of approach, and she is beautifully recorded, but in the last resort this cannot quite compete with the very finest versions.

Thomas Zehetmair's style is curiously restless; his line tends to have subtle dynamic surges, a feeling almost of rocking between phrases, and the effect is at times emotionally jagged; even the famous *Chaconne* of BWV 1004 could be more positive. Yet the pieces that depend on running passage-work (the *Courant* of the *Partita in B minor*, the *Gigue* of the *D minor* or the brilliant Presto of the *G minor Sonata*) are played with a wonderful, lightly articulated bravura which has much imaginative light and shade, while the *Fuga* of the *A minor Sonata* has its simple polyphony well under control without being tense. But in a piece like the *Siciliana*, which precedes that Presto of BWV 1001, the improvisatory restlessness disturbs Bach's underlying serenity, and elsewhere the feeling that the music runs like a mountain stream, over pebbles certainly but essentially flowing onward, is often disturbed in these readings. The recording is close but faithful and gives a very realistic impression against an acoustic which is not too dry.

Sitkovetsky has a beautiful tone and his polished fluency is technically and musically admirable. But everything is too easy-going, there is no sense of grip, of difficulties being surmounted, of a strong forward pulse (Hänssler 92.119). Perlman (❋ EMI 7 49483-2) or Milstein (☞ DG 457 701-2) still remain at the top of the list of recommendations – see our main volume.

(Unaccompanied) *Violin Sonatas Nos. 1–3; Violin Partitas Nos. 1–3;* (i) *Violin Sonatas Nos. 3–4, BWV 1016–17.*

(M) **(*) Ph. (ADD) 464 673-2 (2). Grumiaux ; (i) with Sartori (harpsichord).

(Unaccompanied) *Violin Sonatas Nos. 1–3; & Partitas Nos. 1–3, BWV 1001–6.*

(BB) *(*) Virgin 2 × 1 5 62340-2. Huggett.

Grumiaux's set of the solo *Sonatas* and *Partitas* is available economically on a Philips Duo (438 236-2). His musical authority and purity of intonation impress every bit as much as they did in 1960 when they were made, and the sound has striking realism. There is an aristocratic quality to Grumiaux's playing as well as a natural unforced vitality. Here these performances are offered as one of Philips's '50 Great Recordings' at mid-price with two of the *Sonatas for Violin and Harpsichord* thrown in for good measure. But these were Grumiaux's earlier recordings with Egida Giordani Sartori, which, though his own playing is peerless, were less spontaneous in effect than his later set with Jaccottet (which received a ❋ in our main volume – Philips Duo 454 011-2).

Monica Huggett plays her period instrument with skill and accuracy, but she fails to communicate the inner world of this music. She uses considerable nudgings of rubato and momentary pauses, but the result is curiously uninvolving. Although a piece like the fourth–movement *Double* of the *B minor Partita* offers a beautifully articulated stream of notes, which is technically very impressive, the famous *Chaconne* from the *D minor Partita* is made to sound uninvolved and didactic. She is given first-class recording.

(Unaccompanied) *Violin Sonatas Nos. 1–3, Violin Partitas Nos. 1–3; Violin Sonata No. 3, BWV 1016* (2 versions).

(BB) (***) Naxos mono 8.110918 & 8.110964. Y. Menuhin, with alternatively H. Menuhin or Landowska.

Menuhin's early recordings of the solo *Violin Sonatas* and *Partitas* are also available on Naxos. Ward Marston's transfers are expert, but the sound is not quite as smooth as that transferred by the EMI engineers (who had access to the original masters), and there is slightly more background noise. However, the inclusion of Menuhin's two recordings, made in 1938 and 1944 respectively, of the *E major Violin and Harpsichord Sonata* makes a fascinating comparison, the performance with Landowska's harpsichord slower and heavier in style (especially the *Adagio*) than the fresher version with his sister Hephzibah on the piano.

(Unaccompanied) *Violin Partitas Nos. 2, BWV 1004* (complete); *3 (Minuets I & II only), BWV 1006; Violin Sonatas Nos. 1, BWV 1001; 3, BWV 1005* (complete); (i) *English Suite No. 3 in E, BWV 808: Sarabande; Gavottes Nos. I & II.*

(M) (***) EMI mono 7 64494-2. Heifetz, (i) with Sándor.

Heifetz's Bach was by no means romantic, but his chimerical bowing produces more variety of timbre and subtlety of dynamic shading than would have been likely or possible in Bach's time, while the great *Chaconne* has wonderful detail without losing strength. Such is the spontaneity of effect that the result gives enormous pleasure. The transfer is bright but truthful.

Violin and Harpsichord Sonatas Nos. 1–4, BWV 1014–17.

(BB) *** HM Classical Express HCX 395 7084. Blumenstock, Butt (harpsichord).

In what is presumably to become a complete set, the first instalment from Elizabeth Blumenstock and John Butt is very promising indeed. At the opening *Adagio* of the *B minor Sonata*, BWV 1014, John Butt's introduction is pleasingly free and thoughtful, and the violin entry on a gentle crescendo is just as compelling. Throughout, allegros are engagingly spirited, articulation clean without a hint of didacticism and the interplay between these two artists is constantly stimulating. How delightful is the catchy second movement of the *E major Sonata*, BWV 1016! Elizabeth Blumenstock plays a Strad (and her judicious use of vibrato and refined style are wholly apt for this repertoire); John Butt uses a modern copy of a 1646 Rückers, enlarged in 1780 by Taskin, and the two players are beautifully balanced and recorded. Most enjoyable – highly recommended.

KEYBOARD MUSIC

The Art of Fugue; BWV 1080.

*** MusicMasters 1612 67173-2. Feltsman (piano).

The Art of Fugue, BWV 1080; Partita No. 2 in C min., BWV 826.

(M) **(*) OPS 52-9116/17. Sokolov (piano).

Although he begins gently, Vladimir Feltsman's articulation is at times bold, although it is never

hard-edged. He intersperses the *Canons* individually within the body of the work and makes the very most of dynamic contrast. Yet he can be thoughtfully meditative. Feltsman's interpretation is well thought out and thoroughly convincing. He is very well recorded but offers no coupling.

Sokolov's *Art of Fugue* is entirely pianistic. He is neither pedagogic nor didactic, but his linear clarity is admirable. He uses a wide range of dynamic and one can hear the fullest polyphonic detail, yet the music's underlying expressive character emerges readily. The nineteen *Contrapuncti* are played in order, ending – at the beginning of the second disc – with the unfinished No. 19, presented very slowly. He then groups the *Canons* together and closes the work with a deliberate rallentando. The *C minor Partita* makes a lively and characterful encore.

Chromatic Fantasia & Fugue in D min., BWV 903; 4 Duets, BWV 802–5; Italian Concerto in F, BWV 971; Partita in B min., BWV 831.

❀ (M) *** Decca 4761704. Rousset (harpsichord).

(BB) **(*) Warner Apex 8573 89224-2. Ross (harpsichord).

Christophe Rousset's admirable Bach collection (originally issued on L'Oiseau-Lyre) has been chosen to launch the new mid-priced Universal Classics 'Penguin ❀ Collection', recordings which over the years have earned a personal accolade from one or other of the authors of the *CD Guide*. They are given a handsome livery, each cover framing a miniature reproduction of the original frontispiece, and quoting from our review. Rousset's disc well deserves its place of honour. His playing combines the selfless authority and scholarly dedication of such artists as Gustav Leonhardt and Kenneth Gilbert with the flair and imagination of the younger players, and all the performances here have a taste and musical vitality that reward the listener.

Scott Ross's account of the *Chromatic Fantasia* has less flair than Rousset's. Some may respond to its breadth, emphasized by the full-bodied, resonant harpsichord image. These are undoubtedly fine performances, considered and in excellent style, but at times seemingly a little didactic. They are rewarding, but not a first choice in this repertoire, even at budget price.

Concertos (for solo harpsichord): after Vivaldi, Nos. 1 in D (after Op. 3/9), BWV 972; 2 in C (after Op. 7/2), BWV 973; 4 in G min. (after Op. 4/6), BWV 975; 5 in C (after Op. 3/12), BWV 976; 7 in F (after Op. 3/3), BWV 978; 9 in G (after Op. 4/1), BWV 980; Italian Concerto, BWV 971.

❀ (M) *** Warner Elatus 2564 60362-2. Olivier Baumont (harpsichord).

We are more used to hearing Bach's transcriptions of Italian concertos on the organ, but these works were probably intended for either a harpsichord or even possibly a chamber organ without pedals. In Olivier

Baumont's hands they sound splendid on the harpsichord, full of vitality and vividly coloured. Baumont plays a modern French copy of a German harpsichord 'from the School of Silbermann' of 1735, and it has a particularly effective range of dynamics. He produces some impressively dramatic staccato effects in the slow movement of Op. 4/6, but throughout his playing has irresistible panache. The most famous *Italian Concerto* is used as an encore – and how eloquently Baumont phrases the slow movement. This collection is very enjoyable undeed, a disc to cheer you up on a dull day!

English Suites Nos. 1–6, BWV 806–11.
☙ *** Hyp. **SACD**: SACDA 67451/2; CD: CDA 67451/2. Hewitt (piano).

With her recordings of the *English Suites* Angela Hewitt caps her outstanding series of Bach's keyboard music on the piano. Of course, they are only English in that they were apparently commissioned by an Englishman; otherwise, like Bach's companion *French Suites* they offer the usual collection of dance movements, with a mixture of French, German and Italian influences. However, as Hewitt comments in her accompanying notes, the opening *Preludes* (which she relishes) show Bach at his most imaginative and exploratory. But it is in the *Sarabandes* that she finds a depth of feeling and richness of colour that is possible only on the piano, while the exuberant closing *Gigues* (sample that for No. 4) are sparklingly buoyant and spirited. The recording on CD is first class; we see no reason to prefer the SACD, except for those wanting reproduction in surround-sound.

French Suites Nos. 1–6, BWV 812–17; Suites: in A min., BWV 818a; in E flat, BWV 819a.
**(*) BIS CD 1113/4 (with alternative version of the *Allemande* from the *Suite in E flat, BWV 819a*). Suzuki (harpsichord).

Maasaki Suzuki's performances of the *French Suites* are thoroughly musical and thoughtful and, of course beautifully played. But his restrained introversion at times sometimes seems to rob the music of a degree of vitality, although he is lively enough in the *Gigues* and indeed in the famous *Gavotte* of *Suite No. 5*. But these performances are for collectors who like an essentially intimate approach to this repertoire. The recording, as usual with this BIS series, is most natural and pleasing.

(i) French Suites Nos. 1–6; (ii) English Suite No. 3 in G min., BWV 808; Italian Concerto in F, BWV 971.
(B) **(*) EMI double forte 5 69479–2 (2). (i) Gavrilov (piano); (ii) Bunin (piano).

Andrei Gavrilov's earlier, 1984 set of the *French Suites* is full of interesting things, and there is some sophisticated (not to say masterly) pianism. There is an element of the self-conscious here, but there is also much that is felicitous. To fill up the pair of discs,

Stanislav Bunin's performances of the *Third English Suite* and the *Italian Concerto*, recorded six years later, have been added. His style is bold and direct, less flexible than Gavrilov's approach but totally unselfconscious. Both artists receive excellent recording.

French Suites Nos. 1–6, BWV 812–17 (including 3 additional movements); 18 Little Preludes, BWV 924–8; 930; 933–43; 999; Prelude and Fugue in A min., BWV 894; Sonata in D min., BWV 964.
☙ *** Hyp. CDA 67121/2. Hewitt (piano).

Several readers have pointed out that Angela Hewitt's recording of the *French Suites* appeared without any review in our main volume, as this failed to be carried over from our 1999 edition.

Since then her other Bach recordings have confirmed her natural affinity with the composer and her expertise in this field. Her playing is informed by an intelligence and musicianship that are consistently refreshing. Whether in the *Preludes*, written for Wilhelm Friedmann, or the *Suites* themselves she displays an imaginative vitality of a high order. The recorded sound is very natural.

Goldberg Variations, BWV 988.
*** ECM 472 185-2. András Schiff.
(M) *** DHM/BMG 82876 60146-2. Leonhardt (harpsichord).
**(*) Opus OP 30-84. Hantaï (harpsichord).
**(*) Delos DE 3279. Víníkour (harpsichord).
(B) ** Warner Elatus 2-CD 2564 60010-2 (2). Barenboim (piano) – BEETHOVEN: *Diabelli Variations*. **
(M) ** DG 463 019-2. Gavrilov (piano).

Goldberg Variations; Fughetta in C min., BWV 961; Preludes & Fugues: in A min., BWV 895; D min., BWV 899; E min., BWV 900; F, BWV 901; G, BWV 902.
**(*) Mer. CDA 84291. Cload (piano).

Since he made his first recording of this work for Decca, András Schiff has clearly rethought his approach to the *Goldberg Variations*, playing with a directness and simplicity and with a consistent crispness of articulation that is at times disarming. Occasionally he presses onwards almost too briskly, but there is no lack of underlying flexibility, and this performance, full of spontaneous zest, is very compelling indeed, even if the earlier, more mellow account is not entirely eclipsed. The recording has splendid clarity and presence.

Gustav Leonhardt recorded the *Goldberg Variations* three times, and this last (1978) version, though the most beautifully recorded, will not necessarily enjoy universal appeal. It is an introverted and searching performance, at times very free rhythmically – and almost mannered. The 'Black Pearl' Variation is a case in point, but the reading is so thoughtful that no one can fail to draw some illumination from it. His instrument is a Dowd copy of a Blanchet and is tuned a semitone flat, as opposed to the Skrowroneck copy of a Dulcken at present-day pitch, which he used in his 1967 record for Teldec. The sound is now altogether mellower and more appealing and, though no repeats are observed, this Deutsche Harmonia Mundi version is fresher and more personal than his earlier Das Alte Werk record.

Pierre Hantaï studied with Gustav Leonhardt, so his credentials are impressive. His account of the *Goldberg Variations* has received much praise: 'a happy conjunction of heart and mind' suggested the review in *Gramophone*. The playing is certainly infectiously buoyant and full of life, but his direct manner of presentation and reprise of the *Aria* is borne out by his response to the 'Black Pearl' '*Adagio*, where we feel more expressive flexibility would have been in order. His harpsichord, a Dutch copy of an early eighteenth-century Mietke, is a fine instrument and splendidly recorded.

Jory Vínikour uses an American copy of a 1624 Rückers, which is recorded clearly and cleanly in an attractive acoustic. His playing is alive and has plenty of character; ornamentation is judiciously judged. His inclusion of repeats and choice of tempi mean that this performance, at 85 minutes 39 seconds, runs to a second disc, but the two are offered for the cost of one. There is no doubting the calibre of this playing, but there are a few idiosyncrasies and moments of thoughtful deliberation (Varation 16, for instance), which do not carry the music forward as strongly as with some performances.

Julia Cload observes the repeats in the opening *Aria* but not elsewhere; she therefore finds room for the '*Little*' *Preludes and Fugues*, which she plays appealingly and fluently. Her account of the *Goldberg Variations* is strong and thoughtful, not as inspirational as Tureck's; but some may like its directness of manner. The piano is well recorded, but the ear needs to adjust to the 'empty studio' acoustic.

Barenboim's approach is undoubtedly individual, generally thoughtful and fresh, his pianism well adapted to Bach, with (for the most part) well-chosen tempi, a natural pianistic use of light and shade, and a pleasing linear flow. The inclusion of repeats means that the performance stretches over to a second CD, but the break is well placed, coming after the *Adagio* Variation 25, played very expressively. Then Variation No. 26 seems rather rushed. So this is not a first choice but, if you also want a comparable set of the *Diabelli Variations*, this might be considered. The recording is excellent.

Andrei Gavrilov is a player of astonishing keyboard prowess and there is much that will prompt admiration for both his integrity and articulation. All the same, he makes heavy weather of some of the variations and is, more importantly, handicapped by a less than glamorous recording. There is not enough space round the sound and the instrument is balanced too closely. Angela Hewitt (Hyperion CDA 67305) and Rosalyn Tureck (VAIA 1029)

remain our top recommendations – see the main volume.

Goldberg Variations, BWV 988; Italian Concerto, BWV 971; Partitas Nos. 1–6, & in B min. (French Overture), BWV 825/31.

(M) ★★★ DG (ADD/DDD) Trio 474 337-2 (3). Pinnock (harpsichord).

Trevor Pinnock uses four different harpsichords here, including a recently restored copy of a Rückers for the *Goldberg Variations*, a copy of a Hemsch (tuned to unequal temperament) for the *Italian Concerto* and the six *Partitas*, while the *French Overture* features a copy of a Dulcken. Tempi are generally well judged, rhythms are vital yet free. For the *Goldberg Variations* Pinnock retains repeats for more than half the variations – which seems a fair compromise, in that variety is maintained yet the performnce can be accommodated on a single disc. The playing is again vital and intelligent, with alert, finely articulated rhythm. In the *Partitas* he conveys a sense of pleasure that is infectious, and he has great spirit and panache throughout. The recording is eminently truthful and vivid, a bit close in the B minor *Partita* which, nevertheless, still conveys plenty of expressive feeling.

Partitas Nos. 1–6, BWV 825–30.

(BB) ★★★ Virgin 2 × 1 5 62337-2 (2). Leonhardt (harpsichord).

Leonhardt's set, praised in our main volume, is among the most satisfying versions available, and it is extremely well recorded. The only snag is the absence of repeats, but it remains fully competitive at budget price. Christophe Rousset still remains our first choice (O-L 440 217-2) – see the main volume.

The Well-Tempered Clavier (48 Preludes & Fugues), BWV 846–93 (complete).

(M) ★★★ DG Blue 474 221-2 (Book 1); 474 546-2 (Book 2). Gilbert (harpsichord).

The reissue of Book II (Book I is listed in our main *Guide*) completes Kenneth Gilbert's set. This has long been praised by us for readings that are resilient and individual yet totally unmannered. The recording is excellent too, if rather resonant. This can now be recommended as a first choice among harpsichord versions of the '48', alongside Bob van Asperen's set on Virgin – which, however, has a distinct price advantage.

The Well-Tempered Clavier, Book I, Preludes & Fugues Nos. 1–24, BWV 846–69.

★★(★) HM Mirare MIR 9930 (2). Hantaï (harpsichord).

Born in 1964, Pierre Hantaï has worked with both Gustav Leonhardt and Jordi Savall. He plays the first half of the '48' cleanly and directly, while allowing himself the kind of latitude in the slower movments that one now expects from piano versions. There is a minor degree of nudging linear interference that not all will take to, but this is still very musical playing and it is enjoyable when the recording is so clearly and pleasingly focused.

The Well-Temperered Clavier, Book 1 (excerpts).
** Ondine ODE 1033-2 (2). Mustonen (piano) –
SHOSTAKOVICH: 24 Preludes and Fugues, Op. 87 (excerpts). **

The gifted Finnish pianist Olli Mustonen continues his survey, begun on RCA, interspersing Bach *Preludes and Fugues* with those of Shostakovich, Op. 87. Predictably there is some superb pianism, but the listener's attention tends to gravitate towards the interpreter rather than the composer. His exaggerated staccato playing will strike many as attention-seeking rather than musical, wilful rather than just individual. Of course there are good things, but it is all far too self-aware to give consistent satisfaction.

KEYBOARD RECITAL COLLECTIONS

Adagio in G, BWV 968; Chromatic Fantasia and Fugue (Rust version), *BWV 903a; Clavier-Büchlein: Allemande in G min., BWV 836; Minuets I & III BWV 841 & 843. Partita in A min.* (after *BWV 1004;* arr. Mortensen); *Partita diverse on the Chorale, O Gott, du frommer Gott, BWV 767.*
** Metronome METCD 1956. Hogwood (clavichords).

This collection is entitled 'The Secret Bach' and, including some unfamiliar music among better known pieces, it is something of a disappointment. The accompanying notes quote one of Bach's biographers, J. N. Forkel, as suggesting that Bach found the clavichord 'the best instrument for study and in general for private musical entertainment'. Three clavichords are in use here (by Hass, Bodechtal and Schmahl) but as recorded they sound dull – and so too often does Hogwood's playing. He does not always seem fully involved, and even the virtuosity of the *Chromatic Fantasia* (heard in a slightly modified version), although technically impeccable, fails to project excitingly as one expects.

Arrangements

Sinfonia in D; Siciliano in G min.; Chorales: *Nun komm, der Heiden Heiland; Wachet auf; Ich ruf' zu dir* (arr. Kempff); *Sheep may safely graze* (arr. Mary Howe); *Jesu, joy of man's desiring* (arr. Myra Hess); *Wenn wir in höchsten Nöten sein; Das alte Jahr; Alle Menschen müssen sterben* (arr. Hewitt); *Herzlich tut mich verlangen* (arr. Walton); *Meine Seele erhebt den Herrn* (arr. John Ireland); *O Mensch, bewein dein Sünde gross* (arr. Howells); *Sanctify us by Thy goodness* (arr. Harriet Cohen); *Die Seele ruht in Jesu Händen* (arr. Harold Bauer); *Passacaglia in C min.* (arr. Eugen d'Albert).
**(*) Hyp. CDA 67309. Hewitt (piano).

This collection looks intriguing but is just a little disappointing. Of couse Angella Hewitt's Bach playing is always perceptive, but here there is sometimes a hint of over-characterization. The opening *Sinfonia* is vey bold indeed, as is the *Passacaglia in C minor*, but, as the latter proceeds, in some passages she is almost too gentle. The staccatos at the opening of the *Siciliana* (where the melody itself is played most beautifully) like the accented rhythms in *Wachet auf* seem a shade too precise, though the very clearly focused chorale in *Jesu, joy of man's desiring* works well enough. She is at her very finest when playing very simply, as in Kempff's arrangement of *Ich ruf' zu dir*, Walton's of *Herzlich tut mich verlangen*, and her own of *Alle Menschen müssen sterben*, which ends the programme so serenely.

ORGAN MUSIC

Helmut Walcha's first mono DG Archiv series (incomplete)

Disc 1: Introduction: Demonstration of the registration and improvisation, using the St-Peter-und-Paul-Kirche organ (with commentary in German). *6 Preludes & Fugues, BWV 531–6; Toccata & Fugue (Dorian), BWV 538*. Disc 2: *Fantasias & Fugues, BWV 537 & 542; Fugue, BWV 539; Preludes & Fugues, BWV 541, 543 & 544; Toccata & Fugue, BWV 540.* Disc 3: *Preludes & Fugues, BWV 545–48; 550–551; Fantasia, BWV 562; Toccata, Adagio & Fugue, BWV 564.* Disc 4: *Allabreve, BWV 589; Canzona, BWV 588; Fantasia, BWV 572; Fugue, BWV 578; Passacaglia & Fugue, BWV 582; Pastoral, BWV 590; Toccatas & Fugues, BWV 565–66.* Disc 5: *Trio Sonatas Nos. 1–6, BWV 525–30.* Discs 6–9: *Clavier-Ubung, Part 3: German Organ Mass (Prelude & Fugue, BWV 552; Chorale Preludes, BWV 669–89; 4 Duets, BWV 802–05).18 Leipzig Chorale Preludes, BWV 651–68; Orgelbüchlein, BWV 599–644.* Disc 10: *6 Schübler Chorales; Chorales, BWV 653b, 727, 733, 734 & 736; Fuge on the Magnificat, BWV 733; Fugu on 'Vom Himmel hoch, da komm'ich her', BWV 700; Partita on 'Sei gegrüssset, Jesu gütig', BWV 768; Canonic Variations on 'Vom Himmel hoch'.*
(B) (**(*)) DG mono 474 747-2 (10). Walcha (organs of St-Jacobi-Kirche or St-Peter-und-Paul-Kirche Cappel, Lübeck).

The first three 78 rpm records issued on Deutsche Grammophon's Archiv label in 1947 were of Helmut Walcha playing Bach's six *Schübler Chorales* on the small organ at the St-Jacobi-Kirche in Lübeck. They are included here and are piquantly registered (No. 6, *Kommst du nun*, has a hint of charm – not a quality one usually associates with Walcha's Bach when his playing is so clear, positive and rhythmically clean). He continued with the first and last of the *Trio Sonatas* and the *'Sei gegrüsset' Chorale Variations* (which might better have suited a larger organ).

But when in 1950 and 1952 he went on to record the rest of the Bach organ repertoire which he considered authentic, he turned to the Arp Schnitger organ in the Cappel of the St-Peter-und-Paul-Kirche, including the other four *Trio Sonatas* and the *Canonic Variations on 'Vom Himmel Hoch'*. The latter obviously suit the larger instrument, and the *Sonatas*, divided between the two instruments, make a fascinating aural comparison for, even if they are not as spirited as some versions, they are played very beautifully and are never dull.

By then the LP had arrived, with its background quiet, and the DG engineers found that street noise sometimes compromised the recordings made in the St-Jakobi-Kirche (although such problems do not really emerge here). But the suitability of the St-Peter-und-Paul organ is in no doubt, and this is shown by the introductory demonstration of its registrations included with this set. The only snag is that the commentary is in German and no translation is offered, a most curious omission!

Walcha's Bach recordings continued to be a dominating feature of the Archiv catalogue, so it was not surprising that in 1956 he began to re-record the music in stereo, and the earlier mono recordings were soon eclipsed and all but forgotten. But now they are restored to the public domain and they show Walcha's rigorously austere approach to Bach in perfect focus. He emphatically rejected the idea that this music should be played in the rhythmically free manner that we now take for granted. He believed that such a practice showed a lack of respect for the music's 'unbelievably profound, mysterious and strict pulse'.

The *Preludes and Fugues* gathered together on the first disc readily bear this out with their almost unvarying forward momentum. The *D major* and *G minor* works bring undoubled virtuoso dexterity, which is never made extrovert. The performances on the seond disc continue in the same didactic manner, after a very slow and restrained account of the opening *Fantasia in C minor*.

The massive *G minor Prelude* opens weightily and grandly and the fugue proceeds with clearly articulated deliberation. This is one of Walcha's most impressive performances. Elsewhere, the effect is certainly strong and authoritative, but many listeners will seek greater flexibility.

On the third disc the *Toccata, Adagio and Fugue in C major* is surprisingly lightweight rather than imposing, and for once the closing fugue is rather jolly. The famous *D minor Toccata and Fugue* opens the fourth CD, played directly but more flamboyantly, and the *E major Toccata and Fugue* which follows and the *G minor Fugue* are also rhythmically telling when Walcha's articulation is so clear and positive. Not surprisingly the *Passacaglia and Fugue in C* shows Walcha at his best, with the ever-varying registration consistently ear-tickling. The closing *Pastorale* is also rich in colour.

Alongside the *Trio Sonatas*, Walcha is probably at

his most resourceful in the chorales and chorale variations, of which a great many are included here, spread over discs 6–10. Those within the so-called *German Organ Mass* from the *Clavier-Ubung* are framed by a powerful account of the *St Anne Prelude* and a slow and deliberate performance of the *E flat major Fugue*, BWV 552. The Mass also includes the *Four Duets*, played very precisely and squarely on the harpsichord; and, of the chorale settings included, those for small organ are particularly telling.

But it is the chorales from the *Orgelbüchlein* and *18 Leipzig Chorales* that are most impressive of all: they have great variety of mood, idiom and tempo (especially when different versions of the same chorale are presented together) and they often show a gentle piety, which can be very affecting. All in all, this survey represents a remarkable achievement. Such is the quality of the sound that one's ears hardly register the fact that these are all mono recordings, for they have been splendidly remastered for CD. The documentation too cannot be faulted.

Organ recitals

(i) Disc 1: *Chorale Preludes, BWV 622, 680, 721 & 727; Fugues: in B min. on a theme of Corelli, BWV 579; in G (Jig), BWV 577; Passacaglia & Fugue in C min., BWV 582; Pastorale in F, BWV 590; Prelude and Fugue in G, BWV 541; Toccata & Fugue in D min., BWV 565.*

(ii) Disc 2: *Aria in F* (from CORELLI: *Trio Sonata*), BWV 587; *Chorale Preludes, BWV 657, 719, 731, 734–5; Toccata, Adagio & Fugue in C, BWV 64; Trio Sonata No. 5 in C, BWV 529.*

(BB) ★★★ CfP 5 85630-2 (2). Peter Hurford organs of (i) Martinikerk, Gröningen, Holland; (ii) Ludgerikirche, Norden, Germany.

Having left his complete Decca Bach series long behind him, in 1993–9 Peter Hurford set off on this travels again to record familiar Bach repertoire for EMI. He chose two fine Schnitger organs, one in Gröningen, the other in Norden, both recently restored to their former splendour. If the famous *D major Fugue*, BWV 565, is a fraction less flamboyant here than before, the *Fugue à la Gigue* and *G major Prelude and Fugue* have plenty of character, and the *Toccata, Adagio and Fugue* sounds more sprightly than usual. Characteristically, Hurford brings out a wide range of colour from both instruments, especially in the *Pastorale*, Bach's attractive Vivaldi *Concerto* transcription, and the engaging *Trio Sonata* on the second disc. The chosen *Chorale Preludes* are attractively diverse, sometimes relaxed and thoughtful, at others full of movement: *Nun freut euch*, BWV 734, flows most winningly around the cantus firmus. In the great *C minor Passacaglia and Fugue* that closes the first recital, Hurford demonstrates how magnificently he can hold and build tension when setting off at a measured pace. What a masterpiece this is in his hands! The EMI engineers do him proud with both organs, and it is surprising that this series did not continue.

Chorale preludes: *O Mensch, bewein' dein' Sünde gross, BWV 622; Schmücke dich, o liebe Seele, BWV 654; Wachet auf, ruft uns die Stimme, BWV 645; Fantasia & Fugue in G min., BWV 542; Passacaglia in C min., BWV 582; Prelude & Fugue in A min., BWV 543; Toccata & Fugue in D min., BWV 565.*
(BB) ** EMI Encore (ADD) 5 75215-2. Jacob.

Werner Jacob uses a different organ for each piece, so this is as much a demonstration of different organs as a Bach recital. Certainly, the ubiquitous *D minor Toccata and Fugue*, played with some flair, sounds splendid on the Silbermann instrument at Arlesheim. Jacob plays the chorale preludes reverentially but effectively, his registration unostentatious. The passage-work of the *Prelude and Fugue in A minor* (at St Bavo, Haarlem) is rather blurred, but that comes partly from the style of articulation; it is otherwise a fine performance. The powerfully spacious opening of the *Fantasia and Fugue in G minor* serves to demonstrate the massive tone of the organ of the Marienkirche, Stralsund, but the similar grandeur of the *Passacaglia in C minor*, recorded in Brandenburg, is underlined by Jacob's purposefully deliberate basic tempo. This is an inexpensive way to acquire some fine playing in the German tradition and to sample a number of impressive instruments. The 1970s recordings have transferred well to CD.

VOCAL MUSIC

Complete cantatas: Koopman series with Amsterdam Baroque Chorus & Orchestra on Challenge Classics

Volume I: *Cantatas Nos. 4 (with Appendix: Chorus: Sie nun wieder zufrieden); 31; 71; 106 (Actus tragicus); 131; 150; 185; 196 (Wedding Cantata).*
*** Challenge Classics CC 72201 (3). Schlick, Wessel, De Mey, Mertens.

Volume II: *Cantatas Nos. 12; 18 (with Appendix); 61; 132; 152; 172; 182 (with Appendix); 199; 203: Amore traditore. Quodlibet, BWV 524.*
*** Challenge Classics CC 72202 (3). Schlick, Wessel, Prégardien, Mertens.

Volume III: *Cantatas Nos. 22; 23; 54; 63 (2 versions); 155; 161; 162 (2 versions); 163; 165; 208: Was mir behagt, ist nur die muntre Jagd (Hunt).*
*** Challenge Classics CC 72203 (3). Schlick, Stam, Holton, Bongers, Von Magnus, Scholl, Agnew.

Volume IV: *Cantatas Nos. 198; 201; 204; 209; 211; 214; 215.*
*** Challenge Classics CC 72204 (3). Larsson, Bongers, Grimm, Stam, Von Magnus, De Groot, Agnew, Ovenden, Mertens, Bentvelsen.

Volume V: *Cantatas Nos. 202; 205; 206; 207a; 212; 213.*
*** Challenge Classics CC 72205 (4). Larsson, Rubens, Bongers, Grimm, Von Magnus, Prégardien, Mertens.

Previously available on Erato, but now taken over by Challenge Classics, Ton Koopman's cantata cycle looks set to challenge and indeed surpass the famous Leonhardt–Harnoncourt set on Teldec (and indeed most of his other competitors). These versions all differ in some important respects, and readers will have to decide for themselves how these various factors weigh in their own balance-sheet. First, Koopman favours an intimate approach to choruses – namely one voice to a part – which seems to rob this repertory of some of its sheer majesty and breadth. Second, unlike Leonhardt–Harnoncourt, Koopman opts for female soloists rather than boys, as would have been the case in Bach's day, and he favours mixed rather than solely male choirs. For many this will be a plus point – and it is good news for fans of Barbara Schlick. Third, and again unlike Leonhardt–Harnoncourt, he goes for slightly higher than normal pitch – a semitone above present-day pitch, which, as Christoph Wolff's notes point out, is what Bach used in Mühlhausen and Weimar, brightening the sonority quite a lot. The singing in virtually all the cantatas is pretty impressive and the instrumental playing is of a high order of accomplishment. Those who set store by security of intonation and excellence of ensemble will probably prefer this survey to the earlier set. Moreover, Koopman offers the collector variants and alternative versions, which will again be an undoubted plus.

Koopman's survey is proceeding on largely chronological lines and Volume III includes the delightful secular cantata No. 208, *Was mir behagt, ist nur die muntre Jagd*, which includes '*Sheep may safely graze*'. All these works come from Bach's Weimar years. For the most part the singing here is of a high order of accomplishment – in particular Andreas Scholl and Elisabeth von Magnus, and the instrumental playing is certainly more finished than is often the case in the Teldec set, though here it is by no means always as fresh or secure as on the Japanese series now under way from BIS. In No. 54, *Widerstehe doch der Sände*, Suzuki surpasses Koopman in expressive power, and even when he doesn't the string playing yields in vigour and polish and sonority to the Japanese musicians. Besides offering various appendices, in No. 63, *Christen, ätzet diesen Tag*, and in No. 162, *Ach! ich sehe, jetzt, da ich zur Hochzeit gehe*, Koopman gives alternative versions, giving him an undoubted advantage over the opposition.

The fourth volume is given over to secular cantatas of the Leipzig period (1726–34), most not included in the Teldec survey. Foremost among them is the 1727 cantata, *Lass Fürstin, lass noch einen Strahl*, BWV 198, or the 'Funeral Ode' cantata, composed for the funeral ceremonies to mark the death of Christiane Eberhardine, Queen of Poland and Electoral Princess of Saxony. The noble opening chorus is perhaps wanting in breadth (rhythms are often over-accentuated) – memories of Jürgen Jürgens's 1968 version, also with combined Amsterdam and Hamburg forces, are emphatically not erased – and Koopman's soloists are uneven, particularly Lisa Larsson, whose confidence and intonation are occasionally vulnerable (she is better in BWV 209, *Non sà che sia dolore*). Generally speaking, the men are stronger. Koopman is rather breathless in the opening Sinfonia. All the same, there are many felicities in the set and some expert and beautifully light wind-playing. The recording is absolutely first class.

The fifth volume completes the survey of the Leipzig secular cantatas up to the so-called *Peasant Cantata, Mer hahn en neue Oberkeet*, BWV 212. There is some distinguished singing from Klaus Mertens and Christoph Prégardien and some highly accomplished and felicitous solo instrumental playing (there are some wonderfully poetic oboe obbligatos). Lisa Larsson seems far more at ease in BWV 202, *Weichet nur, betrübte Schatten*, than she was in the earlier volume, though elsewhere intonation occasionally troubles Elisabeth von Magnus. Generally speaking, this gives more consistent pleasure than earlier releases in the series, and the recordings are excellent.

Volumes 6–12 are to be re-released over the coming 12–18 months. But the later volumes, Nos. 13–15, have been given first preference – see below.

Complete Cantatas, Volume XIII: *Cantatas Nos. 1; 33; 38; 62; 92; 93; 96; 122; 133.*
*** Challenge Classics CC 72213 (3). York, Gottwald, Agnew, Mertens, Amsterdam Bar. O, Koopman.

Complete Cantatas, Volume XIV: *Cantatas Nos. 6; 26; 42; 68; 74; 103; 123; 125; 126; 178; Konzertsatz in D, BWV 1045.*
*** Challenge Classics CC 72214 (3). York, Markert, Larsson, Barosz, Gottwald, Dürmüller, Prégardien, Agnew, Gilchrist, Mertens, Amsterdam Bar. Ch. & O, Koopman.

Complete Cantatas, Volume 15: *Cantatas Nos. 3; 28; 85; 87; 108; 110; 128; 146; 168; 175; 176; 183.*
*** Challenge Classics CC 72215 (3). York, Piau, Zomer, Rubens, Barosz, Dürmüller, Prégardien, Agnew, Gilchrist, Mertens, Amsterdam Bar. Ch. & O, Koopman.

Space does not permit the detailed exegesis that this project ideally calls for. With the three volumes listed immediately above, Ton Koopman brings his survey of the Bach cantatas to a successful conclusion. Since he began, Helmuth Rilling has completed his series with the Gächinger Kantorei and the Stuttgart Bach-Collegium on Hänssler, and another complete survey by the Holland Boys' Choir and the Netherlands Bach Collegium directed by Pieter Jan Leusink has appeared on the super-bargain Brilliant label. Both these sets are discussed in our main volume. But

most important of all is a highly distinguished complete cycle that is now well under way from an unlikely source: the Japan Bach Collegium, under Masaaki Suzuki (a pupil of Ton Koopman) on the enterprising BIS label. The latest issues in this series, which we count the finest of all, are discussed below.

Koopman's are cultured performances, not quite as full-blooded as the Japanese cycle with Suzuki, but offering some fine singing and scholarly direction. They include exemplary detailed notes from Christoph Wolff and continue to include alternative versions of some movements that Bach used subsequently. Those who have collected earlier issues in this cycle will know their merits, and these newcomers maintain (and at times surpass) the standards of their predecessors, both artistically and in the refined quality of the recorded sound. Some collectors may be deterred by the fact that one must purchase these in batches of three discs with eleven or twelve cantatas per volume, whereas with the BIS each set can be bought singly. Although the latter remains our first choice, Koopman is highly competitive, and in those parts of the world where Suzuki is not readily available this Challenge coverage is almost every bit as satisfying.

Complete cantatas: BIS Masaaki Suzuki series with Japan Bach Collegium

Cantatas Nos. 7; 20; 94.
*** BIS CD 1321. Nonoshita, Blaze, Kobow, Kooy, Bach Coll. Japan, Suzuki.

Cantatas Nos. 10; 93; 107; 178.
*** BIS CD 1331. Nonoshita, M. White, Sakurada, Kooy, Bach Coll. Japan, Suzuki.

Cantatas Nos. 65; 81; 83; 190.
*** BIS CD 1311. Blaze, Gilchrist, Kooy, Bach Coll. Japan, Suzuki.

The above represent Volumes 21, 22 & 23 in the Japan Bach Collegium's imposing survey with Masaaki Suzuki. All offer generous playing time – though it is not quantity but quality that is the important thing on offer here. All the cantatas on the first two discs belong to the Leipzig cycle of 1724, the bicentenary of the German hymnbook, and are a treasure house of glorious musical invention. Volume 22 introduces a new departure in Bach's cantata output for, instead of illustrating the gospel appointed for the Sunday in question, each is based on one of the famous Reformation hymns and begins with an imposing introductory movement of magisterial contrapuntal mastery. None is more majestic than the opening of *O Ewigkeit, du Donnerwort*, BWV 20, to which Suzuki and his colleagues bring splendid breadth. All are large-scale works with particularly rich sonorities: trumpet, flute and oboe d'amore respectively adding colour to the usual string and continuo forces. Each new volume in this series from Masaaki Suzuki seems to surpass its predecessor and offer performances of total conviction and consummate artistry. The BIS recordings are state-of-the-art, and for many they will remain a first choice.

Other cantata groupings

Cantatas Nos. 2, 20 & 176.

(***) HMC 901791. Zomer, Danz, Kobow, Kooij, Ghent Coll. Voc., Herreweghe.

Two of the soloists (Jan Kobow and Peter Kooij or Kooy) are common to both this and Masaaki Suzuki's version of *O Ewigkeit, du Donnerwort* with the Japan Bach Collegium. These Ghent performances score in terms of breadth and atmosphere, and the quality of both the singing and the instrumental playing is of distinction. The refinement of the phrasing gives much pleasure and satisfaction, as does the excellent recorded sound. Unlike the five-CD Herreweghe box listed below, they are new recordings, and for those not drawn for whatever reason to the various complete sets, this will be a good choice. It should belong in any self-respecting Bach cantata collection.

Festival Cantatas: Nos. 11; 36; 43–4; 57; 61–2; 66; 80; 110; 122; Easter Oratorio; Magnificat in D, BWV 243.

(BB) *** HM 2908135-9 (5). Schlick, Patriasz, Prégardien, Kooy, Mellon, Lesne, Wessel, Taylor, Rubens, Jezovsek, Connolly, La Chapelle Royale, Coll. Voc., Herreweghe.

This five-CD compilation collects 12 festive cantatas, together with the *Magnificat* in its later, more familiar D major version (Herreweghe has recently recorded the E flat) and the *Easter Oratorio*. The performances date from 1990 in the case of the *Magnificat* and *Ein feste Burg ist unser Gott*, BWV 80, through to 1997 in the Advent cantatas, *Schwingt freudig euch empor*, BWV 36, and *Nun komm, der Heiden Heiland* (BWV 61 and 62). The performances have an unfailing elegance and poise, and they are distinguished by fine solo singing and an exemplary feeling for tempo. The Collegium Vocale have refined tone and homogeneity and give much pleasure. The appearance of these discs at so competitive a price enhances a strong basic appeal.

Cantatas Nos. 35; 169; 170.

**(*) Finlandia 3984 25325-2. Groop, Ostrobothnian CO, Kangas.

Monica Groop gives us three solo cantatas for alto, with the important organ obbligato parts played most expertly by Håkan Wikman. The orchestral playing is fresh and has a welcome liveliness to which the recording engineer does justice. Groop is in good voice, though hers is commanding rather than moving singing.

Cantatas Nos. 39; 73; 93; 105; 107; 131.

(B) **(*) Virgin 5 61721 (4). Schlick, Mellon, Lesne, Brett, Kooy, Ghent Coll. Voc. Ch. & O, Herreweghe – *Masses (Missae breves)*. **(*)

These six cantatas are all among Bach's most rewarding works in this genre. With such a starry cast it is not surprising that the solo singing is of the very highest calibre, as is the instrumental playing (on period instruments), especially in the provision of obbligatos. The choral singing is stylishly sympathetic too, and these performances are all warmly enjoyable, with the single proviso that the resonant acoustic (as with the coupled *Missae breves*) takes the edge off the vocal projection and produces just a degree of blandness.

Cantatas Nos. (i) 39, 93 & 107; (ii) 73, 105 & 131; Masses (Missae breves): (iii; iv) in F, A, G min., G, BWV 233/236. Sanctus in D, BWV 238.

(BB) * (**) Virgin 5 62252-2 (4). (i; iii) Mellon, Brett; (i; ii) Crook; (ii; iii) Kooy; (ii) Schlick, Lesne; (iv) Prégardien; Coll. Voc., Ghent, Ch. & O, Herreweghe.

Both discs of cantatas are thoroughly recommendable; indeed the opening chorus of No. 39, *Brich dem Hungrigen dein Brot*, with its engagingly pointed accompaniment for treble recorders and oboes, should prove most inviting for any listener. This is one of Bach's most inspired cantatas, but Nos. 93 and 107, dating from 1724, are also very fine works, their eloquence fully realized by excellent contributions from the soloists and chorus. The cantatas on the second disc include *Aus der Tiefen rufe ich*, BWV 131, one of Bach's earliest, from 1707, and based on Psalm 130, *De profundis*. But it is in no way immature and is very lyrically appealing. It is beautifully sung, and again one notes the expressive intensity of the performance overall. *Herr wir du willst, so schick's mit mir* (No. 73) opens with another striking chorus, instrumentally decorated in Bach's most ingenious manner. But finest of all is *Herr, gehe nicht ins Gericht*, BWV 105, which tells the parable of the unjust steward (St Luke), and here one again notes the sensitive obbligato oboe playing of Marc Ponseele, which distinguishes both CDs and which reaches its zenith in Barbara Schlick's lovely performance of the soprano aria, *Wie zittern und wanken*. Apart from the excellence of the solo singing, one must praise also the fine choral contribution and stylish accompaniments. Herreweghe's pacing cannot be faulted, and the recording has an ideal acoustic so that everything sounds both fresh and warm.

Bach's four short Masses (*Missae breves*), which come in tandem with the cantatas, are also very well sung with comparably excellent solo contributions. The performances are authentic, spirited and stylish. They are certainly warmly enjoyable. But there is a snag. Unlike the cantatas, they have been recorded in a very resonant ecclesiastical acoustic that, while it provides freedom from period-instrument abrasiveness, takes the edge off the choruses, which often sound muddy, and detracts from the presence of the soloists.

Cantatas for the 1st, 2nd and 3rd days of Christmas, Nos. 40; 57; 63; 64; 91; 110; 121; 133; 151.

(M) **(*) Teldec (ADD) 0630 17366-2 (3). Soloists, Ghent Coll. Voc., Leonhardt Consort, Leonhardt; VCM, Harnoncourt.

A gathering of Bach's cantatas for the Christmas season. The ear has to accept moments of less than perfect intonation from the treble soloists of the Vienna Boys' (notably Detlef Bratsch in No. 91), although on the plus side Peter Jelosits makes a fine contribution to No. 63. Similarly among the original instruments, the horns are sometimes wildly astray in their upper harmonics (as in the introduction for the same cantata, *Gelobet seist du, Jesu Christ*). The Ghent chorus are not always absolutely reliable either: they are not completely secure in No. 133; yet they are at their best in No. 151, a splendid cantata. But overall there is much to enjoy here.

(i) *Cantatas Nos. 67; 130. Masses (Missae breves):* (ii) *BWV 233–4;* (iii) *BWV 235–6.*

(B) **(*) Double Decca (ADD) 466 754-2 (2). (i) Ameling, Watts, Krenn, Krause, Lausanne Pro Arte Ch., OSR, Ansermet; (ii; iii) Hickox Singers & O, Hickox, with (ii) Jenkins; (ii; iii) Eathorne, Esswood, Roberts; (iii) Langridge.

In Ansermet's accounts of *Cantatas Nos. 67* and *130*, the orchestra may not be the finest in the world (though the flute playing of André Pepin is certainly in that bracket) and they are hardly 'authentic' (though they are not particularly *Romantic* either), but there is plenty of character here. They are very well recorded and they offer much good singing. Hickox's mid-1970s performances bring more polished orchestral playing, fine singing and excellent recording. BWV 233 and 234 offer many beauties: the *A major Mass*, which draws on *Cantata No. 67* for its *Gloria*, is the more inspired, but it is hard to understand why all four of these works are relatively neglected. The two other *Masses*, BWV 235 and BWV 236, are equally well performed, with the contribution of the choir shining out.

Cantata No. 82: Ich habe genug.

⊶ ❁ (M) (***) EMI mono 6 62807-2. Hotter, Philh. O, Bernard – BRAHMS: *Lieder.* *** ❁

One of the greatest cantata performances ever. Glorious singing from Hans Hotter and wonderfully stylish accompanying from Anthony Bernard and the Philarmonia. This 1950 mono recording was never reissued on LP and it sounds vividly present in its current remastering. Moreover, EMI have found some extra Brahms songs to add to the coupling.

Cantatas Nos. 211 (Coffee Cantata); 212 (Peasant Cantata).

** Analekta Fleur de Lys FL 2 3136. LeBlanc, Polegato, Nils Brown, Tafelmusik, Lamon.

Tafelmusik is one of the liveliest and most musical of period ensembles, whose work we have consistently admired. However, this coupling of two of the most popular Bach secular cantatas does not offer a serious challenge to its main competitors. Brett Polegato conveys some sense of character, but Suzie LeBlanc is no match for Emma Kirkby, and the ensemble's playing is not as alert and sparkling as we have come to expect.

Major choral works

Christmas Oratorio, BWV 248.

(M) ** Virgin 7 59530-2 (2). Schlick, Chance, Crook, Kooy, Ghent Collegium Vocale Ch. & O, Herreweghe.

With a characterful line-up of soloists, notably Howard Crook as the Evangelist and Michael Chance as male alto, Herreweghe offers a lively reading, well recorded, which yields to the finest rivals in the choral singing, not quite as crisply disciplined as it might be. First choice rests with Gardiner (DG 423 232-2).

(i) *Easter Oratorio;* (ii) *Magnificat in D, BWV 243. Cantatas Nos.* (i) *4: Christ lag in Totesbanden;* (ii) *11: Lobet Gott in seinen Reichen (Ascension Cantata); Chorale: Nun ist das Heil und die Kraft* (from BWV 50).

(BB) ** Virgin 2x1 5 61647-2 (2). (i; ii) Van Evera, Trevor, Daniels, Kooy, Thomas; (ii) Kirkby, Tubb, Cable, Crook, Jochens, Charlesworth, Grant; Taverner Cons. & Players, Parrott.

Both sets of performances on Virgin are on a small scale, as Andrew Parrott favours one voice to a part in choruses. Without doubt the effect is refreshingly clear, for the singers are expert and the balance, even with Bach's exultant trumpets, is well managed. The solo singing is always good, often excellent; Caroline Trevor is memorable in the alto solo, *Esurientes implevit bonis*, in the *Magnificat.* The instrumental support too is pleasingly fresh, with fine obbligato playing. But in the end the ear craves more weight.

Mass in B min., BWV 232.

(M) ** DG Double (ADD) 459 460-2. Janowicz, Ludwig, Schreier, Kerns, Ridderbusch, V. Singverein, BPO, Karajan.

Unlike his earlier, EMI set, Karajan's 1974 DG performance is marked by his characteristic smoothness of Bach style – he conveys intensity, even religious fervour, but the sharp contours of Bach's majestic writing are often missing. But there is a strong sense of the work's architecture, and the highly polished surfaces do not obscure the depths of this music.

When released in 1960, Shaw's RCA version was a pioneering set at the cutting edge of authentic performance: a complement of five soloists, a small chorus and orchestra. From a modern point of view, it seems a dated approach to the score, though not with any interpretative extremes, except in its slow tempi, which will seem laboured for most listeners.

The most remarkable thing about this set is the recording: it is astonishingly full and vivid (RCA 09026 63529-2). Gardiner still remains our primary recommendation (DG 415 514-2) – see the main volume.

St John Passion, BWV 245.

- ⊖─➤ (BB) ★★★ Naxos 8.557296 (2). Gilchrist, Barnays, Dougan, Littlewood, Bowman, Beale, Baldy, New College, Oxford, Ch., Coll. Novum, Higginbottom.
- (B) ★★(★) RCA Twofer 74321 49181-2 (2). Augér, Schreier, Ude, Adam, Lorenz, Reiss, Leipzig Thomanerchor & CO, Rotzsch.

The Naxos version of the St John Passion, with the choir of New College, Oxford, at budget price offers an outstanding period performance, which can stand comparison with any in the catalogue. The first distinctive point is that, following Bach's own practice at St Thomas's, only male voices are used, with the soprano arias sung by a boy treble. The choir itself is fresh and bright, singing incisively, with the crowd choruses vividly adding to the drama, helped by the natural balance. Higginbottom's speeds on the fast side follow period practice, except in relatively broad chorales. James Gilchrist is a superb Evangelist, fluent and expressive, and the main quartet of soloists makes a sensitive team, including the confidently firm-toned treble, Joe Littlewood, and the veteran counter-tenor, James Bowman, still in fine voice. The wind instruments of the Collegium Novum have a sharp edge, which brings out the agony implied in the accompaniment to the opening chorus, while the darkness of instrumentation in the great alto aria, Es ist vollbracht, adds to the poignancy of Bowman's singing. However, Suzuki's DVD of the St John Passion (DV-BAJPN) should not be forgotten – see our main volume.

Rotzsch's version was recorded for Ariola in 1975–6 and, using modern instruments, presents a performance that in some ways anticipates period practice, with chorales and recitative generally brisk. The soloists make a strong and characterful team, with Peter Schreier as the Evangelist at his very peak, clear and true and more powerful than most, as well as deeply expressive. It is good too to hear Arleen Augér in the soprano arias. Full, warm sound. A good 'twofer' package.

The alternative Hänssler set under Eckhard Weyand offers a crisp and fresh reading, using modern instruments, very well recorded. The manner is plain, the speeds are well chosen, and it is interesting to hear Christine Schäfer at the very beginning of her career, recorded in 1990. Otherwise, at full price hardly a first choice (CD 98.968).

(i) St John Passion (complete); (ii) St Matthew Passion (complete).

- (B) ★★ Erato 5046 65560-2 (5). De Mey, Schlick, Kooy, Wessel, Mertens; (i) Türk; Netherlands Bach Ch.,(ii) Prégardien, Breda Sacraments Ch., Netherlands Bach Boys' Ch.; (i; ii) Amsterdam Bar. O, Koopman.

Erato have reissued Koopman's Amsterdam recordings of Bach's two key Passion settings at bargain price, each separately documented with full texts, in a slip case; but they are of uneven appeal. The great glory of the St John Passion is the vividly dramatic singing of the choir, very much a protagonist in the drama of the narrative, both in the virtuoso rendering of the turba choruses (one can really imagine an angry mob) and in the freshness of the chorales. The soprano, Barbara Schlick, is pure and silvery, setting the pattern for clear, fresh voices. The other soloists complete a fine team, with Guy de Mey an expressive Evangelist, contrasted with the solo tenor in the arias, Gerd Türk. The Jesus of Peter Kooy is also well contrasted against Klaus Mertens in the arias and incidental roles, though not everyone will like the hooty counter-tenor of Kai Wessel. This was a keen contender on its original, separate issue, but the St Matthew Passion is altogether less successful.

In the St John Passion the chorus is set a little behind the orchestra but still projects well enough, whereas in the St Matthew Passion the Dutch chorus sounds comparatively muddy (especially beside Gardiner's version). The performance too is amiable rather than conveying the fullest tension. The very opening finds Koopman too easy and comfortable, making you register nothing more serious than a dance. However, Barbara Schlick again makes a memorable contribution and Christophe Prégardien also stands out; but otherwise the soloists hardly match Gardiner's team, not even Guy de Mey as the Evangelist.

St Matthew Passion, BWV 244.

- (B) ★★(★) HMX 2901155.57 (3). Crook, Cold, Schlick, Jacobs, Blochwitz, Kooy, Chapelle Royale Ch., Ghent Coll. Mus., Herreweghe.
- (M) ★★ DG (ADD) 463 635-2 (3). Haefliger, Seefried, Töpper, Fischer-Dieskau, Engen, Fahlberg, Munich Bach Ch. & Boys' Ch., Richter.

Herreweghe's 1985 recording (recorded on period instruments at lower pitch), now reissued at bargain price, was not altogether superseded by his later version, discussed in our main volume.

Howard Crook is an excellent, fresh-toned Evangelist, and the other tenor, Hans-Peter Blochwitz, is first rate too. The alto part is taken by the celebrated counter-tenor, René Jacobs, rather hooty in Erbarme dich; but Barbara Schlick, with her bright, clear soprano voice, sings radiantly. The instrumental group plays in authentic style, but not abrasively so; Herreweghe's control of rhythm, however, tends to be too heavy. Chorales are often slow and over-accented, and the heavy stressing also mars the big numbers. Nevertheless this is still impressive overall.

Karl Richter's pioneering 1958 recording for DG Archiv with Munich forces has some fine singing, both from the chorus and from the soloists, who include the young Fischer-Dieskau as baritone soloist. Though Richter represented the authentic cause at the time, using relatively small forces, his speeds are very slow indeed by the standards of period performance today. Though there is a glow and dedication in the music-making, with Ernst Haefliger a radiant Evangelist and Irmgard Seefried producing ravishing sounds, the performance has come to sound stodgy – not just a question of speeds but of rhythmic squareness. Vocally, the disappointment is the fruity contralto, Hertha Töpper, a key soloist in this work. This is now reissued as one of DG's Originals, so that it costs more than its earlier, bargain-priced incarnation, and it is a pity that DG did not choose instead Richter's later, dedicated (1979) version, still rhythmically heavy, but with Janet Baker's singing a crowning glory. However, Gardiner's set on DG remains a first choice (427 648-2).

(i; ii) *St Matthew Passion* (complete). *Suites Nos.*
(ii) *2 in B min., BWV 1067;* (iii) *3 in D, BWV 1068:*
Air (arr. Mahler); (iv) *Concerto in D min., for 2*
violins & orchestra, BWV 1010.

(***) Naxos mono 8.110880–82. (i) Erb, Vincent, Van
   Tulder, Durigo, Ravelli, Schey, Amsterdam
   Toonkunst Ch., Zanglus Boys' Ch.; (ii) Concg. O;
   (iii) New York Philharmonic SO; (ii; iv) with
   Zimmerman, Helman; all cond. Mengelberg.

Here is the famous Palm Sunday 1939 performance of the *St Matthew Passion*, recorded live by the Netherlands Radio, given in the Concertgebouw. Mengelberg's reading, expansively indulging in slow tempi and rallentandos at every imaginable point, is a monument to a tradition now departed. He had conducted this same work in Amsterdam every year from 1899 onwards and, whatever the objections to the style of performance that the modern listener may have, the dedication and intensity are irresistible. Chorales are almost unbelievably slow, with rallentandos added, but the devotional quality is clear; and so it is with the singing both of the fine group of soloists and of the choir. Karl Erb was in his sixties when he sang on this recording, and the voice has its thin patches, but he was still unrivalled in Germany as the Evangelist, moving in his narration. Outstanding among the others is the soprano, Jo Vincent, with the alto, Ilona Durigo, firm and strong too, and Louis van Tulder is an attractively light tenor soloist. The recording, made by Dutch Radio using a process that extended the frequency range usual at that time, has come up very vividly in the Naxos transfer. Mengelberg made substantial cuts in the original performance but, unlike the Philips transfer to CD, which cut still further to fit the work on two discs, this one has the original recording complete. That allows Naxos to add all the other Bach recordings made commercially by Mengelberg between 1929 and 1938, notably a Columbia recording of the *B minor Suite* made in the Concertgebouw in 1931 in surprisingly full and vivid sound, using two (unnamed) flute soloists in unison so as to balance

the large body of strings. In these other Bach recordings speeds are generally not as expansive as those in the *Passion*, with allegros often well sprung. The instrumentalists include Pier van Egmond and the flautist Hubert Barwahser. It first appeared on four Philips LPs and has been expertly restored by Mark Obert-Thorne on these three CDs. The sleeve speaks of it as being 'abridged' but, apart from a cut after the recitative at 49 to the recitative at 53, and the omission of sections 23, 29, 41, 70 and 75, it is complete. In its way it is glorious in much the same way as was Albert Coates' superb pre-war *B minor Mass*, with its rich string sonority, legato phrasing and great tonal warmth. Obert-Thorne is quite right to claim that at its best the sound approaches the level of 'early 1950s tape', which enables us to hear Mengelberg's forces with an often striking presence.

BACH, P. D. Q. (1807–1742?)

The Abduction of Figaro (opera; ed. Peter
Schickele).

*** VAI **DVD** VAIDVD 4251. Kruger, Brustadt, Lloyd,
   Burt, Roy, Ferrante, Walsh, Lehr, Kaemmer, Ford,
   Minnesota Op. Ch., Corpse de Ballet & O, Peter
   Schickele (includes excerpts from *Concerto for
   Diverse Flutes* and 1972 TV Interview: Schickele in
   converstaion with Gordon Hunt).

In the words of Peter Schickele, his amanuensis and creator(?), 'P. D. Q. Bach, is the last and least of Johann Sebastian Bach's twenty-one children, a pimple on the face of music', with the unlikely dates (1807–1742). It is P. D. Q.'s 'masterpiece', *The Abduction of Figaro*, which is recorded here in a 1984 performance. Mr Schickele conducts it vivaciously himself in an undoubtedly first-class live performance by members of the Minnesota Opera.

After the cleverly contrived Overture, the opening scene mirrors that in *Gianni Schicchi*, with the key characters gathered round Figaro's bedside (the doctor dubious as to his survival) singing a preposterous opening ensemble, 'Found a peanut'. But this is immediately contrasted with Susanna's quite touching aria to her husband, 'Stay with me'. This establishes the basic style: Mozartian pastiche, drawing primarily on the five key operas, but also with a dash of *The Pirates of Penzance*, when Captain Kadd arrives and sails off with Figaro, still in his bed.

The sub-plot centres on Donald Giovanni's determination to elude the matrimonial ambitions of the no longer chaste Donna Anna, balanced by the pair of real lovers, the intendingly faithful but thwarted Pecadillo and the worldly-wise Blondie. In the extended final scene of Act II she tells the angrily thwarted Donna Anna, 'You show me a man who is faithful and I'll show you a man that's impotent'. Then she sings her spectacular coloratura aria, *Macho macho*, which begins very like Mozart's *Batti batti* and ends with the abrupt admonition, 'I kid you not'!

Act III, set in *A Magic Forest*, opens with a mock ballet sequence, made the more amusing because, despite various mishaps, it is danced so gracefully by the Minnesota *corpse de ballet*. By now all the principal characters have arrived on Pasha Shaboom's island, and Opec, the amiable male alto equivalent of Osmin, sings an aria that takes us straight into the Pasha's Seraglio, echoed even more recognizably by the Mozartian chorus that follows. Papa Geno and Mama Geno arrive to sing a mock Country-and-Western duet. But it is Schlepporello who stops the show by stealing the pirate treasure and demanding his chance to sing an aria, '*Why oh why?*', before he restores it for the grand finale.

The composer has a remarkable affinity with Mozartian vocal ensemble and part-writing, and this provides charming musical substance to offset the various extravgances and vulgarities of the text. Indeed, much of the P. D. Q. Bach music is memorable. The closing Quartet from Scene 1, *Love is gone*, Pedrillo's charming aria, *Behold Fair Maiden*, in Scene 2, the sparkling Scene 3 Sextet, *What a downer*, are all most enjoyable, while the famous Trio from *Così fan tutte* is obviously the derivation for the delightful quintet and ensemble that ends Act I. The duet, shared by Pecadillo and Donald Giovanni as they survive their shipwreck, *God be praised*, which opens Act II, is no less attractive.

The soloists are all excellent, with Marilyn Brustadt a formidable Donna Anna, and the elusive but warm-voiced Donald Giovanni (Michael Burt) making a splendid duo. Lisbeth Lloyd confidently reaches up into the coloratura stratosphere as the cynical Blondie, and the heady tenor of Bruce Edwin Ford as Pecadillo is a pleasure throughout.

When the curtain falls, we hear what became of all the characters after the story ended, including the surviving Figaro, who 'ended up in Paris where he founded a newspaper'. It is all nonsense – but very enjoyable nonsense, especially if one enters fully into the spirit of Peter Schickele's skilful parody. At the opening of the DVD he introduces, using his characteristic deadpan manner (which we encounter again in the Bonus Interview), his special creation/discovery (?) of the composer's music. However, the weaker humour of the bonus excerpts from the *Gross Concerto for Diverse Flutes*, all of which Schickele plays himself, just about raises a smile, though his intrumental expertise is remarkable.

BACH, Wilhelm Friedemann
(1710–84)

Double Concerto for 2 Harpsichords in D, F.46.

(BB) **(*) Warner Apex 2564 61137-2. Uittenbosch, Curtis, VCM, Harnoncourt – J. C. BACH: *Sinfonia concertante in F* **(*); C. P. E. BACH: *Double Concerto for Harpsichord and Fortepiano* ***; J. S. BACH: *Double Harpsichord Concerto No. 1 in C min etc.* **(*)

Wilhelm Friedemann's *Double Concerto* is a much less remarkable piece than Carl Philipp Emanuel's *Concerto for Harpsichord and Fortepiano*. It is well enough played here, although tuttis are a bit gruff and rather heavily accented. Nevertheless, this bargain disc is generously full and is well worth its modest cost.

Fantasia in C min., F.2; 8 Fugues, F.31; March, F.30; Prelude, F.29; Sonatas: in G, F.7; A min., F.8; Suite in G min., F.24.

⊖– (B) *** HM HMA 1951305. Rousset (harpsichord).

Admirably recorded in 1989, this is a first-class collection of Wilhelm Friedmann's keyboard music to match Harmonia Mundi's companion disc of orchestral repertoire (HMC 901772 – see our main volume). We have already discovered the originality of the *Fantasy in F minor*. If the *A minor Sonata* is rather less innovative, it immediately opens with a flowing and attractive melody which is to be the basis of an elegant *rondeau à la française*. The *Largo* is brief and ruminative, the finale full of infectious imitative bravura. Its companion is more adventurous, with a fantasy-like opening movement, an eloquent central *Lament* and a brilliant Gigue finale in the style of a canon, which even quotes from the eleventh of the *Goldberg Variations*!

The *Suite* has no overture, but a dotted rhythm gives character to the opening *Allemande*, and the *Courante* and *Sarabande* are fully worthy of a son of Johann Sebastian; the following *Presto* and duple-time *Bourrée*, with its two triple-time Minuet-Trios, are no less diverting.

Most remarkable of all are the *Eight Fugues*, their contrapuntal mastery in no doubt, yet each is a striking musical vignette in its own right, with much variety of invention, and the final *F minor Fugue* the most extended. The *Prelude* and dignified little *March* make an attractive interlude and, with characteristically peerless performances from Christophe Rousset (playing a copy of a 1710 Mietke), this is a remarkably satisfying recital, well documented too.

BAGUER, Carlos (1768–1808)

Symphonies Nos. 12 in E flat; 13 in E flat; 16 in G; 18 in B flat.

*** Chan. 9456. LMP, Bamert.

The Catalan composer Carlos Baguer was born in Barcelona and spent his musical life there. The orchestra of the Barcelona Opera gave evening concerts, to which symphonies were introduced in the 1780s, and those of Haydn were to dominate the musical scene from 1782 onwards. Baguer soon adopted the four-movement Haydn pattern, and these symphonies date from a decade later. The craftsmanship is sound but conventional, as is the scoring, although there is some pleasingly assured invention. Although there is a certain warm graciousness to the writing, it is perhaps suprising that there is no local colour and no gypsy influences, not even in the finales. The performances here are nicely turned, and beautifully recorded in the best Chandos manner.

BAINES, William (1899–1922)

The Chimes; Coloured Leaves; Etude in F sharp min.; Idyll; The Naiad; Paradise Gardens; 7 Preludes; Silverpoints; Tides; Twilight Pieces.
*** Priory PRCD 550. Parkin.

William Baines spent his whole life in Yorkshire. It is his piano music for which he is renowned, and this collection explains why. His rhapsodic melodic style is undoubtedly individual and his use of irregular rhythms is so smoothly employed that they seem imperceptible. The greater number of these pieces are pictorial and the harmonic progressions are often quite strikingly effective; but Baines was at his finest when writing reflectively, and the three *Twilight Pieces* are delightful, while the brief *Etude in F sharp minor*, which ends the recital somewhat abruptly, is melodically quite haunting. Eric Parkin proves an ideal advocate of this rewarding music, and he is very naturally recorded.

BAINTON, Edgar (1880–1956)

Symphony No. 2 in D min.
*** Chan. 9757. BBC PO, Handley – CLIFFORD: *Symphony;* GOUGH: *Serenade.* ***

Edgar Bainton was born in London and was a pupil of Stanford. The *Symphony No. 2* is exactly contemporaneous with the Hubert Clifford work with which it is coupled. It is in one movement but falls into a dozen or so short sections, all played without a break. Its outlook is overtly romantic, but whereas Clifford's music has a stronger affinity with, say, Bliss or Walton, Bainton is closer to Arnold Bax. He certainly knows how to score and, although this symphony is uneven in quality of ideas, there is a lot of it that is both inventive and rewarding. A worthwhile and enterprising issue with first-rate playing from the BBC Philharmonic under Handley, and excellent recording.

Miniature Suite (for 2 pianos).
*** Olympia OCD 683. Goldstone and Clement – HOLST: *The Planets, etc.* *** (with BURY: *Prelude and Fugue in E flat;* ELGAR: *Serenade in E min.* ***).

Bainton's charming *Miniature Suite* is played and recorded most persuasively as is the transcription of Elgar's *Serenade.* Frank Bury's *Prelude and Fugue* is equally well crafted and makes an apt and enjoyable bonus. Bury's career was cut sadly short when as a commando he was killed during the Battle of Normandy in 1944.

BALADA, Leonardo (born 1933)

(i) *Cello Concerto No. 2 (New Orleans);* (ii) *Concerto for 4 Guitars and Orchestra; Celebració; Passacaglia.*
(BB) *** Naxos 8.557049. (i) Sanderling; (ii) Versailles Guitar Qt; Barcelona SO & Catalonia Nat. O, Pearce.

Leonardo Balada is a native of Barcelona; he studied at the Conservatorio del Liceu and later at the Juilliard School in New York, where his composition professors included Aaron Copland and Vincent Persichetti. Since 1970 he has been professor of composition at Pittsburgh. Many of his works, including *Torquemada* and the *Concerto for Piano, Winds and Percussion,* have been recorded, mainly on the New World label. His early works blended avant-garde styles with ethnic elements. The *Cello Concerto No. 2 (New Orleans),* superbly played here by its dedicatee, Michael Sanderling, and the *Passacaglia for Orchestra* are recent works, both dating from 2002. The *Concerto for Four Guitars and Orchestra* of 1976 represents the avant-garde side of his personality, while the *Celebració* from 1992, commissioned to mark the millennium of Catalonia, embraces Catalan folk melodies. Those of an exploratory cast of mind should investigate this interesting figure.

BALAKIREV, Mily (1837–1910)

Symphony No. 1 in C; Russia; Tamara (Symphonic Poems).
(BB) *** Regis RRC 1131. USSR State SO, Svetlanov.

Svetlanov's earlier (1974) Russian recording of Balakirev's *First Symphony* brings an interpretation that is little different from his later, Hyperion account with the Philharmonia, except that the performance has more grip and tension. The Russian strings give much pleasure, the wonderfully lyrical slow movement is both atmospheric and warmly relaxed, and the Russian clarinettist plays his solo delightfully. The finale has both striking impetus and gleaming Russian woodwind colour. The recording is rich and well detailed. While Beecham reigns supreme in the symphony, this is still a first-rate bargain, for the two melodically attractive symphonic poems are splendidly done, among the finest in the catalogue, and here the 1978 recording is (if anything) even more vividly colourful. Beecham's disc is available on BBC Legends (BBCL 4084-2) coupled with Borodin and Rimsky-Korsakov – see our main volume.

BANCHIERI, Adriano (1568–1634)

Festino nella sera del giovedì grasso avanti cena, Op. 18; Il Zabaione musicale.
(BB) *** Naxos 8.553785. R. Svizzara (Lugano) Ch., Sonatori de la Gioiosa Marca, Treviso, Fasolis.

Banchieri here presents a pair of musical entertainments built on varied sequences of madrigals. *Il Zabaione musicale* consists of an introduction and three acts, made up of 17 very brief madrigals. The *Festino* – an 'Entertainment for the Eve of Carnival Thursday before Dinner' – is a sequence of 21 very light-hearted madrigals, some of them involving animal and bird noises, as for example the memorable quartet for owl, cuckoo, cat and dog. Diego Fasolis draws superb singing from his Lugano choir, with incisively crisp ensemble, colourfully enhanced by brass and timpani. Excellent recording, made in the studios of Radio Lugano. A splendid example of Naxos enterprise. Full texts and an English translation are provided.

BANKS, Tony (born 1950)

Seven (suite).
(BB) Naxos 8.5547466. LPO, Dixon.

Tony Banks's celebrity is as keyboard player and composer for a celebrated rock group. He has also written several successful film scores, composing from the piano, with the orchestration provided by others. But for the genesis of his first major 'classical' composition, he worked painstakingly alongside arranger Simon Hale to create his suite directly in orchestral terms. The resulting seven movements remain in the style of film music, but show a genuine melodic gift, even if his themes are short-breathed. The snag is the repetition and inflation of the simple basic material, especially in the opening and closing numbers. The first, *Spring Tide*, introduces a kind of sinuous chorale, out of which grows the catchy six-note main motive that dominates the movement and that is built to a big climax, then gently subsiding. *Black Dawn*, which follows ('influenced by the music of Vaughan Williams'), opens darkly on lower strings but flowers expressively as the music moves up to the violins and ends nostalgically.

The *Gateway* begins with a gentle flute solo, and is divertingly scored throughout. The *Ram* then makes a robust contrast, 'more rhythmic and up-tempo', exuberantly repetitive but bringing occasional crudeness in the scoring, as in the combination of strings and trombones. *Earthlight* creates a Romantic pastoral mood and is in the form of simple variations, while *Neap Tide* is more sustained and evocative, characteristically repetitive, but rather affecting.

The final *Spirit of Gravity* is the most extended movement of all, 'travelling through a number of different musical ideas', notably another expanding chorale-like figure, 'only to end up finally where it began'. It is a curiously abrupt close for such an extended movement, but the composer obviously needed to stop. Overall this is an ambitious début, yet one that is, in the main, successful. The LPO under Mike Dixon play the whole work committedly, bringing out any individuality of colouring. The recording is good, not outstanding but acceptably

spacious, and it seems likely that such listener-friendly music has every chance of success with the composer's many admirers.

BARBER, Samuel (1910–81)

Cello Concerto, Op. 22.
*** Naïve V4961. Gastinel, CBSO, Brown – ELGAR: *Cello Concerto.* ***

Like her conductor, Justin Brown, Anne Gastinel is making her début on record, and she couples this fine account of the Barber *Cello Concerto* with a noble and dignified account of the Elgar. Ever since Zara Nelsova's pioneering record with the composer, this has struck us as one of the most enduring and perennially fresh cello concertos of the century, worthy to rank alongside the Shostakovich, and it has been gratifying to note its return to the CD repertoire. This performance was recorded in Birmingham in September 2003. Gastinel is a thoughtful and sensitive artist and her recording is among the very finest now available, although the Wendy Warner/Alsop version on Naxos is also highly recommendable, and for many will have a more suitable coupling (8.559088 – see our main volume). But this new issue does justice to the work's lyricism and freshness and to the gentle melancholy that lies not far beneath the surface at times. Very good sound.

Violin Concerto, Op. 14.
(M) *** Decca 476 17235. Bell, Baltimore SO, Zinman– BLOCH: *Baal Shem*; WALTON: *Violin Concerto.* ***
(M) *** EMI 5 62600-2. Perlman, Boston SO, Ozawa – BERNSTEIN: *Serenade after Plato's 'Symposium'*; FOSS: *3 American Pieces.* ***

Joshua Bell's passionate playing in the Barber, full of tender poetry, is well matched by the excellent orchestra, ripely and brilliantly recorded, with the soloist well forward but not aggressively so. This now takes pride of place. It won the 1998 *Gramophone* Concerto Award and now re-appears at mid-price in Universal's Gramophone Award Collection.

Perlman's outstanding account, both warmly intense and dazzling in the finale, now comes at mid-price as part of the 'Perlman Edition', retaining its two enterprising couplings.

Essays Nos. 2, Op. 17; 3, Op. 47; (i) Toccata Festiva, Op. 36. (ii) Knoxville: Summer of 1915, Op. 24.
(BB) *** Naxos 8.559134. RSNO, Alsop, with (i) Trotter; (ii) Gauvin.

Marin Alsop continues her outstanding series of Barber recordings for Naxos with an attractive group of works, including one of the most popular of all, the evocative setting of a prose poem by James Agee, *Knoxville: Summer of 1915*, with the Canadian soprano, Karina Gauvin, as the opulent soloist. The voice is so rich that the diction is not as clear as it might be, but happily the booklet provides the full text. Alsop's reading brings out the contrasts between the different sections more sharply than usual, and similarly in both of the *Essays* (No. 3 a late work, written in 1976) she highlights contrasts to bring out the feeling in both of compressed symphonic structures. The *Toccata Festiva* for organ and orchestra, written for the unveiling of a new organ for the Philadelphia Orchestra, is an exuberant piece that brings the widest expressive range in the organ part and with the orchestra colourful too; surprisingly, this work is a great rarity on disc, here superbly played and recorded.

Medea (ballet): Suite.

(M) ★★★ Mercury (ADD) [432 016-2].
   Eastman-Rochester O, Hanson – GOULD: *Fall River Legend*, etc. ★★★

Howard Hanson's performance is both polished and dramatic, and the brilliant 1959 Mercury recording has astonishing clarity and vivid presence.

(i) *Symphony No. 1* (in one movement), *Op. 9; Essays for Orchestra, Nos. 1, Op. 12; 2, Op. 17;* (ii) *Music for a Scene from Shelley;* (i) *Night Flight, Op. 19a;* (ii; iii) *Knoxville (Summer of 1915).*

☞ (BB) ★★★ Regis (ADD) RRC 1139. (i) LSO; (ii) Western Australia SO; Measham; (iii) with McGurk.

David Measham proves a splendid advocate of Barber's music, securing passionately committed performances of the *First Symphony* (where at times he brings out its somewhat Waltonian manner) and the powerfully romantic, yet mysterious *Music from Shelley*, an inspired early work from 1933, which ought to be better known. The two *Essays for Orchestra* are also very well played, as is the haunting movement, *Night Flight*, all that the composer originally wanted to survive from the *Symphony No. 2*. This was originally a Unicorn collection, to which the two excellent recordings from Western Australia have been addded, notably Molly McGurk's ravishing account of Barber's Coplandesque setting of *Knoxville*, a prose-poem by James Agee. Framed by a lilting, folk-like melody, it is a young girl's nostalgic reminiscence of 'the time of evening when people sit on their porches, rocking gently and talking gently and watching the street'. A rumbustious interlude pictures a streetcar 'raising its iron moan; stopping, belling and starting', and the soloist rises to an ecstatic climax in evoking the 'blue dew' of the night. Finally the child singer is 'taken in, and put to bed'. A miniature masterpiece, the performance (and recording) here could hardly be more warmly evocative. At budget price this reissue cannot be recommended too highly.

VOCAL MUSIC

Despite and Still (song-cycle), *Op. 41; 10 Hermit Songs, Op. 29; Mélodies passagères, Op. 27; 3 Songs,*

Op. 2; 3 Songs, Op. 10; 4 Songs, Op. 13; 2 Songs, Op. 18; 3 Songs, Op. 45; Beggar's Song; Dover Beach; In the Dark Pinewood; Love at the Door; Love's Caution; Night Wanderers; Nuvoletta; Of That So Sweet Imprisonment; Serenades; A Slumber Song of the Madonna; Strings in the Earth and Air; There's Nae Lark.

(M) ★★★ Decca 474 685-2 (2). Studer, Hampson; Browning or Emerson Qt.

This distinguished (originally DG) set won the *Gramophone* Solo Vocal Award in 1994 and is in every way recommenedable. (It is discussed in greater detail in our main volume.)

BARTÓK, Béla (1881–1945)

Concerto for Orchestra; (i) *Viola Concerto.*

(M) ★★★ Sup. (ADD) SU 3686-2. Czech PO, Ančerl; (i) with Karlovský.

This is the one of the first of a series of recordings made by Karel Ančerl with the Czech Philharmonic Orchestra in the early 1960s that have been transformed by expert remastering (in this instance by Stanislav Sýkora), so that at last we can hear how good the original recordings were. Certainly that applies to this 1963 recording of the *Concerto for Orchestra*, made in the Rudolfinum Studio, Prague, with the violins bright, clear and biting, and with superb inner detail, yet no lack of ambient lustre on the woodwind. It is not the most ruthless performance on record, as one might have expected from one of the most distinguished Slavonic orchestras; rather it is a highly atmospheric and vigorously understanding one, which demonstrates the virtuosity of both the string section and individual players in the way Bartók intended, culminating in a brilliant and exciting account of the finale. This now projects as one of the finest performances in the catalogue and fully deserves its three-star rating.

The coupling of the *Viola Concerto*, a less coherent work, is not quite on this level. The soloist here does not seem able to make a great deal of the first movement, which is perhaps not altogether his fault – the work has since been re-edited by Bartók's son, Peter. But the violist seems much happier in the *Adagio* and finale, although his playing is without a strong personality. However, the recording is well balanced.

(i) *Concerto for Orchestra;* (ii) *Dance Suite; 2 Portraits, Op. 5; Mikrokosmos* (orch. Serly): *Bourrée; From the Diary of a Fly.*

(M) ★★★ Mercury (ADD) [432 017-2]. (i) LSO; (ii) Philh. Hung.; Dorati.

Dorati secures outstandingly brilliant and committed playing from the LSO. The recording, made in Wembley Town Hall, shows characteristic expertise of balance. The rest of the programme was recorded in 1958 in the Grosse Saal of the Vienna Konzerthaus, which affords Dorati's fine orchestra of Hungarian émigrés plenty of body without blurring outlines.

Concerto for Orchestra; Music for Strings, Percussion & Celesta.

(M) ** Orfeo (ADD) C551 011B. Bav. RSO, Kubelik.

Kubelik served as chief conductor of the Bavarian Radio Symphony Orchestra for 18 years, and this account of the *Concerto for Orchestra* was recorded in March 1978 during his tenure; the *Music for Strings, Percussion and Celesta* comes from a guest appearance three years later. There is much to impress, though neither displaces existing recommendations.

Piano Concertos Nos. 1–2.

(M) *** DG 471 360-2. Pollini, Chicago SO, Abbado – STRAVINSKY: *3 Movements from Petrushka.* ***

Pollini's exuberant performances with Abbado, reviewed in our main *Guide*, are now reissued in the 'Pollini Edition' with a Stravinsky coupling instead of Bartók's *Two Portraits*. The two concertos are also available as part of the *Gramophone* Awards Collection on 474 540-2, but apparently without a coupling, as with the original issue.

Piano Concertos Nos. 1–3.

(B) ** Sony SBK 89732. Bronfman, LAPO, Salonen.

These 1996 performances have not taken long to resurface in a more competitive price bracket. Yefim Bronfman is a master pianist and takes all the technical challenges easily in his stride. But the readings as a whole do not take fire in the way that the very finest do. The orchestral playing is cultured rather than characterful, and readers wanting all three concertos on one disc will do better with Schiff at mid-price (Elatus 0927 46735-2) or Kocsis (Philips 446 366-2) or, also at mid-price, Anda (DG 447 399-2).

(i) Piano Concerto No. 3; (ii) Violin Concerto No. 2.

(M) *** Sup. SU 3682-2 011. (i) Bernáthová; (ii) Gertler; Czech PO, Ančerl.

Bernáthová's is an essentially lyrical reading of the *Third Concerto*, but her skittish, lightly pointed articulation is appealing in the outer movements to make a perfect foil for the mood of the *Adagio religioso* slow movement, which is beautifully played and most affecting. This is well coupled with André Gertler's dedicated performance of the *Violin Concerto*, which also strikes a happy balance between romanticism and technical brilliance. Again the opening is light in style with nice, snapping rhythms and crisp accentuation, and in the slow movement Gertler treats the music affectingly as a simple song. In the finale he is most successful in bringing out the scherzando humour. Ančerl's accompaniments are characteristically idiomatic in both works, and this is eminently recommendable, with good, atmospheric 1960s recording naturally transferred to CD.

(i) Piano Concerto No. 3; (ii) Sonata for Two Pianos and Percussion.

(BB) **(*) EMI Encore (ADD) 5 74991-2. Ogdon, (i) Philh. O, Sargent; (ii) Lucas, Holland, Fry – SHOSTAKOVICH: *Piano Concerto No. 2.* ***

Ogdon gives a fine performance of the *Third Concerto*, although Sargent's accompaniment lacks the last degree of brilliance – the result brings out neither the joy nor the poetry of the work at the fullest intensity. The *Sonata for Two Pianos*, however, receives a stimulating performance from the husband-and-wife team: it is not always as sparkling as it might be (the finale runs down a little) but rarely have two pianists achieved such fine technical and emotional rapport in this music.

(i) Viola Concerto; Violin Concertos Nos. 1–2; (ii) Rhapsodies Nos. 1–2 for Violin and Orchestra; (iii) Duos Nos. 28, 31, 33, 36, 41, 42 for 2 Violins. Solo Violin Sonata.

(BB) *** EMI Gemini (ADD) 5 85497-2 (2). Y. Menuhin; (i) New Philh. O, Dorati; (ii) BBC SO, Boulez; (iii) Gotkovsky.

Menuhin, with his strongly creative imagination, plays these concertos with characteristic nobility of feeling, and he and Dorati make much of the Hungarian dance rhythms. There is an appealing, earthy, peasant manner in Menuhin's playing of the *Two Rhapsodies*, which are given an authentic tang, and rather surprisingly this is matched by Boulez's approach, warm, rather than clinical. The great violinist commissioned the *Solo Violin Sonata*, and this is his third recording, made at Abbey Road in 1974/5. The six individually chosen *Duos* make a bonus for what is a very attractive bargain double.

(i) Violin Concerto No. 2. Second Suite for Orchestra (revised, 1943 version).

(M) **(*) Mercury (IMS) (ADD) [434 350-2]. (i) Y. Menuhin; Minneapolis SO, Dorati.

Menuhin's third version of the *Second Violin Concerto* (1957) is much better recorded than either of his earlier records and remains thoroughly worthwhile, with the solo playing demonstrating those special qualities of lyrical feeling and warmth for which he was justly famous. The rare coupling makes this Mercury reissue doubly attractive. The *Second Orchestral Suite* is a colourful, half-hour-long piece in four movements. Dorati is a persuasive advocate, and the characteristically graphic Mercury recording has no lack of primary colours.

(i) Divertimento for Strings; (ii) Music for Strings, Percussion & Celesta; (iii) Sonata for 2 Pianos & Percussion.

**(*) Oxford OOCD-CD2 (1/2) (2). (i; ii) Oxford O da Camera, Sacher; (ii; iii) Fry, Holland; (iii) Berman, Lemin.

In September 1995, within months of his own ninetieth birthday, the commissionee, Paul Sacher, recorded these live performances with the Oxford Orchestra da Camera, and he here introduces each with his own unique commentary in English. At speeds generally broader than usual, these unique performances may lack the vitality and bite of the finest rivals, but they have a compelling warmth and concentration. The two discs may be obtained from the orchestra direct (2 Axtell Close, Kidlington, Oxford).

(i) *The Miraculous Mandarin* (complete); *Hungarian Peasant Songs; Hungarian Sketches; Romanian Folk Dances; Transylvanian Dances.*
*** (M) Ph. 476 17990. (i) Hung. R. Ch., Budapest Festival O, Fischer.

The Miraculous Mandarin (complete); *Music for Strings, Percussion & Celesta.*
** DG (IMS) 447 747-2. Chicago SO, Boulez.

Iván Fischer's account of *The Miraculous Mandarin* is possibly the best ever committed to disc, and certainly the best recorded. The sound is in the demonstration category, with enormous range and depth. It has vivid presence and impact, and the balance is both truthful and refined. The performance has collected golden opinions almost everywhere and has virtuosity, bite and real flair. It won the *Gramophone* Orchestral Award in 1998 and is now reissued at mid-price in Universal's Award Collection: it makes a first-class recommendation for this repertoire.

In his later, DG recording, Boulez takes a characteristically objective view of both works. The playing is brilliant and the recording full and detailed; but with Boulez it is a musical tapestry and not much more. His objectivity works better in the *Music for Strings, Percussion and Celesta*, which begins with the most refined pianissimo.

Rhapsody No. 1 for Cello and Orchestra.
(BB) *** Warner Apex 0927 40600-2. Noras, Finnish RSO, Saraste – ELGAR: *Cello Concerto*; DVORAK: *Cello Concerto.* **(*)

Bartók scored only the first of his two *Rhapsodies* (originally written for violin and piano) for cello and orchestra, and very effective it is on the responsive bow of Arto Noras. The piece is in two sections, *Lassu* and *Friska*, and the contrasts between the lyrical and fiery elements are managed here with aplomb. Good though not oustanding recording, with the cello dominating the sound-picture.

The Wooden Prince (complete); *Music for Strings, Percussion & Celesta.*
(M) **(*) Mercury (ADD) [434 357-2]. LSO, Dorati.

Dorati's performances of both works are brilliantly authentic. *The Wooden Prince* is given a fresh, dynamic reading, vivid in its detail, with the reminders of Stravinsky and the Debussian textures brilliantly caught. The *Music for Strings, Percussion and Celesta* is comparably atmospheric, the playing full of

tension, and Dorati brings out the Hungarian dance inflexions in the finale. The recordings, from 1964 and 1960 respectively, hardly sound their age.

CHAMBER AND INSTRUMENTAL MUSIC

(i; ii) *Contrasts for Clarinet, Violin & Piano;* (ii) *2 Rhapsodies; Romanian Folk Dances.* (Solo) *Violin Sonata.*
(BB) *** Hyp. Helios CDH 55149. Osostowicz, with (i) M. Collins; (ii) Tomes.

Hyperion's distinguished coupling of the Bartók *Contrasts*, with the *Rhapsodies* and the *Sonata for Solo Violin*, now re-emerges on the Helios budget label. All these artists are on excellent form. Krysia Osostowicz is as good as almost any of her rivals in the *Sonata*, and the remainder of the programme is hardly less impressive.

String Quartets Nos 1–6.
(M) *** DG 476 18331. Tokyo Qt.

The DG performances by the Tokyo Quartet bring an almost ideal combination of fire and energy, with detailed point and refinement. The readings are consistently satisfying. Though the polish is high, the sense of commitment and seeming spontaneity are great too. The set now reappears at mid-price in Universal's Award Collection (the Tokyo Quartet won the 1981 *Gramophone* Chamber Music Award).

String Quartet No. 4.
**(*) ECM 465 776-2. Zehetmair Qt (with HARTMANN: *String Quartet No. 1* **(*)).

No quarrels with the Zehetmair's performance of the *Fourth Quartet* (1928), although collectors will probably be more attracted by one of the complete Bartók cycles. The Hartmann coupling, which was written five years later, is an interesting piece and is otherwise not available. However, the disc runs to only 43 minutes, which, at full price, is poor value for money. Three stars for artistic merit, none for economy.

String Quartet No. 5.
(M) (**(*)) Orfeo mono C604031B. Hungarian Qt – SCHUBERT: *String Quartet No. 15.* (**(*))

The Hungarian Quartet made the first commercial recording of the *Fifth Quartet* immediately after the Second World War on four plum-label HMV 78rpm records, but this was never transferred to LP or CD so far as we know. They recorded the complete cycle for DG in 1961, at about the same time as this Munich concert performance. Not quite as finely controlled as their studio recording, it has plenty of intensity. In the absence of their DG set (which may return to the catalogue during the lifetime of this volume) this is a useful reminder of their quality. Decent but not distinguished mono sound.

Portrait, Op. 5/1.

◉ (BB) (★★★) Naxos mono 8.110973. Szigeti, Philh. O, Lambert – BLOCH: *Violin Concerto;* PROKOFIEV: *Violin Concerto No. 1* (★★★). ◉

Szigeti was a stylist and one of the greatest and most individual artists of his day. Not everyone responds to the slightly nasal tone or the nervous vibrato, but there is no questioning the strength of his personality or the quality of his artistry. They are heard to admirable effect in this outstanding account of the first of the Bartók *Portraits*, which he recorded with Constant Lambert on one of his first post-war visits to London. Naxos should reissue the remarkable records he made with Bartók himself in New York.

PIANO MUSIC

Allegro barbaro; 14 Bagatelles; 3 Burlesques; For Children; 4 Dirges; 10 Easy Pieces; 2 Elegies; The First Term at the Piano; 15 Hungarian Peasant Songs; 3 Hungarian Folksongs from the Csík District; Hungarian Folk Tunes; 8 Improvisations on Hungarian Peasant Songs; 9 Little Piece Pieces, Out of Doors; Petite Suite; 3 Rondos on Slovak Folk Tunes; Romanian Christmas Carols; 6 Romanian Folkdances; 2 Romanian Dances; 7 Sketches Suite (with original *Andante*). *Sonata; Sonatina; 3 Studies. Violin Duos* (arr. Sándor): *1, Teasing Song; 17, Marching Song; 35, Ruthenian Kolomejka; 42, Arabian Song; 44, Transylvanian Dance.*

(M) ★★★ Sony SX4K 68275 (4). Sándor.

Older collectors will remember that György Sándor made the very first recording of the *Third Piano Concerto* with Eugene Ormandy and the Philadelphia Orchestra, and he recorded the complete piano music on Vox in the early 1960s. Here he adds a few titles not included in his earlier survey, a short *Andante* originally intended as the second movement of the *Suite*, Op. 14, *The First Term at the Piano* and a suite of songs and dances that he has arranged (very effectively) from Bartók's *Violin Duos*. He does not include the *Mikrokosmos*, which Kocsis has recorded. Sándor of course provides a special authority in this repertoire since he knew Bartók well, and he brings an intuitive understanding to all this music. This playing has a wonderful naturalness and authenticity of feeling and, although it is not quite as magisterial pianistically as the Kocsis discs listed in our main volume, it offers insights that are equally special. The recorded sound is good, though again not the equal of the Philips.

Allegro barbaro; 3 Burlesques; 4 Dirges; 10 Easy Pieces; 3 Hungarian Folksongs from the Csík District 3 Hungarian Folk Tunes; Out of Doors; 2 Romanian Dances.

(BB) ★(★) Naxos 8.555329. Jandó.

Jenö Jandó is a very capable player, though he is far less subtle than Zoltán Kocsis or György Sándor. Part of the problem is the rather closely balanced and bottom-heavy recording but, even making allowances for that, put the *Barcarolla* or *Night Music* from *Out of Doors* alongside that of Kocsis or Sándor and their greater imagination and sensitivity shine through. Idiomatic playing of course, but by no means as impressive as one would expect.

14 Bagatelles, Op. 6; 2 Elegies, Op. 8b; 3 Hungarian Folk tunes; 6 Romanian Folk Tunes; Sonatina.

◉ (M) ★★★ Ph. 476 1657. Kocsis.

This was one of the CDs that R. L. chose as being special among the coverage of Bartók's piano music by Zoltán Kocsis and that Universal have now included in their mid-priced 'Penguin ◉ Collection'. Not only does it have the advantage of state-of-the-art recording quality, but it also has playing which leads the field in subtlety and imagination.

BAX, Arnold (1883–1953)

Christmas Eve; Cortège; Dance of Wild Irravel; Festival Overture; Nympholept; Overture to a Picaresque Comedy; Paean.

(M) ★★(★) Chan. X10158. LPO, Thomson.

Volume 5 in the Chandos series is perhaps for Bax aficionados rather than the general collector. It includes intriguing novelties, but the compilation is uneven in appeal. The *Overture to a Picaresque Comedy* is first-rate Bax, high-spirited and inventive. *Nympholept* means 'possessed by nymphs' and is another imaginative piece. However, *Christmas Eve* is an early work, coming from the Edwardian era, and is less developed and less interesting, while the *Paean* and *Dance of Wild Irravel* may stretch the allegiance of some listeners. The *Festival Overture* dates from 1909, but was revised in 1918 (and as such is recorded here for the first time). It is certainly spirited, if not distinctive. But all the performances here are sympathetic, and very well played and recorded too.

(i) Cello Concerto; (ii) Violin Concerto; (iii) Morning Song (Maytime in Sussex).

(M) ★★★ Chan. X10154. (i) Wallfisch; (ii) Mordkovitch; (iii) Fingerhut; LPO, Thomson.

Chandos is re-grouping its vintage Bax recordings at mid-price, and Volume 1 includes two major concertante works plus the short but attractive *Morning Song*, an aubade for piano and chamber orchestra written to celebrate the twenty-first birthday of Princess Margaret, and subsequently made famous by Harriet Cohen. The *Cello Concerto* is rhapsodic in feeling and Raphael Wallfisch plays it with marvellous sensitivity and finesse, while Lydia Mordkovitch is equally committed to the *Violin Concerto*. This is full of good, easily remembered tunes, yet there is a plangent, bitter-sweet quality about many of its ideas and an easy, Mediterranean-like warmth that is very appealing. All three soloists are given splendid support by the LPO under Bryden Thomson, and the recording sets and maintain high standards for this Bax series.

(i) *Coronation March;* **(ii)** *November Woods;* **(iii)** *Oliver Twist: Fagin's Romp; Finale.* **(iv)** *Tintagel;* **(v)** *Fanfare for the Wedding of Princess Elizabeth.*

(M) (**) Decca mono/stereo 473 080-2. (i) LSO, Sargent; (ii) ASMF, Marriner; (iii) Nat. PO, Herrmann; (iv) LPO, Boult; (v) Philip Jones Brass Ens.

Some good things here, though this collection as a whole feels rather bitty. Boult's classic mono *Tintagel* is lively and highly atmospheric, and though the 1955 sound is slightly limited, it still makes quite an impact. Marriner, hardly a conductor associated with Bax, gives us an effective account of the fine tone-poem *November Woods*, with the haunting, windswept atmosphere well caught in the vivid and warm (Philips) sound, though it does not eclipse Boult's classic Lyrita account (alas no longer current). Sargent's vigorous 1954 recording of the *Coronation March* (mono) is well known, and the seven minutes of music for *Oliver Twist* and the *Fanfare* are pleasing enough. However, this CD, lasting under 49 minutes, is not generous by today's standards, even at mid-price.

Film Music: (i) *Oliver Twist* **(complete original score, prepared Graham Parlett).** *Malta G.C.,* **Part 2:** *Gay March; Quiet Interlude; Work and Play; March.*

*** Chan. 10126. BBC PO, Gamba; (i) with James.

Bax's richly detailed score for David Lean's masterly *Oliver Twist* comes from 1948, during that vintage period in British films when the cream of British composers, including Bliss, Arnold and Walton, were commissioned to provide music of quality that could stand on its own apart from the visual images. Bax's score for *Oliver Twist* is a splendid example, yet it follows the narrative line with the utmost vividness and often with charming detail. In the depiction of Oliver's sleepless night, and again in the amiable depiction of Oliver's happiness at Mr Brownlow's house, Bax writes in effect a concertante piano part, originally written for (and recorded by) Harriet Cohen, but very well played here by Paul James. What is even more impressive is that the writing in the action sequences ('Nancy's hysterical outburst', for instance) never becomes just melodama but retains its quality.

The writing for *Malta G.C.* is less individual but still attractive. It was the composer's first film score, written in 1942 for a Crown Film Unit propaganda short celebrating the island's valour in the face of fierce and protracted air attacks. Only the music for the first reel is included here, but it features a notable *March* with a genuine *nobilmente* theme in the best Elgarian tradition.

The performances under Rumon Gamba are persuasively sympathetic and spontaneous in their narrative flow and are gloriously recorded – just sample the luscious strings in the opening *Prelude* for *Oliver Twist.* Because of this, the previous coupling of these scores, admirably played by the RPO under Kenneth Alwyn, is to some extent displaced, although the Cloud Nine CD (ACN 7012), while offering only a suite from *Oliver Twist,* includes the full score of *Malta G.C.,* otherwise not available.

Golden Eagle; **(i)** *Romantic Overture. Russian Suite;* **(ii)** *Saga Fragment* **(for piano and small orchestra);** **(iii)** *4 Songs: Eternity; Glamour; Lyke-Wake; Slumber Song.*

(M) ** Chan. X10159. LPO, Thomson, with (i) Nunn; (ii) Fingerhut; (iii) Hill.

Bax wrote the incidental music for his brother, Clifford's play, *Golden Eagle* (about Mary, Queen of Scots), which was briefly produced in 1945. Six orchestral numbers survive, of which the closing *Mary Stuart's Prayer* is genuinely touching. The three movements of the *Russian Suite,* all orchestrations of piano pieces, were written as 'symphonic interludes' for Diaghilev's Ballets Russes. As no orchestration of the central *Nocturne* survives, it is here scored by Graham Parlett and is the highlight. The other numbers are more conventional. The *Saga Fragment* (written for Harriet Cohen, but played here with much flair by Margaret Fingerhut) is a transcription of the one-movement *Piano Quartet* of 1922, and to some extent reflects the contrasts of atmosphere – pungent and wistful – of the *First Symphony.* The *Romantic Overture,* written during a visit to Delius in 1926, also has a concertante piano part, but it is overlong and its more striking idea does not appear until towards the end. The *Four Songs* make strange bedfellows and could not be more individually different. Bax wrote the lyrics of the first two (*Glamour* and *Slumber Song*) in 1910, when he fell ardently and hopelessly in love with a young, sylph-like Ukrainian girl, Natalia Skarginsky. He followed her back to Russia, but was rejected. The musical settings came a decade later, with *Glamour* here orchestrated by Rodney Newton. The third song, *Eternity* was a setting of Robert Herrick, while *A Lyke-Wake Border Ballad* uses an anonymous sixteenth-century text. Martyn Hill sings them all sensitively, and throughout the collection the playing of the LPO for Bryden Thomson is exemplary in its commitment and refinement. Altogether Volume 6 of the Chandos series makes an interesting collection, rather than a memorable one.

The Happy Forest; The Garden of Fand; November Woods; Summer Music; Tintagel.

(M) *** Chan. X10156. Ulster O, Thomson.

After Volume 1, Volume 3 is perhaps the most attractive so far of these reissued Chandos Bax compilations in including not only *The Garden of Fand* but also Bax's masterly Cornish evocation, *Tintagel.* The Celtic twilight is ripely and sympathetically caught in the first three items, while *Summer Music,* dedicated to Sir Thomas Beecham and here given its first ever recording, brings an intriguing kinship with the music of Delius. The Chandos recording is superb.

(i; ii) *Eire: I, Into the Twilight; II, In the Faery Hills; III, Rose-Catha.* (iii; ii) *A Legend;* (i; iv) *On the Sea-Shore* (ed. Parlett); (i; ii) *The Tale the Pine Trees Knew.*

(M) *** Chan. X10157. (i) Ulster O, (ii) Thomson; (iii) LPO; (iv) Handley.

Volume 4 brings three tone-poems which form an Irish triology. The first two are filled with typical Baxian Celtic twilight, but the last, *Rose-Catha* (meaning 'battle-hymn') presents the composer in vigorous, extrovert mood, making an excellent contrast. Also included is *The Tale the Pine Trees Knew*, one of the better known as well as one of the most evocative of Bax's tone-poems. All are directed with total sympathy by Bryden Thomson. The prelude, *On the Sea-Shore*, makes a colouful and atmospheric companion in the hands of Vernon Handley, played and recorded with similar warmth and brilliance. A fine disc.

(i) *Mediterranean. Northern Ballads Nos.* (ii) *2 &* (i) *3 (Prelude for a Solemn Occasion).* (ii) *Spring Fire; Symphonic Scherzo.*

(M) *** Chan. X10155. (i) LPO, Thomson; (ii) RPO, Handley.

Volume 2 gathers together some of Bax's shorter, atmospheric and romantic pieces in highly idiomatic performances, notably those from the RPO under Vernon Handley. *Spring Fire* is an early work, but Bax's command of the orchestra is already richly in evidence. The *Second Northern Ballad* is dark and bleak, strongly tied to the landscape of the rugged northern coasts, while the *Third* is another dark and brooding score. The *Symphonic Scherzo* is of less moment than its companions. Thoroughly lifelike and characteristically well-detailed recording from Chandos.

Sinfonietta (Symphonic Phantasy); *Overture, Elegy and Rondo.*

(BB) ** Naxos 8.555109. Slovak PO, Wordsworth.

The *Overture, Elegy and Rondo* comes from 1927, a year after the *Second Symphony*, and the *Sinfonietta* from 1932, the year of the *Fifth*. Neither finds Bax at his most inspired, though the *Sinfonietta* has a fine slow movement. The recordings come from 1987 and were previously offered at full price on Marco Polo. As the playing time of the disc is only 45 minutes, its reappearance on Naxos makes it more competitive. Neither piece is available in alternative versions. The performances are not the last word in polish and the recording does not offer distinguished sound, though it is on the whole acceptable.

Symphonic Variations; Winter Legends (both for piano and orchestra).

(B) *** Chan. 10209X (2). Fingerhut, LPO, Thomson.

It was a sensible idea to pair Bax's two concertante works together as a Chandos bargain Double (two discs for the cost of a single mid-priced record), but why omit the original bonuses of the *Morning Song* and *Saga Fragment?* Nevertheless, Margaret Fingerhut reveals the *Symphonic Variations* to be a work of considerable substance with some sinewy, powerful writing in the more combative variations, thoughtful and purposeful elsewhere. The *Winter Legends* is hardly less impressive; it comes from much the same period as the *Third Symphony*, to which at times its world seems spiritually related. The soloist again proves an impressive and totally convincing advocate, and it would be difficult to imagine the balance between soloist and orchestra being more realistically judged. Indeed, the recording is in the demonstration class – a quite outstanding coupling.

Symphonies Nos. 1–7; Rogue's Comedy Overture; Tintagel.

⊶ ✹ (M) *** Chan. 10122 (5). BBC PO, Handley (set includes free bonus CD of an interview between Vernon Handley and Andrew McGregor).

Vernon Handley has nurtured a life-long ambition to record the seven symphonies of Arnold Bax and, now that Chandos has given him the chance, he has not disappointed us. Generally speaking, this is the most satisfying survey of the cycle we have yet had, and it is difficult to imagine it being superseded. The prodigality of invention in these Bax scores and the luxuriance of their colours and textures are heard to striking effect. Handley holds the scores together very convincingly. His tempi are expertly judged and allow the music to unfold naturally and eloquently. The *Second* (in some ways the most imaginative of them all) comes over impressively (the most satisfying since a memorable broadcast from the BBC Symphony Orchestra under Sir Eugene Goossens in the 1950s), and the *Third* is both tauter yet freer in spirit than any of its rivals, including Barbirolli's wartime pioneering set. Perhaps in the *Fifth* and *Sixth* honours are more evenly divided between Handley and David Lloyd Jones and the Scottish National Orchestra; both show this music in the best possible light. Listening to Handley's *Seventh*, one is forced to question earlier doubts as to its weakness. The overall impression it leaves is much stronger than in Raymond Leppard's deleted Lyrita account or Bryden Thomson's earlier Chandos version, and much the same goes for the *Fourth*, even though this is incontrovertibly the weakest of the seven. The orchestral playing is highly responsive and excels in all departments, and the Chandos BBC recording produces sumptuous tonal results (as one expects from any record bearing the names of Mike George and Stephen Rinker). The aural picture is subtle in colourings, less transparent and defined in detail than the recent Naxos versions, but very satisfying, and it all comes at mid-price together with a rarity from the 1930s, the *Rogue's Comedy Overture*, as well as the (rightly) popular *Tintagel*.

The Naxos recordings are also very competitively priced and enable the collector to build up an imposing number of other orchestral pieces. Those who are not total devotees and who want only some of the symphonies (obviously Nos. 2, 3, 5 and 6) will probaly gravitate towards Lloyd Jones's survey (Nos. 5 and 6 are magnificent) and these are discussed in our main volume. But total Baxians will find this set indispensable. In addition to the performances, there is a commentary on the works by the conductor in interview with Andrew McGregor.

Symphony No. 7; Tintagel.
(BB) **(*) Naxos 8.557145. RSNO, Lloyd Jones.

The *Seventh Symphony* comes from 1939 and was first heard at the New York World Fair that year, conducted by Sir Adrian Boult. It was to be Bax's last symphony and one in which the creative fires seem to burn less intensely than in its two immediate predecessors. David Lloyd Jones makes out a strong case for it and is as persuasive as (or more persuasive than) his predecessors on record. The late lamented Michael Oliver spoke of its first movement as 'an essay on ambiguity ... a complex of unstable components; what appears confidently purposeful at one moment becoming tense later on'. Despite its length (it lasts 42 minutes 20 seconds – Handley is even more leisurely at 44 minutes 02 seconds – and is the longest of the seven), the score is still richly stocked. The recording has been called 'uncongenial' and 'unalluring', which strikes us as harsh, though climaxes do not have the transparency of earlier issues in the series nor the strings quite the bloom. David Lloyd Jones also gives a thoroughly committed account of *Tintagel*.

CHAMBER AND INSTRUMENTAL MUSIC

Cello Sonata in E flat; Cello Sonatina in D; Legend Sonata in F sharp min.; Folk Tale.
** ASV CDDCA 896. Gregor-Smith, Wrigley.

The *Cello Sonata* has many characteristic touches and an imaginative slow movement. Bernard Gregor-Smith and Yolande Wrigley are both highly sensitive and responsive players. In the *Sonata* the recording does not give quite enough back-to-front depth and there is a touch of glassiness about the sound. Things are a bit better in the *Folk Tale* (1920), but the recording is sufficiently wanting in bloom to inhibit a three-star recommendation.

PIANO MUSIC

Apple-Blossom Time; Burlesque; Ceremonial Dance; Country-Tune; Dream in Exile; From 'Salzburg' Sonata; A Hill Tune; In a Vodka Shop; In the Night; Lullaby; Legend; The Maiden with the Daffodil; Mediterranean; A Mountain Mood; Nereid; O Dame get up and bake your pies (Variations on a North Country Christmas Carol); On a May Evening; Paean; The Princess's Rose-Garden (Nocturne); A

Romance; 2 Russian Tone Pictures; Serpent Dance; The Slave Girl; Sleepy-Head; Sonatas Nos. 1–4; Toccata; Water Music; What the Minstrel told us; Whirligig; Winter Waters.
(M) *** Chan. X10132 (4). Parkin.

Eric Parkin proves a sympathetic guide through this repertoire. The smaller pieces are not among Bax's most important works, but in Parkin's hands they certainly sound pleasingly spontaneous. The *Sonatas* are a different matter. They are grievously neglected in the concert hall but are most convincingly presented here. The recording is on the resonant side, but the playing is outstandingly responsive.

BEACH, Amy (1867–1944)

Pastorale for Wind Quintet, Op. 151; String Quartet (in one movement), Op. 89; Violin Sonata, Op. 34; 4 Sketches for Piano: Dreaming (trans. for cello & piano).
*** Chan. 10162. Ambache.

The early *Violin Sonata* of 1897 is characteristically lyrical and very traditional in style, although the *perpetuum mobile* Scherzo brings a distinct personal touch. The slow movement is melodically and harmonically rich, if less individual, but the confident finale establishes the work's distinction, for its secondary theme is memorable. The one-movement *String Quartet*, although begun in 1921 and completed in 1929, was published only after the composer's death. Its character is determined by the three Alaskan folk themes on which it draws. The nostalgic mood created by the simple, poignant chords that dominate the opening *Grave* is dispelled by the central *Più Animato* and *Allegro molto*, but returns hauntingly at the close. The *Pastorale*, which also has a strong personal flavour, was drafted in the same year as the *String Quartet*, but the woodwind scoring was not finalized for another 20 years. It is a charming, gentle, folksy evocation with the balmy atmosphere of a summer afternoon. The arrangement of *Dreaming*, a song without words for cello and piano, gives the cello the gently rhapsodic melodic line, but the piano remains insistent. First-class performances and recording, and worth having for the *String Quartet*, one of Beach's most memorable works.

BECK, Franz Ignaz (1734–1809)

Sinfonias: in B flat; D; G; in D, Op. 10/2; in E, Op. 13/1.
(BB) *** Naxos 8.553790. N. CO, Ward.

Sinfonias: in G min.; E flat; D min., Op. 3/3–5.
(BB) *** CPO 999 390-2. La Stagione, Frankfurt, Schneider.

Franz Ignaz Beck's three-movement *Sinfonias* are concise and sharply characterized, even if they are little more than Italian overtures. The *D major Sinfonia* is the exception, with a Haydnesque pattern of four movements. Ideas are fresh, scoring simple but felicitous. The graceful *Largo* of the *B flat major* work, with its string cantilena floating over a pizzicato bass, is worthy of Boccherini, and the *E major*, Op. 13/1, is a winning little work with a diverting finale. The performances on Naxos could hardly be more persuasive, warmly elegant and full of vitality. The recording, too, is first class.

The CPO disc offers mature later works (especially the *G minor*, with the themes interrelated), which are very much in the Haydn *Sturm und Drang* style. The *D minor Sinfonia* is for strings alone, but the *E flat major*, which has a remarkably searching *Adagio*, uses the horns most effectively as soloists in the *Minuet* and *Trio* and in the closing section of the finale. The period performances here are aggressively full of gusto and vitality, creating a sound-world very different from that on the Naxos collection.

BEECKE, Ignaz von (1733–1803)

String Quartets Nos. 9 in G; 11 in G; 16 in B flat, M.9, 11 & 16.
*** CPO 999 509-2. Arioso Qt.

Ignaz von Beecke is not to be confused with Franz Ignaz Beck, above (although he was an almost exact contemporary). Beecke's string quartets were less well known in his own time than his symphonies. They are finely crafted, cultivated works, which Haydn would surely not have been ashamed to own. The disarming warmth of the opening of the *G major*, M.11 (which is first on the disc), leads to a fine opening movement with two striking themes; the *Minuet* comes second and is equally personable, and after the elegant *Adagio* the finale is as spirited as you could wish. The *B flat Quartet* is in three movements and is hardly less pleasing, with a songful *Adagio* marked *sotto voce*. The companion *G major* work brings a striking minor-key slow movement, opening with a grave slow fugue; the *Minuet* lightens the mood and prepares for a most engaging finale. All three works are thoroughly diverting when played with such warmth, vitality and finesse, and this excellent quartet is very naturally recorded.

BEETHOVEN, Ludwig van
(1770–1827)

Piano Concertos Nos. 1 in C, Op. 15; 3 in C min., Op. 37.
* Ambroisie **DVD** AMI 99403002. Duchable, Ens. de Paris, Nelson.

Piano Concertos Nos. 2 in B flat; 4 in G, Op. 58.
* Ambroisie **DVD** AMI 99403003. Duchable, Ens. de Paris, Nelson.

Piano Concerto No. 5 in E flat (Emperor), Op. 73.
* Ambroisie **DVD** AMI 99403004 (2). Duchable, Ens. O de Paris, Nelson (multiple approaches & angles; with full score; interview with soloist & producers).

When you think that France possesses such formidable pianists as Jean-Philippe Collard and Pascal Rogé, it seems odd that choice here has fallen on François-René Duchable, who only a couple of years ago drew attention to himself by announcing (probably not seriously) his intention to dump his piano into Lake Annecy! These performances are recorded in the sumptuous environment of the Opéra Royal, Versailles, and the last DVD offers an opportunity to follow with the score – but only in individual movements – the slow movement of No. 1 and the finales of Nos. 4 and 5, and to choose the camera angles in the first movements of Nos. 4 and 5 and the finale of No. 3. The video direction is eminently satisfactory but neither the solo playing nor the orchestral support under John Nelson is particularly distinguished. Duchable plays decently, but he consistently offers prose rather than poetry. When you think of the great artists who have recorded this repertoire, what is on offer here is *vin ordinaire*. There is a tour of the Opéra Royal, which is worth taking, and interviews with the artists involved in the enterprise.

(i) *Piano Concertos Nos. 1–5. 7 Bagatelles, Op. 33; 11 Bagatelles, Op. 119; 6 Bagatelles, Op. 126; Fantasia in G min.; 5 Variations on 'Rule Britannia', WoO 79; 7 Variations on 'God Save the King', WoO 78 (i; ii) Choral Fantasia.*
(BB) *** Virgin 5 62242-2 (4). Tan (fortepiano); (i) with LCP, Norrington; (ii) Schütz Ch.

(i) *Piano Concertos Nos. 1–5. Piano Sonata No. 23 (Appassionata), Op. 57.*
(M) *** Warner Elatus 2564 60130-2 (*Nos. 1–2*); 2564 60433-2 (*Nos. 3–4*); 2564 60348-2 (*No. 5 & Piano Sonata 23*). Schiff, Dresden State O, Haitink (available separately).

(i) *Piano Concertos Nos. 1–5; (ii) Choral Fantasia, Op. 80.*
(B) **(*) RCA 82876 55703-2 (3). Ax; (i) RPO, Previn; (ii) NYPO, Mehta.
(M) ** Sup. SU 3540-2. Panenka, Prague SO & (ii) Ch., Smetáček.
(B) *(*) Ph. Trio (DDD/ADD) 470 938-2 (3). Brendel; (i) Chicago SO, Levine; (ii) LPO Ch., LPO, Haitink.

Schiff, with Haitink, offers one of the most refreshing, deeply satisfying Beethoven concerto cycles of recent years, highly praised in our main volume. Since we went to press, all three discs have become available separately on Elatus at mid-price and are thus even more recommendable.

Over the years Melvyn Tan has established an enviable reputation on the fortepiano. His playing has a flair and poetic feeling that are rather special, and this partnership with Norrington in the five

Beethoven concertos has great spontaneity. The first four bring performances of a natural, unselfconscious expressiveness. Even when Tan's speeds for slow movements are very fast indeed, his ease of expression makes them very persuasive, avoiding breathlessness while simultaneously conveying more gravity than one might expect. Tan's individuality comes over unforcedly to make these readings characterful without unwanted wilfulness.

The set is capped by a superb account of the *Emperor* in which Tan displays a poetic fire and brilliance all his own. The reading urgently conveys the feeling of a live performance, and both he and Norrington follow Czerny's brisk (and authoritative) tempo markings. The inspiriting account of the *Choral Fantasia* possesses a mercurial quality and a panache that shows this sometimes underrated work in a new and most positive light. Norrington and the chorus and orchestra are no less persuasive, and R.L. gave this coupling a ✪ on its original, full-priced release. Like the rest of the cycle, the recording is splendidly natural, the piano admirably balanced against the period instruments.

The solo recital that follows is no less distinctive. Tan plays on Beethoven's own Broadwood piano. Expert restoration work reveals an instrument which is richly timbred and full-bodied, far more vibrant than any modern copy. Tan plays these pieces with all the spontaneity and flair that he exhibited in the the concertos, and in the *G minor Fantasy* conveys an improvisatory quality that is very compelling indeed. He could allow himself more time in some of the *Bagatelles*, but there are no real quibbles here in what is a recital of great interest, offering refreshing insights into the sound-world with which Beethoven himself would have been familiar. The recording has striking realism and presence.

Emanuel Ax's boxed set on RCA dates from 1985–6 (although the *Choral Fantasia* was recorded live three years earlier). These are thoughtful, unassertive performances, which in the first two concertos clearly relate the music to Mozart. Previn gives his very musical soloist good support, particularly in the slow movements, which are gentle and touching. Finales are enjoyably brisk and sparkling. The *Third Concerto* is given rather more weight, without ever being forceful: here the finale is more relaxed and measured – pleasingly lyrical in feeling. The *Fourth Concerto* shows these artists at their very best, again warmly lyrical (although the central dialogue could be more dramatic), but the relaxed playing in the *Emperor* makes this a less bitingly compelling version than it can be, with the finale less weighty than usual. Nevertheless this is a most enjoyable set, recorded at Walthamstow (1, 2 & 5) or Abbey Road (3 and 4) with sound that is warmly resonant but clear. The documentation of this bargain reissue is good, and the packaging (as in the rest of RCA's Collections series) is stylishly attractive.

The Supraphon set comes from 1964–71 and made relatively little impact at the time. Jan Panenka is a highly musical player and proves himself a thoughtful Beethoven interpreter. However, he does not have quite the dramatic fire and sense of scale of pianists like Kempff or Leon Fleisher, whose set with Szell and the Cleveland Orchestra also comes from this period and still inspires great admiration. Panenka gives much pleasure all the same, even if others convey a grandeur and power that eludes this combination.

Brendel's 1983 Chicago set of the concertos was intended to prove how much more effective live recording is than studio performances, but the results – recorded at Orchestra Hall, Chicago – belie that, especially compared with his splendid later set with Rattle, which was recorded in the studio, *after* live performances. Anything Brendel does has mastery, but compared with the earlier studio recordings with Haitink and the Concertgebouw this sounds self-conscious and less, rather than more, spontaneous. The recorded sound gives a good sense of presence but is badly balanced, and the loud applause is intrusive.

(i) *Piano Concerto No. 1 in C, Op. 15. Piano Sonatas Nos. 22 in F, Op. 54; 23 (Appassionata) in F min., Op. 57.*

(M) ★★★ RCA (ADD) 82876 59421-2. Richter, (i) with Boston SO, Munch.

Commanding though Sviatoslav Richter's account of the *C major Concerto* is (charismatically conducted by Munch) and a large-scale, compelling reading of the *Piano Sonata No. 22*, it is the electrifying performance of the *Appassionata* that makes this an essential acquisition: it has tremendous range and majesty and is undoubtedly one of the great Beethoven performances on disc. It serves excellently to launch RCA's 'Classic Library' series.

Piano Concerto No. 3; Rondo in B flat, WoO6.

(M) ★(★) DG (ADD) 463 649-2. S. Richter, VSO, Sanderling – MOZART: *Piano Concerto No. 20.* ★★★

Richter's performance, now reissued as one of DG's 'Originals', is too chilly and detached to be wholly convincing. Like Schnabel, Richter takes the slow movement very slowly indeed, but unlike Schnabel he provides little warmth and the result is curiously square. The finale is very hard-driven. The *Rondo* is a different matter. Richter's sparkling account is effortlessly brilliant, but not to the exclusion of all else: there is subtlety here and even a touch of humour, but above all complete spontaneity and a sense of enjoyment throughout. The recording has come up well, with clean piano-tone and a fresh overall balance.

Piano Concertos Nos. 3 in C min., Op. 37; 4 in G, Op. 58.

(M) ★★(★) DG 471 352-2. Pollini, BPO, Abbado.

DG have chosen the later (1992) recordings of Beethoven's *Third* and *Fourth Piano Concertos*, recorded live, for inclusion in the 'Pollini Edition'. On balance, this newer performance of No. 4 has keener concentration than the earlier Vienna account with Boehm, while Pollini's playing in the slow movement of No. 3 is more hushed than before. But the balance of advantage does not always favour the later versions, where the piano sound is often shallower and the orchestral recording tends towards harshness in tuttis, lacking bloom.

Piano Concertos Nos. 3, Op. 37; 4 in G, Op. 58.

(M) ** RCA (ADD) 09026 63078-2. Rubinstein, LPO, Barenboim.

(i) Piano Concerto No. 3 in C min., Op. 37; (ii) Triple Concerto in C, Op. 56.

(BB) (**(*)) Naxos mono 8.110878. (i) Long, Paris Conservatoire O; (ii) Odnoposoff, Auber, Morales, VPO; Weingartner.

Marguerite Long's account of the Third Piano Concerto was made in June 1939 in the relatively dry acoustic of the Théâtre Pigalle in Paris, and it is a great rarity. We do not recall seeing a copy at any time, for it was never issued in England, owing to the outbreak of war. The first-movement tempo, as with all Weingartner performances, seems just right, and Long, who is so closely associated with Ravel and Fauré, proves hardly less at home in Beethoven, though she often makes some expressive hesitations at the beginning of phrases, while Weingartner presses on. She comes to grief early in the restatement of the first movement, but hers is a characterful reading of much style and many unashamedly old-fashioned romantic gestures. One soon gets accustomed to the dryish sound over which Mark Obert-Thorne has obviously laboured long – and successfully. It would be good to have its rival, by Lubka Kolessa (a pupil of Sauer) and the Dresden Staatskapelle under Karl Boehm, back in circulation, for it was a performance of no mean quality. Older readers will have made their first acquaintance of the Triple Concerto via Weingartner's pioneering (1937) account, a wonderful reading that glows with joy and pleasure and that set a standard that was long unsurpassed.

Piano Concerto No. 5 (Emperor); Piano Sonata No. 18, Op. 31/2.

(M) **(*) RCA (ADD) 09026 63079-2. Rubinstein, LPO, Barenboim.

Rubinstein's cycle of Beethoven concertos with Barenboim was recorded in 1975 when the octogenarian pianist was in exuberant mood. The sessions saw each concerto completed more quickly than expected, and much of the drive behind that comes over powerfully, although the slips of finger are too many and too noticeable to allow full enjoyment. It might have been different had Rubinstein not insisted on so close a balance for the piano, which is vividly caught. The accompaniments, beautifully

played by the LPO, are at times masked behind the piano-tone, something this otherwise impressive remastering for reissue in the 'Rubinstein Edition' cannot alter, although the balance is more equal in the sparkling Emperor Concerto. The E flat Sonata makes a fine bonus, full of character, especially the Scherzo and the Presto finale; it was very well recorded (also in 1975).

Piano Concertos Nos. 3 in C min.; 5 in E flat (Emperor).

(M) **(*) Sony (ADD) 512867-2. Serkin, NYPO, Bernstein.

The remastered CD of the 1964 Serkin/Bernstein account of the Third Concerto has improved the sound, which is now relatively spacious. Between them these artists give a super-brilliant performance of the first movement, with strong orchestral accents from Bernstein, which at times almost brutalize the music. The slow movement is serene and poised, but the aggressive feeling returns in the orchestral tuttis of the finale, which are similiarly fierce, partly the effect of the microphones being so close to the violins. Serkin's Emperor is characteristically commanding; the reading is strong and nobly sensitive in the great Adagio. The snag is the rather coarse – if extremely vivid – 1962 recording, which the new transfer is unable to mitigate. However, there is no doubt that this is thrilling music-making, with superb solo playing, and one can adjust to the sound.

Piano Concerto No. 4 in G, Op. 58.

(*) EMI **DVD 492840-9. Rubinstein, LPO, Dorati (with Bonus: CHOPIN: Polonaise in A flat (Heroic)) – MENDELSSOHN: Violin Concerto **; WALTON: Cello Concerto ***.

*** Sup. SU 3714-2. Moravec, Prague Philh. O, Bělohlávek – FRANCK Symphonic Variations ***; RAVEL: Piano Concerto in G **(*).

Rubinstein made a fine recording of the G major Concerto with Josef Krips in New York in the late 1950s – and he recorded three complete cycles in all, playing the Fourth most often. The present performance comes from a Royal Festival Hall concert by the LPO under Antal Dorati in December 1967, when the great pianist was already eighty. Although he was more closely identified in the public mind with Chopin, he was a fine Beethoven interpreter, albeit slightly underrated as a Beethovenian by the wider generality of critics (but not, for example, by the composer and scholar Robert Simpson, who spoke with great admiration of Rubinstein's concerto cycle with Krips). Although this performance does not offer the effortless keyboard mastery of Rubinstein's youth and maturity, it is a valuable document and will be treasured by all admirers of this artist.

This Supraphon CD may seem to offer a very odd coupling, but thanks to the distinctive artistry of the Czech pianist, Ivan Moravec, with his extraordinary clarity of articulation, as well as to the conductor, Jiří

Bělohlávek, the result has an attractive consistency, with each work illuminating the others. In the first movement of the Beethoven, Moravec's crisp enunciation of each note in passage-work that can seem routine makes for sparkling results, with the delicate tracery of the piano part in the recapitulation wonderfully clear. With incisive support from Bělohlávek and the Prague Philharmonia, there is no lack of muscular strength either, with Moravec drawing on a wide tonal range, as he does in his deeply meditative reading of the slow movement. In the finale Bělohlávek matches his soloist in drawing from the Prague Philharmonia comparably transparent textures.

Piano Concertos Nos. 4 in G, Op. 58; 5 in E flat (Emperor).

◉ *** Testament SBT 1299. Richter-Haaser, Philh. O, Kertész.

(BB) **(*) RCA 82876 55267-2. Ax, RPO, Previn.

(BB) ** EMI Encore 5 74721-2. Zacharias, Dresden State O, Vonk.

These noble performances on Testament, like Hans Richter-Haaser's superb Brahms *B flat Concerto* with Karajan, have not enjoyed much exposure since their appearance on LP in the early 1960s. We recall that the late Robert Simpson, who wrote with special insight and authority on Beethoven, spoke of them with awe and in much the same breath as Schnabel and Solomon. They stand the test of time well and deserve the strongest recommendation. This is Beethoven playing of the first order, and we hope that Testament will bring other of Richter-Haaser's records back into circulation. The transfer does the original LPs (which we have long cherished) full justice.

This RCA pairing is taken from the complete set above. The *Fourth Concerto* is outstanding in every way; the *Emperor* is thoughtful rather than forceful, the first movement less of a contest than usual, while the flowing speed for the slow movement and the scherzando quality in the finale make for a comparatively lightweight effect, rather thin of piano tone, powerful though Ax's articulation is.

Christian Zacharias is much admired in Germany, and these well-recorded performances of the *G major* and *Emperor*, made in the late 1980s, have a lot going for them, including supportive playing from the Staatskapelle Dresden and Hans Vonk. The articulation is clean and vital, and there are some sensitive tonal shadings and much pianistic finesse, but in the slow movement of the *Emperor* he lacks real breadth and weight. We are so well served in this that only the most masterly will do.

(i) Piano Concerto No. 4; (ii) Romance No. 2 in F. Symphony No. 5.

(M) (**) Sup. mono (i) Páleníček; (ii) D. Oistrakh; Czech PO, Ančerl.

Josef Páleníček is a fine artist with engagingly nimble fingers and, though this is a comparatively light-weight performance, it is fresh and enjoyable. Not surprisingly, the *Romance* is beautifully played, but it is Ančerl's *Fifth Symphony* that is most impressive here. The first movement develops powerfully and dramatically, with the Czech players in first-rate form. The slow movement has less impetus but plenty of lyrical warmth, and the finale is the most effective movement of all. Altogether a good, stout performance, with the fine mono recording sounding surprisingly modern in Stanislav Sýkora's impressive remastering.

Piano Concerto No. 5 in E flat (Emperor), Op. 73.

(M) *** DG (ADD) 471 351-2. Pollini, VPO, Boehm – MOZART: *Piano Concerto No. 23.* ***

(M) (***) BBC BBCL mono 4074-2. Moiseiwitsch, BBC SO, Sargent – RACHMANINOV: *Piano Concerto No. 2.* (**)

DG have wisely chosen Pollini's earlier analogue recording of the *Emperor* with Boehm for inclusion in the 'Pollini Edition'. Although recorded in the studio, it sounds more spontaneously expressive, with a vein of poetry that is largely missing in the live recording, although there is no lack of energy and power.

Moiseiwitsch's magisterial and noble *Emperor* was recorded only a month before his death. It is not always finger-sure in the finale – he was, after all, 73 – but it has a wisdom and sense of architecture and line that carry all before it. Sargent and the BBC Symphony give excellent support, although the recording does not have the clarity and transparency of a good studio recording of the period. However, connoisseurs of the piano – and of great music-making – should not neglect this opportunity of collecting it.

(i) Piano Concerto No. 5 (Emperor); (ii) Piano Concerto in E flat, WoO 4 (arr. & orch. Willy Hess); (iii) Violin Concerto in D, Op. 61; (iv) Triple Concerto for Violin, Cello & Piano in C, Op. 56.

(B) **(*) Ph. (ADD) Duo 442 580-2 (2). (i) Kovacevich, LSO, C. Davis; (ii) Grychtolowna, Folkwang CO, Dressel; (iii) Krebbers, Concg. O, Haitink; (iv) Szeryng, Starker, Arrau, New Philh. O, Inbal.

Kovacevich's superb (1969) account of the *Emperor* is here part of an attractive Duo compilation, which includes also the early *E flat Piano Concerto* (WoO 4), which the composer wrote when he was only fourteen, here offered in a spirited performance in a reconstruction by Willy Hess. Krebbers's 1974 recording of the *Violin Concerto* is outstanding. In his hands the slow movement has a tender simplicity that is irresistible. The companion account of the *Triple Concerto* with Arrau, Szeryng and Starker is less strongly projected, losing concentration at very unhurried tempi. Yet the set remains highly recommendable.

Piano Concerto No. 5 (Emperor); Grosse Fuge, Op. 133.

(B) ✱✱✱ CfP 585 6162. Kovacevich, Australian CO.

Kovacevich's later, EMI digital version of the *Emperor*, sharper and tauter than the earlier, Philips account, now arrives on Classics for Pleasure (see our main volume).

(i) *Piano Concertos Nos. 1–5.* (ii) *Violin Concerto. Symphonies Nos. 1–9; Overtures: Consecration of the House; Egmont; Leonora No. 3.*

(B) ✱✱(✱) Decca (ADD) 467 892-2 (8). (i) Backhaus;
(ii) Szeryng with LSO; otherwise VPO;
Schmidt-Isserstedt (with Sutherland, Horne, King, Talvela & V. State Op. Ch. in *No. 9*).

Backhaus's authoritative, overtly classical set of the *Piano Concertos* is also available separately (433 891-2 – see our main volume), but Schmidt-Isserstedt's vintage cycle of the symphonies, recorded in the Sofiensaal in the mid- to late 1960s, is new to CD. It presents a consistently musical view, not lacking strength, and without distracting idiosyncrasies. All the symphonies are beautifully played – the character of the VPO coming over strongly – and very well recorded. Apart from the *Pastoral*, clean and classically straightforward, but entirely lacking charm, there is no outright disappointment here, and the series culminates in a splendid account of the *Ninth*, one that does not quite scale the heights but that, particularly in the slow movement and the finale (with outstanding soloists), conveys visionary strength. Szeryng's account of the *Violin Concerto* derives from the Philips catalogue and dates from 1965. His is a strongly lyrical performance, withdrawn in the *Larghetto*, yet creating a dreamy, hushed atmosphere in which the gentle beauty of mood is the highlight of the reading, well supported by his partner.

Violin Concerto in D, Op. 61.

(✱✱✱) Testament mono SBT 1228. Kogan, Paris Conservatoire O, Vandernoot – MOZART: *Violin Concerto No. 5.* (✱✱✱)

✱✱(✱) EMI DVD 490445-9. Grumiaux, O Nat. de l'ORTF, Dorati (with Bonuses:PAGANINI: *Caprice, Op. 1/14;* SAINT-SAENS: *Introduction and Rondo capriccioso* (Ivry Gitlis, Georges Pludemacher); BACH: *Violin Partita No. 2, BWV 1004: Sarabande & Chaconne;* – MENDELSSOHN; Violin Concerto. ✱✱(✱)

(✱✱(✱)) EMI DVD 492834-9. Kogan, O Nat. de l'ORTF, De Froment – *see also under Recitals.*

(BB) ✱(✱) CfP 574 8782. Huggett, OAE, Mackerras – MENDELSSOHN: *Violin Concerto.* ✱(✱)

(i) *Violin Concerto;* (ii) *Romances Nos. 1 in G, Op. 40; 2 in F, Op. 50.*

✱✱ Ph. 462 123-2. Zehetmair, OAE, Brüggen.

Leonid Kogan's mono account of the Beethoven *Concerto* comes from 1957 and, like the Mozart *Concerto* that completes the present CD, was never issued

at the time. Kogan re-recorded the work with Constantin Silvestri two years later in stereo so that, although it was passed for release, it was withheld for obvious reasons. Testament have put us in their debt by issuing it now, for it is a reading of the greatest distinction. It has purity and nobility, as does its successor, but there is a slightly freer quality (Tully Potter's sleeve-note calls it 'carefree') and a spirituality too.

Grumiaux was an aristocrat of violinists, and his tonal refinement and selfless artistry made him quite special. This account of the Beethoven has the breadth and nobility that characterized so much of his work. It was recorded at the Salle Pleyel in February 1965 and, although the sound is somewhat wanting in bloom and climaxes are wanting in transparency, the essential qualities of this great violinist are conveyed. Dorati gets some good playing from the French National Radio Orchestra and, for all the tonal (and occasional visual) blemishes, this gives both pleasure and musical satisfaction.

Kogan made a magnificent recording of the Beethoven with André Vandernoot and the Conservatoire Orchestra, which has of course the benefit of cleaner and better focused sound. This is a rather later performance, made at the Maison de la Radio in March 1966. Kogan's artistry is always in evidence here, and to see as well as hear him live is an illuminating experience. His absorption in his art was total; he made no concessions to showmanship and his platform manner is refreshingly unconcerned with charm. The Orchestre National gets off to an unpromising start with some imperfect wind intonation, but Louis de Froment later draws some sympathetic and supportive playing from this fine orchestra.

The opening timpani strokes are not very arresting in Monica Huggett's 'authentic' version, although later Mackerras achieves incisive enough tuttis. Yet overall this is not a performance that convinces by either its emotional power or its serenity in the slow movement, which is comparatively uninvolving.

Kyung-Wha Chung's 1979 Decca performance is superseded by her later, full-priced, EMI version with Tennstedt, for the earlier account, measured and thoughtful, lacks compulsion thanks to the prosaic conducting of Kondrashin (460 014-2).

The Zehetmair/Brüggen partnership is for authenticists only. The *Romances* are placed first and are far from romantic, with the *G major* very brisk and unbeguiling. So is the opening of the concerto, with the timpani taps very dry, the orchestral exposition strongly accented and dramatically gruff. It is as if Brüggen is not persuaded that this work is the epitome of radiant Beethoven lyricism. Zehetmair uses the first-movement cadenza, with timpani, favoured by Schneiderhan, but plays it as if it were by Paganini, and the great reprise of the main theme is all but thrown away in the closing pages. Fortunately, the *Larghetto* relaxes more, and Zehetmair's playing is often very beautiful, quite ethereal. Brüggen is merely supportive, and the bold gruffness returns to usher in the invigorating finale, again mirrored by the soloist in his cadenza.

First choice among modern recordings rests with Kremer (Teldec 9031 74881-2) or Perlman (EMI 5 66900-2) although Schneiderhan is very special (❂ DG 447 403-2).

Triple Concerto for Violin, Cello & Piano in C, Op. 56.

(M) **★★★** EMI 5 57773-2. Argerich, Capucon, Maisky, Svizzera-Italiana O, Rabinovitch-Barakovsky – SCHUMANN: *Piano Concerto.* **★★★**

(BB) **★★★** DG Entrée 474 569-2. Mutter, Ma, Zeltzer, BPO, Karajan – BRAHMS: *Violin Concerto.* **★★★**

This live recording of the *Triple Concerto*, like the Schumann *Piano Concerto* with which it is coupled, was made at the Lugano Festival, reflecting throughout the magnetism of Martha Argerich, inspiring her two younger colleagues. When the piano part (designed for Beethoven's great patron, the Archduke Rudolph) is the least demanding of the three solo roles, it is remarkable how Argerich still emerges as the obvious leader. Not that the cellist Mischa Maisky is any less characterful; but Argerich's powerful presence seems to modify his customary wilfulness, so that even the great cello melody that opens the slow movement is the more moving for its restraint, with the most delicate tonal shading, while the outer movements have a rare vitality.

The DG version (also available in the Beethoven Edition – see our main *Guide*), enjoyably spontaneous, makes a generous coupling for Mutter's fine account of the Brahms *Violin Concerto*.

Romances for Cello and Orchestra Nos. 1 in G, Op. 40; 2 in F, Op. 50.

★★(*) Orfeo Co80031A. Müller-Schott, Australian CO, Tognetti – HAYDN: *Cello Concerto Nos. 1 & 2.* **★★(*)**

Daniel Müller-Schott is a gifted young cellist (in his mid-twenties when this record was made), who has transcribed the two Beethoven *Violin Romances* for his own instrument – and very successfully too! This is playing of some eloquence and finesse, and the two Haydn concertos that comprise the main works can hold their own with the best of the opposition.

SYMPHONIES

Symphonies Nos. 1–9.

(M) **★(*)** Teldec 3984 27838-2 (6); 8573 83085-2 (1 & 2); 8573 83060-2 (3); 8573 82891-2 (4 & 5); 8573 83061-2 (6); 8573 83062-2 (7 & 8); 8573 83063-2 (9). Berlin State O, Barenboim (with Isokoski, Lang, Gambill, Pape, Berlin State Op. Ch. in *No.* 9).

Symphonies Nos. 1–9; Overtures: Coriolan; Egmont; Fidelio; Leonora No. 3.

★★ DG 439 200–2 (6). BPO, Karajan (with Perry,

Baltsa, Cole, Van Dam, V. Singverein in *No.* 9).

In Karajan's last, digital set, the recording seems to have been affected by the need to make a version on video at the same sessions. The gain is that these performances have keener spontaneity, the loss that they often lack the brilliant, knife-edged precision of ensemble one has come to regard as normal with Karajan. The six discs are now remastered to Digital Gold standards and are offered at a slightly reduced price for the set: six CDs for the price of five.

Barenboim, even more than most of today's conductors, has a lifelong devotion to the work of Furtwängler, a point that is regularly reflected in his current readings of the Beethoven symphonies. Speeds tend to be broad in the Furtwängler manner, often very broad, as in the first movements of the *Eroica* and *Ninth*, and he encourages a fair degree of flexibility within movements. This is the orchestra with which he has worked regularly over his years with the Deutsche Oper in Berlin, and they are certainly responsive to his demands. But what undermines most of these performances is a curious lack of tension. In taking a broad, flexible view, the essential factor, as the finest Furtwängler performances demonstrate, is that the expressive freedom must seem to develop spontaneously. In that Barenboim, while still achieving creditable results, tends to fall short. The result is a series of run-throughs rather than genuine performances, not helped by a rounded recording that could with advantage have been brighter. So this set, whether taken as a whole or sampled individually, can be recommended only to Barenboim devotees.

Muti's Beethoven cycle, like Toscanini's, is beset by problems of recorded sound which are serious, if obviously of a less extreme kind. Even his version of the *Ninth*, the last of the symphonies to be recorded, has sound almost as opaque as the earliest. This is a very serious *Ninth*; but where one expects a Toscaninian spark from Muti to ignite the music, too much of the performance here is rhythmically square and stolid (EMI 5 72923-2).

Symphonies Nos. 1–9; Coriolan Overture.

(BB) **★★★** Warner Apex 2564 60457-2 (5). Sinfonia Varsovia, Y. Menuhin (with Glennon, Schaechter, Janutas, Schollum, Lithuania Kaunas State Ch. in *No.* 9).

Menuhin's set was originally issued in 1995 (on Carlton) to celebrate his eightieth birthday, and it represents the refreshing response of a great interpretative musician who remained perennially young to the very end of his musical life. It helps that five of the nine symphonies (Nos. 1, 2, 4, 5 and 8) were recorded in the Palais de Musique in Strasbourg, a helpful hall. Though the applause that greets the opening of some of the symphonies is irritating (though it is now edited out on the CD containing *Coriolan* and Nos. 4 and 8), the tensions of live performance regularly bring magical results, as in the dedicated, ecstatic performance of the great *Adagio* of the *Ninth*. Often a disappointment in complete cycles, in Menuhin's hands the *Choral Symphony* brings an impressive conclusion to his series.

In the studio performances, as well as those recorded live, Menuhin uses the chamber scale positively, not only clarifying textures but achieving hushed *pianissimos* of ravishing beauty, as in the *Allegretto* of the *Seventh* or in the broken close of the *Eroica* funeral march. Hairpin dynamics are shaded most subtly throughout, and regularly in slow movements Menuhin's cunning in moulding string melodies, born of his violin mastery, is reflected in the imaginative beauty of line. Only in the *Allegretto* of the *Eighth* does he choose a tempo too slow for rhythms to lift.

Allegros generally tend to be on the brisk side, with lightly sprung rhythms adding to the freshness; some of the very fast speeds, as in the finales of Nos. 5 and 7, seem to reflect not so much latter-day period practice as the early influence of Toscanini. Vigorously rejecting the idea of 'fate knocking on the door' at the opening of the *Fifth* means that in this live performance the effect is deliberately understated and the result, for once, is not very cleanly executed. Such flaws are mimimal next to the shining merits of the set. Exposition repeats are observed, and not everyone will object that Menuhuin omits second-half repeats in the Scherzos of Nos. 7 and 9. With recording that puts a fine bloom on the sound without obscuring detail, this is an excellent set for those wanting dedicated performances on a chamber scale, which yet never underplay the strength and power of these masterpieces. The set comes on five individual CDs in jewel cases within a slipcase, and can be ranked alongside those of Rattle, Zinman and Mackerras (see our main *Guide*).

Symphonies Nos. 1–2.

**(*) DG 439 001-2. BPO, Karajan.

Karajan's digital Beethoven series brings some surprisingly slack ensemble in the recording of the first two symphonies. The performances are relaxed in good ways too, with Karajan's flair and control of rhythm never leading to breathless speeds.

Symphonies Nos. 1 in C; 3 in E flat (Eroica).

*** EMI 5 57564-2. VPO, Rattle.

(BB) *** Warner Apex 2564 60452-2. Sinfonia Varsovia, Y. Menuhin.

Recorded live (like the rest of his Vienna cycle), this coupling represents Rattle at his finest. The *First Symphony* brings a powerfully warm and vigorous reading that has the young Beethoven looking forward to the nineteenth century rather than back to tradition, with syncopated cross-rhythms sharply defined and the timpani given prominence. Using Jonathan Del Mar's acclaimed Bärenreiter edition, Rattle takes on board the lessons of period performance without applying them dogmatically. In the

Eroica his tempo for the first movement is fast but allows an infectious lift to rhythms, while in the *Funeral March* he gives full emotional weight to the music in his hushed, spacious reading, very different from the fast-flowing period performances that are short on gravity. In the finale, Rattle relishes the inventiveness of the variations, bringing out a playful element, with rhythms delectably sprung.

The one irritant to Menuhin's performances on Apex is the welcoming applause that comes before the music begins and at the close of No. 1, but not before the opening of No. 3. This is intrusive without the visual element. Otherwise these highly musical performances, strong, but on a convincing chamber scale, are among the most satisfying available, with a dedicated reading of the *Eroica* Funeral March. Warm, well-balanced recording.

Symphonies Nos. 2–4; 6 (Pastoral); 7–9 (Choral); Overture: Leonora No. 3.

(M) ** EMI (DDD/ADD) 5 56837-2 (8). Munich PO, Celibidache (with Donath, Soffel, Jerusalem, Lika, Philharmonic Ch. in *No.* 9) (with SCHUMANN: *Symphony No. 2* **) – BRAHMS: *Symphonies Nos. 1–4; Haydn Variations; German Requiem.* **

Sergiu Celibidache is the latest cult figure, and his followers will eagerly snap up his records in much the same way as do Furtwängler's admirers. Even so, he is too idiosyncratic to gain more than a guarded recommendation.

Symphonies Nos. 2 in D, Op. 36; 5 in C min., Op. 67.

*** EMI 5 57566-2. VPO, Rattle.

As in No. 1, Rattle registers that the *Second Symphony* is a forward-looking work, the biggest symphony written up to that date. In this live recording the first movement is played with great panache; it is fast and swaggering, while the *Larghetto* slow movement is at once fresh and delicately moulded, and the Scherzo and finale are pointed with wit. The *Fifth Symphony* also benefits from being recorded live, with the first movement at once taut, urgent and weighty, with the slow movement bringing high dramatic contrasts, as do all the movements, not least the dramatic account of the finale. In the Scherzo, unlike David Zinman in his Arte Nova set, which also uses the Del Mar edition, Rattle does not take up the option of having the Scherzo and Trio repeated, before the final mysterious and truncated reprise of the Scherzo. Vivid recording, which allows one to hear the piccolo clearly in the finale of the *Fifth*.

Symphonies Nos. 2 in D; 6 in F (Pastoral).

(BB) *** Warner Apex 2564 60453-2. Sinfonia Varsovia, Y. Menuhin.

After the opening applause, Menuhin's reading of the *Second Symphony* is weighty and mature-sounding, the first movement lacking a little in bite but not in buoyancy. The *Larghetto* is nobly phrased, the finale vigorous and high-spirited. Alongside the *Choral*

Symphony, Menuhin's performance of the *Pastoral Symphony* (which opens without applause) crowns his cycle in its sheer lyrical beauty. The chamber scale and the combination of warmth and lightness of touch bring a joyous momentum. The storm bursts in dramatically, and the heartfelt *Shepherds' Thanksgiving* brings a lyrical apotheosis. Satisfyingly full sound, with a natural brilliance.

Symphonies Nos. 2 in D, Op. 36; 7 in A, Op. 92.

(M) (**(*)) BBC mono BBCL 4124-2. Philh. O, Van Beinum.

Eduard van Beinum belonged to the same dedicated school as Weingartner and Sir Adrian Boult, conductors who never sought to impose their personalities and who were first and foremost servants of the composer. To their number might be added Klemperer, for whom van Beinum was standing in for this 1958 concert. The playing recalls the late lamented Peter Stadlen's description of Weingartner's 'lean beef Beethoven' to mind, for it is completely straight and devoid of idiosyncrasy. Van Beinum's Beethoven received both critical and public acclaim and proved to be his London swansong, for he died only five months later. Although the *Second* is a good, straightforward account, the *Seventh* is a performance of some stature and an admirable memorial to an underrated master. Well worth investigating, and decent sound.

Symphony No. 3 (Eroica); Overture: Egmont.

**(*) DG 439 002-2. BPO, Karajan.

The gain in Karajan's last, digital version of the *Eroica* lies most of all in the *Funeral March*, very spacious and intense. The playing lacks something of the knife-edged bite associated with him. The recording is clean and firm, but there is a degree of congestion in big tuttis. An epic reading.

Symphonies Nos. 4 in B flat, Op. 60; 6 (Pastoral).

*** EMI 5 57568-2. VPO, Rattle.

In the *Fourth Symphony* Rattle's live recording brings out the dramatic contrast between the mystery of the slow introduction and the exuberance of the main Allegro. As in the rest of his Vienna cycle, he opts for a more moulded, rather more relaxed manner in the lyrical slow movement than other conductors who have taken note of period performance, while the last two movements are full of Beethovenian swagger. The *Pastoral Symphony* makes a fine coupling in a reading that allows a degree of relaxation in each movement, with speeds on the fast side but not too rigid. The *Peasants' Merrymaking* of the Scherzo is liltingly joyful, leading to a dramatic account of the *Storm* and warm relaxation in the finale.

Symphonies Nos. 4; 8; Coriolan Overture.

(BB) *** Warner Apex 2564 60454-2. Sinfonia Varsovia, Y. Menuhin.

On the reissued Apex CD the opening applause had been edited, and after the not undramatic *Coriolan Overture* the opening of the *Fourth Symphony* is immediately full of tension, the allegro joyful and vigorous without being over-driven, and the rapt *Adagio* played most beautifully. There is lyrical feeling underlying the sprightliness of the Scherzo, and the Trio blossoms. The articulate delicacy from wind and strings alike carries into the finale with its vigorous forward impulse.

The opening movement of the *Eighth* brings more joyous spirits and a most elegant second subject. This elegance also pervades the *Allegretto*, but here Menuhin's pacing is rather too relaxed and there is a lack of rhythmic uplift. However, all is forgiven when the finale erupts with buoyant energy. Again very fine playing, with the widest dynamic range, adds much to the character of the performances, and the spacious yet clear sound-picture is very satisfying.

Symphonies Nos. (i) 5; (ii) 6 (Pastoral).

**(*) DG 439 004-2. BPO, Karajan.

(M) (**(*)) Avid mono AMSC 583. (i) LPO, Weingartner; (ii) VPO, Walter.

Karajan's digital versions of the *Fifth* and *Sixth* present characteristically strong and incisive readings so that the fast speed for the first movement of the *Pastoral* no longer sounds too tense.

Felix Weingartner's *Fifth Symphony*, recorded with the London Philharmonic in 1933, is Beethoven pure and true, straightforward and plain; there is no lack of character and fire. The recording sounds less dated than one might expect, though there is a curious touch of dryness, characteristic of these Avid transfers. Bruno Walter's 1936 account of the *Pastoral*, with the Vienna Philharmonic, is taut and brisk, yet feels expansive. This is a vintage performance, though the strings are not quite sweet enough above the stave.

Symphonies Nos. 5; 7.

(BB) **(*) Warner Apex 2564 60455-2. Sinfonia Varsovia, Y. Menuhin.

(BB) (**) Naxos mono 8.110926. Berlin State Op. O, Richard Strauss.

After the inevitable opening applause, Menuhin opens the *Fifth* unselfconsciously, if not very sharply, immediately setting a brisk tempo for the allegro, which is played comparatively lightly. The *Andante*, too, begins with a sense of delicate lyricism, and it is in the finale that the performance explodes into joyful illumination.

The allegro certainly dances along in the first movement of the *Seventh*, but here the pacing is relatively steady. The *Allegretto* is deeply eloquent and, as in the *Fifth* it is the finale that carries the work to its exhilarating yet weighty conclusion. Playing and recording are well up to standard, though the ensemble could be crisper in the first movevemt of the *Fifth*.

Richard Strauss, long recognized as a great Mozart interpreter, here demonstrates his mastery in relation to Beethoven. Recorded in the 1920s for what was designed as a Beethoven centenary project, these are above all dynamic, bitingly energetic performances, not always well disciplined but always magnetic. That is so despite the astonishingly fluid tempi, rarely staying quite the same for more than a few bars. In the *Fifth* the sound is limited, but the Naxos transfer is undistracting, never getting in the way of the performance.

The *Seventh*, recorded in 1926 just as electrical recording was introduced, comes in drier sound, but the boxiness is something you get used to. Though the second-movement *Allegretto* is rather heavy, the rest is well sprung with a delightfully witty pay-off in the Scherzo. Sadly, the finale brings an enormous cut, designed to fit the movement on to a single 78 side.

Symphony No. 6 (Pastoral).

**(*) Testament SBT2 1217 (2) (with rehearsal). BPO, Klemperer – BACH: *Suite No. 3 in D*; MOZART: *Symphony No. 29.* **(*)

When in May 1964 Otto Klemperer, aged 79, returned to Berlin to conduct the Berlin Philharmonic after a gap of over forty years, the climax of the occasion, rapturously received, came with Beethoven's *Pastoral Symphony*. Only a few weeks earlier, Karajan had also conducted the same players in this very symphony, both live and on disc. As the 45-minute rehearsal sequence on the first disc demonstrates, Klemperer was intent on getting the orchestra to produce a distinctive Klemperer sound, making his version fresher, encouraging each soloist to play out individually, undermining the Karajan technique of blending the woodwind into a homogeneous whole. The result is fresh and dedicated, rustic and refined. The rehearsal sequence is spoken in German, but the booklet provides a helpful summary in English.

Symphonies Nos. (i) 6 (Pastoral); (ii) 8; (ii; iii) 9 (Choral).

(BB) **(*) EMI Gemini (ADD) 5 85490-2 (2). (i) New Philh. O; (ii) LSO; (iii) with Armstrong, Reynolds, Tear, Shirley-Quirk, LSO Ch.; Giulini.

Giulini's is essentially a relaxed, lyrical approach to the *Pastoral Symphony* and, with fine playing from the New Philharmonia and full, atmospheric (1968) Abbey Road recording, the result is warm and attractive. The generally slow tempi will not please everyone and, interpretatively at least, the firmer Klemperer approach (also with slow tempi) is more consistently satisfying. Even so, Giulini's version is certainly enjoyable in its leisured progress.

· Again in the *Choral Symphony* (recorded four years later, in Kingsway Hall) the tempo of the first movement is unusually slow – like Solti, Giulini insists on precise sextuplets for the opening tremolando, with no mistiness – and he builds the architecture relentlessly, finding his resolution only in the concluding coda. The Scherzo is lithe and powerful, with shattering timpani. The slow movement is

warm and Elysian rather than hushed, while the finale, not always quite perfect in ensemble, is dedicatedly intense, helped by fine singing from soloists and chorus alike. The recording is close, immediate and full. The *Eighth Symphony* is less distinguished, but in its lyrical, moulded way remains warmly enjoyable, and the two-disc set is very reasonably priced.

Symphonies Nos. 7 in A, Op. 92; 8 in F, Op. 93.

*** EMI 5 57570-2. VPO, Rattle.

Rattle's live recording brings an account of the *Seventh* that is at once warm and weighty, with the dotted dance-rhythms of the main Allegro of the first movement deliciously pointed, and an element of mystery conveyed in the sudden *pianissimos*. The second-movement *Allegretto* flows easily, marked by sharp *sforzandos* and high dynamic contrasts. The Scherzo, crisply done, has dramatic contrasts too, and the finale is fast – but not so fast as to imperil clarity or rhythmic lift. The *Eighth* brings a joyful performance, conveyed the more clearly in a live recording, with wit in the second-movement *Allegretto* and weight as well as clarity in the outer movements.

Symphonies Nos. (i) 7; (ii) 8; (iii) 9 (Choral).

(B) ** DG Double (ADD) (IMS) 459 463-2 (2). (i) VPO; (ii) Cleveland O; (iii) Donath, Berganza, Ochman, Stewart, Bav. RSO; Kubelik.

Kubelik's *Seventh Symphony*, with the VPO, is beautifully played and well recorded but lacks the drama of his earlier account with the Bavarian RSO. The *Eighth Symphony* receives a robustly enjoyable performance in Cleveland, with the choice of tempi always well judged. For the challenging *Ninth Symphony* Kubelik used his own Bavarian orchestra. It is a warm and understanding performance, leading on consistently to the high spirits of the finale. But there is a missing dimension of conveyed power and greatness here. The performances are recorded well (in the mid-1970s).

Symphony No. 9 in D min. (Choral), Op. 125.

*** EMI 5 57572. Bonney, Remmert, Streit, Hampson, CBSO Ch., VPO, Rattle.

(BB) *** Warner Apex 2564 60456-2. Glennon, Schaechter, Janutas, Schollum, Lithuania Kaunas State Ch., Sinfonia Varsovia, Y. Menuhin.

(**(*)) Testament mono SBT 1332. Giebel, Ludwig, Lewis, Berry, Philh. Ch. & O, Klemperer.

(M) **(*) AVID mono AMSC 591. Hellersgruber, Anday, Maikl, Mayr, V. Srate Op. Ch., VPO, Weingartner.

(M) **(*) DG (ADD) 463 626-2. (i) Seefried, Forrester, Haefliger, Fischer-Dieskau, St Hedwig's Cathedral Ch., BPO, Fricsay.

**(*) (M) RCA (ADD) 09026 63682-2. Marsh, Veasey, Domingo, Milnes, Pro Musica Ch., New England Ch., Boston SO, Leinsdorf (with SCHOENBERG:

Survivor from Warsaw. **(*))

(BB) *(*) RCA 74321 68005-2. Wiens, Hartwig, Lewis, Hermann, Hamburg State Op. Ch., N. German RSO, Wand.

(M) (*) Orfeo mono C533001B. Seefried, Wagner, Dermota, Greindl, V. State Op. Ch., VPO, Furtwängler.

Rattle's live Beethoven cycle with the Vienna Philharmonic is crowned by an outstanding reading of the *Choral Symphony*. Mystery and power are combined in the first movement, with speeds in the Scherzo not so extreme as to undermine rhythmic point. Where throughout his cycle Rattle has taken clear but undogmatic note of the lessons of period performance, in the slow movement of the *Ninth* he allows himself full expansiveness in a refined and dedicated reading, which brings out the contrast between the two variation themes, *Adagio* and *Andante*. Clearly Rattle is unafraid of facing the visionary qualities of this music, so easily minimized by fast speeds. In the finale Rattle benefits from an outstanding quartet of soloists and a warmly robust choir (his own CBSO Chorus). Here more than ever, Rattle gains from the thrust and exhilaration of a live recording, finely balanced.

Though the opening applause is distracting and the first movement is less biting than the rest, the *Choral Symphony* here brings a fitting culmination to Menuhin's cycle, thanks also to the fresh, clear singing of the Lithuanian choir and a young, rather lightweight quartet of soloists. Following the Gardiner thesis, the drum-and-fife sequence in the finale of No. 9 is taken very fast, like a French military march. But with a deeply felt slow movement, this must be counted among the very finest of performances on modern instruments at bargain price.

Recorded by the BBC in November 1961, Klemperer (on Testament) conducts a searingly powerful performance, well worth preserving, even if in mono only; though with surface noise marring the slow movement, it does not displace the 1957 version, also recorded live in the Royal Festival Hall but in stereo, which also appeared on Testament (SBT 1177 – see our main *Guide*). In 1961 Klemperer had just had phenomenal success conducting Beethoven's *Fidelio* at Covent Garden (the opening performance also issued on Testament), and the exhilaration of that achievement is reflected in the *Ninth*, with a ruggedly powerful first movement, a measured but well-sprung Scherzo and a songful slow movement. In all those movements Klemperer is marginally faster than in 1957. Though the finale starts with some untidy ensemble, the electricity of the performance is irresistible, gaining over the 1957 version (and Klemperer's studio version for EMI) in having a finer quartet of soloists.

Fricsay's account of the *Ninth* was the first to come out in stereo in the late 1950s. It is undoubtedly a significant performance, well shaped and full of vitality, though tempi are fairly broad, save in the Scherzo. The *Adagio* is particularly beautiful, and only the finale seems lacking in weight. The recording is well balanced (the soloists forward, but the chorus well in the picture) and sounds remarkably good for its age, and though this is not as recommendable as Karajan or Boehm, it is finer than we had remembered it, and a fair choice for inclusion among DG's 'Originals'. The overture is played as an introduction.

Weingartner's 1935 account of the *Ninth Symphony* was a mainstay of the 78rpm catalogue. It remains impressive, as is his whole cycle, presenting Beethoven truthfully without any intervening filter or interpretative veneer. Weingartner's soloists are also good, particularly the magisterial Richard Mayr. Over sixty years old, it still ranks high among *Ninth*s. The transfer is fair but not outstanding.

Leinsdorf's Beethoven *Ninth* is brilliantly played and recorded, but it misses the heights of the greatest performances. The fill-up is a rarity and surprisingly inappropriate.

Originally issued by EMI, Günter Wand's 1986 version is a rugged interpretation, thrusting and not always very refined. The very opening brings no mystery whatever, with the orchestra recorded close and made thicker through bass-heaviness. However, the Scherzo is wild in its jollity and the drum-and-fife episode of the finale is free and easy, adding to an almost operatic feeling. The ruggedness extends to the slow movement, with the violins of the North German Radio Orchestra not always ideally sweet. At times ensemble is rough, and soloists and chorus are not ideally well drilled. Even at budget price this is far from a top choice, but Wand's admirers should not be too disappointed.

Dedicated as Furtwängler's spacious reading is, the Austrian radio recording from the 1951 Salzburg Festival on Orfeo is too seriously marred by intrusive audience noises and by sour woodwind to provide serious rivalry to Furtwängler's historic Bayreuth performance on EMI from the same summer, in which the soloists are even finer as well.

CHAMBER MUSIC

Cello Sonatas Nos 1–2, Op. 5/1–2; 3, Op. 69; 4–5, Op. 102/1–2; 7 Variations on 'Bei Männern'; 12 Variations on 'Ein Mädchen' both from 'Die Zauberflöte', WoO 66.

(M) (**(*)) Sony mono 515304-2 (2). Casals, Serkin.

These performances come from Prades in 1953, save for the *G minor*, Op. 5, No. 2, and the variations, which were made in Perpignan two years earlier. They are strong, finely shaped accounts that, like the Piatigorsky–Solomon set from the mid-1950s or the Fournier–Schnabel 78s, bring us closer to the spirit of these pieces than most of their successors (Rostropovich and Richter excepted). Serkin is occasionally more aggressive than was Horszowski in their versions; with the latter, one is unaware of the piano's hammers. Some allowances have to be made for the recorded sound, but these transfers are better than any predecessor we have heard.

Cello Sonatas No. 1 in F, Op. 5/1; in E flat, Op. 64 (arr. of String Trio, Op. 3). Variations on Handel's 'See the conqu'ring hero comes', WoO 45.
(BB) ★★★ Warner Apex 0927 49595-2. Karttunen, Hakkila (fortepiano).

Cello Sonatas: No. 2 in G min., Op. 5/2; in F, Op. 17 (trans. of Horn Sonata); 7 Variations on 'Bei Männern, Lelche Liebe fühlen'; 12 Variations on 'Ein Mädchen oder Weibchen'.
(BB) ★★★ Warner Apex 2564 60626-2. Karttunen, Hakkila (fortepiano).

Two discs of Beethoven's works for cello and keyboard, sonatas that were the first of their kind. These Finnish artists play them on instruments of the period, a Benjamin Banks cello from 1770 and a reproduction 1795 Walter fortepiano, and moreover they play them with something of the excitement of first discovery. They have energy, imagination and a fine sense of pace. The recordings, which come from the mid-1990s Finlandia label, also have a lot to recommend them. An admirable supplement to the many accounts of this repertoire recommended in our main volume.

Cello Sonata No. 3 in A, Op. 69.
(M) (★★★) EMI mono 5 67008-2. Casals, Schulhof –
  BACH: (Unaccompanied) *Cello Suite No. 1;*
  BRAHMS: *Cello Sonata No. 2.* (★★★)

For the *A major Sonata*, way back in 1930, Casals chose Otto Schulhof. He is a thoughtful pianist and their playing is wonderfully natural, unforced and musical. The frail, dry sound soon ceases to worry the experienced ear.

Piano Trios Nos. 1–2, Op. 1/1–2; 4, Op. 11.
(BB) ★★★ Warner Apex 2564 60364-2. Trio Fontenay.

The Fontenay performances offer alert and intelligent playing throughout, with attentive phrasing and bright, well-lit recorded sound. If not quite as distinctive as the Ashkenazy/Perlman/Harrell series, it offers excellent value at Apex price.

Piano Trios Nos. 1 in E flat; 3 in C min., Op. 1/1 & 3; 4 in B flat (Ghost), Op. 11.
(BB) ★★ Warner Apex 2564 61366-2. V. Haydn Trio.

The Vienna Haydn Trio is undoubtedly an accomplished ensemble, and for the most part they give good, enjoyable performances, though the slow movement of the *Ghost Trio* is too fast for comfort, and occasionally there is an element of blandness, as in the fluent account of the *C minor Trio*. Although Heinz Medjimorec is a first-class pianist, given the stiff opposition this bargain reissue must be regarded as an also-ran. Not all repeats are observed, but they are included in the first movement of Op. 11. The

recording, though bright and warm, is far from ideal so far as balance is concerned, with the piano tending to dominate the aural picture.

Piano Trios Nos. 5 (Ghost); 6 in E flat, Op. 70/1–2; 7 (Archduke); 8 in E flat, WoO 38; 10 (Variations in E flat), Op. 44; 12 (Allegretto in E flat), Hess 48.
☞ (BB) ★★★ EMI Gemini (DDD/ADD) 5 85496-2 (2). Ashkenazy, Perlman, Harrell.

This generous bargain-priced EMI Gemini compilation (which includes both the *Archduke* and *Ghost Trios*) is drawn from the complete set by these artists, which was made over a period of five years between 1979 and 1984. It has long led the field in this repertoire. The playing is unfailingly perceptive and full of those musical insights that make one want to return to the set. The recording is a shade dry but very present and realistic.

Piano Trios Nos. 5 (Ghost); 7 (Archduke); in E flat (from Septet), Op. 38.
(M) ★★★ EMI 5 62588-2. Perlman, Ashkenazy, Harrell.

The alternative reissue is part of the 'Perlman Edition' and replaces the full-priced disc in our main volume. But the Gemini issue is obviously the one to go for.

Piano Trios Nos. 7 in B flat (Archduke), Op. 97; 12 (Allegretto in E flat, Hess 48); Variations on 'Ich bin der Schneider Kakadu', Op. 121a.
☞ ★★★ Hyp. CDA 67369. Florestan Trio.

We have welcomed in our main volume the earlier Hyperion issue, coupling the two Op. 70 masterpieces from the Florestan Trio (CDA 67327), and this commanding, dramatically conceived account of the *Archduke* is no less superb. Strongly characterized and unfailingly intelligent, this performance can rank among the best to appear for many years, and it is superbly recorded to boot. The fill-up, the *Variations on 'Ich bin der Schneider Kakadu'*, is done with an appealing lightness of touch.

Piano & Wind Quintet in E flat, Op. 16.
(M) ★★(★) Warner Elatus 2464 60445-2. Barenboim, Soloists of Chicago SO — MOZART: *Quintet.* ★★(★)
(M) ★(★) Telarc CD 80114. Previn, V. Wind Soloists — MOZART: *Quintet, K.452.* ★(★)

Barenboim here puts down his baton to join players from the Chicago Symphony Orchestra (Hansjörg Schellenberger, oboe, Larry Combs, clarinet, Dale Clevenger, horn, and Daniele Damiano, bassoon) who distinguish themselves in the engaging interplay of the *Andante*. Barenboim too is in good form – the first movement proceeds jauntily, and the finale is sprightly but nicely relaxed. This is very enjoyable and well recorded. Not a first choice, but fair value at mid-price.

Previn is at his finest in the slow movement, which he opens most persuasively; throughout, his wind colleagues emphasize the work's robust character and the playing fails to sparkle as it should, although the finale goes well enough. The ensemble is good, if not immaculate; the recording, made in a rather resonant acoustic but naturally balanced, is faithful. Even at mid-price, it is hardly a must-have CD, when the Perahia copuling is still available at mid-price (Sony SMK 42099).

Septet in E flat, Op. 20.
(***) Testament mono SBT 1261. Vienna Octet
(members) – SPOHR: Nonet. (***)

An enchanting version of the evergreen Septet from the Vienna Octet: it oozes Viennese charm but is without any cloying sentimentality. Its return to the catalogue is very good news indeed, and it is hoped that other classic accounts from this source are to resurface soon. The 1956 recording is astonishingly warm and vivid (a tribute to whoever made this transfer, as well as to the original Decca engineers). Delightful coupling, too.

Serenade in D, Op. 8 (arr. Matiegka).
*** Mer. CDE 84199. Conway, Silverthorne, Garcia –
KREUTZER; MOLINO: Trios. ***

Beethoven's early Serenade for string trio was arranged for violin, viola and guitar by the Bohemian composer and guitarist Wenceslaus Matiegka. On Meridian, Gerald Garcia has rearranged it for the present delightful combination, offering the violin part to the flute, and giving the guitar a more taxing contribution. As a companion piece for the rare Kreutzer and Molino items, it makes a charming oddity, very well played and warmly recorded.

STRING QUARTETS

String Quartets Nos. 1–16; Grosse Fuge, Op. 133.
(BB) *** ASV Resonance RSB 801 (8). The Lindsays.

The great merit of the earlier Lindsay recordings of Beethoven lies in the natural expressiveness of their playing, most strikingly in slow movements, bringing a hushed inner quality too rarely caught on record. The sense of spontaneity necessarily brings the obverse quality: these performances are not as precise as those in the finest rival sets; but there are few Beethoven quartet recordings that so convincingly bring out the humanity of the writing. They offer superb performances of Op. 59. Their insights are not often rivalled, let alone supassed, in more modern recordings. As to the sound, this set is comparable with most of its competitors and is superior to many; artistically it can hold its own with the best. The Lindsays also get far closer to the essence of the late quartets than most of their rivals, with the benefit of very well-balanced recording. They regularly find tempi that feel completely right, conveying both the letter and the spirit of the music in rich, strong characterization. They are among the finest versions to have been made in recent years and at budget price are outstanding value.

String Quartets Nos. 1–6, Op. 18/1–6.
*** Decca 470 848-2 (2). Takács Qt.
(B) *** EMI 5 62778-2 (2). Alban Berg Qt.

The Takács Quartet in their ongoing Beethoven cycle have now turned to the Op. 18 set and maintain the high standards they have achieved in earlier releases. There are so many splendid sets now on the market – some, like the Quartetto Italiano and the Alban Berg, at highly competitive prices. The Lindsays stretch to a third CD, though they offer the C major String Quintet and the arrangement of Op. 14, No. 1; and the deeply musical accounts by the Leipzig Quartet again involve three CDs, but are available separately. Both sets are both well worth considering. However, those collecting the Takács cycle will know the strength and excellence of this ensemble and their command of nuance, sensitive phrasing and musical architecture. Their sound musical intelligence and freshness of approach are always in evidence, and they are given splendid recorded sound.

The Alban Berg's studio recordings of the Beethoven Quartets in the late 1970s and early 1980s set high standards. This newer set originates from public concerts in 1989 and is, perhaps, an attempt to ensure that the greater intensity and spontaneity generated in the presence of an audience finds its way on to records. Generally speaking, it does; these performances, when listened to alongside the earlier set, on balance are freer and more vital. But the differences are small, and even now there is a feeling of studied perfection of ensemble and sheer beauty of sound that will not strike all listeners as altogether appropriate in this repertoire. However, these performances are not by any means superficial or slick – and admirers of this ensemble need have no hesitation in acquiring them at their new bargain price.

String Quartet No. 1 in F, Op. 18/1.
(**) BBC mono BBCL 4137-2. Smetana Qt – MOZART:
String Quartet No. 20 (**(*)); SMETANA: String
Quartet No. 1. (***)

The Smetana Quartet's performance of Op. 18, No. 1, comes from 1963 when they were at the BBC's Manchester Studios. The sound is in fact better than the Festival Hall Mozart and Smetana performances, made two years later. The slow movement is perhaps a bit fast and almost prosaic, certainly not as searching as such commercial recordings as those of the Végh or the Quartetto Italiano. But, generally speaking, the performance still gives a lot of satisfaction. No exposition repeat in the first movement.

String Quartets Nos. 4–5, Op. 18/4–5; 7; 9 (Rasumovsky), Op. 59/1 &3; 11, Op. 95; 13, Op. 30; 15, Op. 132 Grosse Fugue.
(BB) **(*) Virgin 5 62258-2 (4). Borodin Qt.

Virgin have now combined the Borodin Quartet's recordings in a four-disc budget box. For finesse and beauty of sound their playing is unmatched, even by the Alban Berg. In the early Quartets the elegance and warmth of the playing are an undoubted pleasure; yet, eloquent as it is on the surface, the searching quality that Beethoven calls for is passed by. The playing is not superficial – there is plenty of concentration in the slow movements of both Op. 95 and Op. 132, but at the same time the result is not particularly illuminating either. The *Grosse Fuge* demands and receives great attack and gusto, yet the players are even more in their element in the lighter, substituted finale of Op. 133. The sound is very realistic, and these are the kind of performances that would make a strong impression in the concert hall but that do not resonate in the mind afterwards. Nevertheless, at its modest price this set still offers much to admire and enjoy.

String Quartets Nos. 4; 10 (Harp); 14, Op. 131.
(M) (***) Biddulph mono LAB 056-7. Rosé Qt –
BACH: *Double Concerto*, etc. (***)

These performances bring us as close as we can possibly get to the kind of strongly characterized playing Brahms and Mahler would have heard. The recordings were made in 1930 and 1932, the *C sharp minor* in 1927, and this accounts for the rather primitive sound.

String Quartets Nos. 7 in F; 9 in C (Rasumovsky), Op. 59/1 & 3.
* Chan. 10178. Borodin Qt.

Anyone who has heard the Borodins in the flesh will testify to the particularly sumptuous sonority they produce. It is refined in blend and beautifully balanced, and their ensemble and intonation are impeccable. They were an aristocrat among quartets, unsurpassed in terms of homogeneity and beauty of tone. But, of course, beauty and truth do not always go hand in hand and the search for the former can often mask the latter. Difficult though it is to resist the sheer beauty of the Borodin's playing, there is perhaps more depth to be found in these middle-period masterpieces by the Végh and Talich (and the Lindsays). One is reminded of Robert Simpson's remark about the Alban Berg Quartet in the late 1970s, that 'they were in danger of becoming mere beautifiers of the classics'. On occasion one feels the Borodins are a little too gracious, though there is much here to cherish even so. The finale of Op. 59, No. 3, is pretty dazzling.

String Quartets Nos. 7 in F, Op. 59/1; 10 (Harp) in E flat, Op. 74.
(M) *** Cal. Approche (ADD) CAL 5636. Talich Qt.

String Quartets Nos. 8 in E min., Op. 59/2; 13 in B flat, Op. 130.
(M) *** Cal. Approche (ADD) CAL 5637. Talich Qt.

This is an awkward way of reissuing these celebrated Talich performances, as the *Rasumovskys* would have been far better coupled together. However, the performances are another matter. One is immediately gripped by the purity of sound these artists produce and the effortlessness of their phrasing. As a quartet their ensemble and intonation are impeccable, and they possess both depth of feeling and insight. The readings unfold with a totally unforced naturalness; tempi have the feeling of rightness one recognizes in masterly performances, and the dynamic range is wide without being exaggerated. The sound, as usual with their recordings, is just a little bottom-heavy but otherwise very natural, and, like the Végh, they bring a rich humanity to bear on these masterpieces.

String Quartets Nos. 7 in F (Rasumovsky), Op. 59/1; 11 in F min., Op. 95.
(BB) *** Naxos 8.554181. Kodály Qt.

We have listed several of the Kodály Quartet's Beethoven discs in our main edition, commenting favourably on the performances, the recordings – and the price, which is highly competitive. Both quartets here are very good indeed: thoughtful, decently paced and thoroughly musical accounts, which will give satisfaction.

String Quartets Nos. 9 in C (Rasumovsky), Op. 59/3; 10 in E flat (Harp), Op. 74.
** Praga PR 256014. Vlach Qt.

These Praga performances derive from a complete cycle the Vlach Quartet recorded live in the 1960s for Prague Radio. They have something of the concentration that distinguishes the live performance and naturally are less polished than they would have been had they been made in the recording studio. The sound is a little wanting in bloom, and there is a certain wiriness above the stave. Both are thoroughly musical performances without being among the primary recommendations.

String Quartets Nos. 12–16; Grosse Fuge, Op. 133.
(M) **(*) DG Trio 474 341-2 (3). Emerson Qt.

When the complete Emerson Quartet's recording of the Beethoven cycle of 1994–5 was first issued in 1996, *Gramophone* magazine commented: 'They continually offer new insights into some endlessly enthralling music. Do hear them.' This seems good advice, now they are re-emerging at reduced price, for they have also been praised elsewhere. There are undoubted insights during the course of these performances, and the technical finish of the playing is incredible – amazing, indeed awesome. It goes without saying that there are many incidental beauties too, for the ensemble is immaculate in its precision; its sheer thrust is overwhelming and the DG recording is marvellous. But to our ears the playing concentrates on virtuosity and presentation rather than substance. The group are at their most impressive in the concentration of the last quartets, where their contact with great music is impressive in its unanimity, and this Trio reissue is certainly worth consideration, even if it is by no means a primary choice.

PIANO MUSIC

Piano Sonatas Nos. 1–32; Bagatelles, Opp. 119 & 125.
✹ (B) ✳✳✳ EMI 5 62700-2 (9). Kovacevich.

Piano Sonatas Nos. 1–32; Diabelli Variations.
(M) ✳✳✳ Oehms OCD 229 (10). Perl.

Stephen Kovacevich recorded his Beethoven cycle for EMI between 1992 and 2003 with consistent success, capping the series with an extraordinarily powerful and imaginative account of the *Hammerklavier*. The individual CDs have been highly praised by us, and many as discussed in our main volume. However, some of them have been subsequently withdrawn, so the arrival of the complete set at bargain price is doubly welcome. EMI's recording is of consistently high quality, and this cycle must now be counted a first choice, alongside those by Goode (Nonesuch 7559 79328-2), Kempff (DG mono 447 966-2) and (of course) the pioneering Schnabel readings (EMI mono 7 63765-2).

The young Chilean pianist Alfredo Perl responds superbly to the challenge of a complete Beethoven sonata cycle, giving searching accounts of works both early and late, always fresh and spontaneous-sounding, consistently finding depths of concentration in the most demanding of Beethoven's slow movements. Particularly in the early sonatas, his manner is impulsive, often with allegros fast in a Schnabel manner, yet with technical problems masterfully solved and no fudging of detail. Slow movements by contrast are generally spacious, but not so exaggeratedly so that the music loses momentum or a sense of lyrical line. The cycle is splendidly rounded off in accounts of the late sonatas that transcend everything else, not least the *Hammerklavier*, where the slow movement has a sublime purity. The performance of the *Diabelli variations* is equally commanding and imaginative.

However, although this set was originally issued on Arte Nova at budget price, its reissue at mid-price becomes less competitive when compared with other cycles at bargain price like Kovacevich's or Barenboim's on EMI or Bernard Roberts on Nimbus. The sound is first rate, though inner textures are not always ideally clear, while Perl's use of the pedal is on the generous side, adding to the warmth of the readings. Undoubtedly this Oehms reissue stands alongside the finest surveys of this repertoire, and it is a pity that it is not in a lower price-range. The *Diabelli Variations* (but not the sonatas) are also available separately (OCD 230).

Piano Sonatas Nos. 1–3; 5–7; 16–18; 11; 13; 14 (Moonlight); 16; 17 (Tempest); 18–20; 21 (Waldstein); 23 (Appassionata); 25; 26 (Les Adieux).
(BB) ✳✳✳ EMI 5 62368-2 (5). Tan (fortepiano).

Melvyn Tan began his survey of Beethoven's *Sonatas* using the fortepiano in 1990, continuing in 1991 and 1992; but it was never completed, presumably because of lack of demand, certainly not because of any lack of artistry. Tan has a strong musical personality and in the named middle-period *Sonatas* attacks his instrument with tremendous spirit and flair; every phrase lives, and he is not afraid to present the widest dynamic range. There is consummate artistry and real temperament and fire. Nor is there any want of poetic feeling. In the earlier *Sonatas* he plays with brilliance and sensitivity in equal measure. He uses a copy by Derek Adlam of a Streicher (1814), an instrument for which Beethoven himself expressed a strong preference. The EMI recording is excellent. Even collectors whose taste inclines to the modern piano rather than the fortepiano will surely find both the sounds and musical sense well conveyed here, and perhaps they will be tempted to explore these performances when the cost is so little.

Piano Sonata No. 3 in C, Op. 2/3.
✳✳ Appian Recordings APR 5632. Arrau – BRAHMS: *Piano Sonata No. 3.* (✳)

After he recorded his Beethoven cycle for Philips in 1964–5, Arrau dropped the *C major Sonata*, Op. 2, No. 3, from his active repertoire, taking it up again only at the time of his Prague recital in 1976. In his hands it has a weight and depth almost worthy of middle-period or even late Beethoven. The slow movement has more depth than his earlier, studio account, and the performance holds the listener throughout. Although Solomon played the mercurial finale with greater lightness, this is a performance that is worth hearing. The sound is very acceptable, though it is a bit forward and shallow, but perfectly natural, even if the Czech Radio engineers do not do full justice to the unusually rounded, perfectly focused and rich sonority.

Piano Sonatas Nos. 4 in E flat, Op. 7; 12 in A flat, Op. 26.
(M) ✳✳(✳) BBC mono/stereo BBCL 4064-2.
Michelangeli – DEBUSSY: *Hommage à Rameau* ✳✳(✳); RAVEL: *Gaspard de la nuit* (✳✳✳).

The *Opp. 7* and *26 Sonatas* and the Debussy *Hommage à Rameau* come from a Festival Hall recital that the great pianist gave in 1982. Michelangeli recorded the *E flat Sonata*, Op. 7, for DG, where its 29 minutes were spread over two LP sides. Of the two, this performance sounds the more involving. Michelangeli brings fastidious keyboard articulation and refinement of phrasing to both sonatas here though he remains curiously aloof.

Piano Sonatas Nos. 8 (Pathétique); 14 (Moonlight); 23 (Appassionata).
(BB) ✳✳ CfP (ADD) 575 5612. Chorzempa.

Daniel Chorzempa is best known as an occupant of the organ loft, but here he shows himself equally impressive as a piano virtuoso. His 1971 CfP coupling of Beethoven's three most popular sonatas remains competitive, if lacking a little in sparkle, the interpretations of a very serious young man who knows what he is doing. The simplicity and clarity of his style are well caught in a recording that is notable for its warm sonority.

Piano sonatas Nos. 8 in C min. (Pathétique); 23 in F min. (Appassionata), Op. 57; 31 in A flat, Op. 110.
✪ (M) ★★★ DG (DDD/ADD) 476 2194. Gilels.

If the *Pathétique* does not rank among Emil Gilels's very finest Beethoven performances on record, such are the strengths of his playing that the reading still leaves a profound impression. The account of the *Appassionata* has previously been hailed by us as among the finest ever made, and the 1973 analogue recording is both full and believably present. Op. 110 is given a performance of real stature. Even when Gilels storms the greatest heights in the closing fugue, no *fortissimo* ever sounds percussive or strained. The *Pathétique* and Op. 110 are truthful digital recordings, both made in the Berlin Jesus-Christus-Kirche; the *Pathétique*, made in 1980, has the microphones a bit close, but in No. 31 (dating from five years later) the balance is better judged. An outstanding bargain, all the same. This has now been reissued by Universal as one of the 'Penguin ✪ Collection' at mid-price.

Piano Sonatas Nos. 9–10, Op. 14/1–2.
(M) (★★★) BBC mono BBCL 4126-2. Sviatoslav Richter
   (with CHOPIN: *Etude in F sharp min., Op. 10/4*) –
   SCHUBERT: *Wanderer Fantasy* (★★★);
   SCHUMANN: *Abegg Variations, Op. 1;*
   Faschingsschwank aus Wien (★★).

The two Op. 14 *Sonatas* come from a festival recital in February 1963, two years after Richter's first concert appearances in the West (he had already recorded them commercially for Philips). His very deliberate pace for the *Allegretto* movement of the *E major* lends it a reflective, almost melancholy character, which is unusual, but as always with this great artist his readings are the product of much thought. The mono sound is perfectly acceptable.

Piano Sonatas Nos. 11 in B flat, Op. 22; 12 in A flat, Op. 26; 13 in E flat, Op. 27/1.
(BB) (★★★) Naxos mono 8.110756. Schnabel.

Piano Sonatas Nos. 14 in C sharp min. (Moonlight), Op. 27/2; 15 in D (Pastoral), Op. 28; 16 in G, Op. 31/1.
(BB) (★★★) Naxos mono 8.110759. Schnabel.

Piano Sonatas Nos. 17 in D min. (Tempest), Op. 31/2; 18 in E flat, Op. 31/3; 21 in C (Waldstein), Op. 53.
(BB) (★★★) Naxos mono 8.110760. Schnabel.

Pianistically, these are the reverse of the Pollini sonatas reviewed below. They are full of rough edges and do not aspire to the sheer pianistic perfection and high polish of the great Italian pianist. However, they come closer to Beethoven than has almost any other musician since, and in these excellent transfers

remain an indispensable part of any self-respecting collection.

Piano Sonatas Nos. 13 in E flat; 14 (Moonlight), Op. 27/1–2; 17 in D min. (Tempest), Op. 31/2; 21 in C (Waldstein), Op. 53.
(M) ★★★ DG 471 354-2. Pollini.

Pollini's impeccable keyboard mastery is in evidence throughout these performances – recorded in 1988 (Op. 31/2), 1991 (Op. 27) and 1997 (Op. 53) – though the collection as a whole is a little problematic. The intellectually sombre first movement of the *Moonlight Sonata* will not please all tastes, but Pollini's mood lightens somewhat in the *Allegretto* and in the finale there is a finely judged range of colour and dynamic to make the *Presto agitato* the key point of an unusual but stimulating interpretation. In Pollini's hands, Beethoven's term, *Sonata quasi fantasia*, applies more readily to the *E flat major Sonata*, which comes first on the record. The opening *Andante* is gentle and friendly, but the *Allegro* is brusque and tense, and one welcomes the return to serenity. But this brusqueness reappears in the last two movements, and becomes the work's dominating influence.

The '*Tempest*' Sonata also opens boldly, intensely and apparently impetuously (although everything Pollini does is controlled), but the *Adagio* is poised, and this is a perfectly proportioned account, if one that seems to draw us into its world only sporadically. The *Waldstein* is a live performance (the audience is occasionally restless) and has a spontaneous feeling and a fine sense of pace: in many ways this is the most satisfying performance on the disc. The recording throughout is variable: the engineers do not always allow too much of the ambience of the acoustic to help the sound-picture. Though the effect is not dry, it is rather close. Nevertheless this makes a well-chosen anthology for reissue as part of the 'Pollini Edition'.

Piano Sonatas Nos. 13–14 (Moonlight), Op. 27/1–2; 30 in E, Op. 109.
★ DG 453 457-2. Pires.

Maria João Pires has been much (and rightly) admired in the Mozart concertos and sonatas and in the Schubert *Moments musicaux* and *A minor Sonata*, D.784, she recorded for DG. Her Beethoven recital, on the other hand, is a disappointment: she is for the most part curiously unengaged, and whether in the familiar *Moonlight* or in Op. 109 remains uninvolved and uninvolving. The engineers place her rather close to the microphone.

Piano Sonatas Nos. 22 in F, Op. 54; 23 in F min. (Appassionata), Op. 57 (2 versions); 24 in F sharp, Op. 78 (2 versions); 27 in E min., Op. 90.
(M) ★★ DG 474 451-2 (2). Pollini.

Pollini recorded all four sonatas in the fine acoustic of the Herkulessaal in the Residenz, Munich, during

June 2002, and the sound has impeccable clarity and definition. In addition, we are offered a bonus CD of live performances of Opp. 57 and 78 recorded at the Musikverein in Vienna during the same month. (The little *F sharp major Sonata*, Op. 78, gains in breadth by the observance of both repeats.) However, for all their immaculate pianism there is a want of engagement in all six performances, live or studio, and an unwelcome detachment throughout. Masterly pianism but less masterly as Beethoven.

Piano Sonatas Nos. 29 (Hammerklavier), Op. 106.
(M) **(*) DG (ADD) 474 860-2. Gilels.

Emil Gilels's Olympian *Hammerklavier* was certainly worthy of the *Gramophone* magazine's Instrumental Award in 1984. However, this reissue in the 'Awards Collection' is uncoupled, whereas the same performance is also available as a DG 'Original', coupled with Op. 101 and similarly priced (463 639-2 – see our main volume).

Piano Sonatas Nos. 29 in B flat (Hammerklavier) Op. 106; 30 in E, Op. 109; 31 in A flat, Op. 101; 32 in C min., Op. 111; 6 Bagatelles, Op. 126.
⊶ ❀ (BB) *** EMI Gemini (ADD) 5 85499-2 (2). Eschenbach.

Christoph Eschenbach recorded the *Hammerklavier Sonata* for DG in 1971; it was an impressive account, though it did not survive in the catalogue for very long. He re-recorded it in 1979 for EMI at the Abbey Road Studios with Suvi Raj Grub producing, along with Opp. 109, 110 and 111 and the *Six Bagatelles*, Op. 126. These were not listed in the 1979–82 catalogues (and were not reviewed by *Gramophone* magazine). Nor do they appear to have been issued in the period 1983–99 in Britain. Perhaps they were released on the Continent or there were some contractual problems that stood in their way. Anyway, they are performances of some stature and should be snapped up without delay at this bargain price. The Op. 111 is among the most concentrated, powerfully conceived and sensitive realizations of the score currently before the public and the *Hammerklavier* is no less magisterial and commanding than its DG predecessor. Listening to Beethoven playing of this quality is a wonderfully satisfying experience and, even if you have the fine accounts of these sonatas by Stephen Kovacevich on the EMI label or any of the other classic versions included in our main volume, do not overlook the present set. These are readings of great musical insight that have the strengths of a master pianist combined with the wisdom of a great musician. The recorded sound is very present and lifelike.

Piano Sonatas Nos. 29 (Hammerklavier); 32 in C min., Op. 111.
(M) *** DG (ADD) 471 355-2. Pollini.

When they were first issued in 1977, Joan Chissell spoke of the 'noble purity' of these performances, and that telling phrase aptly sums them up, if also hinting at a missing dimension, which the CD transfer seems to emphasize. The sound has great presence but becomes almost brittle in the *fortissimos* of the *Hammerklavier*, with an adverse effect on the music-making. Pollini's performance is undoubtedly eloquent, and so is Op. 111, which has a peerless authority and power, although there is still a touch of hardness in the sound. However, rather than investing in the present coupling – reissued as part of the 'Pollini Edition' – the great pianist's admirers will probably prefer the set from which it is drawn (also including Opp. 101, 109 and 110), which is available as a two-disc set at a special price.

Piano Sonatas Nos. 30 in E flat, Op. 109; 31 in A flat, Op. 110; 32 in C min., Op. 111.
(M) **(*) Sony (ADD) 512869-2. Serkin.
** BIS CD 1120. Freddy Kempf.

Rudolf Serkin played the last three *Sonatas* in Vienna in October 1987 at the age of eighty-five, and DG subsequently issued an Austrian Radio broadcast of the occasion. There was naturally a certain decline in finesse, and certainly *pianissimo* tone was less in evidence. The present performances come from different periods: Op. 109 was recorded in New York in 1976, Op. 110 in 1971 and Op. 11 in 1967. Unlike Schnabel, Kempff or Arrau, Serkin never did complete Beethoven sonata cycles, feeling always that he was not ready for them, and indeed when he did embark on one in 1971 he did not finish it. There is a commanding rigour and classical feel to his late Beethoven, though he does not always cultivate beauty of tone for its own sake. There are others, such as Gilels, Arrau and Kovacevich, who brought more humanity and pianistic finish to them. Whether or not you respond to Serkin, his is playing of stature; some respected critics have ranked his versions of Opp. 109 and 110 among the very finest. It would not be a first choice; indeed, the opening of the finale of Op. 109 sounds distinctly prosaic. Predictably, the sound shows a very considerable improvement over the original LPs.

Freddy Kempf plays very well and is gifted with good fingers and a good mind. However, the recording, which was made in the former Swedish Royal Academy of Music, tends to be a bit bottom- and middle-heavy, and there is more to this music than this artist uncovers.

Miscellaneous piano music

Allegretto in C min., WoO 53; Andante favori, WoO 57; Für Elise, WoO 59; 6 Variations on an Original Theme, Op. 34.
(B) *** Virgin 2 × 1 5 62233-2 (2). Tan (fortepiano) – SCHUBERT: *Impromptus*, etc. ***

There are no more persuasive performers on the fortepiano than Melvyn Tan. Here he plays a copy by Richard Adlam of an 1814 instrument by Nanette

Streicher, and he brings to these pieces his customary flair and panache. The *F major Variations* come off splendidly: there is plenty of colour and imagination throughout. Despite his rather brisk *Andante favori*, this is a thoroughly enjoyable recital and it is recorded with great realism and presence at The Maltings at Snape.

33 Variations on a Waltz by Diabelli, Op. 120.
(M) (**(*)) Sony mono/stereo 5128662. Serkin.
(B) ** Warner Elatus 2-CD 2564 60010-2 (2). Barenboim (piano) – BACH: *Goldberg Variations.* **

Rudolf Serkin's account of the *Diabelli Variations* was recorded in Marlboro, Vermont, in September 1957; one critic memorably spoke of its 'craggy splendour'. It is indeed a performance of stature, which belonged among the finest of its day. Of course Schnabel's pioneering set still towers above all its successors and, though Kovacevich ranks high – as do Brendel and the young Pole, Piotr Anderszewski (see our main *Guide*) – Serkin still holds an honoured place in the *Diabelli* discography. The *Eleven Bagatelles*, Op. 119, and the *G minor Fantasy* were both recorded in New York, in 1966 and 1970 respectively. They are fine performances and enjoy better sound.

Daniel Barenboim first recorded the *Diabelli Variations* in the late 1960s and he is no stranger to their mystery. His later, Elatus account has much to recommend it, and his admirers need not doubt that he is a thoughtful and serious guide in this masterpiece. There are finer versions, but this one comes coupled with a similarly individual set of the *Goldberg Variations.*

VOCAL MUSIC

Christ on the Mount of Olives, Op. 85.
(BB) *** EMI (ADD) 5 85687-2. Deutekom, Gedda, Sotin, Stadt Bonn Philharmonic Ch., Theaters der Stadt Bonn Ch., Beethovenhalle O, Bonn, Wangenheim.

Recorded in 1969/70 in time for the Beethoven bicentenary, the EMI recording of this neglected oratorio had very limited circulation indeed – never appearing in Britain, for example – and here makes its début on CD in an excellent transfer. This is a piece that centres round the figure of Jesus as he meditates on his predestined fate, with the tenor who sings the role of Christ taking on much the greatest burden. Here Nicolai Gedda is superb, radiant of tone and endlessly perceptive in interpreting the text. The Dutch soprano Cristina Deutekom, bright and flexible, is equally positive as the angelic Seraph visiting Christ. If the edge on her voice occasionally brings moments of stridency, she knows how to shade her tone down in duet to match Gedda, as in the big central duet, *So ruhe denn.* The bass soloist, Hans Sotin, is aptly bluff and forthright in the much smaller role of St Peter. Volker Wangenheim draws a warm, sympathetic performance from his Bonn chorus and orchestra, well recorded in the Beethovenhalle in Beethoven's home city.

Mass in C, Op. 86; Cantatas: Elegischer Gesang, Op. 118; Meeresstille und glückliche Fahrt, Op. 112.
🔑 *** Chan. 0703. Evans, Stephen, Padmore, Varcoe, Coll. Mus. 90, Hickox.

Following up the success of his recordings of Haydn and Hummel Masses, Richard Hickox with a choir of modest size (24 singers) brings out the link between Beethoven's *Mass in C* and those other settings of the Mass also written for the nameday of the Princess Esterházy. Beethoven's *Mass* was initially a failure, condemned by the Prince as 'totally ridiculous', and latterly it has always suffered from being in the shadow of his massive *Missa solemnis* of over a decade later. Yet Hickox consistently brings out the way in which, as in that more ambitious work, Beethoven was rethinking the meaning of each phrase of the liturgy and illustrating it with an electric sense of drama. Even more than John Eliot Gardiner on his rival period performance from DG (431 395-2 – see our main volume), similarly coupled, Hickox brings out the joy of the inspiration, with excellent soloists and a fresh-toned choir, and directs similarly concentrated readings of two brief choral works of 1814, the fine Goethe setting, *Meeresstille und glückliche Fahrt*, and the simple but deeply felt *Elegiac Song* (not offered by Gardiner), which come as welcome couplings.

Missa solemnis, Op. 123.
(BB) *** Naxos 8.557060. Phillips, Redmon, Taylor, Baylon, Van Osdale, Nashville Ch. & SO, Schermerhorn.
(M) ** Warner Elatus 2564 61172-2 (2). Kilberg, Meier, Aler, Holl, Chicago Symphony Ch. & SO, Barenboim.

Kenneth Schermerhorn, best known for his advocacy of twentieth-century music, here demonstrates what power he can bring to Beethoven's supreme choral masterpiece, a work notoriously difficult to interpret. The choral and orchestral sound is full and beefy, reinforcing the thrust of the performance, with the *Credo* at once warm and four-square. Speeds are consistently well chosen, not as fast as those in David Zinman's rival super-bargain issue from Arte Nova, but crisp enough to allow the whole work to be fitted on a single disc. The four soloists are first rate, all with fresh, young-sounding voices, and the enthusiasm of the chorus makes for magnetic singing throughout. The Zinman version on Arte Nova (74321 87074-2 – see our main volume) with its clear, transparent sound may provide more new insights, but the Naxos issue is an equally compelling bargain version.

Barenboim takes a weighty view of the *Missa solemnis*, but the magnificence of the Chicago Symphony Chorus, here trained (as it has been for generations) by Margaret Hillis, is reduced when the recording balance sets it well behind the orchestra. As recorded in Symphony Hall, Chicago, a difficult venue, the sound is not ideally clear, and the occasional flaw in ensemble suggests a live performance, though that is not acknowledged. This is hardly a primary choice, even at mid-price.

OPERA

Fidelio (complete).

(*) DG **DVD 073 052-9. Mattila, Heppner, Struckmann, Lloyd, Pape, Welch-Babidge, Polenzani, Met. Op. Ch. & O, Levine (Dir. Jurgen Flimm; TV Dir.: Brian Large).

⬤ (**(*)) Testament mono SBT 21328 (2). Jurinac, Vickers, Frick, Hotter, Morison, Dobson, ROHCG Ch. & O, Klemperer.

** Teldec 3984 25249-2 (2). Meier, Domingo, Pape, Struckmann, Ikoski, Güra, Deutsche State Op, Berlin Ch. & O, Barenboim.

(BB) (*(*)) Naxos mono 8.110054/5. Flagstad, Kipnis, Huehn, Farell, Laufkötter, Met. Op. Ch. & O, Walter.

(*) EMI 5 57555-2 (2). Denoke, Villars, Held, Polgár, Banse, Trost, Quasthoff, Arnold Schoenberg Ch., BPO, Rattle.

Updated to the present day with warders in US Army uniform and the prisoners chained in cages, Guantanamo Bay-style, Jurgen Flimm's production of Fidelio for the Met., recorded in 2002, is plainly intended to bring home the contemporary associations of Beethoven's opera. As a whole that works effectively, even if the prosaic stage-pictures are not exactly welcoming for video repetition. What is certainly clear is that, with only one flawed member of the cast, and with James Levine at his most intense, tackling a major Beethoven project, the result is an exceptionally powerful reading. Karita Mattila is superb as Leonore, singing with a freedom, beauty and power that cannot be faulted, and though Ben Heppner is in no way a romantic figure he sings with no hint of strain as Florestan. The others sing well too, with Robert Lloyd as Don Fernando made up to look disconcertingly like President George W. Bush. Sadly, the exception is the rough, gritty-toned Pizarro of Falk Struckmann, too often with disagreeable tone singing 'in the cracks' on no recognizable pitch. It takes away some of the impact of the villain of the piece, and the acting in the climactic quartet of Act II, with Struckmann waving a dagger and Leonore finding a revolver only at the last minute, is not as convincing as it might be. But the triumphant finale, as in any great performance of this opera, brings a thrill of excitement and fulfilment.

When Klemperer made his benchmark recording of Fidelio for EMI, he wanted to build on the legendary success of his Covent Garden performances a year earlier, but Walter Legge made changes in the casting, taking only Jon Vickers as Florestan and Gottlob Frick as Rocco. In this superb BBC recording of the first Klemperer performance at Covent Garden in February 1961 we can see just why he wanted his original line-up of singers, for in many ways this even outshines his classic studio recording.

Though inevitably in a live performance the ensemble is not always as polished as in the studio version (now available from EMI in its 'Great Recordings of the Century' series – 5 67364-2), with stage and audience noises intruding at times, the electricity is of an even higher voltage, so that the drama of the piece comes over the more vividly. This is the opposite of the staid Klemperer, with speeds generally a degree faster than in the studio, and though his decision is controversial to include the Leonore No. 3 overture in the once-traditional place just before the finale, the performance of it is hair-raisingly exciting, leaving one agog to hear the sublime sequence of the finale, more than ever under Klemperer emerging as a forerunner of the choral finale of the Ninth Symphony.

When it comes to the cast, Vickers and Frick are if anything even more magnetic than in the studio recording, and the rest of the cast includes at least one singer who totally outshines her studio counterpart, Elsie Morison, whose enchanting portrait of Marzelline makes her EMI rival seem characterless. The casting of the great Wagnerian, Hans Hotter, as Pizarro brings impressive weight to the role, making this arch-villain far more of a threat than he is with the excellent but relatively lightweight Walter Berry on EMI. From the Covent Garden company, John Dobson makes a warmly engaging Jaquino, and Forbes Robinson is a noble Don Fernando, but it is Sena Jurinac singing Leonore for the very first time who sets the seal on the whole performance. She may not have quite the weight as Ludwig on the studio set, but her projection is superb in singing, which combines both brightness and warmth, both noble defiance and womanly compassion. In the excellent Testament transfer the radio sound is astonishingly vivid, with the voices cleanly balanced even when the singers move around on stage.

Rattle's Berlin recording was made at a concert performance in the Philharmonie soon after he had conducted staged performances at the Salzburg Easter Festival in 2003. As his performances at Glyndebourne demonstrated, his approach to the opera is brisk and incisive, with one or two unexpectedly slow speeds for contrast. Yet, with all that preparation. the serious disappointment of this set is that it offers a comfortable run-through rather than a genuinely dramatic experience. Even the Canon Quartet in Act I lacks tension, with none of the rapt mystery it should have. Only at the end of Act II does the performance acquire something of the bite one expects, and even then the opening of the finale is brisk to the point of sounding perfunctory. The cast too is seriously flawed: Angela Denoke with her big, fruity voice is far too approximate in her tuning to be a convincing Leonore, sometimes squally and too often sounding cautious. As Florestan, Jon Villars is a tenor gritty with vibrato, and Alan Held as Pizarro similarly sings between the cracks, with pitch ill-determined. Laszlo Polgár is a lightweight Rocco, making the gaoler a *buffo* character, and Juliane Banse is too mezzo-ish to make a convincing Marzelline. Only Rainer Trost as Jaquino and Thomas Quasthoff come near to matching those in rival casts, and the Arnold Schoenberg Choir sounds surprisingly uninvolved, with ensemble far less crisp than usual.

In Barenboim's version the links are provided in the booklet, and the recording simply omits dialogue, except in passages of accompanied melodrama. The other oddity is that Barenboim prefers the magnificent *Leonore No. 2 Overture* to the usual one for *Fidelio* and he reverses the order of the first two numbers, with Marzelline's little aria coming first. Barenboim is a dedicated Beethoven interpreter, but this is not one of his most inspired recordings. It is worth hearing for Plácido Domingo's heroic account of the role of Florestan, clean and incisive, if strained at times. Waltraud Meier becomes shrill under pressure, and Soile Isokoski with her marked vibrato is a matronly Marzelline. René Pape is an excellent, firm Rocco, but Falk Struckmann is wobbly and strained as Pizarro, and Kwangchul Youn is a lightweight Fernando.

The second Naxos version offers a historic radio recording of a live performance, given in 1940 at the Metropolitan Opera in New York with Bruno Walter conducting and Kirsten Flagstad as Leonore. For many it will immediately be ruled out by the limited, often crumbly sound, even if the performance under Walter is urgently passionate at high voltage. Flagstad naturally dominates the performance vocally, even more vital than in her Salzburg reading under Furtwängler (EMI). Alexander Kipnis as Rocco and Herbert Janssen as Don Fernando stand out among the rest, with the others in the cast generally disappointing.

BELLINI, Vincenzo (1801–35)

Norma (opera; complete).
- ⊕⊸ (M) (***) EMI mono 5 62668-2 [5 62642-2] (2). Callas, Stignani, Picchi, Vaghi, ROHCG Ch. & O, Gui.

Recorded live at Covent Garden in November 1952, this account of *Norma* presents Callas at her very peak and becomes one of EMI's 'Great Recordings of the Century'. She had already sung the role in a dozen places from 1948 onwards, including La Scala, Milan, but her début at Covent Garden marked a new development, with Ebe Stignani, ideally cast as Adalgisa, a splendid foil. More than her studio recordings of the role, this finds Callas in perfect voice, with none of the flaws that developed later in her career, notably unsteadiness under pressure. Here the tone is unmistakable, with the distinctive timbre well caught in a recording that for most of the time

presents the voices vividly, with microphones evidently well placed. Callas's top notes are immaculate, and her coloratura agile, but it is the weight of emotion conveyed that makes this performance unique. Thus, at the start of the duet, *Mira o Norma*, you hear the opening phrase gloriously sung by Stignani in full open tone, with Callas following immediately, shading her tone subtly to add far greater emotional weight. Gui then launches into the brilliant cabaletta at high speed, finding his singers fully equipped to accept the challenge. Interestingly, in the tiny role of Clotilde, companion to Norma, you have Joan Sutherland, then newly recruited to the Covent Garden company: the voice is hardly recognizable, and it might even be that Sutherland the beginner was seeking to match the prima donna next to her as closely as possible. As Pollione, the tenor Mirto Picchi cannot match the women in the cast, but at least he sings with firmer, less strained tone than Mario Filippeschi in Callas's first studio recording of *Norma*, made for EMI in 1954.

BENATZKY, Ralph (1884–1957)

L'Auberge du cheval blanc (operetta; complete).
- (B) ** EMI (ADD) 5 74070-2 (2). Bourvil, Forli, Dens, Ervil, Germain, René Duclos Ch., Paris Conservatoire O, Nuvolone.

The Czech composer Ralph Benatzky had quite a distinguished career in the field of light music and operetta during the first half of the twentieth century and is chiefly remembered for his Johann Strauss pastiche *Casanova* (1928) and, especially, for *The White Horse Inn* (1930). The present operetta enjoyed some success in the 1930s, both in Paris and on Broadway. Its mixture of the styles of operetta and early musical is attractive: there are waltzes alongside the dance rhythms of the day. Highlights include a fully fledged *Tyrolienne* in Act II, along with a drunken version, complete with hiccoughs, in the same act. There is also a lively tango duet and some melting waltzes, some with off-stage choruses. Alas, there are absolutely no texts – nor even notes in English. The performance is quite a good one, with voices suited to this style of music and with lively characterizations. The 1962 recording is vivid, although some voices are very closely miked.

BENDA, František (1709–86)

Violin Concertos: in D; D min.
- (BB) *** Naxos 8.553902. Suk or Pfister, Suk CO, Christian Benda – JAN JIRI BENDA: *Concerto in G.* ***

Of these two concertos, the *D minor* is certainly the finer, for it has a memorably gentle slow movement and a buoyantly lively finale, which Christian Benda and his chamber orchestra relish for its sparkling vitality. Both soloists play most elegantly, and if these works are not highly individual they are both enjoyable when so sympathetically presented. The recording too cannot be faulted.

BENDA, Jan Jiří (1713–52)

Violin Concerto in G.

(BB) *** Naxos 8.553902. Suk, Suk CO, Christian
Benda – FRANTISEK BENDA: *Concertos in D; D min.* ***

Jan Jiří Benda was a member of a celebrated Bohemian family of musicians, and his *G major Concerto* sparkles with vitality in the outer movements (with a faint flavour of Bach) and has a rather fine solo cantila as its centrepiece. Josef Suk is highly sympathetic and dazzles the ear in the sharply pointed rhythms of the finale. Excellent, polished accompaniments and full, natural recording. This disc is well worth its modest cost.

BENDA, Jiří Antonín (1722–95)

Sinfonias Nos. 1 in D; 2 in G; 3 in C; 4 in F; 5 in G; 6 in E flat.

(BB) **(*) Naxos 8.553408. Prague CO, Christian Benda.

Sinfonias Nos. 7 in D; 8 in D; 9 in A; 10 in G; 11 in F; 12 in A.

(BB) **(*) Naxos 8.553409. Prague CO, Christian Benda.

The Bohemian Benda family was something of a musical dynasty in Europe over a period of some 300 years. Jiří's twelve three-movement symphonies are conventional but are kept alive by the rhythmic vigour of the allegros and the graceful but uneventful *Andantes*. Occasionally he features a solo flute or (as in the *Larghetto* of No. 7) a pair of flutes, in No. 9 a songful oboe, and in No. 6, one of the finest of the series, a solo violin takes a concertante role; the scoring for woodwind and horns in the finale is very effective. But the orchestration is seldom a striking feature, and these sinfonias are best approached singly, rather than in a group. Christian Benda is a more recent member of the family clan, and he directs the excellent Prague Chamber Orchestra with vigour and spirit, shaping slow movements with affection. The Naxos recording is admirably fresh and truthful, and the ambience is most pleasing.

VOCAL MUSIC

(i) *Ariadne auf Naxos. Pygmalion.*

(BB) **(*) Naxos 8.553345. Quadlbauer, Uray; (i) Schell; Prague CO, Christian Benda.

Ariadne auf Naxos and *Pygmalion* equally demonstrate Benda's ability to illuminate classical stories,

making the central characters believable. *Pygmalion*, with libretto adapted from a French text of Jean-Jacques Rousseau, is the lighter piece, with a happy ending. Performances under Christian Benda are as impressive as that of *Medea* on the companion disc, but again texts and translations are separated, and no internal tracks are provided. First-rate sound and good acting, though as Pygmalion Peter Uray is not as clear in his delivery as the Ariadne, Brigitte Quadlbauer.

Medea (complete).

(BB) **(*) Naxos 8.553346. Schell & speaking cast, Prague CO, Christian Benda (with J. J. BENDA: *Violin Concerto in G: Grave* ***).

Christian Benda here presents a most characterful and compelling version of what may be counted Jiří Benda's masterpiece, the melodrama *Medea*. Not only is the playing of the Prague Chamber Orchestra tautly committed, the performance offers an impressive team of actors, led by Hertha Schell. Irritatingly, the Naxos booklet gives the German text and English translation on different pages. The fill-up is a treasure. Christian Benda as solo cellist gives a most moving performance of a deeply expressive violin concerto slow movement, as arranged for cello. Excellent sound, with good balance between speaking voices and orchestra.

BENNETT, Robert Russell (1894–1981)

Abraham Lincoln (A Likeness in Symphonic Form); Sights and Sounds (An Orchestral Entertainment).

(BB) ** Naxos 8.5509004. Moscow SO, Stromberg.

Robert Russell Bennett, the orchestrator of many famous musicals, is best known on record for his Gershwin score, the *Symphonic Picture of Porgy and Bess*. The present works show his great orchestral skill, but the quality of the invention does not match the vividly imaginative orchestral sounds. There are longueurs in the four-movement *Lincoln Portrait*, and the various American *Sights and Sounds* are little more than clever orchestral effects. Only the evocation of a *Night Club*, with its saxophone riff, has anything approaching a memorable idea. The orchestral playing and the commitment of the conductor cannot be faulted, nor can the recording. But the result does not encourage repeated listenings.

BENOIT, Peter (1834–1901)

Hoogmis (High Mass).

(BB) * (**) Discover DICD 920178. George, Belgian R. & TV Philharmonic Ch., Koninklijk Vlaams Antwerp Music Conservatoire Ch. & Caecilia Chorale, Gemengd Ars Musica Merksem Ch., Zingende Wandelkring Saint Norbertus Ch., Belgian R. & TV PO, Rahbari.

The bargain Discover label offers a fascinating rarity, the *Hoogmis* (*High Mass*), by the Belgian composer, Peter Benoit, a contemporary of Brahms. Alexander Rahbari's account with the BRTV Philharmonic Orchestra of Brussels and massed choirs, with the tenor, Donald George, taking the solos in the *Benedictus* and *Dona nobis pacem*, has all the thrust you need for an ambitious work lasting 55 minutes, with echoes of Beethoven. The live recording, though atmospheric and full of presence, brings washy sound.

BENTZON, Jørgen (1897–1951)

Divertimento for Violin, Viola & Cello, Op. 2; Intermezzo for Violin & Clarinet, Op. 24; Sonatina for Flute, Clarinet & Bassoon, Op. 7; Variazioni interrotti for Clarinet, Bassoon, Violin, Viola & Cello, Op. 12; (i) *Mikrofoni No. 1, for Baritone, Flute, Violin, Cello & Piano, Op. 44.*

**(*) dacapo 8.224129. Danish Chamber Players; (i) with Bertelsen.

Jørgen Bentzon's music has a clean, fresh, diatonic feel to it, though some of it sounds a bit manufactured. By far the best piece here is the *Mikrofoni*, Op. 44, though it is let down by the solo baritone, and by far the wittiest is the *Variazioni interrotti*.

BERG, Alban (1885–1935)

(i; ii) *Chamber Concerto for Piano, Violin &* 13 *Wind;* (iii) *Violin Concerto (To the Memory of Angel);* (iv) *Lyric Suite:* 3 *Pieces;* 3 *Pieces for Orchestra, Op. 6;* (v; vi) *Adagio* from *Chamber Concerto* (arr. for Violin, Clarinet & Piano); (vii) *Lyric Suite for String Quartet;* (vi) 4 *Pieces for Clarinet and Piano;* (vii) *String Quartet, Op. 3;* (i) *Piano Sonata, Op. 1;* (viii; iv) *Altenberg Lieder, Op. 4;* (ix) *7 Early Songs* (versions with (x) piano; (iv) orchestra; (xi) *4 Lieder, Op. 2;* (xii) *Lieder: An Leukon; Schlieffe mir die Augen beide* (2 settings); (ix; iv) *Der Wein* (concert aria); (viii; iv) *Lulu: Suite (symphonic pieces).* (xiii) *Lulu* (opera; complete). (xiv) *Wozzeck* (complete). (xv) Transcription of Johann STRAUSS Jr: *Waltz: Wein, Weib und Gesang.*

(B) *** DG (ADD/DDD) 474 657-2 (8). (i) Barenboim; (ii) Zukerman, Ens. InterContemporain, Boulez; (iii) Mutter, Chicago SO, Levine; (iv) VPO, Abbado; (v) Kremer, (vi) Meyer, Maisenberg; (vii) LaSalle Qt; (viii) Juliane Banse; (ix) Von Otter; (x) Bengt Forsberg; (xi) Fischer-Dieskau, Reimann; (xii) Marshall, Parsons; (xiii) Stratas, Minton, Schwarz, Mazura, Blankenheim, Riegel, Tear, Paris Op. O, Boulez; (xiv; iv) Grundheber, Behrens, Haugland, Langridge, Zednik; (xv) Boston Symphony Chamber Players.

An impressive and inexpensive collection that should satisfy the most demanding Berg enthusiast. Nearly all these recordings are three star and most are still currently available separately and are praised in our main *Guide*, including the *Chamber Concerto, Violin Concerto, Three Pieces for Orchestra, Lulu Symphonic Suite,* the *Seven Early Songs* and Boulez's pioneering recording of *Lulu.* Abbado's *Wozzeck,* recorded live, has the inevitable drawback of intrusive stage noises and backwardly balanced singers, but is still very compelling.

Among the other recordings, the LaSalle Quartet provide the most persuasive advocacy in the Op. 3 *String Quartet* and *Lyric Suite* arrangement and are vividly recorded. Sabine Meyer's contribution to the works including clarinet is hardly less impressive, and Barenboim, if not quite a match for Pollini, gives a concentrated account of the *Piano Sonata.*

Juliane Banse sings expressively and lyrically in the *Alten-berg Lieder,* atmospherically accompanied by the VPO and Abbado; though some Bergians may prefer tougher, edgier performances, few will resist such a warmly musical response. The contribution of the rich-toned Margaret Marshall and Geoffrey Parsons is hardly less impressive. Fischer-Dieskau with highly sensitive accompaniment from Aribert Reimann is equally communicative in the early Op. 2 *Songs* and the Boston Chamber Players provide an unexpected bonus is Berg's arrangement of a familiar waltz by Johann Strauss.

The documentation is generally very good and includes synopses for the operas but no translations.

Violin Concerto.

*** Warner 2564 60291-2. Hope, BBC SO, Watkins –
BRITTEN: *Violin Concerto.* ***

Alban Berg didn't live to hear his *Violin Concerto* performed, and he was therefore unable to correct a number of errors in the copying of the full score. These have now been corrected from primary sources in the critical edition published by Universal in 1996. It was Daniel Hope who, a year before publication, gave the first performance of the corrected version in Manchester; here, in a warm and purposeful performance, he is the soloist in the first recording of it. He sustains spacious speeds with no sense of self-consciousness, intense and concentrated from first to last, subtly varying his vibrato to heighten emotion, notably in the hushed and tender resolution on the Bach chorale theme, *Es ist genug.* The cellist Paul Watkins proves himself a fine conductor, drawing warmly intense playing from the BBC Symphony Orchestra, helped by full, immediate recording with impressively weighty brass. The Britten *Violin Concerto,* written when the young composer was most influenced by Berg, makes an ideal and unique coupling and another outstanding performance.

Lyric Suite.

(B) *** Nonesuch 7559 79696-2. Upshaw, Kronos Qt.

The Nonesuch disc offers a *Lyric Suite* with a difference and so has a special claim on the collector's allegiance. The work was the outcome of Berg's traumatic relationship with Hanna Fuchs-Robettin and originally included a setting of lines from Baudelaire's *Fleurs du mal* in a German translation by Stefan George ('To you, you sole dear one, my cry rises/Out of the deepest abyss in which my heart has fallen'). The American composer and Berg scholar George Perle has reconstructed the original version of the finale and this is its first recording, very eloquently sung by Dawn Upshaw. The Kronos play with a certain robust intensity and fire (nothing in the least mellifluous here), and they are decently recorded. Since this disc contains only 27 minutes of music, it comes at bargain price.

(i) 4 Pieces for Clarinet & Piano, Op. 5. Piano Sonata.

[M] *** EMI 5 57523-2 (3). Vogt, with (i) Meyer – BRAHMS: *Cello Sonatas* etc.; SCHUMANN: *3 Romanzen* etc. ***

The Berg *Pieces* make an unusual and effective supplement for the Brahms duo items, with the four miniatures inspiring magnetically intense performances from both artists, and Lars Vogt on his own treating the Op. 1 *Sonata* rightly as a post-romantic piece.

Piano Sonata, Op. 1.

** DG 423 678-2. Pollini (with DEBUSSY: *Etudes* **).

Pollini gives an impressive account, as powerful as any on disc, but he is not helped by a clinical, closely balanced recording, and the Debussy *Etudes* with which it is coupled are seriously wanting in atmosphere and poetry.

Lulu (incomplete version).

*(*) RCA 74321 57734-2 (2). Migenes, Adam, Karcyzkowski, Fassbaender, V State Op. O, Maazel.

Maazel's performance was recorded live by Austrian Radio, allowing little bloom on the voices. Even under Maazel there is far too little tension in the orchestral playing, whether in interludes or accompanying the singers. Julia Migenes is characterful in the title-part, treating it in cabaret style, often using plain speech rather than sing-speech. A good cast is largely wasted.

BERKELEY, Lennox (1903–89)

CHAMBER MUSIC

(i; ii) *Horn Trio, Op. 44;* (ii) *Polka;* (iii) *6 Preludes, Op. 23;* (iv) *3 Greek Songs, Op. 38;* (v; vi) *I Sing of a maiden;* (v; vii) *The Lord is my shepherd;* (iv) *5 Poems of W. H. Auden;* (viii) *4 Poems of St Teresa of Avila, Op. 27.*

(M) (***) EMI mono/stereo 5 85138-2. (i) Parikian, Brain; (ii) Smith, Sellick; (iii) Horsley; (iv) Hemsley; Lush; (v) Ch. of King's College, Cambridge; (vi) Willcocks; (vii) Cleobury; (viii) Bowden, Coll. Mus. Londinii, Minchinton.

In the *Horn Trio*, it is the outstanding horn playing of Dennis Brain that one remembers most, with his bubbling stream of virtuosity offering its own pleasures to the listener. The music itself is expertly written and often very beautiful (the *Lento* especially), all in fine (1954) sound. Colin Horsley is excellent in the short but varied *Six Preludes*, which range from thoughtful and lyrical to showy brilliance, and the 1949 sound is very good. The vocal items are superb: the short but haunting *Three Greek Songs* and imaginative *Five Poems of Auden*, both recorded in 1959, make a welcome return to the catalogue. The *4 Poems of St Teresa of Avila* are regarded by some as the composer's finest work: they are varied and imaginative, with Pamela Bowden's rich contralto providing plenty of contrast and emotion in each of the four movements; the searching *If, Lord, thy love for me is strong* makes a dramatic opening item, and it is followed by a musette, *Shepherd, shepherd, hark the calling* and, with its drone in the orchestra, forms a delightfully bucolic number. Next is the simple and gentle *Let mine eyes see thee*, which is followed by *Today a shepherd kith and kin* with its forthright vocal line, with the accompaniment becoming ever more lively and intricate, producing a fine climax. The 1958 sound is excellent and, although the soloist is very closely miked, the sound is warm. The programme ends with a jolly *Polka* (with Cyril Smith and Phyllis Sellick), and the only two stereo items (digital): *I sing of a maiden* and *The Lord is my shepherd*, both beautifully atmospheric works with performances to match.

BERLIOZ, Hector (1803–69)

(i) *Harold in Italy, Op. 16. Les Troyens: Ballet Music.*

☞ (BB) *** LSO Live LSO 0040. (i) Zimmermann; LSO, C. Davis

Recording this Byron-inspired symphony for the third time, Sir Colin Davis demonstrates his supreme mastery as a Berlioz interpreter in a version recorded live, even tauter and more dramatic than his earlier ones made in the studio, with speeds consistently faster, notably in the first movement. Also, the textures are sharper and lighter, partly a question of recording quality, bringing an extra incisiveness. One other benefit of the recording is that the soloist, the magnificent Tabea Zimmermann, is balanced as part of the orchestra instead of being spotlit. The beauty of her tone, with its nut-brown colours down on the C string, is never masked, but at the other end of the spectrum the balance allows *pianissimos* of unrivalled delicacy. The *Ballet Music*, taken from Davis's prize-winning LSO Live version of *Les Troyens*, makes a warmly atmospheric bonus. The disc comes at super-budget price, complete with authoritative notes by David Cairns, and now becomes a primary recommendation.

(i; ii) *Harold in Italy.* (ii) *Overtures: Le Carnaval romain; Le Corsaire; Les Francs-juges; King Lear; Les Troyens (Overture & March); Waverley;* (iii) *Te Deum, Op. 22.*
(M) (***) Sony mono 515300-2 (2). (i) Primrose; (ii) RPO; (iii) Young, LPO Ch., Dulwich College Boys' Ch., D. Vaughan (organ); all cond. Beecham.

Beecham's *Harold in Italy* comes from 1951, only a few years after William Primrose had recorded it with Koussevitzky; the *Te Deum* and the *Overtures* come from 1954. Sir Thomas was a masterly interpreter of Berlioz and during that period had few rivals in this repertoire. Fine though it is, his *Harold* does not quite have the incandescent intensity and power of the Koussevitzky, but in the *Te Deum* and the *Overtures* Beecham has an almost unique feeling for this most original of masters, and the RPO play for him with great finesse and subtlety.

Symphonie fantastique, Op. 14.
(M) **(*) Telarc CD 82014. Cleveland O, Maazel.

Symphonie fantastique; Overtures: Béatrice et Bénédict; Le Carnaval romain.
(BB) ** Warner Apex 8573 89533-2. LPO, Mehta.

Symphonie fantastique; Overtures: Béatrice et Bénédict; Le Carnaval romain; Le Corsaire.
(B) *(*) CfP (ADD) 575 5622. Hallé O, Loughran.

Symphonie fantastique, Op. 14; (i) *Herminie.*
** DG 474 209. Mahler CO & Les Musiciens du Louvre, Minkowski, (i) with Legay.

Symphonie fantastique, Op. 14; (i) *La Mort de Cléopâtre.*
**(*) Ph. 475 095-2. VPO, Gergiev, (i) with Borodina.

Gergiev's reading is above all urgent and weightily dramatic, traditional in not observing the exposition repeat in the first movement and the repeat in the *March to the Scaffold* when arguably such formalities are inappropriate in such a radical work. Not unexpectedly, he also omits the cornets prescribed in the revised score. However, the weight and thrust of Berlioz's dramatic concept come over with thrilling immediacy, and Gergiev draws out the distinctive sound-qualities of the Vienna Philharmonic, recorded in the helpful acoustic of the Musikverein, with ripe horn solos and resonant strings and with waltz rhythms given a Viennese flavour in the second movement, *Le Bal.* The timpani in the fourth movement boom rather too much, but otherwise the sound is full and vivid. The coupling brings Olga Borodina as the powerful soloist in *La Mort de Cléopâtre,* the most adventurous of Berlioz's Prix de Rome entries. It is an early work yet here sounds fully mature and distinctive,

with conductor and soloist underlining the high dramatic contrasts.

Recorded live at the Cité de la musique in Paris, Minkowski's version of the *Symphonie fantastique* strikes new ground in bringing together the talented performers of the Mahler Chamber Orchestra, using modern instruments, and wind-players from Marc Minkowski's period orchestra, Les Musiciens du Louvre. The snag is that he takes so expansive a view of the work that pauses and phrasing too often sound self-conscious, though happily not in the fast movements. Any reservations about the major work are mitigated somewhat by the brilliantly dramatic reading of the rare scène-lyrique, *Herminie,* the second of Berlioz's four entries in the Prix de Rome competition. This setting of a text based on Tasso makes a specially apt coupling, when Berlioz at the very start introduces the theme that later became the *idée fixe* of the *Symphony.* Aurelia Legay, with her warm, cleanly focused soprano, proves an outstanding soloist, intensely dramatic throughout. Let us hope that this can be re-coupled, for Beecham (EMI 5 67971-2) and Sir Colin Davis (Philips 464 692-2) remain unsurpassed in the *Symphonie fantastique* (see our main volume).

Mehta's view of the *Symphonie fantastique* is strong and well sustained, with the LPO playing superbly; but it is not remarkable for poetry. The weighty recording quality reinforces that impression. As fill-up Mehta offers comparably direct and well-played readings of the two overtures, with the weight of the recording helping rather than hindering the mercurial qualities of *Béatrice et Bénédict,* thanks to crisp ensemble. But the performance of the *Symphonie* is not a front runner, even at Apex price.

Maazel's rather plain reading for Telarc compares with the finest rivals only in its spectacular recording of demonstration quality. With no fill-up, the disc has a playing time of only 49 minutes.

James Loughran's Hallé account of the *Symphonie,* which dates from the mid-1970s, is disappointing, heavy in places and rarely really exciting, although there are touches that reveal this conductor's character and freshness of approach. Of the three overtures offered as makeweight, *Le Corsaire* is vivid enough, with a strong contribution from the trombones, but not really exhilarating; the finest performance here is of *Béatrice et Bénédict,* where the lyrical writing shows Loughran and his players at their best. Throughout, the recording is excellent, vivid, yet warm and refined.

On DG, Boulez directs a powerful, sure-footed and beautifully played reading, which is lacking emotional thrust. With rhythms crisp but unsprung, the result is unpersuasive, out of synch with the inspiration of an arch-romantic. The first two sections of *Tristia* are far warmer, but the weirdly atmospheric *Funeral March for the Last Scene of Hamlet* receives a disappointingly plain, detached reading (DG (IMS) 453 432-2).

(i) *Symphonie fantastique;* (ii) *Roméo et Juliette,*
Op. 17.

(M) ** Westminster (ADD) (IMS) 471 242-2 (2). (i) V.
State Op. O, Leibowitz; (ii) Resnik, Turp, Ward, L.
Symphony Ch., LSO, Monteux.

(i) *Symphonie fantastique;* (ii) *Roméo et Juliette*
(excerpts).

(**) Testament mono SBT 1234 (i) French Nat. R. O;
(ii) Paris Opéra O, André Cluytens.

Leibowitz's *Symphonie fantastique* has no pressing
claim to greatness in either performance or execution, and the 1958 recording, while basically full,
suffers from a rather dry and claustrophobic acoustic. Monteux's 1962 *Roméo et Juliette* has a robust,
idiomatic strength, which helps one to forgive some
of the rough patches in the ensemble and recording,
the former indicating a lack of rehearsal. We have
come to expect high standards of refinement and
discipline in this work (set by Munch and Colin
Davis *et al.*), although, of course, any Monteux performance is worth hearing. The CD is well packaged
and includes texts and translations.

The Cluytens performance of the *Symphonie fantastique* is not the same as that included in the 'Great
Conductors' compilation (see Concerts, below) and
derives from a mono recording made in the Salle de
la Mutualité in 1955. It was coolly received in *The
Gramophone* magazine, when it was up against some
pretty formidable compeition. It is well shaped but
not, perhaps, as spontaneous as the concert performance this partnership gave on their Japanese tour,
which the EMI disc includes. Nor is *Roméo seul* and
the *Scène d'amour* as well played as rival versions,
though it has the merit of being straightforward,
unaffected and felt.

CHORAL WORKS

*Le Ballet des ombres, Op. 2; Chanson à boire, Op.
2/5; Chant de chemin de fer, Op. 19/3; Chant
guerrier, Op. 2/3; Chante sacré, Op. 2/6* (versions I &
II); *Le Cinq Mai; Hymne pour la consécration du
nouveau tabernacle; Marche funèbre pour la
dernière scène d'Hamlet; La Mort d'Orfée; La Mort
d'Ophélie; Sara la baigneuse, Op. 11; Scène héroïque
(La Révolution grecque); Tantum ergo
sacramentum; Tristia, Op. 18; Veni Creator Spiritus.*

**(*) EMI 5 57499-2 (2). Villazon, Naouri, Riveno, Les
Eléments Ch., Capitole Toulouse O, Plasson.

Entitled *La Révolution grecque* after the earliest piece
in the collection, Michel Plasson's two-disc survey of
Berlioz's shorter choral works makes a fascinating
study for any lover of Berlioz's music, amplifying the
usual portrait we have from his large-scale works. *La
Révolution grecque*, written in 1825–33 and described
as a *scène héroïque*, harks back to the music of a
generation earlier, inspired by the French Revolution,
a rousing piece in four sections for two basses, chorus and orchestra. It may be less typical of Berlioz
than most of the other works in the collection, but it
still brings many moments forecasting the composer's mature style. *Le Cinq Mai*, written to commemorate the death of Napoleon, is equally rare, part of a
planned major work to celebrate the defeated
Emperor, which Berlioz abandoned. The Op. 2 pieces
are taken from a collection of settings of poems by
the poet Thomas Moore (in translations by Thomas
Gounet), usually given the collective title *Irlande*.
Most of the Op. 2 pieces are simple songs, but
Plasson has here extracted the choral items, which,
like the songs, have piano accompaniment. One of
the weirdest pieces here is the ronde nocturne, *Ballet
des ombres*, and one of the liveliest the *Chants des
chemins de fer*, celebrating the opening of the railway
line from Paris to Lille in 1846. The lovely Hugo
setting, *Sara la baigneuse*, the three movements
labelled *Tristia, Méditation religieuse* and *La Mort
d'Ophélie* and the *Hamlet Funeral March*, are all
relatively well known, here given warmly idiomatic
performances. All these works bear the stamp of
Berlioz's totally original genius, but curiously two of
the later choral works, both settings of Latin for
female chorus, *Veni creator spiritus, a cappella*, and
Tantum ergo, with harmonium accompaniment, are
the least typical. Good, warm sound for most items,
though the piano in the Op. 2 songs is shallow and
clangy.

VOCAL MUSIC

Cantatas: (i) *Herminie;* (ii) *La Mort de Cléopâtre;*
(iii) *La Mort d'Orphée; La Mort de Sardanapale.*

(BB) **(*) Naxos 8.555810. Ch. Régional Nord, O Nat.
de Lille, Régional Nord, Pas-de-Calais, Casadesus;
with (i) Lagrange; (ii) Uria-Monzon; (iii) Vallejo.

It makes an ideal coupling having on a single disc the
four cantatas that the young Berlioz wrote as entries
for the Prix de Rome. The work that finally won him
the prize in 1829, overcoming conservative opposition, was *La Mort de Sardanapale*, though ironically
only a fragment has survived. Ironically too, that
fragment is markedly less original than any of the
earlier works, even if it is well worth hearing for the
hints of Berlioz themes to come. *Herminie*, based on
Tasso's *Jerusalem Liberated*, strikingly uses as a central theme the motif that soon after became the *idée
fixe* of the *Symphonie fantastique*, while *La Mort de
Cléopâtre* even more clearly anticipates the operatic
tone of voice that reached its culmination in *Les
Troyens*. Even the earliest cantata, *La Mort d'Orphée*,
with tenor and a chorus of raging bacchantes, brings
a memorable close, though the soloist, Daniel Galvez
Vallejo, is coarser than either the excellent soprano,
Michele Lagrange, in *Herminie* or the mezzo, Beatrice Uria-Monzon, in *Cléopâtre*, with the Lille
orchestra under Jean-Claude Casadesus warm and
refined.

La Damnation de Faust (complete).

*** Ph. (ADD) 416 395-2 (2). Veasey, Gedda, Bastin,
Amb. S., Wandsworth School Boys' Ch., L.
Symphony Ch., LSO, C. Davis.

(**(*)) BBC mono BBCL 4006/7 (2). Crespin, Turp,
Roux, Shirley-Quirk, L. Symphony Ch., LSO,
Monteux.

Both Nicolai Gedda as Faust and Jules Bastin as
Mephistopheles are impressive in Davis's fine 1974
Philips set. The response of the chorus and orchestra
is highly intelligent and sensitive, and the recording
perspective is outstandingly natural and realistic.

The BBC recording is of a relay from the Royal
Festival Hall on 8 March 1962, and it conveys a real
sense of occasion. The Monteux performance is a
distinguished one with a first-rate cast, and the
sound wears its years very lightly.

(i) *Les Nuits d'été;* (ii) *La Mort de Cléopâtre (Scène
lyrique);* (ii; iii) *Les Troyens: Scenes 2 & 4.*

🌢 (M) *** EMI (ADD) 5 62788-2. J. Baker; (i) New
Philh. O, Barbirolli; (ii) LSO, Gibson; (iii) with
Greevy, Erwen, Howell, Amb. Op. Ch.

The collaboration of Dame Janet Baker at the peak of
her powers and Sir John Barbirolli in what is probably the most beautiful of all orchestral song-cycles
produces ravishing results. The half-tones in the
middle songs are exquisitely controlled, and the ela-
tion of the final song, *L'Ile inconnue,* with its vision of
an idyllic island, has never been captured more rapturously on record. Berlioz's early scena on the death
of a famous classical heroine is also beautifully performed. But even more desirable is Dame Janet's
deeply moving rendering of the concluding scenes of
Berlioz's epic opera. This makes an essential supplement to the complete recording for any dedicated
Berliozian. Baker, helped by a warm and sympathetic
accompaniment under Gibson's direction, allows
herself a range of tone-colour and a depth of expressiveness not matched by Josephine Veasey, the Dido
in the Philips set. Outstanding remastered sound and
full translations are included to make this a worthy
reissue in EMI's 'Great Artists of the Century' series.

Requiem Mass, Op. 5.

(BB) *(*) Naxos 8.554494/5. Schade, Toronto
Mendelssohn Ch. & Youth Ch., Elora Festival O,
Edison.

The chief merits of this disappointing Naxos account
of the Berlioz *Grande messe des morts* – a difficult
work to hold together – are the singing of the
Toronto Mendelssohn Choir, atmospherically
recorded, and of the sweet-toned tenor, Michael
Schade, in the *Sanctus.* Otherwise this is an underpowered reading, lacking the biting intensity of rival
versions, though the recording of the brass in the
Tuba mirum section is rich and ripe. Previn's set
(EMI 5 69512 2) is the one to go for.

Roméo et Juliette.

* Häns. CD 93.005 (2). Denize, Beczala, Lika,
Baden-Baden & Freiburg SW German RSO,
Cambreling – MESSIAEN: *L'Ascension.* *

Roméo et Juliette, Op. 17; Les Nuits d'été, Op. 7.

** DG 474 237-2 (2). Diener, Tarver, Sedov, Cleveland
Ch. & O, Boulez.

Over the years Pierre Boulez has become a far
warmer interpreter of romantic music than when
he started conducting with his crisply fingered
tic-tac instructions. Here he directs a brilliant
account of Berlioz's great dramatic symphony,
remarkable not just for the clarity and precision of
the playing but also for the expressive warmth, with
the fine DG recording bringing out the dynamic
contrasts over the widest range. Yet Boulez's
warmth seems to be inspired more by the instrumental sound itself rather than by the dramatic
situation. Such Berlioz interpreters as Colin Davis
and Charles Dutoit convey even more warmth by
making you visualize the dramatic situations that
Berlioz has chosen from the story, not least in
offstage choral effects. With Boulez, by contrast,
evocation of that kind is far less important than the
pure beauty of the score. This set brings the advantage of a generous and apt coupling in a version of
the song-cycle, *Les Nuits d'été* using the same three
soloists as in the main work, each taking two of the
songs. The bright, warm soprano of Melanie Diener
suits the outer songs well, with Kenneth Tarver
heady and unstrained in the fourth and fifth songs,
Absence and *Au cimetière.* The baritone, Dennis
Sedov, is less convincing in the two darkest songs,
Le Spêctre de la rose and *Sur les lagunes,* partly
because the microphone brings out a distracting
flutter in his voice, a flaw that mars his contribution even more seriously as Friar Laurence in
Roméo et Juliette.

Sylvain Cambreling's version with the SW German
Radio Orchestra of Baden-Baden benefits from
clean, refined sound, but lacks the tautness and
weight that is needed to hold Berlioz's episodic structure together. The playing and singing are worthy,
with the mezzo, Nadine Denize, a characterful soloist; but too often the performance sounds cautious,
lacking the flair necessary in Berlioz. The Messiaen
piece makes a good supplement, but that too sounds
unidiomatic, lacking in tension.

OPERA

Béatrice et Bénédict (complete).

(B) *** Ph. Duo (ADD) 475 221-2 (2). J. Baker, Tear,
Eda-Pierre, T. Allen, Lloyd, Watts, Bastin, Alldis Ch.,
LSO, C. Davis.

Béatrice et Bénédict presents not only witty and brilliant music for the heroine and hero (on Philips,
Janet Baker and Robert Tear at their most pointed)

but also sensuously beautiful passages. First-rate solo and choral singing, brilliant playing, and analogue sound that is refined and clear in texture, bright and fresh, make this a clear first choice for this opera on CD, especially now that it is offered so inexpensively as a Duo.

BERNERS, Lord (1883–1950)

Luna Park; March; (i) *A Wedding Bouquet.*
** Marco Polo 8.223716. (i) RTE Chamber Ch.; RTE Sinf., Alwyn.

Stravinsky spoke of Lord Berners as 'droll and delightful'. Apart from Constant Lambert, he was the only English composer taken up by Diaghilev. *Luna Park* (1930) was written for a C. B. Cochran revue, with choreography by Balanchine. *A Wedding Bouquet* was choreographed by Frederick Ashton and mounted at Sadler's Wells in 1937, with décor and costumes, as well as music, by Berners. This is good light music. Performances are decent, as are the recordings, but the acoustic does not permit tuttis to open out.

Les Sirènes (ballet; complete); *Caprice péruvien; Cupid and Psyche* (ballet suite).
** Marco Polo 8.223780. Blennerhassett, RTE Sinf., Lloyd-Jones.

Les Sirènes was not a great success, and the music, despite some bright moments, does not sustain a high level of invention. The *Caprice péruvien* was put together expertly by Constant Lambert with Berners's help. The ballet *Cupid and Psyche* was another Ashton work, mounted in 1939. Good performances, but not well polished. Again the recordings are wanting in bloom.

Piano music: *Le Poisson d'or; Dispute entre le papillon et le crapaud; The Expulsion from Paradise; Fragments psychologiques; March; 3 Petites marches funèbres; Polka; Valse.* (i) Songs: *A long time ago; Come on Algernon; The Rio Grande; Theodore or The Pirate King; 3 Chansons; 3 English Songs; Lieder Album (3 Songs in the German Manner); Red roses and red noses.*
**(*) Marco Polo 8.22159. (i) Partridge; Vorster.

Lord Berners was a diplomat as well as a musician and was essentially self-taught, but he was the only English composer who was admired by both Diaghilev and Beecham. Both responded to Berners's witty eccentricity and hints of Gallic wit, within a musical style that often retained an underlying Englishness – demonstrated subtly here in the opening *Polka*. Berners was a painter and poet too; the minuscule, lovelorn *Le Poisson d'or* was based on his own poem and has a certain Debussian atmosphere, while the *Trois petites marches* and *Fragments psychologiques* are Satiesque, and not just in their

titles. The longest of the piano pieces is the engagingly nostalgic *Valse.*

Berners's pastiche of German *Lieder* has the piano opening gruffly to contrast a lyrical vocal line, romantically addressing a white pig. The French *chansons*, however, are not parodies but readily idiomatic, with *La Fiancée du timbalier* engagingly spirited. Of the English songs, *Tom Filuter's dialogue* is brilliantly chimerical, and the 1920 set is most winning, especially the opening *Lullaby*. The three later songs of 1921 are a charming rediscovery of the English folk idiom, while the sentimental *Red roses and red noses* has a flowing lyrical line. It is followed by the irrepressible *Come on Algernon*, about the insatiable Daisy, who always 'asked for more!' – a perfect music-hall number, written for the film *Champagne Charlie*, it makes a delightful pay-off to end the recital. Ian Partridge obviously relishes the many stylistic changes like a vocal chameleon, and his words are clear too. Len Vorster backs him up splendidly and is completely at home in the solo piano music. The recording is truthful, and this makes a fine introduction to an underrated composer who has a distinctive voice of his own.

BERNSTEIN, Leonard (1918–90)

✓ *Serenade after Plato's 'Symposium'* (for solo violin, string orchestra, harp & percussion).
*** DG 474 500-2. Mutter, LSO, composer – PREVIN: *Violin Concerto.* ***
(M) *** EMI 5 62600-2. Perlman, Boston SO, Ozawa – BARBER: *Violin Concerto;* FOSS: *3 American Pieces.* ***

Bernstein's five-movement *Serenade*, tautly constructed, makes an excellent coupling for Previn's expansive *Violin Concerto*. Though the title suggests a work less weighty than a full concerto, the opposite is true, when Bernstein found his inspiration in Plato's 'Symposium', with the slow movement, *Agathon*, one of his most profound inspirations, beautifully realized by Mutter and Previn.

Perlman's warmly committed performance of Bernstein's personalized meditation on Plato's *Symposium* now reappears at mid-price as part of the 'Perlman Edition', very attractively coupled.

STAGE WORKS

Candide (final, revised version).
(M) *** DG 474 857-2. Hadley, Anderson, Green, Ludwig, Gedda, D. Jones, Ollmann, L Symphony Ch., LSO, composer.

Bernstein's *Candide* won the *Gramophone* magazine's Music Theatre Award in 1992, hence this reissue in the 'Awards Collection'. It is fully documented.

BERWALD, Franz (1796–1868)

(i; ii) *Piano Concerto in D;* (i; iii) *Duo in D for Violin & Piano;* (i) *Musical Journal: Tempo di marcia in E flat; Piano Piece No. 2: Presto feroce. Rondeau-bagatelle in B flat; Theme & Variations in G min.*
** Genesis (ADD) GCD 111. (i) Erikson; (ii) Swedish RSO, Westerberg; (iii) Grünfarb.

Greta Erikson's 1971 recording of the *Piano Concerto* is serviceable, very nimble and cleanly articulated, but somewhat wanting in poetry. Josef Grünfarb gives a finely turned account of the *D major Duo,* but this partnership is less persuasive than Marieke Blankestijn and Susan Tomes on Hyperion (CDA 66835).

Symphony in A (1820: fragment); *Symphonies Nos. 1–4; Overtures: Estrella di Soria; The Queen of Golconda.*
(M) *** Hyp. Dyad CDD 22043 (2). Swedish RSO, Goodman.

Roy Goodman's set with the Swedish Radio Symphony Orchestra has the advantage of including the early fragment of the *Symphony in A major,* which Berwald completed (it was performed in the same concert as the *Violin concerto* in 1821) but which survives only in fragmentary form. It has been completed – and very well, too – by Duncan Druce, and makes its début on records. It is distinctively Berwaldian, though there are touches of Weber in the opening introduction and of Schubert in the second group. Goodman is always alert and intelligent, though he tends to favour brisk tempi. He starts the *Sinfonie singulière* far too quickly and is forced to pull back when the brass enter. There is a certain loss of breadth here, and again in the *Sinfonie sérieuse.* The *Overture* to *The Queen of Golconda* comes off very well. Berwald's orchestration tends to be top-heavy and the cool acoustic of the Berwald Hall in Stockholm slightly accentuates that.

String Quartet No. 1 in G min.
(M) *** CRD 3361. Chilingirian Qt – WIKMANSON: *String Quartet No. 2* . ***

The Berwald *Quartets* rarely venture into the concert hall outside Scandinavia any more frequently than do the symphonies. There were two quartets from 1818 (the second in B flat does not survive) and two from 1849. In some ways the 1818 *G minor Quartet* is the most interesting of the lot. It is original and forward-looking and, apart from the *Septet,* is the most finished of the works he produced before he went to Berlin in 1829. This reissued performance comes from 1979 and is straightforward, unfussy and faithful, and very well recorded.

BIBER, Heinrich

Mystery (Rosenkranz) Violin Sonatas (complete; with (i) readings from the Rosemary Psalters).
**(*) Avie AV 0038 (2). Pavlo Beznosiuk, Roblo, Chateauneuf, Tunnicliffe; (i) Timothy West (reader).

We have praised Biber's masterly *Rosary Sonatas* in our main volume in connection with the outstanding Virgin recording by John Holloway, Davitt Moroney and Tragicomedia (✿ Virgin 5 62062-2). The present performace is equally fine, if not even finer, and is beautifully recorded in an ideal acoustic. However, it is introduced by and interwoven with a spoken narration by Timothy West of the entire Christian story and, while the narrative is presented with pleasing simplicity and is separately cued, one would not imagine that listeners would want to repeat it at every performance (except, perhaps, as an act of devotion). One can, of course, programme the player to play the music only (the booklet identifies all the musical cues), but that means setting up the CD player especially, and not every listener will want to take the trouble to do this. We hope therefore that Avie will consider a separate issue of the music alone, which could well be a first choice.

Requiem à 15 in A.
(M) *** DHM/BMG 82876 60149-2. Alamanjo, Van der Sluis, Elwes, Padmore, Huijts, Van der Kamp, Netherlands Bach Festival Ch. & O, Leonhardt – STEFFANI: *Stabat Mater.* ***

Leonhardt's account of Biber's *A major Requiem* is very fine indeed. There is no lack of aural spectacle, but the acoustic of Pieterskerk, Utrecht, is ideally free from excessive resonance so that the results are particularly fresh, with remarkably clear detail, yet there is the right warmth of ambience and bloom on the excellent soloists, choir and orchestra alike. The performance has plenty of vitality and, for those interested in having a beautiful setting of the *Stabat Mater* by Biber's contemporary, Agostino Steffani, this is an excellent mid-priced recommendation.

Requiem in F min.; Offertories: Huc Poenitentes; Lux perpetua; Ne cedite mentes; Quo abiit dilectus.
**(*) Ambroisie AMB 9936. Arsys Bourgogne, Cao.

The Arsys Choir of Burundy give a fine, dedicated performance of the *F minor Requiem,* beautifully recorded; the end effect is warm if very slightly bland. The great interest of this disc lies in the first recording of the four beautiful offertories, again very well sung, although the excellent soloists from the choir are not individually distinctive. *Quo abiit dilectus* stands alone in its restrained accompaniment for viols, but the closing *Lux perpetua* for double choir and brass is the most sonorously spectacular.

BILLINGS, William (1746–1800)

Anthems and fuging tunes: *Africa; As the hart panteth; Brookfield; Creation; David's Lamentation; Emmaus; Euroclydon; Hear my Pray'r; I am the Rose of Sharon; Is any afflicted?; Jordan; The Lord is ris'n indeed; O Praise the Lord of Heaven; Rutland; Samuel the Priest (Funeral Anthem); Shiloh.*

☻ (BB) ★★★ HM HCX 3957048. His Majesties's Clerkes, Hillier.

William Billings was a Boston tanner and singing-master who flourished in New England in the years of the emergence of the new American nation, and his anthems and what he engagingly called 'fuging tunes' are wonderfully fresh and appealing. Although usually they are simply structured, they are written in an idiom that has broken away from the sober Lutheran tradition. The opening anthem here, *O Praise the Lord of Heaven*, has a joyous, spirited vigour in its part-writing, and the repeated phrase, 'singing and making melody' which enlivens *Is any afflicted?* avoids any possible hint of sanctimoniousness. Indeed the exuberant sailors' anthem, *Euroclydon*, sounds for all the world like a sea-shanty. Yet *Africa* has a simple, touching melancholy, which reminds one a little of the *Coventry Carol*.

Billings's funeral anthem, *Samuel the Priest*, is similarly touching, but his very characteristic text 'merrily they sing' restores the cheerfulness to *Shiloh*, while the Easter anthem, *The Lord is ris'n indeed*, with its joyful 'Allelujas', is wonderfully direct and exultant. Two of the 'hits' in his own time were the plain one-stanza *Brookfield* and the magnetic, hymn-like *Jordan*; but *Rutland*, often touchingly expressive, brings an almost madrigalesque flavour to the linear interplay. The spirit of this music brings to mind the visually striking white churches of New England rather than the devotional atmosphere of a cathedral. To quote the *Chicago Tribune*, the music is sung with 'impeccable musicianship, full-throated tone, warmth and security of blend and expressive intelligence', and, one might add, with great vitality by His Majestie's Clerkes under Paul Hillier. It is beautifully recorded in a not too reverberant acoustic; the words are clear, but a website address is given from which full texts can be obtained.

BINGE, Ronald (1910–79)

(i) *Elizabethan Serenade;* (ii; iii) *Saxophone Concerto;* (iii) *Saturday Symphony;* (iv) *At the End of the Day; Autumn Dream; Butterflies; Candles on the Table; Farewell Waltz; Fugal Fun; Give Me a Ring; Homeward; Inamorata; The Last of the Clan; I Like Your Smile; The Look in Your Eyes; Man in a Hurry; Miss Melanie; The Moon Looks Down; Morning Light; Perhaps I'm Young; Sailing By; A Scottish Rhapsody; I Sent You Roses; The Sound of Music is Everywhere; A Star is Born; Tango Corto;*

There's a Light in Your Eyes; Under the Sun; Waiting for Moonlight; The Watermill; What Do You Know?; When You are Young.

(M) ★★★ ASV (ADD) CDWLZ 245 (2). (i) Nat. PO, Gerhardt; O, Heller; (ii) Voss; (iii) S German R. O, composer; (iv) Walter Heller & his O; O Raphael, Hotter; or Dreamland O.

Ronald Binge's most famous pieces must be the *Elizabethan Serenade* (which rightly opens disc 1), *Sailing By*, which has been played at the closing of BBC Radio 4, accompanying the Shipping Forecast, since 1973, or the delightful watercolour portrait of *The Water Mill*. As this CD shows, his fund of melody was unquenchable and, with his deftness of orchestration, it resulted in some first-class light classical music of the type that blossomed in the 1950s and 1960s. The *Saxophone Concerto* and *Saturday Symphony* (conducted here by the composer) are much longer than his usual short character-pieces, though they are just as enjoyable. The recordings (mainly from the 1960s) are taken from a variety of sources but mostly feature Walter Heller and his Orchestra. Recommended to all lovers of good tunes. The recordings range from very good to thoroughly acceptable, and it is fascinating to note that the performers of four of the pieces are unknown.

BIZET, Georges (1838–75)

L'Arlésienne: Suites Nos. 1 & 2; Symphony in C; (i) *Carmen: highlights.*

(B) ★★(★) Erato Ultima 0630 18947-2 (2). Strasbourg PO, Lombard; (i) with Crespin, Ply, Pilou, Van Dam, Denize, Carminati, Ch. of Opéra du Rhin.

L'Arlésienne, Suites Nos. 1 & 2; Carmen Symphony (arr. Serebrier).

★★ BIS CD 1305. Barcelona SO and Nat. O of Catalonia, Serebrier.

L'Arlésienne: Suites Nos. 1 & 2; Carmen: Suites Nos. 1 & 2; Ouverture; Patrie (Ouverture dramatique); Scènes bohémiennes; Symphony in C.

(B) ★★(★) Double Decca 475 190-2 (2). Montreal SO, Dutoit.

The Strasbourg performances under Alain Lombard date from the mid-1970s. The two *L'Arlésienne* suites are nicely turned, and the *Symphony* too is alive and well, with an elegant oboe solo in the *Adagio* and an infectiously spirited finale. The analogue sound is full and pleasing, rather than especially brilliant. What makes this Ultima Double especially tempting is the substantial set of highlights from a spontaneously vivid, complete recording of *Carmen*. Régine Crespin is in excellent voice, exuding a sexy sultriness, and she is well partnered by Gilbert Ply, a boldly romantic Don José. Van Dam's vigorous delivery of the 'Toreador's song' certainly carries the day. Lombard directs the proceedings with evident relish, helped by the enthusiasm of the Rhine Opéra Chorus and warmly atmospheric recording with plenty of depth.

An enjoyable and comprehensive collection of Bizet's most popular orchestral works, and some rarer items. In the *Carmen* and *L'Arlésienne Suites*, the playing is elegant and vivid, with superb, demonstration-worthy sound. This Montreal Collection was a top recommendation in its original, single-disc, full-priced format.

However, the second CD, recorded later, which includes the *Symphony*, *Scènes bohémiennes* and the overtures, is not quite so successful. The playing is of good quality, animated and spirited, but the music-making does not possess the charm and sparkle which the best performances (Beecham and Martinon, for example) bring to this repertoire. This music-making is still enjoyable, nevertheless, especially as Decca provide such good sound throughout; but it is a pity that the first CD was not reissued independently.

Unlike Sir Thomas Beecham, the conductor and composer José Serebrier has apparently long been dissatisfied with the conventional orchestral suites drawn from Bizet's *Carmen*, not just on points of orchestration but on the random order of the movements selected. Somewhat self-consciously, his alternative has been to devise a sequence of orchestral movements that broadly follow the development of the plot – though, finding the final death scene inappropriate for orchestral transcription, he has used Carmen's 'Gypsy Dance' instead, from the opening of Act II. So, following the opening *Prélude*, we have a movement called 'The Cavalry', the mustering scene without the chorus of children. After Carmen's *Habanera* and *Seguidilla* a movement called 'Fugato' contains the quarrel music taken from the end of Act I, while the item labelled simply 'Andante cantabile' is the central lyrical solo for Carmen from the Card Scene, and the penultimate movement, 'Wedding', is taken from the opening scene of Act IV.

Serebrier in this performance certainly establishes his main point: that a sequence reflecting the plot of the opera has an extra coherence in its span of 33 minutes, ending with a bang on the 'Gypsy Dance'. Rightly, Serebrier keeps Bizet's original orchestration as far as he is able, but controversially he uses a saxophone for Carmen's vocal part in the *Habanera* and the Card Scene, and it is much more effective in the latter. Though the trombone is a logical choice for Escamillo's vocal part in the 'Toreador's song', set in the correct register, the result rather suggests a bullfighter who is not quite sober. Serebrier draws a compelling performance from the Barcelona Symphony Orchestra, with outstanding wind and brass solos. The two *L'Arlésienne Suites*, crisply done, make an apt enough coupling, all very well recorded, but we feel that most readers will find Bizet's own entr'actes preferable in selecting orchestral music from *Carmen*.

Symphony in C.

(M) ** Sony (ADD) SMK 61830. NYPO, Bernstein – OFFENBACH: *Gaîté parisienne*, etc. ** (with SUPPE: *Beautiful Galathea: overture.* ***)

Bernstein's 1963 performance brings much to enjoy. The finale, in particular, has tremendous brilliance, which is most infectious, and the slow movement is affectionately done. On the downside, the first movement lacks the charm it ideally needs and the recording sounds a bit glassy, though it is better than it was on LP. Stokowski (Sony SBK 48264) or Martinon (DG 469 689-2) are both preferable – see our main volume.

OPERA

Carmen (opera; complete).

** Teldec 0630 12672-2 (3). Larmore, Moser, Gheorghiu, Ramey, Bav. State Op. Ch. & O, Sinopoli.

(BB) (*(*)) Naxos mono 8.110001/2. Swarthout, Kullman, Albanese, Warren, Met Op. Ch. & O, Pelletier.

Sinopoli directs a thoughtful, clean-textured but generally unidiomatic reading of *Carmen*, matched by Jennifer Larmore in the title-role, singing with clear, firm tone, but never sounding sensuous or earthy in the way one requires of this red-blooded character. Thomas Moser as Don José sings cleanly, better served by the microphones than usual, and Samuel Ramey is a heroic Escamillo, though he is not helped in the 'Toreador's song' by Sinopoli's rather slow and detached manner. Most recommendable is the characterful Micaëla of Angela Gheorghiu, but this remains a curiosity of a set.

It would be hard to imagine a less French-sounding account of *Carmen* than the performance given live at the Met. in New York in March 1941, and offered here in a raucous radio recording, close and boxy. Gladys Swarthout is far too little represented on disc, and her magnificent contralto, firm and rich, is an instrument of wonder. The downside is that, though musically her singing is masterly, her characterization resembles Margaret Dumont in a Marx Brothers movie pretending to be a voluptuous young gypsy. Licia Albanese does not sound innocent enough for Micaëla, with the tone not pure enough. Leonard Warren may have been a heroic performer, but the voice with its juddery vibrato too easily comes to sound woolly, not incisive enough for the bullfighter. Only the American tenor Charles Kullman survives the test well, singing with sensitivity and refinement as Don José. The French-Canadian Wilfred Pelletier directs a perfunctory account of the score, with the hard-pressed chorus almost comically unidiomatic. With so many excruciating French accents – and not a single French-speaking singer among the soloists – one wonders why they bothered to use the original language. First choice for *Carmen* rests with Gheorghiu on EMI (5 57434-2) – see our main *Guide*.

Carmen: highlights.

(M) *** EMI 5 57502-2 (from complete recording, with Gheorghiu, Alagna, Hampson, Mula, Ch. & Toulouse Capitole O, Plasson).

(BB) ** EMI Encore CDE5 74955-2 (from complete recording with Bumbry, Vickers, Freni, Paskalis, Paris Opéra Ch. & O, Frühbeck de Burgos).

(M) *(*) Warner Elatus 2564 60804-2. Film soundtrack recording, with Migenes Johnson, Domino, Raimondi, Esham, French R. Ch. & O, Maazel.

We have been enthusiastic about Angela Gheorghiu's Carmen, and she is well matched by Alagna and Hampson, and with Inva Mula an appealingly vulnerable Micaëla (see our main *Guide*). The highlights are generous (70 minutes 31 seconds) and well selected, reflecting all four acts, with an excellent cued synopsis.

Frühbeck de Burgos's account of 1970 was the first to use the original (1875) version of Bizet's score, without the cuts that were made after experience in the theatre, and with spoken dialogue instead of the recitatives, which Guiraud composed after Bizet's early death. The EMI Encore disc offers a comprehensive selection (76 minutes) from a set with a less-than-compelling Carmen in Grace Bumbry, who sings with firm tone but too rarely with musical or dramatic individuality. Vickers makes a strong Don José and Paskalis a rich-toned Escamillo, so with the opera well paced this makes a more than acceptable and well-recorded sampler, even if the synopsis is very sparse.

The glory of the Maazel film version of *Carmen* is the Don José of Plácido Domingo, freer and more spontaneously expressive than in his two previous recordings, not least in the lovely account of the *Flower Song*. Julia Migenes Johnson is a fresh-toned Carmen, not very subtle on detail, but convincing. Ruggero Raimondi as Escamillo is less resonant than usual but sings cleanly, but Faith Esham is a shrill Micaëla. No doubt this will appear complete on DVD in due course, but meanwhile this highlights CD is not especially recommendable: it includes no keyed synopsis.

Carmen: highlights (sung in English).

(B) **(*) CfP (ADD) 585 0082. Johnson, D. Smith, Herincx, Robson, Hynter, Sadler's Wells Opera Ch. & O, C. Davis.

This was one of the most successful Sadler's Wells discs of the 1960s, thanks both to the forceful conducting of Colin Davis and to the rich-voiced, reliable singing of Patricia Johnson as Carmen. Not that Johnson is merely reliable and no more; time and again her phrasing is most imaginative and memorable. It is good that the microphones catch her voice so well, and Donald Smith, the Don José, provides a wonderfully attractive, ringing tone. The selection is

brief (51 minutes) but well made, and the ensemble work has the authentic enthusiasm of a live performance, helped by the vivid sound.

BLISS, Arthur (1891–1975)

CHAMBER MUSIC

Piano Concerto.

✪ (***) British Music Society mono BMS 101 CDH. Mewton-Wood, Utrech SO, Goehr – STRAVINSKY: *Concerto for Piano and Wind* (***); SHOSTAKOVICH: *Piano Concerto No. 1.* (***)

The career of the enormously gifted Australian-born Noel Mewton-Wood was cut tragically short when he committed sucide at the age of 31. Beeecham descibed him as the 'best British talent that I've discovered for years' and Bliss hmself was so impressed with Noel's playing of his *Piano Concerto* that he wrote a sonata especially for him. The *Concerto* was recorded in 1952, and it is a truly prodigious performance, full of flair and with a vein of easy lyricism that invests the slow movement with magical, poetic feeling. There is a real burst of bravura in the first-movement cadenza, and the finale has the kind of impulsive virtuosity that one associates with Horowitz. Alec Robertson, reviewing the original LP in *Gramophone*, said, 'Mewton-Wood gives the performance of his life ... and is evidently at one with the conductor ... and the orchestra sound as if they are enjoying themselves'. Most remarkable of all is the exciting spontaneity of the playing, which sounds for all the world like a live performance. The Concert Hall recording of the orchestra is two-dimensional and lacks body, but the piano is well caught, and one adjusts when Brian Crimp's remastering is clear and clean and the playing so thrillingly compulsive.

Piano Sonata.

** Divine Art 2-5011. Barnard – BUSONI: *24 Preludes.* **

Trevor Barnard played the *Sonata* to Bliss in the late 1950s and the composer made some annotations and corrections in the printed score that are incorporated here. But collectors should note that the Divine Art recording is distinctly monochrome and lacklustre. The Chandos disc is the one to go for (Chan. 8979).

BLOCH, Ernest (1880–1959)

Baal Shem.

*** (M) Decca 476 17235. Bell, Baltimore SO, Zinman – BARBER: *Violin Concerto*; WALTON: *Violin Concerto.* ***

Bloch's own (1939) orchestrations of his three popular Hasidic pieces for violin and piano, *Baal Shem*, offers a fine, unusual makeweight for Bell's prize-winning disc of the Barber and Walton concertos; it won the 1998 *Gramophone* Concerto Award and now re-appears at mid-price in Universal's *Gramophone* Award Collection.

✓ (i) *Violin Concerto; Hebrew Suite for Violin & Orchestra;* (ii) *Schelomo (Hebrew Rhapsody).*
(M) ** Sup. SU 3169-2 011. (i) Bress, Prague SO, Rohan; (ii) Navarra, Czech PO, Ančerl.

Hyman Bress's recording is a thoughtful, ruminative account, well worth hearing and totally unforced. At the time of writing the *Hebrew Suite* is not otherwise available in its orchestral form. André Navarra's 1964 account of *Schelomo* is more high-voltage. Not a first choice, but those investing in these performances will find that there is musical satisfaction to be had here.

Violin Concerto in A min.
⊕ (BB) (***) Naxos mono 8.110973. Szigeti, Paris Conservatoire O, Munch – BARTOK: *Portrait*; PROKOFIEV: *Violin Concerto No. 1* (***). ⊕

Szigeti's pioneering record of the Bloch *Concerto* has long been a classic of the gramophone. So authoritative is it and so revered by violinists that Menuhin waited for almost thirty years before venturing on his recording with Kletzki. Since then there have been few successors, and while Szigeti's 1938 records were transferred to LP in the USA (on Vox Turnabout) this is – unaccountably – its first appearance on CD. A wonderfully serene yet intense performance from both Szigeti and Munch that penetrates to the core of Bloch's masterpiece. Szigeti's nervous vibrato is heard to perfect effect here, as it is in the first of the Bartók *Portraits*, and the classic première recording of the Prokofiev *D major Concerto* with Sir Thomas Beecham and the LPO.

Schelomo (Hebraic Rhapsody) for cello and orchestra.
(M) **(*) Sup. (ADD) SU 3667-2. Navarra, Czech PO, Ančerl – SCHUMANN: *Cello Concerto* **(*); RESPIGHI: *Adagio con variazioni.* ***
** MDG 0321 0215-2. Schmid, NW German PO, Roggen – HONEGGER: *Cello Concerto.* **

André Navarra is a fine cellist and, although he is less commanding than Fournier (DG 457 761-2), his too is a warmly eloquent account, and he is well supported by Ančerl. The remastering has made the solo cello very real and vivid, but the inner orchestral focus is not quite so sharp. Yet the sound remains natural, and for those wanting the couplings this disc is worth considering.

Ulrich Schmid gives a thoroughly idiomatic and well-recorded performance. However, all its rivals offer more generous couplings: at only 42 minutes' playing time, this is not a viable recommendation.

String Quartets, Nos. 1–4.
⊕ (***) Decca mono 475 6071 (2). Griller Qt.

It hard to believe that these performance of Bloch's *String Quartets* (No. 5 had not been written at the time of these recordings) have had to wait so long to appear (although the *Second* was released on Dutton); but it makes their return all the more welcome, especially as these works have been neglected in general. The Griller Quartet were closely associated with Bloch and became his friends and favourite interpreters, with the composer supervising these recordings, made in 1954. Tully Potter's sleeve-note informs us that, after the 1946 première of the *Second Quartet*, Bloch told the Quartet, 'It is a composer's dream come true to hear his work played as you have played it', and he dedicated his *Third Quartet* to them. These are clearly great performances, with any slight faults of intonation made irrelevant in the thrust of the music-making. The *First Quartet* (1916) lasts almost an hour, yet in this magnetic performance it doesn't feel a moment too long; Bloch's wonderfully rich, haunting harmonies are played by the Grillers with spine-tingling concentration, often producing sounds of otherworldly beauty, casting a powerful spell indeed. Tully Potter counts it among *the* great string quartet recordings, with the *Second* not far behind.

BOCCHERINI, Luigi (1743–1805)

(i) *Cello Concertos Nos. 6 in D, G.479; 7 in G, G.480;* (ii) *9 in B flat, G.482; 10 in D, G.483.*
(B) *** Erato Ultima (ADD) 3984 201040-2 (2). Lodéon; (i) Lausanne CO, Jordan; (ii) Bournemouth Sinf., Guschlbauer.

Lodéon's playing is stylish and eloquent, and in the *G major Concerto*, G.480, he is wonderfully fresh and fervent; in his hands the better known *D major Concerto*, G.479 (also recorded by Bylsma and Rostropovich), has tenderness and depth. He is well accompanied by both groups, but the two Lausanne performances (from 1981) have slightly superior sound. The snag to this pair of records is the playing time of only 85 minutes, whereas the competing Bylsma collection manages to get two concertos (G.483 and G.480) and two symphonies on to a single mid-priced CD.

Cello Concertos Nos. 7 in G (G.480); 10 in D (G.483); Sinfonias: in D min. (La casa del diavolo), Op. 12/4; in B flat, Op. 21/5 (G. 497).
⊕ (M) *** DHM/BMG 82876 60150-2. Bylsma, Tafelmusik, Lamon.

Anner Bylsma has already recorded the *G major Concerto* for Teldec within an excellent triptych of concertos on Apex (0927 49805-2 – see our main *Guide*), but this 1989 performance is even finer. Bylsma (a superb cellist) was at his peak, and the slow movement is played with ravishing delicacy, followed by an infectious finale. The *B flat Concerto* has a darker *Andante lentarello* as its centrepiece, phrased with comparable eloquence, and a jolly, horn-led closing *Allegro e con moto*, in which Bylsma's dashing virtuosity is hair-raising. He is lucky to have Jeanne Lamon's Tafelmusik as his accompanying group, one of the most elegant and polished of all period-instrument ensembles. They come into their own in the pair of symphonies, playing with a Mozartian grace and zest; the dancing violins in the *vivace* finale of the *B flat major Symphony* matched by the fierce vigour of the 'furies' in the devilish finale of the D minor work. The recording is absolutely first class.

Symphonies Nos. 8 in A, Op. 15/6 (G.508); 19 in E flat, Op. 35/5 (G.513); 26 in C min., Op. 41 (G.519); 27 in D, Op. 42 (G.520).
(B) **(*) HM Musique d'abord HMA 1951597. Berlin Akademie für Alte Musik.

Four characteristic Boccherini *Symphonies*, given bold and energetic performances by the Berlin Akademie. In the A major work of 1771 Boccherini writes engagingly for the flutes, but the high horns here dominate the *fortissimos*. The string playing in the *Larghetto* is pleasing and, after the Minuet, the work ends with another (*Grave*) slow movement. *No. 19 in E flat* (1782) is a three-movement work with a Minuet finale that hardly sounds like a Minuet at all. Nos. 26 and 27 were written in 1788 and 1789 respectively and are obviously more mature. The *C minor* has a winning *Pastorale* slow movement, sympathetically presented here, and the cascading finale demands and receives considerable virtuosity from the violins, But the *D major* is the finest of the four with a memorable Minuet (with violin obbligato) and a charming, Laendler-like trio, followed by a vigorous finale full of contrasts. The playing throughout lacks neither polish nor strength, but tuttis are gruff, with powerful accents, and at times one wishes the orchestra could relax more and convey a greater sense of elegance, as Tafelmusik do.

CHAMBER MUSIC

Cello Sonatas: in D min., G.2b; in A, G.4; in G, G.5; in A, G.13; in G, G.15; in C min., G.18.
**(*) HM Praga PRD 250 147. Kaňka, Tůma, Hejný.

These Prague recordings feature a full continuo, and the result is like a cello duet accompanied by a (dwarfed) backwardly balanced harpsichord. The playing is eloquent and spirited, but the effect is muddled and much less enjoyable than the splendid Naxos versions.

Guitar Quintets Nos. (i) 4 in D (Fandango), G.448; 9 in C (La riterata di Madrid), G.453. String Quartet in G min., Op. 24/6 (G.194).
**(*) Virgin 5 45607-2. (i) Pinardi, Europa Galante, Biondi.

The Virgin coupling of the *Fandango* and *Riterata di Madrid Quintets* is the most dramatic on record, with Mauro Occhinieri's castanets as spectacular in

the one as the histrionic *crescendo* and *decrescendo* in the other, with the music finally fading away completely into the distance. The playing itself is immensely vigorous, with the cello line at times guttural in its intensity. The snag is the lack of charm (an important feature in Boccherini's music), entirely absent in the *Adagio* of the *G minor String Quartet*. The recording is vividly projected and it is easy to respond to the visceral power of this playing, but this is not the whole story. The Yepes–Melos DG pairing of the two main works may be picturesque rather than theatrically overwhelming, but its elegance is more in keeping with the composer's intentions (DG 449 852-2 – see our main volume).

String Quintets: in A, Op. 10/1; in D min., Op. 18/5; in A (Della disgrazia), Op. 28/2 ; in A, Op. 29/4; in A, Op. 40/4; in F, Op. 41/2.
(***) Testament mono SBT 1245. Quintetto Boccherini.

String Quintets: in F, Op. 11/3; in C min. (Di Nina), Op. 18/1; in D min., Op. 25/1; in C min., Op. 29/2.
(***) Testament mono SBT 1244. Quintetto Boccherini.

String Quintets: in E, Op. 11/5; in D (L'Uccelliera), Op. 11/6; in G, Op. 25/3; in E flat, Op 31/1: Grave in D, (Fandango), Op. 40/2.
(***) Testament mono SBT 1243. Quintetto Boccherini.

For so long dismissed as 'la femme d'Haydn', Boccherini has been underrated and taken for granted. Yet at his finest and most eloquent – and many of these quintets are just that – they show how inventive and poignant he can be. Under the elegant surface, there is a melancholy that is often affecting and, though his music does not show the range and depth of his greatest contemporaries, his art can be deeply rewarding. These mono recordings were all made in the mid-1950s by one of the finest ensembles of the day; they produce a finely balanced sound of great refinement and tonal beauty. This is most civilized music-making and much to be cherished. Each disc is available separately and few collectors having sampled one will be able to resist its companions. Very little allowance need be made for the 1950s recording, and the transfers are eminently truthful and present.

String Quintets: in C, Op. 28/4, (G 310); in C, Op. 42/2 (G 349); (Quintettino) in B min., Op. 42/3 (G 350); in D, Op. 43/2 (G 353).
*** Hyp. CDA 67383. Vanbrugh Qt, with Lester.

The prize-winning Vanbrugh Quartet, with Richard Lester now a seasoned member of the ensemble, continue their exploration of the Boccherini *String Quintets*, using a second cello. The earliest in C major, Op. 28/4, dates from 1779. It opens amiably and is characteristic of the composer's bonhomie, mixed with touches of melancholy, noticeable in the minor-key Trio of the Minuet and the tranquil *Grave*, then offset by the bouncing closing Rondeau. Its companion work in the same key, written a decade later, opens nostalgically, but its congenial Minuet has a catchiness that is similar to the composer's most famous movement in this form, yet again with a minor-key centrepiece. The spirited *Allegro assai* is then followed by a galant finale.

The two-movement *Quintettino* (again from 1789) makes a direct contrast between wistful espressivo and vigorous – but not entirely convincing – jollity. The *D major Quintet*, written a year later, opens positively and follows with graceful Minuet, which leads to a touchingly simple *Andante*; all melancholy is then banished by the good-natured finale. Throughout the four works Boccherini's invention never fails him, and these excellent players relish all the felicities of his writing. Excellent recording.

KEYBOARD MUSIC

6 Duet Sonatas for 2 Harpsichords (from *String Quartets, G.195/200*); *Fandango* (from *String Quintet in D, G. 341*).

(B) ★★ HM HMA 1951233. Christie and Rousset (harpsichords).

These are transcriptions for two harpsichords of string quartets – or rather *quartettinos* (they are in two movements, hence the diminutive) – composed by Boccherini in 1778. They sound less idiomatic in this instrumental form than the *Fandango*, an arrangement of a movement from the *Quintettino*, Op. 40/2, written ten years later. Boccherini himself transcribed it for guitar and quartet. It certainly works more successfully in the keyboard medium than the other quartets. The playing here by a distinguished partnership is lively but closely balanced and is recorded at a high level so that the overall effect is somewhat unremitting.

BOECK, August de (1865–1937)

Symphony in G.

(B) ★★★ Discover DICD 920126. Brussels BRT PO, Rickenbacher – GILSON: *De Zee.* ★★★

The *Symphony in G* of August de Boeck is a ripely exotic work, full of Russian echoes. You might describe it as the Borodin symphony that Borodin didn't write, sharply rhythmic in the fast movements and sensuous in the slow movement, brilliantly orchestrated and full of tunes that are only marginally less memorable than those of the Russian master. Well played and recorded and, at Discover International's bargain price, an ideal disc for experimenting with.

BOËLLMANN, Léon (1862–97)

Cello Sonata in A min., Op. 40; 2 Pieces for Cello & Piano, Op. 31.

★★★ Hyp. CDA 66888. Lidström, Forsberg – GODARD: *Cello Sonata in D min., etc.* ★★★

Boëllmann is best known for his organ music and in particular the *Suite gothique*, whose final Toccata is a familiar *cheval de bataille*. The *A minor Sonata* reveals him to be a cultured and imaginative musician. Mats Lidström and Bengt Forsberg play with such passion and conviction that they almost persuade one that this piece is worthy to rank alongside the Brahms *Sonatas*. The recording is very acceptable, if rather close. Strongly recommended.

BOISMORTIER, Joseph Bodin de (1689–1755)

Ballets de village: Nos. 1–4, Op. 52; Gentillesse No. 5, Op. 45; Sérénade No. 1, Op. 39.

(BB) ★★★ Naxos 8.554295. Le Concert Spirituel, Niquet.

Boismortier's four *Ballets de village* are colourful sets of pastoral dances which make vivid use of rustic instruments – the musette and hurdy-gurdy – with an underlying drone, in concert with wind and string instruments, in continuous lively three-part writing. The three-movement *Gentillesse* is rather more refined. However, the *Sérénade*, Op. 39, with its 18 sections is much more ambitious. Here the texture is based on flutes, violins and oboes. There is an opening *Ouverture* and an extended closing *Chaconne*. In between come more dances, *Gavottes*, a *Gigue*, a *Sarabande*, a fast and piquantly vivacious *Villageoise* introduced by the treble recorder, as well as an *Entrée rustique*, an elegant *Air gracieux*, a charming *Air modéré* and even a *Chœur imaginaire*. Boismortier's invention is unflagging, the instrumental colouring ear-catching, and when played with such authenticity and sparkle this is very attractive, if not to be taken in a continuous sequence. The recording is excellent.

(i) *Bassoon Concerto*; (ii) *Musette (Zampognae) Concerto. Fragments mélodiques* (French dance suite); *Sérénade or Symphonie française No. 2. Stage works: Daphnis et Chloé: Chaconne; Les Voyages de l'amour: Entrées des génies élémentaires.*

(BB) ★★★ Naxos 8.554456. (i) Le Chenadec; (ii) Maillard; Le Concert Spirituel, Niquet.

Naxos at last are filling out a fuller picture of Joseph Bodin de Boismortier, tax collector (for the French Royal Tobacco Company) as well as musician. As this collection shows, he composed with easy facility so that a contemporary writer portrayed him in verse:

Happy is he, Boismortier, whose fertile quill,
Each month, without pain, conceives a new air at will.

The *Bassoon Concerto* shows this facility most agreeably, as does the equally engaging work for musette (Boismortier chose the Italian name to describe the instrument) with its underlying drone. His orchestral palette is shown even more colourfully in the two collections of dances, felicitously and lightly scored for flutes, oboes, hurdy-gurdy, musette and strings. One of his specialities was to write inventive chaconnes in duple instead of triple time. Both the *Fragments mélodiques* and *Sérénade* end with a typical example. But his finale for *Daphnis et Chloé* (which is used to open the concert) is even more individual and deserves to be better known. Most remarkable of all is the *Entrées des génies élémentaires*, a bubbling kaleidoscope of contrasting character dances. Hervé Niquet directs his excellent ensemble with animation and finesse, and both his soloists are in good form. A first-class disc in every way, well worth exploring.

6 Concertos for 5 Flutes, Op. 15/1–6.
(BB) ** Naxos 8.553639. Soloists of Le Concert Spirituel.

Although Boismortier's invention holds up well throughout, his predilection for block chords in slow movements means that the music has relatively little variety of colour. These excellent players blend and match their timbres expertly, often presenting a very homogeneous sound, the effect emphasized by the close balance. A disc to recommend primarily to amateur flautists.

6 Flute Sonatas, Op. 91.
*** Analekta FL2 3008. Guimond, Beauséjour.

Boismortier's Op. 91 is elegant and well crafted, and these sonatas nicely blend French and Italian influences. All except the first, which has an opening *Sicilienne*, are in the fast–slow–fast Italian tradition. They are played beautifully and stylishly by this excellent French-Canadian duo: Claire Guimond on the baroque flute and Luc Beauséjour. They play with an appealing delicacy to charm the ear, yet there is an underlying robustness that makes the music seem far from merely trivial. The recording (as one expects from this Canadian label) is expertly balanced and altogether natural.

(i) *Suites for Solo Flute Nos. 3, 5 & 6;* (ii) *Harpsichord Suites Nos. 1–4* (1731).
(B) *** HM Cal. (ADD) CAL 6865. (i) Urbain; (ii) Lagacé.

(i) *Suites for Solo Flute No. 4; Nos. 3 & 6* (with continuo); (ii) *Harpsichord Suites Nos. 1–4.*
(BB) *** Naxos 8.554457. (i) Savignat, Plubeau; (ii) Martin.

These four *Harpsichord Suites* were Boismortier's only works for harpsichord. They are very much in the style of the *Pièces de clavecin* of Rameau, and Boismortier follows his practice in giving each movement a colourful sobriquet. *La Cavernesque*, which begins the *First Suite*, is aptly titled. The invention is attractive, if perhaps not as individual as with Rameau, although the finale of the last suite shows Boismortier writing a very characterful set of variations. Mireille Lagacé is an excellent advocate and she uses a restored Hemsch, which is truthfully recorded and suits the repertoire admirably. The *First Suite* is also played expertly by Lagacé, and the recording is realistic, provided you turn down the volume. Interleaved with the harpsichord works are three suites for unaccompanied flute. Again the playing is highly responsive, to make this a rewarding concert.

The harpsichord that Béatrice Martin uses on the Naxos disc is not named, but if anything it is an even more attracive instrument that that used by Mireille Lagacé, warmly resonant yet well focused. Anne Savignat plays the charming *Fourth Flute Suite* as a solo work, but in Nos. 3 and 6 she is partnered by Christine Plubeau, who plays a simple bass line on the viola da gamba. Certainly these performances are every bit the equal of those on their Calliope competitor and again make one reflect that the works for harpsichord ought to be far better known.

BOITO, Arrigo (1842–1918)

Mefistofele (complete).
(M) *(*) Sony SM2K 90478 (2). Domingo, Marton, Ramey, Hungarian State Op. Ch. & O, Patanè.

Patanè's is a stiff, rather perfunctory reading of this vivid opera about heaven and hell, not helped by a studio acoustic which, with the chorus cleanly and unatmospherically placed, makes it sound more like an oratorio than an opera. Plácido Domingo sings well, but there is little bloom on the voice and, noble and commanding as Samuel Ramey's performance is, he does not sound sinister. The biggest snag is the singing of Eva Marton, far too heavyweight and unsteady a soprano for Margherita, and hardly better suited to the role of Elena (Helen of Troy) which she doubles – another drawback to the set. Moreover the documentation is unacceptably sparse, with neither libretto nor cued synopsis. First choice for this opera still rests with the vintage Decca recording conducted by Fabritiis, with Pavarotti most seductive and Caballé a fine Elena (410 175-2).

BONONCINI, Giovanni (1670–1755)

Cello Sonata in A min.; Trio Sonata for 2 Violins & Continuo in D min. (i) Cantatas: *Già la stagion d'amore; Lasciami un sol momento; Misero pastorello; Siedi, Amarilli mia.*
*** Virgin 5 45000-2. (i) Lesne; Il Seminario Musicale.

Giovanni Bononcini's cantatas were popular and were published in London in 1721. They reveal their composer to be far more than a mere historical figure. *Lasciami un sol momento* stands out as a particularly moving work, with its melancholy opening aria ('Leave me but for one moment, O bitter memory of my betrayed love') leading to a bravura finale, *Soffro in pace* ('I bear these chains in peace'). The instrumental works are also highly inventive and characterful: the *Lento* of the lively *Trio Sonata* is gently touching and its finale wonderfully spirited. All this music is worth knowing, and the advocacy of these fine artists brings it fully to life. The expressive eloquence of Gérard Lesne's singing could not be more winning, using the most felicitous ornamentation. The recording too is first class.

BORODIN, Alexander (1833–87)

Symphony No. 2 in B min.

(M) *(*) Ph. (ADD) 464 735-2. Concg. O, Kondrashin (with RIMSKY-KORSAKOV: *Scheherazade.* ***)

(BB) *(*) Belair BAM 9724. New Russian O, Poltevsky – RIMSKY-KORSAKOV: *Tsar Saltan: Suite.* ***

Kondrashin's rather brisk live account of the *Second Symphony* has the advantage of fine orchestral playing, though it is let down by some intrusive audience noise and a lapse of intonation in the slow movement. Kondrashin's outstanding *Scheherazade* is a different matter, but fortunately it is also available alternatively coupled with other works by Rimsky-Korsakov (442 643-2 – see our main volume).

At super-bargain price on the Belair label comes Poltevsky's version with an excellent orchestra drawn from a range of Moscow orchestras. Impossibly heavy at the start, with fluctuation of tempo in the first movement, and the other three movements are taken broadly too. A disc worth hearing for an electrifying account of the *Tsar Saltan Suite*.

String Quartets Nos. 1 in A; 2 in D; (i) String Sextet in D min.

*** ASV CD DCA 1143. The Lindsays, (i) with Williams, R. Wallfisch.

The Lindsays add to their repertory of warm, intense recordings this splendid coupling of Borodin's two *String Quartets* alongside a rarity from early in the composer's career, the *String Sextet*, composed in Heidelberg in 1860, of which only two movements survive. It is a most attractive makeweight in which Borodin was plainly seeking to emulate Mendelssohn's masterly *String Octet* with writing similarly light and exuberant. The *Second Quartet*, with its haunting second-movement *Notturno*, has long been a favourite work, but the *First Quartet*, more ambitious in scale, brings similar finesse and melodic warmth. The Lindsays, very well recorded, give glowing, ripely expressive and finely balanced performances that confidently bring out the light and shade of the writing of both scores, as well as a more convincing reading of the *Sextet* than any other we have heard.

The eponymous Borodin Quartet has a special claim on this repertoire and is now to be found on the Chandos mid-price Historic label. But this sumptuously recorded new ASV triptych has splendid eloquence and will probably be a first choice for those readers who are looking for an up-to-date recording.

Prince Igor (complete).

*** Ph. **DVD** 074 173-9 (2). Putilin, Gorchakova, Akimov, Aleksashkin, Vaneev, Borodina, Kirov Ballet Ch. & O, Gergiev (Producer: Paul Smaczny; V/D: Arno Cronvall).

*** Ph. **DVD** 075 099-9 (6). As above – GLINKA: *Ruslan and Ludmilla*; MUSSORGSKY: *Boris Godunov*.

We reported at length (and with much admiration) on Gergiev's three-CD set of *Prince Igor* in our main *Guide*, recorded in the Mariinsky in St Petersburg in 1992. The present production was mounted six years later, in 1998, with a different but equally strong cast. Both Galina Gorchakova and Olga Borodina sing the same roles (Yaroslavna and Konchakova respectively) but the Khan Konchak is Vladimir Vaneev while the performance is dedicated to the memory of the Khan in the earlier set, the incomparable Bulat Minjelkiev; most of the other male roles are differently (but no less superbly) cast. The notes replicate the scholarly account in the CD set of what this edition restores. It includes passages discovered among Borodin's papers that were rejected by Rimsky-Korsakov in his superb edition, and they have been specially orchestrated for this new production by Yuri Faliek. (Rimsky-Korsakov's style and orchestration are very close to Borodin's – and the completion and scoring of Act III was an altogether phenomenal feat on Glazunov's part.) Of Borodin's 20 years of autograph material for the opera, less than a third was included in the published score, and all of that was edited by Rimsky. Some 1,680 bars were the work of Glazunov, who also orchestrated 157 of the 710 pages of full score. Rimsky scored another 368, and only 185 pages remained of Borodin's own scoring. The Gergiev production reverts to a structural outline of 1883, which proposed alternating the Russian and Polovtsian acts. This is not the place to discuss the re-ordering of the material of the opera, but its artistic interest and success are not in question.

The Royal Opera House production from the early 1990s conducted by Haitink was available on video and two LaserDiscs (Decca 071 421-1) and it is well worth seeing for the Igor of Sergei Leiferkus, the Galitsky of Nikola Ghiuselev and Burchuladze's Khan Konchak. However, for obvious reasons it is completely superseded by this superb Philips version. The sets and costumes are sumptuous and the choreography for the *Polovtsian Dances* is that of Fokhine which Diaghilev presented in Paris. The Kirov set is now also included in an attractive package with two other classic productions (presumably at an attractive discount) to mark Valery Gergiev's 25th anniversary at the opera house; those who do not have these performances should take advantage of this. All three are outstanding.

BØRRESEN, Hakon (1876–1954)

At Uranienborg or Tycho Brahe's Dream (ballet); (i) *Romance for Cello & Orchestra. The Royal Guest: Prelude.*

**(*) dacapo 8.224105. Aalborg SO, Hughes; (i) with Brendstrup.

The Royal Guest, a one-act opera from 1919, was Børresen's greatest success, and its *Prelude* whets the appetite. The 12 numbers that constitute the ballet *At Uranienborg or Tycho Brahe's Dream* are given a committed performance, as is the *Romance*, played by Henrik Brendstrup and written in 1908 at the time of the *Second Symphony*. Owain Arwel Hughes and his Aalborg musicians sound as if they are enjoying themselves. But the acoustic of the Aalborg hall is not ideal: the sound is tubby in climaxes and lacks transparency.

Symphonies Nos. 2 in A (The Sea), Op. 7; 3 in C, Op. 21.

*** CPO 999 353-2. Frankfurt RSO, Schmidt.

Both symphonies have a lot going for them. The delightful Scherzo of No. 1 is as transparent in its orchestration as Mendelssohn, and the first movement has a Dvořákian sense of openness and space. Attractive works, not the last word in originality, but presented very persuasively by Ole Schmidt and the Frankfurt Radio Orchestra, and well recorded.

BÖRTZ, Daniel (born 1943)

Trumpet Concerto (Songs & Dances).
*** BIS CD 1021. Hardenberger, Malmö SO, Varga
(with RABE: *Sardine Sarcophagus*; SANDSTROM: *Trumpet Concerto No. 2.* ***)

Börtz's *Trumpet Concerto* is highly imaginative and has a compelling quality, thanks to his feeling for sound and colour, whether or not you respond to the idiom. It is subtitled *Songs and Dances* and is one of four concertos with related titles. Hardenberger is quite stunning, as is the BIS recording. The excellent couplings are included in our main volume.

Sinfonias Nos. 1; 7; Parados; Strindberg Suite.
*** Chan. 9473. Stockholm PO, Rozhdestvensky.

Daniel Börtz is never boring, though his limited range of expressive devices makes it hard to listen to all these pieces straight off, despite the refined sense of orchestral colour. The music is too static, with extensive use of chord-clusters and strong dynamic contrasts, but both the *First* and *Seventh Symphonies* are powerfully atmospheric. The playing of the Stockholm orchestra is superb and the Chandos recording is of demonstration standard: marvellously present, well balanced and realistic.

BOTTESINI, Giovanni (1821–89)

(i) *Double-Bass Concertino in C min.; (i-ii) Duo concertante on Themes from Bellini's 'I Puritani' for Cello, Double-Bass & Orchestra; (i) Elégie in D; (i; iii) Passioni amorose (for 2 double-basses); Ali Baba Overture; Il diavolo della notte; Ero e Leandro: Prelude.*
*** ASV CDDCA 907. (i) Martin; (ii) Welsh; (iii) Petracchi; LSO, Petracchi or (iii) Gibson.

A contemporary said of Bottesini's virtuoso playing, 'Under his bow the double-bass sighed, cooed, sang, quivered,' and it does all those things here on the flamboyant bow of Thomas Martin, himself a musician of the strongest personality. For the *Passioni amorose* the conductor, Francesco Petracchi, exchanges his baton for another bow to join his colleague, establishing a close, decisive partnership. Further contrast is provided in the *Duo concertante* on melodies of Bellini. The programme is interspersed with colourful orchestral miniatures. The *Sinfonia, Il diavolo della notte*, turns naturally from warm lyricism to galloping liveliness, and the brief *Ali Baba Overture* brings a spirited whiff of Rossini. The recording engineers have worked marvels to balance everything so convincingly, and this programme is surprisingly rewarding and entertaining.

Gran duo concertante for Violin, Double-Bass & Orchestra; Gran concerto in F sharp min. for Double-Bass; Andante sostenuto for Strings; Duetto for Clarinet & Double-Bass.
**(*) ASV CDDCA 563. Garcia, Martin, Johnson, ECO, Litton.

The ASV recording combines the *Gran duo concertante* with another *Duetto for Clarinet and Double-Bass*, which Emma Johnson ensures has plenty of personality, though none of this amiable music is very distinctive. The recording is excellent, well balanced and truthful.

Capriccio di bravura; Elegia in Re; Fantasia on 'Beatrice di Tenda'; Fantasia on 'Lucia di Lammermoor'; Grand allegro di concerto; Introduzione e bolero; Romanza drammatica; (i) Romanza: Une bouche aimée.
**(*) ASV CDDCA 626. Martin, Halstead; (i) with Fugelle.

Thomas Martin is a superb virtuoso of the double-bass and he obviously relishes these display pieces, but some of the high tessitura is inevitably uncomfortable. The recording is most realistic.

BOUGHTON, Rutland (1878–1960)

(i) *Oboe Quartet No. 1; 3 Songs without Words (for Oboe Quartet). String Quartets: in A (On Greek Folk Songs); in F (From the Welsh Hills).*

(BB) *** Hyp. Helios CDH 55174. (i) Francis; Rasumovsky Qt.

Nearly all this music is inspired by the countryside, and indeed the folk-styled melodies in the delightful *A major 'Greek' Quartet*, might well have had a British source, rather than a Greek derivation. The second movement of the *F major Quartet* hauntingly evokes the *Landscape from the* (Welsh) *hilltops*. The *Oboe Quartet* has two perky movements and a third, more reflective *Andante con variazione*. Sarah Francis, who has already given us a fine account of Boughton's *First Oboe Concerto* (Helios CDH 55019 – see our main volume), is equally persuasive both here and in the three equally winning *Songs without Words*, opening with an *Andante delicato* and closing sensuously with a *Barcarolle* marked *Andante languido*. The Rasumovsky Quartet gives sympathetic support throughout and, with good, clear recording, this inexpensive disc has much to offer.

BOULEZ, Pierre (born 1925)

CHAMBER MUSIC

Piano Sonata No. 2.

(M) (***) DG (ADD) 471 359-2. Pollini – DEBUSSY: *12 Etudes.* **

'It is the performer's absolute responsibility', Pollini has said, 'to put new music into their programmes ... the only interesting works are those composed in an uncompromisingly modern musical language,' as Beethoven's was in his time. Boulez's *Second Sonata* certainly meets that criterion. Pollini also felt that the hugely destructive energy of the piece also calls up comparisons with late Beethoven, and in particular the *Hammerklavier Sonata*, which is perhaps a little unfortunate. The composer's stated intention was to 'destroy what was first-movement sonata form, to dissolve slow-movement form by means of the trope, to dissolve repetitive scherzo-form by means of variation form, and in the fourth movement to destroy fugal and canonic form'. Indeed in the finale the pianist at one point has an instruction to 'pulverize the sound'.

So, if you like musical disintegration, this is the piece for you, and in the accompanying note Paul Griffiths (the author of a book on Boulez) analyses its content and defines its progress with considerable skill. Pollini truly believes in this sonata, readily demonstrated by the forceful driving momentum of his playing throughout. Its inclusion in the 'Pollini Edition' was therefore inevitable, even though many

listeners
playing is

BOURGAULT-DUCOUDRAY, Louis-Albert (1840–1910)

Rhapsodie cambo

**(*) Marco Polo 8.
FANELLI: *Tableaux
Roman de la Momi*

The impressively named ... composer Louis-Albert Bourgault-Ducoudray is hardly well known today. He was appointed professor of music history at the Paris Conservatoire in 1878, and wrote music throughout his life. His taste for exotic colours and folk tunes is well in evidence in his tone-poem *Rhapsodie cambodgienne* of 1882 (its subtitle is *The Feast of Water*). With colourful orchestration and the use of some genuine Cambodian folk tunes – the second part, the *Fête des Eaux*, is especially enjoyable – it makes an enjoyable seventeen-minute companion to Fanelli's impressive *Tableaux symphoniques*. The recording is good and Adriano is obviously a sympathetic exponent; while the orchestra enter into the spirit, they are not always immaculate in execution, with the strings sounding taxed under pressure. Still, a must for all those with an interest in the byways of French music.

BRADE, William (1560–1630)

Hamburger Ratsmusik: excerpts.

(BB) ***DHM 05472 77476-2. Hespèrion XX, Savall.

Those content with a short selection from this inventive score, including music taken from just the 1609 and 1615 collections, will find this bargain disc most enjoyable.

BRAHMS, Johannes (1833–97)

Academic Festival Overture, Op. 80; Tragic Overture; Variations on a Theme by Haydn, Op. 56a; (i) Rhapsody for Alto, Chorus and Orchestra, Op. 53.

(M) * Decca (ADD) 470 254-2. VPO, Knappertsbusch, (i) with West – WAGNER: *Siegfried Idyll.* *

This programme would have been an attractive addition to the catalogue had the performances been of high calibre, but one cannot believe that Decca thought Knappertsbusch's slow and stodgy Brahms collection was suitable for inclusion in its 'Legends' series for, with its pretty sloppy playing and ponderous tempi, it is not really recommendable at all. The *Rhapsody* is a mite better in some respects, especially as the rarely recorded Lucretia West, with her opulently burnished contralto, will interest collectors of gers. The 1957 sound, ... ot especially ingratiating.

...os. 1 in D min., Op. 15; 2 in B flat,

...dec Ultima 0630 18948-2 (2). Leonskaya;
...ilh. O, Inbal, or Leipzig GO, Masur.
* DG 457 837-2 (2). Pollini, BPO, Abbado.

(i) *Piano Concertos Nos. 1–2.* (ii) *Violin Concerto.*
Symphonies Nos. 1–4. Academic Festival Overture;
Tragic Overture; Variations on a Theme by Haydn.
(B) ** RCA 82876 60388-2 (5). Bav. RSO, C. Davis,
    with (i) Oppitz; (ii) Takezawa.

(i) *Piano Concertos Nos. 1–2. Tragic Overture, Op.*
81; Variations on a Theme of Haydn, Op. 56a.
(B) **(*) DG (ADD) Double 453 067 (2). (i) Pollini;
    VPO; Boehm (*No. 1*) or Abbado (*No. 2*).

(i) *Piano Concertos Nos. 1–2. Tragic Overture;*
Variations on a Theme of Haydn.
(B) *(*) EMI (ADD) 5 72013-2 (2). Arrau; Philh. O,
    Giulini.

(i–iii) *Piano Concertos Nos. 1 in D min., Op. 15;* (i;
iii; iv) *2 in B flat, Op. 83;* (i; v) *Variations & Fugue*
on a Theme by Handel, Op. 24 (orch. Rubbra);
Variations on a Theme by Handel, Op. 56a.
(B) **(*) Double Decca 470 519-2 (2). (i) Ashkenazy;
    (ii) Concg. O; (iii) Haitink; (iv) VPO; (v) Cleveland
    O.

Ashkenazy gives a commanding and magisterial
account of the solo part of the *First Concerto* that is
full of poetic imagination. The *Second Concerto*, with
the VPO, is not as successful. It is spacious in conception and thoughtful in detail, but curiously lacking in
impulse, with cautious speeds, and it is overtly
expressive in the lyrical episodes of the second movement. The slow movement is very beautiful and the
finale offers the proper contrast; but in the last
resort, in spite of the excellent recording, this is
slightly disappointing. For the fill-ups, Ashkenazy
adopts the role of conductor: the *Haydn Variations*
receives an excellent performance in very plush
Cleveland sound – sound that also brings out all the
vibrant colour in Rubbra's extravagant orchestration
of the *Variations and Fugue on a Theme by Handel* – a
substantial bonus – which is similarly well played
and is highly enjoyable. A mixed bag then, but worth
considering by Ashkenazy admirers.

Although Pollini and the Vienna Philharmonic
under Karl Boehm are given finely detailed recording
in the *First Piano Concerto*, other versions (notably
Gilels) provide greater wisdom and humanity. Not
that Pollini is wanting in keyboard command, but he
is a little short on tenderness and poetry. All too
often here he seems to have switched on the auto-
matic pilot and, although the *B flat Concerto* under
Abbado is much fresher and offers some masterly

pianism, there are warmer and more spontaneous
accounts to be had.

DG have also paired together Pollini's two Brahms
concertos, recorded live with Abbado in 1997–8. No. 1
is handicapped by a balance that places the piano
very forward in relation to the orchestra. The *Second
Concerto* is much more acceptable in this respect:
indeed the sound is very satisfactory. The performance too is of some distinction, but this set is poor
value at premium price.

Leonskaya is an impressively direct and powerful
Brahmsian, inclined to be stoic, but also thoughtful
in her lyrical moments. Eliahu Inbal proves a more
successful partner for her than Masur, and the Philharmonia provide a passionate opening for the *D
minor Concerto*, although the secondary material is
much more considered. Overall this is a spacious
rather than a fiery reading and it lacks the electricity
of the finest versions. The *B flat Concerto*, very
broadly conceived, gives an impression of massive-
ness and is even less spontaneous in feeling, although
the finale brings a lighter touch. These artists are
given excellent, modern, digital recording, but their
performances are no match for those of Gilels.

The orchestral music of Brahms, conducted by
Colin Davis, in an attractive bargain box seems a very
good idea in principle, but it is hampered by the
recordings of the *Piano Concertos* played by Gerhard
Oppitz. Oppitz is much admired in Germany, and he
has the technique and dramatic power to cope with
the formidable demands these *Concertos* make. All
the same, an imaginative and poetic dimension is
missing and, despite good playing from the wonderful Bavarian Radio Symphony Orchestra and a warm
acoustic, it is not in the league of the many great
recordings of this repertoire. In the symphonies and
orchestral music Davis offers clean-cut readings,
beautifully played and recorded, fresh and crisp in
outer movements, intense in slow movements, where
he tends to adopt speeds markedly slower than usual.
It is very enjoyable, but not preferable to the best
versions available.

Arrau's first stereo versions for EMI, made at the
beginning of the 1960s, suffer from the feeling of a
lack of affinity with the recording studio that has
often afflicted him in the past. Nor is Giulini the
ideal conductor for him, polished and weighty without being really inspired. Arrau provides some delicious moments in the more graceful passages of No. 1
but is never fiery in the way Curzon, for instance, is
with Szell. The *Second Concerto* has a certain massive
strength, helped by the full-bodied sound, but overall
it hardly adds up to a very convincing performance.
First choice for the paired Brahms Concertos rests
with Gilels (DG 447 446-2).

Piano Concerto No. 1 in D min., Op. 15.
(M) ** Chan. 6621 (2). Margalit, LSO, Thomson (with
    MENDELSSOHN: *Capriccio brillant* **) – SCHUMANN:
    Concerto; SAINT-SAENS: *Concerto No. 2.* **
(M) ** DG 471 353-2. Pollini, BPO, Abbado –

SCHUMANN: *Piano Concerto.* ★★

(BB) ★(★) Naxos 8.554088. Biret, Polish Nat. RSO, Wit
– SCHUMANN: *Introduction & Concert Allegro.* ★★

(i) *Piano Concerto No. 1. 4 Ballades, Op. 10.*

★★ Australian Decca (ADD) 466 724-2. (i) Rubinstein,
Israel PO, Mehta; (ii) Katchen.

(i) *Piano Concerto No. 1. Variations & Fugue on a
Theme by Handel, Op. 24.*

(M) ★★(★) Sony (ADD) 512875-2. R. Serkin; (i) with
Cleveland O, Szell.

As the very opening reveals, Serkin's partnership
with Szell generates the same kind of adrenalin and
ardour as the Decca version with Curzon and the
LSO. The slow movement has fine lyrical feeling, and
the overall reading has a fine grip and is undoubtedly
compelling. Although it does not match the Decca
sound, the 1968 recording has been opened up for
this reissue. The *Handel Variations*, recorded a decade later and also commandingly played (although
not absolutely immaculate technically), is rather
closely balanced in the American manner of the
time.

Rubinstein admirers will be happy to learn that his
1975 Decca recording of Brahms's *First Concerto* has
made it on to CD. With more than a sprinkling of
wrong notes, this can never be a general recommendation, but the character and drive of the man in his
late eighties emerge vividly. To hear such a performance in the concert hall one would readily pay far
more, though here the piano is balanced too forwardly. Katchen's characterfully played and recorded
Ballades make a useful coupling. This CD is nothing
if not a collector's item.

Israela Margalit is a most musical exponent of this
most leonine of concertos, and on the whole Bryden
Thomson proves a sound partner. However, the
sumptuous Chandos recording has the violins backwardly balanced at the very opening, blunting the
orchestral attack. While this account, which has no
lack of poetic feeling, is far more than just an also-
ran and there is much to admire, the overall impression makes it less commanding than the finest
available versions, and its new format is not particularly economical.

Recorded at a concert performance when the Berlin Philharmonic was visiting the Musikverein in
Vienna, Pollini's digital version is handicapped by a
balance that places the piano far too forward. The
pianism impressses, as always, though the overall
effect is marmoreal and ultimately uninvolving.

Idil Biret plays with genuine Brahmsian warmth,
and her pianism is powerful and compelling. The
Polish orchestra is fully committed too. However,
Wit's opening ritornello is romantically wayward,
which prevents any sense of the strong forward
thrust that is so essential in the first movement of
this concerto, and this approach is shared by the
soloist. The slow movement does not lack expressive

warmth, but it is only in the brilliant finale that the
performance is totally convincing. The spacious
recording gives no cause for complaint.

Piano Concertos Nos. (i) *1;* (ii) *2;* (iii) *Violin
Concerto.*

(B) ★★(★) Double Decca (IMS) (ADD/DDD) 453 335-2
(2). (i) Lupu, LPO, de Waart; (ii) Ashkenazy, LSO,
Mehta; (iii) Belkin, LSO, Fischer.

Radu Lupu's approach to the *First Piano Concerto* is
deeply reflective and intelligent, full of masterly
touches and an affecting poetry, which falls short of
the thrusting, combative power of a Serkin or Curzon. Decca produce a particularly truthful sound-
picture. This could be recommended enthusiastically
to those who want a second, alternative view. However, Ashkenazy's account of the *Second Piano Concerto* is less successful, its chief shortcoming being a
lack of tension. On the other hand, Boris Belkin's
performance of the *Violin Concerto* is direct and
spontaneous, a spaciously warm reading that makes
a strong impression. No complaints about the
recorded sound.

Piano Concerto No. 2 in B flat, Op. 83.

★★★ Naïve V4944. Guy, LPO, Berglund.

(M) (★★★) BBC mono BBCL 4125-2. Arrau, SCO,
Gibson – SCHUBERT: *3 Klavierstücke.* (★★★)

(M) ★★(★) DG (ADD) 474 838-2. Anda, PO, Karajan –
GRIEG: *Piano Concerto.* ★★

(BB) ★★ Naxos 8.554089. Biret, Polish Nat. RSO, Wit –
SCHUMANN: *Introduction & Allegro appassionato.*
★(★)

(i) *Piano Concerto No. 2;* (ii) *5 Lieder, Op. 105.*

★★(★) EMI 5 55218-2. Kovacevich; (i) LPO, Sawallisch;
(ii) Murray.

The young French pianist François-Frédéric Guy
caused quite a stir with his Prokofiev at London's
Wigmore Hall a year or two ago, and we hailed his
recording of the *Sixth* and *Eighth Sonatas* in extravagant terms in our main volume as being worthy of
ranking alongside the likes of Richter, Pollini and
Pletnev. This account of the Brahms *B flat Concerto* is
hardly less commanding. It comes from a concert
given at the Royal Festival Hall on 30 May 2003 – and
it is quite simply a straight performance rather than a
compilation drawn from two or more performances.
It can hold its own against the finest – and, having
the electricity of a live occasion, is in some ways to be
preferred to many rivals. Berglund is a supportive
and sympathetic accompanist and audience noises
are unobtrusive. The Festival Hall acoustic does not
flatter the upper strings but, that apart, readers
should find this a most rewarding issue.

Arrau was a masterly interpreter of the Brahms
concertos, often performing both at the same concert. He recorded the *Second* twice during the 1960s
and '70s, once with Giulini and again with Haitink.
This concert performance was given in Glasgow in

1963 and shows him in splendid form: there is a breadth, warmth and luminosity of tone that are peculiar to Arrau at his finest, and an intenstity he brought to everything he did in the concert hall. The mono sound is very faithful and, although the performance does not necessarily add substantially to what we know from his commercial recordings, it is still a worthwhile addition to his concert discography.

The 1968 partnership of Géza Anda and the BPO provides much fine playing from soloist and orchestra alike. The performance opens slowly and is rhapsodically free; it has plenty of impulse and, if Anda is wayward at times, he is always commanding. There is poetry here and undoubted power. The slow movement is often richly eloquent and the finale has a persuasive, lyrical charm. There is much to enjoy, not least in the glorious orchestral response, even if this is not a primary recommendation. The recording is appropriately bold and full, and the balance good, no doubt improved in this new 'Originals' transfer.

After his noble and dedicated account of the *First Piano Concerto* with Wolfgang Sawallisch and the LPO, Stephen Kovacevich's version of its successor brings admiration tinged with disappointment. It does not match this partnership's *First* and does not take wing in quite the same way.

The spacious, boldly romantic approach of Idil Biret and Antoni Wit works much better in the *Second Concerto* than in the *First*, helped by the warmth of the full-bodied recording. There is no doubting the power and virtuosity of the solo playing or the committed response of the Polish orchestra. However, at times the forward momentum of the first movement is inclined to lapse, and Biret in her forcefulness becomes rhythmically heavy. The close of the leisurely *Andante* lacks the concentration necessary to sustain a high level of tension, but the lilting finale is a success.

Violin Concerto in D, Op. 77.

(BB) ✱✱✱ DG Entrée 474 569-2. Mutter, BPO, Karajan – BEETHOVEN: *Triple Concerto.* ✱✱✱

✱✱(✱) DG 457 075-2. Mutter, NYPO, Masur (with SCHUMANN: *Fantasy, Op. 131* ✱✱✱).

(M) ✱✱(✱) Warner Elatus 2564 60806-2. Vengerov, Chicago SO, Barenboim – DVORAK: *Concerto.* ✱✱✱

(BB) ✱✱ RCA 82876 55268-2. Zukerman, LAPO, Mehta – BRUCH: *Concerto No. 1.* ✱✱

(BB) ✱✱ EMI Encore 5 85455-2. F. P. Zimmermann, BPO, Sawallisch – MOZART: *Violin Concerto No. 3.* ✱✱✱

Mutter's early partnership with Karajan proved naturally spontaneous, and her 1981 account of the Brahms *Concerto* has stood the test of time, to make an excellent choice for DG's Entrée label. The performance is also available, coupled with Mendelssohn at mid-price (DG 445 515-2 – see our main volume).

In her New York recording, Anne-Sophie Mutter

cannot quite match the mastery of her early version with Karajan. Her tone, as recorded, is less evenly beautiful, and live performance brings idiosyncrasies and the occasional flaw. It remains an enjoyable, warm-hearted version, recommendable for the unusual Schumann coupling.

We have mixed feeling about Vengerov's Brahms *Violin Concerto* (originally coupled with the *Third Violin Sonata*). For E. G., Vengerov plays not just for display, but with far deeper insights, the inspiration of the moment captured at white heat. Using the widest dynamic and tonal range, this is a performance of extremes, just as felicitous in bravura as in lyrical purity.

R.L., while not denying that Vengerov's technique is dazzling and admitting that he produces a wonderful sound, finds the performance open to the charge of being a bit too gleaming and slick. But it is certainly an account to magnetize the listener.

Zukerman's 1994 recording is better balanced that his 1979 DG version, with a more natural placing of the violin. The power of his playing remains very clear and the reflective quality is all the more intensely conveyed, in a reading regularly marked by poetry. What is less welcome here is the slight edginess in the solo violin sound, missing the roundness that always used to mark Zukerman's tone on disc, and though he is more reflective than before he is also a degree less expansive, with Mehta a rather stiff Brahmsian.

Zimmermann's recording is taken from live performances given in the Philharmonie in Berlin, but only in the finale does this add to the lift and imagination of the reading. Until then his clean, direct approach seems a little too well-mannered for such a bravura work, beautiful as the playing is. Well recorded and coupled with an inspired, quicksilver performance of Mozart, this is fair value but hardly makes a strong contender. First choice rests with Joshua Bell (on Decca 444 811-2).

(i) *Violin Concerto in D, Op. 77;* (ii) *Double Concerto for Violin, Cello & Orchestra, in A min., Op. 102.*

(M) ✱✱✱ RCA (ADD) 82876 59410-2. Heifetz, with (i) Chicago SO, Reiner; (ii) Piatigorsky, RCA Victor SO, Wallenstein.

An excellent and logical coupling of these two vintage accounts for RCA's new 'Classic Library' series. The speeds in all the movements of the *Violin Concerto* may be on the fast side, but Heifetz's ease and detailed imagination make them more than just dazzling, while the central *Andante*, at a flowing speed, is delectably songful. Wallenstein, accompanying the *Double Concerto*, may not quite be in the same league of brilliance as that of Reiner in the *Violin Concerto*, but he nevertheless provides a sympathetic backcloth for the 1960 Heifetz–Piatigorsky partnership. Even if this account does not quite match Heifetz's earlier version with Feuermann, it is still a strong, warm-hearted performance with a strikingly brilliant finale. The sound for both these recordings has been vastly improved in recent incarnations, and this CD certainly retains its classic status.

(i) *Violin Concerto in D, Op. 77*; (ii) *Hungarian Dances Nos. 1, 2, 7 & 9; Sonatensatz in C min. (Scherzo).*

(M) *** EMI 5 62598-2. Perlman; (i) BPO, Barenboim; (ii) Ashkenazy (piano).

Perlman's 1992 'live' recording remains highly recommendable, finding him at his most commanding, powerful and full of nonchalant flair, and conveying an extra warmth of commitment, with no sense that the performance has been achieved too easily. Now, reissued as part of the 'Perlman Edition', it has an apt and delightful collection of encores (recorded a decade earlier, with Ashkenazy an admirable partner). The Joachim arrangements of the four *Hungarian Dances* bring the most carefree playing, but the *Scherzo* is hardly less brilliant.

Violin Concerto (with cadenzas by Busoni, Joachim, Singer, Hermann, Auer, Ysaÿe, Ondricek, Kneisel, Marteau, Kreisler, Tovey, Kubelik, Busch, Heifetz, Milstein, Ricci).

*** Biddulph LAW 002. Ricci, Sinfonia of London, Del Mar.

The veteran Ruggiero Ricci not only gives a strong, assured performance of the concerto, he adds no fewer than 16 cadenzas as well, any of which can be programmed into the main performance on CD. Though Ricci is no longer as fiery or incisive as he once was, his is an attractive performance of the concerto, well recorded.

Double Concerto for Violin, Cello & Orchestra in A min., Op. 102.

(*) EMI **DVD 490449-9. (i) D. Oistrakh, Rostropovich, Moscow PO, Kondrashin – BACH: *Double Violin Concerto*, etc.; MOZART: *Sinfonia concertante.* **(*)

**(*) Testament SBT 1337. Ferras, Tortelier, Philh. O, Kletzki – TCHAIKOVSKY: *Violin Concerto.* **(*)

(M) *(*) BBC (ADD) BBCL 4050-2. Menuhin, Rostropovich, LSO, C. Davis – MENDELSSOHN: *Violin Concerto*; J. S. BACH: *Violin Concerto in E* *(*).

David Oistrakh and Rostropovich were recorded during the Moscow Philharmonic's visit to London in October 1965. It is a highly charged account which shows both artists at their most emotionally intense yet profoundly disciplined. As usual at this period, the camerawork, expertly produced by the young Brian Large, is very restrained, with a limited number of angles and the minimum of visual distraction. Of course the sound is less transparent and present than the commercial records of the period, but this DVD does convey the sense of occasion and musical excitement.

The performance of the *Double Concerto* by Christian Ferras, Paul Tortelier and the Philharmonia Orchestra under Paul Kletzki was recorded at the Kingsway Hall in 1962 and, though it was reissued in a box devoted to Tortelier first in the days of LP and then on CD, it has not been released on one disc. The two French artists have a good rapport and deliver a finely integrated account of the work, and Kletzki gives admirable support. Those who believe that recording has rarely been more natural or truthful than it was in the first few years of stereo will take further solace in the spacious and pleasing sound, excellently remastered by Paul Bailey.

Some imperious and masterly playing from Rostropovich on the BBC disc goes some way towards redeeming a vulnerable performance by Menuhin. The recording comes from a Prom in 1964 and sounds well for its period. However, this is no match for the best now in the catalogue.

Serenades Nos. 1 in D, Op. 11; 2 in A, Op. 16.

(BB) **(*) Warner Apex 2564 61138-2. (i) Royal Stockholm O, A. Davis; (ii) Ens. O de Paris, Jordan.

(M) ** Telarc CD 80522. SCO, Mackerras.

Serenades Nos. 1–2; (i) *Liebeslieder Waltzes, Op. 52 & 65.*

(M) **(*) Orfeo C008 102A (2). VSO, Bertini; (i) with Sieghart, V. Singverein.

Andrew Davis and the Stockholm orchestra give a spirited account of Brahms's masterly early *D major Serenade.* Davis's direction is as sympathetic as the players' response, and the 1998 recording is very good, even if the texture could be more transparent. For the budget reissue it has been joined to Armin Jordan's more mellow performance of the companion A major work, which is a shade less vital, but has a warmly played slow movement, and an engaging closing Rondo. Again the sound, with a nice bloom on the woodwind, is pleasingly full, if not sharply detailed. Excellent value at Apex price.

Gary Bertini's account of the opening movement of the *D major Serenade*, with its rollicking horns, has a boisterous quality which is engaging, and throughout both works he draws much fine playing from the Vienna Symphony Orchestra; the woodwind provide appealing colour. Bertini maintains a good momentum for the *Adagio* slow movements, which is sensible enough, but he captures the relaxed atmosphere better in Op. 16 than in Op. 11. The resonant recording sounds rich-textured at lower dynamic levels, but in *fortissimos* the opulence also brings a touch of heaviness. However, there is much agreeable warmth here and the reissue throws in a second CD with an equally agreeable performance of the seductive *Liebeslieder Waltzes*, liltingly sung by the Vienna Singverein, although Ingrid Sieghart is not a soloist to banish memories of more famous names.

Mackerras's performances of the two *Serenades* are curiously disappointing. They are short of the conductor's usual vigorous enthusiasm and, although they have affectionate touches and are well played, they lack the kind of 'live' spontaneity and warm geniality that makes Tilson Thomas's performances on Sony so persuasive.

(i) *Serenades Nos. 1–2; Academic Festival Overture;* (ii) *Tragic Overture; (i) Variations on a Theme of Haydn; (i, iii) Alto Rhapsody, Op. 53.*

(B) **(*) EMI double forte (ADD) 5 68655-2 (2). (i) LPO; (ii) LSO; (iii) with J. Baker, Alldis Ch.; all cond. Boult.

Sir Adrian Boult's warmly lyrical approach to the two *Serenades* is less ebullient and sparkling than that of Andrew Davis or Bertini, yet he gives pleasure in a different way. Boult's way with these delightful scores is engaging enough to blunt any criticism, when the late-1970s Abbey Road recording is suitably full. What makes this inexpensive double forte reissue even more attractive is the inclusion of Janet Baker's devoted account of the *Alto Rhapsody*, the performance essentially meditative. The *Academic Festival Overture* opens the programme in a rather more extrovert fashion, and the *Variations* are also vividly presented and strongly characterized, the sound here rather more lively. The eloquent *Tragic Overture* also shows Boult as a true Brahmsian. In playing time (just under two hours), however, this is rather less generous than some double fortes.

SYMPHONIES

Symphonies Nos. 1–4.
** DG (ADD) 459 635-2 (3). SW German R. O, Stuttgart, Celibidache.
(M) *(*) Chan. 9776 (4). LSO, Järvi.

Symphonies Nos. 1–4; Academic Festival Overture; Tragic Overture; Variations on a Theme of Haydn.
**(*) Erato 4509 94817-2 (4). Chicago SO, Barenboim.
(BB) ** Ph. Trio 470 942-2 (3). Phd. O, Muti.

Symphonies Nos. 1–4; Academic Festival Overture; Tragic Overture; Variations on a Theme by Haydn; (i) *Alto Rhapsody.*
(M) *** EMI (ADD) mono 5 62742-2 [5 627602] (3). Philh. O, Klemperer; (i) with Ludwig, Phil. Ch.
(BB) *(*) Virgin 5 62081-2 (4). Houston SO, Eschenbach; (i) with Vejzovic & Houston Symphony Male Ch.

Symphonies Nos. 1–4; Variations on a Theme by Haydn; (i) *German Requiem.*
(M) ** EMI (DDD/ADD) 5 56837-2 (8). Munich PO, Celibidache; (i) with Augér, Philharmonic Ch. & Munich Bach Ch. (members) – BEETHOVEN: *Symphonies Nos. 2–4; 6 (Pastoral); 7–8; 9 (Choral); Leonora Overture No. 3* ** (with SCHUMANN: *Symphony No. 2* **).

Klemperer's monumental set – now reissued as one of EMI's 'Great Recordings of the Century' – remains highly desirable. The sound was effectively refurbished (in 1999) for the separate issues of the symphonies, and the commanding strength of these readings continues to recommend them. In that respect No. 1 is unsurpassed; Nos. 2 and 3 may be a trifle austere for some tastes, but their emotional power is in no doubt, and in No. 2 the balance between the lyrical and histrionic elements is held in perfect balance. The combination of gravity and drama in No. 4 makes a continuing impact on almost all listeners (although R.L. confesses that its comparative severity means he has never really enjoyed this *Fourth*). The *Tragic Overture* is done with equal strength, and the *Alto Rhapsody* also shows the conductor at his most masterful and, with Christa Ludwig on fine form, it is a beautifully expressive performance. The *Haydn Variations* is chosen to open the first disc, as it was one of his first (mono) recordings with the Philharmonia, made in 1954; yet the orchestra immediately responds to him, and he enters fully into the spirit of the *Academic Festival Overture*.

Barenboim's inspirational volatility works well in the *Third Symphony*, which does not lose its ongoing purpose and brings beautiful orchestral playing in the central movements. No. 4 is finest of all, a highly concentrated interpretation that moves forward powerfully; even though the tempo for the *Andante* is slow, it is presented ardently and is capped by a gripping performance of the closing *Passacaglia*.

Sergiu Celibidache's DG performances come from his appearances with the Stuttgart Radio (Südfunk) Orchestra in the 1970s. These certainly produce tone of the utmost refinement and subtlety. The sheer intentness of the playing and the tonal sheen produced by the Stuttgart group is nearly always in evidence, but there is a certain want of real forward momentum and of sinew. Beauty rather than truth is dominant. The 1974–6 recordings come up well and there is a bonus rehearsal disc devoted to the first movement of the *Fourth Symphony*.

Celibidache's EMI set boxes all four Brahms symphonies, the *Requiem* and the *Haydn Variations*, and couples them with Schumann's *Second Symphony* and an incomplete Beethoven cycle on eight CDs (not available separately). Celibidache dwells on beauty of sound and refinement of texture. He is happy to pull phrases completely out of shape. In the *Haydn Variations* he is lethargic and at times positively funereal.

The Philips engineers, faced in 1989 with recording in the difficult Philadelphia venue, only gradually overcame their problems. It follows that Muti's set, too, is inconsistent, generally offering crisp, beautifully played readings, which are distinguished without being strongly characterized, occasionally dull and lacking in tension. Individually the most desirable of the four is No. 3 and that would make a fine separate issue with its original coupling, the *Alto Rhapsody*, beautifully sung by Jessye Norman. This has been omitted here to get the set on to three CDs.

Eschenbach's set could compete only if the Houston performances were truly outstanding, which they are not. They are beautifully played and very well balanced and recorded. But Eschenbach, highly musical Brahmsian as he is, has not yet entirely mastered the art of bringing a performance fully to life in the recording studio. Easily the finest performance is of the *Fourth Symphony*, where the tension is consistently maintained and Eschenbach's steady lyrical flow, often impassioned, reminds one of Karl Boehm. One of the highlights of the set is the moving account of the *Alto Rhapsody*. Dunja Vejzovic is in glorious voice and the choral entry is a moment of serene magic, with the Houston chorus beautifully balanced with the solo voice. But as a general recommendation, this Virgin set is a non-starter.

By Järvi's standards, his Brahms cycle is a disappointment, often fussy, sometimes wilful, with playing from the LSO that generally lacks that very quality that marks out most Järvi records: the sense of a genuine performance rather than a studio run-through. Added to that, the Chandos engineers' preference for a wide, reverberant acoustic makes Brahms's heavy orchestral textures sound thick and vague, however great the richness and range of the recording. Originally, each symphony was coupled with a Schumann overture, all of which have now been removed, making each CD particularly ungenerous in playing time. Four discs for the price of two full-price discs is hardly compensation and makes this set a non-starter. However, Karajan's late 1970s recordings on a DG Double (453 097-2) make a 'best buy' for this repertoire.

Symphony No. 1 in C min., Op. 68.

(M) ** DG (IMS) 445 505-2. VPO, Bernstein –
    BEETHOVEN: *Overtures: Coriolan; Egmont.* **

Symphony No. 1 in C min., Op. 68; Academic Festival Overture.

(M) *(*) Warner Elatus 2564 60435-2. Chicago SO, Barenboim.

Symphony No. 1; Variations on a Theme of Haydn.

(BB) **(*) Naxos 8.550278. Belgian R. PO, Brussels, Rahbari.

Symphony No. 1; Tragic Overture.

(BB) *(*) Warner Apex 0927 44351-2. NYPO, Masur.

Opening powerfully with thundering timpani in the manner of Klemperer, though with generally more relaxed tempi, Alexander Rahbari on Naxos gives an account of Brahms's *First* that is certainly recommendable. It is a strong, direct reading, spacious yet with plenty of impetus. A good choice for those with limited budgets, even if there are many finer versions listed in our main *Guide* of all four symphonies.

The finale in Bernstein's version brings a highly idiosyncratic reading, with the great melody of the main theme presented at a speed very much slower than the main part of the movement. In the reprise it never comes back to the slow tempo, until the coda brings the most extreme slowing for the chorale motif. These two points are exaggerations of accepted tradition and, though Bernstein's electricity makes the results compelling (both in the symphony and the overtures), this is hardly a version for constant repetition. The remastered sound is fully acceptable.

Masur is better attuned to the lyrical *Second Symphony* than to No. 1, and despite some first-rate playing from the New York orchestra the result sounds too easy, lacking in tension until the finale.

Barenboim dons his Furtwänglerian mantle for the Elatus account of the *First Symphony*, which, though very well played, suffers from his wilful flexibility and eccentric structural control: at one point in the finale, the great Chicago orchestra is very nearly brought to a dead stop, but it subsequently recovers to end the work very positively.

Symphonies Nos. 1–2; Academic Festival Overture; Tragic Overture.

(B) *(*) Teldec Ultima 8573 84067-2 (2). Cleveland O, Dohnányi.

Dohnányi's reading of the *First Symphony* sets the pattern for his cycle of recordings as a whole: strong and direct, beautifully controlled and finely textured, but rather lacking in the tensions of live communication. The Teldec recording is rich as well as being naturally balanced, finely detailed and full of presence. However, while this is agreeable enough, there are many more distinctive versions available. Moreover, the *Second Symphony* is one in which Dohnányi's direct, slightly no-nonsense approach to Brahms pays fewest dividends. Superbly played and recorded and with speeds impeccably chosen, the performance yet fails to catch fire or give the feeling of anything more than a brilliant run-through.

Symphony No. 2; Academic Festival Overture.

(M) ** DG (IMS) 445 506-2. VPO, Bernstein.

Bernstein in his live recording directs a warm and expansive account, notably less free and idiosyncratic than the *C minor Symphony*, yet comparably rhythmic and spontaneous-sounding. Considering the limitations of a live concert, the recording sounds well. But this is by no means a first choice, even at mid-price.

Symphony No. 2; Tragic Overture.

(M) ** Warner Elatus 2564 60662-2. Chicago SO, Barenboim.

If only the whole *Second Symphony* in this recording had been played like the finale – full of impetus, with the great second subject gloriously re-presented in the recapitulation – then Barenboim's Chicago performance would have been very highly recommendable. But having opened *sotto voce*, the first movement proceeds in its richly moulded, leisurely way, and Barenboim again reduces the momentum at the horn solo towards the end. The central movements are comparably spacious, the tension not consistently maintained, and, while the warm Chicago sound suits this relaxed approach, this is too wilful a reading to be completely satisfying. The *Tragic Overture*, however, responds well to Barenboim's dramatic and lyrical emphases.

Symphonies Nos. 3–4.

(BB) ** DG Eloquence (ADD) 469 756-2. VPO, Boehm.

(BB) ** Warner Apex 09274 9880-2. North West German PO, Lindenberg.

Symphonies Nos. 3–4; (i) Violin Concerto. Variations on a Theme of Haydn.

(B) ** Teldec Ultima 8573 84068-2 (2). Cleveland O, Dohnányi; (i) with Zehetmair.

Dohnányi conducts a clear, direct reading of No. 3, superbly played and recorded. In sound so beautifully balanced, the often thick orchestration is made transparently clear as well as naturally weighty, and this is a version that emphasizes classical values, crisply structured rather than warmly expressive. In the second-movement *Andante*, taken on the slow side, Dohnányi does not entirely avoid squareness, and the horn reprise of the main third-movement theme is forthright rather than affectionate. The opening of the finale lacks mystery, and the hemiola rhythms of the second subject, for all the power of the performance, fail to leap aloft.

The reading of the *Fourth* again brings a strong, finely controlled reading, lacking only occasionally in a flow of adrenalin. The slow movement is hushed and thoughtful, the third clear and fresh in its crisp articulation, while the weight of the finale is well caught – even if it is not thrust home at the close as sharply as it might be. These detailed criticisms are given only to suggest why – with such superlative playing and an irreproachably direct manner, not to mention outstanding sound – these performances finally lack something in Brahmsian magic and memorability.

Similarly Zehetmair's is a warm and thoroughly musical account of the *Violin Concerto*: his timbre is sweet, and both he and Dohnányi, who accompanies sympathetically, offer a good response to Brahmsian lyricism. The Cleveland orchestral playing is beyond criticism and the Teldec sound-balance impressively natural. But other versions of this concerto have a much stronger profile, and this performance fails to resonate in the memory.

Boehm's recordings derive from a 1976 boxed set. The readings are unexpectedly idiosyncratic. Slow movements, in particular, are unusually slow, and indeed there is a general lack of the necessary thrust and impetus in No. 3 until the finale, which then tapers off to a melancholy coda. No. 4 is overall rather more impressive (though not in the same class as Boehm's pre-war 78rpm set with the Saxon State Orchestra). Again the finale sparks into life and

produces a rousing close. Good analogue recording, well transferred to CD; but this coupling is very much an also-ran, even at budget price.

Edouard Lindenberg was a fine musician who began his career in Bucharest with the Philharmonic Orchestra, then settled in Paris in 1947 before becoming a 'nationalized' Frenchman, as the English note puts it. A much respected conductor, particularly in French repertoire (we recall an outstanding Chabrier *Suite Pastorale* from the early 1950s), Lindenberg recorded these performances in 1969, three years before his death, and they are eminently straightforward and decently recorded interpretations which are far from negligible, but in the crowded CD catalogues are less than competitive.

CHAMBER MUSIC

(i) Cello Sonatas Nos. 1–2; Wie Melodien zieht es mir, Op. 105/1; (ii) Clarinet Sonatas Nos. 1–2; Vergebliches Ständchen, Op. 84/4; (iii) Violin Sonatas Nos. 1–3; F.A.E. Sonata: Scherzo, WoO 2.

(M) *** EMI 5 57523-2 (3). Vogt, with (i) Pergamenschikow; (ii) Meyer; (iii) Tetzlaff – BERG: *4 Pieces* etc.; SCHUMANN: *3 Romanzen* etc. ***

In these Brahms duo recordings, made live at the Heimbach Chamber Music Festival in 2002, the pianist Lars Vogt is very much the mastermind, not just because he appears on all three discs, but because he is so much more than an accompanist, regularly the leader of each duo, even with artists as characterful as the clarinettist Sabine Meyer and the violinist Christian Tetzlaff. The cellist Boris Pergamenschikow is a characterful artist too, but Vogt is even more dominant on the cello disc, partly because of a backward balance and partly because Vogt (more than in the other duos) tends to set a fast pace and leave it to the soloist to keep up, as in the finale of the *First Cello Sonata* or the *Allegro appassionato* third movement of Opus 99. The song transcription makes a winning encore, with the Schumann pieces an apt supplement.

Sabine Meyer on the clarinet disc also has a Brahms song as an encore, *Vergebliches Ständchen*, but the brilliant pay-off in the vocal version, with the maiden peremptorily shutting the window in her lover's face, is inevitably less effective when played on the clarinet than when sung. In the two *Clarinet Sonatas* the individual expressiveness of both artists, with free and flexible rubato, is well matched, very much part of the live atmosphere, with Meyer consistently producing her glorious peaches-and-cream tone. Evidently reflecting the order of items in the live concert, the *Second Sonata* comes first on the EMI disc, leading immediately to the two Berg items.

The most satisfying of the three discs is that of the *Violin Sonatas* with Tetzlaff, not just the three numbered ones but also the *Scherzo*, which Brahms contributed to the composite *F.A.E. Sonata* with Schumann and Dietrich, particularly welcome when most rivals do not have that extra item. It is given an exceptionally powerful performance, with cross-rhythms sharply emphatic, and in the numbered sonatas the incisiveness and urgency of both artists makes this a formidable rival to the classic versions. Their speeds are regularly on the fast side, with the opening of the *D minor*, Op. 108, given a hushed, nervy quality that carries one magnetically along in a highly individual reading full of light and shade. Each of the three discs comes in a separate jewel-case, potentially making them available separately in due course.

Cello Sonatas Nos. 1 in E min., Op. 38; 2 in F, Op. 99.

(M) * (**) EMI 5 62741-2 [5 627582]. Du Pré, Barenboim.

(M) **(*) RCA 82876 59415-2. Ma, Ax.

EMI have, understandably, chosen the stereo recordings of the two Brahms *Cello Sonatas* that Du Pré and Barenboim made in 1968, soon after they married, even though the mono versions (available on EMI 5 57293-2 – see our main volume) are more convincingly spontaneous. The studio performances offered here are flawed by Jacqueline du Pré's undeniable stylistic self-indulgence; even if these players tackle the second and more taxing of the sonatas with the sense of heroic size that the music demands, the result is not entirely convincing. This is on the whole the more successful of the two performances. It is hard to accept the blatant changes of tempo between the first and second subjects in the earlier sonata, yet here too there is warmth and flair. The Abbey Road recording is well balanced and realistic, but this is not recommended for those who find themselves resisting the Du Pré–Barenboim brand of romantic expressiveness.

The balance on the Yo-Yo Ma–Emanuel Ax version favours the piano, and Ax sometimes produces too thick a sound in climaxes, while Ma, always sensitive, is smaller in tone. Theirs is an essentially romantic view, and some may find the first movement of the *E minor Sonata* rather too wayward. Ma's *pianissimos* occasionally draw attention to themselves, though the grace and tenderness of his playing are not in question. The claims of these readings reside in their refined lyricism rather than in their muscularity, and these artists have splendid rapport. The RCA recording is truthful, and admirers of this great cellist need not hesitate, especially as this CD now comes at mid-price in the 'Classic Library' series.

Cello Sonata No. 2 in F, Op. 99.

(M) (***) EMI mono 5 67008-2. Casals, Horszowski – BACH: (Unaccompanied) *Cello Suite No. 1 in G*; BEETHOVEN: *Cello Sonata No. 3*. (***)

The celebrated (1936) Paris recording of the Brahms *F major Sonata*, Op. 99, with Casals and Horszowski has had numerous incarnations, most recently on EMI Références, but its splendours do not fade. It remains one of the most moving accounts of this leonine score on disc.

Clarinet Quintet in B min., Op. 115.

(M) * Chan. (ADD) H 10151. Mozkovenko, Borodin Qt – MOZART: *Clarinet Quintet*. **

(i) Clarinet Quintet; (ii) String Quintet No. 2 in G, Op. 111.

** EMI 5 56759-2. (i) Meyer; (ii) Schlichtig; Alban Berg Qt.

Sabine Meyer joins the Alban Berg Quartet for a good rather than outstanding account of the *Clarinet Quintet*, and there are more moving accounts to be had and more memorable versions of the *G major Quintet*.

No date is given for the Borodin recording with Ivan Mozkovenko, but, whatever its provenance, the performance is pretty lugubrious. It is surprising that this wonderful quartet makes such heavy weather of the piece.

Clarinet Sonatas Nos. 1 in F min.; 2 in E flat, Op. 120/1-2.

(M) *** Oehms OCD 232. Manno, Perl.

Ralph Manno has a succulent tone, highly suitable for Brahms. He establishes a strong partnership with Alfredo Perl, and these volatile performances are full of imaginative light and shade. In the *F minor*, the slow movement is freely ruminative, the *E flat major* opens most persuasively and is equally strong on contrast. There is some most winning playing in the *Andante* and the brief finale is full of energy. The well-balanced recording is most realistic and vivid.

Piano Quintet in F min., Op. 34.

(M) **(*) DG (ADD) 474 839-2. Pollini, Italian Qt.

There is some electrifying and commanding playing from Maurizio Pollini, and the Italian Quartet is in eloquent form. The balance, however, is in the pianist's favour, though the effect in this new 'Originals' transfer seems a touch improved over the original (1980) LP release. There are some minor agogic exaggerations but none that should put off admirers of the pianist. However, the playing time of under 44 minutes for this disc undoubtedly will, even if one is hardly short-changed on quality.

Piano Trios Nos. 1 in B, Op. 8; 2 in C, Op. 87.

(BB) *** Warner Apex 2564 61259-2. Trio Fontenay.

Powerful, spontaneous playing with a real Brahmsian spirit, given excellent, modern recording, puts these admirable performances by the Trio Fontenay (originally on Ultima, but now at budget price) at the top of the list.

String Quartet No. 1 in C min., Op. 51; (i) String Quintet in G, Op. 111.

**(*) EMI 5 57661-2. Belcea Qt, (i) with Kakuska.

The Belcea Quartet have rightly collected golden

opinions for their Schubert and Debussy–Ravel couplings. Their approach in the Brahms *C minor Quartet* is less urgent and dramatic than many ensembles: the players' ruminations are gentler and they find both a sense of mystery and a Schubertian grace in its course. At times their *pianissimos* seem a shade exaggerated, but they are consistently imaginative in their approach. In the *G major Quintet* they are joined by Thomas Kakuska of the Alban Berg Quartet, with whom they studied, and they produce a finely shaped, well-thought-out and often searching account of this piece. Not perhaps a first recommendation, for there is a touch of self-awareness about this music-making, but both performances are individual and illuminating. Good recorded sound.

Violin Sonatas Nos. 1 in G, Op. 78; 2 in A, Op. 100; 3 in D min., Op. 108.
(BB) ★ EMI Encore 5 7725-2. Mutter, Weissenberg.

This was one of Anne-Sophie Mutter's earliest recordings for EMI, and this gifted young violinist scores over some rivals by the vividness of the recorded sound. But the attractions of this reissue end there. Her playing is accomplished enough and not wanting in ardour or imagination, but Alexis Weissenberg proves insensitive and lacking in feeling. He conveys little pleasure – and there are few performances in the concert hall or on record that have less magic. Not recommended, even at super-budget price.

Violin Sonatas Nos. (i) 2 in A, Op. 100; (ii) 3 in D min., Op. 108.
(M) ★★★ Warner Elatus 2564 60661-2. Vengerov, (i) Markovich; (ii) Barenboim – ELGAR: *Violin Sonata.* ★★★

Vengerov's partnership with Alexander Markovich works admirably. They both catch the *amabile* of the first movement of the *A major Sonata*, and the Brahmsian mellowness is sustained both in the *Andante tranquillo* and in the easy grace of the *Allegretto grazioso* finale. Yet there is an underlying vitality, and Vengerov rises to the climaxes. The account of the *D minor Sonata* is also very fine, with Vengerov bringing out the mystery of this minor-key work, and with Barenboim at the piano also freely spontaneous. Excellent recording and, while it is a pity that the *First Sonata* could not have been added for this reissue, the coupled performance of the Elgar is passionately convincing.

PIANO MUSIC

Piano music for four hands

German Requiem, Op. 45 (arr. for piano, 4 hands).
(BB) ★★ Naxos 8.554115. Matthies, Köhn.

Brahms's piano-duet arrangement of his great choral work succeeds better than might be expected. Though the whole project may seem odd, what does come out of this warmly expressive performance is the spring-like lyricism of Brahms's writing. On the other hand, having piano tone alone does emphasize the fact that the work is predominantly slow. A curiosity, well recorded.

Solo piano music

4 Ballades, Op. 10; 2 Rhapsodies, Op. 79; Variations and Fugue on a Theme by Handel, Op. 24.
(BB) ★(★) Warner Apex 0927 49986-2. Lubimov.

Alexei Lubimov is nothing if not fleet of finger and eminently vital in his approach to these scores. But the *Handel Variations* are all too over-heated and driven, and the fugue is wanting in grandeur. The two Op. 79 *Rhapsodies* fare better, and there is some expressive, lyrical playing in the *Ballades*. The Erato recording comes from the mid-1990s and is wanting in depth.

3 Intermezzi, Op. 117; 6 Pieces, Op. 118; 4 Pieces Op. 119.
★★★ EMI 5 57543-2. Vogt.

Issued simultaneously with his Brahms duo discs from the Heimbach Chamber Music Festival, Lars Vogt's disc of the three last sets of piano pieces offers a different slant on his Brahms interpretations in a conventional studio recording. There are profound things in these extraordinarily forward-looking late Brahms pieces, and Vogt is a Brahmsian of real quality who is completely inside this repertoire. His speeds, far from being fast, as they tend to be in his live performances, are on the broad side, but his natural warmth and ability to convey the sense of spontaneous invention make these very much a welcome supplement to the festival performances. The EMI disc offers natural, lifelike and wide-ranging recorded sound that does justice to a thoughtful and highly musical artist.

Piano Sonata No. 3 in F min., Op. 5.
(★) HM Appian Recordings APR 5632. Arrau – BEETHOVEN: *Piano Sonata No. 3 in C, Op. 2/3.* ★★

Arrau had a special feeling for the Brahms *F minor Sonata*, and in this 1978 recital at the Avery Fisher Hall he takes more risks than in his fine commercial recording from 1973. The conception is magnificent, but the sound is not. No details are given of its provenance, but the aural image is too ill-focused, clangorous and brittle to emanate from a radio source and it sounds as if it were taken in the wings or in the first few rows. There are far too many microphone bumps. Arrau always had something new to say about great music, but sonic limitations diminish the wider appeal of this reading.

Piano Sonata No. 3 in F min., Op. 5; Capriccio in B min., Op. 76/2; Hungarian Dances Nos. 1 in G min.; 2 in D min.; 3 in F; 6 in D flat; 7 in A; Intermezzo in A min. Op. 76/7.
★★ RCA 82876 52737-2. Kissin.

Masterly and magisterial playing in the *F minor Sonata*, but there is a studied, self-conscious quality about Yevgeni Kissin's playing that is a little disturbing. There is little spontaneity of feeling and not everyone will respond. It is undoubtedly very impressive in its way, but in the sonata readers will be better served by Stephen Hough (Hyperion CDA 67237).

Variations on a Theme of Schumann (trans. for 2 hands by Theodor Kirchner)

** Athene ATHCD 23. Boyde – SCHUMANN: *Impromptus; Variations.* **

Brahms published his variations on the so-called Schumann *Geister variations* for piano duet as Op. 23, and his friend, the composer Theodor Kirchner, transcribed it for solo piano. It comes as the makeweight for an intelligently planned Schumann recital by the German pianist Andreas Boyde. The playing is very convincing but the recording somewhat too close and shallow.

ORGAN MUSIC

11 Chorale Preludes, Op. 122; Chorale Prelude & Fugue on 'O Traurigkeit, O Herzeleid'; Fugue in A flat min.; Preludes & Fugues: in A min.; G min.

(M) ** Simax PSC 1137. Nordstoga (organ of Oslo Cathedral).

As Kåre Nordstoga demonstrates in his flamboyant account of the opening *Prelude in G minor*, the organ at Oslo Cathedral is a magnificent instrument. It is ideal for this repertoire, colourfully resonant yet allowing detail to register clearly, which is especially telling in the *Chorale Preludes*. But, alas, after that brilliant opening, Nordstoga becomes more didactic and favours very steady tempi, especially in the *Fugues*.

VOCAL MUSIC

(i) Alto Rhapsody. Academic Festival Overture.

(M) *** EMI (ADD) 5 62791-2. J. Baker, Alldis Ch., LPO, Boult – SCHUBERT: *Symphony No. 9.* ***

Dame Janet Baker's devoted (1970) recording of the *Alto Rhapsody* with Boult was originally coupled with the *Second Symphony*. Now it comes equally attractively paired with Schubert. The Brahms remains meditative, even though the tempo is unlingering and the manner totally unindulgent. The warm Abbey Road recording is transferred very successfully to CD.

Ave Maria, Op. 12; Nänie, Op. 82; Schicksalslied, Op. 54; (i) Triumphlied, Op. 55.

*** Chan. 10165. Danish Nat. Ch. & SO, Albrecht; (i) with Skovhus.

It is fascinating to find Brahms banging the patriotic drum in his *Triumphlied*, written to celebrate the Prussian victory over the French in 1870 and the establishment of the German empire. Sadly, though the writing is masterly, this three-movement cantata has been neglected over the years, partly for political reasons (though the text is hardly jingoistic, being taken from the Book of Revelations) and partly for the great difficulty for the singers of a piece for eight-part chorus. Albrecht's performance with the Danish National Choir and Orchestra may be less polished than Sinopoli's DG version, but it is markedly warmer and more idiomatic, well coupled with a devotional reading of *Schicksalslied, Song of Destiny* (with a Hölderlin text) and the valedictory *Nänie*. The rare setting of *Ave Maria* for women's voices, an early work, makes a charming supplement.

Lieder: *Auf dem Kirchhofe; Botschaft; Feldeinsamkeit; Minnelied III; Heimweh II (O wüsst ich doch den Weg zurück); Sapphische Ode; Sonntag; Ständchen; Verrat; Wie bist du, Meine Königen; Wie melodien zieht es mir. Wir wandelten; Vier ernste Gesange, Op. 121.*

⊕ ✪(M) (***) EMI mono 6 62807-2. Hotter, Moore – BACH: *Cantata No. 82: Ich habe genug.* (***) ✪

Glorious singing from Hans Hotter, wonderfully accompanied by Gerald Moore. A splendid transfer of the 1950 recordings – an indispensable coupling, with two extra songs included that were not on the old Références CD.

Lieder: *Dein blaues Auge hält; Dort in den Weiden; Immer leiser wird mein Schlummer; Klage I & II; Liebestreu; Des Liebsten Schwur; Das Mädchen; Das Mädchen spricht; Regenlied; Romanzen und Lieder, Op. 84; Salome; Sapphische Ode, Op. 94/4; Der Schmied; (i) 2 Songs with viola, Op. 91; Therese; Vom Strande; Wie Melodien zieht es; Zigeunerlieder, Op. 103.*

(M) *** DG 474 856-2. Norman, Barenboim; (i) with Christ.

Winner of the *Gramophone* Solo Vocal Award in 1983, this delightful and strongly contrasted selection from DG's Lieder Box in the Brahms Edition shows Jessye Norman at her finest. For the CD equivalent of an earlier digital LP, the two *Songs with viola* have been added to make a highlight of the new recital. The task of recording a complete set of women's songs seems in this instance to have added to the warmth and sense of spontaneity of both singer and pianist in the studio, while Wolfram Christ makes a distinguished contribution to Op. 91. The heroic scale of *Der Schmied* is superb, as is the open simplicity of *Zigeunerlieder*, while the gentler songs find the gloriously ample voice exquisitely scaled down. The recording is wonderfully vivid, giving the artists a tangible presence. An outstanding reissue.

Deutsche Volkslieder (42 German Folksong Settings).

(B) **★★★** EMI Gemini (ADD) 5 85502-2 (2). Schwarzkopf, Fischer-Dieskau, Moore.

In Brahms's simple folk-settings no singers in the world can match Schwarzkopf and Fischer-Dieskau in their musical imagination and depth of under-standing. Gerald Moore as ever is the ideal accompa-nist, and the recording quality is natural and vivid, with some enchanting conversation pieces between the soloists. However, no translations are included and no attempt is made to explain the meaning of each song.

German Requiem, Op. 45.

(M) (**★★★**) EMI mono 5 62811-2. Schwarzkopf, Hotter, V. Singeverein, BPO, Karajan.

(M) **★★** Warner Elatus 2564 60434-2. J. Williams, Hampson, Chicago Ch. & SO, Barenboim.

Recorded in October 1947 and issued on ten short-playing 78rpm discs, Karajan's mono version of the *German Requiem* was – surprisingly – the first ever complete recording of this work, and it is fully worthy of inclusion among EMI's 'Great Artists of the Century' series. It was also something of a breakthrough in Karajan's early career. It is in part a tribute to his unique collaboration with Walter Legge, not only that this is a performance – which has been rarely matched since on record, incandes-cent and intense – but that even now the sound has such vivid presence. There is inevitably some surface noise, but nothing too distracting, and the bright-ness and fullness of the sound are astonishing. The chorus is in superb, incisive form, and the two soloists are both at their peak, the young Schwarz-kopf fresh-toned and Hotter far firmer than he later became.

Barenboim's Elatus version from Chicago cannot match his earlier (deleted) recording for DG in intensity. Exceptionally slow speeds make the first two movements sound dull and lacking in bite and tension, not helped by the rather distant balance for the excellent chorus. Thomas Hampson is a splendid baritone soloist, but the warm-toned soprano, Janet Williams, does not sound quite secure. First choice on CD for the *German Requiem* remains with Gar-diner (⊕→ ● Ph. 432 140-2) but there is also a splendid DVD directed by Abbado (TDK DV-MUSIK).

(i) *Vier ernste Gesang (4 Serious Songs), Op. 121;* (ii) *2 Songs with viola, Op. 91.*

(BB) (**★★★**) Regis mono RRC 1153. Ferrier, (i; ii) Spurr, Gilbert – MAHLER: *Kindertotenlieder etc.* (**★★★**) ●

This vintage Kathleen Ferrier record brings together a group of the great contralto's early Decca Brahms recordings from 1949–50, showing the richness of the voice and her natural expressive involvement. These recordings are also available elsewhere, notably in Decca's various Ferrier groupings, but these Regis transfers are appealingly smooth and natural, and the recording is inexpensive.

BREIMER, Peter (20th century)

Songs and Dances of the Silk Road.

(BB) **★★★** Naxos SACD 611082; CD 8.557348. Nishizaki, New Zealand SO, Judd – CHEN GANG: *Butterfly Lovers' Concerto.* **★★★**

The *Songs and Dances of the Silk Road* by the Slovak composer, Peter Breimer, are an obvious coupling for the more famous *Butterfly Lovers' Concerto*, also based on traditional Chinese melodies. There are nine movements, all titles. The first, *A Beloved Rose*, is very seductive, and Nishizaki plays it delightfully; the second, *Half Moon Climbs*, is rather like a film theme. The others are all colourfully inventive, and one of the most attractive is the fifth movement, *Sa li Hong ba*, which opens with a romantic horn solo but is turned into a charming and jaunty dance, led by the soloist. The sixth, *Lan hua hua*, brings a melancholy flute solo, much in the style of *Butterfly Lovers*, and that is no coincidence, as the original folksong tells a similar story of a young girl forced to marry against her wishes. The boldly rhythmic No. 8 is less oriental, including bongo drums, and the final dance begins with a rhythm that would not be out of place in the music of Spain. The perform-ances are excellent, with Nishizaki on top form. James Judd and the New Zealand Symphony Orchestra enjoy their oriental excursion and play spiritedly: their principal flute shows a natural feel-ing for the sinuous Chinese melodies, and the recording is first class.

BRIAN, Havergal (1876–1972)

Symphony No. 1 (Gothic).

(BB) **★★★** Naxos 8.557418/9. Jenisová, Pecková, Dolžal, Mikuláš, Slovak Op. Ch., Slovak Folk Ens. Ch., Lúčnica Ch., Bratislava City Ch. & Children's Ch., Youth Echo Ch., Slovak RSO & PO & Ch., Lénard.

The first of the Havergal Brian symphonies here receives a passionately committed performance from Slovak forces. Despite a few incidental flaws, it conveys surging excitement from first to last, helped by a rich recording, which gives a thrilling impres-sion of massed forces. The final *Te Deum*, alone lasting 72 minutes, brings fervent choral writing of formidable complexity, with the challenge taken up superbly by the Czech musicians. Originally on Marco Polo, this is now a very real bargain in its Naxos reissue.

BRICCIALDI, Giulio (1818–81)

Wind Quintet in D, Op. 124.

(BB) ★★★ Naxos 8.553410. Avalon Wind Quintet –
  CAMBINI: *Wind Quintets Nos. 1–3.* ★★★

Giulio Briccialdi was an Italian flautist of considerable fame during his lifetime. His *Wind Quintet in D
major* is carefree, empty, lightweight – and utterly
charming. It is played expertly by these young German musicians, and the recording is as delightfully
natural as the playing. Well worth its three stars.

BRIDGE, Frank (1879–1941)

*Berceuse; Canzonetta; Rosemary; Suite for Strings;
There is a willow grows aslant a brook; Serenade;
The Two Hunchbacks: Intermezzi. Threads: Andante
and Waltz.*

(BB) ★★★ BMG/RCA 74321 98708-2 (2). Britten Sinf.,
  Cleobury – DELIUS: *Violin Sonatas 1–3* etc. ★★★ ✪

This delightful collection – originally issued on
Conifer – has much in common with similar compilations of the lighter miniatures of Elgar. The beautiful *Suite for Strings* and the inspired Butterworth-like
There is a willow grows aslant a brook are masterpieces, but the vignettes are charming, notably the
Intermezzi from incidental music for a children's
play, *The Two Hunchbacks*, and the gentle *Andante*
and winning little *Waltz* from another play called
Threads. The playing is warmly sympathetic and
polished, and beautifully recorded. The new coupling
is unexpected but welcome.

String Quartet No. 4.

★★★ Redcliffe RR 020. Bochmann Qt (with PURCELL:
  Chacony in G min., ed. Britten ★★★) – BUSH: *Suite
  of Six.* ★★

Frank Bridge's *Fourth Quartet* was written in 1937,
immediately after he had recovered from a very
serious illness, and its atmosphere and character are
undoubtedly influenced by the composer's life-
threatening experience. Yet the Quartet has an almost
Haydnesque classical layout, with the first movement
conceived in sonata form, the second a frail yet
haunting Minuet of contrasting rhythmic simplicity,
and the third combining a brief, deeply felt *Adagio*
and a more unsettled, rondo-like allegro.

  If the jagged opening bleakly presents the basic
musical substance in eleven atonal semitones, the
secondary theme is lyrical and reflective. Both outer
movements are searchingly argued, their harmonic
language uncompromising. Yet there is an overall
tonal core, which gathers influence towards the
work's close, and the music ends positively, as if the
composer had come to terms with his mortality. The
glorious Purcell *Chacony*, in Britten's rich-textured
arrangement, comes as a final encore, presented with
great expressive warmth and dignity; indeed the per-

formances throughout are very fine, while the
recording is of high quality and most realistically
balanced.

BRITTEN, Benjamin (1913–76)

The Building of the House Overture.

(M) ★★★ BBC Legends BBCL 4140-2. New Philh. Ch.
  and O, Giulini – SCHUBERT: *Symphony No. 9*;
  WEBER: *Der Freischütz: Overture.* ★★★

When Giulini made this live recording at the Royal
Festival in January 1968, Britten's overture, written
for the opening of the Snape Maltings, was barely six
months old. It is a dramatic rather than a polished
reading, with the New Philharmonia Chorus brought
in to sing the passages from Psalm 127 that distinguish this energetic but relatively lightweight piece.
An unexpected and valuable addition to Giulini's
discography on this disc, issued to celebrate the
conductor's ninetieth birthday.

Violin Concerto.

★★★ Warner 2564 60291-2. Hope, BBC SO, Watkins –
  BERG: *Violin Concerto.* ★★★

As in the Berg *Concerto*, with which his account of
the Britten is coupled, Daniel Hope sustains broad
speeds in the spacious outer movements, conveying
passionate intensity without expressive exaggeration.
The slow passacaglia of the finale is particularly
moving, from Hope's ethereal first entry to the inner
meditation of the closing pages, while fast music
finds him playing with sharp clarity of articulation.
The cellist Paul Watkins demonstrates his formidable
powers as a conductor, drawing comparably warm,
sympathetic playing from the BBC Symphony
Orchestra, fully and brilliantly recorded.

*(i) Violin Concerto in D min., Op. 15; (ii) Serenade
for Tenor, Horn and Strings, Op. 31.*

(B) ★★ EMI 5 75978-2. (i) Friend, (ii) Partridge, Busch;
  LPO, Pritchard – TIPPETT: *Concerto for Double
  String Orchestra.* ★★

Rodney Friend is an intelligent and thoughtful soloist, but Ian Partridge's account of the *Serenade* suffers
from a reticent balance. The strings are similarly
wanting in presence, and the horn looms too large in
the aural picture.

*Sinfonia da Requiem; Peter Grimes: 4 Sea Interludes
& Passacaglia.*

✪ (M) ★★★ EMI 5 62615-2 [5 62616-2]. LSO, Previn –
  HOLST: *Egdon Heath* etc. ★★★

Previn gives a passionately intense reading of the
Sinfonia da Requiem, the most ambitious of Britten's
early orchestral works, written after the death of his
parents. It is warmer than the composer's own, less
sharply incisive but presenting a valid alternative. So
too in the *Four Sea Interludes*, with Previn springing
the bouncing rhythms of the second interlude – the

picture of *Sunday Morning in the Borough* – even more infectiously than the composer himself. These superb performances are presented in expansive 1970s recordings of demonstration quality. With its new Holst coupling, this is one of Previn's finest CDs, fully worthy of inclusion among EMI's 'Great Recordings of the Century'.

Young Person's Guide to the Orchestra (Variations & Fugue on a Theme of Purcell), Op. 34.
(M) **(*) Virgin 5 61782-2. RLPO, Pešek –
PROKOFIEV: *Peter and the Wolf* (***);
SAINT-SAENS: *Carnival of the Animals* (chamber version). ***

Libor Pešek and the Royal Liverpool Philharmonic Orchestra give a detailed and brilliantly played account of Britten's *Young Person's Guide to the Orchestra*. Tension is comparatively relaxed, but the closing fugue is lively and boldly etched.

CHAMBER MUSIC

(i) *6 Metamorphoses after Ovid;* (i; ii) *Phantasy Quartet* (for oboe, violin, viola & cello), *Op. 2;* (i; iii) *2 Insect Pieces; Temporal Variations;* (iii) *Holiday Diary, Op. 5; Night Piece; 5 Waltzes.*
(BB) *** Hyp. Helios CDH 55154. (i) Francis; (ii) Delmé Qt (members); (iii) Dussek.

Sarah Francis has long had a special association with Britten's oboe music, studying the *Ovid* pieces with the composer himself. She gives strong and distinctive characterizations not only to those six unaccompanied pieces but also to the early *Phantasy Quartet* and to the pieces for oboe and piano as well. Michael Dussek proves a magnetic interpreter of the solo piano music, bringing out the sparkle of the boyhood waltzes (or 'Walztes' as Britten originally called them) and the *Holiday Diary*. He then finds intense poetry and magic in the *Night Piece*, written for the first Leeds Piano Competition, with deliberately awkward keyboard layout.

VOCAL MUSIC

Folksong arrangements: *The ash grove; Avenging and bright; La Belle est au jardin d'amour; The bonny Earl o' Moray; The brisk young widow; Ca' the yowes; Come you not from Newcastle?; Early one morning; The foggy, foggy dew; How sweet the answer; The last rose of summer; The Lincolnshire poacher; The miller of Dee; The minstrel boy; Oft in the stilly night; O Waly, Waly; The plough boy; Le Roi s'en va-t'en chasse; Sally in our alley; Sweet Polly Oliver; Tom Bowling.*
(M) *** Decca 476 1976-2. Pears, Britten.

It is good to have the definitive Pears–Britten collaboration in the folksong arrangements. Excellent, faithful recording, well transferred to CD.

(i) *A Ceremony of Carols; Festival Te Deum; Hymn to St Cecilia;* (ii) *Jubilate Deo;* (i) *Missa brevis in D;* (ii) *Rejoice in the Lamb* (Festival Cantata); *Te Deum in C.*
(M) *** EMI (ADD) 5 62796-2. Soloists, King's College, Cambridge, Ch., (i) Willcocks; (ii) Ledger.

A worthy inclusion in EMI's 'Great Artists of the Century' series. The King's trebles may have less edge in the *Ceremony of Carols* than their Cambridge rivals at St John's College, and the *Missa brevis* can certainly benefit from a throatier sound, but the results here are dramatic as well as beautiful. Philip Ledger's 1974 version of the cantata *Rejoice in the Lamb* has timpani and percussion added to the original organ part. Here the biting climaxes are sung with passionate incisiveness, while James Bowman is in his element in the delightful passage which tells you that 'the mouse is a creature of great personal valour'. The *Te Deum* setting and *Jubilate* make an extra bonus and are no less well sung and recorded.

(i) *A Ceremony of Carols; Hymn to St Cecilia; Hymn to St Peter; Hymn to the Virgin; Te Deum in C.*
(BB) *** ASV Resonance CD RSN 3007. Christ Church Cathedral Ch., Grier; (i) with Kelly.

On ASV Christ Church Cathedral Choir gives attractively vigorous performances, full of the right sort of rhythmic energy for these strongly characterful choral works. There is an earthy quality that reflects the composer's own rejection of over-refined choirboy tone, but the *Hymn to St Cecilia* with its setting of a brilliant Auden poem is a degree too rough, and it loses some impact when the choir is rather backwardly balanced.

(i) *4 Chansons françaises; Les Illuminations;* (ii) *Serenade for Tenor, Horn & Strings.*
(M) **(*) Chan. 10192X. (i) Lott; (ii) Rolfe Johnson, Thompson; RSNO, Thomson.

Felicity Lott gives a strong and sensitive performance of the four *French Songs*, as she does of the other early French cycle on the disc, *Les Illuminations*, bringing out the tough and biting element rather than the sensuousness. Anthony Rolfe Johnson, soloist in the *Serenade*, gives a finely controlled performance, but Michael Thompson is not as evocative in the horn solo as his most distinguished predecessors. Bryden Thomson draws crisp, responsive playing from the SNO, and this is the more attractive at mid-price.

The Holy Sonnets of John Donne, Op. 35; 7 Sonnets of Michelangelo, Op. 22; Winter Words, Op. 52; The Children and Sir Nameless; If it's ever Spring again.
(BB) *** Naxos 8.557201. Langridge, Bedford.

On these reissued 1995/6 recordings, originally available on the Collins label, Philip Langridge gives intense and dramatic performances of the three most important Britten song-cycles with piano, originally written with Peter Pears in mind. With Steuart Bedford, Britten's long-term collaborator, as accompanist, this reading of the Donne sonnet-cycle is marked by high contrasts of dynamic and tone, so that one hears echoes of Peter Grimes's music. In the other two cycles Langridge is just as expressive but is generally lighter in manner, certainly more than Pears in his recordings. Valuably, Langridge adds two more Hardy settings, originally intended for *Winter Words* but that neither fit the main pattern nor quite match the rest in imagination.

St Nicholas, Op. 42.

(M) (***) Decca mono 475 6156. Hemmings, Pears, St John Lehman School, Beccles, Girls' Ch., Ipswich Boys' Ch., Aldeburgh Festival Ch. & O, composer.

With rare exceptions Britten's first recordings of his own works have a freshness amd vigour unsurpassed since. Here is a fine example, which vividly draws on the brightness of boys' voices, not least that of David Hemmings as the youthful *St Nicholas*. The expression may be direct but the emotions behind this work are more complex than one may at first appreciate, and Britten's performance admirably catches the element of vulnerability. The 1955 mono recording still sounds well, but the previous incarnation of this performance (also at mid-price) included also a fine account of *Rejoice in the Lamb* from the same source.

War Requiem, Op. 66.

** Teldec 0630 17115-2 (2). Vaness, Hadley, Hampson, American Boychoir, Westminster Symphonic Ch., NY Philh. O, Masur.

It is always revealing to have non-British performances of British music, and Kurt Masur directs a thoughtful, dedicated reading of the *War Requiem* with three first-rate American soloists. The virtuoso chamber group accompanying the Owen poems is made up of excellent players from the New York Philharmonic, and the choirs cannot be faulted, with the off-stage boys precisely placed. That said, this does not have the dramatic intensity of the finest versions, and the soloists are not helped by a relatively dry acoustic. With no fill-up it makes an expensive purchase compared with the fine Hickox Chandos set (Chan. 8986/4).

OPERA

Billy Budd (original four-act version; complete).

*** Arthaus DVD 100278. Allen, Langridge, Van Allan, Howlett, ENO Ch. & O, Atherton (Director: Albery; V/D: Gavin).

(**) VAIA mono 1034-3 (3). Pears, Uppman, Dalberg, Alan, G. Evans, Langdon, ROHCG Ch. & O, composer.

Tim Albery's production of *Billy Budd* with Thomas Allen powerful in the title-role was one of the classic English National Opera presentations of the 1980s.

This 1988 video version, made originally for BBC Television, with an introduction by Michael Berkeley, vividly captures the intense atmosphere. It is helped by the bare, stylized sets of Tom Cairns and Antony McDonald and by David Cunningham's clever lighting; they have one imagining the scenes with a chilling intensity that a more realistic approach could hardly match. The performance under David Atherton is outstanding, with Philip Langridge as Captain Vere, disguised as E. M. Forster in the solo prologue and epilogue sequences, bringing out the character's scholarly side, interpreting the role in a strikingly different way from Peter Pears, for whom it was written, but just as magnetically. Thomas Allen may in 1988 have seemed rather old for the role of the innocent Billy, but the power not just of his singing but of his acting too, with the voice clear and fresh, makes his performance deeply moving. Just as striking is the venomous figure of Claggart, superbly taken here with terrifying intensity by Richard Van Allan in one of his very finest recorded performances. Barrie Gavin's direction for video adds to the power of the performance with imaginative camera-work. The DVD is provided with plentiful index-points.

Though the sound is very scrubby, disconcertingly so at the very start, the historic recording of the very first performance of the opera in December 1951 is valuable for the fresh, youthful-sounding performance of Theodor Uppman in the title-role, as well as Peter Pears as Captain Vere, clearer and more flexible than in his studio recording of 16 years later. There is no libretto. It is interesting that, though the orchestra sounds dim and limp at the start, Britten as conductor whips up searing tension through the opera.

Owen Wingrave; The Hidden Heart.

*** Arthaus DVD 100 372. Finley, Hellekant, Hill, Savidge, Barstow, Dawson, Gale, Marlton, Westminster Cathedral Ch., Deutches SO, Berlin, Nagano (DVD Dir.: Margaret Williams).

After its first presentation on television, *Owen Wingrave* has been staged regularly, but it works best on the small screen, as this television production, originally made for Channel 4 in Britain, demonstrates. It presents the piece evocatively and convincingly in a setting updated to 1958, with khaki battledress for the soldiers. Surprisingly, it makes Owen's dilemma more convincing than the original over his pacifism and refusal to complete his military studies, with Gerald Finley singing and acting superbly. The unsympathetic fiancée, Kate, also seems a more complex character than before, well taken by Charlotte Hellekant, and the gallery of disagreeable family-members is strongly cast too, notably Martyn Hill as the old, unforgiving Sir Philip Wingrave and Josephine Barstow as Miss Wingrave. Peter Savidge sings well in the role of the tutor, Spencer Coyle, the lone voice of sanity, with Anne Dawson as Mrs Coyle and Hilton Marlton as the wimpish Lechmere. Set mainly in the Wingrave country house, the result is nicely evocative, with the misty ghost scenes sufficiently creepy. With the orchestral score evidently recorded separately by the Deutsches Symphony Orchestra of Berlin under Kent Nagano, the musical results are still well co-ordinated.

What makes this issue especially valuable is that it also contains as an extra the moving film, *The Hidden Heart*, made for Channel 4 by Teresa Griffiths. Subtitled 'A Love Story in Three Pieces', this hour-long film gives a striking portrait of Benjamin Britten from the 1930s onwards, centring on his lifelong love for the tenor, Peter Pears. The discussion of Britten's homosexuality is treated intelligently and sympathetically, with the film's three sections built round three key works, *Peter Grimes* of 1945, the *War Requiem* of 1962 and *Death in Venice* of 1973, his last opera, which, as John Evans of BBC Radio 3 suggests, was the most autobiographical of his works. It consistently comes out that Britten and Pears were in many ways deeply conventional figures, 'like two pre-school masters' as the counter-tenor James Bowman says, with Britten even described as 'straight-laced'. Many of Britten's closest friends and associates give their views, and the film is well illustrated with period clips, not least of Peter Pears singing.

Paul Bunyan (complete).

⊛ (M) *** EMI 5 85139-2 (2). Lawless (spoken part), Dressen, Comeaux, Nelson, Soloists, Ch. & O of Plymouth Music Series, Minnesota, Brunelle.

Aptly, this first recording of Britten's choral operetta comes from the state, Minnesota, where the story is set. When the principal character is a giant who can appear only as a disembodied voice, the piece works rather better on record or radio than on stage. Musically, Britten's conscious assumption of popular American mannerisms does not prevent his invention from showing characteristic originality. Well cast and recorded in clean, vivid sound, with Philip Brunelle a vigorous conductor, this excellent first recording deserves all the prizes it won in its original issue on Virgin Classics.

The Turn of the Screw (complete).

(BB) *** Naxos 8.660109/10. Langridge, Lott, Pay, Hulse, Cannan, Secunde, Aldeburgh Festival Ens., Bedford.

Steuart Bedford's vividly recorded, warmly atmospheric version of *The Turn of the Screw* (originally issued on the Collins label) could not be more welcome in this super-bargain Naxos reissue. Bedford, who took over from Britten himself when the composer could no longer conduct his own recordings, here presents a similarly idiomatic performance with a comparable sharpness and magnetism that, thanks to the spacious recording, brings out the eerie atmosphere of the piece, the quality which originally attracted the young Britten to Henry James's ghost story. The recording also allows one to appreciate the

sharp originality of the instrumentation in what by any standards is the tautest of Britten's operas. The singers too have been chosen to follow the pattern set by the original performers. Langridge here, like Pears before him, takes the double role of narrator and Peter Quint, echoing Pears's inflexions, but putting his own stamp on the characterization. Felicity Lott is both powerful and vulnerable as the Governess, rising superbly to the big climaxes which, thanks to the recording quality, have a chilling impact, not least at the very end. Sam Pay is a fresh-voiced Miles, less knowing than David Hemmings in the Britten set, with Eileen Hulse bright and girlish as Flora. Nadine Secunde is a strong Miss Jessel, and Phyllis Cannan matches up to the strength of her predecessor, Joan Cross. An outstanding set, with the Aldeburgh Festival Ensemble including such fine artists as Jennifer Stinton on the flute, Nicholas Daniel on the oboe, Richard Watkins on the horn and the Brindisi String Quartet.

BROSSARD, Sébastien de
(1655–1730)

Elevations et motets (for 1, 2, or 3 voices): *Festis laeta sonent; O Domine quia refugium; Oratorio seu Dialogus poenitentis animae cum Deo; Psallite superi; Qui non diliget te; Salve Rex Christe; Templa nunc fumet.*

(B) **(*) Opus 111 OP 10002. Rime, Fouchécourt, Honeyman, Delétré, Parlement de Musique, Gester.

Sébastien de Brossard came from Normandy to take a position as Chapel Master at Strasbourg Cathedral. These motets are mainly dialogue cantatas. *O Domine quia refugium* is a fine example, although the expressive and touching *Qui non diliget te* (for which the composer wrote the text) is a solo work, and very beautifully sung by Noémi Rime. The *Dialogue of the repentant soul with God* is shared by soprano and tenor: it is not especially dramatic, but the pace quickens as forgiveness is given. The final work, *Festis laeta sonent cantibus organa* ('May the organ ring out with solemn songs'), is very well sung by the tenor Jean-Paul Fouchécourt; but Brossard's weakness lies in the lack of a more robust spirit to many of these interchanges – surprising from a musician who was an advocate of the introduction of Italian styles into French music. Excellent recording and full texts.

BRUCH, Max (1838–1920)

Violin Concerto No. 1 in G min., Op. 26.

*** Sony SK 67740. Midori, BPO, Jansons –
MENDELSSOHN: *Violin Concerto.* ***

(BB) (***) Naxos mono 8.110977. Milstein, Philharmonic-Symphony O, New York, Barbirolli –
MENDELSSOHN; TCHAIKOVSKY: *Violin Concerto.*
(***)

(BB) ★★ RCA 82876 55268-2. Zukerman, LAPO, Mehta
– BRAHMS: *Concerto.* ★★

It is a tribute to Midori that she can tackle this traditional, much-duplicated coupling with such individuality, particularly when in live recordings her inspired partners are the Berlin Philharmonic under Mariss Jansons. Her first entry in the Bruch is musingly reflective, with the recording heightening contrasts between soloist and orchestra, even though the violin is placed relatively close. The panache of her performance of the first movement is followed by a rapt account of the second. The finale again benefits from bold orchestral playing, with high contrasts setting off the sparkle of the soloist. Here we have a disc that – in the face of formidable competition – remains a clear winner.

Milstein recorded the Bruch Concerto three times; this, his first, made in New York in 1942, sounds remarkably spontaneous and rich-toned. At this time American Columbia were beginning to record on to 33⅓rpm lacquer master discs, after which the approved takes were dubbed on to wax 78rpm discs. Although the resultant 78s were not as impressive as direct-to-wax discs, when they were transferred to LP in the early 1950s there was a much wider frequency range as well as quieter surfaces. The recordings sound as good as 1950s early tape masters. Many critics see the present account as Milstein's finest version of the Bruch: it is certainly exhilarating and wonderfully fresh.

As with the Brahms, with which Zukerman's RCA version is coupled, the violin is placed more naturally than in his earlier, Sony version, also with Mehta conducting. As before, he takes an exceptionally expansive view of all three movements. The big gain in the new version lies in the hushed inner intensity of the reading, helped by the recording balance, and the clarity of articulation in the finale means that he is no less biting. However, this coupling is not a top recommendation, even at budget price.

Violin Concerto No. 2; Scottish Fantasy, Op. 46.
(M) ★★★ EMI (ADD) 5 62589-2. Perlman, New Philh.
O, Lopez-Cobos.

EMI have chosen Perlman's more intimately reflective 1976 New Philharmonia coupling for reissue in the 'Perlman Edition'. His superlative playing invests the first movement of the *Second Violin Concerto* with such warmth that it compares favourably with the more famous, G minor work. In his hands, both the main themes are given a soaring memorability and the coda is exquisitely managed. If the rest of the work has a lower level of inspiration, it is still richly enjoyable, and Perlman's account of the *Scottish Fantasia* is wholly delectable, showing the same degree of stylish lyricism and eloquence of phrasing. The EMI analogue recording is fully worthy of the performances and is well transferred to CD.

BRUCKNER, Anton (1824–96)

Symphonies Nos. 0; 1–9; Overture in G min.
(BB) ★★(★) Decca 475 331-2. Berlin RSO or Concg. O; Chailly.

Chailly's generally impressive Bruckner cycle, recorded over a considerable period from 1985 to 2002, is now available in a bargain box for the first time. While there are reservations about individual discs, there is only one relative failure (No. 1), and overall this is an impressive achievement.

The account of the unnumbered *D minor* (the so-called *Die Nullte*) is more than acceptable; the Berlin Radio Symphony Orchestra respond well to Chailly's direction, and the recording is excellent. The *Overture in G minor* makes a welcome bonus.

Chailly then opts for the 1890/91 version for the *First Symphony*, again using the Berlin RSO. Unusually in this series, the sound has something of the cool transparency of the studio rather than the rich ambience of a cathedral acoustic – though it was in fact recorded in the Jesus-Christuskirche. Impressive sonically, it is wanting in both mystery and spirituality. The textures are well ventilated but do not really glow; it is all very neat and tidy, and very well played, but ultimately one is never drawn into the musical experience.

For the *Second Symphony*, Chailly used the complete Haas Edition. It is a beautifully simple reading, with the slow-movement climax nobly graduated, a strong Scherzo without repeats (the Trio has tuneful charm) and a finale that is not pressed forward ruthlessly but that generates a positive and exciting closing section. The Decca recording is appropriately spacious and luminous.

Vividly recorded and beautifully played, the *Third Symphony* (Berlin RSO), using the 1889 score, has admirable qualities but, by the standards of the finest Bruckner recordings, Chailly's is undercharacterized. This is a broad, spacious view of the work, not unlike Karajan's; but Karajan himself consistently demonstrates his natural mastery in a reading that glows the more intensely, the more spontaneously.

In the *Fourth Symphony*, Chailly has two things in his favour: the incomparable Concertgebouw Orchestra at their most resplendent, and a Decca recording of magnificent opulence. The results are very enjoyable and the reading is far from unimpressive. Perhaps Chailly does not match his greatest rivals in strength of personality, but this account has a great deal to commend it, especially to those who like sound of demonstration quality.

The *Fifth Symphony* receives an outstanding performance, one of the finest in the cycle. The Concertgebouw Orchestra play with sumptuous magnificence, and Chailly's overall control of a work that is noted for its episodic diversity is unerring, moving to an overwhelming final apotheosis. The *Adagio* is very beautiful and never sounds hurried.

The recording is superb, with the brass attacking brilliantly.

The *Sixth Symphony* is refined and powerful at spacious speeds, a performance that is warmly emotional without a trace of sentimentality. In the slow movement as in the first, the extreme *pianissimos* have breathtaking beauty. The pointing of the rhythms in the Scherzo has a Mendelssohnian lightness, and in the finale too, fantasy is set against Brucknerian power. The Concertegebouw Orchestra are on top form and the recording is of demonstration quality.

The *Seventh Symphony*, with the Berlin RSO, is a very fine performance, if perhaps not quite the best available, still excellent by any standards; and in the *Eighth Symphony* Chailly again reinforces his claims to be an outstanding Brucknerian in an incandescent reading, using the Nowak Edition. Despite the refinement of the Concertgebouw playing, the performance conveys an appropriate degree of ruggedness, with a wide dynamic range beautifully caught in the splendid Decca recording. The finale, not as bitingly urgent as it can be, in compensation conveys the composer's joyfully unruly inspiration. That Chailly used the Nowak Edition brings the benefit that, though his speeds are as spacious as you could wish for, the whole symphony is squeezed on to a single CD.

The reading of the *Ninth Symphony* is soberly dedicated, with the Concertgebouw playing superbly. If this spacious view of the finale lacks the concentration of the finest versions, it will be especially enjoyed by those who prefer a more objective approach. Excellent sound, if rather less full-bodied than some from this source.

Symphony No. oo in F min.; Overture in G min.

(M) *** Oehms OC 208. Saarbrücken RSO, Skrowaczewski.

Unlike most cycles of the Bruckner symphonies, Skrowaczewski's with the Saarbücken Orchestra includes this first attempt at writing a symphony, completed in 1863 when the composer was already in his late thirties. It is a fine performance, very well recorded, making an outstanding bargain. The inspiration is fresh and open with many echoes of Mendelssohn and Schumann, but already there are Bruckner fingerprints, notably in the hushed and tender slow movement and the Scherzo with its rugged contrasts. The *Overture in D minor* from the same period makes an ideal fill-up with its mysterious slow introduction leading to a light, Mendelssohnian Allegro. Now reissued on the Oehms label, this series is at mid rather than budget price.

Symphony No. 1 in C min.

(M) *** Oehms OC 210. Saarbrücken RSO, Skrowaczewski.

Skrowaczewski draws dedicated, tautly sprung playing from the Saarbrücken orchestra in what remains a problematic work. At speeds on the fast side, this is a fresh and urgent reading, which yet brings out the hushed intensity of the spacious second movement *Adagio*. Beautifully recorded in a helpful acoustic, it is a match for any version at whatever price.

Symphony No. 1 in C min.; (i) Helgoland.

(M) *(*) Warner Elatus 2564 60436-2. BPO, Barenboim; (i) with Berlin R. Ch., Ernest-Senff Ch.

Barenboim's Elatus version of the *Symphony No. 1* comes with a welcome fill-up in the symphonic chorus, *Helgoland*, but that is one of its few advantages. This is a warm, weighty reading, at times heavy-handed, which does not reveal the Berlin Philharmonic at its polished best. Moreover the recording is rather cloudy in tuttis.

Symphonies Nos. 1 in C min.; 2 in C min. (original versions).

(B) ** Teldec Ultima 0927 41399-2 (2). Frankfurt RSO, Inbal.

Bruckner's *First* is a rather intractable symphony. The composer's restless alternations of heavy tuttis, energetic passages more lightly scored and lyrical blossoming are knitted together less well than in his mature works. Inbal's direct, comparatively brisk approach – with the tempo changes in the first movement convincingly handled – makes quite a good case for the earlier (1866) Linz version, although the lack of opulence in the recording adds to the impression that the end result is lightweight.

In the Frankfurt performance of No. 2, Inbal offers a version that is comparatively close to the 1872 Haas Edition, which, like Tintner's Naxos recording (8.554006), retains the Scherzo and Trio with all repeats and uses the original horn, instead of the clarinet, at the end of the slow movement. The closing string chords are missing here, which brings one up with a start. For the most part the playing is good without being outstanding, and the recording is excellent. However, Tintner's account remains first choice for those seeking the composer's first thoughts.

Symphonies Nos. (i) 1 in C min. (Linz version); 9 in D min.; (ii) Te Deum.

(B) *** Ph. Duo (ADD/DDD) 473 886-2. (i) Concg. O; (ii) Mattila, Mentzer, Cole, Holl, Bav. R. Ch., VPO; Haitink.

This is one of the finest of the reissues from Haitink's analogue Concertgebouw series. The orchestra produces an opulent, deeply Brucknerian sound in the wind department as well as in the strings, and both performances have real stature, with a tremendous grip in the *Ninth* and a vision that penetrates its sense of tragedy and dramatic power as do few others. Even if Haitink misses some of Jochum's mystery and Walter's gentler poetry, his mighty reading still shows the dramatic force of the work. The *Te Deum* is also finely done and makes an added inducement to invest in this coupling.

Symphony No. 2 in C min.
(M) *(*) Warner Elatus 2564 60437-2. BPO,
Barenboim.

Barenboim's most recent version of the *Second Symphony*, recorded at concerts in the Philharmonie in 1997, is no more successful than the companion disc of the *First*. As in that symphony, he opts for the Nowak Edition and the playing is curiously routine and uninspired. The recording too is nothing to write home about.

Symphony No. 3 in D min.
(M) *** Oehms OC 212. Saarbrücken RSO,
Skrowaczewski.

Skrowaczewski offers a mid-priced version of the *Third*, which in both performance and recording rivals any more expensive version. Unlike Tintner he opts for the usual text, following Bruckner's final reworking in his third version of the work. As in Skrowaczewski's other Bruckner recordings now being reissued on the Oehms label, the playing of the Saarbrücken orchestra is strong and intense, with opulent sound to match. So the slow movement is sweet and warm in its lyrical flow, and the finale glows with resplendent brass.

Symphony No. 3 in D min. (1877 version).
(M) **(*) Warner Elatus 2564 60533-2. BPO,
Barenboim.

Barenboim uses the 1877 version of the score, gets impressive results and draws opulent sound from the Berlin Philharmonic, and the recorded sound does them justice. This has considerable passion and musical conviction, and the performance and recording would not disgrace any collector's library. However, it does not have the the same blend of natural eloquence and architectural strength as the Haitink digital Vienna version, nor is it quite as beautifully recorded. That comes with an equally outstanding version of the *Eighth Symphony* on a Philips Duo (470 534-2 – see our main volume).

Symphonies Nos. 3; 4 (Romantic) (original versions: 1873/4).
(B) **(*) Teldec Ultima 8573 87801-2 (2). Frankfurt
RSO, Inbal.

There are three versions of both the *Third* and *Fourth* symphonies. The 1873 version of No. 3 is by far the longest (the first movement alone here lasts 24 minutes). Now that Tintner has chosen it for his Naxos cycle, this pioneering version by Inbal is less important. But the Ultima reissue includes also the *Fourth*, and no one has recorded the 1874 original before. The Scherzo here is a completely different and very fiery movement, and the opening of the finale is also totally different. Inbal's performances are good, paying scrupulous attention to dynamic refinements, while the playing of the Frankfurt Radio Orchestra

shows a keen feeling for atmosphere. The recording is fully acceptable, though the climaxes in No. 4 almost (but not quite) reach congestion. A fascinating reissue, the more attractive with the two discs offered for the price of one.

Symphonies Nos. 3–9; (i) Mass No. 3 in F min.; (ii) Te Deum.
** EMI 5 56688-2 (12). (i) M. Price, Soffel, Straka, Hölle; (i; ii) Munich Philharmonic Ch.; (ii) Price, Borchers; Ahnsjö, Helm, Munich Bach Ch.; Munich PO, Celibidache.

Some good judges have been persuaded by Celibidache's sense of texture and his obvious dedication, but for others the eccentricities place an insurmountable obstacle between the composer and the listener. He manages to linger for more than 100 minutes over the *Eighth Symphony* as opposed to Jochum's or Karajan's 83, and he takes 20 minutes longer than Furtwängler. Likewise his *Ninth* lasts 68 minutes, whereas most interpreters take under the hour. These performances are difficult to grade: for Celibidache devotees they will doubtless rate three stars, since both the orchestral response and the recorded sound are not to be faulted; others, exasperated by his funereal tempi, may not wish to accord them any stars at all!

Symphony No. 4 in E flat (original, 1874 version).
(BB) **(*) Warner Apex 2564 61371-2. Frankfurt RSO, Inbal.

Like the *Third*, there are three versions of the *Romantic Symphony*, and no one had recorded the original version before Inbal. The Scherzo here is a completely different and more fiery movement, and the opening of the finale is also totally different. Inbal's performance is good, with a genuine feeling for the Bruckner idiom, paying scrupulous attention to dynamic refinements. The recording is well detailed, though the climaxes almost (but not quite) reach congestion. A fascinating issue, and especially attractive at budget price.

Symphony No. 4 in E flat (Romantic).
(M) *** Oehms OC 213. Saarbrücken RSO,
Skrowaczewski.
(M) **(*) EMI (ADD) 5 62815-2. Philh. O, Klemperer –
WAGNER: *Siegfried idyll.* ***
(M) ** Warner Elatus 2546 60663-2. BPO, Barenboim.
** Teldec 0630 17126-2. Concg. O, Harnoncourt.
(M) (**) Sup. mono SU 3467-2 001. Czech PO,
Konwitschny.

Skrowaczewski's reading of Bruckner's most popular symphony is characteristically strong and refined, with extreme dynamic contrasts heightened by the excellent recording, so that the crescendo at the start of the finale is exceptionally powerful. Only in the third movement Scherzo does he adopt a tempo at all out of the ordinary, challenging the horns in daringly fast hunting calls, which yet are finely disciplined.

Klemperer's 1965 performance with the Philharmonia is for those primarily seeking architectural strength. The reading is magisterial and the finale has impressive weight and strength. Alongside Jochum's flexible approach, Klemperer's view seems severe, even marmoreal. But there is no question as to its power or the vividness of the remastered EMI recording. It now comes with the bonus of the *Siegfried Idyll*, giving a playing time of 79 minutes.

Barenboim's account with the Berlin Philharmonic is his second reading of the work. This well-recorded version is decent rather than distinguished; it is difficult to find flaws, but at the same time it inspires little enthusiasm. The verdict here is: nothing special.

Harnoncourt's is a relatively objective view of Bruckner, rugged and purposeful, less emotional than most. Dynamic shading is precisely caught, and the Concertgebouw Orchestra plays with typical refinement, with recording to match. But there are many more compelling versions than this.

Konwitschny's reading (using the 1886 score) is above all warmly lyrical, even in the Scherzo (which rather lacks bite and effervescence). The kernel of his reading is the *Andante quasi allegretto*, which is more like an *Andante molto*. But the mono sound is full, and the concentration of the very fine orchestral playing holds the listener, even if the dynamic range is restricted and the brass tuttis are congested.

Symphonies Nos. 4 in E flat; 7 in E.

(B) ** Teldec Ultima 3984 21338-2 (2). NYPO, Masur.

Kurt Masur's New York account of No. 4, recorded live at the Avery Fisher Hall in 1993, has all the breadth and much of the finesse one could ask for. Those with keen memories of the Mehta years can be assured that the orchestra now produces a far more cultured and refined sound. Masur's command of the architecture of the piece is undoubtedly impressive and there is no want of feeling. The weakness lies perhaps in the slow movement, where concentration flags, certainly among the audience. The *Seventh* also comes from a live concert, but it dates from two years earlier, when Masur's relationship with the orchestra was in the bloom of youth and he was working hard to banish the unrefined sonority that was associated with his predecessor. The sound is certainly better blended than before. His opening is very spacious and expansive, with consequent accelerandi later on. The performance is generally more characterful than his Leipzig account and has quite a lot going for it – albeit not quite enough to overcome the unpleasing acoustic of the Avery Fisher Hall, hardly a Bruckner venue. Admirers of this conductor will find the present two-for-the-price-of-one set good value, and it is certainly preferable to its DG competitor; but Giulini is a much stronger recommendation for the *Seventh*, and at mid–price Jochum or Karajan more than hold their own for the *Fourth*.

Symphonies Nos. 4 in E flat (Romantic); 9 in D min.

⊛ (M) *** Sony (ADD) 515302-2 (2). Columbia SO, Walter.

Bruno Walter's recordings of Bruckner's *Fourth* and *Ninth Symphonies* represented the peak of his Indian summer of recordings for CBS in 1959 and 1960; and both sound splendid in this current paired reissue, with glorious strings and richly sonorous brass. Although not quite as impressive as the *Ninth*, the *Fourth* is still a memorable account. Walter makes his orchestra of Californian musicians sound remarkably European in style and timbre, and the superbly played 'hunting' Scherzo is wonderfully vivid. The reading is characteristically spacious. His special feeling for Bruckner meant that he could relax over long musical paragraphs and retain his control of the structure, while the playing has fine atmosphere and no want of mystery.

The *Ninth* is finer still. Walter's mellow, persuasive reading leads one on through the leisurely paragraphs so that the logic and coherence seem obvious where other performances can sound aimless. Perhaps the Scherzo is not vigorous enough to provide the fullest contrast – though the sound here has ample bite – yet it exactly fits the overall conception. The final slow movement has a nobility that makes one glad that Bruckner never completed the intended finale. After this, anything would have been an anticlimax.

Symphony No. 5 in B flat.

(M) ** Ph. (IMS) 464 693-2. Concg. O, Jochum.

Jochum's 1964 Concertgebouw account last appeared on Polygram's super-bargain Belart label. Now it is reissued at mid-price as a very doubtful candidate for inclusion among Philips's '50 Great Recordings'. Jochum's performance undoubtedly has the electricity of live music-making, but the acoustic of the recording is rather confined, with two-dimensional brass sonorities. It was made at a concert in Ottobeuren Abbey in Germany in 1964, yet the string timbre is curiously dry for an ecclesiastical ambience, and most listeners will want a more expansive sound in this work. Sinopoli remains first choice (DG 469527-5).

Symphonies Nos. 5 in B flat; 6 in A (original versions).

(B) *(*) Teldec Ultima 0927 41400-2 (2). Frankfurt RSO, Inbal.

Inbal makes a promising start to the *Fifth Symphony* and gets good playing from the Frankfurt Radio forces. Unfortunately the slow movement is far too brisk to be convincing – lasting 14 minutes as against Jochum's 19 and Karajan's 21. In the *Sixth Symphony* the slow movement is the best part of the performance, with fine string–playing, but the reading overall is a little short on personality. After the *Fifth*, the *Sixth* is probably the least well served of Inbal's cycle, although the recording is full-bodied and spacious and has a dramatically wide dynamic range. But for No. 5 one should turn to Sinopoli (❂ DG 469 527-2) and for No. 6 Chailly (Decca 458 189-2).

Symphony No. 6 in A.

(M) *** EMI (ADD) 5 62621-2 [5 62622-2]. New Philh. O, Klemperer (with Overtures: GLUCK: *Iphigénie en Aulide*; HUMPERDINCK: *Hänsel und Gretel* **).

(M) **(*) Oehms OC 215. Saarbrücken RSO, Skrowaczewski.

Klemperer's 1964 version has been reissued as one of EMI's 'Great Recordings of the Century'. It remains a characteristically strong and direct reading. It is disarmingly simple rather than overly expressive in the slow movement (faster than usual) but is always concentrated and strong, and the finale is held together particularly well. Splendid playing from the New Philharmonia Orchestra, and the Kingsway Hall recording is clear and bright, but even more full-bodied in the present remastering. The two overtures are earlier (1960) and feature the Philharmonia: *Hänsel und Gretel* is richly atmospheric, but the Gluck is heavy-going.

Stanislaw Skrowaczewski has proved himself an impressive Bruckner interpreter. This Arte Nova recording, made in the Saarbrücken Congress Hall in 1997, is very serviceable indeed and Skrowaczewski guides his forces with unerring purpose and nobility. Tempi are well judged throughout and phrases shaped with refinement. The string-tone needs perhaps to be weightier, but this is a very good performance, recommendable alongside Tintner on Naxos, whose account has slightly less gravitas but still has its own appealing individuality.

Symphony No. 7 in E (original version).

(BB) ** Warner Apex 0927 40817-2. Frankfurt RSO, Inbal.

For excellence of orchestral playing and vividness of recording, Inbal's *Seventh* is well up to the standard of his Bruckner series, using the original scores; but the performance itself, although not lacking an overall structural grip, is without the full flow of adrenalin that can make this symphony so compulsive. The great climax of the slow movement is much less telling without the famous contribution from the cymbals.

Symphony No. 7 in E.

(M) *** BBC (ADD) BBCL 4123-2. Philh. O, Giulini – FALLA: *Three-Cornered Hat* (excerpts); MUSSORGSKY: *Khovanshchina: Prelude*. ***

** EMI CMS5 56425-2. CBSO, Rattle.

Giulini's account of the *Seventh Symphony* with the Philharmonia Orchestra comes from the BBC's 1982 Prom season, a performance totally dedicated from beginning to end. Those who were there have not forgotten its breadth and nobility, nor the spirituality of its slow movement. This was the period when the Philharmonia was at its peak, and it is fascinating to

compare this live recording with the studio version that Giulini made for DG with the Vienna Philharmonic later in the 1980s. The Philharmonia playing is just as refined as that of the Viennese, not least the strings, while the live interpretation has an extra intensity and concentration, with speeds consistently faster and more flexible, so that climaxes are all the more thrilling. This ranks among the finest non-studio accounts of this great work, and the sound achieved by the BBC engineers, though not state of the art by the standards of 2004, is very fine indeed, natural in perspective and finely balanced. The Falla fill-up comes from an earlier Prom season (1963) and the *Khovanshchina Prelude* from an Edinburgh Festival concert at the Usher Hall. Strongly recommended.

Rattle's reading of No. 7 brings opulent sound from the Birmingham orchestra, with exceptionally spacious speeds well sustained and with subtle terracing of dynamics. Even so, this is not the most tensely dramatic of Rattle's recorded performances. Recommended to those who value Bruckner for his heavenly length.

Symphony No. 8 in C min. (ed. Haas).

❂ (M) *** DG 476 1654. VPO, Karajan.

(M) **(*) Chan. 7080 (2). LPO, Järvi – REGER: *Variations & Fugue on a Theme of Beethoven*. ***

** Teldec 8573 81037-2. BPO, Harnoncourt.

Karajan's last version of the *Eighth Symphony* is with the Vienna Philharmonic and is the most impressive of them all. The sheer beauty of sound and opulence of texture is awe-inspiring, while never drawing attention to itself; this is a performance in which beauty and truth go hand in hand. The recording is suprior to either of its predecessors in terms of naturalness of detail and depth of perspective. Understandably, Universal have picked it for reissue in their mid-priced 'Penguin ❂ Collection'.

Neeme Järvi's reading with the LPO is warmly spontaneous from first to last, helped by opulent Chandos sound in this 1986 recording. The thrust of argument is conveyed persuasively throughout, as in a live performance, thanks to Järvi's easy control of rubato, with weighty brass set against silky string-tone. The Scherzo is warm, with no hint of menace, and the slow movement cocoons one in a sensuous bath of sound, before the weighty finale, even if the result is not always quite as detailed as in the finest versions. At mid-price with the rare Reger fill-up it is still a good recommendation.

Symphony No. 9 in D min.

(M) ** OC 218. Saarbrucken SO, Skrowaczewski.

(M) (*(*)) Orfeo mono C548001B. Bav. SO, Schuricht.

Skrowaczewski with his Saarbrucken orchestra conducts a clean-cut, strongly structured reading, which yet fails to convey the sort of biting intensity that has marked his finest Bruckner readings with this orchestra. One gets too little feeling of dedication in this unfinished work dedicated to the Love of God. Speeds are unexceptionable and the playing generally refined, but even in the super-bargain category Tintner's Naxos version is far preferable.

Schuricht's Orfeo disc offers a live broadcast reading (in mono only) recorded in the Herkulessaal in Munich in 1963, yet there is too little of the tension one would expect of a live event, even if there are moments of frenetic accelerando, which suggest the inspiration of the moment. Schuricht is better remembered by his studio recordings.

VOCAL MUSIC

Masses Nos. (i) *2 in E min.;* (ii) *3 in F min.;* (iii) *5 Motets: Ave Maria; Christus factus est; Locus iste; Os justi; Virga Jesse;* (iii; iv) *Te Deum.*
(BB) ★★ EMI Gemini (ADD) 5 85508-2. (i) John Alldis Ch., ECO; (ii) Harper, Reynolds, Tear, Rintzler; (iii) New Philh. Ch., (iv) Pashley, Finnilä, Tear, Garrard; (ii; iv) New Philh. O; Barenboim.

Barenboim's approach to the *E minor Mass* and the *Te Deum* is one of dramatic extremes, with meditative passages exceptionally slow and fast passages unusually urgent, the contrasts emphasized by the flamboyant EMI sound with its wide dynamic range. But there is no lack of dynamism and the *Te Deum* is a vivid, boisterous performance, relying not so much on massive choral effects (the recording was done with a comparatively small choir in a smallish church) as on rhythmic energy. The *F minor Mass* is by no means dull or without character but, even more here, one feels that Barenboim does not quite capture the right atmosphere. The motets are well sung; but this is not a first choice for this repertoire.

BUSH, Alan (1900–95)

Cello Sonata, Op. 120; 3 Contrapuntal Studies for Violin and Viola, Op. 13; Phantasy for Violin and Piano, Op. 3; Piano Quartet, Op. 5.
(M) ★★★ Dutton CDLX 7130. London Piano Qt.

Our main volume lists an attractive programme of Bush's chamber music on Meridian, and this new collection from Dutton is, if anything, even more enjoyable. The *Cello Sonata* was written in 1989, sixty years after the other works here, and it shows the mature composer at his finest. Its bold *Allegro energico* immediately establishes the music's strength of purpose, and the expressive *Larghetto molto espressivo*, with its modal harmonic flavour, is memorable in such a sympathetic performance as this by David Kennedy and Philip Fowke. The *Piano Quartet* (1924, revised 1929) is also highly inventive and full of character, its harmonic language individual but never becoming aggressive: its warm underlying lyricism ensures the music's ready communication throughout.

The equally appealing *Phantasy for Violin and Piano* (1923) is similarly lavish in its melodic flow and it brings matching rhythmic freedom, while the three *Contrapuntal Studies* are as aurally enticing as they are skilfully contrived. (They probably date from 1929, the year of Bush's most stimulating chamber work, the *Dialectic* for string quartet.)

All these performances from members of the London Piano Quartet are deeply felt and show how well these four fine artists identify completely with the composer. The recording too, is very lifelike, to make this a most rewarding collection.

Suite of Six, Op. 81.
★★★ Redcliffe RR 020. Bochmann Qt (with PURCELL: *Chacony in G min.*, ed. Britten ★★★) – BRIDGE: *String Quartet No. 4.* ★★★

Dating from 1975, Alan Bush's *Suite of Six* is his final work for string quartet. It is most imaginatively structured and splendidly inventive. An *Introduction* and *Postlude* frame the six central movments, displaying and recalling the six different modes in which they are written. Four are in dance format: a resourceful, imitative *Pavane* with the instruments in pairs, followed by a spirited *Reel*, a snappy *Moto perpetuo* jig and a bold but more lyrical *Sword Dance*. The two slow movements provide serene central interludes, the first an engaging folk-styled Aeolian *Andante*, the second a lovely *Air*. The writing consistently shows the composer at his finest. The Bochmann Quartet give a subtly detailed and expressive performance of high quality, and they are beautifully recorded. The coupled Frank Bridge *Quartet* is a harder nut to crack, but Purcell's *Chacony* makes a heart-warming encore.

Prison Cycle (with Rawsthorne).
★★(★) Campion Cameo 2001. Wells, Swallow – RAWSTHORNE: *Songs* ★★(★); MCCABE: *Folk Songs* ★★★.

Alan Bush contributed three of the five songs that make up the sombre *Prison Cycle*, set to poems by the German socialist poet Ernst Toller, the first and last of which picture him endlessly pacing up and down in his restricted space, and the second in which he dwells on the increasing familiarity and friendliness of all the everyday objects that surround him in his otherwse bare cell. Alison Wells's sympathetic performances are discussed under the Rawsthorne coupling.

BUSONI, Ferruccio (1866–1924)

(i) *Piano Concerto. Fantasia contrappuntistica.*
(B) ★★ Erato Ultima 3984 24248-2 (2). Postnikova; (i) French R. Ch. & Nat. O, Rozhdestvensky.

Postnikova's version of Busoni's ambitious concerto is a curiosity. Her characteristic magic and that of Rozhdestvensky keep tensions sustained for much of the time, despite speeds that by most standards are grotesquely slow, but the result is eccentric. The *Fantasia contrappuntistica* makes a valuable fill-up, but other CD versions have managed to fit the concerto on to a single disc. Recording is good, but the choir in the finale sounds dim. Hamelin's Hyperion version is the one to go for (CDA 67145).

BUXTEHUDE, Diderik
(c. 1637–1707)

CHAMBER MUSIC

(i) *Fried- und Freudenreiche Hinfart, BuxWV 76: Contrapunctus/Evolutio I–II; Klag-Lied; Trio Sonatas, Op. 1/1, 2 & 6, BuxWV 252–3 & 257; Op. 2/3, BuxWV 257; in C & D BWV 266–7;* (ii) (Keyboard) *Ciaccona, BuxWV 160; Passacaglia, BuxWV 161.*

(M) *** DHM/BMG 82876 60151-2. Capriccio Stravagante, Sempé; (ii) Weiss and Sempé (harpsichords).

Here is another useful and characteristic period-instrument selection of Buxtehude's *Trio Sonatas* for those not wanting the complete series. They are very persuasively played by this excellent period-instrument group and include the *D major Sonata*, BuxWV 267, the composer's sole surviving piece of its kind for two bass instruments, here viola da gamba and cello, which enjoy a fascinating interplay. The closing *G major Sonata*, Op. 1/2, is also one of the most attractively inventive of these fertile works. The solemn *Klag-Lied* with the associated *Contrapuncti* (1674) was composed on the death of the composer's father. Of the two keyboard duos, the *Ciaconna* is marginally the more interesting and vital, although the *D minor Passacaglia* may have served as a model for the C minor work of Bach.

BYRD, William (1543–1623)

VOCAL MUSIC

My Ladye Nevells Booke (42 Keyboard pieces) (1591).

❀ (M) *** Decca 476 1530 (3). Hogwood (virginals, harpsichord or chamber organ).

This collection of Byrd's keyboard music was compiled by John Baldwin of Windsor, 'a gentleman of the Chapel Royal', and must be reckoned the finest collection of keyboard music in Europe of the sixteenth century. Christopher Hogwood rings the changes by using a variety of instruments, a virginals, two harpsichords (one Flemish and the other Italian) and a fine chamber organ, all of which he plays with sympathy and vitality. Hogwood's scholarly gifts are shown in the fine notes that accompany the set, but, more important, his masterly keyboard technique and artistic sensitivity are sustained throughout the three CDs (originally four LPs), excellently recorded in the early 1980s. A most enterprising choice for Universal's 'Penguin ❀ Collection', originally issued by L'Oiseau-Lyre, and now appearing on compact disc for the first time.

Psalmes, Sonets and Songs of Sadness (1588): excerpts: *All as at sea; Care for thy soul; Come to me grief; If women could be fair; In fields abroad; Lullaby; The match that's made; O God give ear; O Lord how long?; O that most rare breast; Susanna fair; What a pleasure to have great princes.*

(M) *** Decca (ADD) 475 049-2. Cons. of Musicke, Rooley.

Byrd's *Psalmes, Sonets and Songs of Sadness* of 1588 enjoyed such popularity in their time that they were reprinted twice in their first year of publication. They are more than just a collection of madrigals, as the title suggests, and are given exemplary performances here. Anthony Rooley's fine vocal group is led by Emma Kirkby, and they give many of them as consort pieces, some with the full number of repeated stanzas, which the artists discreetly embellish. This is a first-class reissue, excellently recorded and an invaluable addition to Decca's 'British Music Collection'.

Consort Songs: An aged Dame; Ah silly Soul; All as at a sea; Come to me, grief, for ever; Constant Penelope; How vain the toils; Lullaby: My sweet little Baby; O dear life, when may it be; O God that guides the cheerful Sun; O that most rare breast; Rejoice unto the Lord; Who likes to love; Ye sacred Muses.

☀ *** Hyp. CDA 67397. Blaze, Concordia.

In his preface to *Psalmes, Sonets and Songs of Sadness* (1588) Byrd suggested that his stimulus was 'to perswade everyone to learne how to sing – it is the onely way to know where Nature hath bestowed the benefit of a good voice: which guift is so rare, as there is not one among a thousand that hath it'. Well certainly Robin Blaze 'hath it'; indeed the natural beauty of his vocal colouring stands out among contemporary counter-tenors as being ideal for illuminating these lovely, expressive songs of sadness, like *O dear life, when may it be* (with lute accompaniment) and the two Funeral Consort Songs for Sir Philip Sydney, *Come to me, grief, for ever,* and *O that most rare breast,* and the song of pietie, *How vain the toils that mortal man do take.* Of course there are lighter songs here too, including the jaunty *Who likes to love* (again with lute), while the opening *Rejoice unto the Lord* is full of confidence. But the gem of the collection is also one of the earliest and most extended. *My sweet little Baby* dates from that collection of 1588, and is an entirely delightful Christmas lullaby, which was much and rightly praised by the Earl of Worcester for its immediately communicated beauty. With highly pleasing accompaniments, beautifully balanced, and ravishing singing throughout, this is a record to treasure and draw upon, though not to play all at once.

Masses for 3, 4 and 5 voices; Ave verum corpus; Diffusa est gratia; Magnificat (Great Service); Nunc dimmitis; Prevent us, O Lord; Tristitia et anxuetas; Vigilate.

★★★ Gimell **DVD** GIMDP 901. Tallis Scholars, Philips.

Tudor and Renaissance music is not well represented in the DVD catalogue (understandably so, perhaps) but this, a model of its kind, may encourage others to explore early music. Some of these performances (the *Missa à 3*, and many of the remaining items) are recorded in Tewkesbury Abbey and beautifully filmed by candlelight, while the two remaining Masses were (appropriately enough, given the period) filmed in the Chapel of Merton College, Oxford. As one expects from the Tallis Scholars, these are expert performances, impeccable in intonation and tonal blend. In addition, there is a feature on Byrd. Time was when the BBC would have turned to a leading authority on the music of the period to present such a programme, but this 70-minute feature is fronted by the ubiquitous Charles Hazlewood. Although he is unfailingly pleased with himself, many viewers respond positively to him and the feature is undoubtedly informative.

BYSTRÖM, Oscar (1821–1909)

Symphony in D min.; Andantino; Concert Waltzes Nos. 1 & 3; Overture in D; Overture to Herman Vimpel.

★★ Sterling CDS 1025-2. Gävle SO, Spierer.

Oscar Byström is an interesting figure. He was an accomplished pianist and conductor who, like his fellow Swede Berwald, pursued a career outside music alongside his work as a composer. His *Symphony in D minor* is clearly influenced by Berwald. The second group of the first movement is delightful and the work as a whole has much to commend it. The overtures all come from much the same period and are pleasing, though no one would make great claims for them. They are well served on this CD.

CALDARA, Antonio (c. 1670–1736)

Trio Sonatas: in G min., A & F Op. 2/4, 6 & 8; Ciacona, Op. 2/12; (i) Cantatas: L'anniverario amoroso; La Fama; Vincino a un rivoletto (for alto, violin & cello).

★★(*) ASV Gaudeamus CDGAU 347. Four Nations Ens., Appel; (i) with Lane.

The expert American original-instrument group, the Four Nations, provide an attractively interwoven concert of Caldara's vocal and instrumental music, and their full-voiced mezzo soloist (who sounds more like an alto) contributes stylishly and ardently. The group are at their finest in the splendid instru-

mental *Chaconne* and the beautiful closing cantata, *Vincino a un rivoletto* ('By a stream'), where there are obbligati for both solo violin and cello. The closing (virtual) duet for voice and cello, *Aimé sento il mio core* ('Alas my heart swoons with pain'), beautifully balanced, makes a moving finale. In the *Trio Sonatas* the transparency of string texture is characteristic of period-instrument style, and if Jennifer Lane is less subtle than Gérard Lesne in this repertoire, she communicates readily and with much feeling.

CAMBINI, Giuseppe Maria (1746–1825)

Wind Quintets Nos. 1 in B; 2 in D min.; 3 in F.

(BB) **★★★** Naxos 8.553410. Avalon Wind Quintet – BRICCIALDI: *Wind Quintet in D.* **★★★**

These *Wind Quintets* are doubtless inconsequential, but they are charming, particularly when played so superbly and elegantly by these fine young German musicians. The recording is expertly balanced and very natural. Slight music, but so well served that it will give much pleasure.

CAMPO, Conrado del (1878–1953)

La divina comedia; Evocacion y nostalgia de los molinos de viento; Ofrenda; 6 Little Compositions.

★★★ ASV CDDCA 1100. Gran Canaria PO, Leaper.

Conrado del Campo, unlike his close contemporary, Manuel de Falla, has never been appreciated outside Spain, maybe because his music has few nationalistic flavours, echoing instead such composers as Richard Strauss and Liszt. Adrian Leaper with the Gran Canaria Philharmonic, of which he is principal conductor, here offers an attractive collection, well played, representing the full span of Del Campo's career from *La divina comedia* of 1908, an evocation of Dante's *Inferno* with a warmly lyrical interlude representing Paolo and Francesca, to his last major piece, a 'poetic overture' inspired by the composer's love of windmills, *Molinos de viento*. Completed in 1952, the year before he died, it leads to a passionate climax, while *Ofrenda*, dating from 1934, is equally sensuous, with exotic echoes of Respighi, suggesting that Del Campo could have made his fortune as a Hollywood composer.

CANNABICH, Johann Christian (1731–98)

Symphonies Nos. 47 in G; 48 in B flat; 49 in F; 50 in D min.; 51 in D; 52 in E, Op. 10/1-6.

(BB) **★★★** Naxos 8.554340. Nicolaus Esterházy Sinf., Grodd.

Symphonies Nos. 59 in D; 63 in D; 64 in F; 67 in G; 68 in B flat.
(BB) ★★★ Naxos 8.553960. Lukas Cons., Lukas.

Christian Cannabich was born and made his career in Mannheim, where in 1774 he became conductor of what at that time was the most celebrated orchestra in Europe. Cannabich was to be described by Mozart as the finest conductor he had ever encountered, but he was also a prolific and accomplished, if not always individual, symphonist. His six works published in 1772 as Op. 10 are each in three movements and are effectively scored for flutes (or oboes) and horns. Opening movements are conventional, but the expressively gracious slow movements and lively finales more than compensate, and very soon we encounter the famous Mannheim 'crescendo' (the opening movement of No. 51 provides a very striking example). There are even hints of Mozart. The performances are lively, stylish and well recorded.

The second group of symphonies (though still in three movements) mark a considerable step forward. The scoring of No. 59 uses the oboes more freely as soloists, and its *Andante* is strikingly gracious. But when we reach the dramatic opening of No. 63 the scoring is much more ambitious, using trumpets and timpani, as well as full woodwind, including clarinets. All the celebrated Mannheim effects are here, with an emphatic unison in the introduction, plus the carefully regulated, almost Rossinian crescendos. The lilting oboe melody of the slow movement contrasts with the strong, Mozartian finale.

No. 64 brings more crescendo sequences, and the *Andante* is again very fetching, to be followed by another bold finale, featuring the horns, which are again used most effectively in Nos. 67 and 68. No. 68 begins amiably but energetically, and the solo horns are given the full limelight with the principal theme of the *Andante*. The lighthearted second subject of the finale again demonstrates the variety of Cannabich's invention, and the whole movement displays his deft use of orchestral colour. Viktor Lukas and his Consort give admirable performances, full of life and with the necessary light and shade. They are again very well recorded and this pair of inexpensive discs provides a most stimulating introduction to a composer/conductor justly renowned in his own time.

Flute Quintets, Op. 7/3-6.
★★★ CPO 999 544-2. Camerata Köln.

Cannabich's *Flute Quintets* are for one (or usually two) flutes, violin, viola and cello, and sometimes have optional keyboard parts. The music is elegant, well crafted and charming, if very lightweight, with the 'concertante' flute parts always dominant. Excellent performances here, and natural recording within a pleasing ambience.

CARTELLIERI, Casimir Anton (1772–1807)

Clarinet Concertos Nos. 1 in B flat; 2: Adagio pastorale; 3 in E flat.
★★★ MDG 301 0527-2. Klöcker, Prague CO.

Hardly a household name, Casimir Anton Cartellieri was born in Danzig and eventually found his way to Vienna. His three *Clarinet Concertos* (only the slow movement of the second survives) are expertly laid out for the instrument. While they are not searching or profound, they are astonishingly inventive and full of both charm and wit. Dieter Klöcker and the Prague Chamber Orchestra give thoroughly committed accounts of these delightful pieces, and the MDG recording is immaculate.

(i)*Double Concerto for 2 Clarinets in B flat; (ii) Flute Concerto in G; (i) Movement for Clarinet & Orchestra in B flat.*
★★★ MDG 301 0960-2. (i) Klöcker, Arnold; (ii) Brandkamp; Prague CO.

The *Concerto for Two Clarinets* reaffirms the strong impression made by its companions above. It bubbles over with high spirits and has a strikingly original opening. Klöcker and his pupil, Sandra Arnold, give a masterly account of the piece, and Kornelia Brandkamp is hardly less expert in the diverting and delightful *Flute Concerto*. As always with the Dabringhaus & Grimm label, the recordings are beautifully balanced and very natural. Not great music, perhaps, but very rewarding all the same.

Clarinet Quartets Nos. 1 in D; 2 in E flat; 4 in E flat.
★★★ MDG 301 1097-2. Klöcker, Consortium Classicum.

Those readers who have already discovered Cartellieri's *Clarinet Concertos* will not need persuading to explore these even more delightful companion chamber works. Their style brings an occasional whiff of Mozart but is more *galant* than the music of that master, and there are also touches of the kind of wit one finds in Rossini's *String Sonatas*. Dieter Klöcker plays beguilingly and he is given splendid support from the Consortium Classicum, elegant and fresh, and they are beautifully recorded.

CARTER, Elliott (born 1908)

(i) *Piano Concerto. Holiday Overture; Symphony No. 1.*
(BB) ★★(★) Naxos 8.559151. Nashville SO, Schermerhorn; (i) with Wait.

The three works on the disc in Naxos's enterprising American Classics series make plain the strong contrast between early Carter works, very much in the American open-air tradition developed by Copland and Roy Harris, and the much thornier, more challenging music he came to write from the 1960s onwards. Both the *Holiday Overture* (1945) and the *Symphony No. 1* (1942) are fresh and open in his earlier manner. The *Holiday Overture* is a lively piece and well worth having on disc. The *Symphony* is rewarding, close in idiom to Copland and Piston. Its material is interesting and the feeling for form strong. The disc is worth having for this alone, particularly in this strong, understanding and well-recorded performance, culminating in a sparkling account of the finale. Between those works and the *Piano Concerto* of 1965 (written for the 85th birthday of Stravinsky) Carter concentrated mainly on chamber works, developing the uncompromising personal idiom that has won him universal critical acclaim.

The *Piano Concerto* is pretty rebarbative, highly intricate rhythmically, its ideas firmly embedded in barbed wire and its spikey charms eminently resistible. In short, it is deeply unappealing, even given the virtuosity of the remarkable soloist and the supportive playing of the Nashville orchestra. Other respected musicians feel differently and, at this modest price, collectors can afford to try it for themselves. The pianist, Mark Wait, copes well with the daunting technical problems of the piano writing, well supported by the Nashville orchestra, renowned for its adventurous recordings of modern music. First-rate sound, if with the piano balanced rather too forwardly.

CARWITHEN, Doreen

(1922–2003)

(i) *Concerto for Piano & Strings. Overtures: ODTAA ('One damn thing after another'); Bishop Rock; Suffolk Suite.*

*** Chan. 9524. (i) Shelley; LSO, Hickox.

Doreen Carwithen here emerges as a warmly communicative composer in her own right, owing rather more to Walton's style than to that of her husband (William Alwyn). The two overtures in their vigour and atmospheric colour relate readily to her film music, the one inspired by John Masefield's novel, *ODTAA*, the other inspired by the rock in the Atlantic that marks the last contact with the British Isles, stormy in places, gently sinister in others. The charming *Suffolk Suite* uses melodies originally written for a film on East Anglia. Much the most ambitious work is the *Concerto for Piano and Strings*, with powerful virtuoso writing for the piano set against rich-textured strings. A deeply melancholy slow movement – in which the piano is joined by solo violin – leads to a strong finale which in places echoes the Ireland *Piano Concerto*. Howard Shelley is the persuasive soloist, with Richard Hickox and the LSO equally convincing in their advocacy of all four works. Warm, atmospheric sound.

(i) *Violin Sonata;* (ii) *String Quartets Nos. 1 & 2.*

*** Chan. 9596. (i) Mordkovitch, Milford; (ii) Sorrel Qt.

The *First Quartet*, written in 1948 when she was still a student, firmly establishes Doreen Carwithen's personal idiom, tautly constructed in three movements. The result, identifiably English, yet points forward, though it is only in the *Second Quartet* of 1952, in two extended movements, that one detects a hint that she may have been studying the quartets of Bartók; it comes with warmly expressive performances from the well-matched Sorrel Quartet. The *Violin Sonata*, written later, brings high dramatic contrasts, most strikingly in the central *Vivace*, a *moto perpetuo* in 9/8 rhythm. Lydia Mordkovitch, as ever, proves a passionate advocate, finding a depth and poignancy in the lyrical writing that may reflect her Russian roots. Julian Milford makes an ideal partner, though the piano is rather backwardly balanced. Otherwise the recording is first rate.

CASELLA, Alfredo (1883–1947)

La Giara (Symphonic Suite), Op. 41 bis; Paganiniana (Divertimento for Orchestra), Op. 65; Serenata for Chamber Orchestra, Op. 46 bis.

(BB) ******* Naxos 8.553706. Italian Swiss RSO, Benda.

The performance of *Paganiniana* by the Italian Swiss Radio under Christian Benda is as bright-eyed, polished and sympathetic as its competitor, below. Both the *Serenata*, which is precociously good-humoured (it opens with a droll bassoon solo) and touchingly nostalgic by turns, and the ballet, *La Giara*, are unashamedly eclectic. But Casella has a ready fund of good tunes and they are delectably scored. The ballet also includes a melancholy vocal interlude, *The Story of the Girl Seized by Pirates*, sensitively sung by Marco Beasley, affecting but not in the least sentimental. The recording is first class, vividly atmospheric. This collection is well worth having, but don't play all three works at once.

Paganiniana, Op. 65.

(*******) Testament mono SBT 1017. St Cecilia, Rome, O, Cantelli (with DUKAS: *L'Apprenti sorcier*; FALLA: *Three-cornered Hat*; RAVEL: *Daphnis et Chloé: Suite No. 2.* (*******)).

Paganiniana is a delightful, effervescent score. Cantelli's pioneering record dates from 1949 and comes up sounding very well in a marvellously transferred Testament issue which also offers his 1955–6 Philharmonia recording of the *Daphnis* suite and his 1954 *Three-cornered Hat*. Elegant playing.

PIANO MUSIC

A la manière de ... Op. 17/1 & 2 serie; Barcarola; Berceuse triste; 2 Canzoni popolari italiane; Cocktail's Dance; 2 Contrasts; Inezie, Op. 32; Notturnino; Nove pezzi, Op. 24; Pavane; 2 Ricercari sul nome B-A-C-H; Ricercare sul nome Guido M. Gatti; Sarabande; Sei studi, Op. 70; Sinfonia, Arioso e Toccata; Sonatina, Op. 28; Studio sulle terze maggiori; Toccata; Undici pezzi infantili, Op. 35; Variations sur une Chaconne.

(M) *** Warner (ADD) 0927 47043-2 (3). Lye de Barberiis.

Of the three major Italian composers of the Ottocento – Malipiero, Pizzetti and Casella – the last named was the most active in the cause of contemporary music as a pianist, conductor, teacher and organizer. He studied in Paris with Fauré and rubbed shoulders with the likes of Stravinsky, Ravel and Enescu. Casella was a leading exponent of neo-classicism and a driving force behind the ISCM (International Society for Contemporary Music) and as a pianist he recorded the Bloch *First Piano Quintet* and Roy Harris's *Piano Trio*. He was easily the most influential figure in Italian music between the two world wars, but his own output, which is extensive and of quality, has fallen into neglect. Apart from *Paganiniana*, which has been recorded by Ormandy, Muti and Kondrashin, his *Violin Concerto* was championed by André Gertler on Supraphon and there is a 1936 broadcast, albeit incomplete, of the *Triple Concerto* conducted by Koussevitzky, no less. This three-CD set collects his piano music, and the idiomatic quality of the writing leaves no doubt as to his natural feeling for the keyboard. The idiom is eclectic and the mature style often brittle and dryish, yet his is a cultured, well-stocked musical imagination and the writing is unfailingly inventive, even if it is not a good idea to play too much of it at once. Not great music, perhaps, but eminently intelligent and rewarding – and well played here. Readers who do not want everything can choose the excellent Naxos recital by Luca Ballerini listed below.

11 Children's Pieces, Op. 35; 2 Ricercari on the Name B.A.C.H, Op. 52; 9 Pieces, Op. 24; 6 Studies, Op. 70.

(BB) *** Naxos 8.554009. Ballerini.

What an interesting composer Casella is and how strange that he is so neglected! Like Strauss, his role in the fascist era has attracted the opprobrium of various armchair heroes, usually American academics, who have never faced such realities, but Egon Wellesz, a scholar-composer of proven anti-Nazi credentials, never wavered in his admiration of him. The *Nine Pieces*, Op. 24, are all exploratory in idiom, reflecting the worlds of Stravinsky, Busoni and Ravel. The third, *In modo elegiaco*, even foreshadows the harmonic world of Frank Martin. The *Children's Pieces* of 1920, dedicated to Castelnuovo-Tedesco, are imaginative and full of resource and charm, the last being reminiscent of the circus music of Stravinsky's second *Little Suite*. The *Ricercari on the Name B.A.C.H*, Op. 52, were written for Gieseking in 1932 and are as exploratory in idiom as the charming wartime *Etudes*, Op. 70. Very convincing performances, as intelligent as befits this music, and very well recorded too.

CATOIRE, Georgy (1861–1926)

Piano music: *Caprice, Op. 3; Chants de crépuscule (4 Morceaux), Op. 24; Intermezzo, Op. 6/5; 3 Morceaux, Op. 2; 5 Morceaux, Op. 10; 4 Morceaux, Op. 12; Poème, Op. 34/2; Prélude, Op. 6/2; 4 Préludes, Op. 17; Prélude, Op. 34/3; Scherzo, Op. 6/3; Valse, Op. 36; Vision (Etude), Op. 8.*

*** Hyp. CDA 67090. Hamelin.

Georgy Catoire was born in Moscow to parents of French extraction. His music has been all but forgotten, which makes this dazzling collection of his piano music especially welcome, prompting Marc-André Hamelin to astonishing feats of virtuosity, combined with poetry. Catoire left a big collection of piano miniatures, of which this collection of 28 is an attractive sample. They are played in order of opus number, giving an idea of Catoire's development from echoing Chopin, Liszt and Tchaikovsky to adventuring more towards the world of Wagner and of the French Impressionists. If there is a Russian he echoes, it is Scriabin, and it is the fluency of his writing for the keyboard rather than memorability of material that strikes home, with Hamelin an ideal interpreter. Yet for all these influences, in many ways he is his own man, and his music, particularly the *Morceaux*, is often very seductive. Hamelin also shows how he can tickle the ear with a scherzando lightness, as in the two engaging pieces from Op. 6. This is not a recital to play continuously but, drawn on, it will give much refreshment and pleasure. Hamelin is given an outstandingly natural recording, bright, yet with full sonority and colouring.

CAVALLI, Francesco (1602–76)

La Calisto (complete version; freely arranged by Raymond Leppard).

⊛ (M) *** Decca 476 2176 (2). Cotrubas, Trama, J. Baker, Bowman, Gottlieb, Cuénod, Hughes, Glyndebourne Festival Op. Ch., LPO, Leppard.

No more perfect Glyndebourne entertainment has been devised than this freely adapted version of an opera written for Venice in the 1650s but never heard since. It exactly relates that permissive society of the seventeenth century to our own. It is the more delectable because of the brilliant part given to the goddess, Diana, taken by Dame Janet Baker. In Leppard's version she has the dual task of portraying first the chaste goddess herself, then in the same costume switching immediately to the randy Jupiter disguised as Diana, quite a different character. The opera is splendidly cast. Parts for such singers as James Bowman draw out their finest qualities, and the result is magic. No one should miss Dame Janet's heartbreakingly intense singing of her tender aria *Amara servitù*, while a subsidiary character, Linfea, a bad-tempered, lecherous, ageing nymph, is portrayed hilariously by Hugues Cuénod. The opera has transferred admirably to a pair of CDs, with each of the two acts offered without a break; the recording, made at Glyndebourne, is gloriously rich and atmospheric, with the Prologue in a different, more ethereal acoustic than the rest of the opera. This has now been reissued by Universal as one of the 'Penguin ❂ Collection' – at mid-price and with full documentation included.

CERHA, Friedrich (born 1926)

String Quartets Nos. 1–3; (i) 8 Movements after Hölderlin Fragments for String Sextet.
*** CPO 999 646-2. Arditti Qt; (i) with Kakuska, Erben.

Friedrich Cerha is best known as a champion of the Second Viennese School and as the scholar-composer who completed the third act of Alban Berg's *Lulu*. The three quartets recorded here come from the period 1989–92: the *First Quartet* is subtitled *Maqam*, inspired by Arab music. It makes liberal use of microtones, as does, though to a lesser extent, the minimalist *Second*, inspired by his contact with the Papuan peoples at Sepik in New Guinea. The *Hölderlin Fragments* (1995) are settings for string sextet without voice, though the poems that inspired them are reproduced in the excellent and detailed booklet. The Arditti Quartet play with great expertise and attention to detail, and are vividly recorded. Recommended for those with a special interest in contemporary Austrian music.

CHABRIER, Emmanuel (1841–94)

Bourrée fantasque; España (rhapsody); Joyeuse marche; Suite pastorale; Gwendoline: Overture. Le Roi malgré lui: Danse slave; Fête polonaise.
*** Mercury (ADD) **SACD** 475 6183. Detroit SO, Paray
– ROUSSEL: *Suite.* **(*)

Mercury are bringing out some of their most admired recordings on SACD and, although they are not due to be released until after our book goes to press, we feel sure that listeners will want to be informed of their publication in the autumn of this year. Full reviews of the works listed above can be found in our current main edition. The new format should go some way to further enhance the already spectacular results afforded by the 'Living Presence' technology.

CHADWICK, George (1854–1931)

Serenade for Strings.
*** Albany TROY 033-2. V. American Music Ens., Earle
– GILBERT: *Suite.* ***

This very well-crafted piece by the so-called 'Boston

classicist' gives much pleasure. It is quite beautifully played by this excellent Viennese group, drawn from younger members of the Vienna Symphony Orchestra. The sound too is first rate, a successful example of a 'live recording' bringing no loss in realism and a gain in spontaneity.

CHAMINADE, Cécile (1857–1944)

Music for violin and piano: Capriccio, Op. 18; Rondeau, Op. 97; Sérénade espagnole; Valse carnavalesque, Op. 73. Music for 2 pianos: Danse payenne; Pas des cymbales. Songs: Alleluia; Auprès de ma mie; L'Amour captif; L'Anneau d'argent; Attente (Au pays de Provence); Bonne humeur; Chanson triste; Ecrin; Espoir; L'Eté je voudrais ...; La Lune paresseuse; Malgré nous; Ma première lettre; Menuet; Mignonne; Mots d'Amour; Nice-la-bette; Ronde d'amour; Si j'étais jardinier; Sombrero; Te souviens-tu?; Viens! mon bien-aimé!; Villanelle; Voisinage.
*** DG 471 331-2. Von Otter, Fosberg, Sparf, Jablonski.

Those who associate the Victorian favourite composer Cécile Chaminade with slight, genteel piano pieces will be surprised to find a far greater variety in this winning collection of her songs, as well as pieces for violin and for two pianos. The sparkle and energy of many of them chimes perfectly with the artistry of Anne Sofie von Otter, here at her most vivacious. One may look in vain for any kind of profundity, with the poems chosen by the composer rarely rising above the banal, but the vocal lines are easily elegant and often colourful, and the piano accompaniments unusual and demanding. The picture is completed by equally winning performances of the six instrumental pieces, full of fun and energy.

Piano Trios Nos. 1 in G min., Op. 11; 2 in A min., Op. 34; Pastorale enfantine, Op. 12; Ritournelle; Sérénade, Op. 29 (all 3 arr. Marcus); Serenade espagnole (arr. Kreisler).
*** ASV CDDCA 965. Tzigane Piano Trio.

In these two *Piano Trios* Chaminade confidently controls larger forms, building on a fund of melody. The two central movements of the *Piano Trio No. 1* are charming, a passionately lyrical *Andante* and a sparkling, Mendelssohnian *Scherzo*. The *Piano Trio No. 2*, in three movements, without a *Scherzo*, is weightier, almost Brahmsian, with themes rather more positive. Three of the four miniatures that come as fill-ups have been arranged for trio by the *Tzigane's* pianist, Elizabeth Marcus.

PIANO MUSIC

Air à danser, Op. 164; Air de ballet, Op. 30; Automne; Autrefois; Contes bleus No. 2, Op. 122; Danse créole, Op. 94; Guitare, Op. 32; Lisonjera, Op. 50; Lolita, Op. 54; Minuetto, Op. 23; Pas des

écharpes, Op. 37; Pas des sylphes: Intermezzo; Pierette, Op. 41; 3 Romances sans paroles, Op. 76/1, 3 & 6; Sérénade, Op. 29; Sous le masque, Op. 116; Toccata, Op. 39; Valse arabesque.
*** Chan. 8888. Parkin.

Album des enfants, Op. 123/4, 5, 9 & 10; Op. 126/1, 2, 9 & 10; Arabesque, Op. 61; Cortège, Op. 143; Inquiétude, Op. 87/3; Le Passé; Prelude in D min., Op. 84/3; Rigaudon, Op. 55/6; Sérénade espagnole; Sonata in C min., Op. 21; Les Sylvains, Op. 60; Valse-ballet, Op. 112; Valse brillante No. 3, Op. 80; Valse No. 4, Op. 91.
*** Hyp. CDA 66846. Jacobs.

Arlequine, Op. 53; Au pays dévasté, Op. 155; Chanson brétonne; Divertissement, Op. 105; Etudes de concert, Op. 35: Impromptu; Tarantella. Etude symphonique, Op. 28; Feuillets d'album, Op. 98: Elégie. Gigue in D, Op. 43; Libellules, Op. 24; Nocturne, Op. 165; Passacaille in E, Op. 130; Pastorale, Op. 114; Pièces humoristiques Op. 87: Sous bois; Consolation. Poème romantique, Op. 7; Scherzo-valse, Op. 148; Tristesse, Op. 104; Valse tendre, Op. 119.
*** Hyp. CDA 66706. Jacobs.

Autrefois; Callirhoë; Elévation in E; Etude mélodique in G flat; Etude pathétique in B min.; Etude scholastique; Lisonjera; L'Ondine; Pêcheurs de nuit; Romance; Scherzo in C; Sérénade in D; Solitude; Souvenance; Thème varié in A; Valse romantique; Waltz No. 2.
*** Hyp. CDA 66584. Jacobs.

Artistically these pieces are rather stronger than one had suspected and, although they are by no means the equal of Grieg or early Fauré, they can hold their own with Saint-Saëns and are more inventive than the *Brises d'orient* of Félicien David. There is a quality of gentility that has lent a certain pallor to Chaminade's charms, but both pianists here make out a stronger case for her than most people would imagine possible. Both are well recorded and in this respect there is little to choose between the two. Nor is there much to choose as far as the performances are concerned; both are persuasive, though Parkin has a slight edge over his colleague in terms of elegance and finesse. If you want a single-disc collection you might choose the Chandos disc. If you seek a complete survey, stay with Jacobs.

CHARPENTIER, Marc-Antoine (1643–1704)

Messe de minuit pour Noël (Midnight Mass for Christmas Eve); Dixit Dominus; Te Deum.
(BB) *** Naxos 8.557229. Aradia Ens., Mallon.

Kevin Mallon and his excellent Canadian group, the Aradia Ensemble, give bright, clear readings of two of the most popular of Charpentier's choral works. This period performance of the *Prélude* for the *Te Deum* is very different from the one that used to introduce Eurovision programmes; it is altogether lighter and more joyful, with an exuberant display of timpani at the start and with bright trumpet flourishes throughout. In the *Christmas Mass* Mallon equally brings out the joy of the writing, giving more prominence than usual to the carols that punctuate the *Kyrie*, and springing rhythms infectiously in writing that in many sections offers a thoughtfully original setting of the liturgy. The *Dixit Dominus*, with its unexpectedly gentle minor-key introduction, makes an attractive extra item. Clear, well-balanced sound.

CHAUSSON, Ernest (1855–99)

Poème for Violin & Orchestra.
(M) *** EMI 5 62599-2. Perlman, O de Paris, Martinon (with MASSENET: *Thaïs: Méditation*: Abbey Road Ens., Foster) – RAVEL: *Tzigane*; SAINT-SAENS: *Introduction and Rondo capriccioso etc.* ***
(BB) **(*) CfP 585 6192. Kennedy, LPO, Kamu – TCHAIKOVSKY: *Violin Concerto.* **(*)

Perlman's 1975 account of Chausson's beautiful *Poème*, with the Orchestre de Paris under Martinon, is a classic account by which all newcomers are measured. What a glorious and inspired piece it is when played with such feeling! It now returns to the catalogue at mid-price in the 'Perlman Edition' as part of a particularly distinguished anthology that includes a brilliant account of Ravel's *Tzigane* and the eternally fresh Saint-Saëns pieces so beloved of virtuosi – and of the public too, when played like this. The digital transfer exchanges some of the opulence of the original for a gain in presence (not that Perlman isn't near enough already), but it still sounds full. A luscious account of the Thaïs *Méditation*, recorded digitally two decades later, has now been added.

Nigel Kennedy's version of the *Poème*, unusually expansive and sensuous, with ripe and powerful build-up of climaxes, comes as a welcome, if not very generous, coupling for his warmly romantic reading of the Tchaikovsky *Concerto*, recorded in similarly rich, full sound.

CHEN GANG (born 1935)

The Butterfly Lovers' Concerto.
(BB) *** Naxos SACD 6.110082; CD: 8.557348. Nishizaki, New Zealand SO, Judd – BREIMER: *Songs and Dances of the Silk Road.* ***

The *Butterfly Lovers' Concerto* belongs to China's Communist era, when it was politically correct for a pair of composers to write music together. So in 1959 Chen Yang and his fellow student He Zhanho combined to write a violin concerto using traditional themes. The piece is based on a folk story about a pair of student comrades, one of whom is a girl dressed as a boy. They have to part, her father arranges her wedding and, too late, the hero discovers his comrade is a girl and to be married. Like a true lover he dies of unhappiness. On her wedding day the heroine insists on leaving the bridal procession to mourn at the grave. A thunderstorm breaks out, the grave opens, she leaps in, it closes again, and a rainbow appears in the sky. Two butterflies appear and fly away together, so the lovers are united for ever. It is not easy to relate the music to the narrative except for the engagingly languorous melodies, often heard on the flute as well as the violin, which frame the work and obviously relate to the lovers. There is lively dance music and passages of vigorous melodrama in the central section. But the concerto is beautifully scored, and finally the main romantic theme blossoms, first richly on the strings and then the full orchestra, to show the triumph of true love, before the delicate solo passages return on violin and flute, tenderly reflecting the sadness of the lovers' plight. Takako Nishizaki was the natural choice of soloist for this disarmingly attractive work, for she has recorded it before and became a major star in China, where over three million copies have been sold! She plays it with great tenderness and her slightly fragile (yet warm) timbre surely conjures up the prettiest pair of butterflies.

CHERUBINI, Luigi (1760–1842)

Mass in F (Di Chimay).
★★★ EMI 5 57589-2. Ziesak, Lippert, Abdrazakov, Bav. R. Ch. & SO, Muti.

Riccardo Muti, most persuasive interpreter of Cherubini, follows up his earlier recordings of that neglected composer's choral music with a lively account of the *Mass in F*, which in 1809 broke a creative block then afflicting the composer. In his enthusiasm Cherubini wrote what was then his most ambitious work. It is a massive 75-minute structure that in its inventiveness brings out the drama of the liturgy just as Haydn's last Masses had in the immediately preceding years. Muti's live recording is not always perfectly polished, but in thrust and concentration the performance is most compelling, with the hushed account of the *Crucifixus* bringing rapt choral singing. Characterful soloists too, with the soprano Ruth Ziesak singing radiantly.

CHOPIN, Frédéric (1810–49)

Piano Concertos Nos. 1 in E min., Op. 11; 2 in F min., Op. 21.
(M) ★★(★) EMI ADD 5 67232-2 [567261]. François, Monte-Carlo Op. O, Frémaux.
(B) ★★ Ph. (ADD) 434 145-2. Arrau, LPO, Inbal.
★★ DG 459 684-2. Zimerman, Polish Festival O.

(BB) Hyp. Helios CDH 55180. Demidenko, Philh. O, H. Schiff.

If François's rather grand first entry in the *E minor* is slightly mannered, there is much fine playing here, and the solo contribution in the finales of both concertos often scintillates. Frémaux's accompaniments of outer movements are strong in vitality and certainly supportive in the beautiful *Larghettos*, where again much of the solo playing is persuasive. The remastering of the late–1960s recordings gives both the forwardly placed soloist and the orchestra a vivid presence.

Arrau's performances with Inbal are marred by rubato which at times seems mannered. The early-1970s recording is average (with the piano too forward) and has a surprising amount of tape hiss.

DG marked the 150th anniversary of the composer's death with a newly recorded pairing of the two concertos from Krystian Zimerman. Alas, any sense of momentum or naturalness is submerged by uncharacteristically disruptive rubato. Both concertos are the same – full of intrusive touches and pulled out of shape. Far better to have his earlier set with Giulini and the Los Angeles orchestra: elegant, aristocratic and sparkling (463 622-2).

Nikolai Demidenko produces consistent beauty of sound but his rubati can be disruptive, influenced by moments of disturbing self-consciousness. Probably the best things are in the middle movements, though even these are not always allowed to speak for themselves. Heinrich Schiff gets an excellent response from the Philharmonia Orchestra. For the dedicated admirer of the pianist rather than of the composer.

Piano Concerto No. 2 in F min., Op. 21.
★(★) Decca 467 093-2. Thibaudet, Rotterdam PO, Gergiev – GRIEG: *Concerto.* ★(★)

Of course there are good things in Thibaudet's well-recorded account (among them Gergiev's accompaniment in the slow movement) but they do not add up sufficiently to make a serious challenge to the existing competition. This much-admired (and rightly so) artist does not produce the wonderful range of colour that he has in his pianistic armoury, and the overall impression left is surprisingly anonymous.

PIANO MUSIC

Vladimir Ashkenazy Chopin Edition

Ballades Nos. 1–4; Etudes; Waltzes (complete).
(B) ★★ EMI double forte (ADD) 5 74290-2 (2). Anievas.

Ballades Nos. 1–4; Scherzi Nos. 1–4; Piano Sonatas Nos. 2–3.
(BB) ★★ EMI Gemini 5 85511-2 (2). Ousset.

Agustin Anievas is at his best in the 1966 recording of

the *Etudes*, which remains fresh, with charm and bravura used to bring out a wide range of expression. The *Waltzes* (which include the five posthumous ones) don't have quite the same flair, though there is still much to enjoy, especially in the reflective passages, and the same can be said of the *Ballades* (1975). The recordings are pretty ordinary next to the best ones, but this set is a fair bargain.

Cécile Ousset gives us confident, big-boned surveys of the two *Sonatas*. Some of the tenderness and poetry of the slow movement of the *B minor* (notoriously difficult to bring off) elude her, and there is more virtuosity than grace in the first movement; moreover she is curiously prosaic in the finale of the B flat minor work. In the *Ballades* she has splendid panache, but some ideas are presented in a matter-of fact, rather direct fashion. The four *Scherzi* are powerful and virile, enjoyable in their way but offering few special insights. Overall her playing has undoubted polish and spontaneous brilliance, and she is eminently well recorded, but this issue is not a first recommendation for any of the repertoire offered here.

Berceuse; 12 Etudes, Op. 25; Piano Sonata No. 2, Op. 35.

(M) *** DG (ADD/DDD) 471 357-2. Pollini.

A programme of reissues, specifically designed for the 'Pollini Edition'. Pollini plays the *Berceuse* coolly and elegantly, and with beautiful precision. The *Sonata* is very commanding: the slow movement is particularly fine, and the *Etudes* are masterly. But who would want Op. 25 without Op. 10?

Etudes, Op. 10/1–12; Op. 25/1–12.

**(*) BIS SACD 1390. Kempf.

Ever since becoming the youngest winner of the BBC Young Musician award, Freddy Kempf has gone from strength to strength, and his BIS records have been widely acclaimed. We particularly admired his Rachmaninov and, more recently, Prokofiev. With the two sets of Chopin *Etudes* he comes up against the stiffest competition and in many of them holds his own with the very finest. Overall, however, this is not a set to prefer to those of Perahia, Berezovsky and Pollini (see our main volume). Kempf's playing does not lack fire or poetic sensibility, though not all his interpretative points seem to arise naturally from his music-making but rather seem artificially transplanted (as in Op. 10, No. 11). Yet this survey should be heard, for Kempf has undoubted flair and brilliance to commend him. However, his instrument sounds a shade too bright and glassy.

Mazurkas Nos. 1–58 (complete).

[BB] **(*) EMI Gemini (ADD) 5 86767-2 (2). Smith.

That Ronald Smith's technique is of a high order is evidenced by his numerous Alkan recordings. If there are times, as one listens to his finely drawn account of the Chopin *Mazurkas*, when one would welcome

greater poetic intensity or characterization, these moments are few by comparison with the pleasure this comprehensive and well-recorded set gives, particularly at so reasonable a cost.

Nocturnes Nos. 1–21.

**(*) Hyp. CDA 66341/2. Rév.

Nocturnes Nos. 1–21; Mazurkas Nos. 13 in A min., Op. 17/4; 32 in C sharp min., Op. 50/3; 35 in C min., Op. 56/3; Waltzes Nos. 3 in A min.; 8 in A flat, Op. 64/3; 9 in A flat; 10 in B min., Op. 69/1–2; 13 in D flat, Op. 70/3.

(B) **(*) EMI double forte (ADD) 5 73830-2 (2). Weissenberg.

Lívia Rév is an artist of refined musicianship and impeccable taste, selfless and unconcerned with display or self-projection. Indeed, there are times when she comes too close to understatement. But these are still lovely performances and the recording has great warmth.

Alexis Weissenberg is a thoughtful, serious artist and a natural Chopin player with highly poetic feeling for rubato. But at times he gets impulsively carried away, and occasionally some of the elusive nocturnal quality is lost. The *Mazurkas* too are very volatile, but here the strong rhythmic pointing is more appropriate, and the *Waltzes* sparkle more delicately. Overall one would not want to make too much of Weissenberg's passionate outbursts, for much of his playing is memorably gentle and affecting, helped by a natural piano-sound, which has fine colour and sonority.

24 Preludes, Op. 28; Piano Sonata No. 2 in B flat min., Op. 35; Polonaise in A flat, Op. 53.

** RCA 09026 63535-2. Kissin.

Kissin's new recital offers some masterly, indeed dazzling pianism, but we miss the fresh, spontaneous quality that has distinguished most of his earlier recitals. He makes pretty heavy weather of the *E minor Prelude* (No. 9) though the close RCA balance probably makes him sound heavier than he is.

Piano Sonata No. 3 in B min.; Polonaise No. 6 in A flat, Op. 53.

(B) **(*) EMI Début 5 73500-2. Slobodyanik – SCHUMANN: *Kinderszenen, etc.* **

Alex Slobodyanik is now in his mid-twenties and on the brink of a promising career. His account of the *B minor Sonata* is sensitive and intelligent and, along with the Schumann couplings, serves as an admirable visiting-card for this young artist. At the same time, it does not have quite the strong personality of some of his CD rivals.

Piano Sonata No. 3; Prelude in C sharp min., Op. 45; Scherzo No. 4 in E, Op. 54.

(M) (***) BBC mono/stereo BBCL 4138-2. Perlemuter.

Considering his standing in the musical world, Vlado

Perlumeter made relatively few commercial recordings – a complete Ravel survey for Vox in the mid-1950s and some Fauré and Chopin for Nimbus – so this issue, prompted perhaps by his recent death in his ninety-ninth year, is more than welcome. Born in Lithuania in 1904, Perlumeter came to France as a boy, studying with Cortot and graduating from the Paris Conservatoire when he was fourteen. He shared his master's profound musicality and his indifference to perfectionism. He subsequently became Ravel's only pupil and noted interpreter. He made a number of appearances in the BBC Studios during the Glock era, at the 'Thursday Invitation Concerts' in the Concert Hall, Broadcasting House, or (as here) in the Maida Vale studios. The *Sonata* comes from a 1964 recital and is mono, while the *E major Scherzo* and the *Prelude* (both stereo) are from the early 1970s, when Perlumeter was already in his late sixties. He never set great store by virtuoso display, though he had a formidable keyboard command, and he sought not to dazzle with technical brilliance but to reveal – and this he does. There is some wonderfully perceptive music-making here and the musical importance of this disc is enhanced by exceptionally good notes by Jeremy Siepmann. Strongly recommended.

Waltzes Nos. 1–14; Impromptus Nos. 1–4 (Fantaisie-impromptu)..

(M) *** RCA (ADD) 82876 59422-2. Rubinstein.

Rubinstein's performances of the *Waltzes* have a chiselled perfection, suggesting finely cut and polished diamonds, and his clear and relaxed accounts of the *Impromptus* make most other interpretations sound forced by comparison. The digital remastering has softened the edge of the sound-image, and there is a feeling of added warmth. A vintage Rubinstein reissue, finding a welcome place in RCA's 'Classic Library' series.

Waltzes Nos. 1–19; Impromptus Nos. 1–4 (Fantaisie-impromptu).

(BB) * EMI Encore (ADD) 5 74975-2. Cziffra.

Georges Cziffra's performances date from the 1970s, and although his technique is not in question, there is a feeling of skating on the surface of the music. The effect is exacerbated by the thin, almost brittle quality of the recording, which was poor by 1970s standards, never mind today. With Rubinstein and Lipatti around, this is a non-starter and does scant justice to the artist.

RECITAL COLLECTIONS

Andante spianato et Grande Polonaise brillante, Op. 22; Ballades Nos. 1–4; Fantaisie-Impromptu, Op. 66; Polonaise-fantaisie, Op. 61.

** BIS CD 1160. Kempf.

Having been greatly impressed by his Rachmaninov CD, we approached Freddy Kempf's Chopin with

high anticipation. As in his earlier disc, he plays with great virtuosity, but there are some attention-seeking touches that make the listener more aware of the gifted pianist than of the great composer. They are sufficient to diminish the appeal of this eminently well-recorded issue.

Andante spianato et Grande Polonaise brillante; Fantaisie-Impromptu in C sharp min., Op. 66; 3 Mazurkas, Op. 59; Nocturne in E flat, Op. 9/2; Piano Sonata No. 3 in B min., Op. 58.

*** EMI 5 57702-2. Lim.

The then nineteen-year-old Korean pianist, Dong-Hyek Lim made a strong impression in his debut recital of Chopin, Ravel and Schubert. This appeared in 2003, issued in the 'Martha Argerich Presents' series. He has distinguished himself at the Moscow Competition and in Paris, and was still only nineteen when he recorded this all-Chopin recital at the Abbey Road Studios, thus reaffirming his musical credentials. His range of colour and command of dynamic nuance are masterly and he has a strong and individual musical personality. Apart from his effortless technical fluency, he brings a rich poetic imagination to this music and, in the *Sonata*, no mean command of structure. This is the finest Chopin CD to have appeared for a long time (even in a year that has seen Piotr Anderszewski's fine recital on Virgin, reviewed below) and signals the arrival of an outstanding and exciting pianistic talent. EMI give him an excellent and very natural recording.

Ballades Nos. 3 in A flat, Op. 47; 4 in F min., Op. 52; Mazurkas, Nos. 1–3, Op. 59/1–3; Op. 63; in F min., Op. 68/4; Polonaises Nos. 5 in F sharp min., Op. 44; 6 in A flat (Polonaise héroïque).

*** Virgin 5 45620-2. Anderszewski.

Piotr Anderszewski's Chopin recital has had almost as rapturous a press as his Bach – and with good reason. Along with Dong-Hyek Lim's recital discussed above, it has the right blend of sensibility and poetic feeling with classical finesse. Anderszewski is obviously an artist of quality, whose Chopin has a sense of real flair and vision as well as splendid control.

Ballade No. 3 in A flat, Op. 47; Barcarolle, Op. 60; Berceuse in D flat, Op. 57; Etudes Nos. 13 in A flat; 21 in G flat, Op. 25/1 & 9; Fantaisie in F min., Op. 49; Impromptu No. 1 in A flat, Op. 29; Mazurka No. 13 in A min., Op. 17/4; Nocturnes Nos. 5 in F sharp min., Op. 15/2; 20 in C sharp min., Op. posth.; Preludes: in A flat & C min., Op. 28/17 & 20; Scherzo No. 2 in B flat min., Op. 31; Waltzes Nos. 5 in A flat, Op. 42; 14 in E min. (op. posth.).

(BB) *** Naxos 8.555799. Idil Biret.

Idil Biret's impetuosity and brilliance both combine to make the *E minor Waltz* which opens this recital arresting in its bravura, but she plays with both character and poetry in the *Barcarolle* and the two *Ballades*, while the *Berceuse* has a touching simplicity worthy of a young pupil of Wilhelm Kempff ('Uncle Kempff' as she called him). Indeed, overall this admirably planned recital demonstrates what a natural feeling Biret has for Chopin. Her complete survey is greatly prized in France and the mixture here of *Etudes*, *Preludes* and *Mazurkas* shows her control of colour and rubato in different ways, while the dashing account of the *Scherzo in B flat* demonstrates both her easy virtuosity and her willingness to slip back readily into gentle lyricism. The recording is excellent, with a real sense of presence.

Berceuse in D flat, Op. 57; Impromptus Nos. 1–4 (Fantaisie-impromptu); Sonata No. 3 in B min.
(M) (**(*)) Decca mono 475 6157. Magalov.

Dating from 1954, this Heritage reissue reintroduces Nikita Magalov to the catalogue. This is intelligent and sensitive Chopin playing: the *Berceuse* is one of the finest performances of this elusive piece on record. The four *Impromptus* are played as a set and make very satisfying listening when heard together. The *Sonata* is also very successful, if not quite on the level of Rubinstein or Pollini. The mono recording has warmth as well as clarity.

Mazurkas: in A min., A flat, F sharp min., Op. 59/1-3; Nocturne in F, Op. 15/1; Polonaise in A flat, Op. 53; Scherzo No. 3 in C sharp min., Op. 39; Sonata No. 3 in B min. Op. 58.
** EMI (ADD) 5 56805-2. Argerich.

Argerich's recital is called 'The Legendary 1965 Recording'. It was made at the Abbey Road Studios in June of that year. Hence EMI were never able to issue it for contractual reasons. There are numerous felicities in the *Mazurkas* and the *Nocturne* but Argerich went on to make a finer account of the *B minor Sonata* for DG. The sound is surprisingly shallow and hard.

CIMAROSA, Domenico
(1749–1801)

Overtures: La baronessa Stramba; Cleopatra; Il convito; Il credulo; Il falegname; L'impresario in angustie; L'infedelt´ fedele; Il matrimonia segreto; Il ritorno di Don Calendrino; Le stravaganze del conte; La vergine del sole; Voldomiro.
*(*) Marco Polo 8.225181. Esterházy Sinf., Amoretti.

A disc of Cimorosa's overtures was sorely needed, but this does not fill the gap. The orchestra plays quite well for Alessandro Amoretti, and one enjoys the often witty melodic invention along the way, but it takes a Beecham or a Toscanni – with a first-class orchestra – to transform such works into something special. As it is, the collection here (which includes the first recording of the Vienna version of the *Il matrimonio segreto* overture) only intermittently displays the sparkle of Cimarosa's invention. The

recording is only average, lacking in depth and brilliance in general, with the strings in particular sounding rather thin. At Naxos price it would be more recommendable.

CLEMENTI, Muzio (1752–1832)

(i) *Piano Concerto in C. Symphonies: in B flat & D, Op. 18; Nos. 1 in C; 2 in D; 3 (Great National) in G; 4 in D. Minuetto pastorale; Overtures in C & D.*
(M) ** ASV CDDCS 322 (3). (i) Spada; Philh. O, D'Avalos.

Symphonies: in B flat & D, Op. 18/1-2; Nos. 1-4. Minuetto pastorale; Overtures in C & D.
(M) ** ASV CDDCS 247 (2). Philh. O, D'Avalos.

D'Avalos gets spirited playing from the Philharmonia, though he is not as strong on subtleties of phrasing as Scimone. The ASV performances are now available either in a three-disc set including the *Piano Concerto* (an arrangement of a piano sonata, where Piero Spada appears as the secure and accomplished soloist) or, even more economically, on a pair of CDs without the concerto. The bonus items are common to both.

PIANO MUSIC

Capriccio in B flat; Fantasia with Variations on 'Au clair de la lune', Op. 48; Preludio No. 1 alla Haydn in C; Preludio No. 1 alla Mozart (both from Op. 19); Sonatas: in F min., Op. 13/6; in F, Op. 33/11; in G min., Op. 34/11.
(M) *** Warner Elatus 2564 60676-2. Staier (fortepiano).

The reissue of Andreas Staier's splendid recital on Elatus gives it a fair claim to being the most desirable introduction to the music of Clementi in the catalogue. The anticipation of Beethoven appears in nearly all this music, even in the *Preludio alla Haydn*, although the companion *Prelude* is undoubtedly closer to Mozart, as is the *Capriccio*. The *Sonatas* are all considerable works, and Staier's flexibility of style brings out their individuality strongly.

CLIFFE, Frederic (1857–1931)

Symphony No. 1 in C min., Op. 1; Cloud and Sunshine (Orchestral Picture).
✪ *** Sterling CDS 1055-2. Malmö Opera O, Fifield.

Frederic Cliffe is a name (until now) totally unfamiliar to us. He was born in Bradford in 1857 and is thus contemporary with Elgar. On the staff of the Royal College of Music, he suddenly came to the fore when his *First Symphony* was premièred in 1889, receiving enthusiastic plaudits from every quarter. The symphony is indeed an astonishing achievement for a young composer and gives absolutely no impression of inexperience. It is readily comparable in warmth and constructional skill with, for instance, the *First Symphony* of Gounod, but it has a much greater affinity with the early symphonies of Dvořák.

The stabbing opening duplet leads to a strong opening idea, and the heart-warming secondary theme is to be matched in lyrical memorability with the slow movement, which opens seductively with a cor anglais solo. Its ardent climax is to be later transformed into the powerful close of the finale. There is an engagingly pithy, syncopated Scherzo to separate the first two movements, and the finale has a Mendelssohnian sparkle and grace, producing another endearing secondary melody, and moving through an assured contrapuntal development to its expansively powerful close. The orchestration throughout is vivid, showing a natural flair, especially in its richly Wagnerian scoring for the horns and brass. In short, this is a remarkably inventive and fluent work, which one returns to with much pleasure.

The orchestral picture of *Cloud and Sunshine* is equally confident in its pictorial evocation, if not as memorable thematically as the symphony. Both are played with zest, warmth and spontaneity by the fine Malmö orchestra, under their dedicated and understanding conductor, Christopher Fifield. In his notes he asks the obvious question why Cliffe's music has disappeared into oblivion, suggesting that (alongside the rising dominance of Elgar) the all-powerful Stanford might have been jealous of Cliffe as a highly skilled potential rival. There is more of Cliffe to discover, including a *Violin Concerto*; meanwhile his *Symphony* is well worth acquiring, especially in a performance and recording as red-bloodedly compulsive as this.

CLIFFORD, Hubert (1904–59)

Symphony.
*** Chan. 9757. BBC PO, Handley – BAINTON:
   Symphony No. 2;GOUGH: *Serenade.* ***

Australian born, Hubert Clifford came to England to study at the Royal College of Music in London with Vaughan Williams. He never returned to Australia and, after a spell of teaching, joined the BBC as head of Light Music Programmes. He subsequently became director of music for Alexander Korda. His four-movement *Symphony* is an ambitious score, which runs to 43 minutes. It is compelling, expertly fashioned and vividly scored, even if no distinctive voice emerges. Its idiom at times comes close to the English film music of the 1940s and 1950s. It is well argued, and it would be difficult to imagine a more persuasive and convincing account than the one it receives from the BBC Philharmonic and Vernon Handley or better-recorded sound. An enterprising release.

COATES, Eric (1886–1958)

(i) *By a Sleepy Lagoon;* (ii) *Calling all Workers: March;* (iii) *Cinderella (Phantasy); From Meadow to Mayfair: Suite; London Suite; London again Suite;* (i) *The Merrymakers Overture;* (iii) *Music everywhere: March;* (iii; iv) *Saxo-Rhapsody;* (i) *The Three Bears* (phantasy); (ii) *The Three Elizabeths: Suite;* (i) *The Three Men: Man from the Sea* (only); (iii) *Wood Nymphs (valsette).*
〇━ (B) *** CfP (ADD) 762 5572 (2). (i) LSO,
   Mackerras; (ii) CBSO, Kilbey; (iii) RLPO, Groves; (iv)
   with Brymer.

It is good to welcome back this key collection of the music of Eric Coates, 'the man who writes tunes', much loved by orchestral players as he also writes so gratefully for their instruments, being an ex-orchestral player himself. On the whole, Groves, who has the lion's share of the repertoire here, proves a persuasive advocate, although occasionally his approach is slightly bland. Jack Brymer is the excellent soloist in the *Saxo-Rhapsody*; and the other piece with a diluted jazz element, *Cinderella*, also goes with a swing. However, not surprisingly, the performances from Sir Charles Mackerras and the LSO are even more lively, and there are also several really outstanding ones from the CBSO under Reginald Kilbey. He proves the ideal Coates conductor, with a real flair for catching the sparkle of the composer's leaping allegro figurations, notably in the first movement of *The Three Elizabeths*, where also his shaping of the central, slow movement – one of the composer's finest inspirations, dedicated to the late Queen Mother – has an affectionate grace. The marches are splendidly alive and vigorous. With good transfers this is the best Coates compilation currently available.

COLERIDGE-TAYLOR, Samuel (1875–1912)

4 Characteristic Waltzes, Op. 22; Gipsy Suite, Op. 20; Hiawatha Overture, Op. 30; Othello Suite, Op. 79; Petite Suite de concert, Op. 77; Romance of the Prairie Lilies, Op. 39.
*** Marco Polo 8.223516. Dublin RTE Concert O,
   Leaper.

Coleridge-Taylor wrote much delightful orchestral music, the most famous being the charming *Petite Suite de concert*. The composer's feeling for the genre is also apparent in the *Four Characteristic Waltzes*. Each is nicely coloured: there is a nostalgic *Valse bohémienne*, a countrified *Valse rustique* (the oboe so easily conjuring up the countryside), a stately *Valse de la reine*, and a lively *Valse mauresque*. The *Gipsy Suite* is a piquantly coloured four-movement work of considerable appeal, while the *Othello Suite*, beginning with a lively dance, has an engaging *Willow Song* and ends with a stirring *Military March*. Performances and recording are excellent, and this is altogether a winning if essentially lightweight collection, perhaps more for aficionados than for the general collector.

Violin Concerto in G min., Op. 80.

**(*) Avie AV 0044. Graffin, Johannesburg PO,
Hankinson – DVORÁK: *Violin Concerto.* **(*)

When in 1910 Samuel Coleridge-Taylor went to the United States to conduct his cantata, *Hiawatha*, he was introduced to the great American violinist, Maud Powell. He promised to write a concerto for her, but his first attempt, using spirituals as thematic material, failed to satisfy him or her. His second attempt – with some themes again echoing spirituals – was performed in America in 1912, though the composer was by then too ill to attend, and he died three months later. It is a warmly lyrical work in keeping with his other music, here passionately performed by the excellent French violinist, Philippe Graffin, whose Hyperion recordings of the Saint-Saëns *Violin Concertos* are such a success. Sadly, his virtuosity is not matched by the playing of the Johannesburg Philharmonic, which may be enthusiastic and is forwardly recorded, but which is rough in ensemble. Nevertheless, a welcome rarity. When, after the first performance, the composer was described as 'a coloured Dvořák', the coupling is very apt.

COLES, Cecil (1888–1918)

Behind the Lines (suite): excerpts: Estaminet de Carrefour; Cortège (orch. Brabbins). Overture: The Comedy of Errors; From the Scottish Highlands (suite); Scherzo in A min.; (i) Fra Giacomo (scena for baritone and orchestra); (ii) 4 Verlaine Songs.
*** Hyp. CDA 67293. BBC Scottish SO, Brabbins; with (i) Whelan; (ii) Fox.

Cecil Coles, a close friend of Gustav Holst, died of wounds received on the Somme in April 1918. His career was brief but brilliant, with a period of study from 1908 on a scholarship in Stuttgart, which led to his being appointed assistant conductor at the Stuttgart Royal Opera House. As a bandmaster in the army during the war, he continued to compose, culminating in the suite *Behind the Lines*, from which the two surviving movements are included on this pioneering disc of his music. The scores were hidden away for over 80 years, until they were unearthed by his daughter, Catherine. What immediately strikes one about all the pieces is their confidence and skill, with clean-cut ideas crisply presented and beautifully orchestrated. The bustling *Comedy of Errors Overture* is typical, a piece that deserves to be in the regular repertory; and the dramatic scena, *Fra Giacomo* for baritone and orchestra to a poem by Robert Williams Buchanan, brings out the influence on Coles of Wagner, a melodramatic monologue, positive and red-blooded. The *Scherzo in A minor* is rather more

adventurous stylistically, with its angular brass motif at the start, possibly a movement designed to be included in a full symphony, while the *Four Verlaine Songs*, using English translations, sound more German than French in their warmly romantic idiom. The suite *From the Scottish Highlands*, one of the earliest pieces here, dating from 1906–7, is easily lyrical, with a Scottish folk element, ending with a moving *Lament*; but it is the two movements from *Behind the Lines* that capture the imagination most. The first, *Estaminet de Carrefour*, is a jolly genre piece picturing a typical crossroads tavern, while the final *Cortège*, preserved only in short score and sensitively orchestrated by the conductor, is an elegiac piece that in this dedicated performance has a gulp-in-throat quality, bringing home more than anything the tragedy of a career cut short. Splendid performances throughout, not least from the two singers, and warm, well-balanced recording.

CONFREY, Edward (1895–1971)

African suite; Amazonia; Blue Tornado; Coaxing the Piano; Dizzy Fingers; Fourth Dimension; Jay Walk; Kitten on the Keys; Meandering; Moods of a New Yorker (suite); Rhythm Venture; Sparkling Waters; Stumbling Paraphrase; 3 Little Oddities; Wisecracker Suite.
*** Marco Polo 8.223826. Andjaparidze.

Older collectors will surely remember *Kitten on the Keys* and perhaps *Dizzy Fingers* and *Coaxing the Piano* (all dazzlingly played here). Confrey established his international fame as a precocious virtuoso pianist/composer in the early 1920s. His music has a witty charm and is clearly influenced by French impressionism as well as by Gershwin and the Scott Joplin rags. The Georgian pianist Eteri Andjaparidze gives engagingly sparkling performances of the bravura pieces, including the ingenious closing *Fourth Dimension* with its amazingly virtuosic cross-hand accents, and she is equally at home in the more relaxed ragtime of *Jay Walk*, *Stumbling* and the sauntering gait of *Meandering*. But she also relishes the atmosphere and charm of the gentler pieces among the *Oddities* and the suites (two of the *Moods of a New Yorker* recall the tranquil simplicity of MacDowell's *To a wild rose*). A most entertaining collection, given excellent piano recording.

CONSTANTINESCU, Paul (1909–63)

The Nativity (Byzantine Christmas Oratorio).
**(*) Olympia (ADD) OCD 402 (2). Petrescu, Kessler, Teodorian, Bömches, Bucharest Enescu Ch. & PO, Basarab.

Paul Constantinescu's *Byzantine Christmas Oratorio* is an extended work of some quality in three parts:

Annunciation, Nativity and *The Three Magi*. This impressive performance comes from the late 1970s. Constantinescu writes effectively both for the chorus and for solo voices, and his orchestration too is expert. The soloists are excellent (and in different circumstances might well have made names for themselves outside their native country) and the analogue recording is very good indeed. Readers with an interest in the exotic and a touch of enterprise are recommended to investigate this set.

COPLAND, Aaron (1900–90)

(i) *Clarinet Concerto. Music for the Theatre; Music for Movies;* (ii) *Quiet City.*
**(*) Music Masters 7005-2. (i) Blount; O of St Luke's, Russell Davies; (ii) with Gekker, Taylor.

William Blount is a rich-toned soloist, with spacious, long-drawn phrasing in the opening movement which some might find too languid, contrasting with the brilliant central cadenza and roisterously jazzy finale. The vibrant *Music for the Theatre* with its brash *Prologue* and *Dance* and ironic *Burlesque* nicely offsets the mellower New England evocations of *Music for Movies*, although here *Sunday Traffic* makes another lively contrast and the *Threshing Machines* are very busy too. *Quiet City* is beautifully evoked. This is a reissue of a 1988 CD, but the vivid projection and warmth of the sound suggest more modern provenance.

Statements for Orchestra.
*** Everest (ADD) EVC 9039. LSO, Goossens –
ANTHEIL: *Symphony No. 4.* **(*)

Statements for Orchestra (1934–5), as the bald title suggests, is one of Copland's less expansive works, but its six vignettes, *Militant*, *Cryptic* (hauntingly scored for brass and flute alone), *Dogmatic* (but disconsolate), *Subjective* (an elegiac soliloquy for strings), the witty *Jingo* and the thoughtfully *Prophetic* conclusion, reveal a compression of material and sharpness of ideas that are most stimulating. Goossens's performance is first rate in every way; so is the LSO playing, and the atmospheric (1959) recording sounds hardly dated at all.

Symphony No. 3; Billy the Kid (ballet): Suite.
** Everest (ADD) EVC 9040. LSO, Copland.

Dating from 1959, the composer's first recordings of *Billy the Kid* and his *Third Symphony* (made at Walthamstow) are presented in stereo of sharp clarity with inner detail remarkably clear; the violins, however, are distinctly thin, which makes *fortissimos* sharp-edged, in spite of the basically warm ambience. The LSO are obviously coming fresh to *Billy the Kid*, playing with plenty of rhythmic bite. They give a far less virtuoso performance of the *Symphony*, which is convincing as an expression of emotion in the opening movement and the *Andan-*

tino, but less than perfect in the playing of the brilliant Scherzo.

VOCAL MUSIC

Old American Songs: Sets 1 & 2 (original versions).
** Chan. 8960. White, McNaught (with collection: *American Spirituals; Folk-songs from Barbados and Jamaica* ***).

Characteristically Willard White's opulent bass comes with a pronounced vibrato which on disc tends to get exaggerated. Yet with its helpful acoustic the Chandos recording captures the richness of his voice most attractively, very characterfully black in its evocations.

(i; ii) *Old American Songs (Sets I & II); 12 Poems of Emily Dickinson.* (ii) *4 Piano Blues.*
*** Black Box BBM 1074. (i) Chilcott; (ii) Burnside.

The tragically early death of the soprano Susan Chilcott has sadly robbed us of an outstanding singer, characterful and imaginative. When her voice, clear and fresh, was ideally suited to recording, it is doubly sad that she made far too few recordings. This superb collection of Copland songs, bringing together 25 of his most approachable pieces, plus the *Four Piano Blues*, comes from Iain Burnside's series, 'Voices', for BBC Radio 3, beautifully recorded as well as masterfully performed. Though the *Old American Songs* with their open-air, folk-based inspiration are more readily suited to a man's voice, Chilcott is strong and magnetic in each one, and she equally relishes the touching simplicity of the *Emily Dickinson Poems*, with Burnside the ideal accompanist, crisp and pointed in the songs as well as in his solo pieces.

CORELLI, Arcangelo (1653–1713)

Concerti grossi, Op. 6/1–12.
(M) *** DG 474 907-2. E. Concert, Pinnock.
(B) ** Chan. 6663 (2). Cantilena, Shepherd.

This DG performance of Corelli's masterly set of concertos won the Gramophone Early Music Baroque Award in 1989. Pinnock and his English Concert bring not only an enthusiasm for this music but a sense of grandeur. They are entirely inside its sensibility, and the playing of the concertino group (Simon Standage, Micaela Comberti and Jaap ter Linden) is wonderfully fresh-eyed and alert, yet full of colour. This is most welcome in its new mid-price format.

Corelli's masterly Op. 6 *Concertos* are now generously represented in the bargain range on CD, and although Adrian Shepherd's Cantilena are excellently recorded, their playing is not as polished as that of Marriner and the ASMF (Double Decca 443 862-2). Their approach is genial, but slow movements are sometimes rather lazy-sounding, while the lively music lacks the pointed rhythms characteristic of the best period-instrument performances.

Concerti grossi, Op. 6/1–6.

(B) **(*) HM HCX 3957014. Philh. Bar. O, McGegan.

We are offered only Volume I of McGegan's 1990 complete set of Corelli's *Concerti grossi*, and we must hope that Volume II is to follow, for this makes a good recommendation for those wanting a super-bargain set of the concertos on period instruments. The performances, intimately small-scaled as they are, combine a spirited vivacity with expressive feeling, and although slow movements are moved on more briskly than with Pinnock (who still leads the authentic field) the balance of tempi is generally convincing. One might like rather more textural warmth, but the transparency is appealing and the continuo comes through as it should, and overall the balance is very good.

Concerti grossi, Op. 6/1, 3, 7, 8 (Christmas), 11 & 12.

(M) *** DG 447 289-2. E. Concert, Pinnock.

At mid-price, with the *Christmas Concerto* included, this will admirably suit those collectors who want an original-instrument version and who are content with a single-disc selection.

CHAMBER MUSIC

Violin Sonatas, Op. 5/1–12.

✿ *** HM HMU 907 298.99 (2). Manze, Egarr.

(B) *** Virgin 2 x 1 5 62236-2 (2). Huggett, Meyerson (harpsichord or organ), Cunningham, North.

Corelli's twelve *Violin Sonatas*, Op. 5, were published in 1700. Nos. 1–5 are in five-movement *sonata la chiesa* form, Nos. 7–11 are *sonate da camera*, usually in four movements, although Nos. 10 and 11 each includes a brief additional section. Corelli's invention is inexhaustible and the set closes with perhaps the most celebrated set of variations on the traditional *La Follia* theme. Andrew Manze is in his element here. Dazzling playing on a baroque instrument, with slow movements touchingly lyrical, full of subtle detail, and plenty of gusto and character in allegros, yet with unwanted acerbities banished. Richard Egarr is a true partner, and there are countless felicities. The balance is natural, with the violin obviously dominating, yet the harpsichord comes through.

The writing is basically for two instruments, but Hugget and Meyerson incorporate a variety of continuo group combinations, adding colour with the use of organ as well as harpsichord, cello, archlute, theorbo and guitar. The performances here are as authentic as they are imaginative and stylish, and the recording balance is admirable.

CORIGLIANO, John (born 1938)

Symphony No. 2 for String Orchestra; The Mannheim Rocket.

*** ODE 1039-2. Helsinki PO, Storgårds.

John Corigliano's *Second Symphony*, commisioned by the Boston Symphony Orchestra, draws on his 1996 *String Quartet*, but the adaptation involved rewriting three of the five movements. The opening *Prelude* combines synchronous threads of sound which oscillate hauntingly, leading to a climax and a serene chordal apotheosis. The Scherzo is slashingly aggressive, but the middle section is gentle, bearing a lyrical passacaglia. The *Nocturne* opens ethereally and creates a richly sustained string tapestry to picture a serene Moroccan night, interrupted by a pattern of muezzin calls from the city's many mosques. Then comes a complex *Fugue*, which the composer describes as 'anti-contrapuntal'. He uses a single theme in separate voices moving at different tempi; the work closes with a *Postlude* in valedictory mood, with a high solo violin 'meant to impact a feeling of farewell'. The synchronous sound threads of the *Prelude* return, and the symphony ends as it began, fading into silence. It is a remarkably imaginative piece, not nearly as difficult to follow as it sounds.

The Mannheim Rocket is a phantasmagorical orchestral picture of Baron von Munchausen's Wedding Cake Rocket taking off, but it is also a pun on a musical term made famous by the Mannheim orchestra in the eighteenth century to describe a rising musical sequence that speeded up and grew louder as it went higher. Corigliano quotes the stately opening of a Stamitz *Sinfonia* to lift his rocket clear, but in the end it crashes to the ground, and the piece returns to its Mannhein device for its coda. The performances here are first class and so is the spectacular recording. This is all real music and well worth trying.

CORNELIUS, Peter (1824–74)

Der alte Soldat, Op. 12/1; 3 Chorgesänge, Op. 11; Die Könige, Op. 8/3; Leibe: Ein Zyklus von 3 Chorliedern, Op. 18; 3 Psalmlieder, Op. 13; So weich und warm; Requiem; Trauerchöre, Op. 9; Trost in Tränen, Op. 14; Die Vätergruft, Op. 19.

*** Hyp. CDA 67206. Polyphony, Layton.

Building on the German tradition of amateur choral societies, Peter Cornelius developed the genre of unaccompanied choral pieces like these, starting with the one which became by far the most famous, *Die Könige* ('The Three Kings'). Cornelius, a lifelong devotee of German verse, responded to the words with keen sensitivity, heightening the poems he set to make the genre an equivalent to Lieder, spanning a wide range of moods and atmosphere with beautifully crafted choral effects. Stephen Layton's brilliant group, Polyphony, prove ideal as interpreters, refined on detail, polished in ensemble, while giving thrust and intensity to each item. Beautifully balanced and atmospheric recording to match.

CORRETTE, Michel (1709–95)

6 Organ Concertos, Op. 26.

(B) *** HM (ADD) HMA 195 5148. Saorgin (organ of L'Eglise de l'Escarène, Nice), Bar. Ens., Bezzina.

These lively and amiable *Concertos* are here given admirably spirited and buoyant performances, splendidly recorded using period instruments. The orchestral detail is well observed, and René Saorgin plays vividly on an attractive organ. Michel Corrette's invention has genuine spontaneity, and this makes an enjoyable collection to dip into, though not to play all at one go.

Sonatas: for Bassoon & Continuo: in F & G (Les Délices de la solitude), Op. 20/1 & 5; for Flute & Continuo: in E min.; D min., Op. 13/2 & 4; for Harpsichord & Flute in E min., Op. 15/4; for Oboe & Continuo in D min. (L'Ecole d'Orphée). Suite for Recorder & Continuo in C min. (from Les Pièces, Op. 5). (Harpsichord): Les Amusements du Parnasse: La Furstemberg & Variations; Le Sabotier hollandois & Variations; Premier livre de pièces de clavecin: Suite in D (complete); Suite No. 3 (Les Etoiles): Rondeau, Op. 12 (both from Op. 12).

*** Mer. CDE 84325. Carroll, Rowland, Civil.

The rather agreeable *Oboe Sonata* comes from *L'Ecole d'Orphée*, a violin tutor, and the Op. 5 *Pièces*, from which the *Suite for Recorder and Continuo* is taken, were primarily designated for the musette (an aristocratic set of bagpipes). However, the composer suggested a whole range of alternatives. The versatile and expert Paul Carroll has mastered all the baroque instruments featured in these works and plays each of them with spirit and character. But it is perhaps his harpsichord music for which Corrette is best remembered – and justly so. The *D major Suite* is strikingly inventive. David Rowland plays them on excellent modern copies of two different period instruments, and he is beautifully recorded. The instrumental works, too, are naturally balanced. An entertaining 73 minutes – but not necessarily to be taken all at once.

COUPERIN, François (1668–1733)

KEYBOARD MUSIC

Harpsichord Suites, Book 4, Ordres 21, 24–27.
*** Hyp. CDA 67480. Hewitt (piano).

Angela Hewitt's selection from Book 4 (with the Ordres not played consecutively) is even more enticing than her first collection from Books 2 and 3 (CDA 67440 – see our main volume).

All the pieces have intriguing titles and not all of them are obviously reflected in the mood of the music, though *La Mistérieuse* is certainly atmospheric and *La Muse Victorieuse* is full of self-confidence. Among the most enigmatic are *Les Ombres errantes* ('Wandering souls'), the rondeau *L'Epineuse* ('The Thorny One'), which in the event is most engaging, and the poised and friendly representation of the composer's own name, which may or may not be intended as a self-portrait. *L'Amphibie* is certainly ambitious, a memorable passacaglia minus a ground bass, while *La Petite Pince-sans rire* ('The Straight-faced Wag') is agreeably ironic. The four pieces from the 17th *Ordre* (all in the key of B minor) are kept until last and make a splendidly satisfying closing set. The allemande *L'Esquise* is aptly named, but *Les Pavots* ('The Poppies') and *Les Chinoises* (not at all Chinese) are charming fancies, and the closing *Saillie* ('Leap') serves to end the *Ordre* positively and with satisfying finality. Splendid alive and sensitive performances, really fine recording and excellent documentation.

COWARD, Noël (1899–1973)

Bitter Sweet (musical play).
*** That's Entertainment CDTER 2 1160 (2). Masterson, Smith, Ashe, Maxwell, New Sadler's Wells Opera Ch. & O, Reed.

The idea of writing his pastiche Viennese operetta came to Noël Coward in 1928 after hearing an orchestral selection from *Die Fledermaus* on a gramophone record. Hours later, his car parked on Wimbledon Common under the shade of a huge horse-chestnut tree, the story of its heroine, Sari Linden, was planned and some of the principal melodies began to form in Coward's sub-conscious. The score was finished a year later and the composer relates how the great hit-tune (perhaps the finest sentimental operetta melody written after Lehár's *Merry Widow Waltz*) came to him 'whole and complete', while waiting in a 22-minute traffic-jam in a London taxi.

Bitter Sweet was an enormous sucess in its time, but then it disappeared from the repertoire, although there have been comparatively recent revivals in Plymouth and – very appropriately – Wimbledon. The present re-creation at the New Sadler's Wells Opera, so vividly caught on this recording, could hardly be better cast. Valerie Masterson is a wholly engaging Sari and Martin Smith makes a fine partner in the delicious *Dear little café* and the famous *I'll see you again*. There are lots of fizzing ensembles, not least *Ladies of the Town* (well led by Donald Maxwell) and of course the bouncy *Ta-ra-ra-boom-de-ay*, which few realize derives from this source. But the other great number of the show – Coward at his most endearing – comes from a subsidiary character, the (appropriately named) Manon's sad little soliloquy, *If love were all*, sung with just the right blend of tenderness and philosophical resgination by Rosemary Ashe. Michael Read directs the show with fine spirit and much affection (the orchestral *Bitter Sweet Waltz* has a nice Viennese lilt) and the recording is brightly atmospheric.

COWEN, Frederick (1852–1935)

Symphony No. 3 in C min. (Scandinavian); The Butterfly's Ball: Concert Overture; Indian Rhapsody.
** Marco Polo 8.220308. Slovak State PO (Košice), Leaper.

The *Symphony No. 3* (1880) shows (to borrow Hanslick's judgement) 'good schooling, a lively sense of tone painting and much skill in orchestration, if not striking originality'. But what Cowen lacks in individuality he makes up for in natural musicianship and charm. His best-known work is the *Concert Overture, The Butterfly's Ball* (1901), which is scored with Mendelssohnian delicacy and skill. The *Indian Rhapsody* (1903) with its naive orientalisms carries a good deal less conviction. The performances are eminently lively. The recording is pleasingly reverberant but somewhat lacking in body.

CRESTON, Paul (1906–85)

Symphony No. 5, Op. 64; Invocation and Dance, Op. 58; Out of the Cradle, Op. 5; Partita, Op. 12; Toccata, Op. 68.
(BB) *** Naxos 8.559153. Seattle SO, Schwarz.

Collectors who have his *Second Symphony* will know just how inventive Paul Creston can be and how expertly he writes for the orchestra. The *Toccata* from 1957 has much of the same vitality and rhythmic flair as the symphony, and the wild clarinet solos we recall in the *Second Symphony* resurface here, calling to mind the *Danse générale* from *Daphnis et Chloé*. The *Fifth Symphony* (1956) is a three-movement work, exuberant and full of spirit, and as expertly fashioned as most of Creston's music. *Out of the Cradle* and the *Partita* are early and of lesser interest. Creston was grievously neglected in the 1960s and '70s when tonal composers were considered 'uninteresting' and the likes of Barber patronizingly dismissed. Creston may not be as gifted as the latter, but readers who respond to Barber and Copland will find themselves at home in Creston's world. Splendid performances and recording.

CUI, César (1835–1918)

(i) *Suite concertante (for violin & orchestra), Op. 25. Suite miniature No. 1, Op. 20; Suite No. 3 (In modo populari), Op. 43.*
**(*) Marco Polo 8.220308. (i) Nishizaki; Hong Kong PO, Schermerhorn.

These pieces have a faded period charm that is very appealing (try the *Petite marche* and the equally likeable *Impromptu à la Schumann* from the *Suite miniature*) and are very well played by the Hong Kong Philharmonic. Takako Nishizaki is the expert soloist in the *Suite concertante*. An interesting issue that fills a gap in the repertoire, and very decently recorded too.

Preludes Nos. 1–25.
(BB) **(*) Naxos 8.555567. Biegel.

Of all the members of the 'Kutchka' or 'Mighty Handful' (Balakirev, Borodin, César Cui, Mussorgsky and Rimsky-Korsakov), Cui is by far the least well known. Born in Vilnius, the son of a French officer who had remained in Lithuania after the Napoleonic retreat, he briefly studied with Moniuszko in Warsaw before embarking on a military career (he was an authority on fortifications). His was a talent of minuscule proportions beside those of his four friends, although he was an acerbic, opinionated critic. These *Preludes* have a certain charm, though in *No. 13 in F sharp* the debt to Tchaikovsky is strong – and even stronger in its successor, which is almost a paraphrase of the *Valse à cinq temps* of Tchaikovsky's Op. 72 set. There is also a lot of Schumann and even more Mendelssohn here. Slight and derivative though many of these pieces may be, there is still much worthwhile music among these miniatures, and Jeffrey Biegel gives decent and faithful accounts of them. The recordings come from 1992 and are perfectly acceptable, although the piano has not been perfectly conditioned.

CURZON, Frederick (1899–1973)

The Boulevardier; Bravada (Paso doble); Capricante (Spanish Caprice); Cascade (Waltz); Dance of an Ostracised Imp; Galavant; In Malaga (Spanish Suite); Punchinello: Miniature Overture; Pasquinade; La Peineta; Robin Hood Suite; (i) Saltarello for Piano & Orchestra; Simonetta (Serenade).
*** Marco Polo 8.223425. (i) Cápová; Slovak RSO (Bratislava), Leaper.

The best-known piece here is the *Dance of an Ostracised Imp*, a droll little scherzando. But the *Galavant* is hardly less piquant and charming, the delicious *Punchinello* sparkles with miniature vitality, and the *Simonetta* serenade is sleekly beguiling. Curzon liked to write mock Spanishry, and several pieces here have such a Mediterranean influence. Yet their slight elegance and economical scoring come from cooler climes further north. Both *In Malaga* and the jolly *Robin Hood Suite* are more frequently heard on the (military) bandstand, but their delicate central movements gain much from the more subtle orchestral scoring. The performances throughout are played with the finesse and light touch we expect from this fine Slovak series, so ably and sympathetically conducted by Adrian Leaper. The recording is admirable.

DA CREMA, Giovanni Maria

(died *c.* 1550)

Con lagrime e sospiri (Philippe Verdelot); De vous servir (Claudin de Sermisy); Lasciar il velo (Jacques Arcadelt); O felici occhi mieie (Arcadelt); Pass'e mezo ala bolognesa; Ricercars quinto, sexto, decimoquarto, decimoquinto, duodecimo, tredecimo; Saltarello ditto Bel fior; Saltarello ditto El Giorgio; Saltarello ditto El Maton.

(BB) ★★★ Naxos 8.550778. Wilson (lute) –
   DALL'AQUILA: *Lute Pieces.* ★★★

The pieces here are taken from a *First Lute Book*, which Da Crema published in 1546. The inclusion of the dance movements alongside reflective pieces like *Con lagrime e sospiri* gives variety to an attractive programme, and the *Pass'e mezo ala bolognesa* is rather catchy. The performances are of the highest order, and Christopher Wilson is recorded most naturally. Well worth exploring, especially at such a modest cost.

DA PONTE, Lorenzo (1749–1838)

L'ape musicale.

★★(★) Nuova Era 6845/6 (2). Scarabelli, Matteuzzi, Dara, Comencini, Teatro la Fenice Ch. & O., Parisi.

This greatest of librettists was no composer, but he was musical enough to devise a pasticcio like *L'ape musicale* ('The Musical Bee') from the works of others, notably Rossini and Mozart. The first act – full of Rossinian passages one keeps recognizing – leads up to a complete performance of Tamino's aria, *Dies Bildnis*, sung in German at the end of the act. Similarly, Act II culminates in an adapted version of the final cabaletta from Rossini's *Cenerentola*. The sound is dry, with the voices slightly distanced. The stage and audience noises hardly detract from the fun of the performance.

DALL'ABACO, Evaristo Felice

(1675–1742)

Concerti a quattro de chiesa, Op. 2/1, 4, 5 & 7; Concerti a più instrumenti, Op. 5/3, 5 & 6; Op. 6/5 & 11.

★★★ Teldec 3984 22166-2. Concerto Köln.

Dall'Abaco's foreign travels exposed him to both French and Italian influences, and he draws on them just as it suits him. We also find him astutely keeping up with public taste and subtly modifying his style over the years. Of the four *Concerti a quattro da chiesa*, taken from his Op. 2 (1712), *No. 5 in G minor* is a particularly fine work, worthy of Corelli. The Op. 5 set of *Concerti a più instrumenti* (*c.* 1719) brings predominantly French influences, and very appealing they are. Op. 6 (*c.* 1734) is more forward-looking,

galant in style, with amiable allegros and nicely expressive cantabiles. All in all, this is a most stimulating collection. The Concerto Köln's virtuosity brings a sparkling response, with the group's somewhat abrasive string-timbres infectiously bending to the composer's force of personality. They are splendidly recorded. A real find.

DALL'AQUILA, Marco

(*c.* 1480–1538)

Amy souffrez (Pierre Moulu); La cara cosa; Priambolo; Ricercars Nos. 15, 16, 18, 19, 22, 24, 28, 33, 70 & 101; 3 Ricercar/Fantasias; La Traditora.

(BB) ★★★ Naxos 8.550778. Wilson (lute) – DA CREMA: *Lute Pieces.* ★★★

Marco dall'Aquila was a much-admired Venetian composer/lutenist in his day. These are relatively simple pieces, rhythmically active but often dolorous; *Amy souffrez* and *La cara cosa* are among the more striking, but the *Ricercars* can be haunting too. They are beautifully played by Christopher Wilson, and the recording is admirably balanced.

DAMASE, Jean-Michel (born 1928)

Quintet for Flute, Harp, Violin, Viola & Cello; Sonata for Flute & Harp; Trio for Flute, Harp & Cello; Variations 'Early Music' for Flute & Harp.

★★★ ASV CDDCA 898. Noakes, Tingay, Friedman, Atkins, Szucs.

Jean-Michel Damase was a pupil of Alfred Cortot and Henri Büsser, and his chamber music (and in particular the *Trio for Flute, Harp and Cello* and the *Quintet*) has a fluent, cool charm. It is beautifully fashioned, and those coming to it for the first time will find it very attractive, with touches of Poulenc without his harmonic subtlety. It is nicely played and very well recorded.

DAQUIN, Louis-Claude (1694–1772)

Nouveau Livre de Noëls Nos. 1–12.

★★★ Hyp. CDA 66816. Herrick (organ of Church of St Rémy de Dieppe).

Louis-Claude Daquin was a keyboard prodigy, and at the age of six he is reported to have played for the king, who correctly predicted his later fame. Daquin became organist at Notre Dame in 1735. He is best known for his *Noëls*, which are often used as piquant organ encore pieces. The composer's title page suggests that they could also be played on harpsichord or violins and woodwind; but they were obviously meant primarily for the organ and were intended for performance at Christmas Mass – acting as seasonal voluntaries, usually heard just before midnight.

Each uses a popular melody, to which a cumulative

bravura variation style is applied, with the decoration and variants steadily gaining in pace and brilliance. Above all, performances were required to be buoyant and spirited, as indeed they are here, and Christopher Herrick, who registers a colourfully varied palette, obviously enjoys himself throughout. The Dieppe organ seems an ideal choice (sample Nos. 4, 6 or 10) and it is beautifully recorded. Not a disc to play all at once, but very engaging to dip into.

D'ASTORGA, Emanuele
(c. 1680–1757)

Stabat Mater.

● (M) ★★★ DHM/BMG 82876 60145-2. Monoyios, Mammel, Happel, Balthazar-Neumann Ch., Freiburg Bar. O, Hengelbrock – DURANTE: *Magnificat in B flat*; PERGOLESI: *Confitebor tibi Domine.* ★★★ ●

Baron Emanuele d'Astorga came from the Spanish nobility and was a self-taught composer; he settled for a while in Italy, travelled to London and Lisbon, but eventually returned to his homeland. He led an adventurous life, which was pictured in both a romantic novel and an opera in which the deranged hero is sustained by hearing his own *Stabat Mater*. D'Astorga's setting was justly renowned in its time for its intensity of lyrical feeling and its broad flow of lyrical melody, notably in the solos and duets. Yet, unusually, it ends exultantly, celebrating Christ's 'victory' over the cross, with a lively if unadventurous extended final chorus. The period performance here is in every way persuasive, beautifully sung and played, and directed with much spirit by Hengelbrock. The recording is first class, and texts and translation are included.

DAUVERGNE, Antoine (1713–97)

Concerts de simphonies: Premier Concert in B flat, Op. 3/1; Deuxième Concert in F, Op. 3/2; Quatrième Concert in A, Op. 4/2.

(M) ★★★ Virgin 5 61542-2. Concerto Köln.

Dauvergne's *Concerts de simphonies*, Opp. 3 and 4, are a real find, full of attractive ideas and catchy rhythms. Each begins with an Overture and ends with a Chaconne. One has only to sample the skipping *Andantino* of Op. 3/2, the engaging *Minuetto grazioso* or the penultimate *Presto* (with its fizzing groups of double triplets and double quadruplets) to confirm that Dauvergne is a composer of individuality. The performances here have both grace and much vigour: the period-instrument playing is polished and aurally pleasing, and often has real bravura. The recording too is first class. Well worth seeking out.

DAWSON, William (1899–1990)

Negro Folk Symphony.

★★★ Chan. 9909. Detroit SO, Järvi – ELLINGTON: *Harlem, The River; Solitude.* ★★★

William Dawson began life the son of a poor Alabama labourer, yet he worked his way up to become Director of Music at the Tuskegee Institute. His *Negro Folk Symphony* is designed to combine European influences and Negro folk themes. All three movements are chimerical. The music is rhapsodic and has plenty of energy and ideas, but they are inclined to run away with their composer. Järvi, however, is persuasive and has the advantage of excellent orchestral playing and first-class Chandos sound.

DEBUSSY, Claude (1862–1918)

Concertante and Orchestral Music (almost complete).

(B) ★★★ Chan. X10144 (4). Queffélec, Masters, Bell, King, McChrystal, Ulster O, Y. P. Tortelier.

Chandos have now reissued Yan Pascal Tortelier's undoubtedly distinguished, virtually complete coverage of Debussy's orchestral and concertante music in a bargain box. The first-class recordings generally reflect the state of the art, and there is good documentation. Full details of the contents, which differs slightly from the competing Decca set below, are given on p. 364 of our main volume, and at its new price the set is very recommendable.

(i; ii) *Berceuse héroïque;* (iii) *La Boîte à joujoux* (ballet); *Children's Corner* (both orch. Caplet); (i; iv) *Danse (Tarantelle styrienne);* (i; v; vi) *Danses sacrée et profane for Harp and Strings;* (vii) *Fantaisie for Piano and Orchestra;* (iii) *Images; Jeux;* (i; iv) *Khamma* (orch. Koechlin); (i; vi) *Marche écossaise;* (iii) *Le Martyre de Saint Sébastien* (fragments symphoniques); *La Mer; Nocturnes;* (viii) *Petite suite* (orch. Büsser); (iii) *La Plus que lente* (orch. composer); *Prélude à l'après-midi d'un faune;* (ix) *Prélude: La Cathédrale engloutie* (orch. Stokowski); (viii; x) *Première Rapsodie for Clarinet and Orchestra;* (iii) *Printemps* (orch. Büsser); (viii) *Suite bergamasque: Clair de lune* (orch. Caplet).

(B) ★★(★) Decca 475 313-2 (4). (i) Concg. O; (ii) Van Beinum; (iii) Montreal SO, Dutoit; (iv) Chailly; (v) Vera Badings; (vi) Haitink; (vii) Kars, LSO, Gibson; (viii); SRO, Ansermet; (ix) New Philh. O, Stokowski; (x) Gugholz.

This Decca compilation is based on the outstanding series of recordings of the major works, made in the late 1980s and early 1990s by Dutoit in Montreal, notable both for colourfully expansive recording, richly atmospheric, and the conductor's highly sympathetic approach, vital and flexible yet strong. For the *Berceuse* and the *Danses sacrée et profane* Concertgebouw recordings from the Philips catalogue have been chosen, conducted with great finesse by Eduard van Beinum and Haitink respectively, and for the *Fantaisie for Piano and Orchestra* the soloist is Jean-Randolph Kars, a very persuasive Debussian, given excellent support by Gibson. Ansermet contributes too, and if his *Petite suite* is not as polished as its Chandos competitor, it is certainly vivid. We return to the Concertgebouw Orchestra, this time conducted by Chailly, for the rare *Khamma*, and Stokowski's astonishing orchestration of *La Cathédrale engloutie* makes for an unexpected bonus. Excellent value, although Tortelier's similar but not identical Chandos compilation is more consistent in the quality of the orchestral playing and recording.

6 epigraphes antiques (orch. Ansermet); Jeux.

(***) Testament mono SBT 1324. SRO, Ansermet (with SAINT-SAENS: *Danse macabre*) – DUKAS: *L'Apprenti Sorcier, etc.* **(*).

Ansermet recorded *Jeux* with the *Six Epigraphes antiques* in the early days of LP, re-recording it in stereo five years later. His was only the second recording of the piece to appear (De Sabata's version with the Santa Cecilia Orchestra had appeared on two HMV 78rpm discs in 1947). Although the Suisse Romande Orchestra's wind intonation is not impeccable, it is better than on some issues from the early days of stereo. *Jeux* first appeared in 1953 and the *Six Epigraphes antiques* the following year. Ansermet's scoring is most felicitous. The performances have great atmosphere and real style; and it is good to have the Ansermet account of his own transcription, whose tempi are so perfectly judged and textures so perfectly balanced, back in circulation. Very decent sound. We do not recall these appearing on CD transfers before. A most winning reissue, well worth investigating.

(i) Images; (ii) Jeux; Khamma; (i) La Mer; (ii) Prélude à l'après-midi d'un faune; Printemps. (iii) 2 Arabesques; Children's Corner; Estampes; Images, Book 1; L'Isle joyeuse; Page d'album: Pièce pour le vêtement du blessé; La Plus que lente; Pour le piano; Préludes, Book 1.

(BB) ** Virgin 562261-2 (4). (i) Rotterdam PO; (ii) Finnish RSO; Saraste; (iii) Pommier.

This Virgin collection is inexpensive and represents fair value. In the orchestral items, the Rotterdam acoustic brings an evocative allure to *Images*, which is played very vividly and has both sparkle and atmosphere. *La Mer* brings similar delicacy of detail and no lack of intensity at the close of the *Dialogue de vent et de la mer*. *Jeux* in not in the same league as Haitink's and, apart from a quite impressive account of *Images*, the best thing here is the *Khamma*. Altogether, these performances are eminently serviceable and certainly recommendable, even if there are better individual versions available elsewhere. The piano music offers

accomplished playing from Jean-Bernard Pommier, an intelligent artist with a good feeling for Debussy and excellent technical address. He is often perceptive; but there is strong competition here and, notably in the *Préludes* (where Pommier's bold articulation brings some hardness), the good must yield to the better. The recording is basically truthful, if a little bottom-heavy at times.

Images; La Mer; Nocturnes: Nuages; Fêtes (only); Prélude à l'après-midi d'un faune.

(M) *** RCA (ADD) 82876 59416-2. Boston SO, Munch.

These vintage Munch accounts of Debussy were transformed on CD, with the Boston acoustic now casting a wonderfully warm aura over the orchestra, the sound gloriously expansive and translucent. There is marvellous Boston playing here, especially from the violins. Munch's inclination to go over the top may not appeal to all listeners, but the results are compelling and the orchestral bravura is thrilling. The *Prélude à l'après-midi d'un faune* makes a ravishing interlude, expanding to a rapturous climax. A splendid addition to RCA's mid-priced 'Classic Library' series.

Jeux; Khamma; La Mer; Prélude à l'après-midi d'un faune.

(M) ** Decca (ADD) 470 255-2. SRO, Ansermet.

It was sensible of Decca to choose to use Ansermet's 1957 version of *La Mer* instead of the later, 1964 one: the earlier version has more tension and atmosphere and is better played. His 1958 *Jeux* has plenty of atmosphere and character, too. The rarely heard *Khamma* (orchestrated by Koechlin) is aurally fascinating: the sinister opening of deep woodwinds and pulsating strings is superbly caught by Ansermet and the Decca engineers. Indeed, the analytical quality of these readings is what makes them fascinating and, barring certain lapses of intonation and ensemble from time to time, characteristic of the Swiss orchestra, these performances show Ansermet on top form. The recordings, if a bit thin, have – as always from this source – amazing clarity and vividness.

Le Martyre de Saint Sébastien (symphonic fragments).

** RCA 74321 72788-2. N. German RSO, Wand – MUSSORGSKY: *Pictures at an Exhibition.* **

Günter Wand's account of the four fragments from *Le Martyre de Saint-Sébastien* comes from a concert performance in 1982, and the disc is obviously addressed to Wand fans. The conductor had great feeling for this work, and his is an idiomatic and sympathetic account. However, it is not superior to Barenboim, who offers the complete score, and it comes with yet another *Pictures at an Exhibition*. At 54 minutes and full price, this is unlikely to make the pulse quicken.

Le Martyre de Saint-Sébastien: La Cour des lys; Danse extatique.

*** Arthaus **DVD** 100 314. Rotterdam Philh. O, Gergiev (V/D: Bob van den Burg) – PROKOFIEV: *Scythian Suite;* STRAVINSKY: *Piano Concerto etc.* ***

This DVD shows something of the breadth of Gergiev's musical sympathies (and, in the rehearsal sequences, his charm, which persuades his players to give of their best). He has a geniuine feeling for Debussy and we can imagine him directing a distinguished *Pelléas*.

Le Martyre de Saint-Sébastien: 2 Fanfares & Symphonic fragments; (i) *Nocturnes; Printemps (Symphonic Suite).*

🕪 ✿ (M) *** DG 476 1653. O de Paris; (i) & Ch., Barenboim.

This is one of Barenboim's very finest records and it has been out of the catalogue since the early 1990s. We welcome it back as part of Universal's 'Penguin ✿ Collection'. Its 72 minutes include not only the early *Printemps* and the *Symphonic fragments* from *Le Martyre de Saint-Sébastien* but also his splendid set of *Nocturnes*. The latter performance, though highly individual in its control of tempo, has great fervour: *Sirènes* develops a feeling of soaring ecstasy, and the closing pages with chorus are rapturously beautiful. Comparably, in *Le Martyre* Barenboim succeeds in distilling an intense, rapt quality and brings to life its evocative atmosphere in a way that has not been matched since Cantelli's mono HMV recording. If Barenboim does not expound the score with quite the same delicacy of feeling as Cantelli secured, he still refrains from any expressive indulgence and allows the music to speak for itself. He is no less persuasive in *Printemps* (which had to be re-orchestrated by Henri Büsser – following the composer's instructions – when the original was lost in a fire). This receives a performance as good as any in the catalogue. Barenboim succeeds in balancing intensity with atmospheric feeling, and the result is very persuasive. The 1977/8 recordings, made in either Notre Dame du Liban or the Paris Mutualité, are spacious, rich in texture and well balanced, with good defintion and range, and the CD transfer has refined detail without reducing the allure.

La Mer.

*** Naïve V 4946. O. Nat. de France, Svetlanov – SCRIABIN: *Poème de l'extase.* ***

(M) ** Chan. 6615. Detroit SO, Järvi – MILHAUD: *Suite provençale;* RAVEL: *Boléro; La Valse.* **

The Naïve CD provides an impressive memento of Svetlanov's last visit to France in January 2001, a year before his death. *La Mer* was recorded on 25 January at the Théâtre des Champs-Elysées, and *Le Poème de l'extase* three days later in Nantes. Although he is primarily associated with Russian repertoire, Svetlanov obviously has an intuitive feeling for Debussy's

masterpiece, and he established excellent rapport with these fine players. A very atmospheric account, which is finely paced and superbly played. There would have been room on this 54-minute disc for another piece from these concerts, but doubtless reasons of either time or quality militated against its inclusion. This is a performance of stature, as is that of the Scriabin. An excellent note by Marc Vignal and very good sound.

Neeme Järvi's version of *La Mer* has a fair amount going for it; it has a subtle sense of flow and a good feeling for texture. There are some oddities, including a slowing down in the second part of *De l'aube à midi sur la mer* some way before the passage Satie referred to as 'the bit he liked at about quarter to eleven'. Given the sheer quantity and quality of the competition, however, this is not really a front-runner.

La Mer; Nocturnes.

✿ (M) *** EMI 5 62746-2 [5 627592]. Philh. Ch. & O, Giulini – RAVEL: *Alborada; Daphnis et Chloé: Suite No. 2.* *** ✿

Giulini's early stereo recordings of Debussy (from 1962) remain very distinguished indeed. It would be difficult to fault his reading of *La Mer*, and the *Nocturnes* are played with great delicacy of feeling and refinement of detail. *Nuages* and *Sirènes* are a perhaps a little too dreamy, but they are magically atmospheric, with a fine contribution from the Philharmonia Chorus, which gives the final movement great allure. Both works here are beautifully recorded; indeed, the Kingsway Hall sound is of demonstration quality for its time, and the first-rate CD transfer combines ambience and bloom with inner clarity. The Ravel coupling is equally fine, and this CD is fully worthy of its inclusion among EMI's 'Great Recordings of the Century', ranking alongside Karajan's celebrated DG recordings of *La Mer* and *Daphnis*, with marginally even finer sound.

La Mer; (i) *Nocturnes. Prélude à l'après-midi d'un faune.*

(BB) *** Regis RRC 1177. LSO; (i) L. Symphony Ch.; Frühbeck de Burgos.

Although strong in Mediterranean atmosphere, Frühbeck de Burgos's account of *La Mer* has an underlying grip, so he can concentrate on evocation at the opening and continue to lead the ear on spontaneously. Overall there is plenty of excitement and much subtlety of detail, both here and in the *Nocturnes*, where textures again have the sensuousness of southern climes, and no lack of glitter. The *Prélude à l'après-midi d'un faune* brings lovely, delicate flute-playing from Paul Edmund-Davies and a richly moulded string climax. If these are not conventional readings, they are full of impulse and are superbly recorded.

CHAMBER MUSIC

String Quartet in G min., Op. 10.

** Simax PSC 1201. Vertavo Qt (with GRIEG: *String Quartet* **).

(BB) ** Warner Apex 8573 89231-2. Keller Qt – RAVEL: *Quartet.* **

In neither the Debussy nor the coupled Grieg *Quartet* would the Vertavo Quartet be a first choice, although they make a logical coupling since they share the same key and the Grieg (1878) so clearly influenced the Debussy (1893). The playing is very good but nothing special.

The Keller Quartet is a Hungarian group, formed when the players were still studying at Budapest. They came to wider attention when they won a number of international prizes in 1990. They offer the Debussy and Ravel *Quartets* alone, but their CD is in the lowest price-range. However, they rush and over-dramatize the first movement of the Debussy – in fact, the whole work is rather hurried along, and there is just too much paprika here to make this a three-star recommendation. First choice rests with the Melos Quartet coupled with Ravel (☞ ✿ DG 463 082-2).

Violin Sonata in G min.

(BB) *(*) EMI Encore 5 85708-2. Zimmermann, Lonquich – JANACEK: *Violin Sonata*; RAVEL: *Violin Sonata; Sonate posthume.* *(*)

Frank Peter Zimmermann projects as if he were in a large concert hall and the thoughtful intimacy of this great work eludes him. He plays with virtuosity and expressive warmth, though Alexander Lonquich is sometimes too expressively vehement. Not a realistic choice, in spite of the attractive couplings and the modest price.

PIANO MUSIC

Solo piano music

2 Arabesques; Ballade; Danse bohémienne; Danse (Tarantelle styrienne); Images (1894); Nocturne; Pour le piano; Rêverie; Suite bergamasque; Valse romantique.

(BB) **(*) Regis RRC 1121. Tirimo.

This is a useful and inexpensive collection and Tirimo's playing is distinguished: there is never any doubt as to his Debussian credentials. He plays only the two outer movements of the 1894 *Images*, arguing quite reasonably that the differences between the two versions of the *Sarabande* are only slight. The acoustic of Rosslyn Hill Chapel, Hampstead, is pleasing and allows the sound to expand; but the balance is close and the microphone even picks up the pedal mechanism (try the opening of the *Danse* on track 8). This will worry some listeners more than others, and otherwise this is a fine disc.

2 Arabesques; Berceuse héroïque; D'un cahier d'esquisses; Hommage à Haydn; Images, Books I & II; L'Isle joyeuse; Page d'album; Rêverie.

☞ ✿ (M) *** Decca 475 210-2. Kocsis.

Winner of the *Gramophone* 1990 Instrumental Award, Zoltán Kocsis's Debussy recital, originally issued by Philips, is in every way outstanding. The recording of the piano is still among the most realistic we have heard and artistically this collection is even more distinguished in terms of pianistic finesse, sensitivity and tonal refinement than his earlier, 1983 collection (Philips 412 118-2, now withdrawn).

Children's Corner; Estampes; L'Isle joyeuse; Images I & II; La Plus que lente; Suite bergamasque.

(M) (***) EMI mono 5 62798-2. Gieseking.

A self-recommending disc, drawing on Walter Gieseking's four-disc survey listed in our main *Guide* (EMI 5 65855-2). The mono recordings are of excellent quality.

Estampes; Images (1894); Images I & II.

(BB) ** Warner Apex 7559 79674-2. Jacobs.

Paul Jacobs has an enviable reputation, and his recordings of the *Images* and the *Estampes* have much to recommend them. They were recorded in 1978 in New York, but the sound, though generally acceptable, is a little bottom-heavy at times, unpleasingly so (try *Quelques aspects de 'Nous n'irons plus au bois'*, the third of the 1894 *Images*). It is by no means as refined sonically as, say, Zoltán Kocsis's Debussy records (Philips) or Pascal Rogé (Decca), made only a few years later.

12 Etudes.

(M) ** DG 471 359-2. Pollini – BOULEZ: *Piano Sonata No. 2.* (***)

12 Etudes; Images, Books 1–2.

*** Warner 8573 83940-2. Aimard.

Debussy playing of some stature from Pierre-Laurent Aimard, though his playing does not project the mists and atmosphere of this music so much as its extraordinary colour, inner vitality and originality. The *Images* are vibrant and as good as any in the catalogue, and the musical and technical challenges of the *Etudes* are surmounted with magisterial aplomb. This holds its own even alongside the wonderful Uchida set. Crystalline, clean recording that is in the demonstration category.

In terms of atmosphere and poetic feeling, Pollini is no match for Uchida on Philips (✿ 464 698-2) or indeed for Pierre-Laurent Aimard. He offers impressive and distinguished pianism, but there is little sense of magic, no doubt the fault of the rather close and analytical recording balance. In climaxes there is a certain hardness.

Hommage à Rameau.

(M) **(*) BBC mono BBCL 4064-2. Michelangeli –

BEETHOVEN: *Sonatas Nos. 4 & 12* **(*); RAVEL: *Gaspard de la nuit* (***).

The Debussy *Hommage à Rameau* is beautifully delivered and controlled. It comes with an almost miraculous account of Ravel's *Gaspard*, which alone is worth the price of the disc. The notes by William Robson, Michelangeli's BBC producer, serve to bring the whole occasion vividly to life.

Préludes, Books 1–2 (complete).

(B) **(*) Nonesuch Ultima 7559 79474-2 (2). Jacobs.

Paul Jacobs's choice of occasionally slower tempi means that his complete set of *Préludes* stretches over a pair of CDs, although offered as an Ultima Double. Jacobs's playing is highly evocative, and he can be quirky too, as in the engagingly lighthearted account of *La Danse de Puck*. There is much to appeal here, but in the last resort this Nonesuch set cannot be a top recommendation.

Préludes, Book 1; L'Isle joyeuse.

*(*) (IMS) DG 445 187-2. Pollini.

Maurizio Pollini may be Maurizio Pollini, but only 43 minutes is on the stingy side for a full-price disc. *Ce qu'a vu le vent d'ouest* sounds as if he is attacking Rachmaninov or Prokofiev. There are good things too, and the pianism and control are masterly (as in *Des pas sur la neige*), but generally speaking one remains outside Debussy's world. The recording was made in Munich's Herkulessaal and has abundant clarity and presence.

OPERA

Pelléas et Mélisande (complete).

*** DG **DVD** 073 030-9. Hagley, Archer, Maxwell, Cox, Walker, Welsh Nat. Op. Ch. & O, Boulez (V/D Peter Stein).

Those who did not respond to the *Pelléas* Boulez recorded for CBS in 1970 with George Shirley and Elisabeth Söderström in the title-roles should warm to this 1992 performance directed by Peter Stein with the Welsh National Opera. The production won much acclaim at the time – and rightly so, for it encapsulates the spirit of the *Pelléas* to perfection. Indeed, among the wider *Pelléas* discography it stands high – not far below the Abbado version with Maria Ewing and François Le Roux. (We mentioned it in our main edition, though for some reason it was not listed above the text.) Alison Hagley's *Mélisande* is good to look at as well as to listen to, and both she and her Pelléas, Neill Archer, are totally identified with their characters. They can withstand the most exalted comparisons, and Peter Stein's production, though not sumptuous, is in good style and exemplary taste. During the interludes we can follow the pages of the full score, and in addition we are spared tours of the orchestra pit and shots of a flailing, perspiring maestro – not that Boulez ever does much

of that. Although we never see him, he is the hero of the occasion and, thanks to his direction, the music flows naturally (more so than in the CBS set) and the whole experience resonates in the listener's mind, as do all good accounts of this great work. The Laser-Disc version of the performance was accommodated on three sides but in the DVD, its 158 minutes (four longer than his CBS recording) spill over on to two discs, the second accommodating Act V. Recommended with enthusiasm. It is in almost every respect superior to the rival (1987) account from Lyons, which though expertly conducted by John Eliot Gardiner (who lays out the orchestra as Debussy had done at the first performance), is perversely set in a large drawing room in a château at the end of the nineteenth century. So there is no sense of timelessness, no forest, no sea-shore, no grotto, no sunless castle and no sense of magic or mystery. Why do opera managements tolerate this kind of vandalism and, above all, impertinence?

DE LA BARRE, Michel
(c. 1675–1745)

Flute Suites Nos. 2 in C min.; 4 in G min.; 6 in C; 8 in D; Sonata No. 1 in B flat.

**(*) ASV CDGAU 181. Hadden, Walker, Carolan, Headley, Sayce.

Michel de la Barre played the transverse flute at the Court of Louis XIV with the status of *Flûte de la Chambre*. His suites are among the earliest pieces written for the remodelled instrument, and they have a certain pale charm, balancing a pervading melancholy with brighter, more lively airs, gigues and chaconnes. The charming *Sonata* is for a pair of unaccompanied flutes, the *Suites* for solo flute with continuo, here harpsichord, viola da gamba and theorbo. These expert period-instrument performances are stylishly refined and delicate, and certainly pleasing if taken a work at a time.

DELALANDE, Michel-Richard
(1657–1726)

Premier Caprice ou Caprice de Villers-Cotterêts.

(M) **(*) Erato (ADD/DDD) 2564 60578-2. Ch. Caillard, Jean-François Paillard O, Paillard – LULLY: *Armide; Isis* (extracts). **(*)

Michel-Richard Delalande was closely associated with the courts of Louis XIV (he taught his daughters and was made Master of the King's chamber music in 1685) and Louis XV (he was director of the Royal Chapel in 1714–23), holding in total seven court posts during his lifetime. Delalande extracted music from his elaborate court ballets into suites or symphonies (sometimes called Caprices), which were performed every 15 days during the supper of Louis XIV and Louis XV. This *First Caprice* is named after the *Château de Villers-Cotterêts*, residence of the king's brother, presumably written for some occasion connected with him. This (digital) recording is eminently enjoyable, though Paillard's style, using modern instruments, does seem a little heavy at times, if not enough to seriously mar enjoyment. The music is tuneful and thoroughly entertaining, a nice mixture of lively drums and trumpet numbers with more gently melancholy ones – there is particularly attractive writing for the woodwind (the bassoons and oboes in the *Augmentation, premier air neuf* are delightful). It makes an original bonus for the Lully suites.

De Profundis; Regina coeli; (i) *Sacris solemnis.*

(M) **(*) Erato 2564 60240-2. Lausanne Vocal & Instrumental Ens., Paillard CO, Corboz (i) with Caillat Chorale, Caillat.

Delalande's moving setting of Psalm 129, with its grave introduction, is a most impressive piece. There is real depth here and the performance is committed and eloquent. The earlier *Regina coeli* is the shortest of the composer's *grands motets* and characteristically alternates the soloists (*petite choeur*) with the *grand choeur*, which is especially effective in the final *Alleluia*. The *Sacris solemnis* brings a series of impressive solo arias, a 'nocturne' for bass with a bassoon obbligato, a fine tenor solo with flute and violin accompaniment, and a radiant soprano aria (beautifully sung here) with silvery flute to contrast with the melancholy bassoon. The solos are interwoven with small and large chorus, and the work closes joyfully with the soprano and *grand choeur* together. The performances are excellent and the recordings (from 1970 and 1980 respectively) are transferred most naturally to CD. It is a pity that this rare and rewarding collection is let down by the absence of texts and translations, although there are good notes.

DE LA RUE, Pierre (*c.* 1460–1518)

(i) *Missa de feria; Missa Sancta Dei gentrix;* Motet: *Pater de celis Deus;* (ii) Motets arr. for lute: *O Domine, Jesu Christe; Regina coeli; Salve Regina.*

*** Hyp. CDA 67010. (i) Gothic Voices, Page; (ii) Wilson and Rumsey (lutes).

Pierre de la Rue is still an unfamiliar name, yet he was prolific. His music seems solemn, partly because he is fond of lower vocal ranges, but his ready use of intervals of the third and sixth gives it a harmonic lift and a special individuality. The *Missa de feria* is in five parts and is vocally richer than the more austerely concise *Missa Sancta Dei gentrix* in four; but they are distantly related by sharing an identical musical idea on the words '*Crucifixus*' and '*et resurrexit*'. The canonic imitation that is at the heart of Pierre's polyphony is heard even more strikingly in the superbly organized six-part motet *Pater de celis*

Deus. To provide interludes, Christopher Wilson and his partner play three of his lute-duet intabulations, and their closing *Salve Regina* makes a quietly serene postlude. Christopher Page and his Gothic Voices are thoroughly immersed in this repertoire and period, and these stimulating performances could hardly be more authentic. The recording too is well up to standard.

DELDEN, Lex van (1919–88)

(i) *Concerto for Double String Orchestra, Op. 71; Piccolo Concerto, Op. 67;* (ii) *Musica sinfonica, Op. 93;* (iii) *Symphony No. 3 (Facets), Op. 45.*

* (**) Etcetera stereo/mono KTC 1156. Concg. O; (i) Jochum; (ii) Haitink; (iii) Szell.

The idiom of the Dutch composer, Lex van Delden, is predominantly tonal. The strongest of the works here are the *Third Symphony* and the brilliant *Piccolo Concerto* for twelve wind instruments, timpani, percussion and piano. Van Delden is inventive and intelligent, and these four pieces leave you wanting to hear more. The recordings, which are of varying quality, were made at various times, all in the Concertgebouw Hall and taken from various broadcast tapes, the two concertos conducted by Jochum in 1968 and 1964 respectively (the latter is mono), the *Musica sinfonica* with Haitink in 1969, and the *Third Symphony* with Szell, again mono, in 1957.

DELIUS, Frederick (1862–1934)

Air and Dance for String Orchestra; On Hearing the First Cuckoo in Spring; Summer Evening; Summer Night on the River.

(M) ** Chan. 10174X. LPO, Handley – VAUGHAN WILLIAMS: *Serenade to Music; The Wasps Overture.* **

Handley as an interpreter of Delius generally takes a more direct, less gently lingering view than is common, but here that refusal to sentimentalize – which can miss the more sweetly evocative qualities of the music – goes with the most subtle nuances in performance, fresh as well as beautiful and atmospheric. *Summer Evening* is little more than a salon piece, but is no less attractive for that. The tonal richness of the LPO playing is superbly caught in the outstanding Chandos recording, but this collection plays for only 46 minutes overall, which is ungenerous these days.

(i; ii) *Appalachia;* (iii) *Brigg Fair;* (i; ii) *Hassan: Closing Scene; Irmelin Prelude; Koanga: La Calinda* (arr. Fenby).

(BB) Naxos mono 8.110906. (i) LPO; (ii) BBC Ch.; (iii) Beecham SO; all cond. Beecham.

(i) *Eventyr (Once upon a Time); Hassan: Incidental Music;* (i; ii) *Koanga: Closing Scene;* (iii) *On*

if you respond to the Bloch and Delius concertos, you would find much here to engage your sympathies. The *Cello Concertino* (1930) originally appeared scored for 15 wind instruments, celesta, harp, six double-basses and variously tuned side-drums. The present version is re-scored by his son, Frédéric, for more practical forces; it, too, is imaginative without possessing a strong individual voice. Very good performances and vivid, well-detailed recording.

DIAMOND, David (born 1915)

(i) *Violin Concerto No. 2; The Enormous Room; Symphony No. 1.*
⊕ (BB) ★★★ Naxos 8.559157. (i) Seattle SO, Schwarz, (i) with Talvi.

What a good composer David Diamond is – and how good it is to have the present repertoire reissued on Naxos. Like Barber, Piston and Roy Harris, Diamond was pushed aside in the late 1950s when the march of serialism and post-serialism seemed unstoppable, and Boulez and his followers dismissed such music as irrelevant. However, this generation is returning with a vengeance and Diamond, now eighty-nine, has enjoyed considerable exposure in the last decade or so. The *First Symphony* was composed after the outbreak of war had forced Diamond to abandon his studies with Nadia Boulanger in Paris and return to America. Mitropoulos conducted its première in 1941 and the piece is undoubtedly an auspicious beginning to his impressive symphonic portfolio. The lyrical *Second Violin Concerto* (1947) is a bit Stravinskian with a dash of Walton. It is finely played by the Finnish-born Ilkka Talvi; and the fantasia, *The Enormous Room* (1948), takes its inspiration from the e.e. cummings description of his incarceration in a French detention camp in 1918. The poet described his eighty-by-forty-foot room at La Ferté Macé (shared with many others) as 'filled with a new and beautiful darkness, the darkness of snow outside, falling and falling with the silent gesture which has touched the soundless country of my mind as a child touches a toy it loves'. Diamond's score is rhapsodic in feeling, with orchestral textures of great luxuriance; it is both imaginative and atmospheric, and throughout he is well served by Gerard Schwarz, the Seattle orchestra and the Delos team who originally recorded it. Indeed, the recording is outstanding.

Symphonies Nos. 2 & 4.
(BB) ★★★ Naxos 8.559154. Seattle SO, Schwartz.

In spite of attracting attention after the Second World War, David Diamond's music (with a few exceptions) was grievously neglected in the 1960s and '70s. The *Fourth Symphony* is very diatonic, tonal, impeccably crafted and sophisticated, qualities that were not highly praised at the time. The *Second Symphony* is a large-scale work, lasting nearly three-quarters of an hour, written in 1942–3 at the height of the war, and it has great sweep and power. There is a lot of Roy Harris in the opening measures, and the music unfolds with a similar sense of inevitability and purpose. Overall, his music is less what one might in the vernacular call 'macho'. There are also reminders both of Shostakovich and of the Copland of *Appalachian Spring*. It is beautifully crafted and envinces a continuity of musical thought that defines the real symphonist. These excellent performances were originally recorded by and released on Delos, along with the *Concerto for Small Orchestra*, with the New York Chamber Orchestra, which has, sadly, been removed for its Naxos incarnation. However, at bargain price, with such dedicated and expert playing, all set in a spacious and well-balanced, ventilated acoustic (though some may find it too reverberant), it still represents good value at the asking price.

Symphony No. 8; Suite No. 1 from the Ballet, Tom; (i) *This Sacred Ground.*
(BB) ★★★ Naxos 8.559156. Seattle SO, Schwarz; (i) with Parce, Seattle Girls' Ch. & NorthWest boychoir.

The *First Suite from the Ballet, Tom* inhabits much the same musical world as Aaron Copland. The *Eighth Symphony* makes use of serial technique but will still present few problems to those familiar with Diamond's earlier music, for it remains lyrical and thought-provoking. It culminates in a double fugue of considerable ingenuity. *This Sacred Ground* is a short setting for soloist, choirs and orchestra of the Gettysburg Address, and it may not travel so well. Committed performances and excellent, natural, recorded sound.

DIBDIN, Charles (1745–1814)

(i) *The Brickdust Man* (musical dialogue); (ii) *The Ephesian Matron* (comic serenata); (iii) *The Grenadier* (musical dialogue).
★★★ Hyp. CDA 66608. (i) Barclay, West; (ii) Mills, Streeton, Padmore, Knight; (iii) Bisatt, West, Mayor; Opera Restor'd, Parley of Instruments, Holman.

Dibdin, best known as the composer of *Tom Bowling*, the song heard every year at the Last Night of the Proms, here provides three delightful pocket operas, the shorter ones officially described as musical dialogues and *The Ephesian Matron* as a comic serenata. *The Grenadier* (dating from 1773) lasts well under a quarter of an hour, using a text that is possibly by David Garrick. The brief numbers – duets and solos – are linked by equally brief recitatives, then rounded off with a final trio. The other two pieces are just as delightful in these performances by a group that specializes in presenting just such dramatic works of this period in public. Excellent Hyperion sound.

DOCKER, Robert (1918–92)

(i) 3 *Contrasts for Oboe & Strings;* (ii) *Legend; Pastiche Variations* (both for piano and orchestra); *Air; Blue Ribbons; Fairy Dance Reel; Scènes de ballet; Scène du bal; The Spirit of Cambria; Tabarinage.*

*** Marco Polo 8.223837 Dublin RTE Concert O, Knight; with (i) Presley; (ii) Davies.

Robert Docker is probably best known as a composer of film music (including a contribution to *Chariots of Fire*). His *Legend*, which opens this collection, is a tuneful example of a miniature 'film-concerto'. The closing *Pastiche Variations*, opening with a horn solo, is more expansive and romantic, but witty too. Based on *Frère Jacques*, it has something in common with Dohnányi's *Nursery-Theme Variations*. William Davies proves a most persuasive soloist. In between comes an attractive lightweight suite of *Scènes de ballet*, three engaging *Contrasts for Oboe and Strings* (lovely playing from David Presley), and a series of engaging short pieces. Perhaps the best known is the catchy *Tabarinage*. The delicate *Scène du bal* is a very English waltz despite its French title. There are also some spirited folksong arrangements. *The Spirit of Cambria* (although the composer was a Londoner) was written for St David's Day in 1972 and effectively uses four different traditional Welsh melodies. All this music is played with polish and warmth by the Dublin Radio Orchestra under Barry Knight and is pleasingly recorded.

DONIZETTI, Gaetano (1797–1848)

OPERA

L'elisir d'amore (complete).

(M) **(*) RCA 74321 25280-2 (2). Popp, Dvorský, Weikl, Nesterenko, Munich R. Ch. & O, Wallberg.

(M) **(*) EMI (ADD) 5 65658-2 (2). Carteri, Alva, Panerai, Taddei, La Scala, Milan, Ch. & O, Serafin.

(B) *(*) Ph. Duo 475 442-2 (2). Ricciarelli, Carreras, Nucci, Trimarchi, Riagacci, Turin R. Ch. & O, Scimone.

Wallberg's recording is marked by a charming performance of the role of Adina from Lucia Popp, bright-eyed and with delicious detail, both verbal and musical. Nesterenko makes a splendidly resonant Dr Dulcamara with more comic sparkle than you would expect from a great Russian bass. Dvorský and Weikl, both sensitive artists, sound much less idiomatic, with Dvorský's tight tenor growing harsh under pressure, not at all Italianate, and Weikl similarly failing to give necessary roundness to the role of Belcore.

The La Scala set had a fine cast in its day (1959). Alva is a pleasantly light-voiced and engaging Nemorino. Carteri's Adina ideally should be more of a minx than this, but the part is nicely sung all the same. Panerai as Belcore once again shows what a fine and musical artist he is, and Taddei is magnificent, stealing the show as any Dulcamara can and should. The drawback is Serafin's direction. The La Scala chorus is lively enough, and it is not that the orchestral playing is slipshod, but they provide less sparkle than they should.

Scimone's reissued set from the mid-1980s is disappointing. In a gentle way he is an understanding interpreter of Donizetti, but with a recording that lacks presence, the sound of the chorus and orchestra is slack next to rivals on record, and none of the soloists is on top form, with even Carreras in rougher voice than usual, trying to compensate by over-pointing. Leo Nucci as Belcore also produces less smooth tone than usual, and Domenico Trimarchi as Dulcamara, fine *buffo* that he is, sounds too wobbly for comfort on record. Katia Ricciarelli gives a sensitive performance, but this is not a natural role for her and, unlike Gheorghiu, she does not translate it to her own needs. It is the Gheorghiu–Alagna set on Decca that remains an obvious first choice for this opera, either on DVD (074-103-9) or CD (455 691-2).

Lucia di Lammermoor (complete).

(M) (***) EMI mono 5 62747-2 [5 62764-2] (2). Callas, Di Stefano, Gobbi, Arie, Ch. & O of Maggio Musicale Fiorentino, Serafin.

Callas's earlier (1953) mono set of Lucia (praised in our main edition) was an obvious choice for EMI's 'Great Recordings of the Century', and it has been newly remastered for the reissue. This is a clear first choice for Callas fans.

Maria Stuarda (complete).

(B) ** Ph. Duo 475 224-2 (2). Baltsa, Gruberová, Vermillion, Araiza, Alaimo, Bav. R. Ch., Munich R.O, Patanè.

Giuseppe Patanè in one of his last recordings, made in 1989, conducts a refined account of *Maria Stuarda*, very well sung and recorded. The manner is lighter, the speeds often faster than in its immediate CD rival, and that makes the result less sharply dramatic, a point reflected in the actual singing of Gruberová and Baltsa, which, for all its beauty and fine detail, is less intense than that of Sutherland and Tourangeau on Decca. Whether it is Mary singing nostalgically of home in her first cantilena, or leading the surgingly memorable Scottish prayer in Act III, or even in the confrontation between the two queens, this account keeps a degree of restraint – even in the thrusting insult from Mary to Elizabeth – *Vil bastardo!* Araiza sings well enough as Leicester, but again he gives a less rounded performance than Pavarotti with Sutherland. Not that the rivalry is exact when the Decca set uses a slightly different text. However, Philips offer no translation and the synopsis is not cued. The digital sound is well balanced but there is less sense of presence than in the fine analogue Decca, which remains first choice (425 410-2 – see our main *Guide*).

DOPPER, Cornelis (1870–1939)

Symphony No. 2; Pään I in D min.; Pään II in F min. (symphonic studies).
*** Chan. 9884. Hague Residentie O, Bamert.

Older readers may dimly recall an early recording of Dopper's *Ciaconna gotica*, but apart from that his music has remained unrepresented in the catalogue. Of humble origins, Dopper rose to eminence in Dutch musical life as Mengelberg's assistant at the Concertgebouw, where he conducted the first Dutch performances of Debussy's *La Mer*, Ravel's *Rapsodie espagnole* and Sibelius's *Second Symphony* as well as much else besides. During his lifetime, Dopper's music was championed by Richard Strauss, Monteux and Mengelberg among others. He composed seven symphonies, the *Second* dating from 1903. The writing is cultured in the spirit of Brahms and Dvořák, although the symphony is conservative in idiom, inclined to be diffuse and not exhibiting strong individuality. Nor for that matter do the two *Pääns*, composed during the First World War. Very good performances by the fine Hague Residentie Orchestra under Matthias Bamert. Excellent recording, too, but this is not repertoire that we suspect will invite frequent repetition.

Symphonies Nos. 3 (Rembrandt); 6 (Amsterdam).
*** Chan. 9923. Hague Residentie O, Bamert.

We have already had a fine recording of Dopper's *Second Symphony* from Bamert, but these are both more attractive, and their pervading geniality is endearing. They are not really programmatic: the title of the jolly *Third* (1905) anticipates the third centenary of the birth of the famous Dutch painter in 1906, which was celebrated with major compositions from a number of Dutch composers. The work is pleasingly if conventionally tuneful, with a strong, rhythmic Scherzo; but the finale is perhaps the most striking movement, opening with fanfares, and with a Dvořákian lyrical flavour. The title of the *Amsterdam Symphony* relates to the finale, which celebrates a fair in Amsterdam on the queen's birthday. The Dvořákian flavour persists with the swinging secondary theme and the colourful scoring of the first movement. The contemplative Adagio makes a tranquil interlude before another bustlingly vibrant Scherzo. The engagingly jaunty finale has no lack of picaresque detail, with its popular tunes, the sounds of the bells of the tramcars, and even snatches of the national anthem. This is not great music, but it is certainly entertaining in performances as lively and well played as these. The recording is well up to the house standards, if perhaps a shade over-reverberant.

DOWLAND, J

First Booke of Songes (1597): Unq *Whoever thinks or hopes; My thought* *with hope; If my complaints; Can she excu* *wrongs; Now, O now I must needs part; Dear,* *change; Burst forth my tears; Go crystal tears;* *Think'st thou then by thy feigning; Come away,* *come sweet love; Rest awhile; Sleep wayward* *thoughts; All ye whom Love or Fortune; Wilt thou* *unkind thus leave me; Would my conceit; Come* *again, sweet love doth now invite; His golden locks;* *Awake, sweet love; Come, heavy sleep; Away with* *these self-loving lads.*
⊕ (M) *** Decca (ADD) 475 048-2. Cons. of Musicke, Rooley.

This collection, first issued in 1976, was the first of a continuing series which was to embrace Dowland's entire output. Here Rooley and the excellent Consorte of Musicke have recorded all the contents of the *First Booke of Songes* in the order in which they are published, varying the accompaniment between viols, lute and bass viol, but also offering voices and viols, and even voices alone. There is hardly any need to stress the beauties of the music itself, which is eminently well served by this stylish ensemble, and beautifully recorded.

DRAESEKE, Felix (1835–1913)

(i) Piano Concerto in E flat, Op. 36. Symphony No. 1 in G, Op. 12.
** MDG 335 0929-2. (i) Tanski; Wuppertal SO, Hanson.

Felix Draeseke was best known as a critic and he is scantily represented on CD. The *First Symphony*, composed in 1873, has touches of *Lohengrin* and there are even reminders of Berlioz as well as Schumann and Brahms. The *Piano Concerto* (1885–6) is inevitably Lisztian, though much more conventional. Claudius Tanski makes out a good case for it, and the American George Hanson pilots us through these raffish backwaters with some skill. Decent sound, but not a disc that excites enthusiasm.

DUKAS, Paul (1865–1935)

L'Apprenti Sorcier; La Péri.
**(*) Testament SBT 1324. Paris Conservatoire O, Ansermet (with SAINT-SAENS: *Danse macabre*) – DEBUSSY: *Jeux; 6 Epigraphes antiques, etc.* (***).

Ansermet's first mono recording of *La Péri* comes from 1954. His re-make, with the prefatory *Fanfare* added, dates from 1959 and was one of the demonstration LPs of the day. This earlier account with the Paris Conservatoire Orchestra, which was originally coupled with Rachmaninov's *Isle of the Dead*, omits

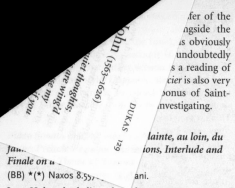

...fer of the
...ngside the
...s obviously
...undoubtedly
...s a reading of
...cier is also very
...onus of Saint-
...nvestigating.

ohn (1563–1626)

...ther thoughts are wing'd
...if you

DUKAS 129

...lainte, au loin, du
Jai... ...ions, Interlude and
Finale on a ...
(BB) *(*) Naxos 8.55/... ...ani.

Jean Hubeau's dedicated performances on Warner Apex carry some authority (he was a pupil of the composer) and are also at bargain price (0927 48996-2 – see our main volume). However, he was seventy at the time of his recording and he does not always show the greatest subtlety in matters of keyboard colour. The French pianist Chantal Stigliani is of Venetian origin and she studied at the Paris Conservatoire and with Yvonne Lefébure. It is clear that she is an artist of quality; her finely played disc would be strongly recommended, were it not for the recording. It is made at the Atelier Philomuses, Paris, which has the acoustic of a broom cupboard. Moreover, she is closely balanced in this claustrophobic environment and the sound is horribly bass-heavy. The playing is much more imaginative than Hubeau's, but the sound really does call for much tolerance.

DUNCAN, Trevor (born 1924)

Children in the Park; Enchanted April; The Girl from Corsica; High Heels; Little Debbie; Little Suite; Meadow Mist; Maestro Variations; Sixpenny Ride; St Boniface Down; La Torrida; Twentieth-century Express; Valse mignonette; The Visionaries: Grand March; Wine Festival.
*** Marco Polo 8.223517. Slovak RSO (Bratislava), Penny.

Trevor Duncan is perhaps best known for the signature-tune to the TV series, 'Dr Finlay's Casebook', the March from the Little Suite, which is offered here along with the other two numbers that make up that suite. But more of his popular pieces are included: the Twentieth-century Express, with its spirited 'going on holiday' feel, the exotic Girl from Corsica, and the tunefully laid-back Enchanted April, which was also used in a television programme. All the music here is nostalgically tuneful, with enough invention of melody and colour to sustain interest. Andrew Penny and the Bratislavan orchestra sound as though they have played it all for years, and the recording is excellent. Full and helpful sleeve-notes complete this attractive collection of good-quality light music.

DUPHLY, Jacques (1715–89)

Pièces pour clavecin: Allemande; La de Belombre; La du Baq; Cazamajor; Chaconne; La Forqueray; La Lanza; Médée; Menuets; La Millettina; Rondeau: Le Pothoüin; La de la Tour; La Tribolet; La de Vaucanson; La de Villeneuve.
** MDG 605 1068-2. Meyerson (harpsichord).

Jacques Duphly published four sets of Pièces de clavecin in Paris between 1744 and 1768. This disc draws on all four collections. The music is finely wrought and vital in spirit, very much in the tradition of Couperin, and Mitzi Meyerson has chosen a well-contrasted and well-planned programme. In her earlier (1988) recital for ASV she used a Goble but here turns to the 1998 copy by Keith Hill of a Taskin, which she used in her recent two-CD set of Forqueray suites. Although she plays with great panache and understanding (her playing could not be more idiomatic), the balance is unpleasingly close and the aural image can only be called overbearing. One quickly tires of the sound though Meyerson's mastery of the style is unfailingly impressive. But the ASV disc is the one to go for.

DUPRÉ, Marcel (1886–1971)

79 Chorales, Op. 28, Nos. 4, 8, 13, 20, 44, 49–51, 67 & 77; Elévation, Op. 2; 15 Pieces, Op. 18; Psalm XVIII, Op. 47.
*** MDG 316 0955-2. Van Oosten (organ).

MDG are in the process of recording Marcel Dupré's complete organ music and this is the fifth volume. The longest piece here is the Op. 18 Versets sur les Vêpres de la Vierge, recorded (like the remainder of his programme) on the Cavaillé-Coll organ at Saint-Ouen, Rouen. This set comes from 1918, and each of its short movements is inspired by the plainchant proper for the sections of the Vespers. Dupré performed them to great acclaim at his London début in 1920, when they were interspersed with liturgical chant, sung by 600 singers assembled by the Gregorian Association. They were originally improvisations, which greatly moved Claude Hoodman Johnson, a founder of Rolls-Royce, who had heard Dupré play them at Notre-Dame and asked him to notate them. They are short, musically unrelated pieces without any trace of 'display', which the Dutch organist Ben van Oosten has recorded at Saint-Ouen, Rouen, where Dupré himself was at one time active. They include some highly expressive and deeply felt music. Van Oosten is organist of the Grote Kirk in Amsterdam, a considerable scholar and author of the standard work on Widor. Admirers of Dupré cannot do much better than explore this and the other records in the series, and the MDG recording is of a high standard.

6 Antiennes pour le Temps de Noël, Op. 48; 79 Chorales, Op. 28, Nos. 21–23, 36–41 & 66; Symphony No. 2, Op. 26; Vision, Op. 44; Zephyrs.

(BB) ** Naxos 8.554542. Baker (organ).

The trouble (if it is a fault) with Marcel Dupré's music is that every piece of substance sounds like a masterly improvisation. Not that this need worry the listener until a long piece such as the *Deuxième Symphonie*, in which a certain want of concentration becomes manifest. George Baker is a committed interpreter but, in spite of the competitive price-tag and decent recording, he must yield to Ben van Oosten's impressive cycle on MDG on artistic grounds.

DURANTE, Francesco (1684–1755)

Magnificat in B flat.

� ❀ (M) *** DHM/BMG 82876 60145-2. Landauer, Oswald, Abele, Balthazar-Neumann Ch., Freiburg Bar. O, Hengelbrock – D'ASTORGA: *Stabat Mater*; PERGOLESI: *Confitebor tibi Domine.* *** ❀

Francesco Durante's briefly succinct setting of the *Magnificat* has been described as 'one of the loveliest works of its kind' and 'the ideal of a musical work of praise'. Durante was apparently by nature taciturn, introverted, and shabby in appearance. Yet he was Pergolesi's teacher and here he shows himself a consummate master of the styles and influences of his time. Moreover, his musical inspiration is in no doubt: the opening and closing choruses are exultantly life-enhancing; the *Et misericordia*, beautifully sung by Bernhard Landauer, is lyrically memorable, as is the tenor/bass duet, *Suscepit Israel*, which is equally touching. Indeed, the performance is first class in every way, with fine contributions from soloists, chorus and orchestra alike, with Thomas Hengelbrock directing the music vividly and sympathetically.

DURUFLÉ, Maurice (1902–86)

Requiem, Op. 9.

**(*) York Ambisonic YORK CD177. White, Martin, Canterbury Cathedral Ch., Flood – FAURE: *Requiem.* **(*)

(i; ii; v) *Requiem, Op. 9*; (iii; iv; v) *Messe cum Jubilo, Op. 11*; (iii) *4 Motets on Gregorian Themes, Op. 10*; (v) (Organ) *Prélude et fugue sur le nom d'Alain, Op. 7.*

⊕ (BB) *** Warner Apex 2564 61139-2. (i) Bouvier, Depraz, Philippe Caillard Ch., LAP; (ii) Stéphane Caillat Ch.; (iii) Soyer; (iv) O Nat. de l'ORTFM; all cond. composer; (v) Duruflé-Chevalier (organ).

Requiem, Op. 9; 4 Motets, Op. 10; (Organ) Prélude et fugue sur le nom d'Alain.

*(*) DG 459 365-2. Bartoli, Terfel, Santa Cecilia Nat.

Ac. Ch. & O, Chung – FAURE: *Requiem.* *(*)

This Apex budget reissue is particularly valuable as it replaces a previous Ultima set and centres on the now familiar *Requiem*, given a spontaneously dedicated performance that blossoms into great ardour at emotional peaks. The less familiar but no less beautiful *Messe cum Jubilo* receives a comparatively inspirational account, its gentler passages sustained with rapt concentration, with beautiful playing from the French Radio Orchestra. The soloists in both works rise to the occasion, and the choral singing combines passionate feeling with subtle colouring: the Chorale Stéphane Caillat are at their finest in the four brief *a cappella* motets, which are no less memorable. The composer proves a splendid exponent of his own works, as does his daughter playing the *Prélude et Fugue* on the organ of Soissons Cathedral. The spaciously atmospheric recordings were made between 1959 (the *Requiem*) and 1971. Not to be missed.

In this Canterbury Cathedral version, helped by exceptionally vivid Ambisonic recording as well as David Flood's direction, the dramatic bite of the Duruflé *Requiem* is brought out in high dynamic contrasts, where often the devotional element is comes over to the exclusion of any dramatic bite. So in the third movement, *Domine Jesu Christe*, the *fortissimo* choral attack is thrilling in the references to the punishments of hell. The sharpness of focus for the choir and accompanying instruments (but not, alas, the baritone soloist, Ian White) goes with a relatively intimate scale, with the brightness of the 18 trebles beautifully caught. More than usual, one registers the differences between this and the Fauré coupling. The version with organ accompaniment is used, which means that one misses the trumpet trimmings of the orchestral version, and Flood opts to have the melody of the *Pie Jesu* sung not by a soloist but by the trebles of the choir.

The characterful contributions of Cecilia Bartoli and Bryn Terfel add to the point of the newest DG coupling with Fauré. Memorably, Terfel gives the *Dies irae* section of the *Libera me* an apt violence. Sadly, the chorus is so dim and distant, with the dynamic range of the recording uncomfortably extreme, that the disc cannot be recommended.

DUŠEK, Franz Xaver (1731–99)

Sinfonias in E flat (Altner Eb3); F (Altner F4); G (Altner G2).

(BB) *(*) Naxos 8.555878. Helios 18, Oschatz.

Part of Naxos's useful '18th Century Symphony' series, these three Dušek symphonies (undated) are pleasing works, with some elegant tunes and nice touches here and there, but the performances, on period instruments, are only just about serviceable, and no more than that, and the dryish sound is not particularly ingratiating.

DUTILLEUX, Henri (born 1916)

Symphonies Nos. 1–2 (Le Double).

(M) ** Warner Elatus 2564 60334-2. O de Paris, Barenboim.

The exhilarating *First Symphony* is not as well served by Barenboim and the Orchestre de Paris as it is on the alternative Chandos coupling of both works by the BBC Philharmonic Orchestra under Yan-Pascal Tortelier (☉➔ ● Chan 9194). In Paris the Scherzo is scrambled and the opening notes of the *Passacaglia* are clipped. Equally the *Second Symphony* is well enough played with an eminently serviceable recording. But the Munch version (below) is far superior.

Symphony No. 2; Métaboles.

(M) *** Erato 2564 60572-2. O Nat. de l'ORTF, Munch – HONEGGER: *Symphony No. 4.* ***

Munch's account of the *Second Symphony*, which he commissioned for the seventy-fifth birthday of the Boston Symphony Orchestra, is in a special category. He was its first interpreter and his performance is not only uniquely authoritative, it is also powerfully evocative. *Métaboles* was commissioned in 1964 by the Cleveland Orchestra, and only three years later was taken into the studio by Munch. In its day the recording was state-of-the-art, and if today it is not quite as fine as Chandos provide for Yan Pascal Tortelier (who also offers No. 1 on Chan. 9194), it still sounds vivid and exhilarating. Munch's account of the Honegger coupling is also outstanding.

DVOŘÁK, Antonín (1841–1904)

Cello Concerto in B min., Op. 104.

(M) **(*) EMI (ADD) 5 62803-2. Du Pré, Chicago SO, Barenboim – SCHUMANN: *Cello Concerto.* **(*)

(B) **(*) Warner Apex 0927 40600-2. Noras, Finnish RSO, Oramo – BARTOK: *Rhapsody No. 1*; ELGAR: *Cello Concerto.* ***

*(*) DG 474 780-2. Maisky, BPO, Mehta – R. STRAUSS: *Don Quixote.* *(*)

(i) *Cello Concerto in B min., Op. 104; Polonaise in A;* (ii) *Rondo in G minor; Silent Woods, Op. 68/5.*

(M) ** Arts 47638-2. Yang, (i) Sinfonica Helvetica; (ii) German CO; all cond. Nowak.

Cello Concerto; Silent Woods, Op. 88.

**(*) Guild GMCD 7253. Kreger, Philh. O, Yu – HERBERT: *Cello Concerto.* **(*)

James Kreger, a pupil of Leonard Rose, won the Piatigorsky Award in his time at Juilliard when he was only 18 years old. He first came to wider notice at the Moscow Tchaikovsky Competition in 1974 and has an impressive *curriculum vitae*. His dedication and artistry come across in this fine Guild version of the *Cello Concerto*, whose slow movement is most eloquent. He is rather too forwardly balanced in comparison with the orchestra and draws out the central section of the first movement rather too much, but this is still a rewarding performance, and the addition of the rarely recorded *Silent Woods* is another plus point. In this coupling with the Victor Herbert *Concerto*, the source of Dvořák's inspiration, he comes into direct competition with Yo-Yo Ma, and some may well prefer Kreger's naturalness of expression. Djong Victorin Yu provides rather routine support, and it is the orchestral response that tips the scales in favour of the Ma performance (discussed in our main *Guide*).

Jacqueline du Pré's celebrated early recording with Barenboim conveys the spontaneous passion that marked her playing in public, and it is a performance that captures very vividly the urgent interpretative flair of both husband and wife, conductor and soloist. Though the exaggeratedly forward balance of the cello remains very noticeble, in the new transfer the sound has filled out nicely and is clearly detailed. The recoupling is also sensible.

The excellent Finnish cellist Arto Noras gives a sensitive reading of the Dvořák *Concerto*, responsively accompanied by Oramo. He is rather too backwardly balanced, but better this than a spotlight, and the orchestra is vividly and warmly caught. There is no lack of vigour, but most impressive are the tender moments, not least the *Epilogue*, raptly done. With fine couplings this is a real bargain.

'Complete Works for Cello and Orchestra' is the bold title of this disc on the Arts label, and some may query the accuracy of that, when it omits the earlier youthful *Cello Concerto*. The argument there no doubt is that Dvořák himself did not orchestrate that early concerto. In any event, the four works on the present disc make a good coupling. Wenn-Sinn Yang, of Taiwanese parentage, was born in Berne, Switzerland, and received his training in Europe, becoming principal cello of the Bavarian Radio Symphony Orchestra at the age of 24. That orchestral experience may account for the fact that there is a degree of reticence in his performances, at times amounting to a lack of bite. The conducting too of Grzegorz Nowak, with the orchestra which he himself founded, occasionally lapses into a rhythmic plod. The *Rondo in G minor* should sparkle more than it does here. That said, there is much in favour of the new issue, for Yang has an immaculate technique, with perfect intonation, and when it comes to Dvořák's warmly melodic writing, he allows himself an element of freedom that gives the performances an extra degree of persuasiveness and individuality, with fine control of tone and dynamic.

Mischa Maisky wears his heart on his sleeve (in fact nearly down to his fingertips) and lacks any kind of expressive reticence. This is an ego-centred performance that, despite good playing from the Berlin Philharmonic and an excellent DG recording, can be recommended only with caution. One critic wrote that he could not imagine returning to this very often. The present listener cannot imagine himself returning to it at all!

(i) *Cello Concerto;* (ii) *Symphony No. 8 in G, Op. 88.*
(M) **(*) RCA (ADD) 82876 55302-2. Boston SO, Munch, (i) with Piatigorsky.

Piatigorsky's classic 1960 account of the *Cello Concerto* emerges again on RCA's Red Seal label – remastered and sounding better than ever – though that cannot alter a balance, which places the cello too close, not always flattering to the soloist. The tuttis are somewhat two-dimensional, though the sound is now fully acceptable. There is no lack of orchestral colour and the acoustic of Symphony Hall is well conveyed behind the music-making. The performance is the very opposite of routine, with Piatigorsky and Munch in complete rapport, producing a totally spontaneous melodic flow. Although there are moments when intonation is less than immaculate, the inspiration of the performance carries the day. The *Symphony* was recorded a year later but sounds better than in earlier transfers. Munch's reading is strongly characterized and, though he occasionally presses hard, the thrust comes from a natural ardour. Some might feel the finale a bit over-driven, but there is plenty of feeling in the slow movement and few would fail to respond to the passionate blossoming in the strings of the inspired lyrical theme that forms the centrepiece of the third-movement *Allegretto*. In short, a fresh, individual account and a desirable coupling.

(i) *Cello Concerto;* (ii) *Symphony No. 9 (From the New World).*
◐─• (BB) *** Apex (ADD) 0927 49919-2. (i) Hoelscher, Hamburg PO, Keilberth; (ii) NW German Philharmonie, Lindenberg.
(M) **(*) DG Entrée 474 167-2. (i) Fournier, BPO, Szell; (ii) Dresden State O, Levine.

This Apex reissue is a real rediscovery. When Ludwig Hoelscher recorded Dvořák's *Cello Concerto* in 1958, he was Germany's leading solo cellist, an artist of the very front rank, with a really big, resonant tone and a big, heroic sense of style to go with it. This performance ranks with the very finest on record, including the famous Rostropovich–Karajan account. With Hoelscher one has a sense of real striving, and that is just how it should be. The passion of the slow movement is conveyed wonderfully, and the orchestral playing is excellent here: witness the famous horn trio. The finale has no less ardour and excitement. The recording, full and warm and vivid, is astonishingly good. If the balance favours the soloist unduly, the tone he gives us is so glorious that one finds it hard to carp over such a matter. Lindenberg's account of the *New World Symphony* is not quite on this level, but it is a direct, persuasively simple reading, again with a beautifully played slow movement. Only the rather

easy-going trio in the Scherzo lets the interpretation down a little, but it is agreeably elegant, and the finale makes amends. Again, good sound (from 1969). This is a bargain disc to seek out, even if duplication is involved.

Fournier's richly distinguished account of the *Cello Concerto*, with Szell an admirable partner, is also available coupled with Kubelik's BPO recording of the *Eighth Symphony* (DG 439 484-2 – see our main volume) and that is, frankly, a better proposition than this alternative Entrée pairing with a good but not distinctive *New World Symphony* from Levine. Its main interest lies in the conductor's rare partnership with the great Dresden Staatskapelle, who certainly play gloriously in the first two movements. But the Scherzo lacks Bohemian rhythmic jauntiness, and the finale is exciting without carrying all before it. Moreover the timpani sound oppressively close in the introduction, and there is no exposition repeat. Nevertheless, the sheer quality of the orchestral playing carries the day.

Piano Concerto in G min., Op. 33.
** Athene CD 21. Boyle, Freiburg PO, Fritzsche – SCHOENFIELD: *Piano Concerto.* **

Andreas Boyle's formidable gifts and keen virtuosity are heard to good effect in Dvořák, but are perhaps not best served by the coupling. Nevertheless this is an impressive performance, but the balance places him so far forward that the Freiburg Orchestra is often masked.

Violin Concerto in A min., Op. 53.
(M) *** Warner Elatus 2564 60806-2. Vengerov, NYPO, Masur – BRAHMS: *Violin Concerto.* **(*)
(BB) (***) Naxos mono 8.110975. Milstein, Minneapolis SO, Dorati – MOZART: *Adagio in E etc.;* GLAZUNOV: *Violin Concerto.* (***)
(*) Sup. SU 3709-2 031. Sporcl, Czech PO, Ashkenazy – TCHAIKOVSKY: *Violin Concerto.* *
**(*) Avie AV 0044. Graffin, Johannesburg PO, Hankinson– COLERIDGE-TAYLOR: *Violin Concerto.* **(*)

(i) *Violin Concerto in A min., Op. 53; Romance in F min., Op. 11;* (ii) *Sonatina in G, Op. 100; 4 Romantic Pieces, Op. 75.*
(M) **(*) EMI 5 62595-2. Perlman, (i) LPO, Barenboim; (ii) Sanders.

Vengerov's live performance (see our main volume) is dazzling, freshly spontaneous and splendidly accompanied by Masur. However, there are some reservations about the new Brahms coupling.

Milstein's account of the Dvořák *Concerto* with Steinberg and the Pittsburgh orchestra enjoyed great and justified celebrity in the early 1960s and reappeared in the six-CD box EMI issued some years ago devoted to his art. This version sounds pretty exhilarating too, and Dorati gets very supportive playing from the Minneapolis orchestra.

The Perlman and Barenboim partnership is at its peak in the both the *Concerto* and the delectable *Romance*, and this coupling remains very competitive, the more so in that this reissue in the 'Perlman Edition' is at mid-price, and now offers the double bonus of the enchanting *Sonatina* plus the hardly less attractive set of *Four Romantic Pieces*. Both are beautifully played and well recorded, save for the imbalance between the celebrated violinist and the more recessed pianist.

The coupling of the Dvořák and Tchaikovsky *Violin Concertos* – two of the finest Slavonic works in the genre – is surprisingly rare, which makes the Supraphon issue very welcome, particularly when the soloist, Pavel Sporcl, is a charismatic violinist, with natural flair and imagination as well as formidable virtuoso technique. It helps that both these performances were recorded live, in the Rudolfinum in Prague, with the electricity of each occasion vividly conveyed. At the end of the Dvořák there is a wild yell of enthusiasm before the applause, suggesting that Sporcl's flamboyant appearance as well as his musical gifts have attracted a youthful following. The Czech audience was obviously roused by hearing so warmly idiomatic a reading of a work that can easily seem wayward. Though in the slow movement Sporcl does not quite match his finest rivals in inner intensity, the finale is delightful, with the Slavonic dance-rhythms lightly sprung.

As in the Coleridge-Taylor *Concerto* with which it is aptly coupled, Philippe Graffin is a warmly committed soloist in the Dvořák, but with flawed orchestral playing, vigorous but rough in ensemble, this version is hardly a strong competitor, except for those wanting the rare work with which it is coupled.

The Golden Spinning Wheel; The Noon Witch; The Water Goblin; The Wild Dove.

⊙━ ⊛ (M) *** Teldec 2-CD 2564 60221-2 (2). Concg. O, Harnoncourt.

Harnoncourt's collection of Dvořák's four most vivid symphonic poems is one of his finest pairs of records and one of Teldec's most realistic recordings. The performances offer superlative playing from the Concertgebouw Orchestra, and Harnoncourt's direction is inspired, lyrical and dramatic by turns, ever relishing Dvořák's glowing scoring for woodwinds and, in the famous *Spinning Wheel*, the horns and, towards the close, a gloriously sonorous passage for the trombones. These are all quite long works and their colourful descriptive narrative means that they need holding firmly together. Harnoncourt does that, yet keeps the narrative flow moving along with an exciting momentum. The end of *The Water Goblin* is superbly melodramatic and *The Golden Spinning Wheel* is unsurpassed on record, even by Beecham. The recording and ambience are so believable that one feels one has the famous Dutch concert hall just beyond the speakers.

Serenade for Strings in E; Serenade for Wind in D min., Op. 44.

(M) *(*) Chan 6678. Philh. O, Warren-Green.

Christopher Warren-Green's rather languorous approach to the work for strings verges dangerously upon the sentimental and, despite glowing sound and fine playing from the Philharmonia strings and wind alike, neither *Serenade* is as effectively characterized as the competition. Warren-Green's earlier Virgin recording with the London Chamber Orchestra is far fresher and, coupled with string works by Suk, Tchaikovsky and Vaughan Williams on a 2x1 Virgin Double (5 61763-2), is also a remarkable bargain.

Slavonic Dances Nos. 1–16, Op. 46/1–8; Op. 72/1–8.

(M) * (**) Mercury (IMS) (ADD) [434 384-2]. Minneapolis (Minnesota) SO, Dorati.

**(*) DG (IMS) 447 056-2. Russian Nat. O, Pletnev.

(M) **(*) Decca (ADD) (IMS) 468 495-2. VPO, Kubelik.

Dorati's performances have splendid brio and Slavonic flair. They are also very well played, and the gentler, lyrical sections are often quite delightful. The snag is the curiously confined recording, full-bodied but somehow unable to expand properly.

Refinement and crispness of ensemble are the keynotes of Mikhail Pletnev's distinctive reading. The approach is at times almost Mozartian in its elegance, with little of the earthier, Slavonic qualities and with even the wildest furiants kept under control and the extrovert joy of the music rather underplayed. Yet consistently Pletnev and his Russian players make one marvel at the beauty of the instrumentation, and this is a disc to give a fresh view of well-loved music. However, the acoustic of the Concert Hall of Moscow Conservatory is not particularly flattering, and competition is strong.

Almost unbelievably, Kubelik's early Vienna Philharmonic recording – the first complete set in stereo – dates from 1955 and was made in the Grosse Saal of the Musikverein, which adds an underlying warmth and atmosphere to a recording that on LP had an unattractively thin upper range. The remastering has greatly improved the sound: the violins still sound pinched, but the effect is less exaggerated. The performances have plenty of vitality and colour, but the Decca reissue is in most respects eclipsed by Kubelik's later, DG version, made 20 years later with the Bavarian Radio Orchestra 457 712-2.

Overture: The Cunning Peasant.

(M) (**) Sup. mono SU 1914 011. Czech PO, Sejna – SKROUP: *The Tinker Overture*; SMETANA: *Festive Symphony*, etc. (***)

The Cunning Peasant is not one of Dvořák's greatest overtures, though Karel Sejna makes the most positive case for it in his mono recording. Acceptable sound and a useful fill-up to Smetana's exhilarating *Festive Symphony*.

Legends, Op. 59; Miniatures, Op. 75a; Notturno in B, Op. 40; Prague Waltzes.

◑─ ✪ ★★★ (M) Ph. 476 2179. Budapest Festival O, Fischer.

The *Legends* are endearing, captivating, gloriously inventive pieces, the charm and character of which are conveyed wonderfully by Iván Fischer and the Budapest Festival Orchestra and recorded as sumptuously as their outstanding Bartók discs. All of these pieces, including the poignant *Notturno* and the delightful *Prague Waltzes*, are performed with great feeling and style and convey Fischer's affection for them. The *Legends* have been well served in the past, and Fischer's version is every bit as idiomatic and better recorded. Now reissued in Universal's 'Penguin ✪ Collection' at mid-price, this recording remains a top recommendation.

SYMPHONIES

Symphony No. 5 in F, Op. 76; Othello Overture; Scherzo capriccioso.

◑─ ✪ (BB) ★★★ EMI Encore 5 85702-2. Oslo PO, Jansons.

Jansons directs a radiant performance of this delectable symphony, and the EMI engineers put a fine bloom on the Oslo sound. With its splendid encores, equally exuberant in performance, this 1989 reissue remains one of the finest Dvořák CDs in the catalogue and is now in addition incredibly inexpensive.

Symphony No. 9 in E min. (From the New World), Op. 95.

**(*) Pentatone SACD PTC 5186 019. Netherlands PO, Kreizberg – TCHAIKOVSKY: *Romeo and Juliet (Fantasy Overture).* **(*)

(M) (***) Teldec mono 8573 83025-2. Concg. O, Mengelberg – FRANCK: *Symphony in D min.* (***)

(BB) ** EMI Encore (ADD) 5 74961-2. New Philh. O, Muti – TCHAIKOVSKY: *Romeo and Juliet.* **(*)

(M) ** Virgin 5 61837-2. Houston SO, Eschenbach (with TCHAIKOVSKY: *Francesca da Rimini* **).

The Netherlands Philharmonic (not to be confused with the Radio Orchestra) was founded as recently as 1986, a merger of the Amsterdam Philharmonic, the Utrecht Symphony and the Netherlands Chamber Orchestra. It boasts a complement of 130 players and claims to be the largest orchestral organization in the country. Jakov Kreizberg has just taken over as chief conductor, prompting the Dutch company Pentatone to make a series of recordings, including this coupling of two favourite works, not otherwise available together on a single disc. The performance of the *New World* is strong and incisive. Kreizberg takes a fresh, direct view. He eases the tempo for the haunting little flute melody of the third subject in the first movement, but that is as near to an idiosyncratic approach as he gets, and in the slow movement he chooses a very spacious, steady pacing, with extremes

of dynamic very well caught by the recording and with the strings admirably refined. Crisp ensemble and articulation mark the Scherzo and finale. Those without the facility of Surround Sound will find the recording coming over at a slightly lower level than usual.

Mengelberg took up his appointment at the Amsterdam Concertgebouw in 1895, only two years after Dvořák had finished his *Symphony, From the New World*. Mengelberg gave its Amsterdam première in 1896. He conducted it with an enormous lyrical intensity, and gets such eloquent playing in these wartime performances that criticism is almost silenced. Both performances here are strongly narrative, so that they totally compel attention throughout, and the expressive self-indulgence of which his detractors complain does not unduly disturb. Such is the dramatic fire and ardour of this playing that most listeners will take his mannerisms in their stride. Mind you, he pulls the contrasting idea of the Scherzo horribly out of shape, and the end of the first movement is rather steeply faded, perhaps to avoid some blemish, but the sound has striking presence and sonority.

Muti's 1976 *New World* is a sweet and amiable performance, unsensationally attractive but hardly memorable. The recording is quite rich and smooth but makes the great cor anglais melody of the slow movement sound a little bland. The price is low but the competition is ferocious. However the Tchaikovsky coupling is very fine.

Eschenbach's reading with the Houston orchestra is strong and often thoughtful, played and recorded with refinement, but it often sounds self-conscious and over-prepared, not at all idiomatic, with a very slow tempo indeed for the *Largo*. That brings out the refined beauty of the Houston string-tone, and generally ensemble is excellent. It would have been much better to have this underappreciated orchestra in music less frequently recorded than the *New World*. Hardly a first choice, but perhaps recommendable to those who want the unusual coupling, although this is not a front-runner either.

CHAMBER AND INSTRUMENTAL MUSIC

Piano Quintet in A, Op. 81; Piano Quartet No. 2 in E flat, Op. 87.

(M) **(*) Warner Elatus 2564 60336-2. Schiff, Panocha Qt.

Both the *Piano Quintet* and the *E flat Quartet*, Op. 87, enjoy distinguished representation on CD, but in only one instance are they coupled together (by Menahem Pressler and the Emerson Quartet on DG 439 868-2 – see our main volume). And so András Schiff and the Panocha Quartet offer a welcome alternative, particularly at so competitive a price. The performances are musical and very well recorded and, though neither is a first choice if price is no object, they are both very enjoyable.

Sextet in A, Op. 48.

(*) Sup. **DVD** SU 7004-2. Augmented Smetana Qt – SMETANA: *String Quartets Nos. 1–2 (plus documentary on the Smetana Quartet).* **(*)**

The *Sextet* makes an admirable fill-up for the two Smetana *Quartets* and is given without intrusive camerawork. Musically very satisfying, though the documentary in which the members of the quartet look back over their career is curiously stiff.

String Quartets Nos. 8 in E flat, Op. 80; 9 in D min., Op. 34.

* Praga HMCD 90. Kocian Qt.

Outstanding performaces from the Kocian Quartet, naturally idiomatic and full of vitality. Both slow movements are played most beautifully, the *Adagio* of the *D minor* is very tender, and both Scherzos have a real Slavonic rhythmic feel. The outer movements of the *E flat major* are particularly appealing. The recording is real and present, perhaps a shade close (there is a hint of shrillness on the violins) but well balanced. This is much more characterful and authentic than the coupling of the same two works by the Chilingirians on Chandos.

VOCAL AND CHORAL MUSIC

Requiem, Op. 89.

(BB) ****** Warner Apex 0927 49922-2. Zylis-Gara, Toczyska, Dvorský, Mroz, Fr. R. Nouvel Philharmonique Ch. & O., Jordan.

Jordan's 1981 Erato version on Apex is weakly characterized by comparison with its competitors, less sharply contrasted in its moods, less idiomatic. Only Zylis-Gara, more incisive than her predecessor, Pilar Lorengar on Decca, might be counted a strong plus point, although the choral singing is quite impressive and the recording is pleasingly atmospheric. However, first choice remains with Fricsay (⊕→ ❂ DG 453073 2).

OPERA

The Jacobin (complete).

(*) Fone **SACD** 024 2 SACD (2). Pivovarov, Werba, Grato, Monogarova, Lehotsky, Panova, Elliot, Wexford Op. Ch., Nat. PO of Belarus, Voloschuk.

It is good to welcome a recording made live at the ever-enterprising Wexford Festival in Ireland. This warmly enjoyable set was recorded at three performances in the tiny Festival Theatre there in 2001, with excellent results. The orchestra as well as many in the cast were drawn from the National Opera of Belarus, Slav performers naturally in tune with this delightful folk-based opera by a Slavonic composer.

Dvořák, intent on developing his international reputation, was initially reluctant to take on a subject that was very much geared to Czech nationalism and village life, like Smetana's *Bartered Bride* in the previous decade. But once he started setting the libretto by Marie Červinková-Riegrová he fell in love with it, and the result is a sparkling score, with a gallery of well-defined characters, an abundance of haunting melody and many exhilarating ensembles.

The title may suggest a seriously political opera, but not so. It is simply that the accusation of being a Jacobin is falsely applied to Bohus, son of Count Vilem, when he returns from a visit to Paris. His accuser is his cousin Adolf, seeking to wrest from him the Count's inheritance. That is the main plot, but the relationship between Jiří, a young gamekeeper, and Terinka, daughter of the local schoolmaster, Benda, tends to take over, when it inspires Dvořák to delectable love music for tenor and soprano, by tradition the central characters in any opera. Needless to say, the problems and obstacles are all eliminated by the end, with the intrigues of the malevolent Adolf defeated. That story reflects the world in which Dvořák grew up, with the portrait of the schoolmaster, for example, directly drawn from his own experience. It gives Dvořák the opportunity to write choruses, folk dances and peasant songs that by rights should have made the opera far more popular than it is in the opera world outside the Czech Republic, an obvious rival to *The Bartered Bride*.

The Wexford performance under the lively direction of Alexander Voloschuk, with no weak link in the cast, captures the folk atmosphere very attractively, with stage effects more vivid than they might have been in the studio and with few disturbing stage noises. As Jiří, Michal Lehotsky has an agreeable, if very Slavonic, tenor, with Mariana Panova bright and clear as Terinka and Alasdair Elliot catching the right idiom in the gift role of her father. The relative dryness of the theatre acoustic in Wexford adds to the clarity without taking bloom away from the voices, with choruses of children as well as adults well caught. The rival Supraphon version under Jiří Pinkas, recorded in Brno in 1977, offers a performance on an altogether bigger scale, but the intimacy of the Wexford production is just as compelling and the performance just as lively. The snag of the Fone set is that, unlike the Supraphon set, it contains no libretto but only a sketchy synopsis, hardly adequate with such an offbeat story.

Rusalka (complete).

(**) TDK **DVD** DV-OPRUS (2). Fleming, Diadkova, Larin, Hawlata, Urbanová, Sénéchal, Deshayes, Paris Nat. Op. Ch. & O., Conlon (Director: Robert Carsen; V/D: Francois Roussillon).

This live recording of *Rusalka*, made in 2002 for French television, offers a DVD of Robert Carsen's Paris Opera production. Like some other DVDs, it permanantly exposes the pitfalls of so many modern opera productions that ignore the intentions of the composer and wilfully place the producer's sometimes bizarre conceits before the needs of the music, distorting the presentation of the principal characters. Here a fine performance is all but ruined by such tasteless visual arrogance.

As in her audio recording for Decca, Renée Fleming confirms her special love for the piece, helped by a supporting cast that could hardly be starrier, with James Conlon a warmly Dvořákian conductor. Fleming is in glorious voice, with the recording balance tending to favour singers rather than the orchestra. Yet there are striking differences in her reading here on stage compared with her studio recording. On stage her expression is far freer, which to a degree brings added warmth but which also makes for singing stylistically far less pure, with sliding between notes and under-the-note attack. When so much is so moving, and Fleming's acting matches her unfailingly heart-felt singing, it may be a minor problem, but on musical grounds the audio version is preferable.

Sergei Larin as the Prince is similarly positive, with his clear Slavonic tenor only occasionally roughening under strain. In Carlsen's modern-dress production, with costumes by Michael Levine, he cuts an even less romantic figure than he might, not helped by his outfits of winter overcoat and trilby, and baggy lounge suit. Larissa Diadkova makes a characterful figure of the witch, Jezibaba, even when in Act III she appears in what initially looks like a padded pulpit, but then in a surreal way turns out to be a vertically upended bed! Franz Hawlata, a fine bass, sings with richness and power as the Water Spirit, an imposing figure even in a lounge suit and wire-framed spectacles. Power and projection also mark the singing of Eva Urbanová as the Prince's seducer, the Foreign Princess, and it is good to have the veteran Michel Sénéchal taking the character role of the Gamekeeper, though both he and the excellent Karine Deshayes as the Kitchen Boy are not helped by the morning dress of tail coat and striped trousers given to all the palace servants. This Paris production with its unflattering modern costumes and prosaic sets – sometimes a bare box, more often a gigantic hotel bedroom – has little magic, despite some clever lighting devised by the director himself. The format is relatively extravagant on two DVDs, with a collection of trailers for other discs from TDK as the only substantial extra. Not recommended. The Decca CD set is in every way a more satisfying musical experience (460 568-2).

The Stubborn Lovers (complete).

*** Sup. SU 3765-2. Janál, Březina, Sýlkorová, Kloubová, Beláček, Prague Philharmonic Ch. & Philh., Bělohlávek.

This sparkling one-act comic opera with an amiably nonsensical plot is guaranteed to delight all lovers of Dvořák's music. In a sequence of 16 brief scenes it gives an amusing picture of village life, mainly in brisk ensembles. A few years before Dvořák wrote it in the autumn of 1874, Smetana's *The Bartered Bride* was given its first performance, and Dvořák follows that iconic example in tone of voice. Yet in keeping with his progressive outlook, this is a piece which links numbers together. This splendid account of an opera otherwise unrecorded, very well sung and played, with Jiří Bělohlávek a most persuasive conductor, makes its mark tellingly, with one winning tune after another from the Overture onwards.

The reluctant lovers of the title are Toník and Lenka, whose parents (Vávra, father of Toník, and Ríhová, mother of Lenka) demand that they marry. Naturally, the young ones want to choose for themselves, but the godfather of both of them, Řeřicha, understands the youngsters better than their parents. He succeeds in making them jealous, demonstrating that they are actually in love with each other, by suggesting that their parents are themselves scandalously intent on marrying across the generations, Vávra with designs on Lenka, Ríhová with Toník. This involves a sequence of farcical overhearings and misunderstandings that, needless to say, are sorted out in the end with little or no pain.

Rather like Alfonso in *Così fan tutte*, Řeřicha is the manipulator, contributing to almost every number, a role strongly taken here by the bass, Gustáv Beláček, coping splendidly with solos rather like patter-songs. The mellifluous light tenor Jaroslav Březina is splendid as Toník, characterizing well and making his change of heart convincing, as Zdena Kloubová does as Lenka when, seeing Toník as the choice of her mother, she wonders why tears have come into her eyes. The respective parents, Vávra and Ríhová, are well taken too, though they have less opportunity to establish positive characters. A welcome rarity.

DYSON, George (1883–1964)

(i) *Cello Sonata*; (ii) *3 Lyrics for Violin & Piano; 3 Violin Pieces. Bach's Birthday; Epigrams for Piano; My Birthday; Prelude & Ballet for Piano; Primrose Mount; Twilight; 3 War Pieces.*

(M) *** Dutton CDLX 7137. Owen Norris, with (i) Spooner; (ii) Juritz.

From a working-class background Dyson won music scholarships to become the leading champion of public school music in the 1920s and subsequently Director of the Royal College of Music. On disc his major works have been well treated, but in this charming collection, master-minded by the pianist, David Owen Norris, quite a different side is revealed, most strikingly in the piano pieces that make up the greater part of the programme. With Owen Norris an ideal interpreter, pointing rhythm and phrase seductively, the wit of the ten tiny *Epigrams* at the start has one appreciating Dyson's lightness of touch. Just as witty are the four pieces entitled *Bach's Birthday*, with counterpoint that strays into atonality, intended as a joke for his friend the pianist and scholar Harold Samuel. *Three War Pieces*, unpublished until now, were written when Dyson was in service in the trenches in the First World War, while other groups of pieces like *Twilight* and *My Birthday* from the 1920s were designed for amateurs to play, as are the two sets of violin pieces.

EBEN, Petr (born 1929)

Job; Laudes; Hommage à Buxtehude.
*** Hyp. CDA 67194. Schiager (organ of Hedvig Eleonora Kykran, Stockholm).

In his homeland this Czech composer of choral and organ music is a famous improviser/recitalist on both organ and piano. Eben is another of the East European musicians who survived Buchenwald concentration camp and emerged with his spirit unbroken. His is undoubtedly a major new voice in the field of organ music – the most exciting since Messiaen. His music is tonal but wholly original in both its complexities and mixed sonorities. Those British music-lovers who think of *Job* as synonymous only with Vaughan Williams must think again. Eben regards its theme of Job as 'the wager between Satan and God on the fate of a human being', and the eight titled movements cover what befalls Job and his personal response, ending with a set of variations on a Bohemian chorale to designate God's blessing, 'for Christ is truly the personification of the innocent sufferer to the very end'. It is an extraordinary work and sonically riveting, as indeed is the four-part *Laudes*, all based on a Gregorian melody, which reflects 'our deep ingratitude to our fellow men and to the world, and above all to its Creator'. The *Hommage à Buxtehude* alternates toccata and fugue and, although based on two quotations from that composer's music, has a quirky rhythmic individuality that would have astonished its dedicatee. This is remarkable music, superbly played and recorded. Just try the very opening of *Job* with its sombrely menacing pedal motif and you will surely want to hear the whole work (some 43 minutes long).

ECKHARD, Johann Gottfried
(1735–1809)

Keyboard Sonatas, Op. 1/1-3; Op. 2/1-2; in G; Menuet d'Exaudet with Variations.
(BB) *** Discovery DICD 920392. Haudebourg (fortepiano).

Johann Gottfried Eckhard's published keyboard sonatas included on this disc are forward-looking and embody expressive and dynamic markings characteristic of the piano. His music is played persuasively by Brigitte Haudebourg and is recorded decently.

EDWARDS, Ross (born 1943)

Piano Concerto.
**(*) Australian ABC Eloquence 426 483-2. Henning, Queensland SO, Fredman – WILLIAMSON: *Double Piano Concerto*; SCULTHORPE: *Piano Concerto.*
**(*)

An enterprising disc of Australian piano concertos. Ross Edwards's example is no masterpiece, but it has a certain enjoyable vitality. The slow movement, using pentatonic scales, gives it a Japanese flavour, and the finale is tuneful and fun. The performance is good, though the recording is only average.

EINEM, Gottfried von (1918–96)

String Quartets Nos. 1, Op. 45; 3, Op. 56; 5, Op. 87.
**(*) Orfeo C 098 101A. Artis Qt.

String Quartets Nos. 2, Op. 51; 4, Op. 63.
**(*) Orfeo C 098 201A. Artis Qt.

Gottfried von Einem came into international prominence in the immediate post-war years when his opera *Dantons Tod* was mounted at the 1947 Salzburg Festival. It is a powerful work whose success put him firmly on the operatic map. In 1938, when he was twenty, he had been arrested by the Gestapo and imprisoned for some months, an experience that inspired his opera, *Der Prozess* ('The Trial'), based on Kafka and premièred in 1953. Several symphonic works were written for American orchestras, including the *Philadelphia Symphony* (1960), but he did not turn to the quartet medium until 1976 when he was in his late fifties. Four others followed, the last in 1991, some five years before his death. Michael Oliver spoke of the *First Quartet* as 'an absorbing, often beautiful and always thought-provoking work', but although there are many felicities in the others none inspires unqualified enthusiasm. They are most expertly crafted, eclectic in idiom, and products of a refined and cultured musical mind. But if the musical idiom is sympathetic and the discourse civilized, the overall impression remains less than the sum of its parts. The Artis Quartet play with total commitment and are truthfully recorded on this CD. There is little here that resonates in the memory.

EISLER, Hanns (1898–1962)

Prelude and Fugue on B-A-C-H for String Trio, Op. 46; String Quartet, Op. 75.
(BB) *** CPO 999 341-2. Leipzig Qt – ADORNO: *String Quartet*, etc. ***

Hanns Eisler wrote relatively little chamber music. The *Prelude and Fugue on B-A-C-H* comes from 1934, the year after he left Berlin for the United States, and the *String Quartet* was written four years later. Rather anonymous music, composed at the time he was renewing his faith in his teacher, Schoenberg.

'Hollywood Songbook'.

(M) *** Decca 475 053-2. Matthias Goerne, E. Schneider.

Hanns Eisler went to Los Angeles but, unlike many, reacted violently against the culture of Hollywood. So it is that the 'Hollywood Songbook', far from being a celebration, is a collection of Lieder reflecting bitterness, cynicism and disillusion. This disc offers a mixed group of 46 brief songs, mainly to words by Bertolt Brecht, which reflect both Eisler's studies with Schoenberg and a desire to communicate directly, standing very much in the central tradition of the German Lied, which Eisler felt was in direct conflict with everything that Hollywood represented. Matthias Goerne, with his incisive baritone and feeling for words, is an ideal interpreter, very well accompanied by Eric Schneider. The collection won the Gramophone's 1999 20th-Century Vocal Award and is now welcome back to the catalogue at mid-price.

ELGAR, Edward (1857–1934)

Cello Concerto in E min., Op. 85.

*** Naïve V 4961. Gastinel, CBSO, Brown – BARBER: Cello Concerto. ***

(B) *** Warner Apex 0927 40600-2. Noras, Finnish RSO, Saraste – BARTOK: Rhapsody No. 1 ***; DVORAK: Cello Concerto **(*).

(i) Cello Concerto in E min., Op. 85. Enigma Variations; Pomp and Circumstances Marches, Op. 39, Nos. 1 & 4.

(BB) **(*) DG 474 561-2. Philh. O, Sinopoli, (i) with Maisky.

Anne Gastinel does not wear her heart on her sleeve but gives an account in which a certain reticence and dignity enhance the all-pervasive melancholy of this glorious score. The performance was recorded in Birmingham in September 2003 and, although it may not be free from blemish, it is a thoughtful and sensitive reading of genuine memorability. Her Barber Concerto, with which this is coupled, is among the very finest committed to disc.

The Finnish cellist Arto Noras, like his Swedish colleague Torleif Thedéen (on BIS 486), seems completely attuned to the Elgar sensibility and gives a moving account of this marvellous work, balancing vigour with a reticent serenity. He is very well accompanied, and this bargain triptych is highly recommendable. Thedéen has a nobility and reticence that are strongly appealing and Noras is hardly less impressive. Neither will disappoint; both enrich and do justice to the Elgar discography.

Mischa Maisky is highly persuasive in the Cello Concerto and, with Sinopoli a willing partner, gives a

warmly nostalgic, if perhaps not absolutely distinctive performance, essentially valedictory in feeling. The slow movement is deeply felt, but not in an extrovert way, and the soloist's dedication is mirrored in the finale. The mood of the Concerto is carried over into the Enigma Variations, where the lyrical variations are expressively relaxed and Nimrod has a simple, direct nobility. Sinopoli avoids the usual speeding up at the end of the finale, the thrust of that and other vigorous climaxes is pressed home passionately. The rich recording adds to the character of the readings, with the Philharmonia playing superbly. With two marches added for this release (not quite so well recorded), this CD is an undoubted bargain.

(i; ii) Cello Concerto. (iii; iv) Violin Concerto; (ii) Cockaigne Overture; In the South (Alassio); Enigma Variations; Froissart Overture; (iii; iv) Salut d'amour; (ii) Serenade for Strings; Symphonies Nos. 1–2.

(B) RCA ** 82876 60389-2 (4). (i) Starker; (ii) LPO; (iii) Zukerman; (iv) St Louis SO; all cond. Slatkin.

János Starker was in his seventies when he recorded the Cello Concerto with Leonard Slatkin, and the performance reflects both his understanding and the intellectual strength that has always marked his playing. In Elgar, his tough, slightly wiry tone goes with a relatively objective approach, with flowing speeds generally kept steady; and Slatkin, as in many of his other Elgar recordings, shows his natural feeling for the idiom. Sadly, in spite of Slatkin's sympathetic direction, Pinchas Zukerman's account of the Violin Concerto is far less involved than his earlier, Sony version. He tends to lack the sheer energy and, to make matters worse, the recording, being set at a distance, lacks body. In the First Symphony Slatkin's credentials as an Elgarian of understanding are very much on display. With bracing tempi, in the manner of Elgar's own performances, Slatkin brings the right sort of surging qualities to the first movement that ideally it needs, helped by brilliant playing from the LPO. The slow movement too is very impressive, though not quite achieving the rapt intensity of the greatest accounts, but noble all the same; the finale is superbly paced and completely satisfying. The account of the Second Symphony is equally splendid, timed beautifully to deliver authentic frissons, and it also has extra power in the finale by the addition of pedal notes on the organ, just before the epilogue – as Elgar once suggested to Sir Adrian Boult. Previously, only Vernon Handley had included them on his equally understanding version on CfP, though Slatkin's version is much more expansive than his. After such stirring accounts of the symphonies, it is sad to report that his reading of Enigma fails to catch fire, with the theme and Nimrod done very sluggishly indeed. Froissart is on the stiff side, but better, and Cockaigne goes reasonably well, but not much more than that. He is, however, back on form for both the

In the South Overture, a fast, bracing performance, often exciting and superbly recorded, and a persuasive reading of the *Serenade for Strings.* A mixed bag, but worth considering.

(i) *Cello Concerto. Falstaff;* (ii) *Romance for Bassoon.* (iii) *Smoking Cantata.*

(M) *** HALLÉ CD HLL 7505 (i) Schiff; (ii) Salvage; (iii) Shore; Hallé O, Elder.

It is quite a coup for Mark Elder in this third Elgar issue on the Hallé's own label to have so masterly a cellist as Heinrich Schiff in the *Cello Concerto.* This is one of the very finest versions ever, in many ways even more impressive than Schiff's earlier version, which was recorded not with a British orchestra but with the Dresden Staatskapelle under Sir Neville Marriner. The new version has even more intensity, with the first movement played with patrician nobility, very Elgarian, yet without inflation. The Scherzo is dazzlingly played, and in the other two movements the reading is markedly different from Schiff's earlier version, with a more flowing speed in the slow movement, less heavy, more songful and just as deeply felt, and a breathtakingly fast account of the main allegro in the finale, crisply articulated and very exciting. *Falstaff* brings a thrustful account that carries one magnetically over the many contrasted sections, giving the illusion of a live performance; and the *Romance for Bassoon* makes an attractive supplement, with Graham Salvage, the orchestra's principal bassoon, as soloist, bringing out the glowing lyricism. As a tiny extra squib comes the first ever performance and recording of one of Elgar's 'japes', a protest for baritone and orchestra against a ban on smoking in the hall, imposed in his home by the composer's host and close friend, Edward Speyer. Only nine bars long, it lasts less than a minute, a Wagnerian flourish to demonstrate Elgar's tongue-in-cheek humour, with Andrew Shore the robust soloist.

(i; ii) *Violin Concerto in B min.;* (iii; iv) *Piano Quintet in A min.;* (v) *String Quartet in E min.;* (i; vi) *Violin Sonata in E min;* (iii) (Piano): *Concert Allegro; Serenade.*

(B) **(*) CfP 585 9082 (2). (i) Bean; (ii) RLPO, Groves; (iii) Ogdon; (iv) Allegri Qt; (v) Music Group of L.; (vi) Parkhouse.

Hugh Bean recorded the *Violin Concerto* in 1972 in the wake of Menuhin's re-recording and, if his performance does not quite match that, it is still a very fine one and – as the splendid opening tutti immediately shows – it is strongly and authoritatively conducted by Sir Charles Groves. There is no question about Bean's technical assurance or his natural identification with the work and, although his performance is more relaxed, less tense than Menuhin's, it has a warmth and simplicity that are disarming, with the first movement's second subject beautifully played, and the serene beauty of the slow movement well caught, followed by a successful finale with some

very fine moments, especially in the closing pages. The EMI recording catches Bean's tonal beauty and gives plenty of body to the orchestra. Not quite a first choice then, but well worth having when the rest of this collection is so desirable, including the *Piano Quintet,* the most ambitious of Elgar's three major chamber works. Its slow movement is among the composer's greatest, and every bar is distinctive and memorable. John Ogdon and the Allegri Quartet give a strong performance, which misses some of the deeper, warmer emotions but which still gives considerable satisfaction. The *String Quartet* is well done too, but not so understandingly as the later account by the Britten Quartet on a budget Regis CD (RRC 1015 – see our main volume). The *Violin Sonata* has both an autumnal quality and a Brahmsian flavour, and it responds to ripe treatment such as Hugh Bean and David Parkhouse provide. The *Concert Allegro* for piano is a valuable oddity, rescued by John Ogdon (the music was long thought to be lost) and splendidly played, while the *Serenade* brings some charming ideas, even if it reveals Elgar's obvious limitations when writing for the keyboard. All these works are well recorded, and this CfP set is more than worth the modest price asked for it.

Chanson de matin; Cockaigne Overture; Enigma Variations, Op. 36* (including the original ending to the *Finale); Serenade for Strings in E min., Op. 20.

(M) *** HALLÉ CD HLL 7501. Hallé O, Elder.

Like Mark Elder's other initial issue on the Hallé label, this one offers a rarity, the original, markedly shorter version of the finale of the *Enigma Variations.* That has long been known to ballet-lovers in the choreographed version of the *Variations,* and though it cannot match the revised and expanded finale it is good to have as an alternative on a separate track. Elder's feeling for the Elgar idiom is unerring, with speeds well chosen not only in the *Variations* but in *Cockaigne, Chanson de matin* and the *Serenade for Strings,* and with the Hallé sound glowingly caught.

Dream Children, Op. 43; Nursery Suite; Wand of Youth Suites Nos. 1 & 2, Op. 1a and 1b.

⊕→ (BB) *** Naxos 8.557166. New Zealand SO, Judd.

It makes an ideal coupling on Naxos to have the two *Wand of Youth Suites,* using themes Elgar had written in boyhood for a family play, alongside his other two works inspired by childhood, *Dream Children* of 1902 and the *Nursery Suite* of 1930, dedicated to the then Duke and Duchess of York and the Princesses Elizabeth (now the Queen) and Margaret Rose. The freshness of inspiration is a delight, superbly brought out in these fine performances from New Zealand, recorded in Wellington in full, well-balanced sound, with James Judd always an idiomatic Elgarian. The *Wand of Youth Suites* in particular range wonderfully wide in mood and invention, culminating in the most brilliant movement of all, *The Wild Bears,* an orchestral showpiece here given a spectacular performance.

Serenade for Strings in E min., Op. 20.

★★ Häns. 93.043. Stuttgart RSO, Norrington – HOLST: *Planets.* ★★

Like Norrington's account of *The Planets*, with which it is coupled, his version of Elgar's *Serenade for Strings* is beautifully played and brilliantly recorded, but lacks something in expressive warmth, a little stiff rather than idiomatic.

Symphony No. 1 in E flat, Op. 55; In Moonlight (Canto Popolare); In the South (Alassio), Op. 50.

(B) Hallé CD HLL 7500. Hallé O, Elder.

This was the first issue on the Hallé Orchestra's own label, and it instantly established what superb standards Mark Elder has been setting in Manchester. This is one of the very finest versions of Elgar's *First Symphony*, of which this orchestra under Hans Richter gave the first performance in 1908. On one hand Elder pays tribute to the Barbirolli tradition, with a natural feeling for the moulding of Elgarian phrases, yet he generally adopts more urgent speeds than his predecessor. The slow movement is ecstatically beautiful, and the finale brings out all the emotional thrust required. It is very well recorded.

Symphonies Nos. 1–2; Cockaigne Overture; Sospiri.

(BB) ★★ EMI Gemini 5 85512-2 (2). LSO, Tate.

Jeffrey Tate conducts the LSO in expansively expressive readings of both symphonies, generally sustaining slow speeds – exceptionally slow in No. 2 – with keen concentration, but letting one or two passages sag. These are warm-hearted performances nevertheless, helped by brilliant playing from the LSO and rich and full if not sharply focused recording. The *Cockaigne Overture* and brief string piece are successful too, but competition is strong and even at bargain price this coupling is hardly a first choice.

CHAMBER AND INSTRUMENTAL MUSIC

Violin Sonata in E min., Op. 82.

(M) ★★★ Warner Elatus 2564 60661-2. Vengerov, Chachamov – BRAHMS: *Violin Sonatas Nos. 2–3.* ★★★

(★★(★)) Testament mono SBT 1319. Rostal, Horsley – DELIUS; WALTON: *Violin Sonatas.* (★★(★))

Originally linked with the Dvořák *Violin Concerto* and now recoupled with Brahms, Vengerov's performance is at once passionate and large scale. He also brings out the thoughtful poetry of the piece, with a vein of fantasy in the elusive slow movement.

Max Rostal, a refugee from Hitler's Germany, became an inspired interpreter of English music, as all three of the *Violin Sonatas* on this fine Testament disc demonstrate. In the Elgar, Rostal is totally idiomatic, with a powerful, thrusting reading of the first movement and an account of the slow movement

that, as with Vengerov, brings out the element of free fantasy. He then plays the finale with a naturally expressive flexibility, which relates the movement more than usual to the accompanied cadenza in the Elgar *Violin Concerto*. The mono recording is on the dry side, but Rostal's refined tone defies the lack of bloom, with Colin Horsley a most responsive partner.

VOCAL AND CHORAL MUSIC

Angelus; Ave Maria; Ave maris stella; Ave verum corpus; Ecce sacardos magnus; Fear not, O land; Give unto the Lord; Great is the Lord; I sing the birth; Lo! Christ the Lord is born; O hearken thou; O salutaris hostia Nos. 1–3.

(BB) ★★★ Hyp. Helios CDH 55147. Worcester Cathedral Ch., Hunt; A. Partington (organ).

In this group of 14 sacred choral works, Dr Donald Hunt, choirmaster of Worcester Cathedral, here provides a refreshing supplement to his fine collection of Elgar part-songs (Hyperion CDA 66271/2 – see our companion volume). Though in the grand setting of Psalm 48, *Great is the Lord*, one misses the impact of a big choir, the refinement of Dr Hunt's singers, their freshness and bloom as recorded against a helpful acoustic are ample compensation, particularly when the feeling for Elgarian phrasing and rubato is unerring. The coronation anthem *O Hearken thou* would also benefit from larger-scale treatment, convincing as this refined performance is; but most of these 14 items are more intimate, and the Worcester performances are near ideal, with clean ensemble, fine blending and taut rhythmic control. Vividly atmospheric recording, which still allows for full detail to emerge.

The Apostles: The Spirit of the Lord is upon me. Ave verum corpus; Ave Marie; Ave Maris stella, Op. 2/1–3; Benedictus. Op. 34/2; Give unto the Lord (Psalm 29), Op. 74; Go Song of mine, Op. 57; Great is the Lord (Psalm 48), Op. 67; The Light of Life, Op. 29: Seek Him that maketh the seven stars; Light of the World. O hearken Thou, Op. 64; O salutaris hostia; Te Deum laudamus, Op. 34/1.

☞ (BB) ★★★ Naxos 8.557288. St John's Cambridge, College Ch., Robinson; J. Vaughan (organ).

This is the last of the series of ten highly successful CDs made by the St John's College Choir under Christopher Robinson, before he retired in 2002. Elgar's shorter Latin settings, *Ave verum corpus, Ave Maria, Ave Maris stella, O hearken Thou* and *O salutaris hostia*, are all quite lovely. The more ambitious *Te Deum* and *Benedictus* was written for the Hereford Three Choirs Festival of 1897 and, like the Psalm setting *Great is the Lord* (first heard at Westminster Abbey in 1912), shows Elgar at full stretch. It is also good to have the serene *Prologue* to *The Apostles* (1903), *The Spirit of the Lord* and, finally, the two memorable excerpts from Elgar's first oratorio, *The Light of Life*, notably the stirring *Light of the world*, which is the exultant closing chorus. Splendid singing throughout and excellent recording make this a collection to treasure.

(i) *Coronation Ode*; (ii) *The Spirit of England, Op. 80; Oh hearken thou (Offertory), Op. 64*; (i) *National Anthem* (arr. Elgar).

(M) ★★★ EMI (ADD/DDD) 5 85148-2. (i; ii) Lott; (i)
Hodgson, Morton, Roberts, Cambridge University
Music Socety, King's College, Cambridge, Ch., New
Philh. O, Band of Royal Military School of Music,
Ledger; (ii) L. Symphony Ch., N. Sinf., Hickox –
PARRY: *I was glad*. ★★★

Ledger is superb in capturing the necessary swagger and panache of the *Coronation Ode*. The 1977 analogue recording, of demonstration quality, is one of the finest made in King's College Chapel – and with extra brass it presents a glorious experience. Excellent singing and playing, though the male soloists do not quite match their female colleagues. A decade later, Hickox conducted a rousing performance of *The Spirit of England*, magnificently defying the dangers of the composer's wartime bombast, adding also a short but telling setting of Psalm 29, composed as the Offertory in the coronation service of King George V in 1911. The London Symphony Chorus is in radiant form, and Felicity Lott is a strong soloist in both major works. First-rate Abbey Road digital sound. The disc opens with Elgar's grandiloquent version of the National Anthem, which includes a last-verse reference to *Pomp and Circumstance No. 1*.

The Dream of Gerontius (complete).

(B) (★★★) CfP mono 585 90422. Lewis, Thomas,
Cameron, Huddersfield Ch. Soc., RLPO, Sargent –
WALTON: *Belshazzar's Feast*. (★★)

Sargent's second mono recording of *The Dream of Gerontius* was chosen by Alec Robertson for inclusion among 'The Great Records'. It was an unfashionable choice, as the accepted view is that Sargent's earlier, 78rpm set (available on Testament SBT 2025 – see our main volume) has a finer cast of soloists and is more inspired. But A. R. thought that this mono LP version had a greater spiritual perception than Sargent's 1945 recording. Here the very opening and the closing pages of both the first and second parts have a rapt intensity that is moving without any hint of emotional indulgence. HMV chose the excerpt of *Go forth upon thy journey* (with John Cameron in superb voice) to include in their original anthology tribute to the work of Sir Malcolm Sargent and this (as does the whole performance) shows an inspiration that the conductor only rarely found in the recording studio. Richard Lewis is a fine Gerontius, and his dialogues with Marjorie Thomas (in the words of Robertson, 'a Rosetti rather than a Rubens angel') have a remarkable beauty and stillness. The one failure in the performance is the 'Demons' Chorus' in which the Huddersfield chorus fail to let themselves go. But everywhere else their singing is

magnificent, and the first-class mono recording is worthy of it.

The Starlight Express (incidental music), *Op. 78*.

(B) ★★★ CfP (ADD) 585 9072. Masterson,
Hammond-Stroud, LPO, Handley.

It has been left to latterday Elgarians to revive a 1916 score (incidental music for a children's play) that was not a success in its day but that reveals the composer at his most charming. On CD in this dedicated reconstruction (without the spoken dialogue) one is conscious of the element of repetition. But the ear is constantly beguiled and the key sequences sugest that this procedure would have won the composer's approval. Much of the orchestral music has that nostalgically luminous quality that Elgarians will instantly recognize. Both soloists are excellent, and the LPO plays with warmth and sympathy. The 1976 recording is excellent and it matters little that, in order to fit the piece complete on to a single CD, some minor cuts have had to be made.

ELLINGTON, Edward Kennedy 'Duke' (1899–1974)

Harlem; The River: suite (orch. Collier); *Solitude* (trans. Morton Gould).

★★★ Chan. 9909. Detroit SO, Järvi – DAWSON: *Negro Folk Symphony*. ★★★

Harlem is a wildly exuberant but essentially optimistic picture of Harlem as it used to be before the drug age. Ellington pictures a parade and a funeral, and ends with riotous exuberance. This is true, written-down, orchestral jazz, more authentic than Gershwin and marvellously played by musicians who know all about the Afro-American musical tradition. The trumpets are terrific.

The River was composed in 1970, intended as music for a ballet with choreography by Alvin Ailey, but this project proved abortive, and Ellington also saw the score as a river journey. The ideas are characteristically varied and imaginative, yet as orchestrated by Ron Collier the seven movements sound like an extended ballet sequence in an MGM film with big-band interludes.

Solitude, which dates from Ellington's Cotton Club days, is much more subtly scored by Morton Gould, and in its orchestral format has a haunting, almost Copland-esque flavour, although it retains Ellington's own musical fingerprints. Splendid recording.

ENESCU, Georges (1881–1955)

Romanian Rhapsody No. 1.

★★★ Mercury (ADD) **SACD** 475 6185. LSO, Dorati –
LISZT: *Hungarian Rhapsodies Nos. 1–6*. ★★(★)

Mercury are bringing out some of their most admired recordings on SACD and, although they are not due to be released until after our book goes to press, we feel sure that listeners will want to be informed of their publication in the autumn of this year. A full review of the work listed above can be found in our current main edition. The new format should go some way to further enhance the already spectacular results afforded by the 'Living Presence' technology.

ENGLUND, Einar (1916–99)

Piano Concertos Nos. 1 & 2; Epinika.
*** Ondine 1015-2. Matti Eaekallio, Tampere PO, Eri Klas.

Einar Englund first made a name in the days of LP with his incidental music to Max Frisch's play *The Great Wall of China*. Afterwards he emerged from relative neglect to really generous exposure. All seven symphonies have been recorded, together with a fair number of his concertos and other pieces. Writing in the early 1970s in *Twentieth Century Composers*, R.L. spoke of him as possessing 'perhaps the most spontaneous and natural gift' of his generation and was impressed by his 'Prokofievian exuberance and skill'. Englund was born in Gotland, the large Swedish island in the Baltic, but settled in Helsinki, where he studied and, after a spell in Tanglewood with Copland, later taught. The idiom owes much to Shostakovich, but his invention is fresh and lively. He was a highly accomplished pianist and wrote for the instrument with great naturalness and flair. The *First Piano Concerto* comes from 1955 and is fluent and likeable. There is plenty of Prokofiev and Shostakovich and there are times when we are fleetingly reminded of Rawsthorne or Britten. In the *Second Concerto*, written nearly twenty years later, the debt to Shostakovich remains strong, and it is musically less interesting and satisfying than No. 1. *Epinika*, written for the first post-war Olympic Games, is a lively and skilfully wrought *pièce d'occasion*. Good performances and recordings, but there is a more than serviceable account of the *First Concerto* on Naxos, coupled with the *Second* and *Fourth Symphonies* (8.553758 – see our main volume).

ENNA, August (1859–1939)

The Little Match Girl (opera); *The Shepherdess and the Chimney-sweep* (ballet for orchestra and narrator).
** CPO 999 595-2. Bonde-Hansen, Sjöbergt, Helmuth, Danish R. Sinf., Zeilinger.

The Danish composer August Enna produced a steady stream of operas and operettas throughout his career that, thanks to his melodic gift and attractive orchestration, earned him considerable success. Alas, by the end of his life his music fell out of fashion, and he died poverty-stricken and disappointed. It is good that CPO has made available these two representative works, based on Hans Andersen fairy-tales, which have never fallen completely out of the Danish repertoire. There is nothing profound here, but *The Little Match Girl* of 1897 has some charming ideas, with the influence of Wagner felt in the style though not in profundity. *The Shepherdess and the Chimney-sweep* has some engaging music, but the prominence (in volume and in quantity) of the narration will surely be too much for English-speaking listeners, although full texts and translations are offered. The performances are sympathetic, but the recording, though acceptable, lacks richness and depth.

ERKEL, Ferenc (1810–93)

Bank Ban.
** Warner 0927-44606-2 (2). Kiss B, Marton, Rost, Hungarian Nat. Ch. & Millennium O, Pal.

Central to the repertory in Hungary are two nineteenth-century operas by Ferenc Erkel, both on historic themes, *Hunyadi Laszlo* and this one, *Bank Ban*, first heard in 1861 when the composer was fifty. Set in the early thirteenth century, it tells of squabbles and conspiracies at the court of King Endre II, prompting Erkel to produce a score full of rousing melodies that echo early Verdi but with a Hungarian flavour, as in the colourful *Csárdás*. This recording, made to go with a film of the opera, brings vigorous conducting from Tamas Pal, with chorus and orchestra both excellent. In the title role of Bank (a Hungarian contraction of Benedict) the baritone, Attila Kiss B, is firm and incisive, though the other principals are disappointing, with Eva Marton as the scheming Queen Gertrud raw of tone and Andrea Rost as Bank's wife too fluttery. The bass Kolos Kovats as the king is wobbly and ill-focused, and the tenor Denes Gulyas as the evil Otto is strained and coarse. Nevertheless, a welcome rarity.

EYCK, Jakob van (1590–1657)

Der Fluyten Lust-hof (excerpts).
*** Astrée E 8588. Feldman, Marq, Lislevand.

Jakob van Eyck was blind but, as his tombstone stated: 'What God took from his eyes he gave back in his ear'. He played the recorder 'like a bird' in the local park, to the delight of the weekend promenaders. *Der Fluyten Lust-hof*, published in two volumes, dates from the middle of the seventeenth century. Van Eyck wrote divisions and improvisations on famous tunes of the time, most of which came from France and England – half a dozen of Dowland's most famous numbers are featured. Jill Feldman sings with engaging purity of line and tone, and she has a knack for simple embellishment. The intimacy of the performances is nicely reflected in the recording.

FALLA, Manuel de (1876–1946)

El amor brujo (complete).

(M) **(*) BBC (ADD) BBCB 8012-2. Reynolds, ECO, Britten (with TCHAIKOVSKY: *Francesca da Rimini; Romeo and Juliet* **).

Britten conducts a warmly evocative reading of the Falla ballet. Not only does he bring out the atmospheric beauty of the writing, he characteristically points rhythms in a seductively idiomatic way, as in his treatment of the haunting *Pantomime*. Anna Reynolds may not sound very Spanish, but she too is warmly responsive and characterful. However, the Tchaikovsky coupling ultimately lacks the kind of strong adrenalin flow so essential in this repertoire.

Nights in the Gardens of Spain.

** Arthaus DVD 100 034. Barenboim, Chicago SO, Domingo – SIBELIUS: *Violin Concerto.* ** (Producer: Bernd Hellthaler; V/D: Bob Coles).

A 1997 recording, made while the Chicago orchestra was in Germany. On the face of it, this should have strong claims on the collector, a master-pianist as soloist and a great Spanish singer-now-conductor on the podium. Yet despite the latter, the performance is curiously wanting in mystery and atmosphere, and one remains untransported to the magical Sierra de Córdoba. Barenboim plays with his customary aplomb, and the video direction is expert and unobtrusive. The encores, the *Ritual Fire Dance* and *The Magic Circle* from *El amor brujo*, come off well under Barenboim's baton.

The Three-Cornered Hat (ballet): *Miller's Dance, Danse finale.*

*** BBC (ADD) BBCL 4123-2. Philh. O, Giulini – BRUCKNER: *Symphony No. 7*; MUSSORGSKY: *Khovanshchina: Prelude.* ***

The Falla dances, recorded live, make a lively contrast to Giulini's dedicated reading of Bruckner's *Seventh Symphony*, the main work on the disc.

La vida breve (complete).

(BB) ** Naxos 8.660155 (2). Sánchez, Valls, Nafé, Echeverría, Baquerizo, Suárez, Cid, Sanz, Reyes (guitar), Prince of Asturias Foundation Ch., Asturias SO, Valdés.

Having an idiomatic account of Falla's colourful opera, well cast and well recorded, makes a good bargain on the Naxos label, even if there is a serious lack of tension in much of the performance. It does not help that the story of the love between the gypsy girl Salud and Paco from a well-to-do family is too naive to be convincing. Even when Salud at the climax commits suicide in despair when Paco returns to his intended bride, neither the singer nor the orchestra sounds very involved. In the central part, Ana Maria Sánchez has a warm, well-focused voice with the right mezzo tinge, and she sings intelligently

but conveys little sense of drama. As Paco, Vincente Ombuena Valls is well cast, with his pleasing, fresh tenor, while among the others Alicia Nafé is most characterful as Salud's grandmother. The two *Dances* that come as orchestral showpieces betray the relative slackness of the rest in the way they immediately raise the tension. The earlier version with Victoria de los Angeles as Salud is clearly preferable and it comes at mid-price, but in a two-disc set, coupled with *El amor brujo* and *The Three-cornered Hat* ballets (EMI 5 67587-2 [567590-2] – see our main volume).

FANELLI, Ernest (1860–1917)

Tableaux symphoniques d'après 'Le Roman de la Momie'.

**(*) Marco Polo 8.225234. Drahosova, Slovak RSO, Adriano – BOURGAULT-DUCCOUDRAY *Rhapsody cambodgienne.* **(*)

Hardly a well-known name now, but French composer Ernest Fanelli belongs to one of the great might-have-beens: if only he was born in a different time and under a different set of circumstances, he might be better known now, for he was undoubtedly a composer of some originality. It was Pierné who, in 1912, on inspecting a score submitted by Fanelli as a specimen of his musical handwriting for a job as copyist, was impressed by the music itself (Fanelli submitted his score without telling Pierné that he had written it), commenting that it 'contained all the principles and all processes of modern music used by the recognized masters of today' – remarkable, as the work was written some 29 years earlier. Through Pierné, Fanelli secured performances of some of his music, giving the composer a brief period of interest in the music world. Adriano is a strong advocate of Fanelli, and in the sleeve-notes he suggests that Fanelli invited a certain amount of jealousy from Debussy, who once walked out of a room on hearing some of Fanelli's 'advanced' harmonies; interestingly, Ravel apparently said, 'now we know where his [Debussy's] impressionism comes from'. Fanelli's life was undoubtedly difficult, and he died disillusioned and embittered. All that aside, on the strength of this disc, Adriano's championing of him is certainly worthwhile: *Le Roman de la Momie* (*Romance of the Mummy*) (1883–6) was inspired by the exotic novel of the same name by Théophile Gautier, who filled his short novel with vivid depictions of Egyptian landscapes, costumes and locations – an ideal frame for Fanelli's 'Tableaux symphoniques' (the second part of the score, *Fête dans le palais du Pharon*, is dedicated to Gautier's daughter). While it is not true to say that Fanelli has an instantly distinctive voice, his music, with the aid of a large orchestra (including a wordless soprano vocalise in Part I of *Thèbes*), enters the worlds of Rimsky-Korsakov, Ravel and Respighi, as well encompassing whole-tone scales and polytonality. The score has plenty of atmosphere and builds up to powerful climaxes: at times the score is reminiscent of film music – an exotic/gothic production of the golden era (such as the opening of the *Fête danse le palais du Pharon*, for example) but is none the worse for that. It all makes for fascinating listening, and anyone interested in the by-ways of French music should explore this disc, especially with its rare coupling. Adriano gives an enthusiastic performance, the only reservation being that the string-tone could be sweeter, especially above the stave where they are taxed at times; the playing is not always as immaculate as it might be. The recording is well detailed and quite decent. As Adriano writes – and it must be stressed that it was he, not the writer of this note, who wrote it – 'Gautier's Mummy, in fact, returns again'!

FARNON, Robert (born 1917)

A la claire fontaine; Colditz March; Derby Day; Gateway to the West; How Beautiful is Night; 3 Impressions for Orchestra: 2, In a Calm; 3, Manhattan Playboy. Jumping Bean; Lake in the Woods; Little Miss Molly; Melody Fair; Peanut Polka; Pictures in the Fire; Portrait of a Flirt; A Star is Born; State Occasion; Westminster Waltz.
*** Marco Polo 8.223401. Slovak RSO (Bratislava), Leaper.

Farnon's quirky rhythmic numbers, *Portrait of a Flirt*, *Peanut Polka* and *Jumping Bean*, have much in common with Leroy Anderson in their instant memorability; their counterpart is a series of gentler orchestral watercolours, usually featuring a wistful flute solo amid gentle washes of violins. *A la claire fontaine* is the most familiar. Then there is the film music, of which the *Colditz March* is rightly famous, and the very British genre pieces, written in the 1950s. All this is played by this excellent Slovak orchestra with warmth, polish and a remarkable naturalness of idiomatic feeling. The recording is splendid, vivid, with the orchestra set back convincingly in a concert-hall acoustic.

(i) *Canadian Caravan;* (ii) *Gateway to the West; High Street; How Beautiful is Night; Huckle-Buckle; In a Calm; Journey into Melody; Jumping Bean; Manhattan Playboy; Melody Fair; Mountain Grandeur; Ottawa Heights; Peanut Polka; Portrait of a Flirt; Sophistication Waltz; A Star is Born; State Occasion; String Time; Taj Mahal;* (i) *Willie the Whistler.*
(BB) (***) Naxos mono 8.110849. Orchestras conducted by (i) Williams; (ii) composer.

These recordings date mainly from the late 1940s and offer a ring of authenticity that instantly takes one back to that era. The fleetness of the string-playing in, for example, *Portrait of a Flirt* is inimitable, while the use of subtle *portamento* is an art now all but lost. Elsewhere, one readily responds to the nostalgic atmosphere of these recordings, with the quiet *How*

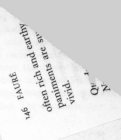

Beautiful is Nig... hypnotic quality. more imperially maybe not now pol *Mahal* follows. Care tering of these track Chappell Library reco worth the very modes excellent, too.

FARRANCE, Louise (1804–75)

Piano Quintets Nos. 1 in A min., Op. 30; 2 in E, Op. 31.
*** ASV CDDCA 1122. London Schubert Ens.

Louise Farrance studied with Reicha, Hummel and Moscheles and became the only woman professor of the piano at the Paris Conservatoire during the nineteenth century. She composed prolifically for the piano, but her output includes three symphonies, which were given in Paris, Brussels, Geneva and Copenhagen during her lifetime, as well as a quantity of chamber music. She has fallen from view: the *Everyman Dictionary of Music* does not mention her, nor do Michael Kennedy's *Oxford Dictionary* or Alison Latham's *Oxford Companion*. All the same, there does seem to be an upsurge of interest in her on CD: two of the symphonies have been recorded, as have the *Nonet*, the *Sextet for Wind and Piano* and two of her piano trios. The *Piano Quintet in A minor* comes from 1839 and was her first chamber work of any kind, its successor following a year later. Both are scored for the same forces as the Hummel *Quintet* and the Schubert *Trout*. Although her musical language owes much to Haydn and Hummel, there are elements of Weber, Spohr and Mendelssohn to be found, and there is considerable harmonic subtlety in her writing. Good playing from the London Schubert Ensemble and truthful recording.

FASCH, Johann (1688–1758)

Bassoon Concertos: in C; D min. Concerto in A (for Violin Obbligato) in A. Double Oboe Concertos: in G; in E flat; in C min. Overture in G.
*** CPO 777 015-2. Azzolini, Skuplik, La Stravaganza, Köln.

A delightful collection from the German composer Johann Fasch. These lively and inventive works are thoroughly entertaining, the composer bridging the gap between the baroque and classical eras, clearly pushing forward new ideas, with some often bold writing, most notably in the woodwind department. The orchestra clearly relish the music and revel in the brilliance of the writing. The double concertos are especially enjoyable and there is little here that falls below a high standard. One takes pleasure in the bold array of colour and sound that the soloists produce –

for its own sake. The accom-
...erb and the recording is sharply

...os: in B flat, FWV N:B2; in D min., FWV
...d2; in F, FWV N:F2; in G min., FWV N:g1; Trio
Sonatas: in D min., FWV N:d1; in G min., FWV
N:g2; in F, FWV N:F6.
** HM HMC 905251. Arfken, Brüggemann, Agrell &
    continuo.

Fasch, a contemporary of J. S. Bach, wrote in a *galant*
manner without the lively polyphonic interest of his
most famous contemporary. These are agreeable
works, but the oboes generally play together in simple harmony, while the part-writing and imitation
are comparatively ingenuous. The music is pleasing
but no more. The recording closely integrates the
instruments – a degree more separation would have
been welcome.

FAURÉ, Gabriel (1845–1924)

CHAMBER MUSIC

*Piano Quartets Nos. 1 in C min., Op. 15; 2 in G min.,
Op. 45; Piano Quintets Nos. 1 in D min., Op. 89; 2 in
C min., Op. 115.*
(B) *** Double Decca 475 187-2 (2). Rogé, Ysaÿe Qt.
(B) *(*) Erato Ultima 8573 84251-2 (2). (i) Hubeau,
    Gallois-Montbrun, Lequien, Navarra; (ii) Hubeau,
    Via Nova Qt.

It goes without saying that Pascal Rogé and the Ysaÿe
Quartet give performances of great finesse and sensitivity. On the first CD they are more successful in the
Quintet No. 1 than in the early *Quartet No. 1*, where
they must yield to Domus (Hyperion), who find
greater delight and high spirits in the Scherzo. The
recording here is very good, though there is an
occasional moment when the reverberant acoustic
affects the focus. The *Second Quintet* and *Quartet*
were recorded in a different location a year later –
though, curiously, the aural image is still not quite
perfect: Rogé is just that bit too much to the fore, and
the quartet is not set in an ideal focus. That said, the
playing of all concerned is excellent, alive and subtle,
with expert and sensitive contributions from the
distinguished pianist. The musical values of these
performances sweep aside any of the slight reservations concerning the sound, especially as this set is
offered so inexpensively.

These performances originally appeared in the
1970s as part of a five-LP Erato set, which was
subsequently issued on three CDs. They were displaced in the late 1970s by Jean-Philippe Collard's set
with the Parrenin Quartet, which is currently not
available. Jean Hubeau was a distinguished professor
at the Paris Conservatoire and recorded the complete
Fauré piano music in the early 1970s. These accounts,
though serviceable and reasonably priced, lack the

sensitivity and finesse of their best modern rivals.

*(i; ii) Piano Trio, Op. 120; Après un rêve (arr. for
piano trio by Eguchi); (i) Violin Sonata No. 1 in A,
Op. 11; Andante, Op. 25. Berceuse, Op. 28; Masques
et bergamasques: Clair de lune, Op. 46/2 (arr.
Périlhou); Pelléas et Mélisande: La Fileuse (arr.
Auer); Sicilienne. Morcea a lecture a vue; Romance,
Op. 28; Serenade Toscane (arr. Ronchini).*
*** Vanguard ATM-CD 1239. Shaham; with (i) Eguchi,
    (ii) Brinton Smith.

Gil Shaham, among the most inspired violinists of
his generation, here offers what he describes as a
'Fauré Album'. Two major works, the *First Violin
Sonata*, ardently lyrical, and the *Piano Trio*, one of
the finest of the late chamber works, are comple-
mented by eight shorter pieces, including some
favourites. *Après un rêve* comes in an arrangement
for piano trio, and other songs arranged for violin
and piano include *Clair de lune* and *Serenade
Toscane*. There are also two numbers from Fauré's
incidental music for Maeterlinck's *Pelléas et
Mélisande*, not just the popular *Sicilienne* but a spectacular arrangement of *La Fileuse* by the teacher and
virtuoso, Leopold Auer, in which the muted violin
imitates a spinning-wheel. Shaham plays with a phenomenal range of tone and dynamic, consistently
caressing the ear. In the two major works too his free
expressiveness brings a winning sense of spontaneity,
well matched by the pianist, Akira Eguchi.

*Violin sonatas Nos. 1 in A, Op. 13; 2 in E min., Op.
108; Andante, Op. 75; Berceuse, Op. 16; Morceau de
concours – Romance, Op. 28.*
&— ❂ (M) *** Decca 476 2180. Amoyal, Rogé.

Readers wanting a modern recording of the two
Fauré *Violin Sonatas* need look no further. Pierre
Amoyal and Pascal Rogé play them as to the manner
born. As one would expect, they are totally inside the
idiom and convey its subtlety and refinement with
freshness and mastery. There are admirable alternatives from Grumiaux and Crossley at mid-price and
from Krysia Osostowicz and Susan Tomes, but
Amoyal and Rogé more than hold their own against
them and throw new light on the three slight miniatures that they offer as a bonus. Impeccable recording, too. A lovely disc, now available at mid-price in
Universal's 'Penguin ❂ Collection'.

VOCAL MUSIC

Requiem, Op. 48.
**(*) York Ambisonic YORK CD177. Rawlins, White,
    Martin, Canterbury Cathedral Ch. & O, Flood –
    DURUFLE: *Requiem.* **(*)
** René Gailly CD 87 162. Coppé, Van der Crabben,
    Capella Brugensis, Coll. Brugense, Peire –
    POULENC: *Organ Concerto.* **
*(*) DG 459 365-2. Bartoli, Terfel, Santa Cecilia Nat.

Ae. Ch. & O, Chung – DURUFLE: *Requiem.* ★★

(i) *Requiem.* (ii; iii) *Après un rêve, Op. 7/1;* (ii) *Dolly (Suite), Op. 56;* (ii; iii) *Elégie, Op. 24;* (ii; iv) *Pavane, Op. 50.*

(BB) ★★(*) DG Entrée 474 562-2. (i) Battle, Schmidt, Philh. Ch. & O, Giulini; (ii) Boston SO, Ozawa; (iii) Eskin; (iv) Tanglewood Festival Ch.

(i–iii) *Requiem, Op. 48. Mélodies:* (i; iv) *Aurore; Chanson d'amour; La Fée aux chansons; Notre amour; Le Secret;* (ii; iv) *Chanson du pêcheur; En sourdine; Fleur jetée; Nell; Poème d'un jour, Op. 21; Le Voyageur.*

(BB) ★★ RCA 82876 55303-2. (i) Bonney; (ii) Hagegård; (iii) Tanglewood Festival Ch., Boston SO, Ozawa; (iv) Warren Jones (piano).

The York Ambisonic engineers project the Canterbury Cathedral Choir and Orchestra, as well as the powerful organ, with an impressive weight and immediacy, with the performances unaffected by cloudy reverberation despite being recorded in the Cathedral. John Rutter's edition is used, which restores the original modest orchestration with no orchestral violins, only a solo violin, and four each of violas and cellos, plus single double-bass. The baritone soloist is very much part of the choir, hardly at all separated from his colleagues and not well focused. One big advantage is that the intimacy of scale comes over clearly, while the sharpness of focus for the choir and accompanying instruments also brings out the differences between the two works, where mistier sound tends to twin them very closely. Thanks to David Flood's direction as well as to the recording, the drama is underlined in high dynamic contrasts, where often in both works the devotional element is brought out to the exclusion of any dramatic bite. The treble soloist, Joseph Rawlins, is bright and fresh in the *Pie Jesu.*

Giulini with large-scale Philharmonia forces adopts consistently slow speeds and a very reverential manner in the *Requiem.* That view usually makes the work too sentimental, but Giulini's care for detail in textures and his unexaggerated expressive style keep the result hushed and prayerful rather than sugary, with warm, atmospheric recording to match. Kathleen Battle sings with glowing warmth in the *Pie Jesu,* sounding sumptuous but not really in style. One might have expected Ozawa's characteristic reticence to be highly suitable for Fauré, but in the rest of the items on this CD his understatement perhaps goes a shade too far at times. The *Pavane* is almost certainly sung in French, though the words are inaudible, partly because of the Boston resonance; the choral embroidery, however, adds an agreeable touch of vitality to a rather solemn performance. The music-making springs to life in the delectable opening movement of *Dolly,* and Ozawa's performance has the deftest touch throughout; the second movement, *Mi-a-ou* (fortunately not as onomatopoeic as it

sounds), is delightful, and the gay finale, *Le Pas espagnol,* is worthy of Sir Thomas himself; indeed, this was the most attractive recorded account (it dates from 1986) since Beecham's and, like the rest of the Ozawa items, it is very pleasingly recorded within a warm concert-hall ambience. A mixed but worthwhile bargain.

Ozawa uses the full score. His performance is gentle and recessive, although the performers (including the fine Boston orchestra) rise to the climaxes. The reverberation of Symphony Hall bathes the chorus in a hazy glow of resonance which suits the music but blurs the focus. However, many may like the ecclesiastical, cathedral-like effect, and it ensures that the closing *In Paradisum* is tenderly ethereal. The two sensitive soloists provide the couplings, two separate groups of Fauré songs, also over-resonantly recorded (in Massachusetts and Sweden respectively) – here the piano is adversely affected. Barbara Bonney responds to Fauré's muse very pleasingly (her lively *La Fée aux chansons* and the touching *Le Secret* are highlights), Håkan Hagegård less so – his style is very forthright.

The Bruges performance uses the version from 1893 with chamber forces and is free from the glamour of star soloists or instrumentalists. It has the affecting simplicity you would expect to find in any university city performance. Hilde Coppé's *Pie Jesu* has great purity. Overall this is not accomplished enough to be a first recommendation, but the absence of star quality is not in itself a handicap. Decent recording.

On the latest DG coupling with Duruflé Myung-Whun Chung's speeds are often excessively slow, challenging even Bartoli's control in the *Pie Jesu.* The characterful singing of both soloists has to be balanced against dim and distant choral sound and an excessively wide dynamic range in the recording. Not recommended. First choice rests with John Rutter's inspired account of Fauré's original 1893 score with the Cambridge Singers (COLCD 109 – see our main volume).

FEINBERG, Samuil (1890–1962)

Piano Sonatas Nos. 1–6.
★★★ BIS CD 1413. Samaltanos (*Nos. 1, 4 & 5*) & Sirodeau (*Nos. 2, 3 & 6*).

Samuil Feinberg is known as one of the greatest Soviet pianists of his day. In their anthology of the Russian Piano School issued in the mid-1990s, BMG/Melodiya included Feinberg playing his transcriptions of Bach organ pieces and some Mozart sonatas. He was a noted Bach interpreter and in his notes Christophe Sirodeau, one of the two pianists on this CD, writes that in 1958–9 Feinberg was the second pianist to record Bach's complete '48', the first being Edwin Fischer. (In fact, Rosalyn Tureck recorded a set in the early 1950s, recently reissued on DG, but let that pass.) Feinberg also championed Prokofiev,

Debussy and Scriabin – his interpretation of the *Fourth Sonata* was much admired by Scriabin himself. As a composer, Feinberg wrote mainly for the piano and for the voice. During the first half of his creative life (1910–33) his output was virtuosic, rich in contrasts and (to quote Sirodeau) 'imbued with a symbolist fragility that owes something to Scriabin'. Later his style became increasingly diatonic in much the same way as had Miaskovsky and Prokofiev. Anyway, the six *Sonatas* recorded here (there are 12 in all, together with three piano concertos) come from the period 1914–23 and, with the exception of the *Third* (1916), are all in one movement and short. No. 3 takes 23 minutes but the remainder, except for No. 6, last less than ten minutes. They are all very well played and recorded.

FERNSTRÖM, John (1897–1961)

Wind Quintet, Op. 59.
*** Phono Suecia PSCD 708. Amadé Wind Quintet –
KALLSTENIUS: *Clarinet Quintet, Op. 17*; KOCH:
Piano Quintet. ***

Although John Fernström was a prolific composer, much of his energy and time was consumed by work with orchestras and choirs in southern Sweden. However, the *Wind Quintet* is well fashioned and civilized. The playing of the Amadé Quintet has plenty of finesse and elegance and scores over its Oslo rival on Naxos.

FERRANTI, Marco Aurelio Zani de (1801–78)

Exercice, Op. 50/14; Fantaisie variée sur le romance d'Otello (Assisa a piè), Op. 7; 4 Mélodies nocturnes originales, Op. 41a/1-4; Nocturne sur la dernière pensée de Weber, Op. 40; Ronde des fées, Op. 2.
*** Chan. 8512. Wynberg (guitar) – FERRER:
Collection. ***

Simon Wynberg's playing fully enters the innocently compelling sound-world of this Bolognese composer; it is wholly spontaneous and has the most subtle control of light and shade. Ferranti's invention is most appealing, and this makes ideal music for late-evening reverie; moreover the guitar is most realistically recorded.

FERRER, José (1835–1916)

Belle (Gavotte); La Danse de naïades; L'Etudiant de Salamanque (Tango); Vals.
*** Chan. 8512. Wynberg (guitar) – FERRANTI:
Collection. ***

José Ferrer is a less substantial figure than Ferranti, but these four vignettes are almost as winning as that

composer's music. The recording has striking realism and presence.

FESCA, Alexander (1820–49)

Septets Nos. 1 in C min., Op. 26; 2 in D min., Op. 28.
(M) *** CPO 999 617-2. Linos Ens.

Alexander Fesca's two *Septets* were written in the first half of the 1840s, each lasting around 35 minutes. While hardly profound masterpieces – though their minor key gives them a nice dash of gravitas – they are tunefully entertaining and fluent, with the composer obviously knowing how to please an audience. There are plenty of nice touches to keep the listener's ear tickled, and, as quoted in the excellent sleeve-notes (by a contemporary critic in Fesca's day), '[this music] belongs to a field of higher, nobler entertaining music'. The performances here are superb, fluent and stylish, with a recording to match. Recorded in 2001, it is now offered at mid-price.

FESCA, Friedrich Ernst (1789–1826)

Symphonies Nos. 2 in D, Op. 10; 3 in D, Op. 13; Overture: Cantemire.
*** CPO 999 869-2. N. German R. Philharmonie, Beermann.

Friedrich Ernst Fesca, like other composers of his generation, was overshadowed by Beethoven, and works like these disappeared from programmes after the 1840s. The two symphonies recorded here, the *Second* composed between 1809 and 1813 and the *Third* in 1816, hardly deserve to be as forgotten as they are – or, at least, were. These are very much works at the beginning of the romantic era: they are full of energy and spirit, with the influence of Beethoven most strongly felt. With outer movements of brawling vigour and driving Scherzos contrasting with slow movements that sustain their tension – these works should be explored by anyone interested in this ever-expanding era. The *Cantemire Overture* (one of two operas he composed) makes an enjoyable bonus. The performances and recording are excellent.

FIBICH, Zdeněk (1850–1900)

Symphonies Nos. 1 in F, Op. 17; 2 in E flat, Op. 38.
(BB) ** Naxos 8.553699. Razumovsky SO, Mogrelia.

The Naxos issue of the first two symphonies offers fresh, clean-cut performances with transparent textures, making an attractive bargain issue, though they pale beside Järvi's Chandos performances (Chan. 9682).

FILS, Anton (1733–60)

Symphonies in A; C; D; E flat; G min.
*** CPO 999 778-2. Orfeo Bar. O, Gaigg.

Here is another composer emerging from eighteenth-century obscurity (this time from Bavaria), and with the opening of the *Symphony in C*, with its dramatic *crescendi*, it comes as no surprise to find that he was very much part of the Mannheim music scene. Interestingly, unlike many composers from this period, Fils's music came into fashion just after his death. Perhaps its freshness, with pleasing folk-music elements, especially in some snappy rhythmic patterns, made it stand out. The minuets in general have a charmingly rustic dance quality, and the *Prestissimo* finale of the *A major Symphony* interrupts its headlong rush with a very characteristic sequence, complete with bass-drone. The finale of the *D major Symphony* displays the composer's ability to build up tension steadily, starting off with unison strings, and includes a particularly striking pedal point (on violas) lasting some 26 bars. The poignant oboe solo in the minuet of the *C major Symphony* is another highly attractive episode. Indeed all these symphonies are melodically appealing and lively, and the *G minor Symphony* is particularly exhilarating. The Orfeo Barockorchester plays excellently under Michi Gaigg: the string ensemble is elegantly pointed, and the often piquant woodwind writing is delightfully brought out. The recording is both warm and vivid.

FINZI, Gerald (1901–56)

(i; ii) *Clarinet Concerto;* (iii) *Eclogue;* (iv) *Forlana* (arr. Ashmore); (v) *Magnificat;* (ii) *New Year Music: Nocturne. Romance* (for strings); (vi) *Earth and Air and Rain;* (vii) *In terra pax;* (viii) *Let us garlands bring;* (ix) *Dies Natalis;* (x) *Amen* (from *The Full, Final Sacrifice*).
🎵 (B) *** Decca 476 2163 (2). (i) A. Marriner; (ii) ASMF, N. Marriner; (iii) Lane, ECO, Daniel; (iv) Johnson, RPO, Reynolds; (v) City of L. Sinf., Hickox; (vi) Luxon, Willison; (vii) Crabtree, Sweeney, Waynflete Singers, Winchester Cathedral Ch., Bournemouth SO, Hill; (viii) Terfel, Martineau; (ix) Langridge, LSO, Hickox; (x) New College, Oxford, Ch., Higginbottom.

The account of the *Clarinet Concerto* (originally Philips) is a particularly sensitive one: Marriner *père* is an admirable partner and secures some ravishingly gentle playing from the ASMF in the *Adagio*, and the finale lilts engagingly. The lyrical *Nocturne* flows in the finest pastoral tradition, and Marriner's account of the eloquent if brief *Romance for Strings* is second to none (all deriving from the same Philips CD). Piers Lane's excellent version of the *Eclogue*, in fine Decca sound, will give much pleasure, as will Richard

Hickox's performance of *Dies Natalis*, which brings a notably sensitive and passionate soloist in Philip Langridge. The Christmas work, *In terra pax*, opens atmospherically with the baritone's musing evocation of the pastoral nativity scene, admirably sung by Donald Sweeney. Then comes a burst of choral splendour at the appearance of the Angel of the Lord, and after her gentle declaration of the birth of Christ comes an even more splendid depiction of the 'multitude of the heavenly host', magnificently sung and recorded, and the music returns to the thoughful and recessed mood of the opening. The boldly set *Magnificat* of 1951 was an American commission and it receives a strongly convincing performance. It is a pity that there was room only for the brief *Amen* from *Lo, the Full, Final Sacrifice*, but on these generously filled CDs there wasn't room for anything else. In *Earth and Air and Rain*, Finzi's distinctive setting of Hardy, there is sometimes a flavour of Vaughan Williams, and in *When I set out for Lyonnesse* a distinct reminder of Stanford's *Songs of the Sea* emerges. But in the touching *Waiting both* and the dramatic *Clock of the years* Benjamin Luxon demonstrates the versatility of Finzi's word-settings. Excellent accompaniments from David Willison – his gentle postlude for the finale song, *Proud songsters*, ends the cycle movingly. The five Shakespearean settings, *Let us garlands bring*, are just as memorable in their contrasted ways, and they are beautifully sung by Bryn Terfel. All in all, this is a thoroughly worthwhile compilation, and the recordings are excellent throughout.

FIORILLO, Federigo (1755– after 1823)

Violin Concerto No. 1 in F.
(B) *** Hyp. Helios CDH 55062. Oprean, European Community CO, Faerber – VIOTTI: *Violin Concerto No. 13*. ***

Fiorillo's *Concerto* is charmingly romantic. Adelina Oprean's playing can only be described as quicksilver: her lightness of bow and firm, clean focus of timbre are most appealing. She is given a warm, polished accompaniment, and the recording is eminently truthful and well balanced.

FISCHER, Johann Caspar Ferdinand (c. 1670–1746)

Musical Parnassus, Volume 1: Suites Nos. 1-6 (Clio; Calliope; Melpomène; Thalia; Erato; Euterpe).
(BB) *** Naxos 8.554218. Beauséjour (harpsichord).

J. C. F. Fischer is remembered for his *Ariadne musica* (1715), a series of 20 preludes and fugues, each in a different key, thus anticipating Bach's *Wohltemperierte Klavier*. His role in music history was to fuse the style of the Lullian suite with the classical core of dance suite movements favoured by Froberger. He published his *Musicalischer Parnassus* in 1738, which comprises nine suites named after the Muses. The first six are included on this disc and are often fresh and inventive, rarely routine. The Canadian Luc Beauséjour plays them with some flair and is very vividly recorded.

FORQUERAY, Antoine (1671–1745)

(i) *Pièces de Viole*; (ii) *Pièces de clavecin.*

(M) *** DHM/BMG 82876 60165-2. (i) Bernfield; (ii) Sempé.

Antoine Forqueray was a younger contemporary of Marin Marais and enjoyed a reputation as one of the greatest gamba players of his day, though he responded more favourably to the Italian music of his time (Corelli and Vivaldi) than did Marais. This record constrasts some of his character pieces with the harpsichord transcriptions made by his son, Jean-Baptiste (1699–1782), and published in 1747, two years after his death. The latter was also a formidable player; indeed it has been suggested that the father's denunciation of him to the Paris Police for 'gambling, womanising and theft', when he was beginning to establish himself in the 1720s, was in part motivated by jealousy of his enormous talent! The transcriptions are, as such things should be, re-creations and remarkably free rhythmically. Nor is there a hint of rigidity in Skip Sempé's performances; they have all the expressive freedom and poetic feeling that the music calls for. The music has an intimacy and character that is beguiling, and Jay Bernfeld's playing has a comparable instinctive artistry. Both players are well served by the engineers who do not attempt to make either instrument larger than life. This is one of the most rewarding reissues in the current Deutsche Harmonia Mundi mid-priced series.

FOSS, Lucas (born 1922)

3 American Pieces.

(M) *** EMI 5 62600-2. Perlman, Boston SO, Ozawa – BARBER: *Violin Concerto*; BERNSTEIN: *Serenade after Plato's 'Symposium'.* ***

Foss's Coplandesque pieces are a bonus for the two key works of Barber and Bernstein, and it is good that this uniquely valuable triptych is now offered at mid-price.

FRANÇAIX, Jean (1912–97)

(i) *Piano Concertino. Les Bosquets de Cythère; Les Malheures de Sophie.*

*** Hyp. CDA 67384. (i) Cassard; Ulster O, Fischer.

We still have a very special affection for the Mercury performance of the *Piano Concertino* by the composer's daughter, Claude Françaix, and we hope Universal will find a way to reissue this in the UK. Meanwhile, this new account by Philippe Cassard on Hyperion is to be warmly welcomed. The first movement *Presto* is exhilaratingly brisk, yet Cassard's articulation is immaculate, and the other three movements are full of the delicacy and charm for which the work is celebrated, especially the whimsical finale.

Les Bosquets de Cythère might have been a ballet but is in essence a suite of waltzes. The island of Cythère was traditionally the birthplace of Aphrodite and it is celebrated as the home of intoxicating sensual pleaure. This is hinted at daintily in several of the gentler movements, such as the sadly fragile portrait of *Aminte délaissée, Le Consolateur facétieux*, and *Subtile tendresse*, with its echoes of Ravel. Yet the rumbustious *Introduction à la vie joyeuse* has something of the spirited *galanterie* of Milhaud.

Les Malheurs de Sophie depicts the misadventures of the ill-behaved three-year-old heroine and her cousin, Paul, who is two years older. Although the ballet opens boisterously, there are many exquisite touches to show the composer's affection for his heroine, including the idyllic *Andante tranquillo* that opens the Second Tableau and the charming *Allegretto* that opens the Third, while the *Pas de deux of Sophie and Paul* is ingenuously lighthearted. Like the other works here, the score is played with great affection and elegant attention to detail by the Ulster Orchestra under Thierry Fischer, and the Hyperion recording is in the demonstration class.

CHAMBER MUSIC

8 Bagatelles for Piano Quintet; Dixtuor for Wind Quintet and String Quintet; Divertissement for Piano Trio; Nonette after the Quintet, K.452, of Mozart; String Quartet; (i) Theme and Variations for Clarinet and Piano; (ii) Violin Sonatine.

*** Disques Concord Erol ER 96004 (2) L'Octuor de France (members), composer (piano); with (i) Sajot; (ii) Naganuma.

The Octuor de France under the direction of the composer, who also participates vividly on the piano, provide here an admirably represenative collection of Françaix's chamber music written over five decades. The *String Quartet* (1934), like the well-known *Piano Concertino*, is small-scale but delightfully so, apparently slight, and certainly amiable, but with a touching *Andante* and a sparkling pizzicato Scherzo, full of syncopations, followed by a simpler *moto perputuo* finale with a tranquil coda, with something of the luminosity of Ravel.

The early *Divertissement* was written like a concerto grosso a year later, but here, in the 1974 revision, a piano replaces the orchestral ripieno and the result is delightfully insouciant. The bustling finale is very French in its uninhibited animation, yet the

Andante again has a gentle inner feeling, which is to return touchingly in the last movement before the closing whirlwind.

The violin *Sonatine* (1934) has a will-o'-the-wisp precocity, yet once more there is an underlying lyrical tractability. A set of variations as its centrepiece produces a kaleidoscope of unpredictable moods and much dashing bravura from both participants. Similarly, the *Clarinet Variations* bring a series of brief, spirited vignettes, full of charm, with the witty *Tempo di Valzer* particularly catchy.

Turning now to the pair of late works, we find the subdivided first movement of the *Dixtnor* (1987) opening with a seductively lazy *Larghetto tranquillo*, then moving into a similarly easy-going allegro. The lightweight Scherzo chortles in 3/8 time and almost becomes a waltz, and the finale combines pastoral and folksy elements. The *Eight Bagatelles* of 1980 are in the composer's kaleidoscopic vignette style, and include two rather spare but expressive solo movements for viola and cello, before the penultimate poignant graduated crescendo in which all the partcipants gradually join, with the composer's skittish mood reappearing in the finale.

The *Nonette* is a fairly straightforward transcription of Mozart's *Piano and Wind Quintet*, K.452, for four wind instrunments and string quintet, including a double bass. Françaix takes some liberties and the atmosphere is more romantic than the original, but the Mozartian spirit remains predominant, and there is plenty of charm. All the performances here are of the highest order, and the recording too is first class. But this is a set to be dipped into rather than taken in a single draught.

FRANCK, César (1822–90)

Symphonic Variations for Piano & Orchestra.
★★★ Sup. SU 3714-2. Moravec, Prague Philh. O,
  Bělohlávek – BEETHOVEN: *Piano Concerto No. 4*
  ★★★ RAVEL: *Piano Concerto in G* **★★**(★).

As in his transparent account of the Beethoven *G major Concerto*, Moravec's ability to convey expressive warmth without exaggeration comes out in the Franck *Symphonic Variations*, with the improvisatory writing for the soloist sounding totally natural and spontaneous in free rubato. The faster variations bring bright, clear textures, not just in the piano part but also in the orchestral writing, with Bělohlávek drawing the most responsive playing from the orchestra he founded.

(i) *Symphonic Variations for Piano and Orchestra*;
(ii) *Symphony in D minor.*
(★(★)) Testament mono SBT 1237. (i) Ciccolini, Paris
  Conservatoire O; (ii) French Nat. R. O; Cluytens –
  D'INDY: *Symphonie sur un chant montagnard
  français.* (★★)
Both the *Symphony* and the *Variations symphoniques*

were recorded in the Théâtre des Champs-Elysées in 1953, although the former is much better balanced. Cluytens gives a dignified and finely shaped account of the piece, which is well worth hearing, even if the Orchestre National de la Radiofusion Française does not always produce a refined tone and the sound is a bit two-dimensional. The *Variations symphoniques* are well played by Aldo Ciccolini, but unfortunately the sound is dryish and the piano is too forwardly balanced to do full justice to the soloist's tone.

Symphony in D min.
(M) (**★★★**) Teldec mono 8573 83025-2. Concg. O,
  Mengelberg – DVORAK: *Symphony No. 9 (From
  the New World).* (**★★★**)

When Mengelberg took up his appointment at the Amsterdam Concertgebouw in 1895, both the Franck *Symphony* and the *New World* were new music, and although the Franck had been composed in 1888 it was not published until the mid-1890s, when it soon appeared at a Concertgebouw concert. Mengelberg conducted it with an enormous lyrical ardour and gets such responsive playing from his wartime orchestra that criticism is almost silenced. His Franck last appeared in the 1980s (Philips 416 214-2), although this was a broadcast from October 1940, a month before the present commercial recording was made. Bryan Crimp's transfer reveals a sound that is extraordinarily vivid and rich for its period. Of course, the same agogic mannerisms that are so characteristic of this conductor are in evidence, but we have to say that such is the dramatic fire and fervour of this playing that most listeners will surely be willing to take them in their stride.

*Symphony in D min.; Psyché : Four Orchestral
Extracts.*
B→ **★★★** Avie AV 003. Strasbourg PO, Latham-König.

Jan Latham-König's account of the Franck *Symphony* is the finest to have appeared for some years. It is superbly played by the Strasbourg orchestra, but the interpretation is by by means conventional. Latham-König daringly uses constantly varying tempi and the widest dyamic range. His reading is wayward but full of warmth, and he keeps a splendid grip on the structure; the passionate outburst of excitement as the secondary theme swings into the listener's presence is visceral. The *Allegretto* makes a gentle, serene interlude; but the forward sweep of the finale is again interrupted as earlier themes are recalled, and the very close proves a most satisfying culmination. He then offers Franck's second orchestral version of *Psyché* (omitting the chorus), which is essentially a tone-poem in four sections. The radiant opening (*Le Sommeil de Psyché*), rapturously phrased on the clarinet, is followed by the most lustrous string-playing, which languorously captures the music's sensuous evocation. After the 'awakening breezes' of what acts as a Scherzo, the thrilling climax of the third section, *Le Jardin d'Eros*, is later to be ardently capped by the strings in a mood of 'ravishing luxuriance and ecstatic fulfilment', to quote Julian Haylock's sleeve-note. The recording is spaciously spectacular – very much in the demonstration bracket.

CHAMBER MUSIC

Cello Sonata in A min.; (i) Panis Angelicus; Le Sylphe.
(**) Hyp. CDA 67376. Isserlis, Hough, (i) with Evans –
RACHMANINOV: *Cello Sonata*, etc. (**)

As in the great Rachmaninov *Sonata*, with which it is coupled, this Hyperion cello version of the Franck *Violin Sonata* suffers from the dimness of the record-ing, which seriously undermines here the expressive-ness and bite of Steven Isserlis and Stephen Hough that normally mark their work. The two songs, beau-tifully sung by Rebecca Evans, are a small compensa-tion.

Violin Sonata in A min.
**(*) EMI 5 57505-2. Capucon, Gurning –
RACHMANINOV: *Cello Sonata*. **(*)

Renaud Capucon and Alexandre Gurning give a big-scale, warmly expressive reading of the Franck *Violin Sonata*. If not perhaps a first choice, it is magnetically made the more dramatic by being recorded live. Well coupled with the Rachmaninov *Cello Sonata*, played by Capucon's brother, Gautier.

FRASER-SIMPSON, Harold
(1872–1944)

The Maid of the Mountains (with James W. Tate).
*** Hyp. CDA 67190. Kelly, Maltman, George, Suart, Burgess, Maxwell, Gamble, New L. Light Op. Ch. & O, Corp.

The history of successful musicals is always fascinat-ing and *The Maid of the Mountains* is no exception. Although it has a famous score accredited to Fraser-Simpson, including such a key number as the splen-did 'Love Will Find a Way', when it was on its out-of-town try-out at the Prince's Theatre, Man-chester, in 1916, its female lead, José Collins, decided that the score did not have enough popular hits. So her stepfather, James W. Tate, came to the rescue and wrote three of the show's most catchy numbers, 'A Paradise for Two', 'A Bachelor Gay' and the duet, 'When You're in Love'. The result was a resounding success, and the show played for 1,352 performances, its run ending only when its leading lady decided that enough was enough! It is a winningly light-hearted, cosy score and still holds up well in the amateur theatre. But it is good to have such a lively professional account as this, from principals and excellent chorus alike, conducted by Ronald Corp, with a consistently vivacious spirit and clear words. The one slight snag is that the heroine, Teresa, sung

by Janis Kelly, has a rather close, soubrettish vibrato. However, Richard Suart shines in the relatively small part of Tonio, with his Gilbertian solo, 'I Under-stood', and the charming duet with Vittoria (Sally Burgess), 'Over Here and Over There', which also has a G&S flavour. Excellent recording and a full libretto.

FRØHLICH, Johannes (1806–60)

Symphony in E flat, Op. 33.
*** Chan. 9609. Danish Nat. RSO, Hogwood – GADE: *Symphony No. 4.* ***

This delightful disc resurrects a long-buried work, which proves far more than just a curiosity. Johannes Frederik Frohlich was one of the fathers of Danish music. He wrote his *Symphony* in 1833, but it was so poorly played it sank without trace and was never given again. Yet this is a totally refreshing, beautifully written work, not unlike the symphonies of another Scandinavian, Berwald; it also owes much to Weber. The writing is inventive and full of character, and the Danish Radio Orchestra under Christopher Hog-wood play it with both spirit and conviction. It is well coupled here in splendid performances with the best-known symphony by another Dane, Niels Gade, devoted follower of Mendelssohn. Good recording too, if not Chandos's very finest.

FROST, Stephen (born 1959)

(i; ii) Bassoon Concerto; (iii) Oboe Concerto; (ii; iv) The Lesson.
**(*) Chan. 9763. (i) Birkeland; (ii) Bournemouth SO; (iii) Elmes, Ens. 2000; (iv) Bergset; cond. Harrison.

The work for oboe is undoubtedly the finer of these two concertos, succinctly inventive. The *Bassoon Concerto* is perhaps somewhat over-extended as its genial opening toccata gives way to a long central soliloquy, decorated with percussion but also featur-ing a solo piano, which is to provide a link into the energetic finale. Both soloists are excellent players, and the performances overall are of high quality. *The Lesson* is a floating vocal melisma using the poem by W. H. Auden. The speaker is placed within the orchestra and no attempt is made to focus the words sharply (and no text is included) so one assumes they are merely a starting point for a piece that is above all evocative. Excellent recording.

FRY, William Henry (1813–64)

The Breaking Heart; Niagara Symphony; Overture to Macbeth; Santa Claus (Christmas Symphony).
(BB) **(*) Naxos 8.559057. RSNO, Rowe.

William Henry Fry has a distinct place in the history of American music, for as an academic, critic and composer he was the first native-born American to write for a large symphony orchestra and also the first to write a grand opera. His music is innocently tuneful, though its roots are firmly in the European, rather than in native American soil. The longest work here is the *Santa Claus, Christmas Symphony*, written in 1853 and lasting just under 27 minutes. It is an ingenuous, episodic work, originally performed with a detailed programme of the Christmas story. The writing has a certain period charm and, if it doesn't always hold the listener's full attention, there are some attractive episodes. The finale features a sleigh-ride, followed by shimmering strings ushering in *O Come All Ye Faithful*, which is thundered out at the end.

The *Niagara Symphony* brings some quite startling passages depicting the famous Falls, with strings scurrying about in watery cascades, and with no fewer than eleven timpani to ram the effect home. This is real tempest music – and with a reflective chorale in the middle for contrast. *The Breaking Heart* is a rather sentimental 10-minute piece, which includes a lilting waltz theme, while the melodramatic *Overture to Macbeth* seems to have borrowed some of *Niagara*'s swirling strings at one point. The performances are enthusiastic, though there are signs that more rehearsal time would have been desirable. The recording is satisfactory, but this is hardly an indispensable issue.

FUX, Johann Joseph (1650–1741)

Il Concentus musico instrumentalis: Overtures (Suites) Nos. 2 in B flat; 4 in G min. Overtures (Suites) in B flat; D min.
(M) *** Van. 99705. Il Fondamento, Dombrecht.

Il Concentus musico instrumentalis, 1701: Serenada à 8 for 2 clarinos, 2 oboes, bassoon, 2 violins, viola and continuo; Rondeau à 7 for violino piccolo, bassoon, violin, 3 violas and continuo; Sonata à 4 for violin, cornet trombone, dulcian and organ.
(BB) *** Warner Apex 2564 60449-2. VCM, Harnoncourt.

Fux wrote a great many overtures or suites that combine the French and Italian styles, of which the present four are lively and quite colourful examples. They have a good deal in common with similar works of Telemann, even if not nearly so skilfully scored. Il Fondamento, a period-instrument group under Paul Dombrecht, bring these works to life quite vividly. They are agreeably recorded, though the sound could ideally be more transparent. But the thickness of texture is partly caused by the doubling up in the scoring, with the wind playing in tutti with the strings.

Harnoncourt's selection was originally issued on Telefunken's Das Alte Werk series in 1970. Fux's *Serenada à 8* takes its time – it has sixteen movements – but is amazingly inventive. It was written for the Habsburg emperor's son in 1701 as an outdoor enter-

tainment. There is some highly original writing for the high trumpets, and a most beautiful Minuet. The *Sonata* is texturally even more aurally intriguing. Indeed, by the time one has heard this CD through, one is tempted to dismiss the common view of Fux as a dull academic. There is nothing academinc about the music, and for that matter nothing dull about the performancs. Excellent recording.

GABRIELI, Giovanni (1557–1612)

Music for Brass, Vol. 2: Canzon La Spirita à 4; Canzon à 12; Canzon II; Canzon III; Canzon V; Canzon VI; Canzon XII; Canzon XVI à 12; Canzon primi toni à 8; Canzon Seconda à 4; Canzon Terza à 4; Sonata XVIII; Sonata XIX; Sonata Octavi Toni à 12.
(BB) *** Naxos 8.553873. LSO Brass, Crees.

Music for Brass, Vol. 3: Canzon IV; Canzon X; Canzon XV; Canzon Primi Toni à 10: Canzon in Echo Duodecimi Toni à 10; Canzon Duodecimi Toni à 10 No. 2; Canzon Prima; Canzon Quarta à 4; Canzon Quarti Toni à 15; Canzon Septimi Toni à 8 No. 1; Sonata XX; Sonata XXI (with organ).
(BB) *** Naxos 8.554129. LSO Brass, Crees.

The London Symphony Orchestra Brass under Eric Crees continue their excellent Naxos series. The *Canzon in Echo Duodecimi Toni à 10* in Volume 3 is obviously the most spectacular piece, but the paired *Sonatas XX* and *XXI* (with organ) thrillingly combine rich sonorities with complex decoration, and in Volume 2 there are several very striking pieces, notably *La Spiritata* and *Canzon XVI à 12*, which closes the disc.

GADE, Niels (1817–90)

Symphony No. 4 in B flat, Op. 20.
*** Chan. 9609. Danish Nat. RSO, Hogwood –
FROLICH: *Symphony*. ***

In this best known of his eight symphonies, as in most of his works, Gade charmingly echoes Mendelssohn. Very well played and recorded, it makes an excellent coupling for the delightful, long-buried Frohlich symphony. The performance does not supplant Neeme Järvi, coupled with the *Third*, which has more transparent, better-balanced recorded sound. All the same, a very recommendable disc, for the coupling is delightful.

GALBRAITH, Nancy (born 1951)

Piano Concerto No. 1.
*** Ocean OR101. Zitterbart, Cincinnati CO, Lockhart
– ALONSO-CRESPO: *Overtures & Dances from Operas*. ***

The first movement of Nancy Galbraith's attractively colourful concerto uses what she calls 'sensuous rhythmic pulses' in the orchestra, minimalist style, from which the piano regularly surfaces in a concertante manner. In the atmospherically lyrical slow movement the piano achieves an essentially reflective solo role, before the orchestra reasserts its dominance in a driving, energetic, toccata-like finale which has quite haunting lyrical interludes. This is writing that communicates directly to the listener. The performance here is persuasively full of life and colour, and the recording is excellent.

GANNE, Louis (1862–1923)

Les Saltimbanques (operetta; complete).

(BB) **(*) EMI (ADD) 5 74079-2 (2). Mesplé, Lublin, Amade, Calàs, Tirmont, Benoit, René Duclos Ch., LOP, Marty.

Louis Ganne is hardly a well-known figure now, but in his day he had quite a successful career in Paris, both as a conductor and as a composer of music theatre, operetta, salon pieces and songs. His best music is light and catchy, though it is mainly *Les Saltimbanques* ('The Travelling Entertainers') that now keeps his name alive and that also shows his particular facility for dance and march rhythms. Written in collaboration with Maurice Ordonneau in 1899, *Les Saltimbanques* quickly became a popular favourite throughout France. The story centres on Suzanne, a foundling taken in by a travelling circus, who, by the end of the work in true operetta fashion, discovers her noble origins and is free to marry the man she loves. The novel circus backdrop and romantic intrigue were constructed with elements of both *opéra comique* and operetta, and the result is a score of much charm. This 1968 performance is probably the only one we'll get, so it's just as well it's a good one. Mady Mesplé has exactly the right, perky timbre for the part of the heroine, Suzanne, very French-sounding and characterful, while Claude Calàs as her tenor lover, André de Langeac, is light-voiced, but sensitive and convincing. The rest of the cast does not disappoint, especially the lively chorus. Jean-Pierre Marty conducts with enthusiasm, well contrasting the racy numbers with the gently lilting rhythms, and his Lamoureux orchestra, with its French-sounding brass, is good too. The recording is reasonably vivid and full for its period, although a little strident at times. The only real reservation about this bargain set is that it comes with no texts or translations.

GARDINER, Henry Balfour (1877–1950)

Humoresque; The Joyful Homecoming; Michaelchurch; Noel; 5 Pieces; Prelude; Salamanca; Shenandoah & Other Pieces (suite).

*** Continuum (ADD) CCD 1049. Jacobs.

Balfour Gardiner was at his finest in miniatures, and his writing has an attractive simplicity and innocence. Most of this music is slight, but its appeal is undeniable when it is presented with such authority and sympathy. It is very well recorded indeed.

GARDNER, John (born 1917)

(i) *Flute Concerto, Op. 220. Half-Holiday Overture, Op. 52; Irish Suite, Op. 231; Prelude for Strings, Op. 148a; Sinfonia piccola for Strings, Op. 47; Symphony No. 3 in E min., Op. 189.*

(M) *** ASV CDWHL 2125. Royal Ballet O, Sutherland, (i) with Stinton.

John Gardner was born in Manchester. After service in the RAF he joined the staff at St Paul's Girls' School at Hammersmith (following in famous footsteps). His *First Symphony* was premièred at the Cheltenham Festival in 1951, and the opera *The Moon and Sixpence* at Sadler's Wells in 1957.

The catchy *Half-Holiday Overture* doesn't go on a moment too long. The *Flute Concerto*, written for Jennifer Stinton in 1995, has a relaxed, conversational opening movement, followed by a poignant *Nocturne*, and the rondo finale gives the flute plenty of opportunities for sparkling virtuosity.

The *Third Symphony* suggests influences from Shostakovich, which persist in the solemn, threnodic *Adagio*. The finale restores the mood of genial humanity. The elegiac *Prelude for Strings* derives from a string quartet.

Most successful of all is the *Sinfonia piccola*. The *Andante* proves to be a searching passacaglia, always a source of stimulation in the hands of a fine composer. The finale has a touch of Britten's *Simple Symphony* about it. The *Irish Suite* genially celebrated the composer's eightieth birthday. Fine performances and an excellent recording serve to recommend this collection well, and congratulations to ASV for issuing it at mid-price.

GATES, Philip (born 1963)

Airs & Graces; Clarinet Sonata; Flute Sonata; Danzas del Sud; Mood Music; Rio Bound.

**(*) Shellwood Productions SWCD 15. Way, Kelly, Clarke, Willox, composer.

Philip Gates obviously has a special feeling for the flute and is clearly influenced by twentieth-century French writing for this instrument, including the jazzy inflexions. The engagingly cool nostalgia of the central movement of his *Sonata* has a few unpredictable interruptions from the piano, for which Gates also writes very naturally. The finale's rhythmic influences are Latin-American. The six *Airs and Graces* are lightweight vignettes, the most striking being *At Loch Leven* (with its Scottish snap in the melody) and the neatly syncopated *Rag-a-muffin*. The *Clarinet Sonata* flows amiably, with a bluesy central *Cantabile*; but it is the snappy finale that stands out. *Rio Bound* makes a good final encore. The *Mood Music* pieces for alto-saxophone are less striking. The *March Hare* gambols robustly, but *Sax-Blue* and *Soft-Shoe* are too predictable. The performances are excellent and so is the recording.

GAUARNIERI, Camargo
(1907–93)

Symphonies Nos. 1; 4 (Brasília); Abertura Festiva.
*** BIS CD 1290. São Paulo SO, Neschling.

The Brazilian Camargo Gauarnieri was the oldest son of a poor family; his parents quickly recognized his musical gifts, moving to São Paulo so as to provide him with a good musical education. Later he was able to continue his studies both in France and in the United States. He was the most important Brazilian composer after Villa-Lobos, as well as being an influential musical educator. Young pianists have long been familiar with his *Piano Sonata*, a standby at auditions and competitions. The present disc includes the first recordings of his *First Symphony*, dedicated to Koussevitzky, and his *Fourth*, dedicated to Bernstein. Both were recorded in São Paulo by the excellent São Paulo Symphony Orchestra conducted by John Neschling. Engaging, inventive, well-wrought music, well worth investigating.

GAUBERT, Philippe (1879–1941)

Flute Sonatas Nos. 1–3; Madrigal; Orientale; 3 Aquarelles for Flute, Cello & Piano; Pièce romantique for Flute, Cello & Piano.
**(*) Deux-Elles DXL 923. Thomas, Shaw, Scott.

Philippe Gaubert was a virtuoso flautist and composed extensively for the instrument. This anthology shows his refinement of craftsmanship and freshness of inspiration. Not great music but full of Gallic charm, which is well conveyed in these accomplished performances by Kathryn Thomas and Richard Shaw, who are joined in the 3 *Aquarelles* and the *Pièce romantique* by the cellist Phoebe Scott. Decently recorded, even if the acoustic is over-reverberant.

Music for Flute and Piano: Sonatas Nos. 1–3; Sonatine. Ballade; Berceuse; 2 Esquisses; Fantaisie; Nocturne et allegro scherzando; Romance; Sicilienne; Suite; Sur l'eau.
*** Chan. 8981/2. Milan, Brown.

Gaubert had a genuine lyrical gift and his music has an elegance and allure that will captivate. He is eminently well served by Susan Milan and Ian Brown, and they are well balanced by the Chandos engineers. Truthful sound; civilized and refreshing music, not to be taken all at one draught but full of delight.

GAY, John (1685–1732)

The Beggar's Opera (complete; arr. Britten).
(M) *** Decca 473 088-2 (2). Murray, Langridge, Kenny, Rawnsley, Lloyd, Collins, Aldeburgh Festival Ch. & O, Bedford.

What Britten has done is to take the simple melodies assembled by Gay and treat them to elaborate, very Britten-ish accompaniments and developments that go even further in individuality than his folksong settings. It becomes very much a twentieth-century piece, starting with an overture that is pure Britten, with Gay tunes woven in. *Fill Every Glass* is then no longer a simple drinking-song but a slow contrapuntal movement, and *The Modes of the Court*, to the tune of 'Lilliburlero', becomes another elaborate mosaic. Conversely, some nostalgic arias, like *O What Pain it is to Part*, are done briskly, even abrasively.

Under Steuart Bedford this first recording is based on a staged presentation, given at The Maltings during the Aldeburgh Festival, with Declan Mulholland as an Irish beggar bluffly introducing the entertainment. Philip Langridge sings clearly and incisively as Macheath, portraying him very much as a gentleman, and Robert Lloyd is outstanding as Peachum, dark and resonant, a bluff Cockney. The team is a strong and characterful one, though neither Ann Murray as Polly Peachum nor Yvonne Kenny as Lucy Lockit is caught very sweetly. Britten's distinctive orchestration, one instrument per part, is well played by a distinguished group, including Jennifer Stinton on the flute, Nicholas Daniel on the oboe and Richard Watkins on the horn. Excellent sound, good direction of the well-edited spoken dialogue by Michael Geliot. Now offered at mid-price, it is far more than a curiosity.

GERMAN, Edward (1862–1936)

Berceuse; The Conqueror; Gipsy Suite; Henry VIII: 3 Dances. Merrie England: Suite. Nell Gwyn: Suite. Romeo and Juliet: Suite. Tom Jones: Waltz.
*** Marco Polo 8.223419. Czecho-Slovak RSO (Bratislava), Leaper.

Richard III Overture; The Seasons; Theme & 6 Diversions.
** Marco Polo 8.223695. RTE Concert O, Penny.

Symphony No. 2 in A min. (Norwich); Valse gracieuse; Welsh Rhapsody.
*(*) Marco Polo 8.223726. Nat. SO of Ireland, Penny.

Of the three Edward German CDs listed above, the first is definitely the one to go for. These suites essentially consist of a string of piquant, rustic-type dances of considerable charm. Most of the composer's most famous numbers are here: the items from *Merrie England* and *Henry VIII*, the pseudo-exotic *Gipsy Suite*, the memorable *Waltz* from *Tom*

Jones, plus a few rarities. All of it is effectively presented by the ever-reliable Adrian Leaper, and his Bratislava orchestra play as though they were from the home counties. Definitely an enticing collection in Marco Polo's valuable British Light Music series, most of which shows this composer at his best.

German's 'symphonic suite', *The Seasons*, is appealingly tuneful, colourfully orchestrated and enjoyable. The darker colours in *Autumn* provide a certain gravitas, while *Winter* has plenty of scurrying strings and woodwind to paint the scene. If the *Richard III Overture* is no towering masterpiece, it is not dull either, and it has enough ideas and a certain Romantic sweep to keep it going. A robust theme in D minor on the brass opens the *Theme and Six Diversions*, and the ensuing variations are enjoyable and nicely varied. The caveat is that, although the music is well conducted and played with enthusiasm, the orchestra is a bit scrawny in the string department. Nor is the recording first class – it lacks richness and bloom. But the music's character does come through.

The *Second Symphony* was commissioned by the Norwich Festival (hence its title, 'Norwich') in 1893. It has a certain charm – the spirits of Mendelssohn and Dvořák vaguely hover around in the background – but in the last resort the writing fails to be memorable. The charming *Valse gracieuse* and the deservedly well-known *Welsh Rhapsody* show the composer on better form. The performances are committed, but the sound is only average.

PIANO MUSIC

Concert Study in A flat; Elegy in C min.; First Impromptu in E min.; Graceful Dance in F; Humoresque in E; Intermezzo in A min.; Mazurka in E; Melody in D flat; Melody in E flat; Polish Dance in E; Rêverie in A min.; Tarantella in A min.; Valse-caprice in A; Valse fantastique; Valsette in E min.
** Marco Polo 8.223370. Cuckston.

These piano miniatures show Edward German at his best. This is unpretentious music of much charm and piquancy. The minor-key works are nostalgically disarming: sometimes quite serious, such as the seven-minute *Elegy in C*; sometimes carefree, like the *Tarantella*; but nothing outstays its welcome. Alan Cuckston's performances are good, but not outstanding, and the piano tone is a little harsh, perhaps because of the dry acoustic. Enjoyable and recommendable, nevertheless.

Merrie England (complete; without dialogue).
(B) * (**) CfP Double 575 767-2 (2). McAlpine, Bronhill, Glossop, Glynne, Sinclair, Kern, Rita Williams Singers, O, Collins.

Although this recording dates from 1960, it cannot compare in stereo sophistication with EMI's *Beggar's Opera* of five years earlier. All the solo voices are close-miked, usually in an unflattering way, and too often they sound edgy, while the chorus is made artificially bright; the orchestra is lively enough, but the violins are thin. However, it must be said that Michael Collins directs the proceedings in an attractively spirited fashion. Among the soloists, Howell Glynne is splendid as King Neptune, and Monica Sinclair sings with her usual richness and makes *O peaceful England* more moving than usual. Patricia Kern's mezzo is firm and forward, while William McAlpine as Sir Walter Raleigh sings with fine, ringing voice. The Rita Williams Singers are thoroughly professional even if just occasionally their style is suspect. However, another recording seems unlikely so this is acceptable, *faute de mieux*.

GERSHWIN, George (1898–1937)

An American in Paris.
(M) ** DG (ADD) 463 665-2. San Francisco SO, Ozawa – RUSSO: *3 Pieces for Blues Band and Symphony Orchestra*, etc. **

There is a softness of focus in Ozawa's 1976 account of the Gershwin work that takes away the necessary bite, and although the recording sounds fine in its new 'Originals' transfer, this is far from a top choice. The rarer couplings are the main interest of this release.

Rhapsody in Blue.
(M) **(*) Decca 430 726-2. K. and M. Labèque, Cleveland O, Chailly – ADDINSELL: *Warsaw Concerto*; GOTTSCHALK: *Grand Fantasia*; LISZT: *Hungarian Fantasia*; LITOLFF: *Scherzo*. (***)

Although the Labèque duo play charismatically, their account is made somewhat controversial by the addition of an improvisatory element (more decorative than structural). However, the playing does not lack sparkle and the recording is first class.

(i) *Rhapsody in Blue* (orchestral version); (ii) *Rhapsody in Blue* (piano solo version); *Preludes for Piano. Songs: Do it again; I'll build a stairway to paradise; I got rhythm; Liza; The man I love; Nobody but you; Oh, lady be good; Somebody loves me; Swanee; Sweet and low down; 'Swonderful; That certain feeling; Who cares?*
(B) ** Sony (ADD) SBK 89369. (i) Entremont; Philadelphia O, Ormandy; (ii) Watts.

Philippe Entremont's account of the *Rhapsody in Blue* with Ormandy is bright and attractive, marred only by the recording, which sounds over-bright and brittle in the upper register. Only the keenest Gershwin collector is likely to want the solo piano version, even though André Watts's performance is thoughtful as well as brilliant. However, the songs are ever attractive, even without the vocals, and these assured if sometimes wilful performances have plenty of life. The recording (no dates given) is a little hard, but acceptable. But one needs to turn to Bernstein (Sony SMK 63086) or Wayne Marshall (Virgin 5 62056-2) for the main Gershwin repertoire (see our main *Guide*).

Arrangements of Songs: *Embraceable you; Fascinatin' rhythm; A foggy day; Funny Face; He loves and she loves; I got rhythm; Liza; Love is here to stay; The man I love; Nice work if you can get it; Oh, Lady be good; Soon; Summertime; 'S wonderful; They all laughed; They can't take that away from me.*

(BB) *** EMI Encore (ADD) 5 85081-2. Y. Menuhin & Stéphane Grappelli.

This is an attractive bargin re-assembly of the Gershwin numbers taken from the vintage Menuhin–Grappelli series of studio collaborations, recorded during the 1970s and early 1980s, in which two distinguished musicians from different musical backgrounds struck sparks off each other to most entertaining effect. The songs are all famous and the treatments highly felicitous. The sound has excellent presence.

PIANO MUSIC

Piano Rolls

'*The Piano Rolls*' Vol. 2: FREY: *Havanola.* CONRAD/ROBINSON: *Singin' the blues.* GERSHWIN: *From now on.* AKST: *Jaz-o-mine.* SILVERS: *Just snap your fingers at care.* KERN: *Whip-poor-will.* GERSHWIN/DONALDSON: *Rialto ripples.* PINKARD: *Waitin' for me.* WENDLING/WILLS: *Buzzin' the bee.* C. SCHONBERG: *Darling.* BERLIN: *For your country and my country.* MORRIS: *Kangaroo hop.* MATTHEWS: *Pastime rag No. 3.* GARDNER: *Chinese blues.* SCHONBERGER: *Whispering.* GRANT: *Arrah go on I'm gonna go back to Oregon.*

** None. 7559 79370-2. Gershwin.

As can be seen, Volume 2 includes music by others, and few of these numbers even approach the quality of Gershwin's own output. But it is all played in good, lively style, although one senses that Gershwin was doing a professional job rather than acting as an enthusiastic advocate, and some pieces come off more appealingly than others. Frankly, much of this is cocktail bar music, although Chris Schonberg's *Darling* is a rather effective exception. Again the recording cannot be faulted.

Piano Duet

***An American in Paris* (original 2-piano version)**

(BB) ** EMI Encore 5 75224-2. K. & M. Labèque – GRAINGER: *Fantasy on Gershwin's 'Porgy and Bess'.* **

The Labèque sisters here present the first recording of the composer's two-piano score of his famous overture, in which several brief passages are included that were later cut in the orchestral score. There is plenty of freshness and bite in the performance, if not much warmth, and the recording is to mathc: bright to the point of aggressiveness. But the CD is now offered at budget price.

I Got Rhythm Variations; 2nd Rhapsody; 2 Waltzes.* Arrangements: *Blue Monday; Embraceable you; Our love is here to stay.

(BB) ** EMI Encore 5 74729-2. K. and M. Labèque.

The Labèque sisters have previously recorded piano-duet versions of the *Piano Concerto* plus the *Rhapsody in Blue*, and these will probably follow the present collection on EMI's Encore label. Here their usual exuberant brashness of style is matched by bright, almost metallic piano-timbre, and no one could complain of a lack of jazzy impetus – indeed the effect is often dazzling, although also a little wearing without the orchestral cushion in the two main works. The song arrangements (*Blue Monday* uses the same material that Gershwin features in *Lullaby for Strings*) have a less aggressive, more sophisticated charm that is highly communicative.

GESUALDO, Carlo (*c.* 1561–1613)

Leçons de tenèbres: Responsories for Maundy Thursday.

🔑 *** Signum SIGCD 048. King's Singers.

Gesulado's *Responses for Holy Week* of 1611, with their surprising chromatic dissonances, are among the most remarkable and original of all *Tenèbre* settings. We already have a fine performance of them from Alfred Deller's Consort on Harmonia Mundi (HMA 190220), but this new, ground-breaking account from the King's Singers is even more expressively powerful. Immediately, as *In Monte Oliveti* opens, the King's Singers demonstrate a very flexible approach to tempo and dynamic that is to characterize their whole performance. The impeccable intonation and tonal matching also give a special richness to the chordal writing; and its moments of dissonance and the drama of *Amicus meus osculi* ('the betrayal with a kiss') and *Judas mercantor pessimus* are very tangible. The performance closes simply with the chant, *Christus factus est*, and this is treated as a brief recessional. In short, this is a superbly sung performance, expressively poignant but dramatic too, which brings a new dimension to this remarkable music; and the recording is outstanding.

GETTY, Gordon (born 1933)

***The White Election* (song-cycle).**

*** Delos D/CD 3057. Erickson, Guzelimian.

The simple, even primitive, yet deeply allusive poetry of Emily Dickinson is sensitively matched in the music of Gordon Getty. Here he tackles a sequence of

32 songs, building them into an extended cycle in four linked parts 'to tell Emily's story in her own words'. If at times the tinkly tunes seem to be an inadequate response to profound emotions, the total honesty of the writing disarms criticism, particularly in a performance as dedicated and sensitive as this, with Kaaren Erickson a highly expressive artist with a naturally beautiful voice. The pianist too is very responsive.

GHEDINI, Giorgio Federico
(1892–1965)

Violin Concerto (Il belprato); Musica da concerto for Viola, Viola d'amore and Strings.

*(*) Essay CD 1075. Tenenbaum, Pro Musica Prague, Kapp – SIBELIUS: 6 Humoresques. *(*)

Giorgio Federico Ghedini belongs to the generation that came to the fore in Italy in the wake of Pizzetti and Malipiero. In the 1950s the *Concerto dell'Albatro* (1945), generally regarded as his finest work, was periodically broadcast, but he has since fallen out of the repertory. Yet he was a prolific composer: his output includes an opera on *Billy Budd* (1949), based on Melville with a libretto of Quasimodo – two years before Britten's opera of the same name. The *Concerto for Violin and Strings (Il belprato)* (1947) and the *Musica da concerto for Viola, Viola d'amore and Strings* (1953) are well worth getting to know, or would be if the performances had greater charm and were better recorded. The second movement of *Il belprato* is imaginative, even if it is reminiscent of the slow movement of the Prokofiev *G minor Violin Concerto*. Mela Tenenbaum is not particularly well served by the engineers and does not seem to possess a particularly beautiful tone; the recording is close, dry and two-dimensional. This disc is useful as a reminder that, apart from Ghedini, there is a lot of Italian repertoire waiting to be explored: Casella's *Violin Concerto*, Pizzetti's *Symphony in A* and the Petrassi *Piano Concerto*.

GIBBONS, Orlando (1583–1625)

Consorts for Viols: Fantasies a 3, Nos. 1–4; Fantasies a 6, Nos. 1–5; In Nomines a 5, Nos. 1–2. Keyboard Pieces arranged for Viols: Fantasia; Galliard; Go from my Window; Pavan; Pavan Lord Salisbury; Peascod Times. Vocal works arranged for Viols: Hosanna to the son of David; O Lord, in thy wrath. The Silver Swan.

⊙━ *** Avie AV 0032. Phantasm.

The *Fantasies* for viol consort by Orlando Gibbons are among the most sublime works in the string repertory, leading on to the *Fantasias* of Purcell, even breathing the same air as the late Beethoven *Quartets*. Sadly, on disc they have too often been treated to performances that slice your ears off in period abra-

siveness; happily, the group, Phantasm, is different, at once authoritative and beautifully matched. The complexity of the *Fantasies in six parts*, presented here as a cohesive group, is astonishing both in rhythm and in counterpoint, and the two six-part *In Nomines*, more austere, have a similar intensity. Four *Fantasies in three parts* demonstrate Gibbons's contrapuntal mastery just as clearly. Quoting the composer, Phantasm supplement this music written specifically for viols with transcriptions of such keyboard pieces as the superb *Lord Salisbury Pavan*, as well as three of Gibbons's greatest vocal pieces, the anthems *O Lord, in thy wrath* and *Hosanna to the Son of David*, as well as the lovely madrigal, *The Silver Swan*. Well-balanced sound, though with a limited dynamic range.

GILBERT, Henry (1868–1928)

Suite for Chamber Orchestra.

*** Albany TROY 033-2. V. American Music Ens., Earle – CHADWICK: Serenade for Strings. ***

Henry Gilbert belonged to a time when almost all musical influences came from Europe and the American public did not value the output of its indigenous composers. This *Suite*, which is harmonically innocuous but has an agreeable nostalgic languor, has something in common with Delius's *Florida Suite*, although Gilbert's invention is less indelible. An excellent performance here from members of the Vienna American Ensemble, who are completely at home in the music, as well they might be. The recording is excellent.

GILLES, Jean (1668–1705)

Messe des Mortes (Requiem Mass).

⊙━ (BB) *** Warner Apex 2564 61260-2. Azema, Nirouër, Hite, Mason, Aix-en-Provence Festival Ch., Sagittarius Vocal Ens., Provençaux Ens. de Tambours, Boston Camerata, Cohen.

Gilles's *Requiem*, which for many years was a favourite work in France, was rejected by the two families who originally commissioned it, so Gilles decreed that it should be used for his own funeral. So great was the regional pride in eighteenth-century Provence that the work was often heard alongside the *Requiem* of Campra, with alternating movements from each!

The music is preceded by an introductory drum processional, gradually approaching, here provided by the Provençal Ensemble of Tambours, and they end the work with an equally atmospheric recessional. (A solo tambour also heads the *Communion*.) This was obviously intended to simulate the local custom of giving the open coffin a *tour de ville* before burial. In the interests of complete authenticity, the present performance also interpolates the liturgical chants in their appropriate places in the Mass, solemnly and resonantly sung by members of the Sagittarius Ensemble.

Gilles carries over the introductory march rhythm into the extended *Introit* which, like the splendid *Sanctus* and touchingly beautiful *Agnus Dei*, gives the soloists much that is rewardingly florid and expressively beautiful to sing. The solo team here rises to the occasion, each individually first class and working eloquently together. The chorus writing too is imaginative and demanding, and the Provençal choir is excellent, crisply directed by Joël Cohen, while the period-instrument accompaniment could hardly be more stylishly involved in the proceedings. Most attractive of all is to have this authentic performance so well recorded in Aix-en-Provence Cathedral, where the composer began his musical career as a choirboy and subsequently learned his craft as a composer. Altogether, this Apex reissue cannot be recommended too highly.

GILSON, Paul (1865–1942)

De Zee (suite).
(B) *** Discover DICD 920126. Brussels BRT PO, Rickenbacher – DE BOECK: *Symphony in G.* ***

Like August de Boeck, also represented on this disc, Paul Gilson was a Belgian composer, born in 1865. His suite, *De Zee*, like de Boeck's *Symphony*, is full of Russian echoes. It is a series of four seascapes halfway between Wagner's *Flying Dutchman* and Debussy's *La Mer*, with Rimsky-Korsakov's *Scheherazade* mixed in. Well played and recorded and, at Discover International's bargain price, an ideal disc for experimenting with.

GINASTERA, Alberto (1916–83)

Estancia (ballet suite); *Panambi* (choreographic legend).
*** Everest (ADD) EVC 9007. LSO, Goossens –
   ANTILL: *Corroboree;* VILLA-LOBOS: *Little Train of the Caipira.* **(*)

Both these brightly hued scores bring a high standard of invention. *Panambi* is the earlier – written when the composer was only twenty. It opens with a haunting picture of *Moonlight on the Panama*, and the *Lament of the Maidens* is gently touching, while the *Invocations of the Powerful Spirits* and *Dance of the Warriors* are powerfully primitive. *Estancia* dates from a slightly later period. Again the scoring is exotic and impressive, and the lively dances are full of primeval energy, notably the closing *Malambo*, while the lovely *Wheat Dance* brings another nostalgic interlude. The performances are in every way first class and the atmospheric recording brilliantly captures the composer's imaginatively varied soundworld.

GIORDANO, Umberto (1867–1948)

Andrea Chénier.
*** Warner NVC Arts **DVD** 5050466-8357-2-7. Tomowa-Sintow, Domingo, Zancanaro, ROHCG Ch. & O, Rudel (V/D: Humphrey Burton).

Dating from 1985, the DVD of Michael Hampe's production offers a traditional staging that vividly captures the atmosphere of Giordano's melodramatic presentation of Revolutionary France. Under the experienced conducting of Julius Rudel, the three principal characters are powerfully drawn, all three at the peak of their powers. Plácido Domingo cuts a flamboyant figure as Chénier, with the widest range of tone and expression in his key monologues. Though Anna Tomowa-Sintow's creamy soprano grows a little rough under pressure, she makes a tenderly sympathetic Maddalena; but it is Giorgio Zancanaro as Gérard who emerges as the most powerful figure, singing gloriously and bringing out the more human side of this revolutionary leader, convincingly making the transition from the defiant flunky he is in Act I. Other roles are well taken, too. No booklet is provided and no synopsis, with no indication on the box who is singing which roles.

Fedora (complete).
(M) ** Sony (ADD) SM2K 91138 (2). Marton, Carreras, Kincses, Hungarian R. & TV Ch. & O, Patanè.

On Sony, Eva Marton is aptly cast as Fedora, the Romanov princess, but in a work that should sound sumptuous it is not a help that the voices are placed forwardly, with the orchestra distanced well behind. The balance exaggerates the vibrato in Marton's voice, but it is a strong, sympathetic performance; Carreras, too, responds warmly to the lyricism of the role of the hero, Loris, giving a satisfyingly forthright account of the key aria, *Amor ti vieta*. The rest of the cast is unremarkable, and Patanè's direction lacks bite, again partly a question of orchestral balance. The other snag is inadequate documentation, offering neither libretto nor a cued synopsis. The Decca set with Olivero and Del Monaco is the one to turn to (433 033-2).

GLAZUNOV, Alexander (1865–1936)

Violin Concerto in A min., Op. 82.
(M) *** EMI 5 62593-2, Perlman, Israel PO, Mehta –
   SHOSTAKOVICH: *Violin Concerto No. 1 etc.* ***
(BB) (***) Naxos mono 8.110975. Milstein, RCA Victor SO, Golschmann – DVOŘÁK: *Violin Concerto;* MOZART: *Adagio in E etc.* (***)

The command and panache of Perlman are irresistible in this showpiece concerto, and the whole performance, recorded live, erupts into a glorious account of the galloping final section in playing to match that of the supreme master in this work, Heifetz. The acoustic of the Mann Auditorium in Tel Aviv is not an easy one for the engineers, and tuttis are rather rough, but this is more atmospheric than most from this source.

Milstein brings a special authority to the Glazunov *Violin Concerto*, as he played it under the composer's baton in 1915, many times during his youth, and at his American début concert in 1928 with the Philadelphia Orchestra under Stokowski. He recorded it, with Beecham conducting, in 1934 and again in 1951 with the RCA Victor Symphony Orchestra and Steinberg. No one plays it with greater virtuosity, aristocratic finesse or tonal beauty, and we would decline to choose one from among the five recordings he made. All of them show this enchanting work as the masterpiece it is and they both exhilarate and move the listener.

String Quartets: Nos. 3 in G (Slave), Op. 26; 5 in D min., Op. 70.

*** MDG 603 1236-2. Utrecht Qt.

We wrote with enthusiasm about the Utrecht Quartet's recording of the Gretchaninov *Quartets* (see our main *Guide*) and this newcomer, coupling the *Third* and *Fifth* Glazunov *Quartets*, deserves no less warm a welcome, particularly as this is announced as Volume 1. The *Third Quartet* occupied Glazunov from 1886–8 when he was still in his early twenties and shortly before he started work on his *Third Symphony*; and the *Fifth* followed a decade later, in 1898, between the *Sixth* and *Seventh Symphonies*. This is eminently civilized music and is both played and recorded well.

GLIÈRE, Reinhold (1875–1956)

The Bronze Horseman: Suite; (i) Horn Concerto, Op. 91.

** Chan. 9379. (i) Watkins; BBC PO, Downes.

The Bronze Horseman is not great music – nor, for that matter, is the *Horn Concerto*. Richard Watkins is a fine soloist in the latter; Downes gets good rather than really distinguished playing from the BBC Philharmonic, though the recording is excellent.

Octet, Op. 5; Sextet, Op. 11.

*** MDG 308 1196-2. Berlin Philharmonic String Octet.

Although he is best known for the huge *Il'ya Mouramets Symphony* and his ballet *The Red Poppy*, Glière's chamber-music output was also extensive. His music is firmly rooted in the great post-nationalist Russian style, and as a teacher he exerted a great influence on Miaskovsky, Khachaturian, Lev Knipper and the eleven-year-old Prokofiev. His *Octet* comes from 1900, when the composer was in his mid-twenties, and the *Sextet*, his third essay in the medium, was composed five years later. Both works

show a mastery not only of the genre (Glière was a fine violinist) but the impeccable craftsmanship that one would expect from a pupil of Taneyev, while the melodic ideas are both beautifully fashioned and finely paced. Everything unfolds as you feel it should, there is a keen sense of forward movement and nothing outstays its welcome. The spiritual world is that of Borodin and Glazunov, even if the thematic ideas do not have the former's distinction. The Berlin Philharmonc String Octet play with enthusiasm and persuasiveness, and the MDG sound is very lifelike. An appealing and welcome issue.

GLINKA, Mikhail (1804–57)

Polka No. 1 (orch. Balakirev); Spanish Overtures Nos. 1 (Jota aragonesa); 2 (Summer Night in Madrid); Waltz Fantasia; Ivan Susanin (A Life for the Tsar): Overture. Prince Kholmsky: Overture and Entr'actes to Acts II–IV; Ruslan and Ludmilla: Overture; Chernamor's March.

(BB) *** Regis (ADD/DDD) RRC 1142. USSR SO & Bolshoi Theatre O, Svetlanov.

These Russian recordings have been selected from a two-disc Melodiya set that last appeared on BMG/RCA. The performances embrace a considerable time-span (1963–84). The playing of the USSR Symphony Orchestra, which provides the majority of the items, is nothing if not expert and idiomatic, and the remastered recordings, though variable in quality, are generally very good indeed.

CHAMBER MUSIC

Grand Sextet in E flat.

(BB) *** Hyp. Helios CDH 55173. Capricorn – RIMSKY-KORSAKOV: *Quintet for Piano & Wind.* ***

The engaging Capricorn performance of Glinka's *Sextet* for piano, string quartet and double-bass is even more welcome on Hyperion's budget Helios label.

PIANO MUSIC

Volume 1: Variations on an Original Theme in F; Variations on the Romance 'Benedetta sia la madre'; Variations on Two Themes from the Ballet, 'Chao-Kang'; Variations on 'The Nightingale' (by Alabyev); Variations on a Theme from 'Anna Bolena' (by Donizetti); Variations & Rondino brillante on a Theme from the Opera, 'I Capuleti e i Montecchi' (by Bellini); Variations on a Theme from 'Faniska' (by Cherubini); Variations on the Russian Folk song 'In the shallow valley'.

** BIS CD 980. Ryabchikov.

All these variations were written when the composer was in his twenties. Ryabchikov suggests, in his thorough and authoritative notes, that 'the music is full of tenderness and expression, elegant simplicity and nobility'. Although he plays with evident feeling, he is handicapped by a rather forward recording. When he is playing above *forte* there is a touch of glare. The recording was made in Moscow, not by the familiar BIS team, and produced by the pianist himself.

Volume 2: Andalusian Dance, Las Mollares; Bolero; Contredanse, La Couventine; Contredanse in G; Cotillon in B flat; A Farewell Waltz; French Quadrille; Galop; Grande valse in G; 6 Mazurkas; Polka; Polonaise in E; The Skylark (trans. Balakirev); *Tarantella; Valse-favorite; Valse mélodique; Variations on a Theme by Mozart; Variations on the Terzetto from the Opera 'A Life for the Tsar'* (trans. Alexandr Gourilyov).
** BIS CD 981. Ryabchikov.

Victor Ryabchikov's second survey of Glinka's piano music includes a supplement of three alternative versions of the *Variations on a Theme by Mozart*, plus Balakirev's transcription of *The Skylark*, made a few years after Glinka's death, and the *Variations on the Terzetto from the Opera 'A Life for the Tsar'* transcribed by Alexandr Gourilyov. No masterpieces are uncovered among these salon pieces, though there are some attractive numbers such as the *Bolero* and *A Farewell Waltz*. These are the kind of dances that you might have heard at any ball in Russia, and Ryabchikov plays them in the order you might have heard them in at such a function. Three-star playing and clear, rather forward recording made in the Melodiya Studios in Moscow, but distinctly one-star music.

OPERA

Ruslan and Ludmilla (complete).
⊛— *** Ph. **DVD** 075 096-9 (2). Ognovienko, Netrebko, Diadkova, Bezzubenkov, Gorchakova, Kirov Op. Ch. & O, Gergiev – (Producer Wilson; V/D: Hulscher) (Bonuses: **Gergiev:** 'Introducing Ruslan' and 'Catching up with Music' – biographical tour).
*** Ph. **DVD** 075 099-9 (6). As above – BORODIN: *Prince Igor;* MUSSORGSKY: *Boris Godunov).*

The CDs of the opera are reviewed in our main edition. The set also appeared in a Deluxe Limited Edition, which had the CDs as well as a video, all handsomely presented. The performance was recorded at the Mariinsky Theatre, St Petersburg, in February 1995, and its musical merits need little further elaboration. The Ludmilla, Anna Netrebko, makes a particularly strong impression with her purity of tone and expressive power. Nor are Vladimir Ognovienko as Ruslan and Galina Gorchakova as Gonislava less impressive, though it is in the vitality and distinction of Gergiev's conducting that the main strength lies. There is much refinement and

sensitivity from all concerned and a vivid sense of that fairy-tale quality that makes its charm pretty irresistible. It now appears on two sharply defined and colourful DVDs with Acts I–III on the first and Acts IV and V on the second disc. In addition there are two bonuses, the first an introduction to the opera of some 18 minutes and a 50-minute feature about Gergiev. The staging is colourful, if at times a bit static, and the whole production will give much pleasure. Good essays in English, French and German, from different authorities (and subtitles in Italian, Spanish and Mandarin). *Ruslan* is a great work, and this version will delight all who invest in it. The discs are also included in the excellent Philips set, 'The Glory of Russian Opera'.

GLUCK, Christophe (1714–87)

Iphigénie en Tauride (complete).
⊛— ✱ (M) *** Ph. 476 171-2 (2). Montague, Aler, Allen, Argenta, Massis, Monteverdi Ch., Lyons Op. O, Gardiner.
(M) *(*) Sony SM2K 90463 (2). Vaness, Surian, Allen, Winbergh, La Scala, Milan, Ch. & O, Muti.

Gardiner's electrifying reading of *Iphigénie en Tauride* is a revelation. Though his Lyons orchestra does not use period instruments, its clarity and resilience and, where necessary, grace and delicacy are admirable. Diana Montague in the name-part sings with admirable bite and freshness and Sir Thomas Allen is an outstanding Oresté, characterizing strongly but singing with classical precision. John Aler is a similarly strong and stylish singer, taking the tenor role of Pylade. The recording is bright and full. A well-chosen inclusion for Universal's 'Penguin ✱ Collection'.

Muti's set, recorded live at La Scala in 1992, is a big-scale version, a possible alternative for those who insist on modern rather than period instruments. Muti's taut direction is comparably dramatic, but with beefy orchestral sound and close-up recording it is an overweight performance that misses the essential elegance of Gluck in its lack of light and shade. Vaness's dramatic timbre is apt, but the microphone catches a flutter in the voice. Thomas Allen as Oreste is telling (as he is for Gardiner) but, thanks to the recording, his subtler shading is missing and Gösta Winbergh as Pylade sings with fine ringing tones yet lacks subtlety and variety. Moreover, the set's documentation, as in the rest of this Sony series, is hopelessly inadequate, providing neither libretto nor cued synopsis. Gardiner's set on Philips is the one to go for.

GODARD, Benjamin (1849–95)

Cello Sonata in D min., Op. 104; 2 Pieces for Cello & Piano, Op. 61.
*** Hyp. CDA 66888. Lidström, Forsberg –

BOELLMANN: *Cello Sonata in A min.*, etc. ★★★

An interesting and compellingly played disc of off-beat repertoire. Benjamin Godard was a pupil of Vieuxtemps. His *D minor Sonata* is very much in the Schumann–Brahms tradition and is beautifully crafted and powerfully shaped, as are the *Aubade and Scherzo*. Mats Lidström and Bengt Forsberg play with such passion and conviction that they almost persuade you that this piece is worthy to rank alongside the Brahms sonatas. The recording is just a trifle on the close side, but it produces eminently satisfactory results. Strongly recommended.

GOETZ, Hermann (1840–76)

Francesca da Rimini: Overture. Spring Overture, Op. 15; (i) *Nenie, Op. 10;* (i; ii) *Psalm 137, Op. 14.*
(B) ★★ CPO 999 316-2. (i) N. German R. Ch.; (ii) Stiller; N. German R. PO, Hanover, Albert.

Hermann Goetz was born in the same year as Tchaikovsky. The best piece here is *Nenie*, which has a strong sense of purpose and a genuine lyrical flow. The *Francesca da Rimini Overture* comes from an opera its composer left unfinished. The musical language is very much in the tradition of Mendelssohn and Spohr, but the invention is of some quality, even if a little bland. Good performances from all concerned and decently balanced, well-rounded sound.

GOLDSCHMIDT, Berthold (1903–96)

(i) *String Quartets Nos. 2-3;* (ii) *Letzte Kapitel;* (iii) *Belsatzar.*
★★★ Largo LC 5115. (i) Mandelring Qt; (ii) Marks; (ii; iii) Ars-Nova Ens., Berlin, Schwarz.

Berthold Goldschmidt was hounded from Nazi Germany in 1935 and settled in London. This disc collects his *Letzte Kapitel* for speaker and an instrumental ensemble, very much in the style of Kurt Weill, and the *Second Quartet*, which has something of the fluency of Hindemith. It is an excellently fashioned piece with a rather powerful slow movement, an elegy subtitled *Folia*. The CD is completed by *Belsatzar*, an *a cappella* setting of Heine, and the *Third Quartet*, a remarkable achievement for an 86-year-old, the product of a cultured and thoughtful musical mind. The performances are dedicated, the recordings satisfactory.

GOLIGHTLY, David (born 1948)

Symphony No. 1; 3 Seascapes.
★★★ ASC CDCS 38. Prague PO, Sutherland.

It may seem extraordinary, but David Golightly's *Symphony No. 1*, written over a period of four years, was commissioned by and dedicated to Middles-brough F. C. and its chairman, Steve Gibson. Essentially programmatic, it is effectively wrought with a first movement founded on a rhythmic ostinato (*Resoluto marcato*) 'for those who strive, knock hard on the door of fate', the Scherzo reflecting the lively optimism of visits to Wembley, the eloquent and imaginatively scored slow movement reflecting the pain of defeat in an idiom that reminded the writer a little of the spacious string-writing of Howard Hanson. The finale is a jaunty populist march, exotically scored, with the two-part structure reflecting the two halves of the game. The orchestral fanfares depict the team scoring. It is a happy, extrovert inspiration and receives a fine performance under Gavin Sutherland in Prague, and a full-blooded recording. The three *Seascapes* further demonstrate Golightly's vivid orchestral skill, using well-known folk-themes, like *Shenandoah*. The disc is available from Modrana Music Publishers Ltd, tel. 01625 875389, or Disk Imports Ltd, tel. 0161 491 6655.

GÓRECKI, Henryk (born 1933)

'*World of Górecki*': (i) *Lerchenmusic, Op. 53:* 2nd movement only; (ii; iii) *Old Polish Music;* (iv) *Symphony No. 3: Finale;* (ii; v) *Totus Tuus;* (i) *Kleines Requiem für eine Polka, Op. 66:* 2nd and 3rd movements only.
(B) ★★ Decca 470 128-2. (i) Schoenberg Ens., De Leeuw; (ii) Nelson; (iii) Czech PO; (iv) Warsaw PO, Kord; (v) Prague Ph. Ch.

Here is a sampler obviously designed to tempt listeners to explore beyond the *Third Symphony* (originally issued by Philips), the popular third movement of which became such a hit. It is here coupled with other, generally more demanding works. Only the vigorous second movement and the infectiously jazzy finale of the *Little Requiem* are included and are well performed on this 1995 recording (again with a Philips source). *Totus Tuus* and the *Old Polish Music* emanate from a 1993 Argo CD. The latter work is perhaps the most striking, effectively contrasting both lullaby and medieval organum, while the *a cappella Totus Tuus* is a beautifully reflective piece of choral writing. The *Lerchenmusic* movement is quite effective in a quasi-Bartókian way, if without that composer's individuality. A fair collection then, although fewer, but complete, works would have been a better proposition for the serious collector. Excellent sound and performances.

GOTTSCHALK, Louis (1829–69)

Grand Fantasia Triumfal for Piano & Orchestra.
(M) ★★★ Decca 430 726-2. Ortiz, RPO, Atzmon –
ADDINSELL: *Warsaw Concerto* ★★★; GERSHWIN: *Rhapsody* ★★(*) (with LISZT: *Hungarian Fantasia* ★★★; LITOLFF: *Scherzo* ★★★).

Gottschalk's *Grand Fantasia* has naïvety, and a touch of vulgarity too, but the performers here give it an account that nicely combines flair and a certain elegance, and the result is a distinct success.

(i; ii) *Grande Tarantelle for Piano & Orchestra;* **(ii)** *Symphony No. 1 (A Night in the Tropics);* **(iii)** *Music for one piano, four hands: L'Étincelle; La gallina; La jota aragonesa; Marche de nuit; Orfa; Printemps d'amour; Radieuse; Réponds-moi; Ses yeux; Souvenirs d'Andalousie; Tremolo.* **(2 pianos):** *The Union* **(concert paraphrase on national airs).**

(M) *** Van. (ADD) 08.4051 71. (i) Nibley; (ii) Utah SO, Abravanel; (iii) List, with Lewis or Werner.

With nearly 77 minutes of music this well-recorded Vanguard reissue makes an ideal introduction to Gottschalk's music. The *Grande Tarantelle* has a very catchy main theme; the two-movement *Night in the Tropics* uses its title of 'symphony' very loosely. The second movement is a kind of samba, rhythmically very winning. The music for piano, four hands, is played with flair and scintillating upper tessitura. The opening arrangement of *La jota aragonesa* heads an ear-tickling programme, with a touch of wit in the piece called *Tremolo*. When the participants move to two pianos for *The Union* concert paraphrase, the acoustic expands and the effect is properly grand. The orchestral recordings date from 1962, the piano pieces from 1976, and the sound is excellent throughout.

PIANO MUSIC

Piano music for 4 hands: (i) *Le Bananier (Chanson nègre), Op. 5; La Gallina (Danse cubaine), Op. 53; Grande tarantelle, Op. 67; La jota aragonesa (Caprice espagnol), Op. 14; Marche de nuit, Op. 17; Ojos criollos (Danse cubaine – Caprice brillante), Op. 37; Orfa (Grande polka), Op. 71; Printemps d'amour (Mazurka–caprice de concert), Op. 40; Réponds-moi (Danse cubaine), Op. 50; Radieuse (Grand valse de concert), Op. 72; La Scintilla (L'Etincelle – Mazurka sentimentale), Op. 21; Ses yeux (Célèbre polka de concert), Op. 66.* **Solo piano music:** *Le Banjo; Berceuse (cradle song); The Dying Poet (meditation); Grand scherzo; The Last Hope (religious meditation); Mazurka; Le Mancenillier (West Indian serenade); Pasquinade caprice; Scherzo romantique; Souvenirs d'Andalousie; Tournament galop; The Union: Concert Paraphrase on National Airs (The Star-Spangled Banner; Yankee Doodle; Hail Columbia).*

(B) ** Nim. NI 7045/6 (2). Marks, (i) with Barrett.

Much of Gottschalk's music exists in alternative two- and four-handed arrangements, and Alan Marks and Nerine Barrett make an effervescent Gottschalk partnership in the latter, playing the more dashing pieces to the manner born. The drawback is that this very personable piano duo are recorded – realistically

enough – in an empty, resonant hall, and although one adjusts, the effect is not advantageous.

The solo recital is still resonant, but not exaggeratedly so, and Alan Marks plays with considerable flair: the *Souvenirs d'Andalousie* glitters with bravura, his felicity of touch and crisp articulation bring much sparkle to the *Grand scherzo* and *Scherzo romantique*, while he sounds like a full orchestra in the *Tournament galop*. Most importantly, there is not a hint of sentimentality in *The Dying Poet* or *The Last Hope*, the composer's most famous piece. For those wanting an inexpensive survey of Gottschalk, this Nimbus Double will serve well enough, but the Hyperion series is artistically and sonically preferable.

Complete solo piano music: 'An American Composer, bon Dieu!'

Volume 1: *Le Bananier (Chanson nègre), Op. 5; Le Banjo; Chanson de Gitano; Columbia (Caprice américain), Op. 34; Danza, Op. 33; Le Mancenillier, Op. 11; Mazurka; Minuit à Seville, Op. 30; Romanze; Souvenir de la Havana (Grand caprice de concert), Op. 39; Souvenir de Porto Rico, marche des Gibaros, Op. 31; Les Yeux créoles (Danse cubaine), Op. 37; Union (Paraphrase de concert), Op. 48.*

*** Hyp. CDA 66459. Martin.

Gottschalk invented the conception of the composer/recitalist in America, just as Liszt had in Europe. As a touring virtuoso he had great audience appeal, and if his music is lightweight it is well crafted and tuneful, paying homage to both Liszt and Chopin. Its exotic folk-influences are drawn colloquially and naturally from the Deep South, with syncopated rhythms the strongest feature.

Philip Martin's continuing complete survey on Hyperion is in every way distinguished. He is naturally sympathetic to the transatlantic idioms, yet he treats the music as part of the romantic mainstream, bringing out its various derivations. He plays with elegance, brilliance, style and, above all, spontaneity. He is very well recorded in an ideal acoustic. In Volume 1 he closes with the celebrated and grandiose *Union (Paraphrase de concert)*, which Gottschalk, a dedicated abolitionist, played for President Lincoln and his First Lady in 1864.

Volume 2: *Ballade; Berceuse, Op. 47; Caprice polka; Grand scherzo, Op. 57; La jota aragonesa (Caprice espagnol), Op. 14; Manchega (Etude de concert), Op. 38; Marche de nuit, Op. 17; Miserere du Trovatore (paraphrase de concert), Op. 52; Pasquinade (caprice), Op. 59; Polkas: in A flat; in B flat. La Savane (Ballade créole), Op. 3; Scherzo romantique; Souvenirs d'Andalousie (Caprice de concert), Op. 22; Souvenir de Lima (Mazurka), Op. 74; Suis-moi! (Caprice), Op. 45; Ynés.*

*** Hyp. CDA 66697. Martin.

The *Paraphrase of Verdi's Miserere* all but upstages Liszt. One can imagine how the composer's contemporary audiences would have loved its melodrama, while both the *Jota aragonesa* and the similar *Souvenirs d'Andalousie* are *tours de force* of extrovert dexterity. The *Caprice polka* is polished and sparkling, while the *Souvenir de Lima* returns to an engagingly Chopinesque idiom. Again, a very good recording.

Volume 3: *Bamboula (Danse des nègres), Op. 2; La Chute des feuilles (Nocturne), Op. 42; The Dying Poet* (Meditation); *Hercule (Grande étude de concert); Murmures éoliens; O ma charmante, épargnes-moi (Caprice); Gottschalk's Melody; Grand fantaisie triomphale sur l'hymne national Brésilien; The Last Hope; Symphony No. 1 (La Nuit des tropiques):* 1st movement: *Andante* (arr. Napoleão); *Tournament galop.*
*** Hyp. CDA 66915. Martin.

The Dying Poet and *The Last Hope* – which the composer described, tongue in cheek, as a '*succès de larmes*' (tears) – are treated with a nice discretion. *Hercule* (given a striking march theme with simple decorative variants) is built to a fine rhetorical climax, as is the slow movement of the *Symphony No. 1* (in this not entirely advantageous transcription). The closing, very orchestral *Tournament galop* is superbly thrown off. It has a Rossinian vivacity, but its roulades are very much Gottschalk's own.

Volume 4: *Apothéose (Grande marche solennelle), Op. 29; La Colombe (petite polka), Op. 49; Fantôme de bonheur (Illusions perdues), Op. 36; Forest Glade Polka (Les Follets), Op. 25; La Gitana (Caprice caractéristique), Op. 35; La Moissonneuse (Mazurka caractéristique), Op. 8; Morte!! (Lamentation), Op. 55; Ossian (2 Ballades), Op. 4/1-2; Pensée poétique; Polonia, Op. 35; Reflets du passé, Op. 28; La Scintilla (L'Etincelle: Mazurka sentimentale), Op. 20; Ricordati (Nocturne, méditation, romance), Op. 26; Le Songe d'une nuit d'été (Caprice élégant), Op. 9; Souvenir de Cuba (Mazurka), Op. 75.*
*** Hyp. CDA 67118. Martin.

If you decide to explore this enjoyable Hyperion survey, Volume 4 is a good place to start, for much of its content is little known and every piece is enjoyable. The Lisztian *Le Songe d'une nuit d'été,* the thoughtful *Pensée poétique, La Scintilla* (with its iridescence) all have great charm. *Morte!!* brings an elegiac contrast and has a distinctly sentimental ambience. *Polonia* is a jolly peasant dance, while the *Forest Glade Polka* curiously anticipates the music of Billy Mayerl, and there is a flamboyant closing *Apothéose,* which takes a fair time to reach its zenith, but proceeds to do so with panache.

Volume 5: *Ballade No. 8; Bataille; La Chasse du jeune Henri; El Cocoyé; Marguerite; Orfa Polka; Polka de salon; Rayons d'azur; Réponds-moi (Dí que sí); Sospiro; Tremolo.*
*** Hyp. CDA 67248. Martin.

Philip Martin here continues his inestimable series,

playing Gottschalk with such musical feeling that he makes writing that is ingenuous and designed solely to tickle the ear sound worthy of the concert hall. Such are the opening waltzes, *Sospiro* and the very engaging *Marguerite.* The *Etude de concert* has a very striking opening theme, but its treatment is perhaps rather over-extended. The rag-like *Réponds-moi* (originally written for four hands) and *El Cocoyé,* with their Cuban rhythms, are quintessential Gottschalk, but the Chopinesque *Solitude* and the *Eighth Ballade* are both based on pleasingly serene melodies, while the ingenious *Tremolo* and the polka *Razons d'azur,* with its leggiero repeated notes, are both delectably virtuosic (and delightfully played here). The other polkas, notable *Orfa,* have much charm. The closing *Chasse du jeune Henri* is based on Méhul's overture to his otherwise discarded opera and soon intrigues the ear with its catchy, galloping motive. Altogether a fascinating programme, very well played and recorded.

Volume 6: *Caprice élégiaque; Le Carnaval de Venise* (with Variations); *Colliers d'or; Danse des sylphes; Danse ossianique; La Favorita: Grand fantaisie triomphale; Impromptu; Jeunesse; Marche funèbre; Printemps d'amour; Le Sourire d'une june fille; Vision.*
*** Hyp. CDA 67349. Martin.

Volume 6 begins with an elaborate and scintillating treatment of the *Carnival of Venice,* followed by a droll little *Funeral March* , which Philip Martin plays charmingly. The rippling *Vision* and pretty little mazurka, *Printemps d'amour,* are more characteristic, and the *Caprice élégiaque* and *Colliers d'or (deux mazurkes)* are Chopinesque, but the very pleasing *Danse ossianique* has an even stronger flavour of that composer. The *Sylphs* dance to glittering runs in the piano's highest register, and 'The Maiden's Blush' (*Le Sourire d'une jeune fille*) was just made for Gottschalk to turn into a cute little waltz. Last comes the grandly introduced Donizetti fantasia to make a lyrically tuneful and virtuosic finale, which is presented with aplomb by Philip Martin, who continues to show such a natural flair for this writing and never makes it sound cheap.

Bamboula; Le Bananier; Le Banjo; The Dying Poet; The Last Hope; The Maiden's Blush; Ojos criollos; Pasquinade; La Savane; Souvenir de Porto Rico; Suis-moi!; Tournament galop.
(M) *** Van. (ADD) 08.4050.71 [OVC 4050]. List.

Eugene List made this repertoire very much his own in the USA in the late 1950s and early 1960s, and his performances are second to none. The glittering roulades in *Le Bananier* and *Ojos criollos* are brought off with unaffected brilliance, and the plucking imitations at the close of *The Banjo* are equally successful. The pieces with sentimental titles are more appealing than their names might suggest, and the *Tournament galop* closes the recital at an infectious canter. The recording dates from 1956 but doesn't sound its age at all: it is very well balanced and realistic.

Bamboula; Le Banjo; Le Bananier; The Dying Poet; L'Etincelle; La Gallina; La jota aragonesa; Manchega; Pasquinade; La Savane; Souvenirs d'Andalousie; Souvenir de Porto Rico, Marche ds Gibaro; Suis-moi!; Tremolo; Tournament Galop; The Union: Paraphrase de Concert on the national airs, Star-Spangled Banner, Yankee Doodle and Hail Columbia.

⊕━ (BB) *** Naxos 8.559145. Licad.

If you want a single representative disc of Gottschalk's music, this is it. Cecile Licad is right inside this repertoire. She obviously enjoys every bar and conveys her enthusiasm to us, playing with character, polish and rhythmic gusto. *Le Banjo*, which opens the programme, has great zest, *Bamboula* (the 'Danse de nègres') thumps vigorously, and the *Tournament Galop* chases along with infectious bravura. Yet *Le Bananier* has an almost sinuous charm and *La Savane* is played with winning delicacy. Even *The Dying Poet* is made to sound delicate rather than too overtly sentimental, partly because here, as elsewhere, Licad's rubato is naturally spontaneous. The idiomatic feeling of *La jota aragonesa* and of the two *Souvenirs* is striking, for she has a real feeling for Spanish and Afro-Caribbean rhythms. The programme closes with the spectacular *Union Paraphase*, presented with genuine bravdo. Very well recorded, this disc is irresistible.

GOUGH, John (1903–51)

Serenade for Small Orchestra.
*** Chan. 9757. BBC PO, Handley – BAINTON: *Symphony No. 2 in D min.*; CLIFFORD: *Symphony.* ***

John Gough worked for a time as a studio manager or balance engineer in the BBC and was later Pacific Service Music Organizer during the war years. After the war he became a features producer during the period when that BBC department was at the height of its fame. The short but charming *Serenade for Small Orchestra* reveals a genuine creative talent and was written in 1931 for Hubert Clifford's wedding. Exemplary playing and first-rate recorded sound.

GOULD, Morton (1913–96)

Fall River Legend: Suite; Spirituals for String Choir & Orchestra.
(M) *** Mercury (ADD) [432 016-2].. Eastman–Rochester SO, Hanson – BARBER: *Medea: Suite.* ***

The composer's orchestral suite from the ballet is brightly played by the Eastman–Rochester Orchestra under the highly sympathetic Howard Hanson, who also gives an outstandingly vibrant account of the *Spirituals*. The 1959–60 Mercury recording has astonishing clarity, range and presence.

GOUNOD, Charles (1818–93)

(i) *Petite symphonie in B flat for Wind;* (ii) *Messe solennelle de Sainte-Cécile.*
(BB) ** EMI Encore 5 74730-2. (i) Hallé O (members), Barbirolli; (ii) Lorengar, Hoppe, Crass, Duclos Ch., Paris Conservatoire O, Hartemann.

Barbirolli's account (from the 1960s) of Gounod's witty and charming *Petite symphonie* still sounds well. The performance has plenty of character, yet a suitably light touch, and Barbirolli's affection is obvious. The Hallé players are in good form.

One also welcomes back to the catalogue Jean-Claude Hartemann's performance of this highly attractive Victorian Mass. The *Credo* is the part to sample first, a rollicking setting with more than a hint of a Beatles tune; and Gounod, having invented such a good tune, has no inhibitions about using it. Whatever the rhythms of the words, he brings it back whenever he wants to, ending with a very secular-sounding augmentation, almost in Hollywood style. If that is the most vulgar movement, it is also the most enjoyable. The rest is agreeable without being terribly memorable. This Paris performance is capable without being very distinguished and the recording is only fair, but at super-budget price this disc is worth exploring.

GRAF, Friedrich (1727–95)

6 Flute Quartets.
*** MDG 311 0520-2. Hünteler, Festetics Qt (members).

Friedrich Hartmann Graf began his musical career as a timpanist in the band of a Dutch regiment but, after being wounded in battle and taken prisoner, decided to turn to the more peaceful flute. He developed into a virtuoso, becoming a colleague of Telemann in Hamburg in 1759. In his six quartets for flute, violin, viola and cello (dating from around 1775) the flute dominates, but the ensemble is elegantly integrated. They are gently melodious and full of charm and, taken one at a time, make very pleasing listening. The performances here are beautifully turned and perfectly balanced in a warm acoustic. Undoubtedly lightweight, but beguiling.

GRAINGER, Percy (1882–1961)

PIANO MUSIC

Fantasy on Gershwin's 'Porgy and Bess' (arr. for piano duet).
(BB) ** EMI Encore 5 75224-2. K. & M. Labèque –

GERSHWIN: *An American in Paris.* ★★

The Labèque sisters in their tough brilliance bring out the strong dramatic contrasts of Grainger's two-piano arrangement of passages from *Porgy and Bess*, a piece more obviously pianistic than the composer's own two-piano version of *An American in Paris*, with which it is coupled. A fair coupling, recorded with a brightness that threatens to become aggressive, with the occasional clattery quality still apparent in its new bargain incarnation.

VOCAL MUSIC

Folksong Arrangements: The Bride's Tragedy (for chorus & orchestra); *Brigg Fair* (for tenor & chorus); *Danny Deever* (for baritone, chorus & orchestra); *Father and daughter* (*A Faeroe Island dancing ballad*; for 5 solo narrators, double chorus, & 3 instrumental groups); *I'm seventeen come Sunday* (for chorus, brass & percussion); *Irish tune from County Derry* (*Londonderry air*; for wordless chorus); *The Lost lady found; Love verses from The Song of Solomon* (for tenor & chamber orchestra); *The merry wedding* (*Bridal dances*; for 9 soloists, chorus, brass, percussion, strings & organ); *My dark-haired maiden* (*Mi nighean dhu*; for mixed voices); *Scotch strathspey and reel – inlaid with several Irish and Scotch tunes and a sea shanty* (orchestral version); *Shallow Brown* (for solo voice or unison chorus, with an orchestra of 13 or more instruments); *The Three Ravens* (for baritone solo, mixed chorus & 5 clarinets); *Tribute to Foster* (for vocal quintet, male chorus & instrumental ensemble).

🕭 (M) ★★★ Decca 475 213-2. Soloists, Monteverdi Ch., English Country Gardiner O, Gardiner.

It would be difficult to imagine a more exhilarating disc of Grainger's music than this (originally Philips) collection of 'Songs and Dancing Ballads', which won the *Gramophone*'s Choral Award in 1996. John Eliot Gardiner met the eccentric composer as a child and has become devoted to his music. The variety is astonishing, even among the folksong settings, which often use melodies transcribed from original sources by Grainger himslf. Gardiner singles out the hypnotically measured sea-shanty *Shallow Brown* as the most 'searingly original' of Grainger's works and the most haunting. The performance here backs that up, with furious tremolandos from guitars and banjos, which Grainger called 'wogglings'. The richest, most exotic piece is the setting of *Love verses* from the Song of Solomon, while the longest and most elaborate items bring astonishingly original effects for both voices and orchestra, the richly evocative *Tribute to Stephen Foster* and the setting of a mock Scottish ballad by Swinburne, *The Bride's Tragedy*, which Grainger described as a pained 'grumble-shout'. All 14 items, many of them first-ever recordings, bring typically quirky inspirations, superbly interpreted. Even if the

choir's attempts at various dialects, from Mummerset onwards, may not be to everyone's taste, the virtuosity of the singing is breathtaking. The bitter element in some of the numbers provides a clue to the inspiration that fired Grainger, as in the grim setting of Kipling's *Danny Deever*, with its refrain, 'Oh they're hanging Danny Deever in the morning'. Echoing Mahler in its subject, it is far more angry. Superb sound, though (because of the complexity of textures) words are often inaudible. Full text and really oustanding notes – a model of what documentation should be.

GRAUN, Carl Heinrich (1704–59)

Cleopatra e Cesare (opera): 'Great arias'.
(M) ★★★ HM HMT 7901 602. Williams, Vermillion, Dawson, Gambill, RIAS Chamber Ch., Concerto Köln, Jacobs.

Taken from a complete three-disc set, recorded in Berlin in 1995, this generous, 77-minute collection of overture and ten arias plus two ensembles is consistently refreshing. In this selection, fast arias predominate – no doubt a wise choice – with all the principals singing most stylishly, with clean, agile attack, not least Janet Williams and Iris Vermillion in the twin title-roles, as well as Lynne Dawson, singing most beautifully as Cornelia, widow of Pompey. Williams is sweetly affecting in her big Act III aria, and Vermillion with her firm, strong mezzo makes a most characterful Caesar. Under René Jacobs, a sensitive director, there is no weak link in the rest of the cast either, and recorded sound is nicely balanced to convey an apt scale for this music.

GRAUPNER, Christoph (1683–1760)

Double Flute Concerto in E min., GWV.321; Overtures in E flat, GWV.429; in E, GWV.439; Sinfonias in D, GWV.538; in G, GWV.578.
★★★ MDG 341 1121-2. Nova Stravaganza.

MDG has a knack of finding these previously forgotten baroque composers. German-born Graupner was prolific, writing 113 symphonies, 50 concertos, 80 suites (overtures), operas and cantatas, as well as a vast amount of chamber music. The works recorded here are typical, showing both imagination and individuality. The three-movement *Sinfonias* demonstrate the composer's adventurous spirit, with plentiful ideas: the *Sinfonia in D* has a charming flute duet in the central movement, while the finale is both vivacious and fresh. The *G major Sinfonia* uses its two horns to good effect in the first movement, rather like a hunting concerto, contrasting with its minor-keyed central movement and the elegant, if more formal, minuet finale. Again in the *Double Flute Concerto*, while there are two quite substantial fast movements, the minor key ensures that the writing is not entirely frivolous, and the finale, with its interplay between the two soloists, is especially infectious. The *Overture/Suites* are in the late-baroque style, featuring dance movements but beginning with a more substantial introduction. They are agreeable enough, though not as striking as their companion works. Excellent performances and recording.

GREGSON, Edward (born 1945)

***Blazon;* (i) *Clarinet Concerto;* (ii) *Violin Concerto. Stepping Out* (for string orchestra).**

*** Chan. 10105. (i) Collins; (ii) Charlier; BBC PO, Brabbins.

Edward Gregson is Principal of Manchester's Royal Northern College of Music, but there is no suspicion of academia here; instead, a highly individual composer emerges who writes in the mainstream of twentieth-century English music, notably Walton, Malcolm Arnold and Vaughan Williams. He shows a genuine orchestral flair, and distinctive melodic gifts. The two concertos are both most rewarding, and that for the clarinet is as strikingly individual as any written for this instrument in the latter years of the twentieth century.

But the CD opens with *Blazon* (1992), a smaller-scale concerto for orchestra, brimful of energy and ideas. Opening and closing with royal brass fanfares, it features each orchestral group in turn, underwritten with a striking lyrical theme that acts an an anchor. Gregson favours lively moto perpetuo allegros, which thrust his music vibrantly forward, contrasted with chorale-like melodies with a modal essence.

The splendid *Clarinet Concerto* (1994) opens with the soloist reflectively exploring the work's basic material, and this rumination gestates the spiritedly impetuous, rhythmically spiky main themes. The work's beautiful second half begins ethereally with *pianissimo* high strings and creates magical textures and an atmosphere of profound, moving serenity. But the dynamism of the first part returns, and from this previous material Gregson fashions a richly heart-warming melody, which becomes a satisfying resolution. The concerto is brilliantly, sensitively and exuberantly played by Michael Collins.

Each movement of the *Violin Concerto* (1999) is prefaced by lines of poetry, but these prove to be only a series of inspirational stepping-off points. Certainly the brashly, almost vulgarly sardonic waltz climax of the first movement does catch something of the decadent atmosphere of Oscar Wilde's *The Harlot's House.* But the kernel of the work is the Elysian, mystical slow movement, inspired by Paul Verlaine's *Chanson d'automne,* warmly and delicately played by Olivier Charlier. The Irish reel of the athletically vigorous finale is then at one with the words of W. B. Yeats ('And the merry love the fiddle, And the merry love to dance'). The soloist leads the dance uninhibitedly, even drawing on the blazing energy of the ideas we first heard at the climax of *Blazon.*

Stepping Out (1996) for string orchestra briefly visits the world of John Adams, but the work's succinct polyphonic second section brings a spontaneous lyrical momentum all Gregson's own, and the colourful individuality of the richly coloured orchestral detail in all three works proves the composer's orchestral resourcefulness. Any of these pieces would be sure to create a great impression at a Prom, especially if directed as spontaneously as they are here by Martyn Brabbins. The recordings are vivid and warmly atmospheric; moreover Olivier Charlier's small, sweet violin-image is perfectly balanced in the *Violin Concerto,* while Michael Collins easily dominates the work for clarinet. The collection is highly recommendable if you care about contemporary British orchestral music.

GRIEG, Edvard (1843–1907)

Piano Concerto in A min., Op. 16.

🔑 ✿ *** EMI 5 57562-2. Andsnes, BPO, Jansons – SCHUMANN: *Piano Concerto.* *** ✿

(M) ** DG (ADD) 474 838-2. Anda, PO, Kubelik – BRAHMS: *Piano Concerto No. 2.* **(*)

*(*) Decca 467 093-2. Thibaudet, Rotterdam PO, Gergiev – CHOPIN: *Piano Concerto No. 2.* *(*)

(BB) * EMI Encore (ADD) 5 74732-2. Cziffra, New Philh. O, Cziffra Jr – RACHMANINOV: *Piano Concerto No. 2.* *

It was with the Grieg, coupled with a fine Liszt *A major Concerto,* that Leif Ove Andsnes, most celebrated of Norwegian pianists and among the most sensitive of young artists, made his concerto début in 1990 on the Virgin label. This new version, recorded live in Berlin, is just as spontaneous-sounding, with soaring flights of imagination. The performance is also a degree more urgent than in his 1990 recording, while the Berlin Philharmonic is at its warmest under Mariss Jansons. This is a conductor for whom any trace of routine is alien, and who so often illuminates familiar terrain; equally, the freshness of approach that distinguishes Andsnes's performances in the concert hall is well in evidence here. His virtuosity is commanding, but it is never at the expense of tenderness and poetic feeling; he is an aristocrat among pianists and has the gift of bringing new and deeper insights (listen to the slow movement) without any loss of spontaneity or the slightest trace of artifice. The Schumann too brings glorious playing from both soloist and orchestra, with both offering warm, clear sound. Even alongside Stephen Kovacevich's much admired coupling, this new issue stands out: in short, this is a gramophone classic for the present decade.

Anda's 1963 account, promoted to the 'Originals'

series, is more wayward than some, but it is strong in personality and has plenty of life. Kubelik's accompaniment is also very good and, although the sound is a bit dated, it is more than acceptable. However, this is hardly a first recommendation for this much-recorded concerto.

Thibaudet's very routine performance disappoints. There are good things, notably Gergiev's contribution in the slow movement, but for the most part Thibaudet's playing is curiously monochrome and overall this never fully springs to life.

Cziffra's account of the Grieg from the early 1970s is singularly disappointing. There are moments of poetry here, but the too leisurely first movement does not hold the listener's attention and the performance overall fails to make a strong impression. The backward balance of the orchestra and the indifferent sound, shallow and thin, does not help matters. There are too many outstanding versions of this concerto to make this worth considering, even at its modest cost, especially as the coupling is hardly better.

(i) *Piano Concerto. Lyric Suite; Peer Gynt Suites Nos. 1–2.*

(M) ** Chan. 10175X. (i) Fingerhut; Ulster O, Handley.

Margaret Fingerhut has eloquently championed Bax on the Chandos label (see above) and has put us in her debt with other keyboard rarities. With the Grieg *Concerto* she enters a more competitive field and gives a thoughtful and musicianly reading that holds a fine balance between the work's virtuosic and poetic elements. Her first-movement cadenza shows tenderness as well as brilliance, as indeed does the slow movement. Only in the finale does she fall short of distinction, if we compare her, say, to Stephen Kovacevich; even so, the slow middle section has many felicitous touches and this is a far from negligible account. With its attractive couplings, this disc would seem an attractive proposition for the smaller collection, yet Vernon Handley is not at his happiest and most perceptive in the *Peer Gynt Suites*, with the *First* failing to take off and the *Second* occasionally somewhat overblown. But he gets generally sympathetic and responsive playing from the Ulster Orchestra and is very well recorded.

Lyric Suite, Op. 54; Norwegian Dances, Op. 35; Symphonic Dances, Op. 64.

**(*) BIS SACD 1291. Bergen PO, Ruud.

This is rather less successful than the earlier Grieg disc from Bergen under Ole Kristian Ruud, devoted to music of 1864–8 (the *Concert Overture, In Autumn,* the *C minor Symphony* and the *Piano Concerto* – BIS CD 1191; see our main volume). The sound is first rate, well defined and full-bodied, and captures the excellent acoustic of the Grieg Hall with great realism. For the most part the Bergen orchestra play with the naturalness and eloquence we associate with this repertoire – and with them. But the phrasing in the

second of the *Norwegian Dances* is a little too 'knowing' and *Shepherd Boy* in the *Lyric Suite* is too slow and affected. Neeme Järvi takes 4 minutes 14 seconds over this as opposed to Ruud's 5 minutes 31 seconds! As far as the *Symphonic Dances* are concerned, Sakari Oramo's account with the CBSO on Erato (8573 82917-2) is fresher and more direct in utterance. All the same, Ruud draws some highly responsive playing from his fine orchestra, and the sound is quite sumptuous.

CHAMBER MUSIC

Cello Sonata in A min., Op. 36; Intermezzo in A min.

(B) ** Virgin 5 62203-2. Mørk, Thibaudet – SIBELIUS: *Malinconia, etc.* **

On Virgin the *Cello Sonata* is paired with the rather Schumannesque *Intermezzo in A minor*, which Grieg composed in 1866 for his cello-playing brother. Truls Mørk plays with finesse and good poetic feeling; but Jean-Yves Thibaudet, for all his flair and sensitivity, proves somewhat overbearing. The balance favours him excessively, with the result that Mørk's tone sounds very small.

PIANO MUSIC

Lyric Pieces, Opp. 12/8; 38/1 & 6; 43/1 & 2; 47/1, 3 & 7; 54/3–4; 57/4, 5 & 6; 62/4; 68/2; 71/2–3.

(B) *** CDK CDKM 1003. Pletnev.

It is good to see this masterly Grieg recital return to circulation, as it contains playing of great poetic feeling and keen sensibility. It was briefly available on Melodiya in the late 1980s and, though by no means the equal of Gilels's famous anthology on DG (449 721-2) in terms of recorded sound, was artistically a worthy successor. His *Klokkeklang* ('Bell Ringing') has a remarkable range of colour and dynamics, even though it is not as slow and mysterious as his BBC broadcast of much the same period. There are many individual insights: the quality of the *pianissimo* tone in *Hemmelighed* ('Secrecy'), Op. 57, No. 4, is a case in point, and the poignancy of *Hjemve* ('Homesickness') is eloquently conveyed. As usual with Pletnev nothing is routine and there is a concentration that gives these miniatures a freshness and depth that few artists can match. Even if you have the Gilels and Andsnes anthologies, you should not miss this. One had forgotten just how good this revealing recital is. If the distinction of the playing is not matched by the quality of the recorded sound, it is still eminently serviceable.

Lyric Pieces, Opp. 12/1; 38/1; 43/1–2 & 6; 47/2–4; 54/1, 3–5; 57/6; 62/4 & 6; 65/5–6; 68/2–3 & 5; 71/1–4, 6–7.

(BB) ** Regis RRC 1071. Austbø.

Born in Norway but now based in Amsterdam,

Håkon Austbø enjoyed success in Paris, where he won the Ravel Competition, and in Royan, where he won the Messiaen Competition. He is best known for his advocacy of the French master as well as Scriabin, and his command of keyboard colour and his wide dynamic range are impressive. There is no lack of tonal sophistication here, although he is rather too forwardly balanced; but, for all his unfailing accomplishment and sensitivity, he lacks the naturalness of utterance and freshness of vision that such rivals as Gilels, Andsnes and Pletnev bring to this repertoire. Theirs is the art that conceals art.

VOCAL MUSIC

Haugtussa (song-cycle), Op. 67; 6 Songs, Op. 48; Songs: Beside the stream; Farmyard song; From Monte Pincio; Hope; I love but thee; Spring; Spring showers; A swan; Two brown eyes; While I wait; With a waterlily (sung in Norwegian).

⊶ ❁ (M) ✱✱✱ DG Dig. 476 18157. Von Otter, Forsberg.

This recital of Grieg's songs by Anne Sofie von Otter and Bengt Forsberg is rather special. Von Otter commands an exceptionally wide range of colour and quality, and in Forsberg she has a highly responsive partner. Altogether a captivating recital, and beautifully recorded, too; it rightly won the *Gramophone* Solo Vocal Award in 1993 and was also the magazine's 'Record of the Year'. It now reappears in Universal's '*Gramophone* Award Collection' at mid-price, with full documentation included.

Haugtussa, Op. 67; 6 Songs to Poems by A. O. Vinje, Op. 33.

✱(✱) NMA 3. Kringelborn, Martineau.

Haugtussa ('The Mountain Maid') includes the greatest of Grieg's songs and has been well served on record (Flagstad recorded it no fewer than three times). Solveig Kringelborn prefaces the cycle with *Ku-Lok* ('Cow Call') one of the five songs Grieg omitted when he finally published the set – and a very effective opening it makes to the disc. Hers is a strong musical personality, and she commands much vocal beauty, even if her expressive characterization is at times exaggerated. For example, she does not allow a song like *Blåbær-Li* ('Blueberry Slope') to speak for itself: she is too self-aware, almost arch in her approach. Throughout she gets admirable support from Malcolm Martineau. The *Twelve Settings of Aasmund Olavson Vinje*, which Grieg published as Op. 33, were composed 15 years earlier, in 1880, and are among his most poetic utterances for voice: their intensity of feeling is unmistakable. Again one is struck by the tonal beauty Kringelborn commands, but for many listeners she will seem just a bit too self-conscious, though the recording is very natural and lifelike. However, this is no match for the fine version by Anne Sofie von Otter and Bengt

Forsberg on DG, which, in terms of interpretative insight and a natural unforced eloquence, remains unchallenged.

GRIFFES, Charles Tomlinson
(1884–1920)

Bacchanale; Clouds; The Pleasure-Dome of Kubla-Khan; (i) Poem for Flute and Orchestra. 3 Tone-Pictures (The Lake at Evening; The Vale of Dreams; The Night Winds); The White Peacock. (ii) 3 Poems of Fiona McLeod (The Lament of Ian the Proud; The Dark Eyes to Mine; The Rose of the Night).

⊶ (BB) ✱✱✱ Naxos 8.559164. Buffalo PO, Falletta; with (i) Wincenc; (ii) Quintiliani.

This invaluable disc gives a warm and colourful portrait of this late-romantic American composer, sadly short lived. It includes not only his three best-known orchestral works, but a clutch of rarities as well, otherwise unavailable on disc. Most of these started as piano pieces, which Griffes orchestrated, yet such was the composer's mastery over evocative tone-painting that one would never guess that. Griffes was the first US composer to respond to the call of Impressionism. In 1903 he studied in Berlin with Humperdinck, turned his main interest towards composition and returned four years later to the United States, taking a job as a music teacher. The shimmering beauty of his writing matches that of Debussy on the one hand, Delius on the other, with his inspiration regularly coming from English literature, Coleridge in *Kubla Khan*, Fiona McLeod (William Sharp) in *The White Peacock*, as well as in the three songs, and W. B. Yeats in the first of the *Three Tone Pictures*. Apart from Debussy and Ravel, Griffes was drawn to Mussorgsky and Scriabin, as well as to oriental music. *The White Peacock* (1915) comes from a suite for piano (*Four Roman Sketches*), which he later scored for orchestra. *The Pleasure-Dome of Kubla Khan* (1919) and the *Poem for Flute and Orchestra* (1918) are probably his masterpieces. Performances here are outstanding and very well recorded, with JoAnn Falletta as music director of the Buffalo Philharmonic drawing refined and atmospheric performances from her players, with Barbara Quintiliani as the bright soloist in the songs and Carol Wincenc, principal flute in the orchestra, a most sympathetic soloist in the *Poem*. This fine compilation fills an important gap in the catalogue.

GRØNDAHL, Agathe Backer
(1847–1907)

6 Etudes de concert, Op. 11; 3 Etudes, Op. 22; 3 Morceaux, Op. 15; 4 Sketches, Op. 19; Suite, Op. 20.
✱✱✱ BIS CD 1106. Braaten.

Four years younger than Grieg, Agathe Grøndahl

died only a few weeks before him. The annotator does her cause no service by placing her music on a level with Grieg and Kjerulf, for although she was much respected in her day as a concert pianist well beyond Scandinavia, her music has never escaped the shadows of Mendelssohn and Schumann. The folk-influenced Norwegian accents that inspired Nordraak, Grieg and Svendsen held little attraction for Grøndahl. Bernard Shaw hailed her as a great pianist and found some individuality in the songs but little in the piano pieces. On this disc they range from the *Concert Studies*, Op. 11, of 1881, her first published composition, through to the *Trois études*, Op. 22, of 1888; they are written capably but are wanting in originality. Geir Henning Braaten plays splendidly and is given an excellent BIS recording.

GUBAIDULINA, Sofia
(born 1931)

In Croce for Bayan & Cello; Seven Last Words for Cello, Bayan & Strings; Silenzio for Bayan, Violin & Cello.

(BB) ★★★ Naxos 8.553557. Moser, Kliegel, Rabus, Camerata Transsylvanica, Selmeczi.

In Croce is an arrangement of a work for cello and organ, composed in 1979 and arranged for bayan or push-button accordion in 1993. The *Seven Last Words*, composed in 1982 for cello, accordion and strings, is probably the best entry-point into Gubaidulina's strange world, mesmerizing for some, boring for others. Maria Kliegel is an intense and powerful cellist, and Elsbeth Moser is a dedicated player long associated with this repertoire. Good recorded sound.

GYROWETZ, Adalbert (1763–1850)

Symphonies: in E flat; F, Op. 6/2-3; in D, Op. 12/1.
★★★ Chan. 9791. LMP, Bamert.

The Bohemian composer Adalbert Gyrowetz, a talented contemporary of Haydn and Mozart, outlived both of them. The Gyrowetz symphonies are delightful, full of characterfully individual invention, with Gyrowetz adding *galant* touches of his own. The engaging bravura horn solo in the Trio of the Minuet of Op. 6/2 is truly Bohemian, as is the genial opening movement of Op. 6/3, while the *Andante* soon produces a winning arioso for the oboe, followed by a bouncing half Scherzo, half Ländler and a Haydnesque finale. There are catchy ideas too in the *Andante* of the later *D major Symphony* and again in the nicely scored finale. In short, these are most enjoyable works and they are played (on modern instruments) with great elegance and sparkle and are beautifully recorded. Well worth seeking out.

HADLEY, Henry Kimball
(1871–1937)

The Culprit Fay (Rhapsody), Op. 62; The Ocean, Op. 99; Symphony No. 4 in D min., Op. 64.
(BB) ★★(★) Naxos 8.559064. Ukraine Nat. SO, McLaughlin Williams.

Another issue in Naxos's enterprising American Classics series. Hadley's music is very much in the European Romantic tradition, and the 1921 tone-poem, *The Ocean*, is full of melodrama, thundering timpani and sea effects (the poem on which it is based is included in the sleeve-notes). Though this style of writing is not too far away from a Hollywood film score of the 1930s or '40s, it is no less effective for that, especially when it is so colourfully orchestrated. *The Culprit Fay*, wth its evocative string-writing at the opening, portrays the magical, airy quality of Joseph Drake's poem depicting the adventures of a fairy. There is more attractive colouring in this delicate, animated score, and it sustains its 15 minutes remarkably well. The *Fourth Symphony* was composed for the Norfolk, Connecticut Festival and was first performed in 1911. It comes with a programme portraying different parts of America (the four movements are entitled *North*, *South*, *East* and *West*) though, curiously, the second movement is described as an 'Oriental tone-picture' and is predictably exotic. If far from a masterpiece, it is entertaining and ingenuously tuneful. The performances here are enthusiastic, and the recording vivid, though the violins tend to sound a bit under-nourished above the stave.

HAHN, Reynaldo (1875–1947)

Le Bal de Béatrice d'Este (ballet suite).
(BB) ★★★ Hyp. Helios CDH 55167. New L. O, Corp – POULENC: *Aubade; Sinfonietta.* ★★★

This excellent performance and recording of Hahn's charming pastiche is welcome back to the catalogue on Hyperion's budget label.

Nocturne in E flat for Violin and Piano; Piano Quartet No. 3 in G; Romance; Si mes vers avaient des ailes (trans. for cello and piano); Soliloque et Forlane for Viola and Piano; Violin Sonata in C.
★★★ Hyp. CDA 67391. Room-Music.

Recent years have brought a welcome resurgence of interest in Reynaldo Hahn, for we have had generous attention paid not only to the songs but also to such chamber works as the *F sharp minor Piano Quintet* and the *String Quartets*. Stephen Coombs, who is the pianist of Room-Music, has proved a persuasive advocate of the composer in the *Piano Concerto* and the *Quintet* (see our main volume) and here he plays with great sensitivity and intelligence. So, too, do his companions, the violinist Charles Sewart, violist

Yuko Inoe and Philip de Groote, cellist of the Chilingirian Quartet. The *C major Violin Sonata* of 1926 breathes much the same air as the Fauré of the *Piano Quartets* and the *A major Sonata*; and much the same goes for the shorter pieces: the *Romance* and the *Nocturne*. Both come from the first decade of the last century and the charming *Soliloque et Forlane* from 1936.

The *Piano Quartet No. 3* was composed on the composer's return to France.

He had been forced to flee Paris in 1940 as he was part-Jewish – though he was born in Venezuela – and he spent the war in the somewhat safer environment of Cannes. But this work reflects nothing of the darkness of the times. Its slow movement has all the enchantment of a balmy Mediterranean night. Jeremy Filsell's note speaks of the 'uncomplicated and radiant freshness' of Hahn's music. It has fluency and grace, and an innocent delight in life. Hahn's own transcription for cello and piano of the setting of Victor Hugo's *Si mes vers avaient des ailes*, which he had composed when he was thirteen, acts as a kind of encore to the recital.

PIANO MUSIC

L'Album d'un Voyageur: Orient. Premières Valses; Portraits de peintres, d'après les poésies de Marcel Proust; Sonatine.
** ProPiano 224538. Favre-Kahn.

Best known for the songs (and increasingly for his chamber music), Reynaldo Hahn composed prolifically for the piano, for which he wrote some 120 pieces, few of which have made it to the catalogue. There is a touching quality and an innocence about many of these salon pieces composed during the period 1898–1909, and Laure Favre-Kahn conveys their grace well. She comes from Arles and studied at conservatories in Avignon and Paris. Still in her mid-twenties, she attracted attention at Carnegie Hall in 2001, and this valuable CD was the result. Unfortunately, she is balanced far too closely and recorded in a claustrophobic studio environment, and the sound is a genuine handicap. Even played at a fairly low level, it is impossible to escape the bottom-heavy sound. This is a great pity, since this charming music and sensitive pianist deserve better. There are no alternatives except in the *Sonatine* and one of the *Portraits de peintres*. Although all the pieces are slight, the engaging *Ninette* or the simple yet affecting *Berceau* from the *Premières Valses* have tremendous charm, and the haunting *Watteau* portrait from the *Portraits de peintres, d'après les poésies de Marcel Proust* (in one way not recommended since, once heard, it is difficult to get out of one's head) makes this disc well worth getting. *En caïque* from the *Album d'un voyageur* shows much inventiveness and great feeling for the atmosphere of the Bosporus and the Middle East. Recommended, with the obvious caution about the sound but with no caution about the merits of the music or its interpreter.

HANDEL, George Frideric
(1685–1759)

Ballet Music: *Alcina: Overture; Acts I & III: Suites. Il pastor fido: Suite. Terpsichore: Suite.*
(M) *** Warner Elatus (ADD) 2564 60335-2. E. Bar. Sol., Gardiner.

John Eliot Gardiner is just the man for such a lightweight programme. He is not afraid to charm the ear, yet allegros are vigorous and rhythmically infectious. The bright and clean recorded sound adds to the sparkle and the quality is first class. A delightful collection, and very tuneful too.

Concerti grossi, Op. 3/1–6 (including) 4b, HWV 312–7.
(M) *** Warner Elatus (ADD/DDD) 2564 6028-2. VCM, Harnoncourt.

This Elatus set is among the most endearing of Harnoncourt's earlier, authentic performances of baroque music. In Op. 3, tempi tend to be relaxed, but the performances are very enjoyable in their easy-going way; the ripe, fresh colouring of the baroque oboes, played expertly and expressively, is most attractive to the ear, and the string-sound is unaggressive. The recordings were made in the Vienna Casino Zögernitz between 1971 and 1981. Curiously, string tuttis are a little dry, although the overall effect is quite spacious and the inner detail excellent. Not a first choice perhaps, but the whole effect is distinctive.

Concerti grossi, Op. 3/1–6; Concerto grosso in C (Alexander's Feast); (i) *Music for the Royal Fireworks; Water Music* (complete).
(BB) *(*) Virgin 2x1 5 61656-2 (2). Linde Consort; (i) with Cappella Coloniensis.

These are good, quite well-characterized performances, nicely recorded, but not much more than that. This repertoire is richly covered by excellent authentic and modern-instrument versions, so we must relegate this Virgin Double – despite its bargain price – to the second division.

(i) *Concerti grossi, Op. 3/1–6;* (ii) *Water Music: Suites 1–3.* (complete).
(B) ** Erato Ultima 3984 24243-2 (2). (i) Les Musiciens du Louvre, Minkowski; (ii) Amsterdam Bar. O, Koopman.

In Minkowski's set of the *Concerti grossi* the original wind instruments at times steal so much of the limelight from the strings that one has the impression that these are solo concertos for oboe or, in the case of No. 3, recorder and flute. In No. 6 the organ dominates. String textures are bright and transparent, with the lightest possible sonority, and the continuo comes through intimately. With brisk allegros that are always alert and vivacious, the effect here is of hearing a completely new series of concertos.

Koopman's approach to the *Water Music*, again using period instruments, also brings an individual approach. In the first, *F major Suite*, it is not until the third-movement *Allegro*, with the entry of the horns, that the music becomes robust. The second suite places elegance of style first and foremost, and the effect, engaging as it is in its way, seems more like eighteenth-century French court music. The opening of the third, *D major Suite* has a ceremonial feeling, but overall this has the character of a chamber performance.

Concerti grossi, Op. 6/1–10.
(B) **(*) EMI double forte (ADD) 5 73344-2 (2). Bath Festival CO, Menuhin.

(i) *Concerti grossi, Op. 6/11–12; Water Music (Suites 1–3; complete);* (ii) *Violin Sonatas, Op. 1/3, 10, 12–15.*
(B) **(*) EMI double forte (ADD) 5 73347-2 (2). (i) Bath Festival CO, Menuhin; (ii) Menuhin, Malcolm, Gauntlet.

Menuhin gave us the first complete stereo set of Op. 6 in the early 1960s, recording the later concertos first and working backwards. He used a modest body of strings, and during the sessions it was suggested to the artists that a double continuo might be used, as was Handel's practice. But this does not appear to happen until what was originally the third LP, containing Nos. 1, 2, 4, and 5 (in this reissue the works are presented in a straightforward numerical sequence). In consequence, the performances of the first two concertos – the last to be recorded – are the finest of the set, both buoyant and rich in expressive feeling; the harpsichord contribution comes through splendidly. In the later concertos the harpsichord continuo is too backwardly balanced. But they are still very enjoyable.

For the *Water Music* Menuhin used a new edition especially prepared by Neville Boyling, and his genial approach again demonstrates the humanity and freshness that always informed his music-making, with excellent playing and lively spontaneity throughout. Both recordings have been admirably transferred to CD. The Opus 1 *Violin Sonatas* were pioneering authentic versions, vital and stylish, using a well-balanced continuo (Ambrose Gauntlet, viola da gamba, and George Malcolm, harpsichord). But here the CD transfer makes Menuhin's violin-timbre sound slightly edgy. The 1963 Abbey Road recording is warm, fresh and clear in its new CD transfer.

Concerti grossi, Op. 6/1–4; Concerto grosso in C (Alexander's Feast).
* Virgin 5 45348-2. OAE, McGegan.

Nicholas McGegan's Virgin Veritas disc was the first instalment of a most enjoyable new period-instrument set; however, so far, the rest of the con-

certos have not materialized. Above all, the playing appealingly combines rhythmic vitality with a graceful warmth in slow movements, while Handel's fugal passages are spirited and joyous. The concertino (Elizabeth Wallfisch, Catherine Mackintosh, Alison Bury and Susan Sheppard) play most beautifully, without a suspicion of edginess. In the infectious account of the *Alexander's Feast Concerto*, the ripieno is further augmented, but textures remain fresh. The Abbey Road recording has just the right degree of resonance.

Concerti grossi, Op. 6/1, 2, 6, 7 & 10.
(B) **(*) HM HMA 1951507. Les Arts Florissants, Christie.

For some reason Christie also never completed his set of Op. 6, the present selection dating from 1995. The performances are vivid and athletic, helped by clean, transparent recording, with no lack of body and with the concertino and ripieno clearly defined. The playing in slow movements is refined and there is no lack of expressive feeling, but the overall result is less involving than with Turovsky and, although allegros are spirited, there is more to this music than these performers discover. First choice for a complete set of Handel's Op. 6 rests with I Musici di Montréal directed by Turovsky (⊖→ Chandos 9004/6).

Concerto grosso in G min., Op. 6/6; (i) *Il duello amoroso (HWV 2).*
(M) ***** DHM/BMG 82876 60157-2. Freiburg Bar. O, Von der Goltz; (i) with Argenta, Chance – PURCELL: *Dioclesian* excerpts. *****

As we know from their outstanding DVD of the Bach *Brandenburgs*, the Freiburg Baroque Orchestra is outstanding among period-instrument ensembles, and their account of the *G minor Concerto grosso* (using oboes as well as strings) is full of character. It acts here as an enticing prelude to Handel's Italian cantata, *Il duello amoroso*, probably written (in Rome) in 1708. Its engaging dialogue represents the efforts of the shepherd Daliso (Michael Chance) to win back his unfaithful beloved, the nymph Amarilli (Nancy Argenta). At the close she tells him abruptly, 'Don't beg for my love any more. No, you haven't got the torch to light my fire.' The performance of this light-hearted lovers' tussle is admirable and very well recorded.

(i) *Harpsichord Concerto, Op. 4/6. Suite No. 15: Air & Variations.*
(**(*)) Biddulph mono LHW 032. Landowska; (i) with O, Bigot – BACH: *Concerto No. 1 in D min.* (**); HAYDN: *Concerto in D, etc.* (***)

We more usually hear this concerto on the organ or harp, but Wanda Landowska makes a fairly good case for the harpsichord, although her predilection towards grandeur means that her presentation is on the heavy side. The *Air and Variations* is played with much character and is made to be every bit as memorable as *The Harmonious Blacksmith.* The recording is vivid throughout and very well transferred.

Organ Concertos: Op. 4/1–3; (i) Op. 4/4; (ii) Op. 4/6. Op. 7/1–6.

** Hyp. CDA 67291/2. Nicholson, Brandenburg Cons., Goodman; (i) with Clare College Ch., Cambridge; (ii) Kelly (harp).

Besides using Handel's own organ (still in excellent condition) in St Lawrence, Whitchurch, at Canons, near Edgware, north of London, the Nicholson–Goodman set offers a novelty in including Op. 4/4 in a 1737 version where Handel concluded the finale with an *Alleluia* chorus from *Athalia*, an eccentric idea that in the event is effective enough. Op. 4/6 is heard in the arrangement for harp, and the performance lacks charm. In any case the performances here are at times curiously didactic. The crisp rhythms with which these works abound and that should sound amiably jaunty, are often here just that bit too rigid. Both playing and recording are otherwise fresh, but the competition is fierce and this is far from a first choice, which rests with Koopman (⊕→ ⦿ Erato 0630 17871-2 – see our main *Guide*).

Organ Concertos, Op. 4/2; Op. 7/3–5; in F (The Cuckoo and the Nightingale).

(M) *** DG 447 300-2. Preston, E. Concert, Pinnock.

This is more generous than the previous (full-price) sampler from Preston's series with Pinnock. Both performances and sound are admirably fresh.

Music for the Royal Fireworks; Water Music (complete).

(BB) ** RCA 82876 55304-2. Paillard CO, Paillard.

Music for the Royal Fireworks; Water Music (complete); (i) Il trionfo del Tempo e del Disinganno: Sonata.

(B) ** CfP (ADD) 574 8812. Virtuosi & Wind Virtuosi of E., Davison; (i) with Kynaston (organ).

The Classics for Pleasure reissue of the complete *Water Music* is not only less expensive than many of its competitors but is a great deal more generous. It not only includes the *Fireworks Music,* but throws in for good measure the sonata that Handel wrote for his allegorical oratorio, *Il trionfo del Tempo e del Disinganno,* which is used to accompany Bellezza (who represents Beauty) when she is enticed into the Palace of Pleasure. It is an engaging miniature, with an obbligato organ part, and is given a very spirited account here. Davison employs additional wind for his performance of the *Royal Fireworks Music,* but the result rather lacks weight in the bass, although the playing is fresh and stylish and the recording crisply immediate. His authenticity of style is carried over into the *Water Music,* which is well played and recorded.

Re-recording the music digitally in 1990, Paillard

and his Chamber Orchestra fail to match the vitality and sparkle of their earlier, Erato analogue version. This is agreeable enough and is well recorded, but there is an element of routine in the playing. The earlier Apex is the one to go for (0927 48685-2 – see our main volume), but first choice for a modern instrument coupling of the *Fireworks* and *Water Music* rests with the Orpheus Chamber Orchestra on DG Entrée (474 166-2).

VOCAL MUSIC

Alexander's Feast; Concerto grosso in C (Op. 3/4b).

(M) ** Teldec (ADD) 3984 26796-2 (2). Palmer, Rolfe Johnson, Roberts, Stockholm Ch., VCM, Harnoncourt.

Harnoncourt's 1978 recording of *Alexander's Feast* is variably successful. The team of soloists is first rate, with Felicity Palmer, Anthony Rolfe Johnson and Stephen Roberts all stylish, although Palmer's line is not always even and Roberts is too light of voice for the magnificent *Revenge, Timotheus cries.* The Stockholm Choir is consistently lively, a splendid ensemble, and the Concentus Musicus play with excellent precision, but the edginess that comes with authentic performance of this vintage (the horns sound awkward) is often disconcerting, albeit generally well served by the recording. It also seems perverse to include the *Concerto grosso* from Op. 3 as a fill-up, rather than the obvious choice of the concerto that carries the name of the vocal work. This *is* included by Gardiner in his complete recording of the oratorio (Ph. 422 053-2 – see our main *Guide*).

(i; ii) Amarilli vezzosa (Il duello amoroso). Clori, mia bella Clori; (i) O come chiare e belle (Italian Cantatas).

(BB) *** Hyp. Helios CDH 55136. Kwella, L. Handel O, Darlow; with (i) Fisher, (ii) Denley.

The team that recorded the highly successful Hyperion issue of Handel's *Aminta e Fillide* here tackles three more cantatas from Handel's Italian period. The most ambitious work here is *O come chiare e belle,* a half-hour piece with allegorical overtones using three voices and written to compliment Pope Clement XI during the War of the Spanish Succession. As in most of the cantatas, some of the ideas are familiar from later versions, as in the aria, *Tornami a vagheggiar,* later used in *Alcina,* and here brilliantly sung by Gillian Fisher. The two shorter cantatas are equally charming, *Clori, mia bella Clori* for solo voice, the other a duet for soprano and contralto, well sung by Patrizia Kwella and Catherine Denley. Though Denys Darlow does not always lift rhythms enough, the freshness of the music is well caught.

Athalia (oratorio; complete).

(M) *** Decca 475 207-2 (2). Sutherland, Kirkby, Bowman, Jones, Rolfe Johnson, Thomas, New College, Oxford, Ch., AAM, Hogwood.

Hogwood's splendid set is cast from strength, with Dame Joan Sutherland's richly vibrant singing contrasting with the pure silver of Emma Kirkby, not to mention the celestial treble of Aled Jones in the role of the boy-king, Joas. Christopher Hogwood and his Academy are on top form too, and this recording, praised in our main volume, is now deservedly reissued as winner of *Gramophone*'s 1987 Choral Award.

Belshazzar (oratorio; complete).

⊶ (B) *** DG Trio 477 037-2 (3). Rolfe Johnson, Augér, Robbin, Bowman, Wilson-Johnson, E. Concert Ch. & O, Pinnock.

Handel modified *Belshazzar* over the years, and Pinnock has opted not for the earliest but for the most striking and fully developed text. The cast is starry, with Arleen Augér at her most ravishing as the Babylonian king's mother, Nitocris, Anthony Rolfe Johnson in the title-role, James Bowman as the prophet Daniel and Catherine Robbin as King Cyrus, all excellent. Full, well-balanced sound. This reissued Trio is a real bargain.

(i) *Coronation Anthems* (complete); **(ii)** *Dixit Dominus.*

(M) ** EMI Encore (ADD) 5 85454-2. King's College, Cambridge, Ch., ECO; (i) Ledger; (ii) Zylis-Gara, J. Baker, Lane, Tear, Shirley-Quirk, Willcocks.

Ledger (in 1982), using what by name are the same forces as his predecessor, Sir David Willcocks, on Decca, directs a reading that favours measured speeds, but though the choir is small the recording balance, in excellent digital sound, has the voices standing out clearly to reinforce the weight of the reading. This is a valid alternative version, for though it is perhaps not as exciting as its main competitors, it has both modern strings and admirable detail. *Dixit Dominus* was recorded a decade earlier, and this performance too is alive and spirited. But here one senses that the performers are not completely inside the work and the security that comes with complete familiarity is not always present. The intonation of the soloists is not above reproach, and the trio *Dominus a dextris* is not very comfortable, while the chorus seems not completely happy with the virtuoso running passages a little later. Willcocks might have achieved more security had he been content with a slightly slower pace. There is vigour and enthusiasm here but not always the last degree of finesse. The recording is atmospheric, and digital remastering has brought a sharper focus with hardly any loss of weight.

(i) *Funeral Anthem for Queen Caroline: The Ways of Zion do mourn;* **(ii)** *Utrech Te Deum.*

(BB) ** Warner Apex (ADD/DDD) 2564 61142-2. (i) Burrowes, Brett, Hill, Varcoe, Monteverdi Ch. & O, Gardiner; (ii) Palmer, Lipovšek, Langridge, Equiluz, Moser, Naumann, Arnold Schoenberg Ch., VCM, Harnoncourt.

Queen Caroline – whom Handel had known earlier as a princess in Hanover – was the most cultivated of the royal family of Hanover, and when she died in 1737 he was inspired to write a superb cantata in an Overture (Sinfonia) and eleven numbers. Gardiner directs a performance that brings out the high contrasts implicit in the music, making it energetic rather than elegiac. Excellent work from soloists, chorus and orchestra alike, all very well recorded. Handel later used the material for the first act of *Israel in Egypt*, and Erato have also coupled the piece with the complete recording of that work. However, here it is paired with the *Utrecht Te Deum*, which Handel wrote before coming to London, as a sample of his work. Harnoncourt's account offers a quite different style from Gardiner's, and in a relatively intimate acoustic he sometimes presents allegros briskly and lightly. But that is the exception; elsewhere speeds are slow and heavy, rhythms leaden, with the chorus efficient enough, but lacking the brightness and rhythmic spring that Gardiner finds in the companion work. The characterful solo singing – the murky-sounding contralto apart – makes some amends but the sound is dryish, and this cannot be counted one of Harnoncourt's more convincing ventures in the studio.

Messiah (complete).

(B) ** Virgin 5 62004-2 (2). Kirkby, Van Evera, Cable, Bowman, Cornwell, Thomas, Taverner Ch. & Players, Parrott.

(M) ** Westminster (ADD) 471 232-2 (3). Alarie, Merriman, Simoneau, Standen, V. Ac. Chamber Ch., V. State Op. O, Scherchen.

(B) * Teldec Ultima 0630 18952-2 (2). Gale, Lipovšek, Hollweg, Kennedy, Stockholm Chamber Ch., VCM, Harnoncourt.

Andrew Parrott assembled a fine team of performers, as well as his own Taverner Choir and Players, on his 1989 set. Emma Kirkby is even more responsive than she was on her earlier recording for Oiseau-Lyre; but, for all its merits, the performance lacks the zest and the sense of live communication that mark out a version like Pinnock's, another period performance that also dares to adopt slow, expressive speeds for such arias as *He was despised* and *I know that my Redeemer liveth*. Even at bargain price this is not a strong contender.

Hermann Scherchen's version is fascinatingly eccentric, notable for his erratic choice of tempi, and it is a pity that (because of a playing time of well over three hours) it comes on three mid-priced CDs, for it is a real collector's item. So we have *And the Glory of the Lord* slow and steady, while *And He shall purify* is so fast that it becomes a choral scramble, and *For unto us a Child is born* and *All we like sheep* are similarly brisk and lightly articulated, attractively so, but severely straining the resources of the Vienna Academy Choir. Scherchen has fine soloists, two of them outstanding. Beginning with a memorable

Ev'ry valley, Léopold Simoneau's tenor contribution is very fine indeed, and throughout there is some exquisite soprano singing from Pierrette Alarie. *I Know that my Redeemer liveth* is very slow but very pure and true, and wonderfully sustained, with the orchestral accompaniment partly restricted to soloists from the first desks. *Since by man came death*, which follows, sustains the rapt atmosphere, with a spurt of energy to follow, and Richard Standen's *The trumpet shall sound* is full of robust vigour. Nan Merriman sings most sensitively too, but not all will take to her close vibrato in *He was despised*. But when Scherchen is slow he is usually very slow and, while the effect is touching in *And with His stripes we are healed*, the adagio tempo for the closing *Amen* is grotesque, providing easily the longest performance on record – taking over eight minutes to reach its marmoreal conclusion. The 1959 recording, made in the Mozartsaal of the Vienna Konzerthaus, is excellent, spacious and well transferred, giving a natural bloom to the voices, a good overall balance and a warm-textured orchestral sound.

Nikolaus Harnoncourt's version was compiled from two public concerts in Stockholm in 1982, with ill-balanced sound that puts the choir at a distance, making it sound even duller than it is. With the exception of Elizabeth Gale, the soloists are poor, and Harnoncourt's direction lacks vigour. This cannot even begin to match Scherchen's version on Westminster, let alone the top recommendations. There are plenty of outstanding versions of *Messiah* toted in our main volume with Pinnock (DG 423 630-2) and Suzuki standing out (✿ BIS CD 891/892).

Ode for St Cecilia's Day.

(M) *** DG Blue 474 549-2. Lott, Rolfe Johnson, Ch. & E. Concert, Pinnock.

(BB) ** Naxos 8.554752. Mields, Wilde, Alsfelder Vokalensemble, Concerto Polacco, Helbich.

Trevor Pinnock's account of Handel's magnificent setting of Dryden's *Ode* comes near the ideal for a performance using period instruments. Not only is it crisp and lively, it has deep tenderness too, as in the lovely soprano aria *The complaining flute*, with Lisa Beznosiuk playing the flute obbligato most delicately in support of Felicity Lott's clear singing. Anthony Rolfe Johnson gives a robust yet stylish account of *The trumpet's loud clangour*, and the choir is excellent, very crisp of ensemble. Full, clear recording with voices vivid and immediate.

Recorded in a church in Templin, Germany, the Naxos version of the *St Cecilia Ode* brings a lightweight performance, marked by some sprightly singing and playing in faster movements but with some damagingly sluggish accounts of recitative and the central soprano aria, *What passion cannot music raise*, as well as the final aria with chorus, *As from the powers*. The most celebrated movement is the aria for tenor with chorus, *The trumpet's loud clangour*, and that is admirably bright and resilient, with its 'double

double double beat', with Mark Wilde the fresh, clear soloist. The bright, pure soprano is Dorothee Mields, and though the chorus is rather backwardly balanced, this adds to the liveliness of the two fast numbers to which it contributes.

Saul (oratorio; complete).

*** DG 474 510-2 (3). Neal Davies, Scholl, Padmore, Gritton, Argenta, Agnew, Lemalu, Gabrieli Consort and Players, McCreesh.

Central to the success of Paul McCreesh's version of *Saul* is the warmly characterful singing of the counter-tenor Andreas Scholl, in the role of David, in effect the central character in this dramatic oratorio even more than the king himself. McCreesh favours speeds on the fast side, only occasionally sounding too rushed, and his excellent cast responds well, with the chorus singing with crisp ensemble, strong and incisive. That said, none of the other soloists quite matches their counterparts on the rival Gardiner version on Philips (426 265-2 – see our main volume), a recording made live in Gottingen in 1989 and still sounding well, with an acoustic less reverberant than that of All Saints, Tooting, where this DG Archiv recording was made. So Neal Davies as Saul is less cleanly focused than Alastair Miles on Philips, and Neil Mackie is fresher and firmer as the High Priest than Paul Agnew here, while even Nancy Argenta as Saul's daughter, Michal, sounds less sweet than usual, hardly a match for Lynne Dawson on Philips. The tautness of McCreesh's direction and the precision of the choral singing, all the crisper in a studio performance, make it a strong alternative, but the Gardiner version remains first choice.

OPERA

Ariodante (complete).

(M) *** Ph. Trio (ADD) 473 955-2 (3). J. Baker, Mathis, Burrowes, Bowman, Rendall, Ramey, L. Voices, ECO, Leppard.

Leppard's strongly cast recording of *Ariodante*, with Dame Janet Baker outstanding in the title-role, now returns as a mid-priced Trio, which means that it is without a translated text, and a cued synopsis is offered as a poor alternative. In all other respects it is an outstanding set (discussed in our main volume).

Giulio Cesare (complete).

**(*) DG 474 210-2 (3). Mijanovic, Kožená, Von Otter, Hellekant, Bejun Mehta, Ewing, Bettini, Ankaoua, Musiciens du Louvre, Minkowski.

Minkowski's version of what is arguably Handel's greatest opera was recorded live at a concert performance in Vienna. That adds to the dramatic impact of a long and varied piece, helped by a strong and distinguished cast of soloists. As he establishes in the Overture, Minkowski prefers speeds on the fast side, sometimes very fast, with playing clear and clipped from the Musiciens du Louvre. That regularly sets a challenge to his singers as well as the players, very well taken. So Cleopatra's first aria in Act I sounds rushed despite the brilliant, characterful singing of Magdalena Kožena, and sadly her second Act I aria is cut. Otherwise, hers is a commanding performance, deeply moving in her big lyrical numbers, *V'adoro pupille* and *Piangero*, for which Minkowski allows full warmth and tenderness at aptly spacious speeds. Marijana Mijanovic sings powerfully in the title-role, with Anne Sofie von Otter a poised Sesto and Charlotte Hellekant a firm, clear Cornelia. This now provides a fair alternative to the outstanding Jacobs version on Harmonia Mundi (HMX 2901 385/7), which has a fuller text and a price advantage and is often more sympathetically paced, with Jennifer Larmore as Caesar and Bernarda Fink as Cornelia even more compelling than the singers here.

Imeneo (complete).

*** CPO 999 915-2 (2). Hallenberg, Stojkovic, Thornhill, Stiefermann, Chung, Cologne Vocal Ens., Capella Augustina, Spering.

This late opera by Handel, one of the last two Italian operas he ever wrote, has been inexplicably neglected on disc, and this lively version, recorded in Cologne in collaboration with West German Radio, admirably fills the gap, well sung and well played, even if Andreas Spering's direction brings some plodding continuo. The story is relatively simple, with Princess Rosmene saved from the pirates by Imeneo (the Italian for Hymen) and demanding her hand in reward, even though she is still in love with Tirinto. Gratitude prevails in the end over love, to the despair of Tirinto. The story inspires Handel to a sequence of fine numbers, notably for Rosmene and Tirinto. The scoring is light, with the story moving easily and with Rosmene in Act II given a fine, thoughtful arioso and later a stormy aria. Johanna Stojkovic sings strongly, bright and clear in the most taxing divisions, while Anna Hallenberg as Tirinto is equally commanding with her warm, firm mezzo, rising superbly to the challenge of her big showpiece aria, *Sorge nell'alma*, which anticipates *Why do the nations* in *Messiah*. Finer still is her tragic minor-key aria in Act III, *Pieno il core*, by far the most extended number. Also impessive is the trio for Rosmene and the rival suitors, while Rosmene's final aria is the most original of all, with curious stops and starts, and bald octave writing in the accompaniment. The original version of the text is used, with the role of Imeneo taken by a baritone – impressively sung by Kay Stiefermann – where Handel's revision for Dublin uses a tenor instead. Clear, well-balanced sound.

Semele (slightly abridged).

**(*) Pierre Vernay PV 704021/2 (2). De Niese, Miller, Innes, Laurens, Fournier, Agnew, Palacio, May, Opera Fuoco Ch. & O, Stern.

This new set of *Semele* from the French label Pierre Vernay, with a strong cast and period orchestra directed by the American David Stern, by rights should fill an obvious gap, but, like Gardiner's Erato set, it offers a cut text, with both of Athamas's arias cut, as well as a couple of choruses, Juno's aria in Act III and Cupid's delightful aria in Act II. Immediately in the Overture Stern reveals his preference for daringly fast speeds, with scampering triplets to challenge the players to the limit. It is very much the same with the vocal numbers following, when again high speeds are allied to a winning lightness of touch. This is helped by the intimate acoustic, with limited forces involved. One benefit is that the performance comes, like Gardiner's, on two discs instead of the three for Nelson's DG version using modern instruments, Acts I and II on the first disc (75 minutes) and Act III, longer than the other two, on the second disc (50 minutes).

Stern's cast may not be as characterful as those of its rivals, and half of the singers are Francophone rather than English-speaking. Yet the mezzo, Guillemette Laurens, makes a most striking Juno, totally convincing. One marvels at the idiomatic way she presents the formidable goddess as she uses her wiles to persuade Semele to make her life-threatening request to Jupiter: that he should appear to her not in human form but as a god. The bright, fresh-toned Danielle De Niese makes an innocent-sounding Semele, relishing the challenge of such big numbers as *Endless pleasure* at the end of Act I and *Myself I shall adore* in Act III. Though the microphone catches some shrillness in places, she is amazingly agile, apparently unfazed by Stern's hectic speeds. Paul Agnew as Jupiter offers similar virtuosity in coping with rapid divisions. Happily, as in Semele's sleep aria, the conductor relaxes persuasively for *Where'er you walk*. The others in the cast are comparably agile, though Susan Miller as Iris is unpleasantly edgy. Jonathan May doubles as both Cadmus and Somnus, more convincing in the latter role. The Scottish soprano Louise Innes, light and fresh as Semele's sister, Ino, makes her mark positively, and the warm-toned counter-tenor Sebastien Fournier, stylish as Athamas, makes one regret the loss of his arias. The excellent chorus is only twelve singers strong. An interesting and always refreshing alternative to existing versions. First choice still goes to Nelson's DG set (🔊 435 382-2).

VOCAL COLLECTIONS

Opera Arias from: *Agrippina; Orlando; Partenope; Rinaldo; Serse.*

(BB) **(*) Warner Apex 2564 60519-2. Horne, Sol. Ve., Scimone.

Here is a dazzling demonstration of Marilyn Horne singing a varied compilation of Handel arias to set beside her wider-ranging collection listed in our Vocal Recitals section, below. The flexibility of her voice in scales and trills and ornaments of every kind remains formidable, and the power is extraordinary down to the tangy chest-register. The voice is spotlit against a reverberant acoustic. Purists may quesion some of the ornamentation, but voice-fanciers will not worry.

HANSON, Howard (1896–1981)

Symphonies Nos. 1 in E min. (Nordic), Op. 21; 2 (Romantic), Op. 30; (i) Song of Democracy.
⊖→ *** Mercury (ADD) **SACD** 475 6181.
    Eastman-Rochester O, composer; (i) with Eastman School of Music Ch.

Mercury are bringing out some of their most admired recordings on SACD and, although they are not due to be released until after our book goes to press, we feel sure that listeners will want to be informed of their publication in the autumn of this year. Full reviews of the works listed above can be found in our current main edition. The new format should go some way to further enhance the already spectacular results afforded by the 'Living Presence' technology.

HARTMANN, Emil (1836–98)

(i) Cello Concerto in D min., Op. 26. Hakon Jarl (symphonic poem); Hærmædene på Helgeland: Overture.
**(*) Danacord DACOCD 508. (i) Dinitzen; Danish PO, South Jutland, Wallez – J.P.E. HARTMANN: *Overtures.* **(*)

Emil Hartmann was naturally overshadowed in Denmark by his father, Johann Peter Emilius, who, fearing accusations of nepotism, did virtually nothing to further his son's career. He studied first with his father in Copenhagen and then in Leipzig, subsequently becoming organist at the Christianborg Slotskirke (Palace Church). He made more of a name in Germany, particularly as a conductor, where three of his seven symphonies were performed. The *Cello Concerto* is a relatively short piece, perhaps reminiscent in style of Saint-Saëns. The disc also affords an opportunity for contrasting the two composers' approach to the overture: Emil's *Overture* to Ibsen's *Hærmædene på Helgeland* is probably the most successful here.

Piano Concerto in F min., Op. 47.
*(*) Danacord DACOCD 581. Marshev, Danish PO, South Jutland, Aeschbacher – WINDING: *Piano Concerto,* etc. **(*)

Emil Hartmann's *Piano Concerto*, composed in 1889, is perhaps less interesting than the *Cello Concerto* (reviewed above) and is too strongly reminiscent of Weber and Schumann to speak with a strongly individual voice. However, the Russian-born Oleg Mar-

shev plays with such ardour and authority (and is so well supported by the Danish orchestra) that one is almost persuaded that it is better than it is. Three stars for the pianist but not for the work, which comes with a concerto by his brother-in-law, August Winding.

HARTMANN, Johann Peter Emilius (1805–1900)

4 Caprices, Op. 18/1; 6 Characteerstykker med indledende Smaavers of H. C. Andersen, Op. 50; Etudes instructives, Op. 53; Fantasiestücke, Op. 54; 2 Pièces caractéristiques, Op. 25; 6 Tonstücke in Liederform, Op. 37.
**(*) dacapo 8.224162. Gade.

These miniatures by Niels Gade's long-lived father-in-law are well served by Nina Gade. This is not great music, but it has a certain period charm and has not been recorded before.

Overtures: En efterårsjagt, Op. 63b; Hakon Jarl, Op. 40.
**(*) Danacord DACOCD 508. Danish PO, South Jutland, Wallez – EMIL HARTMANN: *Cello Concerto,* etc. **(*)

Though little played nowadays, J. P. E. Hartmann composed one fine opera, *Liden Kirsti*, and wrote excellently for the orchestra. He became Niels Gade's father-in-law in the 1850s, and one of his descendants, albeit remotely, was Niels Viggo Bentzon. These two concert overtures make an admirable introduction to his work as well as a useful foil to the *Cello Concerto* by his son, Emil.

The Valkyrie, Op. 62.
** CPO 999 620-2 (2). Frankfurt RSO, Jurowski.

Written for Bournonville, Hartmann's ballet has a pretty lurid scenario, with plenty of blood and thunder. However, *The Valkyrie* remains curiously bland and tame, and its melodic ideas are obstinately unmemorable. Good playing and recording, and Bournonville fans will surely want it, but the music itself does not represent Hartmann at his best and we would hesitate to press its claims on non-specialists.

HARTY, Hamilton (1879–1941)

A Comedy Overture; (i) Piano Concerto; (ii) Violin Concerto; (iii) In Ireland (Fantasy); An Irish Symphony; (ii) Variations on a Dublin Air. With the Wild Geese. (iv) The Children of Lir; Ode to a Nightingale. Arrangement: The Londonderry Air.
(M) *** Chan. 10194X (3). (i) Binns; (ii) Holmes; (iii) Fleming, Kelly; (iv) Harper; Ulster O, Thomson.

Bryden Thomson's reissued box gathers togther Harty's orchestral and concertante works with great success. The *Piano Concerto* has strong Rachmaninovian influences, and if the *Violin Concerto* is less individual it is often touched with poetry. The *Irish Symphony*, built on traditional themes, is best known for its Scherzo, entitled *A Fair Day*, but it is brilliantly scored and enjoyable throughout, and the other works are all full of attractive Irishry. Performances are highly sympathetic and there is high standard of digital sound throughout. The three discs are no longer available separately.

HASSE, Johann (1699–1783)

(i; ii) *Aria 'Ah Dio, ritornate' from La conversione di San'Agostino* for viola da gamba and harpsichord; (iii; i; ii) *Flute Sonata in B min., Op. 2/6;* (ii) *Harpsichord Sonata in C min. Op. 7/6;* (iv; i-iii) Cantatas: *Fille, dolce mio bene; Quel vago seno, O Fille;* Venetian ballads: *Cos e' sta Cossa?; Grazie agli inganni tuoi; No ste' a condanare; Si' la gondola avere', non crie'.*

(M) *** CRD 3488. (i) Headley; (ii) Proud; (iii) Hadden; (iv) Baird.

The cantatas here are written in a pastoral style, with important flute obbligatos (a legacy from Frederick II). They show much charm and distinct expressive feeling, and Julianne Baird has exactly the right voice for them, with a freshness of tone and purity of line matched by the right degree of ardour. The *Harpsichord Sonata*, alternating fast and slow movements, is inventive and good-humoured, and the *Aria* for viola da gamba readily shows the composer's operatic style, while the Venetian ballads that close this elegantly performed and very well-recorded concert are also full of character, cultivated rather than folksy in their more popular idiom.

HAYDN, Josef (1732–1809)

Cello Concertos Nos. 1 in C; 2 in D, Hob VIIb/1–2.
**(*) Orfeo C08003iA. Müller-Schott, Australian CO, Tognetti – BEETHOVEN: *Romances Nos. 1 & 2.* **(*)
*(*) Transart TR 121. Haimovitz, O de Bretagne, Stefan Sanderling – MOZART: *Flute Concerto No.2* (arr. for cello). *(*)

The cellist Matt Haimovitz first came to prominence on disc in recordings of Lalo and Saint-Saëns concertos for DG with Levine and the Chicago Symphony Orchestra, and since then has done a number of solo recordings of twentieth-century works, also for DG. Here he gives impressive performances, recorded live, of the two Haydn *Cello Concertos*, marred by rhythmically stodgy playing in the slow movements and thin orchestral sound. Set in a dry acoustic, the sound exposes limitations in the playing of this chamber orchestra based in Brittany, here recorded in Rheims. Though this full-price issue cannot compare with the finest discs coupling the two Haydn concertos, it has the unique plus-point of offering as a bonus the first ever recording of George Szell's realization of Mozart's *D major Flute Concerto* as a cello concerto.

Daniel Müller-Schott is in his late twenties and hails from Munich, but he has already appeared as a soloist with most of the major European orchestras as well as the Philadelphia Orchestra. He is obviously a thoughtful and intelligent musician and he gives highly accomplished accounts of the *C major* and *D major Concertos* with the Australian Chamber Orchestra, led by Richard Tognetti. In both concertos he plays cadenzas he has written in collaboration with Heinrich Schiff and Steven Isserlis, who has placed his 1740 Venetian instrument by Domenico Montagnan at Müller-Schott's disposal. We do not care for the exaggerated *pianissimos* in which he indulges, but in other respects he is very stylish. He plays his own transcription of the two Beethoven *Romances* with an appropriate lyrical ardour. While these performances do not displace Isserlis (RCA 09026 68578-2), Wispelwey (CCS 7392) or Jacqueline du Pré (EMI 5 66896) as listed in our main volume, they have a lot going for them. The recordings, made in Nimbus's Monmouthshire studio, are very truthfully balanced. First choice remains with Steven Isserlis and Roger Norrington and they also include the *Sinfonia concertante* (⊕→ RCA 09026 68578-2).

(i) *Harpsichord Concerto in D, Hob XVIII/11. Sonata No. 36 in C sharp min.; Minuet; German Dance No. 5 (Ballo tedesco).*
(***) Biddulph mono LHW 032. Landowska; (i) with O, Bigot – BACH: *Harpsichord Concerto No. 1 in D min.* (**); HANDEL: *Concerto, Op. 4/6, etc.* (**(*))

With neatly scaled playing from Landowska, and a crisp, clean accompaniment from Bigot, the Haydn concerto is much more attractive than its heavyweight Bach coupling, and the encores too are very pleasing, especially the sharply rhythmic *German Dance*. The recording is surprisingly good (a bit thin on violin timbre, but not unpleasantly so) and this is a most refreshing view of Haydn, dating from 1937.

Piano Concertos: in F, Hob XVIII/3; in D, Hob XVIII/11.
(M) ** Guild GMCD 7206. Thew, Zürich Camerata, Tschupp – KUHN: *Concierto de Tenerife.* **

The Guild issue is a memorial to the American pianist Warren Thew, who lived in Zürich from 1956 until his untimely death in 1984. He was a composer and the author of around 200 poems in the Romansh language, which were published posthumously in 2000 to much acclaim. In the two Haydn concertos he is unfailingly musical and sensitive, though the Camerata Zürich is no match for the Norwegian Chamber Orchestra (and for Leif Ove Andsnes on EMI 5 56960-2). The recording from 1972 is acceptable and well balanced, but wanting in range and freshness.

(i) *Piano Concertos in G, F, & D, Hob XVIII/4, 7 &*
11. Piano Sonatas Nos. 33, Hob XVI/20; 60 (English),
Hob XVI/50; 62, Hob XVI/52; Andante & Variations
in F min., Hob XVII/6.

⊖➞ (BB) ★★★ Virgin 4-CD 5 62259-2 (4). Pletnev; (i)
Deutsche Kammerphilharmonie – MOZART: *Piano*
Concertos Nos. 9, 20, 23 & 24. ★★★

Of the three concertos recorded here, the *F major*,
Hob XVIII/7, is not authentic, and the early *G major*,
Hob XVIII/4, is also of doubtful provenance. In both
pieces, however, Mikhail Pletnev offers playing of
great character and personality. He obviously enjoys
a splendid rapport with the Deutsche Kammerphilharmonie, and the colour and feeling he discovers in
these pieces are still a source of wonder on
re-listening to the performances. The sonatas too are
full of personality and character. The *C major*, the
so-called *English Sonata*, is given with great elegance
and wit, and the great *E flat Sonata*, Hob XVI/52, is
magisterial. The playing has a masterly authority and
Pletnev is well recorded throughout. Now coupled in
a super-bargain box with hardly less memorable
accounts of four Mozart piano concertos, this is well
worth considering, even if duplication is involved.

Piano Concerto in D, Hob XVIII:11.

(M) ★★ EMI (ADD) 5 62823-2. Michelangeli, Zurich
CO, De Stoutz– MOZART: *Concertos Nos. 13 & 23.*
(★★)

Curiously detached playing from Michelangeli
diminishes the appeal of this reissue. The great pianist adds to the range of the keyboard and thickens
various chords. The piano tone could be fresher and,
despite the contribution of the Zurich orchestra
under Edmond de Stoutz, which is lively enough, this
issue cannot be counted a great success.

(i) *Trumpet Concerto in E flat. Sinfonia concertante.*

(BB) ★★★ DG (DDD/ADD) 474 567-2. COE, Abbado, (i)
with Herseth – VIVALDI: *The Four Seasons.* ★★★

Abbado conducts the Chamber Orchestra of Europe
in a winning performance of the *Sinfonia concertante*
– the violinist and cellist just as stylish as their wind
colleagues who have appeared as soloists on several
CDs – this issue even outshines other excellent versions from Vienna and London with more mature
soloists. The *Trumpet Concerto* is not quite in the
same class, lacking the last ounce of character; but it
is spirited enough, is well played and recorded and is
certainly enjoyable. The coupling is a highly distinguished account of Vivaldi's *Four Seasons*. For the
Trumpet Concerto, see under Håkan Hardenberger in
the Concerts section below (❂ Ph. Duo 464 028-2).

SYMPHONIES

The Nimbus complete set of Haydn Symphonies is
reissued on Brilliant Classics 9925 (33 CDs) at budget
price but the individual boxes are still available at

mid-price in their original formats and are discussed
and listed individually below.

Symphonies Nos. 1–20.

(M) ★★(★) Nim. NI 5426/30(5). Austro-Hungarian
Haydn O, Fischer.

The Nimbus project of recording all the Haydn symphonies on modern instruments in the Haydnsaal of
the Esterházy Palace brings playing that is fresh yet
warm, with the considerable reverberation adding to
the weight and scale of the earlier symphonies in a
manner that some ears will relish but others may
find too opulent. In the accompanying notes the
conductor, Adám Fischer, comments that the chosen
orchestra, which is made up of players from Vienna
and Budapest, carries forward the tradition of
Austro-Hungarian music-making. The playing itself
is warm and elegant, and time and again in these
early symphonies the ear enjoys the finesse of this
music-making and its ripeness of texture, with the
rich-toned Viennese horns soaring out over the
strings when given an opportunity to do so. The
woodwind are sprightly and offer plenty of colour,
and in Nos. 6–8 the various orchestral solos are taken
with distinction. The conductor's speeds are moderate. Slow movements are gracious and phrasing is
cultivated; minuets are courtly and finales lively and
resilient, without being rushed. The sound itself is
rich in ambience and easy to enjoy, for it does not
cloud.

Symphonies Nos 21; 22 (Philosopher); 23–5; 26
(Lamentatione); 28–9; 30 (Alleluia); 31 (Horn
Signal); 32–7; 38 (Echo); 39; Symphonies A & B.

❂ (M) ★★★ Nimbus NI 5683/7 (5). Austro-Hungarian
Haydn O, Fischer.

Adám Fischer's set of earlier Haydn symphonies caps
his achievement for Nimbus in a series of astonishingly perceptive performances, very strongly characterized, played with great finesse, with Fischer
showing a remarkable ear for detail. Many of these
works cannot be dated with certainty, although we
know that Nos. 21–24 were written in 1764. We can
sense Haydn continually experimenting with his
orchestral forces. Fischer gives all three on a chamber
scale, slow movements are delicate and graceful, and
allegros (taken fast) bubble over with vitality, notably
the finales, with brilliant writing for horns and
oboes. Indeed, so sharply pointed and vibrant are
allegros throughout this set that at times one feels
that Haydn's later *Sturm und Drang* period is being
anticipated.

The best-known work in this group, subtitled *Philosopher* (with its potent scoring of pairs of cor
anglais and horns), is outstanding, as is the later
account of the remarkable *Lamentatione* (No. 26)
with its raw emotional vitality and deeply expressive
Adagio. Nos. 28–31 can be dated to 1765. Each is
individual: there is brilliant trumpet playing to open
the *'Alleluja' Symphony* (the reason for the nickname

obvious), while in the *Horn Signal* the four horns blaze away gloriously. There are more exuberant horn contributions in Nos. 35 and 36, and 37 is all but dominated by the timpani. No. 38 is a particularly fine work, with a charming *Andante* with delicate echo effects, and virtuoso oboe parts in the Minuet's Trio, against economical string pizzicati.

Most striking of all is No. 39 (1766–7), with Haydn again using four horns dramatically. The opening movement with its false starts and a finale bursting with impetuous passion are clearly looking to the future. The superb orchestral playing throughout this set is something to revel in, and Adám Fischer's vital, imaginative approach ensures that there is not a dull bar anywhere. The transparent textures and sharp rhythmic springing (in the Minuets especially) bring a style of performance that has the best of both worlds, period and modern. The recording too is outstanding, full and clearly detailed.

Symphonies Nos. 40–54.

(M) *** Nim. NI 5530/4 (5). Austro-Hungarian Haydn O, Fischer.

In Volume 3 of his ongoing series, Adám Fischer homes in on the *Sturm und Drang* works, but he is working in numerical order, so he includes one or two other symphonies, though none that is not full of stimulating ideas (the theme and variations that forms the *Andante* of *L'Imperiale* is sheer delight). The orchestral playing is consistently warm and committed and of course there is none of the astringency of texture one expects with Hogwood, or squeezed violin phrasing that Brüggen and others insist is authentic. The result is richly enjoyable, and slow movements in particular consistently gain from such a dedicated orchestral response. The *Adagio* opening of *La Passione* is gentle yet intensely concentrated in feeling, and the following *Allegro di molto* is crisp, fast and biting. Minuets are faster and racier than with Dorati, with plenty of dynamic contrasts – and finales, if helter-skelter, still retain an elegant poise. The unnamed *C major Symphony* (No. 50) and the following *B flat major* work are among the finest performances here, splendidly characterful – and in the *Adagio* of the latter there is a glorious horn solo, followed by the graceful *Allegretto* finale. The Viennese elegance of phrasing, and polish combined with sparkle, often reminds one of Beecham in its friendly listener-appeal. The recording is first class, full and warm, with a natural concert-hall ambience.

Symphonies Nos. 43; 44; 49; 52 in C min.; 59; 64 (Tempora mutantur).

(B) *** Nim. NI 7072/3 (2). Austro-Hungarian Haydn O, Fischer.

This Nimbus Double, centring on the *Sturm und Drang* era, makes a splendid sampler for Adám Fischer's Haydn cycle, played on modern instruments. Fischer is often at his most imaginatively

persuasive in these works, and both orchestral playing and recording are first class. The slow movements of the *Mercury* and *Trauer* symphonies are both very beautiful, while the *Adagio* opening of *La Passione* is gentle yet intensely concentrated in feeling, and the following *Allegro di molto* is crisp, fast and biting. In the notes we are told by David Threasher that the nickname of No. 64 (*Tempora mutantur*) is based on a couplet by the Welsh epigrammist John Owen, which was used as an inscription on clocks and sundials.

Symphonies Nos. 55–69.

(M) *** Nim. NI 5590/4 (5). Austro-Hungarian Haydn O, Fischer.

With Adám Fischer a dedicated advocate, inspiring fresh, persuasive playing from his hand-picked orchestra, there is no slackening of standards in this fourth volume of Nimbus's Haydn cycle. This group of works follows up the *Sturm und Drang* sequence with symphonies regularly related to Haydn's theatre music, at times with eccentric effects, as in the six-movement *Il distratto*, No. 60, or No. 67 with its *col legno* and hurdy-gurdy effects. In the helpful acoustic of the Haydnsaal of the Esterházy Palace at Eisenstadt, the sound is at once warmly atmospheric and intimate, with high contrasts of dynamic and texture. Continuing to use modern rather than period instruments, but with limited string vibrato and with Viennese oboes and horns standing out distinctively, these are recordings to challenge the long-time supremacy of Dorati's pioneering Decca set. In important ways, not just in the extra fullness of the digital sound, the new performances improve on the old, notably in the brisker speeds for Minuets. Fischer generally tends to prefer speeds in slow movements a fraction more flowing than those of Dorati, while outer movements are regularly a degree more relaxed. Thanks to Fischer's springing of rhythm, speeds never drag, even if those dedicated to period practice might well prefer the more hectic *Prestos* and *Prestissimos* of the earlier set. These are performances that register Haydn's humour more clearly, even in the *Sturm und Drang* symphonies here, Nos. 58 and 59 (*The Fire*).

Symphonies Nos. 70–81.

*** Nim. NI 5652/5 (4). Austro-Hungarian Haydn O, Fischer.

With the exception of No. 72, which probably dates from the 1760s, Volume 5 of Adám Fischer's ever more attractive survey contains works written more or less consecutively during a compact period of just over four years (1778–82). Robbins Landon has emphasized that generally these are much more courtly works than their *Sturm und Drang* predecessors, and No. 79 is a characteristically elegant example.

No. 70 is not. It opens very dramatically and bursts with energy, then changes mood completely, before its minor-key slow movement, which is a set of double variations. The brilliantly contrapuntal finale, based on a repeated note motif, also opens in the minor key and develops into a remarkable triple fugue. No. 71 brings another striking opening movement, which may have been written earlier than the other three, and also has a very beautiful *Adagio*.

Symphony No. 72 immediately recalls the *Horn Signal Symphony*, and the scoring for four horns is certainly virtuosic, with bravura upward scales and roulades in the first movement, which even today remain fiendishly difficult. The *Andante* is a concertante movement featuring solo violin and flute, and the finale, another *Andante*, offers more solo playing (including a double-bass contribution) within an enchanting set of variations. No. 73 is the best known. Its slow movement offers more variations, this time on a song, *Gegenliebe*. The finale with its main hunting theme on horns and trumpet gives the symphony its title (*La Chasse*).

But what will continually strike the non-specialist listener when listening through these ever-diverting works is their wide range of mood, particularly in the two minor-key symphonies (Nos. 78 and 80). Development sections give a flashing reminder of Haydn's most concentrated manner. Kaleidoscopic sequences of keys whirl the argument in unexpected directions (especially in No. 80), while slow movements are winningly diverse. The *Adagio cantabile* of No. 74, the *Poco Adagio (Andante con variazioni)* of No. 75, the *Adagio* of No. 76 and the memorable flowing melody of No. 77 are all highly rewarding examples.

Haydn was incapable of being boring, and some of these works are in every way remarkable in their forward-looking progressions, often anticipating Mozart's most visionary works. The modern-instrument performances here combine vitality, intensity and warmth in ideal proportions, and the recording reveals the full detail of Haydn's very felicitous scoring, besides having an attractive overall bloom.

Symphonies Nos. 82–87 (Paris Symphonies).

(M) **(*) Nim. NI 5419/20 (2). Austro-Hungarian Haydn O, Fischer.

The expansive sound of the Austro-Hungarian Orchestra suits the *Paris Symphonies*. *La Poule* and *La Reine* (with its rhythmically powerful opening movement) both show Fischer and his players at their best, and finest of all is one of the least known, *Symphony No. 84 in E flat*, with another remarkably original first movement. Slow movements are warm and poised: the *Largo* of No. 86 is particularly successful, as is the light-hearted trio of its Minuet, with a vigorous finale, lightly articulated, to round the work off. The sound is always satisfyingly full-bodied, with the violins resonantly rich. The weighty bass is not always absolutely clean, but generally the effect is very believable.

Symphonies Nos. 88–92; Sinfonia concertante in B flat for Violin, Cello, Oboe, Bassoon & Orchestra.

(M) ** Nim. NI 5417/8 (2). Austro-Hungarian Haydn O, Fischer.

As with the other issues in this Nimbus series, the recording is full and pleasing, but here the warm resonance prevents sharpness of detail and also has the effect of blunting the string articulation. Too often one feels the need for more bite in Allegros. Tempi are almost always relaxed, so that the famous slow movement of *No. 88 in G*, warmly expressive as it is, very nearly drags, although Fischer brings off the *Adagio* of the *Oxford Symphony* beautifully. Throughout, Minuets are very stately indeed, but finales dance gracefully and opening *Adagios* are warmly expressive; yet in the end there is an absence of conveyed exhilaration. The *Sinfonia concertante* included on the second disc is a particularly pleasing performance, with most sympathetic solo playing.

Symphonies Nos. 93–104 (London Symphonies).

(M) **(*) Nim. NI 5200/4 (5). Austro-Hungarian Haydn O, Fischer.

With three symphonies apiece on the first two discs of the five-disc Nimbus set, Fischer's cycle of all twelve *London Symphonies* makes a neat and attractive package, with consistently fresh, resilient and refined performances. Though these works were first given in the intimate surroundings of the Hanover Square Rooms in London, they were very quickly heard in this much grander setting, and the performances reflect the fact, with broad speeds and weighty tuttis made weightier by the reverberant Nimbus recording. Such a movement as the lovely *Adagio* of No. 102 with its soaring melody is given added beauty by the ambience and slow speed. The set can be warmly recommended to most who resist period performance when, even at broad speeds, rhythms are light and resilient. Never sounding breathless, Fischer's Haydn consistently brings out the happiness of the inspiration. These are very much performances to relax with.

Other miscellaneous symphonies

Symphonies Nos. 22 in E flat (Philosopher); 23 in G; 24 in D; 25 in C.

(BB) *** Hyp. Helios CDH 55116. Hanover Band, Goodman.

Goodman's account of the *Philosopher*, with its pair of cor anglais, is predictably bold and rhythmic, with an exhilarating finale (superb horn triplets!) to cap what has gone before. Opening No. 23 with horn whoops, Haydn seems determined that its first movement should not fall flat after that famously spectacular work, and the four-note groups that dominate the finale have a similar rhythmic sharpness. The dramatic contrasts of the first movement of No. 24 are offset by a delicate Adagio with a cantabile flute solo. No. 25 has a briefly pensive introduction but is most notable for its hectic final Presto. Again brilliant, highly persuasive performances and excellent recording.

Symphonies Nos. 30 in C (Alleluja); 53 in D (L'Imperiale); 69 in C (Loudon).

⊕━ (BB) ★★★ Warner Apex 2564 60520-2. VCM, Harnoncourt.

Here is another outstandingly vibrant Harnoncourt triptych of named Haydn symphonies to set beside his Elatus disc of Nos. 31, 59 and 73 (2564 60033-2 – see our main volume). The first movement of No. 30 is based on an *Alleluia* that formed part of the Mass for Easter week. The work features unusually prominent writing for the trumpets in the outer movements, and in the charming *Andante* there are important solo parts for flute and oboes, played most delicately here. No. 53 has a vigorous first movement with dancing strings, and the *Andante* features characteristically inventive variations on one of the composer's most engaging themes. The finale recorded here, although effectively vigorous, is comparatively straightforward and (according to Robbins Landon) may not have been Haydn's own composition, but written by a pupil under the composer's surpervision. Yet in Harnoncourt's hands it makes a convincing conclusion.

The sobriquet of No. 69, *Loudon*, was appended by Haydn himself and celebrates a highly successful field marshal of that name. The vigorous rhythms of the opening movement certainly have a military flavour, yet the slow movement (*Un poco adagio, più tosto Andante*) has a contrasting elegant gentility. But it is the unpredictable finale with its fiercely contrasting dynamics (and a violin solo to introduce the return of the main theme) that gives the work its individuality. All three performances here are quite splendid, with outstandingly brilliant playing from the Vienna strings. This is music-making that makes an unanswerable case for playing Haydn on period instruments. The recording is first class, the resonant acoustic seems just right.

Symphonies Nos. (i) 44 (Mourning); 45 (Farewell); 49 (La Passione); (ii) 55 (Schoolmaster); 80; (i) 88; 92 (Oxford); 93; 94 (Surprise); 95; (i) 96 (Miracle); (ii) 97; (i) 98; 99; (ii) 100 (Military); (i) 101 (Clock); (ii) 102; 103 (Drum Roll); 104 (London).

(M) (★) DG mono/stereo 471 256-2. (i) V. State Op. O; (ii) VSO; Scherchen.

Haydn and his fans owe much to Westminster Records and Hermann Scherchen for recording so much of Haydn's music at a time when there was comparatively little available. The bulk of this set was recorded between 1950 and 1953, the exception being the stereo recording of No. 45; the quality of the sound is generally good throughout for its period, all reasonably full and warm and well balanced. As for the performances, they will appeal mainly (possibly only) to Hermann Scherchen fans. With Haydn, this

conductor's usual trick of playing the fast movements very fast and the slow very slow has been tapered (slightly). Be that as it may, the introduction of No. 99 is still slow, but the ensuing allegro is up to 'authentic' speeds, if not to the best precision of execution. The finale of the *Clock*, though, seems extremely slow by today's standards (the 'tick-tock' in the slow movement needs a good wind-up too); in fact, the slow movements in general are too slow for modern ears, as are the Minuets, not to mention the slow introductions: a presentiment that ponderousness is never far away. The fast passages generally come off best, and when things click into place – as in the *Military Symphony* (described overenthusiastically on the box as the 'Classic' account) – the music-making comes to life. But what makes this set unrecommendable is the general quality of the orchestral playing; like many European orchestras during this time, they still hadn't quite recovered from the ravages of the war: the intonation of the woodwind and brass is often vague, to say the least, and the string playing is far from the last word in precision. The opening movement of No. 102 produces some really uningratiating sounds, with very tatty playing indeed, and that is by no means an isolated example. The stereo *Farewell Symphony*, in good sound, offers better orchestral playing and is perhaps the best performance here; in the famous finale, each player says 'Auf Wiedersehen' as he leaves – a nice touch – but not enough to recommend this set, in which much of the playing is simply not acceptable by modern standards.

Symphonies Nos. 82 (The Bear); 83 (The Hen); 84; 85 (La Reine); 86; 87 (Paris).

(B) ★★ Decca (ADD) 470 062-2 (2). SRO, Ansermet.

(M) ★★ Sony (ADD) SM2K 89566 (2). NYPO, Bernstein.

Both Ansermet and Bernstein offer traditional, pre-authentic, yet certainly individual accounts of the six *Paris Symphonies*. Ansermet directs strong, direct readings, a touch cool, with the Minuets weightier than we expect today, but with the outer-movement Allegros robustly spirited. The Swiss conductor is always stimulating to hear in matters of detail, and the performances have plenty of character, showing his commitment to the composer. Accepting that the SRO does not possess the finesse of the VPO, this set will reward the conductor's admirers (and perhaps surprise others), especially as the 1962 sound is warm and vivid and the price modest.

Bernstein offers equally characterful performances, full of life and zest, with greater warmth and more sophisticated orchestral playing than Ansermet's. Bernstein has greater dynamic nuance too, and again shows much attention to detail. The main snag is the recording, which, though basically full and vivid, offers rather strident strings when under pressure, and the whole sound-picture is not as ingratiating as the Decca set. At mid-price, it is hardly a bargain, nor do Sony opt for the more convenient slim-line packaging.

Symphonies Nos. 85 in B flat (La Reine); 86 in D.
(BB) **(*) Warner Apex 2564 60451-2. St Paul CO, Wolff.

The excellent St Paul Chamber Orchestra give polished, animated accounts of two of the finest *Paris Symphonies*. No. 85 *(La Reine)* includes the slow-movement variations on *'La petite gentille et jeune Lisette'*, so admired by Queen Marie-Antoinette, here played most elegantly. The *Capriccio* slow movement of No. 86 is perhaps a little staid, but the finale is infectiously spirited. Excellent, natural recording with the concert-hall acoustic on the resonant side, adding to the weight of the first movement of the D major work.

Symphonies Nos. 88–91; 92 (Oxford).
(BB) ** Virgin 2×1 5 61567-2 (2). La Petite Bande, Kuijken.

Kuijken's performances of this nicely balanced group of key Haydn symphonies have many of the qualities that made his set of the *Paris Symphonies*, also on Virgin, so winning. Yet with a gap of two years, and a change of orchestra to La Petite Bande, come differences that weigh significantly against this reissue. For these rather later symphonies, Kuijken has abandoned the use of harpsichord continuo, and his preference for very measured speeds in slow movements leads him to at least one serious miscalculation. At a funereal pace he makes the heavenly *Largo* of No. 88 far too heavy, seriously holding up the flow of the great melody with over-emphasis and exaggerated pauses. The sound is warm and well balanced, though violins could be better defined in tuttis; but overall this is something of a disappointment when compared with Kuijken's earlier achievement.

Symphony No. 92 (Oxford); (i) Arianna a Naxos (Cantata); Scena di Berenice.
(*) BBC Opus Art **DVD OA 0831 D. (i) Bartoli; VCM, Harnoncourt at the 2001 Syriarte Festival, Graz, Austria (includes discussion of the music of Haydn between Bartoli and Harnoncourt, and a brief depiction of the Festival) (TV Director: Brian Large).

We already have a Decca recording of *Arianna a Naxos* by Cecilia Bartoli with András Schiff, but this splendidly sung version with string accompaniment is even more telling, even though the orchestral transcription was not Haydn's own. Moreover, the performance is especially vivid in the singer's visual presence, while Harnoncourt accompanies with great sensitivity.

The equally inspired *Scena di Berenice* is set to a text taken from Metastasio's *Antigono*. It has a direct affinity with *Arianna*, as its heroine has to come to terms with the fatal wounding of her lover and asks God to increase her suffering so that death will claim her. Bartoli's performance is again very moving, and

is most expressively accompanied. The two vocal items are preceded by a vibrant performance of Haydn's *Oxford Symphony* which, like *Arianna*, was very well received during Haydn's visits to London in the 1790s. This is a characteristic Harnoncourt performance with a rather gruff, even abrasive, first movement that not all will take to. He is more persuasive in the central movements, and the sparkling finale is a joy. Certainly the performance gains from watching the conductor, whose facial expressions are so mobile; and in Brian Large's directions the camerawork cannot be faulted. The bonuses include a fascinating dialogue between the conductor and singer, who discuss Haydn and his music, and a brief look at the Festival founded by Harnoncourt in Graz, with a little music from a novel instrumental group.

Symphonies Nos. 94 (Surprise); 96 (Miracle); 103 (Drum Roll).
(M) **(*) Warner Elatus 2564 60337-2. Concg. O, Harnoncourt.

Symphonies Nos. 95 in C min.; 97 in C; 98 in B flat.
(M) *** Warner Elatus 2564 60438-2. Concg. O, Harnoncourt.

Harnoncourt is nothing if not wide-ranging in his Haydn interpretations: the vigorous and polished Concertgebouw playing, with hard-driven allegros and contrasting moments of great delicacy, is certainly never dull. Although the readings bring characteristic gruffness, they have great character. Accents are stronger than ever, and in the *Andante* of the *Surprise*, after the orchestra has fined down to a *pianissimo* for the repetition of the opening phrase, not only is there one loud explosive interruption, but others follow, and the climax is spectacular. Then the Minuet whirls along at a forceful, rhythmic one-in-a-bar. If one accepts the sheer weight of the *fortissimo* tuttis, the *Miracle* is another impressive reading, with the secondary theme of the opening movement elegant enough. Here the Minuet is not pressed as hard, with the fizzing energy released in the finale. Nos. 97 and 98 are similarly compelling. The most notable eccentricity is at the opening of the *Drum Roll*, which is an arresting volley of 'drumshots', which return at the close of the movement, not at all what Haydn intended! Yet the performance overall combines characteristic vigour with moments of graciousness. (This reissue replaces Ultima 3984 21337-2, listed in our main *Guide*.)

Symphonies Nos. 93–104 (London Symphonies).
(B) **(*) Decca 475 551-2 (4). LPO, Solti.

A very welcome return to Solti's survey of the *London Symphonies*. While Solti's way is very different from Beecham's and he can be a bit uptight for Haydn, some of these works really glow in his hands, with the coupling of Nos. 93 and 99 (recorded in 1987) proving the pick of the set. (They received a ❂

from us on their initial release.) Solti's manner in this pairing is sunny and civilized; there is no lack of brilliance – indeed, the LPO are consistently on their toes – but the music-making is infectious rather than hard-driven. The lovely slow movement of No. 93 has both delicacy and gravitas, and that of No. 99 is serenely spacious. The Minuets are shown to have quite different characters, and the finales sparkle in the happiest manner. However, the earliest symphonies recorded (1981) were the *Miracle* and the *Clock*, and, although brilliantly played, they were rather too taut to convey all Haydn's charm. Again, in Nos. 102 and 103, recorded a year later, even though the beauty and refinement of the LPO and the fine Decca recording cannot help but give pleasure, the tensions speak of the twentieth century rather than the eighteenth, with even the lovely *Adagio* of No. 102 failing quite to relax. In the *Surprise* and *Military Symphonies* (recorded in 1984), the conductor again stresses the brilliance and fire of the outer movements, which are a bit hard-driven, but there is no lack of *joie de vivre*. The recordings, hitherto excellent, here approach demonstration standard in fullness and transparency, and this is even more striking in Nos. 95 and 104. Here (in 1986), Solti found the perfect balance between energy and repose. The pacing is admirable and the LPO playing is smiling and elegant, yet full of bubbling vitality. No. 95 has a striking sense of cohesion and purpose, and there are few finer versions of No. 104. Throughout, Solti uses a full body of strings and all the resources of modern wind instruments with the greatest possible finesse, yet the spontaneity of the music-making is paramount. The final release, of Nos. 97 and 98, was in 1992, and maintained the balance between Solti's boundless energy and Haydn's warmth and humour. The twelve symphonies, now released in a bargain box (on four instead of five CDs), makes a very attractive set, for the qualities of the playing outweigh the points of criticism, and this is music-making of strong personality.

Symphonies Nos. 93–98 (London Symphonies).

☺– (BB) *** EMI mono Gemini (ADD) 5 85770-2 (2). RPO, Beecham.

This first collection is of Beecham's earlier mono recordings; they sound admirably full-bodied and have been transferred amazingly successfully, and we see no reason to put brackets round the stars. The performances are just as sensitive and invigorating as the later ones, below.

Symphonies Nos. 99–104 (London Symphonies).

☺– (BB) *** EMI Gemini (ADD) 5 85513-2 (2). RPO, Beecham.

The art of phrasing is one of the prime secrets of great music-making, and no detail in Beecham's performances of the *London Symphonies* goes unattended. They have also great warmth, drama too, and perhaps a unique geniality. The sound throughout is

full and fresh (it's the 1992 remastering), with plenty of body, sweet violin-timbre and no edge. The performances possess an inner life and vitality that put them in a class of their own and are wonderful value in this bargain Gemini-double format.

Symphonies Nos. 99 in E flat; 101 in D (Clock).

(M) **(*) Warner Elatus 2564 61175-2. Cong. O, Harnoncourt.

An effective recoupling. Although the interpretations still have their eccentricities – the opening to the finale of the *Clock*, for instance, is surprisingly slack – this is Harnoncourt's Haydn at its most stimulating. In period-performance style, first movements are fierce and emphatic, and Minuets are treated as Scherzos with rhythms clipped, but their Trios are full of character. The *Adagio* of No. 99 is leisurely but well sustained and beautifully played (woodwind as well as strings distinguish themselves throughout both works), and the *Andante* of the *Clock* is genially relaxed. Excellent recording, with the Concertgebouw acoustic adding weight.

Symphonies Nos. 102 in B flat; 104 in D (London).

(M) ** Warner Elatus 2564 60659-2. Concg. O, Harnoncourt.

Harnoncourt's eccentricity rears its head in this coupling of two of Haydn's late and great symphonies. In period-performance style, the first movements of both symphonies are fierce and emphatic, and the glorious *Adagio* of No. 102 is clipped and short winded. The Minuets of both symphonies are strongly accented and are treated briskly like Scherzos. Yet the opening of the Trio of No. 102 is surprisingly slack. While this is music-making of a powerful persuasion, very well played and recorded, it cannot receive a strong general recommendation.

CHAMBER MUSIC

8 Notturni for the King of Naples, Hob II/25–32 (Nos. 1–6 only, Hob II/25–6; 29–32)

(M) ** CPO 999 741-2. Consortium Classicum, Klöcker.

These eight divertimenti, in three or four movements (although No. 6 has only two), were commissioned by King Ferdinand IV of Naples and written for the lira organizzata or, rather, a pair of them, for the king played in duet with his friend Norbert Hadrava, an Austrian diplomat. The lira comprised a keyboard and a revolving wheel and was really a modified hurdy-gurdy. It seems a pity that someone could not have managed a reconstruction of this seemingly fascinating instrument. Haydn's original scoring was for two lire, two horns, two clarinets (or, later, violins), two violas, and cello (later with double-bass added). He thought sufficiently well of the works and brought them to London with him to play at the Salomon Concerts in 1791, with the lira parts given to flutes, or flute and oboe, and the clarinet parts for practical reasons allotted to violins, which also have independent solo roles in Nos. 7 and 8. This is the nearest Haydn came to writing wind divertimenti of the calibre of those by Mozart, and although this music is slight, it has much charm, with particularly sprightly finales, including a jolly fugue for No. 5. (The last movement of No. 6 is lost, although the engaging *Andante* makes up for it.) No. 8 with a slow introduction before the first-movement *Allegro* is like a miniature symphony without a minuet, and H. C. Robbins Landon has declared the touching *Adagio* as being the greatest single movement of the whole set.

Dieter Klöcker on CPO gets round the textural problem by using a pair of chamber organs placed to the left and right of his wind and string ensemble (two violas and a double-bass), to give an antiphonal effect. The result is piquantly appealing at first, but the continuing use of the upper range of the organs loses its novelty after a time, although the music-making itself is elegant and pleasing. In any case this CPO set is incomplete.

String quartets

String Quartets Nos. 44–49, Op. 50/1–6.

⊕→ * ASV Gold GLD 4007 (1–3); GLD 4008 (4–6). The Lindsays.

The Lindsays' set of Op. 50, superbly played and recorded, arrived just as we were going to press. Their approach is less mellow, less affectionate than that of the Kodály Quartet (Naxos 8.553983/4) who are not surpassed, but the playing is very stimulating indeed.

String Quartets Nos. 57–59, Op. 54/1–3.

***** HM Aeon AECD 0313, Ysaÿe Qt.

These Ysaÿe performances can rank with the very best. Playing and ensemble are first class and there is plenty of warmth: the *Adagio* of the *C major*, Op. 54/2, is particularly fine, and the finale is most impressively handled. The slow movement of the *E major*, too, is beautifully judged, and the finale is both graceful and spirited. Excellent, well-balanced recording and a friendly atmosphere to make this a most enjoyable disc.

String Quartets Nos. 63, 65 & 68, Op. 64/1, 3 & 6.

***** Astrée E 8886. Mosaïques Qt.

Immaculate period-instrument performances from the Mosaïques, with absolutely no rough edges. They are beautifully played in every respect, but are a little cool by the side of the Lindsays. However, admirers of 'authentic' Haydn will find this well up to standard, and the recording is very lifelike.

String Quartets Nos. 67 in D (Lark), Op. 64/5; 76 in D min. (Fifths), Op. 76/2; No. 81 in G, Op. 77/1.

⊕→ * HM HMC 901823. Jesusalem Qt.

The Jerusalem Quartet is a first-class group and they give outstanding performances of these three master-pieces. In the *D major*, the 'Lark' soars aloft sweetly and disarmingly, and after a beautifully played *Adagio* the finale has the lightest possible touch. The first movement of the *Fifths* is faster than usual, but convincingly so, and the following *Andante* is delightfully elegant. Similarly, the opening movement of the *G major* dances along with engaging rhythmic pointing, and the *Adagio* that follows is comparably searching. The recording is beautifully balanced and sounds very real in a most suitable acoustic. Highly recommended (alongside the Lindsays on ASV).

String Quartet No. 74 in G min., Op. 74/3.

(M) ***** Cal. Approche CAL 5242. Talich Qt –
MOZART: *String Quartets Nos. 16 & 17.* *****

The *Quartet in G minor*, Op. 74/3 (dedicated to Count Apponyi), is one of Haydn's greatest quartets. It brings a very beautiful, serenely introspective *Largo assai* in which, in this searching Talich performance, one has the feeling of eavesdropping on private music-making. After the blithe Minuet, the finale is engagingly light and spirited. Superb playing and most natural recording, which applies also to the Mozart coupling.

String Quartets Nos. 75–80, Op. 76/1–6; 81–2, Op. 77/1–2; 83, Op. 103.

(M) ***** DG (ADD) Trio 471 762-2 (3). Amadeus Qt.

Haydn's late quartets have much the same expansiveness and depth as the symphonies, and here the Amadeus succeed in conveying both their intimacy and their sense of scale. The recordings are bright and truthful. Those who invest in this Trio will find much to reward them, though in Op. 76 the Kodály Quartet are even finer. However, the Amadeus accounts of the two Op. 77 *Quartets* are outstanding, as is the unfinished *D minor*, Op. 103. They are on their finest form here. There is a sense of spontaneity as well as a genuine breadth to these readings. The recordings have a warm acoustic and plenty of presence.

PIANO MUSIC

Keyboard (Divertimento) Sonatas Nos. 1–20, Hob XVI/1–16 & G1; D1; 17–18, Hob Es2 & 3; 19, Hob XVI/47; 20, Hob XVI/18.

(M) ***** BIS CD 1293/4 (3). Brautigam (fortepiano).

With this volume, the ninth in his Haydn survey, Ronald Brautigam turns to the early 'Divertimeno' sonatas that were written in the 1750s and '60s for the clavichord or harpsichord. Brautigam uses a forte-piano, a copy by Paul McNulty of a mid-1790s instrument by Walther. Many of the earlier sonatas are of little consequence and Haydn did not include them in his list of complete keyboard works that he made for Breitkopf. The more individual sonatas, such as the *E minor, No. 19*, Hob XVI/47, and the *B flat, No. 20*, Hob XVI/18, come from the 1760s and are played with imagination and delicacy. Overall, the short sonatas that predominate in this three-CD set are not the most substantial or satisfying of Haydn's keyboard output and the discs are primarily of value in completing the picture. Good playing and exemplary recording, but ultimately the set is for completists.

Piano Sonatas Nos. 32 in G min., Hob XVI/44; 33 in C min., Hob XVI/20; 53 in E min. Hob XVI/34; 54 in G, Hob XVI/40; 58 in C, Hob. XVI/48.

(M) **★★★** Warner Elatus 2564 60677-2. Schiff.

Piano Sonatas Nos. 59–62, Hob XVI/49–52; Fantasia in C, Hob XVII/4.

(M) **★★★** Warner Elatus 2564 60807-2. Schiff.

András Schiff's Haydn recordings are comparatively recent and were much acclaimed when they first appeared in 1999. They are now released at mid-price. Recorded in the Berlin Teldec studios by Christopher Raeburn, one of Decca's most distinguished producers, this is a collection issue of high quality – and it comes with the original essays by Misha Donat.

Piano Sonatas Nos. 47 in B min., Hob XVI/32; 53 in E min., Hob XVI/34; 56 in D, Hob XVI/42; Adagio in F, Hob XVII/9; Fantasia in C, Hob XVII/4.

✿ (M) **★★★** Ph. 476 1715-2. Brendel.

Here is a Haydn recital about which we waxed enthusiastic when it first appeared in the 1980s. The disc was soon withdrawn (although the recordings remained available in a boxed set), but now happily Universal have reissued it at medium price as part of the 'Penguin ✿ Collection'. Brendel's performances are marvellously held together, self-aware at times, as many great performances are, but inspiriting and always governed by the highest intelligence. The *B minor Sonata* has a *Sturm und Drang* urgency, and Brendel's account has vitality and character. Moreover, the recording is splendidly realistic.

Other piano music

Adagios: in G, Hob XV/22II & F, Hob XVII/9. Allegrettos: in G, Hob XVII/10 & Hob III/411V (authentic version of the finale of the String Quartet in G, Op. 33/5). Andante and Variations in: A, Hob XVII/A3; F min., Hob XVII/6; D, Hob XVII/7; B flat, Hob XVII/12. Andantino (Allegretto) with Variations in A, Hob XVII/8; Aria with Variations in C, Hob XVII/15; Ariettas with 12 Variations in E flat, Hob XV11/3 & A, Hob XVII/2. Capriccio in G, Hob XVII/1 'Acht Sauschneider müssen seyn'; 6 Easy Variations in C, Hob XVII/5; Fantasia in C, Hob XVII/4; 12 German Dances, Hob IX/12; Il Maestro e lo Scolare in F, Hob XVIIa/1; Kontretanz, Hob XXXI/c:17b; March, Hob. VIII/3/3bis; 2 Marches (for Sir Henry Harpur), Hob

VIII/1; 12 Minuets: Hob IX/3, 8 & 11. Variations in G on the Hymn, 'Gott erhalte Franz, den Kaiser', Hob III/77II; 20 Variations in G, Hob XVII/2.

★★★ BIS CD 1323/4 (3). Brautigam (fortepiano).

This is the tenth and penultimate survey of Haydn's keyboard music by Ronald Brautigam (only the keyboard arrangement of *The Seven Last Words* remains). Its contents range from the remarkable *Andante con variazioni in F minor* with its wide range of feeling to the delightful *Deutsche Tänze*, which older collectors will remember from Mogens Wöldike's 78rpm set (now on the Dutton label). The diversity and range of Haydn's invention never fail to surprise and delight. As always, Brautigam's playing has an irresistible vitality and finesse – and Ingo Petry's recording (he also serves as the pupil in *Il Maestro e lo Scolare*) is excellently balanced.

VOCAL MUSIC

Arianna a Naxos (cantata).

(B) **★★★** EMI Début 5 85559-2. Coote, Drake – MAHLER: *Das Knaben Wunderhorn* (excerpts), etc.; SCHUMANN: *Frauenliebe und Leben.* **★★★**

Haydn's dramatic scena has already been recorded with distinction by Cecilia Bartoli (Decca 440 297-2) and Anne Sofie Von Otter (DG 447 106-2), and it was also one of Dame Janet Baker's party-pieces in recitals. Here the mezzo Alice Coote offers a comparably stylish performance, which stands well against this formidable competition, with her wide range of dynamic and tone-colour adding to the drama. This is one of the very finest of EMI's admirable Début series, though – as with other EMI issues of Lieder at budget price – no texts or translations are given.

The Creation (Die Schöpfung; in German).

☛ **★★★** DHM/BMG 82876 58340-2 (2). Röschmann, Schade, Gerhaher, Arnold Schoenberg Ch., VCM, Harnoncourt.

Celebrating their fiftieth anniversary at the Musikvereinsaal in Vienna, Nikolaus Harnoncourt and the Concentus Musicus give an incandescent account of Haydn's *Creation*, recorded live. This warm and dramatic reading is very different from the very scholarly and sometimes abrasive performances that marked much of the early work of the Concentus Musicus, admirable as it always was. Harnoncourt, benefiting from his wide experience conducting orchestras of every kind in a wide range of repertory, here inspires a natural warmth that infects all the performers, the outstanding Arnold Schoenberg Choir as well as the three splendid soloists, the soprano Dorothea Röschmann at once full and clear, the tenor Michael Schade heady and unstrained and the finely focused bass Christian Gerhaher plainly benefiting from his experience as a Lieder singer. The live atmosphere adds to the dramatic bite of the performance from the start, with period players in a substantial body bringing out the daring originality of such passages as the *Chaos Prelude*. The recording, well forward with weighty brass, adds to the drama, not least with the great entry of the chorus on the word, *Licht* ('Light'), thrillingly powerful. A triumphant celebration of 50 years' achievement.

The Seasons (complete; in English).

(B) *** Somm Beecham (ADD) 16-2 (2). Morison, Young, Langdon, Beecham Choral Soc., RPO, Beecham.

Beecham recorded *The Seasons* in its entirety between 1956 and 1958, yet he had only once conducted a complete concert performance (at the Edinburgh Festival in 1950). He preferred instead to conduct individual movements, of which *Spring* was his favourite. But it is a work that suited his personality, and his interpretation combines vigour with an affectionate warmth.

Nevertheless, Beecham's approach to Haydn's score was somewhat cavalier. He used orchestrations of the keyboard accompaniments for the recitatives, and (as with his RCA recording of Handel's *Messiah*) added percussion effects, including cymbals. A bell was added to the horns striking eight o'clock in *Summer*, and extra shots to the bass's hunting aria in *Autumn*. Yet he obviously revelled in Haydn's expressive tone-painting and he chose a fine solo team, led by Elsie Morison, who sings with tender flexibility and charm. The fresh-voiced tenor, Alexander Young, and the vibrant bass, Michael Langdon, are equally strong, and the three singers match their voices very musically in the various trios. The choral singing is not as polished as we would expect today from an entirely professional chorus, but the hearty vigour and commitment carry the day, while the RPO, and especially the strings, play with both warmth and stylish delicacy of feeling. In short, this is as spirited and individual as one would expect from Beecham, and the early Abbey Road stereo is full and clear. The remastering cannot be faulted, and a full text is provided of Dennis Arundell's new translation, which was especially commissioned for this recording.

OPERA

(i) *Armida;* (ii) *La fedeltà premiata;* (iii) *Orlando paladino;* (iv) *La vera costanza* (all complete).

(B) *** Ph. (ADD) 473 476-2 (10). (i) Burrowes, Ramey, Leggate; (i; iii; iv) Ahnsjö; (i; iv) Norman, Rolfe Johnson; (ii) Terrani, Landy, Von Stade, Titus, Cotrubas, Alva, Mazzieri, SRO Ch.; (ii; iv) Lövaas; (iii) Augér, Ameling, Killebrew, Shirley, Luxon; (iii; iv) Trimarchi; (iv) Donath, Ganzarolli; Lausanne CO, Dorati.

(i) *L'incontro improvviso;* (ii) *L'infedeltà delusa;* (iii) *L'isola disabitata;* (iv) *Il mondo della luna* (all complete). (v) Cantata: *Miseri noi! misera patria;*

Petrarch's Sonnet from 'Il Canzionieri': Solo e pensoso. (vi) *Terzetto and* (vii) *Aria from* PASTICCIO: *La Circe, ossia L'isola incantata. Arias for:* (viii) *Acide e Galatea.* (ix) SARTI: *I finti erede.* (x) TRAETTA: *Ifigenia in Tauride.* (xi) BIANCHI: *Alessandro nell'Indie.* CIMAROSA: *I due supposti conti.* GAZZANIGA: *L'isola di Alcina.* GUGLIELMI: *La Quakera spiritosa.* PAISIELLO: *La Frascatana.*

(B) *** Ph. (ADD) 473 851-2 (10). (i) Luxon, M. Marshall, D. Jones, Prescott; (i; ii; vi; x) Ahnsjö; (i; iii) Zoghby; (i, iv) Trimarchi; (ii) Hendricks; (ii; iv; v; vii; xi) Mathis; (ii; vi; vii; ix) Baldin; (ii; vi; viii) Devlin; (iii) Lerer; (ii; iv) Alva, Bruson; (iv) Von Stade, Augér, Valentini, Terrani, Rolfe Johnson; Lausanne CO, Dorati.

Haydn is not celebrated as an operatic composer, yet in many ways his contribution to this genre is underrated, and for those drawn to Dorati's vintage series, these two boxes, each of ten CDs, in the Philips bargain Collector's Edition, provide an economical way to explore this repertoire. Each opera is also available separately and is discussed individually in our companion volume. With fine soloists there is much here to delight the ear, and Dorati conducts brightly and resiliently; although he tends to flag in the recitatives, these performances still offer much to relish. Indeed, after each fairly conventional overture, the vocal writing flows forward enticingly, with many a sparkling reminder of Mozart. One can imagine how much these works must have been enjoyed at Esterházy. The presentation offers good documentation, but keyed synopses in place of full libretti. Also included is an additional programme of miscellaneous arias by Haydn and substitution arias by other composers, the latter (for the most part) sung by Edith Mathis. The analogue recording from the late 1970s is excellent and the CD transfers first class. Try the first box and you will surely want the second.

HEADINGTON, Christopher
(1931–96)

(i) *Piano Concerto;* (ii) *The Healing Fountain;* (iii) *Serenade for Cello & String Orchestra.*

*** ASV CDDCA 969. Britten Sinfonia, Cleobury, with (i) Fergus-Thompson; (ii) Carwood; (iii) Baillie.

The Healing Fountain was composed in 1978 'in memoriam Benjamin Britten' and is a 26-minute cycle for high voice and chamber orchestra, comprising settings of Auden, Sassoon, Wilfred Owen, Thomas Moore and Shelley. It is expertly fashioned and often imaginative, though it is perhaps a little too close for comfort to the Britten idiom – indeed it quotes from *Peter Grimes, Death in Venice* and the underrated *Nocturne*. The *Piano Concerto* was begun the following year but was put aside until 1991. Although it is not as haunting or personal as the *Violin Concerto*, Headington's masterpiece, it is a strong piece, well structured and rewarding. The composer was an excellent pianist and his writing for the instrument is exhilarating and adroit. Those who respond to, say, Prokofiev or Britten will find much to admire here. The *Serenade* is the most recent work, and was commissioned by Julian Lloyd Webber and premièred by him in 1995. Fine and committed performances and very good recording too.

HEBDEN, John (1712–65)

6 Concertos for Strings (ed. Wood).
**(*) Chan. 8339. Cantilena, Shepherd.

These concertos are Hebden's only known works, apart from some flute sonatas. Although they are slightly uneven, at best the invention is impressive. The concertos usually feature two solo violins and are well constructed to offer plenty of contrast. The performances here are accomplished, without the last degree of polish but full of vitality.

HEINICHEN, Johann David
(1683–1729)

Dresden Concerti: in C, S 211; in G, S 213; in G (Darmstadt), S 214; in G (Venezia), S 214; in G, S 215; in F, S 217; in F, S 226; in F, S 231; in F, S 232; in F, S 233; in F, S 234; in F, S 235. Concerto movement in C min., S 240; Serenata di Moritzburg in F, S 204; Sonata in A, S 208.
(M) *** DG 474 892-2 (2). Col. Mus. Ant., Goebel.

Johann David Heinichen, a contemporary of Bach, was a Dresden court musician and the concertos here were intended for the (obviously excellent) Dresden court orchestra. It is the orchestral colour that makes these concertos so appealing rather than their invention, which is more predictable. Goebel's Cologne forces obviously relish the delicacy of Heinichen's wind scoring and his neat and busily vital allegros. The lollipop of the set is the *Pastorell* second movement of the *C major Concerto*, Seibel 211, with its piquant drone (track 5 of the second CD). It is immediately followed by a peaceful *Adagio* for flute and strings and a sparkling finale. This set is now re-issued at mid-price celebrating its winning *Gramophone* magazine's Non-Vocal Baroque Award in 1993.

Dresden Concerti: in A min., S 212; in E min., S 218; in E min., S 222; in D, S 225; in G min., S 237; in G min., S 238.
**(*) CPO 999 637-2. Fiori Musicale, Albert.

It is fortunate that the present issue from Thomas Albert and his Bremen group involves no duplication of items in the DG set, and so for those who have the Archiv recordings this will be a welcome supplement, though it must be said that the playing is by no means as accomplished or elegant as that of the Cologne group.

HENZE, Hans Werner (born 1926)

VOCAL MUSIC

(i) *3 Dithyramben;* (ii) *Ode to the Westwind;* (iii) *5 Neapolitan Lieder.*
(BB) ** Arte Nova 74321 89404-2. Saarbrücken RSO;
   (i) Wich; (ii) Rivinius, Saarbrücken RCO,
   Skrowaczewski; (iii) Hermann, Halffter.

Henze's music is not well served on bargain disc, so this issue should be welcome, even if the welcome must be qualified. The good news – in that it is not otherwise recorded and is also by far the best thing on the disc – is the *Drei Dithyramben* with its Italianate warmth and strong atmosphere. In the *Ode to the Westwind* the cellist is rather too far forward and in the *Neapolitanische Lieder*, one of Henze's most approachable and charming scores, Roland Hermann is less subtle and less varied in tonal colour than in the pioneering Fischer-Dieskau recording from the 1950s. The balance in all three pieces is less than ideal, and in the *Ode to the Westwind* the sound is opaque. Recommended at the price for the *Drei Dithyramben.*

Die Bassariden (opera; complete).
(M) (**(*)) Orfeo mono C605032I (2). Driscoll,
   Paskalis, Lagger, Melchert, Dooley, Meyer, V. State
   Op. Ch., VPO, Dohnányi.

Although his orchestral and instrumental work is well represented in the catalogue, Henze's operas, which occupy a central position in his output, are not. *The Bassarids* comes from 1965, three years after his successful collaboration with Auden and Chester Kallman in *Elegy for Young Lovers*. It was recorded commercially with a strong cast, including Kenneth Riegel as Dionysus, Andreas Schmidt as Pentheus and Berlin Radio forces under Gerd Albrecht on Schwann Musica Mundi. It comes chronologically midway between the *Fifth* and *Sixth Symphonies* of 1962 and 1969. In many ways it represents a synthesis of Henze's symphonic and operatic writing, its single 2½-hour act being divided into four movements: a first-movement sonata form, a Scherzo, an Adagio and a passacaglia finale. The plot (after Euripides's *The Bacchae*) concerns the conflict between Pentheus, the new king of Thebes, and the god Dionysus, and the king's subsequent murder at the hands of Dionysus's drunken followers, among them Pentheus's own mother. It contains some of Henze's most imaginative and compelling invention. This Orfeo performance is of the première on 6 August 1966 and is an impressive one. Loren Driscoll's Dionysus is perhaps not quite as imposing as Kenneth Riegel's in the slightly later (deleted) recording made for Koch under Gerd Albrecht, but he is very good indeed, and the remainder of the cast could hardly be bettered. Christoph von Dohnányi gets first-class results from the Vienna Philharmonic. The recording is pretty monochrome but generally well balanced, and it makes an important contribution to the Henze discography.

HERBERT, Victor (1859–1924)

Auditorium Festival March; Columbus Suite; Irish Rhapsody; Natoma: excerpts.
**(*) Marco Polo 8.225109. Slovak RSO (Bratislavia), Brion.

The longest piece here, the *Columbus Suite*, was also the composer's last major work and was premièred in 1903. Its four movements are all descriptive and have mild moments of interest (the *Murmurs of the Sea* brings nice orchestral effects), but it's all a bit thin really. The other works are more enjoyable. The *Irish Rhapsody*, with its haunting Irish folk-tunes running throughout and alternating pastoral and vigorous episodes, is really quite fun. The selections from *Natoma* – Herbert's one foray into grand opera – sound like a mixture of Wagner and Hollywood, with a tango halfway through! Its musical inspiration, the music of Native Americans, gives it an additional dash of local colour. The *Auditorium Festival March* (1901) is an exuberant piece quoting extensively from *Auld Lang Syne*, which sounds ready made for a Hollywood film of the 1930s. Enthusiastic performances and acceptable recording.

Cello Concerto No. 2 in E min., Op. 30.
**(*) Guild GMCD 7253. Kreger, Philh. O, Yu –
　DVORAK: *Cello Concerto; Silent Woods.* **(*)

James Kreger's dedication and artistry come across in this fine version of Victor Herbert's *Cello Concerto*, coupled with the Dvořák concerto, which inspired it. He comes into direct competition with Yo-Yo Ma with Kurt Masur and the New York Philharmonic and, although there is much to be said for Kreger's naturalness of expression, Masur provides stronger support than Djong Victorin Yu (Sony SK 67173).

HERZOGENBERG, Heinrich
(1843–1900)

Legends, Op. 62; Piano Quartet in B flat, Op. 95; String Trio in F, Op. 27/2.
(M) *** CPO 999 710-2. Frölich, Belcanto Strings.

Heinrich von Herzogenberg was born in Vienna, but was descended from a French aristocratic family. A connoisseur of Baroque music, a conductor of the Leipzig Bach-Verein and then a professor of composition at the Berlin Hochschule, he figures prominently in biographies of Brahms and of Clara Schumann. His wife, Elisabet, became a close confidante of Brahms in his later years. The centenary of his death was in 2000, and the appearance of this record serves to fill in our picture of him. All three pieces are so indebted to Brahms in their musical

language that they can only *just* be said to lead an independent life. They are played very well by these artists, and the recording is lifelike and well balanced.

HESS, Nigel (born 1953)

East Coast Pictures; Global Variations; Thames Journey; Scramble!; Stephenson's Rocket; (i) *To the Stars!. The TV Detectives; The Winds of Power.*
**(*) Chan. 9764. L. Symphonic Wind O, composer;
　(i) with children from Daubney Middle School, Bedford.

Nigel Hess has made his name primarily as a composer for television and theatre. He knows how to score, and he has a ready fund of melody. This is demonstrated in *The TV Detectives*, which brings together five rather striking TV themes, including 'Dangerfield', 'Wycliffe' and 'Hetty Wainthrop Investigates'. Of the concert music here, easily the most impressive piece is the flamboyant *To the Stars!*, which gets a real lift-off from the vocal energy of the children of Daubney Middle School. *Thames Journey* opens with trickling woodwind at its source, like Smetana's *Vltava*, and then introduces a Wiltshire folk melody on the horn as its main theme; but overall it is little more than a well-crafted pot-pourri, with *Greensleeves* and later *The Lass of Richmond Hill* also introduced. The three *East Coast Pictures* evoke the eastern seaboard of the USA, but are curiously without any strong American colouring. *Stephenson's Rocket* is rugged and vigorous, but not much of a train imitation. *The Winds of Power* is more evocative but rather loosely held together. *Scramble!* is more succinct and celebrates the Battle of Britain vividly enough. Indeed, all these works have plenty of vitality, even if they are not really distinctive. They are brilliantly played here under the composer, and are given excellent Chandos sound.

HIGDON, Jennifer (born 1962)

Concerto for Orchestra; Cityscape.
⊶ ✪ *** Telarc CD 80620. Atlanta SO, Spano.

Here, bursting upon us with her dazzling *Concerto for Orchestra*, is a new American composer with the kind of immediacy and communicative force that are all too rare in the concert hall today. Serialism is forgotten: this is music of immediate appeal in its melodic lines, its rich palette of colour and its inherent vitality. Ned Rorem, Jennifer Higdon's teacher and mentor, has placed her foremost among today's American women composers, and it is no wonder that, when her *Concerto* was premièred by the Philadelphia Orchestra, it brought a roaring ovation from the audience. It is an astonishing alive and fertile work in five movements, summoned by bells, and opening with a whirlwind on the strings, soon joined by woodwind, and introducing glowing brass sonorities. The second movement is a sprightly Scherzo, first with witty pizzicatos; then the strings take up their bows athletically, the animation undiminished. The third movement, which is most imaginatively scored, introduces each section of the orchestra in turn, with the string chords giving a distinct whiff of Copland (which is to return in the finale). The fourth belongs to the percussion. With sounds both exotic and ear-tweaking, it gathers momentum, helped by the drummers, to lead to the exhilarating finale with its stabbing rhythmic ostinato on the violins, which becomes more and more jubilant.

Cityscape, commissioned by the orchestra, is a portrait of Atlanta, first its vibrant *Skyline*, the centrepiece a haunting pastoral evocation as the 'river sings a song to the trees', and finally a kaleidoscopic evocation of the city's main thorougfare – *Peachtown Street* – with its swiftly changing evocations and unrelenting, unstoppable energy, even including a dynamic fugato.

The performances here are outstanding, the *Concerto* resplendent with orchestral virtuosity, the *Cityscape* conveying an unmistakable American panorama. The Telarc engineers rise to the occasion, yet they have the advantage of the superb acoustics of Atlanta's Symphony Hall, which gives a radiance to the quiet strings and bloom to both woodwind and brass, within a realistically spacious overall sound-picture.

HILDEGARD of Bingen
(1098–1179)

(i) *Ordo Virtutum;* (ii) *In Portrait.*

🔑 ❀ *** BBC **DVD** Opus Arte OA 0874 D (2). (i) Boothroyd, Hancorn, Mayfield, Chamber Op. Ch., Vox Animae, Fields, Adams, Devine (Directors: Michael Fields & Evelyn Tubb).

Hildegard was not only the most remarkable 'Renaissance woman' of the twelfth century, she was one of the most remarkable women (or men) of all time. Confidante of popes, she was a genius in almost every field – composer, playwright, author, poet, artist, theologian, philosopher, visionary and prophet. She believed in the 'web of creation to which all creatures belong'; she compared 'the great love of the Creator and creation to the same love and fidelity with which God binds man together'; and she taught that the world should be enjoyed by man and woman together – 'Only thus is the earth fruitful'. Her views were so remarkable in their time that it is a wonder they could be expressed and survive. Because her mystic visions (in which she believed that God was communicating directly to her) were accepted by the Church as genuine, her power was remarkable and far-reaching. Moreover, she could speak plainly to those in authority above her and her criticisms would be accepted.

Her extraordinarily sung and spoken mystery play, *Ordo Virtutum* ('The Play of the Virtues') celebrates her philosophy, based on the love of God and the enjoyment of life, alongside resistance to sin. Even with the music alone (which has been imaginatively recorded by Sequentia) this is a remarkable achievement, but to see it played out in glowing colours, imaginatively performed and beautifully sung, partly outside and partly inside, in splendidly chosen natural settings, adds an extra dimension to the drama, particularly in the dramatic passages in Scenes I and IV, where the Devil enters. He contests the value of the fear of God and the virtue of chastity, to receive the neat reply that chastity produced 'one man who bound himself to humankind'. The music, simple but soaring monody but with sparingly used harp, recorder and percussion accompaniments, is very beautiful in itself; its flowing lines haunt the memory and it is radiantly sung, while the drama of the piece comes over splendidly.

The accompanying second CD includes a compulsive BBC 'Omnibus' dramatization of Hildegard's early life, before she set up her own order; and no better choice for the role of Hildegard could have been found than Patricia Routledge, who conveys her humility in the face of God and her determination in the face of man (and woman) and the warmth and spiritual essence of her character. This is a film to watch more than once, so it makes an ideal counterpart to the music, which one can return to again and again. The additional items include 'A Real Mystic' (an interview and lecture with Professor Matthew Fox, author of *Illuminations*, supplemented with an illustrative art gallery tour), while Mary Grabowsky considers Hildegard's spiritual significance for the twenty-first century. This DVD Double is a truly remarkable achievement, but it also surely points the way to the manner of biographical publishing in the future.

Symphoniae (Spiritual Songs).

(M) *** DHM/BMG 82976 60152-2. Sequentia, Thornton; Bagby.

This is a further reissue of Sequentia's very first collection, made in 1979. The collection divides into two groups – the first celebrating female divinities such as Mary, Ursula and her accompanying virgins, and even Wisdom, considered a type of feminine deity and for which Hildegard wrote one of her most eloquent tributes. The second group is of laudatory pieces – for the Apostles (a responsory, introduced with a plaintive flute solo), for the Holy Confessors, for the Patriarchs and Prophets, and for the Martyrs. In this last, remarkable piece the upper vocal line moves over a sustained lower note. The freshness of the singing here and the considerable instrumental interest makes this one of the most imaginatively conceived of the series.

***Vision* (The music of Hildegard; arranged and recomposed by Richard Souther).**

* (**) EMI 5 55246-2. Van Evera, Sister Fritz (with

chorus, instrumental contributions & synthesized rhythm).

Richard Souther's way-out recomposed versions are precociously and recklessly inauthentic, even including instrumental numbers (*The living light*, and *Only the Devil laughed* are typical titles). The sophisticated rock style amplifies the music's sensuous, hypnotic, melodic flow, adding all kinds of extra-instrumental vocal and synthesized nourishment, with echo-chamber effects plus exotic live percussion. But Souther is obviously deeply involved in this very personal enterprise, and he has the advantage of the illustrious singing of Emily Van Evera, who really understands this repertoire, having also recorded it under authentic circumstances. Her beautiful voice is close-miked, 'pop style', unabashedly flattered with an acoustic halo. The programme opens with *O virga ac diadema purpure regis*, included on the Naxos disc (8.550998 – see our main *Guide*), but the effect is extravagantly different. Certainly the emotional power of the music and its innate melodiousness project vividly. The CD's title number, *Vision* (*O Euchari*) (also included in Jeremy Summerly's programme on Naxos) is heard twice, ending the programme in a more elaborate, extended version. This is a disc to either wallow in or hate. Full translations are included.

HINDEMITH, Paul (1895–1963)

'Hindemith Conducts Hindemith' (complete DG recordings):

Amor und Psyche: Overture; Concerto for Orchestra, Op. 38; (i) *The Four Temperaments (Theme and Variations for Piano and Strings);* (ii) *Konzertmusik for Harp, Piano & Strings, Op. 49. Symphonic Dances; Symphonic Metamorphoses on themes of Carl Maria von Weber; Symphony (Die Harmonie der Welt); Symphony (Mathis der Maler).*

🔾 (★★★) DG mono 474 770-2 (3). BPO, composer; with (i) Otte; (ii) Haas.

Hindemith made a number of records for Deutsche Grammophon in the early 1950s, before transferring his allegiance to EMI. All of them are collected in this invaluable boxed set. Some of them have been in the CD catalogue, but works like the exhilarating *Symphonic Dances*, the *Konzertmusik for Harp, Piano and Strings*, and the *Harmonie der Welt Symphony* have not been in currency since the days of vinyl. DG certainly lavished first-class sound on them and the *Mathis Symphony* and the *Weber Metamorphoses* are impressively detailed and full-bodied, given their date. Those who have treasured their LPs of these pieces can rest assured that a great deal of trouble has been taken over these transfers, and it is particularly good to have Hindemith's own thoughts on the *Harmonie der Welt Symphony*, one of his greatest works. We must hope that EMI will be prompted to

reissue the *Sinfonia serena* and the *Clarinet Concerto* with the Philharmonia Orchestra. Meanwhile, do not hesitate or procrastinate! Get this while the opportunity still exists and before it succumbs to deletion.

Cello Concerto.

(M) ★★(★) BBC mono BBCL 4133-2. Tortelier, BBC SO, Downes – SCHUMANN: *Cello Concerto.* ★★(★)

Paul Tortelier's account of the *Cello Concerto* comes from a 1967 TV broadcast from the BBC Maida Vale studios in which Tortelier gave a masterclass on the piece, an excerpt from which is included on this disc. Tortelier was a consistent champion of this concerto and played it with the composer himself. This is a highly persuasive account to which we would have accorded three stars, were it not for the rather opaque, monochrome sound of Maida Vale Studio 1. But this should be recommended for the artistry and conviction of both the soloist and the BBC Symphony Orchestra under Downes.

(i) *Organ Concerto;* (ii) *Organ Sonatas, Nos. 1–3.*

(BB) ★★★ Warner Apex (ADD) 2564 60227-2. (i) Heiller, Austrian RSO, Hórvat; (ii) Ullmann.

A most valuable reissue, particularly at so competitive a price. The *First* and *Second Organ Sonatas* come from 1937 and they are both exhilarating and masterly, and are beautifully laid out for the instrument. The *Third Sonata* was written shortly after Hindemith had settled in Yale. Apart from Messiaen, nobody composed more idiomatically for the instrument in the 1930s and '40s. The *Organ Concerto* is not to be confused with the last of the *Kammermusik* of 1927, but is the larger-scale four-movement score, commissioned by the New York Philharmonic in 1962 and which was to prove the composer's last work. The performance by Anton Heiller and Austrian Radio forces under Milan Hórvat is authoritative and well recorded, and the sonatas are also finely played on the organ of the Brucknerhaus, Linz. Very good value for money.

Piano Concerto.

★★(★) First Edition (ADD) LCD 002. Luvisi, Louisville O, Smith (with LAWHEAD: *Aleost* ★(★)) – ZWILICH: *Symphony No. 2.* ★★

Although the newer recording of Hindemith's *Piano Concerto* on CPO 999 078-2 (see our main volume) upstages this earlier recording by Lee Luvisi and the Louisville Orchestra, they nevertheless give a very good account of themselves and are more than adequately recorded.

Mathis der Maler (symphony); *Symphonic Metamorphoses on Themes by Weber; Neues vom Tage (News of the Day): Overture.*

(B) ★★ Virgin 5 61922-2. Bamberg SO, Rickenbacher – MAHLER: *Blumine; Totenfeier; etc.* ★★

Rickenbacher's are straightforwardly strong and very serious-minded performances, not helped by a recording that is well balanced but rather opaque. His lighter novelty is the brief overture to an early 'comic' opera, *Neues vom Tage*, which generates plenty of sardonic energy, introduces a melancholy lyrical theme, becomes more exotic, and ends rumbustiously, but heavily. The main interest of this reissue is the Mahler couplings.

CHAMBER MUSIC

(i) *Alto Saxophone Sonata;* (ii) *Bass Tuba Sonata;* (iii) *Bassoon Sonata;* (iv) *Morgenmusik;* (v) *Trio;* (vi) *Trombone Sonata;* (vii) *Trumpet Sonata.*
**(*) BIS (ADD) CD 159. (i) Savijoki, Siirala; (ii) Lind, Harlos; (iii) Sonstevold, Knardahl; (iv) Malmö Brass Ens.; (v) Pehrsson, Jonsson, Mjönes; (vi) Lindberg, Pöntinen; (vii) Tarr, Westenholz.

The *Alto Saxophone Sonata* and the *Alto Horn Sonata* are the same work. The *Recorder Trio* is expertly played, as is the exhilarating *Morgenmusik* for brass, not to mention the inventive *Bassoon Sonata*. However, the BIS recordings are rather closely balanced, though not disturbingly so.

Kleine Kammermusik for Wind Quintet, Op. 24/2.
*** Nimbus NI 5728. V. Quintet – LIGETI: *6 Bagatelles;* NIELSEN: *Wind Quintet.* ***

The Vienna Quintet fully convey the wit and lightness of touch that distinguish Hindemith's writing in this entertaining *Kleine Kammermusik*. We are well served in this repertoire, but the 'quintett.wien' as they call themselves are as good as the very best. The playing is a delight from first to last and is beautifully recorded in the Wiener Konzerthaus. The coupling, too, is logical in giving us an exact contemporary, the Nielsen *Wind Quintet*.

String Quartets Nos. 1 in C, Op. 2; 2 in F min., Op. 10; 3 in C, Op. 16; 4, Op. 22; 5, Op. 32; 6 in E flat; 7 in E flat.
(B) *(*) CPO 999 287-2 (3). Danish Qt.

The Hindemith quartets are not generously represented in the catalogue, so this issue is (on the face of it) particularly welcome. It also includes an early quartet (Op. 2) composed in 1915 and not recognized in the published order of the scores. Accordingly, what we have always known as the *Sixth Quartet in E flat* of 1945 becomes the *Seventh*, and each of its predecessors adds one. Unfortunately, the Danish Quartet will not win over the unconverted, nor will they give much comfort and joy to those who like this repertory. Their playing lacks authority and is wanting in tonal finesse and colour.

Viola Sonata in F, Op. 11/4.
*(*) Olympia OCD 625. Bashmet, Richter (with BRITTEN: *Lachrymae; Viola Sonata* *(*)).

Distinguished playing, as you would expect from these artists, who were recorded live in Germany in 1985. But the sound is distinctly unappealing, too close and hard.

HOFFMANN, E. T. A. (1776–1822)

(i) *Harp Quintet;* (ii) *Piano Trio (Grand) in E;* (iii) *6 Duettini Italiani* (for soprano, tenor and piano).
*** CPO 999 309-2. (i) Moretti, Parisii Qt; Beethoven Trio, Ravensburg; (iii) Mields, Kabow, Brunner.

E. T. A. Hoffmann is indelibly linked to Offenbach's *Tales of Hoffmann*, but it is good that recordings of his music emerge from time to time. CPO have made a speciality of recording music of the early romantic era, and they always seems to come up trumps. And so they have here, in this well-produced CD, with copious and informative sleeve-notes. The *Piano Trio* of 1809 is the most meaty work here, with robust themes and dynamic contrasts; it is clear that, as on all composers of this period, Beethoven has made his influence felt here. Some will count it a weak point that it lacks a proper slow movement with an ensuing central emotional core, which we have come to expect. However, there is plenty to enjoy in the lively writing and enthusiastic playing throughout its 22 minutes. The *6 Duettini italiani*, written in 1812, with their simple and attractive vocal lines in the Italian manner, enter into the world of the fashionable drawing-room: there is lovely interplay between the tenor and soprano parts, and they are eminently entertaining: it would make a good novelty to hear in a live recital.

The *Harp Quinet* is an undemanding charmer; with its minor-key, florid writing, it is most ingratiating, with an especially attractive finale. The performances and recording are all first class.

HOFFMEISTER, Franz (1754–1812)

Clarinet Quintets: in A; B flat; D; E flat.
*** CPO 999 812-2. Klöcker, Vlach Qt, Prague.

Hoffmeister's *Clarinet Quintets* bubble on amiably for the duration of this 75-minute CD. There is nothing deep or profound here, but this is *galant*, light music of quality, well constructed and brimming with geniality and melodic resource. The first three *Quintets* are in three movements, each with a fairly substantial first movement, a simple *Adagio*, and fizzing finales, either allegros or Minuets. The *Adagio* of the *D major Quintet* is one of the few places where a minor key is allowed in for any length of time, and the *E flat Quintet* breaks with tradition by having five movements, but maintains the appeal of its companions. Performances are first rate, with creamy-toned Dieter Klöcker taking all the virtuosity in his stride. The recording, too, is warm and well balanced.

HOFMANN, Leopold (1738–93)

Sinfonias: in B flat; in C; in D; in F; in F.
(BB) **(*) Naxos 8.553866. N. CO, Ward.

Leopold Hofmann was one of the earliest composers who consistently wrote four-movement symphonies with both a slow introduction and minuets. He preceded Haydn in this respect. Incidentally, for a brief period in 1791 Mozart acted as an assistant to him, doubtless in the hope of receiving preferment when Hofmann died. The five symphonies recorded here show him to be lively and fresh, though no one could pretend that his music plumbs great depths – or indeed is consistently interesting. The performances are very alert and sprightly, but the recording, though distinguished by clarity and presence, is handicapped by a rather dry acoustic.

HOL, Richard (or Rijk) (1825–1904)

Symphonies Nos. 1 in C min.; 3 in B flat, Op. 101.
* (**) Chan. 9796. Hague Residentie O, Bamert.

The son of an Amsterdam milkman, Richard (or Rijk) Hol was an influential figure in the second half of the nineteenth century, both as a conductor and as a teacher. He was prolific, and like Brahms he wrote four symphonies, but they are nearer to Schumann in their musical ethos, although the scoring owes more to Brahms and Mendelssohn, who provided the inspiration for the engaging Scherzo that is the highlight of the later, B flat major work. The melodic invention is somewhat conventional but is lyrical and pleasing throughout each symphony here. R. L. feels that, whatever may be said of his originality or importance, Hol was a *real* symphonist who has total command over his material and has a sense of architecture and pace. For E. G., the orchestral writing is attractive, but the musical material hardly deserves such extended treatment, with too many passages depending on empty gestures, with trite repetitions and sequences, and melodies that turn back on themselves. For I. M. this is not music he would wish to return to very often. However, we are all agreed that the performances, from a first-class orchestra who are naturally at home in the repertoire, are warmly sympathetic, and the full-bodied Chandos sound presents the composer's orchestration persuasively.

HOLBROOKE, Joseph (1878–1958)

The Birds of Rhiannon, Op. 87; The Children of Don: Overture, Op. 56; Dylan: Prelude, Op. 53.
** Marco Polo 8.223721-2. Ukraine Nat. SO, Penny.

In Holbrooke's opera *The Children of Don* (the first of a trilogy) neither overture nor prelude offers particularly memorable or individual ideas and, generally speaking, inspiration is pretty thin. There are touches of Wagner in the former but the musical language is predominantly diatonic, particularly in the tone-poem, *The Birds of Rhiannon*. The longest piece is the *Prelude* to *Dylan*, which is pretty undistinguished stuff. The performances sound a bit under-rehearsed but are adequate (some may find the horn vibrato a bit excessive) and the recording is decent.

(i) *Piano Quartet in G min., Op. 21;* (ii) *String Sextet in D, Op. 43;* (iii) *Symphonic Quintet No. 1 in G min., Op. 44.*
** Marco Polo 8.223736. New Haydn Qt. with (i; iii) Hegedüs; (ii) Papp, Devich.

Although the music here never falls below a certain level of melodic fluency and is expertly crafted, little of it remains in the memory. The *String Sextet* makes the most immediate and positive impact but, after the CD has come to an end, one realizes why Holbrooke has not stayed the course. The fine Hungarian ensemble play these pieces with appropriate conviction and ardour. Decent recording, much better than for the orchestral disc.

HOLMBOE, Vagn (1909–96)

Chamber Concertos Nos. 8 (Sinfonia concertante), Op. 83; 10 (Woodwind, Brass and Gut), Op. 40; Concerto giocondo e severo, Op. 132; Den Galsindede Tyrk (The ill-tempered Turk): Ballet Suite, Op. 32b.
*** BIS CD 917. Aalborg SO, Arwel Hughes.

The *Eighth Chamber Concerto* was one of the first of Holmboe's orchestral works to be given in England (by Harry Newstone and the Haydn Orchestra). It belongs in a set of twelve chamber concertos composed during 1939–50 (a thirteenth followed in 1955). There is a strongly neo-classical flavour to both scores, and those who enjoy the exhilarating *Fifth Symphony* will derive much pleasure from both, and particularly the resourceful theme-and-variations that comprise the second movement of the *Eighth*. Good though the complete survey by the Danish Radio Sinfonietta is on dacapo (see our main volume), these performances and above all the recordings are even finer.

In the *Concerto giocondo e severo* of 1977, Holmboe returned to the genre and produced a short work of just over ten minutes, which is scored for much larger forces than its predecessors but which has much of their ambience and spirit and is every bit as rewarding. Holmboe composed little for the stage, though there is an opera, *Kniven* ('The Knife') – and his ballet *Den Galsindede Tyrk* ('The Ill-tempered Turk'), based on a Thousand-and-One-Nights theme by the Danish author and illustrator Axel Salto, which occupied him in 1942–4, was never mounted. In 1970 Holmboe returned to the score and fashioned a five-movement work of quality from the original, recasting and rescoring much of it. In a tribute in the journal *Nordic Sounds* the Canadian scholar Paul Rapaport wrote of Holmboe as 'a noble and wondrous composer', and here is another disc to bear witness to that. As his BIS cycle of the symphonies has shown, Owain Arwel Hughes and his fine Aalborg musicians are completely attuned to Holmboe's world and the recording has all the realism, clarity and presence one has come to expect from BIS and Robert Suff. Recommended with all possible enthusiasm.

HOLMÈS, Augusta (1847–1903)

Andromeda (symphonic poem); *Ireland* (symphonic poem); (i) *Ludus pro patria: Night & Love. Overture for a Comedy; Poland* (symphonic poem).

*** Marco Polo 8.223449. Rheinland-Pfalz PO, Friedmann; (i) Davin.

Augusta Holmès was from an Anglo-Irish family that had settled in France. She was a person of remarkable gifts for, apart from her musical talents, she was an accomplished painter and wrote well. Although the *Overture for a Comedy* (1876) is trite, *Andromeda* is quite striking. It is by far the best piece on the disc, and the best scored, though limitations in Holmès's technique are evident. But this is music of much interest – and its composer was obviously no mean talent. She has been well served by the Rheinland-Pfalz Philharmonic under Samuel Friedmann. The recordings, too, are eminently satisfactory.

HOLST, Gustav (1874–1934)

Egdon Heath; The Perfect Fool (Ballet Suite).

⊶ (M) *** EMI 5 62615-2 [5 626162]. LSO, Previn – BRITTEN: *Sinfonia da Requiem* etc. *** ●

Previn's account of *Egdon Heath* is full of dark intensity and his *Perfect Fool* ballet suite makes a colourful, extrovert contrast. First-class recording makes this an excellent bonus for Previn's outstanding Britten coupling.

The Planets (suite), *Op. 32.*

(M) *** Decca 476 17242. Montreal Ch. & SO, Dutoit.
(M) ** RCA 74321 68018-2. Philh. O, Slatkin (with VAUGHAN WILLIAMS: *Fantasia on Greensleeves*, etc. **(*))
** Häns. 93.043. Stuttgart RSO (with Ch.), Norrington – ELGAR: *Serenade for Strings.* **

(i) *The Planets* (Suite); *Beni Mora* (Oriental Suite); (ii) *The Perfect Fool* (Ballet Suite).

(B) *** CfP 585 9132. (i) BBC SO; (ii) RPO; Sargent.

Charles Dutoit's natural feeling for mood, rhythm and colour, so effectively used in his records of Ravel,

here results in an outstandingly successful version of *The Planets*, both rich and brilliant, and recorded with an opulence to outshine almost all rivals. It is remarkable that, whether in the relentless build-up of *Mars*, the lyricism of *Venus*, the rich exuberance of *Jupiter* or in much else, Dutoit and his Canadian players sound so idiomatic. It won the *Gramophone* Engineering Award in 1987, as well it might, and now appears in Universal's '*Gramophone* Awards Collection' at mid-price.

The EMI engineers have freshened the quality of Sargent's early stereo recordings on Classics for Pleasure, made in Kingsway Hall in the late 1950s and Abbey Road in 1961, so that they hardly sound dated at all, and have still plenty of spectacle. Sir Malcolm introduced many of us to *The Perfect Fool* and, like *The Planets*, his performance is full of character. *Mars*, taken fast, like *Uranus*, has plenty of clarity and bite and the organ pedals come through well in the sombre portrayal of *Saturn*, while the central tune in *Jupiter* is given special dignity. Sargent is equally at home in *Beni Mora*, an attractively exotic piece that shows Holst's flair for orchestration in a different but equally vivid way. Altogether a splendid collection, showing Sargent at his most charismatic

Slatkin's recording dates from 1996 and has the benefit of first-class orchestral playing and recording. He brings out much of the beauty and detail of the work if, ultimately, the reading does not convey the full magical qualities that the score possesses. *Mercury* is certainly fleet and light, but *Jupiter*, the 'Bringer of Jollity', feels a little earth-bound. *Saturn* and *Neptune*, too, seem just that bit too slow and uncelestial in Slatkin's hands, whereas in other accounts, Boult's for example, the otherworldly qualities of the score are conveyed much more mystically.

Very well played and recorded, with complex textures clarified, Norrington's reading of *The Planets* is of interest as an example of a German orchestra tackling English music, but the result is literal rather than idiomatic. *Mars* is very slow and emphatic, leading to an account of *Venus* that is steady and meticulous rather than poetic. *Mercury* and *Jupiter* then sound a little cautious, with the big tune of *Jupiter* not as legato as usual, with detached phrasing. The other three movements at steady speeds are also too metrical to convey the evocative overtones that Holst requires, though the offstage chorus (unnamed) sings most beautifully in the final movement, *Neptune*.

The Planets (original version for 2 pianos); *Cotswolds Symphony: Elegy: In Memoriam William Morris* (original version for 2 pianos).

*** Olympia OCD 683. Goldstone and Clemmov – ELGAR: *String Serenade;* BAINTON: *Miniature Suite* *** (with BURY: *Prelude & Fugue in E flat* ***).

On Olympia it comes as a surprise to find how

effective the score sounds on two pianos. *Mars*, grumbling ominously in the bass, certainly does not lack menace or power at its climax, *Venus* has remarkable translucence, and if nimble pianism cannot match a delicate string tracery in *Mercury*, *Saturn* is highly evocative. *Jupiter* is ebullient enough, although the performers here choose to play the famous central tune quite slowly and almost elegiacally, and to good effect. *Uranus* opens baldly and strongly, then is made to dance along spiritedly. Altogether a great success. The *Elegy*, part of the neglected *Cotswolds Symphony*, stands up well on its own.

VOCAL MUSIC

Part Songs: *Ave Maria; Bring us in good ale; Diverus and Lazarus; Home they brought her warrior dead; I love my love; In youth is pleasure; I sow'd the seeds of love; Jesu, Thou the Virgin-born; Light leaves whisper; Lullay my liking; Mae 'nghariad i'n Fenws; Matthew, Mark, Luke and John; Now sleeps the crimson petal; Of one that is so fair and bright; O spiritual pilgrim; O swallow, swallow; The Song of the Blacksmith; The splendour falls; Spring; Summer; Swansea Town; Sweet and low; Tears, idle tears; Terly, terlow; There was a tree; This I have done for my True Love; A Welcome Song.*

⊕ (BB) ******* Hyp. Helios CDH 55171. Holst Singers, Layton (with Theodore, Truman, Williams).

A wholly delightful collection: it has so many treasures and the music and singing (and recording) are of such quality that, as the original *Gramophone* review rightly commented, it is 'a joy to listen through without interruption'. The sheer technical excellence of the singing is remarkable, as is Stephen Layton's absolute control: the blending peeerless, partly because the choir's intonation is absolutely secure.

The programme opens with carols (the eight-part double-choir setting of *Ave Maria* has an extraordinarily rich interplay of harmony, and the two linked numbers – *A Welcome Song* and *Terly terlow* – both with David Theodore (oboe) and Robert Truman (cello) – are enchanting. The programme then become more robust with *Bring us in good ale* and a strophic *Diverus and Lazarus*, the tune of which we know so well from the Vaughan Williams stringpiece. Another passage which has been used elsewhere (this time by Holst himself, in one of the *Military Band Suites*) pictures the syncopated hammering of *The Song of the Blacksmith* with its refrain, *Kiki, kikki, kang, kang*, which sounds for all the world like 'Chitty, chitty, bang, bang', and with the same rhythm.

The group of settings from Tennyson's *The Princess* was written for schoolgirl singers, but you would never guess that. The radiant *Sweet and low* and *The splendour falls* have superbly evocative

imitative effects, spectacularly echoing into the distance, the latter ending with the repeated word 'dying' fading away, rather like *Neptune* in *The Planets*. The lovely *Now sleeps the crimson petal* brings delightful overlapping of parts, and the unpronounceable Welsh folksong translates as 'My sweetheart's like Venus'. *There was a tree*, richly expanded, brings ever-varying tempo changes. Holst's imagination knows no bounds and this is altogether a superb reminder of his remarkable versatility.

HOLT, Simon (born 1958)

... era madrugada ...; Shadow Realm; Sparrow Night; (i) *Canciones.*
*** NMC D008. (i) Kimm; Nash Ens., Friend.

Regularly Simon Holt has found inspiration in Spanish sources, particularly Lorca, and two of these four pieces are fine examples – *... era madrugada ...*, a sinister evocation of a Lorca poem about a man found murdered in the hour just before dawn (*madrugada*). Like the other three pieces, it was written for the Nash Ensemble, who here under Lionel Friend respond superbly to Holt's virtuoso demands. Fiona Kimm is the formidable mezzo soloist in three Spanish settings, *Canciones*; but rather more approachable are the two highly atmospheric instrumental works, *Shadow Realm* and *Sparrow Night*, which round the disc off. These two also bring sinister nightmare overtones. The superb recording is engineered by Holt's fellow-composer, Colin Matthews.

HOLTEN, Bo (born 1948)

(i) *Clarinet Concerto* (1987); (ii) *Sinfonia Concertante for Cello & Orchestra* (1985–6).
*** Chan. 9272 (i) Schou; (ii) Zeuten; Danish Nat. RSO; cond. (i) Panula; (ii) Graf.

Bo Holten's *Clarinet Concerto* is certainly appealing. The *Sinfonia Concertante* comes from a broadcast of 1987 and is long on complexity (36' 6") and short on substance, but there are sufficient moments of poetic vision to encourage one to return to it. It is played with great zest and conviction by Morten Zeuten (cellist of the Kontra Quartet), and the recording has exemplary presence and clarity.

HONEGGER, Arthur (1892–1955)

Cello Concerto.
** MDG 0321 0215-2. Schmid, NW German PO, Roggen – BLOCH: *Schelomo.* ******

Ulrich Schmid and the Nordwestdeutsche Philharmonie under the Swiss conductor Dominique Roggen give a dedicated account of Honegger's delightful *Cello Concerto*. All the same, at only 42 minutes' playing time, this would be distinctly uncompetitive even at bargain price, let alone premium rate.

Symphonies Nos. 1–5; Pacific 231.

(BB) ** EMI Gemini (ADD) 5 85516-2 (2). Toulouse Capitole O, Plasson.

Michel Plasson has the advantage of fine recordings from the late 1970s, and the spacious acoustics of the Toulouse Halle-aux-Grains seem right for the music. However, the performances do not have the panache and virtuosity that make Karajan's coupling of Nos. 2 and 3 (DG 447 435-2) so memorable, or the character of Munch's account of No. 4; at times, in the most searing music, one feels a lack of grip and emotional intensity. Nevertheless, there are some fine moments here, and Plasson finds much of the charm in *No. 4*, even if the Scherzo of the *Fifth Symphony* sounds rather tame. One other point: in the *Symphony for Strings* (the *Second*) the trumpet for which Honegger called to strengthen the chorale, but which he did not regard as mandatory, is omitted. The CD transfers are natural in balance and enhance the sound, which has plenty of ambience.

Symphony No. 4 (Deliciae Basiliensis).

(M) *** Erato 2564 60572-2. O Nat. de l'ORTF, Munch – DUTILLEUX: *Symphony No. 4; Métaboles.* ***

Munch's account of the *Symphony 'Deliciae Basiliensis'*, based on Swiss folksongs, the chimes, the Basler Morgenstraich and so on, is indeed a delight, and this version is arguably still the best. Its appearance at budget price makes for an outstanding bargain.

Jeanne d'Arc au bûcher.

♦→ ✸ (M) *** DG 476 16502. Keller, Wilson, Escourrou, Lanzi, Pollet, Command, Stutzman, Aler, Courtis, R. France Ch., Fr. Nat. O, Ozawa.
** Cascavelle VEL 3024 (2). Petrovna, Lonsdale, Dominique, Maîtrise des Haute-de-Seine, Ch. de Rouen-Haute-Normandie, O Symphonie Français, Petitgirard.

Honegger's 1935 setting of the Claudel poem is one of his most powerful and imaginative works, full of variety of invention, colour and textures. It is admirably served by these forces, and in particular by the Joan of Marthe Keller. The singers, too, are all excellent and the Choir and the six soloists of the Maîtrise of Radio France are as top-drawer as the orchestra. The DG engineers cope excellently with the large forces and the acoustic of the Basilique de Saint-Denis. This now reappears at mid-price among Universal's 'Penguin ✸ Collection'.

Though strong on atmosphere, Laurent Petitgirard on Cascavelle takes a rather measured approach. Although he gets generally good results from his forces and has the benefit of first-rate recorded sound, Ozawa is to be preferred both artistically and

as a recording. The Cascavelle set offers two booklets, one in French, the other in German, with 36 pages of artist and session photos but no translations into English, Italian or Spanish. DG offered a four-language booklet as well as an authoritative note by Harry Hallbreich. That set also accommodates the work on one CD, while this new version from Cascavelle runs to two. Of course, this extraordinary piece still casts a strong spell and if you can't find the Ozawa this is better than nothing.

HOTTETERRE, Jacques
(1674–1763)

(i) 6 Trio Sonatas, Op. 3; (ii) Suite for 2 Treble Recorders without Continuo in D min., Op. 4.

(M) ** Teldec (ADD) 3984 26797-2. (i) Boeke, Van Hauwe, Möller, Van Asperen; (ii)Brüggen, Boeke.

All the music gathered here was published in 1712. The *Trio Sonatas* are agreeable enough and are variously scored for pairs of treble recorders or voice flutes (Nos. 2 and 5), of which the latter works come off best here. Truth to tell, although the performances are authentic, complete with *notes inégales* (where the first note of two successive quavers is lengthened and the second correspondingly shortened), the sounds produced by Kees Boeke and Walter van Hauwe are somewhat pale. Their music-making is completely upstaged by the *Suite sans continuo*, where the far stronger personality of Frans Brüggen dominates the proceedings and brings this fine work vividly to life, especially its key movement, a splendid closing *Passacaille*. The recording is forward but truthful. This reissue would have been more enticing in Teldec's budget range.

HOWELLS, Herbert (1892–1983)

Clarinet Sonata; A Near-Minuet for Clarinet & Piano; Prelude for Harp; Rhapsodic Clarinet Quintet; Violin Sonata No. 3.

(BB) *** Naxos 8.557188. Mobius.

Howells's *Rhapsodic Quintet* for clarinet and string quartet is one of the most beautiful clarinet works of the twentieth century, a piece written in 1919 which brought the young composer immediate recognition. Robert Plane, the clarinet of the talented group Mobius, plays with a ravishing range of tone and natural warmth, well supported by the string quartet led by Philippe Honore. Plane is also the brilliant soloist in Howells's even more ambitious *Clarinet Sonata* of 1946, a work in two extended movements (one predominantly reflective, one fast), more angular and percussive than one expects from Howells. Honore is the violinist with the pianist Sophia Rahman in the powerful *Violin Sonata No. 3*, written for Albert Sammons in 1923 after a visit by the composer to Canada, inspired by the rugged grandeur of the

Rockies. The *Prelude for Harp* and the *Near-Minuet for Clarinet and Piano* are attractive make-weights for a superb disc, compelling in every way and vividly recorded.

Violin Sonatas Nos. 1 in E, Op. 18; 2 in E flat, Op. 26; 3 in E min., Op. 38; Cradle Song, Op. 9/1; 3 Pieces, Op. 28.

✪ (BB) *** Hyp. Helios CDH 55139. Barritt, Edwards.

A truly outstanding disc, missed by us when it first appeared in 1993. The three *Violin Sonatas* come from an intensely creative period. The *First* (1917) was originally entitled *Phantasy Sonata* but was later (during 1919) revised. In four movements, it opens delicately and romantically, darkens a little in the *Meno mosso*, then, after a brief, unbridled *Scherzo*, ends in ravishing tranquillity. The *Second*, although in only three movements, is a bigger work both emotionally and in its overall span and bold forward impulse. Rhapsodically lyrical, with a lovely, simple, folk-like slow movement, it bursts into sparkling vitality in the finale. The *Third Sonata* maintains the English pastoral character in its underlying lyricism, but erupts with energy in the pizzicato centrepiece, which carries through into the restless finale: both are marked *assai ritmico*. The main theme of the delightful *Cradle Song* is rather like a Slavonic folk-tune, and while the first two of the *Three Pieces* are richly English in feeling, the haunting finale is actually based on a Russian folksong. Paul Barritt and Catherine Edwards are right inside this music and play together with a passionate and moving single voice; moreover, they are superbly balanced and recorded. The ✪ is for the sheer pleasure this record brings when it is played straight through – such is the variety of the music, with the splendid *Second Sonata* rightly coming last.

HUME, Tobias (c. 1575–1645)

Captain Humes Poeticall Musick (1607) (music for viols, lute and voice).

(BB) *** Naxos 8.55416/7 (available separately). Les Voix Humains.

Tobias Hume was a mercenary who served in both the Swedish and Russian armies. Relatively little is known about him. The dedications of his two collections, the *First Part of Ayres* (1605) and the *Poeticall Musick* (1607), were designed to court favour, the first from the Earl of Pembroke. He was a champion of the viol as opposed to the lute, and the pieces recorded here vindicate him. It is obvious that he was an accomplished composer, and this excellently recorded Canadian ensemble prove persuasive advocates. A most enjoyable and welcome addition to the catalogue.

HUMFREY, Pelham (1647–74)

Verse Anthems: By the Waters of Babylon; Have Mercy on Me, O God; Hear, O Heav'ns; Hear my Crying, O God; Hear my Prayer, O God; Lift up your Heads; Like as the Hart; O give thanks unto the Lord; O Lord my God.

⊖ (BB) *** HM HMX 2907053. Deam, Minter, Covey-Crump, Potter, David Thomas, Clare Coll., Cambridge, Ch., Romanesca, McGegan.

Here yet another name from the past emerges as a remarkably strong musical personality. Pelham Humfrey (or Humphrey) began his career as a chorister at the Chapel Royal, and he made such an impression that he was sent abroad at the expense of the royal purse of Charles II to study in France and Italy. After more than one visit he returned as a Gentleman of the Chapel Royal and, when the incumbent died in 1672, he took over as Master of the Choristers. He married, and his short life ended at the age of 27. He brought back from Italy (and from Lully in France) a thorough absorption of the operatic style, and his verse-anthems are remarkably dramatic and powerfully expressive, using soloists almost like operatic characters. *By the Waters of Babylon* and, especially, *O Lord my God* are very striking indeed. Nicholas McGegan's fine performances reflect this histrionic dimension, helped by his soloists who at times approach stylistic boundaries in their performance of what is essentially devotional music, even if intensely felt. Nevertheless, no one could say that these authentic performances are in any way dampened by scholarly rectitude. With a highly sensitive instrumental contribution from the excellent Romanesca, this collection (about half of Humfrey's surviving output) is very freshly recorded, and this bargain reissue is strongly recommended to the adventurous collector.

HUMMEL, Johann (1778–1837)

Amusement for Piano & Violin in F min., Op. 108; Violin Sonatas: in F, Op. 5/2; C, Op. 14; Variations 'alla Monferina' in D, Op. 54 for Piano & Cello.

*** Mer. CDE 84439. Triangulus.

The title 'Amusement' for the first of the four works on this Meridian disc could not be more apt. This is in effect a compact sonatina for violin and piano, which brings out the open, unpretentious qualities of Hummel's writing at their most appealing The outer movements are built on tinkling tunes (the finale in jaunty polka-rhythm), while the slow movement is a song without words in all but name, with a reminder not just of Mendelssohn but of Bellini. Though longer and structurally more elaborate, the other two *Sonatas* are hardly more ambitious, two works similarly designed to entertain without making too many demands on the listener. The Op. 5 work, an early piece, again has a song without words for its slow movement and another jaunty finale. The Op. 14 is just as charming, with the slow movement, similarly songful, this time in a yearning minor key.

The *Variations 'alla Monferina'* for cello and piano, varied and inventive, have a haunting little refrain in 6/8 which recurs at various points. After ten variations the piece is rounded off with a galloping 6/8 coda. Though Alison Moncrieff's cello is not helped by the recording, which underlines some minor flaws, this is another engaging example of Hummel's attractive and undemanding writing. In both the works with violin and those with cello, Lyn Garland at the piano is the prime mover, as Hummel would have expected, always fresh and lively.

Missa Solemnis in C; Te Deum.

⊕━ (BB) ★★★ Naxos 8.557193. Wright, McKendree-Wright, Power, Griffiths, Tower Voices, New Zealand SO, Grodd.

Following Richard Hickox's brilliant Chandos issue of two Hummel Masses (Chan. 0681 – see our main volume) comes more evidence of the vigour that this neglected composer brought to his choral works. On the recommendation of Haydn he was carrying on the tradition of writing annual Masses for Prince Esterházy, demonstrating what a sense of drama he had in illustrating the liturgy, masterly in counterpoint and orchestration, never resorting to notespinning, as he often does in his keyboard writing. Here with New Zealand forces, including the brilliant professional chamber choir, Tower Voices, we have the longest of Hummel's five Masses in coupling with an electrifying setting of the *Te Deum*. Both were written in 1806, and one is constantly reminded that this was the period of the Napoleonic wars, when each of these works so often features martial music with fanfares, trumpets and drums. Unlike most Anglican settings, this *Te Deum* ends on a grand *fortissimo*. A thrilling issue, all the more recommendable at super-bargain price.

CHAMBER MUSIC

Piano Sonatas Nos. 3 in F min., Op. 20; 4 in F sharp min., Op. 81; 6 in D, Op. 106.

⊕━ ★★★ Hyp. CDA 67390. Hough.

Johann Nepomuk Hummel, renowned as one of the greatest pianists of his day, wrote a series of works to celebrate his own virtuosity – not just piano concertos (already recorded by a number of pianists, including Stephen Hough) but sonatas, of which nine are for solo piano. These three, arguably the finest of the series, generally avoid the empty passage-work which sometimes mars the concertos, and Hough gives the most characterful performances, beautifully recorded. The most radical of the three, written in 1819, is in F sharp minor, in which

Hummel fully embraces the new romantic movement, with a first movement that brings a very free rendering of sonata form, full of contrasts and surprises, built on a striking, angular main theme. The slow movement after a weighty introduction then anticipates Chopin's *Nocturnes*, leading to an energetic Slavonic dance finale. *No. 4 in D* marks a return to a more classical manner, at times like Weber, with a fast mazurka for Scherzo, while *No. 3 in F minor* of 1807 has a quirkiness typical of the composer, with a central slow movement marked to be played 'majestically'. In its way this makes as much of a discovery as Richard Hickox's revelatory recordings of Hummel *Masses*.

HUMPERDINCK, Engelbert
(1854–1921)

The Canteen Woman (Die Marketenderin): Prelude. The Merchant of Venice: Love Scene. Moorish Rhapsody: Tarifa (Elegy of Summer); Tangier (A Night in a Moorish Coffee-house); Tetuan (A Night in the Desert). The Sleeping Beauty: Suite.

★★(★) Marco Polo 8.223369. Slovak RSO (Bratislava), M. Fischer-Dieskau.

The Love scene from *The Merchant of Venice* ('On such a night') is beautiful but rather over-extended, and all three sections of the *Moorish Rhapsody* are much too long (the composite piece lasts some 32 minutes). The opening of the *Summer Elegy* begins with raptly ethereal writing for the violins, but the jolly Moorish coffee-house sequence sounds as if the restaurant has been leased from the owner of a Bavarian bierkeller. The Slovak performances under Martin Fischer-Dieskau (the famous Lieder singer's grandson) are not ideally polished but have freshness and vitality, while the Marco Polo recording is open and reasonably full.

Hansel and Gretel (complete; in English).

⊕━ (B) ★★★ CfP (ADD) 5 75993-2 (2). Kern, Neville, Howard, Hunter, Herincx, Robinson, Sadler's Wells Op. O, Bernadi (with WAGNER: *Siegfried Idyll*: L. Sinf., C. Davis ★★★).

This was the first full-length Sadler's Wells Opera recording in English, and it proved to be one of the finest of all the company's ventures into the recording studio. It was also the first complete foreign opera in English on record since way back in the days of early operatic 78s. EMI used their then (1964) new 'ambionic' technique with feedback, bringing extra reverberation to the comparatively dry No. 1 Studio at Abbey Road. The result is warm and atmospheric and not at all artificial sounding.

As for the performance, it is in every way successful, and the clear English words undoubtedly enhance one's enjoyment at every point, with no musical loss. The singing is full of zest, with Patricia Kern and Margaret Neville as the two children in splendid voice (and vocally well differentiated). Rita Hunter and the richly resonant Raimund Herincx are strongly cast as Mother and Father, and the smaller parts of the Dew Fairy (Jennifer Eddy) and Sandman (Elizabeth Robinson) are delightfully sung. Ann Howard makes a characterful and believable Witch. But the overall achievement relies much on the Canadian conductor, Mario Bernadi, who not only keeps the narrative flow sparklingly alive, but also ensures that the orchestra consistently excels itself. The English text rises over the ripe orchestral sound, and altogether this is just as rewarding as any of the German-language versions, and altogether more accessible (for there is an excellent synopsis). With room to spare on the second CD, EMI remind us of the Wagnerian affinities of Humperdinck's score by including Colin Davis's 1960 Sinfonia of London recording of the *Siegfried Idyll*, a real performance and enjoyable for its simplicity and eloquence, although the sound is a little dated. The opera is not to be missed.

IBERT, Jacques (1890–1962)

Bacchanale; Divertissement; Escales; Ouverture de fête; Symphonie marine.
(BB) ✶ Naxos 8.554222. LOP, Sado.

Sado's *Divertissement* is without the sheer champagne fizz of Martinon's old – but exceptionally vivid – Decca recording (currently withdrawn). *Escales* also suffers from comparison with more magical accounts already available (from Munch and Paray) and, while the *Symphonie marine* is a rarity, it is musically rather thin. The *Ouverture de fête* is enjoyable enough but does rather outstay its welcome. The recording is quite good and the CD is cheap but is difficult to recommend even so.

Flute Concerto.
✶✶✶ EMI 5 57563-2. Pahud, Tonhalle O, Zinman – KHACHATURIAN: *Flute Concerto.* ✶✶✶

Emmanuel Pahud and the Zurich Tonhalle Orchestra under David Zinman give the most virtuosic and stylish account of Ibert's delightful *Flute Concerto*. No need to hesitate if you accept the coupling, for not only is the performance outstanding but so, too, is the recorded sound.

INDY, Vincent d' (1851–1931)

(i) *Fantasy on French Popular Themes* (for oboe & orchestra), *Op. 31. Saugelfleurie* (Legend after a Tale by Robert de Bonnières); *Tableaux de voyage, Op. 36; L'Etranger: Prelude to Act II. Fervaal: Prelude to Act I.*
✶✶ Marco Polo 8.223659. (i) Cousu; Württemberg PO, Nopre or (i) Burfin.

The tone-poem *Saugelfleurie*, based on a tale by

Robert de ... *age* and the ... music of qu... seeds of popu... *populaires fran...* fervent charm w... ances of all these p... distinction but are ... too, is eminently s... French music need n...

Symphonie sur un chan... (Symphonie cévenole).
(✶✶) Testament mono SBT ... iccolini, Paris Conservatoire O, Cluytens – FRANCK: *Symphonic Variations; Symphony.* (✶(✶))

As with the Franck *Variations symphoniques*, d'Indy's *Symphonie sur un chant montagnard français* (sometimes known as the *Symphonie cévenole*) was recorded in the Théâtre des Champs-Elysées in 1953, and suffers from too forwardly balanced a soloist and a dryish acoustic. The playing of Aldo Ciccolini is sensitive, and André Cluytens is very supportive.

IRELAND, John (1879–1962)

CHAMBER MUSIC

Violin Sonatas Nos. 1 in D min.; 2 in A min.; Bagatelle; Berceuse; Cavatina; The Holy Boy.
(BB) ✶✶✶ Hyp. Helios CDH 55164. Barritt, Edwards.

Paul Barritt and Catherine Edwards make an effective partnership and give very persuasive accounts of both these fine sonatas. An excellent, well-balanced recording earns this a strong recommendation to those wanting just this repertoire alone on a single (budget) disc.

IVES, Charles (1874–1954)

(i) *New England Holidays Symphony. Three Places in New England;* (i) *They are there!*
▶ ✿ (M) ✶✶✶ Decca 476 153-2. (i) Baltimore SO Ch.; Baltimore SO, Zinman.

Opening with the exuberantly spectacular Sousa-esque choral march *They are there!* (a true lollipop if ever there was one), this is now the finest CD coupling of Ives's two key masterworks, the *New England Symphony* and *Three Places in New England*. The orchestral playing is splendid: the quiet, gentle evocations raptly sustained by the strings and woodwind, the multitude of quotations wittily evoked, and the polyphonic and polytonal clashes are all presented with great vigour and panache. The vivid Decca recording is truly in the demonstration class, handling the complicated sound-pictures with remarkable clarity, yet within a spacious ambience. The brief entry of the Baltimore Symphony Chorus

200 JANÁČEK
at the close of Thanksgiving moment
truly arresting moment

...and *Forefathers' Day* is a

dental music for a play by Gerhardt Hauptmann, *Schluck und Jau*. Mackerras describes it as 'a peculiar play whose subject matter bears a great resemblance to Beckett's *Waiting for Godot*'. The first of the two completed movements brings some intriguing echoes of the fanfares in the *Sinfonietta*, and the second in 5/8 time is equally original in its unexpected instrumentation, with deep trombones and stratospheric violins, light and exciting, with a brassy climax. The suite taken from *The Cunning Little Vixen*, consisting of virtually the whole of Act I without the voices, is here given in Janáček's own sharply original orchestration, whereas generally the smoothed-over version of Vaclav Talich is used. Best of all, the two central orchestral works, the *Sinfonietta* and *Taras Bulba*, come in live recordings which, spurred on by a Czech audience, are magnetic, flowing lightly and flexibly, building up in excitement. Mackerras has recorded both these works before with great success, but these latest versions are even warmer and more idiomatic, crowning the whole collection, helped by full and spacious recording.

...CEK, Leoš (1854–1928)

...HAMBER MUSIC

(i) *Concertino for piano and seven instruments;* (ii) *Sinfonietta; Taras Bulba.*
☐━ ✪ *** (M) *** DG 476 2196. (i) Firkušný, Bav. RSO (members); (ii) Bav. RSO; Kubelik.

A quite outstanding bargain triptych that would make a worthwhile addition to any collection, large or small. Kubelik has a special feeling for this repertoire, and he partners Rudolf Firkušný in a thoroughly idiomatic account of the *Concertino*, with the dialogue between keyboard and sparsely scored accompaniment both plangent and witty. *Taras Bulba*, with its unpleasant scenario of death and torture, is powerfully evoked, with a discerning balance between passion and subtlety. The organ part is integrated into the texture most delicately in the first section, yet adds grandiloquence to the work's triumphant apotheosis, with its vision of a triumphant Cossack future. Virtuoso playing from the Bavarian orchestra throughout, with much excitement generated in the last two sections. The orchestra is hardly less impressive in the *Sinfonietta* (and particularly so in the central movements), while at the opening and close of the work the spacious acoustic of the Munich Herculessaal is especially suited to the massed brass effects. The vintage (1970) recording has been superbly remastered and sounds amazingly fresh. It is now reissued as part of Universal's mid-price 'Penguin ✪ Collection'.

Sinfonietta; Taras Bulba; Jealousy Prelude; The Cunning Little Vixen: Suite. Káta Kabanová: Overture & Interludes. Sárka Overture. Schluck und Jau (incidental music): excerpts: Andante & Allegretto.
*** Sup. SU 3739-2 (2). Czech PO, Mackerras.

No one can match Sir Charles Mackerras as an inspired and dedicated advocate of the music of Janáček. Issued to celebrate the 150th anniversary of the composer's birth, this collection neatly encompasses the whole span of his career. *Sarka*, his first opera, is represented by the *Overture* in an excerpt from Mackerras's revelatory complete recording, issued two years ago, and the *Káta Kabanová* excerpts (including the two delightful little *Interludes* that Mackerras himself discovered in Prague) similarly come from his complete recording of 1997. The other items all come in completely new recordings, with the Czech Philharmonic responding warmly in what may well be Mackerras's very last Janáček recordings. Apart from *Jealousy*, the original prelude to *Jenůfa*, the rarity in the collection is the very last orchestral music that Janáček wrote, two pieces from the inci-

Violin Sonata.
*** HM HMC 901793. Faust, Kupiec —
LUTOSLAWSKI: *Partita; Subito;* SZYMANOWSKI: *3 Mythes.* ***
**(*) Avie AV0023. Gleusteen, Ordonneau —
PROKOFIEV: *Violin Sonata No. 1;*
SHOSTAKOVICH: *19 Preludes.* **(*)
(BB) *(*) EMI Encore 5 85708-2. Zimmermann, Lonquich — DEBUSSY: *Violin Sonata;* RAVEL: *Violin Sonata; Sonata posthume.* *(*)

The programme on the Harmonia Mundi disc may seem an odd mixture, but it works well. Quite apart from all three composers having a Slavonic background, the performances bring out unexpected similarities, not just between the Janáček and Szymanowski, both dating from 1915, but with the much more recent Lutoslawski *Partita* of 1984. There is a spontaneous sense of fantasy in all these performances which lightly brings out the quirky side of the Janáček, and also does similarly in some passages of the Lutoslawski *Partita*, while the pianist Ewa Kupiec matches Isabelle Faust in drawing out the atmospheric beauties of Szymanowski's *Three Mythes*. The Janáček makes a sharp opening item that in the hands of these performers flows on naturally as though they are improvising it with its potentially awkward tremolos and trills in the first movement and the odd, fragmentary interjections so typical of Janáček. In the lyrical *Ballata* second movement, Isabelle Faust's *pianissimo* playing is breathtaking.

The similarly mixed bag of Slavonic works on the Avie disc makes an impressive showcase for the talents of the Canadian-born violinist, Kai Gleusteen, and his French accompanist, Catherine Ordonneau. Their account of the quirky Janáček *Violin Sonata* is most compelling, though Faust brings out the fantasy more clearly in this highly original work. In a relaxed manner, with pure violin tone, Gleusteen brings the work closer than usual to the central repertory, finding fire in the energetically folk-based third movement. The recording, one of a series made in the 'inspirational and innovative working space' of Crear, on the west coast of Scotland, is on the reverberant side, thanks to the large, bare studio where it was made, but there is no lack of detail.

Frank Peter Zimmermann projects this wonderful *Sonata* with conviction, though his accompanist is not exactly the last word in sensitivity. Not really recommendable, despite the attractive couplings and the modest price.

PIANO MUSIC

Along an Overgrown Path: Books I & II; In the Mists; A Recollection; Piano Sonata (1.X.1905).
✱ (✱✱) ECM 461 660-2. Schiff.

András Schiff has great feeling for this repertoire and plays with enormous sensitivity and insight. But the recorded sound poses a real problem: there is a fair amount of reverberation, which at times smudges detail, and the instrument appears bass-heavy, ill-defined and thin on top. Readers should stick with Firkušný (DG 449 764-2) or Andsnes (Virgin 5 61839-2).

OPERA

✓ *The Cunning Little Vixen* (sung in English).
(M) **✱✱✱ Chan. 3101 (2). Watson, Allen, Tear, Knight, Howell, ROHCG Ch. & O, Rattle.**

Reissued in Chandos's 'Opera in English' series, the Rattle set is ideal for anyone wanting the opera in English. It gains from having been recorded as a spin-off from a highly successful Covent Garden production with the same excellent cast. In interpretation, Rattle's approach provides a clear contrast with that of Sir Charles Mackerras on his classic Decca version with the Vienna Philharmonic and a Czech cast (417 129-2). Where Mackerras characteristically brings out the sharp, angular side of Janáček's writing, the distinctively jagged element, Rattle's manner is more moulded, perhaps more immediately persuasive if less obviously idiomatic. The recording is beautifully balanced, with the new Chandos transfer a degree more open on top and cleaner in texture than the EMI, important in the ensembles. What matters is that the words in both are ideally clear, with excellent diction from everyone.

Jenůfa (sung in English).
(M) **✱✱✱ Chan. 3106 (2). Watson, Barstow, Wedd, Robson, Davies, WNO Ch. & O, Mackerras.**

Based on the acclaimed production of *Jenůfa* from Welsh National Opera, Sir Charles Mackerras's Chandos set offers an important alternative to the classic, prize-winning version he conducted in 1982 for Decca. The first obvious difference is the use of English in this issue in the Peter Moores Foundation's 'Opera in English' series. The translation by Edward Downes and Otakar Kraus works very well, even though the sumptuous Chandos recording places the voices a little further back than the Decca version does, with many words less clear. The benefit of the Chandos sound is that the colour and originality of Janáček's orchestral textures come over even more vividly than on the brilliant Decca set, at once opulent and well defined, with each strand clarified and the exotic percussion effects brought out. Helped by a few sound-effects, the result is generally more atmospheric.

In international terms the Welsh National Opera Orchestra may be no match for the Vienna Philharmonic on Decca, but their experience of this opera in the pit ensures not only that the playing is finely honed but that there is an extra idiomatic warmth, born of long experience, while reflecting the insights of the conductor. Using, as before, the original scoring of the so-called Brno version, without the radical re-orchestration imposed by Karel Kovarovic, Mackerras takes a marginally broader view than last time, remaining just as powerful and dramatic.

When it comes to the rival casts, they are both very strong, with no weak links. If it was luxury casting to have Elisabeth Söderström in the title-role on Decca, Janice Watson on Chandos has just as beautiful a voice, sounding more aptly young, fresh and girlish, and deeply expressive too. As the Kostelnicka, Dame Josephine Barstow presents a striking contrast to her Decca opposite number, Eva Randová, Wagnerian in richness and power. Barstow's voice is edgier and more abrasive, and with that she conveys not only the obsessive side of this powerful character but an element of vulnerability, apt for the story. The two tenor roles are also very well taken, with Peter Wedd as Steva and Nigel Robson as Laca nicely contrasted, effectively bringing out the sharp differences of character between the half-brothers. Elizabeth Vaughan as Grandmother Buryja and Neal Davies as the Foreman complete a formidable line-up of principals. Not surprisingly, words are much clearer from the male singers than from the female. The Chandos set does not include the extra items on the earlier Decca – the discarded Prelude Jealousy and Kovarovic's version of the opera's conclusion – but the final duet between Jenůfa and Laca is even more tender than it was in the Vienna performance, bringing out all the subtlety of Janáček's evocative writing.

The Makropulos Affair.
⊶ ✿ ✱✱✱ Warner DVD 0630 14016-2. Silja, Begley, Braun, Shore, LPO, A. Davis (Director: Nikolaus Lehnhoff; V/D: Brian Large).

The Makropulos Affair is Janáček's penultimate opera, and it is a masterpiece. It had an almost definitive performance on Decca with Elisabeth Söderström in one of her greatest roles as the 337-year-old heroine, Emilia Marty, and with the Vienna Philharmonic under Sir Charles Mackerras in superb form (430 372-2 – see our main volume). Now comes the 1995 Glyndebourne production by Nikolaus Lehnhoff, whose *Káta Kabanová* we so much admired, and with an astonishingly powerful account of the heroine from Anya Silja. In fact, it is difficult to flaw this production on any count. It is excellently cast, with Kim Begley as Gregor, Viktor Braun as Pruš and Andrew Shore as Dr Kolenaty, and it is conducted with a sense both of atmosphere and of pace by Sir Andrew Davis. He is hardly less idiomatic and sensitive than Mackerras. Those who were privileged to see this will not forget the excellence of the staging either, but above all the commanding portrayal of Emilia by Silja. As usual, Brian Large brings everything to the screen with scrupulous care and taste to make this a very special contribution to the Janáček DVD discography. A small but tiresome point: Warner's presentation is virtually non-existent and does not even run to a full cast-list.

JÄRNEFELT, Armas (1869–1958)

Berceuse; Korsholm; Ouverture lyrique; Praeludium; The Promised Land (Det förlovade landet): Suite; The Song of the Crimson Flower (Sången om den eldröda blomman).
** Sterling CDS-1021-2. Gävle SO, Koivula.

Järnefelt is best remembered nowadays for two light classics, the *Berceuse* and *Praeludium*, which still delight music-lovers. He was one of the first Nordic composers to write for the cinema: *The Song of the Crimson Flower* dates from 1919. All this music is direct in feeling and has a touch of nobility. It is national-romantic in character, not dissimilar to, say, Sibelius's *King Christian II* music. It is appropriate that it should be played by a Swedish orchestra, as he adopted Swedish nationality in the 1920s. Hannu Koivula's conducting disappoints. There is not enough charm in these performances. Worth hearing all the same.

Songs: (i) *A Dreamer's Song to Life; A Flower is Purest when Blossoming; To the Kantele; Lullany to Breaker; The Poor One; Rock, O Cradle; Summer Shore; On Sunday; Twilight; When all the clocks have struck twelve; You;* (ii) *Dream; A Fiddling and Dancing Tune; My Hope; The Lark; Sing, sing! Soft, soft; At Sunset; Sunshine.*
*** Ondine ODE 1029-2. (i) Nylund; (ii) Hynninen; Paananen.

Armas Järnefelt, four years younger than his brother-in-law Sibelius, outlived him by one year. (The family enjoyed a high profile: the father was governor of Kuopio, and his sons were all gifted artistically, Eero being a fine painter and Arvid a dramatist. Their only sister, Aino, was highly cultured and a good linguist.) Armas studied with Busoni during his Helsinki years and later with Massenet at Paris. As a conductor Järnefelt introduced the Wagner operas to Finland and in 1907 went to the Royal Opera in Stockholm, making a reputation as a fine Beethoven conductor and an authoritative Sibelius interpreter. In all there are some 60 songs of which 22 are given here. All of them are short – indeed, half are less than two minutes long, very much in the national romantic-vein idiom. Unusually for the period, half are to Finnish rather than Swedish texts. (The Järnefelts were keen advocates of the Finnish language, which during the nineteenth century enjoyed a subservient status to Swedish.) Although Järnefelt is not a great song composer, these are invariably well fashioned. Songs like *Skymning* ('Twilight'), the Fröding setting *I solnedsgången* ('At Sunset') and *Unelma* ('Dream') have a great simplicity and directness.

Although Jorma Hynninen has lost the youthful timbre and bloom we remember from his records of *Kullervo* and his Kilpinen recitals, he still sings with his usual intelligence and refinement, and he still gives pleasure. Camilla Nylund is a fresh-toned and appealing interpreter, and they are well served by their accompanist and recording team.

JENNER, Gustave (1865–1920)

Piano Quartet in F; String Quartets Nos. 1–3; (i) *Trio for Piano, Clarinet & Horn in E flat.*
*** CPO 999 699-2. Mozart Piano Qt (members); (i) with Pencz, Darbellay.

We don't know much about Gustave Jenner (born in Keitum on the Island of Sylt), though the insert notes are helpful. However, it is the music that matters, and this is another of CPO's interesting discoveries. The *Piano Quartet* begins with a lovely sweeping figure and the secondary theme is no less beguiling. The slow movement quotes Schubert's *Piano Trio in B flat* and is most attractively decorated. The lively Scherzo is then followed by a theme and variations with a diverting Hungarian sequence. The three *String Quartets* are very much in the tradition of Jenner's teacher and mentor, Brahms. They are quite spontaneous, with plenty of amiable ideas. Occasionally, too, there are darker, Hungarian colourings, notably in the *G minor Quartet*. The *Third Quartet* has a particularly attractive finale, witty and energetic and lyrically quite seductive. Though not in the league of the Brahms *Horn Trio* (Brahms apparently did not care too much for it), Jenner's differently scored work is notable for the facility and vigour of the writing, rather than any deeper qualities. But this remains an enjoyable enough collection of chamber rarities, and the performances and vivid sound make the very most of the music's felicities.

JOEL, Billy (born 1949)

Fantasies & Delusions for Solo Piano: Air (Dublinesqe); Aria (Grand Canal); Fantasy (Film Noir); Invention in C min.; Reverie (Villa d'Este); Soliloquy (On a Separation); Suite; Waltzes 1–3.
★★★ Sony SK 86397. Joo.

Billy Joel is a talented composer in the world of 'pop' music but here, in the most cultivated manner, he turns to music of a more permanent kind. His brief but memorable *Invention* certainly turns our thoughts to Bach and Scarlatti, but, although his skilful piano writing is thoroughly eclectic, Chopin is the predominating influence, especially in the *Third* of the three charming *Waltzes*, each quite different; and the *Aria* (subtitled *Grand Canal*) is like an extended nocturne. The closing, nostalgic *'Dublinesque' Air*, with its quirky mood-changes, is also most winning. Richard Joo maintains a sense of improvisatory spontaneity throughout the recital – Joel could hardly have a more persuasive advocate – and the recording is excellent. What a pity the documentation consists only of photographs and titles.

JONES, Daniel (1912–93)

String Quartets Nos. 1–8.
★★★ Chan. 9535 (2). Delmé Qt.

The *First Quartet* is a particularly impressive work, with a certain cosmopolitanism and a distinctly French tinge to its atmosphere. But Jones is always his own man. No. 2 is exploratory and has a characteristically concentrated *Lento espressivo*. Nos. 3–5 are distinguished by seriousness of purpose and fine craftsmanship. And for the most part this is more than just expertly fashioned music: it is unflamboyant, but all three works are of substance. The last three quartets are even more succinct (each lasting about a quarter of an hour). No. 6 marked the 250th birthday of Haydn and uses two of that master's themes. Its mood is strongly focused, moving from a solemn introduction (and back again) via the Haydnesque Scherzo and a simple slow movement. No. 7 is masterly, intensely concentrated: its central movement is marked *Penseroso*. The last quartet, full of memorable ideas, was left unfinished; it was skilfully completed from the composer's sketches by Giles Easterbrook. Appropriately, it has a hauntingly elegiac close. It is played here with enormous dedication and, like No. 7, holds the listener in a powerful emotional spell. A fitting conclusion to a splendid series, given definitive readings from a quartet closely identified with the music, and first-class Chandos sound.

JONES, Sidney (1861–1946)

The Geisha (complete).
★★★ Hyp. CDA 67006. Watson, Maltman, Walker, Suart, New L. Light Op. Ch. & O, Corp.

The Geisha makes a delightful, innocent romp, helped by a sparkling performance under Ronald Corp. Jones and his librettist, Owen Hall, sought to follow up the success of Gilbert and Sullivan's *Mikado*. The formula worked so well that this Japanese musical play ran for two years. Granted that Jones cannot match Sullivan in finesse or tuneful memorability, this has a striking sequence of numbers with such off-beat titles as *The amorous goldfish* and *The interfering parrot*. The choruses also work splendidly. Though Lillian Watson's bright soprano grows edgy at the top, she is charming as the heroine, Mimosa, and though Christopher Maltman's baritone grows gritty and uneven under pressure, he makes a dashing hero. Best of all is Sarah Walker, with her voice as rich and firm as ever, relishing the idiom, just as she does in cabaret songs. Richard Suart is ideal in the comic role of Wun-Hi.

JOSQUIN DESPREZ (died 1521)

Missa Hercules Dux Ferrariae; Miserere mei Deus.
Motets: *Absolom, fili mi; Ave Maria gratia pleni; De profundis clamavi; In te Domine speravi per trovar pietà; Pater noster/Ave Maria; Tu solus qui facis mirabilia; Veni, Sancti Spiritus.* Chansons: *Le Déploration de la mort de Johannes Ockeghem (Nymphes de bois); El grillo; En l'hombre d'ung buissonet au matinet; Je me complains; Je ne me puis tenir d'aimer; Mille regretz; Petite camusette; Scarmella va alla guerra – Loyset Compère: Scaramella fa la galla.* GOMBERT (attrib. JOSQUIN): Motet: *Lugabet David Absolon.*
(BB) ★★★ Virgin 2×1 5 62346-2 (2). Hilliard Ens., Hillier.

The Hilliard Ensmble find the full measure of Josquin's Mass, *Hercules dux Ferrariae*, probably written just before the composer's appointment to Ferrara in 1505, and featuring a cantus based on the letters of the work's title, paying homage to the composer's future employer, Duke Ercole d'Este. The performance revels in the rich flowing lyricism of the *Kyrie* and *Agnus Dei*, whose second section includes a fascinating three-in-one canon, yet bringing passionate ardour to the climaxes of the *Sanctus* and *Benedictus*.

Both the *Pater noster/Ave Maria* and the masterly *Miserere mei Deus* – a setting of Psalm 50, actually commissioned by the duke – are taken slowly and serenely. Some might feel that, particularly in the latter, the music might have been pressed forward more strongly, but the underlying intensity is well sustained and there is no lack of light and shade. One can understand, after listening to the dedicated

Hilliard account, why the deeply expressive *Lugabet David Absalon* was attributed to Josquin, although it was probably written by Nicolas Gombert, and the first disc ends with a gloriously blended and ideally paced performance of the beautiful *Tu solus qui facis mirabilia*.

We have had the collection of motets and chansons on the second disc before (see our main volume). The motets are sung with dignity and feeling, but the chansons display infinite variety and colour. *Petite camusette* ('Little Snubnose') has a winning charm to set against the deeply touching *Mille regretz*, while the sparkling Italian frottola, *Scaramella va' alla guerra* and the witty portrait of a cricket, *El grillo*, show Josquin in lighter vein. The disc ends movingly with an elegiac tribute to Ockeghem, who succeeded Josquin in Ferrara after only a year, only to perish later in the plague. The collection of motets and chansons was recorded in London's Temple Church in 1983, the Mass and other items in the Priory Church of St Mary and St Blaise in Boxgrove, Chichester, in 1989. Expertly balanced and eminently truthful, they make an admirable pair (at budget price) to kindle the enthusiasm of the uninitiated as will few other Josquin compilations. But it is a pity there are no texts and translations.

KABALEVSKY, Dmitri (1904–87)

Symphonies Nos. 1 in C sharp min., Op. 18; 2 in C min., Op. 19.
** Olympia OCD 268. Szeged PO, Acél.

Kabalevsky's *First Symphony* unfolds naturally and the musical procedures have real dignity, even if some of the material of the finale is banal. The *Second Symphony* is both more individual and tautly argued. Good, though not first-class, performances from the Szeged Philharmonic Orchestra under Erwin Acél; however, the recording is handicapped by a rather cramped and constricted acoustic.

(i) Symphony No. 4 in C min., Op. 54; (ii) Requiem, Op. 72.
** Olympia (ADD) OCD 290 (2). (i) Leningrad PO; (ii) Levko, Valaitis, Moscow Artistic Educational Institute Ch., Moscow SO; Kabalevsky.

The *Fourth Symphony* is a rather conventional work which goes through the correct motions of sonata form, but the ideas are only intermittently engaging; indeed, many border on the commonplace. The *Requiem* is a more rewarding piece, even if much of it is hard work. But the longueurs are offset by some moving passages and a genuine, unforced dignity that grips the listener. The sound in the *Requiem* is very good indeed for the period – and the place.

KAJANUS, Robert (1856–1933)

Sinfonietta in B flat, Op. 16; Finnish Rhapsody No. 1 in D min., Op. 5; Kullervo's Funeral March, Op. 3; (i) Aino (Symphonic Poem for male chorus and orchestra).
*** BIS CD 1223. Lahti SO, Vänskä, (i) with Helsinki University Ch.

As a conductor Kajanus was Sibelius's most fervent advocate, interpreting all his major works and directing those premières that the composer himself didn't conduct. He made the first recordings of four of the symphones (Nos. 1, 2, 3 and 5) as well as *Pohjola's Daughter*, *Tapiola* and *Belshazzar's Feast* with the LSO. It was he who founded the Helsinki Orchestra and over the years also introduced unfamiliar new music to Finnish audiences, César Franck and Ravel and, in the 1920s, Stravinsky and Hindemith. It was a performance that Kajanus gave in Berlin of his *Aino Symphony* (or, rather, Symphonic Poem for male chorus and orchestra) that inspired Sibelius to compose his *Kullervo Symphony*. Before Sibelius burst on the scene with *Kullervo* and *En Saga*, Kajanus made a considerable name for himself as a composer, but his energies became increasingly consumed by conducting. His music is typical of the national romanticism of the period and, although few would make great claims for its individuality, it is always finely crafted and, in the case of the *Sinfonietta* of 1915, often arresting. Osmo Vänskä and the Lahti orchestra play it with fervour and conviction, and the BIS team serves them well.

KALLSTENIUS, Edvin (1878–1963)

Clarinet Quintet, Op. 17.
*** Phono Suecia PSCD 708. Andersen, Lysell Qt – FERNSTROM: *Wind Quintet*; KOCH: *Piano Quintet*. ***

Edvin Kallstenius was ignored in his lifetime by the record companies and his neglect by Swedish Radio was almost total. After his studies in Germany he pursued a career as a conductor, and during the 1930s he was a music librarian of Radiotjänst, as the Swedish Radio was then known. The *Clarinet Quintet* was written in 1930 and is neo-Romantic in outlook, generally Brahmsian with a touch of Reger. It is a pleasing work but does not make a really strong impression in spite of an excellent performance by Niklas Andersen and the Lysell Quartet and a first-class recording.

KÁLMÁN, Emmerich (1882–1953)

Countess Maritza: highlights (in English).
**(*) TER CDTER 1051. Hill-Smith, Remedios,

Livingstone, Moyle, Rice, Martin, Barber, Bullock, New Sadler's Wells O, Wordsworth.

Set in the Hungarian countryside, *Countess Maritza* gave Kálmán plenty of chances to display his skill in writing memorable numbers with a Hungarian flavour. The plot is slight, but the nostalgic *Luck is a Golden Dream*, sung by Lynn Barber as a gypsy girl, sets the scene, followed by the delightful *How Do You Do*, characterfully sung by Count Tassilo, the opera's hero, with children's chorus. But the score's highlight must be the evocative *Vienna mine*, one of the composer's most catchy melodies, although Remedios has not quite the easy smoothness of a Tauber to make it as captivating as it might be. Marilyn Hill-Smith as the Countess, singing with her customary style, is charming in the sentimental duet with the Count, *Be Mine, my Love*, as well as in the aria, *Set the Gipsy Music Playing* – another popular hit. The opera ends with a swinging waltz. Barry Wordsworth conducts securely and catches the spirit of Kálmán's world with a fair degree of success. The recording, though perhaps not ideally atmospheric, is reasonably full and bright. The English translation works with varying degrees of success, but operetta fans should not be too disappointed.

Die Csárdásfürtin (The Csárdás Princess).
(M) **(*) Oehms OC 201. Serafin, Bothmer, Grotrian, Eröd, Mörbisch Festival Ch. & O, Bible.

It is easy to see why *Die Csárdásfürtin* (dating from 1913–15) is generally regarded as Kálmán's finest operetta. The opening immediately launches into a delightfully Hungarian-sounding aria for the heroine, Sylvia, with an exhilarating *Csárdás* chorus. In fact, the melodies come thick and fast and the story, involving a cabaret singer and a prince, brings many opportunities for vivacious duets, cabaret arias, as well as some splendid waltzes, be they lively or pensive. Kálmán has much in common with Lehár, although his style is more robust, with a touch of Offenbach thrown in. He is never more alluring than in such numbers as the waltz-duets, *Heller Jubel* and *Tanzen möcht ich*. The grand finales of each act are very spirited, but the trace of melancholy which runs through parts of the score is said to be the result of the death of the composer's brother halfway through the work's composition.

Martina Serafin proves a spirited Sylvia, and if at times she is a little shrill, the lively numbers such as *O jag dem Glück nicht nach* are dispatched with spirit. Edwin Ronald makes an attractive Prince with his light but secure tenor, and the rest of the cast provides ebullient support. The recording is warm and well balanced, but it is a little confined in the upper register, failing to open out as it should. Only a German text is provided (the dialogue is omitted in this recording) but the CD is offered at mid-price.

KARAMANOV, Alemdar
(born 1934)

Symphonies Nos. 20 (Blessed are the Dead); 23 (I am Jesus).
(M) ** Olympia OCD 486. USSR SO, Fedoseyev.

Alemdar Karamanov is another recent discovery among Russian composers. He is of a strongly religious temperament, and his music earned the allegiance of Shostakovich, who hailed him as 'one of the most original and unique composers of our time'. The present symphonies come from a cycle of six (Nos. 18–23) on the theme of the Apocalypse, written between 1976 and 1980. The music has a certain ecstatic voluptuousness that is reminiscent of Scriabin, but there are also touches of Shostakovich, Rachmaninov and Glière. Karamanov is very imaginative, though a streak of sentimentality comes to the surface – fairly often in the case of No. 20. The USSR Symphony Orchestra produce rather crude tone at times and there are moments when the wind intonation is flawed. There is a certain pervading sameness about the hot-house atmosphere of this writing and the Szymanowski-like textures, and both symphonies sound very similar. One wonders how well they will wear on repetition. There is, however, no question as to their interest.

KARLOWICZ, Mieczyslaw
(1876–1909)

Bianca da Molina (Symphonic Prologue); Rebirth Symphony; Serenade.
*** Chan. 10171. BBC PO, Noseda.

Mieczyslaw Karlowicz, killed in an Alpine avalanche at the age of 32, might well have developed into a major figure in Polish music. Though these are all early works, written or conceived when he was still studying in Berlin, they have an individuality and richness of invention that are immediately attractive. *Bianca da Molina*, the symphonic prologue for a play, opens magically with shimmering strings and brassy fanfares, anticipating Respighi's *Pines of Rome* by two decades. Karlowicz's orchestral mastery shines throughout. The four movements of the *Serenade* have a winning lightness of touch, with a haunting waltz as third movement, while the *Rebirth Symphony*, much weightier, relates to Tchaikovsky on the one hand, to Richard Strauss on the other, but remains individual in its structure, warmly lyrical, built on memorable themes. Those who feel at home in the musical world of Suk or Novák will respond to his musical language and will lose no time in investigating this successor. Under Gianandrea Noseda the BBC Philharmonic gives strong, persuasive performances, opulently recorded.

Violin Concerto in A, Op. 8.
*** Hyp. CDA 67389. Little, BBC Scottish SO,

Brabbins – MOSZKOWSKI: *Violin Concerto* etc.
***

Like the works on Noseda's Chandos disc, this *Violin Concerto* demonstrates the mastery of this sadly short-lived composer. Written in 1902, it marked a turning point in Karlowicz's career, a piece which – in an inspired performance like this from Tasmin Little – emerges as a long-neglected masterpiece. It may bring echoes of Tchaikovsky, not least in the glowing horn motif at the very start (like the opening of the *First Piano Concerto* in reverse), but Karlowicz's personal tone of voice, strong and inventive, with one striking theme after another, is securely established in each well-constructed movement, all superbly orchestrated, not least for the brass section. Warm, vivid sound. With the Moszkowski works, a valuable addition to Hyperion's 'Romantic Violin Concerto' series.

KELLY, Bryan (born 1934)

(i) *Crucifixion. Missa brevis; Magnificat from the Emanuel Evening Service; Like as the Hart; O Clap your Hands; Praise his Name in the Dance; The Lovely Lady.*
*** Priory PRCD 755. (i) Manahan Thomas, Mulroy; Clare College, Cambridge, Ch., Brown, Reid (organ).

Bryan Kelly was born in Oxford, trained as a boy chorister at Worcester Cathedral and later studied with Gordon Jacob, Herbert Howells and Nadia Boulanger, a heady mix of influences, well absorbed. He now lives in France.

It is good to have a *Crucifixion* setting so powerful and immediate in its appeal, completely removed from the Victorian heritage of Stainer, while still featuring simple sung chorales. The work's radiantly pungent choral opening is underpinned by highly individual organ writing, which is later to demand great bravura in describing the disciples' panic. The bold contrasts between soprano and tenor soloists are a strong feature of a work which intersperses biblical texts with poems by George Herbert, the librettist, Anne Ridler and W. H. Auden's 'Shield of Achilles', and the touching solo dialogue, *A Ragged Urchin*, makes a poignant interlude after Jesus' final cry of despair to God.

Kelly's *Missa brevis* is equally compelling, with another brilliant contribution from the organ in the *Gloria in excelsis*, with the chorus later joyfully moving into waltz tempo without a suggestion of triviality. But the *Agnus Dei* ends the work in serenity. The exuberant *Magnificat* is trumped in rhythmic energy by *Praise His Name in the Dance*, and while *O Clap your Hands* is more tranquil, the use of a 5/8 time signature gives the melodic lines a subtle lift. Neither the lovely medieval carol setting, *The Lovely Lady Sat and Sang*, nor the passionate closing, *Like as the Hart*, is in the least predictable, but both show the composer at his imaginative best. The Clare College

Choir have a famous association with John Rutter, and under their current conductor, Timothy Brown, they are just as naturally at home in this moving, highly communicative music, which they sing with great freshness, vigour and beauty, while the organist John Reid's contribution is in every way admirable. They are excellently recorded and those looking for choral music which tweaks the ear but which remains melodic in the best sense will find this a most rewarding collection.

KETÈLBEY, Albert (1875–1959)

Aberfoyle (Waltz); Cockney Suite; Danse à la tarentelle; A Desert Romance; Fiddle Fun; Gallantry; In a Camp of the Ancient Britons; Jungle Drums; Mind the Slide; A Musical Jigsaw; Sunset Glow; (i) *With Honour Crowned;* (ii) *Blow, blow, thou winter wind;* (iii) *I call you from the shadows.*
(BB) (***) Naxos mono 8.110869. Various orchestras, all cond. composer, except (i) Massed Bands of the Aldershot & Eastern Commands, Seymour; (ii) with Allen; (iii) Kingston.

This collection and its companions below are extraordinary 'period pieces', mementoes of popular music styles in the early years of the century, before the Jazz Age took over. In spite of the primitive recording quality, the vibrancy of the music-making leaps out from these historic performances, even on the very early ones, the earliest being the *Danse à la tarentelle* from 1909, played by the 'Empire Symphony Orchestra'. By the later 1920s, recording techniques had improved considerably, so that the drums in *Jungle Drums* (a delightful bit of 'exotic' nonsense) recorded in 1929 come over reasonably well. One must have a heart of stone not to respond to the ingenuous, rose-coloured portrayal of pre-war London in the *Cockney Suite* – blatant nostalgia as it is. There is all sorts of fun and games to be had after this: *Mind the Slide* (recorded 1916) features some wacky trombone-sliding, and with plenty of whistles too, the atmosphere of the music hall not far away. *Fiddle Fun* (violinist unknown, Ketèlbey at the piano, recorded 1915), a *fantasia burlesca* (or 'musical switch'), features all sorts of well-known tunes melded kaleidoscopically together. More ingenious still is *A Musical Jigsaw* (recorded 1923), which comprises some 53 'famous themes' (cut to 44 on this recording), often incongruously following one another. Among the vocal items, Norman Allen is stirring in *Blow, blow, thou winter wind* (recorded 1923), while Morgen Kingston in *I call you from the shadows* evokes such period atmosphere that it's easy to drift back to 1912, when it was recorded. Many of the other numbers, such as *Sunset Glow* (from the early 1920s), *A Desert Romance* (1923) and *Gallantry* (from 1940), recreate the light music style of their eras, while the *Aberfoyle Waltz* shows Ketèlby in Johann Strauss mode. The disc ends with the stirring *With Honour Crowned: Processional March*, with the

Massed Bands of the Aldershot and Eastern Commands, conducted by Leslie Seymour – the sharp rhythms compensating for the rather thin (1936) sound. This CD is a genuine collector's item, with Naxos's transfers generally satisfactory and the sleeve-notes informative.

(i) *Bells Across the Meadow;* (i; v) *A Dream of Christmas;* (i) *In a Fairy Realm: Suite;* (ii; vi) *In a Monastery Garden;* (i) *In a Persian Market;* (iii; vii) *In the Mystic Land of Egypt;* (iv; vii) *The Sacred Hour;* (i; viii) *Sanctuary of the Heart;* (i; ix) *Wedgwood Blue;* (ix; x) *Algerian Scene* (for violin and piano). Songs: (i; xi) *Fairy Butterfly; King Cupid.*

(BB) (★★★) Naxos mono 8.110848. O cond. (i) composer; (ii) Geehl; (iii) Prentice; (iv) Dawson; with (v) Easton; (vi) Natzke; (vii) Noble; (viii) Walker; (ix) composer (piano); (x) Sandler (violin); (xi) Smithson.

A fascinating disc. Albert Ketèlbey's picture-postcard music can be curiously haunting, and here one recalls Noël Coward's observation on the potency of cheap music, especially when there are such starry names on the cast list. These historic performances, largely under the direction of the composer, are imbued with the atmosphere of pre-war England. Florence Smithson, a famously agile soprano notable for her incredibly high notes, flutters through the mists of time in the charming *Fairy Butterfly*, and both this and *King Cupid* are great fun to hear, though her final high notes defeat the 1917 acoustic recording. The rest of the items, from the late 1920s and early 1930s, bar the odd crumbly passage, sound much better, with presence and plenty of warmth and atmosphere. *In a Monastery Garden* is eloqently sung by Oscar Natzke, and the famously full and clear bass-baritone of Peter Dawson rings out in *The Sacred Hour*. One readily enters into *The Mystic Land of Egypt* (with Dennis Noble appearing from a distance and gradually getting nearer) or the exotic imagery of the anglicized *Persian Market*, the composer's most famous number. With the composer at the piano, the salon pieces *Wedgwood Blue* and *Algerian Scene* (with Albert Sandler, the 'King' of the Palm Court) have a distinctive faded charm, glowingly sentimental like *A Dream of Christmas* and *In a Fairy Realm*. Another nostalgic bargain.

Canzonetta; Christmas; In Holiday Mood; Knights of the King; The Phantom Melody; Silver-Cloud; A Sunday Afternoon Rêverie; Tangled Tunes: Parts 1–4; A Vision of Fujiu-San; Wildhawk; Wonga; (i; ii) *In a Monastary Garden;* (i) *Men of England (A Short Patriotic Ode);* (iii) *My heart still clings to you.*

(BB) (★★★) Naxos mono 8.110870. O, cond. composer, with (i) Chorus; (ii) Walker; (iii) Coyle.

More vintage Ketèlbey, beginning with the highly patriotic *Men of England* (recorded 1929), the sort of music that it would be very hard to bring off today, but here sounding absolutely convincing. *In Holiday Mood* (recorded 1938) similarly belongs to a long-gone age: the *Down the Stream* central section with its gently meandering strings is very seductive, especially when the celesta joins in at the end. The *Four Tangled Tunes* (recorded 1914) is another musical *mélange*, ingeniously put together, and once more it calls for some major detective work to name all the themes used. *A Sunday Afternoon Rêverie* is based on the musical notes 'DECCA', 'in appreciation' of that company, featuring Ketèlbey's music on Radio Luxembourg, which Decca were sponsoring. Several famous numbers are included here, such as *The Phantom Melody* (played by Jean Schwiller on the cello, recorded 1912) and *Silver-Cloud* (recorded 1913), with its beating drums setting the scene for this 'Indian Maiden's Song'. Exoticism of this kind is also found in *Wonga* (recorded 1916) and *Wildhawk* (recorded 1913), as well as in *The Vision of Fuji-San*, with its cymbals, gongs and harp (1933). Of the vocal items, *My heart still clings to you* (from 1913) suffers a bit sonically, though it is easy to respond to *In a Monastery Garden* (1927), sung by Nellie Walker: not a dry eye in the house! Naturally, some of the earliest recordings sound rather thin, occasionally affected by swish (such as *Tangled Tune No. 1*), but the transfers are good, with the music fighting through the years. These three Naxos discs may be preposterous, but they are surely fascinating!

The Adventurers: Overture. Bells across the Meadow; Caprice Pianistique; Chal Romano; The Clock and the Dresden Figures; Cockney Suite, excerpts: *Bank Holiday; At the Palais de Danse. In a Monastery Garden; In the Moonlight; In a Persian Market; The Phantom Melody; Suite Romantique; Wedgwood Blue.*

★★ Marco Polo 8.223442. Slovak Philharmonic Male Ch., Slovak RSO (Bratislava), Leaper.

The Marco Polo collection has the advantage of modern, digital recording and a warm concert-hall acoustic, and the effect is very flattering to *In a Monastery Garden*. Adrian Leaper's performance is romantically spacious and includes the chorus. If elsewhere his characterization is not always as apt as Lanchbery's (see below), this is still an agreeable programme. It offers several novelties and, though some of these items (for instance *The Adventurers Overture*) are not vintage Ketèlbey, there is nothing wrong with the lively Slovak account of the closing *In a Persian Market*, again featuring the chorus.

(i) *'Appy 'Ampstead;* (ii) *Bank Holiday; Bells Across the Meadows;* (i) *By the Blue Hawaiian Waters;* (ii) *The Clock and the Dresden Figures; Dance of the Merry Mascots; In a Chinese Temple Garden; In a Monastery Garden;* (i) *In the Moonlight;* (ii) *In the Mystic Land of Egypt;* (i) *A Passing Storm on a*

Summer Day; (ii) *In a Persian Market;* (i) *The Phantom Melody;* (ii) *Sanctuary of the Heart; With Honour Crowned.*

(M) ** Decca mono/stereo 473 720-2. (i) New SO, Robinson; (ii) Dale, Reeves, Ambrosian Ch., L. Promenade O, Faris.

The Faris recordings (originally on Philips) date from 1982 and are digital. But although they include vocal contributions, they lack the flair of the very best performances in this repertoire; occasionally the slower numbers drag a bit, although the collection is enjoyable enough. The recording is also acceptable, but lacks a bit of sparkle on top. The early Robinson performances, though mono, have more dash and brilliance in the lively numbers, as well as more atmosphere in the evocative pieces. The mono sound here is very bright, but reasonably full and warm.

'Appy 'Ampstead; Bells across the Meadows; In a Chinese Temple Garden; In a Monastery Garden; In a Persian Market; In the Mystic Land of Egypt; The Phantom Melody; Sanctuary of the Heart; Wedgwood Blue.

(M) *** Decca (ADD) 444 786-2. RPO & Ch., Rogers (with *Concert of Gypsy Violin Encores:* Sakonov, L. Festival O. ***)

Eric Rogers and his orchestra present the more famous pieces with both warmth and a natural feeling for their flamboyant style, and the tunes throughout come tumbling out, vulgar but irresistible when played so committedly. The birds twittering in the monastery garden make perfect 'camp' but the playing is straight and committed, and the larger-than-life Phase Four recording suits the music admirably. Moreover, it was a happy idea to couple this programme with a collection of Hungarian gypsy fireworks and other favourite lollipops, played with great panache by Josef Sakonov.

Bells Across the Meadow; Chal Romano (Gypsy Lad); The Clock and the Dresden Figures; In a Chinese Temple Garden; In a Monastery Garden; In a Persian Market; In the Moonlight; In the Mystic Land of Egypt; Sanctuary of the Heart.

(B) *** CfP (ADD) CD-CFP 4637. Midgley, Temperley, Pearson (piano), Amb. S., Philh. O, Lanchbery (with LUIGINI: *Ballet Egyptien* ***).

A splendid collection in every way. John Lanchbery uses every possible resource to ensure that, when the composer demands spectacle, he gets it. In *In the Mystic Land of Egypt*, for instance, uses soloist and chorus in canon in the principal tune (and very fetchingly too). In the *Monastery Garden* the distant monks are realistically distant, in *Sanctuary of the Heart* there is no mistaking that the heart is worn firmly on the sleeve. The orchestral playing throughout is not only polished but warm-hearted: the middle section of *Bells across the Meadow*, which has a delightful melodic contour, is played most

tenderly and loses any hint of vulgarity. Yet when vulgarity is called for, it is not shirked – only it's a stylish kind of vulgarity! The recording is excellent, full and brilliant. Luigini's *Ballet Egyptien* is equally successful.

KHACHATURIAN, Aram
(1903–78)

Flute Concerto.

*** EMI 5 57563-2. Pahud, Tonhalle O, Zinman – IBERT: *Flute Concerto.* ***

Emmanuel Pahud and the Zurich Tonhalle Orchestra under David Zinman give a pretty dazzling account of Jean-Pierre Rampal's transcription of the Khachaturian *Violin Concerto.* If you like the concerto in this particular form, not only is the performance outstanding, so also is the recorded sound.

Violin Concerto in D min., Op. 47.

*** HM Naïve V 4959. Sergey Khachaturian, Sinfonia Varsovia, Krivine – SIBELIUS: *Violin Concerto.* ***

Violin Concerto in D min.; Concerto-Rhapsody for Violin and Orchestra.

(BB) **(*) Naxos 8.555919. Martin, Ukraine Nat. SO, Kuchar.

The young Sergey Khachaturian has already made his name with performances in Europe and Tokyo of this very underrated concerto. He has found an ideal partner in Emmanuel Krivine, who brings out all the colourfully imaginative orchestral detail to match the soloist's commanding lyrical flow, especially in the unforgettable, sinuous main theme of the first movement. The *Andante* produces another haunting Armenian melody, and the soloist phrases it exquisitely, then ruminates poetically until, with the reprise, Krivine produces the composer's thrillingly brash orchestral cimax, and the movement ends gently. The finale sets off with tremendous gusto and, when the winding melody of the first movement reappears, soloist and orchestra are perfectly integrated. With splendid recording, spacious, open and wide-ranging, this highly spontaneous account now goes to the top of the list of modern recordings of this rewardingly melodic concerto.

The Romanian-born Mihaela Martin and the Ukraine National Symphony Orchestra, directed by Theodor Kuchar, also play the concerto very sympathetically. Martin has a rich timbre, and the sinuous melodies, especially that of the *Andante*, sit warmly on her bow, and there is no lack of impetus and energy in the finale. Orchestra and soloist are well balanced and recorded, but there is a studio-ish feel to the recording and the overall effect has less flair. However, she also gives us the much rarer 1992 *Concert-Rhapsody*, written for Leonid Kogan (whose recording of the regular *Violin Concerto* was given a

✪ in our main volume – RCA 09026 63708-2). It has to be said that this is a less inspired work, with much less memorable invention; but Martin and Kuchar make as strong a case for the piece as possible, and their performance is very successful.

Greeting Overture; Festive Poem; Lermontov Suite; Ode in Memory of Lenin; Russian Fantasy.
** ASV CDDCA 946. Armenian PO, Tjeknavorian.

Although it has plenty of characteristic Armenian colour, most of this music is routine Khachaturian, or worse: the *Festive Poem* (at nearly 20 minutes) is far too inflated for its content, and the *Ode to Lenin* is an all too typical Soviet tribute. The sub-Rimskian finale of the *Lermontov Suite* is by far the best movement. The *Russian Fantasy* uses an agreeable folk-like melody, but we hear it repeated too often before the final quickening. Good performances, but the resonant recording is acceptable rather than sparkling.

VOCAL MUSIC

Ballad of the Motherland (Maybe somewhere the sky is blue); 3 Concert Arias; Ode to Joy (The Spring Sun Rises); Poem; March of Zangezur.
*(*) ASV CDDCA 1087. Amirkhanian, Hatsagortsian, Vardouhi Khachaturian, Armenian PO, Tjeknavorian.

Although the performances are adequate, none of this is first- or even second-class Khachaturian, although the three *Concert Arias* show a genuine operatic flair, essentially Armenian in flavour, but with a hint of Puccini too. Hasmik Hatsagortsian sings them passionately and convincingly. The *Ballad of the Motherland* was given its Russian première by six basses in unison! Here Mourad Amirkhanian sings alone, longing for his homeland. The 1936/7 *Ode to Stalin* is here revised and renamed innocuously *Poem*. It consists of a very long orchestral prelude, followed by a brief patriotic chorus with quite a good tune. The *Ode to Joy* opens with a rather engaging 16-bar *moto perpetuo* on the violins; the mezzo soloist enters with an ardent soliloquy on the joys of spring; then the chorus enters and enthusiastically takes up the melody in popular Soviet style. Texts and translations are provided only for the *Concert Arias*.

KILPINEN, Yrjö (1892–1959)

(i) *Fjeldlieder.* (ii) *Elegie an die Nachtigall, Op. 21/1; Lieder der Liebe, Op. 61; Lieder um den Tod, Op. 62; Marienkirche zu Danzig im Gerüst; Mondschein; Der Skiläufer; Spielmannslieder, Op. 77; Venezianisches Intermezzo; Vergissmeinnicht, Op. 39.*
✪ (B) (***) Dutton mono CDBP 9741. (i) Berlin State Op. O, Hanns Udo Müller; (ii) Hüsch, M. Kilpinen.

Kilpinen is really a connoisseur's composer who has never attracted much popular attention, but his stature far outstrips his meagre representation on CD, and the finest of his songs withstand comparison with Wolf, whose successor he was at one time proclaimed. This 1934 anthology by the incomparable Gerhard Hüsch, accompanied by Kilpinen's daughter Margareta, was recorded by Walter Legge for his HMV subscription Society series. Musically, Kilpinen remained aloof from contemporary trends and his harmonic vocabulary does not go much beyond Wolf, and yet at his best he creates a strangely distinctive world. He is a master of the vignette and distils a powerful atmosphere and a keen psychological intensity with the greatest economy of means. He wrote 767 songs in all, though a good proportion of his output remains in manuscript. This classic pre-war set appeared in 1936, two years after the records were made, with an edition limited to 400, each set autographed by the composer. 'Colour is the element of music most likely to fade,' Kilpinen once declared, and he shunned the rich harmonic textures of the National Romantic tradition for monochrome, Mussorgskian intensity. The third song, *Der Tod und der einsame Trinker* ('Death and the Solitary Drinker'), of the *Lieder um den Tod* is an astonishing example of his directness and vividness. Death is a figure of terror and the drunk of incoherence, and Hüsch's portrayal of the two characters sends shivers down the spine. These are marvellous and rewarding songs and Hüsch's interpretations have a distinction and intensity that not even Jorma Hynninen has surpassed. An indispensable classic set, expertly transferred.

KNUSSEN, Oliver (born 1952)

(i) *Horn Concerto, Op. 28. Flourish with Fireworks, Op. 22; Music for a Puppet Court, Op. 11; Two Organa, Op. 27; "... Upon One Note' (Fantasia after Purcell); The Way to Castle Yonder, Op. 21a.* (ii) *Whitman Settings, Op. 25a.*
*** DG 474 322-2. L. Sinf., composer, with (i) Tuckwell; (ii) Shelton.

This collection of seven of Oliver Knussen's shorter works, brilliantly performed and recorded under his own baton, consistently brings out his fascination with original and exotic orchestral sounds. The very opening *Fanfare with Fireworks*, written for Michael Tilson Thomas's first concert as music director of the LSO, brings magical textures, with sidelong references to Stravinsky's early piece, *Fireworks*, a favourite of Tilson Thomas's. *The Way to Castle Yonder* re-cycles three evocative passages from Knussen's opera for children, *Higglety Pigglety Pop*, and the *Horn Concerto* that he wrote for Barry Tuckwell in 1994 exploits the solo instrument in gloriously ripe sounds, with the longest of the four compact movements, *Fantastico*, bringing the most exuberant fantasy, designed to make full use of the acoustic of the

Sun Tory Hall in Tokyo, which sponsored the commission. Tuckwell's playing, recorded in 1995, is masterly.The two *Organa* exploit medieval techniques, and *Music for a Puppet Court*, using two antiphonal chamber orchestras, is developed from puzzle-canons attributed to the Tudor composer John Lloyd. Most challenging is the final item, the *Whitman Settings* written for Lucy Shelton, the soloist on this disc, with the angular vocal line obscuring rather than illuminating the four short poems on big themes. Brilliant playing from the London Sinfonietta, matched by full, immediate sound.

KOCH, Sigurd von (1889–1919)

Piano Quintet.
★★★ Phono Suecia PSCD 708. Negro, Lysell Qt –
FERNSTROM: *Wind Quintet.* KALLSTENIUS:
Clarinet Quintet **★★★**.

Little known outside Sweden, Sigurd von Koch was active as an author and painter as well as a composer. His *Piano Quintet* dates from 1916, and despite its length it is the least substantial work among these rarities. Its phrase structure tends to be square, and there is too much sequential repetition. It is played elegantly by Lucia Negro and the Lysell Quartet but is wanting in real personality and substance.

KODÁLY, Zoltán (1882–1967)

(Unaccompanied) *Cello Sonata Op. 8.* (i) *Cello Sonata* (for cello and piano), Op. 4.
★★★ Sup. SU 3515-2. Barta, (i) with Cech – NOVAK:
Cello Sonata. **★★★**

Kodály's *Solo Cello Sonata* is among the strongest, most searching of all his works, arguably the finest of all works for unaccompanied cello since Bach's *Suites*, and here it receives a performance of exceptional power, precision and clarity from the Czech cellist Jiří Barta. More than most rivals, he is able to keep a steady tempo and to clarify textures with clean attack on double stopping, all seemingly without strain. Deeply reflective, the intensity of his performance never flags, with a rare depth of concentration in the darkly intense central Adagio. In the Allegro finale, with its folk-dance rhythms, he is volatile and thrusting, again using a formidable range of dynamic, well caught in the recording. In both movements of the Op. 4 *Sonata*, the opening *Fantasia* as well as the weighty finale, Barta and his pianist, Jan Cech, make the switches of speed seem natural as though part of an improvisation, and the folk element is aptly heightened by an element of rawness, with the players striking sparks off each other in fiery fantasy. The Novák *Sonata* makes a welcome and substantial supplement.

KOLESSA, Mykola (born 1903)

Symphony No. 1.
★★ ASV CDDCA 963. Odessa PO, Earle – SKORYK:
Carpathian Concerto, etc. **★★**

Mykola Kolessa is the grand old man of Ukrainian music. The *First* of his two symphonies was composed in 1950 in the immediate wake of the Zhdanov affair, when any sense of harmonic adventure was discouraged. This piece at times sounds like Glière or Arensky. It is expertly written and is easy to listen to, but it could just as well have been composed in the 1890s. Very well played and recorded. The pieces by Kolessa's pupil, Myroslav Skoryk, are more interesting.

KOMZÁK, Karel (1850–1905)

Edelweiss Overture; Der letzte Gruss Galopp; Louise de Lavallière (Air). Marches: *Echtes Wiener Blut; Erzherzog Rainer; Thun-Hohenstein.* Polkas: *Am Gardasee; Heitere Stunden; Volapük.* Waltzes: *Bad'ner Mädl'n; Maienzauber; Neues Leben; Phantome.*
★★(*) Marco Polo 8.225175. Razumovsky SO, Pollack.

Czech composer Karel Komzák was not only an organist for a lunatic asylum in Prague but also founded, in the same city, an orchestra in which Dvořák played the viola. He then became a highly successful band-master, travelling throughout Austria. He wrote around 300 works, to which this CD is an ideal introduction. It includes a nice mixture of marches, waltzes and polkas, as well as a more substantial overture. Though not quite in the Johann Strauss league, it is all tuneful music of charm, and is well played and recorded here.

KOPPEL, Herman D. (1908–98)

Symphonies Nos. 3, Op. 39; 4, Op. 42.
★★★ dacapo 8.226016 Aalborg SO, Atzmon.

Herman D. Koppel was among those Danes who made the crossing to Sweden when the Nazis gave the order to round up the Jews in 1942. He spent the rest of the war in Sweden where the *Third Symphony* was written. He wrote his *First* in his early twenties and its successor in 1943 during the Nazi occupation (dacapo 8.224205 – see our main volume) and subsequently disowned them. But they are well worth hearing for all that. He was enormously productive, with seven symphonies to his credit as well as five piano concertos, a highly imaginative cello concerto written for Erling Bløndal-Bengtsson, and five quartets. But Koppel is primarily a symphonist, as the two works recorded here show. There is a real sense of movement and a feeling that we have embarked on a voyage; there is breadth, a sense of organic cohesion

LAJTHA, László (1892–1963)

Hortobágy, Op. 21; Suite No. 3, Op. 56; Symphony No. 7, Op. 63 (Revolution Symphony).
**(*) Marco Polo 8.223667. Pécs SO, Pasquet.

László Lajtha was one of the leading Hungarian composers and scholars to emerge after the generation of Bartók and Kodály. Indeed, as an exact contemporary of Honegger and Milhaud, he is separated from his compatriots by a mere decade. The *Seventh Symphony* is a well-wrought and eclectic score that is worth hearing, even if it does not possess the concentration or profile one expects of a major symphonist. The suite from *Hortobágy*, a memorable film set in the plains of Hungary, and the *Two Symphonic Portraits* are effectively scored but their material is insufficiently distinctive. Good performances and recording.

LALO, Edouard (1823–92)

Cello Concerto No. 1 in D min., Op. 33.
(BB) ** Warner Apex (ADD) 2564 60709-2. Navarra, LOP, Munch – SAINT-SAENS: *Cello Concerto No. 1.* **

André Navarra is very forwardly balanced in the Warner (originally Erato) recording but, with Munch securing some good, lively playing from his Lamoureux orchestra, it is an enjoyable, characterful account. Not a top choice, but worth considering at bargain price.

(i) *Cello Concerto in D min.;* (ii) *Symphonie espagnole, Op. 21.*
(B) *(*) Erato (ADD) 2564 60226-2. (i) Lodéon, Philh. O, Dutoit; (ii) Amoyal, Monte-Carlo Op. O, Paray.

This musically attractive issue is marred by the variable and badly balanced sound. Lodéon's performance of the *Cello Concerto* is thoroughly recommendable, with the Philharmonia under Dutoit providing excellent support. Unfortunately, the early 1980s recording was not one of Erato's best. The soloist is balanced very forwardly, and the orchestra, given a middle and bass emphasis, is muddy and opaque, although the violin timbre remains sweet. Amoyal gives an enjoyably warm and polished account of the *Symphonie espagnole*, rhythmically infectious and with many a seductive turn of phrase, but here the very early 1970s recording is thin and the soloist unnaturally forward.

LAMBERT, Constant (1905–51)

(i) *Piano Concerto (for piano & 9 players);* (ii) *Horoscope (ballet suite);* (ii; iii) *The Rio Grande.*
(M) **(*) Decca 473 424-2. (i) Stott; (ii) D. Jones, BBC Singers; BBC Concert O, Wordsworth.

With bright, forward recording this account of *The Rio Grande* is rather more aggressive than the Hyperion one (CDA 66565 – see our main *Guide*) and is a degree more literal, less idiomatic in its interpretation of jazzy syncopations, but the power and colour of the writing come across with fine bite and clarity. In the ballet suite from *Horoscope* there is one more movement than Lambert ever recorded, the *Palindromic prelude*, less striking than the other movements but still beautifully written. Here again Wordsworth and the BBC Concert Orchestra are a degree more literal than Lambert himself was in jazz-rhythms. Kathryn Stott with members of the orchestra gives splendid point to the angular *Concerto* for piano and nine players, where the emotional element is much more severely repressed than in the other works on the disc. This is now reissued at mid-price in Decca's British Music Collection and is worth considering for the *Piano Concerto* alone.

LAMOND, Frederic (1868–1948)

Symphony in A, Op. 3; Overture: Aus dem Schottischen Hochlande, Op. 4; Sword Dance.
*** Hyp. CDA 67387. BBC Scottish SO, Brabbins – D'ALBERT: *Overture: Esther.* ***

Frederic Lamond was one of the most distinguished interpreters of Beethoven's piano music in the early years of the last century, making a number of impressive recordings. Born in the Glasgow area, he came from a poor family but, thanks to the dedication of his father, a Scottish weaver who devoted himself to local music-making, and helped also by an older brother and sister, he was able to study in Germany and to get to know Liszt and Brahms among others. It is sad that, once he achieved success as a pianist, he never continued composing, for these are strong, inventive works, built on memorable themes, superbly orchestrated. Thanks to vigorous, finely judged performances by Brabbins and the BBC Scottish Orchestra, they make a powerful impact, with the four movements of the *Symphony* well contrasted. There are obvious influences – from Beethoven in the energetic Scherzo and, above all, from Brahms in the finale, which starts with a barefaced crib from the *Second Symphony* – but the fluency and confidence of the writing with the occasional hint of a distinctive Scottish flavour make such echoes of little importance. The *Overture* is similarly inventive, with some glorious writing for the horns, and the *Sword Dance*, a Scottish reel using drone basses, makes one curious about the opera from which it is taken. Though these performances were recorded in the difficult acoustics of Usher Hall in Edinburgh, the engineers have produced excellent sound.

LAMPE, John Frederick (1702/3–51)

(i; ii) *Pyramus and Thisbe* (A mock opera); (ii; iii) *Flute Concerto in G (The Cuckoo).*

*** Hyp. CDA 66759. (i) Padmore, Bisatt, (ii) Opera Restor'd, Holman; (iii) Brown.

Pyramus and Thisbe, written in 1745, is a reworking of the entertainment given by the rude mechanicals in Shakespeare's *Midsummer Night's Dream*, with the role of the heroine, Thisbe, taken not by a man but by a soprano. The Opera Restor'd company, with Jack Edwards as stage director, here present it complete with spoken Prologue for several attendant characters. Following the overture come 16 brief numbers, with the score edited and completed by the conductor, Peter Holman. Mark Padmore is outstanding as Pyramus, with Susan Bisatt a fresh-toned Thisbe. The warm, immediate recording brings out the distinctive timbre of the period instruments, notably the braying horns. As an agreeable makeweight, the disc also offers Lampe's only surviving independent orchestral work, the *G major Flute Concerto*, with its three crisp movements lasting little more than 5 minutes.

LANE, Philip (born 1950)

3 Christmas Pictures; Cotswold Dances; Diversions on a Theme of Paganini; Divertissement for Clarinet, Harp & Strings; London Salute; A Maritime Overture; 3 Nautical Miniatures for Strings; Prestbury Park.

*** Marco Polo 8.225185. Royal Ballet Sinfonia, Sutherland.

Philip Lane is best known for his valuable reconstructions of film scores. His own music is tuneful and entertaining, nostalgic and very much in the British light music tradition. He offers a new slant on the Paganini theme, which has enticed so many composers before him, and the result is very enjoyable. His quietly charming set of *Cotswold Dances*, some delicately piquant writing in the *Divertissement for Clarinet, Harp and Strings*, and robust nautical writing interspersed with more melancholy sections in the *Maritime Overture*, all catch and hold the ear. The *Sleighbell Serenade*, the first of the *Three Christmas Pictures*, is his best-known work, but the central *Starlight Lullaby* is very attractive too, rather in the manner of film music. Gavin Sutherland has proved himself in this field before, and he does so again here, with the Royal Ballet Sinfonia showing an appropriately light touch. The recording and presentation are both excellent too.

LANGFORD, Gordon (born 1930)

Colour Suite: Pastorale & March; Fanfare & Ceremonial Prelude; (i) *Concertino for Trumpet.* *Greenways; Hippodrome Waltz; 4 Movements for Strings;* (ii) *A Song for All Seasons* (for piano & orchestra). *The Spirit of London Overture; Suite of Dances No. 1.*

*** Chan. 10115. BBC Concert O, Gamba; with (i) Steele-Perkins; (ii) Stephenson.

Gordon Langford had a traditional musical training at the Royal Academy, he gained orchestral experience as pianist with pier and spa orchestras, and later toured as a trombonist in the pit of an opera company. He subsequently worked for the BBC and provided orchestrations for London-produced musicals. Like Eric Coates, with whom he has much in common, Langford's orchestral scoring is winningly adroit, and the two excerpts from the *Colour Suite* show it at its most richly hued. The opening *Fanfare and Ceremonial Prelude* is contrastingly flamboyant, Elgarian/Waltonesque in derivation, with an agreeable, all-but-*nobilmente* tune in the middle.

The *Trumpet Concertino*, which Crispian Steele-Perkins plays with panache, is both cheerful and lyrical, and has an audacious freshness. The stylish, neo-classical *Movements for Strings* are introduced by a dancing, airy-textured, opening movement, contrasting with a hauntingly delicate and agreeably atmospheric *Andante* and a pastiche Minuet. The *Song for All Seasons*, with its concertante piano (the nimble William Stephenson), has a syncopated rhythmic condiment but a lyrical core, while the *Suite of Dances* is very English, with its quaintly piping opening theme and wistful Waltz, followed by a sultry Tango and a sparkling, folksy Gigue. *Greenways* is charmingly sentimental, remembering closed railway lines, while *The Spirit of London* (very Eric Coatesian) is rumbustious and full of Cockney spirit. So too is the *Hippodrome Waltz*, composed for the BBC Concert Orchestra, which played in a north London theatre of that name, where the composer saw Christmas pantomimes as a child. All this very friendly and tuneful music is splendidly played by the BBC Concert Orchestra under Rumon Gamba and is superbly recorded. Recommended.

LASSUS, Orlandus (c. 1532–94)

Chansons and Morescas: *Allala, pia Calia; Canta Giorgia; Cathalina; Chi chilichili?; Elle s'en va; En un chasteau; Fuyons tous l'amour le jeu; Hai, Lucia; Je l'ame bien; Las! me faut-il; Lucescit jam o socii; Lucia, celu; Mais qui pourroit estre celuy; La Nuict froide et sombre; O foible esprit; O Lucia; Si du malheur; Une Jeune Moine est sorti du couvent; Une Puce j'ay dedans l'oreille; Un Triste Coeur; Vignon, vignon, vignette.* (i) Lute pieces: *J'ay un mary; Quand mon mary vient de dehors; Le Tems peult bien.*

(B) ****(*)** HM Musique d'abord HMA 1951391. Ens. Janequin, Visse; (i) Bellocq (lute).

This delightful collection of chansons and morescas, with three short lute pieces acting as a central interlude, show an entirely different Lassus from the more familiar composer of deeply devotional church music. Even though they were published in Paris as late as 1581, they were written in his youth, and are expressive and humorous by turns. *Si du malheur* and *Un Triste Coeur* are full of melancholy, while the title of *La Nuict froide et sombre* speaks for itself. But even in his mature years Lassus could be a humorist, and the lighthearted works, inspired by the spirit of the *commedia dell'arte*, show that readily. They include morescas – villanellas with texts parodying African dialect, characterized by quirky rhythms, a swift interplay of voices, and often sudden changes of tempo. *Cathalina, Chi chilichili? Cucurucu* and *Hai, Lucia* are engaging examples, sung here with vivacious aplomb, while in *Lucescit jam o socii*, the four voices sing alternately in Latin and French. The great drawback to this reissue is that the texts are provided without translations and the notes do not tell the listener what the songs are about. This is a quite unforgivable omission, when the performances are so idiomatic and lively. The recording too is vividly atmospheric.

Missa pro defunctis (Requiem) à 5; (i) Alma Redemptoris mater à 6; (i) Ave Maria à 5; (i; ii) Magnificat (Praeter rerum serium) à 6. O bone Jesu à 4.
(M) *** DHM/BMG (ADD) 82876 60153-2. L. Pro Cantione Antiqua, Turner; with (i) Hamburg Wind Ens. für Alte Musik; (ii) Coll. Aur. (members).

Lassus's *Requiem à 5* of 1580 stays close to the Gregorian chants for the *Missa pro defunctis*, with the setting often allotting a simple *cantus firmus* to the solo tenor. The choral contribution brings much rich homophony, reaching a celestial climax in the *Offertorium, Domine Jesu Christe*, with the following *Sanctus* serene and the rest of the Mass maintaining this deeply moving but tranquil mood.

The large-scale *Magnificat* of 1582 uses Josquin's motet, 'Praeter rerum serium' as its model: it is powerfully sustained and richly scored, here using cornets and trombones to fill out the textures. They are retained in the two motets, *Alma Redemptoris mater* and *Ave Maria*, with the comparatively gentle unaccompanied *O bone Jesu* providing an expressive interlude. Superb singing and playing throughout, under the wise directing hand of Bruno Turner, and wonderfully sonorous recording in an ideal ambience make this a collection to cherish.

LECUONA, Ernesto (1895–1963)

Danzas Afro-Cubanas; Gardenia; Noche de Estrellas; Porcelana china (Danza de muñecos); Polka de los Enanos; (i) Rapsodia Cubana. Valses fantásticos; Vals del Nilo; Yo te quiero siempre.
** BIS CD 794. Tirino, (i) with Polish Nat. RSO, Bartas.

Ernesto Lecuona hailed from Cuba and made a career for himself outside Latin and Central America. With the exception of the *Rapsodia Cubana*, which is conspicuously slight in invention, this is light music in the Latin-American style but distinguished by an inventive and resourceful use of rhythm. Thomas Tirino's pianism is equal to its demands, although this recording – which emanates from New York and Katowice, not BIS's usual venues – is not three-star. Nor is the music; however, although it is all very limited, there are rewarding moments of sophistication.

LE FLEM, Paul (1881–1984)

Symphony No. 4; (i) Le Grand Jardinier de France (film music). 7 Pièces enfantines; Pour les morts (Tryptique symphonique No. 1).
** Marco Polo 8.223655. Rhenish PO, Lockhart, (i) with Nopre.

Paul Le Flem is another French composer who is emerging from the shadows into which he has been so prematurely cast. The *Fourth Symphony* bears witness to an amazing creative vitality, when one thinks that its composer was just ninety years young at the time (1971–2). (As his dates will show at a glance, he lived to be 103.) The *Sept Pièces enfantines* is an orchestral transcription of a set of children's pieces for piano, and *Le Grand Jardinier de France* is a film score. Both have a certain charm and would have more, had the orchestra been allowed more rehearsal. Wind intonation is not always flawless. Le Flem is not, perhaps, a major personality, but the *Fourth Symphony* is in its way quite remarkable and, had the performance greater finesse, the disc would have rated a three-star recommendation.

LEHÁR, Franz (1870–1948)

Overtures: Clo-clo; Der Göttergatte. Die lustige Witwe. Waltzes: Adria; Altwiener; Grützner; Valse Boston (Wilde Rosen).
**(*) CPO 999 891-2. Berlin RSO, Jurowski.

These are large-scale performances of generally little-known Lehár, with the exception of the *Merry Widow Overture* (here in the composer's 1940 version). The less well-known concert waltzes are enjoyable, with a lovely robust theme in the *Altwiener Liebeswalzer Waltz*, with some felicitous writing throughout. It is hard to understand why the *Grützner Waltz*, with its beautiful opening building up to a fine waltz, very much in the Strauss tradition, was never published. The *Valse Boston* dispenses with the Strauss-like introduction and replaces is it with a short *maestoso* to call the dancers to the floor. The overtures to *Clo-Clo* and *Der Göttergatte* are lively works and full of delightful ideas, as is the *Adria Waltz*, with a short but exhilarating introduction leading quickly to another good waltz tune (there is also an especially attractive minor-key waltz in this one). It is all very enjoyable, and the orchestra play to the manner born. The only reservation is the recording, which, although it allows details to emerge well, is just a bit too reverberant.

(i) *The Count of Luxembourg*: highlights; (ii) *The Land of Smiles*: highlights; (iii) *The Merry Widow*: highlights.

(B) ** CfP (ADD) 575 9962 (2). (i–iii) Bronhill; (i) Jason, Fyson, McCarthy Singers, Studio 2 Concert O; (ii) Craig, Fretwell, Grant, Sadler's Wells Op. O; (i; ii) cond. Tausky; (iii) Round, McAlpine, Lowe, Sadler's Wells Op. Ch. & O, Reid.

The Sadler's Wells pioneering recording of *The Merry Widow* in English was made in 1958 after a triumphant season in the West End. It is perfectly true that this performance does not have an *echt*-Viennese flavour but, using an admirable new translation by Christopher Hassall, and with the excellent June Bronhill both stylish and charming in the lead, this can stand quite proudly alongside Stolz's Decca Viennese set with Hilde Gueden on Decca (458 549-2 – see our main *Guide*), which was recorded at about the same time. However, although the English words (which are splendidly clear) immediately convey the point of the lighter numbers, somehow the Viennese singers can manage to convey the humour with voice inflexions alone. The Sadler's Wells cast is strongly characterized; only in Howard Glynne's Baron Zeta is there a suspicion of Gilbert and Sullivan. Thomas Round is an appropriately raffish Danilo, although it is a pity that the recording tends to accentuate the unevenness in his voice. William McAlpine as Camille de Rosillon comes over much better, and his *Red as the Rose* is exquisitely sung. The chorus is outstandingly good and these excerpts are most entertaining: the March-Septet is a riot (if a well-drilled riot), and William Reid conducts with sensitivity, obvious affection and a real feeling for the music's idiom. This is a 'Made in Britain' *Merry Widow*, but none the worse for that, and the recording is vividly atmospheric.

The Land of Smiles (again in an English version by Christopher Hassall) was recorded the following year and, if the music and performance are not quite on the level of *The Merry Widow*, there are some delightful numbers and the company sings them with an engaging freshness, if not always with the authentic Viennese ring. Here June Bronhill takes the supporting role of Mi (the heroine's sister), and though Elizabeth Fretwell is less rich-timbred she sings sweetly enough. Charles Craig, as ever, is outstanding as Sou-Chong, with his rich, fine tenor voice sounding out gloriously in 'You are my heart's delight' (with different words) in a way that makes one forget how hackneyed it has become. The recording has a good balance between brilliance on

the one hand and warmth and resonance on the other and, as with *The Merry Widow*, the CD transfer is exellent.

The Count of Luxembourg was recorded a decade later and, even though June Bronhill is most engaging as Juliette and she also sings the operatic role of Angèle Didier, this is generally less distinguished. The translation by Basil Hood and Adrian Ross, has little of Christopher Hassall's flair, and although Tausky conducts just as understandingly as he does in *The Land of Smiles*, and Neville Jason makes an engaging Count, the singing overall is less impressive than before. The recording was originally made in EMI's hi-fi-conscious Studio 2 system; although the CD transfer has managed to smooth some of the original edginess, the effect is often unflattering to the voices. Nevertheless, these excerpts offer a successful reminder of a neglected score with some good numbers, and altogether this inexpensive two-CD reissue makes a good sampler of a Sadler's Wells vintage period.

The Land of Smiles (Das Land des Lächelns); The Merry Widow (Die lustige Witwe) (both complete in German).

(M) (***) EMI mono 5 85822-2 (2). Schwarzkopf, Kunz, Gedda, Loose, Philh. Ch. & O, Ackermann.

It was the Ackermann mono sets of *The Land of Smiles* and *The Merry Widow* in the early 1950s which established a new pattern in recording operetta, treating it with all the care for detail normally lavished on grand opera. The result brought heightened character, both dramatic and musical, with high polish and sharp focus the order of the day. As Hanna Glawari in *The Merry Widow* (which she was to record again in stereo) Schwarzkopf has both sparkle and youthful vivacity, and the *Viljalied* – ecstatically drawn out – is unique. Some may be troubled that Kunz as Danilo sounds older than the Baron (Anton Niessner), but it is still a superbly characterful cast.

The Land of Smiles has a comparably glamorous roster, and if here Gedda does not have quite the passionate flair of Tauber in his famous *Dein ist mein ganzes Herz*, his thoughtful artistry matches a performance which effortlesssly brings out the serious parallels without weighing the work down. Schwarzkopf and Kunz again sing delectably, and the CD transfers are lively and full of presence. Dialogue is included, but separately cued.

The Merry Widow (La Veuve joyeuse): sung in French.

(B) *(*) EMI (ADD) 5 74094-2 (2). Dax, Dens, Lafaye, Mallabrera, Benoit, Grigoriou, Pruvost, René Duclos Ch., Paris Conservatoire O, Leenart.

With its Parisian setting, it might seem appropriate to sing *The Merry Widow (La Veuve joyeuse)* in French and with a largely French cast. But the recording, dating from 1967, inclines to harshness at times. It is vivid enough, the spoken dialogue – brightly delivered – comes over clearly, and the conducting is spirited, as is the performance. But much of the singing is less than ideal, especially that of the heroine, Micheline Dax, who sounds a rather faded widow, not at all ingratiating, which is a major flaw in this operetta. So the set is really of curiosity value only, especially as there are no texts or translations included; indeed, there is no documentation in English whatsoever.

Excerpts from: *Eva (Prelude); Das Fürstenkind; Frasquita (in English & German); Friederike; Giuditta; Das Land des Lächelns* (in German & English); *Die lustige Witwe; Paganini* (in German & English); *Der Rastelbinder; Schön ist die Welt; Der Zarewitsch; Zigeunerliebe*. Selections: 'Lehár memories I & II'.

(M) (*(*)) EMI mono 5 67652-2. Tauber (with various orchestras and conductors).

Why is it that almost alone among singers who recorded in the 1920s and 1930s Richard Tauber's records suffer from so much distortion, insecurity and vocal blasting, immediately obvious in his famous opening number, *Dein ist mein ganzes Herz*, from *Das Land des Lächelns*, and which persists almost continually through all his German recordings? And the orchestral sounds are pretty appalling too (even when Franz Lehár himself conducts the *Vorspiel* from *Eva*).

Fortunately, the English records from the 1940s, made at Abbey Road, emerge relatively unscathed, notably *You are my heart's delight* with a schmaltzy, gentle reprise; and many will relish the duets with Evelyn Laye from *Paganini*. For Tauber admirers there is much to treasure here, providing allowances are made for the sound; others should approach this set with caution.

Arias from: *Frasquita; Friederike; Giuditta; Die lustige Witwe; Paganini; Schön ist die Welt; Der Zarewitsch*. Overtures: *Das Land des Lächelns; Zigeunerliebe. Suite de dance.*

(**(*)) CPO mono 999 781-2. Pfahl, Wittrisch, Reichssender Saarbrücken O, composer.

This CD opens with a broadcast from German Radio introducing this June 1939 concert, designed to promote tuneful and edifying music to the German public girding up for war. At that time, Gustav Kneip was in charge of organizing such patriotic events, and it was he who was able to secure two of the most famous artists around to take part in the programme recorded here, preserved on shellac disc and found, quite recently, in the recording archive of the Reich Radio Society. The performances ooze period nostalgia, with Lehár extracting a large helping of sentimentality from his orchestra, as well as plenty of robust energy in the lively passages, with the idiomatic use of portamenti adding to the period flavour. Margaret Pfahl was a popular coloratura

soubrette, and although she is obviously not at her best here (there is an obtrusive vocal wobble) she sings with much character. Marcel Wittrisch's contribution has a style and energy often missing in operetta recitals today, but he is capable of singing softly too – the high cadence at the end of the *Zarewitsch* is a delight, and the tenderness of the *Friederike* aria is also most affecting. With the composer directing, the Overtures are enjoyable too, especially *Zigeunerliebe* with its Hungarian flavour, and the *Suite de dance* is an unexpected bonus. The transfers seem to be very satisfactory, being warm and reasonably vivid. The wonder is the discs survived at all!

LEIFS, Jón (1899–1968)

Baldr, Op. 34.
*** BIS CD 1230/1. Guðbjörnsson, Schola Cantorum, Iceland SO, Kropsu.

The Icelandic composer Jón Leifs studied in Germany and remained there with a Jewish wife and two daughters until he was able to take refuge in Sweden in 1944. *Baldr* is a 'choreographic drama in two acts' which draws on the *Prose Edda*, written in 1220 by Storri Sturluson. It relates the struggle between Baldr, the son of Odin and the fairest of the gods, and Loki, the personification of evil. Leifs began the score in 1943 when he was still in Nazi Germany (where Loki ruled), finishing it in 1947, the year in which Mount Hekla erupted: the final movement is called *Volcanic Eruption and Atonement*. In *Baldr* Leifs goes even further than he did in earlier works: the wind section includes *lurs* (primitive horns), and to the percussion he adds anvils, cannons, rocks, metal chains and so on – not to mention organ and carillons! Aspirins must have been in brisk demand in Reykjavik after this performance! Imposing though it is, Leifs's primitivism may strain the patience of some listeners: the brutal, repetitive pounding rhythms and the crude *fortissimos* prompt longing for some variety of pace and rhythm, but at the same time there are many imaginative and even beautiful episodes that reward perseverance. Enough of his music is recorded to leave no doubt that Leifs is distinctive – a maverick, no doubt, but powerful nevertheless, and as unlike anyone else as the Icelandic landscape is unlike anywhere else! The present performance is totally committed and convincing, while the recording is pretty amazing and of demonstration quality.

LEIGHTON, Kenneth (1929–88)

Piano Quartet in 1 Movement (Contrasts & Variants), Op. 63; Piano Quintet, Op. 34; Piano Trio, Op. 46.
*** Mer. CDE 84465. Markham, Edinburgh Qt.

We have already had a fine recording of the *Piano*

Trio of 1965, and the *Piano Quartet* and *Quintet* confirm what a strongly individual contribution Kenneth Leighton has made to mid-twentieth-century English chamber music. Both establish his concentrated polyphonic style and the stuctural unity of his conceptions, the early *Piano Quintet* of 1959 growing out of a four-note theme at the opening, which returns in the finale as a splendidly developed *Passacaglia.* The elegiac *Adagio* contrasts with a vibrant Scherzo to match that in the *Piano Trio.* The single-movement *Piano Quartet* of 1972 is a concentrated kaleidoscope of mood and tempo contrasts, yet ends in calm serenity, confirming the underlying lyricism of all Leighton's music. The performances are first class. These artists are thoroughly inside this music and their playing is deeply felt, displaying the viruosity only possible from great familiarity, with the pianist Robert Markham making a strikingly brilliant contribution to the Scherzo.

VOCAL MUSIC

Crucifixus pro nobis; An Easter Sequence; Evensong Services: Magnificat & Nunc Dimittis; Magnificat & Nunc Dimittis (Collegium Magdalenae Oxoniense); Give Me the Wings of Faith; Rockingham: Chorale Prelude on 'When I Survey the Wondrous Cross'; Veni, creator spiritus; What Love of this is thine?
(BB) *** Naxos 8.555795. Durrant, Oxley,
  Steele-Perkins, Whitton, St John's College,
  Cambridge, Ch., Robinson.

Anglican church music has never had more persuasive advocates on disc than Christopher Robinson and the brilliant choir he trained at St John's College, Cambridge. Sadly, Robinson has now retired, bringing the inspired Naxos series to an end, but this collection of the church music of Kenneth Leighton is perhaps the finest of all, brilliantly sung and recorded with brightness and warmth. Leighton was steeped in the Anglican tradition in his youth as a cathedral chorister, and he contributed to its repertory throughout his life. There are two settings here of the Evening Canticles, framing the sequence, one for Magdalen College, Oxford (1959), and the *Second Service* (1971) composed in memory of the organist Brian Runnett, who died tragically in his mid-thirties. They are among the most powerful since those of Herbert Howells, vividly and thoughtfully illustrating each verse, the *Second Service* ending with a hushed *Gloria.* The *Easter Sequence,* with trumpet obbligato, here played superbly by Crispian Steele-Perkins, is wonderfully written for trebles, and the cantata, *Crucifixus pro nobis,* using seventeenth-century texts by Patrick Carey and Phineas Fletcher, is a movingly spare and compressed setting of the Passion story. Composed for the Choir of New College, Oxford, it is a setting of four metaphysical poems, for tenor, choir and organ. With James Oxley the sensitive tenor soloist, it comes over as a work of real substance and deserves the widest dissemination.

Christopher Whitton, the responsive organist, has his solo item in *Rockingham,* based on the hymn, 'When I Survey the Wondrous Cross'. Leighton is a fine and unjustly neglected composer whose music has vitality and eloquence and impeccable craftsmanship. Robinson obtains very good singing from St John's College Choir and the acoustic of St John's College Chapel is splendidly captured in this fine Naxos recording.

LEMBA, Artur (1885–1960)

Symphony in C sharp min.
*** Chan. 8656. SNO, Järvi (with Concert: *'Music from Estonia'*: Vol. 2 ***).

Lemba's *Symphony in C sharp minor* was the first symphony ever to be written by an Estonian. It sounds as if he studied in St Petersburg: at times one is reminded fleetingly of Glazunov, at others of Dvořák (the Scherzo) – and even of Bruckner (at the opening of the finale) and of Elgar. This is by far the most important item in an enterprising collection of Estonian music.

LEWIS, Michael J. (born 1939)

Film scores: *Julius Caesar; The Medusa Touch; The Naked Face; 92 in the Shade; North Sea Hijack; The Rose and the Jackal; Sphinx; The Stick Up; Theatre of Blood; The Unseen; Upon this Rock; The Madwoman of Chaillot; The Hound of the Baskervilles.*
*** Pen Dinas PD 951. Berlin R. SO, Los Angeles Ens.,
  composer.

Welsh-born Michael J. Lewis (currently based in Los Angeles) first came to notice with his 1969 score for *The Madwoman of Chaillot,* the highlight of which is the romantic *Aurelia's Theme,* though the *Palais de Chaillot,* with its battery of percussion instruments, shows the composer's knack for vibrant, atmospheric writing. The brooding evocation of Dartmoor is well conveyed in *The Hound of the Baskervilles,* while the exotically perfumed score to *Sphinx* uses authentic Eastern instruments alongside a full modern symphony orchestra. Lewis's ability to create an atmosphere of menace showed his mastery in the genre of horror films. *The Unseen,* a now largely forgotten B-movie, owes almost all its success to the background music. The simple yet affecting *Love Theme* and *Romance* are included here. *The Medusa Touch* gets the full Gothic treatment, and the dramatic *Destruction of Cathedral* (London's Westminster Cathedral, no less), with its driving rhythms and organ, is very effective. One of the most enjoyable items, however, is the score to *Theatre of Blood,* in which a Shakespearean actor (outrageously hammed up by Vincent Price) wreaks revenge on all his critics by despatching them to gory deaths which correspond with the plays in which his performances were lambasted. The mixture of humour and horror is underlined in the score; the opening theme begins on a single mandolin but soon expands into a full-blooded, sweeping statement, while the fugal *Duel* (perhaps, uniquely, the only duel on film ever fought on a trampoline) is not meant to be taken too seriously. Lewis possesses a distinctive voice, and this CD, with excellent performances in good sound, will be savoured by film buffs and is worth exploring by anyone interested in film music in general.

LIADOV, Anatol (1855–1914)

(i) *Baba Yaga, Op. 56; The Enchanted Lake, Op. 62; Kikimora, Op. 63;* (ii) *8 Russian Folksongs.*
(BB) **(*) Naxos 8.550328. Slovak PO, (i) Gunzenhauser; (ii) Jean (with Concert: 'Russian Fireworks' ***).

It is good to have inexpensive recordings of these key Liadov works, particularly the *Russian Folksongs*, eight orchestral vignettes of great charm, displaying a winning sense of orchestral colour. The performances are persuasive, and the digital recording is vivid and well balanced.

LIBERT (or LIEBERT), Reginaldus (born *c.* 1425/35)

Missa de Beata Virgine; Kyrie à 4.
*** Lyrichord LEMS 8025. Schola Discantus, Moll.

Like Dufay's *Missa Sancti Jacobi*, Libert's Marian Mass has the distinction of being one of the earliest to survive that includes settings of both the Ordinary and Proper. Moreover, the Mass is made cohesive by being based on a very striking, melismatic cantus firmus, which is always recognizable as it usually appears in the upper voice, decorated with ornamental notes. The three-voiced counterpoint is comparatively simple, with the third voice subordinate to the upper parts, enriching the sonority. Even so, the *Credo* is powerful and ambitious, followed by a particularly fine *Sanctus*. In short, this is an appealing and memorable work, and the performance here is an eloquent one, with well-judged pacing. With the addition of the separate four-part *Kyrie*, this disc includes all the music positively attributed to Libert. The recording is first class, made in a spacious acoustic, and the documentation very good, except that for the text and translation of the *Kyrie* and *Gloria* we are referred to another Lyrichord issue (LEMS 8010), a curious proposition, as we are not told any more about this CD. The presentation also associates Libert's Mass with Jeanne d'Arc, and gives her biography, but although she was a contemporary of the composer and this music, there is no other connection.

LIGETI, György (born 1923)

6 Bagatelles for Wind Quintet.
*** Nimbus NI 5728. V. Quintet – HINDEMITH: *Kleine Kammermusik*; NIELSEN: *Wind Quintet.*
***

The Vienna Quintet give as persuasive an account of the lighthearted 1953 *Bagatelles* as any we have had in the past. They are subtle, witty and effervescent and, a delight from first to last – and they are beautifully recorded in the Wiener Konserthaus.

LISZT, Franz (1811–86)

(i) *Piano Concertos Nos. 1–2; Fantasia on themes from Beethoven's 'The Ruins of Athens'; Grande fantasie symphonique on themes from Berlioz's 'Lélio'; Hungarian fantasia for Piano & Orchestra; Malédiction; Totentanz.* Piano transcriptions: SCHUBERT: **Wanderer Fantasy**; WEBER: **Polonaise brillante.** Symphonic Poems: *Ce qu'on entend sur la montagne; Die Ideale; Festklänge; 2 Episodes from Lenau's 'Faust'; Héroïde funèbre; Hamlet; Hungaria; Hunnenschlacht; Mazeppa; Mephisto Waltz No. 2; Orpheus; Les Préludes; Prometheus; Tasso; Von der Wiege bis zum Grabe;* (ii) *Dante Symphony;* (iii) *A Faust Symphony.*
(BB) *** EMI (ADD) 5 85573-2 (7). Leipzig GO, Masur, with (i) Béroff; (ii) Leipzig St Thomas Cho; (iii) Leipzig R. Ch. Male Voices.

Kurt Masur's Liszt survey is perhaps his finest recorded legacy, and it is now issued complete on seven CDs, in superb new transfers – a remarkable bargain. Béroff has won acclaim for his virtuosic technique and his refined poetic sense, and these recordings show him to be a Lisztian of flair. His accounts of the much-recorded *Concertos* can hold their own with most of the competition: there is nothing routine or slapdash here, but remarkable technical prowess. These are exhilarating performances, and they are given the extra attraction of fine orchestral playing and vivid (late 1970s) recording.

The same comments also apply to the other concertante works here: they are all played impressively, with ample brilliance, yet musical and stylish. As for the tone-poems, barring certain individual accounts, these 1970s performances sweep the board in almost every respect. If some of the early works suffer from formal weakness and (for some ears) lack of melodic distinction, Masur makes the strongest possible case for them, with works such as *Festklänge* emerging much more strongly than usual. Elsewhere – in *Hamlet*, the *Héroïde funèbre* and *Prometheus* for example – there is plenty to admire. *Hamlet* has great dramatic intensity and Masur is a vivid and sympathetic exponent throughout. *Die nächtlichw Zug*, the first of the *Two Episodes from Lenau's 'Faust'*, has an intense, brooding atmosphere. The performances – and, whatever one may think of it, this music – cast a strong spell and, with rare exceptions, Masur proves as persuasive an advocate as any on record; the well-known tone-poems – such as *Mazeppa* and *Les Préludes* – emerge as strongly as ever. The rich sonority on the lower strings, the dark, perfectly blended woodwind tone and the fine internal balance of the Leipzig Gewandhaus Orchestra hold the listener's attention throughout – for in the weaker pieces Liszt needs all the help his interpreters can give him. Only in *Orpheus* does Masur let us down: he breezes through it at record speed and misses the endearing gentleness that Beecham brought to it in the early 1960s. In the two *Symphonies* Mazur is impressive, though even in the *Gretchen* movement of the *Faust Symphony* he again moves things on, albeit not unacceptably, and there is no want of delicacy or ardour. Masur's *Faust Symphony* can certainly hold its own, and the same can be said of the *Dante Symphony*. The recordings are well balanced and refined throughout, emerging fresher than ever on CD. Liszt's influence was enormous in his lifetime – on Wagner, the Russians, the French – and listening again to these recordings, one realizes that his musical personality has lost none of its magnetism.

Piano Concertos Nos. 1–2; Hungarian Fantasia; Totentanz.

(B) ** EMI Encore (ADD) 5 74736-2. Cziffra, O de Paris, Cziffra Jr.

(i) *Piano Concertos Nos. 1–2;* (ii) *Hungarian Rhapsody No. 4; Les Préludes, G.97.*

(BB) * (**) DG Entrée (ADD/DDD) 474 563-2. (i) Berman, VSO, Giulini; (ii) VPO, Sinopoli.

(i) *Piano Concertos Nos. 1 in E flat; 2 in A;* (ii) *Malédiction;* (iii) *Dante Sonata* (orch. Lambert).

(B) (***) Dutton mono CDBP 9742. (i) Sauer, Paris Conservatoire O, Weingartner; (ii) Osborn, Boyd Neel SO, Boyd Neel; (iii) Kentner, Sadler's Wells O, Lambert.

(i) *Piano Concertos Nos. 1–2; Piano Sonata in B min.*

(M) *(*) Sony SMK 89880. Ax; (i) Philh. O, Salonen.

This Dutton reissue is of special documentary interest. Emil Sauer and Felix Weingartner were the last surviving members of Liszt's circle so they knew his musical intentions well. Their recording of the two *Concertos* was made in two sessions in December 1938 in the somewhat unglamorous acoustic of the Rue d'Albert studios in Paris. The sound is a bit dry and wanting in transparency, but it affords a rare opportunity to relish the artistry of Sauer, then seventy-six but still a commanding, authoritative virtuoso. Franz Osborn (1905–55) gave us the very first recording of the *Malédiction*, which comes from 1945, his only appearance as a concerto soloist on records. (Egon Wellesz used to speak of his late

Beethoven sonatas, Opp. 109–111, with awe – he was not a pupil of Schnabel for nothing – but, alas, he never recorded them.) The sound is very natural indeed for the period and the playing magisterial. So, too, is Louis Kentner's *Dante Sonata* in the arrangement that Constant Lambert made of *Après une lecture de Dante*. Again, the 1940 recording wears its years lightly in this fine Dutton transfer. A valuable set that all Lisztians will want.

These father-and-son performances on EMI Encore (the father being the pianist) emanate from the early 1970s. The playing has some flair and character, but the recording in the concertos lets the side down – the sound is opaque and shallow, with the piano inclining to brittleness. Although the *Hungarian Fantasia* and *Totentanz* have greater vividness, they are still not ideal. EMI list 12 tracks in the booklet, but in reality we have only one track per piece.

Lazar Berman's 1976 recording of the concertos has the advantage of Giulini's sensitive and masterly accompaniment with the Vienna Symphony Orchestra, and even if you feel that these scores hold no surprises for you, try listening to this CD. Berman's playing is consistently poetic and he illuminates detail in a way that has the power to touch the listener. Some of his rapt, quiet tone would not register without the tactful assistance of the DG engineers, who enable all the detail to 'tell', but the balance is most musical and well judged. A very thoughtful account of No. 1 and a poetic reading of No. 2 make this a desirable CD of this repertoire. Giulini keeps a strong grip on the proceedings and secures an excellent response from his players. If they don't eclipse the greatest performances of these works, they remain distinguished accounts.

Sinopoli offers highly polished accounts of the *Rhapsody* and tone-poem, often very beautiful but lacking the unbridled enthusiasm which this music ideally needs. In the *Hungarian Rhapsody*, the orchestra almost grinds to a halt in the passages leading up to the faster gypsy dancing music, in theory providing contrast, but in effect sounding mannered. That said, with the rich, bright, digital recording, and with superb orchestral playing, these performances are not without enjoyment – but Karajan and Stokowski really know how make this music go.

Emanuel Ax and the Philharmonia Orchestra under Esa-Pekka Salonen combine to give a rumbustious and lyrically appealing account of the *First Concerto*, with plenty of brilliance from the soloist and full-blooded recording to match. They are less successful in creating atmosphere at the opening of No. 2 – which is always more elusive – although the performance picks up tension as it continues. Ax's interpretation of the *Sonata*, however, is disappointingly melodramatic and artificially brillant, showing little feeling for its unique combination of romanticism and structural cohesion. The recording here does not flatter the piano.

(i; ii) *Piano Concerto No. 1 in E flat*; (iii; iv)
Hungarian Fantasia; (iv) *Hungarian Rhapsodies
Nos. 2, 4 & (i) 6*; (v) *Mephisto Waltz No. 1*; (iv) *Les
Préludes*; (i) *Piano Sonata in B min.*; (vi)
Bénédiction de Dieu dans la solitude; (vii) *Feux
follets; Harmonies du soir.*

(BB) ** DG Panorama (ADD) 469 151-2 (2). (i)
    Argerich; (ii) LSO, Abbado; (iii) Cherkassky; (iv)
    BPO, Karajan; (v) Ashkenazy; (vi) Arrau; (vii)
    Richter.

Argerich and Abbado are in very good form in the *E
flat Concerto* and the recording is excellent. Equally
compelling are Karajan's *Hungarian Rhapsodies Nos. 2*
and *4* (the 6th is for piano solo, excitingly done by
Argerich) and *Les Préludes* – all deservedly famous
recordings. Cherkassky's glittering account of the
Hungarian Fantasia is another highlight, and the solo
items from Ashkenazy and Arrau are all worth having.
The Richter performances are live and date from the
late 1950s, but the much poorer sound and unbelievably noisy audience preclude much enjoyment.

Hungarian Rhapsodies Nos. 1–6.

(*) Mercury (ADD) **SACD 475 6185. LSO, Dorati – –
    ENESCU: *Romanian Rhapsody No. 1.* ***

Mercury are bringing out some of their most
admired recordings on SACD and, although they are
not due to be released until after our book goes to
press, we feel sure that listeners will want to be
informed of their publication in the autumn of this
year. Dorati's is undoubtedly the finest set of *Hungarian Rhapsodies*. He brings out the gypsy flavour
and, with lively playing from the LSO, there is both
polish and sparkle. The new format should go some
way to further enhance the already spectacular
results afforded by the 'Living Presence' technology.

Hungarian Rhapsodies Nos. 1–6; Hunnenschlacht; Mazeppa; Mephisto Waltz No. 1; Les Préludes.

(M) ** Westminster (ADD) 471 237-2 (2). V. State Op.
    O, Scherchen.

Scherchen's recordings date from the late 1950s but
sound surprisingly full and refined for their age.
They contain their fair share of the characteristically
eccentric tempi for which this conductor is famous,
but at times he coaxes surprisingly subtle detail from
these scores, while the fast passages generate plenty
of excitement. Not a top choice in this repertoire but
a characterful and interesting one. A pity the disc
isn't at bargain price.

SYMPHONIC POEMS

Les Préludes.

(BB) **(*) EMI Encore 5 85460-2. Phd. O, Muti –
    RAVEL: *Boléro* *(*); TCHAIKOVSKY: *1812.* *(**)

Muti has the full measure of *Les Préludes*, catching its
breadth as well as its exuberance, with the Philadelphia Orchestra on top form. This is the most succesful of the three showpieces on this inexpensive
reissued CD and, while the early digital recording
shows that the engineers were striving for brilliance
rather than sonority, the result is still impressive and
certainly exciting.

PIANO MUSIC

Années de pèlerinage, 1st Year, Switzerland (complete).

(M) *** Decca 457 206-2. Bolet.

Winner of the *Gramophone* Instrumental Award in
1985, this reissued recording of the Swiss pieces from
the *Années de pèlerinage* represents Jorge Bolet at his
very peak, in many ways even transcending his masterly achievement in other discs in the series, with
playing of magical delicacy as well as formidable
power. So *Au bord d'une source* brings pianism limpid in its evocative beauty. The piano sound is outstandingly fine, set against a helpful atmosphere, and
gaining greatly from its complete background
silence.

Recital: Années de pèlerinage: Au bord d'une source. Concert Studies 1–2: Waldesrauschen; Gnomenreigen. Concert Paraphrase: Les Patineurs (Illustration No. 2 from Meyerbeer's 'Le Prophète'); Etudes de Concert: La leggierezza; Un sospiro; Paganini Etudes Nos. 2 in E flat; 3 (La campanella); 5 (La Chasse). Etudes d'exécution transcendante: Feux follets.

(**) Pearl mono GEM 0148. Kentner – BARTOK:
    Piano Concerto No. 3, etc. (*)

The Liszt performances come from 78rpm records
made between 1937 and 1949 for the Columbia DX
label. Louis Kentner was a Lisztian of great distinction, and these old discs testify to his finesse and
sensitivity. Decent transfers, but the Bartók coupling
is much less recommendable.

Ballade No. 2; Harmonies poétiques et religieuses: Bénédiction de Dieu dans la solitude. Mephisto Waltz No. 1; Sposalizio; En rêve; Schaflos!; Unstern!

(M) *** Oehms OCD 228. Perl.

The Chilean pianist Alfredo Perl has already made a
powerful impact on disc with his superb complete
cycle of the thirty-two Beethoven sonatas for the
midpriced label Oehms. Here, in playing equally
commanding, he tackles Liszt, making an imaginative choice of pieces, four of them substantial, three
of them miniatures. In his rapt concentration Perl
brings weight to Liszt's sequential arguments, underlining the link between the magnificent *Ballade* over
its 15-minute span and Liszt's sonata in the same key.
Even more expansive is the surgingly lyrical *Bénédiction*, with the first *Mephisto Waltz* bringing virtuoso
fireworks at the end. Excellent, well-balanced sound.

12 Etudes d'exécution transcendante.

* (**) Naïve **DVD** DR 2104 AV103. Berezovsky.

Recorded live at La Roque d'Anthéron, France, 6 August 2002 (V/D: Andy Sommer).

12 Etudes d'exécution transcendante; Mephisto Waltz No. 1.

(M) *** EMI mono 5 62799-2. Cziffra.

Boris Berezovsky's account of the *Transcendental Studies* is stunning. Ever since we first encountered him playing the Beethoven *G major Concerto* at Leeds, this pianist has never ceased to amaze by his sheer virtuosity, imagination and musicality. Although this is remarkable musically, the video direction greatly diminishes the listener's pleasure. The camera shots are often very close, concentrating on a narrow area of the keyboard, restlessly changing and generally attracting attention to the camera itself. It must have been a hot evening, as Berezovsky perspires profusely and the camera dwells on beads of sweat that gather on the pianist's nose. There is some tiresome mixing of images in *Feux follets*, and admiration for the sheer musical wizardry is tempered by exasperation at the unmusical prduction. Three stars and a bouquet for the playing but a brickbat for the visual direction. So intrusive and irritating is the latter that many will find it difficult to go on watching. However, fortunately, Berezovsky's complete CD recording of the *Etudes* is available on Warner Elatus (2564 60125-2).

Cziffra's chimerically brilliant set of the *Etudes d'exécution transcendante* was recorded in faithful if slightly restricted mono sound in the Hungaraton studio in 1956. The result is strikingly fresh and the easy technical dexterity is astonishing, as it is too in the *Mephisto Waltz*. Georges Cziffra was then at the height of his powers, so this a predictable reissue to include in EMI's series of 'Great Artists of the 20th Century'.

Piano Sonata; 2 Legends (St Francis of Assisi Preaching to the Birds; St Francis of Paola Walking on the Waves); Scherzo & March.

(BB) *** Hyp. Helios CDH 55184. Demidenko.

Nikolai Demidenko's is a keenly dramatic and powerfully projected account of the sonata that has the listener on the edge of his or her seat. It must be numbered among the finest performances he has given us. The excitement and virtuosity are second to none and almost call to mind Horowitz: his playing can be measured against that of Brendel and Pletnev. He has the advantage of exceptionally vivid recorded sound, and the remainder of the recital goes equally well.

Piano Sonata in B min.; La Lugubre Gondola.

(M) *** DG 471 358-2. Pollini – SCHUMANN: *Fantasy in C; Arabesque.* ***

It is good that DG have restored Pollini's riveting 1989 account of the Liszt *B minor Sonata* to the catalogue for the 'Pollini Edition'. It is a performance of real vision, which combines powerful emotional feeling with astonishing bravura; moreover Pollini's structural grasp is consummate, moving unerringly to the closing pages, with the concentration never slipping. *La Lugubre Gondola* makes a curious encore but its darker atmosphere is well caught, and there are no complaints about the recording.

VOCAL MUSIC

Lieder: *Der Alpenjäger; Anfangs wollt ist fast verzagen; Angiolin dal biodo crin; Blume und Duft; Comment, disaient-ils; Die drei Zigeuner; Du bist wie eine Blume; Der du von dem Himmel bist; Enfant, si j'étais roi; Ein Fichtenbaum steht einsam; Es muss ein Wunderbares sein; Es rauschen die Winde; Der Fischerknabe; Gastibelza; Gestoren war ich; Der Hirt; Hohe Liebe; Ich möchte hingeln; Ihr Glocken von Marling; Im Rhein, im schönen Strome; In Liebeslust; J'ai perdu ma force; Klinge leise, mein Lied; Lasst mich ruhen; Die Lorelei; Morgens steh'ich auf und frage; Oh! Quand je dors; O Lieb, so lang; Petrarch Sonnets Nos. 1–3; Schwebe, schwebe blaues Auge; S'il est un charmant gazon; Die stille Wasserose; Des Tages laute Stimmen schweigen; La Tombe et la rose; Der traurige Mönch; Über allen Gipfeln ist Ruh; Die Vätergruft; Vergiftet sind meine Lieder; Le Vieux Vagabond; Wer nie sein Brot; Wieder möcht ich dir begegnen; Wie singt die Lerche schon.*

(M) *** DG 474 891-2 (3). Fischer-Dieskau, Barenboim.

As in a number of other fields Liszt has been severely under-appreciated as a song composer. The reissue of this collection of 43 songs plus an accompanied declamation, which won the *Gramophone* Solo Vocal Award in 1981 and is now on three mid-priced CDs instead of four LPs, should do something to right the balance. Fischer-Dieskau, so far from making such an enormous project sound routine, actually seems to gain inspiration and intensity with the concentration; for example, the most famous of the songs, the *Petrarch Sonnets*, are here even more inspired than in his previous performances. The sheer originality of thought and the ease of the lyricism – not least in *O Lieb*, which everyone knows as the famous piano solo, *Liebestraume No. 3* – are a regular delight, and Barenboim's accompaniments could hardly be more understanding, though Liszt presented surprisingly few virtuoso challenges to the pianist. The recording is excellent.

Lieder: *Comment, disaient-ils; Die drei Zigeuner; Ein Fichtenbaum steht einsam; Enfant, si j'étais roi; Es muss ein Wunderbares sein; Oh, grand je dors; S'il est un charmant gazon; Über allen Gipfeln ist Ruh; Vergiftet sind meine Lieder.*

(M) *** Decca 474 536-2. Fassbaender, Gage – R. STRAUSS: *Lieder.* ***

Coupled with an equally characterful collection of Strauss songs, Brigitte Fassbaender's Liszt selection richly deserved to win the Solo Vocal prize in the *Gramophone* awards in 1987. This is singing which, in its control of detail, both in word and in note, as well as in its beauty and range of expression, is totally commanding. There are few women Lieder singers in any generation who can match this in power and intensity, with each song searchingly characterized. Fassbaender proves just as much at home in the four Victor Hugo settings in French as in the German songs. Sensitive accompaniment and well-placed recording.

Christus (oratorio).

(BB) ★★★ Warner Apex 2564 61167-2 (3). Valente, Lipovšek, Lindroos, Krause, Slovak Philharmonic Ch., Rotterdam PO, Conlon.

Liszt's *Christus* is less an oratorio than an episodic sequence of contrasted pieces, many of them very beautiful, inspired by the person of Christ. It is not part of the scheme to personify Christ in the way that Bach does in the Passions, but to intersperse devotional hymns – such as *The Three Kings* or the carol-like *O filii et filae* – between atmospheric scene-paintings such as *The Beatitudes* or *The Miracle Depicting Christ Walking on the Waters*. James Conlon and his Rotterdam forces give a dedicated reading, full of warmth and understanding. The liveliness of the acoustic and the distancing of the sound may obscure some detail, but this is an account, recorded at a live concert, that brings out the beauties and expressiveness of the writing to the full. Tiny mishaps, inevitable in a live performance, are not likely to undermine enjoyment, and the reissue is very reasonably priced.

LOURIÉ, Arthur (1892–1966)

(i) String Quartets Nos. 1–3 (Suite); (ii) Duo for Violin & Viola.

★★(★) ASV CDDCA 1020. (i) Utrecht Qt; (ii) Koskinen, Raiskin.

The three quartets were composed in quick succession: the *First* is a two-movement piece lasting half an hour, whose first movement (nearly 20 minutes) is very amorphous and wanting in concentration. The *Second Quartet* (1923) is a much shorter, one-movement work with a hint of Stravinskian neo-classicism and humour. But it is the economical and well-wrought *Duo for Violin and Viola* that is most Russian. The *Third Quartet* (1924), subtitled *Suite* (its movements are called *Prélude*, *Choral*, *Hymne* and *Marche funèbre*), save for the last movement does not make as strong an impression as *A Little Chamber Music* from the same year. Nevertheless this is an interesting byway, explored with great dedication by these players.

LULLY, Jean-Baptiste (1632–87)

Divertissements Nos. 1–3 (arr. Sempé).

(M) ★★ DHM/BMG 82876 60154-2. Laurens, Capriccio Stravagante, Sempé.

Skip Sempé and his chamber group have already given us a recommendable CD of the music of Buxtehude, but this collection of the music of Lully is rather disappointing. Sempé is attempting to recreate the evening concerts at the Versailles court enjoyed by the nobility, featuring a small ensemble plus a celebrated soloist. The three 'Divertissements' draw on music from several of Lully's tragédies lyriques, including *Amadis*, *Psyché* and *Armide*, but the authentic string-textures here are too meagre to bring out the richness of the expressive writing and, although the mezzo-soprano soloist Guillemete Laurens understands the style of the music and sings expressively, her full-bodied voice, with ample vibrato, will please some ears more than others. Overall these performances fail to seduce the ear. Texts and translations are provided.

Dies irae; Te Deum.

(BB) ★★(★) Warner Apex 2564 61369-2. J. Smith, Bessac, Vandersteene, Devos, Huttenlocher, Vocal Ens. 'A Cœur Joie' de Valance, Paillard CO, Paillard.

The *Dies irae* is written for double choir, and the antiphonal dialogue between the two groups is a vital part of Lully's musical architecture. Paillard makes no attempt to divide his forces, relying mainly on the contrast with the solo group. It is a noble piece, encapsulating a mood of dark melancholy, and it makes the strongest impression here. The performance itself is suitably restrained and dignified, with a totally dedicated contribution from the soloists. The effect has a striking elegiac beauty. The sudden choral interjections at a faster pace are convincingly managed. The coupled *Te Deum*, which dates from 1677, is probably Lully's best-known sacred piece. It is a creation of genuine splendour and breadth, rather than the general-purpose pomp often favoured by Lully and his followers. Like the *Dies irae*, the work makes effective use of the contrast between soloists, chorus and orchestra, and François Paillard and his vocal forces give a thoroughly committed and eloquent account of the piece, and the orchestra accompanies impressively. The analogue recording is eminently satisfactory in both works; the overall balance is good and the CD transfer is well managed. Paillard does not offer the last word on either work, but the record is worth having, especially at so modest a price. Incidentally, it was while conducting the *Te Deum* that Lully vigorously brought the heavy stick that served to mark the beat down on his right foot; gangrene eventually set in, and he died a couple of months later.

Armide; Isis (extracts).

(M) ★★(*) Erato (ADD/DDD) 2564 60578-2. Ch.
Caillard, Jean-François Paillard O, Paillard –
DELALANDE: *Premier Caprice.* ★★(*)

A very pleasing selection from *Armide* and *Isis*,
recorded in 1972. While the performances lack the
bite one would undoubtedly get from an authentic
performance today, under Paillard these do not lack
life and character. There is a nice balance between the
orchestral and choral writing, and all the music is of
Lully's best inventive quality. *Le Sommeil de Renaud*
from *Armide* is very much the sort of thing that
Beecham might have selected as one of his lollipops,
while the *Choeur des trembleurs* from *Isis*, with its
staccato 'trembling' chorus echoed in the orchestra,
makes an enjoyable novelty number, and it is followed by a charming if melancholy *Rondeau 'Plains
de lo'*. The sound is good, if a little reverberant,
slightly blunting some of the sharpness.

LUMBYE, Hans Christian
(1810–74)

The complete orchestral works

Volume 1: *Amélie Waltz; Britta Polka; Artist Dreams
Fantasia; Cannon Galop; Champagne Galop;
Columbine Polka-mazurka; Copenhagen Steam
Railway Galop; Dagma Polka; Deborah Polka
Mazurka; King Christian IX's March-past; Otto
Allin's Drum Polka; Queen Louise Waltz; Saecilie
Waltz; Salute to August Bournonville Galop; A
Summer Night at the Mön Cliffs Fantasia; (Berlin)
Vauxhall Polka.*

★★ Marco Polo 8.223743. Tivoli SO, Bellincampi.

Volume 2: *Amanda Waltz; Camilla Polka; Crinoline
Polka-mazurka; The Dream after the Ball;
Goodnight Polka; King Carl XV's March-past; A
Little Ditty for the Party Galop; Master Erik's Polka;
Military Galop; Minerva Polka; Regatta Festival
Waltz; Rosa and Rosita Waltz; Salute to Capri Polka;
Victoria Bundsen Polka-mazurka; Victoria Galop;
Wally Polka.*

★★ Marco Polo 8.223744. Tivoli SO, Bellincampi.

Volume 3: *Amager Polka, No. 2; Carnival Joys;
Pictures from a Masquerade; Concert Polka for 2
Violins; Festival Polonaise in A; The Guardsmen of
Amager: Finale-galop; New Year Greeting March;
Ornithobolaia Galop; Sounds from Kroll's Dance
Hall; Tivolis Concert Salon Galop; Tivoli Volière
Galop; Torchlight Dance.*

★★ Marco Polo 8.225122. Tivoli SO, Bellincampi.

Following on from their monumental Strauss Edition, Marco Polo now turn their attention to the
'Strauss of the North', Hans Christian Lumbye. The
first three volumes are sympathetically and enjoyably played, but the recordings are not ideal: they

are too reverberant and backwardly balanced, taking away some of the warm intimacy, as well as the
sparkle, this music should ideally have. But collectors who wish to explore this composer's output in
depth will find much to enjoy here. Like the
Strausses, Lumbye's fund of melody is seemingly
inexhaustible, and the various novelty pieces are
often delightful. Much of the writing has a robust
quality which is most infectious, and the orchestration is always colourful. These Marco Polo discs,
despite the too-resonant sound, will certainly give
pleasure.

Volume 5: *Artist Carnival Locomotive Galop;
Caroline Polka Mazurka; In the Dusk (Fantasy);
Fountain Waltz; Hesperus Waltz; Jenny Polka; Marie
Elisabeth Polka; Memories of Vienna, Waltz; The
Night before New Year's Day (Polka Mazurka);
Regards to the Ticket-Holders of Tivoli (March);
Salute March of King Frederik VII; The Sleigh Ride
(Galop); Telegraph Galop.*

★★★ Marco Polo 8.225171. Tivoli SO, Vetö.

Volume 5 in Marco Polo's Lumbye edition seems to
offer marginally richer sound than earlier volumes,
and the performances are excellent. There are plenty
of things to delight here: the *Sleigh Ride* sounds
suitably festive, with its dashing runs up and down
the scale, whips and bells, while the full-length concert waltzes, such as *Memories from Vienna* and the
Hesperus Waltz, provide more substantial fare as well
as much charm and elegance. *The Night before New
Year's Day* charmingly alternates the major and
minor keys, while *In the Dusk* is a charming pastoral
evocation of a peaceful evening, which gradually
becomes more and more animated, though it ends, 'à
l'invitation to the dance', as peacefully as it began.
There are some novelties here, too: the *Telegraph
Galop*, reflecting rivalry between two orchestras,
opens with a couple of wallops on the bass drum and
is a communication between both groups, who
'telegraph melodies' to each other, sometimes in
different keys, though finally coming together – an
amusing idea skilfully realized. This is one of the best
CDs in the series.

ŁUTOSŁAWSKI, Witold
(1916–94)

(i; ii) *Cello Concerto;* (ii) *Postlude No. 1;* (iii)
Preludes and Fugue for 13 Solo Strings; (iv) *String
Quartet;* (v; ii) *Paroles tissées;* (ii; vi) *3 Poèmes
d'Henri Michaux;* (vii; ii) *5 Songs for Soprano &
Orchestra (The Sea; Storm; Winter; Knights; Church
Bells).*

⊶ (B) ★★★ EMI Gemini (ADD) 5 85773-2 (2). (i)
Jablonski; (ii) Polish R. Nat. SO; (iii) Polish CO; all
cond. composer; (iv) Alban Berg Qt; (v) Louis
Devos; (vi) Kraków R. Ch.; (vii) Lukomska.

This valuable collection was recorded under the auspices of the composer in the Polish Radio Studios in Kraków in 1976–7, with the *String Quartet* added much later, in 1995. Roman Jablonski's account of the *Cello Concerto* still stands up well against the competition, though it is not a first choice. The searching *Seven Preludes and Fugue for Strings* (1970–72) show the mature Lutosławski and are vividly played by the Polish orchestra, as is the short, elliptical *Postlude* (1958). The choral *Poèmes d'Henri Michaux* date from the early 1960s. With their variety of effects, including whispering and syllabic monotones, the writing readily contrasts with the atmospheric *Paroles tissées* ('Woven Words') with its mystical feeling and remarkable word-imagery. The equally atmospheric *Five Songs* (written in 1957 and orchestrated the following year) find a highly sympathetic and idiomatic soloist in Halina Lukomska, with the texturally intriguing accompaniments catching the ear quite as much as the vocal line.

In his two-movement *String Quartet* Lutosławski tells us that he uses 'chance elements to enrich the rhythmic and expressive character of the music without in any way limiting the authority of the composer over the final shape of the piece'. Whatever its merits, it has a highly developed and refined feeling for sonority and balance, the main movement sounding all but orchestral at times, and generally speaking it succeeds in holding the listener in a performance and recording as compelling as this. Altogether this inexpensive survey offers a well-conceived demonstration of the composer's breadth of achievement. As might be expected, performances are of a generally high standard and the analogue recordings have been transferred very well to CD.

Partita; Subito.

*** HM HMC 901793. Faust, Kupiec – JANACEK: *Violin Sonata*; SZYMANOWSKI: 3 *Mythes*. ***.

Spicing up this Slavonic mixed bag, Lutosławski's *Subito* is a showpiece full of manic energy, quirky and fragmentary, inspiring Isabelle Faust and Ewa Kupiec to a dazzling performance. The five-movement *Partita*, which Lutosławski originally wrote for Pinchas Zukerman and Marc Neikrug, makes a powerful concluding item. Structurally, the composer may have had baroque models in mind, but stylistically this is well removed from regular neo-classicism, like the other pieces on the disc, making formidable technical demands in the quirkiness of the writing over the widest dynamic and tonal range.

LYAPUNOV, Sergei (1859–1924)

Piano Concertos Nos. 1 in E flat min., Op. 4; 2 in E, Op. 38. Rhapsody on Ukrainian Themes, Op. 28.

*** Hyp. CDA 67326. Milne, BBC Scottish SO, Brabbins.

It is to the *Etudes d'éxecution transcendante* that one's thoughts turn when Lyapunov's name is mentioned. The *First Piano Concerto* of 1890 is much earlier and, although it was published in Berlin in the mid-1890s and was frequently played in the decade or so after its composition (its première was conducted by Balakirev and the pianists who took it up included Josef Hofmann), this is its first commercial recording. Like so much of the music of the post-nationalist generation, its debts are to Borodin and Balakirev, the keyboard writing showing the Lisztian sympathies of its composer. Along with the Rachmaninov *Second Concerto*, the Arensky *D minor Trio* and Scriabin's *Third* and *Fourth Sonatas*, it was awarded a Belaiev Glinka prize in 1904 and, although in terms of originality and musical substance it does not belong in their company, it is far too good to languish unplayed. Although Lyapunov never escaped the influence of Balakirev to develop a strong individual creative personality, his writing is unfailingly accomplished and satisfying. Both the remaining works have been recorded, the *Ukrainian Rhapsody* by Michael Ponti (Vox) and the *Second Concerto* of 1909 more recently by Howard Shelley (Chandos). All three pieces offer civilized pianistic discourse and will reward the interest of all who love Russian music of this period. Hamish Milne's aristocratic playing and effortless virtuosity give much delight, though in the *Second Concerto* (Chan. 9808) Shelley has perhaps greater dash and imagination. The orchestral playing under Martyn Brabbins is eminently supportive and the balance between soloist and orchestra could not be better judged. There are excellent and authoritative notes by Edward Garden.

LYATOSHYNSKY, Boris (1895–1968)

Symphony No. 1 in A min., Op. 2; Overture on 4 Ukrainian Themes, Op. 20; Poem of Reunification, Op. 40.

*** Russian Disc RDCD 11055. Ukrainian State SO, Gnedash.

Symphonies Nos. 2, Op. 26; 3 in B min., Op. 50.

*** Marco Polo 8.223540. Ukrainian State SO, Kuchar.

Symphonies Nos. 4 in B flat min., Op. 63; 5 in C ('Slavonic'), Op. 67.

*** Marco Polo 8.223541. Ukrainian State SO, Kuchar.

Symphony No. 4 in B flat min., Op. 63; (i) On the Banks of the Vistula, Op. 59; (ii) Lyric Poem.

** Russian Disc RDCD 11062. Ukrainian State SO, Blazhkov, with (i) Sirenko; (ii) Glushchenko.

Lyatoshynsky began writing his *First Symphony* immediately after the First World War, and it is a well-crafted, confident score that inhabits the world of Russian post-nationalism, Strauss and Scriabin. It abounds in contrapuntal elaboration and abundant orchestral rhetoric. The *Second Symphony* followed in 1936, but its air of pessimism did not sit well in post-*Lady Macbeth* Russia. Although the *Third Symphony* (1951) tries hard to be a good Soviet symphony, it does not wholly ring true.

The *Fourth Symphony* (1963) is more directly Shostakovichian than its predecessors. Its middle movement depicts what must be a mysterious, chimerical city to a Ukrainian, namely Bruges. There is striking use of bells and celesta, and at times a suggestion of Messiaen. The *Fifth (Slavonic)* certainly pays tribute to his master, Glière, in using the *Rus* theme, *Il'ya Mourametz*, as well as a wide variety of Russian, Bulgarian and Serbian liturgical melodies. It aspires to explore the common roots of the Slavonic peoples; hence its title. There are many touches of colour and some token modernity, but basically this looks back to earlier masters.

Those with exploratory tastes will find much to interest them in these symphonies, provided they are not expecting masterpieces. As far as performances are concerned, the Ukraine orchestra obviously is inside this music, and none of the playing is second rate. The Marco Polo recordings are more than marginally superior to the Russian Disc, and the performances sound much better rehearsed than is usually the case with this label, while the odd fillers on the Russian Discs are not of sufficient interest to tip the scales in their favour.

MAAZEL, Lorin (born 1930)

(i) *Music for Cello & Orchestra;* (ii) *Music for Flute & Orchestra;* (iii) *Music for Violin & Orchestra.*
*** RCA 09026 68789-2. (i) Rostropovich; (ii) Galway; (iii) composer; Bav. RSO, Post.

The austere titles of these works of Lorin Maazel – products of his increased activity as a composer in the mid-1990s – belie the fact that Maazel is at root a late romantic, working to no formula but expressing what he feels, often lyrically, always with colour and fine feeling for orchestral timbres. The most outward-going of the three is the flute piece for James Galway, reflecting the dedicatee's flamboyant character as an artist. It ends with a big cadenza, accompanied by percussion, leading into a brilliant coda heightened by blatant brass. The cello piece written for Rostropovich is the most demanding of the three, an extended half-hour made up of eight contrasted sections, one developing from the other and ending, as the work began, with a darkly reflective coda. Maazel wrote the violin piece for himself to play, dedicating it to his wife, who inspired it. Again the music is largely reflective, ending on an epilogue marked 'tranquillo', which yet includes a pained climax. Excellent performances and recording.

MCCABE, John (born 1939)

CHAMBER MUSIC

3 Folk Songs, Op. 19: Johnny was gone for a soldier; Hush-a-ba Birdie; John Peel: (for tenor, clarinet and piano).
*** Campion Cameo 2001. Hindmarsh, Turner, Cuckson – BUSH: *Prison Cycle;* RAWSTHORNE: *Songs.* **(*)

The *Three Folk Songs,* by John McCabe, very well sung by Martin Hindmarsh, have a neatly tailored clarinet obbligato, and the recital closes with a droll arrangement of *John Peel,* with its witty hornpipe pay-off.

MACHY, Sieur de (died c. 1692)

Pièces de viole (1685): Suites 1–3.
(M) *(*) Astrée (ADD) ES 9946. Savall.

Little is known about Sieur de Machy (or Demachy) except that his published *Viol Suites* predated the first publication of the Marais suites by a year. They are the usual collection of Allemandes, Courantes, Sarabandes, Gavottes, Gigues and Minuets, but so freely improvisational is the style of Savall's performances that their rhythmic profile is often all but lost. This is simple music, and it needs a direct, clearly rhythmic approach. An interesting but essentially disappointing reissue (from the late 1970s).

MAHLER, Gustav (1860–1911)

Symphonic movements: *Blumine; Totenfeier; Symphony No. 10: Adagio.*
(B) ** Virgin 5 61922-2. Bamberg SO, Rickenbacher – HINDEMITH: *Mathis der Maler,* etc. **

Blumine is comparatively well known as the movement Mahler intended for his *First Symphony* and then omitted. *Totenfeier* ('Funeral Rites'), written in 1888, was an amalgam of symphonic poem and funeral march, which gestated into the first movement of the *Second (Resurrection) Symphony* without being greatly altered, except in detail. The Bamberg orchestra under Karl Anton Rickenbacher give sympathetic performances of these two movements and an eloquent account of the well-known Adagio from the *Tenth.* They are well recorded, but this seems to be a reissue for dedicated Mahlerians rather than the general collector.

Symphonies Nos. 1 (including Blumine); 2–9 (complete); 10 (Adagio).
** Chan. 9572 (12). Copenhagen Boys' Ch., Danish Nat. Ch. & RSO, Segerstam (with Kilberg, Dolberg in Nos. 2 & 8; Gjevang in Nos. 3 & 8; Johansson in No. 4; Nielsen, Majken, Bonde-Hansen, Sirkiä, Hynninen, Stabell, BPO Ch. in No. 8).

The main advantages of the Chandos set are fine playing by a clearly committed and dedicated orchestra and superbly rich and expansive recording, notably the brass and chorus in the powerful finale of the *Resurrection Symphony*, although the vocal balance in No. 8, as so often, is less than ideal. Segerstam's is a very relaxed view of Mahler, and he takes us through the Mahlerian pastoral scenery as in an affectionate guided tour. Immediately in the *First Symphony* one notices a lack of grip in the opening evocation, and throughout the series the relaxed tempi and Segerstam's lack of firmness mean that although the playing itself is committed and always sensitive there is a loss of sustained intensity. Inner movements are often delightfully coloured, and the famous *Adagio* of the *Fifth Symphony* is warmly atmospheric but very laid back. Similarly Segerstam opens the *Fourth* in the most coaxing manner but remains very relaxed, and the explosive *fortissimo* of the slow movement could be more biting. In the great *Adagio* of the *Ninth* there is the widest range of dynamic and some beautiful *pianissimo* playing, but the final pull of tension from the conductor which makes for a compellingly great performance is missing. The layout too is less than ideal, with the first five symphonies not coming in numerical order, so initially finding one's way about the twelve CDs takes some care.

Symphonies Nos. 1; 3 in D min.

(B) ** RCA High Performance (ADD) 09026 63469-2 (2). BSO, Leinsdorf.

Neither of the Leinsdorf performances is completely recommendable. The *First* is hard driven, almost brutal, in no sense Viennese, and lacking in atmosphere, yet one cannot deny that it is exciting at times. He is more successful in the *Third*, where his straightforward approach makes for more convincing results. The recordings (from 1962 and 1966) are very up-front, brilliant in hi-fi terms, though not a genuine concert image. One still turns to Solti for No. 1 (Decca 458 622-2) and Rattle for No. 3 (EMI 5 56657-2).

Symphony No. 2 in C min. (Resurrection).

●→ ✪ (M) (***) BBC Legends (mono) BBCL 4163-2. Woodland, Baker, BBC Ch. & Choral Soc., LSO, Stokowski.

(M) (***) Testament (Mono) SBT2 1320 (2). Stader, J. Baker, St Hedwig's Cathedral Ch., BPO, Barbirolli.

(B) ** Sony SB2K 89784 (2). Marton, Norman, V. State Op. Konzertvereinigung, VPO, Maazel.

For the first ever Prom performance of the *Resurrection Symphony*, William Glock, as BBC Controller of Music, made a shrewd choice in Leopold Stokowski (in 1963 then aged 81), still only an occasional visitor to his native country. It was a triumph, for here was a larger-than-life reading of an apocalyptic work. The response of the audience at the end was so prolonged and so enthusiastic that, against the strict Prom rule of the time, Stokowski gave an encore, repeating the final visionary choral sequence. Even critics who generally dismissed Stokowski as a publicity-seeker were bowled over, recognizing that here was music-making of exceptional power and intensity.

Now at last on disc in this BBC Legends recording of the broadcast, we have the legend vividly confirmed, for though the sound is in mono the immediacy and sense of presence, as well as the atmosphere of the hall, are vividly caught: full, bright and clear, giving the illusion of stereo. As issued on Testament, Barbirolli's rich and powerful reading of this same work with the Berlin Philharmonic is very compelling, yet the impact of the Stokowski performance is even greater, with Janet Baker again the dedicated mezzo soloist, this time joined by the fresh-toned Rae Woodland. Stokowski is more urgent than Barbirolli, lighter in the second-movement *Andante*, more sinister in the Scherzo, leading to a shattering rendering of the *Judgement Day* finale, with the BBC Chorus, Choral Society and attendant choirs as intense in their dedicatedly hushed singing as in the extrovert power of the climaxes. It makes an overwhelming experience, marred only slightly by inevitable audience noises.

Barbirolli's long-buried radio recording from Berlin will be a revelation even to the many admirers of this great Mahlerian. In 1965, a year after he had conducted a historic studio recording of Mahler's *Ninth Symphony*, he returned to the Berlin Philharmonic for this concert performance of the *Resurrection Symphony*, and the result is electrifying from beginning to end. Helped by full, vividly immediate sound, this is an impassioned, freely volatile performance, massively powerful in the outer movements while setting in contrast the 'Wunderhorn' playfulness of the third movement against the darkness of the *Urlicht* slow movement, sung by Dame Janet Baker with heartfelt intensity. The vision of Judgement Day in the long choral finale is then cataclysmic, so shattering that one readily forgives the out-of-time chimes at the very end. Just too long for a single CD, this issue is offered on two discs for the price of one.

With full recording, clear and atmospheric, and no lack of presence, Maazel's mid-1980s Vienna version brings impressively weighty accounts of the vocal passages in the last part of the symphony, the vision of Judgement Day. But even there Maazel's preference for a very steady pulse, varied hardly at all by rubato and tenuto, married to exceptionally slow speeds, undermines the keen intensity of the performance. Rhythmically, the first movement becomes leaden and, paradoxically with this orchestra, the Viennese element in Mahler is minimized.

(i) Symphony No. 3. Kindertotenlieder.

(B) ** Sony SB2K 89893 (2). Baltsa, VPO, Maazel; (i) with V. Boys' Ch.; V. State Op. Ch.

As in his other Mahler recordings with the Vienna Philharmonic, Maazel draws beautiful, refined playing from the orchestra; however, at a time when a spacious approach to this symphony has become the norm, he outdoes others in his insistence on slow speeds until the very measured gait for the finale comes to sound self-conscious, lacking a natural forward pulse. His soloist, Agnes Baltsa, adds to the appeal of this bargain reissue by the heartfelt simplicity of her approach to the *Kindertotenlieder*, where Maazel's accompaniment is again sympathetic and warmly supportive. However, for the *Symphony* Rattle remains first choice (EMI 5 56657-2).

Symphony No. 4 in G.

(M) *** RCA (ADD) 82876 59413-2. Blegen, Chicago SO, Levine.

(B) ** CfP (ADD) 574 8822 [574882]. M. Price, LPO, Horenstein.

** DG (IMS) 463 257-2. Banse, Cleveland O, Boulez.

James Levine draws a superlative performance from the Chicago orchestra, one which bears comparison with the finest versions, bringing out not merely the charm but also the deeper emotions. The subtlety of his control of tempo, so vital in Mahler, is superbly demonstrated and, though he may not quite match the nobility of Szell's famous analogue Sony version in the great slow movement, he has the advantage of a more modern (1975) recording. Judith Blegen makes a fresh, attractive soloist, and this is a thoroughly worthwhile addition to RCA's mid-priced 'Classic Library' series, even if it does not replace Szell (Sony SBK 46535).

Horenstein's many admirers will probably be tempted by the CfP reissue of his 1970 recording with the LPO and Margaret Price. Yet his characteristic simplicity of approach here seems too deliberate (the rhythms of the second movement, for instance, are curiously precise) and even the great slow movement sounds didactic, though it is not without atmosphere. The solo singing in the finale is beautiful but cool, in line with the rest of the interpretation. The recording, made in Barking Town Hall (produced by John Boydon), is forwardly balanced, so the CD transfer reveals excellent detail and certainly the sound is vivid, full and rich.

Nothing could be further removed from the warmth of Fritz Reiner (see below) than Pierre Boulez's account of the *Fourth Symphony* with the Cleveland Orchestra and Juliane Banse as soloist in the finale. It is a generally brisk, rather understated performance that takes a cool, analytical view of Mahler. The result lacks spontaneity except in the slow movement, where Boulez's simple dedication conveys a depth of feeling rather missing in the rest.

(i; ii) Symphony No. 4; (iii) Kindertotenlieder; (i; iv) Das Lied von der Erde.

(B) **(*) RCA (stereo/mono) 74321 845992-2. (i) Chicago SO, Reiner; (ii) with Della Casa; (iii) Anderson, San Francisco SO, Monteux; (iv) Forrester, Lewis.

Reiner's version of the *Fourth Symphony* dates from 1958, though it is exceptionally vivid and bright, its detailed sound naturally glowing from within Chicago's Orchestra Hall, even if in the present transfer it lacks the fullest amplitude. The performance is wayward, but lovingly so, and everything Reiner does sounds spontaneous. There is a mercurial quality in the first movement and plenty of drama, too; the second movement is engagingly pointed but with a balancing warmth, and the Viennese influence is strong. The slow movement has striking intensity, with its rapt closing pages leading on gently to the finale, where Lisa Della Casa, in ravishing voice, matches Reiner's mood.

Reiner's approach to *Das Lied von der Erde* is cooler, but he follows the letter of the score exactly. For instance, at the climactic point of the closing *Abschied*, Reiner and Maureen Forrester create considerable tension with their gentle tenderness, and if the whispered murmurs of 'Ewig' at the close have not the heart-searching intensity that others have found, their deliberate understatement may be nearer to the meaning of the poem. Forrester is on top form throughout, and if Richard Lewis is not quite her match, he is imaginative and musicianly. The recording has the same qualities as the symphony. *Kindertotenlieder* dates from 1950, and while the mono recording is exceptionally clear and vivid, its up-front perspective is rather unyielding, with some of the woodwinds glaringly forward – the oboist in *Wenn dein Mütterlei*, for instance, sounds as if he is performing a concerto. The performance, with Marian Anderson's rich contralto instantly conveying the emotional intensity of the poems, is one of much character. Monteux is sensitive, too, though once again the bright recording robs the reading of some of its atmospheric beauty. No texts are provided for this release.

(i; ii) Symphony No. 4; (iii) Das Lied von der Erde; (i; iv) Rückert Lieder.

(B) **(*) DG (ADD/DDD) 469 304-2 (2). (i) BPO, Karajan; (ii) Mathis; (iii) Fassbaender, Araiza, BPO, Giulini; (iv) Ludwig.

With playing of incomparable refinement – no feeling of rusticity here – Karajan directs a performance of compelling poise and purity, not least in the slow movement, with its pulse very steady indeed, most remarkably at the very end. Karajan's view of the finale is gentle, wistful, almost ruminative, with the final stanzas very slow and legato, beautifully so when Edith Mathis's poised singing of the solo is finely matched. Not that this quest for refinement means in any way that joy has been lost in this performance, and the 1979 recording is excellent. Karajan is no less sensitive in his 1975 recording of the *Rückert Lieder*, and his accompaniment is perfectly matched with Christa Ludwig's beautiful singing in these fine, positive performances.

Giulini's 1984 performance of *Das Lied von der*

Erde is a characteristically restrained and refined reading. With Francisco Araiza a heady-toned tenor rather than a powerful one, the line '*Dunkel ist das Leben*' in the first song becomes unusually tender and gentle, with rapture and wistfulness the keynote emotions. In the second song Brigitte Fassbaender gives lightness and poignancy rather than dark tragedy to the words '*Mein Herz ist müde*'; and even the final *Abschied* is rapt rather than tragic, following the text of the poem. Not that Giulini fails to convey the breadth and intensity of Mahler's magnificent concept, and the playing of the Berlin Philharmonic could hardly be more beautiful. The only snag to this Panorama release is the absence of texts, but it is an inexpensive way to acquire some wonderful Mahler performances.

Symphonies Nos. (i) 4 in G; 5 in C sharp min.
(B) ** Ph. Duo 475 445-2 (2). BPO, Haitink; (i) with McNair.

Haitink's later (1992) Berlin Philharmonic recording of the *Fourth Symphony* is a warm, highly polished reading that can hardly be faulted, except that it rather misses the innocent freshness lying behind this of all Mahler's symphonies. In the slow movement this seems a poised rather than a rapt performance: very beautiful, but not as moving as it can be. The child-heaven finale too is smoother than usual, with Sylvia McNair the light and boyish soloist. The *Fifth* is also less than ideal: imposing, very expansive, especially the *Adagietto*, which is very slow, though offset by the bucolic flavour of the Scherzo, and the finale well controlled but somehow heavy-handed. Marvellous playing throughout, of course, and fine recording, but this Duo is not a top recommendation.

(i) Symphonies Nos. 4; (ii) 5 in C sharp min.
(B) ** Double Decca 458 383-2 (2). (i) Stahlman, Concg. O; (ii) Chicago SO; Solti.

Solti's earlier Concertgebouw performance of the *Fourth Symphony* is disappointing. It is extremely well balanced as a recording, but the conductor is not altogether happy in the first movement and, besides a wilfulness of style, there are dull patches which he is unable to sustain with any richness of emotional expression. He does the finale best, and here Sylvia Stahlman sings charmingly. The opening *Funeral March* sets the tone of his reading of the *Fifth*. At a tempo faster than usual, it is wistful rather than deeply tragic, even though the dynamic contrasts are superbly pointed, and the string-tone could hardly be more resonant. In the pivotal *Adagietto* too, Solti secures intensely beautiful playing, but the result lacks the 'inner' quality one finds so abundantly in Barbirolli's interpretation. Full-bodied if slightly over-reverberant recording.

Symphonies Nos. (i; ii; iii) 4 in G; (i; ii) 5 in C sharp min.; (iii; iv) Lieder und Gesäng aus der Jugendzeit.
(M) (**) Sony mono 515301-2. (i) NYPO; (ii) Walter; (iii) Halban; (iv) Walter (piano).

Recorded in New York in 1945, Bruno Walter's performance was – astonishingly – the first ever complete recording of Mahler's most popular symphony to be issued commercially. Interpretatively, the *Fourth* still has much to show any rival, with delicately pointed rhythms and easily flexible speeds that consistently sound idiomatic. He brings out the pure joy behind the inspiration, culminating in the child-heaven finale, performed with delicious jauntiness. The aptly boyish-sounding soloist, Desi Halban, is not well focused in the recording, but her voice is caught with more presence in the original fill-up, eight of Mahler's 'Youth' songs, *Aus der Jugendzeit*, with Walter accompanying on the piano. Recorded in a dry acoustic, Halban (daughter of the celebrated soprano, Selma Kurz) is made to sound a little edgy under pressure, but the latest transfer catches her voice freshly enough. Walter's playing, however, is often rhythmically lumpy, not nearly as persuasive as his conducting. The closely balanced recording allows little dynamic range, with *pianissimos* eliminated and the high strings thin and peaky in the symphony. But the woodwind have lustre, and for its age it has reasonable body and clarity.

Walter followed up his recording of the *Fourth* with this account of the *Fifth*, another persuasive reading, marked by fine rhythmic pointing and natural expressiveness. It is transferred (evidently from the original 78s, not from tape) with a good body of sound, but again with a limited dynamic range. Even so, the celebrated *Adagietto* – taken much faster than has become customary – has an easy warmth, which makes one recognize it as idiomatic, naturally and unselfconsciously flexible in a song-like way. Mahler, one imagines, would have wanted it like this and might well have objected to the extra weight and depth which latter-day slow readings bring. The ensemble is not always perfect – as at the end of the finale – and the recording gives even more of an unwanted edge to the high violins; but this remains a classic reading that is welcome back in the catalogue.

Symphony No. 5 in C sharp min.
(B) *** CfP 585 6222. RLPO, Mackerras.
(B) ** Sony SBK 89289. VPO, Maazel.

With brilliant, refined playing from the Liverpool orchestra in warm, well-detailed sound, the Mackerras 1990 version is a match for almost any in the catalogue, and easily leads the lower-priced CDs. Mackerras in his well-paced reading sees the work as a whole, building each movement with total concentration. There is a thrilling culmination on the great brass chorale at the end, with polish allied to purposefulness. Barbirolli in his classic reading may find more of a tear-laden quality in the great *Adagietto*, but Mackerras, with fewer controversial points of intepretation and superb sound from producer Andrew Keener and balance engineer, Mike Clements is very recommendable indeed.

Maazel draws superb playing from the VPO. His is a direct, unexaggerated approach, refreshing and clear, but, particularly in the slow movement, he misses the depth and emotional intensity that are essential elements in Mahler. A good recording, and it is inexpensive, but that's not enough in this fiercely competitive area.

(i) *Symphony No. 5;* (ii; iii) *Lieder eines fahrenden Gesellen;* (ii; iv) *Des Knaben Wunderhorn.*

(BB) ** Virgin 2x1 5 61507-2 (2). (i) Finnish RSO, Saraste; (ii) Murray; (iii) RPO, Litton; (iv) Allen, LPO, Mackerras.

Saraste and the Finnish Radio Orchestra offer a refined and well-paced reading of the *Fifth* which gives a relatively lightweight view of the symphony. Rhythms are beautifully sprung, and the *Adagietto* is the more tenderly moving for being a degree reticent and understated. The recording is refined to match, warm and naturally balanced. On the second disc Ann Murray gives a warmly responsive account of *Lieder eines fahrenden Gesellen,* and is particularly touching in the two outer songs. She is joined by Thomas Allen in *Des Knaben Wunderhorn,* directed with imagination and character by Mackerras. Two of the highlights are Allen's noble *Rheinlegendchen,* and Murray's ravishing performance of the closing song, *Wo die schönen Trompeten blasen,* here a solo rather than a duo. The recording is warmly resonant and spacious.

Symphony No. 5; (i) *Das Lied von der Erde.*

(B) ** EMI double forte (ADD/DDD) 5 74849-2 (2). LPO, Tennstedt, (i) with Baltsa, König.

Tennstedt takes a ripe and measured view of Mahler's *Fifth* (recorded in 1978), and though his account of the lovely *Adagietto* lacks the fullest tenderness (starting with an intrusive balance for the harp), this is an outstanding interpretation, thoughtful on the one hand, impassioned and expressive on the other. The recording is warm and full. The coupling of *Das Lied von der Erde* is less successful. Though Tennstedt's interpretative insight is never in doubt, the tension behind the performance is relatively low, not helped by the recorded sound, which is lacking in bass and with a relatively narrow dynamic range. The moments of hushed intensity, of which there are many, notably in the long final *Abschied,* fail to create the necessary heart-stilling effect. In that the choice of Agnes Baltsa as mezzo soloist is in good measure to blame. Not only is her tone often made impure with pronounced vibrato, words are so heavily inflected that the oriental detachment implied in the poems is completely missing. For all the expressive weight of the mezzo songs, the singing should be poised if the full emotion is to be conveyed. Klaus König is a clear-toned Heldentenor, strained at times at the top but always well focused, though he too misses the Mahlerian magic. No texts are provided.

Symphony No. 6 in A min.

(***) Testament mono SBT 1342. BPO, Barbirolli.

Testament here follows up its Barbirolli version of Mahler's *Second* with his 1966 account of the enigmatic *Sixth Symphony* in another radio recording, again with the Berlin Philharmonic in superb form. It is a reading markedly faster than Barbirolli's studio recording of the following year, and it builds to a full-blooded account of the long finale, bringing out its fantasy as well as its power. The mono sound cannot compare with that of the studio version (EMI 5 69349-2), but the impact of the whole is comparably great.

Symphony No. 8 (Symphony of 1000).

🔑 ✪ (M) *** DG 476 2198. Studer, Blasi, Jo, Lewis, Meier, Nagai, Allen, Sotin, Southend Boys' Ch., Philh. Ch. & O, Sinopoli.

** RCA 09026 68348-2(2). Marc, Sweet, Norberg-Schulz, Kasarova, Liang, Heppner, Leiferkus, Pape, Bayerischen Rundfunks Ch., Berlin Rundfunkchor, Stuttgart Südfunk Ch., Tölz Boys' Ch., Bav. RSO, C. Davis.

(**) Orfeo mono C 519 992 B. Coertse, Zadek, West, Malaniuk, Zampieri, Prey, Edelmann, Konzertvereinigung, Singverein, Wiener Sängerknaben, VPO, Mitropoulos.

Giuseppe Sinopoli crowns his Mahler cycle with the Philharmonia in a ripely passionate account of this most extravagant of the series, recorded with a richness and body that outshine any digital rival. In vividness of atmosphere it is matched only by Solti's magnificent analogue version, recorded in Vienna (see our main *Guide*). Sinopoli, highly analytical in his methods and flexible in his approach to speed, here conveys a warmth of expression that brings joyful exuberance to the great outburst of the opening *Veni creator spiritus.* It builds into one of the most thrilling accounts ever, helped by a superb team of soloists and incandescent choral singing, recorded with fine weight and body. In the long second movement and its setting of the closing scene of *Faust,* Sinopoli's approach is almost operatic in its dramatic flair, magnetically leading from one section to another, with each of the soloists characterizing strongly. As in the first movement, the chorus sings with fine control and incandescent tone, from the hypnotic first entry through to a thrilling final crescendo on '*Alles vergangliche*'. It is now available at mid-price, being part of Universal's 'Penguin ✪ Collection'.

Sir Colin Davis has the benefit of the wonderful Bavarian orchestra, who play with great eloquence and commitment, and excellent engineering from his RCA team. There is some very fine choral singing and the sweep and grandeur of Mahler's vision come over clearly. But the performance is flawed by some of the female singers. The soloists are too close to the microphone and are uneven, in what is otherwise a well-balanced sound-picture. Alessandra Marc's vibrato is intrusive, and neither Sharon Sweet nor Ning Liang gives much pleasure.

Dimitri Mitropoulos's acclaimed 1960 account of the *Eighth Symphony*, with a fine line-up of soloists, choirs and the Vienna Philharmonic, will doubtless be sought after by Mahlerians and Mitropoulos admirers alike. This great conductor possessed a selfless dedication to whatever work he was performing, and this certainly shines through. Artistic considerations aside, the ORF (Austrian Radio) recording lets it down. One has only to compare the sound their engineers achieved with the vivid stereo that BBC engineers produced for Horenstein in 1959 to realize how inadequate is the present engineering.

Symphony No. 9 in D min.

🔑 (M) *** DG 474 537-2. BPO, Karajan.
** DG 457 581-2. Chicago SO, Boulez.

Karajan's second digital recording of Mahler's *Ninth* was the *Gramophone's* 'Record of the Year' in 1984. The performance transcended Karajan's analogue version of only two years earlier and, with full, spacious recording, became one of the conductor's finest achievements on record. It is very welcome back to the catalogue at mid-price.

Boulez's grasp of the work's architecture is impressive and he charts this territory with unfailing clarity and intelligence, without fully revealing its spiritual landscape. He seems determined to give us the facts without the slightest trace of hysteria, and his objectivity makes for a thought-provoking reading. He draws from the Chicago orchestra the most powerful playing – strong, resonant and seamless – with DG's immediate recording adding to the impact.

***Symphony No. 10 in F sharp (Unfinished)* (revised performing edition by Deryck Cooke).**

(B) **(*) CfP 585 9012. Bournemouth SO, Rattle.

With a digital recording of outstanding quality, Simon Rattle's vivid and compelling reading of the Cooke performing edition did much to convince that a remarkable revelation of Mahler's intentions was achieved in this painstaking reconstruction. While the Bournemouth orchestra plays with dedication (marred only by the occasional lack of fullness in the strings) and this recording makes for an excellent and genuine bargain, Rattle's newer, full-priced version with the Berlin Philharmonic Orchestra (EMI 5 56972-2) is finer in every respect.

VOCAL MUSIC

Kindertotenlieder; 3 Rückert Lieder: (Ich atmet' einen linden Duft; Ich bin der Welt abhanden gekommen; Um Mitternacht).

🔑 ❁ (BB) (***) Regis mono RRC 1153. Ferrier, VPO, Walter – BRAHMS: *Vier ernste Gesang* etc. (***)

Kathleen Ferrier's radiant *Kindertotenlieder* (from 1949) are wonderfully moving, and the three *Rückert Lieder* from 1952, heartfelt and monumental, are magically intense, with Bruno Walter and the Vienna Philharmonic Orchestra adding a special affectionate glow to the music-making. Indeed, the orchestra sounds far better here than on the original Decca LPs. These two artists worked wonderfully well together and this Regis coupling, transferred warmly and smoothly, is a very real bargain.

Des Knaben Wunderhorn: Das irdische Leben; Nicht wiedersehen!; Rheinlegendchen; Urlicht. 4 Rückert Lieder.

(B) *** EMI Debut 5 85559-2. Coote, Drake – HAYDN: *Arianna a Naxos*; SCHUMANN: *Frauenliebe und leben.* ***

This is one of the finest issues in EMI's excellent Debut series, with the mezzo Alice Coote boldly choosing challenging repertory that will be widely associated with Janet Baker. The voice may not have the velvety warmth of the latter, but the range of tone and dynamic, down to breathtaking pianissimos, could not be more distinctive. Here, in four of the five *Rückert Lieder*, her performances are so magnetic that for once one hardly misses the orchestra, with Julius Drake the most sympathetic accompanist. A pity that, as in other EMI issues of Lieder in this series, no texts or translations are given.

Lieder eines fahrenden Gesellen; Lieder und Gesänge (aus der Jugendzeit); Im Lenz; Winterlied (**).

🔑 ❁ (BB) *** Hyp. Helios CDH 55160. J. Baker, Parsons.

Janet Baker presents a superb collection of Mahler's early songs with piano, including two written in 1880 and never recorded before, *Im Lenz* and *Winterlied*; also the piano version of the *Wayfaring Lad* songs in a text prepared by Colin Matthews from Mahler's final thoughts, as contained in the orchestral version. The performances are radiant and deeply understanding from both singer and pianist, well caught in atmospheric recording. A heart-warming reissue.

***Des Knaben Wunderhorn*: excerpts and other Lieder, including *Lieder und Gesäng aus der Jugendzeit: Ablösung in Sommer; Aus! Aus!; Des Antonius von Padua; Fischpredigt; Frülingsmorgen; Lied des Verfolgten' im Turm; Lob des hohen Versandes; Revelge; Rheinlegendchen; Starke Einbildungskraft; Der Tambourg'sell; Zu Strassburg auf der Schanz; Wo die schönen Trompeten blasen; Das himmlische Leben; Das irdische Leben; Urlicht* (with Interviews).**

(*) TDK **DVD DV-TTTH-EUR. Hampson, Rieger.

This admirably sung recital, filmed live with six cameras in the elegant surroundings of the Théâtre Musical de Paris Châtelet, demonstrates once again the difficulty of presenting this kind of programme on DVD. Let it first be said that Thomas Hampson sings with great intensity, a natural feeling for the words and music, and he characterizes strongly. His performances of *Der Tambourg'sell* (darkly histrionic), *Wo die schönen Trompeten blasen* (touchingly tender) and *Das himmlische Leben* – which we know from the *Fourth Symphony* – (full of innocent charm) are instances of his identification with Mahler, which is shared by his superb accompanist Wolfram Rieger whose total absorption in the music is a pleasure to watch. But while the perspectives change, the principal camera dwells too often on the singer's face in close-up, and his highly dramatized facial expressions (obviously sincere, but often held self-consciously at the end of a song) become difficult to watch – one wishes one was at a greater distance, and sometimes needs to shut one's eyes.

The songs are imaginatively divided into three groups, 'Fables and Parables of Nature and Man', 'Humoresques and Ballads – Scenes of Separation and War' and 'Ballads and Allegories – Transcendence of Life'. Each group is introduced and analysed by the singer; moreover, he interrupts each section at least twice to make further intellectualized comments, and he is big on the 'transcendence of life'. Whether one would want to hear his remarks, however informed and thoughtful, more than once is open to doubt. Of course, they are separately cued and can be programmed out, but it would have been far better to have these dissertations at the beginning and end of the recital. One receives a far more intuitive feeling about the music by watching the pianist, who is extraordinarily expressive, especially when he is playing a prelude or a postlude to a song. The recording is technically and visually of high quality.

(i) Des Knaben Wunderhorn (song-cycle); (ii) Lieder eines fahrenden Gesellen; 11 Lieder und Gesäng aus der Jugendzeit; 4 Rückert Lieder.

(M) **(*) Sony (ADD) 515303-2 (2). (i) Ludwig, Berry; (ii) Fischer-Dieskau; Bernstein (piano).

Where the *Wunderhorn* songs sung by Christa Ludwig and Walter Berry keep constantly in touch with the folk inspiration behind them, the other groups with Fischer-Dieskau bring an even more sophisticated partnership beween pianist and singer. It is true that even in the *Wunderhorn* songs Bernstein allows himself the most extreme rubato and tenuto on occasion. With the Fischer-Dieskau performances, both singer and pianist adopt a far more extreme expressive style all through, responding to each other in an almost impressionistic way, notably in the *Four Rückert Lieder*, which inspire the singer to velvety legato. The eleven 'Youth' songs here sound quite different from the Halban–Walter recording, coupled with the *Fourth* and *Fifth Symphonies*, with *Scheiden und Meiden* given with exhilarating bounce, and with a song such as *Nicht wiedersehen* treated expansively. Taken almost twice as slowly as on the Walter version, it evokes a totally different, magical world. These 1968 recordings have been out of the

catalogue for some time and are very welcome back, completing a collection which is a valuable supplement to Bernsein's Mahler recordings as a conductor.

Das Lied von der Erde.

(M) ** Orfeo C 494 001B. Jänicke, Elsner, Stuttgart RSO, Fischer-Dieskau.

** Sony SK 60646. Domingo, Skovhus, LAPO, Salonen.

(M) (*) Sony (ADD) SMK 89567. Ludwig, Kollo, Israel PO, Bernstein.

(i; ii) Das Lied von der Erde; (i) Rückert Lieder: Ich bin der Welt abhanden gekommen. Symphony No. 5 in C sharp min.: Adagietto.

(BB) (**) Naxos mono 8.110850. VPO, Walter, with (i) Thorborg; (ii) Kullman.

The account on Orfeo is of special interest in that Dietrich Fischer-Dieskau conducts rather than sings. The soloists are two German singers of the younger generation – Yvi Jänicke and one of Fischer-Dieskau's pupils, Christian Elsner – who are accompanied by the Stuttgart Radio Orchestra. It goes without saying that Fischer-Dieskau knows what this music is all about, but he is a little sluggish in *Der Einsame im Herbst*, though not as slow as the classic Bernstein version in which he sang. A good performance, but not the outstanding experience one might have expected. Decent sound.

Salonen chooses speeds faster than usual, but gives a warmly sympathetic and sensitive reading which brings out the full emotion of the writing. There are good precedents on record for an all-male *Das Lied*. Plácido Domingo in Heldentenor mode produces a gloriously firm and full tone, but the subtler shadings required in Lieder-singing, even with orchestra, rather elude him. Bo Skovhus, following Mahler's option of using a baritone in place of the mezzo, has rarely sounded so clear and true on disc, subtly shading his tone, singing with perfect diction. The recording places the soloists well forward, with the orchestra in soft focus behind so that the violins, though refined, lack body.

Bruno Walter's 1936 recording of Mahler's *Das Lied von der Erde* was made live, with fine soloists, even if they do not quite match Kathleen Ferrier and Julius Patzak on Walter's later Decca recording. Warmly idiomatic, it atmospherically captures the feeling of a great occasion in this new transfer. The Naxos disc of Bruno Walter's pre-war Mahler recordings from Vienna duplicates the Dutton issue of the same live recordings, but the transfers give less body to the orchestral sound. It also lacks some of the clarity and immediacy of the Dutton issue and has higher background hiss. In addition, the Dutton offers an extra item, one of the other *Rückert Lieder*, *Ich atmet' einen Linden duft*, recorded by Charles Kullman in London with Sargent conducting, using an English translation.

Bernstein, Ludwig and Kollo have all appeared earlier in other versions of *Das Lied von der Erde*, but the conjunction of the three in this 1972 Israeli performance did not produce extra illumination – rather the reverse. The recording, idiosyncratically balanced and put together from a series of live performances, didn't rival the best performances then, and it doesn't now.

Levine, in what is claimed to be a live recording, conducts a heavy-handed account of *Das Lied*, weighty and often contrived, lacking flow. Neither soloist is helped by the very close balance. Jessye Norman sounds self-conscious in her detailing, missing the mystery of the final song, and Siegfried Jerusalem is less subtle than he can be (DG 439 948-2).

MANZONI, Giacomo (born 1932)

Masse: Omaggio a Edgard Varèse

(M) *** DG 471 362-2. Pollini, BPO, Sinopoli – NONO: *Como una ola de fuerza y luz*; ... *soffrte onde serene*.

Manzoni might be broadly classified as a follower of Luigi Nono, a teacher and critic as well as a composer, so the present recoupling in the 'Pollini Edition' is very appropriate. *Masse* has nothing to do with church liturgy, but refers to measures or quantities, and in its tribute to Varèse follows up a scientifically based mode of thought which proves surprisingly dramatic and colourful. Only the piano part has much in the way of melodic interest, and Pollini exploits it for all he is worth, not least in the elaborate cadenza-like passages. Sinopoli too, in what (in 1982) was his first major recording, already revealed his feeling for texture and dynamic which has since made his conducting so memorable.

MARKEVITCH, Igor (1912–83)

(i) *Piano Concerto. Icare*; (ii) *Cantate*.

**(*) Marco Polo 8.225076. Arnhem PO, Lyndon-Gee, with (i) Van den Hoek; (ii) Oostenrijk, Nederlands Concertkoor, Amsterdam (men only).

Before becoming a conductor in the years immediately after the Second World War Markevitch was known first and foremost as a composer who occasionally appeared as a conductor, primarily of his own music. As a youth he was Diaghilev's last protégé, and the great impresario brought the seventeen-year-old to London in 1929 to give the first performance of his *Piano Concerto*. This is derivative, with lots of Stravinsky and the motoric rhythms of Prokofiev in the outer movements; the slow movement is by far the most memorable. The soloist, Martijn van den Hoek, is a magnificent artist whose neglect by the gramophone companies has been puzzling. The *Cantate* for solo soprano, male chorus and orchestra was composed after Markevitch received news of Diaghilev's death. He asked Cocteau to com-

pose the ... Pigalle in ... a work of ... opening has ... grosso about ... tive piece. *Icare* ... of 1932 written w... written for Serge L... mounted the ballet. ... of imagination, thoug... awkwardness rhythmica... ... e any of the earlier discs in th... ... get it. The music is of great interest an... ...gh the orchestral playing lacks the last degree ... polish, the recording is eminently acceptable.

234 MARSH

Rébus; Hymnes.

*** Marco Polo 8.223724. Arnhem PO, Lyndon-Gee.

Rébus was written in 1931 for Massine, though he never mounted or danced it. No less an authority than Henri Prunières hailed it as a work of genius: it is certainly an interesting piece of immense talent. *Hymnes* was completed in 1933, though the final section, *Hymne à la mort*, was not added until 1936. There is much Stravinsky in the very imaginative *Prélude* and *Pas d'acier* in the first section, *Hymne au travail*, and a strong sense of atmosphere in *Hymne au printemps*. This CD gave us much pleasure and is well worth investigating; good recorded sound too.

(i) *The Flight of Icarus*; (ii) *Galop*; (iii) *Noces*; (iv) *Serenade*.

*** Largo 5127. (i) Lyndon-Gee, Lang, Gagelmann, Haeger; (ii) Markevitch Ens., Köln; (i; iii; iv) Lessing; (iv) Meyer, Jensen.

Noces, for piano, was composed in 1925 when Markevitch was only thirteen, and it was on the strength of this and a *Sinfonietta* that Diaghilev was prompted to take him up. The young composer-conductor was only twenty when he composed *L'Envoi d'Icare*, which Lifar commissioned but subsequently never produced. It is heard here not in its orchestral form but in the transcription for two pianos and percussion. *Noces*, neatly played by Kolja Lessing, is close to the world of Poulenc and Satie, and it is obvious that Markevitch knew his Ravel. The *Serenade* is akin to the Milhaud of the *Petites symphonies*, and there is tremendous energy and a lot of Stravinsky in *L'Envoi d'Icare*. This disc gives an insight into his talent and musicianship which will be of interest to all those who care about the Diaghilev years and Paris between the wars.

Vuca Lorenzo il Magnifico; Psaumes.

*** Marco Polo 8.223882. Shelton, Arnhem PO, Lyndon-Gee.

Markevitch's vocal symphony, *Lorenzo il Magnifico*, sets poems by Lorenzo de' Medici. It is said to be his masterpiece, and it is not only highly imaginative but

pace and feeling of
... om 1933 when Markevitch
... enjoyed a *succès de scandale* at
... werful stuff, rather Milhaudesque at
... the same time evidence of a distinctive
... iginal mind. Lucy Shelton sings the demand-
... solo part well in both scores, and the playing and
recording are eminently serviceable. Markevitch is a
composer of substance and some distinction.

MARSH, John (1752–1828)

*Symphonies Nos. 1 in B flat (ed. Robins); 3 in D; 4 in
F; 6 in D; A Conversation Symphony for 2
Orchestras (all ed. Graham-Jones).*
** Olympia OCD 400. Chichester Concert,
Graham-Jones.

John Marsh was innovative: because of the continuing influence of Handel the symphony format was
not fashionable in England at that time. For the most
part they each consist of three short movements and,
while the tunes sometimes have a whiff of Handel,
there is a strong element of the English village green.
The *Conversation Symphony* does not divide into two
separate ensembles but makes contrasts between
higher and lower instrumental groupings. Five of his
works are presented here with enthusiasm by an
aptly sized authentic Baroque group; they play well
and are quite effectively recorded.

MARSHALL-HALL, G. W. L.
(1862–1915)

Symphony in E flat; Symphony in C: Adagio.
**(*) Move MD 3081. Queensland Theatre O,
Bebbington.

Born in London, Marshall-Hall studied under Parry
and Stanford and his first song-cycle received an
enthusiastic review from George Bernard Shaw. In
1892 he settled in Australia, where he became the first
Professor of Music at Melbourne University. His *E
flat Symphony* was premièred by Sir Henry Wood in
London and by Nikisch in Berlin, before lapsing into
obscurity. While highly eclectic and often Brahmsian,
it still remains very much his own, and has plenty of
attractively flowing ideas. The first movement surges
along, the central *Largamente* is appealingly lyrical
and expertly scored, and the rondo finale ends confidently. The *Adagio sostenuto* from the earlier *C minor
Symphony* is gently elegiac, again attractively orchestrated. Both works are well played and quite persuasively directed by Warren Bebbington, although one
feels at times that they need a stronger forward pulse.
But this well-recorded CD is still enjoyable and
appears on a bargain label in Australia. (Its publisher
can be reached on www.move.com.au.)

MARTIN, Frank (1890–1974)

*(i) 3 Chants de Noël; 3 Minnelieder; (ii) 6
Monologues from 'Jederman' (Everyman); (iii)
Poèmes de la mort.*
*(*) Cantate C 58013. (i) Thomas-Martin, Kroupa; (ii)
Arendts, Kroupa; (iii) Arendts, Schildt & various
artists.

The *Six Everyman Monologues* are among Frank
Martin's finest works, and indeed among the greatest
song-cycles of the twentieth century. They are heard
here in their monochrome form (voice and piano)
rather than in the composer's wonderful orchestration, and derive from a 1998 Sender Freies Berlin
broadcast. The performance, too, is a bit monochrome and not to be preferred to José van Dam
(Virgin 5 61850-2) or David Wilson-Johnson (Chandos 9411), who are much more imaginative (alongside Fischer-Dieskau, whose DG disc is deleted). The
post-war *Trois chants de Noël* for soprano, flute and
piano have charm, though the *Drei Minnelieder*,
written in the wake of the *Mystère de la Nativité*, have
more depth. The *Poèmes de la mort* are composed for
three male voices and the unusual combination of
three electric guitars. The sonority is highly distinctive in Martin's hands and the songs are of both
originality and quality. Decent broadcast performances but, at 48 minutes, very short measure.

MARTINŮ, Bohuslav (1890–1959)

*The Amazing Flight (Podivuhodný Let); On tourne!
(Natáči se!); La Rêvue de cuisine (Kuchynska
Revue).*
☯ *** Sup. SU 3749-2. Czech PO, Hogwood.

Christopher Hogwood made an earlier record of *La
Rêvue de cuisine* with the Saint Paul Chamber
Orchestra on an all-Martinů record for Decca which
lasted only a very short time in the catalogue. The
piece stands up rather well against *La Création du
monde* or any other of Milhaud's jazz-inspired
pieces, and Martinů's 'Charleston' is particularly
infectious. The present CD arrived without any
documentation, save for the bare titling in Czech. In
his Grove VI article on Martinů Brian Large lists
Báječný let of 1927 as a mechanical ballet without
dancers: 'báječný' and 'podivuhodný' are synonyms
(like 'incredible' and 'amazing'). The only other ballet
from 1927 that he lists is *On tourne!*, whose Czech
name is *Natáči se! La Rêvue* is well represented on
CD, but the present performance is second to none,
if not a first choice. The Czech Philharmonic play
every note with great zest. Neither of the other 1927
ballets was performed at the time and both contain
music of real quality, imaginative invention and outstanding charm even by Martinů's standards. *Natáči
se!* is quite irresistible in its freshness and innocence,
and its seventh movement, once played, is difficult if

not impossible to get out of one's head. And what harmonic subtlety there is elsewhere in this wonderfully inventive and imaginative score. This is music which infectiously communicates its love of life and high spirits – and leaves you feeling better! Very good and well-detailed recorded sound.

Concerto grosso; Overture for Orchestra; The Parables; Rhapsody for Large Orchestra; Sinfonia concertante for 2 Orchestras.
*** Sup. SU 3743-2. Czech PO, Bělohlávek.

These recordings come from the late 1980s: the *Overture*, *Rhapsody* and *Parables* were originally issued together, while the *Concerto grosso* and *Sinfonia concertante* came with another piece, the *Tre Ricercari* (on a not so well-filled disc). This coupling is much better value. The set of *Parables* is among the composer's last works and is vintage Martinů. It is some four years later than the more celebrated *Frescoes of Piero della Francesca* but is in no way inferior to them in terms of invention and fantasy. The *Rhapsody* of 1928 was written for Koussevitzky, but the *Sinfonia concertante* and the *Concerto grosso* are both from the 1930s and are good examples of Martinů's neo-baroque style. The *Overture* is much later and comes from the period of the *Sixth Symphony* (*Symphonies fantastiques*) though it is much less imaginative and inventive. It is something of a rarity, and this is the only recording currently available. The resonant acoustic of the Dvořák Hall of the Rudolfinum, Prague, slightly muddies detail, but this will not put off admirers of the composer, for the performances by the Czech Philharmonic under Jírí Bělohlávek are exhilarating and idiomatic. The artwork (including the CD label itself) has a childlike, paintbox quality that is highly attractive.

3 Frescoes of Piero della Francesca.
(**) Orfeo mono C 521 991B. VPO, Kubelik (with TCHAIKOVSKY: Symphony No. 6 (**)).

Martinů dedicated the *Three Frescoes of Piero della Francesca*, one of his most inspired and colourful scores, to Rafael Kubelik. This performance, recorded at the 1956 Salzburg Festival, was its première (Kubelik recorded them commercially on a mono HMV LP not long afterwards but that did not survive very long in the catalogue). His reading of the first movement is fractionally more measured than we often get nowadays and gains in its breadth. The mono sound is not bad for its period but this, of course, is a score which benefits from good modern sound. The Tchaikovsky coupling is not distinctive.

Symphonies Nos. 1–6.
🎵➝ (M) *** BIS CD 1371/2. Bamberg SO, Neeme Järvi.

BIS have now put Järvi's set of the six *Symphonies* in a box, with the three CDs offered for the price of two, making a clear first choice for modern recordings of this repertoire (see our main volume).

Symphonies Nos. 2 & 4.
(BB) ** Naxos 8.553349. Nat. SO of the Ukraine, Fagen.

These are both radiant symphonies, life-enhancing and infectious in their rhythmic vitality and luminous textures. The playing of the Ukraine orchestra is lively, and the recording is well lit and full of inner detail. All the same, they are not in the same league as Järvi or, in the case of No. 4, Bělohlávek, which will give greater long-term satisfaction.

Symphony No. 5.
** CBC Records (ADD) PSCD 2021. Toronto SO, Ančerl (with BEETHOVEN: Symphony No. 6 **).

A pity that another Martinů work could not have been found for this Canadian CD, as it would make a more logical coupling than Beethoven's *Pastoral Symphony*, which is well played but in no way outstanding. Ančerl's Multisonic version of the Martinů is among the best recordings of the piece and has more breadth and sense of mystery than this Toronto account from 1971. The latter is rather fast: Ančerl takes 26 minutes 22 seconds as opposed to 30 minutes 22 seconds in 1955. There is plenty of commitment and enthusiasm from the orchestra, and the CBC sound is decent if a little top-heavy.

MASCAGNI, Pietro (1863–1945)

Le maschere (complete).
(M) * Warner Fonit 0927 43298-2 (2). Felle, Gallego, La Scola, Sabbatini, Dara, Chausson, Teatro Comunale di Bologna Ch. & O, Gelmetti.

Over ten years before Strauss brought *commedia dell'arte* characters on to the operatic stage in *Ariadne auf Naxos*, Mascagni attempted a more direct approach in a full *commedia dell'arte* presentation, complete with Prologue as introduction. *Le maschere* appeared in January 1900, the same month as Puccini's *Tosca*. Such was Mascagni's fame after *Cavalleria rusticana* that no fewer than six world premières were organized on the same night in the principal Italian opera-houses. Except in Rome, where Mascagni was himself conducting to a polite reception, the performances were all fiascos, with audiences rowdily unsympathetic, even in Milan with Toscanini conducting and Caruso singing.

This live recording, made in 1988, helps to explain why. The score is skilfully written, with light textures and tripping rhythms, as one would anticipate with such a subject, but without the luscious tunes and big emotional moments that audiences had come to expect of Mascagni. One can understand audiences growing impatient, even if the total and immediate condemnation suggests some plotting.

Under Gelmetti the Bologna performance is competent enough, with a reasonable provincial cast, but what seriously minimizes enjoyment is the balance of the voices. Most of the time they are so distanced, the characters seem to be off-stage. Recommended only to Mascagni devotees.

MASSENET, Jules (1842–1912)

(i) *Piano Concerto in E flat. Année passées, Nos. I–IV; 2 Berceuses; 6 Danses; Devant la Madonne; 7 Improvisations; 3 Marches; Musique pour bercer les petits enfants; Papillons noirs, Papillons blancs; Première suite; Toccata; Valse folle; Valse très lente; La Vierge: galiléenne.*

(BB) ** EMI Gemini (ADD) 585517-2 (2). Ciccolini, (i) with Monte Carlo Nat. Op. O, Cambreling.

Massenet's *Piano Concerto in E flat* has perhaps the manners of Saint-Saëns, but he does not posses that composer's flair in this genre. There are some nice things in it though, the Hungarian colourings of the first and last movements especially so. This performance is lively and enjoyable, a little dry in sound, but reasonably vivid. Stephen Coombs's new Hyperion account is finer, however, but that is at full price and differently coupled. The bulk of this two-CD set comprises Massenet's piano works, most of it salon music. This is lightweight repertoire, but it has a certain charm running throughout the best pieces; with some lively character dances and nostalgic sentimental ones – including the lovely *Elégie* – it makes for excellent light listening. The piano image is well focused, if the acoustic is a bit dry.

OPERA

Cendrillon (complete).

(M) ** Sony (ADD) SM2K 91178 (2). Von Stade, Gedda, Berbié, Bastin, Welting, Amb. Op. Ch., Philh. O, Rudel.

Julius Rudel directs a most winning performance of Massenet's Cinderella opera, very much a fairy story in which the magic element is vital. The opera follows Charles Perrault's famous narrative closely enough, but adds a few extra twists of its own. The Fairy Godmother is a sparkling coloratura (here Ruth Welting) and Cendrillon a soprano in a lower register. Federica Von Stade gives a characteristically strong and imaginative performance, untroubled by what for her is high tessitura. The pity is that the role of the Prince, originally written for soprano, is here taken by a tenor, Nicolai Gedda, whose voice is no longer fresh-toned. Jules Bastin sings most stylishly as Pandolfe, Cinderella's father, and the others make a well-chosen team. The recording is vivid and spacious. The only snag, a fairly big one, is the absence of either a libretto or a cued synopsis.

Esclarmonde (complete).

(B) *** Decca Trio 475 50129 (3). Sutherland, Aragall, Tourangeau, Davies, Grant, Alldis Ch., Nat PO, Bonynge.

Joan Sutherland is the obvious diva to encompass the demands of great range, great power and brilliant coloratura of the central role of *Esclarmonde*, and her performance is in its way as powerful as it is in Puccini's last opera. Aragall proves an excellent tenor, sweet of tone and intelligent, and the other parts are well taken too. Richard Bonynge draws passionate singing and playing from chorus and orchestra, and the recording has both atmosphere and spectacle to match the story, based on a medieval romance involving song-contests and necromancy. This has now been reissued on a Decca Trio, and although only a synopsis is included, it makes a fine bargain for those wanting to explore Massenet's lesser-known operas.

Manon (complete).

*** TDK **DVD** DVOPMANON (2). Fleming, Alvarez, Chaignaud, Sénéchal, Paris Nat. Op. Ch. and O, Lopez-Cobos (Dir.: Deflo; DVD Dir.: François Roussillon).

Recorded in 2001, Gilbert Deflo's production for the National Opera in Paris offers a production with no 'concept' pretensions, refreshingly direct in its presentation of the story over the five acts, using apt in-period costumes set in contrast with the simple stylized sets, both designed by William Orlandi. The undistracting simplicity of the sets, merely suggesting the broad outlines of buildings and rooms, has the big advantage of allowing swift scene-changes in this long and complex piece. The casting of the three principals is outstanding. Renée Fleming not only sings superbly, she acts with total conviction, brilliantly making the transition from the vivacious seventeen-year-old of Act I, inexperienced yet wilful, to the mature, even more wilful figure of the later acts, making one understand her dilemma over her love for Des Grieux. It is a commanding performance, well matched by the upstanding, slightly awkward Des Grieux of Marcelo Alvarez, also singing splendidly with a wide tonal range down to a fine head-voice in *Ah fuyez douce image*. Equally fine is the magnificent singing of the baritone Jean-Luc Chaignaud, a handsome, swaggering figure who sings with a virile firmness and no hint of strain, readily commanding the stage. With Jesus Lopez-Cobos drawing idiomatic playing and singing from chorus and orchestra, it makes a splendid addition to the DVD catalogue.

Le Roi de Lahore (complete).

✪ (M) *** Decca 476 1705 (2). Sutherland, Lima, Milnes, Ghiaurov, Morris, Tourangeau, L. Voices, Nat. PO, Bonynge.

It is good to have this fine set restored to the catalogue at mid-price in Universal's 'Penguin ✪ Collection'. *Le Roi de Lahore* was Massenet's first opera for the big stage of L'Opéra in Paris and marked a turning point in his career, even introducing the supernatural, with one act set in the Paradise of

Indra. The characters may be stock figures out of a mystic fairytale, but in the vigour of his treatment Massenet makes the result red-blooded in an Italianate way. This vivid performance under Bonynge includes passages added for Italy, notably a superb set-piece aria which challenges Sutherland to some of her finest singing. Sutherland may not be a natural for the role of the innocent young priestess, but she makes it a magnificent vehicle with its lyric, dramatic and coloratura demands. Luis Lima as the King is somewhat strained by the high tessitura, but his is a ringing tenor, clean of attack. Sherrill Milnes as the heroine's wicked uncle sounds even more Italiante, rolling his 'r's ferociously; but high melodrama is apt, and with digital recording of demonstration splendour and fine perspective this shameless example of operatic hokum could not be presented more persuasively on CD.

Thaïs (complete).
(M) ** EMI 5 65479-2 (2). Sills, Milnes, Gedda, Van Allan, John Alldis Ch., New Philh. O, Maazel.

Thaïs is an exotic period-piece, set in Egypt in the early Christian era. Sentimental as the plot is, it inspired Massenet to some of his characteristically mellifluous writing, with atmospheric choruses and sumptuous orchestration. Maazel's conducting is crisply dramatic (and he plays the violin solo himself most tastefully in the famous *Méditation*). The casting is good, except for the heroine. Beverly Sills has a bright, almost brittle voice, and here it sounds neither seductive nor idiomatic. She is at her best as the reformed Thaïs in the later scenes. Sherrill Milnes is a powerful but conventional Athanaël, and, though Nicolai Gedda as Nicias sings with his usual intelligence, it is not a young enough voice for the role. A good, warm recording, well transferred on to CD, and with a complete text and translation. But first choice rests with the Decca set with Renée Fleming and Thomas Hampson (466 766-2).

Werther (complete).
(B) *** Ph. 475 496-2 (2). Carreras, Von Stade, Allen, Buchanan, Lloyd, Children's Ch., ROHCG O, C. Davis.
(M) **(*) EMI (ADD) 5 62627-2 [5 62630-2] (3). Gedda, De los Angeles, Soyer, Benoit, Grigoriou, Mallabrera, Mesplé, ORTF Children's Ch., O de Paris, Prêtre.

Although the EMI recording of *Werther* (5 56820-2) with the formidable partnership of Alagna and Gheorghiu, and conducted by the always sympathetic Antonio Pappano, remains first choice for this opera, Sir Colin Davis's mid-priced alternative is also highly recommendable, with Frederica Von Stade an enchanting Charlotte, matched by Thomas Allen as her husband, Albert, and Isobel Buchanan as her sister, Sophie. The recording was outstanding enough to win the *Gramophone*'s Engineering Award for 1981; but in this reissue the break between the two discs

remains badly placed in the middle of a key scene in Act II between Werther and Charlotte. A full text and translation are still provided.

Victoria de los Angeles's golden tones, which convey pathos so beautifully, are ideally suited to Massenet's gentle melodies and, although she is recorded too closely (closer than the other soloists), she makes an appealing heroine. Gedda, too, makes an intelligent romantic hero, though Prêtre's direction could be more subtle. This set now reappears, excellently remastered, as one of EMI's 'Great Recordings of the Century', and while it has now been outclassed by EMI's newest recording with Gheorghiu and Alagna, it still has much going for it as a reminder of past glories.

MATTEIS, Nicola (c. 1640–c. 1714)

Ayres for the Violin, Book I: *Suite in C min.*; Book II: *Suite in G min.*; Book IV: *Suites in A; C; G min.; D min.*
(B) HM HCX 3957067. Arcadian Academy.

Not a great deal is known about Nicola Matteis. Born in Naples, he apparently came to England in 1670 and later had considerable success as a solo violinist/guitar player, then married a wealthy widow and 'took a great house' in Norfolk. His *Suites of Ayres for the Violin* date from the 1670s and 1680s and are either solo or trio sonatas. Each suite is in essence a set of variations, for the same musical material undergoes many melodic and rhythmic transformations with diverting results. In every case there is an opening *Preludio*; then follows a series of brief vignettes exploiting various dance movements – Giga, Minuet, Ricercata, Corrent, Sarabanda – plus slow and fast sections, grounds, fugues and *Arie amarosi*. McGegan and his Arcadian Players respond with spontaneous vitality and revel in the music's undoubted fantasy. The recording, although a bit edgy on top, is otherwise vivid.

MAW, Nicholas (born 1935)

(i) *Dance Scenes*; (ii) *Odyssey*.
(M) *** EMI 5 85145-2 (2). (i) Philh. O, Harding; (ii) CBSO, Rattle.

Spanning an hour and 40 minutes, Nicholas Maw's panoramic *Odyssey* has been counted the biggest continuous orchestral piece ever written, and its gestation came over a period of 13 years, between 1972 and 1985. As in Mahler, if not so readily, one comes to recognize musical landmarks in the six substantial movements. The slow movement alone lasts over half an hour, while the allegros bring a genuine sense of speed, thrusting and energetic. It was at Rattle's insistence that this superb recording was made at live concerts. The result is astonishingly fine, with the engineers totally disguising the problems of recording in Birmingham Town Hall.

The *Dance Scenes* of 1995 could hardly be more different. Lightweight but never trivial, it is a buoyantly spirited work, brilliantly scored and full of readily accessible melodic lines and ideas. The influence of Walton is predominant, but the four dances are full of personality and individually attractive. They obviously appealed to the Philharmonia players, whose advocacy has both polish and sparkle. The Abbey Road recording is first class.

MAXWELL DAVIES, Peter
(born 1934)

Sinfonia; Sinfonia concertante.
(BB) *** Regis RRC 1148. SCO, composer.

A welcome bargain reissue. In his *Sinfonia* of 1962 Peter Maxwell Davies took as his inspiration Monteverdi's *Vespers* of 1610, and the dedication in this music, beautifully played by the Scottish Chamber Orchestra, is plain from first to last. The *Sinfonia concertante* is a much more extrovert piece for strings plus solo wind quintet and timpani. In idiom this is hardly at all neo-classical and, more than usual, the composer evokes romantic images, as in the lovely close of the first movement. Virtuoso playing from the Scottish principals, not least the horn. Well-balanced recording too.

(i) *Antechrist;* (i; ii) *Missa super 'L'Homme armé';*
(iii) *Second Fantasia on John Taverner's 'In nomine';*
(iv) *Seven In Nomine;* (v) *Lullaby for Ilian Rainbow;* (i; vi) *From Stone to Thorn; Hymn to St Magnus;* (vi) *O magnum mysterium.*
⊕➡ (M) *** Decca (ADD) 475 6166 (2). (i) Fires of London, composer; (ii) V. Redgrave (speaker); (iii) New Philh. O, Groves; (iv) London Sin., Atherton; (v) Walker (guitar); (vi) Thomas (soprano); Cirencester Grammar School Ch. & O, composer.

Much of Maxwell Davies's creative energy has been projected towards writing works for the two overlapping groups which he formed and directed, first the Pierrot Players and later the Fires of London. The latter recorded four characteristic works in 1973 (of which three are included here, *Hymnos* being omitted for reasons of space) which they regularly performed at their concerts, starting with *Antechrist*, a sort of exuberant overture. *L'Homme armé*, a more extended but comparable work, similarly working on a medieval motif, is also most approachable, while *From Stone to Thorn*, a work much thornier in argument, directly displays the formidable talents of – among others – the soprano Mary Thomas. Two years later, the Fires of London recorded the *Hymn to St Magnus*, a powerful and uncompromising piece lasting over 36 minutes, one of the finest works inspired by the composer's flight to Orkney. Living there alone when he wrote this music, based on a twelfth-century hymn about St Magnus (martyred in

1137), he reflected the Orkney landscape and weather in his music. For all the complexity of its intellectual base, it has an immediacy of impact that is most compelling in this peformance under the composer's direction. The soprano soloist, Mary Thomas, helps to build the concentration, particularly in the hypnotic repetitions of the plea, *St Magnus, pray for us* (in Latin), which punctuate the long third movement.

The original (1975) review of *The Second Fantasia on John Taverner's 'In nomine'* noted, 'In an age of crabbed inspiration on the one hand, uncharted wildness on the other, it is remarkable that a composer making no concessions should argue strongly, satisfyingly and movingly over a span of 40 minutes, using the conventional symphony orchestra and producing something totally original and new.' The first public performance required an introductory lecture from the conductor (Pritchard) but, on repeated hearing, the logic in its 13 sections is plain enough. Some of the music was used later in *Taverner*, the opera about the composer whose *In nomine* forms the basis of this work. Groves's 1972 performance, in good sound, is not ideally incisive or polished; but anyone willing to accept a challenge will find this work very rewarding. *O magnum mysterium* was written for the Cirencester Grammar School, where the composer once taught, and his pupils sing this brilliantly imaginative cantata with skill and enthusiasm, while the school orchestra provides an exotic accompaniment. Good (1962) sound.

This excellent Maxwell Davies anthology is especially valuable for including *Seven in Nomine*, released for the first time. It is an early work, starting life as a composition exercise when the composer was at Princeton University in 1963–4, but eventually forming this composition after a commission by the Melos Ensemble, who gave the work its première. Opening with a string quartet version of John Taverner's organ *In nomine*, followed by his own *In nomine*, its seven movements are full of the composer's fascinating experiments in textures and form, often reflecting and using music from the sixteenth and seventeenth centuries. The 1979 performance under David Atherton is excellent. All in all, this is an ideal introduction to Maxwell Davies's music, and represents superb value for money.

(i; ii) *Mass;* (i) *Missa parvula. Dum complerentur; Veni Sancta Spiritus.* Organ pieces: (i) *Reliquit domum meum; Veni Creator Spiritus.*
*** Hyp. CDA 67454. Westminster Cathedral Ch., Baker; with (i) Quinney; (ii) Houssart (organ).

Maxwell Davies wrote his two strongly contrasted settings of the Mass for Westminster Cathedral Choir in 2002 and 2003, both of them among his most approachable works. Where the *Missa parvula* is a setting for boys' voices in unison with organ accompaniment, the *Mass* is for full choir and with organ accompaniment involving a second instrument in two of the sections. The lyrical directness of the *Missa parvula*, with the final *Agnus Dei* sounding almost like a carol, is immediately attractive, touching in its simplicity. Maxwell Davies, with roots in medieval music, tends to avoid making the liturgy dramatic, so that even the setting of *Et resurrexit* in the *Credo* hardly stands out from the lyrical flow. Similarly, in the *Mass* for full choir, using a much more elaborate idiom, the composer even more strikingly draws on medieval techniques, basing it on two Whitsun plainsong chants. The result is altogether darker, even violent at times, thanks to powerful organ writing, with the *Gloria* the longest and most elaborate movement, the *Sanctus* bringing a triumphant setting of *Hosanna*. Originally, Maxwell Davies intended to keep this as a *Missa brevis*, without a *Credo*, but then was persuaded to set the *Credo* after all, contrasting it with the rest with voices in forthright unison. In this setting, as in the *Missa parvula*, there is no change of pace for *Crucifixus* and *Et resurrexit*, but the simple dedication is most moving. Complementing the two settings of the Mass come two motets, *Veni Sancta Spiritus*, slow and devotional, and *Dum complerentur*, a Pentecostal piece involving triumphant 'Alleluias', and two organ pieces, the valedictory *Reliquit domum* and the penitential *Veni Creator Spiritus*. As in his previous Westminster recordings for Hyperion Martin Baker draws radiant singing from his fine choir, atmospherically recorded.

MAYERL, Billy (1902–59)

Aquarium Suite; Autumn Crocus; Bats in the Belfry; Four Aces Suite: Ace of Clubs; Ace of Spades. 3 Dances in Syncopation, Op. 73; Green Tulips; Hollyhock; Hop-o'-my-thumb; Jill All Alone; Mistletoe; Parade of the Sandwich-board Men; Sweet William; White Heather.
*** Chan. 8848. Parkin.

Eric Parkin obviously enjoys this repertoire and plays the music with much sympathy and vivacious rhythmic freedom. His programme is well chosen to suit his own approach to Mayerl's repertoire, and this Chandos record is certainly very enjoyable as he is very well treated by the recording engineers.

MEDTNER, Nikolai (1880–1951)

Forgotton Melodies, Cycles I & II, Opp. 38/39.
(B) ** Arte Nova 74321 93121-2. Ossipova.

An inexpensive introduction to Medtner is very welcome for there is no doubting the eloquence and beauty of this music. Irina Ossipova is a respected teacher in the Moscow Conservatoire and obviously a fine player. The playing is just a little short on poetry and no one who has heard such distinguished figures as Hamelin in this repertoire will find this of comparable quality.

MELARTIN, Erkki (1875–1937)

(i) *Violin Concerto, Op. 60. Sleeping Beauty (Suite), Op. 22; Suite lyrique No. 3 (Impressions de Belgique).*
** Ondine (ADD) ODE 923-2. (i) Storgårds; Tampere PO, Segerstam.

Ten years younger than Sibelius, Erkki Melartin's music shows a considerable lyrical talent and expertise in writing for the orchestra. The *Violin Concerto* (1910–13) has a lot going for it and John Storgårds takes its formidable difficulties in his stride. At one point its slow movement even brings Delius to mind. The atmospheric *Suite lyrique* is a set of six impressionistic sketches inspired by a visit the composer made to Bruges in 1914, and the incidental music to Topelius's play, *The Sleeping Beauty*, dates from 1910. Decent recording, but the Tampere orchestra is a bit too raw-toned and ill-tuned to do this music full justice. Worth hearing all the same.

MENDELSSOHN, Felix (1809–47)

Piano Concerto in A min; (i) Double Concerto for Violin & Piano.
** Teldec 0630 13152-2. Staier, Concerto Köln; (i) with Kussmaul.

As these boyhood concertos were first heard in the Sunday salons of the composer's banker father, it is logical that they should be recorded here not just on period instruments but with a small band of strings – in places one instrument per part. What is less welcome is that the strings of Concerto Köln are too acid-sounding even by period standards. By contrast, the solo violinist, Rainer Kussmaul, plays with rare freshness and purity, allowing himself just a measure of vibrato, and if Staier takes second place, that is not just a question of balance between the violin and an 1825 fortepiano, but of the young composer's piano writing, regularly built on passage-work – often in arpeggios – rather than straight melodic statements. That also applies to the piano writing in the solo concerto, and it is striking that a clear progression is revealed between 1822, the date of the solo concerto, and March 1823, when the double concerto was completed in time for his 14th birthday.

Piano Concerto No. 1 in G min., Op. 25.
*** DG 474 291-2. Lang Lang, Chicago SO, Barenboim
 – TCHAIKOVSKY: *Piano Concerto No. 1.* **(*)

Lang Lang in his native China first tackled the Mendelssohn concerto when he was only seven, since when it has become a favourite work of his. As in the Tchaikovsky, the close balance of the piano establishes this as a big-scale performance, with the minor-key bite of the opening strongly presented. In the slow movement he opts for a tempo on the broad side, lessening its role as a song without words. With sparkling playing, the performance erupts into a winningly joyful account of the finale. A rare and attractive coupling for the distinctive account of the Tchaikovsky.

Violin Concertos in D min. (for Violin & Strings); in E min., Op. 64.

(BB) *(*) EMI Encore 5 74739-2. Zimmermann, Berlin RSO, Albrecht.

Though it makes an apt and attractive coupling to have Mendelssohn's great *E minor Violin Concerto* coupled with his youthful essay in the genre, Zimmermann's disc has to be approached with caution. It is in the major work that he falls short. Not helped by a close balance which exaggerates the soloist's tonal idiosyncrasies, the violin sound has a distinct edge, with the melodic line often gulpingly uneven. The second subject then gives respite, but the slow movement is ungainly, and only in the finale does the playing sound happy and relaxed – though even there Zimmermann does not compare with the finest versions. Though in the youthful concerto the slow movement is delightfully persuasive, the outer movements fail to sparkle as they should. Apart from the distractingly close balance of the soloist, the sound is full and firm.

Violin Concerto in E min., Op. 64.

*** Sony SK 67740. Midori, BPO, Jansons – BRUCH: *Violin Concerto No. 1.* ***

**(*) EMI DVD 490445-9. Grumiaux, O. Nat. de l'ORTF, Rosenthal (with BACH: *Violin Partita No. 2, BWV 1004: Sarabande & Chaconne.* BLOCH: *Baal Shem: Il Nigun* (with André Chometon) – BEETHOVEN: *Violin Concerto.* **(*)

(M) *** EMI (ADD) 5 62591-2. Perlman, LSO, Previn – TCHAIKOVSKY: *Concerto.* **(*)

(BB) (***) Naxos mono 8.110977. Milstein, Philharmonic-Symphony O, New York, Barbirolli – BRUCH: *Violin Concerto No. 1;* TCHAIKOVSKY: *Violin Concerto.* (***)

(B) **(*) Discover DICD 920122. Bushkov, Slovak New PO, Rahbari (with TCHAIKOVSKY: *Concerto* **).

(M) *(*) BBC (ADD) BBCL 4050-2. Menuhin, LSO, C. Davis – BACH: *Violin Concerto, No. 2;* BRAHMS: *Double Concerto.* *(*)

(B) *(*) CfP 574 8782. Huggett, OAE, Mackerras – BEETHOVEN: *Violin Concerto.* *(*)

It is surprising that Midori has taken so long to record this traditional coupling, but the wait has been worth it when, in live performances with Jansons and the Berlin Philharmonic at their most inspired, the results are so distinctive, at once thoughtful and detailed yet youthful-sounding too. The moment in the first movement when the soloist for a moment relaxes on a downward arpeggio brings a breathtaking *pianissimo*, always a fine testing-point. Recorded live, Midori and Jansons convey urgency, heightening climaxes with a hint of

accelerando, so that in all three movements Midori's overall timings are relatively fast, with the central *Andante* flowing freely. In the finale the urgency brings extra excitement, with a consistent sense of freely spontaneous expressiveness.

The Grumiaux DVD account of the Mendelssohn *Concerto* was made in the Palais de la Méditerranée in Nice in January 1961. In his day Grumiaux was an aristocrat of violinists, and his tonal refinement and selfless artistry made his achievement quite special. The sound is somewhat wanting in bloom and climaxes are wanting in transparency, but the essential qualities of this great violinist emerge in this work and in the various shorter pieces listed above. The Paganini was an encore at the Mendelssohn concert, while the Bach and Bloch pieces were recorded variously at the ORTF studios and in the Netherlands.

Perlman's 1972 recording was very highly regarded in its day. He gives a performance as full of flair as almost any, and he is superbly matched by the LSO under Previn, at that time at their very peak. With ripe recording, this remains competitive in its mid-priced reissue in the 'Perlman Edition', although the Tchaikovsky coupling is not quite its match.

Milstein made four recordings of the Mendelssohn, and this, his first, comes from May 1945, shortly after the war in Europe had come to an end. There is a sense of exhilaration and a freshness that is very persuasive and the engineers capture Milstein's tone with great fidelity. Just before (and through) the war American Columbia recorded on to 33⅓rpm lacquer master discs, after which the approved takes were dubbed on to wax 78rpm discs. Although the resultant 78s were not as impressive as direct-to-wax discs, when they were transferred to LP in the early 1950s there was a much wider frequency-range as well as quieter surfaces. The recordings sound as well as 1950s early tape masters. Mark Obert Thorne's transfers are exemplary; the performance, which (unless we are much mistaken) has not been available on LP or CD since the 1950s, should be snapped up, particularly at so competitive a price.

Evgeny Bushkov is a pupil of Leonid Kogan, and he prepares and plays the secondary theme of the opening movement with appealing tenderness. The *Andante* has a matching simplicity and the finale no lack of bravura and fire. He is well accompanied, and the recording, made in the Concert Hall of Slovak Radio, Bratislava, is full and well balanced. Not a first choice, however, for the coupled Tchaikovsky *Concerto* sounds less spontaneous.

In his BBC recording of the Mendelssohn *Concerto* Menuhin is on rather better form than in the Brahms coupling with Rostropovich. All the same this is not one of the most successful of the BBC 'Legends' series.

Monica Huggett's 'authentic' version is a disappointment. Without a memorably lyrical slow movement, any recording of this concerto is a non-starter.

Violin Concerto in E min.: 1st movement only.

** EMI **DVD** 492840-9. Heifetz, Bell Telephone Hour O, Voorhees (with Bonus: DEBUSSY: *La fille aux cheveux de lin*; DINICU: *Hora staccato*) –
BEETHOVEN: *Piano Concerto No. 4* **(*); WALTON: *Cello Concerto.* ***

The recording of the Mendelssohn first movement calls for some tolerance; the playing of Heifetz, on the other hand, beggars belief. The recording comes from an early American TV programme called the 'Bell Telephone Hour', on which Heifetz periodically appeared. Among his instruments Heifetz possessed the 1742 Guarneri del Gesù on which Félicien David gave the première of Mendelssohn's concerto! The DVD celebrates the Million Dollar Trio (Heifetz, Rubinstein, Piatigorsky), though they are not heard playing together but only separately.

(i) Overtures: *Calm Sea and a Prosperous Voyage; The Hebrides (Fingal's Cave); Ruy Blas;* (ii) *A Midsummer Night's Dream: Overture and Incidental Music: Scherzo; Intermezzo; Notturno; Wedding March.*

(BB) (*) Naxos 8.554433. Slovak PO; (i) Bramall; (ii) Dohnányi.

Leaden performances, with no magic, flair or sparkle, and with a recording to match.

Symphonies for Strings Nos. 1, 4, 6, 7 & 12.
(M) **(*) Warner Elatus 2564 60353-2. Concerto Köln.

Symphonies for Strings Nos. 2, 3, 5, 11 & 13.
(M) **(*) Warner Elatus 2564 60440-2. Concerto Köln.

This pair of discs completes the separate reissue of the Concerto Köln's set of the *String Symphonies.* (Nos. 8–10 are listed in our companion volume – 2564 60124-2). These are excellent period-instrument performances, very well recorded, but they would have been even more attractive on the budget Apex label.

Symphonies Nos. 1–5 (complete).
(BB) **(*) Arts 47620/2 (3). SO de Madrid, Maag (with Valente, Suárez, Calderon, Orfeón Donostiarra in No. 2).

When Peter Maag conducted a vintage (1960) Decca version of the *Scottish Symphony*, long regarded as a classic, it is good that at the end of his career he was able to record a complete Mendelssohn symphony cycle. These are generally light, resilient performances that bring out the joy of Mendelssohn's inspiration, his youthful exuberance. On this showing the Madrid Symphony Orchestra has some impressive wind and brass soloists and refined strings, with rhythms elegantly pointed, and with everyone responding well to the challenge of Maag's very fast speed in such a movement as the *Saltarello* finale of the *Italian Symphony*, a genuine *Presto.* The recording also helps to clarify textures, with impressive weight given to the brass in the *Reformation Sym-*

phony. Sadly, Mendelssohn's choral symphony, No. 2, *The Hymn of Praise*, is markedly less successful than the rest, partly because this is an ambitious work that needs full weight, but more particularly because the soloists are disappointing, with the first soprano edgy and the tenor strained. Even so, at bargain price this is a set well worth considering by collectors who have relished Maag's justly famous early Decca disc.

Symphonies Nos. 3 in A min. (Scottish); 4 (Italian).
(BB) *** ASV Resonance CD RSN 3018. O of St John's, Lubbock.
(BB) ** EMI Encore 5 74965-2. LPO, Welser-Möst.

Lubbock's coupling of the *Scottish* and *Italian Symphonies* makes an outstanding super-bargain reissue, offering performances of delightful lightness and point, warmly and cleanly recorded. The string section may be of chamber size but, amplified by a warm acoustic, the result sparkles, with rhythms lifted exhilaratingly. The slow movements are both on the slow side but flow easily with no suspicion of sentimentality, while the *Saltarello* finale of the *Fourth*, with the flute part delectably pointed, comes close to Mendelssohnian fairy music.

Welser-Möst's are light, consciously controlled readings, very well paced, fresh and unsentimental. He brings out the finesse of the playing of the LPO, of which he had recently become music director, helped by slightly distant recording. The strings lead the ensemble in refinement, with the splendid LPO horns cutting through the texture well, though the big horn whoops in the coda of the *Scottish* are disappointingly thin and uninvolving. Elsewhere, too, Welser-Möst's concern for refinement means that in places the performances fail to lift in the way they would in a concert hall. He observes the exposition repeat in the first movement of the *Italian*, but not in the *Scottish*. Even in the bargain range this is not really competitive.

Symphony No. 4 (Italian).
(B) *** Decca Penguin 460 643-2. San Francisco SO, Blomstedt – SCHUBERT: *Symphony No. 8.* **

Blomstedt's 1990 recording is one of the very finest. Not only does he choose ideal speeds – not too brisk in the exhilarating first movement, nor sentimental in the slow one – he conveys a feeling of spontaneity throughout, springing the rhythms infectiously. The recording is outstanding, but it is a pity that the original coupling of an equally fine performance of the *Scottish Symphony* was replaced with Schubert's *Unfinished*, which is considerably less successful. The personal commentary is by John Guare.

CHAMBER MUSIC

String Quartets Nos. 1 in E flat, Op. 12; 2 in A min., Op. 13.
(BB) **(*) EMI Encore 5 85693-2. Cherubini Qt.

*String Quartets Nos. 2; 4 in E min., Op. 44/2; 2
Pieces, Op. 81/1–2.*

✶(✶) Chan. 955. Sorrel Qt.

These were the initial recordings in the Cherubini
Mendelssohn cycle, with the *Second Quartet* coming
first in 1989 and the *First* following a year later. The
playing is most accomplished and certainly ardent,
though they are occasionally guilty of being a bit
self-conscious, notably in the *A minor*. Dynamic
markings here are slightly exaggerated, and some
might feel that the opening of the finale is over-
dramatized. The *E flat Quartet* is simpler in style and
both are warmly and naturally recorded.

The Sorrel Quartet do not produce a really beautiful sound or enough polish to be convincing candidates in these pieces. Excellent recording.

*String Quartets Nos. 5 in E flat, Op. 44/3; 6 in F
min., Op. 80; Scherzo & Theme and Variations,
Op. 81.*

✶✶✶ MDG 307 1056-2. Leipzig Qt.

We have admired earlier issues in this Leipzig Mendelssohn Quartet series (see our main edition) and
this final instalment (coupling the superb *E flat
Quartet*, the last of the Op. 44 series, and the *F minor*,
Op. 80) is if anything even finer than its companions.
Chorley pronounced the Op. 80 quartet 'one of the
most impassioned outpourings of sadness existing in
instrumental music', composed after the death of the
composer's beloved sister, Fanny, and the Leipzig
Quartet conveys its intensity and concentration with
surpassing eloquence. Their performances serve as a
reminder that this is great music which is all too
often taken for granted by critics. We are well served
in this repertoire, with the Ysaÿe (Decca) and Cherubini Quartet (EMI) having much to recommend
them, but the Leipzig is the most impressive and
convincing of all in this coupling and calls for a
strong recommendation.

Violin Sonatas: in F min., Op. 4; in F (1838).

(M) ✶✶✶ Decca 474 690-2. Mintz, Ostrovsky.

Mendelssohn was only fourteen when he composed
the *F minor Sonata*, but even so it is not wanting in
individuality and is much more than a youthful
exercise. The 1838 *Sonata* comes from Mendelssohn's
productive Leipzig period. The performances are
beyond reproach; the playing of both artists is a
model of sensitivity and intelligence, the recording is
absolutely first class, and the CD understandably
won the *Gramophone* Chamber Award in 1988.

VOCAL MUSIC

*Lieder: Andres Maienlied (Hexenlied); Auf Flügeln
des Gesanges; Erster Verlust; Es weiss und rät es doch
keiner; Frage; Frühlingsglaube; Frühlingslied;
Geständnis; Gruss; Die Liebende schreibt; Mädchens*

*Klage; Maienlied; Minnelied; Der Mond; Nachtlied;
Neue Liebe; Schilflied; Suleika (Ach, um deine
feuchten Schwingen); Suleika (Wes bedeutet die
Bewegung?); Sun of the Sleepless!; There be none of
Beauty's Daughters; Volkslied; Das Waldschloss;
Wanderlied.*

(BB) ✶✶✶ Hyp. Helios CDH 55150. M. Price, Johnson.

A wholly delightful collection, in many ways even
more revealing than Dame Janet Baker's shorter survey (on EMI 5 73836-2, combined with songs by Liszt
and Schumann), which is praised in our main *Guide*.
Once again there is a delightfully light touch to the
famous 'On Wings of Song', (*Auf Flügeln*). *Frühlingslied* ('Spring Song') is equally appealing, and
Minnelied soars. The vivid portrayal of a witches'
dance (*Hexenlied*) and *Neue Liebe* with its 'riding
elves in the moonlight' are both very much in the
spirit of the *Midsummer Night's Dream* music, even if
the former, with the fiendishly complex piano part so
brilliantly played by Graham Johnson, has a slightly
sinister air. In between comes the lovely *Gruss*, a
gentle 'Greeting'.

Perhaps the Goethe settings do not quite match
those of Schubert, but the two *Suleika* settings are
among the highlights of the recital and *Erster
Verlust* is ravishing. It is followed by *Volkslied*,
which is set with touching Mendelssohnian simplicity. The novelty is Graham Johnson's discovery of
the two Byron settings in English, of which *Sun of
the Sleepless!* is especially appealing. Then comes
Mendelssohn's sole setting of Schiller, *Mädchens
Klage*, showing the composer at his most imaginative, as do the four Eichendorf songs which end the
recital (the piano introduction to the dramatic *Das
Waldschloss* recalls Schubert's *Winterreise*). In short,
this is a particularly rewarding collection, with
Margaret Price and her partner Graham Johnson in
splendid form and made vividly present by the
recording. Even though this is a bargain reissue, full
texts and translations are provided, plus excellent
notes by Richard Wigmore.

Elijah (complete).

(BB) ✶✶(✶) Warner Elatus 2564 60534-2 (2). Miles,
Donath, Van Nes, George, Klein, Leipzig MDR Ch.,
Israel PO, Masur.

Masur as a Mendelssohnian consistently eliminates
any hint of sentimentality, but in *Elijah* his determination to use a new broom involves many fast speeds
that fail to let this dramatic music blossom, not least
in the exuberant final chorus. Yet anyone wanting a
fine, modern, digital recording, using the German
text, crisply and urgently done, should not be too
disappointed, particularly when Alastair Miles sings
so freshly and intelligently in the title-role. Another
incentive, too, is its new bargain price, complete with
texts and translations.

MERCADANTE, Saverio
(1795–1870)

Sinfonia caratteristica; Sinfonia fantastica; La danza; (i) *Fantasia on 'Lucia di Lammermoor' for Cello & Orchestra; Fantasia on Themes from Rossini's Stabat Mater; Il lamento di Bardo.*
*(*) Fonit. O Philharmonia Mediterranea, De Filippi.

The *Sinfonia caratteristica* is delightful, very like a Rossini overture, and almost as tuneful and witty, even if Mercadante can't quite manage an authentic 'crescendo'. The episodic *Sinfonia fantastica* is less remarkable, and *Il lamento di Bardo* is melodramatic, if rather endearingly so. *La danza* is not nearly as infectious and catchy as Rossini's famous piece, and is rather like second-class ballet music; the two *Fantasias* need bolder advocacy than they receive here: the solo cello in *Lucia di Lammermoor* is wan and low-profiled. The orchestra play well enough and are pleasingly recorded, but only in the first piece does Luigi De Filippi display the kind of flair the programme needs throughout.

MERIKANTO, Aarre (1893–1958)

Andante Religioso; 4 Compositions for Orchestra; Lemminkäinen, Op. 10; Pan, Op. 28; Scherzo.
** Ondine ODE 905-2. Tampere PO, Ollila.

Lemminkäinen comes from 1916, when Merikanto was finishing his studies in Moscow, and is derivative (Russian post-nationalism, Sibelius and a dash of Scriabin). *Pan* is more radical and is highly imaginative with an evocative and powerful atmosphere. The *Four Compositions for Orchestra* come from the 1930s, as does the *Scherzo*. Good performances and decent recording, though the Tampere studio is a bit on the dry side.

(i) *Piano Concertos Nos. 2 & 3; 2 Studies for Small Orchestra; 2 Pieces for Orchestra.*
** Ondine ODE 915-2. (i) Raekallio; Tampere PO, Ollila.

Although neither of the piano concertos is the equal of the *Second Violin Concerto*, they are both inventive and rewarding. The middle movement of the *Third Piano Concerto*, with its strong evocation of nature, is one of Merikanto's most haunting inspirations. The orchestral pieces are less interesting. Matti Raekallio is a very capable player, and the Tampere orchestra, though obviously a provincial band, copes well under Tuomas Ollila. The sound is synthetic, with little front-to-back perspective. Worth investigating all the same.

MESSIAEN, Olivier (1908–92)

L'Ascension.
* Häns. CD 93.005 (2). Baden-Baden & Freiburg SW

German RSO, Cambreling – BERLIOZ: *Roméo et Juliette.* *

Messiaen's four symphonic meditations make an unusual supplement for Cambreling's version of the Berlioz, but similarly bring a performance conscientious rather than convincing, lacking tension. First-rate, refined recording.

Turangalîla Symphony.
(M) *** RCA (ADD) 82876 59418-2. Yvonne & Jeanne Loriod, Toronto SO, Ozawa.

Ozawa's performance comes from 1967, but you would never guess that from the brilliantly atmospheric sound, which is just as vivid as some of the newer versions, such as Nagano's Erato version, and has that bit more warmth and atmosphere. Yvonne Loriod's piano is placed too forward, but her contribution is undoubtedly seminal, and the overall balance is otherwise well managed. The performance itself is brilliantly played: it has plenty of electricity, and a warm sensuality too. It was and remains one of Ozawa's best recordings and is now economically reissued on a single CD as part of RCA's 'Classic Collection'. However, Previn's version (available both on an audio DVD and as part of an EMI double forte, coupled with Poulenc concertos) remains first choice and costs about the same (see our main volume).

PIANO MUSIC

Catalogue d'oiseaux (complete); *La Fauvette des jardins.*
(M) **(*) DG Trio 474 345-2 (3). Ugorski.

It is good to have such a bold, powerful and essentially Slavonic approach to Messiaen's multi-faceted evocations of birdsong heard against graphically depicted landscapes, often rough-hewn, with all the extravagance of nature. It is impossible not to respond to such vivid pictorialism, even if Anatol Ugorski's approach is essentially extrovert and at times almost melodramatic in its dynamism and sense of contrast. This would make a spectacular impression at a live performance, but under domestic circumstances the greater intimacy and the less flamboyant, more subtle approach of Peter Hill on Regis and Håkan Austbø on Naxos are more satisfying. The DG recording is very immediate, which is not necessarily an advantage when Ugorski's playing creates its own presence.

ORGAN MUSIC

Volume 1: *Apparition de l'église éternelle; Le Banquet céleste; La Nativité du Seigneur.*
(M) *** Priory PRCD 921. Weir.

Volume 2: *Méditations sur le mystère de la Sainte Trinité.*

☐━➤ (M) ✶✶✶ Priory PRCD 922. Weir.

Volume 3: *Les Corps glorieux; Messe de la Pentecôte.*

☐━➤ (M) ✶✶✶ Priory PRCD 923. Weir.

Volume 4: *L'Ascension; Livre d'orgue.*

☐━➤ (M) ✶✶✶Priory PRDC 924. Weir.

Volumes 5 & 6: *Livre du Saint Sacrement.* Early Pieces: *Diptyque; Monodie; Offrande au Saint Sacrement; Prélude; Verset pour la Fête de la Dédicace.*

☐━➤ (M) ✶✶✶ Priory Double PRDC 925/6. Weir.

Gillian Weir's magnificently recorded coverage of Messiaen's organ music dates from 1994. It was recorded on the superb organ of Aarhus Cathedral, Denmark, in association with BBC Radio 3, and was originally issued on Collins – to be withdrawn only too swiftly when that label disappeared. On its original issue it received an extraordinary number of accolades, both for Gillian Weir's astonishing virtuosity and control, and indeed for the demonstration quality of the recording. Now it returns on Priory, and its excellence is confirmed. Like Jennifer Bate, Weir was a personal friend and confidante of the composer, and the authority and conviction of her playing shines out through the entire project: its concentration and power are immediately apparent in the opening *Apparition de l'église éternelle*, while *Le Banquet céleste* and the remarkably diverse *Le Corps glorieux* show the strength of her characterization. Only in the *Méditations sur le mystère de la Saint Trinité* does one feel that, although she still holds the music in a firm grip, her approach is a little static. But this remains very compelling, if only for the rich and sometimes piquant palette of sound she commands on her Danish organ. The records are available individually at mid-price (with the fourth and fifth discs together, treated as a double), whereas Bate's recording is on the budget Regis label (see our main volume). But Gillian Weir's set is in every way a recommendable alternative, and it is well documented, including her personal reminiscences of the composer.

Three of the five early works (several only recently discovered), which have been added to Volume 6, were recorded as recently as 2003.

MIASKOVSKY, Nikolay

(1881–1950)

Violin Concerto.

(BB) ✶✶✶ Naxos 8.557194. Grubert, Russian PO, Yablonsky – VAINBERG: *Violin Concerto.* ✶✶✶

The Lithuanian violinist Ilya Grubert offers the Miaskovsky *Concerto* coupled enterprisingly with the Vainberg and at a remarkably competitive price.

Oistrakh's pioneering version (superbly transferred on Pearl) is mandatory listening, for he more than anyone is so perfectly attuned to the warmth and lyricism of this glorious piece. Grubert plays it with appropriate affection and grace, and he is well supported by his Russian players. At the price this must be self-recommending, and readers who have not acquired the even finer Repin version (Philips 473 343-2 – see our main volume), should lose no time in snapping this up.

Symphonies Nos. (i) *1 in C min., Op. 3;* (ii) *19 in E flat for Wind Band, Op. 46.*

✶✶(✶) Russian Disc (ADD) RDCD 11 007. (i) USSR MoC SO, Rozhdestvensky; (ii) Russian State Brass O, Sergeyev.

Miaskovsky's *First Symphony* is a student work, very much in the received tradition. It is obvious from the very start that Miaskovsky was a composer who could think on a big scale. The *Nineteenth Symphony in B flat* for military band is a slighter piece, worth hearing for its inner movements, a wistful *Moderato* and a well-written *Andante*. The *First Symphony* is well played by the Ministry of Culture Orchestra under Gennady Rozhdestvensky, though the brass sound a bit raw, as indeed do the upper strings. The *Nineteenth* is played with great brio and genuine affection. The less-than-three-star recording-quality should not deter collectors from investigating this work.

Symphonies Nos. 2 in C sharp min.; 10 in F min., Op. 30.

✶✶(✶) Orfeo C496991A. V. RSO, Rabl.

The *Second Symphony* comes from 1912, when Miaskovsky was still a student (he turned to music at a relatively late stage), and breathes much of the same air as Scriabin, Rachmaninov and Glière (he was a pupil of the last). The *Tenth* (1927) is a more radical piece with greater contrapuntal density, which in its level of dissonance shows the influence of his lifelong friend, Prokofiev. The playing of the Austrian Radio Orchestra under Gottfried Rabl is serviceable rather than distinguished, and the recording is a bit resonant, but there are no alternative versions currently available.

MIELCK, Ernst (1877–99)

Symphony in F min., Op. 4; (i) *Concert Piece in E min. for Piano & Orchestra, Op. 9.*

✶✶ Sterling CDS 1035-2. (i) Pohjola; Turku PO, Lintu.

Ernst Mielck's *Symphony*, Op. 4, preceded Sibelius's *First* by two years, and its success is said to have acted as a spur to that great composer to complete his own. It is a four-movement work, some 40 minutes in length. Although it begins promisingly, neither of its main ideas can lay claim to any strong personality, though there is a genuine sense of form. Probably the best movement is the lyrical and endearing slow movement. By and large it offers promise rather than fulfilment. The Turku orchestra under Hannu Lintu plays decently. The *Concert Piece*, Op. 9, is rather dreadful, though the central *Largo* has some poetic writing. A valuable release, which will be of interest to Sibelians in deepening their historical perspective about his background, but Mielck is no Arriaga.

MILHAUD, Darius (1892–1974)

L'Apothéose de Molière, Op. 286; Le Bœuf sur le toit, Op. 58; (i) Le Carnaval d'Aix, Op. 83b; Le Carnaval de Londres.
〇━ (BB) ★★★ Hyp. Helios CDH 55168. (i) Gibbons; New L. O, Corp

Le Carnaval d'Aix is a delight from start to finish and very expertly played by Jack Gibbons and the New London Orchestra under Ronald Corp. They also convey the Satie-like circus-music of *Le Bœuf sur le toit* and are equally at home in the rest of the programme. Very good recording too. A real bargain.

Suite provençale.
(M) ★★ Chan. 6615. Detroit SO, Järvi – DEBUSSY: *La Mer*; RAVEL: *Boléro; La Valse.* ★★

Järvi's *Suite provençale* is very well played in Detroit and is well recorded too, but this captivating score needs greater lightness of touch if it is to charm the listener as it should. Not a first choice, and it must be conceded that neither *La Mer* nor the Ravel pieces are front-runners either, although all have their merits.

Symphonies Nos. 1 (1939); 2 (1944); Suite provençale.
✪ (M) ★★★ DG 476 2197. Toulouse Capitole O, Plasson.

In the inter-war years Milhaud was known for his little three-minute symphonies, and it was not until he was in his late forties that he embarked on a full-scale essay in the form. This was in response to a commission from the Chicago Symphony Orchestra, and he subsequently recorded the work with the Columbia Broadcast Orchestra in the early days of LP. Those who possess that disc or the LP of the *Second* made by Georges Tzipine will not only know how richly imaginative, melodically inventive and rewarding these scores are; they will also be puzzled as to why they have not entered the repertoire. Sample the fourth movement, *Avec sérénité*, of the *Second* and you will see just how sunny, relaxed and easy-going this music is; try also the slow movement of the *First* for its powerful, nocturnal atmosphere. The Orchestre du Capitole de Toulouse and Michel Plasson play these melodious scores with total commitment, and they convey their pleasure in rediscovering this music. The recording is very natural, with a refined tone and well-balanced perspective, by far the most successful sound to have been captured in the

Salle-aux-Grains by any engineering team to date. The delightful *Suite provençale* is as good as a holiday in the south of France – and cheaper! It is now available at mid-price for the first time as one of Universal's 'Penguin ✪ Collection'.

MINKUS, Léon (1826–1917)

Don Quixote (ballet; original, 1869 version).
(BB) ★★(★) Naxos 8.557065/66 (2). Sofia Nat. Op. O, Todorov.

As one would expect from a ballet by Minkus, *Don Quixote* is full of lively dances and attractive melodies, all of it well crafted and colourfully orchestrated, if without the genius of Tchaikovsky and Delibes. That said, it makes for undemanding, entertaining listening, with its dashes of Spanish colouring (the Spanish dances are especially attractive) and plenty of character dances, such as the *Sailor's Dance* in Act II, to enjoy. The performance is lively and sympathetic and the recording reasonably good (it lacks a certain richness), but they do not quite possess the flair which Bonynge and Decca brought to this repertoire. At the price, admirers of both light music and ballet should not hesitate: there is plenty to enjoy here.

MOERAN, Ernest J. (1894–1950)

(i) Cello Concerto; (ii; iii) Violin Concerto; (iii) 2 Pieces for Small Orchestra: Lonely Waters; Whythorne's Shadow.
〇━ (M) ★★★ Chan. 10168X. (i) Wallfisch, Bournemouth Sinf., Del Mar; (ii) Mordkovitch; (iii) Ulster O, Handley.

This a straight reissue of an outstanding coupling reviewed in our main volume, with the original superb recording sounding better than ever.

Symphony in G min.; Overture for a Masque; (i) Rhapsody for Piano & Orchestra.
〇━ (M) ★★★ Chan. 10169X. (i) Fingerhut; Ulster O, Handley.

To meet the competition from Naxos, Chandos have reissued at mid-price Vernon Handley's compelling performance of a favourite symphony (praised in our main volume), plus the tunefully folksy *Rhapsody*, with the exuberant, syncopated *Overture* thrown in for good measure. (It was commissioned during the Second World War by Walter Legge for ENSA as entertainment for the troops.) An outstanding disc in every way, with the superb recording sounding better than ever.

(i) Fantasy Quartet for Oboe & Strings; (ii) String Quartet No. 2 in A min.; (iii) Violin Sonata.
(M) ★★★ Chan. 10170X. (i) Francis, English String Qt (members); (ii) Melbourne Qt; (iii) Scott, Talbot.

Sarah Francis's admirable account with the English String Quartet of Moeran's folk-influenced *Fantasy Quartet*, an attractively rhapsodic single-movement work, is here re-coupled with the *String Quartet in A minor* of 1921, together with the more intense and forward-looking *Violin Sonata* (written a year later). The performance from Donald Scott and John Talbot is full of rough-hewn energy, with plenty of contrast in the central *Lento*. While the Maggini–Naxos coupling with the earlier *E flat Quartet* is more logical (8.554079), the Chandos disc is very attractive in its own right.

MOLINO, Francesco (1775–1847)

Trio, Op. 45.
*** Mer. CDE 84199. Conway, Silverthorne, Garcia –
BEETHOVEN: *Serenade;* JOSEPH KREUTZER:
Grand Trio. ***

Italian-born, Molino first settled in Spain before going on to London and Paris, where he built a reputation as a violinist and guitarist. Undemanding music to complete a charming disc for a rare combination. First-rate playing and recording.

MOMPOU, Federico (1893–1987)

COMPLETE PIANO MUSIC

Cants Mágics; Charmes; Dialogues; Fêtes lointaines; Impresiones intimas; Pessebres; Préludes; Scènes d'enfants; Souvenirs de l'Exposistion; Surburbis; 3 Variations; Variations sur un thème de Chopin.
(B) **(*) Nimbus NI 5724/7 (4). Jones.

Martin Jones has already given us some fine records, including a first-rate set of the piano music of Percy Grainger. Now he turns to another miniaturist. Born in Barcelona, Mompou studied in Paris and his music is a fascinating mixture of Catalan and French influences, though in its colouring and textures the French influence is strong. There are plenty of fine individual CDs of this composer's music, but for collectors who want to explore the entire repertoire, Jones is a sound guide, at home in its diverse moods and colours. One feels at times he could be more chimerical and seek more translucent textures, but his simplicity of approach is a plus point and, with truthful recording, this can certainly be recommended to musical explorers.

MONDONVILLE, Jean-Joseph Cassanéa de (1711–72)

6 Sonates en symphonies, Op. 3.
(M) *** DG Blue 474 550-2. Les Musiciens du Louvre, Minkowski.

This entirely captivating set of *Symphonies* confirms Mondonville as a great deal more than a historical figure. They originated as sonatas for violin and obbligato harpsichord in 1734, but the composer later skilfully orchestrated them. Each is in three movements, with an expressively tuneful centrepiece framed by sprightly allegros. Their invention is consistently fresh, and they are played here with great élan and spontaneity and are beautifully recorded. This now reappears competitively priced on DG's Archive Blue label. Highly recommended.

MONIUSZKO, Stanislaw (1819–72)

The Haunted Manor (opera; complete).
(M) *** EMI 5 57489-2 (2). Kruszewski, Hossa, Lubańska, Stachura, Nowacki, Toczyska, Polish Nat. Op. Ch. & O, Kaspszyk.

Moniuszko, the leading Polish romantic after Chopin, is generally remembered, if at all, by his opera *Halka*, a tragic story set against a peasant background. Yet in almost every way *The Haunted Manor*, one of the hidden treasures of Polish opera, is more original, more inventive and, above all, more attractive with its tuneful sequence of ensembles. Two shuddering chords at the very start reflect the title, but then the first scene sets quite a different tone of voice in a rousing military ensemble, when two brothers, Stefan and Zbigniev, on leaving their comrades, swear they will never marry, so as always to be ready to fight for their country. They find their match when they visit an old friend of their father, Miecznik, the Sword-Bearer, and meet his two daughters, Hanna and Jadwiga, each intent on finding a husband. The manner is as close to Gilbert and Sullivan as to Smetana, with a dash of Donizetti thrown in. A fortune-telling scene prompts a charming duet and ensemble for women's voices, when the sisters learn that they will marry soldiers. After that the main haunting scene anticipates the G. & S. 'Ghosts' High Noon Scene' in *Ruddigore*, with portraits coming to life. The big difference is that this is no genuine haunting but simply a ruse by Hanna and Jadwiga, themselves taking the place of the portraits. The brothers wake up to the fact that they are both in love, Stefan with Hanna, Zbigniev with Jadwiga. Though the plot rather rambles about towards the end, the dénouement is helped by the unexpected arrival of a crowd of party guests, which, however implausibly, gives Moniuszko the excuse to insert a big Mazurka number for the full ensemble, guaranteed to bring the house down.

Though ensembles predominate, each of the main characters is given a big showpiece aria. The one for Hanna is particularly impressive, with its Donizettian coloratura brilliantly sung by the bright-toned Iwona Hossa. Anna Lubańska with her firm, warm mezzo is also impressive as Jadwiga; but the casting of the two brothers is not so strong, with the lusty tenor Dariusz Stachura strained as Stefan, not attacking notes cleanly, and Piotr Nowacki as Zbigniev happier in fast music than sustained melody. Best of all is Adam Kruszewski in the central role of the host, Miecznik, the Sword-Bearer, a fine baritone with a timbre not unlike Sir Thomas Allen's. Add on a few *buffo* characters and a formidable aunt figure, strongly taken by Stefania Toczyska, and you have a splendidly successful entertainment, with superb playing and singing from the Polish National Opera Chorus and Orchestra, dynamically conducted from first to last by Jacek Kaspszyk.

MONTEMEZZI, Italo (1875–1952)

L'amore dei tre re (complete).

(M) **(*) RCA (ADD) 74321 50166-2 (2). Moffo, Domingo, Elvira, Siepi, Davies, Amb. Op. Ch., LSO, Santi.

(M) (**(*)) Warner Fonit mono 8573 87487-2 (2). Bruscantini, Petrella, Berdini, Capecchi, RAI Ch. & O of Milan, Basile.

Italo Montemezzi, one of Puccini's young successors, delivered this lurid melodrama based on a play by Sem Benelli, and the obvious dramatic echoes of *Tristan* and *Pelleas* combined with a red-blooded, lyrical score brought it success. What it lacks, compared to Puccini – let alone to Wagner or Debussy – are memorable ideas. Nevertheless, with colourful scoring and an economical structure it makes easy listening. The 1977 recording with Nello Santi a thrustful conductor makes as good a case for the piece as one is likely to get. Anna Moffo is an old-sounding if dramatic Fiora, but Plácido Domingo is in glowing form as Avito, and Cesare Siepi vividly heightens the melodrama as Archibaldo. As Manfredo, the baritone Pablo Elvira sings with firm, clean attack, as does Ryland Davies in the role of the castle guard, Flaminio. Full, warm, well-balanced sound. Synopsis and libretto with translation are provided but no background information on the work or the composer.

Recorded for Cetra in Milan in 1950 in collaboration with Italian Radio, the mono recording of Montemezzi's one operatic success brings a red-blooded, idiomatic account of a piece cherished in America as well as Italy, largely through the initial advocacy of Toscanini. It says much for the conductor, Arturo Basile, that he drives the piece so strongly through a tale of such improbable blood and thunder, helped by a strong cast. Central to the success of the performance is the singing of Sesto Bruscantini as the barbarian king, Archibaldo, who forces his daughter, Fiora, to marry the unfortunate Manfredo, before malevolently rooting out her passionate affair with her true love, Avito, with widespread carnage at the end. Bruscantini, only thirty-one at the time, sings with commanding power in this villainous role, cutting a very different figure from his classic Figaro, which became such a favourite at Glyndebourne. Clara Petrella sings sensitively as Fiora, well matched

against her lover, Avito, sung by Amedeo Berdini, with the young Renato Capecchi making Manfredo into a believable character. The mono recording is very limited but catches voices well. Though the later stereo version with Moffo and Domingo must take priority, this one from a company of singers and players familiar with the music is both convincing and enjoyable in putting over such outrageous hokum. An Italian libretto is provided but no translation, only multi-lingual synopses.

MONTEVERDI, Claudio (1567–1643)

Madrigals, Books 1 (1587); 2 (1590); 3 (1592); 6 (1614) (all complete); 7, excerpts: *Tempo la cetra; Tirsi e Clori.* 8: *Madrigali guerrieri; Madrigali amorosi;* Opera-ballets: *Il ballo dell ingrate; Il combattimento di Tancredi e Clorinda; Volgendo il ciel* (1638) (complete).

(BB) **(*) Virgin 5 62268-2 (7). Kirkby, Tubb, Nichols, Agnew, King, Ewing and soloists, Cons. of Musicke, Rooley.

Anthony Rooley recorded almost all the Monteverdi Madrigals between 1990 and 1996, mostly for EMI (as listed here), but for Books 4–5 he turned to L'Oiseau-Lyre, and these recordings are now available on a reissued Double, together with two items from Book 7 and two from Book 8 (455 718-2 – see our main volume). Rooley additionally recorded for L'Oiseau-Lyre ten further madrigals from Book 7 (1619) with instrumental accompaniments, under the title 'Madrigal erotici'. These are currently withdrawn, but Regis have reissued a further collection of six more from Book 7, which first appeared on Carlton, including duets featuring Emma Kirkby and Evelyn Tubb (RRC 1060 – again, see our main volume).

Two-thirds of the texts in Book 1 are concerned with love's disappointments, the words full of torments, which gives Monteverdi plenty of opportunity for expressive dolour. Though these early madrigals are usually brief and without the sharp poignancy of the later examples, there is much here that is imaginative and there is consistent lyrical beauty. This first disc also includes two excerpts from Book 7, including the charming pastoral ballet, *Tirsi e Clori,* written for the Mantuan court and extolling the the joys of requited love and faithfulness. Book 2 is also more simple in its appeal and imagery than the later writing but, like Book 1, it all comes to life freshly, including the very effective Tasso settings.

With Books 3 and 4 we move to some of Monteverdi's finest madrigals, often dazzling, in which his originality began to make itself felt to the full. Moreover these are masterly performances, the flexibility and control of dramatic contrasts conveying consistent commitment. Book 6 includes the five-part transcription of of the *Lamento d'Arianna* and *Zefiro torno,* two of the composer's masterpieces, and also works from Monteverdi's years at Mantua.

Monteverdi published his ambitious Volume 8 after a long gap in his madrigal output. It includes one of the very greatest examples in *Lamento della ninfa*, in what the composer described as the *stille rappresentativo* or theatre style, plus the well-known opera-ballets. The performances here continue to be polished and distinctive, and the cast-list is strong; but Andrew King is the narrator in *Combattimento*, and his approach is less than robustly full-blooded in the way the narrative demands.

For the most part, however, this reissued collection represents a considerable achievement for Rooley and his singers and instrumentalists, with first-class recording throughout. The set is most inexpensive, but the documentation is sparse, with no texts and translations.

Missa di capella á 4; Missa de capella in Illo tempore á 6; Motets: Cantata Domine; Domine, ne in furore (both á 6).
(BB) *** Hyp. Helios CDH 55145. The Sixteen, Christophers; Phillips (organ).

Two of Monteverdi's three surviving settings of the Mass make a splendid coupling on Hyperion's Helios budget label, along with two magnificent motets, both of which (like the *Mass in illo tempore*) are in six parts. Harry Christophers draws superb singing from his brilliant choir, highly polished in ensemble, but dramatic and deeply expressive too, suitably adapted for the character of each Mass-setting, when the four-part Mass involves stricter, more consistent contrapuntal writing and the six-part, in what was then an advanced way, uses homophonic writing to underline key pasages. In the latter, the incisiveness and clarity of articulation of the Sixteen add enormously to the dramatic bite. Vivid, atmospheric recording.

Sacred Music, Vol. I: Beatus vir I; Christe redemptor omnium; Confitebor Primo; Dixit [Dominus] Primo; Laudate Dominum omnes gentes; Laudate pueri Primo; Magnificat Primo; Messa à 4.
*** Hyp. CDA 67428. Outram, Covey-Crump, Mulroy, Auchincloss, Daniels, Gilchrist, Harvey, Evans, King's Consort Ch. & O, King.

When Monteverdi's Marian *Vespers* of 1610 have won such wide appreciation, not least on disc, it is strange than his other church music has been relatively neglected. Here Robert King with his King's Consort follows up the success of his big Purcell series with the first in a Monteverdi cycle, also for Hyperion. The eight items offered here all come from the great 1640 collection, *Selva morale e spirituale*, six Psalm settings associated with Christmas Vespers (including the haunting *Beatus vir*) plus the magnificent setting of the *Magnificat in eight parts* and the *Mass in four parts 'da capella'*, harking back to an earlier polyphonic style. In a recording made in St Jude's, Hampstead, King achieves a fine spread of vocal and instrumental sound as well as clarity, with instru-

mental accompaniment in the *Mass* as well as in the rest.

OPERA

Orfeo (opera; complete).
** Virgin 5 45642-2 (2). Bostridge, Dessay, Coote, Gens, Ciofi, Maltman, Agnew, European Voices, Les Sacqueboutiers, Le Concert d'Astrée, Haïm.
(M) ** Teldec (ADD) 2292 42494-2 (2). Kozma, Hansmann, Berberian, Katanosaka, Villisech, Van Egmond, Munich Capella Antiqua, VCM, Harnoncourt.
(BB) ** Naxos 8.554094-2 (2). Carmignani, Pennichi, Frisani, Pantasuglia, Capella Musicale di San Petronio di Bologna, Vartolo.

With an exceptionally starry cast led by Ian Bostridge in the title-role, Emanuelle Haïm's Virgin recording has much in its favour, recorded in the helpful acoustic of the Lebanese church in Paris. Directing from the continuo keyboards (harpsichord, organ and regal), Haïm is an energetic interpreter, tending to prefer fast speeds, while the singers characterize vividly. Impressive as Bostridge's virtuoso performance is in Orfeo's big Act III solo, *Possente spirto*, persuading Charon to let him cross the Styx, he is in danger of over-interpreting each word. Next to such a comparably starry version as John Eliot Gardiner's on DG Archiv (419 250-2) the singers here, like Bostridge, tend to underline heavily in their expressive phrasing so that at times this sounds like a performance of a nineteenth-century opera rather than one from 1607. Natalie Dessay, in the allegorical role of La Musica, the first solo singer one hears, adds to that impression with her fruity soprano, very different from the voices of most period singers. Patrizia Ciofi as Euridice, Véronique Gens as Proserpina and Alice Coote in the small but significant role of the Messenger are all strong artists too, technically perfect, but they too follow the same performing style, with the line-up of men also strong if not quite so characterful. Though the strings of Le Concert d'Astrée tend to be edgy in a way that most period bands have abandoned, the freshness of the whole set is certainly attractive. But first choice rests with Pickett's L'Oiseau-Lyre set with John Mark Ainsley in the title-role and Catherine Bott outstanding as La Musica and Prosperina.

In Harnoncourt's version, the ritornello of the Prologue might almost be by Stravinsky, so sharply do the sounds cut. He is altogether more severe than John Eliot Gardiner. In compensation, the simple and straightforward dedication of this performance is most affecting, and the solo singing, if not generally very characterful, is clean and stylish. One exception is Cathy Berberian as the Messenger. She is strikingly successful and, though differing slightly in style from the others, she sings as part of the team. Excellent recording. The extra clarity and sharpness of focus – even in large-scale ensembles – add to the abrasiveness from the opening *Toccata* onwards, and the 1968 recording sounds immediate and realistic.

With some first-rate solo singing and a restrained, scholarly approach, there is much to enjoy in the Naxos version. However, Sergio Vartolo's speeds are consistently slow. Alessandro Carmignani is a fine, clear Orfeo, coping splendidly with all the technical problems, and his singing in the big solos has a dedicated intensity, but at such slow speeds there is a sleepwalking quality in the results, however beautiful. More seriously, the exchanges between characters never have the dramatic intensity needed. In the instrumental numbers the strings are often uncomfortably edgy. It is as well that full text and translation are provided, when the CD tracks on the disc are radically different from those indicated in the booklet. Clear, well-balanced sound, recorded in the theatre of Puy-en-Velay in France. However, first choice rests with Pickett, with John Mark Ainsley in the title role (O-L 433 545-2).

MORLEY, Thomas (1557–1603)

Ayres and Madrigals: *Absence, hear thou my protestation; Arise, awake; Besides a fountain; Deep lamenting; Fire and lightning; Hard by a crystal fountain; Hark! Alleluia; In every place; Mistress mine; No, no, no, Nigella; O grief ev'n on the bud; Phyllis I fain would die now; Singing alone; Sleep slumbr'ing eyes; Stay heart, run not so fast; With my love.*

(M) *** Decca 476 1971. Consort of Musicke, Rooley.

Morley is generally thought of as a lesser figure than his contemporaries, even though he was the pioneering English madrigalist. This CD should do something to modify the picture of him for, although the lighter *canzonetti* and *balletti* based on Italian models (and in particular Gastoldi) are in evidence, there are more searching and thoughtful pieces. *Deep lamenting, grief betraying* is one such piece, and there are others which make one feel that the range of Morley's musical personality has not been adequately reflected heretofore. This is an interesting and attractive recital and has the benefit of well-projected performances and good recorded sound.

MOSONYI, Mihály (1815–70)

(i) *Piano Concerto in E min.;* (ii) *Symphony No. 1 in D.*

** Marco Polo 8.223539. (i) Körmendi, Slovak State Philh. O (Košice); (ii) Slovak RSO (Bratislava); Stankovsky.

Despite his English origins, Mosonyi is thought of as one of the most representative nineteenth-century Hungarian composers – apart, of course, from the more obvious major figures, Liszt and Erkel. The *Symphony No. 1 in D* is an early work, composed in his late twenties and modelled on the Viennese classics in general and Beethoven in particular. The *Piano Concerto in E minor*, which comes from about the same time, shows the influence of Chopin and Weber. If, like the symphony, it is not strong on individuality, it is at least well-crafted, well-bred music and well worth an occasional airing. Klára Körmendi is the fluent soloist, and she receives decent orchestral support from Robert Stankovsky and his Slovak forces.

MOSZKOWSKI, Moritz
(1854–1925)

Violin Concerto in C, Op. 30; Ballade in G min., Op. 16/1.

*** Hyp. CDA 67389. Little, BBC Scottish SO, Brabbins – KARLOWICZ: *Violin Concerto.* ***

The Moszkowski *Violin Concerto*, first heard in 1883, may not be as inspired as the Karlowicz concerto with which it is coupled, but it delivers many striking ideas over its 34-minute span, from the attractively offbeat opening onwards. The jolly, gallumping first theme in compound time hardly sounds promising material for a 15-minute symphonic movement, but Moszkowski clearly demonstrates how unfair it is that he has regularly been dismissed as merely a composer of miniatures. As in the Karlowicz, Tasmin Little and Martyn Brabbins are most persuasive interpreters, with the playing from the BBC Scottish Orchestra both polished and warmly expressive, which no doubt reflects ample rehearsal time. The *Ballade*, Moszkowski's first orchestral work, developed from a piece for violin and piano, similarly ranging and wide in expression, makes an ideal filler. Full, warm sound, recorded in Caird Hall, Dundee.

Piano Music: Air de ballet, Op. 36/5; Albumblatt, Op. 2; Au crépuscule, Op. 68/3; Barcarolle from Offenbach's 'Contes d'Hoffmann'; Chanson bohème from Bizet's 'Carmen'; Danse russe, Op. 6/4; En autumne, Op. 36/4; Expansion, Op. 36/3; La Jongleuse, Op. 52/4; Minuetto, Op. 68/2; Nocturne, Op. 68/1; Poème de Mai, Op. 67/1; Près de berceau, Op. 58/3; Rêverie, Op. 36/2; Serenata, Op. 15/1; Tarantella, Op. 27/2; Valse mignonne.

(BB) **(*) Hyp. Helios CDH 55141. Tanyel.

Pieces like *Au crépuscule* have a certain sub-Lisztian charm, *La Jongleuse* is an engaging *moto perpetuo*, and *Près de berceau* is the epitome of a salon piece. Setya Tanyel characterizes the music sympathetically, but she is hard put to sustain interest through a 69-minute recording of genre pieces that are heard most effectively as encores at the end of a more substantial programme. The *Air de ballet* is an ideal example, with its brilliant filigree at the close, which sparkles readily in her hands. Truthful recording.

MOYZES, Alexander (1906–84)

Down the River Vah, Suite for Large Orchestra, Op. 26; Germer Dances, Suite for Large Orchestra, Op. 51; Pohronie Dances, Suite for Large Orchestra, Op. 43.

*(*) Marco Polo 8.223278. CSR SO (Bratislava), Lenárd.

This disc contains some attractive dances and colourful (not over-extended) tone-poems, which, although not great music, are yet not unappealing. Their Slavonic flavour and vivid orchestration, with considerable rhythmic interest, help to hold the listener's attention. The performances are enthusiastic, but the orchestral playing and especially the 1989 sound (which produces a scrawny effect at times) are not very inviting. At Naxos price this would be worth considering for the rare repertoire, but its full-price tag gives one pause.

Symphonies Nos. 11, Op. 79; 12, Op. 83.

** Marco Polo 8.225093. Slovak RSO, Slovák.

Moyzes established himself as a pioneer of Slovak national music, and both these works mix Slovakian elements into the Western Romantic tradition. Nothing is remotely atonal: it is all approachable, melodic and boldly coloured. The *Eleventh Symphony* dates from 1978 and begins ominously with repeated timpani strokes, but, from the *Allegro* onwards, the composer's penchant for lively folk material soon emerges. There is no lack of energy. The *Twelfth Symphony* was the composer's last work and follows the conventional pattern of its predecessor. The opening movement (after a slow introduction) is a kind of *moto perpetuo*, which the composer suggested represented 'contemporary living – with everyone running and hurrying, always on the move'. The central slow movement is powerfully reflective, and the finale has plenty of robust vitality. The performances are excellent, and if neither the orchestral playing nor the sound is first class, they are more than satisfactory.

MOZART, Wolfgang Amadeus (1756–91)

SYMPHONIES

Symphony in F, K.19a; Symphonies Nos. 1 in E flat, K.16; 4 in D, K.19; 5 in B flat, K.22; 6 in F, K.43; 7 in D, K.45; 7a in G (Alte Lambacher), K.45a; in B flat, K.45b; 8 in D, K.48; 9 in C, K.73; 10 in G, K.74; in F, K.75; in F, K.76; in D, K.81; 11 in D, K.84; in D, K.95; in C, K.96; in D, K.97; in C, K.102; 12 in G, K.110; 13 in F, K.112; 14 in A, K.114; in D, K.120 & 121; 15 in G, K.124; 16 in C, K.128; 17 in G, K.129; 18 in F, K.130; 19 in E flat, K.132; 20 in D, K.133; 21 in A, K.134; in D, K.161; 22 in C, K.162; 23 in D, K.181; 24 in B flat, K.182; 25 in G min., K.183; 26 in E flat, K.184; 27 in G, K.199; 28 in C, K.200; 29 in A, K.201; 30 in D, K.202; 31 in D (Paris), K.297; 32 in G, K.318; 33 in B flat, K.319; 34 in C, K.338; 35 in D (Haffner), K.385; 36 in C (Linz), K.425; 38 in D (Prague), K.504; 39 in E flat, K.543; 40 in G min., K.550; 41 in C (Jupiter), K.551.

⊕→ (BB) *** EMI 5 85589-2 (11). ECO, Tate.

Jeffrey Tate's survey of the Mozart *Symphonies* is one of the finest things he has done for the gramophone. Recorded over a long period, from 1984 to 2003, his inspiration remained constant. He entered at the deep end by recording Nos. 40 and 41 first, and they remain impressive accounts. In the *Jupiter*, the apt scale of the ECO allows the grandeur of the work to come out fully: on the one hand it has the clarity of a chamber orchestra performance, but on the other, with trumpets and drums, its weight of expression never underplays the scale of the argument, which originally prompted the unauthorized nickname. In both symphonies exposition repeats are observed in outer movements, particularly important in the *Jupiter* finale, which, with its miraculous fugal writing, bears even greater argumentative weight than the first movement, a point firmly established by Tate. Those who like a very plain approach may find his elegant pointing in the slow movements excessive, but Tate's keen imagination on detail, as well as over a broad span, consistently conveys the electricity of a live performance. The recording is well detailed, yet has pleasant reverberation. Both the *Linz* and the *Prague* receive strong but elegant performances, bringing out the operatic overtones in the latter, not just in the *Don Giovanni*-like progressions in the slow introductions but also in the power of the development section and in the wonder of the chromatic progressions in the slow movement, as well as the often surprising mixture of timbres. In the *Linz* Tate is attractively individual, putting rather more emphasis on elegance and finding tenderness in the slow movement, taken (like the adagio of the *Prague*) at a very measured speed.

The first three CDs in the box set are new recordings (2003) and concentrate on his earliest symphonies, including many of the unnumbered symphonies; these early works are full of vitality (even if the authenticity of a couple of them is doubtful): Tate finds a fresh exhilaration in these scores in which the young Mozart was finding his feet, exploring possibilities all the time. There is a surprising variety in these very early works, often pointing to his future brilliance in the opera house.

The follow-up three-disc set comprises Nos. 13–24, written before Mozart's first out-and-out masterpiece among the symphonies (No. 25). The set also includes some of the rarer early unnumbered works, usually adaptations of early opera overtures, and all of them colourful pieces.

Moving forward, from No. 25 onwards, itself very well done, Tate's detailed articulation and fine detail are always telling. In all these works he provides a winning combination of affectionate manners, freshness and elegance. (By the way, the alternative movements, originally included in this middle-batch of symphonies, have been excised on this bargain-box release.) The recordings are fresh and warm throughout this set, which is strongly recommended to those who want authentic modern-instrument performances of the Mozart cycle, and it is especially attractive at super-bargain price.

Symphonies Nos. 18 in F, K.130; in D, K.141a; 19 in E flat, K.132; 20 in D, K.133; 21 in A, K.134; in D, K.135; 26 in E flat, K.161a; 27 in G, K.161b; 22 in C, K.162; 23 in D, K.162b; 24 in B flat, K.173dA.

(M) ★★★ Decca (ADD) 476 17181 (3). AAM, Schröder; Hogwood.

This was the first box of the Academy of Ancient Music's issue of the complete recording of Mozart symphonies using authentic texts and original instruments – and very invigorating it proved. The variety of scale as well as of expression makes it a very refreshing collection, particularly as the style of performance, with its non-vibrato tang, sharply picks out detail of texture rather than moulding the sound together. The recording is excellent, and the CD transfers are bright and clean. The set won the *Gramophone*'s Early Music Award in 1979 and now reappears in the *Gramophone* Awards Collection at mid-price.

Symphonies Nos. 25 in G min., K.183; 26 in E flat, K.184; 28 in C, K.200; 29 in A, K.201; 35 (Haffner) in D, K.385; 36 (Linz) in C, K.425; 38 (Prague) in D, K.504; 39 in E flat, K.543; 40 in G min., K.550; 41 (Jupiter) in C, K.551.

(B) ★★ Teldec 5046 68288-2 (4). Concg. O, Harnoncourt.

Nikolaus Harnoncourt's Mozart, for all its merits, is nothing if not wilful. He made his survey of the later Mozart symphonies between 1983 and 1988, turning from conducting an ensemble of original instruments to the glory of the Concertgebouw Orchestra and establishing his personality immediately, with strong, even gruff accents, yet at times with an approach which (notably in slow movements, with speeds rather slower than usual) is relatively romantic in its expressivness. He consistently secures fine playing, and the Teldec engineers reward him with bright, clear, yet resonant sound. However, the results are of mixed appeal. No. 25 is very purposeful indeed: it opens aggressively, but the lovely slow movement lacks serenity. The unsuppressed energy in the finale brings guttural tuttis.

The opening of No. 26 is comparably pungent, tuttis emphatic and heavy, and the first movement of No. 28 is more *Molto* than *Allegro spiritoso*. Although here the gentle, muted strings in the *Andante* are beautiful, there is a feeling of restlessness too. The last two movements are crisp and fast: the finale

combines lightness of articulation and great energy. No. 29 brings erratic tempi and very bold contrasts in the first movement; in the slow movement there is the most delicate string-playing, but the steady momentum reduces the feeling of repose. The performance of the *Haffner* is refreshingly direct, certainly dramatic, marked by relative unforced tempi; but charm is somewhat missing. In the *Linz* Harnoncourt observes even more repeats than are marked in the regular scores, making it a more expansive work than usual. The *Prague* is generally very successful, superbly played, and Harnoncourt is very generous with repeats (it runs for 38 minutes). Tempi are again erratic in No. 39 (the Minuet is rushed), although the first movement of this symphony is well judged; *No. 40 in G minor* has an unsettled mood overall (hardly Mozartian), with the slow movement very brisk. The *Jupiter* offers superbly disciplined playing, although the results are on the heavy side and the inclusion of all repeats gives an overall playing time of nearly 42 minutes. Nevertheless, for those wanting to try Harnoncourt's way with Mozart, this inexpensive four-CD set, which includes four of the original six CDs in the series, is fair value.

Symphonies Nos. 25 in G min., K.183; 29 in A, K.201; 35 (Haffner); 36 (Linz); 38 (Prague); 39 in E flat; 40 in G min.; 41 in C (Jupiter).

☛ (M) ★★★ DG Trio 474 349-2 (3). VPO, Bernstein.

Bernstein's recordings of Mozart's last and greatest symphonies were taken from live performances between 1984 and 1986, although the two early masterpieces now included in this Trio, which are equally successful (especially the beautifully played No. 29), date from 1990. All have the added adrenalin that is expected (but not always achieved) in live performances. Besides the electricity, Bernstein's Mozart also has breadth and style; only occasionally (as in No. 39) does a suspicion of self-consciousness affect the interpretation. But pacing is consistently well judged, except sometimes in finales, where the VPO are kept very much on their toes with speeds that are perilously brisk. For those not seeking the astringencies of 'authenticity' this is a fine, modern set, with more vitality and charisma than most alternatives. The sound is full and well balanced. The separate issue of Nos. 40 and 41 received a ● in our companion volume.

Symphony No. 29 in A, K.201.

★★(★) Testament SBT2 1217 (2). BPO, Klemperer – BACH: *Suite No. 3 in D*; BEETHOVEN: *Symphony No. 6 (Pastoral).* ★★(★)

In May 1964 Otto Klemperer, aged 79, returned to Berlin to conduct the Berlin Philharmonic in three works that were favourites with him, and he won a rapturous reception. It was over 40 years since his first appearance with the Berlin Philharmonic, and he seemed determined above all to get Karajan's orchestra to produce a distinctive Klemperer sound.

Though the Mozart brings characteristically broad speeds, it erupts into an exuberant account of the finale. First-rate transfers of radio sound.

Symphonies Nos. 35 in D (Haffner); 41 (Jupiter).
(BB) ** EMI Encore 5 85696-2. ASMF, Marriner.

With allegros on the brisk side, yet with rhythms well poised and with immaculate, totally unmannered phrasing, Marriner's 1984 coupling of the *Haffner* and *Jupiter Symphonies* offers direct, unidiosyncratic Mozart. Crisp and polished as the playing is, some may find the performances lacking just a little in both spontaneity and touches of individuality, next to the most magnetic readings, but there are no complaints about the sound, which is forward and full, but not aggressive.

Symphony No. 36 in C (Linz), K.425.
(M) ** BBC (ADD) BBCL 4055-2. LSO, Barbirolli – R.
  STRAUSS: *Ein Heldenleben.* **

From Barbirolli a big-band performance in the old manner – and none the worse for that! However, it must be admitted that Sir John was not in his usual robust form when this concert was recorded, and there is not much evidence of the elegance and élan which distinguished his finest work.

Symphonies Nos. 36 (Linz); 39; Overtures: Così fan tutte; Le nozze di Figaro.
** Guild GMCD 7172. Bournemouth Sinf., Frazor.

These Bournemouth performances of a pair of favourite symphonies offer a model combination of warmth, elegance and finesse, though there is drama too, especially when the timpani open No. 39 so boldly. The recording is most naturally balanced. The overtures are neatly done, though they could have a shade more sparkle. But this is an enjoyable programme, showing the conductor and orchestra as natural Mozartians.

Symphonies Nos. 38 (Prague); 39; 40; 41 (Jupiter).
(B) ** Virgin 2x1 5 62010-22. L. Classical Players, Norrington.

Norrington's readings have many individual points of detail, which – even if not all are convincing – bring the sense of a fresh approach, and his players are certainly at one with him. Exposition repeats are included throughout, and after a strong, grave introduction the first movement of the *Prague* is taken at a lively but not exaggerated pace, and if tuttis are somewhat fierce the second subject has warmth and elegance. The *Andante* too flows agreeably and the finale has plenty of energy and bite. *No. 40 in G minor* opens briskly but is so lightly articulated that there is no sense of hurry until the slow movement, which is surely not relaxed enough. The Minuet is curiously mellow and unpointed, but the finale combines neatness with energy.

However, on the second disc the measured introduction to No. 39 is so fast that it is barely recogniz-

able. The result is again refreshingly different but totally misses the grandeur which is implicit in the piece. Other speeds are disconcertingly fast too, although the central movements of the *Jupiter* flow agreeably and the finale, if explosive, certainly has weight. Those who want period performances of these masterpieces that are characterful rather than purely tasteful will find Norrington's way specific, but less eccentric than, say, Harnoncourt. He is very well recorded. However, collectors wanting outstanding versions of Mozart's late symphonies (Nos. 35, 36, 38 and 39–41) should turn to Virgin's five-disc super-bargain box, where Menuhin's performances with the Sinfonia Varviso are outstanding in every way (5 61678-2 – see our main volume).

CHAMBER MUSIC

Clarinet Quintet in A, K.581.
** Chan. H 10151. Mozkovenko, Borodin Qt –
  BRAHMS: *Clarinet Quintet.* *

Recorded in 1969, this is an eminently satisfactory account of the *Quintet* without in any way achieving the distinction one would expect from so celebrated an ensemble. The Brahms coupling is pretty lugubrious and diminishes the competitiveness of the issue.

(i) Clarinet Quintet; (ii) Violin Sonatas Nos. 24, K.376; 33, K.481.
(M) *** Cal. Approche (ADD) CAL 5628. (i) Zahradnik, Talich Qt; (ii) Messiereur, Bogunia.

The *Clarinet Quintet* is exquisitely done. Bohuslav Zahradnik's contribution has much delicacy of feeling and colour; he is highly seductive in the slow movement, and even in the finale the effect is gentle in the most appealing way without any loss of vitality. The recording balance is exemplary. The two *Violin Sonatas* are also beautifully played in a simple, direct style that is wholly persuasive. The recording is clearly detailed and well balanced, if slightly more shallow.

Divertimento No. 17 in D, K.334 (chamber version).
(**) Pearl mono GEM 0129. Vienna Octet (members) – SCHUBERT: *Piano Quintet (Trout).* (**)

In the 1955 edition *The Record Guide* gave both the recordings on the Pearl disc two stars, their highest accolade. The Mozart appeared in one of Decca's earliest LP supplements at the end of 1950. The second repeat of the Trio in the Minuet is not observed and there are two cuts in the finale, one of them substantial and both unwelcome. But those who recall the Vienna Octet's broadcasts and records of this period will relish the elegance and grace of their playing. Roger Beardsley has gone to great trouble in his remastering to do justice to these performances. He claims that now for the first time they can be heard to far better effect than in the early

1950s, and those who recall hearing them will recognize a great improvement.

Piano Quartets Nos. 1 in G min., K.478; 2 in E flat, K.493.

(BB) ** Naxos 8.554274. Menuhin Festival Piano Qt.

Piano Quartets Nos. 1–2. Rondo in A min., K.411.

(M) ** RCA (ADD) 09026 63075-2. Rubinstein, Guaneri Qt (members).

The Menuhin Festival Piano Quartet is an international ensemble with an excellent German pianist, Friedemann Rieger, an American violinist, Nora Chastain, the Scottish-born violist, Paul Coletti, and a French cellist, Francis Gouton. They give very spirited accounts of both quartets, observing not only the exposition but also second-time repeats in the first movements, though the brilliant pianist is a little monochrome. They are not as tonally subtle as our first recommendations, but the acoustic in which they are recorded is a bit dry and so does not flatter them.

The pity is that Rubinstein's bright and invigorating playing and indeed the string-timbre of the members of the Guarneri Quartet have been given artificial brightness and their forwardness exaggerated by the recording balance. The mercurial re-creation of two of Mozart's most delectable chamber works is here in the hands of a pianist who is nothing if not an individualist, and the liveliness of Rubinstein – even in his eighties enjoying himself with fellow-musicians – is ample reason for hearing this coupling, even if the string sound is not wholly congenial.

Piano & Wind Quintet in E flat, K.452.

(M) **(*) Warner Elatus 2464 60445-2. Barenboim, Soloists of Chicago SO – BEETHOVEN: Quintet. **(*)

(M) *(*) Telarc CD 80114. Previn, V. Wind Soloists – BEETHOVEN: Quintet, Op. 16. *(*)

Barenboim shares Mozart and Beethoven with members of his Chicago orchestra, and the result is undoubtedly fresh and vital. But his comparatively brisk approach to the first movement misses the feeling of relaxation that this music ideally needs, and although the players work very well together elsewhere, and especially in the pert finale, this well-recorded performance is not a first choice.

Previn leads admirably throughout this performance of one of the most engaging of Mozart's chamber works, but the wind support is robust rather than refined. The opening of the slow movement brings elegant playing from the pianist but a heavy response from his colleagues. Previn articulates the engaging main theme of the finale most attractively, and here the effect is very spirited. The resonant acoustic tends to spread the sound, but the balance is quite well managed. This CD is not strongly recommended. First choice rests with Perahia (Sony SMK 42099).

String quartets

String Quartets Nos. 3, K.156; 14, K.387; 15, K.421.

⊶ (M) *** Cal. Approche (ADD) CAL 5241. Talich Qt.

String Quartets Nos. 8–12, K.168–172.

⊶ (M) *** Cal. Approche (ADD) CAL 5247. Talich Qt.

String Quartets Nos. 16, K.428; 17 (Hunt), K.458.

⊶ (M) *** Cal. Approche (ADD) CAL 5242. Talich Qt. – HAYDN: String Quartet No. 74. ***

The prize-winning recordings by the Talich Quartet are here reissued in their previous couplings. As we have commented before, their playing is immaculate in ensemble and they have a special kind of shared intimacy which yet is immediately communicative. They are the soul of finesse and make music with expressive simplicity, while bringing vitality to allegros and conveying a consistent feeling of spontaneous vitality throughout. They are naturally balanced. The analogue recordings have not been further remastered and remain beautiful, very warm and smooth on top, slightly middle- and bass-orientated. There are few records of Mozart's Quartets to match these.

String Quartets Nos. 14–19 (Haydn Quartets).

(M) ** Decca Trio 473 963-2 (3). Ysaÿe Qt.

The performances by the Ysaÿe Quartet are by no means to be dismissed, but they are in the last resort disappointing. The G major is more closely balanced than the D minor, and on the second disc this also seems to apply, if to a lesser extent, when comparing the Hunt with K.428. The playing in K.387 is what the French call nerveux and there is little sense of space in the faster movements or of repose in the slow movement. In the first movement of the D minor the players' feelings do not seem to be engaged, and there is a similar impression in the Andante con moto of K.428, although they are at their most impressive in the calm atmosphere of the Adagio of the Hunt. The Dissonance Quartet opens well, but the slow movement is bland and here, as in K.464, the resonant sound brings inflated textures. The playing is most enjoyable in the finale of the A major work, which is very spirited.

String Quartets Nos. 14–19 (Haydn Quartets); 20–21(Hoffmeister); 22–3 (Prussian).

⊶ (M) *** Warner Elatus (ADD) 2-CD 2564 60678-2 (2) (Nos.14–17 & 20); 2564 60809-2 (2) (Nos. 18–19; 21–3). Alban Berg Qt.

These splendid recorded performances derive from the set made by the Alban Berg Quartet in the latter half of the 1970s, available on four CDs and highly praised by us in our main volume (4509 95495-2). This pair of separate reissues is most welcome.

String Quartets Nos. 14–16; 17 (Hunt); 18; 19
(Dissonance) (Haydn Quartets); 20 (Hoffmeister);
21–23 (Prussian Nos. 1–3); (i) String Quintets Nos. 3
in C, K.515; 4 in G min., K.516; (ii) Piano Concerto
No. 12 (for piano & string quartet), K.414 (K.385);
Piano Quartet No. 2 in E flat, K.493.

(BB) **(*) EMI 5 85581-2 (7). Alban Berg Qt., with (i)
M. Wolf; (ii) Brendel.

This later EMI Alban Berg survey was made between
1986 and 1989, and in 1990 Brendel joined them for
the pairing of the *A major Piano Concerto,* K.414, and
the *E flat Piano Quartet,* and this coupling is the
highlight of the set. Not surprisingly the group are at
their finest in the six *Haydn Quartets,* playing with a
complete integration of texture and much subtlety of
light and shade. (The opening of the *Dissonance
Quartet* has remarkable atmosphere.) Their warmth
is unquestioned; however, although there is much
elegance and many delicate touches, sometimes there
is a passionate forcefulness, an almost orchestral style
which all but robs the music of its natural intimacy.

In the *Hoffmeister* and *Prussian Quartets* the playing brings sumptuous tone and the greatest polish,
but everything sounds a bit overnourished. As quartet playing this is all beyond reproach, and undoubtedly gives pleasure; but these players do not always
bring Mozart's musical essence to the listener in the
way that they undoubtedly intend, although the
recording is excellent.

Markus Wolf joins them in the pair of *String
Quintets,* and again they have the benefit of a warm
acoustic environment; they are forwardly placed,
which serves to underline their rich sonority and
tonal body. Again their playing commands much
admiration, but they rarely seem to penetrate far
below the music's surface. There is little of the
inwardness, spirituality or poignancy that one
finds, for instance, in the Grumiaux versions on
Philips.

In the string quartet version of the concerto,
Mozart made no change to the score, simply pointing out that the wind parts could be omitted, and
that those for strings could be played by four solo
instruments. The concerto works surprisingly well
in this chamber version, with Brendel more relaxed
than in his Philips recording of the full concerto,
with delightful interplay between piano and quartet.
The rapt *Andante* brings playing of Beethovenian
gravity. The *Piano Quartet* brings a performance
equally illuminating, with Brendel at his most sparkling in the finale, helped by the bright, immediate
recording.

String Quartet No. 15 in D min., K.421.

(B) *** EMI Début 5 85638-2. Atrium Qt –
   SHOSTAKOVICH: *String Quartet No. 7;*
   TCHAIKOVSKY: *String Quartet No. 3.* ***

The present disc is part of the invaluable EMI Début
series and serves as a visiting card for the young
Atrium String Quartet. They hail from St Petersburg

and were the winners of the 2003 London International String Quartet; they were coached by Iosif
Levinzon, the cellist of the Taneyev Quartet. Their
programme is intelligently chosen, not just as a vehicle for their artistry, but as repertoire useful for the
collector. They play Mozart K.421 – the only one of
his *Haydn Quartets* in a minor key – with much
understanding and sympathy, and they penetrate the
underlying melancholy of the *Andante* to telling
effect. Throughout their recital they play with great
finesse and tonal beauty, and EMI have given them
first-rate recorded sound.

String Quartets Nos. 15 in D min., K.421; 16 in E flat,
K.428; 17 in B flat (Hunt); 18 in A, K.464; 19 in C
(Dissonance); 20 in D (Hoffmeister), K.499; 21 in D,
K.575; 22 in B flat, K.589; 23 in F, K.590 (Prussian
Nos. 1–3); (i) String Quintets Nos. 2 in C , K.515; 3 in
G min., K.516; 5 in D, K.593; 6 in E flat, K.614.

✪ (M) (***) DG Westminster mono/stereo 474
   000-2. Amadeus Qt, (i) with Aronowitz.

These legendary recordings were made for the Westminster label in the early days of mono LP, beginning
in 1951 – three years after the Amadeus Quartet's
Wigmore Hall début – and continuing in 1954, 1955
and 1957 (the *D major Quintet,* which is stereo). The
venues chosen – London's Conway Hall, Hampstead
Parish Church, Abbey Road Studios, the Beethoven-
saal in Hanover and the Hamburg-Blankenese Studio
– each provided a pleasing acoustic, and the sound is
real and vivid, a little forward, but not excessively so.
The performances are very distinguished – indeed
thrilling – wonderfully natural and spontaneous. The
group's cellist, Martin Lovett has commented: 'They
were probably the best of us because we were so fresh
and keen.' That is certainly true; later recordings by
this group may show keener insights gained from
experience, but here the response to the music is
instinctive and wonderfully vibrant. Even if tempi
are sometimes pressed hard, the effect is often
inspired, and that applies equally to the warmth and
delicacy of the relaxed slow movements. The vibrato
which always characterized their playing is never
overdone. Indeed these performances, to quote Tully
Potter, who wrote the accompanying biographical
notes, 'still have the power to amaze'. The box is
described as a 'limited edition' so an early purchase is
essential.

String Quartet No. 20 in D (Hoffmeister), K.499.

(M) (**(*)) BBC mono BBCL 4137-2. Smetana Qt –
   BEETHOVEN: *String Quartet No. 1 (**);*
   SMETANA: *String Quartet No. 1. (***)*

The performance of the *Hoffmeister Quartet,* K.499,
comes from a BBC relay from the Royal Festival Hall
in June 1965. The mono sound is very good indeed, if
slightly dry. The playing of the Smetanas has polish,
ardour and freshness, and there is not the slightest
touch of routine. Recommended.

String Quartets Nos. 20 (Hoffmeister), K.499; 21, (Prussian No. 1) K.575; (ii) Violin Sonata No. 17, K.296.

⊶ (M) ★★★ Cal. Approche CAL 5244. Talich Qt.

String Quartets Nos. 22 in B flat (Prussian No. 2), K.589; 23 in F (Prussian No. 3), K.590; Adagio and Fugue in C min., K.546..

⊶ (M) ★★★ Cal. Approche CAL 5245. Talich Qt.

The Talich couplings of the *Hoffmeister* and *Prussian Quartets* are digital and the recording is brighter and more present than in the earlier *Quartets*. The playing has comparable sensibilty and plenty of vitality.

Concertos

Adagio for Violin and Orchestra in E, K.261; Rondo for Violin and Orchestra in C, K.373.

(BB) (★★★) Naxos mono 8.110975. Milstein, RCA Victor SO, Golschmann – DVOŘÁK; GLAZUNOV: *Violin Concerto.* (★★★)

These Mozart pieces are given with all the elegance and finesse – and purity – that Milstein commanded, and make a splendid foil to the Dvořák and Glazunov *Concertos*.

Flute Concerto No. 2 in D (arr. Szell for cello).

★(★) Transart TR 121. Haimovitz, O de Bretagne, Sanderling – HAYDN: *Cello Concertos Nos. 1–2.* ★(★)

The conductor George Szell had the idea that Mozart's *Oboe Concerto*, K.314, later rejigged by Mozart himself as the *D major Flute Concerto*, was originally written for cello. He transcribed the outer movements very effectively, but then found the slow movement unsuitable for cello adaptation. Instead, for a slow movement he used the *Andante in A*, K.470, for violin and orchestra, written much later, in 1785, transcribing the solo part for cello. When K.470 is a rarity, a piece thought to have been written as a substitute slow movement for a Viotti concerto, it makes an apt enough choice, even if the inconsistency of style is immediately evident. In this live recording Haimovitz gives a strong, sympathetic performance of this composite cello concerto, sadly marred by the same flaws of dry sound and insecure orchestral playing as the two Haydn concertos on the disc.

Flute concertos

Flute Concertos Nos. 1–2, K.313/4; (i) Flute and Harp Concerto in C, K.299.

(M) ★★★ RCA 82876 59409-2. Galway, ASMF, Marriner, (i) with Robles.

(BB) ★★(★) Naxos 8.557011. Gallois, Swedish CO, (i) with Pierre.

James Galway and his favourite harpist partner, Marisa Robles – always characterful – take an expansive, warmly expressive view of the slow movement of the *Flute and Harp Concerto*. As in previous recordings with Galway, she also matches him in a delightfully bouncy account of the finale, sharper in focus than Pahud on EMI. In the solo concertos too, Galway takes an expansive, expressive view of the slow movements and a winningly relaxed one of the allegros. Fine recording and a useful addition to RCA's mid-priced 'Classic Library'.

Patrick Gallois is a delightful player, as is obvious in the Rondos of both solo concertos. But, surprisingly, the playing of the Swedish Chamber Orchestra is on the heavy side, not helped by the resonance of Örebro Concert Hall, which also affects the harp focus. So while these are stylish and enjoyable performances, they lack the lightness of touch that Galway, Robles and Marriner bring to them.

Piano concertos

Piano Concertos Nos. 9 in E flat (Jeunehomme), K.271; 20 in D min., K.466; 23 in A, K. 488; 24 in C min., K. 491.

⊶ (BB) ★★★ Virgin 4-CD 5 62259-2 (4). Pletnev, Deutsche Kammerphilharmonie – HAYDN: *Piano Concertos & Sonatas.* ★★★

Pletnev and the Deutsche Kammerphilharmonie have obviously established a close rapport, and each of these performances is individually and positively characterized. The *Jeunehomme* certainly sounds youthful, bringing crisp, precise articulation in the first movement and a poised *Andante*, yet with real expressive depth, followed by a brisk, attractively jaunty finale. The cadenzas are Mozart's own.

The uneasy, *sotto voce* opening of the *D minor*, K.466, is full of underlying tension, which is maintained throughout the strong tuttis, but Pletnev relaxes completely for the delicate lyrical secondary theme and again in the *Romance*, bringing some exquisite articulation to the outer sections and a perfectly judged centrepiece. In this concerto he uses Beethoven's cadenzas, which bring a sudden striking change of mood in the finale, otherwise lighthearted, and with some fine wind playing from the orchestra. In Pletnev's hands the slow movement of K.488 is among the most beautiful on record, the finale the most rushed. Here he returns to Mozart's cadenzas. But in the *C minor Concerto* (K.491) he is again intensely dramatic, Beethovenian in feeling and powerful in conception: his own first-movement cadenza looks even more forward into the nineteenth century; and there is commanding playing from all concerned. Excellent recording throughout. This now comes recoupled in a budget box with equally impressive performances of piano concertos and sonatas of Haydn. It makes a fascinating set, well worth exploring, even if this involves duplication.

Piano Concertos Nos. (i) 9, K.271; (ii) 20, K.466.

(M) (★★(★)) Sony mono/stereo 512863-2. Serkin; with (i) Marlboro Festival O, Schneider; (ii) Phd. O, Ormandy.

In his last years, Rudolf Serkin embarked on a Mozart concerto cycle with Abbado for DG which were remarkable for an artist of his age. They were generally well received, but by comparison with his earlier achievements as a Mozartian they struck us as at times just a shade didactic, even ponderous. The *Jeunehomme Concerto*, with the Marlboro Festival Orchestra under the violinist Alexander Schneider, comes from 1956, while the *D minor* with Ormandy and the Philadelphia Orchestra was recorded in 1951, in the first years of the LP. In the 1950s Serkin's Mozart still had some of the lightness of touch and style that distinguished his pre-war collaboration with Adolf Busch. The sound is a bit opaque but there is no doubting the distinction of the music-making – not least on the part of that generally underrated maestro Ormandy.

Piano Concertos Nos. 11 in F, K.413; 12 in A, K.414; 13 in C, K.415 (chamber versions).
*** Hyp. CDA 67358. Tomes, Gaudier Ens.

Mozart himself arranged the orchestral parts of these concertos for chamber forces, the first three of the masterly sequence of piano concertos that he wrote for Vienna. These works have been recorded in chamber form before, but this time, even though a double-bass is added to the usual string quartet, the result is lighter and more intimate than in previous versions, helped by a clear, dry, recording acoustic. There are few recording pianists to match Susan Tomes in clarity of articulation, and here she leads performances which sparkle from beginning to end, with every note cleanly defined. Speeds are relatively fast, with slow movements kept moving to bring out their soaring lyricism.

Piano Concertos Nos. 13, K.415; 14 in E flat, K.449; 23 in A, K.488.
(BB) **(*) Warner Apex 2564 60448-2. Pires, Gulbenkian Foundation CO of Lisbon, Guschlbauer.

Maria João Pires, in a triptych of her earliest recordings (1973–4) for Erato, plays with spirit and taste as well as immaculate small-scale fingerwork. She plays the lovely slow movement of K.488 delicately and gently, yet she sparkles in the finale. Her playing at that time reminds one a little of Ingrid Haebler's earliest records for Vox, and she offers many personal insights. Barenboim, for instance, may inflect the second theme of the first movement of K.415 with greater imagination, but Pires holds her own elsewhere. Guschlbauer gives her most musical support and provides robust orchestral tuttis in the outer movements of the two early concertos. The recording can hardly be faulted, for the engineers provide a realistic balance and the sound is warm and pleasingly intimate. An enjoyable bargain.

Piano Concertos Nos. 13, K.425; 23, K.488.
(M) (**) EMI mono 5 62823-2. Michelangeli, Alessandro Scarlatti O, Caracciolo – HAYDN: *Piano Concerto No. 11.* **

Immaculate pianism from Michelangeli, of course, but the playing in the *C major Concerto* seems a little studied, with some curious accenting. However, the simplicity of his approach in the *A major Concerto* brings its own rewards, and if the *Adagio* is a trifle cool the finale has an attractive rhythmic lift, thanks at least in part to Franco Caracciolo's contribution with the Alessandro Scarlatti Orchestra. Good, faithful, mono recording.

Piano Concertos Nos. 16 in D, K.451; 24 in C min., K.491; 25 in C, K.503; 26 in D (Coronation), K.537; 27 in B flat, K.595.
(B) **(*) Double Decca 475 181-2 (2). Schiff, Camerata Academica des Mozarteum, Salzburg, Végh.

András Schiff's recordings with Sándor Végh and the Camerata Academica of the Salzburg Mozarteum were made at various times between 1989 and 1994. The playing has exemplary taste and is distinguished by refined musicianship, though the recording balance tends to place Schiff's Bösendorfer rather distantly in an acoustic that may perhaps be a touch too resonant for some collectors. Schiff eschews a wide range of dynamics and conveys splendid intimacy in his dialogue with Végh and his players. There is a wonderful unanimity of phrasing and musical thinking from the strings and some superb wind playing, every note finely placed and every phrase shaped with keen sensitivity. One snag is that the rare *D major Concerto*, K.451, is split between the two CDs.

Piano Concertos Nos. 18 in B flat, K.456; 19 in F, K.459; Rondo in D, K.382.
⌐ ✿ (M) *** Warner Elatus 2564 60810-2. Barenboim, BPO.

Barenboim immediately puts his personal seal on this CD with his captivating account of the *D major Rondo*, a work of much charm but also repetitive, which lends itself to flexibility. Here, by imaginative variation of tempo and dynamic, it sounds wonderfully fresh. But so do both the Concertos. They are brimming over with Barenboim's joy in the music, with delightfully sprung rhythms and winningly felicitous slow movements, especially that for K.456 with its reminder of Barbarina's little aria in *Le nozze di Figaro*. The totally infectious finales end each work in a mood of blissful happiness, especially the *B flat major Concerto*, which is a live performance of special zest. The Berlin Philharmonic respond to Barenboim's flair and affectionate elegance with especially elegant woodwind playing, and the recording balance could not be improved on. A treasure of a disc – and Barenboim uses Mozart's own cadenzas.

(i; ii) Piano Concerto No. 19, K.459; (i; ii; iii) Double Piano Concerto in E flat, K.365; (i; iv) Triple Piano Concerto in F, K.242.
(BB) *(*) EMI Encore (ADD) 5 85456-2. (i) Hephzibah Menuhin, (ii) Bath Festival O; (iii) Fou Ts'ong ; (iv) Yaltah & Jeremy Menuhin , LPO; all cond. Yehudi Menuhin.

This family compilation from the 1960s is something of a disappointment. Hephzibah's performance of the *F major solo Concerto* is heavy-handed, her playing marred by some insensitive phrasing, and this cannot compare with other recommended versions. The *Double* and *Triple Concertos* are somewhat more successful, yet it is surprising that there is not more of a conveyed sense of enjoyment and high spirits. The playing is quite polished, but the *E flat Concerto* is careful rather than spontaneous, and K.242, not one of Mozart's best works, also lacks sparkle.

Piano Concerto No. 20 in D min., K.466.

(M) *** DG (ADD) 463 649-2. S. Richter, Warsaw PO, Wislocki – BEETHOVEN: *Piano Concerto No. 3; Rondo.* *(*)

Richter proves his virtuosity by restraint, and this is the quality running right through his extremely fine performance of the *D minor Concerto*. He lets Mozart's music speak for itself, but whether in the choice of tempo, a touch of rubato or some finely moulded phrase, his mastery is always apparent. The slow movement is beautifully shaped, its opening theme phrased with perfect grace, and the closing pages are exquisite. The buoyancy of the finale is a joy. Wislocki and the Warsaw orchestra provide an accompaniment of character, and although the recording sounds dated in the matter of string-tone, the piano image remains realistic. This reissue is fully worthy to take a place among DG's 'Originals', and it is a pity that the coupling is so disappointing.

Piano Concertos Nos. 20, K.466; 21 in C, K.467.

(BB) ** EMI Encore 5 74741-2. Zacharias, Bav. RSO, Zinman.

Christian Zacharias is a much-admired Mozartian in Germany. He is an artist of strong classical instinct, although less impressive in the variety and subtlety of keyboard colour he has at his command. These performances are thoroughly acceptable, but neither account challenges existing recommendations.

Piano Concertos Nos. 20, K.466; 23 in A, K.488; 24 in C min. K.491; 25 in C, K.503.

(BB) *** Virgin 2x1 5 62343-2 (2). Tan (fortepiano), LCP, Norrington.

Melvyn Tan radiates delight in what he is doing, and the playing here has both imagination and poise. The fortepiano may be less able than a modern concert grand to convey the dark *Don Giovanni* colourings of the *D minor Concerto*, K.466, and the tragic overtones of the slow movement of the *C minor* (No. 24), where Tan does not help himself by adopting a rather brisk tempo; but these readings have an impressive flair. He tries not to see the *C minor Concerto* through Beethovenian eyes and approaches it with great freshness, shaping the finale with subtlety and finesse, and he is equally thought-provoking in the *C major* (No. 25). The London Classical Players under Norrington are generally supportive, playing with poise and grace, and the naturally balanced EMI recording does justice to their artistry.

Piano Concertos Nos. 20, K.466; 25, K.503 (arr. Hummel).

*** BIS CD 1147. Shiraga, with Wiese, Clemente, Benyi.

Odd as it may seem to record such arrangements as these when there are so many recordings of these great concertos in their original form, these fine performances from Fumiko Shiraga, fresh and perceptive, give us important insights into performance practice in Mozart's time and after. These arrangements by Hummel are quite different from Mozart's own arrangements of his concertos, K.413, 414 and 415, which with string accompaniment retain the feeling of concertos; these Hummel arrangements are in effect self-sufficient piano transcriptions of the whole work, with flute, violin and cello added simply as trimmings. The piano enters instantly and is never silent for a single bar, the other instruments often simply doubling the lines in the piano part. The big loss is that there is no sense of a new arrival when the piano takes up the solo part after the opening tutti; one simply hears two versions of the exposition section. The slow movements of both works give the most striking instances of Hummel's performance practice, when he radically elaborates what is in the published scores with ornamentation and modified passage-work. Hummel's modifications of the solo part of K.503 are particularly relevant when, as a boy, he was studying with Mozart at the very time the concerto was written; and for many years after that it became a favourite party-piece for him in his career as a virtuoso pianist. The modifications to the solo part in the fast outer movements are fascinating but less striking, and it is worth noting how elaborate are the cadenzas which Hummel provides, longer than many. With clear sound tending to favour the piano rather than the attendant instruments – all very well played by distinguished performers – these are consistently refreshing performances.

Piano Concertos Nos. 21, K.467; 22 in E flat, K.482.

⊶ (M) *** EMI (ADD) 5 62750-2 [5 62767-2]. Fischer, Philh. O, Sawallisch.

Annie Fischer's vintage coupling was much treasured when it first appeared in 1959 on a mono LP and, while the general style of performance of Mozart concertos in recent years has tended to become more robust, Miss Fischer's gentle, limpid touch, with its frequent use of half-tones, still gives much pleasure. The slow movements of both concertos are beautifully done, and the pianist's intimate manner is often shared by the Philharmonia wind soloists, who offer playing of polish and delicacy. Sawallisch's contribution is also considerable, and his firm directing hand ensures that neither performance becomes effete. These are essentially small-scale readings, and the refined approach does not reduce the opportunities for displaying sparkle in finales. Fischer's silken touch is higly persuasive and the recording is nicely balanced, the piano full in tone, and the orchestra does not sound too dated. An obvious candidate for EMI's 'Great Recordings of the Century'.

Piano Concertos Nos. 22, K.482; 23, K.488.
(M) **(*) Warner Elatus 2564 61174-2. Barenboim, BPO.

These come from Barenboim's digital re-recordings of the key Mozart Concertos with the Berlin Philharmonic, directed from the keyboard in the early 1990s, playing most expressively for him. The *E flat major Concerto* is the more rewarding of the two performances here, the *Andante* obviously deeply felt, and the finale, in which Barenboim chooses to play an abridged version of a cadenza by Edwin Fischer, agreeably lighthearted. However, the lovely *Adagio* of the *A major*, which is very leisured, is self-conscious and this performance is less spontaneous-sounding overall. Both recordings are very well balanced.

Piano Concerto No. 23, K.488.
(M) *** DG 471 351-2. Pollini, VPO, Boehm –
BEETHOVEN: *Piano Concerto No. 5 (Emperor)*. ***

This is one of the finest CDs in the 'Pollini Edition'. He gives a superbly poised account of the *A major Concerto*, with a vibrant sense of line. Every phrase here seems to speak, and everything is admirably paced. He is given excellent support from Boehm and the Vienna orchestra and the analogue recording is warm, well detailed and finely balanced, and has transferred very well to CD.

Piano Concertos Nos. (i) 24, K.491; (ii) 27, K.595.
(M) (**) Orfeo mono C 536001B. Casadesus, VPO, with (i) Mitropoulos; (ii) Schuricht.

Any reminder of Casadesus's artistry is to be welcomed: his stature as a Mozartian was unquestioned, and his concerto recordings with George Szell were legendary in their day. The value of the present issue is somewhat diminished, however, by the inferior quality of the Austrian Radio recordings. The *C minor*, K.491, with Mitropoulos at the helm of the Vienna Philharmonic, comes from a Salzburg Festival performance in 1956 but sounds thin and shallow, almost as if it had been made on a domestic tape recorder. The *B flat*, K.595, made in 1961 with Schuricht, is better, but only marginally so. Casadesus is on characteristically good form in both works, but the disc's sonic limitations call for much tolerance.

(i) Piano Concerto No. 26, K.537; (ii) Concert Rondos for Piano and Orchestra Nos. 1 in D, K.382; 2 in A, K.386; (i; iii) Double Piano Concerto in E flat, K.365.
(M) **(*) DG mono 474 611-2. Seeman, (i) BPO; (ii) Bamberg SO; (iii) with Foldes.

These mono recordings date from the early 1950s and were originally reviewed by us in the very first *Penguin Guide to Bargain Records*. About the solo concertos we said: 'An outstanding *Coronation*, with well-rounded piano tone in proportion to the work and its accompaniment.' Carl Seeman brings freshness and clarity to the finale especially and the *Concert Rondo in D major*, written to replace the rondo of an early D major concerto, is a treasure. If anything, the *A major Rondo* added here is even more elegant. Seeman's style is precise but totally Mozartian.

About the *E flat Double Concerto* (differently coupled on its original issue) we had more reservations concerning the orchestral accompaniment, but suggested that 'the pianists play it with enthusiasm and a high degree of competence'. It is perhaps a little humourless, but the finale is infectious. The recording of the pianos remains excellent; the orchestral sound is a little rougher here.

Piano Concertos Nos. 26, K.537; 27, K.595.
☛ (M) *** Warner Elatus 2564 60679-2. Barenboim, BPO.

This 1988–9 coupling from Barenboim is first class in every way, beautifully played, with warm, vigorous accompaniments from the Berlin Philharmonic which do not sound inflated. There is a hint of sobriety in both slow movements, but they are both memorable and each is perfectly offset by the lighthearted contrast of the finale which follows. A most enjoyable coupling, drawn from a highly distinguished cycle.

Violin concertos

Violin Concertos Nos. 1–5; 6, K.268; 7, K.271a; in D (Adelaide; harmonized & orch. Marius Casadesus), K.Anh.294a; (i) Concertone in C for 2 Violins, Oboe, Cello & Orchestra, K.190. Divertimento No. 15 in B flat, K.287; Serenade No. 7 in D (Haffner): 2nd–4th movements only; (ii) Sinfonia concertante for Violin, Viola & Orchestra in E flat, K.364.
(BB) ** EMI 5 85030-2 (5). Yehudi Menuhin, Bath Festival. O, or Menuhin Festival. O (K.271a & K.Anh. 294a); with (i) Lysy, Dobson, Simpson; (ii) Barshai.

These recordings nearly all date from the early 1960s, although K.271a and the so-called '*Adelaide*' *Concerto* were added a decade later, and the sound is fuller in consequence. This particular pairing is apt, for each is of doubtful origin, though both Blüme and Einstein suggest that No. 7 is largely the work of Mozart. It seems likely that he began it, lost interest in it and left it for someone else to finish off. Menuhin is just the artist to give these works persuasive performances, also inspiring his Festival Orchestra to accompany him with an infectious spring. Fascinatingly he uses cadenzas by Enescu in No. 7 and by Hindemith in the *Adelaide*. No. 6 is almost certainly the work of another composer, but if it is accepted by the listener simply as a late-eighteenth-century work of better than average quality, the music is agreeable enough, and Menuhin's affectionate warmth makes the most of it.

In the five authentic concertos Menuhin uses cadenzas of his own, and many may feel that they are not Mozartian. Otherwise these performances give an engaging sense of musicians making intimate music together for the joy of it. One is always conscious that this is the phrasing of a master musician who can also provide the lightest touch in finales, which are alert and extrovert. In the *Concertone* Mozart put his own fingerprint on the oboe part, which, in Michael Dobson's expert hands, has nearly as much to offer the listener as the contribution from the two solo string players. The snag is that the remastering does not flatter the original recordings. Throughout the stereo has a bright sheen and the orchestral violins are made to sound thin and glassy above the stave.

For the *Divertimento* Menuhin uses a chamber orchestra rather than a chamber ensemble, yet the group is of Mozartian size and cannot be faulted in terms of style; and Menuhin makes a good job of the demanding solo fiddle section in the *Theme and Variations*. The performance is responsive and spontaneous, and the recorded sound is more agreeable than in the concertos.

In the *Sinfonia concertante* Menuhin and Rudolf Barshai make a fine team with happily similar views, but again the transfer does not flatter the orchestral strings. The inclusion of only the three concertante movements (the second-movement *Andante*, followed by the *Minuet* and *Trio* and *Rondo*) from the *Haffner Serenade* makes for a curious omission, particularly as Menuhin successfully recorded the whole work, and the fifth disc, on which these excerpts appear, plays for only 57 minutes. Nevertheless, at bargain price this set might be worth considering for the three rare works of doubtful lineage. But it is a pity that the transfers were not better managed.

Violin Concertos Nos. (i) *1 in B flat, K.207;* (ii) *2 in D, K.211; 4 in D, K.218;* (i) *Adagio in E, K. 261.*
⊕━ (M) *** EMI 5 62825-2. Mutter; (i) ASMF, Marriner; (ii) Philh. O, Muti.

Anne-Sophie Mutter made her Mozartian début with Karajan on DG with a famous youthful coupling of the *G major* and *A major Violin Concertos* (K.216 and K.219). She then went on, in 1981, to record the two *D major Concertos* for EMI with a different orchestra and conductor, and the results were hardly less successful. A decade later, changing conductors once again, she provided a delightful successor, offering the *B flat Concerto*, with a quicksilver finale, and an exquisite account of the *Adagio in E major*. Throughout these performances she was given very sensitive support from both Muti and Marriner. Her playing combines purity and classical feeling, delicacy and incisiveness, and is admirably expressive. Its freshness is also most appealing. Moreover, the digital

recording is consistently good, the images clearly defined and the balance very satisfactory. This reissue in EMI's 'Great Artists of the Century' series is a record to treasure.

Violin Concerto No. 3 in G.
(BB) *** EMI Encore 5 85455-2. F. P. Zimmermann, BPO, Sawallisch – BRAHMS: *Violin Concerto.* **

With the string complement of the Berlin Philharmonic aptly reduced and with Sawallisch at his most sparkling, Zimmermann's studio recording of Mozart's *G major Concerto* is a delight, with a quicksilver lightness in the outer movements and a compelling repose and concentration in the central Adagio. In its own right this is superb music-making, but it was perverse to couple it with Brahms rather than with other violin concertos of Mozart.

Violin Concerto No. 5 in A, K.219.
(***) Testament mono SBT 1228. Kogan, Paris Conservatoire O, Vandernoot – BEETHOVEN: *Violin Concerto.* (***)

Leonid Kogan recorded this glowing account of the Mozart in the same year, 1957, as the Beethoven *Concerto* with which it is coupled. Like the Beethoven, it was never issued at the time, being overtaken by the advent of stereo. Testament put us in their debt by issuing it now, for it is a reading of much distinction and great purity of feeling. Good sound, too.

(i) *Concertone in C. K.190;* (ii) *Sinfonia concertante, K.364.*
⊕━ ✿(M) *** DG 476 1651. Perlman, Zukerman, Israel PO, Mehta.

The DG version of the *Sinfonia concertante* is in a special class and is an example of 'live' recording at its most magnetic, with the inspiration of the occasion caught on the wing. Zubin Mehta is drawn into the music-making and accompanies most sensitively. The *Concertone* is also splendidly done; the ear notices the improvement in the sound-balance of the studio recording of this work. But the *Sinfonia concertante*, with the audience incredibly quiet, conveys an electricity rarely caught on record. An outstanding addition to Universal's 'Penguin ✿ Collection'.

Divertimenti and serenades

Divertimento No. 17 in D, K.334.
(*) Sony DVD SVD 46388. BPO, Karajan – Richard STRAUSS: *Also sprach Zarathustra.* *

By the time Karajan conducted these two celebratory concerts he was already ailing, as one registers from his painful progress to the podium each time; but, once there, the electric intensity of his conducting is as striking as ever. This last of the *Divertimenti* that Mozart wrote for Salzburg – for two horns and strings – was the first of the two items in a Berlin Philharmonic concert celebrating the city's 750th anniversary. Karajan gives brightly refreshing accounts of the outer movements, and determinedly traditional readings of the three middle movements omitting the march movement, K.445, latterly thought to belong to the piece. The celebrated Minuet, which comes third, prompts Karajan to a reading so slow and moulded one is reminded of Beecham's more eccentric interpretations of Mozart. The orchestra responds with total loyalty, and the wit and exhilaration of the finale make a delightful conclusion.

Wind divertimenti and serenades

Serenades Nos. 6 in D (Serenata notturna), K.239; 7 in D (Haffner), K.250.

(BB) **(*) Warner Apex 2564 60712-2. Amsterdam Bar. O, Koopman.

Koopman's account of the *Haffner* is bold and his accents robust, especially in Minuets; indeed, the energetic timpani are little short of explosive. But he has an excellent violin soloist in Pavlo Beznosiuk, and he ensures that the delectable *moto perpetuo* sparkles daintily. The extra transparency means that detail registers throughout. The timpani again come through strongly but cleanly in the *Serenata notturna* and they tend to dominate aurally, but the string playing remains elegantly turned.

Sinfonia concertante for Violin, Viola & Orchestra in E flat, K.364.

**(*) EMI DVD 490449-9. I. Oistrakh, D. Oistrakh, Moscow PO, Menuhin – BACH: *Double Violin Concerto*, etc.; BRAHMS: *Double Concerto* . **(*)

Mozart's heavenly *Sinfonia concertante* is wonderfully played by Oistrakh *père et fils* at the Royal Albert Hall in September 1963 when the Moscow Philharmonic was on tour here, and in this item Menuhin rather than Kondrashin conducts. It is a valuable document and is splendidly produced by Anthony Craxton with appropriately discreet camerawork. David Nice's notes speak of 'the elegance and focused tone David Oistrakh draws from the viola', and this is a joy in itself. A moving record, in spite of the inevitable limitations of the sound.

(i; ii) Sinfonia concertante for Violin, Viola & Orchestra, K.364; (iii) Sinfonia concertante for Oboe, Clarinet, Horn, Basooon & Orchestra, K.297b; (i) Violin Concerto No. 5 (Turkish), K.219; Divertimento for Strings, K.136; Serenade No. 13 (Eine kleine Nachtmusik); Symphony No. 29 in A, K.201.

(B) **Virgin 2×1 5 62212-2. (i) Warren-Green; (ii) Chase; (iii) Hunt, Collins, Thompson, Alexander; LCO.

This inexpensive reissue offers an unfortunately chosen pairing. The performances of the two *Sinfonias concertantes* are highly recommendable. In K.364 Christopher Warren-Green and Roger Chase provide a characteristically vital account of Mozart's inspired work for violin and viola: speeds for fast movements are brisk but gain in freshness when they never sound rushed. In suitable contrast the *Andante* is slow and warmly expressive, yet without a trace of sentimentality. The coupling of K.297b is even more delectable, and it would be hard to imagine a more persuasive team of wind players than those here. Gordon Hunt and Michael Collins phrase with the kind of magic one would expect from a Beecham performance, and their partners, Michael Thompson (horn) and Meyrick Alexander (bassoon), are hardly less impressive. Both performances are very satisfying, with full-timbred sound from soloists and orchestra alike.

Unfortunately, the coupled collection comprising the *Violin Concerto, Divertimento, Serenade* and the *A major Symphony* was one of Warren-Green's rare disappointing records, made during his early tenure leading the London Chamber Orchestra. The playing is as polished as ever, but tempi are so brisk that the effect is at times almost perfunctory, particularly in the *Violin Concerto*, which is undoubtedly played brilliantly. EMI should reissue the *Sinfonias concertantes* separately.

ORGAN MUSIC

Andante in F, K.616; Adagio & Allegro in F min., K.594; Fantasia in F min. (Adagio & Allegro), K.608 (all for musical clock); Allegro in G (Veronese), K.72a; Gigue in G, K.574; (i) Epistle Sonatas: in F, K.244; in C, K.328.

(BB) ** Teldec (ADD) 0630 17371-2. Tachezi (organ of Basilika Maria Treu, Vienna); (i) with Alice and Nicholas Harnoncourt and Pfeiffer.

Mozart is never really thought of as a composer for the organ, but he loved its challenge and, whenever he travelled, always made a point of seeking out a local instrument. The problem for us was that he liked best of all to improvise and seldom wrote anything down. Until now, the only 'organ works' we have had on record have been the three pieces he wrote for Count Deym's mechanical organ attached to a clock. Mozart had no opinion of the mechanism for which his music was commissioned and is known to have wished the pieces were intended for a large instrument. To these Herbert Tachezi adds a brief *Allegro* and an attractive *Gigue*, plus two of the *Epistle Sonatas*, in which he is joined by the Harnoncourt Trio. The performances overall are acceptable and well registered, but there is nothing distinctive about this record, although the sound is excellent.

PIANO MUSIC

Piano Sonatas Nos. 15 in F, KV 533/494; 16 in C, K.545; 17 in B flat, K.570; 18 in D, K.576.

**(*) Avie AV 0025. Haefliger.

Andreas Haefliger is an artist of calibre who gives splendidly vital accounts of these sonatas. He does not bring the same variety of keyboard colour and dynamic nuance or poetic feeling as do the likes of Perahia or Pletnev, but he has sobriety and an undoubted sense of style and unfailing musicianship. However, these four works are not otherwise available together on a single CD, and it remains a satisfying collection and benefits from excellent recorded sound.

SACRED VOCAL MUSIC

(i; ii) *Mass No. 16 in C (Coronation), K.317; Vesperae solennes de confessore, K.339;* (ii) *Ave verum corpus, K.618;* (iii) *Exsultate jubilate, K.165.*
(M) ** Warner Elatus 2564 61298-2. (i) Rodgers, Von Magnus, Protschka, Polgár, Arnold Schoenberg Ch.; (ii) V. Hofburgkapelle Choral Scholars; (iii) Bonney; VCM, Harnoncourt.

Harnoncourt is not entirely logical in using period instruments but including women rather than boy trebles in the choir. As usual, accents are strong, dynamic contrasts are exaggerated and phrasing is somewhat eccentically moulded. Joan Rodgers is a fine soprano soloist in both works (although Barbara Bonney takes over bracingly in the *Exsultate jubilate*). The recording has plenty of atmosphere but could be more clearly defined.

Mass No. 19 (Requiem) in D min., K.626.
(BB) ** Warner Apex (ADD) 8573 89421-2. Ameling, Scherler, Devos, Soyer, Gulbenkian Foundation, Lisbon, Ch. & O, Corboz.

(i) *Mass No. 19 (Requiem). Adagio & Fugue, K.546.*
⊶ (M) *** Decca 475 205-2. M. Price, Schmidt, Araiza, Adam, Leipzig R. Ch., Dresden State O, Schreier.
(M) ** DG (ADD) 463 654-2. BPO, Karajan; (i) with Lipp, Rössl-Majdan, Dermota, Berry, V. Singverein.

Peter Schreier's outstanding 1984 recording won a *Gramophone* Choral Award. Since then his performance has not been surpassed and is now most welcome back into the catalogue. It is a forthright reading, bringing strong dramatic contrasts and marked by superb choral singing and a consistently elegant and finely balanced accompaniment. The recording is exceptionally well balanced and the orchestral detail emerges with natural clarity. Margaret Price in the soprano part is as fine as any yet heard on record, and the others make a first-rate team, if individually more variable. Only in the *Kyrie* and the final *Cum sanctis tuis* does the German habit of using the intrusive aitch intrude. Altogether this is the most satisfying modern-instrument version now available of the standard Süssmayr score of Mozart's valedictory choral work, and it is splendidly recorded.

Karajan's earlier (1962) recording was a strange choice for reissue as one of DG's 'Originals'. There is nothing legendary here except Karajan's remarkably suave view of Mozart's valedictory work. Here detail tends to be sacrificed in favour of warmth and atmosphere. The solo quartet are wonderfully blended, a rare occurrence in this work above all, and though the chorus lacks firmness of line they are helped out by the spirited playing of the Berlin Philharmonic. However, both Karajan's later (1976) analogue and newest digital version are greatly preferable. The *Adagio and Fugue* offered as a makeweight, with glorious Berlin string-tone, is both refined and expansive.

Michel Corboz, an excellent choral conductor, directs a nicely scaled performance and gets some fine, and often fervent, singing from his Lisbon choir. His concern for detail is admirable. Elly Ameling is outstanding in a variable quartet of soloists, but the performance ultimately lacks the last degree of thrust, particularly in the closing *Lux aeterna*.

OPERA

Don Giovanni (complete).
(M) **(*) Ph. Trio 473 959-2 (3). Allen, Sweet, Mattila, Alaimo, Araiza, Lloyd, McLaughlin, Otelli, Amb. Op. Ch., ASMF, Marriner.
(M) ** RCA 74321 57737-2 (3). London, Della Casa, Jurinac, Kunz, Dermota, Seefried, Berry, Weber, V. State Op. Ch. & O, Boehm.
** Decca 455 500-2 (3). Terfel, Fleming, Murray, Pertusi, Lippert, Groop, Scaltriti, Luperi, L. Voices, LPO, Solti.
(M) ** Virgin 5 61601-2 (3). Schmidt, Yurisich, Halgrimson, Dawson, Mark Ainsley, Argenta, Finley, Miles, Schütz Ch. of L., L. Classical Players, Norrington.
(M) * Virgin 5 45425-2 (3). Mattei, Cachemaille, Remigio, Gens, Padmore, Larson, Fechner, Gudjon Oskarsson, Aix-en-Provence Academy Ch., Mahler CO, Harding.

Marriner's Trio reissue has the benefit of outstandingly fine recorded sound, full and well balanced. His direction is well paced and resilient, with far keener feeling for dramatic pacing than his earlier recording of *Figaro*. Vocally, the star is Thomas Allen as the Don, even more assured than he was for Haitink in the EMI Glyndebourne version. The others make a strong team, with Simon Alaimo an attractive, young-sounding Leporello, though Sharon Sweet is occasionally raw-toned as Donna Anna. There is no libretto, only a keyed synopsis, and overall this is far from being a primary choice.

The Boehm RCA version, recorded live by Austrian Radio and given in German, is a historic curiosity – a performance that in 1955 marked the reopening of the Vienna State Opera. Vocally, it is worth hearing for the contributions of the three women principals, with Lisa della Casa creamy-toned as Donna Anna, Sena Jurinac at her magical peak as Donna Elvira and Irmgard Seefried the most charming of Zerlinas. George London is a strong but sour-toned Giovanni. The others are not at their finest either, not helped by the dry acoustic and odd balances.

Recorded live at the Royal Festival Hall in London in October 1996, Solti's version is disappointing despite the promising cast-list. It lacks the keen electricity that marks his live recording of *Così fan tutte*, and not one of the singers is on top form. Even Renée Fleming's beautiful voice sounds clouded, and Ann Murray as Elvira is seriously strained. Monica Groop as Zerlina, sweet enough in her arias, is edgy elsewhere, while Roberto Scaltriti is a gritty Masetto and Michele Pertusi often rough as Leporello. Bryn Terfel, so inspired a Leporello, proves an unpersuasive lover, with the tone tending to become unfocused. Dryish sound.

Sir Roger Norrington's version provides a period performance which ingeniously offers the alternative of playing the original Prague version or Mozart's revision for Vienna. This it does by having long sections on separate tracks, instead of tracking each individual number. The snag is that if you want to find a particular aria, it is far less convenient, and many numbers are duplicated when there are alternative sections for Prague or Vienna. Sadly, the singing cast cannot match that in the Gardiner set. Though Lynne Dawson as Elvira, John Mark Ainsley as Ottavio, Gregory Yurisich as Leporello and Alastair Miles as the Commendatore all sing impressively, they hardly outshine their DG opposite numbers, and most of the others fall seriously short, including Andreas Schmidt as an ill-focused Don and Amanda Halgrimson as a shrill Donna Anna. Good, well-balanced sound.

Recorded live at the 1999 Aix-en-Provence Festival, Daniel Harding's reading is an extraordinary exercise in speed. To describe it as perfunctory is to underestimate the impact of speeds that reduce the soloists to a gabble and that prompt the Mahler Chamber Orchestra to produce sounds that would seem scrawny even from an unreconstructed period band, not helped by a recording that lacks body. The cast, mainly of promising young soloists, is almost completely defeated by such wilfulness from the conductor, with even the stylish and characterful Véronique Gens sounding underpowered and uncomfortable. Only the experienced Gilles Cachemaille survives the experiment with any success, a winning and warm Leporello. Giulini, Gardiner and Krips all offer outstanding versions of this opera, discussed in our main volume.

Don Giovanni (Prague & Vienna versions; complete).
(BB) ** Virgin 5 66267-2 (5). Schmidt, Yurisich, Dawson, Halgrimson, Argenta, Mark Ainsley, Finley, Miles, L Schütz Ch., LCP, Norrington – *Die Zauberflöte*. *

Norrington's version not only provides a period-instrument performance which on the orchestral side outshines earlier authentic versions (though not the newer Gardiner set) but that also ingeniously offers the alternative of hearing the original Prague score of the opera, alongside Mozart's revision for Vienna. But this is not done in the ideal way of laying out the tracks of the two versions (where they differ) side by side. Instead, the first two CDs present the opera as it would have been heard at the first performance in Prague in 1787, and the third offers the additional numbers and amendments that Mozart provided for the Vienna première the next year. So in order to switch between the two you need a pair of CD players, and many numbers are duplicated. A fascinating experiment, nevertheless, but sadly the singing cast cannot match the very finest versions. Though Lynne Dawson as Elvira, John Mark Ainsley as Don Ottavio, Gregory Yurisich as Leporello and Alastair Miles as the Commendatore all sing impressively, most of the others fall seriously short, including Andreas Schmidt as an ill-focused Don, and Amanda Halgrimson as a shrill Donna Anna. This set is now offered very inexpensively indeed (if without a libretto or cued synopsis), but it comes in harness with an unrecommendable account of *Die Zauberflöte*.

Don Giovanni (highlights).
*(*) Telarc CD 80442 (from complete set with Skovhus, Lott, Corbelli, Brewer, SCO, Mackerras).

Mackerras's 1995 recording of *Don Giovanni* is vividly dramatic and perfectly paced, with modern instruments echoing period practice. The teamwork is excellent, but individually the casting is flawed, so the performance is better approached through a highlights disc. This one is generous enough (77 minutes), although the booklet offers only historical notes on the opera and a synopsis which is uncued, which is surely unacceptable for a full-priced CD. In any case Bo Skovhus as the Don may be seductive in expression but his vocal focus too often grows woolly under pressure. Felicity Lott, as recorded, is in disappointing voice as Elvira, not nearly as sweet as usual, and there is too much acid in the soprano tones of Christine Brewer as Donna Anna, though Christine Focile makes a characterful Zerlina. The sound has a pleasing ambience but does not provide much sparkle.

Die Entführung aus dem Serail (complete).
(M) *** Oehms OCD 249 (2). Haberman, Ellen, Bezcala, Kalchmair, Ringelhahn, Linz Landestheater Ch. Linz Bruckner O, Sieghart.
(M) (**) DG (IMS) mono 457 730-2 (2). Stader, Streich, Haefliger, Greindl, Vantin, Berlin RIAS Chamber Ch. & SO, Fricsay (with *Exsultate, jubilate*, K.165 ***).
** Telarc CD 80544 (2). Kodalli, Groves, Rancatore, Rose, Atkinson, Tobias, SCO, Mackerras.

With an excellent cast of young singers the Oehms

(originally Arte Nova) set offers an outstanding version of *Entführung* to rival almost any in the catalogue. With Martin Sieghart a crisp and urgent conductor, stylistically impeccable, drawing fine playing from the Linz Bruckner Orchestra, the performance gains from having been recorded in conjunction with live performances on stage, a point consistently reflected in the interplay between the soloists. Ingrid Habermann is a formidable Konstanze, fresh and clear, bright in coloratura yet creamy of tone in lower registers, undaunted by the demands of *Martern aller Arten*. The American Donna Ellen is a lively Blonde with clear, unstrained top register. The Polish tenor Piotr Bezcala is a stylish, honey-toned Belmonte, with power as well as lyric beauty, only occasionally lachrymose in attack, while Oliver Ringelhahn is a well-contrasted Pedrillo, though pushed to the limit in his big Act II aria, *Frisch zum Kampfe*. Best of all is the Osmin of Franz Kalchmair, whose firm, dark bass copes masterfully with every demand of the role, cleanly focused from top to bottom. Still youthful-sounding, he yet conveys a compelling portrait of this prickly character. Good sound, though the spoken dialogue (well edited) is not consistent. Now at mid-price, the set comes with full libretto, including English translation.

Though lacking in body, the mono sound for Fricsay's recording brings splendid detail, with voices well caught. Fricsay characteristically opts for fast, generally refreshing speeds and crisp attack, though Konstanze's great aria of lamentation, *Traurigkeit*, lacks tenderness. Maria Stader is appealing in that role, even though the sweet voice grows less secure on top. Haefliger as Belmonte brings weight but little lyrical beauty. Greindl is a strong but often gritty Osmin and Martin Vantin a boyish Pedrillo, while the finest singing comes from Rita Streich as Blonde. The dialogue is mainly spoken by actors. *Exsultate, jubilate*, with Stader, makes a welcome fill-up.

Recorded for the soundtrack of a film of *Entführung*, *Mozart in Turkey*, the Telarc version conducted by Sir Charles Mackerras offers lively conducting and a young-sounding cast. The modest string band is set in contrast against prominent percussion, with wind and brass also well to the fore. As in his other Mozart with the Scottish Chamber Orchestra, Mackerras introduces elements of period practice in light, fast allegros, fierce at times, though in slow music he allows ample relaxation. Paul Groves is a fresh, clear-toned Belmonte, not quite free enough at the very top, and Yelda Kodalli a bright, clear Konstanze, as impressive in her tender account of *Traurigkeit* as in the bravura of *Martern aller Arten*. As Blonde, Desirée Rancatore is agile too but, as recorded, there is a distracting flutter in the voice. The Osmin of Peter Rose is vocally impressive but sadly undercharacterized. There may be a point in making Osmin more serious than usual, but with the voice sounding far too young there is little or no comedy, and no feeling of anger in his rages. Lynton Atkinson makes a sparky Pedrillo, even if the voice is distractingly similar to that of Groves as Belmonte. Excellent singing from the chorus and lively playing from the orchestra. Clear recording, rather drier than some from this source. This is acceptable enough but hardly a primary recommendation.

Le nozze di Figaro (complete).

(BB) (**(*)) Naxos mono 8.110206/7. Mildmay, Helletsgruber, Rautawaara, Domgraf-Fassbänder, Henderson, Nash, Glyndebourne Festival Ch. & O, Busch.

(B) ** Ph. Trio 475 61118 (3). Popp, Hendricks, Baltsa, Van Dam, Raimondi, Amb. Op. Ch., ASMF, Marriner.

(BB) *(*) EMI (ADD) 585520-2 (2). Evans, Fischer-Dieskau, Harper, Blegen, Berganza, Finnilä, Fryatt, John Aldis Ch., ECO, Barenboim.

At the beginning of June 1934, only a few weeks after the very first Glyndebourne Festival, work was started on this pioneering recording of *Figaro*. It was recorded and later issued by HMV on short-playing 78rpm discs in batches, arias separate from ensembles, and surprisingly the finished set omitted *secco* recitatives. Even so, with a classic cast the performance is well worth hearing, for, though in the Naxos transfer the orchestra is relatively dim, the voices come over well. Willi Domgraf-Fassbänder, father of Brigitte, is the most characterful Figaro, a dominant personality, even if his Italian is idiosyncratic. Audrey Mildmay, wife of John Christie, founder of Glyndebourne, is a charming, refined Susanna, nicely contrasted with Aulikki Rautawaara as the Countess. It is good too to have Heddle Nash in the comic role of Basilio, not a side of his work generally heard on disc, and Roy Henderson is characterful too as the Count, if a little stiff, stressed as he is by the high tessitura of his big aria and, like the others, by the often hectic speeds demanded from the overture onwards by the inspired Fritz Busch. A historic document well worth investigating at Naxos price.

After his sparkling set of the other Figaro opera, Rossini's *Barbiere di Siviglia*, Sir Neville Marriner this time in Mozart falls down on his dramatic timing, and the result fails to lift. As an instance, the delicious duet between Susanna and the Count at the beginning of Act III, *Crudel! perche finora*, is made lugubrious thanks to Raimondi, who is then superbly well focused in his big aria. Though Lucia Popp gives a deeply felt performance as the Countess, the strain on the voice tends to imperil the legato. Barbara Hendricks makes an attractively girlish Susanna and Van Dam a formidable Figaro, though one inclined to be too emphatic, not comic; even *Non più andrai* is too heavy. The final disappointment of the set is Marriner's failure to convey the necessary sense of resolution in the closing scene, with little or no poignancy conveyed. Despite the excellent recording in both formats, this could not be a first choice, even at bargain price.

For so lively a Mozartian, Barenboim takes a strangely staid view of *Figaro*. This EMI set was recorded soon after live performances at the Edinburgh Festival in 1976 and with substantially the same cast. Though recitatives are sharp enough, the result lacks sparkle, despite the characterful – if at times unsteady – Figaro of Sir Geraint Evans, in a classic characterization. The others too, on paper a fine, starry team, fail to project at full intensity, often thanks to slow speeds and unlifted rhythms. Those interested in individual singers might consider this set (especially at bargain price), but there are far finer versions than this. A synopsis is included, but nothing else. Readers need to consult our main volume for recommendations for this opera.

Le nozze di Figaro (highlights).

(BB) ** EMI Encore 5 74745-2 (from complete recording with Allen, Battle, M. Price, Hynninen, Murray, V. State Op. Ch., VPO, Muti).

Recorded in 1986, the Muti Vienna selection is disappointing for the cloudiness of the recording; and the singing, from a starry line-up of soloists, is very variable. Commanding as Thomas Allen is as Figaro, this is not a comic figure, dark rather, and less than winning. Kathleen Battle is a sparkling Susanna, but Margaret Price's Countess is not as nobly distinctive as she might be, and Ann Murray makes a somewhat edgy Cherubino. Muti's pacing is sometimes too fast to convey a feeling for the comedy. This 70-minute selection gives a good idea of the character of the set, but the sparse synopsis is barely adequate.

Idomeneo (sung in English).

(M) *** Chan. 3103 (2). Ford, Montague, Evans, Patterson, Davies, Gedda, Bayley, Opera N. Ch. & O, Parry.

On Chandos, the performance of *Idomeneo* in English works surprisingly well. The translation has been done very capably by David Parry, whose conducting brings out both the power and the originality of this great example of an *opera seria* which in every way transcends the limitations of the genre. The overture instantly establishes the vigour and weight of the performance, which yet allows clean textures, so that the excellent wind-playing of the Opera North Orchestra is caught vividly. The text is basically that of the original Munich production, with the role of Idamante taken by a high voice, but with substantial cuts to allow the whole opera to be fitted on two very well-filled discs. Both of Arbace's arias disappear (a pity, when Ryland Davies is strongly cast as the High Priest) as well as one of Idamante's and one of Idomeneo's in Act III.

In the title-role, Bruce Ford's distinctive tenor is powerfully expressive, even if his rapidly flickering vibrato does tend to obtrude in the more lyrical passages. The cast of women is outstanding, with Rebecca Evans as Ilia and Diana Montague as Idamante as mellifluous a duo as one could imagine,

deeply expressive, too. Susan Patterson is well contrasted as Electra, with her rather harder soprano suiting the aggressive side of the character. The drama of the piece is consistently brought out, not least in the thrilling close of Act II with its storm music, and in the climactic quartet of Act III. Having the veteran Nicolai Gedda in the cameo role of the Voice of Neptune is also a welcome plus-point. The vivid Chandos recording brings excellent balances between voices and orchestra, with words admirably clear. Mozart's score has never sounded fresher.

Il sogno di Scipione.

(*) Astreé E 8813 (2). Hartelius, Larsson, Brandes, Ford, Workman, Ovenden, Cremonesi, Louvre Ch. & O, Freiburger Bar. O, Goltz.

Described as an 'azione teatrale', *Il sogno di Scipione* was first performed at the installation of Hieronimus Colloredo as Prince-Archbishop of Salzburg in 1772, having first been conceived as a celebratory piece for his predecessor, who promptly died. Like most early Mozart operas, it is an attractive trifle that only occasionally reveals the full individuality of the genius who was emerging. Sadly, this live recording, made in the Stravinsky Auditorium in Montreux in September 2000, is far too flawed to recommend beside the existing set in the Philips Mozart Edition. This new one uses period instead of modern instruments, but the style is rough and abrasive, and it is made worse by the unpleasantly dry acoustic. That also affects the voices, with only two of the soloists rising above the elimination of bloom, the radiant Malin Hartelius as Costanza and Christine Brandes as Licenza. All the others, including the distinguished tenor Bruce Ford, sound gritty or unsteady. The lumpish conducting of Gottfried von der Goltz does not help.

Zaïde (complete).

(B) *** HM HMX 2907205. Dawson, Blochwitz, Bär, Lippert, Purves, AAM, Goodwin.

Written in 1779–80, *Zaïde* is a singspiel on a 'Turkish' subject, which Mozart failed to complete, not because he lacked inspiration but because it was overtaken by the project to write his other 'Turkish' opera, *Die Entführung*. As the Mozart scholar Neal Zaslaw puts it in his note, it is 'a masterpiece in the making truncated by circumstances', containing 70 minutes of inspired music recognizably from the same period as *Idomeneo* as well as *Entführung*. Though it lacks an overture, the opening establishes its originality with a brief introduction from the tenor narrator leading to a melodrama spoken by that same singer in his role as Gomatz, the hero of the story. Mozart also introduces the second act with another melodrama, a unique device in his operas. In Act I the first full aria is for the soprano taking the name-part, *Ruhe sanft*, one of the loveliest arias that even Mozart ever wrote; and the rest of the work as far as it was completed includes a duet, a trio (ending

Act I) and a final quartet, as well as arias for all the main characters.

Paul Goodwin directs the Academy of Ancient Music and a very talented quintet of soloists in an almost ideal performance. It was recorded in Paris soon after live performances, with Lynne Dawson singing ravishingly, not least in a heavenly account of *Ruhe sanft*. Hans Peter Blochwitz as Gomatz sings with a heady beauty, nicely contrasted with the other tenor in the cast, Herbert Lippert, also free of strain in the role of Sultan Soliman, compassionate as his counterpart is in *Entführung*. Here, as in *Entführung*, you have a character called Osmin, very much a sketch for the fully developed comic figure in the later opera, well sung here by the bass-baritone Christopher Purves. As Allazim, the Sultan's favourite slave, Olaf Bär sings with all his characteristic sensitivity.

Die Zauberflöte (complete).

❂ (M) (★★★) DG mono 476 1752 (2). Stader, Streich, Fischer-Dieskau, Greindl, Haefliger, Berlin RIAS Ch. & SO, Fricsay.

(B) ★★ Double Decca 448 734-2 (2). Gueden, Lipp, Simoneau, Berry, Böhme, Schoeffler, V. State Op. Ch., VPO, Boehm.

(BB) ★ Virgin 5 66267-2 (5). Upshaw, Rolfe Johnson, Hoch, Hauptmann, Schmidt, Pierard, De Mey, L. Schütz Ch., LCP, Norrington – *Don Giovanni* (Prague & Vienna Versions). ★★

Fricsay's recording has been treasured by us since the early days of LP. It is an outstandingly fresh and alert *Die Zauberflöte*, marked by generally clear, pure singing and well-sprung orchestral playing at generally rather fast speeds which yet never sound rushed. It deserves its place within Universal's 'Penguin ❂ Collection' at the same time serving to remind us that our ❂ was inadvertently omitted when it was listed in our main *Guide*! Now it is restored. Maria Stader and Dietrich Fischer-Dieskau phrase most beautifully, but the most spectacular singing comes from Rita Streich as a dazzling Queen of the Night, and the relatively close balance of the voice gives it the necessary power such as Streich could convey less readily in the opera house. Ernst Haefliger, too, is at his most honeyed in tone as Tamino, and only the rather gritty Sarastro of Josef Greindl falls short – and even he sings with a satisfying dark resonance. This was the first version to spice the musical numbers with brief sprinklings of dialogue, just enough to prevent the work from sounding like an oratorio. Even including that, DG have managed to put each of the acts complete on a single disc.

The principal attraction of this Double Decca reissue from the earliest days of stereo, apart from its modest cost, is the conducting of Karl Boehm. That might well be counted recommendation enough, in spite of the absence of dialogue, particularly when the Tamino of Léopold Simoneau and the Papageno of Walter Berry are strongly and sensitively sung and

Wilma Lipp proves an impressive Queen of the Night. But the rest of the singing is variable, with Hilde Gueden a pert, characterful Pamina, unhappy in the florid divisions, and Kurt Böhme a gritty and ungracious Sarastro. The new cued synopsis is a great improvement on the previous reissue and includes new documentation intended to offer a helpful guide for the newcomer to the opera.

Norrington in a 1991 period performance linked his recording with a live concert, but left too long a period between them, so that the sparkle of a live event disappeared. Fast speeds become fierce and unsmiling when rhythms can no longer be lifted seductively. The cast is strong but far from ideal, with Cornelius Hauptmann unstylishly wobbly as Sarastro. This now comes inexpensively linked to a combination of the Prague and Vienna versions of *Don Giovanni*, about which there are also reservations, though that set is the more successful of the two. The documentation is sparse, without even a cued synopsis.

Recitals

Arias and Duets from: *Così fan tutte; Davidde Penitente; Don Giovanni; Die verstellte Gärtnerin.* Arias: *Mentre ti lascio, o figlia; Misero! O Sogno ... Aura che intorno spiti; Per pietà, non ricercate; Si mostra la sorte; Un bacio la mano.*

★★★ DHM/BMG 82876 55782-2. Christoph Genz, Stephan Genz, La Petite Bande, Kuijken.

The tenor Christoph Genz and his baritone brother Stephan are among the most interesting young German singers of their generation; here, in a recording made in Spain, they offer a series of eleven arias, tricked out with the only two duets that Mozart wrote for tenor and baritone, both from *Così fan tutte*, shorter than most of the items here. The selection ranges wide, including not only popular favourites like Ferrando's *Un'aura amorosa* from *Così*, elegantly done, and Don Giovanni's Serenade, but rarities like the more extended aria that Mozart gave to Guglielmo in *Così* and *Per pieta*, an aria that Mozart wrote to be inserted in an opera by Pasquale Anfosso. Excellent as the performances are, the snag is that the closeness of the recording takes away some of the bloom on the voices, occasionally bringing a hint of roughness.

Arias from: (i) *La clemenza di Tito;* (ii) *Così fan tutte; Don Giovanni;* (i) *Lucio Silla; Mitrate, rè di Ponto;* (i) *Le nozze di Figaro; Zaïde; Die Zauberflöte.*

(B) ★★★ CfP 585 9022. SCO, with (i) Murray; cond. Leppard; (ii) Allen; cond. Armstrong.

Dating from 1984, when both singers were in their prime, this is one of the most delectable collections of Mozart arias ever assembled on a single disc. Sir Thomas Allen has the lion's share, and he is in superb form in the four *Figaro* arias and in Papageno's pair from *Die Zauberflöte*. His honeyed legato in *Deh vieni alla finestra* from *Don Giovanni* is matched by the sheer gusto of *Finch'han dal vino*. To conclude, there are two rarer excerpts from *Zaïde*, and the engaging *Un bacio di mano*, an insertion aria which Mozart wote for Pasquale Anfossi's *Le gelosie fortunate* in 1788. Ann Murray then takes over for splendidly sung excerpts from *La clemenza di Tito* (*Parto parto*, with the clarinet obbligato stylishly played by Lewis Morrison) and the spectacular *Lungi da te, mio bene* from *Mitridate, rè di Ponto*, with a fine horn obbligato from Frank Lloyd, who also stays around to contribute similarly to the Handelian encore, *Va tacito e nascosto* from Act I of *Giulio Cesare*, which is equally impressive. With stylish accompaniments from the Scottish Chamber Orchestra under Sir Richard Armstrong or Raymond Leppard, and warm, natural recording, which (because of the skill of the balance engineer, Stuart Eltham) is kind to both voices. At Classics for Pleasure price this is quite irresistible.

MUDARRA, Alonso (1510–80)

Music in Tablature for Vihuela & Voice, Book 3 (1546)
(M) *** Astrée ES 9941. Figueras, Hopkinson Smith.

The collection here (taken from the last of Mudarra's set of three Books) is also the third known collection of music for vihuela (following publications by Luis Milán and Luis de Nárvaez). In this repertoire Montserrat Figueras is in her element, singing these simple but beautiful melodies without artifice. She is accompanied by what many reference books have described as an obsolete instrument, the guitar's lute-like predecessor. But Hopkinson Smith plays four vihuelas (all modern reproductions) to accompany these captivating, folk-like *romances* and *villancicos*. The singing is quite lovely. A cherishable disc, beautifully recorded and with full translations included.

MUFFAT, Georg (1653–1704)

Concerti grossi Nos. 1 in D min. (Good News); 2 in A (Watchful Heart); 3 in B (Convalescence); 4 in G min. (Sweet Sleep); 5 in D (The World); 6 in A min. (Who is This?).
(BB) ** Naxos 8.555096. Musica Aeterna Bratislava, Zajíeek.

Concerti grossi Nos. 7 in E (Delight of Kings); 8 in F (Noble Coronation); 9 in C min. (Sad Victory); 10 in G (Perseverance); 11 in E min. (Madness of Love); 12 in G (Propitious Constellations).
(BB) ** Naxos 8.555743. Musica Aeterna Bratislava, Zajíeek.

The 12 *Concerti grossi* of Muffat are inventive works, in which the influences of both Corelli and Lully are much in evidence. There is plenty to enjoy in these pieces, written for court entertainment, which are melodic and well contrasted, with a few unexpected quirks of harmony and rhythm adding spice. The performances are good ones, stylish and lively, with attractive embellishments, but the recording is rather strident, with the strings not very ingratiating – the effect becomes a little tiring after a while. However, this pair of CDs come at a modest price and the repertoire is certainly worth exploring. Incidentally, the intriguing titles have little to do with the actual music, but refer to the occasions of their first performances.

MUSSORGSKY, Modest (1839–81)

Night on the Bare Mountain; Pictures at an Exhibition; Boris Godunov: Symphonic Synthesis. Khovantschina, Act IV: Entr'acte (all arr. & orch. Stokowski).
*** DG 457 656-2. Cleveland O, Knussen.

Oliver Knussen is a devotee both of Mussorgsky's music and of the conducting of Leopold Stokowski, who was a family friend when Oliver was a boy. That makes him an ideal interpreter of these colourful Stokowski arrangements, recorded in 1995–6, but not issued until 2004. Koussevitzky, who commissioned the Ravel transcription of the *Pictures*, retained exclusive performance rights for a number of years, so Stokowski created his own score, leaving out *Tuileries* and *The Market-Place at Limoges* for not very convincing reasons. Although he draws on Ravel in using a squeaking solo trumpet in *Samuel Goldenberg and Schmule*, much else is different and he opens the first *Promenade* with strings and low woodwind, in place of the brass. Knussen makes sure the effect has dignity and that the score's richness of colour is displayed throughout, for example in the serenade of *The Old Castle*, where the solo is given to the melancholy cor anglais.

As we discovered in Walt Disney's *Fantasia*, Stokowski's *Night on the Bare Mountain* is malevolently spectacular. He said that he went back to the 'original orchestration' – but which is that? Rimsky's version was based on Mussorgsky's revision for use in *Sorochinsky Fair*, which is vocal, and this was also apparently used by Abbado for his marvellous Sony Berlin Philharmonic recording (though uncredited on the disc). Anyway, Stokowski's transcription is splendidly played here, with a tolling bell left resonating at the close.

The *Symphonic Synthesis* from *Boris Godunov* fully captures the dramatic essence of the opera; the portrayal of the monks chanting may be romanticized, but it is genuinely evocative, and the two closing scenes (featuring the Idiot's warning and the death of Boris) also come off with moving narrative effect on the orchestra alone. But perhaps the most telling of Stokowski's Mussorgsky 'operatic scenas' is the entr'acte to *Khovanshchina*, scored with glowing richness. Knussen's performances are both powerful and polished, but a direct comparison with the Chandos disc of the identical coupling reveals how much fuller the Chandos sound is, weightier and more immediate with exceptionally powerful brass (Chan. 9445). One of the few marked interpretative contrasts is in *Bydlo*, the Polish ox-cart movement of *Pictures*, which Knussen takes unusually fast (too fast?), making the ox-cart move briskly, where Bamert makes it lumber along, as one expects it to do.

***Pictures at an Exhibition* (orch. Ravel).**

(BB) *** DG Entrée (ADD/DDD) 474 564-2. Chicago SO, Giulini – RIMSKY-KORSAKOV: *Scheherazade*. *

(B) ** CfP 575 5642. LPO, Pritchard – PROKOFIEV: *Romeo and Juliet*: highlights. **

** RCA 74321 72788-2. N. German RSO, Wand – DEBUSSY: *Le Martyre de Saint Sébastien*. **

Giulini's successful (1977) account of the *Pictures* was made with the Chicago Symphony Orchestra – the orchestra with which Reiner made his classic account. While not quite in that league, this is certainly excellent by any standards, with a vivid and atmospheric recording. Unfortunately, it is coupled with a lumbering (digital) *Scheherazade*.

A well-characterized account under Pritchard in which the personality of the orchestra comes over strongly, the players obviously enjoying themselves and their own virtuosity. The well-detailed 1970 recording, made in Barking Town Hall, makes every detail of the orchestration clear against a pleasing ambience, and the building up of *The Great Gate of Kiev* sequence provides an impressive finale.

Günter Wand's account comes from a concert performance given in 1999 at the Musikhalle in Hamburg and must be addressed primarily to his wide circle of admirers. It is undoubtedly good but comes somewhat illogically with the four fragments from Debussy's *Le Martyre*. At 54 minutes this strikes us as a non-starter: it would not be really competitive at the price of a Naxos issue.

***Pictures at an Exhibition* (original piano version).**

* Hyp. CDA 67018. Demidenko – PROKOFIEV: *Romeo & Juliet: 10 Pieces*, etc. **

No doubts about Demidenko's virtuosity and keyboard command here, or the excellence of the Hyperion sound. There are doubts, however, about many of the highly idiosyncratic touches, which are so pervasive that he attracts more attention to himself than to Mussorgsky!

OPERA

***Boris Godunov* (complete).**

🔑 *** Ph. **DVD** 075 089-9 (2). Lloyd, Borodina, Steblianko, Leiferkus, Kirov Op. Ch. & O, Gergiev (Producer: Andrei Tarkovsky; V/D: Humphrey Burton).

*** Ph. **DVD** 075 099-9 (6). As above – BORODIN: *Prince Igor*; GLINKA: *Ruslan & Ludmilla*).

We have discussed this classic Tarkovsky production at some length and with much enthusiasm in our main edition. Londoners will have had the chance of renewing acquaintance with it as it was revived by the Royal Opera House in the 2004 season and will, we hope, be returning in future seasons. It is now included in an attractive package with two other classic productions (presumably at an attractive discount) to mark Valery Gergiev's 25th anniversary at the Kirov, and those who do not have these performances should take advantage of this. All three performances are outstanding.

***Boris Godunov* (arr. Rimsky-Korsakov).**

(B) **(*) Decca (ADD) 472 495-2 (3). Ghiaurov, Vishnevskaya, Spiess, Maslennikov, Talvela, V. Boys' Ch., Sofia R. Ch., V. State Op. Ch., VPO, Karajan.

With Ghiaurov in the title-role, Karajan's superbly controlled Decca version, technically outstanding, came far nearer than previous recordings to conveying the rugged greatness of Mussorgsky's masterpiece. Only the Coronation scene lacked something of the weight and momentum one ideally wants. Vishnevskaya was far less appealing than the lovely non-Slavonic Marina of Evelyn Lear on EMI, but overall this Decca set had much more to offer. However, Gergiev's recording of the original version makes a clear first choice for this opera, so Decca have now sensibly reissued this at bargain price, although with only a synopsis; the text and translation is available only on a CD-ROM.

Khovanshchina: Prelude.

*** BBC (ADD) BBCL 4123-2. Philh. O, Giulini – BRUCKNER: *Symphony No. 7*; FALLA: *Three-Cornered Hat* (excerpts). ***

In his live recording Giulini draws refined, evocative playing from the Philharmonia, an atmospheric supplement to the Bruckner *Symphony*, the main work.

***Khovanshchina* (complete).**

🔑 *** Arthaus **DVD** 100 310 (2). Ghiaurov, Atlantov, Marusin, Shaklovity; Burchuladze, Shemchuk, Slovak Phil. Ch., V. Boys' Ch.; V. State Op. Ch. & O, Abbado (Stage/Video Director: Kirchner).

This recording was made at the same time as the DG three-CD set (429 758-2), namely in September 1989. There are some differences in cast: to name the most important, the late Aage Haugland who was Ivan Khovansky is sung (wonderfully, too) by Nicolai Ghiaurov, Vladimir Popov's Prince Golitsin is replaced by Yuri Marusin and the Marfa of Marjana Lipovšek by Ludmila Shemchuk. Otherwise the performance does not differ from the rightly admired CD set. Those who know the rival Gergiev set made in 1991 (or who saw the production during the Kirov season at Covent Garden in 2002) should still investigate the present issue as they differ textually. Abbado's version is essentially the Shostakovich version (based on Pavel Lamm's 1929 edition) though he lightens some of the scoring and discards the triumphant ending in Act V with the return of the *Preobrazhensky March* in favour of the finale prepared by Stravinsky. Rimsky-Korsakov's marvellous orchestration is rejected as too sumptuous these days, and his corrections of Mussorgsky's harmony are seen as too academically correct. And with the beautiful, tragic music of Abbado's ending the strength and dignity of the Old Believers is reinforced. Gergiev's version occupied four LaserDisc sides and three CDs, and it cannot be long before it is transferred to DVD. His production is traditional (and none the worse for that) and has an outstanding Ivan Khovansky in the late Bulat Minzhilkiev, a superb Prince Golitsin in Vladimir Galusin and a gloriously refulgent Marfa in Olga Borodina. It has splendid tension, and Gergiev is masterly. However, Abbado, who has for so long been Mussorgsky's most eloquent champion among Western conductors of his generation, is even more electrifying. There is an intensity here, and a mastery both of pace and of climax. The playing of the Vienna orchestra is exquisite in the quieter episodes and sumptuous in tone throughout. There is simply no question of its superiority over the Kirov orchestra (though the choral singing in the Gergiev version is arguably superior). The recording for Abbado, too, is superbly balanced and defined. Above all, the performance has a commanding assurance and compelling power: sample the first act, and the next 3½ hours are gone. The presentation was a very strong element of the DG set, with a remarkable survey by Richard Taruskin of the historical background to the work and a careful table of the manuscript sources. None of this is to be found in the DVD package, but there is a short essay and a synopsis of the plot. Visually the production is good to look at, and the camera is expertly directed and always where the viewer wants it. This is a mandatory choice for all lovers of Russian opera. And if the Gergiev set appears on DVD during the lifetime of this book, get that too for the sake of Bulat Minzhilkiev's Prince Khovansky – and much else besides!

MUSTONEN, Olli (born 1967)

(i) *Triple Concerto for Violins & Orchestra. Frogs Dancing on Water Lilies*; (ii) *Petite Suite for Cello & Strings. Nonets Nos. 1 & 2.*

*** Ondine ODE 9742. (i) Pekka & Juaakko Kuusisto, Batiashvili; (ii) Rousi; Tapiola Sinf., composer.

The Finnish pianist Olli Mustonen has made a name for himself as a gifted if somewhat idiosyncratic composer. His *Triple Concerto* for three violins and orchestra is a neo-Baroque pastiche. There is a strong element of pastiche too in the *Nonet No. 1*, whose Scherzo trips along like Mendelssohn with great delicacy and lightness. The *Petite Suite for Cello and Strings* has something of the naturalness and charm of Gunnar de Frumerie's *Pastoral Suite*. Mustonen does not have a strongly individual voice (to put it mildly) and limits himself to a limited range of musical devices, but the naïveté and directness of it all are undoubtedly likeable. Very good playing and recording.

MYSLIVEČEK, Josef (1737–81)

Symphonies: F26 in C; F27 in A; F28 in F; F29 in D; F30 in B flat; F31 in G.
⊞ *** Chan. 10203. LMP, Bamert.

The lively violin concertos of the Czech composer Josef Mysliveček have become relatively well known, thanks to a number of recordings, but his symphonies have been almost completely neglected on disc. This delightful set of six, never previously recorded, was published in London in 1772, having been written for an expatriate British nobleman, Earl Cowper, living in Florence. Mysliveček left his native Prague in 1763 in his mid-twenties, having earlier worked in his family's milling business. He remained in Italy for most of the rest of his life, writing not only some 45 symphonies, many concertos and copious chamber music, but nearly 30 operas. All six of the present set of symphonies are in conventional three-movement form, fast–slow–fast, each lasting around ten minutes. What distinguishes all six from dozens of symphonies of the period is the liveliness and memorability of each movement, with the music never for a moment outstaying its welcome or falling into routine. The scoring is for two oboes, two horns and strings, with the last of the set in particular bringing some striking horn-writing. Fresh, lively performances, recorded in full, atmospheric sound.

NEPOMUCENO, Alberto (1864–1920)

Galhofeira, Op. 13/4; Improviso, Op. 27/2; Nocturnes: Nos. 1 in C; 2 in G (for the left hand); 5 Pequenas peças (for the left hand); Nocturne, Op. 33; Sonata in F min., Op. 9; Suite antiga, Op. 11.
** Marco Polo 8.223548. Guimarães.

Alberto Nepomuceno has every right to be called the father of Brazilian music. He was active as a teacher and for a time was director of the National Institute of Music in Rio de Janeiro, helping the youthful Villa Lobos. Although he composed in most genres, little of his output has been recorded, so this disc of his piano music is welcome. Much of it is derivative – Brahmsian or Schumannesque – but it shows him to be far from negligible. Morever there is a trace of the kind of popular Brazilian music that fascinated Milhaud in his *Saudades do Brasil*. The *Cinco pequenas peças* and the *Nocturnes* of 1919 were both written for Nepomuceno's daughter, who was born without a right arm. Maria Inês Guimarães is not the most imaginative of pianists and is somewhat wanting in finesse, but those with a taste for off-beat repertoire may find this worth investigating.

NEVIN, Arthur (1871–1943)

From Edgeworth Hills.
*** Altarus AIR-CD 9024. Amato – E. NEVIN: *A Day in Venice*, etc. ***

Arthur Nevin was without his older brother's melodic individuality, but he wrote spontaneously and crafted his pieces nicely. The most striking number of *From Edgeworth Hills* is the tripping *Sylphs*, very characteristic of its time, while *As the Moon Rose* has an agreeably sentimental tune, and the picaresque *Firefly* sparkles nicely here. *Toccatella* is rhythmically a bit awkward but is quite a showpiece, and Donna Amato plays it with real dash. Excellent recording.

NEVIN, Ethelbert (1862–1901)

A Day in Venice (suite), *Op. 25; Etude in the Form of a Romance; Etude in the Form of a Scherzo, Op. 18/1-2; May in Tuscany* (suite), *Op. 21; Napoli (En passant), Op. 30/3; Mighty Lak' a Rose* (after the transcription by Charles Spross); *O'er Hill and Dale* (suite); *The Rosary* (arr. Whelpley); *Water Scenes, Op. 13.*
*** Altarus AIR-CD 9024. Amato – A. NEVIN: *From Edgeworth Hills.* ***

Ethelbert Nevin was born in Edgeworth, Pennsylvania, scored his first great success when *Narcissus* became a world-wide hit, and *The Rosary* was Nevin's other success, with the sheet music selling over a million copies in the decade following its publication in 1898. Donna Amato grew up in the area where Nevin was born, and she takes care not to sentimentalize these genre pieces, which can be just a little trite but also quite engaging. *Mighty Lak' a Rose*, another favourite, retains all its charm. The recording is clear and natural in a pleasing acoustic.

NIELSEN, Carl (1865–1931)

(i) *Commotio, Op. 48;* (ii) *Violin Sonata No. 2 in G min., Op. 35;* (i) *7 Early Songs* (all orch. Holten).
*(*) Danacord DACOCD 588. (i) Hansen; (ii) Bonde-Hansen; Odense SO, Holten.

These three works come from different periods of Nielsen's life. The early songs have a touching and artless simplicity that is quite special and that is lost in these orchestrations. At times *Æbleblomst* ('Appleblossom'), which has great purity and tenderness,

acquires a Mahlerian lushness that changes its character. So, too, does *I Seraillets Have* ('In the Garden of the Seraglio'). Nor is the scoring always that expert: *Irmelin Rose* sounds crude. Bo Holten's orchestration of *Commotio* (1931) completely transforms its character. Instead of enhancing its majesty and splendour, it thickens Nielsen's textures; the overall effect sounds cumbersome, laboured and overblown, completely at variance with the clarity and grandeur of the original. The *G minor Violin Sonata* of 1912 is one of the composer's strangest and most haunting pieces, but its essential inwardness and feel of strangeness are lost. The character of the opening of the finale is changed beyond recognition. It all serves to show that Nielsen's thinking was keenly attuned to the medium in which it sought expression. Decent performances and recording, but not really recommendable.

Violin Concerto, Op. 33.
** EMI 5 56906-2. Znaider, LPO, Foster (with BRUCH: *Violin Concerto No. 1 ** *).

Nikolaj Znaider comes from Denmark but is of Russian parentage and made a very strong impression at the 1999 Ysaÿe Competition in Brussels, taking the first prize in a very strong field. His Nielsen concerto is very well thought out and fervent, though it lacks the total conviction and white-hot inspiration that Cho-Liang Lin and Salonen bring to it. He has very good support from Lawrence Foster and the LPO, but he is slightly self-aware and reluctant to let go. The Bruch concerto is also ardent but in the last resort not distinctive. Cho-Liang-Lin gives the performance of this work which stands above all others (Sony SK 44548).

Symphonies Nos. 1 in G min., Op. 7; 2 in B min. (Four Temperaments), Op. 16.
*(*) Finlandia 8573 85574-2. Finnish RSO, Saraste.

There is some very good playing from the Finnish Radio Orchestra, and Saraste is generally attentive to detail and free from any kind of interpretative point-making. At the same time it makes a less strong impression than his powerful accounts of the *Fourth* and *Fifth Symphonies*. Tempi are generally well chosen (even if some may find Saraste fractionally on the fast side in the third movement of No. 1 and distinctly so in the finale of No. 2). Elsewhere, as in the finale of No. 1, he sets off at exactly the right stride. But the first movement of the *Four Temperaments* is coarse rather than choleric and its second theme wanting in nobility, as is the slow movement. The phlegmatic movement is a bit short on charm. Competition in both works is pretty stiff, and readers will find more recommendable versions listed in our main volume, notably Blomstedt's complete Decca set on a pair of Doubles (460 985-2 and 460 988-2).

Symphonies Nos. 2 (Four Temperaments), Op. 16; 5, Op. 50.
** BIS CD 1289. BBC Scottish SO, Vänskä.

On the BIS CD the first movement of the *Second Symphony* needs to move a shade faster if it is to convey the choleric temperament, and the finale could also move with a brisker stride. Part of the problem with both performances is that the strings are wanting in the richness and weight that distinguish rival accounts. Decent, but not in any way outstanding, recorded sound.

(i) *Symphonies Nos. 3 (Espansiva); 4 (Inextinguishable).*
(M) **(*) Warner Elatus 2564 60432-2. (i) Kaappola, Kortekangas; Finnish RSO, Saraste.

** BIS CD 1209. BBC Scottish SO, Vänskä, (i) with Komsi, Immler.

Saraste and the Finnish Radio Orchestra capture to perfection the explosive character of the opening of No. 4 and, although there are moments when one feels that the current could flow with a higher charge, for the most part the performance is splendidly shaped and impressively executed. The *Sinfonia espansiva*, too, opens with a powerful impetus, and the first movement maintains its forward impulse, while Saraste finds Sibelian affinities in the *Andante pastorale*. The vocal soloists are not too forwardly balanced, although some might find the soprano's vibrato a little too prominent. The finale opens nobly and closes with fierce eloquence. While not perhaps a first choice, this coupling is certainly compelling throughout.

Vänskä's *Espansiva* is curiously uninvolving and wanting in fire. He has not inspired his players as he did in his Sibelius cycle at Lahti. The *Fourth Symphony*, however, is another matter. This is a vital performance in every way and conveys the splendour of Nielsen's visionary score. In this the Finnish conductor gets almost everything right, though his strings could do with greater weight and body of tone. Curiously, the BIS recording, judged by the exalted standards of the house, is serviceable rather than distinguished.

CHAMBER MUSIC

String Quartets Nos. 1; 4; Little Suite for Strings (arr. Zapolski).
* Chan. 9635. Zapolski Qt.

String Quartets Nos. 2 in F min., Op. 5; 3 in E flat, Op. 14.
*(*) Chan. 9817. Zapolski Qt.

The Zapolski Quartet is so concerned with projecting Nielsen's ideas that the music is never allowed to speak for itself. Those who know these delightful works will view both performances with some impatience, though the playing as such is accomplished and the recording more than acceptable. Just try the scherzo movement of the *E flat Quartet* and you can see for yourself. The directness of utterance of Nielsen's ideas is undermined by over-sophisticated

expressive exaggeration. Perhaps the group is not quite as intrusive as it was in the *F major Quartet*, Op. 44, but it is still too studied and self-aware. Fortunately, the Oslo Quartet is available at a third of the price.

Wind Quintet, Op. 43.
*** Nimbus NI 5728. V. Quintet – HINDEMITH: *Kleine Kammermusik*; LIGETI: *6 Bagatelles.* ***

The Vienna Quintet – or, to give it its chosen website name, the 'quintett.wien' – give us a totally fresh and delightful account of the Nielsen, which proves, as do its two companions, a delight from start to finish. Beautifully cultured playing which reveals their affection for this piece. Perhaps the earthiness of some of the finale's variations eludes them, but this is a small reservation. There is no harm in seeing Nielsen attired in his Sunday best or having black Copenhagen coffee with schlagobers. The recording, made in the Wiener Konzerthaus, is first class. This displaces the Athena Quintet and the various Scandinavian ensembles from Bergen to Jutland who have recorded it, though the pioneering Copenhagen Wind Quintet, for whom Nielsen wrote the piece, is in a special category.

PIANO MUSIC

Chaconne; Dream of Merry Christmas; Festival Prelude; Humoresque-bagatelles, Op. 11; Piano Pieces for Young & Old, Op. 53; 3 Pieces, Op. 59; 5 Pieces, Op. 3; Luciferian Suite, Op. 45; Symphonic Suite, Op. 8; Theme & Variations, Op. 40.
(B) ** Danacord DACOCD 498/499 (2). Miller.

Chaconne; Humoresque-bagatelles; Luciferian Suite; Piano Music for Young & Old, Books I–II; 5 Pieces, Op. 3; 3 Pieces, Op. 59; Symphonic Suite, Op. 8; Theme & Variations, Op. 40.
*(*) da capo 8.224095/6 (2). Koppel.

Mina Miller is an American academic who edited the texts of the piano music for the Wilhelm Hansen Edition in 1981 and subsequently recorded them for Hyperion in 1986, of which this is a Double reissue. She really understands what this music is about but does not command the keyboard authority or range of sonority of an Andsnes.

Apart from his distinction as a composer, Herman Koppel's interpretations of Nielsen provide a link with the composer, for as a young man of 21, he played for him. He recorded the *Chaconne* and the *Theme and Variations* in 1940, and again in 1952, in the early days of LP, when he also committed the *Suite*, the *Three Piano Pieces*, Op. 59, and other important works to disc. The present set was recorded in 1982–3, when he was in his mid-seventies and beyond his prime. There is insufficient subtlety in tonal colour and dynamic shading.

VOCAL MUSIC

Songs, Op. 4; 6; 10; Bow Down Your Head Now;
Bright are the Leaves in the Woods Now; Flower;
Maskerade: Duet. Nature Study; Italian Pastoral
Aria; Oft am I Glad; Oh, Strange Evening Breezes.
*** dacapo 8.224218. Dam-Jensen, Lassen, Staerk.

Nielsen's songs may not have the psychological subtlety of Kilpinen or the nature mysticism of Sibelius,
but within this repertory they have been surpassed in
neither artistry nor beauty and subtlety of vocal
colour. They stem from the directness and simplicity
of Danish folksong and the songs of Nielsen's precursor, C. F. E. Weyse. All of them are strophic and fresh,
touching and heart-warming. No doubt the wonderful records made in the 1940s by Aksel Schiøtz served
to inhibit Danish singers from trespassing on this
repertory, for the LP and CD eras have done nothing
like justice to their genius, though all the Nielsen
songs have been recorded at one time or another. But
now at long last comes a new record that presents
these captivating songs in a worthy manner and well
recorded. Inger Dam-Jensen captures their special
character splendidly, and she has excellent support
from the pianist Ulrich Stærk. Her choice ranges over
the whole of Nielsen's career, from the Opp. 4 and 6
collections of 1891 through to the *Italian Pastoral* of
1931. There is also a short duet from the opera
Maskerade in which she is partnered by Morten Ernst
Lassen. Strongly recommended.

OPERA

Maskarade (complete).
◉→ (M) ******* Decca 475 214-2 (2). Haugland, Resmark,
Henning, Jensen, Skovus, Kristensen, Ravn,
Bonde-Hansen, Rørholm, Danish Nat. R. Ch. & SO,
Schirmer.

Ulf Schirmer's outstanding recording of this
neglected but appealing opera won the *Gramophone*'s
20th-Century Opera Award in 1999, so it now reappears at mid-price. It is discussed in more depth in
our main volume, but it can be recommended unre-
servedly.

NIELSEN, Ludolf (1876–1939)

String Quartets Nos. 2 in C min., Op. 5; 3 in C, Op.
41.
**(*) CPO 999 698-2. Aros Qt.

Ludolf Nielsen formed and played in a string quartet
in his younger days, and his *Second Quartet* of 1903–4
is beautifully crafted and effortlessly fluent. It is
cyclic in layout, its language owes much to Svendsen
and shows a natural feeling for form. There is a
certain dignity and nobility that compensate for a
lack of personality and depth. The slow movement of
the *Third*, however, is a moving and eloquent lament,

written on the death of the composer's parents in
1919. Civilized and cultured music, which gives pleasure, even though the Aros Quartet are not the last
word in polish or tonal blend. Still, these are very
acceptable performances, and very well recorded.

Symphony No. 1 in B min. Op. 3; Fra Bjærgene
(From the Mountains: Symphonic Suite), Op. 8.
** da capo 8.224093. Danish PO, Cramer.

Ludolf Nielsen was eleven years younger than his
famous namesake and, like his exact contemporary,
Hakon Børresen, a pupil of Svendsen. His *First Sym-*
phony (1903) has real symphonic feeling and a natural grasp of form. The ideas have a touch of Bruckner
and of Carl Nielsen too, and it is obvious that Ludolf
possessed an original mind. The Danish Philharmonic is the South Jutland Orchestra, based at
Odense, and the playing under the German conductor Frank Cramer is perfectly acceptable, though the
recording is not top-drawer. Both the *Symphony* and
the *Suite*, Op. 8, are well worth investigating.

Symphony No. 3 in C, Op. 22; Hjortholm, Op. 53.
** da capo 8.224098. Bamberg SO, Cramer.

There are six Nielsens other than the famous Carl in
the record catalogues, and even one who shares his
first name. Like his colleague Hakon Børresen, who
has been receiving attention of late, Carl Henrik
Ludolf Nielsen was eleven years younger than his
celebrated countryman. He was both eclectic and
prolific, with some 200 works to his credit, and he
served for a time in the viola section of the Tivoli
Orchestra and later as its conductor. From 1926 until
his death in 1939 Nielsen was with the Danish Radio,
planning the programmes of its newly founded
orchestra. Whatever his limitations, he has the
breadth of a symphonist. His *Third Symphony* (1913)
is generally post-romantic with touches of Bruckner
and the occasional reminder of the late Dvořák tone-
poems and of Wagner. However, the work is overlong
and not free from bombast. Nielsen was not a great
original, but his craftsmanship is expert and his
discourse civilized. The tone-poem *Hjortholm*, written in the early 1920s, does not fulfil the promise of
its opening. Well-prepared performances and acceptable recording, even if it is wanting the last ounce of
transparency.

(i) *Violin Sonatas Nos. 1 in A, Op. 9; 2 in G min.,*
Op. 35. Prelude & Presto, Op. 52 (for solo violin);
Prelude & Theme with Variations, Op. 48 (for solo
violin).
*** BIS CD 1284. Demertzis, with (i) Asteriadou.

The *Violin Sonatas* are relatively neglected, though
they are both fine works; the *G minor*, composed just
before the First World War, is one of his best pieces.
Nielsen, himself an accomplished violinist, spent
some time as a young man in the Royal Danish
Orchestra. In addition to the two sonatas, we have
two other works for violin alone. It was when he was

shown the *First Sonata* that the Hungarian violinist Emil Telmányi made contact with the composer and later became his son-in-law. Nielsen composed two extended works for solo violin for him, the *Prelude and Theme with Variations* from 1923 and the *Prelude and Presto*, composed five years later. Georgios Demertzis and Maria Asteriadou do the sonatas justice and the former tackles the formidable difficulties of the two solo works with aplomb. This well-recorded CD fills an important gap in the Nielsen discography.

NONO, Luigi (1924–90)

(i) *Como una ola de fuerza y luz* (for soprano, piano, orchestra & tape). ... *soffrte onde serene* (for piano & magnetic tape).
(M) *** DG (ADD) 471 362-2. Pollini; (i) with Slava Taskova, Bav. RSO, Abbado) – MANZONI: *Masse: Omaggio a Edgard Varèse.* ***

Like Henze, Nono was much influenced by the Cuban revolution. *Como una ola de fuerza y luz*, a large-scale work involving sumptuous sound, is among the direct inspirations. It involves electronic devices, with blocks of sound and a hammering piano soloist (what a waste to use Pollini!) subjected to electronic treatment – not music in the conventional sense at all, but, with superb recording, it certainly makes an impression.

... *soffrte onde serene* represents Nono's personal response to the playing of Pollini, his sympathy and admiration heightened by family bereavements suffered by composer and pianist. The concentration of the performance helps one to make light of the difficulty of the idiom. This repertoire is not for everyone, but it is well worth investigating by those for whom the possibilities of electronic exploration are of interest. Certainly there are no complaints about the skill and dedication of the recording producer and engineers.

NØRHOLM, Ib (born 1931)

Symphonies Nos. (i) *4 (Décreation), Op. 76. 5 (The Four Elements), Op. 80.*
** Kontrapunkt CD 32212. (i) Pavlovski, Dahlberg, Høyer, Nørholm, Danish Nat. R. Ch.; Danish Nat. RSO, Serov.

The *Fourth Symphony (Décreation)* is highly self-conscious – the sub-title itself, *Moralities* or *There may be Many Miles to the Nearest Spider*, puts you in the picture, although there are many imaginative touches during its course. Sadly, inspiration is intermittent and the work as a whole is deficient in thematic vitality. There is a lot going on but very little actually happens. The *Fifth Symphony (The Four Elements)* is better, though again its neo-expressionism outstays its welcome. The perform-ances under Eduard Serov are obviously committed, and in the *Fourth* the composer himself is the narrator. Decent recording.

NORMAN, Ludwig (1831–85)

Symphonies Nos. 1 in F min., Op. 22; 3 in D min., Op. 58.
*(*) Sterling CDS 1038-2. Nat. SO of South Africa, Eichenholz.

Ludwig Norman was an interesting figure in Swedish musical life. A champion of Berwald, whose influence can be discerned in the *First Symphony*, he was much drawn to the world of Schumann and Mendelssohn. The former remains the dominant influence not only here but elsewhere in his output. Unfortunately, the orchestral playing is wanting in finish and the strings are particularly scruffy. There is little space in which the tutti can expand and the texture lacks transparency.

NOVÁK, Vitězslav (1870–1949)

Cello Sonata, Op. 68.
*** Sup. SU 3515-2. Barta, Cech – KODALY: *Cello Sonatas.* ***

As a powerful supplement to Kodály's two cello masterpieces, Jiří Barta and Jan Cech offer one of Vitězslav Novák's late works, written in 1941 during the Nazi occupation of Czechoslovakia. As Novák explained, it represented an eruption of hatred against the invaders and their tyranny. Though it may not quite match the two Kodály works in emotional power, the darkness and intensity of the writing over the closely argued single movement – bringing together elements of a multi-movement sonata structure – are most impressive, particularly in a performance as commanding as this.

NYSTEDT, Knut (born 1915)

Apocalypse Joannis.
**(*) Simax PSC1241 (2). Julsrud, Gilchrist, Oslo Ch. & PO, Remmereit.

The Norwegian composer Knut Nystedt, now in his late eighties, is best known for his choral music. He was for many years conductor of the Norsk Solistkor and as the opus number of *Apocalypse Joannis* shows (115 on the cover and 155 inside the booklet!) he is nothing if not prolific. The present work was written in response to a commission from the Oslo Philharmonic to mark his eighty-fifth birthday in 2000. It is inspired by texts from the Revelation of St John the Divine; but unlike, say, Hilding Rosenberg's *Johannes Uppenbarelse*, which is half-oratorio half-symphony, this divides into three purely orchestral movements, plus a finale for two soloists, chorus and orchestra lasting the best part of an hour (though it seems longer). For a composer in his eighties, it is undoubtedly quite an achievement. The musical language is eclectic and the writing effective and often imaginative (the third movement 'he is the Word which came forth from silence' is a case in point) and there is no doubting his skill in handling his forces. Nystedt's orchestration is masterly and resourceful, and there is a strong atmosphere at times and some arresting musical ideas. However, not all this music is touched with distinction, and to be frank the musical personality is not quite big enough to sustain a canvas of these dimensions. But we are glad to have heard the piece, and there are no quarrels with the quality of the performance or recording.

Canticles of Praise: Kristnikvede; A Song as in the Night.

** Simax PSC 1190. Bergen Cathedral Ch. & O, Magnersnnes.

The *Kristnikvede* or *Canticles of Praise* was commissioned in 1995 to commemorate Olav Trygvason's arrival in Norway in AD 995 and its conversion to Christianity; *A Song as in the Night* was written for a Swedish choral society in the university city of Uppsala. Nystedt's musical language is very direct in utterance, diatonic and well written. He knows exactly what voices can do. There is a faint wisp of Stravinsky and Honegger too. Worthwhile music decently performed, though the choir is not in the first flight and neither is the orchestra. But Nystedt is a composer of substance.

OFFENBACH, Jacques (1819–80)

Gaîté parisienne (ballet, arr. Rosenthal; complete).

(B) ** EMI Encore (ADD) 5 85066-2. Monte Carlo Op. O, Rosenthal – WALDTEUFEL: *Waltzes*. ***

Gaîté parisienne (ballet; complete); Offenbachiana (both arr. Rosenthal).

(BB) ** Naxos 8.554005. Monte-Carlo PO, Rosenthal.

As in his later version for Naxos, Rosenthal's mid-1970s EMI recording, though sometimes idiomatically persuasive, has not the glamour and verve of the finest versions, notably those of Fiedler and Karajan. However, those attracted to the four Waldteufel *Waltzes* may well prefer this EMI coupling to *Offenbachiana*.

Naxos must have felt that it was quite a feather in their cap to get Manuel Rosenthal to record his own arrangements of these two Offenbach ballets. But alas, as he proved with his previous recording for EMI, he is a less inspiring conductor than he is an arranger. He obviously chooses ballet dance tempi, and while the orchestra responds with playing of elegance and polish and the wind soloists are all very good, the absence of uninhibited zest is a great drawback, especially in the famous final *Can-can*.

Gaîté parisienne (ballet; excerpts); Orpheus in the Underworld: Overture.

(M) ** Sony (ADD) SMK 61830. NYPO, Bernstein – BIZET: *Symphony in C* ** (with SUPPE: *Beautiful Galathea: Overture* ***).

Bernstein's quite enjoyable performance of excerpts from *Gaîté parisienne* dates from 1969, and would be more recommendable if the ballet were recorded complete and the sound was less brash. The *Orpheus in the Underworld* overture comes off well, and the (1967) recording is richer here than in *Gaîté parisienne*. The Suppé Overture is superbly done.

OPERA

La Belle Hélène (complete).

(B) ** EMI (ADD) 5 74085-2 (2). Millet, Burles, Benoit, Dens, Ch. & L.O.P., Marty.

Jean-Pierre Marty's 1970 recording is fair value at its bargain price, although no texts are provided. He has the advantage of a largely French cast, who generally sing their parts well enough and with character, but Danièle Millet is not the equal of either Norman or Lott in the other available sets (see our main *Guide*). The recording is acceptable and would be recommendable enough were it not for the Plasson and Minkowski versions, which outclass it in every way and are well worth the extra outlay.

Les Contes d'Hoffmann (complete).

*** Warner **DVD** 0630 19392-2. Domingo, Serra, Baltsa, Cotrubas, Evans, Nimsgern, Ghiuselev, Lloyd, ROHCG Ch. & O, Prêtre (V/D: Brian Large).

The Warner DVD offers a 1981 performance at Covent Garden with Plácido Domingo ideally cast in the name-part, singing and acting superbly in John Schlesinger's production, here imaginatively directed for video by Brian Large. Georges Prêtre conducts an idiomatic performance, using the traditional score, with the climactic sextet as part of the Venice Act, which comes second in the sequence, leaving the Antonia Act till last and making the epilogue the briefest of afterthoughts.

Like the production, sets and costumes, the casting is lavish, with separate star singers for roles normally doubled up between the acts. Effective as all the performances are, the very length of the cast list makes it most regrettable that the box contains no booklet and little information, not even a cast list. One simply has to rely on the visual credits at the end. Luciana Serra is bright and agile as the doll, Olympia, though edgy as recorded, while Agnes Baltsa is an imperious Giulietta in the Venice Act, tough and characterful with her tangy mezzo, and Ileana Cotrubas is charming and touching as Antonia. Among those outstanding in the character roles are Geraint Evans as Coppelius, Robert Tear as Spalanzani, and Nicola Ghiuselev as Dr Miracle. The sound is a little dry and is distracting in the context.

Les Fées du Rhin (complete).

⋆⋆⋆ Accord 472 920-2 (3). Schörg, Gubisch, Beczala, Jenis, Klaveness, Pepper, R. Letton Ch., Montpellier Nat. O, Layer.

When, in 1863, Offenbach was commissioned to write an opera by the director of the Hofoper in Vienna (Offenbach's operettas were hugely popular in Vienna at that time) he leapt at the chance, always wishing to write something more serious than operettas. The result was *Les Fées du Rhin*, or *Die Rheinnixen*, of which this CD set (sung in German) is its first recording. Into this work Offenbach poured everything that embodied German romanticism: from ruined castles by midnight, to soldiers, village maidens, the Rhine, of course (with its water-sprites, pixies and elves) – and even psychic shock is included! Add to this elements of grand opera, French and Italian opera, and just about everything else you can think of, and the result is a Weber-cum-Offenbach mélange. If the story is a typical example of operatic hokum, one forgives its excesses for the sake of the music, which contains some excellent Offenbach tunes; and if the spirit of operetta is never too far away, there is more dramatic writing than you might expect from this source – some of the arias and duets are really quite impressive; with plenty of splendid ensembles and vibrant choruses (as well as a delightful ballet and *grande valse*) there is plenty of spectacle too. The cast in this live (2002) recording is generally very good. The heroine, Armgard, sung by Regina Schörg, copes well with the coloratura passages: her aria in Act I, *There, where the ancient oaks and dark pine trees grow*, is a good example of Offenbach creating a gently eerie effect with wordless coloratura passages appearing throughout the song. It is curiously memorable; later, when she is forced to sing for the solders, she delivers some even more impressive coloratura, before dropping down dead – or at least appearing to do so. The hero, Franz, a light tenor sung by Piotr Beczala, has an attractive voice, coping reasonably well in the high passages and singing with sensitivity when called for; he is well contrasted with the baritone of Dalibor Jenis, his rival, in splendid full-blooded voice. Armgard's mother, Hedwig, sung by Nora Gubisch, is a fine mezzo, and the rest of the cast is good. That the whole thing works is a tribute to Friedemann Layer, who draws an excellent response from his orchestra. The sound is very acceptable too, with very little noise from the audience; and full texts and translations are provided.

La Fille du tambour major (complete).

(B) ⋆⋆(⋆) Accord/Universal (ADD) 461 673-2 (2). Harbell, Arnaud, Musy, Pondeau, Mallabrera, Light, Ch. & O, Blareau.

La Fille du tambour major was one of Offenbach's best later works, closer to the spirit of a light *opéra-comique* than some of his more savage *opéras-bouffes* (the spirit of Donizetti's *La fille du Régiment* is also echoed here). It fizzes with good tunes and wit, and so does this 1962 performance. As one might expect, it is full of 'military' numbers, with plentiful use of snare drum and the like; the finales build up to a frenzy of excitement, with Acts II and III ending with the exhilarating opening tune of the *Overture*. (On the opening night, the audience rose to its feet when, in the finale, the exciting brassy *Chant du départ* – a patriotic song indelibly linked with Napoleonic victories – was thundered out on the stage, causing the audience to go wild with excitement: a brilliant *coup de théâtre* of which Offenbach was master.) Character numbers abound, such as a 'Donkey' song in which the owner sings of the virtues of the animal that pulls her cart: he had a good heart ('there are few men on earth that can say as much'), and an undefiled heart ('there are few women who can boast that'), all supported by 'Hee-haws' from the chorus; there is a splendid waltz, well up to Offenbach's best standard, and a dashing *Tarentella* which opens Act III; there is even a 'migraine' song! The drawback for non-French speakers is that there are no texts and translations, not even a synopsis, and there is quite a bit of spoken dialogue (performed with exceptional liveliness). The soloists are excellent, full of character, with Richard Blareau keeping the fun going all the way through. The sound, considering its provenance, is excellent: bright and vivid, only lacking the depth of a modern recording. A must for Offenbachians.

La Grande Duchesse de Gérolstein (complete).

(B) ⋆⋆ Accord/Universal (ADD) 465 871-2 (2). LaFaye, Raynaud, Aubert, Bedex, Asse, Terrasson, Ch. & O, Hartemann.

Along with *Orphée aux enfers* and *La Vie parisienne*, *La Grande Duchesse de Gérolstein* represents the best of Offenbach's exhilarating satires, this time its target being the military. It is crammed full of his best tunes, sparkling ensembles and arias, with rousing choruses and with the score laced with piquant wit and sparkle; it is in many ways the most consistently enjoyable of all his *opéras-bouffes*. This recording dates from 1966 and has the obvious advantage of an all-French, idiomatic cast. The performance is a good one, though it does not quite possess the fizz of *La Fille du tambour major* on the same label. The rather dry, unflattering sound does not help matters, although everything is reasonably vivid, especially the (lively) spoken dialogue, which sounds dubbed on afterwards. One drawback for non-French speakers is that there are no texts and translations, not even a synopsis, and there's quite a bit of spoken dialogue: one really does need to know what is going on to appreciate fully this marvellous piece of froth. The version ideally to wait for, not currently available, is Sony's glittering version with the delicious Régine Crespin in the title-role, conducted by Plasson. Until that arrives, this makes a serviceable stop-gap.

Orpheus in the Underworld (highlights in English).
** TER CDTER 1134. Kale, Watson, Angas, Squires,
   Bottone, Pope, ENO Ch. & O, Elder.

After listening to Plasson's recording of *Orphée*, this version, based on ENO's production of the mid-1980s, now seems rather flat and dated, with Public Opinion obviously based on the then current prime minister. Those who saw and enjoyed the show will get more out of this than those who did not, for while there is plenty of knock-about British humour, little of Offenbach's French champagne comes through here. Indeed, this kind of performance, when even Bonaventura Bottone's hilariously camp portrait of prancing Mercury is not nearly so much fun when simply heard, ideally needs a DVD.

ONSLOW, Georges (1784–1853)

String Quintets in B flat, Op. 33; in E min., Op. 74.
**(*) MDG 603 1233-2. Ens. Concertant Frankfurt.

String Quintets in A min., Op. 34; G, Op. 35.
*** MDG 603 1253-2. Quintett Momento Musicale.

Georges Onslow was one of the few French composers of his generation who wrote a substantial amount of chamber music, which represents his largest body of work. His quartets and quintets were published in his lifetime and reached a wide audience in their day, although they were sometimes criticized for a certain emotional coolness, even blandness. The Ensemble Concertant are not quite as sweet-sounding as the Quintett Momento Musicale and don't seem to have the music quite under their belts as do their rivals. They still make a good case for the Op. 33 (1827–8) and Op. 74 (1847) *Quintets*, the latter being the more seductive. However, all these works, and especially those in the hands of the Quintett Momento Musicale, emerge as fresh, well-constructed pieces, generally in classical tradition, not always strikingly individual but unfailingly enjoyable. The *Adagio* movements are beautifully poised, while the lively outer movements have plenty of life – the *Presto* of the Op. 35 is especially enjoyable and inventive. Both CDs are beautifully recorded by MDG.

Grand Septet, Op. 79 (for flute, oboe, clarinet, horn, bassoon, double-bass & piano); *Grand Sextet, Op. 77b* (for flute, clarinet, bassoon, horn, double-bass & piano).
(BB) **(*) Warner Apex 0927 49536-2. Nielson
   Quintet, with Marder, Hubeau.

These two works were written during Onslow's last creative period, both dating from 1849, though the *Sextet* was a transcription of the *Nonet*, Op. 77, for strings, published the previous year. Both are quite substantial works, lasting over half an hour, and are eminently entertaining in their bright and breezy way. The 1992 performance is good one, though occasionally it is possible to imagine more polished

accounts. The recording is vivid, if a little unyielding – it's a tad dry and also quite closely miked, thus limiting the full dynamic range of the performance. However, these are comparatively minor points overall, and this disc, at its low price, is worth considering.

ORFF, Carl (1895–1982)

Carmina Burana.
(M) *** RCA (ADD) 82876 59417-2. Mandac, Kolk,
   Milnes, New England Conservatory Ch. & Children's
   Ch., Boston SO, Ozawa.
(B) ** Decca Penguin (ADD) 460 646-2. Burrows,
   Devos, Shirley-Quirk, Brighton Festival Ch., RPO,
   Dorati.

Ozawa's earlier version of *Carmina Burana* is strong and incisive, bringing out the bold simplicity of the score with tingling immediacy, rather than dwelling on its subtlety of colour. The soloists, too, are all characterful, especially Sherrill Milnes. The tenor Stanley Kolk sounds a little constrained with his *Roast Swan*, but otherwise the solo singing is always responsive. Overall, this is a highly effective account, if not a first choice. Full texts and translations have now been included in this mid-price release (unlike previous incarnations), making it now fully recommendable in RCA's mid-priced 'Classic Library' series.

Dorati's version was recorded in the Kingsway Hall in 1976 in Decca's Phase Four system. The result is a beefy, vibrant account with good singing and playing. Despite some eccentric speeds, Dorati shows a fine rhythmic sense, but the performance cannot match the best available. The remastered recording brings a bold impact in *fortissimos*, but the quieter, more atmospheric passages are less cleanly defined. Now reissued on the bargain Penguin Classics label with an essay by John Berendt, it hardly makes a primary choice, which rests with the EMI recording made in Toulouse and conducted by Michel Plasson (5 57197-2).

PACIUS, Fredrik (1809–91)

Kung Karls Jakt (King Charles's Hunt; opera: complete).
(M) *** Finlandia 1576 51107-2. Törnqvist, Lindroos,
   Krause, Grönroos, Jubilate Ch., Finnish Nat. Op. O,
   Söderblom.

Fredrik Pacius became known as 'the father of Finnish music', for he brought the Finnish capital, then a provincial backwater, into contact with the mainstream of European music. His opera *King Charles's Hunt* brings pretty simple musical ideas. Some are pleasant, but there is little evidence of much individuality. There is some fine singing from Pirkko Törnqvist as the fisherman's daughter, Leonora, from

Peter Lindroos as her fiancé, and from Walton Grön-roos as the coup leader, Gustaf Gyllenstjerna. The young King is a speaking role. Much care has been lavished on the production and Ulf Söderblom holds things together admirably. No masterpiece is uncovered, but it will be of interest to collectors with a specialist interest in the beginnings of opera in the northern countries.

PAGANINI, Niccolò (1782-1840)

Violin Concertos Nos. '0' in E (orch. Mompellio); 2 in B min.
(M) * (**) EMI 5 57150-2. Accardo, O da Camera Italiana.

Violin Concertos Nos. 1 in D, Op. 6; 3 in E.
(M) * (**) EMI 5 57151-2. Accardo, O da Camera Italiana.

Violin Concertos Nos. 4 in D min.; 5 in A min. (orch. Mompellio).
(M) * (**) EMI 5 57152-2. Accardo, O da Camera Italiana.

Phonè Italia have prevailed on Accardo to re-record the Paganini concertos and have provided what is described as an additional work, discovered in London as recently as 1972. The manuscript for the so-called No. '0' was scored for guitar accompaniment, which has been filled out and orchestrated very convincingly by Federico Mompellio. However, this is in fact the same concerto as the posthumous No. 6 included by DG. It almost certainly dates from just before the *First Concerto*, and it might be regarded as a model for that familiar piece, for it has a rather similar (if not so memorable) lyrical secondary theme in the first movement and plenty of solo display in the finale.

Accardo's consummate technique and his persuasive musical response are as impressive as ever, as are his dazzling fireworks. The finales of Nos. 1 and 2 have great flair. He also directs the orchestral accompaniments, and very impressively too. The snag is the recording, which spotlights the solo violin and brings an unwanted excess of digital brilliance to the orchestra, which fiercens the orchestral strings in all the *fortissimos*. There is plenty of weight but the upper range is often unagreeably shrill. The DG set is the one to go for.

Violin Concerto No. 1 in D, Op. 6.
(M) *** EMI (ADD) 5 62594-2. Perlman, RPO, Foster
 – SARASATE: *Carmen Fantasy* etc. ***

Perlman's famous 1971 recording returns at mid-price in the 'Perlman Edition', with two extra Sarasate items added. Provided one does not feel strongly about the traditional cuts in the Paganini, this performance remains unsurpassed.

PALESTRINA, Giovanni Pierluigi da (1525–94)

Canticum Canticorum; 8 Madrigali spirituali (from Book I).
(BB) ** Virgin 2×1. 5 62239-2 (2). Hilliard Ens., Hillier.

The 29 motets Palestrina based on the *Canticum Canticorum* (Song of Songs) include some of his most inspired writing; all are for five voices. Into these impassioned texts with their strongly erotic overtones, Palestrina poured music of great feeling, remarkable beauty and finish of workmanship. The *Song of Songs* has always been regarded as a symbolic illustration of 'the happy union of Christ and His Spouse', the Spouse being the Church, more specifically the happiest part of it, namely perfect souls, every one of which is His beloved. These are beautifully shaped performances, with refined tonal blend and perfect intonation, but they are comparatively remote and ultimately rather cool in emotional temperature. Earlier recordings have, with success, adopted a more fittingly expressive and sensuous approach. The second CD includes also eight Petrarch settings from the *First Book of Madrigals*.

Music for Advent and Christmas: *Missa Hodie Christus natus est.* **Motets:** *Alma redemptoris mater; Canite tube; Deus tu converses; Christus, redemptor omnium; Hodie Christus natus est; Magnificat Primi toni; O admirabile commercium; O magnum mysterium; Tui sunt coeli.*
*** Hyp. CDA 67396. Westminster Cathedral Ch., Baker.

Westminster Cathedral Choir under its latest choirmaster, Martin Baker, goes from strength to strength. This is a thrilling recording of Palestrina's music for the Christmas season, centring not just on the Mass, *Hodie Christus natus est*, but on the motet on which the Mass is based. Vividly set against the cathedral acoustic, warm but clear, it brings out better than most rival versions the exuberance of the cries of *Noe* ('Noel') that dramatically punctuate the piece, reflecting individual joy in welcoming the birth of Christ. The eight other items, all relating to Advent and Christmas, culminate in the *Magnificat Primi Toni* with its rich textures, framed before and after by the plainsong antiphon, *Hodie Christus natus est*.

PARRY, Hubert (1848–1918)

VOCAL MUSIC

I was glad (from Psalm 122).
(M) *** EMI (ADD) 5 85148-2. Cambridge University Music Society, King's College, Cambridge, Ch., New Philh. O, Ledger – ELGAR: *Coronation Ode* etc. ***

This expansive version of Parry's most popular

church anthem makes an excellent coupling for Elgar's patriotic ceremonial music. Splendid recording too.

PÄRT, Arvo (born 1935)

(i) *Cantus in memory of Benjamin Britten;* (ii) *Festina lente;* (i) *Fratres* (for string orchestra & percussion); *Summa* (for string orchestra) (iii) *Fratres; Spiegel im Spiegel* (both for violin & piano); (iv) *The Beatitudes for Choir & Organ; Magnificat;* (iv) *7 Magnificat Antiphons; Summa.*

(B) *** CfP 585 9142. (i) Estonian Nat. SO, Järvi; (ii) Bournemouth Sinf., Studt; (iii) Little, Roscoe; (iv) King's College, Cambridge, Ch., Cleobury; (v) Varsai Singers, Backhouse.

An admirable and enterprising compilation from Classics for Pleasure, gathered from a number of sources to tempt those who have not sampled this Estonian composer's highly individual sound-world with its tintinabulation (ringing bells). In the two works for violin and piano, Tasmin Little holds the listener's attention by the intensity of her commitment and the powerful projection of her playing. *Summa* is heard in two versions, the choral one being a fresh and carol-like setting of the Creed, and this leads naturally into the brief but concentrated *Magnificat Antiphons*, with the Seventh the longest and most telling. Pärt's comparatively static *Magnificat* relies on intensity of sonority rather than movement; his better-known *Beatitudes*, gentle and rippling, is regularly pierced by dissonance, with the organ entering briefly and unexpectedly at the end to add a florid postlude and then disappear into infinity. Fine, idiomatic performances throughout and excellent recording.

PERGOLESI, Giovanni (1710–36)

Confitebor tibi Domine.

✿ (M) *** DHM/BMG 82876 60145-2. Monoyios, Landauer, Balthazar-Neumann Ch., Freiburg Bar. O, Hengelbrock – DURANTE: *Magnificat in B flat*; D'ASTORGA: *Stabat Mater.* *** ✿

Pergolesi's little-known setting of Psalm 110 immediately arrests the attention with its richly eloquent choral opening, but later it depends upon the solo soprano, who has a dialogue with the chorus in the *Confessio*, and the solo alto, whose *Sanctum et terrible* and *Intellectus bonus* create the work's expressive climax. Both Ann Monoyios and Bernhard Landauer rise to the occasion here, as does the chorus in the closing *Gloria Patri* and *Sicut erat*. The excellent period-instrument Freiburg Baroque Orchestra are notable for their characterful contribution to the *Sanctum*. In short, this performance, directed with life and spirit by Thomas Hengelbrock, is first class in every way, and so is the recording. Highly recommended.

La Morte de San Giuseppe (oratorio).

(M) ★ Warner Fonit 0927 43308 (2). Farruggia, Manca di Nissa, Angeles Peters, Pace, Naples Alessandro Scarlatti R. & TV O, Panni.

The autograph score of Pergolesi's oratorio has only recently come to light in the New York Pierpont Library, which acquired it from a European dealer. It is a splendid work, but the present recording will not do. The singing of Maria Angeles Peters in the role of San Michelle is insecure to say the least and suffers from poor intonation. A delightful aria like *Appena spira aura soave* ('As soon as the gentle breeze blows') needs a voice like Emma Kirkby's. The contralto, Bernadette Manca di Nissa, who takes the part of Maria Santissima, is much stronger, but Patrizia Pace in the demanding coloratura role of Amor is not always accurate either, and Michele Farruggia as San Giuseppe is only adequate. Panni gets a lively and stylish response from the excellent orchestra and the digital recording is excellent, but this can only serve as a stopgap until something better comes along.

PETTERSSON, Allan (1911–80)

Barfota sånger (Barefoot Songs); 6 Songs.

** CPO 999499-2. Groop, Garben.

These songs come from the war years when Pettersson was working as an orchestral player. The *Barefoot Songs* precede any of his seventeen symphonies and are of the utmost simplicity. They are all strophic, and few last more than a couple of minutes. They are superbly sung by Monica Groop, but not even she and her expert pianist can disguise their naïvety and in some cases emptiness. Admirers of the composer may not find their charms so eminently resistible or the melodic invention so unmemorable.

PHILLIPS, Montague (1885–1969)

Arabesque; Moorland Idyll; The Rebel Maid: 4 Dances. Revelry Overture; A Shakespearean Scherzo (Titania and her Elvish Court); Sinfonietta; A Surrey Suite; Symphony in C min.

(M) *** Dutton CDLX 7140. BBC Concert O, Sutherland.

Montague Phillips's name has often popped up on ASV's series of light classics recordings, and it is good that he has a disc devoted to himself. It gets off to an exhilarating start with the *Revelry Overture* of 1937, a lively six-minute piece encompassing many attractive ideas, all brightly orchestrated. The *Four Dances* from his comic-opera *The Rebel Maid* are very much in the vein of Edward German and Sullivan – and none the worse for that – with their rustic atmosphere also pervading other numbers, including the pleasing *Moorland Idyll*, which has a lilting middle section in the manner of Dvořák. The two movements which make up the *C minor Symphony* (first heard in 1912) include *A Summer Nocturne*, showing the composer in a rather deeper emotional mood, while *A Spring Rondo* is in a more characteristic and lighter vein (the other two movements of the *Symphony* have yet to be reconstructed). The *Arabesque* of 1927 has an appealing Russian flavour, while the *Shakespearean Scherzo*, a lively and inventive mini tone-poem, is very enjoyable too. Although written during wartime Britain in 1943, the *Sinfonietta* is stiff-upper-lip heroic music rather than reflecting the horrors of war, and the slow movement is agreeably nostalgic. The Scherzo finale has a curious march motif in the middle section, which fades out on muted brass, though the work ends triumphantly. Lewis Foreman, the writer of the notes, suggests that the composer was saying in 1943, 'keep your spirits up, we've almost made it'. Excellent performances, as usual from Gavin Sutherland, well known from his ASV recordings, but here on one of Dutton's discs, superbly engineered.

PISTON, Walter (1894–1976)

Symphonies Nos. 2; 6.
⊖—▪ (BB) ✲✲✲ Naxos 8.559161. Seattle SO, Schwarz.

Make no mistake, these are superb works and they are interpreted here with total dedication and eloquence. Michael Tilson Thomas's Boston account of the *Second Symphony* for Deutsche Grammophon is no longer in circulation, though Leonard Slatkin's *Sixth* with the St Louis orchestra is still to be had. Even so, this competitively priced coupling makes as good an entry point into Piston's musical world as any – almost as good as the *Fourth*, which we highlighted in our main volume. On its original Delos release an additional work, the *Sinfonietta*, was included but is omitted here.

PIZZETTI, Ildebrando (1880–1968)

(i) *Piano Concerto. Preludio per Fedra;* (ii) *Sinfonia del fuoco* (from the film score *Cabiria*).
✲✲ Marco Polo 8.225058. Schumann Philh. O, Caetani, with (i) Stefani; (ii) Statsenko, Städtischer Op. Ch., Chemnitz.

The present issue brings the eloquent Act I *Prelude* to the opera Pizzetti composed with Gabriele d'Annunzio, plus the *Sinfonia del fuoco*, drawn from the incidental music Pizzetti wrote in 1914 for an elaborate production of *Cabiria* (again with d'Annunzio) in which silent film was used. But the most substantial work is the *Piano Concerto*, 'Song of the High Seasons', of 1930. It is a little overripe perhaps, and at times even rather like Rachmaninov. The soloist Susanna Stefani acquits herself well. The *Fedra* prelude is the finest thing here and the Robert Schumann Philharmonie of Chemnitz give decent,

serviceable performances. However, at less than 50 minutes' playing time this CD is over-priced.

PONCHIELLI, Amilcare
(1834–86)

La Gioconda: Dance of the Hours.
✲✲✲ Testament (ADD) SBT 1327. Philh. O, Mackerras –
VERDI: *Overtures and ballet music;*
WOLF-FERRARI: *Overtures, Intermezzi & Dances.*
(✲✲✲)

With the Philharmonia Orchestra in superb form, Mackerras brings refinement and point to his performance of Ponchielli's *Dance of the Hours*, without loss of sparkle.

PÓRARINSSON, Leifur
(1934–c. 1994)

A Dream of the House; In Cyprus; Rent; Spring in my Heart; (i) *Angelus Domini; Styr: Notturno Capriccioso.*
✲✲ Smekkleysta SMK 27. Reykjavík CO; (i) Gunnarsdóttir.

Born in 1934, Leifur Pórarinsson studied in Vienna in the mid-1950s with Hanns Jelinek, a pupil of Alban Berg, and then with Wallingford Riegger and Gunther Schuller in the United States. He subsequently lived for some years in Denmark and, in the early 1990s, in Nicosia. In his work there are traces of Bartók, Stravinsky and Schoenberg, and his adherence to serial technique remained strong until the very end. He died in the mid-1990s, though the notes do not give the exact date. This CD collects six pieces for various chamber combinations; they are eclectic in spirit and idiom, and show a keen aural imagination and an awareness of sonority. (*Rent* is so called because it was a commission from the Örebro Orchestra, which paid his rent for a month!) Among the strongest pieces here is *Angelus Domini*, a setting of Laxness's translation of a medieval Latin poem published in his novel, *The Great Weaver of Kashmir*. All six pieces are resourceful and well crafted, though it is possible to imagine more polished performances. Accomplished and often arresting music, then, albeit one in which it is difficult to discern a strongly distinctive voice.

POULENC, Francis (1899–1963)

(i; ii) *Aubade;* (i; iii) *Concert champêtre for Harpsichord & Orchestra;* (i; ii) *Piano Concerto;* (i; iii; iv) *Double Piano Concerto in D min.;* (i; iv) *Organ Concerto;* (i) *Sinfonietta.* Vocal Music: (vi) *Ave verum corpus; Chanson à boire for male choir a cappella; 7 Chansons; 8 Chansons françaises* (both for mixed choir a cappella; *Exsulate Deo; Figure humaine;* (i; vii; viii) *Gloria;* (vi) *Laudes de Saint*

Antoine de Padoue; (i; viii) *Litanies à la Vierge noire;* (vi) *Mass in G;* 4 *Motets pour un temps de Noël;* 4 *Motets pour un temps de pénitence;* 4 *Petites prières de Saint François d'Assise; Salve Regina;* (i; vii; viii) *Stabat Mater;* (vi) *Un Soir de neige.*

�») (BB) ✱✱✱ EMI 5 62384-2 (5). (i) City of L. Sinfonia, Hickox, with (ii) Pommier; (iii) Cole; (iv) Queffélec; (v) Weir; (vi) The Sixteen, Christophers; (vii) Dubosc; (viii) Westminster Singers.

This budget-priced collection is of high quality and serves admirably for collectors wanting both the concertante and choral music of Poulenc. Jean-Bernard Pommier gives a thoroughly idiomatic and incisive account of the *Aubade,* but the *Piano Concerto* receives rather laid-back treatment with the gamin-like charm of the opening not fully realized. Yet, both Pommier and Anne Queffélec play the *Concerto for Two Pianos* to the manner born. They have the measure of the pastiche Mozart slow movement and the quasi-gamelan first. Maggie Cole then produces a splendidly idiomatic performance of the charming *Harpsichord Concerto,* and so does Gillian Weir in the *Organ Concerto.* However, the balance in the *Concert champêtre* is less than ideal: the harpsichord occupies an appropriately small space, but the wind (and, more particularly, the percussion) are far too prominent. Hickox conducts throughout with aplomb and gives an affectionate and charming account of the *Sinfonietta.* Excellent recording throughout.

Turning to the choral music, the performances from Harry Christophers and The Sixteen (which include the *Figure humaine* for double choir, the *Mass,* and some of the composer's most celebrated a cappella motets) are beautifully sung and can be strongly recommended both on artistic grounds and for the excellence of the sound. The collection of larger-scale works includes the arch-like *Litanies à la Vierge noire,* ravishingly sung by the Westminster Singers, rising to a splendid central climax and back. The combination of the well-known *Gloria,* with what Lionel Salter has described as its 'Stravinskian acerbities', with the less familiar but just as inspired *Stabat Mater* is equally fine. The chorus is confident and firm, and Catherine Dubosc is a warm-toned soloist. In the *Gloria,* although there is plenty of bite, some of Hickox's tempi are on the slow side; even so, he makes them seem convincing. The City of London Sinfonia plays beautifully throughout. The recording is excellent. This set is an undoubted and genuine bargain.

Aubade; Piano Concerto; (i) *Double Piano Concerto in D min.*

☛ ✱✱✱ RCA 82876 60308-2. Le Sage, Liège PO, Denève; (i) with Braley.

After the ambivalent mood of the opening *Toccata,* Poulenc's *Aubade* ('an allegory of women and feminine solitude') is a series of brief vignettes, witty, audacious and melancholy by turns, and at the close the plaintive *Variation for Diana* (the unwillingly chaste heroine of the piece) leads on to a gentle, melancholy *Adieu,* which almost becomes a *marche funèbre.*

The easy-going charm of the opening of the *Piano Concerto* is also admirably caught, the *Andante* wistfully romantic and the skittish finale making a perfect foil. Both are played with style and panache by Eric le Sage, persuasively accompanied by Stéphane Denève.

Frank Braley enthusiastically joins the team for the *Double Piano Concerto,* which opens at high speed, with exhilarating, almost reckless dash, so the contrast of the gentle quasi-Mozartian pastiche of the *Larghetto* is the more enticing. More fireworks in the finale, which brings virtuosic precision of articulation from the soloists, yet keeps its élan. All in all, a very successful, consistently diverting triptych, very well (if resonantly) recorded.

(i) *Aubade. Sinfonietta.*

(BB) ✱✱✱ Hyp. Helios CDH 55167. New L. O, Corp – HAHN: *Le Bal de Béatrice d'Este.* ✱✱✱

The *Sinfonietta* is a fluent and effortless piece, full of resource and imagination, and Ronald Corp and the New London Orchestra do it proud. Julian Evans is an alert soloist in the *Aubade:* his is a performance of real character and, though less well balanced than the *Sinfonietta,* his account can hold its own artistically with the competition. The Hahn rarity with which it is coupled enhances the interest and value of this reissue.

Bucolique (from *Variations sur le nom de Marguerite Long);* (i) *Concert champêtre.* 2 *Marches et un intermède; Fanfare; Pièce brève sur le nom d'Albert Roussel; Sinfonietta; Suite française.*

☛ ✿ (M) ✱✱✱ Decca 476 2191. (i) Rogé; French Nat. O, Dutoit.

The major works here are the *Sinfonietta* and the *Concert champêtre.* The *Sinfonietta,* commissioned to mark the first anniversary of the BBC's Third Programme and dedicated to his fellow composer, Auric, comes off marvellously. For those who entertain doubts as to its quality, this version by Charles Dutoit and the Orchestre National de France should be mandatory listening; it is certainly among the most persuasive accounts in the catalogue. In the *Concert champêtre* Pascal Rogé proves as fine a clavecinist as pianist and his account, equally strong on charm and elegance, ranks high among present recommendations. The smaller pieces greatly enhance the already strong attractions of this disc. All of them are imaginative, none more so than *Bucolique* from the *Variations sur le nom de Marguerite Long.* The excellence of the performances is matched by first-rate and meticulously balanced Decca sound. It now returns to the catalogue at mid-price with Universal's 'Penguin ✿ Collection'.

(i; ii) *Concert champêtre for harpsichord & piano;*
(i; iii) *Double Piano Concerto in D min.; (i–iv)*
Organ Concerto in G min.

(M) (★★★) EMI mono/stereo 5 62647-2 [5 62649-2]. (i)
Paris CO, Cond. (i) Dervaux; with (ii) Van de Wiele;
(iii) Février; composer (iv) Duruflé; cond. Prêtre.

This is the première recording of the *Organ Concerto*
(which first appeared on LP in harness with the
Gloria) and the very first LP account of the *Concerto
champêtre* (written in the late 1920s for Landowska)
with Aimée van de Wiele, and the *Concerto for Two
Pianos* with Jacques Février, both recorded in 1957.
This was briefly available to special order and was
chosen for inclusion in the four-CD box of Poulenc's
complete works that EMI issued to mark the centenary of his birth in 1999. It was rapidly superseded by
the 1962 stereo version with the same soloists but
with Georges Prêtre conducting, and the latter was
chosen for reissue during the LP years. To be frank,
apart from the greater amplitude of stereo there is
not a great deal to choose between them, and in
some ways Van de Wiele's first recording has marginally greater character. In any event this present issue
with Duruflé's authoritative account of the *Organ
Concerto*, made in the presence of the composer, is
thoroughly recommendable in every way and the
sound, exceptional in its day, is still first class. A
worthy addition to EMI's 'Great Recordings of the
Century'.

Concerto in G min. for Organ, Strings & Timpani.
★★ René Gailly CD 87 162. Michiels, Brugense Coll.,
Peire – FAURE: *Requiem.* ★★

Ignace Michiels is an excellent soloist for the Brugense performance, and the orchestra has plenty of
fire. However, it is obvious that there are few players,
and there is a want of body and weight. Not a first
choice, although the Fauré is not unappealing.

(i) *Suite française; (ii) Cello Sonata; (iii) 3
Mouvements perpétuels; (iv) Ave verum; Exsultate
Deo; 4 Motets pour le temps de Noël; 4 Petites
prières de Saint François d'Assise; Salve Regina.*
(M) ★★ ASV Platinum PLT 8515. (i) London Wind O;
(ii) Wallfisch, York; (iii) Bennett, Wynberg; (iv) Joyful
Company of Singers.

Raphael Wallfisch's account of the *Cello Sonata* was
recorded as recently as 2000 and, as you would
expect, he turns in a good performance. But next to
Fournier's EMI version, this newcomer sounds more
efficient than inspired. Perhaps the effect is exacerbated by the recording, which tends to iron out the
dynamic range, and the piano-tone is not especially
rich. The choral items, too, are quite well done, but
there is also plenty of competition here (see our
main volume) and in terms of ensemble, chording
and tonal blend they do not match other recommendations. The *Suite française* is admirably fresh, and
the familiar *Mouvements perpétuels* are beautifully

played and recorded. But this collection is not especially enticing.

PIANO MUSIC

Piano duet

(i) *Music for piano, 4 hands: L'Embarquement pour
Cythère; Sonata.* Solo piano music: *Bourrée au
Pavillon d'Auvergne; Française; Humoresque; 3
Intermezzi; Mélancolie; 3 Mouvements perpétuels; 3
Novelettes; Pastourelle; 3 Pièces; Presto in B flat;
Suite in C; Suite française; Valse in C; Villageoises.*
(BB) ★★ EMI Encore (ADD/DDD) 5 85457-2. Tacchino,
(i) with Février.

This is all delightful music and it is crisply played by
Gabriel Tacchino, although he tends to favour brisk
tempi. He is at his best in the six *Villageoises*, which
are witty and brittle and with a general feeling of
pastiche. The three *Intermezzi* are agreeably romantic, while much of the other music, although slight, is
curiously haunting. Many of the pieces (the *Suite
française* for instance) have a delicately observed
period flavour as well as Poulenc's sophisticated harmonic sense. The piano-sound, whether analogue or
digital, is acceptable but a bit shallow. Tacchino characterizes strongly and the piano timbre does not
help. He is joined by Jacques Février in the four-
handed music, which is thoroughly idiomatic but
less strong on charm. This is fair value, but there are
finer versions of this repertoire available if you pay a
little more.

Solo piano music

*Improvisations Nos. 1–3; 6–8; 12–13; 15; Mouvements
perpétuels; 3 Novelettes; Pastourelle; 3 Pièces; Les
Soirées de Nazelles; Valse.*
☷ ✿ ★★★ Decca 475 042-2. Rogé.

On its first issue in 1988 this collection won the *Gramophone's* Instrumental Award and a ✿ from us – which
we now restore. This music is absolutely enchanting,
full of delight and wisdom; it has many unexpected
touches and is teeming with character. Pascal Rogé is a
far more persuasive exponent of it than any previous
pianist on record; his playing is imaginative and
inspiriting, and the recording is superb.

CHORAL MUSIC

Sacred Music: *Ave verum corpus; Exsulate Deo;
Laudes des Saint Antoine de Padoue; (i) Litanies à la
vierge noire. 4 Motets pour un temps de Noël; 4
Motets pour un temps de Pénitence; Salve Regina;*
Secular Music: *Chanson à boire; 7 Chansons (1936);
8 Chansons françaises (1945); Figure humaine; Un
Soir de neige.*
(BB) ★★(★) EMI Gemini 5 85776-2 (2). Groupe Vocale
de France, Alldis; (i) with Alain (organ).

Recognizing the need for a French chamber choir to match the great international choirs, the Groupe Vocale de France was formed in 1976 by the City of Paris and the French Ministry of Culture, under Marcel Couraud. The result was these two recorded collections: the sacred, recorded in 1981 in L'Eglise Saint Germain, and the secular, recorded six years later in the Salle Wagram. This is all music that ideally needs French voices, and John Alldis has trained his French group splendidly so that they combine precision and fervour with a natural feeling for the words.

In the sacred concert the soaring *Ave Verum* is matched by the exhilaration of the *Exsultate Deo* and the originality of the *Litanies* with its stabbing bursts of organ tone. The *Salve Regina* is very fine too, and the four *Christmas Motets* which close the first disc have the right extrovert joyfulness and sense of wonder. The recording is made within an ecclesiastical ambience, yet the definition is admirable.

Alas, the secular music was balanced less satisfactorily and the effect sounds rather synthetic. Nevertheless the performances are expert enough and, although the acoustic is dryish, this shorter selection is worth having at so modest a cost, even if no texts and translations are included.

OPERA

La Voix humaine.

(M) *** Warner Elatus 2564 60680-2. Migenes, O Nat. de France, Prêtre.

Julia Migenes's dramatic and moving performance of Poulenc's theatrical telephone monologue, *La Voix humaine*, is the finest modern version on record. In our main volume it is linked with the cantata, *Figure humaine*, and with some a cappella motets, but this separate issue is most welcome.

PREVIN, André (born 1929)

Violin Concerto.

*** DG 474 500-2. Mutter, LSO, composer –
  BERNSTEIN: *Serenade after Plato's 'Symposium'.*
  ***

André Previn wrote his *Violin Concerto* in 2001 on commission from the Boston Symphony Orchestra for the violinist Anne-Sophie Mutter in the months leading up to their marriage. Starting with a melody as luscious as anything in the Korngold *Concerto*, a work they had already performed together, he makes it clear in the lyricism which invades each of the three movements that this is love music. Mutter responds accordingly with magical playing, making each phrase distinctive while also relishing the challenge of the bravura writing. The hushed ending of the third movement, a set of variartions on a nursery theme that Previn as well as Mutter knew in child-

hood, is breathtaking. At 40 minutes the Previn work may be dangerously expansive, but the performance is magnetic, and the coupling of Bernstein's *Plato Serenade* makes an excellent foil, most persuasively done.

PROKOFIEV, Serge (1891–1953)

(i) *Autumn, Op. 8; Dreams, Op. 6; Cello Concertino in G min., Op. 132;* (ii; iii) *Piano Concertos Nos. 1–5;* (iii; iv) *Violin Concertos Nos. 1 in D, Op. 19; 2 in G min., Op. 63;* (i) *The Prodigal Son, Op. 46; 2 Pushkin Waltzes, Op. 120;* (i; v) *Sinfonia concertante in E min. Op. 125;* (i) *Symphonies Nos. 1–7; Waltzes, Suite, Op 110; The Year 1941, Op. 90;* (iii) *Sonata for Solo Violin, Op. 115.*

(BB) ** Naxos White Box 8.509001 (9). (i) Nat. O of the Ukraine, Kuchar; (ii) Paik; (iii) Polish Nat. R.O, Wit; (iv) Papavrami; (v) Rudin.

On the face of it a bargain, even if few of these performances would be a first choice. The symphonies do not compete with many of their CD rivals: the *Classical Symphony* is very heavy-handed and the quality of the playing is not particularly distinguished in the remainder. There are some deeply felt things in the *Sixth*, whose tempi are eminently well judged, but the horns call for some tolerance. Kuchar gives us the post-war version of the *Fourth Symphony* but he also includes *The Prodigal Son*, from which the original Op. 47 drew so heavily. The *Piano Concertos* are much more successful. Kun Woo Paik is an impressive and commanding soloist who is thoroughly inside the idiom. His virtuosity is imposing and he enjoys excellent support from the Polish National Radio Orchestra under Antoni Wit. In the *Violin Concertos* Tedi Papavrami proves a formidable soloist. Brought up in Albania, he became a pupil of Pierre Amoyal and an admired competition winner; he has real temperament and lyrical feeling. With Alexander Rudin we return to the Ukraine orchestra, who are not the most subtle of accompanists, but the Russian cellist is a powerful player and, although this is not a flawless reading, he brings conviction and feeling to the score. A serviceable box and a useful introduction to this fascinating repertoire.

Cinderella (ballet; complete), *Op. 87.*

** CPO 999610-2 (2). Cologne WDR SO, Jurowski.

Michail Jurowski's recording of *Cinderella* is in no sense the equal of his account of *The Tale of the Stone Flower* with the Hanover Radio Philharmonic Orchestra, which was distinguished by refined orchestral playing and a pleasingly natural sound. It is soon evident that the characterization and the quality of the orchestral playing do not begin to approach either Pletnev or Previn. This is a studio performance with no sense of the footlights or atmosphere. Good though the Cologne orchestra is, the LSO outclass it in every way, as do the Cleveland

Orchestra for Ashkenazy. Moreover, these competitors offer more music.

Cinderella (ballet; complete), Op. 87; Summer Night: Suite, Op. 123.

🕪 ✪ (M) *** DG 476 2233 (2). Russian Nat. O, Pletnev.

Here is playing of terrific life, lightness of touch, poetic feeling and character. Quite simply the best-played, most atmospheric and affecting *Cinderella* we have ever had on disc. We found its effect tremendously exhilarating and have had difficulty in stopping playing it! Don't hesitate – it is on every count one of the great recordings of the 1990s and is now available at mid-price, for the first time, in Universal's 'Penguin ✪ Collection'.

Chout (ballet; complete), Op. 21.

🕪 *** CPO 999 975-2. WDR SO, Cologne, Jurowski.

Michail Jurowski and the Cologne Radio Orchestra continue their survey of the Prokofiev ballets with one of the most neglected and rewarding. *Chout* ('The Buffoon'), which Diaghilev mounted in 1921, did not enjoy the success its score deserved, though the music was not slow to reach the gramophone. It is a deliciously scored and inventive work with relatively few longueurs. Albert Wolff recorded a suite from it before the war, and in 1962 Rozhdestvensky did the most extensive recording up to that time, omitting some of the entr'actes. His version ran to just over 37 minutes while Jurowski's newcomer runs to nearly 57. He and his team maintain the high standards that he achieved in *The Stone Flower*, and Prokofiev admirers who want every note and every repeat need not hesitate. The NordWestDeutscher Rundfunk recording is to a very high standard in terms of clarity and definition.

(i) Concertino in G min. for Cello & Orchestra, Op. 132 (completed and orch. Kabalevsky & Rostropovich); (ii) Piano Concertos Nos. 1–5; (iii) Violin Concertos Nos. 1–2; (i) Sinfonia concertante for Cello & Orchestra, Op. 125.

🕪 (M) *** Decca Trio (ADD/DDD) 473 259-2 (3). (i) Harrell, RPO, Ashkenazy; (ii) Ashkenazy (piano), LSO, Previn; (iii) Bell, Montreal SO, Dutoit.

The *Cello Concertino*, inspired by Prokofiev's collaboration with Rostropovich in Op. 125, is a comparatively slight piece, but it is very well played by Lynn Harrell. He gives an even more impressive account of the *Sinfonia concertante* and he sounds as if he is relishing the numerous challenges to his virtuosity that this score poses. His playing of the cadenza in the middle movement (fig. 18 in the score and the ensuing paragraphs) is pretty stunning and Ashkenazy draws strongly characterized playing from the RPO. Turning to the keyboard, Ashkenazy then offers vintage, authoritative accounts of the five *Piano Concertos*, which have been much praised by

us. (These are also available separately – see our main volume.)

Employing a measure of emotional restraint and an exceptionally pure tone, Joshua Bell completes this outstanding anthology with ravishingly beautiful accounts of both *Violin Concertos*, heightening the light and shade in the great lyrical passages to contrast with the formidable bravura writing, which finds him at his most commanding. Others, like Chung, may find darker emotions here but, with outstanding recording throughout, this compilation is very recommendable indeed.

(i) Concertino in G min. for Cello & Orchestra, Op. 132 (completed and orch. Kabalevsky & Rostropovich); Sinfonia concertante in E min. for Cello & Orchestra, Op. 125; (ii) Cello Sonata in C, Op. 119.

(M) (**) Revelation mono RV10102. Rostropovich, (i) USSR SO, Rozhdestvensky; (ii) Richter.

Rostropovich's performances of this coupling were made at public concerts in 1964 and 1960 respectively (the performance is a composite one). Some allowance must be made for the sound here and in the 1951 recording of the *Cello Sonata*, once briefly available on the Monitor label, but what a performance!

Violin Concerto No. 1 in D, Op. 19.

✪ (BB) *** Naxos mono 8.110973. Szigeti, LPO, Beecham – BARTOK: *Portrait*; BLOCH: *Violin Concerto*. (***) ✪

Szigeti's pioneering version of the Prokofiev *D major Concerto* with Sir Thomas Beecham and the LPO captures the bitter-sweet intensity of this magical score to perfection. The demonic brilliance of the Scherzo has never been surpassed, even by such great soloists as Oistrakh and Milstein, and the sense of character throughout is superb. Szigeti was a strongly individual artist, and the partnership with Sir Thomas and the LPO brings altogether special results.

(i) Violin Concertos Nos. 1–2; (ii) Sonata for 2 Violins.

(M) *** EMI (DDD/ADD) 5 62592-2. Perlman, with (i) BBC SO, Rozhdestvensky; (ii) Zukermann.

Perlman's 1980 performances bring virtuosity of such strength and command one is reminded of the supremacy of Heifetz. Though the EMI recording has warmth and plenty of bloom, the balance of the soloist is unnaturally close, which has the effect of obscuring important melodic ideas in the orchestra behind mere passagework from the soloist, as in the second subject of the *First Concerto*'s finale. Nevertheless, in their slightly detached way these performance are impossible to resist as, apart from the balance, the recording is excellent. The *Double Violin Sonata* (added for this reissue) dates from 1932, when Prokofiev was still living in Paris and is lyrical in feeling, offering both depth and charm. The playing is excellent – as one has every right to expect from this partnership.

(i) *Violin Concerto No. 1. Symphony No. 1 (Classical); 16 Visions Fugitivies, Op. 22 (arr. Barshai).*
* Chan. 9615. (i) Grubert; Moscow CO, Orbelian.

All these pieces date from 1917 but, the *Classical Symphony* apart, they receive pretty lacklustre performances. Ilya Grubert undergoes too close a scrutiny from the recording engineers, and in the *Visions fugitives* their American conductor sets somewhat slow tempi. Subfusc recording.

Violin Concertos Nos. (i) *1 in D, Op. 19*; (ii) *2 in G min., Op. 63*; (iii) *Violin Sonata No. 2 in D, Op. 94a.*
(BB) *** EMI Encore 5 85458-2. Zimmermann, with (i) BPO, Maazel; (ii) Philh. O, Jansons; (iii) Lonquich.

These performances were recorded in 1987 and 1991 and the disc is drawn from a two-CD set in which Frank Peter Zimmermann played all Prokofiev's output for the violin, including the sonata for solo violin and for two violins. Zimmermann gives strong, eloquent accounts of the concertos, and they have no want of character. Those who know either of Heifetz's accounts of the *G minor Concerto* will find this just a bit lacking in sarcasm and bite, but there is no doubting the fine musicality and accomplishment of this performance and its companions. Not to be preferred to Oistrakh, Milstein or Kyung-Wha Chung where these are available, but well worth considering, given the competitive price and the excellence of the sound.

(i) *Dreams, Op. 6*; (ii) *Lieutenant Kijé* (suite); *Love for Three Oranges* (suite); (iii) *The Stone Flower, Op. 118* (ballet; excerpts); (iv) *Visions fugitives, Op. 22* (arr. Barshai). (ii; v) *Alexander Nevsky, Op. 78.*
(BB) **(*) Double Decca (ADD/DDD) 473 277-2 (2). (i) Concg. O, Ashkenazy; (ii) Montreal SO, Dutoit; (iii) SRO, Varviso; (iv) ASMF, Marriner; (v) van Nes, Montreal Ch.

Dutoit's Prokofiev, as one would expect, is more than competent and is worth hearing, though he is not uniformly successful here. *Alexander Nevsky* opens atmospherically and, with characteristically good St Eustache sound, Prokofiev's abrasive scoring ensures that the effects are suitably ominous. But overall Dutoit's reading lacks the necessary pungency, and the *Battle of the Ice* sequence fails to grip, despite the spectacular Decca engineering. The highlight of the performance is Jard van Nes's moving solo contribution, and the closing section produces the proper grandeur and sense of triumphant exultation. The *Lieutenant Kijé* and *Love of Three Oranges* suites find the conductor back on form and are very enjoyable. Varviso's excepts from *The Stone Flower* are highly enjoyable too, even if the Swiss orchestra is hardly the last word in orchestral brilliance; it has plenty of character and the 1966 sound is exceptionally warm

and vivid. *Dreams* was composed in 1910 while Prokofiev was still a student. It is an atmospheric piece, indebted to Debussy and early Scriabin; it is very well played by Ashkenazy and is recorded in warm, digital sound. New to CD is Marriner's 1972 account of Barshai's brilliant string arrangements of Prokofiev's piano pieces for his Moscow Chamber Orchestra. The ASMF clearly relish the ingenuity of the transcription, which makes them sound like original string music, and the sound is warm and atmospheric.

The Prodigal Son, Op. 46; Le Pas d'acier, Op. 41 (ballets; complete).
*** CPO 999 974-2. West German RSO, Cologne, Jurowski.

Michael Jurowski made a strong impression with his recording of *The Stone Flower* ballet, recorded with the Hanover orchestra (CPO 999 385-2 – see our main volume) and the present release is no less satisfying. *The Prodigal Son*, on which Prokofiev drew for the *Fourth Symphony*, is a fine work which the Royal Ballet revived early in 2004 as part of its Balanchine triple bill. *Le Pas d'acier* is a little earlier and is an inventive and characterful work, designed to shock Paris audiences in the manner of the *Second Symphony*. Neither work is generously represented in the catalogue, so this well-played and -recorded newcomer deserves a welcome. It is as good as any of the (admittedly few) alternatives.

Peter and the Wolf, Op. 67.
(***) Pentatone PTC 5186. Sophia Loren, Russian Nat. O, Nagano (with BEINTUS: *Wolf Tracks* (narrated Bill Clinton); includes spoken prologue and epilogue in Russian by Mikhail Gorbachev).
(M) Virgin VM5 61782-2. Henry, RLPO, Pešek –
BRITTEN: *Young Person's Guide* **(*);
SAINT-SAENS: *Carnival of the Animals* (chamber version). ***

Sophia Loren's most engaging narration of *Peter and the Wolf* has universal appeal. Children will surely love its warmth and innocence, and adults will appreciate the way this fine actress identifies so charmingly with the story. She keeps closely to the text, yet her little personal touches add to the friendliness of her story-telling. She is helped by Kent Nagano's attentive yet relaxed pacing, and some strikingly picaresque characterizations by the orchestral soloists, especially the cat – so feline and sneaky on the clarinet. (The solo describing the dash up the tree, with its closing cadential near-'miaow', is a winning touch.) Grandfather too is chipper yet persuasive in his authority on the bassoon, and the oboe's melancholy is very affecting at the very close when Sophia's last words are so gentle and sympathetic. She will make any child face the situation that the duck alive inside the wolf brings a dilemma virtually impossible to resolve.

The coupling offers an anodyne retelling of the

story in a completely new narrative by Walt Kraemer to suit 'wolf-friendly' sensibilities, backed with a pleasant but wishy-washy score by Jean-Pascal Beintus which adds virtually nothing to the narrative. The narration of the tale by Bill Clinton, though undoubtedly sympathetic, becomes increasingly and embarrassingly sentimental, and the otherwise admirable moral, 'The time has come to leave the wolves alone' is underlined *ad nauseam*. Mikhail Gorbachev provides a (fortunately brief) Prologue, Intermezzo and Epilogue in Russian, which is then spoken in translation by Sergei Markov. These cliché-ridden comments are pointless, and one wonders why the Russian ex-president could not have managed to speak his political benedictions in English. Each of the major participants is donating his or her royalties to the charity of choice, including of course the Wolf Conservation Center. Indeed, the Wolf himself is quoted in the booklet as saying, 'Everyone, including you dear listener, has made a contribution to a better future for wolves, and all the noble creatures on our planet'. Even so, this part of the CD is quite impossible to recommend.

Lenny Henry's colloquial narration is enthusiastic, clear and communicative. Children will certainly respond to his individual 'voices' for the characters in the tale and also his additional vocalized effects. But the record's appeal is reduced to virtually nil by the extraordinarily inept new instrumental characterization for each of the characters in the tale. The piece was specifically designed by Prokofiev to introduce young listeners to the orchestral palette, and the dumbing-down here robs his score of its primary purpose, plus almost all its elegance and wit. Peter stays with the strings; but, instead of a flute, the bird is portrayed by a Chinese 'mouth organ', the duck is a squealing Catalan 'tiple'. Even more unfortunately, the wolf is represented by three very bland accordions; and, worst of all, the engagingly feline clarinet with which Prokofiev identified the cat is changed to an oboe d'amore in order to produce a semblance of a 'miaow'.

Romeo and Juliet, Op. 64: (ballet; highlights).

(B) ** CfP 575 5642. LPO, Pritchard – MUSSORGSKY: *Pictures at an Exhibition*. **

Pritchard's selection is not always predictable in its content, but it follows the narrative until the fight between Tybalt and Mercutio, then moves straight to the *Death of Juliet*. He is rhythmically positive, yet most effective in the gentler lyrical music, as is shown by his sensitive rubato in the atmospheric introduction, and his picture of *Juliet as a Young Girl*, delicately evoked. The LPO play with colour and commitment, although the passion of the lovers has been depicted with even greater intensity in other selections. The 1975 recording, made in Barking Town Hall, is certainly vivid.

Romeo and Juliet (ballet; excerpts including *Suites Nos. 1–3*).

** DG 453 439-2. BPO, Abbado.

Romeo and Juliet (ballet): Suites Nos. 1 & 2, Op. 64.

(BB) ** EMI Encore CDE5 75227-2. Oslo PO, Jansons.

Abbado's selection from *Romeo* has some exemplary playing from the Berlin Philharmonic, and the DG engineers offer us very well-balanced recorded sound. This 70-minute anthology is assembled from the three published concert suites, as well as the ballet itself. Everything is well shaped and finely characterized, but Salonen's Berlin Philharmonic selection has greater atmosphere and dramatic flair.

Jansons secures playing of alert sensibility, discipline and refinement from the Oslo Philharmonic and has the advantage of a naturally balanced and vividly present recording, but the performance as a whole is wanting in a sense of the theatre. The best buy for this music remains Salonen on Sony (SBK 89740).

Scythian Suite, Op. 20 (with rehearsal).

*** Arthaus **DVD** 100 314. Rotterdam PO, Gergiev (with DEBUSSY: *Le Martyr de Saint-Sébastien*). (Director: Rob van der Berg. V/D: Peter Rump.) – STRAVINSKY: *Piano Concerto*, etc. ***

Apart from performing it, Gergiev here discusses the *Scythian Suite* and its composer, championing the score with much eloquence. There are few pieces in twentieth-century music that are as imaginative as its third movement, *Night*, or as inventive as the first, *The Adoration of Vélèss and Ala*, with its extraordinary lush contrasting group. Gergiev's performance has great fervour and eloquence, and it is good to hear him speak of the music with such warmth in the accompanying hour-long documentary. This includes some valuable archive material of Prokofiev himself and a contribution from his second son, the painter Oleg (who is also now no longer with us). The camera-work is unobtrusive and intelligent, though – as so often – one could do without some of the aerial shots of the orchestra. The *Scythian Suite* is difficult to balance, and some of the detail emerges in greater prominence than the main lines; but for the most part the sound balance is vivid and very present. The Debussy excerpts from *Le Martyr de Saint-Sébastien* are also most impressively played and recorded. This is an outstanding and invaluable DVD that is hugely enjoyable.

SYMPHONIES

Symphonies Nos. 1–7; Lieutenant Kijé: Suite.

(B) * DG 463 761-2 (4). BPO, Ozawa.

Ozawa's BPO set of Prokofiev symphonies is a non-starter. The performances are well played, but are very routine: without looking at the documentation, it would be hard to recognize this celebrated orchestra, which here produces a general-purpose sonority which Karajan would never have countenanced in his day. *Lieutenant Kijé* is sadly lacking in sparkle. Järvi's set on Chandos (8931/4) is the one to have.

Symphonies Nos. 6 in E flat, Op. 111; 7 in C sharp min., Op. 131.

(M) * Warner Elatus 0927 49826-2. Fr. Nat. O, Rostropovich.

These performances formed part of the Warner Prokofiev Centenary set and are discussed in detail in our main volume. Rostropovich makes heavy weather of both masterpieces, and even at mid-price they are not really recommendable.

CHAMBER MUSIC

Cello Sonata in C, Op. 119.

⊶ (BB) *** Double Decca 473 807-2 (2). Harrell, Ashkenazy – RACHMANINOV: *Cello Sonata*, etc.; SHOSTAKOVICH: *Cello Sonata*, etc. ***

Prokofiev's *Cello Sonata* is the product of his last years and, like the *Sinfonia concertante*, was inspired by the playing of the young Rostropovich. The excellent account from 1988 remains one of the top recommendations; readers will find Lynn Harrell and Vladimir Ashkenazy wholly satisfying on all accounts. The rest of the programme is equally fine.

Violin Sonata No. 1 in F min., Op. 80.

**(*) Avie AV0023. Gleusteen, Ordronneau – JANACEK: *Violin Sonata*; SHOSTAKOVICH: *19 Preludes from Op. 34*. **(*)

The Prokofiev *Violin Sonata No. 1*, much less well-known than No. 2, is a more elusive work than its successor, with its dark and ruminative *Andante* first movement. Even more than in the Janáček and Shostakovich works, Kai Gleusteen is in his element, and so is Catherine Ordronneau, bringing out the often violent contrasts in the writing, as well as the fantasy of the *Andante* third movement and the power and ebullience of the two fast movements, the second and the finale. It's is a pity that Gleusteen and Ordronneau did not devote themselves entirely to Prokofiev and give a complete survey of his violin-and-piano music. The recording, one of a series made in Crear on the west coast of Scotland, is on the reverberant side, thanks to the large, bare studio in which it was made, but there is no lack of detail.

Violin Sonatas Nos. (i; ii) 1 in F min., Op. 80; (iii; iv) 2 in D, Op. 94; (i; iii) Sonata for 2 Violins, Op. 36.

(BB) *** Warner Apex 2564 60623-2. (i) Jaakko Kuusisto; (ii) Paananen; (iii) Pekka Kuusisto; (iv) Kerppo.

Both Jaakko and Pekka Kuusisto produce playing with a youthful ardour and vitality that is refreshing. This (originally Finlandia) Apex reissue ranks among the best, yet it is now very inexpensive. Anyone investing in it is unlikely to be disappointed.

PIANO MUSIC

10 Pieces from Romeo and Juliet, Op. 75; Toccata in D min., Op. 11.

** Hyp. CDA 67018. Demidenko – MUSSORGSKY: *Pictures*. *

No doubts about Demidenko's virtuosity and keyboard command, particularly in the *Toccata*, or the excellence of the Hyperion sound. His playing in the *Romeo and Juliet* often delights, but there are exasperating mannerisms that attract attention to the pianist rather than to Prokofiev.

Piano Sonatas Nos. 1 in F min., Op. 1; 6 in A, Op 82; 7 in B flat, Op. 83; Toccata in C, Op. 11.

*** BIS CD 1260. Kempf.

Freddy Kempf's Prokofiev has a lot going for it and finds him totally inside the idiom. He has all the technical address, flair and temperament this music needs. At present the sonatas are uncommonly well served on record – in the *Sixth* we were much impressed both with Pogorelich's outstanding version (● DG 463 678-2) and the recent and exciting François-Frédéric Guy account, coupled with *No. 8* (Naïve V 4898) and in the *Seventh* with Pletnev (coupled with *Nos. 2 & 8* on DG 457 588-2). All these are discussed in our main volume. Kempf doesn't displace any of them, but his playing is satisfying and his admirers need not hesitate.

Piano Sonatas Nos. 4 in C min., Op. 29; 6 in A, Op. 82; 10 Pieces from 'Romeo and Juliet', Op. 75.

● *** Warner 2564 61255-2. Lugansky.

Dazzling playing from Nikolai Lugansky, performances that stand out even in exalted company. The *Sixth Sonata* is the most exciting and authoritative now before the public and supersedes the likes of Pogorelich and Kissin in musical insight and virtuosity. The *Romeo and Juliet Pieces* have equal mastery and fascination. Remarkable Prokofiev playing, wonderful in terms of characterization and effortless virtuosity.

Piano Sonata No. 7 in B flat, Op. 83.

(BB) *(*) Warner Apex 0927 40830-2. Sultanov – RACHMANINOV: *Piano Sonata No. 2*; SCRIABIN: *Piano Sonata No. 5*. *(*)

A strongly muscular and powerful account of the *Seventh Sonata* comes from Alexei Sultanov, although it is too crude and aggressive to disturb allegiance to such recommendations as Argerich, Pollini and Pletnev.

OPERA

The Fiery Angel (complete).

● *** (M) Ph. 476 18263 (2). Gorchakova, Leiferkus, Pluzhnikov, Ognovanko, Kirov Op. Ch. & O, Gergiev.

Gergiev's recording with Kirov forces is very fine.

From the very outset the style is declamatory in a way that recalls Mussorgsky. The vocal line is largely heightened speech, but Prokofiev does provide a series of leitmotivs, which are identified with characters or situations in the opera. Indeed, in terms of fantasy and sheer imaginative vision, *The Fiery Angel* reaches heights which Prokofiev never surpassed, and its atmosphere resonates for a long time. This Philips live recording, with full, forward sound, avoids most of the snags of a recorded stage-performance. Above all, it offers in the singing and acting of Elena Gorchakova in the central role of Renata, the hysterical woman obsessed by demons, one of the most compelling operatic performances in years, with the timbre of the voice often sensuously beautiful, even when stretched to the limit. Sergei Leiferkus as Ruprecht with his clear, firm baritone is also ideally cast. The remainder of the cast, from the Landlady of Evgenia Perlasova to the resonant Inquisitor of Vladimir Ognovanko, are absolutely first class, while the Kirov team provides outstanding, always idiomatic and individual performances in smaller roles. Gergiev proves an inspired conductor who secures orchestral playing of great dramatic eloquence. There are the inevitable stage noises, but any snag is quickly forgotten. The CD set won the 1996 *Gramophone* Opera Award and is now re-issued at mid-price in Universal's *Gramophone* Awards Collection, representing supreme value as texts and translations are included.

PUCCINI, Giacomo Sr (1712–81)

Messa di Requiem. Overtures: Lucio Giunio Bruto; Marzio Coriolano.

(BB) *** Arte Nova 74321 98497-2. Morgan, Kenny, Cornwell, Thomas, Kantorei Saarlouis, Ens. UnaVolta, Fontaine.

The celebrated Giacomo Puccini was the last in a line of composers, starting with another Giacomo, born in 1712, his great-great-grandfather. As this fine setting of the *Requiem* demonstrates, he was a notable figure in eighteenth-century Italian music, one who (like his descendant) was not afraid to cherry-pick his ideas. Here his elaborate contrapuntal writing for double choir harks back to an earlier generation, with clashing discords based on suspensions, such as one finds in Purcell's choral music, and chromatic sequences refreshing to the modern ear, all set against elegant baroque solos, well sung by the stylish quartet of British-based soloists. The two overtures, too, written for the secular oratorios celebrating the city of Lucca's annual elections, are lively and refreshing, with vigorous performances, cleanly recorded.

PUCCINI, Giacomo (1858–1924)

Adagietto; Preludio; Scherzo (all for orchestra); *Corazzata Sicilia; Scossa elettrica* (both for wind). Vocal music: (ii) *Cessato il suon' dell'armi (cantata)*; (i) *Ecce Sacerdos Magnus; Inno a Roma*; (i; iii) *Motetto per San Paulino; Requiem*; (i; iv) *Salve Regina*; (i; v) *Vexilla Regis; Manon Lescaut*, Act II: *Prelude*. (vi) *Turandot*, Act III: *Finale* (ed. Berio).

*** Decca 478 320-2. Giuseppe Verdi SO, Chailly, with
(i) Giuseppe Verdi Ch.; (ii) Calleja; (iii) Mastromarino; (iv) Taigi; (v) De Thierry (organ); (vi) Urbanova, Fantosh, Volonte, Luperi.

All but one of the items on this 'Discovery' disc are pieces incidental to Puccini's career, whether from his early years as a student, or short, occasional pieces written later for specific purposes; all of them are fascinating for giving us fresh insights into the composer's development. The final item on the disc is by far the most important, Luciano Berio's completion of Act III of the unfinished last opera, *Turandot*. Like Franco Alfano, who made the regular completion, Berio used the composer's sketches for that unfinished ending, but the results are very different, not least in having a hushed, downbeat ending. That ending may be totally justified dramatically, but it is unsatisfying compared with Alfano's knockout blow in the choral reprise of *Nessun dorma*. Surprisingly, though the orchestral accompaniment is quite different, with a substantial orchestral interlude in the middle, the vocal lines of Turandot and Calaf in their duet are remarkably close to those in the Alfano, both following Puccini's sketches. Turandot's solo, *Del primo pianto*, then begins with the same melodic line, but quickly becomes impassioned, and Calaf's *Il mio mistero* also keeps the same vocal line. After Turandot and Calaf's final brief exchange, there is only a gentle easing into silence.

Seven of the 13 remaining items also come in première recordings. They include Puccini's first two surviving works, both written during his schooldays, the *Preludio a orchestra*, which charmingly turns into a Viennese-style waltz, and the *Motetto per San Paulino*, bold and brassy, with a long baritone solo in the middle (rather roughly sung by Alberto Mastromarino). *Vexilla Regis* for men's chorus and organ also dates from the composer's schooldays. At the other end of Puccini's career comes the untypical *Inno a Roma* of 1919, his last completed work, later notoriously adopted by Mussolini's fascists using different words. The *Scherzo* of 1882–3 and the *Salve Regina*, from his student years in Milan, both provided material for his first opera, *Le Villi*, and the tenderly beautiful *Adagietto for Small Orchestra* from the same period was used for Fidelia's aria in Act III of his second opera, *Edgar*.

Other little gems include two pieces for wind band, *Corazzata Sicilia*, a development of the march at the end of Act II of *La Bohème* using material from earlier in the act (the work of a bandmaster) and *Scossa elettrica* ('Electric Shock'), a lively fragment of 1899 with jaunty syncopations, written for a convention of telegraphists. By far the weakest piece, the cantata of 1877, *Cessato il suon*, discovered only in 2003, is one for which the vocal line had to be invented.

Chailly draws excellent performances from his various artists, with generally fresh, alert singing from soloists and chorus, and the one complaint is that, though the notes by Dieter Schickling (author of the comprehensive Puccini catalogue) are very informative, the lack of texts for the vocal items is a serious omission.

OPERA

La Bohème (complete).

(M) ** RCA (ADD) 09026 63179-2 (2). Moffo, Tucker, Costa, Merrill, Tozzi, Rome Op. Ch. & O, Leinsdorf.

(BB) (**) Naxos mono 8.110072/3. Albanese, Gigli, Menotti, Poli, Baronti, Baracchi, La Scala, Milan, Ch. & O, Berrettoni.

(M) (**) Nim. mono NI 7862/3. Albanese, Gigli, Poli, Menotti, Baracchi, Baronti, La Scala, Milan, Ch. & O, Berrettoni.

(B) ** Naxos 8.660003/4. Orgonasova, Welch, Gonzales, Previati, Senator, Slovak Philharmonic Ch., Slovak RSO (Bratislava), Humburg.

On the Leinsdorf set Anna Moffo is an affecting Mimì, Mary Costa a characterful Musetta, while Merrill and Tozzi provide strong support. Tucker gives a positive characterization as Rodolfo, though he has lachrymose moments. Sadly, Leinsdorf's rigid direction, with speed fluctuations observed by instruction and never with natural expression, sets the singers against a deadpan, unsparkling accompaniment. Dated recording, impressively remastered.

Gigli was always at his most winning in the role of Rodolfo in *La Bohème*, and here opposite Licia Albanese he is the central focus of a warmly enjoyable version, recorded in 1938 at La Scala. Gigli indulges at times in his cooing manner, but it is a powerful as well as a charming assumption, with humour well caught. In the next decade Albanese was Toscanini's choice for Mimì, and she went on singing the role at the Met. in New York until the mid-1960s, a role she made her own. The others are reliable if not comparably characterful, with Umberto Berrettoni as conductor. First-rate Naxos transfers from 78s.

The Nimbus transfer process works well here too, with plenty of body in the sound, without too much masking of reverberation, and with a bloom on the voices. The glory of the set is Gigli's Rodolfo, with a chuckle in the voice bringing out the fun, and he uses his pouting manner charmingly, with the occasional sob adding to the charm. He adds little touches, as when he murmurs '*Prego*' when ushering Mimì out, before she discovers she has lost her key. He dwarfs the others, with even Albanese a little shrill as Mimì.

Well played and atmospherically recorded, the Naxos version under Humburg offers an outstanding performance by Luba Orgonasova as Mimì. The creamy quality of the voice, coupled with her warm expressiveness and her vocal poise, brings out the tenderness of the character to the full; it is a pity that none of the others matches her. Jonathan Welch as Rodolfo and Fabio Previati as Marcello are both strained and unsteady at times, while Carmen Gonzales tries too hard as Musetta. First choice for this opera rests with Pappano on EMI (5 56120-2) – see our main volume.

La Bohème (highlights).

(B) ** Penguin Decca 460 617-2 (from complete recording with Tebaldi, Bergonzi; cond. Serafin).

(M) (**) EMI mono 5 66670-2 (from complete recording with Callas, di Stefano; cond. Votto).

(BB) ** EMI Encore (ADD) 5 74984 2 5. Scotto, Kraus, Milnes, Neblett, Plishka, Manuguerra, Amb. Op. Ch., Trinity Boys' Ch., Nat. PO, Levine.

The sets of excerpts from the Tebaldi and Callas recordings are little more than samplers. Although both include the Love duet from Act I, and the closing scene, the overall playing time is only 54 minutes for the EMI disc, and a minute or so more for the Decca. There is a cued synopsis for Callas, but the Decca selection offers merely a very brief cued narrative summary. However, the one compensation here is the usual Penguin Classics author's note, which is written most engagingly by Rabbi Lionel Blue.

With Levine's 1979 complete set currently unavailable, collectors might consider this highlights disc, even though the singing is flawed. Alfredo Kraus's relatively light tenor is no longer as sweet as it was and Scotto is not flatteringly recorded here. Milnes make a a powerful Marcello and Neblett a strong Musetta, but Levine could be more persuasive in the big melodies.

Edgar (complete).

*** Naïve V4957. Varady, McCormick, Tanner, Jenis, Cigni, R. France Ch. & O, Levi.

After the success of his first opera, *Le Villi*, Puccini's publisher, Giulio Ricordi, kept faith with his young discovery, even though it was five years before he completed his next opera, *Edgar*. Puccini's big mistake was to retain the services of the same librettist, Ferdinando Fontana. Where the story of *Le Villi* is very simply told, telescoping much of the action and with motivation clear and direct despite the supernatural element, *Edgar* has a much more elaborate story, with absurd developments that no composer could make convincing. So the hero, Edgar, at the climax of Act I, for no evident reason burns down his own house, and in Act III, just as implausibly, he stages his own funeral, with a suit of armour in place of the body.

Where the faithful heroine, Fidelia, is a tenderly sympathetic character, her rival, Tigrana, as the name might suggest, is a fire-eater, modelled on Carmen. Evil through and through, she remains one-dimensional, making Edgar's sudden passion for her seem at best capricious. However, the score of *Edgar* brings important developments in Puccini's technique as a composer, through-composed, merging arias and ensembles.

Like the recording of *Le Villi*, also from French Radio (see below), this one of *Edgar* scores in the refinement of the sound. Julia Varady as Fidelia and Carl Tanner in the title-role of Edgar are both outstanding, allowed a range of expression largely denied to their rivals on Maazel's Sony version, which suffers from aggressively close-up sound. Mary Ann McCormick as Tigrana is well contrasted with Varady, with her firm, clear mezzo finely controlled. Clean-cut singing too from Dalibor Jenis as Frank and Carlo Cigni as Gualtiero, with excellent choral work from the Choir of Radio France, whose choirmaster is the great Norbert Balasch. Yoel Levi proves a warmly understanding Puccinian, pointing rhythms and phrases with natural sympathy.

La fanciulla del West (The Girl of the Golden West; complete).

☞ (M) *** DG (ADD) 474 840-2 (2). Neblett, Domingo, Milnes, Howell, ROHCG Ch. & O, Mehta.
(M) (*(*)) Warner Fonit mono 8573 87488-2 (2). Gavazzi, Campagnano, Savarese, Caselli, RAI Ch. & O of Milan, Basile.

On DG, Mehta's manner – as he makes clear at the very start – is on the brisk side, even refusing to let the first great melody, the nostalgic *Che faranno i viecchi*, linger into sentimentality. Sherrill Milnes as Jack Rance makes that villain into far more than a small-town Scarpia, giving nobility and understanding to the Act I arioso. Domingo, as in the theatre, sings heroically, disappointing only in his reluctance to produce soft tone in the great aria, *Ch'ella mi creda*. The rest of the team is excellent, not least Gwynne Howell as the minstrel who sings *Che faranno i viecchi miei*; but the crowning glory of a masterly set is the singing of Carol Neblett as the Girl of the Golden West herself, gloriously rich and true, with formidable attack on the exposed high notes. Full, atmospheric recording to match, essential in an opera that is full of evocative offstage effects. With its new 'Originals' transfer and at a new mid-price, with texts and translations included, this set deserves upgrading to a full three stars.

Recorded in 1950 for Cetra in collaboration with Italian Radio, this Warner Fonit set was the first ever commercial recording of *La fanciulla del West*, an opera for long unfairly ignored outside Italy. It yields to later versions both in recorded sound – limited mono with clear voices but dim orchestra – and in the casting, which features a team of singers from a generation that built up opera in Italy after the war

without making an impact outside. All the principals have powerful voices but, as recorded, their singing is fluttery, maybe in part a question of recording balance. What makes the performance convincing nonetheless is the conducting of Arturo Basile, totally idiomatic, pressing home the great lyrical and dramatic moments with a conviction born of familiarity. An Italian libretto is provided, but no translation. A historic document rather than a serious contender. First choice among stereo versions still rests with the Decca Tebaldi set (421 595-2), which itself might almost be regarded as historic were not the Decca recording so spectacular, denying its age.

Gianni Schicchi (complete).

☞ (M) *** EMI 5 62777-2. Gobbi, De los Angeles, Del Monte, Montarsolo, Rome Op. Ch. & O, Santini
– VERDI: *Don Carlo; Simon Boccanegra* excerpts. ***
(M) ** Orfeo (ADD) C546 001B. Fischer-Dieskau, Schary, Mödl, Ahnsjö, Thaw, Fahberg, Auer, Engen, Grumbach, Wewezow, Bav. State Ch. & O, Sawallisch.

Tito Gobbi's classic assumption of the role of Gianni Schicchi has dominated the catalogue (as part of a complete recording of *Il Trittico*) since the earliest days of LP and it was a splendid idea for EMI to reissue it separately to represent Gobbi in their 'Great Artists of the Century' series. He gives an amazing performance. Though his incomparable baritone is not by nature comic-sounding, he is unequalled as Schicchi, sardonically manipulating the mourning relatives of Buoso Donati as he frames a new will for them. Puccini, the master of tragedy, here emerges as a supreme master of comic timing too. De los Angeles is charmingly girlish as Lauretta and the supporting cast is excellent. The early (1959) stereo is remarkably vivid and atmospheric, and there is a good cued synopsis.

Gianni Schicchi recorded live in German makes little sense outside Germany, but this is well worth hearing for the powerful contribution of Dietrich Fischer-Dieskau in the title-role. He takes a freer view than you would expect of so meticulous a musician, resorting to parlando at times, but in that he is responding to the joy of the piece as a member of a strong team. The trouble is that Gunther Rennert's lively production involves stage noises – often sounding louder than the music. The balance of voices is very variable, too, with the orchestra set behind. One result of the dryness and Sawallisch's incisive conducting is that the dissonant modernity of Puccini's writing in places is brought out the more. Fischer-Dieskau is well supported by a delightful pair of young lovers. As Lauretta, Elke Schary is fresh and girlish, ending her celebrated aria (in German *O du, mein lieber Vater*) with a tender diminuendo. As Rinuccio, the Swedish tenor Claes-Haakan Ahnsjö sings with a bright, clear tone. Among the others one cherishes most of all the characterful contribution of Martha Mödl, then over sixty, as a formidable Zita.

Madama Butterfly (complete).

(M) **(*) Sony (ADD) SM2K 91135 (2). Scotto, Domingo, Knight, Wixell, Amb. Op Ch., Philh. O, Maazel.

(M) (*) Warner Fonit mono 0927 43551-2 (2). Petrella, Tagliavini, Taddei, Cetra Ch., RAI SO of Turin, Questa.

Eleven years after her EMI recording of *Butterfly* with Barbirolli (5 67885-2 [567 888-2] – see our companion volume), Renata Scotto recorded the role again, this time with Maazel, and the years brought nothing but benefit. The voice – always inclined to spread a little on top at climaxes – had acquired extra richness by the late 1970s and was recorded with a warmer tonal bloom. In perception too, Scotto's singing is far deeper, most strikingly in the heroine's *Un bel dì*, where the narratve leads to special intensity on the words '*Chiamerà Butterfly, della lontana*'. Maazel is warmly expressive without losing his architectural sense; he has not quite the imaginative individuality of Barbirolli, but this is both powerful and unsentimental, with a fine feeling for Puccini's subtle orchestration. Other contributions are incidental, even Plácido Domingo, who sings heroically as Pinkerton, but arguably makes him too genuine a character for such a cad. Wixell's voice is not ideally rounded as Sharpless, but he sings most sensitively, and Gillian Knight makes an expressive Suzuki. Among the supporting cast, Malcolm King as the Bonze is outstanding in a good team. The recording is rich and warm without having the bloom of Karajan's Decca set, and the voices are balanced relatively (though not uncomfortably) close. But the main snag of this reissue is the incredibly sparse documentation, without either libretto or cued synopsis – just a list of track titles!

Recorded in 1954, the old Cetra set of *Butterfly*, now reissued on Warner Fonit, brings perfunctory conducting from Angelo Questa and a flawed cast. Ferruccio Tagliavini as Pinkerton sets out loud and hectoring in the opening scene, only to be transformed by the sight of Butterfly, becoming from then on seductively honey-toned. Giuseppe Taddei is an impressive Sharpless, while Clara Petrella is an idiomatic if hardly distinctive Butterfly. Not a viable set with its limited, mono sound, with voices balanced so close that even Goro sounds loud. Freni, Pavarotti and Karajan still lead the field in this opera (Decca 417 577-2 – see our main *Guide*).

Tosca (complete).

☞ (BB) (***) EMI mono 5 85644-2 (2). Callas, di Stefano, Gobbi, Calabrese, Mercuriali, La Scala, Milan, Ch. & O, de Sabata.

(BB) (***) Naxos mono 8.110256–57 (2). Callas, di Stefano, Gobbi, Calabrese, Mercuriali, La Scala, Milan, Ch. & O, de Sabata.

(BB) (**) EMI mono 5 62675-2 (2). Callas. Cioni, Gobbi, ROHCG Ch. & O, Cillario.

(M) (**) RCA mono 09026 63305-2 (2). Milanov, Björling, Warren, Rome Op. Ch. & O, Leinsdorf.

(BB) (**) Naxos mono 8.110096-97 (2). Caniglia, Gigli, Borgioli, Dominici, Tomei, Rome Op. Ch. & O, Fabritiis.

(M) (**) Warner Fonit mono 8573 87479-2 (2). Frazzoni, Tagliavini, Guelfi, RAI Ch. & O of Turin, Basile.

(M) * Sony M2K 91175 (2). Marton, Carreras, Pons, Hungarian State R. & TV Ch. & O, Tilson Thomas.

EMI's super-bargain transfer of the classic Callas–Gobbi set with de Sabata conducting is designed to outclass the rival set from Naxos. As well as being packaged much more attractively, it brings a transfer which, taken from the original tapes, has the voices brighter and more immediate than on the Naxos set. Though painstakingly transferred from a series of different LPs, with minor imperfections ironed out, the Naxos set brings few advantages. Though it is claimed that the EMI transfers have been made at the wrong pitch, there is no evidence that La Scala was using a relatively high pitch, such as is normal in the United States (where the transfers were made), and most ears will hardly detect a difference. The immediate impact of the voices on EMI will for most be the deciding factor. Neither set has a libretto, but both helpfully provide a detailed synopsis linked to the index points on the disc.

Recorded at Covent Garden two years after Callas's classic studio recording of *Tosca* conducted by de Sabata, this alternative set, recorded live in 1954, makes a fascinating supplement but cannot in any way compare in quality. EMI make an apology for the technical imperfections of the sound, often cloudy and with odd balances and inevitable audience noises; and that will deter many. Yet Callas heard live, free and imaginative in one of her finest roles, is certainly worth an airing, and though Cillario cannot compare with de Sabata, he directs a powerful performance with Gobbi also at his finest and Renato Cioni a competent if not inspired Cavaradossi.

At mid-price Leinsdorf's version will be of principal interest to admirers of the veteran singer in the cast. Jussi Björling was at the peak of his fame as Cavaradossi. Though Zinka Milanov was past her best and was sometimes stressed by the role, there is much beautiful singing here from a great soprano who recorded all too little. Leonard Warren was another characterful veteran, but the furry edge to the voice makes him a less-than-sinister Scarpia.

It is rare for a recording of *Tosca* to centre round the tenor taking the role of Cavaradossi, rather than round Scarpia or Tosca herself, yet here Gigli at the height of his fame in 1938 is manifestly the main focus. He does not disappoint, making the hero a more rounded, more human character than is common, with fun and playfulness well caught as well as pathos. Maria Caniglia was a last-minute choice when Iva Pacetti proved unavailable, and though it is not a searching portrayal of the jealous opera-singer, it is a vocally strong and purposeful one, with the occasional edge on the voice apt enough. Armando Borgioli as Scarpia is reliable vocally rather than characterful, with Oliviero de Fabritiis pacing the score well in a full, red-blooded reading. Excellent CD transfers, mastered by Ward Marston, with voices very well caught indeed. The two discs include a 50-minute supplement taken from a version of *Tosca* recorded in French in 1931, an abridged version on seven 78rpm discs chiefly valuable for the enchanting portrayal of Tosca by Nino Vallin, very feminine and seductive. The others are no match for her – Enrico de Mazzei self-indulgent as Cavaradossi and Paul Payan as Scarpia not remotely sinister. One does not regret that the hero's two big arias are both omitted from this supplement.

Though the historic mono recording from Warner Fonit is uncompetitive in a crowded field, it is worth hearing for the mellifluous Cavaradossi of Ferruccio Tagliavini, at his peak in 1956 when the recording was made. Also for the stentorian Scarpia of Gian Giacomo Guelfi, dark and powerful rather than convincingly villainous. It was recorded for Cetra by Italian Radio, which accounts for the absence of stereo in a 1956 recording, but the voices are well caught. The Tosca of Gigliola Frazzoni is totally idiomatic but not very distinctive.

Eva Marton makes a coarse and often unsteady Tosca on the Sony version. José Carreras sings well as Cavaradossi, but not as well as on his two previous versions for Karajan and Sir Colin Davis. Juan Pons is a lightweight Scarpia, not sinister enough. Such vocal shortcomings undermine the thrust of Tilson Thomas's direction, and the documentation includes neither libretto nor cued synopsis, making it an unrecommendable version all round.

Turandot (complete).
*(*) RCA 74321 60617-2 (2). Casolla, Larin, Frittoli, Maggio Musicale Fiorentino Ch. & O, Mehta.
(M) *(*) Sony (ADD) SM2K 90444 (2). Marton, Carreras, Ricciarelli, Kerns, V. State Op. Ch. & O, Maazel.

The RCA recording offers a strong performance under Zubin Mehta in beefy, if at times abrasive, sound, with ample space round the voices. The casting of the principals is seriously flawed. Sergei Larin sings with fine dramatic thrust, though his voice grows strained towards the end. Giovanna Casola has a big voice with a pronounced flutter, so that the tone grows sour, and at the top pitching becomes vague under stress, so that *In questa reggia* ends with a squeal. Barbara Frittoli is even less well cast as Liù, with her heavy vibrato and reluctance to sing softly.

Turandot brings the warmest and most sensuous performance in Maazel's Sony Puccini series, thanks in good measure to its being a live recording, made in September 1983 at the Vienna State Opera House. Applause and stage noises are often distracting, and the clarity of CD tends to make one notice them even more. Recording balances are often odd, with Carreras – in fine voice – suffering in both directions, sometimes disconcertingly distant, at others far too close. Katia Ricciarelli's Liù is predictably heavyweight, though the beat in her voice is only rarely apparent. The strengths and shortcomings of Eva Marton as the icy princess emerge at the very start of *In questa reggia*. The big, dramatic voice is well controlled, but there is too little variation of tone, dynamic or expression; she rarely shades her voice down. In the closing act, during the Alfano completion, Marton's confidence and command grow impressively, with her heroic tone even more thrilling. But the presentation of this reissue prevents any kind of general recommendation. Not only are there no dividing bands within the acts, but no libretto is provided either, nor any kind of cued synopsis, and only a single paragraph to summarize the plot! The Decca set with Sutherland and Pavarotti still leads the field (414 274-2 – see our main *Guide*).

Le Villi (complete).
*** Naïve V4958. Diener, Machado, Tézier, David, French R. PO, Guidarini.

Puccini wrote his first opera, *Le Villi*, using a story similar to that of Adam's ballet, *Giselle*: the faithless lover finally destroyed by the ghostly spirit of the beloved who has died of a broken heart. Puccini composed it in 1883 for the Sonzogno competition for one-act operas, an annual event later won by Mascagni with *Cavalleria rusticana*. Puccini's effort was instantly rejected, largely because his manuscript score, written in haste, was so hard to read. Luckily, he was given a second chance, and the first performance in 1884 was an instant success, winning him a contract with Italy's leading publisher, Giulio Ricordi.

This French Radio recording scores impressively over Maazel's Sony version (MK 76890) in the refinement of the sound, which in turn brings out the subtleties of the fine singing from all the principals. Where the Sony set has the characterful Tito Gobbi as the male narrator, the new one has a woman, Sylvie David, lighter and more conversational. Marco Guidarini proves a very convincing Puccinian, bringing out the dramatic bite of the orchestral showpieces, as well as moulding the big melodies affectionately. The Sony set (MK76890 – discussed in our main *Guide*) has Lorin Maazel conducting, but he is not helped by the closeness of the Sony sound, which at times makes him sound too aggressive. Equally Renato Scotto is not flattered by the closeness, and though both she and Plácido Domingo as Roberto are more characterful than Melanie Diener and Aquiles Machado on the new disc, the refinement of sound helps to make the fresh, sensitive singing of the newcomers just as enjoyable. Equally Ludovic Tezier is clear and direct as Anna's father Guglielmo.

COLLECTIONS

Arias: (i) *La Bohème: Sì mi chiamano Mimì; Donde lieta uscì. Gianni Schicchi: O mio babino caro. Madama Butterfly: Un bel dì; Con onor muore. Manon Lescaut: In quelle trine morbide; Sola perduta. Suor Angelica: Senza mamma. Turandot: Signore ascolta!; In questa reggia; Tu che del sei cinta.* Duets: (ii; iii) *La Bohème: O soave fanciulla;* (ii; iv) *Madama Butterfly: Vogliateme bene;* (ii; v) *Tosca: Non la sospiri.* Aria: *Vissi d'arte.*

(M) (★★★) EMI mono/stereo 5 62794-2. Callas; with (i) Philh. O, Serafin; (ii) La Scala, Milan O; (iii) Votto; with Di Stefano; (iv) cond. Karajan, with Gedda; (v) De Sabata; with Di Stefano.

The first eleven items here formed Callas's first EMI recital, recorded in mono in Watford Town Hall in September 1954. Now reissued to represent the diva among EMI's 'Great Artists of the Century', it brings a classic example of her art. She was vocally at her peak. Even when her concept of a Puccinian 'little woman' has eyes controversially flashing and fierce, the results are unforgettable, never for a moment relaxing on the easy course, always finding new revelation, whether as Turandot or Liù, as Manon, Mimi or Butterfly. The other items, mostly duets, come from her complete sets, including her famous and indispensable portrayal of Tosca, conducted by Victor de Sabata. The transfers are excellent, well balanced but with the voice always vividly projected.

Arias and Duets: *La Bohème: Donde lieta usci; Si,mi chiamano Mimì.* (ii) *Canto d'anime.* (i) *Gianni Schicchi: O mio babbino caro. Madama Butterfly: Intermezzo Atto II, Parte seconda; Un bel dì vedremo. Manon Lescaut: In quelle trine morbide; Intermezzo Act III; Sola perduta, abandonnata.* (ii) *Morire.* (i) *La Rondine: Ch'il bel sogno di Doretta.* (ii) *Sole e amore.* (i) *Suor Angelica: Senza Mamma, o bimbo. Tosca: Vissi d'arte. Turandot: Signore ascolta; Tu che di gel sei cinta. Le Villi: Se come voi.*

(M) ★★★ Warner Elatus 2564 60681-2. Te Kanawa; (i) Nat. Op. de Lyons, Nagano; (ii) Vignoles (piano).

This is a Puccini disc with a difference. Besides the usual operatic excerpts, it includes three Puccini songs of which one, *Sole e amore*, is particularly enticing. Rightly Dame Kiri sings it not as an opera excerpt *manqué* but – encouraged by Roger Vignoles's imaginative accompaniment – as the trivial album-leaf intended. Those three songs with piano provide a welcome variety in a Puccini collection which, avoiding Minnie and Turandot, might have lacked contrast. Tosca's *Vissi d'arte* comes as an introduction, but then the ordering is chronological. The orchestra interludes from *Manon Lescaut* and *Butterfly* are beautifully done, but more songs with piano would have been preferable. With a recording lacking in bloom on top, the voice is not quite as creamy as it once was, if still very beautiful.

PURCELL, Henry (1659–95)

INSTRUMENTAL MUSIC

Chaconne in G min. for 2 Violins & Continuo; Anthems: *Blow up the Trumpet in Zion; My Heart is Inditing; O God, Thou art my God; O God, Thou has Cast me out; Remember not, Lord, our Offences; Rejoice in the Lord Alway.*

(BB) ★★★ Warner Apex (ADD) 2564 60821-2. Bowman, Rogers, Van Egmond, King's College, Cambridge, Ch., Leonhardt Consort, Leonhardt.

An attractive collection from the late 1960s, which happily blends scholarship and spontaneity. The instrumental ensemble uses period instruments and playing style, and the character of the sound is very distinctive. Not all the anthems have instrumental accompaniments – Purcell sometimes uses the organ, at others bass continuo – but they are all very well sung, with the characteristic King's penchant for tonal breadth and beauty. Excellent recording.

Gardiner Purcell Edition

(i) Disc 1: *Come, Ye Sons of Art Away; Funeral Music for Queen Mary (1695).* (ii) Disc 2: *Ode on St Cecilia's Day (Hail! Bright Cecilia).* (iii) Disc 3: *The Indian Queen (incidental music).* (iv) Disc 4: *The Tempest (incidental music).*

☞ (M) ★★★ Erato 5046 68281-2 (4). (i) Lott, Brett, Williams, Allen, Equale Brass Ens.; (ii) Gordon, Elliott; (ii; iii) Stafford, (ii; iii; iv) Jennifer Smith, Varcoe, Elwes, Thomas; (iii) Fisher, Hill; (iii; iv) Hardy; (iv) Hall, Earle; (i–iv) Monteverdi Ch. & O, Gardiner.

Originally issued to commemorate the tercentenary of Purcell's death, Gardiner's distinguished early series of Erato recordings from the 1970s and 1980s now reappears as a pair of four-disc sets, each disc packaged separately in its jewel-case (the choral works with texts) and presented together in a slip-case. The individual CDs are not now available separately.

Come, Ye Sons of Art, the most celebrated of Purcell's birthday odes for Queen Mary, is splendidly coupled here with the unforgettable funeral music he wrote on the death of the same monarch. With the Monteverdi Choir at its most incisive and understanding the performances are exemplary, and the recording, though balanced in favour of the instruments, is clear and refined. Among the soloists Thomas Allen is outstanding, while the two counter-tenors give a charming performance of the duet, *Sound the Trumpet*. The *Funeral usic* includes the well-known *Solemn March* for trumpets and drums, a *Canzona* and simple anthem given at the funeral, and two of Purcell's most magnificent anthems setting the *Funeral Sentences*. Recording made in 1976 in Rosslyn Hill Chapel, London.

Gardiner's characteristic vigour and alertness in Purcell come out superbly in the delightful record of the 1692 *St Cecilia Ode* – not as well known as some of the other odes he wrote, but a masterpiece. Soloists and chorus are outstanding even by Gardiner's high standards, and the recording is excellent. Recording made in 1982 in the Barbican Concert Hall, London.

The Indian Queen is fully cast and uses an authentic accompanying baroque instrumental group. The choral singing is especially fine, with the close of the work movingly expressive. John Eliot Gardiner's choice of tempi is apt and the soloists are all good, although the men are more strongly characterful than the ladies; nevertheless the lyrical music comes off well. The recording is spacious and well balanced, and was made in 1979 in Henry Wood Hall, London.

Whether or not Purcell wrote this music for *The Tempest* (the scholarly arguments are still unresolved), Gardiner demonstrates how delightful it is, a masterly collection, in performances both polished and stylish and with excellent solo and choral singing. At least the overture is clearly Purcell's, and that sets a pattern for a very varied collection of numbers, including three *da capo* arias and a full-length masque celebrating Neptune for Act V. The 1979 recording, made in London's Henry Wood Hall, is full and atmospheric; the words are beautifully clear, and the transfer to CD is admirably natural.

Dioclesian: Overture and excerpts.

(M) *** DHM/BMG 82876 60157-2. Argenta, Chance, Freiburg Bar. O, Von der Goltz – HANDEL: *Concerto grosso, Op. 6/6* etc. ***

Those not wanting the entire masque shold be well satisfied with this overture and set of songs and dances, presented with great zest by the superb Freiburg Baroque Orchestra, with excellent soloists in Michael Chance and Nancy Argenta. The *Chaconne* is beautfully played and the Second Music, which ends the selection, is particularly lively. Excellent couplings and first-class recording make this a highly recommendable reissue.

(i) *The Indian Queen* (incidental music); (ii) *King Arthur* (complete).

🔑 ✽ (M) *** Decca 476 1552 (2). (i) Cantelo, W. Brown, Tear, Partridge, Keyte, St Anthony Singers, ECO, Mackerras; (ii) Morison, Harper, M. Thomas, Whitworth, W. Brown, Galliver, Cameron, Anthony, Alan, St Anthony Singers, Philomusica of L., Lewis.

It was a happy idea of Universal to pair these comparatively early but outstanding Purcell recordings to include in their 'Penguin ✽ Collection'. *The Indian Queen* (originally issued on L'Oiseau-Lyre) dates from 1966, and the recording from a vintage era remains first rate. With stylish singing and superb direction and accompaniment (Raymond Leppard's harpsichord continuo playing must be singled out), this is an invaluable reissue. Charles Mackerras shows himself a strong and vivid as well as scholarly Purcellian. The Rosette, however, is for the pioneering 1959 set (also Oiseau-Lyre) of *King Arthur*, fully worthy to stand alongside the companion recording of *Dido and Aeneas*, made three years later. Here the success of the interpretation does not centre on the contribution of one inspired artist, but rather on teamwork among a numer of excellent singers and on the stylish and sensitive overall direction of Anthony Lewis. Oiseau-Lyre's excellent stereo also plays a big part. A very happy example is the chorus *This Way, That Way*, when the opposing spirits (good and evil) make a joint attempt to entice the King, while the famous freezing aria will surely send a shiver through the most warm-blooded listener.

(i) *Ode for the Birthday of Queen Mary* (1694): *Come, Ye Sons of Art Away; Ode for St Cecilia's Day: Welcome to All the Pleasures. Of Old when Heroes Thought it Base (The Yorkshire Feast Song).* (ii) *Dido and Aeneas* (complete); (iii) *Dioclesian* (masque); (iv) *King Arthur* (complete); (v) *Timon of Athens* (masque).

(B) *** DG 474 672-2 (5). (i) J. Smith, Chance, Wilson, Richardson, Mark Ainsley, George ; (ii) Von Otter, Dawson, Varcoe, Rogers; (iii) Monoyios, Agnew, Edgar-Wilson, Gadd, Birchall, Wallington, Foster; (iii; iv) Argenta, Bannatyne-Scott; (iv) Perillo, Gooding, MacDougall, Tucker, Finley; E. Concert & Ch., Pinnock.

Pinnock's is a somewhat arbitrary collection, but the standard of performance and recording is very high and this set represents excellent value. He directs exuberant performances of Purcell's two most celebrated odes; the weight and brightness of the choral sound go with infectiously lifted rhythms, making the music dance. The soloists are all outstanding, with the counter-tenor duetting of Michael Chance and Timothy Wilson in *Sound the Trumpet*, delectably pointed. The coupling, the neglected *Yorkshire Feast Song*, is full of wonderful inspirations, like the tenor and counter-tenor duet, *And Now When the Renown'd Nassau* – a reference to the new king, William III.

The performance of *Dido and Aeneas* is more controversial, presented as a court entertainment rather than as a school-sized entertainment in Dr Josias Priest's girls' establishment in Chelsea; but though the reading is not as inspired as many that Pinnock has given us, the scale is attractive. Both Anne Sofie von Otter and Lynne Dawson have voices that are at once warm and aptly pure for authentic performance. Von Otter as Dido, both fresh and mature-sounding, sings her two big arias with a combination of weight, gravity and expressive warmth which is yet completely in scale. The final lament, while faster than in traditional performances, still conveys the full tragic intensity of this epic in microcosm.

Much more questionable is the casting on the male side, and that includes a tenor taking the role of the Sorceress. Nigel Rogers, not in his sweetest voice, takes that role as well as that of the Sailor. Confusingly, almost immediately after the Sailor's jolly song at the start of Act III, Rogers reappears as the Sorceress in a quite different mood, making much too quick a change. Stephen Varcoe is a rather unheroic-sounding Aeneas, but the chorus of the English Concert produces fresh, alert singing. Instead of a repetition of the final chorus, Pinnock opts for an instrumental reprise to provide an epilogue.

Dioclesian and *Timon of Athens*, both sets of theatre music including masques, were recorded in tandem. Pinnock presents both works on a slightly larger (but not inflated) scale than either Gardiner on Erato or Hickox on Chandos, often more weighty to match a bigger, warmer (though not over-reverberant) acoustic. In keeping with this, he is more warmly expressive, and often adopts broader speeds, which allow him to spring rhythms the more infectiously, more clearly introducing an element of sparkle and humour. He includes the extra song in Act III of *Dioclesian*, 'When I First Saw', and certainly here the effervescence of Purcell's inspiration in one of his finest collections of theatre music is consistently compelling.

King Arthur follows on after *Dido and Aeneas*, opening with the *Chaconne* and making a break between CDs at the end of Act I. The performance is praised in our main volume: Linda Perillo makes a charming Philidel; Brian Bannatyne-Scott and Nancy Argenta are equally memorable, and the chorus and orchestra sing and play throughout with consistent vitality.

VOCAL MUSIC

Odes for Queen Mary's Birthday: Come Ye Sons of Art; Love's Goddess Sure was Blind; Now Does the Glorious Day Appear.

(M) ** Virgin 5 61844-2. Gooding, Bowman, Robson, Crook, Wilson-Johnson, George, OAE Ch. & O, Leonhardt.

A happy triptych on Virgin, but Leonhardt's personality is firmly stamped on all three works here. The orchestral texture has the less than fully nourished sound of period stringed instruments, and Leonhardt's jogging rhythm at the opening of *Now Does the Glorious Day Appear* seems a little too circumspect for that joyful ode. Indeed, his sobriety tends to override the music's character. He has a splendid chorus and superb soloists, and they are in excellent voice. James Bowman stands out, as does Julia Gooding (most winning, both in *Love's Goddess Sure* and in her lovely duet with the oboe, *Bid the Virtues*, in *Come Ye Sons of Art*). But Leonhardt's restraint prevents Purcell's inspired settings from taking the fullest flight.

The Complete Secular Solo Songs:

Volume 1: *Ah, how pleasant 'tis to love; Amidst the shades and cool refreshing streams; Beneath a dark and melancholy grove; Beware, poor shepherds; Cease anxious world, your fruitless pain; Draw near you lovers; How I sigh when I think of the charms of my swain; I loved fair Celia; Farewell, all joys; If music be the food of love; Let each gallant heart; Love, thou canst hear, tho' thou art blind; Musing on cares of human fate; My heart, whenever you appear; O! fair Cedaris, hide those eyes; On the brow of Richmond Hill; Pastora's beauties when unblown; Rashly I swore I would disown; See how the fading glories of the year; Since the pox of the plague; They say you're angry; A thousand sev'ral ways I tried; This poet sings the Trojan wars; Urge me no more; What hope for us remains now he has gone; While Thirsis, wrapp'd in downy sleep; Whist Cynthia sung, all angry winds lay still; Ye happy swains, whose nymphs are kind.* (CDA 66710)

Volume 2: *Ah! cruel nymph; Celia's fomd, too long I've lov'd her; Fairwell ye rocks, ye seas and sands; Fly swift ye hours; Gentle shepherds, you that know the charms* (Pastoral elegy on the death of John Playford); *How delightful's the life of an innocent swain; If grief has any pow'r to kill; Hears not my Phyllis how the birds* (The knotting song); *High on a throne of glitt'ring ore; If music be the food of love; Incassum, Lesbia* (Queen's Epicidium); *In vain we dissemble; I love and I must; I resolve against cringing and whining; I take no pleasure in the sun's bright beams; Love arms himself in Celia's eyes; Love's pow'r in my hear shall find no compliance; Not all my torments can your pity move; Phyllis, talk no more of passion; Scarce had the rising sun appear'd; She that would gain a faithful lover; She who my poor heart possesses; Through mournful shades and solitary groves; Since one poor view has drawn my heart; Sylvia, now your scorn give over; What a sad fate is mine; When all her languishing eyes said love; When first my sheperdess and I; When my Aemelia smiles; Who but a slave can well express.* (CDA 66720)

Volume 3: *Amintas, to my grief I see; Amintor, heedless of his flocks; Ask me to love no more; Bacchus is a pow'rdivine; Corinna is divinely fair; Cupid, the slyest rogue alive; The fatal hour comes on apace; From silent shades; He himself courts his own ruin; I came, I saw and was undone; If music be the food of love* (3rd version); *If pray'rs and tears; In Cloris all soft charms agree; Let formal lovers still pursue; Let us, kind Lesbia, give way; Love is now become a trade; Lovely Albina's come ashore; No, to what purpose should I speak?; O solitude, my sweetest choice; Olinda in the shades unseen; Phyllis I can ne'er forgive it; Pious Celinda goes to prayers; Sawney is a bonny lad; Spite of the godhead; Sylvia, 'tis true you're fair; When Stephen found his passion vain; Who can behold Florella's charms; Young Thirsis'fate.* (CDA 66730)

Volumes 1–3 (complete).

(M) *** Hyp. CDS 44161/3 (3). Bonney, Gritton, Bowman, Covey-Crump, Daniels, George, King's Consort, King.

Originally issued on three separate CDs, this boxed collection brings obvious advantages, not least in the alphabetical index provided of the 87 songs. It is good, for example, to be able instantly to compare the three different settings of *Music for a while*, each on a different disc. The second and best-known version is a revision of the first (both for tenor, elegantly sung here by Rogers Covey-Crump), whereas the third is quite different, a free-ranging arioso setting of the same text by Henry Heveningham, taking the first line from Shakespeare's *Twelfth Night*. Barbara Bonney sings it exquisitely, and all the soloists here are excellent, with Robert King with his Consort, notably on bass viols and theorbo, providing most sympathetic accompaniment. Not included are Purcell's bawdy songs and catches, usually for multiple voices.

STAGE WORKS AND THEATRE MUSIC

Dido and Aeneas (complete).

*** Virgin 5 45605-2. Graham, Bostridge, Tilling, De Boever, Palmer, Daniels, Agnew, European Voices, Le Concert d'Astrée, Haïm.

(BB) ** Warner Apex 8573 89242-2. Troyanos, Stilwell, Johnson, Ch. & CO, Leppard.

With an exceptionally strong line-up of soloists, Emanuelle Haïm directs a most distinctive period performance of *Dido and Aeneas*, with even the tiny role of the Spirit taken by a star singer, the countertenor David Daniels. The instrumental accompaniment is weightier than usual, helped by the immediate recording-balance, and that matches the thrustful manner of Haïm, strong and purposeful if occasionally challenging her singers and players uncomfortably. By contrast, in the brief chorus, *Cupid only throws the dart*, she is curiously slow and laboured. More aptly, she also adopts broad speeds in Dido's two big arias, *Ah Belinda* and the final *Lament*. There and throughout, Susan Graham as Dido sings with warm, full tone, and though some may resist the idea of a tenor taking the role of Aeneas, Ian Bostridge too characterizes strongly and darkens his voice more than usual. More controversially, as in Haïm's Virgin recording of Monteverdi's opera *L'Orfeo*, she encourages these and other soloists to lean into notes and phrases in search of expressive warmth, rather than attacking cleanly, as one expects in a period performance. It is a mannerism that many will welcome rather than resist, and Felicity Palmer as a larger-than-life Sorceress quickly makes one forget any expressive idiosyncrasy in the vividness of her characterization. Camilla Tilling as Belinda and Paul Agnew as the Sailor both sing strongly too, and the chorus, European Voices, under the direction of Simon Hasley, is crisp and alert. But first choice among recordings of this opera still rests with Dame Janet Baker and Anthony Lewis (Decca 466 387-2).

Leppard directs a consistently well-sprung and well-played performance, as one would expect, but the overall impression is disappointing, largely because the climax of the opera fails to rise in intensity as it should. Tatiana Troyanos, stylish elsewhere, misses the tragic depth of the great lament of Dido, and without that focus the impact of the rest falls away. However, it is interesting to have a baritone (Richard Stilwell), instead of a tenor, singing the *Sailor's song*. The recording is excellent.

QUILTER, Roger (1877–1953)

(i) *A Children's Overture;* (ii) *3 English Dances; Where the Rainbow Ends* (Suite). (iii) *The Fuchsia Tree; Now sleeps the crimson petal; Weep you no more.* (iv) *Come away, death;* (v) *7 Elizabethan Lyrics;* (vi; vii) *Go, lovely rose. It was a lover and his lass* (two versions, with viii; ix & x); (viii; ix) *Love's Philosophy;* (xi) *Non nobis, Domine;* (iv) *Now sleeps the crimson petal;* (vi; ix) *O mistress mine.*

⊶ (M) *** EMI (ADD/DDD) 585149-2. (i) Light Music Soc. O, Dunn; (ii) N. Sinf., Hickox; (iii) Hough; (iv) Bostridge, Drake; (v) Allen, Parsons; (vi) Harvey; (vii) Byfield; (viii) J. Baker; (ix) Moore; (x) Lott, Murray, Johnson; (xi) Finchley and Barnet & District Ch. Societies, Central Band of the RAF, Wallace.

Beginning with Quilter's masterly *A Children's Overture*, in Sir Vivian Dunn's bright if not distinctive performance from 1969, this well-planned anthology is a worthy tribute to this master of unpretentious composition. Richard Hickox's digital accounts of the *Three English Dances* and *Where the Rainbow Ends* are charmingly done, fully revealing all the rustic qualities of 'olde England'. There are some real gems among the vocal items: Janet Baker bringing characteristic vocal richness to *Love's Philosophy*, and *It was a lover and his lass*, which is also heard in a quite different and equally delightful version with Felicity Lott and Ann Murray in duet. Baritone Trevor Harvey invests passion rather than finesse in *O mistress mine*, but sings *Go, lovely rose* with more tenderness. In Ian Bostridge's two numbers, the sheer beauty of his tenor makes one readily forgive any reservations concerning over-interpretation – and what lovely songs they are, too. With three very attractive piano pieces, finely played by Stephen Hough, and a rousing performance of *Non nobis, Domine*, this CD is thoroughly recommendable. The sound-quality throughout is excellent, only the Frederick Harvey items from the mid-1960s sounding a bit dated.

RABAUD, Henri (1873–1949)

Divertissement sur des chansons russes, Op. 2; Eglogue, Op. 7; Mârouf, savetier du Caire: Dances;

Symphonic Poem after Lenau's Faust (Procession nocturne), Op. 6; Suites anglaises Nos. 2–3.

** Marco Polo 8.223503. Rheinland-Pfalz PO, Segerstam.

The *Eglogue* was Rabaud's first orchestral piece and derives its inspiration from the first *Eclogue* of Virgil. The dances from *Mârouf, savetier du Caire* have an appropriately oriental flavour since the opera itself is based on an episode from the *Arabian Nights*. The *Procession nocturne* is a tone-poem based on the same Lenau poem which inspired Liszt's *Nächtlige Zug* and is the most atmospheric of the pieces on this disc. The *Suites anglaises* are arrangements of Byrd, Farnaby and other Elizabethan composers that Rabaud made for a 1917 production of *The Merchant of Venice*. Like Roger-Ducasse, Rabaud's music is not strongly personal, but it is distinctly Gallic and well worth investigating. Segerstam and his orchestra show a real sympathy with this turn-of-the-century French repertoire, and they are decently recorded too.

RACHMANINOV, Sergei
(1873–1943)

Caprice bohémien, Op. 12; The Isle of the Dead, Op. 29; Prince Rostislav; The Rock, Op. 7; Scherzo in D min.

*** Chan. 10104. Russian State SO, Polyansky.

All these orchestral pieces turn up from time to time as couplings for the symphonies, though the tone-poem, *Prince Rostislav*, is more of a rarity. The *Scherzo* is Rachmaninov's earliest orchestral score, dating from 1888, when he was sixteen, while *The Isle of the Dead* is one of his greatest. In the latter Polyansky does not displace Pletnev (DG) among modern recordings or the composer himself, but he is certainly competitive and has this music in his blood. The recording is perhaps a bit too reverberant, but no reader wanting this repertoire should be put off, for the performances are all vivid.

The Isle of the Dead, Op. 29; The Rock, Op. 7; Symphonic Dances, Op. 45.

(BB) **(*) Warner Apex 2564 60958-2. Royal Stockholm PO, A. Davis.

Sir Andrew Davis gets good results from the Royal Stockholm Philharmonic Orchestra, who play very well indeed, and the recordings have admirable clarity and warmth. If neither *The Isle of the Dead* nor the *Symphonic Dances* – though eminently enjoyable – are really as distinguished as the best of their rivals, the bargain price-tag is very much in their favour.

CONCERTOS

Piano Concertos Nos. 1–4; Rhapsody on a Theme of Paganini.

(M) **(*) Danacord DACOCD 582-583 (3). Marshev, Aarhus SO, Loughran.

(i) *Piano Concertos Nos. 1–4; Rhapsody on a Theme of Paganini. Piano Sonata No. 2 in B flat, Op. 36; Variations on a Theme of Corelli, Op. 42.*

(M) *** Decca Trio (ADD) 473 251-2 (2). Ashkenazy, (i) with LSO, Previn.

Ashkenazy's highly praised set of the four Rachmaninov Concertos is also available on a Double Decca (444 839-2) and in a six-disc bargain box, which also includes the *Paganini Rhapsody*, the *Second Piano Sonata* and the *Corelli Variations*, plus other music, including the *Suites for 2 Pianos* (● 455 234-2). However, if you just want the items listed above, this Trio offers excellent value.

Oleg Marshev, born in Baku, a Russian-trained virtuoso who earlier recorded a whole series of adventurous discs for Danacord – Emil von Sauer, Strauss, Rubinstein, as well as Prokofiev and Liszt – here goes on to central, much-duplicated repertory, emerging as a formidable contender if hardly an outright winner. These are broad-brush readings in many senses. The speeds are generally broader than usual – with No. 2 taking over five minutes longer than in some vintage versions – but with his weight and power Marshev sustains broad tempi well, only occasionally letting the music run the risk of sounding plodding, as in the slow movement of No. 2 and at the start of the *Third Concerto*. Yet the thrust and intensity of his performances consistently carries one along, with full, forward recording-balance adding to the power. It also allows one to appreciate Marshev's clarity of articulation in Rachmaninov's brilliant passage-work. The downside is that the weight of the recording in heavy-textured passages tends to obscure inner detail. It also tends to downplay the poetic side of these heartfelt warhorses. Marshev's control of rubato is always fluent and idiomatic, conveying spontaneity of feeling, but others are even freer, and the absence of a true *pianissimo* makes the slow movements in particular sound a little heavy-handed in comparison with the finest versions. Loughran draws comparably powerful playing from the excellent Aarhus Symphony Orchestra, with a fine sheen on the strings, its most outstanding section. The broad speeds mean that the set has had to spread to three discs, but they come at mid-price. However, first choice for the four concertos still remains with Ashkenazy and Previn.

Piano Concertos Nos. 1 in F sharp min., Op. 1; 2 in C min., Op. 18.

*** DG 459 643-2. Zimerman, Boston SO, Ozawa.

Krystian Zimerman is an aristocrat among aristocrats of the piano and his playing is never less than awesome. These performances have been showered with so many plaudits and critical accolades that they must be regarded as self-recommending. Of course, like everything Zimerman does, they are touched by distinction, but for all the admiration they inspire, there is just a trace of self-possession about them: one would welcome greater emotional abandon.

Feeling does not always seem to arise spontaneously. But this is playing at an exalted level and many readers may not respond in this way – and most critics we have read certainly have not. Good orchestral support from Ozawa and the Boston orchestra, and very vivid and present recording.

Piano Concerto No. 2 in C min., Op. 18.

(BB) ** Warner Apex 0927 40835-2. Sultanov, LSO, Shostakovich – TCHAIKOVSKY: *Piano Concerto No. 1.* **

(M) (**) BBC BBCL mono 4074-2. Moiseiwitsch, BBC SO, Sargent – BEETHOVEN: *Piano Concerto No. 5.* (***)

(BB) ** EMI Encore 5 85705-2. Weissenberg, BPO, Karajan– TCHAIKOVSKY: *Piano Concerto No. 1.* *(*)

(B) * EMI Encore (ADD) 5 74732-2. Cziffra, New Philh. O, Cziffra Jr – GRIEG: *Piano Concerto.* *

Sultanov's recording was made in the immediate aftermath of his success at the eighth Van Cliburn Competition. There is plenty of exuberance and brilliance and an impressive range of tonal colour. Whatever reservations one may have, this is an eminently serviceable account, even if this would hardly be a first choice. The balance places the soloist too far forward, and the recording does not do justice to the LSO strings, which sound lustreless.

Rachmaninov thought Moiseiwitsch one of his finest interpreters, and this performance from a 1956 Prom serves as a reminder of his stature. Moiseiwitsch was seventeen years younger than the composer and grew up in his shadow. He is certainly steeped in both his spiritual and sound world, even if, in the heat of live performance, he was prone to the odd split note. But by this time, when he was in his sixties, he unaccountably appeared less in the concert hall than he had during the 1940s, and this inevitably took its toll. There are plenty of insights into this piece that the gladiatorial virtuosi of the present day do not bring, and he is given excellent support from Sir Malcolm Sargent, a fine concerto accompanist. Unfortunately, the sound is wanting in transparency and range and comes close to distortion in climaxes. All the same, this is an invaluable musical document, which all who care about the piano should investigate.

The Weissenberg–Karajan partnership dates from 1972. The performance rises splendidly to the climaxes, notably in the first movement and finale, but elsewhere tension is less consistently sustained. Weissenberg's thoughtful manner often seems too deliberate, although the slow movement produces some hushed playing which has undoubted magnetism. Taken as a whole, even though the recording is vivid, this is not entirely satisfying, and the new Tchaikovsky coupling provided for this reissue is even less so.

Though not entirely lacking poetic feeling, Cziffra's early 1970s account brings a general lack of passion and brilliance (mainly the fault of the conductor), though the finale does catch fire in the right places. The sound is below 1970s standards, with the orchestra sounding scrawny at times. Not recommended, even at budget price, with so much white-hot competition.

Piano Concerto No. 2; Rhapsody on a Theme of Paganini.

(B) ** CfP 585 6232. Fowke, RPO, Temirkanov.

Philip Fowke gives tasteful, well-mannered performances, ultimately lacking the bravura needed in both these display works, although the recording is excellent. However, Martino Tirimo's excellent coupling of the same two works on the same label offers far more red-blooded performances, also in first-rate digital sound (CD-CFP 9017 – see our main *Guide*).

Piano Concertos Nos. (i) 2; (ii) 3.

(BB) **(*) RCA (DDD/ADD) 82876 55269-2. (i) Douglas, LSO, Tilson Thomas; (ii) Janis, Boston SO, Munch.

** BIS CD 900. Ogawa, Malmö SO, Arwel Hughes.

The main interest here is Byron Janis's very fine first (1958) recording of the *Third Concerto* with Munch. He was to re-record it later even more successfully with Dorati for Mercury, and the earlier account produces a somewhat less full-bodied piano image; but the balance is acceptable within the warm Boston acoustic, and somehow the timbre seems right for Janis's comparatively brisk tempo for the main theme of the first movement. His approach is often impetuous, spontaneously so, but the contrast with the second subject is convincingly made and the reading has an underlying lyricism. Munch is a sympathetic partner. He contributes a strong surge of romanticism to the *Adagio*, and the performance brings some dazzling solo playing in the last movement with a particularly exciting close.

Unfortunately, Barry Douglas's digital recording of the *Second Concerto* (made 34 years later) does not take off in the same way. It would be an exaggeration to call it prosaic, but it is less imaginative or tonally refined than one would expect from a Tchaikovsky Competition winner. No quarrels with the excellent orchestral playing or the fine recorded sound.

Norika Ogawa is a cultured and musical artist but she does not have quite the tempestuous, barnstorming brilliance that any pianist aspiring to the *Third Piano Concerto* must command if he or she is to convince. She gives us the bigger cadenza, which seems to have replaced the more exhilarating one that Rachmaninov and Horowitz recorded. This is all rather low-voltage, though the Malmö orchestra under Owain Arwel Hughes are very supportive and the BIS recording is first class.

Piano Concertos Nos. (i) 2; (ii) 3. Preludes: in C sharp min., Op. 3/2; in E flat, Op. 23/6.

🔵— *** Mercury SACD (ADD) 470 639-2. Janis, with (i) Minneapolis SO; (ii) LSO; Dorati.

Mercury are bringing out some of their most admired recordings on SACD and, although they are not due to be released until after our book goes to press, we feel sure that listeners will want to be informed of their publication in the autumn of this year. Full reviews of the works listed above can be found in our current main edition. The new format should go some way to further enhance the already spectacular results afforded by the 'Living Presence' technology.

(i) *Piano Concertos Nos. 2; 3. Rhapsody on a Theme of Paganini. Elégie, Op. 3/1; Etudes-tableaux, Op. 39/3 & 5; Moments musicaux, Op. 16/3–6. Preludes, Op. 23/1, 2, 5 & 6; Op. 32/12.*

(B) **(*) EMI Gemini 5 85779-2 (2). Gavrilov; (i) with Phd. O, Muti.

Andrei Gavrilov recorded the solo items together in Moscow in 1984, the *Third Concerto* in Philadelphia in 1986, following on with the *Second* and the *Paganini Rhapsody* three years later. There is some pretty remarkable solo playing here, especially in the stormy *B flat major Prelude*, while the *G sharp minor* from Op. 32 has a proper sense of fantasy. More prodigious bravura provides real excitement in the *F sharp minor Etude-tableau*, Op 39/3, and in the *E minor Moment musical*, while Gavrilov relaxes winningly in the *Andante cantabile* of Op. 16/3 and *Elégie*. Sometimes his virtuosity almost carries him away, and the piano is placed rather near the listener, so that we are nearly taken with him, but there is no doubt about the quality of this recital.

Before this, EMI had issued a remarkable Melodiya LP of Gavrilov's incandescent first recording of the *Third Concerto*, made at the time of the Tchaikovsky competition, which was rightly acclaimed as a truly memorable reading, strong and passionate, with the finale offering a thrilling display of bravura. The new account with Muti still offers some dazzling playing, with Gavrilov again using the longer, more complex first-movement cadenza to powerful effect and creating a thrilling climax to the finale. But overall the reading is more idiosyncratic and, although the lyrical waywardness is warmly sustained, the end result is less authoritative than the earlier version.

In neither the *C minor Concerto* nor the *Rhapsody on a Theme of Paganini* does Gavrilov bring the distinction he commanded in his earlier recordings. There is plenty of flamboyant virtuosity and all these Philadelphia performances have a finely shaped orchestral response from the Philadelphia Orchestra under Muti, and the recording is excellent. But there is a self-regarding brilliance from the pianist (noticeable immediately at the opening of the *Paganini Rhapsody*) that is not wholly pleasing. There is certainly no lack of adrenalin or charisma, but his account of the *D minor Concerto*, made in the 1970s, has a naturalness of utterance that is less apparent here.

Piano Concerto No. 3 in D min., Op. 30.

⊶ (B) (***) RCA mono 82876 56052-2 (2). Horowitz, RCA Victor SO, Reiner– TCHAIKOVSKY: *Piano Concerto No. 1; Recital: 'Legendary Recordings'.* (***)

(i) *Piano Concerto No. 3. Etudes tableaux, Opp. 33/1–3; 39/6.*

(M) **(*) EMI 5 62837-2. Andsnes; (i) with Oslo PO, Berglund.

(i) *Piano Concerto No. 3. Prelude in B flat, Op. 23/2; Vocalise, Op. 34/14.*

** RCA 09026 61548-2. Kissin; (i) Boston SO, Ozawa.

Horowitz's 1951 RCA account with Reiner now reappears, coupled with his earlier (1941) version of the Tchaikovsky *First Concerto* with Toscanini. The Rachmaninov performance is full of poetry yet, like the Tchaikovsky, it is electrifying in its excitement. In spite of its dated sound (restricted but within a much warmer acoustic than the Tchaikovsky coupling) and a less than ideal balance, its magic comes over, and it is to be preferred to his later performance with Ormandy. The recital added to make a two-disc bargain double is assembled from various individual mono records mainly from the same era, but with a few items from the 1970s and 1980s.

Leif Ove Andsnes offers cultivated playing in the *D minor Concerto*, which was recorded at a public concert in Oslo in 1995. As always, he brings finesse and a refined musicianship to all he does, and the *Etudes tableaux* are touched with distinction. Berglund is supportive and free from egotism, but he does not draw from the Oslo players the refined sonority which Jansons commands. Nevertheless, the many admirers of the young Norwegian pianist will feel that this is a worthy representation of his art in EMI's 'Great Artists of the Century' series.

Kissin's opening is very measured and at low voltage. The pianism is superbly elegant, but one can easily feel that it is curiously judicious, given the incandescence this artist can command. Yet there are a number of poetic insights which almost persuade the listener that the slow tempo is justified. The record is assembled from live performances and the piano timbre is at times discoloured. Ozawa gets decent rather than distinguished results from the orchestra, which, as recorded, is curiously veiled and badly wanting in transparency at the top.

(i) *Piano Concerto No. 3 in D min., Op. 30. Piano Sonata No. 2 in B flat min., Op. 36.*

(M) * (**) RCA (ADD) 82876 59411-2. Horowitz, (i) with NYPO, Ormandy.

Horowitz's legendary association with Rachmaninov's *D minor Concerto* daunted even the composer. Horowitz made it virtually his own property over half a century. In January 1978 he was persuaded to re-record the work in stereo, this time at a live concert, with Ormandy drawing a committed and romantically expansive accompaniment from the New York Philharmonic Orchestra. Perhaps just a little of the old magic is missing in the solo playing, but it remains prodigious and Horowitz's insights are countless. Not all the playing is immaculate and there is some rhythmic eccentricity in the finale, but the communicative force of the reading is unquestionable. The snag is the recording, which was originally very dry and clinical, the piano timbre lacking bloom. For CD, the remastering has altered the sound-picture radically, considerably softening the focus, to bring a more romantic aura to the music-making. The result is that at lower dynamic levels the image appears to recede. The effect is disconcerting, but one can adjust to it, and certainly the effect is more agreeable than the 'bare bones' of the original LP's sound-quality. The *Sonata* comes from a live concert in 1980 and is also pretty electrifying. Horowitz plays the conflation he made (and of which Rachmaninov approved) of the 1913 original and the 1931 revision, plus a few further retouchings he subsequently added. An indispensable part of any Rachmaninov collection, which, in its remastered form, sounds better than it has before. Nevertheless, the earlier, mono account with Reiner is an even finer reading, even if it cannot match this later version in sound-quality.

SYMPHONIES

Symphony No. 1; The Isle of the Dead.

(BB) ★★★ EMI Encore 5 85459-2. St Petersburg PO, Jansons.

Mariss Jansons and his St Petersburg musicians do not wear their hearts on their sleeves, but they give a totally committed and finely shaped performance of the *First Symphony*. Jansons maintains a firm hold over the architecture of the piece and produces playing of great poetic feeling. *The Isle of the Dead* is highly atmospheric, a convincing and indeed haunting performance. The recording is beautifully natural, with transparent string-sound and plenty of space around the instruments and with no want of presence. A very satisfying reissue and a real bargain.

Symphony No. 2 in E min., Op. 27.

(BB) ★ Naxos 8.554230. Nat. SO of Ireland, Anissimov.

Symphony No. 2; (i) 3 Russian Songs, Op. 41.

★(★) Chan. 9665. Russian State SO, Polyansky; (i) with Russian State Symphonic Capella.

Valéry Polyansky's account is far from negligible, but it is equally far from distinguished. The most attractive feature of the disc is the Op. 41 set of *Three Russian Songs*, a glorious triptych, full of character, which are given decent, full-blooded performances.

Though the Naxos version is well played and recorded, the conductor, Alexander Anissimov, tends to make heavy weather of the outer movements, with boldly underlined rubato in the big melodies and

with a final climax in the fourth movement which fails to lift as it should. Even in the super-bargain category there are preferable, more idiomatic versions, including the earlier Naxos issue with Gunzenhauser, which also boasts *The Rock* as a coupling.

Symphony No. 3 in A min.; Symphonic Dances.

(BB) ★★★ EMI Encore 5 62809-2. St Petersburg PO, Jansons.

This fine coupling of the *Third Symphony* and the *Symphonic Dances* last appeared in a six-CD set of all three symphonies and the four piano concertos with Mikhail Rudy as soloist (EMI CZS5 75510-2). Although the concertos have distinct merits, they do not really displace such magnificent versions as Ashkenazy and Previn with the LSO or Jean-Philippe Collard, Plasson and the Toulouse orchestra. Jansons's account of the *Third Symphony*, however, is arguably the finest of the three (though his version of the *First* runs it close). It still sounds very good indeed and, although in this coupling Pletnev (DG 457 598-2) has a special feeling for the Rachmaninov sonority and plasticity of melodic line, Jansons has the merit of superb recorded sound and a competitive price-tag. Not everyone will warm to everything Pletnev does (the slow episode in the finale is very slow) though the *Symphonic Dances* are masterly. In any event, the Jansons is strongly recommended.

CHAMBER MUSIC

Cello Sonata in G min., Op. 19.

★★(★) EMI 5 57505-2. Capucon, Zilberstein – FRANCK: *Violin Sonata.* ★★(★)

Cello Sonata in G min., Op. 19; Lied; Melody on a Theme by Rachmaninov (arr. Altschuler/ Hayroudinoff); *2 Pieces, Op. 2; Prelude, Op. 23/10; Vocalise.*

★★(★) Chan. 10095. Ivashkin, Hayroudinoff.

Cello Sonata in G min.; Oriental Dance, Op. 2/2; Prelude, Op. 2/1.

(★★) Hyp. CDA 67376. Isserlis, Hough – FRANCK: *Cello Sonata, etc.* (★★)

Cello Sonata in G min.; 5 Pieces for Cello & Piano: Oriental Dance, Op. 2/2; Prelude, Op. 2/1; Romance; Vocalise, Op. 34/14 (with ALTSCHULLER: Mélodie).

🔊 (BB) ★★★ Double Decca 473 807-2 (2). Harrell, Ashkenazy – PROKOFIEV: *Cello Sonata;* SHOSTAKOVICH: *Cello Sonata, etc.* ★★★

Lynn Harrell and Vladimir Ashkenazy give an impassioned, full-throated account of the glorious *Cello Sonata* and they capture its melancholy perfectly. They are very well attuned to its sensibility and to the affecting drama of the smaller pieces. The Decca recording is in the high traditions of the house; the balance and perspective are completely natural. An outstanding bargain in the Double Decca series.

Alexander Ivashkin and Rustem Hayroudinoff give us the complete works for cello and piano, though it is only the *Sonata* that really counts. The *Two Pieces* of Op. 2 (a *Prelude* and *Danse orientale*) are very appealing, as is the slightly earlier *Lied*, written when Rachmaninov was seventeen. But the remainder are arrangements. Ivashkin produces a beautifully burnished, lustrous tone, and the playing of this duo is highly cultured. One would at times welcome more abandon in the second movement. One respected critic wrote that 'everything on this CD is mahogany brown and as mellow as a fine brandy' – nothing wrong with that, one might think. It is all thoroughly enjoyable and well (if forwardly) recorded, but for those wanting just the *Sonata* this is probably not a first choice.

The cellist Gautier Capucon, less well known than his violinist brother, Renaud, gives a bold, big-scale performance of the Rachmaninov *Sonata*, with the big exposition repeat observed. Even though the reading is extrovert rather than thoughtful, with the piano-playing splashy at times, this is a most warmly enjoyable version, helped by being recorded live.

On Hyperion, in the Rachmaninov as in the cello version of the Franck, the expressiveness and subtlety of Steven Isserlis and Stephen Hough is seriously and – unexpectedly with such a duo – undermined by the dim recording, making the music seem small-scale and lacking in bite.

PIANO MUSIC

Piano duet

Suites Nos. 1–2, Opp. 5 & 17; Symphonic Dances Op. 45.
** Sony SK 61767. Ax, Bronfman.
(B) ** Warner 0927 49611-2. Argerich, Rabinovitch.

Emanuel Ax and Yefim Bronfman have impressive technical address, but they are curiously unresponsive to the atmosphere engendered by these glorious pieces. These artists relish the bright surfaces without penetrating much further.

Very good recorded sound in this Warner coupling, which conveys the full range of touch and colour and has just the right amount of atmosphere. In the *First Suite* Argerich and Rabinovitch strive a bit too hard for effect and don't get far under the surface. The *Second Suite* and the *Symphonic Dances* are less self-conscious, but readers who want this repertoire are really far better off musically with the Ashkenazy and Previn set on Decca (444 845-2).

Solo piano music

Piano Sonata No. 2 in B flat min., Op. 36.
(BB) *(*) Warner Apex 0927 40830-2. Sultanov –
PROKOFIEV: *Piano Sonata No. 7*; SCRIABIN:
Piano Sonata No. 5. *(*)

Even at its modest price, Alexei Sultanov's Apex CD

is of questionable value. There is no want of virtuosity, but it is of the designed-to-dazzle variety. Sultanov gives a pretty aggressive account of the *Sonata*, very brightly lit and fiery. Some readers may respond more warmly to his showmanship than others, but he is essentially brilliant but brash and no challenge to the top recommendations.

OPERA

(i) *Aleko;* (ii); *Francesca da Rimini;* (iii) *The Miserly Knight.*
☚ (B) *** DG Trio 477 041-2 (3). Levitsky, Kotscherga, Von Otter; (i; ii) Guleghina, Leiferkus; (ii; iii) Larin, Aleksashkin; (iii) Chernov, Caley, Gottenburg SO, Järvi.

DG recorded all three of Rachmaninov's operas in 1996, issuing them in a box, then followed up with three separate issues at full price. Now, they return to the catalogue as a bargain Trio, but without texts and translations. Rachmaninov wrote the one-act *Aleko* (based on Pushkin) when he was still a teenager, completing it (with orchestration) in only seventeen days. It is rather like a Russian-flavoured *Cavalleria rusticana*, with the hero murdering his unfaithful sweetheart and her lover, but musically it brings echoes of Borodin, notably in evocative choruses like Polovtsian dances. Distinctive Rachmaninov fingerprints are few, but the result is most attractive, particularly in a performance like this, ideally cast, with Sergei Leiferkus a commanding Aleko and Neeme Järvi a warmly persuasive conductor.

Francesca da Rimini comes from 1906 and, like *The Miserly Knight*, shows something of the effect Bayreuth had on him. The opera is encumbered by an unsatisfactory libretto by Modest Tchaikovsky, but there is some glorious music and some fine singing from Maria Guleghina as Francesca and Sergei Leiferkus as Lanciotto Malatesta, the jealous husband. Sergei Larin makes a convincing Paolo, and the Gothenburg Orchestra and Chorus again respond magnificently to Neeme Järvi. The recording quality is quite outstanding.

The Miserly Knight, to a Pushkin text, contrasts the old knight, whose devotion to gold is total, and his son, who eyes his father's fortune enviously. The famous soliloquy, arguably Rachmaninov's finest dramatic scena, is powerfully done by Sergei Aleksashkin, who succeeds in winning us over to the Knight. Sergei Larin is hardly less convincing as his son, Albert. The outstanding recording and the fine orchestral playing make this a most desirable set.

RAFF, Joachim (1822–82)

Symphony No. 1 in D (An das Vaterland), Op. 96.
(BB) ** Naxos 8.555411. Rhenish PO, Friedman.

Symphony No. 2 in C, Op. 140; Overtures: Macbeth; Romeo and Juliet.

(BB) ** Naxos 8.555491. Slovak State PO (Košice), Schneider.

Symphonies Nos. 3 in F (Im Walde), Op. 153; 10 in F min. (Zur Herbstzeit), Op. 213.

** Marco Polo 8.223321. Slovak State PO (Košice), Schneider.

Symphonies Nos. 3; 4 in G min., Op. 167.

(BB) **(*) Hyp. Helios CDH 55017. Milton Keynes City O, Davan Wetton.

Symphonies Nos. 4; 11 in A min. (Winter), Op. 214.

*(*) Marco Polo 8.223529. Slovak State PO (Košice), Schneider.

Symphony No. 5 in E (Lenore), Op. 177; Overture, Ein feste Burg ist unser Gott, Op. 127.

*(*) Marco Polo 8.223455. Slovak State PO (Košice), Schneider.

Raff enjoyed enormous standing during his lifetime, though nowadays he is best remembered for a handful of salon pieces. However, he composed no fewer than eleven symphonies between 1864 and 1883, some of which have excited extravagant praise. Yet generally speaking, Raff's music is pretty bland, if far from unambitious.

As we commented in our main *Guide*, his *First Symphony* (*An das Vaterland*) takes itself very seriously and its 70-minute duration invites longueurs. However, now it has been reissued at Naxos price admirers of this uneven composer might feel it is worth trying. It is well enough played and recorded. Although the *Symphony No. 2 in C* – also well played and recorded – has a certain charm, it is predominantly Mendelssohnian and, while outwardly attractive, it remains pretty insubstantial.

The *Third (Im Walde)* and *Tenth Symphonies* are now available on Naxos and might be a good starting point for collectors wishing to explore this repertoire.

Of the eleven symphonies it is the *Fifth (Lenore)* which has captured the imagination of many. No doubt this may be accounted for by the somewhat macabre programme that inspired its finale. Although the symphony itself is more inspired than some of its companions (it has a particularly eloquent slow movement), it does need rather better advocacy than it receives from the Slovak Philharmonic under Urs Schneider. The Overture, *Ein feste Burg ist unser Gott*, is hardly sufficient to tip the scales in its favour.

The *Eleventh Symphony in A minor* was left incomplete on Raff's death in 1882 and is not otherwise available; the *Fourth* of 1871, available on the Hyperion version under Hilary Davan Wetton, is insufficiently persuasive. This music has moments of charm but is essentially second-rate and must have the most expert advocacy and opulent recorded

sound if it is to be persuasive; neither of these two versions is really first class. One needs a Beecham to work his magic on these scores. In these performances they are merely amiable but insignificant.

RAMEAU, Jean Philippe

KEYBOARD MUSIC

Music for Harpsichord: *Book I* (1706); *Pièces de clavecin* (1724); *Nouvelles Suites de pièces de clavecin* (c. 1728); *5 Pièces* (1741); *La Dauphine* (1747).

🎵 (M) *** Decca 475 493-2 (2). Rousset (harpsichord)

Christophe Rousset's coverage of Rameau's keyboard music deservedly won the *Gramophone's* Baroque Non-Vocal Award in 1992. Rousset's playing is marvellously persuasive and vital, authoritative and scholarly, yet fresh and completely free from the straitjacket of academic rectitude. The recording is excellent and this is most welcome, back in the catalogue at mid-price.

RAUTAVAARA, Einojuhani
(born 1928)

Piano Concertos Nos. 2; 3 (Gift of Dreams). Isle of Bliss.

(BB) **(*) Naxos 8.557009. Mikkola, Netherlands RSO, Klas.

Neither concerto is new to the catalogue and No. 3 has been recorded by Vladimir Ashkenazy, who commissioned it. It takes as a starting point the composer's 1978 Baudelaire setting, *Le Mort des pauvres*, in which the words '*le don des rêves*' occur: hence the sub-title. Both here and in the *Isle of Bliss*, written three years earlier and inspired by the Finnish poet Aleksis Kivi, one is reminded a lot of Honegger: Rautavaara's use of triads moving in contrary motion and his refined harmonic sense have more parallels with the French/Swiss master than with the Sibelius tone-poems to which it has been compared. But even if the music unfolds effortlessly and envelops the listener in its world, there is little real melodic distinction. The *Second Piano Concerto* comes from the late 1980s and is imaginative. The rippling piano figuration of the opening is effective, though the middle movement is lacking in concentration. All the same, this is good value for those wanting to sample these pieces.

VOCAL MUSIC

(i) *Canción de nuestro tiempo.* (ii) *In the Shade of the Willow.* (i; iii) *True and False Unicorn.*

*** Ondine ODE 1020-2. (i) Kortekangas, Rissanen, Salomaa; (ii) Huhta; Finnish R. Chamber Ch., (iii) with SO, Nuoranne.

The three works on this disc are all from the last decade, the earliest being the *Canción de nuestro tiempo* from 1993, and the setting of James Broughton's *True and False Unicorn*, though first planned in 1971, was not finally realized until 2000. It is a 45-minute work, often inventive and imaginative, and nearly always compelling (one or two passages called to mind the Frank Martin of *The Tempest* in its harmonic language and colouring), though the *Horn and Hounds* section with its quotations including '*God save the Queen*' does not really come off. However, the writing is always effective and the Holstian opening of *Mon seul désir*, the closing section of the piece, is rather haunting. The other two pieces are for voices alone and exhibit much command of vocal resource and colour. The *Canción de nuestro tiempo*, to three Lorca poems, is highly inventive, and the Aleksis Kivi settings, *In the Shade of the Willow*, prove admirable vehicles for the virtuosity of the Finnish Radio Chamber Choir and their soloists. Rautavaara's later music is always approachable (occasionally to the point of blandness). These pieces invariably hold the attention without necessarily striking the resonances that compel you to revisit it often. A worthwhile issue.

RAVEL, Maurice (1875–1937)

Alborada del gracioso; Daphnis et Chloé: Suite No. 2.
⊕ (M) ★★★ EMI 5 62746-2 [5 627592]. Philh. O, Giulini
– DEBUSSY: *La Mer; Nocturnes.* ★★★ ⊕

Giulini's 1959 accounts of these two key works are justly celebrated. They are not only among the most polished Ravel performances on record (the solo flute playing in *Daphnis* is quite ravishing), but they are also richly sensuous, with the most refined detail and an exquisite feeling for atmosphere. The *Alborada* has great rhythmic flair and the sumptuous Kingsway Hall recordings reveal remarkable inner clarity as well as giving the orchestra a glowing overall bloom, which the CD transfer captures perfectly. The Debussy couplings are no less distinguished, and this is truly a 'Great Recording of the Century'.

Alborada del gracioso; Ma mère l'Oye (complete ballet); Le Tombeau de Couperin; Valses nobles et sentimentales.
☞– ⊕ (M) ★★★ Decca 475 043-2. Montreal SO, Dutoit.

As we commented when this CD was first issued (without the *Alborada*) to win the *Gramophone* Engineering Award in 1985, a few bars of *Ma mère l'Oye* leave no doubt as to its quality. The sound is transparent and refined, the textures beautifully balanced, with translucent detail and firm focus. The performances, too, are wonderfully refined and sympathetic. *Ma mère l'Oye* is ravishingly beautiful, its special combination of sensuousness and innocence perfectly caught. The *Alborada*, recorded at the same

time, glitters: within the St Eustache acoustic it has a clarity and depth of perspective to match the elegant *Tombeau de Couperin* and a no less distinguished account of the *Valses*. An outstanding reminder of Decca's supreme technical and musical achievement in the early days of the compact disc (two decades ago!).

Boléro.
(BB) ★(★) EMI Encore 5 85460-2. Phd. O, Muti –
LISZT: *Les Préludes* ★★(★); TCHAIKOVSKY:
1812. ★ (★★)

Muti sets a measured tempo and almost lingers in his expressive treatment of the opening statements of the theme, against the clear side-drum snares. But by the time the climax is in sight, the upper range has harshened and the strings are glassy: the final *fortissimo* is very fierce indeed.

Boléro; Daphnis et Chloé (ballet): Suite No. 2. Pavane pour une infante défunte; Ma mère l'Oye (ballet): suite. La Valse.
☞– ★★★ Telarc CD 80601. Cincinnati SO, Järvi.

An outstanding collection in every way, gloriously recorded in the rich ambience of Cincinnati's Music Hall. Paavo Järvi secures performances which are beautifully played, affectionately detailed, warmly sensuous and radiantly textured (especially *Ma mère l'Oye*, which is more romantic than usual). The brightly paced *Boléro* and the expansive but equally magnetic *La Valse* both move to thrilling climaxes, the former with a characteristically spectacular bass drum. The wide dynamic range increases the drama of the interpretations – and indeed the spectacle of the demonstration-standard sound. Highly recommended.

Boléro; La Valse.
(M) ★★ Chan. 6615. Detroit SO, Järvi – DEBUSSY: *La Mer*; MILHAUD: *Suite provençale.* ★★

Järvi's *La Valse* opens atmospherically but is fairly brisk and not without its moments of exaggeration – indeed, affectation unusual in this conductor. There is no lack of tension, either here or in *Boléro*, although this is not a first choice for either piece. Very natural recorded sound.

Piano Concerto in G.
★★(★) Sup. SU 3714- 2 031. Moravec, Prague Philh.,
Bělohlávek– BEETHOVEN: *Piano Concerto No. 4*;
FRANCK: *Symphonic Variations.* ★★★

The lightness and clarity typical of the veteran Czech pianist Ivan Moravec brings out the neo-classical element in the Ravel *G major Concerto*. In the first movement the contrast is heightened between the rapid passage-work of the main *allegro* sections and the lyricism of the broadly expressive *andante* passages, with Bělohlávek colourfully touching in the jazz influences. The slow movement is at once poised, rapt and poetic, the more moving for the degree of understatement, and Moravec characteristically manages a velvety legato with only the lightest use of the pedal. In the reprise of the main melody the cor anglais is then far too backward when it takes up the theme, an inconsistency untypical of a generally well-balanced recording. In the extrovert finale Bělohlávek more than ever relishes the jazz element, while Moravec brings his usual clarity to the rushing figuration.

Piano Concerto in G; Piano Concerto in D for the Left Hand.

(M) *(*) EMI 5 66905-2 [566957]. François, Paris Conservatoire O, Cluytens.

Samson François has good analogue sound in his favour. But the choice of this pairing for EMI's 'Great Recordings of the Century' series is surely misguided, however much affection the French may feel for the soloist. Samson François was not always a particularly sensitive player and there is little to recommend in his efficient but prosaic performance of one of Ravel's most magical works. Fortunately, his spirited account of the *Left-hand Concerto* is more competitive. The piano is forwardly balanced, but not at the expense of orchestral detail.

Daphnis et Chloë (complete ballet); Ma mère l'Oye: Suite.

(*(*)) Testament mono SBT 1264 Fr. Nat. R. O, Ingelbrecht.

The complete *Daphnis* was recorded in 1953, not long after Ansermet's pioneering LP, and a year or so before Munch's famous Boston Symphony LP. It does not withstand comparison with either of them, in terms of either conception or execution. The playing of the Orchestre National is at times scruffy, and there is none of the distinctive authority that can be discerned in other recordings by this (rightly) admired conductor. The Testament transfer does its best for a recording that fell far below the standard the French engineers gave André Cluytens. Most (if not all) of Testament's issue from this period in the French recording industry is self-recommending, but this is an exception.

Ma mère l'Oye: Suite; La Valse

** Chan 9799. Danish Nat. RSO, Termirkanov – TCHAIKOVSKY: *The Nutcracker.* ** (with GADE: *Tango: Jalousie*).

It is difficult to know quite for whom this recording is designed. Recordings of the *Ma mère l'Oye* suite and *La Valse* are hardly in short supply and most collectors will want a more logical coupling than bits of Act II of *Nutcracker*. Including the Gade item was a curious idea. No complaints about the sound.

CHAMBER MUSIC

Tzigane for Violin & Orchestra.

(M) *** EMI (ADD) 5 62599-2. Perlman, O de Paris,

Martinon (with MASSENET: *Thaïs: Méditation*) – CHAUSSON: *Poème*; SAINT-SAENS: *Havanaise* etc. ***

Perlman's classic 1975 account of Ravel's *Tzigane* returns to the catalogue as part of the 'Perlman Edition'. It is marvellously played: the added projection of CD puts the soloist believably at the end of the sitting-room. The opulence of his tone is undiminished by the remastering process, and the orchestral sound retains its atmosphere while gaining in clarity.

String Quartet in F.

(BB) ** Warner Apex 8573 89231-2. Keller Qt – DEBUSSY: *Quartet.* **

The Keller Quartet are tauter and more dramatic than some of their rivals but, for all its merits, their performance does not match those rivals in terms of subtlety and tonal finesse. First choice rests with the Hagen Quartet on DG 437 836-2 or, at mid-price, the Melos Quartet on DG 463 082-2 – see our main volume.

Violin Sonata; Sonata posthume.

(BB) *(*) EMI Encore 5 85708-2. Zimmermann, Lonquich – DEBUSSY, JANACEK: *Violin Sonata.* *(*)

A commanding account of the *Sonata*, which is not as full of charm as it should be. Frank Peter Zimmermann plays with virtuosity and warmth, though Alexander Lonquich is not the most sensitive of partners. Readers who recall Augustin Dumay and Jean-Philippe Collard on this label will wonder why EMI's choice fell on these recordings.

(i; ii) Violin Sonata (1897); Violin Sonata in G; Tzigane; (i; iii) Sonata for Violin & Cello; (i; ii) Berceuse sur le nom de Gabriel Fauré; Kaddish; Pièce en forme de habanera.

⊖ (M) *** Decca 475 486-2. (i) Juillet; (ii) Rogé; (iii) Mørk.

This highly distinguished reissue won the *Gramophone* Chamber Music Award in 1997. These performances are predictably cultured and beautifully recorded, and the *Tzigane* is a version with a difference in that Rogé uses a piano luthénal (an instrument modified to sound like a cimbalom, which was used in the first performance in 1922). Strongly recommended, and the more so at mid-price.

PIANO MUSIC

Solo piano music

Gaspard de la nuit.

⊖ (M) (***) BBC mono BBCL 4064-2. Michelangeli – BEETHOVEN: *Sonatas Nos. 4 & 12*; DEBUSSY: *Hommage à Rameau.* (**(*))

Gaspard comes from a recital given in the Concert

Hall of Broadcasting House in 1959, and those who were fortunate enough to be there were electrified by Michelangeli's playing. The very opening of *Ondine* is not as hushed (the marking is *pianopianissimo*) as it seemed at the time, but everything else is magical. *Le Gibet* is fantastically controlled and full of atmosphere and *Scarbo* is dazzling and sinister – it must be one of the greatest performances it has ever received. The mono sound is strikingly well transferred and infinitely better than earlier, unauthorized LP versions that have been in currency.

OPERA

L'Enfant et les sortilèges.

☰— (M) *** DG 474 890-2. Ogéas, Collard, Berbié, Sénéchal, Gilma, Herzog, Rehfuss, Mauranne, Fr. R. Ch. & Boys' Ch., Fr. R. O, Maazel.

It is good that DG have reissued Maazel's delightful recording of *L'Enfant et les sortilèges* as a separate disc, as it won the *Gramophone* Award for Remastered CDs in 1989. However, those seeking the companion CD of *L'Heure espagnole* will find that DG's two-disc set includes also Maazel's outstanding recordings of Rimsky-Korsakov's *Capriccio espagnol* and Stravinsky's *Le Chant du rossignol*, two classics of the gramophone from the early days of stereo (449 769-2 – see our main volume).

RAWSTHORNE, Alan

(1905–71)

(i) Piano pieces: *Ballade in G sharp min.; Valse.* Songs: (ii) *Carol; 2 Fish;* (iii) *3 French Nursery Songs; Precursors; Prison Cycle* (with Alan Bush); (iv) *Scena Rustica* (for soprano & harp); (ii) *2 Songs for tenor & piano: (Away delights; God Lyaeus);* (iii) *Tzu-Yeh Songs.*

(*) Campion Cameo 2001. (i) Cuckson; (ii) Hill; (iii) Wells; (ii; iii) Swallow; (iv) Buckle, Wakeford – BUSH: *Prison Cycle (3 Songs)* **(*); MCCABE: *3 Folk Songs.* *

As Trevor Holst suggests in the accompanying notes, one thinks of Rawsthorne primarily as an orchestral and instrumental composer, so it is not remarkable that although all these settings bring appealingly melodic vocal lines, the musical kernel of each song is usually within the piano accompaniments, here so responsively played by Keith Swallow. The evocative opening *Prison Cycle*, with the settings shared by Rawsthorne and Bush, sets poems by the German Socialist poet Ernst Toller, who was imprisoned by the Nazis and who committed suicide in 1939. The soprano soloist Alison Wells (singing in German) sombrely evokes his claustrophobic imprisonment ('Six steps forward, Six steps back'), and the pleasure of seeing a pair of swallows perching on the barred window of his cell – before they are shot by the prison guards.

The mood is then lightened by five *Tzu-Yeh Songs*, translations from the Chinese, which have minimal oriental musical influence but much charm, as indeed have the *Three French Nursery Songs*, all of which show Alison Wells at her best, as does the richly lyrical MacNeice setting, *Precursors*. But the *Scena Rustica*, which offers an intimate dialogue for soprano and harp, suits Judith Buckle's voice less well, mainly because of an intrusive vibrato.

Of the tenor songs the gentle *Carol* and the boisterous medieval *Two Fish* ('the adult'rous Sargus' and 'the constant Cantharus') show Martyn Hill in good form. Two early piano pieces, played simply by Alan Cuckson, act as an interlude, before the sparkling tenor triptych, *Three Folk Songs* by John McCabe, closes the recital. Good recording, but made in a less than ideal ecclesiastical acoustic with the microphones fairly close and not always flattering the singers.

REED, W. H. (1875–1942)

Andante con moto; Andante tranquillo; 2 Chinese Impressions; Fantaisie brillante; The Gentle Dove (Welsh Folksong); Lento and Prelude; Luddi Dance; On Waterford Quay (An Irish Impression); Punjabi Song; Reverie; Rhapsody for Viola and Piano; Rhapsody in E min. for Violin and Piano; Spanish Dance (Fragment); Toccata.

(M) *** Dutton CDLX 7135. Gibbs, Mei-Loc Wu.

This Dutton compilation is illustrated with an engaging picture of W. H. Reed and Elgar, two English gentlemen complete with walking sticks, standing on the bank of the River Severn. Reed was a great friend of Elgar as well as being his musical colleague and adviser, and he assisted Elgar with violin figuration for the latter's *Concerto* and chamber music. He was well equipped to do so as leader of the London Symphony Orchestra from 1912 to 1935, as a Professor of the Violin at the Royal College of Music, and as a composer of unadventurous, but very well-written music of his own, in which the violin (or viola) took the leading role. Many of these pieces are romantic vignettes, which have something in common with Kreisler's miniatures, if without being quite so sharply memorable. But they include a pair of more ambitious *Rhapsodies* and a lighthearted, dancing *Andante tranquillo*, all of which display an easy-going fluency and genuine musical craftsmanship. The more extended *Fantaisie brillante*, with its agreeable central *Andante* and virtuoso moto perpetuo finale, was dedicated to Reed's teacher, Emile Sauret.

The advocacy here of the sweet-toned Robert Gibbs, partnered by Mary Mei-Loc Wu (who is much more than an accompanist), is very persuasive throughout this programme, and they play the longer works with conviction and style. But the genre pieces are also often appealing and are thrown off with aplomb. The *Toccata* has a cascading, Elgarian felicity, the *Chinese Impressions* are quaint without being trivial, while the *Punjabi Song* is quite memorable in its simplicity, and the *Luddi Dance* is certainly catchy. Excellent recording too, natural and very well balanced.

REGER, Max (1873–1916)

Variations & Fugue on a Theme of Beethoven, Op. 86.

(M) *** Chan. 7080 (2). LPO, Järvi – BRUCKNER: *Symphony No. 8.* **(*)

Terminally ill, in his last years Reger concentrated on composition, here orchestrating eight of the twelve variations of a work he originally scored for two pianos. The result is a brilliant, sharply characterized piece with obvious echoes of Brahms, a fine companion for Reger's two better-known sets of variations on themes of Mozart and Hiller, and an attractive coupling for Järvi's warm-hearted reading of the Bruckner, now at mid-price. Rich 1986 Chandos sound.

(Unaccompanied) Cello Suites Nos. 1 in G; 2 in D min.; 3 in A min., Op. 131c.

(M) *** Oehms OC 235. Schiefen.

A pupil of Maurice Gendron and Siegfried Palm, Guido Scheifen is now in his early thirties and proves an authoritative and persuasive advocate of the three Reger *Cello Suites*, Op. 131c. These were composed immediately before the *Variations and Fugue on a Theme by Mozart* and were modelled on Bach, whom they at times paraphrase. Not essential listening perhaps, but played like this they are quite impressive and they are well recorded too.

RESPIGHI, Ottorino

(1879–1936)

Adagio con variazioni (for Cello & Orchestra).

(M) *** Sup. (ADD) SU 3667-2. Navarra, Czech PO, Ančerl – BLOCH: *Schelomo*; SCHUMANN: *Cello Concerto.* **(*)

Respighi's short but charming set of variations shows the composer on top form. It is an Italianate equivalent of Tchaikovsky's *Rococo Variations* and has a burst of almost Russian romantic expressiveness to make a sunset-like ending. Navarra plays it very beautifully, and both his timbre and the orchestra are greatly enhanced by the current remastering.

Ancient Airs and Dances: Suites Nos. 1–3.

⊶ ✿ *** Mercury **SACD** (ADD) 470 637-2. Philh. Hungarica, Dorati.

Mercury are bringing out some of their most admired recordings on SACD and, although they are not due to be released until after our book goes to press, we feel sure that listeners will want to be informed of their publication in the autumn of this year. We are particularly excited to learn that the suites from the *Ancient Airs and Dances* are to be released on SACD, the enhanced format giving even more lifelike reproduction.

La Pentola magica (ballet); arr. of BACH: *Prelude and Fugue in D*; arr. of ROSSINI: *La Boutique fantasque.*

*** Chan. 10081. BBC PO, Noseda.

As his orchestral showpieces demonstrate, Ottorino Respighi was among the greatest orchestrators ever, and here, showing off his brilliance, he sumptuously transforms other composers' music. His sparkling arrangements of Rossini's late inspirations, the 'Sins of Old Age', which make up the ballet *La Boutique fantasque*, have long been popular, here inspiring an exhilarating performance from Gianandrea Noseda and the BBC Philharmonic, richly recorded. *La Pentola magica* ('The Magic Pot'), is a ballet score which remained unpublished until after the composer's death, drawing on rare Russian sources in a gentle sequence of ten brief movements, again beautifully orchestrated. The *Prelude and Fugue in D*, the most spectacular item, is an exuberant realization of Bach's organ original, which, far from imitating the organ, pulls out all the orchestral stops in a resounding display.

Violin Sonata in B min.

⊶ (M) *** Decca 474 558-2. Chung, Zimerman – R. STRAUSS: *Violin Sonata.* ***

Winner of *Gramophone*'s Chamber Music Award in 1990, these performances have never been surpassed. Kyung-Wha Chung is at her best, and Krystian Zimerman brings an enormous range of colour and dynamics to the piano part – the clarity of his articulation in the *Passacaglia* is exceptional. Excellent recording, too.

REVUELTAS, Silvestre (1899–1940)

La Coronela (ballet; orch. Moncada; arr. Limantour); *La noche de los Mayas* (arr. Limantour); *Sensemayá.*

(BB) *** Naxos 8.555917. Aguascalientes SO, Mexico, Barrios.

The Mexican composer and violinist Silvestre Revueltas is essentially remembered for his colourful tone-poems, which are strongly influenced by Mexican folk music. His music is approachable: rhythmic, vibrant, even gaudily orchestrated, often with strong elements of popular Hispanic–American cultures in scores which also have strands of Stravinsky, Prokofiev and Chavez. The popular *Sensemayá* (1938), based on a poem by the Afro-Cuban revolutionary Nicolás Guillén, is about the killing of a snake. It is an exciting work, notable for its battery of drums and terrific rhythmic drive, building up to a huge climax, and here heard in its orchestral (as opposed to the original vocal and orchestral) form. *La noche des los Mayas* ('The Night of the Mayas') was written for a 1939 film; it forms the colourful 30-minute suite assembled by the composer José Yves de Limantour in 1960 recorded here. In the (unfinished) ballet *La Coronela*, written in 1960, Revueltas's obvious rhythmic flair produces some excellent, spikily balletic numbers, with the emphasis on rhythm and bold colour rather than long melodic lines. Not that there are no tunes: *Don Ferruco's Nightmare* starts out as a lovely Waltz and gets gradually more quirky as it goes on. Vibrant recording to match the performances.

REYNOLDS, Alfred (1884–1969)

Alice Through the Looking Glass: Suite. The Duenna: Suite of Five Dances. Festival March; Marriage à la mode: Suite. Overture for a Comedy; 3 Pieces for Theatre; The Sirens of Southend; The Swiss Family Robinson: Swiss Lullaby and Ballet. The Taming of the Shrew: Overture. 1066 and All That: Suite (inc. Ballet of the Roses). The Toy Cart: Suite.
**(*) Marco Polo 8.225184. Royal Ballet Sinf., Sutherland.

Born in Liverpool, the son of waxwork museum proprietors, Alfred Reynolds studied music in Liverpool, Heidelberg, and then for six years in Berlin under the guidance of Humperdinck. His name is largely associated with the stage, with much of the music here written as incidental for plays. It is all spontaneously tuneful in the best British light music tradition, occasionally more substantial, but never attempting profundity. The more substantial overtures are highly enjoyable: the *Overture for a Comedy* has some diverting episodes and, like the rest of the programme, makes one nostalgic for the past. *Alice Through the Looking Glass* features some nice, piquant numbers (especially the *Jabberwocky* and *March of the Drums*), and Reynolds's interest in eighteenth-century music is felt sporadically throughout the programme, including the *Entr'acte* from *The Critic* (*Three Pieces for Theatre*), a charming minuet with a gentle hint of pomposity. The excerpts from his most famous work, *1066 and All That*, are highly enjoyable, as is the splendidly rousing *Festival March*. Dance rhythms make up a fair proportion of the music – a lively tarantella here, a nostalgic waltz there, plus a rustic jig and a Spanish fandango. Gavin Sutherland is as reliable as ever in securing the right style from his orchestra, though occasionally the sound isn't as sweet as it might be. Lovers of light music should consider this CD, as Alfred Reynolds deserves to be remembered.

REZNIČEK, Emil von (1860–1945)

Raskolnikov (Phantasy Overture); (i) *Schlemihl (A Symphonic Life Story).*
*** CPO 999 795-2. WDR SO, Cologne, Jurowski, (i) with Yamamasu.

It is good to hear more music from the composer of the brilliant *Donna Diana Overture*, and it is immediately striking to hear Richard Strauss parallels (a composer who often entrusted performances of his tone-poems to Reznic̆ek), notably in *Schlemihl (A Symphonic Life Story)*, first performed in 1912. It is loosely autobiographical, and the sleeve-note writer at one point suggests that it might be titled 'Not a Hero's Life'. The events of this 45-minute work (which contains plenty of hints of Mahler, Wagner and Shostakovich, along with Strauss) are written out in exhaustive detail, down to the last minute, and are included in the extensive booklet. In its way it makes enjoyable listening, especially with Reznic̆ek's gift for bright orchestration, and with seemingly every conceivable emotion and orchestral gesture contriving to make an appearance. This committed performance makes a good case for it, though Nobuaki Yamamasu is a little unsteady in his short solo. The 22-minute *Raskolnikov Overture* (1932) has some good passages in it, but in its meandering way it does not always sustain interest. However, the performance is excellent. Good recording.

RIES, Ferdinand (1784–1838)

Symphonies Nos. 1 in D, Op. 23; 2 in C min., Op. 80.
*** CPO 999 716-2. Zürich CO, Griffiths.

Ferdinand Ries was a pupil and protégé of Beethoven. The latter entrusted the second performance of his *Third Piano Concerto* to the youngster and also allowed him to write his own cadenza. Ries was in his mid-twenties when he wrote the first of his eighteen symphonies in 1809 (the year of the Siege of Vienna) and the *Second in C minor* was written and first given in 1814 in London, where Ries spent the best part of a decade. It enjoyed much exposure during Ries's lifetime, and although the shadow of his master (and especially the *Eroica*) is strikingly in evidence, it is by no means wanting in quality. Ries is a fine craftsman and has good taste and an inventive lyrical vein. This music serves to show that if Beethoven loomed head and shoulders above his contemporaries, they were still far from negligible. Both symphonies are the product of a fine musical intelligence and offer civilized discourse. Persuasive performances and decent recording from the Zürich orchestra under Howard Griffiths.

Symphony No. 4 in F, Op. 110; 6 in D, Op. 146.
*** CPO 999 836-2. Zürich CO, Griffiths.

Another excellent find from MDG, who have been

kindly resurrecting composers obscured in the shadow of Beethoven: Fesca, Onslow, Spohr and now Ferdiand Ries. Ries, composer, pianist and conductor, wrote some eighteen symphonies, of which the two recorded here make a good coupling. He was a pupil of Beethoven, who is alleged to have remarked that Ries 'imitates me too much', a remark – whether it was made or not – which has some justification; it would be pretty strange if there were not an element of imitation from a pupil of Beethoven, so powerful his influence was (and is!): the Scherzo of the *Fourth Symphony* is pure Beethoven, almost a crib. Even if no masterpieces have been uncovered, with their lively and melodic writing it is hard not to enjoy these two works, written in 1818 and 1822 respectively, both coming up freshly in these enthusiastic and sympathetic performances. Curiously, in the *Sixth Symphony*, Ries employs a *Menuetto* rather than more 'modern' Scherzo – and a very attractive one it is too; in the finale (which has a lovely, jaunty recurring tune), a battery of 'Turkish' instruments is recruited – bass drum, cymbals and triangle – to give an extra splash of colour, very exotic for its day. The sound is excellent and, as usual with CPO, the sleeve-notes are highly informative.

RIISAGER, Knudåge (1897–1974)

(i) *Concertino for Trumpet & Strings, Op. 29. Darduse, Op. 32; Slaraffenland (Fools' Paradise): Suites Nos. 1 & 2; Tolv med Posten, Op. 37.*

*** Marco Polo 8.224082. (i) Hardenberger; Hälsingborg SO, Dausgaard.

Knudåge Riisager is best known for his neoclassical works from the 1930s, and all the music on this CD comes from that decade. *Fools' Paradise* has a fair amount of circus-like music *à la manière de* Satie and Milhaud, but the touching lyricism of *Prinsesse Sukkergodt* ('Princess Sweets') is captivating. The whole work has bags of charm and deserves the widest currency. Håkan Hardenberger is in good form in the *Concertino*, though the orchestral support could have greater lightness of touch and finesse. *April* from *Tolv med Posten*, on the other hand, has much elegance. Readers who investigate this CD will find little depth but much to entertain them. Generally good performances under Thomas Dausgaard but rather bass-light sound.

Erasmus Montanus Overture, Op. 1; Etudes (ballet: complete); *Qarrtsiluni, Op. 36.*

*** Chan. 9432. Danish Nat. RSO, Rozhdestvensky.

Both the *Etudes* and *Qarrtsiluni* are classics of the Danish ballet. Knudåge Riisager's admiration for *Les Six* is evident in the elegance and wit that distinguish the *Etudes* (1948), a pastiche based on Czerny, and *Qarrtsiluni* (1938). There is a zest and sparkle about his music, though it neither aims for nor has any great depth. The attractive *Erasmus Montanus Over-*

ture is a highly accomplished first opus, neatly performed and superbly recorded.

RIMSKY-KORSAKOV, Nikolay (1844–1908)

(i) *Christmas Eve (Suite); Le Coq d'or: Suite.* (ii) *Fantasia on Serbian Themes, Op. 6; Fairy-Tale (Skazka), Op. 29; Overture on Russian Themes, Op. 20;* (i) *Sadko, Op. 5; Scheherazade, Op. 35; Song of India (from Sadko);* (ii) *Symphonies Nos. 1, Op. 1; 2 (Antar); 3, Op. 32;* (i) *The Tale of Tsar Saltan: Suite & Flight of the Bumble-Bee;* (ii) *The Tsar's Bride: Overture.*

(BB) **(*) Brilliant 99934 (4). (i) Armenian PO, Tjeknavorian; (ii) Philh. O or LSO, Butt.

This inexpensive Brilliant compilation is on the face of it a most attractive survey of Rimsky's orchestral works, but in the event it is uneven in appeal. Two of the four CDs, which include a seductive *Scheherazade* and lustrous, sparking accounts of many of the shorter works, are played with much élan by the Armenian Philharmonic Orchestra under Loris Tjeknavorian and given first-class sound. The other pair of discs features the Philharmonia or London Symphony Orchestra, directed by Yondani Butt. Here the orchestral playing itself is refined and colourful, but the lack of vitality or a powerful forward drive in the *First* and *Third Symphonies* is a drawback, while in *Antar* it is only the central movements that spring powerfully to life. The shorter pieces are more successful, but the Armenian performances have far more red-blooded Russian character. The two CDs conducted by Tjeknavorian are still available on ASV (see our companion volume) and will perhaps be later reissued in a lower price range.

Fairy Tale (Skazkà), Op. 29; Fantasia on Serbian Themes, Op. 6; Legend of the Invisible City of Kitzh (symphonic suite); The Maid of Pskov (Ivan the Terrible): Suite.

(BB) ** Naxos 8.553513. Moscow SO, Golovchin.

This is a very attractive compilation containing some of Rimsky's lesser-known music, often languorous in feeling and displaying a characteristically glowing orchestral palette. The Moscow Symphony Orchestra are obviously at home in this repertoire and they play it very beguilingly (apart from occasional rasping trombones), and the recording is warmly atmospheric. But the effect is very relaxed and in music which is atmospherically sustained one needs more internal tension. The narrative of *Skazka*, too, lacks a positive momentum. Even so, this is still desirable and worth its modest price.

Scheherazade (symphonic suite), Op. 35.

(M) (***) Cala (ADD) CACD 0536. LSO, Stokowski (with rehearsal sequence) – TCHAIKOVSKY: *Marche slave.* **(*)

(BB) ★ DG Entrée (ADD/DDD) 474 564-2. BPO,
Maazel – MUSSORGSKY: *Pictures at an Exhibition.*
★★★

Scheherazade; Capriccio espagnol, Op. 34; Tsar Saltan: Flight of the Bumble-Bee.
★★ Teldec 0630 17125-2. NYPO, Masur.

Scheherazade; Russian Easter Festival Overture.
★★ Telarc CD 80568. Atlanta SO, Spano.

On his visits to England in the 1960s, Leopold
Stokowski, always adventurous over recording techniques, became fascinated with the Phase Four system developed by the Decca engineers, and in 1964
he went to Kingsway Hall to make this spectacular
recording of a favourite work of his. At 82 he was still
at the height of his powers, and the result is even
more thrillingly high-powered than the multiple versions he had already put on disc and the one which
(11 years later) he was to make for RCA. The warmth
and drama of this evocative programme piece have
never been conveyed more vividly, and in this excellent CD transfer, using original material, the sound
never for a moment betrays its age. This Cala version
comes with fascinating couplings: the thrilling live
performance of Tchaikovsky's *Marche slave* that
Stokowski conducted as an encore at his ninetieth
birthday concert in London, with a spoken introduction by himself, and, fascinatingly, four substantial
clips from the rehearsals the conductor took in the
Phase Four sessions on *Scheherazade*. As he says,
'Music is not mechanism,' and every note he conducted confirms that.

Robert Spano in his first recording as music director draws clean, polished playing from the Atlanta
orchestra, which yet lacks the forward thrust and
improvisatory freedom needed in the episodic structure of *Scheherazade*. The violin soloist, Cecylia Arze-
wski, similarly plays with precision but too stiffly.
The *Russian Easter Festival Overture*, too, brings a
note of caution. The Telarc recording is unobtrusively brilliant, with brass very well caught.

Though Masur's *Scheherazade* was recorded live,
there is little or no rush of adrenalin. Ensemble is
phenomenally precise, with the cleanest articulation,
and Masur's control is so complete that even the
rhapsodic solos, both from the solo violin and from
the woodwind, have little feeling of freedom. The
approach is similar in the *Capriccio espagnol*, fast and
fierce, missing jollity. Some may find the results of
Masur's approach refreshing, and the *Flight of the
Bumble-Bee* does bring a dazzling performance, full
of wit and fun, but there is a missing dimension here.

There is nothing to detain the collector in Maazel's
digital DG version. The playing of the Berlin Philharmonic Orchestra is, of course, peerless, and in the
slow movement they make some gorgeous sounds,
though the the acoustics of the Philharmonie are not
entirely flattering on CD. But Maazel's spacious reading is simply lacking in electricity. A pity, as the
coupling is a good one.

Symphony No. 2 (Antar); Russian Easter Festival Overture.
➑─ (BB) ★★★ Hyp. Helios CDH 55137. Philh. O,
Svetlanov.

It goes without saying that the Philharmonia Orchestra under Svetlanov produce an excellent account of
Rimsky-Korsakov's colourful score and there is no
want of atmosphere or spirit in their playing. Moreover, they are given excellent recorded sound by the
Hyperion team. The performances themselves are
not superior to those on the two-CD set from the
Gothenburg orchestra under Neeme Järvi, but at its
new budget price this reissue can receive an unre-
seved recommendation, even if the playing time is
still a bit short – a mite under 50 minutes.

Tsar Saltan: Suite
★★★ Belair BAM 9724. New Russian O, Poltevsky –
BORODIN: *Symphony No. 2 in B min.* ★(★)

The young Russian, Oleg Poltevsky, conducts this
hand-picked Russian orchestra in an electrifying
account of the colourful *Tsar Saltan* music, well
recorded. An excellent, if ungenerous coupling for a
rather ponderous reading of the Borodin.

Piano & Wind Quintet in B flat.
(BB) ★★★ Hyp. Helios CDH 55173. Capricorn –
GLINKA: *Grand Sextet in E flat.* ★★★

Capricorn's sparkling account of Rimsky's youthful
Quintet for piano, flute, clarinet, horn and bassoon is
all the more welcome at budget price, particularly as
it is very well recorded.

RODGERS, Richard (1902–79)

Ballet Scores: Ghost Town; On Your Toes: La Princess Zenobia; Slaughter on Tenth Avenue.
★★★ TER CDTER 1114. O, Mauceri.

Richard Rodgers often wrote quite extensive ballets
for his Broadway output, the best known being
Slaughter on Tenth Avenue, first heard in the 1936
musical *On Your Toes*, which also presented *La
Princess Zenobia* for the first time. However, *Ghost
Town*, an American folk ballet about the Gold Rush,
was commissioned by the Ballet Russe de Monte
Carlo in 1939 and produced at the Metropolitan
Opera that year. All three ballets have their fair share
of good tunes – *Slaughter on Tenth Avenue*, easily the
best of them, has three superb melodies (among
Rodgers's finest) – and there is no doubting that the
colourful orchestrations of Hans Spialek go a large
way towards making these scores as sparkling as they
are. The performances under John Mauceri are first
rate, as is the vivid and bright recording, which
admirably catches the Hollywoodesque orchestrations. The fine orchestra is presumably a pick-up
ensemble, as, curiously, it is not credited with a
name.

Carousel (film musical).

*** EMI (ADD) 5 27352-2. Film soundtrack recording with MacRae, Jones, Mitchell, Ruick, Turner, Rounseville, Christie, 20th Century Fox Ch. & O, Newman.

The King and I (film musical).

*** EMI (ADD) 5 27351-2. Film soundtrack recording with Nixon/Kerr, Brynner, Gordon/Moreno, Saunders, Fuentes/Rivas, 20th Century Fox Ch. & O, Newman.

Oklahoma! (film musical).

*** EMI (ADD) 5 27350-2. Film soundtrack recording with MacRae, Jones, Greenwood, Grahame, Nelson, Steiger, 20th Century Fox Ch. & O, Newman.

In these days when so many twentieth-century composers of so-called 'serious' music and opera seem unwilling, or unable, to write hummable melodies, it seems worth while to celebrate again the achievement of three great Rodgers and Hammerstein musicals of the 1940s and early 1950s. The sheer tunefulness of the music is of the kind which, once lodged in the memory, is impossible to erase. And Richard Rodgers had the good fortune to collaborate with a librettist who showed not only a natural feeling for a melodic line, but also an inspired ear for the vernacular. The Rodgers and Hammerstein love songs communicate directly and universally, while in the case of 'I can't say no' and 'With me it's all er nothin'' (from *Oklahoma!*) there is an attractive colloquial realism. When Carrie Pipperidge (Barbara Ruick) in *Carousel* sings her charming song about her beloved fisherman, Mr Snow, she tells us engagingly 'my heart's in my nose', while 'June is bustin' out all over' conveys the burgeoning fecundity of spring with an elemental exuberance seldom matched elsewhere.

In *The King and I* author and composer were faced with a seemingly unromantic widow-heroine, who had become an impecunious schoolteacher. Yet in 'Hello young lovers' (with its graceful shifts between duple and waltz time) they triumphed over the problem with one of their loveliest songs, as Anna remembers and communicates her past happiness with her husband, Tom. Later, the underlying tension between Anna and the King underpins the apparently lighthearted number, 'Shall we dance'.

In short, these are masterly scores, with masterly lyrics and, as the recent outstanding National Theatre revival of *Oklahoma!* demonstrated, this is a work of classic stature, with much greater depth of characterization than had been hitherto realized.

We discussed the original Capitol soundtrack LPs of these three spectacular wide-screen movies in the very first volume of our hardback *Stereo Record Guide* (1960), where our response was mixed. In spite of often surprisingly good stereo effects, the sound was often coarse, and unnecessary musical cuts were made. The new digital transfers show how extraordinarily rich and vivid was the quality of the original

film tracks, and what gorgeous sounds were made by the superb 20th Century Fox studio orchestra under Alfred Newman. The chorus is pretty good too.

The dubbing of Deborah Kerr's songs in *The King and I* by the sweet-voiced Marni Nixon, and Tuptim's 'We kiss in the shadow' by the sultry Leonora Gordon (originally undisclosed) is now part of the current documentation, although Rita Moreno herself narrates the highly dramatic ballet sequence, *The Small House of Uncle Tom*. In *Carousel* and *Oklahoma!* Gordon MacRae and Shirley Jones make a delightfully fresh-voiced pair of lovers, and the smaller parts are all full of character.

Much that was previously omitted has now been restored, including items which did not appear in the final edited films. This means that there is a good deal of repetition and reprises. Never mind, these three discs are very enjoyable, and you may even find yourself humming along. The documentation is excellent, so a final word from Oscar Hammerstein about the gestation of the famous *Carousel Waltz* seems appropriate: 'I'd become weary – and am still weary – of the sound that comes out of an orchestral pit during the "Overture". All you can hear is the brass, because you never have a sufficient number of strings; and the audience must make a concerted effort to pick up any melody that is not blasted. I wanted to avoid this. I wanted people to start paying attention to what came out of the pit with the very first sound they heard.' He succeeded.

'*Rodgers & Hammerstein Songs*' from: *Allegro; Carousel; The King and I; Me and Juliet; Oklahoma!; The Sound of Music; South Pacific; State Fair.*

*** DG 449 163-2. Terfel, Opera North Ch., E. N. Philh., Daniel.

Bryn Terfel masterfully embraces the Broadway idiom, projecting his magnetic personality in the widest range of songs, using a remarkable range of tone, from a whispered head voice (as he does magically at the end of 'Some enchanted evening') to a tough, almost gravelly *fortissimo* at climaxes, from the biting toughness of 'Nothing like a dame' or Billy Bigelow's big soliloquy in *Carousel* (using a very convincing American accent) to the warmth of 'If I loved you' and 'You'll never walk alone' (with chorus). Specially welcome are the rarities, including one number from *Me and Juliet* and four from the stylized and underprized *Allegro*, including the powerfully emotional 'Come home'. With excellent sound and fine playing from Opera North forces under Paul Daniel, this is a wide-ranging survey. It deserves the widest circulation.

RODRIGO, Joaquín (1902–99)

Naxos Complete Rodrigo Edition

Naxos has embarked on the most comprehensive survey of Rodrigo's music available today and is now up to Volume 8. These Naxos recordings are all good, to varying degrees, though the most popular works are usually available in superior performances. However, for the serious Rodrigo collector, the series represents value for money, and the sound is usually full and vivid, although occasionally the orchestral playing proves not quite as fine as it might be, even at budget price.

Complete Orchestral Works, Vol. 1: *Soleriana* (ballet, arr. from Soler's keyboard music); *5 Piezas infantiles; Zarabanda lejana y Vallancico.*

(BB) **(*) Naxos 8.555844. Asturias SO, Valdés.

Rodrigo's delightfully imagined eighteenth-century picture of Spain is the essence of *Soleriana*, which is based on the keyboard works of Antonio Soler and consists of eight dances, lasting some 40 minutes in all. The *Pastoral* has a lovely melancholy beauty, though most of the movements are relatively lively and portray a picturesque, rococo image of the local scene in music, which displays both charm and piquancy. The *Zarabanda lejana* ('Distant Sarabande') is a haunting work, its two movements displaying some lovely string-writing, and the highly engaging *Cinco piezas infantiles* are characteristically brightly coloured. The performances are good; the massed strings sound a bit thin above the stave, but the overall sound-picture is very acceptable.

Complete Orchestral Works, Vol. 2: (i) *Concierto Andaluz for 4 Guitars and Orchestra;* **(ii)** *Concierto de Aranjuez; Fantasía para un gentilhombre.*

(BB) **(*) Naxos 8.555841. Asturias SO, Valdés, with (i) EntreQuatre Guitar Qt; (ii) Gallén.

The popular *Concierto de Aranjuez* and *Fantasía para un gentilhombre* are given very decent performances, but they lack the last ounce of polish and, in terms of recording and performance, cannot match the very best versions, such as Bonell–Dutoit on Decca. The *Concerto Andaluz*, with its *Tempo di boléro* opening movement and use of Andalusian folk tunes, makes an enjoyable companion-piece.

Complete Orchestral Works, Vol. 3: (i) *Concerto in modo galante* (for cello & orchestra); *Concierto como un divertimento* (for cello & orchestra); **(ii)** *Concierto de estío* (for violin & orchestra); *Cançoneta* (for violin & string orchestra).

(BB) *** Naxos 8.555840. Castile and León SO, Darman, with (i) Polo; (ii) Ovrutsky.

Volume 3 plunges into rarer Rodrigo: in the jolly *Concerto in modo galante*, written in 1949 for cellist Cassadó, Rodrigo's easy-going manner has an eighteenth-century Spanish spirit. The *Concierto como un divertimento*, written in 1981, is another agreeable cello concerto, peppered with all sorts of Spanishry and brightly orchestrated; the slow movement features the cello playing against flute, clarinet and celesta, creating a very pleasing effect. Rodgrio looked to Vivaldi (in structural form, at least) in his

Concierto de estío for violin and orchestra: the two lively outer movements are separated by an especially attractive central Siciliana *adagio*. The *Cançoneta for Violin and String Orchestra* is short and pleasurable.

Complete Orchestral Works, Vol. 4: (i) *Concierto para piano y orquesta* (rev. Achúcarro). *Homenaje a la tempranica; Juglares; Música para un jardín; Preludio para un poema a la Alhambra.*

(BB) **(*) Naxos 8.557101. Castile and León SO, Darman, (i) with Ferrandiz.

Starting dramatically, the *Concierto para piano y orquesta* soon enters familiar Rodrigo territory, with some attractive episodes, but not really having enough inspired music to sustain its 30 minutes. The *Música para un jardín*, written in 1935, depicts the growth of a garden throughout the year. It's a slight work, with one or two nice touches, but hardly another *Nights in the Gardens of Spain*. More successful and more deeply reminiscent of Falla is the *Preludio para un poema a la Alhambra*, a mini tone-poem: 'At twilight, the guitar sighs, and beyond, almost within the Alhambra, rings out the rhythms which drive the dance.' It was first performed in 1930. Similarly, the *Homenaje a la tempranica* and *Juglares* find the composer at his best in short, undemanding movements. Lively performances and good sound.

Complete Orchestral Works, Vol. 5: *Concierto Madrigal; Concierto para una fiesta.*

(BB) **(*) Naxos 8.555842. Gallén, Clerch, Asturias SO, Valdés.

The *Concierto Madrigal*, a suite of movements with the common link of the Renaissance madrigal *O felici ocche*, is one of the composer's finest compositions, with a real piquancy. It has been recorded several times of course, and this performance is a good, warmly relaxed one, though other versions, such as the Yepes on DG, are livelier, with more character and flair. The *Concierto para una fiesta* has a slow movement not unlike that of the *Concierto de Aranjuez*, if not so inspired. The outer movements are predictably tuneful and undemanding. The orchestral playing and the recordings are both up to standard.

Complete Orchestral Music Vol. 6: *A la busca del más allá; Dos danzas españolas; Palillos y panderetas; Per la flor del lliri blau; Tres viejos aires de danza.*

(BB) ** Naxos 555962. Castile and León SO, Darman.

Plenty of light, undemanding Spanishry here, not all of it showing the composer at his best, some of the movements here being a bit noisy and empty (the opening of *Palillos y panderetas*, for example), and showing melodic weakness. The pair of *Spanish Dances* are pleasing enough, and so too are the three *Traditional Dance Airs* (*Tres viejos aires de danza*).

For the Flower of the Blue Lily (*Per la flor lliri blau*) is a colourful tone-poem dating from 1936 and is admirably inventive. *A la busca del más allá* ('In Search of What Lies Beyond') was written in 1976 in response to a commission from the Houston Symphony Orchestra, and dedicated to NASA. It is undoubtedly one of the composer's most modern-sounding works, with the orchestra's fullest resources used to good effect, though there is no great substance in the work. The performances are enthusiastic, but the violin sound is somewhat under-nourished when exposed, with signs of under-rehearsal in a few sloppy entries. Otherwise, good sound.

Complete Orchestral Music, Vol. 7: *Cántico de San Francisco de Asis; Himnos de los neófitos de Qumrán; Música para un códice salmantino; Retable de Navidad.*

(BB) ** Naxos 8.557223. Lojendio, Prieto, Marchante, Allende, Rubiera, Comunidad Ch. & O, Encinar.

Volume Seven concentrates on Rodrigo's works for chorus and orchestra. *Retablo de Navidad* (*Christmas Carols and Songs*) (1952) are really simple folksongs dressed up in orchestral colours, but with more restraint than one expects from this composer. *Himnos de los neófitos de Qumrán* (*Hymns of the Neophytes of Qumran*), for three sopranos, male chorus and chamber orchestra, using texts from the Dead Sea scrolls, was written in 1975. Here the composer reduces the orchestral forces to a minimum, and it is hard to guess that this was written by Rodrigo – it has a far more eerie sound-world than usual. A more familiar style returns for *Música para un códice salmantino*, a commission by Salamanca University in 1953, though its 11 minutes (for bass soloists and mixed chorus) are not especially gripping, and the chorus is not especially refined. The *Cántico de San Francisco de Asis* ('Canticle of St Francis of Assisi') was written in 1982 to mark the 800th anniversary of the birth of the saint. As ever with this composer, it has some good episodes, though it only just holds the listener's interest through its (almost) 19 minutes. Again the recording is good but, like the orchestral playing, not exceptional, and the chorus is a bit approximate at times. Texts and translations are helpfully included.

Complete Orchestral Music, Vol. 8: (i) *Concierto pastoral* (for flute & orchestra); *Fantasía para un gentilhombre* (arr. Galway for flute & orchestra). *Dos miniaturas andaluzas; Adagio para instrumentos de viento.*

(BB) ** Naxos 8.557801. Asturias SO, Valdés, (i) with G'froerer.

Top-notch light music in the form of Rodrigo's *Fantasía para un gentilhombre*, but here presented in Sir James Galway's arrangement for flute and orchestra. It is an enjoyable performance, even if it doesn't quite gel in the way the best performances do: occa-

sionally the soloist's playing seems a bit too literal, not helped by the closely miked flute, robbing the music of some of its dynamic range. The *Concierto pastoral* is another of the composer's best works, undemanding but inventive, and the *Dos miniaturas andaluzas* make an attractive five-minute bonus. The *Adagio para instrumentos de viento* ('Adagio for Wind Instruments') features unexpectedly loud and lively music for an adagio!

(i) *Concierto Andaluz;* (ii; iii) *Concierto de Aranjuez;* (ii–iv) *Concierto madrigal;* (v) *Concierto pastoral;* (vi) *Concierto serenata;* (ii; vii) *Fantasía para un gentilhombre;* (ii) *Entre olivaras.*

(B) ** DG Panorama (ADD/DDD) 469 190-2 (2). (i) Los Romeros, San Antonia SO, Alessandro; (ii) Yepes; (iii) Philh. O, Navarro; (iv) with Monden; (v) Gallois, Philh. O, Marin; (vi) Zabaleta, Berlin RSO, Märzendorfer; (vii) ECO, Navarro.

The duet *Concierto madrigal*, with Yepes and Monden, is most enjoyable, with each of the twelve miniatures which make up the work springing readily to life. Yet Yepes's account of the *Concierto de Aranjuez* – the most famous piece here – lacks sparkle in the outer movements, and the DG sound is rather lacklustre. Yepes's *Fantasia para un gentilhombre* has more character and refinement, and the *Concierto Andaluz* for four guitars, recorded much earlier, is immediately more vivid and open, if a bit astringent, the performance more spontaneous. The *Concierto pastoral* is brilliantly played and recorded (digitally), but the highlight of the set is the delightful *Concierto serenata*, given an ideal performance and recording.

ROMAN, Johan Helmich
(1694–1758)

(i) *Violin Concertos in D min.; E flat; F min. Sinfonias in A; D & F.*

*** BIS CD 284. (i) Sparf; Orpheus Chamber Ens.

Of the five *Violin Concertos*, the three recorded here are certainly attractive pieces, particularly in such persuasive hands as those of Nils-Erik Sparf and the Orpheus Chamber Ensemble, drawn from the Stockholm Philharmonic. None of the *Sinfonias* have appeared on disc before. Very stylish and accomplished performances, which are scholarly in approach.

Drottningholm Music; Little Drottningholm Music.

(BB) *** Naxos 8.553733. Uppsala CO, Halstead.

Little Drottningholm Music; Sjukmans Music; (i) *Piante amiche.*

*** Musica Sveciae MSCD 417. (i) Nilsson; Stockholm Nat. Museum CO, Génetay.

In 1744 Johan Helmich Roman wrote 24 pieces celebrating the marriage of the future King of Sweden to a daughter of Frederick the Great of Prussia. From first to last they are full of delightful invention, starting with a swaggering Allegro (which, like other movements, owes something to the example of Handel's *Water Music*), and ending with a bouncy *vivace* Jig. Halstead also includes eight extra pieces, written to be used in reserve at the wedding, under the title *Little Drottningholm Music*. Unlike the recording on Musica Sveciae, Halstead's Naxos version – just as exhilarating, often at brisker speeds – uses period instruments to bring out the great variety of instrumental colour. Fresh, lively performances and excellent sound.

Génetay offers all 17 dances of the *Little Drottningholm Music* plus the somewhat earlier *Sjukmansmusiquen*, which has no less appeal. The performances by the Stockholm National Museum Orchestra convey real pleasure in the music-making. The disc includes a short cantata probably (but not certainly) by Roman, *Piante amiche*, which is attractive whatever its authenticity, and nicely sung too by Pia-Maria Nilsson. The recorded sound is well balanced and truthful.

6 Assaggi (solo violin).
*** Nytorp 9902. Ringborg.

As a young violinist in the Swedish Royal Orchestra, Roman was sent to study in England, where he played briefly in Handel's opera orchestra at the King's Theatre. He possessed much individuality and resource, even though here he is much indebted to Geminiani, Tartini and, above all, Handel. Tobias Ringborg is the first to record all six of the *Assaggi* ('essays' or 'attempts') for solo violin, which leave no doubt as to his familiarity with and mastery of contemporary technique, multiple stopping, etc. Technical matters apart, he reveals the extent of his inventive resource and imagination. He plays with great authority, and we doubt that his compelling accounts of these suites will be surpassed easily. They are excellently recorded.

(i) Assaggi for Violin in A, in C min. & in G min., BeRI 301, 310 & 320; (i; ii) Violin & Harpsichord Sonata No. 12 in D, BeRI 212; (ii) Harpsichord Sonata No. 9 in D min., BeRI 233.
*** Cap. (ADD) 21344. (i) Schröder; (ii) Sönnleitner.

The *Assaggi* ('essays') recorded here often take one by surprise, particularly when played with such imagination as they are by Jaap Schröder. The *Harpsichord Sonata* is also more inward-looking than many others of Roman's pieces, and the only work that one could possibly describe as fairly predictable is the opening *Sonata for Violin and Continuo*. Excellent performances and recording, as well as exemplary presentation.

ROMBERG, Andreas (1767–1821)

String Quartets, Op. 1/1–3.
**(*) MDG 307 0963-2. Leipzig Qt.

String Quartets, Op. 2/2; Op. 16/2; Op. 30/2.
*** MDG 307 1026-2. Leipzig Qt.

Romberg was a celebrated violinist, admired by both Haydn and Beethoven. His three Op. 1 *Quartets* date from between 1794 and 1796 and are very much after the style of Haydn. Although they leave no doubt as to his expertise, next to the Viennese masters this is small talk – amiable and pleasing, but unmemorable. The Leipzig Quartet is such a superb ensemble and so thoroughly musical that the disc gives pleasure nonetheless.

The Op. 2 *Quartets* come from 1797–9 and show an intimate knowledge of, and admiration for, Haydn's quartets, and indeed are dedicated to 'l'homme de génie à l'immortel Haydn'. The Op. 16 *Quartets* come from 1804–6 and the Op. 30 set from 1806–10. After Romberg's death, his quartets fell into oblivion, for they do not blaze a trail as those of Haydn and Beethoven did. But they are none the less urbane, inventive and civilized, and well worth getting to know, particularly in these unforced and musical performances. Exemplary recording.

ROMBERG, Sigmund (1887–1951)

The Student Prince (musical play/operetta; complete).
*** TER CDTER 1172 (2). Bailey, Hill-Smith, Montague, Rendall, Ambrosian Ch., Philh. O, Edwards.

The Student Prince (orchestrated by Emil Gerstenberger) is Romberg's most famous score and was first performed in New York in 1924. The story of a young prince who falls in love with a barmaid but is forced to give her up for the sake of duty gives it a bittersweet quality, while Romberg's music all but redeems its sentimentality. The melodic invention is very strong indeed, with colourful orchestrations adding to the impact, and this (1990) recording presents the music complete for the first time on CD. John Owen Edwards directs an enthusiastic yet polished performance, and with a fair sprinkling of star performers, notably Marilyn Hill-Smith as the heroine Kathy – completely at home in this repertoire – and David Rendall as her lover, the result is most enjoyable. There are excellent contributions, too, from Norman Bailey and Diana Montague, and the heady if somewhat dated atmosphere of the operetta-musical play style of the 1920s is vividly conveyed.

ROPARTZ, Joseph Guy (1864–1955)

(i) *Le Miracle de Saint-Nicolas.* (ii) *Psalm 136;*
Dimanche; Nocturne; Les Vêpres sonnent.
(BB) *** Naxos 8. 555656. (i) Solistes de la Maîtrise de
R. France, Lebrun (organ); (ii) Papis, Henry, Le
Texier, Ile de France Vittoria Regional Ch., O
Symphonique et Lyrique de Nancy, Piquemal.

Ropartz has been rather overshadowed by Magnard,
and while neither is in the front rank of French
masters, both are rewarding. The longest piece on the
disc is *Le Miracle de Saint-Nicolas* of 1905 for soloists,
children's voices (here the excellent Solistes de la
Maîtrise de Radio-France), organ, piano and orchestra. The *Psalm 136* dates from 1897 and the *Nocturne*
and *Les Vêpres sonnent* from 1926–7. They are dignified and rather beautiful pieces with more than a
touch of d'Indy and Fauré to commend them, and in
the case of *Les Vêpres sonnent* echo the *Sirènes* of
Debussy's *Nocturnes*. This recording from the mid-
1990s first appeared on Marco Polo but its competitive price renders it much more attractive. The
performances are eminently serviceable, though the
Choeur Régional Vittoria d'Ile de France is at times a
little vulnerable in terms of focus and blend. The
repertoire will be new to most readers and will
delight many who do not realize how touching and
appealing this music is.

ROREM, Ned (born 1923)

Songs: *Alleluia; Clouds; Do I love you more than a*
day?; Early in the morning; Little elegy; Far far
away; Ferry me across the water; For Poulenc; For
Susan; I am rose; I will always love you; I strolled
across an open field; A journey; Jeannie with the
light brown hair; Look down fair moon; The Lordly
Hudson; Love; Now sleeps the crimson petal; Ode; O
do not love too long; O you, whom I often and
silently come; Orchids; Santa Fé, Op. 101/Nos. 2, 4, 8
& 12; The serpent; The tulip tree; Sometimes with
one I love; Stopping by woods on a snowy evening;
To a young girl; That shadow, my likeness.
*** Erato 8573 80222-2. Graham, Martineau.

Ned Rorem spent many of his formative years in
Paris during the 1950s, when he came to know
Poulenc and Auric, but he never lost the American
flavour that makes his style so distinctive. This
recital, encompassing settings of English, American
and French verse, gives a good idea of his melodic
resource and feeling for words. His songs, such as
the *Santa Fé* series and the setting of Tennyson's
Now sleeps the crimson petal, bear witness to a rich
imagination and a marvellous feel for both the
voice and the piano. Susan Graham does them all
proud, and Malcolm Martineau gives impeccable
support.

ROSENBERG, Hilding (1892–1985)

PIANO MUSIC

Improvisationer; Plastiska Scener; Små
föredragsstudier; Sonatas Nos. 1 & 3.
** Daphne 1001. Widlund.

Sonatas Nos. 2 & 4; Sonatina; Suite; Tema con
variazioni.
** Daphne 1003. Widlund.

The musical quality of Rosenberg's piano music is
variable: the cosmopolitan influences are obvious
and Rosenberg is at his best in the smaller-scale
miniatures such as the *Små föredragsstudier* ('Small
Performing Studies'). He obviously knew his Ravel
and Honegger, and in the *Largamente* from the *Plas-*
tiska Scener there are hints of Schoenberg. The *Third*
Sonata in particular is arid and its companions are
not uniformly rewarding. But the smaller pieces are
well worth having and, like the sonatas, are new to
the catalogue. Mats Widlund is a dedicated advocate
and the recordings are very natural.

ROSETTI, Antonio (c. 1750–92)

Flute Concertos in C, RWV C16; F, RWV C21; G,
RWV C22; G, RWV C25.
*** Orfeo C095 031A. Meier, Prague CO.

These flute concertos, agreeably elegant and melodic,
each lasting 18 or 19 minutes, with lively outer movements flanking slow movements of pastoral charm,
receive their première recording here. The performances (on modern instruments) are as unselfconscious as the music itself and give unfailing pleasure.

ROSLAVETS, Nikolai (1881–1944)

Cello Sonatas Nos. 1 & 2; Dance of the White Girls;
Meditation; 5 Preludes for Piano.
*** Chan. 9881. Ivashkin, Lazareva.

Roslavets was one of the leading avant-garde figures
in the 1920s Soviet Union and the first to experiment
with atonality. He soon fell foul of official orthodoxy,
and, while his work was known in specialist quarters,
he never gained wide recognition in either the Soviet
Union or the West. In fact he is known for his
reputation rather than the music itself.

The *Dance of the White Girls* is an early piece with
a strong whiff of impressionism, while the two one-
movement *Cello Sonatas* and the *Meditation* come
from the early 1920s. Alexander Ivashkin speaks of
the *Second* as a mixture of late Scriabin and early
Messiaen, and the *Five Preludes for Piano* are certainly indebted to Scriabin's Op. 74. Both the cellist
and pianist make out a strong case for this music,
and they are well served by the recording.

Piano Trios Nos. 2–4.
** Teldec 8573 82017-2. Fontenay Trio.

The Fontenay give a strong account of the three *Trios* but, interesting though this music is, it conveys little real feeling of mastery.

ROSSI, Luigi (1597–1653)

Orfeo (opera; complete).
(M) **(*) HM HMX 2901358.60 (3). Mellon, Zanetti, Piau, Favat, Fouchécourt, Salzmann, Corréas, Deletré, Les Arts Florissants, Christie.

Luigi Rossi's *Orfeo* has a much more complex classical story than the Monteverdi, yet in its artificial way it is less effectively dramatic. Even so, it offers such incidental delights as a slanging match between Venus (enemy of Orfeo, when he represents marital fidelity) and Juno. That hint of a classical send-up adds sparkle, contrasting with the tragic emotions conveyed both in Orfeo's deeply expressive solos and in magnificent Monteverdi-like choruses. William Christie draws characteristically lively and alert playing from Les Arts Florissants, but his cast is not as consistent as those he usually has in his Harmonia Mundi recordings. Too many of the singers sound fluttery or shallow, and even Agnès Mellon as Orfeo is less even and sweet of tone than usual. Nevertheless this remains a most welcome recording of an important rarity, and at bargain price, with full libretto and translation included, it is well worth considering.

ROSSINI, Gioachino (1792–1868)

La Boutique fantasque (ballet; complete; arr. Respighi).
*** Chan. 10081. BBC PO, Noseda – RESPIGHI: *La Pentola magica*, etc. ***

Noseda's sparkling account of the famous Rossini/Respighi ballet is complete and is splendidly recorded. It is discussed under Respighi above, where it is combined with other spectacular Respighi arrangements. However, Ansermet's vintage mono account of *La Boutique* with the LSO (which is not quite complete) remains very special and is available on SOMMCD 027 – see our main *Guide*.

String Sonatas Nos. 1–3; (i) *Andante & Theme with Variations in E flat for Clarinet & Orchestra;* (ii) *Une Larme for Double Bass.*
(BB) ** Naxos 8.554418. Hungarian Virtuosi, Benedek; with (i) Szepesi; (ii) Buza.

String Sonatas Nos. 4–6; (i) *Variations in C for Violin & Small Orchestra.*
(BB) ** Naxos 8.554419. Hungarian Virtuosi, Benedek; with (i) Szenthelyi.

The Naxos performances are very well played, warm and elegant enough, but surprisingly, with a Hungar-

ian virtuoso group, have neither fizz not wit. Of the extra items the *Variations* for clarinet has an attractively jocular finale. There are no complaints about the recording, but first choice rests with Marriner (⊖→ Double Decca 443 838-2).

String Sonatas Nos. 1–5 (arr. for wind quartet by Berr).
(BB) ** Naxos 8.554098. Michael Thompson Wind Qt.

The considerable charm of Rossini's delightful early *String Sonatas* is the more remarkable when one realizes that they are the work of a 12-year-old: their invention is consistently on the highest level and their bubbling humour is infectious. This wind arrangement adds another dimension to these works and is highly enjoyable, with the quartet of soloists (horn, flute, clarinet and flute) providing felicitous interplay, and it shows considerable resource of colour with only four instruments. The performances here are spontaneous, stylish and lively, with plenty of sparkle. Alas, the very forward recording is set in a too dry and un-atmospheric acoustic, and the effect is rather unyielding after a while, with a lack of bloom and an inadequate ambience.

VOCAL MUSIC

Missa di Milano; Petite messe solennelle (1867 orchestral version).
(B) *** Ph. Duo 475 230-2 (2). Mentzer, Giménez, Bostridge, Alaimo, Ch. & ASMF, Marriner.

This reissued 1995 recording of Rossini's *Missa di Milano* is a real find. It is not really a complete Mass but the assembly of a *Kyrie, Gloria* and *Credo* probably composed independently before 1808. They are three separate manuscripts held in the Milan Conservatory (hence the title) but they fit together convincingly. They are well sprinkled with the musical fingerprints of the youthful, zestful Rossini, notably the crescendo in the *Gloria in excelsis Deo*, the nimble *Laudamus*, the lighthearted *Domine Deus*, and the *Qui tollis* with violin obbligato, very well sung here by Susanne Mentzer, who is even more impressive than the full-toned operatic soprano, Susann Mentzner. The closing repeated *Amen* has an irresistible exuberance. The performance could hardly be better, full of jubilation, with the chorus singing lustily and the excellent soloists, including an early recorded contribution by Ian Bostridge, whose vocal personality comes over more robustly than we expect now.

Comparable praise applies to Marriner's account of the orchestral version of the *Petite messe solennelle*, which may not be as winningly coloured as the original score for two pianos and harmonium, but is very enjoyable in its own right. Marriner strikes a happy balance between the swingingly exuberant *Cum sancto spiritus*, and the more serious mood of the closing *Agnus Dei* – beautifully sung here. Excellent recording makes this a reissue to cherish.

OVERTURES

Overtures: *Armida; Il barbiere di Siviglia; Bianca e Faliero; La cambiale di matrimonio; La Cenerentola; Demetrio e Poblibio; Edipo a Colono; Edoardo e Cristina;* (i) *Ermione; La gazza ladra; L'inganno felice; L'Italiana in Algeri; Maometto II; Otello.* (ii) *Ricciardo e Zoraide; La scala di seta; Semiramide; Le siège de Corinthe; Il Signor Bruschino; Tancredi; Il Turco in Italia; Torvaldo e Dorliska; Il viaggio a Reims; William Tell. Sinfonia al Conventello; Sinfonia di Bologna.*

(M) *** Ph. Trio (ADD) 473 967-2 (3). ASMF, Marriner; (i) with Amb. S.

Marriner's reissued Trio spans all Rossini's overtures, but one must remember that the early Neapolitan operas, with the exception of *Ricciardo e Zoraide* and *Ermione,* make do with a simple Prelude, leading into the opening chorus. *Ricciardo e Zoraide,* however, is an extended piece (12 minutes 25 seconds), with the choral entry indicating that the introduction is at an end. *Maometto II* is on a comparable scale, while the more succinct *Armida* is an example of Rossini's picturesque evocation, almost like a miniature tone-poem. Twenty-four overtures plus two sinfonias make a delightful package in such sparkling performances, which eruditely use original orchestrations. Full, bright and atmospheric recording, spaciously reverberant, admirably transferred to CD, with no artificial brilliance.

Overtures: *Il barbiere di Siviglia; La Cenerentola; La gazza ladra; L'Italiana in Algeri; La scala di seta; Semiramide; Il Signor Bruschino; Tancredi; William Tell.*

(M) *** EMI (ADD) 5 62802-2. Philh. O, Giulini.

Giulini's performances, recorded between 1959 and 1964, derive from two LP sources and now appear on a single CD (77 minutes 33 seconds) for the first time. They offer characteristically refined Philharmonia playing, with the conductor's careful attention to detail balanced by a strong sense of drama. Although they are not the most genial accounts on record, they are strong in personality. The performance of *William Tell* is outstanding for the beauty of the cello playing at the opening and the affectionate shaping of the pastoral section, while the introduction to *La scala di seta* is very fast indeed, and the following allegro is also swiftly paced, but the Philharmonia playing is always immaculate. Bright, vivid sound, with the date of the earlier recordings showing in the rather thin upper-string *fortissimos.* But the ear soon adjusts when the performances are so characterful.

Overtures: *Il barbiere di Siviglia; La Cenerentola; L'Italiana in Algeri; La scala di seta; Il Signor Bruschino; Tancredi; William Tell;* (i) *Il barbiere di Siviglia:* excerpts.

(B) (*) EMI Encore 5 74752-2. Stuttgart RSO, Gelmetti; (i) with Hampson, Mentzer.

Gelmetti races off with the opening string flourish of *La scala di seta,* the effect unpleasingly gabbled. The rest of the performance is fast and hard pressed, with little of the wit allowed to bubble to the surface (and with some disagreeable stresses on the violin phrase around 3 minutes 40 seconds). A similar pattern emerges with the rest of the programme, with generally charmless playing. *Il barbiere* sounds really quite brutal, and the elegant string opening of *Il Signor Bruschino* is also rushed. The famous *galop* in *William Tell* is curiously four-square and has nothing of the exhilarating verve which, for example, Marriner (Philips) and Abbado (DG) generate. The recording is vivid, but this disc is a non-starter – even with three celebrated *Il barbiere* excerpts thrown in.

OPERA

Il barbiere di Siviglia (complete).

(BB) * EMI (ADD) 585523-2 (2). Sills, Gedda, Milnes, Capecchi, Raimondi, Barbieri, John Aldis Ch., LSO, Levine.

Levine conducts vigorously in his EMI version, but the singing of neither Beverly Sills nor Nicolai Gedda can be recommended with any enthusiasm, the one unpleasant in tone, for all its brilliance, the other seriously strained – a reminder, no more, of what Gedda's voice once was. Sherrill Milnes makes a strong, forthright Figaro, in every way the centre of attention here, and Ruggero Raimondi is a sonorous Basilio. Even though it is now offered at bargain price, in good mid-1970s sound, this set can hardly be recommended with such strong competition around. A synopsis is included. First choice rests with Patanè's Decca set with Cecilia Bartoli as Rosina (425 520-2).

La Cenerentola (complete).

(M) *(*) Sony (ADD) SM2K 90419 (2). Valentini Terrani, Araiza, Trimarchi, Dara, Ravaglia, West German R. Ch., Capella Coloniensis, Ferro.

On Sony, Gabriele Ferro, one of the ablest of Rossini scholars, who earlier recorded *L'Italiana in Algeri* impressively, conducts an easy-going, but at times pedestrian account of *La Cenerentola,* well played and well sung, but lacking some of the fizz essential in Rossini. Even the heroine's final brilliant aria hangs fire, and that despite warm, positive singing from Lucia Valentini Terrani, whose stylish contribution is spoilt only by a high quota of intrusive aitches. The rest of the cast is strong and, apart from the backward placing of the orchestra, the digital transfer is full and realistic. However, as in the other operas in this series of Sony reissues, the documentation is unacceptably sparse, with neither libretto nor cued synopsis. Bartoli's DVD dominates recordings of *La Cenerentola* (Decca 071 444-9).

Guglielmo Tell (*William Tell;* abridged; in Italian).

(M) (*) Warner Fonit mono 8573 87489-2 (3). Taddei,

Carteri, Sciutti, Filippeschi, Tozzi, Corena, RAI Ch. & O of Turin, Rossi.

Where most of the 1950s Cetra recordings in collaboration with Italian Radio were made in the studio like other commercial issues, this one of Rossini's last and longest opera, recorded in a single day, seems to have been a one-off studio performance, with all the flaws that entailed. Beginning with an excruciating cello solo, the celebrated Overture brings the most rough-and-ready playing, even if the out-of-tuneness may in part be a result of 'wow' on the tape. While the whole performance has energy, it remains too rough for comfort, though several individual performances stand out, notably the magnificent singing of Giuseppe Taddei in the title-role, rich and firm, heroic in every way. The young Graziella Sciutti in the *travesti* role of Tell's son, Jemmy, is also impressive, powerful in the scene in Act III, following the celebrated archery test. Giorgio Tozzi and Fernando Corena are also singers who stand out, and Mario Filippeschi, in the principal tenor role of Arnoldo, sings incisively with cleanly focused tone, even if under strain at times. Sadly, Rosanna Carteri, one of the principal Italian sopranos of the day, sounds too unsteady for comfort. The text is the much-cut version in general use in Italy. The voices come off best in the limited recording. As with others in this series, a libretto is provided but not a translation.

L'inganno felice (complete).

*(*) Claves CD 50-9211. De Carolis, Felle, Zennaro, Previato, Serraiocco, ECO, Viotti.

L'inganno felice is stylishly and energetically conducted by Viotti with sprung rhythms and polished playing, but with a flawed cast. As the heroine, Amelia Felle is agile but too often raw-toned, even if on occasion she can crown an ensemble with well-phrased cantilena. As the hero, Bertrando, Iorio Zennaro has an agreeable natural timbre, but his tenor is not steady enough and strains easily. The *buffo*, Fabio Previato, is the soloist who comes closest to meeting the full challenge. The recorded sound has a pleasant bloom on it, but the orchestra is too recessed, and though the recitatives are briskly done, with crisp exchanges between the characters, the degree of reverberation is a serious drawback.

Maometto II (complete).

(B) ★★★ Ph. Trio 475 50921-2 (3). Anderson, Zimmermann, Palacio, Ramey, Dale, Amb. Op. Ch., Philh. O, Scimone.

Claudio Scimone's account of *Maometto II* has Samuel Ramey magnificently focusing the whole story in his portrait of the Muslim invader in love with the heroine. The other singing is less sharply characterized but is generally stylish, with Margarita Zimmermann in the *travesti* role of Calbo and June Anderson singing sweetly as Anna. Laurence Dale is excellent in two smaller roles, while Ernesto Palacio mars some fresh-toned singing with his intrusive

aitches. Excellently recorded, this is well worth exploring at bargain price, even though only a synopsis is included.

Otello (complete).

(B) ★★★ Ph. Duo (ADD) 475 448-2 (2). Carreras, Von Stade, Condò, Pastine, Fisichella, Ramey, Amb. S., Philh. O, López-Cobos.

The libretto of Rossini's *Otello* bears remarkably little resemblance to Shakespeare – virtually none at all until the last act. It is some tribute to this performance, superbly recorded and brightly and stylishly conducted by López-Cobos, that the line-up of tenors is turned into an asset, with three nicely contrasted soloists. Carreras here is at his finest – most affecting in his recitative before the murder, while Fisichella copes splendidly with the high tessitura of Rodrigo's role, and Pastine has a distinct timbre to identify him as the villain. Frederica von Stade pours forth a glorious flow of beautiful tone, well matched by Nucci Condò as Emilia. Samuel Ramey is excellent too in the bass role of Elmiro. It makes an undoubted bargain at its new price; its cost, alas, precluding the possibility of including text and translation.

The Thieving Magpie (complete; in English).

(M) ★★★ Chan. 3097 (2). Cullagh, Banks, Bickley, White, Smythe, Purves, Geoffrey Mitchell Ch., Philh. O, Parry.

This is one of the very finest of the many Opera in English recordings promoted by the Peter Moores Foundation. David Parry draws sparkling performances from his excellent cast of singers, as well as from the Philharmonia Orchestra. Using a lively translation by Jeremy Sams, the performance makes light of the improbablities of the plot, which has its unpleasantly dark element when the heroine is threatened with death after being accused of stealing one of her mistress's silver spoons. The culprit is of course the magpie of the opera's title, and all turns out well in the end. The set gains enormously from having been made in the wake of a stage production at Garsington Manor in 2002, also conducted by Parry. As he points out in a note, the full score is unmanageably long, which has entailed some cutting of the piano recitative (almost certainly not by Rossini) and of some inessential numbers, no doubt originally included to placate certain solo singers. As Parry claims, the arias that are dramatically less essential tend to be those least interesting musically. As it is, the piece moves swiftly along, with the Irish soprano Majella Cullagh as the heroine, Ninetta, and Christopher Purves as the Mayor, her employer, outstanding both musically and dramatically with cleanly focused singing. It helps no doubt that they both took part in the Garsington production, but the others are first rate too, with the tenor Barry Banks as the hero, Giannetto, Susan Bickley as the Mayor's wife Lucia, Russell Smythe as Ninetta's father and John Graham-Hall as the pedlar, Isacco. Full, well-balanced sound, recorded in the Blackheath Concert Halls.

ROTT, Hans (1858–84)

Symphony in E.

(BB) *** Hyp. Helios CDH 55140. Cincinnati Philh. O, Samuel.

It is astonishing to encounter in Hans Rott's *Symphony* ideas that took root in Mahler's *First* and *Fifth* symphonies. Structurally the work is original, each movement getting progressively longer, the finale occupying nearly 25 minutes. But the music is full of good ideas and, anticipations of Mahler apart, has a profile of its own. The Cincinnati Philharmonia are a student orchestra who produce extraordinarily good results under Gerhard Samuel. The recording is good. Readers should investigate this bargain reissue.

ROUSSEL, Albert (1869–1937)

***Bacchus et Ariane, Op. 43: Suites 1 & 2;* (i) *Aeneas* (ballet; complete).**

⊶ ❁ (M) *** Erato (ADD) 2564 60576-2. O Nat. de l'ORTF, Martinon, (i) with Ch.

Praise be! Erato have at last released Martinon's classic (1969) version of *Bacchus et Ariane* on CD. It is a thrilling performance and, compared with Dutoit's version on the same label, finds the latter sounding tame by comparison. Martinon's energy and momentum do not smudge Roussel's dense orchestration, and there is both inner life and outer drive here: the quiet passages are held raptly, with both tension and atmosphere. Splendid remastered sound, too, much better than it ever was on LP. The coupling of *Aeneas* (a much rarer work) is ideal. It was composed after *Bacchus* and based on a libretto by the Belgian poet Joseph Weterings, depicting the destiny of the founder of Rome; it is hardly less compelling and is undeniably powerful. It is laid out in Roussel's characteristic rich textures and orchestrated sumptuously, with the chorus playing an important role. There is no lack of vigorous imagination, both rhythmically and harmonically during its 40 minutes, ending with a triumphant hymn 'to his glory and the glory of Rome'. The only reservation is that *Aeneas* has only one cue. But, along with Munch's accounts of the *Third* and *Fourth Symphonies* on Erato, this is a must for anyone remotely interested in this composer.

Le Festin de l'araignée, Op. 17; Symphony No. 2 in B flat, Op. 23.

⊶ (M) *** Erato (ADD) 2564 60577-2. O Nat. de l'ORTF, Martinon.

Martinon fully captures the brooding atmosphere of Roussel's *Second Symphony*, and from the very opening bars the listener's attention is caught and held. This is one of the most gripping accounts available, with the richness of the writing and its inner vitality fully realized, ensuring total conviction. The lighter scoring of the magical *Le Festin de l'araignée* provides the perfect contrast, and the ballet receives a similar, totally idiomatic performance, with all the subtleties and nuances vividly caught. The remastered sound is very good for its date (1969) and this CD should be snapped up quickly: for some reason these outstanding Martinon performances never seem to stay in the catalogue for long.

Suite in F, Op. 33.

(*) Mercury (ADD) **SACD 475 6183. Detroit SO, Paray – CHABRIER: *Bourrée fantasque*, etc. ***

Mercury are bringing out some of their most admired recordings on SACD and, although they are not due to be released until the autumn of this year, we feel sure that listeners will want to be informed of their publication in advance. The new format should go some way to further enhance the already spectacular results afforded by the 'Living Presence' technology.

RUBINSTEIN, Anton (1829–94)

Piano Concertos Nos. 1 in E, Op. 25; 2 in F, Op. 35.

** Marco Polo 8.223456. Banowetz, Czech State PO, A. Walter.

Piano Concertos Nos. 3 in G, Op. 45; 4 in D min., Op. 70.

** Marco Polo 8.223382. Banowetz, Slovak State PO (Košice), Stankovsky.

Piano Concerto No. 5 in E flat, Op. 94; Caprice russe, Op. 102.

**(*) Marco Polo 8.223489. Banowetz, Slovak RSO (Bratislava), Stankovsky.

Rubinstein was the first composer of concertos in Russia and was enormously prolific. His *First Piano Concerto in E major*, dating from 1850, is greatly indebted to Mendelssohn though it is more prolix. The *Third Piano Concerto in G* (1853–4) is more concentrated, and there is a recording of the *Fourth in D minor* (1864) by his pupil, Josef Hofmann; no later pianist has equalled that. By the mid-1860s Rubinstein's perspective had broadened (rather than deepened), and the *Fifth Piano Concerto in E flat* (1874) is an ambitious piece, longer than the *Emperor* and almost as long as the Brahms *D minor*. No doubt its prodigious technical demands have stood in the way of its wider dissemination. It has all the fluent lyricism one expects of Rubinstein, though most of its ideas, attractive enough in themselves, overstay their welcome.

Joseph Banowetz has now recorded all the concertos for Marco Polo and, although the orchestral support and the recording do not rise much above routine, there is nothing ordinary about Banowetz's pianism. The *Fifth*, at least, is worth investigating (for the *Fourth*, one should turn to Cherkassky). The *Caprice russe* was written four years after the concerto, but the fires were obviously blazing less fiercely. All the same, this is an issue of some interest, and the solo playing has conviction.

Symphony No. 1, Op. 40; Ivan the Terrible, Op. 79.
(BB) ★(★) Naxos 8.555476. Slovak State PO (Košice), Stankovsky.

Naxos are presumably going to reissue on their bargain label all six of the Rubinstein symphonies previously available at full price on Marco Polo (They were originally discussed in our 1996 edition.) The *First* – a young man's work – comes from 1850 and is coupled with the tone-poem *Ivan the Terrible* of 1869, which draws its inspiration from the same source as did Rimsky-Korsakov's opera of the same name (also known as *The Maid of Pskov*). Tchaikovsky, incidentally, made the piano score of it. Rubinstein's language is completely and utterly rooted in Mendelssohn, and David Brown's verdict on the *Second Symphony (Ocean)* as 'watery and Mendelssohnian' applies equally here. Music of lesser stature calls for interpreters of quality and flair if it is to have the slightest chance of success, and neither of these performances is much more than routine. However, given the modest outlay involved, readers may be inclined to give these pieces a try.

Symphony No. 3 in A, Op. 56; Eroica Fantasia, Op. 110.
(BB) ★ Naxos 8.555590. Slovak RSO, Stankovsky.

The *Third Symphony* is not endowed with ideas of interest or even with personality, and although it is not entirely without merit it is mostly predictable stuff. The playing by the Bratislava Radio Orchestra is fairly routine and Robert Stankovsky brings few insights to the score. The *Eroica Fantasia*, as its high opus number suggests, is a later and, if anything, less inspired work.

Symphony No. 4 in D min. (Dramatic), Op. 95.
(BB) ★ Naxos 8.555979. Slovak PO, Stankovsky.

The Rubinstein symphonies are perhaps more enticing on a budget label. The *Fourth*, the *Dramatic* of 1874, runs to some 65 minutes and is not a strong work. Its thematic substance is pretty thin and, despite its epic proportions, there is little sense of sweep or consistency of inspiration. The performance is acceptable but no more, as is the recording.

Piano Sonatas Nos. 1 in E min., Op. 12; 2 in C min., Op. 20; 3 in F, Op. 41; 4 in A min., Op. 100.
(B) ★★★ Hyp. Dyad CCD 22007 (2). Howard.

Leslie Howard proves highly persuasive in all four works. The 1981 recordings sound excellent, and this set is more enticing as a Dyad, with two discs offered for the price of one. Returning to these works, one is surprised to find how enjoyable the music is, with some good lyrical ideas, phrased romantically, to balance the arrestingly flamboyant rhetoric which Leslie Howard obviously relishes.

RUSSO, William (born 1928)

3 Pieces for Blues Band & Symphony Orchestra; Street Music, Op. 65.
(M) ★★ DG (ADD) 463 665-2. Siegel-Schwall Band, San Francisco SO, Ozawa – GERSHWIN: *An American in Paris.* ★★

William Russo has been an assiduous advocate of mixing jazz and blues traditions with the symphony orchestra, and *Street Music* has its attractive side. But despite the presence of Corky Siegel on harmonica, it is no more successful at achieving genuine integration than other pieces of its kind, and its half-hour span is far too long for the material it contains. The 1976 recording is excellent, though the close focus for the harmonica makes for some unattractive sound from Mr Siegel. *Three Pieces for Blues Band* represents another vigorous attempt at barrier-leaping and will appeal to those who like such mixtures. To others it is likely to seem both over-sweet and over-aggressive (rather like the 1972 sound, which is both rich and fierce). Still, this is rare repertoire, although a curious choice for DG's 'Originals' label.

SABATA, Victor de (1892–1967)

Gethsemani; Juventus; La notte di Plàton.
★★★ Hyp. CDA 67209. LPO, Ceccato.

Most conductors from Furtwängler to Pletnev compose, though few reach the record catalogues. As you might expect, Victor de Sabata shows himself a master of the orchestra and these scores have the opulence and extravagance of Respighi and Strauss. The three pieces recorded here comprise the bulk of his orchestral output. *Juventus* (1919) was championed by Toscanini and its two companions are also virtuoso orchestral showpieces. *La notte di Plàton* (1923) is an evocation of Plato's last feast and its opening portrayal of night is highly imaginative. So is *Gethsemani* (1925), which makes some use of Gregorian melody. The LPO under Aldo Ceccato respond well to these scores, as will those who take the trouble to investigate this impressively recorded disc.

SÆVERUD, Harald (1897–1992)

(i) Oboe Concerto, Op. 15. Symphony No. 5 (Quasi una fantasia), Op. 16; Entrata regale, Op. 41; Sonata Giubilata, Op. 47.
★★★ BIS CD 1162. (i) Hunt; Stavanger SO, Ruud.

Sæverud used to show his visitors newspaper caricatures of himself as a drayhorse, and this note of self-mockery can be clearly discerned in his music. RL was privileged to visit him from time to time and, apart from showing this caricature, he liked to give his visitors a small cow-bell! In this continuation of the BIS survey of Sæverud's music the *Fifth Symphony* (1941), composed a year after the Nazi invasion, is coupled with the *Oboe Concerto* of 1938 and a couple of later occasional pieces. The *Concerto* was first given in 1939 at Gothenburg, the most enterprising and outward-looking of the Scandinavian music centres, but the composer revised it in 1953, when the two outer movements were shortened. It is an inventive and spirited work, excellently played by Gordon Hunt and the Stavanger orchestra, and this CD supplants the earlier (1983) version with Erik Niord Larsen and the Oslo Philharmonic under Mariss Jansons, once available on Norwegian Philips. The *Fifth Symphony* is perhaps the least satisfying of the wartime trilogy: the powerful, lyrical *Sixth Symphony* (*Sinfonia dolorosa*, 1942) and its successor, *Salmesymfoni* (1944–5), both display a stronger feeling for structure and sense of the Norwegian landscape. Although it caused a great stir at its first performance under the composer's own baton, the *Fifth* is too short-breathed to carry symphonic conviction, even though it is unfailingly vital. This and the two occasional pieces that complete the disc are well served by Ole Kristian Ruud and his Stavanger players.

Just a reminder that there is a rival account by the Bergen orchestra and Dmitri Kitajenko on Simax PSC 3124, a two-CD set which offers symphonies (Nos. 4, 6, 7 and 8) plus the irresistible *Galdreslåtten* and the far from irresistible *Rondo Amoroso*. Three stars for the recorded sound and the performances, but not for the symphony itself.

SAINT-SAËNS, Camille

(1835–1921)

Cello Concerto No. 1 in A min., Op. 33.

(BB) ** Warner Apex (ADD) 2564 60709-2. Navarra, LOP, Munch – LALO: *Cello Concerto.* **

(i) ***Cello Concerto No. 1; Suite, Op. 16;*** (ii) ***Allegro appassionato, Op. 43; Carnival of the Animals: The Swan's Romance No. 1 in F; Cello Sonata No. 1.***

** DG (IMS) 457 599-2. Maisky, (i) Orpheus CO; (ii) Hovora.

Mischa Maisky plays with great virtuosity and brings splendid vitality as well as brilliance to the quicker movements of the *A minor concerto*. But for all his virtuosity and beauty of tone, expressive exaggeration is not alien to his nature and he is prone to emote heavily at the slightest pretext. Of course he makes a glorious sound, and the Orpheus Chamber Orchestra play with splendid attack. One longs for the finesse and understatement of a Fournier.

As in the Lalo coupling, Navarra is too forwardly balanced, sometimes masking the orchestral detail, which is a pity as the playing of the Lamoureux Orchestra is lively and characterful. However, at bargain price, this CD is worth considering as the overall effect is enjoyable.

Piano Concertos Nos. 1 in D, Op. 17; 2 in G min., Op. 22; 3 in E flat, Op. 29; 4 in C min., Op. 44; 5 in F (Egyptian), Op. 103.

(B) * Sony (ADD) SB2K 89977 (2). Entremont, O du Capitole Toulouse, Plasson.

Entremont is a vigorously persuasive interpreter of French music, but here he is let down by the recording. As with other reissues in the 'Essential Classics' series, Sony is coy about the recording date, but '1989' is given on the disc itself and '2002' on the back of the insert listing. However, in reality the recording dates from the late 1970s and did less than justice to the soloist's gentler qualities, with the forward balance reducing the dynamic range. The CD remastering has made matters worse, with orchestral tuttis sounding crude and fierce and no bloom given to the piano, which becomes clattery and aggressive under pressure. Stephen Hough's complete set on Hyperion leads the field (🔑 ❁ CDA 67331/2 – see our main volume).

Piano Concerto No. 2 in G min., Op. 22.

(M) ** Chan. 6621 (2). Margalit, LSO, Thompson (with MENDELSSOHN: *Capriccio brillant* **) – BRAHMS: *Concerto No. 1;* SCHUMANN: *Concerto.* **

Israela Margalit's version of the concerto has no want of abandon, but it lacks the aristocratic distinction that Rubinstein brings to it. The recording is resonant, but the piano is rather forward in the aural picture. The two-CD format does not enhance the attractions of this reissue.

(i) ***Violin Concerto No. 3 in B min., Op. 61; Havanaise, Op. 83; Introduction & Rondo capriccioso, Op. 28;*** (ii) ***Le Déluge: Prelude***

(BB) ** EMI 585699-2. Dumay, Monte Carlo PO; with (i) Yazaki; (ii) Rosenthal. (with FAURE: *Berceuse;* LALO: *Symphonie espagnole: Intermezzo.* **)

The characteristic Monte Carlo acoustic isn't always ideal, and here the soloist is placed a bit too far forward. But these straightforward, idiomatic accounts of works for violin and orchestra (recorded in 1983) with admirable pacing and plenty of life are all enjoyable, even if some other versions of this much-recorded repertoire offer even greater polish. The three short items conducted by Rosenthal don't have quite the same level of tension as the rest of the programme, but it is good that the comparatively rare *Prelude* to *Le Déluge*, with its violin obbligato, is included.

Havanaise, Op. 83; Introduction & Rondo capriccioso, Op. 28.

🔑 (M) *** EMI (ADD) 5 62599-2. Perlman, O de

Paris, Martinon (with MASSENET: *Thaïs: Méditation*) –
CHAUSSON: *Poème*; RAVEL: *Tzigane*. ★★★

Perlman plays these Saint-Saëns warhorses with special panache and virtuosity; his tone and control of colour in the *Havanaise* are ravishing. The digital remastering brings Perlman's gorgeous fiddling right into the room, at the expense of a touch of aggressiveness when the orchestra lets rip, but the concert-hall ambience prevents this from being a problem.

Javotte (ballet; complete); *Parysatis* (ballet;
introduction & 3 scenes).
★★(★) Marco Polo 8.223612. Queensland O, Mogrelia.

It is a pity that Saint-Saëns did not write more ballet music outside his operas – his natural gift for melody and colour suits the medium perfectly. *Javotte* (1896) seems to be his only full-length ballet, and one can find out very little about its history. Nothing is mentioned in the booklet, although a detailed synopsis is provided. The rustic story, in the manner of *La Fille mal gardée*, provided plenty of opportunity for Saint-Saëns to prove that at the end of his career he had lost none of his ability for writing witty and tuneful music, all of it charmingly orchestrated. Curiously, the composer regarded this work as 'the *post scriptum* to my musical career', though in the event it proved nothing like it. The eight-minute *Parysatis* suite, incidental music for the play first performed in 1902, shows the composer in exotic mode, reflecting the imported nature of both the story and the country, Egypt, where the music was mainly written (during 1901). Excellent performances, though the recording is pretty average: the strings lack glow, with Saint-Saëns's colours slightly muted by the sound in general.

(i) *Symphonies Nos. 1 in E flat, Op. 2; 2.* (ii) *Piano
Concerto No. 4;* (i) *La Jeunesse d'Hercule;* (iii) *Le
Rouet d'Omphale.*
(B) ★★ Erato Ultima (ADD/DDD) 3984 24236-2 (2). (i)
VSO, Prêtre; (ii) Duchable, Strasbourg PO, Lombard;
(iii) O Nat. de l'ORTF, Martinon.

This Ultima double is attractive in assembling very serviceable performances of the composer's two lesser-known published symphonies (useful for those who already have No. 3), plus one of the most attractive of the piano concertos, and the seldom-heard *La Jeunesse d'Hercule*. Prêtre does not quite match Martinon's flair in the symphonies, but he gets some refined playing from the VPO in the central movements (the two Scherzi are highlights), and he finds a pleasing energetic lightness for the first-movement fugato and the tarantella-finale of the *Second*. Duchable then opens the *C minor Concerto* pleasingly (what a seductive work it is!) and the solo playing is never thoughtless or slipshod. Yet his bold assertiveness later in the work brings a hint of aggressiveness to music that should above all captivate the listener with its charm. *La Jeunesse d'Hercule* is quite strongly characterized, if a bit

melodramatic; then Martinon's extremely vivid *Le Rouet d'Omphale*, Op. 31, arrives to show us what the earlier performances lacked in natural spontaneity and panache.

Symphony No. 3 in C min., Op. 78.
(★) Testament mono SBT 1240. Roget, Paris
Conservatoire O, Cluytens – FAURE: *Requiem.* (★)

(i) *Symphony No. 3;* (ii) *Danse macabre; Le Déluge:
Prelude, Op. 48; Samson et Dalila: Bacchanale.*
(M) ★★★ DG Entrée (ADD) 474 612-2. (i) Litaize,
Chicago SO; (ii) O de Paris., Barenboim.

Barenboim's inspirational 1976 performance of the *Symphony* glows with warmth and vitality from beginning to end and has now, understandably, been reissued as one of DG's 'Originals'. Among the three attractive bonuses is an exciting account of the *Bacchanale* from *Samson and Dalila*. However, although the remastering has brought an excitingly vivid impact, especially in the finale of the *Symphony*, the effect is not entirely advantagous. While detail is sharper, the massed violins sound thinner and less natural at *fortissimo* level.

André Cluytens recorded Saint-Saëns's *Third Symphony* at the Salle de la Mutualité in 1955 – and, of course, in mono. Cluytens gives a generally well-paced and finely conceived account of it, although the playing of the Paris Conservatoire Orchestra falls short of distinction.

CHAMBER MUSIC

Carnival of the Animals (chamber version).
(M) ★★★ Virgin 5 61782-2. Nash Ens. – BRITTEN:
Young Person's Guide to the Orchestra ★★(★);
PROKOFIEV: *Peter and the Wolf.*

The Nash performance of the *Carnival of the Animals* is first class, but the performance of *Peter and the Wolf* is a non-starter.

SALIERI, Antonio (1750–1825)

Overtures: *L'Angiolina, ossia Il matrimonio per
sussurro; Armida; Axur, re d'Ormus; Cesare in
Farmacusa (Tempesta di mare); Les Danaïdes; Don
Chisciotte alle nozze di Gamace; Eraclito e
Democrito; La grotta di Trofonio; Il moro; Il ricco
d'un giorno; La secchia rapita; Il talismano.*
(★★) Marco Polo 8.223381. Czech-Slovak RSO
(Bratislava), Dittrich.

In his day Salieri was a highly successful opera composer in both Vienna and Paris, and this collection of overtures covers his output from the one-act opera-ballet *Don Chisciotte* of 1770 to *L'Angiolina, ossia Il matrimonio per sussurro* of 1800, of which a complete recording exists. The overtures are often dramatic, *Armida* and *Les Danaïdes* especially so, while *La grotta di Trofonio* begins by depicting the magician's cave where the two male heroes are put under a spell to interchange their characters, much to the annoyance of their prospective brides. *Cesare in Farmacusa* is entirely taken up by the standard opening storm sequence. Elsewhere there are plenty of bustle and vigour, and some agreeable lyrical ideas, but also much that is conventional. The performances are lively and well played but not distinctive, and the recording is more than acceptable. But this cannot match the Chandos collection and would have been more attractive as a budget Naxos issue.

'The Salieri Album': Arias from: *La cifra; La fiera Venezia; La finta scena; La grotta di Trofonio; Palmira, regina di Persia; Il ricco d'un guirno; La secchia rapida.*
** Decca 475 100-2. Bartoli, OAE, Fischer.

It is astonishing when this adventurous disc contains so much imaginative, brilliant and characterful singing, exploiting rare repertory, that it opens with an aria from Salieri's opera, *La secchia rapida*, in which Cecilia Bartoli's performance can only be described as grotesque. With fluttery tone she attacks this bravura piece with ugly squawking. That will be enough to turn off many listeners, but the rest is never less than characterful, often exciting and occasionally moving, even if some of the more demanding of these 13 arias bring some fluttering and roughness of tone that Bartoli would earlier have avoided. Though Salieri's inspiration may be thin compared with that of Mozart, these pieces are consistently lively and inventive, and Bartoli proves a passionate advocate, vigorously accompanied by Adám Fischer and the Orchestra of the Age of Enlightenment. Notes and full texts are provided in a handsome booklet.

SANTOS, Joly Braga (1924–88)

Symphonies Nos. 3 & 6.
*** Marco Polo 8.225087. Neves, São Carlos Theatre Ch., Portuguese SO, Cassuto.

José Manuel Joly Braga Santos is the leading Portuguese symphonist of his day. His *Third Symphony*, composed in 1949, when he was in his mid-20s, is strongly modal in idiom, with a strong sense of forward movement and a powerful feeling for architecture. It is imaginatively scored and at times suggests Vaughan Williams, and even at one point in the slow movement (about two and a half minutes in) the Shostakovich of the *Fifth Symphony*. The *Sixth Symphony* (1972) is a one-movement work with a closing choral section. The first two-thirds are purely orchestral and more expressionist in their musical language, non-tonal but without being dodecaphonic, the choral part being tonal. Very good performances and recordings.

SARASATE, Pablo (1844–1908)

Carmen Fantasy, Op. 25; Introduction et Tarantelle, Op. 43; Zigeunerweisen.
(M) *** EMI (ADD/DDD) 5 62594-2. Perlman, Abbey Road Ens., Foster – PAGANINI: *Violin Concerto No. 1.* ***

Perlman's *Carmen Fantasy* makes a dazzling encore for his unsurpassed account of the Paganini *Concerto*, and for this reissue in the 'Perlman Edition' EMI have added dazzling accounts of two other showpieces, the *Introduction et Tarantelle* and *Zigeunerweisen*, recorded digitally in 1995, in which Perlman's tone is even more luscious.

SARMANTO, Heikki (born 1939)

'Meet the Composer': (i; ii) *Kalevala Fantasy: Return to Life;* (iii) *Max and the Enchantress; Sea of Balloons;* (iv; v; ii) *Suomi (A Symphonic Jazz Poem for Orchestra);* (iii; vi) *The Traveller: Northern Atmosphere.* (Instrumental): (iv; vii) *Distant Dreams: Tender Wind. Pan Fantasy: The Awakening; In the Night.* (Vocal) (viii) *Carrousel;* (ix) *Light of Love;* (x) *New England Images;* (xi; iii) *New Hope Jazz Mass: Have Mercy on Us.* (x) *Northern Pictures.*
(B) ** Finlandia 0630 19809-2 (2). (i) UMO Jazz O; (ii) dir. composer; (iii) Heikki Sarmanto Ens.; (iv) with Aaltonen; (v) with O; (vi) with Pantir, Rainey; (vii) composer (keyboards); (viii) Merrill, Tapiola Sinf., Zito; (ix) Parks, McKelton, Opera Ebony, Haatanen; (ix; x) Sarmanto Jazz Ens.; (x) Finnish Chamber Ch., Eric-Olof Söderström; (xi) Hapuoja, Gregg Smith Vocal Qt, Long Island Symphonic Choral Assoc., Smith.

Heikki Sarmanto firmly 'eludes all attempts at categorization,' writes Antti Suvanto in his notes for this set. Sarmanto was a theory pupil of Joonas Kokkonen, and he went on to further studies in the United States. The main influence on the music that represents him here is Duke Ellington, though few of the pieces here rival his model. He is accomplished and inventive, though the choral pieces really do strike us as having more facility than taste. There is some good playing from the various artists involved, and Sarmanto is obviously a skilled as well as a prolific musician. On the whole, however, his music strikes us as deeply unappealing.

SATIE, Erik (1866–1925)

PIANO MUSIC

Piano, Four Hands: *Aperçus désagréables; La Belle excentrique; En habit de cheval (Divertissement); 3 Morceaux en forme de poire; 3 Petites pièces montées.* Solo Piano Music (early pieces): *Allegro (1884); Fantaisie-Valse; Valse-ballet (both 1885). Avant-dernières pensées. Caresse; Carnet d'esquisses et de croquis* (both ed. Cadby); *Chapitres tournés en tous sens; Croquis et agaceries d'un gros bonhomme en bois; Danse de travers No. 2* (ed. Caby); *9 Danses gothiques; Eginhard; Descriptions automatiques; Embroyens desséchés; Fête donnée par les Chevaliers Normands en l'Honneur d'une jeune Demoiselle (XI siècle); Enfantins: 1, Menus propos enfantins; 2, Enfantillages pittoresques; 3, Peccadilles importunes; 4: 3 Nouvelles enfantines. Le Fils des étoiles; 3 Gymnopédies; 6 Gnossiennes; Heures séculaires et instantanées; Jack-in-the-Box; Je te veux; Musiques intimes et secrètes* (ed. Cadby); *La Nazaréen; 5 Nocturnes; Nouvelles pièces froides; Ogives; Les Pantines dansent; Passacaille; 12 Petits chorals* (ed. Cadby); *Petite ouverture à danser; Petite musique de clown triste* (both ed. Cadby); *Le Piccadilly; Pièces froides I & II; Le Piège de Méduse. Le Poisson rêveur; 6 Pièces de la période 1906–13* (both ed. Cadby); *La Porte héroïque du ciel; Poudre d'or; Préludes flasques (pour un chien); Prélude et tapisserie; Premier Menuet à Claude Dubosq; Première Pensée Rose + Croix. Prière* (fragment); *Rêverie du pauvre* (both ed. Cadby); *2 Rêveries nocturnes* (ed. Cadby); *3 Sarabandes; Sonatine bureaucratique; Sonneries de la Rose + Croix; Sports et divertissements; 3 Valses distinguées du précieux dégouté; Véritables préludes flasques (pour un chien); Verset laïque & somptueux; Vexations; Vieux sequins et vieilles cuirasses.*

(BB) **(*) EMI 5 85602-2 (5). Ciccolini, (i) with Tacchino.

Aldo Ciccolini's first set of recordings of Satie's piano music, made between 1967 and 1971, did much to awaken the wider public's awareness of this composer's art. Then the French pianist went on re-record the majority of the pieces, between 1983 and 1986, enlisting Gabriel Tacchino in the four-hand works. The later coverage is pretty comprehensive, including the very early and posthumously published works – in some cases employing Robert Cadby as editor. The music is grouped on each disc broadly in chronological order, so we discover that the famous *Gymnopédies* (1888) are among the composer's earliest inspirations. Few of the pieces are more than a couple of minutes long, so listening to them in bulk is like gorging on canapés or petits-fours. But for all the delight Satie takes in shocking the musical establishment, an inner stillness and purity lie at the centre of his art, which in the right hands can be very touching. Ciccolini's devotion to the composer and the comprehensive nature of his enterprise must be warmly acknowledged. If you want virtually all Satie, this set (which replaces the six-disc edition listed in our main volume) is eminently serviceable and often a good deal more than than that, though the recorded sound is variable. Moreover, although this is a bargain box, there is good back-up documentation provided by James Harding.

SCHARWENKA, Franz Xaver
(1850–1924)

Piano Concertos Nos. 2 in C min., Op. 56; 3 in C sharp min., Op. 80.

*** Hyp. CDA 67365. Tanyel, Hanover R. Philharmonie des NDR, Strugala.

These two concertos bristle with technical challenges of which Seta Tanyel makes light. She has long championed this composer, and her fine records for the defunct Collins label are now resurfacing on Hyperion. She is fully equal to their technical demands and takes them comfortably in her stride, although she is not quite in the same league as Stephen Hough, whose recording of the *Fourth* on this label rightly won such acclaim. The *Second Concerto* comes from 1880, and the debt to both Chopin and Hummel can be clearly discerned. Eighteen years separate the two concertos, seven of which Scharwenka spent in the United States. He gave the first performance of the *Third* in Berlin in 1899 to much acclaim – understandably so, given the quality of the central *Adagio.* Tanyel not only copes with the virtuoso demands of Scharwenka's writing but is a very musical player. Excellent support from Tadeusz Strugala and the Hanover Radio Orchestra, and a first-class (1996) recording.

SCHMIDT, Franz (1874–1939)

(i) *Quintet in B flat for Clarinet, Piano & Strings;* (ii) *3 Fantasy Pieces on Hungarian National Melodies.* (Piano) *Romance in A; Toccata in D min..*

** Marco Polo 8.223415. Ruso, with (i) Janoska, Török, Lakatos; (i; ii) Slávik.

The *Quintet*, like so much of Schmidt's music with piano, was composed with the left-handed pianist Paul Wittgenstein (brother of the philosopher) in mind. The piano part was subsequently rearranged for two hands by Friedrich Wührer. Its character is predominantly elegiac; it was composed after the death of Schmidt's daughter and can best be described as having something of the autumnal feeling of late Brahms, the subtlety of Reger and the dignity and nobility of Elgar or Suk. The players sound pretty tentative at the very start but soon settle down, though their tempo could with advantage have been slower. All the same it is a thoroughly sympathetic, recommendable account. The *Drei Phantasiestücke* and the two piano pieces, the *Romance* and the *D minor Toccata,* are earlier and less interesting, though they are well enough played.

Das Buch mit sieben Siegeln (The Book with 7 Seals).

☛ (BB) *** EMI Gemini 85782-2 (2). Oelze, Kallisch, Andersen, Odinius, Pape, Reiter, Bav. R. Ch. & SO, Welser-Möst; Winklhofer (organ).

This newest version of Schmidt's *Book with Seven Seals* was recorded live by EMI in the Herculessaal in 1997 and is played by the magnificent Bavarian Radio Orchestra with the Bavarian Radio Chorus under Franz Welser-Möst, who shows great sympathy for the score. The soloists are excellent, and this now supplants both Harnoncourt's account with the Vienna Singverein and the VPO on Teldec, and also the earlier Calig version of 1996. However, no texts are included.

SCHNITTKE, Alfred (1934–98)

Concerto for Piano and Strings; (i) Concerto for Piano Four Hands & Chamber Orchestra.
(M) ** Warner Elatus 0927 49811-2. Postnikova, (i) with Irena Schnittke; L. Sinf., Rozhdestvensky.

Authoritative performances of two very thin pieces. In the *Concerto for Piano Four Hands* the quality of the musical invention is far from distinguished and, without putting too fine a point upon it, the *Concerto for Piano and Strings* is pretty empty. The playing time of the disc is 47 minutes, but it seems much longer. Victoria Postnikova plays with taste and authority as, in the *Concerto for Piano Four Hands*, does the composer's widow. The recording comes from the early 1990s and is very acceptable.

SCHOECK, Othmar (1886–1957)

(i) Horn Concerto, Op. 65. Prelude for Orchestra, Op. 48; (ii) Serenade for Oboe, Cor Anglais & Strings, Op. 27. Suite in A flat for Strings.
** CPO 999 337-2. (i) Schneider; (ii) Zabarella, Zuchner; Coll. Musik, Winterthur, Albert.

The major work here is the five-movement *Suite in A flat for Strings*, which Schoeck composed in 1945. Although it is not quite as poignant as *Sommernacht*, there is some imaginative and expressive writing. The second movement, *Pastorale tranquillo*, has that sense of melancholy and nostalgia so characteristic of Schoeck. In it he imagined 'the peace and deep stillness of the forests'. The slightly later *Concerto for Horn and Strings* (1951) is well played by Bruno Schneider and is an appealing piece that will strike a responsive chord among all who care for late Strauss. The *Serenade for Oboe, Cor Anglais and Strings* is a five-minute interlude which Schoeck composed for a much-truncated production of his opera, *Don Ranudo*, at Leipzig in 1930. The *Prelude for Orchestra* serves as a reminder that Schoeck was at one time a pupil of Reger. Its textures lack transparency, but this is in part due to the rather opaque recording, made in a radio studio. It is perfectly acceptable, but the strings could do with more bloom and tuttis need to open out a little more.

Violin Sonatas: in D, Op. 16; in E, Op. 46; in D, WoO22; Albumblatt, WoO70.
** Guild GMCD7142. Barritt, Edwards.

The two *D major Violin Sonatas* come from the first decade of the last century. The student essay of 1905 is of lesser interest, but Op. 16 has a strong vein of lyricism and a characteristic warmth of invention. The *Sonata in E major*, Op. 46, of 1931 inhabits a totally different world. Its musical language is less immediate and in this respect could possibly be compared with late Fauré, though there is no resemblance in idiom. Paul Barritt and Catherine Edwards give very capable and sensitive performances and, were the recording a little more spacious and less forward, this would gain three stars.

3 Lieder, Op. 35; 6 Lieder, Op. 51; Das Wandsbecker Liederbuch, Op. 52; Im Nebel; Wiegenlied.
** Jecklin JD677-2. Banse, Henschel, Rieger.

Das Wandsbecker Liederbuch is a latter-day equivalent of the Hugo Wolf Songbooks; they offer a portrait of a poet (in this case Mathius Claudius) rather than a thematically connected cycle, and the songs, though highly conservative in idiom, are full of subtleties and depth, as indeed are the remaining songs on this CD. They are decently sung and recorded, and admirers of Schoeck's art need not hesitate.

SCHOENBERG, Arnold (1874–1951)

Pelleas und Melisande (Symphonic Poem), Op. 5.
*(*) DG (IMS) 469 008-2. Berlin Deutsche Op. O, Thielemann – WAGNER: *Siegfried Idyll.* *(*)

Christian Thielemann is an outstanding conductor but sometimes an intrusive interpreter who is loth to allow the music to unfold naturally. There is too much expressive exaggeration here, and although the playing of the orchestra of the Deutsche Oper is fine, this mannered account does not begin to challenge the classic Karajan account.

(i) Piano Concerto. Piano Music: 3 Pieces, Op. 11; 6 Little Pieces, Op. 19; 5 Pieces, Op. 23; 2 Pieces, Op. 33a & b; Suite, Op. 25.
(M) **(*) D G (DDD/ADD) 471 361-2. Pollini, (i) with BPO, Abbado – WEBERN: *Variations for Piano.* ***

Pollini is very persuasive in the *Piano Concerto*; his account has all the pianistic mastery one would expect and much refinement of keyboard colour, but he is not helped by a rather claustrophobic recording that is wanting in real transparency. Abbado gives devoted support and the Berlin orchestra play splendidly. In the solo piano music Pollini again plays with enormous authority and refinement of dynamic nuance and colour, making us perceive this music in a totally different light from other performers. Here the sound is excellent, very slightly on the dry side, but extremely clear and well defined.

Gurrelieder.

(M) ★★(★) Ph. 475 455-2 (2). McCracken, Norman, Troyanos, Werner Klemperer, Tanglewood Festival Ch., Boston SO, Ozawa.

Ozawa's gloriously opulent live performance *Gurrelieder*, with a ravishing contribution from Jessye Norman, won the *Gramophone* Choral Award in 1979. It is not now a first choice, with Rattle (EMI 5 57303-2) and Sinopoli (Teldec 4509 98424-2) leading the list of current recommendations, but its price advantage and the inclusion of text and translation certainly make it more competitive, even though the recording is obviously not up to the finest studio standards. However, it is also available on a Philips Duo which includes the *Chamber Symphony No. 1* as a bonus, though omitting the libretto (464 736-2 – see our main *Guide*).

Variations for Orchestra, Op. 31; Verklaerte Nacht, Op. 4.

☗ ✪ (M) ★★★ DG 476 2201. BPO, Karajan.

Karajan's version of *Verklaerte Nacht* is altogether magical and very much in a class of its own. There is a tremendous intensity and variety of tone and colour: the palette that the strings of the Berlin Philharmonic have at their command is altogether extraordinarily wide-ranging. Moreover, on CD the sound is firmer and more cleanly defined, and this is now a mid-priced bargain on Universal's 'Penguin ✪ Collection'.

SCHOENFIELD, Paul (born 1947)

Piano Concerto (Four Parables).

★★ Athene CD 21. Boyde, Dresden SO, Nott – DVORAK: *Piano Concerto.* ★★

The American composer Paul Schoenfield is now in his fifties and has made few inroads into the concert hall outside the USA. This CD is of the 1998 European première of his *Piano Concerto (Four Parables)*, which draws on a variety of styles – popular music, vernacular and folk traditions and 'the normal historical traditions of cultivated music often treated with sly twists'. It has some degree of flair, but from the multiplicity of styles no distinctive personality emerges. Very brilliant playing from the talented Andreas Boyde but this is not music which arouses enthusiasm.

SCHREKER, Franz (1878–1934)

Ekkehard Overture; Fantastic Overture; Die Gezeichneten: Prelude. Der Schatzgräber, Act III: Interlude. Das Spielwerk: Prelude.

(BB) ★★ Naxos 8.555246. Slovak PO, Seipenbusch.

Prelude to Memnon; Romantic Suite.

(BB) ★★ Naxos 8.555107. NOe. Tonkünstler O, Vienna, Mund.

Both these issues first appeared on Marco Polo in the late 1980s, when Schreker's representation in the catalogue was relatively meagre. It is, of course, useful to have these (on the whole) adequate performances at bargain price, but it would be idle to pretend that they are of the highest order. Neither the Slovak Philharmonic under Edgar Seipenbusch nor the NOe. (Lower Austrian) Tonkünstler Orchestra with Uwe Mund are the equal of the BBC Philharmonic, nor do the recordings approach the Chandos Schreker series. On the Slovak disc neither the *Ekkehard Overture* nor the *Fantastic Overture* is the best Schreker; they are, in fact, less than distinguished. The Prelude to *Die Gezeichneten* is another matter, although the playing has more guts than finesse. The Chandos account of the *Romantic Suite* under Valery Sinaisky knocks spots off the Viennese rival and is altogether richer and more enjoyable. Incidentally, the *Prelude to Memnon* is identical to the *Prelude to a Drama* on Chan. 9797.

Der Geburtstag der Infantin.

★★ Edition Abseits ED A013-2. Berlin Kammersymphonie, Bruns – TOCH: *Tanz-Suite, Op. 30.* ★★

This is a first recording of the original (1910) version of Schreker's dance pantomime on Oscar Wilde's short story, *The Birthday of the Infanta*. It surfaced during the 1980s in a Vienna Archive, having been misfiled. Good playing and recording.

SCHUBERT, Franz (1797–1828)

ORCHESTRAL MUSIC

Symphonies Nos. 1–6; 8 (Unfinished); 9 (Great).

☗ (BB) ★★★ Warner Apex 2564 60532-2 (5). Sinfonia Varsovia, Y. Menuhin (disc 5 includes conversation in German: Menuhin/Jurgen Seeger).

Menuhin's more recent (1997) IMG set of the Schubert *Symphonies*, now reissued on Apex, offers performances electrically tense, generally at brisk speeds, with an easy feeling for Schubertian lyrcism, helped by alert, warmly responsive playing from this leading Polish chamber orchestra and full, immediate recording. With Menuhin there is no question of the early symphonies – boyhood works often described as Haydnesque – being mistaken for eighteenth-century music. Modest in scale, these are interpretations that yet bite home with Beethovenian power. With the last two symphonies the result is equally fresh, with fast, steady speeds and high contrasts. Most radical of all is the *Great C major*, brisk and urgent. The disappointment is that the supplementary conversation is in German only.

Symphonies Nos. 1 in D, D.82; 4 in C min. (Tragic).

(BB) ★★(★) Warner Apex 2564 60527-2. Sinfonia Varsovia, Y. Menuhin.

Menuhin's *First Symphony* opens weightily (partly the effect of the resonant recording), but the allegro, fast and resilient, is graceful as well as lively, and the *Andante* has characteristic warmth. As throughout the cycle, the Minuet is briskly characterful and the finale captivates with energetic lightness of articulation from the strings. The *Tragic Symphony* opens powerfully, yet again the main allegro, like the finale, is resilient as well as boldly forward-looking, and the slow movement nobly expressive. The Trio of the Minuet is most engagingly done. The sound is full-bodied, with tuttis not completely transparent, but this is certainly a very recommendable series in the budget range.

(i) *Symphony No. 1*; (ii) *Marche militaire, Op. 51/1*; (iii) Overtures: *Fierrabras; Des Teufels Lustschloss*; (iv) *4 Waltzes & 4 Ecossaises* (2 sets).
** Australian Decca Eloquence 466 908-2. (i) Israel PO, Mehta; (ii) VPO, Knappertsbusch; (iii) VPO, Kertész; (iv) Boskovsky Ens.

Mehta is no Beecham, but his account of the *First Symphony* is a fresh, straightforward account which gives pleasure. The Israeli orchestra lacks something in polish. But there are no such problems for the ensuing Viennese recordings, which give this bargain disc its appeal. Knappertsbusch's noble and trusty account of the *Marche militaire*, and the little-known overtures under Kertész are always a joy to hear. *Des Teufels Lustschloss* is a juvenile work. *Fierrabras* is more melodramatic, but lively in invention. To cap an imaginative programme, Boskovsky gives delectable accounts of the charming dance pieces, and all are well recorded.

Symphonies Nos. 2 in B flat; 6 in C.
(BB) *** Warner Apex 2564 60529-2. Sinfonia Varsovia, Y. Menuhin.

Menuhin's coupling is outstanding in every way, with first-movement allegros swiftly paced and fizzing with vitality. Both *Andantes* are beautifully played, each elegant and poised. With vigorous Scherzi (winning Trios) and jaunty finales, these performances are hard to beat, full of Schubertian character. The orchestral playing is first class, glowing and vivacious, and the recording is both full and transparent.

Symphonies Nos. 3 in D; 5 in B flat; 8 in B min. (Unfinished).
(BB) *** Warner Apex 2564 60530-2. Sinfonia Varsovia, Y. Menuhin.

A truly outstanding triptych from Menuhin at his most inspired. No. 3 is bold, strong and forward-looking, yet the first movement's second subject could not be more enticingly Schubertian, and the *Allegretto* is delightful, as is the Trio of the vigorously rhythmic Scherzo. No. 5 too, has both strength and grace, although some listeners may feel that Menuhin moves the *Andante* on too briskly. However, one soon adjusts, for this is a movement that can too easily drag. The *Unfinished* then emerges as the most

powerful, most romantic of the cycle, the *sotto voce* lower strings at the opening full of mystery and the climaxes thrillingly Beethovenian in their power; the second movment is then perfectly balanced in its lyrical serenity, while retaining its emotional puissance. Again superb playing from the Sinfonia Varsovia and first-rate recording.

Symphony No. 8 in B min. (Unfinished), D.759.
(M) ** DG (ADD) 463 609-2 (2). Chicago SO, Giulini – MAHLER: *Symphony No. 9*. **
(B) ** Decca Penguin 460 643-2. San Francisco SO, Blomstedt – MENDELSSOHN: *Symphony No. 4 in A (Italian)*. ***

There are some very good things in Giulini's deeply felt 1978 reading of the *Unfinished*, with much carefully considered detail. But the Mahler coupling is not a prime recommendation.

Blomstedt's account of the *Unfinished* is beautifully played, but only in the second movement does the performance glow as it should – the first movement is rather uneventful. The recording is excellent. The accompanying essay in the Penguin Classics CD is by John Guare.

Symphonies Nos. 8 (Unfinished); 9 in C (Great).
⊶ ❂ (M) *** Decca (ADD) 476 1551. (i) VPO; (ii) LSO; Krips.
(M) ** Sony (ADD) SMK 61842. NYPO, Bernstein.

Krips recorded the *Unfinished* in the very early days of mono LP, a gentle, glowing performance; and here, in 1969 with the VPO, he directs an unforced, flowing and wonderfully satisfying account, helped by excellent playing and splendid Sofiensaal recording, produced by Christopher Raeburn. This makes a splendid coupling for Krips's much earlier LSO recording of the *Ninth*, which has long been counted by us as one of his very finest records, perhaps *the* finest. The performance similarly has a direct, unforced spontaneity, which shows Krips's natural feeling for Schubertian lyricism at its most engaging. An ideal candidate for Universal's mid-priced 'Penguin ❂ Collection'.

Bernstein gives a dramatic account of the *Unfinished*, with a great surge of energy in the first-movement development. Yet there is lyrical warmth too and at times a sense of mystery. The playing of the NYPO is first class and the recording from 1963 is acceptable. The account of the *C major Symphony* is less consistent. There is plenty of vitality, but it lacks the unforced spontaneity which can make this symphony so exhilarating. The finale charges along like a runaway express train, exciting and brilliant, yes, but a bit charmless too.

Symphony No. 9 in C (Great), D.944.
⊶ (M) *** RCA 82876 59425-2. BPO, Wand.
(M) *** EMI (ADD) 5 62791-2. LPO, Boult – BRAHMS: *Alto Rhapsody; Academic Festival Overture*. ***

(BB) ★★★ Warner Apex 2564 60531-2. Sinfonia Varsovia, Y. Menuhin.

(M) ★★★ BBC Legends BBCL 4140. LPO, Giulini –
BRITTEN: *The Building of the House Overture*;
WEBER: *Der Freischütz: Overture.* ★★★

(M) ★★ Sup. (ADD) SU 3468-2 011. Czech PO, Konwitschny.

Günter Wand offers a visionary account of Schubert's *Great C major Symphony*, taken from superbly played, live, Berlin performances, glowingly recorded. Consistently he makes the playing sound spontaneous, even in the tricky problems of speed changes inherent in this work. In the manner of his generation, he does not observe exposition repeats in the outher movements or second-half repeats in the Scherzo, but this is a beautifully co-ordinated, strong and warm reading, well worthy of reissue in RCA's mid-priced 'Classic Library' series.

Older readers will welcome back to the catalogue this splendidly wise and magisterial account from the doyen of British conductors. There is not a whit of hyperbole; indeed, Sir Adrian's tendency to understate is evident in the slow movement, just as his feeling for the overall design is undiminished. The LPO respond with playing of high quality and the 1972 Kingsway Hall recording (like the Brahms coupling) is transferred admirably to CD.

Most listeners will surely do an aural double-take at the astonishing speed of the opening horn solo of Menuhin's highly individual and original interpretation. Yet the movement moves forward in a single thrust, gathering power, energy and momentum to its thrilling coda. The *Andante con moto* is also brisker than usual, but it comes naturally within Menuhin's conception, and the Scherzo rollicks forcefully and genially before the closing *Allegro vivace* sweeps all before it, the trombones helping to drive the music onwards. The sheer exuberance of this performance all but negates the idea of a work of 'heavenly' length and, with such vigour and zest, it is impossible to be bored for a moment, even if you resist the conception. Marvellous playing and splendid recording, leaving the listener on a high.

Giulini's live recording of Schubert's great *C major Symphony* was made at the Royal Festival Hall in London in May 1975, the principal work in one of the BBC Legends reissues celebrating the conductor's ninetieth birthday. It is a powerful reading, well recorded in full-bodied stereo. In the first two movements Giulini's speeds are broader than usual, so that he manages generally to avoid the traditional if unmarked speed-changes of most performances. So it is that in the slow movement he builds the central climax relentlessly with no speeding up; but then, for the yearning cello melody which follows, he does allow himself a degree of broadening, phrasing with characteristic warmth. The Scherzo is then infectiously sprung and the finale is beautifully articulated, even at high speed. As well as the two overtures, the extra items include a brief clip from a

BBC interview, emphasizing the spiritual quality Giulini finds in music.

Konwitschny's *Ninth* dates from 1962. It is a straightforward, simple and warmly relaxed reading, Viennese in feeling. In that, it has a good deal in common with Krips's early Decca version with the VPO, although without the level of concentration that makes that performance so totally compelling; Konwitschny is more easy-going. The first movement's development has a pleasing jaunty progress and the return to the opening theme is deftly managed. The *Andante* is beautifully played (the principal oboe's contribution a highlight). Only the Scherzo, with all repeats included, brings a nagging suggestion of 'heavenly length', and the finale, although not pressed hard, makes an agreeable conclusion. The analogue recording is warm and naturally balanced.

CHAMBER MUSIC

(i) *Arpeggione Sonata in A min., D.821* (arr. for cello); (ii) *Piano Quintet in A (Trout).*

(BB) ★★(★) RCA (ADD/DDD) 822876 55270-2. (i) Harrell, Levine; (ii) Ax, Guarneri Qt (members), Julius Levine (double bass).

We have long praised Lynn Harrell's 1976 recording of the *Arpeggione Sonata* in partnership with James Levine. It is a refreshingly unmannered account and yet full of personality. Vital, sensitive playing, excellently recorded. It now comes coupled with a *Trout*, recorded digitally a decade later, yet less well balanced. The piano dominates throughout, not least because of the strong, though very musical contribution of Emanuel Ax. The leader of the Guarneri Quartet is backwardly balanced and his timbre is small, yet this adds to the intimacy of what is undoubtedly a lively performance, with sympathtic accounts of both the *Andante* and Variations.

Octet in F, D.803.

(M) ★★(★) Cal. CAL 9314. Octuor de France.

A beautifully played and naturally recorded performance of the *Octet* from the French ensemble on Calliope, notable for its warmth and simplicity, and also for fine contributions from the clarinettist, Jean-Louis Sajot, and the horn player, Antoine Degremont. The overall effect is warmly spontaneous but there is no coupling, so the disc cannot be a top recommendation. The performance by the Vienna Octet coupled with Spohr remains first choice (466 580-2 – see our main *Guide*).

Piano Quintet in A (Trout), D.667.

(M) ★★(★) Sony (ADD) 512872-2. R. Serkin, Laredo, Naegele, Parnas, J. Levine – SCHUMANN: *Piano Quintet.* ★★(★)

(★★) Pearl mono GEM 0129. Panhofer, Vienna Octet (members) – MOZART: *Divertimento No. 17.* (★★)

The Serkin performance is distinguished, with some

spontaneous if idiosyncratic playing from the master pianist. As a performance this is worth considering in the mid-price range, but the recommendation must be qualified, because the string tone of the 1967 recording is somewhat hard.

The *Record Guide* gave the early Decca mono recording on the Pearl disc two stars – in those days the Guide listed only two versions! The *Trout* was reissued on Decca's Ace of Clubs economy label in the early 1960s, by which time Curzon's set with the same artists had supplanted it. Curzon brings greater subtlety and tonal refinement to the piano part, though Panhofer has undeniable sparkle and style. The original sounded wiry and unpleasing (particularly in its ACL format), but Roger Beardsley has gone to great trouble to find a stylus that would do justice to these performances. The sound is far richer and better defined. An affecting reminder of performance style fifty years back and well worth hearing fifty years on! But András Schiff and the Hagen Quartet give an outstanding modern performance again on Decca (458 608-2 – see our main *Guide*).

(i) *Piano Quintet in A (Trout). String Quartets Nos. 13 in A min., D.804; 14 (Death and the Maiden); 15 in G, D.887;* (ii) *String Quintet in C, D.956.*

(M) ** EMI (ADD) 5 66144-2 (4). Alban Berg Qt, with (i) Leonskaja, Hörtnagel; (ii) Schiff.

The Alban Berg *Trout* (in which the quartet are joined by Elisabeth Leonskaja and Georg Hörtnagel) brings keen disappointment. Despite the excellence of the recording and some incidental beauties, it remains a curiously uninvolving performance with routine gestures. The *A minor Quartet*, however, is beautifully managed, though the slow movement is very fast indeed. The exposition repeat is omitted in the first movement of *Death and the Maiden*, but otherwise this, too, is a very impressive performance. The playing is breathtaking in terms of tonal blend, ensemble and intonation throughout both these works; if one is not always totally involved, there is much to relish and admire. In the *G major* the Alban Berg players are most dramatic. They are strikingly well recorded, and beautifully balanced; but the sense of over-projection somehow disturbs the innocence of some passages. In the great *C major Quintet*, where they are joined by Heinrich Schiff, they produce a timbre which is richly burnished and full-bodied. Once more there is no first-movement exposition repeat, but theirs is still a most satisfying account, strongly projected throughout. The recording is admirable, but as a collection this is a mixed success.

Piano Trio No. 2 ; Notturno, D.897.

*(*) ECM 453 300-2. Schneeberger, Demenga, Dähler.

The fine players on ECM do not help themselves by choosing an all too leisurely tempo in the first movement. They are just a shade ponderous and heavy-handed at times in both pieces, though the actual quality of the recorded sound is more than serviceable. One needs to turn to the Beaux Arts Trio on Philips (438 700-2 – see our main *Guide*).

String quartets

String Quartets Nos. 10 in D, D.87; 14 (Death and the Maiden).

⊖– (M) *** Cal. Approche CAL 5234. Talich Qt.

The Talich Quartet do not wear their hearts on their sleeves: the intensity of their performance of *Death and the Maiden* comes from within. There is a profundity in the theme and variations of the *Andante* which, together with the richness of texture that they create, is wonderfully heart-warming. The performance of the earlier *D major Quartet* is hardly less fine: more volatile, with the spirited finale concluding the disc unforgettably. Superb recording; string quartet discs do not come any better than this.

String Quartets Nos. 13 in A min., D.804; 14 (Death and the Maiden), D.810; 15 in G, D.887; (i) *String Quintet in C, D.956.*

(BB) **(*) EMI Gemini (ADD) 5 85526-2 (2). Hungarian Qt; (i) with Varga.

This economical EMI package brings all Schubert's last masterpieces in this genre. The performances have been in circulation on a number of occasions, most recently in the 'Rouge et Noir' series. The *Death and the Maiden* and the *A minor Quartet* were recorded in 1958, the early days of stereo (the former appeared in this country on the Vox label), while the *G major Quartet*, recorded in the Salle Wagram, comes from 1968, and the *Quintet*, with the fine Hungarian cellist László Varga as second cello, is from 1970. They are eminently serviceable performances, which will give pleasure even if – in the *Quartets* at least – they do not displace the Quartetto Italiano on Philips.

String Quartet No. 15 in G, D.887.

(M) (**(*)) Orfeo mono C604031B. Hungarian Qt – BARTOK: *Quartet No. 5.* (**(*))

This performance comes from a concert given at the Salzburg Mozarteum in August 1961, some seven years before the Hungarian Quartet's commercial recording at the Salle Wagram. The live occasion prompts playing of tremendous intensity and heartfelt feeling. This has a higher emotional temperature than the latter, but the more refined EMI stereo recording will probably incline most readers towards the studio set, though the mono sound is perfectly acceptable.

Violin Sonatinas, Nos. 1–3; Fantasy in C, D.934.

(BB) * (**) Naxos 8.550420. Kang, Devoyon.

Korean-born Dong-Suk Kang plays with style and panache and is given excellent support by Pascal Devoyon. Neither is well served by the recording, however, made in a cramped studio that robs the piano-tone of some of its timbre, while the close balance does less than complete justice to the sound this fine violinist makes in the flesh. Nevertheless it still gives pleasure. Performances three star; the recording one.

PIANO MUSIC

Piano music for four hands

Allegro moderato & Andante, D.968; Divertissement on Original French Themes, D.823; 2 Ecossaises, from D.783; Fantaisie, D.48; Marche héroïque in C, D.602/2.
** Olympia OCD 677. Goldstone, Clemmow (with
SCHUMANN: *Polonaises Nos. 7 in G min.; 8 in A flat
**).

16 Deutscher Tänze from D.783; Fugue in E min., D.952; Grande marche et trio in B min., D.819/3; Marche héroïque in B min., D.602/1; Overture in G min., D.668; 2 Polonaises in D min., D.824/1 & D.599/1; Sonata in B flat, D.617; Variations on a Theme from Hérold's Opera Marie, D.908.
** Olympia OCD 676. Goldstone, Clemmow (with
SCHUMANN: *Polonaise No. 6 in E **).

Deutscher Tanz in C, D.783/9; Fantaisie, D.9; Grande marche héroïque, D.885; 2 Marches caractéristiques, D.886; Duo in A min. (Lebensstürme), D.947; Polonaise in E, D.824/6; D.599/3; Variations on a French Song, D.624.
** Olympia OCD 675. Goldstone, Clemmow (with
SCHUMANN: *Polonaise No. 5 in B min. **).

Fantaisie, D.1; Grande marche funèbre in C min., D.859; Grande marche et trio in D, D.819/4; 2 Ländler in C min. & C, D.814/3 & 4; March in G (Kindermarsch), D.928; Polonaise in D, D.824/4; Variations on an Original Theme in A flat, D.813.
** Olympia OCD 674. Goldstone, Clemmow (with
SCHUMANN: *Polonaise No. 4 in B flat **).

Deutscher Tanz in E flat, D.783/8; Divertissement à la hongroise, D.818; Grande marche et trio in G min., D.819/2; 2 Ländler in E flat & A flat, D.814/1 & 2; 3 Marches militaires, D.733; Polonaises in A, D.824/5; B flat, D.618a, Sketches (realized by Goldstone); Rondo in A, D.951.
** Olympia OCD 673. Goldstone, Clemmow (with
SCHUMANN: *Polonaise No. 3 in F min. **).

The Anthony Goldstone and Caroline Clemmow partnership are a husband-and-wife team who give eminently musical and shapely accounts with plenty of sensitive observation. They can be confidently recommended (save for the recorded sound, which is not of uniform quality) but not in preference to their EMI rivals, who have the advantage of also being less expensive. The Schumann *Polonaises* are rarer repertoire and make acceptable bonuses for each disc.

Fantasia in F min., D.940; German Dance & 2 Ländler, D.618; 3 Marches héroïques, D.602; Overture in F; Variations on an Original Theme, D.968a.
(BB) *** Naxos 8.554513. Jandó, Kollar.

The Hungarian pianist Jenö Jandó first made his mark on disc when he recorded all 32 of Beethoven's *Sonatas* for Naxos, fresh, totally unmannered performances that were among the early treasures of that bargain label. Here, with his colleague Zsuzsa Kollar, he gives a similarly magnetic reading of what by any reckoning is the greatest of all piano duets, Schubert's haunting *F minor Fantasia*, with its inspired telescoping of a four-movement structure. With Jandö and partner, nothing distracts one from the beauty of Schubert's writing, and the lesser pieces, including the dramatic *Overture in F* and some delectable dances and marches, have comparable freshness, cleanly recorded.

Solo piano music

Allegretto in C min., D.915; 3 Klavierstücke, D.946; Piano Sonata No. 20 in A, D.959.
(M) *** DG 471 356-2. Pollini.

DG have reissued the *A major Sonata* alone in their 'Pollini Edition'. The playing is characteristically strong. But his admirers will surely prefer the alternative mid-priced disc combining D.958 and D.959 (DG 427 327-2 – see our main volume).

Fantasia in C (Wanderer Fantasy), D.760; Piano Sonata No. 19 in G, D.894.
(BB) *(*) Warner Apex 0927 40831-2. Leonskaja.

Even at budget price Elisabeth Leonskaja's account of the *Wanderer Fantasy* and the *G major Sonata*, D.894, would not be a strong recommendation. There is something four-square about her playing, and she does not fully convey the vulnerability and tenderness of Schubert's art. The Teldec recording is a bit hard, which does not help.

Imprompus Nos. 1–4, D.899; 5–8, D.935; 3 Klavierstücke, D.946; 6 Moments musicaux, D.780.
(B) *** Virgin 2 × 1 5 62233-2 (2). Tan (fortepiano) –
BEETHOVEN: *Allegretto*, etc. ***

Schubert on the fortepiano is, of course, quite unlike the Schubert we know from the modern pianoforte. Melvyn Tan's playing is refreshingly unmannered and for the most part very persuasive: he is at pains to avoid any sentimentality, yet he succeeds in conveying the music's tenderness. He has the measure of the scale of the *F minor Impromptu*, D.935/1, and brings both dramatic fire and poetic feeling to it. He is arguably a shade too brisk in D.935/4 and in the *B flat major*, D.935/3, but throughout there are valuable insights. In the *Moments musicaux* he has remarkable feeling for colour and never approaches the music with any excess of that judicious reverence which distinguishes some musicians using period instuments. His Schubert is consistently spirited and fresh and, throughout, this stimulating and lively playing casts new light on the composer. The recording is excellent.

3 Klavierstücke, D.946.
(M) (***) BBC mono BBCL 4125. Claudio Arrau – BRAHMS: *Piano Concerto No. 2.* (***)

Arrau's magisterial artistry is captured here in the BBC's Maida Vale Studios in 1959. These are searching accounts, which should be eagerly snapped up by admirers of Arrau. The later Schubert box that Philips issued in the 1990s did not include these pieces.

Piano sonatas

Piano Sonatas Nos. 7 in E, D.568; 16 in A min., D.845.
(BB) *(*) Naxos 8.553099. Jandó.

These are decent performances from Jenö Jandó but ultimately plain and unmemorable. Not a patch on Schiff, Kempff or Lupu.

Piano Sonatas Nos. 13 in A, D.664; 20 in A, D.959.
(BB) ** Warner Apex 0927 40832-2. Leonskaja.

The two *A major Sonatas* coupled here find Elisabeth Leonskaja much more attuned to the Schubertian sensibility, though in neither would her performances be a first choice. Were this on the shelf alongside the likes of Lupu, Brendel or Kempff, it would be to them rather than to Leonskaja that you would turn.

Piano sonatas Nos. 16 in A min., D.845; 18 in G, D.894.
🔑 ✿ (M) *** Decca (ADD) 476 2182. Lupu.

Radu Lupu's version of the *A minor Sonata* of 1825 is searching and poetic throughout. He brings tenderness and classical discipline to bear on this structure, and his playing is musically satisfying in a very Schubertian way. The coupling is hardly less fine, a superb reading, relatively straight in its approach but full of glowing perception on points of detail; moreover, the exposition repeat is observed in the first movement. The analogue recordings date from 1975 and 1979 respectively and are of Decca's finest, with timbre of warm colour yet with a striking sense of presence overall. A fully worthy addition to Universal's 'Penguin ✿ Collection' (at mid-price).

Piano Sonatas Nos. 19–21; Allegretto in C min., D.915; 3 Klavierstücke, D.944.
(M) *** DG 474 613-2 (2). Pollini.

Piano Sonatas Nos. 19–21; 4 Impromptus, D.899.
🔑 (B) *** Double Decca 475 184-2 (2). Schiff.

In his note András Schiff calls Schubert's last three sonatas 'among the most sublime compositions written for the instrument' – and he plays them as if they are too. There is formidable competition, particularly in the *A major* and great *B flat Sonata* from Perahia, Kempff and Kovacevich, but admirers of the present fine artist can rest assured that the finesse and insight of his playing are undiminished. The bold drama of the *C minor* work is set in contrast with the more ruminative approach to the *B flat Sonata.* Excellent, truthful recording.

In Pollini's hands the three last sonatas emerge as strongly structured and powerful, yet he is far from unresponsive to the voices from the other world with which these pieces resonate. Perhaps with his perfect pianism he does not always convey a sense of human vulnerability, as have some of the greatest Schubert interpreters, but this pairing is certainly worthy of inclusion among DG's 'Originals'.

Piano Sonata No. 15 in C, D.840 – see under *Winterreise.*

Piano Sonatas Nos. 15 in C (Relique), D.840; 21 in B flat, D.960.
(M) **(*) Sony mono/stereo 512874-2. Serkin.

Although he opens the *B flat major Sonata* persuasively, Rudolf Serkin's rugged, less lyrical manner in Schubert will not be to all tastes, but it is undeniably strong in impact. The slow movement is squarer and less flowing than usual, and the interpretation registers the mature, uncompromising response of an artist intent on reading his Schubert very directly, and less intent on beguiling his audience. But there is no question of the patrician character of both these readings. The two-movement *C major Sonata* was recorded (in mono) in 1955, twenty years before the *B flat major*, and with very much the same positive manner, although the *Andante* has an apealing simplicity. In both, the recording is close, strikingly present, but rather hard.

Piano Sonatas Nos. 20 in A, D.959; 21 in B flat, D.960.
🔑 *** HM HMC 901800. Lewis.

In the 2001–2 Wigmore Hall season Paul Lewis played a complete cycle of the Schubert *Sonatas* and in doing so received the South Bank Television Award for 2003. His performances of both these late masterpieces are completely individual and deeply felt, using the widest range of colour and dynamic and great variety of articulation. At one moment his playing is touchingly gentle, thoughtful and introspective, at others intensely dramatic; yet the result sounds totally spontaneous, as at a live recital. These are among the most stimulating and thoughtful Schubert performances of the last few years, and they are very well recorded. A disc to seek out, even if you already have this repertoire played by other, more famous names.

Piano Sonata No. 20 in A, D.959; 4 Impromptus, D.935/1–4.

(M) **(*) Sony (ADD) 512873-2. Serkin.

A much-praised performance in its day (1966), Rudolf Serkin's account of Schubert's *A major Sonata* seems somewhat less sensitive than one remembers and expects from an artist of this stature, although it has some moments of appealing lyricicm. His command of the structure of the work is impressive enough, but *fortissimos* are rather hard (partly the fault of the recording) and one would have liked more finesse in the phrasing. The *Impromptus*, recorded 13 years later, are a different matter, undoubtedly distinguished, and the recording, if slightly dry, is truthful and sounds even better in its new transfer. Serkin's manner may be more severe than Brendel's or Perahia's, but the playing is searching and has memorable insights. There is a sense of stature here, while the songful character of the writing is conveyed without a trace of sentimentality. The range of dynamic is matched by Serkin's sense of colour; the classical authority is balanced by the natural spontaneity of the music-making.

Piano Sonata No. 21 in B flat, D.960; Allegretto in C min., D.915; 6 Moments musicaux, D.780.

⊕–→ ✿ (M) *** EMI 5 62817-2. Kovacevich.

Piano Sonata No. 21 in B flat, D.960; Impromptus Nos. 1–4, D.935.

(M) ** Warner Elatus 0927 49838-2. Barenboim.

Stephen Kovacevich made a memorable recording of the great *B flat major Sonata* for Hyperion which (in our 1988 edition) we called 'one of the most eloquent accounts on record of this sublime sonata and one which is completely free of expressive point-making. It is an account which totally reconciles the demands of truth and beauty.' One could well say the same of the later (1994) EMI version though, if anything, it explores an even deeper vein of feeling than its predecessor. Indeed, it is the most searching and penetrating account of the work to have appeared in recent years and, given the excellence and truthfulness of the recording, must carry the strongest and most enthusiastic recommendation. It certainly ranks Kovacevich among the 'Great Artists of the Century', and for this reissue EMI have added the six *Moments musicaux* which he recorded six months later, also at Abbey Road, and which have comparable insights.

Barenboim's are live performances at the Vienna Musikverein in 1992, marking the fortieth anniversary of the pianist's debut there and his own fiftieth birthday. There is some point-making in the sublime *B flat Sonata* (the C sharp minor theme which opens the slow movement would be more effective if given without expressive underlining). Of course there are perceptive and insightful touches, but on the whole this does not do full justice to this exalted Schubertian, nor really does the recording quality. The *Impromptus* fare better and have a welcome spontaneity.

Wanderer Fantasy in C, D.760.

(M) (**) BBC mono BBCL 4126-2. Richter (with CHOPIN: *Etude in F sharp min., Op. 10/4*) – BEETHOVEN: *Piano Sonatas Nos. 9–10*; SCHUMANN: *Abegg Variations etc.* **

The *Wanderer Fantasy* was one of the first works that Richter took into his repertoire while he was still studying with Neuhaus and it is, as one might expect, a performance of stature. Richter himself said that it was only in later life that he succeeded in playing it with the freedom it needs. Such are its almost orchestral demands that Schubert himself broke down when he came to the concluding fugue. Richter recorded it commercially in 1963 (it was reissued in harness with the Dvořák *Piano Concerto* in the 'Great Recordings of the Century' on EMI 5 66895-2); but the present magisterial account has the compelling quality of a live concert occasion. Very acceptable sound, although the EMI studio recording is finer still.

VOCAL MUSIC

Miscellaneous vocal recitals

Lieder: (i) *An die Musik; An Sylvia; Auf dem Wasser zu singen; Ganymed; Gretchen am Spinnrade; Im Frühling; Die junge Nonne; Das Lied im Grünen; Der Musensohn; Nachtviolen; Nähe des Geliebten; Wehmut;* (ii) *Der Einsame; Die Forelle; Heidenröslein; Der Jüngling an der Quelle; Liebe schwärmt auf allen Wegen; Liebhaber in allen Gestalten; Seligkeit; Litanei; Ungeduld; Die Vögel;* (iii) *An mein Klavier; Erlkönig.*

⊕–→ ✿ (M) (***) EMI mono/stereo 5 62754-2 [5 62773-2]. Schwarzkopf, with (i) Fischer; (ii) Moore; (iii) Parsons.

Elisabeth Schwarzkopf had her doubts about taking many of the Schubert songs into her repertoire, most of which she felt were more suitable for the male voice; but the present survey includes some of those for which she felt a strong personal identification, including *Gretchen am Spinnrade* and the passionate *Die junge Nonne*. The main group here is drawn from an elysian selection she put on disc at the beginning of her recording career in partnership with Edwin Fischer, who was at the end of his life. In spite of her reservations about lack of experience in this repertoire (in the early 1950s), she and Fischer create a magical partnership, full of intimate intercommunication, with even the simplest of songs inspiring intensely subtle expression from singer and pianist alike. Though Fischer's playing is not immaculate, he left few recordings more endearing than this, and Schwarzkopf's colouring of word and tone is masterly. So it is in the other songs now added to further extend this survey of her Schubertian career. Among the items accompanied by Gerald Moore, *Die Vögel* and *Liebhaber in allen Gestalten* date from 1948, *Litanei* and *Ungeduld* from 1954, and the others from 1965/6, including the two final songs accompanied by Geoffrey Parsons, of which *Erlkönig* was one of her favourites. With excellent transfers – the sound surprisingly consistent – and full texts and translations included, this collection makes an obvious choice for inclusion among EMI's 'Great Artists of the Century'.

'Favourite Lieder': ***An Sylvia; Auf der Bruck; Bei dir allein; Du bist die Ruh'; Der Einsame; Freiwilliges Versinken; Gondelfahrer; Die Götter Griechenlands; Gruppe aus dem Tartarus; Heidenröslein; Himmelsfunken; Im Haine; Der Jüngling an der Quelle; Lied eines Schiffers; Nachtviolen; Prometheus; Ständchen; Die Sterne; Waldesnacht; Der Wanderer an den Mond.***

(B) *** CfP 585 6182. Keenlyside, Martineau.

The velvety beauty of Simon Keenlyside's cleanly focused baritone goes with fresh, thoughtful readings of 20 favourite songs, perfectly judged, with ever-sensitive accompaniment from Malcolm Martineau. Now at bargain price, this disc makes another outstanding Schubert Lieder recommendation, which includes one or two unusual songs among many favourites.

Song-cycles

Die schöne Müllerin **(song-cycle),** ***D.795.***

(M) *** Decca 475 211-2. Schreier, Schiff.

Rarely has a pianist played Schubert accompaniments with such individuality as András Schiff in this 1991 *Gramophone* award-winning performance of *Die schöne Müllerin.* He brings new illumination in almost every phrase, so that in *Wohin?* he transforms the accompaniment into an impressionistic fantasy on the flowing stream, and his rhythmic pointing regularly leads the ear on, completely avoiding any sense of sameness in the strophic songs. Peter Schreier, here challenged to produce his most glowing tone, matches his partner with his brightly detailed singing, transcending even his earlier versions of this favourite cycle, always conveying his response so vividly that one clearly registers his changes of vocal expresion from line to line. At times the voice develops a throaty snarl, purposely so for dramatic reasons. Outstandingly warm and well-balanced recording makes this mid-priced reissue very desirable.

Schwanengesang; 5 Lieder: Am Fennster; Herbst; Sehnsucht; Der Wanderer an den Mond; Wiegenlied, D.867.

🔑 ⚙ (M) *** Decca 474 535-2. Fassbaender, Reimann.

Winner of the *Gramophone* Solo Vocal Award in 1992, Brigitte Fassbaender's performance of *Schwanengesang* remains uniquely distinctive. Discussed in our main volume, it now makes a welcome reissue at mid-price.

(i; ii) ***Winterreise, D.911;*** **(ii)** ***Piano Sonata No. 15 in C, D.840.***

(M) *** Ph. 475 490-2 (2). (i) Schreier; (ii) Richter.

Winterreise (song-cycle), D.911.

(M) *** EMI (ADD) 562784-2. Fischer-Dieskau, Moore.

** EMI CDC5 56445-2. Hampson, Sawallisch.

(BB) ** Naxos 8.554471. Trekel, Eisenlohr.

For their reissue in the 'Great Artists of the Century' series EMI have chosen Dietrich Fischer-Dieskau's 1962 *Winterreise,* which combines direct power of expression with rich vocal power. A great performance which has the virtue of striking freshness from singer and pianist alike. The recording scarcely shows its age. A full text and translation are included.

Recorded live in the newly restored Semper Opera House in Dresden just after its reopening in February 1985, Peter Schreier's is an inspired version of *Winterreise*: dramatic, outstandingly beautiful and profoundly searching in its expression, helped by magnetic, highly individual accompaniments from Richter, a master of Schubert. Speeds are not always conventional, indeed they are sometimes extreme – but this only adds to the vivid communication which throughout conveys the inspiration of the moment. Rarely has the agonized intensity of the last two songs been conveyed so movingly on record, the more compellingly when the atmosphere of a live occasion is so realistically captured; it is a small price to pay that the winter audience makes so many bronchial contributions. A more serious snag is that the cycle (which is usually contained on a single CD) spreads over to a second, thanks to the slow speeds. It is surprising that for this reissue celebrating a Solo Vocal Award by the *Gramophone* in 1986, the recording was not remastered to fit on a single disc – for with modern technology that would almost certainly be possible.

Though the Schubert *C major Sonata* brings a comparably inspired performance from Richter (recorded live at Leverkusen in (then) West Germany in December 1979), not everyone will want the coupling. The sound in the *Sonata* recording – though, like the song-cycle, it has striking presence – is drier but is less troubled by audience noise.

SCHUMANN, Clara (1819–96)

4 Songs, Op. 12.

*** Philadelphia Orchestral Association POA 2003 (3). Hampson, Sawallisch – R. SCHUMANN: *Violin Concerto; Symphonies Nos. 1–4,* etc. **(*)

The songs by Clara Schumann find Thomas Hampson in superb form, communicating vividly with every word, flawlessly supported by Wolfgang Sawallisch on the piano.

SCHUMANN, Robert (1810–56)

Cello Concerto in A min., Op. 129.

(M) **(*) Sup. (ADD) SU 3667-2. Navarra, Czech PO, Ančerl – BLOCH: *Schelomo* **(*); RESPIGHI: *Adagio con variazioni.* ***

(M) **(*) EMI (ADD) 5 62803-2. Du Pré, New Philh. O, Barenboim – DVOŘÁK: *Cello Concerto.* **(*)

(M) **(*) BBC BBCL 4133-2. Tortelier, BBC SO, Dorati: – HINDEMITH: *Cello Concerto.* **(*)

André Navarra on his day is one of the most commanding of cellists and his performance here has real personality, rivalling some versions on dearer labels. The Supraphon sound has been made more vivid by the remastering, with the cello focus real and present, and the orchestra caught warmly and naturally.

Jacqueline du Pré's spontaneous style is well suited to this most recalcitrant of concertos and the slow movement is particularly beautiful. As in the coupling, the partnership with Daniel Barenboim is very successful, and the remastered 1968 recording has brought a firmer orchestral focus to match the realistic cello timbre.

Paul Tortelier's account comes from the dryish BBC Maida Vale studios in 1962 and the sound is perhaps less appealing than in many recordings from this label, though the ear quickly adjusts. It is a very spontaneous and finely shaped performance, which admirers of the great French cellist will want to have. The BBC Symphony Orchestra under Antal Dorati responds with vital and sensitive playing, and it comes with a fine account of Hindemith's *Cello Concerto* written in 1940.

(i) Cello Concerto (ii) 3 Fantasiestücke, Op. 73; 3 Romanzen, Op. 94.

(***) Testament mono SBT 1310. Gendron, SRO, (i) Ansermeti (ii) Français – TCHAIKOVSKY: *Variations on a Rococo Theme.* (***)

It is hard to believe that the Testament recording of the *Cello Concerto* is over half-a-century old for it has great freshness and presence. Maurice Gendron was rather overshadowed by his countrymen and contemporaries, Pierre Fournier and Paul Tortelier, but he was no less eloquent an artist and had much of the former's aristocratic finesse and the latter's intensity. His playing was quite personal and his tonal burnish reflects (as Tully Potter puts it in an excellent note) his admiration for Feuermann. When it first appeared, the authors of *The Record Guide* spoke of it as by far the best of the versions then available, and even if such master-cellists as Fournier and Rostropovich had not then committed it to disc, Gendron's remains an impressive account, well worth reviving. It makes its first appearance on CD. The Opp. 73 and 94 pieces, recorded in 1952, originally appeared coupled with Schubert's *Arpeggione Sonata* and serve as a reminder of the refined musicianship of the elegant composer-pianist, Jean Français.

(i) Cello Concerto in A min., Op.129; (ii; iii) Piano Concerto in A min., Op.54; (iv) Symphony No. 1 in B flat (Spring); (ii) Arabeske in C, Op. 18; Fantasia in C, Op. 17; (v) Kinderszenen, Op. 15.

(B) ** DG Panorama (ADD/DDD) 469 199-2 (2). (i) Rostropovich, Leningrad PO, Rozhdestvensky (ii) Pollini; (iii) BPO, Abbado; (iv) VPO, Bernstein. (v) Pollini; (v) Kempff.

This Panorama Schumann compilation is drawn exclusively from Deutsche Grammophon. The earliest recording is the *Cello Concerto*, performed by Rostropovich and Rozhdestvensky in 1960, and the most recent is the *A minor Piano Concerto*, which Pollini made almost 30 years later. It is difficult to flaw DG's choice of the former, but the *Piano Concerto* is more questionable. It makes only intermittent contact with Schumann's sensibility. Pollini's recording of the *C major Fantasia* enjoys classic status. The *Kinderszenen* comes from 1973 when Kempff was in his late seventies. From the symphonies DG's choice has fallen on the *Spring Symphony*; here Kubelik or Karajan would surely have stronger musical claims than Bernstein, who is intrusive at times and pushes the first movement rather hard.

Piano Concerto in A min., Op. 54.

🔔 ✹ *** EMI 5 57562-2. Andsnes, BPO, Jansons – GRIEG: *Piano Concerto.* *** ✹

EMI 5 57773-2. Argerich, Svizzera-Italiana O, Rabinovitch-Barakovsky – BEETHOVEN: *Triple Concerto.* ***

(M) **DG 471 353-2. Pollini, BPO, Abbado – BRAHMS: *Piano Concerto No. 1.* **

((M) ** Chan. 6621 (2). Margalit, LSO, Thompson (with MENDELSSOHN: *Capriccio brillant* **) – BRAHMS: *Concerto No. 1;* SAINT-SAENS: *Concerto No. 2.* **

The Schumann and Grieg *Concertos* make a perfect coupling since the one is modelled on the other. As a student at Leipzig, Grieg had fallen under Schumann's spell and had heard Clara Schumann playing her husband's *Concerto*. The Schumann is new to Andsnes's discography and is a performance of the highest poetic feeling and distinction. Like the Grieg, it brings glorious playing from both soloist and the orchestra under Jansons, a performance similarly combining spontaneity and concentration, dedication and poetry, with no hint of self-consciousness or routine. The pianistic virtuosity is commanding but never overrides tenderness. A performance of both authority and nobility, recorded in particularly lifelike and well-balanced sound. A classic version for our time.

EMI's live recording of the Schumann, made at the Lugano Festival, has a rare vitality, thanks to the vividly characterful playing of Martha Argerich. This account may not be as polished as Argerich's studio version, when impulsively she keeps taking her conductor by surprise, but the magnetism of her playing is here irresistible, with high dramatic contrasts between sparkling virtuosity and yearning lyricism. With the Beethoven *Triple Concerto*, similarly animated, as an unusual coupling, this makes an attractive recommendation.

Pollini's 1990 account is not without tenderness and poetry (witness the slow movement) but he is at times rather business-like and wanting in freshness. He is handicapped by a rather unventilated recorded sound and an inconsistent balance (the piano sounds further back in the slow movement by comparison with the first). But this is not nearly as fine as the live performance with Karajan, included as a bonus disc with the 'Pollini Edition' and not available separately.

Israela Margalit brings no lack of warmth or poetic feeling to the concerto, but she is somewhat idiosyncratic. The central A flat section of the first movement is very measured and she is not averse to point-making by means of rubati. The recording is resonant, with the piano well forward. This offers no serious challenge to the front-runners in the catalogue, and the two-disc format is uneconomical.

Introduction & Allegro appassionato in G, Op. 92.
(BB) *(*) Naxos 8.554089. Biret, Polish Nat. RSO, Wit
– BRAHMS: *Piano Concerto No. 2.* **

As with the companion work below, Biret's playing is romantically full-blooded, and she receives warm support from Wit and the Polish orchestra. However, a tighter overall grip would have made the performance even more effective. No complaints about the recording, which is resonantly full and well balanced.

Introduction & Concert-allegro, Op. 134.
(BB) ** Naxos 8.554088. Biret, Polish Nat. RSO, Wit –
BRAHMS: *Piano Concerto No. 1.* *(*)

Idil Biret plays with no mean virtuosity and brilliance, and this performance is more successful than its coupling. The recording is spacious.

SYMPHONIES

(i; ii) Violin Concerto in D min. (i) Symphonies Nos. 1–4; Manfred Overture; (iii) Andante & Variations.
**(*) Philadelphia Orchestral Association POA 2003 (3). (i) Phd. O, Sawallisch; (ii) with Kavakos; (iii) Sawallisch, with Buchbinder and orchestral soloists
– C. SCHUMANN: 4 Songs, Op. 12. ***

In tribute to Wolfgang Sawallisch at the end of his ten years as music director, the Philadelphia Orchestra has published these live recordings of Schumann, made at concerts over his last season. For some 30 years Sawallisch's Dresden recordings of the Schumann symphonies for EMI (5 67268-2) have established themselves as benchmark versions, and the simple message here is that, with fuller, clearer, weightier digital sound, these new Philadelphia versions have every advantage, carrying exactly the same authority as before, enhanced by modern recording. These are the first issues of recordings made in the

orchestra's fine new Verizon Hall, at once warm and clear. Sawallisch, like other great conductors, has long made nonsense of the old idea that Schumann's orchestration is thick and opaque and, even more than the more reverberant Dresden recordings, these new ones bear that out. At the very start in the slow introduction of the *Spring Symphony, No. 1*, the separation of the wind solos, the terracing of texture, is more clearly brought out, and the rhythmic spring in the main *allegro* is all the more infectious. Differences are slight, and broadly Sawallisch's approach to each of the symphonies remains very much the same, if with a tendency for speeds, fast and slow, to be not quite so extreme.

The third disc in the Philadelphia set is a mixed bag. After the incandescence of the symphonies, the relatively low-key account of the *Manfred Overture* is a disappointment. There is a similar lack of bite in the first movement of the *Violin Concerto*, despite the commanding virtuosity of Leonidas Kavakos. The slow movement is then beautifully tender and songful, leading to a bright, clean reading of the finale. For the other items Sawallisch demonstrates his mastery as a pianist. The 19-minute *Andante and Variations* involve the odd ensemble of two pianos, two cellos and horn, which works surprisingly well, and Sawallisch with his pianist colleague, Rudolf Buchbinder, and three fine Philadelphia players conveys the joy of such corporate music-making. Yet it is perhaps a pity that this Philadelphia set does not concentrate on just the symphonies.

Symphonies Nos. 1–4.
☞ (BB) *** Arte Nova 8287657743-2 (2). Zurich Tonhalle O, Zinman.

Symphonies Nos. 1–4; Scherzo in G min. (ed. Draheim).
**(*) Classico CLASSCD 431/2. Czech Chamber PO, Bostock.

As in his outstanding cycle of the Beethoven symphonies, David Zinman with the Tonhalle Orchestra offers modern-instrument performances which have taken on board the lessons learned from period-instrument performances. With speeds on the fast side, these are all readings which, with excellent sound, are at once fresh, resilient and transparent, defying the old idea of Schumann's thickness of orchestration. Among digital sets there is no finer cycle, whatever the price.

It is fascinating to hear the versions of the symphonies that Douglas Bostock has recorded for Classico with the Czech Chamber Philharmonic Orchestra using a very modest band of strings recorded in a modestly sized hall. It is he too who orchestrated the extra item, the *Scherzo in G minor*. It makes an attractive miniature. In the regular symphonies the interpretative approach is consistently plain, almost metrical at times, with melodies less affectionately phrased than they might be. These are not in any way chilly readings, and they will appeal to anyone who wants a lighter approach to these works. First choice still rests with Karajan (DG 429 672-2 – see our main *Guide*).

Symphonies Nos. 1 in B flat (Spring), Op. 38; 4 in D min., Op. 120; Konzertstück for 4 Horns & Orchestra in F, Op. 86.

(M) *** DG 474 551-2. ORR, Gardiner.

These recordings were orginally part of a three-CD set (currently withdrawn), which included both versions of the *Fourth Symphony*. This mid-price release gives us the familiar (1851) version of the *Fourth*, less bold than the original version, but still striking in this vivid performance. The *Spring Symphony*, too, is fresh and dynamic, and full of energy. But perhaps the most fascinating work here is the 1841 *Konzertstück for four horns*, virtually unplayable in Schumann's own time, but presented here with extraordinary panache, with the ORR soloists breathtaking in their virtuosity.

(i) *3 Romanzen (for cello & piano), Op. 94; Fantasiestücke, Op. 73.*

(M) *** EMI 5 575523-2 (3). Vogt, (i) with Pergamenschikow – BERG: *4 Pieces;* etc.; BRAHMS: *Cello Sonatas* etc. ***

The two sets of cello pieces (Op. 94 quite a rarity when played on the cello) make an apt coupling for the two Brahms *Cello Sonatas*. It is welcome to find in these live performances from the Heimbach Chamber Music Festival that both cellist and pianist relax more in this songful music than in the major works.

CHAMBER MUSIC

Piano Quintet in E flat, Op. 44.

(M) **(*) Sony (ADD) 512872-2. Serkin, Budapest Qt – SCHUBERT: *Piano Quintet (Trout).* **(*)

On Sony there is some masterly playing from Serkin, though the intonation of the Budapest Quartet is not above suspicion and their tone not of the warmest. But this remains a performance of stature, even if the sound is less than ideal.

PIANO MUSIC

Abegg Variations, Op. 1; Faschingsschwank aus Wien, Op. 26.

(M) (**) BBC mono BBCL 4126-2. Sviatoslav Richter (with CHOPIN: *Etude in F sharp min., Op. 10/4)* – BEETHOVEN: *Piano Sonatas Nos. 9–10;* SCHUBERT: *Wanderer Fantasy.* (**)

It was with an LP of Schumann's *Waldszenen* and some of the *Fantasiestücke* on DG that Richter first made his entry into the catalogues. His affinity with the composer is soon communicated, though the bronchial audience is tiresome. As always with this

great artist, his readings are the product of much thought and the mono sound is perfectly acceptable.

Arabeske, Op. 18; Bunte Blätter; Etudes symphoniques, Op. 13 (1832 & 1852 versions, with 1873 appendix); Fantasie in C, Op. 17.

~~B~~ *** DG 474 817-2. Pletnev.

Mikhail Pletnev has a uniquely distinctive keyboard sonority and his pianistic prowess is almost unrivalled. He gave three of the *Bunte Blätter* and the *C major Fantasy* at the Barbican Centre in London early in 2003, which viewers of BBC Four will have seen. Wonderful though his pianism is, it must be conceded that the *C major Fantasy* has some disruptive agogic touches, which impair its natural flow. Even so, Pletnev has remarkable powers of artistic persuasion and his Schumann has a compelling quality that mainly silences some of the doubts listeners may initially feel. This finely recorded issue should be heard by all Schumanniacs for, although Perahia remains a first choice, Pletnev always has interesting thoughts, whatever the repertoire he chooses.

Arabeske, Op. 18; Blumenstücke, Op. 19; Davidsbündlertänze; Etudes symphoniques, Op. 13.

(M) *** Warner Elatus 0927 49612-2. Schiff.

András Schiff opts for the original (1837) *Davidsbündlertänze*, rather than the more usual 1851 revision. Admittedly the differences are not earth-shattering, but the fewer repeats ensure the greater freshness of the ideas. Each of the pieces is strongly characterized and played with appropriate ardour. In the *Etudes symphoniques* he chooses the generally used late version of 1852 (posthumously revised to restore two rejected earlier numbers). The *Arabeske* and the *Blumenstücke* complete a satisfying and competitively priced recital.

Arabesque, Op. 18; Fantasy in C, Op. 17.

(M) *** DG (ADD) 471 358-2. Pollini – LISZT: *Sonata; La Lugubre gondola.* ***

Pollini's 1973 account of the *C minor Fantasy* is most distinguished. It is as fine as Richter's, and the playing throughout has a command and authority on the one hand and deep poetic feeling on the other that instantly capture the listener spellbound. The *Arabesque*, too, is impressively played. The recording is good if not outstanding, but, with its riveting Liszt coupling, this is one of the very finest reissues in the 'Pollini Edition'.

Carnaval, Op. 9; Fantasiestücke, Op. 12; Papillons, Op. 2.

(M) ** Somm SOMMCD 024. Lazaridis.

George-Emmanuel Lazaridis was perhaps unwise to choose this very demanding Schumann programme for his début CD. The moments of gentle poetry show that he has a feeling for the composer, even if his tempi and phrasing are somewhat indulgent, especially in *Papillons*. But for the most part his impulsive tendency to press ahead, seeking to convey a spontaneous forward impulse, serves Schumann less well. Even in *Carnaval*, the most successful performance here, one sometimes feels the piano hammers being applied too percussively, although the playing has plenty of spirit. Fine recording, its brightness partly accounted for by Lazaridis's bold articulation.

Impromptus on a Theme of Clara Wieck, Op. 5; Variations on a Theme of Beethoven; Variations on an Original Theme (Geistervariationen); Variations on a Theme of Schubert.

** Athene ATHCD 23. Boyde – BRAHMS: *Variations on a Theme of Schumann.* **

An intelligently planned recital, which brings repertoire little-known even to those who know their Schumann. The ten *Impromptus on a Theme of Clara Wieck* of 1833 are well represented in the catalogue but the remainder are relatively neglected. The Beethoven variations of 1830 are based on the slow movement of the *Seventh Symphony*. The *Geistervariationen* was Schumann's very last work. Andreas Boyde has reconstructed the *Variations on a Theme of Schubert*, which Schumann began in 1829 and to which he returned five years later. Accomplished but not highly sensitive playing, though this impression may in part be due to the close and two-dimensional recording.

Kinderszenen, Op. 15; Papillons, Op. 2.

(B) ** EMI Début 5 73500-2. Slobodyanik – CHOPIN: *Piano Sonata No. 3*, etc. **(*)

Alex Slobodyanik's accounts of both *Papillons* and *Kinderszenen* are undoubtedly sensitive and distinguished by great beauty of touch. There are many imaginative touches but the performance is somewhat marred by moments of affectation, from which the Chopin is relatively free.

VOCAL MUSIC

Frauenliebe und Leben, Op. 42.

(B) *** EMI Debut 5 85559-2. Coote, Drake – HAYDN: *Arianna a Naxos*; MAHLER: *Das Knaben Wunderhorn* (excerpts), etc. ***

EMI's Debut series has brought to disc a formidable list of young artists, but none finer than the mezzo, Alice Coote. Her choice of repertory could hardly be more challenging, inviting instant comparison with recordings by Dame Janet Baker at her very finest. Coote's voice may not have the velvety warmth of Dame Janet, but in its firmness and clarity it is strikingly distinctive, with a wide dynamic range perfectly controlled down to *pianissimos* of breathtaking intensity. One of Baker's very first recordings was of this Schumann song-cycle, and Coote comes very near that model in depth and range of feeling, with words finely pointed. A pity that, as in other EMI issues of Lieder in this series, no texts or translations are given.

Scenes from Goethe's Faust.

⦿ (M) *** Decca (ADD) 476 1548 (2). Harwood, Pears, Shirley-Quirk, Fischer-Dieskau, Vyvyan, Palmer, Aldeburgh Festival Singers, ECO, Britten.

Britten's outstanding 1972 performance (see our main volume) now reappears in Universal's 'Penguin ⦿ Collection' at mid-price with full documentation included.

SCHUSTER, Joseph (1748–1812)

Demofoonte (opera; complete).

*** BMG/RCA 74321 98282-2 (2). Post, Mields, Melnitzki, Waschinski, Buchin, Kobow, Schafferer, La Ciaccona, Rémy.

Dresden-based throughout his career, Joseph Schuster had his training as an opera composer during several extended visits to Italy. He became court composer in Dresden in 1777, a much-respected figure. Having had early success writing *opera buffa*, he turned to *opera seria*, with *Demofoonte* appearing in 1786 while he was on one of his trips to Italy. To a libretto by Metastasio already set by Paisiello a couple of years earlier, Schuster decks the improbable story in an attractive series of lively and inventive numbers. The oracle has placed on the realm of King Demofoonte a curse: a virgin must be sacrificed each year as long as a usurper sits on the throne. The heroine, Dircea, daughter of the King's chief minister, Matusio, is secretly married to the King's eldest son, Timante, and that leads to her being condemned as the victim. The twists in the plot are many and complex, before the necessary happy ending is achieved through a double switch of parentage, a twist worthy of W.S. Gilbert.

In this recording, made in the Bavarian Music Academy, the period-performance group La Ciaccona, under Ludger Rémy, brilliantly brings out the strong colouring of Schuster's instrumental writing, with braying horns rasping away in almost every number from the hunting-rhythms of the Overture onwards, and with oboes adding bite. The casting is good, with Dorothee Mields sweet and tender as well as agile as Dircea, and with Joerg Waschinski, accurately described as a male soprano, taking on the formidable castrato role of Timante, her lover. Two incidental castrato roles are well taken by male altos, Werner Buchin and Bernhard Schafferer, though Marie Melnitzki's soprano (as recorded) sounds unpleasantly thin and shallow. Both the tenor roles are very well sung, with Andreas Post as Demofoonte and Jan Kobow equally fresh and unstrained as the minister, Matusio. Schuster's limitation is that, lively as his writing is in general, he seems to find it hard to express deep emotion. When the ill-fated Dircea sings the aria *Padre perdona*, it is only the first few bars that express pathos, before the aria switches to a jolly allegro. Deeper feelings tend to be consigned to recitative; disappointingly, the opera ends on a sequence of *secco* recitative, with only a final march from the orchestra to round things off. A welcome rarity nevertheless, well recorded.

SCHÜTZ, Heinrich (1585–1672)

Motets: *Auf dem Gebirge; Der Engel sprach; Exultavit cor meum; Fili mi Absolon; Heu mihi Domine; Hodie Christus natus est; Ich danke Dir Herr; O quam tu pulchra es; Die seele Christi; Helige mich; Selig sind die Todten; Was mein Gott will.*

⊕➔ (BB) ★★★ Regis (ADD) RRC 1168. Esswood, Keven Smith, Elliott, Griffet, Partridge, Etheridge, George, Pro Cantione Antiqua, L. Cornet & Sackbut Ens., Restoration Ac., Fleet.

An eminently useful and well-recorded super-bargain anthology of Schütz motets that offers such masterpieces as *Fili mi Absolon* (for bass voice, five sackbuts, organ and violone continuo) and the glorious *Selig sind die Todten* in well-thought-out and carefully prepared performances under Edgar Fleet. These accounts have a dignity and warmth that make them distinctive. Moreover, the CD sound is excellently managed, rich and clear.

Musicalische Vesper.

★★★ MDG 332 1170-2. Kölner Kammerchor, Coll. Cartusianum, Neumann.

Taking Monteverdi's great 1610 set of *Vespers* as a model, Peter Neumann with his talented Cologne period group has here devised a thrilling German equivalent to Monteverdi's masterpiece, using appropriate Psalm settings and antiphons from Schütz's principal collections. So it is that we can appreciate with fresh ears some of the most inspired church music that Schütz ever wrote, given new perspectives when set against the model of Monteverdi. Vespers and Matins were the only elements of the Catholic liturgy fully retained in the Lutheran church, so that Schütz, who was studying in Venice with Giovanni Gabrieli just when Monteverdi published his work, was inspired to write church music which directly echoed his example, clearly designed for great cathedrals. The German sequence also gains greatly in cohesion from being relatively compact, at just over an hour, ending with a glorious setting of the *Magnificat*. The Psalm settings leading up to that are drawn from such collections as the composer's *Psalms of David* and *Symphoniae Sacrae*, some items already well known on disc, but others not otherwise available. Peter Neumann draws singing and playing from his Cologne forces of spectacular precision and clarity, and he gains greatly from the brilliant engineering of the record company, MDG, which, using only two channels, yet gives a vivid illusion of surround sound.

The Seven Words of Jesus on the Cross. Magnificat. Motets: *Ach, Herr, du Schöpfer aller Ding; Adjuro vos; Anima mea; Die mit Tränen säen; Erbarm dich mein, o Herre Gott; Meine Seele erheben den Herren; Quemadmodum desiderat.*

(B) ★★ HM HMA 1951255. Soloists, Clément Janequin Ens., Les Saqueboutiers de Toulouse, Visse.

Schütz's *Seven Last Words* is a comparatively short work (17 minutes) and takes up only a small part of this programme, although the front of this Musique d'abord CD does not make this clear. After the *Introitus*, seven sentences of text (taken from Schuruck's *Book of Saints and Martyrs* of 1617) are given meditatively to a tenor, alternated with the four Evangelists (different solo voices), who briefly narrate the Gospel story, with brass accompaniment.

The concert opens with a Latin *Magnificat* setting, again alternating brass and solo voices, but sounding more like a secular madrigal than a religious celebration. The *madrigal spirituel, Ach, Herr, du Schöpfer aller Ding,* is also sung slowly and serenely. The excerpts from the *Symphoniae sacrae,* too, might again have been more spirited, although the closing concerted number from the *Psalmen Davids* is livelier. The actual singing here is of a high standard, and the brass-playing is superb, but one feels that the music-making could have been more eloquently extrovert. The recording is excellent, but only texts and no translations are provided. A fascinating disc, just the same.

Sinfonae Sacrae, Op. 6/2–13, 15, 17–19, SWV 258–269, 271, & 273–5.

⊕➔ (BB) ★★★ Warner Apex 2564 61143-2. Dietschy, Bellamy, Lurens, Zaepfel, Elwes, Guy de Mey, Fabre-Garrus, Les Saqueboutiers de Toulouse.

Schütz's 20 *Sinfoniae Sacrae* of 1629 (of which 16 are included here) are the result of the Dresden composer's second visit to Italy in 1628, when he was strongly influenced by Monteverdi and the Italian *concertato* style. These pieces fascinatingly combine voices and instruments in a single texture, usually with an interweaving interplay, and rarely with the instruments acting just as an obbligato. The performances are eminently stylish and freshly spontaneous, and the instrumentalists are expert – and, moreover, they play in tune. The balance is beautifully judged, with voices and instruments within the same perspective, and the recording is wholly realistic.

SCOTT, Cyril (1879–1970)

(i) *Piano Concerto No. 2; Neptune (Poem of the Sea);* (ii) *Symphony No. 3 (The Muses).*

★★★ Chan. 10211. BBC PO, Brabbins; with (i) Shelley; (ii) Huddersfield Ch. Soc.

It is good to have at last a really representative disc of Cyril Scott's major orchestral works. The *Piano Concerto* has been recorded before (by John Ogdon for

Lyrita in 1975), but the present performance by Howard Shelley is every bit as convincing and is certainly compelling. Although it has undoubted atmosphere, its shifting moods and rhapsodic chromaticism will not be to all tastes. The interplay between soloist and orchestra is not a clearly determined dialogue (it is rather like a baroque ritornello concerto, where soloist and accompanist play alternating passages). In the first movement, tempi fluctuate and there is a curious passage marked *Nobilmente tranquillo*, yet the nobilmente is elusive. After the brief slow movement (*Tranquillo pastoral*) the finale brings more contrasting episodes and, because of this, its *energico* easily dissipates.

The *Symphony No. 3*, subtitled *The Muses*, is not very coherent in symphonic terms either, although it has four clearly defined movements, devoted to 'Epic Poetry and Tragedy', 'Comedy and Merry Verse', 'Love and Poetry' and, finally, the 'Muse of Dance and Song'. It is scored for a huge orchestra, including a large percussion section with a wind machine, and in the finale a vocalising choir. The broad-spanned, powerfully dramatic first movement, although it opens gently on four muted violins, soon expands into a vast and complex score, with distinct reminders not only of Debussy's *La Mer* but also of Ravel's *Daphnis et Chloé*. The Scherzo becomes more like a bacchanale and the spirit of its title seems evasive. The slow movement is even more enigmatic, its melodic lines elusive, suggesting that love too is elusive. The finale opens dramatically with pounding timpani, and the spirit of the dance is orgiastic, the chorus becoming wilder and wilder, like the wailing of dervishes. But the movement reaches a positive if brief conclusion on a triumphant C major, and the listener is left breathless.

Undoubtedly the most succesful work here is *Neptune* (*Poem of the Sea*). Here the constantly changing moods and tempi certainly evoke the restless ocean. No specific programme is intended, though the original plan was to descibe the *Titanic* disaster pictorially. In response to criticism, Scott removed almost all the tangibly descriptive passages. Perhaps this is a pity, but the present work remains very evocative, and it is more cohesive than its two companions. It still depicts a central storm sequence and, after a despondent passage for three bassoons, the work ends with an elegiac lament, the sea now once again calm, creating a mood of twilight brooding.

The performances are very fine, Chandos has provided its most spectacular sound and, for all its diffuseness of ideas, Scott's music undoubtedly has a haunting quality which makes one want to return to it.

SCRIABIN, Alexander (1872–1915)

(i) *Piano Concerto in F sharp min., Op. 20. Poème de l'extase, Op. 54.* (i; ii) *Prometheus (Le Poème du feu), Op. 60. Rêverie, Op. 24. Symphonies Nos.* (ii; iii) *1, Op. 26. 2; 3 (Le Divin Poème).*

(M) **(*) Decca Trio 473 971-2 (3). Deutsches SO, Berlin, Ashkenazy; with (i) Jablonski; (ii) Berlin R. Ch.; (iii) Balleys, Larin.

(i) *Piano Concerto in F sharp min., Op. 20; Le Poème de l'extase, Op. 54;* (i; ii) *Prometheus.*

** DG (IMS) 459 647-2. (i) Ugorski; (ii) Chicago Symphony Ch.; Chicago SO, Boulez.

Ashkenazy's set of the Scriabin *Symphonies* is also available on a Double Decca, together with his highly charged Berlin Radio version of the *Poème de l'extase* (460 299-2). They are beautifully recorded; the performances shimmer with sensuality, but are lacking in the last degree of dramatic intensity. The same comments apply here to the *Piano Concerto*, in which Jablonski is a sympathetic if rather self-effacing soloist (he is not very forwardly balanced). Nevertheless he and Ashkenazy find plenty of romantic poetry in the music, especially in the slow movement, and with such good sound this is certainly enjoyable.

However Ashkenazy's earlier performances of the *Concerto* and *Prometheus* (in which he takes the solo piano role) are finer still, and for the symphonies first choice rests with Muti's mid-priced EMI set (5 67720-2).

Boulez's second recording of *Le Poème de l'extase* is short on ecstasy and not too strong on poetry either; ultimately it is analytical and detached. Boulez does restrain Anatole Ugorski's propensity to pull things out of shape, and both the *Piano Concerto* and *Prometheus* receive straightforward and at times elegant performances with excellent recorded sound. All the same, this is not a first choice for any of these pieces.

Le Poème de l'extase.

*** Naïve V 4946. O Nat. de France, Svetlanov – DEBUSSY: *La Mer.* ***

An impressive memento of Svetlanov's last visit to Paris. He has, of course, recorded the *Poème de l'extase* commercially with the USSR Symphony Orchestra for Melodiya, and a 1968 performance at the Proms with the same orchestra has appeared on the BBC 'Legends' label (see our main volume, p.1196) coupled with Rimsky's *Scheherazade*. If anything, this is even finer, for he seems to have established an excellent rapport with this great French orchestra, and he casts a powerful spell. A fine account, which comes with a no less atmospheric *La Mer.* Very good recorded sound.

Symphony No. 3 (Le Divin Poème); Le Poème de l'extase.

(M) ** Warner Elatus 2564 60812-2. O de Paris, Barenboim.

Barenboim's performances were recorded live at the Salle Pleyel, Paris, in 1986 and 1987. The *Symphony* sprawls in his hands and is far from a first choice, although the Orchestre de Paris plays with evident relish. The *Poème de l'extase* is much more successful, a ripely atmospheric reading emphasizing the composer's debt to Wagner, and to *Tristan* in particular. The orchestra produces warm, well-integrated textures, and that is stressed by the mellow, slighty recessed quality of the recording.

PIANO MUSIC

Piano Sonatas Nos. 1–10; Piano Sonata in E flat min. (1887–9); Sonata fantaisie in G sharp min.
(B) **(*) DG Trio 477 049-2 (3). Szidon.

Roberto Szidon recorded all ten *Sonatas* as well as the two early *Sonatas* and the Op. 28 *Fantasy* in 1971, and this DG Trio offers the whole set at bargain price. Szidon seems especially at home in the later works. His version of the *Black Mass Sonata* (No. 9) fares best and conveys real excitement. At its new price this is an attractive reissue and can be considered alongside Ashkenazy, who only offers the basic ten works (Decca 452 961-2), and John Ogdon, who offers extra music (EMI 5 72652-2). But first choice rests with Marc-André Hamlin on Hyperion (CDA 67121/2), who commands the feverish intensity that Scriabin must have.

Piano Sonata No. 5 in F sharp, Op. 53.
(BB) *(*) Warner Apex 0927 40830-2. Sultanov –
  PROKOFIEV: *Piano Sonata No. 7*;
  RACHMANINOV: *Piano Sonata No. 2.* *(*)

Alexei Sultanov has great brilliance and a formidable technical address, which is heard to considerable effect here. But the concentration is largely on virtuosity, dazzle and gloss.

SCULTHORPE, Peter (born 1929)

Piano Concerto.
**(*) Australian ABC Eloquence 426 483-2. Fogg, Melbourne SO, Fredman – EDWARDS: *Piano Concerto* **(*); WILLIAMSON: *Concerto for 2 Pianos* **(*).

In many ways, Sculthorpe's *Piano Concerto* is the most difficult of the three works to get to grips with on this Australian Eloquence CD. Written during a very sad time in the composer's life, its mood reflects that. It is not a virtuosic showpiece for the pianist, but stands as an interesting modern concerto that repays listening. The performance here is excellent and the recording acceptable.

SEGERSTAM, Leif (born 1944)

Symphonies Nos. (i) 21 (September; Visions at Korpijärvi); (ii) 23 (Afterthoughts, Questioning Questionings).
**(*) Ondine ODE 928-2. (i) Finnish RSO; (ii)

Tampere PO (both without conductor).

There are some refined and sensitive touches in the course of these shapeless and sprawling pieces. They seem more like the improvisational sketches a composer makes prior to composition than the finished work of art. There is no feeling of a distinctive musical personality. The heavily scored and seemingly interminable tutti subdue and overpower the listener but the overall impact is underwhelming. Very good performances and excellent recording. If you try these pieces, you may like them more than we do.

SEIBER, Mátyás (1905–60)

String Quartet No. 3 (Quartetto lirico).
(M) (***) EMI mono 5 85150-2. (i) Amadeus Qt –
  TIPPETT: *String Quartet No. 2, etc.* (***)

Hungarian composer Matyas Seiber's *Third String Quartet* was completed in 1951 and dedicated to the Amadeus Quartet, who recorded this performance in 1954. It employs serial technique, with plenty of glissandi and *sul ponticello*, and if this style will not be to all tastes the music obviously springs from intense emotion, although it is the Tippett *String Quartet No. 2* on this CD which communicates more readily. This performance is a very good one indeed, and one enjoys the often very beautiful sounds for their own sake. The recording is astonishingly rich and full, with virtually no background noise at all.

SEIXAS, Carlos de (1704–42)

Harpsichord Concerto in A; Sinfonia in B flat; Keyboard Sonatas Nos. 1, 16, 32–3, 42, 46–7, 57, 71 & 79.
*** Virgin 5 45114-2. Haugsand, Norwegian Bar. O.

The Portuguese composer Carlos de Seixas is revealed here as having a distinct musical personality, and the jolly outer movements of his *A major Concerto* – separated by only a brief Adagio – are enjoyably spirited in the hands of Ketil Haugsand, who also conducts the excellent period orchestral group. The *Sinfonia* is essentially an Italian overture with a fast closing minuet, and the *Keyboard Sonatas* also show Italian influences. The earlier works are in a single movement, but the last three are more ambitious. This is not great music but always inventive and very personable, and it is effectively presented here and very well recorded.

SEREBRIER, José (born 1938)

(i) *Partita (Symphony No. 2); Fantasia; Winterreise;*
(ii) *Sonata for Solo Violin.*
*** Reference RR 90 CD. (i) LPO, composer; (ii) Acosta.

The *Partita* (or *Symphony No. 2*) is attractive and its exuberant finale sparkles with Latin-American dance rhythms. The *Fantasia for Strings* convincingly combines energy with lyricism, while *Winterreise* titillates the listener's memory by ingeniously quoting, not from Schubert, but from seasonal inspirations of Haydn, Glazunov and Tchaikovsky's *Winter Daydreams Symphony*, using all three snippets together, plus the *Dies irae* at the climax. The *Solo Violin Sonata* is unashamedly romantic and very well played, as are the orchestral works under the composer. An enterprising and worthwhile issue.

SÉVERAC, Déodat de (1872–1921)

Cerdaña (5 Etudes pittoresques pour le piano); En Languedoc.

☙— (BB) ✶✶✶ Naxos 8.555855. Masó.

Aldo Ciccolini's set of Déodat de Severac's music has much to commend it (EMI 5 72372-2 – see our main volume), but three CDs may be too many for some collectors. Jordi Masó's lucid and sensitive accounts will make an excellent introduction to this delightful composer. His playing is finely characterized and there is a subtle use of keyboard colour. Good sound, too.

SGAMBATI, Giovanni (1841–1914)

Piano Concerto in G min., Op. 15; Overture Cola di Rienzo; Berceuse-rêverie, Op. 42/2 (orch. Massenet).
✶✶✶ ASV CDDCA 1097. Caramiello, Nuremberg PO, Ventura.

Giovanni Sgambati grew up in Rome as a musical prodigy. But from his earliest years he was not interested in Italian opera, his tastes turning instead to the music of the nineteenth-century German masters. He conducted the first Italian performances of the *Eroica Symphony* and *Emperor Concerto*, and in 1886 premièred Liszt's *Dante Symphony*. All these influences can be found in his music, yet he was his own man, and his *Piano Concerto* is a real find, genuinely inspired, with the solo part marvellously conceived to work in harness with the orchestra, both heroically and poetically. The concerto opens not with a grand gesture, but evocatively and thoughtfully, and a little forlornly. The piano entry is bold and strong, but soon slips into the lyrical secondary material, which it decorates with brilliant roulades. The movement is on the largest scale and produces continuous rhapsodical mood changes, a remarkable variety of invention and orchestral re-colourings, always holding the listener by its flowing spontaneity and structural security. Schumann and Brahms hover over the remaining two movements. The *Andante* is like an intermezzo, at first hesitant, but soloist and woodwind soon enter into a gentle romantic dialogue. The finale opens on the brass and soon galumphs away

with a syncopated theme, but with underlying lyrical warmth to counter the coruscating brilliance of the solo writing. Altogether it is a splendid work, and it could hardly be played with more confidence and understanding than it is here by Francesco Caramiello in his excellent Nuremberg orchestral partnership with Fabrizio Ventura.

It is they who then give a completely convincing account of the Lisztian symphonic poem, which is designated the *Cola di Rienzo Overture*. One of the composer's earliest works, written in 1866, it opens with appealingly romantic melodic evocation and proceeds to describe an undocumented narrative, often excitingly, sometimes melodramatically, but with lovely orchestral colouring and powerful expressive feeling. The closing section is quite haunting. The delightful *Berceuse-Rêverie*, originally a piano piece, but lusciously scored by Massenet, makes a delightful closing lollipop. With first-class recording, this disc is really worth exploring; the concerto is as fine as any in Hyperion's 'Romantic Piano Concerto' series.

SHCHEDRIN, Rodion (born 1932)

Piano Concerto No. 2.
✶✶✶ Hyp. **SACD**: SACDA 67425; CD: CDA 67425. Hamelin, BBC Scottish SO, Litton –
SHOSTAKOVICH: *Piano Concertos Nos. 1–2.* ✶✶✶

The *First* of Shchedrin's concertos was a graduation piece from 1954, very much in the Kabalevsky or Khachaturian mould. In the *Second Concerto* in 1966, Shchedrin experimented with 12-note technique and jazz. It teems with energy and there is some pretty angular keyboard writing, though much of the activity seems to be to little purpose. Shchedrin himself recorded it with Svetlanov in the late 1970s, but this newcomer supersedes it in sheer virtuosity and panache, not to mention the clarity and presence of the Hyperion recording.

SHEBALIN, Vissarion (1902–63)

(i) *Concertino for Violin & Orchestra, Op. 14/1;* (ii) *Concertino for Horn & Orchestra, Op. 14/2;* (iii) *Sinfonietta on Russian Folk Themes, Op. 43;* (iv) *Symphony No. 5, Op. 56.*
✶✶ Olympia stereo/mono OCD 599. (i) Shulgin, USSR Academic SO Ens., Provatorov; (ii) Afanasiev, USSR R. and TV SO, Anosov; (iii) USSR R. and TV SO, Gauk; (iv) USSR State SO, Svetlanov.

The most important work here is the well-structured and finely crafted *Fifth Symphony*, composed in the last year of Shebalin's life. It is well worth investigating, though Shebalin's is not a strongly individual voice, even if his music is cultured and thoughtful. Svetlanov's is a live performance from 1963, recorded in mono. The two Op. 14 *Concertinos* come from the turn of the 1920s and 1930s and reflect the more outward-looking spirit of Soviet music at the time – there are reminders of Hindemith and contemporary French music. These are both stereo recordings, well played, though the solo horn has an obtrusive rubato. The horns produce a pretty blowsy sonority in the *Sinfonietta*, here heard in a 1954 mono recording. Composed in 1949-51, it is a perfunctory, second-rate piece. An interesting issue just the same.

SHOSTAKOVICH, Dmitri
(1906–75)

Cello Concerto No. 1 in E flat, Op. 109.

🎗 (M) (★★★) BBC Legends mono BBCL 4143-2.
   Rostropovich, Leningrad PO, Rozhdestvensky –
   TCHAIKOVSKY: *Symphony No. 4.* (★★★)

Rostropovich's recording of the *Cello Concerto* with Ormandy and the Philadelphia Orchestra was 'rush-released' by CBS and appeared only a few days before this live performance introduced the score to the concert hall in the UK. The recording comes from the Usher Hall during the 1960 Edinburgh Festival and has all the power and authority of the commercial recording plus the additional excitement of what was obviously an important musical occasion.

The Times 'special Correspondent', whose by-line disguised the identity of William Mann, is quoted by the notes as saying that 'Rostropovich's tone has to be heard to be believed, so mighty is its strength, so richly varied its colour, and so beautiful its quality throughout its range. His technique is that of the effortless kind that enables him to carry out every feat of bowing, chording or violin-like dexterity with thought not for the means but only the artistic end' – and the virtuosity and tonal homogeneity of the Leningrad Philharmonic is astonishing. An exceptionally compelling musical document, coupled with an equally high-voltage account of Tchaikovsky's *Fourth Symphony*, given 11 years later at the Royal Albert Hall.

(i) *Cello Concerto No. 2; Symphony No. 12 (The Year 1917), Op. 112.*

★★ Chan. 9585. (i) Helmerson; Russian State SO, Polyansky.

This fine Swedish cellist plays with eloquence and authority in the *Second Cello Concerto* but the orchestral response is a little disappointing. Moreover, the *Twelfth Symphony* calls for the advocacy of an outsize personality if it is to make a really positive impression.

Piano Concerto No. 1 for Piano, Trumpet & Strings, Op. 35.

★★★ EMI 5 56760-2. Andsnes, Hardenberger. CBSO, Järvi (with BRITTEN: *Piano Concerto*; ENESCU: *Legend for Trumpet and Piano* ★★★).

(★★★) British Music Society mono BMS 101 CDH.

Mewton-Wood, Sevenstern, Concert Hall O, Goehr – BLISS: *Concerto* (★★★) ✹; STRAVINSKY: *Concerto for Piano and Wind.* (★★★)

The Britten coupling of Andsnes's recording was discussed in our main volume, but the Shostakovich review was inadvertently omitted. This performance with Håkan Hardenberger and the CBSO under Paavo Järvi comes from a live concert and has virtuosity and poetry, and it is very well recorded indeed. Its couplings are particularly valuable, too, and for those wanting the *First Concerto* alone this is a prime choice. Marc-André Hamelin's new Hyperion disc (see below) is a formidable challenger, but Hardenberger is the more subtle and aristocratic trumpeter, as one can hear also in the Enescu *Legend*.

The Shostakovich concerto was the last commercial recording made by Noel Mewton-Wood, in 1953, and the sound is the finest of the three concertos reissued on this British Music Society CD, the orchestral strings lustrous in the delicately romantic *Largo*, warm and full in the *Moderato* and with plenty of bite in the outer movements, with Harry Sevenstern's crisply articulated trumpet-playing cleanly caught. The performance is full of wit, gently ironic in the first movement, sharply brilliant in the dazzlingly played finale.

Piano Concerto Nos. (i) 1 for Piano, Trumpet & Strings in C min., Op. 35. 2 in F, Op. 102.

🎗 ★★★ Hyp. **SACD**: SACDA 67425; CD: CDA 67425.
   Hamelin, (i) O'Keeffe; BBC Scottish SO, Litton –
   SHCHEDRIN: *Piano Concerto No. 2.* ★★★

Marc-André Hamelin gives a vibrant, superbly articulate and dazzling account of both *Concertos*. These are stunning performances, which fully deserve the plaudits that have been showered on them. The listener is on the edge of the seat throughout, with both poetic insights and the right kind of excitement. Both works are splendidly characterized, though the trumpeter really rather overdoes things in the 'Poor Jenny is a Weeping' section of the finale. The recording, made in the Caird Hall, Dundee, is in the demonstration class. There is no better version of the two piano concertos coupled together on the market.

Piano Concertos: Nos. (i) 1 for Piano, Trumpet & Strings in C min., Op. 35; (ii) 2 in F, Op. 102. 3 Fantastic Dances, Op. 5; Preludes and Fugues, Op. 87 Nos. 1 in C; 4 in E min.; 5 in D; 23 in F; 24 in D min.

(M) (★★(★)) EMI mono 5 62646-2 [5 62648-2].
   Composer, with (i) Vaillant; (ii) O DE L'ORTF, Cluytens.

Shostakovich made his mono recordings of the two piano concertos and the solo piano pieces in Paris in 1958. In his youth he was an accomplished player and was good enough to enter the first Warsaw Piano Competition in 1924, though he did not gain a prize. By the time he made these recordings his keyboard prowess had passed its peak and he did not play very much in public. Despite intensive practice he was not totally in command (he was experiencing a mysterious and debilitating weakness of the right hand – as well as his usual nerves), but the performances are still valuable in giving an authoritative idea of his own conception of his music. He gets a supportive accompaniment from Cluytens and the French National Radio Orchestra. The concertos appeared in EMI's 'Composer as Performer' series but, if memory does not deceive, the mono sound is improved in Simon Gibson's new transfer for the 'Great Recordings of the Century'.

Piano Concerto No. 2 in F, Op. 102.

(BB) *** EMI Encore (ADD) 5 74991-2. Ogdon, RPO, Foster – BARTOK: Piano Concerto No. 3, etc. **(*)

John Ogdon, at the height of his powers, gives a splendidly idiomatic account of this concerto written originally for Shostakovich's son, Maxim. The playing is full of character, the outer movements striking for their wit and dash, and the beautiful slow movement richly romantic without being sentimentalized. This remains one of the finest versions available, and the 1971 sound is excellent.

Violin Concerto No. 1 in A min., Op. 99.

**(*) Simax PSC 1159. Tellefsen, RPO, Berglund – BACH: Violin Concerto No. 2. **(*)

Arve Tellefsen gives a fine account of the concerto and brings fine musicianship and no lack of passion to it. Berglund proves a supportive accompanist and the RPO play well for him. Moreover the sound is very well balanced. But this is not a first choice.

(i) Violin Concerto No. 1 in A min., Op. 99; (ii) 3 Violin Duets.

(M) **(*) EMI (DDD/ADD) 5 62593-2. Perlman, with (i) Israel PO, Mehta; (ii) Pinchas Zukerman – GLAZUNOV: Violin Concerto. **(*)

Perlman's version of the Shostakovich First Violin Concerto was recorded live in the Mann Auditorium in Tel Aviv, and though that involves some roughness in the sound, particularly in tuttis, the flair and electricity of this modern wizard of the violin are more compellingly caught. Excitement is the keynote: Perlman and Mehta put the work in the light of day and, in the two fast movements and the cadenza, that brings tremendous dividends. There is no violinist in the world who can quite match Perlman in sheer bravura, particularly live, and the ovation which greets this dazzling performance of the finale is richly deserved. Yet some of the mystery and fantasy which Russian interpreters have found – from David Oistrakh onwards – is missing, and the close balance of the solo instrument, characteristic of Perlman's concerto recordings, undermines hushed intensity. The three Violin Duets which act as an encore are entertaining trifles (there is a salon piece, a gavotte and some waltzes), all betraying some

measure of wit. They are, of course, marvellously played.

The Limpid Stream (complete ballet; revised Rozhdestvensky).

** Chan. 9423. Stockholm PO, Rozhdestvensky.

Shostakovich's ballet enjoyed much the same fate as Lady Macbeth of the Mtsensk District for, after a successful run of eight months, The Limpid Stream was denounced in Pravda. It is not vintage Shostakovich nor complete, for as presented here it is a revision by Rozhdestvensky. Some of the numbers are familiar from The Bolt, but there is nothing that is as good as, say, the polka from The Age of Gold. Good recording, and the playing is very good if a little wanting in abandon.

(i) Symphony No. 5; (ii) Hamlet (film incidental music), Suite, Op. 116.

⊕– (M) *** RCA (ADD/DDD) 82876 55493-2. (i) LSO, Previn; (ii) Belgian RSO, Serebrier.

Previn's celebrated RCA version, dating from early in his recording career (1965), remains at the top of the list for this often recorded symphony, sounding excellent in this new transfer. This is one of the most concentrated and intense readings ever, superbly played by the LSO at their peak. In the third movement, Previn sustains a slower speed than anyone else, making it deeply meditative in its dark intensity, while the build-up in the central development section brings playing of white heat. The bite and urgency of the second and fourth movements are irresistible. Only in the hint of tape-hiss and a slight lack of opulence in the violins does the sound fall short of the finest modern recordings, but it is more immediate than many more modern versions. The coupling is appropriate. Hamlet obviously generated powerful resonances in Shostakovich's psyche and he produced vivid incidental music: the opening Ball scene is highly reminiscent of Romeo and Juliet. The playing of the Belgian Radio Orchestra under Serebrier is eminently serviceable without being really distinguished but, with an atmospheric recording, this 28-minute suite makes a considerable bonus.

Symphony No. 6, Op. 54; (i) The Execution of Stepan Razin, Op. 119.

** Chan. 9813. Russian State SO, Polyansky; (i) with Lochak, Russian State Symphonic Capella.

Valery Polyansky has given us some splendid things, but his account of the Sixth Symphony does neither him nor Shostakovich full justice. The performance is touched by routine. The Execution of Stepan Razin is given with much greater character, and Polyansky has greater conviction than in the symphony; but although Anatoly Lochak is a fine soloist, memories of Vitaly Gromadsky with Kondrashin in 1966 are not banished.

Symphony No. 10 in E min., Op. 93.

(M) **(*) Elatus 2564 60660-2 Leningrad PO,

Mravinsky (with WAGNER: *Tristan: Prelude and Liebestod* ★★(★)).

Mravinsky conducted the work's première. His Erato recording was made at a 1976 concert performance and it has no want of intensity or power. The recording is less than ideal, but this is a performance to reckon with, and the Wagner bonus (also recorded live, two years later) also rises to a passionate climax.

Symphony No. 11 (The Year 1905), Op. 103.
(M) ★★ Warner Elatus 2564 60443-2. Nat. SO of Washington, Rostropovich.

There is atmosphere in Rostropovich's account with the Washington orchestra but, as can easily happen in this score, the listener can soon wool-gather if the conductor does not have tremendous grip. The out-of-tune timpani have been commented on elsewhere, but for many this will not be as disturbing as the lack of narrative drive. No challenge here to the finest versions.

Symphony No. 15; (i) *Cello Concerto No. 1.*
★(★) Chan. 9550. (i) Helmerson; Russian State SO, Polyansky.

Valery Polyansky and the Russian State Symphony give a straightforward but ultimately rather undistinguished account of the *Fifteenth Symphony*. The slow movement in particular is lacking in atmosphere. In the *First Cello Concerto*, the distinguished Swedish soloist plays well, but ensemble is not impeccable.

CHAMBER MUSIC

(i) *Cello Sonata in D min., Op. 40; Moderato* for cello & piano; (ii) *Piano Quintet;* (iii) *2 Pieces.*
☉➔ (BB) ★★★ Double Decca 473 807-2 (2). (i) Harrell; (i; ii) Ashkenazy; (ii; iii) Fitzwilliam Qt –
PROKOFIEV: *Cello Sonata;* RACHMANINOV: *Cello Sonata,* etc. ★★★

Lynn Harrell and Vladimir Ashkenazy give a convincing account of the *Cello Sonata*, though they slow down rather a lot for the second group of the first movement. All the same, their brisk tempo and their freedom from affectation are refreshing. The short *Moderato* for cello and piano was discovered in the Moscow State Archives only in the 1980s; it could at some stage have been intended for the *Sonata* itself, though its brevity and its quality make one doubtful. The *Piano Quintet*, with Ashkenazy and the Fitzwilliam Quartet, cannot be seriously faulted and withstands comparison with the illustrious Richter and Borodin Quartet version, and the recording is superb. With the highly attractive *Two Pieces* – the first mysteriously haunting, the second delightfully quirky – also included, this set, with its excellent couplings, is an undoubted bargain.

Piano Quintet in G min., Op. 57; Piano Trio No. 2 in E min., Op. 67.
☉➔ (M) ★★★ Warner Elatus 2564 60813-2. Leonskaja, Borodin Qt.

Previously paired on Ultima with the last *String Quartet*, Op. 144, these inspired performances (reviewed in our main volume) can be cordially welcomed as a separate issue.

Piano Trios Nos. 1, Op. 8; 2 in E min., Op. 67; (i) *7 Romances to Poems by Alexander Blok, Op. 127.*
★(★) Orfeo C465 991A. Munich Piano Trio; (i) Ablaberdyeva.

Although obviously a highly accomplished ensemble, the Munich Piano Trio do not convey much of the atmosphere of the eerily enigmatic and powerful *E minor Trio*, Op. 67, and Alla Ablaberdyeva is not wholly successful in the *Romances to Poems by Alexander Blok*.

String Quartet No. 7 in F sharp min., Op. 108.
(B) ★★★ EMI Début 5 85638-2. Atrium Qt – MOZART: *String Quartet No. 15;* TCHAIKOVSKY: *String Quartet No. 3.* ★★★

The *Seventh Quartet* serves as a visiting card for the young Atrium String Quartet from St Petersburg. They were the prize-winners of the 2003 London International String Quartet and were coached by Iosif Levinzon, the cellist of the Taneyev Quartet. Their programme is intelligently chosen, not just as a vehicle for their artistry, but as repertoire useful for the collector. Despite its brevity (it lasts some 13 minutes) the Shostakovich is a work of both substance and concentration, and the Atrium play it as well as any in the catalogue – no mean compliment when you look at the competition. They make a beautiful sound, and the EMI team captures it with distinction.

Viola Sonata.
★(★) Olympia OCD 625. Bashmet, Richter (with BRITTEN: *Lachrymae*) – HINDEMITH: *Viola Sonata.* ★(★)

A partnership between Bashmet and Richter that excites the highest expectations in this repertoire proves disappointing. Recorded live in Germany in 1985, the forward balance and unpleasant acoustic rob this record of much of its value. The sound is too close and hard.

19 Preludes, from Op. 34 (arr. Tikanov for violin & piano).
★★(★) Avie AV0023. Gleusteen, Ordronneau – JANACEK: *Violin Sonata;* PROKOFIEV: *Violin Sonata No. 1.* ★★(★)

The transcription of Shostakovich's *Preludes* for violin and piano works surprisingly well in this mixed bag of Slavonic works. The composer himself gave full approval to this arrangement of his original piano versions, readily persuaded by his friend, Dmitri Tikanov, a violinist as well as a composer. Tikanov was leader of the Beethoven Quartet for over half a century, the group that gave the first performances of all but the last of the Shostakovich Quartets. He chose 19 out of the *24 Preludes*, putting them in a different order and concentrating on those that were the most melodic. The result is that, though the violin versions bring out the lyrical element more clearly, they sound less sharply original, if still very characteristic of Shostakovich. Kai Gleusteen plays them with obvious love, giving extra power to some of the more dramatic preludes.

Preludes and Fugues, Op. 87/1–9, 12, 15–17 & 19 (arr. Alban Wesly).
**(*) MDG 619 1185. Calefax Reed Quintet.

The *Preludes and Fugues* are intelligently arranged, most expertly played and superbly recorded. The Calefax give us 14 (just over half) of the set, omitting those that are too pianistic. Readers should turn first and foremost to Tatiana Nikolaeva in this repertoire (Regis RRC 3005 – see our main volume) though there are other highly desirable alternatives. This does not strike us as one of them. This will doubtless attract some wind enthusiasts, but it is of somewhat specialist and limited appeal.

PIANO MUSIC

Aphorisms, Op. 13; 3 Fantastic Dances, Op. 5; Lyric Waltz (from *Dances of the Dolls*); *Nocturne* (from *The Limpid Stream*); *Piano Sonata No. 2, Op. 61; 5 Preludes; Short Piece & Spanish Dance* (from *The Gadfly*).
*** Decca SACD 470 469-2. Ashkenazy.

Although he was an accomplished pianist, Shostakovich wrote comparatively little for his instrument. Apart from the two concertos and the music on the present disc, there are only the *First Sonata*, the *Preludes*, Op. 34, and the Op. 87 *Preludes and Fugues*. Vladimir Ashkenazy is a trusted guide in this repertoire and benefits from outstanding and natural recorded sound. His version of the *Sonata* does not efface memories of the classic Gilels account (or, way back in the days of LP, Menahem Pressler) but, as one would expect, there are none of the affectations of Mustonen's recent Op. 87, to which we have just been listening, but an appropriate dedication to and respect for the composer's intention.

Aphorisms, Op. 13; 3 Fantastic Dances, Op. 5; Piano Sonata No. 1; 24 Preludes, Op. 34.
(BB) *** Naxos 8.555781. Scherbakov.

Beautifully recorded at Potton Hall in Suffolk, Konstantin Scherbakov gives thought-provoking and wonderfully controlled accounts of the Op. 34 *Preludes*. By comparison with Nikolayeva he is at times a little too sophisticated in matters of tonal finesse, and dynamic markings are a shade exaggerated; but this has such imaginative and masterly pianism that readers can afford to overlook the occasional affectation (which we have not encountered in this artist before). He plays the whole recital with the keyboard mastery we associate with him. Strongly recommended.

24 Preludes, Op. 34.
(M) *** Decca 475 212-2. Mustonen – ALKAN: *25 Preludes.* ***

Of the recordings of the Shostakovich *Preludes*, Op. 34, currently available, the Decca record by the Finnish pianist Olli Mustonen is as strong as any, although since this record won its *Gramophone* Instrumental Award in 1992, Hyperion have issued another outstanding set by Tatiana Nikolayeva (CDA 66620 – see our main volume). However, Mustonen scores over his rivals by offering an apt Alkan rarity, the *25 Preludes*, Op. 34, some 47 minutes of highly interesting music, which makes a highly satisfying coupling, very well recorded.

24 Preludes; Piano Sonata No. 2, Op. 61.
** Cyprès CYP 2622. Schmidt.

Johan Schmidt is a young Belgian pianist with good fingers and clean articulation. He is fluent and intelligent but is let down by the synthetic-sounding recording, which is very two-dimensional. The piano is too close and the acoustic dry.

24 Preludes & Fugues, Op. 87: excerpts.
** Ondine ODE 1033-2 (2). Mustonen (piano) – BACH: *Well-Tempered Clavier, Book 1: excerpts.* **

Olli Mustonen intersperses the Shostakovich *Preludes and Fugues* with those of Bach. His playing is impressive, yet we find the result curiously unsatisfying, in that he seems very concerned with personal point-making rather than letting the music speak for itself.

24 Preludes & Fugues, Op. 87, Nos. 2–4, 8–10, 14–16, 20–22.
*(*) RCA 74321 61446-2 (2). Mustonen (with BACH: *Preludes & Fugues* *(*)).

Olli Mustonen has again chosen here a dozen of the Shostakovich Op. 87 set of *Preludes and Fugues* and juxtaposes them with half of *Book I* of the Bach *Well-Tempered Clavier*. The eccentricities – exaggerated staccatos picked from the keyboard – and his narcissistic attention-seeking detract from the half of Shostakovich he does give us.

SIBELIUS, Jean (1865–1957)

Andante festivo for Strings; Canzonetta, Op. 62a; The Dryad, Op. 45/1; Dance Intermezzo, Op. 45/2; In Memoriam, Op. 59; 4 Legends, Op. 22; Pan and Echo, Op. 53a; Romance in C for Strings, Op. 42; Spring Song, Op. 16; Suite Mignon for 2 Flutes & Strings, Op. 98a; Suite champêtre for Strings, Op.

98b; The Tempest: Prelude; Suites Nos. 1 & 2, Op.
109/1–3; Valse romantique, Op. 62b.

(BB) **(*) EMI Gemini (ADD) 5 85532-2 (2). RLPO,
Groves.

This Gemini double draws together the recordings
Sir Charles Groves made of rare Sibelius miniatures
in the early 1970s. Much of this is lightweight Sibelius, but none the worse for that when it is so beautifully played. However, *The Dryad*, which comes from
the same period as the *Fourth Symphony*, is rather
impressive. *Spring Song* is an early piece and not
particularly strong, yet its sonority catches the ear
readily. The two *Suites*, Op. 98 are charming, and so
are the *Canzonetta, Dance Intermezzo* and *Valse
romantique*. The better-known *Romance in C* is most
eloquently played, as is the *Andante festivo*, while *In
Memoriam* has nicely judged gravitas. Always a sympathetic Sibelian, Groves succeeds in generating both
atmosphere and tension in the *Four Legends*, which
are often exciting, even if they could not be considered a primary recommendation. The same comment applies to the music from *The Tempest*. In *The
Oak-tree* and *The Chorus of the Winds* Groves fails to
distil the magic that distinguished Beecham's famous
mono set, but the performances are by no means to
be dismissed. The recording is well balanced and
vividly detailed, and its warmth of sonority is striking, with rich string-textures – some of the recordings were originally made in quadraphony.
Altogether this inexpensive reissue gives considerable
pleasure, not least because of the splendid sound.

Violin Concerto in D, Op. 47.

*** HM Naïve V 4959. Sergey Khachaturian, Sinfonia
Varsovia, Krivine – KHACHATURIAN: *Violin
Concerto*. ***

(M) *** EMI (ADD) 5 62590-2. Perlman, Pittsburgh
SO, Previn – KORNGOLD: *Concerto*; SINDING:
Suite. ***

** Arthaus **DVD** 100 034. Vengerov, Chicago SO,
Barenboim – FALLA: *Nights in the Gardens of
Spain*. ** (Producer: Bernd Hellthaler; V/D Bob
Coles.)

(M) *(*) RCA (ADD) 82876 59419-2. Perlman, Boston
SO, Leinsdorf – TCHAIKOVSKY: *Violin Concerto*.
*(*)

(i; ii) *Violin Concerto in D min., Op. 47; (iii) En
saga, Op. 9; (ii) Finlandia, Op. 26; Karelia Suite,
Op. 11.*

(BB) ** CfP (ADD) 575 5662. (i) Sarbu; (ii) Hallé O,
Schmidt; (iii) RSNO, Gibson.

Sergey Khachaturian comes from a famous Armenian musical family and in 2000 he won first prize in
the Jean Sibelius competition in Helsinki. His
account of the *Concerto*, although opening ethereally,
is full of Slavic feeling, with the slow movement
passionately intense. It is a powerfully spontaneous
performance, very well accompanied by the excellent
Polish Sinfonia Varsovia, and excellently recorded.

The coupling is an outstanding account of the
(underrated) Khachaturian *Violin Concerto*.

Perlman's second (1978) version is now restored to
the catalogue in the 'Perlman Edition'. Here he plays
the work as a full-blooded virtuoso showpiece, and
the Pittsburgh orchestra under Previn support him to
the last man and woman. In the first movement his
tempo is broader than that of Heifetz, and in the rest
of the work he is more expansive than he was on the
earlier record. This new version takes 32 minutes,
whereas the Boston performance took 29 minutes 15
seconds. Perlman is at his stunning best in the first
cadenza and he makes light of the fiendish difficulties
with which the solo part abounds. He takes a conventional view of the slow movement, underlining its
passion, and he gives an exhilarating finale. As usual
with this artist, the balance places him rather forward,
but the sound is marvellously alive, the CD transfer
making the forward balance even more apparent.

A 1997 recording made while the Chicago orchestra and Vengerov were in Germany. Pretty stunning
virtuosity and much *zigeuner* brilliance and glitz,
though much less of the silvery, aristocratic restraint
that is called for in the slow movement. But if you
warm to this glamorous player – and he has a strong
following – this DVD can be recommended. Barenboim accompanies sensitively and Vengerov dashes
off the Bach *Sarabande* from the *D minor Partita* and
the *Third Solo Sonata (Ballade)* of Ysaÿe as encores.

Eugene Sarbu is a Romanian artist who made his
recording of the Sibelius *Concerto* in 1980, when he
was in his early thirties. His vibrato is a little wide
and intonation is not always impeccable though he
has plenty of dash and power. He makes the most of
every expressive point and underlines romantic fervour rather than spirituality. His is a *zigeuner*-like
approach without the purity and refinement of tone
which are ideal – and which emerge in Cho-Liang
Lin and Kyung-Wha Chung. There is a nobility in
this music which Sarbu does not always convey, but
he is well supported by the Hallé, who give Ole
Schmidt sensitive and responsive playing, and they
are heard to great effect in the *Karelia* and *Finlandia*
couplings. Gibson's atmospheric RSNO *En saga*
(recorded in 1974) has been added as a makeweight
for this reissue. Sarbu is a formidable artist and this
vibrant collection is good value.

Perlman's performance on RCA is a good one, but
this reading has neither the character nor the personality of his later, EMI version. The over-bright sound
and the close balance of the soloist don't help matters
either.

*Dance Intermezo, Op. 45/2; The Dryad, Op. 45/1;
Karelia: Overture; King Christian II (suite), Op. 27;
Pan and Echo, Op. 53a; Spring Song, Op. 16; The
Wood-Nymph, Op. 15.*

*(*) Finlandia 0927 49598-2. Kuopio SO, Satu.

Since its first recording in 1996 by Osmo Vänskä and
the Lahti Orchestra, Sibelius's tone-poem *The Wood-*

Nymph (Skogsrået) has had little attention. Sibelius thought sufficiently well of it to programme to conduct it alongside the *First Symphony* in 1899, and it was given again during his seventieth-birthday celebrations in 1935. Although most Sibelians knew of the piece, the autograph long remained undisturbed in Helsinki University Library. Stylistically it inhabits the same world as the *Karelia* music and the *Lemminkäinen Legends*. The middle section has great beauty and is quite unlike anything else in Sibelius's output. It is certainly of greater substance than the *Spring Song (Vårsång)*. The Kuopio Orchestra consists of some 45 musicians, much the same size as the forces Sibelius himself would have had at his disposal at the turn of the century, and Shuntaro Satu gets vigorous and enthusiastic playing from them. But the strings are wanting in body and tonal lustre, and this seriously diminishes pleasure. Readers wanting *The Wood Nymph* are advised to stick with the interestingly coupled BIS disc (BIS CD 815 – see our main volume). Sensitive though these readings are, they do not present a challenge to alternative versions.

(i) *En Saga, Op. 9; Finlandia, Op. 26; Karelia Suite, Op. 11;* (ii) *Legend: The Swan of Tuonela.*

(B) ★★★ Ph. Eloquence 468 201-2 (2). Philh O, Ashkenazy; (ii) ASMF, Marriner – GRIEG: *Holberg Suite* etc. ★★

Ashkenazy's superb (Decca) Sibelius recordings – a fresh-sounding yet exciting *Finlandia*, an impressively evocative *En Saga* and an enjoyably vivid *Karelia Suite* – remain top choices, and the early digital recordings are superb in every way. Marriner's *Swan of Tuonela* is most sensitive, with the cor anglais solo beautifully played by Barry Griffiths. However, the Grieg couplings are not quite so recommendable.

Six Humoresques, Opp. 87 & 89.

★(★) Essay CD 1075. Tenenbaum, Pro Musica Prague, Kapp – GHEDINI: *Violin Concerto,* etc. ★(★)

Sibelius was toying with the idea of a second violin concerto in 1915, and it is not too fanciful to imagine that some of its ideas could have found their way into the two sets of *Humoresques*. They are rarely heard in the concert hall, thanks partly to their dimensions and the technical demands they make. Mela Tenenbaum is no match for the likes of Dong-Suk Kang (BIS CD 472), Aaron Rosand or Accardo (now deleted). She inserts all sorts of little expressive hesitations and does not produce a particularly beautiful sound, though to be fair the close balance and unglamorous studio acoustic do not help her. The liner notes are uninformed on matters Sibelian and are marred by factual errors. Nor are they well written: we learn at one point that Sibelius at the time of the *Humoresques* 'found himself prematurely obsolesced'!

4 Legends, Op. 22; Night Ride and Sunrise, Op. 55.

(M) ★★(★) Warner Elatus 2564 60621-2. Toronto SO, Saraste.

Saraste re-recorded the *Four Legends* in 1998, only six years after his set with the Finnish Radio Orchestra for RCA, and it is reasonable to wonder whether we need his views on this wonderful score again so soon! However, while his 1992 recording was very good, it must be admitted that this Canadian account is better in both the quality of the orchestral playing and the recorded sound. Like Sakari on Naxos, Saraste reverses the order of the two central movements and those who wish to follow Sibelius's wishes have to programme their machines accordingly (tracks 1, 3, 2, 4). No lack of atmosphere all the same, particularly in *Lemminkäinen in Tuonela*, and no want of passion, even if Saraste does not match the urgent momentum and level of excitement in *Lemminkäinen's Homeward Journey* that Beecham, Segerstam or Vänskä achieve, and *Night Rise and Sunset* sounds pedestrian by the side of Sir Colin Davis.

SYMPHONIES

Symphonies Nos. 1–7; (i) *Kullervo. The Bard, Op. 22; Finlandia, Op. 26; Karelia Suite, Op. 11; Kuolema: Valse triste. 4 Legends, Op. 22; Night Ride and Sunrise, Op. 55; The Oceanides, Op. 73; Pohjola's Daughter, Op. 49; Rakastava Tapiola, Op. 112.*

⊶ (B) ★★★ RCA 828 765 5706-2 (7). LSO, Sir Colin Davis.

Symphonies Nos. 1–7.

(M) (★★) Finlandia mono 3984-22713-2 (3). Stockholm PO, Ehrling.

★(★) Finlandia 3984-23389-2 (4). COE, Berglund.

Symphonies Nos. 1–2, 4–5.

(B) ★(★) Finlandia Ultima 0630 18962-2 (2). Finnish RSO, Saraste.

Symphonies Nos. 3; 6–7; (i) *Kullervo Symphony.*

(B) ★★ Finlandia Ultima 3984 21348-2 (2). Finnish RSO, Saraste; (i) with Groop, Hynninen, Polytech Ch.

Sir Colin Davis's set of the *Symphonies* has now been reissued together with his other major LSO recordings of the principal orchestral works. The excellence of the LSO playing is matched by the consistently fine RCA recordings, made in the Blackheath Concert Halls, Watford Town Hall or Walthamstow, between 1992 and 2000. It is a totally authoritative survey, and nearly all the symphonic poems are of a similar calibre, with the magical account of *The Bard, Night Ride and Sunrise, The Oceanides* and a riveting *Tapiola* standing out. A set which should be at the centre of any representative Sibelius collection.

On Finlandia comes the very first survey of the symphonies, which dates from 1952–3 and was conducted by Sixten Ehrling. Their handsome sleeves are reproduced here. (Incidentally, the original LPs speak of the 'Stockholm Radio Symphony Orchestra'.) Sibelius himself is said to have heard and liked them. Ehrling is an admirably sound interpreter. In the first two symphonies the playing has more temperament than polish. In the *Third*, Ehrling – giving the symphony its first recording since the pioneering Kajanus set – is more measured than Collins, who set very brisk tempi in both the first and second movements. The *Fourth* is impressively dark, and in the *Fifth* the transition between the body of the first movement and its Scherzo section is well negotiated. Not a real challenge to Collins, but though it lacks finesse and has some vulnerable wind intonation, it provides an interesting insight into how these symphonies sounded at the time.

Berglund's survey is available not only as a complete set but also broken down into separate formats. Nos. 1–3 are offered together on two discs: 3984-23388-2; Nos. 4 and 6 on 0630 14951-2; and Nos. 5 and 7 on 0630 17278-2. They are the product of an enthusiastic collaboration with the Chamber Orchestra of Europe. Berglund knows this music as intimately as anyone alive. He offers the scores plain and unadorned. There are good things, namely a sober and vigorous *Third* and a finely paced and sensitively moulded *Sixth*, as well as one or two ugly details, such as the ungainly stress he gives to the rhetorical string passage in the first movement of the *Second* (1 minute 35 seconds, five bars before letter B). One has to decide whether these performances, good though they are, convey enough new insights to justify displacing his earlier cycles with the Bournemouth and Helsinki orchestras. Those earlier sets, though they have solid merits, fall short of the ideal in terms of poetic imagination, but the same goes for this new set. In some ways Berglund's very first, 1969 recording of the *Fourth Symphony*, issued in 1973, remains the freshest and most keenly felt of his Sibelius recordings!

The pair of Finlandia Ultima Doubles offers all seven symphonies in performances recorded while the Finnish Radio Symphony Orchestra was in St Petersburg during the summer of 1993. It was only three or four years earlier that Saraste recorded a complete cycle for RCA with the same orchestra. None of these performances seems to mark an advance on that studio set, though at times there is the excitement generated in the concert hall to spice up the music-making. Although there are good things here, including a fine account of the *Fourth*, there is nothing really special, and the *Third Symphony* is hopelessly rushed. However, the second of the two Ultima sets includes the *Kullervo Symphony*, which was the finest performance in the cycle. It has a more urgent sense of movement and a greater dramatic intensity than most of its major competitors, and it has excellent soloists. We hope this will become available separately on Warner's bargain Apex label.

Symphonies Nos. (i) *1–3;* (ii) *4–7.*

(M) **(*) DG Trio ADD 474 353-2 (3). (i) Helsinki R.O or (No. 2) BPO, Okko Kamu; (ii) BPO, Karajan.

As Karajan did not record a complete Sibelius cycle in the 1960s for DG, that company has created the present Trio by ingeniously filling in the missing early works with performances from Okko Kamu recorded in the early 1970s. Alas, the resulting collection is far from ideal, for the account of No. 1 rarely rises above the routine, and in No. 2 Kamu indulges in some impulsive touches – the odd speed-up or slow-down. These are not destructive, and the Berlin Philharmonic provides highly polished and superbly refined playing. The pick of Kamu's three performances is undoubtely the *Third*, which still has strong claims to be considered among the finest on record. Tempi are well judged and the atmosphere is thoroughly authentic, particularly in the slow movement, whose character seems to have eluded so many conductors. The recordings, whether made in Berlin or Helsinki, are excellent and most musically balanced.

When one turns to the last four symphonies, one moves into an inspired Sibelian world, with Karajan securing playing of astonishing tonal beauty and virtuosity from the Berlin Philharmonic and performances of great intensity and power. The most obvious way to acquire them is with the separate DG, mid-priced couplings of Nos. 4 and 7 (439 527-2 – given a ✪ in our companion volume) and 5 and 6 (439 982-2).

Symphonies Nos. 2; 5 in E flat, Op. 82.

(BB) * Warner Apex. 8573 88434-2. Finnish RSO, Saraste.

Saraste's performances are well played and acceptably recorded, but considering these were concert performances there is a remarkable absence of real grip and forward thrust here.

Symphonies Nos. 4 in A min., Op. 63; 6 in D min., Op. 104.

✪ (M) *** DG (ADD) 476 220-2. BPO, Karajan.

Karajan's nearly 40-year-old recording of the *Fourth Symphony* is a performance of real stature, notable for its great concentration and tension. It is coupled with a glorious account of the *Sixth Symphony*, which remains almost unsurpassed among modern versions. Although these recordings do not have quite the range of the very best newer versions, the sound is considerably improved now over earlier releases, and this readily finds its place in Universal's 'Penguin ✪ Collection'.

(i) *Symphony No. 7 in C, Op. 105;* (ii) *Pohjola's Daughter; Swan White: The Maiden with the Roses. Tapiola.*

(BB) (***) Naxos mono 8.110168. (i) BBC SO; (ii) Boston SO; Koussevitzky (with GRIEG: *The Last Spring* (***)).

Koussevitzky's pioneering (1933) recording of the *Seventh Symphony* with the then newly formed BBC Symphony Orchestra has rarely been challenged and never surpassed and, together with his *Pohjola's*

Daughter and *Tapiola* from 1936 and 1939 respectively, is among the classics of recorded music. One critic spoke of the Boston Symphony Orchestra under Koussevitzky as one of the great achievements of Western civilization and, listening to them in these splendid new transfers, this scarcely seems an exaggeration.

CHAMBER MUSIC

(i) Music for Cello & Piano: *Canzonetta, Op. 62a. King Christian II: Elegie. Malinconia, Op. 20; 2 Pieces, Op. 77; 4 Pieces, Op. 78; Romance for Strings in C, Op. 42; Rondino Op. 81/2; Valse romantique, Op. 62b; Valse triste, Op. 44/1.* (ii) Music for Violin & Piano: *Sonatina in E, Op. 80;* (iii) *Berceuse, Op. 79/6; Danse caractéristique, Op. 116/1 & 2. 4 Pieces, Op. 78; 4 Pieces, Op. 81; 4 Pieces, Op. 115; Scène de danse.*

(B) ** Finlandia 0927 41355-2 (2). (i) Sariola, Liu; (ii) Arai, Tateno; (iii) Yaron, Sharon.

Sibelius was of course an accomplished violinist in his youth and never lost his feeling for the instrument. The two CDs here collect performances made in 1976–7 (the first CD) and 1985 in the case of the the second. Most of the violin pieces, with the exception of Opp. 115 and 116, come from the war years, when Sibelius was cut off from the great European orchestras and from his livelihood, namely his royalties from Breitkopf in Leipzig. He wrote a large number of instrumental pieces to generate the income his isolation cost him. In the first decade of the century Breitkopf also published arrangements of some of his smaller orchestral scores (the *Elégie* from *King Christian II* was made by the conductor, Georg Schnéevoigt). Most of the pieces on the second CD played by Raimo Sariola were composed for violin and piano or for violin or cello and piano, and some can be heard in both forms. Although many of these pieces are slight, they are (for the most part) of quality and are presented as such.

Malinconia, Op. 20; 2 Pieces, Op. 77; 4 Pieces, Op. 78.

(B) ** Virgin 5 62203-2. Mørk, Thibaudet – GRIEG: *Cello Sonata in A min.*, etc. **

Like Grieg, Sibelius also had a cello-playing brother, which is probably why the Opp. 77 and 78 pieces for violin and piano are marked as playable by the cello. *Malinconia* was written for the cellist and conductor Georg Schnéevoigt and his wife Sigrid, and is emphatically not top-drawer Sibelius. Truls Mørk and Jean-Yves Thibaudet play these pieces well enough, but the balance is unsatisfactory and favours the pianist excessively, with the result that Mørk's tone sounds very small.

Piano Trios in A min.; in A min. (Hafträsk); in G for 2 Violins & Piano; Piano Trio movements: Allegro in C; Andantino in A; Allegro in D; Andante –

Adagio – Allegro maestoso; Minuet in D min.; Minuet in F for 2 Violins & Piano; Moderato in A min.

*** BIS CD 1282. Kuusisto, Vänskä, Ylönen. Gräsbeck.

All these pieces are still unpublished and the autographs are in Helsinki University Library. All are new to the catalogue and will naturally be of keen interest to Sibelians. They were all composed in Sibelius's late teens, before he began his formal studies in Helsinki with Wegelius. In his study of Sibelius's juvenilia John Rosas quotes Sibelius's secretary, Santeri Levas, as saying that in all his correspondence with the Sibelius Museum in Turku (Åbo), the composer was at pains to emphasize that these chamber works were *neither to be published nor performed – even after his death!* This CD brings to the attention of the wider musical public music that has been available heretofore only to scholars. The opening of the family vaults has revealed the full extent of the composer's early activity, which finds him flexing his creative muscles in the shadow of the Viennese masters. The earliest work is the *G major Trio* for two violins and piano, a fluent and attractive piece, which reflects Sibelius's own youthful experience as a player. As always, the writing is well schooled though the ideas give scant indication of what was to come. Perhaps the most striking work is the *A minor Trio* of 1884, whose provenance Folke Gräsbeck explores in his well-researched notes. It owes something to Haydn in its layout, and its *Trio* has distinctly rustic accents. The *Andantino in A major* of 1886 is a rather lovely piece, too. No one would make exaggerated claims for these pieces, some of which have scant merit; but to observe the composer's complete ban on them would have deprived us of the opportunity of hearing at first hand the extraordinary transformation of Sibelius's talent into genius only a half a dozen years later. The performances are alert and intelligent and the recording exemplary and wonderfully present.

Piano Trios in D (Korpo) (1887); *in C, (Lovisa). Alla Marcia in C; Andantino in G min.; Allegretto in A flat; Allegro in D min. (completed Aho); Allegretto in E flat (completed Kuusisto).*

*** BIS CD 1292. Kuusisto, Ylönen, Gräsbeck.

The second volume of music for piano trio covers the period 1887–95 and thus follows chronologically on the first. Together they represent Sibelius's complete output in this medium for, although he never returned to it in later life, the piano trio was almost his favourite chamber form in the 1880s. The 'Lovisa' *Trio*, so called because it was written in the family summer home in Lovisa, is available in two alternative versions, but otherwise this music is all new. The 'Korpo' *Trio* (1887) is by far the most substantial piece here running to over 35 minutes. Korpo is an island in the southwest archipelago of Finland, and the estate on which the manor house (designed by Charles Bassi and reproduced on the sleeve) is where Sibelius composed his *Trio*. Few coming to it with innocent ears would guess the identity of the composer but it evinces a natural feeling for form. There are other rarities too, some of which are in fragmentary form. The most engaging is the *March in C major*, which almost calls to mind the Saint-Saëns of the *Carnival of the Animals*! Expert performances.

String Quartet in D min. (Voces intimae), Op. 56.
**(*) HM HMA 1951671. Melos Qt – VERDI: *String Quartet*. **(*)

The Melos Quartet give an impeccably well-turned-out performance of *Voces intimae* and one which will give satisfaction to their admirers. It does not displace the New Helsinki Quartet (Finlandia 0927 40872-2) – and briefly returning to it, we were reminded of how the famous Budapest version of 1933 remains incomparable (Bidduph LAB 098). The recording is very truthful but (at 50 minutes or so) the issue is short measure, given its price-tag.

PIANO MUSIC

10 Bagatelles, Op. 34; Barcarole, Op. 24/10; Esquisses, Op. 114; Kyllikki, Op. 41; 5 Pieces, Op. 75; Piano transcriptions: Finlandia, Op. 26; Valse triste, Op. 44/1.
(***) Ondine ODE 847-2. Gothoni.

Gothoni makes the most of every expressive gesture and every gradation of keyboard colour, without indulging in any exaggeration. These performances make out a stronger case for Sibelius's piano music than almost any other. Unfortunately, they are badly let down by the recording, which is reverberant and clangorous; the piano itself hardly sounds in ideal shape. A pity about the sound.

VOCAL MUSIC

Finlandia (version for orchestra and mixed chorus); Homeland (Oma maa), Op. 92; Impromptu, Op. 19; (i) Snöfrid, Op. 29; Song to the Earth (Maan virsi), Op. 95; Song to Lemminkäinen, Op. 31; Väinö's Song, Op. 110.
** Ondine ODE 754-2. (i) Rautelin (reciter); Finnish Nat. Op. Ch. & O, Klas.

While most of Sibelius's songs are to Swedish texts, the choral music is predominantly Finnish. *Oma maa* ('Homeland') is a dignified and euphonious work and includes a magical evocation of the wintry nights with aurora borealis and the white nights of midsummer. *Väinö's Song* is an appealing piece which bears an opus number between those for *The Tempest* and *Tapiola* – though it is not really fit to keep them company. The performances and the recording are decent rather than distinguished.

Songs

Complete Songs: 5 Christmas Songs, Op. 1; Arioso, Op. 3; 5 Songs of Runeberg, Op. 13; 7 Songs, Op. 17; Jubal, Teodora, Op. 35; 6 Songs, Op. 36; 5 Songs, Op. 37; 5 Songs, Op. 38; 6 Songs, Op. 50; 8 Songs of Josephson, Op. 57; 4 Songs, Op. 72; 6 Songs, Op. 86; 6 Songs of Runeberg, Op. 90; Serenade (1888); Segelfahrt (1899); Souda, souda, sinisorsa (1899); Hymn to Thaïs (1900); Erloschen (1906); Narcissen (1918); Små flickorna (1920); King Christian II, Op. 27; Serenade to the Fool. Pelléas et Mélisande, Op. 46; Les Trois Soeurs aveugles. Two Songs from 'Twelfth Night', Op. 60.
⊕–➤ ✿ (M) *** Decca (ADD) 476 17259 (4). Söderström, Krause, Ashkenazy or Gage; Bonell (guitar).

Many of these songs had never been recorded before this collection arrived and won the 1985 *Gramophone* Solo Vocal Award. Sibelius the symphonist has, understandably enough, overshadowed the achievement of the song composer. Indeed, in the past his songs have been written off by many music-lovers whose knowledge of them does not extend far beyond the popular handful: *Black Roses, The Maid Came from her Lover's Tryst* (*Flickan kom ifrån sin älsklings möte*) and *Sigh, Sedges, Sigh* (*Säv, säv, susa*). As with Grieg, the most popular of his songs are not necessarily the best and may have served to hinder the collector from exploring the rest. Another cause for their neglect is the relative inaccessibility of the Swedish language as far as non-native singers are concerned, for again (like those of Grieg or Mussorgsky) the songs of Sibelius do not sound well in translation. Only a handful (quite literally five) of the songs are in Finnish; the bulk are inspired by the great Swedish nature romantics: Runeberg, Rydberg, Fröding and Tavaststjerna. Apart from the familiar handful, there are so many riches here to take one by surprise: songs like *Soluppgang* ('Sunrise') and *Lasse Liten* ('Little Lasse') are finely characterized, with some of the concentration and atmosphere one finds in his finest miniatures. *På verandan vid havet* ('On a Balcony by the Sea'), more familiar from Flagstad's recording, is almost a miniature tone-poem; it shows a very different side of the Sibelius world and its dark, questioning lines look forward to the bleak contours and landscape of the *Fourth Symphony*. Both *Autumn evening* (*Höstkväll*) and *On a Balcony by the Sea* are great songs by any standards and can be mentioned in the most exalted company, but neither is new to record, whereas both *Jubeland* and *Teodora*, the two songs comprising Op. 35, were, at the time of this set's original release. The first, *Jubel*, is to a poem of the Swedish poet and painter, Josephson, who inspired the Op. 58 settings. As so often in Sibelius, the piano part is fairly simple, and the burden of the musical argument rests with the voice – the reverse of Wolf. But what a vocal part it is! It ranges with great freedom over a compass of almost two octaves;

indeed, so intense is this writing and that of its companion, *Teodora*, and so full of dramatic fire that, in spite of *The Maiden in the Tower*, one wonders whether Sibelius could not have become an operatic composer. *Teodora* will come as a revelation to many Sibelians, for in its over-heated expressionism it comes close to the Strauss of *Salome* and *Elektra*. Krause is superb here and indeed throughout this set. The vast majority of these songs falls to him and Irwin Gage, the remaining dozen or so coming from Södeström and Ashkenazy. Krause's voice has lost some of its youthful freshness and bloom, but none of its black intensity. If you put his earlier accounts of, say, *Vilse* ('Astray') or *Narcissen* ('Narcissus'), both delightful songs, alongside the new, you will notice the firmer focus of the voice in the earlier items, but you will find this offset by the keener interpretative insight and feeling for their character in the complete set. The performances throughout are authoritative and majestic. Apart from Swedish and Finnish, Sibelius set a number of German poets before the First World War. They are not in the same class as the best of the Runeberg settings, but none of them is second rate: *Im Feld ein Mädchen singt* is undoubtedly an eloquent song. However, the real masterpiece in this set is its companion, *Die stille Stadt*, which has the concentration of mood and the strong atmosphere of a miniature tone-poem; indeed, its serenity, beauty of line and sense of repose mark it out from the others. It is a song of great distinction and refinement of feeling. The Op. 61 set, composed in close proximity to the *Fourth Symphony*, has some of Sibelius's most searching thoughts. One song here is grievously neglected; it alone is almost worth the price of this set: *Låndsamt som kvällsyn* ('Slowly as the Evening Sun'), which haunts the listener with its intensity and concentration of mood. It is a setting of Karl August Tavaststjerna, to whom Sibelius turns for four other poems in this set. None is quite so searching and inward in feeling, but nevertheless they all find the composer at his most individual. *Romeo*, for example, is a most subtle and brilliant song, which shows that he knew his Debussy well; and the *Romans* has strong atmosphere too. (His diaries from this period record that Sibelius had been studying both Debussy and Rachmaninov.) This is one of the pleasures of this set, that one finds new delights in the songs each time one turns to them, and a piece that one at first thought unremarkable turns out to be very special. In terms not just of ambition but also of achievement, this set is a landmark recording. Very few of the songs (*Segelfahrt* is an example) are wanting in interest; most of them are very rewarding indeed, and there are many more masterpieces than is commonly realized. This is a veritable treasure-house which will be a revelation to many who think they already know their Sibelius. Music lovers should be very grateful to Universal Classics for making this set available again (it has previously been issued on CD only in Japan), and is now released on their *Gramophone* Award Collection at mid-price with – thank heavens – full

texts and translation. Anyone who cares about Sibelius and songs simply must seek out this set.

SILLÉN, Josef Otto af (1859–1951)

(i) *Violin Concerto in E min.; Symphony No. 3 in E min.*

** Sterling CDS 1044-2 (i) Bergqvist; Gävle SO, Nilson

Josef Otto af Sillén is a very minor figure and is not listed in Grove or Bakers, nor even in Sohlman, the Swedish equivalent. As a young man he pursued a military career and then turned to insurance, while at the same time being active in the Philharmonic Society: he was briefly in charge of the Stockholm Opera and held a court appointment as a royal chamberlain. He composed for much of his life, though performances were not always under his own name as he felt his aristocratic name might work to his disadvantage. His *Violin Concerto* probably dates from the early 1920s, and he wrote the *Third Symphony* in his late seventies (it was premièred in 1937). A musician of culture rather than originality, he conveys little feeling of real mastery. The *Violin Concerto*, dedicated to his daughter, Greta af Sillén Roos, an Auer pupil who, alas, never played it, opens like Bruch, and in the symphony there is a lot of Tchaikovsky: the Scherzo is Mendelssohnian, albeit somewhat heavy-handed. There are moments here and there which are rather endearing. Christian Bergqvist is the persuasive soloist in the concerto and the performance and recording are perfectly acceptable. Of interest for its curiosity value.

SILVESTROV, Valentin (born 1937)

Metamusik (Symphony for Piano & Orchestra); Postludium.

*** ECM 472 081-2. Lubimov, V. RSO, R. Davies.

Silvestrov has been hailed in extravagant terms as one of the legends of the former Soviet avant garde: David Fanning called his *Fifth Symphony* one of 'the best-kept secrets of the ex-Soviet symphonic repertoire', and nominated it as 'the finest symphony composed in the former Soviet Union since the death of Shostakovich'. The notes speak of the relationship between the two pieces as that of a sketch and its execution. The earlier *Postludium* for piano and orchestra, now almost 20 years old, is the terser; the *Metamusik* of 1992 lasts nearly 50 minutes! It casts a strong spell and the heady atmosphere is tremendously powerful; one's thoughts turn to late Scriabin or the most hothouse Szymanowski, though they sound positively austere by comparison! Whether or not you respond to Silvestrov, there is no doubting the qualities of imagination and the richness of invention that his music possesses. The scoring, particularly in the bass end of the spectrum, is wonderfully rich and the heavy, dark and oppressive textures are at times almost suffocating. The post-Scriabinesque moments are offset by the occasional dreamlike (some might say sickly) hints of Mahlerian warmth. This is strong stuff, an undeniably powerful vision to which listeners will react strongly. As with any composer of vision, Silvestrov creates a world that is distinctively his own, though not everyone will want to enter it and some ears may have difficulty sitting this music out! Expert and authoritative playing, and superb recorded sound.

SINDING, Christian (1856–1941)

Suite in A min., Op. 10.

(M) ★★★ EMI (ADD) 5 62590-2. Perlman, Pittsburgh SO, Previn– KORNGOLD; SIBELIUS: *Concertos.* ★★★

Heifetz recorded this dazzling piece in the 1950s, and it need only be said that Perlman's version (restored to the catalogue as part of the 'Perlman Edition') is not inferior. The blend of archaism and fantasy in Sinding's *Suite* sounds distinctly Scandinavian of the 1890s yet is altogether fresh and quite delightful. Such is the velocity of Perlman's first movement that one wonders whether the recording transfer is playing at the right speed. Stunning virtuosity and vivid recording.

SKORYK, Myroslav (born 1938)

Carpathian Concerto; Hutsul Triptych.

★★ ASV CDDCA 963. Odessa PO, Earle – KOLESSA: *Symphony No. 1.* ★★

Myroslav Skoryk teaches composition at Lvov and has a considerable output to his credit, including two piano concertos, two violin concertos and a good deal of music for the theatre. The *Hutsul Triptych* (1965) derives from a score Skoryk composed for the film, *Shadows of Forgotten Ancestors*, by Sergei Paradhzhanov. It is colourful, often atmospheric and inventive, not unlike some Shchedrin. The *Carpathian Concerto* (1972) is an expertly scored orchestral piece with strong folkloric accents – and some cheap orientalism. Not a good piece nor strongly individual, but the centrepiece of the *Hutsul Triptych* is worth hearing.

SKROUP, František (1801–62)

The Tinker Overture.

(★★) Sup. mono SU 1914 011. Czech PO, Sejna – DVORAK: *The Cunning Peasant Overture* (★★); SMETANA: *Festive Symphony*, etc. (★★★)

The author of the sleeve-note speaks of 'the stunning melodic spontaneity' of Skroup's *The Tinker Overture*, which is no small claim. It is not a bad piece, but its melodic invention, while pleasant, is far from

stunning. Sejna's performance is marvellously spirited, but the recording was made in 1951 and is rather thin on top.

SMETANA, Bedřich (1824–84)

Festive Symphony in E, Op. 6; Festive Overture, Op. 4.

(M) (★★★) Sup. stereo/mono SU1914 011. Czech PO, Sejna – DVORAK: *Cunning Peasant Overture*; SKROUP: *The Tinker Overture.* (★★)

Smetana's *Festive* or *Triumphal Symphony* from 1853 is best known for its effervescent Scherzo, which is often performed on its own. It is also by far the best of the four movements. Karel Sejna's account was recorded in 1966, though the orchestral texture is so well balanced that it can hold its own with more modern recordings. The *Festive Overture*, Op. 4, recorded in 1955, is amazingly good for its period.

Má Vlast (complete).

(BB) ★★★ Virgin 5 62204-2. RLPO, Pešek.

Má Vlast; The Bartered Bride: Overture; 2 Dances.

(B) ★★ Teldec Ultima 3984 28174-2 (2). Frankfurt RSO, Inbal.

Pešek's idiomatic and finely played account of *Má Vlast* is now happily separated from the less attractive Dvořák coupling listed in our main volume and, offered at budget price, becomes much more competitive. It is very well played and recorded.

The Teldec digital recording is strikingly fine and this is music where the vividly coloured and well-balanced, clear sound can be especially telling. The orchestral playing is first class too, and Inbal's reading is dramatic. However, the overall playing-time of the performance, at around 78 minutes, means that it would have fitted on to a single CD, and the *Bartered Bride* bonus is hardly generous.

Má Vlast: From Bohemia's Woods and Fields; Vltava; Vyšehrad. The Bartered Bride: Overture & Dances.

(BB) ★★★ DG 474 565-2. VPO, Levine.

The three *Má Vlast* excerpts, taken from Levine's complete set, are quite splendid, full of momentum and thrust, aptly paced, with much imaginative detail. The opening of *Vyšehrad* immediately shows the impulse of the music-making, yet it is warmly romantic too; while the two most famous pieces, *Vltava* and *From Bohemia's Woods and Fields*, are full of flair and are most beautifully played. The *Bartered Bride Overture* and *Dances* are highly infectious: Levine offers the usual numbers, plus the *Skocná*. The sound is full-blooded and vivid, with a wide amplitude and range to give the music plenty of atmosphere. A good bargain for those just wanting the popular numbers of *Má Vlast*.

Má Vlast: Vltava.

(M) (★★★) EMI mono 5 62790-2. VPO, Furtwängler –
R. STRAUSS: *Death and Transfiguration* etc. (★★★)

Furtwängler's recording of *Vltava* was made in the
Musikvereinsaal in 1951 with Walter Legge producing,
a guarantee of a finely balanced musical sound which
does justice to the tonal finesse of the Vienna orchestra. It serves as an introduction and makeweight to
three Strauss tone-poems that were given performances of commanding eloquence and which remain
in the memory long after the record ends.

CHAMBER MUSIC

(i) *Piano Trio in G min., Op. 15;* (ii) *Fantasy on a
Bohemian Song; From my Homeland.*

(M) ★★ Sup. (ADD) SU 3449-2 131. (i) Klánsky; (i; ii)
Pavlík, Jerie.

Idiomatic performances on Supraphon of the *G
minor Piano Trio* and of the *Fantasy on a Bohemian
Song* and *From my Homeland*, both for violin and
piano. Decent recording, too, but at only 47 minutes'
playing time, it is hardly good value, even at mid-
price.

*Memories of Bohemia in the Form of Polkas, Op. 12;
Op. 13; 3 Poetic Polkas, Op. 8; Polkas in F min.; A; E;
G min.; 3 Salon Polkas, Op. 7.*

★★ Teldec 3984 21261-2. Schiff.

This issue serves as a reminder of the excellence and
freshness of Smetana's keyboard music. Two-thirds
of his output is for the piano. András Schiff is as
sympathetic an interpreter as one could wish for, but
the attractions of the disc are somewhat diminished
by the claustrophobic acoustic, which lends a brittle
tone to the instrument.

String Quartet No. 1 in E min. (From My Life).

(M) (★★★) BBC mono BBCL 4137-2. Smetana Qt –
BEETHOVEN: *String Quartet No. 1* (★★); MOZART:
String Quartet No. 20. (★★(★))

The performance of the *E minor Quartet (From my
Life)* comes from a BBC relay from the Royal Festival
Hall in June 1965, and the mono sound is very
acceptable indeed. The Smetanas recorded it commercially, but their playing here has equal polish,
ardour and freshness. Recommended, alongside the
best of its rivals.

*String Quartets Nos. 1 in E min. (From my Life); 2 in
D min.*

★★ Sup. 3740-2. Skampa Qt.

Forty-six minutes is not generous playing time for a
full-price CD, even if the performances are really
outstanding. Most rivals manage to offer a coupling;
the Lindsays give us some Dvořák pieces. The
Skampa recorded *No. 2*, coupling it with Beethoven's
Op. 95 and a couple of Dvořák waltzes, way back in
the mid-1990s, but the present issue was made in

2003 and should surely accommodate more.
Although this group is highly regarded among Czech
quartets, their account of the *E minor Quartet* falls
short of distinction when placed alongside the Alban
Berg or the Hollywood (on Testament). The *Second* is
another matter, and receives a performance of quality. However, the Supraphon recording is curiously
dry and for those wanting both Quartets the Lindsays remains first choice (ASV CDDCA 777).

*String Quartets Nos. 1 in E min. (From my Life); 2 in
D min.* (plus Documentary).

★★(★) Sup. **DVD** SU 7004-2. Smetana Qt – DVORAK:
Sextet in A. ★★(★)

From the Smetana Quartet, straightforward performances and equally straightforward presentation
for the camera. Perhaps they are not quite as fresh as
the recordings they made commercially in the 1960s
or the BBC broadcast reviewed below, but they still
bring a special authority to this repertoire. However,
the documentary in which the members of the quartet look back over their career is curiously stiff and it
is difficult to imagine oneself replaying it. Recommended for the performances, however.

SMYTH, Ethel (1858–1944)

*Piano Sonatas Nos. 1 in C; 2 in F sharp min.; 3 in D;
2 Canons; Aus der Jugendzeit! (To Youth!); 4
Four-part Dances; Invention in D; Piece in E;
Preludes & Fugues: in F sharp; in C. Suite in E;
Variations in D flat on an Original Theme.*

★★ CPO 999 327-2 (2). Serbescu.

The *C major Sonata* was Dame Ethel's first composi-
tion when she arrived to study in Leipzig in July 1877.
It is a promising work, opening agreeably and with a
gentle funeral march for its *Adagio* slow movement,
which Liana Serbescu plays touchingly. The *Second
Sonata* also has a pleasing but less distinctive
Andante, and the *Third* is notable for its lively closing
Scherzo. However, it cannot be said that any of these
works is very distinctive, although the neo-classical
Suite is jolly, with an engagingly soft-centred Minuet.
The extended *Variations*, 'of an exceedingly dismal
nature' according to the composer, are indeed rather
heavy-going, although the theme itself is agreeable
enough. There are immediate reminders of Brahms
in the third and fourth of the *Four-part Dances*,
which open the collection, and the two very successful *Preludes and Fugues* which close the second CD
successfully evoke the world of Mendelssohn. All this
music is played sympathetically and is well recorded,
but none of it is likely to re-enter the repertoire.

SOLER, Antonio (1729–83)

*Harpsichord Sonatas Nos. 1; 15; 18; 19; 43; 54; 85; 90;
91; 101; 110.*

(BB) Naxos 8.553462. Rowland (harpsichord).

Harpsichord Sonatas Nos. 16; 17; 35; 42; 46; 52; 83; 87; 92; 106; 116.

(BB) ✷✷ Naxos 8.553463. Rowland (harpsichord).

Harpsichord Sonatas Nos. 28; 29; 32; 33; 34; 50; 55; 57; 69; 93; 117.

(BB) ✷✷ Naxos 8.553464. Rowland (harpsichord).

A new series of the Soler keyboard sonatas from Naxos is played with sensibility and often real panache by Gilbert Rowland on a modern copy of a French two-manual harpsichord. The snag is that while he is truthfully and not too forwardly recorded, the acoustic of Epsom College Concert Hall (Surrey) is over-resonant and spreads the sound somewhat uncomfortably in the fast bravura passages. In the more reflective minor-key works (*17 in D minor* and *52 in E minor*, for instance) there are no grumbles, and often the brilliance of the playing (as in the romping *No. 43 in G*, the sparkling *No. 69 in F* and *No. 106 in E minor*, with its crisp articulation) projects through the resonance. The discs have really excellent documentation, describing each individual work in detail.

SORABJI, Khaikhosru (1892–1988)

Fantaisie Espagnole; Fantasiettina sul nome illustre dell'egregio poeta Christopher Grieve ossia Hugh M'Diarmid (Tiny Little Fantasy on the Illustrious Name of the Distinguished Poet Christopher Grieve, i.e. Hugh M'Diarmid); Fragment for Harold Rutland; Gulistán (The Rose Garden): Nocturne for Piano; Introito and Preludio-Corale from Opus Clavicembalisticum; Le Jardin parfumé (Poem for Piano); Nocturne: Djâmî. 3 Pastiches: Chopin's Valse, Op. 64/1; Habanera from Bizet's Carmen; Hindu Merchant's Song (Rimsky-Korsakov). Piano Pieces: In the Hothouse; Prelude, Interlude & Fugue; Toccata. Quaere relique hujus materiei inter secretiora; St Bertrand de Comminges: 'He was Laughing in the Tower'; Valse Fantasie (Hommage à J. Strauss).

✷✷✷ British Music Society BMS 427-9 (3). Habermann
(with HABERMANN: *A la manière de Sorabji: 'Au clair de la lune'* ✷✷✷).

This three-CD set collects the remarkable recordings that Michael Habermann has made of Sorabji's piano music over the years. It is well known that after a performance of his *Opus Clavicembalisticum* Sorabji banned further performance of his music – or, rather, insisted that it should be given only with his expressed permission. Yonty Solomon in Britain and Michael Habermann in America were his chosen interpreters. Habermann proves an extraordinarily persuasive advocate of this music: he has all the virtuosity it needs, as well as the musical and imaginative insight. When Sorabji played his *First Sonata* to Busoni in London in 1919, Busoni observed that it was like 'a tropical forest' and it is for its luxuriant,

hothouse textures that it has gained a reputation. The *Fantaisie espagnole* (1918) is an extraordinarily fantastic evocation of the sights and sounds of Spain and *Le Jardin parfumé*, which earned Delius's admiration, has all the sensuous loveliness of the latter but with an added vivid luxuriance of texture and colour. Sorabji's musical world derives inspiration from Busoni, Scriabin and middle-period Szymanowski, and some have seen it as foreshadowing Messiaen. (He had little time for Messiaen, as R.L. can testify; having written without enthusiasm about one of Messiaen's larger works, he received a card from Sorabji memorably describing the French master as 'Scriabinated Franck'). Be that as it may, these three discs leave no doubt as to the uniqueness and originality of Sorabji's music. Habermann's excellent notes are worth quoting for they sum the composer up well: 'The interaction of imaginative rhythms, melodies, harmonies and textures in his music is fascinating – perhaps even awe-inspiring. Moods are varied. The nocturnal pieces explore mystical trance states. The energetic pieces grab the listener by their sheer obstinacy and determination, and massive climaxes encompass the entire arsenal of the piano (and pianist).' Habermann is a splendid exponent of the pyrotechnical wizardry and the richness of imagination of these scores, and he gives us an admirable entry point into Sorabji's world. The recordings are eminently acceptable.

SOUSA, John Philip (1854–1932)

The Bride Elect (including ballet: People Who Live in Glass Houses); El Capitan; Our Flirtations.

✷✷(✷) Marco Polo 8.223872. Razumovsky SO, Brion.

John Philip Sousa's Band was the first great commercial success of American popular music. Sousa became its primary focus in the last decade of the nineteenth century. He toured the American continent every year, and took his Band across the Atlantic on four European tours in the first five years of the new century. His quick marches and two-steps (danced as well as marched to) had a unique transatlantic rhythmic vitality. One tends to forget that Sousa wrote things other than marches, and here we have some music from his operettas. Though successful in their day, like so many other stage works of their kind they did not have the staying power of Gilbert and Sullivan, but the dances and incidental music from them remain fresh. *The Bride Elect* was written in 1897, but Sousa's ballet *People Who Live in Glass Houses* was used in the 1923 revival and is included here. It seems like a ballet for alcoholics, with its dances entitled *The Champagnes, The Rhine Wines, The Whiskies ('Scotch, Irish, Bourbon and Rye!')*, and is highly entertaining. The waltzes and marches from *El Capitan* and *Our Flirtations* are enjoyable too, and display imaginative touches of orchestration. Keith Brion, musicologist, Pops Director of the Harrisburg Symphony, also leads his own touring Sousa band, so it is not surprising that he is thoroughly at home in this repertoire. Under his direction the Razumovsky orchestra plays this music brightly and idiomatically, and the recording is good.

Caprice: The Coquette; Circus Galop; The Gliding Girl (tango); *The Irish Dragoon: Myrrha Gavotte; On Wings of Lightning; Peaches and Cream* (foxtrot); *Presidential Polonaise; 3 Quotations; Sandalphon Waltzes; Silver Spray Schottische.* **Marches:** *Belle of Chicago; Fairest of the Fair; Federal; Gladiator; Hail to the Spirit of Liberty; Venus.*

**(*) Marco Polo 8.223874. Razumovsky SO, Brion.

The present Sousa survey provides a fair degree of variety by including an attractive *Gliding Girl* tango, a flimsy *Caprice* and a disarming *Gavotte*, plus a slightly grander *Presidential Polonaise*, as well as the usual marches and waltzes at which Sousa excelled. As usual on this label, helpful notes are included, and this CD should not disappoint those drawn to this repertoire.

Colonial Dames Waltz; Humoresque on Gershwin's *Swanee; Looking Upwards* (suite). **Marches:** *Daughters of Texas; Foshay Tower; Hail to the Spirit of Liberty; Hands across the Sea; Imperial Edward; Invincible Eagle; Kansas Wildcats; Manhattan Beach; Power and Glory.*

(BB) *** Naxos 8.559058. Royal Artillery Band, Brion.

Naxos provide here a superb new collection of Sousa's wind band music, presented with tremendous vigour and panache by the Royal Artillery Band, directed by Keith Brion, who knows just how to play this repertoire. The old favourites – as well as some of the rarer items – come up as fresh as paint. The recording is very good – perhaps a little lacking in opulence, but vivid enough.

Dwellers of the Western World (suite); *Humoresque* on Gershwin's *Swanee; Humoresque* on Kern's *Look for the Silver Lining; The Irish Dragoon: Overture; Rêverie: Nymphalin; Semper fidelis; Songs from Grace and Songs for Glory.* **Marches:** *Bullets and Bayonets; The Daughters of Texas; Jack Tar; Invincible Eagle; Power and Glory; Stars and Stripes Forever.*

** Marco Polo 8.223873. Slovak RSO (Bratislava), Brion.

Opening with the bright and breezy *Irish Dragoon Overture*, the ensuing programme is laced with bracing marches, but balanced out with more reflective music, such as the *Rêverie*, and fantasias on famous popular songs, plus arrangements of popular religious themes. The three movements of *The Dwellers of the Western World* are entitled *Red Man, White Man* and *Black Man*. This is agreeable enough with its dashes of folksy colour, though much of the writing is less than first rate. Keith Brion persuades his Slovak orchestra to play it all convincingly

enough, while the famous *Stars and Stripes Forever* generates plenty of gusto. The sound is fully acceptable, but lacks ultimate range and richness. The documentation is good.

MARCHES

The Complete 116 Known Published Marches.

☛ *** Walking Frog Records (ADD) WFR 300 (5). Detroit Concert Band, Smith (available from PO Box 680, Oskaloosa, Iowa 52577, USA www.walkingfrog.com).

We are greatly indebted to an American reader who not only pointed out the omission of this key set of recordings from our survey, but subsequently arranged for Walking Frog Records (wonderful name) to send us the CDs for review. Their excellence is almost beyond compare. The Detroit Band is a superb ensemble in all departments, and Leonard B. Smith (distinguished cornet soloist and ex-member of the Goldman Band and later the US Navy Band) proves to be an outstandingly persuasive exponent of Sousa marches. In his hands they swing along without any feeling of being pressed too hard; indeed, their gait and their sheer bonhomie bring an instant smile of pleasure. The playing is not only crisp and polished, but it has a consistent zest and spontaneity.

The recordings too are consistently demonstration-worthy. We were not surprised to discover that they have analogue masters. They were made between 1973 and 1979 in the main auditorium of the Masonic Temple in Detroit, Michigan, using a classic stereo microphone coverage without gimmicks, and the recording team was led by none other than Jack Renner (of Telarc); his colleagues were Robert Woods and James Schulkey. Tony Schmitt's digital remastering for CD calls for equal praise: nothing has been lost. The percussion (wonderful snare drums) and the full, clear bass line are equally real. As the documentation truly claims: the sound you hear is what the listener would hear having 'the best seat in the house'.

We have not space to list the entire contents, but each of these five CDs is led by one of the most famous marches: Volume 1, *The Thunderer*; Volume 2, *El Capitan*; Volume 3, *The Washington Post*; Volume 4, *Hands across the Sea*; while Volume 5 offers a double whammy, opening with a riveting *Semper fidelis*, with a splendidly built climax, and ending with the greatest march of all, *The Stars and Stripes Forever*. This is music-making that cannot but help but cheer you up.

The Complete Commercial Recordings of 60 Marches by the Sousa Band (1897–1930).

(**(*)) Crystal CD 461-3 (3). Introductory speech by Sousa. Sousa Band, Sousa; Pryor; Higgins; Rodgers; Shillkret; Bourdon; Herbert L. Clarke; Edwin G. Clarke; Pasternack.

Sousa himself briefly introduces this anthology, in a recording taken from a 1929 NBC broadcast celebrating his seventy-fifth birthday, and he follows, of course, by conducting *The Stars and Stripes Forever*. These recordings, made over a period of 33 years, are an integral part of the history of the gramophone, for before the coming of the electric process a woodwind and brass concert band was the only instrumental ensemble which could be captured with a reasonable degree of realism by the acoustic recording process.

If the recordings deriving from early 7-inch Berliner discs are often of very poor quality, with more background noise than music, a cheerful 1899 record of *The Mikado March* (well laced with Sullivan tunes), conducted by Arthur Pryor, is an honourable exception, and Sousa's own later RCA recordings are often of surprising fidelity. In his historical note, Keith Brion reminds us that the musicians used for these RCA Camden sessions included many members of the Philadelphia Orchestra, plus a smattering of Sousa Band players who lived in the Philadelphia area.

Arthur Pryor usually got good results, too, although not all the playing here is immaculate. The ensemble slips badly at the opening of *Jack Tar*, yet the performance is redeemed by the middle section, which briefly quotes the *Sailor's Hornpipe* and has almost hi-fi percussion effects. However, the recordings Sousa himself made in 1917–18 bring some particularly crisp ensemble and tempi that, in *Sabre and Spurs* and *Solid Men to the Front*, for instance, are surprisingly relaxed.

Joseph Pasternack, who conducted the band in the 1920s, also did not press forward as forcefully as some modern American performances do, but followed Sousa's style, with a swinging pace that would have been ideal for marching. Rosario Bourdon, who followed in the late 1920s (and had the benefit of fuller, though not necessarily clearer electric recording), added a little more pressure, and Arthur Pryor, who has the last word here with a 1926 Camden recording of *The Stars and Stripes*, certainly doesn't look back: the piccolo solo is a joy. Excellent documentation, with photographs

Marches: *The Ancient and Honorable Artillery Company; The Black Horse Troop; Bullets and Bayonets; The Gallant Seventh; Golden Jubilee; The Glory of the Yankee Navy; The Gridiron Club; High School Cadets; The Invincible Eagle; The Kansas Wildcats; The Liberty Bell; Manhattan Beach; The National Game; New Mexico; Nobles of the Mystic Shrine; Our Flirtation; The Piccadore; The Pride of the Wolverines; Riders for the Flag; The Rifle Regiment; Sabre and Spurs; Sesqui-centennial Exposition; Solid Men to the Front; Sound off.*
⊖→ ★★★ Mercury (ADD) **SACD** 475 6182. Eastman Wind Ens., Fennell.

Fennell's collection of 24 Sousa marches derives from vintage Mercury recordings of the early 1960s. The performances have characteristic American pep and natural exuberance; the zestfulness of the playing carries the day. One of the more striking items is *The Ancient and Honorable Artillery Company*, which incorporates *Auld lang syne* as its middle section. Reissued as an SACD, it sounds even better than in its former incarnation on CD.

Marches: *The Beau Ideal; The Belle of Chicago; The Black Horse Troop; The Charlatan; The Crusader; Daughters of Texas; The Diplomat; El Capitan; The Fairest of the Fair; Le Flor de Sevilla; From Maine to Oregon; The Gallant Seventh; The Gladiator; The Glory of the Yankee Navy; Golden Jubilee; The Gridiron Club; Hail to the Spirit of Liberty; Hands Across the Sea; The High School Cadets; The Invincible Eagle; Jack Tar; Kansas Wildcats; King Cotton; The Lambs; The Legionnaires; The Liberty Bell; Manhattan Beach; Marquette University; The National Game; New York Hippodrome; The Northern Pines; Nobles of the Mystic Shrine; On the Campus; Powhatan's Daughter; The Pride of the Wolverines; The Rifle Regiment; The Royal Welch Fusiliers; Semper fidelis; Solid Men to the Front; Sound Off; The Stars and Stripes Forever; The Thunderer; The Washington Post.*
⊖→ (BB) ★★★ EMI Gemini 5 85535-2 (2). Band of HM Royal Marines, Lt-Col. Hoskins.

Originally issued on three CDs, these are the most convincing performances of Sousa marches yet to appear from a British Band. Lt.-Col. Hoskins liltingly catches their breezy exuberance and his pacing is consistently well judged. While many of the favourites are included, there is plenty of unfamiliar material here too; while the music-making still retains the sense that the performances emanate from this side of the Atlantic, the Royal Marines Band plays with style as well as enthusiasm. The digital recording is very much in the demonstration class. EMI have a long history of recording military bands and know how to balance them properly; the result is stirringly realistic, with cymbal transients telling and the side-drum snares crisp without exaggeration. Excellent value.

SPERGER, Johannes (1750–1812)

Symphonies in B flat; C; F.
(BB) ★★ Naxos 8. 554764. Musica Aeterna Bratislava, Zajíček.

Johannes Sperger was a famous double-bass player in his day and, apart from appearing as a soloist, found his main livelihood playing in various court orchestras, including that of the Cardinal Primate of Hungary. His symphonies are stylized works in three movements, the centrepiece in one instance here being a simple *Andante*; in each of the other two it is a *Minuet* and *Trio*. The most striking movement is the first of the *F major*, relatively (only relatively) strong and turbulent. But these are in essence undemanding works, well crafted, but with nothing very individual to say, and they never reveal that their composer was a virtuoso of the double-bass. They are very well played by this excellent period-instrument chamber orchestra, and the recording cannot be faulted. But, alas, Johannes Sperger deserves his obscurity.

SPOHR, Ludwig (1784–1859)

Nonet in F, Op. 31.

(★★★) Testament mono SBT 1261. Augmented Vienna Octet – BEETHOVEN: *Septet.* (★★★)

It is good to see this 1952 Decca recording of Spohr's delightful *Nonet* – full of tunes and good humour – return to the catalogue. The playing here is superb, full of unforced charm, with a lovely Viennese glow. The transfers are excellent, the mono sound unbelievably warm and rich for the period.

STANFORD, Charles (1852–1924)

(i) *Piano Concerto No. 2, Op. 126; Down among the Dead Men, Op. 71. Irish Rhapsodies Nos. 1; 2 (The Lament for the Son of Ossian);* (ii) *3 (for Cello & Orchestra); 4 (The Fisherman of Loch Neagh and What He Saw); 5;* (iii) *6 (for Violin & Orchestra).*
(M) ★★★ Chan. X10116 (2). (i) Fingerhut; (ii) Wallfisch; (iii) Mordkovitch; Ulster O, Handley.

This is a further re-coupling and replaces Chan. 7002/3 in our main volume. Stanford's ambitious *Second Piano Concerto*, although in three rather than four movements, is a work on the largest scale, recalling Brahms's *B flat Concerto*. Yet Stanford asserts his own melodic individuality and provides a really memorable secondary theme for the second movement, even if the finale is perhaps a little inflated. Margaret Fingerhut is a first-rate soloist, both here and in her apt and entertaining account of the *Down among the Dead Men Variations*, for Stanford was a dab hand at this format. The new coupling is with the six *Irish Rhapsodies* (two of them also concertante pieces with highly responsive soloists), which are the more impressive when heard as a set. They too are splendidly played and recorded.

STEFFANI, Agostini (1654–1728)

Stabat Mater.
(M) ★★★ DHM/BMG 82876 60149-2. Alamanjo, Van der Sluis, Elwes, Padmore, Van der Kamp, Netherlands Bach Festival Ch. & O, Leonhardt – BIBER: *Requiem à 15 in A.* ★★★

Agostino Steffani was diplomat and priest as well as a composer, but his music has a strongly individual character. His serene, melancholy *Stabat Mater* has moving and expressive content and much imaginative word-setting, while the *Cujus animam* and *Pro peccatis* are glorious in their expressively rich harmonies. The solo writing is imaginative and the layering of parts in the closing *Quando corpus*, which gathers pace as it proceeds, is very telling. The performance could hardly be bettered, with soloists and chorus equally dedicated. First-rate recording.

STENHAMMAR, Wilhelm (1871–1927)

(i) *Allegro brillante in E flat; Allegro ma non tanto;* (ii; iii) *Violin Sonata in A min., Op. 19;* (iii) *Piano Sonata in A flat, Op. 12.*
★★ BIS CD 764. (i) Tale Qt (members); (ii) Olsson; (iii) Negro.

All this music comes from the 1890s, before Stenhammar's personality was fully formed. The *A flat Sonata*, written in the same year (1895) as the better-known and somewhat Brahmsian *Three Fantasies*, Op. 11, though derivative has some pleasing invention and a good feeling for form. Lucia Negro plays it with great authority and sensitivity. The *Violin Sonata* comes from 1899 and was written for Stenhammar's chamber-music partner, the composer Tor Aulin. The *Allegro ma non tanto* is the first movement of a projected piano trio (1895); and little is known about the even earlier *Allegro brillante* fragment. The pianist, who is unfailingly responsive, rather swamps her partners here and in the *Violin Sonata*, thanks to a less than satisfactory balance.

STEVENSON, Ronald (born 1928)

Passacaglia on D.S.C.H.
⊖ ★★★ Divine Art 25013. McLachlan.

It was the appearance of John Ogdon's remarkable LP set of the *Passacaglia on D.S.C.H.* in 1967 that alerted collectors to Ronald Stevenson's music. He composed the *Passacaglia* between 1960 and 1962 and, like Sorabji's *Opus clavicembalisticum* or Busoni's *Fantasia contrappuntistica* (Stevenson is a keen and persuasive advocate of that composer), it is something of a *tour de force*. It is a mighty set of variations on the four-note motif D-S-C-H derived from Shostakovich's monogram, lasting without a break for some 80 minutes. Later on in the score Stevenson introduces another four-note anagram, B-A-C-H, perhaps a reference to Busoni's *Fantasia contrappuntistica*. When he presented Shostakovich with the score at the 1962 Edinburgh Festival, he said that the combination of Russian and German motifs symbolized his hope that the two nations, and mankind generally, would live in harmony. The twelfth section cleverly alludes to the microtonal scale of the Highland bagpipes and incorporates a seventeenth-century Pibroch *Cumha ne Cloinne* ('Lament for the Children') and there is a formidable climactic triple fugue in which the *Dies irae* surfaces. In the 1960s Sir William Walton hailed the pieces as 'really tremendous – magnificent – I can't remember having been so excited by a new work for a very long time'. Murray McLachlan is an impressive exponent of this score and he is very well recorded. (Some years ago he recorded the two piano concertos that Stevenson wrote at about this time, so he is completely attuned to this music.) An earlier version by Raymond Clarke (Marco Polo 8.223545), though a formidable musical achievement, is rather let down by the boxy recording, and neither of the composer's own accounts is easily available.

STRADELLA, Alessandro
(1644–82)

San Giovanni Battista (oratorio).
🔾 ✪ (M) *** Warner Elatus 2564 60444-2. Bott, Batty, Lesne, Edgar-Wilson, Huttenlocher, Musiciens du Louvre, Minkowski.

Stradella's oratorio on the biblical subject of John the Baptist and Salome is an amazing masterpiece and offers unashamedly sensuous treatment of the story. Insinuatingly chromatic melodic lines for Salome (here described simply as Herodias's daughter) are set against plainer, more forthright writing for the castrato role of the saint, showing the composer as a seventeenth-century equivalent of Richard Strauss. There is one amazing phrase for Salome, gloriously sung here by Catherine Bott, which starts well above the stave and ends after much twisting nearly two octaves below with a glorious chest-note, a hair-raising moment, Herod's anger arias bring reminders of both Purcell and Handel, and at the end Stradella ingeniously superimposes Salome's gloating music and Herod's expressions of regret, finally cutting off the duet in mid-air as Charles Ives might have done, bringing the whole work to an indeterminate close. Quite apart from Catherine Bott's magnificent performance, at once pure and sensuous in tone and astonishingly agile, the other singers are most impressive, with Gerard Lesne a firm-toned countertenor in the title-role and Philippe Huttenlocher a clear if sometimes gruff Herod. Marc Minkowski reinforces his claims as an outstanding exponent of period performance, drawing electrifying playing from Les Musiciens du Louvre, heightening the drama. Excellent sound. Not to be missed – especially at mid-price.

STRAUS, Oscar (1870–1954)

Marches: *Einzugs; Bulgaren; Die Schlossparade. Menuett à la cour.* Polka: *G'stellte Mäd'ln. Rund um die Liebe* (Overture); Waltzes: (i) *L'Amour m'emporte. Alt-Wiener Reigen; Eine Ballnacht; Der Reigen; Didi;* (i) *Komm, komm, Held meiner Träume; Tragante; Valse lente; Walzerträume.*
*** Marco Polo 8.223596. (i) Kincses; Budapest Strauss SO, Walter.

Although Oscar Straus is no relation to the famous Strauss family, his style of writing echoed theirs, also absorbing influences from Lehár. His great hit was the operetta, *A Waltz Dream* (1907), which had a first run in Vienna of 500 performances. His *Walzerträume* is deftly based on the main theme from the operetta, and the *Einzugs-Marsch* comes from the same source. But he could also manage a neat polka and score it very prettily, as is instanced by *G'stellte Mäd'ln*, while the *Alt-Wiener Reigen Waltz* is also full of charm and is played here very seductively. *Komm, komm, Held meiner Träume* is, of course, the famous 'Come, Come, my Hero', which comes from a parody operetta based on George Bernard Shaw's *Arms and the Man*. In 1908 it was a flop in Vienna, under its title *Der tapfere Soldat* ('The Brave Soldier') but was a resounding success in England and the USA later, when its title was changed to *The Chocolate Soldier* and its hit song took the world by storm. It is nicely sung here in soubrette style by Veronika Kincses. After the Second World War, Straus wrote an engaging hit, sung first by Danielle Darrieux in a 1952 French film, *Madame de ...*, and here by Kincses, and he capped his movie career with a Parisian-style waltz, *Der Reigen*, for the famous Max Ophüls film, *La Ronde*, the song eventually becoming better-known than the movie. The programme opens with a pot-pourri overture irresistibly full of sumptuous and lighthearted melody. It is infectiously played here, like the rest of the programme, by the first-class Budapest Strauss Symphony Orchestra, conducted with affection and great élan by Alfred Walter – easily the best CD he has made so far. The recording, too, is gorgeously sumptuous, and this is a marvellous disc to cheer you up on a dull day. Highly recommended.

STRAUSS Family, The

Strauss, Johann Sr (1804–49)

Strauss, Johann Jr (1825–99)

Strauss, Josef (1827–70)

Strauss, Eduard (1835–1916)
(all music listed is by Johann Strauss Jr unless otherwise stated)

Strauss, Johann Sr: The Complete Edition

Volume 1: *Alte und neue Tempête* (includes: *Altdeutscher Postertanz; Altvatr Galoppade; Altvater Marsch; Sauvage*). Galops: *Alpenkönig, Op. 7/1–2; Champagner; Schauer; Seufzer; Stelldichein.*

Waltzes: *Döblinger Réunion; Gesellschafts; Kettenbrücke; Täuberin; Wiener-Carneval; Wiener Launen.*
*** Marco Polo 8.225213. Camerata Cassovia, Pollack.

Marco Polo's all-embracing survey of the music of the Strauss family now turns to the least-known repertoire of all, that written by Johann Senior, beginning in the third decade of the nineteenth century. Until the arrival of Johann the Elder, Viennese dance music had been in the hands of Joseph Lanner, and Johann began his career as a viola player in Lanner's small café orchestra. But he was already composing and arranging, and although his *Täuberin-Walzer* of 1826, published as his Op. 1, was not his very first waltz, no earlier examples have survived and it is now regarded as his first major composition. It has distinct charm but is of modest scale, and with the solo violin introducing the main theme a Ländler flavour remains, as it does in the *Döblinger Réunion-Walzer*, written for Lanner's ensemble that same year, and very simply scored for flute, two clarinets, two horns, trumpet and strings.

But in 1827 Strauss struck out on his own and gave his first concert with his own orchestra at the Zu den zwei Tauben (Two Doves tavern). No doubt *Täuberin* was included in that programme. The agreeable *Vienna-Carnival Waltz* appeared the following year and was intended as a tribute to Weber, who had just died. It quotes from an aria from *Oberon*, but its style remains predictable.

The *Alpine Galop* (which appears here in two versions, differently scored, brought about by a change of the composer's publisher) spiritedly connects a series of motives from Wenzel Müller's incidental music for play of the time, but the *Champagne Galop* of 1828 has rather more individuality and its principal motif was quoted by the composer again in his later waltz of the same name.

But it is with the *Kettenbrüke Waltz* that Strauss (then still only 24) gives us his first really striking string of tunes to establish a format which was to be the pattern for the finest Viennese works in this form. Similarly, the *Seufzer-Galoppe*, sparkles with personality, and appropriately it originally included a vocal 'sigh' in which the breathless dancers were invited to join. Its scoring, although still modest in scope, is certainly vivid, and the *Stelldichein-Galoppe* with its bouncing horn theme is also charmingly infectious. Perhaps most fascinating of all is Strauss's 1827 pot-pourri of old and new dances, individually primitive but agreeably diverse and including the *Old German Pillow Dance*, a round dance for courting couples, which Tchaikovsky included in the Act I party scene of his *Nutcracker Ballet*.

Christian Pollack is a master of this repertoire and his Camerata Cassovia gives a perfect simulation of the small Viennese ensembles of the period. They play with a polished, infectious stylishness that gives much pleasure, and they are well recorded in a pleasing acoustic.

Volume 2: Galops: *Carolinen; Chineser; Erinnerungs; Gesellschafts; Kettenbrücke.* Ländler: *Die so sehr beliebten Erinnerung.* Waltzes: *À la Paganini; Die beliebten Trompetenwalzer; Champagne; Fort nacheinander! Krapfen-Waldel; Lieferung der Kettenbrücke Lust-Lager.*
*** Marco Polo 8.225252. Camerata Cassovia, Pollack.

Volume 2 remains mainly in the more intimate world of Viennese Schrammeln music, scored for modest resources, which spawned the early Strauss output. Paganini caused a sensation when he visited Vienna in March 1828, so Strauss's *Paganini* selection begins with *La Campanella* (which was the talk of the city) but after that is a rather routine affair. The highlights are the relatively familiar *Chinese Galop* with its piquant piccolo and the lesser-known *Carolinen* and *Kettenbrücke Galops*, which both have infectious galloping rhythms. *Erinnerungs* is bouncy too. The *Die so sehr beliebten Erinnerung* Ländler, charmingly scored, shows that Johann Senior was still happiest in this earlier triple-time format. The 'Popular Trumpet Waltz' is enterprising only for the signal calls from its named brass soloist, but *Fort nacheinander* ('Off after One Another!'), as the title suggests, is the most varied and inventive waltz here. Fine performances from Pollack and his chamber group.

Volume 3: *Contredanses par Jean Strauss.* Galops: *Einzugs; Hirten; Sperl; Ungarische Galoppe oder Frischka Nos.1–3; Wettrennen; Wilhelm Tell.* Waltzes: *Es ist nur ein Wien! Frohsinn im Gebirge; Hietzinger-Reunion* (or *Weissgärber-Kirchweih-Tänz) Josephstädler; Es ist nur ein Wein!; Dies Verfassers beste Laune.*
*** Marco Polo 8.225253. Slovak Sinf., Zilina, Märzendorfer.

By 1829 Strauss's scoring was growing more ambitious, and the lively 'There is Only One Vienna! Waltz' is given its winning character from its chirpy scoring for a pair of clarinets and a flute (besides two horns and a trumpet), while the delectable *Hirten-Galoppe* expands the orchestral complement to flute, oboe, bassoon, two clarinets, two horns (used simply and effectively) plus a pair of trumpets; and the *Races Galop* uses the brass wittily. The *Hietzinger-Reunion-Walzer* returns to a simple, Ländler style, but retains the fuller scoring. The *William-Tell Galoppe* is an unashamed crib, but skilfully put together; while the three *Hungarian Dances* draw on the same material used by Brahms. The finest of the waltzes here is appropriately 'The Composer's Best Fancy', but this collection is most notable for its galops, in particular the irresistible *Sperl*, which is delightfully scored and draws on a familiar Rossini motif to spirited effect. The *Contredanses for Jean Strauss* is a quadrille, drawing on lively French melodies but retaining much of the Viennese Schrammeln style, even when the music is fully scored. Excellent performances throughout, even if the playing is spirited rather than very polished.

Volume 4: *Cotillons on Motives from Bellini's opera, 'La Straniera'; Schwarz'sche Ball-Tänz in Saul zum Sperl (Cotillons based on Motives from Auber's 'La Muette de Portici')*. Galops: *Galop Nos. 1 & 2 from Auber's 'La Muette de Portici'; Fortuna; Venetianer.* Polkas: *Charmant; Launen.* March: *Wiener Bürger-Marsch No. 1: Original Parademarsch.* Waltzes: *Bajaderen; Heiter auch in ernster Zelt; Hof-Ball-Tänzer; Das Leben ein Tanz oder Der Tanz ein Leben!; Vive la Danse!*
*** Marco Polo 8.224254. Slovak Sinf., Zilina, Märzendorfer.

The cotillons from Auber's *La Muette de Portici* open zestfully with the jolly tune, famous from the Overture, better known as *Masaniello*. You can't go wrong with Auber, and this is most enjoyable, as are the pair of galops using material fom the same opera. The carefree *Bajaderen-Walze*, equally agreeable, draws on Auber's *Le Dieu et la Bayadère*. The *Charmant Polka* really is charming, and this extends to the lighthearted waltz, *Viva la Danse!* The follow-up was 'Cheerful too, at a serious time', badly needed in Vienna, as in 1830 the Danube flooded its banks and in 1831 the city was suffering a cholera epidemic. *Das Leben ein Tanz* thus opens mournfully on the brass to signify Strauss's acknowledgement of the disaster, but the waltz itself is lighthearted. The cheerful *Parade March* of 1832 must also have been much appreciated. We move on to 1834 for the delicately effervescent *Venetian Galope* which completes a particularly generous programme.

Johann Strauss Jr: The Complete Edition

All played by the CSSR State PO (Košice) unless indicated otherwise)

Vol. 1: Mazurka: *Veilchen, Mazur nach russischen motiven.* Polkas: *Fledermaus; Herzenslust; Zehner.* Quadrilles: *Debut; Nocturne.* Waltzes: *Bei uns z'Haus; Freuet euch des Lebens; Gunstwerber; Klangfiguren; Maskenzug française; Phönix-Schwingen.*
**(*) Marco Polo 8.223201. A. Walter.

Vol. 2: *Kaiser Franz Josef 1, Rettungs-Jubel-Marsch.* Polkas: *Czechen; Neue Pizzicato; Satanella; Tik-Tak.* Polka-Mazurka: *Fantasieblümchen.* Quadrilles: *Cytheren; Indra.* Waltzes: *Die jungen Wiener; Solonsprüche; Vermälungs-Toaste; Wo die Zitronen blüh'n.*
** Marco Polo 8.223202. A. Walter.

Vol. 3: Polkas: *Aesculap; Amazonen; Freuden-Gruss; Jux; Vergnügungszug.* Quadrilles: *Dämonen; Satanella.* Waltzes: *Berglieder; Liebslieder; Lind-Gesänge; Die Osterreicher; Wiener Punsch- Lieder.*
**(*) Marco Polo 8.223203. A. Walter.

Vol. 4: Polkas: *Bürger-Ball; Hopser; Im Krapfenwald'l (polka française); Knall-Kügerin;*

Veilchen. Marches: *Austria; Verbrüderungs.* Quadrille: *Motor.* Waltzes: *Dividenden; O schöner Mai!; Serail-Tänze.*
**(*) Marco Polo 8.223204. Edlinger.

Vol. 5: *Russischer Marsch Fantasie.* Polkas: *Eilsen (polka française); Heiligenstadt Rendezvous; Hesperus; Musen; Pariser.* Quadrille: *Sur des airs français.* Waltzes: *Italienischer; Kennst du mich?; Nachtfalter; Wiener Chronik.*
*** Marco Polo 8.223205. O. Dohnányi.

Vol. 6: *Caroussel Marsch.* Polkas: *Bluette (polka française); Camelien; Warschauer.* Quadrilles: *Nach Themen französischer Romanzen; Nordstern.* Waltzes: *Concurrenzen; Kuss; Myrthen-Kränze; Wellen und Wogen.*
** Marco Polo 8.223206. O. Dohnányi.

Vol. 7: *Deutscher Krieger-Marsch; Kron-Marsch.* Polkas: *Bacchus; Furioso; Neuhauser.* Polka-Mazurka: *Kriegers Liebchen.* Quadrille: *Odeon.* Waltzes: *Ballg'schichten; Colonnen; Nordseebilder; Schnee-Glöckchen; Zeitgeister.*
**(*) Marco Polo 8.223207. Polish State PO, O. Dohnányi.

Vol. 8: *Banditen-Galopp; Erzherzog Wilhelm Genesungs-Marsch.* Polkas: *Leichtes Blut; Wiedersehen; Pepita.* Quadrilles: *Nach Motiven aus Verdi's 'Un ballo in maschera'; Saison.* Waltzes: *Cagliostro; Carnevals-Botschafter; Lagunen; Die Sanguiniker; Schallwellen.*
**(*) Marco Polo 8.223208. Polish State PO, O. Dohnányi

This extraordinary Marco Polo enterprise – to record the entire output of the Strauss family – began in 1988. All these initial volumes centre on the music of Johann Junior. Johann and his orchestra were constantly on the move and, wherever they travelled to play, he was expected to come up with some new pieces. While obvious 'hits' and favourites stayed in the repertoire, often the novelties were treated as ephemeral and in many instances only the short piano-score has survived. It was necessary – for the purpose of the recording – to hire professional arrangers to make suitable orchestrations; from these, new orchestral parts could be copied. Such is the perversity of human experience that quite regularly the original orchestral parts would suddenly appear for some of the pieces – after the recording had been made! It is therefore planned to have an appendix and to re-record those items later, from the autographs. So far the recordings have been made in Eastern Europe. Apart from cutting the costs, the Slovak Bohemian tradition provides a relaxed ambience, highly suitable for this repertoire. Much of the music is here being put on disc for the first time, and indeed the excellent back-up documentation tells us that three items on the first CD were part of the young Johann's first concert programme: the *Gunst-*

werber ('Wooer of Favour') *Waltz, Herzenslust* ('Heart's Desire') polka and, even more appropriately, the *Debut-Quadrille*, so that makes Volume 1 of the series something of a collectors' item, while Volume 3 also seems to have above-average interest in the selection of its programme.

Evaluation of these recordings has not been easy. The first three CDs were made by the Slovak State Philharmonic under Alfred Walter. The mood is amiable and the playing quite polished. With the arrival of Richard Edlinger and Oliver Dohnányi on the scene, the tension seems to increase, and there is much to relish. Of this second batch we would pick out Volumes 5, 7 and 8, all representing the nice touch of Oliver Dohnányi, with Volume 5 perhaps a primary choice, although there are many good things included in Volume 8.

Vol. 9: *Habsburg Hoch! Marsch; Indigo-Marsch.* Polkas: *Albion; Anen; Lucifer.* Polka-Mazurka: *Nachtveilchen.* Quadrille: *Festival Quadrille nach englischen Motiven.* Waltzes: *Carnevalsbilder; Gedanken auf den Alpen; Kaiser.*
** Marco Polo 8.223209-2. Polish State PO, Wildner.

Vol. 10: *Pesther csárdas.* Polkas: *Bauern; Blumenfest; Diabolin; Juriston Ball.* Quadrille: *Nach beliebten Motiven.* Waltzes: *Feuilleton; Morgenblätter; Myrthenblüthen; Panacea-Klänge.*
** Marco Polo 8.223210. Polish State PO (Katowice), Wildner.

Vol. 11: *Revolutions-Marsch.* Polkas: *Frisch heran!; Haute-volée; Hermann; Patrioten.* Polka-Mazurka: *Waldine.* Quadrilles: *Die Afrikanerin; Handels-élite.* Waltzes: *Aus den Bergen; Donauweibchen; Glossen; Klänge aus der Walachei.*
**(*) Marco Polo 8.223211. A. Walter.

Vol. 12: *Krönungs-Marsch.* Polkas: *Auora; Ella; Harmonie; Neues Leben (polka française); Souvenir; Stürmisch in Lieb' und Tanz.* Quadrille: *Fest.* Waltzes: *Aus den Bergen; Donauweibchen; Glossen; Klänge aus der Walachei.*
**(*) Marco Polo 8.223212. A. Walter

Vol. 13: *Egyptischer Marsch; Patrioten-Marsch.* Polkas: *Demolirer; Fidelen; Nur fort!; Tanzi-bäri; was sich liebt, neckt sich (polka française).* Quadrilles: *Nach Motiven aus der Oper 'Die Belagerung von Rochelle'; Neue Melodien.* Waltzes: *Sirenen; Thermen; Die Zillerthaler.*
**(*) Marco Polo 8.223213. A. Walter

Vol. 14: *Romance No. 1 for Cello & Orchestra.* Polkas: *Champagne; Geisselhiebe; Kinderspiele (polka française); Vöslauer.* Quadrilles: *Bal champêtre; St Petersburg (Quadrille nach russischen Motiven).* Waltzes: *Du und du; Ernte-tänze; Frohsinns-spenden; Grillenbanner; Phänomene.*
**(*) Marco Polo 8.223214. A. Walter

Vol. 15: *Jubelfest-Marsch.* Polkas: *Bijoux; Scherz.* Polka-Mazurkas: *Lob der Frauen; La Viennoise.* Quadrilles: *Alexander; Bijouterie.* Waltzes: *Die Jovialen; Kaiser-Jubiläum; Libellen; Wahlstimmen.*
** Marco Polo 8.223215. CSR SO (Bratislava), Wildner.

Vol. 16: *Fürst Bariatinsky-Marsch.* Polkas: *Brautschau (on themes from Zigeunerbaron); Eljen a Magyar!; Ligourianer Seufzer; Schnellpost; Studenten. La Berceuse Quadrille; Zigeuner-Quadrille (on themes from Balfe's 'Bohemian Girl').* Waltzes: *Bürgerweisen; Freuden-Salven; Motoren; Sangerfährten.*
**(*) Marco Polo 8.223216. A. Walter

With Volume 9, we move to Poland and a new name, Johannes Wildner. He has his moments, but his approach seems fairly conventional. He does not make a great deal of the famous *Emperor Waltz*, which closes Volume 9, although he does better with *Gedanken auf den Alpen*, another unknown but charming waltz. Alfred Walter – who began it all – then returns for Volumes 11–14. Of this batch, Volume 11 might be singled out, opening with the jolly *Hermann-Polka*, while the *Klänge aus der Walachei, Aus den Bergen* ('From the Mountains') and *Donauweibchen* ('Nymph of the Danube') are three more winning waltzes; but the standard seems pretty reliable here, and these are all enjoyable discs. Volume 16 has another attractive batch of waltzes, at least two winning polkas and a quadrille vivaciously drawing on Balfe's *Bohemian Girl*. It also includes the extraordinary *Ligourian Seufzer-Polka*, in which the orchestra vocally mocks the Ligourians, a despised Jesuitical order led by Alfonso Maria di Ligouri. Another good disc.

Vol. 17: *Kaiser Franz Joseph-Marsch.* Polkas: *Armen-Ball; 'S gibt nur a Kaiserstadt! 'S gibt nur a Wien; Violetta (polka française).* Quadrille: *Melodien.* Waltzes: *Adelen; Bürgersinn; Freiheits-Lieder; Windsor-Klänge.*
*** Marco Polo 8.223217. CSR SO (Bratislava), Eschwé.

Vol. 18: *Alliance-Marsche; Studenten-Marsch.* Polkas: *Edtweder-oder!; Invitation à la polka mazur; Leopoldstädter; Stadt und Land; Cagliostro-Quadrille.* Waltzes: *Grössfürstin Alexandra; Lava-Ströme; Patronessen; Die Pulizisten; Rathausball-Tänz.*
**(*) Marco Polo 8.223218. A. Walter.

Vol. 19: *Hoch Osterreich! Marsch.* Polkas: *Burschenwanderung (polka française), Electro-magnetische; Episode (polka française).* Quadrilles: *Le Premier Jour de bonheur; Opéra de Auber; Seladon.* Waltzes: *Dorfgeschichten (im Ländlerstil); Novellen; Rosen aus dem Süden; Seid umschlungen, Millionen; Studentenlust.*
**(*) Marco Polo 8.223219. A. Walter.

Vol. 20: *Dinorah-Quadrille nach Motiven der Oper,*
'Die Wallfahrt' nach Meyerbeer.
Kaiser-Jäger-Marsch. Slovianka-Quadrille, nach
russischen Melodien. Polkas: *Auf zum Tanze; Herzel.*
Polka-Mazurkas: *Ein Herz, ein Sinn; Fata Morgana.*
Waltzes: *Aurora-Ball-Tänze; Erhöhte*
Schwärmereien (concert waltz).
** Marco Polo 8.223220. A. Walter.

Vol. 21: *Ottinger Reiter-Marsch.* Polkas: *Figaro*
(polka française); Patronessen (polka française);
Sans-souci. Polka-Mazurka: *Tändelei.* Quadrilles:
Orpheus; Rotunde. Waltzes: *Cylcoiden; G'schichten*
aus dem Wienerwald; Johannis-Käferin.
** Marco Polo 8.223221. Wildner.

Vol. 22: *Klipp-Klapp Galopp. Persischer Marsch.*
Polkas: *L'Inconnue (polka française); Nachtigall.*
Polka-Mazurka: *Aus der Heimat.* Quadrilles:
Carnevals-Spektakel; Der lustige Krieg. Waltzes:
Controversen; Immer heiterer (im Ländlerstil);
Maxing-tänze; Ninetta.
** Marco Polo 8.223222. Wildner.

Vol. 23: *Deutschmeister-Jubiläumsmarsch.* Polkas:
Maria Taglioni; Die Pariserin (polka française);
Rasch in der Tat! Polka-Mazurka: *Glücklich ist, wer*
vergisst. Quadrilles: *Le Beau Monde; Indigo.*
Waltzes: *Gross-Wien; Rhadamantus-Klänge;*
Telegramme; Vibrationen; Wien, mein Sinn!
** Marco Polo 8.223223. Wildner.

Vol. 24: *Gavotte der Königin. Viribus unitis, Marsch.*
Polkas: *Demi-fortune (polka française);*
Heski-Holki; Rokonhangok (Sympathieklänge); So
ängstlich sind wir nicht! Polka-Mazurka: *Licht und*
Schatten. Quadrille: *Streina-Terrassen.* Waltzes:
Idyllen; Jux-Brüder; Lockvögel; Sinnen und Minnen.
** Marco Polo 8.223224. A. Walter.

Volume 17 introduces another new name, Alfred
Eschwé. It is a particularly good collection, one of the
highlights of the set, and is beautifully played. Volume 18 brings back Alfred Walter and another very
good mix of waltzes and polkas. Johannes Wildner
then directs Volumes 21–23, and it must be said that
the middle volume shows him in better light than the
other two, and with a well-chosen programme.

Vol. 25: *Grossfürsten Marsch.* Polkas: *Bonbon (polka*
française); Explosions; Lustger Rath (polka
française); Mutig voran!. Polka-Mazurka: *Le*
Papillon. Quadrilles: *Künstler; Promenade.* Waltzes:
Frauen-Käferin; Krönungslieder; Spiralen; Ins
Zentrum!
** Marco Polo 8.223225. Wildner.

Vol. 26: *Es war so wunderschön Marsch.* Polkas:
Elektrophor; L'Enfantillage (polka française); Gut
bürgerlich (polka française); Louischen (polka

française); Pásmán. Quadrilles: *Industrie; Sofien.*
Waltzes: *Juristenball-Tänze; Künstlerleben; Pasman;*
Sinngedichte.
*** Marco Polo 8.223226. Austrian RSO, Vienna,
Guth.

Vol. 27: *Spanischer Marsch.* Polkas: *Drollerie;*
Durch's Telephon; Express; Gruss an Wien (polka
française). Polka-Mazurka: *Annina.* Quadrilles:
Künstler; Sans-souci. Waltzes: *Aeolstöne; Souvenir*
de Nizza; Wein, Weib und Gesang;
Frühlingsstimmen.
❂ *** Marco Polo 8.223227. Austrian RSO, Vienna,
Guth.

Vol. 28: *Freiwillige vor! Marsch (1887). Frisch in's*
Feld! Marsch. Polkas: *Unter Donner und Blitz;*
Pappacoda (polka française). Polka-Mazurkas:
Concordia; Spleen. Quadrille: *Tête-à-tête.* Waltzes:
Einheitsklänge: Illustrationen; Lebenswecker;
Telegraphische Depeschen.
** Marco Polo 8.223228. Wildner.

Vol. 29: *Brünner-Nationalgarde-Marsch. Der lustig*
Krieg, Marsch. Polkas: *Die Bajadere; Hellenen;*
Secunden (polka française). Polka-Mazurka: *Une*
bagatelle. Quadrille: *Waldmeister.* Waltzes:
Deutsche; Orakel-Sprüche; Schatz; Tausend und eine
Nacht; Volkssänger.
** Marco Polo 8.223229. A. Walter.

Vol. 30: *Fest-Marsch. Perpetuum mobile.* Polkas:
Alexandrinen; Kammerball; Kriegsabenteuer; Par
force! Quadrille: *Attaque.* Waltzes: *Erinnerung an*
Covent Garden; Kluh Gretelein; Luisen-Sympathie-
Klänge; Paroxysmen; Reiseabenteuer.
** Marco Polo 8.223230. A. Walter.

Vol. 31: *Napoleon-Marsch.* Polkas: *Husaren;*
Taubenpost (polka française); Vom Donaustrande.
Polka-Mazurka: *Nord und Süd.* Quadrilles:
Bonvivant; Nocturne. Waltzes: *Gambrinus-Tänze;*
Die ersten Curen; Hochzeitsreigen; Die
Unzertrennlichen; Wiener Bonbons.
** Marco Polo 8.223231. A. Walter.

Vol. 32: *Wiener Jubel-Gruss-Marsch.* Polkas: *Auf der*
Jagd; Olge; Tritsch-Tratsch. Polka-Mazurka: *An der*
Wolga. Quadrilles: *Methusalem; Hofball.* Waltzes:
Fantasiebilder; Ich bin dir gut!; Promotionen.
Wiener Blut.
** Marco Polo 8.223232. Wildner.

Volume 26 brings another fresh name, Peter Guth,
and fresh is the right word to describe this attractive
programme. From the bright-eyed opening, *Elektro-*
phor Polka schnell, this is winningly vivacious music-
making, and the waltz that follows, *Sinngedichte*,
makes one realize that there is something special
about Viennese string-playing, for this is the orchestra of Austrian Radio. Volume 27 features the same
orchestra and conductor and opens with the delecta-

ble *Künstler-Quadrille.* After the aptly named *Droll-erie* polka comes the *Aeolstöne* waltz with its portentous introduction, and the waltz itself is heart-warming. The *Souvenir de Nizza* waltz is hardly less beguiling; and *Wine, Women and Song* and, to end the disc, *Frühlingsstimmen* – two top favourites – simply could not be better played. These two Peter Guth CDs are the finest of the series so far, and we award a token Rosette to the second of the two, although it could equally apply to its companion. After those two marvellous collections it is an anticli-max to return to the following volumes. There is much interesting music here, but the performances often have an element of routine.

Vol. 33: *Saschen-Kürassier-Marsch.* Polkas: *Etwas kleines (polka française); Freikugeln.*
Polka-Mazurka: *Champêtre.* Quadrilles: *Bouquet; Opern-Maskenball.* Waltzes: *Abschieds-Rufe; Sträusschen; An der schönen blauen Donau; Trau, schau, wem!.*
** Marco Polo 8.223233. Wildner.

Vol. 34: (i) *Dolci pianti* (Romance for Cello & Orchestra). *Im russischen Dorfe, Fantasie* (orch. Max Schönherr). *Russischer Marsch. Slaven-potpourri.* Polkas: *La Favorite (polka française); Niko.* Polka-Mazurka: *Der Kobold.* Quadrille: *Nikolai.* Waltzes: *Abschied von St Petersburg; Fünf Paragraphen.*
*** Marco Polo 8.223234. Slovak RSO (Bratislava), Dittrich, (i) with Sikora.

Vol. 35: *Zivio! Marsch.* Polkas: *Jäger (polka française); Im Sturmschritt! Die Zeitlose (polka française).* Polka-Mazurka: *Die Wahrsagerin.* Quadrilles: *Der Blits; Der Liebesbrunnen.* Waltzes: *Accelerationen; Architecten-Ball-Tänze; Heut' ist heut' Königslieder.*
** Marco Polo 8.223235. Wildner.

Vol. 36: *Matador-Marsch.* Polkas: *Bitte schön! (polka française); Diplomaten; Kreuzfidel (polka française); Process.* Polka-Mazurka: *Der Klügere gibt nach.* Quadrilles: *Elfen; Fledermaus.* Waltzes: *D'Woaldbuama (im Ländlerstil)* (orch. Ludwig Babinski); *Extravaganten; Mephistos Höllenrufe; Neu-Wien.*
** Marco Polo 8.223236. A. Walter.

Among the following batch, the CD that stands out features another new name, Michael Dittrich. Work-ing with the Slovak Radio Symphony Orchestra, he produces a splendid collection to make up Volume 34. The flexible handling of the *Slav Pot-pourri* shows his persuasive sympathy for Strauss, while the *Fünf Paragraphen* waltz has an equally delectable lilt. There is great charm in the elegant *La Favorite* polka and the *Abschied von St Petersburg* waltz has a nicely beguiling opening theme.

Vol. 37: *Triumph-Marsch* (orch. Fischer). Polkas: *Das Comitat geht in die Höh!; Sonnenblume; Tanz mit dem Besenstiel!* (all arr. Pollack); (i) *Romance No. 2 in G min. for Cello & Orchestra, Op. 35* (arr. Schönherr). Quadrilles: *Die Königin von Leon* (arr. Pollack); *Spitzentuch. Neue Steierische Tänze* (orch. Pollack); *Traumbild II.* Waltzes: *Jugend-Träume* (orch. Pollack); *Schwungräder.*
*** Marco Polo 8.223237. Pollack; (i) with Jauslin.

Volume 37 is among the most interesting and worth-while issues so far. It includes the waltz with which the nineteen-year-old Johann Junior created his first sensation at Zum Sperlbauer in Vienna. He had taken over the orchestra's direction in February 1845, and during a summer's night festival in August of that same year *Jugend-Träume* was introduced. It received five encores! The waltz is entirely character-istic, opening with a lilting theme on the strings and moving from one idea to another with the easy facility that distinguishes his more famous waltzes. Christian Pollack is a Strauss scholar, and in almost every case here he has worked from piano scores or incomplete scoring. Particularly delectable is the set of *New Styrian Dances*, seductively written in the Ländler style of Lanner's *Steyrische Tänze.* Here an almost complete piano version was available, while the orchestral parts end with the third dance; Pollack has therefore scored the fourth dance (very convinc-ingly) in the style of the other three. While the *Romance for Cello and Orchestra* is agreeably slight, the other striking novelty here is *Traumbild II,* a late domestic work in two sections, the first of which is a gentle and charming 'dream-picture' of Strauss's wife, Adèle; the second shows the other side of her nature – more volatile and capricious. Both are in waltz time. Christian Pollack is not just a scholar but an excellent performing musician, and the playing here is polished, relaxed and spontaneous in an agreeably authentic way.

Vol. 38: *Wiener Garnison-Marsch* (orch. Babinski); *Ninetta-Galopp.* Polkas: *Damenspende; Lagerlust; Maskenzug* (2nd version); *Nimm sie hinn!; Zehner* (2nd version). Quadrilles: *Eine Nacht in Venedig; Serben* (orch. Babinski). Waltzes: *An der Elbe; Faschings-Lieder* (orch. Kulling); *Leitartikel.*
**(*) Marco Polo 8.223238. A. Walter.

An der Elbe is a real find among the waltzes, a charming melodic sequence with a striking introduc-tion. But the *Ninetta-Galopp* with its perky main theme and swirling woodwind answer has the poten-tial to become a Strauss lollipop, while the more sedate *Maskenzug-polka française* closes the pro-gramme engagingly. This is one of Alfred Walter's better programmes, nicely played and well recorded.

Vol. 39: *Ninetta-Marsch.* Polkas: *I Tipferl; Sylphen; Unparteiische Kritiken.* Quadrilles: *Jabuka; Slaven-Ball* (both orch. Pollack). Quodlibet: *Klänge* *aus der Raimundzeit.* Waltzes: *Abschied; Irenen* (orch. Babinski); *Hell und voll.*

**(*) Marco Polo 8.223239. Pollack.

The two most interesting items here both date from Johann's last years, the *Abschied* ('Farewell') *Waltz* and the *Klänge aus der Raimundzeit* (1898), an affectionate pot-pourri, including tunes by Johann Senior and Lanner. Johann originally called this good-humoured quodlibet *Reminiscenz. Aus der guter alten Zeit* ('from the good old days'). The score of the waltz is written in the composer's own handwriting; his widow, Adèle, offered it to be performed posthumously in 1900. The *I Tipferl-polka française* is based on a popular comic song from Strauss's *Prinz Methusalem*, and the couplet: 'The man forgot – the little dot, the dot up on the i!' is wittily pointed in the music. Christian Pollack directs excellent performances of all the music here which, although of varying quality, is never dull.

Vol. 40: *Hochzeits-Praeludium.* Polkas: *Herzenskönigin; Liebe und Ehe; Wildfeuer.* Quadrilles: *Ninetta; Wilhelminen* (orch. Babinski). Waltzes: *Heimats-Kinder* (orch. Babinski); *The Herald* (orch. Schönherr); *Irrlichter; Jubilee* (orch. Cohen).

*(*) Marco Polo 8.223240. Slovak RSO (Bratislava), Bauer-Theussl.

Vol. 41: March: *Wo uns're Fahne weht.* Polkas: *Newa; Shawl.* Quadrilles: *Martha; Vivat!.* Waltzes: *Burschen-Lieder; Gedankenflug; Lagunen. Traumbild* (symphonic poem). *Aschenbrödel (Cinderella): Prelude to Act III.*

** Marco Polo 8.223241. Slovak RSO (Bratislava), Dittrich.

Vol. 42: *Hommage au public russe.* March: *Piccolo.* Polkas: *An der Moldau; Auroraball; Grüss aus Osterreich; Sängerlust; Soldatespiel.* Waltzes: *Gartenlaube; Hirtenspiele; Sentenzen.*

**(*) Marco Polo 8.223242. Slovak RSO (Bratislava), Pollack.

For Volumes 40 to 42 Christian Pollack returns, but we also meet a new conductor, Franz Bauer-Theussl. As it turns out, the music-making in Volume 40 under Bauer-Theussl immediately proves heavy-handed in the opening waltz, and the feeling throughout is that he is conducting for the commercial ballroom rather than the concert hall. As Pollack demonstrates in Volume 42, much more can be made of relatively strict tempo versions than Bauer-Theussl does with the *Irrlichter* and *Herald* Waltzes. The *Jubilee Waltz* was written for the Strausses' Amerian visit in 1872, when in Boston he conducted its première, played by a 'Grand Orchestra' of 809 players, including 200 first violins! With this kind of spectacle it is not surprising that he chose to end a not particularly memorable piece by including a few bars of the American national anthem in the coda.

Without being exactly a live wire, Michael Dittrich makes a good deal more of Volume 41. He is able to relax and at the same time coax the orchestra into phrasing with less of a feeling of routine, as in the *Shawl-Polka*, which lilts rather nicely, and the comparatively sprightly *Vivat!* Dittrich fails to make a great deal of the one relatively well-known waltz here, *Lagunen*, but he manages the *Aschenbrödel Prelude* colourfully and does very well indeed by the *Traumbild I* ('Dream Picture No. 1'), a warmly relaxed and lyrical evocation, quite beautifully scored. It was written towards the end of the composer's life, for his own pleasure.

But when we come to Volume 42, so striking is the added vivacity that it is difficult to believe that this is the same orchestra playing. The opening *Piccolo-Marsch* and the *Auroraball polka française* are rhythmically light-hearted, as are all the other polkas in the programme, and if the *Hirtenspiele* (or 'Pastoral play') *Waltz* is not a masterpiece, it is still freshly enjoyable in Pollack's hands, despite the demands of a ballroom tempo. The *Gartenlaube-Walzer* is a real find; it has a charming introduction with a neat little flute solo, then the opening tune, lightly scored, is very engaging indeed. It is a great pity that Marco Polo did not hire the services of Christian Pollack much earlier in the series. Even the recording sounds better focused here.

Vol. 43: *An dem Tanzboden* (arr. Pollack); *Reitermarsch.* Polkas: *Herrjemineh; Postillon d'amour; Die Tauben von San Marco.* Quadrilles: *Simplicius; Des Teufels Antheil* (arr. Pollack). Waltzes: *Trifolien; Walzer-Bouquet No. 1; Wilde Rosen* (arr. Babinski & Kulling).

**(*) Marco Polo 8.223243. Pollack.

Vol. 44: Polkas: *Auf freiem Fusse; Nur nicht mucken* (arr. Peak); *Von der Börse.* Quadrilles: *Hinter den Coulissen; Monstre* (with J. STRAUSS SR). *Maskenfest; Schützen* (with J. and E. STRAUSS). Waltzes: *Altdeutscher* (arr. Pollack); *Aschenbrödel (Cinderella); Strauss' Autograph Waltzes* (arr. Cohen).

** Marco Polo 8.223244. Pollack.

Vol. 45: Ballet music from *Der Carneval in Rom* (arr. Schönherr); *Ritter Pásmán. Fest-Marsch. Pásmán-Quadrille* (arr. Pollack); *Potpourri-Quadrille; Zigeunerbaron-Quadrille.* Waltzes: *Eva; Ischler.*

**(*) Marco Polo 8.223245. A. Walter.

With Christian Pollack directing with his usual light touch, Volume 43 is one of the best of the more recent Marco Polo issues, even if the *Walzer-Bouquet* is less winningly tuneful than its title suggests. *Wilde Rosen* is rather better, though not really memorable like *An dem Tanzboden* ('On the Dance Floor'), which was inspired by a painting. It is a real lollipop with a charming introduction (with clarinet solo) and matching postlude. The main waltz-tune is captivating and Pollack plays it exquisitely. Strauss originally intended to feature a zither in his scoring, but later indicated a pair of flutes instead, which sound delightful here. This is a prime candidate for a New Year concert. The polkas and *Simply Delicious Quadrille* are amiably diverting too, but the *Trifolien Waltz*, though lively enough, is a run-of-the-mill piece.

Volume 44 includes the brief (three-minute) but pleasant *Altdeutscher Waltz*, arranged by the conductor, and the relatively familiar *Aschenbrödel*, which is attractive but not one of Strauss's vintage waltzes. As usual with Pollack, the various quadrilles and polkas are agreeably relaxed but never dull, and the recording is up to standard.

Alfred Walter returns to conduct Volume 45, and he is at his finest in the lively and tuneful waltz that is the central movement of the *Ritter Pásmán Ballet*. The other ballet music, from *Der Carneval in Rom*, is scored by Schönherr – and very vividly too. The *Eva Waltz* is brief but delightfully graceful; *Ischler*, however, is more conventional. The quadrilles are nicely managed and the sound is very good.

Vol. 46: March: *Vaterländischer.* **Polkas:** *Pawlowsk; Pizzicato* (with Josef); *Probirmamsell.* **Quadrilles:** *Marien; Annika.* **Romance:** *Sehnsucht.* **Waltzes:** *Cagliostro; Engagement; Greeting to America.* (i) **Gradual:** *Tu qui regis totum orbem.* SCHUMANN (arr. J. Strauss): *Widmung.*
★★★ Marco Polo 8.223246. Slovak RSO (Bratislava), Dittrich; (i) with Slovak Philh. Ch. (members).

Michael Dittrich is on top form in Volume 46 of this ongoing series, opening vivaciously with a musical switch in march form, beginning with the *Radetzky* 'fanfare' and proceeding to quote intriguing snippets from all kinds of sources, including the Austrian national anthem. The *Greeting to America Waltz* has a very appropriate and recognizable introduction and is as attractive as the delightfully scored *Engagement Waltz*, also written for America. The *Marien-Quadrille* is another charmer, and we learn from the excellent notes that the famous *Pizzicato Polka*, a joint effort between Johann and Josef, was composed in Pavlovsk on a Russian tour in 1869. The transcription of Schumann's love song, *Widmung*, was made by Johann in 1862 as a tribute to his new bride, Jetty, who was a singer, but the *Romance* (*Sehnsucht*) was written as a more robust cornet solo. The Gradual, *Tu qui regis totum orbem* ('Thou who rulest the whole world'), is a surprise inclusion from the eighteen-year-old composer – an offertory sung in conjunction with the performance of a Mass by his teacher, Professor Dreschler – and very pleasing it is. The concert ends with one of the deservedly better-known waltzes, taken from the operetta *Cagliostro in Wien* and played in an elegantly vivacious but nicely flexible style, like the rest of this very appealing programme, one of the very best of the Marco Polo series. The recording is excellent.

Vol. 47: Ballet music from *Die Fledermaus;* **from** *Indigo und die vierzig Räuber* (arr. Schönherr). *Eine Nacht in Venedig: Processional March.* GOUNOD (arr. J. Strauss): *Faust (Romance). Quadrille on themes from 'Faust'.* **Marches:** *Kaiser Alexander Huldinungs; Kaiser Frans Joseph Jubiläums; Der Zigeunerbaron.* **Waltzes:** *Coliseum Waltzes; Farewell to America; Sounds from Boston.*
★★★ Marco Polo 8.223247. Bratislava City Ch., Slovak RSO, Wildner.

This is another very attractive compilation with many beguiling novelties. After the brief but lively march from *Der Zigeunerbaron* comes *Farewell to America*, an agreeable pastiche waltz, which waits until its coda to quote *The Star-spangled Banner*. The following *Faust Romance* is a robust flugelhorn solo, based on an aria which was later to disappear from Gounod's revision of his score. The lively *Quadrille*, however, includes many favourite tunes from the opera and climaxes genially with the *Soldiers' Chorus*. Strauss's own ballet-music, written to be played during Orlofsky's supper party in *Die Fledermaus*, is today almost always replaced by something briefer. It includes a number of short national dances (not forgetting a *Schottische*) and the *Bohemian Dance* is in the form of a choral polka, actually sung here ('Marianka, come here and dance with me'), while the Hungarian finale reprises the music from Rosalinde's *Csárdás*. On the other hand, Schönherr's audaciously scored (some might say over-scored) 11-minute *mélange* of tunes from *Indigo and the Forty Thieves* is at times more like Offenbach than Strauss: it coalesces the good tunes and presents them in a glittering kaleidoscope of orchestral colour. The engaging *Coliseum Waltzes* that follow uncannily anticipate the *Blue Danube*, complete with an opening horn theme. *Sounds from Boston*, written for the composer's Boston visit in 1872, is another pastiche waltz of considerable charm, resulting as much from its delicacy of scoring as from its ready melodic flow: the orchestra parts were discovered, hidden away in the music library of the Boston Conservatory. The ideas come from earlier waltzes and almost none of them are familiar. All this music is liltingly and sparklingly presented by the Slovak Radio Orchestra, and no one could accuse the conductor, Johannes Wildner, of dullness.

Vol. 48: Complete Overtures, Vol. 1: *Concert Overture: Opéra comique* (arr. Pollack). *Intermezzo from 'Tausend und eine Nacht'.* **Overtures:** *Blindekuh; Cagliostro in Wien; Der Carneval in Rom; Die Fledermaus; Indigo und die vierzig Räuber. Prince Methusalem; Das Spitzentuch der Königen.*
★★(★) Marco Polo 8.223249. A. Walter.

Collections of operetta overtures are almost always entertainingly tuneful, and this one is no exception. It begins with a curiosity that may or may not be authentic, an *Overture comique* written by the young

Johann Jr for large harmonium (a kind of orchestrion) and piano, and afterwards arranged by the Strauss scholar, Fritz Lange, for violin and piano. None of the ideas it contains can be traced to the composer's notebooks, but the piece is attractive and is well put together in the form of a concert overture. It is heard here in a new arrangement (following the Lange manuscript) by Christopher Pollack. *Indigo und die vierzig Räuber* ('Indigo and the Forty Thieves') is also interesting in that Strauss omits the waltz rhythm altogether, which makes its lightly rhythmic progress seem rather Offenbachian. The *Intermezzo* from *Thousand and One Nights* is a just favourite, although Walter's languorous performance could use a little more lift, and *Die Fledermaus* is a fairly routine performance. However, Walter conducts the other overtures very agreeably and makes the most of their pretty scoring. The waltzes are always coaxed nicely, particularly that in *Cagliostro in Wien*, and the playing has charm; yet one feels that some of the livelier ideas might have been given a bit more zip.

Vol. 49: Complete Overtures, Vol. 2: *Aschenbrödel (Cinderella): Quadrille.* Overtures: *Die Göttin der Vernunft (The Goddess of Reason); Der lustige Krieg. Jabuka: Prelude to Act III. Eine Nacht in Venedig: Overture* and *Prelude to Act III.* Overtures: *Simplicius; Waldmeister; Der Zigeunerbaron.*
**(*) Marco Polo 8.223275. A. Walter.

Alfred Walter's second collection of overtures has distinctly more sparkle than the first. He is always good with waltzes and there are quite a few here, if only in snippet form. The pair included in *A Night in Venice* are presented with appealing delicacy, while *The Goddess of Reason* brings a waltzing violin solo complete with cadenza and, at the close, another waltz which swings splendidly. *Zigeunerbaron* is the best-known piece here, and it is laid out elegantly and is beautifully played. But Walter is inclined to dally by the wayside: in the theatre a performance like this would not hold the attention of the audience. *Simplicius* is much more lively, with a march near the beginning, and *Waldmeister* has real verve, with the horns skipping along nicely towards the end. What one rediscovers on listening through this pair of discs is not only the fecundity of Johann's invention and the charm of his orchestration, but also the felicitous way he turns a pot-pourri into a naturally spontaneous sequence of ideas. The recording throughout both collections is first class, spacious and with a ballroom warmth.

Vol. 50: (i) *Am Donaustrand;* (i) *Erste Liebe (Romanze); Erster Gedanke;* (i) *Ein gstanzi von Tanzl; Die Fledermaus; Csárdás. Frisch gewagt* (Galop); *Da nicken die Giebel* (Polka-Mazurka); *Die Göttin der Vernunft* (Quadrille); (i) *Dolci pianti.* Waltzes: (i) *Frühlingstimmen;* (i) *King Gretelein;*

Nachgelassener; Odeon-Waltz; (i) *Wo die Citronen blüh'n;* (i) *Wenn du ein herzig Liebchen hast.*
*** Marco Polo 8.223276. (i) Hill Smith; Slovak RSO (Bratislava), Pollack.

Marilyn Hill Smith was on hand for this collection, so one wonders why the opening *Csárdás* from *Die Fledermaus* is the orchestral version (arranged by Hans Swarowsky); but the excellent Christian Pollack makes a good case for it, his ebb and flow of mood and tempo very engaging. Hill Smith sings a number of items, and her light soubrette is just right for this repertoire. She presents *Wo die Citronen blüh'n* with much vivacity and is hardly less sparkling in the famous *Voices of Spring*. Moreover she offers as a charming vignette *Dolci pianti* (a song that Strauss composed for his singer-wife, Jetty) for which she has also provided the accompanying translation. The rest of the programme is agreeable, but there are no lost masterpieces here. Pollack makes the most of the waltzes and is especially characterful in the polka-mazurka, *Da nicken die Giebel*, which sounds a bit like a slow waltz with extra accents. Again, first-rate recording.

Vol. 51: *Auf der Alm* (Idyll); *Fürstin Ninetta* (Entr'acte). Galop: *Liebesbotschaft.* (i) Choral polka: *Champêtre (Wo klingen die Lieder).* Polka-Mazurka: *Promenade-Abenteuer.* (ii) *Romance No. 2 for Cello & Orchestra.* Choral waltz: (i) *An der schönen, blauen Donau.* Waltzes: *Centennial; Enchantment; Engagement; Farewell to America; Manhattan; Tauben.* Songs: (iii) *Bauersleut' im Künstlerhaus; D'Hauptsach* (both arr. Rott).
✹ *** Marco Polo 8.223279. Slovak RSO (Bratislava), Cohen; with (i) Slovak Philharmonic Ch.; (ii) Tvrdik; (iii) Eröd.

It is rather appropriate that Volume 51 should be special, and so it is. It opens with the enchanting choral *Polka mazurka champêtre*, introduced by the horns and gloriously sung by a male chorus with a nicely managed diminuendo at the coda. And it ends with Strauss's masterpiece, the *Blue Danube*, also for male-voice choir and sung with an infectious lilt, to leave the listener in high spirits. All the other half-dozen waltzes here are virtually unknown, and every one is delightful. The opening strain of *Manhattan* is ear-catching and Cohen later (rarely in this series) indulges himself in some affectionate rubato, which is most seductive. The *Centennial* and the (well-named) *Enchantment Waltzes* are again most affectionately presented, and their beguiling introductions are in each case followed by a string of good tunes. The *Engagement Waltz* opens more grandly, but then the atmosphere lightens, and there is plenty of sparkle. *Farewell to America* (a pot-pourri) brings the American national anthem delicately and nostalgically into the coda. The *Romance No. 2 for Cello and Orchestra*, tastefully played by Ivan Tvrdik, is surprisingly dolorous at its opening, then produces a romantic flowering, before ending nostalgically. The *Liebesbotschaft Galop* then arrives to cheer us all up, and it is followed by yet another unknown waltz, *Tauben*, in which Cohen coaxes the opening quite ravishingly. Of the two brief baritone solos, the second, *D'Hauptsach*, has a most pleasing melody. No other record in the series so far offers such a fine package of unexpected delights or more hidden treasure, and there could be no better advocate than the present conductor, Jerome Cohen. He has the advantage of spacious, naturally balanced recording. A Rosette then for the sheer enterprise of the first half-century of this series and also for the special excellence of this collection with its discovery of six remarkably fine waltzes.

Pot-pourris, Vol. 1: *Cagliostro in Wien; Indigo und die vierzig Räuber; Der lustige Krieg; Eine Nacht in Venedig; Prinz Methusalem; Das Spitzentuch der Königin.*
⋆(⋆) Marco Polo 8.225074. Pollack.

Pot-pourris, Vol. 2: *Fürstin Ninetta; Die Göttin der Vernunft; Jabuka (Das Apfelfest); Ritter Pásmán; Simplicius.*
⋆(⋆) Marco Polo 8.225075. Pollack.

Even today, selections from musical shows are the mainstay of the bandstand, and so it was in the days of the Strauss family. However, although they include a fair smattering of good tunes, some of the pot-pourris here outlast their welcome (*Indigo und die vierzig Räuber* runs for over 18 minutes) and the scoring of the vocal numbers is seldom very imaginative. Curiously, even Christian Pollack, usually an inspired Straussian, is below his best form, and he fails to make a case for them. In the end this becomes nothing more than wallpaper music. So this pair of discs, although well enough played, is of documentary interest only.

OTHER COLLECTIONS

Galops: *Banditen; Cachucha.* Marches: *Egyptyscher; Kaiser Franz Josef.* Polkas: *Annen; Auf der Jagd; Eljen a Magyar; Fata Morgana; Furioso; Tritsch-Tratsch.* Quadrille nach Motiven der Operette 'Der lustige Krieh'. Waltzes: *An der schönen blauen Donau; Morgenblatter; Rosen aus dem Süden; 1001 Nacht; Wiener Blut; Wiener Bonbons.* JOSEF STRAUSS: Polkas: *Farewell; Die Libelle; Moulinet; Ohne Sorgen.* Waltzes: *Aquarellen; Perlen der Liebe.* EDUARD STRAUSS: March: *Weyprecht-Payer.* Polka: *Saat und Ernte.* Waltzes: *Leuchkäferin; Schleier un Krone.*

(B) ⋆⋆ Chan. 6687 (2). Johann Strauss O, Rothstein.

This generous two-disc compilation is assembled from recordings made between 1981 and 1992. It includes a number of attractive novelties, among them rare items from Josef and Eduard, although Josef's *Perlen der Liebe* is a shade disappointing.

Otherwise there is no lack of spontaneity here: the polkas are infectious and cheerful, there is no lack of lilt in the waltzes, and the bright digital sound has plenty of bloom. However, good though Rothstein is, he does not equal John Georgiadis among other British conductors in this repertoire.

Banditen-Galopp; Quadrille nach Motiven der Operette. Marches: *Egyptischer; Kaiser Franz Josef.* Polkas: *Annen-Polka; Auf der Jagd; Eljen a Magyar; Fata Morgana; Furioso-Polka quasi Galopp; Tritsch-Tratsch; Unter Donner und Blitz.* Waltzes: *An der schönen, blauen Donau; Morgenblätter; Rosen aus dem Süden; Tausend and eine Nacht; Wiener Blut; Wiener Bonbons.* EDUARD STRAUSS: *Weyprecht-Payer* (march); *Saat und Ernte* (polka). Waltzes: *Leuchtkäferin; Schleir und Krone.* JOSEF STRAUSS: Polkas: *Die Libelle; Farewell!; Moulinet; Ohne Sorgen.* Waltzes: *Aquarellen; Perlen der Liebe.* J. STRAUSS SR: *Cachucha-Galopp.*

(M) ⋆⋆(⋆) Chan. (ADD) 7129 (2). Strauss O, Rothstein.

These are relaxed, enjoyable performances, which are hard to fault. If they lack the Viennese distinction of Boskovsky or the individuality of Karajan, the varied programme, with plenty of novelties, makes up for it. There are several agreeable surprise items in this two-CD set, and the sound is very good.

OPERA AND OPERETTA

Die Fledermaus (complete).
(B) ⋆⋆(⋆) Decca (ADD) 473 499-2. Janowitz, Holm, Kmentt, Kunz, Waechter, Windgassen, V. State Op. Ch., VPO, Boehm.
(M) (⋆⋆) RCA mono 74321 61949-2. Gueden, Streich, Waechter, Zampieri, Berry, Stolze, Kunz, Klein, Ott, Meinrad, V. State Op. Ch. & O, Karajan.
(M) ⋆(⋆) DG (ADD) 457 765-2 (2). Varady, Popp, Prey, Kollo, Weikl, Rebroff, Kusche, Bav. State Op. Ch. & O, C. Kleiber.

It is good to have a reissue of Karl Boehm's 1971 *Fledermaus*, not previously issued on CD. Boehm conducts with great warmth and affection, and the recording was made without dialogue, which many will prefer. The stars of the performance are undoubtedly Gundula Janowitz, in rich voice as Rosalinde, and Renate Holm as Adèle. The male principals are rather less impressive, and the use of a male Orlovsky has less dramatic point on record than it would on stage. Windgassen, who assumes this role, is vocally here much inferior to, say, Brigitte Fassbaender. But there is much to enjoy, and the vintage Decca recording was made in the Sofiensaal. As with other reissues in Universal's 'Compact Opera Collection', the complete text and translation are available separately on a CD-ROM.

Recorded live by Austrian Radio at the Vienna State Opera on New Year's Eve, 1960, the RCA set gives a vivid picture of the event, warts and all. For the non-German speaker, the acres of dialogue will be a serious deterrent, notably in Act III with only 15 minutes of music out of 40. This is still a cherishable issue for capturing the atmosphere and special flavour of a great Viennese occasion. Hilde Gueden is the complete charmer (as on her early Decca set, a very Viennese heroine), with Walter Berry as Falke, Giuseppe Zampieri as Alfred and Peter Klein as Dr Blind, also relishing the comedy all the more. The party junketings in Act II include not just Erich Kunz singing the *Fiakerlied* by Gustav Pick, but a special guest, Giuseppe di Stefano, singing *O sole mio* and Lehár's *Dein ist mein ganzes Herz* (Italy's tribute to Vienna prompting wild cheering). Also a ten-minute ballet, *Schottisch, Russisch, Hungarisch und Polka*.

The glory of the Kleiber set is the singing of the two principal women – Julia Varady and Lucia Popp, magnificently characterful and stylish as mistress and servant – but much of the set is controversial, to say the least. Carlos Kleiber is certainly exciting at times and rejects many older conventions in performing style, which some will find refreshing, but he is not at all easy-going. Other conductors allow the music's intrinsic charm to bubble to the surface like champagne; with Kleiber, one feels the charm, if one can call it that, being rammed down one's throat. But that is nothing compared to the falsetto of Ivan Rebroff, which has to be heard to be believed – it sounds grotesque and is likely to put most listeners off this recording. Full texts and translations are included. But first choice still rests with Previn's set with Dame Kiri Te Kanawa as Rosalinde (Ph. Duo 464 031-2 – see our main *Guide*).

STRAUSS, Josef (1827–70)

Josef Strauss: The Complete Edition

Vol. 1: Polkas: *Angelica; Bauern; Eislauf; Etiquette; Moulinet; Thalia*. March: *Galenz. Kakadu-Quadrille*. Waltzes: *Fantasiebilder; Marien-Klänge; Wiegenlieder*.
** Marco Polo 8.223561. Budapest Strauss SO, A. Walter.

Vol. 2: *Amazonen-Quadrille*. Polkas: *Arabella; Diana; Genien; Stiefmütterchen; Sturmlauf; Sympathie*. Schottischer Tanz. Waltzes: *Petitionen; Tranz-Prioriräten*: arr. of SCHUMANN: *Träumerei*.
** Marco Polo 8.223562. Slovak State PO (Košice), A. Walter.

Vol. 3: *Avantgarde March*. Polkas: *Gnomen; Die Lachtaube; Die Naïve; Ohne Sorgen; Sport*. Quadrilles: *Caprice; Flick-Flock*. Waltzes: *Assoziationen; Ernst und Humor; Mai-Rosen*.
** Marco Polo 8.223563. Slovak State PO (Košice), A. Walter.

It is good to see Marco Polo now exploring the output of Josef Strauss, of which we know remark-

ably little. Indeed almost all the items in this first volume are completely unfamiliar. Alfred Walter's easy-going style permeates the whole programme, and most of the polkas are left badly needing a more vital pacing. The waltzes are lilting in a lazy way: Walter shapes the evocative opening of *Fantasiebilder* rather beautifully, helped by polished and sympathetic playing from a group of Hungarian players. *Wiegenlieder* ('Cradle Songs') is another waltz which opens very enticingly and ought to be better known: it has a charming main theme and is nicely scored. The closing *Eislauf Polka*, so very like the writing of Johann Junior, ends the concert spiritedly, and this well-recorded disc has great documentary interest, while the back-up notes are equally praiseworthy.

In Volume 2, Walter introduces two more waltzes which are fully worthy of Johann Jr; *Petitionen* is particularly inventive. The polkas are amiable, with *Diana* aptly introduced by the horns. They are, as usual, played in a relaxed dance tempo: the most successful is the charming, Ländler-like *Stiefmütterchen*. The Schumann arrangement is very straightforward and adds little or nothing to the original piano piece: Walter presents it without any attempt at romantic subtlety.

Volume 3 opens with a sprightly march (not too heavily articulated), but the highlights are the *Assoziationen* and *Ernst und Humor* waltzes and the *Sport Polka*, played here with great spirit. Of the two waltzes the latter ('In a serious and light-hearted manner') has some interesting changes of mood, with modulations to match. It ought to be at least as well known as the closing (and justly renowned) *Ohne Sorgen Polka*, which the Slovak players present with much enthusiasm, including the vocal interpolations. Excellent recording.

Vol. 4: March: *Osterreichischer Kronprinzen*; Polkas: *La Chevaleresque; Jockey; Schlarffen; Titi; Wiener Leben*. Quadrilles: *Genovefa; Turner. Ständchen*. Waltzes: *Freudengrüsse; Frohes Leben; Vereins-Lieder*.
**(*) Marco Polo 8.223564. Slovak RSO (Bratislava), Dittrich.

Josef usually proves most reliable in his polkas, and *Schlarffen* is one of his finest, while the *Titi Polka* is delicious, with the portrait of that pretty bird implied in the scoring rather than with any imitations. Both are very infectious as presented here by the excellent Michael Dittrich, and the better-known *Jockey* bursts with vivacity. The *Turner Quadrille* is also captivating in its swinging rhythm, with some whistling piccolo embroidery near the close. The waltzes *Vereins-Lieder* and *Freudengrüsse*, however, are lighthearted without being truly memorable. *Frohes Leben* has more striking ideas. The programme ends with a simple *Serenade* that might or might not have been intended as a tribute to Wagner.

Vol. 5: *Defilier* (March); Polkas: *Die Gazelle; Maiblümchen; Die Marketenderin; Mignon;*

Vorwärts. Quadrilles: *Csikos; Die Grossherzogin von Gerolstein.* Waltzes: *Dynamiden (Geheime Anziehungskräfte); Flammen; Huldigungslieder.*
**(*) Marco Polo 8.223565. Slovak State PO (Košice), Pollack.

The very fetching *Die Grossherzogin Quadrille* gets this programme off to a good start. In English, of course this comes out as *The Grand Duchess of Gerolstein* and the piece is an agreeable pot-pourri of the many excellent tunes from Offenbach's operetta, presented one after another with little or no attempt at tailoring and with brief pauses in between. Pollack (as elsewhere) chooses a dancing tempo and one wants to get up and join in. The polka, *Marketenderin* ('Camp Follower' – in this case a vivacious lady, generous with her favours), is charming too, though it reminds the listener a little of a more famous piece by Johann. *Vorwärts* ('Forward') then goes with a swing and is delightfully scored – one of Josef's very best. *Mignon* is very catchy too, and *Die Gazelle* has something of the grace of its title. Of the three waltzes included here, there is one masterpiece: *Dynamiden*, with its ravishing cantabile, is fully worthy of Johann, and it is beautifully played. *Huldigungslieder* also begins impressively and has a rather good opening waltz-tune, but it is slightly less memorable overall. *Flammen* surprises the listener by opening with a fast, polka-like introduction. The main strain is very agreeable and there are some engagingly fresh ideas later on. Pollack takes the polka-mazurkas at dance tempi with a strong accent on the first beat, which is obviously authentic; but for concert perfomance a slightly faster tempo might have been more effective, and this applies especially to *Maiblümchen*, which closes the concert. Nevertheless this is one of the most rewarding Josef Strauss collections so far in the series.

Vol. 6: March: *Victor.* Polkas: *Carrière; Causerie; Figaro; Joujou; Tanz-Regulator; Waldröslein. Musen Quadrille.* Waltzes: *Die Industriellen; Krönungslieder; Nilfluthen.*
**(*) Marco Polo 8.223566. Slovak State PO (Košice), Georgiadis.

Of the three waltzes here, the first, *Die Industriellen*, is marginally the most beguiling, and Georgiadis has its measure, both at the lilting opening tune and in its engaging secondary scalic figure, which rises and falls in a busy little group of notes. *Nilfluthen* ('Nile Waters') was written for the Concordia Ball, held during the celebrations for the opening of the Suez Canal (Emperor Franz Josef was there). It, too, has a nifty main theme and there is nothing in the least Egyptian about its style. *Krönungslieder* opens with a regal fanfare (it celebrated a royal political settlement in 1867 between the Austrian Empire and Hungary, when the emperor and empress were crowned in Budapest); but after that it is a routine sequence. Of the polkas, the *Causerie* ('Chatting') is the most ingenuously charming, while *Carrière* is one of

Josef's most infectious galops. John Georgiadis is thoroughly at home here, and this music is all stylishly presented and again very well recorded.

Vol. 7: March: *Erzherzog Karl.* Polkas: *Bouquet; Frohsinn; Irenen; Jucker.* Polka mazurs: *Die Idylle; Minerva.* Quadrille: *Parade.* Waltzes: *Friedenspalmen; Hesperus-Bahnen; Streichmagnete.*
** Marco Polo 8.223567. Slovak State PO (Košice), Eichenholz.

Volume 7 opens winningly with the *Jockey Polka*, and the hardly less engaging *Parade Quadrille*. Here Mika Eichenholz displays a light rhythmic touch and the Slovak State Philharmonic continue to be thoroughly at home. The *Streichmagnete Waltz* has a beguilingly delicate introduction and its main theme does not disappoint, but the following ideas are more conventional. *Friedenspalmen* and the very agreeable *Hesperus-Bahnen* also open atmospherically and in the former a fine stream of melodies follows, and it ought to be much better known. Eichenholz, who adopts a lazy, Viennese waltz style, readily responds to it. If he is less impressive in the two polka mazurs, which tend to hang fire, the *Irenen Polka* which ends the programme is delightfully pert.

Vol. 8: Polkas: *Die Amazone; Arm in Arm; En passant; Mailust; Saus und Braus; Seraphinen; Sylphide.* Quadrille: *Debardeurs.* Waltzes: *Die Clienten; Expensnoten; Wiener Stimmen.*
** Marco Polo 8.223568. Slovak State PO (Košice), Eichenholz.

This collection is mainly of documentary interest. The various polkas proceed in leisurely fashion, and it is not until the waltzes, *Die Clienten* and *Expensnoten*, that the music rises much above routine formulas. Eichenholz indulges them in his casual manner, and also the seductive *Arm in Arm* polka masur, which follows, while *Wiener Stimmen* lilts most engagingly of all, with the main theme nicely lifted. Any of these items could be very impressive in the hands of a great conductor.

Vol. 9: March: *Deutscher Union.* Polkas: *Adamira; Eingesendet; Lieb' und Wein; Masken; Die Spinnerin; Zephir.* Quadrille: *Bivouac.* Waltzes: *Deutsche Sympathien; Rudolphsklänge; Studententräume.*
*** Marco Polo 8.223569. Slovak State PO (Košice), Pollack.

Not surprisingly, with Christian Pollack in charge this is one of the best if not *the* best of Marco Polo's Josef Strauss series. The opening *Adamira Polka* sparkles with life and the following *Bivouac-Quadrille* bounces along infectiously. These performance are in a completely different class from those directed by Mika Eichenholz, and all three waltzes glow with rhythmic and melodic life. The introduction to *Studententräume* is quite enchanting. Indeed this collection continually shows that at its best Josef's invention, craftsmanship and orchestration could readily match that of his brother, Johann. Splendid playing and first-class recording make this a disc to treasure.

Vol. 10: Polkas: *Abendstern; For Ever; Grüss an München; Harlekin; Heiterer Muth; Herzbleamerl; Nachtschatten.* Quadrille: *Touristen.* Waltzes: *Herztöne; Wiener Fresken; Wiener Kinder.*
*** Marco Polo 8.223570. Slovak State PO (Košice), Pollack.

The performances in Volume 10 are just as vivacious as those in Volume 9, and though the opening of the *Wiener Kinder Waltz* is not helped by its rather fruity horn solo, Pollack is persuasive enough when the waltzes proper begin, even if the tunes are not top drawer. The following series of polkas all sail along gaily and the two remaining waltzes are rather more striking, especially *Wiener Fresken.* The other highlight is the bouncing *Touristen-Quadrille.* Everything is played with affection and strong rhythmic character.

Vol. 11: Polkas: *Bon-bon; Die Emancipirte; Lust-Lager; Schwalbenpost; Die Schwätzerin; Victoria.* Quadrilles: *Dioscuren; Les Géorgiennes.* Waltzes: *Gedenkblätter; Hochzeits-Klänge; Maskengeheimnisse.*
**(*) Marco Polo 8.223571. Razumovsky SO, Eschwé.

There is nothing that really stands out in Volume 11, although the *Schwalbenpost Polka* is jolly enough, and there are some nice touches of orchestral colour throughout (notably in the *Schwätzerin Polka Masur*). Eschwé is a more flexibly imaginative conductor than Eichenholz, but he does not have the natural flair of Pollack. He makes the most of the *Maskengeheimnis* and *Hochzeits-Klänge Waltzes*, both pleasing, if not in the first flight, and is pleasingly elegant in the *Victoria-polka française*, while the closing *Lust-Lager* is engagingly vivacious.

Vol. 12: March: *Schützen.* Polkas: *Allerlei; Amaranth; Frisch auf!; Laxenburger; Une Pensée; Schabernack.* Quadrille: *Herold.* Waltzes: *Helenen; Schwert und Leyer; Tanzadressen an die Preisgekrönten.*
*** Marco Polo 8.223572. Slovak State PO (Košice), Pollack.

Christian Pollack returns for Volume 12, as is immediately obvious from the spirited and vivid opening *Herold-Quadrille*, which is fully worthy of Johann and very elegantly scored. Pollack also again brings a lilting sweep to the string-tunes in all three waltzes. *Schwert und Leyer* opens melodramatically, but then a very seductive melody steals in on the strings. *Tanzadressen an die Preisgekrönten* is another of Josef's best, and *Helenen* with its chattering opening flutes is a real charmer. There is a high proportion of the slower polkas in the collection, of which the closing polka masur, *Une Pensée*, has a string of tunes

rather like a waltz. The playing has a pleasingly urbane finish.

Vol. 13: *Phönix-Marsch.* Polkas: *Extempore; Farewell; Matrosen; Wiener.* Polka-Mazurka: *Die Galante.* Quadrilles: *Toto; Turnier.* Waltzes: *Deutsche Grüsse; Herbstrosen; Wintermärchen.*
** Marco Polo 8.223573. Slovak State PO (Košice), Dittrich.

Michael Dittrich brings zest to the opening march and sparkle to the polkas, and he shapes the three waltzes affectionately. But he is just a little too relaxed to realize their full potential, even though they are beautifully played, and the recording is well up to the usual standard of this fine series. The closing *Turnier-Quadrille* is an infectious highlight.

Vol. 14: Polkas: *Auf Ferienreisen; Bellona; Künstler-Grüss; Neckerei; La Simplicité; Springinsfeld; Die Tänzerin.* Quadrille: *Blaubart.* Waltzes: *Disputationen; Die guten, alten Zeiten; Die Zeitgenossen.*
** Marco Polo 8.223574. Slovak State PO (Košice), Dittrich.

Volume 14 opens with a vivacious account of the spirited *Auf Ferienreisen Polka* and is also notable for the *Bluebeard-Quadrille*, an engaging Offenbach pot-pourri, neatly scored, with plenty of familiar tunes, where Dittrich, too, is at his best. But again he makes too little of the three waltzes, being content to play them through *a tempo*.

Vol. 15: *Hesperus-Ländler.* March: *Ungarischer Krönungsmarsch.* Polkas: *Amouretten; Gedenke mein!; Plappermäulchen; Winterlust.* Polka-Mazurkas: *Die Nasswalderin; Vielliebchen.* Quadrille: *Theater.* Waltzes: *Combinationen; Lustschwärmer; Mein Lebenslauf ist Lieb' und Lust.*
** Marco Polo 8.223575. Slovak State PO (Košice), Kulling.

Two famous numbers stand out here: the *Plappermäulchen Polka*, played here with considerable gusto, and the waltz *Mein Lebenslauf ist Lieb' und Lust*, which is given a routine performance. Indeed Arthur Kulling is another conductor who is better in the bright work than in coaxing the waltzes. The very agreeable Ländler is also rather heavily presented. The *Theatre Quadrille* includes melodies from operas and operettas by Verdi, Suppé and Meyerbeer, among others, and as usual is nicely orchestrated. But Kulling does not make a great deal of it.

Vol. 16: March: *Schwarzenberg-Monument.* Polkas: *Fashion; Freigeister; In der Heimat; Punsch; Die Schwebende; Wilde Rose.* Quadrilles: *Lancer; Schäfer.* Waltzes: *Ball-Silhouetten; Frauenwürde; Wiener Couplets.*
** Marco Polo 8.223618. Slovak State PO (Košice), Kulling.

Kulling opens with a rhythmically buoyant account

of the march, the polkas have life and charm, and the two quadrilles are elegant enough. All three waltzes here are among Josef's most appealing (often with a strong whiff of Johann) and *Frauenwürde* has a most enticing opening. They are well played, have a relaxed rhythmic feeling, and lilt warmly, but Pollack would surely have given them even more personality. As always in this series, the recording ambience is very pleasing.

Vol. 17: March: *Wallonen.* **Polkas:** *Edelweiss; Feurfest!; Jocus; Die Sirene; Tag und Nacht; Verliebte Augen.* **Quadrille:** *Policinello.* **Waltzes:** *Dorfschwalben aus Osterreich (Village Swallows); Perlen der Liebe; Sphären-Klange (Music of the Spheres).*
** Marco Polo 8.223619. Slovak State PO (Košice), Märzendorfer.

Ernst Märzendorfer presents all the polkas here pleasingly enough. The opening *Die Sirene* is charming, and the famous *Feuerfest!* has gusto. The *Policinello-Quadrille* (complete with a brief chorus near the end) is winningly sprightly, and he also finds a nice bouncy rhythm for the *Wallonen-Marsch*, which is really a lilting two-step. But although the two great waltzes, *Music of the Spheres* and the chirping *Village Swallows* are nicely introduced, once the music gets under way, routine sets in, and *Perlen der Liebe* is at times mannered. Good playing and excellent recording.

Vol. 18: March: *Armee.* **Polkas:** *Brennende Liebe; Gurli; Im Fluge; Die Libelle; Rudolfsheimer.* **Quadrilles:** *Colosseum; Sturm.* **Waltzes:** *Aquarellen; Die Ersten nach den Letzten; Normen.*
*** Marco Polo 8.223619. Slovak State PO (Košice), Geyer.

There is an engaging story about the composition of *Die Ersten nach den Letzten*, one of Josef's best waltzes, and a real find. In August 1853 'Pepi' Strauss, as he was affectionately known, found himself obliged to direct the orchestra for the first time, because his brother was recuperating after a serious illness. For the same reason he had also to provide a waltz for the occasion. Determined that his substitute musical directorship should not be permanent, he called the waltz *Die Ersten und Letzen* ('The First and the Last'). But the piece, published as his Op. 1, enjoyed considerable success, and he was unable to maintain his resolve. Thus, with a hint of irony, but also with a twinkle, he called his Op. 12 (above) *The First after the Last. Normen* ('Standards') is also a very attractive piece, with a chirruping main theme and plenty of good ideas. Geyer is a much more persuasive advocate than many of his colleagues, and with some perky polkas (*Gurli,* the lilting *Rudolfsheimer,* and *Im Fluge* among the most characteristic), the justly celebrated *Aquarellen,* and a pair of attractive quadrilles, this is one of the best discs in the series.

Although the crispness of ensemble is very striking, in Karl Geyer's collection there is also a feeling of a rhythmic straitjacket. This applies particularly to the quadrilles. Yet if you don't mind the articulated precision, Geyer presents the waltzes with plenty of sparkle, and there are three good ones here, two quite unfamiliar. After the introduction *Normen* takes off very seductively. The opening *Armee-Marsch* suits Geyer very well, but his *pièce de résistance* is the closing polka, *Im Fluge,* which bursts into the room and has enormous energy and projection. The recording is excellent.

Vol. 19: *Benedek-Marsch.* **Polkas:** *Dornbacher; Eile mit Weile; Nymphen; Sehnsucht; Souvenir; Die tanzende Muse.* **Quadrille:** *Folichon.* **Waltzes:** *Consortien; Frauenblätter; Musen-Klänge.*
**(*) Marco Polo 8.223621. Slovak State PO (Košice), Hilgers.

Walter Hilgers is most welcome on the podium. If he does not quite match Christian Pollack (see below) he gets good ensemble and articulates crisply, yet relaxes more flexibly than Geyer, so that the polka-mazurkas and quadrilles have their full Viennese charm. All three waltzes are well worth having on disc. Hilgers coaxes the beguiling opening of *Musen-Klänge* ('Music for the Muses') bewitchingly, and there is a nice lift for the charming *Frauenblätter* ('Women's Magazines'). The opening of *Consortien* is again most pleasingly shaped and the waltz itself, written for a gathering of prominent industrialists in 1869, is unexpectedly lighthearted and full of good things. Incidentally, Hilgers takes all the repeats, so each of the three waltzes plays for over ten minutes, without outlasting their welcome.

Vol. 20: *Liechtenstein-Marsch.* **Polkas:** *Cupido; Dithyrambe; Frauenherz; Künstler-Caprice; Pêle-mêle; Vélocipède.* **Quadrille:** *Pariser.* **Waltzes:** *Actionen; Delirien; Flattergeister; Wiener Bonmots.*
*** Marco Polo 8.223622. Slovak State PO (Košice), Pollack.

This is perhaps the most delightful of the Josef Strauss collections so far. Not only does it include a most winning account of his greatest waltz, *Delirien,* but the lighthearted *Flattergeister* ('Social Butterflies'), after a robust introduction, opens the main waltz sequence with a lilting tune on the violins (fully worthy of Johann) and brings a stream of attractive ideas. *Wiener Bonmots,* too, chirps wittily. Christian Pollack again shows himself a master of Viennese rhythmic inflexion and the slower polka-mazurkas are even more seductive than the sparkling *Pell-Mell* and the fizzingly brilliant *Vélocipède.* The Slovak orchestra are clearly on their toes and enjoying the dance, and the bright recording has a pleasing ambience.

Vol. 21: *Andressy-Marsch* (arr. Pollock). **Ländler:** *Waldbleamin.* **Polkas:** *Buchstaben; Flora;*

Immergrün; Lebensgeister; Steeple Chase.
Quadrilles: *Stegreif; La Périchole.* Waltzes: *Günstige Prognosen; Die Vorgeiger.* Arr. of MENDELSSOHN: *Song without Words No. 1.*
** Marco Polo 8.223623. Slovak State PO, Dittrich.

Michael Dittrich conducted Volumes 13 and 14 of the Marco Polo Josef Strauss series and he shows here, as he did then, that he is happiest in the polkas – which dominate the present collection – but less imaginative with the waltzes. There are only two of them, neither especially memorable as presented here: *Die Vorgeiger* ('The Leading Violinists') and the appropriately mellow *Favourable Prognosis*, written in 1863 for a medical ball attended by the male students at the University of Vienna (females were not admitted until nearly the turn of the century). Apart from the lively if unsubtle pot-pourri of tunes from Offenbach's *La Périchole*, the highlights here are the delightful Ländler, *Waldbleamin* ('Forest Flowers'), which deserve to be rescued from oblivion, and Josef's charming arrangement of an unidentified *Song without Words* of Mendelssohn.

Vol. 22: *Einzugs-Marsch.* Polkas: *Elfen; Die Kosende; Lock; Patti.* Quadrilles: *Rendezvous; Sofien.* Waltzes: *Flimserin; Die Sonderlinge; Die Veteranen; Die Zufälligen.*
*** Marco Polo 8.223624. Slovak State PO, Geyer.

There are four fine waltzes here and *Die Veteranen* was dedicated to Field Marshal Count Radetzky, for whom Johann Senior wrote his most famous march. The brassy two-in-a-bar opening is appropriate, and indeed *Die Sonderlinge* and *Die Zufälligen* also have lively introductions, not in waltz time. They are both attractive, but the most pleasing of all, *Die Flimserin* ('Sequins'), opens most delicately and has a seductive principal melody. As we have already discovered in Volume 18, Karl Geyer is a much more persuasive exponent of these pieces than many of his colleagues, and each of these waltzes has an agreeable rhythmic lift and lilt, while the polkas and quadrilles also have plenty of life. One of the best discs in the series.

Vol. 23: *Fest-Marsch.* Polkas: *Aus dem Wienerwald; Cabriole; Concordia; Vergissmeinennicht.* Quadrilles: *Crispine; Kadi.* Waltzes: *Heiden-Gedichte; Neue Welt-Bürger; Zeitbilder.*
** Marco Polo 8.223625. Slovak State PO (Košice), Müssauer.

Manfred Müssauer is a promising newcomer, and he directs Volume 23 spiritedly. All three quick-waltzes are fresh and lively, but none is a masterpiece. *Heiden-Gedichte* ('Heroes' Poems') originally had a ceremonial connection, and opens with robust fanfares. Müssauer makes the most of it and provides an effective accelerando at the end. He also brings out the striking contribution of the horns in *Zeitbilder*, and we would like to hear him conduct some more seductive waltzes. The opening *Cabriole Polka* is vivacious, but here it is the quadrilles which contain the

most engaging music. Good playing and recording, but none of these pieces shows Josef at his best.

Vol. 24: *March: Unbekannter* (arr. Pollock); Polkas: *Amanda; Aus der Ferne; Blitz; Cyclopen.* Quadrille: *Fortunio* (arr. Pollack). Waltzes: *Die Ersten und Letzten; Glückskinder; Liebesgrüsse; Sternschnuppen; Transactionen.*
*** Marco Polo 8.223626. Slovak State PO (Košice), Pollack.

Christopher Pollack, the finest conductor in this series, returns to direct Volume 24 and is quite seductive at the openings of *Liebesgrüsse*, *Glückskinder* and *Sternschnuppen* ('Shooting Stars'), which are among the composer's most charming waltzes. The 'Unknown March' is a very jaunty early work, discovered among the composer's effects after he died. In a letter to his publisher, Josef told how he composed the engaging *Quadrille*, drawing on three Offenbach operettas, *Fortunio*, *Magellone* and Pan eavesdropping on the lovers, *Dapnnis et Chloé*. 'Beginning at four o'clock,' he continued 'I finished it completely by 7.30, including everything. I sat down again and completed the arrangements precisely at eight o'clock.' But the star of the present collection is *Transactionen*, one of the finest of all Josef's waltzes.

Vol. 25: *Albumblatt: Mein Schönes, Wein.* Polkas: *Euterpe; Margherita; Pauline; Die Soubrette; Die Windsbraut.* Quadrille: *Faust.* Waltzes: *Heilmethoden; Hesperus Balltänz; Soll und Haben; Die Tanzinterpellanten.*
*** Marco Polo 8.223664. Slovak State PO (Košice), Dittrich.

Michael Dittrich directs the polkas with charm and he creates an anticipatory, atmospheric opening for *Soll und Haben*, but the waltz themes are then run-of-the-mill. With the *Faust Quadrille* we return to a kaleidoscope of melody, nicely presented, and the two remaining waltzes are both attractive. *Die Soubrette* rounds the collection off nicely.

Vol. 26: March: *Prince Eugen.* Polkas: *Gallopin; Mille fleurs* (2 versions); *Sturm; Tarantel.* Potpourri: *Das musikalische Osterreich.* Quadrille: *Bachanten.* Waltz: *Die Zeisserin.*
**(*) Marco Polo 8.223679. Slovak State PO (Košice), Pollack.

Although the *Gallopin* and (especially) the *Sturm Polkas* are very jolly, the most attractive piece here is *Das musikalische Osterreich*, a 20-minute pot-pourri with pleasingly diverse orchestration and a nice use of the horns. It is a varied collection of Austrian national airs and dances, with the *Radetzky March* intertwined with the Emperor's Anthem in the coda. The *Prinz Eugen-Marsch* is more pompously Austrian, with an attractive trio. The *Die Zeisserin Waltz* is agreeable but not one of Josef's finest, and the *Bachanten Quadrille* and *Mille fleurs Polka* (which we hear in two, very similar, versions) are agreeable but not distinctive. However, Christian Pollack's direction of the Slovak orchestra is of a consistently high calibre, and the recording is well up to standard.

STRAUSS, Richard (1864–1949)

An Alpine Symphony; Der Rosenkavalier: Suite.
** DG 469 519-2. VPO, Thielemann.

Thielemann's are live recordings made in the Grosser Saal of the Musikverein in October 2000, offering brilliant VPO playing, and these performances certainly do not lack tension. However, in the *Alpine Symphony* the conductor's scrupulous concern for pictorial detail means that we receive a series of vividly colourful pictures of each segment of the ascent and descent, rather than an overall impression of a continuing journey, although the closing nocturnal sequence is movingly gentle. The digital recording is very spectacular, immensely so in the *Thunderstorm* sequence, but the ear senses the presence of the close microphones, so a natural concert-hall effect is less readily conveyed. The *Rosenkavalier Suite* is again superbly played, but its sensory romantic atmosphere, and the perception of a lilting masquerade, eludes Thielemann. Moreover, the vivid recording lacks the necessary lusciousness of string texture.

(i) *An Alpine Symphony;* (ii) *Also sprach Zarathustra;* (i) *Death and Transfiguration; Don Juan; Ein Heldenleben;* (ii) *Festliches Praeludium, Op. 61; Der Rosenkavalier: waltzes from Act III. Salome: Dance of the Seven Veils; Till Eulenspiegel.*
(B) * (**) DG mono/stereo 463 190-2 (3). (i) Dresden State O, (ii) BPO; Boehm.

Boehm's Strauss is impressive, and this bargain box, comprising some mono but mainly stereo recordings, is a fine tribute to his natural affinity with this composer. *An Alpine Symphony, Don Juan* and *Ein Heldenleben* are mono, but are excellent performances: it is Boehm's attention to detail which one most enjoys, though there is excitement too, even if this music ideally requires stereo to make its full impact. The rest of the performances are stereo. *Also sprach Zarathustra* dates from 1958 and the sound is good if a little thin; it is a spacious and satisfying account, with splendid playing to support the conductor's conception. The rustic portrayal of *Till* and the *Waltzes* from *Der Rosenkavalier* are both effective, as is the highly sensuous account of *Salome's Dance.* The *Prelude,* written in 1913 for the opening of the Konzerthaus in Vienna, is a fascinating bonus: it is a somewhat inflated work, for organ and a huge orchestra, in which the composer piles sequence upon sequence to produce a climax of shattering sonority. Boehm manages to give the work a dignity not really inherent in the music. All these were recorded a few years after *Also sprach Zarathustra* and have fuller sound. For *Death and Transfiguration,*

Boehm's 1972 live Salzburg Festival recording was used; it is a performance of excitement and strong tensions (despite a couple of irritating coughs at the beginning), even if the recording is slightly overweighted at the top. At bargain price, this set is worth considering, and an essential purchase for admirers of this distinguished conductor.

An Alpine Symphony; Death and Transfiguration; Don Juan; Ein Heldenleben.
(M) ** Chan. 10199 X (2). RSNO, Järvi.

Neeme Järvi's version of the *Alpine Symphony* is roundly enjoyable, ripely recorded in a helpfully reverberant acoustic; his approach is warm and genial, if without the electricity of the finest performances. *Ein Heldenleben* is strongly characterized, warmly sympathetic, with the RSNO giving a powerful thrust throughout, lacking only the last degree of refinement in tone and ensemble. There are few complaints to be made about *Don Juan,* even if, again, it is not quite in the league of the very best versions available. *Death and Transfiguration* comes off very well, with the RSNO standing up remarkably well by comparison with its Dresden and Berlin rivals – one of Järvi's best Strauss performances.

Also sprach Zarathustra, Op. 30.
*** Sony **DVD** SVD 46388. BPO, Karajan– MOZART: *Divertimento No. 17.* **(*)

By the time Karajan conducted the concert celebrating the 750th anniversary of the founding of Berlin, he was already ailing, as one registers from his painful progress to the podium each time; once there, however, the electric intensity of his conducting never falters in passionate commitment to this great Strauss work, always a favourite of his. It is as though he realizes that this may be the last time he will ever conduct it. Though the hushed close makes this a subdued sort of celebration. Karajan's control is emphasized in the total silence at the end, until his subtle signal of release for the applause to begin, at which the audience responds with fervour. One myth which the performance tends to undermine is that Karajan consistently had his eyes shut when conducting. There are certainly moments when that happens, but in this work above all, his eye, when you see it, drills like a gimlet, ever observant. It is a help that the DVD offers ample index points separating the sections. This DVD is short measure but is still indispensable.

(i) *Also sprach Zarathustra, Op. 30;* (ii) *Don Juan, Op. 20;* (iii) *Salome: Dance of the Seven Veils, Op. 54.*
(BB) **(*) DG 474 566-2. (i) NYPO; (ii) Dresden State O; (iii) Deutsche Oper, Berlin, O; Sinopoli.

Sinopoli is at his most warmly and passionately persuasive in this Strauss triptych and all three orchestras play with virtuosity and conviction. But in *Also sprach Zarathustra* the conductor's special relationship with the New York Philharmonic is let down by the recording, brilliant and spectacular but harsh in *fortissimos*. The Dresden and Berlin acoustics are more sympathetic, and both *Don Juan* and the *Dance of the Seven Veils* have very powerful climaxes.

Also sprach Zarathustra; (i) Don Quixote. Macbeth; Sinfonia domestica; Till Eulenspiegel.

(M) ** Chan. 10206 X (2). RSNO, Järvi, (i) with Wallfisch.

Neemi Järvi's well-regarded Strauss recordings, dating from the 1980s, are now being released at mid-price in slim-line packaging. Although this is a step in the right direction, they are competing with Karajan and Reiner – as well as Kempe's magnificent Dresden survey – and are therefore not the value they might once have been. *Also sprach Zarathustra* is one of the least successful performances in his Strauss survey for Chandos. The reverberant acoustic (characteristic of Caird Hall in Dundee) here muddies the sound without giving it compensating richness. *Till* is much better, however, and Järvi brings out the work's joy admirably. The *Sinfonia domestica* is a good-natured and strongly characterized account, gutsy and committed to remove any coy self-consciousness from this extraordinarily inflated but delightful musical portrait of Strauss's family life. *Macbeth*, not one of Strauss's masterpieces, gets as good a performance here as you're likely to get.

Also sprach Zarathustra, Op. 30; Ein Heldenleben, Op. 40.

☛ (***) Testament mono SBT 1183. VPO, Krauss.

Clemens Krauss brings the heroic sweep, the contrasts and delicacy of texture and the breadth of *Ein Heldenleben* before one's eyes. There is a nobility here (and, for that matter, in *Zarathustra* too) that not every Strauss conductor conveys. Straussians will naturally have Karajan, Reiner and Kempe in this repertoire, but Krauss still has special claims on the serious collector and he has a warmth and humanity that are enormously rewarding.

Le Bourgeois Gentilhomme: Suite, Op. 60. Sinfonia domestica, Op. 53.

☛ (***) Testament mono SBT 1184. VPO, Krauss.

Remarkably few allowances need be made for the 1951 recording of the *Sinfonia domestica*, a Cinderella among Strauss tone-poems and curiously unloved. If any performance should transform its status, this is it. Krauss had given it its Viennese première in 1922, and this was its first (and for many years only) LP recording. The authors of *The Record Guide* noted that many critics 'have been so bothered by the mundane details of the programme that they have failed to appreciate the beauties as well as the dazzling cleverness of the score'. There have been impressive versions from Reiner, Karajan, Kempe, Sawallisch and others; this one has a special authenticity of feeling and richness of response that disarm

criticism. Krauss conducted many early performances of the suite from *Le Bourgeous Gentilhomme* and this unforgettable (1952) account has wonderful lightness of touch and delicacy of feeling. Its charm is quite irresistible. This ranks alongside the great recordings by Fritz Reiner and Sir Thomas Beecham.

Death and Transfiguration; Don Juan; Till Eulenspiegel.

☛ (M) (***) EMI mono 5 62790-2. VPO, Furtwängler – SMETANA: Vltava. ***

Don Juan and *Till Eulenspiegel* come from 1954, some months before the onset of deafness brought Furtwängler's career to an end, while *Death and Transfiguration* was recorded in Vienna in 1950. They are performances of commanding stature and have the glowing sonorities, naturalness of utterance and mastery of pace that characterized Furtwängler at his best. The EMI recordings still sound glorious despite their age, though climaxes in *Death and Transfiguration* are distinctly opaque; Walter Legge produced the 1950 sessions and Laurance Collingwood the 1954 ones, and it is hard to imagine any mono discs of *Don* and *Till* being better balanced or more natural. Of course, they were soon superseded by the Karajan records, but these earlier performances have a special place in any Strauss collection.

Death and Transfiguration; Metamorphosen for 23 Solo Strings.

✹ ☛ (M) *** DG 474 889-2. BPO, Karajan.

Karajan's digital coupling of *Death and Transfiguration* and the *Metamorphosen* is one of his very finest records and deservedly won the *Gramophone* Orchestral Award in 1983. This famous CD (discussed in our main volume) is now available at mid-price.

Don Juan, Op. 20; Till Eulenspiegel. Op. 28; (i) Don Quixote.

(***) Testament mono SBT 1185. (i) Fournier, Moraweg; VPO, Krauss.

A magnificent *Don Quixote* from Clemens Krauss and his eminent soloist which encapsulates the essence of Strauss's score. RL recalls Egon Wellesz in the early 1950s singing the praises of Krauss as a Straussian ('unsurpassed even by Sir Thomas Beecham'), and this performance with that aristocrat of cellists, Pierre Fournier, has a special nobility and authority. Both *Don Juan* and *Till Eulenspiegel* were recorded in 1950 (the *Don Quixote* in 1953) and are superbly characterized. In the latter, Krauss clearly does not regard this as just a conductor's showpiece but puts characterization before orchestral display.

Don Quixote, Op. 35.

*(*) DG 474 780-2. Maisky, B. PO, Mehta – DVOŘÁK: Cello Concerto. *(*)

Don Quixote is so richly eloquent a score that its narrative needs no expressive adornment. As in the Dvořák *Concerto*, Mischa Maisky is all too prone to wear his heart on his sleeve and he emotes all too readily. When there are so many marvellous versions around there is no reason for this to detain readers, good though the Berlin orchestra's playing and the DG recording are.

Ein Heldenleben, Op. 40.

(M) ** BBC (ADD) BBCL 4055-2. LSO, Barbirolli – MOZART: *Symphony No. 36 (Linz).* **

This BBC recording from 1969 documents one of Sir John's last concert appearances. Made in the Royal Festival Hall, it shows considerable vitality and zest, although it is far from being an ideal testimony to his art and career. The sound is very good and not greatly inferior to that in the studio recording.

(i) Ein Heldenleben; (ii) Till Eulenspiegel; (iii) Salome: Dance of the Seven Veils.

(B) (***) Dutton CDBP 9737. (i) Bav. State O; (ii) Berlin State Op. O; (iii) BPO; composer.

Dutton has already put us in his debt with a superb transfer of the 1941 *Alpine Symphony* that Strauss recorded for Electrola (CDBP 9720 – see our main volume). Later the same year Strauss returned to DG to record this wonderfully humane account of *Ein Heldenleben* with the Munich orchestra. Siemens had developed a new recording process which extended the frequency range, and no previous transfer has ever reproduced its sound quite so vividly. The playing Strauss produces is characterized by such unforced virtuosity and naturalness of feeling that it is put quite in a class of its own. Even if you possess Karajan, Kempe and Beecham, this is a mandatory purchase, for it really carries the ring of truth. *The Dance of the Seven Veils* and *Till Eulenspiegel* both come from the late 1920s and are less revelatory.

Violin Sonata in E flat, Op. 18.

🔾━ (M) *** Decca 474 558-2. Chung, Zimerman– RESPIGHI: *Violin Sonata.* ***

Among modern violinists Kyung-Wha Chung is *primus inter pares*, and her version of the *Sonata* also scores over rivals in the power and sensitivity of Krystian Zimerman's contribution and the excellence of the (originally DG) recording. There is, however, a cut of 42 bars in the coda of the first movement (Universal Edition) which appears to be sanctioned, as Heifetz also observed it in his recording.

VOCAL MUSIC

Songs: Ach, was Kummer, Qual und Schmerzen; Allerseelen; Blauer Sommer; Cäcilie; Des Dichters Abendgang; Einerlei; Ich wollt ein Sträusslein binden; Leises Lied; 3 Lieder Der Ophelia, Op. 67; Meinem Kinde; Morgen!; Muttertändelei; Die Nacht; Das Rosenband; Ruhe, meine Seele!; Schlechtes

Wetter; Ständchen; Der Stern; Die Verschwiegenen; Waldseligkeit; Wiegenlied; Winterweihe; Die Zeitlose; Zueignung.

** ASV CD DDCA 1155. Lott, Johnson.

A disc of Strauss songs sung by Dame Felicity Lott accompanied by Graham Johnson is self-recommending, and there is much to enjoy on this issue, recorded in 2002. Lott's insights and those of her accompanist are consistently revealing, not least in the three Ophelia songs, which come at the climactic point of the recital, just before the final item, *Morgen*. She and Johnson bring out the other-worldly quality which Strauss evokes in these offbeat evocations of Ophelia's madness. The snag is that the odd recording quality is not kind to the singer's voice, betraying the fact that her characteristic creamy sound-quality is not as pure as it once was, with vibrato often intrusive. More seriously, the odd recording-balance is flattering neither to the singer nor to the pianist, with a slight distancing in an odd acoustic that makes one want to clear away a gauze.

Lieder: Allerseelen; Am Ufer; Aus den Lindern der Trauer; Heimkehr; Liebeshymnus; Lob des Leidens; Madrigal; Morgen Die Nacht; Winternacht; Zueignung.

(M) *** Decca 474 536-2. Fassbaender, Gage – LISZT: *Lieder.* ***

Coupled with an equally perceptive group of Liszt songs, Fassbaender's Strauss selection, winner of the *Gramophone* Solo Vocal Award for 1987, brings singing of exceptional command and intensity; always she communicates face to face, and the musical imagination – as in the very slow account of the popular *Morgen* – adds to the sharply specific quality she gives to each song. The voice is beautiful as recorded, but that beauty is only an incidental. Warmly understanding accompaniment; well-balanced recording.

(i) 4 Last Songs; (ii) Arabella (opera): excerpts. (i) Capriccio (opera): Closing Scene.

(M) (***) EMI mono 5 85825-2. Schwarzkopf, Philh. O; (i) Ackermann; (iii) Felbermeyer, Metternich, Prüglhüf, Dickie, Berry, Von Matačić.

This a a straight reissue of 5 6795-2 highly praised in our main volume. However, there are no texts or translations.

(i) Four Last Songs; Orchestral Lieder: Befreit; Cäcilie; Muttertändelei; Waldseligkeit; Wiegenlied. Der Rosenkavalier: Suite.

(M) ** RCA 82876 59408-2. (i) Fleming; Houston SO, Eschenbach.

Renée Fleming with her rich, mature soprano gives warmly sympathetic readings of the *Four Last Songs*, thrilling in climaxes as the voice is allowed to expand and full of fine detail, even if these readings lack the variety of a Schwarzkopf. The five separate orchestral Lieder also bring a wide expresive range, with *Wald-*

seligkeit beautifully poised, and ending boldly on *Cäcilie*. The singer is not helped by the way Eschenbach makes the accompaniments seem a little sluggish, polished though the playing is. Something of the same lack of thrust marks his account of Strauss's own arrangement of the *Rosenkavalier* excerpts, despite beautiful playing from the Houston orchestra. How much more welcome it would have been to have extra items from the singer.

Lieder: *Allerseelen; All' mein' Gedanken; Befreit; Cäcilie; Efeu; Heimliche Aufforderung; Herr Lenz; Hochzeitlich; Junggesellenschwur; Liebeshymnus; Mein Auge; Meinem Kinde; Nachtgang; Nichts; Das Rosenband; Sehnsucht; Ständchen; Traum durch die Dämmerung; Waldseligkeit; Wasserrose; Weihnachtsgefühl; Winternacht.*

⊕➙ (B) ✱✱✱ CfP 585 9032. Keenlyside, Martineau.

Simon Keenleyside follows up the success of his fine Schubert recital (now also reissued on CfP) with this excellent collection of Strauss Lieder, beautifully sung, again with Malcolm Martineau a most sensitive accompanist. Try the highly distinctive, intimate reading of *Ständchen* ('Serenade'), with Keenlyside singing almost in a half-tone and with Martineau playing magically. The fine-spun legato of *Waldseligkeit* and the poise of *Meinem Kinde* are equally impressive. Keenleyside uses a head voice for the gentle top notes of *Allerseelen* ('All Saints' Day') but then finds plenty of power, sharply focused, in songs like *Befreit*. The sequence is rounded off with two exhilarating songs, *Cäcilie* and *Herr Lenz* (with its pun on the name Strauss – nosegay). No texts are provided in its new Classics for Pleasure release; even so, it is well worth its bargain price.

OPERA

Die Aegyptische Helena (complete).
✱✱✱ Telarc CD 80605 (2). Voigt, Tanner, Shafer, Grove, Robertson, NY Concert Chorale, American SO, Botstein.

If till now *Die Aegyptische Helena* has failed to make its mark in the regular repertory, the fault lies rather with the libretto of Hugo von Hofmannsthal than with the music of Strauss. It is a point that comes over vividly with this Telarc version, made live in New York in 2002, the finest yet. This is the third of a trilogy of marriage operas, following up the massively symbolic *Die Frau ohne Schatten* and the lightly autobiographical *Intermezzo*. Hofmannsthal's suggestion was to write an opera about the mythical Helen after she returned from Troy to Menelaus, the husband she had left, though the failure to make Menelaus into a rounded character tends to undermine that, even in face of the sensuous warmth of Strauss's score. Even so, the role of Menelaus is arguably the finest he ever gave to a tenor, very well sung here by Carl Tanner. The relationship between Helen and the Egyptian princess and sorceress Aithra is far more revealing, prompting Strauss into the sort of duetting between sopranos that drew from him so much of his finest operatic inspirations. What the New York recording triumphantly brings out is the melodic richness of Strauss's score. It has even been described as a bel canto opera, though that is to underestimate the complexity of the work's structure, wonderfully crafted throughout, with orchestral writing of a richness that even Strauss never surpassed. Where the conductor, Leon Botstein, scores even over Antal Dorati in the previous studio recording, made for Decca, and over Josef Krips in the live recording of 1970 from the Vienna State Opera (RCA) is the extra warmth he finds in the score, helped by rich, digital sound, with the engineers overcoming the acoustic problems of recording in the Avery Fisher Hall in Lincoln Center. The new set also scores heavily over those previous versions in not having Gwyneth Jones in the title-role, always given to squally moments. This time it is Deborah Voigt, whose richness and command are a joy, with even the most challenging top notes firm and pure. She is well matched by Celena Shafer as Aithra, singing with consistent freshness and clarity. Jill Grove is the wonderfully resonant contralto in the improbable role of the Omniscient Seashell (adviser to Aithra), with Christopher Robertson as Altair, prince of the Atlas Mountains, and Eric Cutler as his son, Da-ud.

Arabella (complete).
✱✱✱ Warner **DVD** 0630-16912-2. Putnam, Brocheler, Rolandi, Sarfaty, Korn, Lewis, Bradley, LPO, Haitink (Dir.: John Cox; DVD Dir.: John Vernon).

The Warner DVD offers a live recording of a classic Glyndebourne production of *Arabella* with handsome, realistic sets by Julia Trevelyan Oman. In this 1984 performance Bernard Haitink, then music director at Glyndebourne, draws ravishing playing from the LPO in support of an outstanding cast with not a single flaw. Ashley Putnam makes a tall and imposing Arabella, at once pretty and girlishly eager, yet with a natural dignity and a vocal command that makes her performance magnetic, with the set-piece solos and duets deeply moving. Opposite her, John Brocheler is a formidable Mandryka, handsome and heavily bearded, with a clean-cut voice that has just a hint of grit in it, aptly so. As Zdenka Gianna Rolandi cuts a vivacious, eager figure, even if her tiny stature next to the imposing Putnam makes it unlikely that even the simple-minded Matteo (superbly sung by Keith Lewis) would mistake her for Arabella even in bed. As Arabella's parents, Regina Sarfaty and Artur Korn both characterize well, and Gwendolyn Bradley makes the most of the brief if spectacular role of the Fiakermilli in Act II. John Vernon's video direction, using many helpful close-ups, adds to the impact. The irritation of this issue is that the printed documentation does not include a list of cast and characters: that appears only on screen at the end, as each character takes a bow. It is inadequate too that only the briefest synopsis is given on the box, with no booklet provided.

Ariadne auf Naxos (complete).

** DG DVD 073 028-9. Norman, Battle, Troyanos, King, Netwig, Dickson, Laciura, Met. Op. Ch. & O, Levine (V/D: Brian Large).

There is some impressive singing in this 1988 Metropolitan production of *Ariadne*. Levine's DG recording of the opera had been made only a year earlier in Vienna with Anna Tomowa-Sintow as Ariadne, Agnes Baltsa as the Composer and Kathleen Battle as Zerbinetta. Jessye Norman had only recently recorded the title-role with Masur for Philips, and Tatiana Troyanos had been the Composer in Solti's Decca set from the late 1980s. Recordings of *Ariadne* are legion and some (like the Karajan, Kempe and Solti versions) are in their way indispensable, but there is only one DVD alternative, marvellously conducted by Sir Colin Davis but in an intrusively updated production. This is straight and unfussy in its staging, and the video production by Brian Large could not be more expert and unobtrusive (save for one or two close-ups of Norman's larynx. Troyanos's Composer is quite superb, and neither Battle nor Norman can be faulted vocally, even if some will find the former's charm a bit overdone. No complaints about the men either, even if James King's Bacchus is a mite strained on some of his top notes. James Levine is a fine musician, but the orchestral playing has all too little of the finesse and subtlety of Kempe or Karajan and the orchestral textures are nowhere near as refined as they achieve.

Capriccio (complete).

*** Arthaus DVD 100 354. Te Kanawa, Hagegard, Troyanos, Braun, Kuebler, Keenlyside, Sénéchal, Travis, San Francisco Op. O, Runnicles (Dir. Lawless; DVD Dir.: Maniura).

With evocative sets by Mauro Pagano and in-period eighteenth-century costumes by Thierry Bosquet, Stephen Lawless's production for the San Francisco Opera will delight traditionalists. In this live (1993) performance, Donald Runnicles is the deeply sympathetic conductor inspiring an outstanding cast with no weak link. Kiri Te Kanawa not only sings gloriously with a continuous flow of full, warm sound, she acts most movingly. Vivacious at the start of this 'conversation piece', her deepening of feeling is vividly conveyed, first when she hears the sonnet written for her, and then throughout in the way she uses her deep-set, haunted eyes with their hooded lids, fully exploited in Peter Maniura's video direction. Håkan Hagegard as the Count, her brother, is a big, burly figure, bumbling enough in his overacting to make the rehearsal scene with Tatiana Troyanos as a characterful Clairon both funny and believable. The rival duo of poet and composer is superbly taken by

David Kuebler as Flamand and Simon Keenlyside as Olivier, vocally and visually handsome, with Victor Braun as La Roche, Maria Fortuna and Craig Estep as the Italian soprano and tenor ideally cast, and with even the role of the Major Domo very strongly sung by Dale Travis, and with the veteran Michel Sénéchal masterly in the cameo role of the prompter, Monsieur Taupe. For sheer Straussian beauty, evocatively presented, it would be hard to match the rendering here of the final scene. First-rate sound and excellent documentation in the accompanying booklet, as usual with Arthaus DVDs.

Elektra (complete).

(B) ** Ph. Duo 464 985-2 (2). Behrens, Ludwig, Secunde, Ulfung, Hynninen, Matthews, Tanglewood Festival Ch., Boston SO, Ozawa.

Ozawa's version of *Elektra* was recorded at live performances of the opera in Boston in 1988, using stage cuts. Its great glory is the singing of Hildegard Behrens in the name-part, perhaps finer here than she has ever been on record. Hers is a portrayal that movingly brings out the tenderness and vulnerability in this character, as well as the unbalanced ferocity. She it is – with Christa Ludwig a marvellous foil as Klytemnestra, searingly intense, letting out a spine-chilling off-stage scream at her murder – who provides the performance's dramatic tension, rather than the conductor. Though this is a live recording, it lacks the very quality which may justify the inevitable flaws in such a project: an underlying emotional thrust. The tension-building passage leading to Elektra's recognition of Orestes is plodding and prosaic and, against radiant singing from Behrens in the carol of joy which follows, the orchestra might as well be playing a Bruckner slow movement, for they provide no emtional underpinning of this supreme moment of fulfilment after pain. The other soloists are disappointing, even Jorma Hynninen, who is dry-toned and uningratiating as Orestes. Ragnar Ulfung as Aegistheus is also dry-toned, aptly if unpleasantly so, and Nadine Secunde is far too wobbly as Chrysothemis. Voices are well caught, but the orchestral sound is again too dry to bring out the glory of Strauss's orchestration. First choice still rests with Sinopoli (● DG 453 429-2 – see our main volume).

Die Liebe der Danae (complete).

*** CPO 999 967-2 (3). Grundheber, Schöpflin, McNamara, Uhl, Zach, Chafin, Behle, Fleitmann, Kiel Op. Ch. & PO, Windfuhr.

Recorded live at the Kiel Opera in April 2003, the CPO set of this late opera of Strauss, mingling the two gold-related Greek legends of Midas and Danae, follows on the success of this same company's recording of Alfano's *Cyrano de Bergerac*. It comes into direct competition with the Telarc version under Leon Botstein, also recorded live but in a concert performance. Where the account under Ulrich

Windfuhr consistently scores is in the dramatic bite of the performance, with singers on stage conveying each confrontation of character more convincingly than is ever likely in a concert performance. The recording helps, made by the engineers of North German Radio. Though the voices on stage are balanced in front of the orchestra, they are well separated, and the extra bloom on the orchestral sound compared with the rather boxy sound on Telarc makes all the difference in this luscious score with its evocative passages like the 'golden rain' interlude in Act I. Though Botstein is a formidable Straussian, Windfuhr is even more warmly idiomatic, conveying a surge of warmth at the big climaxes, and his singers too seem to understand the idiom far more clearly than their American counterparts. Standing out from an excellent cast is the magnificent Jupiter of Franz Grundheber, weightily Wagnerian like a latter-day Wotan; and Robert Chafin in the tenor role of Midas is also splendid. Manuela Uhl as Danae has a bright, clear soprano, which she shades down seductively in gentler passages such as the meeting with Midas, but she tends to sound inflexible under pressure. Her counterpart on Telarc is sweeter and easier on the ear. Though in precision of ensemble the chorus on stage cannot match the American chorus in concert, the singers regularly convey an extra warmth in compensation, adding to the impact of the big choral moments.

Der Rosenkavalier (complete).

(M) ** DG (ADD) 463 668-2 (3). Schech, Seefried, Streich, Böhme, Fischer-Dieskau, Unger, Wagner, Dresden State Op. Ch., Saxon State O, Dresden, Boehm.

There is much that is very good indeed about the Boehm Dresden performance. Yet here is undoubtedly a set that elusively fails to add up to the sum of its parts. It is partly Boehm's inability to generate the sort of power and emotional tension that are so overwhelming in the Karajan–Schwarzkopf set on EMI. More importantly, the Feldmarschallin of Marianne Schech is decidedly below the level set by Seefried as Octavian and Streich as Sophie. Schech just does not have the strength of personality that is needed if the opera's dramatic point is to strike home. We cannot feel the full depth of emotion involved in her great renunciation from the performance here. Kurt Böhme is a fine Ochs and the recording is appropriately rich, but in almost every way the EMI set provides a more convincing experience – and how fine that is (5 67605-2 [5 67609-2] – see our main *Guide*).

Salome (complete).

(M) *(*) Sony SM2K 90450 (2). Marton, Weikl, Zednik, Fassbaender, Lewis, BPO, Mehta.

(M) (**(*)), Decca mono 475 6087 (2). Goltz, Kenny, Patzak, Dermota, Braun, VPO, Krauss.

Mehta's set brings a supreme performance from Brigitte Fassbaender as Herodias, dominating all her scenes. Otherwise the rest of the cast and the Sony recording are disappointing. Above all, the wobbly, ill-focused singing of Eva Marton in the title-role puts the set out of court. In the theatre her sheer volume might make her performance exciting, but on disc the microphone is unforgiving in showing up the unevenness of vocal production. She conveys a compelling lasciviousness in the final scene, but Bernd Weikl is disappointing as Jokanaan, sounding too old; and even the glorious sounds of the Berlin Philharmonic are dimmed by the distancing of the recording, blunting the impact of this highly charged work. Moreover, as with the rest of this Sony reissue series, the documentation is without either libretto or cued synopsis.

The glory of the Decca set, dating from 1954, is the loving direction from Clemens Krauss, the composer's close friend. The drawback is the unlovely performance of the heroine's music by Christel Goltz, who was a magnetic artist in the opera house but with a voice that took very badly to the microphone. Even so, with Patzak and Dermota in the cast the performance was certainly worth putting on Decca's excellent 'Original Masters' series, especially as all of Krauss's 1950s Decca recordings (courtesy of Testament Records) are now available. The sound has emerged well on CD, the orchestral sound not especially rich but good enough for its vintage (without the harsh quality which affects some Decca mono recordings from this period) and with the voices well caught and with surprisingly little distortion. There are no texts, but most collectors will already have a version of *Salome* with one. What a great conductor Krauss was!

STRAVINSKY, Igor (1882–1971)

Apollo (ballet; complete); (i) *Capriccio for Piano and Orchestra. Le Chant du rossignol; Circus Polka;* (ii) *Concerto for Piano & Wind;* (iii) *Violin Concerto. Petrushka* (complete; original (1911) ballet); *Symphony in E flat, Op. 1; Symphony in C; Symphony in Three Movements;* (iv) *Symphony of Psalms;* (iv; v) *Oedipus Rex.*

(B) ** Chan. 6654 (5). SRO, Järvi, with (i) Tozer: (ii) Berman; (iii) Mordkovitch; (iv) Chamber Ch., Lausanne Pro Art Ch., Société Ch. de Brassus; (v) Schnaut, Svensson, Amoretti, Grundheber, Kannen, Rosen, Plat.

Neeme Järvi offers typically red-blooded readings in his five-disc collection of symphonies, concertos and ballets, plus *Oedipus Rex*. His performances do not always have the refinement and sharpness of focus that one ideally wants, but the thrust of the music comes over convincingly, even if some of the slow movements – as in the *Symphony in Three Movements* – grow curiously stodgy rhythmically at relatively slow speeds. However, the *Violin Concerto* is beautifully played by the warm-toned Lydia Mordkovitch, with the romantic expressiveness of the two central *Arias* an apt counterpart to the vigour and panache of the outer movements. The string playing in *Apollo* has plenty of warmth, and Järvi's vivid *Petrushka* is particularly winning. Using the 1911 score, he finds an attractive sparkle at the opening and in the *Shrovetide Fair*, with the *Russian Dance* given a superb bounce. Some of the subtlety of Stravinsky's scoring in the central tableaux may be missing, but such characterful playing is most attractive, both here and in the *Circus Polka* on the same disc. Generally speaking the symphonies and concertos are all very successful in their outer movements and disappointing in their slow ones, and both Geoffrey Tozer and Boris Berman are convincingly muscular soloists in the two concertante works with piano. The performance of the youthful *Symphony*, Op. 1, is particularly convincing in its warmth and thrust. *Oedipus Rex*, with a good narrator in Jean Piat, receives the same sort of full-blooded approach, but the cast is uneven, with Gabriele Schnaut wobbly and shrill as Jocasta and with *pianissimos* sadly lacking, partly a question of recording balance. The sound throughout the five discs is generally warm and full, although the resonance means that inner detail often lacks sharpness of focus, and in the *Symphony of Psalms* the chorus is rather backwardly balanced. The texts for the vocal items are not included, but these CDs remain individually available at mid-price (including texts, where applicable).

(i) *Apollo; Dumbarton Oaks Concerto; Concerto in D; (ii) Le Chant du rossignol; Symphony in C; Symphony in Three Movements.*

(BB) *(*) Virgin 5 62022-2 (2). Saraste, with (i) Scottish CO; (ii) Finnish RSO.

There is nothing really wrong with the Scottish performances but, on the other hand, there is nothing especially brilliant about them either. The Scottish Chamber Orchestra offer some impressive and sometimes beautiful playing in *Apollo*, but in some of the slow sections of the score the tension is not well maintained. The neo-classical *Concertos* are quite lively, but their effect is dampened down by the rather over-reverberant acoustic. *Le Chant du rossignol*, which opens the Finnish CD, is played with considerable finesse, but here the sound is undistinguished, with a limited dynamic range, the bright orchestral colours blunted by the flat, underrecorded sound. The two *Symphonies* suffer much the same fate.

(i) *Piano Concerto; Fireworks.*

*** Arthaus DVD 100 314. (i) Toradze; Rotterdam PO, Gergiev (with DEBUSSY – *Le Martyre de Saint-Sébastien* ***) (Director: Rob van der Berg. V/D: Peter Rump) – PROKOFIEV: *Scythian Suite*, Op. 20 (with Rehearsal). *** ●

Alexander Toradze is as impressive an exponent of Stravinsky as he was of the Prokofiev concertos he recorded with Gergiev and the Kirov Orchestra for Philips, and while the main interest of this DVD is the Prokofiev coupling, this well-planned concert is very rewarding throughout and stimulating to watch.

Concerto for Piano & Wind.

(***) British Music Society mono BMS 101 CDH. Mewton-Wood, Hague Residentie O, Goehr – BLISS: *Concerto* *** ●; SHOSTAKOVICH: *Piano Concerto No. 1.* (***)

Edward Sackville West placed this record as one of two recordings that serve as the 'best memorial of his [Mewton-Wood's] style', and certainly the partnership here with Walter Goehr is very impressive indeed. It is the central *Largo* one especially remembers, wonderfully cool and beautiful, immediately offset by the brilliance of the finale. In reviewing the original LP in *Gramophone* Lionel Salter wrote: 'Clarity and balance of forces here are exemplary; but what takes one's breath away is the uncanny and faultless accuracy in this very taxing work.' The recording of the piano is very good, and the orchestra has more body than in the Bliss coupling.

(i) *Ebony Concerto; L'Histoire du soldat* (ballet suite); *Octet for Wind; Symphonies of Wind Instruments;* (ii) *Piano Rag-Music;* (ii; iii) *Ragtime for 11 Instruments.*

(M) ** Sup. SU 3168-2 911. (i) Prague Chamber Harmony, Pešek; (ii) Novotný, (iii) Zlatnikova.

These Prague performances from the 1960s are no match for the finest versions in their characterisation and finesse or the quality of the recorded sound. However, given the moderate price-tag, they remain very serviceable.

The Firebird (complete); *Le Chant du rossignol; Fireworks; Scherzo à la russe.*

●━ ● *** Mercury (ADD) **SACD** 470 643-2. LSO, Dorati.

Mercury are bringing out some of their most admired recordings on SACD and, although they are not due to be released until after our book goes to press, we feel sure that listeners will want advance warning of their publication in the autumn of this year. The new format should go some way to further enhance the already spectacular results afforded by the 'Living Presence' technology.

The Firebird (complete); *4 Etudes; Petrushka* (1947 version; complete); *Scherzo à la russe* (2 versions: for jazz band; for orchestra); *Symphony in 3 Movements.*

(BB) **(*) EMI Gemini 5 85538-2 (2). CBSO, Rattle.

Strong, clean and well played, Rattle's CBSO version of *The Firebird* is forthright and positive rather than atmospheric, looking forward to the *Rite of Spring* rather than back to Russian nationalism. So the lovely melody of Khorovod, the *Round Dance of the Princesses*, has a plain, folk-like quality, and *Kastchei's Dance*, firmly controlled, is straightforward and direct, not as fiercely exciting as it can be. The recording is warm and full, but this is not one of Rattle's most inspired recordings. His reading of *Petrushka* brings out the sturdy jollity of the ballet, contrasting it with the poignancy of the puppet's own feelings. The full and brilliant recording here is beefy in the middle and bass, and Rattle and his players benefit in clarity by their use of the 1947 scoring, finely detailed to bring out many points that are normally obscured. In the *Symphony in Three Movements*, done with comparable power, colour and robustness, Rattle brings out the syncopations and pop references with great panache. The two versions of the *Scherzo à la russe* then make a fascinating comparison – both given with Rattle's usual flair, infectiously bouncy. The *Four Studies* provide another light-hearted makeweight.

Firebird Suite (1919 version); *The Rite of Spring.*
** Delos DE 3278. Oregon SO, DePreist.

The Oregon Symphony under James DePreist give a sumptuously romantic account of the *Firebird Suite*, helped by the warm acoustics of the Baumann Auditorium, at the George Fox University in Newberg. But although the mystic atmosphere of the lyrical pages of *The Rite of Spring* is hauntingly conveyed, the score's inherent violence and sacrificial brutality are under-emphasized, and there is a lack of pungent rhythmic bite. The composer's own recordings of *The Firebird* and *The Rite of Spring* dominate this repertory (Sony SMK 89875 – see our main *Guide*).

Complete ballets: *The Firebird; Petrushka; The Rite of Spring; Fireworks; Scherzo fantastique.*
(B) ★ Erato/Teldec Ultima 0630 18964-2 (2). Philh. O, Inbal.

This Ultima CD is a non-starter. With the three main ballets generating a very low voltage and smooth rather than vivid sound, there is little drama and excitement to be found here. Inbal's very metrical view of the *Rite* may be valid in principle, but the music sounds too safe in practice. Not recommended.

Petrushka (1911, original version).
(M) (*) Westminster mono 471 245-2. RPO, Scherchen
– HONNEGER: *Chant de joie*, etc. (*(*))

With a sprinkling of Scherchen eccentricities to remind one who is at the helm, it is hard to recommend his otherwise rather flaccid 1954 account to the general collector with so many excellent and less idiosyncratic performances available.

Petrushka (1911 score; complete); *The Rite of Spring.*
(BB) ** RCA 74321 68020-2. RPO, Temirkanov.

Petrushka (ballet; complete 1947 version); *The Rite of Spring; Circus Polka.*
(B) ** Australian Decca Eloquence (ADD) 460 509-2. LAPO, Mehta.

(i) *Petrushka* (1947 score); (ii) *The Rite of Spring; Fireworks, Op. 4.*
(M) ** RCA (ADD) 09026 63311-2. (i) Boston SO; (ii) Chicago SO, Ozawa.

There is nothing intrinsically wrong with Yuri Temirkanov's 1988 readings of these two masterful scores – they are well played and well recorded – but there is nothing especially outstanding about them either. *Petrushka* lacks the character of the best performances, and although there is some nice detail in *The Rite*, it lacks the sheer overwhelming impact that the score should generate.

Mehta's Los Angeles *Rite of Spring*, despite extreme tempi, some very fast, others slow, is an interesting and individual reading, very well recorded. *Petrushka* is played superbly, but lacks the character of the finest versions. What makes it compelling, in its way, is the astonishingly brilliant recording, which startlingly brings the Los Angeles orchestra into your sitting room. The *Circus Polka* makes a sparkling bonus, but this CD is primarily recommendable to audiophiles.

Recorded in 1968 and 1969 respectively, Ozawa's accounts of *Petrushka* and *The Rite of Spring* are unequal in appeal. *Petrushka* is a lightweight interpretation in the best sense, with Ozawa's feeling for the balletic quality of the music coming over, sometimes at the expense of dramatic emphasis. However, he is at times too dainty, and the underlying tension suggesting the strong feelings of the puppet characters is not always apparent. There are certainly more earthy accounts of *The Rite of Spring* available, even if the Chicago acoustic adds to the weight of the performance. Curiously, the early *Fireworks*, which one would have thought suited Ozawa's talents best of all, sounds rather aggressive.

PIANO MUSIC

3 Movements from Petrushka.
(M) *** DG (ADD) 471 360-2. Pollini– BARTOK: *Piano Concertos Nos. 1–2.* ***

Pollini's electrifying performance of Stravinsky has here been (less suitably) recoupled with Bartók's *Piano concertos* instead of other twentieth-century piano music.

SULLIVAN, Arthur (1842–1900)

Symphony in E (Irish); Imperial March; Overture in C (In Memoriam); Victoria and Merrie England Suite.
** CPO 999 171-2. BBC Concert O, Arwel Hughes.

On CPO the first movement of the *Irish Symphony* obstinately refuses to take off and, as Owain Arwel Hughes observes the exposition repeat, its 16 minutes' length seems like a lifetime. The other movements are rather more successful, but in almost every way this performance is inferior to the new Chandos version. The other items here pass muster, with the ballet suite easily the most enjoyable item, especially the finale, *May Day Festivities*, which might well have been an undiscovered interlude from *The Yeomen of the Guard*.

The Savoy Operas

The Savoy Operas: (i) *The Gondoliers;* (ii) *HMS Pinafore;* (iii) *Iolanthe;* (iv) *The Mikado;* (v) *Patience;* (vi) *The Pirates of Penzance;* (vii) *Ruddigore;* (viii) *Trial by Jury;* (ix) *The Yeomen of the Guard* (all without dialogue). Orchestral Music: (x) *Cello Concerto in D* (reconstructed Mackerras & Mackie); (xi) *Overtures: Cox and Box; Di ballo; Princess Ida.* (xii) *In Memoriam;* (xiii) *Symphony in E (Irish);* (xii) *The Merchant of Venice: Suite. The Tempest* (incidental music): *Suite.*

(BB) *** EMI (ADD/DDD) 5 74468-2 (16). (i) Graham; (i; vi) Milligan; (i; iii; v; ix) Young; (i; iv; ix) G. Evans; (i; ii; iv; vi–ix) Lewis; (i–iv; vi; viii; ix) Cameron; (i–ix) Brannigan, Morison; (i–vi; ix) Thomas; (i–vii; ix) Sinclair; (ii; iii; v–viii) G. Baker, (iii) Cantelo; (iii; vi) Harper; (iii; iv) Wallace; (v) Shaw, Anthony, Harwood, Harper; (vii) Blackburn, Bowden, Rouleau; (ix) Dowling; Glyndebourne Festival Ch., Pro Arte O, Sargent; (x) Lloyd Webber, LSO, Mackerras; (xi) Pro Arte O or BBC SO, Sargent; (xii) CBSO, Dunn; (xiii) RLPO, Groves.

At long last the distinguished Sargent EMI series of the Savoy Operas is back in the catalogue. They are not available separately, but this generously filled box is at super-budget price and is first-class value for money. The performances are uniformly notable for the quality of the soloists (and, indeed, the excellent chorus). Sargent was a long-experienced advocate and he conducts with consistent authority, if not always with the 'first-night' zest that Isidore Godfey managed consistently to achieve in his D'Oyly Carte recordings.

The Gondoliers is a case in point. Sargent chose a curiously slow tempo for the *Cachucha*, while the long opening scene is rather relaxed and leisurely. At the entrance of the Duke of Plaza Toro (Sir Geraint Evans, no less) things wake up considerably and Owen Brannigan, whose larger-than-life vocal personality dominates the whole series, is a perfectly cast Don Alhambra. Edna Graham only sang in this one recording, but she is a charmingly small-voiced Casilda, and there is much else to enjoy.

It was to Owen Brannigan's credit that, little as he has to do in *HMS Pinafore* without the dialogue, he conveys the force of Dick Deadeye's personality so strongly. George Baker is splendid as Sir Joseph and John Cameron, Richard Lewis and (especially) Monica Sinclair as Buttercup make much of their songs. Elsie Morison is rather disappointing: she spoils the end of her lovely song in Act I by singing sharp. The whole of the final scene is musically quite ravishing, and if Sir Malcolm fails to find quite all the

wit in the music he is never less than lively.

There is much to praise, too, in *Iolanthe*. The climax of Act I, the scene in which the Queen of the Fairies lays a curse on members of both Houses of Parliament, shows most excitingly what can be achieved with the 'full operatic treatment'. George Baker is an excellent Lord Chancellor: the famous *Nightmare Song* is very well and clearly sung; however, for some ears John Cameron's dark timbre may not readily evoke an Arcadian Shepherd. The two Earls and Private Willis are excellent, and all of Act II – except perhaps Iolanthe's recitative and ballad near the end (which is always a bit of a problem) – goes well. The famous Trio with the Lord Chancellor and the two Earls is a joy.

The Sargent set of *The Mikado* was the first to be recorded, in 1957, but it has been given remarkable vividness and presence by the digital remastering. The grand operatic style for the finales of both acts, the trio about the 'death' of Nanki-Poo, and the glee that follows are characteristic of the stylish singing, even if the humour is less readily caught than in the D'Oyly Carte version. Owen Brannigan makes a fine Mikado, but the star performance is that of Richard Lewis, who sings most engagingly throughout as Nanki-Poo. Elsie Morison is back on form as a charming Yum-Yum, and Monica Sinclair is a generally impressive Katisha, although she could sound more convinced when she sings 'These Arms shall Now Enfold You'.

Patience was one of the great successes of the Sargent cycle. It is pity that there is no dialogue, which is so important to establish the character of Bunthorne, the 'fleshly poet'. But there is more business than usual from this EMI series and a convincing theatrical atmosphere. The chorus is a strong feature throughout, and Elsie Morison's Patience, George Baker's Bunthorne and John Cameron's Grosvenor are all admirably characterized, while the military men are also excellent.

Once again in *Pirates*, the EMI recording has more atmosphere than usual, and the performance is (for the most part) highly successful, stylish as well as lively, conveying both the fun of the words and the charm of the music. Undoubtedly the star of this piece is George Baker: he is a splendid Major-General, and Owen Brannigan is his inimitable self as the Sergeant of the Police, a role he was surely born to play. The performance takes a little time to warm up, and in 'Poor Wandering One', Mabel's opening cadenza, Elsie Morison, is angular and over-dramatic. However, elsewhere she is much more convincing, especially in the famous duet, 'Leave Me not to Pine Alone'. The choral contributions are pleasingly refined yet have no lack of vigour. 'Hail Poetry' is resplendent, while the choral finale is vigorously done and with a balance which allows the inner parts to emerge effectively.

In most respects *Ruddigore* crowned the EMI series. Sargent's essentially lyrical approach brings out the associations this lovely score has with Schubert.

The performance is beautifully sung. Perhaps George Baker sounds a little old in voice for Robin Oakapple, but he manages his 'character' transformation later in the opera splendidly. Pamela Bowden is a first-class Mad Margaret, and her short Donizettian scene is superbly done. Equally Richard Lewis is an admirably bumptious Richard. Owen Brannigan's delicious Act II duet with Mad Margaret has irresistible gentility. The drama is well managed too; the scene in the picture gallery (given a touch of added resonance by the recording) is effectively sombre. Altogether a superb set, probably unsurpassed on record.

Sargent's *Trial by Jury* (with George Baker as the Judge) is by general consent the best there is, splendidly spirited and very well sung and recorded; and *The Yeomen of the Guard* is also very fine. The trios and quartets with which this score abounds are most beautifully performed and skilfully balanced, and the ear is continually beguiled. Owen Brannigan's portrayal of Wilfred again comes up trumps, and Monica Sinclair is a memorable Dame Carruthers. The finales to both acts have striking breadth, and the delightfully sung trio of Elsie, Phoebe and the Dame in the finale of Act II is a charming example of the many felicities of this set. 'Strange Adventure', too, is beautifully done. There is very little feeling of humour, but the music triumphs and, as with the rest of the series, the sound is excellent, with fine presence and definition.

It might have been better had EMI not included the fillers which accompanied the individual issues of the operas. The most interesting and most disappointing is the *Cello Concerto*, written when Sullivan was nineteen, after he returned from study in Leipzig. It was given a few performances and then forgotten. In 1964 the one surviving score was destroyed in the fire at Chappell's publishing house; but the work was reconstructed in the late 1980s with the help of the solo cello part. Sadly, the end result hardly justifies such labours. Curiously proportioned, with the first movement too brief for any symphonic pretensions and with themes less than memorable, it is a lightweight divertissement, pleasant but undistinguished. However, Julian Lloyd Webber and Mackerras, very well recorded, do all they can to give the flimsy inspiration some bite.

The *Symphony* is a far better proposition, pleasingly lyrical, with echoes of Schumann as much as the more predictable Mendelssohn and Schubert. The jaunty *Allegretto* of the third movement with its 'Irish' tune on the oboe is nothing less than haunting. Groves and the RLPO give a fresh and affectionate performance, and the 1986 recording has emerged freshly on CD.

The pair of Shakespeare-inspired suites are also well worth having. The longer selection from *The Tempest* dates from 1861, the same year as the *Cello Concerto*, but shows distinctive flair and orchestral confidence. The shorter *Merchant of Venice Suite* was composed five years later; almost immediately, the writing begins to anticipate the lively style which was so soon to find a happy marriage with Gilbert's words. The performance here is highly infectious and the sound is first class. Of the overtures, *Di ballo* is the most useful, well worth having in Sargent's performance, but *In Memoriam*, a somewhat inflated religous piece, written for the 1866 Norwich Festival, is for Sullivan aficionados only.

(i) *Iolanthe* (complete, without dialogue). (ii) *Pineapple Poll* (ballet, arr. Mackerras: complete).

(BB) (**) Naxos mono 110231/2. (i) Green, Halman, Mitchell, Drummond-Grant, Styler, Osborn, Thornton, Morgan, D'Oyly Carte Op. Ch. & O, Godfrey; (ii) Sadler's Wells O, Mackerras.

The joy of this 1951 recording (one of the last of the first Decca series) is of course Martyn Green's Lord Chancellor, particularly when set against Ella Halman's resonantly fruity Queen of the Fairies, one of her most celebrated characterizations. Although ensemble is not always ideally polished, the performance is certainly spirited and is at its best in the long Act I Finale. Margaret Mitchell's Phyllis is certainly fresh and Ann Drummond-Grant sings Iolanthe's Act II aria very touchingly, so there is much to enjoy. But the transfer retains the accentuated treble that dogged the Ace of Clubs mono LPs, and this makes the orchestral violins thin and shrill and even affects the voices at times. Mackerras's early recording of *Pineapple Poll* is more successfully transferred.

Patience (complete, without dialogue).

(BB) (***) Naxos mono 8.11023. Green, Mitchell, Styler, Fancourt, Pratt, Osborn, Griffiths, Halman, Drummond-Grant, Harding, D'Oyly Carte Op. Ch. & O, Godfrey.

The quality of the Naxos transfer of the 1951 *Patience* is unbelievably better than the companion set of *Iolanthe*, and the performance is much more polished, from the lively Overture onwards. Darrell Fancourt is magnificent as Colonel Calverly (wonderful diction) and almost – but not quite – upstages Martyn Green's memorable Bunthorne. Margaret Mitchell's Patience is fresh and charming, if perhaps a little over-sophisticated, as Alan Styler's Grosvenor is a shade precious. But Ella Halman is a splendid Lady Jane, and her duet with Bunthorne, 'So Go to Him and Say to Him', is a highlight. Throughout the chorus is excellent and the whole performance is full of spirit. Alongside *The Mikado* it was one of the very finest of Godfrey's first series of recordings for Decca and in this excellently managed and well-documented Naxos reissue is very enjoyable indeed.

The Yeomen of the Guard (complete, without dialogue).

(BB) (**) Naxos mono 8.110293/4 (2). Green, Fancourt, Watson, Osborn, Harding, Drummond-Grant, Halman, D'Oyly Carte Ch. & New Promenade O, Godfrey (with orchestral selections from the operas: British Light SO, Moore *).

This was another of the best of Decca's first-generation mono sets of the Savoy Operas, recorded in the summer of 1950. Dominated by Martyn Green's inimitable Jack Point, it is strongly cast, with Ella Halman at her commanding best as Dame Carruthers, Richard Watson a formidable Wilfred Shadbolt and Darrel Fancourt in the relatively minor role of Sergent Merryll. Ann Drummond-Grant returned to the company that year to sing the mezzo role of Phoebe very stylishly. (She was to take over the principal contralto roles the following year, when Halman retired.) Muriel Harding is a charming Elsie and the merits of the female cast as a team come out attractively in the closing numbers of Act II, 'A Man who would Woo a Fair Maid', 'When a Wooer Goes a Wooing', and the infinitely touching finale, when Martyn Green shows he can play a tragic role, without overdoing the sentiment, as well as a comic one. (His patter songs are all irresistible.) Godfrey conducts with his usual dedication and vitality, and the chorus sings ardently (the opening of Act II is especially fine). If the ensembles are not always immaculate, that shows the recording conditions of the time, with limited rehearsal and a scratch orchestra. Excellent, vivid mono sound, splendidly transferred: every word is clear. The nostalgic orchestral selections from six operas which follow (including, surprisingly, an excerpt fom *Utopia Ltd*) come from 1935 78s on the Columbia label. The ensemble is very small, with single wind and brass, reminiscent of a pier orchestra, but Stephen Moore's conducting is lively enough and the studio-ish recording is incredibly good and expertly remastered: one could hardly guess the recording date, except that occasionally one can hear some background rustle.

SUPPÉ, Franz von (1819–95)

Complete overtures

Vol. 1: Overtures: *Carnival; Die Frau Meisterin; Die Irrfahrt um's Glück (Fortune's Labyrinth); The Jolly Robbers (Banditenstreiche); Pique Dame; Poet and Peasant; Des Wanderers Ziel (The Goal of the Wanderers). Boccaccio: Minuet & Tarantella. Donna Juanita: Juanita march.*

★★ Marco Polo 8.223647. Slovak State PO (Košice), A. Walter.

Vol. 2: Overtures: *Beautiful Galatea (Die schöne Galatea); Boccaccio; Donna Juanita; Isabella; Der Krämer und sein Kommis (The Shopkeeper and His Assistant); Das Modell (The Model); Paragraph 3; Tantalusqualen. Fatinitza March.*

★★ Marco Polo 8.223648. Slovak State PO (Košice), A. Walter.

Vol. 3: Overtures: *Fatinitza; Franz Schubert; Die Heimkehr von der Hochzeit (Homecoming from the Wedding); Light Cavalry; Trioche and Cacolet;*

Triumph. Boccaccio: March. Herzenseintracht polka; Humorous Variations on 'Was kommt dort von der Höhv'; Titania Waltz.

★★ Marco Polo 8.223683. Slovak State PO (Košice), A. Walter.

Alfred Walter's performances here are unsubtle, but they have a rumbustious vigour that is endearing and, with enthusiastic playing from the Slovak orchestra, who are obviously enjoying themselves, the effect is never less than spirited. Many of the finest of the lesser-known pieces are already available in more imaginative versions from Marriner. But Walter has uncovered some attractive novelties, as well as some pleasing if inconsequential interludes and dances. On Volume 1 *Carnival* (nothing like Dvořák's piece), opens rather solemnly, then introduces a string of ideas, including a polka, a waltz and a galop. *Des Wanderers Ziel* begins very energetically and, after brief harp roulades, produces a rather solemn cello solo and brass choir; later there is an attractive lyrical melody, but there are plenty of histrionics too, and the dancing ending brings distinctly Rossinian influences.

In Volume 2 *Isabella* is introduced as a sprightly Spanish lady, but Viennese influences still keep popping up, while *Paragraph 3* summons the listener with a brief horn-call and then has another striking lyrical theme, before gaiety takes over. *Der Krämer und sein Kommis* proves to be an early version (the ear notices a slight difference at the dramatic opening) of an old friend, *Morning, Noon and Night in Vienna*. *Donna Juanita* brings a violin solo of some temperament; then, after some agreeably chattering woodwind, comes a grand march.

On the third CD, *Trioche and Cacolet* immediately introduces a skipping tune of great charm and, after another of Suppé's appealing lyrical themes, ends with much rhythmic vigour. The biographical operetta about *Schubert* opens with an atmospheric, half-sinister reference to the *Erlkönig* and follows with further quotations, prettily scored; however, the writing coarsens somewhat vulgarly at the end. But the prize item here is a set of extremely ingenious variations on a local folksong, which translates as *What comes there from on high?* It seems like a cross between 'A Hunting we will Go' and 'The Grand Old Duke of York'.

Vol. 4: Overtures: *Dame Valentin oder Frauenräuber und Wanderbursche; Dolch und Rose oder Das Donaumädchen; Der Gascogner; Die G'frettbrüderln; Die Hammerschmidin aus Steiermark oder Folgen einer Landpartie; Kopf und Herz; Reise durch die Märchenwelt; Unterthänig und Unabhängig; Zwei Pistolen.*

★★(*) Marco Polo 8.223865. Slovak State PO (Košice), Pollack.

The intriguing titles here provide the entrée to music of much charm and inexhaustible melody – little of the music here is dull. The opening *Der Gascogner*

('The Man from Gascogny') begins with a rather haunting series of held notes on the horn, and the melodramatic opening of *Dolch und Rose* ('The Dagger and the Rose') is not quite what we expect from this composer. *Dame Valentin oder Frauenräuber* ('Dame Valentin or Lady Robber') has a piquant opening, complete with triangle, before melting into some delightful melodies, including, of course, some spirited waltzes and galops. There is plenty to enjoy here, especially some of Suppé's more ambitious writing – *Reise durch die Märchenwelt* ('Journey through the World of Fairies') has passages which sound almost Wagnerian. The performances here are sympathetic, although the recording lacks ideal richness.

Overtures: Beautiful Galatea; Boccaccio; Light Cavalry; Morning, Noon and Night in Vienna; Pique-Dame; Poet and Peasant.

🎵 *** Mercury (ADD) **SACD** 470 638-2. Detroit SO, Paray – AUBER: *Overtures*. *** ⬤

Mercury are bringing out some of their most admired recordings on SACD and, although they are not due to be released until after our book goes to press, we feel sure that listeners will want to be informed of their publication in the autumn of this year. Full reviews of the works listed above can be found in our current main edition. The new format should go some way to further enhance the already spectacular results afforded by the 'Living Presence' technology.

SVENDSEN, Johann Severin
(1840–1911)

Symphony No. 2; Carnival in Paris, Op. 9; Norwegian Artists' Carnival, Op. 14; Norwegian Rhapsody No. 2, Op. 19; (i) Romance in G, for Violin & Orchestra, Op. 26.

** Chatsworth FCM 1002. Stavanger SO, Llewelyn; (i) with Thorsen.

Decent performances from Stavanger of the *Second Symphony* and other popular Svendsen pieces under the Welsh conductor, Grant Llewelyn. The strings do not have the depth of sonority of their immediate rivals, but the orchestra plays with freshness and enthusiasm.

String Quartet in A min., Op. 1; (i) String Quintet in C, Op. 5.

*** CPO 999 858-2. Olso String Qt, (i) with Graggerud.

Two early works, composed while Svendsen was at the Leipzig Conservatoire. Both show a natural feeling for form and an unfailing sense of proportion. Svendsen thinks in long musical paragraphs, and his ideas have a strong, lyrical momentum as well as astonishing assurance and freshness. Both Op. 1 and Op. 5 were coupled together many years ago by the Hindar Quartet, but these Oslo players have much greater tonal blend and refinement, as well as unanimity of attack. Two delightful and rewarding scores that have been absurdly neglected, now very persuasively played and well recorded.

SWEELINCK, Jan (1562–1621)

Allein Gott in der Höh sei Ehr; Ballo del granduca; Christe qui lux est et dies; Echo Fantasia (Ionian); Engelsche Foruyn; Erbarme dich mein; Est-ce Mars?; O Herre Gott; Fantasia (a-Phrygian); Fantasia Chromatica; Ich ruf zu dir, Herr Jesu Christ; Ick voer al over Rhijn; Ik heb den Heer lief (Psalm 116); Malle Sijmen; Mein junges Leben hat ein End; More palatino; Nun freut euch, lieben Christen gemein; Onder een linde groen; Ons is gheboren een kindekijn; Onse Vader hemelrijck; Pavana hispanica; Pavana Lachrimae; Pavana Philippi; Poolsche dans; Ricerar (Aeolian); Toccata (Ionian).

🎵 *** Hyp. CDA 67421/2 (2). Herrick (organ of the Norrfjärden Kyrka, Norrfjärden, Piteå, Sweden).

Sweelinck exerted enormous influence during his lifetime, and his keyboard music was in turn much influenced by the English composers of the day. Ton Koopman has recorded his complete keyboard music on four modestly priced CDs (Philips 468 417-2 – see our main edition), and that must remain the cornerstone of any collection. Christopher Herrick has chosen the organ of the Norrfjärden Kyrka, Piteå, on the northeastern coast of Sweden. It is based on a reconstruction of the 1609–84 organ of the Tyskakyrkan in Stockholm, an instrument closely associated with one of Sweelinck's pupils. Herrick is completely attuned to the flavour and style of this repertoire and draws a consistently characterful sound from this lovely instrument. Koopman notwithstanding, collectors should investigate this fine set of a composer who remains seriously underrated outside the Netherlands. The recording is in the best traditions of the house.

SZYMANOWSKI, Karol
(1882–1937)

(i; ii) Concert Overture, Op. 12; (iii; iv) Harnasie, Op. 55; Symphonies Nos. (i; ii) 2 in B flat, Op. 19; (i; iv–vi) 3 (Song of the Night), Op. 27; (i; v; vii) 4 (Symphonie concertante), Op. 60. (viii) 20 Mazurkas for Solo Piano, Op. 50/1 & 2. Theme & Variations for Solo Piano, Op. 3.

(BB) **(*) EMI Gemini (ADD) 585539-2 (2). (i) Polish R. Nat. SO; (ii) Kaspszyk; (iii) Bachleda, Kwasny, Polish R. O of Kraków, Wit; (iv) Polish R. Ch. of Kraków; (v) Semkow; (vi) Ochman; (vii) Paleczny; (viii) Blumenthal.

This is an excellent and inexpensive way to explore this often marvellous composer. The *Second Sym-*

phony is not as rewarding as the *Third*, but it is unusual in form: there are only two movements, the second being a set of variations, culminating in a fugue. The influences of Richard Strauss and Scriabin are clearly audible, if not altogether assimilated. The *Third Symphony (Song of the Night)*, however, is one of the composer's most beautiful scores, with a heady, intoxicated – and intoxicating – atmosphere. These performances date from 1982, and they remain full and atmospheric, even if the quality of the orchestral playing, though good, has been superseded in more recent versions (the vibrato on the brass instruments will not be to all tastes). The gripping account of the ambitious *Concert Overture*, which sounds for all the world like an undiscovered symphonic poem by Richard Strauss, is highly enjoyable. In the *Symphonie concertante*, Piotr Paleczny is no mean artist and he has all the finesse and imagination as well as the requisite command of colour that this work calls for; Wit provides him with admirable support, and this 1979 account, as a whole, makes a stronger impression than the more recent Naxos version, similarly priced. *Harnasie* is also very successful; it reflects Szymanowski's discovery of the folk music of the Tatras. It calls for large forces, including a solo violinist as well as a tenor and full chorus, and poses obvious practical production problems. As always with this composer, there is a sense of rapture, the soaring, ecstatic lines and the intoxicating exoticism that distinguish the mature Szymanowski, and it comes across most tellingly here. The sound is spaciously wide-ranging and full, but it is made a bit fierce on top by the CD mastering. Blumenthal's accounts of the piano items are reasonably persuasive, though they are sound rather than inspired performances; however, they make a nice bonus.

(i) *Violin Concertos Nos. 1–2*; (ii) *Symphony No. 4 (Symphonie concertante)*.
🔲 *** EMI 5 57777-2. (i) Zehetmair; (ii) Andsnes; CBSO, Rattle.

Thomas Zehetmair's deeply felt versions of the two *Violin Concertos* are now joined by Leiv Ove Andsnes's outstanding account of the *Symphonie concertante*. Both he and Rattle capture the sensuous luminosity of the central movement, and Rattle unleashes the wildness of the finale with great vigour. Throughout, the CBSO conjures up the exotic Szymanowskian sound-world, and the engineers deliver spectacularly wide-ranging recording.

CHAMBER MUSIC

3 Mythes, Op. 30.
*** HM HMC90 1793. Faust, Kupiec – JANACEK: *Violin Sonata*; LUTOSLAWSKI: *Partita*, *Subito*. ***

The Szymanowski *Mythes* (dating from 1915, like the Janáček *Sonata*), bring a sharp contrast with the rest of this mixed bag in the shimmeringly evocative opening of *The Fountain of Arethusa*, at once reflective and urgent, here presented with a magical lightness by the pianist as well as the violinist, who produce magical *pianissimos*. The mystery, the ethereal quality, in these three classically inspired pieces is beautifully brought out, when the technical demands on the violinist can easily result in heavy-handed, earthbound playing. That applies not only to the first two pieces but to the energetic third piece, *Dryades et Pan*, with its buzzing trills suggesting insect music.

PIANO MUSIC

20 Mazurkas, Op. 50; 2 Mazurkas, Op. 62; 4 Polish Dances; Valse Romantique.
*** Hyp. CDA 67399. Hamelin.

The Szymanowski *Mazurkas* are late works and are among his best and certainly his most haunting piano pieces. They are without doubt the finest mazurkas after Chopin. Their inward qualities and their sense of mystery elude many pianists, but Marc-André Hamelin gives as perceptive and authoritative an account of these extraordinary pieces as any. In this music Szymanowski was entering new territory, and their significance in his development cannot be underestimated. Hyperion give Hamelin natural and truthfully balanced sound, and no readers interested in this once neglected but now rightly appreciated master should overlook this fine issue.

TALLIS, Thomas (*c.* 1505–85)

Complete music, Vol. 6: Music for a Reformed Church: *The First (Dorian) Service; Responses & Collects for Christmas Eve Evensong & Easter Matins.* **Anthems:** *O Lord give thy Holy Spirit; Purge me, O Lord; Remember not, O Lord God; O Lord in thee is all my trust; Out of the Deep; Verily, verily I say unto you. 9 Tunes from Archbishop Parker's Salter.*
*** Signum SIGCD 022. Chapelle du Roi, Dixon.

Volume 6 of the excellent Signum coverage of Tallis's output is devoted to music which he composed for use in the reformed services promulgated by *The Booke of the Common Prayer*, which came into effect in 1549, here presented in the normal liturgical sequence. Much of the music is simple and homophonic, but it has an unadorned beauty of its own. The anthems are richer in the interplay of parts but are still brief, and the collection ends with the nine even briefer psalm-tune harmonizations which Tallis contributed to Archbishop Matthew Parker's *Psalter*, published in about 1567. The beautiful, serene singing of the Chapelle du Roi under Alistair Dixon holds the listener's attention throughout, especially when the recording has such a full and pleasing ambience.

Complete music, Vol. 7: Music for Queen Elizabeth: Motets: *Absterge Domine; Derelinquit impius; Discomfort them O Lord; Domine, quis habitat; In ieiunio et fletu* (low & high versions); *In manus tuas; Laudate Dominum; Mihi autem nimis; Miserere nostri; O nata lux de lumine; O sacrum convivium; O salutaris hostia; Salvator mundi I & II; Spem in alium* (40-part Motet).

*** Signum SIGCD 029. Chapelle du Roi, Dixon.

Elizabeth was the fourth monarch to sit on the throne in Tallis's lifetime, and Tallis was by then in his sixties. Undoubtedly both greatly regretted the destruction of choir books and partbooks of the older generations of church music which the Reformation had brought about. Both composer and monarch also appear to have been equally determined that the new Elizabethan Latin motets should seek new expressive approaches, while drawing on the best of the past. The resulting style of the writing, using both liturgical and non-liturgical texts, combines serenity with comparative simplicity, without loss of expressive ardour. Their success is confirmed by the fact that cathedral musicians fitted English words to much of Tallis's music. *Absterge Domine* therefore also becomes *Discomfort them O Lord*. The two Psalm settings included, *Domine, quis habitat* (Psalm 15) and the shorter but no less impressive *Laudate Dominum* (Psalm 117), are both memorable, and often Tallis has a way of catching the ear with a soaring opening phrase, as in both settings of *Salvator mundi*, and particularly in the beautiful *Salutaris hostia*. The most celebrated of these motets is of course *Spem in Alium*, with its incredibly dense part-writing still able to astonish the ear. It was first heard in the early 1570s and remains one of the greatest achievements of English vocal music. It is sung gloriously here, its ebb and flow and rich climaxes splendidly controlled by Alistair Dixon, and the recording throughout combines fullness of ambience with reasonable detail considering the ecclesiastical acoustic.

Motets: *Audivici vocem de celo; Candidi facti sunt Nazarei eius a 5; Dum transisset sabbatus; Gaude gloriosa, Dei Mater; Hodie nobis celorum rex; Homo quidam fecit cenam magnam; Honor, virtus et potestas; In jejunio et fletu; In pace in idipsum; Lamentations of Jeremiah I & II; Loquebantur variis linguis; Miserere nostri; O nata lux de lumine; O sacrum convivium; Salvator mundi I & II; Spem in alium; Suscipe quaeso Domine; Te lucis ante terminum (Procul recedante somnia) I; Videte miraculum.*

(B) *** Virgin 2x1 5 62230-2 (2). Taverner Consort, Parrott.

The Taverner style is brighter and more abrasive than we are used to in this often ethereal music but, apart from the scholarly justification, the polyphonic cohesion of the writing comes over the more tellingly. Our listing is in alphabetical order, but the programme – as presented here – was planned as two separate collections, the first disc containing Tallis's most elaborate and most celebrated choral piece, the 40-part motet, *Spem in alium*, as well as nine other magnificent responsories, some of them – like *Videte miraculum* and *Dum transisset sabbatus* – almost as extended in argument. The second of the two discs has two magnificent *Lamentations of Jeremiah* as well as an even more expansive motet, which Tallis wrote early in his career, *Gaude, gloriosa, Dei Mater*, and a number of the shorter *Cantiones sacrae*. This reissue is warmly recommendable and very well recorded.

TANEYEV, Sergei (1856–1915)

Symphonies Nos. (i) *2 in B flat* (ed. Blok); (ii) *4.*
** Russian Disc (ADD) RD CD11008. (i) USSR R. & TV Grand SO, Fedoseyev; (ii) Novosibirsk PO, Katz.

In the *Fourth Symphony* Arnold Katz and the Novosibirsk orchestra give a spirited, characterful reading, which can hold its own against Järvi's excellent account. The recording is very good, though not quite in the three-star bracket. This version of the *Second Symphony in B flat* seems to be identical with Fedoseyev's 1969 LP; climaxes are a bit raw and raucous. The performance itself is satisfactory, and there is at present no alternative.

TARTINI, Giuseppe (1692–1770)

Violin Concertos in C, D.2; F, D.67; A, D.96; A min. (A Lunardo Venier), D.115; B min., D.125.
🔊 (BB) *** Warner Apex (ADD) 2564 60152-2. Toso, Sol. Ven., Scimone.

Tartini is a much underrated composer, as the many beautiful slow movements of these concertos will readily show. Pierre Toso, who recorded a number of them in the early 1970s responds with admirable feeling, his timbre consistently sweet. The *Adagio* of the C major, D.2 (*Se mai saprai*), is particularly beautiful, but for Toso the 'senza splendor' of the concerto's finale is not ostentatious. Yet his approach is consistently stylish and pleasing: the *Adagio* of the *A major* is most gracious, and the *Largo/Andante* finale (which has the inscription 'Flow bitter tars until my anguish is consumed') is movingly played. No less touching is the *Larghetto* of the *B minor Concerto*, which brings another inscription, '*Lascia ch'io dica addio*', while the *Andante cantabile* of the *F major* is a charming siciliano with the indication '*Misterio anima mea*'. Scimone and I Solisti Veneti accompany sympathetically and, while the balance tends to favour the solo violin a little, it otherwise produces excellent results, with the overall sound most natural and pleasing.

TAVENER, John (born 1944)

(i) *Angels;* (ii) *Collegium regale: Magnificat & Nunc Dimmitis;* (i; iii) *God is with us (A Christmas Proclamation);* (iv) *Funeral Ikos; 2 Hymns to the Mother of God; The Lamb;* (i) *Lament of the Mother of God;* (i) *Song for Athene;* (v) *The Protecting Veil* (excerpt): 1st section only.

𝄆━ (B) *** CfP 585 9152. (i) Winchester Cathedral Ch., Hill; (ii) King's College, Cambridge, Ch., Cleobury; (iii) with Kendall, Dunnet (organ); (iv) Vasari Singers, Backhouse; (v) Isserlis, LSO, Rozhdestvensky.

Like the companion Classics for Pleasure introduction to the music of Arvo Pärt, this compilation draws on a number of similar sources, all of high quality, both musically and as recordings. The items from the Vasari Singers include Tavener's justly famous and haunting carol, *The Lamb.* Jeremy Backhouse enhances his performance with an effective ritardando at the end of each verse, while he links the melancholy simplicity of the *Funeral Ikos* naturally to the ethereality of the *Two Hymns to the Mother of God.* The items from the Winchester choir conducted by David Hill (with David Dunnet at the organ in *God is with us*) are all atmospherically recorded: each one presents a sharply distinctive vision, culminating in the magnificent Christmas proclamation, *God is with us.* The choir then closes the programme with the beautiful and intense *Song for Athene*, heard at the funeral of Princess Diana. However, it seems a curious idea to include only the first section from Tavener's most famous instrumental work, *The Protecting Veil*, impressive though it is in the performance from Steven Isserlis, conducted by Rozhdestvensky.

TCHAIKOVSKY, Peter (1840–93)

Concert Fantasy, Op. 56; Piano Concertos Nos. 1–3.
𝄆━ (BB) **(*) EMI Gemini 85540-2 (2). Donohoe, Bournemouth SO, Barshai.

Peter Donohoe's account of the *B flat minor Concerto*, although thoroughly sympathetic and spaciously conceived, lacks the thrust and indeed the electricity of the finest versions. The *Third Concerto* is altogether more successful, dramatic and lyrically persuasive, and held together well by Barshai. The *Concert Fantasia* is even more in need of interpretative cohesion. A little more poise would have been welcome, but there is no denying the spontaneous combustion of the music-making here, and the recording – but for a little too much resonance for the solo cadenza in the opening movement – is effectively spectacular. But what makes this inexpensive Gemini Double distinctive is the inclusion of Donohoe's much praised account of the *Second Concerto*, which was given a ● on its original separate

issue and deserves to retain it. This superb recording of the full original score in every way justifies the work's length and the unusual format of the slow movement. Its extended solos for violin and cello are played with beguiling warmth by Nigel Kennedy and Steven Isserlis. The first movement goes with splendid impetus, and the performance of the finale is a delight from beginning to end. Donohoe plays with infectious bravura, and he is well supported by sparkling playing from the Bournemouth orchestra under Barshai.

Piano Concerto No. 1 in B flat min., Op. 23.
𝄆━ (B) (***) RCA mono 82876 56052-2. Horowitz, NBC SO, Toscanini – RACHMANINOV: *Piano Concerto No. 3; Recital: 'Legendary RCA Recordings'.* (***)
(*) DG 474 291-2. Lang Lang, Chicago SO, Barenboim – MENDELSSOHN: *Piano Concerto No. 1.* *
(BB) ** Warner Apex 0927 40835-2. Sultanov, LSO, Shostakovich – RACHMANINOV: *Piano Concerto No. 2.* **
(BB) *(*) EMI Encore 5 85705-2. Weissenberg, O de Paris, Karajan – RACHMANINOV: *Piano Concerto No. 2.* **

Horowitz's reading of the *Tchaikovsky Concerto* with his father-in-law, Toscanini, is well known from various issues and reissues, but this is the 1941 performance given at Carnegie Hall, even faster and more exciting than the better-known 1943 version. The playing is not always immaculate, but it is wonderfully incisive in articulation. The sound is confined, with shallow piano-timbre, but acceptable This now comes coupled on a bargain double with his unsurpassed 1951 version of the Rachmaninov *Third Concerto* and a recital assembled mainly from miscellaneous 78rpm discs of the same era, but with a few more recent recordings added.

Recorded in Chicago's Orchestra Hall in 2003, Lang Lang's performance bears out the glowing reports of his youthful brilliance and sensitivity. He is totally at ease, if with breathtaking virtuosity, in the notorious bravura passages of the Tchaikovsky; his tempos tend to be broader than usual, only occasionally sounding self-conscious, for in general he is masterly in his control of rubato. The opening instantly establishes this as a big-scale performance, strongly rhythmic and sharply accented, though – with the piano balanced close – the big melody on the first violins sounds surprisingly weak, hidden behind the pianist's monumental chords: the reason for our reservation, when this is one of the composer's most eloquent themes. The outer sections of the slow movement, like the lyrical passages of the first movement, are daringly broad, with Barenboim helping to sustain tension, while in the finale Lang Lang, again encouraged by Barenboim, himself a keyboard virtuoso, varies the tempo boldly, while sustaining a purposeful thrust. The Mendelssohn makes an unusual but attractive coupling.

There is some fiery playing from Alexei Sultanov, which testifies to a considerable technique; but compare his handling of the *prestissimo* episode in the slow movement with someone like Argerich and he emerges as rather coarse-grained, and the second group of the finale is crudely handled. However, there is much more that excites admiration, and it is only the indifferent accompanying and the less than ideal recording balance that inhibit a strong recommendation, even at bargain price.

The Weissenberg–Karajan account dates from 1970. The opening is very slack and, while the languorous approach to the *allegro* finds the poetic element of the secondary material, the main climax of the first movement lacks impetus and thrust. The *Andante cantabile* too is similarly lacking in magnetism, and even at budget price this coupling with Rachmaninov provides no real competition. Indeed, alongside Horowitz the Weissenberg Tchaikovsky performance sounds positively anaemic.

(i) *Piano Concerto No. 1;* (ii) *Violin Concerto in D, Op. 35.*

*** Pentatone **SACD**/CD PTC 5186 022. (i) Lugansky; (ii) Tetzlaff; Russian Nat. O, Nagano.

(BB) ** EMI Encore (ADD) 7243 574591 2 9. (i) Cziffra, Philh. O, Vandernoot; (ii) Kogan, Paris Conservatoire O, Silvestri.

Nicolai Lugansky was a pupil of Tatiana Nikolaeva, and his is a far from barnstorming performance of the *B flat minor Concerto.* The famous opening is broad and weighty, and the vividly Russian first subject of the allegro is given a bold, rhythmic character, yet it is not pressed too hard. In both the exposition and recapitulation the beauty of the lyrical secondary material is relished, the link with Tchaikovsky's *Romeo and Juliet* made obvious, and the puissant cadenza is explored in all its detail. The timing of this first movement is remarkably different (21 minutes 37 seconds) from the famous thrusting 1941 Horowitz/Toscanini version (17 minutes 30 seconds), but the power of the music is not diminished. The *Andantino,* introduced exquisitely by the flute, is played by Lugansky with comparable delicacy, followed by a scintillating central scherzando section. The finale then bursts forth with irrepressible impetus, the Russian orchestral players surging into their tuttis with a passionate, dancing abandon. But the secondary melody steals in quite wistfully and when, near the close, it reappears – after the pianist has made his thundering re-entry – Nagano broadens the tempo massively, to make a hugely positive climax. Some of the forward impetus is lost, but Lugansky's bravura is thrilling, and the coda would certainly bring the house down at a concert.

In his warmly romantic but never sentimental account of the *Violin Concerto,* Tetzlaff's beguiling introduction of the two main themes is invested with a natural lyrical feeling, and he bounces his bow with engaging lightness in the key passage, which Hanslick famously described as 'beating the violin black and blue', while – as in the work for piano – the cadenza becomes a highlight of the first movement. Nagano follows the flowing cantabile style of his soloist, yet he brings a surge of rhythmic energy when Tchaikovsky turns the main theme into an exuberant polacca; the recapitulation then brings a wonderfully warm reprise, with a gently ecstatic climax, followed by a quicksilver coda. Not surprisingly, the orchestral colouring of the slow movement is very Russian, and this ripely nostalgic palette carries through to the contrasting woodwind interludes in the exuberant finale. Tetzlaff's bravura playing, almost unbelievably polished and secure, is thrilling in its sparkling virtuosity, the closing bars dazzling in their exuberance. Excellent recording, and a realistic balance here; although in the companion concerto the piano is much more forward, right in front of the listener, very real and tangible.

In the famous Tchaikovsky warhorse, Cziffra displays a prodigious technique, but during the first movement he and Vandernoot seem not wholly to agree on the amount of forward thrust the music needs and, despite the use of Kingsway Hall, the strings tend to shrillness. Kogan's performance of the *Violin Concerto* is a different matter. Enjoyment and spontaneity are written in every bar of his interpretation. His account of the finale is especially infectious, with a lilt to the rhythm to really make it a Russian dance. In the first two movements, where he and Silvestri are more concerned with the architecture, he is steadier, but the build-up of tension when the main theme is developed is most exciting through his very refusal to slacken the basic speed. His tone is gloriously rich, and only occasionally does he mar a phrase with a soupy swerve. He rarely achieves a true *pianissimo,* but that may be the fault of the early stereo recording, which is very good, fuller and warmer than many Paris issues of this period.

Violin Concerto in D, Op. 35.

*** Sup. SU 3709-2. Sporcl, Czech PO, Bělohlavek– DVORAK: *Violin Concerto in D.* **(*)

(BB) (***) Naxos mono 8.110977. Milstein, Chicago SO, Stock – BRUCH: *Violin Concerto No. 1;* MENDELSSOHN: *Violin Concerto.* (***)

(M) **(*) EMI (ADD) 5 62591-2. Perlman, Phd. O, Ormandy – MENDELSSOHN: *Concerto.* ***

(BB) **(*) CfP 585 6192. Kennedy, LPO, Kamu – CHAUSSON: *Poème.* **(*)

**(*) Testament SBT 1337. Ferras, Philh. O, Silvestri – BRAHMS: *Double Concerto.* **(*)

(M) *(*) RCA (ADD) 82876 59419-2. Perlman, Boston SO, Leinsdorf – SIBELIUS: *Violin Concerto.* *(*)

The Dvořák and Tchaikovsky *Violin Concertos* are among the most striking ever to come from Slavonic composers, written within a year of each other; yet strangely they have rarely if ever been coupled on disc. That apt and attractive linking of the two works is more than enough to earn a recommendation for this new Supraphon issue, particularly when the young Czech virtuoso Pavel Sporcl is a colourful, charismatic artist. It helps that the performances were recorded live, in the Rudolfinum in Prague, with the electricity of each occasion vividly conveyed. Sporcl brings not only dashing virtuosity but tonal variety and tender expressiveness to the Tchaikovsky, with speed changes always sounding natural and spontaneous. The central *Canzonetta* has a hushed poignancy, with the recording beautifully capturing the subtlety of Sporcl's *pianissimo* playing. In the finale his clarity of articulation is a delight, with the coda irresistibly exciting.

Milstein recorded the Tchaikovsky in Chicago in March 1940 with Frederick Stock, an underrated maestro (as indeed was his successor, Desiré Defauw). It is a more classical reading than his later versions, though the finale is a remarkably dashing *tour de force* on the part of soloist and orchestra. The recording is also very fine, for at this time American Columbia had begun to record on to 33⅓rpm lacquer master discs. The recordings sound as well as 1950s early tape masters. This may not be Milstein's best account of the Tchaikovksy, but it has a lot going for it, and comes with two superb performances of the Bruch and Mendelssohn *Concertos*.

The expressive warmth of Perlman's 1978 recording goes with a very bold orchestral texture from Ormandy and the Philadelphia Orchestra. The focus of sound is not quite as clean as this work ideally needs, but Perlman's panache always carries the day.

Nigel Kennedy gives a warmly romantic reading of the Tchaikovsky *Concerto*, full of temperament with one of the most expansive readings of the first movement ever put on disc. In ample sound, it is consistently beguiling, though equally its idiosyncrasies will not please everyone. Slow as Kennedy's basic tempo for the first movement is, he takes every opportunity to linger lovingly. The result would sound self-indulgent, except that Kennedy's total commitment vividly conveys the impression of a live experiance, naturally free in expression. For all its many *tenutos* and *rallentandos*, he is not sentimental and his range of tone is exceptionally rich and wide, so that the big moments are powerfully sensual. The *Canzonetta* is taken at a flowing speed, while the finale brings extremes of expression similar to those in the first movement. Okko Kamu and the LPO are recorded in exceptionally rich and full sound, and the playing is excellent. But their style does not always match that of the soloist; it sometimes sounds a little stiff in the tuttis, though the final coda is thrilling. A bargain at its new, CfP price.

Christian Ferras recorded his better-known account of the Tchaikovsky *Concerto* with Karajan for DG in 1967, but he made this version earlier in his short career, in 1957 with Constantin Silvestri and the Philharmonia. This shines perhaps with less lustre but has greater feeling and individuality. Some col-

lectors worry at Ferras's rather sinewy nervous vibrato – though it was surely less worrying than Francescatti's; but by any standards this is a performance natural in style and direct in utterance which finds the Philharmonia responding to their soloist with playing of great enthusiasm and fire. The *Concerto* is erroneously described as being in D minor, an unusual slip for Testament, whose presentation is always scrupulous.

Perlman provides a good performance, but, in a field as competitive as this, his RCA version cannot figure high in the lists of recommendations. As in the Sibelius coupling, his later, EMI recording is far preferable. First choice for the Tchaikovsky is with Repin coupled with Miaskovsky (Ph. 473 343-2 – see our main *Guide*).

1812 Overture, Op. 49.

(BB) *(**) EMI Encore 5 85460-2. Phd. O, Muti –
LISZT: *Les Préludes* **(*); RAVEL: *Boléro*. *(*)

Muti gives an urgent, crisply articulated account of *1812*, concentrated in its excitement. The Philadelphia Orchestra takes the fast speed of the main allegro in its stride, and the coda produces a spectacularly thrilling climax. Those who enjoy the bass drum will find it very much in evidence here, and the sonics include a mêlée of bells and an impressive cannonade at the close. The snag lies in the fierceness of the early digital recording of the strings above the stave, the brilliance artificially achieved.

Festival Overture on the Danish National Anthem, Op. 15; (i) Hamlet: Overture & Incidental Music, Op. 67a.

(M) *** Chan. X10108. (i) Kelly, Hammond-Stroud; LSO, Simon.

Tchaikovsky himself thought his *Danish Festival Overture* superior to the *1812*, and though one cannot agree with his judgement it is well worth hearing. The *Hamlet Incidental Music*, however, shows the composer's inspiration at its most memorable. The *Overture* is a shortened version of the *Hamlet Fantasy Overture*, but much of the rest of the incidental music is virtually unknown, and the engaging *Funeral March* and the two poignant string elegies show the composer at his finest. *Ophelia's Mad Scene* is partly sung and partly spoken, and Janis Kelly's performance is most sympathetic, while Derek Hammond-Stroud is suitably robust in the *Gravedigger's Song*. A translation of the vocal music is provided. It is sung in French (as in the original production of *Hamlet*, performed in St Petersburg). The digital recording has spectacular resonance and depth to balance its brilliance, and there are excellent notes by Noel Goodwin.

Francesca da Rimini.

(M) ** Virgin 5 61837-2. Houston SO, Eschenbach –
DVORAK: *Symphony No. 9 (From the New World)*.
**

Eschenbach's performance of *Francesca da Rimini* has similar qualities to those in the Dvořák symphony with which it is coupled. With clean textures and ensemble, with rhythms crisply resilient and with the brass section gloriously ripe, it is a refreshing performance, which yet lacks Tchaikovskian passion. It makes a generous and unusual fill-up for the *New World Symphony*.

Manfred Symphony, Op. 58.
(*(*)) Testament mono SBT 1129. Fr. Nat. R. O, Silvestri (with LISZT: *Tasso.* ★★★)

In the earlier *Manfred* Symphony he recorded with the Orchestre National de France, Silvestri tarted up Tchaikovsky's orchestration, but it is not that so much as the moments of sour intonation and agogic distortion that diminish the appeal of his recording. The Bournemouth broadcast is to be preferred (see our main *Guide*), but the Testament does have the benefit of a first-class fill-up in Liszt's *Tasso*.

Manfred Symphony (abridged); Romeo and Juliet (Fantasy Overture).
(M) (★★(*)) Music and Arts mono CD 4260. NBC SO, Toscanini.

Toscanini had an on–off relationship with Tchaikovsky, first introducing many of his works to Italy in the 1890s but later losing interest in the Russian composer for more than 30 years. It was with *Manfred*, in 1933, that his interest revived and he conducted it several times, recording it for RCA in 1949. However, the present recording was made during a January 1953 concert, broadcast within the flattering acoustics of Carnegie Hall, so different in ambience from his infamous broadcasting studio. However, Toscanini took Tchaikovsky too seriously when the composer not only fell out of love with his own work, but said so. Toscanini used this as an excuse to truncate the piece, making major cuts, mostly in the outer movements. Certainly *Manfred* does suffer from a certain amount of inflation, and there is no doubt that the Toscanini version is more succinct than the composer's original. It makes a powerful impact throughout, even if the cymbal clashes the conductor added in the last seven bars of the coda of the first movement may not be to all tastes. Yet adrenalin runs free and the performance is undoubtedly thrilling, while the lyrical music (especially in the centrepiece of the Scherzo) shows the conductor's affection and warmth in a very positive and endearing way. The orchestral playing itself is not always as immaculate as we expect from Toscanini, but its passionate thrust carries the listener along with it. Moreover, the actual sound is amazingly good, with a richness and depth that are only too rare in this conductor's recordings.

Romeo and Juliet dates from only two months later and shows Toscanini and his orchestra right back on form; indeed, this is a splendid performance, as perceptively structured as it is exciting, and again the

sound is remarkably full-bodied. With all the reservations, this is a Toscanini reissue with a wide appeal, for all its idiosyncrasies.

Marche slave.
– ★★★
(M) ★★(*) Cala (ADD) CACD 0536. LSO, Stokowski – RIMSKY-KORSAKOV: *Scheherazade*. (★★★)

This Cala version of Stokowski's Phrase Four account of the Rimsky-Korsakov comes with this thrilling live performance of Tchaikovsky's *Marche slave*, given as an encore at his ninetieth birthday concert in London, with a spoken introduction by himself. It even outshines his studio recording in high-voltage electricity.

Stokowski's *Marche slave* was recorded live at the Royal Albert Hall in 1972. It is charismatic, very Russian in feeling, but with an unexpected elegance and charm in the Trio and the captivating coda, in which Stokowski holds back the flow of adrenalin until the thrilling *accelerando* at the closing section. The sound of the strings is a bit fierce, but the recording overall is forwardly vivid.

The Nutcracker; Sleeping Beauty; Swan Lake (ballets; complete).
(B) ★★ RCA 82876 55707-2 (6). St Louis SO, Slatkin.

Slatkin recorded the three great Tchaikovsky ballets over seven years, from the middle and late 1980s to the early 1990s, with uneven success. In *The Nutcracker* his brightly paced reading keeps the action moving in Act I, and the orchestral playing has plenty of character throughout. Other versions have more charm but are not more vivid. The lively St Louis recording, though spacious, is a little lacking in sumptuousness and richness of woodwind colour, but here Slatkin's vitality is a plus point.

The same briskness of approach works less well in *Swan Lake*; these are far from ballet tempi, and the relative thinness of the RCA sound, with dry violin timbre, is unalluring, increasing the feeling of unyielding forward motion.

Sleeping Beauty, the last to be recorded, in 1990–91, offers superior sound-quality, fuller than the earlier *Nutcracker*, with the hall ambience well conveyed. Here the vitality is less pressured, while there is plenty of drama and colour, and the Act III *Divertissement* brings both sparkle and grace. But the sound lacks that degree of glowing warmth and expansiveness in the bass that one would expect from, say, a Decca recording of this repertoire. Previn or Bonynge prove more satisfying guides in this repertoire.

The Nutcracker (excerpts).
★★ Chan. 9799. Danish Nat. RSO, Temirkanov – RAVEL: *Ma mère l'Oye (suite); La Valse* ★★ (with GADE: *Tango Jalousie*).

This CD offers only some of *The Nutcracker*, and the Ravel coupling is hardly a rarity. The fine Danish

Radio Orchestra plays excellently, but Temirkanov is, as so often, all too idiosyncratic. No complaints about the sound.

The Nutcracker: Suite; The Sleeping Beauty
(excerpts); Swan Lake (excerpts).
(B) ** Decca Penguin (ADD) Classics 460 639-2. SRO, Ansermet.

What we have from Ansermet is a pretty meagre selection of excerpts (60 minutes – similar to the previous LP), which fails to convey the full effect he achieved in the complete sets from which these are taken. The late-1950s recordings, despite some tape hiss, are excellent (especially in The Nutcracker and The Sleeping Beauty). The contributory essay is by Sir Roy Strong.

Romeo and Juliet (fantasy overture).
(BB) **(*) EMI Encore (ADD) 5 749641-2. Philh. O, Muti – DVORAK: Symphony No. 9 (From the New World). **

In his Philharmonia period Muti was an outstanding Tchaikovskian, and his 1977 Romeo and Juliet is a very fine performance, full of imaginative touches. The opening has just the right degree of atmospheric restraint and immediately creates a sense of anticipation; the great romantic climax is noble in contour yet there is no lack of passion, while the main allegro is crisply and dramatically pointed. The repeated figure on the timpani at the coda is made to suggest a tolling bell and the expressive woodwind that follows gently underlines the feeling of tragedy. The recording is good although rather light in the bass, and it is a pity that the coupling is not a performance of distinction.

Romeo and Juliet (fantasy overture).
**(*) Pentatone SACD PTC 5186 019. Netherlands PO, Kreizberg – DVOŘÁK: Symphony No. 9 (From the New World). **(*)

A strong, incisive performance of Tchaikovsky's Romeo and Juliet to match the Dvořák Symphony, very well played and brilliantly recorded. The SACD is compatible and, if played on a normal CD player, reproduces at a slightly lower level than usual.

The Sleeping Beauty, Op. 66 (ballet; complete).
(BB) **(*) EMI Gemini (ADD) 5 85788-2 (2). LSO, Previn.

With warm, polished orchestral playing and recording to match (though it expands at climaxes), Previn conveys his affection throughout; but too often – in the famous Waltz, for instance – there could be more sparkle. On the other hand, the Panorama shows Previn and the LSO at their very best, the tune floating over its rocking bass in the most magical way. There is also much delightful wind-playing but, with Previn's tempi sometimes indulgently relaxed, it has been impossible to get the complete recording on a pair of CDs and the penultimate number (29) in

Act III (included in the original three-disc LP issue) has been cut. Never mind, the CD transfer of the 1974 Abbey Road recording is admirable, and with such a flow of marvellous tunes and inspired orchestral colouring this makes very relaxing listening. And the set is very inexpensive.

Souvenir de Florence, Op. 70.
*** Channel Classics SACD: CCS SA 21504. Amsterdam Sinf., Thompson – VERDI: String Quartet. ***

The Amsterdam Sinfonietta, formerly called the Nieuw Sinfonietta Amsterdam, here offers outstanding performances of two works originally written for solo strings which, played like this by a string orchestra, are if anything even more impressive. This was Candida Thompson's first recording with them after she was appointed the Sinfonietta's leader/conductor, and the unanimity of the playing, the immaculate precision of ensemble, is phenomenal, yet it is never a cold precision. The warmth of the performances is just as remarkable, with the bounding rhythms of the first movement of the Tchaikovsky – one of his most purely happy inspirations – given an exuberant thrust. That goes with total homogeneity in the subtle shaping of rubato, so that in that first movement the entry of the second subject brings a pianissimo which is ravishing in its tenderness. The slow movement too has a breathtaking purity. The resonance of the playing is also exceptional too, involving a strikingly wide dynamic range and a meticulous observance of markings. The opulent recording helps, with a helpful ambience allowing ample detail, with the opportunity of 'surround sound' if you have the additional speakers.

Swan Lake, Op. 20 (ballet; complete).
(BB) **(*) EMI Gemini 5 85541-2 (2). Phd. O, Sawallisch.

Sawallisch directs Tchaikovsky's greatest ballet score with pleasing freshness, and the Philadelphia Orchestra play superbly. But, as so often in the past, they are let down by the choice of venue for the recording, in this instance the Memorial Hall, Fairmount Park, whose apparently intractible acoustics have led to close microphone placing, creating an unnatural effect. There is no lack of atmosphere, but very soon it becomes apparent that fortissimos are unrefined, with fierce cymbals, grainy violins, even an element of harshness. This orchestra's fine string section does not sound like this at a concert. Yet there is much to enjoy: the first and most famous Waltz is played gorgeously, and how engaging are the Cygnets, tripping in very precisely, while in the famous Pas de deux of Odette and the Prince the violin and cello duet brings ravishingly serene yet voluptuous solo playing. There are many instances of Sawallisch's nicely judged pacing and the consistently responsive solo playing, while the thrilling final climax (with gorgeously full horn-tone at the restatement of the famous *idée fixe*) makes an overwhelming apotheosis, even if the shrillness added to the violins, who play with enormous fervour, is not a plus factor. A very stimulating set, nevertheless, and singularly inexpensive in this reissued format.

Variations on a Rococo Theme for Cello & Orchestra, Op. 33.

(***) Testament mono SBT 1310. Gendron, SRO, Ansermet – SCHUMANN: *Cello Concerto* etc. (***)

When it first appeared in 1954, the authors of *The Record Guide* spoke of 'a wonderful display of consummate cello playing' and indeed so it is! Although Maurice Gendron was rather overshadowed in the 1950s and 1960s by Fournier and Tortelier, he was no less eloquent an artist, who brought an aristocratic finesse and tonal richness to everything he did. The virtuosity is effortless and his phrasing seamless; Gendron's artistry gives unalloyed pleasure. As always with this label, the transfer does justice to the 1953 Decca recording.

SYMPHONIES

Symphonies Nos. 1–6; Capriccio italien; Fatum; Francesca da Rimini; Marche slave; Romeo and Juliet (Fantasy Overture); Swan Lake (ballet suite).

(B) ** RCA 82876 55781-2 (6). RPO, Temirkanov.

Temirkanov is a wilful Tchaikovskian. In concert his free approach on questions of tempo, with exaggerated speed-changes, can result is exciting performances. In the studio it is harder to get the necessary adrenalin working, and, even with the RPO in first-rate form, the wilfulness quickly comes to sound mannered or contrived, not spontaneous. These discs are inexpensive but can be recommended only to devotees of the conductor. Jansons (Chandos 8672/8) or Karajan (DG 429 675-2) both offer far superior cycles.

Symphony No. 1 (Winter Day Dreams); Francesca da Rimini.

(BB) * Warner Apex 2564 61141-2. Leipzig O, Masur.

Though there is something to be said for bringing out the symphonic weight of Tchaikovsky's writing, Masur and his superb Leipzig orchestra with their smooth manner and rhythmically four-square approach go too far in removing all hints of Slavonic temperament. Even in this first and lightest of the Tchaikovsky cycle, the result is heavy, and *Francesca da Rimini* also lacks excitement.

Symphony No. 4 in F min., Op. 36.

(M) (***) BBC Legends mono BBCL 4143-2. Leningrad PO, Rozhdestvensky – SHOSTAKOVICH: *Cello Concerto No. 1.* (***)

A particularly valuable reminder of the days when orchestras from the then Soviet Union were heard relatively rarely in the West. This high-voltage account of the *Fourth Symphony* was recorded at one of three Promenade Concerts this great orchestra gave in the 1971 season, and it has the compelling quality and excitement that live music-making generates. The BBC recording does justice to the rich sonority this great orchestra produced at that period.

Symphony No. 5; Romeo and Juliet (Fantasy Overture).

⊖─☐ *** HM HMU 907381. RPO, Gatti.

Daniele Gatti offers a fine new recording of Tchaikovsky's *Fifth*, helped by some superb playing from the RPO, especially the brass and woodwind. Gatti often chooses tempi that are brisker than usual and that are closer to the composer's own metronome markings. The result in the first movement, with crisp rhythmic pointing, is an invigorating forward thrust from beginning to end, with the primary second subject theme on the violins romantic in its rubato, rather than impassioned, as with Gergiev. The elegiac melancholy of the slow movement, with its evocative horn solo most sensitively played by Martin Owen, brings climaxes which are spaciously affecting but not as passionately overwhelming as with Gergiev, the forceful interruptions of the motto theme less histrionic, and the movement brings a gently touching close. The Waltz is elegant and graceful, with neatly decorative violins, a contrasting interlude before the excitingly strong, direct finale. Here the brass is crisp and urgent, especially in the repeated reprise of the Fate theme, which is very sharply focused. Once again Gatti takes the movement forward in a single sweep, with free-running adrenalin, pausing only briefly to reflect Tchaikovsky's moment of self-doubt before pressing onwards to the triumphant coda with its blazing trumpets.

The outstanding live performance from Gergiev and the Vienna Philharmonic is not upstaged, but Gatti's account is thoroughly satisfying too, and there is both depth of feeling and unquenchable energy in the RPO playing. Moreover, whereas the Philips disc is uncoupled with a playing time of only 46 minutes, Gatti offers in addition a superb account of *Romeo and Juliet*. The romantic theme for the lovers is ushered in within a magical *pianissimo*, followed by the most delicately lovely moonlight sequence, and the central climax is thrilling. The love theme then blossoms gloriously and overwhelmingly in a great curving sweep of string-tone. The Abbey Road recording throughout both symphony and overture is excellent, full-bodied, with vivid, weightily sonorous brass.

Symphony No. 6 (Pathétique); Swan Lake (ballet): Suite.

** Ph. 446 725-2. Saito Kinen O, Ozawa.

Characteristically, Seiji Ozawa brings out the balletic overtones in Tchaikovsky's symphonic masterpiece, a point emphasized by having the *Swan Lake* coupling. With him the start of the symphony is deceptively light, not ominous, and the sweet beauty of the Saito Kinen string playing adds to the feeling of poise and control. With exceptionally clean ensemble, even the central development section has no hint of hysteria. Taken very fast, the third-movement march is so light it might almost be fairy music, opening out brilliantly as the march develops. The ballet suite, by contrast, comes in an understated performance, less alert than that of the symphony. The Japanese recording enhances the refinement and transparency of the playing.

CHAMBER MUSIC

String Quartets Nos. 1–3; (i) Souvenir de Florence (String Sextet), Op.70.
(B) **(*) Nim. NI 5711/2. Schubert Qt.

The Nimbus set from the early 1990s has been issued as a two-for-the-price-of-one Double. The Franz Schubert Quartet are throughly sympathetic and produce smooth, beautifully balanced sound and good ensemble. Indeed, this is one of the best chamber-music recordings Nimbus have given us. All the same, the performances yield to the Borodin versions on Teldec (4509 90422-2) made at about the same time – see our main volume.

String Quartet No. 3 in E flat min., Op. 30.
(B) *** EMI Début 5 85638-2. Atrium Qt – MOZART: *String Quartet No. 15;* SHOSTAKOVICH: *String Quartet No. 7.* ***

The *E flat minor Quartet* is strongly elegiac in feeling, and was dedicated to the memory of Ferdinand Laub, who led the first performances of Tchaikovsky's *First* and *Second Quartets.* The performance serves as recording début for the young Atrium String Quartet from St Petersburg (their teacher was Iosif Levinzon, cellist of the Taneyev Quartet). Their programme is admirably chosen. Like its immediate predecessor, the *Quartet* is a rarity in the concert hall, though it has strong musical claims on the music lover. The Atrium play it as well as any of the many ensembles in the catalogue: their performance is deeply felt, they make a beautiful sound and the EMI team serve them well. Strongly recommended.

PIANO MUSIC

Piano Music: *Piano Sonata in G, Op. 37; Deux morceaux; Dumka (Scène rustique russe); Méditation; Nutcracker Suite: Andante maestoso* (arr. Pletnev); *Valse; Valse-Scherzo No. 1.*
*** EMI 5 57719-2. Uehara.

Ayako Uehara was the first prize winner in the Tchaikovsky Competition of 2002, placing her in the company of Vladimir Ashkenazy, Andrei Gavrilov and Mikhail Pletnev. She was in fact the first woman to gain this distinction, as well as the first Japanese

pianist. This recital shows her to be a sympathetic as well as brilliant exponent of Tchaikovksy. In the *Sonata* she has awesome competition from the likes of Richter and Pletnev; though they are not superseded, she is certainly a serious contender in this repertoire and, moreover, is blessed with an excellent recorded sound.

TCHEREPNIN, Alexander
(1899–1977)

Piano Concertos Nos. 2, Op. 26; 4 (Fantaisie), Op. 78; Magna mater, Op. 41; Symphonic Prayer, Op. 93.
*** BIS CD 1247. Ogawa, Singapore SO, Lan Shui.

Tcherepnin bridged so many different musical cultures. He grew up in St Petersburg, from which he was forced to flee during the Revolution: first to the Georgian capital of Tbilisi and subsequently to Paris in 1921. His career as a pianist-composer took him to many parts of the world, and he spent some time teaching in Shanghai. The *Piano Concerto No. 2* is 'European' in style, while the *Fourth Concerto,* written shortly before he emigrated to the USA, is full of Chinese influence. Neither *Concerto* is new to the catalogue but the present versions supersede their predecessors. Eminently serviceable recording.

Symphony No. 4; Romantic Overture, Op. 67; Russian Dances, Op. 50; Suite for Orchestra, Op. 87.
**(*) Marco Polo 8.223380. Czech-Slovak State PO (Košice), Yip.

The *Fourth Symphony* is among Tcherepnin's finest works. Written in the mid-1950s, it is colourful and tautly compact, neo-classical in idiom, very well organized and full of lively and imaginative musical invention. The *Suite,* Op. 67, is less individual and in places recalls the Stravinsky of *Petrushka* and *Le Chant du rossignol.* Like the much earlier *Russian Dances,* it is uneven in quality but far from unattractive. The *Romantic Overture* was composed in wartime Paris. Generally good performances, decently recorded too under the young Chinese conductor Wing-Sie Yip, who draws a lively response from her players.

TELEMANN, Georg Philipp
(1681–1767)

Concertos in B flat for 3 Oboes, 3 Violins & Continuo, TWV 44:43; F for Recorder, Bassoon & Strings; for 4 Violins in G, TWV 40:201. Overture in F for 2 Horns & Strings, TWV 44:7.
(BB) *** Warner Apex 2564 60523-2. Soloists, VCM, Harnoncourt.

When this collection was first issued on LP in 1966 on Telefunken's Das Alte Werk label we suggested it was one of the best Telemann discs in the catalogue, and it still is. The *Overture* featuring a pair of solo horns (natural horns are used here) shows the composer at his most characteristic, using all the open notes possible on these valveless instruments with striking melodic ingenuity. In the *B flat Concerto* the oboes also sound splendidly in tune, which was not always the case with earlier recordings using baroque instruments, and phrasing is alive and sensitive. In the *Concerto for Recorder and Bassoon*, featuring Frans Brüggen and Otto Fleischmann as soloists, the combination of woody bassoon timbre and the piping recorder is most effective. Indeed, all the performances here are extremely fine; the recording, made in a warm acoustic, is excellent, and at budget price this disc still deserves a strong recommendation.

Don Quixote (Suite burlesque in G); Concerto in D for 2 Violins & Bassoon; Overtures in B min.; G.

*** Chan. 0700. Coll. Mus. 90, Standage.

The descriptive *Don Quixote* burlesque is well covered in the catalogue, but this account from Collegium Musicum 90 is among the best; and the other two *Suites*, if not especially individual, are very well played too. The engaging little *Concerto in D* with its string–bassoon solo interplay is also played and recorded most elegantly.

CHAMBER MUSIC

***Der getreue Music-Meister* (complete).**

🔑 ✿ (M) *** DG 476 1852 (4). Mathis, Töpper, Haefliger, Unger, McDaniel, Würzburg Bach Ch., Instrumental soloists, including Linde, Tarr, Melkus, Schäffer, Van der Ven, Ulsamer.

We award a ✿ for sheer enterprise to DG's Archiv division for recording (in 1966–7) a 'complete' version of Telemann's *Der getreue Music-Meister* ('The Constant Music Master'), which has been called the first musical periodical. Other composers were invited to contribute, thus the present box includes a lute piece by Weiss, a *Gigue sans basse* by Pisandel and an ingenious choral canon by Zelenka. There is also a great deal of refreshing instrumental music of Telemann with the widest variety of instrumentation, with various combinations of recorder, flute, oboe, chalumeau, bassoon, trumpet and various stringed instruments, including a *Burlesque suite* for two violins ingeniously depicting scenes from *Gulliver's Travels*. The operatic arias from *Eginhard*, *Belsazar* and *Sacio* are of considerable interest, while the comic fable from *Aesopus* concerns 'The she-goat's wooing of the lion'. Sixty-two pieces are recorded here. Performances are almost invariably of excellent quality, and Edith Mathis and Ernst Haefliger stand out among the vocal soloists. Excellent documentation includes full vocal texts. The recording sounds delightfully fresh and natural, and it is now most welcome back to the catalogue in Universal Classics' 'Penguin ✿ Collection' at mid-price.

Fantasias for Solo Treble Recorder in C; D min.; G min.; A min.; B flat, TWV 40/2, 4, 9, 11 & 12. Sonatas for Treble Recorder & Continuo: Essercizii musici. Sonatas in C, TWV 41:C5; D min., TWV 41:d4; Der getreue Music-Meister: Canonic Sonata in B flat, TWV 41:B3; Sonatas in C, TWV 41:C2; F, TWV 41:F2; F min., TWV 41:f1.

(BB) *** Warner Apex 2564 60368-2. Brüggen, Bylsma, Leonhardt.

The 12 solo *Fantasias* were actually written for transverse flute, but Frans Brüggen plays them very effectively on the treble recorder, transposing them up a minor third in order to do so. The *Sonatas for Treble Recorder and Continuo* are all most winning and well chosen to show the composer at his most inventive, and are played with breathtaking virtuosity and a marvellous sense of style. The sound is excellent.

***Paris Flute Quartets Nos. 1–6* (1730) (for flute, violine, viola da gamba & continuo).**

🔑 *** HM HMC 901787. Freiburg Bar. Cons.

The splendid Freiburg Baroque Consort (including the exceedingly nimble flautist Karl Kaiser), drawn from the excellent orchestra of that name, give first-class period-instrument performances of these delightful works, and the recording is excellent. An outstanding disc in every way.

Sonatas Corellisante Nos. 1–6; Canonic Duos Nos. 1–4.

** Chan. 0549. Standage, Comberti, Coe, Parle, Coll. Mus. 90.

The six (Trio) *Sonatas Corellisante* of 1735 are not transcriptions, as might at first be expected, but original works 'in the Italian style', although it is essentially an overlay rather than intrinsic to Telemann's invention. Frankly, this is too often routine and fails either to sparkle or to have the sunshine sonority of the real thing. Perhaps it might sound better on the fuller sound of modern instruments. These performances are alert but hardly beguiling, and the simpler *Canonic Duos*, which are played with sprightly vivacity, completely upstage them.

KEYBOARD MUSIC

6 Overtures for Harpsichord, TWV 32:5/10.

(M) ** CPO 999 645-2. Hoeren (harpsichord).

Telemann's six *Overtures* were published between 1745 and 1749. Each is in three movements, beginning grandly in the French style (the rhythm dotted) and moving on to a toccata-like fugato. The central movement is usually marked *Largo e scherzando*, and each work ends with a lovely presto. This layout was regarded as a feature of the 'Polish style', often incorporating local rhythmic influences, for Telemann said: 'A Polish song sets the whole world a-jumping.' Harald Hoeren plays boldly on a modern copy of a Flemish harpsichord from around 1750. He is suitably vigorous in allegros, yet is inclined to be rhythmically metric elsewhere.

VOCAL MUSIC

Orpheus (Die wunderbare Beständigkeit der Liebe).
(B) ★★★ HM HMX 2901618/19 (2). Röschmann, Trekel, Ziesak, Kiehr, Güra, Poulenard, Müller-Brachmann, Köhler, RIAS Kammerchor, Akademie für Alte Musik, Berlin, Jacobs.

Subtitled *The Marvellous Constancy of Love*, Telemann's gloss on the Orpheus story is a lively example of his operatic writing, only recently brought out of the cupboard, thanks to various gaps in the surviving score being filled by likely material from other works. In collaboration with two Telemann scholars, René Jacobs has made the necessary inserts with the full surviving libretto as guide, and the result is very convincing. Brisk arias predominate, with the cosmopolitan side of musical life in Hamburg reflected in Telemann's use of French and Italian in various arias as a contrast to the basic German of most arias and the intervening recitative. When, having lost Eurydice a second time, Orpheus laments his fate, his aria, *Fliesst ihr zeugen*, is solemn rather than deeply emotional, the sort of piece that Telemann might have included in one of his religious works. The distinctive point of the story is that Orasia, Queen of Thrace (superbly sung here by Dorothea Röschmann), is the key character, with predatory intent seeking to have Eurydice killed so that she can herself marry her beloved Orpheus. When in Act III he finally rejects her, in anger she orders her Bacchantes to kill him, only to regret it in the final scene. Generally the treatment is relatively lighthearted, with even Orpheus's plea to Pluto in the Underworld scarcely passionate and with Pluto a jolly rather than a sinister character. Very well played and recorded and with an excellent team of soloists, this makes a delightful entertainment. The role of Orpheus is strongly taken by the baritone Roman Trekel, with the tenor Werner Güra as his friend and companion, Eurimides, and with Hanno Müller-Brachmann as Pluto, both first rate. Ruth Ziesak makes a delightfully fresh-toned Eurydice, sadly killed off well before the end of Act I. A welcome rarity, full of lively ideas characteristic of this prolific composer.

TIPPETT, Michael (1905–98)

Concerto for Double String Orchestra.
(B) ★★ EMI 5 75978-2. LPO, Pritchard – BRITTEN: *Violin Concerto, etc.* ★★

An eminently serviceable account of Tippett's rightly popular score comes from Sir John Pritchard and the LPO. Enjoyable, like the Britten couplings, but without being in any way a first choice.

(i) *String Quartet No. 2 in F sharp;* (ii; iii) *Boyhood's End; The Heart's Assurance;* (ii; iv) *Songs for Ariel.*
(M) (★★★) EMI mono/stereo 5 85150-2. (i) Amadeus Qt; (ii) Pears; (iii) Wood; (iv) Britten – SEIBER: *String Quartet No.3.* (★★★)

A fascinating disc in which some historic Decca recordings (the vocal items) seem to have escaped on to EMI. *Boyhood's End* is a setting of a passage from W. H. Hudson's autobiography, *Far Away and Long Ago*. Its evocation of Hudson's boyhood past – seen from the perspective of him as an old man – in which he recalls his fear of losing his close contact with nature is subtly done, with the vocal line in very expressive arioso style, with much florid decoration. There is great atmosphere, too, with Pears making the very most of all the nuances. *The Heart's Assurance* occupies very much the same world, though with even more brilliant and difficult accompaniments, and the tragic spirit of the poems is beautifully caught. These historic recordings (Pears premièred both these works) dating from 1953 suffer from a little distortion, but are perfectly acceptable. The three short *Songs for Ariel*, written for a 1962 production of *The Tempest*, are short but effective, and are recorded here in stereo. Tippett's *Second String Quartet*, with its opening movement rich in polyphony, a very haunting fugal second movement, a bracing Scherzo and the emotional fervour of the finale, has much to recommend it. This very eloquent performance, in amazingly good (1954) sound, makes a welcome return to the catalogue. An important historical disc, with an unusual coupling.

VOCAL MUSIC

(i) *A Child of Our Time;* (ii) *5 Negro Spirituals.* Choral music: *Magnificat and Nunc Dimittis; 4 Songs from the British Isles. Bonny at Morn; Dance, Clarion Air; Lullaby; Music; Plebs angelica; The Source; The Weeping Babe; The Windhover.*
⊙━ (M) ★★★ Decca (ADD) 473 421-2. (i) J. Norman, J. Baker, Cassilly, Shirley-Quirk, BBC Singers, BBC Ch. Soc., C. Davis; (ii) Oxford Schola Cantorum, Cleobury.

Sir Colin Davis's Philips account of *A Child of Our Time*, though more detached in style with a fairly old recording, offers a sharply focused performance with by far the finest quartet of soloists on record. Davis's speeds tend to be on the fast side, both in the spirituals and the other numbers. He may miss some of the tenderness; by avoiding all suspicion of sentimentality, however, the result is incisive and very powerful, helped by excellent solo and choral singing. This is now reissued in Decca's British Music Collection with more choral music added, recorded three years later in Oxford for the Argo label. This demonstrates the awkward quality in the composer's choral writing: the music rarely progresses in anything like a predictable way. However, the Oxford Schola Cantorum has the music's full measure under Cleobury, and they sound fresh and spontaneous. Always Tippett has some illumination of words, whether in Edith Sitwell (*The Weeping Babe*), Yeats (*Lullaby*) or more traditional texts. The spirituals from *A Child of Our Time* are duplicated here, to make an apt conclusion, though out of context they do not sound as effective as in the oratorio.

TJEKNAVORIAN, Loris
(born 1937)

Piano Concerto, Op. 4.
*** ASV CDDCA 984. Babakhanian, Armenian PO, composer – BABADZHANIAN: *Heroic Ballade; Nocturne.* ***

A highly coloured work, very much in the tradition of Khachaturian, but rather more dissonantly pungent, Tjeknavorian's *Fourth Concerto* certainly makes an immediate impact on the listener. There is a central pianistic soliloquy at the centre of the first movement, sinuously Armenian in flavour, which leads to a huge climax, ridden by the pianist's thundering bravura, before the wildly obstreperous orchestra returns to add to the mêlée. Introduced by a yearning horn theme, the *Andante* wears its romantic heart on its sleeve, even though the soloist ruminates; and the rumbustious, syncopated finale also has a sinuous lyrical interlude, before the orchestra returns for the riotous race to the winning post. Babakhanian is surely an ideal soloist, producing explosions of virtuosity whenever needed, yet persuasively sensitive to the work's lyrical side. With the composer conducting and the orchestra on their toes, the result surely is definitive, for the recording is extremely vivid.

TOCH, Ernst (1887–1964)

Tanz-Suite, Op. 30.
** Edition Abseits EDA013-2. Kammersymphonie Berlin, Bruns – SCHREKER: *Der Geburtstag der Infantin.* **

Ernst Toch's *Dance Suite* comes from 1923. It is an expertly crafted piece, inventive and resourceful. The playing of the Kammersymphonie Berlin under Jürgen Bruns is first rate, and the recording is eminently serviceable.

TOMLINSON, Ernest (born 1924)

Aladdin: 3 Dances (Birdcage Dance; Cushion Dance; Belly Dance); Comedy Overture; Cumberland Square; English Folk-Dance Suite No. 1; Light Music Suite; Passepied; (i) Rhapsody & Rondo for Horn & Orchestra. Brigadoon; Shenandoah (arrangement).
*** Marco Polo 8.223513. (i) Watkins; Slovak RSO (Bratislava), composer.

The opening *Comedy Overture* is racily vivacious, and there are many charming vignettes here, delectably tuneful and neatly scored, and the pastiche dance movements are nicely elegant. The *Pizzicato humoresque* (from the *Light Music Suite*) is every bit as winning as other, more famous pizzicato movements, and in the *Rhapsody and Rondo* for horn Tomlinson quotes wittily from both Mozart and Britten. The composer finally lets his hair down in the rather vulgar *Belly Dance*, but the concert ends well with the charming *Georgian Miniature*. The playing is elegant and polished, its scale perfectly judged, and the recording is first class.

An English Overture; 3 Gaelic Sketches: Gaelic Lullaby. Kielder Water; Little Serenade; Lyrical Suite: Nocturne. Nautical Interlude; 3 Pastoral Dances: Hornpipe. Silverthorne Suite; 2nd Suite of English Folk Dances; Sweet and Dainty; arr. of Coates: The Fairy Coach; Cinderella Waltz.
*** Marco Polo 8.223413. Slovak RSO (Bratislava), composer.

Ernest Tomlinson's orchestral pieces charm by the frothy lightness of the scoring. The winningly delicate *Little Serenade*, which opens the disc, is the most famous, but the gentle, evocative *Kielder Water*, the captivating *Canzonet* from the *Silverthorne Suite* and the *Nocturne* are hardly less appealing. *Love-in-a-mist* is as intangible as it sounds, with the most fragile of oboe solos, and it is not surprising that *Sweet and Dainty* has been used for a TV commercial. There is robust writing, too, in the *Folk Dance Suite* – but not too robust, although the jolly *English Overture* begins with *Here's a Health unto His Majesty* and certainly does not lack vitality. The music is played with much grace and the lightest possible touch by the remarkably versatile Slovak Radio Orchestra under the composer, and the vivid recording has delightfully transparent textures, so vital in this repertoire.

TORCH, Sydney (1908–90)

All Strings and Fancy Free; Barbecue; Bicycle Belles; Comic Cuts; Concerto Incognito; Cresta Run; Duel for Drummers; Going for a Ride; London Transport Suite; Mexican Fiesta; On a Spring Note; Petite Valse; Samba Sud; Shooting Star; Shortcake Walk; Slavonic Rhapsody; Trapeze Waltz.
*** Marco Polo 8.223443. BBC Concert O, Wordsworth.

Sydney Torch worked frequently with the BBC Concert Orchestra (the orchestra on this CD), and for many he is remembered for his weekly broadcasts 'Friday Night is Music Night'. The *London Transport*

Suite was commissioned by the BBC for their Light Music festival of 1957 and was inspired by the withdrawal of the 'Brighton Belle' on the London-to-Brighton railway service. Each of its three movements represents a mode of transport: *The Hansom Cab, Rosie, the Red Omnibus* and *The 5:52 from Waterloo*. All the music here is tuneful, at times wistful and nostalgic, at others bright and breezy – *All Strings and Fancy Free* is both. *Barbecue* sounds like a Scottish snap, while the *Trapeze Waltz* is reminiscent of the circus music of Satie. The *Concerto Incognito* is very much in the *Warsaw Concerto* mould, and the *Petite Valse* (also with piano) is more robust than its title suggests. The *Mexican Fiesta* and *Samba Sud* produce some fine local colour and are very jolly, while the *Slavonic Rhapsody* (with two pianos) is a fun work, drawing on the music of Rimsky-Korsakov, Tchaikovsky, Knipper, Borodin and Khachaturian, to form an entertaining if outrageous pastiche. The longest work is the *Duel for Drummers*, which, as its title suggests, is a *tour de force* for the percussion department; it has some ideas which are reminiscent of Eric Coates and a few surprises, including a cockerel crowing, and a desert-island storm in the central movement. It ends with a lively *galop*. Barry Wordsworth conducts with flair, and the recording is excellent.

TUBIN, Eduard (1905–82)

Symphonies Nos. 9 (Sinfonia semplice); 10; 11.
*** Alba ABCD 172. Estonian Nat. SO, Volmer.

It is good that there should be an alternative to Neeme Järvi's fine cycle of the symphonies on BIS. This did not include the one-movement *Eleventh Symphony*, left incomplete on Tubin's death, though Paavo Järvi subsequently recorded it for Virgin. Both the *Ninth* and *Tenth* belong among Tubin's very finest works, and the former is particularly haunting. The first 541 bars of No. 11 were completed and fully scored, and the Estonian-born Canadian composer Kaljo Raid scored the remaining 70-odd measures. Arvo Volmer conducted its première in Tallinn in 1988 and recorded it in the early 1990s (on Koch). The present recordings were made in 2002 and are strong performances, not superior to Järvi in Nos. 9 and 10, but worthy of recommendation alongside them.

TURNAGE, Mark-Anthony
(born 1960)

Scorched (with John SCOFIELD).
*** DG 474 729-2. Scofield, Patitucci, Erskine, Frankfurt RSO, HR Big Band, Wolff.

In sound that comes up and hits you, *Scorched* is a prime example of 'musical fusion', with Mark-Anthony Turnage developing jazz pieces by the American guitarist and composer, John Scofield, using not only a jazz trio (led by Scofield on a prominent electric guitar) but a big band and symphony orchestra. The title itself, *Scorched*, was designed to reflect that: SCofield ORCHestratED. The result, recorded live at the Alte Oper in Frankfurt and later developed by Turnage and Scofield, is certainly ear-catching, with most of the 14 pieces – some separate and some linked – vigorously upfront, with Scofield's playing magnetic, but including strongly contrasted pieces for strings. The wildest piece of all, which rounds off the concert, is improbably called *Protocol*. Recommended for anyone who, like Turnage from a classical base, is fascinated by jazz.

TURNBULL, Percy (1902–76)

Piano music: Character Sketches Nos. 2–4 & 7; 3 Dances; Fantasy Suite; 3 Miniatures; Pasticcio on a Theme by Mozart; 2 Preludes; Sonatina; 3 Winter Pieces.
*** Somm SOMMCD 1015. Jacobs.

Percy Turnbull, born in Newcastle upon Tyne, is yet another of the lost generation of English composers whose virtually forgotten music is now being rescued by the gramophone. His student contemporaries at the Royal College of Music included Tippett, Maconchy and Rubbra, yet at the time (the early 1920s) his talent shone out from among them. He was a fine pianist and is a natural-born composer of piano music, his style a beguiling diffusion of many influences, from Delius and John Ireland in England, to Fauré and Ravel among his French contemporaries. Yet his musical personality has its own individuality and his writing gives great refreshment and pleasure, his style notable for its gentle colouring, clarity and lightness of texture, without any hint of triviality.

The delightful *Pasticcio on a Theme of Mozart* displays his classical background, for each of the 12 variations absorbs the manner of another composer, from Bach to Brahms, Fauré and Ravel to Delius and Bartók. The *Sonatina* is entirely his own, moving from gentle English lyricism to a witty, syncopated finale. The other miniatures continually delight the ear and the *Three Winter Pieces* (1956), which were his last completed works for piano, are typical of his easy and innocent inventiveness at its most sophisticated and communicative. Throughout, Peter Jacobs is an admirable and persuasive advocate, and he is beautifully recorded. Well worth exploring.

VAINBERG, Moishei (1919–96)

Violin Concerto.
(BB) *** Naxos 8.557194. Grubert, Russian PO, Yablonsky – MIASKOVSKY: *Violin Concerto.* ***

The Lithuanian violinist Ilya Grubert on Naxos

couples Miaskovsky's glorious concerto with the relatively little known concerto of Mieczyslaw (or Moishei) Vainberg, composed in 1958 for Leonid Kogan. His pioneering Melodiya account (still available on Olympia OCD 622) has a special authority, but Grubert is hardly less persuasive and the competitive price may well encourage collectors, who have hesitated to acquire the Kogan, to investigate this. The concerto owes a lot to Shostakovich, but an individual voice can be discerned as one comes closer to it.

Sinfonietta No. 1, Op. 41; Symphony No. 5, Op. 76.
★★★ Chan. 10128. Polish Nat. RSO, Chmura.

Most of Vainberg's symphonies have been recorded at one time or another. Probably the best entry point into the cycle is the succinct *Fourth*, which Kondrashin recorded in the 1960s (see our main volume); it has wit, style and a splendid sense of forward movement. There are touches of Hindemith, Prokofiev and even Mahler. All the symphonies we have heard also betray a debt to Shostakovich, without being entirely overwhelmed by him. The *Fifth* is a long piece dating from 1962, and it holds the listener even when it doesn't wholly satisfy him or her. The slow movement is a little too long, given the quality of its ideas, but generally speaking the work has considerable power and eloquence. It has thoroughly committed players in Gabriel Chmura and his fine Polish orchestra – and superb Chandos recording. The *Sinfonietta No. 1* (1948) makes use of Jewish melodies, which Vainberg fashions in a style influenced by Bartók. Well worth investigating. Incidentally, Vainberg is variously transliterated as Vaynberg or Weinberg, though Chandos opts for the latter (as in the most recent Grove).

Piano Sonatas Nos. 1, Op. 5; 2, Op. 8; 3, Op. 31; 17 Easy Pieces, Op. 34.
★★ Olympia OCD 595. McLachlan.

Piano Sonatas Nos. 4, Op. 56; 5, Op. 58; 6, Op. 73.
★★ Olympia OCD 596. McLachlan.

Vainberg's output was extensive (22 symphonies and some 17 string quartets), but he wrote very little for the piano. He was a good pianist himself and a duet partner of Shostakovich on occasion. The first two sonatas come from the early 1940s and are close in idiom to Prokofiev and Shostakovich. The *Third Sonata* and the *17 Easy Pieces* are both post-war (1946). The impressive *Fourth Sonata* (1955) enjoyed the advocacy of Gilels, who recorded it two years after its composition (he had also given the earlier sonatas in recital programmes). Its two successors are strong, well-wrought pieces, and the *Fifth* has an imposing, well-argued *Passacaglia*, but after the *Sixth* (1960) Vainberg seems to have abandoned the medium. The enterprising Murray McLachlan's commitment to, and belief in, the present repertoire is never in doubt. He is recorded in Gothenburg – not in the Concert Hall, unfortunately, but the university's hall – and although the sound is satisfactory it is not as open or fresh. All the same, those whose appetite has been aroused by the *Fourth Symphony* or the late *Chamber Symphonies* will want to explore these for themselves. The notes by Per Skans are very informative.

VALEN, Fartein (1887–1952)

(i) *Violin Concerto;* (ii) *Symphony No. 1;* (iii) *Le Cimetière marin, Op. 20;* (iv) *Nachtstücke; Ode to Solitude, Op. 35; Pastorale, Op. 11; Song without Words.*
★★★ Runegrammofon RCD 2013. (i) Tellefsen, Trondheim SO, Ruud; (ii) Bergen PO, Ceccato; (iii) Oslo PO, Caridis; (iv) Torgersen.

The Norwegian composer Fartein Valen enjoyed cult status for a few years after the Second World War, but interest has waned since his death in the early 1950s. He grew up in Madagascar, where his father was a missionary, and he studied philology and languages before turning to music. As early as the 1920s he developed a kind of 12-note technique, but for much of his life he was something of an outsider in Norwegian music. At times there is a strong sense of nature and refinement of texture, as if he were a mildly atonal Delius; at others there is a feeling of claustrophobia, as if the fjords are shutting out light. After a time the ear tires of the concentration of activity above the stave.

The *Violin Concerto* is Valen's masterpiece; it is short and intense and, like the Berg concerto, an outpouring of grief on the death of a young person. It ends like the Berg by quoting a Bach chorale. Incidentally, Valen was adamant that he had never heard the Berg. (Music did not travel easily in 1940, and Valen lived in a particularly isolated part of Norway.) His own concerto is played marvellously here by Arve Tellefsen.

The longest work here is the *First Symphony*, which began life as a piano sonata but reached its definitive orchestral form two years later in 1939. The textures are fairly dense, though the opening of the second movement is an exception: the pale, luminous colouring is distinctly northern. *Le Cimetière marin* is one of the better known of Valen's works and is highly evocative. All are given well-prepared and dedicated performances and eminently serviceable recordings, made between 1972 and 1997. The presentation is impossibly pretentious. The CD label contains no information of any kind and appears to come from the Tate Modern: the front cover reads 'fartein valen – the eternal' (all lower case) and the backing slip gives, in absolutely microscopic print, the titles of the works – again lower case, black on a darkish red. You need to consult the booklet for track information, which is all in funereal black. That apart, this anthology serves as a useful introduction to this intriguing composer.

VALI, Reza (born 1952)

(i) *Flute Concerto;* (ii) *Deylámân;* (iii) *Folksongs.*
(BB) **(*) Naxos 8.557224. Boston Modern O, Rose;
with (i) Almarza; (ii) Bárbát; (iii) Baty.

Persian composer Reza Vali's *Flute Concerto*, written
in 1998, uses the technique involving the playing of
the flute and singing simultaneously, bringing out
the overtones and altering the timbre of the instrument in order to imitate the sound of the Persian
bamboo flute (the ney). There is quite a lot of
Persian 'mood' music here, but also some more jolly
sections too: not a profound work, but quite an
entertaining modern concerto, even if the 17 minutes
of the final movement are too long. In the *Folksongs*,
which are based on Persian folk music, the vocal line
is bolstered by Vali's brightly colourful accompaniments (the third movement is a lament, full of bells
and gongs, and lots of references to birds, appropriate for a piece composed in memory of Olivier
Messiaen). *Deylámân* (1995), named after a region in
northwest Persia, employs two Persian instruments,
the ney (or, rather, the flute imitating it here, as in
the *Flute Concerto*, above) and the bárbát (or oud, a
short-necked lute) and uses a mode which originates
(and is named after) that region. It is a curious (if
not terribly gripping) work, with more exotic 'mood'
music, beginning and ending all very mysteriously
with what the composer describes as a special type of
'Persian polyphony', in between which there are
quotes from various classical composers: Beethoven,
Bruckner, Mahler and Wagner, though why is not
explained. The performances and recording are first
class.

VAŇHAL, Jan (1739–1813)

*Symphonies: in A min. (Bryan a2); in C (Sinfonia
Comista); in D min. (Brian d1); in E min. (Bryan
e1); in G min. (Bryan g1).*
(M) **(*) Warner Elatus 2564 60340-2. Concerto Köln.

Vaňhal (or Wanhal, as he himself signed his name)
was born in Bohemia but spent the greater part of
his life in Vienna, where these works were composed
during the 1760s and 1770s. This was the period of
the so-called *Sturm und Drang* symphonies, works in
a minor key with a keen, driving intensity, of which
Haydn's *La Passione* is a good example. Vaňhal's
symphonies were widely heard at this time, and the
great French Mozart scholar Georges de Saint-Foix
cited his *D minor Symphony* (albeit not the one on
this disc) as an influence on Mozart's little *G minor
Symphony*, K.183. These are works of vivid and lively
invention, which also embrace a wide diversity of
approach. The *C major Sinfonia Comista*, one of the
later symphonies, differs from its companions in its
richness of scoring and its programmatic inspirations. The Concerto Köln play with tremendous

spirit, enthusiam and style, but the recording is too
forwardly balanced so that tuttis are at times a little
rough. Not that this greatly inhibits a three-star
recommendation for what is a very interesting
recording of repertoire which is not otherwise available at present.

VARÈSE, Edgar

Tuning Up; Amériques (original version); *Arcana;
Dance for Burgesses;* (i) *Density 21.5. Déserts;* (ii)
Ecuatorial; (iii; iv) *Un grand sommeil noir* (original
version). (iii) *Un grand sommeil noir* (orch.
Beaumont); *Hyperprism; Intégrales; Ionisation;* (v;
vi) *Nocturnal, Octandre;* (v) *Offrandes; Poème
électronique.*
⊶ ✪ (M) *** Decca 475 487-2 (2) Concg. O or
ASKO Ens., Chailly; with (i) Zoon, (ii) Deas; (iii; iv)
Delunsch, (iv) Kardoncuff; (v) Leonard; (vi) Prague
Philharmonic Male Ch.

This comprehensive coverage of the music of Varèse
was given the 1999 *Gramophone* Award for
Twentieth-Century Music. It is reviewed in depth in
our main volume and remains an indispensable cornerstone of any comprehensive collection. All the
performances here are superbly definitive, and this
excellently recorded set will be hard to surpass.

VAUGHAN WILLIAMS, Ralph (1872–1958)

*Fantasia on a Theme by Thomas Tallis; In the Fen
Country;* (i) *The Lark Ascending. Norfolk Rhapsody
No. 1;* (ii) *On Wenlock Edge* (cycle).
(M) **(*) EMI 5 85151-2. (i) Chang; (ii) Bostridge;
LPO, Haitink.

An appealing anthology assembled from fill-ups
originally offered with Haitink's set of the symphonies. The comparatively rare *Norfolk Rhapsody* is
particularly welcome when it is so beautifully played.
In the *Tallis Fantasia*, Haitink's straight rhythmic
manners make the result sensitively unidiomatic, but
very powerful in its monumental directness, helped
by a recording of spectacular range. Sarah Chang
proves an intensely poetic soloist in *The Lark Ascending*, volatile at the start in the bird-like, fluttering
motif and magnetically concentrated to match. With
Ian Bostridge the sensitive, honey-toned soloist, the
six songs of the Housman cycle make a welcome
closing section. First-class recording throughout.

The Lark Ascending.
(M) *** EMI 5 62813-2. Kennedy, CBSO, Rattle –
WALTON: *Viola Concerto; Violin Concerto.* ***

Originally paired with Kennedy's second recording of
the Elgar *Concerto*, this spacious and inspirational
account of Vaughan Williams's evocative piece makes
a fine bonus for the two Walton concertos chosen to

represent Nigel among EMI's 'Great Artists of the Century'. It is beautifully recorded.

Serenade to Music (orchestral version): The Wasps Overture.

(M) ** Chan. 10174X. LPO, Handley – DELIUS: *Air and Dance; On Hearing the First Cuckoo in Spring*, etc. **

Exceptionally well recorded, Handley's readings of *The Wasps Overture* and the *Serenade to Music* is its orchestral version are most sympathetically done and, although the *Serenade* lacks a dimension without voices, it is most persuasive and is beautifully played by the LPO. However, at 46 minutes overall, this mid-priced reissue is distinctly ungenerous.

SYMPHONIES

(i) Symphonies Nos. 1–9; (ii) Concerto Academico in D min.; (iii) Tuba Concerto in F min.; 3 Portraits from Elizabeth in England; The Wasps: Overture.

⊖ ⚙ (B) *** RCA 82876 55708-2 (6). LSO, Previn; with (i) Harper, Shirley-Quirk, Amb. S., L. Symphony Ch., R. Richardson (speaker); (ii) J. O. Buswell; (iii) J. Fletcher.

Previn recorded the Vaughan Williams *Symphonies* over a five-year span from 1968 to 1972, and his achievement in this repertoire represented a peak in his recording career at that time. Here the nine symphonies plus their original fill-ups have been neatly compressed on to six CDs. The most striking performances are those which were recorded last, Nos. 2, 3 and 5; for these Previn achieves an extra depth of understanding, an extra intensity, whether in the purity of *pianissimo* or the outpouring of emotional resolution. For the rest there is only one performance that can be counted at all disappointing, and that is of the symphony one might have expected Previn to interpret best, the taut and dramatic *Fourth*. Even that is an impressive account, if less intense than the rest. Otherwise, the great landscape of the whole cycle is presented with richness and detail in totally refreshing interpretations, brilliantly recorded and impressively transferred to CD. The extra items are worth having too, notably the two concertos with responsive soloists.

Symphony No. 4 in F min..

(M) (***) Cala mono CACD 0528. NBC SO, Stokowski – ANTHEIL: *Symphony No 4* (***); BUTTERWORTH: *Shropshire Lad*. (**)

The only time that Stokowski ever conducted Vaughan Williams's provocative *Fourth Symphony* was in March 1943, when this high-powered, red-blooded reading was recorded, the first to be made outside Britain. The violently dissonant opening is broad and emphatic, leading to a warm, passionate account of the lyrical second subject, and throughout the performance one marvels that Stokowski could draw sounds from the NBC Orchestra so different from those the same players produced under Toscanini. The chill and poignancy of the slow movement and the bluff humour of the *Scherzo*, each strongly characterized, lead to a comparably positive account of the finale, making one regret that Stokowski never returned to this work. The sound, limited in range, is yet satisfyingly full-bodied.

Symphonies Nos. (i) 4 in F min.; (ii) 6 in E min.; (i) Fantasia on a Theme of Thomas Tallis.

⊖ (B) (***) Retrospective Sony mono/stereo RET 011. NYPO, (i) Mitropoulos; (ii) Stokowski.

This outstanding coupling of Vaughan Williams's two most abrasive symphonies demonstrates what idiomatic power and brilliance American musicians could bring to this music, and the *Tallis Fantasia* brings no less understanding. The remastered recordings sound excellent. A first-class bargain.

Symphonies Nos. 6 in E min.; 8 in D min.; (i) Nocturne

*** Chan. **SACD** CHSA 5016; CD CHan. 10103. LSO, Hickox; (i) with Roderick Williams.

As in the rest of this Vaugham Williams Cycle, Richard Hickox draws warmly idiomatic playing from the LSO in this coupling of Nos. 6 and 8. He is particularly fine in the deidcated slow finale of No. 6 with its visionary overtones; yet in the first three movements of that darkly intense work the abrasiveness of the writing is a little muted, thanks to the mellow recording acoustic of All Saints' Tooting. It does not help either that the transfer level is on the low side, so that the heavy brass passages, for all their weight, lack something in bite. In No. 8 the acoustic is less of a problem, even if the Scherzo for wind alone could be even more jaunty. The slow movement for strings brings tender refinement and the rumbustious finale a swaggering conclusion. The *Nocturne* for baritone and orchestra makes a most valuable supplement. Written in 1908 but not discovered till 2000, it is a warmly evocative setting of the composer's favourite Walt Whitman. He was about to study with Ravel in Paris, but demonstrates here what mastery he already had over orchestral colour, giving forecasts of *A London Symphony*.

Symphony No. 6 in E min

(**(*)) Cala mono CACD 0537. NYPO, Stockowski (with TCHAIKOVSKY: *Romeo and Juliet* (abridged version). MOZART: *Symphony No 35 (Haffner)*. Thomas Jefferson SCOTT: *From the Sacred Harp*. WEINBERGER: *Schwanda the Bagpiper: Polka & Fugue* (**).

This is the same recorded performance of the Sixth Symphony as is available on Retrospective Sony, but the 1949 Carnegie Hall recording is vastly improved in the present transfer, with fuller textures and a more realistic conveyance of the Carnegie Hall ambience. The performance has a riveting foward impetus and, characteristically, Stokowski relishes the big tune on the strings in the first movement; but the slow movement is controversially fast. Also, whether the couplings offered here can match the appeal of Mitropoulos's *Fourth Symphony* and *Tallis Fantasia* on Sony is doubtful. The *Haffner* is Stokowski's only recording of any Mozart symphony: it is certainly lively and has a beautifully pointed *Andante* and a sparkling finale. But it suffers badly from audience noises. *Romeo and Juliet* is well played but hardly riveting, and the recording lacks range. Moreover, Stokowski substitutes a quiet ending for the composer's dramatic final chords, doubtfully claiming that such an alteration had Tchaikovsky's sanction. Thomas Jefferson Scott's folksy *From the Sacred Harp* is hardly one of the conductor's major discoveries, but the Weinberger *Polka and Fugue* is certainly successful, and the only time Stokowski conducted any music by this composer. Good transfers, but not really a satisfying collection, except perhaps for the Stokowski aficionado.

OPERA

Hugh the Drover (complete).

(M) *** Hyp. Dyad CDD 22049 (2). Bottone, Evans, Walker, Van Allan, Opie, New L. Children's Ch., Corydon Singers & O, Best.

Hyperion's excellent version of *Hugh the Drover* (see our main volume) now appears at mid-price, where it currently has no competition and can be cordially recommended.

The Poisoned Kiss (complete).

*** Chan. **SACD** 5020 (2); CD 10120 (2). Jo Watson, Gilchrist, Helen Stephen, Williams, N. Davies, Collins, Adrian Partington Singers, BBC Nat. O of Wales, Hickox.

When in 1927 Vaughan Williams began writing *The Poisoned Kiss*, his forgotten opera, he was already at work on his Falstaff work, *Sir John in Love*, and was beginning to make sketches for *Job*. Consistently this far-fetched setting of a fairy-tale reflects the exuberance of his inspiration, yet that subject and its treatment explains why *The Poisoned Kiss* has been so consistently neglected, not just in performance but on disc too, for this is its very first complete recording. Evelyn Sharp, sister of Cecil Sharp, leader of the folksong movement, wrote a libretto based on short stories by Richard Garnett and Nathaniel Hawthorne; it centres round a beautiful princess who lives on poison. The trouble is that the treatment of that idea both in the plot and, even more seriously, in deplorably bad versification, undermines the lightness originally intended. Sharp and the composer had in mind among other sources the operettas of Gilbert and Sullivan, yet the choice of anachronisms is never pointed in a Gilbertian way. Despite two bouts of revision, in 1936 and 1955, there are still too many unfunny lines.

This recording helps towards rehabilitating the opera by eliminating virtually all the spoken dialogue, including it merely in the libretto, printed in shaded sections. Prefacing the libretto comes a very helpful detailed synopsis, describing each of the 39 numbers and the story in between. One trouble is that neither Vaughan Williams nor Sharp could quite work out the right balance between comedy and the central romance, the love between Tormentilla, brought up on poison by her magician father, Dipsacus, and Prince Amaryllus, son of the Empress Persicaria. Despite the irritations of the libretto, repeated hearings bring out how rich this score is in vintage Vaughan Williams inspiration, with mere doggerel prompting one delectable musical idea after another, and with each number beautifully tailored, never outstaying its welcome. Plainly, Vaughan Williams took the story of forbidden love much more seriously than he perhaps realized even himself. The inspiration never flags, charm predominating, with tenderly beautiful melodies like that in the Act I duet of Amaryllus and Tormentilla, *Blue Larkspur in a Garden*, and a surgingly emotional climax in the ensemble which crowns Act II, when their love leads passionately to the poisoned kiss and the threat of death to Amaryllus.

Whatever the obvious shortcomings of the piece, no lover of Vaughan Williams's music should miss hearing this wonderful set, with a strong and characterful cast superbly led by Richard Hickox, and with warmly atmospheric sound enhancing the musical delights. Janice Watson as Tormentilla sings with sweetness and warmth, while giving point to the literally poisonous side of the character, and James Gilchrist makes an ardent Amaryllus, with Pamela Helen Stephen as Angelica and Roderick Williams totally affecting in their love music, given many of the most charming moments of all. Neal Davies is firm and strong as the magician, Dipsacus, and, though the Empress does not arrive until Act III, she then dominates things, following the G&S tradition of formidable contraltos: in that role the veteran Anne Collins is aptly larger than life. The incidental trios of Hobgoblins and Mediums are also cast from strength with leading singers, the chorus is fresh and bright, and the BBC National Orchestra of Wales plays throughout with winning warmth. Outstandingly atmospheric recording, specially on SACD.

VELASQUEZ, Glauco (1884–1914)

Album-leaves Nos. 1–2; Brutto Sogno; Canzone Strana; Danse de silphes; Devaneio; Divertimento No. 2; Impromptu; Melancolia; Minuetto e Gavotte Moderni; Petite Suite; Prelúdios Nos. 1–2; Prelúdio e Scherzo; Rêverie; Valsa lenta; Valsa romântica.
*** Marco Polo 8.223556. Sverner.

Glauco Velasquez was an illegitimate child, born in Naples to a Brazilian mother and fathered by a Portuguese singer. When their relationship collapsed, his mother took the boy to Brazil, where he was brought up in ignorance of his father's identity. He soon showed musical aptitude, and by his mid-twenties he had attracted some attention in musical circles with his piano miniatures, recorded here. Their heady melancholy, often in Scriabinesque chromatic writing, is most beguiling. Clara Sverner brings out the personality and charm, and they are very well recorded.

VERDI, Giuseppe (1813–1901)

The Lady and the Fool (ballet; arr. Mackerras); Overtures: Alzira; La forza del destino; Nabucco.
(***) Testament mono/stereo SBT 1326. Philh. O, Mackerras.

In the mid-1950s, when all these recordings were made, Charles Mackerras was regularly brought in to conduct sessions with the Philharmonia if one of Walter Legge's stars of the period, Klemperer, Giulini or others, cancelled a scheduled engagement. Regularly, the results were not just excellent musically but brilliant as recordings too, a point brought out in these fine Testament transfers. Three of Verdi's finest overtures come in a coupling with the ballet score, The Lady and the Fool, which Mackerras drew from the lesser-known operas of Verdi. To choreography by John Cranko, it tells the story of the beautiful La Capricciosa choosing the clown, Moondog, as her lover in preference to three rich and eligible suitors. Mackerras's aim was to follow up the brilliant success of his earlier ballet score, Pineapple Poll, which in a very similar way uses material drawn from Sullivan's operettas and other works. This is the only complete recording ever made, demonstrating what a superb sequel it is. Not only has Mackerras drawn on dozens of delectable Verdian ideas, he has woven them into a scintillating tapestry. Ingeniously, Mackerras often superimposes one theme contrapuntally on another, just as Sullivan did in some of his most brilliant ensembles. Some of the movements draw on as many as six or seven different operas over a brief span. The orchestration too is far more adventurous than the originals, while remaining broadly faithful to Verdi's distinctive timbre. Though the recording is in mono only, the sense of presence is most impressive, at least as vivid as in the stereo recordings of the three overtures which come as bonus to the 50-minute ballet, all of them combining brilliance and expressive warmth.

Ballet music from: (i) Il trovatore; I vespri siciliani; (ii) Otello; (i) Overture: Luisa Miller.
(***) Testament (ADD) SBT 1327. Mackerras with (i) Philh. O; (ii) Rohcg O – PONCHIELLI: La Gioconda: Dance of the Hours ***; WOLF-FERRARI: Overtures, Intermezzi and Dances (***)

This mixed bag of Mackerras's recordings from the mid-1950s has as its centrepiece his brilliant record-

ings of the Luisa Miller Overture and three examples of the ballet music which Verdi provided for Paris productions of his operas. It is striking, even in the Otello ballet music with its corny orientalism, how Verdi regularly harks back to a much earlier, less sophisticated style than he uses in the main body of the opera in question, perhaps a reflection on Parisian taste. The results may have their banalities – even the more ambitious Four Seasons, written for the original production of Les Vêpres siciliennes – but Mackerras's springing of rhythm and the sparkle of the Philharmonia playing fully bring out their unassuming delights. He is helped by the finely balanced stereo sound in all but the Otello music, which curiously seems only ever to have been issued on a 45rpm EP.

String Quartet in E min. (arr. for string orchestra).
*** Channel Classics SACD: CCS SA 21504.
Amsterdam Sinf., Thompson – TCHAIKOVSKY: Souvenir de Florence. ***

The Amsterdam Sinfonietta, recording for the first time under its new name and with its new leader/conductor Candida Thompson, plays with phenomenal unanimity, demonstrating what gains there are in having a full string orchestra performing the Verdi String Quartet. As in the Tchaikovsky Souvenir de Florence, with which it is aptly coupled, speeds are ideally chosen, with the second movement clearly an Andantino, light and elegant, and the chattering quavers of the fugal finale shaped more clearly. The thrust and warmth of the performance is enhanced by the wide dynamic range of the playing, well caught in the opulent recording (with the option of 'surround sound').

String Quartet in E min.
**(*) HM HMA 1951671 Melos Qt – SIBELIUS: String Quartet in D min. **(*)

This distinguished ensemble give a suitably well-turned-out performance of the Verdi, though they tend to underplay its pure lyricism. We are not so well served in this repertoire at present that new Verdi Quartets can be lightly passed over. The recording is truthful but with the Voces intimae as its sole companion, the 50 minutes or so of this issue makes for relatively short measure.

CHORAL MUSIC

Requiem Mass.
** DG (IMS) 439 033-2 (2). Tomowa-Sintow, Baltsa, Carreras, Van Dam, V. State Op. Konzertvereinigung, VPO, Karajan.
(M) ** Sony (ADD) SM2K 89579 (2). Arroyo, Veasey, Domingo, Raimondi, LSO Ch. & O, Bernstein.

Requiem Mass. La forza del destino: Overture.
(M) (**(*)) BBC Legends mono BBCL 4144-2 (2). (i) Ligabue, Bumbry, Kónya, Arié, Philh. Ch.; Philh. O,

Giulini (also Interview: Giulini in Conversation wih Michael Oliver).

Carlo-Maria Giulini's performances of the Verdi *Requiem* in the early 1960s have long been counted legendary. In 2000, BBC Legends issued his Prom performance of August 1963 on CD, even more intense than his classic studio recording for EMI (5 68615.2 – see our main *Guide*). Six months later he performed the *Requiem* once more, again with Philharmonia forces, but this time at the Royal Festival Hall and with a starrier international quartet of soloists. This second live recording comes as a valuable supplement, though it hardly replaces the earlier BBC version. Sadly, it comes in mono only, with the dry Festival Hall acoustic unhelpful, not nearly as warm or atmospheric as the stereo recording from the Prom. The biting drama of Giulini's performance comes over thrillingly, but with some harshness in such passages as the *Dies irae*, and, though the singing of the international quartet is more strongly characterized than that of the fine British one at the Prom, they are no more imaginative. The *Overture* makes a good supplement, and Michael Oliver's interview with Giulini on the subject of recording is more valuable still (how easy to create a 'beautiful corpse' in the studio, he says), but the extras on the rival BBC version are much more generous (BBCL 4029-2).

Though Karajan's smooth style altered relatively little after his earlier version, the overall impression in his later DG set is fresher, though as transferred the recording is inconsistent. Even with 'original image bit reprocessing' improving the focus and impact, the sound is not impressive. Though Tomowa-Sintow's un-Italian soprano sometimes brings a hint of flutter, she sings most beautifully in the final rapt account of *Libera me*.

Bernstein's 1970 *Requiem* was recorded in the Royal Albert Hall. By rights, the daring of the decision should have paid off, but with close balancing of microphones the result is not as full and free as one would expect. Bernstein's interpretation remains persuasive in its drama, exaggerated at times, maybe, but red-blooded in a way that is hard to resist. The quartet of soloists is particularly strong. At mid-price, with no coupling, many may feel this is a bit expensive these days.

OPERA

Aroldo (complete).

(M) *(*) Sony SMK 90469 (2). Caballé, Cecchele, Lebherz, Pons, NY Oraorio Soc., Westminster Choral Soc., NY Op. O, Queler.

Aroldo is Verdi's radical revision of his earlier, unsuccessful opera, *Stiffelio*. He translated the story of a Protestant pastor with an unfaithful wife into this tale of a crusader returning from the Holy Land. Less compact than the original, it contains some splendid new material, such as the superb aria for the heroine, beautifully sung by Caballé; the final scene too is quite new, for the dénouement is totally different. The storm chorus (with echoes of *Rigoletto*) is most memorable – but so are the rum-ti-tum choruses common to both versions. The recording of a concert performance in New York is lively, though the tenor is depressingly coarse. Moreover, no libretto is provided, and the documentation does not even provide a cued synopsis. The Philips set with Neil Schicoff and Carol Vaness is far preferable (462 512-2 – see our main *Guide*).

Don Carlo (complete).

(BB) **(*) Naxos 8.660096/8. Cleveman, Ryhänen, Mattei, Rundgren, Martinpelto, Tobiasson, Sörensen, Hedlund, Wallén, Leidland, Royal Swedish Op. Ch. & O, Hold-Garrido.

Edited together from three live performances, the Naxos set offers a lively, incisive account of the five-act version of *Don Carlo*, with the Swedish Opera's Spanish music-director, Alberto Hold-Garrido, drawing out the formidable talents of his company in a warmly idiomatic reading. It is the more impressive that this is a repertory performance without imported stars. Hillevi Martinpelto, commanding as Elisabetta, and Peter Mattei, the powerful Rodrigo, have both had great success outside Sweden, not least on disc, but the others in the cast equally demonstrate the company's tradition, ever since the days of Jussi Björling and Birgit Nilsson, in encouraging singers with firm, clear voices at a time when too many ill-focused wobblers are being accepted elsewhere.

In the title-role, Lars Cleveman may not be a match for such a star as Plácido Domingo in imagination, but this is a fresh, gripping performance which in Carlo's duets with Rodrigo can live up to almost any comparison. As Philip II, Jaakko Ryhänen sings magnificently, movingly so in his monologue, carrying on the Finnish tradition of Martti Talvela, while Ingrid Tobiasson makes a feisty Eboli. The only snag is that the singers so impress the Stockholm audience that the performance is frequently interrupted by applause. It is a tribute to the singers that even with close-up sound, set in a relatively dry acoustic and with the orchestra forwardly placed, there is no roughness in the singing, just evidence of well-honed technique. As usual with this opera – of which Verdi devised four alternative versions, four-act and five-act – the text is an amalgam, mainly drawn from the 1886 Modena version with a shortened Fontainebleau scene preceding the final revision of the other four acts, and with elements of the original Paris version brought in. An outstanding bargain issue that even includes the full Italian libretto. However, the Warner DVD with Alagna, Hampson and Van Dam, conducted by Pappano, should not be forgotten (0630 16318-2 – see our main *Guide*).

(i) Don Carlo, Act III, Scene 2; (ii) Simon Boccanegra, Act I, Scene 2.

(M) *** EMI 5 62777-2. Gobbi, (i) Filippesci; (ii) De los Angeles; (i) Rome Op. O, Santini – PUCCINI: Gianni Schicchi. ***

Rodrigo in Don Carlo and his golden-voiced Simon Boccanegra were two of Tito Gobbi's most famous roles, and they are well celebrated in this dramatic pair of excerpts, with honeyed support from De los Angeles as Amelia and Mario Filippesci as Don Carlo. Texts and translations are included.

Falstaff (complete).

(M) **(*) Sony (ADD) SM2K 91181 (2). Fischer-Dieskau, Panerai, Ligabue, Sciutti, Oncina, Resnik, Rössl-Majdan, V. State Op. Ch., VPO, Bernstein.

(M) ** RCA 09026 60705-2 (2). Panerai, Titus, Sweet, Kaufmann, Horne, Lopardo, Bav. R. Ch. & RSO, C. Davis.

It is remarkable that Bernstein's mid-1960s set, with Fischer-Dieskau in the title-role, has been out of the catalogue for so long. Now its reissue is flawed by Sony's inept presentation, without either a libretto/translation (so essential in this opera), or even a cued synopsis. Nevertheless, collectors will surely want to snap it up before it disappears again. It is based on a production at the Vienna State Opera, and the fleetness of execution at hair-raisingly fast speeds suggests that Bernstein was intent on out-Toscanini-ing Toscanini. The allegros may be consistently faster than Toscanini's, but they never sound rushed, and always Bernstein conveys a sense of fun, while in relaxed passages, helped by warm Viennese sensitivity, he allows a full rotundity of phrasing, at least as much as any rival. It does not really matter here, any more than it did with the Toscanini set, that the conductor is the hero rather than Falstaff himself.

Fischer-Dieskau does wonders in pointing the humour. In his scene with Mistress Quickly arranging an assignation with Alice, he can inflect a simple 'Ebben?' to make it intensely funny, but he finally suffers from having a voice one inevitably associates with baritonal solemnity, whether heroic or villainous. Just how noble Falstaff should be is a matter for discussion.

The others are first rate – Panerai singing superbly as Ford, Ilva Ligabue as Mistress Ford, Regina Resnik as Mistress Quickly, and Graziella Sciutti and Juan Oncina as the young lovers. Excellent engineering (by a Decca recording team) together with effective remastering have produced a very satisfactory sound-balance. But this set is let down by its inadequate documentation.

While many will welcome the return to the catalogue of Sir Colin Davis's RCA set for the fine performance of Rolando Panerai, strong and resonant in the title-role, the reverberant acoustic remains a problem in an opera where inner clarity is so important. Here the resonance, though flattering

to the voices, confuses detail (with even the semiquaver figure of the opening barely identifiable), making it harder for the fun of the piece to come over. Davis, as he has shown many times at Covent Garden, is masterly in his Verdian timing, but the result here lacks sparkle: it is all too serious and Germanic. Alongside Panerai the cast is a good one, including another veteran, Marilyn Horne, producing stentorian tones as Mistress Quickly. Sharon Sweet is a forceful Alice, with Julie Kaufmann as Nanetta well matched against Frank Lopardo's Fenton, stylish in Verdi as he was in Rossini. Yet with such sound the recording has distinct limitations. A full libretto/translation is included, but the set appears to be at full price in the USA, which would make it distinctly uncompetitive. In any case, the DG set with Bryn Terfel and conducted by Abbado remains the primary recommendation (471 194-2 – see our main Guide).

La forza del destino (1862 version; complete).

(M) *** DG 474 903-2 (3). Plowright, Carrres, Bruson, Burchuladze, Baltsa, Pons, Amb. Op. Ch., Philh. O, Sinopoli.

Sinopoli's performance is notable for the creamy soprano of Rosalind Plowright, Agnes Baltsa's splendidly assured Preziosilla and Paata Burchuladze's resonant portrayal of the Padre Guardiano. Carreras also contributes strongly if not without a sense of strain at times. Although this recording won the Gramophone Opera Reward in 1987, it is not now a first choice – which still lies with Levine's RCA set, with Leontyne Price and Domingo (74321 39502-2 – see our main Guide).

Macbeth (1847 version; complete).

*** Opera Rara ORCV 301 (2). Glossop, Hunter, Tomlinson, Collins, BBC Singers & Concert O, Matheson.

What till now have been seriously neglected on disc have been Verdi's first thoughts, the versions of operas which he went on to revise, none more radically than his first Shakespearean venture, Macbeth. This fascinating recording of the original version will be a revelation to most Verdians. Taken from a BBC studio broadcast of 1979, masterminded by the Verdi scholar Julian Budden, it demonstrates very clearly how many of the most strikingly original passages were already there in Verdi's first version. Act I is already in place as we know it, with just a few tiny changes, and Lady Macbeth's great sleepwalking scene of Act IV, one of the most memorable passages of all, is already fully developed. Yet the revisions, involving almost a third of the score, are radical, the more strikingly so as the opera progresses. So in Act II, instead of the dramatic aria, La luce langue, Lady Macbeth sings a more conventional display piece which, like her Brindisi later in the act, involves a jolly oompah rhythm, while in Act III, the scene of Macbeth's hallucinations is quite different. Act IV is what Verdi changed most. Here it opens with a bold chorus involving a big tune sung in unison on the lines of *Va pensiero*, the chorus of Hebrew Slaves from *Nabucco*. Like almost all of Verdi's other first thoughts, it is not as refined musically as the magnificent chorus of lamentation with which it was replaced in 1865, but stylistically it is more consistent with the rest of the opera. The final scene too is quite different in this first version. A sequence of fanfares instead of a fugato represents the battle, with the whole opera ending on a death scene for Macbeth instead of a victory chorus.

This set is the more cherishable when the performance, incisively conducted by John Matheson, is so strongly cast. In this version the central roles of Macbeth and Lady Macbeth are vocally even more demanding than in Verdi's revision, and the baritone, Peter Glossop, here gives a searingly powerful performance as Macbeth. Rita Hunter is equally commanding as Lady Macbeth, as for her massive soprano, Wagnerian in scale, is surprisingly flexible in coloratura, with a perfectly controlled trill. The young John Tomlinson is magnificent as Banquo, and the tenor Kenneth Collins makes a fine MacDuff.

Otello (complete).

*** DG **DVD** 073 092-9. Domingo, Fleming, Morris, Bunnell, Croft, Anthony, Metropolitan Ch. & O., Levine (Producer: Louisa Briccetti; V/D: Brian Large).

(B) **(*) Decca 473 502-2 (2). Cossutta, M. Price, Bacquier, V. Boys' Ch., V. State Op.Ch., VPO, Solti.

It is good to have so telling a reminder on DVD of Plácido Domingo's masterly assumption of the role of Otello: commanding in every way, particularly when at the Met. in New York in 1996 he was singing opposite Renée Fleming as Desdemona, then at her freshest and purest, yet also with power, looking and sounding girlish. James Levine's direction is high-powered from beginning to end, matching the singing of his principals, controlling the massive forces provided in this lavish production directed by Elijah Moshinsky with sets by Michael Yeargan and costumes by Peter J. Hall. Though James Morris is not the most sinister of Iagos, his singing is clean and firm, well varied in the two big monologues of Act II. Excellent singing too from Jane Bunnell as a very positive Emilia and Richard Croft as Cassio, a tenor well contrasted with Domingo. The only bonuses on DVD are a picture gallery and trailer.

The warmth and tenderness of Solti's Vienna reading of *Otello* as well as its incisive sense of drama take one freshly by surprise. The recording is bright and atmospheric to match. As Desdemona Margaret Price gives a ravishing performance, with the most beautiful and varied tonal quality allied to deep imagination. Carlo Cossutta as Otello is not so characterful a singer, but he sings sensitively with clear, incisive tone. Gabriel Bacquier gives a thoughtful, highly intelligent performance as Iago, but he is disappointingly weak in the upper register. This was originally re-issued as a Double Decca but now reappears in Universal's Compact Opera Collection, which means it has a synopsis and the libretto/translation is only available via a CD-ROM.

Simon Boccanegra (1857 version; complete).

**(*) Opera Rara ORCV 302 (2). Bruscanti, Ligi, Turp, Elvin, Howell, Hudson, BBC Singers, BBC Concert O, Matheson.

The revision of *Simon Boccanegra* which, prompted by Boito's rewriting of the libretto, Verdi produced in 1881 has now firmly been accepted as one of the composer's supreme masterpieces, defying the old idea that it could never be popular. This valuable Opera Rara issue, like that company's recording of the original version of Verdi's *Macbeth*, is taken from a BBC recording made in 1976. The sound is satisfyingly vivid and well balanced, and the performance under John Matheson is warmly idiomatic, with the BBC Concert Orchestra rivalling the work of the other BBC orchestras. Casting is strong, with Sesto Bruscantini (towards the end of his career) as characterful as ever, with the voice still lyrical, set in striking contrast against the powerful Fiesco of the bass, Gwynne Howell, singing magnificently. Josella Ligi, little known on disc, makes an appealing Amelia, with the Canadian tenor André Turp singing strongly as Gabriele.

Even so, the set is rather of specialist than of general interest, when in every significant way, certainly at every key moment in the involved story, this first version is disappointingly conventional. So even the great Recognition scene, when Boccanegra realizes that Amelia is his daughter, fails in its timing and structure to have the overwhelming impact of the revised version, and the scene which was later replaced by the great Council Chamber scene seems astonishingly flat and perfunctory by comparison. One of the passages omitted in the revision is a cabaletta for Amelia, attractive enough but dramatically inappropriate; and Amelia's lovely nocturnal aria lacks the evocative orchestral introduction and distinctive accompaniment which make it so striking in the revision. Roger Parker's essay in the lavish booklet and libretto makes as strong a case as possible for this first version as being more consistent stylistically, but then fails to specify the differences with the revision, a sad omission. Even so, dedicated Verdians will welcome the chance to study just how Verdi translated a relatively workaday example of his music into a towering masterpiece.

La traviata (complete).

(M) *(*) Sony SM2K 90457 (2). Fabbricini, Alagna, Conti, La Scala, Milan, Ch. & O, Muti.

Response to Muti's Sony version will depend greatly on the ear's response to the voice of Tiziana Fabbricini as Violetta. Its Callas-like tang goes with many of the same vocal flaws which afflicted that supreme diva, but Fabbricini has nothing like the same musical imagination or charisma. The effort is hardly worth it for, although she produces one or two impressive top notes in *Sempre libera* at the end of Act I, the edge on the voice is genuinely unattractive. Muti, always a taut Verdian, does not pace the opera any more sympathetically here than in his earlier, EMI set, and in a live performance the flaws of ensemble are distracting, with the dry La Scala acoustic generally unhelpful, despite clever balancing by the Sony engineers. Paolo Conti is a strong, smooth-toned Germont but not very imaginative, and the main enjoyment in the set comes from the fresh, virile singing of the tenor Roberto Alagna as Alfredo. However, this is another of those Sony reissues with neither a libretto nor a cued synopsis. The Decca DVD (071 431-9) with Gheorghiu, Lopardo and Nucci, conducted by Solti, leads the field – see our main *Guide*.

La traviata (highlights).

(BB) ** EMI Encore (ADD) 5 74760-2 (from complete recording, with Sills, Gedda, Panerai, John Alldis Ch., RPO, Ceccato).

Beverly Sills makes an affecting Violetta, producing much lovely singing, although when she is pressed her voice grows shrill and unfocused. The character of an older woman knowing what suffering is to come remains firm, however, and with a fine Alfredo in Gedda this is a very acceptable set of highlights, when Panerai is a strong-voiced, if not subtle Germont and Aldo Ceccato proves an alert and colourful conductor. The RPO play well for him, and the closely miked recording is almost too vivid in its CD transfer. It is a pity that the selection (only 59 minutes) is not more generous, and the synopsis is sparsely inadequate.

Il trovatore (complete).

(BB) (***) Regis mono RRC 2060 (2). Milanov, Björling, Warren, Barbieri, Moscona, Robert Shaw Ch., RCA Victor O, Cellini.

(BB) ** Arte Nova (ADD) 74321 72110-2 (2). Bogza, Svetanov, Alperyn, Morosow, Bratislava Nat. Op. Ch., Bratislava Slovak RSO, Anguelov.

(B) *(*) Double Decca 460 735-2 (2). Sutherland, Pavarotti, Wixell, Horne, Ghiaurov, L. Op. Ch., Nat. PO, Bonynge.

(*) Sony S2K 89533 (2). Frittoli, Licitra, Urmana, Nucci, La Scala Ch. & O, Muti.

The classic RCA recording of 1952, with four of the reigning stars of the Metropolitan Opera at their peak, has already appeared on Naxos (8.110240/41 – see our main *Guide*). But this new Regis transfer seems to us to give the voices marginally more presence, although there is not a great deal in it, and the Naxos sound is a little more rounded. Both sets are very enjoyable indeed, so choice can be made by considering whether or not you require the Naxos bonus of six Yugoslavian folksongs sung by Milanov.

Incidentally, our review omitted to mention the superb contribution of Nicola Moscona as Ferrando in the opera's first scene.

The Arte Nova version, an enjoyable super-bargain issue, stems from a live concert performance, well recorded, with a good team of young soloists and fresh, vigorous playing and singing from the Bratislava choir and orchestra under the conductor Ivan Anguelov. This may not be a subtle performance, but the dramatic bite of a live occasion, well rehearsed, comes over very well. Anda-Louise Bogza makes a strong, vehement Leonora with plenty of temperament, and Boiko Svetanov as Manrico sings with clean, firm tone, if explosively from time to time. Shining out even from the others is Graciela Alperyn as Azucena, with a firm, strong mezzo and a splendid chest register, well controlled, attacking notes fearlessly. As the Conte di Luna, Igor Morosow is strong and clear except under strain on top. A full libretto in Italian is provided, but no translation.

Bonynge in most of his opera sets has been unfailingly urgent and rhythmic, but his account of *Il trovatore* is at an altogether lower level of intensity. Nor does the role of Leonora prove very apt for Sutherland late in her career; the coloratura passages are splendid, but a hint of unsteadiness is present in too much of the rest. Pavarotti for the most part sings superbly, but he falls short in, for example, the semiquaver groups of *Di quella pira* and, like Sutherland, Marilyn Horne as Azucena does not produce a consistently firm tone. Wixell as the Count sings intelligently, but a richer tone is needed. The CD transfer cannot be faulted.

When there are many fine versions of this opera, it seems a waste to have a live recording from Muti and La Scala forces which might just pass muster in a radio broadcast, but which is far too flawed for repeated listening. Even Barbara Frittoli is well below form as Leonora, not as steady as usual, and though Salvatore Licitra as Manrico has a ringing tenor, he uses it with little subtlety, while Leo Nucci is a mere shadow of his former self, singing coarsely throughout, too often failing to pitch notes at all, resorting to a sort of sing-speech. By far the best soloist is Violeta Urmana as Azucena, even if she sounds too young for the role. Muti is at his least sympathetic, forcing the pace so as to make the music sound breathless and brutal, and though five performances were edited together for the recording, the musical imprecisions and stage noises counterbalance any of the advantages of a live event. The sound too has little bloom on it.

COLLECTIONS

Choruses from: *Aida; La battaglia di Legnano; Don Carlos; I Lombardi; Macbeth; Nabucco; Otello; Il trovatore.*

(BB) ** Warner Apex 0927 40836-2. St Cecilia Ch. & O, Rizzi.

These are certainly very well-sung accounts of Verdi's most popular choruses, but Rizzi concentrates on refinement rather than on drama. The result lacks the raw energy that can make these warhorses so exciting. Compared with Decca's rival (1960s) recording with the same orchestra under Franci (now on Opera Gala 458 237-2), these digital performances feel a little anaemic. Side by side, the ubiquitous *Anvil Chorus* and *Grand March* from *Aida* sound tame compared to the Decca set, which has more character and excitement. Even if there is some tape hiss, the Decca sound is palpably more vivid and theatrical too, and if it costs a little more, there are almost 15 minutes' extra music, and full texts and translations are provided.

VERHULST, Johannes (1816–91)

Symphony in E min., Op. 46; Overtures in B min., Op. 2; C min. (Gijsbrecht van Aemstel); D min., Op. 8.
*** Chan. 10179. Residentie O, The Hague, Bamert.

Bamert has given us much attractive music in his Dutch music survey on Chandos (notably the music of Voormolen, Chan. 9815), and here is another excellent addition. Verhulst occupied an important position in Dutch musical life for many years, although his intrinsic conservatism in the face of the 'new' music of Liszt and Wagner ultimately led to his withdrawal from musical life, both voluntarily and not, and he died, embittered and increasingly forgotten. However, there is nothing embittered in his music: the composer who most readily springs to mind in the 1841 E minor Symphony is Mendelssohn (the finale reminds one especially of the *Octet*), though Schubert and Schumann are here too. It is full of vitality and good tunes among its drama and is well worth anyone's 35 minutes. The three early *Overtures*, though not quite as inspired as the *Symphony*, have the same qualities and are all highly enjoyable. Warm Chandos sound makes this an excellent CD for anyone who responds to music of the first half of the nineteenth century.

VILLA-LOBOS, Heitor (1887–1959)

Bachianas Brasileiras No. 2: The Little Train of the Caipira.
(*) Everest (ADD) EVC 9007. LSO, Goossens – ANTILL: *Corroboree* **(*); GINASTERA: *Estancia; Panambi.* *

It is good to have a recommendable mid-priced version of Villa-Lobos's engaging tone-picture of a little country train in São Paulo, Brazil, with Brazilian percussion instruments suggesting train noises. The performance is excellent and the recording vivid, if slightly over-resonant, with a slight edge to the violins.

PIANO MUSIC

As três Marias; Bachianas Brasileiras No. 4: Preludio. Prole do bèbe (The Child's Doll): Suite; Rudepoèma.
(BB) **(*) Warner Apex (ADD 0927 40837-2). Freire.

Excellent playing and eminently satisfactory recording of some delightfully colourful piano music. But at 40 minutes the measure is short, even at Apex price.

VIOTTI, Giovanni Battista (1755–1824)

Violin Concerto No. 13 in A.
(BB) *** Hyp. Helios CDH 55062. Oprean, European Community CO, Faerber – FIORILLO: *Violin Concerto No. 1.* ***

Viotti wrote a great many violin concertos in much the same mould, but this is one of his best. Adelina Oprean's quicksilver style and light lyrical touch give much pleasure – she has the exact measure of this repertoire and she is splendidly accompanied and well recorded. The measure, though, is short.

VIVALDI, Antonio (1675–1741)

Il Cimento dell'armonia e dell'inventione (12 Concertos), Op. 8; La Cetra (12 Concertos), Op. 9.
⊕─ (BB) *** Virgin 5 62260-2 (4). Huggett & Soloists, Raglan Baroque Players, Kraemer.

Anyone wanting *Il Cimento dell'armonia* (including a highly recommendable set of *The Four Seasons*) and *La Cetra* together, admirably played on period instruments, could hardly better this Virgin budget box. Monica Huggett has already give us *La Stravaganza* on Oiseau-Lyre (although this currently awaits reissue) and her Vivaldian credentials are impeccable. The present performances are so accomplished and in such good style that they are unlikely to be surpassed by other authentic-instrument versions. She is in excellent form throughout and her virtuosity always appears effortless. Notably in *The Four Seasons*, her expressive flexibility extends to quite personal touches of rubato, which some might find a little mannered, but they give her solo playing added individuality. The Raglan Baroque Players are of the same size as the Academy of Ancient Music and some players are common to both groups. First-class recording throughout.

The Four Seasons, Op. 8/1–4.
(BB) *** Regis RRC 1160. Laredo, SCO (with *Concert – String Masterpieces* *** – see below).
(BB) **(*) DG (ADD/DDD) 474 567-2. Kremer, LSO, Abbado – HAYDN: *Trumpet Concerto*, etc. ***

The Four Seasons, Op. 8/1–4; Double Violin Concerto in G, RV 516; Double Concerto for Violin & Oboe Concerto in F, RV 548.

(M) *** DG 474 616-2. Standage, E. Concert, Pinnock.

The Four Seasons, Op. 8/1–4; Triple Violin Concerto in F, RV 551; Quadruple Violin Concerto in B min., RV 580.

✪ (M) *** Ph. 476 1716. Accardo & soloists with CO.

Salvatore Accardo's is a version with a difference. Recorded in live performances at the 1987 Cremona Festival, it is of particular interest in that Accardo uses a different Stradivarius for each of the four concertos – period instruments with a difference! Thanks to this aristocrat of violinists, the sounds are of exceptional beauty, both here and also in the two multiple concertos which are added as a bonus. The performances are much enhanced, too, by the imaginative continuo playing of Bruno Canino. The recording itself is a model of fidelity and has plenty of warmth; it must rank very high in the Vivaldi discography and now justly reappears as part of Universal's 'Penguin ✪ Collection'.

Trevor Pinnock directs his 1981 Archiv version from the keyboard, with Simon Standage leading the English Concert. Although a relatively intimate sound is produced, their approach is certainly not without drama, while the solo contributions have impressive flair and bravura. The overall effect is essentially refined, treating the pictorial imagery with subtlety. The result finds a natural balance between vivid projection and atmospheric feeling. With two highly attractive (if not generous) double concertos added to this mid-priced Originals release – all in fine sound – authenticists should be well satisfied.

Jaime Laredo's performance with the Scottish Chamber Orchestra – originally issued on Carlton – was always one of the most recommendable lower-priced versions, and now it comes with a well-chosen collection of baroque string lollipops, which is excellent in every way (see Concerts). The performance of *The Four Seasons* has great sponaneity and vitality, emphasized by the forward balance, which is nevertheless admirably realistic, as the bright upper range is balanced by a firm, resonant bass. Laredo plays with bravura and directs polished, strongly characterized accompaniments. Pacing tends to be on the fast side; although the reading is extrovert and the lyrical music – played responsively – is made to offer a series of interludes to contrast with the vigour of the allegros, the effect is exhilarating rather than aggressive. A first-class bargain.

In the DG version with Gidon Kremer and the LSO under Claudio Abbado, it is obvious from the first bar that Abbado is the dominating partner. This is an enormously vital account, with great contrasts of tempo and dynamic. The dramatization of Vivaldi's detailed pictorial effects is extremely vivid. The vigour of the dancing peasants is surpassed by the sheer fury and violence of the summer storms. Yet

the delicacy of the gentle zephyrs is matched by the hazy somnolence of the beautiful *Adagio* of *Autumn*. After a freezingly evocative opening to *Winter*, Abbado creates a mandolin-like pizzicato effect in the slow movement (taken faster than the composer's marking) to simulate a rain shower. The finale opens delicately, but at the close the listener is almost blown away by the winter gales. Kremer matches Abbado's vigour with playing that combines sparkling bravura and suitably evocative expressive moments. Given the projection of a brilliantly lit recording, the impact of this version is considerable. Leslie Pearson's nimble continuo, alternating organ and harpsichord, sometimes gets buried, but drama rather than subtlety is the keynote of this arresting account. The 1982 analogue recording has been effectively remastered for CD, sounding fresh and clean, its brilliance very apparent. Well worth considering at its new bargain price and with attractive couplings.

Bassoon Concertos, RV 471/473; 481/2; 484; 491/497; 499/500; 503/4.

🕭⟶ (B) *** Ph. Duo 475 233-2 (2). Thunemann, I Musici.

Apart from the complete cycle by Daniel Smith on ASV, which has some rough edges, this is the most comprehensive (and economical) survey of Vivaldi's bassoon concertos on CD. Moreover (as we commented in our main volume, discussing the separate issues from which this Duo is compiled), Klaus Thunemann makes every work seem a masterpiece. His virtuosity is remarkable and it is always at the composer's service, while the polish of the playing is matched by its character and warmth. I Musici are on their finest form, and all the slow movements here are touchingly expressive, with Thunemann's ease of execution adding to the enjoyment. With the Philips recording in the demonstration bracket, this reissue demonstrates just how well Vivaldi's music can sound on modern instruments.

Concerto funèbre con molti istromenti for muted oboes, Chalumeaux (Salmoè), Violin & Viola da gamba; Double Concertos: for Violin & Cello in F (Il Proteo o sia il mondo al rovescio); for Violin & Viola da gamba in A, RV 546; Triple Concertos for 2 Violins & Viola da gamba: in D min., RV 565; in G min., RV 578; Concerto for 4 Violins & Cello in B Min. RV 580.

🕭⟶ *** Alia Vox AV 9835. Savall & soloists, Le Concert des Nations.

This splendid collection centres on the vibrant presence of Jordi Savall, who contributes instrumentally to half the concertos included here, and directs them all. The highly original *Funeral Concerto* (based on a *Sinfonia* from the opera *Tito Manlio*) creates most colourful sonorities by including muted oboes, tenor chalumeaux, and three viole'all'inglese. The 'Il Proteo' (upside-down) concerto is written with the violin solos written in the bass clef while the cello reads from the treble clef. This is a joke aimed at the players, for it makes no difference to the resulting sound. These are all aurally fascinating works, and they are superbly played and recorded, with characteristic Savall gusto in allegros and warmly lyrical slow movements.

Mandolin Concertos in D, RV 93; C, RV 425; (i) Double Mandolin Concerto in G, RV 332; Concerto for 2 Flutes, 2 Chalumeaux, 2 Violins ('In tromba marina'), 2 Mandolins, 2 Theorbos & Cello in C, RV 558.

⊖⊸ (BB) ★★★ Warner Apex 2564 61264-2. Orlandi; (i) Frati; soloists, Sol. Ven., Scimone.

It is good to have a budget CD with excellent performances of the two solo *Mandolin Concertos* and the *Double Mandolin Concerto*, presented with style and delicacy and with the colourful *Concerto con molti istromenti* thrown in for good measure. The recording is very good indeed.

Violin Concertos: L'estro armonico, Op.3/3; (i) 5, 6, 9 & 12. Il cimento dell'armonia e dell'invenzione, Op. 8/7, 9 & 12. Double Concertos: (i) for 2 Violins, RV 529; (ii) for Violin & Cello, RV 547 & 547; (iii) for Violin and Oboe, RV 548; (iv) for Violin & Organ, RV 541 & 542.

(BB) ★★★ EMI Gemini 5 85544-2 (2). Y. Menuhin, Polish CO, Maksymiuk; with (i) Chen; (ii) Mørk; (iii) Black; (iv) Bell.

This reissue combines two CDs (from 1986 and 1990 respectively) which we have not encountered before, to make a most attractive pairing, especially at budget price. The first combines four solo violin concertos from *L'estro armonico* with three from *Il cimento dell'armonia e dell'invenzione* (missing out, of course, the first four, which are known as *The Four Seasons*). They are all fine works and Menuhin is in excellent form; his expressive playing is often very beautiful indeed. Moreover, Jerzy Maksymiuk directs lively and stylish accompaniments. These are modern-instrument performances of high quality, but the crisp rhythms and bright, clean recording offer no suggestion of inflation.

The second collection, which Menuhin directs from the bow, concentrates on double concertos and includes the A major work from *L'estro armonico*, Op. 3/5. With Truls Mørk an erstwhile partner, the two concertos with cello are certainly enjoyable, and the combination of violin and organ also brings a most engaging interplay. But it is the B flat *Concerto for Violin and Oboe* that is most winning of all, and here Neil Black makes a truly memorable contribution.

VOCAL MUSIC

Vespers for the Assumption of the Virgin Mary (arr. Alessandrini).

★★★ Opus 111 OP 30383 (2). Bertagnolli, Invernizzi, Simboli, Mingardo, Ferrarini, Bellotto, De Secondi, Concerto Italiano, Alessandrini.

Taking Monteverdi's great 1610 set of *Vespers* as a model, Rinaldo Alessandrini, in collaboration with the scholar Frederic Delamea, has devised a sequence of Psalm settings and antiphons parallel to Monteverdi's, choosing works by Vivaldi such as might have been used for the Vespers service. Though Vivaldi never wrote music for the vast basilica of St Mark's in Venice, as Monteverdi had done a century earlier, he did write Psalm settings employing double choirs, works which cry out for spatial separation. Starting with a double concerto as overture with similarly divided forces, Alessandrini has included in the sequence such masterly examples of Vivaldi's church music as the *Dixit Dominus* (Psalm 109), *Lauda Jerusalem* (Psalm 147) and the superb *Magnificat* setting, RV 610a, rounded off with a cantata for solo contralto with two orchestras, *Salve Regina*. It makes a most compelling sequence. The challenge of over two and a half hours of music prompts Alessandrini to draw from his choir and period orchestra, Concerto Italiano, consistently fresh and incisive performances, brilliantly recorded. The soloists have bright, clear voices, apt for this music, with none of the vocal fruitiness typical of Italian singers.

OPERA

Opera Overtures: Armida al campo d'Egito; Arsilda, regina di Ponto; Bajazet (Tamerlano); Dorilla in Tempe; Farnace; Giustino; Griselda; L'incoronazione di Dario; L'Olimpiade; Ottone in Villa; La verità in cimento.

(BB) ★★★ Warner Apex 2564 60537-2. I Sol. Ven., Scimone.

Vivaldi's 'opera overtures' were conceived as sinfonias, scarcely related to the character of each work. But these 11 make a lively and surprisingly varied collection, splendidly played and recorded. But it may be as well not to play them all in sequence.

WAGNER, Richard (1813–83)

American Centennial March (Grosser Festmarsch); Kaisermarsch; Overtures: Polonia; Rule Britannia.

(BB) ★★ Naxos 8.555386. Hong Kong PO, Kojian.

The *Polonia Overture* (1836) is the best piece here. Although its basic style is Weberian, there is a hint of the Wagner of *Rienzi* in the slow introduction. The *Grosser Festmarsch (American Centennial March)* was commissioned from Philadelphia, and for this inflated piece Wagner received a cool five thousand dollars! The *Rule Britannia Overture* is even more overblown, and the famous tune, much repeated, outstays its welcome. The *Kaisermarsch* is also empty and loud. The Hong Kong orchestra play all this with great enthusiasm, if without much finesse. The recording is vividly bright, but on CD it is not a priority item, even for the most dedicated Wagnerian. However, at the Naxos price it is more enticing for the curious collector than the original issue was on Marco Polo.

(i) *Die Feen: Overture. Grosser Festmarsch (American Centennial March); Huldigungsmarsch; Kaisermarsch; Das Liebesverbot: Overture.* (ii) *Lohengrin: Preludes to Acts I & III. Die Meistersinger: Preludes to Acts I & III; Dance of the Apprentices; Finale.Tannhäuser: Overture. Tristan und Isolde: Prelude.*
(BB) ★★ Virgin (ADD/DDD) 5 62034-2 (2). (i) R. France PO; (ii) LSO; Janowski.

This two-CD compilation combines two unequal Wagner collections. One CD contains a not terribly distinguished group of operatic preludes and orchestral excerpts, but they generate no real excitement or tension, and the digital recording is disappointing. But the paired CD, recorded by EMI in 1972, makes this collection worth considering. It consists of early, rarely heard works and occasional pieces, none of them great music, but all of them at the very least interesting. Indeed, it is quite a surprise to hear Wagner's music sounding not too different from Offenbach, as in the racy *galop* – complete with glittering castanets – which opens the *Overture Das Liebesverbot* (a failed Wagner operetta, dating from 1836). Elsewhere, the marches such as the *Huldigungsmarsch (Homage March)* and the *Grand Festival March* (written to celebrate the centenary of American independence in 1876) have a pomp more associated with Meyerbeer, while *Die Feen* resides in the world of Weber. It is all eminently enjoyable and enthusiastically played by the LSO, with the analogue recording much more vivid than its digital companion.

Symphony in C.
(BB) ★★ Warner Apex 2564 60619-2. Norwegian R.O, Rasilainen – WEBER: *Symphonies Nos. 1 & 2.* ★★

A useful and inexpensive way to explore Wagner's early *Symphony*, composed at the age of nineteen, and very much indebted to Beethoven and even Mendelssohn. It's no masterpiece, of course, but fascinating to hear and reasonably rewarding. The performance and recording are good, but not outstanding.

Siegfried Idyll.
(M) ★★★ EMI (ADD) 5 62815-2. Philh. O, Klemperer – BRUCKNER: *Symphony No. 4.* ★★★
★(★) DG (IMS) 469 008-2. Berlin Deutsche Oper O, Thielemann – SCHOENBERG: *Pelleas und Melisande.* ★(★)
(M) ★ Decca (ADD) 470 254-2. VPO, Knappertsbusch – BRAHMS: *Academic Festival Overture,* etc. ★

Klemperer (like Solti) favours the original chamber-orchestra scoring, and the Philharmonia players are very persuasive, especially in the score's gentler moments. However, the balance is forward and, although the 1962 sound is warm, the ear craves greater breadth of string-tone at the climax.

The playing of the Orchestra of the Deutsche Oper, Berlin, is fine, but why does Thielemann not allow the music to unfold naturally? He is given to somewhat intrusive expressive exaggeration. Good, though not outstanding sound.

Nothing special at all about Knappertsbusch's 1955 mono *Siegfried Idyll*, either in the playing or the sound, which is below Decca's best efforts. This reissue does nothing at all for its famous conductor's reputation.

Siegfried Idyll; A Faust Overture; Gotterdämmerung: Siegfried's Rhine Journey. Lohengrin: Prelude to Act III. Overtures: Die Meistersinger; Rienzi.
(M) ★★(★) RCA 82876 59414-2. BPO, Maazel.

For the Berlin Philharmonic's Wagner programme directed by Lorin Maazel, now reissued as part of the 'Classic Collection', RCA has returned to the Berlin Jesus-Christus-Kirche, where so many of the orchestra's most celebrated recordings were made. The *Siegfried Idyll* is beautifully played, the ebb and flow of tension admirably controlled, and the closing section quite lovely. *Rienzi* and the *Lohengrin Third Act Prelude* are vivid and brilliant, and the *Faust Overture* has plenty of character. But in the *Prelude to Die Meistersinger*, which Maazel paces convincingly, the ear craves rather more amplitude in the recording itself, in a deeper, more resonant bass. The principal horn (who also contributed impressively to the *Siegfried Idyll*) plays with panache (slightly distanced) in the closing *Siegfried's Rhine Journey* which, after an atmospheric opening and a sudden, impulsive accelerando, certainly makes a spectacular and gripping end to the concert. The digital sound-picture is cleanly focused, fresh, clear and well balanced, but a little more reflection of the hall acoustics would have made the recording even finer.

ORCHESTRAL EXCERPTS AND PRELUDES FROM THE OPERAS

Der fliegende Holländer: Overture. Götterdämmerung: Siegfried's Funeral Music; Finale. Die Meistersinger: Prelude, Act I. Tristan und Idolde: Preludes, Acts I & III; Liebestod. Die Walküre: The Ride of the Valkyries.
(BB) ★★(★) DG Entrée 474 568-2. O de Paris, Barenboim.

Barenboim's is a warm and sympathetic collection of overtures and preludes, plus the instrumental version of Isolde's *Liebestod*. The only snag is that the Paris orchestra – particularly its brass section, with its excessive vibrato – does not sound quite authentic, and the acoustic is not always helpful, failing to give the necessary resonance to the deeper brass sounds. These recordings derive from two LPs dating from 1983–4, though it's a pity there was no room for the delightful rarity included on one of the LPs, *La Descente de la Courtille*, a jolly processional piece sounding more like Offenbach and great fun.

(i) *Der fliegende Höllander: Overture.* (ii) *Götterdämmerung: Dawn; Siegfried's Rhine Journey & Funeral March.* (i) *Lohengrin: Prelude to Act III. Die Meistersinger: Preludes to Acts I & III. Tannhäuser: Overture and Venusberg Music. Die Walküre: Ride of the Valkyries.*

(B) ** CfP (DDD/ADD) 575 5682. LPO, (i) Elder; (ii) Rickenbacher.

Most of the excerpts here are conducted by Mark Elder, who provides well-played but unmemorable performances, brightly but not particularly richly recorded. The *Ride of the Valkyries* comes off best, but it seems a curious plan to include the *Venusberg Music* from *Tannhäuser* without the chorus. The *Götterdämmerung* excerpts conducted by Karl Anton Rickenbacher, added as a makeweight, are altogether superior, and it was a pity that EMI did not choose to reissue the complete collection from which they derive, instead of the Elder disc.

Overtures: Der fliegende Holländer; Die Meistersinger. Lohengrin: Preludes to Acts I & III; (i) *Tannhäuser: Overture and Venusberg Music. Tristan und Isolde: Prelude & Liebestod.*

⊖━ (M) *** EMI 5 62756-2 [5 62771-2]. BPO, Karajan; (i) with Deutsch Op. Ch.

All in all, Karajan's 1974 collection is perhaps the finest single disc of miscellaneous Wagnerian overtures and preludes in the catalogue, recommendable alongside Szell's Cleveland collection of orchestral music from the *Ring*. Karajan's CD is fully worthy of inclusion as one of EMI's 'Great Recordings of the Century'. The body of tone produced by the Berlin Philharmonic gives a breathtaking amplitude at climaxes and the electricity the conductor generates throughout the programme is unforgettable. Also available on a spectacular DVD (DVC4 92397-9), this much less expensive CD can be recommended with equal enthusiasm.

(i) *Götterdämmerung: Siegfried's Rhine Journey & Funeral March;* (ii) *Die Meistersinger: Prelude to Act III; Procession of the Meistersingers;* (iii) *Das Rheingold: Entrance of the Gods into Valhalla;* (ii) *Rienzi: Overture. Tristan und Isolde: Prelude and Liebestod. Die Walküre:* (ii) *Magic Fire Music;* (iii; iv) *Ride of the Valkyries.*

(M) * (**) RCA (ADD) 82876 55306-2. Stokowski, with (i) LSO; (ii) RPO; (iii) Symphony of the Air; (iv) Arroyo; Ordassy; Parker.

Three orchestras are here unified by Stokowski's brand of magnetism. At a flick of the wrist, he creates electric tension, the dynamic contrasts and climaxes

made more all the more effective when heard alongside the richly sensuous playing in the slow numbers, with the conductor adopting tempos which might seem indulgent in less gifted hands. The opening of the *Die Meistersinger Prelude* is rich in Wagnerian amplitude, while the *Tristan Prelude and Liebestod* is glowingly atmospheric in the high strings. The *Entry of the Gods into Valhalla* and a vocal version of the *Ride of the Valkyries* are predictably exciting, as is the *Rienzi Overture*, which builds up to a fine climax. The two *Götterdämmerung* items with the LSO bring a real frisson, with *Siegfried's Funeral March* suitably sombre and the dramatic interjections from the full orchestra powerfully placed. The sound is surprisingly uniform throughout the programme (dating from between 1961 and 1974), generally full and certainly vivid, but not always refined, with the brass coarsening under pressure, though Stokowski's string sonorities come over well.

OPERA

Die Meistersinger von Nürnberg (complete).

(*) Arthaus **DVD 100 122. Doese, McIntyre, Frey, Pringle, Doig, Shanks, Gunn, Allman, Australian Op. Ch., Elizabethan PO, Mackerras (Producer/Director Peter Butler & Virginia Lumsden; V/D: Michael Hampe).

(M) (**(*)) Andante mono AND-3040 (4). Nissen, Reining, Wiedemann, Noort, Thorborg, Ch. & VPO, Toscanini.

** Teldec 3984 29333-2 (4). Holl, Seiffert, Magee, Schmidt, Wottrich, Bayreuth Festival Ch. & O, Barenboim.

Recorded in 1990 in the relatively small opera-theatre of the Sydney Opera House, this Australian Opera production brilliantly overcomes the limitations of a theatre with very little space in the wings and orchestra pit and a relatively dry acoustic. Only in the overture and the orchestral link into the final scene of Act III does the relative thinness of the string-sound obtrude, and even then the electricity and vitality of Sir Charles Mackerras's conducting makes one readily forget any shortcomings. The production by Michael Hampe is very traditional, with sets by John Gunter which exploit the depth of the stage rather than its width, and ethnic German costumes by Reinhard Heinrich. The acting too is geared to old conventions, at times obtrusively so when viewed close on video (as when the girl–boy apprentices scamper about), but Donald McIntyre is magnificent as Sachs, both vocally and dramatically, and the Swedish soprano Helena Doese is radiant as Eva, with her creamy soprano flawlessly even, most moving in the great quintet of Act III. After a rather rough start, Paul Frey emerges as an engaging Walther, rising to the challenge of the Prize Song with little strain, and the other principal tenor, Christopher Doig, effortlessly sails through the lighter role of David. Rosemary Gunn projects firmly and strongly as Magdalena, and John

Pringle is a splendidly prim Beckmesser, singing and acting most convincingly. The test of any *Meistersinger* comes in the emotional impact of the big moments, and here, thanks to excellent singing and masterly conducting, the impact of Wagner's great score catches you as it would in the theatre. A booklet is included with ample information and a good essay, with copious index points on the two DVDs.

When Toscanini's commercial recordings never included a complete Wagner opera, it is exciting to get a flavour of what it was like to attend one of his legendary Salzburg Festival performances. Dating from 1937, this one of *Meistersinger* demonstrates very clearly how at that period Toscanini was far from rigid in his conducting, with the high-voltage electricity of the moment leading him forward in urgency, while equally letting him and his performers expand in warmth. Hans Hermann Nissen makes a noble Sachs, as he does on EMI's historic Boehm recording of Act III made at the same period, and Maria Reining is a touching Eva, far fresher than in her later recordings. The others make a fine team. The radio sound is very limited, with the orchestra thin and dry. For most of the time the voices come over well, but they periodically fade into the distance, with the balances of voices on stage variable. Happily, the long first scene of Act III comes over best, no doubt the result of forwardly placed scenery. The wonder is that the CD transfer by Ward Marston does so much to make the sound acceptable, with Andante offering its typically luxurious packaging.

Recorded live at the 1999 Bayreuth Festival, Barenboim's version starts well with a thrustful account of the Overture, helped by full, immediate sound, but problems develop rapidly from then on, with the orchestra close but the voices set in a far more spacious acoustic, with the chorus distant and ill-defined. Too often over the great span of the three acts, Barenboim's direction grows uncharacteristically stodgy and square, with jog-trot rhythms evenly stressed. Vocally the great glory of the set is the singing of Peter Seiffert as Walther, amply heroic in scale but clear-toned and never strained. His feeling for words is always illuminating, and his performance is crowned by a superb account of the Prize Song in Act III. Emma Magee is an impressive Eva too, the voice warm, the manner fresh and girlish. Both of them are sharply contrasted with the pedestrian Hans Sachs of Robert Holl, lacking weight, with the voice no longer cleanly focused and with little feeling for the character. This is a dull dog of a Sachs with little or no sense of humour. Andreas Schmidt sings well as Beckmesser in a clean-cut, unexaggerated reading, but that minimizes the sparkle of the inspiration.

Tannhäuser (Dresden version; complete).
(B) **(*) Ph. (ADD) 473 505-2 (3). Windgassen, Waechter, Silja, Stolze, Bumbry, Bayreuth Festival (1962) Ch. & O, Sawallisch.
** Teldec 8573 88064-2 (3). Seiffert, Eaglen, Meyer,

Hampson, Deutsche Op. Ch., Berlin State O, Barenboim

Sawallisch's version, recorded at the 1962 Bayreuth Festival, comes up very freshly on CD. Though the medium brings out all the more clearly the thuds, creaks and audience noises of a live performance (most distracting at the very start), the dedication of the reading is very persuasive, notably in the Venusberg scene, where Grace Bumbry is a superb, sensuous Venus, and Windgassen – not quite in his sweetest voice, often balanced rather close – is a fine, heroic Tannhäuser. Anja Silja controls the abrasiveness of her soprano well, to make this her finest performance on record, not ideally sweet but very sympathetic. Voices are set well forward of the orchestra, in which strings have far more bloom than brass; but the atmosphere of the Festspielhaus is vivid and compelling throughout. This now reappears as an impressive bargain in Universal's 'Compact Opera' Collection, the only snag being that the documentation includes only a synopsis, and the libretto and translation are available only via an additional CD-ROM.

This Teldec set does not add up to the sum of its parts. Though the casting is starry, arguably as fine a team as could be assembled today, and Barenboim's credentials as a Wagnerian have long been tested at Bayreuth and elsewhere, the performance lacks the dramatic thrust needed to bring together one of the more problematic of Wagner's operas. For many it will be in the set's favour that the text used is the original Dresden form with the more elaborate version of Act I Scene 2, the big duet between Tannhäuser and Venus, taken from the much later Paris version. It does not help that Barenboim's speeds tend to be on the slow side, yet with little of the hushed tension that marks his finest Wagner performances, while occasionally by contrast he will choose a frenetic speed. The impression is of a carefully prepared studio run-through, and indeed the solo singing is beautifully controlled as though for a concert, so when Thomas Hampson as Wolfram sings his song to the evening star the emphasis is on beauty of tone and phrase. In the title-role Peter Seiffert sings with clean, firm projection with no sign of strain, yet the sound is hardly beautiful and his vocal acting is unconvincing. Waltraud Meyer is a formidable Venus, but again the sound as recorded is unrelenting rather than sensuous. Jane Eaglen as Elisabeth controls her massive soprano well, but one really wants a more tender, lyrical sound. The recording, faithful enough, tends to confirm the feeling of a concert performance.

Tristan und Isolde (complete).
☞ (BB) (***) EMI mono 5 85873-2 (4). Flagstad, Suthaus, Thebom, Greindl, Fischer-Dieskau, Phil., Furtwängler.
(BB) (**(*)) Naxos 8.110321 (4) Flagstad, Suthaus, Thebom, Greindl, Fischer-Dieskau, Phil., Furtwängler.

(*) Hardy **DVD (ADD) HCD4009 (2). Nilsson,
Vickers, Hesse, Rundgren, Berry, New Philh. Ch., O
Nat. de l'ORTF, Boehm.

Furtwängler's classic (1952) version of *Tristan* has
already appeared at mid-price in EMI's 'Great
Recordings of the Century' series, but to forestall the
imminent transfer of the same recording by Naxos,
this super-budget version was issued, minus libretto
but with a very detailed synopsis linked to copious
index points on the discs. The mono sound is amazingly full and immediate, transferred from the original tapes with more presence than the Naxos version
and with less background noise.

In default of the EMI super-budget version, the
Naxos set in the same price-bracket, lovingly transferred from carefully chosen LPs, offers a good alternative, not quite so vivid, also without a libretto and
with fewer index points linked to the synopsis.

The DVD on the Hardy label offers a live recording made at the Orange Festival in France in July
1973, with the title-roles taken by the unchallenged
leaders among Wagner singers of the day, Birgit
Nilsson and Jon Vickers, with Karl Boehm conducting. That line-up alone makes this well worth investigating, and Nikolaus Lehnhoff's simple, stylized
staging in the great amphitheatre at Orange is undis-
tractingly effective. The circular stage contains
merely two curved stairways, moved around in different positions for each act. It matters little that in
Act I there is no hint of a ship or the sea; thanks to
the music and the singing, one simply imagines the
necessary scene. Nilsson and Vickers may not be the
greatest actors, statuesque rather than dynamic, but
their vocal command is irresistible, with not a hint of
strain from either of them. Among the others Ruth
Hesse is an uneven Brangäne, but both Walter Berry
as Kurwenal and Bengt Rundgren as King Mark are
superb, as commanding as Nilsson and Vickers. The
chorus is the visiting New Philharmonia of London
but, thanks to the staging, they are never visible. The
big disappointment is that the video sound is so
limited and thin, not nearly as full as one might have
expected of a 1973 recording. The presentation,
mostly in Italian, is also limited, with a simple leaflet
giving an outline background to the opera and a
simple synopsis.

WAGNER, Siegfried (1869–1930)

Die Heilige Linde (opera; complete).

*** CPO 999 844-2 (3). Wegner, Schellenberger, Lukic,
George, Scharnke, Kruzel, Horn, Heidbüchel,
Halmai, West German RSO, Cologne Ch. & O,
Albert.

It says much for Siegfried Wagner that, even in face
of the towering position held by his father, he was
still determined to become a composer himself. *Die
Heilige Linde* ('The Holy Linden Tree'), first heard in
1924, is the fourteenth of his 16 operas, with a sub-

stantial *Prelude* generally counted one of his finest
works. The easy tunefulness of the very opening
instantly establishes that the musical idiom preferred
by the son is more straightforwardly diatonic, not
nearly so radical as the chromatic style his father
developed. One might relate it to the music of
Humperdinck, or among Richard Wagner's works,
Die Meistersinger, with a similar concern for German
folksong.

That is apt, for this involved tale from the third
century A.D., telling of Arbogast, king of a German
tribe, his wife Hildegard, and Fritigern, son of the
king of a neighbouring tribe. The villain is Philo,
described as a soldier instigator, in fee to the Roman
Emperor, intent on getting Arbogast to forge an
alliance with Rome. The second act, lighter and
brighter than the first and third, is set in that city, but
throughout the opera the involved story prompts the
composer to produce an attractive series of episodes,
colourfully orchestrated with some fine choral passages, which yet fail to add up dramatically. It makes
agreeable listening, but the ends of the first two acts
bring no sense of drama, and the end of the whole
opera, when Arbogast has been killed in battle, is
effective as a warmly patriotic ensemble rather than
as a dramatic resolution.

Recorded in Cologne in collaboration with West
German Radio, this CPO recording offers a warmly
idiomatic performance under Werner Andreas Albert,
very well sung. As Arbogast, John Wegner exploits a
clear, forthright baritone, with Dagmar Schellenberger fresh and firm as Hildegard, and the tenor
Schorsten Scharnke aptly heroic as Fritigern, the role
with which the composer identified. As the sinister
Philo, Volker Horn characterizes well with his bleating
voice. The booklet contains a complete libretto and
translation, with various essays and background material, but no synopsis of the difficult plot.

Sternengebot (opera; complete).

*(*) Marco Polo 8.225150-51 (2). Kruzel, Roberts, Lukic,
Horn, Kinzel, Wenhold, Sailer, Bav. Ch. & Youth O,
Albert.

Tutored in composition by Humperdinck, Siegfried
Wagner wrote no fewer than 18 operas, some of them
unfinished, which rather than echoing his father's
music turn rather to the example of his tutor in
easily romantic fairy-tale pieces. This one, *The Commandment of the Stars*, completed in 1906, draws on
astrology in its story from the age of chivalry, dated
around the time of King Henry the Fowler. The
writing is easily lyrical, far less radical than that of his
father, but with the occasional nod of acknowledgement to Richard's example in his own, very
involved libretto, as for example in the tournament
for the heroine's hand, when the hero, Helferich, is
defeated.

Apart from a thinness on exposed violins, the
playing of the Bavarian Youth Orchestra is strong
and expressive under the vigorous direction of

Werner Andreas Albert, helped by full, clear recording. The role of Helferich is well taken by the tenor Volker Horn, if with some strain at times. Sadly, the other soloists are disappointing, notably Ksenija Lukic as the heroine, Agnes, whose shrill hooting tone in her opening scene is almost comical, even though she later improves slightly. In the principal baritone roles Karl-Heinz Kinzel as Adalbert and Andre Wenhold as Kurzbold are both very uneven. It is good to have on disc such a major score of Siegfried Wagner, but this set has to be approached with caution. A German libretto is provided, but no English translation, only a detailed synopsis.

WALDTEUFEL, Emile (1837–1915)

Polkas: *Les Bohémiens; Retour des champs; Tout ou rien.* Waltzes: *Ange d'amour; Dans les nuages; España; Fontaine lumineuse; Je t'aime; Tout-Paris.*
** Marco Polo 8.223438. Slovak State PO (Košice), Walter.

Polkas: *Camarade; Dans les bois; Jeu d'esprit.* Waltzes: *Bien aimés; Chantilly; Dans tes yeux; Estudiantina; Hommage aux dames; Les Patineurs.*
** Marco Polo 8.223433. Slovak State PO (Košice), Walter.

Polkas: *L'Esprit français; Par-ci, par-là; Zig-zag.* Waltzes: *Hébé; Les Fleurs; Fleurs et baisers; Solitude; Toujours ou jamais; Toujours fidèle.*
**(*) Marco Polo 8.223450. Slovak State PO (Košice), Walter.

Invitation à la gavotte; Polkas: *Joyeux Paris; Ma Voisine.* Waltzes: *Pluie de diamants; Les Sirènes; Les Sourires; Soirée d'été; Très jolie; Tout en rose.*
** Marco Polo 8.223441. Slovak State PO (Košice), Walter.

Béobile pizzicato. Polka-Mazurka: *Bella.* Polka: *Château en Espagne.* Waltzes: *Acclamations; La Barcarolle; Brune ou blonde; Flots de joie; Gaîté; Tout à vous.*
**(*) Marco Polo 8.223684. Slovak State PO (Košice), Walter.

Grand vitesse galop. Mazurka: *Souveraine.* Polka: *Les Folies.* Waltzes: *Amour et printemps; Dolorès; Mello; Mon rêve; Pomone; Sous la voûte étoilée.*
** Marco Polo 8.223451. Slovak State PO (Košice), Walter.

Galop: *Prestissimo.* Polkas: *Bella bocca; Nuée d'oiseaux.* Waltzes: *Au revoir; Coquetterie; Jeunesse dorée; Un Premier Bouquet; Rêverie; Trésor d'amour.*
** Marco Polo 8.223685. Slovak State PO (Košice), Walter.

Grand galop du chemin de fer. Polkas: *Désirée; Jou-jou* (all arr. Pollack). Waltzes: *La Berceuse: Entre nous; Illusion; Joie envolée; Mariana; Sur le plage.*
** Marco Polo 8.223686. Slovak State PO (Košice), Walter.

Waldteufel's music, if not matching that of the Strauss family in range and expressive depth, has grace and charm and is prettily scored in the way of French ballet music. Moreover, its lilt is undeniably infectious. The most famous waltz, *Les Patineurs,* is mirrored in style here by many of the others (*Dans les nuages,* for instance), and there are plenty of good tunes. *Pluie de diamants,* with lots of vitality, is among the more familiar items, as is the sparkling *Très jolie,* but many of the unknown pieces are equally engaging. Like Strauss, Waldteufel usually introduces his waltzes with a section not in waltz-time, and he is ever resourceful in his ideas and in his orchestration. The polkas are robust, but the scoring has plenty of character. The performances here are fully acceptable.

March: *Kamiesch* (arr. Pollack). Polkas: *Bagatelle; En garde!; Trictrac.* Waltzes: *Etincelles; Idyll; Naples; Nid d'amour; Roses de Noël; La Source.*
**(*) Marco Polo 8.223688. Slovak State PO (Košice), Walter.

For this latest in the ongoing Marco Polo series, Christian Pollack made the arrangement of the opening *Kamiesch March* and one could wish he had also conducted the disc, for Alfred Walter is often rather metrical. Yet he opens the charming *Bagatelle* and *Trictrac Polkas* flexibly enough and the closing polka militaire, *En garde!,* suits him admirably. But the main attraction here is the inclusion of half a dozen waltzes, most of them unknown. Walter opens each affectionately enough (none actually begins in waltz tempo), is distinctly beguiling in both *Nid d'amour* and *Roses de Noël* and phrases the horn solo at the beginning of *Naples* very pleasingly. When each gets under way he is spirited; but a little more subtlety, a little less gusto, would have been welcome. Nevertheless the Slovak playing is full of spirit and the recording excellent.

Waltzes: *Acclamations; España; Estudiantina; Les Patineurs.*
(B) ** EMI Encore (ADD) 5 85066-2. Monte Carlo PO, Boskovsky – OFFENBACH *Gaîté Parisienne* (ballet). **

It is good to have this inexpensive reissue of Boskovsky's performances, well recorded in 1976. *Les Patineurs* is the composer's finest waltz, and it is the highlight here, given a splendidly affectionate and sparkling account. *Estudiantina* is similarly vivacious, and *Acclamations* opens very invitingly too; in *España* one feels that Boskovsky could have alluded more subtly to Chabrier's original.

WALLACE, William Vincent
(1812–65)

Celtic Fantasies: Annie Laurie; Auld Lang Syne and The Highland Laddie; The Bard's Legacy; Charlie is my Darling and The Campbells are Coming; Coolun, Gary Owen and St Patrick's Day; Homage to Burns: Impromptu on Somebody and O for Ane and Twenty Tam; Kate Kearney and Tow, row, row; The Keel Row; The Last Rose of Summer; The Meeting of the Walters and Eveleen's Bower; Melodie Irlandaise; The Minstrel Boy and Rory O'More; My Love is like a Red Red Rose and Come o'er the Stream Charlie; Comin' through the Rye; Robin Adair; Roslin Castle and A Highland Lad my Love was Born; Ye Banks and Braes.

(M) ** Cala CACD 88042. Tuck.

William Wallace was born in Waterford, Ireland, and began his career as a bandmaster, later concentrating on the violin, leading the Adelphi Theatre Orchestra in Dublin. In 1829 he heard Paganini and was so mesmerized that he 'stayed up all night' practising that composer's more dashing pieces. When he went to Tasmania (for his health) in 1836, his virtuosity caused a sensation and, moving on to Sydney, he was dubbed the 'Australian Paganini'. He subsequently travelled the world; in New Orleans he met and befriended Gottschalk, and in the early 1840s his playing was to be acclaimed in New York, Boston and Philadelphia. But when he returned to London in 1845 he made his name not with his fiddling, but with his first opera, *Maritana*, the work by which he is now chiefly remembered, although his ballads and songs also became very popular. His *Celtic Fantasias* for piano, based on traditional melodies, are little more than eloborate arrangements, with bravura embellishments which add little except surface gloss. Rosemary Tuck plays them with accomplished sympathy, but cannot make them more than showpieces: the tunes are far more indelible than Wallace's embellishments. She is well recorded.

WALTON, William (1902–83)

(i) *Anniversary Fanfare; Coronation Marches: Crown Imperial; Orb and Sceptre; (ii; v) Cello Concerto; (v) Symphony No. 1 in B flat min.; (iii–v) Belshazzar's Feast; (iv; v) Coronation Te Deum.*

(B) ** Chan. 2-for-1 (ADD/DDD) 241-10 (2). (i) Philh. O, Willcocks; (ii) Kirshbaum; (iii) Milnes; (iv) RSNO Ch.; (v) RSNO, Gibson.

The *Anniversary Fanfare* is designed to lead directly into *Orb and Sceptre*, which is what it does here. However, the Kirshbaum–Gibson reading of the *Cello Concerto* is disappointing, lacking the warmth, weight and expressiveness that so ripe an example of late romanticism demands. And while Gibson's is a well-paced, convincingly idiomatic view of the *First*

Symphony, ensemble is not always bitingly precise enough for this darkly intense music (malice prescribed for the Scherzo, melancholy for the slow movement). The recording is first rate, but with less body than usual from Chandos and with timpani resonantly obtrusive. Gibson's view of Walton's brilliant oratorio *Belshazzar's Feast* tends towards brisk speeds, but is no less dramatic for that. It remains individually competitive, particularly with so magnificent a baritone as Sherrill Milnes as soloist, but overall this is not one of the more enticing issues in Chandos's 2-for-1 series.

Cello Concerto.

☦― *** EMI **DVD** 492840-9. Piatigorsky, BBC SO, Sargent – MENDELSSOHN: *Violin Concerto* **; BEETHOVEN: *Piano Concerto No. 4.* **(*)

Walton's *Cello Concerto* was commissioned by Piatigorsky, who subsequently premièred and recorded it with the Boston Symphony and Charles Munch. This was its British première, at the Royal Albert Hall in February 1957 with Sir Malcolm Sargent conducting the BBC Symphony Orchestra, whose chief conductor he still was. Those who remember hearing the broadcast or who were fortunate enough to have been there will find Piatigorsky's aristocratic account a particularly moving document; and those coming to it without any nostalgic baggage can hardly fail to respond to his blend of virtuosity and restraint. The camerawork is pleasingly restrained and totally free from the intrusive changes of perspective that are inescapable nowadays.

Viola Concerto; Violin Concerto.

(M) *** EMI 5 62813-2. Kennedy, RPO, Previn – VAUGHAN WILLIAMS: *The Lark Ascending.* ***

Kennedy's achievement in giving equally rich and expressive performances of both works makes for an ideal coupling, helped by the unique insight of André Previn as Waltonian. Kennedy on the viola produces tone as rich and firm as on his usual violin. The Scherzo has never been recorded with more panache than here, and the finale brings a magic moment in the return of the main theme from the opening, hushed and intense. In the *Violin Concerto* too, Kennedy gives a warmly relaxed reading, in which he dashes off the bravura passages with great flair. He may miss some of the more searchingly introspective manner of Chung in her 1971 version, but there are few Walton records as richly rewarding as this, helped by warm, atmospheric sound, and with the bonus of Vaughan Williams's *Lark Ascending* this makes an excellent representation for Nigel Kenndy among EMI's 'Great Artists of the Century'.

Violin Concerto.

☦― (M) *** Decca 476 17235. Bell, Baltimore SO, Zinman – BLOCH: *Baal Shem*; BARBER: *Violin Concerto.* ***

From an American perspective, Walton's *Violin Con-*

certo can well be seen as a British counterpart of the Barber, similarly romantic, written at exactly the same period. This prize-winning Decca disc has Bell giving a commanding account of the solo part, even matching Heifetz himself in the ease of his virtuosity. Playing with rapt intensity, Bell treats the central cadenza of the first movement expansively, making it more deeply reflective than usual. Rich and brilliant sound, with the violin balanced forward, but not aggressively so. It won the 1998 *Gramophone* Concerto Award and now reappears at mid-price on Universal's *Gramophone* Award Collection.

(i; ii) *Violin Concerto: Andante tranquillo;* (ii) *Crown Imperial;* (iii) *Façade* (excerpts); (ii) *Henry V: Charge and Battle Musico;* (iv) *Portsmouth Point Overture;* (v) *Symphony No. 2: Passacaglia;* (vi) *5 Bagatelles for Guitar;* (vii) *Belshazzar's Feast* (excerpts); (viii) *Set Me as a Seal upon thine Heart.*
(B) *(*) Decca (ADD/DDD) 470 127-2. (i) Little; (ii) Bournemouth SO, Litton; (iii) Ashcroft, Irons, L. Sinf., Chailly; (iv) LPO, Boult; (v) RPO, Ashkenazy; (vi) Hallé; (vii) LPO Ch. & O, Solti; (viii) Moule, Kendall, Winchester Cathedral Ch., Wayneflete Singers, Hill.

This ill-advised collection in Decca's 'World Of' composer anthologies is much too piecemeal to be satisfying. Boult's mono *Portsmouth Point Overture,* an early 1954 recording, is an obvious piece for inclusion, and the Litton items are well performed in digital sound. The *Façade* excerpts are acceptable, but hardly compare with the Collins–Sitwell complete version. The guitar *Bagatelles* are very well played, but it is frustrating that we are offered only one movement from Tasmin Little's fine performance of the *Violin Concerto.* The programme ends with excerpts from Solti's lively 1977 *Belshazzar's Feast,* which should tempt any listener to explore the complete work. But this is not really the way to approach Walton's music.

Violin Sonata.
(**(*)) Testament mono SBT 1319. Rostal, Horsley – DELIUS: *Violin Sonata No. 2;* ELGAR: *Violin Sonata in E min.* (**(*))

The Walton *Violin Sonata* was still only five years old when Max Rostal and Colin Horsley made this recording for the fledgling Argo company. The original interpreters, Menuhin and Louis Kentner, had already recorded it for EMI, but Rostal, German-born but the most understanding interpreter of English music, and Horsley are even more persuasive, with Rostal overcoming the problems of the dry acoustic, subtly shading his tone as in the haunting recollection of the main theme in the coda of the first movement. Opting generally for faster speeds than Menuhin, Rostal then holds the argument together more tautly in the long set of variations that make up the second movement, playing with rapt concentration, not least in his warmly

persuasive reading of the seventh and last variation, *Andante tranquillo.* The clarity of the clean, fresh Testament transfer quickly allows one to forget the sonic limitations.

Belshazzar's Feast.
(B) (**) CfP mono 585 9042. Milligan, Huddersfield Ch. Soc., RLPO, Sargent – ELGAR: *The Dream of Gerontius.* (***)

Sargent was present at the gestation of *Belshazzar's Feast* and conducted the first performance at the Leeds Festival in 1931, thereafter making it his own for a considerable period. His interpretation is authoritative, but he does not seem to have taken care over detail for this 1958 recording. (Among other things, the anvil to represent the God of Iron is missing.) The rich acoustic of Huddersfield Town Hall adds weight to the sound but robs the choral words of any kind of clarity and bite. James Milligan is a strong soloist, the orchestra plays very well indeed, and the recording is impressively transferred to CD, but overall this was not a jewel in Sargent's choral crown.

(i) *Belshazzar's Feast. Coronation Marches: Crown Imperial; Orb and Sceptre.*
(BB) ** Naxos 8.555869. (i) Purves, Lindley, Laudibus, Huddersfield Ch. Soc., Leeds Philharmonic Soc. Ch.; English N. Philh., Daniel.

The Huddersfield Choral Society made the very first, ground-breaking recording of *Belshazzar's Feast* in 1943 at the height of the Second World War. Here on Naxos, today's choir returns to Walton's colourful masterpiece, joined not only by colleagues from Leeds but by the chamber choir, Laudibus, yet the impression on disc – with the singers set very much behind the orchestra – is regrettably not of massed choirs. That is a disappointment in what in so many ways is a powerful reading, with Paul Daniel a vigorous and generally idiomatic Waltonian, as he has demonstrated in his earlier Walton recordings for Naxos. The vividness of the orchestral sound is most impressive, notably the brass, a valuable asset in this highly coloured work, and the choral balance certainly improves in the central sections, involving praise to the Gods and the actual feast. Yet in the closing, exuberant chorus, *Then Sing Aloud,* the trouble is intensified, for distancing brings disconcertingly cloudy textures, not helped by the extraordinarily fast tempo that Daniel adopts, which also minimizes the rhythmic lift of the jazzy syncopations. Unlike the chorus, the baritone soloist, Christopher Purves, is balanced close, and is generally clean of attack. Andrew Davis with the BBC Singers and Chorus on the rival super-bargain version on Warner Apex (0927 444 394-2 – see our main volume) has choral sound both clearer and more powerful, and that disc also offers a fine performencs of *Job.* The two *Coronation Marches* on Naxos make a comparably ungenerous coupling. Taken from a 1996 disc of Prom favourites, they are very well played and recorded.

WASSENAER, Unico Wilhelm

Concerti armonici Nos. 1–6.
⊕ (BB) *** Hyp. Helios CDH 55155. Brandenburg Cons., Goodman.

These splendid concertos, once attributed to Palestrina, are almost on a par with the *Concerti grossi* of Handel, and they could hardly be better played or recorded than they are here. This bargain reissue sweeps the board (see our main *Guide*).

WATERHOUSE, Graham
(born 1962)

(i) *Celtic Voices, Op. 36/1;* (i;ii) *Chieftain's Salute;* (iii) *Hale Bopp, Op. 36/2;* (iv) *Hymnus, Op. 49;* (i) *Jig, Air & Reel, Op. 8;* (iv) *Mouvements d'Harmonie, Op. 29;* (i) *Sinfonietta.*
*** Mer. CDA 84510. (i) ECO, Traub; (ii) with Waller; (iii) Funnel (treble); (iv) Endymion Ens.

The novelty here is the opening *Chieftain's Salute*, a spectacular concertante work for 'great highland bagpipe' (played with much panache by Graham Waller) and strings. After the introductory 'Scottish Snap', the distant piper moves forward to a set of variations on the seventeenth-century lament, *Lady Doyle's Salute*. Most dramatic is the piquant harmonic clash between the pipes, with their three underlying drones, and the orchestra, which increases as the piper comes nearer, to produce a lively Scottish jig, before the return of the Lament as he departs.

In the works for strings, Graham Waterhouse writes very much within the broad tradition of English string music in a harmonic style that is essentially diatonic, but, by injecting pungent atonal dashes, the composer brings stimulating touches of abrasiveness to the textures. The deftly concise *Sinfonietta* has athletic and delectably astringent outer movements framing a neo-romantic *Adagio* and a fiddle-dominated folksy Scherzo. *Celtic Voices* similarly balances bravura with even warmer lyricism by adding a harmonic flavour of the Phrygian mode.

Hale Bopp mystically celebrates the appearance of the famous comet, then, after gaining momentum, introduces the melody, 'How Brightly Shines the Morning Star', sung hauntingly in the distance by a boy treble, acccompanied by just four string players. Waterhouse's writing for woodwind and horns in the *Mouvements d'Harmonie* has a distinct Gallic flavour, harmonically tangy, while the grave chorale of *Hymnus* recalls a famous carol. The concert ends richly with comparatively simple arrangements of three famous folk tunes, *Roger de Coverley*, the ravishing *Star of the County Down* and the sparkling *Devil among the Tailors*. First-rate playing throughout and

excellent recording, bright but with an attractively spacious acoustic, which adds to the distinction of this collection, another memorable example of Meridian's current exploration of twentieth-century British composers.

WAXMAN, Franz (1906–67)

Film Music: Suites: (i) *The Bride of Frankenstein;* (ii) *The Invisible Ray; Prince Valliant; Rebecca; Suspicion; Taras Bulba.*
*** Silva Screen FILMCD 726. Westminster PO, Alwyn; (ii) City of Prague PO, Bateman.

With a flamboyant introduction that sweeps one into 1930s Hollywood, *The Bride of Frankenstein* – regarded by many as one of the finest 'horror' films ever made – is one of Waxman's most imaginative scores, very colourfully orchestrated, including the use of an ondes martenot – the effect provided here by a synthesizer – to create supernatural effects. There are moments of wit and parody too (Gounod's *Faust* crops up), and one especially enjoys the *Minuet*, most charmingly orchestrated by Clifford Vaughan. As an organist himself, he uses that instrument most effectively, especially in the the delightfully quirky *Danse macabre* – a number that should have a lease of life on its own. Kenneth Alwyn and his orchestra fully re-create the music's evocation.

The more famous suites from *Prince Valliant*, *Taras Bulba* and *Suspicion* are included, as well as *Rebecca* (Waxman's most hauntingly memorable score) and the less familiar *The Invisible Ray*, with the suite assembled by the composer's son, John Waxman. Many of the Waxman manuscripts did not survive, and here Stephen Bernstein orchestrated it completely by ear after listening to the film's soundtrack. Very good performances, and excellent sound too.

WEBER, Carl Maria von (1786–1826)

(i) *Clarinet Concertos Nos. 1 in F min.; 2 in E flat;* (ii) *Konzertstück in F min. for Piano & Orchestra;* (iii) *Invitation to the Dance* (orch. Berlioz), *Op. 65; Overtures: Abu Hassan;* (iv) *Euryanthe; Der Freischütz; Oberon.* (v) *Symphony No. 1 in C., Op. 19;* (vi) *Clarinet Quintet.*
(B) ** Ph. Duo (ADD) 462 868-2 (2). (i) Michallik, Dresden State O, Sanderling; (ii) Magaloff, LSO, C. Davis; (iii) LSO, Mackerras; (iv) Concg. O, Dorati; (v) New Philh. O, Boettcher; (vi) Stahr, Berlin Philharmonic Octet (members).

The two *Clarinet Concertos* are well played by Oskar Michallik, with good support from Sanderling and the fine Dresden orchestra. But, as in Herbert Stahr's Berlin account of the *Quintet*, these artists are at their best in slow movements. Elsewhere, though thoroughly musical, the playing could do with more dash. However, Magaloff's poised and well-characterized account of the *Konzertstück* is most satisfying, well recorded and altogether one of the best versions on the market. The two performances under Mackerras are also a delight: *Abu Hassan* light and sparkling, and an elegant *Invitation to the Dance*. But in the other three overtures, the Concertgebouw string sound as recorded is brilliant to the point of fierceness and the effect is to emphasize Dorati's concentration on drama rather than atmosphere (though there is some beautiful horn playing). However, the engaging *First Symphony* is well served both by the New Philharmonia and by Boettcher, who favours a weighty approach but does not lack a lighter touch when needed. Overall this is fair value.

Symphonies Nos. 1 in C, J.50; 2 in C, J.51.

(BB) ** Warner Apex 2564 60619-2. Norwegian R. O, Rasilainen – WAGNER: *Symphony in C.* **

An inexpensive way of acquiring Weber's two very attractive *Symphonies*, with a Wagner curiosity. The performances are lively and committed, but the recording is not much above average.

OPERA

(i) *Abu Hassan. Symphony No. 1 in C.*

🔊— *** DHM/BMG 054 72 7779-2. (i) Völz, Dürmüller, Stojkovic, Selig, Werk Ruhr Ch.; Cappella Coloniensis of West Deutsche TV & R. Weil.

Abu Hassan is a delightful one-act opera, an early work written in 1811, which, like Mozart's *Entführung*, exploits the fashion for 'Turkish' subjects. In a crisp series of brief numbers – two choruses, two arias, two duets and two trios – it lasts a mere 50 minutes, allowing it to be coupled in this sparkling performance with Weber's equally delightful *Symphony No. 1*. Using period instruments, Bruno Weil gives the score all the lightness and transparency it needs, with a first-rate trio of soloists, all with clear, fresh voices, plus a Narrator who doubles in the role of the Caliph. The only snag for the non-German speaker is that the spoken dialogue separating the musical numbers may prove excessive, but there is generous indexing of tracks to allow it to be omitted, and the well-planned booklet gives German text and English translation. The *Symphony* too gains in point and transparency in this lively performance with period instruments.

Der Freischütz (complete).

(B) ** Double Decca (ADD) 460 194-2 (2). Behrens, Donath, Kollo, Moll, Brendel, Meven, Bav. R. Ch. & SO, Kubelik.

Kubelik takes a direct view of Weber's high romanticism. The result has freshness but lacks something of dramatic bite and atmosphere. There is far less tension than in the finest versions, not least in the Wolf's

Glen scene, which in spite of the full-ranging 1979 recording seems rather tame. The singing is generally good, René Kollo as Max giving one of his best performances on record, but Hildegard Behrens, superbly dramatic in later German operas, here as Agathe seems clumsy in music that often requires a pure lyrical line. The bargain price (without texts) makes the set reasonable value, but the Keilberth mid-priced EMI set is altogether finer (769342-2).

Der Freischütz: Overture.

(M) (***) BBC Legends mono BBCL 4140. New Philh. O, Giulini – BRITTEN: *The Building of the House Overture*; SCHUBERT: *Symphony No. 9.* ***

Recorded in mono at the Royal Festival Hall in December 1970, Giulini's reading of the Weber overture brings a performance of extremes, at once dedicated and dramatic, a valuable addition to the conductor's discography on this disc issued to celebrate his ninetieth birthday.

WEBERN, Anton (1883–1945)

Variations for Piano, Op. 27.

(M) *** DG (ADD) 471 361-2. Pollini– SCHOENBERG: *Piano Concerto & solo piano music.* **(*)

Weber's highly concentrated set of *Variations for Piano* (in three sections), lasting only six minutes, are very impressive in Pollini's hands and make a well-chosen bonus for his coverage of Schoenberg's piano music.

WEILL, Kurt (1900–50)

The Rise and Fall of Mahagonny (complete).

(M) ** Sony SM2K 91184 (2). Lenya, Litz, Günter, Mund, Gollnitz, Sauerbaum, Markwort, Roth, Murch (speaker), NW German R. Ch. & O, Brückner-Rüggeberg.

Though Lotte Lenya, with her metallic, rasping voice, was more a characterful *diseuse* than a singer, and this bitterly inspired score had to be adapted to suit her limited range, it remains a most memorable performance. The recording lacks atmosphere, with voices (Lenya's in particular) close balanced. Yet even now one can understand how this cynical piece caused public outrage when it was first performed in Leipzig in 1930. The one great drawback to this reissue is the lack of any documentation except a single paragraph giving a summary of the plot.

WEISSENBERG, Alexis
(born 1929)

(i) *4 Improvisations on Songs from La Fugue. Le Regret; Sonata en état de jazz.*

* (**) Nim. NI 5688. Mulligan; (i) with Walden.

As with other composer-pianists who have a wide repertoire, Weissenberg's own music does not project a strong individuality. La Fugue was a musical comedy for which he wrote the score in Paris in the 1960s. It was revived as a 'surrealistic musical' in Darmstadt in 1992, with the new name Nostalgia. The first of the Four Improvisations is a jazzy, jittery tarantella, brilliantly played here; the other three bear out the title admirably, with Frank Walden on saxophone joining the pianist to create the smoky, late-evening atmosphere in the second piece, Mon destin. Le Regret is also written in a gentle, improvisatory style, which seems to be the composer's forte, for it is the third movement of the Jazz Sonata, the rather haunting Reflets d'un blues, which is the most beguiling. The other three, which in turn supposedly embody the spirit of the tango, charleston and samba, are somewhat intractable, and not very successful in their evocation, although the final Provocation de samba is the most rhythmically inventive. Weissenberg could not have a more committed advocate than Simon Mulligan, who plays with great flair and conviction, and is very well recorded. But this is not a disc for the general collector.

WELLESZ, Egon (1885–1974)

Die Bakchantinnen.

*** Orfeo Musica Rediviva C136012H (2). Mohr, Burt, Stamm, Alexander, Barainsky, Breedt, Aschenbach, Gottschick, Berlin R. Ch., Deutsches SO, Albrecht.

During the 1920s and 1930s Wellesz was better known as an operatic musicologist than as a composer. In England, to which he came at the time of the Anschluss, it was his eminence as a scholar in the field of early Christian and Byzantine hymnology and as a historian of opera that overshadowed his creative work. It was for his research on Giuseppe Bonno (a contemporary of Gluck), Cavalli and Venetian opera, Antonio Cesti and the development of opera and oratorio in Vienna that his reputation rested. True, Oxford put on his charming opera Incognita in a student performance under Sir Jack Westrup in 1951, but otherwise, apart from the rare broadcast from Austria, his operas remain unknown. His symphonies remain unrecorded, and Die Bakchantinnen is the first of his operas to reach CD.

He wrote five operas between 1921 and 1931, and Die Bakchantinnen, for which he supplied his own libretto in 1930, was his last. Premièred in Vienna under Clemens Krauss the following year, it leaves no doubts about his mastery of dramatic pacing and momentum nor about the quality of his musical imagination. Wellesz's musical language is tonal and direct in appeal, and though he was close to the Schoenberg–Berg–Webern circle (he was Schoenberg's first biographer), he is very different from them. He is a master of the orchestra and writes effectively for the voice, as in Agave's exchanges with Ino in Act II. Almost the most impressive thing is the extensive (and often high-

lying) choral writing. The choir plays a prominent role throughout, and Wellesz's choral writing is consistently powerful. What impresses – more than the dramatic characterization – is the sense of line, which is so much stronger than in Schreker, whose refined palette and exotic scoring are far removed from his world. Unlike Schreker, Wellesz never set great store by pure harmonic effect. Melodic lines are often angular but always move purposefully, and there is atmosphere and a strong responsiveness to dramatic mood. The cast is strong, in particular Roberta Alexander's Agave, even if Thomas Mohr's Dionysos shows the occasional sign of strain. The chorus and orchestra give a good account of themselves under Gerd Albrecht. The recording balance is well judged and the overall sound is very good. The notes are in German and English, but not in French, and the libretto is not offered in translation. Let us hope that Orfeo will go on to record Alkestis and the often enchanting Incognita.

Prospero's Spell (Prosperos Beschwörungen), Op. 53;
(i) Violin Concerto, Op. 84.

*** Orfeo C478 981A. V. RSO, Albrecht; (i) with Löwenstein.

Egon Wellesz pursued a dual career as a scholar and composer. Prosperos Beschwörungen (1935) is a highly imaginative score; Wellesz had toyed with the idea of writing an opera on The Tempest but these five orchestral pieces were the result. They are quite individual, though they are closer to Hindemith than to the Second Viennese school. The Violin Concerto (1961) is a made of sterner stuff and it provides a formidable challenge to the soloist, to which Andrea Duka Löwenstein rises triumphantly. Good playing from the ORF (Oesterreiches Rundfunk) or Vienna Radio Orchestra under Gerd Albrecht. Good sound, though perhaps a little studio bound.

Symphonies Nos. 2 in E flat (English), Op. 65; 9, Op. 111.

*** CPO 999 997-2. V. RSO, Rabl.

The first issue in the Wellesz symphony series brought us Nos. 4, 6 and 7. During the 1920s and '30s his work as a scholar – he was a leading authority on Baroque opera, on Byzantine and early Christian hymnology, and Professor of Musicology in Vienna – consumed much of his energies. His main creative preoccupation at that period and after he settled in Oxford in 1938 was with opera but wartime conditions and the British indifference to opera led to a creative hiatus. He did not turn to the symphony until he was sixty in 1945. No. 2 dates from 1947–8 and was first given in Vienna under Karl Rankl. RL recalls hearing the BBC première by the BBC Symphony Orchestra under Sir Adrian Boult (though he does not recall it ever being called 'The English'). Its subtitle apparently derived from the fact that Wellesz had steeped himself in English literature at the time of its competition. It is the longest of the nine and is consistently tonal, and the theme of its Scherzo stays with you, once heard. The *Ninth* comes from 1970, when Wellesz was eighty-five, and shows him losing none of his mastery, despite his frail health. Wellesz was also a master of the orchestra (his musical calligraphy, incidentally, resembled Strauss in its clarity) and he understood the symphonic process inside out. Gottfried Rabl and the Vienna Radio Symphony Orchestra do justice to these scores, and the recording is admirably balanced.

WERT, Giaches de (1535–96)

Madrigals: *Ahì, come soffirò; Amor che sai; L'anima mia ferita; Con voi giocando, Amor; Crudelissima doglia; Del vago Mincio; Dica chi vuoi; Dolci spoglie; Forsennata grivada; Giunto a la tomba; Io non son però; M'ha punt'Amor; Misera, che farò; Non sospirar, pastor; Nova amor, nove fiamme, e nova legge; Occhi, de l'alma mia; O come vaneggiate, Donna; Questi odorate fiori; Soccorete, bem mio; Solo e pensoso; Sorgi e rischiara; Vago augeletto; Vezzosi augeli; Voglia mi vien; Voi ch'ascoltate.*

(B) **(*) HM HMX 2901621. Cantus Cöln, Junghänel.

Giaches de Wert was one of the most notable of the Flemish composers who travelled abroad to work in Italy. He was Monteverdi's predecessor in Mantua at the court of Count Alfonso. Over half a century, between 1558 and 1608, he published 16 books of madrigals, and the present well-contrasted selection dips into nearly all of them, but concentrates mainly on Book 7, published in 1581. The opening madrigal, *Vezzosi augelli* ('Graceful Birds among the Green Branches') is charmingly light-hearted, but many of the other settings are concerned with the trials and disappointments of love. *Forsenatta grivada 'O te che porte'* ('Frantically she cried: "O you who bear away part of me with you"') is passionately declamatory and strongly sung here, but *Dolci spoglie* and *Misera, che farò* are very doleful indeed. Yet there is light relief too, and *Con voi giocando, Amor* is a charming scherzando. As in a previous (deleted) selection from Anthony Rooley's Consort of Musicke, De Wert certainly emerges here as a composer of expressive depth and personality, with a fine feeling for words. The Cologne performances, like their English predecessors, are richly blended, expressive and animated. Perhaps they are a shade too refined, not Italianate enough in feeling, but they are still very enjoyable, and are excellently recorded.

WEYSE, Christoph Ernst Friedrich (1774–1842)

Sovedrikke (The Sleeping Draught).
**(*) da capo 8.224149. Soloists, Sokkelund Ch., Danish R. Sinf., Bellincampi.

The Sleeping Draught was mounted in 1809 to great acclaim: the present issue is its first recording and indeed the first of any of Weyse's operas. The action is not easily summarized and calls for nine characters who are all pretty two-dimensional. There is scant opportunity for characterization and perhaps the most impressive things are the multi-movement finales: that of the first act runs for some 19 minutes. The cast is generally very good and the singing never falls below a decent level of accomplishment, and the sole aria (a kind of catalogue aria) of the baritone Guido Paëvatalu gives much pleasure. The Danish Radio Sinfonietta under Giordano Bellincampi are lively and enthusiastic, and the recording is eminently well balanced and warm. It comes with extensive and authoritative essays by Jørgen Hansen on the historical background and the development of the singspiel in Denmark as well as on Weyse himself. *Sovedrikke* is a fresh and pleasing entertainment for which few would make great claims but which has a lot of charm and is well worth hearing.

Symphonies Nos. 1 in G min., DF117; 2 in C, DF118; 3 in D, DF119.
**(*) da capo 8.224012. Royal Danish O, Schønwandt.

The example of Haydn affected Weyse strongly, and the minor-key symphonies in particular are reminiscent of Haydn's *Sturm und Drang* symphonies. Michael Schønwandt gives vital yet sensitive accounts of all three symphonies and is well served by the engineers. This lively music is worth investigating.

Piano Sonatas Nos. 5 in E; 6 in B flat; 7 in A min.; 8 in G min.
** da capo 8.224140. Trondhjem.

The German-born Weyse played a key role in the development of song in Denmark, but he was also a fine pianist and, among other things, introduced some of the Mozart concertos to Copenhagen. These sonatas come from 1799, though the *Eighth in G minor* was not published until 1818. They are very much in the tradition of Clementi, Haydn and C. P. E. Bach, whose pupil Weyse nearly became. The *Eighth* even suggests the Beethoven of Op. 26. They employ a limited range of pianistic devices but have a certain grace. Thomas Trondhjem gives very acceptable performances and is decently recorded.

WHITLOCK, Percy (1903–46)

Ballet of the Wood Creatures; Balloon Ballet; Come Along, Marnie; Dignity and Impudence March. The Feast of St Benedict: Concert Overture. Holiday Suite; Music for Orchestra: Suite. Susan, Doggie and Me; Wessex Suite.
**(*) Marco Polo 8.225162. Dublin RTE Concert O, Sutherland.

Percy Whitlock's style is attractive and easy-going, with quite imaginative orchestration and nice touches everywhere. The marches are jolly and the waltzes nostalgic – *The Ballet of the Wood Creatures* is especially charming. Gavin Sutherland directs the RTE Orchestra with his usual understanding. The sound is good, but occasionally the strings sound a little scrawny (the opening of *Waltz* in the *Holiday Suite*, for example).

WIDOR, Charles-Marie (1844–1937)

Symphonies Nos. 3 in E min., Op. 13/2: excerpts: Prélude; Adagio; Finale. 4 in F min., Op. 13/4; 9 (Gothique), Op. 70.
(M) ★★★ Warner Elatus (ADD) 2564 60341-2. Alain (Cavaillé-Coll organ of L'Eglise St-Germain, St Germain-en-Laye).

In the hands of Marie-Claire Alain, the St-Germain organ sounds very orchestral, and the colouring of the gentle *Adagio* (a perpetual canon) of the *Third Symphony*, and the *Andante cantabile* of No. 4 are quite haunting. The spectacular Wagnerian finale of this *E minor Symphony* (played in the revised, 1901 version) with its cascading sextuplets is not musically as well focused as the more famous *Toccata*, which closes its successor, but it sounds very exciting here and, as it ends gently, the opening *Toccata* of No. 4 makes a bold contrast. The *Gothic Symphony* has a notable third movement in which a Christmas chant (*Puer natus est nobis*) is embroidered fugally. The final section is a set of variations, and the Gregorian chant is reintroduced in the pedals. These are classic performances, given spacious, analogue sound, with just a touch of harshness to add a little edge to *fortissimos*.

WIKMANSON, Johan (1753–1800)

String Quartet No. 2 in E min., Op. 1/2.
(M) ★★★ CRD 3361. Chilingirian Qt – BERWALD: *String Quartet No. 1.* ★★★

Johan Wikmanson is even more neglected than Berwald – though more understandably so. He spent some 30 years working for the Royal Lottery in Sweden and studied with both Kraus and the Abbé Vogler. He attained some eminence as an organist, translated Tartini's *Traité des agréments de la musique* into Swedish, and towards the end of his short life became Director of the Swedish Royal Academy of Music's conservatory. His three quartets are all modelled on Haydn and were published thanks to the latter's acceptance of their dedication. While the Chilingirians do not always observe every dynamic nuance of the 1970 Critical Edition, they play the work with genuine commitment and, in the case of the slow movement, charm – though it is for the interesting 1818 Berwald *Quartet* that collectors will investigate this. The 1979 recording stands up well.

WILLIAMS, John (born 1932)

Film Music: *Close Encounters of the Third Kind; E.T.; Raiders of the Lost Ark; Star Wars Trilogy; Superman* (with COURAGE: *Star Trek: theme*).
(M) ★★(★) Telarc CD 80094. Cincinnati Pops O, Kunzel.

The Telarc recording is certainly spectacular and the concert has a synthesized prologue and epilogue to underline the sci-fi associations. The inclusion of the famous *Star Trek* signature theme (a splendid tune) is wholly appropriate. The orchestra plays this music with striking verve, and the sweeping melody of *E.T.* is especially effective; but the overall effect is very brash, with the microphones seeking brilliance in the sound-balance (though for some that will be its attraction).

WILLIAMS, Charles (1893–1978)

The Bells of St Clements; Blue Devils; Cross Country; Cutty Sark; Destruction by Fire; Devil's Galop; (i) *The Dream of Olwen. The Girls in Grey; High Adventure (Friday Night is Music Night); The Humming Top; Jealous Lover; Little Tyrolean; London Fair; Model Railway;* (i) *The Music Lesson. The Night Has Eyes; Nursery Clock; The Old Clockmaker; Rhythm on Rails; Sally Tries the Ballet; Starlings; Throughout the Years; The Voice of London; Young Ballerina (The Potter's Wheel).*
(M) ★★★ ASV WHL 2151. BBC Concert O, Wordsworth,
  (i) with Elms.

Rather like Henry Mancini and his *Pink Panther* theme, if Charles Williams had written only *Devil's Galop* (aka the *Dick Barton* theme), he would certainly be remembered, and it is brilliantly done here. Older listeners will surely recognize *Girls in Grey* and *The Potter's Wheel* from early 1950s television, and also *High Adventure* (used for *Friday Night Is Music Night* on Radio 2). Film buffs will know the themes from *The Apartment* and the pseudo-romantic piano concerto *The Dream of Olwen* – not in the league of the *Warsaw Concerto* but curiously haunting nevertheless, and certainly more durable than the film for which it was written (*While I Live*). Williams wrote a great deal of attractive, unpretentious music, much of included on this generously filled CD. There are plenty of 'character' numbers, such as *The Music Lesson*, with metronome and scales interspersed with a most attractive theme, and the *The Nursery Clock*, a perky little vignette, just on the right side of twee. *The Little Tyrolean* gently evokes the world of the Strauss family, while *The Humming Top* is reminiscent of Bizet's *Jeux d'enfants*. England of the 1950s is evoked in *Cross Country* (1954) and *London Fair* (1955), while railway travel of the period is recalled in *Model Railway* (1951) and the even better remembered *Rhythm on the Rails* (1950). *The Bells of St Clements* is a charming fantasy based on the popular nursery rhyme, while the composer is in more dramatic mode for *Destruction by Fire*, depicting the wartime Blitz. In the 1960s, Oxford University invited Williams to receive an honorary doctorate. He declined, considering himself unworthy. It's hard to imagine too many composers of popular music doing that today! Recording and performances are both excellent.

WILLIAMSON, Malcolm
(1931–2003)

Double Concerto for 2 Pianos & Strings.
**(*) Australian ABC Eloquence 426 483-2.
  Williamson, Campion, Tasmanian SO, Tuckwell –
  EDWARDS: *Piano Concerto* **(*); SCULTHORPE:
  Piano Concerto. **(*)

Williamson's *Concerto for Two Pianos* has been recorded before (by EMI), but that is not currently available. This performance of this distinctive, but fairly tough – though by no means unapproachable – work is committed, well performed and reasonably well recorded, and is part of a valuable trilogy of rare concertos.

WINDING, August (1835–99)

Piano Concerto in A min., Op. 19; Concert Allegro in C min., Op. 29.
**(*) Danacord DACOCD 581. Marshev, Danish PO,
  South Jutland, Aeschbacher – E. HARTMANN:
  Piano Concerto. *(*)

August Winding belonged to Grieg's circle of Copenhagen friends (Grieg introduced his *Overture to a Norwegian Tragedy* to Christiania, as Oslo was then known). He studied with Gade, Reinecke and Dreyschock and had a flourishing but short career as a virtuoso pianist before a nervous complaint in his arm forced him to give up concert work. His *Piano Concerto* shares the same key but not the same opus number as the Grieg. The concerto is small talk, very derivative and much indebted to Gade and Mendelssohn. It has a certain charm, even if the ideas are pretty unmemorable. The *Concert Allegro* is eminently Schumannesque, but is so brilliantly played by the Russian virtuoso Oleg Marshev and the Danish orchestra that one is almost tempted to believe that it is better than it is. Winding shares the disc with his brother-in-law, Emil Hartmann.

WOLF, Hugo (1860–1903)

Italienisches Liederbuch (complete).
🎵 (M) ★★★ EMI (ADD) 5 62650-2 [5 62651-2].
  Schwarzkopf, Fischer-Dieskau, Moore.

The classic Schwarzkopf–Fischer-Dieskau set now reappears – rightly – as one of EMI's 'Great Record-

ings of the Century'. Few artists today can match the searching perception of these two great singers in this music, with Fischer-Dieskau using his sweetest tones and Schwarzkopf ranging through all the many emotions inspired by love. Gerald Moore is at his finest, and the well-balanced (1969) recording sounds better than ever.

WOLF-FERRARI, Ermanno
(1876–1948)

The Jewels of the Madonna: Dances and Intermezzi.
School for Fathers: Overture & Intermezzo.
Susanna's Secret: Overture.
(★★★) Testament mono SBT 1327. Philh. O, Mackerras
  – PONCHIELLI: *La Gioconda: Dance of the Hours*
  ★★★; VERDI: Overtures and ballet music. (★★★)

As the opening section in this mixed bag of Mackerras's recordings from the 1950s, the charming Wolf-Ferrari pieces are delectably done, not just popular favourites like the overture to *Susanna's Secret* and the second *Intermezzo* from *The Jewels of the Madonna*, but the other miniatures too. The mono recording is clear and well balanced.

YSAŸE, Eugène (1858-1931)

6 Sonatas for Solo Violin, Op. 27.
🎵 (BB) ★★★ Naxos 8.555996. Kaler.
(M) ★★★ Oehms OC 236. Schmid.

As is well known, the six sonatas Ysaÿe published in 1924 were written for the six greatest virtuosi of the day: Szigeti, Kreisler, Enescu, Jacques Thibaud and (less well remembered nowadays) Manuel Quiroga and Matthieu Grickboom. They are held in special regard by violinists who enjoy overcoming the technical challenges they pose. Ilya Kaler was a gold medallist in the Sibelius, Paganini and Tchaikovsky competitions and is a virtuoso of the first order. These are commanding accounts, which characterize the particular qualities of each *Sonata* to impressive effect; even if it did not enjoy a competitive price advantage it would be our preferred first choice.

No one investing in Benjamin Schmid's recording (and the outlay is modest) will be disappointed, for these performances are full of imagination and this is satisfying in its own right. However, Kaler makes one see these pieces in a fresher light.

ZELENKA, Jan (1679–1745)

Missa Dei Filii, ZWV 20; Litaniae Laurentanae, ZWV 152.
🎵 (M) ★★★ DHM/BMG 82876 60159-2. Argenta,
  Chance, Prégardien, G. Jones, Stuttgart Chamber
  Ch., Tafelmusik, Bernius.

This fine reissue offers not only one of Zelenka's late

masses, but also a splendid *Litany*, confirming him – for all the obscurity he suffered in his lifetime – as one of the most inspired composers of his generation. The *Missa Dei Filii* ('Mass for the Son of God') is a 'short' Mass, consisting of *Kyrie* and *Gloria* only. Some of the movements into which the two sections are divided are brief to the point of being perfunctory, but the splendid soprano solo in the *Christe eleison* points forward to the magnificent setting of the *Gloria*, in which the first two sections and the last are wonderfully expansive, ending with a sustainedly ingenious fugue. It seems that Zelenka never heard that Mass, but his *Litany*, another refreshing piece, was specifically written when the Electress of Saxony was ill. Zelenka, like Bach, happily mixes fugal writing with newer-fangled concertato movements. Bernius provides well-sprung support with his period-instrument group, Tafelmusik, and his excellent soloists and choir.

I Penitenti Sepolcro del Redentore (The Penitents at the Tomb of the Redeemer).

(M) **★★★** Sup. SU 3785-2. Kožena, Prokeš, Pospíšil, Capella Regia Musicalis, Hugo.

Thanks to a series of fine recordings, mainly of his instrumental music, Jan Dismas Zelenka has at last, two and a half centuries late, come to be appreciated as one of the most original composers among Bach's contemporaries. Bach himself understood that this second of Zelenka's oratorios, written in 1736 but apparently never performed then, hardly matches his instrumental music in daring; nevertheless its five arias and linking recitatives are both lively and inventive. The poem of Stefano Palavicini, with an Italian text, brings linked meditations from three biblical figures, not just Mary Magdalene and St Peter from Christ's own lifetime but his ancestor, the Psalmist, King David. When the arias are extended pieces, drama plays little part in the piece, and this performance recorded in Prague in 1994, is not helped by the rather colourless timbre of the tenor Martin Prokeš as King David, making the first aria with its da capo repeat seem very long indeed. The mezzo, Maddalena Kožena, then at the beginning of her career, is quite different, singing superbly in Mary's two big arias well as the recitatives, already an outstanding artist. As St Peter Michael Pospíšil sings vehemently in his characterful defiance aria, *Lingua perfida*, condemning the slander which made this outspoken disciple deny Christ, at the expense in places of clean vocalising. A fascinating rarity.

ZIEHRER, Carl Michael
(1843–1922)

Auersperg-Marsch; Landstreicher-Quadrille. Polkas: *Burgerlich und romantisch; Pfiffig; Die Tänzerin;*

Loslassen! Waltzes: *Clubgeister; Diesen Kuss der ganzen Welt; Libesrezepte; Osterreich in Tönen; Wiener Bürger.*

★★(★) Marco Polo 8.223814. Razumovsky Sinfonia, Walter.

Fächer-polonaise; Mein Feld ist die Welt-Marsch. Polkas: *Endlich allein! Im Fluge; Lieber Bismarck, schaukle nicht; Matrosen.* Waltzes: *Heimatsgefühle; Herreinspaziert!; Sei brav; In der Sommerfrische; Tolles Mädel.*

★★(★) Marco Polo 8.223815. Razumovsky Sinfonia, Dittrich.

Ziehrer's style is very much in the Johann Strauss tradition but, unlike many of Strauss's rivals, Ziehrer's music has a distinctive, robust quality, probably attributable to his career as a military band leader for many years. His music overflows with tunes, is thoroughly entertaining, and will disappoint no one who responds to the Viennese tradition.

Volume 1 opens with his most famous piece, *Wiener Bürger*, a delightful waltz that rivals the best of Strauss. The *Die Tänzerin* polka uses as its basis themes from the opera of the same name – to invigorating effect; the *Landstreicher-Quadrille* is composed in the same way, and contains some particularly jaunty numbers. Not surprisingly, Ziehrer was adept at writing marches, and the *Auersperg-Marsch* is one of his best – it had to be repeated several times at its première. The almost forgotten *Osterreich in Tönen Waltz (Melodies of Austria)* is another highlight: all its melodies are in fact original, but it has an agreeably localized ethnic flavour.

Volume 2 offers more of the same: it begins with the fine *Herreinspaziert Waltz*, which soon lunges into a richly contoured theme to rival *Wiener Bürger*. The *Fächer* ('Fan') polonaise is memorable, and is still used to introduce the prestigious annual Philharmonic Ball in Vienna. The polkas are wittily crafted, and none of the waltzes here is without at least one memorable theme. The *Tolles Mädel* ('Crazy Girl') waltz even begins to look forward to the American musical and is a winner in every way, as is the *Sei brav* ('Be Good') waltz – a lively confection of music from Ziehrer's operetta *Fesche Geister* ('Lively Spirits').

The performances from both conductors are lively and sympathetic, the recordings bright and vivid (the second disc a little less so), and the sleeve-notes helpful and informative.

Marches: *Auf! in's XX; Freiherr von Schönfeld; Wen mann Geld hat, ist man fein!* Polkas: *Ballfieber; Ein Blich nach Ihr!; Cavallerie; Wurf-Bouquet.* Styrien Tänze: *D'Kermad'ln;* Waltzes: *Auf hoher See!; Gebirgskinder; Ich lach'!; O, dies Husaren!; Zichrereien.*

★★★ Marco Polo 8.225172. Razumovsky Sinfonia, Pollack.

Volume 3 is easily the finest Ziehrer collection so far, and one laments again that Christian Pollack, who is a master of Viennese rhythmic inflexion, did not direct the other two (and indeed all the Strauss family collections). The three marches have a lighthearted zest (*Wenn man Geld hat* almost sounds like Lehár). *Auf hoher See* opens with a trumpet/cornet solo, and not surprisingly the brass take the lead in the *Cavallerie Polka*, while the *Ballfieber* polka français is also most beguiling, and Pollack's bold accents in *Wurf-Bouquet* add lift rather than heaviness. The charming waltzes bounce along engagingly. *O, dies Hasaren!* has been rescued from its surviving piano score and orchestrated jointly by Martin Uhl and Pollack with idiomatic skill; and how beautifully Pollack opens the *Gebirgskinder*, with a zither solo reminiscent of Johann's *Tales from the Vienna Woods*. Indeed this is another of Ziehrer's waltzes with a string of melodies all but worthy of that master. The orchestra responds with lilt and sparkle throughout, and the recording cannot be faulted.

ZWILICH, Ellen (born 1939)

Symphony No. 2.

** First Edition LCD 002. Louisville O, Leighton Smith
  – HINDEMITH: *Piano Concerto* **(*) (with
  LAWHEAD: *Aleost* *(*)).

Ellen Taaffe Zwilich was a pupil of Dohnányi. Her *First Symphony* (1982) won a Pulitzer Prize and prompted the San Francisco Orchestra to commission the *Second Symphony* in 1985. The work is called a 'cello symphony', since the cellos play a dominant role in the musical argument. The invention is solid and well argued, rather than inspired; it is music that commands respect, though it is not easy to discern a voice of strong individuality. Good playing and decent recording.

CONCERTS OF ORCHESTRAL AND CONCERTANTE MUSIC

Art of conducting

'*The art of conducting*': Vol. 1: '*Great conductors of the past*' (Barbirolli, Beecham, Bernstein, Busch, Furtwängler, Karajan, Klemperer, Koussevitzky, Nikisch, Reiner, Stokowski, Richard Strauss, Szell, Toscanini, Walter, Weingartner): BRUCKNER: *Symphony No. 7* (rehearsal) (Hallé O, Barbirolli). GOUNOD: *Faust: ballet music* (with rehearsal) (RPO, Beecham). Silent film (BPO, Nikisch). Richard STRAUSS: *Till Eulenspiegel* (VPO, Richard Strauss). WEBER: *Der Freischütz: Overture* (Paris SO, Felix Weingartner). WAGNER: *Tannhäuser: Overture* (Dresden State O, Fritz Busch). MOZART: *Symphony No. 40* (BPO, Bruno Walter). BRAHMS: *Symphony No. 2* (rehearsal) (Vancouver Festival O, Bruno Walter). BEETHOVEN: *Egmont: Overture; Symphony No. 9* (Philh. O, Klemperer). WAGNER: *Die Meistersinger: Overture.* SCHUBERT: *Symphony No. 8* (Unfinished). BRAHMS: *Symphony No. 4* (both rehearsals) (BPO, Furtwängler). VERDI: *La forza del destino: Overture; La Traviata: Coro di zingarelle.* RESPIGHI: *The Pines of Rome* (NBC SO, Toscanini). PURCELL (arr. Stokowski): *Dido and Aeneas: Dido's lament.* RESPIGHI: *The Pines of Rome* (BBC SO). TCHAIKOVSKY: *Symphony No. 5* (NYPO) (all cond. Stokowski). BEETHOVEN: *Egmont overture* (Boston SO, Koussevitzky). TCHAIKOVSKY: *Violin Concerto* (Heifetz, NYPO, Reiner). BEETHOVEN: *Symphony No. 7* (Chicago SO, Reiner). BRAHMS: *Academic Festival Overture.* BEETHOVEN: *Symphony No. 5* (Cleveland O, Szell). BEETHOVEN: *Symphony No. 5.* DEBUSSY: *La Mer* (BPO, Karajan). SHOSTAKOVICH: *Symphony No. 5* (rehearsal and performance) (LSO). MAHLER: *Symphony No. 4* (VPO) (both cond. Bernstein). BEETHOVEN: *Symphony No. 9* (Philh. O, Klemperer). (Commentary by John Eliot Gardiner, Isaac Stern, Jack Brymer, Beecham, Menuhin, Oliver Knussen, Suvi Raj Grubb, Szell, Walter, Klemperer, Hugh Bean, Werner Thärichen, Richard Mohr, Stokowski, Julius Baker, Karajan).
⚙ ✱✱✱ Teldec **DVD** 0927 42667-2.

This extraordinary DVD offers a series of electrifying performances by the great conductors of our century, all seen and heard at their very finest. Enormous care has been taken over the sound, even in the earliest recordings, for it is remarkably full-bodied and believable. But most of all it is to watch conductors weaving their magic spell over the orchestra which is so fascinating. And sometimes they do it imperceptibly, like Richard Strauss conducting *Till Eulenspiegel* with apparent nonchalance, yet making music with the utmost aural vividness; Fritz Busch creating great tension in Wagner; Bruno Walter wonderfully mellow in Brahms; Klemperer in Beethoven hardly moving his baton and yet completely in control; Furtwängler rehearsing the finale of Brahms's *Fourth Symphony* with a tremendous flow of adrenalin; Toscanini the martinet in Verdi; Stokowski moulding gloriously beautiful sound with flowing movements of his hands and arms; and, most riveting of all, Bernstein creating enormous passion with the LSO in Shostakovich's *Fifth Symphony*.

Of the many commentaries from other artists and various musicians, the experience of Werner Thärichen stands out. He was participating in a Berlin performance when he suddenly realized that the sound around him had changed: it had become uncannily more beautiful. Not understanding why, he looked to the back of the hall . . . and saw that Furtwängler had just walked in. The great Nikisch is seen conducting (on silent film) but not heard – and no one knows what the music was!

The collection opens fascinatingly with Toscanini (1952), Karajan (1957), Klemperer and Szell (1961) heard consecutively conducting an excerpt from Beethoven's *Fifth Symphony*.

Ančerl, Karel

SHOSTAKOVICH: *Festive Overture.* NOVAK: *In the Tatra Mountains.* KREJCI: *Serenade.* JANACEK: *Taras Bulba.* MACHA: *Variations on a Theme by and on the Death of Jan Rychlík* (all with Czech PO). SMETANA: *Má Vlast: Vltava.* DVORAK: *Slavonic Dance No. 8, Op. 46/8* (with VSO). *Symphony No. 8 in G.* (with Concg. O. MARTINU: *Symphony No. 5* (with Toronto SO).

(B) (★★★) EMI mono/stereo 5 75091-2 (2).

The earliest recording in this Ančerl anthology is the Novák, made in 1950 and familiar to LP collectors from the old mono Supraphon catalogue. It sounds very good here, though naturally it is lacking in transparency of a more modern recording. The *Serenade for Orchestra* of Iša Krejči is extrovert and diatonic; the composer was a school friend of Ančerl and, subsequently, a colleague in pre-war Prague Radio. Recorded in 1957, it is unremittingly cheerful but completely unmemorable. The transfer of Ančerl's classic (1959) account of *Taras Bulba* is excellent and the *Variations on a Theme by and on the Death of Jan Rychlík* by Otmar Mácha – whose representation in the catalogue is slender – is rather haunting. The 1958 *Vltava*, recorded in Vienna, is first rate both as performance and as sound. The Dvořák *Eighth Symphony* is relatively late, coming from a 1970 guest appearance with the Concertgebouw, and there is a bright and vital account of the Martinů *Fifth Symphony* from a 1971 Toronto concert. Even if the quality of the Canadian strings is not as fine-grained or as well blended as the Czech Philharmonic in the earlier commercial records, this still well worth having. The presentation is exemplary, with authoritative notes from Patrick Lambert. Incidentally there is a misprint on the back of the disc, which gives Ančerl's date of death as 1967.

Argenta, Ataúlfo

LISZT: *A Faust Symphony.* RAVEL: *Alborada del gracioso.* FALLA: *El amor brujo* (with Ana Maria Iriate; all with Paris Conservatoire O). SCHUBERT: *Symphony No. 9 in C (Great)* (with O des Cento Soli).

(B) (★★(★)) EMI mono/stereo 5 75097-2 (2).

Whether or not this set does full justice to Ataúlfo Argenta is a moot point. His mono account of the *Faust Symphony* was made in 1955 without the choral ending Liszt added later. It was soon superseded by the Beecham, which was in stereo and which had Liszt's choral afterthoughts. This is a performance of some merit but it does not have the imaginative flair and dramatic fire of Argenta's *Symphonie fantastique*, which soon acquired cult status after its appearance in 1958. (It was even reissued in an LP custom pressing a few years ago.) His Schubert *Great C major* with the Orchestre des Cento Soli, made for the Club Français du Disque and available in England only from one of the then emerging LP clubs, was also stereo. It is a spirited account though not perhaps with the natural flair he brought to early twentieth-century music, as evinced in the 1951 *El amor brujo* (mono) and the Ravel. Sadly, his early death at only forty-four brought to an end a career of already some fulfilment but even more exceptional promise.

Barbirolli, Sir John

ELGAR: *Enigma Variations.* RAVEL: *Ma Mère l'Oye* (suite) (both with Hallé O). WAGNER: *Die Meistersinger: Prelude* (with LSO). MAHLER: *Symphony No. 2 (Resurrection)* (with Donath, Finnilä, Stuttgart R. Ch. & SO). PUCCINI: *Madama Butterfly: Love Duet* (with Scotto, Bergonzi, Rome Opera O).

(B) (★★★) EMI mono/stereo 5 75100-2 (2).

This valuable set brings out of limbo Barbirolli's 1956 Pye version of Elgar's *Enigma Variations* – his first in stereo but largely forgotten thanks to the excellence of his EMI recording of six years later – and offers for the first time a radio recording from Stuttgart of a Mahler symphony Barbirolli never otherwise put on commercial disc, No. 2. This radio recording of the Mahler dates from April 1970, the year Barbirolli died, and although dynamic contrasts tend to be ironed out a little, the warmth and concentration of Barbirolli in Mahler come over from first to last, leading up to a thrilling account of the choral finale, with the re-creation of Judgement Day thrillingly caught. The acoustic seems to open up the moment the voices enter, with the excellent soloists, Helen Donath and Birgit Finnilä, and the massed chorus all sounding full and vivid. The *Meistersinger Prelude*, recorded by EMI the previous year with the LSO, brings a weighty reading at broad speeds. After that the Pye recordings both of *Enigma* and of the Ravel *Mother Goose Suite* are more limited in different ways. The Ravel brings up-front sound with good, bright reproduction of percussion. In the Elgar the playing may not be as refined as in the much-loved EMI stereo version with the Philharmonia of 1962, but the Hallé with Barbirolli somehow convey an extra emotional tug, whether in *Nimrod* or the passionate climax of the finale. As a welcome supplement comes the heart-warming extract from Barbirolli's Rome recording for EMI of Puccini's *Madama Butterfly* with Renata Scotto and Carlo Bergonzi, as loving an account of the Act I duet as you will ever hear.

Beecham, Sir Thomas

ROSSINI: *Overture: William Tell.* DVORAK: *Legend in G, Op. 59/2.* WEBER: *Der Freischütz: Overture.* DELIUS: *Appalachia* (with Cuthbert Matthews and Royal Opera Chorus) (all with LPO). WAGNER: *Das Rheingold: Entry of the Gods into Valhalla* (with Walter Widdop, Theo Hermann & soloists). MOZART: *Divertimento No. 15 in B flat, K.287: Theme and Variations; Minuet* (only). RIMSKY-KORSAKOV: *Symphony No. 2 (Antar), Op. 9.* MENDELSSOHN: *Songs Without Words Nos. 44 & 45, Op. 102/3* (orch. Del Mar). TCHAIKOVSKY: *Symphony No. 4 in F min., Op. 36.* HANDEL: *Amaryllis (Suite, arr. Beecham): Sarabande* (all with RPO).

(B) (★★★) EMI mono/stereo 5 75938-2 (2).

An impressive selection of recordings made in 1934/5 with the LPO and between 1947 and 1957 with the RPO. There were 17 78-r.p.m. side takes for the opening *William Tell Overture* and the earliest three have been chosen here for their extra spontaneity, yet the string playing in the very spirited galop is flawless. The ensemble in the Dvořák *Legend* is not quite so fine (it was never issued) and the horns are not immaculate in *Der Freischütz.* But this is a live performance, recorded in the Queens Hall in 1935 alongside *Appalachia,* which displays all the Beecham Delian magic in the atmospheric horn solos at the very opening, and later in some fine *pianissimo* choral singing. An exciting finale triumphs over the two-dimensional sound, with shrill violins. It is good to have the Wagner excerpt (with text and translation included), notable mainly for Walter Widdop's memorable contribution as Loge, and the two movements from the Mozart *Divertimento* are engagingly urbane.

Beecham's warmly sensuous, richly coloured, yet highly animated 1951 performance of *Antar* is unsurpassed and, together with his thrilling reading of Tchaikovsky's *Fourth Symphony,* provides the highlight of the set. Fortunately both recordings offer glowing sound, with alluring strings and rich colouring given to the RPO woodwind. Curiously, only the first movement of the Tchaikovsky *Fourth* was recorded in stereo, in the Kingsway Hall in 1958. It sounds marvellous. But the other three movements do not disappoint, recorded a year earlier in Paris in the resonant Salle Wagram. Beecham's reading is full

of individual touches (with some lovely gentle woodwind and string playing in the first movement's second subject), but they never hold back the music's spontaneous onward flow. The close of the *Andantino* is particularly beautiful, and after the vibrant pizzicato the finale generates plenty of excitement.

Two of Mendelssohn's *Songs Without Words,* charmingly scored by Norman Del Mar, make an elegant interlude between the two symphonies, and Sir Thomas's own arrangement of the lovely *Sarabande* from Handel's *Amaryllis Suite* makes a fitting final encore.

Beinum, Eduard van

THOMAS: *Mignon: Overture.* SCHUBERT: *Symphony No. 6 in C.* BRAHMS: *Symphony No. 2 in D.* NICOLAI: *The Merry Wives of Windsor: Overture.* R. STRAUSS: *Don Juan.* RIMSKY-KORSAKOV: *Scheherazade* (all with Concg. O). ELGAR: *Cockaigne Overture* (with LPO).

(B) (★★(★)) EMI mono 5 75941-2 (2).

Eduard van Beinum inherited the Concertgebouw Orchestra from Mengelberg immediately after the war, and he also became a regular visitor to London, becoming conductor of the LPO for a time (1950–53). He made numerous commercial records in Amsterdam, including some memorable Bruckner with Decca and then with Philips. Like Sir Adrian Boult, he was dedicated to the letter and the spirit of the score; expressive self-indulgence and interpretative flamboyance were foreign to his muse. As this compilation shows, he never fell below a high standard and (despite assertions to the contrary) was rarely dull. He recorded the Brahms *First* no fewer than three times, but the Brahms *Second* and *Don Juan* are live performances, made when the Concertgebouw Orchestra was visiting Stuttgart (he never recorded any Strauss commercially).

Boult, Sir Adrian

BERLIOZ: *Rob Roy Overture.* TCHAIKOVSKY: *Suite No. 3 in G: Theme and Variations.* WALTON: *Portsmouth Point: Overture.* SCHUMANN: *Symphony No. 4 in D min.* SCHUBERT: *Symphony No. 4 in C min.* SIBELIUS: *The Tempest, Prelude* (all with LPO). FRANCK: *Symphony in D min.* (with L. Orchestral Soc.). BEETHOVEN: *Coriolan Overture* (with New PO). WOLF: *Italian Serenade* (with PO).

(B) ★★★ EMI 5 75459-2 (2).

This EMI series usually mixes live or studio performances that are not otherwise available with commercial recordings; but the set devoted to Sir Adrian Boult does not include any of his concerts with the BBC Symphony Orchestra which ought to survive in the BBC's Archives. Instead it concentrates on the commercial LPs he made for Pye or Nixa, which he made in his sixties with the LPO. The Franck is given an unsentimental and well-held-together reading and the players were drawn from various London orchestras, including the Philharmonia. He recorded *Portsmouth Point* on a 10-inch HMV record before the war and remade it with the LPO for Decca, but this 1967 account comes from a series of recordings made for the World Record Club, as do the Franck and Schubert symphonies. The Schumann symphony is no less finely shaped and sounds very good indeed – and in every way an improvement over the original LPs. Sir Adrian was much underrated in both Berlioz and Sibelius. He never recorded the symphonies commercially but made a fine set of the tone-poems in 1956, also including this powerfully atmospheric *Tempest Prelude*, which did not last very long in the catalogue. A useful set that pays tribute to a master conductor whose interpretative range went much further than Elgar and Vaughan Williams. Very good transfers by Paul Baily.

Busch, Fritz

BEETHOVEN: *Leonora Overture No. 2.* BRAHMS: *Tragic Overture; Symphony No. 2.* HAYDN: *Sinfonia concertante in B flat.* MENDELSSOHN: *Symphony No. 4 in A (Italian).* MOZART: *Symphony No. 36 in C (Linz).* WEBER: *Overture, Der Freischütz* (all with Danish State RSO). R. STRAUSS: *Don Juan* (with LPO).

(B) (***) EMI mono 5 75103-2 (2).

It is a revelation that Fritz Busch, the musical founder of Glyndebourne and normally regarded as just a Mozartian, conveys such authority in this wide range of works. They are superbly played, consistently reflecting the joy that the players had in renewing their relationship with a conductor who, from 1933, when he was sacked by the Nazis from his post in Dresden, was their great orchestral trainer in the classical and romantic repertory.

With the exception of the Strauss *Don Juan*, which was made in 1936 with the LPO, all these performances come from 1947–51, the heyday of the Danish State Radio Symphony Orchestra, which Busch brought to a level unrivalled in the other Scandinavian countries. They had greater personality as well as greater virtuosity and finesse than the Stockholm and Oslo orchestras of the day, as witness the 1949 *Linz Symphony* (the 78s were treasurable and still are) and the superb Brahms *Second Symphony*, which is also available on the Dutton anthology issued to mark the orchestra's 75th anniversary; the Dutton transfer is in every way superior. This is also valuable for the first reissue of the Haydn *Sinfonia concertante in B flat*, which features their celebrated oboist, Waldemar Wolsing, and three other first-desk players. The *Leonora No. 2 Overture* and the *Italian Symphony* are new to the catalogue and come from a 1950 concert in Copenhagen.

Cluytens, André

BIZET: *Symphony in C.* BERLIOZ: *Symphonie fantastique* (with French RO). DEBUSSY: *Images* (with Paris Conservatoire O). MUSSORGSKY: *Boris Godunov: Coronation Scene* (with Christoff, Sofia Opera Ch.). RAVEL: *La Valse* (with Philh. O). SCHUMANN: *Manfred Overture.* WAGNER: *Lohengrin, Act III: Prelude* (with BPO).

(B) *** EMI (ADD) 5 75106-2 (2).

As far as British and American audiences are concerned, André Cluytens (pronounced Klwee-tunss) came to prominence only in the early 1950s: he accompanied Solomon in the *Second* and *Fourth* Beethoven *Concertos* in 1952, but he made few appearances in England, although he was the first Belgian conductor to appear at Bayreuth (in 1955). Bizet was one of the first composers he recorded, and his 1953 account of the *Symphony in C* with the Orchestre National de la Radiodiffusion Française was highly thought of in its time – and rightly so. There is a straightforward quality about it, totally unconcerned with effect. It is also available in Testament's Bizet anthology. Also included here is the Coronation Scene from Mussorgsky's *Boris Godunov* with Boris Christoff in the title-role – naturally in Rimsky-Korsakov's opulent scoring – and a relatively little-known account of *La Valse* with the Philharmonia Orchestra from 1958, which is more polished than his later recording, although the warmer acoustic of the Salle Pleyel shows the Parisians to better advantage.

The highlights of the set are the atmospheric accounts of the Debussy *Images*, quite unjustly overshadowed at the time by the Monteux (though that was admittedly better played) and the *Symphonie fantastique*, a different account from that issued on Testament. This was recorded at a 1964 concert in Tokyo while the Conservatoire Orchestra was on tour, and is new to the catalogue. A strongly narrative performance, it grips and holds the listener, not so much through its virtuosity as through its sense of forward movement and line. Cluytens knew what this music was all about, and though it lacks the polish of the very finest versions, there is a splendid sense of involvement. A most valuable issue, which gives a good picture of a much underrated maestro.

Coates, Albert

WEBER: *Oberon Overture.* LISZT: *Mephisto Waltz No. 1.* BORODIN: *Symphony No. 2 in B min.* RIMSKY-KORSAKOV: *Mláda: Procession of the Nobles.* MUSSORGSKY: *Sorochinsky Fair: Gopak.* TCHAIKOVSKY: *Francesca da Rimini.* RAVEL: *La Valse.* WAGNER: *Tannhäuser Overture; Das Rheinhold: Entry of the Gods into Valhalla. Die Walküre: Magic Fire Music. Götterdämmerung: Siegfried's Rhine Journey* (all with LSO).

HUMPERDINCK: *Hänsel und Gretel: Overture.* R. STRAUSS: *Death and Transfiguration.* WAGNER: *Tristan und Isolde: Love Duet* (with Frida Leider, Lauritz Melchior, Berlin State Op. O).

(B) (★★★) EMI mono 5 75486-2 (2).

Albert Coates was old enough to have met Tchaikovsky when he was a small boy and to have studied composition with Rimsky-Korsakov. He began his career on the podium in Elberfeld, Mannheim and Dresden, before conducting *Siegfried* in St Petersburg, where he was immediately engaged by the Imperial Opera House. After the First World War he began his long assocation with the London Symphony Orchestra, which he had first conducted in 1910. After 1926, pretty well all his HMV records were made with them, though he was in demand as a guest conductor on the continent, in America and the Soviet Union. All these performances come from 1926–32 and display much of the zest and fire for which he was celebrated. The Borodin *Second Symphony* was for long the classic of its day, and as he championed so much Russian music and made a first recording of Tchaikovsky's *Polish Symphony*, it is a pity that his pioneering (1932) set of Prokofiev's *Le Pas d'acier*, which sounds quite astonishing for its day, was not included. This is a valuable reminder of a conductor of stature whose work spanned the first decades of the century. Good transfers and excellent notes by Alan Sanders.

Golovanov, Nikolai

GLAZUNOV: *Symphony No. 6.* LISZT: *Symphonic Poems: Festklänge; Héroïde funèbre; Mazeppa; Orpheus; Prometheus.* MENDELSSOHN: *A Midsummer Night's Dream: Overture; Scherzo.* TCHAIKOVSKY: *1812 Overture* (all with Moscow RSO).

(B) (*) EMI mono 5 75112-2 (2).

Nikolai Golovanov, an exact contemporary of Prokofiev, brought the Moscow Radio Orchestra to a high pitch in the difficult post-war years. He gets playing of much sensitivity and vitality from the strings in Glazunov's endearing *Sixth Symphony* – a very spirited account. In the Liszt tone-poems the playing is handicapped by ill-tuned, raw wind tone and blowsy horns. He sets a very fast tempo for the Mendelssohn *Scherzo*, and the results sound scrambled. The recording quality ranges from the just acceptable to the rough.

Kleiber, Erich

BEETHOVEN: *Symphony No. 6 (Pastoral), Op. 68* (with Czech PO). DVORAK: *Carnaval Overture.* MOZART: *Symphony No. 40 in G min., K. 550.* JOSEF STRAUSS: *Waltz: Spharenklänge.* JOHANN STRAUSS JR: *Der Zigeunerbaron Overture* (all with LPO); *Du und Du Waltz* (with VPO). SCHUBERT: *Symphony No. 5 in B flat.* R. STRAUSS: *Till Eulenspiegel* (with N. German R. O).

(B) (★★★) EMI mono 5 75115-2 (2).

Often the most valuable items on the two-disc sets so far issued in this EMI 'Great Conductors' series are radio recordings never previously published. In the superb set representing the work of Erich Kleiber (father of the elusive Carlos Kleiber, and, many would say, even greater), the most exciting performances are indeed those on radio recordings. The recording he made with the Czech Philharmonic in Prague in 1955 (less than a year before his death) of Beethoven's *Pastoral Symphony* is at once glowingly incandescent and refined, with radiant string tone and rollicking Czech wind and horn playing in the Scherzo. Kleiber's readings for North German Radio of Schubert's *Fifth Symphony* and Strauss's *Till Eulenspiegel* are also outstanding, the Schubert sunny and full of character, the Strauss racily exciting. Though the transfer engineers have not tamed the fierce string sound of the Decca recordings included here, it is good to have from that source Kleiber's powerful, dramatic reading of Mozart's *G minor Symphony*, No. 40, and engaging trifles by the other Strausses, presented with warmth and a degree of indulgence.

Koussevitzky, Serge

BEETHOVEN: *Symphony No. 5 in C min.* (with LPO). SIBELIUS: *Symphony No. 7* (with BBC SO). HARRIS: *Symphony No. 3.* TCHAIKOVSKY: *Symphony No. 5 in E min.* RACHMANINOV: *The Isle of the Dead* (all with Boston SO).

(B) (★★(★)) EMI mono 5 75118-2 (2).

The two discs devoted to Serge Koussevitzky are variable in content, but among the treasures is the revelatory first recording, made live with the BBC Symphony in 1933, of Sibelius's *Seventh Symphony*. By comparison his 1934 studio recording of Beethoven's *Fifth* with the LPO is disappointingly heavy, while all the rest, recorded later with his own Boston Symphony Orchestra, bring superb playing, not least in Roy Harris's powerful, single-movement *Third Symphony*. This account of Rachmaninov's *Isle of the Dead*, never issued in Europe in the 78 era, even rivals the composer's classic account.

Malko, Nicolai

BORODIN: *Symphony No. 2.* DVORAK: *Symphony No. 9 (New World).* GLINKA: *Ruslan and Ludmilla – Overture.* PROKOFIEV: *Symphony No 7.* RIMSKY-KORSAKOV: *Tsar Sultan: Dance of the Tumblers.* SUPPE: *Poet and Peasant: Overture.* TCHAIKOVSKY: *Nutcracker: excerpts.* (all with

Philh. O). HAYDN: *Symphony No. 92* (with Royal Danish O). NIELSEN: *Maskarade: Overture* (with Danish State R. O).

(B) (★★★) EMI mono/stereo 5 75121-2 (2).

Nicolai Malko conducted the première of Shostakovich's *First Symphony* in 1926 and was an eminent teacher, numbering Evgeni Mravinsky among his pupils. But when Soviet policy towards the Arts became less liberal, he decided to emigrate and take his chance as a freelance conductor. His recording career began in the days of shellac, and the present compilation ranges from Nielsen's *Maskarade Overture* (1947), thoroughly idiomatic and vital, through to Prokofiev's *Seventh Symphony* (1955) and Glinka's *Ruslan Overture* (1956), a spirited account but not breathless and headlong. He is at his best in Borodin's *Second Symphony* (the second of his two recordings) and the Prokofiev *Seventh Symphony*, whose first British performance he gave. Both have great clarity of texture and momentum, and in charm and finesse the *Seventh* has rarely been equalled. His Haydn with the Royal Danish Orchestra ('Det Kongelige') has great lightness of touch and, in the finale, wit. There is not the slightest trace of affectation, and the same goes for the *New World Symphony*, which is not a great performance, perhaps, but is lively and enjoyable. Malko was not a charismatic conductor, but he was always at the service of the composer and not his own ego. The sound is consistently good for its period.

Markevitch, Igor

CHABRIER: *España* (with Spanish R. & TV SO). DEBUSSY: *La Mer.* GLINKA: *A Life for the Tsar: Overture and 3 Dances* (with LOP). RAVEL: *Daphnis et Chloë: Suite No. 2* (with Hamburg NDR O). R. STRAUSS: *Till Eulenspiegel* (with French Nat. R. O). TCHAIKOVSKY: *Manfred Symphony* (with LSO). VERDI: *La forza del destino: Overture* (with New Philh. O).

(B) ★★ EMI (ADD) 5 75124-2 (2).

An enormously gifted man and a composer of substance, Igor Markevitch gave us relatively few great recordings. His first *Rite of Spring* was certainly one, and his Berwald symphonies with the Berlin Philharmonic were very fine, too. None of the performances here falls below a certain standard, but nearly all have been surpassed elsewhere: his somewhat cool *Manfred Symphony* is not a patch on the electrifying Toscanini, Jansons or Pletnev accounts, and his *Daphnis* is no match for the likes of Ormandy or Karajan. As is the case with other issues in this series, the performances derive not only from commercial recordings but from broadcasts. Trouble has been taken over the transfers, so Markevitch's admirers need not hesitate on that score.

Mitropoulos, Dimitri

MAHLER: *Symphony No. 6* (with West German RSO, Cologne). BERLIOZ: *Roméo et Juliette: excerpts.* DEBUSSY: *La Mer.* R. STRAUSS: *Salome: Dance of the 7 Veils* (with NYPO).

(B) (★★(★)) EMI mono 595471-2 (2).

The Mahler symphony comes from a 1959 concert in the WestDeutscher Rundfunk studio in Cologne, a year before the conductor's death. This was a period when the Mahler symphonies were rarities and the LP catalogue listed only one commercial recording of the *Sixth* (by the Rotterdam Philharmonic Orchestra under Eduard Flipse on Philips). As one might expect, Mitropoulos brings great intensity and tremendous grip to this mighty score. The New York recordings were made when he was conductor-in-chief of the Philharmonic: the Debussy in 1950, the Berlioz in 1952 and the Strauss four years later. All were issued in the USA and the Berlioz appeared on a 10-inch Philips LP in Britain. Both that and the Debussy were still to be found in specialist outlets in Britain in the 1970s. The recorded sound is very much of its day but the performances are pretty electrifying.

Munch, Charles

SAINT-SAËNS: *La Princesse jaune: Overture.* MENDELSSOHN: *Octet: Scherzo* (❀). MARTINU: *Symphony No. 6 (Fantaisies symphoniques).* PROKOFIEV: *Romeo and Juliet: excerpts.* BEETHOVEN: *Symphony No 9 in D min. (Choral)* (with L. Price, Forrester, Poleri, Tozzi, New England Conservatoire Ch.; all with Boston SO). BERLIOZ: *Le Corsaire Overture* (with Paris Conservatoire O). BIZET: *Symphony in C* (with Fr. Nat. R. O).

(B) (★★★) EMI mono/stereo 5 75477-2 (2).

This is of exceptional interest in that it restores to circulation the Martinů *Sixth Symphony (Fantaisies symphoniques)*, written for Munch, which has never been available in Britain on CD. (Indeed, we are not sure that it was ever available in stereo.) The 1956 recording which was rather hard in its mono LP form has splendid tonal refinement and openness. It is superbly balanced and has good detail and a wonderful sense of space. It is the definitive performance and recording, if there could ever be such a thing. The collection ranges from a 1948 *Corsaire* with the Orchestre de la Société des Concerts du Conservatoire to the 1966 Bizet *Symphony*. (It would have been good if his fine *Queen Mab Scherzo* from the same period could have been included, or his glorious Mendelssohn *Reformation Symphony*, but perhaps next time . . .).

Ormandy, Eugene

BRAHMS: *Symphony No. 4.* RACHMANINOV:
Symphony No. 2. SIBELIUS: *Legend:
Lemminkäinen's Homeward Journey, Op. 22/4.*
WEBERN: *Im Sommerwind* (all with Phd. O).
KABALEVSKY: *Colas Breugnon: Overture.* R.
STRAUSS: *Don Juan* (both with Bav. RSO).

(B) ★★★ EMI (ADD) 5 75127-2 (2).

All these recordings, except for the brilliantly played
Kabalevsky *Colas Breugnon Overture* and Strauss's
Don Juan, are with the Philadelphia Orchestra, over
whose fortunes Ormandy presided for the best part
of half a century. Since theirs was one of the most
prolific recording partnerships, selection must have
presented a problem, although it is natural that
Rachmaninov, with whom Ormandy was so closely
associated, should feature. He recorded that composer's *Second Symphony* four times, and it is the fourth
version, in which he opened out all the old traditional cuts, that is offered here. The 1973 performance
sails forth with consistent ardour, but for all the
splendour of the rich, massed Philadelphia strings,
the continuous intense expressiveness, with relatively
little light and shade, almost overwhelms the listener.
What a pity the 1956 CBS version was not chosen,
cuts and all, for that is much fresher and more
spontaneous sounding.

The performance of Brahms's *Fourth Symphony,*
another work that Ormandy recorded more than
once, brings a similar problem. The performance has
great forward thrust, and the passionate progress of
the music certainly holds the listener, but at the end
one is left emotionally spent, craving more subtle
detail and greater dynamic contrast.

Ormandy's recordings of Shostakovich's *First* or
Fifteenth, both peerless, his wonderful Prokofiev *Fifth*
or either of his magical accounts of the *Daphnis et
Chloé Suite No. 2* would have done his art greater
justice.

Undoubtedly the highlight of the first disc is
Webern's rarely heard early work, *Im Sommerwind,*
an evocation of a summer day spent in the countryside. Its vivid impressionism obviously fired
Ormandy, and he conducted its première in 1962.
The recording followed a year later, and like most
first recordings the performance has constant freshness and is most stimulating and enjoyable. Fortunately, the second disc closes with an excerpt from
the *Lemminkäinen Legends* of Sibelius, one of
Ormandy's finest late recordings for EMI, dating
from 1978. Throughout these Philadelphia sessions
the sheer orchestral opulence and dazzling virtuosity
of the players and the control exercised by this great
conductor (whose powers were so often taken for
granted in his lifetime) still put one under his spell,
and the sound is certainly full blooded.

For the brashly exciting Kabalevsky overture and
Strauss's *Don Juan* Ormandy turned to the Bavarian
Radio Symphony Orchestra, and in an exciting live
recording of Strauss's tone-poem they provide a balance between passion and strong characterization.

Schuricht, Carl

BEETHOVEN: *Symphony No. 1 in C* (with Paris
Conservatoire O). BRUCKNER: *Symphony No. 8 in
C min.* MENDELSSOHN: *Overture: The Hebrides.*
MOZART: *Symphony No. 35 in D (Haffner).*
SCHUBERT: *Symphony No. 8 (Unfinished)* (all with
VPO).

(B) ★★★ EMI (ADD) 5 75130-2 (2).

Carl Schuricht was a conductor of the old school, a
wholly dedicated and thoughtful musician, unconcerned with image or publicity. Although Testament
reissued his glorious Bruckner *Ninth* with the Vienna
Philharmonic some years back (in a special vinyl
pressing), his *Eighth* (in the Haas Edition) with the
same orchestra has not been available since the 1960s.
It never received its proper due at the time, but it is
every bit as glorious a performance, finely proportioned and noble, and sounds pretty sumptuous in
this splendidly restored 1963 recording. It can challenge many of its more celebrated rivals. Yet, starting
with an account of Mendelssohn's *Hebrides Overture*
that is thrusting and not at all atmospheric, there is a
penny-plain element in Schuricht's approach to these
masterpieces that makes one hanker after more idiosyncratic touches. In Schubert's *Unfinished Symphony,* recorded for Decca in 1956, there is none of
the magic one finds, for example, in the earlier Decca
mono version from Josef Krips and the Vienna Philharmonic. As in the Mendelssohn, Schuricht is
strong and rugged with no attempt at charm, and it
is much the same in both Mozart's *Haffner Symphony*
and Beethoven's *First;* there is no lingering by the
wayside. That comes closer to latterday taste than the
more romantically expressive manner often favoured
at the time, with the slow movement of the
Beethoven crisp and clean with relatively little
moulding. When Schuricht varies tempo, it tends to
be towards an accelerando rather than an easing up,
with the fundamental impression being one of ruggedness, with textures clarified. Except for the
Beethoven, all these performances are with the
Vienna Philharmonic.

Szell, George

AUBER: *Fra Diavolo: Overture.* DVORAK: *Symphony
No. 8 in G.* DELIUS: *Irmelin: Prelude.* ROSSINI:
L'Italiana in Algeri: Overture (all with Cleveland
O). DEBUSSY: *La Mer.* TCHAIKOVSKY: *Symphony
No. 5* (with West German RSO, Cologne). WAGNER:
Die Meistersinger: Prelude. Josef STRAUSS: *Delirien
Waltz* (with NYPO).

(B) ★★★ EMI (ADD) 5 75963-2 (2).

The Dvořák symphony is the version EMI recorded three months before Szell's death in 1970. The sound is more spacious and natural than the quality which the CBS engineers used to give him in Cleveland. This is one of Szell's finest performances, he gives the phrases time to breathe, the slow movement is relaxed and has charm (not a quality one normally associates with him), and he never rushes the music, either in the Scherzo or in the finale. In short, a lovely performance and arguably the best thing in the set. The two live studio performances come from Cologne: the Tchaikovsky *Symphony* was recorded in 1966 and *La Mer* four years earlier. They bear all the hallmarks of the conductor: finely balanced textures, clarity, excellence of execution and a complete absence of interpretative idiosyncrasy. We don't associate Szell with Delius, but the inclusion of his 1956 account of the *Prelude to Irmelin*, played with a fine sense of atmosphere, serves as a reminder that he spent 1937–9 in Glasgow as conductor of the BBC Scottish Orchestra. A valuable set.

Walter, Bruno

BEETHOVEN: *Symphony No. 6 in F (Pastoral).*
MAHLER: *Symphony No. 5: Adagietto.*
Kindertotenlieder: Nun will die Sonn' so hell aufgeh'n (with Ferrier) (all with VPO). BRAHMS: *Symphony No. 2 in D* (with NYPO). HAYDN: *Symphony No. 92 in G (Oxford).* J. STRAUSS: *Die Fledermaus: Overture* (both with Paris Conservatoire O). MOZART: *Le nozze di Figaro: Overture.* WAGNER: *Die Meistersinger: Overture; Die Walküre: Act II, Scene 5* (with Lehmann, Melchior & soloists) (both with British SO).

(B) (★★★) EMI mono 5 75133-2 (2).

The value of this Bruno Walter set lies in its pre-war rarities: his 1936 account of the Beethoven *Pastoral*, which has great freshness and warmth, and one of the Haydn symphonies he recorded in 1938 during his days with the Paris Conservatoire, a performance of great elegance, treasured by all who have them in their shellac form. The radiance of the *Adagietto* from Mahler's *Fifth Symphony* is richly caught in a reading that is by no means slow – it had to fit on two 78-r.p.m. sides! – yet because of the expansive phrasing, it still sounds relaxed, and the recording is remarkably warm and spacious.

Walter's partnership with Kathleen Ferrier was certainly worth remembering, and she is in superb voice in this finely transferred excerpt from the *Kindertotenlieder*. Walter also championed Wagner on his regular London visits, and his *Meistersinger*

overture, where the sound is less flattering, comes from 1930, as does the *Figaro* overture, brilliantly done by the British Symphony Orchestra. The excerpt from *Die Walküre* with Lotte Lehmann and Lauritz Melchior among others is almost worth the price of the whole disc. The only post-war recording is a fine New York Brahms *Second* from 1946 – once again given a first-class transfer. Definitely worth having, not least for the sake of the *Pastoral*, which he never surpassed.

Weingartner, Felix

BEETHOVEN: *The Creatures of Prometheus Overture, Op. 63* (with VPO). *Symphony No. 2 in D* (with LSO). BERLIOZ: *Marche troyenne.* WAGNER: *Rienzi Overture* (with Paris Conservatoire O). WEBER/BERLIOZ: *Invitation to the Dance.* BRAHMS: *Symphony No. 3 in F, Op. 90.* MOZART: *Symphony No. 39 in E flat, K.543.* WAGNER: *Siegfried Idyll.* LISZT: *Les Préludes; Mephisto Waltz* (all with LPO).

(B) (★★★) EMI mono 5 75965-2 (2).

Weingartner is thought of as the supreme classicist, the conductor who served (in Peter Stadlen's memorable phrase) 'lean-beef' Beethoven in Vienna's Sunday morning concerts. His Beethoven, now restored on the Naxos Historical label, is pretty well unsurpassed, and the LSO records of the *Second Symphony* are included here, 'a paradigm of Weingartner's greatness', as the notes put it. The Brahms *Third Symphony*, recorded with the LPO in 1938, is wonderfully sinewy but at the same time warm, and the remaining performances have the ring of truth. Here is a conductor who is totally dedicated and self-effacing. Though he was not identified with Berlioz, his *Marche troyenne* serves as an admirable reminder of his credentials in this repertoire: he made an impressive recording of the *Symphonie fantastique* with the LSO in the late 1920s, though the sound was distinctly frail. No quarrels with any of the sound here – quite the reverse. *Les Préludes* and the *Mephisto Waltz* were recorded with the LSO during the war (Weingartner was based in Basle during his last decades). His Liszt carries a special authority as he was close to the composer during 1883–6. As Christopher Dyment's authoritative notes remind us, Weingartner was known as the 'prince of guest conductors', for he appeared with most major European orchestras after his long tenure of the Vienna Philharmonic, and this set offers examples of his work in London and Paris as well as Vienna. Very successful transfers.

Other Concerts

Academy of Ancient Music, Christopher Hogwood

PACHELBEL: *Canon & Gigue.* HANDEL: *Water Music: Air. Berenice: Overture; Minuet; Gigue.* VIVALDI: *Flute Concerto in G min. (La notte), Op. 10/2.* BACH: *Christmas Oratorio, BWV 248: Sinfonia. Quadruple Harpsichord Concerto in A min., BWV 1065.* CORELLI: *Concerto grosso (Christmas Concerto), Op. 6/8.* A. MARCELLO: *Oboe Concerto in D min.*

(M) **(*) O-L ADD/DDD 443 201-2.

It seems a curious idea to play popular baroque repertoire in a severe manner; Pachelbel's *Canon* here sounds rather abrasive and lacking in charm. But those who combine a taste for these pieces with a desire for authenticity should be satisfied. The selection for this reissue has been expanded and altered. Handel's *Queen of Sheba* no longer arrives – and she is not missed (for she was much more seductive in Beecham's hands) – and the highlight of the original, full-priced compilation (a pair of Gluck dances) is no longer present! Instead, we get several new items taken from another Academy of Ancient Music compilation of baroque music associated with Christmas, notably Corelli's splendid Op. 6/8, in which the playing has a suitably light touch, and Vivaldi's engaging *La notte Flute Concerto*, while Bach's *Quadruple Harpsichord Concerto* substitutes for the famous Vivaldi work for four violins (Op. 3/10). On the whole an enjoyable mix. The new playing time is 67 minutes.

Academy of St Martin-in-the-Fields, Sir Neville Marriner

'The Best of the Academy' SUPPE: *Overture: Light Cavalry.* GRIEG: *2 Elegiac Melodies, Op. 34; Holberg Suite, Op. 40: Prelude.* TCHAIKOVSKY: *Andante cantabile (from String Quartet No. 1).* DVORAK: *Nocturne in B, Op. 40.* PONCHIELLI: *La Gioconda: Dance of the Hours.* NICOLAI: *The Merry Wives of Windsor: Overture.* FAURE: *Pavane, Op. 50.* BOCCHERINI: *String Quintet in E, Op. 13/5: Minuet.* WAGNER: *Siegfried Idyll.* HANDEL: *Solomon: Arrival of the Queen of Sheba.* J. S. BACH: *Cantata No. 208: Sheep may safely graze; Cantata No. 147: Jesu, joy of man's desiring; Christmas Oratorio:*

Pastoral Symphony. HANDEL: *Berenice: Minuet; Messiah: Pastoral Symphony.* SCHUBERT: *Rosamunde: Entr'acte No. 3 in B flat.* GLUCK: *Orfeo ed Euridice: Dance of the Blessed Spirits.* BORODIN: *String Quartet No. 2 in D: Nocturne.* SHOSTAKOVICH: *The Gadfly: Romance.* MUSSORGSKY/RIMSKY-KORSAKOV: *Khovanshchina: Dance of the Persian Slaves.* RIMSKY-KORSAKOV: *Tsar Saltan: The Flight of the Bumble-bee. The Snow Maiden: Dance of the Tumblers.*

(B) *** CfP 585 6242 (2).

This reissued CfP bargain double draws on the contents of three different (HMV) digital collections, recorded between 1980 and 1987. The first included the *Siegfried Idyll*, in which Marriner uses solo strings for the gentler passages, a fuller ensemble for the climaxes, here passionately convincing. Delicately introduced by the harp and the gentle striking of the morning hour, the account of the *Dance of the Hours* has characteristic finesse and colour, while there is comparably gracious phrasing in *The Merry Wives of Windsor Overture*. The other, mainly gentle, pieces by Tchaikovsky, Fauré, Boccherini and Grieg are given radiant performances. To open the second disc, Handel's *Queen of Sheba* trots in very briskly and here the noble contour of Handel's famous *Berenice* melody is the first thing to strike the ear; but it is the Schubert *Entr'acte* from *Rosamunde* and the passionately expressive Borodin *Nocturne* that resonate in the memory. With the Shostakovich *Barrel Organ Waltz* providing a touch of piquancy and Mussorgsky's *Persian Slaves* suitably sinuous and sentient, this makes a most agreeable entertainment, ending with gusto with Rimsky's *Tumblers*. The digital sound is excellent throughout.

'*Fantasia on Greensleeves*': VAUGHAN WILLIAMS: *Fantasia on Greensleeves; The Lark Ascending* (with Iona Brown); *English Folksongs Suite.* WARLOCK: *Serenade; Capriol Suite.* GEORGE BUTTERWORTH: *A Shropshire Lad; Two English Idylls; The Banks of Green Willow.* DELIUS: *A Village Romeo and Juliet: The Walk to the Paradise Garden. Hassan: Intermezzo and Serenade. A Song before Sunrise; On Hearing the First Cuckoo in Spring; Summer Night on the River; La Calinda.* ELGAR: *Serenade for Strings, Op. 20; Sospiri for Strings, Harp and Organ; Elegy for Strings, Op. 58; The Spanish Lady (suite); Introduction and Allegro, Op. 47.*

🎵 (B) *** Double Decca (ADD) 452 707-2 (2).

This exceptionally generous programme, mainly of English pastoral evocations but including Iona Brown's Elysian account of *The Lark Ascending* and Elgar's two string masterpieces in not wholly idiomatic but very characterful performances, is self-recommending, for the Academy are thoroughly at home here and play with consistent warmth and finesse, while the vintage Decca sound never disappoints. Marvellous value for money.

'*English Classics*': VAUGHAN WILLIAMS: *Fantasia on Greensleeves; English Folksong Suite* (trans. Gordon Jacob). ELGAR: *Serenade for Strings, Op. 20.* BUTTERWORTH: *The Banks of Green Willow.* WARLOCK: *Capriol Suite.* DELIUS: *On Hearing the First Cuckoo in Spring; The Walk to the Paradise Garden.*

(B) ★★★ Decca Penguin Classics (ADD) 460 637.

These recordings are rarely out of the catalogue, and rightly so. They are lovely performances and show the Academy on vintage form; there is much subtlety of detail here as well as striking commitment and depth of feeling, and although the recordings range from 1967–81, they are all rich and full. Reissued on the Penguin Classics label, they come with a personal appraisal by Jim Crace. However, the fuller selection on the Double Decca above is an even more attractive proposition.

'A Celebration': VIVALDI: *The Four Seasons: Spring.* HANDEL: *Water Music: Suite No. 2 in D.* BACH: *Brandenburg Concerto No. 4 in G.* AVISON: *Concerto grosso No. 7 in G min.* BOYCE: *Symphony No. 5 in D.* MOZART: *Eine kleine Nachtmusik.* BIZET: *Symphony in C.* WAGNER: *Siegfried Idyll.* BRAHMS: *Hungarian Dance No. 5.* ROSSINI: *Overture: William Tell.* BEETHOVEN: *Wellington's Victory.* BARBER: *Adagio for Strings.* FALLA: *Ritual Fire Dance.* DELIUS: *The Walk to the Paradise Garden.* VAUGHAN WILLIAMS: *Fantasia on a Theme by Thomas Tallis.* WALTON: *Sonata for Strings.* TIPPETT: *Fantasia Concertante on the Theme of Corelli* (includes a bonus DVD with: TCHAIKOVSKY: *Serenade for Strings in C, Op. 48.* GRIEG: *At the Cradle, Op. 68/5; Holberg Suite, Op. 40*).

(M) ★★(★) Ph. (ADD/DDD) 475 6117 (3).

So vast and ubiquitous is Sir Neville Marriner's output, it is only too easy to take for granted what he has contributed to the recorded repertoire. Yet this three-CD set offers plenty of evidence as to why he has been such a successful recording artist: the classic account of the Bizet *Symphony* remains one of the best ever recorded – it has all the polish and elegance characteristic of vintage ASMF records of the early 1970s: the slow movement has a delectable oboe solo and the finale is irrepressibly high-spirited. Walton expanded his *Sonata for Strings* at the suggestion of Marriner in 1947, and for the bigger ensemble Walton tautened the argument, while expanding the richness of texture, frequently relating the full band to the sound of four solo instruments. Though something of the acerbity of the original is lost, the result was another in the sequence of great British string works, warmly romantic in lyricism in the first and third movements, spikily brilliant in the Scherzo and finale. The performance here is superb, as is the 1973 recording, and it makes its CD début. From the same Argo era there are vintage performance of Delius's *A Walk to the Paradise Garden* and Tippett's *Corelli Variations*, as well as a compilation disc devoted mainly to some of his classic Argo baroque recordings (Vivaldi, Bach, Avison, Boyce and Handel) which remain as fresh-sounding as ever. Understandably, Universal wanted to include some of his later, digital accounts on Philips and, while these are very good by any standards, they don't quite capture the magic of the earlier ones: the *Tallis Fantasia*, for example, is beautiful but lacks the last degree of emotional intensity. Similarly too, while the original Argo recording of Barber's *Adagio* received a ✿ in our main volume; the later, digital version featured here does not have the gripping intensity of that classic account. The same comments also apply to the *Siegfried Idyll*, which is again very beautiful but does not create the emotional pull of the very best accounts. Unexpectedly included is Beethoven's *Wellington's Victory* (recorded 1990) with a battery of sound effects. That goes well, as does a warm and vividly recorded *Eine kleine Nachtmusik*, dating from 1984, and the *William Tell Overture* also finds the conductor on top form, with the finale going like the devil. The bonus DVD, '*From Penshurst Place, 1989*', offers attractive music-making from Marriner and the ASMF, but also lots of pretty film of the countryside. It is a bit twee, really, and when the orchestra plays outside, after the Tchaikovsky, with the sound dubbed on afterwards, the effect is not quite so convincing. Still, as a free bonus DVD it's acceptable, and it does include, of course, some gorgeous music. A good, enjoyable collection, if not quite full to the brim with the very best that Marriner has given us.

Algarve Orchestra, Alvaro Cassuto

ARRIAGA: *Overture: Los esclavos felices; Symphony in D.* SEIXAS: *Sinfonia in B flat.* CARVALHO: *Overture: L'amore industrioso.* MOREIRA: *Sinfonia.* PORTUGAL: *Overture: Il Duca di Foix.*

(BB) ★★(★) Naxos 8.557207.

An attractive collection of Spanish and Portuguese music from the eighteenth century, the most famous work being Arriaga's splendid *D major Symphony*, along with his delightfully bubbly *Los esclavos felices Overture*. The *Sinfonia* of Moreira is another highlight, with its sunny Italian disposition, qualities also found in Portugal's *Il Duca di Foix Overture*. The rest of the programme is similarly pleasing and undemanding. The performances are lively, and if sometimes (such as in the *Los esclavos Overture*) the strings are not quite able to take the fast tempi in their stride, it is a minor point compared to the overall vitality and enjoyment of the music-making. Good sound.

American masterpieces

'*American masterpieces*' (with (i) Cleveland O, Louis Lane; (ii) Phd. O, Eugene Ormandy; (iii) NYPO, André Kostelanetz): (i) BERNSTEIN: *Candide: Overture.* (ii) IVES: *Variations on 'America'.* (iii) William SCHUMAN: *New England Triptych.* (ii) BARBER: *Adagio for Strings.* GOULD: *American Salute.* (iii) GRIFFES: *The Pleasure Dome of Kubla Khan.* (ii) MACDOWELL: *Woodland Sketches: To a Wild Rose.* (iii) GERSHWIN: *Promenade.* (ii) GOTTSCHALK: *Cakewalk: Grand Walkaround* (arr. Hershy Kay). (i) BENJAMIN: *Jamaican Rumba.* RODGERS: *On Your Toes: Slaughter on 10th Avenue.* Virgil THOMSON: *Louisiana Story* (film score): *Arcadian Songs and Dances.*

(B) **(*) Sony (ADD) SBK 63034.

Not everything here is a masterpiece, and Arthur Benjamin, who makes the wittiest contribution, was an Australian! But there are some obvious favourites included and one or two novelties, among them the attractively folksy *Arcadian Songs and Dances* of Virgil Thomson, affectionately directed in Cleveland by Louis Lane. He is well recorded, and so, on the whole, is Ormandy, who presents the Ives *Variations* with charm as well as panache, while the Philadelphia strings are powerfully eloquent in Barber's *Adagio* and warmly persuasive in MacDowell's engaging *To a Wild Rose.* Kostelanetz conducts with plenty of personality and zest and is at his best in the Gershwin *Promenade* and the touching central movement of Schuman's *New England Triptych.* But here the up-front recording of the NYPO is overlit and the climaxes of the otherwise atmospheric *Kubla Khan* sound aggressive. A stimulating programme, just the same.

André, Maurice (trumpet)

Trumpet Concertos (with BPO, Karajan): HUMMEL: *Concerto in E flat.* Leopold MOZART: *Concerto in D.* TELEMANN: *Concerto in D.* VIVALDI: *Concerto in A flat* (ed. Thilde).

(M) **(*) EMI (ADD) 5 66909-2 [5 66961].

A key collection of trumpet concertos, brilliantly played by André. His security in the upper register in the work by Leopold Mozart and the fine Telemann concerto is impressive, with Karajan and the BPO wonderfully serene and gracious in the opening *Adagio* and the *Grave* slow movement of the latter. The jaunty quality of the Hummel is not missed, and the finale of this work, taken at breakneck pace, is cer-

tainly exhilarating, while the cantilena of the *Andante* is nobly contoured.

The Vivaldi work is arranged from the *Sonata in F major for violin and continuo*, RV 20, and makes a very effective display piece. The 1974 recording has generally been well transferred to CD. Although the trumpet timbre is very bright and the violins are not absolutely clean in focus, there is plenty of ambience. However, this reissue has a playing time of only 47 minutes and hardly seems an apt choice for EMI's 'Great Recordings of the Century' series.

'*Trumpet concertos*' (with ASMF, Marriner): STOLZEL: *Concerto in D.* TELEMANN: *Concerto in C min.; Concerto in D for Trumpet, 2 Oboes and Strings* (with Nicklin and Miller). VIVALDI: *Double Trumpet Concerto in C, RV 537* (with Soustrot); *Double Concerto in B flat for Trumpet and Violin, RV 548* (with I. Brown).

(B) *** EMI Red Line (ADD) 569874.

Maurice André is peerless in this kind of repertoire and the accompaniments under Marriner are attractively alert and stylish. The Academy provides expert soloists to match André on the concertante works by Telemann (in D) and Vivaldi (RV 548) which come together towards the end and offer much the most interesting invention. The concerto by Stölzel is conventional, but has a fine slow movement. Throughout, André's smooth, rich timbre and highly musical phrasing give pleasure. The recording is first class, with the CD adding extra definition and presence.

Music for trumpet and organ (with Jane Parker-Smith or Alfred Mitterhofer): CHARPENTIER: *Te Deum: Fanfare.* ALBINONI: *Adagio* (arr. Giazotto). BACH: *Violin Partita in E: Gavotte & Rondeau. Orchestral Suite No. 3: Air. Cello Suite No. 4: Bourrée. Cantata No. 147: Chorale: Jesu, joy of man's desiring.* CLARKE: *Trumpet Voluntary.* SENAILLE: *Allegro spiritoso.* STANLEY: *Trumpet tune.* BACH/GOUNOD: *Ave Maria.* MOZART: *Exsultate jubilate: Alleluja.* PURCELL: *The Queen's dolour* (aria). Music for trumpet and orchestra: HANDEL: *Concerto in D min.* (arr. Thilde from *Flute Sonata in B min.*). ALBINONI: *Concertos: in B flat and D, Op. 7/3 & 6* (arr. of Oboe Concertos). TELEMANN: *Concerto in D for Trumpet and Oboe* (all with ECO, Mackerras). HERTEL: *Concerto in E flat.* HAYDN: *Concerto in E flat.* TELEMANN: *Concerto in F min.* (arr. of Oboe Concerto). ALBINONI: *Concerto in D min.* (arr. of *Chamber Sonata for Violin and Continuo, Op. 6/4*). ALESSANDRO MARCELLO: *Concerto in C* (originally for oboe) (all with LPO, Jesús López-Cobos).

(B) *** EMI Double fforte (ADD) 5 73374-2 (2).

Both these discs open with a series of famous tunes arranged for trumpet and organ, which for baroque repertoire works well enough. Played with rich tone, cultured phrasing, and, when needed, dazzling bravura, they are sumptuously presented, if you don't mind an excess of resonance. The programme begins with a larger-than-life account of the famous Charpentier *Te Deum*, and includes Clarke's famous *Voluntary* and the comparable trumpet piece by Stanley.

But otherwise the repertoire ranges wide, encompassing music originally written for other, very different instruments. These include pieces by Bach for solo violin and cello, by Albinoni and others for oboe, a famous bassoon encore by Senaillé and even (in the case of Mozart) a display-piece for the soprano voice. But André's presentation is so assured that one could be forgiven at times for thinking that they were actually conceived for the trumpet. Indeed the Bach *Gavotte* and *Rondeau* are most attractive on the trumpet.

Much the same applies to the concertos. The first group, vivaciously conducted by Mackerras, includes an ingenious Handel concoction, which even brings a brief reminder of the *Water Music*, and the Telemann multiple concerto is also very diverting. Then André negotiates the Hertel concerto, with its high tessitura, with breathtaking ease.

The second group, also given lively accompaniments, by the LPO under López-Cobos, are particularly successful, with the famous Haydn concerto most elegantly played, and in the transcriptions of works by Albinoni and Marcello slow movements are warmly phrased and André's stylishness and easy execution ensure the listener's enjoyment. Throughout, the analogue recording from the mid- to late 1970s is of high quality and very well transferred to CD. It is a pity that room was not found for the Hummel concerto, but this is undoubtedly excellent value.

'The Trumpet Shall Sound' (A 70th Birthday Tribute): TELEMANN: *Concertos: in E min., TWV51:e1; in G, TWV Anh.51:G1; in C min., TWV51:c1.* HANDEL: *Concertos Nos. 1 in B flat, HWV 301; 2 in B flat, HWV 302a; 3 in G min., HWV 287; Messiah: The Trumpet Shall Sound* (with Franz Crass, bass) (all with Munich Bach O, Karl Richter). Joseph HAYDN: *Concerto in E flat.* Michael HAYDN: *Concerto in D.* Franz Xaver RICHTER: *Concerto in D* (all with Munich CO, Hans Stadlmair). Alessandro SCARLATTI: *Sinfonia Concertata con ripieni No. 2 in D for Flute, Trumpet & Strings* (with Hans-Martin Linde, flute, & Zurich Coll. Mus.). VIVALDI: *Double Trumpet Concerto in C, RV 537.* BUONAVENTURA: *Sonata No. 1 in C for Trumpet & Organ* (with Hedwig Bilgram, organ). TORELLI: *Concerto in D.* STOLZEL: *Concerto in D.* TELEMANN: *Concerto Sonata in D, TWV44:1* (all with ECO, Mackerras).
(B) ★★(*) DG Double (ADD) 474 331-2 (2).

DG have gathered together on this Double all Maurice André's recordings made for that label between 1965 and 1977, with splendidly sustained solo playing throughout. It includes, of course, the greatest trumpet concerto of all, by Haydn, and here André takes the *Andante* in a rather leisurely fashion; but he is gracious and serene, and most listeners will respond to his elegance. Michael Haydn's concerto, a two-movement concertante section of a seven-movement *Serenade*, has incredibly high tessitura but, characteristically, André reaches up for it with consummate ease. Most of the Baroque concertos (notably those by Telemann and Handel) were originally written for oboe, tempering virtuosity in outer movements with very agreeable central *Andantes*, but André makes them sound custom-made for the trumpet. The Torelli (with its fine slow movement) is an exception. In the Vivaldi *Double Concerto* André plays both solo parts (by electronic means). The *Sonata* by Giovanni Bonaventura Viviani (1638–c. 1692) is a very attractive piece, comprising five brief but striking miniatures, each only a minute or so in length. Alessandro Scarlatti's engaging *Sinfonia* is also in five movements and incorporates a solo flute; the latter is all but drowned out in the *Spiritoso* first movement but takes the solo role in the two brief *Adagios* (the second quite touching); the trumpet returns to echo the flute in the central *Allegro*, and they share the *Presto* finale. The recording usually catches the solo trumpet faithfully throughout, but the earlier, Munich recordings show their age in the string-tone and occasionally a certain lack of refinement, though those conducted by Stadlmair are smoother. The later recordings with Mackerras and the ECO are obviously more modern.

Argerich, Martha (piano), with other artists

Martha Argerich Collection.
(M) ★★(*) DG ADD/DDD 453 566-2 (11).

Volume I: *Concertos*: BEETHOVEN: *Piano Concertos Nos. 1 in C, Op. 15; 2 in B flat, Op. 19* (with Philh. O, Sinopoli). CHOPIN: *Piano Concertos Nos. 1 in E min., Op. 11* (with LSO, Abbado); *2 in F min., Op. 21.* SCHUMANN: *Piano Concerto in A min., Op. 54* (both with Nat. SO, Rostropovich). TCHAIKOVSKY: *Piano Concerto No. 1 in B flat min., Op. 23* (with RPO, Dutoit). LISZT: *Piano Concerto No. 1 in E flat* (with LSO). PROKOFIEV: *Piano Concerto No. 3 in C, Op. 26.* RAVEL: *Piano Concerto in G* (with BPO) (both cond. Abbado).
(M) ★★(*) DG ADD/DDD 453 567-2 (4).

The chimerical volatility of Martha Argerich's musical personality comes out again and again in this impressive survey of her recorded repertory. Her ability in concertos to strike sparks in a musical partnership with the right conductor (Giuseppe Sinopoli in Beethoven and Abbado in Chopin's *First Concerto*) brings characteristically spontaneous music-making, bursting with inner life.

If Chopin's *F minor Concerto*, recorded ten years later in 1978, is rather less successful, she is back on form again in Tchaikovsky (with Dutoit), to produce a performance which has a genuine sense of scale and which balances poetry with excitement. Her temperament takes less readily to the Schumann *Concerto* (here with Rostropovich), a performance which has dynamism, vigour and colour, and delicacy in the slow movement, but which does not quite capture the work's more refined romantic feeling in the outer movements.

Yet her Liszt *E flat Concerto* is surprisingly restrained, gripping without any barnstorming. She is perhaps at her very finest in Prokofiev's *Third Concerto* and hardly less impressive in the Ravel *G major*, a performance full of subtlety, but vigorous and outgoing too. Abbado was again her partner in the three last-mentioned works and together they found a rare musical symbiosis. DG have generally given Argerich's concertos excellent recording, and there is nothing here which will not provide stimulating repeated listening. All these performances (except the Chopin *Second Concerto*) are discussed in greater depth under their composer entries in our main volume.

Volume II: Chopin and Bach: CHOPIN: *Piano Sonatas Nos. 2 in B flat min., Op. 35; 3 in B min., Op. 58; Barcarolle in F sharp, Op. 60; Scherzos Nos. 2 in B flat min., Op. 31; 3 in C sharp min., Op. 39; 24 Preludes, Op. 28; Preludes in C sharp min., Op. 45; in A flat, Op. posth.; Andante spianato & Grande polonaise brillante, Op. 22; Polonaise No. 6 in A flat, Op. 53; Polonaise-Fantaisie in A flat, Op. 61; 3 Mazurkas, Op. 59.* BACH: *Toccata in C min., BWV 911; Partita No. 2 in C min., BWV 826; English Suite No. 2 in A min., BWV 807.*

(M) **(*) DG (ADD) 453 572-2 (3).

Argerich's accounts of the two Chopin *Sonatas* are fiery, impetuous and brilliant, with no want of poetic vision to discommend them. Both, however, have a highly strung quality that will not be to all tastes. The *Preludes* show Argerich at her finest, full of individual insights. The *Scherzo No. 3* and *Barcarolle* are taken from her remarkable début LP recital of 1961 and are very impetuous indeed, and are also less easy to live with. She seems not to want to provide a firm musical control, but is carried away on a breath of wind. Many of the other pieces are played splendidly, with the *Scherzo No. 2* impressively demonstrating her technical command. Her Bach, too, is lively but well conceived. The digital remastering gives the piano-image striking presence, and the recording is resonant and full in timbre, although at *fortissimo* levels the timbre becomes hard.

Volume III: Music for piano solo and duo: SCHUMANN: *Kinderszenen, Op. 15; Kreisleriana, Op. 16; Piano Sonata No. 2 in G min., Op. 22.* LISZT: *Piano Sonata in B min.; Hungarian Rhapsody No. 6.* BRAHMS: *Rhapsodies, Op. 79/1–2.* PROKOFIEV: *Toccata, Op. 11.* RAVEL: *Gaspard de la nuit; Jeux d'eau; Sonatine; Valses nobles et sentimentales. Ma*

Mère l'Oye; Rapsodie espagnole (arr. 2 pianos & percussion). BARTOK: *Sonata for 2 Pianos & Percussion* (with Freire, Sadlo, Guggeis). TCHAIKOVSKY: *Nutcracker Suite, Op. 71a* (arr. 2 pianos). RACHMANINOV: *Symphonic Dances for 2 Pianos, Op. 45* (with Economou).

(M) **(*) DG ADD/DDD 453 576-2 (4).

The third box contains much of interest. There is no doubting the instinctive flair or her intuitive feeling for Schumann. However, she is let down by an unpleasingly close recording of *Kinderszenen* and *Kreisleriana*. Her Ravel again shows her playing at its most subtle and perceptive, yet with a vivid palette, even if at times a little more poise would be welcome. Taken from her début recital of 1961, the Brahms *First Rhapsody* is explosively fast; then suddenly she puts the brakes on and provides most poetic playing in the central section. Such a barnstorming approach is more readily at home in the Prokofiev *Toccata*, and she goes over the top in the Liszt *Hungarian Rhapsody* with a certain panache.

In the Liszt *Sonata*, although the playing demonstrates an impressively responsive temperament, the work's lyrical feeling is all but submerged by the brilliantly impulsive virtuosity. The Ravel arrangements (with percussion!) are done with eminently good taste, restraint and musical imagination but, all the same, is there a need for them at all? They are more interesting to hear once or twice than to repeat.

The Bartók, though, has tremendous fire and intensity. The aural image is very good and discreetly balanced. The Tchaikovsky *Nutcracker* arrangement of Nicolas Economou works well. The playing is of a very high order. The Rachmaninov *Dances* are played with great temperament, and everything is marvellously alive and well thought out. There is much sensitivity and a lively sense of enjoyment in evidence, as well as great virtuosity. The recording is good.

Arrau, Claudio (piano)

BEETHOVEN: *Piano Concerto No. 4 in G, Op. 58* (with Dresden State O, C. Davis). *Diabelli Variations; Piano Sonata No. 26 in E flat* (Les Adieux), *Op. 81a; 30 in E, Op. 109. Violin Sonata No. 1 in D, Op. 12/1* (with Arthur Grumiaux). BRAHMS: *Piano Concerto No. 1 in D min., Op. 15* (with Concg. O, Haitink). *Piano Sonata No. 2 in F sharp min., Op. 2.* CHOPIN: *Ballades, Nos. 1–4; Barcarolle in F sharp, Op. 60; Fantaisie-Impromptu in C sharp min., Op. 66; Impromptus Nos. 1–3, Op. 29, 36 & 51; Scherzos Nos. 1–4.* MOZART: *Fantasias in D min., K.397, & C min., K.474; Rondo in A min., K.511.* SCHUMANN: *Fantaisie in C, Op. 17; Humoreske in B flat, Op. 20; Nachtstücke, Op. 23.* LISZT: *Piano Concerto No. 2 in A* (with LSO, C. Davis). *Etudes d'exécution transcendante; Réminiscences de Simone Boccanegra; Sonata in B min.; Vallée d'Obermann.* SCHUBERT: *Sonata No. 19 in C min., D.958;*

Allegretto in C min., D.915; 3 Klavierstücke, D.946.
BACH: *Partita No. 5 in G, BWV 829.* DEBUSSY:
*Préludes, Book 2; La plus que lente; Valse
romantique.*

(B) (***) Ph. mono/stereo 471 461-2 (10).

A compilation to mark the centenary of Arrau's birth
in 1903 which collects some of his very finest records.
Those who have acquired some or many of them will
have to make up their own minds as to whether this
box offers a sensible investment, but there is no
question as to the musical stature of this great artist.
The first disc includes a rarity, the *Diabelli Variations*
that Arrau recorded in New York in 1952 (it was
issued in England on the Brunswick label), which has
not been in currency for many years. The Beethoven
G major Concerto with Sir Colin Davis and the
Dresden orchestra of 1984 is among the most recent.
The two sonatas, Opp. 81a and 109, are superb examples of his art, though the *Hammerklavier* was among
the most searching. The Brahms *D minor Concerto*
with Haitink and the Concertgebouw is magisterial
(its slow movement particularly inspired) and the
Liszt and Schumann are hardly less worthy of inclusion. It is good to see the Second Book of Debussy
Préludes included, for we were much impressed by
them when they appeared in the early 1980s. All in
all, there are some magisterial performances here
that will give pianists and music-lovers alike much
food for thought.

Ashton, Graham (trumpet)

CD 1 (with Irish Chamber Orchestra): PURCELL:
Trumpet Sonata in D. CORELLI: *Trumpet Sonata in
D.* VIVALDI: *Double Trumpet Concerto* (with
Ruddock). TELEMANN: *Trumpet Concerto in D.*
ALBINONI: *Trumpet Sonatas Nos. 1 in C; 2 in D.*
STRADELLA: *Sinfonia 'Il Barcheggio' in D.* TORELLI:
Sonata No. 5 for Trumpet and Strings in D.
HANDEL: *Suite for Trumpet and Strings in D.*

CD 2 (with John Lenehan (piano)): MAXWELL
DAVIES: *Trumpet Sonata.* JOLIVET: *Heptade for
Piano and Percussion* (with Gregory Knowles,
percussion). NYMAN: *Flugal Horn & Piano Sonata.*
HENZE: *Sonatina for Solo Trumpet.* BERIO:
Sequenza X for Solo Trumpet. FENTON: *Five Parts of
the Dance.*

(BB) ** Virgin 2x1 5 62031-2 (2).

This inexpensive set combines two recital CDs, one
devoted to baroque trumpet repertoire, the other to
more contemporary works. The baroque items are
well enough played by the soloist, but his orchestral
support is indifferent, and the reverberant recording
is poorly detailed. The avant-garde works on the
second CD are altogether more sharply performed
and are given better sound. Maxwell Davies's *Trumpet Sonata* echoes the layout of the baroque concertos, though the harmonic language is of an entirely

different world. Jolivet's *Heptade* has a battery of
percussion instruments to support the myriad effects
the soloist achieves on his instrument, and after this
generally spiky work, Michael Nyman's lyrical writing is welcome. The longest piece here is Berio's
Sequenza. It is everything one expects of this composer, and if there is no melody to speak of, the
effects are aurally fascinating, even if some may feel
that twenty minutes of them is too much of a good
thing. Fenton's *Five Parts of the Dance* begins rather
hauntingly, with the trumpet placed in the distance,
and the ensuing movements with piano and percussion are quite imaginative. This set will be of greatest
appeal to those interested in the contemporary items
(which would be better off on a separate issue and
with more helpful documentation).

Ballet Music

'Fête du Ballet' (played by the ECO, LSO, New
Philh. O, ROHCG O, Bonynge): ROSSINI: *Matinées
musicales; Soirées musicales; William Tell: Ballet
Music.* CHOPIN: *Les Sylphides.* STRAUSS (arr.
Desormière): *Le Beau Danube.* SAINT-SAENS: *The
Swan.* TCHAIKOVSKY: *Pas de deux* from *The Black
Swan, Sleeping Beauty* and *Swan Lake; Melody;
December.* RUBINSTEIN: *Danses des fiancées de
Cachemir.* CZIBULKA: *Love's Dream after the Ball.*
KREISLER: *The Dragonfly.* ASAFYEV: *Papillons.*
LINCKE: *Gavotte Pavlova.* DELIBES: *Naïla:
Intermezzo.* CATALANI: *Loreley: Danza delle
Ondine.* KUPRINSKI: *Polish Wedding.* TRAD.:
Bolero, 1830; Mazurka. DRIGO: *Le Flûte magique:
Pas de trois; Le Réveil de Flore; Pas de deux* from *Le
Corsaire, Diane et Actéon* and *La Esmeralda.*
MINKUS: *Pas de deux* from *La Bayadère, Paquita*
(including *Grand pas*) and *Don Quixote.* ADAM:
Giselle (excerpts). LOVENSKJOLD: *La Sylphide: Pas
de deux.* PUGNI: *Pas de quatre.* HELSTED: *Flower
Festival at Genzano: Pas de deux.* MASSENET: *Le
Cid: ballet music; La Cigale: Valse très lente; Le Roi
de Lahore: Entr'acte (Act V)* and *Waltz (Act III);
Méditation de Thaïs; Cendrillon; Scènes alsaciennes;
Scènes dramatiques.* MEYERBEER: *Les Patineurs.*
LUIGINI: *Ballet égyptien.* AUBER: *Pas classique;
Marco Spada; Les Rendez-vous.* THOMAS: *Françoise
de Rimini.* SCARLATTI: *The Good-humoured
Ladies.* DONIZETTI: *La Favorite: Ballet Music.*
BERLIOZ: *Les Troyens: Ballet Music.* LECOCQ (arr.
Jacob): *Mam'zelle Angot.* OFFENBACH: *La Papillon:
Suite.* BURGMÜLLER: *La Péri.*

❂ (BB) *** Decca (ADD/DDD) 468 578-2 (10).

This set is a perfect and well-conceived tribute to
Richard Bonynge's indefatigable quest to resurrect
forgotten treasures: it's a feast of some of the most
delightful and piquant ballet music of the (mainly)
nineteenth century. It includes two major ballets not
released on CD before: Auber's *Marco Spada*, which
is full of the catchy tunes we know from his overtures, and Burgmüller's *La Péri*, a work seeped in the

romantic ballet tradition. Other highlights include Lecocq's deliciously witty *Mam'zelle Angot*; the rarely heard and effervescent *Le Beau Danube*; Luigini's *Ballet égyptien* (still the only recording of the complete work and originally part of a two-LP set, 'Homage to Pavlova', of which all the charming vignettes are included here); the only recordings of Auber's *Pas classique* and *Les Rendez-vous*; plus a string of vivacious and colourful *pas de deux*. Other unexpected delights are the perky *Bolero, 1830*; the once-popular coupling of *Le Cid* and *Les Patineurs* ballet music (here in exceptionally vivid sound); the luscious *Waltz* from Massenet's *Le Roi de Lahore*; the same composer's *Scènes dramatiques* (first time on CD) and *Scènes alsaciennes*, along with the sparkling *March of the Princes* from *Cendrillon*. Bonynge's supremacy in this repertoire is obvious: through his well-sprung rhythms and elegant pointing of the melodic line, the music glows. With excellent sleeve notes and vintage Decca sound, this set is highly recommended.

'*Bonynge Ballet Festival*' (played by LSO or Nat. PO):

Volume 1: WEBER (orch. Berlioz): *Invitation to the dance*. CHOPIN (arr. Douglas): *Les Sylphides*. J. STRAUSS JR (arr. Gamley): *Bal de Vienne*. LUIGINI: *Ballet égyptien*.

Volume 2: TRAD. (arr. O'Turner): *Bolero 1830*. PUGNI: *Pas de quatre*. MINKUS: *La Bayadère* (excerpts). DRIGO: *Pas de trois*. ADAM: *Giselle* (excerpts). LOVENSKJOLD: *La Sylphide* (excerpts).

Volume 3: '*Homage to Pavlova*': SAINT-SAENS: *The Swan*. TCHAIKOVSKY: *Melody; Noël*. RUBINSTEIN: *Danses des fiancées de Cachemir*. CZIBULKA: *Love's dream after the ball*. KREISLER: *The Dragonfly (Schön Rosmarin)*. ASAFYEV: *Papillons*. LINCKE: *Gavotte Pavlova (Glowworm Idyll)*. DELIBES: *Naïla: Intermezzo*. CATALANI: *Danza delle Ondine*. KRUPINSKI: *Mazurka (Polish Wedding)*.

Volume 4: '*Pas de deux*': AUBER: *Pas classique*. MINKUS: *Don Quixote: Pas de deux; Paquita: Pas de deux*. TCHAIKOVSKY: *The Nutcracker: Pas de deux. Sleeping Beauty: Pas de deux*. DRIGO: *Le Corsaire: Pas de deux; La Esmeralda; Pas de deux*. HELSTED: *Flower Festival at Genzano*.

Volume 5: '*Ballet music from opera*': ROSSINI: *William Tell*. DONIZETTI: *La Favorita*. GOUNOD: *Faust; La Reine de Saba (waltz)*. MASSENET: *Ariane; Le Roi de Lahore*. BERLIOZ: *Les Troyens*. SAINT-SAENS: *Henry VIII*.

*** Australian Decca (ADD/DDD) 452 767-2 (5).

This less comprehensive set of Richard Bonynge's ballet recordings also includes much music not otherwise available. Volume 1 has two rarities: *Bal de Vienne* – a particularly felicitous arrangement of Johann Strauss's lesser-known works, with an

exhilarating finale, and (surprisingly) the only complete recordings of Luigini's delightful *Ballet égyptien* (Fistoulari only recorded the four-movement suite).

Volume 2 draws from Bonynge's '*The Art of the Prima Ballerina*' set: each of the rarities by Minkus, Drigo and Pugni has at least one striking melody, and all are vivacious and colourfully orchestrated; the *Bolero 1830* is short but piquant.

Volume 3, '*Homage to Pavlova*', is more reflectively nostalgic and has delightful rarities: many are just salon pieces but show their worth when played so beautifully on a full orchestra.

Volume 4's collection of *Pas de deux* is both elegantly and robustly enjoyable, with the Auber, Minkus and Drigo numbers especially lively and memorable.

Volume 5 comprises generally better-known ballet music from operas. It includes the lovely Massenet ballet music from *Le Roi de Lahore*, which starts off ominously in a minor key, before a theme, magically introduced on the saxophone, builds up into a magnificent full orchestral waltz swirling around the whole orchestra. *The Dance of the Gypsy* from Saint-Saëns's *Henry VIII* is another gem: it begins sinuously, but ends in a jolly *valse macabre*.

This is music in which Bonynge excels: he has exactly the right feel for it and produces an infectious lift throughout. The recordings are in Decca's best analogue tradition – vivid, warm and full (though a few are from equally vivid digital sources), and all sound pristinely fresh in these transfers. With full sleeve-notes included, this is a splendid bargain collection of highly entertaining music well worth seeking out.

Baltimore Symphony Orchestra, David Zinman

'*Russian sketches*': GLINKA: *Overture: Ruslan and Ludmilla*. IPPOLITOV-IVANOV: *Caucasian Sketches*. RIMSKY-KORSAKOV: *Russian Easter Festival overture*. TCHAIKOVSKY: *Francesca da Rimini, Op. 32. Eugene Onegin: Polonaise*.

**(*) Telarc CD 80378.

Opening with a fizzingly zestful performance of Glinka's *Ruslan and Ludmilla overture*, with impressively clean articulation from the violins, this remarkably well-recorded concert of Russian music readily demonstrates the excellence of the Baltimore Symphony in every department.

The *Caucasian Sketches* are a disappointment, but only because Zinman's conception of the evocative first three movements (*In the Mountain Pass, In the Village* and *In the Mosque*) is too refined, not Russian enough in feeling; but the famous *Procession of the Sardar* has plenty of piquant colour and impetus. *Francesca da Rimini* brings the most brilliant playing and the middle section, with its rich, Tchaikovskian woodwind palette, is glowingly beautiful. However, the impact of the closing pages here depends more on the spectacular Telarc engineering than on the conductor, who does not generate the necessary degree of passionate despair in the work's great climax. Rimsky-Korsakov's *Russian Easter Festival overture* is a different matter, generating considerable excitement. It is superbly done, with lustrous colours from every section of the orchestra and a memorable solo contribution from the trombones (who are also very impressive in *Francesca*). The recording here is very much in the demonstration bracket and shows Telarc engineering at its most realistic, thrilling in its breadth and body of orchestral tone, with excellent detail and a convincing presence in a natural concert-hall acoustic.

Barbirolli, Sir John (cello), and conducting various orchestras

'*Glorious John*': Barbirolli centenary collection (1911–69): Disc 1: (1911–47): VAN BIENE: *The Broken Melody* (Barbirolli, cello). MOZART: *String Quartet in E flat, K.428: Minuet* (with Kutcher Qt). MASCAGNI: *Cavalleria rusticana: Santuzza's aria* (with Lilian Stiles-Allen). VERDI: *Otello: Niun me tema* (with Renato Zanelli). PUCCINI: *Tosca: Tre sbirri, una carozza* (with Giovanni Inghilleri). JOHANN STRAUSS JR: *Die Fledermaus: Brother dear and sister dear*. SAINT-SAENS: *Valse-caprice, Op. 76* (with Yvonne Arnaud, piano). BALFE: *The Bohemian Girl: Overture* (with SO). COLLINS: *Overture*. WEINBERGER: *Christmas* (with NYPO). WEBER: *Euryanthe: Overture*. DELIUS: *Walk to the Paradise Garden* (with VPO). .

Disc 2: (1948–64) (all with Hallé O): STRAVINSKY: *Concerto in D*. MOZART: *Cassation in G, K.63: Andante; Divertimento No. 11 in D, K.251: Minuet*. GRIEG, arr. Barbirolli: *Secret*. VILLA-LOBOS: *Bachianas brasileiras No. 4*. FALLA: *Seguidilla murciana* (with Marina de Gabarain). LEHAR: *Gold and Silver Waltz*. BACH, arr. Barbirolli: *Sheep may Safely Graze*. BERLIOZ: *Damnation of Faust: rehearsal sequence*. Interview: Barbirolli and R. Kinloch Anderson.

(B) (***) Dutton mono/stereo CDSJB 1999 (2).

It was Vaughan Williams who referred to Barbirolli as 'Glorious John', hence the title of this budget-priced compilation to celebrate the great conductor's centenary: twenty historic items, five of them previously unpublished, plus a rehearsal sequence and an interview full of reminiscences. From 1911 you have the eleven-year-old Giovanni Barbirolli playing the cello, swoopy but perfect in intonation.

As a budding conductor he accompanies star soloists, including Yvonne Arnaud in Saint-Saëns's charming *Valse-caprice*, while items from his under-

prized New York period include a delightful Weinberger piece, otherwise unavailable, *Christmas*. Also unexpected is Barbirolli's pioneering account with the Hallé of Stravinsky's *Concerto in D*, recorded in 1948, two years after the work first appeared. And how revealing to have the Vienna Philharmonic heartfelt in Delius's *Walk to the Paradise Garden*!

The rehearsal of the *Dance of the Sylphs* dates from 1957, and in many ways most endearing of all is the 1964 conversation between the gravel-voiced Barbirolli and his recording producer Roland Kinloch Anderson, covering such subjects as Mahler, the Berlin Philharmonic and Elgar – a splendid portrait.

'*A Barbirolli Collection*' (with Hallé O, LSO, Philh. or New Philh. O): BRITTEN: *Violin Concerto* (original version; with Theo Olof). HEMING: *Threnody for a Soldier Killed in Action*. RUBBRA: *Symphony No. 5; Loth to Depart* (mono 5 66053-2). DELIUS: *Brigg Fair; La Calinda; In a Summer Garden; Fennimore and Gerda: Intermezzo. Hassan: Intermezzo and Serenade* (with Robert Tear); *Irmelin Prelude; Late Swallows; On Hearing the First Cuckoo in Spring; A Song before Sunrise; A Song of Summer; Summer Night on the River; A Village Romeo & Juliet: Walk to the Paradise Garden. Appalachia* (with Jenkins, Amb. S.) (5 65119-2) (2). ELGAR: *Symphony No. 1; Cockaigne Overture* (7 64511-2); *Symphony No. 2; Sospiri; Elegy* (7 64724-2); *Cockaigne; Froissart; Pomp and Circumstance Marches 1–5* (5 66323-2); *Enigma Variations; Falstaff* (5 66322-2); *Dream of Gerontius* (with J. Baker, R. Lewis, Kim Borg, Hallé Ch., Sheffield Philharmonic Ch., Amb. S.) (5 73579-2) (2). *Introduction and Allegro; Serenade for Strings; Cockaigne Overture*. VAUGHAN WILLIAMS: *Sinfonia Antartica* (with M. Ritchie, Hallé Ch.); *Oboe Concerto* (with Evelyn Rothwell); *Tuba Concerto* (with Philip Catelinet); *Fantasia on Greensleeves; 5 Variants on Dives and Lazarus; The Wasps Overture* (mono 5 66543-2) (2). *A London Symphony (No. 2)*. IRELAND: *A London Overture* (5 65109-2). VAUGHAN WILLIAMS: *Symphony No. 5*. BAX: *Tintagel* (5 65110-2).

(BB) *** EMI mono/stereo 5 75790-2 (13).

Barbrolli's super-bargain box offers a baker's dozen of highly desirable CDs, all of which are available separately and are reviewed under their composers in our main volume, and a number of which (Elgar and Delius) are also included in other, comparable, budget collections. Notable here is the inclusion of two important Vaughan Williams reissues in a Double-CD package of Barbirolli's première mono recordings, including the *Sinfonia Antartica* and the *Oboe Concerto* (with Evelyn Rothwell), coupled with Elgar string music, and Barbirolli's warmly passionate stereo version of the *Fifth Symphony*, coupled with an unforgettable performance of Bax's *Tintagel*.

Baroque music

'*Music of the Baroque*' (played by: (i) Orpheus CO; (ii) Simon Standage; (iii) David Reichenberg; (iv) Trevor Pinnock (harpsichord); (v) English Concert Ch.; (vi) English Concert, Trevor Pinnock; (vii) Söllscher (guitar), Camerata Bern, Füri; (viii) Hannes, Wolfgang & Bernhard Läubin, Simon Preston, Norbert Schmitt): (i) HANDEL: *Solomon: Arrival of the Queen of Sheba.* (vi) *Water Music: Allegro – Andante; Air; Bourrée; Hornpipe.* (i) *Xerxes: Largo.* (v, vi) *Messiah: Hallelujah Chorus.* (vi) *Music for the Royal Fireworks: La Réjouissance.* (iii; iv; vi) *Oboe Concerto No. 1 (Adagio; Allegro).* (vi) *Concerto grosso, Op. 6/12 in B min. (Aria; Larghetto e piano).* (i) PACHELBEL: *Canon in D.* (viii) MOURET: *Rondeau.* J. S. BACH: (i) *Jesu, joy of man's desiring.* (vi) *Brandenburg Concerto No. 3 in G (Allegro).* PURCELL: *Sound the trumpet, sound.* (ii; vi) VIVALDI: *The Four Seasons: Winter (Largo).* (vii) *Lute Concerto in D (Largo).* (i) ALBINONI (arr. GIAZOTTO): *Adagio in G min.* CORELLI: *Christmas Concerto, Op. 6/8 (Allegro; Pastorale; Largo).* (iv) DAQUIN: *Le Coucou.*

(B) *** DG 449 842-2.

This 75-minute concert draws on various digital recordings made during the 1980s to make a most agreeable entertainment. The various items have all been issued previously, and their performance pedigrees, on either modern or original instruments, cannot be gainsaid. The opening *Arrival of the Queen of Sheba* and the elegantly played Pachelbel *Canon* feature the Orpheus Chamber Orchestra, but Pinnock's suite from the Handel *Water Music* is equally persuasive in demonstrating the advantages of period instruments in baroque repertoire. Such contrasts are aurally stimulating and, with plenty of favourite items included, this makes a very successful bargain sampler, when all the music is consistently well played and recorded. However, the lack of proper documentation is a drawback: the two excellent vocal soloists in Purcell's *Sound the trumpet* are unnamed.

BBC Philharmonic Orchestra, Matthias Bamert

'*Stokowski Encores*': HANDEL: *Overture in D min.* GABRIELI: *Sonata piano e forte.* CLARKE: *Trumpet Prelude.* MATTHESON: *Air.* MOZART: *Rondo alla turca.* BEETHOVEN: *Adagio from Moonlight Sonata.* SCHUBERT: *Serenade.* FRANCK: *Panis Angelicus.* CHOPIN: *Funeral March.* DEBUSSY: *The Girl with the flaxen hair.* IPPOLITOV-IVANOV: *In the manger.* SHOSTAKOVICH: *United Nations March.* TCHAIKOVSKY: *Andante cantabile.* ALBENIZ: *Festival in Seville.* SOUSA: *The Stars and Stripes forever.* (all arr. Leopold Stokowski).

*** Chan. 9349.

However outrageous it may seem to take a tiny harpsichord piece by a contemporary of Bach and Handel, Johann Mattheson, and inflate it on full strings, the result caresses the ear, and the Chandos engineers come up with recording to match. Amazingly, Mozart's *Rondo alla turca* becomes a sparkling moto perpetuo, Paganini-like, with Stokowski following Mozart himself in using 'Turkish' percussion, *Entführung*-style.

The opening *Adagio* of Beethoven's *Moonlight Sonata* with lush orchestration then echoes Rachmaninov's *Isle of the Dead*, with menace in the music. Stokowski's arrangement of the Handel *Overture in D minor* (taken from the *Chandos Anthem No. 2*) is quite different from Elgar's transcription of the same piece, opulent in a different way, with timbres antiphonally contrasted.

If Bamert cannot match the panache of Stokowski in the final Sousa march, *The Stars and Stripes forever*, that is in part due to the recording balance, which fails to bring out the percussion, including xylophone. The least attractive item is Schubert's *Serenade*, given full Hollywood treatment not just with soupy strings but with quadruple woodwind trilling above. Hollywood treatment of a different kind comes in the *United Nations March* of Shostakovich, in 1942 used as the victory finale of an MGM wartime musical, *Thousands Cheer*. Stokowski promptly cashed in with his own, non-vocal arrangement. A disc for anyone who likes to wallow in opulent sound.

BBC Philharmonic Orchestra, Yan Pascal Tortelier

'*French Bonbons*': Overtures: ADAM: *Si j'étais roi.* AUBER: *Le cheval de bronze (The bronze horse).* HEROLD: *Zampa.* MAILLART: *Les dragons de Villars.* THOMAS: *Mignon: Gavotte.* OFFENBACH: *La Belle Hélène* (arr. Haensch); *Contes d'Hoffmann: Entr'acte & Barcarolle.* CHABRIER: *Habanera; Joyeuse marche.* GOUNOD: *Marche funèbre d'une marionette.* MASSENET: *Thaïs: Méditation* (with Yuri Torchinsky, violin; both with Royal Liverpool PO Ch.). *Mélodie: Elégie* (with Peter Dixon, cello); *Les erinnes: Tristesse du soir. La Vierge: Le dernier sommeil de la Vierge.*

⊶ *** Chan. 9765.

As Sir Thomas Beecham well knew, there is something special about French orchestral lollipops and this is a superb collection, beautifully played and given demonstration-standard recording – just sample the brass evocation of Maillart's Dragoons, and in *La Belle Hélène*, which is played with much warmth and style. Gounod's whimsical *Funeral march of a marionette*, which Hitchcock has made famous, is delightfully done, and the other bandstand overtures have plenty of sparkle and zest, yet are not driven too hard – the galop which climaxes *The Bronze Horse* is exhilaratingly jaunty. Highly recommended.

BBC Symphony Orchestra, Sir Adrian Boult

'*Boult's BBC Years*': BEETHOVEN: *Symphony No. 8 in F, Op. 93*. HUMPERDINCK: *Overture: Hansel and Gretel*. TCHAIKOVSKY: *Capriccio italien, Op. 45; Serenade for strings, Op. 48*.

(***) Beulah mono 1PD12.

These recordings return to the catalogue for the first time since the days of shellac and will almost certainly be new to the majority of younger collectors. The Beethoven is a strong, sturdy performance which gives a good idea of the excellence of the BBC Symphony Orchestra in the early days of its existence. It comes from 1932 and the strings produce an opulent, weighty sound without having the opaque quality they developed in the post-war years. The recording is not at all bad for the period, and the transfer does it justice. The Tchaikovsky *Serenade* was recorded five years later in the same Abbey Road studio but with the acoustic sounding much drier. A patrician account with no nonsense about it that may since have been surpassed by many other great partnerships but which will give pleasure to those old enough to remember Sir Adrian's pre-war and wartime broadcasts. The Colston Hall, Bristol, in which the orchestra recorded the *Capriccio italien* in 1940, has the richer acoustic, and the performance combines dignity and freshness.

BBC Symphony Orchestra & Chorus, Sir Andrew Davis

'*Last Night of the Proms 2000*' BACH: *Fantasia and Fugue in C min., BWV 537*. MOZART: *Violin Concerto No. 4 in D, K.218* (with Hahn, violin). R. STRAUSS: *Salome: Dance of the 7 Veils: Final Scene* (with Eaglen, soprano). SHOSTAKOVICH: (orch. McBurney) *Jazz Suite No. 2*. GRAINGER: *Tribute to Foster* (with Watson, Murray, Spence, Tear, Davies). DELIUS: *A Village Romeo and Juliet: Walk to the Paradise Garden*. ELGAR: *Pomp & Circumstance March No. 1*. WOOD: *Fantasia on British Sea Songs*. ARNE: *Rule Britannia!* (with Eaglen). PARRY: (orch. Elgar): *Jerusalem. National Anthem* (with Introductions, Interviews with Soloists, Laying of the Wreath; Speech by Sir Andrew Davis and presentation by Nicholas Kenyon. Producer: Peter Maniura).

*** BBC **DVD** WMDVD 8001-9.

Watching an old Last Night of the Proms programme on DVD might seem like eating half-warmed-up soup, but the year 2000 had some special claims – not just marking the Millennium but also in celebrating Sir Andrew Davis. He said goodbye after eleven consecutive Last Nights, as well as giving his final concert as Chief Conductor of the BBC Symphony Orchestra. The programme itself reflects

Davis's own preferences, when, as he explains in an interview, three of his favourite composers are represented: Elgar, with his sumptuous arrangement of Bach organ music, the *Fantasia and Fugue in C minor*; Mozart, with the *Violin Concerto No. 4 in D* featuring the brilliant young American, Hilary Hahn, as soloist; and Richard Strauss, with the *Dance of the Seven Veils* and the final scene from *Salome*, in which Jane Eaglen is the soprano, producing the most opulent tone, a commanding figure in every way.

Special facilities on the DVD consist of options on subtitles and an ability to limit the playing to music only, without introductions. What is infuriating and pure sloppiness over the transfer, however, is that tracking is so limited, so that the Mozart *Violin Concerto*, 25 minutes long, is on a single track, with no separation of movements.

BBC Symphony Orchestra & Chorus, Sir Andrew Davis (with other artists)

'*Prom at the Palace*': The Queen's Golden Jubilee Concert: WALTON: *Anniversary Fanfare*. HANDEL: *Music for the Royal Fireworks*: excerpts (both with Band of Royal Marines, Col. Richard Waterer). *Coronation Anthem: Zadok the Priest*. BIZET: *Carmen: Micaëla's Aria*. GERSHWIN: *Porgy and Bess: Summertime* (Dame Kiri Te Kanawa). TRAD., arr. BURTON: *2 Spirituals* (London Advent Chorale, Ken Burton). MESSAGER: *Solo de Concours for Clarinet and Piano* (Julian Bliss, Ashley Wass). HOLST: *The Planets: Jupiter*. TCHAIKOVSKY: *Swan Lake; Black Swan pas de deux* (danced by Roberto Bolle & Zenaida Yanowsky). ROSSINI: *Il barbiere di Siviglia: Largo al factotum*. GERMAN: *Merrie England: The Yeomen of England* (Sir Thomas Allen). ARNOLD: *Irish Dance; 2 Scottish Dances; Welsh Dance*. VILLA-LOBOS: *Bachianas Brasileiras No. 1* (Rostropovich & Cellos of LSO). PUCCINI: *Tosca: Vissi d'arte; 'E lucevan le stelle*. VERDI: *La traviata: Brindisi* (Angela Gheorghiu & Roberto Alagna). ELGAR: *Pomp and Circumstance March No. 1*. ARNE: *God Save the Queen*. (DVD introduced by Michael Parkinson. TV Producer: Ben Weston; Director: Bob Coles. DVD Producer: James Whitbourn.)

*** BBC Opus Arte **DVD** OA 0844 D. CD: VTCDX 42.

The DVD offers a straight repeat of the BBC's television relay of the concert in the grounds of Buckingham Palace, celebrating the Queen's Golden Jubilee in June 2002. Introduced by Michael Parkinson, it offers a sequence of short items, not all of them predictable, performed by an excellent choice of artists, with none of the media-boosted, middle-of-the-road performers who in too many so-called classical events represent a degrading of standards. Gheorghiu and Alagna may have been glamorized, but in musical terms they are outstanding, and here offer arias from Puccini's *Tosca* and the *Brindisi* duet from Verdi's *La Traviata*. Sir Thomas Allen, as well as singing Figaro's aria from Rossini's *Barbiere*, gives the *Yeomen of England* from Edward German's *Merrie England*, nowadays a rarity, and as an encore to Micaëla's aria from Bizet's *Carmen* Dame Kiri Te Kanawa sings *Summertime* from Gershwin's *Porgy and Bess*. A charming interlude has the 13-year-old clarinettist Julian Bliss performing a *Solo de Concours* by Messager (an item that specially delighted the Queen) and Rostropovich with the cellos of the LSO plays the *Prelude* from Villa-Lobos's *Bachianas Brasileiras No. 1*, not on the outdoor stage but more intimately in the Music Room of Buckingham Palace. In the Ballroom of the Palace, the dancers Roberto Bolle and Zenaida Yanowsky perform the *Black Swan pas de deux* from Tchaikovsky's *Swan Lake*, and Sir Andrew Davis and the BBC Symphony Orchestra crown their many contributions with Handel's *Fireworks Music*, joined by the Royal Marines Band and prompting a cracking firework display in *La Réjouissance* just as dusk gives way to night. The concert ends in true Proms-style with *Land of Hope and Glory* and the *National Anthem*. Though the amplified sound is aggressive at times, the wonder is that it comes over so well.

The CD version simply includes most of the musical items with the Parkinson introductions omitted as well as the *Fireworks Music*.

BBC Symphony Orchestra, Jac van Steen

'British Film Scores': BRITTEN: *Love from a Stranger.* GERHARD: *This Sporting Life.* LUTYENS: *The Skull.* RODNEY BENNETT: *The Return of the Soldier.*
★★★ NMC D 073.

Benjamin Britten's scores for pre-war GPO documentary films have long been recognized – notably the two with words by Auden, *Night Mail* and *Coal Face* – but his one score for a feature film, the thriller *Love from a Stranger*, has been buried for almost 70 years. The six fragments on this fascinating disc show that, even working at high speed, he wrote music consistently striking and inventive. Temperamental, he swore afterwards he would never again have anything to do with the film world (nor did he), when in addition to cuts being made, some of his music was ditched. The other three composers are all serialists, with the exiled Catalan, Roberto Gerhard, a strange choice for David Storey's *This Sporting Life*, with its background of mining and rugby league football. The result is fluent if unrelievedly dark. Elisabeth Lutyens, equally uncompromising in her idiom, is much more attuned to the needs of the medium in the horror film, *The Skull*, at once vigorous and sinister. Richard Rodney Bennett, far more adaptable, remains one of our most successful film composers, here splendidly represented by his evocative music for Alan Bridge's neglected film, *The Return of the Soldier*, an adaptation of a novel by Rebecca West. Excellent performances throughout, well recorded.

Beckett, Edward (flute), London Festival O, Ross Pople

'Fantaisie' (Romantic French flute music): HUE: *Gigue; Nocturne.* VILLETTE: *Complainte.*
SAINT-SAENS: *Romance, Op. 37; Odelette, Op. 162.*
RAVEL: *Pièce en forme de habanera (orch. Hoérée).*
GODARD: *Suite, Op. 116.* BUSSER: *Andalucia, Op. 86.*
FAURE: *Fantaisie, Op. 111.* PERILHOU: *Ballade.*
WIDOR: *Suite for Flute & Piano, Op. 34: Scherzo; Romance* (orch. Beckett & Widor).
★★★ Black Box BBM 1049.

French composers instinctively write flute music to tickle the ear, with Gallic elegance in the way of the *Gigue* and *Nocturne* of Georges Huë. His sprightly *Gigue* blithely erupts with triple-tongued bravura, while the *Nocturne*, a languorous barcarolle, is hardly less enticing.

The most subtle music here is by Fauré and Ravel, but Pierre Villette's *Complainte* has a Ravelian atmosphere and a gentle melancholy. The two morceaux by Saint-Saëns are characteristically charming, with *Odelette* bringing a brief central burst of virtuoso roulades. On the other hand, Benjamin Godard's *Suite* is very operatic: one could imagine the pirouetting opening *Allegretto* and the chirruping *Waltz* being used as a duet with a coloratura soprano; in between comes the ingenuous *Idylle* to remind us that Godard was the composer of the *Berceuse de Jocelyn*.

Büsser's *Andalucia* has Mediterranean charm and a whiff of voluptuousness, though it remains more French than Spanish, and Widor's *Scherzo* and *Romance* display a thistledown lightness, unexpected from an organ composer. Edward Beckett, Irish born, yet a pupil of Rampal, has a lovely tone and phrases with style. He is persuasively accompanied by Pople, but the orchestra has comparatively little to contribute, except support. The sound is warmly atmospheric, the flute not too forward. Altogether a most enticing lightweight collection.

Bergen Philharmonic Orchestra, Dimitri Kitaienko

'French & Russian Orchestral Favourites': DUKAS: *The Sorcerer's Apprentice.* RAVEL: *Ma Mère l'Oye Suite; Boléro.* DEBUSSY: *Prélude à l'après-midi d'un faune.* MUSSORGSKY: *Night on the Bare Mountain* (original version). LIADOV: *The Enchanted Lake; 8 Russian Folk Songs; Kikimora; A Musical Snuffbox; Baba-Yaga.* STRAVINSKY: *The Firebird* (suite, 1919); *4 Norwegian Moods.*
(BB) ★★ Virgin 2x1 5 61901-2 (2).

This is an attractive programme, but the two CDs were recorded five years apart, in 1991 and 1996 respectively, and are uneven in appeal. The inclusion of the original score of Mussorgsky's *Night on a Bare Mountain* is particularly welcome. It is much cruder, more rambling than Rimsky's later revision, but it sounds strikingly primitive and bizarrely individual. The opening Dukas showpiece is glowingly animated, and the works by Debussy and Ravel also come off well. The approach is direct and atmospheric, while *Boléro* moves forward to produce a strong climax. On the second disc, however, while Kitaienko's Liadov performances are not without atmosphere, they lack sparkle. Stravinsky's *Norwegian Moods* bring a pleasingly folksy evocation, but the *Firebird Suite*, though similarly colourful, seriously lacks a vibrant dramatic profile. The recording is pleasingly colourful and evocative, but this is not distinctive music-making.

Berlin Philharmonic Orchestra, Claudio Abbado

'New Year's Gala 1997': BIZET: *Carmen:.* excerpts (with Von Otter, Alagna, Terfel). BRAHMS: *Hungarian Dance No. 5 in G min.* FALLA: *El amor brujo; Ritual Fire Dance.* RACHMANINOV: *Rhapsody on a Theme of Paganini.* (with Pletnev). RAVEL: *Rhapsodie espagnole.* SARASATE: *Carmen Fantasy, Op. 25* (with Shaham).
*** Arthaus **DVD** 100 026.

A concert that takes Bizet's *Carmen* as a theme, or point of departure. The sound is very good indeed and naturally balanced, and the camerawork discreet and unobtrusive. The excerpts from the opera come off very well, but easily the best thing on the disc is the *Paganini Rhapsody*, played effortlessly by Mikhail Pletnev. Rachmaninov playing does not come better than this. It is every bit as strongly characterized and brilliant in execution as his CD recording and must be numbered among the very finest on disc. The individual variations do not have access points. Gil Shaham's performance of the Sarasate *Fantasy* is also played with virtuosity and panache. A rather strangely designed programme, but well worth having, purely for the sake of Pletnev's dazzling Rachmaninov.

'New Year's Gala Concert' (with Swedish R. Ch.): BRAHMS: *Hungarian Dances Nos. 1, 5, 7, 10, 17, 21; Gypsy Songs, Op. 103; Liebesliederwalzer Nos. 1, 2, 4, 5, 6, 8, 9, 11; Es tont ein voller, Op. 17.* BERLIOZ: *Hungarian March.* RAVEL: *Tzigane* (with Maxim Vengerov); *La Valse.*
*** Arthaus **DVD** 100 042.

The Berlin Philharmonic in this 'New Year's Gala' puts up a direct challenge to Vienna, using Brahms pieces very much as the Vienna Philharmonic uses Johann Strauss, concentrating on the *Hungarian Dances* and the *Liebesliederwalzer.* As in Vienna it makes for a fun occasion, with Abbado at his most relaxed, smiling as he conducts. The theme of dances and gypsy tunes then extends to Ravel in two major items, *Tzigane* and *La Valse*, while Berlioz is finally brought in with the *Hungarian March* from the *Damnation of Faust* as an obvious equivalent of Vienna's *Radetsky March*, though happily no one in the Berlin audience dares to clap to it.

One great bonus of this programme is the inclusion of Maxim Vengerov as a masterly soloist in the *Tzigane*, as well as in Brahms's *Hungarian Dance No. 7*, which comes as his encore. Just as striking is the contribution of the Swedish Radio Chorus, not just visually with the ladies sporting velvet stoles over their black dresses in brightly contrasted primary colours, but in their obvious affection for Brahms. The *Liebeslieder Waltzes* are charmingly done, as is the lovely song for women's chorus with horn and harp accompaniment, *Es tont ein voller*, though one is sorry not to have the other three songs in that Opus 17 group. The only extra item is a brief tourist sequence on Berlin and its attractions, *Kunst und Genuss* ('Arts and Delights').

Berlin Philharmonic Orchestra, Daniel Barenboim

New Year's Eve Concert in the Philharmonie: *'Invitation to the Dance'*: BACH: *Orchestral Suite No. 3: Gavotte.* MOZART: *Divertimento No. 17 in D, K.334: Menuetto; Rondo for Piano and Orchestra, K.382* (with Barenboim, piano). VERDI: *Aida: Dance of the Moorish Slaves.* TCHAIKOVSKY: *The Nutcracker: Waltz of the Flowers.* SIBELIUS: *Kuolema: Valse triste.* Johann STRAUSS, Jr: *Kaiser (Emperor) Waltz; Unter Donner und Blitz (Thunder and Lightning) Polka.* ❂ KODÁLY: *Dances from Galánta.* BRAHMS: *Hungarian Dance No. l.* SALGÁN; *A fuego lento (Tango).* DE ABREU & OLIVEIRA: *Tico Tico.* CARLI: *El firulete.*
*** TDK **DVD** DV-SG 2001;105184-9. (Director Hans Hulscher.)

This is the Berlin Philharmonic's equivalent of the Vienna New Year Concert, and very enjoyable it is. The music is all strikingly well played, and in the Mozart *Rondo*, with its neat interchanges between piano and orchestra of a simple but most engaging theme, Barenboim directs from the piano. Tchaikovsky's *Waltz of the Flowers* is lush but a trifle cosy, but it sparks up nicely for the coda, and the following *Valse triste* is played very beautifully indeed. Then suddenly, and electrifyingly, the music-making is transformed with a superb, wonderfully spontaneous performance of Kodaly's *Dances from Galánta.* The musicians play with enormous intensity, the lyrical solos richly glowing, with even a brief flash of irony at one point. Barenboim's up-and-down conducting style is transformed with kinetic energy, and one can feel his powerful communicative force. The tension builds up and the end is riveting, and superbly timed. The audience reaction is tumultuous, as well it might be. This is a wonderful example of the way a DVD can be far more exciting than a CD. You sit in your chair and the full force of the inspirational playing jumps out and engulfs you thrillingly. Whew!

After that, the popular encores seem a little cheap, until the electricty sparks again in the *Thunder and Lightning Polka*, and the concert ends with Brahms, played with great warmth. Fortunately, the recording is in the demonstration bracket, and the camera is almost always in the right place. A very entertaining DVD, both to enjoy and to demonstrate to your friends.

'1997 *European Concert at the Opéra Royal de Château de Versailles*': RAVEL: *Le tombeau de Couperin.* ✪ MOZART: *Piano Concerto No. 13 in C, K.415* (with Barenboim, piano). BEETHOVEN: *Symphony No. 3 in E flat (Eroica).*
*** TDK **DVD** DV-VERSA.

Another oustanding example of the way DVD video can enhance one's enjoyment of a live concert. All the performances here are of the highest calibre, and although the cameras are at times restless, and the back-of-the-hall perspective is too distant, the close-ups of the conductor and players communicate the music visually as well as aurally, with members of the orchestra projecting as individual personalities. Ravel's *Le tombeau* is played with engaging freshness and luminous beauty, and one identifies especially here with the principal oboe.

One turns the disc over for Barenboim's *Eroica*, which is very strong indeed, the climaxes gripping, the Funeral March powerfully moving. In the Scherzo the horns dominate visually, as they should, and the finale, with its visually fascinating variations and fugue, ends the work with an explosion of joy.

But the highlight of the concert is the captivating account of the early Mozart *Concerto*, when Barenboim, like the composer before him, directs from the keyboard. Here the empathy between soloist and players is magical and this communicates to the viewer, raptly so in the concentration of the lovely slow movement and the light-hearted finale, with its intriguing changes of tempo and mood. The recording throughout is first class, very naturally balanced with a dramatic but not exaggerated dynamic range, and a full, clean bass response. The piano too is naturally focused. This is a DVD to return to, and it is enhanced by the glorious visual backcloth of the Opéra Royal de Château de Versailles.

'1998 *Concert at the Berlin State Opera, Unter den Linden*': BEETHOVEN: *Symphony No. 8 in F.* SCHUMANN: *Konzertstück in F for 4 Horns & Orchestra, Op. 86* (with Dale Clevenger, Stefan Dohr, Ignacio Garcia, George Schreckenberger, horns). LISZT: *Les Préludes.* WAGNER: *Die Walküre: Ride of the Valkyries.*
*(*) TDK **DVD** DV-LINDE.

After Barenboim's 1997 Berlin Philharmonic concert at the Opéra Royal de Château de Versailles this is a great let-down. It opens with a comparatively routine account of Beethoven's *Eighth Symphony*, while Liszt's *Les Préludes* is lacking in flamboyance and adrenalin, though in both the Berlin Philharmonic playing cannot be faulted for poor tone or ensemble. The great highlight of the concert is the superb performance of the Schumann *Konzertstück for Four Horns*. This work is not only technically very demanding, but lies very high in the horn register, with continually repeated passages where the soloists are taken up into the the stratosphere, which is very tiring on the horn-player's lip muscles, something Schumann did not seem to understand. With fine players a studio recording is feasible as the work can be recorded in sections. But this is a live performance by a superb quartet, led by Dale Clevenger, one of America's most distinguished orchestral principals, and the spirited bravura of all four players (to say nothing of their stamina) throughout the work's 21 minutes is as exhilarating as it is astonshing, while Barenboim accompanies zestfully. The horn quartet returns for the final item in the programme and lines up behind the orchestra as the extras in Wagner's *Ride of the Valkyries*. But that performance, well played as it is, only serves to emphasize the other drawback to the audio recording throughout this DVD – its very limited dynamic range. This has a damping-down effect in both the Beethoven and Liszt, and when the extra brass is visibly seen to enter in Wagner's famous galloping show piece and the music fails to increase in volume, the effect is bizarre.

Berlin Philharmonic Orchestra, Plácido Domingo

'*Spanish Night*': CHABRIER: *España.* LINCKE: *Berliner Luft.* LUNA: *Cancion Espanola.* SERRANO: *Romanza.* TORROBA: *La Petenara* (all with Ana Maria Martinez). MASSENET: *Thaïs: Méditation.* SARASATE: *Carmen Fantasy; Zigeunerweisen* (all with Sarah Chang). MONCAYO: *Huapango.* RIMSKY-KORSAKOV: *Capriccio espagnol.* J. STRAUSS JR: *Spanish March.* VIVES: *Fandango.*
*** TDK Euro Arts **DVD** 10 5123 9.

The Waldbühne (Woodland Stage) in Berlin where the open-air concert on this DVD took place in July 2001 is like a cross between the concert venue at Kenwood in north London and the Hollywood Bowl. With an audience of 22,000 this performance rounded off the orchestra's season and, following tradition, ended with Lincke's rousing Prussian song, *Berliner Luft*, with Domingo finally persuaded to sing as well as conduct, and with the audience flashing lights and waving sparklers. The focus of the whole event this time was Spanish, with Plácido Domingo as conductor putting together a delightful sequence of Spanish-inspired pieces, including three songs from his favourite genre of the distinctive Spanish form of operetta, the zarzuela, in which Martinez's warm, throaty soprano is ideal.

Sarah Chang makes just as glamorous a figure, playing with masterly point in the two Sarasate works, *Zigeunerweisen* and the *Carmen Fantasy*, as well as sweetly and tenderly in the *Méditation* from Massenet's *Thaïs*. Besides the purely Spanish items, such orchestral show pieces as Chabrier's *España* and Rimsky-Korsakov's *Capriccio espagnol* are self-recommending, and loyally Domingo includes a colourful piece, *Huapango*, by the Mexican composer Moncayo, well worth hearing. Of particular interest is the rarity by Johann Strauss, the *Spanish March*, with its sharply varied sections. One of the 'Special Features' of the disc is an interview session with both Chang and Domingo. Considering how dry the sound can be in the open air, the quality here is first rate, no doubt helped by the canopy over the orchestra resembling an extended crusaders' tent.

Berlin Philharmonic Orchestra, Wilhelm Furtwängler

Wartime Concerts, 1942–4

Vol. 1: BEETHOVEN: *Coriolan Overture, Op. 62; Symphonies Nos. 4, 5 & 7; Violin Concerto* (with Röhn). HANDEL: *Concerto grosso in D min., Op. 6/10.* MOZART: *Symphony No. 39 in E flat, K.543.* SCHUBERT: *Symphony No. 9 in C (Great).* WEBER: *Der Freischütz: Overture.*

(B) (★★★) DG mono 471 289-2 (4).

Vol. 2: BRAHMS: *Piano Concerto No. 2 in B flat, Op. 83* (with Fischer). BRUCKNER: *Symphony No. 5 in B flat.* RAVEL: *Daphnis et Chloé: Suite No. 2.* SCHUMANN: *Cello Concerto in A min., Op. 129* (with de Machula); *Piano Concerto in A min., Op. 56* (with Gieseking). SIBELIUS: *En saga.* R. STRAUSS: *Don Juan, Op. 20; Till Eulenspiegel, Op. 28; Symphonia Domestica, Op. 53.*

(B) (★★★) DG mono 471 294-2 (5).

Hans Werner Henze once recalled how during the war he came to associate music-making with danger, having played chamber music with some Jewish friends who were in continual fear of discovery and arrest. And there is certainly a heightened intensity and an urgent, emotional charge about performances given in wartime conditions, as we can hear in the astonishing recordings Furtwängler made with the Berlin Philharmonic in 1942–4, which DG have just repackaged. British Intelligence was puzzled by the sheer quality of wartime German broadcast concerts, which were technically far ahead of their time, thanks to the excellence of the recordings, which were made on 14-inch reels of iron-oxide tape running at 30 inches per second. There are perform-

ances of great stature in these inexpensive boxes, including a Brahms *Second Piano Concerto* with Edwin Fischer, and an imposing Mozart *Symphony No. 39 in E flat*, as well as repertoire that one does not associate with Furtwängler: Sibelius's *En saga*, full of atmosphere and mystery, and a magical account of the Second Suite from Ravel's *Daphnis et Chloé*. Strauss's *Symphonia Domestica*, Furtwängler's only recording of a longer Strauss tone-poem, is superbly shaped and vividly characterized: it comes from the last concert before the Philharmonie was destroyed by Allied bombs. The other work in the same 1944 concert was the Beethoven *Violin Concerto*, seraphically played by the Berlin Philharmonic's leader, Erich Röhn – a very special performance indeed. Not everything is inspired (Gieseking's Schumann *Concerto* is curiously prosaic by his standards), but there is much that is, including an incandescent and noble Bruckner *Fifth Symphony*, and some powerful Beethoven.

Berlin Philharmonic Orchestra, Mariss Jansons

'A *Night of Encores: Summer Concert at the Berlin Waldbühne*' (with Vadim Repin, violin): MONIUSZKO: *Halka: Mazurka.* WIENIAWSKI: *Polonaise, Op. 4.* TCHAIKOVSKY: *Souvenir d'un lieu cher: Mélodie. Valse-Scherzo, Op. 34. The Nutcracker: Pas de deux.* Ruperto Chapi Y LORENTE: *Overture: Le revoltosa.* LYAN JOON KIM: *Elegy.* LUMBYE: *Champagne Galop.* TOYAMA: *Dance of the Celestials.* SIBELIUS: *Kuolema; Valse triste.* ELGAR: *Wand of Youth; Wild Bears.* WAGNER: *Lohengrin: Prelude to Act III.* KREISLER: *Tambourin Chinois.* GARDEL: *Por una cabezza.* PAGANINI: *The Carnival of Venice* (with encore). ZIEHRER: *Wiener Burger.* MASCAGNI: *Cavalleria Rusticana: Intermezzo.* DVORAK: *Slavonic Dance No. 15 in C, Op. 72/7.* BIZET: *L'Arlésienne: Farandole.* MASSENET: *Le Cid: Aragonaise; Navarraise.* LINCKE: *Frau Luna: Berliner Luft.*

★★(★) TDK **DVD** T0513-9; DV-WBONE (Producer: Dorothy Dickmann; Director: Bob Coles).

The Berlin Walbühne is a huge open space, able to take a very large audience indeed, with the orchestra accommodated in a shell. As some of the distant shots demonstrate, if you are at the back, the orchestra is very far away indeed. Presumably there is amplification for the audience: what we hear is not an open-air sound; instead, there is an agreeable ambience. The programme offers a nice mixture of favourites and novelties. The *Overture Le revoltosa* has attractive writing for the woodwind and bouncy dance rhythms, Lyan Joon Kim's *Elegy* has a rich melody introduced on the cor anglais and taken up warmly by the strings. Toyama's *Celestials* dance nostalgically and gracefully on the flute, and Lumbye's *Champagne Galop* is complete with a 'popping cork'.

The standard items in the programme are very well played indeed, with Elgar's *Wild Bears* a rumbustious novelty. The soloist Vadim Repin has plenty of chances to show his virtuosity and his warm, lyrical playing in the two Tchaikovsky miniatures. *The Carnival of Venice* is treated as a fun piece but, as the camera is not in right place, the DVD viewer misses the joke. Otherwise the camera angles are well managed, and this is undoubtedly a very enjoyable concert of its kind.

Berlin Philharmonic Orchestra, Herbert von Karajan

'*New Year's Eve Concert, 1985*': LEONCAVALLO: *I Pagliacci: Intermezzo.* LISZT: *Hungarian Rhapsody No. 5 in E min.* PUCCINI: *Manon Lescaut: Intermezzo.* RAVEL: *Boléro.* WEBER: *Overture: Der Freischütz.*

★★★ Sony **DVD** SVD 46402.

The passion behind Karajan's conducting in this celebratory concert comes over very clearly on DVD, as though he realizes that this may be the last time he ever conducts these favourite works. That gives an emotional tug to such a piece as the *Interlude* from Puccini's *Manon Lescaut*, where his facial expression, generally grim and mask-like, clearly indicates the depth of his feelings, always a great interpreter of this composer. Unlike the New Year's Day concerts in Vienna, the New Year's Eve events in Berlin span the widest range of repertory. This time he starts with the Weber overture, not just refined and beautifully shaded but with high dramatic contrasts. The two Italian opera interludes follow, with Karajan quickly silencing threatening applause between them, leading to an affectionately lyrical reading of the least Hungarian and least dramatic of Liszt's *Hungarian Rhapsodies*. The final item, which inevitably brings the house down, is Ravel's *Boléro*, offering a superb demonstration not just of the virtuosity of individual players and of the different sections in this great orchestra but also of the deftness of the television directors, picking out the relevant players in close-up. If Karajan's reading of this obsessively repetitive piece is far less boring than it can be, the explanation lies not just in the technical brilliance of the players but in the subtlety of the conductor's pointing of rhythm, lifting music that can so easily become merely metrical. Significantly, for this piece Karajan abandons his baton, merely giving restrained indications with gesturing hands.

Overtures and Intermezzi: JOHANN STRAUSS JR: *Overture: Zigeunerbaron.* MASSENET: *Thaïs: Méditation* (with Anne-Sophie Mutter, violin). CHERUBINI: *Overture: Anacréon.* WEBER: *Overture: Der Freischütz.* SCHMIDT: *Notre Dame: Intermezzo.* PUCCINI: *Suor Angelica: Intermezzo; Manon Lescaut: Intermezzo.* MASCAGNI: *L'amico Fritz:*

Intermezzo. HUMPERDINCK: *Overture: Hänsel und Gretel.* MENDELSSOHN: *Overture: The Hebrides (Fingal's Cave).*

(BB) ★★ EMI Encore (ADD/DDD) 5 74764-2.

A curiously planned programme. It opens with a brilliantly played and indulgently seductive account of the *Gypsy Baron Overture*; then comes the *Méditation* from *Thaïs* (a young Anne-Sophie Mutter the gentle soloist) played very romantically, immediately followed by Cherubini's *Anacréon Overture*. The performances of the Weber and Humperdinck overtures are disappointing, the first lacking electricity, the second charm. Best are the intermezzi, played with the utmost passion. The digital recording here is very brightly lit and there is a fierce sheen on the strings, but the closing *Fingal's Cave Overture* is played most beautifully, generating plenty of excitement, its effect enhanced by the resonantly spacious acoustic.

CHOPIN: *Les Sylphides* (orch. Roy Douglas). DELIBES: *Coppélia: Ballet Suite.* GOUNOD: *Faust: Ballet Music and Waltz.* OFFENBACH: *Gaîté parisienne* (ballet, arr. ROSENTHAL): extended excerpts. TCHAIKOVSKY: *Sleeping Beauty: Suite.* PONCHIELLI: *La Gioconda: Dance of the Hours.*

🔗 ⊙ ★★★ DG (ADD) 459 445-2 (2).

This scintillating collection of ballet music is superbly played, and every item shows Karajan and his great orchestra at their finest. The very beautiful performance of Roy Douglas's exquisite arrangement of *Les Sylphides* – with its ravishing string playing and glowingly delicate woodwind solos – has never been matched on record. It is also available on a single bargain disc together with the exhilaratingly racy *Gaîté parisienne* selection (which includes most of the ballet) and the *Coppélia Suite*; but the latter is cut. The missing movements are restored here and sound marvellous, as does the vivacious *Faust Ballet Music* and *Waltz*, the latter played with irresistible panache. Another riveting moment comes in the thrilling crescendo at the climax of the *Introduction* to the *Sleeping Beauty Ballet Suite*, yet there is much elegance and delicacy of colour to follow. The closing *Dance of the Hours* – so affectionately phrased – also sparkles as do few other recorded performances, and throughout, these excellent CD transfers demonstrate DG's finest analogue quality from the 1960s and 1970s.

WEBER: *Invitation to the Dance.* BERLIOZ: *Damnation de Faust: Ballet des Sylphes; Menuet des feux follets.* LISZT: *Mephisto Waltz.* SMETANA: *The Bartered Bride: Furiant, Polka & Dance of the Comedians.* BORODIN: *Prince Igor: Polovtsian Dances.* VERDI: *Othello: ballet music.* PONCHIELLI: *La Gioconda: Dance of the Hours.*

(M) ★★★ DG (ADD) 474 617-2.

With panther-like smoothness, Karajan and his Berlin orchestra purr their way through these popular orchestral pieces. Not that in their smoothness they lack vitality: the lively numbers are superbly done too (the Liszt is wonderfully romantic in style); indeed, these are vintage performances in every respect, with every item given the full Karajan treatment – even the hardly subtle Verdi ballet music is given greater dignity than usual, and the result is highly enjoyable. The delicacy of the strings in the *Invitation to the Dance* and the *Ballet des Sylphes* is spine-tingling, while *The Dance of the Hours* have never passed the time more magically. Well-remastered sound from 1971. This CD is worth anyone's money.

Berlin Philharmonic Orchestra and (i) Wind Ensemble, Herbert von Karajan

Christmas Concert: CORELLI: *Concerto grosso in G min. (Christmas), Op. 6/8.* MANFREDINI: *Concerto grosso in C (Christmas), Op. 3/12.* LOCATELLI: *Concerto grosso in F min., Op. 1/8.* TORELLI: *Concerto a 4 (Pastorale), Op. 8/6.* (i) Giovanni GABRIELLI: *Canzona a 8.* SCHEIDT: *In dulci jubilo.* ECCARD: *Chorales: Vom Himmel hoch, da komm ich her; Es is ein Ros entsprungen.* GRUBER: *Stille Nacht.*

(M) ** DG 474 556-2.

Karajan's '*Christmas Concert*' combines a collection of Christmas concertos, played exquisitely (especially the *Pastorales*) in the conductor's perfumed baroque style, interspersed with more robust items from the Berlin Philharmonic Wind Ensemble. However, the lack of bite in the faster movements of the string works, partly brought about about by the balmy resonance of the 1970s analogue recording, damps down the music's vitality. Karajan is pictured looking grey and old in a series of family snapshots with his wife.

Berlin Philharmonic Orchestra, Georges Prêtre

'*Concert at the Waldbühne*': BERLIOZ: *Overture: Le carnaval romain.* BIZET: *Carmen Suite; L'Arlésienne: Farandole.* DEBUSSY: *Prélude à l'après-midi d'un faune.* RAVEL: *Concerto for Piano Left Hand* (with Leon Fleischer). *Boléro.* JOHANN STRAUSS SR: *Radetzky March.* (Director & Video Director: Hans-Peter Birke-Malzer.)

*** TDK **DVD** DV-WBFRN.

This is a 1992 outdoor concert recorded at the Waldbühne in Berlin with the Berlin Philharmonic in splendid form under the vivacious Georges Prêtre. The Berlioz *Carnaval romain* is wonderfully spirited and there seems to be an excellent rapport between the Berliners and their French guest. The DVD is worth acquiring for the rare opportunity of seeing and hearing Leon Fleischer play the Ravel *Left Hand*

Concerto with impressive authority. The camerawork is unobtrusive and expert.

Berlin Philharmonic and Israel Philharmonic Orchestras; Zubin Mehta

'*Joint Concert, Tel Aviv (1990)*': BEN-HAIM: *Symphony No. 1, 2nd Mov.: Psalm.* SAINT-SAENS: *Introduction & Rondo capriccio, Op. 28* (with Hagner, violin). WEBER: *Clarinet Concertino in E flat, Op. 67* (with Kam, clarinet). RAVEL: *La Valse.* BEETHOVEN: *Symphony No. 5.*

*(*) Arthaus **DVD** 100 068.

The visit of the Berlin Philharmonic had been keenly awaited in Tel Aviv, and this joint concert in the Mann Auditorium should have been an electrifying occasion. The two soloists are very good, and there is some excellent orchestral playing, with the two orchestras combined in the *Psalm* and the Beethoven and sounding pretty splendid in the Ravel, in spite of the less than ideal acoustics. However, the account of Beethoven's *Fifth* simply fails to spark into life until the finale, and even then it is hardly earth-shaking. Certainly the DVD gives one a sense of being there, but the concert remains a disappointment.

Berlin State Opera Orchestra, Daniel Barenboim

'*Berliner Luft*' (Gala Concert from the State Opera, Unter den Linden): NICOLAI: *Overture: The Merry Wives of Windsor.* MOZART: *Don Giovanni: La ci darem la mano* (with Pape, Röschmann). SAINT-SAENS: *Introduction & Rondo capriccioso, Op. 28* (with Christ, violin). TCHAIKOVSKY: *Swan Lake: Dance of the Little Swans* (with ballet); *Waltz.* SHOSTAKOVICH: *Tahiti Trot.* WEILL: *Berlin im Licht* (Gruber, Barenboim, piano). KOLLO: *Untern Linden* (Vocal Ens.). LINCKE: *Glow-Worm Idyll* (Nold); *Berliner Luft.* J. STRAUSS JR: *Unter Donner und Blitz.*

*** Arthaus **DVD** 100 094.

This is obviously the Berliners' equivalent of the Last Night of the Proms and the well-dressed audience clearly have a wonderful evening. The DVD has tremendous spirit and atmosphere, Barenboim and the orchestra are obviously enjoying themselves and there are even magicians doing party tricks to add to the revels. Everyone joins in the closing popular numbers, and although it is not as uninhibited as at the Proms (the audience is much older for one thing), it is still very infectious and enjoyable. The recording obviously came from a broadcast, for it is compressed here and there, but it does not affect the sense of spectacle. One could criticize the cameras for being too volatile in moving around the orchestra, but it suits the occasion, especially in the delightful account of Shostakovich's *Tahiti Trot* (based on Vincent Youmans's *Tea for Two*).

Bezaly, Sharon (flute), Tapiola Sinfonietta, Kantorow

GOUNOD: *Concerto for Flute and Small Orchestra.* DEVIENNE: *Flute Concerto No. 7 in E min.* SAINT-SAENS: *Airs de ballet d'Ascanio: Adagio & Variation; Odelette; Romance; Tarentelle* (for flute, clarinet and orchestra). FAURE: *Fantaisie.*
*** BIS CD 1359.

A delightful disc this, with Sharon Bezaly on sparkling form. The longest work here is Devienne's *Flute Concerto*, most appealing in its minor-keyed *galant*-style writing – elegant melody interspersed with not-too-serious drama, and a lilting finale. Fauré's *Fantaisie* is as beautiful as ever, and one doesn't resent Yoav Talmi giving it – with the aid of added final chords – a more emphatic ending than Fauré wrote. Both the Gounod *Concertino* and the Saint-Saëns *Romance* are slight, but utterly charming – and the same goes for the latter's *Odelette*, written just a year before the composer's death. However, the six-minute *Tarentelle* is perhaps the gem of these rarer works, with flute and clarinet skipping along together over the tarantella rhythm with infectious insouciance. Although Bezaly is quite closely recorded, the sound is full and rich, as well as cleanly focused. Jean-Jacques Kantorow conducts with both enthusiasm and sensitivity throughout, adding much to the success of this disc.

Bolister, Ruth (oboe), Elgar Chamber Orchestra, Stephen Bell

English Oboe Concertos: JACOB: *Oboe Concerto No. 1.* ELGAR: *Soliloquy* (orch. Jacob). HOLST: *A Fugal Concerto for Flute and Oboe* (with Kate Hill, flute). Eugene GOOSSENS: *Concerto in One Movement.* VAUGHAN WILLIAMS: *Concerto in A min.*
⚫ *** ASV CDDCA 1173.

This is just about the most desirable collection of English oboe concertos in the catalogue. Ruth Bolister's delicate timbre and refined phrasing are captivating throughout, and especially so in the delicate Elgar *Soliloquy* (a fragment of an *Oboe Suite*, scored by Gordon Jacob). His own *First Concerto* is the most substantial work in the programme, and is given its première here. It was written for Evelyn Rothwell, and in Bolister's hands the neo-classical first movement is most diverting and the yearning *Andante* quite lovely. In the Holst *Fugal Concerto*, Kate Hill's contribution is equally felicitous; the opening *Moderato* brings a perky interplay and the *Adagio*, with its flowing line reminding one of Bach,

has surely never been played more beautifully on record, capped by the witty, folksy finale. The Goossens *Concerto*, succinctly structured, is yet a kaleidoscope of diverse invention, its spicy and unpredictable moments of astringency aurally stimulating and making a foil for the other music here; the piece has a sombre lyrical core, yet it ends genially. The closing work by Vaughan Williams then makes a delightful finale, its pastoral feeling perfectly caught. Throughout Stephen Bell's accompaniments with the excellent Elgar Chamber Orchestra could not be more stylish or polished, with the string playing especially fine; the lustrous recording, warm, natural and transparent, is very much in the demonstration bracket. Very highly recommended.

Bonynge, Richard

MASSENET: *Cigale* (ballet, with Nat. PO); *Fantasy for Cello and Orchestra* (with Silberman, SRO). Songs: *Les amoureuses sont des folles; Ce que disent les cloches; Elle s'en est allée; L'éventail; Je t'aime; L'âme des fleurs; La mélodie des baisers; Nuit d'Espagne; On dit! Passionnément; Pensée d'automne; Le petit Jésus; Pitchounette; Printemps dernier; Rose d'Octobre; Le sais-tu?; Sérénade d'automne; Souhait; Souvenance; Les yeux clos* (with Huguette Tourangeau, Bonynge, piano). AUBER: *Cello Concerto No. 1* (arr. Gamley). POPPER: *Cello Concerto in E min., Op. 24* (with Silberman, SRO). J. C. BACH: *Sinfonia concertante in C* (for flute, oboe, violin, cello & orchestra); *Symphony in E flat, Op. 9/2.* SALIERI: *Double Concerto in C* (for flute and oboe); *Sinfonia in D (Veneziana)* (with ECO). 'Arias from Forgotten Operas': *Arias from:* BALFE: *Ildegonda nel Carcere.* BIZET: *Djamileh.* DONIZETTI: *L'assedio di Calais.* AUBER: *Le cheval bronze.* MASSENET: *Hérodiade.* VERDI: *Oberto.* VACCAI: *Giulietta de Villars.* MAILLART: *Les Dragons de Villars* (with Huguette Tourangeau, SRO). 'Arie Antiche': MARTINI: *Piacer d'amor.* SARTI: *Lungi dal caro bene.* BONONCINI: *Deh più a me non v'ascondete.* HANDEL: *Verdi prati, selve amene.* A. SCARLATTI: *Le violette.* GLUCK: *Divinités du Styx; Frondi tenere Ombra mai fù; O del mio dolce ardor.* PAISIELLO: *Chi vuol la zingarella; Nel cor più non mi sento.* PERGOLESI: *Stizzoso, mio Stizzoso.* CIAMPI: *Tre giorni son che Nina.* VIVALDI: *O del mio dolce ardour* (with Renata Tebaldi, New Philh. O).
⚫ *** Universal Classics Australian Heritage (ADD) ABC 475 070-2 (4).

A diverse collection, to say the least, with the attraction that much of it has never been released on CD before. One of the most striking LPs to be transferred is Huguette Tourangeau's vividly recorded 1970 recital disc, 'Arias from forgotten operas'. Hers was a controversial voice in some ways, but a distinctive and characterful one: rare qualities these days. The vivid colour photograph on the original LP sleeve (reproduced in the booklet) certainly suggests an artistic personality of character, and the recital does not disappoint. The dark, lower register of the voice, with its ability to bring a sudden change of character to the melodic line, coupled to the crisp, accurate coloratura of the upper register, is especially effective in the Donizetti excerpt (which has a swinging *cabaletta*), while the dramatic bite and secure technical control make the very most of the opening Balfe aria, which is of unexpectedly high quality. Bizet's lyrical scene is beautifully sung, and the excerpt from Vaccai's *Giulietta e Romeo* is very attractive too.

One of the highlights here is a vivacious aria by Maillart, which has a finale worthy of Offenbach, and another is the little-known but sparkling aria from Auber's *Le Cheval de bronze*. Enjoyable as is the excerpt from Verdi's *Oberto*, not even the exciting *stretta* in the orchestra near the end of the aria prepares one for Tourangeau's unexpected and thrilling final D – electrifying in its impact.

If her style is unashamedly histrionic in style for the bold romantic arias, she is wonderfully intimate in Massenet's charming songs. Here, in this 1975 recital disc, she knows just how to inflect her voice in the right way to bring out the full range of colour in these varied mélodies, from the playful *Pitchounette* to the long sweeping phrases in such songs as *Sérénade d'automne*. Three are hightened by cello obbligati, which brings an added frisson, especially effective in the impassioned *Je t'aime!* Other highlights include *Ce que disent les cloches*, with its haunting, bell-like accompaniment (superbly done by Bonynge throughout), and Massenet's *Nuit d'Espagne*, which uses the delightful *Air de ballet* from his *Scènes pittoresques*, with a suitably Spanish accompaniment, to great effect.

The third vocal LP included here was Renata Tebaldi's final recording, *Arie Antiche*, recorded in 1973. It was a clever programme in choosing songs which did not tax a great voice that was no longer in its prime. However, Tebaldi's artistry – and her (and Bonynge's) love for the music – is never in doubt, and Douglas Gamley's ear-tickling (if not exactly authentic) orchestrations are a delight. Throughout the programme, Tebaldi maintains a beautiful legato line in both the dramatic and pastoral items, and in Vivaldi's melancholy *Piango, gemo, sospiro*, she draws the voice into the deep, chest mezzo to great effect. Two favourites are included: the well-known *Plaisir d'amour* and the delightful Paisiello song, *Nel cor più non mi sento*, with flutes adding rustic piquancy, as they do in the Bononcini aria.

In the orchestral items, the highlight is undoubtedly Massenet's ballet *Cigale* (1978), full of memorable tunes, colourfully orchestrated and brilliantly played and recorded. Of the three *Cello Concertos*, Auber's is a pleasing work of which the jolly finale is the most enjoyable movement; the Popper is nicely lyrical too and, once again, the rustic-sounding finale is the best. But the finest of the trio is Massenet's: its richly lyrical nature, very rhapsodic in feeling, is

obviously by the composer of *Manon*. There are many delights along the way, not least the gypsy-flavoured passage in the central movement, a jaunty gavotte, its quirky harmonies adding to the memorability of the piece.

The baroque and classical items are all extremely well played and recorded. They are fresh and enjoyable, and Salieri's *Double Concerto* is a real charmer of a work. The vigorous writing of J. C. Bach can't fail to give pleasure, even if these works are not in the authentic style of today (they were recorded in the late 1960s). Our ✪ is given to this set for two reasons: as an overall accolade to Richard Bonynge, who has been indefatigable over the past 40 years in bringing out so many enterprising recordings, orchestral and operatic, and for Huguette Tourangeau's brilliant recital. The sleeve-notes are lavish, although no texts are provided. Although this is an Australian issue it seems to be readily available in the UK.

Boskovsky Ensemble, Willi Boskovsky

'*Viennese Bonbons*': J. STRAUSS SR: *Chinese Galop; Kettenbrücke Waltz; Eisele und Beisele Sprünge; Cachucha Galop*. J. STRAUSS JR: *Weine Gemüths Waltz; Champagne Galop; Salon Polka*. LANNER: *Styrian Dances; Die Werber & Marien Waltzes; Bruder Halt Galop*. MOZART: *3 Contredanses, K.462; 4 German dances, K.600/1 & 3; K.605/1; K.611.* SCHUBERT: *8 Waltzes & Ländler.*
(M) *** Van. (ADD) 8.8015.71 [OVC 8015].

This is a captivating selection of the most delightful musical confectionery imaginable. The ensemble is a small chamber group, similar to that led by the Strausses, and the playing has an appropriately intimate Viennese atmosphere. The transfer is impeccable and the recording from the early 1960s, made in the Baumgarten Hall, Vienna, is fresh, smooth and clear, with a nice bloom on sound which is never too inflated.

Boston Symphony Orchestra, Serge Koussevitzky

COPLAND: *El salón México*. FOOTE: *Suite in E min., Op. 63*. HARRIS: *Symphony (1933); Symphony No. 3.* MCDONALD: *San Juan Capistrano – Two Evening Pictures.*
(M) (***) Pearl mono GEMMCD 9492.

Koussevitzky's performance of the Roy Harris *Third Symphony* has never been equalled in intensity and fire – even by Toscanini or Bernstein – and Copland himself never produced as exhilarating an *El salón México*. The Arthur Foote *Suite* is unpretentious and has great charm. Sonic limitations are soon forgotten, for these performances have exceptional power and should not be missed.

PROKOFIEV: *Symphony No. 1 in D (Classical), Op. 25; Chout, Op. 21 bis: Danse finale.* SHOSTAKOVICH: *Symphony No. 9 in E flat, Op. 70.* TCHAIKOVSKY: *Francesca da Rimini, Op. 32.*

(***) Biddulph mono WHL 058.

Koussevitzky is in a class of his own. His premier recordings have great freshness and authority. His Shostakovich *Ninth Symphony*, recorded in 1946–7, was a rarity and never appeared in Britain in the days of shellac. The pre-war set of the Prokofiev *Classical Symphony* has even greater sparkle than the 1947 version included here, but this will do very nicely too! An electrifying *Francesca da Rimini*. Very good notes by David Gutman and decent transfers by Mark Obert-Thorn.

Boston Symphony Orchestra, Charles Munch

SAINT-SAËNS: *Symphony No. 3.* IBERT: *Escales.* D'INDY: *Symphonie sur un chant montagnard (Symphonie cévénole)* (with Nicole Henriot-Schweitzer). FRANCK: *Symphony in D min.* ROUSSEL: *Bacchus et Ariane: Suite No. 2.* HONEGGER: *Symphony No. 5 (Di Tre Re).*

(BB) (***) RCA mono/stereo 74321 98715-2.

This is one of the 50-odd two-CD Artistes-Repertoires series that RCA France are marketing, and it collects well-known recordings from Munch's Boston years including a brilliant (1952) mono record of Honegger's *Fifth Symphony* which still remains unsurpassed, an exhilarating *Suite* from *Bacchus et Ariane* (with which it was originally coupled), as well as other classic French scores including an atmospheric and seductive *Escales*. The set is decently transferred and well worth acquiring if you haven't already got these recordings, though the presentation is printed in minuscule type. The notes are in French only, but that should not deter the serious collector.

Bournemouth Sinfonietta, Richard Studt

English String Music: BRITTEN: *Variations on a Theme of Frank Bridge, Op. 10.* HOLST: *St Paul's Suite, Op. 29/1.* DELIUS: *2 Aquarelles.* VAUGHAN WILLIAMS: *5 Variants of Dives and Lazarus.* WARLOCK: *Capriol Suite.*

(BB) *** Naxos 8.550823.

This is the finest of the concerts of string music recorded for Naxos by Richard Studt and the excellent Bournemouth Sinfonietta. The Britten *Frank Bridge Variations* is particularly memorable, showing easy virtuosity yet often achieving the lightest touch, so that the Vienna waltz movement sparkles in its delicacy. The *Funeral March* may not be so desper-

ately intense as Karajan's famous mono version with the Philharmonia, but it is still very touching; and the following *Chant* is ethereal in its bleakly refined atmosphere.

The sprightly Holst *St Paul's Suite* and Warlock's *Capriol*, agreeably robust, could hardly be better played, while Vaughan Williams's *Dives and Lazarus* is especially fresh and conveys the famous biblical story of the rich man and the beggar most evocatively, especially in the very beautiful closing section, when Lazarus finds himself in heaven. The recording, made in St Peter's Church, Parkstone, is full-bodied, immediate and real – very much in the demonstration bracket.

20th-century String Music: BARTOK: *Divertimento.* BRITTEN: *Simple Symphony, Op. 4.* WALTON: *2 Pieces from Henry V: Death of Falstaff (Passacaglia); Touch her Soft Lips and Part.* STRAVINSKY: *Concerto in D.*

(BB) ** Naxos 8.550979.

This is the least successful of the three concerts of string music recorded by Naxos in Bournemouth. The Sinfonietta players do not sound completely at ease in the shifting moods of the Bartók *Divertimento* and their ensemble could be crisper in the Stravinsky *Concerto*. The *Simple Symphony* comes off brightly, with a gently nostalgic *Sentimental Sarabande* and a brisk, alert finale, but the *Playful Pizzicato* could be more exuberant, especially in its famous trio which the composer wrote so joyously. The two Walton pieces are warmly atmospheric, and there are no complaints about the sound.

Scandinavian string music: GRIEG: *Holberg Suite.* DAG WIREN: *Serenade, Op. 11.* SVENDSEN: *2 Icelandic Melodies; Norwegian Folksong; 2 Swedish Folksongs, Op. 27.* NIELSEN: *Little Suite in A min., Op. 1.*

(BB) *** Naxos 8.553106.

The liltingly spontaneous account of the Dag Wirén *Serenade* ensures a welcome for this enjoyable collection of Scandinavian music. The performance of Grieg's perennially fresh *Holberg Suite* is hardly less successful in its combination of energy and polish, folksy charm and touching serenity in the famous *Air*. Nielsen's *Little Suite* also has plenty of style and impetus, the changing moods of the finale neatly encompassed. The Svendsen folksong arrangements belong to the 1870s. The two *Icelandic Melodies* are melodically robust but the *Norwegian Folksong* is gentler and quite lovely. Yet it is the second of the two *Swedish Folksongs* that most reminds the listener of Grieg. All are played with a natural expressive feeling, and the recording, made in the Winter Gardens, Bournemouth, has a fine, full sonority to balance its natural brilliance.

Brain, Dennis (horn)

BEETHOVEN: *Horn Sonata in F, Op. 17* (with Denis Matthews). MOZART: *Horn Concertos Nos. 2 in E flat, K.417* (with Philh. O, Susskind); *4 in E flat, K.495* (with Hallé O); *Horn Quintet in E flat, K.407* (with Griller Q). RICHARD STRAUSS: *Horn Concerto No. 1 in E flat, Op. 11* (with Philh. O, Galliera).

(M) (**(*)) Pearl mono GEM 0026.

Dennis Brain recorded the Beethoven *Sonata* with Denis Matthews in February 1944 on a simple, valved Boosey and Hawkes French horn (which legend has it cost £12). Because of its valve system, this was a more flexible instrument than the Viennese hand-horns used in Mozart's own time, but also a more imperfect one, with a few insecure upper harmonics. Brain's timbre is unique, his articulation is endearingly musical, his technique phenomenal but never showy; even so, there is the occasional slightly insecure note. Yet the passagework in both Beethoven and Mozart is full of imaginative touches. In the Beethoven *Sonata* Denis Matthews provides an elegant Mozartian-styled partnership, his lightness of touch balancing nicely with Brain's elegance. How beautifully they exchange the question and answer of the briefly melancholy *Andante* and then launch into the robust finale so spiritedly!

The programme opens with the lovely Mozart *Quintet* (recorded eight months later). The Grillers play very sweetly and adroitly for the dominating horn, and the finale sparkles, but remains elegant. The two Mozart concertos followed. K.495 came first in 1943 (with the Hallé Orchestra – the strings in rather indifferent form, conducted by their leader, Laurence Turner), K.417 (with the Philharmonia under Susskind) in 1946. In both, Brain's phrasing of the lovely slow-movement melodies is Elysian and the jaunty finale of K.417 remains unforgettable. When he came to re-record the Mozart *Horn Concertos* with Karajan in 1953 (reissued in EMI's 'Great Recordings of the Century' series – 5 66898-2) he had adopted the wide-bore German double horn, which has a fatter, more spreading sound, not a timbre Mozart would have recognized. So there is a case for preferring Brain's earlier performances because Mozart simply sounds better on the narrower-bore instrument, and that is not to disparage the marvellous playing on the Karajan disc.

It is not certain which instrument Brain used for the present 1947 recording of the Richard Strauss, but the playing is wonderfully ebullient and crisply articulated, all difficulties swept aside: it sounds like a French rather than a German horn. The effect is to echo the work's Mozartian inspiration, and in the great soaring romantic theme at the centre of the slow movement – here, unfortunately affected by intrusive, uneven, scratchy surface noise – the lyrical surge is thrilling but not inflated, and this is one of his very finest solo performances on record. The Pearl transfers are faithful and agreeable (there is no edginess on the strings). But it surely ought to have been possible to diminish the background surface noise.

Brass Partout

'*Playgrounds for Angels*': GRIEG: *Sorgemarsj over Rikard Nordraak*. NYSTEDT: *Pia Memoria*. RAUTAVAARA: *A Requiem in our Time; Playgrounds for Angels*. SIBELIUS: *Overture in F min.; Allegro; Andantino and Menuett; Förspel (Preludium); Tiera*.

*** BIS CD 1054.

Brass Partout (or rather brass partout, all fashionably lower case), is a virtuoso group of brass and percussion players, drawn from the Berlin Philharmonic and other major German orchestras. The disc takes its title from the ingenious piece the Finnish composer Einojuhani Rautavaara composed for the Philip Jones Brass Ensemble. The *Requiem in our Time* put Rautavaara on the map in 1953 and is only available in one other version.

All the Sibelius rarities are from 1889, before *Kullervo*, except only *Tiera* (1899). They fill in our picture of his growth during those formative years, though none is a masterpiece. The splendid *Pia Memoria*, a requiem for nine brass instruments by the Norwegian, Knut Nystedt, has nobility and dignity. So, too, does Grieg's *Sorgemarsj over Rikard Nordraak* to whose strains the composer himself was buried. The playing is pretty stunning and so, too, is the superb BIS recording.

British Light Music

'*British Light Music*' (with (i) **Light Music Society O, Sir Vivian Dunn;** (ii) **Pro Arte O, George Weldon;** (iii) **Studio Two Concert O, Reginald Kilbey;** (iv) **Eric Coates and his O**): (i) DUNCAN: *Little Suite: March.* CURZON: *The Boulevardier.* BINGE: *The Watermill.* DOCKER: *Tabarinage.* HOPE: *The Ring of Kerry Suite: The Jaunting Car.* (ii) COATES: *Springtime Suite: Dance in the Twilight.* COLLINS: *Vanity Fair.* CURZON: *Punchinello: Miniature Overture.* TOMLINSON: *Little Serenade.* BINGE: *Miss Melanie.* Alan LANGFORD: *Waltz.* BAYCO: *Elizabethan Masque.* DEXTER: *Siciliano.* Haydn WOOD: *Moods Suite: Joyousness.* (iii) *Paris Suite: Montmartre.* BINGE: *Elizabethan Serenade.* VINTER: *Portuguese Party.* OSBORNE: *Lullaby for Penelope.* FARNON: *Portrait of a Flirt.* HARTLEY: *Rouge et noir.* (iv) COATES: *Impression of a Princess; Wood Nymphs; The Dam Busters March.*

(M) *** EMI stereo/mono 5 66537-2.

Obviously inspired by the great success of the programmes of British light music recorded (at premium price) by Ronald Corp for Hyperion, EMI have delved into their archives and brought out this equally attractive selection, drawing on four different sources, all of the highest quality. Moreover this EMI CD is offered at mid-price and includes 76 minutes of ear-catching melody. The obvious favourites are here, from Ronald Binge's famous *Elizabethan Serenade* to his delectable vignette evoking *The Watermill*, Anthony Collins's *Vanity Fair* (the popularity of which he valued above his fame as a conductor) and Robert Farnon's witty *Portrait of a Flirt*.

But also included are many more novelties of equal charm: Bayco's winning pastiche, *Elizabethan Masque*, Binge's wistful portrait of *Miss Melanie*, Alan Langford's pastel-shaded *Waltz*, Harry Dexter's lilting *Siciliano*, Leslie Osborne's gently touching *Lullaby for Penelope*, and the delicious Irish whimsy of Peter Hope's *Jaunting Car*. To bring lively contrast come Robert Docker's roisterous *Tabarinage* and Gilbert Vinter's equally vivacious *Portuguese Party*. The stereo recordings, made at Abbey Road between 1963 and 1970, are excellent and very pleasingly transferred. Appropriately, the programme opens and closes with the music of Eric Coates, and the last three items are conducted by the composer, ending with a vigorous account of *The Dam Busters March*. These are mono recordings, but of high quality.

'*British Light Music*' (played by the Slovak or Czecho-Slovak Radio Symphony Orchestra, Andrew Penny, Adrian Leaper (with male chorus), Ludovit Raijter or Ernest Tomlinson; BBC Concert Orchestra, Kenneth Alwyn; Dublin RTE Concert Orchestra, Ernest Tomlinson or Proinnsias O Duinn):

Volume 1: COATES: *By the Sleepy Lagoon.* QUILTER: *Children's Overture.* ADDINSELL: *Film music: Tom Brown's Schooldays.* CURZON: *Robin Hood Suite.* Haydn WOOD: *Sketch of a Dandy.* DUNCAN: *Little Suite.* COLLINS: *Vanity Fair.* KETELBEY: *Suite romantique.* (8.554709).

Volume 2: KETELBEY: *In a Monastery Garden.* FARNON: *Colditz March.* GERMAN: *Gypsy Suite.* Haydn WOOD: *Roses of Picardy; Serenade to Youth.* DUNCAN: *Enchanted April.* CURZON: *La Pienneta.* QUILTER: *Rosmé Waltz.* ELLIS: *Coronation Scot.* (8.554710).

Volume 3: ADDINSELL: *Film music: Goodbye Mr Chips.* GERMAN: *Romeo and Juliet* (incidental music): *Suite.* DUNCAN: *20th-century Express.* Haydn WOOD: *The Seafarer.* FARNON: *Pictures in the Fire.* COATES: *The Selfish Giant.* QUILTER: *As You Like It: Suite.* BENJAMIN: *Jamaican Rumba.* KETELBEY: *Bells across the Meadow.* (8.554711).

Volume 4: ADDINSELL (arr. Roy Douglas): *Warsaw Concerto.* BATH: *Cornish Rhapsody.* Richard

Rodney BENNETT: *Murder on the Orient Express: Theme and Waltz.* Charles WILLIAMS: *Dream of Olwen* (with Philip Fowke). FARNON: *Lake in the Woods; Westminster Waltz.* DUNCAN: *Girl from Corsica; Visionaries' Grand March.* CURZON: *Bravada: Paso doble.* Haydn WOOD: *Evening Song.* TOMLINSON: *Little Serenade.* (8.554712).

Volume 5: COATES: *Dam Busters March.* ADDINSELL: *Film music: Fire over England.* GERMAN: *Nell Gwynn: 3 Dances; Tom Jones: Waltz.* KETELBEY: *In the Moonlight.* BINGE: *Elizabethan Serenade.* FARNON: *Peanut Polka.* QUILTER: *3 English Dances.* WOOD: *May-Day Overture.* MAYERL: *Marigold.* KETELBEY: *In a Persian Market.* (8.554713).

(BB) ★★★ Naxos 8.505147 (5).

Unlike the Naxos set of 'British orchestral masterpieces' below, in which five existing CDs are offered in a slipcase, '*The Best of British Light Music*' has been specially compiled, with items selected from a number of Naxos CDs. It offers a wide selection, well over five hours of music, so is less selective than the full-priced Hyperion CDs of the New London Orchestra under Ronald Corp. The NLO are also rather more characterful and even better recorded (see below) but the Naxos set remains excellent value. Although Kenneth Alwyn directs most of the film music, much of the rest is played, surprisingly idiomatically, by the Slovak Radio Symphony Orchestra, usually conducted by Adrian Leaper, although Ernest Tomlinson directs his own music (including his delicate lollipop, *Little Serenade*). The highlights include Roger Quilter's lovely *Children's Overture*, Anthony Collins's *Vanity Fair* (which he greatly prized), Binge's *Elizabethan Serenade* and *Sailing By*, Benjamin's *Jamaican Rumba* and mostly familiar items by Eric Coates. Robert Farnon is well represented by *Colditz*, his charming *Westminster Waltz* and the catchy *Peanut Polka*, as well as two rather effective tone-pictures, *Lake in the Woods* and *Pictures in the Fire*, and there are other obvious hits like Vivian Ellis's *Coronation Scot* and of course the 'film concertos'. Not everything else is quite so memorable, but Edward German, Haydn Wood and Ketèlbey are all well represented and everything is brightly played and well recorded. The five records come for the price of four, and all are quite well documented.

'*British Light Music Festival*' (played by various orchestras & conductors): FANSHAWE: *Fanfare To Planet Earth; Millennium March.* LANGFORD: *Petite Promenade.* HOPE: *Irish Legend; Petit Point; Playful Scherzo; Ring of Kerry.* TOMLINSON: *Cantilena.* ABBOTT: *London Fragments.* TURNER: *Countrywise; Passepied des enfants.* KELLY: *Dance Suite; Comedy Film.* LYON: *Dance Prelude; Divertimento.* VINTER: *April Shower; March Winds; Mayflowers; Song – Dance Suite; Tenderfoot.* JOSEPHS: *Aeolian Dance; Ecossaise; March Glorious.*

ARNOLD: *Sarabande*. DYER: *Marche Vive*. PERRY: *Lonely Journey*. DRING: *Danza Gaya*. SAUNDERS: *Badinage; Kanikani*. DOCKER: *Commemoration March*.

(M) **(*) ASV (ADD) CDWLS 250 (2).

An excellent anthology of performances drawn from various sources, mainly from the 1960s, though David Fanshawe's were recorded as recently as 2000. All of the music is in the best British light-music tradition, which flourished especially well in the 1950s and 1960s. If it is not all first rate, it is often nostalgically enjoyable just the same. Helpful sleeve-notes, as usual from this source.

'Halcyon Days: A Treasury of British Light Music': PHILIPS: *Hampton Court Overture*. DELIUS: *2 Aquarelles*. TOMLINSON: *Cantilena*. RUTTER: *Vivace*. BRIDGE: *Miss Melanie*. DAVIES: *RAF March Past*. WARLOCK: *4 Folksong Preludes*. J. GARDINER: *Half Holiday*. VAUGHAN WILLIAMS: *Fantasia on Greensleeves*. ELGAR: *The Spanish Lady (Suite), Op. 90*. FIELD: *Rondo*. HOROVITZ: *Sinfonietta*. ARNOLD: *The Padstow Lifeboat*. ANSELL: *Plymouth Hoe*. Haydn WOOD: *London Landmarks*. MORLEY: *Rotton Row*. COATES: *By the Sleepy Lagoon; The Dam Busters March; Halcyon Days; London Suite*. LANE: *3 Spanish Dances; Suite of Cotswold Folk Dances* (excerpts). GLYN: *Anglesey Seascapes* (excerpts). CURZON: *March of the Bowmen*. GOODWIN: *City of Lincoln March*. MACCUNN: *Land of the Mountain and Flood Overture*. HARTY: *Londonderry Air*. CHARLES WILLIAMS: *The Devil's Galop; Girls in Grey; High Adventure*. BINGE: *Sailing By; The Watermill*. MATHIESON: *Loch Laggan*. GOODALL: *Ecce Homo; Psalm 23*. ADDINSELL: *Southern Rhapsody*. JOSEPHS: *March Glorious*. LEWIS: *An English Overture*. WALTON: *Spitfire Prelude and Fugue*. MONTGOMERY: *Carry On Suite*. ERIC ROGERS: *Carry On Up the Khyber* (arr. Sutherland). BLAKE: *Andante Expressivo*. FANSHAWE: *Tarka the Otter*. GRAY: *The African Queen*. BLEZARD: *Caramba*. SMYTH: *2 Interlinked French Melodies*. SAUNDERS: *Kanikani*. KELLY: *Divertissement*. RODNEY BENNET: *Suite Française*. SUMSION: *A Mountain Tune*. HOPE: *4 French Dances*. LANGFORD: *Petite Promenade*. MACDONALD: *Cuban Rondo*. VINTER: *Song – Dance Suite*. ADDINSELL: *Greengage Summer* (excerpts). TCHAIKOVSKY (arr. Wilkinson): *Beatlecracker Suite*. ARNOLD: *Sarabande*. GORDON: *2 Dances*. DRING: *Danza Gaya*. TOYE: *The Haunted Ballroom*. READE: *2 Dances*. LYON: *3 Dances*. STANFORD: *Celestial Fire* (excerpts). JOSEPHS: *Aeolian Dances*.

(B) *** ASV (ADD/DDD) WLS 501 (5).

A positive cornucopia of British light music, taken from the myriad of CDs in the ASV White Line catalogue, mostly conducted by Gavin Sutherland, along with Barry Wordsworth, Kenneth Alwyn, *et al.*,

and a sprinkling of vintage performances from the 1960s. With compositions ranging from Elgar and Dame Ethel Smyth, right up to the *Carry On* films, there is no lack of variety here, with pretty much all the famous numbers – *The Devil's Galop, Sailing By*, the *Dam Busters March*, etc., included. The pleasure of this set lies in rediscovering so much long-forgotten, undemanding and tuneful music which has slipped from the repertoire over the years but has been rescued, on recordings at least, for the twenty-first century. The five CDs are very well planned, mixing the more substantial compositions of Mac-Cunn and Walton and the like with the various suites, overtures, dances and novelty numbers, with the sound consistently fine. This feast of light music is a great way to acquire a lot of good tunes in one go!

'British Orchestral Masterpieces'

'British Orchestral Masterpieces' (played by (i) RSNO; (ii) E. N. Philh. O; (iii) David Lloyd-Jones; (iv) Paul Daniel; (v) with Tim Hugh (cello): (i; iii) BAX: *Symphony No. 1; The Garden of Fand; In the Faery Hills*. (ii; iii) BLISS: (v) *Cello Concerto. Music for Strings, Op. 54; 2 Studies, Op. 16*. ELGAR: *Falstaff, Op. 68; Elegy, Op. 58; The Sanguine Fan (ballet), Op. 81*. (i; iii) HOLST: *Beni Mora; Egdon Heath; Fugal Overture; Hammersmith*; (v) *Invocation for Cello and Orchestra. Somerset Rhapsody*. (ii; iv) WALTON: *Symphony No. 1; Partita*.

(BB) *** Naxos 8.505154 (5).

With the five CDs offered for the price of four, this is an exceptionally successful anthology and a self-recommending bargain of the highest order. All these discs have been reviewed before. The Bax collection is the only one about which there are any reservations and these are minor, mostly concerning the recording, which is not as full and forward as usual from this source, with the solo cello rather backwardly balanced in the *Concerto*. Hugh's reading is reflective to match. Poetry rather than power is the keynote, centring on the *Larghetto* slow movement. In the Bax, David Lloyd-Jones draws warmly sympathetic performances from the RSNO, most impressively recorded, and the RSNO play extremely well for him. Tim Hugh is again a most responsive soloist in the rare Holst *Invocation*, with the rest of the Holst items hardly less distinguished. Lloyd-Jones's account of *Falstaff* brings tinglingly brisk tempi tempered by a highly idiomatic ebb and flow of rubato, and *The Sanguine Fan* is equally persuasive, alongside a touching account of the Elgarian *Elegy*. To cap the set comes Paul Daniel's outstanding version of the Walton *Symphony*, as bitingly intense as almost any in the catalogue, with the joyful *Partita* hardly less stimulating.

Camden, Anthony (oboe)

Italian Oboe Concertos (with City of London Sinfonia, Nicolas Ward): CIMAROSA, arr. Arthur BENJAMIN: *Concerto in C.* BELLINI: *Concerto in E flat.* RIGHINI: *Concerto in C.* FIORILLO: *Sinfonia concertante in F* (with Julia Girdwood). CORELLI, arr. BARBIROLLI: *Concerto in A.*
PERGOLESI/BARBIROLLI: *Concerto in C min.*
(BB) **(*) Naxos 8.553433.

This collection recalls the series of outstanding recordings made by Evelyn Rothwell for Pye/PRT with her husband, Sir John Barbirolli, conducting. He specially arranged the highly engaging pastiche works of Corelli and Pergolesi for her to play and put his signature firmly on the *Sarabanda* of the Corelli *Concerto*, which he scored as a duet for oboe and cello, his own instrument. Lady Barbirolli's recordings have just been restored to the catalogue, but at full price.

Meanwhile these sympathetic and stylishly played performances from Anthony Camden will suffice admirably, particularly at Naxos price. He has a most attractive timbre, and Nicholas Ward's accompaniments are impeccable. There are two very small reservations. The Fiorillo *Sinfonia concertante*, which features a pair of oboes (the second part is neatly managed by Julia Girdwood), although nicely written for the two soloists, is very conventional in its material and the first movement is a shade too long. The other point concerns the delightful five-note opening phrase of Arthur Benjamin's delicious Cimarosa confection, which Camden plays curiously lethargically, echoed by Ward. It is a small point, but Lady Barbirolli's account still lingers in the memory. The Naxos recording is excellently balanced and truthful.

'The Art of the Oboe' (with (i) London Virtuosi, John Georgiadis; (ii) City of L. Sinfonia, Nicholas Ward): (i) ALBINONI: *Oboe Concertos: in C, Op. 7/12; in D min., Op. 9/2; in C, Op. 9/5.* (ii) HANDEL: *Concerto No. 3 in G min.; Rondo in G; Rigaudon.*
RIGHINI: *Idomeneus Concerto.* CORELLI: *Concerto.*
CIMAROSA: *Concerto in C min.* BELLINI: *Concerto in E flat.*
(BB) *** Naxos 8.553991.

This collection again has something in common with Evelyn Rothwell, Lady Barbirolli's collection of oboe concertos with her husband directing, but has the advantage of modern digital sound of high quality. Anthony Camden is a first-class soloist and these are vividly played performances, stylishly accompanied by both groups. Camden's tempi are not always quite so apt as his predecessor but slow movements are always sensitive and finales sparkle. Most enjoyable.

Capella Istropolitana, Adrian Leaper

'English String Festival': DOWLAND: *Galliard a 5.*
ELGAR: *Elegy, Op. 58; Introduction and Allegro, Op. 47; Serenade, Op. 20.* BRIDGE: *Lament.* PARRY: *An English Suite; Lady Radnor's Suite.*
(BB) **(*) Naxos 8.550331.

It is fascinating and rewarding to hear these excellent Slovak players turn their attention to essentially English repertoire, and with a considerable degree of success. The brief Dowland *Galliard* makes a strong introduction, and the attractive pair of neo-Baroque Parry suites of dance movements, played with warmth, finesse and spirit, are given bright and lively sound. In the Elgar *Introduction and Allegro* the violins above the stave have their upper partials over-brilliantly lit by the digital recording, the focus not quite sharp; but otherwise the sound is full, with plenty of resonant ambience. The playing is strongly felt, but the fugue is a bit too measured, and the great striding theme, played in unison on the G string, could also do with more pace, especially when it returns. Otherwise this is persuasive, and the *Serenade* is presented simply, combining warmth and finish. At super-bargain price, this is worth exploring.

Capuçon, Renaud (violin)

'Le Boeuf sur le toit' (with Bremen Deutsche Kammerphilharmonie, Harding): BERLIOZ: *Rêverie et caprice.* MASSENET: *Thaïs: Méditation.*
MILHAUD: *Le Boeuf sur le toit, Op.58.* RAVEL: *Tzigane.* SAINT-SAENS: *Danse macabre; Havanaise; Introduction and Rondo capriccioso; Etudes, Op. 52* (arr. YSAYE): *En forme de valse.*
*** Virgin 5 45482-2.

This is a violin-and-orchestra recital with an attractive theme that fills a neat gap. Featuring the brilliant young French virtuoso, Renaud Capuçon, masterly throughout, this collection of short concertante pieces by French composers offers such predictable items as the Massenet *Méditation*, the Ravel *Tzigane* and the Saint-Saëns *Havanaise* and *Introduction and Rondo capriccioso*, but also includes the less well-known Berlioz piece and other related items. *Danse macabre* makes an obvious extra, although it features the solo violin more as an orchestral leader than as a main soloist, while the fourth Saint-Saëns item, described as *Valse-caprice* on the disc, is an arrangement made by Ysaÿe of the most popular of Saint-Saëns's piano études.

Most intriguing is the longest item, which provides the title for the whole disc, *Le Boeuf sur le toit*. This is one of two current versions of the arrangement which Milhaud himself made for the violinist, René Benedetti, of his Brazilian-inspired 'cinema-fantasy'.

He characteristically takes the opportunity to emphasize the bizarre character of this suite of jazzy dances with its rondo theme inspired by Charlie Chaplin, making the solo violin the prime mover in bringing out the comic 'wrong-note' writing and clashing polytonality. Capuçon and Harding together make a strong case for this alternative version, relishing to the full the wit of the piece.

Casals, Pablo (conductor & cello)

SCHUBERT (with Prades Festival O): *Symphony No. 5 in B flat. String Quintet in C, Op. 163, D.956* (with Stern, Schneider, Katims, Tortelier).

(M) (★★★) Sony mono SMK 58992 [id.].

The Schubert *Fifth Symphony*, recorded in 1953, omits the first-movement exposition repeat but, as with everything this great musician does, is full of musical interest. It has not been issued in the UK before, eclipsed by the later (and perhaps even finer) performance by the 1970 Marlboro Orchestra in stereo. However, this earlier account boasts a particularly eloquent reading of the slow movement. The Casals account of the sublime Schubert *C major String Quintet* has rarely been absent from the catalogue: it first appeared on Philips and then CBS, and is too familiar to require detailed comment. Recorded in 1952, it sounds as marvellous as ever. This coupling is surely a must for all Casals admirers.

Chang, Sarah (violin), Berlin Philharmonic Orchestra, Plácido Domingo

'Fire and Ice': BACH: *Orchestral Suite No. 3 in D, BWV 1068: Air.* BEETHOVEN: *Romance No. 2 in F, Op. 50.* DVORAK: *Romance in F min., Op. 11.* MASSENET: *Thaïs: Méditation.* RAVEL: *Tzigane.* SARASATE: *Concert Fantasy on Carmen, Op. 25; Zigeunerweisen, Op. 20.*

★★★ EMI 5 57220-2.

Don't be put off by the silly title of the disc – 'Fire and Ice'! We have here a collection of rightly popular violin virtuoso pieces played with terrific panache and splendid style by this still young player. It is only ten years since Chang's last record of the Sarasate, although it was made some years earlier (when she was nine) and played on a smaller-sized instrument. Since then she has gone on to record concertos by Paganini, Tchaikovsky, Sibelius and Vieuxtemps, all of which have been acclaimed. In the early 1990s Miss Chang was hailed by Menuhin as 'the most ideal violinist I have ever heard', and now, ten years later, her prowess and virtuosity are never in doubt here. Those attracted to this repertoire can be assured that the playing from all concerned is pretty dazzling, and there are no reservations about the quality of the

recording, made in the Philharmonie, Berlin. The balance is very acceptable and places the soloist firmly in the spotlight without in any way allowing her to mask the orchestral detail.

Chicago Symphony Orchestra

Historic Telecasts, Volume 1 (1954): **Fritz Reiner**

BEETHOVEN: *Symphony No. 7 in A, Op. 92; Egmont Overture, Op. 84.* HANDEL: *Solomon: Arrival of the Queen of Sheba.*

(★★★) VAI Video VAI 69601.

Historic Telecasts, Volume 2 (1961): **Georg Szell**

MUSSORGSKY: *Prelude to Khovanshchina.* BEETHOVEN: *Symphony No. 5 in C min., Op. 67.* BERLIOZ: *Le Carnaval romain Overture, Op. 9.*

(★★★) VAI Video VAI 69602.

Historic Telecasts, Volume 3 (1962): **Leopold Stokowski**

BACH, arr. Stokowski: *Toccata and Fugue in D min.* BRAHMS: *Variations on a Theme of Haydn (St Anthony chorale).* RIMSKY-KORSAKOV: *Capriccio espagnol, Op. 34.*

(★★★) VAI Video VAI 69603.

Historic telecasts, Volume 4 (1961): **Pierre Monteux**

BEETHOVEN: *Symphony No. 8 in F, Op. 93.* WAGNER: *Die Meistersinger: Prelude to Act III.* BERLIOZ: *Le Carnaval romain Overture, Op. 9.*

(★★★) VAI Video VAI 69604.

The above four videos are even more valuable than the wider but more piecemeal coverage of the '*Art of Conducting*', above. They offer us four great conductors at the height of their powers directing a great orchestra, and every performance is memorable. We even have a chance to compare Szell's and Monteux's interpretations of Berlioz's supreme orchestral masterpiece, *Le Carnaval romain*, Szell the more electrifying, Monteux the more colourful.

These telecasts are part of a series inaugurated in Chicago in 1951 (under Kubelik). But when Reiner took over the orchestra in 1953 the programmes were extended to 45 minutes, broadcast first on Sunday afternoons, and subsequently (in 1959) at 8 p.m. on Sunday evenings, with Deems Taylor as initial host. The list of guest conductors who joined the series is wide-reaching, including Barbirolli, Beecham, Copland, Hindemith, Martinon, Munch and Previn. Announcements and commentaries are omitted from the published videos and the music is presented without introductions.

It was right that Reiner should carry on the series, at a live concert in Symphony Hall in 1954. With the bold swathe of his strong, clear up-and-down beat, a serious mien, and frowning gaze, he establishes total control of the orchestra. Although the early recording quality brings the usual sound-track discoloration of woodwind upper partials, with moments of distortion in the wide amplitude of string sound, the warmth of the playing projects readily, as does its spontaneous feeling (after the single hour-long run-through rehearsal, which was standard for the series).

It is a pity that no Richard Strauss was included, but the Beethoven performances generate enormous electricity. The camera-work is fairly primitive, and it is interesting that the producer misses the dominating role of the horns in the thrilling furioso close of the outer movements of the *Seventh Symphony* and focuses instead on the woodwind, whereas in *Egmont* the horn section is portrayed at the key moments. Reiner, stiff and unrelenting in manner throughout, permits himself a half smile to acknowledge the applause, and even gives the oboes a bow – after the Queen of Sheba has arrived and departed rather fiercely.

Szell's clear beat is hardly less concentrated, achieving extraordinary precision and powerful clipped rhythms in Beethoven's *Fifth*; but he uses his left hand much more subtly than Reiner. It is a great performance, creating and gathering intensity in a formidable progress to its gripping finale. The first-movement repeat is observed (as it is later by Monteux in the *Eighth*) and the strings flowingly decorate the main theme of the slow movement with appealing warmth. Before that comes the evocatively detailed Mussorgsky *Khovanshchina Prelude*, with the delectable Rimsky-Korsakov orchestration glowing in the coda, and the following Berlioz overture is quite riveting in its orchestral bravura, almost upstaging the symphony in sheer adrenalin.

Reiner, Monteux and Szell conduct from memory, but Stokowski uses scores throughout, even in his famous Bach arrangement. Here the remarkably imaginative orchestration is made to seem the more vivid by camera close-ups, which even feature the glockenspiel and show the great horn entry at the climax of the fugue, before the thrilling upward rushes of strings. Where his colleagues favour batons, Stokowski uses his ever-supple hands to shape the music. This means slightly less precision of ensemble in the Bach (where he is concerned with the range of sonority and colour) but not in the Brahms, a richly idiomatic account, in no way idiosyncratic, although the lyrical warmth of the string writing is brought out in the closing variations. Rimsky's *Capriccio* is then played with enormous virtuosity (especially at the close) and the camera relishes the opportunity to portray each of the orchestral soloists in turn. As with the Szell concert, this is a studio recording, with a much drier acoustic, but the middle strings still glow as Stokowski coaxes their phrasing affectionately.

For the Monteux concert we return to Symphony Hall, with an audience, and this tape offers the best sound of the four – warm and well-detailed. Monteux's dapper, genial manner is deceptive, yet it brings the most relaxed atmosphere of all and at one endearing moment the camera catches one of the violin players on the back desks turning to his companion and smiling. The performance of Beethoven's *Eighth* is superb, polished, wonderfully detailed, and with a perfectly judged forward flow. When Monteux wants to be forceful he clenches his left fist, and the result catches the music's full intensity without fierceness. The glorious horn playing (on which the camera dwells indulgently) gives great warmth and nobility to the following Wagner *Prelude*, and the Berlioz overture ends the programme with a fizzing burst of energy at its very close.

Historic Telecasts, Volume 5 (1963): Charles Munch

RAMEAU/D'INDY: *Dardanus Suite.* BERLIOZ: *Les Troyens: Royal Hunt and Storm.* RAVEL: *Valses nobles et sentimentales; La Valse.*
(***) VAI Video VAI 69605.

Historic telecasts, Volume 6 (1963): Paul Hindemith

HINDEMITH: *Concert Music for Strings and Brass.* BRUCKNER: *Symphony No. 7: first movement* (only). BRAHMS: *Academic Festival Overture.*
⚫ (***) VAI Video VAI 69606.

Historic Telecasts, Volume 7 (1961): George Szell

MOZART: *Overture: Le nozze di Figaro; Violin Concerto No. 5 in A (Turkish), K.219* (with Erica Morini). BEETHOVEN: *Overture: Leonora No. 3.*
(***) VAI Video VAI 69607.

This second batch of videos includes the most valuable of all, a video of Paul Hindemith conducting 'live' in Chicago's Orchestra Hall, where understandably the privileged audience give him a hero's welcome. With his lips pursed seriously throughout, and using a clear, purposeful stick technique, he directs an electrifying account of his own *Concert Music for Strings and Brass*, with the Chicago strings and brass responding with the most glorious sounds. One might even use the adjective voluptuous in relation to the strings, except that, rich though the textures are, Hindemith's lyricism remains sinewy – for that is its strength. The fugato (nicely observed by the camera) also has splendid bite. He also conducts a superbly paced account of the first movement of Bruckner's *Seventh*, full of humanity. This follows a brief filmed interview when he is suitably articulate on the music's universality to a not very imaginative TV interviewer. The closing overture, spacious and exciting, is richly Brahmsian. The sound really is remarkably good.

By the side of this, Munch's concert is just a shade disappointing. The Rameau/D'Indy suite is elegant enough, but, lacking the incandescence of a Beecham touch, sounds anachronistic, and the *Royal Hunt and*

Storm, beautifully played as it is, takes a little while to warm up. However, the climax when it comes does not disappoint (with the camera-work among the brass adding a great deal to the visual effect), and the closing horn solo is poetically atmospheric. The Ravel performances are warmly idiomatic, but here the sound lacks enough transparency to bring out the lustrous detail.

Szell, after a brilliant, if ungenial *Nozze di Figaro Overture*, has the advantage of a very stylish soloist, Erica Morini, in Mozart's most popular violin concerto. She plays with beautful tone, splendid assurance and a disarming simplicity of line, and only the three cadenzas (rather too much of a good thing) give any cause for criticism. *Leonora No. 3* makes a meticulously detailed but exciting finale. Good sound, with the solo violin well caught, although balanced very forwardly.

Chicago Symphony Orchestra, Daniel Barenboim or Pierre Boulez

'*Musik Triennale Cologne 2000*'

DVD 1 (cond. Pierre Boulez): BERG: *Lulu Suite.* DEBUSSY: *Le jeu d'eau; 3 Ballades de François Villon* (with Christine Schäfer). STRAVINSKY: *The Firebird* (ballet; complete).
*** DVD TDK DV-MTKBO.

DVD 2 (cond. Daniel Barenboim). BOULEZ: *Notations I–IV.* CARLI: *El firulete.* DEBUSSY: *La Mer.* FALLA: *El sombrero de tres picos (The Three-cornered Hat* (ballet; complete; with Elisabete Matos).
*** DVD TDK DV-MTKBA.

In April 2000 the Chicago Symphony Orchestra visited the Cologne Triennial Music Festival of 20th-century Music, with these two concerts conducted respectively by Pierre Boulez and Daniel Barenboim. On each DVD comes a ten-minute excerpt, one following from the other, of a conversation between the two conductors, both of them worthwhile supplements. The music-making in both concerts is persuasive, brilliant and warm, the more compelling when seen as well as heard.

It is Barenboim who conducts the Boulez work, the one example of music from after the Second World War. Not that these four *Notations* are typical of Boulez when they are basically orchestrations, made in maturity with revisions and development, of early piano pieces he wrote as a student of René Leibowitz. The first, with its evocative orchestral writing, here sumptuously performed, has one thinking of Debussy, while the energetic fourth piece brings echoes of *The Rite of Spring*, with Barenboim momentarily echoing Boulez's crisp 'tic-tac' style of conducting. The Barenboim programme then goes on to a sensuous account of Debussy's *La Mer* and a

vigorously dramatic one of the complete Falla ballet, with the Chicago players warmly idiomatic in the Spanish dance-rhythms. Elisabete Matos is the fine mezzo soloist in the vocal introduction, with the members of the orchestra enthusiastically clapping and shouting '*Ole!*' They equally let their hair down when, at the end of the concert, Barenboim concedes an encore, a jolly dance by José Carli, *El firulete*, a frill or bit of nonsense.

The Boulez offering is even more striking, when Christine Schäfer is such an inspired soloist both in Berg's *Lulu Suite* and in the Debussy songs with orchestral accompaniment. Schäfer not only sings Lulu's Song in the second movement but the lament of Countess Geschwitz after Lulu's murder in the final movement, though she does not attempt a scream at the moment prescribed. When heard live, Schäfer's voice may seem relatively small, but as balanced here it is full, firm and sensous, ideal both for Berg in such a warm performance and for Debussy in the subtleties of the *Villon* songs with their echoes of early music. A pity though that the camera often takes you so close to her you practically see down to her tonsils. The orchestral sound is full-bodied on both discs, with solo instruments brought forward in reflection of the camera-work. An auspicious introduction to twentieth-century music on DVD.

Chicago Symphony Orchestra, Sir Thomas Beecham

HAYDN: *Symphony No. 102 in B flat.* MOZART: *Symphony No. 38 in D (Prague), K.504.*
** NCV Arts Video 8573 84095-3.

DELIUS: *Florida Suite: By the River.* HANDEL, **arr.** BEECHAM: *Love in Bath* (Suite). MENDELSSOHN: *Hebrides Overture.* SAINT-SAENS: *Le Rouet d'Omphale.*
** NCV Arts Video 8573 84096-3.

Beecham is not generously represented on film, and these performances given in Chicago in March 1960 are the only colour images to survive. The colour is admittedly not very good; nor, for that matter, is the sound. Moreover, the dynamic range is not as wide as we are accustomed to in Beecham's commercial recordings, so the rapt magical *pianissimo* tone is less in evidence. Of course, there are moments when the Beecham magic works, but they surface only intermittently. The camera-work is rather stiff and wooden, with none of the flexibility you would expect from a BBC telecast of the period. We often focus on lines of string players, and Beecham himself gets far less attention from the camera than one might expect. Recommended, then, but with only modified rapture.

Chicago Symphony Orchestra, Carlo Giulini

'The Chicago Recordings': MAHLER: *Symphony No. 1 in D.* BERLIOZ: *Roméo et Juliette, Op. 17:* orchestral music. BEETHOVEN: *Symphony No. 7 in A, Op. 92.* BRUCKNER: *Symphony No. 9 in D min.* BRAHMS: *Symphony No. 4 in E min., Op. 98.* STRAVINSKY: *Firebird Suite (1919); Petrushka Suite (1947).*
(M) *** EMI 5 85974-2 (4).

To mark the great Italian conductor's ninetieth birthday EMI have collected the recordings he made with the Chicago Symphony Orchestra in 1969–71 (save for the Bruckner *Symphony*, which comes from 1976). They have been out of circulation since the days of LP, apart from the Beethoven and Bruckner symphonies, which have briefly appeared on CD. They are all performances of some stature, in particular the collection of orchestral excerpts from *Romeo and Juliet*, which alone is worth the price of the set. This is playing of rapt poetic feeling and intensity, which shows the Chicago orchestra at its very finest. The Bruckner *Ninth*, too, is very fine and arguably more spontaneous than the later, DG account with the Vienna Philharmonic, though the orchestral playing was particularly sumptuous. The sound in most of these recordings is very vivid and truthfully balanced, though we regret that EMI have split the Berlioz over two discs, though that matters less perhaps than putting the first movement of the Brahms on disc 3 and the rest on disc 4. Never mind, these are very impressive performances and it is good to have them all back.

Chicago Symphony Orchestra, Fritz Reiner

ROSSINI: *Overture: La gazza ladra.* HAYDN: *Symphony No. 88 in G.* BEETHOVEN: *Symphony No. 7 in A, Op. 92.* WEBER: *Invitation to the Dance.* J. STRAUSS JR: *Emperor Waltz.* LISZT: *Mephisto Waltz No. 1.* R. STRAUSS: *Don Juan.* RAVEL: *Rapsodie espagnole.* BARTOK: *Hungarian Sketches.*
⊷ (B) *** RCA (ADD) 74321 84219-2 (2).

An ideal compilation for those wish to explore Fritz Reiner's Chicago recordings from the early stereo era, many of which remain top recommendations. Here we have a glittering *Rapsodie espagnole*, a dashing *Don Juan* and a powerful Beethoven *Seventh*. Reiner was also master of the lighter repertoire, and his Strauss waltzes and Rossini overtures are always a joy to hear; his Haydn is full of character, too. Indeed, all these performances have this conductor's magnetism stamped on them, and new listeners will understand why he has a cult following. The recordings all have the vivid Chicago ambience, though in these new transfers some can be bit aggressive under pressure. Notes about the music and conductor are included.

Chicago Symphony Orchestra, Frederick Stock

WAGNER: *Die Meistersinger Overture.* BRAHMS: *Hungarian Dances Nos. 17-21.* GOLDMARK: *In the Springtime Overture.* SUK: *Fairy tales: Folkdance (polka).* GLAZUNOV: *Les Ruses d'amour: Introduction and Waltz.* TCHAIKOVSKY: *Symphony No. 5 in E min.* PAGANINI: *Moto perpetuo, Op. 11* (orch. Stock). WALTON: *Scapino: Comedy Overture.* DOHNANYI: *Suite for Orchestra, Op. 19.* R. STRAUSS: *Also sprach Zarathustra.* STOCK: *Symphonic Waltz. Op. 8.*
✹ (M) (***) Biddulph mono WHL 021/22.

Frederick Stock, born in Germany in 1872, studied composition and violin at the Cologne Conservatoire; among his teachers was Humperdinck, and Mengelberg was a fellow student. He began his career as an orchestral violinist, and in 1895 he emigrated to America to join the ranks of the Chicago Symphony as a viola player. The orchestra was then four years old. In 1905 he was hired on a temporary basis as its musical director; but he stayed on for nearly forty years until he died in October 1942.

He built the orchestra into the splendid ensemble which Fritz Reiner was eventually to inherit and established its world reputation, especially for its brass playing, although (on the evidence of these recordings) the strings were equally impressive. Like Reiner, he had the advantage of the marvellous acoustics of Chicago's Symphony Hall in which to make his records, which, alongside Stokowski's Philadelphia recordings, are technically among the finest to come out of America in the late 1920s.

Indeed, the sound in Tchaikovsky's *Fifth* (1927) is so warm and full-bodied that in no time at all one forgets one is listening to an old recording and simply revels in the rich string patina and fine woodwind colours (heard at their best in the elegantly played waltz movement). The brass come fully into their own in the finale. Stock's interpretation is endearingly wilful, very like Mengelberg's more famous reading, which was made only six months later. Stock pulls back at the entry of the secondary group in the first movement. The effect is emphasized because of a side change but is consistent in the recapitulation. The slow movement is very much *con alcuna licenza* (Tchaikovsky's marking) and the horn soloist must have needed immense nerve to sustain his great solo at the chosen spacious tempo. But Stock has that supreme gift of being able to create the feeling of a live performance while making a recording, and this *Fifth*, for all its eccentricities, is very enjoyable. The finale has the traditional cut which was so often observed at that time, but the effect is seamless and the final brass peroration has only ever been topped by Stokowski's 78-r.p.m. Philadelphia set.

The programme opens with a thrillingly sonorous account of *Die Meistersinger Overture* (1926), with the tension held right to the end, in spite of the big rallentando at the majestic reprise of the introductory 'fanfare'. The Brahms dances, played with virtuosity and considerable panache, were recorded in 1925 but never issued, and both the Suk *Polka* (1926) and the charming Glazunov *Waltz* (1929) show the colourful palette of Stock's Chicago woodwind section, while Goldmark's *In the Springtime Overture* sounds uncommonly fresh in this early (1925) performance. The Dohnányi suite too (1928) is stylishly and pleasingly done, with nice touches of wit and plenty of lilt in the waltz featured in the closing movement, where Stock handles the tempo changes with affectionate sophistication. But here for some reason the recording is very closely miked and dry; was it actually recorded in Symphony Hall, one wonders, for there is little ambient effect?

Stock's most famous record is of Walton's *Scapino Overture*, which he commissioned for the orchestra's fiftieth-anniversary celebrations. It is played here with fizzing virtuosity and much élan and is particularly valuable in being the only existing recording of Walton's original score before the composer made his revisions. This and an equally brilliant account of Paganini's *Moto perpetuo*, deftly played in unison by the orchestral violins, were recorded in 1941, the sound brightly lit (the violins are closely miked in the Paganini) but retaining underlying warmth.

The set ends appropriately with a work indelibly associated with Chicago because of Reiner's superb, later, stereo version: Strauss's *Also sprach Zarathustra*. But Stock's account certainly does not come under its shadow. The spectacular opening is remarkably well caught and the passion of the violins is thrilling. This was made in 1940, and here the Columbia engineers made a compromise between brilliance and richness of timbre, with the hall ambience adding a natural breadth. The range of dynamic is striking, and Stock's reading must be placed among the finest, for it is seemingly completely spontaneous, yet splendidly controlled and shaped. The orchestral concentration is held at the highest level throughout, and particularly so during the darkly dormant section of the score on the lower strings associated with '*Science*' and the later passage on the high violins; Stock then follows with an exciting accelerando to reach the spectacular climax in '*The Convalescent*'. He maintains this thrust through to the closing pages, with the tolling bell coming through plangently, and the coda very touching. Then for an encore the conductor provides a charmingly tuneful *Symphonic Waltz* of his own composition, endearingly inflated but not boring when presented with such zest, and sumptuously recorded in 1930. Yet there is nothing 'historic' about live music-making of this calibre,

and this fascinating set is very highly recommended. It certainly does Stock's reputation full justice.

(i) Chicago Symphony Orchestra, Frederick Stock; (ii) Cincinnati SO, Eugene Goossens

English Music: (i) BENJAMIN: *Overture to an Italian Comedy.* ELGAR: *Pomp and Circumstance March No. 1.* (ii) VAUGHAN WILLIAMS: *A London Symphony* (No. 2; original version); WALTON: *Violin Concerto* (with Jascha Heifetz (violin))
(★★★) Biddulph mono WHL 016.

This superbly transferred Biddulph issue celebrates the fact that some of the very finest recordings of British music have come from America. Heifetz's historic first recording of the Walton *Violin Concerto* is imaginatively coupled with the only recording ever made (also by Goossens and the Cincinnati orchestra, immediately following the Walton sessions in 1941) of the 1920 version of Vaughan Williams's *London Symphony*. As welcome fill-ups come Elgar's *Pomp and Circumstance No. 1* and Arthur Benjamin's *Overture to an Italian Comedy*, brilliantly played by the Chicago orchestra under Frederick Stock.

Chung, Kyung Wha (violin)

'*The Great Violin Concertos*': MENDELSSOHN: *Concerto in E min., Op. 64* (with Montreal SO, Dutoit). BEETHOVEN: *Concerto in D, Op. 61* (with VPO, Kondrashin). TCHAIKOVSKY: *Concerto in D, Op. 35.* SIBELIUS: *Concerto in D min., Op. 47* (both with LSO, Previn).
(B) ★★(★) Double Decca ADD/DDD 452 325-2 (2).

This Double Decca begs comparison with Grumiaux's Philips Duo, called, more sensibly, '*Favourite Violin Concertos*' (see below). Grumiaux offers Brahms instead of Sibelius and concentrates on repertoire in which his refined, poetic style produces satisfying results in all four works. Chung only scores three out of four. Her collection is let down by the 1979 account of the Beethoven which, measured and thoughtful, lacks the compulsion one would have predicted, due largely to the often prosaic conducting of Kondrashin. There is poetry in individual movements – the minor-key episode of the finale, for example, which alone justifies the unusually slow tempo – but, with too little of the soloist's natural electricity conveyed and none of her volatile imagination, it must be counted a disappointment, despite the first-class digital sound.

The Mendelssohn, made two years later, could not be more different. Chung favours speeds faster than usual in all three movements and the result is sparkling and happy, with the lovely slow movement fresh and songful, not at all sentimental. With warmly sympathetic accompaniment from Dutoit and the Montreal orchestra, amply recorded, the result was one of her happiest recordings.

The Sibelius/Tchaikovsky pairing (from 1970) is highly praised in our main volume. She brings an equally sympathetic and idiomatic response to both concertos, and Previn's accompaniments are of the highest order. The latter is a much better investment than the latest format, unless the Mendelssohn is essential.

Cincinnati Pops Orchestra, Erich Kunzel

'*Favourite Overtures*': SUPPE: *Light Cavalry; Poet and Peasant.* AUBER: *Fra Diavolo.* HEROLD: *Zampa.* REZNICEK: *Donna Diana.* OFFENBACH: *Orpheus in the Underworld.* ROSSINI: *William Tell.*
*** Telarc CD 80116.

In this spectacularly recorded (1985) collection of favourite bandstand overtures the playing has fine exuberance and gusto (only the galop from *William Tell* could perhaps have had greater impetus) and the resonant ambience of Cincinnati's Music Hall lends itself to Telarc's wide-ranging engineering, with the bass drum nicely caught. Perhaps the opening of *Fra Diavolo* would have benefited from a more transparent sound, but for the most part the opulence suits the vigorous style of the music-making, with *Zampa* and the Suppé overtures particularly successful.

'*Pomp and Pizazz*': J. WILLIAMS: *Olympic Fanfare.* SUK: *Towards a New Life.* ELGAR: *Pomp and Circumstance March No. 1.* IRELAND: *Epic March.* TCHAIKOVSKY: *Coronation March.* BERLIOZ: *Damnation de Faust: Hungarian March.* J. F. WAGNER: *Under the Double Eagle.* FUCIK: *Entry of the Gladiators.* SOUSA: *The Stars and Stripes Forever.* HAYMAN: *March Medley.*
*** Telarc CD 80122.

As enjoyable a march collection as any available, with characteristically spectacular and naturally balanced Telarc recording, with its crisp transients and wide amplitude. The performances have comparable flair and sparkle. The inclusion of John Ireland's comparatively restrained *Epic March* and the Tchaikovsky *Coronation March*, with its piquant trio and characteristic references to the Tsarist national anthem, makes for attractive contrast, while the Hayman medley (including *Strike up the Band, 76 Trombones, South Rampart Street Parade* and *When the Saints go Marching in*) makes an exuberant, peppy closing section. By comparison the Berlioz *Rákóczy March* is quite dignified. The sound is in the demonstration class. Most entertaining.

'*Symphonic spectacular*': SHOSTAKOVICH: *Festival Overture, Op. 96.* WAGNER: *Die Walküre: Ride of the Valkyries.* FALLA: *El amor brujo: Ritual Fire Dance.* BIZET: *L'Arlésienne: Farandole.* JARNEFELT: *Praeludium.* CHABRIER: *España.* TCHAIKOVSKY: *Marche slave, Op. 31.* HALVORSEN: *Entry of the Boyars.* ENESCU: *Romanian Rhapsody No. 1, Op. 11.* KHACHATURIAN: *Gayaneh: Sabre Dance.*
*** Telarc CD 80170.

With spectacular recording, well up to Telarc's best standards, this is a highly attractive collection of orchestral lollipops. Everything is played with the special flair which this orchestra and conductor have made their own in this kind of repertoire. Most entertaining, and technically of demonstration standard.

'*The Fantastic Leopold Stokowski*' (transcriptions for orchestra): BACH: *Toccata & Fugue in D min., BWV 565; Little Fugue in G min., BWV 578.* BOCCHERINI: *Quintet in E flat: Minuet.* BEETHOVEN: *Moonlight Sonata: adagio sostenuto.* BRAHMS: *Hungarian Dance No. 6.* DEBUSSY: *Suite bergamasque: Clair de lune. Prélude: La Cathédrale engloutie.* ALBENIZ: *Fête-Dieu à Seville.* RACHMANINOV: *Prelude in C sharp min., Op. 3/2.* MUSSORGSKY: *Night on the Bare Mountain; Pictures at an Exhibition: The Great Gate of Kiev.*
● (M) *** Telarc CD-80338.

Stokowski began his conducting career in Cincinnati in 1909, moving on to Philadelphia three years later; so a collection of his orchestral transcriptions from his first orchestra is appropriate, particularly when the playing is so committed and polished and the recording so sumptuous. Indeed, none of Stokowski's own recordings can match this Telarc disc in sheer glamour of sound. The arrangement of *La Cathédrale engloutie* is very free and melodramatically telling. Most interesting is *Night on the Bare Mountain*, which has a grandiloquent brass chorale added as a coda. Any admirer of Stokowski should regard this superbly engineered CD as an essential purchase. It is now reissued with two extra items added, the Brahms *Hungarian Dance No. 6* and Stokowski's extraordinary transcription of *The Great Gate of Kiev* from Mussorgsky's *Pictures at an Exhibition*. Kunzel has the advantage of Telarc's bass-drum recording, and at the very close there is a highly imaginative added touch as the old magician introduces an evocation of Moscow cathedral bells.

City of Prague Philharmonic Orchestra, Gavin Sutherland

Music from the '*Carry On*' films: *Carry on Camping; Carry on Suite* (music from *Carry on Sergeant, Teacher* and *Nurse*); *Carry on Cabby; Carry on Cleo; Carry on Jack; Carry on Behind; Raising the Wind; Carry on at Your Convenience; Carry on Up the Khyber; Carry on Doctor Again.*
(M) *** ASV CDWHL 2119.

Some readers may raise a quizzical eyebrow at the

inclusion of this collection, for the famous 'Carry On' series of films is the epitome of British vulgarity. Yet their incidental music shows the British light-music tradition at its best. The early scores were written by Bruce Montgomery (*Carry on Teacher, Nurse, Cabby*, etc.) where a flavour of the late 1950s is evoked: the main '*Carry On*' theme is unashamedly jazzy, yet has a central counter-theme which is delightfully nostalgic and totally British. For the later films, Eric Rogers took over – he peppered the films with quotes from famous classical pieces, whilst his own melodies are distinctly appealing, reflecting the 'swinging sixties'. The *Carry on Camping* and *Carry on Doctor* suites are perhaps the best, not just for their vivaciousness, but also for the remarkably piquant and deft orchestration throughout. *Carry on at Your Convenience* evokes the production line of a toilet-bowl factory, and the Prague orchestra respond with enthusiasm (the timpani are especially impressive); then there is an unexpectedly charming romantic passage which is quite touching, before the riotous ending. The imperial opening music of *Carry on Up the Khyber* (perhaps the wittiest of the series) is strongly characterized, and the *Carry on Cleo* suite, with a Hollywood-style opening march à la Rosza, is also effective. Altogether the invention is surprisingly varied. The orchestra perform as though they have played it all their lives, no doubt a tribute to the conductor, Gavin Sutherland, and the producer, Philip Lane. The recording is also superb. Thoroughly recommended for those on the 'Carry On' wavelength, and for other lovers of this musical genre who are simply curious.

'British by Arrangement': TCHAIKOVSKY: *Beatlecracker Suite* (arr. Wilkinson). BORODIN: *Nocturne* (arr. Sargent). GRAY: *The African Queen: Suite* (arr. Lane). LANE: *Mendelssohniana*. PRAETORIUS: *Dances from Terpsichore* (arr. Lane). DONIZETTI: *Donizetti Variations* (arr. Irving).

(M) ** ASV WHL 2142.

The *Beatlecracker Suite* is an ingenious – if curious – working of Beatles' themes in the style of Tchaikovsky. It was written at the suggestion of the ballet star, Doreen Wells, for her personal use and is recorded here in its expanded eight-movement form. Whatever one thinks of the result, it is cleverly done, a homage to both Tchaikovsky and the Beatles. Philip Lane's *Mendelssohniana* for strings (based on his *Children's Pieces*) is distinctly attractive, as is his colourful arrangement of Praetorius's *Dances from Terpsichore*, which is audaciously un-period in style. Allan Gray's amalgam of romantic themes from the film *The African Queen* makes another unexpected item, though here the high strings sound pinched and under-nourished at times; and a similar problem affects the lovely Borodin *Nocturne*. Donizetti wrote much jolly and vivacious ballet music, and this suite, the *Donizetti Variations*, as arranged by Robert Irving, is certainly enjoyable, even if the performance

lacks the brilliance of Antonio de Almeida's Philips recording with the Philharmonia Orchestra (now on a bargain Duo release). Good performances and recording, as one expects from this source, but the exposed strings do sound uncomfortable from time to time.

'British Light Music Discoveries', Vol. 5: HOPE: *Kaleidoscope*. FOX: *A Pastoral Reflection*. LEWIS: *Inauguration*. LYON: *Adagio Serioso; Rondoletta*. DOUGLAS: *Music for Strings*. G. SUTHERLAND: *Capriol Overture*. HANDEL (arr. BARBIROLLI): *Clarinet Concerto*. TOYE: *The Haunted Ballroom: Waltz*. PITFIELD: *Overture on North-Country Tunes*.

(M) **(*) ASV WHL 2144.

Peter Hope's colourful *Kaleidoscope* is aptly described by Philip Lane, the disc's producer, as 'a mini-concerto for orchestra', and this disc offers a varied programme of mainly rare items. It is good that we can hear something of Gavin Sutherland's own compositions, with his tunefully attractive *Capriol Overture* of 2001. John Fox's *Pastoral Reflection* and David Lyon's *Adagio Serioso* offer a quiet nostalgia, though the latter's *Rondoletta* is a contrastingly bright and perky number. Entertaining, too, is Barbirolli's arrangement of Handel to form this clarinet concerto, originally written for oboe. Of the other works, Thomas Pitfield's *Overture on North-Country Tunes* offers some familiar, attractively scored folk tunes; Paul Lewis's *Inauguration* is suitably festive, but with more reflective interludes; while Brian Douglas's *Music for Strings* is more unusual in drawing its influences from Elizabethan church music. Geoffrey Toye's lovely *Haunted Ballroom Waltz* is hardly a rarity, but its inclusion here is a highlight. Excellent performances and recording, but with the violins sounding a bit taxed in the upper registers under pressure.

City of Prague Philharmonic Orchestra, with (i) Gavin Sutherland or (ii) Christopher Phelps

'Entente Cordiale': (i) WARLOCK: *Capriol Suite* (orchestral version). SMYTH: *Two Interlinked French Melodies*. HOPE: *4 French Dances*. JONGEN: *2 Pieces, Op. 53a*. LECOCQ: *The Lady and the Maid: Overture*. LEWIS: *A Paris*. GABRIEL-MARIE: *Mireio (Suite Provençale)*. (ii) FRANCK: *Choral No. 2 in B min*. (orch. Phelps).

(M) *** ASV CD WHL 2147.

A typically felicitous programme from ASV, opening with a robust performance of Warlock's splendid *Capriol Suite*, in full orchestral dress. Peter Hope's *Four French Dances* similarly employ ancient dance-metres, dressed up in modern orchestrations.

Jean Gabriel-Marie's *Mireio*, incidental music written in 1930 for an adaptation of a poem by Paul Giran (which also was the basis of Gounod's *Mireille*), is all prettily rustic-sounding, slight but undeniably charming. The *Lady and the Maid Overture* is not quite authentic Lecocq: it was put together by Havelock Nelson, using various scores found in Cramer's *Opéra-Comique Cabinet*, mainly using a work by Lecocq called *My New Maid*. It makes an enjoyable three minutes and sounds like a number left over from *La Fille de Madame Angot*. Dame Ethel Smyth's *Two Interlinked Melodies* feature genuine folk melodies: the first 'Melody' is a Burgundian vintage song, the second is Breton in origin, and they make for pleasing listening. Joseph Jongen's *Two Pieces* were originally organ works, somewhat impressionistic in style, and this is also true in their orchestral guise: the first, *Chant de mai*, is essentially a solo line with accompaniment, and has an appealingly quirky nature which is nicely contrasted with the more robust *Menuet-Scherzo*. By far the longest track on this disc (and rather more serious than the rest of the programme) is an arrangement of César Franck's organ *Choral No. 2 in B minor* for full orchestra. It is an excellent arrangement, with Christopher Phelps capturing the sound-world of Franck admirably, and is most enjoyable, especially for those who enjoy Stokowski-like transcriptions. The performances and recordings, while they do not have the last word in refinement, are still very good.

Cleveland Symphonic Winds, Fennell

'*Stars and Stripes*': ARNAUD: *3 Fanfares.* BARBER: *Commando March.* LEEMANS: *Belgian Paratroopers.* FUCIK: *Florentine March, Op. 214.* KING: *Barnum and Bailey's Favourite.* ZIMMERMAN: *Anchors aweigh.* J. STRAUSS SR: *Radetzky March.* VAUGHAN WILLIAMS: *Sea Songs; Folksongs Suite.* SOUSA: *The Stars and Stripes Forever.* GRAINGER: *Lincolnshire Posy.*
*** Telarc CD 80099.

This vintage collection from Frederick Fennell and his superb Cleveland wind and brass group is one of the finest of its kind ever made. Severance Hall, Cleveland, has ideal acoustics for this programme and the playing has wonderful virtuosity and panache. Add to all this digital engineering of Telarc's highest calibre, and you have a very special issue.

(Royal) Concertgebouw Orchestra, Eduard van Beinum

The Radio Recordings: ANDRIESSEN: *Miroir de Peine* (with Kolassi); *Symphony No. 4.* BACH: *Cantata No. 56* (with Harrell); *Clavier Concerto in D min., BWV 1052* (with Lipatti); *Double Concerto in C min., BWV 1060* (with van Beinum, den Hertog). BADINGS: *Cello Concerto No. 2* (with Leeuwen Boomkamp). BARTOK: *Concerto for Orchestra.* BEETHOVEN: *Egmont Overture, Op. 84; Piano Concerto No. 3 in C min., Op. 37* (with Solomon); *Violin Concerto in D, Op. 61* (with Francescatti). BRAHMS: *Symphony No. 1 in C min., Op. 67.* DEBUSSY: *La Mer; Images pour orchestre; Printemps.* DIEPENBROCK: *Te Deum* (with Spoorenberg, Merriman, Haefliger, Bogtman; Toonkunstkoor Amsterdam). ESCHER: *Musique pour l'esprit en deuil.* FRANCK: *Psyché* (excerpts); *Symphonic Variations* (with Hengeveld). HENKEMANS: *Viola Concerto* (with Boon). LISZT: *Piano Concerto No. 2 in A* (with Pembauer). RUDOLF MENGELBERG: *Salve Regina* (with van der Sluys). MOZART: *Violin Concerto No. 4 in D, K.218* (with Menuhin). PIJPER: *Symphony No. 3.* RAVEL: *Daphnis et Chloé: Suite No. 2; Piano Concerto in G* (with de Groot). REGER: *Eine Ballet Suite, Op. 130.* RESPIGHI: *Fountains of Rome.* SCHOENBERG: *5 Orchestral Pieces, Op. 16.* SCHUBERT: *Der Hirt auf dem Felsen* (with Vincent). STEPHAN: *Musik für Geige und Orchester* (with Kulenkampff). STRAVINSKY: *Firebird Suite.* TCHAIKOVSKY: *Romeo and Juliet (Fantasy Overture); Symphony No. 4 in F min.* VERDI: *Don Carlos: Dormirò sol nel manto mio regal* (with Christoff).

DVD: BEETHOVEN: *Symphony No. 3 in E flat (Eroica).*
(**(*)) One for You Q-Disc (mono) 97015 (11 CDs + 1 DVD).

Eduard van Beinum presided over the Concertgebouw Orchestra in the post-war years when Willem Mengelberg was in disgrace because of his collaboration with the Nazis. Van Beinum was a most civilized and selfless artist, who never enjoyed the renown of some of his contemporaries but who, like Sir Adrian Boult in England, put the cause of the composer above all else. Although the Dutton label has brought us transfers of the *Symphonie fantastique*, the Brahms *First Symphony* and his amazing Bartók *Concerto for Orchestra*, this 11-CD set enables a generation for whom he is only a name to assess the quality of his contribution to Dutch musical life. Enterprising collectors will welcome the opportunity of having such rarities as Willem Pijper's *Third Symphony*, the *Fourth* of Hendrik Andriessen and the *Viola Concerto* of Hans Henkemans, all of which are rewarding scores (neither the Pijper nor the Henkemans is otherwise available). Van Beinum was a conductor of classical instinct, whose performances are perfectly straight yet infused with poetic feeling. Of particular interest are the concerto appearances of Solomon and Dinu Lipatti and, in the Bach *C minor Concerto* for two pianos, van Beinum himself. What a fine Debussy conductor he was too. This valuable set also comes with a black-and-white DVD of the *Eroica Symphony*, gripping and exhilarating, recorded from a TV broadcast in May 1957, which gives a rare glimpse of his technique and mastery. Naturally, the quality of these radio recordings, which come from the late 1940s and early 1950s, is variable, although generally much better than you might reasonably expect. Well worth investigating and with an admirably annotated 150-page booklet in five languages.

(Royal) Concertgebouw Orchestra, Bruno Walter

MAHLER: *Symphony No. 4 in G* (with Schwarzkopf). BRAHMS: *Symphony No. 4 in E min., Op. 98.* MOZART *Symphony No. 40 in G min., K.550.* STRAUSS *Don Juan.*
(**) Music & Arts mono CD 1090.

Music & Arts offers the whole of a 1952 Bruno Walter/Concertgebouw concert with Elisabeth Schwarzkopf. Egon Wellesz, who often heard Mahler conducting in the first decade of the last century, spoke of the composer as having 'the fire and electricity of Toscanini and the warmth of Bruno Walter', and it was Walter he thought of as being, as it were, the keeper of the seal. Even now, when there is a superabundance of CDs of the *Fourth Symphony*, Walter's Mahler is still something special and carries an authenticity of feeling that comes across half a century. The sound is not up to the standard of commercial recordings of the 1950s but is perfectly adequate.

Concerto Copenhagen, Andrew Manze

'*Swedish Rococo Concertos*' (with soloists): AGRELL: *Flute Concerto in B minor* (with Bania); *Oboe Concerto in B flat* (with Henriksson). Heinrich Philip JOHNSEN: *Double Bassoon Concerto in F* (with Klingfors & Beuse). Ferdinand ZELLBELL: *Bassoon Concerto in A minor: Allegro.* (with Klingfors). (v) *Cello Concerto in D* (with Åkerberg).
*** Musica Sveciae Dig. MSCD 411.

These composers inhabit the outer fringes of the catalogue. None is represented by more than one work. Heinrich Philip Johnsen (1717–79) was born in northern Germany and came to Stockholm with his princely employer, Adolf Frederik of Holstein-Gottorp, who was elected to the Swedish throne. Johan Agrell (1701–65) was born in Sweden but spent the bulk of his life in Germany, and of the three only Ferdinand Zellbell (1719–80) was born, bred and died in Sweden.

  With the exception of the Handelian *Oboe Concerto* of Agrell, all these pieces are in manuscript. The *F major Concerto for Two Bassoons* by Heinrich Philip

Johnsen is rather delightful. It is fresh and entertaining, and played with polish and elegance. (Johnsen enjoys the distinction of having written an opera, *The Bartered Bride*.)

  Zellbell was a pupil of Roman and went to Hamburg, where he studied with Telemann, and to Hanover, where in 1741 he composed this cello concerto. He spent the bulk of his life in Stockholm, where he succeeded to his father's position as organist of the Storkyrkan (cathedral) but he was unpaid for many years and died heavily in debt. The movement from his *A minor Concerto* is a witty piece, and the *Cello Concerto* is inventive and at times touching. Andrew Manze and the Concerto Copenhagen give first-class support to the talented soloists and the aural perspective is eminently truthful. Impeccable scholarly notes by Martin Tegén.

Crowther, Jill (oboe), English Northern Philharmonia, Alan Cuckson

'*English Oboe Concertos*': HURD: *Concerto da camera.* LEIGHTON: *Concerto, Op. 23.* BLEZARD: *2 Celtic Pieces.* GARDNER: *Concerto, Op. 193.* LANE: *3 Spanish Dances.*
(M) *** ASV CDWHL 2130.

A highly delectable collection of oboe concertos by twentieth-century English composers, immediately inviting, full of melody, and diverse enough to make a stimulating concert. Jill Crowther, principal of the Royal Ballet Orchestra and subsequently of the RPO, is a highly sensitive artist with an agreeably succulent tone which she can fine down with the utmost delicacy, as in the solo filigree of the opening movement of the very striking Gardner *Concerto*, heard against a backcloth of dancing violins. Michael Hurd's *Concerto da camera* is romantically rich-textured, but its English pastoralism soon peeps through, and the syncopated finale is infectiously winning. Kenneth Leighton's work is altogether more searching (and affecting), with an unusual degree of angst for an oboe concerto. The elegiac slow movement has a bleak flavour of Shostakovich; however, the clouds lift for the finale. The two *Celtic Pieces* of William Blezard are hauntingly folksy, and Philip Lane's *Spanish Dances* close the concert in holiday mood by taking the listener into a diverting Mediterranean atmosphere. Excellent, spacious recording well balanced, although the high violins are not always in perfect focus.

Curzon, Clifford (piano)

BEETHOVEN: *Piano Concerto No. 5 (Emperor) in E flat, Op. 73* (with LPO, Szell). TCHAIKOVSKY: *Piano Concerto No. 1 in B flat, Op. 23* (with New SO, Szell). SCHUBERT: *4 Impromptus, D.935; Piano*

Sonata No. 17 in D, D.850. FRANCK: *Symphonic Variations.* LITOLFF: *Concerto Symphonique: Scherzo* (with LPO, Boult). FALLA: *Nights in the Gardens of Spain* (with New SO, Jorda). RAWSTHORNE: *Piano Concerto No. 2* (with LSO, Sargent). MOZART: *Piano Concertos Nos. 23 in A, K.488; 27 in B flat, K.595* (with VPO, Szell).

⊕ (B) ★ (★★) Decca mono/stereo 473 116-2 (4).

The two volumes dedicated to Clifford Curzon in Decca's 'Original Masters' series are very special indeed. One must acknowledge Raymond McGill who, as Product Manager for the series, has ensured that all these boxes contain skilfully chosen repertoire to show Curzon at his most characteristic, including some rare performances. In this case, we have two magnificent Mozart *Piano Concertos*, K.488 and K.595, which have never been released before. Curzon was notoriously fussy – even neurotic – about what was released on LP, and if he felt they were not good enough, they could not be issued, however ureasonable their rejection seemed to be. But it really is hard to know why he withheld these two recordings. His playing is as stylish as ever, aristocratic and elegant, framed by Szell's alert and sympathetic accompaniments, more relaxed than one might expect from this conductor. The opening allegros are perfectly proportioned, full of little felicities which delight the ear, though never fussy in detail; the finale of K.595 has a wonderfully lilting quality, and the playing throughout sparkles.

It is as rare as it is rewarding to hear Curzon in twentieth-century repertoire, and the inclusion of Rawsthorne's vigorously inventive *Second Piano Concerto* is especially welcome. It was written for the Festival of Britain and recorded in 1951, and it is given a highly persuasive performance, with Curzon bringing out all the colour and vitality of the writing. The sound is vivid for its period, too. Other classic mono recordings include the 1949 *Emperor Concerto* where, bar the odd bit of distortion, the sound is good, with the performance more fiery under Szell than in Curzon's later, stereo account with the magisterial Knappertsbusch. The Tchaikovsky concerto with Szell is also arguably more successful than the later, stereo version with Solti – fine though that is – in as much as soloist and conductor are seemingly more in tune with one other here, and the sound is again excellent for its vintage (1950). In the *Nights in the Gardens of Spain*, Curzon excels with his ability to change in a flash from the flamboyant to the introspective. This dates from a year later and, with bright mono sound – full of colour and atmosphere – it makes a welcome return to the catalogue, as do the poised, masterly accounts of the Schubert *Impromptus* (1952), recorded in a studio-ish acoustic but with reasonably full sound. Back in stereo, we have a glittering account of the Litolff *Scherzo*, Franck's *Symphonic Variations* – still among the best versions available – and a spontaneously relaxed account of

Schubert's *D major Sonata*, D.850 – all classics of the gramophone.

Decca recordings, Volume 2: 1941–1972: SCHUBERT: *4 Impromptus, D.899; Piano Sonata No. 21 in B flat, D.960.* MOZART: *Piano Concertos Nos. 23 in A, K.488; 24 in C min., K.491* (with LSO, Josef Krips). BRAHMS: *Piano Concerto No. 1 in D min., Op. 15* (with Concg. O, Eduard van Beinum). *Piano Sonata No. 3 in F min., Op. 5; Intermezzi: in E flat, Op. 117/1; in C, Op. 119/3.* GRIEG: *Piano Concerto in A min., Op. 16* (with LSO, Anatole Fistoulari). DVORAK: *Piano Quintet in A, Op. 8.* FRANCK: *Piano Quintet in D min.* (with V. Philharmonic Qt).

⊶ ⊕ (M) ★★★ Decca mono/stereo (ADD) 475 084-2 (4).

This treasurable second anthology, which won the *Gramophone* 'Historical Instrumental Award' in 2003, surveys some of the very finest of Clifford Curzon's recordings for Decca made over three decades, including the early Schubert *Impromptus* (1941) and the remarkably beautiful performances of the two Mozart *Piano Concertos* (1953) with Josef Krips. Curzon was to record them again later in stereo, but the *C minor* (No. 24) in particular, with its exquisite *Larghetto*, remains very special. It appears here in its first international CD release.

Curzon was also to record the Brahms and Grieg *Concertos* again in stereo, the Brahms famously with Szell in 1962. But the earlier account with Van Beinum is no less fine, if different in character, less pungently arresting, more warmly relaxed, the music's nobility brought out, especially in the slow movement. With the Grieg, Fistoulari proved a volatile partner, and again the slow movement is memorable, although in this instance the later, stereo version with Fjelstad brought a specially idiomatic character to the orchestral playing. Both these earlier performances (from 1951) are also appearing on CD for the first time.

In chamber music Curzon's playing was no less magnetic, and the stereo coupling of the utterly seductive Dvořák and Franck *Piano Quintets* was another landmark; the stereo recordings, made in the Sofiensaal (in the early 1960s), still sound very impressive.

But it is the Brahms and Schubert *Sonatas* that sum up perfectly all that is uniquely cherishable in Curzon's art. The playing has great humanity and freshness. Both interpretations are wonderfully sensitive and totally spontaneous-sounding; yet in the Brahms, despite the underlying intensity, nothing is overstated, and in the Schubert, (as with the *Impromptus*) detail is finely drawn but never emphasized at the expense of the architecture as a whole. The stereo recording too is first class and balanced most naturally. A set (described as a Limited Edition) which is not to be missed.

Czech Philharmonic Orchestra, Gerd Albrecht

HAAS: *Studies for String Orchestra.* SCHULHOF: *Symphony No. 2.* ULLMANN: *Symphony No. 2.* KLEIN: *Partita for Strings.*
★★★ Orfeo C 337941 A.

Like the issues in Decca's *Entartete Musik* series, this Orfeo disc features music dismissed by the Nazis as decadent, all here by Jewish composers from Czechoslovakia slaughtered in the Holocaust. Pavel Haas, often counted as Janáček's most important pupil, wrote his *Studies* in Theresienstadt, the prison camp where the Nazis assembled Jewish intellectuals, later to be killed in death camps. Tautly argued in four sections lasting eight minutes, it was given its first performance in the camp under one of the then inmates who happily managed to survive, Karel Ančerl, later the conductor of the Czech Philharmonic. Albrecht and today's Czech Philharmonic bring out the vitality of the writing, with no hint in it of self-indulgence or self-pity. This is a composer writing in sight of death simply because he has to, relishing a last opportunity.

The *Symphony No. 2* of Erwin Schulhof was written in 1932, long before the Germans invaded Czechoslovakia, a work very much of its period with a charming *Scherzo alla Jazz* influenced by Stravinsky's *Soldier's Tale*. The *Symphony No. 2* of Viktor Ullmann, also in four crisp movements, was one of no fewer than twenty-five works that he wrote in Theresienstadt, including the opera *The Emperor of Atlantis*, also on disc. Though he was a pupil of Schoenberg, he here returned to tonality, communicating directly.

The youngest of the four, Gideon Klein from Moravia, more specifically drew inspiration from folk roots, very much in the way that Bartók did in Hungary. His *Partita for Strings*, like the Pavel Haas *Studies*, has darkness in it, notably in the central variation movement, but here too the piece culminates in a mood of energetic optimism, a heartwarming expression of defiance. Very well played and recorded, the four works are the more moving for giving only momentary hints of what the composers were going through. First-rate sound.

Czech Philharmonic Orchestra, Karel Ančerl

Overtures: SHOSTAKOVICH: *Festive Overture, Op. 96.* MOZART: *Die Zauberflöte.* BEETHOVEN: *Leonora No. 3.* WAGNER: *Lohengrin: Prelude to Act I.* SMETANA: *The Bartered Bride.* GLINKA: *Ruslan and Ludmilla.* BERLIOZ: *Le Carnaval romain.* ROSSINI: *William Tell.* WEBER/BERLIOZ: *Invitation to the Dance.*
(M) ★★★ Sup. (ADD) SU 3689-2.

Karel Ančerl and the Czech Philharmonic Orchestra have never sounded better on record than in this thrilling collection of overtures. Admirably played and recorded in the Prague Rudolfinum Dvořák Hall, in the early to mid-1960s, the recording is now so expertly transferred (by Stanislav Sýcora) to CD that the sound at times reaches demonstration quality. The excessive resonance that had previously dogged Supraphon recordings is now controlled, yet the hall ambience remains. The witty Shostakovich *Festive Overture* sparkles irresistibly, followed by a crisply stylish *Zauberflöte* and a compulsive *Leonora 3*, where the allegro skips along unstoppably to reach a powerful climax at the coda. Not surprisingly, *The Bartered Bride* has a real Slavonic fizz: those stabbing string entries are superbly clear, and *Ruslan and Ludmilla* demonstrates similar virtuosic élan, yet with the lyricism nicely balanced. For some reason, one has to turn up the volume slightly for the virtuosic *Le Carnaval romain*, and then down a little for the superb *William Tell*, elegant at the opening, chirping merrily in the pastoral scene, and with barnstorming trombones at the close. Only the *Lohengrin Prelude* is a fraction below par, yet it is still well played and has a fine climax. The elegant Weber/Berlioz piece acts as a successful opening *Invitation to the programme*.

Damiens, Alain (clarinet), Ensemble InterContemporain, David Robertson

'*American Clarinet*': ELLIOTT CARTER: *Concerto; Gra for Solo Clarinet.* STEVE REICH: *New York Counterpoint for Clarinet and Tape.* HOWARD SANDCROFT: *Tephillah for Clarinet and Electronics.* ADAMS: *Gnarly Buttons for Clarinet and Small Orchestra* (with André Troutlet, clarinet).
★★★ Virgin 5 45351-2.

Elliott Carter's *Concerto* is written in six sections, for different instrumental groups (percussion, strings, woodwind and so on). In a live performance the soloist moves among them. The music is characteristically complex and unpredictable, yet has a strong lyrical core. The solo *Gra* is more fragmented. Reich's *New York Counterpoint* is written in eleven clarinet parts, only one of which is live. The soloist plays with his own recordings, which are held in endless ostinato loops. There are three movements, and the last has syncopated jazz inflections. The composer demands a performance 'without charm', but the end result is very diverting. Sandcroft's *Tephillah* is based on Hebrew chant, although its fragmentation means that you might not guess it! The soloist is 'electronically' shadowed. By the side of these works John Adams's *Gnarly Buttons* is positively traditional, readily communicative, with a central *Hoe down*, and the lyrical finale melodically haunting, with the soloist providing a burst of virtuosity to dominate a surge of energy near the close. The vivid performances throughout this anthology certainly illustrate the pluralism of twentieth-century American music.

Daniel, Nicholas (oboe), Peterborough String Orchestra

Italian Oboe Concertos: VIVALDI: *Concerto in C, RV 44.* ALBINONI: *Concerto in D min., Op. 9/2.* BELLINI: *Concertino in E flat.* MARCELLO: *Concerto in D min.* CIMAROSA: *Concerto in C* (arr. Arthur Benjamin).

(BB) **(*) Hyp. Helios CDH 55034.

All the music here is tunefully undemanding, with the minor-key concertos adding a touch of expressive gravitas. Arthur Benjamin's arrangement of the charming Cimarosa concerto is always a delight, and the lovely Bellini *Concertino* sounds like one of his operatic arias arranged for oboe – complete with cabaletta finale. Nicholas Daniel is closely miked, but he is a stylish performer and draws lively support from the Peterborough orchestra. The disc plays for just under 55 minutes, but is offered at budget price.

Danish State Radio Symphony Orchestra

'75th Anniversary Concert': BRAHMS: *Symphony No. 2* (cond. Busch). HAYDN: *Symphony No. 91 in E flat; 12 German Dances* (cond. Wöldike). BEETHOVEN: *Funeral March.* NIELSEN: *Overture Maskarade.* DEBUSSY: *Prélude à l'après-midi d'un faune.* SÆVERUD: *Galdreslåtten.* STRAVINSKY: *Suite No. 2* (cond. Malko). GLINKA: *Ruslan and Ludmilla: Overture* (cond. Dobrowen). LUMBYE: *Dream Pictures.* NIELSEN: *At the Bier of a Young Artist* (cond. Grøndahl). RIISAGER: *Trumpet Concertino* (with Eskdale; cond. Jensen). NIELSEN: *Little Suite for Strings* (cond. Tuxen). MOZART: *Divertimento No. 12 in E flat, K.252* (orchestral wind soloists).

❄ (B) (***) Dutton mono 2CDEA 5027 (2).

Issued to celebrate the splendid Danish orchestra's 75th anniversary, these excellent recordings, mainly from the late 1940s, demonstrate what a superb band had developed in Copenhagen during and just after the Second World War. The late 1940s and early 1950s were the heyday of the orchestra, and the acoustic of the Concert Hall of the Radio House was, before its later refurbishment, altogether superb, bright yet warm and full bodied.

Nikolai Malko's account of the Stravinsky *Suite No. 2* and Sæverud's *Galdreslåtten* were demonstration 78-r.p.m. discs in their day, and this early 1950s account of Brahms's *Second Symphony*, urgent and direct under Fritz Busch's direction, was a revelation (particularly its thrilling finale), at a time when choice was limited to Beecham, Weingartner or Stokowski. In his admirable note Lyndon Jenkins

calls it 'civilized, exhilarating, yet full of humanity'. The sound, as transferred by Dutton, is still vivid, as it is in all these varied items.

Mogens Wöldike's wonderfully sprightly and stylish recording of Haydn's *Symphony No. 91 in E flat* is its first and arguably best recording, not even forgetting Jochum's glorious version with the Bavarian Radio Orchestra from 1958, while the little Riisager *Trumpet Concertino* is a delight, as is Nielsen's vigorous *Overture to Maskarade*. The *Deutsche Tänze* are absolutely captivating.

The *Funeral March* is, incidentally, a transcription and transposition Beethoven made of the first movement of the *Sonata in A flat,* Op. 26, for the play, *Leonora Prohaska.* As far as we know, neither the Haydn nor the Brahms symphonies was ever transferred to LP and make their first appearance since the 1950s. The same goes for most of the other material.

The original sound is so good that collectors will be amazed at its quality and presence. The transfers are really excellent with no trace of surface noise, although with a fractional loss of the body compared with the originals, which were probably bottom-heavy. A very special set, which for those who do not know these performances will bring unexpected musical rewards and which deserves the widest currency.

Davies, Philippa (flute), Thelma Owen (harp)

'The Romance of the Flute and Harp': HASSELMAN: *La source, Op. 44; Feuilles d'automne.* GODARD: *Suite, Op. 16: Allegretto.* GODEFROID: *Etude de concert.* FAURE: *Berceuse, Op. 16; Impromptu, Op. 86.* DOPPLER: *Mazurka.* MENDELSSOHN: *Spring Song, Op. 62/3.* THOMAS: *Watching the Wheat.* SAINT-SAENS: *Carnival of the Animals: The Swan.* BIZET: *Fair Maid of Perth: Intermezzo.* PARISH-ALVARS: *Serenade.* DEBUSSY: *Syrinx; Suite bergamasque: Clair de lune.*

(BB) *** Regis RRC 1085.

An unexpectedly successful collection which effectively intersperses harp solos with music in which the flute takes the leading role. The playing is most sensitive and the recording is very realistic indeed. The programme, too, is well chosen and attractively laid out and is fairly generous in playing time (59 minutes). Highly recommended for a pleasant summer evening.

Detroit Symphony Orchestra, Neeme Järvi

'Favourite Encores': CHABRIER: *Fête polonaise.* GLINKA: *Kamarinskaya; Valse fantaisie.* SIBELIUS: *Andante festivo for strings.* BOLZONI: *Minuet.* DVORAK: *Humoresque.* DARZINS: *Valse*

mélancolique. ELLINGTON: *Solitude* (trans. for strings). SHOSTAKOVICH: *The Gadfly: Romance.* MUSSORGSKY: *Gopak.* DEBUSSY: *Suite bergamasque: Clair de lune.* SCHUMANN: *Abendlied, Op. 107/6.* MEDINS: *Aria.* GERSHWIN: *Promenade: Walking the Dog.* SOUSA: *The Stars and Stripes Forever.*

(M) **(*) Chan. 6648.

The acoustics of Detroit's Orchestra Hall, made famous by the Mercury engineers at the end of the 1950s, remain impressive and the Detroit orchestra is flattered here by opulently glowing sound, which especially suits the Glinka pieces and the lovely Sibelius *Andante festivo.* The rest of the programme is rather slight, consisting entirely of lollipops, some well known, plus a few engaging novelties. All are presented with Järvi's customary flair and are very well played. If you enjoy this kind of concert, there is no need to hesitate, for the programme is generous at 73 minutes.

Detroit Symphony Orchestra, Paul Paray

'*French Opera Highlights*': HEROLD: *Overture: Zampa.* AUBER: *Overture: The Crown Diamonds.* GOUNOD: *Faust: Ballet Suite; Waltz* (from Act II). SAINT-SAENS: *Samson et Dalila: Bacchanale.* BIZET: *Carmen: Danse bohème.* BERLIOZ: *Les Troyens: Royal Hunt and Storm.* MASSENET: *Phèdre: Overture.* THOMAS: *Mignon: Gavotte.*

(M) *** Mercury (ADD) [432 014-2].

Paul Paray's reign at Detroit tempted the Mercury producers to record a good deal of French music under his baton, and here is a good example of the Gallic verve and sparkle that were achieved. The only disappointment is the unslurred horn phrasing at the magical opening and close of the *Royal Hunt and Storm.* This and its companion CD are not now available in the UK.

'*Marches and Overtures à la française*': MEYERBEER: *Le Prophète: Coronation March.* GOUNOD: *Funeral March for a Marionette.* SAINT-SAENS: *Marche militaire française; Marche héroïque.* DE LISLE: *La Marseillaise.* Overtures: ADAM: *Si j'étais roi.* BOIELDIEU: *La Dame blanche.* ROSSINI: *William Tell.* OFFENBACH: *La belle Hélène; Orpheus in the Underworld. Contes d'Hoffmann: Barcarolle, etc.*

(M) **(*) Mercury (ADD) [434 332-2].

A generous and flavourful Gallic concert, recorded in three different Detroit venues, with acoustics not entirely flattering to the orchestra, who nevertheless always play splendidly. The Adam and Boieldieu overtures need the glow of Kingsway Hall: here the resonance of Cass Technical High School slightly clouds detail. The marches and the Offenbach items were recorded in 1959 in Old Orchestral Hall, and the

sound is more expansive. The most memorable pieces are the wittily engaging Gounod (always to be remembered as Alfred Hitchcock's TV signature-tune) and the spirited *Belle Hélène* overture, not put together by the composer, but none the worse for that. Throughout, the élan of the playing always brings enjoyment, and the virtuosity of the fiddles in the *William Tell* galop is exhilarating.

Du Pré, Jacqueline (cello)

'*The Art of Jacqueline du Pré*' (with (i) LSO, Sir John Barbirolli; (ii) RPO, Sir Malcolm Sargent; (iii) New Philh. O; (iv) Chicago SO; (v) ECO; (vi) Daniel Barenboim; (vii) Valda Aveling; (viii) Gerald Moore; (ix) Ernest Lush; (x) Steven Bishop): (i) ELGAR: *Cello Concerto in E min., Op. 85.* (ii) DELIUS: *Cello Concerto.* (iii; vi) SAINT-SAENS: *Cello Concerto No. 1 in A min., Op. 33.* (iv; vi) DVORAK: *Cello Concerto in B min., Op. 104; Waldesruhe, Op. 68.* (iii; vi) SCHUMANN: *Cello Concerto in A min., Op. 129.* (i; vii) MONN: *Cello Concerto in G min.* HAYDN: *Cello Concertos: in* (i) *C and* (v; vi) *D, Hob VIIb/1-2.* (vi) CHOPIN: *Cello Sonata in G min., Op. 65.* (vi) FRANCK: *Cello Sonata in A.* (viii) FAURE: *Elégie in C min., Op. 24.* (viii) BRUCH: *Kol Nidrei, Op. 47.* BACH: *(Unaccompanied) Cello Suites Nos. 1-2, BWV 1007/8.* (ix) HANDEL: *Cello Sonata in G min.* BEETHOVEN: (vi) *Variations in G min. on Judas Maccabaeus: See the conqu'ring hero comes, WoO 45;* (x) *Cello Sonatas Nos. 3, in A, Op. 69; 5 in D, Op. 102/2.* (vi) *Variations on Themes from 'The Magic Flute': 7 Variations in D, WoO 46 (Bei Männern, welche Liebe fühlen); 12 Variations in F, 66 (Ein Mädchen oder Weibchen).*

(B) *** EMI (ADD) 5 68132-2 (8).

Admirers of this remarkably gifted artist, whose career ended so tragically, will welcome this survey of her major recordings, made over the incredibly brief period of a single decade. Her first recordings (1961) have a BBC source and her last (the Chopin and Franck *Sonatas*) were made at Abbey Road in 1971. But of course she made her real breakthrough in 1965 with the justly famous Kingsway Hall recording of the Elgar *Concerto* with Barbirolli. Some items included here are not otherwise currently available and, with excellent transfers, this set is an admirable and economical way of exploring her art. There are good, if brief, notes and some heart-rending photographs showing this young prodigy playing with characteristic concentration and joyously in conversation with her equally young husband, Daniel Barenboim.

Cello Concertos: BOCCHERINI: *Concerto in B flat* (arr. GRUTZMACHER). HAYDN: *Concertos in C & D, Hob VIIb/1-2* (with ECO, Barenboim or LSO, Barbirolli). SCHUMANN: *Concerto in A min., Op. 129.* SAINT-SAENS: *Concerto No. 1 in A min., Op. 33* (with New Philh. O, Barenboim). DVORAK: *Concerto in B min., Op. 104; Silent Woods, Op. 68/5* (with Chicago SO, Barenboim). DELIUS: *Concerto* (with RPO, Sargent). MONN: *Concerto in G min.* ELGAR: *Cello Concerto in E min., Op. 85* (both with LSO, Barbirolli). RICHARD STRAUSS: *Don Quixote, Op. 35* (with New Philh. O, Boult).

(B) *** EMI (ADD) 5 67341-2 (6).

Those not wanting the chamber music on the above eight-disc coverage of the 'Art of Jacqueline du Pré', will find that this six-disc set is no less desirable, adding as it does the Boccherini/Grützmacher *Concerto*, most endearingly played, plus the recently remastered 1968 *Don Quixote* (with Boult), which is particularly fine. Good transfers and excellent value.

'*A Lasting Inspiration*' (with Daniel Barenboim, cond. or piano): BOCCHERINI: *Cello Concerto in B flat* (arr. GRUTZMACHER). DVORAK: *Cello Concerto (Adagio); Silent Woods, Op. 68/5.* HAYDN: *Cello Concerto in C.* BEETHOVEN: *Piano Trio No. 5 in D (Ghost), Op. 70/1; 7 Variations on 'Bei Männern'* (both with Pinchas Zukerman). BRAHMS: *Cello Sonata No. 1 in E min., Op. 38.* FRANCK: *Sonata in A* (arr. DELSART) *(Allegro ben moderato).*

(M) **(*) EMI (ADD) 5 66350-2 (2).

A medium-priced anthology that is self-recommending if the more comprehensive programme is of appeal. The chamber-music performances have the same qualities of spontaneity and inspiration that have made du Pré's account with Barbirolli of Elgar's *Cello Concerto* come to be treasured above all others. Any tendency to self-indulgence, plus a certain leaning towards romantic expressiveness, is counterbalanced by the urgency and intensity of the playing. In the Brahms *Sonata* it is hard to accept the blatant change of tempo between first and second subjects, but here too there is warmth and flair. If some find du Pré's approach to Haydn too romantic, it is nevertheless difficult to resist in its ready warmth. The Beethoven *Ghost Trio* is comparably individual and inspirational. The sound-quality is fairly consistent, for all the remastered transfers are successful.

Eastman-Rochester Orchestra, Howard Hanson

American Orchestral Music: BARBER: *Capricorn Concerto, Op. 21* (with Joseph Mariano (flute), Robert Sprenkle (oboe), Sidney Mear (trumpet)). PISTON: *The Incredible Flutist* (ballet suite). GRIFFES: *Poem for Flute and Orchestra.* KENNAN: *3 Pieces.* MCCAULEY: *5 Miniatures for Flute and Strings* (all with Joseph Mariano (flute)). BERGSMA: *Gold and the Señor Commandante* (ballet suite).

(M) *** Mercury (ADD) [434 307-2].

A first-rate concert of pioneering recordings, made

between 1957 and 1963. The collection is worth having for Barber's *Capricorn Concerto* alone, a less characteristic work than, say, any of the *Essays for Orchestra*, or the solo concertos. Walter Piston's ballet *The Incredible Flutist* comes from 1938 and the suite is one of the most refreshing and imaginative of all American scores.

Griffes' *Poem* with its gentle, shimmering textures is French in feeling but is thoroughly worthwhile in its own right. Joseph Mariano is an excellent soloist, as he is in the more simplistic but engaging *Miniatures* of the Canadian William McCauley (born 1917). Kent Kennan's *Three Pieces* are clearly influenced by the ballet music of Stravinsky. Bergsma's ballet is rather noisy at times, and fails to be memorable, though brightly scored. Excellent performances throughout and typically vivid Eastman-Rochester sound.

American Orchestral Music II: MCPHEE: *Tabuh-Tabuhan (Toccata for Orchestra).* SESSIONS: *The Black Maskers (suite).* Virgil THOMSON: *Symphony on a Hymn Tune; The Feast of Love* (with David Clatworthy).

(M) *** Mercury (ADD) [434 310-2].

McPhee's *Tabuh-Tabuhan*, written in 1936, uses Balinese music for its main colouring and rhythmic background. Roger Sessions' *Black Maskers suite* was written as incidental music for a play by Andreyev about devil worship and the Black Mass, but it is not in the same class as, say, Prokofiev's *Scythian Suite*. This is no fault of the performance or recording. The Virgil Thomson *Symphony*, although based on hymn-like material, is attractively quirky (reflecting the composer's Parisian years, the influence of Les Six, and Satie in particular). The cantata *The Feast of Love* could hardly be more contrasted in its warmly flowing lyricism, a heady setting of an anonymous Latin love poem. The poet revels in the erotic joys of love, and the composer and his excellent soloist are obviously delighted by the voluptuous feeling of the words. As always, the vintage Mercury sound is vivid with colour.

American Music: MOORE: *Pageant of P. T. Barnum.* CARPENTER: *Adventures in a Perambulator.* Bernard ROGERS: *Once upon a Time (5 Fairy Tales).* Burrill PHILLIPS: *Selection from McGuffey's Reader.*

(M) *** Mercury (ADD) [434 319-2].

John Alden Carpenter's suite was a favourite of American audiences before the Second World War and is diverting and often charming. The idiom is amiably innocuous but surprisingly seductive, not least the closing number, *Dreams*. Douglas Moore's *Pageant of P. T. Barnum* is hardly less accessible, with its engaging portraits of Jenny Lind, General and Mrs Tom Thumb and Joice Heth, a negress who was supposedly 160 years old!

Bernard Rogers's set of *Five Fairy Tales* is scored with whimsical charm. William Holmes McGuffey's

Readers formed the staple textbook diet of school-children in mid-nineteenth-century America. The gently nostalgic second movement of Burrill Phillips's *Selection* pictures John Alden and Priscilla (who sailed on the *Mayflower*), and the noisy finale depicts Paul Revere's midnight ride. If this is perhaps the least memorable of the four works included here, its composer sums up rather succinctly the ethos of the whole programme. The performances are affectionate and committed throughout and the early stereo (1956–8) remarkably truthful. The above three CDs are now withdrawn in the UK.

Eastman-Rochester Orchestra or Philharmonia, Howard Hanson

'*Music for Quiet Listening*': John LA MONTAINE: *Birds of Paradise, Op. 34* (with the composer, piano). GRIEG: *Elegiac Melody: The Last Spring.* LIADOV: *The Enchanted Lake; Kikimora.* Charles Martin LOEFFLER: *2 Rhapsodies: L'Etang (The Pool); La Cornemuse (The Bagpipe)* (with Sprenkle (oboe); Tursi (viola); Basile (piano)). HANSON: *Fantasy Variations on a Theme of Youth* (with Burge (piano)).

(M) *** Mercury (ADD) [434 390-2].

Under a rather deceptive title, Wilma Cozart-Fine, the Mercury producer, has gathered together an exceptionally imaginative compilation which is considerably more than the sum of its individual musical components. John La Montaine's *Birds of Paradise* is eclectic but ear-tickling, and it is recorded with that glittering sharpness of focus and bold colouring for which the Mercury engineers were justly famous. With the composer at the (concertante) piano, its opening evokes Messiaen and its close Debussy. Prefaced by a quotation from Wilfred Owen, it is artfully crafted and imaginatively scored, and not too long.

A particularly eloquent account of Grieg's most beautiful *Elegiac Melody* is then followed by vividly atmospheric accounts of two of Liadov's most memorable orchestral miniatures.

The orchestra then stays silent while Robert Sprenkle (a piquant-timbred oboist), Francis Tursi and Armand Basile present Charles Martin Loeffler's engaging – indeed haunting – pair of rhapsodic miniatures. Loeffler was concertmaster of the Boston Symphony but resigned from his first desk in 1903 to devote himself to composition. (He was born in Alsace and before his Boston appointment had played as a member of the court orchestra of a Russian nobleman, wintering in Nice and spending the summers at Lake Lugano!) His elegantly fastidious style is undoubtedly Gallic, and these two pieces are more subtly written and offer a far wider range of invention than their titles suggest.

The programme ends with a set of variations for piano and orchestra by Howard Hanson, full of lyrical warmth and imbued with that strongly personal, nostalgically Nordic melodic imprint which makes this splendid composer's music so striking. It is gloriously played and richly recorded.

(i) Eastman-Rochester Pops Orchestra, or (ii) Eastman Wind Ensemble, Frederick Fennell

'*Fabulous Marches*': (i) WALTON: *Orb and Sceptre.* BEETHOVEN: *The Ruins of Athens: Turkish March.* SIBELIUS: *Karelia Suite: Alla marcia.* BORODIN: *Prince Igor: March.* SCHUBERT: *Marche militaire.* GRIEG: *Siguard Jorsalfar: Homage March.* WAGNER: *Tannhäuser: Grand March;* (ii) *Rienzi: Overture. Parsifal: Good Friday music.*

(M) *** Mercury (ADD) [434 394-2].

An invigoratingly robust collection. It begins with a stirring account of Walton's *Orb and Sceptre*, made all the more exciting by the brilliant Mercury sound, and the piquant little Beethoven march which follows is toe-tappingly catchy. If the *Karelia Suite March* takes a little while to warm up, the following Borodin piece grips from the word go (it sounds a bit sinister too) with well-pointed, vibrant strings.

Schubert's *Marche militaire* is briskly done, and the Grieg and Wagner marches are most enjoyable. Two Wagner pieces, very effectively arranged for wind band, have been added to the original LP collection, and make an excellently played and unusual bonus. The 1959/60 recording is spectacular in the Mercury manner, closely miked, a bit dry, a bit of tape-hiss, but remarkable even by modern standards. If the programme appeals, go ahead.

(i) Eastman-Rochester Pops Orchestra, or (ii) London Pops Orchestra, Frederick Fennell

'*Popovers II*': (i) RACHMANINOV: *Prelude in G min.* GLIERE: *Russian Sailors' Dance.* WEINBERGER: *Schwanda: Polka and Fugue.* (ii) RODGERS: *Carousel Waltz.* MASSENET: *Le Cid: Aubade; Aragonaise.* BOLZONI: *Minuet.* GERMAN: *Henry VIII: Dances.* BENJAMIN: *Cotillon Suite.* ROSSINI: *William Tell: Passo a sei.* RIMSKY-KORSAKOV: *Dance of the Tumblers; Procession of the Nobles.*

(M) ** (ADD) Mercury [434 356-2].

A good collection of sweetmeats, made all the more enjoyable by the inclusion of rarities: Arthur Benjamin's *Cotillon Suite* is a collection of eighteenth-century airs and ballads in modern orchestral dress, and is charmingly rustic. German's once-popular *Henry VIII Dances* conjure up a similarly rural scene, whilst Bolzoni's *Minuet* is neatly elegant. Fennell's direction is vivacious throughout (though not always producing perfection in ensemble, especially in the Eastman-Rochester recordings), notably in the spectacular numbers of Rimsky-Korsakov, Glière and Weinberger.

The two excerpts from the *Le Cid* ballet music leave one hankering after the complete suite. The one great snag to this disc is the quality of the recording – it is vivid and bright in the Mercury manner, but doesn't allow for any real *pianissimos*, with the upper strings inclining to shrillness in high registers, especially in the earlier (1959) American recordings (the London ones date from 1965). An enjoyable collection all the same. But like most of the Eastman discs above, this has been withdrawn in the UK.

Eastman Wind Ensemble, Frederick Fennell

American Wind Band Music: MORTON GOULD: *West Point (Symphony for Band).* GIANNINI: *Symphony No. 3.* HOVHANESS: *Symphony No. 4, Op. 165* (cond. A. Clyde Roller).

(M) ** Mercury (ADD) [434 320-2].

Fine playing, but the music here is often too inflated to give pleasure on repetition. Gould's *West Point Symphony* is in two movements, *Epitaphs* (which at 11 minutes 55 seconds is far too long) and *Marches*. The *Symphony No. 3* of Vittorio Giannini improves as it proceeds: the Scherzo and finale are the most interesting movements and the most attractively scored. Best by far is the Hovhaness *Symphony No. 4* (admirably directed by A. Clyde Roller) with its bold, rich, brass sonorities in the slower outer movements contrasting with marimba, vibraphone and other tuned percussion instruments in the central *Allegro*. Splendid sound, too.

Music from Ballet and Opera:
SULLIVAN/MACKERRAS: *Pineapple Poll: Suite* (arr. DUTHOIT). ROSSINI/RESPIGHI: *La Boutique fantasque: Suite* (arr. Dan GODFREY). GOUNOD: *Faust: Ballet Suite* (arr. WINTERBOTTOM). WAGNER: *Lohengrin: Prelude to Act III; Bridal Chorus* (arr. WINTERBOTTOM); *Elsa's Procession* (arr. CAILLIET). *Das Rheingold* (arr. Dan GODFREY).

(M) ** Mercury (ADD) [434 322-2].

Although played with characteristic Eastman verve, this is essentially a programme for admirers of wind band transcriptions – here mostly traditional scorings by prominent British military band arrangers. Little of this music gains from its loss of string textures, and the famous Rossini/Respighi *Boutique fantasque* lacks sumptuousness. All this would be entertaining on the bandstand, but at home the ear craves the full orchestra.

'Hands across the Sea – Marches from Around the World': SOUSA: *Hands across the Sea; The US Field Artillery; The Thunderer; Washington Post; King Cotton; El Capitan; The Stars and Stripes Forever.*

GANNE: *Father of Victory (Père de la victoire).* Mariano SAN MIGUEL: *The Golden Ear.* TIEKE: *Old Comrades.* PROKOFIEV: *March, Op. 99.* HANSSEN: *Valdres March.* Davide DELLE CESE: *Inglesina.* COATES: *Knightsbridge.* MEACHAM: *American Patrol.* GOLDMAN: *On the Mall.* MCCOY: *Lights Out.* KING: *Barnum and Bailey's Favourite.* ALFORD: *Colonel Bogey.* KLOHR: *The Billboard.*

(M) *** Mercury (ADD) [434 334-2].

March records don't come any better than this, and nor does military/concert-band recording. The sparkling transients at the opening of *Hands across the Sea* and the peppy spirit of the playing (as with all the Sousa items, and especially *The Stars and Stripes Forever*) give the listener a real lift, while the French *Father of Victory* and German *Old Comrades* are just as full of character. The Prokofiev is as witty as you like, and Fennell shows he understands the more relaxed swagger of the British way in *Colonel Bogey*. First rate – but, with a 65-minute programme, this needs to be taken a march or two at a time, unless you want to fall out with the neighbours – this is not a CD to reproduce gently!

'Spirit of '76': Music for Fifes and Drums based upon the Field Music of the US Army: Drum Solo (2 versions); *The Camp Duty; Marching Tunes* (6 versions); *Service Calls; Traditional Fife and Drum Duets.* *'Ruffles and Flourishes': Music for Field Trumpets and Drums based upon the Field Music of the US Armed Forces:* Music for Rendering Honours (3 versions); *Marching Tunes and Inspection Pieces* (15 versions); *Drum solo; Bugle Calls for the US Army* (excerpts).

(M) *** Mercury (ADD) [434 386-2].

The sound-quality of this CD is remarkably vivid, often startling, as though the cavalry is just about to burst into your sitting room; it was recorded in 1956 and it a wonderful tribute to the engineering of Mercury at that time. The 66 tracks cover American military music from the time of the Revolutionary War to the Civil War; the first half is fife and drum music, and the second group is for trumpets and drums. This is certainly not a disc to be played all in one go, with its lack of instrumental variety and brevity of duration (one piece lasts eight seconds!). Some collectors might feel that it is not a disc to play at all! It is, none the less, a fascinating project. Frederick Fennell takes you through the music in a detailed booklet essay and generates plenty of electricity throughout the programme with his battery of percussion instruments. An eccentrically enjoyable disc then, but for whatever reason you buy it, it is hoped that you have tolerant neighbours. As most American readers will probably know, a similar two-CD collection called *'The Civil War'* is also available in the USA [Mercury 432 591-2] which is just as startling and has one of the most detailed booklets in the history of the compact disc. If the above disc appeals, then so will that.

Ehnes, James (violin), Orchestre Symphonique de Québec, Yoav Talmi

'*French Showpieces: Concert Français*':
SAINT-SAENS: *Introduction and Rondo capriccioso.*
BERLIOZ: *Le Corsaire: Overture; Rêverie et Caprice.*
CHAUSSON: *Poème.* DEBUSSY: *Tarantelle Styrienne.*
MILHAUD: *Le Boeuf sur le toit (cinéma fantasie).*
MASSENET: *Thaïs: Méditation.*
*** Analekta Fleur de Lys FL 2 3151.

By a remarkable coincidence James Ehnes and the Quebec Symphony Orchestra under Yoav Talmi have recorded a very similar programme to the young French virtuoso, Renaud Capuçon with the Bremen Chamber Philharmonique (see above) featuring *Le boeuf sur le toit* in the weird but ear-tweaking jazzy arrangement of this Brazilian-inspired 'cinema-fantasy' which Milhaud himself made for the violinist, René Benedetti. James Ehnes plays the solo part with much dash and relish and the Quebec orchestra obviously enjoy its more outlandish elements and witty polytonal acerbity.

Ehnes is also a memorable soloist in the two Saint-Saëns showpieces, with dazzlingly brilliant articulation of the pyrotechnics and a seductive response to the lyrical melodies, a response which he also extends to an all but voluptuous account of Chausson's *Poème*. For all his extrovert bravura he is above all a very stylish player, which shows in the Berlioz and Massenet pieces. His timbre is not as expansive as some, but perfectly formed and nicely coloured, with a wide range of dynamic: his intonation is impeccable, his playing involved and involving, the result is very appealing indeed. The orchestra also show their paces not only in the lively accompaniments but in a wildly uninhibited account of Berlioz's *Le Corsaire Overture* and are no less exhilarating in the Debussy *Danse*.

Elizabethan serenade

'*Elizabethan Serenade*' (played by (i) Slovak RSO, Penny; (ii) Czecho-Slovak RSO, Leaper; (iii) RTE Concert O or Czecho-Slovak or Slovak RSO, Tomlinson; (iv) Slovak RSO, Carpenter): (i) COATES: *By the Sleepy Lagoon*; (ii) *London Suite: Knightsbridge March. Dam Busters March.* CURZON: *Robin Hood Suite: March of the Bowmen.*
KETELBEY: *Bells Across the Meadows; In a Monastery Garden; In a Persian Market* (both with chorus). (iii) ELLIS: *Coronation Scot.* (ii) Haydn WOOD: *Sketch of a Dandy*; (iii) *Roses of Picardy.* (ii) FARNON: *Westminster Waltz.* (i) DUNCAN: *Little Suite: March.* (iii) BINGE: *Sailing By; Elizabethan Serenade.* BENJAMIN: *Jamaican Rumba.*
TOMLINSON: *Little Serenade.* WHITE: *Puffin' Billy.*
(ii) GERMAN: *Tom Jones: Waltz.* (iii) COLLINS: *Vanity Fair.* (iv) MAYERL: *Marigold.*
(BB) *** Naxos 8.553515.

This Naxos collection is in effect a super-bargain sampler for a worthwhile (full-priced) Marco Polo Light Music composer series, and it inexpensively duplicates a great deal of the repertoire included on other, similar programmes by various orchestras (see above and below). Our allegiance to their excellence remains, but the strong appeal of the present collection is obvious. The performances are a little more variable but are always very good, and those conducted by Ernest Tomlinson, who includes his own delightful *Little Serenade*, are excellent, notably Edward White's *Puffin' Billy*, Arthur Benjamin's *Jamaican Rumba* and the morceau by Anthony Collins. There are no complaints about the recording either. Excellent value.

English Chamber Orchestra, Daniel Barenboim

English Music (with (i) Black; (ii) Zukerman):
DELIUS: *On Hearing the First Cuckoo in Spring; Summer Night on the River; 2 Aquarelles; Fennimore and Gerda: Intermezzo.* VAUGHAN WILLIAMS: *Fantasia on Greensleeves;* (i) *Oboe Concerto;* (ii) *The Lark Ascending.* WALTON: *Henry V* (film incidental music): *Passacaglia; The Death of Falstaff; Touch her Soft Lips and Part.*
(M) *** DG (ADD) 439 529-2.

We have always had a soft spot for Barenboim's warmly evocative ECO collection of atmospheric English music. Even if the effect is not always totally idiomatic, the recordings have a warmth and allure that are wholly seductive.

English Chamber Orchestra, Richard Bonynge

'*Handel Overtures and Overtures of the 18th century*': HANDEL (ed. Bonynge): *Solomon: Overture and Arrival of the Queen of Sheba. Overtures: Berenice; Teseo; Ariodante; Jephtha (Sinfonia); Esther; Rinaldo* (with *March and Battle*); *Sosarme; Faramondo; Judas Maccabaeus; Radamisto; Arminio; Deidamia; Scipio; Belshazzar (Sinfonia); Julius Caesar* (with Act I *Minuet*); *Semele: Sinfonia* (Act II). *18th-century Overtures*:
J. M. KRAUSS: *Olympia.* Florian GASSMANN: *L'amore artigiano.* BOIELDIEU: *Zoraime et Zulnar.*
Ferdinando PAER: *Sargino.* GRETRY: *Le Magnifique.* SACCHINI: *La Contadina in Corte (Sinfonia).*
HAYDN: *Orlando Paladino.* SALIERI: *La fiera di Venezie.*
*** Double Decca (ADD) 466 434-2 (2).

This remarkably generous Double (150 minutes) covers the contents of three LPs from 1968–71. The Handel collection may include the *Arrival of the Queen of Sheba*, but much of the rest has been left unheard, and all credit to Bonynge for resurrecting it with such vigour. Handel's cosmopolitan qualities give such music the benefit of all the traditions of the time – French finesse, Italian elaboration, English plain-spokenness. Bonynge uses his scholarship to produce results that are the very opposite of the dry-as-dust approach which can affect hard-line authenticists.

He may use double-dotting, *notes inégales* and added *appoggiaturas* beyond what other scholars would allow, but the baroque elaboration is justified in the exuberance of the end result. The rarities included here are all delightful and if the English Chamber Orchestra fields a larger body of strings than we expect today, the playing is splendidly alert, and the recording is exceptionally vivid.

The overtures by lesser names are much less inspired, but they undoubtedly have an aural fascination. *Olympia* is like Gluck without the inspiration, and *L'amore artigiano* is conventional, if with an attractive middle section. *Zoraime et Zulnar*, an early work of Boieldieu, shows something of the wit and melodic flair of the better-known overtures. But *Sargino* is altogether more striking, offering more in the way of memorable tunes, and a distinct flavour of Rossini.

Grétry's *Le Magnifique*, if somewhat optimistically titled, is also quite memorable. Unexpectedly opening with a side-drum like Auber's *Fra Diavolo*, it gradually builds up to its middle section, a hauntingly serene and rather beautiful minor-keyed passage, before concluding as it began in military style. The Salieri piece, too, is pleasingly fresh, helped like the rest by first-class advocacy from conductor, orchestra and recording engineers alike. The CD transfers are excellent.

English Chamber Orchestra, Sir Benjamin Britten

'English Music for Strings': PURCELL (ed. Britten): *Chacony in G min.* ELGAR: *Introduction & Allegro, Op. 47.* BRITTEN: *Prelude & Fugue for Strings, Op. 47; Simple Symphony, Op. 4.* DELIUS: *2 Aquarelles.* BRIDGE: *Sir Roger de Coverley for String Orchestra.*
〇━ ● (M) ★★★ Decca (ADD) 476 1641.

This rich-toned recording, still sounding extraordinarily real and vivid, was surely a prime candidate for reissue in Universal Classics' mid-priced 'Penguin ●' Collection. It was one of the first made at The Maltings, Snape, in 1968 (although the *Prelude and Fugue*, which has been added to fill out the CD, dates from three years later). The warm acoustic gives the strings of the English Chamber Orchestra far greater weight than you would expect from their numbers. Britten drew comparably red-blooded playing from

his band, whether in his own *Simple Symphony* (a performance unsurpassed on disc), the engaging Bridge dance or the magnificent Purcell *Chacony*, which has never sounded more imposing. It is good to find him treating his own music so expressively. In the Delius, the delicacy of evocation is delightful, while the Elgar is in some ways the most interesting performance of all, moving in its ardour yet with the structure of the piece brought out far more clearly than is common. An indispensable reissue to set alongside Barbirolli's coupling of the string music of Elgar and Vaughan Williams.

'Britten at the Aldeburgh Festival': BEETHOVEN: *Coriolan Overture.* DEBUSSY: *Prélude à l'après-midi d'un faune.* HAYDN: *Symphony No. 95 in C min.* MENDELSSOHN: *Overture: Fingal's Cave.* MOZART: *Symphony No. 35 in D (Haffner).*
(M) ★★(★) BBC Music (ADD) BBCB 8008-2.

Though this is a strange mixture, Britten as conductor brings to each item a striking freshness, giving a vivid idea of the electricity he conveyed in his performances at the Aldeburgh Festival. Mendelssohn's *Hebrides Overture* – the item which opens the sequence – is urgent and vigorous, giving a storm-tossed view of the Hebrides, while bringing out the strength of the musical structure. That and the Beethoven overture, given a similarly alert and dramatic reading in a 1966 performance at Blythburgh church, are especially valuable, as Britten otherwise made no commercial recordings of either composer's music.

The Debussy too is wonderfully fresh, with Richard Adeney's mistily cool flute solo at the start, presenting the whole score with a rare transparency, leading to a passionate climax. The recording, also made at Blythburgh, is a degree more immediate, less atmospheric than those from the Maltings, but the extra impact is an advantage – as it is in Britten's account of the Haydn symphony, which in its C minor angularity at the start has the biting toughness of *Sturm und Drang*. Mozart's *Haffner Symphony*, recorded in the Maltings in 1972, brings sound rather less focused than on the rest of the disc, but it is an amiable performance, energetic in the outer movements, warmly affectionate in the slow movement.

English Northern Philharmonia, David Lloyd-Jones

'Victorian Concert Overtures': MACFARREN: *Chevy Chase.* PIERSON: *Romeo and Juliet, Op. 86.* SULLIVAN: *Macbeth.* CORDER: *Prospero.* ELGAR: *Froissart, Op. 19.* PARRY: *Overture to an Unwritten Tragedy.* MACKENZIE: *Britannia, a Nautical Overture, Op. 52.*
(BB) ★★★ Hyp. Helios CDH 55088.

Sir George (Alexander) Macfarren (1813–87) was an English composer of Scottish descent who taught at and eventually became Principal of the Royal Academy of Music. His music was very successful in its day; he was a distinguished early editor of Purcell's *Dido and Aeneas* and of major stage works of Handel. Many of his own operas were produced in London, including one based on the story of Robin Hood.

A CD showing us a wider range of his music is overdue; meanwhile he makes a strong contribution to this collection of Victorian concert overtures with *Chevy Chase*, a spirited, tuneful piece that was admired by Mendelssohn. Pierson's *Romeo and Juliet* hardly explores its theme with any substance but Frederick Corder's *Prospero* has a certain flamboyant gravitas. Mackenzie's *Britannia* is a pot-boiler featuring a borrowed tune now famous at the Proms. Against all this and more, Elgar's *Froissart* stands out as the early masterpiece it was. The whole concert is persuasively performed by the excellent Northern Philharmonia under the versatile David Lloyd-Jones, and this reissue is even more tempting at budget price.

(i) English Chamber Orchestra, Paul Tortelier; (ii) Northern Sinfonia, Jean-Bernard Pommier

'*French Impressions*': Disc 1: (i) DEBUSSY: *Petite Suite: En bateau. Prélude a l'après-midi d'un faune.* FAURE: *Pavane, Op. 50; Elégie, Op. 24* (with Tortelier, cello). PIERNE: *Marche des petits soldats.* MASSENET: *Thaïs: Méditation* (with (violin). *La Vierge: Le dernier sommeil de la Vierge.* SATIE: 2 *Gymnopédies* (arr. Debussy). SAINT-SAENS: *Le Cygne* (Tortelier & Reeves, piano). TORTELIER: *Valse, Alla Maud* (Paul & Maud Tortelier).

Disc 2: (ii) DEBUSSY: *Petite Suite* (orch. Büsser). FAURE: *Ballade for Piano and Orchestra* (with Pommier, piano); *Masques et bergamasques* (suite). RAVEL: *Pavane pour une infante défunte; Ma Mère l'Oye: suite.*

(BB) **(*) Virgin 2 x 1 5 62182-2 (2).

These two collections were recorded separately in 1987 and 1988, but they combine rather pleasingly. The recordings, made at Abbey Road and supervised by Andrew Keener, are of excellent quality and, as it happens, both programmes open seductively with *En bateau* from Debussy's *Petite Suite*. Paul Tortelier's collection with the English Chamber Orchestra of evocative French lollipops is perhaps not distinctive but is very well played, featuring various fine solo contributions.

The more substantial programme from Bernard Pommier and the Northern Sinfonia brings warm, rather laid-back performances, wanting the last degree of intensity; yet the slightly hazy sound-picture gives an appealing palette of French impressionistic colours. Debussy's *Petite Suite* perhaps needs a slightly stronger profile, and the central dance movements of *Masques et bergamasques*, like the *Ballade for Piano and Orchestra* (in which Pommier moves over to the keyboard), are very relaxed too. But *Ma Mère l'Oye* glows beguilingly – *Le Jardin féerique* is quite lovely – and the refined orchestral playing gives pleasure throughout. The documentation, however, is very sparse.

English Northern Philharmonia Orchestra, David Lloyd-Jones

'*English String Miniatures*', Volume 2: BRIDGE: *Sally in our Alley; Cherry Ripe; Sir Roger de Coverley.* ELGAR: *Sospiri.* Haydn WOOD: *Fantasy Concerto.* IRELAND: *The Holy Boy.* VAUGHAN WILLIAMS: *Charterhouse Suite.* DELIUS: *Air and Dance.* WARLOCK: *Serenade for the 60th Birthday of Delius.* BUSH: *Consort Music.*

(BB) *** Naxos 8.555068.

A wholly delightful record, even more winning than the highly recommendable Volume 1 from the same source, in which Lloyd-Jones conducted the Royal Ballet Orchestra (Naxos 8.554186 – see below). Opening with Frank Bridge's exquisitely tender arrangement of *Sally in our Alley*, followed by the charmingly witty *Cherry Ripe*, Lloyd-Jones moves on to give a very touching performance of Elgar's lovely *Sospiri*, then brings a comparable delicacy of feeling to John Ireland's *Holy Boy*. The Haydn Wood *Fantasy-Concerto* is in the best tradition of lyrical English string music and has a splendidly pulsing finale, with a memorable secondary tune. The title of Vaughan Williams's *Charterhouse Suite* reflects the composer's schooldays. It was originally written for piano, and has been effectively orchestrated by James Brown. It is unassertive, the pastoral *Slow Air* engagingly English, with a lively closing *Pezzo ostinato*. Warlock's *Serenade* and Delius's *Air and Dance* are so alike in harmonic character that they might well have been written by the same composer. Geoffrey Bush's *Consort Music* is not remoted Elizabethan, but it is very entertaining, especially the quirky *Caprice* and the lusciously expansive *Cradle Song*. The spiritedly robust finale is highly contagious. Then Bridge's *Sir Roger de Coverley* ends the programme with sparkling virtuosity, with *Auld Lang Syne* making a surprise appearance at the close. Altogether a marvellous concert, given first-class recording – a splendid bargain by any standards.

European Community Chamber Orchestra, Eivind Aadland

'*Concertos for the Kingdom of the Two Sicilies*': A. SCARLATTI: *Concerto No. 6 in E* (for strings).

Sinfonia di concerto grosso No. 12 in C min.
PERGOLESI: *Flute Concerto in G* (both with Giulio
Viscardi). PORPORA: *Cello Concerto in G* (with
Giovanni Sollima). DURANTE: *Concerto per
quartetto No. 1 in F min.*
(BB) *** Hyp. Helios CDH 55005.

This most engaging and beautifully recorded collection is centred on Naples, the musical focus of the
so-called 'Two Sicilies', which once embraced southern Italy. The programme is lightweight but played –
on modern instruments – with an airy lightness.
Whereas Scarlatti's E major work is a concerto
grosso, the *Sinfonia di concerto* features a solo flute
and matches the concerto attributed to Pergolesi in
charm, when the flute playing is so nimble. In Porpora's *Cello Concerto* (again with an impressive soloist)
exuberantly vivacious *Allegros* frame an eloquent
central *Largo*. Durante's splendid little concerto
grosso has a sombre introduction and is comparatively serious in mood; even the *Amoroso* third movement, using the solo quartet, is touching rather than
romantic, but the tension lifts in the gay, rhythmically pointed finale. Excellent value.

European Union Chamber Orchestra, Dmitri Demetriades

'*The Concerto in Europe*': PAISIELLO: *Harp
Concerto in D.* GRETRY: *Flute Concerto in C.*
GARTH: *Cello Concerto No. 2 in B flat.* STAMITZ:
Viola Concerto in D, Op. 1.
(BB) **(*) Hyp. Helios CDH 55035.

A collection of quietly attractive and tuneful, rarely
heard concertos. The Paisiello *Harp Concerto*, originally a keyboard work, is graceful and elegant, with a
touching central movement and a jolly, if brief,
finale. Grétry's operatic leaning is felt at the opening
of his *Flute Concerto*, and at intervals throughout; the
central movement flirts with minor keys, but it is
generally a sunny work. The English are represented
by a cello concerto by John Garth: it is an interesting
piece with some robust cello writing, stylistically a bit
earlier than the other concertos (more baroque in
flavour) but no less enjoyable for that. Stamitz's *Viola
Concerto* is the most substantial work, with some
nice ideas, especially in the slow movement, and has
secured a place in the viola concerto repertoire. The
performances and recordings are good, though at
times a hint of blandness creeps in. The CD, which
plays for just under an hour, is worth considering if
the programme appeals.

Fernández, Eduardo (guitar), English Chamber Orchestra

Guitar Concertos: RODRIGO: *Concierto de Aranjuez.*
CASTELNUOVO-TEDESCO: *Concerto No. 1 in D, Op.*
99 (both cond. Martinez). GIULIANI: *Concerto in A,
Op. 30.* VIVALDI: *Concerto in D, RV 93* (both cond.
Malcolm). PONCE: *Concierto del sur.* VILLA-LOBOS:
Concerto (both cond. Enrique Garcia Asensio).
ARNOLD: *Concerto.*
(B) **(*) Double Decca 455 364-2 (2).

There are few guitar concertos to match the effective-
ness of the jazz-inflected piece by Malcolm Arnold.
Fernández is in his element in this work, making the
haunting melody of the first movement's second subject warm and not sentimental, echoed by the glowing ECO strings, while the full depth of the blues-
inspired slow movement is also movingly conveyed.
Yet outer movements are fizzingly vital, the playing
spikily incisive in bringing out the jazz overtones.

As we have said elsewhere, Fernández is a musician's guitarist whose playing is consistently refined
and sensitive, and he is again at his most inspired in
the concertos by Ponce and Villa-Lobos, creating
magical evocation in the atmospheric slow movements, where Enrique Garcia Asensio is a persuasive
partner.

The Giuliani and Castelnuovo-Tedesco concertos
are presented with warm, refined elegance; the
Andantino of the latter is made to sound charmingly
ingenuous, and the Vivaldi too brings refinement
rather than extrovert brilliance. It is in the most
famous concerto of all, the Rodrigo *Concierto de
Aranjuez*, that some listeners may feel Fernández falls
short in his total unwillingness to treat the music as a
vehicle for extrovert display. The beautiful *Adagio* is
unusually ruminative, but the outer movements, too,
are comparatively laid back, delicate in feeling, yet by
no means lacking in vitality. We found all the music-
making here most refreshing, and certainly the Decca
digital recording is consistently well balanced and of
the highest quality.

Flute concertos

MOZART: *Flute Concertos Nos. 1 in G, K.313; 2 in D,
K.314* (with Bennett, ECO, Malcolm). VIVALDI:
Flute Concerto in C min., RV 441; J. S. BACH: *Flute
Concerto in G min., from BWV 1056* (with William
Bennett), attrib. GRETRY: *Flute Concerto in C* (with
Monteux) (both with ASMF, Marriner). CIMAROSA:
Concerto in G for 2 Flutes (with Aurèle &
Christiane Nicolet); C. P. E. BACH: *Flute Concerto
in D min., Wq. 22* (with Nicolet) (both with
Stuttgart CO, Münchinger). SALIERI: *Concerto for
Flute and Oboe in C* (with Adeney, Brown, ECO,
Bonynge).
(B) *** Double Decca (ADD) 460 302-2 (2).

William Bennett's recordings of the two Mozart concertos are second to none, and the recordings which
Marriner accompanies so stylishly (Vivaldi, Bach and
Grétry) are equally enjoyable. The double concertos,
by Cimarosa and Salieri, bring a fair amount of

elegant chatter, but there is nothing here which fails to please, and the recording is consistently of Decca's vintage analogue standard.

Foundation Philharmonic Orchestra, David Snell

WILLIAMS: *Tuba Concerto* (with Easler).
TAILLEFERRE: *Harp Concerto* (with Dall'olio).
TOMASI: *Saxophone Concerto* (with Ashby).
MAYUZUMI: *Xylophone Concertino* (with May).
**(*) ASV CDDCA 1126.

An enterprising, if uneven, disc of twentieth-century concertos. There cannot be too many xylophone concertos; that by the Japanese composer Toshirô Mayuzumi dates from 1965, and although no master-piece, it has its entertaining moments, if inevitably it sounds a bit 'Tom and Jerryish' at times. John Williams wrote his *Tuba Concerto* in 1985. His attractive film-music style provides a backcloth for his unusual soloist, though the piece is musically pretty thin, especially the slow middle section, which goes on for too long. Henri Tomasi's *Saxophone Concerto* of 1949 is more substantial; its full, colourful orchestration has atmosphere and imagination, suggesting at times a score for a *film noir* of the 1940s. But perhaps the best concerto here is Germaine Tailleferre's unpre-tentious work for harp of 1928, a piece that mixes impressionistic and classical influences with much charm. The performances cannot be faulted, the recording is good, and if the strings occasionally sound a little undernourished, the actual balance is well judged.

François, Samson (piano)

LISZT: *Piano Concertos Nos. 1 in E flat; 2 in A* (with Philh. O, Silvestri). PROKOFIEV: *Piano Concertos Nos. 3 in C, Op. 26; 5 in G, Op. 55* (with Philh. O, Rowicki); *Piano Sonata No. 7 in B flat, Op. 83.* SCHUMANN: *Piano Concerto in A min. Op. 54* (with French Nat. R. O, Kletzki).

(B) *(*) EMI (ADD) 5 74324-2 (2).

Samson François enjoyed legendary status in his native France, although his undoubted talents were offset by a tendency to disregard dynamic markings under *piano* and sometimes under *forte*, which made for unsubtle results. The Schumann, recorded in 1958, conveys little of the freshness or delicacy of this masterpiece. We have no recollection of either the Liszt or the Prokofiev *Fifth Concerto*, recorded in 1960 and 1963 respectively, appearing in the UK. Muscular and decently recorded performances, but there were much finer accounts of all these pieces in the catalogue at the time. Recommendable only to admirers of François.

(i) French Radio Orchestra, (ii) Philharmonia Orchestra, Igor Markevitch

PROKOFIEV: (i) *Love for 3 Oranges (suite), Op. 33;* (ii) *Le Pas d'acier (suite), Op. 41;* (i) *Scythian Suite, Op. 20.* STRAVINSKY: (i) *Le Baiser de la fée (Divertimento);* (ii) *Petrushka: Suite;* (i) *Pulcinella (suite);* (ii) *The Rite of Spring.*

(B) (**(*)) EMI mono/stereo 5 69674-2 (2).

Igor Markevitch was the last and most unusual of Diaghilev's protégés and married the daughter of his first, Nijinsky. Markevitch's career initally took off as a composer and pianist. However, after the end of the Second World War, during which he served in the Italian resistance, he gave up composition to concen-trate on conducting full time. He was an excellent ballet conductor whose cool elegance can be readily observed in these recordings. His mono (1952) account of *Le Sacre* with the Philharmonia Orchestra caused quite a stir in its day, but this 1959 stereo re-make, undertaken at very short notice when Klemperer was taken ill, has much to recommend it, even if the former has perhaps the greater atmos-phere.

Markevitch gets good results from the Philharmo-nia Orchestra throughout and a very professional response from the French Radio Orchestra, which was in better shape than the Conservatoire Orchestra at this period. *Le pas d'acier* is a rarity these days and is hardly ever encountered in the concert hall; it sounds to excellent effect here. The Paris recordings come from 1954-5 and the Philharmonia *Petrushka* and *Pas d'acier* from 1954. Only the 1959 *Le Sacre* is in stereo.

Fricsay, Ferenc

'A Life in Music' (with BPO, or Berlin RIAS SO):
BEETHOVEN: *Symphony No. 1 in C.*
MENDELSSOHN: *Midsummer Night's Dream: Overture and Incidental Music* (with Streich, Eustrati, Berlin RIAS Ch.; all with BPO).
PROKOFIEV: *Symphony No. 1 in D (Classical).*
MAHLER: *Rückert Lieder* (with Forrester).
TCHAIKOVSKY: *Symphony No. 6 in B min. (Pathétique).* ROSSINI–RESPIGHI: *La Boutique fantasque.* RIMSKY-KORSAKOV: *Scheherazade. Concertante works:* FALLA: *Nights in the Gardens of Spain.* FRANÇAIX: *Concertino for Piano and Orchestra.* HONEGGER: *Concertino for Piano and Orchestra.* FRANCK: *Symphonic Variations.* RACHMANINOV: *Rhapsody on a Theme of Paganini* (all five with M. Weber). VON EINEM: *Dantons Tod: Interlude.* HINDEMITH: *Symphonic Dances.* HARTMANN: *Symphony No. 6.* MARTIN: *Petite Symphonie Concertante* (with Hertzog, Kind, Helmis). HAYDN: *The Seasons (Die Jahreszeiten)*

(with Stader, Haefliger, Greindl & St Hedwig's Cathedral Ch.). Johann Sr & Jr and Josef STRAUSS: *Waltzes and Overtures* (all above with Berlin RIAS SO).

(B) (★★★) DG 474 383-2 (9).

Some years ago Deutsche Grammophon issued a ten-CD box devoted to Ferenc Fricsay – plus a bonus rehearsal disc of Smetana's *Vltava*. Readers who have it may easily be tempted to brush the present nine-CD set aside, fearing that it would entail inevitable duplication. But DG have kept faith with collectors by ensuring that there is none. Even Gottfried von Einem, represented in the larger box by his *Piano Concerto* and *Ballade for Orchestra*, is appropriately (since he conducted the opera's première) served by the inclusion of the *Interlude* from *Dantons Tod*. Many performances that have been out of circulation for many years, like the Frank Martin *Petite Symphonie Concertante* or the *Sixth Symphony* of Karl Amadeus Hartmann, make a long overdue and welcome comeback. Honegger's delightful and unjustly neglected *Concertino for Piano and Orchestra* and Jean Françaix's captivating essay in that form are expertly handled. The earliest performances here (the Martin and *Midsummer Night's Dream* music with the Berlin Philharmonic) are from 1950; the noble account of Haydn's *Die Jahreszeiten* with a particularly distinguished line-up of soloists was made in 1961, only 14 months before his death. And of course his Tchaikovsky *Pathétique* should not be forgotten, the recording with which he created such a sensation when Deutsche Grammophon began issuing mono LPs in the UK. This set is not to be missed and its contents are to be treasured.

Fröst, Martin (clarinet), Malmö Symphony Orchestra, Lan Shui

Clarinet Concertos: ARNOLD: *Concerto No. 2, Op. 112.* COPLAND: *Concerto for Clarinet and String Orchestra, with Harp and Piano.* HINDEMITH: *Concerto.*

★★★ BIS CD 893.

Three first-class performances of three outstanding twentieth-century concertos, all originally written for Benny Goodman. Fröst is an eloquently spontaneous soloist, stealing in gently against a magical orchestral *pianopianissimo* at the opening of the Copland; and he is equally at home in Hindemith's more sinewy lyricism. Both he and the persuasive conductor, Lan Shui, obviously relish the verve and energy of the Malcolm Arnold *Concerto* and they play the slow movement very seductively, before romping away into the rooty-tooty finale, with its audacious orchestral whoops, the kind of music to bring the house down at a Promenade concert. The recording is splendid in every way and this can receive the strongest recommendation.

Galway, James (flute)

'*Pachelbel's Canon and other Baroque Favourites*' (with various orchestras & conductors): VIVALDI: *Concerto in D (Il Gardellino), Op. 10/3:* 1st & 2nd movts. *Four Seasons: Spring* (arr. GALWAY). TELEMANN: *Suite for Strings in A min.: Réjouissance; Polonaise.* PACHELBEL: *Canon.* HANDEL: *Sonatas in A min., Op. 1/4:* 4th movt; *in F, Op. 1/11: Siciliana; Allegro* (both with Cunningham, Moll). *Solomon: Arrival of the Queen of Sheba* (arr. GERHARDT). *Messiah: Pifa (Pastoral Symphony). Xerxes: Largo.* BACH: *Suites Nos. 2 in B min., BWV 1067: Minuet & Badinerie; 3 in D, BWV 1068: Air. Trio Sonata No. 2 in G, BWV 1039:* 4th movt (with Kyung Wha Chung, Moll, Welsh); *Flute Sonatas Nos. 2 in E flat, BWV 1031: Siciliano* (with Maria Graf, harp); *4 in C, BWV 1033:* 2nd movt (arr. GERHARDT for flute & O). *Concerto in E min., BWV 1059/35* (ed. Radeke): 3rd movt. ALBINONI: *Adagio.* QUANTZ: *Concerto in C: Finale.* MARAIS: *Le Basque* (arr. GALWAY/GERHARDT).

★★★ BMG/RCA DDD/ADD 09026 61928-2.

If the famous Bach *Air* from BWV 1068 is spun out somewhat romantically and the *Siciliano* from BWV 1031 (with harp accompaniment) is too solemn, Handel's famous *Largo* is gloriously managed, completely vocal in feeling. Galway certainly dominates Pachelbel's *Canon* in a way not intended by the composer, but his elegant line and simple divisions on the lovely theme are very agreeable.

Any of the composers included here would surely have been amazed at the beauty of his tone and the amazing technical facility, always turned to musical effect. He is a wonderful goldfinch in Vivaldi's Op. 10/3, while Gerhardt's arrangement of Handel's *Arrival of the Queen of Sheba*, which exchanges oboes for flutes, is ear-tickling. The engaging Quantz concerto movement is as sprightly in the strings (of the Württemberg Chamber Orchestra) as it is in the felicitously decorated solo part. The Bach and Handel sonata excerpts are refreshing and the (Handel) Siciliana from Op. 1/11 is matched in pastoral charm by the beautiful account of the *Pifa* from *Messiah*, but is not more engaging than the lollipop of the whole concert: the delicious *Le Basque* of Marais, one of Galway's most endearing arrangements. The recording naturally balances the soloist forward, but the sound is first class throughout. This is a full-price record but it includes 68 minutes of entertainment, perfect for a fine summer evening.

'*Dances for Flute*' (with Nat. PO, Gerhardt or Mancini; I Solisti di Zagreb, Scimone; The Chieftains; RPO, Myung-Whun Chung; and other artists): GODARD: *Waltz.* CHOPIN: *Minute Waltz in D flat, Op. 64/1.* DEBUSSY: *La plus que lente; Petite suite: Ballet.* J. S. BACH: *Suite No. 2, BWV 1067: Polonaise; Menuet; Badinerie.* TRAD.: *Crowley's Reel; Brian Boru's March; Belfast Hornpipe.*

KHACHATURIAN: *Waltz; Sabre Dance.*
MERCADANTE: *Concerto in D: Polacca.* MANCINI:
Pie in the Face Polka; Pennywhistle Jig. RODRIGO:
Fantasia para un gentilhombre: Canario.
BENJAMIN: *Jamaican Rhumba.* MOZART:
Divertimento in D, K.334: Menuetto. VIVALDI:
Concerto in D (Il Gardellino): Cantabile. DINICU:
Hora staccato. GOSSEC: *Tambourin.* KREISLER:
Schön Rosmarin.
*** BMG/RCA (ADD) 09026 60917-2.

Galway can certainly make his flute dance – often in
scintillating fashion. This collection is essentially for
the sweet-toothed, but its consummate artistry is
remarkable: just sample the delicious opening
Godard *Waltz*. The traditional pieces are especially
enjoyable, and two real lollipops are the Mercadante
Polacca (from a virtually forgotten concerto) and the
(Beechamesque) Gossec *Tambourin*. We also have a
soft spot for Mancini's *Pennywhistle Jig*. Good sound
and 64 minutes of music.

Il Giardino Armonico, Giovanni Antonini

'*The Italian Bach in Vienna*': J. S. BACH: *Double
Clavier Concerto in C, BWV 1061; Triple Clavier
Concerto in D min., BWV 1061* (both with Katia and
Marielle Labèque (fortepianos); BWV 1061 also
with Danone (harpsichord)). C. P. E. BACH:
Sinfonia in G, Wq.182/1. VIVALDI: *Il cimento
dell'armonia e dell'inventione: Violin Concerto in D
min., Op. 8/7, RV 242* (with Onofri (violin)).
(*) TDK **DVD DV-BACON.

The Musikverein provides at attractive backcloth and
an appealing ambience for this programme which
centres on the music of Bach and Vivaldi. The novelty here is the performance of Bach's *Triple Keyboard
Concerto* on a pair of fortepianos plus a harpsichord,
which works surprisingly well. With a microphone
given to each soloist, the engineers are able to achieve
a satisfactory balance, but the snag in the *Double
Concerto,* with such a close balance and the two
keyboards side by side, is that the movement of
Bach's solo line from one fortepiano to another is
achieved electronically, and the effect is curiously
unnatural. Moreover the close balance reveals an
obbligato vocalise from one of the soloists, very
audible in the Adagio of BWV 1061. The performances are certainly brilliant, with both finales very
lively indeed. Enrico Onofri (the orchestra's leader)
also plays with much bravura in the Vivaldi *Concerto,*
especially in his first-movement cadenza, but his
performance is without charm.

Il Giardino Armonico and its young and dynamic
conductor, Giovanni Antonini, have made their
name by a bravura period-instrument style, and that
is very much to the fore in the *G major Sinfonia* of
C. P. E. Bach, visually overflowing with energy, with
sharply articulated, very brisk outer movements and

staccato articulation in the *Poco Adagio*. But their
ensemble cannot be faulted and no one could suggest
their music-making was lacking in spirit.

CASTELLO: *Sonata concertante, Op. 2/4 & 10.*
MARINI: *Sonata, 'Sopra la Monica'.* MERULA:
Ciaconna. SPADI: *Dominuzione;* SOPRA: *Anchor
che co'l partire.* VIVALDI: *Lute Concertos in D, RV
93; in D (Il giardellino), Op. 10/3. Recorder Concerto
in G min. (La notte), RV 104.*
* Arthaus **DVD** 100 010.

Il Giardino Armonico is a brilliant group which
performs this repertoire with stunning virtuosity and
imagination. Musically, there are no quarrels here
except, perhaps, for the over-bright sound. Moreover,
the DVD facilities offer the scores, though when they
are superimposed the visual image is masked –
indeed, it virtually disappears. The text in the Vivaldi
is, of course, the Ricordi short score. Although the
performances are expert enough, though very
brightly recorded, the visual direction is irritatingly
hyperactive. The musicians are superimposed on all
sorts of Sicilian backdrops but never for more than a
few seconds at a time. The empty 'cleverness' of the
director, who cannot leave anything to speak for
itself, is very tiresome to start with and insufferable
after a few minutes. Two stars for the brilliant if
exhibitionist music-making, but none for the distracting visual antics.

Glennie, Evelyn (percussion)

'*Rebounds*' (with Scottish CO, Daniel): MILHAUD:
Concerto pour batterie et petite orchestre. RODNEY
BENNETT: *Concerto for Solo Percussion and
Chamber Orchestra.* ROSAURO: *Concierto para
marimba e orquestra de cordas.* MIYOSHI: *Concerto
for Marimba and Strings.*
*** BMG/RCA 09026 61277-2.

Here is a chance for Glennie to show what she can do
with more ambitious concert music – although, of
course, there are popular influences and jazz rhythms
in the works by both Richard Rodney Bennett and
Rosauro. Bennett even offers an aleatory element for
the percussionist. But his concerto is imaginatively
thought out and has plenty of atmosphere and colour. The Milhaud concerto (its title sounds so much
more inviting in French) is a most spontaneous
piece, without fireworks but very effectively written.

Other than that, the most enjoyable work here is
the tuneful four-movement concerto by the Brazilian
Ney Rosauro, with a haunting *Lament* for the slow
movement, an engaging *Dança*, followed by an
imaginative finale. The *Miyoshi Marimba* concerto is
in a kaleidoscopic single movement. All these works
are brilliantly played and the collection is much more
diverse and entertaining than one might expect. The
recording engineers have a field day, yet they do not
try to create exaggerated effects.

Gould, Glenn (piano)

Glenn Gould Edition

BACH: *Harpsichord Concertos Nos. 1–5; 7, BWV 1052–6 & BWV 1058* (with Columbia SO, Bernstein (No. 1) or Golschmann).

(M) (**) Sony mono (No. 1)/stereo SM2K 52591 (2).

BACH: *Fugues, BWV 953 & BWV 961; Fughettas, BWV 961 & BWV 902; 6 Little Preludes, BWV 933–8; 6 Partitas, BWV 825–30; Preludes, BWV 902 & 902/1a; Prelude and Fugue, BWV 895; 2 Preludes & Fughettas, BWV 899–900.*

(M) (**) Sony (ADD) SM2K 52597 (2).

BACH: *Well-tempered Clavier, Book I, Preludes and Fugues Nos. 1–24, BWV 846–69.*

(M) (**) Sony (ADD) SM2K 52600 (2).

BACH: *Well-tempered Clavier, Book II, Preludes and Fugues Nos. 25–48, BWV 870–93.*

(M) (**) Sony (ADD) SM2K 52603 (2).

BEETHOVEN: *7 Bagatelles, Op. 33; 6 Bagatelles, Op. 126; 6 Variations in F, Op. 34; 15 Variations with Fugue in E flat (Eroica), Op. 35; 32 Variations on an Original Theme in C min., WoO 80.*

(M) (**) Sony (ADD) SM2K 52646 (2).

BRAHMS: *4 Ballades, Op. 10; Intermezzi, Op. 76/6–7; Op. 116/4; Op. 117/1–3; Op. 118/1, 2 & 6; Op. 119/1; 2 Rhapsodies, Op. 79.*

(M) (**) Sony ADD/DDD SM2K 52651 (2).

Glenn Gould is an artist who excites such strong passions that guidance is almost superfluous. For his host of admirers these discs are self-recommending; those who do not respond to his pianism will not be greatly interested in this edition. For long he enjoyed cult status, enhanced rather than diminished by his absence from the concert hall. There is too much that is wilful and eccentric in these performances for any of them to rank as a sole first recommendation. Yet if for his devotees virtually all his recordings are indispensable, for the unconverted a judicious approach is called for. There is no questioning Gould's keyboard wizardry or his miraculous control of part-writing in Bach, for which he had much intuitive feeling. The majority of his Bach discs evidence strong personality and commitment throughout, even though the tiresome vocalise (which became an increasing source of frustration, particularly later in his recording career) is a strain. However, the sound generally has insufficient freshness and bloom, and the eccentricity (some might say egocentricity) of some of Gould's readings and the accompanying vocalise are often quite insupportable.

Grafin, Philippe (violin), Ulster Orchestra, Thierry Fischer

'Rare French Works for Violin and Orchestra':
FAURE: *Violin Concerto in D min., Op. 14.*
SAINT-SAENS: *Morceau de concert, Op. 62.* LALO: *Fantasie norvégienne.* GUIRAUD: *Caprice.* LALO: *Guitarre, Op. 28.* CANTELOUBE: *Poème.*
*** Hyp. CDA 67294.

This attractive compilation is worth having for the Fauré *Concerto* alone, which the composer never completed. The existing two movements are full of delightful ideas and Philippe Grafin is a most sympathetic exponent. The Saint-Saëns *Morceau* is a working of the *Caprice brillant* for violin and piano and shows all the composer's tuneful facility and flair. Lalo's *Fantaisie norvégienne* uses what he thought was a folksong, but was in fact a melody of Grieg's – and a very delightful one too. *Guitarre* is essentially an instrumental piece, engaging enough, and orchestrated by Pierné for his own use as an encore. It recalls the *Symphonie espagnole*, but is altogether slighter. The surprise here is the two-movement *Caprice* of Ernest Guiraud, who we remember as the composer of recitatives for Bizet's *Carmen*. The gently seductive *Andante* is followed by a sparkling *Allegro appassionato*, after the fashion of the Saint-Saëns *Introduction and Rondo capriccioso*. The Canteloube *Poème* is passionately languorous, richly orchestrated: its composer was afraid his scoring was too opulent and would drown its soloist, but that is not a problem here and one revels in its sumptuousness and orchestral colour. Altogether a most worthwhile collection, very well played and recorded.

Grumiaux, Arthur (violin)

'Favourite violin concertos' (with (i) Concg. O; (ii) New Philh. O; (iii) Sir Colin Davis; (iv) Bernard Haitink; (v) Jan Krenz): BEETHOVEN: (i; iii) *Concerto in D; (i; iv) Romance No. 2 in F.* (ii; iii) BRAHMS: *Concerto in D.* (ii; v) MENDELSSOHN: *Concerto in E min.* TCHAIKOVSKY: *Concerto in D.*
☞ ✿ (B) *** Ph. Duo (ADD) 442 287-2 (2).

Another extraordinary Duo bargain set from Philips, containing some of the great Belgian violinist's very finest performances. He recorded the Beethoven twice for Philips, and this is the later account from the mid-1970s with Sir Colin Davis. Grumiaux imbues this glorious concerto with a spirit of classical serenity and receives outstanding support from Davis. If we remember correctly, the earlier account with Galliera had slightly more of a sense of repose and spontaneous magic in the slow movement, but the balance of advantage between the two versions is very difficult to resolve, as the Concertgebouw recording is fuller and richer and (even if there is not absolute orchestral clarity) there is less background noise.

The performance of the Brahms, it goes without saying, is full of insight and lyrical eloquence, and again Sir Colin Davis lends his soloist the most sympathetic support. The (1973) account of the Mendelssohn is characteristically polished and refined, and Grumiaux, even if he does not wear his heart on his sleeve, plays very beautifully throughout: the pure poetry of the playing not only lights up the *Andante* but is heard at its most magical in the key moment of the downward arpeggio which introduces the second subject of the first movement.

Similarly in the Tchaikovsky his playing – if less overtly emotional than some – has the usual aristocratic refinement and purity of tone to recommend it. His reading is beautifully paced and has a particularly fine slow movement; both here and in the brilliant finale he shows superb aplomb and taste. With excellent accompaniments in both works from Krenz, this adds to the attractions of the set, for the 1970s recording has a wide range and is firmly focused in its CD format.

Concert (with LOP, Rosenthal): LALO: *Symphonie espagnole, Op. 21.* SAINT-SAENS: *Introduction and Rondo capriccioso, Op. 28; Havanaise, Op. 83.* CHAUSSON: *Poème, Op. 25.* RAVEL: *Tzigane.*

**(*) Australian Ph. Eloquence (ADD) 462 579-2.

A worthwhile collection of French music. Grumiaux's playing is always individual, not showy or extrovert, but with plenty of colour and relaxed bravura. The orchestral support is lively and sympathetic, and lets the soloist dominate in the right way. The Lamoureux Orchestra is not the most refined of instruments but is reasonably stylish, with a French timbre which is nice to hear in these conformist times. The recording is a little thin-sounding (it dates from the mid-1960s), but is acceptable and well balanced.

Hallé Orchestra, Sir John Barbirolli

BAX: *Oboe Quintet* (arr. Barbirolli; with Evelyn Rothwell). VAUGHAN WILLIAMS: *Symphony No. 8 in D min.* DELIUS: *On Hearing the First Cuckoo in Spring.* RAWSTHORNE: *Street Corner Overture.* WALTON: *Coronation March: Crown Imperial.* ELGAR: *Land of Hope and Glory* (with Kathleen Ferrier & Hallé Ch.). *National Anthem* (with Trumpeters & Band of Royal Military School of Music, Kneller Hall).

(M) (***) BBC mono/stereo BBCL 4100-2.

On the BBC Legends label these radio recordings of British music, all but one from the late 1960s, offer a delightful selection of Barbirolli favourites, including his own arrangement of Bax's *Oboe Quintet* for oboe and strings, with his wife Evelyn Rothwell as the expressive soloist. Written for Rothwell's teacher,

Leon Goossens, it originally involved writing for the string quartet that Barbirolli found awkward with its double-stopping, something that his arrangement clarifies. Vaughan Williams's *Eighth Symphony*, dedicated to him as 'Glorious John', was always a work he specially enjoyed, and this live performance from a 1967 Prom is both broader and warmer than his studio recording, if not quite so clean of texture. That and Rawsthorne's rumbustious *Overture, Street Corner*, are the only stereo recordings here. Walton's *Crown Imperial* is also given with plenty of panache, and Delius's *First Cuckoo* could not be more warmly done. The National Anthem, recorded at the same Royal Albert Hall concert, is an oddity, with voices inaudible, and *Land of Hope and Glory*, also taken very slowly, is a much older recording, taken from a severely damaged shellac disc, with Kathleen Ferrier the radiant soloist. This was recorded at the opening of the rebuilt Free Trade Hall in Manchester in 1951.

BEETHOVEN: *Symphony No. 7 in A, Op. 92.* MOZART: *Symphony No. 35 in D (Haffner);* WAGNER: *Siegfried Idyll.*

(M) (**(*)) BBC Legends stereo/mono BBCL 4076-2.

Barbirolli never made a commercial recording of Beethoven's *Seventh Symphony* (in fact he recorded only Nos. 1, 3, 5 and 8), so this Festival Hall account is more than welcome. One senses straight away that there is a strong personality in command, and one that is wholly dedicated to Beethoven. In this mighty work Sir John is totally straightforward and unfussy, yet attentive to every detail of phrasing, and there is a fine sense of momentum. The only slight reservation lies in the finale, which is not quite headlong enough. But this is a performance of stature, and the sound is remarkably good for its period and venue: the balance is excellently judged, with every detail coming across, even if tuttis sound a bit fierce. The Mozart symphony has plenty of spirit and warmth; tempi are brisk but the phrasing is always alive. The Albert Hall sound, though not as finely detailed or as present as in the Beethoven, is more than acceptable. Sir John also never recorded the *Haffner Symphony* for his record companies, nor did he commit the *Siegfried Idyll* to disc. As you would expect, he shapes it beautifully, though the playing is generally less polished than in either of the symphonies. The strings sound vinegary at times, although their quality and timbre were not flattered by the acoustic of the BBC Manchester Studios. The mono recording is less rich and detail less transparent. All the same, this set is a valuable addition to the Barbirolli discography.

'*Barbirolli at the Opera*': RICHARD STRAUSS: *Die Liebe der Danae* (symphonic fragments; arr. Krauss); *Der Rosenkavalier: Suite.* WEBER: *Der Freischütz; Euryanthe: Overtures.* VERDI: *La traviata: Preludes to Acts I & III.* MOZART: *Le nozze di Figaro: Overture.* WAGNER: *Lohengrin: Preludes to Acts I & III.*

(M) (***) Dutton Lab. mono CDSJB 1004.

Hearing these glowing performances, full of Barbirollian expressiveness and panache, brings home how sad it is that he recorded so few complete operas in the studio. It is tantalizing to realize what a great interpreter of Rosenkavalier he would have been, when his account of the much-maligned suite is so warm and persuasive, a première recording of 1946. Every item demonstrates the quality of the Hallé as trained by Barbirolli in the immediate post-war period, notably the strings. The Dutton transfers are first rate, though the original recordings used here were obviously more limited than those on some earlier Barbirolli Society issues, and this collection is too highly priced.

'Hallé Favourites – 2': SUPPÉ: *Overture: The Beautiful Galatea.* TURINA: *Danzas fantásticas.* CHABRIER: *España.* LEHAR: *Gold and Silver Waltz.* SIBELIUS: *Valse triste.* WALDTEUFEL: *The Skaters' Waltz.* GRIEG: *Two Elegiac Melodies; Peer Gynt Suite No. 1.*

(M) (★★★) Dutton Lab. mono/stereo CDSJB 1013.

Some of the recordings here have an EMI mono source from the 1950s; the rest, including the Sibelius and Grieg items (which are particularly warmly played), were early stereo with a Pye source. All the transfers are up to Dutton's standard and Chabrier's *España* and the two waltzes have plenty of lilt and sparkle. It is a pity that – as it is sponsored by the Barbirolli Society – this disc is comparatively expensive.

'Barbirolli's English Music Album': BARBIROLLI: *An Elizabethan Suite.* BAX: *The Garden of Fand.* BUTTERWORTH: *A Shropshire Lad.* ELGAR: *Three Bavarian Dances: Lullaby. Enigma Variations.* IRELAND: *The Forgotten Rite; Mai-Dun; These Things Shall Be* (with Parry Jones, tenor, Hallé Ch.). PURCELL (arr. BARBIROLLI): *Suite for Strings.* VAUGHAN WILLIAMS: *Fantasia on Greensleeves; Fantasia on a Theme by Thomas Tallis.*

(M) (★★★) Dutton mono CDSJB 1022 (2).

The long-buried treasure here is Barbirolli's very first recording of Elgar's *Enigma Variations*, never previously issued. As Michael Kennedy's authoritative note explains, it was recorded in Manchester in May 1947, only months before he went on to make his first published recording in October of that year, an inexplicable duplication when if anything this earliest version is even finer than the published one, certainly more spontaneously expressive at key points such as *Nimrod* and the finale variation, while the opening statement of the theme is more flowing and less emphatic.

There is much else to cherish on the two discs for any devotee of English music, let alone Barbirolli enthusiasts. The two Vaughan Williams items, the *Tallis Fantasia* dating from 1946 and *Greensleeves* from 1948, both recorded in Houldsworth Hall, Manchester, have never previously appeared on CD, and

both are very welcome. In mono sound they may be less rich-textured than Barbirolli's stereo remakes, but the *Tallis Fantasia*, featuring a vintage quartet of Hallé principals, separates the quartet more clearly from the main body than the version with the Sinfonia of London, and again is more warmly expressive. The extra lightness of *Greensleeves* too sounds more easily spontaneous.

Those performances are contained on the second of the two discs, with the shorter works of Bax, Butterworth and Ireland on the first. The exotic orchestration of Bax's *The Garden of Fand* is well detailed, as are the evocative textures of the Butterworth orchestral rhapsody, recorded for Pye like Barbirolli's own *Elizabethan Suite*, all of them stereo recordings. The EMI mono recordings of the two Ireland orchestral pieces, dating from earlier, have comparable weight. In the Ireland choral work, *These Things Shall Be*, the dynamic range is again wider than one expects in mono recordings of this vintage. The performances all have a passionate thrust typical of Barbirolli, with the tenor, Parry Jones, and the Hallé Chorus matching the orchestra in their commitment. The two suites devised by Barbirolli himself emerge as curiosities in an age devoted to period practice. It is striking that Purcell survives the romanticizing involved rather better than Byrd, Farnaby and Bull.

Hälsingborg Symphony Orchestra, Okko Kamu

'Swedish Orchestral Favourites': SODERMAN: *Swedish Festival Music.* STENHAMMAR: *The Song (cantata): Interlude.* LARSSON: *Pastoral Suite; A Winter's Tale: Epilogue.* PETERSON-BERGER: *Frösöblomster: 4 Pieces.* ALFVEN: *Roslagspolka; Midsummer Vigil; Gustavus Adolphus II Suite.* WIREN: *Serenade for Strings: Marcia.*

(BB) ★★★ Naxos 8.553115.

A useful anthology of popular favourites from the Swedish repertory, nicely played by the Hälsingborg orchestra and Okko Kamu, which should have wide appeal, not only in but outside Sweden. The playing is lively, the performances of the Alfvén and Lars-Erik Larsson pieces are as good as any in the catalogue, the recording is excellent and the price is right.

Hanover Band, Graham Lea-Cox

18th-Century British Symphonies: ABEL: *Symphony in E, Op. 10/1.* ARNE: *Symphony No. 4 in C min.* COLLETT: *Symphony in E flat, Op 2/5.* ERSKINE: *Periodical Overture No. 17 in E flat.* MARSH: *A Conversation Symphony in E flat.* SMETHERGELL: *Symphony in B flat, Op. 5/2.*

✿ ★★★ ASV CDGAU 218.

This collection of six British symphonies dating from

the late eighteenth century could not be more refreshing, brilliantly played and recorded. Hardly anything is known of John Collett, not even his dates, but his four-movement *Symphony in E flat, Op. 2/5*, published in 1767, is a delight, its eager energy echoing the new Mannheim school, with brazen horn writing. His patron, Thomas Erskine, the Earl of Kelly, studied for years in Mannheim, but his *Periodical Overture No. 17*, briefer and bluffer, is less striking. It is in three movements only, as are all the rest, including John Marsh's elegant *Conversation Sinfonie* for two orchestras from 1778, which was influenced by J. C. Bach. With such bright, carefree inspiration running through all these works, the old idea that Handel stifled British composers needs revising.

Hanslip, Chloé (violin)

'Chloé' (with LSO, Mann): PAGANINI (arr. KREISLER): *La Campanella*. BLOCH: *Nigun*. GADE: *Capriccio*. J. WILLIAMS: *Theme from 'Schindler's List'*. MUSSORGSKY (arr. Rachmaninov & Ingman): *Gopak*; BRUCH: *Adagio appassionato*. GLAZUNOV: *Meditation*. TCHAIKOVSKY: *Valse-scherzo*. SHOSTAKOVICH: *The Gadfly: Romance*. SARASATE: *Romanza andaluza*. WAXMAN: *Carmen Fantasy*.
★★★ Warner 8573 88655-2.

Chloé Hanslip was 13 years old when she recorded this impressive recital disc. Although there is only limited evidence of distinctive artistry, it makes a formidable display, very well recorded. Hanslip, born and brought up in Surrey, gives formidably mature performances of all 11 pieces here, marked by dazzling virtuosity, flawless intonation, phenomenal attack in virtuoso showpieces like the Sarasate, and, above all, a genuine depth of expression that is sensitively matched to the style of each piece. So in Bloch's *Nigun*, with its subtitle of improvisation, she is uninhibitedly free in her warm phrasing, freer than in the Shostakovich, where the haunting melody is played with tender restraint. What are especially welcome are the rarities. Bruch's *Adagio appassionato*, written in 1891, the same year as the third violin concerto, is a violin equivalent of *Kol Nidrei*. Niels Gade's *Capriccio*, too, which was written in his sixties and has rarely appeared on disc, is here played with all the sparkle that is slightly lacking from the brilliant but literal account of the opening item, Kreisler's arrangement of the Paganini *Campanella* study, which is a little too metrical. By contrast, Tchaikovsky's *Valse-scherzo*, another rarity, sounds a little unsteady, with tenutos not quite spontaneous sounding.

Hardenberger, Håkan (trumpet)

'Famous Classical Trumpet Concertos': HUMMEL: *Concerto in E*. HERTEL: *Concerto No. 1 in E flat*. STAMITZ: *Concerto in D*. HAYDN: *Concerto in E flat*

(all with ASMF, Marriner). RICHTER: *Concerto in D*. Leopold MOZART: *Concerto in D*. MOLTER: *Concerto No. 1 in D*. Michael HAYDN: *Concerto No. 2 in C* (all with LPO, Howarth). CORELLI: *Sonata for Trumpet, 2 Violins and Continuo*. ALBINONI: *Concerto in B flat, Op. 7/3* (with I Musici). ALBINONI/GIAZOTTO: *Adagio in G min*. CLARKE: *Trumpet Tune* (attr. PURCELL). BACH: *3 Chorale preludes*. BACH/GOUNOD: *Ave Maria* (all with Simon Preston, organ).
🔗 ✪ (B) **★★★** Ph. Duo 464 028-2 (2).

This is simply the finest collection of concertante music for trumpet in the catalogue. Hardenberger's playing in the famous Haydn concerto, with his noble line in the *Andante* no less telling than his sparkling bravura in the finale, is matched by his account of the Hummel which he plays in E, rather than the expected key of E flat, which makes it sound brighter than usual. Neither he nor Marriner misses the galant lilt inherent in the dotted rhythm of the first movement, while the slow-movement cantilena soars beautifully over its jogging pizzicato accompaniment, and the finale captivates the ear with its high spirits and easy virtuosity. The Stamitz concerto is a comparatively recent discovery. The writing lies consistently up in the instrument's stratosphere and includes some awkward leaps. It is inventive, however, notably in the exhilarating finale. There is no lack of panache here or in the lesser concerto by Hertel, and throughout Marriner's accompaniments are consistently elegant and polished. Apart from these obvious highlights there is much to enjoy in the lesser works too. The wealth of melody is apparent, and if not all the music here is in the masterpiece league, it is played as if it were. Hardenberger is as brilliant in the fast movements as he is sensitive in the slow ones, and his phrasing and tone are superb in both. In the two attractive baroque concertos by Albinoni and Marcello he plays with similar flair and gleaming tone, and he is a dab hand at embellishment, without overdoing things. The recordings and accompaniments are comparably fine, and it is difficult to imagine a better programme of this kind at any price.

Harle, John (saxophone), Academy of St Martin-in-the-Fields, Sir Neville Marriner

DEBUSSY: *Rapsodie for Alto Saxophone and Orchestra*. IBERT: *Concertino da camera*. GLAZUNOV: *Concerto*. Rodney BENNETT: *Concerto*. HEATH: *Out of the Cool*. VILLA-LOBOS: *Fantasia*.
(B) **★★★** EMI Red Line 5 72109.

A first-class disc in every way. These are all attractive and well written for their instrument, and John Harle is its master. The Debussy, Ibert and Glazunov are all works well worth getting to know. The recording is excellent.

Harp Concertos

Harp Concertos (played by: (i) Robles; (ii) ASMF, Brown; (iii) Ellis, LSO, Bonynge; (iv) Tripp, Jellinek, VPO, Münchinger; (v) Philh. O, Dutoit): (i; ii) BOIELDIEU: *Harp Concerto in C.* DITTERSDORF: *Harp Concerto in A* (arr. PILLEY). (iii) GLIERE: *Harp Concerto, Op. 74.* (i; ii) HANDEL: *Harp Concerto, Op. 4/6.* (iv) MOZART: *Flute and Harp Concerto in C, K.299.* (i; v) RODRIGO: *Concierto de Aranjuez.*

(B) *** Double Decca (ADD) 452 585-2 (2).

Boieldieu's *Harp Concerto* has been recorded elsewhere but never more attractively. The (originally Argo) recording is still in the demonstration class and very sweet on the ear. Dittersdorf's *Harp Concerto* is a transcription of an unfinished keyboard concerto with additional wind parts. It is an elegant piece, thematically not quite as memorable as Boieldieu's, but captivating when played with such style. Glière's is an unpretentious and tuneful work, with Osian Ellis performing brilliantly. Excellent (1968) Kingsway Hall recording.

Handel's Op. 4/6 is well known in both organ and harp versions. Marisa Robles and Iona Brown make an unforgettable case for the latter by creating the most delightful textures while never letting the work sound insubstantial. The ASMF accompaniment, so stylish and beautifully balanced, is a treat in itself, and the recording is well-nigh perfect. The much earlier, Vienna recording of Mozart's *Flute and Harp Concerto* is played stylishly and has stood the test of time, the recording smooth, full, nicely reverberant and with good detail. Refinement and beauty of tone and phrase are a hallmark throughout, and Münchinger provides most sensitive accompaniments.

The glowing acoustic of St Barnabas's Church, London, creates an attractively romantic aura for Marisa Robles's magnetic and highly atmospheric account of the composer's own arrangement for harp of his *Concierto de Aranjuez*. Robles is so convincing an advocate that for the moment the guitar original is all but forgotten, particularly when, with inspirational freedom, she makes the beautiful slow movement sound like a rhapsodic improvisation. It is a haunting performance, and the digital sound is first rate. Altogether an excellent anthology; however, the Boieldieu, Dittersdorf and Handel concertos on the first disc are also available separately at mid-price, and we gave a Rosette to this disc in our main volume (Decca 425 723-2).

Hauk, Franz, Ingolstadt Philharmonic, Alfredo Ibarra

Music for Organ and Orchestra (Klais Organ in Liebfrauenmünster Ingolstadt): WIDOR: *Symphony No. 3 for Organ and Grand Orchestra, Op. 42.* JONGEN: *Alleluja, Op. 112; Hymne, Op. 78* (both for organ and orchestra). Horatio PARKER: *Organ Concerto in E flat, Op. 55.*

**(*) Guild GMCD 7182.

In terms of sheer hyperbole Widor does this better than almost anyone. His *G minor concertante Symphony* is made up from two solo organ symphonies: the spectacular outer movements, including the brilliant closing *Toccata*, well laced with brass, are drawn from the *Sixth*, Op. 42/2, and the central *Andante* from the *Second*, Op. 13/2, composed ten years earlier.

The Jongen works are both lyrically colourful. The nobilmente *Alleluja* was composed to inaugurate a new organ in the concert hall of Belgian Radio in 1940, and with its closing fanfares sounds rather like wartime film music. The *Hymne* (for organ and strings) is a threnody of some character, well sustained and making a welcome contrast with the surrounding flamboyance.

The American Horatio Parker earned the contempt of his pupil Charles Ives for 'imposing second-hand German romanticism on the patriots of New England'. But his readily tuneful if at times overblown edifice is endearing for its somewhat sentimental romantic feeling, symbolized by the violin and horn solos in the *Andante*. The work was modelled on a concerto of Rheinberger, and its third-movement *Allegretto* is also lightly scored and has charm. The finale includes a fugato, a vigorous pedal cadenza, a bit like a recitative, and a resounding close to bring the house down. Here the final cadence echoes away in the long reverberation period of the Liebfrauenmünster. The organ itself is a magnificent beast and is played with great bravura and expressive flair by Franz Hauk; the orchestra accompany with spirit and enthusiasm, even if at times they are all but drowned in the resonant wash of sound. The recording copes remarkably well, although it is hardly refined.

'*Triumphal Music for Organ and Orchestra*': GOUNOD: *Fantaisie on the Russian National Hymne; Suite concertante.* DUBOIS: *Fantaisie triomphale.* GUILMANT: *Adoration.* GIGOUT: *Grand choeur dialogue.*
*** Guild GMCD 7185.

Gounod's *Fantaisie* on the Tsarist anthem is imposing enough, if a bit repetitive. The Dubois *Fantaisie* is suitably grand and pontifical, to be followed by Guilmant's very romantic *Adoration*, a rather beautiful soliloquy for organ and strings. After more pomp from Gigout, we return to Gounod, and an amiably attractive four-movement suite, with hunting horns setting off the jolly Scherzo, followed by a songful *Andante* (nicely registered here). But, not surprisingly, it is the catchy vivace finale that steals the show: a bouncy tune that could become a hit if it got more exposure. It is most winningly played and completes an attractive concertante programme that does not rely on decibels for its main appeal. The

performances are excellent and here the very reverberant acoustic seems for the most part under control.

Heifetz, Jascha (violin)

'*Centenary Memorial Edition*' (1901–2001):
BEETHOVEN: *Concerto* (with NBC SO, Toscanini).
BRAHMS: *Concerto*. PROKOFIEV: *Concerto No. 2,
Op. 63* (both with Boston SO, Koussevitzky).
SIBELIUS: *Concerto* (with LPO, Beecham).
GLAZUNOV: *Concerto*. TCHAIKOVSKY: *Concerto.*
WIENIAWSKI: *Concerto No. 2*. VIEUXTEMPS:
Concertos Nos. 4, Op. 31; Op. 37. ELGAR: *Concerto*
(both with LSO, Sargent). SAINT-SAENS:
Introduction & Rondo capriccioso (all with LPO,
Barbirolli). *Havanaise*. SARASATE: *Zigeunerweisen*
(both with LSO, Barbirolli). WALTON: *Concerto*
(original version; with Cincinnati SO, Goossens).
BRAHMS: *Double Concerto for Violin & Cello* (with
Feuermann, O, Ormandy). BRUCH: *Scottish
Fantasia* (with RCA Victor SO, Steinberg).
MENDELSSOHN: *Concerto, Op. 64*. MOZART:
Concertos Nos. 4, K.218 (both with RPO, Beecham);
5 (Turkish), K.219 (with LPO, Barbirolli).
GRUENBERG: *Concerto, Op. 47* (with San Francisco
SO, Monteux). WAXMAN: *Carmen Fantasy* (with
RCA Victor O, Voorhees).

(BB) (★★★) Naxos mono 8.107001 (7).

The seven Naxos discs of Heifetz's mono recordings
of concertos are available in a boxed set as above, as
well as separately. The transfers are of a good standard, mellower than the RCA originals, although the
EMI alternative remastering is rather more sophisticated, and the EMI separate discs have less background hiss. They are also far more expensive. This
Naxos box is certainly highly recommendable in its
own right.

'*Heifetz the Supreme*': BACH: (Unaccompanied)
Violin Partita No. 2, BWV 1004: Chaconne.
BRAHMS: *Violin Concerto in D, Op. 77.*
TCHAIKOVSKY: *Violin Concerto in D, Op. 35* (with
Chicago SO, Fritz Reiner). BRUCH: *Scottish Fantasy,
Op. 46* (with New SO of London, Sargent).
SIBELIUS: *Violin Concerto, Op. 47* (with Chicago
SO, Hendl). GLAZUNOV: *Violin Concerto, Op. 82*
(with RCA Victor SO, Hendl). GERSHWIN
(transcribed Heifetz): *3 Preludes* (with Brooks
Smith, piano).

(M) ★★★ RCA (ADD) 74321 63470-2 (2).

For once the hyperbole of a record company's title is
not exaggerated: truly Heifetz is the supreme virtuoso among violinists, and this generously compiled
two-disc set shows him at his very finest. The performance of the great Bach *Chaconne* is not only
technically phenomenal, it has an extraordinary
range of feeling and dynamic, while Heifetz exerts a
compelling grip over the structure. The perform-

ances of the five concertante works (discussed more
fully in our main volume) are not only inspired and
full of insights, they show how well Heifetz chose his
accompanists, notably Fritz Reiner in Brahms and
Tchaikovsky. Sargent too gives most sensitive support in the Bruch *Scottish Fantasy* – the atmospheric
opening is most evocative. Finally come the dazzling
and touching Gershwin showpieces, showing that
quicksilver bow arm at its most chimerical, even if
here the recording is much too closely observed.

'*The Unpublished Recordings*': BEETHOVEN:
Romances Nos. 1 and 2. LALO: *Symphonie espagnole*
(both with Philh. O, Susskind). CHAUSSON: *Poème*
(with San Francisco SO, Monteux).

(★★★) Testament mono SBT 1216.

It seems astonishing that any recordings by Heifetz,
let alone performances as fine as these, should have
slipped through the net and never been issued. The
Lalo and Beethoven were recorded at EMI's Abbey
Road studios in June 1950, just at the time when the
long-time alliance between EMI in Britain and RCA
Victor in America was slackening. Heifetz went on to
record both the *Romances* and the Lalo again for
RCA in America the following year, but the EMI
sound is warmer and more helpful to the violin. In
both (with the central *Intermezzo* of the Lalo omitted, as was then the custom) Heifetz also sounds
more flexibly spontaneous. The Chausson, with
Monteux and the San Francisco orchestra, was
recorded by RCA five years earlier, in 1945, with
limited sound and a dry, unhelpful acoustic, making
even Heifetz's violin-tone sound rather fizzy at the
start, and with the orchestra backwardly placed. The
performance itself is magnificent, warmly expressive,
with the structure tautly held together.

(i) Hilversum Radio PO or (ii)
London Symphony Orchestra,
Leopold Stokowski

(i) FRANCK: *Symphony in D min*. RAVEL: *L'éventail
de Jeanne*. (ii) CHOPIN: *Mazurka in A min., Op.
17/4* (orch. Stokowski). MESSIAEN: *L'Ascension.*
DUPARC: *Extase* (orch. Stokowski).

(M) ★★ Cala CACD 0526.

These recordings were made in the early 1970s in
Decca's hi-fi-conscious Phase Four system, and the
exaggerated sound goes with the flamboyance of
Stokowski's interpretations. The Franck *Symphony* is
the most controversial reading on this disc. The
conviction with which Stokowski moulds a romantic
symphony like this is always striking. But here, by
underlining the vulgarities in this score which most
conductors seek to conceal, the overall balance of the
work is disturbed, and the reading is less than satisfying. Of course it has its moments, but Stokowski
too often ventures perilously close to the cliff edge.
The Hilversum orchestra does not have the virtuosity

of the LSO in the companion pieces, but plays with energy as well as warmth. The rest of the programme is much more successful. After the Ravel *Fanfare* which is startling in its vividness, the following Chopin and Duparc pieces are richly atmospheric and show Stokowski at his most magical. Messiaen's *L'Ascension* is an early work, written first for organ, but then orchestrated in 1935 with a different third movement. Stokowski is characteristically persuasive in developing the smooth flow of the music, though some will object to the opulence of the sound he (and the engineers) favour in the sweet meditation for strings alone, *Prayer of Christ ascending to the Father*.

Hofmann, Josef (piano)

'*The Complete Josef Hofmann*', Vol. 2 (with Curtis Institute Student O, cond. Reiner or Hilsberg): BRAHMS: *Academic Festival Overture.* RUBINSTEIN: *Piano Concerto No. 4 in D min.* CHOPIN: *Ballade No. 1 in G min., Op. 23; Nocturne in E flat, Op. 9/2; Waltz in A flat, Op. 42; Andante spianato et Grande polonaise brillante in E flat, Op. 22* (2 versions); *Nocturne in F sharp, Op. 15/2; Waltz in D flat, Op. 64/1; Etude in G flat, Op. 25/9; Berceuse in B flat, Op. 57; Nocturne in C min., Op. 48/1; Mazurka in C, Op. 33/3; Waltz in A flat, Op. 34/1.* HOFMANN: *Chromaticon for Piano & Orchestra* (2 versions). MENDELSSOHN: *Spinning Song in C, Op. 67/4.* RACHMANINOV: *Prelude in G min., Op. 23/5.* BEETHOVEN–RUBINSTEIN: *Turkish March.* MOSZKOWSKI: *Caprice espagnole, Op. 37.*
✪ (★★★) VAI Audio mono VAIA/IPA 1020 (2).

Josef Hofmann's amazing 1937 performance of Rubinstein's *Fourth Piano Concerto* has long been a much-sought-after item in its LP format, and those who possess it have treasured it. The performance was attended by practically every pianist around, including Rachmaninov and Godowsky. (It was the latter who once said to a youngster who had mentioned a fingerslip in one of Hofmann's recitals, 'Why look for the spots on the sun!') In no other pianist's hands has this music made such sense: Hofmann plays his master's best-known concerto with a delicacy and poetic imagination that are altogether peerless.

Olin Downes spoke of his 'power and delicacy, lightning virtuosity and the capacity to make the keyboard sing, the richness of tone colouring and incorruptible taste'. The 1937 concert included the Brahms overture, a speech by Walter Damrosch, the incomparable performance of the Rubinstein concerto and, after the interval, a Chopin group. One is tempted to say that the *G minor Ballade* has never been surpassed. The second CD includes four later items, recorded in 1945. Once again – and it can't be said too often – the Rubinstein is phenomenal.

Horowitz, Vladimir (piano)

'*The First Recordings*': CHOPIN: *Etude in F, Op. 10/8; Mazurka No. 21 in C sharp min., Op. 30/4.* DEBUSSY: *Children's Corner: Serenade for the Doll.* SCARLATTI: *Capriccio in E, L. 375.* BIZET/HOROWITZ: *Variations on Themes from 'Carmen'.* DOHNÁNYI: *Capriccio (Concert Etude in F min., Op. 28/6).* LISZT: *Concert Paraphrase of Schubert's Liebesbotschaft; Paganini Etude No. 5 in E (La chasse); Valse oubliée No. 1.* LISZT/BUSONI: *Paganini Etude No. 2 in E flat (Octave).* RACHMANINOV: *Piano Concerto No. 3 in D min., Op. 30* (with LSO, Coates).
(BB) (★★★) Naxos mono 8.110696.

Horowitz's pioneering 1930 account of the Rachmaninov *Third Concerto* with Albert Coates conducting the LSO last appeared on the Biddulph label (coupled with Rachmaninov's own version of the *Second* with Stokowski). An earlier transfer on EMI Références came in a three-CD set with all his recordings from 1930–51. This Naxos transfer comes with the early records Horowitz made for Victor between 1928–30, when he would have been twenty-five to twenty-seven. When in 1928 he first ran through the concerto, with Rachmaninov at the second piano, the composer famously told friends that 'Horowitz pounced with the voraciousness of a tiger: he swallowed it whole'. One can hear this in the Coates partnership – and even more, perhaps, in the electrifying 1941 account with Barbirolli on APR. The Coates version (with its memory lapse in the finale to testify that Horowitz was after all human) is so well known as to need no further comment, except to say that Coates is a marvellously supportive accompanist and that the Obert-Thorn transfer is very successful. It is good to have the cadenza Rachmaninov himself played, too, rather than the combative (and ugly) one now generally favoured by pianists. Three of the other pieces here have never been released before: two of them, *Liebesbotschaft* and the 1838 version of *La chasse*, Horowitz dropped from his repertoire after 1930. Obert-Thorn uses vinyl pressings for the unpublished takes and has taken great trouble over the transfer. A feast of superb playing from a unique pianist and an invaluable supplement to the Horowitz discography.

'*Legendary RCA Recordings*': RACHMANINOV: *Piano Concerto No. 3* (with RCA SO, Reiner); TCHAIKOVSKY: *Piano Concerto No. 1* (with NBC SO, Toscanini): Recital: CHOPIN: *Polonaise-Fantaisie; Mazurka in C sharp min., Op. 30/4. Nocturne in E flat, Op. 9/2.* SCHUMANN: *Kinderszenen: Träumerei. Sonata No. 3 in F min., Op. 14: Wieck Variations.* SCRIABIN: *Preludes: in D flat, Op. 48/3; in G flat, Op. 11/13; in F sharp min., Op. 15/2; Etude in D sharp min., Op. 18/12.* MOSZKOWSKI: *Etincelles.* BIZET: *Variations on a*

Theme from 'Carmen'. PROKOFIEV: *Toccata*.
CLEMENTI: *Sonata, Op. 47/2: Rondo*. POULENC:
Presto. RACHMANINOV: *Prelude in G, Op. 32/5*.
Domenico SCARLATTI: *Sonatas, L. 189 & L. 494*.
LISZT: *Mephisto Waltz*.
☞ (B) (★★★) RCA mono 82876 56052-2 (2).

The two famous concerto performances are discussed under their respective composer entries. The
solo recital is of hand-picked items spanning Horowitz's RCA recording career after the early years.
Most were recorded between 1947 and 1957, although
the beautifully played Rachmaninov *Prelude*, Schumann's *Wieck Variations* and the dazzling Liszt
Mephisto Waltz come from the late 1970s, and the
Scarlatti *Sonatas* and Scriabin *D sharp minor Etude*
from the early 1980s. There is some prodigious virtuosity here, notably in the Bizet, Clementi and Poulenc encores, but some lovely lyrical playing too, in
Schumann and Rachmaninov, and delectable delicacy of articulation in Scarlatti. The sound for the
most part is very acceptable.

Hungarian State Orchestra, Mátyás Antal

'*Hungarian Festival*': KODALY: *Háry János: Suite*.
LISZT: *Hungarian Rhapsodies for Orchestra Nos. 1, 2
& 6* (arr. DOEPPLER). HUBAY: *Hejre Kati* (with
Ferenc Balogh). BERLIOZ: *Damnation de Faust:
Rákóczy march*.
(BB) ★★★ Naxos 8.550142.

The Hungarian State Orchestra are in their element
in this programme of colourful music for which they
have a natural affinity. There are few more characterful versions of the *Háry János Suite* and Hubay's
concertante violin piece, with its gypsy flair, is similarly successful, even if the violin soloist is not a
particularly strong personality. The special interest of
the Liszt *Hungarian Rhapsodies* lies in the use of the
Doeppler orchestrations, which are comparatively
earthy, with greater use of brass solos than the more
sophisticated scoring most often used in the West.
The performances are suitably robust and certainly
have plenty of charisma. The brilliant digital recording is strong on primary colours but has atmosphere
too, and produces plenty of spectacle in the Berlioz
Rákóczy march.

Jansen, Janine (violin), Royal Philharmonic Orchestra, Barry Wordsworth

KHACHATURIAN: *Masquerade: Nocturne*. RAVEL:
Tzigane. SAINT-SAENS: *Havanaise; Introduction
and Rondo capriccioso*. SHOSTAKOVICH: *The
Gadfly: Romance*. TCHAIKOVSKY: *Swan Lake:*

Danse russe. VAUGHAN WILLIAMS: *The Lark
Ascending*. John WILLIAMS: *Schindler's List: Theme*.
★★(★) Decca 475 011-2.

This brilliant young Dutch violinist made an impressive British début, playing *The Lark Ascending* at the
second Prom of 2003. She is an artist of exceptional
magnetism, as this mixed bag of a recital demonstrates in every item, from her flamboyant account of
the *Danse russe* from *Swan Lake* onwards. With close
recording balance for both orchestra and soloist,
these are larger-than-life performances, with the two
Saint-Saëns showpieces, *Havanaise* as well as the
Introduction and Rondo capriccioso, prompting the
widest expressive and dynamic range. Vaughan Williams's *Lark Ascending* is fresh and open rather than
meditative, while Ravel's *Tzigane* in its concentration
has the feeling of an improvisation. It will be good to
hear Jansen in more substantial works.

Jensen, Thomas (conducting various orchestras)

'*Scandanavian Classics*' (with (i) Copenhagen PO,
(ii) Royal Danish O; (iii) Tivoli Concert Hall O;
(iv) Eskdale; (v) Danish State R. O; (vi) Andersen):
(i) GADE: *Echoes of Ossian Overture, Op. 1*. J. P. E.
HARTMANN: *Triumphal March of the Nordic Gods*.
HENRIQUES: *Voelund the Smith: Prelude*.
HOFFDING: *Det er ganske vist (Once Upon a Time)*.
LANGE-MULLER: *Prelude to Renaissance*. NIELSEN:
(ii) *Little Suite for Strings, Op. 1; Helios Overture,
Op. 17*; (iii) *Saul & David, Act II Prelude*. RIISAGER:
Little Overture for Strings; (iv; v) *Concertino for
Trumpet and Strings*; (ii) *Slaraffenland (Fools'
Paradise)*. (iii) SIBELIUS: *Finlandia, Op. 26; Valse
triste, Op. 44/1; Valse lyrique, Op. 96a*. (v; vi)
SVENDSEN: *Romance for Violin and Orchestra, Op.
26*. TARP: *Mosaik Suite*.
(★★★) Danacord mono DACOCD 523/524 (2).

Thomas Jensen's post-war Nielsen LPs are well represented on CD. This generously filled two-CD set
collects some of his pre-vinyl records from the late
1930s and 1940s, including Nielsen's *Little Suite for
Strings*, Op. 1, eloquently played by the Royal Danish
Orchestra, and the *Helios Overture*. Jensen himself
played under Nielsen and also heard Sibelius conduct
Finlandia and *Valse triste* when he visited Copenhagen in 1925 to give the first Danish performance of
the *Seventh Symphony*. His pioneering (1939) account
of Svendsen's *Romance* with Carlo Andersen, leader
of the Royal Orchestra, as soloist – recorded, incidentally, the day before the German invasion of Poland –
is refreshingly free from cloying sentiment. It is a
measure of the popularity of Riisager's *Slaraffenland
(Fools' Paradise)* in the 1940s that there were two
versions of it on 78s. *Slaraffenland* inhabits the
vaudeville world of Satie or *Les Six* and was perhaps
an echo of the days Riisager spent in Paris in the
1920s. (Jensen's 1937 recording omits three move-

ments.) George Eskdale, whose Haydn concerto was one of the mainstays of the shellac catalogue, recorded Riisager's *Concertino for Trumpet and Strings* in 1949, and it was not seriously challenged until Håkan Hardenberger came along. Finn Høffding, whose pupils, incidentally, included Vagn Holmboe, lived to be 98 and is best known by his short tone-poem, *Det er ganske vist*, a brilliant orchestral showpiece, which, in a just world, would be a well-known repertory piece. Not everything here is of interest: the *Prelude* to *Vølund Smed* by Fini Henriques is pretty thin stuff, and the same goes for the Lange-Müller and J. P. E. Hartmann pieces. A very welcome issue all the same, with admirably straightforward, no-nonsense transfers.

Johnson, Emma (clarinet)

Disc 1: Concertos (with ECO): MOZART: *Concerto in A, K.488* (cond. Leppard). CRUSELL: *Concerto No. 2 in F min., Op. 5.* BAERMANN (attrib. WAGNER): *Adagio in D* (both cond. Groves). ARNOLD: *Concerto No. 2, Op. 115* (cond. Bolton).

Disc 2: Recital: READE: *The Victorian Kitchen Garden (suite)* (with Kanga, harp). RIMSKY-KORSAKOV: *Flight of the Bumblebee.* RACHMANINOV: *Vocalise, Op. 34/12.* MILHAUD: *Scaramouche.* SATIE: *Gymnopédie No. 1.* GERSHWIN (arr. COHN): *3 Preludes.* MACDOWELL (arr. ISAAC): *To a Wild Rose.* BLAKE: *The Snowman: Walking in the Air.* BENJAMIN: *Jamaican Rumba* (all with Drake, piano). SCHUMANN: *Fantasiestücke, Op. 73.* DEBUSSY: *La fille aux cheveux de lin.* RAVEL: *Pavane pour une infante défunte* (with Black, piano). FINZI: *5 Bagatelles, Op. 23* (with Martineau, piano).

(M) *** ASV CDDCS 238 (2).

Emma Johnson's recording of Bernhard Crusell's *Second Concerto* made her a star and earned a Rosette for the original disc (ASV CDDCA 559), coupled with Baermann's rather beautiful *Adagio* (once attributed to Wagner) and music of Rossini and Weber. In return she put Crusell's engagingly light-weight piece firmly on the map, and later went on to record its two companion works (ASV CDDCA 784 – see our main volume). Here it comes coupled with Malcolm Arnold and her magnetic performance of the greatest clarinet concerto of all, by Mozart.

The solo pieces on the second CD derive from several compilations recorded over the last decade, two of which are listed below under Instrumental Recitals. But many will find the present collection works well as an ongoing recital, as it covers such a wide range. Highlights include her heartfelt account of the Schumann *Fantasy Pieces*, and the 5 *Bagatelles* of Gerald Finzi. The charming – almost Ravelian – douceur of Paul Reade's *Victorian Kitchen Garden Suite* is matched by the simplicity of MacDowell's *To a Wild Rose*; and the famous *Snowman* theme is

hauntingly presented. There is plenty of virtuosity too – *Scaramouche* is uninhibitedly scatty – the rhythmic sparkle here and in the *Jamaica Rumba* is delightful, and Rimsky's *Bumblebee* is almost jet-propelled. The various pianists all accompany help-fully and the recording is excellent.

Kam, Sharon (clarinet)

'American Classics' (with LSO, Gregor Buhl): BERNSTEIN: *Prelude, Fugue and Riffs.* COPLAND: *Clarinet Concerto.* GERSHWIN: *Summertime; They all Laughed; The Man I Love; I Got Rhythm.* GOULD: *Derivations for Clarinet and Band.* ARTIE SHAW: *Clarinet Concerto.*

(*) Teldec 8573 88482-2.

This unique collection of American works involving the clarinet is brilliantly performed, but the record-ing is so unrelentingly aggressive that it makes you feel you are shut up in a matchbox with a group of very loud and persistent performers. The acoustic of the Olympic Studios in London is close and dry, which may suit jazz, the music which inspires all these items; but they are works which demand more subtlety, with light and shade and a dynamic more varied than perpetual *fortissimo*. For all the virtuosity and understanding of idiom from Sharon Kam, it is hard to enjoy these performances. Even in the won-derfully smoochy melody which opens the *Clarinet Concerto*, written by Copland for Benny Goodman, Kam's playing is made to sound sour and unpleasant, with any sort of expressiveness undermined. The LSO strings equally are made to sound thin and dry. The Bernstein *Prelude, Fugue and Riffs* is certainly energetic, but misses any finer qualities. The second of the four movements of Morton Gould's *Deriva-tions* is a 'slowly moving contrapuntal blues', but it is made to sound neither warm nor moving but depressingly arid. Rhythmic control in the fast music here and throughout the disc cannot be faulted, but how wearing it all is. A pity, when not only the Gould but a work like Artie Shaw's *Clarinet Concerto* – conventional in its style but a skilful mix of jazz and classical procedures – are rarities in the classical catalogue.

Karajan Edition (EMI)

The Berlin years

BEETHOVEN: *Piano Concertos Nos. 3 in C min., Op. 37; 5 in E flat (Emperor), Op. 73.*
Alexis Weissenberg, BPO ((ADD) 5 66091-2).

BEETHOVEN: (i) *Piano Concerto No. 4 in G, Op. 58;* (ii) *Triple Concerto in C, Op. 56.*
(i) Alexis Weissenberg; (ii) David Oistrakh,
  Rostropovich, Richter; BPO ((ADD) 5 66092-2).

MOZART: *Symphonies Nos. 40; 41 (Jupiter).
Rehearsal extracts.*

BPO ((ADD) 5 66100-2).

Karajan's period with EMI, after he had left Decca, was less consistently successful than his later, DG era, when he probably reached the peak of his recording career. Some collectors will resist the sumptuous orchestral sound he was given in the works of Mozart, where we are now accustomed to more transparent textures. In the Beethoven concertos he was not well partnered by Weissenberg. These recordings are separate issues and rate between two and three stars.

King, Thea (clarinet)

'*The Clarinet in Concert*': BRUCH: *Double Concerto in E min. for Clarinet, Viola and Orchestra, Op. 88* (with Imai). MENDELSSOHN: *2 Concert Pieces for Clarinet and Basset Horn in F min., Op. 113; in D min., Op. 114* (with Dobrée). CRUSELL: *Introduction and Variations on a Swedish Air, Op. 12* (all 4 works with LSO, Francis). SPOHR: *Variations in B flat for Clarinet and Orchestra on a Theme from Alruna.*
RIETZ: *Clarinet Concerto in G min., Op. 29.*
SOLÈRE: *Sinfonie Concertante in F for 2 Clarinets* (with Dobrée). HEINZE: *Konzertstück in F* (all with ECO, Judd or Litton).

(B) ★★★ Hyp. Dyad CDD 22017 (2).

A thoroughly engaging programme of little-known music (the Bruch is not even listed in the *New Grove*), all played with skill and real charm, and excellently recorded. The Bruch *Double Concerto* is particularly individual, but the two attractive Mendelssohn concert pieces (each in three brief movements) and the quixotic Crusell *Variations* are by no means insubstantial. They are discussed more fully under their composer entries in our main volume. The novelties on the second disc are slighter but no less entertaining: the jaunty Spohr *Variations* followed by the galant concerto by Julius Rietz (1812–77) with its engaging lyrical flow. In Etienne Solère's *Sinfonie concertante*, one cannot help but smile at the garrulous chatter between the two solo instruments, which evokes the clinking of teacups, while Gustav Heinze's warmly tuneful *Konzertstück* has a jocular, Hummelian finale to match the bouncing closing Rondeau of the Solère. The playing brings many chortling roulades and a seductive timbre from the ever-stylish Thea King, and Georgina Dobrée is a nimble partner in the *Sinfonie concertante*. The accompaniments are excellent too, while the recording has fine range and presence.

Kleiber, Erich

'*Decca Recordings, 1949–1955*': BEETHOVEN:
Symphonies Nos. 3 in E flat (Eroica), Op. 55; (2

versions, with Concg. O and VPO); *5 in C min., Op. 67; 6 in F (Pastoral), Op. 68* (both with LPO); *7 in A, Op. 92* (with Concg. O); *9 in D min. (Choral), Op. 125* (with Gueden, Wagner, Dermota, Wever, Singverein der Gesellschaft der Musikfreunde, VPO). WEBER: *Symphony No. 1 in C, Op. 19.*
MOZART: *Symphonies Nos. 39 in E flat, K.543; 4 German Dances* (with Cologne RSO); *40 in D min., K.550* (with LPO). SCHUBERT: *Symphony No. 9 in C (Great), D.944.*

(M) (★★(★)) Decca mono 475 6080 (6).

Kleiber's series of legendary Beethoven recordings was one of the highlights of the early LP era: indeed, the 1953 performance of the *Fifth Symphony* was virtually top choice until his son Carlos made his famous stereo version for DG, recording some 20 years later. Erich Kleiber's vision of Beethoven is profoundly classical, taut but never hard-driven, and he always leaves the listener feeling that his is the only possible way of playing these masterpieces. If many European orchestras in the immediate post-war period and up to the mid-1950s were not at their peak, any blemishes are swept away by the power of the music-making. Two versions of the *Eroica* are included here; the Vienna account dates from 1955 but was not issued until 1959 because the woodwind balance was imperfect and the horns were also backward. That said, no other apologies need be made, and the spacious acoustics of the Musikvereinsaal spread the sound and help cushion the rather thin violins above the stave. The performance is in every way outstanding – even more intense and dramatic than his earlier, Concertgebouw version (good though it is to have and to compare) – and it includes the repeat of the exposition in the first movement, making the whole structure more powerfully monumental. The electricity of the performance is maintained throughout, with the *Funeral March* deeply felt, the mood lightened in the Scherzo, and the finale making an apotheosis.

Decca released Erich Kleiber's 1953 accounts of the *Fifth* and *Sixth Symphonies* on CD in 1987, but this new transfer is much better, with greater warmth and richness. The *Seventh* was recorded in 1950 and is a little thin in sound, with the string-tone a shade astringent, as many recordings of this period were, but not too bad. In the slow movement Kleiber uses a controversial pizzicato ending, a curious effect (also adopted by his son); the Scherzo has an exhilarating bounce, and throughout this symphony the right sort of tension is maintained.

The *Choral Symphony* dates from 1952 and, with an excellent team of soloists, has the same clear-eyed conception as the rest of the symphonies.

Mozart's *Symphony No. 40* dates from 1949, and here the string-sound is both richer and warmer than in the Beethoven – no doubt largely thanks to the (much missed) Kingsway Hall acoustics. The performance is spontaneous and has the humanity and life for which Kleiber was famous. The orchestral playing is not immaculate: the horns in the third movement and the discipline in the finale can be faulted, but the music-making, as always here, is so alive and sympathetic to make one forgive all.

Symphony No. 39 and the *Four German Dances*, along with the charming Weber *Symphony*, derive from a recorded live broadcast dating from 1956, and although the sound-quality (and sometimes the playing) is not of the best, the music-making is alive, even though the *Four German Dances* are taken a bit too fast: the famous sleigh ride is positively reckless!

The sound, too, in Schubert's *Great C major Symphony*, also taken from a live broadcast in 1953, is not ingratiating (nor is one of the horn notes in the terrifyingly exposed introduction, which goes a little sharp near the end – we are so used to it being heard in perfect studio conditions), but it is good to have Kleiber's impressive conception all the same; unlike many conductors who vary the tempi of this work throughout, especially those who are romantically inclined, Kleiber manages to vary the tension without any slowing down or speeding up and he achieves the same result with no violation of the score whatsoever. The strength of Kleiber's interpretation comes over again and again with a multitude of interpretative problems solved as if they didn't exist. If only he had recorded the work a few years later in stereo with the VPO, it would surely be a legendary account, never out of the catalogue. An important historical set.

Koussevitzky, Serge (double-bass and conductor), see also under Boston Symphony Orchestra

Collection (with (i) Pierre Luboshutz; (ii) Boston SO; (iii) Bernard Zighera, Pierre Luboshutz): BEETHOVEN: (i) *Minuet in G* (arr. Koussevitzky) (ii) *Symphony No. 6 in F (Pastoral)*. (iii) ECCLES: *Largo*. (i) LASKA: *Wiegenlied*. (ii) KOUSSEVITZKY: *Concerto, Op. 3: Andante; Valse miniature*. JOHANN STRAUSS JR: *Wiener Blut; Frühlingsstimmen*.
(M) (★★★) Biddulph mono WHL 019.

In his youth and before he was established as a conductor of international celebrity, Koussevitzky was regarded as the greatest double-bass virtuoso of the age. In 1928–9, in his mid-fifties, he was enticed into the New York studios to record the above with the pianist Bernard Zighera, but he then re-recorded everything with Pierre Luboshutz the following year. These performances confirm that he brought to the double-bass the same lyrical intensity and feeling for line and sonority that distinguished his conducting.

Judging from the two concerto movements included here, he was no great composer, but the 1928 recording of the *Pastoral Symphony* with the Boston Symphony Orchestra is little short of a revelation. As an interpretation it feels just right; generally speaking, it is brisk but totally unhurried, each phrase wonderfully shaped. Given the fact that he never lingers, the paradox is that this performance seems strangely spacious. One young and knowledgeable collector to whom we played this thought it quite simply 'among the best *Pastorals* ever'; moreover the recorded sound is remarkable for its age and comes up very freshly. This disc, though comparatively expensive, is worth it.

Kraggerud, Henning (violin), Razumovsky Symphony Orchestra, Bjarte Engeset

'*Norwegian Violin Favourites*': BULL: *The Herd-girl's Sunday; La Mélancholie* (arr. Kraggerud); *Concerto in E min.: Adagio*. SINDING: *Suite im alten Stil, Op. 10*. SVENSEN: *Romance in G, Op. 26*. HALVORSEN: *Norwegian Dances 1-2; Maiden's Song; The Old Fisherman's Song; Wedding March; Andante religioso*. GRIEG: *I Love Thee* (arr. Kraggerud); *Elegiac Melody: The Last Spring*.
(BB) ★★★ Naxos 8.554497.

Ole Bull, born in Bergen in 1810, was a virtuoso of the traditional Norwegian 'Hardanger' fiddle, which he took to Europe, where he achieved a considerable success in Paris. He was one of the first gatherers of Norwegian folk tunes, which he used in his own music. The opening piece here, *The Herd-girl's Sunday*, with its charming melancholy, is characteristic, but the touching *Adagio* from his *Violin Concerto* shows that he also used his folk material more ambitiously and his influence remained. The best-known piece here, Svensen's disarmingly memorable *Romance*, although more sophisticated in construction, is in a similar melodic vein. Johan Halvorsen continued this tradition and his miniatures are equally attractive, as is the Sinding *Suite*. Henning Kraggerud plays a modern violin, and invests all these pieces with a simplicity of style and a beauty of tone that gives great pleasure, ending with two Grieg favourites, including a transcription of his most famous song. With excellent accompaniments and a most natural sound-balance this collection gives much pleasure.

Krips, Josef (with various orchestras)

MOZART: *Symphonies Nos. 31 in D (Paris), K.297; 39 in E flat, K.543; 40 in G min., K.550* (with LSO); *41 in C (Jupiter)* (with Israel PO). BRAHMS: *Symphony No. 4 in E min., Op. 98*. SCHUBERT: *Symphony No. 8 (Unfinished)*. SCHUMANN: *Symphony No. 4 in D min., Op. 120*. MENDELSSOHN: *Symphony No. 4 (Italian)*. DVORAK: *Cello Concerto in B min., Op. 104* (with Nelsova; all with LSO). BEETHOVEN: *Ah!*

Perfido!. R. STRAUSS: *Salome: Closing Scene* (both with Borkh). TCHAIKOVSKY: *Symphony No. 5 in E min., Op. 64.* HAYDN: *Symphonies Nos. 94 in G (Surprise); 99 in E flat.*

(B) (**) Decca mono/stereo 473 121-2 (5).

This is a disappointing set which does not do Krips full justice. It is not the fault of the (mostly mono) Decca recordings, which are of quality and have been well transferred. But in the 1950s Krips seemed to be able to create spontaneous vitality in his studio recordings only sporadically. Of the Mozart *Symphonies*, the *Paris* is the most lively; but No. 39 is routine. The *Fortieth in G minor* is just about adequate, but the tension in the *Jupiter*, recorded in Israel, is again held very slackly. The slow movement refuses to blossom, while the finale lacks grip. The Brahms *Fourth Symphony* is more successful. It is a straightforward, no-nonsense reading, and the first two movements are very satisfying, with Krips showing that the emotion of the slow movement can speak for itself. But the Scherzo is too strait-laced and the passacaglia finale hardly has the strength that the greatest conductors have brought to it.

The *Unfinished* is one of the highlights of the collection, finely played and full of drama and atmosphere, to anticipate Krips's later, outstanding, stereo version. He also offers a colourful and lively account of Mendelssohn's *Italian Symphony*, making the most of the flowing, sunlit phrases. The LSO plays the tarantella finale with great gusto and crisp staccato – a performance that is as alive to colour as it is to rhythm. The Schumann *Fourth* is also animated, if lightweight.

Zara Nelsova is the passionate soloist in the Dvořák *Cello Concerto*, producing a gloriously radiant sound at any speed, and at any part of the compass. But Krips's accompaniment is far behind her in quality – though, fortunately, not as regards ensemble. So with the soloist carrying the day, this is still very enjoyable. The vocal items with Inge Borkh depend on how you take to this very individual voice, but when we move on to the Vienna Philharmonic's Tchaikovsky *Fifth* – superbly recorded – the symphony refuses to hang together properly under Krips's baton, and the result is frankly dull.

Fortunately, the paired Haydn *Symphonies*, the *Surprise* and No. 99, show Krips back on top form. They are played in the very finest Viennese manner. Krips extracts the very best from his players, and his performances are matched by excellent, early stereo recording, and an ideal balance between wind and strings. Perhaps the performances reach their peak in the beautiful slow movment of the *E flat Symphony* (No. 99), which is especially rich in melodic ideas and in depth of musical thought, but the *Surprise*, too, is highly infectious, and the bright, vivid sound presents both works in their best light.

Larrocha, Alicia de (piano)

'The Art of Alicia de Larrocha' (with various orchestras and conductors):

Disc 1: BACH: *Italian Concerto in F, BWV 971; French Suite No. 6 in E, BWV 817; Chorales: Beloved Jesus, We Are Here; Sanctify Us with thy Goodness* (both arr. Cohen). *Chaconne in D min. from BWV 1004* (arr. Busoni). *Concerto No. 5 in F min., BWV 1056.* HAYDN: *Concerto in D, Hob XVIII/2* (both with London Sinf., David Zinman).

Disc 2: HAYDN: *Andante with Variations in F min., Hob XVII/6.* MOZART: *Sonatas: in A, K.331; in D, K.576.* BEETHOVEN: *7 Bagatelles, Op. 33.* MENDELSSOHN: *Variations sérieuses, Op. 54.*

Disc 3: CHOPIN: *24 Preludes, Op. 28; Berceuse, Op. 57; Piano Concerto No. 2 in F min., Op. 21* (with SRO, Comissiona).

Disc 4: LISZT: *Sonata in B min.* SCHUBERT: *Sonata No. 21 in B flat, D.960; Impromptu in A flat, D.899/4.*

Disc 5: SCHUMANN: *Fantaisie in C min., Op. 17; Allegro, Op. 8; Romance, Op. 28/2; Concerto in A min.* (with RPO, Dutoit).

Disc 6: SOLER: *Sonatas: in G min., SR 42; in D min., SR 15; in F, SR 89.* TURINA: *Zapateado, Op. 8/3.* GRANADOS: *Danzas españolas, Book 2; El pelele.* MONTSALVATGE: *Sonatina para Yvette.* MOMPOU: *Prélude 7 (for Alicia de Larrocha).* ALBENIZ: *Tango, Op. 165/2; Iberia, Book 1.* FALLA: *Fantasia béatica.*

Disc 7: FALLA; *Nights in the Gardens of Spain* (with SRO, Comissiona). KHACHATURIAN: *Concerto* (with LPO, Frühbeck de Burgos). RAVEL: *Piano Concerto for the Left Hand* (with LPO, Foster).

(B) **(*) Decca (ADD/DDD) 473 813-2 (7).

The 2002/3 concert season marked Alicia de Larrocha's eightieth birthday and also her farewell to the concert hall, so Decca's anthology covering her peak years from 1970 onwards is opportune. She usually combined the gift of spontaneity in the studio with excellent support from the Decca engineers. However, at times she could be idiosyncratic, and not all the recordings chosen here show her at her very best.

The programme opens well with her solo Bach recital, for the most part recorded in Decca's West Hampstead studio in 1970. The sound is clear and clean, reflecting her simple style and her desire to present Bach effectively in pianistic terms. The great *Chaconne*, however, recorded two years later in Kingsway Hall, is expansive and romantically very free, reflecting her response to the transformation of Busoni's flamboyant transcription. Then in the Haydn *Concerto*, which completes the first disc, her crisp, clean articulation obviously seeks to evoke the fortepiano, and the sharp rhythmic snap of the 'gypsy' finale is a joy, when David Zinman's accompaniment is excellent and the scale of the recording is so well judged.

She was a natural classicist and Haydn's *Andante and Variations* are thoughtfully played, while in the Mozart *Sonatas* her balance betwen warmth and poise shows a ready sensibility; phrasing is always intelligently pointed and there is an admirable sense of flow. She is equally accomplished in the Mendelssohn *Variations sérieuses*, but here some of her rubati are a shade unconvincing, and this comment could also be applied to her set of Chopin *Préludes*. Yet there is some poetic and imaginative playing too, and the *F minor Concerto* is also attractive and poetic; throughout, the analogue recording is first class.

The Liszt *Sonata* brings some formidable playing, yet, for all the many perceptive touches, she is a little too idiosyncratic for her reading to be included among the finest available versions. However, her performance of the great *B flat major Sonata* of Schubert shows her at her finest. The heart of her reading lies in the slow movement, played introspectively with great poetic feeling. Her poise and crisp articulation in the final two movements also give much pleasure, and if she is rather less successful than, say, Curzon or Kempff in finding the spiritual serenity of the large span of the first movement, hers is still a memorable account, beautifully recorded.

The Schumann *Fantasia in C minor* again brings a very personal reading, perhaps too personal, yet there are many good things in its favour. She is very relaxed indeed in the *A Minor Concerto,* and there are more touches of wilfulness, as in the ritenuto before the recapitulation of the first movement. Poetry is certainly not absent: the interchanges between piano and clarinet are beautifully done, but the lack of overall vitality becomes enervating in the finale, where the basic tempo is too lazy to be convincing.

The encores on the sixth disc are entirely delightful; the *Sonatas* of Soler and the works of Turina, Granados, Albéniz and Falla are her home teritory, and Mompou's *Seventh Prelude* was written for her. The final disc brings a distinguished account of Ravel's *Left-Hand Concerto* and an unsurpassed reading of Falla's *Nights in the Gardens of Spain*, and she then makes the slow movement of the Khachaturian *Concerto* sound evocatively like Falla. The finale too is infectiously jaunty. Not so the first movement, however, which is disappointingly slack in rhythm at a dangerously slow tempo.

The seven records in their cardboard sleeves each carry a different photograph of the pianist, taken over the years during which the recordings were made, which will make this set doubly attractive for her admirers.

Lawson, Colin (clarinet or basset horn), Parley of Instruments, Peter Holman

'*English Classical Clarinet Concertos*': JOHN MAHON: *Concerto No. 2 in F; Duets Nos. 1 & 4 in B flat for 2 Basset Horns* (with Harris). J. C. BACH: *Concerted Symphony in E flat.* JAMES HOOK: *Concerto in E flat.*
** Hyp. CDA 66869.

The clarinet (invented around 1700) did not achieve a strong solo profile until well into the eighteenth century, and even then it was not favoured by amateurs. Mozart remains the only composer of that period to have written really great music for it. Thus, even more than in his companion disc of violin concertos (listed under Wallfisch), Peter Holman has had to scrape the barrel a bit and even include a *Concerted Symphony* by J. C. Bach, which in the event is the most enterprising work here but which features (besides a pair of clarinets) two oboes, a bassoon and two horns. It has a very striking first movement and a touching *Larghetto*, which opens with a bassoon solo; the flute then takes over, and the clarinets enter much later. The most unusual scoring is in the closing Minuet, where in the Trio the woodwind take over entirely.

John Mahon's *Duos* for basset horns are agreeable but sub-Mozart. His *Concerto*, however, goes even further than the contemporary violin concertos (see below), by using a complete Scottish folksong for his ingenious *Andante* and another popular tune (*The wanton God*) for the Rondo finale. James Hook's *Concerto* has little that is individual to say in its conventional and rather long opening movement, yet it includes the prettiest roulades for the clarinet soloist. However, the composer reserves the real fireworks for the final Rondo, especially in the spectacular closing episode, introduced by the horns, where the clarinet ripples hectically up and down its register in a quite abandoned manner. Colin Lawson is fully equal to such bravura and he plays with fine style throughout. Holman provides excellent accompaniments, but it is a pity that the music itself is so uneven.

Lefèvre, Alain (piano), Quebec Symphony Orchestra, Yoav Talmi

20th-Century Piano Concertos: MATHIEU: *Concerto de Québec.* ADDINSELL: *Warsaw Concerto.* GERSHWIN: *Concerto in F.*
** Analekta AN 29814.

André Mathieu's *Concerto de Québec*, written in 1943, in time for the composer's fourteenth birthday, exists in six different scores (!), out of which Alain Lefèvre has fashioned this performing version. It is prodominently romantic, with the undoubtedly memorable slow movement sounding very like film music, yet somehow curiously distinctive in its melodic lyricism. The finale has a perkily rhythmic main theme, and again brings a memorable secondary idea with a distinctly Rachmaninovian flavour, and its passionate climax on the strings is truly in the Rachmaninov/Tchaikovsky concerto tradition. This is not great music, but it is very persuasively played here: Lefèvre is obviously committed to the music and Talmi provides excellent support.

The *Warsaw Concerto* is given an expansive, at times very languorous performance, again very well played, and certainly producing a luscious climax. But some may want more ongoing thrust in the performance overall. Similarly the first movement of the Gershwin is very relaxed, not without its nice touches of rhythmic pointing, but minus the exhilaration one expects from North American performances. This means that the evocative slow movement, warmly played though it is, does not bring the proper degree of contrast, and it is in the zestful finale that Gershwin's witty crossover rhythms come fully into their own. The recording is very good without being in the demonstration bracket.

Leningrad Philharmonic Orchestra, Evgeni Mravinsky

'*Mravinsky in Prague*': BARTOK: *Music for Strings, Percussion and Celesta.* SHOSTAKOVICH: *Symphonies Nos. 5 in D min., Op. 47; 6 in B min., Op. 54; 11 in G min. (The Year 1905), Op. 103; 12 (The Year 1917), Op. 112; Violin Concerto No. 1 in A min., Op. 77* (with Czech PO & D. Oistrakh). PROKOFIEV: *Symphony No. 6 in E flat min., Op. 111.*
(★★★) (M) HM/Praga mono/stereo PR 256016/19 (4).

The performances in this set have been issued previously in various combinations and formats. The first disc couples the Bartók and the Shostakovich *Fifth* in 1967 performances recorded at the Prague Spring Festival. The *Music for Strings, Percussion and Celesta* has suitable intensity, although not as much as that in the Shostakovich *Eleventh Symphony*, recorded in the same year, which occupies the third CD. This is one of the finest performances Mravinsky gave on disc, and it is played flat out with such electricity that criticism is silenced. The second CD brings a 1955 performance of the *Sixth Symphony*, a work he did with extraordinary concentration. It is not the equal of his Melodiya version from the 1960s and, quite apart from the limited mono sound, suffers from intrusive audience noise. The *Twelfth Symphony* comes from 1962, the same year as his Melodiya recording, and he gives it with 500 per cent conviction and frenetic but wonderfully controlled energy. The Shostakovich *First Violin Concerto* with David Oistrakh comes fresh from the press as it were, in 1957, when the piece was being introduced to the world, and, like its pioneering accounts under Mitropoulos and Mravinsky himself, is in mono. His first mono version of the Prokofiev *Sixth* was a classic of the LP catalogue, and this 1967 version, though not perhaps as intense, is still one of the most impressive on CD. The sound is of variable quality throughout, but the playing is mostly in a class of its own.

Leonhardt, Gustav ((i) harpsichord (ii) cond.), Orchestra of the Age of Enlightenment

'*Portrait*': BACH: (i) *English Suite No. 3, BWV 808; Partita No. 1, BWV 825;* (ii) *Double Harpsichord Concerto No. 2 in C, BWV 1061* (with van Asperen, Amsterdam). C. P. E. BACH: *Hamburg Sinfonia, Wq. 183/2.* PURCELL: *Ode for Queen Mary: Love's Goddess Sure was Blind* (with Gooding, Bowman, Robson, Wilson-Johnson and OAE Ch.).
(M) ★★(★) Virgin 5 61400-2.

Leonhardt opens ebulliently with the *G minor English Suite* and he is also at his thoughtful best in the *B flat Partita.* The *Double Harpsichord Concerto* is lively too, although here the resonant acoustic means that the overall sound-picture is less than ideally clear in focus. The other highlight is the lively C. P. E. Bach *Sinfonia,* with its remarkably colourful, though brief, central *Adagio.* The single vocal item, the Purcell *Ode,* brings distinguished solo singing and refined detail, but could ideally be more robust in feeling. Readers wanting to sample Leonhardt's special contribution to the world of baroque music would do better to choose from his own Teldec Edition below, under Instrumental Recitals.

Lindberg, Christian (trombone)

American Trombone Concertos (with BBC Nat. O of Wales, Llewellyn): CHAVEZ: *Concerto.* ROUSE: *Concerto in Memory of Leonard Bernstein.* Augusta Read THOMAS: *Meditation.*
(★★★) BIS CD 788.

By the time he started writing his *Concerto,* Chavez was already in the terminal stages of cancer and his wife had just died. The work opens with an extended morose soliloquy in which the orchestra provides dissonantly pungent support; at times the pacing quickens, but the disconsolate atmosphere remains and, though some percussive intrusions towards the end provide more lively contrast, this music undoubtedly brings longueurs and is essentially depressing.

The *Meditation* by Augusta Read Thomas opens much more positively, with the soloist proceeding over a series of lively orchestral interjections. Bell effects (echoed by the strings) and a percussive spicing add variety, and there is a final eruption of energy. But the meagre musical invention is unenticing.

Easily the finest work here is the concerto by Rouse, which, though darkly atmospheric, readily holds the listener most compellingly. The music climbs up from the lower depths (the opening evocation rather like that at the beginning of the Ravel *Left-hand Piano Concerto*). After an exciting climax the soloist has a ruminative cadenza, before dashing off in a dazzling Scherzo (superb bravura from Lindberg), with the orchestra just about managing to keep up, yet doing so with some panache. There is a series of hair-raising orchestral explosions, followed by a mêlée of urgently volatile brass figurations, which then die away slowly, leading to the touching finale, marked *Elegiaco, lugubre*.

This is designated by Rouse as a memorial to Leonard Bernstein and quotes what is described as the 'Credo' theme from Bernstein's *Third (Kaddish) Symphony*. The movement has an unrelenting thrust and the central orchestral declamation of grief makes a powerful statement, before the soloist steals in with his own gentle and moving valedictory lament. Then, Orpheus-like, he returns into the depths. Superb solo playing throughout this disc, and very fine recording. But the Rouse is the only piece here of real memorability, and it badly needs new couplings.

Classical Trombone Concertos (with Australian Co, Richard Tognetti): Michael HAYDN: *Concerto in D.* Leopold MOZART: *Concerto in D.* WAGENSEIL: *Concerto in E flat.* ALBRECHTSBERGER: *Concerto in B flat.* LINDBERG: *Dreams of Arcadia* (for flute and orchestra) (Bezaly, Swedish CO, Lindberg). GOTHE: *Prelude and Dance* (Swedish Wind Ensemble, Lindberg).
★★★ BIS CD 1248.

These concertos by Michael Haydn and Leopold Mozart are *not* transcriptions of horn concertos, they are genuine classical trombone concertos, almost certainly written for a celebrated Austrian trombone virtuoso, Thomas Gschladt, who was a contemporary and friend of horn player Joseph Leutgeb, for whom Mozart wrote his four horn concertos. The presence of lip trills in the solo parts fooled scholars, as they were not thought possible on a trombone. But subsequently it became clear that such trills were indeed part of the eigthteenth-century trombonist's expertise and, as Christian Lindberg demonstrates here with flair, he positively relishes them.

Michael Haydn's *Concerto* dates from 1764 and was almost certainly written for Gschladt. It consists of three movements of a ten-movement work which included a solo trombone in three of them, and was later published as a *Divertimento in D*. The brilliant opening *Allegro spiritoso* is very spirited, the thoughtful central *Andantino* (with plenty of trills) was admired by Mozart, and it is followed by a sprightly closing *Presto*, where the orchestra's principal horn (probably Leutgeb at the first performance) joins the trombone in amiable duetting.

Leopold Mozart's three concertante movements are also part of a larger work, a *Serenade* which already (in 1755) had two movements for trumpet, to which (on hearing Gschladt play) Leopold added three more especially for this astonishing early virtuoso. He included a spectacular cadenza in the first movement and an all but Romantic central *Andante*, which Lindberg plays very beautifully. The closing *Presto* skips along winningly and the clipped solo articulation here is most diverting.

Wagenseil's *Two Movements for Trombone* are of more doubtful origin (although Gschladt may have been associated with their provenance). They are agreeable enough, the first a modest march, the second more animated and demanding. But neither this nor the three-movement *Concerto* by Johann Albrechtsberger rises much above a routine level, except for the brief, jolly finale of the latter, which would make a good encore.

Christian Lindberg's performances of all four works are outstanding. He shows total mastery of his instrument and his virtuosity is audacious, while his elegant phrasing and stylish use of dynamic contrast conquers the more conventional writing. The accompaniments from Richard Tognetti and his Australian Chamber Orchestra are admirable, and the recording is most convincingly balanced. The two bonus items are samplers of two other CD collections, where Christian Lindberg takes over the conductor's podium. The excerpt from his own concertante work for flute (sensitively played by Sharon Bezaly) introduces some seductive bird-sounds; the *Prelude and Dance* by Mats Larsson Gothe is altogether less genial, rhythmically persistent but with a wide range of sonority and colour. It is presented with great conviction, and both are very well recorded.

Lipatti, Dinu (piano)

'*The Legacy of Dinu Lipatti*' (with Boulanger; Philh. O, Zürich Tonhalle O, Lucerne Festival O; Galliera, Ackermann, Karajan): BACH: *Chorale, Jesu, Joy of Man's Desiring* (arr. HESS, from BWV 147); *Chorale Preludes, BWV 599 & 639* (both arr. BUSONI); *Partita No. 1, BWV 825; Siciliana* (arr. KEMPFF, from BWV 1031). D. SCARLATTI: *Sonatas, Kk. 9 & 380.* MOZART: *Piano Concerto No. 21 in C, K.467; Piano Sonata No. 8 in A min., K.310.* SCHUBERT: *Impromptus Nos. 2–3, D.899/2 & 3.* SCHUMANN: *Piano Concerto in A min., Op. 54.* GRIEG: *Piano Concerto in A min., Op. 16.* CHOPIN: *Piano Concerto No. 1 in E min., Op. 11; Barcarolle, Op. 60; Etudes, Op. 10/5 & 25/5; Mazurka No. 32, Op. 50/3; Nocturne No. 8, Op. 27/2; Piano Sonata No. 3 in B min., Op. 58; Waltzes Nos. 11–4.* LISZT: *Années de pèlerinage, 2nd Year: Sonetto 104 del Petrarca.* RAVEL: *Alborada del gracioso.* BRAHMS: *Waltzes (4 hands), Op. 39/1–2, 5–6, 10, 14–15.* ENESCU: *Piano Sonata No. 3 in D, Op. 25.*
۞ (M) (★★★) EMI mono 7 67163-2 (5).

This set represents Lipatti's major recording achievements. Whether in Bach (*Jesu, joy of man's desiring* is unforgettable) or Chopin – his *Waltzes* seem to have grown in wisdom and subtlety over the years – Scarlatti or Mozart, these performances are very special indeed. The remastering is done well, and this is a must for anyone with an interest in the piano.

Lloyd Webber, Julian (cello)

'*Favourite Cello Concertos*': DVORAK: *Concerto in B min., Op. 104* (with Czech PO, Neumann). TCHAIKOVSKY: *Variations on a Rococo Theme* (original version), *Op. 33* (with RPO, Cleobury). FAURE: *Elégie, Op. 24.* SAINT-SAENS: *Concerto No. 1 in A min., Op. 33; Allegro appassionato, Op. 43* (with ECO, Yan Pascal Tortelier). *Carnaval des animaux: Le cygne* (with ECO, Cleobury). ELGAR: *Concerto in E min., Op. 68* (with RPO, Menuhin); *Romance in D min., Op. 62* (with ASMF, Marriner); *Idylle, Op. 4/1* (arr. for cello and organ). ALBINONI: *Adagio* (arr. GIAZOTTO). SCHUMANN: *Kinderszenen: Träumerei* (arr. PARKER). BACH: *Cantata No. 147: Jesu, Joy of Man's Desiring.* RIMSKY-KORSAKOV: *Flight of the Bumblebee.* BACH/GOUNOD: *Ave Maria* (all with ECO or RPO, Cleobury). Julian LLOYD WEBBER: *Jackie's Song.* (M) *** Ph. (ADD) 462 115-2 (2).

Lloyd Webber is at his finest in the Elgar *Concerto*. Nor is there any lack of intensity in the Dvořák, a strong and warmly sympathetic reading. He has the advantage of Menuhin to direct the RPO most idiomatically in the former, and the Dvořák specialist, Neumann, with the Czech Philharmonic to accompany him in the latter. The Czech orchestral attack has fine bite and the clipped style of articulation brings out the folk element. The horn soloist plays the great second-subject melody with a degree of vibrato but he is a fine artist, and Lloyd Webber's playing is marked by a ripe, rich tone. Intonation is excellent, but the soloist's occasional easing of tempi may not appeal to some listeners.

Both Saint-Saëns works are played with considerable virtuosity, and again there is the advantage of a first-class accompaniment, from Yan Pascal Tortelier and the ECO. Tchaikovsky's original score is used for the *Rococo Variations*, which is presented affectionately and elegantly. All in all, if the various encores also appeal, this is an attractive enough package, very well recorded in Philips's most natural manner. *Jackie's song*, Lloyd Webber's catchy little tribute to Jacqueline du Pré, is added as an ardent postscript.

'*Cello Moods*' (with RPO, James Judd): FRANCK: *Panis angelicus.* ELGAR: *Chanson de matin; Salut d'amour.* Julian LLOYD WEBBER: *Jackie's song.* DEBUSSY: *Rêverie.* BACH: *Suite No 3: Air.* MASSENET: *Thaïs: Méditation.* CACCINI: *Ave Maria.* BORODIN: *Nocturne.* GLAZUNOV: *Mélodie, Op. 20/1.* CHOPIN: *Nocturne, Op. 9/2.* BOCCHERINI: *Cello Concerto: Adagio.* RHEINBERGER: *Cantilena.* BRUCH: *Kol Nidrei.* *** Ph. 462 588-2.

Decorated with extraordinary artwork by Jane Powell which shows an unclothed cellist covered only with shadowy music staves (the cello hiding any suggestion of immodesty), this collection of lollipops is obviously aimed at the crossover market. The playing is of high quality, with none of these famous tunes sentimentalized. Franck's *Panis angelicus* and Massenet's *Méditation* here sound almost noble on the cello. The other highlights are the charming Glazunov *Mélodie*, the Rheinberger *Cantilena*, and the very eloquent Max Bruch *Kol Nidrei*. If you enjoy this kind of programme it couldn't be better played or recorded.

London Gabrieli Brass Ensemble, Christopher Larkin

Original 19th-century Music for Brass: BEETHOVEN: *3 Equales for 4 Trombones.* CHERUBINI: *Trois pas redoublés et la première marche; Trois pas redoublés et la seconde marche.* DAVID: *Nonetto in C min.* DVORAK: *Fanfare.* LACHNER: *Nonet in F.* RIMSKY-KORSAKOV: *Notturno for 4 Horns.* SIBELIUS: *Overture in F min.: Allegro; Andantino; Menuetto; Praeludium.* *** Hyp. CDA 66470.

'*From the Steeples and the Mountains*': IVES: *From the Steeples and the Mountains; Let there be Light.* BARBER: *Mutations from Bach.* HARRIS: *Chorale for Organ and Brass.* VIRGIL THOMSON: *Family Portrait.* COWELL: *Grinnell Fanfare; Tall Tale; Hymn and Fuguing Tune No. 12; Rondo.* GLASS: *Brass Sextet.* RUGGLES: *Angels.* CARTER: *A Fantasy upon Purcell's Fantasia about One Note.* (BB) *** Hyp. Helios CDH 55018.

It is difficult to decide which of these two programmes is the more enterprising and the more rewarding. If you are responsive to brass sonorities and you acquire one of them, you will surely want its companion. Beethoven's *Equales* were used at the composer's funeral. They are brief, but noble and dignified. The Sibelius suite is folksy, uncharacteristic writing, but has genuine charm.

The second concert opens and closes with the always stimulating music of Charles Ives. *From the Steeples and the Mountains* is scored for four sets of bells, trumpet and trombones, and its effect is clangorously wild! Elliott Carter's Purcell arrangement also has tolling bells, and is quite haunting. Of the other pieces the most striking is the Barber *Mutations*, which draws on the chorale *Christe du Lamm Gottes* to highly individual effect. Most passionate of all is Ruggles's pungently compressed, muted brass *Angels*, yet the piece is marked 'Serene'! The brass playing throughout the two discs is as communicative as it is expert and the recording is splendidly realistic and present.

London Baroque, Terence Charlston (harpsichord/chamber organ)

'The Trio Sonata in 17th-Century England':
GIBBONS: *3 Fantasias a 3.* COPRARIO: *Fantasia Suite.* LAWES: *Sett No. 1.* JENKINS: *Fancy & Ayre; Fantasia a 3.* LOCKE: *Suite in D min.* SIMPSON: *(Suite) in D.* BLOW: *Ground in G min.; Sonata in A.* PURCELL: *Sonata XX in D.*
**(*) BIS CD 1455.

A well-played and -recorded collection of trio sonatas from the seventeenth century. It is all gently pleasing but, with a preponderance of generally quite slow music, not desperately exciting. The chamber organ contributions in some of the items make for a nice tonal contrast, and overall this makes for ideal 'relaxing' listening, perhaps best not played all in one go.

London Philharmonic Orchestra, Sir Thomas Beecham

HANDEL, arr. Beecham: *The Great Elopement* (ballet). HAYDN: *Symphony No. 97 in C.* MOZART: *Serenade (Eine kleine Nachtmusik); La clemenza di Tito: Overture.*
(**) Biddulph mono WHL 041.

BEETHOVEN: *Symphony No. 4 in B flat, Op. 60.* MOZART: *Die Entführung aus dem Serail: Overture.* SCHUBERT: *Symphony No. 6 in C, D.589.*
(**) Biddulph mono WHL 042.

BERLIOZ: *Les Troyens: Royal Hunt and Storm; Trojan March.* BORODIN: *Prince Igor: Overture.* MENDELSSOHN: *Symphony No. 5 in D min. (Reformation), Op. 107.* RIMSKY-KORSAKOV: *May Night: Overture.* TCHAIKOVSKY: *Eugene Onegin: Waltz; Polonaise.*
(**) Biddulph mono WHL 043.

These three discs are most welcome for filling in the least-known period of Beecham's recording activities, towards the end of the Second World War, working with the newly self-governing LPO, before he founded the RPO. These recordings had a sadly brief period in the catalogue and, unlike Beecham's pre-war recordings, have remained in limbo ever since.

The second of the three discs, coupling Mozart, Beethoven and Schubert, is the most substantial. Beecham's account of Beethoven's *Fourth Symphony* – a work he never returned to on record – has great flair and vitality, with fierceness set alongside

elegance. The *Entführung Overture* here is very similar to the one in his classic recording of the complete opera, but with a concert ending.

This 1944 version of Schubert's *Sixth* was a first recording, differing from his RPO remake in that the outer movements are faster, and the middle two broader, notably the *Andante.* On the first disc, the finale of *Eine kleine Nachtmusik* in this 1945 version is more an *Allegretto* than an *Allegro*, idiosyncratically slow but deliciously sprung. In the *Clemenza overture*, originally issued by Victor, not HMV, Beecham takes a lightweight view, as though this is early Mozart, but the Haydn *97th Symphony* comes in a typically alert reading, with fierceness and elegance set in contrast, rather as in the Beethoven. The Biddulph transfers here lack sufficient body to sustain the top emphasis. That is very evident when one compares this transfer of the Handel–Beecham *Great Elopement* recording with the Dutton version.

On the third disc the sound for the Beecham lollipops – delectably done – is still thin, but the 1945 version of Mendelssohn's *Reformation Symphony* is generally better, with the brass full, bright and well separated, and with gentle string *pianissimos* (as in the '*Dresden Amen*') beautifully caught. A valuable trio of discs which should be considered by Beecham devotees despite the reservations over the transfers and the fact that they are not inexpensive.

(i) London Philharmonic Orchestra or (ii) BBC Symphony Orchestra, Sir Thomas Beecham

(i) RIMSKY-KORSAKOV: *May Night Overture.* BERLIOZ: *The Trojans: Royal Hunt and Storm; Trojan March.* MENDELSSOHN: *Symphony No. 5 in D min. (Reformation), Op. 107.* BORODIN: *Prince Igor: Overture.* (ii) SIBELIUS: *Karelia Suite, Op. 11.* REZNICEK: *Donna Diana: Overture.*
(B) (***) Dutton Lab mono CDEA 5508.

All these excellent transfers come from 1945, before Beecham had formed the RPO. The *Royal Hunt and Storm* from the *The Trojans* and Rimsky-Korsakov's *May Night Overture* are characteristic of Beecham, and his guest appearances with the BBC Symphony Orchestra produced excellent accounts of the *Intermezzo* and *Alla marcia* from the *Karelia Suite* and the delightful *Donna Diana Overture* of Reznicek, which has not appeared before. Was its release delayed because, a year or so later, Karajan recorded it with the Vienna Philharmonic for Columbia? Sir Thomas's account of the *Reformation Symphony* does not, however, show him at his very best (the *Allegro vivace* movement is just a bit too fast). Excellent transfers.

London Philharmonic Orchestra, Sir Adrian Boult

'The Boult Historic Collection'

George BUTTERWORTH: *A Shropshire Lad* (rhapsody); *The Banks of Green Willow* (idyll). BAX: *Tintagel* (tone-poem). HOLST: *The Perfect Fool* (ballet suite). VAUGHAN WILLIAMS: *Old King Cole* (ballet). ELGAR: *Chanson de nuit; Chanson de matin, Op. 15/1–2.*
(BB) (***) Belart mono 461 354-2.

Butterworth's two beautiful evocations of the English countryside have wonderful delicacy of texture and feeling, while Bax's *Tintagel* is both evocative and passionately full-blooded at its climax. Holst's *Perfect Fool* ballet suite sounds remarkably fresh and vivid, and Vaughan Williams's *Old King Cole* (taken from another ballet, of 1923) is both jolly and boisterous, as befits the image of that famous nursery-rhyme monarch. Elgar's paired miniatures of morning and night have characteristically affectionate warmth, and here the full ambience of the recording might almost be mistaken for stereo.

London Symphony Orchestra, Karl Boehm

'In Salzburg 1973/7': BEETHOVEN: *Symphony No. 7 in A.* BRAHMS: *Symphony No. 2.* MOZART: *Symphonies Nos. 28 in C, K.328; 38 in D (Prague); Violin Concerto No. 7 in D, K.271* (with Szeryng, violin); SCHUMANN: *Symphony No. 4; Piano Concerto in A min.* (with Gilels, piano); Richard STRAUSS: *Death and Transfiguration.*
(M) **(*) Andante RE-A-4030 (4).

It was the most unexpected of musical love-affairs – between Karl Boehm, fierce upholder of the German-Austrian tradition, and the London Symphony Orchestra, in 1973 riding high to the point of arrogance. The rehearsal of the very first item, Brahms's *Second Symphony*, set the pattern, and after the concert, which also included Mozart's *Haffner Symphony* and the doubtfully authentic *Violin Concerto No. 7*, with Henryk Szeryng as soloist, the message came back from Boehm that he had rarely known an orchestra so warmly responsive. He conducted the LSO again on their next Salzburg visit in 1975, and a third time in 1977, by which time the love affair had so developed that the players voted to have the old man as their honorary president.

Those seminal occasions are now preserved on these four discs in excellent transfers of Austrian Radio recordings. Consistently there is an extra warmth and a degree more flexibility in the performances compared with those that Boehm made in the studio, usually with the Berlin Philharmonic or the Vienna Philharmonic. In the Brahms (which

Boehm never recorded in the studio) the recording reveals a crescendo of tension, while Boehm's Mozart with the LSO is lighter and more elegant than in his studio recordings, and in Beethoven's *Seventh Symphony* the Salzburg performance is markedly more joyful in the fast movements and less square in the *Allegretto* slow movement. In Schumann's *Fourth Symphony* Boehm's measured speeds are controlled so subtly that again squareness is avoided, while Emil Gilels gives a warmly magisterial account of the *A minor Piano Concerto*, crisply lightened in the central intermezzo. Strauss's *Death and Transfiguration*, in the 1977 concert, has an irresistible glow. What consistently emerges throughout is not just the brilliance of the LSO woodwind and brass but the refinement and the resonance of the strings.

London Symphony Orchestra, Antal Dorati

ENESCU: *Romanian Rhapsody No. 2.* BRAHMS: *Hungarian Dances Nos. 1–7; 10–12; 15; 17–21; Variations on a Theme of Haydn, Op. 56a.*
(M) ** Mercury (ADD) [434 326-2].

Dorati is completely at home in the Enescu *Second Rhapsody* (played passionately – but, as music, not nearly as memorable as No. 1) and the Brahms *Hungarian Dances*, where he captures a true Hungarian spirit. When he takes a piece faster than expected, one does not feel he is being wilful or intent on showing off, but simply that he and his players are enjoying themselves. If the delicious rubato in No. 7 does not spell enjoyment, one would be very surprised. The recording, made at either Watford or Wembley, sounds firmer and cleaner than on LP. The *Variations* are enjoyable but not distinctive.

London Symphony Orchestra, Skitch Henderson

'Children's Classics' PROKOFIEV: *Peter and the Wolf, Op. 67* (narrative revised). SAINT-SAENS: *Carnival of the Animals* (with verses by Nash, and animals from the London Zoo; both with Lillie). TRAD. (arr. Sharples): 'Uncle Ken's Nursery Rhymes' (with McKellar, and orchestral accompaniment directed by Sharples).
**(*) Australian Decca Eloquence (ADD) 466 673-2.

This collection includes a fascinating early LP version of *Peter and the Wolf* involving a 'cabaret act' by Beatrice Lillie to words by 'Bidrum Vabish' (a pseudonym for John Culshaw), full of asides and additions like 'The cat climbed up the tree *before you could say Prokofiev'.* The original LP was most notable for the correspondence it provoked (after the record's review in *The Gramophone*) between Mr Culshaw Vabish and Vetrov Hayver (Guess who!). Curious older readers are referred to the issues of

November and December 1960.

The orchestral part of the performance is rather less than distinguished, but the conductor adopts a determined and unflagging pace, and after all it is Miss Lillie's record, and its enjoyment depends on whether or not you take to her rather arch contribution and the new text which she undoubtedly points up in lively fashion, as she does with the words (by Ogden Nash) which are a superfluous addition to Saint-Saëns's witty menagerie.

The grafted-on animal noises which set the scene for the *Carnival* were recorded at London Zoo: the lion's roar at the beginning is startling to say the least! What also makes this disc of interest is that Julius Katchen and Gary Graffman, no less, are the pianists, and the Decca sound from the early 1960s, which is remarkably vivid. The fill-up is a charming medley of the A–Z of nursery rhymes, inimitably sung by Kenneth McKellar, with nicely detailed orchestral accompaniments by Robert Sharples – it will appeal to children of all ages. A collectors' item.

London Symphony Orchestra, Sir Georg Solti

'*Romantic Russia*': GLINKA: *Ruslan and Ludmilla Overture.* MUSSORGSKY: *Khovanshchina: Prelude; Night on the Bare Mountain* (arr. RIMSKY-KORSAKOV). BORODIN: *Prince Igor: Overture and Polovtsian Dances* (with LSO Ch.). TCHAIKOVSKY: *Symphony No. 2 (Little Russian), Op. 17* (with Paris Conservatoire O).

✪ (M) ★★★ Decca Legends (ADD) 460 977-2.

This was a demonstration record in its day and the analogue recording remains of Decca's vintage quality, with marvellous detail and a warm ambience. The account of the *Ruslan and Ludmilla Overture* is justly famous for its sheer brio, and Solti's *Polovtsian Dances* are as exciting as any in the catalogue with a splendid contribution from the LSO Chorus. The *Prince Igor Overture* is warmly romantic, yet has plenty of fire and spontaneity, and a lovely horn solo. *Night on the Bare Mountain* makes a forceful impact, but brings a tender closing section.

Solti also recorded the evocative *Khovanshchina Prelude* with the Berlin Philharmonic Orchestra around the same time, and that had marginally more lustre, but the LSO create plenty of atmospheric tension. The performance of Tchaikovsky's *Little Russian Symphony* has been added for this reissue. It dates from the late 1950s and the recording is noticeably less opulent. After a commanding opening, there is no lack of vitality, and the delightful slow movement is affectionately shaped. The Scherzo lacks something in elegance and charm (partly the fault of the French orchestral playing) but the finale certainly does not lack adrenalin. Overall this is surprisingly memorable and makes a splendid addition to Decca's 'Legends' series.

(i) London Symphony Orchestra; (ii) Royal Philharmonic Orchestra, (iii) Anatole Fistourlari; (iv) Gaston Poulet

'*French Favourites*': (i; iii) POULENC: *Les Biches (ballet suite).* (ii-iii) *Aubade* (choreographic concerto for piano and 18 instruments). DEBUSSY: *Fantaisie for Piano and Orchestra* (both with Jacquinot, piano). (i; iv) RAVEL: *Alborada del gracioso; Une barque sur l'océan.*

(B) ★★★ Dutton Lab. mono CDEA 5501.

Here are some splendidly fresh performances from the early-1950s Parlophone label. Expert and attractive accounts of *Alborada del gracioso* and *Une barque sur l'océan* from the LSO under Gaston Poulet are coupled with two Poulenc works: a sparkling and vivacious *Les Biches* from Fistoulari and the same orchestra, and a captivating *Aubade* with Fabienne Jacquinot. She is hardly less persuasive in Debussy's neglected *Fantaisie*, both with the RPO (billed on the LP at the time, as older collectors will remember, as the Westminster Symphony Orchestra for contractual reasons). In any event, these are thoroughly delightful performances and few allowances need be made, for the recorded sound is little short of amazing.

Long Beach Symphony Orchestra, JoAnn Falletta

'*Impressions of the Sea*': MENDELSSOHN: *The Hebrides Overture (Fingal's Cave).* DEBUSSY: *La Mer.* LIADOV: *The Enchanted Lake.* BRIDGE: *The Sea (suite).* DEBUSSY: *Prélude: La Cathédrale engloutie* (arr. BUSSER).

★★★ LBSO 6698-1.

It is good to find an orchestra of this calibre, under the excellent JoAnn Falletta, producing playing of such high quality, especially in an often thrilling and certainly evocative account of *La Mer* where the body of orchestral tone is most impressive. Liadov's *Enchanted Lake* is also atmospherically evoked, but best of all is Frank Bridge's *Suite* with the opening *Seascape* and penultimate *Moonlight* scenes pictured with memorable vividness of colour. Finally comes Henri Büsser's orchestration of Debussy's *La Cathédrale engloutie*, not as outrageously original as the celebrated Stokowski version, but still imaginative, and richly sonorous in its scoring. The recording is excellent, spacious and well detailed. The CD is available from the orchestra direct, whose website is www.lbso.org

Los Angeles Philharmonic Orchestra, Zubin Mehta

'*Spectacular orchestral showpieces*': HOLST: *The Planets*. RICHARD STRAUSS: *Also sprach Zarathustra*. JOHN WILLIAMS: Film scores: *Close Encounters of the Third Kind (suite); Star Wars (suite)*.

(B) **(*) Double Decca (ADD) 452 910-2 (2).

Zubin Mehta's set of *Planets* ranks high in stellar splendour and has been a demonstration record since it was first issued on LP in 1971. The performance is strongly characterized and splendidly played. It is discussed more fully under its composer entry in our companion volume, where it is paired with Holst's *Perfect Fool* suite. However, hi-fi buffs will surely think this Double Decca set well worth considering with such appropriate couplings. In the never-to-be-forgotten opening of *Also sprach Zarathustra* Mehta has the distinction of stretching those famous first pages longer than any rival. From the start, this 1969 recording was also plainly intended for demonstration with its extrovert sonic brilliance, and as such it succeeds well; but other versions are more interesting interpretatively.

Mehta is a good, even a passionate Straussian, but he is a forceful rather than an affectionate one. The two John Williams film scores were recorded later, in 1977, and again offer a spectacular sound-stage. However eclectic the inspiration, both scores are undeniably attractive and each draws considerable appeal from the imaginative orchestration. The music from *Star Wars* forms a definite suite of six movements; the shorter piece from *Close Encounters* is continuous and essentially atmospheric. Both are very well played in Los Angeles and, if Mehta's approach has an element of hyperbole, in *Star Wars* the Hollywoodian theme picturing Princess Leia includes a horn solo which is played quite gorgeously, while the closing section has an appropriate swagger.

Los Angeles Philharmonic Orchestra or Chamber Orchestra, Zubin Mehta

'*Concertos in Contrast*' (with soloists): HAYDN: *Trumpet Concerto in E flat*. VIVALDI: *Piccolo Concerto in A min., P.83*. WEBER: *Concertino for Clarinet and Orchestra, Op. 26*. WIENIAWSKI: *Polonaise de concert, Op. 4; Scherzo-Tarantelle, Op. 16*. BLOCH: *Schelomo* (with Janos Starker (cello), Israel PO).

**(*) Australian Decca Eloquence (ADD) 466 683-2.

Contrasting concertos indeed – but the programme works. All are played with polish and sparkle, with the soloists (except in *Schelomo*) principals of the Los Angeles orchestra. The Wieniawski showpieces are brilliant rarities, and the delightful Weber piece has all the melodic freshness of his better-known concertos. The famous Haydn and Vivaldi concertos receive beefy performances, but not at all heavy, and it is a pleasure to hear them in such a rich sound. The recordings throughout are particularly full, though the Israeli strings in *Schelomo* cannot quite match those of the American orchestra. But the performance with Starker is very fine indeed.

Ma, Yo-Yo (cello)

'*Great Cello Concertos*': HAYDN: *Concerto in D, Hob VIIb/2* (with ECO, Garcia). SAINT-SAENS: *Concerto No. 1, Op. 33* (with O Nat. de France, Maazel). SCHUMANN: *Concerto in A min., Op. 129* (with Bav. RSO, Colin Davis). DVORAK: *Concerto in B min., Op. 104* (with BPO, Maazel). ELGAR: *Concerto in E min., Op. 85* (with LSO, Previn).

(M) *** Sony DDD/ADD M2K 44562 (2).

An enticing mid-priced package, offering at least two of the greatest of all cello concertos, in Yo-Yo Ma's characteristic and imaginative refined manner. Only the performance of the Haydn gives cause for reservations and these are slight; many will enjoy Ma's elegance here. He is also lucky in his accompanists, and the CBS sound gives no reasons for complaint.

Marches

'*40 Famous Marches*' (played by various ensembles, including the Philip Jones Brass, VPO, Boskovsky and Knappertsbusch, Curley, organ): ALFORD: *Colonel Bogey*. C. P. E. BACH: *March*. BEETHOVEN: *Turkish March*. BERLIOZ: *Damnation de Faust: Hungarian March*. BIZET: *Carmen: Marche des contrebandiers*. BLISS: *Things to Come: March*. CHABRIER: *March joyeuse*. CLARKE: *Trumpet Voluntary*. COATES: *The Dambusters March*. ELGAR: *Pomp and Circumstance Marches Nos. 1 and 4 in D*. FUCIK: *Entry of the Gladiators*. GOUNOD: *Funeral March of a Marionette*. HANDEL: *Occasional Oratorio: March. Rinaldo: March. Saul: Dead March*. KARG-ELERT: *March triomphale*. MENDELSSOHN: *Athalie: War March of the Priests. Midsummer Night's Dream: Wedding March*. MEYERBEER: *Coronation March*. NIELSEN: *Oriental Festive March*. PROKOFIEV: *The Love for 3 Oranges: March*. PURCELL: *Funeral March*. RIMSKY-KORSAKOV: *The Procession of the Nobles; The Tale of Tsar Saltan: March*. SCHUBERT: *March militaire*. SIBELIUS: *Karelia Suite: All marcia*. SOUSA: *Stars and Stripes Forever; Washington Post*. J. STRAUSS JR: *Egyptian March; Jubel March; Napoleon March; Persian March; Russian March; Spanish March*. J. STRAUSS SR: *Radetzky March*. TCHAIKOVSKY: *The Nutcracker: March Miniature*.

VERDI: *Aida: Grand March.* WAGNER: *Tannhäuser: Grand March.* WALTON: *Crown Imperial (Coronation march).*

⊶ (B) ★★★ Double Decca (ADD) 466 241-2 (2).

Most of the obvious marches are here, but this splendid collection is made all the more interesting by a shrewd choice of imaginative repertoire and performance, often in unexpected arrangements – the Philip Jones Brass Ensemble in the *Aida* and *Tannhäuser* marches (played with considerable brilliance), Carlo Curley's organ arrangement of Beethoven's *Turkish March*, and so on. Highlights include a string of J. Strauss's most exotic marches (*Egyptian, Persian, Russian* and *Spanish*) under Boskovsky, a crisply executed example from *The Tale of Tsar Saltan* by Martinon, Ansermet's hi-fi demonstration version of Chabrier's *Marche joyeuse*, a simple but striking march by C. P. E. Bach, arranged by the late Philip Jones, and many others. The Nielsen march is another unexpected choice, and no Decca collection of marches would be complete without Knappertsbusch's noble account of the *March militaire*. This is one of the best collections of its kind, and with recordings ranging from good to spectacular it will not fail to lift the spirits.

Markevitch, Igor (conducting various orchestras)

BEETHOVEN: *Symphony No. 3 in E flat (Eroica), Op. 55* (with Symphony of the Air). *Symphony No. 6 in F (Pastoral), Op. 68; Overtures: Coriolan; Leonore No. 3; Fidelio; Zur Namensfeier, Op. 115; Consecation of the House.* BIZET: *Suite: Jeux d'enfants.* BRAHMS: *Symphonies Nos. 1 in C min., Op. 68; 4 in E min., Op. 90; Tragic Overture.* DEBUSSY: *La Mer.* GOUNOD: *Symphony No. 2 in E flat.* GLUCK: *Sinfonia in G.* HAYDN: *Sinfonia concertante in B flat, Hob. I:105.* MOZART: *Symphony No. 38 (Prague).* SCHUBERT: *Symphony No. 3 in D, D.200.* TCHAIKOVSKY: *Francesca da Rimini Op. 32.* WAGNER: *Preludes: Lohengrin: Acts I & III; Tannhäuser: Overture and Bacchanale* (all with LOP). BRAHMS: *Alto Rhapsody, Op. 53* (with Arkhipova). KODÁLY: *Psalmus Hungaricus, Op. 13* (with Ilosfalvy; both with Russian State Ac. Ch., USSR State SO). CIMAROSA: *Double Concerto for 2 Flutes in G* (with Nicolet, Demmler). MOZART: *Symphonies Nos. 34; 35 (Haffner).* TCHAIKOVSKY: *Symphony No. 6 in B min. (Pathétique).* WAGNER: *Siegfried Idyll* (all with BPO).

(B) ★★★ DG 474 400-2 (9).

Markevitch's eminence as a conductor was a postwar phenomenon. Before the war he was known primarily as a composer and composer–conductor, making his début as a teenager with his *Piano Concerto* during Diaghilev's last London season (see Composer section of this edition). During the war he took part in the Italian resistance, but after the early 1940s his creative fires had burned out. It was Nadia Boulanger who encouraged him to take up conducting, and this occupied him until deafness struck him in the last years of his life. He conducted in Berlin, Paris, Moscow, London and Stockholm; and his repertoire was exploratory, ranging from Berwald to Roussel. This set includes almost all the Berlin Philharmonic recordings that have not been available from other sources. The notes speak of his translucent and intense dramatic style and his generally unsentimental approach. At times this led some listeners to find him 'cool' in some of the cycle of Tchaikovsky symphonies he recorded with the LSO for Philips – but this stricture certainly does not apply to his 1953 *Pathétique* included here. His Brahms *Alto Rhapsody* with Irina Arkhipova at her prime is very powerful, as is his very dark *Tragic Overture*. His Gounod *E flat Symphony* has charm, a quality which we don't normally associate with him; and the clarity of his mind is evident in the Debussy he also recorded with the Orchestre Lamoureux de Paris. There are some memorable things here, and this impeccably produced set provides a valuable opportunity to rediscover a many-faceted and highly individual artist.

Marsalis, Wynton (trumpet)

Trumpet Concertos (with ECO or Nat. PO, Raymond Leppard): PURCELL: *The Indian Queen: Trumpet Overture.* HAYDN: *Concerto in E flat.* HUMMEL: *Concerto in E.* FASCH: *Concerto in D for Trumpet and 2 Oboes.* MOLTER: *Concerto No. 2 in D.* TORELLI: *2 Sonatas à 5 for Trumpet and Strings in D, t.v. 3 & 7.*

⊶ ⊛ (M) ★★★ Sony SMK 89611.

The brilliant American trumpeter, Wynton Marsalis, recorded the Haydn, Fasch and Hummel concertos with the ECO over a period of a week in 1993 at St Giles Church, Cripplegate, in London. The playing is as expert and stylish as we have come to expect from this remarkable player. His approach is just a little cool, but none the worse for that, for there is also admirable poise, and in the finale of the Hummel he lets himself go with the most infectious bravura. Incidentally, there is no improvising in cadenzas: 'I don't feel comfortable enough to improvise in music of this period', Marsalis told us in the notes with the original full-priced issue.

The other recordings date from a year later, with the Purcell *Trumpet Overture* from *The Indian Queen* used to open the programme arrestingly. So often in a trumpet anthology the ear wearies of the timbre, but never here. Marsalis scales down his tone superbly to match the oboes in the delightful Fasch *Concerto* (especially as they are backwardly balanced) and he plays the *Sonatas* of Torelli with winning finesse. The recording gives him a striking (but not too exaggerated) presence in relation to the orchestra, making the trumpet very tangible, especially in the upper tessitura of the Molter *Concerto*, where the solo playing makes the hairs at the nape of one's neck tingle.

Mewton-Wood, Noel (piano)

BEETHOVEN: *Piano Concerto No. 4 in G, Op. 58* (with Utrecht SO, Goehr); *Violin Sonata No. 8 in G, Op. 30/3*. ALBENIZ (arr. Kreisler): *Malagueña* (both with Haendel). CHOPIN: *Tarantelle in A flat, Op. 43*. WEBER: *Piano Sonata No. 1 in C, Op. 24*. LISZT: *Années de pèlerinage: Petrarch Sonnets Nos. 44 & 104*. TCHAIKOVSKY: *Piano Concerto No. 2 in G, Op. 44* (with Winterthur SO, Goehr). SHOSTAKOVICH: *Concerto No. 1 for Piano, Trumpet & Strings, Op. 35* (with Sevenstern, Concert Hall SO, Goehr). SCHUMANN: *Kinderszenen, Op. 15*. BUSONI: *Violin Sonata No. 2 in E min., Op. 36a* (with Rostal). TIPPETT: Songs: *Boyhood's End; The Heart's Assurance* (with Pears).

✪ ★★★ Australian Universal Heritage ABC Classic mono 461 900-2 (3).

An invaluable reissue, impressively produced and presented, this three-CD set comprises one of three in the launch of the Australian Heritage Series. No effort has been spared in presentation, and the set pays tribute to an almost forgotten but outstanding artist, Noel Mewton-Wood. Born in Melbourne, Australia, he had a highly successful career in England, favoured by, among others, Beecham, Sargent, Henry Wood and Britten. His recordings have long been sought after by collectors, and this anthology presents him in solo and concertante repertoire. Several performances are especially worth pointing out: his sleight of hand in one of the silveriest performances of the Beethoven *G major Violin Sonata* on record, with a 13-year old Ida Haendel; a magnificent Beethoven *Fourth Concerto*; a corruscating Shostakovich *Concerto* (the finale is electrifying); two searing Liszt *Petrarch Sonnets*; and a memorable recording of *Kinderszenen* (though with some surface noise) never before issued. The two Tippett song-cycles were the first recordings of any of the composer's vocal works (originally issued on Argo) with Peter Pears sounding admirably fresh and Mewton-Wood's accompaniments full of insight. His playing is consistently suffused with vitality and warmth, ranging from the imperceptibly delicate to the overwhelmingly powerful. Tchaikovsky's *Second Concerto*, brought off with enormous aplomb, is highly charged emotionally and remains among the finest versions available. The sound ranges from acceptable to good, but this set is indispensable and well worth seeking out.

Minimalism

'The World of Minimalism': GLASS: *'Heroes' Symphony: V2 Schneider* (with American Composers O, Davies). REICH: *Drumming*: excerpts (with Steve Reich and Musicians). MORAN: *Points of Departure* (with Baltimore SO, Zinman). FITKIN: *Frame* (Fitkin and Sutherland). ADAMS: *Shaker Loops: Shaking and Trembling* (with San Francisco SO, de Waart). NYMAN: *The Cook, the Thief, his Wife and her Lover: Memorial* (Michael Nyman Band). RILEY: *In C* (with Davidson-Kelly, Harris, Heath, Richter, Strawson, Wood).

(M) ★(★★) Decca (ADD/DDD) 470 125-2.

Minimalist music has a small yet sturdy following, but some of the music here will test all but its most devoted advocates. The excerpts from Steve Reich's *Drumming* falls into the 'stuck in groove' category, which may be hypnotic to some but is undoubtedly monotonous to others. Fitkin's *Frame*, played on two keyboards, merely grates from the first note. Repetition is taken to extreme in Riley's infamous *In C* – a 20-minute composition, based on the repeated playing of the octave C, for concert grand and upright piano, Rhodes piano, two harpsichords and vibraphone. Moran's mythical ballet *Points of Departure* offers far more attractive and colourful symphonic scoring and, like Glass's *V2 Schneider*, sounds not unlike many contemporary American film-scores. Nyman's *Memorial* is perhaps the most approachable work here, with an easy listening quality that has made his film music so successful. However, it is John Adams who shines as the strongest and most original composer in this collection. Superb recordings and, as far as one can tell, performances.

Minneapolis Symphony Orchestra, Antal Dorati

Concert: GERSHWIN: *An American in Paris*. COPLAND: *Rodeo (4 Dance Episodes)*. SCHULLER: *7 Studies on Themes of Paul Klee*. BLOCH: *Sinfonia breve*.

(M) ★★ Mercury (ADD) [434 329-2].

This is a disappointing collection, a rare occurrence for this label. Dorati's *Rodeo* lacks the incandescent vitality of Bernstein's electrifying New York version, and Gershwin's *American in Paris* doesn't suit the Hungarian conductor too well either (try the big blues tune at its trumpet entry). The almost overdetailed recording does not help, either here or in Bloch's rather dry *Sinfonia breve*, which needs richer string-textures. It is highly suitable for Schuller's sharply etched *Seven Studies on Themes of Paul Klee* but, brilliantly though this is played, the music itself does not live up to the promise of titles like *The twittering machine* and *Little blue devil*.

ALBENIZ: *Iberia* (suite, orch. Arbós). FALLA: *La vida breve: Interlude and Dance*. MUSSORGSKY: *Khovanshchina: Prelude; Dance of the Persian Slaves*. SMETANA: *The Bartered Bride: Overture and 3 Dances*.

(M) ★★ Mercury (ADD) [434 388-2].

The Northrop Auditorium in Minnesota never proved an ideal venue acoustically for the Mercury recording team. Although the sound is not without warmth and the woodwind have bloom, there is an underlying acoustic dryness. Using the favoured M56 Telefunken microphones, closely placed, this produced an unattractive glare, even a fierceness in *fortissimos*, an artificial brilliance likely to appeal only to hi-fi buffs. Of course, the somewhat brash Arbós scoring in *Iberia* does not help, and certainly Dorati catches the sinuous Spanishry of this music. He is equally vital in the rest of the programme, which is all brilliantly played; but easily the highlight here is Mussorgsky's highly atmospheric *Khovanshchina Prelude*. With its orchestration expertly touched in by Rimsky-Korsakov, it magically pictures the sun rising over the Kremlin. Although the timbre of the orchestra's principal oboe is not opulent, this is one of the most evocative accounts in the CD catalogue, and here the recording cannot be faulted.

Minnesota Orchestra, Eije Oue

'*Orchestral Fireworks*': KABALEVSKY: *Overture Colas Breugnon.* Deems TAYLOR: *Through the Looking Glass: Looking Glass Insects.* RIMSKY-KORSAKOV: *Tsar Sultan: Flight of the Bumblebee.* LISZT: *Les Préludes.* BRAHMS: *Hungarian Dance No. 3 in F.* DINICU: *Hora staccato.* DVORAK: *Slavonic Dance, Op. 71/2.* JARNEFELT: *Praeludium.* BERLIOZ: *Damnation de Faust: Danse des sylphes.* KLEMPERER: *Merry Waltz.* CHABRIER: *Habanera.* RAVEL: *Boléro.*
*** Reference Dig. RR-92 CD.

From the evidence of this enjoyable concert the Minneapolis Orchestra is in excellent shape under its new conductor, Eije Oue, and they play with refinement as well as virtuosity. *Les Préludes*, for instance, is a particularly impressive performance, entirely without vulgarity, with a dignified opening, yet the closing pages generate much excitement and the final peroration is really powerful. The slightly bass-heavy recording adds to the weight of the piece. And how warmly and elegantly does the orchestra play the Brahms and Dvořák dances, while the slinky Chabrier *Habanera* is very seductive. An attractive novelty here is the Deems Taylor *Scherzo*, reminiscent of early Stravinsky, but very colourful in its own right.

Hora staccato and Rimsky's *Bumblebee* are both played with the lightest touch, the orchestral virtuosity sparkling throughout, while it is good to welcome the charming Jarnefelt *Praeludium*. But the surprise is the Klemperer *Waltz*, turned into a real lollipop, and more persuasive here than the conductor/composer's own version. *Boléro* is very well played indeed (the opening woodwind solos especially so), but it is also very relaxed until a sudden burst of adrenalin at the close. The recording is spacious and full, with warn, pleasing string-quality, but the bass is at times a trifle boomy.

Molnar, Jozsef (alphorn)

Alphorn Concertos (with Capella Istropolitana or Slovak PO, Urs Schneider): LEOPOLD MOZART: *Sinfonia pastorella.* JEAN DAETWYLER: *Dialogue avec la nature; Concerto.* FERENC FARKAS: *Concertino rustico.*
(BB) *** Naxos 8. 555978.

The Alphorn (pictured on the front of the CD) has a fine fat timbre, but its natural harmonics produce a basic range of only five notes. Leopold Mozart uses them robustly in various permutations and most successfully in his ingenuously jolly rondo finale. But a good deal of the melodic action goes on in the orchestra, and the *Andante* omits the soloist altogether. For all its naïveté the result is rather endearing.

The *Concerto rustico* of Ferenc Farkas is much more ingenious in using and extending the instrument's range. The slow movement, *Rubato, a piacere*, is surprisingly successful in its doleful *espressivo*, unashamedly featuring the instrument's out-of-tune harmonics, and in the finale the alphorn almost manages a tune rather like a garbled version of '*Poor Jennie is A-weeping*'.

The Swiss composer, Jean Daetwyler, gets round the minimalistic problem even more enterprisingly by adding in a piccolo to portray the birds in his *Dialogue avec la nature*, while his orchestral scoring is rich in atmosphere and colour. The alphorn and piccolo duet together piquantly in the charming rondo finale, which is not too extended.

Daetwyler's four-movement *Concerto* is much more ambitious, opening with a soliloquy taking his soloist up to his highest harmonics, and, like Farkas, not shunning those notes that are inherently out of tune. Again the tangy orchestral colouring makes a rich backcloth for the soloist, especially in the razzle-dazzle *Scherzo* and the *Misterioso pastorale*. The *Furioso* finale makes even more virtuoso demands, which Jozsef Molnar clearly relishes. Indeed his playing throughout is astonishingly secure and full of character. The accompaniments are supportive and the recording excellent. This is a collection which would have been a doubtful recommendation at its original Marco Polo premium price, but on Naxos it is well worth trying – although not all at once!

Musica da Camera, Robert King

Baroque Chamber Works: BACH: *Cantata No. 42: Sinfonia.* CORELLI: *Concerto grosso in G min. (Christmas), Op. 6/8.* PACHELBEL: *Canon and Gigue.* HANDEL: *Concerto grosso in B flat, Op. 3/2.*

VIVALDI: *L'Estro armonico: Concerto in D min., Op. 3/11.* ALBINONI (**arr.** GIAZOTTO): *Adagio for Organ and Strings.*
*** Linn CKD 012.

An exceptionally successful concert of baroque music, with a very well-chosen programme, presented on an authentic scale, with what appears to be one instrument to a part. Phrasing is thoroughly musical and the intimacy and transparency of sound are achieved without loss of sonority or disagreeable squeezing of phrases. The familiar *Largo* of the Corelli *Christmas Concerto* is particularly fresh, and the opening of the famous Pachelbel *Canon* on a sombre solo bass-line is very telling. The colour of the lively Bach and Handel works (using wind as well as strings) is attractively realized. Excellent, realistic recording.

I Musici

ALBINONI: *Adagio in G min.* (**arr.** GIAZOTTO).
BEETHOVEN: *Minuet in G, WoO 10/2.*
BOCCHERINI: *Quintet in E, Op. 11/5: Minuet.*
HAYDN (**attrib.**): *Quartet, Op. 3/5; Serenade.*
MOZART: *Serenade No. 13 in G (Eine kleine Nachtmusik), K.525.* PACHELBEL: *Canon.*
*** Ph. (IMS) 410 606-2.

A very enjoyable concert, recorded with remarkable naturalness and realism. The effect is very believable indeed. The playing combines warmth and freshness, and the oft-played Mozart *Night music* has no suggestion whatsoever of routine: it combines elegance, warmth and sparkle. The Boccherini *Minuet* and (especially) the Hoffstetter (attrib. Haydn) *Serenade* have an engaging lightness of touch.

Mutter, Anne-Sophie (violin)

MOZART: *Violin Concertos Nos. 2 in D, K.211; 4 in D, K.218* (with Philh. O, Muti). BACH: *Concertos Nos. 1 in A min., BWV 1041; 2 in E, BWV 1042; Double Violin Concerto in D min., BWV 1043* (with ECO, Accardo). LALO: *Symphonie espagnole, Op. 21.* SARASATE: *Zigeunerweisen, Op. 20* (with O Nat. de France, Ozawa).
(M) ******* EMI 5 65538-2 (3).

Anne-Sophie Mutter followed up her celebrated early coupling of Mozart's *G major*, K.216, and *A major*, K.219, *Violin Concertos* (now reissued as a DG Original – see under the Composer entry in our main volume) with the two *D major Concertos* on HMV, and a different orchestra and conductor. The results are hardly less successful. Her variety of timbre as well as the imagination of her playing is extremely compelling, and while the degree of romantic warmth she adopts in her Bach playing is at odds with today's 'authentic school', her performance of the slow movement of the *E major Concerto* is finer

than almost any other version except Grumiaux's, with marvellous shading within a range of hushed tone.

Accardo's accompaniment here (as throughout the collection) is splendidly stylish and alert. In principle the slow movement of the *Double Concerto* – where Accardo takes up his bow to become a solo partner, scaling down his timbre – is too slow, but the result could hardly be more beautiful, helped by EMI recording which gives body to the small ECO string band. The account of Lalo's Spanish showpiece makes an excellent foil, with its dazzling display of bravura offset by Mutter's delicacy of phrasing, although there is no lack of passionate eloquence in the central movements. Here the balance is a shade too forward, and the digital recording brings a touch of digital edge to the sound. The Sarasate offers more violinistic fireworks, but some may find Mutter's playing of the famous principal lyrical melody a little chaste. Overall, however, this makes a fine showcase for a splendid artist.

'*Carmen-fantasie*' (with VPO, James Levine):
SARASATE: *Zigeunerweisen; Carmen Fantasy.*
WIENIAWSKI: *Légende.* TARTINI: *Sonata in G min. (Devil's trill).* RAVEL: *Tzigane.* MASSENET: *Thaïs: Méditation.* FAURE: *Berceuse.*
*** DG 437 544-2.

This is an unashamedly fun record, with Mutter playing with freedom and warmth and obviously enjoying herself. Comparing the *Carmen Fantasy* of Sarasate with Perlman shows Mutter as equally sharp in characterization, yet in the end Perlman's easy style is the more beguiling. But Mutter's Ravel *Tzigane* is made stunningly Hungarian in its fiery accelerando at the end, while Tartini's famous *Devil's Trill Sonata* is played as a virtuoso piece, rather than placed back in the eighteenth century – no harm in that in the present context. The recording is vividly close.

Nakariakov, Sergei (trumpet)

Concertos (with Lausanne CO, López-Cobos):
JOLIVET: *Concertino for Trumpet, Piano and Strings* (with Markovich, piano). HUMMEL: *Concerto in E flat.* HAYDN: *Concerto in E flat.* TOMASI: *Concerto in D.*
(M) ******* Warner Elatus 0927 49831-2.

The very gifted young Russian trumpeter makes a brilliant contribution to the Jolivet *Double Concerto*. His partner, the pianist Alexander Markovich, plays very well too, but the balance is less than ideal. Yet, at under ten minutes, the work does not outstay its welcome and it has a catchy, angular main theme. The Tomasi solo concerto is more kaleidoscopic, with lyrical and rhythmic elements alternating and a whiff of jazz in the melodic style.

In the Haydn and Hummel *Concertos* Nakariakov

does not quite match the famous Hardenberger performances, and the orchestral playing in Lausanne is serviceable rather than outstanding. Nakariakov plays the Hummel in the key of E flat, rather than the brighter E major favoured by Hardenberger, but both this and the Haydn bring a superb solo contribution from the young Russian virtuoso, and the lovely *Andante* of the latter work is memorably warm and graceful, before a sparkling finale which matches that of the Hummel in high spirits.

'*No Limit*' (playing trumpet and flugel horn, with Philh. O, Ashkenazy; arrangements by Nakariakov & Dokshitser): SAINT-SAENS: Trumpet: *Introduction and Rondo capriccio.* GERSHWIN: *Rhapsody in Blue.* Flugel horn: TCHAIKOVSKY: *Andante cantabile; Variations on a Rococo Theme.* BRUCH: *Canzone.* MASSENET: *Thaïs: Méditation.*

(★★★) Teldec 8573 80651-2.

Sergei Nakariakov's tone is so beautiful, his phrasing so naturally musical, his virtuosity so effortless and dazzling, that he almost reconciles one to these arrangements. Certainly the Saint-Saëns displaypiece is presented with great flair – and Nakariakov's breathtakingly fast tonguing at the close is extraordinary.

But Tchaikovsky's *Andante cantabile*, on the flugel horn instead of the cello, just will not do. For all the warmth of line and tasteful vibrato, the atmosphere of the bandstand remains. The *Rococo Variations* works rather better, played very stylishly, with the melodic line here often lying higher up. But again it sounds far better on a cello.

Max Bruch's *Canzone* and Massenet's '*Méditation*' are effective enough, and undoubtedly Nakariakov is a natural in Gershwin, where he returns to the trumpet. It is a brilliant performance, with a strong jazzy inflection. The instrument's middle and lower range is used to good effect, and there is a touch of humour when the bassoon makes a solo entry. The big tune is introduced delicately and played with a cup mute; but in the following string climax the saxes fail to come through (if they are there). Throughout Ashkenazy provides good support, although the balance makes his contribution no more than an accompaniment. But that Gershwin opening should have been left to the clarinet.

NBC Symphony Orchestra, Guido Cantelli

'*The NBC Broadcasts 1951*': BARTOK: *Concerto for Orchestra.* BRAHMS: *Tragic Overture.* DEBUSSY: *Le martyre de Saint-Sébastien: Symphonic Fragments.* GHEDINI: *Concerto dell'Albatro* (with Mischakov, Miller, Balsam, Grauer). GILLIS: *Prairie Sunset.* MENDELSSOHN: *Symphony No. 4 (Italian).* MOZART: *Le nozze di Figaro: Overture. Symphony No. 29 in A, K.291.* RAVEL: *La Valse; Pavane pour*

une infante défunte. ROSSINI: *Overture: The Siege of Corinth.* SCHUBERT: *Symphony No. 2 in B flat, D.125.* STRAVINSKY: *Fireworks.* VIVALDI: *Concerto grosso in A min., Op. 8/3* (with Mischakov, Hollander).

(M) (★★★) Testament mono SBT4 1336 (4).

On these four discs we have broadcasts from five concerts Cantelli conducted in New York with the NBC Symphony Orchestra, four in January 1951 and one in the December of that year. None are from the notoriously dry Studio 8-H; the January concerts are from the Manhattan Center and the December one from Carnegie Hall. Although the set includes pieces that he recorded commercially, such as the *Italian Symphony* and the *Symphonic Fragments* from *Le martyre de Saint-Sébastien* (which incidentally was broadcast by the BBC Third Programme as a tribute during the evening after his death was announced), he never recorded the Bartók *Concerto for Orchestra* or the *Concerto dell'Albatro* by his compatriot and teacher, Giorgio Federico Ghedini. The Bartók is atmospheric and sensual. Ghedini's almost forgotten score used to be broadcast quite frequently in the 1950s; with its austere neo-classicism and eloquence (the idiom is indebted to Bartók, Hindemith and Frank Martin) it is very well served by the orchestra and its fine soloists. The quotations from Melville featured in the finale are spoken in the civilized American English which was in wide currency in the 1950s. The Schubert *Second Symphony* is absolutely exhilarating and wonderfully light and vibrant. Cantelli's NBC producer was Don Gillis (of *Symphony No. 5-and-a-half* fame) whose short *Prairie Sunset* makes a welcome appearance. Leaving aside the quality of the playing, the mono recordings are a very pleasant surprise and have been expertly remastered by Paul Baily.

NBC Symphony Orchestra, Arturo Toscanini

'*The Immortal Toscanini*': WAGNER: *Lohengrin: Preludes to Acts I & III. Siegfried: Forest Murmurs. Tristan und Isolde: Vorspiel und Liebestod. Die Walküre: The Ride of the Valkyries.* BRAHMS: *Variations on a Theme by Haydn.* R. STRAUSS: *Till Eulenspiegel.* TCHAIKOVSKY: *Nutcracker Suite, Op. 71a.* MUSSORGSKY: *Pictures at an Exhibition.* DUKAS: *L'apprenti sorcier.* ROSSINI: *William Tell: Overture.*

(B) (★★(★)) RCA mono 74321 84220-2 (2).

These 1950s performances give an excellent idea of Toscanini's legendary, often electrifying style, as well as RCA's notoriously dry Studio 8-H acoustics. The Wagner items display his special brand of electricity, especially the *Lohengrin Preludes* and the soaringly intense *Tristan Liebestod*, and although the dynamic range is compressed the sound is surprisingly good. In his view of the Mussorgsky–Ravel score he is at his least sympathetic in the statement of the opening *Promenade*, not only rigidly metrical but made the coarser by the cornet-like trumpet tone. Otherwise the orchestral playing has virtuoso brilliance and many of the individual movements are done with greater understanding – for example, the *Ballet of the Unhatched Chicks* – but too often Toscanini's lack of warmth undermines the character of this rich score. However, he is on top form for the *Sorcerer's Apprentice*, creating memorably translucent textures at the opening and then setting off with great dash at the entry of the main theme – in that respect the performance is unique. The *William Tell Overture* was recorded in Carnegie Hall, and although closely miked the acoustic has obvious ambient advantage, and the performance is undoubtedly exciting, with a tautly exciting final gallop. The *Nutcracker Suite* receives a bright, crisp performance, even if the *Sugar Plum Fairy* might have danced with more lightness and grace. The straightforward account of the Brahms *Variations* has more drive than charm, though it is undoubtedly exciting. So is *Till Eulenspiegel*, which receives a well-characterized and sharply dramatic performance – the maestro on top form. The transfers are generally excellent.

'*Great Symphonies*': MOZART: *Symphony No. 40 in G min., K.550.* HAYDN: *Symphony No. 94 in G (Surprise).* CHERUBINI: *Symphony in D.* SCHUMANN: *Symphony No. 3 in E flat (Rhenish), Op. 97.* DVORAK: *Symphony No. 9 (New World), Op. 95.*

(B) (**(*)) RCA mono Twofer 74321 59481 (2).

This may be a mixed bag of symphonies, classical and romantic, but each one demonstrates the electrical intensity of Toscanini's conducting. Even in the new transfers the Haydn and Mozart sound rather thin as well as harsh, and the Cherubini, one of his most celebrated records, is only a little better. The two romantic symphonies on the other hand benefit greatly, with a sense of space and full-bodied sound, notably in the 1949 recording of Schumann, the earliest here.

Neveu, Ginette (violin)

Concert: BRAHMS: *Violin Concerto* (with Philh. O, Dobrowen). CHOPIN: *Nocturne No. 12 in C sharp min.* FALLA: *Danse espagnole.* RAVEL: *Tzigane.* SUK: *4 Pieces.* DINICU: *Hora staccato* (with Jean Neveu, piano).

(B) (***) Dutton mono CDEP 9710.

No sooner had Ginette Neveu established her claims as a great artist, mainly in her recordings in the immediate post-war period, than she was taken from us, together with her brother, Jean, in a tragic air accident. It makes these fine recordings the more precious, and they have been superbly transferred by Dutton, with the Brahms *Violin Concerto* sounding a

degree more refined than in the earlier, EMI transfer. Some of Neveu's recordings of the other items are new to CD, as for example the imaginative *Four Pieces* of Suk, with Neveu displaying her virtuoso flair in such showpieces as Dinicu's *Hora staccato*.

New London Orchestra, Ronald Corp

'*British Light Music Classics*': Vol. 1: COATES: *Calling All Workers.* TOYE: *The Haunted Ballroom.* COLLINS: *Vanity Fair.* FARNON: *Jumping Bean.* BAYNES: *Destiny.* CURZON: *The Boulevardier.* LUTZ: *Pas de quatre.* BINGE: *The Watermill; Elizabethan Serenade.* WILLIAMS: *The Devil's Galop.* GIBBS: *Dusk.* WHITE: *Puffin' Billy.* KETELBEY: *Bells across the Meadows.* Charles WILLIAMS: *The Old Clockmaker.* JOYCE: *Dreaming.* ELLIS: *Coronation Scot.* ANCLIFFE: *Nights of Gladness.*

*** Hyp. CDA 66868.

Almost as soon as it was issued, Ronald Corp's stylish and beautifully played collection of inconsequential but engaging English miniatures rose up and held its place in the bestseller lists. This was the kind of music that used to be heard on seaside piers and which was played by spa orchestras in the years between the two World Wars – orchestras that have long since disappeared.

The robust *Nights of Gladness* (1912) was composed by Charles Ancliffe on return from service as a bandmaster in India, while Sydney Baynes's *Destiny Waltz*, from the same year, has a cello solo which, years later, was played by Sir John Barbirolli at Hallé balls; Archibald Joyce's *Dreaming* dates from the previous year, while two other hauntingly atmospheric pieces, *Dusk* by Armstrong Gibbs and Geoffrey Toye's *Haunted Ballroom*, were both written in 1935. Vivian Ellis's *Coronation Scot*, a catchy sound-picture of a steam locomotive, dates from 1939 and became famous when it was used as the signature tune for BBC radio's 'Paul Temple' detective series. More recently, Ronald Binge has added his engaging *Elizabethan Serenade* (1951) and a delicate portrait of *The Watermill* (1958). It was the famous Sibelius conductor, Anthony Collins, who wrote the delectable morsel, *Vanity Fair*, and he once said in a radio interview that he valued its composition above all his other achievements 'because it will keep my name alive long after my records have been forgotten'. The affectionate, polished performances here will certainly help to do that: they give much pleasure, and Tony Faulkner's recording balance is beautifully judged.

'*British Light Music Classics*', Vol. 2: COATES: *London Suite: Knightsbridge.* FLETCHER: *Bal masqué.* BUCALOSSI: *Grasshopper's Dance.* Arthur WOOD: '*The Archers' Theme': Barwick Green.*

HARTLEY: *Rouge et Noir*. FARNON: *Peanut Polka; Westminster Waltz*. FRANKEL: *Carriage and Pair*. Haydn WOOD: *The Horse Guards, Whitehall (Down Your Way Theme)*. DUNCAN: *Little Suite: March (Dr Finlay's Casebook Theme)*. BINGE: *Sailing By*. VINTER: *Portuguese Party*. RICHARDSON: *Beachcomber*. FINCK: *In the Shadows*. DOCKER: *Tabarinage*. KETELBEY: *Sanctuary of the Heart*. ELGAR: *Carissima*. Charles WILLIAMS: *Girls in Grey*. WHITE: *The Runaway Rocking Horse*. CURZON: *Robin Hood Suite: March of the Bowmen*.
★★★ Hyp. CDA 66968.

Ronald Corp's second collection of popular evergreens is just as delightful as the first, for the supply of catchy and popular numbers shows no sign of drying up. Radio and television signature-tunes provide the cornerstones, with *Barwick Green (The Archers)* by Arthur Wood pointing the way, a piece inspired not by the West Country or the fictional world of Ambridge, but by a village near Leeds. From Eric Coates's *Knightsbridge March* onwards, chosen in the early 1930s to introduce the pioneering radio magazine programme *In Town Tonight*, here is a rich source of nostalgia, including Haydn Wood's *Horse Guards March (Down Your Way)*, Ronald Binge's *Sailing By* (Radio 4 signing off) and Trevor Duncan's catchy *March (Dr Finlay's Casebook)*, which reminds one a little of the *Marcia* of Dag Wirén and is here played most delicately.

What comes out from every one of these 20 pieces is not just their catchy memorability and tunefulness, but the brilliance and subtlety of the instrumentations. They are full of the sort of effects that only a really practical musician, close to players, could think up; and they are here made the more enjoyable by the warmth and clarity of the sound. It is welcome that Elgar is this time included with one of his lesser-known pieces, *Carissima*, not to mention Ben Frankel with the jaunty *Carriage and Pair*, with its clip-clopping rhythm vividly evoking the period Parisian atmosphere of the film *So Long at the Fair*. A must for anyone at all given to nostalgia.

'*British Light Music Classics*', Vol. 3: Haydn WOOD: *Montmartre*. Clive RICHARDSON: *Melody on the Move*. Trevor DUNCAN: *The Girl from Corsica*. LionelMONCKTON: *Soldiers in the Park*. FelixGODIN: *Valse septembre*. BINGE: *Miss Melanie*. Ivan CARYLL: *Pink Lady Waltz*. FARNON: *Portrait of a Flirt*. DEXTER: *Siciliano*. KETELBEY: *In a Persian Market* (with chorus). JackSTRACHEY: *Theatreland*. ArchibaldJOYCE: *Songe d'automne*. VivianELLIS: *Alpine Pastures*. TOMLINSON: *Little Serenade*. MELACHRINO: *Woodland Revel*. TOLCHARD EVANS: *Lady of Spain*. ANCLIFFE: *Smiles, then Kisses*. TORCH: *On a Spring Note*. COATES: *Rediffusion March: Music Everywhere*.
★★★ Hyp. CDA 67148.

Volume 3 is well up to the standard of its attractive predecessors, warmly and sparklingly played, with the orchestra clearly enjoying the melodic profusion. Haydn Wood's opening *Montmartre* would cheer anyone up, and the following *Melody on the Move* and *In the party mood* maintain the spirited forward momentum. Many of the later items are justly famous. No collection of British light music would be complete without Ketèlbey, and the New London Light Opera Chorus makes a lusty contribution in the *Persian Market*.

Farnon's *Portrait of a Flirt*, Harry Dexter's delectably fragile *Siciliano* and Tomlinson's equally charming *Little Serenade* are all winningly personable, while Melachrino's *Woodland Revel* begins wittily with a simple interplay on a melodic fragment, which then flowers romantically, generating a rumbustious climax. The Ancliffe waltz is delightfully English in rhythmic inflection, and after Sidney Torch's catchy reminder of spring, Eric Coates provides a rousing conclusion. The recording is crisp and clear within a pleasingly warm ambience. Most refreshing.

'*European Light Music Classics*': JESSEL: *Parade of the Tin Soldiers*. LEHAR: *Gold and Silver* (waltz). PIERNE: *Album pour mes petits amis: Marche des petits soldats de plomb*. Johann STRAUSS JR: *Tritsch-Tratsch Polka*. LINCKE: *Glow Worm Idyll*. ALFVEN: *Swedish Polka*. GOUNOD: *Funeral March of a Marionette*. WALDTEUFEL: *The Skaters Waltz*. HEYKENS: *Serenade*. PADILLA: *El relicaro*. BECUCCI: *Tesoro mio!* HELLMESBERGER: *Ball Scene*. WEINBERGER: *Schwanda the Bagpiper: Polka*. FETRAS: *Moonlight on the Alster*. HALVORSEN: *Entry of the Boyars*.
★★(★) Hyp. CDA 66998.

Although there is much to enjoy here, this is a less enterprising collection than usual in this series. The highlights are what one might call the Palm Court trifles, the two evocations of miniature soldiers (Pierné's unmistakably French), Lincke's exquisite *Glow Worm Idyll*, the Heykens *Serenade* and the *Entry of the Boyars*, which is most winningly played. *Moonlight on the Alster*, too, is a famous waltz by an unfamous composer and Waldteufel's *Skaters* are always welcome. But why choose the *Tritsch-Tratsch Polka* and *Gold and Silver*, which are readily available elsewhere; the latter is one of Barbirolli's specials? Performances and recordings are pretty well up to standard.

'*American Light Music Classics*'; SOUSA: *Washington Post*. Kerry MILLS: *Whistling Rufus*. GOULD: *American Symphonette No. 3: Pavane*. Felix ARNDT: *Nola (A silhouette)*. PRYOR: *The Whistler and his Dog*. Leroy ANDERSON: *Belle of the Ball; Plink, plank, plunk*. TRAD.: *The Arkansas Traveller (The Old Fiddler's Breakdown)*. BRATTON: *Teddy Bears' Picnic*. MACDOWELL: *Woodland Sketches: To a Wild Rose*. HOLZMANN: *Blaze Away!* FRIML: *In Love (Chanson)*. Raymond SCOTT: *The Toy Trumpet*. GERSHWIN: *Promenade*. HERBERT: *Babes in Toyland: March of the Toys.* ROSE: *Holiday for Strings.* NEVIN: *Water Scenes: Narcissus.* Don GILLIS: *Symphony No. 5½ (A Symphony for Fun).* RODGERS: *Carousel Waltz.*

*** Hyp. CDA 67067.

The surprise here is instantly to recognize so many catchy tunes, and then find they come from the other side of the Atlantic. After the familiar Sousa march (played with spirit and a touch of panache, rather than Yankee pizazz), Kerry Mills's *Whistling Rufus,* with its cakewalk rhythm, is unmistakably American. Abe Holzmann's *Blaze Away!,* complete with piccolo solo, is equally identifiable. So is the engaging Gould *Pavane* and the two witty Leroy Anderson encore pieces, while the New Yorker Edward MacDowell's tender little portrait of a wild rose, delightfully played here, remains his most famous piece. But *Nola, The Whistler and his Dog* (complete with 'bark-ing' coda), *Narcissus* and David Rose's winning pizzi-cato *Holiday for Strings* all seem so familiar that they feel more like local items.

The *Teddy Bear's Picnic,* was an American instru-mental piece but became a British song, and a huge hit in England. Rudolf Friml's *Chanson (In Love)* also became famous when words were added to it – for its appearance in the Hollywood film *The Firefly,* and it was renamed the *Donkey Serenade.* I. M. has a treas-ured childhood memory of seeing another 1930s film, *Babes in Toyland,* in which Laurel and Hardy helped to defeat the evil Bogeymen to the strains of Victor Herbert's famous *March.* In that instance the toy soldiers were six feet tall, as Stanley, who had ordered them for Father Christmas, unfortunately got the measurements wrong! The music sounds as piquant as ever. Don Gillis's *Symphony for Fun* doesn't seem as audacious as it once did, but it still enjoyably bears out its descriptive title. As in the rest of this splendid Hyperion series, performances are as polished as they are spontaneous, and the recording is first class.

(i) New Philharmonia Orchestra, (ii) London Symphony Orchestra, Richard Bonynge

'*Overtures and Ballet Music of the Nineteenth Century*':

Disc 1: (i) Overtures: AUBER: *Marco Spada; Lestocq.* ADAM: *Giralda; La Poupée de Nuremburg.* LECOCQ: *La Fille de Madame Angot.* THOMAS: *Mignon.* PLANQUETTE: *Les Cloches de Corneville.* BOIELDIEU: *Le Calife de Bagdad; La Dame blanche.* (ii) Ballet Music: MEYERBEER: *Le Prophète: Coronation March.* MASSENET: *La Navarraise: Nocturne.* GOUNOD: *La Reine de Saba, Act II: Waltz.* BIZET: *Don Procopio, Act II: Entr'acte.*

Disc 2: (ii) Overtures: DONIZETTI: *Roberto Devereux.* ROSSINI: *Torvaldo e Dorliska.* MAILLART: *Les Dragons de Villars.* OFFENBACH: *La Fille du tambour-major.* VERDI: *Giovanna d'Arco.* HEROLD: *Zampa.* WALLACE: *Maritana.* AUBER: *La Neige. Ballet Music:* MASSENET: *Cherubin, Act III: Entr'acte. Don César de Bazan: Entr'acte Sevillana. Les Erinnyes: Invocation.* GOUNOD: *Le Tribut de Zamora, Act III: Danse grecque.* SAINT-SAENS: *Henry VIII, Act II: Danse de la gypsy.* DELIBES: *Le Roi l'a dit, Act II: Entr'acte.*

☛ ❀ *** Double Decca (ADD) 466 431-2 (2).

By delving further into the back catalogue, Decca have come up with an even more delectable collec-tion of overtures and orchestral sweetmeats than in the companion ECO eighteenth-century compila-tion, above. The programme is again based on three Bonynge LPs, two from the LSO and one from the New Philharmonia Orchestra, again from the late 1960s and early 1970s. The format of the nineteenth-century overture is a pretty standard one, usually a potpourri, but sometimes more sophisticated in lay-out, as with Thomas's *Mignon* and, to a lesser extent, Hérold's *Zampa.* But it is the tunes that count.

Of the three Auber overtures *Marco Spada* has a wonderfully evocative opening, suggesting a sunrise, before bursting champagne-like into one of his typi-cal galloping allegros; *Lestocq* contains a memorably wistful tune for the oboe, while *La Neige,* more subtle than usual, shows the composer's gift for writing catchy tunes quite early in his career. Adam's *Giralda* and *La Poupée de Nuremburg* display all the delicacy and skill we know from his ballet scores; the former features glittering castanets, the latter an unexpected passage for string quartet. Boieldieu's charming *La Dame blanche* is as light as thistledown and *The Caliph of Bagdad* has never sounded more resplend-ent. Lecocq's *La Fille de Madame Angot* is quite delicious.

Among the LSO performances, *Maritana* stands out. Bonynge does this gorgeously, the melodramatic opening arresting, and the shaping of the hit tune '*Scenes that are Brightest*' lusciously presented. Ros-sini's *Torvaldo e Dorliska* is interesting in including the second subject of the *Cenerentola Overture,* while Donizetti's *Roberto Devereux* flagrantly draws on 'God Save the King'. Offenbach's winning *La Fille du tambour-major,* piquantly scored, ends with an exu-berant can-can played with superb gusto.

We also turn to the LSO for the ballet music. Besides a brilliant account of Meyerbeer's *Coronation March,* there is a series of delightful *bon bouches* including a famous Massenet cello solo (the *Invoca-tion* from *Les Erinnyes*) and the *Nocturne* from *La Navarraise.* Gounod's *Grande valse* from *La Reine de Saba* sounds as though it has been left over from the *Faust* ballet music, while Saint-Saëns's *Gypsy Dance* from *Henry VIII,* with its ominous timpani strokes, turns into a tuneful valse-macabre. The programme ends with a charming pastiche *Minuet* from Delibes's

Le Roi l'a dit. Bonynge is a complete master of this repertoire, which he clearly loves, and all this music is so chic and poised in his hands and so brilliantly played and recorded, that enjoyment is assured.

New World Symphony, Michael Tilson Thomas

CHAVEZ: *Symphony No. 2 (Sinfonia india).* COPLAND: *Danzón cubano.* ROLDAN: *Suite de 'La rebambaramba'.* REVUELTAS: *Sensemayá.* CATURLA: *Tres danzas cubanas.* ROLDAN: *Ritmica V.* PIAZZOLLA: *Tangazo.* GINASTERA. *Estancia, Op. 8a: 4 Dances.*

★★★ Australian Decca Eloquence (ADD) 467 603-2.

This disc seems to have had a short life in its full-price incarnation, but returns in Australian Decca's Eloquence series. It demonstrates a titillating mixture of South American influences, from the unashamedly jazzy *Danzón cubano* of Copland to more substantial works, such as Chávez's *Second Symphony*. Its exotic rarities include Revueltas's *Sensemayá.* This has a delightfully quirky opening with the bass drum, gong and bassoon; then an ever-increasing collection of instruments create an impressive cumulative effect. The longest work here is *Tangazo*, first heard in 1988. A celebration of the famous South American dance, it begins slowly and broodingly, but gradually becomes more vigorous and sensual. All the music here is colourful and vivid, and the performances and recordings are excellent.

New York Philharmonic Orchestra, Leopold Stokowski

'*1947–49 Columbia Recordings and Live Broadcasts*': VAUGHAN WILLIAMS: *Symphony No. 6.* TCHAIKOVSKY: *Romeo and Juliet.* MOZART: *Symphony No. 35 (Haffner).* SCOTT: *From the Sacred Harp.* WEINBERGER: *Schwanda the Bagpiper: Polka and Fugue.*

(★★★) Cala mono CACD 0537.

The main item here is the electrifying account of Vaughan Williams's *Sixth Symphony*, which Stokowski recorded in New York in February 1949, only nine months after the first performance – a première recording made ahead even of EMI's first version with Sir Adrian Boult. Stokowski's speeds are consistently on the fast side, but that brings a thrilling intensity, magnetic from first to last. This has appeared on CD from Sony, but the Cala version, with digital mastering by Paschal Byrne and Craig Thompson, brings sound more vivid and more open. This version of the Tchaikovsky overture, recorded in New York in November 1949, is similarly high-powered, marked by Stokowski's preference for a *pianissimo* ending, avoiding the *fortissimo* chords added by the composer. The *Haffner Symphony*, brisk

and alert in the outer movements, is, amazingly, the only commercial issue of Stokowski conducting a Mozart symphony, taken from a broadcast in November 1949 with obviously rougher sound than in the Columbia studio recordings. The swaggering account of the Weinberger showpiece is also taken from a broadcast, while the piece by Thomas Jefferson Scott is based on two Southern American hymns which the composer found in a collection called *The Sacred Harp* and which Stokowski encouraged him to write. A recording of the broadcast was put on a wartime V-disc, distributed for entertaining members of the American forces, few of which have survived.

Noras, Arto (cello), Finnish Radio Symphony Orchestra, Oramo or Saraste; Norwegian RSO, Rasilainen

DVORAK: *Cello Concerto (with Finnish RSO, Oramo).* DUTILLEUX: *Cello Concerto (Tout un monde lointain).* ELGAR: *Cello Concerto.* LALO: *Cello Concerto in D min.* SAINT-SAENS: *Cello Concerto No. 1.* BARTOK: *Rhapsody No. 1 (originally for violin and O) (all with Finnish RSO, Saraste).* SHOSTAKOVICH: *Cello Concertos Nos. 1 & 2.* RICHARD STRAUSS: *Romanze in D (1883) (with Norwegian RSO, Rasilainen).*

(B) ★★★ Finlandia 3984 26836-2 (3).

This fine collection of cello concertos comes in just one of the many bargain boxes issued to celebrate the twentieth anniversary of the Finlandia label. The Finnish cellist Arto Noras makes an outstanding soloist in this wide range of works, with his impressive technique, flawless intonation and firm, full tone. In generous couplings the Elgar *Concerto*, dedicatedly done, is just one of eight full concertos, all excellently performed in fresh, clear interpretations, as well as shorter works by Bartók and Strauss. Brilliant, full sound.

Northern Ballet Theatre Orchestra, Pryce-Jones

Twentieth-century English Ballets: FEENEY: *Cinderella.* MULDOWNEY: *The Brontës.* Carl DAVIS: *A Christmas Carol.*

(BB) ★★★ Naxos 8.553495.

This enterprising disc is of music taken from full-length ballet scores commissioned by the Northern Ballet Theatre. The most instantly appealing work is Carl Davis's *A Christmas Carol*, delightfully nostalgic with its mixture of sentimental and vigorous numbers – these include a lively, rustic-sounding dance as some poor Londoners try to keep themselves warm. It is an appealing score, with much piquant orchestration and a neat use of the harpsichord. Davis introduces well-known Christmas carols to present the story of Scrooge in a fresh way.

Philip Feeney's *Cinderella* is more severe, reflecting the story as told by the Brothers Grimm, rather than the more romanticized version by Perrault. Feeney uses a battery of percussion instruments to tell the tale, and the result lacks really memorable tunes. But it is not at all dull and has plenty of rhythm and colour. The *Courtly Dances* begin with an array of bells, percussion instruments and a gong, then the composer switches to the harpsichord halfway through to striking effect. *The Red Ball*, where the prince introduces himself, is quirky in a haunting way, and the finale brings an up-beat conclusion.

The Brontës, with music by Dominic Muldowney, is a series of vignettes portraying the Brontë family, as seen through the eyes of the father, Revd. Patrick Brontë, who outlived all his six children. The opening *Toy Soldiers' Fantasy* is charming, with its trumpet fanfares set against a robust marching tune; *The Moors* and *Wuthering Heights* numbers are appropriately broody, while *Charlotte in Brussels* is a jaunty little waltz with witty writing throughout the orchestra. It is thoroughly entertaining. The performances and recording are outstanding.

Northern Philharmonia Orchestra of England, Leeds Festival Chorus, Paul Daniel

'*Rule, Britannia – The Last Night of the Proms*': WALTON: *Coronation Marches: Crown Imperial; Orb and Sceptre.* PARRY: *Jerusalem.* ELGAR: *Enigma Variations: Nimrod. Pomp and Circumstance March No. 1.* WOOD: *Fantasia on British Sea Songs* (including *Rule, Britannia*). ARNOLD: *Overture Tam O'Shanter.* PARRY: *I was Glad.*

(BB) **(*) Naxos 8.553981.

If it seems a little perverse to record such a programme without the contribution of the Prommers and the heady last-night atmosphere, it has to be said that this is a very good concert in its own right, and the Leeds Chorus makes an impressive contribution in *Rule, Britannia* and especially in the reprise of the great *Pomp and Circumstance* melody (which is the more effective at Paul Daniel's spacious tempo). The two Walton marches have panache and Arnold's *Tam O'Shanter* is splendidly done. Here the recording is of spectacular demonstration quality. Excellent value.

Northern Sinfonia, David Lloyd-Jones

'*English String Miniatures*': HOPE: *Momentum Suite.* BRIDGE: *2 Pieces* (arr. Hindmarsh). CARSE: *2 Sketches.* TOMLINSON: *Graceful Dance.* HOLST: *A Moorside Suite.* DELIUS: *2 Aquarelles.* LEWIS: *English Suite.*

(BB) *** Naxos 8.555070.

Another enterprising programme of light but never trivial English music, all with a distinct pastoral feel. In Philip Hope's *Momentum Suite* the first movement, *Dance*, a lively rustic-sounding piece, has an especially attractive middle section, while the last movement, which gets faster and faster, gives the work its title. Paul Lewis's *English Suite* balances its lively *March, Jig* and *Jaunt* movements with a reflective *Meditation*. The two Frank Bridge *Pieces* are highly contrasted. The humour of the *Scherzo Phantastick* comes over well in Paul Hindmarsh's arrangement, including the 'sneeze' at the end of the mock *Trio* section; the *Valse-intermezzo* is delightful, too. *A Northern Dance* from Adam Carse's *Two Sketches* has a quite haunting melancholy feel (with a tune rather similar to 'Danny Boy'). Tomlinson's *Graceful Dance* is slight, but pleasing. The better-known Holst and Delius works are beautifully played, with the *Nocturne* from Holst's *A Moorside Suite* especially atmospheric. The recording is resonant but well detailed, and the performances are first class, as one might expect from Lloyd-Jones and his excellent northern players. Strongly recommended at super-bargain price.

Oistrakh, David (violin)

'*The Originals*' (with (i) VSO; (ii) Igor Oistrakh; (iii) RPO, Goossens; (iv) Dresden State O, Konwitschny): BACH: (i) *Violin Concertos Nos. 1 in E; 2 in A min;* (ii-iii) *Double Violin Concerto in D min., BWV 1041-3.* (iii) BEETHOVEN: *Romances Nos. 1 in G, 2 in F, Opp. 40 & 50.* (iv) BRAHMS: *Violin Concerto, Op. 77.* TCHAIKOVSKY: *Violin Concerto, Op. 35.*

(M) (***) DG stereo/mono 447 427-2 (2).

In 'The Originals' series at mid-price, DG here offers reissues of classic Oistrakh recordings, unavailable for years in any format. Rarest are the 1954 mono recordings of the Brahms and Tchaikovsky *Concertos*, more relaxed, more volatile readings than those Oistrakh recorded later in stereo. Oistrakh moves effortlessly from dashing bravura to the sweetest lyricism, the complete master.

The Bach and Beethoven offerings are hardly less welcome. Allowing for the practice of the time, these Bach performances are all strong and resilient, consistently bringing out the sweetness and purity of Oistrakh's playing, not least in the rapt accounts of the slow movements. Directing the Vienna Symphoniker from the violin, Oistrakh may make the tuttis in the two Bach solo concertos rather heavy, but he then transforms everything the moment he starts playing. The Bach *Double Concerto* with Oistrakh father and son, accompanied by Goossens and the RPO, is more magnetic still, and they accompany him no less sympathetically in the warm, poised readings of the two Beethoven *Romances*.

Concertante Works and Duos (with Igor Oistrakh): VIVALDI: *Concerto grosso in A min., Op. 3/8* (with RPO). SARASATE: *Navarra, Op. 33* (with Leipzig GO, Konwitschny). BACH: *Sonata for 2 Violins and Harpsichord in C, BWV 1037* (with Pischner, harpsichord). HANDEL: *Sonata for 2 Violins and Harpsichord in G min., Op. 2/7*. BENDA: *Trio Sonata in E* (both with Yampolsky, piano). WIENIAWSKI: *3 Etudes-caprices for 2 Violins, Op. 18*.
(M) (***) DG mono/stereo 463 616-2.

The second Oistrakh reissue in DG's 'Originals' series, again joining father and son, gathers together an oddly assorted programme of recordings made in 1957/8 and 1960, with (surprisingly) only the Vivaldi item in stereo, although the sound throughout is very good indeed. The Bach hardly needs recommendation, the Handel *Sonata* is a gem, and even the Benda – a slight but pleasing work – has its moments.

Orchestre National de France, Charles Munch

'*Hommage à Charles Munch*'.

BEETHOVEN: *Symphonies Nos. 4 in B flat; 7 in A; Overture: Consecration of the House* (*(*) V 4825).

BERLIOZ: *Symphonie fantastique, Op. 14; Overtures: Le Corsaire, Op. 21; Benvenuto Cellini, Op. 23* (* V 4826).

BRAHMS: *Symphony No. 2 in D, Op. 73*. SCHUMANN: *Symphony No. 4 in D min., Op. 120* (** V 4827).

DEBUSSY: *Images: Iberia; La Mer; Fantaisie for Piano and Orchestra* (with Nicole Henriot) (** V 4828).

FRANCK: *Symphony in D min*. FAURE: *Pelléas et Mélisande: suite* (** V 4829).

HONEGGER: *Symphony No. 1*. DUTILLEUX: *Symphony No. 2* (**(*) V 4830).

HONEGGER: *Symphonies Nos. 2 (for strings and trumpet obbligato); 5 (Di tre re); Le chant de Nigamon; Pastorale d'été* (** V 4831).

ROUSSEL: *Symphonies Nos. 3 in G min., Op. 42; 4 in A, Op. 53; Bacchus et Ariane: suite No. 2* (** V 4832).

'*Hommage à Charles Munch*' (complete).
(BB) ** Auvidis Valois (ADD) V 4822 (8) (with the

complete set: SIBELIUS: *Legends: The Swan of Tuonela; Lemminkäinen's Return*).

An eight-CD set called *Hommage à Charles Munch* commemorates his work with the Orchestre National after his return from Boston. If you buy the whole set – and it is very inexpensive – you get a 1964 recording of two of the *Four Legends*, made while the orchestra was on tour in Finland. The discs are available separately and bring some outstanding performances, albeit in variable sound.

The Beethoven *Fourth* (V 4825) was recorded in Stockholm on the same Scandinavian tour; and the *Seventh* and, appropriately enough, *The Consecration of the House* come from the inaugural concert in the *Maison de la Radio* in Paris in 1963. Not first-class but acceptable sound, as is the Berlioz (V 4826). The *Symphonie fantastique*, recorded in a rather dry acoustic in Lisbon in 1963, is a bit hard-driven, as was his Boston account. *Un bal* is horribly rushed.

Good though his Franck, Brahms and Schumann may be, it was for his Honegger and Roussel that Munch is best remembered. Always a champion of good contemporary music, he conducted the Honegger and Dutilleux (V 4830) in 1962. Both works are closely associated with Boston. Koussevitzky commissioned the Honegger *First Symphony* (along with the Roussel *Third*) for the 50th anniversary of the founding of the Boston Symphony and Munch conducted the première of the Dutilleux *Symphony* during his Boston years. The Honegger recording is not absolutely first class – a bit strident and narrower in frequency range than some of its companions – but the Dutilleux is very good, and what a performance!

Two other Honegger symphonies, Nos. 2 and 5 (V 4831), come from performances taken from the orchestra's 1964 European tour, the *Symphony for Strings* in San Sebastián in Spain and the *Fifth* from Helsinki. The early *Le chant de Nigamon*, an amazingly original piece, was recorded at the Théâtre des Champs-Elysées two years earlier and, though not first-class sound, is perfectly acceptable (it briefly captures the conductor's vocalise!). Neither of the symphonies is superior to his Boston performances from the 1950s and the rather shrill-sounding *Symphony for Strings* is nowhere near as impressive as his 1969 EMI recording with the Orchestre de Paris. The Helsinki recording of the *Fifth* sounds better.

The Roussel *Third* (V 4832) has plenty of drive, too, but the recording balance is poor. It comes from the 1964 Edinburgh Festival and the string melody at the opening has to struggle to make itself heard against the percussive accompaniment. The *Fourth Symphony*, recorded two years later at the Théâtre des Champs-Elysées, is better, though the *Bacchus et Ariane* suite, whose provenance is not given, is more transparent and present than either. Munch was closely identified with Roussel all his life and, though this disc is better than nothing, if you can get hold of his commercial recording of the symphonies on Erato they are better served in terms of sound. All the same, despite its sonic limitations this is a set to have. Munch was a conductor of stature and his work with the Orchestre National is well worth commemorating.

Ormandy, Eugene (conductor and violinist)

'*The Art of Eugene Ormandy*': Ormandy as violinist: RIMSKY-KORSAKOV: *Le Coq d'Or: Hymn to the Sun. Sadko: Song of India.* Victor HERBERT: *Mlle. Modiste: Kiss Me Again.* DRDLA: *Souvenir.* DVORAK: *Humoresque.* Ormandy and his Salon O: BRAHMS: *Hungarian Dance No. 2 in D min..* HOSMER: *Southern Rhapsody.* With Dorsey Brothers' Concert O: COSLOW–SPIER–BRITT: *Was it a Dream?.* With Minneapolis SO: ZEMACHSON: *Chorale and Fugue in D min., Op. 4.* ZADOR: *Hungarian Dance.* GRIFFES: *The Pleasure Dome of Kubla Khan, Op. 8.* HARRIS: *When Johnny Comes Marching Home.* With Phd. O: BARBER: *Essay No. 1, Op. 12.* MENOTTI: *Amelia Goes to the Ball: Overture.* MIASKOVSKY: *Symphony No. 21 in F sharp min., Op. 51.* RICHARD STRAUSS: *Symphonia domestica, Op. 53.* With Yeend, Beech, Coray, Kullman, Harrell, London, Los Angeles Ch., Hollywood Bowl SO: (vi) MAHLER: *Symphony No. 8: 1st movt only.*

(***) Biddulph mono WHL 064/5.

This two-disc set gives a fascinating profile of Ormandy's early career. He arrived in America seeking a career as a violinist and in the first five tracks we hear him as a good deal more than capable in that role. These recordings, dating from the 1920s, have a warm nostalgic glow and the sound is generally good.

His next progression was conducting light classical and salon music for radio, of which there are three examples from the late 1920s, including a characteristic 1920s account (with vocals) of *Was it a dream?*

Ormandy's great turning point came when he stood in for Toscanini, who sudddenly pulled out of a Philadelphia Orchestral engagement and Ormandy took over. His concerts were a triumph and, thanks to a talent scout, resulted in a series of recordings with the Minneapolis Symphony Orchestra , of which four (from the mid-1930s) are included here. The repertoire is comparatively rare today, which makes their inclusion valuable, especially as they are so enjoyable.

But it is the Philadelphia recordings which are the glories of this set: Barber's *Essay No. 1* has rarely been equalled in performance, while the Menotti overture is brilliant as it could be. The Miaskovsky is magnetic in concentration and atmosphere, and one just has to hear the sumptuous string-tone to appreciate why the Philadelphia sound is legendary. The *Symphonia domestica* is also perceptively characterized and, again, there is something quite magnetic about the performance.

The first movement of Mahler's *Eighth Symphony* is an interesting reminder of Ormandy's pioneering importance in this repertoire, but the recorded sound, from a live broadcast in 1948, leaves something to be desired. A fascinating collection just the same, with helpful sleeve-notes and convenient slimline packaging.

Osipov State Russian Folk Orchestra, Vitaly Gnutov

'*Balalaika Favourites*': BUDASHIN: *Fantasy on 2 Folk Songs.* arr. GORODOVSKAYA: *At Sunrise.* KULIKOV: *The Linden Tree.* OSIPOV: *Kamarinskaya.* MIKHAILOV/SHALAYEV: *Fantasy on Volga Melodies.* ANDREYEV: *In the Moonlight; Under the Apple Tree; Waltz of the Faun.* SOLOVIEV/SEDOY: *Midnight in Moscow.* TCHAIKOVSKY: *Dance of the Comedians.* SHISHAKOV: *The Living Room.* arr. MOSSOLOV: *Evening Bells.* arr. POPONOV: *My Dear Friend, Please Visit Me.* RIMSKY-KORSAKOV: *Flight of the Bumblebee.*

✪ (M) ★★★ Mercury 432 000-2.

The Mercury recording team visited Moscow in 1962 in order to make the first recordings produced in the Soviet Union by Western engineers since the Revolution. The spirit of that unique occasion is captured wonderfully here – analogue atmosphere at its best. The rippling waves of balalaika sound, the accordion solos, the exhilarating accelerandos and crescendos that mark the style of this music-making: all are recorded with wonderful immediacy. Whether in the shimmering web of sound of *The Linden Tree* or *Evening Bells*, the sparkle of the folksongs or the sheer bravura of items like *In the Moonlight*, which gets steadily faster and louder, or in Rimsky's famous piece (sounding like a hive full of bumblebees), this is irresistible, and the recording is superbly real in its CD format.

Overtures

'*Famous Overtures*': BIZET: *Carmen: Prélude.* BEETHOVEN: *Egmont; Fidelio.* BRAHMS: *Academic Festival Overture.* BERNSTEIN: *Candide* (with Met. Op. O, VPO or LSO, Bernstein). ROSSINI: *Il barbiere di Siviglia.* MUSSORGSKY: *Khovanshchina: Prelude.* MOZART: *Le nozze di Figaro* (with COE, VPO or V. State Op. O, Abbado); *Die Zauberflöte* (with VPO, Karajan). VERDI: *La traviata: Act I Prelude.* WEBER: *Der Freischütz* (with Bav. State Op. O, Kleiber). OFFENBACH: *Orpheus in the Underworld.* J. STRAUSS JR: *Die Fledermaus.* SUPPE: *Light Cavalry* (with BPO, Karajan). REZNICEK: *Donna Diana* (with Gothenberg SO, Järvi). GLUCK: *Orfeo ed Euridice* (with E. Bar. Sol., Gardiner). MENDELSSOHN: *A Midsummer Night's Dream.* GERSHWIN: *Cuban Overture* (with Chicago

SO, Levine). VERDI: *La forza del destino.* WAGNER: *Die Meistersinger von Nürnberg* (with O de Paris, Barenboim). GLINKA: *Ruslan and Ludmilla* (with Russian Nat. O, Pletnev).

⊕━ (B) ★★★ DG Panorama (ADD/DDD) 469 322-2 (2).

An outstandingly imaginative collection, with the advantage of a pair of discs that range widely and imaginatively which includes many outstanding performances. Karajan's sumptuously played Suppé and Offenbach overtures are more sophisticated than many accounts (if less visceral in their excitement); Bernstein's swaggering, though comparatively measured account of the *Carmen Prelude* and his warmly personal readings of the Beethoven and Brahms overtures are distinctive, not to mention his own scintillating *Candide* overture. Pletnev's vibrant *Ruslan and Ludmilla* and Abbado's sparkling Rossini and Mozart items are most enjoyable, as is the latter's hauntingly atmospheric account of the *Khovanshchina Prelude*, one of the high points of the collection. Gardiner's period-instrument account of Gluck's *Orfeo ed Euridice* is another highlight, as are Kleiber's *Der Freischütz* and Järvi's *Donna Diana*, a happy, light-hearted foil. The recordings, mainly digital, range from very good to excellent. This is the best compilation of its kind in the catalogue.

Paris Conservatoire Orchestra, Albert Wolff

MASSENET: *Scènes alsaciennes; Scènes pittoresques.* Overtures: ADAM: *Si j'étais roi.* AUBER: *Le domino noir.* HEROLD: *Zampa.* REZNICEK: *Donna Diana.* SUPPE: *Pique Dame.*

★★(★) Testament (ADD) SBT 1308.

Never mind the bracket round the third star – that merely acknowledges the odd orchestral blemish – for this disc offers full three-star enjoyment. These recordings from the 1950s simply ooze with a Gallic style of orchestral playing which has now all but disappeared, with performances of much character and personality. Just listen to the delicious way Wolff points the strings in *Si j'étais roi*, and the genial vitality which pervades the music-making throughout – a long way from the bland brilliance of many of today's performances. The Massenet *Suites* could hardly sound more picturesque – why are these charming works so rarely heard nowadays? – and the sound of the French orchestra, especially the brass, makes one regret the more or less uniform quality of international orchestras today. Even the obvious fluff in the brass in *Zampa* [3'25"] seems to add to the charm of this disc. The overtures, originally released in 1958 under the title 'Overtures in Hi-Fi', have never sounded better, full and vivid, with only a certain tubbiness betraying their age. The Massenet items were recorded in 1955 and the excellent sound-quality, though a bit thin by modern standards, is

even more remarkable. Well done to Testament for restoring these recordings to us, and hopefully more will follow.

Perkins, Laurence (bassoon)

Bassoon Concertos (with Manchester Camerata, Douglas Boyd): M. HAYDN: *Concertino in B flat.* MOZART: *Concerto.* STAMITZ: *Concerto.* WEBER: *Concerto; Andante and Rondo ungarese.*
★★★ Hyp. CDA 72688.

If the bassoon has often been cast as the clown of the orchestra, the five concertante works on this disc demonstrate how much wider its role is, with Laurence Perkins as soloist bringing out the tender beauty of the muted slow movement of the Mozart *Bassoon Concerto*, an early work too often dismissed, but full of charm. The Stamitz *Concerto*, elegant in the slow movement, vigorous in the outer movements, is equally attractive, and the two Weber concertante works show him in relaxed mood, with the *Hungarian Rondo* and the finale of the *Concerto* winningly rumbustious. The *Concertino* by Michael Haydn is the slow movement of one of his orchestral *Serenades*. Perkins, with his crisp articulation, brings out the fun in much of the inspiration as well as the lyrical beauty, warmly accompanied by the Manchester Camerata (of which he is principal bassoon) under another leading wind-player, the oboist, Douglas Boyd.

Perlman, Itzhak (violin)

'The Perlman Edition':

BEETHOVEN: *Piano Trios Nos. 5 (Ghost); 7 (Archduke); in E flat (from Septet), Op. 38* (with Ashkenazy & Harrell) (5 62588-2).

BRUCH: *Concerto No. 2; Scottish Fantasy, Op. 46* (with New Philh. O, Lopez-Cobos) (5 62589-2).

KORNGOLD: *Concerto in D, Op. 35.* SIBELIUS: *Concerto in D min., Op. 47.* SINDING: *Suite in A min., Op. 10* (with Pittsburgh O, Previn) (5 62590-2).

MENDELSSOHN: *Concerto in E min., Op. 64* (with LSO, Previn). TCHAIKOVSKY: *Concerto in D, Op. 35* (with Phd. O, Ormandy) (5 62591-2).

PROKOFIEV: *Concertos Nos. 1–2* (with BBC SO, Rozhdestvensky). *Sonata for 2 Violins* (with Zukerman) (5 62592-2).

GLAZUNOV: *Concerto in A min., Op. 82.* SHOSTAKOVICH: *Concerto No. 1 in A min., Op. 99* (with Israel PO, Mehta); *3 Violin Duets* (with Zukerman) (5 62593-2).

PAGANINI: *Concerto No. 1 in D, Op. 6.* SARASATE: *Carmen Fantasy, Op. 25; Introduction et Tarantelle, Op. 43; Zigeunerweisen* (with RPO or Abbey Road Ens., Foster) (5 62594-2).

DVORAK: *Concerto in A min., Op. 53; Romance in F min., Op. 11* (with LPO, Barenboim); *Sonatina in G, Op. 100; 4 Romantic Pieces, Op. 75* (with Sanders, piano) (5 62595-2).

'Encores' (with Sanders, piano) (5 62596-2).

'Tradition': Familiar Jewish Melodies (with Zohar, clarinet, and Israel PO, Seltzer) (5 62597-2).

BRAHMS: *Concerto in D, Op. 77* (with BPO, Barenboim). *Sonatensatz in C min. (Scherzo); Hungarian Dances Nos. 1, 2, 7 & 9* (with Ashkenazy, piano) (5 62598-2).

CHAUSSON: *Poème.* RAVEL: *Tzigane.* SAINT-SAENS: *Introduction and Rondo capriccioso, Op. 28; Havanaise, Op. 83* (with O de Paris, Martinon). MASSENET: *Thaïs: Méditation* (with Abbey Road Ens., Foster) (5 62599-2).

BARBER: *Concerto, Op. 14.* BERNSTEIN: *Serenade after Plato's Symposium.* FOSS: *3 American Pieces* (all with Boston SO, Ozawa) (5 62600-2).

KREISLER: *Encores: Andantino in the Style of Martini; Caprice Viennoise; Liebesleid; Recitative & Scherzo capriccioso, Op. 6; Schön Rosmarin; Siciliano & Rigaudon in the Style of Francoeur; Tempo di minuetto in the Style of Pugnani. Syncopation; Toy Soldiers' March; Tambourin chinoise.* Arrangements: ALBENIZ: *Tango.* CHAMINADE: *Sérénade espagnole.* DVORAK: *Slavonic Dances Nos. 2 in E min.; 3 in G; Songs My Mother Taught Me.* GLUCK: *Mélodie.* GRAINGER: *Molly on the Shore.* GRANADOS: *Spanish Dance No. 5.* CHOPIN: *Mazurka No. 45 in A min., Op. 67/4.* LEHAR: *Frasquita: Serenade.* SCHUMANN: *Romance in A, Op. 94/2* (with Sanders, piano) (5 62601-2).

BACH: *Concertos Nos. 1 in A min., BWV 1041; 2 in E, BWV 1042; Double Concerto in D min., BWV 1043* (with Zukerman, ECO, Barenboim). *Concerto for Violin and Oboe in C min., BWV 1060* (with Black (oboe), Israel PO) (5 62602-2).

(B) *** EMI (ADD/DDD) 5 85083-2 (15).

Itzhak Perlman was born in Tel Aviv in 1945; he taught himself to play the violin and, despite being stricken by polio (and thus obliged always to play sitting down), he began his concert career at the age of ten. Undoubtedly the supreme master of his instrument in our time, he has seemed a natural successor to Heifetz, and has recorded virtually all the key concertos for his instrument with consistent success. If his technique is dazzling, it is always put at the service of the composer, and his extraordinary sophistication of bow technique and rich yet often

subtle control of colour and dynamic often add a new dimension to music which we know well. He chose always to make his recordings in a microphone spotlight, which detracts to some extent from the orchestral balance; but in the end the listener is disarmed by the glorious sounds he conjures from his 1714 Stradivarius violin.

He worked with many different conductors on record, but undoubtedly his most successful concerto records were made mainly with André Previn, while he has a similarly close relationship with Pinchas Zukerman in instrumental music. The somwehat self-effacing Samuel Sanders was his chosen accompanist in solo repertoire, and they achieved a genuine duo in music in which the piano played an equal role with the violin. Each of these CDs is available separately at mid-price and (apart from the two recital collections) each is reviewed separately under its various conposer entries. All in all, this slip-case compilation – the CDs are in separate jewel-cases – is a fabulous achievement; the current transfers, even if at times the analogue recordings have lost just a little of their atmospheric allure, are generally excellent.

'A la carte' (with Abbey Road Ens., Foster): MASSENET: *Thaïs: Méditation.* GLAZUNOV: *Mazurka-Obéreque; Méditation, Op. 32.* RACHMANINOV: *Vocalise, Op. 34/14.* SARASATE: *Zigeunerweisen, Op. 20; Introduction and Tarantelle, Op. 43.* RIMSKY-KORSAKOV: *Russian Fantasy* (arr. KREISLER). TCHAIKOVSKY: *Scherzo, Op. 42/2* (orch. Glazunov). WIENIAWSKI: *Légende, Op. 17.* KREISLER: *The Old Refrain; Schön Rosmarin.*

**(*) EMI 5 55475-2.

Perlman is in his element in this luscious concert of mostly Russian lollipops – although, as it happens, the most delectable playing of all comes in the Sarasate *Zigeunerweisen.* But the pieces by Glazunov, Tchaikovsky's sparkling *Scherzo* and the Rimsky-Korsakov *Fantasy* also show the extraordinary range of colour and sheer charisma of this fiddling. Alas, as always, the violin is too closely balanced, and this is most disadvantageous in the Wieniawski *Légende,* which loses much of its romantic atmosphere. Perlman's closing solo encore, Kreisler's *Schön Rosmarin,* ends the programme with extraordinary panache. Otherwise Lawrence Foster accompanies discreetly.

'Concertos from my Childhood' (with Juilliard O, Foster): RIEDING: *Violin Concerto in B min., Op. 25.* SEITZ: *Schuler-Konzert No. 2, Op. 13* (orch. ADOLPHE). ACCOLAY: *Violin Concerto No. 1 in A min.* BERIOT: *Scenes de ballet, Op. 100.* VIOTTI: *Violin Concerto No. 22 in A min.*

*** EMI 5 56750-2.

Itzhak Perlman here returns in nostalgia to the concertos which, from the age of six onwards, helped to shape his phenomenal technique. None of this is great music, not even the longest and best-known piece, the Viotti *Violin Concerto No. 22*. But playing with obvious love, Perlman brings out freshness and sparkle in each of them. He turns even passing banalities into moments of joy. Oscar Rieding and Friedrich Seitz are so obscure that even their dates seem to be unknown, yet their miniature concertos here are totally charming, with Perlman springing rhythms infectiously. The student orchestra plays brilliantly too.

'*Encores*' (with Sanders, piano): NOVACEK: *Perpetuum mobile*. BEN-HEIM: *Berceuse sfradite*. DEBUSSY: *La Fille aux cheveux de lin*. SARASATE: *Zapateado*. PONCE: *Estrellita*. MOSZKOWSKI: *Guitarre, Op. 45/2*. CHOPIN: *Nocturne in E flat, Op. 55/2*. POULENC: *Presto*. SAINT-SAENS: *Le Cygne*. PARADIES: *Toccata*. ELGAR: *La Capricieuse*. FOSTER: *Old Folks at Home*. VIEUXTEMPS: *Souvenir d'Amérique*. PARADIES: *Sicilienne*. RAFF: *Cavatina, Op. 85/3*. SARASATE: *Malagueña, Op. 21/1; Caprice basque, Op. 24; Romanza andaluza, Op. 22/1*.

(M) *** EMI 5 62596-2.

Perlman's supreme mastery of the violin has never been demonstrated more endearingly than in this collection of encores, recorded over two decades between 1972 and 1989. Brilliant showpieces vie with gentler inspirations which touch the heart by their refined delicacy, like the performance of Ben-Heim's dainty *Berceuse* and Debussy's delicate evocation of *La Fille aux cheveux de lin* with their veiled tonal beauty – framed as they are by Nováček's dazzling *Perpetuum mobile* and Sarasate's coruscating *Zapateado*. The wistful sentimentality of Ponce's *Estrellita* (which actually derives from a forgotten violin concerto) is perfectly caught, while Poulenc's spiccato *Presto* and the Paradies *Toccata* similarly offer contrast to a charmingly fragile portrayal of *Le cygne*.

Tully Potter in the notes tells us that Elgar's *La capricieuse* 'demands a good up-bow staccato': it is managed here with aplomb, while the Paradies *Sicilenne* and the more luscious Raff *Cavatina* make a charming foil for the witty Vieuxtemps *Souvenir d'Amérique*, which must surely raise a smile of recognition. The recital ends with Spanishry: three pieces by Sarasate, with whom Perlman has already shown a great affinity in his recordings of the concertante *Carmen Fantasy* and *Zigeunerwiesen*. Samuel Sanders accompanies with discretion but is a true partner where necessary. For the most part he is backwardly balanced, but he makes his initial entry strongly, before Perlman, in the opening *Perpetuum mobile*. The recording is very truthful and immediate.

'*Tradition*': Familiar Jewish Melodies (with Israel Zohar, clarinet, and Israel PO, Seltzer): *A Yiddishe Mamme; As der Rebbe Elimelech is gevoyrn asoi freylach; Reyzele; Oif'n Pripetchik brennt a feier; Doyna; Rozhinkes mit Mandelen; Oif'n Weyg steyt a Boim; A Dudele; Viahin soll ich geyn?*

(M) *** EMI 5 62597-2.

Perlman spent his childhood years in Israel, and this affectionately played programme reflects his familiarity with traditional Jewish melodies, always warmly seductive in melodic outline and 'poised', as Tully Potter comments in the notes, 'between joy and sadness, sentiment and sentimentality'. There are also the occasional accelerando features that we recognize from the Brahms *Hungarian Dances*. Dov Seltzer has scored these pieces concertante fashion, but leaving plenty of opportunities for Perlman to carry the luscious melodies, gently and tastefully (as in *Oif' Weyg steyt a Boim*). The principal clarinettist of the Israel Philharmonic also makes a modest solo contribution to three numbers. However, despite the conductor's surname, his chosen programme concentrates on slow, languorous melodies, rather than adding an element of sparkle. The recording is richly textured, with Perlman flatteringly profiled.

'*Virtuoso Violin*': SARASATE: *Carmen Fantasy, Op. 25* (with RPO, Foster); *Zigeunerweisen, Op. 20* (with Pittsburg SO, Previn). *Music for Violin and Piano* (with Sanders): *Malagueña & Habanera, Op. 21/1–2; Romanza Andaluza, Op. 22; Playera & Zapateado, Op. 23; Caprice basque, Op. 24; Spanish Dance, Op. 26/8*. FALLA: *Suite populaire espagnole* (arr. KOCHANSKI). GRANADOS: *Spanish Dance*. ALBENIZ: *Malagueña, Op. 165/3* (both arr. KREISLER). HALFFTER: *Danza de la Gitana* (arr. HEIFETZ).

(BB) *** EMI Encore (ADD) 5 74765-2.

Here is a recital for violin and piano, originally more appropriately entitled 'Spanish Album', framed by two of Perlman's most successful concertante recordings of Sarasate, the dazzling *Carmen Fantasy* and the equally beguiling *Zigeunerweisen*. Perlman is a violinist who on record demonstrates his delight in virtuosity in every phrase he plays. Yet he can also refine his timbre to be magically beguiling, as in the gentle *Asturiano* from Falla's *Suite populaire espagnole*. There are few more joyful records of violin fireworks than this, and the recording projects his playing vividly throughout, although the sound is a bit over-bright.

'*The Art of Itzhak Perlman*' (with Israel PO, Mehta; Pittsburgh SO, Previn; LPO, Ozawa; RPO, Foster; also Ashkenazy, Canino, Sanders, Previn (piano) and other artists): BACH: *Concerto, BWV 1056; Partita No. 3, BWV 1006*. VIVALDI: *Concerto, RV 199*. MOZART: *Oboe Quartet, K.370*. BRAHMS: *Sonata No. 3; Hungarian Dances 1–2, 7 & 9*. SINDING: *Suite, Op. 10*. WIENIAWSKI: *Concerto No. 1*. SIBELIUS: *Concerto*. KHACHATURIAN: *Concerto*. KORNGOLD: *Concerto*. STRAVINSKY: *Suite italienne*. ANON.: *Doyna*. YELLEN/POLLACK: *My Yiddishe Momma*. FOSTER (arr. HEIFETZ): *The Old Folks at Home*. PONCE (arr. HEIFETZ): *Estrellita*. JOPLIN: *The Rag-time Dance; Pineapple Rag*. SMETANA: *Z domoviny*. KREISLER: *Liebesfreud; Liebesleid*. RACHMANINOV (arr. PRESS/GINGOLD):

Vocalise. GRAINGER: *Molly on the Shore.* PREVIN:
Look at him; Bowing and Scraping. TRAD. (arr.
KREISLER): *Londonderry Air.* SARASATE: *Carmen
Fantasy.*

(M) ✱✱✱ EMI ADD/DDD 7 64617-2 (4).

This box contains a feast of this great violinist's
recordings. He made the choice himself and, while
the concertos, particularly the Wieniawski, Sibelius,
Khachaturian and Korngold (and not forgetting the
dazzling concertante *Carmen Fantasy* of Sarasate or
the *Suite* of Sinding), are all indispensable, the
shorter pieces on the last disc just as readily display
the Perlman magic. They include the delectable jazz
collaboration with Previn, the beautifully played
Kreisler encores, and many popular items which are
readily turned into lollipops. The stylish account of
the Stravinsky *Suite italienne* which ends disc three is
also one of the highlights of the set. For the most
part the recordings have the violin very forwardly
balanced, but that was Perlman's own choice; the
sound is otherwise generally excellent. The discs are
also currently available separately at mid-price.

'*Great Romantic Violin Concertos*' (with (i) Chicago
SO or (ii) Philh. O, Giulini; (iii) Concg. O, Haitink;
(iv) RPO, Foster; (v) Phd. O, Ormandy): (i)
BRAHMS: *Concerto in D, Op. 77.* (iii) BRUCH:
Concerto No. 1 in G min., Op. 26. (ii) BEETHOVEN:
Concerto in D, Op. 61. (iv) PAGANINI: *Concerto No.
1 in D, Op. 6.* (iii) MENDELSSOHN: *Concerto in E
min., Op. 64.* (v) TCHAIKOVSKY: *Concerto in D, Op.
35.*

(M) ✱✱(✱) EMI ADD/DDD 7 64922-2 (3).

These major Perlman recordings include his earlier
(1980) studio recording of the Beethoven *Concerto*; it
is among the most commanding of his readings and
the element of slight understatement, the refusal to
adopt too romantically expressive a style, makes for a
compelling strength, perfectly matched by Giulini's
thoughtful, direct accompaniment. The (1976)
Brahms is also a distinguished performance, again
finely supported by Giulini, this time with the Chicago orchestra, a reading of darker hue than is customary, with a thoughtful and searching slow
movement rather than the autumnal rhapsody which
it so often becomes. The (1983) Bruch *G minor
Concerto* must be counted a disappointment, however, not helped by the harsh, early digital recording
which gives an edge to the solo timbre. The performance is heavily expressive and, like the Mendelssohn
(recorded at the same time), is not nearly as spontaneous as Perlman's earlier, analogue recording with
Previn. The Paganini (1971) is one of Perlman's very
finest records and, although the traditional cuts are
observed, the performance has irresistible panache
and has been transferred to CD very well. In the
Tchaikovsky (1978) the soloist is placed less aggressively forward than is usual. Perlman's expressive
warmth goes with a very bold orchestral texture from
Ormandy and the Philadelphia Orchestra. However,

admirers of these artists are unlikely to be disappointed.

'*Cinema Serenade*': Film Themes (with Pittsburgh
SO, Williams): TEMPERTON/ROSENBAUM: *The
Color Purple.* GARDEL: *Scent of a Woman (Tango).*
ELMER BERNSTEIN: *The Age of Innocence.* JOHN
WILLIAMS: *Far and Away; Sabrina; Schindler's List.*
LEGRAND: *The Umbrellas of Cherbourg.* PREVIN:
The Four Horsemen of the Apocalypse. JOHN
BARRY: *Out of Africa.* BONFA: *Black Orpheus.*
✱✱✱ Sony SK 63005.

Over the centuries all the great violin virtuosi have
indulged themselves with the popular tunes of the
day, and in our time quite a few of the best of them
come from film-scores. Perlman relishes their melodiousness, playing them with an easy sophistication
and an unashamed tonal succulence. He is immediately beguiling in the title theme from *The Color
Purple* and then dances to the tango rhythms of *Pur
una cabeza* from *Scent of a Woman.*

Most of these concertante arrangements have been
skilfully managed by John Williams, and in his own
score for *Far and Away* he has created a sparkling
scherzando to offset the lyrical melody. *Il Postero* and
Sabrina bring a more delicate charm, but Elmer
Bernstein's music for *The Age of Innocence* and John
Barry's score for *Out of Africa* develop a Hollywoodian orchestral opulence. The engaging tune
Michel Legrand was inspired to write for *The
Umbrellas of Cherbourg* seems custom-made for Perlman's stylish languor, and for contrast *Black Orpheus*
brings a more intimate duet for violin and guitar.

But our own favourite is the charmingly romantic
music Andrea Morricone wrote for *Cinema Paradiso*,
a nostalgic score for one of the more memorable
films of the last decade. But there is too little of it,
and there would have been room for more. Throughout, the easy bravura and panache of the solo playing
recall Heifetz, and Williams and the excellent Pittsburgh orchestra provide spectacular accompaniments. The recording is spacious with Perlman (as
usual), upfront in a spotlight; the orchestra is full
and warm, but could be better focused.

Petri, Michaela (recorder)

'*The Ultimate Recorder Collection*': VIVALDI: *The
Four Seasons: Spring* (with Guildhall String Ens.,
Malcolm). *Concerto in D (Il gardellino), Op. 10/3:
Finale. Concerto in G min. (La Notte), Op. 10/2, RV
439.* SAMMARTINI: *Recorder Concerto in F* (all with
Moscow Virtuosi, Spivakov). SATIE: *Gymnopédie
No. 1.* GLUCK: *Orfeo: Melody & Dance of the Blessed
Spirits.* BACH: *Suite in D, BWV 1067: Air.*
SCHEINDIENST: *Variations.* TARTINI: *Sonata in G
min. (Devil's trill).* KOPPEL: *Nele's dances Nos.
15–18.* JACOB: *An Encore for Michaela* (all with
Hannibal, arr. for recorder and guitar). GRIEG: *Peer
Gynt: Solveig's Song; Anitra's Dance.* Lyric pieces:

Butterfly; Little Bird, Op. 43/1 & 4; March of the Trolls, Op. 54/3; Once Upon a Time, Op. 71/1; 2 Norwegian Dances, Op. 35/1-2 (all arr. Langford). KOPPEL: *Moonchild's Dream: Conclusion.* ARNOLD: *Recorder Concerto, Op. 133: Lento.* CHRISTIANSEN: *Dance suite, Op. 29: Molto vivace* (all with ECO, Okko Kamu). HANDEL: *Sonata in G min., Op. 1/2.* BACH: *Sonata in E flat* (transposed G), *BWV 1031* (with Jarrett, harpsichord). TELEMANN: *Trio Sonata No. 3 in F min.* (with Hanne Petri, harpsichord, David Petri, cello). *Sonata No. 5 in D min. for 2 Recorders* (with Selin). CORELLI: *Concerto grosso, Op. 6/8 (Christmas): Finale including Pastorale* (with Nat. PO, Neary). BACH: *Cantata No. 140: Chorale: Wachet auf* (with Westminster Abbey Ch., Ross, organ; cond. Neary).
(B) ** RCA Twofer 74321 59112-2 (2).

This is a collection that will best appeal to amateur recorder players, and might make a good birthday present for a young beginner, who will surely be impressed by Michaela Petri's easy virtuosity and will respond to a string of such famous melodies. Not all of them transcribe too well, and many are far more effective on the instruments for which they were written. Vivaldi's *Spring* from *The Four Seasons* is indestructible, but Bach's famous *Air* sounds puny, while Grieg's *Second Norwegian Dance* is much better suited to the oboe. However, there is quite a lot of genuine recorder repertoire here, stylishly presented, which hopefully should tempt any budding young soloist to explore further. The recording balance is generally well managed and the effect is truthful and not overblown.

Philadelphia Orchestra, Wolfgang Sawallisch

Stokowski Orchestral Transcriptions: BACH: Chorales from Cantatas: *Sheep may Safely Graze; Wachet auf; Ein' feste Burg ist unser Gott. Toccata and Fugue in D min., BWV 565.* BOCCHERINI: *Minuet, Op. 13/5.* BEETHOVEN: *Piano Sonata No. 14 (Moonlight):* 1st movt. CHOPIN: *Prelude in E min., Op. 28/4.* FRANCK: *Panis angelicus.* TCHAIKOVSKY: *Andante cantabile, Op. 11; At the Ball* (with Lipovšek). DEBUSSY: *Suite bergamasque: Clair de lune. Prélude: La Cathédrale engloutie.* RACHMANINOV: *Prelude in C sharp min., Op. 3/2.*
(BB) **(*) EMI Encore 585672-2.

Though Stokowski's own recordings, even those he made in extreme old age, generally have a degree more flair and dramatic bite than any of these from the latter-day Philadelphia Orchestra, this makes a fine tribute from the great orchestra he created. The selection of items is an attractive one, not least the Tchaikovsky song orchestration, with Marjana Lipovšek an aptly Slavonic-sounding soloist, though balanced too close.

Sawallisch brings out the evocative magic of Stokowski's impressionistic view of the *Moonlight Sonata* movement, and *Clair de lune* is similarly free in its expressiveness. With warm, resonant sound, firmer in the bass than usual from this source, this makes a sumptuous collection, even if some will prefer the brighter, sharper focus of rival Stokowski collections, such as Kunzel's on Telarc or Bamert's on Chandos. It is worth noting that Bamert's even more generous selection of 15 encore pieces overlaps in only three items, and it includes more fun pieces. However, they are much more expensive.

Philadelphia Orchestra, Leopold Stokowski (see also under Stokowski Decca recordings below)

'*Fantasia*': BACH, orch. Stokowski: *Toccata and Fugue in D min.* DUKAS: *L'Apprenti sorcier.* MUSSORGSKY, arr. Stokowski: *Night on the Bare Mountain.* STRAVINSKY: *The Rite of Spring.* TCHAIKOVSKY: *Nutcracker Suite.*
(M) (***) Pearl mono GEMMCD 4988.

A self-recommending disc. *The Rite of Spring* comes from 1929–30 and the *Nutcracker* from as early as 1926, though one would never believe it. Everything Stokowski did at this period was full of character, and the engineers obviously performed miracles. The latest recording is Stokowski's amazing arrangement of *Night on the Bare Mountain*, which dates from 1940. Such is the colour and richness of sonority Stokowski evokes from the fabulous Philadelphians that surface noise and other limitations are completely forgotten. The transfers are very good.

'*Philadelphia Rarities*' (1928–1937): arr. STOKOWSKI: *2 Ancient Liturgical Melodies: Veni, Creator Spiritus; Veni, Emmanuel.* FALLA: *La vida breve: Spanish Dance.* TURINA: *Gypsy Dance, Op. 55/5.* DUBENSKY: *Edgar Allan Poe's 'The Raven'* (narr. de Loache). arr. KONOYE: *Etenraku: Ceremonial Japanese Prelude.* MCDONALD: *The Legend of the Arkansas Traveller; The Festival of the Workers (suite): Dance of the Workers. Double Piano Concerto* (with Behrend & Kelberine). EICHHEIM: *Oriental Impressions: Japanese Nocturne. Symphonic Variations: Bali.* SOUSA: *Manhattan Beach; El Capitan.*
(M) (***) Cala mono CACD 0501.

All these recordings show what splendid recorded sound Stokowski was achieving in Philadelphia as early as 1929. The opening Stokowski liturgical arrangements show how that master of orchestral sonority could make liturgical chants his very own, with a discreet tolling bell to indicate their source. Falla's *Spanish Dance* shows him at his most sparklingly chimerical. Dubensky's music does not add a great deal to Edgar Allan Poe, but the narrator, Benjamin de Loache, certainly does, presenting the narrative with the essentially genial, melodramatic lubricity of Vincent Price.

Hidemaro Konoye and Stokowski and his players conspire between them to provide an extraordinarily authentic Japanese sound in *Etenraku*, and then in *The Legend of the Arkansas Traveller* we have a complete change of local colour for Alexander Hilsberg's folksy, sub-Country-and-Western violin solo. Henry Eichheim's Japanese and Balinese impressions are suitably exotic, but not music one would wish to return to. As for Harl McDonald's *Double Piano Concerto*, the piano writing is splashy and the finale is spectacularly based on the *Juarezca*, a jazzy Mexican dance. The two soloists provide convincing, extrovert dash, and Stokowski obviously revels in what Noël Coward might have described as 'potent cheap music' if with nothing like the melodic appeal of Coward's own work. The two Sousa marches have both poise and élan, but here the sound is barely adequate – not the fault of the CD transfer. The programme lasts for 78 minutes and Stokowksi aficionados need not hesitate.

Philadelphia Orchestra, or (i) Minneapolis Orchestra, Eugene Ormandy

BEETHOVEN: *Piano Concertos Nos. 3 in C min., Op. 37* (with Arrau); *4 in G, Op. 58* (with Casadesus). BARBER: *Essay No. 1 for Orchestra, Op. 12.* BRAHMS: *Double Concerto in A min., Op. 102* (with Heifetz & Feuermann). BRUCKNER: *Symphony No. 7 in E.* DVORAK: *Cello Concerto in B min., Op. 104* (with Piatigorsky). (i) GRIEG: *Piano Concerto in A min., Op. 16* (with Rubinstein). GRIFFES: *The Pleasure Dome of Kubla Khan, Op. 8.* (i) MAHLER: *Symphony No. 2 in C min. (Resurrection)* (with Frank, O'Malley Gallogly; Twin City Symphony Ch.). MIASKOVSKY: *Symphony No. 21 in F sharp min. in One Movement, Op 51.* MUSSORGSKY: *Pictures at an Exhibition* (orch. Caillet). RACHMANINOV: *Piano Concertos Nos. 1 in F sharp min., Op. 1; 3 in D min., Op. 30* (with composer). RAVEL: *Piano Concerto for the Left Hand* (with Casadesus). (i) SCHOENBERG: *Verklaerte Nacht, Op. 4.* SIBELIUS: *Symphony No. 1 in E min., Op. 39; Legend: Lemminkäinen's Homeward Journey, Op. 22/4.* RICHARD STRAUSS: *Don Quixote, Op. 35* (with Feuermann); *Symphonia domestica, Op. 53.* TCHAIKOVSKY: *Piano Concerto No. 1 in B flat min., Op. 23* (with Levant); *Symphony No. 6 in B min. (Pathéthique).*
(BB) (★★★) Brillante Maestro (mono) 205236/240-303 (10).

This is an amazing cornucopia of classic performances given by the Philadelphia Orchestra, presided over by Eugene Ormandy. The Minneapolis Orchestra is represented by the electrifying 1935 Mahler *Second Symphony* and the 1934 Schoenberg *Verklaerte Nacht*, its première recording in the version

for full strings. The earliest of the Philadelphia performances are *The Pleasure Dome of Kubla Khan* (1934) and the Bruckner *Seventh Symphony* (1935), the last being the Tchaikovsky *B flat minor Concerto* with Oscar Levant. Speaking of which, what a line-up of soloists is on offer: Jascha Heifetz and Emanuel Feuermann in the Brahms, and the legendary 1940 *Don Quixote* also with Feuermann. Those who remember the Mahler will know how dramatic and intense was this performance. It is particularly good to have Robert Casadesus in Beethoven's *G major Concerto* and Louis Caillet's scoring of *Pictures at an Exhibition* recorded in 1937. Some of these performances (the Barber *Essay for Orchestra* and the Miaskovsky *Symphony*) are already available in alternative transfers, but many are not. As far as we know, the *Verklaerte Nacht* makes its first appearance since the 1930s. It was a much-sought-after import after the war and commanded what was then an astronomic price: £1 a disc! The whole treasure-house of ten CDs is marketed at under £20 (£2 a disc, each of which would encompass eight or nine 78s). Generally speaking the transfers are serviceable rather than distinguished: the Schoenberg does not noticeably improve on the original shellac discs, and the Rachmaninov concertos are not better than either the RCA or Naxos transfers. No matter; this is an incredible bargain, and some of the performances are alone worth the price of the whole box. Ormandy was taken for granted in the 1950s and 1960s, but he got a wonderful sound from his Philadelphia Orchestra; none of these performances falls below distinction.

Philharmonia Orchestra, Constant Lambert

'The Last Recordings': CHABRIER (orch. Lambert): *Ballabile.* SUPPE: *Overtures: Morning, Noon and Night in Vienna; Pique dame.* WALDTEUFEL: *Waltzes: Estudiantina, Les patineurs, Pomone, Sur la plage.* WALTON: *Façade Suites Nos. 1 and 2.*
(M) (★★★) Somm Celeste mono SOMMCD 023.

This charming disc offers a generous collection, very well transferred, of the recordings Constant Lambert made just before his death. Lambert's flair as a ballet conductor is reflected in all the items here. Whether in Waldteufel waltzes, Suppé overtures or the orchestral *Façade* pieces (source of the highly successful ballet) Lambert is masterly at giving a spring to the dance-rhythms, while never indulging excessively in rubato. Lambert rivals even the composer himself in bringing out the fun of *Façade*. He was, after all, almost the work's surrogate creator – the friend of Walton who, alongside him, discovered the joys of jazz and syncopated rhythms in the early 1920s. It is remarkable too that even with the limitations of mono recording of 1950 Lambert keeps textures ideally clear and transparent, helped by the refined playing of the Philharmonia Orchestra, adding to the freshness of all these performances. As part of the documentation, Alan Sanders provides a most illuminating essay on Lambert's life and recording career.

Philharmonia Orchestra, Nicolai Malko

BORODIN: *Prince Igor: Overture; Polovtsian Dances; Polovtsian March. Symphony No. 2 in A min.*
RIMSKY-KORSAKOV: *Maid of Pskov (Ivan the Terrible): Overture.* LIADOV: *8 Russian Folksongs.*
GLAZUNOV (with Sokolov and Liadov): *Les vendredis: Polka.*
(**) Testament mono/stereo SBT 1062.

Nicolai Malko, from 1926 the chief conductor of the Leningrad Philharmonic and the first interpreter of Shostakovich's *First Symphony*, made all too few recordings; though some of these with the Philharmonia lack tautness, his feeling for the Slavonic idiom is unerring. This reading of the *Prince Igor Overture* is light and transparent (in newly unearthed stereo) but lacks dramatic bite, and so do the *Polovtsian Dances*, polished but not involving. The *Polovtsian March* is quite different: a tense, swaggering performance which reveals the true Malko. Then after an amiable, low-key account of the first movement of the Borodin *Symphony*, the Scherzo second movement brings a virtuoso performance. Best of all is the Rimsky-Korsakov overture, in full-bodied stereo. After a relaxed, colourful account of the Liadov *Folksongs*, the corporately written *Polka* makes a charming encore, an Elgarlike salon piece.

Philharmonia Orchestra, Igor Markevitch

'*Orchestral Portrait*': BARTOK: *Dance Suite.* RAVEL: *La valse.* SATIE: *Parade.* BUSONI: *Tänzwalzer.*
LIADOV: *Kikimora.* CHABRIER: *Le roi malgré lui: Fête polonaise.* LISZT: *Mephisto Waltz.*
(***) Testament (mono) SBT 1060.

The seven varied items here make an illuminating portrait of a conductor who at the time seemed destined to be more central in the world of recording than he became. With immaculate transfers, the 1950s mono recordings have astonishing vividness and presence. In the effervescent account of Satie's *Parade* (sadly cut in the last movement) the brass and percussion (including the celebrated typewriter) have wonderful bite, and so have the joyful brass fanfares at the start of the Chabrier *Polonaise*, done in Viennese style. Perhaps most vivid of all is the virtuoso performance of the *Mephisto Waltz*.

Pierlot, Pierre (oboe)

'*The Magic of the Oboe*' (with Sol. Ven., Scimone; or Paillard CO, Paillard): VIVALDI: *Concertos in C, RV 452; F, RV 455.* ALBINONI: *Concerto a cinque in D min., Op. 9/2.* CIMAROSA: *Concerto* (arr. BENJAMIN). ZIPOLI: *Adagio for Oboe, Cello, Organ and Strings* (arr. GIOVANNINI). MARCELLO: *Concerto in C min.* BELLINI: *Concerto.*
(M) *** Erato 4509 92130-2.

For once, a record company's sobriquet for a collection does not disappoint: this is indeed a magical and very generous (74 minutes) collection, well recorded. One might say the cream of baroque oboe concertos are included here, and Benjamin's arrangement of the *Concerto* by Cimarosa with its delightful central *Siciliano* and spiccato finale is as engaging as any. The Albinoni and Marcello *Concertos* have memorable slow movements, too, and the Bellini a catchy Polacca finale. The novelty is Zipoli's *Adagio*, sumptuously arranged by Francesco Giovannini after the manner of Giazotto's 'Albinoni *Adagio*'. It doesn't quite come off, but it is a very near miss. Throughout, Pierlot's sweet, finely focused timbre and graceful phrasing are a constant pleasure.

Pollini, Maurizio (piano)

'The Pollini Edition'

BARTOK: *Piano Concertos Nos. 1–2* (with Chicago SO, Claudio Abbado). STRAVINSKY: *3 Movements from Petrushka* (471 360-2).

BEETHOVEN: *Piano Concertos Nos. 3–4* (with BPO, Abbado) (471 352-2).

BEETHOVEN: *Piano Concerto No. 5 (Emperor).*
MOZART: *Piano Concerto No. 23 in A, K.488* (with VPO, Karl Boehm) (471 351-2).

BEETHOVEN: *Piano Sonatas Nos. 13 in E flat; 14 (Moonlight), Op. 27/1–2; 17 in D min. (Tempest), Op. 31/2; 21 in C (Waldstein), Op. 53* (471 354-2).

BEETHOVEN: *Piano Sonatas Nos. 29 (Hammerklavier); 32 in C min., Op. 111* (471 355-2).

BOULEZ: *Sonata No. 2.* DEBUSSY: *12 Etudes* (471 359-2).

BRAHMS: *Piano Concerto No. 1 in D min., Op. 15.*
SCHUMANN: *Piano Concerto in A min., Op. 54* (with BPO, Abbado) (471 353-2).

CHOPIN: *Berceuse; 12 Etudes, Op. 25; Piano Sonata No. 2, Op. 35* (471 357-2).

LISZT: *Sonata in B min.; La Lugubre gondola.*
SCHUMANN: *Fantasy in C, Op. 17; Arabesque, Op. 18* (471 358-2).

MANZONI: *Masse: Omaggio a Edgard Varèse* (with BPO, Giuseppe Sinopoli). NONO: *Como una ola de fuerza y luz* (with Taskova, Bav. RSO, Abbado); . . . *soffrte onde serene* (471 362-2).

SCHOENBERG: *The works for Solo Piano; Piano Concerto* (with BPO, Abbado). WEBERN: *Variations for Piano, Op. 27* (471 361-2).

SCHUBERT: *Piano Sonata No. 20 in A, D.959; Allegretto in C min., D.915; 3 Klavierstücke, D.946* (471 356-2).

Bonus CD: CHOPIN: *Piano Concerto No. 1 in E min., Op. 11* (with Warsaw PO, Katlewicz). SCHUMANN: *Piano Concerto in A min., Op. 54* (with VPO, von Karajan).

(B) **(*) DG (ADD/DDD) 471 363-2 (12 + bonus CD).

Pollini's impeccable keyboard mastery dominates this collection. His Beethoven recordings have been highly praised, yet they have had variable success on records. Here DG have chosen the later (1992) recordings of Beethoven's *Third* and *Fourth Piano Concertos*, recorded live. But the balance of advantage does not always favour these later versions, and wisely Pollini's earlier, analogue recording of the *Emperor* with Boehm has been preferred, for although it is a studio recording it is seemingly more spontaneously expressive.

When they were first issued in 1977, Joan Chissell spoke of the 'noble purity' of Pollini's performances of the late Beethoven *Sonatas*, and that telling phrase aptly sums them up, if also hinting perhaps at a missing dimension of deep feeling which the CD transfer seems to emphasize. Yet Pollini's performances are undoubtedly eloquent and have great authority and power. His Chopin playing is cool and elegant, his Schubert strong and commanding. Both have superb precision, but his technical mastery is even more impressive in the music of Liszt. With any minor reservations noted, taken overall this collection is very impressive, with his records of twentieth-century repertoire outstanding in every way. Yet in some ways the bonus CD is finest of all, combining a spendid account of Chopin's *E minor Concerto* with a superb performance of the Schumann *Piano Concerto* in which his partnership with Karajan produces results that are dazzling, touchingly poetic and, above all, freshly spontaneous. All the recordings here are also available separately and each is discussed under its composer listing.

Radio Television Eireann Concert Orchestra, Dublin, Ernest Tomlinson

'*British Light Music - Miniatures*': COLLINS: *Vanity Fair.* LUBBOCK: *Polka Dots.* GIBBS: *Dusk.* FRANKEL: *Carriage and Pair.* ELLIS: *Coronation*

Scot. BENJAMIN: *Jamaican Song; Jamaican Rumba.* DOCKER: *Tabarinage.* ELGAR: *Beau Brummel.* DEXTER: *Siciliano.* WARNER: *Scrub, Brothers Scrub!* JACOB: *Cradle Song.* ARNE, arr. TOMLINSON: *Georgian Suite: Gavotte.* VINTER: *Portuguese Party.* TOYE: *The Haunted Ballroom* (concert waltz). WHITE: *Puffin' Billy.* MELACHRINO: *Starlight Roof Waltz.* RICHARDSON: *Beachcomber.*

**(*) Marco Polo 8.223522.

Anthony Collins was right to be proud of his delightful vignette, 'Vanity Fair', for its theme is indelible, and it comes up very freshly here in a programme of unassuming orchestral lollipops, including many items with almost equally catchy musical ideas, even a *Gavotte* by Thomas Arne, arranged by the conductor to sound just a little like a caricature. The tunes are usually pithy and short, like Harry Dexter's daintily wispy *Siciliano*, but sometimes the writing is gently evocative, like the two romantic waltzes, *Dusk* by Armstrong Gibbs, and Geoffrey Toye's *Haunted Ballroom*, and Gordon Jacob's delicate *Cradle Song.*

Novelties like Benjamin Frankel's clip-clopping *Carriage and Pair*, Edward White's *Puffin' Billy*, and Ken Warner's moto perpetuo, *Scrub, Brothers Scrub!* readily evoke the world of Leroy Anderson, while Clive Richardson's quirky *Beachcomber* makes one want to smile. The conductor, Ernest Tomlinson, understands that their very slightness is part of the charm of nearly all these pieces, and he presents them with a simplicity that is wholly endearing. The only relative disappointment is Vivian Ellis's wittily evoked *Coronation Scot*, which needs much more verve than it receives here. Good playing and good recording, although the acoustic effect becomes noticeably more brash for the second item, Mark Lubbock's breezy *Polka Dots.*

Radio France Philharmonic Orchestra, Yutaka Sado

'French Spectacular': DUKAS: *The Sorcerer's Apprentice.* BIZET: *Carmen: Suites Nos. 1 & 2* (excerpts); *L'Arlésienne: Suites Nos. 1 & 2* (excerpts). OFFENBACH: *Gaîté parisienne* (excerpts).

(M) *(*) Warner Elatus 2564 61357-2.

The *Sorcerer's Apprentice* is well played but lacks a real sense of calamity and excitement. The Bizet excerpts go well enough, but the complete suites would be better, especially as the Offenbach excerpts lack the essential effervescence they need. Good sound.

Rahbari, Sohre (saxophone), Belgian Radio and TV Orchestra, Brussels, Alexander Rahbari

Music for Saxophone and Orchestra: MILHAUD: *Scaramouche (suite).* GLAZUNOV: *Concerto in E flat,*

Op. 109. DEBUSSY: *Rapsodie.* IBERT: *Concertino da camera.* MUSSORGSKY: *Pictures at an Exhibition: The Old Castle.* SOHRE RAHBARI: *Japanese Improvisation for Solo Saxophones.*

(BB) ** Naxos 8.554784.

The Ibert is the most successful piece here, and the concertante version of *Scaramouche* works well too, with its lively quotation of 'Ten green bottles', but the Glazunov rather outstays its welcome. Sohre Rahbari is a fine player and responds to Debussy's exoticism with an attractive freedom of line. Alexander Rahbari is at his best and the Belgian orchestra gives quite persuasive support, although their playing could be more refined. The recording is good, but rather resonant. Value for money, but not distinctive.

Rampal, Jean-Pierre (flute)

'*20th-century Flute Masterpieces*' (with (i) LOP, Froment; (ii) O de l'ORTF, Martinon; (iii) LOP, Jolivet; (iv) Robert Veyron-Lacroix): (i) IBERT: *Concerto.* (ii) KHACHATURIAN: *Concerto* (arr. from *Violin Concerto*). (iii) JOLIVET: *Concerto.* (iv) MARTINU: *Sonata.* HINDEMITH: *Sonata.* PROKOFIEV: *Sonata in D.* POULENC: *Sonata.*

(M) **(*) Erato (ADD) 2292 45839-2 (2).

The concertos on the first CD have less than perfectly focused orchestral strings, and the Khachaturian arrangement is dispensable. But the Ibert *Concerto* is winning and the more plangent Jolivet not inconsiderable. The highlights of the collection are all on the second disc, three out of the four of them inspired works, delightfully written for the instrument and marvellously played. Only the first movement of the Hindemith is a bit below par in its utilitarian austerity; the cool slow movement and more vigorous finale have something approaching charm. The Prokofiev *Sonata* (also heard in a version for violin – but the flute is the original) is a masterpiece, and Rampal makes the very most of it. Then comes the delightful Poulenc piece with its disarmingly easy-flowing opening, delicious central cantilena and scintillating finale with hints of *Les Biches*. The recording of the sonatas, made in 1978, is vividly firm and realistic. If this set is reissued later on a Bonsai Duo, it will be well worth seeking out.

Reilly, Tommy (harmonica)

'*Harmonica Concertos*' (with (i) Munich RSO, Gerhardt; (ii) Basel RSO, Dumont; (iii) SW German R. O, Smola; (iv) Munich RSO, Farnon; (v) Farnon O, Farnon): (i) SPIVAKOVSKY: *Harmonica Concerto.* (ii) ARNOLD: *Harmonica Concerto, Op. 46.* (iii) VILLA-LOBOS: *Harmonica Concerto.* (iv) MOODY: *Toledo (Spanish fantasy).* (v) FARNON: *Prelude and Dance.*

*** Chan. 9248.

This is most attractive. The Spivakovsky is a particularly winning piece, with a catchy tune in the first movement, rather like a Leroy Anderson encore, a popular, romantic central interlude, marked *Dolce*, and a delicious moto perpetuo finale. Not surprisingly, the Malcolm Arnold is very appealing too, one of this composer's best miniature concertos, written in 1954 for the BBC Proms. The Villa-Lobos, written in 1955, should be much better known. Scored for a small orchestra of strings, single wind, harp, celesta and percussion, it has a neo-classical character. It produces a quite lovely melody for the *Andante*; only the finale, which moves along at a genial pace, has piquant hints of the composer's usual Brazilian preoccupation. James Moody's *Spanish Fantasy* might be described as good cheap music, and it offers the soloist a glittering chance to demonstrate his bravura with infectious panache. Farnon's hauntingly nostalgic *Prelude and Dance* (a charmingly inconsequential little waltz) brings a felicitous interleaving of both themes. The recording balance is surely as near perfect as one could wish.

Ricci, Ruggiero (violin)

'*Decca Recordings, 1950–59*': PAGANINI: *Violin Concertos Nos. 1 in D, Op. 6; 2 (Campanella) in B min., Op. 7* (with LSO, Collins); *24 Caprices for Solo Violin, Op. 1.* RAVEL: *Tzigane* (with SRO, Ansermet). R. STRAUSS: *Violin Sonata in E flat, Op. 18.* WEBER: *6 Sonatas Progressives, J99–104* (with Bussotti). SARASATE: *Fantasia on Bizet's 'Carmen', Op. 25; Zigeunerweisen, Op. 20.* SAINT-SAENS: *Havanaise, Op. 83; Introduction & Rondo capriccioso, Op. 28* (with LSO, Gamba). LALO: *Symphonie espagnole, Op. 21* (with SRO, Ansermet). HINDEMITH: *Solo Violin Sonatas, Op. 31/1 & 2.* PROKOFIEV: *Solo Violin Sonata, Op. 115.* KHACHATURIAN: *Violin Concerto* (with LPO, Fistoulari).

(B) * (**) Decca mono/stereo 475 105-2 (5).

It is good that Ruggiero Ricci has been included in the 'Original Masters' series. He was an important recording artist in the early years of the Decca company, and this set, compiled by Raymond McGill, contains a wide range of both expected and unexpected items. The *Paganini Caprices* are the mono accounts dating from 1950, rather than Ricci's later stereo version (already released). It is fascinating to compare the two versions, some numbers faster in one, slower in the other, though the later accounts shave off around 4 minutes from the overall time. However, this mono set – in vividly bright, if rather dry sound – emerges as the fresher of the two, and it is now available on CD for the first time. The Paganini *Concertos* are brilliantly done, full of life, with Ricci making the most of Paganini's *bel canto*-like melodies, as well as the dazzling virtuosity of the bravura writing. Anthony Collins's lively and stylish accompaniments are of enormous help. The mono sound (1955) is strikingly full and vivid, but of course the soloist is very closely miked.

The pianist Carlo Bussotti is the accompanist for the unexpected repertoire on the third disc, with the Strauss *Violin Sonata* a good if not totally convincing account, and the rare Weber *Sonatas Progressives* one of this set's highlights: charming, unpretentious works, with delightful melodic invention. The sound for this disc is a little two-dimensional, but more than acceptable. Ricci's 1960 (stereo) recital of twentieth-century solo violin works stands up very well: the Prokofiev *Sonata* is the most approachable by reason of its neo-baroque spirit and easy contours; and if the Hindemith *Sonatas*, as always, show the workings of a vigorous and inventive mind, the music does not readily hold the attention throughout.

Ricci's classic (1956) account of the Khachaturian *Concerto* is still one of the best-sounding and most exciting versions today, with Fistoulari's lively and incisive support. Ricci again provides plenty of colour and sparkle in Lalo's *Symphony espagnole* and Ravel's *Tzigane*, even if the ensemble of Ansermet's Suisse Romande Orchestra at that time was hardly the last word in refinement. Ricci's classic accounts of the Sarasate and Saint-Saëns showpieces with the LSO and Gamba are characteristically brilliant, sounding as fresh and exciting as ever: in terms of bravura these 1959 versions remain in the first division.

Roscoe, Martin (piano), Guildhall Strings, Robert Salter

'*Peacock Pie*': JACOB: *Concertino*. ARMSTRONG GIBBS: *Concertino; Peacock Pie (suite)*. ROOTHAM: *Miniature Suite*. MILFORD: *Concertino in E*. DRING: *Festival Scherzo*.

*** Hyp. CDA 67316.

A wholly delectable disc of piano concertinos with string orchestra, very English in character. The opening work by Gordon Jacob, characteristically well crafted, sets the scene with its spirited neo-classical outer movements, and a delicate morsel of a central *Andante*. Armstrong Gibbs opens and closes his *Concertino* (written at Windermere, in the Lake District, in 1942) jauntily and is more romantic in the *Andante*, which yet has an English pastoral flavour. *Peacock Pie* is no less infectious, taking its title and inspiration from Walter de la Mare's book of rhymes; again the lyrical style is folksy, but the central picture of a *Sunken Garden* is mysteriously evocative and the *Ride-by-Nights* finale gallops along with witches in mind, although there is nothing spooky in the music. Cyril Rootham's *Miniature Suite* is again very English in atmosphere, with a dainty opening *Allegretto*, a tripping third movement in a neatly contrived 5/4 rhythm and a distinct folksong idiom coming to the fore in the finale. Robin Milford's

Concertino has a pleasing insouciance and a charming siciliano as its central *Poco adagio*, which is recalled in the last movement. Madeleine Dring's *Festival Scherzo* makes a sparkling, debonair encore. Performances are light-hearted and polished, and beautifully recorded.

Rostropovich, Mstislav (cello and conductor)

'*The Russian Years*' (1950–1974)

SHOSTAKOVICH: *Cello Concertos Nos. 1 in E flat, Op. 107* (with Moscow PO, Rozhdestvensky); *2 in G, Op. 126* (with USSR State SO, Svetlanov). *Cello Sonata in D min., Op. 40* (with composer, piano). KABALEVSKY: *Cello Sonata in B flat, Op. 71* (with composer, piano). KAREN KHACHATURIAN: *Cello Sonata* (with composer, piano).

(M) (**(*)) EMI mono 5 72295-2 (2).

In 1997 EMI marked the 70th birthday of Mstislav Rostropovich with an ambitious, celebratory survey called 'The Russian Recordings – 1950–74', which consisted of 13 discs (EMI CZS5 72016-2, now withdrawn) from which the present two-CD set is drawn. Rostropovich chose them himself from archival recordings in Russia. All the performances are three star, but the sound does not always do justice to his glorious tone.

EMI 5 72295-2 concentrates on Shostakovich and includes a 1961 concert performance of the *First Cello Concerto* and the very first performance of the *Second*, in 1966, given under Svetlanov and in the presence of the composer, who was celebrating his 61st birthday. The accompanying sonatas were all recorded with their respective composers, though no date is given for the Shostakovich. Rostropovich recalls that some tempi are on the brisk side: 'it was a beautiful day and Shostakovich was anxious to visit friends in the country'. The performance sounds identical to the one issued in the USA in 1958 on the Monitor label (MC 2021), though the sound has been rebalanced.

'*Slava 75*' (*75th Birthday Edition*): Cello: BACH: *Suite No. 3 in C BWV 1003*. HAYDN: *Concertos Nos. 1–2* (with ASMF). DVORAK: *Concerto* (with LPO, Giulini). BEETHOVEN: *Triple Concerto, Op. 56* (with Oistrakh, Richter, BPO, Karajan). Conducting: DVORAK: *Symphony No. 9 (New World)* (LPO). GLINKA: *Overture: Ruslan and Ludmilla; Valse-fantaisie*. BORODIN: *In the Steppes of Central Asia* (O de Paris). SHOSTAKOVICH: *Symphony No. 8* (Nat. SO of Washington).

(M) **(*) EMI (ADD/DDD) 5 67807-2 (4).

This is a more ambitious coverage than that offered by DG below and, while its range is wider, not everything shows the great Russian musician at his finest and most illuminating. He is at his most brilliant and responsive in Bach's *Third Cello Suite*, and the recording is vividly present. The pair of Haydn concertos bring comparable virtuosity and, even if his style is rather romantic, it is only too easy to be seduced by such genial and commanding music-making. The Beethoven *Triple Concerto* is a classic account which remains unsurpassed, and the 1969 recording, made in the Berlin Jesus-Christus-Kirche, is generous in resonance and yet remains clear. It is rightly one of EMI's 'Great Recordings of the Century'. The Dvořák *Concerto* is another matter. Although it is beautifully recorded, it is much too indulgently idiosyncratic to be really satisfying for repeated listening.

Turning now to Rostropovich as conductor, we find his interpretations consistently more wilful than his solo playing. He directs the weightiest reading possible of the *New World Symphony*. The very opening chords of the slow introduction suggest an epic view, and from then on, with generally expansive tempi, the performance presents this as a genuine 'Ninth', a culmination to the cycle. In the first movement the exposition repeat brings a slight modification of treatment the second time round, and some will resist such inconsistencies as this. The conscious weight of even the *Largo* is controversial too, though in all four movements Rostropovich contrasts the big tuttis – almost Straussian at times – with light pointing in woodwind solos. The recording is richly ample to match, and certainly this account is an engulfing experience.

Of the Russian items, the most attractive is the Glinka *Valse-fantaisie*, which is both elegant and lilting; the *Ruslan Overture* is very well played too but lacks the kind of zest which makes it unforgettable. *In the Steppes of Central Asia* is poetically shaped, but here the kind of heaviness experienced in the *New World Symphony* returns in the brass, the phrasing becomes too broad and the music's onward flow loses its simple forward impetus.

Fortunately the Shostakovich *Eighth* is in every way a success. This is a Teldec recording, licensed to EMI for the occasion, and here Rostropovich's intensity and that of his American players does not spill over into excess. This is a gripping account that can rank alongside the best performances one has heard on or off record – Mravinsky, Rozhdestvensky, Kondrashin and the excellent Haitink – and it is very well recorded too.

'Rostropovich Mastercellist (Legendary Recordings 1956–1978)': DVORAK: *Concerto.* TCHAIKOVSKY: *Andante cantabile for Cello and String Orchestra* (with BPO, Karajan). SCHUMANN: *Concerto* (with Leningrad PO, Rozhdestvensky). GLAZUNOV: *Chant du ménestral* (with Boston SO, Ozawa). RACHMANINOV: *Cello Sonata, Op. 19; Vocalise, Op. 34/14.* CHOPIN: *Introduction and Polonaise brillante, Op. 3.* SCHUBERT: *Impromptu in D flat, D. 899/3.* SCHUMANN: *Kinderszenen: Träumerei* (all with Alexander Dedyukhin, piano).

♦━ (M) *** DG stereo/mono DG 471 620-2 (2).

Of the two celebratory compilations issued to celebrate Rostropovich's 75th birthday, the DG two-disc package is undoubtedly the one to go for, unless you already have his incomparable 1969 recording of the Dvořák *Concerto* with Karajan or indeed the hardly less memorable account of the Schumann, imaginative and ever-communicative. The slighter, nostalgic Glazunov piece is also disarmingly attractive, and the great cellist can be readily forgiven for indulging himself a little in two of Tchaikovsky's loveliest lyrical melodies which together form the *Andante cantabile*. But what makes this programme even more enticing and valuable is the inclusion of the works with piano.

Recorded in Warsaw in 1956, with Alexander Dedyukhin, who was Rostropovich's regular partner in recitals over many years, these pieces have not been published in the UK before. They include a truly outstanding account of Rachmaninov's *Cello Sonata*, a romatically vibrant work in which a stream of irrepressible lyrical melodies constantly rise to the surface and blossom. Rostropovich plays with a rapt delicacy of feeling, his timbre in the upper range quite lovely, his phrasing at times slightly more restrained than in later years, echoed by the ever-poetic Dedyukhin.

However, there is plenty of flair and gusto in the Chopin *Introduction and Polonaise brillante*, and here the pianist lets himself go brilliantly in the more extrovert bravura. The encores are played affectionately, with the Schubert *Impromptu* (transcribed first by Heifetz and then arranged by Rostropovich) quite unlike the piano original. The recordings are mono and truthful, closely but faithfully balanced.

Rotterdam Philharmonic Orchestra, Valéry Gergiev

STRAVINSKY: *Fireworks. Piano Concerto* (with Toradze). PROKOFIEV: *Scythian Suite, Op. 20* (with Rehearsal Feature). DEBUSSY: *Le Martyre de Saint-Sébastien: Symphonic Fragments.* (Director: Rob van der Berg. Video Director: Peter Rump.)
✪ *** Arthaus **DVD** 100 314.

The concert itself is just under an hour but the DVD also includes a rehearsal feature in which Gergiev discusses Prokofiev and the *Scythian Suite*. What a relief to find a conductor championing this score with such eloquence! For too long it has been compared unfavourably with *The Rite of Spring* by English and American critics when no such comparison is called for. There are few pieces in twentieth-century music that are as imaginative as its third movement, *Night*, or as inventive as the first, *The Adoration of Véless and Ala*, with its extraordinarily lush contrasting group (fig. 8 onwards). There have been some fine CD versions, by Markevitch and Abbado, albeit none with the fervour of Koussevitzky and Désiré Defauw in the late 1940s. Gergiev comes nearest to them in his fervour and conviction, and it is good to hear him speak of the music with such warmth in the accompanying hour-long documentary. This includes some valuable archive material of Prokofiev himself and a contribution from his second son, the painter Oleg. (The programme was recorded in 1997, some time before Oleg's death.) The concert itself is imaginatively planned and Alexander Toradze is as impressive an exponent of the Stravinsky *Concerto* as he was of the Prokofiev concertos he recorded with Gergiev and the Kirov Orchestra for Philips. The camera-work is unobtrusive and intelligent, though one could do without some of the aerial shots of the orchestra. The *Scythian Suite* is difficult to balance, and some of the detail emerges in greater prominence than the main lines, but for the most part the sound-balance is vivid and very present. This is an outstanding and valuable issue that is hugely enjoyable.

Rousseau, Eugene (saxophone), Paul Kuentz Chamber Orchestra, Kuentz

Saxophone Concertos: IBERT: *Concertino da camera for Alto Saxophone and 11 Instruments.* GLAZUNOV: *Alto Saxophone Concerto in E, Op. 109.* VILLA-LOBOS: *Fantasia for Soprano Saxophone, 3 Horns and String Orchestra.* DUBOIS: *Concerto for Alto Saxophone and String Orchestra.*

(M) ★★★ DG (ADD) 453 991-2.

An enterprising anthology. The Glazunov is a late work and the best known and most often recorded of the pieces here. However, both the Villa-Lobos *Fantasia* and the Ibert *Concertino da camera* are as appealing and exotic, and there is much to give pleasure. The longest work is the *Concerto for Alto Sax* by Max-Pierre Dubois, a pupil of Milhaud: fluent, well crafted and civilized. Eugene Rousseau is an expert and persuasive soloist and the recording, which dates from the early 1970s, is first class.

Royal Academy of Music Symphonic Winds, Keith Bragg

'Sounding Out': MOZART: *Serenade No. 10 in B flat (Gran Partita), K.161.* R. STRAUSS: *Sonatina No. 2 in E flat for Wind (The Happy Workshop).* BEETHOVEN: *Symphony No. 7* (arr. for wind ensemble).

★★ Royal Academy of Music RAM 020 (2).

It seems strange that the Royal Academy of Music Symphonic Winds chose to record a programme that would not fit on a single CD. But as it happens, by far the most impressive performance here is of the genial Richard Strauss *Sonatina* (more a wind symphony – 35 minutes long) which is alone on the second disc

(presumably with the two CDs offered for the cost of one). This is in every way a 'happy workshop'. The opening movement has great vigour and spirit, yet every detail of its complex scoring comes through, every sonority is beautifully judged. The *Andantino* has genuine charm (an unexpected dimension with Richard Strauss) and the Minuet has just the right touch of robust humour. The dazzling yet essentially lyrical finale brings some aurally captivating woodwind textures. An appealing lyrical feeling predominates, even when considerable virtuosity is demanded and provided. There is some particularly fine playing from the clarinets and much nimble bravura from the horns, the solo flute and oboe. The climax is joyously resounding, to cap a superb account overall.

Alas, the rest of the programme is less appealing. Clearly Keith Bragg (the Academy's Professor of the Piccolo) has trained his players to a very high standard of excellence, but in Mozart he favours a very brisk, direct performance style that fails to to capture the convivial spirit of the great *B flat major Serenade*, and in the finale his tempo is simply too fast to find the music's wit. The *Allegretto* of the Beethoven symphony is pressed on somewhat unrelentingly and, while the Scherzo is infectious, the finale, although undoubtedly physically exciting, is *vivace* rather than *con brio*. Throughout, the Royal Academy of Music Symphonic Winds is a very impressive ensemble indeed, both in matching of timbres and in solo individuality, but in the Mozart *Serenade* they do not seem to be encouraged to play with a great deal of personal flexibility. The recording is excellent.

Royal Ballet Orchestra, David Lloyd-Jones

'English String Miniatures', Volume 1: RUTTER: *Suite.* ORR: *Cotswold Hill Tune.* MELACHRINO: *Les jeux.* DODD: *Irish Idyll.* ARMSTRONG GIBBS: *Miniature Dance Suite.* CORDELL: *King Charles's Galliard.* LYON: *Short Suite.* DOUGLAS: *Cantilena.* LANE: *Pantomime.*

(BB) ★★★ Naxos 8.554186.

A delightful collection. John Rutter shows how artfully he can write for strings, using traditional tunes: the invigorating *A-Roving*, the gentle *I Have a Bonnet Trimmed with Blue*, the touchingly simple *O, Waly, Waly* and the fizzing energy of *Dashing Away with the Smoothing Iron.* Much of the other music is permeated with influences from British folksong. Orr's *Cotswold Hill Tune* and Charles Peter Dodd's flimsy *Irish Idyll* have much in common melodically, while George Melachrino's *Les jeux* makes an engaging contrast, a gossamer dance tapestry, alternating with a semi-luscious lyrical tune. Frank Cordell's melancholy *Galliard*, of noble contour, and the *Miniature Dance Suite* of Armstrong Gibbs both have a hint of the pastiche flavour of Warlock's *Capriol Suite*. The serene *Aria*, the penultimate movement of the equally attractive *Short Suite* of David Lyon, shares an evocative link with the longer, gentle *Cantilena* of Roy Douglas. Philip Lane's *Pantomime* is another three-movement miniature suite of dainty charm and energy: its bouncing closing *Vivace* ends the concert winningly. Performances are persuasively polished and vivacious, and the Naxos recording is excellent: this disc is rewarding value for money.

Royal Ballet Orchestra, Andrew Penny

'*Welsh Classical Favourites*': WILLIAMS: *Fantasia on Welsh Nursery Rhymes.* WALFORD DAVIES: *Solemn Melody.* WALTERS: *Overture Primavera; A Gwent Suite.* ROBERTS: *Pastorale.* HODDINOTT: *Folksong Suite.* BURTCH: *Aladdin: Overture.* MATHIAS: *Serenade.* PARROTT: *Fanfare Overture (for a Somerset Festival).*

(BB) ★★★ Naxos 8.225048.

The Welsh have a long and enduring vocal and choral heritage. But only in the twentieth century has there been an orchestral tradition, and so Welsh folk melodies had not received the concert-hall exposure of comparable English tunes. Then, in 1940, Grace Williams completed her *Fantasia*, using eight very attractive ideas, arranging them into a kind of pot-pourri, winningly scored. Walford Davies had preceded her in the 1930s, and he left us the famous hymn-like *Solemn Melody*. Trevor Roberts's delicate *Pastorale* readily evokes the Pembrokeshire countryside, with a lovely oboe solo and an expressive string climax, somewhat in the manner of George Butterworth. Alun Hoddinott's *Folksong Suite* is similarly felicitously scored. Mervyn Burtch's *Aladdin* concert overture has a syncopated main theme of considerable character, and Gareth Walters's vigorous spring-inspired overture is hardly less spontaneously inventive. The colourful orchestration of the latter's set of dances is matched in the extrovert finale of Mathias's *Serenade*, where the main theme is presented in constantly changing colours, and in the exuberant opening and closing movements of the Walters *Gwent Suite*. All this music is vividly played by Penny and his Royal Ballet Orchestra and given excellent recording, with a flattering ambience. The disc is generously full and good value. Worth exploring.

Royal Ballet Sinfonia, Gavin Sutherland

'*Brian Kay's British light Music Discoveries*': ARNOLD: *The Roots of Heaven Overture.* ALWYN: *Suite of Scottish Dances.* SARGENT: *An Impression on a Windy Day.* PARKER: *Overture: The Glass Slipper.* LANGLEY: *The Coloured Counties.* JACOB: *Overture: The Barber of Seville Goes to Town.* JOHNSTONE: *Tarn Hows (Cumbrian Rhapsody).* LANGFORD: *Two Worlds (Overture).* RODNEY BENNETT: *Little Suite.* DYON: *Joie de vivre.*

(M) ★★★ ASV CDWHL 2113.

Brian Kay (of BBC Radio 3) has certainly made some felicitous discoveries here: this is a most entertaining programme, summed up perfectly by Ernest Tomlinson's quoted definition of light music as 'where the melody matters more than what you do to it'. There are plenty of melodies here, and the opening rumbustious Malcolm Arnold *Overture* (a concert work based on film music) has a characteristic share. William Alwyn's *Scottish Dances* are charmingly scored, with *Colonel Thornton's* elegant *Strathspey* a highlight. Sir Malcolm Sargent's breezy Scherzo *An Impression on a Windy Day* follows, and after the frothy *Glass Slipper Overture*, James Langley's *Coloured Counties* (which describes the spectacular English view from Bredon Hill) brings an engaging oboe solo. Gordon Jacob's pastiche is agreeable enough and the whimsy of Langford's *Two Worlds Overture* leads neatly into Sir Richard Rodney Bennett's *Little Suite* with its charming bird-imagery and delicate *Ladybird Waltz*. The only disappointment is Maurice Johnstone's *Tarn Hows*, a pleasantly evocative pastoral idyll, but unworthy of that man-made gem, up in the hills above Hawkshead, perhaps the most beautiful tarn in the whole English Lake District.

British Light Music: ARNOLD: *Little Suite No. 4, Op. 80a* (orch. Lane). BLEZARD: *The River.* CRUFT: *Hornpipe Suite.* FENBY: *Overture: Rossini on Ilkla Moor.* WARREN: *Wexford Bells – Suite on Old Irish Tunes.* BUTTERWORTH: *The Path across the Moors.* HEDGES: *An Ayrshire Serenade, Op. 42.* LEWIS: *An English Overture.* LANE: *Suite of Cotswold Folkdances.*

(M) ★★★ ASV CDWHL 2126.

An excellent collection of British light music, all imbued with a strong rustic flavour, and valuable for rarities. Adrian Cruft's *Hornpipe Suite* is nautically enjoyable, with each dance nicely contrasted; Raymond Warren's *Wexford Bells Suite* draws on traditional melodies, yet with modest orchestral forces, each movement nicely atmospheric.

Arthur Butterworth's *The Path across the Moors* is highly enjoyable – its title perfectly describing its content – and Fenby's witty *Rossini on Ilkla Moor* gives us an idea of what Rossini might have sounded like had he been a Yorkshireman! Robustly enjoyable is *An English Overture* by Paul Lewis, written in 1971 for the opening of Westward TV in the west of England; it uses folksongs from that area.

William Blezard's *The River* is a beautiful, haunting, slightly melancholy piece, while Anthony Hedges's three-movement *Ayrshire Serenade*, with its breezy outer movements and nostalgic centrepiece, is a good find. Philip Lane's superb arrangements and reconstructions of film music are greatly valued, and it is good to hear some of his own music: his suite of *Cotswold Folkdances* is piquantly orchestrated, as is his arrangement of Arnold's *Little Suite*. Gavin Sutherland understands exactly how this music should go, and the recording is excellent.

'British Light Music Discoveries, Vol. 4': RUTTER: *Partita.* RODNEY BENNETT: *Suite française.* ARNOLD: *The Padstow Lifeboat: March.* FANSHAWE: *Fantasy on Dover Castle.* BLEZARD: *Battersea Park Suite.* HURD: *Dance Diversions.* LEWIS: *Miniature Symphony.*
(M) *** ASV CDWHL 2131.

John Rutter's opening *Partita* is comparatively ambitious, with a gently elegiac *Aria* framed by a brightly syncopated *Vivace* – perhaps a shade overlong – and a finale which unashamedly borrows the celebratory regal manners and characteristic harmonic progressions of Walton's *Crown Imperial.* Less imposing but no less appealing is Rodney Bennett's charming *Suite française*, which uses traditional French melodies made distinctive by refined, often Ravelian scoring.

Arnold's exuberant *Padstow* march brings an almost bizarre domination from the local foghorn, while David Fanshawe's historical evocation of *Dover Castle*, although impressively scored, is not underpinned by really memorable musical material. That could not be said of William Blezard's *Battersea Park*, which vividly evokes the Festival of Britain funfair of the early 1950s, which he enjoyed with his children. *On the Lake* and *Child asleep* make charming nostalgic interludes.

Charming ideas are certainly not lacking in Michael Hurd's set of five *Dance Diversions*, often pastel-coloured and reminding one a little of the Malcolm Arnold *English Dances*. Each of the four movements of Paul Lewis's *Miniature Symphony* lasts barely over a minute, and this piece is most memorable for its finale – a galumphing horn tune. Excellent performances and first-rate recording, but overall this programme seems a little lacking in more robust items.

'British Light Overtures': BLEZARD: *Caramba.* BLACK: *Overture to a Costume Comedy.* LANGLEY: *Overture and Beginners.* DUNHILL: *Tantivy Towers.* CHAPPELL: *Boy Wizard.* CARROLL: *Festival Overture.* HURD: *Overture to an Unwritten Comedy.* MONCKTON: *The Arcadians* (arr. Wood). LANE: *A Spa Overture.* PITFIELD: *Concert Overture.* LEWIS: *Sussex Symphony Overture.*
(M) *** ASV CD WHL 2133.

A very promising start to an ASV series of British light overtures and including a modern recording of Stanley Black's delightful *Overture to a Costume Comedy*, a work of considerable charm, deftly scored. But there are many such delights in this programme: Michael Hurd's *Overture to an Unwritten Comedy* was written in 1970, yet sounds as though it could slot into an Ealing comedy of the

1950s. Lionel Monckton's *The Arcadians* is particularly tuneful and lively, while William Blezard's *Caramba*, which opens the programme, has a distinct Latin-American flavour, and is well laced with rumba rhythms. Thomas Pitfield's *Concert Overture*, the longest work here, makes charming use of French folk tunes (real or not) and is prettily orchestrated. Paul Lewis describes his *Sussex Symphony Overture* as 'seven minutes of joyful noise with a quiet bit in the middle'. This refers to some lovely nostalgic episodes, very imaginatively orchestrated, and proves that there are still composers who can write tunes (it was composed in 2000). Even more recent is Herbert Chappell's *Boy Wizard* overture from 2001, which is great fun. Philip Lane's *A Spa Overture* dates from 1982 and was written for the Cheltenham Ladies' College. It creates a romantic picture of that town, with a middle section evoking the spirit of Edward Wilson, Cheltenham's Antarctic explorer, whose statue looks down on the main Promenade. James Langley's *Overture and Beginners* has a theatrical atmosphere and a galumphing main theme. Thomas Dunhill's *Tantivy Towers* (reconstructed by Philip Lane from the piano score, plus a tape of a BBC broadcast from the 1970s) well captures the spirit of the early 1930s, when it was written. Gavin Sutherland secures an excellent response from the orchestra, and the sound is just right for the music: bright, not too reverberant, warm, with plenty of detail emerging. Most entertaining!

'British Light Overtures, Vol. 2': ANSELL: *Plymouth Hoe (A Nautical Overture).* GOW: *Overture One-Two-Five.* RODNEY BENNETT: *Farnham Festival Overture.* ALWYN: *The Moor of Venice.* J. GARDINER: *A Scots Overture.* GRYSPEERDT: *The Lamprey.* HOPE: *Scaramouche.* HEDGES: *A Cleveland Overture.* GLYN: *A Snowdon Overture.*
(M) *** ASV WHL 2137.

The second volume of British overtures kicks off with John Ansell's briny *Plymouth Hoe Overture*, full of traditional sea-songs and ending with Arne's *Rule Britannia*. From the sea we move to the land-locked railway with David Gow's *One-Two-Five Overture*, written in 1976 to celebrate the launch of British Rail's 125 train. But there have been more memorable musical evocations of the railways from other composers. Richard Rodney Bennett's unpretentious *Farnham Festival Overture* is not unrelated to his film music, and none the worse for that: the main theme is particularly winning. Gareth Glyn's *A Snowdon Overture* is the longest and most recent work here (2001), pleasingly episodic, with an evocatively nostalgic middle section. Anthony Hedges' *Cleveland Overture* was written 'to provide a showpiece for the enthusiasm, exuberance and artistry of the Cleveland Youth Orchestra players', and here its five minutes' playing time tests the resources of the Royal Ballet Sinfonia. They come through with flying colours, as they do in the spirited *Scaramouche Overture* of Peter Hope and John Gardiner's equally lively *Scots Overture*, featuring bagpipe tunes, brightly orchestrated.

William Alwyn's *The Moor of Venice* – a character study of Othello, and more of a mini tone-poem – was originally a piece for brass band, but it is here heard in Philip Lane's excellent orchestral arrangement, moving from the stormy music which heralds Othello himself to the melancholy of Desdemona's haunting 'Willow Song'. Not a masterpiece, perhaps, but, like the rest of this composer's music, very well crafted. Sympathetic performances throughout and bright recording.

'*British Light Overtures, Vol. 3*': CURTIS: *Open Road.* BLYTON: *The Hobbit.* PHILLIPS: *Hampton Court.* FOX: *Summer Overture.* MONTGOMERY: *Overture to a Fairy Tale.* SAUNDERS: *Comedy Overture.* QUILTER: *A Children's Overture.* LANE: *Celebration Overture.* LANGLEY: *The Ballyraggers.* TAYLOR: *The Needles.*

(M) **(*) ASV WHL 2140.

The obvious highlight of the third volume in ASV's enterprising 'British Light Overtures' series is Roger Quilter's enchanting *Children's Overture*, a brilliant weaving together of the finest nursery rhyme tunes you can think of, superbly orchestrated and wonderfully crafted, not for a second outstaying its 11-minute duration. None of the rest of the music here is of this inspirational quality, although Matthew Curtis's breezy *Open Road*, as its title suggests, effectively evokes a feeling of driving away from it all – even if its sense of freedom gives the impression of driving in the 1950s rather than in 2004!

Bruce Montgomery (who wrote the music to the early *Carry On* films) is represented by his *Overture to a Fairy Tale*, a substantial work, completed in 1946, in which the spirit of Elgar is pleasingly evoked. Carey Blyton (nephew of the children's author, Enid Blyton) has chosen *The Hobbit* for his miniature, whizzing through the characters of the J. R. R. Tolkein classic in four and a half minutes – quite different in character from the recent blockbuster films! Montague Phillips's *Hampton Court Overture* is light-heartedly regal in spirit, while John Fox's *Summer Overture* has an especially attractive middle section, flanked by lively but less distinctive outer sections. Philip Lane's *Celebration Overture* lives up to its name in style, if perhaps not entirely in content, and Adam Saunders' *Comedy Overture* would not sound out of place as background to a 1950s Ealing comedy. Nor, for that matter, would James Langley's *The Ballyraggers*. (A Ballyragger is a person who indulges in violent language, practical jokes and horseplay.) But this scallywag music is no match for Malcolm Arnold's *Beckus the Dandipratt*. The most recent work here is Matthew Taylor's *The Needles* (2001), which is a pretty empty, orchestral showpiece. Indeed, quite a lot of the music on this disc has an element of routine, despite the usual sympathetic advocacy and bright recording (with the upper strings sounding a little under-nourished at times).

'*British String Miniatures, Vol. 1*': WALTERS: *Divertimento.* ELGAR: *Elegy.* ROBERTS: *Suite.* DELIUS: *2 Aquarelles* (arr. Fenby). HEDGES: *Fiddler's Green.* WALTON: *Henry V: The Death of Falstaff; Touch Her Soft Lips and Part.* ADDISON: *Partita.*

(M) **(*) ASV WHL 2134.

ASV's prodigious White Line series has now tapped into the rich vein of British string music and has come up with three programmes which attractively mix the familiar with the unfamiliar, often exploring byways of this repertoire with entertaining results. Apart from the well-known Elgar, Delius and Walton items here (all receiving sensitive performances), the majority of the items in Volume 1 are rarities. Gareth Walters' *Divertimento* is an inventive five-movement suite, lively and expressive by turns. Michael Roberts's *Suite* draws on music written for TV in the 1960s and 1970s, all tuneful and easy-going. John Addison's *Partita*, by contrast, is much grittier, but appealing in its amalgam of Englishness with a touch of acerbity. Anthony Hedges' *Fiddler's Green* was written as recently as 2001, but it slots in well to the light music world of the 1950s. Splendid performances and recordings, the strings only slightly taxed in high-lying fast passages.

'*British String Miniatures, Vol. 2*': PURCELL: *Set of Act Tunes and Dances* (arr. Bliss). WARLOCK: *Serenade for the Birthday of Frederick Delius.* GLYN: *Anglesey Sketches.* DELIUS: *Air and Dances.* CURTIS: *Serenade.* ELGAR: *The Spanish Lady (Suite), Op. 69.* LANE: *Serenata concertante.*

(M) *** ASV WHL 2136.

Volume 2 carries forward the repertoire combination of Volume 1, with Bliss's slight but charming arrangements of Purcell's *Act Tunes and Dances* and better-known items such as Elgar's engaging music for *The Spanish Lady*, and the very welcome Delius and Warlock miniatures – all lovingly played here. Matthew Curtis's *Serenade* is a further fine example of English string writing, as are the *Anglesey Sketches* of Gareth Glyn. Philip Lane's *Serenata concertante* was originally a brass band piece, but it is doubly effective in this string arrangement, written in the manner of an eighteenth-century *concerto grosso*, with a string quartet concertino contrasting with the ripieno of the main body of strings. Its slow central movement is especially haunting and, with fine playing and recording, this is one of the most rewarding of Gavin Sutherland's exploratory compilations.

'*British String Miniatures, Vol. 3*': VINTER: *Entertainments.* ELGAR: *Sospiri.* WARLOCK: *4 Folksong Preludes.* FOX: *Countryside Suite.*

MARSHALL: *Elegy*. CYRIL SCOTT: *First Suite for Strings*. WALTERS: *Sinfonia breve*.
(M) ★★★ ASV WHL 2139.

With only Elgar's *Sospiri* really well known, this is perhaps the most enterprising of Gavin Sutherland's collections of English string music. The programme gets off to a bright and breezy start with Gilbert Vinter's *Entertainments*, originally a brass band work, but sounding very much at home here. It includes an amusing *Taproom Ballad*, with a solo viola portraying a somewhat inebriated singer. Philip Lane's transcription from piano to strings of Peter Warlock's haunting *Folksong Preludes* is just as telling in its new format, while John Fox's *Countryside Suite* is very much music of the open air – a pastoral suite, dating from 1975. A valedictory mood comes with Haigh Marshall's deeply felt *Elegy*, dedicated to the memory of Sir John Barbirolli, but contrast is again provided by Cyril Scott's folksy *First Suite for Strings*, written in the composer's highly chromatic style and wittily including 'Oh, dear, what can the matter be' in the finale. Gareth Walters' *Sinfonia breve* is the longest and most recent work (1998) in the programme, the 'breve' acknowledging that it has only three movements instead of the usual four of the classical symphony. The writing is more abrasive than the rest of the programme, not so obviously tuneful, but making an agreeably astringent diversion and a satisfying end-piece. Throughout the programme there is some especially delightful string-playing from the Royal Ballet Sinfonia, and this disc is well worth seeking out.

'British Clarinet Concertos' (with Scott, clarinet): PAUL: *Clarinet Concerto*. HOROVITZ: *Concertante for Clarinet and Strings*. WOOLFENDEN: *Clarinet Concerto*. BUSH: *Rhapsody for Clarinet and Strings*. MACDONALD: *Cuban Rondo*. CRUFT: *Concertino for Clarinet and Strings*. RIDOUT: *Concertino for Clarinet and Strings*.
(M) ★★(★) ASV WHL 2141.

All the works here are rarities and are presented on CD for the first time. Scottish composer Alan Paul's *Concerto* (1958) is dedicated to Jack Brymer. It begins with a tuneful opening movement, followed by a richly romantic central *Adagio* and a jolly finale, with some pleasing touches of baroque pastiche, as well as a lilting waltz. But its overall profile is not very individual. Geoffrey Bush's nostalgically dreamy *Rhapsody* (1940), however, is one of the disc's highlights. It has a haunting atmosphere, which is not matched in Joseph Horovitz's similarly paced *Concertante for Clarinet and Strings* of 1948. By the side of this, Adrian Cruft's reflective (1955) *Concertino* is quite compelling, well constructed and with plenty of imaginative touches. It is a more interesting work than Guy Woolfenden's *Concerto* (1985) which, though amiable enough, is not really memorable. Alan Ridout's *Concertino* (1978) is short and pleasing, and Malcolm MacDonald's *Cuban Rondo* (1960)

makes an enjoyable lollipop, with an appropriate Cuban percussion backing. Excellent performances from soloist and orchestra alike, and very good recording; but most of this music is pleasing without being really distinctive.

'English Recorder Concertos' (with Turner, recorder): GARDINER: *Petite Suite, Op. 245*. MCCABE: *Domestic Life*. LAWSON: *Song of the Lesser Twayblade*. LEIGHTON: *Concerto, Op. 88*. LANE: *Suite champêtre*. MELLERS: *Aubade*. MILFORD: *2 Pipe Tunes* (arr. Lane). KAY: *Mr Pitfield's Pavane*. DODGSON: *Concerto Chacony*.
(M) ★★★ ASV WHL 2143.

Opening with John Gardiner s delightful *Petite Suite*, this disc of English recorder concertos proves unexpectedly diverting. There are plenty of similarly attractive concertante pieces here: Philip Lane's *Suite champêtre*, Wilfrid Mellers' colourfully scored *Aubade* (which has some lovely sonorities, especially in the *Cantilena*), and Robin Milford's *Two Pipe Tunes*, simple but effective as heard in Philip Lane's arrangement.

There is nothing like a chaconne for bringing out the best in a composer, and Stephen Dodgson's *Concerto Chacony*, with its baroque overtones, is an intriguing score, as is Kenneth Leighton's *Concerto*, one of the finest works included. It is especially notable for its vivid harpsichord writing, neatly played by Keith Elcombe. Indeed, at times it seems almost like a harpsichord concerto!

John McCabe aptly describes his *Domestic Life* as 'a very light *pièce d'occasion*', while *The Song of the Lesser Twayblade* of Peter Lawson was written in 2000 as part of a series of musical portraits dedicated to the 48 wild orchids of Britain. It is easy-going and agreeably evocative, rather in the manner of film music. Norman Kay's *Mr Pitfield's Pavane* also has its moments. Excellent performances from John Turner, backed up by the ever-reliable Gavin Sutherland, and very good sound too, with a convincing balance; plus useful and copious notes by the brilliant soloist.

'British Film Composers in Concert': PARKER: *2 Choreographic Studies; Thieves' Carnival*. LUCAS: *Ballet de la reine*. COLLINS: *Eire Suite*. MONTGOMERY: *Scottish Aubade; Scottish Lullaby*. Eric ROGERS: *Palladium Symphony*.
(M) ★★★ ASV WHL 2145.

It is almost always rewarding to hear film-music composers' concert music. Both Bruce Montgomery and Eric Rogers are famous for their background music for the *Carry On* films, but here their style is more reflective than expected. Montgomery's Scottish works are actually derived from his film-scores and are vignettes, giving a popular romantic evocation of picturesque Caledonia, well leavened with attractive folk themes in nicely clothed orchestrations. Rogers' *Palladium Symphony*, on the other hand, was inspired by his experiences as an orchestral pit player, but the feeling throughout its four movements is one of nostalgia for a past era, rather than a gaudy musical representation of the musical hall. Clifton Parker's *Thieves' Carnival Overture* is light-heartedly swashbuckling, while his two very pleasing *Choreographic Studies – Alla spagnola* and *Alla cubana* – create local colour without recourse to a battery of percussion instruments. Leighton Lucas's unrealized ballet on the subject of Queen Mary, *Ballet de la reine*, appealingly infuses sixteenth-century styles with modern, piquant orchestrations. Last and not least is Anthony Collins' *Eire Suite*, full of Irish whimsy, and especially infectious in the *Fluter's Hooley (Reel)*. Excellent recording to match the highly persuasive performances.

Royal Ballet Sinfonia, John Wilson

'*Scottish Light Music*': DAVIE: *Royal Mile.* DODS: *Highland Fancy.* HAMILTON: *Scottish Dances.* MACCUNN: *The Land of the Mountain and Flood (overture); Highland Memories.* MATHIESON: *From the Grampians (suite).* ORR: *Fanfare and Processional; Celtic Suite.* ROBERTON: *All in the April Evening.*
(M) ★★★ ASV CDWHL 2123.

What a good idea to assemble a disc of comparatively rare light Scottish music, which with its characteristic folksy influences proves most entertaining. The most famous piece here, MacCunn's *The Land of the Mountain and Flood Overture*, begins the programme robustly, while the same composer's *Highland Memories* (1897) for strings offers contrast: two rather nostalgic movements followed by a more lively *Harvest Dance* (which is curiously reminiscent of the second movement of Schubert's *Ninth Symphony*). Muir Mathieson is widely known for his work in countless films and the opening of the *Grampians Suite* (1961) could well begin some Scottish swashbuckler; the rest of the *Suite* is thoroughly diverting too.

Buxton Orr's *Fanfare and Processional* (1968) is more angular than its companion pieces, while in his *Celtic Suite* (1968), a four-movement work using dance rhythms as a basis, he pays tribute to his Celtic origins (the last movement, *Port-a-Beul*, means 'mouth music'). Cedric Thorpe Davie's robustly enjoyable *Royal Mile* (recorded complete for the first time) is subtitled 'a coronation march' and was written in 1952 for one of a series of concerts leading up to that celebrated event. Iain Hamilton's *Scottish Dances* were, like Sir Malcolm Arnold's, composed for the BBC Light Music Festival and premièred on St Andrew's Day, 1956. They are comparably enjoyable. Marcus Dods' amusing *Highland Fancy* and Sir Hugh Roberton's touching *All in the April Evening* complete the programme. Full marks for an original collection, committed performances, a vibrant recording – and all at mid-price.

Royal Ballet Sinfonia, Barry Wordsworth

'*Tribute to Madame*': Ballet Music; BLISS: *Checkmate.* BOYCE-LAMBERT: *The Prospect Before Us.* GORDON: *The Rake's Progress.* TOYE: *The Haunted Ballroom.*
(M) ★★★ ASV CDWHLS 255.

'Madame' was of course Dame Ninette de Valois, the 'mother' of British ballet, and she is rightly celebrated with these fine scores by Bliss and Gavin Gordon and Constant Lambert's elegant pastiche drawing on the music of Boyce. The surprise is Toye's *Haunted Ballroom*, much more than just a (very memorable) waltz. First-class performances and fresh, bright recording.

'*Tribute to Sir Fred*': MESSAGER: *Les deux pigeons* (arr. Lanchbery). LISZT: *Dante Sonata* (arr. Lambert). RAWSTHORNE: *Madame Chrysanthème* (ballet). COUPERIN: *Harlequin in the Street* (arr. Jacob).
(M) ★★(★) ASV CDWLS 273 (2).

These four contrasting ballets are gathered together here as a tribute to their choreographer, Sir Frederick Ashton. *Les Deux Pigeons* is a charming score, and it is brightly played in a slightly truncated version by John Lanchbery (the complete original version is offered by Bonynge on Decca). Liszt's *Dante Sonata* is very telling in Lambert's orchestration, sounding very gothic in its high-flown romanticism. *Madame Chrysanthème* is presented here complete, rather than the suite we know from the old EMI recording conducted by the composer. Rawsthorne's vividly energetic score was first performed in 1955. It is colourfully orchestrated, featuring a large percussion section, including piano, and beginning unusually and hauntingly with a wordless mezzo-soprano voice. The music is full of imaginative touches, with subtle devices used to evoke the oriental flavour of the story. Much lighter in tone is *Harlequin in the Street*, with Couperin's short pieces strung together in Gordon Jacob's colourful and witty orchestrations. The performances throughout are lively and sympathetic, bar the odd slip in the orchestra, and the recorded sound is vivid, though the strings lack richness in the upper register – the violins sound a little pinched at times.

(i) Royal Ballet Sinfonia or (ii) BBC Concert Orchestra, Barry Wordsworth

'*British Light Music, Volume 3*': (i) ARNOLD: *HRH The Duke of Cambridge March, Op. 60a.* KELLY: *Divertissement.* LAMBERT: *Elegiac Blues.* LYON: *3 Dances.* RAWSTHORNE: *Overture for Farnham.* (ii)

LAMBERT: *Romeo and Juliet: Second Tableau.*
MARTELLI: *Promenade.* STANDFORD: *Celestial Fire.*
(M) ★★★ ASV CD WHL 2128.

This concert gets off to a rousing start with a swaggering march by Sir Malcolm Arnold, complete with a stirring central theme. Much of this music comprises short dance movements and, as such, makes attractive, undemanding listening. Constant Lambert's *Romeo and Juliet* is a shade more serious to balance the programme; it has a particularly haunting *Adagietto*, and elsewhere Lambert shows much imagination as well as wit. Martelli's cheeky *Promenade* almost sounds as though it has come out of a *Carry On* film, while the old dance forms parodied by David Lyon, Bryan Kelly and Patric Standford all have piquant charm. There is enough quirky writing, wit and humour to hold the listener's attention, and this disc of rarities is certainly recommendable.

Royal Philharmonic Orchestra, Sir Thomas Beecham

DVORAK: *Symphonic Variations, Op. 78.*
BALAKIREV: *Tamara (Symphonic Poem).*
RIMSKY-KORSAKOV: *Le Coq d'Or: Suite.*
☛ (M) (★★★) Sony mono SMK 91171.

This repertoire is indelibly associated with Beecham. His *Islamey* is unsurpassed in its exotic allure, while *Le Coq d'Or* glitters iridescently and his portrait of the Queen of Chemaka is radiantly sensuous. The underrated Dvořák *Variations* are vividly characterized and here the hitherto excellent mono recording sounds very like stereo in its ambient warmth.

Royal Philharmonic Orchestra, Sir Charles Groves

'*English String Masterpieces*': ELGAR: *Serenade for Strings, Op. 20.* BRITTEN: *Variations on a Theme by Frank Bridge, Op. 10.* VAUGHAN WILLIAMS: *Fantasia on a Theme by Thomas Tallis.* TIPPETT: *Fantasia Concertante on a Theme of Corelli.*
✿ (BB) ★★★ Regis RRC 1138.

With gloriously full and real recording, providing the most beautiful string-textures, this is one of Sir Charles Groves's very finest records, and it makes a worthy memorial to the achievement of the closing decade of his long career. The RPO players give deeply felt, vibrant accounts of four great masterpieces of English string music.

Royal Philharmonic Orchestra, Adrian Leaper

'*Orchestral Spectacular*': CHABRIER: *España.*
RIMSKY-KORSAKOV: *Capriccio espagnol.*

MUSSORGSKY: *Night on the Bare Mountain* (arr. Rimsky-Korsakov). BORODIN: *Prince Igor: Polovtsian Dances.* RAVEL: *Boléro.*
(BB) ★★★ Naxos 8.550501.

Recorded in Watford Town Hall by Brian Culverhouse, this concert would be highly recommendable even if it cost far more. All these performances spring to life, and the brilliant, full-bodied sound certainly earns the record its title. The brass in the Mussorgsky/Rimsky-Korsakov *Night on the Bare Mountain* has splendid sonority and bite, and in the *Polovtsian Dances* the orchestra 'sings' the lyrical melodies with such warmth of colour that the chorus is hardly missed. Leaper allows the *Capriccio espagnol* to relax in the colourful central variations, but the performance gathers pace towards the close. Chabrier's *España* has an attractive rhythmic lilt, and in Ravel's ubiquitous *Boléro* there is a strong impetus towards the climax, with much impressive playing on the way (the trombone solo, with a French-style vibrato, is particularly strong).

Royal Philharmonic Orchestra, Barry Wordsworth

'*British Light Classics*': ARNOLD: *English Dance, Set 2, Op. 33/1.* COATES: *Calling All Workers; The Dam Busters March; The Sleepy Lagoon.* A. WOOD: *Barwick Green.* ELLIS: *Coronation Scot.* Haydn WOOD: *The Bandstand, Hyde Park.* BATH: *Cornish Rhapsody.* FARNON: *Portrait of a Flirt; Westminster Waltz.* DUNCAN: *Little Suite: March.* C. WILLIAMS: *Devil's Galop; Heart O' London; Rhythm on Rails.* BENJAMIN: *Jamaican Rumba.* WHITE: *Puffin' Billy.* COLLINS: *Vanity Fair.* ELGAR: *Chanson de nuit.*
★★(★) Warner 2564 61438-2.

A very well-played collection of British light classics in warm and detailed sound: the percussion is clear and sharp, and the strings and brass are warm and vivid. These are essentially genial performances, and if other versions have offered more sheer excitement one finds oneself readily responding to the warmth of the music-making. Almost everything here is well known, from Arthur Wood's *Barwick Green* (*The Archers* theme), to Anthony Collins's delicious *Vanity Fair*. There is a lovely swagger in *The Bandstand* of Haydn Wood and no lack of drive in Charles Williams's inspired *Devil's Galop*, which ends the CD. If the programme appeals, don't hesitate.

Salvage, Graham (bassoon)

Bassoon Concertos (with Royal Ballet Sinfonia, cond. (i) Sutherland (ii) Butterworth): (i) FOGG: *Concerto in D.* ADDISON: *Concertino.* HOPE: *Concertino.* (ii) A. BUTTERWORTH: *Summer Music, Op. 77.*
(M) ★★★ ASV CD WHL 2132.

The three concerto/concertinos by John Addison, Eric Fogg and Peter Hope are all most enjoyable and are played with elegance, warmth and style by Graham Salvage, an outstandingly sensitive soloist, with lively and sympathic accompaniments from Gavin Sutherland and the Royal Ballet Sinfonia. The Addison *Concertino* opens in a mood of gentle melancholy, soon wittily dispelled but returning later, and is quietly enjoyable. It is notable for the droll waltz that forms the second movement and the humorously quirky finale. Fogg's *Concerto* (1931) is essentially light-hearted and rhythmically sparkling, although there is a balancing dolour and solemnity in the central movement. The first-movement cadenza is too long, but the rest of the movement, like the finale, is certainly entertaining. Peter Hope's *Concertino*, written as recently as 2000, opens in a mood of romantic reverie. It is rather like a period-film score (the composer worked with John Williams and James Horner), with gentle string ostinatos creating a haunting evocation, contrasted with a more lively middle section. But it has a blues centrepiece, replete with a 'walking bass' and vibraphone, while the finale delectably evokes a Latin-American fiesta.

But these very personable works are completely upstaged by Arthur Butterworth's masterly *Summer Music*, written in 1985, which is discussed under its separate composer entry. This work alone is well worth the cost of this disc. You will surely be drawn back to it, as we were. The other very entertaining pieces make an attractive programme overall. The performances and recordings are excellent, and this is a valuable addition to the catalogue.

Sargent, Sir Malcolm

'*Sir Malcolm Sargent conducts British music*' (with (i) LPO; (ii) LSO; (iii) Mary Lewis, Tudor Davies & O; (iv) Royal Choral Soc.; (v) New SO): (i) HOLST: *Perfect Fool: Suite.* (ii) BRITTEN: *Young Person's Guide to the Orchestra.* (iii) VAUGHAN WILLIAMS: *Hugh the Drover: Love Duet.* ELGAR: (iv) *I Sing the Birth*; (ii) *Pomp & Circumstance Marches Nos. 1 & 4.* (v) COLERIDGE TAYLOR: *Othello: Suite.* (ii) BAX: *Coronation March.*

(★★★) Beulah mono 1PD13.

Sargent was at his finest in this repertory, and it is very welcome to have his personal electricity so vividly conveyed throughout the disc, and most of all in the recording, taken from the sound-track of the original COI film, of Britten's *Young Person's Guide*. The optical transfer by Martin Sawyer produces far more vivid and satisfyingly weighty results than one would ever expect. The *Love duet* from *Hugh the Drover* was recorded in 1924 in limited pre-electric sound, but the Elgar part-song, recorded live at the Royal Albert Hall in 1928, also soon after the first performance, is vividly atmospheric. The *Othello Suite* of Coleridge Taylor, another première

recording, is a sequence of brief genre pieces, with recording more than lively and colourful enough to make one forget the high surface-hiss. The three marches at the end were recorded for the Queen's coronation in 1953, with Sargent taking an uninhibitedly broad view of the great tunes in both the Elgar favourites, and with Bax doing a fair imitation of Walton.

Schuricht, Carl (conductor)

'*The Decca Recordings, 1949–1956*': BEETHOVEN: *Symphonies Nos. 1 in C, Op. 21; 2 in D, Op. 36* (with VPO); *5 in C min., Op. 67* (with Paris Conservatoire O). MENDELSSOHN: *Overtures: The Hebrides (Fingal's Cave); Calm Sea and Prosperous Voyage; The Fair Melusine; Ruy Blas* (with VPO). BRAHMS: *Piano Concerto No. 2 in B flat, Op. 83* (with Backhaus, VPO); *Violin Concerto in D, Op. 77* (with Ferras, VPO); *Symphony No. 2 in D, Op. 73.* SCHUMANN: *Overture, Scherzo and Finale, Op. 52; Symphonies Nos. 2 in C, Op. 61; 3 (Rhenish) in E flat, Op. 97* (with Paris Conservatoire O). SCHUBERT: *Symphony No. 8 in B min. (Unfinished)* (with VPO). TCHAIKOVSKY: *Capriccio italien; Suite No. 3 in G: Theme and Variations* (with Paris Conservatoire O).

(M) (★★) Decca mono 475 6074 (5).

It is good that Decca have devoted one of their 'Original Masters' boxes to Carl Schuricht, for many of these recordings haven't been in circulation since their last resurrection on Ace of Clubs LPs, of which they formed a large part. Straight away one notices the sharp difference in the sound of the orchestras between those recordings made in Vienna and those in Paris, with the latter's distinctive reedy oboes and the brass with pronounced vibrato, characteristics all now gone. Character these French performances may have, but not orchestral brilliance: the Schumann symphonies are given straightforward accounts, but the playing lacks polish throughout. The *Rhenish*, curiously, isn't as well recorded as the *Second*, though it dates from a year later (1953); in the finale of the *Rhenish*, Schuricht does not adopt the usual rallentando at the end of the final movement with the glorious brass chords, but he cranks up the tempo at the end, which is unexpected but quite exciting. In Brahms's *Second Symphony*, Schuricht's sense of rhythm is more erratic than usual; nor is the *Violin Concerto* the most exciting or imaginative version from this period, and the 1954 sound is also below Decca's best. All are back on form for the 1952 account of the *Second Piano Concerto*, always a work which Backhaus did well (he later made an even finer account in stereo with Boehm), even if the strings sound a bit papery. 'Good but not outstanding performances' was how the 1966 *Penguin Guide* described the Mendelssohn overtures when they lived on ACL 33, and that assessment holds, pleasant though it is to hear them again (*Ruy Blas* and *Calm*

Sea come off best). Beethoven's *First Symphony* is unfussy and direct, but the 1952 recording is not terribly comfortable, the strings rather too bright and acidic. The *Fifth*, recorded in 1949, is better recorded, sounding good for its age, and the performance is direct and honest – if again not the last word in precision of ensemble and intonation. As for the Tchaikovsky items (in quite vivid (1952) sound), *Capriccio italien* is quite exciting (and what vibrato on the opening brass fanfare!), but in the *Theme and Variations* the playing of the woodwind lets things down too much for comfort, though the performance itself goes quite well. The *Unfinished Symphony*, recorded in 1957, is excellent and was much admired in its day; it is an affectionate reading, warmly played (the best playing and recording in this set) with a good forward impulse. In short, recommendable to admirers of Schuricht interested in his historical performances, rather than to the general collector, and certainly not a choice for those who insist on flawless orchestral refinement!

Scottish Chamber Orchestra, Jaime Laredo

'*String Masterpieces*': ALBINONI: *Adagio* (arr. Giazotto). HANDEL: *Berenice: Overture. Solomon: Arrival of the Queen of Sheba.* BACH: *Suite No. 3, BWV 1068: Air. Violin Concerto No. 1 in A min., BWV 1041: Finale* (with Laredo, violin). PACHELBEL: *Canon in D.* PURCELL: *Chacony; Abdelazar: Rondeau.*

(BB) ★★★ Regis RRC 1160 (with VIVALDI: *The Four Seasons* ★★★ – see above).

An excellent popular collection, the more attractive for being at budget price and coupled with a first-rate performance of Vivaldi's *Four Seasons*. The playing of the Scottish Chamber Orchestra is alive, alert, stylish and committed, without being overly expressive; yet the famous Bach *Air* has warmth and Pachelbel's *Canon* is fresh and unconventional in approach. The sound is first class, spacious and well detailed but without any clinical feeling. The Purcell *Rondeau* is the tune made familiar by Britten's *Orchestral Guide*; the superb *Chaconne* is presented with telling simplicity.

Serenades for Strings

Israel PO: DVORAK: *Serenade in E, Op. 22* (cond. Kubelik). TCHAIKOVSKY: *Serenade in C, Op. 48* (cond. Solti). ASMF, Marriner: ELGAR: *Serenade in E min., Op. 20.* WARLOCK: *Serenade.*

★(★) Australian Decca Eloquence (ADD) 466 665-2.

Decca's early recordings in Israel were not of their finest vintage, suffering from the difficult hall acoustics, and this 1958 pairing of the Dvořák and Tchaikovsky *Serenades* with the Israeli orchestra

sounds a bit aggressive and bright in the upper registers, and rather tubby in the bass. Kubelik is sensitive and musical in the Dvořák, and the performance emerges fresher than we had remembered. Solti's hurricane-like Tchaikovsky has to be heard to be believed – the finale almost flies off with the gale. However, Marriner's trusty accounts of the Elgar and Warlock are always a joy to hear, and here the recorded sound is beautiful.

Slovak Philharmonic Orchestra

'*Russian Fireworks*' (cond. (i) Hayman; (ii) Jean; (iii) Gunzenhauser; (iv) Halász): (i) IPPOLITOV-IVANOV: *Caucasian Sketches: Procession of the Sardar.* (ii) LIADOV: *8 Russian Folksongs.* KABALEVSKY: *Comedians' Galop.* MUSSORGSKY: *Sorochintsy Fair: Gopak. Khovanshchina: Dance of the Persian Slaves.* (iii) LIADOV: *Baba Yaga; The Enchanted Lake; Kikimora.* (iv) RUBINSTEIN: *Feramor: Dance of the Bayaderes; Bridal Procession. The Demon: Lesginka.* (ii) HALVORSEN: *Entry of the Boyars.*

(BB) ★★★ Naxos 8.550328.

A vividly sparkling concert with spectacular digital sound, more than making up in vigour and spontaneity for any lack of finesse. The Liadov tone-poems are especially attractive and, besides the very familiar pieces by Ippolitov-Ivanov, Halvorsen and Mussorgsky, it is good to have the Rubinstein items, especially the *Lesginka*, which has a rather attractive tune.

Slovak State Philharmonic Orchestra (Košice), Mika Eichenholz

'*Locomotive music (A musical train ride), Vol. 1*': LANNER: *Ankunfts Waltz.* JOHANN STRAUSS SR: *Reise Galop; Souvenir de Carneval 1847 (quadrille); Eisenbahn-Lust (waltz).* HOYER: *Jernban Galop.* JOHANN STRAUSS JR: *Reiseabenteuer Waltz.* MEYER: *Jernvägs-Galop.* EDUARD STRAUSS: *Glockensignale Waltz; Mit Dampf Polka; Lustfahrten Waltz; Tour und Retour Polka.* JOSEF STRAUSS: *Gruss an München Polka.* GRAHL: *Sveas helsning till Nore Waltz.* LUMBYE: *Copenhagen Steam Railway Galop.*

★★ Marco Polo 8.223470.

'*Locomotive music, Vol. 2*': LANNER: *Dampf Waltz.* FAHRBACH: *Locomotiv-Galop.* JOHANN STRAUSS JR: *Wilde Rosen Waltz; Vergnügungszug Polka; Spiralen Waltz; Accelerationen Waltz.* GUNGL: *Eisenbahn-Dampf Galop.* EDUARD STRAUSS: *Polkas: Reiselust; Ohne Aufenthalt; Treuliebchen; Ohne Bremse; Von Land zu Land; Bahn frei; Feuerfunken Waltz.* ZIEHRER: *Nachtschwalbe Polka.*

★★ Marco Polo 8.223471.

This seems a happy idea on which to base a two-CD collection of Viennese-style dance music, but in the event the only piece which celebrates the effect of a train journey really successfully is the *Copenhagen Steam Railway Galop*. The Slovak performance has rather a good whistle but seems more concerned with rhythm than with charm and cannot compare with the account included in the splendid Unicorn collection of Lumbye's dance music, so beautifully played by the Odense Symphony Orchestra under Peter Guth (DKPCD 9089 – see our main volume). The first Marco Polo disc opens with Lanner's *Ankunfts* ('Arrival') *Waltz*, which ironically dates from before the railway had even arrived in Vienna. It is enjoyable for itself; the other highlights are more descriptive. Frans Hoyer's *Jernban Galop* makes a fair shot of a train starting up and has a rather engaging main theme, while Jean Meyer's *Jernvägs-Galop* follows Lumbye's pattern of an elegant opening and a whistle start, with the side-drum snares giving a modest railway simulation. This too is attractive melodically, but the coda is too abrupt. Eduard Strauss's *Mit Dampf Polka* has a rather half-hearted whistle but plenty of energy, and his *Lustfahrten Waltz* is lyrically appealing.

The second disc opens with Lanner again, but the *Dampf* refers to the steam of a coffee house! It is followed by Fahrbach's jolly *Locomotiv-Galop*, where the effects are minimal and primitive. However, Joseph Gungl does better, with an opening whistle which returns on a regular basis against supporting bass-drum beats. Johann Strauss's *Vergnügungszug Polka* concentrates on the exhilaration of a day out on an excursion train, but Eduard Strauss's *Bahn frei*, comparably zestful, manages a cleverly brief introductory train imitation, and *Ohne Aufenthalt* has a gentle bell to set off. If most of this repertoire is unadventurous in terms of evocation, it is all tuneful and brightly presented; the playing is not without finesse and has plenty of zest, and the orchestra is very well recorded – and not in a train shed either. But these are full-priced CDs and plainly one is not travelling in a first-class carriage with the VPO.

Steele-Perkins, Crispian (trumpet)

'Six Trumpet Concertos' (with ECO, Anthony Halstead): J. HAYDN: *Concerto in E flat.* TORELLI: *Concerto in D.* M. HAYDN: *Concerto No. 2 in C.* TELEMANN: *Concerto for Trumpet, 2 Oboes and Strings.* NERUDA: *Concerto in E flat.* HUMPHRIES: *Concerto in D, Op. 10/12.*
(BB) *** Regis (ADD) RRC 1053.

Collectors who have relished Håkan Hardenberger's famous collection of trumpet concertos might well go on to this equally admirable concert, which duplicates only the Joseph Haydn – and that in a performance hardly less distinguished. Crispian Steele-Perkins has a bright, gleaming, beautifully focused timbre and crisp articulation, with easy command of the high tessitura of the Michael Haydn work and all the bravura necessary for the sprightly finales of all these concertos. His phrasing in the slow movement of Joseph Haydn's shapely *Andante* is matched by his playing of the *Largo* of the Neruda and the *Adagio-Presto-Adagio* of the Torelli, another fine work. Anthony Halstead with the ECO gives him warmly sympathetic support. The recording balance gives the soloist plenty of presence, but the orchestra is recorded rather reverberantly, an effect similar to that on the Hardenberger record.

Stinton, Jennifer (flute)

20th Century Flute Concertos (with SCO, Bedford): NIELSEN: *Flute Concerto.* HONEGGER: *Concerto da camera for Flute, Cor Anglais and Strings* (with Brown, cor anglais). IBERT: *Flute Concerto.* POULENC: *Flute Sonata* (orch. Berkeley).
(BB) *** Regis RRC 1126.

Honegger's *Concerto da camera* comes from the same period as the *Fourth Symphony*, and the slow movement is strikingly reminiscent of it. It is an enticing work and very nicely played (with a most sensitive cor anglais contribution from Geoffrey Brown), as is the Poulenc, an effective transcription by Lennox Berkeley of the *Sonata for Flute and Piano*. The Nielsen, too, is a fine performance, although its contrasts could be more strongly made. Ibert's charming and effervescent piece comes off even better, though the orchestral playing is not particularly subtle. The whole concert is beautifully recorded, and this remains a very enjoyable concert, well worth exploring at budget price.

Stockholm Sinfonietta, Esa-Pekka Salonen

'*A Swedish Serenade*': WIREN: *Serenade for Strings, Op. 11.* LARSSON: *Little Serenade for Strings, Op. 12.* SODERLUNDH: *Oboe Concertino* (with A. Nilsson). LIDHOLM: *Music for Strings.*
**(*) BIS CD 285.

The most familiar piece here is the Dag Wirén *Serenade for Strings*. Söderlundh's *Concertino for Oboe and Orchestra* has a lovely *Andante* whose melancholy is winning and with a distinctly Gallic feel to it. It is certainly played with splendid artistry by Alf Nilsson and the Stockholm Sinfonietta. The Lidholm *Music for Strings* is somewhat grey and anonymous, though it is expertly wrought. Esa-Pekka Salonen gets good results from this ensemble and the recording lives up to the high standards of the BIS label. It is forwardly balanced but has splendid body and realism.

Stockholm Sinfonietta, Jan-Olav Wedin

'Swedish Pastorale': ALFVEN: The Mountain King, Op. 37: Dance of the Cow-girl. ATTERBERG: Suite No. 3 for Violin, Viola and String Orchestra. BLOMDAHL: Theatre Music: Adagio. LARSSON: Pastoral Suite, Op. 19; The Winter's Tale: 4 Vignettes. ROMAN: Concerto in D for Oboe d'amore, String Orchestra and Harpsichord, BeRI 53. ROSENBERG: Small Piece for Cello and String Orchestra.
*** BIS CD 165.

In addition to affectionate accounts of the Pastoral Suite and the charming vignettes for The Winter's Tale, the Stockholm Sinfonietta include Atterberg's Suite No. 3, which has something of the modal dignity of the Vaughan Williams Tallis Fantasia. It has real eloquence and an attractive melancholy, to which the two soloists, Nils-Erik Sparf and Jouko Mansnerus, do ample justice. The Blomdahl and Roman works are also given alert and sensitive performances; they make one realize how charming they are. Hilding Rosenberg's piece is very short but is rather beautiful. A delightful anthology and excellent (if a trifle closely balanced) recording. Confidently recommended.

Stokowski, Leopold (with various orchestras)

'Decca Recordings 1965–1972': Orchestral transcriptions: BACH: Toccata and Fugue in D min., BWV 565; Well-Tempered Clavier: Prelude in E flat min., BWV 853. Chorales: Mein Jesu was für Selenweh, BWV 487; Wir glauben all'einen Gott, BWV 680. Easter Cantata: Chorale: Jesus Christus, Gottes Sohn, BWV 4. Passacaglia and Fugue in C min., BWV 582. RACHMANINOV: Prelude in C sharp min. (all with Czech PO). BYRD: Earl of Salisbury Pavan; Galliard (after Tregian). CLARKE: Trumpet Voluntary (with Snell, trumpet). SCHUBERT: Moment musical in F min., D.780/3. CHOPIN: Mazurka in A min., Op. 17/4. TCHAIKOVSKY: Chant sans paroles, Op. 40/6. DUPARC: Extase (with LSO). DEBUSSY: La cathédrale engloutie (with New Philh. O). TCHAIKOVSKY: Symphony No. 5, Op. 64. BERLIOZ: Symphonie fantastique (with New Philh. O Damnation de Faust: Ballet des Sylphes. SCRIABIN: Poème de l'extase. ELGAR: Enigma Variations (with Czech PO). FRANCK: Symphony in D min. RAVEL: L'éventail de Jeanne (with Hilversum R. PO). Daphnis et Chloé: Suite No. 2. (with LSO Ch.). STRAVINSKY: Firebird Suite (1919 version). DEBUSSY: La Mer; Prélude à l'après midi d'un faune. MESSIAEN: L'Ascension: 4 Méditations symphoniques (all with LSO).
(B) **(*) Decca (ADD/DDD) 475 145-2 (5).

The five Stokowski CDs included here were all made in Decca's hi-fi-conscious Phase 4 system which, by close microphoning and the use of a 20-channel mixer, created exceptionally vivid projection and detail. None was more spectacular than the 1968 Kingsway Hall Symphonie fantastique, with the New Philharmonia Orchestra, in which the brass have satanic impact in the Marche au Supplice and finale. The performance is as idiosyncratic as it is charismatic and is thrilling in every way. Stokowski's warmth of phrasing is aptly romantic, but generally the most surprising feature is his meticulous concern for the composer's markings. The Danse des Sylphes makes a ravishing encore.

Elgar's Enigma Variations also shows Stokowski at his most persuasive, richly phrased by the Czech players and completely spontaneous-sounding. Equally, the Czech account of Scriabin's Poème de l'extase (edited from more than one performance) has all the passionate commitment of the live concert hall, with the ebb and flow of tension and the flexibility of the phrasing again captured compellingly.

Among the LSO recordings, La Mer has surprisingly slow basic tempi, but the effect is breathtaking in its vividness and impact, and the Prélude à l'après-midi d'un faune is richly languorous, yet has a wonderful intensity. The account of the second Daphnis et Chloé Suite is comparably glowing, with sumptuous playing, and the multi-channel technique is used here to produce exactly the right disembodied, ethereal effect for the offstage chorus. Stokowski takes the choral parts from the complete ballet and adds a fortissimo chord at the very end; but after such involving music-making few will begrudge him that.

The Firebird Suite is similarly sumptuous, and the gentler music shows the wonderful luminosity Stokowski could command from a first-class orchestra. Rich-textured violins dominate the beginning of the final climax. Messiaen's L'Ascension is tonally hardly less opulent, yet Stokowski is characteristically persuasive in developing the smooth flow of the music. Though some may feel that the final sweet meditation for strings alone, Prayer of Christ ascending to the Father, lacks true spirituality, it is played very beautifully.

The most controversial performance here is of Tchaikovsky's Fifth Symphony. Although there is no doubting the electricity of the music-making, Stokowski tends to languish rather than press forward. Yet he also creates some thrilling climaxes and certainly holds the listener throughout. However, he makes a number of small cuts in the outer movements, and dispenses with the pause before the finale. In the César Franck Symphony the Hilversum orchestra plays with tremendous energy and warmth. The problem is that Stokowski's reading, though moulded with conviction, underlines vulgarities in the score that most conductors try to minimize.

The transcriptions, without which no Stokowski anthology would be complete, range from thrilling technicolor Bach to the extraordinarily imaginative arrangement of Debussy's *La cathédrale engloutie*, which has a wholly different sound-world from the original piano version. The sheer force of Stokowski's orchestral personality makes all this music very much his own.

Stuttgart Radio Symphony Orchestra, Sir Georg Solti

'*Solti in Rehearsal*': BERLIOZ: *Damnation of Faust: Hungarian March.* WAGNER: *Overture: Tannhäuser.*
*(**) Arthaus DVD 101068.

These rehearsal sequences, recorded in black and white in 1966 (Wagner) and 1968 (Berlioz) give an illuminating idea of Sir Georg Solti's approach at that period when, in his mid-fifties, he was emerging as one of the world's leading conductors. Though his reputation at that time – at least with British orchestral players – was one of impatience and even irascibility, the opposite is the case here. The vast majority of his instructions involve subtle gradations, a dominant concern not with the brilliant or extrovert qualities one might have expected, but with the shading of *pianissimos* and the moulding of legato phrases.

So in the *Tannhäuser Overture* he spends almost all of the 45 minutes of the first rehearsal sequence getting the slow introduction as he wants it, notably the hushed opening on the horns, then letting the players off the rein with a cry of release when the great trombone theme enters. He also makes a point of quoting, when the relevant theme arrives, the words of Tannhäuser himself in the opera, that the burden of his sins is weighing him down. The fast sections he tends to leave alone in his instructions, relying on fierce information from his baton.

The Berlioz similarly finds Solti concentrating on refined points, and charmingly he goes into some detail about how Berlioz was given the theme by Liszt and was instantly magnetized. It is, Solti explains, an old Hungarian song of liberation, a joyful march associated with Rákóczy as a freedom fighter. That leader failed – but then, 'Hungarians always fail', says Solti with a grin.

The big limitation, needless to say, is that the rehearsal sequences are conducted in German. Though, as always with DVDs, one has the option of having subtitles in English, the translation involved inevitably dilutes the experience. The performances themselves are as polished and refined as the rehearsals promise. The only surprise is that at the end of each performance the applause is so feeble.

Swedish Chamber Orchestra, Petter Sundkvist

'*Swedish Orchestral Favourites, Vol. 2*': LARSSON: *Lyric Fantasy, Op. 54; Little Serenade, Op.12; Adagio for String Orchestra, Op. 48.* FRUMERIE: *Pastoral Suite, Op. 13b* (with Lindloff). BLOMDAHL: *The Wakeful Night: Adagio.* ATTERBERG: *Suite No. 3 for Violin, Viola and Orchestra, Op. 19/1* (with Tröback & Persson). RANGSTROM: *Divertimento elegiaco for Strings.*
(BB) *** Naxos 8.553715.

All the music on this inexpensive issue exerts a strong appeal. It is worth the modest outlay for just Atterberg's poignant *Suite No. 3 for Violin, Viola and Orchestra*, Op. 19, which is one of his most poignant utterances, and for Gunnar de Frumerie's perennially fresh *Pastoral Suite* for flute and strings. Having been resistant over the years to Rangström's overblown symphonies but captivated by his songs, it is also a pleasure to welcome a new account of the *Divertimento elegiaco*, whose eloquence is well conveyed in this fine performance. Indeed, throughout this disc the Swedish Chamber Orchestra under Petter Sundkvist are first class.

Swedish Radio Symphony Orchestra, Sergiu Celibidache

DVORAK: *Cello Concerto in B min., Op. 104* (with du Pré). FRANCK: *Symphony in D min.* HINDEMITH: *Mathis der Maler Symphony.* SHOSTAKOVICH: *Symphony No. 9 in E flat, Op. 70.* SIBELIUS: *Symphonies Nos. 2 in D, Op. 43; 5 in E flat, Op. 82.* R. STRAUSS: *Don Juan, Op. 20; Till Eulenspiegel, Op. 28.*
*(**) DG (ADD) (IMS) stereo/mono 469 069-2 (4).

There are some good things here, and Jacqueline du Pré's many admirers will welcome the fiery eloquence this partnership brings to the Dvořák *Cello Concerto* (although this is available separately). After the war Celibidache was briefly with the Berlin Philharmonic, but he spent most of his time with radio orchestras, which could afford to indulge his inordinate and demanding rehearsal schedules. During the late 1960s he brought the Swedish Radio Orchestra to a high level of accomplishment, and these performances, made at various times between 1965 and 1971, show the refinement and sophistication of texture and sonority as well as the fine tonal blend he achieved. Celibidache may be idiosyncratic – some find his interpretations impossibly egocentric – but at its best his work could be tremendously vibrant. These performances are much more recommendable than some of his Stuttgart recordings, although they are by no means free from affectation. The Sibelius *Fifth Symphony* is curiously fascinating. His admirers will doubtless want this, but for others a certain caution may be advisable, particularly as the set is at premium price.

Symphonies: 'Great Symphonies'

BEETHOVEN: *Symphony No. 5 in C min., Op. 67* (Philh. O, Ashkenazy). BRAHMS: *Symphony No. 3 in F, Op. 90.* DVORAK: *Symphony No. 9 in E min. (From the New World), Op. 95.* (VPO, Kertész). HAYDN: *Symphony No. 94 in G (Surprise)* (Philh. Hungarica, Dorati). MENDELSSOHN: *Symphony No. 3 in A min. (Scottish), Op. 56* (LSO, Abbado). MOZART: *Symphony No. 40 in G min., K.550* (VPO, Karajan). SAINT-SAENS: *Symphony No. 3 in C min. (Organ), Op. 78* (LAPO, Mehta). SCHUBERT: *Symphony No. 9 in C (Great), D.944* (Israel PO, Mehta). SIBELIUS: *Symphony No. 7 in C, Op. 105* (VPO, Maazel). TCHAIKOVSKY: *Symphony No. 4 in F min., Op. 36* (LSO, Szell).

**(*) Australian Decca ADD/DDD 466 444-2 (5).

This set contains two really outstanding recordings: Szell's Tchaikovsky *Fourth* and Maazel's Sibelius *Seventh*, with the Kertész *New World* not far behind. There is nothing substandard about anything else in this set either – most of the performances are well worth hearing, not least Ashkenazy's superbly recorded Beethoven *Fifth*, Dorati's Haydn *Surprise* and Mehta's vintage Decca version of the Saint-Saëns *Organ Symphony*. He is less successful in Schubert's *Ninth*. The set includes excellent sleeve-notes.

Tancibudek, Jiri (oboe)

HAYDN: *Oboe Concerto in C, Hob. VIIg/C1* (with Adelaide CO, Duvall). MARTINU: *Oboe Concerto for Small Orchestra* (with Adeleide SO, Shapirra). BRITTEN: *6 Metamophoses after Ovid.* FELD: *Sonata for Oboe and Piano* (with Blumenthal). SUTHERLAND: *Sonatina for Oboe and Piano* (with Stokes).

**(*) Australian Universal Heritage ABC Classics (ADD) 461 703 2.

Part of the brief of the Australian Heritage series is to include recordings by important Australian residents even if they were not Australian born. One such is oboist Jiri Tancibudek, who was principal oboist for the Czech Opera and then the Czech Philharmonic under Kubelik. The Second World War caused him and his family to flee in a desperate night-time trek across the mountains, and they finally settled in Australia. This anthology is valuable for his agile playing of the Martinů *Oboe Concerto*, a work dedicated to him, as well as the Bartók-influenced *Sonatine* for oboe and piano by the Australian composer Margaret Sutherland, although the Haydn *Concerto* and the Britten pieces also receive fine performances. The 1970s sound is good, but not outstanding.

Thames Chamber Orchestra, Michael Dobson

'*The Baroque Concerto in England*' (with Black, Bennett): ANON. (probably HANDEL): *Concerto grosso in F.* BOYCE: *Concerti grossi in E min. for Strings; in B min. for 2 Solo Violins, Cello and Strings.* WOODCOCK: *Oboe Concerto in E flat; Flute Concerto in D.*

(M) *** CRD (ADD) CRD 3331.

A wholly desirable collection, beautifully played and recorded. Indeed, the recording has splendid life and presence and often offers demonstration quality – try the opening of the Woodcock *Flute Concerto*, for instance. The music is all highly rewarding. The opening concerto was included in Walsh's first edition of Handel's Op. 3 (as No. 4) but was subsequently replaced by another work. Whether or not it is by Handel, it is an uncommonly good piece, and it is given a superbly alert and sympathetic performance here. Neil Black and William Bennett are soloists of the highest calibre, and it is sufficient to say that they are on top form throughout this most enjoyable concert.

Tokyo Metropolitan Orchestra, Ryusuke Numajiri

'*Japanese Orchestral Favourites*': TOYAMA: *Rhapsody for Orchestra.* KONOYE: *Etenraku.* IFUKUBE: *Japanese Rhapsody.* AKUTAGAWA: *Music for Symphony Orchestra.* KOYAMA: *Kobiki-Uta for Orchestra.* YOSHIMATSU: *Threnody to Toki for String Orchestra and Piano, Op. 12.*

(BB) *** Naxos 8.555071.

There are now plenty of CDs devoted to British light classics, but this one of Japanese favourites is the first of its kind. It is everything one imagines Japanese light orchestral music to be: full of glittering percussion instruments, folk melodies and dance rhythms interspersed with more exotic elements. All these composers are professionals, writing for a modern symphony orchestra, so the music is well constructed and readily accessible. It is all entertainingly colourful, and well worth Naxos price for anyone wanting something fresh and off the beaten track. The performances and recordings are first class.

Toulouse Capitole Orchestra, Michel Plasson

French Symphonic Poems: DUKAS: *L'Apprenti sorcier.* DUPARC: *Lénore; Aux étoiles.* FRANCK: *Le Chasseur maudit.* LAZZARI: *Effet de nuit.* SAINT-SAENS: *Danse macabre.*

**(*) EMI 5 55385-2.

An interesting and (on the whole) successful programme, let down by the brilliant but unbeguiling account of *The Sorcerer's Apprentice*. There is more fun in this piece than Plasson finds. Similarly, the humour of *Danse macabre* is not within Plasson's perceptions, although he gives an excitingly dramatic account of the piece and there is a seductive violin solo from Malcolm Stewart. There is plenty of gusto in *Le Chasseur maudit*, where the opening horn-call is arresting, the chase is properly demonic and the malignant middle section masterful, when Christian stalwarts are sinisterly warned of the Satanic welcome waiting for those choosing the hunt rather than the church for their Sunday morning occupation.

Hardly less telling is Duparc's *Lénore*, an equally melodramatic scenario (also espoused by Liszt, with narrative included). This concerns a ghoulish midnight embrace with a skeleton after the eager heroine has been carried off on horseback by her dead lover. But the two most memorable pieces here are the radiantly serene *Aux étoiles* ('The astral light of dawn'), also by Duparc, and – most haunting of all – Sylvio Lazzari's impressionistic *Effet de nuit*, with its bleakly sinuous evocation on the bass clarinet of the scaffold silhouetted in the rain against the darkening evening sky. Its climax depicts 'three ghastly prisoners marching dejectedly' in the pitiless downpour, urged on by 225 halberdiers. The recording is excellent: spacious, yet vivid; it is a shame about *L'Apprenti sorcier*.

Trumpet: 'The Sound of the Trumpet'

'*The Sound of the Trumpet*': CLARKE: *Trumpet Voluntary*. M.-A. CHARPENTIER: *Te Deum: Prelude* (arr. Hazel). PURCELL: *Trumpet Tune and Air* (arr. Hurford) (all with Hurford, organ, Michael Laird Brass Ens.). HAYDN: *Trumpet Concerto in E flat* (Stringer, trumpet, ASMF, Marriner). BACH: *Christmas Oratorio: Nun seid ihr wohl gerochen* (arr. Reeve). SCHEIDT: *Galliard battaglia*. HANDEL: *Occasional Oratorio: March* (arr. Hazel); *Royal Fireworks Music: Overture* (arr. & cond. Howarth) (all with Philip Jones Brass Ens.); *Messiah: The Trumpet Shall Sound* (with Howell, bass). VIVALDI: *Double Trumpet Concerto in C, RV 537* (with Wilbraham, Jones, trumpets). HUMMEL: *Trumpet Concerto in E* (with Wilbraham, trumpet) (all three with ASMF, Marriner). STANLEY: *Trumpet Tune in D* (arr. Pearson; with Pearson, organ). ARBAN: *Carnival of Venice* (arr. & cond. Camarata; L. Festival O) (both with Wilbraham, trumpet).
🔘 ✹ (M) ★★★ Decca (ADD/DDD) 476 1644.

The Decca production team are particularly adept at compiling an anthology like this, and there is simply no better single-disc recommendation for those who enjoy the sound of trumpets – regal and exciting –

on the lips of true virtuosi. Such indeed are John Wilbraham and the individual players of the Michael Laird and Philip Jones Ensembles (especially in Elgar Howarth's highly effective brass arrangement of the *Overture* from Handel's *Royal Fireworks Music*). The popular favourites by Jeremiah Clarke, once attributed to Purcell, and Purcell's own *Trumpet Tune and Air* are equally appealing. Wilbraham's account of the Hummel *Concerto* is among the finest ever recorded, elegant in the slow movement and with the finale sparkling irresistibly. Marriner and the ASMF, during their vintage period, accompany with comparable polish, as they do Alan Stringer, who plays the Haydn *Concerto* excellently, with a bolder and more forthright open timbre which is undoubtedly authentic. Peter Hurford, when he participates, is similarly stylish. Almost every item here is a winner, and the stereo interplay in Scheidt's *Galliard battaglia* is indicative of the demonstration standard of many of the recordings included. The programme ends with a dazzling display from John Wilbraham in Camarata's lollipop arrangement of the most famous of all cornet solos, Arban's variations on the *Carnival of Venice*. It is an excellent and unexpected addition to Universal's 'Penguin Rosette' Collection and, especially at mid-price, fully deserves its accolade.

Tuckwell, Barry (horn), Academy of St Martin-in-the-Fields, Sir Neville Marriner or (i) English Chamber Orchestra

Horn Concertos: TELEMANN: *Concerto in D*. CHERUBINI: *Sonata No. 2 in F for Horn and Strings*. Christoph FORSTER: *Concerto in E flat*. WEBER: *Concertino in E min., Op. 45*. Leopold MOZART: *Concerto in D*. Giovanni PUNTO: *Concertos Nos. 5 in F; 6 in E flat; 10 in F; 11 in E*. (i) Michael HAYDN: *Concertino in D* (arr. SHERMAN). (i) Joseph HAYDN: *Concerto No. 1 in D*.
🔘 ✹ (B) ★★★ EMI Double fforte (ADD) 5 69395-2 (2).

Barry Tuckwell readily inherited Dennis Brain's mantle and held his place as Britain's pre-eminent horn player for several decades before finally retiring in 1997. This EMI Double fforte set celebrates his supreme achievement in nearly a dozen of the finest concertos for his instrument; the Tuckwell recordings of the key works by Wolfgang Amadeus and Richard Strauss are of course available elsewhere. His supreme mastery and ease of execution, his natural musicality and warm lyricism of line – to say nothing of his consistent beauty of tone – make every performance here memorable, and he has the advantage of polished, graceful accompaniments from the ASMF under Marriner, except in the works by Michael and Joseph Haydn, in which he directs the ECO himself with comparable elegance.

The *Concerto* of Telemann opens with a catchy

moto perpetuo, despatched with aplomb; then comes a fine *Adagio* which often moves to the very top of the horn's upper range, before the tension is released in the buoyant finale. The Cherubini *Sonata* opens with a melancholy *Largo*, then erupts into joyous high spirits, while the racing opening arpeggios of the *Concerto* by Leopold Mozart and the tight trills in the finale (with harpsichord echoes) are managed with comparable exuberance. The Weber is an attractively diverse and extensive (17 minutes) set of variations and includes a good example of horn 'chords', where the soloist plays one note and hums another; it also has an exceptionally joyful finale.

One of the novelties is a delightful concerto by the virtually unknown Christoph Forster (1693–1745) with its amiably jogging first movement marked *Con discrezione* and its brief, disconsolate *Adagio* followed by a closing Rondo in which, though the clouds clear away, the lyrical feeling remains. In some ways, most striking of all is the collection of four concertos by the Bohemian virtuoso Giovanni Punto, a successful and highly cultivated composer whose music is enjoyably distinctive, a mixture of Mozartian influences and Hummelian *galanterie*. The individual CD of these four works was issued to celebrate Barry Tuckwell's fiftieth birthday, and the performances show him at his finest. The recording throughout is of EMI's finest analogue quality, and the remastering retains the warmth and beauty of the originals.

Turner, John (recorder), Royal Ballet Sinfonia, Gavin Sutherland or Edward Gregson

English Recorder Music for Recorder and Strings: LANE: *Suite ancienne.* ARNOLD: *Concertino, Op. 41a.* PITFIELD: *Concerto for Recorder, String Orchestra and Percussion; 3 Nautical Sketches.* GREGSON: *3 Matisse Impressions.* LYON: *Concertino.* PARROTT: *Prelude and Waltz.* BULLARD: *Recipes.*
*** Olympia OCD 657.

Who could have guessed that eight concertante works for recorder and strings would have been so entertainingly diverse? Philip Lane's *Suite* in the olden style is unrepentant pastiche with an irresistibly exuberant finale (*Beau Brummel's Bath Night*). Arnold's *Concertino* is even more quirky, with a haunting central *Chaconne*. Thomas Pitfield was a distinguished Professor of Composition at the Royal Manchester College and subsequently the Royal Northern College of Music, and his *Concerto*, which uses both treble and descant recorders, moves easily from English pastoralism to a *Tarantella* dance finale.

The *Nautical Sketches* draw on sea-shanties with equally light touch. Edward Gregson cleverly catches the mood of three Matisse paintings: the evocative style is predictably French but also individual. David Lyon's *Concertino* is the most recent work (1999) and its wry opening movement nicely offsets the delicacy

of the haunting central waltz. Parrott's *Prelude* opens more abrasively, bringing a welcome astringency, then he relents into another delectably embroidered waltz. Bullard's very entertaining *Recipes* certainly titillates the palette, with a *Barbecue Blues* wittily followed by a *Prawn* habanera, and, after a Chinese *Special Chop Suey*, ends with a circus galop enthusiastically celebrating *Fish and Chips*.

The invention of all these works is consistently diverting and, with a masterly soloist in John Turner, excellent accompaniments from the Royal Ballet Sinfonia under Gavin Sutherland (or Gregson, who conducts his own work), this is very enjoyable throughout and highly recommendable.

'Twilight Memories'

'Twilight Memories': WILLIAMSON: *Curtain Up.* WILLIAMS: *They Ride by Night; The Young Ballerina.* YORKE: *Fireflies.* ELLIS: *Muse in Mayfair.* TORCH: *Fandango; Wagon Lit* (with Queen's Hall Light O, Sydney Torch). VAUGHAN WILLIAMS: *Sea Songs: Quick March* (with New Concert O). FLETCHER: *Fiddle Dance; Folk Tune* (with Jay Wilbur O). COATES: *The 3 Bears: Waltz* (with Queen's Hall Light O, composer). STRACHEY: *Ascot Parade.* BRIDGEWATER: *Prunella.* WHITE: *Caprice for Strings.* W. COLLINS: *Cumberland Green.* BANTOCK: *Twilight Memories* (L. Promenade O, W. Collins). RICHARDSON: *Shadow Waltz.* CAMPBELL: *Cloudland.* MORLEY: *Mock Turtles.* SIDAY: *Petticoat Lane.* MACKINTOSH: *Strings on Wings* (with Queen's Hall Light O, King). CURZON: *Dance of an Ostracised Imp* (New Concert O, Wilbur). MILNER: *Downland* (with L'Orchestra de Concert, O'Henry). FARNON: *Goodwood Galop.* THOMAS: *Looking Around* (with Queen's Hall Light O, Farnon).
(M) (*******) ASV mono CDAJA 5419.

Another collection of vintage nostalgia, dating from the late 1940s. The programme opens appropriately with Lambert Williamson's *Curtain Up*, a charming example of period writing, and a lively account of the *Quick March* from Vaughan Williams's *Sea Songs* follows. Percy Fletcher's *Folk Tune*, a piece of much charm, and Sidney Torch's catchy percussion rhythms in the jazzy *Fandango* are offset by Richardson's dainty *Caprice for Strings*. Farnon's *Goodwood Galop* races along without a care in the world, and Angela Morley shows her gift for orchestral colour in the amusing *Mock Turtles*. Peter Yorke's *Fireflies* with its scurrying woodwind writing brings slinky strings into the middle section. Walter Collins's *Cumberland Green* is another joyful piece of tuneful writing, while Bantock's *Twilight Memories*, which gives this collection its title, is a rather haunting waltz. The recordings vary in quality, though none is below a decent standard for the period, and this disc is certainly recommended to those collectors with a nostalgic affection for the British light music tradition.

Vengerov, Maxim (violin)

'*Vengerov and Virtuosi*' (with Papian, piano, or Virtuosi): BAZZINI: *Le Ronde des lutins, Op. 25.* BRAHMS: *Hungarian Dances Nos. 1, 5 & 7.* DVORAK: *Humoresque No. 7 in G flat.* KHACHATURIAN: *Gayaneh: Sabre Dance.* MASSENET: *Thaïs: Méditation.* MONTI: *Csárdás.* NOVACEK: *Perpetuum mobile.* PONCE: *Estrellita.* RACHMANINOV: *Vocalise, Op. 34/14.* TCHAIKOVSKY: *Souvenir d'un lieu cher, Op. 42.* SCHUBERT (arr. Wilhelmi): *Ave Maria.*
*** EMI 5 57164-2.

With its odd accompaniment from Vengerov's chosen band of 11 Russian solo violins and piano, recorded live in the Musikvereinsaal in Vienna in April 2001, Vengerov's recital of violin lollipops is very much a fun record for those with a sweet tooth. The opening item, Rachmaninov's *Vocalise*, heavily inflected, leads to an account of Ponce's *Estrellita* that echoes Palm Court in its sweetness. Vengerov, full of spontaneous flair and encouraged by a live audience, allows himself extreme rhythmic freedom. Cheering greets the last item, Monti's famous *Csárdás*, with a big laugh from the audience as Vengerov plays around with bird imitations, but otherwise there is little evidence of the audience's presence. Tempo changes in almost every bar witness a young violinist at the peak of his form, enjoying himself from first to last in music that is undemanding on the ear if not on the technique, and outrageously showing off in a way that for many will be very endearing. Not that the playing is extrovert all the time. Vengerov's account of the *Méditation* from Massenet's *Thaïs* conveys a rare depth of feeling, making it more than just a lyrical interlude. Curiously, the coagulation of 11 solo violins often sounds rather like an accordion.

Vienna Philharmonic Orchestra, Valéry Gergiev

'*Salzburg Festival Concert*': PROKOFIEV: *Symphony No. 1 in D (Classical) Op. 25.* SCHNITTKE: *Viola Concerto* (with Yuri Bashmet). STRAVINSKY: *The Firebird* (complete ballet). plus feature: Stravinsky and Prokofiev (Gergiev) and Schnittke (Bashmet). (Director/Video Director: Brian Large.)
*** TDK **DVD** DV-VPOVG.

Gergiev and the Vienna Philharmonic are recorded at the Salzburg Festival in 2000 in an all-Russian programme. The excellence of the performances is enhanced by the visual direction, which, as so often with Brian Large, directs the listener's eyes where his ears want them to be. Gergiev has an excellent rapport with his Viennese players, and *The Firebird*, for which most collectors will want this concert, is

impressive both musically and, thanks to an excellent balance, aurally. There are times when one feels he could give his players just a little more time (the *Dance of the Princesses*) and conversely the first movement of the Prokofiev feels a little staid. However, for the most part these are very fine readings, with superb playing from the Viennese.

Schnittke's *Viola Concerto*, completed not long before his stroke, is generally thought to be among his most powerful compositions. Yuri Bashmet, who is the dedicatee, has recorded the concerto twice before, with Rozhdestvensky and Rostropovich. It is made up of two *Largos* surrounding a fast central movement, the mood swinging between a pensive brooding and a kind of frenetic activity. Whether one warms to Schnittke or not, it is a powerfully communicative performance. The TDK notes, incidentally, tell us that the '*Firebird Suite* exists in three versions ... the second, *to be heard in the present recording* contains only seven numbers of the original 19 in the two-act (sic!) ballet version'. Not so, fortunately! The title-page lists the 19 numbers of the full version and it is the complete score that is recorded here. TDK must look to their presentation.

Vienna Philharmonic Orchestra, Nikolaus Harnoncourt

'*Vienna New Year's Concert 2001*': J. STRAUSS SR: *Radetzky March* (original and revised versions). J. STRAUSS JR: *Overture: Eine Nacht in Wien* (Berlin version). Polkas: *Electrofor; Electro-magnetic; Vergnügungzug (Excursion Train); Der Kobold; Luzifer.* Waltzes: *Morgenblätter; Seid umschlungen Millionen; An der schönen Blauen Donau (Blue Danube).* JOSEF STRAUSS: Polkas: *Harlekin; Ohne Sorgen.* Waltz: *Dorfschwalben aus Osterreich (Village Swallows).* LANNER: *Jägers Lust (galop); Die Schonbrunner Waltz; Steyrische Tanze.*
*** Teldec 8573 83563-2.

Harnoncourt may still be best known as a pioneer of period performance, but he is also dedicatedly Viennese, someone who as a young cellist once played in the orchestra. True to character, he introduces a fair sprinkling of novelties, starting with the original version of what by tradition has become the concert's final encore, the *Radetzky March*. Far more plainly orchestrated, it offers little rivalry for the established version. Other items new to the concerts include the *Electro-magnetic Polka* and *Electrofor Polka*, nicely contrasted, and the Polka-mazurka, *Der Kobold* ('The Goblin'), with charming pizzicato effects and a *pianissimo* coda. The three items by Joseph Lanner, stylistically well differentiated, celebrate that composer's bicentenary and include a jolly rarity, *Jägers Lust* ('Huntsman's Delight'), with hunting horns prominent and a shot simulated by the timpani. In a fascinating note on the history of the concerts the orchestra's chairman, Dr Clemens Hellberg, makes an illuminating comment on Harnoncourt from the players' point of view: that they were delighted to 're-examine the Philharmonic's Strauss tradition through the eyes of this analytical yet so impulsive conductor'. A vintage year, presented in sparklingly clear sound.

Vienna Philharmonic Orchestra, Herbert von Karajan

'*The Great Decca Recordings*': BRAHMS: *Symphonies Nos. 1 in C min., Op. 68; 3 in F, Op. 90; Tragic Overture, Op. 81.* HAYDN: *Symphonies Nos. 103 in E flat (Drumroll); 104 in D (London).* MOZART: *Symphonies Nos. 40 in G min., K.550; 41 in C (Jupiter), K.551.* TCHAIKOVSKY: *Romeo and Juliet (fantasy overture); Nutcracker Suite; Swan Lake (ballet): Suite; Sleeping Beauty (ballet): Suite.* ADAM: *Giselle (ballet; abridged).* BEETHOVEN: *Symphony No. 7 in A, Op. 92.* DVORAK: *Symphony No. 8 in G, Op. 88.* GRIEG: *Peer Gynt (incidental music): Suite No. 1; Suite No. 2: Ingrid's Lament; Solveig's Song.* HOLST: *The Planets (suite), Op. 31.* JOHANN STRAUSS JR: *Die Fledermaus: Overture and Ballet Music. Der Zigeunerbaron: Overture. Polkas: Annen; Auf der Jagd. Waltz: Geschichten aus dem Wiener Wald.* JOSEF STRAUSS: *Delirien Waltz.* RICHARD STRAUSS: *Till Eulenspiegel; Salome: Dance of the 7 Veils. Don Juan, Op. 20; Also sprach Zarathustra, Op. 30.*

(B) **(*) Decca (ADD) 448 042 (9).

Following directly on after his EMI Philharmonia recordings with Walter Legge, Karajan's five-year Decca period with the Vienna Philharmonic – master-minded by producers John Culshaw and Erik Smith – lasted from 1959 until 1964. Though the epithet 'great' can be applied to only a handful of the recordings in this box, almost all of them have far more character and musical appeal than many of the more anonymous records flooding the present-day CD market. Certainly Karajan's 1960 *Romeo and Juliet* stands the test of time, not only for its passion but also for its delicacy of feeling in the 'moonlight' music; and his virtually complete (1961) recording of Adam's *Giselle* (with sumptuous sound still approaching demonstration standard) shows what a fine ballet conductor he was, the playing combining affectionate warmth, elegance and drama.

The suites from the three Tchaikovsky ballets have comparable panache and generate considerable excitement; apart from the rather plangent timbre of the VPO's principal oboe, they have plenty of glowing colour, with the *Panorama* from *Sleeping Beauty* endearingly suave and the final climax from *Swan Lake* riveting in its histrionic power. The *Nutcracker Suite* has more vivid characterization than the later, Berlin Philharmonic, account, with the *Waltz of the Flowers* lilting agreeably. The remastering scores over

the analogue DG versions in its greater ambient depth.

The excerpts from *Peer Gynt* bring the freshest response from the VPO, with gusty Trolls galloping into the *Hall of the Mountain King*, and *Solveig's song* radiantly beautiful. Again, the 1961 Decca recording stands up well alongside the later, DG analogue version (which we count as marginally the most alluring of his three stereo accounts) and in many ways is superior in body and naturalness. As for *The Planets*, dating from that same vintage year, this is certainly a great performance, with *Mars* among the most thrilling ever put on disc. With whining Wagnerian tubas it makes a terrifying impact; then *Venus* follows, transmuted into sensuous balm – the Venus of gentle ardour rather than mysticism. *Jupiter* is bucolic and breezy, the Vienna strings bringing their own characteristic tone-colour to the big central tune. *Saturn* with its slow, sad march and *Uranus* with superb VPO brass are no less outstanding, and the wordless chorus at the end of *Neptune* is more atmospheric than in almost any other version. The analogue recording is so stunningly vivid that it could have been made yesterday.

Karajan never surpassed his 1960 VPO collection of overtures, polkas and waltzes by Johann and Josef Strauss until he came to make his wonderful (DG) 1987 New Year concert with the same orchestra. His later, BPO records sound glossy by comparison, yet here his rhythmic touch is unerring in the two overtures, while the polkas have all the flair you could ask for. However, the highlight is the highly seductive account of *Tales from the Vienna Woods*, played most beautifully, an account which may have been equalled, but has never been surpassed.

The superlative performances of the Richard Strauss tone-poems are hardly less remarkable, and they sound wonderfully fresh. In this repertoire no one can quite match Karajan in the panache and point of his conducting. This programme is available separately in Decca's Legends series and is discussed above under its Composer entry.

In the symphonic repertoire the results are less even. Of the two Haydn *Symphonies*, No. 103 is more urbane than No. 104, though both offer enjoyably polished VPO playing: there is plenty of robust vigour in the latter and both slow movements are beautifully shaped. The same comments might apply to Mozart's *Fortieth* and *Jupiter Symphonies*. In the G minor every detail remains beautifully in place, each phrase nicely contoured and in perspective. Beautifully articulate, this performance has genuine dramatic power, even though one feels that it all moves within carefully regulated limits. The reading of the *Jupiter* is strong and direct and has breadth as well as warmth. Exposition repeats are observed in the first movements of each symphony, but not in the finale of the *Jupiter*.

Of the two Brahms *Symphonies*, No. 1 gives the impression of being over-rehearsed. Its pacing does not always seem spontaneous, with an overall lack of tension; though towards the end of the finale Karajan cannot help creating genuine excitement, this is dissipated in a very slow chorale reference in the coda. The *Third* is much more successful. Here is another case in which the Vienna performance rivals the quality of the later, DG Berlin version. In both, Karajan takes the opening expansively; in both, he omits the exposition repeat. The third movement, too, is very slow, but the overall reading has plenty of grip and tension, and the Decca recording has a fuller and more resonant bass than the DG, and this well suits Brahms.

The recording of Beethoven's *Seventh* is also full-bodied, though not as fine as that for the Dvořák *Eighth*. 1961 was certainly a vintage year for the Decca engineers. The Beethoven performance is massive rather than incandescent and refuses to catch fire or grip the listener emotionally. The Dvořák is another matter, a most winning performance with superb orchestral playing. There are moments of slight self-indulgence in the Trio of the Scherzo, but the result is delectable when the Vienna strings are at their creamiest; overall, this account blends polish and spontaneity in almost equal measure. The orchestra are clearly enjoying themselves, and so do we.

Vienna Philharmonic Orchestra, Rudolf Kempe

'*The Vienna Philharmonic on Holiday*': MASCAGNI: *Cavalleria rusticana: Intermezzo.* PONCHIELLI: *La Gioconda: Dance of the Hours.* SCHMIDT: *Notre Dame: Intermezzo.* GOUNOD: *Faust: Waltz.* BAYER: *Die Puppenfee: Suite.* OFFENBACH: *Orpheus in the Underworld: Overture.* GOTOVAC: *Ero the Joker (dance).* SCHUBERT: *Rosamunde: Overture (Die Zauberharfe); Entr'acte in B flat; Ballet in G.* GLUCK: *Orfeo et Euridice: Dance of the Blessed Spirits.*

*** Testament (ADD) SBT 1127.

It is good to be reminded so vividly of an aspect of Rudolf Kempe's mastery too easily forgotten – his Beechamesque charm in light music. Waltz rhythms are given a delicious lilt, not just in Viennese items like the delightful Josef Bayer suite, *Die Puppenfee*, but in Gounod too, with Kempe bringing out the delicacy as well as the vigour. Kempe's use of rubato is often extreme – arguably too much so in the Schubert *Rosamunde* music – but it never fails to be winning in a very Viennese way, as in the rare Franz Schmidt *Intermezzo*. The Ponchielli, once so popular, now neglected, sparkles with uninhibited joy, as does the Offenbach, and it is good to have such a rarity as the *Kolo* by the Zagreb conductor and composer Jakob Gotovac, rhythmic and colourful. The recordings were all made in the Musikvereinsaal in Vienna in December 1961, with the glowing EMI recording well caught in Testament transfers which bring out both warmth and depth of focus.

Vienna Philharmonic Orchestra, Riccardo Muti

'*New Year's Concert, 2004*': J. STRAUSS JR: Waltzes: *Accelerationen; An der schönen, blauen Donau. Champagne Polka; Die Fledermaus: Csádás. Es war so wunderschön March; Im Sturmschritt Polka; Satanella Polka; Das Sitzentuch der Königin Overture; Zigeunerin Quadrille.* J. STRAUSS SR: *Beliebte-Sperl Polka; Cachucha-Galopp; Frederika Polka; Indianer Galopp; Philomelen Waltz; Radetzky March.* LANNER: *Hofball-Tänze Waltz; Tarantel Galopp.* JOSEF STRAUSS: *Eislauf Polka; Sphären-Klänge Waltz; Stiefmütterchen Polka.* EDUARD STRAUSS: *Mit Vergnügen Polka.*

*** DG **DVD** 073 097-9 (Video Director: Brian Large); CD 474 900-2 (2).

It is fascinating how the New Year's Day concert in Vienna seems to mellow even the severest disciplinarians among conductors. Lorin Maazel has never been so warm as when conducting this annual event; and here Riccardo Muti once again presents his programme with an authentic Viennese glow. The concert in 2004 was designed to celebrate the bicentenary of Johann Strauss I, father of the waltz-king we most revere. Normally the final encore, the *Radetzky March*, is his most notable contribution, but on the first of these two discs we have four rare pieces by him, including the delectable *Philomela Waltz*, leading to two seductive items by his contemporary, Joseph Lanner, presented with an endearing, gentle touch of Viennese schmalz in the more modest Schrammeln style that we remember from the early recordings of the Boskovsky Ensemble.

Johann Strauss II and his siblings, Josef and Eduard, take over again in the second half, with more rarities and an ecstatic account of the *Sphärenklänge Waltz*, to match an equally ravishing account of the *Accelerationen Waltz* in the first half, where the increase of tempo at the opening is managed most engagingly.

While the *Champagne Polka* fizzes appropriately, it cannot be said that visually the 2004 concert is as electrifying as Harnoncourt's 2003 proceedings (see our main volume, p. 1264). Muti's visual image is dapper; curiously, his bespectacled countenance reminds one a little of Glenn Miller, although there is nothing jazzy about his affectionately cultivated conducting style. With Brian Large in command, the camera angles are almost always impeccable and only very occasionally do we leave the auditorium. With DVD one feels part of the proceedings, and the sound is excellent. There are optional filmed sequences of the Vienna State Opera Ballet for *Accelerations* and the *Champagne Polka;* and for Josef Strauss's *Eislauf Polka*, we are offered a choice of figure-skating impressions. But it is much more rewarding to watch and be caught up in the music-making itself.

Vienna Philharmonic Orchestra, Seiji Ozawa

'*New Year Concert 2002*': JOHANN STRAUSS SR: *Beliebte Annen Polka, Radetzky March.* JOHANN STRAUSS JR: *Carnevalbotschafter Waltz; Zivio! March; Kunstlerleben Waltz; Die Fledermaus Overture; Perpetuum mobile; Elisen-Polka; Waltz: Wiener Blut; Tik-tak Polka; Waltz: An die schönen Blauen Donau.* JOSEF STRAUSS: *Die Schwatzerin, Vorwarts!, Arm in Arm, Aquarellen Waltz, Die Libelle, Plappermaulchen, Im Pfluge.* HELLMESBERGER: *Danse diabolique.* (Video Director: Brian Large).
*** TDK **DVD** Mediactive DV-WPNK02.

With a large Euro sign in flowers on the organ pipes behind the orchestra in the Vienna Musikvereinsaal, this was a special New Year's concert, signalling the arrival that day of the new currency. One of the extra items in the 'Special Features' section of the disc is an alternative version of Johann Strauss's *Perpetuum mobile*, showing what is described as the 'Dance of the Machines' with illustrations of Euro notes being printed and Euro coins being minted and stamped. Other additional items include alternative accounts of the *Blue Danube*, with the ballet company of the Vienna State Opera, and of two polkas, *Beliebte Annen* by Johann Strauss Senior and the *Elisen Polka* by Junior, with the Spanish Riding School performing wonders of equitation, a delightful extra.

Those extra items allow the main concert to be presented with no visual distraction from shots of the players, conductor, hall and audience, with almost every advantage for the DVD over the equivalent CD. Quite apart from the bonus of visual presentation the DVD offers five numbers omitted from the CD – two pieces by Josef Strauss, celebrating his 175th anniversary, the polkas *Arm in Arm* and *Im Pfluge*, and three Johann Jr numbers, the *Carnevalbotschafter Waltz*, the *Beliebte Annen Polka* and *Perpetuum mobile*.

Ozawa at his most relaxed is naturally idiomatic in his pauses and warm rubato, helped by not using a baton, relying on the innate expressiveness of the Viennese players to mould in perfect time. More than anyone since Karajan in his single New Year concert, Ozawa controls the clapping of the audience, limiting it to the proper passages in the final *Radetzky March*. The international credentials of the orchestra are demonstrated in the multilingual new year greetings from a dozen and more players, just before the traditional *Blue Danube*.

(i) Vienna Philharmonic Orchestra, or (ii) Berlin Philharmonic Orchestra, Bruno Walter

(i) MAHLER: *Symphony No. 4 in G* (with Seefried).
(ii) R. STRAUSS: *Don Juan.*
(**) Urania mono URN 22156.

One of the glories of the post-war catalogue was Mahler's *Fourth Symphony* with Bruno Walter and the New York Philharmonic. Although the *Second* and *Ninth Symphonies* had been available, the latter, together with a Vienna *Das Lied von der Erde*, was a Society issue, available only by subscription. The appearance of the *Fourth* enthused music-lovers, but Walter's singer was Desi Halbein, whose colouring and timbre were somewhat uninviting. The Urania set comes from 1950 and has a rich-toned Irmgard Seefried and the Vienna Philharmonic. There is another Walter recording with her in New York in 1953, while Music & Arts (see above) offers a 1952 live Concertgebouw recording with Elisabeth Schwarzkopf.

Virtuosi di Praga, Oldřich Vlček

Music for Strings: GRIEG: *Holberg Suite.* RESPIGHI: *Ancient Airs and Dances: Suite No. 3.* ELGAR: *Serenade in E min., Op. 20.* ROUSSEL: *Sinfonietta, Op. 52.*
(BB) **(*) Discover DICD 920236.

The Prague Virtuosi are an expert body of soloists who command an impressive sonority in spite of their modest size (here 11 players). Some ears might feel that the Elgar *Serenade* lacks ripeness of Elgarian feeling, yet the *Larghetto* is tenderly affecting. Equally, the Respighi suite of *Ancient Airs* sounds fresher, less anachronistically voluptuous than usual. The chamber scale suits the *Holberg Suite* admirably, with plenty of energy and bite. But undoubtedly the most effective performance here is the Roussel *Sinfonietta*, bracingly astringent and grippingly vital.

Wallfisch, Elizabeth (violin), Parley of Instruments, Peter Holman

'*English Classical Violin Concertos*': JAMES BROOKS: *Concerto No. 1 in D.* THOMAS LINLEY JR: *Concerto in F.* THOMAS SHAW: *Concerto in G.* SAMUEL WESLEY: *Concerto No. 2 in D.*
**(*) Hyp. CDA 66865.

Peter Holman and his Parley of Instruments expend much energy and Elizabeth Wallfisch considerable musical sensibility to bring these concertos from the late eighteenth century fully to life. They succeed admirably in that, working hard over music which is usually felicitous and always well crafted but too often predictable. In first movements one keeps getting the impression of second-rate Haydn. However, the opening movement of the James Brooks *Concerto* is amiably pleasing in its melodic contours and offers the soloist plenty of lively bravura. Its brief *Largo affettuoso* is agreeable too, and the dancing finale sparkles on the Wallfisch bow, and she produces a neat cadenza.

Thomas Linley offers a *galant* Moderato first movement, another all-too-brief but graceful slow movement with a nice rhythmic snap; the finale is a charming gavotte. But Thomas Shaw goes one better in his *Adagio*, creating the best tune on the disc, for his slow movement, again with a Scottish snap, is most winning, very like a folksong. The finale bounces and the horns hunt boisterously. Wesley's first movement is vigorous and assured, if too long; and in the slow movement a pair of the orchestral violins join the soloist in a trio. The finale is very jolly and buoyant. The recording is excellent and, dipped into, this collection will give pleasure, providing you do not expect too much.

'Wedding Classics'

'Wedding Classics': MENDELSSOHN: *Midsummer Night's Dream: Wedding March* (OAE, Mackerras). ALBINONI: *Adagio* (L. CO, Warren-Green). FAURE: *Pavane* (City of L. Sinf., Hickox). MARCELLO: *Oboe Concerto: Adagio* (Ray Still, L. Academy, Stamp). MOZART: *Ave verum Corpus* (with Schütz Ch.). PURCELL: *The Fairy Queen, Part II: Overture* (both with LCP, Norrington). *The Indian Queen: Trumpet Overture.* PACHELBEL: *Canon.* HANDEL: *Messiah: Hallelujah Chorus; Dixit Dominus: excerpt.* BACH: *Jesu, joy of Man's desiring* (all by Taverner Players & Ch., Parrott). *Suite No. 3: Overture; Air; Gavottes I & II* (ECO, Ledger); *Wedding Cantata (No. 202): Gavotte* (Nancy Argenta, Ens. Sonnerie, Huggett). BARBER: *Agnus Dei* (arr. of *Adagio for Strings*) (Winchester Cathedral Ch., Hill). MOZART: *Alleluia* (Monika Frimmer); *Serenata notturna: Minuet* (Lausanne CO, Y. Menuhin). BACH/GOUNOD: *Ave Maria* (Sister Marie Keyrouz, Auvergne CO, Van Beck). ROSSINI: *Petite Messe solennelle: Prelude religioso* (Wayne Marshall, organ). RACHMANINOV: *Gloria in excelsis* (Swedish R. Ch., Kaljuste). FRANCK: *Cantabile for organ* (Nicholas Danby). HAYDN: *The Seasons: excerpt* (La Petite Bande, Kuijken). FALLA: *Three-Cornered Hat (ballet): Miller's Dance* (Aquarius, Cleobury). HOLST: *The Planets; Venus* (RLPO, Mackerras). GRIEG: *Olav Trygvason: excerpts* (Trondheim Ch. & SO, Ruud). BORODIN: *Prince Igor: Polovtsian Dance* (RLPO Ch. & O, Mackerras). POULENC: *Organ Concerto: excerpts* (Weir; cond. Hickox). ORFF: *Carmina Burana: O Fortuna* (Bournemouth Ch. & SO, Hill).

(B) ** Virgin 2x1 5 61890-2 (2).

This curious Virgin collection of wedding music ('spiritual, contemplative or festive') was originally compiled in 1989, which perhaps accounts for the omission of the Widor *Organ Toccata.* But one wonders where music from Falla's *Three-Cornered Hat* ballet or Grieg's *Olav Trygvason* will fit into an English wedding celebration? However, there are quite a number of more suitable items, and the performances and recordings are of a high standard. No doubt the inclusion of Orff's *O Fortuna* as the final item is intended to celebrate the 'luck' of the bride, and she will be glad to know that Holst's *Venus* represents 'the bringer of peace' rather than extramarital temptation.

Williams, John (guitar)

'The Seville Concert' ((i) with Orquesta Sinfónica de Sevilla, José Buenagu): ALBENIZ: *Suite españolas: Sevilla; Asturias.* BACH: *Lute Suite No. 4, BWV 1006a: Prelude.* D. SCARLATTI: *Keyboard Sonata in D min., Kk. 13* (arr. WILLIAMS). (i) VIVALDI: *Concerto in D, RV 93.* YOCUH: *Sakura Variations.* KOSHKIN: *Usher Waltz, Op. 29.* BARRIOS: *Sueño en la Floresta.* (i) RODRIGO: *Concierto de Aranjuez: Adagio.*

*** Sony SK 53359.

With so much reappearing from the Julian Bream archive, it is good to have a first-rate, modern recital from the estimable John Williams. It was recorded in Spain (in the Royal Alcázar Palace) as part of a TV programme, which accounts for its hour-long duration and the inclusion of the ubiquitous Rodrigo *Adagio* as the closing item. The recording is very realistic and present, yet the balance is natural and the effect not jumbo-sized. John Williams's intellectual concentration is as formidable as his extraordinary technique. This playing comes as much from the head as from the heart. He is first rate in the Bach and brings a sense of keyboard articulation to the engaging *D minor Sonata* of Scarlatti (who was Bach's almost exact contemporary). His strength is felt in the flamenco accents of Albéniz's *Asturias*; a sense of the darkly dramatic is powerfully conveyed in Koshkin's *Usher Waltz* (after Edgar Allan Poe). Yet his playing can be charmingly poetic, as in the delicate account of the *Largo* of the Vivaldi concerto; touchingly gentle, as in Yocuh's charming pentatonic evocation of cherry blossoms; or thoughtfully improvisational, as in the Barrios *Sueño en la Floresta.*

Zabaleta, Nicanor (harp)

Harp concertos: (i) BOIELDIEU: *Harp Concerto in 3 tempi in C* (with Berlin RSO, Märzendorfer). SAINT-SAENS: *Morceau de concert in G, Op. 154.* TAILLEFERRE: *Concertino for Harp and Orchestra* (with ORTF, Martinon). RAVEL: *Introduction and*

Allegro for Harp, Flute, Clarinet and String Quartet (with members of the Kuentz CO).

(M) **(*) DG (IMS) (ADD) 463 084-2.

Two rarities – the Tailleferre and Saint-Saëns – make this collection interesting. Germaine Tailleferre's *Concertino* dates from 1927 and contains influences of Ravel, Poulenc and even Stravinsky peeping over the composer's shoulder. It is elegantly written and not without its own degree of urbanity, even if the lyrical element is comparatively diffuse. The three movements have an attractive impetus, with the jolly finale developing real exuberance. Saint-Saëns's *Morceau de concert* was written when he was 83 years old. Its four miniature movements – the dainty Scherzo only runs for 1'54" – have a structure which has much in common with that of the *Second Piano Concerto*. But the work's charm rests on its delicacy of texture and the skill with which the accompaniment is tailored, so that it supports but never overwhelms the soloist. Yet the invention has characteristic facility. Both performances are superb, with Martinon providing stylish accompaniments in good (1969) DG sound. The Ravel and Boieldieu performances are both stylish, but neither is quite the finest available, and the sound is not ideally full either. A pity that the Ginastera *Concerto*, originally on the Martinon disc, was dropped, for this disc plays for under 65 minutes.

INSTRUMENTAL RECITALS

The Art of the Piano

'*The Art of the Piano*': *Great Pianists of the 20th Century*: (Paderewski; Hofmann; Rachmaninov; Moiseiwitsch; Horowitz; Cziffra; Myra Hess; Rubinstein; Planté; Cortot; Backhaus; Edwin Fischer; Gilels; Richter; Michelangeli; Gould; Arrau).

(*) Warner/NVC Arts **DVD 3984 29199-2; Video 3984 29199-3.

This fascinating DVD and video is in the line of '*The Art of Conducting*'. Unfortunately it is musically flawed because so many of the most interesting visual images are taken from old films and cinema sound-tracks which, with their inherent unsteadiness and fluctuations of timbre and pitch, have in the past been notoriously unkind to the piano. Most of the examples here offer marbled tone and harmonic distortion to varying degrees. However, the video's introduction still brings a spectacular display of technical wizardry. We see and hear a kaleidoscope of stormy performances of Beethoven's *Appassionata Sonata* edited together in a rapid ongoing sequence, with Solomon first (in 1956), swiftly followed by Arrau (1983), then Dame Myra Hess (1945), Sviatoslav Richter (1992) and finally the aristocratic Artur Rubinstein (1975). Even with such short snippets, the different pianistic personalities of the five players emerge vividly.

We next focus on Paderewski, Prime Minister as well as a somewhat eccentric musician, but an artist whose personal magnetism projected strongly. Like Liszt, whose music he plays, he was irresistible to women; hence his success in a 1936 Hollywood movie, *Moonlight Serenade*. Josef Hofmann, a legend among fellow pianists, is much more patrician: his approach to the ubiquitous Rachmaninov *C sharp minor Prelude* has no nonsense about it. Rachmaninov follows on, playing his own music with natural authority, and then we meet one of his greatest contemporary interpreters, Moiseiwitsch. A pity there is not more of the *Second Piano Concerto* (conducted by Constant Lambert) as the plum-label HMV records of this work were considered by some collectors even finer than the composer's own set with Stokowski.

The extraordinary dash of Horowitz (filmed in the Carnegie Hall in 1968) is seen in Scriabin and Bizet, his hands (to quote Támás Vásáry) 'like race horses!' virtually matched by those of the underrated Cziffra in Liszt.

Dame Myra Hess always felt intimidated by the recording studio, but here her performance of the first movement of Beethoven's *Appassionata Sonata* (of which we have previously heard a brief excerpt) demonstrates the full power and concentration of her live performances. Rubinstein follows magisterially with Chopin's *A flat Polonaise* (in 1953), then creates magic in the closing pages of the first movement of Beethoven's *Fourth Concerto*, with Antal Dorati 15 years later; and here the recording is faithful enough to make a real highlight.

But perhaps it is Cortot who provides the most intriguing cameo in the first part of the video. We see and hear him playing *The poet speaks* from *Kinderszenen* to a 1953 masterclass, commenting throughout Schumann's intimate reverie, and suggesting that the performer's aim should be 'to dream the piece rather than play it'.

Backhaus (filmed during his Decca recording sessions) now plays the slow movement of his favourite concerto, Beethoven's *Fourth*. He quotes Hans Richter who called it the 'Greek' concerto. In this central movement, Backhaus tells us, 'Orpheus pleads to set Eurydice free; he meets with fierce resistance before his entreaties are answered'.

We move on to Edwin Fischer's pioneering Bach with its 'luminous' sound-quality and intellectual spontaneity and then meet a very young Gilels in a Soviet wartime propaganda film playing Rachmaninov to a carefully staged group of Russian service personnel. Cut to his electrifying and extraordinarily imaginative 1959 performance of the cadenza from the first movement of Tchaikovsky's *B flat minor Piano Concerto* (conducted by André Cluytens). This is followed immediately by Sviatoslav Richter, with his 'overwhelming presence' and extraordinary visceral bravura in the finale of the same work, and a comparable 'transcendental virtuosity' in a performance of Chopin's *Revolutionary* study.

After that, Michelangeli's narcissistically self-aware keyboard personality makes a strange contrast, but his immaculate performance of a Scarlatti sonata is blurred by poor sound. Glenn Gould makes his entry playing Bach eccentrically, with intrusive vocalise, but is then heard at his most magnetically inspirational in partnership with Bernstein in the closing part of the first movement of the *D minor Clavier Concerto*, where he is totally absorbed in creating an extraordinary diminuendo. But it is Claudio Arrau who has the last word, and he is just as articulate talking about music-making as he is at the keyboard, where his closing except from

Beethoven's last, *C minor, Piano Sonata* is played with a beauty and concentration to transcend the recorded sound.

The Art of the Violin

'The Art of the Violin' by Bruno Monsaingeon.

With Elman, Enescu, Ferras, Francescatti, Goldstein, Grumiaux, Heifetz, Kogan, Kreisler, Menuhin, Milstein, Neveu, Oistrakh, Rabin, Stern, Szeryng, Szigeti, Thibaud, Ysaÿe; and with commentaries by Perlman, Gitlis, Haendel, Hahn, Rostropovich and Menuhin.

*** Warner/NVC Arts **DVD** 5 8573-85801-2.

Bruno Monsaingeon made a strong impression with his revealing studies of Sviatoslav Richter and David Oistrakh. As a glance at the list of artists here shows, he offers a glimpse of some of the great violinists of the last century and includes archival footage that will not only be new to many but, since some has only just come to light, new to all.

Virtuosity is common to all and transcendental in many, but it is the originality of their sound-world that is at the centre of Monsaingeon's opening argument, which explores the expressive individuality and sonority of great violinists. No one listening to Szigeti or Kreisler, Oistrakh or Elman – and above all Heifetz – is ever in the slightest doubt as to who was playing. There are excellent commentaries by Itzhak Perlman, Ida Haendel and the splendid Ivry Gitlis; only Hilary Hahn is completely out of her depth in their company.

There is rare footage of Thibaud and Ginette Neveu playing the closing bars of the Chausson *Poème* in Prague and an interesting montage of part of the Mendelssohn *Concerto* in which the soloists (Oistrakh, Stern, Christian Ferras, Milstein, Menuhin, Grumiaux, Heifetz and Elman) change, thus bringing home their differences in tonal production and their rich diversity of approach.

Other rarities include a glimpse of Ysaÿe from 1912, looking like an emperor! This thoughtful and intelligent production can be warmly recommended. Incidentally, on the credits nearly every European TV station is listed as supporting this venture, but neither the BBC nor Channel 4 is among them – further evidence, perhaps, of the declining cultural ambition of British television in the last decade.

Other Instrumental Recitals

Amadeus Quartet

Westminster, DG and EMI Recordings (1951–7):
HAYDN: *The Seven Last Words of our Saviour on the Cross. String Quartets Nos. 57 in G; 58 in C, Op. 54/1–2; 67 in B flat, Op. 64/3; 72 in C; 74 in G min. (Rider), Op. 74/1 & 3; 81 in G, Op. 77/1; 83 in B flat, Op. 103.* HOFFSTETTER: *String Quartet in F (Serenade)* (attrib. HAYDN, *Op. 3/5*). SCHUBERT: *String Quartets Nos. 10 in E flat, D.87; 8 in B flat, D.112; 13 in A min., D.804; 14 in D min. (Death and the Maiden); 15 in G, D.887; Quartettsatz, D.703.* MENDELSSOHN: *Capriccio in E min., Op. 81.* BRAHMS: *String Quartets Nos. 1 in C min.; 2 in A min., Op. 51/1–2; 3 in B flat, Op. 67.*
⊶ ✪ (B) (★★★) DG mono 474 730-2 (7).

These superb performances were originally issued on either the Westminster or DG labels, and were recorded at Conway Hall, in Hanover's Beethoven-saal, or by an EMI recording team at Abbey Road. The performances are of consistently superb quality (*The Seven Last Words* of Haydn is particularly fine), immaculate in ensemble and with a freshness, intensity and spontaneity which the Amadeus players did not always maintain in their later, stereo recordings for DG. Their Haydn *Quartets* are wonderfully refreshing, their Schubert appealingly combines drama with humanity, and their Brahms has the lyric feeling and warmth that make this composer special. The recordings, partly mono, partly stereo, have only the slightest hint of thinness on top, and plenty of body, and the acoustic has a pleasing spaciousness. A superb set in every way.

Amato, Donna (piano)

'*A Piano Portrait*': LISZT: *Hungarian Rhapsody No. 2* (cadenza by Rachmaninov); *Consolation No. 3; Liebestraum No. 3.* DEBUSSY: *Arabesque No. 1; Suite bergamasque: Clair de lune. Préludes: La Fille aux cheveux de lin; La Cathédrale engloutie.* RAVEL: *Pavane pour une infante défunte.* GERSHWIN: *3 Preludes; Rhapsody in Blue* (solo piano version). Song transcriptions: *The Man I Love; Swanee; Oh, Lady be Good; I'll Build a Stairway to Paradise; 'S Wonderful; I got Rhythm.*
★★★ Olympia OCD 352.

The young American pianist Donna Amato here proves her mettle in standard repertoire and, more importantly, confirms her ability to create 'live' performances in the recording studio. None of the readings is routine or conventional: the Liszt *Consolation* has an attractive simplicity and the famous *Liebestraum*, while not lacking romantic impulse, has an agreeable lack of gush. Her Debussy is particularly impressive: the *Arabesque* has a lightly chimerical variety of touch and colour and the two most famous pieces are made to seem refreshingly unhackneyed. The highlight, however, is *La cathédrale engloutie*, an unforgettably powerful evocation, played quite superbly. She is, not surprisingly, completely at home with Gershwin. The song transcriptions are splendidly stylish and sparkling and her solo account of the *Rhapsody in Blue* is highly idiomatic. In its strong, natural impulse and rhythmic freedom it can be spoken of in the same breath as Bernstein's version, although it has completely its own character. Donna Amato's style is not that of a Horowitz, and so it was perhaps a pity she chose to open with the Liszt *Hungarian Rhapsody*, which would have been better placed later on in the programme, while the Ravel *Pavane* is a little too sober; but as a whole this 76-minute recital, recorded very realistically indeed in Salen Church Hall, Ski, Norway, is most enjoyable.

Anda, Géza (piano)

Edinburgh Festival Recital, 23 August 1955:
BEETHOVEN: *Piano Sonata No. 7 in D, Op. 10/3.* SCHUMANN: *Etudes symphoniques, Op. 13.* BARTOK: *Suite, Op. 14.* BRAHMS: *Variations on a Theme by Paganini, Op. 35.*
(M) (★★★) BBC mono BBCL 4135-2.

Géza Anda made a number of records on the blue Columbia label during the 1950s, including a memorable 'Bartók For Children', before migrating to Deutsche Grammophon in the 1960s. (His Bartók and Schumann have reappeared in excellent transfers on the Testament label.) This BBC recording was made when he was at the height of his powers and brings an account of the *Etudes symphoniques* that does him – and Schumann – proud, and the Bartók *Suite* is hardly less fine. The recording shows its age a little, but the recital offers playing of such pianistic finesse and poetic feeling that few will be troubled by sonic shortcomings.

Anderson, John (oboe), Gordon Back (piano)

'*Capriccio*': PONCHIELLI: *Capriccio*. HUE: *Petite pièce*. PALADILHE: *Solo*. KALLIWODA: *Morceau de salon, Op. 228*. PASCULLI: *Concerto sopra motivi dell'opera 'La Favorita' di Donizetti*. FAURE: *Pièce*. DONIZETTI: *Solo*. SCHUMANN: *3 Romances, Op. 94*. FRANCK: *Pièce No. 5*. SINIGAGLIA: *Variations on a Theme of Schubert, Op. 19*.

(M) **(*) ASV CDWHL 2100.

The three *Romances* by Schumann are the highlight of the programme: they have more substance than the rest and are beautifully played, while Sinigaglia's ingenious variations on one of Schubert's most charming melodies make for an engaging finale. The decoratively florid *Capriccio* of Ponchielli which opens the recital receives the most stylish bravura from the soloist; but it is completely inconsequential. The *Petite pièce* of Georges Hüe is more distinctive and Paladilhe's *Solo* (in fact a duo with piano) is amiable too, as is the Kalliwoda *Morceau*, although it is rather longer than a morceau.

When we come to Pasculli's cleverly contrived fantasia on Donizetti's *La Favorita*, the tunes are more indelible, and the resulting virtuosity is impressive. Donizetti's own *Solo* is another attractive miniature, as is the lilting Franck *Pièce*. John Anderson is a first-rate oboist and he is persuasively supported throughout by Gordon Back. The recording is very real and immediate. But this lightweight 75-minute concert needs to be dipped into rather than taken all at once.

Andreasen, Henri Wenzel (flute), Anna Oland (piano)

Flute music of the Danish Golden Age: HARTMANN: *Sonata in B flat, Op. 1; Prelude in G min*. FROLICH: *Sonata in A min*. WEYSE: *Rondeau in D min*. KUHLAU: *Duo brillant, Op. 110/1*.

(BB) *** Naxos 8.553333.

The Danish Golden Age is, roughly speaking, the period of the artists C. W. Eckersberg and Christen Købke (the first half of the nineteenth century) and it was then that the present repertoire was composed. It is best summarized as slight but pleasing music, and the performances are alert and fresh with good, bright – but not overbright – sound.

Andsnes, Leif Ove (piano)

'*The Long, Long Winter Night*': GRIEG: *Norwegian Folksongs, Op. 66; Peasant Dances, Op. 72*. TVEITT: *Fifty Folktunes from Hardanger, Op. 150*. JOHANSEN: *Pictures from Nordland: Suite No. 1, Op. 5*. VALEN: *Variations for Piano, Op. 23*. SÆVERUD:

Tunes and Dances from Siljustøl, Opp. 22, 24, 25; Peer Gynt: Hymn against the Boyg, Op. 28.

✪ *** EMI 5 56541-2.

A recital of unusual excellence and distinction from Leif Ove Andsnes, devoted to his fellow countrymen. The disc takes its title, 'The Long, Long Winter Night', from one of the *Hardanger Folktunes* by Geirr Tveitt. His programme ranges widely from some of the late and extraordinarily characterful *Slåtter* or *Peasant Dances* of Grieg to the *Variations* by Fartein Valen, the pre-war Norwegian apostle of dodecaphony. Grieg's biographer David Monrad Johansen (best known perhaps for his tone-poem, *Pan*) is represented by two early piano pieces that are of more than passing interest. He also includes seven of the Op. 150 set of *Hardanger Folktunes*, which could be as popular here as they are in Norway if they were given the chance.

Although his symphonies are now gaining ground on CD, Harald Sæverud was arguably at his best as a miniaturist, and Andsnes gives us a handful of his distinctive, original *Slåtter og stev fra Siljustøl*, which have such winning titles as 'The cotton grass plays on a moonbeam fiddle' (variously translated as 'The windflowers twiddle the moonbeam fiddle'). He also includes *Kjæmpeviseslåtten* ('The Ballad of Revolt') that came to symbolize Norwegian resistance to the Nazis during the occupation. A well-planned and imaginative recital, and an exhibition of masterly pianism. Very good recording indeed.

Antonelli, Claudia (harp)

Music for Harp and Violin: CLEMENTI: *Andante and Variations*. VIOTTI: *Harp Sonata*. POLLINI: *Capriccio and Aria with Variations; Theme and Variations*. ROSSINI: *Allegretto; Harp Sonata; Violin and Harp Sonata*. DONIZETTI: *Violin and Harp Sonata* (both with Alberto Ambrosini, violin). BOCHSA: *Fantasia on Bellini's 'I Capuleti e Montecchi'*. ROCCHIS: *Fantasia on Bellini's 'Casta Diva'*.

(BB) * Naxos 8.554252.

For the most part this is prettily attractive music, the most substantial work being the 16-minute Viotti *Sonata*, which gives the programme a bit of weight. Claudia Antonelli plays well enough, though from time to time a hint of blandness creeps in, and, although the two short sonatas with violin add tonal variety, Alberto Ambrosini's timbre is hardly beautiful, with unstable intonation, and one or two really disagreeable passages. The harp is recorded adequately, but with the higher registers leaning towards harshness.

Argerich, Martha (piano)

CHOPIN: *Scherzo No. 3 in C sharp min., Op. 39; Barcarolle in F sharp min., Op. 60*. BRAHMS: 2

Rhapsodies, Op. 79. PROKOFIEV: *Toccata, Op. 11.*
RAVEL: *Jeux d'eau.* LISZT: *Hungarian Rhapsody No.
6; Piano Sonata in B min.*

(M) (**) DG 447 430-2.

This particular 'Legendary Recording' in DG's series
of 'Originals' presents Argerich's remarkable début
LP recital, recorded for DG in 1961. The phenomenal
technique (she was twenty-one at the time) is as
astonishing as the performances are musically exasperating. This artist's charismatic impulsiveness is
well known, but in presenting Chopin and Brahms
she is too impetuous by half, although *Jeux d'eau*
brings a certain Ravelian magic. The Liszt *Sonata* has
been added on; it dates from a decade later and yet
again, although the bravura is breathtaking and there
is no lack of spontaneity, the work's architecture and
indeed its breadth are to some extent sacrificed to the
insistent forward impulse of the playing. Good but
not exceptional recording, a bit hard in the Liszt,
though that may well reflect faithfully the percussive
attack of Argerich's powerful hands.

'Live from the Concertgebouw 1978 & 1979': BACH:
*Partita No. 2 in C min., BWV 826; English Suite No.
2 in A min., BWV 807.* CHOPIN: *Nocturne No. 13 in
C min., Op. 48/1; Scherzo No. 3 in C sharp min., Op.
39.* BARTOK: *Sonata.* GINASTERA: *Danzas
argentinas, Op. 2.* PROKOFIEV: *Sonata No. 7, in B
flat, Op. 83.* D. SCARLATTI: *Sonata in D min.,
Kk.141.*

*** EMI 5 56975-2.

CD 2: RAVEL: *Sonatine; Gaspard de la Nuit.*
SCHUMANN: *Fantaisiestücke, Op. 12.*

*** EMI 5 57101-2.

Electrifying playing, even by Argerich's own standards. The Prokofiev *Seventh Sonata* is given with
demonic abandon, and the commanding performances by Horowitz, Pollini and Pletnev seem almost
measured by comparison. The Bartók is hardly less
astonishing, and the same must be said of Ginastera's
Danzas argentinas. The Scarlatti is wonderfully
elegant, and the Bach and Chopin are gripping. Fine
though her studio recordings are, these have an
inflammable quality that is special. The recordings
are a bit forward, but with playing like this, who
cares!

Art of Brass, Copenhagen

'From the Merry Life of a Spy' (Music for Brass
Quintet): HOLMBOE: *Quintets Nos. 1, Op. 79; 2, Op.
136.* NORHOLM: *From the Merry Life of a Spy. Op.
156.* NORDENTOFT: *3 Studies.* JORGENSEN: *Quintet.*
ANDRESEN: *3 Norwegian Dances.*

*** dacapo 8.226001.

The Art of Brass, Copenhagen, was formed in 1996
and won first prize in the Eighth International Brass
Quintet Competition in Narbonne four years later.

Small wonder, for they are technically immaculate
and their virtuosity is lightly worn in this record of
Danish music for brass. By far the most substantial
pieces here are the two *Brass Quintets* by Vagn Holmboe, the *First* commissioned in 1960 by the New
York Wind Quintet and the *Second* written in 1979
for the tenth anniversary of the Copenhagen Brass
Quintet. The writing is masterly and always both
individual and vital. The disc takes its title, *'From the
Merry Life of a Spy'*, from Ib Nørholm's short piece
whose inspiration derives, the composer tells us,
from the many different muting possibilities of the
ensemble, which prompted him to try and write a
spy story on the John Le Carré model 'with a hush-
hush conspiracy in the first movement and a shoot-
out in the last'. The *Three Norwegian Dances* of 1990
by Mogens Andresen are inventive and entertaining
(the composer, born in 1945, is himself a trombonist)
and the companion pieces, the amiable wartime
Quintet by Axel Jørgensen and the far less amiable
Studies by Anders Nordentoft, complete a stimulating and brilliantly played disc.

Barere, Simon (piano)

'The Complete HMV Recordings, 1934–6': LISZT:
*Etude de concert (La leggierezza), G.144/2. Années de
pèlerinage, 2nd Year (Italy): Sonetto 104 del
Petrarca, G.161/5. Gnomenreigen, G.145/2;
Réminiscences de Don Juan, G.418 (2 versions);
Rapsodie espagnole, G.254; Valse oubliée No. 1,
G.215.* CHOPIN: *Scherzo No. 3 in C sharp min., Op.
39; Mazurka No. 38 in F sharp min., Op. 59/3; Waltz
No. 5 in A flat, Op. 42.* BALAKIREV: *Islamey (2
versions).* BLUMENFELD: *Etude for the Left Hand.*
GLAZUNOV: *Etude in C, Op. 31/1.* SCRIABIN: *Etudes:
in C sharp min., Op. 2/1; in D sharp min., Op. 8/12
(2 versions).* LULLY/GODOWSKI: *Gigue in E.*
RAMEAU/GODOWSKI: *Tambourin in E min.*
SCHUMANN: *Toccata in C, Op. 7 (2 versions).*

❀ (***) Appian mono CDAPR 7001 (2).

This two-CD set offers all of Barere's HMV recordings, made in the mid-1930s, including the alternative
takes he made in the studio. What can one say of his
playing without exhausting one's stock of superla-
tives? His fingerwork is quite astonishing and his
virtuosity almost in a class of its own. The set contains an absolutely stunning account of the *Réminiscences de Don Juan*, and his *Islamey* knocks spots off
any successor's in sheer virtuosity and excitement; it
is altogether breathtaking, and much the same might
be said of his *Rapsodie espagnole*. Nor is there any
want of poetry – witness the delicacy of the Scriabin
C sharp minor Etude or Liszt's *La leggierezza*. Readers
wanting to investigate this legendary artist should
start here. One of the most important functions of
the gramophone is to chart performance traditions
that would otherwise disappear from view, and this
set is one to celebrate.

Barrueco, Manuel (guitar)

'*Cuba!*': LECUONA: *La Comparsa; Dana Lecami; A la Antiga.* BROUWER: *Preludio; Rito de los Orisbas.* FARINAS: *Cancón triste; Preludio.* UBIETA: *New York Rush (Theme from El Super).* ANGULO: *Cantos Yoraba de Cuba.* ARDEVOL: *Sonata.*

(M) **(*) EMI 5 56757-2.

Manuel Barrueco, Cuban by birth, is clearly at home in this late-evening programme of mostly gentle music. The three opening Lecuona pieces are totally seductive, as is Brouwer's lovely *Preludio* and the haunting *Theme from El Super*, which is built on a rhythmic bass ostinato of Caribbean extraction. Even the series of nine brief vignettes which make up Angulo's *Cantos Yoraba*, and which are based directly on folk melodies, are primarily evocative (No. 4, *Borotití*, is like a berceuse). And it is only in Ardévol's *Sonata* with its central variations and vibrant closing *Danza* that the music becomes really animated.

This is maintained in the closing group of five Dances and Evocacións from Brouwer's *Rito de los Orisbas*, which bring plenty of chances for rhythmic bravura. (They should have been individually cued, however.) Barrueco plays with a spontaneous, ruminative style, and he is most naturally recorded (at Abbey Road).

VILLA-LOBOS: *Preludes Nos. 1–5; Chôros No. 1 in E min.* BROUWER: *Danza caracteristica; Canticum; Canción de cuna (Berceuse); Elogio de la danza; Ojos brujos; Guajira criolla. Julián orbon: Preludio y danza.*

(M) *** EMI 5 66576-2.

The Cuban guitarist Manuel Barrueco is the latest star in the line of great guitarists which began with Segovia and includes, of course, both John Williams and Julian Bream. His breadth of repertoire is remarkable and his playing is often electrifying, yet showing the most subtle imaginative touches in the control of rhythm, colour and dynamics. Barrueco is naturally at home in the music of his compatriots Leo Brouwer and the young Julián Orbon. The latter was a pupil of Aaron Copland, but his *Preludio y danza* comes nearer to the world of Villa-Lobos, with which Barrueco also has a ready affinity.

The Brouwer pieces, including the *Canticum* (dazzlingly vibrant and evocative by turns), the deliciously seductive *Canción de cuna*, the haunting *Elogio de la danza* and the *Guajira criolla* with its enticing opening pizzzicatos (violin style), are all marvellously done. Barrueco is perhaps not quite as winningly flexible as Bream in the famous *Third Prelude* of Villa-Lobos, but he makes No. 4 totally his own with a magical vibrato on the repeated tenutos. The *Chôros* is played with engaging intimacy, and the recording cannot be faulted.

FALLA: *The Three-cornered Hat: Night; Miller's Dance; Dance of the Corregidor; Dance of the Miller's Wife. Omaggio per chitarra (Scritto per le tombeau de Debussy).* PONCE: *Sonatina meridional.* RODRIGO: *Invocación y danza (Homenaje a Manuel de Falla); 3 Piezas españolas.*

(M) *** EMI 5 66577-2.

What comes over here is not just the (often unostentatious) dazzling bravura and the evocative feeling, but the appealingly warm intimacy with which Barrueco communicates so directly to the listener. He finds all the colour and flamenco rhythms in Falla's *Three-cornered Hat* ballet music without ever going over the top; but he is at his very finest in the delicate nocturnal evocation of Rodrigo's very personal tribute to Falla. Falla's own *Homenaje* for *Debussy* flashes vibrantly, as does the *Zapateado* finale of the Rodrigo *Spanish Pieces*; but, for all the astonishing technical mastery of this playing, one always feels that Barrueco is looking beneath the music's surface and seeking to find added depth and atmosphere. If you enjoy Spanish guitar music, this recital is unmissable.

Bate, Jennifer (organ)

'*From Stanley to Wesley*' (Eighteenth-century organ music on period instruments from Adlington Hall, the Dolmetsch Collection, St Michael's Mount, Kenwood House, Killerton House, Everingham Chapel).

(BB) **(*) Regis RRC 5002 (5).

Volume 1: READING: *Airs for French Horns & Flutes.* STANLEY: *Voluntaries, Op. 5/7 & 10; Op. 6/5 & 8; Op. 7/3.* HANDEL: *Fugues in G min.; in B flat.* ROSEINGRAVE: *Voluntary in G min.* TRAVERS: *Voluntary in D min. & major.* WALOND: *Voluntary in A min.* RUSSELL: *Voluntary in E min.* S. WESLEY: *Short Pieces Nos. 7 & 12; Voluntary, Op. 6/1.*

(BB) *** Regis RRC 1113.

Volume 2: GREENE: *Voluntary in C min.* STANLEY: *Voluntaries, Op. 5/6 & 9; Op. 6/7 & 9; Op. 7/2.* HANDEL: *Voluntary in C; Fugue in A min.* LONG: *Voluntary in D min.* WALOND: *Voluntary in B min.* NARES: *Introduction & Fugue in F.* RUSSELL: *Voluntary in A min.* S. WESLEY: *Short Piece No. 9 in F; Voluntaries, Op. 6/3 & 9.*

Volume 3: GREENE: *Voluntary in B min.* STANLEY: *Voluntaries, Op. 6/1, 6 & 10; Op. 7/1 & 6.* WALOND: *Voluntary in G.* HANDEL: *Fugue in B min.; Voluntary in C.* BURNEY: *Voluntary No. 1: Cornet Piece in C.* RUSSELL: *Voluntary in A.* DUPUIS: *Voluntary in B flat.* S. WESLEY: *Short Pieces Nos. 6 & 8; Voluntary, Op. 6/6.*

(BB) **(*) Regis RRC 2058 (2).

Volume 4: CROFT: *Voluntary in D.* GREENE: *Voluntary in E flat.* STANLEY: *Voluntaries, Op. 5/1 & 8; Op. 6/4; Op. 7/8.* WALOND: *Voluntary in G.* HANDEL: *Fugue in C min.; Voluntary in G min.*

BURNEY: *Fugue in F min.* KEEBLE: *Select Piece No. 1 in C.* S. WESLEY: *Voluntary, Op. 6/10.*

Volume 5: BOYCE: *Voluntary in D.* STANLEY: *Voluntaries, Op. 6/2; Op. 7/4, 7 & 9.* STUBLEY: *Voluntary in C.* HANDEL: *Fugue in G; Voluntary in C.* ROSEINGRAVE: *Fugue No. 8 in E min.* HERON: *Voluntary in G.* RUSSELL: *Voluntary in F.* HOOK: *Voluntary in C min.* S. WESLEY: *Voluntaries in B flat; in E flat, Op. 6/7.*

(BB) **(*) Regis RRC 2059 (2).

Jennifer Bate's survey of eighteenth-century English organ music uses six different organs from stately homes to secure maximum variety of presentation. But these instruments are without pedals, and each produces a sonority that is relatively light-textured, bright and sweet. The five programmes are each made up in the same way, usually opening with a voluntary by Maurice Greene (or alternatively Croft or Boyce), then offering a clutch of voluntaries by John Stanley, followed in most cases by music by Walond and Handel, among others, and usually ending with pieces by Samuel Wesley.

None of these are great composers, save Handel of course, and his chosen examples are extremely minor works. Jennifer Bate did much initial research into available instruments before undertaking the original project for Unicorn, and she plays all this music in impeccable style and is beautifully recorded. So the particular attractions of each volume depend on the items included. Easily the most engaging are the works which use cornet or trumpet stops, which are colourful and jolly, while the *Vox humana* stop, as in the finale of Stanley's Op. 6/5 of the first disc, is also ear-tickling.

Indeed the first volume is a good place to start, with Op. 5/7 by the same composer also quite engaging. The voluntaries are usually in two sections, but William Russell's E minor piece is in three, with an imposing opening, and the fugue used as a centrepiece. Samuel Wesley's *Short Piece No. 12* is a contrapuntal moto perpetuo.

The second volume offers more examples of Stanley's ready facility, notably Op. 7/2 and Op. 5/6, but on the whole this is a less interesting programme than the third, which again shows Stanley at his more inventive in Op. 7/1, while Op. 6/1 begins with a pleasing *Siciliano*, and the trumpet theme of Op. 6/6 might have been written by Purcell. Handel's *Voluntary in C* brings an attractive interplay of parts in its second movement, while Burney's *Cornet Piece* has a whiff of the *Hallelujah Chorus*.

In Volume 4 Jennifer Bate registers Stanley's Op. 5/8 with piquant skill (this is a three-part work), and Volume 5 brings new composer names, adding music of Heron, Hook and Stubley, although the idiom remains much the same. Volume 1, however, is the CD to try first, and if you enjoy this go on to the two-CD set including Volumes 3 and 4. But only the dedicated enthusiast attracted by the sounds of early English organs will want the complete set, for much of the music here is conventional.

Beaux Arts Trio

'*1967–74 Recordings*': MENDELSSOHN: *Piano Trios Nos. 1 in D min., Op. 49; 2 in C min., Op. 66.* SCHUMANN: *Piano Trios Nos. 1 in D min., Op. 63; 2 in F, Op. 80; 3 in G min., Op. 110.* CLARA SCHUMANN: *Piano Trio in G min., Op. 17.* CHOPIN: *Piano Trio in G min., Op. 8.* TCHAIKOVSKY: *Piano Trio in A min., Op. 50.* SMETANA: *Piano Trio in G min., Op. 15.* IVES: *Piano Trio.* SHOSTAKOVICH: *Piano Trio No. 2, Op. 67.*

(B) *** Ph. (ADD) 475 171-2 (4).

It is right that the achievement of the Beaux Arts Trio in the late 1960s and early 1970s should be celebrated. The Schumann *Piano Trios*, for instance, were recorded in 1971, and still remain the safest recommendation in this repertoire, sounding good over 30 years later. Following on in the same year, Clara Schumann's attractive *G minor Piano Trio*, though not in the same league as her husband's, is still very welcome. If in the past we have favoured the EMI Chung/Tortelier/Previn version of the Mendelssohn *D minor Trio* – one of his most richly inspired chamber works – the Beaux Arts are hardly far behind, with playing that is always splendidly alive and musical. Chopin's *Piano Trio* is an early work and not wholly characteristic, but it would be hard to imagine a more persuasive performance. The original coupling of the Smetana *Piano Trio* is included and is given powerful advocacy here; the 1970 sound remains fresh and vivid. It is good, too, to hear the Beaux Arts Trio in some twentieth-century repertoire, and the 1974 pairing of Ives and Shostakovich was an apt choice. Written between 1904 and 1911, Ives's *Piano Trio* is a powerful and memorable work, ending with a strikingly beautiful *Moderato* movement. There is a fascinating contradiction between the superb polish of the Beaux Arts ensemble and the characteristic oddity of Ives's inspiration, with its separation of individual parts. But the result here is splendidly convincing, with the toughness of the first movement and the exuberance of the central Scherzo (a typical collage of popular tunes) presented at full intensity. The Beaux Arts also give a pure and intense reading of the Shostakovich *Piano Trio No. 2*, in which all the technical difficulties are overcome. The Scherzo has rarely if ever been played so fast as here, and certainly not with the same meticulous ensemble – a tribute to the players' collective virtuosity, developed over many years of corporate performance. The Tchaikovsky *Trio* is as polished and eloquent as one would expect, though some collectors may prefer a bolder approach. On the whole an impressive achievement, with the excellent recordings impressively transferred throughout.

Belgian Wind Quintet

'*Summer Music*': BEETHOVEN: *Wind Quintet in E flat.* HOLST: *Wind Quintet in A flat, Op. 14.* BARBER: *Summer Music, Op. 31.* ARRIEU: *Quintet in C.*

(BB) *** Discover DICD 920322.

A delightful collection, well worth its modest price. The many felicities of the Barber *Summer Music* are matched by those of the much less familiar work of Holst, contemporary with the *Military Band Suites.* Claude Arrieu (born 1903) also writes very engagingly: his *Quintet* is both elegant and witty. The playing of the Belgian group is polished and spontaneous, and they are very well recorded.

Bennett, Richard Rodney (piano)

'*British Piano Music of the '20s & '30s*': MAYERL: *Marigold; Punch; Ace of Hearts; Antiquary; Shallow Waters; Printer's Devil; Sleepy Piano; Railroad Rhythm.* BLISS: *The Rout Trot.* Gerrard WILLIAMS: *Déjeuner dansant: Valsette brute; Raguette extra-sec.* GOOSSENS: *Folk-tune.* WALTON (arr. Rodney Bennett): *Façade: Old Sir Faulk.* LAMBERT: *Elegiac Blues; Elegy. Concerto for Piano and 9 Players* (with members of the English Sinfonia, Dilkes).

(M) **(*) EMI (ADD) 5 65596-2.

Constant Lambert's *Concerto for Piano and Nine Players* presents a clever marriage between neo-classical and jazz manners. In a poor performance the work can seem very dry indeed, but here (in 1974) Richard Rodney Bennett makes the music sparkle with wit, pointing the rhythms with subtle nuances that bring it to life. The sleight-of-hand pay-off endings to each movement are delectably done. The couplings could hardly be more apt: a collection of short pieces by Lambert and others with direct debts to jazz. The main addition to the original LP is eight characteristic pieces by Billy Mayerl – including his most famous, *Marigold.* Their carefree jazz style is neatly brought out by the pianist, even though here the piano is too backwardly balanced. Lambert's *Elegiac Blues* is rather leisurely, but very expressive, while the *Elegy,* which is more ambitious in scale, is less sharply inspired. The two miniatures by Gerrard Williams are slight but attractive. But every item here has a point: Bliss's piece is like a cross between Scott Joplin and Grainger's *Country Gardens,* while Walton's *Old Sir Faulk* shines out as the finest example of all in this tiny but delightful genre. A most enjoyable collection which fully conjures up the spirit of the 1920s and '30s, and the sound, with the caveat about the (1975) Mayerl pieces already mentioned, is remarkably good.

Bergen Wind Quintet

BARBER: *Summer Music, Op. 31.* SÆVERUD: *Tunes and Dances from Siljustøl, Op. 21a.* JOLIVET: *Serenade for Wind Quintet with Principal Oboe.* HINDEMITH: *Kleine Kammermusik, Op. 24/2.*

*** BIS CD 291.

Barber's *Summer Music* is a glorious piece dating from the mid-1950s; it is in a single movement. Sæverud's *Tunes and Dances from Siljustøl* derive from piano pieces of great charm and sound refreshing in their transcribed format. Jolivet's *Serenade* is hardly less engaging, while Hindemith's *Kleine Kammermusik,* when played with such character and finesse, is no less welcome. Throughout, the fine blend and vivacious ensemble give consistent pleasure.

Bliss, Julian (clarinet), Julien Quentin (piano)

POULENC: *Sonata.* MESSAGER: *Solo de concours.* HOROVITZ: *Sonatina.* JEANJEAN: *Clair matin* (Idylle). FRANÇAIX: *Tema con variazioni.* MARTINU: *Sonatina.* BASSI: *Concert Fantasia on Motives from Verdi's 'Rigoletto'.*

(B) *** EMI Début 5 85639-2.

EMI's Début series performs an invaluable service in providing young artists with a CD visiting-card, though Julian Bliss, at only fourteen, has already attracted attention with appearances at the 'Prom at the Palace' in 2002, and he has played with various orchestras: the Tokyo Symphony, the Zurich Chamber, Bergen Philharmonic and the BBC Symphony Orchestra. His programme is intelligently planned and is worth having for the Poulenc and Martinů sonatas alone. They are played with great spirit and elegance, as are the Françaix *Concertino* and Joseph Horovitz's engaging *Sonatina.* He apparently caused a stir with the Messager test-piece at the Prom, understandably so. His partner, Julian Quentin, is a highly gifted player and will hopefully go on to make a strong solo career himself. Very well-balanced sound.

Bok, Henri (bass clarinet), Rainer Klaas (piano)

20th-century Music for Bass Clarinet and Piano: HINDEMITH: *Sonata.* SCHOECK: *Sonata, Op. 41.* SLUKA: *Sonata.* REHAK: *Sonnet III.* HEUCKE: *Sonata, Op. 23.* SOLL: *Lumen.*

*** Clarinet Classics CC 026.

A remarkably stimulating collection with a group of four diverse sonatas which between them explore every lyrical and virtuosic possibility of the bass clarinet's colour spectrum and virtuosic range. From Hindemith comes an unexpectedly enticing mixture of wit and wan pastoralism, while Rehak's *Sonnet III* is a darkly atmospheric interlude before the most ambitious piece here, by Stefan Heucke. It is in three sections, a *Ballade*, an extraordinary set of central *Variations*, full of original and unexpected rhythms and sounds, followed by a plangent closing *Elegie*. Soll's *Lumen* then acts as a lighter, entertaining encore. The performances throughout are in every way superb and the recording excellent.

Bowyer, Kevin (organ)

'*A Feast of Organ Exuberance*' (Blackburn Cathedral organ): LEIDEL: *Toccata Delectatione, Op. 5/35.* SWAYNE: *Riff-Raff.* BERVEILLER: *Suite; Cadence.*
(M) *** Priory Dig. 001.

The spectacular sound made by the magnificent 1969 Walker organ in Blackburn Cathedral is well demonstrated by this first-rate recital. Leidel is from the former East Germany, and his acknowledged influences from Messiaen and Scriabin are well absorbed into his own style. The *Toccata for Pleasure* is titillating in its colouring and certainly exuberant in its extravagant treatment of its basic idea, which goes far beyond the minimalism achieved by many of his contemporaries. Giles Swayne is Liverpool-born and his quirky *Riff-Raff*, in the words of the performer, suggests 'isolated flashes of light of varying intensity'. Berveiller comes from the traditional French school of Dupré. His *Suite* is eminently approachable music, with a whimsical second-movement *Intermezzo* to remain in the memory, and a smoothly rich *Adagio*, before the Widorian finale. His *Cadence* provides a lightweight but by no means trivial encore. What one remembers most of all from this concert is the magnificent sonority of the organ, beautifully captured within its natural ambience, and that in itself shows how well composers and performer have combined their talents.

Brain, Dennis (horn)

Chamber Music. BEETHOVEN: *Piano and Wind Quintet in E flat, Op. 16* (with Dennis Brain Wind Ensemble). BRAHMS: *Horn Trio in E flat, Op. 40* (with Salpeter & Preedy). DUKAS: *Villanelle.* MARAIS: *Le Basque* (both with Parry). MOZART: *Horn Quintet in E flat, K.407* (with English String Qt).
☛ ✹ (M) (***) BBC mono BBCL ADD 4048-2.

This is an indispensable record which does full justice to the art of Dennis Brain in the key classical chamber works featuring the horn. The undoubted highlight of the programme is the Beethoven *Piano and Wind Quintet* in which Dennis shows himself to be the perfect chamber-music partner who yet cannot help drawing the ear at every entry.

This recording (like the Dukas and Marais) was made in the Ulster Hall at the 1957 Edinburgh Festival, in front of a live audience. But they are mercifully unintrusive, and the balance is quite perfect. The recording too is astonishingly real and immediate. It might even be stereo: one can visualize the five players sitting just behind one's speakers: Leonard Brain (oboe), Steven Waters (clarinet), Cecil James (who is recognizably playing a French bassoon), Wilfrid Parry (piano) and, of course, Dennis. The blending is nigh perfect, and Parry's pianism is not only the bedrock of the performance, but the playing itself is very elegant and communicative, particularly the way in which the players echo one another in the development section of the first movement – and how splendidly they play the coda (with a superb flourish of triplets from the horn).

The Mozart *Horn Quintet* is hardly less felicitous. Brain has warm support from the English String Quartet, notably in the lovely slow movement, but here his playing consistently dominates the ensemble, particularly in the joyful closing Rondo. Needless to say, the performance of the Brahms *Horn Trio* is very fine indeed. The withdrawn atmosphere of the slow movement created by the horn's gentle soliloquy is unforgettable; and again the infectious hunting-horn whooping of the finale carries all before it. The recording is distanced in a resonant acoustic and is not ideally clear, but one soon forgets this. Brain's ardour all but convinces us that the Dukas *Villanelle* is first-rate music, and he uses Marais's sprightly *Le Basque* as a witty encore, his articulation dazzling in its easy poise.

BEETHOVEN: *Sextet in E flat for String Quartet & 2 Horns, Op. 81b* (with Civil & English String Qt). SCHUBERT: *Auf dem Strom* (with Pears, Mewton-Wood). HAYDN: *Horn Concerto No. 1* (with BBC Midland O, Wurmser). MOZART: *Wind Divertimento (Sextet) No. 14 in B flat, K.270.* IBERT: *3 Pièces brèves.* MILHAUD: *La Cheminée du roi René* (with Brain Wind Quintet). Arnold COOKE: *Arioso and Scherzo* (with Carter String Trio). Illustrated talk: Dennis Brain demonstrates the sounds of different horns.
(M) (**(*)) BBC mono BBCL 4066-2.

It is the three recordings by the Dennis Brain Wind Quintet (Brain himself, Gareth Morris, Leonard Brain, Stephen Waters and Cecil James) which make this collection indispensable. The delectable Mozart *B flat Divertimento* could not sound fresher, and the geniality of Ibert's witty *Trois Pièces brèves* and Milhaud's *Cheminée du roi René*, with its piquant Provençal colouring, is sheer delight. In the Beethoven *Sextet* Dennis chooses to play the second horn part, giving Alan Civil the upper line: the result is a felicitously characterful bravura interplay, well supported by the English String Quartet. Unfortunately the recording of the Haydn *Concerto*, which Dennis plays with characteristic finesse and spirit, produces severe harmonic distortion which gets worse as the work proceeds. However, in the attractive occasional piece by Arnold Cooke the sound is excellent.

In Schubert's *Auf der Strom*, Brain and Pears offer a memorable partnership, but here the voice is rather too closely miked, and Noel Mewton-Wood's piano contribution is relegated to the background, although artistically he remains very much in the picture. As a bonus Dennis gives an engagingly laid-back demonstration of the different timbres of an 1812 French hand-horn, a modern Alexander wide-bore double horn, and – on his lips – an amazingly effective 'garden' hosepipe. He ends with the *Prologue* from Britten's *Serenade*, played on the hand-horn, which demonstrates – as the composer intended – the horn's not-quite in-tune upper harmonics.

Bream, Julian (guitar or lute)

🔴 '*The Julian Bream Edition*' (BMG/RCA).

The Julian Bream Edition once ran to some thirty CDs, representing three decades of a remarkably distinguished recording career. Bream has now moved over to EMI; now all but two CDs remain. The Elizabethan lute songs are listed under Peter Pears among Vocal Recitals.

Bream, Julian (lute)

Volume 1. '*The Golden Age of English Lute Music*': Robert JOHNSON: 2 *Almaines; Carman's Whistle.* John JOHNSON: *Fantasia.* CUTTING: *Walsingham; Almaine; Greensleeves.* DOWLAND: *Mignarda; Galliard upon a Galliard of Daniel Bachelar; Batell Galliard; Captain Piper's Galliard; Queen Elizabeth's Galliard; Sir John Langton's Pavan; Tarleton's Resurrection; Lady Clifton's Spirit.* ROSSETER: *Galliard.* MORLEY: *Pavan.* BULMAN: *Pavan.* BACHELAR: *Monsieur's Almaine.* HOLBORNE: *Pavan; Galliard.* BYRD: *Pavana Bray; Galliard; Pavan; My Lord Willoughby's Welcome Home.*

(M) ★★★ BMG/RCA (ADD) 09026 61584-2.

Bream is a natural lutenist and a marvellously sensitive artist in this repertoire, and here he conjures up a wide range of colour, matched by expressive feeling. Here Dowland is shown in more extrovert mood than in many of his lute songs, and overall the programme has plenty of variety. The CD combines two recitals, the first 15 items recorded by Decca in London in September 1963, and the rest of the programme in New York City two years later. The recording is exemplary and hiss is minimal.

Bream, Julian (guitar)

'*Guitarra*' (Music of Spain): MUDARRA: *Fantasias X & XIV.* Luis DE MILAN: *Fantasia XXII.* Luis DE NARVAEZ: *La canción del Emperador; Conde claros.*

Santiago de murcia: Prelude & Allegro. BOCCHERINI: *Guitar Quintet in D, G.448* (arr. for 2 guitars): *Fandango.* SOR: *Gran solo, Op. 14; Variations on a Theme of Mozart, Op. 9; Fantasie, Op. 7; Sonata, Op. 25: Minuet.* AGUADO: *Rondo in A min., Op. 2/3.* TARREGA: *Study in A; Prelude in A min.; Recuerdos de la Alhambra.*

(M) ★★★ BMG/RCA (DDD/ADD) 09026 61610-2.

An admirable survey covering 400 years and featuring several different instruments, all especially built by José Ramanillos and including a Renaissance guitar and a modern classical guitar. Bream's natural dexterity is matched by a remarkable control of colour and unerring sense of style. Many of the earlier pieces are quite simple but have considerable magnetism. The basic recital was recorded digitally in 1983 at Bream's favourite venue, Wardour Chapel, Windsor, and is laid out chronologically. Two additional Sor items, the *Fantasie*, Op. 7, and the *Minuet* from Op. 25, were made 18 years earlier in New York and, as they are analogue, have sensibly been added at the end.

'*Popular Classics for Spanish Guitar*': VILLA-LOBOS: *Chôros No. 1; Etude in E min.* TORROBA: *Madroños.* TURINA: *Homenaje a Tárrega, Op. 69: Garrotín; Solearas. Fandanguillo.* ALBENIZ: *Suite española, Op. 47: Granada; Leyenda (Asturias).* FALLA: *Homenaje pour le tombeau de Debussy.* TRAD., arr. LLOBET: *Canciones populares catalanas: El testament d'Amelia.*

(M) ★★(★) RCA (ADD) 09026 68814-2.

This outstanding early recital, recorded at Kenwood House in 1962, was one of Bream's very finest LP collections. The electricity of the music-making is consistently communicated, and all Bream's resources of colour and technical bravura are brought into play. The Villa-Lobos pieces are particularly fine, as is the Turina *Fandanguillo* (which comes at the end), and the Albéniz *Leyenda* is a *tour de force* and makes an almost orchestral effect. The recording (originally produced by James Burnett, with Bob Auger the engineer) has been splendidly remastered for RCA's 'Living Stereo' series (the equivalent of Decca's 'Classic Sound') and Bream is given a remarkable presence, with the analogue background noise all but vanquished. However, the playing time is only 42 minutes, while that earlier reissue included most of the present items, plus a great deal more music.

'*Baroque Guitar*': SANZ: *Pavanos; Canarios.* J. S. BACH: *Prelude in D min., BWV 999; Fugue in A min., BWV 1000; Lute Suite in E min., BWV 996.* SOR: *Fantasy and Minuet.* WEISS: *Passacaille; Fantaisie; Tombeau sur la mort de M. Comte de Logy.* VISEE: *Suite in D min.*

(BB) ★★★ RCA Navigator (ADD) 74321 24195-2.

This is a shorter version of the baroque recital which formed Volume 9 of the 'Julian Bream Edition'. It still includes well over an hour of music as Bream's superb account of Bach's *E minor Lute Suite* has been added. The recording is very natural, and this makes a fine recital in its own right, realistically recorded. A very real bargain in RCA's bargain-basement Navigator series.

Bream, Julian (guitar and lute)

'*The Ultimate Guitar Collection*' ((i) with Monteverdi O, Gardiner): (i) VIVALDI: *Lute Concerto in D, RV 93* (ed. Bream). Lute Pieces: CUTTING: *Packington's Round; Greensleeves.* DOWLAND: *A Fancy (Fantasia).* Guitar Pieces: SANZ: *Canarios.* M. ALBENIZ: *Sonata in D* (arr. PUJOL). I. ALBENIZ: *Suite española, Op. 47: Cataluña; Granada; Sevilla; Cádiz; Leyenda (Asturias). Mallorca, Op. 202. Cantos de España: Córdoba, Op. 232/4.* FALLA: *Three-cornered Hat: Miller's Dance.* TARREGA: *Recuerdos de la Alhambra.* VILLA-LOBOS: *Chôros No. 1; Preludes Nos. 1 in E min.; 2 in D.* RODRIGO: *En los trigales;* (i) *Concierto de Aranjuez; 3 Piezas españolas.* GRANADOS: *Cuentos para la juventud: Dedicatoria. Tonadilla: La Maja de Goya. Danzas españolas Nos. 4 (Villanesca); 5 (Valses poéticos).*

⊕ ✹ (B) ★★★ RCA (DDD/ADD) 74321 33705-2 (2).

The extraordinary achievement of RCA's 'Julian Bream Edition' is admirably summed up by this inexpensive pair of CDs which include two and a half hours of the most popular repertoire for guitar, plus a small group of lute pieces for good measure. There is not a single item here that is not strong in musical personality, and every performance springs vividly and spontaneously to life. John Eliot Gardiner provides highly distinguished accompaniments for the two justly famous concertos by Vivaldi (for lute) and Rodrigo (for guitar).

The first of the two CDs provides a well-planned historical survey, opening with Elizabethan lute music and progressing through to include three magnetic pieces by Villa-Lobos. Highlights include an electrifying performance of Falla's *Miller's Dance* from *The Three-cornered Hat* and, of course, the most famous guitar piece of all, the *Recuerdos de la Alhambra* of Tárrega.

The second collection, which is entirely digital (from 1982–3), concentrates mainly on Isaac Albéniz and Granados (not forgetting the superb accounts of the *Córdoba* by the former and the *Danza española No. 5* by the latter, which are highly praised in our Composer section). It ends appropriately with Rodrigo's *Tres Piezas españolas*, with its remarkable central *Passacaglia*. The recordings are of the highest quality and are excellently transferred to CD.

Bream, Julian and John Williams (guitar duo)

'*Together*': Disc 1: CARULLI: *Serenade in A, Op. 96.* GRANADOS: *Danzas españolas: Rodella aragonesa;*

Zambra, Op. 37/6 & 11. ALBENIZ: *Cantos de España: Bajo la palmera, Op. 232/3. Ibéria: Evocación.* GIULIANI: *Variazioni concertanti, Op. 130.* JOHNSON: *Pavan & Galliard* (arr. BREAM). TELEMANN: *Partie polonaise.* DEBUSSY: *Rêverie; Children's Corner: Golliwog's Cakewalk. Suite bergamasque: Clair de lune.*

Disc 2: LAWES: *Suite for 2 Guitars* (arr. BREAM). CARULLI: *Duo in G, Op. 34.* SOR: *L'encouragement, Op. 34.* ALBENIZ: *Cantos de España: Córdoba, Op. 232/4. Suite española: Castilla (Seguidillas).* GRANADOS: *Goyescas: Intermezzo* (arr. PUJOL). *Danzas españolas: Oriental, Op. 37/2.* FALLA: *La vida breve: Spanish Dance No. 1.* RAVEL: *Pavane pour une infante défunte.* FAURE: *Dolly (suite), Op. 56* (both arr. BREAM).

(B) ★★★ RCA (ADD) 74321 20134-2 (2).

The rare combination of Julian Bream and John Williams was achieved by RCA in the studio on two separate occasions, in 1971 and 1973, providing the basic contents of these two recitals. Further recordings were made live in Boston and New York in 1978, during a North American concert tour.

Curiously, it is the studio programmes which seem the more spontaneous, and Fauré's *Dolly Suite*, which sounds a little cosy, is the only disappointment (it also brings some audience noises). Highlights are the music of Albéniz and Granados (notably the former's haunting *Evocación* from *Ibéria*, and *Córdoba*, which Bream also included on a very successful solo recital). The transcription of the *Goyescas intermezzo* is also very successful, as is Debussy's *Golliwog's cakewalk*, in a quite different way. Giuliani's *Variazioni concertanti*, actually written for guitar duo, brings some intimately gentle playing, as does the Theme and variations which forms the second movement of Sor's *L'encouragement*, while the *Cantabile* which begins this triptych is delightful in its simple lyricism.

The Carulli *Serenade* opens the first recital very strikingly, while on the second disc the performance of Ravel's *Pavane*, very slow and stately, is memorable. The Elizabethan lute music by Johnson and Lawes and the Telemann *Partie polonaise* (written for a pair of lutes) bring a refreshing change of style in what is predominantly a programme of Spanish music. The concert ends with Albéniz's *Seguidillas*, and an appropriately enthusiatic response from the audience. With the overall timing at a very generous 149 minutes, the pair of discs comes for the cost of a single premium-priced CD and can be recommended very strongly indeed. This is music-making of the very highest order, and the CD transfers bring fine presence and a natural balance.

Brodsky Quartet

'*Music from Vienna, Volume I*': SCHOENBERG: *String Quartet in D.* WEBERN: *Langsamer Satz (Slow Movement).* ZEMLINSKY: *String Quartet No. 1 in A.*

(M) *** Van. 99208.

In the first of two discs titled 'Music from Vienna', the Brodsky Quartet have devised a fascinating grouping of early works by musical pioneers which give little idea of radical developments to come. The Schoenberg offers a surprising range of Dvořákian echoes from the opening onwards, and Dvořák is one of the influences too in the early Zemlinsky *Quartet*, again with Brahms part of the mixture. The Webern (dated 1905, the same year as his earliest atonal works) is even more ripely romantic, with echoes of Schoenberg's *Verklärte Nacht* and little astringency. The Brodsky Quartet give flawless performances, at once stirring and subtle, with superbly polished ensemble in deeply expressive music. For Volume 2, see our main volume under composers Korngold and Kreisler.

Brüggen, Frans (recorder)

'*The Frans Brüggen Edition*' (complete)
(M) *** Teldec/Warner 4509 97475-2 (12).

Volume 1: TELEMANN (with Bylsma, Leonhardt): *Essercizii musici: Sonatas in C, TWV 41:c5; in D min., TWV 41:D4. Fantasias in C, TWV 40:2; in D min., TWV 40:4; in F, TWV 40:8; in G min., TWV 40:9; in A min., TWV 40:11; in B flat, TWV 40:12. Der Getreue Music-Meister: Canonic Sonata in B flat, TWV 41:b3; Sonatas in C, TWV 41:c2; in F, TWV 41:f2; in F min., TWV 41:F1* (4509 93688-2).

Volume 2: *Italian Recorder Sonatas* (with Bylsma, Leonhardt): CORELLI: *Sonatas: in F, Op. 5/4; La Follia (Variations in G min.), Op. 5/12.* BARSANTI: *Sonata in C.* VERACINI: *Sonatas in G; in A min.* (1716). BIGAGLIA: *Sonata in A min.* CHEDEVILLE: *Sonata in G min., Op. 13/6.* MARCELLO: *Sonata in D min., Op. 2/11* (4509 93669-2; currently not available).

Volume 3: *English Ensemble Music* (with Boeke, van Hauwe, Bylsma, Leonhardt, Consort): HOLBORNE: *Dances and Airs.* TAVERNER: *In nomine.* TYE: *In nomine (Crye).* BYRD: *In nomine; The Leaves be Green.* Thomas SIMPSON: *Bonny Sweet Robin.* MORLEY: *La Girandola; Il Lamento; La Caccia.* JEFFREYS: *Fantasia.* PARCHAM: *Solo in G.* Robert CARR: *Divisions upon an Italian Ground.* William BABELL: *Concerto in D.* PEPUSCH: *Sonata in F.* PURCELL: *Chaconne in F* (4509 97456-2; currently not available).

Volume 4: *Early Baroque Recorder Music* (with Boeke, van Hauwe, Bylsma, Möller, van Asperen, Leonhardt): Jacob VAN EYCK: *Batali; Doen Daphne d'over schoonne Maeght; Pavane Lachryme; Engels Nachtegaeltje.* FRESCOBALDI: *Canzon: La Bernadina.* Giovanni Paolo CIMA: *Sonatas in D & G.* Giovanni Battista RICCIO: *Canzon in A; Canzon in A (La Rosignola).* SCHEIDT: *Paduan a 4 in D.* ANON.: *Sonata in G* (4509 97466-2).

Volume 5: *Late Baroque Recorder Music* (with van Wingerden, Boeke, van Hauwe, Vester, Tromp, Pollard, Bylsma, Möller, Leonhardt, van Asperen): TELEMANN: *Quartet in D min., TWV 43:D1.* FASCH: *Quartet in G.* LOEILLET: *Quintet in B min.* QUANTZ: *Trio Sonata in C.* Alessandro SCARLATTI: *Sonata in F.* Johann MATTHESON: *Sonata No. 4 in G min.* (4509 97467-2; currently not available).

Volume 6: *French Recorder Suites* (with Boeke, Harnoncourt, Bylsma, Leonhardt): Charles DIEUPART: *Suites in G min. & A.* HOTTETERRE: *Suite No. 1* (4509 97468-2).

Volume 7: *French Recorder Sonatas* (with Boeke, van Hauwe, Bylsma, Leonhardt): Philibert DE LAVIGNE: *Sonata in C (La Barssan).* BOISMORTIER: *Sonata in F.* PHILIDOR: *Sonata in D min.* Louis-Antoine DORNEL: *Sonata (a 3 Dessus) in B flat.* François COUPERIN: *Le Rossignol-en-amour* (4509 97469-2; currently not available).

Volume 8: VIVALDI: *Chamber Concertos* (with Schaefleit, Fleischmann, Harnoncourt, Pfeiffer, Harnoncourt, Leonhardt): *in C, RV 87; in D, RV 92 & RV 94; in G min., RV 105; in A min., RV 108; in C min., RV 441; in F, RV 442* (4509 97470-2; currently not available).

Volume 9: HANDEL: *Recorder Sonatas* (with Harnoncourt, Bylsma, Harnoncourt, Leonhardt, Tachezi): *in G min., HWV 360; in A min., HWV 362; in C, HWV 365; in F, HWV 369, Op. 1/2, 4, 7 & 11; in F, HWV 389, Op. 2/4. Fitzwilliam Sonatas Nos. 1 in B flat, HWV 377; 3 in D min., HWV 367a* (4509 97471-2; currently not available).

Volume 10: TELEMANN: *Concertos and Orchestral Music* (with VCM, Harnoncourt): *Concertos in C; à 6 in F; Suite (Overture) in A min., TWV 55:A2* (4509 97472-2).

Volume 11: J.S. BACH: *Chamber and Orchestral Music* (with van Wingerden, Stastny, Leonhardt, Harnoncourt, Leonhardt, Tachezi): *Concertos in A min., BWV 1044; in F, BWV 1057; Sonata Concerto from Cantata No. 182; Sonatina from Cantata No. 106; Trio Sonata in G, BWV 1039* (4509 97473-2; currently not available).

Volume 12: *Recorder Sonatas and Concertos* (with Vester, Harnoncourt, Harnoncourt, Bylsma,

Leonhardt, Tachezi, VCM; Amsterdam CO):
LOEILLET: *Sonata in C min.; Sonata in G.*
SAMMARTINI: *Concerto in F.* HANDEL: *Trio Sonata in B min.* NAUDOT: *Concerto in G.* TELEMANN: *Double Concerto in E min.* (4509 97474-2).

Frans Brüggen is perhaps the greatest master of the recorder of the post-war era. In his hands phrases are turned with the utmost sophistication, intonation is unbelievably accurate and matters of style exact. There is spontaneity too and, with such superb musicianship and the high standard of recording we have come to expect from the Teldec Das Alte Werk series, these reissues in Brüggen's own special edition can almost all be recommended without reservation. He is equally at home in early or late baroque music. Throughout the collection, Frans Brüggen and his estimable colleagues demonstrate various period instruments; Anner Bylsma, Gustav Leonhardt and Bob van Asperen are present to provide a distinguished continuo, while Harnoncourt and the Vienna Concentus Musicus and Schröder's Amsterdam Chamber Orchestra are available for authentic concerto accompaniments. As we go to print, the complete set is still available but most of the individual issues are deleted and are marked as such.

Volume 1 is a single-disc anthology of Telemann's chamber music. Brüggen plays with his usual mastery and, as one would expect from Gustav Leonhardt's ensemble, the performances have polish and authority, and they are excellently recorded.

Volume 2 with its collection of Italian recorder sonatas is surely a perfect sampler for the whole edition, for it gives the opportunity for this king of recorder players to demonstrate his expertise and musicianship to maximum effect, admirably partnered by Anner Bylsma and Gustav Leonhardt. Corelli puts the famous 'Follia' melody through all possible hoops and Brüggen obliges with nimble virtuosity. The Veracini works are also primarily for violin, though the recorder is an optional alternative for the *G major Sonata.* All this music is played with exemplary skill, but this indidvidual disc is deleted.

The collection of English ensemble music which constitutes Volume 3 is particularly diverting, opening with Holborne's *Suite of Dances and Airs* which alternates recorder and viols. The several *In nomines* are all differently scored and are very different in character too, while the folksong arrangements by Byrd and Simpson are touching. The *Solo* (Suite) by Andrew Parcham, the *Divisions* of Robert Carr and Pepusch's *Sonata* are all engaging and are played with characteristic skill and musicianship so that only occasionally does the ear detect the limitations of early instruments. Alas, also now deleted.

Volume 4 introduces works by Jacob Van Eyck, which are unaccompanied but are aurally titillating, particularly the primitive *Batali* with its 'bugle' calls, while the florid upper tessitura of *Engels Nachtegaeltje* really takes wing. The Frescobaldi *Canzon* and the works by Cima and Riccio use an organ and cello

continuo, and the delightful *La Rosignola* is for recorder trio with cello and harpsichord.

Late-baroque chamber music is represented on Volume 5, with works by Alessandro Scarlatti, Telemann and Johann Mattheson standing out, while Volume 6 brings entertainingly elegant and tuneful *Suites* by Dieupart (a French-born musician who taught in London around 1700 and whose harpsichord music influenced Bach) and Hotteterre (known as Le Romain). These suites are very much cast in the style favoured by Telemann, with an *Overture* and a collection of dances. (Volume 5 is also deleted.)

Volume 7 concentrates on French recorder sonatas and brings another vivid nightingale evocation – *Le Rossignol-en-amour*, by François Couperin. (Also deleted.)

Volumes 8–10 are composer collections of music by Vivaldi, Handel and more Telemann, all discussed in detail under their Composer entries, in our main volume. Volume 11, offering a Bach collection, is the only relative disappointment. Two of the major works here are transcribed, and BWV 1044 comes off more effectively than BWV 1057. Best is the *Trio Sonata in G*, BWV 1039, although the two cantata excerpts are pleasing. Unfortunately, only Volume 10 is still available individually.

A final excellent sampler is provided by the collection of *Recorder Sonatas* and *Concertos* which makes up Volume 12, featuring a chamber ensemble and both the Amsterdam Chamber Orchestra and the Vienna Concentus Musicus. The Telemann *Double Concerto in E minor for Recorder and Flute* is a particularly fine one, and the dulcet duet in the slow movement begins rather like Handel's *Where'er you Walk.* The Sammartini *Concerto* has an unexpectedly solemn *Siciliano* for its slow movement. The Handel *Trio Sonata* is a splendid work, and the two Loeillet *Sonatas* are light and airy and full of charm, while even the less striking Naudot piece emerges as music of character. All these performances are outstandingly successful.

The recordings were nearly all made during the 1960s, with a few dating from the following decade, and they are of the highest quality, as are the vivid CD transfers. Documentation is very good.

Byzantine, Julian (guitar)

ALBENIZ: *Rumores de la Caleta; Suite española No. 1; Torre bermeja.* TORROBA: *Madroños.* TARREGA: *La Alborada; Capricho árabe.* LAURO: *Vals venezolano No. 3.* VILLA-LOBOS: *Chôros No. 1 in G; 5 Preludes; Study No. 1 in E min.* RODRIGO: *En los trigales.* BORGES: *Vals venezolano.* GRANADOS: *Adaluza.* MALATS: *Serenata española.* FALLA: *The Three-cornered Hat: Corregidor's Dance; Miller's Dance.*

(B) **(*) CfP (ADD/DDD) 575 140-2.

Julian Byzantine is a thoroughly musical player; his

rubato and control of light and shade are always convincing. The playing may lack the last degree of individuality and electricity, and sometimes the listener may feel that the flow is too controlled, not absolutely spontaneous, but this remains an impressive recital, generous and varied in content and well recorded.

Campoli, Alfredo (violin)

'*Homage to Kreisler*' (with Gritton; or Wada, piano): KREISLER: *Praeludium and Allegro; Liebeslied; Liebesfreud; Polichinelle-serenade; Schön Rosmarin; Caprice viennois; Tamborin chinois; Rondo on a Theme by Beethoven; La Chasse; La Gitana.* Arrangements: PADEREWSKI: *Minuet in G.* WIENIAWSKI: *Caprices: in E flat; A min.* GRANADOS: *Dance espagnole.* TARTINI: *Variations on a Theme of Corelli.* ALBENIZ: *Tango.* BRAHMS: *Waltz in A flat.* YAMADA: *Akatonbo; Jogashima no ame.* BACH: *Arioso.* SCHUBERT: *Ave Maria.* MOZART: *Divertimento No. 17: Rondo.*

(***) Australian Decca Eloquence mono/stereo 466 666-2.

This disc not only pays 'Homage to Kreisler', but also to Alfredo Campoli. None of the music here is deeply profound, but it is all very entertaining – whether it be breathtakingly showy or charmingly sentimental. Many of Kreisler's encore hits are included and Campoli's performances are full of flair, while the Decca recordings, both mono and stereo, are all characteristically vivid, though the stereo brings greater depth and richness.

Cann, Claire and Antoinette (piano duo)

'*Romantic Favourites on 2 Pianos*': SAINT-SAENS: *Danse macabre.* DEBUSSY: *Petite suite.* TCHAIKOVSKY (arr. CANN): *Nutcracker Suite: excerpts.* BRAHMS: *Variations on a Theme of Haydn (St Anthony Chorale), Op. 56b; Waltzes, Op. 39/1–2, 5–6, 9–11 & 15.* MACDOWELL (arr. NIEMANN): *Hexentanz.* LISZT (arr. BRENDEL): *Hungarian Rhapsody No. 2.*

◉ (M) *** Apollo Recordings ARCD 961.

We are glad to welcome the début recital of the Cann duo back to the catalogue. With the demise of the Pianissimo label it was unavailable for some time but it now returns on the Apollo label, distributed in the UK by Canterbury Classics. It is difficult to imagine a more scintillating piano duet record than this. Saint-Saëns's skeletons – summoned by an evocative midnight bell – dance as vigorously as do MacDowell's witches in the brilliant *Hexentanz*, while Debussy's delightful *Petite suite* – played here very effectively on two pianos, rather than with four hands on one – is full of charm. The Cann sisters then produce a rich-textured fullness of tone for the Brahms *Haydn Variations*, which are every bit as enjoyable here as in their orchestral dress. Most remarkable of all are the excerpts from the *Nutcracker Suite*, conceived entirely pianistically and glittering with colour. Indeed, the *Sugar Plum Fairy* has a much stronger profile than usual and the *Chinese Dance* an irresistible oriental glitter. The *Hungarian Dances* bring beguiling variety of mood and texture and display an easy bravura, ending with a lovely performance of the famous *Cradle Song (No. 15 in A flat)*, while the dazzling Liszt *Hungarian Rhapsody* ends the recital with great exuberance and much digital panache. The recording, made in Rosslyn Hill Chapel, is exceptionally real and vivid, and is ideally balanced.

'*Fantasy – Classics on 2 Pianos*': RIMSKY-KORSAKOV (arr. RACHMANINOV): *Flight of the Bumblebee.* RACHMANINOV: *Rhapsody on a Theme of Paganini: Variation No. 18.* TCHAIKOVSKY (arr. RACHMANINOV): *Sleeping Beauty: Suite.* ELLIOT: *Berceuse pour deux.* RAVEL: *Ma Mère l'oye (excerpts).* BORODIN (arr. CANN): *Polovtsian Dances.* OWENS: *Pianophoria No. 3.* GERSHWIN (arr. GRAINGER): *Fantasy on 'Porgy and Bess'.*

*** Apollo ARCD 011.

A delightful and generous follow-up recital. There is plenty of virtuosity and, as usual with this very musical duo, they are especially enjoyable when playing transcriptions; both the *Sleeping Beauty Suite* and the *Polovtsian Dances* are sparkling examples. Elliot's *Berceuse* is quite memorable, but Owens' *Pianophoria* seems to meander. However, Grainger's Gershwin *Fantasy* ends the programme with much flair. Excellent recording.

Capuçon, Renaud and Gautier (violin and cello)

'*Face à Face*' (Duos for Violin and Cello): HALVORSEN: *Passacaille after Handel (Suite No. 7 in G min.).* KODALY: *Duo, Op. 7.* TANGUY: *Sonata for Violin and Cello.* SCHULHOFF: *Duo.* GHYS/SERVAIS: *Variations brillantes sur 'God Save the King', Op. 38.*

*** Virgin 5 45576-2.

A showcase for the Capuçon brothers, who hail from Chambéry and who have won various prestigious awards and competitions. Renaud studied with Stern, Shlomo Mintz and Dumay, while the cellist Gautier won the André Navarra prize in Toulouse. It is not perhaps ideal as a calling-card, as it would have been if it had been able to include the Ravel *Sonata*, which they recorded on an earlier Virgin anthology. They are impressive artists and their programme is rewarding, particularly the Kodály *Duo* and Halvorsen's engaging *Variations*.

Casals, Pablo (cello)

BEETHOVEN: *Cello Sonatas Nos. 1–5, Op. 5/1–2; Op. 69; Op. 102/1–2; 7 Variations on 'Bei Männern' (from Mozart's 'Die Zauberflöte'), WoO 46; 12 Variations on 'Ein Mädchen' (from Mozart's 'Die Zauberflöte'), WoO 66* (with Serkin).

(M) (**) Sony mono SM2K 58985 (2).

These Casals accounts of the Beethoven *Cello Sonatas* come from 1953 and 1958 and exhibit strong personality but less finish, understandably so when one considers that by the latter date Casals was approaching eighty. In spite of the keyboard expertise of Serkin, these performances do not match his performances with Horszowski, made between 1931 and 1938 and now reissued on EMI, coupled with the Brahms *Second Cello Sonata*, in which the pianist is Otto Schulhof, an altogether excellent mid-price set (CHS5 65185-2).

BRAHMS: *Piano Trio No. 1 in B, Op. 8* (with Dame Hess, Stern); *String Sextet No. 1 in B flat, Op. 18* (with Stern, Schneider, Katims, Thomas, Foley).

(M) (***) Sony mono SMK 58994.

The Brahms performances, the *B major Trio*, Op. 8, and the *B flat Sextet*, Op. 18, are hardly less celebrated. The *Trio* with Isaac Stern and Myra Hess is a noble and beautifully phrased performance. The majestic and passionate account of the *Sextet* enjoyed cult status in France and elsewhere when it was used in Louis Malle's 1958 film, *Les amants*; and it remains a classic of the gramophone – one of the artistic peaks of the Casals Edition.

Cherkassky, Shura (piano)

'80th Birthday Recital from Carnegie Hall': BACH (arr. BUSONI): *Chaconne.* SCHUMANN: *Symphonic Etudes, Op. 13.* CHOPIN: *Nocturne in F min., Op. 55/1; Tarantelle, Op. 43.* IVES: *3-Page Sonata.* HOFMANN: *Kaleidoscope, Op. 40/4.* PABST: *Paraphrase on Tchaikovsky's 'Eugene Onegin'.* GOULD: *Boogie Woogie Etude.*

(M) *** Decca 475 040-2.

It is rare for a miscellaneous piano recital, even a live one, to win a *Gramophone* award, but Cherkassky did so in 1993 with his 80th-birthday programme at Carnegie Hall. The content has a wide range, including several novelties, and the Bach/Busoni *Chaconne* and Schumann *Symphonic Studies* show him at his most commanding. There are few examples of a live recital captured more succssfully on disc than this, and the Decca recording is most real and vivid.

Clarion Ensemble

'Trumpet Collection': FANTINI: *Sonata; Brando; Balletteo; Corrente.* MONTEVERDI: *Et e pur dunque vero.* FRESCOBALDI: *Canzona a canto solo.* PURCELL: *To Arms, Heroic Prince.* A. SCARLATTI: *Si suoni la tromba.* BISHOP: *Arietta and Waltz; Thine Forever.* DONIZETTI: *Lo L'udia.* KOENIG: *Posthorn Galop.* ARBAN: *Fantasia on Verdi's 'Rigoletto'.* CLARKE: *Cousins.* ENESCU: *Legende.*

✪ *** Amon Ra (ADD) CD-SAR 30.

The simple title 'Trumpet Collection' covers a fascinating recital of music for trumpet written over three centuries and played with great skill and musicianship by Jonathan Impett, using a variety of original instruments, from a keyed bugle and clapper shake-key cornopean to an English slide trumpet and a posthorn. Impett is a complete master of all these instruments, never producing a throttled tone; indeed, in the Purcell and Scarlatti arias he matches the soaring soprano line of Deborah Roberts with uncanny mirror-image precision. Accompaniments are provided by other members of the Clarion Ensemble. The Frescobaldi *Canzona* brings a duet for trumpet and trombone, with a background harpsichord filigree, which is most effective. With demonstration-worthy recording, this is as enjoyable as it is interesting, with the *Posthorn Galop* and Arban's *Rigoletto Variations* producing exhilarating bravura.

Cleobury, Stephen (organ of King's College, Cambridge)

'Organ Favourites': VIERNE: *Carillon, Op. 31/21.* BACH: *Toccata and Fugue in D min., BWV 565; Chorale Preludes: Herzlich tut mich verlangen, BWV 727; In dulci jubilo, BWV 808.* MESSIAEN: *L'Ascension: Transports de joie.* PRIZEMAN: *Toccata.* KARG-ELERT: *Nun danket alle Gott, Op. 65/69.* MENDELSSOHN: *Sonata in D min., Op. 65/6: Finale. Prelude and Fugue in C min., Op. 37/1.* LISZT: *Prelude and Fugue on BACH.* PACHELBEL: *Ciacona in F min.* JONGEN: *Chant de mai, Op. 53/1.* WIDOR: *Symphony No. 5: Toccata.*

(B) **(*) CfP 585 6172.

A well-balanced and generous recital. Perhaps the opening Vierne *Carillon* does not suit the King's College organ as well as it would a Cavaillé-Coll instrument, but the Messiaen *Transports de joie* certainly does, and so does the engaging *Chant de mai* of the Belgian composer, Joseph Jongen. Cleobury is flamboyant enough in Liszt, using the widest dynamic range, but the most famous Bach *D minor Toccata and Fugue* (which the accompanying notes suggest may not be by Bach at all!) is a rather laid-back performance which some listeners might find a bit tame. The *Chorale Preludes*, however, are beautifully played and Cleobury makes Robert Prizeman's *Toccata* (familiar as the signature-tune for the BBC's *Songs of Praise*) into a catchy neo-lollipop. His closing Widor *Toccata* is magnificent in every way. The recording cannot be faulted and this is excellent value.

Cohler, Jonathan (clarinet)

'*Cohler on Clarinet*' (with Gordon, piano):
BRAHMS: *Sonata No. 1 in F min., Op. 120/1.* WEBER:
Grand duo concertante, Op. 48. BAERMANN:
Quintet No. 3, Op. 23: Adagio (arr. for clarinet &
piano). SARGON: *Deep Ellum Nights (3 Sketches).*
*** Ongaku 024-101.

This fine collection marks the recording début of an
outstanding, Boston-born, American clarinettist. He
has a splendid technique and a lovely tone, and he is
already master of an extraordinarily wide range of
repertoire. The opening Brahms *F minor Sonata* is a
supreme test, and he passes with distinction. The
Weber *Grand duo concertante* is suitably good-
natured, with a songful central cantilena and plenty
of wit in the finale.

The Baermann *Adagio* shows how ravishingly
Cohler can shape a melting legato line with a breath-
catching *pianissimo* at its peak. He then throws his
hat in the air in the three exuberant *Sketches* of
Simon Sargon, where sultry melodic lines are interrupted by all kinds of jazzy glissandos and uninhibited syncopations, notably an explosive burst of
energy intruding into the *Quiet and easy* central
section. The finale is like a flashy cakewalk. The
recording is truthful, but the piano is placed behind
in a too resonant acoustic (the empty Paine Concert
Hall at Harvard University), which is a tiresome
misjudgement. Even so, Judith Gordon provides
sympathetic support, and the playing more than
compensates.

'*More Cohler on Clarinet*' (with Hodgkinson,
piano): BRAHMS: *Sonata No. 2 in E flat, Op. 120/2.*
POULENC: *Sonata.* SCHUMANN: *Fantasiestücke, Op.
73.* MILHAUD: *Sonatina, Op. 100.* STRAVINSKY: *3
Pieces* (for solo clarinet).
*** Ongaku 024-102.

Cohler's second disc is much more satisfactorily balanced. His excellent partner, Randall Hodgkinson, is
fully in the picture. The opening of the Brahms *E flat
Sonata* is agreeably warm and relaxed, and the
Theme and variations finale brings a pleasing interplay between the two artists. Poulenc's *Sonata* is
beautifully done, the lovely *Romanza (Très calme)* is
cool in the way only a player who knows about jazz
can manage, while the fizzing finale also brings a hint
of rapture in its contrasting lyrical theme. The
warmth of the Schumann pieces, for which Cohler
imaginatively modifies his timbre, contrasts with the
outrageous Milhaud *Sonatina*, with both outer
movements marked *Très rude* but the *Lent* centrepiece quite magical. The three dry Stravinsky fragments make a perfect close to a disc which is
outstanding in every way.

Coletti, Paul (viola), Leslie Howard (piano)

'*English Music for Viola*': BRITTEN: *Elegy for Solo
Viola.* VAUGHAN WILLIAMS: *Romance.* CLARKE:
Lullaby No. 1; Morpheus; Sonata. GRAINGER: *Sussex
Mummers' Carol; Arrival Platform Humlet for Solo
Viola.* BAX: *Legend.* BRIDGE: *Pensiero; Allegro
appassionato.*
(BB) *** Hyp. Helios CDH 55085.

This attractive and important collection went unno-
ticed on its first issue and we are happy now to give it
the strongest recommendation as an unmissable bargain. Paul Coletti is a first-rate violist and a fine
artist, and he opens with an intensely compelling
account of the *Elegy* which Britten wrote when he
was only sixteen, but which was only recently discovered and premièred at the Aldeburgh Festival in 1984
by Nobuko Imai. The moving Vaughan Williams
Romance was another posthumous discovery, found
among the composer's effects after his death.

Like Vaughan Williams, Bax had a special feeling
for the viola and his elegiac *Legend* is imbued with a
mysterious Celtic atmosphere. The two folk inspirations of Grainger certainly suit the viola's rich cantilena, and Frank Bridge's *Pensiero* and *Allegro
appassionato* make a perfect foil for each other. But
the major work here and the most ambitious (21
minutes long) is Rebecca Clarke's three-movement
Sonata. Not for nothing is the first movement
marked *Impetuoso*, and this mood interrupts and
engulfs the lyrical *Adagio* finale. Here (as elsewhere),
Leslie Howard proves his mettle. Clarke's two shorter
pieces, the lovely *First Lullaby* and the similarly
reflective *Morpheus*, are, like the *Sonata*, underpinned with English pastoral feeling. All in all a most
stimulating and rewarding programme, played with
great commitment by both artists, and vividly
recorded.

Cortot, Alfred (piano), Jacques Thibaud (violin), Pablo Casals (cello)

BEETHOVEN: *Variations on 'Ich bin der Schneider
Kakadu'.* HAYDN: *Piano Trio No. 39 in G (Gypsy).*
SCHUBERT: *Piano Trio No. 1 in B flat.*
(BB) (***) Naxos 8.110188

Although the piano trio Alfred Cortot formed with
Pablo Casals and Jacques Thibaud was perhaps the
most famous pre-war trio, it was extraordinarily
short lived – in fact it lasted barely a decade, unlike
the Beaux Arts, which cover the best part of half a
century, and (again unlike them) had a small repertoire and made few records. The claims of their solo
careers meant that they had virtually stopped playing
together by the mid-1930s. They are technically
immaculate, supremely lyrical and with a spontaneity of feeling underpinned by firm yet flexible

rhythm. Ward Marston's transfers give these exalted performances a new lease of life.

Crabb, James and Geir Draugsvoll (accordions)

Début Recital: STRAVINSKY: *Petrushka* (ballet; complete). MUSSORGSKY: *Pictures at an Exhibition* (both arr. CRABB/DRAUGSVOLL).
(B) ★★(*) EMI Début 5 69705-2.

It seems impossible to believe that Stravinsky's brilliantly scored ballet, played on a pair of piano accordions, could sound remarkably like the orchestral version; but this phenomenal transcription brings all the colours of the Stravinskian palette vividly before the listener. Only the bold sound of unison horns and the bite of massed strings eludes these virtuosi, and they bring the ballet's drama and pathos fully to life. This is an extraordinary listening experience. Mussorgsky's *Pictures at an Exhibition* is equally ingenious but is far less consistently effective, for one's ear is used to bold brass sonorities and spectacle. *Catacombs* and the big finale do not really come off, although the grotesque *Baba-Yaga* certainly does, played with proper rhythmic venom; otherwise the most effective pictures are those in which we normally expect woodwind chattering: *Tuileries, Limoges* and the cheeping chicks. Nevertheless it's a good try, and the playing itself has astonishing bravura. Well worth sampling on EMI's bargain Début label. The recording cannot be faulted.

Curley, Carlo (organ)

'*Toccata: Organ Favourites*' (organ of Girard College Chapel, Philadelphia): BACH: *Toccata and Fugue in D min., BWV 565; Cantata No. 22: Subdue us by thy Kindness; Suite No. 3 in D: Air. Cantata No. 147: Jesu, Joy of Man's Desiring. Cantata No. 140: Wachet auf. Cantata No. 29: Sinfonia in D.* ALBINONI, arr. GIAZOTTO/CURLEY: *Adagio.* GUILMANT: *March on a Theme by Handel, Op. 15.* SOLER/BIGGS: *Emperor's Fanfare.* SCHUBERT, arr. CURLEY: *Ave Maria.* KARG-ELERT: *Chorale Improvisation: Now Thank We all our God (Trauung, Taufe, Emtefest).* LIDON: *Sonata on the First Tone.* SAINT-SAENS: *Carnival of the Animals: The Swan.* DUSSEK, arr. THALBEN-BALL: *Andante in F.* MOZART: *Fantasia in F min., K.608.* WIDOR: *Organ Symphony No. 5: Toccata.* STANLEY: *Suite in D: Introduction & Trumpet Tune, Op. 6/6.* MULET: *Tu es Petrus.* VIERNE: *Carillon de Westminster.* BEETHOVEN, arr. CURLEY: *Ruins of Athens: Turkish March.* SCHUBERT: *Moment Musical in F min.* HANDEL: *Concerto in F, Op. 4/5: Allegro* (both arr. CURLEY). RACHMANINOV, arr. BIRD: *Vocalise.* BOELLMANN: *Suite gothique, Op. 25.* HOLST: *The*

Planets: Jupiter (theme, arr. CURLEY). SOUSA, arr. CURLEY: *Washington Post.*
(B) ★★★ Double Decca 458 364-2 (2).

On the original issue which contained the *Emperor's Fanfare* (an anachronistic but irresistible arrangement of Soler's music by E. Power Biggs, which provides an opportunity for great splashes of throaty timbre and uses the powerful *Tuba mirabilis* stop) the flamboyant Carlo Curley described with engaging enthusiasm the organ he plays here: 'Nearly one hundred feet from the [Girard] Chapel's marble floor and above the vast, coffered ceiling, entirely covered incidentally with real gold leaf, the organ, all thirty-five metric tonnes, and with 6,587 handmade pipes, is miraculously suspended. In a chapel so cavernous, and with such remarkable reverberation, it is well nigh impossible to identify the source of the sound.'

Yet the Decca (Argo) engineers manage to provide an excellent focus and capture the extremely wide range of Curley's playing with precision at both ends of the spectrum. The performances are full of drama and temperament, unashamedly romantic, yet very compelling. A great deal of this music is not ideally suited to the organ but Curley's panache almost convinces one that it is, and this collection cannot fail to entertain any organ fancier when the recording is so spectacularly vivid.

Curzon, Clifford (piano)

'*Edinburgh Festival Recital*': HAYDN: *Andante and Variations in F min.* LISZT: *Années de pèlerinage: Sonetto del Petrarca No. 104; Berceuse* (2nd version); *Valse oubliée No. 1; Piano Sonata in B min.;* SCHUBERT: *Impromptus, D.899/2, 3 & 4.*
(M) (★★★) BBC Legends mono BBCL 4078-2.

When Clifford Curzon was always so reluctant to work in the recording studio, such a collection as this of live performances is most treasurable, despite any flaws. Curzon's account of the Liszt *Sonata*, given at the 1961 Edinburgh Festival, has obvious slips of finger but is even more persuasively spontaneous than the Decca studio version of only a couple of years later. The impulsive energy lets us appreciate a side of Curzon's genius rarely revealed in his official recordings, the daring of the virtuoso. As for the other Liszt items, they reveal Curzon's magic at its most intense, so that in the *Petrarch Sonnet* his velvet legato has one imagining a voice singing the words. In the Haydn *Variations*, a piece that can seem too formal and painstaking, Curzon similarly finds sparkle and fantasy, and the Schubert *Impromptus* – for him core repertory – show him at his happiest, though his breathtakingly fast tempo for No. 2 with its rippling scales in triplets may initially seem disconcerting. The singing legato of No. 3 is then all the more soothing, and the textural contrasts of No. 4 the more dramatic. The mono sound may be limited but is very acceptable. An excellent note by Jonathan Dobson movingly quotes a remark made by Curzon in 1981 that in his boyhood playing the piano became 'a lonely child's retreat from a happy family'. That sense of wonder was a quality he kept throughout his life.

Daniel, Nicholas (oboe), Julius Drake (piano)

– see below under Snowden, Jonathan (flute).

Danish Radio Wind Quintet

NIELSEN: *Wind Quintet, Op. 43.* MORTENSEN: *Wind Quintet.* JERSILD: *Serenade for Wind Quintet.* WELLEJUS: *Wind Quintet.*
*** dacapo 8.224151.

Recordings of the Nielsen *Quintet*, all variously coupled, are relatively plentiful. The fine wind players of the Danish Radio Orchestra give an expertly shaped and well-characterized account of the piece. In the finale the clarinet variation was not more vividly portrayed even by Aage Oxenvad himself, whose character it was supposed to enshrine. The expressive emphasis a few bars into the first movement and some rather too affectionate phrasing in the Trio of the minuet must be mentioned, but one cannot imagine them causing serious concern. The Nielsen can be recommended alongside the Oslo Quintet on Naxos. Jørgen Jersild was born in 1913 and spent some years in France, studying briefly with Roussel. The *Serenade* (1947) confirms the positive impression so much of his music makes; it is impeccably crafted, intelligent and of some wit. The *Quintet* of 1944 by Otto Mortensen (1907–86) is pleasing, not wildly original perhaps, but civilized. The same goes for Henning Wellejus's slight and short *Quintet* from the mid-1960s. The performances are carefully prepared and strongly profiled, and the disc is worth having for the Nielsen and the Jersild. Good recording.

Claude Debussy Wind Quintet

'*The New Interpreters*': LIGETI: *6 Bagatelles; 10 Pieces.* JANACEK: *Mládi; Concertino* (with Cassard, piano, Martinez & members of Parish Qt).
(B) *** HM HMN 911624.

Anyone who thinks of Ligeti as a 'difficult' composer should sample this infectious performance of the *Six Bagatelles*, especially the riotous élan of the opening *Allegro con spirito* and the more wry wit of the finale. There is unexpected melodic charm too in the *Allegro grazioso* (No. 3), and the sombre tribute to Bartók is darkly memorable. The *Ten Pieces* are thornier, but still stimulating. The penultimate number is marked *Sostenuto stridente* and the finale *Presto bizzare*, but the music remains ear-catching.

The two better-known Janáček works are also played with keen rhythmic feeling and, although this is in essence a sampler, it makes a highly enjoyable concert; the recording gives these excellent players a very tangible presence within a nicely judged acoustic.

Demidenko, Nikolai (piano)

'*Live at Wigmore Hall*': VORISEK: *Fantasia in C, Op. 12.* HAYDN: *Variations in F min., Hob XVII/6.* D. SCARLATTI: *Sonatas, Kk. 11, 377.* SCHUMANN: *Variations on a Theme of Clara Wieck.* MENDELSSOHN: *Fantasy in F sharp min., Op. 28.* KALKEBRENNER: *Nocturne in A flat, Op. 129.* LISZT: *Concert Paraphrase of Beethoven's 'An die ferne Geliebte'.* BERG: *Sonata in B min., Op. 1.* BUXTEHUDE/PROKOFIEV: *Prelude & Fugue in D min., BuxWV 140.* GUBAIDULINA: *Ciacona.* LISZT: *Funérailles.* SCHUBERT: *Impromptu, D.899/4.*
(B) **(*) Hyp. Dyad CDD 22024 (2).

With the advantage of the superb Wigmore Hall acoustics, Nikolai Demidenko, recorded live at a series of concerts between January and June 1993, comes over charismatically, and the programme is certainly diverse. Mendelssohn's *Fantasy* could hardly be played more brilliantly and this set, which has received an enthusiastic press, is a must for the pianist's admirers, even if perhaps the general collector would not be drawn to hearing some of this music very often. The Liszt/Beethoven song-cycle transcription, for instance, has not very much to offer compared with a vocal version. The Gubaidulina *Ciacona* is a stunning, indeed overwhelming, example of extrovert bravura and (like the spectacular Liszt *Funérailles*) receives a deserved ovation. But it leaves the listener somewhat battered! One welcomes the simpler appeal of the Schubert *Impromptu* with which the recital closes.

Drake, Susan (harp)

'*Echoes of a Waterfall*': HASSELMANS: *La Source, Op. 44; Prelude, Op. 52; Chanson de mai, Op. 40.* ALVARS: *Divertissement, Op. 36.* GODEFROID: *Bois solitaire; Etude de Concert in E flat min., Op. 193.* GLINKA: *Variations on a Theme of Mozart.* THOMAS: *Echoes of a Waterfall; Watching the Wheat; Megan's Daughter.* SPOHR: *Variations on 'Je suis encore', Op. 36.*
(BB) *** Hyp. Helios CDH 55128.

The music here is lightweight but full of charm. Susan Drake is a beguiling exponent and her technique is as impressive as her feeling for atmosphere. Those intrigued by the title of the collection will not be disappointed by the sound here (the recording is excellent) which balances evocation with a suitable degree of flamboyance when the music calls for it. The evocation of watery effects is certainly picturesque in the Hasselmans *La Source* and Thomas's *Echoes of a Waterfall* (which is exquisitely played), while the Spohr and (especially) the Glinka *Variations* have considerable musical appeal. So have the arrangements of Welsh folk tunes. The definition is very good, while the acoustic remains warmly resonant. A most enjoyable disc.

'Arabesque': (Romantic Harp Music of the 19th Century): DEBUSSY: *Arabesque No. 1; La Fille aux cheveux de lin.* HASSELMANS: *Feux follets (Will-o'-the-Wisp).* TRAD.: *All Through the Night* (arr. Drake). PARISH-ALVARS: *Romance in G flat, Op. 48/3; La Mandoline, Op. 84.* SCHUBERT: *Ave Maria.* ZABEL: *Am Springbrunnen, Op. 23; Marguerite douloureuse au rouet, Op. 26.* POSSE: *Variations on The Carnival of Venice.* ANON.: *Romance (Jeux interdits).* DIZI: *Etude No. 21.* SAINT-SAENS: *Le Cygne (The Swan,* arr. Hasselmans).

(BB) **(*) Hyp. Helios CDH 55129.

Susan Drake's second recital, although attractive, is not quite as successful as her first, and the recording, though still warmly atmospheric, has a mistier focus. Having said this, many of the items are very attractive, not least her free approach to Debussy's *Arabesque*, with its element of fantasy, and her exquisite portrayal of *The Girl with the Flaxen Hair.* The Parish-Alvars miniatures, and the delightful Hasselmans *Feux follets* are also very pleasing, and if the anonymous *Romance* is more familiar as a guitar solo, it is equally effective on the harp, as is, more surprisingly, her arrangement of Saint-Saëns's gliding *Swan.*

Duo Mandala (Alison Stephens (mandolin), Lauren Scott (harpsichord))

'Tapestry': CONNOR: *Krug.* DAWES: *3 Pieces for Mandolin & Harp.* MITCHELL-DAVIDSON: *Tapestry.* SUTTON-ANDERSON: *Mandalas.*
*** Black Box BBM 1088.

All the works here have been written especially for this remarkable duo – the gentler harp contrasting and blending with the more tangy mandolin – an ear-tickling texture, with surprising potetntial for variety. Bill Connor's minimalist *Krug* is dominated by a single rhythmic idea, in circlar momentum. The *Three Pieces* of Julian Dawes bring first a mellow *Waltz*, drawing for its mood on Satie's most famous *Gymnopédie*, and the rhapsodic *Phantasy* which follows is ingeniously based on a pair of decorated arpeggio chords; the third piece is a dazzling carillon.

David Sutton-Anderson's aurally intriguing set of eight *Mandalas* is the centrepiece of the programme. Each is brief and concentrated, and together they display a magically glowing range of textures and colours with an exotic flavour of orientalism. A 'Mandala' is a Buddhist symbol of both a deity and

the universe itself. It is essentially contemplative, and this mood is immediately created by the work's mysterious opening, with its suggestion of water droplets. The second piece is lively and explorative; the third, featuring the solo mandolin, is improvisational. The delectable No. 4 is like an angelic music-box, while No. 5 contrasts resonant harp chords with glittering mandolin figurations. No. 6 is more meditative, but using a wide variety of textures; No. 7 darts about iridescently, and at the close the work returns to its opening idea, culminating in a mood of gentle serenity.

Paul Mitchell-Davidson's colourful four-movement suite, *Tapestry*, is more richly romantic, especially in the opening *Dance of Limewood, Smile of Ash*, and the moments of 'polytonal dissonance' in the jumpy second movement tickle the ear rather than bringing discomfort, even in the atonal obbligato for the central processional Chopinesque chorale. The closing *Full Moon Rising Red* is the most virtuosic and complex, demanding great bravura from the players to sustain its kaleidoscopic mood-changes. But they do so with panache. The whole programme is brilliantly played, providing a continuing sense of spontaneity, and given a recording that is extremely real and present. A most stimulating CD!

Duo Reine Elisabeth (Wolfgang Manz and Rolf Plagge)

Russian music for two pianos: STRAVINSKY: *Petrushka.* SCRIABIN: *Romance in A min.* SHOSTAKOVICH: *Concertino, Op. 94.* RACHMANINOV: *6 Morceaux, Op. 11.*
(BB) *** Discover DICD 920150.

Petrushka has plenty of colour and a surprising degree of charm; the finale swings along infectiously. The melodically lavish, early Scriabin *Romance* then contrasts aptly with the wittily audacious Shostakovich *Concertino*, which has the temerity to open with an echo of the slow movement of Beethoven's *G major Piano Concerto.* The six Rachmaninov *Morceaux* are strongly and colourfully characterized, and their diversity gives much pleasure. In short, Wolfgang Manz and Rolf Plagge create an impressive artistic symbiosis, playing with spontaneity as well as commanding impressive technical resource. Very good recording too – not too reverberant. A bargain.

Du Pré, Jacqueline (cello)

BACH: *Cello Suites Nos. 1 in G; 2 in D min., BWV 1007–8.* BRITTEN: *Cello Sonata in C, Op. 65 (Scherzo and Marcia)* (with Kovacevich). FALLA: *Suite populaire espagnole.* BRAHMS: *Cello Sonata No. 2 in F, Op. 99.* HANDEL: *Sonata in G min.* (all with Lush). F. COUPERIN: *Treizième concert (Les goûts-réunis)* (with Pleeth).

(B) (★★★) EMI Double fforte mono 5 73377-2 (2).

Here are some of the radio performances which Jacqueline du Pré gave in her inspired teens. Her 1962 recordings of the first two Bach *Cello Suites* may not be immaculate, but her impulsive vitality makes phrase after phrase at once totally individual and seemingly inevitable. In two movements from Britten's *Cello Sonata in C*, with Stephen Kovacevich as her partner, the sheer wit is deliciously infectious, fruit of youthful exuberance in both players. The first of the two discs is completed by Falla's *Suite populaire espagnole*, with the cello matching any singer in expressive range and rhythmic flair. The second has fascinating Couperin duets played with her teacher, William Pleeth; the Handel *Sonata* is equally warm and giving. Best of all is the Brahms *Cello Sonata No. 2*, recorded at the 1962 Edinburgh Festival.

Fanning, Diana (piano)

'*Musical Treasures*': JANACEK: *On an Overgrown Path* (1911). DEBUSSY: *L'isle joyeuse.* CHOPIN: *Piano Sonata No. 3 in B min., Op. 58.*
★★★

The American pianist Diana Fanning is a member of the music faculty at Middlebury College in Vermont and also a well-known soloist and chamber-music performer in her native state. She has that special gift of being able to bring music spontaneously to life in the recording studio. The highlight of this recital is a splendidly alive and romantically compelling account of the Chopin *B minor Sonata*, which exerts more magnetism than many accounts by more famous artists. Her account of *L'isle joyeuse* is compellingly exciting too, and yet *On an overgrown path* has a pleasingly poetic intimacy. The recording is real and vivid, the ambience attractive, although a shade over-resonant for the fullest detail to emerge in the Debussy piece. The CD appears to have no catalogue number, but is available direct from Franck Publications, PO Box 96, Middlebury, Vermont 05753, USA.

Fergus-Thompson, Gordon (piano)

'*Reverie*': DEBUSSY: *Rêverie; Arabesque No. 1; Suite bergamasque: Clair de lune.* SCRIABIN: *Etude, Op. 42/4.* BACH: *Chorales: Wachet auf* (trans. Busoni); *Jesu, Joy of Man's Desiring* (trans. Hess). GLINKA: *The Lark* (trans. Balakirev). GODOWSKY: *Alt Wien.* SAINT-SAENS: *The Swan* (arr. GODOWSKY). SCHUMANN: *Arabeske in C, Op. 18; Kinderszenen: Träumerei.* BRAHMS: *Intermezzo in A, Op. 118.* GRIEG: *Lyric Pieces: Butterfly, Op. 43/1; Nocturne, Op. 54/4.* RAVEL: *Le tombeau de Couperin: Forlane. Pavane pour une infante défunte.*

(M) ★★★ ASV CDWHL 2066.

This 76-minute recital fills a real need for a high-quality recital of piano music for the late evening, where the mood of reverie is sustained without blandness. Gordon Fergus-Thompson's performances are of high sensibility throughout, from the atmospheric opening Debussy items to the closing Ravel *Pavane.* Perhaps his Bach is a little studied but the rest is admirably paced, and the two favourite Grieg *Lyric Pieces* are particularly fresh. Excellent recording.

Fernández, Eduardo (guitar)

'*The World of the Spanish Guitar*': ALBENIZ: *Sevilla; Tango; Asturias.* LLOBET: *6 Catalan Folksongs.* GRANADOS: *Andaluza; Danza triste.* TARREGA: *Estudio brillante; 5 Preludes; Minuetto; 3 Mazurkas; Recuerdos de la Alhambra.* SEGOVIA: *Estudio sin luz; Neblina; Estudio.* TURINA: *Fandanguillo; Ráfaga.*

(M) ★★★ Decca 433 820-2.

Fernández is most naturally recorded in the Henry Wood Hall. His programme is essentially an intimate one and centres on the highly rewarding music of Tárrega, although opening colourfully with items from Albéniz's *Suite española.* The Llobet group of *Folksongs,* and Segovia's hauntingly atmospheric *Neblina* ('Mist'), make further highlights. Later there is bravura from Turina, notably the spectacular *Ráfaga* ('Gust of wind') but even here, though the playing is vibrant, there is no flashiness. With an hour of music and digital sound, this well-chosen programme is excellent value.

Fischer, Annie (piano)

BRAHMS: *Piano Sonata No. 3 in F min., Op. 5.* BARTOK: *15 Hungarian Peasant Songs.* LISZT: *3 Etudes de concert.* DOHNANYI: *Rhapsody in C, Op. 11/3.*

(M) (★★★) BBC mono BBCL 4054-2.

Annie Fischer is captured here in an Usher Hall recital at the 1961 Edinburgh Festival, albeit in mono sound. She was an artist of great musical insight who steeped herself in each composer's sound-world. Probably the best thing is the Bartók, which has never been played with greater imagination or sympathy (except, perhaps, by Kocsis). The Dohnányi encore is a delight. Such is the quality of Fischer's playing that the odd smudge or finger-slip to which she was prone in the concert hall do not disturb more than marginally.

Fretwork

'*In nomine*': 16th-century English Music for Viols: TALLIS: *In nomine a 4, Nos. 1 & 2; Solfaing song a 5; Fantasia a 5; Libera nos, salva nos a 5.* TYE: *In*

nomine a 5 (Crye); In nomine a 5 (Trust).
CORNYSH: *Fa la sol a 3.* BALDWIN: *In nomine a 4.*
BULL: *In nomine a 5.* BYRD: *In nomine a 4, No. 2.*
Fantasia a 3, No. 3. TAVERNER: *In nomine; In*
nomine a 4. PRESTON: *O lux beata Trinitas a 3.*
JOHNSON: *In nomine a 4.* PARSONS: *In nomine a 5;*
Ut re mi fa sol la a 4. FERRABOSCO: *In nomine a 5;*
Lute fantasia No. 5; Fantasia a 4.
*** Amon Ra (ADD) CD-SAR 29.

This was Fretwork's début CD. The collection is not
so obviously of strong popular appeal as the later
collections for Virgin but is nevertheless very rewarding and distinguished, and it includes the complete
consort music of Thomas Tallis. The sound is naturally pleasing in a fairly rich acoustic and readers can
be assured that there is no vinegar in the string-
timbre here; indeed, the sound itself is quite lovely in
its gentle, austere atmosphere.

'*Heart's Ease*': HOLBORNE: *The Honiesuckle;*
Countess of Pembroke's Paradise; The Fairie Round.
BYRD: *Fantasia a 5 (Two in One); Fancy in C.*
DOWLAND: *Mr Bucton, His Galliard; Captaine*
Digorie Piper, His Galliard; Lachrimae Antiquae
Pavan; Mr Nicholas Gryffith, His Galliard. BULL:
Fantasia a 4. FERRABOSCO: *In nomine a 5.*
GIBBONS: *In nomine a 5; Fantasia a 4 for the Great*
Dooble Base. LAWES: *Airs for 2 Division Viols in C:*
Pavan of Alfonso; Almain of Alfonso. Consort Sett a
5 in C: Fantasia; Pavan; Almain.
*** Virgin 7 59667-2.

An outstanding collection of viol consort music from
the late Tudor and early Stuart periods; the playing is
both stylish and vivacious, with a fine sense of the
most suitable tempo for each piece. The more lyrical
music is equally sensitive. This is a tuneful entertainment, not just for the specialist collector, and Fretwork convey their pleasure in all this music. The
William Byrd *Fancy* (from *My Ladye Nevells Booke*) is
played exuberantly on the organ by Paul Nicholson,
to bring some contrast before the closing Lawes
Consort Sett. The recording is agreeably warm, yet
transparent too.

'*Portrait: Music for Viols*' ((i) with Chance
(counter-tenor), Wilson (lute), Nicholson (organ)):
BYRD: *Pavan a 6; Galliard a 6; (i) Come to Me,*
Grief for Ever; Ye Sacred Muses. BEVIN: *Browning a*
3. GIBBONS: *Go from My Window a 6; Fantasy a 6;*
In nomine a 5. DOWLAND: *Lachrimae Antiquae;*
Lachrimae Coacte; Mr John Langtons Pavan; The
Earl of Essex Galliard; Mr Henry Noell his Galliard.
(i) *Lasso vita mia.* LAWES: *Pavan a 5 in C min.;*
Fantasy a 6 in F; Aire a 6 in F min. HOLBORNE: *The*
Honiesuckle; The Fairie-Round.
(M) *** Virgin 5 61402-2.

A quite outstanding concert, with the consort music
nicely leavened by three vocal solos. Much of the
atmosphere is melancholic, but with the arrival of
the two dances by Holborne the mood (and timbre)

changes completely, while the following Dowland
Galliards, if less upbeat, bring yet another change of
character. The two vocal highlights are by Byrd,
Come to me, grief for ever, in which he outflanks
Dowland in dolour, and the beautiful *Ye sacred*
muses, both sung ravishingly by Michael Chance.
Lawes's *Pavan a 5 in C minor* which follows embroi-
ders a particularly memorable theme and features
the use of the chamber organ subtly to fill out the
sonority, as it does the touching Gibbons *In nomine a*
5, while in the Lawes *Fantasy a 6* the organ has a
delicate contrapuntal role. Excellent – if close –
recording.

Friedman, Ignaz (piano)

Vol. 1: LISZT: *Concert Paraphrase of Schubert's*
'*Hark Hark, the Lark*'. CHOPIN: *Ballade in A flat,*
Op. 47/3; Etudes, Op. 10/7 & 12 (Revolutionary); Op.
25/6; Mazurka in D; Mazurka in B min.; Mazurkas
in D, Op. 33/2; C sharp, Op. 63/3; Minute Waltz;
Preludes in D flat, Op. 25/15 (Raindrop); E flat, Op.
28/19; Waltz in A min., Op. 34/2.
GAERTNER-FRIEDMAN: *Viennese Dance No. 1.*
HUMMEL: *Rondo in E flat.* MOZART: *Rondo alla*
Turca. SCARLATTI: *Pastorale.* MOSZKOWSKI:
Serenata, Op. 15/1. MENDELSSOHN: *Scherzo in E*
min., Op. 16/2. BEETHOVEN: *Sonata No. 14 in C*
sharp min. (Moonlight), Op. 27/2. LISZT/BUSONI:
La Campanella. FRIEDMAN: *Elle danse, Op. 10.*
(BB) (***) Naxos mono 8.110684.

Vol. 2: MENDELSSOHN: *Scherzo in E min., Op. 16/2.*
FRIEDMAN: *Elle danse, Op. 10; Marquis et*
Marquise; Tabatière à musique. BEETHOVEN: *Piano*
Sonata No. 14 in C sharp min. (Moonlight), Op.
27/2. CHOPIN: *Berceuse, Op. 57; Etudes: in G flat,*
Op. 10/5 & Op. 25/9; Mazurka in B flat, Op. 7/1;
Polonaise in A flat, Op. 53; Sonata No. 2 in B flat
min., Op. 35: Funeral March and Finale. GRIEG:
Piano Concerto in A min. (with O, Gaubert).
RUBINSTEIN: *Romance in E flat, Op. 44/1.* SUK:
Suite, Op. 21: Minuet. MITTLER: *Music Box for the*
Little Nana, Op. 2/2.
(BB) (***) Naxos mono 8.110686.

Vol. 3: CHOPIN: *Mazurkas: in B flat, Op. 7/1; in A*
min., Op. 7/2; in F min., Op. 7/3; in B flat, Op. 24/4;
in D, Op. 33/2; in B min., Op. 33/4; in C sharp, Op.
41/1 (twice); in A flat, Op. 50/2; in C sharp min., Op.
63/3; in C, Op. 67/3; in A min., Op. 67/4; in A min.,
Op. 68/2; Polonaise in B flat, Op. 71/2.
GLUCK/BRAHMS: *Gavotte.* GLUCK/FRIEDMAN:
Menuet (Judgement of Paris). LISZT: *Concert*
Paraphrase of Schubert's 'Hark Hark, the Lark'.
SCHUBERT/FRIEDMAN: *Alt Wien (plus Friedman*
talking about Chopin (from New Zealand Radio,
1940)).
(BB) (***) Naxos mono 8.110690.

When Ignaz Friedman first approached Leschetizky

in 1901, the great pianist, then a seventy-year-old, advised him to give up any thought of being a pianist. Naturally he was fired to pursue his goal and perfect his technique, and he was eventually acknowledged as being among Leschetizky's greatest pupils. There is the very occasional reminder that articulation is less than perfect but, the odd inaccuracy apart, this is fabulous playing. The rich and subtle range of sonority he could produce from the instrument is splendidly conveyed in Ward Marston's superb transfers. In terms of virtuosity, Friedman was one of the old school and he did not hide just how masterly was his technique. Listen to his extraordinary brilliance and, above all, delicacy in Liszt's *La Campanella*. Delicacy and imagination are there in abundance, and the three discs offer a treasure house of great playing. Friedman recorded only one concerto, the Grieg, which is let down by poor piano sound and less than distinguished orchestral support from an unnamed ensemble under Philippe Gaubert. But these are records that no piano buff will want to pass over.

Fromentin, Lawrence and Domenique Plancade (piano duo)

Début: 'French Piano Duets': POULENC: *Sonata*. DEBUSSY: *Petite suite.* RAVEL: *Ma Mère l'oye suite.* FAURE: *Dolly (suite), Op. 56.* BIZET: *Jeux d'enfants* (complete).

(B) *** EMI Début 5 72526-2.

Lawrence Fromentin and Domenique Plancade, both Gold Medal winners at the Paris Conservatoire and pupils of Pascal Devoyon, decided to join together as a duo in 1992, and this is their recording début. The results are very impressive indeed. They encompass the wide stylistic contrasts of their programme with sympathy and panache, from the brittle wit of Poulenc and its underlying innocence, to the exquisitely delicate Ravelian atmosphere of *Ma Mère l'oye* and the gentle charm of Fauré's *Dolly*. Debussy's *Petite suite* is winningly spontaneous, while the perceptively characterized *Jeux d'enfants* of Bizet is the more valuable for being complete, including all 12 movements, not just those familiar in the orchestral suite. The recording is excellent. A genuine bargain in every sense.

Galimir Quartet

BERG: *Lyric Suite.* MILHAUD: *String Quartet No. 7 in B flat.* RAVEL: *String Quartet in F.*

(**) Rockport RR 5007.

Like the Hagens, the Galimir was a family *Quartet,* founded in 1929 by Felix Galimir with his three sisters. They recorded the Milhaud and Ravel quartets in 1934 in the presence of their respective com-posers, and the *Lyric Suite* in 1935 just before Berg's death. Felix Galimir emigrated to the United States just before the outbreak of the Second World War and taught at the Juilliard School until his death. The performances naturally carry authority, though the somewhat dry acoustic of the Berg calls for tolerance. The present transfer of the latter is much better than the Continuum version coupled with Louis Krasne's broadcast of the *Violin Concerto*, with Webern conducting.

(i) Goldstone, Anthony & (ii) Caroline Clemmow (piano duo)

'*Explorations*': (i; ii) LEIGHTON: *Prelude, Hymn & Toccata, Op. 96.* HOLST: *Japanese Suite, Op. 33 (for 2 pianos).* STEVENSON: *2 Chinese Folk-Songs* (for piano duet). Solo piano music: HEDGES: (i) *Sonata, Op. 53;* (ii) *3 Explorations, Op. 45; 5 Aphorisms.*
*** Divine Art 25024.

The key work here is Kenneth Leighton's *Prelude, Hymn and Toccata*, an immensely impressive and commanding antiphonal work for two pianos. The *Hymn*, on which Leighton provides a kind of fantasia, is 'Abide with me', but it is so heavily disguised that one has to listen out for it as it enters. After its serene close comes the *Toccata*, erupting into a characteristically powerful and abandoned *Presto precipitoso* climax, and ending with surprising abruptness. The works by Anthony Hedges are also exploratory and stimulating, the *Explorations* based on a single concentrated motif, the *Aphorisms* producing a fine *Lento* slow movement, and the *Sonata* (also with a memorable *Adagio*) concentrated in structure, with the brilliant Rondo finale nostalgically recalling material from the first two movements, before the animated closing section. Lighter, exotic contrast is provided by the enticing oriental pastiches of Holst and Stevenson, with the latter's *Song of the Crab Fisher* something of a lollipop. Altogether a stimulating collection, played with commitment and understanding by these two fine artists, and very well recorded.

Goossens, Leon (oboe)

'*The Goossens Family*' (with Lloyd, piano, Marie & Sidonie Goossens, harps, Fitzwilliam Qt): BACH: *Easter Oratorio: Sinfonia.* SOMER-COCKS: *Three Sketches: No. 1.* STANTON: *Chanson pastorale.* RICHARDSON: *Scherzino.* HENSCHEL: *Shepherd's Lament.* PITFIELD: *Rondo Lirico.* HUGHES: *Bard of Armagh.* DUNHILL: *Romance.* BOYCE: *Matelotte.* FINZI: *Interlude.* KREIN: *Serenade for Oboe & 2 Harps.* NICHOLAS: *Melody.* SAUNDERS: *A Cotswold Pastoral.* ELGAR (arr. Jacob): *Soliloquy* (with Bournemouth Sinf., Del Mar).

(M) *** Chan. (ADD) 7132.

This touching tribute to Leon Goossens, a superstar among oboists long before that term was invented, is the more welcome when he made relatively few recordings over his long career. The harpists, Marie and Sidonie Goossens, accompany their brother in two of the most charming items, the Krein *Serenade* and Morgan Nicholas's *Melody*, but the rest of the programme is devoted to Leon. These are mainly recordings (first issued on RCA in the late 1970s) which Goossens made after his amazing rehabilitation following a serious car accident. Although the technical facility may not be quite the same as earlier, the warmth of tone and the ability to charm are undiminished. That he was in his late seventies at the time only adds to the marvel. The two most extended items are the *Soliloquy* which Elgar wrote for Goossens right at the end of his life, and the Finzi *Interlude*, superbly played by the Fitzwilliam Quartet, with contrasted sections covering a wide emotional range. Specially welcome is the carefree little *Rondo* by Thomas Pitfield with its witty pay-off.

Green, Gareth (organ)

English Organ Music (organ of Chesterfield Parish Church): LANG: *Tuba Tune, Op. 15.* HOWELLS: *3 Psalm Preludes, Op. 32.* ELGAR: *Sonata No. 1, Op. 28.* VAUGHAN WILLIAMS: *Rhosymedre (Hymn Prelude).* WHITLOCK: *Hymn Preludes: on Darwell's 148th; on Song 13.* COCKER: *Tuba Tune.*
(BB) *(*) Naxos 8.550582.

The organ as recorded here has no clarity of profile, and even the two characterful *Tuba Tunes* fail to make their full effect. The sound in the *Hymn* and *Psalm Preludes* is washy and indistinct. Gareth Green plays the early Elgar *Sonata* very well but it makes an impact only in its more powerful moments, and it is difficult to find a volume level which reveals the unfocused, quieter detail while not having the climaxes too loud.

Grumiaux, Arthur (violin), István Hajdu (piano)

'*Favourite Violin Encores*': PARADIS: *Sicilienne.* MOZART: *Rondo, K.250; Divertimento in D, K.334: Minuet.* GLUCK: *Mélodie.* GRANADOS: *Danza española No. 5.* KREISLER: *Schön Rosmarin; Liebesleid; Liebesfreud; Rondino on a Theme of Beethoven; Andantino in the Style of Padre Martini.* VERACINI: *Allegro; Largo* (arr. CORTI). VIVALDI: *Siciliano* (arr. from Op. 3/11). LECLAIR: *Tambourin.* BEETHOVEN: *Minuet in G.* SCHUBERT: *Ave Maria; Ständchen.* DVORAK: *Humoresque in G flat, Op. 101/7; Songs My Mother Taught Me, Op. 55/4; Sonatine in G, Op. 100: Larghetto.* MASSENET: *Thaïs: Méditation.* TCHAIKOVSKY: *Valse sentimentale, Op. 51/6.* ELGAR: *La Capricieuse.*

FAURE: *Après un rêve, Op. 7/1; Les berceaux, Op. 23/1.* ALBENIZ: *Tango, Op. 165/2.* PONCE: *Estrellita.* SIBELIUS: *Nocturne, Op. 51/3.* PERGOLESI: *Andantino.* SCHUMANN: *Kinderszenen: Träumerei.* BACH/GOUNOD: *Ave Maria.* PAGANINI: *Sonata No. 12 in E min., Op. 3/6.* WIENIAWSKI: *Souvenir de Moscou, Op. 6.* RAVEL: *Pièce en forme de habanera; Tzigane.* SARASATE: *Zigeunerweisen, Op. 20/1.* FIOCCO: *Allegro.* BLOCH: *Baal Shem: Nigun.* KODALY: *Adagio.*
(B) *** Ph. Duo (ADD) 446 560-2 (2).

Marvellous fiddler as he is, Grumiaux is not an extrovert in the manner of a Perlman who likes to dazzle and be right on top of the microphones; instead, these are essentially intimate performances. Yet when fire is needed it is certainly forthcoming, as in the superb account of Ravel's *Tzigane*. But Grumiaux is completely at home in what are mostly elegant *morceaux de concert*, and especially the Kreisler encores. He brings a particularly nice touch of rubato to *Schön Rosmarin* and produces a ravishingly stylish *Liebesleid*, while the *Andantino in the Style of Martini* is engagingly ingenuous. Schumann's *Träumerei* is made to sound as if originally conceived as a violin solo. The *Méditation* from *Thaïs* is delectably romantic without being oversweet, and the following *Valse sentimentale* of Tchaikovsky has just the right degree of restraint.

But Grumiaux's simplicity of style is heard at its most appealing in Wieniawski's *Souvenir de Moscou*, with its warm melody elegantly decorated and then let loose in a burst of Paganinian fireworks. István Hajdu accompanies with comparable taste, notably in Bach's unwitting contribution to Gounod's *Ave Maria*, while his simple introduction to Elgar's *La Capricieuse* is a model of how to set the scene for a salon piece of this kind. He is equally helpful in echoing Grumiaux in Schubert's lovely *Serenade* and in his discreet backing for Ponce's gently voluptuous *Estrellita*. The recording is most natural, without any edginess on the violin-tone, and the piano is pleasingly balanced within a warm acoustic.

Hamelin, Marc-André (piano)

'*Live at Wigmore Hall*': BEETHOVEN (arr. ALKAN): *Piano Concerto No. 3:* first movt. CHOPIN (arr. BALAKIREV): *Piano Concerto No. 1: Romanza.* ALKAN: *3 Grandes études.* BUSONI: *Sonatina No. 6 (Chamber Fantasy on 'Carmen').* MEDTNER: *Danza festiva, Op. 38, No. 3.*
☰ ✿ *** Hyp. CDA 66765.

This is among the most spectacular piano issues of the last decade. It captures live one of the programmes given in June 1994 at Wigmore Hall by the French-Canadian pianist Marc-André Hamelin, in a series called 'Virtuoso Romantics'. Bizarre as the mixture is, it works magnificently, thanks not only to Hamelin's breathtaking virtuosity, finger perfect, but to his magnetism. As well as the *Trois Grandes études* of Alkan, he plays Alkan's arrangement of the first movement of Beethoven's *Third Piano Concerto*. Thanks to his sharp clarity, one marvels afresh at the purposefulness of the writing, and he revels in Alkan's manic six-minute cadenza, which in dotty inspiration even quotes the finale of Beethoven's *Fifth Symphony*. Balakirev's arrangement of the Romanza from Chopin's *First Piano Concerto* then offers yearning poetry, with two flamboyant display-pieces as encores: Busoni's *Carmen Fantasy* and Medtner's *Danza festiva*.

'*Kaleidoscope*': woods: *Valse phantastique*. behr (trans. rachmaninov): *Polka de W.R.* hofmann: *Kaleidoskop; Nocturne*. hamelin: *Etudes Nos. 3 (d'après Paganini-Liszt) & 6 (Esercizio per pianoforte)*. blumenfeld: *Etude pour la main gauche seule*. offenbach: *Concert Paraphrase of 'The Song of the Soldiers of the Sea'*. massenet: *Valse folie*. moszkowski: *Etude in A flat min, Op. 72/13*. poulenc: *Intermezzo in A flat*. godowsky: *Alt Wien*. michalowski: *Etude d'après l'Impromptu en la bémol majeur de Fr. Chopin*. lourie: *Gigue*. blanchet: *Au jardin du vieux sérail, Op. 18/3*. casella: *2 Contrastes*. vallier: *Toccatina*. glazunov (trans. hamelin): *Petit adagio*. kapustin: *Toccatina*.
★★★ Hyp. CDA 67275.

This collection of encores, most of them rarities, is a box of delights, with Marc-André Hamelin bringing out the fun as well as the brilliance. Consistently, one marvels that ten fingers can possibly play the notes involved, when the virtuosity demanded is almost beyond belief. Yet Hamelin is masterly at bringing out the wit of each piece, as in the opening item by a virtually unknown composer, Edna Bentz Woods, with waltz rhythms naughtily pointed. Hamelin's own tribute to Scarlatti in his *Etude No. 6* is in fact an amusing parody, very much tongue-in-cheek, and it is pure fun to have the American Marines' Hymn (drawn from Offenbach) elaborated as a virtuoso keyboard study. Hamelin also brings out the keyboard magic of such a piece as Blanchet's evocation of the garden of the seraglio or the transcription from Glazunov's ballet, *The Seasons*, with beauty as well as brilliance part of his message. Vivid recorded sound.

Hardenberger, Håkan (trumpet)

'*The Virtuoso Trumpet*' (with Pöntinen): arban: *Variations on Themes from Bellini's 'Norma'*. francaix: *Sonatine*. tisne: *Héraldiques*. honegger: *Intrada*. maxwell davies: *Sonata*. rabe: *Shazam!*. hartmann: *Fantasia brillante on the Air 'Rule, Britannia'*.
★★★ BIS CID 287.

This collection includes much rare and adventurous repertoire, not otherwise available and very unlikely to offer frequent access in live performance. Moreover, Hardenberger plays with electrifying bravura in the Maxwell Davies *Sonata* and the virtuoso miniatures. Antoine Tisné's five *Héraldiques* are eclectic but highly effective on the lips of such an assured player; *Scandé* and the following *Elégiaque* are notably characterful. But easily the most memorable item is the Françaix *Sonatine* (originally for violin and piano) in which two delicious brief outer movements frame a pleasing central *Sarabande*. Honegger's improvisatory *Intrada* is an effective encore piece. The recording is eminently realistic, with the CD giving superb presence.

Hausmusik

Chamber Music Collection: mozart: *String Quintets Nos. 2 in C, K.515; 3 in G min., K.516*. beethoven: *String Quintet in C, Op. 29. Septet in E flat, Op. 20*. schubert: *Piano Quintet in A (Trout), D.667*. hummel: *Piano Quintet in E flat, Op. 87* (with Cyril Huvé, fortepiano). schubert: *Octet in F, D.803*. mendelssohn: *String Quintet No. 1 in A, Op. 18; Octet for Strings, Op. 20*.
✹ (BB) ★★★ EMI 5 62352-2 (5).

Hausmusik were one of EMI/Virgin's key period-instrument chamber-music groups in the early 1990s, and then curiously they disappeared from view. This highly recommendable collection begins with outstanding performances of two of the finest of the Mozart *String Quintets*. As the very opening of the *C major* demonstrates, their playing brings a wonderfully light rhythmic touch and is remarkably airy in texture. The first movement of the *G minor* is managed no less beautifully. Slow movements have a movingly restrained espressivo, withdrawn but without a feeling of austerity; the *Adagio* of the *G minor* is hauntingly dark in its gentle melancholy. Finales bounce along joyfully and, although different in character, these performances are every bit as rewarding as those on modern instruments.

Hausmusik's version of the Beethoven *Septet* is also outstanding among period performances, presenting a refreshing, lively view with the advantage of extra clarity in textures and pointed rhythms. The strings are light, tangy without abrasiveness, and the wind characterfully contrasted. The *String Quintet* is equally fresh, and Hausmusik's performance of the Schubert *Octet* is so winning that it can be recommended as a top choice, even to those who do not normally follow the cult of authenticity. This time the group includes such imaginative wind players as the clarinettist Anthony Pay shaping the opening solo of the *Adagio* slow movement with heavenly phrasing, and the fine horn-player Anthony Halstead is hardly less impressive. Speeds are rarely extreme, allowing full, open expressiveness, as in the *Adagio*; allegros are generally easy enough to allow a delectable rhythmic spring. The pointing is the more infectious when period string-playing allows textures to be so transparent. There are few Schubert performances that so consistently convey the joys of spring, and this one received a Rosette on its first appearance.

The *Trout Quintet* is less easy-going. The pianist Cyril Huvé leads strongly and rhythmically; while, as always, textures are agreeably translucent, especially striking in the *Andante*, one feels the players could relax more. Although this account has fine impetus, there is less Schubertian charm than in the *Octet*. The Hummel *Piano Quintet* is much more successful: here the energy of the performance pays dividends in the lively outer movements, and there is a nice romantic touch in the brief *Largo*, before the highly animated closing Rondo.

The Mendelssohn *Octet* is coupled with another miraculous masterpiece of Mendelssohn's boyhood. In both, the period instruments give extra weight to the lower lines, compared with the violins, with the extra clarity intensifying the joyfulness of the inspiration. Most reveaing of all is the way that the last two movements of the *Octet*, the feather-light Scherzo and the dashing finale, with their similar figuration, are presented in contrast, the one slower and more delicately pointed than usual, the other more exhilarating at high speed. The recording and balance are in the hands of Mike Hatch and Mike Clements, which automatically implies high standards, and this budget-priced set is very recommendable indeed.

Headington, Christopher (piano)

British Piano Music of the 20th Century: BRITTEN: *Holiday Diary.* DELIUS: *3 Preludes.* ELGAR: *Adieu; In Smyrna; Serenade.* HEADINGTON: *Ballade-image; Cinquanta.* IRELAND: *The Island Spell.* MOERAN: *Summer Valley.* PATTERSON: *A Tunnel of Time, Op. 66.*
*** Kingdom KCLD 2017.

The novelties here are fascinating. The Delius *Preludes* (1923) have much of the luminous atmosphere of the orchestral music, while Britten's *Holiday Diary* (what a happy idea for a suite!), written when he was just twenty, is most winning. The Elgar pieces are well worth having, and Headington again reveals himself as an appealing composer. Both his pieces were written for fiftieth-birthday celebrations and the *Ballade-image* expressly seeks to conjure up an atmosphere combining the influences of Chopin and Debussy. It is most engaging. John Ireland's *Island Spell* is beautifully played. A 69-minute recital which is skilfully planned to be listened to in sequence. Good, if not outstanding, recording.

Heifetz, Jascha (violin)

'*The Legendary Heifetz*' (with Bay or Sandor, piano): BAZZINI: *La Ronde des lutins, Op. 25.* WIENIAWSKI: *Scherzo-tarantelle in G min., Op. 16.* DEBUSSY: *L'enfant prodigue; Prélude.* ALBENIZ: *Suite española: Sevillañas.* ELGAR: *La Capricieuse, Op. 17.* MOSZKOWSKI: *Guitarre, Op. 45/2.* FALLA: *Danza española No. 1.* Cyril SCOTT: *Tallahassee Suite: Bygone Memories.* DOHNANYI: *Ruralia hungarica, Op. 32a: Gypsy Andante.* CASTELNUOVO-TEDESCO: *Valse.* POULENC: *Mouvements perpétuelles No. 1.* VIVALDI: *Sonata in A, Op. 2/2.* PAGANINI: *Caprice, Op. 1/13.* BACH: *English Suite No. 3 in G min., BWV 808: Gavottes Nos. 1 & 2 (Musette).* FRANCK: *Sonata in A: First Movement Mosso* (with Rubinstein).
(M) (**) EMI mono 5 67005-2.

Although the playing here offers the sophistication of bow-arm technique, and fabulous assurance for which Heifetz is famous, the recorded sound detracts very considerably from the listener's pleasure. All these recordings were made at Abbey Road (for the most part in 1934, and a few in 1937) but they are a credit neither to the original EMI engineers nor to the current EMI remastering process. The acoustic is dry, the violin uncomfortably close to the microphone, minimizing the breadth of tone, making it sound top-heavy and peaky. It is surely possible to do better than this! As it is, the extraordinary virtuosity of *La ronde des lutins*, Wieniawski's *Scherzo-tarantelle* and famous *Hora staccato*, the veiled beauty of tone in the Debussy *Prélude* to *L'enfant prodigue* and the evocation of Cyril Scott are all but lost. The Vivaldi *Sonata*, superbly stylish, and the excerpt from the Franck *Sonata* (with Rubinstein) seem almost to triumph over the sound, but, even so, one needs to replay this disc with the aural equivalent of top-quality dark glasses to enjoy the music-making.

Hilton, Janet (clarinet), Keith Swallow (piano)

'*Rhapsodie*': POULENC: *Clarinet Sonata.* RAVEL: *Pièce en forme d'habanera.* DEBUSSY: *Première rhapsodie.* SAINT-SAENS: *Clarinet Sonata, Op. 167.* ROUSSEL: *Aria.* MILHAUD: *Duet concertante, Op. 351.*
(M) ** Chan. 6589.

There are some highly beguiling sounds here, and the languorous style adopted throughout is emphasized by the reverberant acoustic which is less than ideal, creating the feeling of an empty hall. The Ravel and Debussy are given an evocative sentience and the Poulenc comes off very well too; overall, however, there is a feeling that a little more vitality and a more sharply focused sound-picture would have been advantageous.

Horowitz, Vladimir (piano)

Complete DG Recordings: BACH/BUSONI: *Chorale Prelude, Nun komm, der Heiden Heiland.* MOZART: *Piano Sonatas: in B flat, K.281; in C, K.330; in B flat, K.333. Adagio in B min., K.540; Rondo in D, K.485; Piano Concerto No. 23 in A. K.488* (with La Scala, Milan, O, Giulini). CHOPIN: *Mazurkas: in A min., Op. 17/4; in C sharp min., Op. 30/4; in F min., Op. 7/3. Scherzo No. 1 in B min., Op. 20; Polonaise No. 6 in A flat, Op. 53.* SCHUBERT: *Impromptus: in A flat, D.899/4; in B flat, D.935/3. Marche militaire in D flat, D.733/1. Moment musical in F min., D.780/3; Piano Sonata No. 21 in B flat, D.960.* LISZT: *Consolation No. 3 in D flat; Impromptu (Nocturne) in F sharp; Valse oubliée No. 1; Soirées de Vienne: Valses-Caprices Nos. 6, 7 & 8; Années de pèlerinage: Sonetto 101 del Petrarca. Concert Paraphrase of Schubert's 'Ständchen'.* SCHUMANN: *Novelette in F, Op. 21/1; Kreisleriana, Op. 16; Kinderszenen, Op. 15 (complete) & excerpt: Träumerei.* RACHMANINOV: *Preludes: in G sharp min., Op. 32/12; in G, Op. 32/5; Polka de W. R.* SCRIABIN: *Etude in C sharp min., Op. 2/1; in D sharp min., Op. 8/12.* MOSZKOWSKI: *Etude in F, Op. 72/6; Etincelles, Morceau caractéristique, Op. 36/6.* D. SCARLATTI: *Sonatas: in B min., Kk. 87; in E, Kk. 135; in E, Kk. 380.*

(B) *** DG 474 370-2 (6).

This set of six CDs collects all the recordings Horowitz made for Deutsche Grammophon between 1985 and 1989, when he was in his early eighties. The first was made in his Manhattan home and is taken from the soundtrack of the video, 'Vladimir Horowitz – The Last Romantic'. Other recordings come from Moscow, Vienna and Milan. Although, judged by the standards of the youthful Horowitz, there is less of the demonic virtuoso, there is still plenty of brilliance, combined with introspective sensitivity. We have lavished plaudits on each of these recordings in their first incarnations. There is much vintage Horowitz: the Bach/Busoni arrangement, which he had not committed to disc since his 1947 RCA recording, has a seamless legato that is almost in a class of its own. Some of the stormier passages in *Kreisleriana* are not as effortless as they would have been in his youth, but it is still an astonishing achievement. Some have complained that, in his desire to shed new light, there are touches that are a little forced. Yet he evokes a Schumann who sounds wholly possessed. And as Joan Chissell so aptly put it, his Scriabin *Etude in D sharp minor* 'shows how he can still kindle glowing embers into scorching flame'. The Scarlatti and Mozart are marked by exquisite delicacy, and his feeling for sonority and his magisterial authority leave a profound impression. And it is good to hear the great pianist in truthful recorded sound. This is a set to cherish – and in its new edition a bargain as well.

Recital: BACH/BUSONI: *Chorale Prelude: Nun komm, der Heiden Heiland.* MOZART: *Piano Sonata No. 10 in C, K.330.* CHOPIN: *Mazurka in A min., Op. 17/4; Scherzo No. 1 in B min., Op. 20; Polonaise No. 6 in A flat, Op. 53.* LISZT: *Consolation No. 3 in D flat.* SCHUBERT: *Impromptu in A flat, D.899/4.* SCHUMANN: *Novellette in F, Op. 21/1.* RACHMANINOV: *Prelude in G sharp min., Op. 32/12.* SCRIABIN: *Etude in C sharp min., Op. 2/1.* MOSZKOWSKI: *Etude in F, Op. 72/6* (recording of performances featured in the film *Vladimir Horowitz – The Last Romantic*).

*** DG (IMS) 419 045-2.

Recorded when he was over eighty, this playing betrays remarkably little sign of frailty. The Mozart is beautifully elegant and the Chopin *A minor Mazurka*, Op. 17, No. 4, could hardly be more delicate. The only sign of age comes in the *B minor Scherzo*, which does not have the leonine fire and tremendous body of his famous 1950 recording. However, it is pretty astonishing for all that.

'*The Studio Recordings*': SCHUMANN: *Kreisleriana, Op. 16.* D. SCARLATTI: *Sonatas in B min., Kk. 87; in E, Kk. 135.* LISZT: *Impromptu (Nocturne) in F sharp; Valse oubliée No. 1.* SCRIABIN: *Etude in D sharp min., Op. 8/12.* SCHUBERT: *Impromptu in B flat, D.935/3.* SCHUBERT/TAUSIG: *Marche militaire, D.733/1.*

*** DG (IMS) 419 217-2.

The subtle range of colour and articulation in the Schumann is matched in his Schubert *Impromptu,* and the Liszt *Valse oubliée* offers the most delicious, twinkling rubato. Hearing Scarlatti's *E major Sonata* played with such crispness, delicacy and grace must surely convert even the most dedicated authenticist to the view that this repertoire can be totally valid in terms of the modern instrument. The Schubert–Tausig *Marche militaire* makes a superb encore, played with the kind of panache that would be remarkable in a pianist half Horowitz's age. With the passionate Scriabin *Etude* as the central romantic pivot, this recital is uncommonly well balanced to show Horowitz's special range of sympathies.

'*The Indispensable Horowitz*': CHOPIN: *Polonaise-fantaisie in A flat, Op. 61; Scherzi Nos. 1 in B min., Op. 20; 2 in B flat, Op. 31; Etudes in C sharp min., Op. 10/4; in C sharp min., Op. 25/7; Nocturnes in B, Op. 9/3; in C sharp min., Op. 27/1; in E min., Op. 72/1; Barcarolle, Op. 60; Polonaise in A flat, Op. 53; Ballade No. 1 in G min., Op. 23.* D. SCARLATTI: *Keyboard Sonatas, Kk. 87, 127 & 135.* RACHMANINOV: *Humoresque, Op. 10/5; Preludes in G min., Op. 23/5; in G, Op. 32/5; Barcarolle, Op. 10/3.* MOSZKOWSKI: *Etincelle, Op. 36/6; Etude in F, Op. 72/6.* LISZT: *Hungarian Rhapsodies Nos. 2 & 15 (Rákóczy March)* (both arr. HOROWITZ); *Mephisto Waltz No. 1.* BIZET/HOROWITZ: *Variations on a Theme from 'Carmen'.* SCRIABIN: *Etudes: in C*

sharp min., Op. 2/1; in B flat min., Op. 8/7; in D sharp min., Op. 8/12; in C sharp min., Op. 42/5.
SOUSA/HOROWITZ: *The Stars and Stripes Forever.*
☙ ☀ (B) ★★★ RCA stereo/mono, 74321 63471-2 (2).

The notes with this remarkably generous collection include a quote from Neville Cardus, who once described Horowitz as 'the greatest pianist alive or dead'. Later he added that this comment 'perhaps was not positive enough about pianists still unborn'. His eulogy still holds true at the time of writing, and the programme here demonstrates why. If you look for astonishing, barnstorming virtuosity you will find it in Horowitz's own *Carmen Variations*, the Liszt *Hungarian Rhapsody* 'arrangements' or the closing *Stars and Stripes*; but if you seek bravura delicacy, the Moszkowski *F major Etude* is a supreme example, while his Scarlatti is unforgettable. Romantic poetry constantly illuminates his Chopin (the *Barcarolle* and *G minor Ballade* are especially memorable) and his Rachmaninov (the *G major Prelude* is exquisite), while throughout this is playing of unique distinction which offers infinite rewards.

Scriabin, another of Horowitz's special composers, is generously represented, not only by Horowitz's favourite, *D sharp minor Etude* (taken from a 1982 live recital) but also by the more prolix *C sharp minor*, recorded three decades earlier. What is surprising is the fairly consistent quality of the sound: one of the earliest mono recordings (from 1950), of Scriabin's Op. 2/1, is remarkably warmly coloured. Of course, the later, stereo recordings are ever finer, as the commanding opening *Polonaise-fantaisie* of Chopin (1982) readily shows. But on sonic grounds there is little to criticize; artistically this pair of discs are in a class of their own.

Horszowski, Mieczyslaw (piano)

J.S. BACH: *French Suite No. 6 in E, BWV 817.*
BEETHOVEN: *Piano Sonata No. 6 in F, Op. 10/2.*
SCHUMANN: *Papillons, Op. 2; Kinderszenen: Träumerei.* CHOPIN: *Etude in F min., Op. 25/2; Impromptu in F sharp, Op. 36; Nocturne in E flat, Op. 9/2; Scherzo No. 1 in B min., Op. 20; Waltz in C sharp min., Op. 64/2.*
☀ (M) ★★★ BBC BBCL (ADD) 4122-2.

Extraordinary playing. This is a recording of a recital given in London's Wigmore Hall on 21 June 1990, when Horszowski was two days short of his 98th birthday. The playing is radiant and the quality of sound he produces has an almost disembodied, luminous quality that was so special. Older collectors will remember the famous Vox LPs he made of the *Hammerklavier Sonata* and the *Diabelli Variations*, and they will find that he was still active and better than ever, forty years later. As those who heard his wonderful Szymanowski *Mazurkas* at Aldeburgh seven years earlier will remember, there is not the

slightest trace of age in his playing. Magical playing that is to be treasured.

Hough, Stephen (piano)

'*Piano Album*':

Disc 1: MACDOWELL: *Hexentanz, Op. 12.* CHOPIN: *Chant polonaise No. 1.* QUILTER: *The Crimson Petal; The Fuchsia Tree.* DOHNÁNYI: *Capriccio in F min., Op. 28/8.* PADEREWSKI: *Minuet in G, Op. 14/1; Nocturne in B flat, Op. 16/4.* SCHLOZER: *Etude in A flat, Op. 1/2.* GABRILOVICH: *Mélodie in E; Caprice-burlesque.* RODGERS: *My Favourite Things.* WOODFORDE-FINDEN: *Kashmiri Song.* FRIEDMAN: *Music Box.* SAINT-SAENS: *Carnival of the Animals: The Swan* (arr. GODOWSKY). ROSENTHAL: *Papillons.* GODOWSKY: *The Gardens of Buitenzorg.* LEVITZKI: *Waltz in A, Op. 2.* PALMGREN: *En route, Op. 9.* MOSZKOWSKI: *Siciliano, Op. 42/2; Caprice espagnol, Op. 37.*

Disc 2: CZERNY: *Variations brillantes, Op. 14.* LEVITZKI: *The Enchanted Nymph.* SCHUMANN: *Der Kontrebandiste.* RUBINSTEIN: *Melody in F.* LIEBERMANN: *Gargoyles, Op. 29.* REBIKOV: *The Musical Snuffbox.* RAVINA: *Etude de style (Agilité), Op. 40/1.* WOODFORDE-FINDEN: *Till I Wake.* QUILTER: *Weep You No More.* RODGERS: *March of the Siamese Children.* MOSZKOWSKI: *Valse mignonne; Serenata, Op. 15/1.* BACH: *Violin Sonata No. 2: Bourrée.* GODOWSKY: *Erinnerungen.* BIZET: *L'Arlésienne: Adagietto.* TAUSIG: *Ungarische Zigeunerweisen.*
(BB) ★★★ Virgin 5 61498-2 (2).

There are few young pianists who can match Stephen Hough in communicating on record with the immediacy and vividness of live performance; this dazzling two-disc recital of frothy showpieces presents the perfect illustration. Indeed, this Virgin Classics bargain Double captures more nearly than almost any other recent record – even those of Horowitz – the charm, sparkle and flair of legendary piano virtuosos from the golden age of Rosenthal, Godowsky and Lhévinne.

So many of the items are frivolous that it may be surprising that any serious pianist can stomach them; yet on the first disc the very opening item, MacDowell's *Hexentanz* ('Witches' dance'), launches the listener into pure pianistic magic, and the second, with Czerny's fizzing *Variations brillantes*, similarly offers totally uninhibited playing, with articulation and timing that are the musical equivalent of being tickled up and down the spine.

One would hardly expect Hough's own arrangements of sentimental little songs by Roger Quilter and Amy Woodforde-Finden to be memorable – yet, in their tender expressiveness, they are most affecting. In the grand tradition, Hough does a Valse-caprice arrangement he himself has made of *My Favourite*

Things from *The Sound of Music*, as well as an equally attractive but simpler arrangement of Rodgers's *March of the Siamese Children*. Firework pieces by Rosenthal and Moszkowski, among others, go along with old-fashioned favourites like Paderewski's *Minuet in G*, Rubinstein's *Melody in F* (here sounding fresh and unfaded) and Godowsky's arrangement of the Saint-Saëns *Swan*.

Not all of Lowell Liebermann's *Gargoyles* are menacing (there is a charming *Adagio semplice*) but the *Feroce* marking for the closing number is pungently realized. Then follow two different miniature portrayals of a *Musical Snuffbox*, the first, by Vladimir Rebikov, not a whit less delightful than the more famous version by Liadov. The programme ends with an arresting account of Tausig's *Ungarische Zigeunerweisen*. Altogether it is a feast for piano lovers, very well recorded: the first disc in 1986 (in London and New York), the second in 1991 using the BBC's Manchester studio.

'*New Piano Album*': LISZT: *Concert Paraphrase of Schubert: Soirées de Vienne.* SCHUBERT (arr. GODOWSKY): *Moment Musical in D min., D.780/3; Die schöne Müllerin: Morgengrüss.* GODOWSKI: *Alt Wien.* MOSZKOWSKI: *Etincelle, Op. 36/6.* PADEREWSKI: *Mélodie in G flat, Op. 16/2.* CHAMINADE: *Pierrette (Air de ballet), Op. 41; Autrefois, Op. 87/4.* KALMAN (arr. HOUGH): *Hello Young Lovers; Carousel Waltz.* TRAD. (arr. HOUGH): *Londonderry Air.* RACHMANINOV: *Humoresque, Op. 10/5; Mélodie, Op. 3/3* (revised, 1940 version). TCHAIKOVSKY: *Humoresque, Op. 10/2.* TCHAIKOVSKY, arr. WILD: *Swan Lake: Pas de quatre.* TCHAIKOVSKY/PABST (arr. HOUGH): *Sleeping Beauty Paraphrase.*
★★★ Hyp. CDA 67043.

In his latest collection, Stephen Hough demonstrates yet again the flair with which he tackles trivial party pieces like the 20 varied items here. Such encore material has in his hands a sparkle and point that magick the ear, whether in the virtuoso display of pieces by Godowsky, Moszkowski and Rachmaninov or in the loving lyricism of pieces by Chaminade, Kalman and others. As well as offering two witty showpieces of his own, Hough also plays his arrangements of two Richard Rodgers numbers and the *Londonderry Air*. Among the four Tchaikovsky items, it is good to have the haunting little *Humoresque*, best known through Stravinsky's ballet, *The Fairy's Kiss*. Vivid sound.

'*English Piano Album*': RAWSTHORNE: *Bagatelles.* REYNOLDS: *2 Poems in Homage to Delius; 2 Poems in Homage to Fauré.* HOUGH: *Valses enigmatiques Nos. 1–2.* ELGAR: *In Smyrna.* BANTOCK: *Song to the Seals.* BOWEN: *Reverie d'amour, Op. 20/2; Serious Dance, Op. 51/2; The Way to Polden, Op. 76.* BRIDGE: *The Dew Fairy; Heart's Ease.* LEIGHTON: *6 Studies (Study-Variations), Op. 56.*
★★★ Hyp. CDA 67267.

This recital disc from Stephen Hough has a different aim from his previous collections of charmers, starting with four gritty and tough miniatures of Rawsthorne, thoughtful and intense, balanced at the end by Kenneth Leighton's *Study Variations*. Those do not make for easy listening either, inspiring Hough to superb pianism over six sharply characterized pieces, at times echoing Bartók in their angry energy, at others full of fantasy, with the second a slow and concentrated piece full of harmonic clusters, and with the final *Study* a breathtaking virtuoso exercise. What all these very varied items demonstrate is Hough's profound love of keyboard sound and textures, and his rare gift of bringing out the full beauty of that sound. His own pieces, the two *Valses enigmatiques*, each based on his own initials linked to those of friends, both bear that out, the one with light textures, the other with Debussian parallel chords. He also offers a warmly sympathetic arrangement of a song he recorded earlier with the tenor, Robert White, on a Hyperion disc of ballads, Bantock's *Song to the Seals*.

It is evidence too of Hough's wizardry that he makes the Elgar piece, *In Smyrna*, sound so bewitching, with echoes of the lovely solo viola serenade in the overture, *In the South*, written some two years before in 1903 and also with a Mediterranean inspiration. The four pieces by Stephen Reynolds, two with echoes of Delius, two of Fauré, are consciously relaxed exercises outside the composer's more astringent idiom. The two pieces by Frank Bridge bring out his love of delicate keyboard textures, while the three York Bowen pieces are simple and song-like, using an almost cabaret-style of piano writing. In all this music Hough's magic is presented in full, clear Hyperion sound.

Hurford, Peter (organ)

'*Great Romantic Organ Works*' (played on organs at Ratzeburg Cathedral, the Royal Festival Hall, in the Basilica of Saint-Sermin, Toulouse): WIDOR: *Symphony No. 5: Toccata; Symphony No. 6, Op. 42: Allegro.* FRANCK: *Chorals Nos. 1–3; Pièce héroïque.* MENDELSSOHN: *Preludes and Fugues: in C min., Op. 37/1; D min., Op. 37/3; Sonata in A, Op. 65/3.* GIGOUT: *10 pièces: Scherzo.* KARG-ELERT: *March triomphale: on 'Nun danket alle Gott'.* VIERNE: *24 pièces en style libre: Berceuse. Symphony No. 1, Op. 14: Final.* BRAHMS: *Choral Preludes: Es ist ein Ros entsprungen; Herzlich tut mich verlangen; Schmücke dich.* LISZT: *Prelude and Fugue on B-A-C-H.* SCHUMANN: *Four Sketches, Op. 58/4: Allegretto.* REGER: *Introduction and Passacaglia in D min.* BOELLMAN: *Suite gothique, Op. 25.*
(B) **★★★** Double Decca 466 742-2 (2).

A self-recommending set of organ favourites at bargain price in splendid digital sound, for the most part played on the magnificent organ at Ratzeburg Cathedral. Not many collections of Romantic organ music match this in colour, breadth of repertoire and brilliance of performance. Hurford's playing defies all considerations of Victorian heaviness, and the programme includes many key repertoire works. You cannot go wrong here.

'Organ Favourites': Sydney Opera House organ: BACH: Toccata and Fugue in D min., BWV 565; Jesu, Joy of Man's Desiring. ALBINONI: Adagio (arr. GIAZOTTO). PURCELL: Trumpet Tune in D. MENDELSSOHN: A Midsummer Night's Dream: Wedding March. FRANCK: Chorale No. 2 in B min. MURRILL: Carillon. WALFORD DAVIES: Solemn Melody. WIDOR: Organ Symphony No. 5: Toccata. Royal Festival Hall organ: FRANCK: Pièce héroïque. Ratzeburg Cathedral organ: BOELLMANN: Suite gothique.

(B) **(*) Decca 452 166-2.

Superb sound here, wonderfully free and never oppressive, even in the most spectacular moments. The Widor is spiritedly genial when played within the somewhat mellower registration of the magnificent Sydney instrument (as contrasted with the Ratzeburg Cathedral organ), and the pedals have great sonority and power. The Murrill Carillon is equally engaging alongside the Purcell Trumpet Tune, while Mendelssohn's wedding music has never sounded more resplendent. The Bach is less memorable, and the Albinoni Adagio, without the strings, is not an asset to the collection either. The Pièce héroïque and the Suite gothique have been added for the Eclipse reissue.

Isbin, Sharon (guitar)

'Latin Romances': de la MAZA: Zapateado. RODRIGO: Invocación y Danza. BARRIOS: La Catedral. ABREU: Quejas (Lament). JOBIM: Estrada do Sol. TARREGA: Capricho árabe. BROUWER: El Decameron negro. VILLA-LOBOS: Sentimental Melody; Etude No. 8. ALBENIZ: Mallorca; Asturias.
(BB) *** Virgin 2x1 5 61627-2 (2) (with RODRIGO: Concierto de Aranjuez; Fantasia para un gentilhombre ***. SCHWANTNER: From afar . . . (fantasy) **).

Sharon Isbin is a masterly guitarist and has inherited Segovia's gift of achieving natural spontaneity in the recording studio, so that this solo recital is consistently fresh and communicative, the playing brilliant and evocative by turns. Rodrigo's Invocación y Danza and Tárrega's Capricho árabe are only two of the familiar pieces which project magnetically, as does the Albéniz Asturias, which ends the recital so vibrantly. The novelty is The Black Decameron of Leo Brouwer, a programmatic triptych which is sharply characterized and atmospherically realized. Isbin is given great presence by the recording, and he plays the key Rodrigo concertante works with no less distinction. The Schwantner piece is less recommendable, but this two-disc set remains a bargain.

Isoir, André (organ)

French Renaissance Organ Music (Koenig organ at Bon Pasteur, Angers): Bransles, Galliards and other dances by GERVAIS; FRANCISQUE; ATTAIGNANT. JANEQUIN: Allez my fault. SANDRIN: Quand ien congneu. Eustache du CAURROY: Fantaisie sur une jeune fillette. ATTAIGNANT: 3 Versets du Te Deum; Prélude aux treize motets; Kyrie cunctipotens. Fantaisies by GUILLET; LE JEUNE; RACQUET. RICHARD: Prélude in D min. THOMELIN: Duo. LA BARRE: Sarabande. Henri du MONT: Prélude No. 10 in D min.; Pavane in D min. ANON.: Fantaisie; Ave Maris Stella. ROBERDAY: Fugue et caprice No. 3 in C; Fugues Nos. 10 in G min.; 12 in D.
(M) *** Cal. CAL 6901.

The Angers organ has a spicy régale stop which is used tellingly in several of the dance movements included in the programme, notably Gervaise's Bransle de Bourgogne and a Basse dance, Bransle and Gaillarde of Attaignant and also in Sandrin's Quand ien congneu. A warmer palette is found for Eustache du Caurroy's agreeable Fantaisie sur une jeune fillette. This is a French equivalent to the divisions found in Elizabethan music, whereas the piquant Fantaisie sur orgue ou espinette of Guillaume Costeley is very succinct. Attaignant's Kyrie cunctipotens and the Third Fantaisie of Charles Guillet are essentially chorale preludes, as is the more elaborate Fantaisie of Charles Racquet, but the Second Fantaisie of Claude Le Jeune, a remarkable piece, anticipates the chorale variations of Bach, but using two different fugal subjects. Joseph Thomelin's (two-part) Duo is a winning miniature and Joseph de la Barre's Sarabande also has a gentle charm, while the three Fugues of François Roberday show impressive craftsmanship. No. 12, which ends the recital resplendently, is a good example of Isoir's imaginative registrations, which find ear-tickling contrasts between the plangent and mellow timbres that this organ offers, while the music is kept very much alive. A generous (76 minutes) and stimulating recital, although not to be played all at one sitting.

Isserlis, Steven (cello)

'Cello World' (with Adès, Cole, Tilson Thomas, Moore): BEETHOVEN: Andante and Variations. SCHUMANN: Violin Sonata: Intermezzo. FAURE: Morceau de concours. LEONARD: L'âne et l'ânier. DVORAK: Romantic Piece. SEIBER: Dance Suite (all arr. ISSERLIS). DEBUSSY: Nocturne et Scherzo. BERLIOZ: La Captive. TAVENER: The Child Lives (both with Lott). SAINT-SAENS: Le Cygne. VILLA-LOBOS: O canto do cisne negro. MARTINU: Duo. RACHMANINOV: Lied. SCRIABIN: Romance. POPPER: Dance of the Elves. ISSERLIS: Souvenir russe. TSINTSADZE: Chonguri. VINE: Inner World.
*** RCA 09026 68928-2.

This is a cello recital with a difference, attractive in an off-beat way. The last and longest item, *Inner World*, by the Australian Carl Vine, is for amplified cello with electronic support, a cult piece, modern but not difficult. Otherwise, there are only two regular cello showpieces: Saint-Saëns's *Swan*, exquisitely portrayed, and Popper's *Dance of the Elves*, with Isserlis flamboyant. The Beethoven *Variations*, with harpsichord accompaniment, were transcribed from a *Sonatina for Mandolin and Piano* (1796), but most of the transcriptions are from violin originals, including the comic Leonard piece, full of ever more exaggerated hee-haws, set against the carter's song in the middle. In most items, Thomas Adès is the inspired accompanist, and inspired too is the accompaniment by Maggie Cole, relishing the witty 1920s parodies in Matyas Seiber's *Dance Suite*. The two items with Felicity Lott bring extra freshness and beauty, not just in the Berlioz song but also in the Tavener piece with accompaniment for cello alone. First-rate sound.

(i) Jackson, Francis (organ of York Minster), (ii) Michael Austin (organ of Birmingham Town Hall)

'*Pipes of Splendour*': (i) COCKER: *Tuba Tune.* PURCELL: *Trumpet Tune and Almand.* JACKSON: *Division on 'Nun Danket'.* LEIGHTON: *Paean.* DUBOIS: *Toccata in G.* GUILMANT: *Allegretto in B min., Op. 19.* GIGOUT: *Scherzo in E.* MULET: *Carillon-Sortie.* (ii) REGER: *Toccata and Fugue in D min./major, Op. 59/5–6.* DUPRE: *Prelude and Fugue in B, Op. 7.* FRANCK: *Final in B flat.*
(M) *** Chan. (ADD) 6602.

It was Francis Jackson who made Cocker's *Tuba Tune* (with its boisterous, brassy principal theme) justly famous, and it makes a splendid opener. But the entire programme shows that it is possible to play and record an English organ without the result sounding flabby. The *Toccata* of Dubois is very winning and, in its quieter central section, the detail is beautifully clear, as it is in the charming Guilmant *Allegretto* and the lightly articulated Gigout *Scherzo*. Mulet's *Carillon-Sortie* rings out gloriously and Leighton's *Paean* brings a blaze of tone. The items played in Birmingham by Michael Austin are no less stimulating, especially the two French pieces, which have a fine piquant bite, while the Reger isn't in the least dull. Superb transfers of demonstration-standard analogue recording from the early 1970s.

Jacoby, Ingrid (piano)

MUSSORGSKY: *Pictures at an Exhibition.* PROKOFIEV: *Piano Sonata No. 7.* TCHAIKOVSKY: *The Seasons*: excerpts.
*** Dutton CDSA 6802.

There are few keyboard warhorses to compare with Mussorgsky's *Pictures at an Exhibition*. Quite apart from the virtuoso demands of piano writing with its chunky chords that rarely fit under the fingers, there is always the colourful rivalry of the ever-popular orchestral arrangement by Ravel. It says much not just for the brilliant technique but also the artistry of the American pianist, Ingrid Jacoby, that she so clarifies textures, with pedal lightly used, making the writing seem far more pianistic than usual, yet retaining the vivid pictorial detail and the tension and excitement of the final sequence leading to the culminating evocation of *The Great Gate at Kiev*. The Prokofiev *Sonata*, another warhorse, arguably his most striking piano work, demands great virtuosity, yet brings similar clarity and incisiveness, with four of the most memorable movements from Tchaikovsky's suite, *The Seasons*, as an agreeable interlude. Exceptionally vivid piano-sound.

John, Keith (organ)

'*Great European Organs No. 10*': Tonhalle, Zurich: MUSSORGSKY (trans. John): *Pictures at an Exhibition.* ALAIN: *3 Danses (Joies; Deuils; Luttes).*
*** Priory PRCD 262.

Keith John has made his own transcription of Mussorgsky's *Pictures* – and pretty remarkable it sounds. Only the pieces like *Tuileries* that require pointed articulation come off less well than on orchestra or piano, but *Gnomus* and *Bydlo* and, especially, the picture of the two Polish Jews are all remarkably powerful, while the closing sequence of *Catacombs*, *The Hut on fowl's legs* and *The Great Gate of Kiev* are superb. The three Alain pieces make a substantial encore. This is as much a demonstration CD as an orchestral version of the Mussorgsky.

'*Great European Organs No. 26*': Gloucester Cathedral: STANFORD: *Fantasia and Toccata in D min., Op. 57.* REGER: *Prelude and Fugue in E, Op. 56/1.* SHOSTAKOVICH: *Lady Macbeth of Mtsensk: Passacaglia.* SCHMIDT: *Chaconne in C min.* RAVANELLO: *Theme and Variations in B min.*
*** Priory PRCD 370.

Keith John, having shown what he can do with Mussorgsky, turns his attention here to little-known nineteenth- and twentieth-century organ pieces. The programme is imaginatively chosen and splendidly played – indeed, the bravura is often thrilling – and most realistically recorded on the superb Gloucester organ. Both the Schmidt *Chaconne* and Ravanello *Theme and Variations* are fine works, and the Shostakovich *Passacaglia*, an opera entr'acte, was originally conceived as a work for organ.

'*Toccata!*' (organ of St Mary's, Woodford): BACH/BUSONI: *Partita No. 2 in D min., BWV 1004: Chaconne* (trans. K. John). BACH/RACHMANINOV:

Partita No. 3 in E, BWV 1006: suite (trans. K. John). GUILLOU: *Sinfonietta.* HEILLER: *Tanz-Toccata.*
(M) ★★★ Priory PRCD 002.

It was a most imaginative idea to use Busoni's arrangement of Bach's famous *D minor Partita for Unaccompanied Violin* as a basis for an organ transcription, and the result is like nothing you have ever heard before – especially when Keith John gets cracking on the pedals. The three excerpts from the *E major Partita* (as originally transcribed by Rachmaninov) are hardly less successful: how well the opening *Prelude* sounds on the organ, and one can forgive Keith John's affectionately mannered touch on the famous *Gavotte*. We then have a dramatic, almost bizarre change of mood and colour with Jean Guillou's 'neoclassical' (more 'neo' than 'classical') *Sinfonietta*. Even though it opens with a Bachian flourish, its colouring and atmosphere are highly exotic, the austere central *Allegretto* leading to a somewhat jazzy but naggingly insistent, partly contrapuntal and plangent *Gigue*. Heiller's *Tanz-Toccata*, with its complex rhythms and chimerical changes of time-signature, finally brings a positive link with Stravinsky's *Rite of Spring* during the insistent motoric final pages. After his remarkable Bach performances, Keith John's kaleidoscopic registration here shows how adaptable and versatile is the modern (1972) organ at St Mary's, Woodford.

Johnson, Emma (clarinet)

'*A Clarinet Celebration*' (with Back, piano): WEBER: *Grand duo concertante; Variations concertantes.* BURGMULLER: *Duo.* GIAMPIERI: *Carnival of Venice.* SCHUMANN: *Fantasy pieces, Op. 73.* LOVREGLIO: *Fantasia de concerto, La Traviata.*
★★★ ASV CDDCA 732.

ASV have reissued and repackaged Emma Johnson's outstanding 72-minute collection, dating from 1990. It is still at full price but is worth it. These are party pieces rather than encores, all of them drawing electric sparks of inspiration from this winning young soloist. Even in such virtuoso nonsense as the Giampieri *Carnival of Venice* and the Lovreglio *Fantasia* Johnson draws out musical magic, while the expressiveness of Weber and Schumann brings heartfelt playing, with phrasing creatively individual. Gordon Back accompanies brilliantly, and the sound is first rate.

'*British Clarinet Music*' (with Martineau (piano); (i) Howard (soprano)): IRELAND: *Fantasy Sonata in E flat.* VAUGHAN WILLIAMS: *6 Studies in English Folksong;* (i) *3 Vocalises for Soprano Voice and Clarinet.* BAX: *Clarinet Sonata.* BLISS: *Pastoral;* (i) *2 Nursery Rhymes.* STANFORD: *Clarinet Sonata.*
★★★ ASV CDDCA 891.

Stanford's *Sonata* has the usual Brahmsian flavour but uses an Irish lament for the expressive central *Adagio*; then the finale has the best of both worlds by combining both influences. Vaughan Williams's *Six Studies in English Folksong* (1927) are beguilingly evocative, while the *Vocalises* for soprano voice and clarinet are brief but rather touching; they were written in the last year of the composer's life. Both the Bax two-movement *Sonata* and the Ireland *Fantasy Sonata* are fine works, and Bliss's *Pastoral* is wartime nostalgia, written while the composer was in France during the First World War. Needless to say, Emma Johnson plays everything with her usual spontaneity and musicianship, and she has a fine partner in Malcolm Martineau, while Judith Howard's contribution is pleasingly melismatic. Excellent, atmospheric recording, made in the London Henry Wood Hall.

Kang, Dong-Suk (violin), Pascal Devoyon (piano)

French Violin Sonatas: DEBUSSY: *Sonata in G min.* RAVEL: *Sonata in G.* POULENC: *Violin Sonata.* SAINT-SAENS: *Sonata No. 1 in D min.*
⊶ (BB) ★★★ Naxos 8.550276.

One of the jewels of the Naxos catalogue, this collection of four of the finest violin sonatas in the French repertoire is self-recommending. The stylistic range of this partnership is evident throughout: they seem equally attuned to all four composers. This is warm, freshly spontaneous playing, given vivid and realistic digital recording in a spacious acoustic. A very real bargain.

Katchen, Julius (piano)

The Art of Julius Katchen

Volume 1: BEETHOVEN: *Piano Concertos Nos. 1–3; 5 (Emperor), Rondo in B flat for Piano and Orchestra* (with LSO, Piero Gamba).
(B) ★★★ Double Decca 460 822-2 (2).

Volume 2: BEETHOVEN: *Piano Concerto No. 4, Op. 58* (with LSO, Gamba); *Choral Fantasia, Op. 80* (also with LSO Ch.). MOZART: *Piano Concertos No. 13 in C, K.415* (with New SO of London, Maag); *20 in D min., K.466; 25 in C, K.503* (with Stuttgart CO, Karl Münchinger).
(B) ★★★ Double Decca 460 825-2 (2).

Volume 3: BRAHMS: *Piano Concertos Nos. 1* (with LSO, Monteux); *2* (with LSO, Ferencsik). SCHUMANN: *Piano Concerto in A min.* (with Israel PO, Kertész); *Fantasia in C, Op. 17.*
(B) ★★★ Double Decca 460 828-2 (2).

Volume 4: LISZT: *Piano Concertos Nos. 1–2* (with LPO, Argenta). *Mephisto Waltz No. 1; Harmonies poétiques et religieuses: Funérailles; Hungarian*

Rhapsody No. 12. GRIEG: *Piano Concerto in A min., Op. 16* (with Israel PO, Kertész). BALAKIREV: *Islamey.* MUSSORGSKY: *Pictures at an Exhibition.*
(B) *** Double Decca stereo/mono 460 831-2 (2).

Volume 5: TCHAIKOVSKY: *Piano Concerto No. 1 in B flat min., Op. 23.* LISZT: *Hungarian Fantasia* (both with LSO, Gamba). PROKOFIEV: *Piano Concerto No. 3 in C, Op. 26* (with LSO, Kertéz). RACHMANINOV: *Piano Concerto No. 2 in C min., Op. 18* (with LSO, Solti). *Rhapsody on a Theme of Paganini, Op 43.* DOHNANYI: *Variations on a Nursery Theme* (both with LPO, Boult).
(B) *** Double Decca mono/stereo 460 834-2 (2).

Volume 6: GERSHWIN: *Piano Concerto in F* (with Mantovani and his Orchestra). BARTOK: *Piano Concerto No. 3.* RAVEL: *Piano Concerto in G; Piano Concerto for the Left Hand* (all with LSO, Kertész). BRITTEN: *Diversions for Piano (left hand) and Orchestra, Op. 21* (with SO, composer).
(B) *** Double Decca 460 837-2 (2).

Katchen's very distinguished 15-year recording career spanned the end of the mono LP era and the first decade of stereo. He was for most of that time Decca's star pianist, and these six Double Deccas are part of a complete survey of his Decca recordings on a series of well-filled Doubles with the brightly lit transfers adding to the vividness, and the piano timbre of consistent high quality. However, as yet, the last two volumes are only available in their original Australian issues. Katchen's range of repertoire was as wide as his technique was brilliant, and he never delivered an unstimulating or unspontaneous performance. For his concerto recordings Decca provided him with a fine roster of conductors. The unexpected choice of Mantovani for the early LP of Gershwin's *Concerto in F* worked quite well, for he had fine soloists in his orchestra, and many will relish the compilations offered here on Volumes 5 and 6, particularly as the wonderfully imaginative performance of Britten's *Diversions* (with the composer conducting) is an indispensable highlight.

In the Beethoven concertos Katchen's partnership with Gamba worked particularly well, and the performances are fresh and commanding. Tempi are often on the fast side, but Katchen keeps a classical firmness and provides the necessary contrast in relaxed, poetic accounts of slow movements and sparkling readings of finales. In No. 1 he uses the longest and most impressive of Beethoven's own cadenzas for the first movement. The opening atmosphere of No. 4 is beautifully caught, while the *Emperor* is characteristically full of animal energy. The first and last movements are taken at a spanking pace, but not so that Katchen sounds at all rushed. Plainly he enjoyed himself all through, and in the very relaxed slow movement he seems to be coaxing the orchestra into matching his own delicacy, with the tension admirably sustained. The *Rondo* and the

Choral Fantasia, too, are both very successful.

In the Brahms *First Concerto* the solo playing is superb, especially in the first movement, and Katchen is well partnered by Monteux (with the LSO), as he is by Ferencsik in No. 2, where he again gives an impassioned and exciting account of the solo piano part, here combining tremendous drive with the kind of ruminating delicacy Brahms so often calls for. These recordings are less successfully balanced than the Beethoven. However, in the Grieg and Schumann *Concertos* the sound is clear and brilliant, with both performances strong, any willfulness tempered by a natural flexibility and the feeling for the music's poetry. Kertész provides plenty of life in the accompaniments. In Schumann, Katchen's virtuosity does not eschew romantic charm, the first movement more rhapsodical than usual, and throughout there is a pervading freshness. The Mozart performances, with Münchinger not always an ideally resilient conductor, yet have character (as does the solo sonata), and in the *D minor* there is strength as well as plenty of life and spirit.

In Liszt, Katchen is in his element. He is superb in the *E flat Concerto* and by any standards these are commanding performances. The Bartók, Prokofiev and Ravel *Concertos* are among his finest records, with Kertész especially compelling in his native Hungarian music, the playing combining intensity with brilliance and sparkle, and the Rachmaninov and Dohnányi performances are hardly less celebrated. The Tchaikovsky *Piano Concerto* offers equally prodigious pianism, but is alas mono, and although the recording is basically rich and full, and the piano timbre is real and well balanced, the high violin timbre is thin and glassy, though not disastrously so, except perhaps at the very opening. Some might feel that in the finale Gamba broadens the reprise of the grand tune rather more than necessary. An exciting account just the same. Of the other solo performances Katchen's almost unbelievable technique is well demonstrated in Balakirev's *Islamey.* Even in an age of technicians few pianists could play the piece like this. The *Mephisto Waltz* and Mussorgsky *Pictures* are also pretty remarkable, but in the latter the rather dry mono sound does not help Katchen to colour the music as he might. *Goldenberg and Schmuyle* and the *Chicks* are highlights, but the finale could ideally be more expansive.

Volume 7: BEETHOVEN: *Piano Sonatas Nos. 23 in F min. (Appassionata), Op. 57; 32 in C min., Op. 111. 33 Variations on a Waltz by Diabelli, Op. 129; 6 Bagatelles, Op. 126; Polonaise in C, Op. 89.*
MOZART: *Piano Sonatas Nos. 13 in B flat, K.388; 16 in C, K.545.* .
*** Australian Decca Double mono/stereo 466 714-2 (2).

Katchen recorded his impressive (mono) *Appassionata* in 1956 and his sparkling account of the *Diabelli Variations* (a work that proved ideal for his pianistic talents) in 1961, but Opus 111 dates from the year before his death. Already the cancer which would kill him was taking its toll, for the playing, although still prodigious, is no longer immaculate. But the performance has great power, total spontaneity and a profound searching inner quality in the *Adagio*. The Mozart sonatas, also from 1956 and mono, are sheer delight, wonderfully crisp and stylish, yet with just the right degree of underlying expressive feeling. All the recordings have come up well and Katchen is given a very real presence.

Volume 8: SCHUBERT: *Fantasy in C (Wanderer), D.760.* SCHUMANN: *Carnaval, Op. 9; Toccata in C, Op. 7; Arabeske in C, Op. 18.* DEBUSSY: *Suite bergamasque: Clair de lune.* FALLA: *El amor brujo: Ritual Fire Dance.* CHOPIN: *Piano Sonatas Nos. 2 in B flat min. (Funeral March), Op. 36; 3 in B min., Op. 58; Fantaisie-impromptu, Op. 66; Polonaise No. 6 in A flat (Heroic), Op. 53.* MENDELSSOHN: *Rondo capriccioso, Op. 14.* LISZT: *Concert Paraphrase of Mendelssohn's 'On Wings of Song'.* BACH, arr. HESS: *Jesu, Joy of Man's Desiring.*
★★★ Australian Decca Double mono/stereo 466 717-2 (2).

Volume 8 is another Double showing the remarkable range of a great pianist who died sadly young at the age of 42. The performance of *Carnaval* is striking for its skittishness as well as its infinite variety of mood and colour, while the *Arabeske* has a delightful sense of fantasy. The *Wanderer Fantasia* also shows both Katchen's imaginative range and his feeling for Schubert. But what stands out here is the Chopin, powerful yet with a natural lyrical feeling. His virtuosity comes into play too in the dazzling account of the *Fantaisie-impromptu*, while the finale of the *B flat minor Sonata* is quite breathtaking in its evenness and clarity, and the *Scherzo* of the *B minor* is just as remarkable in its clean articulation. Yet both slow movements are deeply felt. The famous *A flat Polonaise* is arresting and the two Mendelssohn pieces which follow show in turns sparkling dexterity and an unsentimentally bold romantic impulse, while Debussy's *Clair de lune* has an exquisite simplicity. The sound throughout is excellent.

Kayath, Marcelo (guitar)

'*Spanish Guitar Music*': TARREGA: *Prelude in A min.; Capricho arabe; Recuerdos de la Alhambra.* GRANADOS: *La Maja de Goya.* ALBENIZ: *Granada; Zambra; Granadina; Sevilla; Mallorca.* TORROBA: *Prelude in E; Sonatina; Nocturno.* RODRIGO: *Zapateado.* TRAD.: *El Noy de la mare.*
(BB) ★★★ Regis RRC 1122.

Following the success of his first Latin-American recital (see below), Marcelo Kayath gives us an equally enjoyable and spontaneous Spanish collection, full of colour. By grouping music by several

major composers, he provides a revealing mix. The three fine Tárrega pieces include the famous *Recuerdos*, played strongly; then come five of Granados's most evocative and tuneful geographical evocations, while the Tórroba group includes the attractive three-movement *Sonatina*. After the vibrant Rodrigo miniature, he closes with the hauntingly memorable *El Noy de la mare*. The recording affords him a realistic presence in a pleasing acoustic.

'*South American Guitar Classics*': PONCE: *Valse; Preámbulo e allegro; Gavotte.* PIAZZOLA: *La muerte del angel.* BARRIOS: *Mazurka appassionata; Danza Paraguaya; Tremolo, Una limosna por el amor de Dios; Tango No. 2; Study in A (Las abejas); Vals, Op. 8/3; Choror de Saudade; Julia Florida.* LAURO: *Vals Venezolanus No. 2; El negrito; El marabino.* REIS: *Si eia preguntar.* VILLA-LOBOS: *5 Preludes.*
(BB) ★★★ Regis RRC 1149.

Marcelo Kayath's inspirational accounts of the Villa-Lobos *Preludes* can stand comparison with the finest performances on record, and he is equally at home in the extended programme of the distinctive music of Barrios, playing with the lightest touch and a nice feeling for rubato, notably so in the *Vals*. He is a fine advocate too of the engaging Lauro pieces. Indeed, he plays everything here with consummate technical ease and the most appealing spontaneity. The recording, made in a warm but not too resonant acoustic, is first class.

Kempff, Wilhelm (piano)

'*Classic Archive*': *Recitals at the Paris ORTF, and Besançon:* SCHUMANN: *Arabeske in C, Op. 18; Papillons, Op. 2; Davidsbündlertänze, Op. 6.* BEETHOVEN: *Piano Sonatas Nos. 14 in C sharp min. (Moonlight), Op. 27/2; 17 in D min. (Tempest), Op. 31/2; 27 in E min., Op. 90.*
✿ ★★★ EMI **DVD** DVB 490447-9. (Directors: Gérard Herzog, Denise Billon, Claude Ventura & Yvonne Courson). Bonus: SCHUMANN: *Novelleten, Op. 21/1.* BARTOK: *Out of Doors, Nos. 4 & 5* (Dino Ciani).

This DVD is pure gold. Even though the Schumann items (from 1961 and 1963) and the Beethoven *Tempest Sonata* (1969) are in black and white, the latter has a brief voice-over as Kempff begins to play, and by some oversight the recording misses out most of the exposition of the first movement, yet the visual images are very remarkable; and when we see the *Moonlight Sonata* and the *E minor*, Op. 90, in colour, the effect is totally compelling. As we guessed from his records, Kempff's concentration is visionary: he is utterly held inside the music; there is absolutely no attempt to play to the audience. He plays for the composer, his *pianissimos* raptly gentle, his *fortissimos* unexpectedly strong. His affinity with both Schumann and Beethoven is legendary, and now we can enjoy the unassertive genius of his art and watch his curiously stubby fingers coaxing magical sounds from the keyboard. His face is often almost expressionless, yet with just occasionally a hint of a smile of pleasure at a special turn of phrase or modulation. The recording is generally very good, catching a full range of dynamic, and the camera angles are simple, with the changes of perspective sensibly managed. There is a curious black-and-white bonus of Dino Ciani playing (and playing very well) Schumann and Bartók, but neither the photography or the sound is distinguished.

Recital in Queen Elizabeth Hall, London, 5 June 1969: BACH: *Chromatic Fantasia and Fugue, BWV 903.* BEETHOVEN: *Sonata No. 22 in F, Op. 54.* SCHUBERT *Sonata No. 11 in F min., D.625; 3 Klavierstücke, D.946; Impromptus Nos. 3 & 4, D.899/3–4.*

(M) *** BBC (ADD) BBCL 4045.

This recital was one of the finest examples of Kempff's inspired pianism that London ever heard. He was still at the height of his powers, and inspiration did not desert him on this occasion. Brendel spoke of his *cantabile* with reverence as being the essence of his art, which made him such a great Schubert interpreter and makes his *Klavierstücke* so special. (Oddly enough, the cover does not refer to the *F minor Sonata*.) But the Bach and Beethoven are hardly less magnificent, and they enhance the value of this invaluable BBC archive series. This playing really is the stuff of legends.

Piano Transcriptions (arr. Kempff): BACH: *Chorale Preludes: Es ist gewisslich an der Zeit, BWV 307 & 734; Nun komm der Heiden Heiland, BWV 659; Befehl du deine Wege, BWV 727; In dulci jubilo, BWV 751; Wachet auf, BWV 140; Ich ruf' zu dir, BWV 639; Jesus bleibet meine Freude, BWV 147/6. Cantatas Nos. 29: Sinfonia, BWV 147: Herz und Mund und Tat und Leben: Jesu, Joy of Man's Desiring. Flute Sonata in E flat, BWV 1031: Siciliano. Harpsichord Concerto No. 5 in F min., BWV 1056: Largo.* HANDEL: *Minuet in G min.* GLUCK: *Orfeo ed Euridice: ballet music.* J. S. BACH: *English Suite No. 3 in G min.; French Suite No. 5 in G, BWV 816.*

**(*) Australian DG Eloquence (ADD) 457 624-2.

The Kempff magic is never entirely absent from any of this pianist's recordings, but some may feel that it makes its presence felt rather unevenly in this recital. Several of the *Chorale Preludes* are played in a rather studied way. The presentation of *Wachet auf* is very firm and clear, and the background embroidery precisely articulated, and *Jesu, Joy of Man's Desiring* has more extrovert projection than usual. The *Siciliano* from BWV 1031, however, is given an appealing lyrical flow, and the *Orfeo* excerpts are very beautiful. For this bargain release, the *English Suite No. 3* and the *French Suite No. 5* have been added, and they are first class in every way.

Kennedy, Nigel (violin), Lynn Harrell (cello)

Duos for Violin and Cello: RAVEL: *Sonata.* HANDEL: *Harpsichord Suite No. 7 in G min.: Passacaglia* (arr. HALVORSEN/PRESS). KODALY: *Duo.* BACH: *2-Part Invention No. 6 in E.*

⊕--➔ ✲ *** EMI 5 56963-2.

An extraordinarily successful collaboration between the extrovert Kennedy and the more reticent Harrell, in which the listener has the constant impression of inspirational live intercommunication, and no suggestion whatsoever of the recording studio. The Ravel *Sonata* opens with disarming simplicity and immediately takes off, producing an enormous intensity of feeling – whether in the sheer gutsy energy and fireworks of the *Très vif Scherzo*, or the veiled delicacy of the slow movement, begun very gently by Harrell.

The playing in the first movement of the masterly Kodály *Duo* is so closely and powerfully intertwined, so completely integrated in its ebb and flow of phrasing, dynamic and tension, that it is as if violin and cello were the flip sides of the same coin. The superb Handel *Passacaglia* is played with confident and captivating bravura and the programme ends coolly and satisfyingly with simple Bach polyphony, the interchange quite perfectly balanced. The recording is forward and gives the illusion of an extremely vivid presence, within an open acoustic.

King, Thea (clarinet), Clifford Benson (piano)

English Clarinet Music: STANFORD: *Sonata, Op. 29.* FERGUSON: *4 Short Pieces, Op. 6.* FINZI: *5 Bagatelles, Op. 23.* HURLSTONE: *4 Characteristic Pieces.* HOWELLS: *Sonata.* BLISS: *Pastoral.* REIZENSTEIN: *Arabesques.* COOKE: *Sonata in B flat.*

(B) *** Hyp. Dyad CDD 22027 (2).

This Hyperion Dyad aptly combines two separate recitals, now offered for the price of one. They were recorded at the beginning of the 1980s and are in many ways complementary. Stanford's *Clarinet Sonata* is clearly influenced by Brahms but has plenty of character of its own. The other works on the first disc are all appealingly communicative, lighter in texture and content, but well crafted.

The second CD opens with the Howells *Sonata*, among the finest written since Brahms, a warmly lyrical piece in two extended movements that bring out the instrument's varied colourings. Bliss's early *Pastoral* follows, thoughtful and unassuming, improvisatory in feeling. Reizenstein's short piece then acts as an interlude before the Cooke *Sonata*, strong but undemanding, with a darkly nostalgic *Adagio* and a chirpy finale. Thea King's warm, naturally expressive playing makes her an ideal advocate, not only for the music, but for her instrument; and her partner, Clifford Benson, is no less eloquent. Smooth, natural, analogue recording.

Kipnis, Igor (harpsichord)

'First Solo Recordings (1962)': BACH: French Suite No. 6 in E, BWV 817; Fantasia in G min., BWV 917; Prelude, Fugue and Allegro in E flat, BWV 998. Toccata in E min., BWV 914. HANDEL: Suite No. 5 in E (HWV 430). SOLER (attrib.): Fandango in D min. DUSSEK: The Sufferings of the Queen of France.
*** VAI Audio VAIA 1185.

With a photo of the young Kipnis as the frontispiece, this superb recital demonstrates a prodigious keyboard talent, and playing that is thoughtful, scholarly yet alive. His Bach is of a high calibre, and equally impressive is the Handel suite (which includes a breathtaking account of the Harmonious blacksmith). Soler's extended Fandango is equally brilliant and diverting, and he ends with his own edition of Dussek's vividly pictorial programmatic fantasia, describing the suffering, imprisonment and execution of Marie Antoinette – played with great imaginative flair, and bravura. The harpsichord is not named, but it is a most attractive instrument, with a wide range of colour, and is most naturally recorded.

Kissin, Evgeni (piano)

'Carnegie Hall Début' (30 September 1990), Highlights: LISZT: Etude d'exécution transcendante No. 10; Liebestraum No. 3; Rhapsodie espagnole. SCHUMANN: Abegg Variations, Op. 1; Etudes symphoniques, Op. 13; Widmung (arr. LISZT).
*** BMG/RCA 09026 61202-2.

Evgeni Kissin has phenomenal pianistic powers; this is a tour de force not only in terms of technical prowess but also in sheer artistry. Both sets of Schumann Variations are remarkable. The Liszt Rhapsodie espagnole is played with superb bravura. Kissin's range of colour and keyboard command throughout are dazzling. The Carnegie Hall was packed and the recording balance, while a bit close, is perfectly acceptable. The excitement of the occasion is conveyed vividly.

BEETHOVEN: Piano Sonata No. 14 in C sharp min. (Moonlight), Op. 27/2. BRAHMS: Variations on a Theme of Paganini, Op. 35. FRANCK: Prélude, chorale et fugue.
*** RCA 09026 68910-2.

Strongly projected playing from this outstanding (and still young) artist. There is impressive concentration in the Beethoven, an effortless virtuosity in the Brahms, and great poetic feeling in the Franck. Everything here bears witness to a powerful musical mind allied to consummate pianistic mastery. Excellent recorded sound.

Kocsis, Zoltán (piano)

BEETHOVEN: Sonata No. 27 in E min., Op. 90. SCHUBERT: Sonata No. 7 in E min., D.566. BARTOK: Sonata, Sz80; For Children: excerpts. KURTAG: Games: excerpts. LISZT: Hungarian Rhapsody No. 5 in E min.; Années de pèlerinage: Les Jeux d'eau à la Villa d'Este. Sunt lacrymae rerum; Czárdás macabre. (Recorded live at La Roque d'Anthéron, France, 29 July 2002. (Video Director: János Darvas.)
*** Naïve DVD DR 2100 AV103.

Kocsis may have lost his youthful appearance but certainly none of his ability to mesmerize an audience. At 90 minutes this recital is more generous in length than Lugansky's but no less rewarding musically. Recorded at La Roque d'Anthéron in the heart of Provence when Kocsis had just turned fifty, his Bartók has tremendous fire and virtuosity, while the Beethoven and Schubert exhibit a satisfying blend of classicism and sensitivity. The Liszt, too, has effortless technique and naturalness of utterance to commend it. As with the other recitals we have heard in this series, the sound has superb clarity and definition, and the camerawork is altogether exemplary. A most worthwhile issue that can be recommended to all admirers of this artist and to all lovers of the piano.

Kogan, Leonid (violin)

'Classic Archive': BACH: Violin Partita in D min., BWV 1004: Sarabande. HANDEL: Violin Sonata in E, HWV 373. DEBUSSY: Beau soir. SHOSTAKOVICH: Preludes, Op. 24/10, 15, 16 & 24 (with Andrei Mytnik). BRAHMS: Hungarian Dance No. 17. PAGANINI: Cantabile. FALLA: Suite populaire espagnole (with Naum Walter, piano). LECLAIR: Sonata for 2 Violins in C, Op. 3/3 (with Elizaveta Gilels-Kogan).
(***) EMI DVD 492834-9 – BEETHOVEN: Violin Concerto. (**(*))

This is even more rewarding than the Beethoven Concerto, because the BBC recordings from 1962 do full justice to the great tonal refinement Kogan commanded. They were produced by Walter Todds, whose direction of the cameras is a model of unobtrusiveness and discretion. The Handel has seamless phrasing and a musicality that is a joy in itself, and Beau Soir and the four Shostakovich Preludes in Dmitri Tziganov's transcriptions are no less beguiling. Andrei Mytnik is a splendid partner, and the overall sound is hardly less refined in the 1968 Paris recordings (Brahms, Falla and Paganini). Kogan's stage presence may lack charm but he saves that quality for his music-making. There is a bonus in the form of a 1963 recording of a Leclair *Sonata for Two Violins* which he recorded with his wife (the sister of Emil Gilels). There is a good accompanying essay from Tully Potter.

Koh, Jennifer (violin), Reiko Uchida (piano)

'*Violin Fantasies*': Ornette COLEMAN: *Trinity.* SCHOENBERG: *Phantasy, Op. 47.* SCHUBERT: *Fantasy in C, D.934.* SCHUMANN: *Fantasie in C, Op. 131.*
*** Cedille CDR 90000 073.

Jennifer Koh, winner of the 1994 Tchaikovsky Competition, offers an unusual and attractive grouping of works, based on the idea of a Fantasy, the most flexible of forms. The warmth and imagination of her playing consistently illuminate pieces that by the very freedom of their structure need a positive hand to hold them together. This she does admirably, with the help of an ideally matched partner in the pianist, Reiko Uchida, wonderfully crisp and agile in piano writing that is not always grateful for the player. The Schubert, with its central set of variations on the song, 'Sei mir gegrüsst', fares least well, partly because of the ungainly piano part; but that leads to magnetic, often passionate accounts of the other three pieces. The Schumann *Fantasie in C* was one of his last works, written for the young Joachim, and here played in the composer's own piano transcription of the orchestral part, while Schoenberg's *Phantasy* was the last of his instrumental works, for which the piano part was added almost as an afterthought. *Trinity*, for unaccompanied violin, has the jazz musician Ornette Coleman forsaking his usual idiom in a lyrical meditation with folk-like overtones. Excellent recording.

Kremer, Gidon (violin)

Violin Sonatas: BEETHOVEN: *Sonatas Nos. 1–9* (complete). SCHUMANN: *Sonatas Nos. 1–2.* BARTOK: *Sonata for Violin and Piano No. 1.* JANACEK: *Sonata.* MESSIAEN: *Theme and Variations for Violin and Piano.* PROKOFIEV: *Sonatas Nos. 1–2; 5 Mélodies, Op. 35 bis* (all with Argerich). BRAHMS: *Sonatas Nos. 1–3.* BUSONI: *Sonata No. 2 in E min., Op. 36a* (both with Afanassiev). Richard STRAUSS: *Sonata in E flat, Op. 18* (with Maisenberg).
(B) ** DG 474 648-2 (8).

Kremer's partnership with Martha Argerich proved to be very propitious in Beethoven and Schumann, and their volatile Beethoven cycle is highly praised in our main volume, notably for its freshness and spontaneity, as are the Schumann *Sonatas*, which are reflective and mercurial by turns.

The triptych of Bartók, Janáček and Messiaen is

also very successful, the Bartók played with great expressive intensity, enormous range of colour and effortless virtuosity, while the Janáček again displays great imaginative intensity and power. The Messiaen *Variations*, an early work, is rarer, and here the music's fervour is well captured.

However, these artists are less successful in Prokofiev, where subtle differences of dynamics or characterization do not detain them more than cursorily and Prokofiev's lyricism takes second place to considerations of virtuosic display. The recordings, however, are excellent.

For the Brahms and Busoni *Sonatas* Kremer formed a partnership with Valery Afanassiev which proved much less fortunate. Not that there is any doubt as to their artistry and accomplishment, but their approach is so studied as to be self-conscious; in the opening of the *A major Sonata*, for example, the playing has enormous tonal refinement, but the expressive hesitations in the lead into the second subject group are surely excessive. The first three minutes of the *G major* are beautifully played, it is true, but the way in which these artists hold back just before the end of the exposition through to the return of the G major theme is unacceptably wilful. There is little difference between the *Allegro* and the ensuing *Adagio* of the *G minor*, so disruptive are the rubati and so slow the tempi that the music is robbed of any sense of forward movement.

These artists then follow on with another indulgent performance – of Busoni's *Second Sonata*, which is a one-movement piece, dating from 1898, with a *Langsam* opening (though not as langsam as it is in their hands), a *Presto*, and a most beautiful *Andante* section leading to a set of variations, where they are heard at their best.

Fortunately, Kremer's partnership with Oleg Maisenberg in the Richard Strauss *Sonata* is more successful. If these artists fail to find the fullest romantic intensity which distunguishes both the Repin/Berezovsky and Kyung Wha Chung versions, their performance is still enjoyable – and especially so in the brilliant finale. As throughout, the recording is excellent, but this compilation is difficult to recommend as a whole, except to Kremer's admirers.

Labèque, Katia and Marielle (piano duo)

'*Encore!*': A. BERIO: *Polka; Maria Isabella (Waltz); La Primavera (Mazurka).* BACH: *Jesu, Joy of Man's Desiring* (arr. HESS). GERSHWIN: *Preludes Nos. 1–3; Promenade (Walking the Dog).* STRAVINSKY: *Tango; Waltz.* L. BERIO: *Wasserklavier.* BRAHMS: *Waltz in A flat.* TCHAIKOVSKY: *The Seasons: June.* BERNSTEIN: *West Side Story: Jets' song; America.* JOPLIN: *Bethena (Ragtime Waltz); The Entertainer.* JAELL: *Valse.* BARTOK: *New Hungarian Folksong.* SCHUMANN: *Abendlied.*
*** Sony SK 48381.

The Labèque sisters have never made a better record than this; the playing scintillates, especially the Bernstein and Stravinsky items, while the Labèques' Scott Joplin is admirably cool and the account of Myra Hess's arrangement of the famous Bach chorale is gentle and quite beautiful. Luciano Berio's evocative *Wasserklavier* is a real lollipop, but the surprise is the selection of four catchy and often boisterous pieces by his grandfather, Adolfo, a church organist 'of doubtful faith' (according to his grandson); Luciano gives his imprimatur to the lively Labèque performances, even while he feels that their 'modern and uninhibited pianism' might not have suited his more conventional grandfather.

Landowska, Wanda (harpsichord)

'*Portrait*': F. COUPERIN: *La favorite; Les moissonneurs; Les Langueurs-Tendres; Le Gazouillement; La Commère; Le Moucheron; Les Bergeries; Les Tambourins; Les Fastes de la grande ménestrandise; Le Dodo, ou l'amour au berceau; Musette de Taverny; Les Folies françaises ou les Dominos; Les Calotins et les calotines; Les Vergers fleuris; Soeur Monique.* RAMEAU: *Suite in G min.* BACH: *Goldberg Variations, BWV 988.* HANDEL: *Suites Nos. 2 in F, HWV 427; 5 in E, HWV 430; 7 in G min., HWV 432.*

(M) (★★★) Grammofono 2000 mono AB 78715/6.

It is good to have a representative collection of the art of Wanda Landowska, who put the harpsichord back on the musical map in the twentieth century. She was not the first to try to do so; Violet Gordon Woodhouse actually made earlier acoustic recordings of some distinction, but it was Landowska's larger-than-life personality that soon made her a star. She gave her first performances on this instrument in 1903, and she toured Europe over the next two decades, visiting the United States from 1923 onwards. She persuaded Falla and Poulenc to write concertos (in 1926 and 1927 respectively) and had Pleyel build a large, modern instrument especially for her concerts.

Yet, as is readily apparent here, in the music of Couperin and Rameau she could articulate with the greatest delicacy (*La Poule* is delightful), and she kept her big guns in reserve for appropriate moments. Her *Goldberg Variations* was rightly celebrated, the playing robust when required but suitably restrained at other times. Her overall timing is surprisingly close to Leonhardt's but her approach, without any loss of seriousness of purpose, is freer and more imaginative, and her reprise of the *Aria* reminds one of Rosalyn Tureck in its delicacy of feeling.

The recordings of French music were made in 1934, the *Goldberg* in 1933, and the quality is excellent, although in the French *pièces de clavecin* there are pitch differences between some items. The Handel *Suites* are a little more variable in sound, but still impressive, and in No. 5 *The Harmonious Blacksmith* (1935) strikes his anvil at first robustly but later with

varying degrees of delicacy: there is no more spontaneous account in the catalogue. In the *Overture* which opens Handel's *Seventh Suite*, Landowska flamboyantly sounds like a full orchestra, and she plays the closing *Passacaglia* with similar satisfying weight, but in between there is a wider range of dynamic. Above all, this great artist communicated her joy in everything she played, and these excellent transfers ensure that we fully share it.

Larrocha, Alicia de (piano)

'*Favourite Spanish encores*': Mateo ALBENIZ: *Sonata in D.* Isaac ALBENIZ: *Recuerdos de viaje: Puerta de tierra (Bolero); Rumores de la caleta (Malagueña), Op. 71/5–6; Pavana capricho, Op. 12; España: Tango; Malagueña, Op. 165/2–3. Suite española: Sevilla, Op. 47/2.* SOLER: *Sonatas: in G min.; D.* GRANADOS: *Danzas españolas: Nos. 5, Andaluza (Playera); 7, Valenciana (Calesera).* TURINA: *Danzas gitanas: Sacromonte, Op. 55/5. Danzas andaluzas: Zapateado, Op. 8/5.* MONTSALVATGE: *Concierto breve* (with RPO, Frühbeck de Burgos).

(M) ★★★ Decca (IMS) (ADD) 467 687-2.

An entirely delightful collection of lightweight Spanish keyboard music, played with such skill and simplicity that even the slightest music never becomes chocolate-boxy. The eighteenth-century classicism of the sonatas by Soler and Mateo Albéniz makes a splendid foil for the warmer romanticism of Isaac Albéniz and the vivid colours of Granados and Turina. The recording, made in the Kingsway Hall in 1976, offers very lifelike piano-tone, warm and natural. For the highly appropriate reissue in their 'Legends' series, Decca have added Xavier Montsalvatge's *Concierto breve*, which is dedicated to Alicia de Larrocha. She plays it here with authority and conviction and is sympathetically accompanied by the RPO under Frühbeck de Burgos. The work has great facility and an attractive rhythmic flair, and if its thematic substance is less than really distinguished, it is certainly pleasing, and the piquant finale comes off with exotic dash. The sheer quality of de Larrocha's playing makes for attractive listening, particularly when the sound is spectacularly brilliant in the way of Decca's vintage analogue recordings of the mid-1970s. Like the solo recital, it is splendidly transferred to CD.

LaSalle Quartet

Chamber Music of the Second Viennese School: BERG: *Lyric Suite; String Quartet, Op. 3.* SCHOENBERG: *String Quartets: in D; No. 1 in D min., Op. 7; No. 2 in F sharp min., Op. 10/3* (with Price); *No. 3, Op. 30; No. 4, Op. 37.* WEBERN: *5*

Movements, Op. 5; String Quartet (1905); *6*
Bagatelles, Op. 9; String Quartet, Op. 28.
(M) *** DG (IMS) 419 994-2 (4).

DG have compressed their 1971 five-LP set on to four
CDs, offering them at a reduced and competitive
price. They have also retained the invaluable and
excellent documentary study edited by Ursula
Rauchhaupt – which runs to 340 pages! It is almost
worth having this set for the documentation alone.
The LaSalle Quartet give splendidly expert performances, even if at times their playing seems a little
cool; and they are very well recorded. An invaluable
issue for all who care about twentieth-century music.

Lawson, Peter, and Alan MacLean
(piano duet)

English Music for Piano Duet: BERNERS: *Valses*
bourgeoises; Fantasie espagnole; 3 Morceaux.
LAMBERT: *Overture* (ed. Lane); *3 Pièces nègres pour*
les touches blanches. RAWSTHORNE: *The Creel.*
WALTON: *Duets for Children.* LANE: *Badinages.*
*** Troy TROY 142.

This collection centres on Lord Berners, who had a
recurring twinkle in the eye and loved to parody;
moreover his inspiration regularly casts a glance in the
direction of Satie and Poulenc, as the *Trois Morceaux*
readily demonstrate. Both Walton and Constant Lambert were his friends, admired his individuality and
came under his influence. Lambert's *Trois Pièces*
nègres have a Satiesque title, yet they are all the composer's own work: the *Siesta* is quite haunting and the
catchy *Nocturne* brings sparkling Latin-American
rhythmic connotations, far removed from Chopin.

The four engaging Rawsthorne miniatures,
inspired by Izaak Walton's *Compleat Angler*, fit
equally well into the programme. The Walton *Duets*
for Children have a disarming simplicity and often a
nursery rhyme bounce: *Hop Scotch* is particularly
delightful, and vignettes like *The Silent Lake* and
Ghosts will surely communicate very directly to
young performers. Walton's final *Galop* was arranged
by Philip Lane, who also provides four of his own
pieces to close the concert with a strongly Gallic
atmosphere. The performances by Peter Lawson and
Alan MacLean are strong on style yet also convey
affection. Excellent recording in a nicely resonant but
not muddy acoustic.

Leach, Joanna (piano)

'*Four Square*': SOLER: *Sonata No. 90 in F sharp.*
HAYDN: *Sonata in C, Hob XVI/1.* J.S. BACH: *Partita*
No. 1 in B flat: Prelude; Minuets I & II; Gigue.
MOZART: *Fantasia in D min., K.397; Sonata No. 11 in*
A, K.331. SCHUBERT: *Impromptu in A flat, D.899/4.*
MENDELSSOHN: *Songs Without Words, Op. 19/1.*
*** Athene CD 3.

There is no more convincing fortepiano recital than
this. Joanna Leach uses an 1823 Stodart with its
effectively dark lower register for the Soler *Sonata*,
then plays the same instrument later to show its
attractive upper range in an almost romantic performance of Mozart's *Fantasia in D minor*; she ends
the recital with the *A major Sonata*, K.331, with the
introductory variations particularly inviting. For the
Haydn, she chooses a 1789 Broadwood, a more brittle
sound, and for the Bach a very effective 1787 instrument made by Longman & Broderip. In the Schubert
and Mendelssohn pieces an 1835 D'Almaine brings us
that bit nearer a modern piano. Fine performances
throughout, and excellent recording. A fascinating
way of discovering what the modern piano's ancestors could do best.

Léner Quartet

HAYDN: *String Quartets: Nos. 76 in D min., Op.*
76/2: Andante; 77 in C (Emperor), Op. 76/3; 79 in D,
Op. 76/5 (2 versions).
(**) Rockport mono RR 5004.

HAYDN: *String Quartets Nos. 17 in F, Op. 3/5* (2
versions); *67 in D (Lark), Op. 64/5: Minuet.*
MOZART: *Divertimento No. 17 in D, K.334* (with
Aubrey & Dennis Brain).
(**) Rockport mono RR 5006.

SCHUBERT: *Octet in F, D.803* (with Draper, Aubrey
Brain, Hinchcliff, Hobday). SCHUMANN: *String*
Quartet No. 3 in A, Op. 41/3.
(**) Rockport mono RR 5008.

MOZART: *Oboe Quartet in F, K.370* (with
Goossens); *String Quartet No. 17 in B flat (Hunt),*
K.458; String Quintet No. 3 in G min., K.516 (with
d'Oliviera).
(**) Rockport mono RR 5010.

These are the first four CDs in what is to be a
complete reissue of all the Léner Quartet recordings
on CD. The scale of the enterprise is daunting, as the
Léners recorded no fewer than 210 shellac discs. The
planners of the series estimate that the final set will
run to 30 CDs. Only a few of their recordings are
currently available: the Brahms *Quartets*, the Mozart
and Brahms *Clarinet Quintets* and the Mozart *Oboe*
Quartet with Leon Goossens (also included here).
The Léners began recording in 1924 and were the first
to record a complete Beethoven cycle. One unusual
feature of this venture is to juxtapose their acoustic
recordings with later, electrical versions on the same
CD. The first disc brings Haydn's *Emperor Quartet*,
Op. 76, No. 3, made in 1935, and contrasts their 1924
and 1928 versions of the *D major Quartet*, Op. 76, No.
5. Similarly, the third disc brings two versions of the
Op. 3, No. 5 (now attributed to Roman Hofstetter).

Those who think of the Léner as oversweet in tone
with too much vibrato and cloying portamento

should hear the *Hunt Quartet*, recorded in 1924. The sound is frail and wanting in body, but the quartet's purity of style is quite striking. Later on, in the 1930s, Jenö Léner developed a much wider vibrato, witness the *D major Divertimento*, K.334, from 1939 (with Aubrey and Dennis Brain) and again in the *G minor Quintet*, K.516, of 1930, with Louis d'Oliviera as second viola. Contrasts between their approach in the same works are often quite marked. In the first movement of Op. 3, No. 5 they are faster in their 1924 acoustic recording, although the famous *Serenade* movement is slower in 1928 and much pulled around. The Schumann Quartet in A, Op. 41, No. 3, is wonderfully rhapsodic in feeling, with little sense of the bar-line. Indeed, this is the sort of approach that seems totally idiomatic. Léner shows great imagination and poetic feeling in the *Adagio*, and there is an aristocratic poise that distinguishes his playing throughout. His style is very personal, whether or not you like it, and, on its own terms, is completely natural in approach, with, above all, no playing to the gallery. The Schubert *Octet*, with such distinguished figures as Charles Draper and Aubrey Brain, has some lovely playing, though the sound is pretty frail. Allowances have to be made for the actual quality, but then that is the case throughout the set. Robert Philip in his *Grove* article rightly speaks of the 'unusually homogeneous blend' of the Léners and the 'extraordinary smoothness and finish of their performances'. What is equally striking are their matchless sense of legato, a sophisticated lyricism (some might say over-sophisticated) and a generally unhurried and civilized approach. An important project.

Leonhardt Consort, Gustav Leonhardt (director, and playing: harpsichord, organ, virginal, viol)

Leonhardt Edition

Gustav Leonhardt has made an exceptionally distinguished contribution to period-instrument performances of baroque music. During the 1960s he directed and performed in many first recordings for Das Alte Werk label, and it was appropriate that Teldec celebrated the fortieth anniversary of that label with a 21-disc Leonhardt Edition. The excellent Ensemble which bears his name always sought to make a sound which, although transparent, also had body, as well as being in believable period style. Similarly for his own many keyboard recordings, he chose instruments which would colour the music pleasingly as well as authentically.

Leonhardt's scholarship, his understanding of the finer points of baroque performance detail, not least ornamentation, showed a remarkable combination of musicality and scholarship. If his readings sometimes erred on the side of literal directness and sobriety, he could never be accused of self-regarding eccentricity, and it is apt that these reissued records

should carry with their documentation printed tributes from such current experts in the period-instrument field as Bob van Asperen and Ton Koopman. The set as a whole is now deleted but many of discs are still available separately.

BACH: **Harpsichord Concertos** (with (i) Brüggen (flute), Leonhardt (violin); (ii) Müller; (iii) Uittenbosch; (iv) Curtis; (v) van Wering). *Concertos*: (i) *in A min., for Flute, Violin and Harpsichord, BWV 1044; Nos. 2 in E; 3 in D; 4 in A; 5 in F min., for Solo Harpsichord, BWV 1053–6; 6 for Harpsichord and 2 Recorders in F, BWV 1057; 7 in G min.; 8 in D min., for Solo Harpsichord, BWV 1058–9; Double Harpsichord Concertos Nos.* (ii) *1 in C min., BWV 1060;* (iii) *2 in C, BWV 1061;* (ii) *3 in C min., BWV 1062;* (iii-iv) *Triple Harpsichord Concertos Nos. 1 in D min.; 2 in C, BWV 1063–4;* (ii-iii; v) *Quadruple Harpsichord Concerto in A min., BWV 1065.*

(M) *(*) Teldec (ADD) 3984 21350-2 (3).

The one clear drawback to this Edition as a complete set (apart from the curious omission of the *First Concerto*, BWV 1052) is Leonhardt's set of harpsichord concertos; this has many fine qualities, including Brüggen's contribution (immediately apparent in the *A minor Concerto*, BWV 1044), but it is surprisingly lacking in imagination and spontaneity. The recording is warm and resonant (comparable with the sound we usually expect from the Collegium Aureum) and reproduces smoothly, but inner clarity leaves much to be desired and the keyboard reproduction in the multiple concertos is much too opaque. In the solo works Leonhardt's steady – at times seemingly unrelenting – progress in allegros wearies the ear and, although he can be sensitive enough in slow movements (witness the famous *Largo* of the *F minor Concerto*), this is very disappointing, all things considered.

BACH: *Quodlibet*, **Canons, Chorales, Songs and Keyboard Works** (with Bylsma (cello), Giebel, Gilles, van t'Hoff, Runge): *Canons in 2 Parts, BWV 1075; in 7 (8) Parts, BWV 1078; in 4 Parts, BWV 1073; in 4 (5) Parts, BWV 1077;* (Keyboard) *Capriccio in B flat (sopra la lontananza del suo fratello dilettissimo), BWV 992; Preludes: in F, BWV 927; in E, BWV 937; in G min., BWV 929; in D, BWV 925; in C, BWV 939; Fugue in C, BWV 952; Prelude and Fugue in A min., BWV 895; Prelude and Fughetta in D min., BWV 899; Suite in F min., BWV 823. Quodlibet, BWV 524.* Arias: *Erbauliche Gedanken eines Tobackrauchers, BWV 515a; Gieb dich zufrieden und sie stille, BWV 511; Vergiss mein nicht, mein allerliebster Gott! BWV 505. Chorales: O Herzensangst, o Bangigkeit und Zagen! BWV 400; Nicht so traurig, nicht so sehr, BWV 384; Dir, dir Jehova, will ich singen, BWV 452; Was betrübst du dich, mein Herze, BWV 423; Wer nur den lieben Gott lässt walten (3 versions), BWV 691, BWV 434.*

(M) *** Teldec (ADD) 3984 21354-2.

Much of this material comes from Anna Magdalena's *Klavierbüchlein*, intended for use by Bach's sons: keyboard pieces, together with simple chorales and songs for domestic entertainment rather than public performance. They show another side of Bach, as a genial but painstaking family man, and the music brings out the best in Leonhardt, who plays the brief keyboard pieces in an appropriately light-hearted manner.

He gives a colourful account of the designedly programmatic *Capriccio in B flat* ('On the departure of a beloved brother'), personally announcing the title of each section in German. The brief *Canon in 2 parts* wittily introduces a recorder, while the *Canon in 7 (8) parts* fills out quickly and ends in mid-air.

The arias and chorales are agreeably outgoing. In *So oft ich meine Tobacks-Pfeife* (subtitled 'The edifying thoughts of a tobacco-smoker') Bert van t'Hoff (or Peter Runge – it is not quite clear which) genially reflects on Bach's 'contented puffing on my small pipe', while the serene *Gieb dich zufrieden und sie stille* ('Be of good cheer and hold your peace') is sung delightfully by Agnes Giebel. The chorale *Was betrübst du dich, mein Herz* ('Why are you sad, my heart?') touchingly appears to reflect on a family crisis.

But the highlight of the concert is the *Quodlibet* ('As you wish') for vocal quartet, which by definition is an informal, light-hearted piece, but here is a true musical joke, originally intended for performance at a wedding. The manuscript is incomplete (both the beginning and the end are missing) but what there is (about 10 minutes) is set to outrageous words which flit from image to image, not unlike Gilbert's famous Nightmare song, and ending with the observation, 'Oh what a delightful fugue this is!' The whole piece is captivating, especially when sung so freshly. To end the collection, Leonhardt returns to his more didactic Bach keyboard style for BWV 823, BWV 895 and BWV 899, but the closing *Fughetta* of the latter work is pleasingly jaunty. The recording throughout is excellent, and altogether this is a most entertaining concert.

English Consort and Keyboard Music: DOWLAND: *Pavan in C.* LAWES: *Suites Nos. 1 in C min.; 2 in F; Sonata No. 7 in D min.; Suite No. 3 in B flat: In nomine.* COPRARIO: *Fantasia; Suite.* BYRD: *Pavan; Galliard; Fantasia No. 3.* Thomas SIMPSON: *Ricercar: Bonny Sweet Robin.* Thomas LUPO: *Fantasia.* BYRD: *Pavan; Galliard; Miserere.* MORLEY: *Nancie; Fantasia.* John BULL: *Hexachord Fantasia; The Duchesse of Brunswick's Toye.* William RANDALL: *Dowland's Lachrymae; Galliard: Can't She Excuse my Wrongs.* TOMKINS: *Pavan; Galliard; A Sad Pavan for these Distracted Times.* GIBBONS: *Pavan.* FARNABY: *Fantasia; Spagnioletta.* William TISDALE: *Mrs Katherin Tregians Pavan.* ANON.: *A Toye.*

(M) ★★★ Teldec (ADD) 3984 21760-2 (2).

This two-CD compilation draws on three Das Alte Werk LPs from 1965–6 and 1970, and the result is an unusually comprehensive survey which gives an excellent overall picture of the various composers writing music in Elizabethan and Jacobean England. The programme opens appropriately with Byrd, a consort *Pavane*, and later we are to have a harpsichord *Pavane and Galliard* and two consort *Fantasias*. In between come the highly individual *Suites* of William Lawes, who was a member of the Chapel Royal and a very considerable contributor to early seventeenth-century consort music. His *In nomine* (taken from the *Third Suite*) is particularly eloquent. But the surprise is perhaps the music of William Coprario (Cooper), whose *Fantasia* (for two violins, viola, viol and cello) is very striking indeed, to be followed by a tuneful and light-hearted *Suite in Three Parts* and the equally engaging *Ricercar on Bonny Sweet Robin* by Thomas Simpson.

The first CD ends with Lupo's *Fantasia*, another piece of real quality. There could perhaps be more ornamentation in these performances, but on the whole they are in excellent taste and style. There is nothing anaemic about the string textures, nor are they edgy, while the playing itself has plenty of life and spirit. The recording is impeccable.

The music of Byrd again opens the second disc with a consort pavane and galliard to introduce his beautiful *Miserere*, which is most touchingly played by Leonhardt on a chamber organ. He continues with a series of keyboard pieces, alternating harpsichord (choosing between two different instruments) and virginal. All come from the Fitzwilliam Virginal Book, except for the Gibbons *Pavane* and the two pieces by Randall. Predictably fine are the Bull *Fantasia* and the three pieces by Thomas Tomkins: here Leonhardt changes instruments for the third, *A Sad Pavane for these Distracted Times.* Farnaby's jolly *Spagnioletta* makes a spirited contrast and the programme ends with an encore – a brief, anonymous *Toye*.

Consort Music: BIBER: *Harmonia artificiosa-ariosa: diversi mode accordata: Partita No. 3 in A; Mensa sonora: Part 3; Fidicinium sacro-profanum: Sonatas 3–6.* MUFFAT: *Armonico tributo: Sonata No. 2 in G min.* ROSENMULLER: *Sonata No. 7 a 4.* SCHEIDT: *Paduan a 4.* SCHMELZER: *Sacro-profanus concentus musicus: Sonatas Nos. 7, 9.*

(M) ★★★ Teldec (ADD) 3984 21761-2.

It was Leonhardt who introduced us (in the late 1960s) to much of Biber's instrumental music, the excellence of which is only now being fully explored. The best-known set is the *Harmonia artificiosa-ariosa*, a collection of seven *Partitas* or suites for strings (published posthumously), and here we are offered the *Third* with its remarkable finale, an elaborately decorated *Chaconne/Canon*.

The *Mensa sonora* sonatas (from 1680) are – as the title suggests – essentially homophonic, more concerned with richness of texture and harmony than with contrapuntal ingenuity. Again we are offered *Partita III*, in five movements, written for a modest chamber ensemble and continuo. The music is warmly expressive: even the fourth-movement *Chaconne* is mellow.

Four of the twelve *Fidicinium sacro-profanum Sonatas* follow. They were published three years later and are scored for 2 violins, 2 violas, 2 cellos and continuo. As their title suggests, contrast is the order of the day, with the expressive movements quite dolorous, while allegros are lively and light-hearted. The *Sixth Sonata* (the last here) opens quite solemnly, and Leonhardt fills out the texture with an organ continuo.

The following Muffat *Sonata* opens even more sombrely, but it becomes an inventive series of linked movements alternating Grave slow sections with buoyant allegros. The two Schmelzer *Sonatas* (1662) for two violins, viola and continuo seek contrast in the same way as Biber's music and are similarly entitled *Sacro-profanus concentus musicus*. They are of high quality, as is the briefer work by Johann Rosenmüller and the stately *Paduan* (Pavane) of Samuel Scheidt. As can be seen, all this music, much of which is well off the beaten track, comes from the same fertile period, and Leonhardt and his players (six in all) are persuasive advocates. They use period instruments which are tuned to seventeenth-century pitch, but the sounds they make are full-timbred, and expressive phrasing is not eccentric but warmly musical.

FROBERGER: **Organ and Harpsichord Works: Organ:** *Capriccio II; Fantasia III; Toccata XI alla levazione; Ricercar II; Canzona II.* **Harpsichord:** *Toccata IX; Suite XVIII; Toccata XVIII; Suite XII.*

(M) ★★★ Teldec (ADD) 3984 21762-2.

Froberger was a pupil of Frescobaldi and one of the most exploratory and inward-looking composers of the seventeenth century. Leonhardt, who is an authoritative guide, offers here two groups of pieces, the first five played on the now familiar eighteenth-century organ (at the Waalse Kerk, Amsterdam), and the second group on a modern harpsichord, copied from an Italian instrument from the same period. The opening organ *Capriccio* is joyously buoyant, but the *Chorale fantasia* is more thoughtful and in its steady progress anticipates Bach. The *Toccata alla levazione* has much of Frescobaldi's improvisatory feeling, while the *Ricercar II* brings a remarkably solemn profundity. The *Harpsichord Suites*, skilfully decorated, are more lively and outgoing and readily show the composer's resourceful melodic and harmonic flair. Most striking is the opening movement of the *Twelfth Suite*, which laments the death of King Ferdinand IV in 1654. The closing *Sarabande* has comparable regal dignity. Excellent recording of both instruments.

MONDONVILLE (with Frydén): *Violin Sonatas Op. 3, Nos. 1 in G min.; 2 in F; 3 in B; 4 in C; 5 in G; 6 in A.*

(M) ★★(★) Teldec (ADD) 3984 21765-2.

Mondonville's *Violin Sonatas* are important in that they helped the development away from the violin-plus-continuo style to the form as we know it today. Thus both instruments are given proper 'solo' parts to play, and they are often very florid parts. One might be forgiven for occasionally thinking that the composer had forgotten himself and allotted two accompaniment parts instead! But generally the music is inventive enough, and the disc has real historical interest in demonstrating the duet sonata when ideas concerning the marriage of two instruments were very much in the melting pot. Opus 3 dates from about 1734 and predates by 14 years the fascinating Opus 5 set, which also includes the human voice and which is listed and discussed in our main volume. The recording here, made in 1966, is good but is rather more forward than the earlier (1963) recording by these same artists of the Bach *Violin and Harpsichord Sonatas*. This means that the full timbre of Lars Frydén's baroque violin is less flattered, although he can still be serenely expressive in the *Arias* which form the slow movements – witness the fine flowing melody of *No. 4 in C major* – and Leonhardt's harpsichord (a Kirckman, made in London in 1766) is a little sharp-toned. But the two instruments are generally well balanced – and the players seem pretty sure of themselves. Tempi are often brisk and very lively (try the infectious *Giga* finale of that same *C major Sonata*).

Organ and Harpsichord Music: F. COUPERIN: *Messe à l'usage ordinaire des Paroisses: Offertoire sur les grands jeux. L'Art de toucher le clavecin: 8 Préludes.* Alessandro POGLIETTI: *Ricercar primi toni.* Nicolas DE GRIGNY: *Cromorne en taille à deux parties.* RAMEAU: *Pièces de clavecin.* ANON.: *Daphne; Resonet in laudibus.*

(M) ★★(★) Teldec (ADD) 3984 21766-2.

This collection creates a stimulating variety of timbres and textures from the various keyboard instruments which Leonhardt chooses. He first seeks a French association rather than a specific French accent in presenting the Couperin *Offertoire* rather grandly on the Müller organ at the Waalse Kerk (or French church) in Amsterdam, which dates originally from 1680. The instrument has clarity and all the necessary bite in the reeds. He then plays eight *Préludes* from *L'Art de toucher le clavecin* very stylishly and pleasingly on a copy of a Rück harpsichord by an eighteenth-century Dresden maker, C. A. Gräbner, which works equally well.

The solemn *Ricercar* by Alessandro Poglietti, an influential Italian who became organist at the Viennese Imperial Chapel, follows on yet another organ, which it suits admirably. Leonhardt then returns to Amsterdam to find an engaging registration for

Nicolas de Grigny's gentle *Cromorne en taille.*

According to the documentation, the same Rück/ Gräbner harpsichord is used for the six *Pièces de clavecin* of Rameau as for the Couperin *Préludes,* but the recordings were made two years apart and the Rameau (from 1962) is mono, and is less easy on the ear: brighter, harsher and at times even clattery. But one soon adjusts, and the effect is certainly lively and characterful. The anonymous portrait of *Daphne* has a gentle melancholy, and for this Leonhardt uses a noticeably mellower 1648 Ruckers, a stereo recording of five years later, closing with the divisions on *Resonet in laudibus* played on the deliciously reedy Arp Schnitger organ at Noordbroek, Gronigen. Most entertaining.

PURCELL: **Anthems, Instrumental Music and Songs (with Leonhardt Consort):** Anthems (with Bowman, Rogers, van Egmond, King's College Cambridge Choir, Willcocks): *Rejoice in the Lord Alway; Blow Up the Trumpet in Sion; O God, Thou Art my God; O God, Thou Hast Cast Us Out; My Heart is Inditing; Remember Not, Lord, Our Offences.* Consort music: *Chacony in G min.; Overture in D min.; Pavan in B flat; Overture (with Suite) in G; Pavan in A min.; Fantasia (Chaconne): 3 Parts on a ground in D; Overture in G min.; Pavan of 4 parts in G min.; Sonata in A min.; Ground in D min.* Harpsichord music: *Suite in D; Sefauchi's Farewell in D min.; A New Ground in E min.* Songs: *Fly Swift, Ye Hours; The Father Brave; Return, Revolting Rebels* (with van Egmond, Leonhardt Consort). Consort music: *Fantasia a 4 No. 7* (Brüggen Consort).

✹ (M) ★★★ Teldec (ADD) 3984 21768-2 (2).

This Purcell collection is the pick of the bunch and should not be missed. The anthems are all very well sung indeed, with the King's College Choir's penchant for tonal breadth and beauty. Not all of them have instrumental accompaniments, but those that do enjoy a distinctive sound, with period instruments used in such a way that the performances overall happily blend scholarship and vigour, warmth and spontaneity. The recordings were not made at King's College, but in Holland, in 1969, and the acoustic is ideal, not too resonant, so that the effect is uncommonly fresh and clear. The delightful *Blow Up the Trumpet in Sion* has splendid antiphonal effects which remind one of Purcell's famous directional chorus in *King Arthur.* But the highlight must be *My Heart is Inditing,* an extended work, also for double chorus, in which the polyphony is a thing of wonder. It is superbly integrated and the choir conclude with a very beautiful performance of the unaccompanied *Remember Not, Lord, Our Offences.*

Leonhardt's excellent Dutch ensemble experiences no difficulty in getting right inside the spirit of Purcell's instrumental music, which they perform with admirable taste and finesse of style. The *Fantasia on a Ground,* a brilliant work exploiting the special sound of three violins above a repeated bass motive, is one of the best-recorded versions of this piece, as is that of the famous *Chacony in G minor.* The two *Overtures* are less familiar; while they may not rank, like the *Pavans* and *Sonatas* here, among Purcell's best music, it is good to have them in such neat and sparkling performances, and Leonhardt's intepretations of the harpsichord solos leaves little to be desired. The stereo sound from the late 1960s is warm and lively, and very successfully transferred.

Organ and Harpsichord Music: **Organ:** REINCKEN: *An den Wasserflüssen Babylon.* SCHEIDEMANN: *Praeambulum in D.* BACH: *Prelude and Fugue in D min., BWV 539.* **Harpsichord:** BOEHM: *Suites Nos. 6 in E flat; 8–9 in F min.* HANDEL: *Suite No. 8 in F min.* J. C. BACH: *Sonata in D, Op. 5/2.*

(M) ★★★ Teldec (ADD) 3984 21769-2.

Johann Adam Reincken was a famed improviser, and Bach travelled to Hamburg to hear him play. Not surprisingly, his *Chorale Fantasia* on *An den Wasserflüssen* is an ingeniously crafted work that projects readily in Leonhardt's fine performance. The following *D minor Prelude and Fugue* of Bach might have been moved on a little more swiftly, yet Leonhardt certainly holds the listener's attention at his chosen pace.

He then turns to the harpsichord for the three attractive *Suites* of Georg Böhm (French in form and layout, but German in sensibility) and the splendid work of Handel, and he closes with a remarkably modern-sounding *D major Sonata* of J. C. Bach, with its pair of *Allegro di molto* movements (played with great flair), followed by a closing minuet. Leonhardt uses two different organs and (more importantly) three different harpsichords: two copies and, for the J. C. Bach work, an original instrument made in London in 1775. The basic sound of each is quite different (the Boehm and Handel *Suites* appear to be very good mono recordings), and Leonhardt makes the most of his colouristic opportunities. The balance is close, but otherwise the CD transfer produces first-class results. Very stimulating.

Harpsichord and Consort Music: FRESCOBALDI: *Toccata settima; Toccata undecima in C; Canzona terza; Toccata in G; Fantasia sesta sopra doi soggetti; 5 Galliards.* TURINI: *Sonata in A.* CACCINI: *Amarilli mia bella.* Biagio marini: *Balletto secondo a tre & a quattro.* D. SCARLATTI: *Sonatas in A min., Kk. 3: Presto; in D min., Kk. 52: Andante moderato; in E, Kk. 215: Andante; in E, Kk. 216: Allegro.*

(M) ★★★ Teldec (ADD) 3984 21770-2.

Another very enjoyable recital, in which Leonhardt uses four different early harpsichords. Frescobaldi's music suits him admirably, for he obviously relishes its improvisational freedom of style and its ability to take the listener by surprise. Alternating an Italian instrument and a sonorous London Kirkman, he plays the *Toccatas* with an entirely appropriate freedom and is equally appealing in the *Canzona*; it is only in the *Fantasia* that he progresses somewhat deliberately. But he finds an appropriately buoyant rhythmic touch for the five brief *Galliards*. Turini's *Trio Sonata*, alternately expressive and vigorous, makes a strong contrast, played with elegance and spirit, while the following *Amarilli mia bella* of Caccini has a certain lovelorn air when played so responsively on a fine Ruckers.

The Ensemble returns for Marini's ballet suite, which has a surprisingly grave concluding *Pretirata*. The programme ends with nicely turned performances of four choice keyboard *Sonatas* of Scarlatti, using a characterful instrument made by R. Schütz of Heidelberg. These appear to be more mono recordings (from 1962) but of high quality. The closing work in *E major*, Kk. 216, with its swirling bravura scales, is particularly engaging.

Lidström, Mats (cello), Bengt Forsberg (piano)

'*Smorgásbord*': KORNGOLD: *Mummenschant; Romance Impromptu in E flat.* GRAINGER: *Sussex Mummers' Christmas Carol.* SIBELIUS: *Rondino; Berceuse.* GODOWSKY: *Larghetto lamentoso.* JONGEN: *Valse; Habanera.* MONTSALVATGE: *Canto negro.* HALFFTER: *Habanera.* MOERAN: *Prelude.* KREISLER: *Liebesleid.* SCRIABIN: *Poème in F sharp, Op. 32/1; Romance in A min.* MARTINU: *Arabesque No. 1.* TORTELIER: *Pishnetto.* HAGG: *Andante; Albumblatt.* LENNOX BERKELEY: *Andantino, Op. 21/2a.* LIDSTROM: *The Sea of Flowers is Rising Higher (Elegy).* RAMEAU: *Air vif; 'Torture d'Alphise'.* TILLE: *Courante.* OFFENBACH: *Souvenir du val, Op. 29/1.* FAURE: *Pièce (Papillon), Op. 77.* STENHAMMAR: *Adagio.*

*** Hyp. CDA 67184.

This fine Swedish partnership has given us some enterprising issues, ranging from Saint-Saëns to Boëllmann and Benjamin Godard, but on this disc they assemble some 25 *bonnes bouches* lasting in all not much longer than an hour. They call it '*Smörgåsbord*' (the table of Scandinavian hors d'oeuvres that used to precede but sometimes also comprises the main course) although many of the pieces here, such as Ernesto Halffter's *Habanera* and Kreisler's *Liebesleid* could just as well be petits fours. In any event, whether they be sweet or savoury, they are all delicious as served here. As a glance at the listing above shows, their choice of repertoire is highly enterprising and ingenious. The thought of hearing so many miniatures puts one in mind of Bernard Shaw's celebrated remark about Grieg: 'His sweet but very cosmopolitan modulations, and his inability to get beyond a very pretty snatch of melody do not go very far with me – give me a good, solid, long-winded classical lump of composition with time to go to sleep and wake up two or three times in each

movement.' Well, there is no time to doze off here, and no inducement to do so either. Everything is compellingly and exquisitely played, and beautifully recorded too. Almost all these pieces are worthwhile, though one is not altogether sure about Lidström's own work, written soon after the death of Diana, Princess of Wales. But that is the single exception and this is a highly enjoyable issue.

Lim, Dong-Hyek (piano)

CHOPIN: *Ballade No. 1 in G min., Op. 23; Etude in C, Op. 10./1; Scherzo No. 2 in B flat min., Op. 31.* RAVEL: *La Valse* (trans. composer); SCHUBERT: *Four Impromptus, D.899/1–4.*

✪ (M) *** EMI 5 67933-2.

Magnificent! This recital by the South Korean pianist Dong-Hyek Lim is as virtuosic as were some of his footballing countrymen at the World Cup. He was seventeen last year when this recital was recorded, and is presently studying in Moscow with Lev Naumov. From the very first bar to the last, he has the listener in his grip, such is the strength of his musical personality. A real artist and not just a brilliant pianist, he brings a commanding narrative power to this repertoire. The Chopin is electrifying, sensitive, poetic and has an authority that is unexpected in one so young, and the Schubert has depth and poignancy. He is one of the artists who appear under Martha Argerich's banner and has the same youthful flair she had at the beginning of her career as well as ardour, effortless technique and sensitivity.

Lipatti, Dinu (piano)

Besançon Festival Recital (1950): BACH: *Partita No. 1 in B flat, BWV 525.* MOZART: *Piano Sonata No. 8 in A min., K.310.* SCHUBERT: *Impromptus, D. 899/2 & 3.* CHOPIN: *Waltzes Nos. 1; 3–14.*

(M) (***) EMI mono 5 62819-2.

Like Lipatti's representation in EMI's 'Great Recordings of the Century' (see below) these recordings derive from the pianist's Besançon Festival recital, and the incomplete set of the Chopin *Waltzes* has been added from the same source, the recording different from the complete set, recorded by Walter Legge in a Geneva studio.

Recital: BACH: *Partita No. 1 in B flat, BWV 825. Chorale Preludes: Nun komm, der Heiden Heiland; Ich ruf zu dir, Herr Jesu Christ; Jesu, Joy of Man's Desiring. Flute Sonata No. 2 in E flat, BWV 1031: Siciliana* (arr. KEMPFF). D. SCARLATTI: *Sonatas, Kk. 9 & 380.* MOZART: *Sonata No. 8 in A min., K.310.* SCHUBERT: *Impromptus, in E flat; G flat, D.899/2–3.*

(M) (***) EMI mono 5 66988-2 [5 67003-2].

No collector should overlook this Lipatti CD. Most of

the performances derive from the pianist's last recital in Besançon and have scarcely been out of circulation since their first appearance in the 1950s: the haunting account of the Mozart *A minor Sonata* and the Bach *B flat Partita* have both had more than one incarnation on LP and CD. The Schubert *Impromptus* are equally treasurable, and the Scarlatti *Sonatas* have been added for the present reissue in EMI's 'Great Recordings of the Century' series. The remastering is well done; and one notices that, among his other subtleties, Lipatti creates a different timbre for the music of each composer.

Recital: CHOPIN: *Sonata No. 3 in B min., Op. 58.*
LISZT: *Années de pèlerinage; Sonetto del Petrarca No. 104.* RAVEL: *Miroirs: Alborada del gracioso.*
BRAHMS: *Waltzes, Op. 39/1, 2, 5, 6, 10, 14 & 15* (with Boulanger). ENESCU: *Sonata No. 3 in D, Op. 25.*
(M) (***) EMI mono 5 67566-2 [567567-2].

The Chopin *Sonata*, the Liszt and the Ravel were recorded in 1947–8, the Brahms *Waltzes*, with Nadia Boulanger, as long ago as 1937; while the Enescu *Sonata* comes from a 1943 wartime broadcast from Swiss Radio. The Chopin is one of the classics of the gramophone and it is good to have it again on CD. The Brahms *Waltzes* are played deliciously, with tremendous sparkle and tenderness; they sound every bit as realistic as the post-war records. The Enescu *Sonata* is an accessible piece with an exuberant first movement, a rather atmospheric *Andantino* and a sparkling finale, and that too sounds fresher in this latest transfer, though not as impressive as the Brahms. A must for all those with an interest in the piano and an obvious 'Great Recording of the Century'.

Little, Tasmin (violin), Piers Lane (piano)

'*Virtuoso Violin*': KREISLER: *Prelude and Allegro in the Style of Pugnani; Caprice viennois.* BRAHMS: *Hungarian Dances Nos. 1 & 5.* SHOSTAKOVICH: *The Gadfly: Romance.* DRIGO: *Valse bluette.* FIBICH: *Poème.* FALLA: *La vida breve: Spanish Dance.*
WIENIAWSKI: *Légende, Op. 17.* SARASATE: *Introduction and Tarantelle, Op. 43.* BLOCH: *Baal Shem: Nigun.* DEBUSSY: *Beau soir.*
RIMSKY-KORSAKOV: *Flight of the Bumblebee* (both arr. HEIFETZ). DELIUS: *Hassan: Serenade* (arr. TERTIS). KROLL: *Banjo and Fiddle.* RAVEL: *Tzigane.*
(B) *** CfP 574 9492.

A pretty dazzling display of violin fireworks from a brilliant young fiddler who conveys her delight in her own easy virtuosity. The opening Kreisler pastiche, *Prelude and Allegro*, is presented with real style, and later the *Caprice viennois* has comparable panache and relaxed charm. The schmaltzy daintiness of Drigo's *Valse bluette* is followed by an unexaggerated but full-timbred warmth in Fibich's *Poème*. The gypsy

temperament of the Falla and the ready sparkle of Sarasate's *Tarantelle* and Kroll's *Banjo and Fiddle* are offset by the lyrical appeal of the more atmospheric pieces. The violin is very present – perhaps the microphones are a fraction too close, but the balance with the piano is satisfactory and there is not an exaggerated spotlight here.

Lloyd Webber, Julian (cello)

'*British Cello Music*' ((i) with McCabe, piano): (i) RAWSTHORNE: *Sonata for Cello and Piano.*
ARNOLD: *Fantasy for Cello.* (i) IRELAND: *The Holy Boy.* WALTON: *Passacaglia.* BRITTEN: *Tema (Sacher); Cello Suite No. 3.*
*** ASV CDDCA 592.

A splendid recital and a most valuable one. Julian Lloyd Webber has championed such rarities as the Bridge *Oration* at a time when it was unrecorded and now devotes this present issue to British music that needs strong advocacy; there is no alternative version of the Rawsthorne *Sonata*, in which he is most ably partnered by John McCabe. He gives this piece – and, for that matter, the remainder of the programme – with full-blooded commitment. Good recording.

'*British Cello Music*', Vol. 2 (with McCabe, piano): STANFORD: *Sonata No. 2, Op. 39.* BRIDGE: *Elegy; Scherzetto.* IRELAND: *Sonata in G min.*
✪ *** ASV CDDCA 807.

The Stanford *Second Cello Sonata* (1893 – written between the *Fourth* and *Fifth Symphonies*) is revealed here as an inspired work whose opening theme flowers into great lyrical warmth on Lloyd Webber's ardent bow. The focus of the recording is a little diffuse, but that serves to add to the atmosphere. Ireland's *Sonata*, too, is among his most richly inspired works, a broad-spanning piece in which ambitious, darkly intense outer movements frame a most beautiful *Poco largamente*. Again Lloyd Webber, who has long been a passionate advocate of the work, conveys its full expressive power. The Bridge *Elegy* (written as early as 1911) is another darkly poignant evocation, which points forward to the sparer, more austere style of the later Bridge, and the *Scherzetto* (even earlier, 1902) makes a winning encore: it should ideally have been placed at the end of the recital. John McCabe is a sympathetic partner – in spite of the balance – but this collection offers what are among Lloyd Webber's finest performances on disc.

London Wind Trio

'*20th-century Miniatures*': IBERT: *5 Pièces en trio.*
MILHAUD: *Pastorale; Suite d'après Corrette, Op.*

161b. TOMASI: *Concert champêtre.* POULENC: *Sonata for Clarinet and Bassoon.* VILLA-LOBOS: *Trio.*

(M) ******* Somm SOMMCD 013.

The personnel of the London Wind Trio consists of Neil Black, Keith Puddy and Roger Birnstingl, who are as adroit individually as they are perfectly matched as a team. They give attractively deft and fresh performances of these finely crafted French works, conveying their enjoyment of the music's melodic felicity. The wit, charm and nostalgia of Ibert's *Cinq Pièces* contrast with Milhaud's *Pastorale*, which is more brazenly prolix, yet his *Suite d'après Corrette* has an ingenuous simplicity, while offering a neat condiment of dissonance in its Menuet, before the chirping of 'Le coucou'.

No less diverting is the cheeky Poulenc duo *Sonata* with its rueful central 'Nocturne' (*très doux*). Tomasi's rustic *Concert champêtre* is hardly less engaging, with its droll *Nocturne* temporarily interrupting the good humour before the folksy closing 'Vif'. The Villa-Lobos *Trio* is the most ambitious piece, fascinatingly intricate in its rhythmic and harmonic texture, evoking the exotic, vividly colourful sounds of the Brazilian jungle, with the central *Languissamente* a darker, but still restless, tropical nocturnal. It is played with great character and unforced virtuosity. The well-balanced, natural recording gives these artists a fine presence, and altogether this is a most diverting and rewarding recital.

Lugansky, Nikolai (piano)

BRAHMS: *6 Pieces, Op. 118.* WAGNER: *Götterdämmerung Paraphrase* (arr. Lugansky). RACHMANINOV: *Moment Musical in E min., Op. 16/4; Preludes, Op. 23/5 & 7.* (Recorded live at La Roque d'Anthéron, France, 6 August 2002. Video Director: Pernoo).

*** Naïve **DVD** DR 2105 AV103.

Very impressive playing by this masterly Russian pianist. His Brahms is thoughtful and full of musical insight, while the highly successful Wagner transcription (which includes *Siegfried's Journey down the Rhine*, the *Funeral March* and the closing *Immolation*) is imaginative and compelling. The three Rachmaninov pieces serve as a reminder that among pianists of his generation Lugansky is second to none. This recital was captured live at the piano festival at La Roque d'Anthéron, near Aix-en-Provence; the camera-work is unobtrusive and the sound excellent.

McLachlan, Murray (piano)

Piano Music from Scotland: SCOTT: *8 Songs* (trans. Stevenson): *Since all Thy Vows, False Maid; Wha is That at my Bower-door?; O Were my Love yon Lilac Fare; Wee Willie Gray; Milkwort and Bog-cotton; Crowdieknowe; Ay waukin, O; There's News, Lasses, News.* CENTER: *Piano Sonata; 6 Bagatelles, Op. 3.; Children at Play.* STEVENSON: *Beltane Bonfire. 2 Scottish Ballads: The Dowie Dens O Yarrow; Newhaven Fishwife's cry.*

✿ ******* Olympia OCD 264.

Francis George Scott (1880–1958) was a prolific and striking composer of songs and Ronald Stevenson's very free transcriptions, somewhat after the fashion of Liszt's concert paraphrases, are imaginatively creative in their own right. Ronald Center's *Piano Sonata* is restless and mercurial, lacking much in the way of repose, but the joyous syncopations of the first movement are infectious and the work is a major contribution to the repertory and not in the least difficult to approach. The *Six Bagatelles* are even more strikingly diverse in mood. *Children at Play* is an enchanting piece, with a musical-box miniaturism of texture at times, yet the writing is by no means inconsequential. All this music is played with commitment and considerable bravura by Murray McLachlan, who is clearly a sympathetic exponent, and the recording is extremely vivid and real. Our Rosette is awarded not just for enterprise, but equally from admiration and pleasure.

Mayer, Albrecht (oboe), Markus Becker (piano)

COSSART: *Liebesgedicht, Op. 23/4.* DAELLI: *Fantasy on Themes from Verdi's 'Rigoletto'.* KOECHLIN: *Le Repos de tityre – Monodie, Op. 216/10.* NIELSEN: *2 Fantasy Pieces, Op. 2.* SCHUMANN: *Abendlied, Op. 107/6; Ihre Stimme, Op. 96/3; Romanzen, Op. 94; Stille tränen, Op. 35/10.* YVON: *Sonata in F.*

✿ (B) ******* EMI Début 5 73167-2.

Albrecht Mayer is an artist of exceptional quality and his partnership with Markus Becker the meeting of true minds. Their playing on this EMI Début recital gives enormous pleasure for its subtlety, refinement and musicianship. Their choice of repertoire is unfailingly enterprising and the Schumann and Nielsen are played as well as we have ever heard. Mayer is principal oboe of the Berlin Philharmonic and will obviously be one of the great players of the next decade or so. Excellent recording.

Melos Ensemble

18th- and 19th-century Chamber Music: MOZART: *Piano and Wind Quintet in E flat, K.452.* BEETHOVEN: *Piano and Wind Quintet in E flat, Op. 16; Sextet in E flat for 2 Horns, 2 Violins, Viola & Cello, Op. 81b; March for Wind Sextet in B flat, WoO 29; Rondino in E flat, WoO 25; Duo No. 1 for Clarinet and Bassoon, WoO 27.* SCHUMANN: *Fantasiestücke for Clarinet and Piano, Op. 73.*

Märchenerzählungen, Op. 132. BRAHMS: *Clarinet Quintet in B min., Op. 115.* REGER: *Clarinet Quintet in A: 2nd Movt: Vivace.*

(B) ★★★ EMI Double fforte (ADD) 5 72643-2 (2).

This collection, like its companion below, dates from the late 1960s when the Melos Ensemble gathered together some of London's finest orchestral musicians to make a series of recordings for EMI. There is plenty of individual personality in the music-making here, but how beautifully these fine musicians blend together as a group! The polished elegance and charm of their playing cannot be heard to better effect than in the Mozart *Piano and Wind Quintet*, dominated by the splendid musicianship of the pianist, Lamar Crowson, and with some particularly felicitous oboe playing from Peter Graeme. Its Beethoven successor follows on naturally, played with a lighter touch than usual to emphasize the Mozartian influences.

The *Sextet* brings some splendid bravura from the two horn players, Neil Sanders and James Buck, while the *March* (for wind alone) is very jolly. The *Duo* for clarinet and bassoon is now thought not to be by Beethoven but is very agreeable nevertheless. Schumann's rarely heard *Märchenerzählungen* ('Fairy-tales') is late (1853) and is almost unique in being scored for the same combination as Mozart's *Trio* for clarinet, viola (here Gervase de Peyer and Cecil Aronowitz) and piano. The *Fantasiestücke*, for clarinet and piano, was written four years earlier. Both performances are persuasively warm and mellow, although Lamar Crowson again achieves a strong backing profile. For all their lyricism, these artists don't miss Schumann's marking, '*mit Feuer*', in the finale of Op. 73, and the second movement of Op. 132 is strongly accented to make a bold contrast with the flowingly romantic third, before the similarly bold finale. Gervase de Peyer then relaxes completely to present an essentially lyrical view of the Brahms *Clarinet Quintet*. It is a lovely performance, achieving a wistful nostalgia in the slow movement, but it is perhaps in the rippling execution of the arpeggios of the finale that his playing is particularly individual. The Reger lollipop *Scherzo*, which acts as an encore, may be as light as thistledown, but its central *Trio* has a beguiling richness of style in the post-Brahms tradition. All the recordings were made at Abbey Road, and the sound is excellent throughout; only in the Beethoven *Sextet* is there a hint of thinness in the violins. Overall this will give much refreshment and pleasure.

20th-century Chamber Music. RAVEL: *Introduction and Allegro for Flute, Clarinet, Harp and String Quartet.* POULENC: *Trio for Oboe, Bassoon and Piano; Sonata for Clarinet and Bassoon.* FRANCAIX: *Divertissement for Oboe, Clarinet and Bassoon; Divertissement for Bassoon and String Quintet.* MILHAUD: *Suite for Violin, Clarinet and Piano.* BARTOK: *Contrasts for Violin, Clarinet and Piano.*

SKALKOTTAS: *Octet; 8 Variations on a Greek Tune.* KHACHATURIAN: *Trio for Clarinet, Violin and Piano.* PROKOFIEV: *Overture on Hebrew Themes.*

(B) ★★★ EMI Double fforte (ADD) 5 72646-2 (2).

If anything, the Melos survey of twentieth-century music is even more enjoyable than their classical programme. It opens with Ravel's sublime *Septet* (with Richard Adeney, Gervase de Peyer and Osian Ellis in the lead). The performance is very fine indeed, and the 1967 Abbey Road recording is that bit warmer and smoother than their earlier version for Oiseau-Lyre/Decca, even if that might have a degree more subtlety (Decca 452 891-2). Both the Poulenc pieces are delightful, particularly the delicious *Trio for Oboe, Bassoon and Piano*, which has an admirably dry wit and unfailing inventiveness; the playing is above reproach. The two *Divertissements* of the always elegant Jean Françaix have much inconsequential charm, and the *Ouverture* and *Finale* of the irrepressible Milhaud *Suite* sparkle lustrously, while the inner movements produce an engaging, gentle melancholy. The other masterpiece here is the Bartók *Contrasts*, for the same combination as the Milhaud but of altogether stronger fibre. Both are played superbly. The works by the neglected Greek composer Nikolaos Skalkottas (a Schoenberg pupil who died not long after the Second World War) show a fairly strong personality, the *Octet* abrasively neo-classical, and both pieces revelling in a mordant harmonic dissonance. The surprise is Khachaturian's remarkably cultivated *Trio*, laced with attractively sinuous Armenian ideas. Finally comes Prokofiev's *Overture on Hebrew Themes*, another highly spontaneous piece, presented with real style. The recording is excellent throughout.

Menuhin, Yehudi and Stéphane Grappelli (violins)

'*Menuhin and Grappelli play*' (with rhythm group; Alan Clare Trio; Orchestral Ensemble; cond. Nelson Riddle and Max Harris): GERSHWIN: *Fascinatin' rhythm; Soon; Summertime; Nice work if you can get it; Embraceable you; Liza; A foggy day; 'S wonderful; The man I love; I got rhythm; He loves and she loves; They can't take that away from me; They all laughed; Funny face; Our love is here to stay; Lady be good.* STRACHEY: *These foolish things.* RASKIN: *Laura.* HARBURG & DUKE: *April in Paris.* KOSMA, PREVERT & MERCER: *Autumn leaves.* DUKE: *Autumn in New York.* BERLIN: *Cheek to cheek; Isn't this a lovely day; Change partners; Top hat, white tie and tails; I've got my love to keep me warm; Heat wave.* KERN: *The way you look tonight; Pick yourself up; A fine romance; All the things you are; Why do I love you?* PORTER: *I get a kick out of you; Night and day; Looking at you; Just one of those things.* RODGERS & HART: *My funny Valentine;*

Thou swell; The lady is a tramp; Blue room. GADE: *Jealousy.* CARMICHAEL: *Skylark.*

(B) *** EMI Double fforte (ADD/DDD) 5 73380-2 (2).

The partnership of Menuhin and Grappelli started in the television studio, many years before Menuhin was ennobled. Their brief duets (tagged on to interviews) were so successful that the idea developed of recording a whole recital (and then several), with each maestro striking sparks off the other in style, but matching the other remarkably closely in matters of tone and balance. One of the secrets of success of this partnership lies in the choice of material. All these items started as first-rate songs, with striking melodies which live in whatever guise, and here with ingenious arrangements (mostly made by Max Harris, but some by Nelson Riddle) which spark off the individual genius of each violinist, acting as a challenge, and inviting the players' obvious enjoyment. The result is delightful, particularly in numbers such as *Pick yourself up*, where the arrangement directly tips a wink towards Bachian figuration. The CD transfers are immaculate and the high spirits of the collaboration are caught beautifully.

Michelangeli, Arturo Benedetti
(piano)

Recital in the RTSI Auditorium, Lugano, Switzerland on 7 April 1981: BEETHOVEN: *Piano Sonatas Nos. 11 in B flat, Op. 22; 12 in A flat, Op. 26.* SCHUBERT: *Piano Sonata No. 4 in A min., D.537.* BRAHMS: *4 Ballades, Op. 10.*

*** Euro Arts TDK **DVD** 10 5231 9 DV MPSR (TV Director: János Darvas).

It is really something to come almost face to face with this legendary pianist and to realize that the sense of aloofness that his recordings often engender is indeed part of his personality. As for instance here, when he takes his bow impassively at the end of the recital. The programme too demonstrates his apparent degree of involvement, less so in Beethoven's Op. 26, which offers beautiful, refined pianism but in which the *March funèbre* seems almost stoic, although the Scherzo is lively enough. The more extrovert account of the *B flat Sonata*, Op. 22, communicates more directly: here the *Adagio* has feeling as well as refinement, and he almost gets carried away in the closing Rondo.

But when he begins the early Schubert *A major Sonata*, one is immediately conscious of being in the presence of a great artist, not least in the beautifully articulated *Allegretto* which is utterly enchanting. The Brahms *Ballades*, too, from the very opening of the *First in D minor*, command the attention and hold the listener raptly in their spell.

The colour photography is excellent and the camera angles well judged, not intrusive, with the changes of shot always achieved at appropriate moments in the music. The close-ups subtly reveal the pianist's degree of involvement in his facial gestures, which communicate to us, even though he is always totally absorbed in the music. The piano sound lacks a little in range, but is real – full in sonority and timbre. Altogether a success: Michelangeli admirers need not hesitate.

BEETHOVEN: *Piano Sonatas Nos. 4 in E flat, Op. 7; 12 in A flat, Op. 26.* DEBUSSY: *Hommage à Rameau.* RAVEL: *Gaspard de la nuit.*

(M) *** BBC Legends (ADD) BBCL 4064-2.

The Ravel *Gaspard de la nuit* has been in circulation on various labels, most recently in the Philips 'Great Pianists of the Twentieth Century' series. Recorded in the Concert Hall of Broadcasting House in 1959, it was a legendary account of *Gaspard* which left all who heard it spellbound. But, of course, there have been many *Gaspards*: the balance renders Michelangeli's enormous dynamic range less wide than usual (the opening of *Ondine* is not as *pianissimo* as one remembers it being in the Concert Hall). Those who recall Michelangeli's marmoreal account of the *E flat Sonata*, Op. 7, which bestrode two sides of a DG LP way back in the early 1970s, will find the 1982 Festival account more involving – but then, it had to be! Generally speaking, Michelangeli is commanding in both *Sonatas* and produces some lovely sounds in the Debussy *Hommage à Rameau*. Admirers of the great pianist will want this, and the sound is very acceptable indeed.

BACH/BUSONI: *Chaconne from Violin Partita No. 2 in D min., BWV 1004.* BRAHMS: *Variations on a Theme by Paganini, Op. 35.* SCHUMANN: *Carnaval, Op. 9. Album für die Jugend, Op. 68, excerpts: Winterzeit I & II; Matrosenlied.*

(M) ** EMI mono/stereo 5 62740-2 [5 62757-2].

'Few pianists have provoked greater awe and controversy than Michaelangeli,' writes Bryce Morrison in his note for this reissue among EMI's 'Great Recordings of the Century', 'through his crystalline perfection, controversy through interpretations that ranged from the chilly to the sublime.' One could add to this, interpretative linear eccentricity, which rears its head here both in Schumann and the otherwise very impressive Brahms *Variations*. The *Chaconne* is certainly a remarkable display of freely romantic Bach and some prodigious pianism, even if the recording is only fair. But the Schumann performances are strangely idiosyncratic. Beautiful pianism, of course (and good recording), but far from self-effacing. The opening of *Carnaval* is portentous and there is far too little spontaneity. Of all the recordings of this work by major arists this is the least consistent, and the excerpts from the *Album für die Jugend* could ideally sound more light-hearted.

SCARLATTI: *Keyboard Sonatas: in D min., Kk. 11; B flat, Kk. 172; B flat; Kk. 332.* BEETHOVEN: *Piano*

Sonata No. 32 in C min., Op. 111. CLEMENTI: *Piano Sonata in B flat, Op. 12/1.* CHOPIN: *Piano Sonata in B flat min., Op. 35.*

(M) (**(*)) BBC mono BBCL 4128-2.

Michelangeli recorded Op. 111 for Decca in the early 1960s, but this studio recording was made in 1961 at the BBC's Maida Vale studios some few years later. Magisterial pianism, but we somehow remain outside Beethoven's world (as we did in the commercial recording). All the same, the piano sound is remarkably good for its age. The Scarlatti, Clementi and Chopin are another matter, and no admirer of great piano playing should miss them.

Miolin, Anders (ten-stringed guitar)

'*The Lion and the Lute*': WALTON: *5 Bagatelles.* RAWSTHORNE: *Elegy.* LENNOX BERKELEY: *Sonatina, Op. 51; Theme and Variations, Op. 77.* TIPPETT: *The Blue Guitar.* BRITTEN: *Nocturnal, Op. 70.*

*** BIS Dig. CD 926.

Anders Miolin, born in Stockholm, designs his own guitars, allowing a greater compass and creating a richer palette. That is well borne out here by this unsurpassed collection of British twentieth-century guitar music; indeed, the colour inherent in the five Walton *Bagatelles* has never glowed so brightly, and this comment might also be applied to the whole programme, so attractively recorded in an open acoustic. The Rawsthorne *Elegy* is darkly expressive and both the Tippett and Britten works are highly charged and atmospheric. The Tippett was inspired indirectly by a Picasso painting, which stimulated Wallace Stevens to write a poem called 'The man with the blue guitar'. The Britten night music is a set of seven variations and a passacaglia on Dowland's song *Come Heavy Sleep*. Both make considerable imaginative as well as technical demands on the player, and they could hardly be more persuasively presented or recorded. If you enjoy guitar music, this is not to be missed.

Mitchell, Madeleine (violin), Andrew Bell (piano)

English Violin Sonatas: GOOSSENS: *Sonata No. 1 in E min., Op. 21.* HURLSTONE: *Sonata in D min.* TURNBULL: *Sonata in E min.*

(M) *** Somm SOMMCD 031.

Of these three fine *Violin Sonatas* (all new to CD) that by Eugene Goossens (1918) is the most commanding. The style is thoroughly romantic, but Goossens also draws eclectically on the musical background of the period. Yet the music's underlying lyrical feeling predominates, and there is fine craftsmanship too, as in the beautifully managed close of the first movement. The *Adagio* features an appealing

folk theme, and the sparkling *Con brio* finale centres on a lolloping principal rhythmic figure, also with a folksy flavour. There is also a passionate secondary melody to again bring contrast. The piano writing throughout the work is just as demanding as the violin contribution, and both these artists enter fully into the music's spirit, as they do in the other two works included here.

Hardly less appealing is the Hurlstone *D minor Sonata* of 1897, comparably lyrical and inventive and bringing another sprightly scherzando finale (which again produces a memorable second subject). Percy Turnbull's *E minor Sonata* of 1925 also has a friendly opening movement: its *Andante* is thoughtful, and the lively finale is imbued with a Ravelian purity of feeling in the piano writing, with the violin soaring freely above in richly lyrical response. In short these works make a most attractive triptych, and the recording is excellent, naturally balanced and clear within a warm acoustic.

Mogilevsky, Alexander (piano)

BACH, arr. SILOTI: *Prelude in B min.* BRAHMS: *Fantasias, Op. 116/2, 4 & 5.* PROKOFIEV: *Sonata No. 7.* SCHUMANN: *Kinderszenen.*

(M) *(*) EMI 5 67934-2

Alexander Mogilevsky is one of the young artists to enjoy the advocacy of Martha Argerich in EMI's mid-price series. Born in Odessa twenty-five years ago he is Moscow-trained and has already appeared at the Théâtre du Châtelet in Paris and at the Wigmore Hall. He possesses excellent fingers and an impressive range of keyboard colour but he is far from self-effacing in his approach to these pieces. In the three Brahms *Intermezzi* from the *Fantasien*, Op. 116 he produces beautifully inward, withdrawn sound and the intrusive rubati which are so ruinous in Schumann's *Kinderszenen* are less disturbing. Nothing is left to speak for itself in the Schumann, which is at times unbearably affected, and even in the slow movement of the Prokofiev *Seventh Sonata* he manages to insert all sorts of little expressive hesitations into the melodic line. The recording, made in the studios of Radio della Svizzera Italian in Lugano, is excellent.

Moiseiwitsch, Benno (piano)

1938–1950 Recordings: MUSSORGSKY: *Pictures at an Exhibition.* BEETHOVEN: *Andanti favori, WoO 57; Rondo in C, Op. 51/1.* WEBER: *Sonata No. 1: Presto; Invitation to the Dance* (arr. TAUSIG). MENDELSSOHN: *Scherzo in E min., Op. 16.* SCHUMANN: *Romanzen: No. 2, Op. 28/2.* CHOPIN: *Nocturne in E flat, Op. 9/2; Polonaise in B flat, Op. 71/2; Barcarolle, Op. 60.* LISZT: *Liebestraum No. 3; Etude de concert: La leggierezza. Hungarian Rhapsody No. 2 in C sharp min. Concert Paraphrase* of Wagner's 'Tannhäuser' Overture. DEBUSSY: *Pour le piano: Toccata. Suite bergamasque: Clair de lune. Estampes: Jardins sous la pluie.* RAVEL: *Le tombeau de Couperin: Toccata.*

(**(*)) APR mono CDAPR 7005 (2).

Moiseiwitsch never enjoyed quite the exposure on records to which his gifts entitled him, though in the earlier part of his career he made a great many. Later, in the electrical era, he was a 'plum-label' artist and was not issued on the more prestigious and expensive 'red label'. In this he was in pretty good company, for Solomon and Myra Hess were similarly relegated. This anthology gives a good picture of the great pianist in a wide variety of repertory: his *Pictures at an Exhibition*, made in 1945, was for some time the only piano version; and those who identify him solely with the Russians will find his Chopin *Barcarolle* and Debussy *Jardins sous la pluie* totally idiomatic. The transfers are variable – all are made from commercial copies, some in better condition than others.

Moore, Gerald (piano)

'A Tribute to Gerald Moore': Moore (piano), with Goossens (oboe), Yehudi Menuhin (violin), Barenboim (piano), de Peyer (clarinet), du Pré (cello): BACH: *Siciliano.* WEBER: *Variations on a Theme from 'Silvana'.* FAURE: *Elégie.* RAVEL: *Pièce en forme de habanera.* DEBUSSY: *La fille aux cheveux de lin.* DVORAK: *Slavonic Dance in G min.*

(M) *** EMI (ADD) 5 67990-2 (2).

As a follow-up to the Lieder recital which marked Gerald Moore's official retirement in 1967, EMI devised another tribute, with Moore in partnership with ten artists he specially admired, five singers and five instrumentalists, ending with fellow-pianist Daniel Barenboim, with whom he plays Dvořák's vigorous *G minor Slavonic Dance*. At Barenboim's insistence, Moore played primo, so that he could for once play the tune. All these great artists were inspired to give inspired performances, matching Moore's accompaniment. Especially moving is Jacqueline du Pré's moving account of Fauré's *Elégie*. Unlike the 1967 Lieder recital, this fascinating collection has been neglected on CD, making it the perfect fill-up for the two-disc version of the recital in EMI's 'Great Recordings of the Century' series.

Mordkovitch, Lydia (violin), Gerhard Oppitz (piano)

BRAHMS: *Violin Sonatas Nos. 1–3.* PROKOFIEV: *Violin Sonatas Nos. 1–2.* SCHUBERT: *Fantasie in C, Op. post. 159 D.934; Violin Sonata in A, Op. post. 162 D.574.* R. STRAUSS: *Violin Sonata in E, Op. 18.* SCHUMANN: *Violin Sonatas Nos. 1–2.* FAURE: *Violin Sonata in A, Op. 13.*

(M) ** Chan. 6659 (4).

Chandos has collected Lydia Mordkovitch's sonata recordings made with Gerhard Oppitz in the 1980s into this one bargain box. It is an inexpensive way of acquiring this artist's often exciting violin playing, very Russian, full of temperament, and never dull. The Brahms *Sonatas* are without question among the finest performances of this repertoire, with Mordkovitch's imaginative and subtle phrasing a constant source of pleasure. Both she and Oppitz give authoritative and perceptive accounts of all three *Sonatas*, which could almost be a top choice, were it not for the over-reverberant sound. If her accounts of the Prokofiev *Sonatas* do not displace versions by Oistrakh and Perlman, they can be placed alongside them. These are thoughtful readings with vital contributions from both partners. They have the measure of the darker, more searching side of the *F minor*, and are hardly less excellent in the companion work. The recording is excellent and the insights both artists bring to this music make these performances well worth exploring. The popular Fauré *Sonata* is given a sensitive account by Mordkovitch, but her other-worldly, disembodied *pianissimo* tone does not always draw comparable playing from the pianist, though the acoustic may have posed problems. All the same, the performance gives pleasure. The Strauss *Sonata* is certainly compelling, though here too the recording, which tends to make the piano a little overpowering, is not ideal. The Schubert pieces receive lovely performances, though yet again the over-reverberant recording, which draws attention to the fact that it was recorded in an empty church, does not help – for this is above all intimate music, and the sound – which even blurs details in places – precludes that. The quality for the Schumann is much better, and one enjoys the rich colours Mordkovitch finds in these richly rewarding *Sonatas*.

Mutter, Anne-Sophie (violin)

'Tango, Song and Dance' (with André Previn or Lambert Orkis, piano): PREVIN: *Sonata drammatica; Tango, Song & Dance.* FAURE: *Violin Sonata No. 1.* Music by: BRAHMS; GERSHWIN; KREISLER.

**(*) DG 471 500-2.

Celebrating the marriage of Anne-Sophie Mutter and André Previn, this collection of songs and dances, for which Previn's *Tango, Song and Dance* provides the title, is as near as anything to a direct expression of love. Mutter is inspired to play with uninhibited freedom, both with her new husband (in Heifetz's Gershwin arrangements as well as his own piece) and with Lambert Orkis, her accompanist in the other pieces. The Fauré *Violin Sonata No. 1* is the most substantial work, like the rest at once songful and dance-like, and Previn's three-movement *Sonata drammatica*, written for Mutter in 1996, starts like Piazzola observed through a distorting lens, before developing into a haunting song and a final jazz-based dance, 'like Boogie on speed' as Mutter says. Three of Brahms's *Hungarian Dances* are so uninhibitedly free that rhythms are undermined, but the three Kreisler pieces are magnetic.

Nakariakov, Sergei (trumpet), Alexander Markovich (piano)

'*Trumpet Works*': GERSHWIN: *Rhapsody in Blue* (arr. DOKSHITSER). ARENSKY: *Concert Waltz.* ARBAN: *Carnival of Venice.* RAVEL: *Pavane pour une infante défunte.* BERNSTEIN: *Rondo for Lifey.* GLAZUNOV: *Albumblatt.* STOLTE: *Burleske.* HARTMANN: *Arbucklenian Polka.* FIBICH: *Poème.* RIMSKY-KORSAKOV: *Flight of the Bumblebee.* DINICU: *Hora staccato.* GLIÈRE: *Valse.* RUEFF: *Sonatina.*
*** Teldec 9031 77705-2.

An astonishing CD début by a brilliant Russian schoolboy virtuoso, barely fifteen at the time. Nakariakov's supreme command of the instrument is matched by instinctive musicality and taste. He manages to sound suitably transatlantic in an incredible full-length arrangement of Gershwin's *Rhapsody in Blue*, and is even better in Bernstein's entertainingly ebullient *Rondo for Lifey*. Lovely tone and simplicity of line make Fibich's *Poème* sound appealingly restrained, and in the bandstand variations by Arban and Hartmann the playing is stylishly infectious. Highlights are Stolte's witty *Burleske* and the very considerable *Sonatina* by Jeanine Rueff in which trumpeter and pianist, as elsewhere, make a genuine partnership. But for ear-tickling bravura try Dinicu's *Hora staccato*, which surely would have impressed Heifetz. Excellently balanced and realistic recording.

ARBAN: *Variations on a Theme from Bellini's 'Norma'; Variations on a Tyrolean Song.* BIZET, arr. WAXMAN: *Carmen Fantasy.* BRANDT: *Concert Piece No. 2.* FALLA: *Spanish Dance.* FAURE: *Le réveil.* PAGANINI: *Caprice, Op. 1/17; Moto perpetuo, Op. 11.* SARASATE: *Zigeunerweisen, Op. 20/1.* SAINT-SAENS: *Le Cygne.*
**(*) Teldec 4509 94554-2.

Sergei Nakariakov exhibits some stunning technique in his second Teldec recital, coupling various trifles, including Franz Waxman's *Carmen Fantasy* and Paganini's *Moto perpetuo*, as well as the remainder of his programme. He was only seventeen when this recording was made and, although not many will want to hear more than a few of these pieces at a time, there is much to enjoy. He is a veritable Russian Håkan Hardenberger, save for the fact that, on the evidence of this disc, he does not always command the latter's extraordinary variety of tonal colour or his impeccable taste.

Navarra, André (cello), Erika Kilcher (piano)

Recital: Sonatas by: LOCATELLI; VALENTINI; BOCCHERINI: *in A & G.* GRANADOS: *Goyescas: Intermezzo.* FALLA: *Suite populaire espagnole* (arr. Maurice MARECHAL). NIN: *Chants d'Espagne: Saeta; Andalousie.*
(M) *** Cal. (ADD) CAL 6673.

Navarra's recital dates from 1981 and shows this fine cellist in top form. He is splendidly partnered by Erika Kilcher, who, although she is backwardly balanced in relation to the up-front cello (recorded somewhat dryly), makes a highly artistic contribution with her sympathetic accompaniments. This is immediately noticeable in the splendid opening sonata of Locatelli. But it is the four-movement work by Giuseppe Valentini which is the highlight of the Italian repertoire, a most engaging piece with an elegant *Gavotte* and an aria-like *Largo*, framed by two energetic outer movements in which Navarra's spiccato-like articulation of moto perpetuo allegros is most infectious. He is equally at home in the Spanish half of the programme, and Kilcher joins him in providing colourful characterization of the five miniatures which make up the Falla suite. In the second of the two Nin pieces, *Andalousie*, Navarra's cello sounds like a larger-than-life Spanish guitar. However, it is a pity that the documentation does not identify the Italian sonatas more positively.

New Century Saxophone Quartet

'*Main Street USA*': GOULD: *Pavane. Main Street Waltz; Main Street March.* GERSHWIN: *Promenade; Three Quartet Blues; Merry Andrew. Porgy and Bess: Clara, Clara; Oh, I got plenty o' nuttin'; Bess, you is my woman now; Oh, I can't sit down; It ain't necessarily so; Summertime; There's a boat dat's leavin' for New York; Oh Lawd, I'm on my way.* BERNSTEIN: *West Side Story: I feel pretty; Balcony scene; Tonight; Cha-cha/Meeting scene; Jump; One hand, one heart; Gee, officer Krupke; Scherzo; Somewhere.*
*** Channel Classics CCS 9896.

Uncommonly fine playing, with superbly blended timbres and a subtly appealing melodic lead from Michael Stephenson on the soprano saxophone, means that this collection of famous show melodies is very appealing. Gould's delightful *Pavane* is presented with a neat degree of whimsy and the three Gershwin instrumental numbers have a pleasing sophistication. Stephenson's line in the songs is quite remarkably vocal in feeling. 'It ain't necessarily so' recalls Fats Waller, and the Balcony scene from *West Side Story* is really touching. Steven Kirkman gives admirably restrained support on percussion, when needed, and the balance and recording could hardly be bettered.

Nishizaki, Takako (violin)

'*Romantic Violin Favourites*': trans. Kreisler (with Harden, piano): SCHUBERT: *Rosamunde: Ballet Music.* BIZET: *L'Arlésienne: Adagietto.* RIMSKY-KORSAKOV: *Le coq d'or: Hymn to the Sun. Sadko: Hindu Song. Scheherazade: Oriental Dance.* DVORAK: *Songs my Mother Taught Me.* GLUCK: *Orfeo ed Eurydice: Dance of the Blessed Spirits.* HAYDN: *Piano trio in G: Hungarian Rondo. Austrian Imperial Hymn.* MOZART: *Haffner Serenade: Rondo.* SCHUMANN: *Romance, Op. 94.* GRIEG: *Lyric Piece: To the Spring.* RAMEAU: *Tambourin.* GRAINGER: *Molly on the Shore.* TRAD.: *Song of the Volga Boatmen; Londonderry air.*
(BB) **(*) Naxos Dig. 8.550125.

'*Violin Miniatures*' (with Jandó, piano): KREISLER: *Schön Rosmarin; Rondino; Liebesleid; Liebesfreud; Caprice viennois.* RACHMANINOV: *Rhapsody on a Theme by Paganini: Variation No. 18.* FIBICH: *Poème.* ELGAR: *Salut d'amour.* GRANADOS: *Spanish Dance: Andaluza, Op. 37/5.* BRAHMS: *Hungarian Dance No. 1.* SCHUBERT: *Moment Musical in F min.* DVORAK: *Humoresque, Op. 101/7; Slavonic dance No. 1 in G min.* (all trans. Kreisler). BOCCHERINI: *Minuet.* DEBUSSY: *Clair de lune.* MASSENET: *Thaïs: Méditation.* TCHAIKOVSKY: *Chant sans paroles, Op. 2/3; Chanson triste, Op. 40/2.*
(BB) **(*) Naxos 8.550306.

Takako Nishizaki is a highly accomplished player who has recorded prolifically on the Marco Polo and Naxos labels. She has recorded Mozart sonatas with Jenö Jandó and a host of rare works, from Respighi's *Concerto gregoriano* to César Cui's *Suite concertante.* She delivers these miniatures with considerable charm and aplomb. Good recording – no one investing in these CDs is likely to be disappointed and, were there not even more virtuosic and authoritative versions in the catalogue, they would warrant an unqualified three stars.

O'Dette, Paul (lute)

'*Alla Venetiana*': DALZA: *Pavana alla veneziana; Saltarello; Piva I; Piva II; Piva III; Ricercar; Calata ala spagnola ditto terzetti; Tastar de corde – Recercar dietro; Pavana alla ferrarese; Saltarello.* ANON., arr. DALZA: *Laudate Dio.* CAPIROLA: *Recercar primo; Recercar secondo; Recercar quinto; Non ti spiaqua l'ascoltar; La vilanela; Padoana belissima; Spagna seconda; Tientalora (Balletto da ballare).* VAN GHIZEGHEM: *De tous bien playne; De tous bien playne nel ton del primo recercar.* CARA: *O mia ciecha, e dura sorte.* PESENTI: *Che farala.* SPINACINO: *Recercare I; Recercare II.* MARTINI: *Malor me bat.* JOSQUIN DESPREZ: *Adieu mes amours; Qui tolis pechata mondi.*
📻 *** HM HMU 907215.

The expert lutenist Paul O'Dette seldom disappoints. He draws here mainly on the very first Venetian books of solo lute music to be published, by Francesco Spinacino (1507) and Joan (Zuan) Ambrosio Dalza (1508). Lively dance pieces by the latter, who has a comparatively strong musical personality, are used to frame this varied 73-minute programme. The early repertory comes in three main categories, the improvisatory ricercare, and arrangements of vocal music and dances. O'Dette shows himself a master of the ruminative improvisatory style, but adding some splendid bravura flourishes, as in the first of Spinacino's *Recercare*; and his virtuosity is just as striking in the *Spagna seconda* of Capirola and Dalza's sparkling *Calata ala spagnola* (which must have been a hit in its day).

One of the most touching pieces is Martini's melancholy *Malor me bat*, which is followed by a most extrovert *Piva* by Dalza, and the darker mood then returns with the reflective anonymous *Laudate Dio.* Capirola's haunting *La vilanela* is matched by the two reflective vocal transcriptions from Josquin Desprez.

This discerningly selected recital is beautifully played and recorded, and admirably documented. A sample page (in colour) from Capirola's richly illuminated Lute Book is upstaged by the frontispiece (taken from a miniature by Philippe de Mazerolles) elegantly picturing a Venetian brothel. A colourfully garbed lutenist is accompanying the less venial pleasures: the naked men are clearly enjoying themselves, the young ladies are hardly more modest in their apparel, but look more circumspect.

Ogden, Craig (guitar), Alison Stephens (mandolin)

'*Music from the Novels of Louis de Bernières*': VIVALDI: *Concerto in C, RV 425* (arr. BEHREND). HUMMEL: *Mandolin Concerto in G: Andante with Variations.* GIULIANI: *Grand duo concertante.* PERSICHINI: *Polcha variata.* CALACE: *Amor si culla, Op. 133.* PALUMBO: *Petite bolero.* SAGRERAS: *El Colibri (The Humming Bird).* LAURO: *4 Venezuelan Waltzes.* BARRIOS: *Choro de Saudade; Las Abejas.* LLOBET: *El noi de la mare; El testament d'Amelia; El mestre.* ANON.: *Mis dolencias.* Celedonio ROMERO: *Suite andaluza: Soleares.* TURINA: *Homenaje a Tárrega: Soleares.*
*** Chan. 9780.

Not many gimmicky discs work as well as this. It makes a delightful mixture having the metallic 'plink plonk' of the mandolin set against the rich twanging of the guitar. The author of *Captain Corelli's Mandolin* has helped the two talented young performers here, Craig Ogden and Alison Stephens, in making a wide selection of music from Vivaldi to Villa-Lobos, mainly of works specifically mentioned in de Bernières' novels – not just *Captain Corelli's Mando-*

lin but also the Latin trilogy – as well as of related pieces. Starting with Vivaldi's *Mandolin Concerto* with the string accompaniment arranged for solo guitar, each of the 23 items is a charmer, not least those from unknown composers like Persichini, Calace and Sagreras.

Ogdon, John and Brenda Lucas
(pianos)

RACHMANINOV: *Suites for 2 Pianos Nos. 1 (Fantasy), Op. 5; 2 in C, Op. 17; Six Pieces for Piano Duet, Op. 11; Polka italienne.* ARENSKY: *Suite for 2 Pianos, Op. 15.* KHACHATURIAN: *Sabre Dance.* SHOSTAKOVICH: *Concertino, Op. 94.* DEBUSSY: *Petite Suite; Fêtes.* BIZET: *Jeux d'enfants.*
(B) **(*) EMI (ADD) Double fforte 5 69386-2 (2).

John Ogdon and Brenda Lucas's readings of the two Rachmaninov *Suites*, not ideally imaginative but enjoyable nevertheless, are aptly coupled with other duet recordings made by them, including the delightful Arensky *Suite* which includes the famous waltz. It is good too to have the long-neglected *Concertino* of Shostakovich and the anything-but-neglected *Sabre Dance*, which is rather heavy-going here. However, the Debussy *Petite suite* is very engaging, and most valuable of all is the complete recording of Bizet's *Jeux d'enfants* – all twelve movements. Only the five included by the composer in his orchestral suite are at all well known, and many of the others are equally charming, not least the opening *Rêverie (L'Escarpolette)*, the *Scherzo (Les chevaux de bois)* and the *Nocturne (Colin-Mainard* – 'Blind man's buff'). Fine ensemble and sparkling fingerwork, but just occasionally a touch of rhythmic inflexibility. Good, mid-1970s recording.

Oslo Wind Ensemble

Scandinavian Wind Quintets: FERNSTROM: *Wind Quintet, Op. 59.* KVANDAL: *Wind Quintet, Op. 34; 3 Sacred Folktunes.* NIELSEN: *Wind Quintet, Op. 43.*
(BB) ** Naxos 8.553050.

A super-bargain account of the Nielsen Quintet, more relaxed in its tempi and measured in approach than the account by the Scandinavian Quintet on Marco Polo. Very decently recorded, too. The Swedish musician John Fernström was a prolific composer whose output runs to 12 symphonies and much else besides. He was for years solely represented in the catalogue by a *Concertino for Flute, Women's Choir and Small Orchestra*. This *Wind Quintet* is not quite so charming, but is well worth hearing – as, for that matter, is the *Wind Quintet* by the Norwegian Johan Kvandal, a thoughtful figure who is a composer of imagination and substance.

Paik, Kun Woo (piano)

Recital: LISZT: *Années de pèlerinage: Au bord d'une source; Au lac de Wallenstadt; Les jeux d'eau à la Villa d'Este. Harmonies poétiques et religieuses: Bénédiction de Dieu dans la solitude. Liebestraum No. 3; Mephisto Waltz No. 1; Hungarian Rhapsody No. 12; Variations on B-A-C-H.* French music: POULENC: *Nocturnes Nos. 1, 5 & 6; Presto; Improvisations Nos. 10, 12 & 15; Intermezzo No. 2; Mouvements perpétuels Nos. 1–3.* DEBUSSY: *Pour le piano; Suite bergamasque: Clair de lune.* SATIE: *Gnossiennes Nos. 4 & 5; Ogives Nos. 1–2; Descriptions automatique: Sur un vaisseau; Sur un casque. Chapitre tourné en tous sens: Celui qui parle trop. Croquis et agaceries d'un gros bonhomme en bois: Españaña. Embryons desséchés: D'Edriophtalma; De Podophtalma. Gymnopédies Nos. 1–3.*
(BB) *** Virgin Classics 2×1 5 61757-2 (2).

This Virgin 2×1 reissue pairs two outstanding individual recitals, a distinguished Liszt collection already discussed under the composer, and the present grouping of French repertoire, which is slightly more idiosyncratic, even including individual movements from suites of miniatures meant to be played as a group. However, the mixture works well when the playing is consistently magnetic. There is much to relish, notably Poulenc's *Mouvements perpétuels* and indeed other pieces by this composer. Kun Woo Paik's withdrawn performance of *Clair de lune* is a little indulgent and the *Gnossiennes* also find him a shade mannered, while the *Gymnopédies* are very languorous. But the outer movements of Debussy's *Pour le piano* bring some electrifying bravura and his imagination is given full rein in the quirkier Satie miniatures. There are 154 minutes of music here and, even if the back-up documentation is fairly sparse, the value is obvious, for the recording is excellent.

Parker-Smith, Jane (organ)

'*Popular French Romantics*' (organ of Coventry Cathedral): WIDOR: *Symphony No. 1: Marche pontificale. Symphony No. 9 (Gothique), Op. 70: Andante sostenuto.* GUILMANT: *Sonata No. 5 in C min., Op. 80: Scherzo.* GIGOUT: *Toccata in B min.* BONNET: *Elfes, Op. 7.* LEFEBURE-WELY: *Sortie in B flat.* VIERNE: *Pièces de fantaisie: Clair de lune, Op. 53/5; Carillon de Westminster, Op. 54/6.*
*** ASV CDDCA 539.

The modern organ in Coventry Cathedral adds a nice bite to Jane Parker-Smith's very pontifical performance of the opening Widor *March* and creates a blaze of splendour at the close of the famous Vierne *Carillon de Westminster*, the finest performance on record. The detail of the fast, nimble articulation in the engagingly Mendelssohnian *Elfes* of Joseph Bonnet is not clouded; yet here, as in the splendid Guilmant *Scherzo* with its wider dynamic range, there is also a nice atmospheric effect. Overall, a most entertaining recital.

'*Popular French Romantics*', Vol. 2 (organ of Beauvais Cathedral): FRANCK: *Prélude, fugue et variation, Op. 18.* GUILMANT: *Grand choeur in D* (after Handel). MULET: *Carillon-Sortie.* RENAUD: *Toccata in D min.* SAINT-SAENS: *Prelude and Fugue.* VIERNE: *Symphony No. 1: Finale. Stèle pour un enfant défunt.* WIDOR: *Symphony No. 4: Andante and Scherzo.*
★★★ ASV CDDCA 610.

With his *Prelude and Fugue*, Saint-Saëns is in more serious mood than usual but showing characteristic facility in fugal construction; Widor is first mellow and then quixotic – his *Scherzo* demands the lightest articulation and receives it. High drama and great bravura are provided by the Vierne *Finale* and later by Albert Renaud's *Toccata* and Henri Mulet's *Carillon-Sortie*, while Franck's *Prélude, fugue et variation* and the poignant Vierne *Stèle pour un enfant défunt* bring attractive lyrical contrast: here Jane Parker-Smith's registration shows particular subtlety. The organ is splendidly recorded.

Peyer, Gervase de (clarinet), Gwenneth Pryor (piano)

French Music for Clarinet and Piano:
SAINT-SAENS: *Sonata, Op. 167.* DEBUSSY: *Première rhapsodie; Arabesque No. 2; Prélude: La Fille aux cheveux de lin.* POULENC: *Sonata.* SCHMIDT: *Andantino, Op. 30/1.* RAVEL: *Pièce en forme de habanera.* PIERNE: *Canzonetta, Op. 19.*
⊕━ ✪ ★★★ Chan. 8526.

A gorgeous record. The Saint-Saëns *Sonata* is an attractively crafted piece, full of engaging invention. Poulenc's *Sonata* is characteristically witty, with contrast in its lovely central *Romanza* (*très calme*); and the other short pieces wind down the closing mood of the recital, with de Peyer's luscious timbre drawing a charming portrait of *The Girl with the Flaxen Hair* before the nimbly tripping closing encore of Pierné. This is a quite perfect record of its kind, the programme like that of a live recital and played with comparable spontaneity. The recording is absolutely realistic; the balance could hardly be improved on.

Pinnock, Trevor (harpsichord or virginals)

'*At the Victoria and Albert Museum*': ANON.: *My Lady Wynkfylds Rownde.* BYRD: *The Queens Alman; The Bells.* HANDEL: *Harpsichord Suite No. 5 in E.* CROFT: *Suite No. 3 in C min.* ARNE: *Sonata No. 3 in G.* J. C. BACH: *Sonata in C min., Op. 5/6.*
(M) ★★★ CRD (ADD) CRD 3307.

Trevor Pinnock recorded for CRD before he moved over to the DG Archiv label and this was his first solo recital, made at the Victoria and Albert Museum using virginals and other period harpsichords. He opens with three very colourful pieces played on an instrument originally belonging to Queen Elizabeth I, who was an accomplished virginals player. It is in splendid condition and has a most attractive sound. Pinnock plays it with enthusiasm and his performance of Byrd's extraordinarily descriptive *The Bells* is a *tour de force*. For the rest of the recital he uses two different harpsichords. His style in the works of Handel, Croft, Arne and J. C. Bach is less flamboyant, more circumspect, but the music is strongly characterized and boldly recorded. The Handel suite is the one which has the *Harmonious blacksmith* as its finale, which is played with considerable flair.

Pletnev, Mikhail (piano)

'*Hommage à Rachmaninov*': RACHMANINOV: *Variations on a Theme of Corelli, Op. 42; 4 Etudes-tableaux, Op. 39/5; Opp. 44/6, 8–9.* BEETHOVEN: *Piano Sonata No. 26 (Les Adieux), Op. 81a.* MENDELSSOHN: *Andante cantabile & Presto agitato; Andante & Rondo capriccioso, Op. 14.* CHOPIN: *Andante spianato et Grande polonaise brillant, Op. 22.*
✪ ★★★ DG 459 634-2.

Way back in 1982, when Pletnev was in his early twenties, Dr Mark Zilberquist (in *Russia's Great Modern Pianists*) noted the young pianist's affinities with his aristocratic and patrician compatriot, Rachmaninov: 'discreet, reserved, outwardly restrained in showing emotion'. Pletnev certainly has something of the same commanding keyboard authority, the extraordinary range of colour and clarity of articulation of Rachmaninov. This recital is recorded at Rachmaninov's own summer home, the Villa Senar on the Vierwaldstätter See, near Lake Lucerne, using the composer's newly restored American Steinway. The playing is breathtaking, worthy of the composer at his best, and dazzling but never ostentatious. The delicacy of the Mendelssohn and the introductory *Andante cantabile* to the Chopin is magical. A quite exceptional recital even by the standards of this exceptional pianist.

'*Carnegie Hall Recital*' (1 November 2000): BACH/BUSONI: *Chaconne in D min., BWV 1004.* BEETHOVEN: *Sonata No. 32 in C min., Op. 111.* CHOPIN: *4 Scherzi: Op. 20; Op. 31; Op. 39; Op. 54.* Plus encores: BALAKIREV: *Islamey.* MOSZKOWSKI: *Etude de virtuosité, Op. 72/6.* RACHMANINOV: *Etude-tableau, Op. 39/5.* SCARLATTI: *Sonata in D min., Kk 9.* SCRIABIN: *Poème, Op. 32/1.*
✪ ★★★ DG 471 157-2 (with encores bonus CD).

Mikhail Pletnev made his Carnegie Hall début when he was in his early forties, relatively late in his career, but the wait should not have disappointed his many American admirers. 'He links arms with such stalwarts of the Russian school as Horowitz, Richter and Gilels,' wrote the *New York Times*, and his programme has all the dazzling command and authority, not to mention virtuosity, we would expect. The Beethoven Op. 111 *Sonata* has tremendous power and concentration and comes up sounding altogether fresh, while the four Chopin *Scherzi*, which comprised the second half, are quite thrilling and brought the house down. The five encores that followed come on an extra CD, and the *Islamey* belongs among the great performances of this work. Some recital this, and very decently recorded too!

Pollini, Maurizio (piano)

STRAVINSKY: *3 Movements from 'Petrushka'.* PROKOFIEV: *Piano Sonata No. 7 in B flat, Op. 83.* WEBERN: *Variations for Piano, Op. 27.* BOULEZ: *Piano Sonata No. 2.*

(M) *** DG 447 431-2.

The Prokofiev is a great performance, one of the finest ever committed to disc; and the Stravinsky *Petrushka* is electrifying. Not all those responding to this music will do so quite so readily to the Boulez, fine though the playing is; but the Webern also makes a very strong impression. This is the equivalent of two LPs and is outstanding value. It is a natural candidate for reissue in DG's set of 'Originals' of legendary performances.

Preston, Simon (organ)

'The World of the Organ' (organ of Westminster Abbey): WIDOR: *Symphony No. 5: Toccata.* BACH: *Chorale Prelude, Wachet auf, BWV 645.* MOZART: *Fantasia in F min., K.608.* WALTON: *Crown Imperial* (arr. MURRILL). CLARKE: *Prince of Denmark's March* (arr. PRESTON). HANDEL: *Saul: Dead March.* PURCELL: *Trumpet Tune* (arr. TREVOR). ELGAR: *Imperial March* (arr. MARTIN). VIERNE: *Symphony No. 1: Finale.* WAGNER: *Tannhäuser: Pilgrims' Chorus.* GUILMANT: *March on a Theme of Handel.* SCHUMANN: *Study No. 5* (arr. WEST). KARG-ELERT: *Marche triomphale (Now Thank We All Our God).*

(M) *** Decca (ADD) 430 091-2.

A splendid compilation from the Argo catalogue of the early to mid-1960s, spectacularly recorded, which offers 69 minutes of music and is in every sense a resounding success. Simon Preston's account of the Widor *Toccata* is second to none, and both the Vierne *Finale* and the Karg-Elert *Marche triomphale* lend themselves admirably to Preston's unashamed flamboyance and the tonal splendour afforded by the Westminster acoustics. Walton's *Crown imperial*, too, brings a panoply of sound which compares very

favourably with an orchestral recording. The organ has a splendid trumpet stop which makes both the Purcell piece and Clarke's *Prince of Denmark's March*, better known as the 'Trumpet Voluntary', sound crisply regal.

Prometheus Ensemble

'French Impressions': RAVEL: *Introduction & Allegro for Harp, Flute, Clarinet and String Quartet.* DEBUSSY: *Danses sacrée et profane; Sonata for Flute, Viola and Harp.* ROUSSEL: *Serenade.* *** ASV CDDCA 664.

This young group gives eminently well-prepared and thoughtful accounts of all these pieces. The *Danse sacrée* and *Danse profane* sound particularly atmospheric and the Debussy *Sonata* is played with great feeling and sounds appropriately ethereal. The Roussel, too, is done with great style and, even if the *Introduction and Allegro* does not supersede the celebrated Melos account, the Prometheus do it well.

Purcell Quartet, Purcell Band, with Robert Wooley (harpsichord)

'La Folia (Variations on a Theme)': CORELLI: *Violin Sonata in D min., Op. 5/12.* MARAIS: *Les folies d'Espagne.* VIVALDI: *Trio Sonata in D min. (Variations on 'La Folia'), Op. 1/12 (RV 63)* (Purcell Quartet). GEMINIANI: *Concerto grosso (La Folia)* (after Corelli) (Purcell Quartet & Purcell Band). Alessandro SCARLATTI: *Toccata No. 7 (Primo tono): Folia.* C. P. E. BACH: *12 Variations on Folies d'Espagne, Wq.118/9 (H.263)* (Wooley).

⊙ *** Hyp. CDA 67035.

Just as the chanson *L'homme armé* was popular among composers as a basis for Mass settings in the fifteenth and early sixteenth centuries, so at the very end of the seventeenth and throughout the eighteenth, *La Folia* was in constant use for instrumental variations. The word '*folia*' is Portuguese in origin and means 'empty-headed', but also refers to a dance in triple time, which originated around the same time as that famous chanson. It changed its rhythmic accents over the years, and the special character of the format we now recognize seems to have first come into use by Lully for an oboe tune around 1672.

Corelli probably appropriated it from Lully in 1700, resourcefully turning the piece into a chaconne, but Marais probably beat him to it: even though his *Folies d'Espagne* was not published until 1701, it was probably written some years earlier. Thereafter composers seemed to almost fall over each other to put it to good use in their instrumental music. The above six listings are excellent examples, among which Vivaldi's highly entertaining *Trio Sonata* stands out alongside Carl Philipp Emanuel Bach's superb set of variations for the keyboard, which ought to be much better known. But all the versions here are stimulating, and played with fine, expressive vitality. The recording too is excellent. This is not a recital to play continuously, but, dipped into a version at a time, it will give much pleasure.

Puyana, Rafael (harpsichord)

'*The Golden Age of Harpsichord Music*': ANON.: *My Lady Carey's Dompe.* BULL: *Les Buffons; The King's Hunt.* PEERSON: *The Primerose; The Fall of the Leafe.* BYRD: *La Volta.* PHILIPS: *Pavana dolorosa; Galliard dolorosa.* BESARD: *Branle Gay.* L. COUPERIN: *Tombeau de M. de Blancrocher; Pavane.* FRANCISQUE: *Branle de Montiradé.* BACH: *Keyboard Concerto in D min., after Marcello.* FREIXANET: *Sonata in A.* M. ALBENIZ: *Sonata in D.* CHAMBONNIERES: *Le Moutier* (after Louis Couperin). RAMEAU: *Gavotte et Doubles.* DIEUPART: *Passepied.* F. COUPERIN: *La Pantomime.*

⚙ (M) ★★★ [Mercury 434 364-2].

If you think you don't enjoy listening to the harpsichord, Rafael Puyana, who was a pupil of Landowska, will surely persuade you otherwise in this remarkably diverse, 75-minute recital, for he is a supreme master of his instrument. He plays a large, modern, double-keyboard Pleyel harpsichord (replicating one of Landowska's own instruments). In his bravura hands it produces an astonishingly wide range of dynamic, colour and sonority, no better demonstrated than in the *Gavotte et Doubles* of Rameau, which is a continuously inventive set of variations, running on for about ten minutes. Puyana effectively uses every possible device to divert his listeners, to say nothing of demonstrating his own dexterity, which he does again more simply in the engagingly brief *Passepied* of Charles Dieupart (who died in 1740). Martin Peerson's modest variations on a popular song of the period, *The Primerose*, and his more dolorous evocation of *The Fall of the Leafe* both feature the highly effective dynamic contrasts which this instrument can provide.

The programme opens with the piquant *My Lady Carey's Dompe*, a lollipop if ever there was one, presented with great panache. John Bull's divisions on *Les Buffons* and *The King's Hunt* have never sounded more vital, while Puyana's account of the charming *La Volta* of William Byrd makes one appreciate why it was reputedly a favourite dance of Queen Elizabeth I. Perhaps Puyana goes over the top a bit in his robust presentation of the pieces by Peter Philips, and he plays Bach's *Concerto in D minor* (supposedly after Alessandro Marcello, but sounding more like Vivaldi) in such a robust manner that it is almost as if he were sitting at the keyboard of an organ. But the crisply articulated *Sonata* of Freixanet is very effective indeed, and the *Sonata* of Mateo Albéniz is a *tour de force*.

The instrument's resonant lower octave is really

made to tell in Louis Couperin's *Tombeau*; while the elegant *Le Moutier* of Jacques Champion de Chambonnières brings a nice sonic contrast on three different levels, within a time period of just over two minutes. The Mercury recording is real and vivid, but please don't set the volume level too high. Alas, this disc has now been withdrawn in the UK.

Ragossnig, Konrad (Renaissance lute)

'*Renaissance Lute Music*': Disc 1: England: DOWLAND: *King of Denmark's Galliard; Lachrimae antiquae pavan; Fantasia; My Lady Hunsdon's Puffe; Melancholy Galliard; Mrs Winter's Jump; Semper Dowland, semper dolens; Earl of Essex his Galliard; Forlorne Hope Fancy.* BATCHELAR: *Mounsiers almaine.* BULMAN: *Pavan.* CUTTING: *Almain; Greensleeves; Walsingham; The Squirrel's Toy.* ANON.: *Sir John Smith his Almain.* MORLEY: *Pavan.* JOHNSON: *Alman.* HOLBORNE: *Galliard.* Italy: CAPIROLA: *Ricercars 1, 2, 10 & 13.* SPINACINO: *Ricercar.* Francesco da MILANO: *Fantasia.*

Disc 2: Italy (continued): MOLINARO: *Fantasias 1, 9 & 10. Saltarello – Ballo detto Il Conte Orlando – Saltarello.* BARBETTA: *Moresca detta le Canarie.* TERZI: *Ballo tedesco e francese – Tre parti di gagliarde.* NEGRI: *La spagnoletto – Il bianco fiore.* Santino Garsi de PALMA: *Aria del Gran Duca – La Cesarina – La Mutia – La ne mente per la gola – Gagliarda Manfredina – Ballo del Serenissimo Duca di Parma – Corenta.* Spain: MILAN: *Pavanas 1–6; Fantasias 10–12 & 16.* MUDARRA: *Pavana de Alexandre; Gallarda; Romanesca: O guárdame las vacas; Diferencias sobre Conde claros; Fantasia que contrahaze la harpa en la manera de Luduvico.* Luis de NARVAEZ: *Diferencias sobre Guádame las vacas; Milles regres. La canción des Emperador del quarto tono de Jusquin; Fantasia; Baxa de contrapunto.*

Disc 3: Poland & Hungary: CEDA: *Praeludium; Galliarda 1 & 2; Favorito.* ANON.: *Balletto Polacho.* POLAK: *Praeludium.* DLUGORAJ: *Chorea polonica.* BAKFARK: *Fantasia; Finale; Villanella; Finale; Kowaly; Finale; 4 Fantasies.* Germany: JUDENKUNIG: *Hoff dantz.* NEWSIDLER: *Ellend bringt peyn; Der Juden Tantz; Preambel; Welscher tantz Wascha mesa.* Landgraf Moritz von HESSEN: *Pavane.* ANON.: *Der gestraifft Danntz – Der Gassenhauer darauff.* WAISSEL: *Fantasia; Deutscher Tantz.* OCHSENKHUN: *Innsbruck, ich muss dich lassen.*

Disc 4: Netherlands: ADRIAENSSEN: *Fantasia; Courante; Branle simple de Poictou.* HOWET: *Fantasie.* SWEELINCK: *Psalms 5 & 23.* Joachim van den HOVE: *Galliarde.* VALLET: *Prelude; Galliarde; Slaep, soete, slaep.* France: ATTAIGNANT: *Chansons: Tant que vivray; Destre amoureux. Basse dances: Sansserre; La Magdelena. Branle gay: C'est mon amy; Haulberroys.* Adrien le ROY: *Passemeze.*

BALLARD: *Entrée de luth; Corante; Branle de village.* BESARD: *Branle; Gagliarda; Branle gay; Gagliarda vulgo dolorata; Allemande; Air de cour: J'ai trouvé sur l'herbe assise; Volte; Branle – Branle gay; Guillemette; Ballet; Pass' e mezo; Chorea rustica.*

❀ (M) *** DG (ADD) 476 1840 (4).

This admirable four-disc Archiv set gives us a comprehensive survey of the development of lute music throughout Europe in the fifteenth, sixteenth and the first half of the seventeenth century. English lute music came to its peak at the end of the Elizabethan and beginning of the Jacobean eras and is well represented by that master of melancholy, John Dowland – although he could also be spirited, witness *My Lady Hunsdon's Puffe*. But the oldest-known (written-down) lute music came from Italy, and the remarkably flexible *Ricercars* of Vincenzo Capirola (born in 1474) make an ideal example of music which is essentially improvisatory in feeling yet settling down into formal shape. The equivalent of the lute in Spain was the vihuela de mano (an ancestor of the guitar), and it was in Spain that the variation form was born, using the term 'diferencias'. Here, besides the solemn music and dances, we have fine examples of *Diferencias* by Mudarra and Narvaéz.

Polish and Hungarian lute music is comparatively little known, but, as the four late-sixteenth-century pieces by Diomedes Cato demonstrate, its manner closely reflects the Renaissance style in the rest of Europe. The Hungarian, Valentin Bakfark, however, is revealed as a composer of considerable individuality and his two *Villanellas* are particularly haunting. The German repertoire, too, is particularly strong in character and it brings some novelties, like Newsidler's extraordinarily exotic *Juden Tanz*. In the Netherlands programme, Sweelinck's music (two beautiful Psalm evocations) catches the ear, while the *Galliarde* and the touching *Slaepe, sote slaep* draw the listener's attention to his little-known contemporary, Nicolas Vallet.

The programme of French music which concludes the survey is hardly less rich in fine invention, and this is obviously because Pierre Attaignant and Robert Ballard were publishers first and foremost, and they both obviously had an ear for a hit number. Thus all the anonymous pieces listed under their names are full of character: sample the *Branle gay: C'est mon amy*, the charming *La Magdalena* or the rustic *Branles de village* with its drone imitation suggesting a hurdy-gurdy. Jean-Baptiste Besard, however, was an outstanding French lutenist (also a doctor of law and a physician) and his music is of the highest quality: the *Gagliarda vulgo dolorata, Air de cour, J'ai trouvé sur l'herbe assise, Branle gay* and sad little *Guillemette* can be spoken of in the same breath as the best Dowland pieces. Throughout his long programme, recorded between 1973 and 1975, Konrad Ragossnig plays with impeccable style. His spontaneous feeling brings all this music vividly to life and his variety of timbre and subtle use of echo dynamics always intrigue the ear. The recording is very fine indeed, giving his period lute a natural presence and very slightly more body than RCA provide for Julian Bream, who nevertheless can continue to be recommended alongside the present set: he is especially at home in the English repertoire. Ragossnig's set is now available in Universal's 'Penguin Rosette' Collection and is especially welcome at mid-price, with full documentation.

Rév, Lívia (piano)

'*For Children*': BACH: *Preludes in E, BWV 939; in G min., BWV 930.* DAQUIN: *Le Coucou.* MOZART: *Variations on 'Ah vous dirai-je maman', K.265.* BEETHOVEN: *Für Elise.* SCHUMANN: *Album for the Young, Op. 63: excerpts.* CHOPIN: *Nocturne in C min., Op. posth.* LISZT: *Etudes, G. 136/1 & 2.* BIZET: *Jeux d'enfants: La Toupie.* FAURE: *Dolly: Berceuse.* TCHAIKOVSKY: *Album for the Young, Op. 39: Maman; Waltz.* VILLA-LOBOS: *Prole do bebê: excerpts.* JOLIVET: *Chansons naïve 1 & 2.* PROKOFIEV: *Waltz, Op. 65.* BARTOK: *Evening in the Country; For Children: excerpts.* DEBUSSY: *Children's Corner: excerpts.* MAGIN: *3 Pieces.* MATACIC: *Miniature Variations.*

*** Hyp. CDA 66185.

A wholly delectable recital, and not just for children either. The whole is more than the sum of its many parts, and the layout provides excellent variety, with the programme stimulating in mixing familiar with unfamiliar. The recording is first class. Highly recommended for late-evening listening.

Reykjavik Wind Quintet

Jean-Michel DAMASE: *17 Variations.* DEBUSSY (arr. BOZZA): *Le petit nègre.* FAURE (arr. WILLIAMS): *Dolly Suite: Berceuse, Op. 56/1.* FRANCAIX: *Quintet No. 1.* IBERT: *3 Pièces brèves.* MILHAUD: *La Cheminée du Roi René, Op. 205.* PIERNE: *Pastorale, Op. 14/1.* POULENC (arr. EMERSON): *Novelette No. 1.*
*** Chan. 9362.

Another delightful recital for late-night listening. Elegant, crisp playing from this accomplished Icelandic ensemble. The Damase *Variations* are delightful, as indeed are the Françaix and Milhaud pieces, and the Chandos recording is in the best traditions of the house.

'*Nordic Music for Wind Quintet*': RASMUSSEN: *Quintet in F.* LARSSON: *Quattro tempi (Divertimento), Op. 55.* NIELSEN: *Quintet, Op. 43.* HALLGRIMSSON: *Intarsia.*
*** Chan. 9849.

The *Quintets* by Peter Rasmussen and Haflidi Hall-grímsson are new to CD. Rasmussen comes between

Gade and Nielsen, though if you heard this music without knowing what it was, you could be forgiven for thinking it was by Reicha and Danzi or one of their contemporaries. It is well written for the instruments but pleasingly inconsequential. Haflidi Hallgrímsson, who was born in 1941, is Icelandic. His *Intarsia* is a witty and inventive score, expertly laid out for wind. Its title derives from knitting, and the ideas bubble away in a diverting and inventive way. Well worth trying out. Lars-Erik Larsson's evocation of the four seasons, *Quattro tempi*, is an imaginative and individual score. This version more than holds its own against the earlier (1983) version by the Stockholm Wind Quintet (Caprice). With the Nielsen *Quintet*, competition is very stiff, and though the Reykjavik players do it well, the Oslo Quintet (Naxos) and the Wind Quintet of the Danish Radio Orchestra (dacapo – see above) have the greater personality and finesse. Enjoyable and recommendable, though the sound is a bit upfront.

Ricci, Ruggiero (violin), Louis Persinger or Ernest Lush (piano)

PAGANINI: *Witches Dance, Op. 8; Fantasia on the G string after Rossini's 'Mosè in Egitto'; Moto perpetuo in C; Variations on 'Nel cor più mi sento' from Paisiello's 'La Molinara'; Variations on 'God Save the Queen'; La Campanella (from Violin Concerto No. 2); Sonata No. 12 in E min, Op. 3/6; I Palpiti: Variations after Rossini's 'Tancredi'* (arr. KREISLER). WIENIAWSKI: *Scherzo-Tarantelle in G min.* ELGAR: *La Capricieuse.* VECSEY: *Caprice No. 1 (Le vent).* KROLL: *Banjo and Fiddle.* CHOPIN: *Nocturne No. 20 in C sharp min.* (arr. MILSTEIN). SMETANA: *Má Vlast: Andantino.* SARASATE: *8 Spanish Dances; Caprice basque; Introduction et Tarantelle; Zigeunerweisen; Jóta Aragonesa.* SUK: *Burleska.* ACHRON: *Hebrew Melody.* HUBAY: *The Zephyr.* MOSZKOWSKI: *Guitarre.* BAZZINI: *La Ronde des lutins: scherzo fantastique.*

(B) ★★★ Double Decca mono/stereo 458 191-2 (2).

Ricci gives us a dazzling display of violin pyrotechnics in all these pieces which are much prized by violinists from Heifetz downwards – music to show off the virtuoso possibilities (and improbabilities) of the instrument, and this they surely do. Ricci uses every trick in the book to make one gasp at the sheer technical brilliance – try the final Bazzini number first, and then the music of Sarasate, in which he was a specialist. The mono sound is naturally a little thin, but has transferred very well to CD, and half the programme is in excellent stereo. As much of this repertoire is rare in the concert hall these days, this collection is especially valuable, and this is now available as a Double Decca, thanks to Australian Decca (who compiled the original issue). Thoroughly recommended.

Richter, Sviatoslav (piano)

Recital: BACH: *Well-tempered Klavier: Preludes and Fugues Nos. 1–6, BWV 846–53.* HAYDN: *Piano Sonata in G min.* SCHUBERT: *Allegretto in C min., D.915; Ländler in A, D.366.* CHOPIN: *Polonaise-fantaisie, Op. 61; Etudes: in C; in C min. (Revolutionary), Op. 10/7 & 12.* SCHUMANN: *Abegg Variations, Op. 1.* DEBUSSY: *Estampes; Préludes: Voiles; Le Vent dans la plaine; Les Collines d'Anacapri.* SCRIABIN: *Sonata No. 5 in F sharp min., Op. 53.* RACHMANINOV: *Prelude in G sharp min., Op. 32/12.* PROKOFIEV: *Visions fugitives, Op. 22/3, 6 & 9; Sonata No. 8 in B flat, Op. 84.*

☞ ✿ (M) ★★★ DG (ADD) 476 2203 (2).

This remarkable Richter treasury collects many of the stereo recordings he made for DG (or which were licensed to DG) between 1962 and 1965. They are all of good quality and often the sound is excellent, if a little dry. The recordings, taken from live recitals during his Italian tour, bring a cough or two. The opening Bach *Preludes and Fugues* immediately bring rapt concentration. The Chopin selection opens with a wonderfully poetic account of the *Polonaise-fantaisie*, and the *Revolutionary Study* is almost overwhelming in its excitement. The audience noises may be found intrusive both here and in the superb Debussy performances, yet *Jardins sous la pluie* is quite magical, as is the gentle exoticism of *Pagodes* (both from *Estampes*). Richter's Schumann is no less special, and in the delicious account of the Schubert *Ländler* one can sense the smile in his eyes. Both in the Scriabin and Prokofiev *Sonatas* it is the powerful dynamism of Richter's technique that projects the music so vividly, but of course there is much poetic feeling too. An inexpensive cross-section of his art, this could hardly be bettered. A splendid addition to Universal's 'Penguin Rosette' Collection, at mid-price.

'*Sviatoslav Richter in the 1950s*', Volume 1: PROKOFIEV: *Cinderella: 5 Pieces. Visions fugitives, Op. 22: excerpts; Piano Sonata No. 7 in B flat, Op. 83.* SCHUMANN: *Toccata in C, Op. 7.* DEBUSSY: *Images, Book II: Cloches à travers les feuilles* (2 performances). CHOPIN: *Etudes in C & E* (2 performances), *Op. 10/1 & 3.* RACHMANINOV: *Preludes: in F sharp min., Op. 23/1; in B flat, Op. 23/2; in D, Op. 23/4; in G min., Op. 23/5; in C min., Op. 23/7; in A flat, Op. 23/8; in A, Op. 31/9; in C, Op. 32/1; in B flat min., Op. 32/2; in F, Op. 32/7; in B min., Op 32/10; in G sharp min., Op. 32/12; in G sharp min., Op. 32/15.* TCHAIKOVSKY: *Piano Sonata in G, Op. 37.* LISZT: *Valse oubliée No. 1.*

(M) (★★★) Parnassus mono PACD 96-001/2 (2).

We owe this double-pack of Richter to the dedication of some enthusiasts who have tracked down a considerable number of live performances from the 1950s, before his star had risen in the West, recordings which have never been issued before. The unsigned liner-note claims that Richter was at this time 'perhaps even more of a virtuoso than the more mature artist' and that 'he was more willing to dazzle audiences with his facility'. Another claim the producer makes, and one that must be upheld, is that 'the recorded sound while not the ultimate in fidelity is superior to what we might have expected from early Russian tapes'.

The first CD brings some dazzling Prokofiev, recorded in Moscow in April 1958. The transcriptions from *Cinderella*, the excerpts from *Visions fugitives* and the *Seventh Sonata* are little short of amazing. (The sonata was recorded two months before the BMG/Melodiya version made at a recital in the Great Hall of the Moscow Conservatoire, and is every bit as electrifying, though the BMG is better recorded.) The producer's claim that Richter took more risks in this concert performance of the Schumann *Toccata* than in the safer but still stunning DG studio recording later the same year is also on target.

The Tchaikovsky *G major Sonata*, Op. 37, comes from another Moscow recital, in December 1954, two years before the BMG account, as do two other pieces also played at that later recital, the *Cloches à travers les feuilles* and the Chopin *E major Study*, Op. 10, No. 3. Richter also recorded the Tchaikovsky *Sonata* in the studio in the mid-1950s (it was issued in the UK on Parlophone). We would not wish to choose between the two presently before the public; what is undeniable is that both are pretty sensational. (There are some barely discernible bumps in the slow movement but the transfers are otherwise excellent.) So, for that matter, are the 13 Rachmaninov *Preludes* in this recital. What pianisim!

'*Sviatoslav Richter in the 1950s*', Volume 2:
MUSSORGSKY: *Pictures at an Exhibition.*
SCHUMANN: *Abegg Variations, Op. 1; 3 Fantasiestücke, Op. 12; Humoreske in B flat, Op. 20.* SCRIABIN: *12 Preludes, Op. 11; Sonatas Nos. 2 in G sharp min., Op. 19; 6, Op. 62.* TCHAIKOVSKY: *Piano Concerto No. 1 in B flat min., Op. 23* (with USSR State SO, Rachlin).

(M) (**(*)) Parnassus mono PACD 96-003/4 (2).

The earliest performances here are the Mussorgsky *Pictures* and the Scriabin *Sixth Sonata*, which come from a 1952 Moscow recital. The BMG/Melodiya account comes from 1958, the same year as the famous Sofia recital, while their recording of the Scriabin comes from three years later, in 1955. The other Scriabin repertoire, along with the Schumann pieces, come from June 1955 and the Tchaikovsky concerto with Nathan Rachlin from 1957. Though the playing is again dazzling, the orchestral recording is coarse and climaxes discolour, and in the climaxes the engineers can be heard reducing the level to avoid overloading. Apart from this, Richter is in a class of his own, and *aficionados* will surely want this.

'*In Memoriam - Legendary Recordings (1959–1962)*':
BACH: *Well-tempered Clavier, Book I: Preludes and Fugues Nos. 1, 4–6 & 8, BWV 846, 849–51 & 853.*
HAYDN: *Sonata in G min., Hob XVI/44.* CHOPIN: *Ballades Nos. 3 in A flat, Op. 47; 4 in F min., Op. 52; Polonaise-fantaisie in A flat, Op. 61; Etudes in C; C min. (Revolutionary), Op. 10/1 & 12.* SCHUBERT: *Allegretto in C min., D.915. Ländler, D.366/1, 3 & 4–5.* SCHUMANN: *Abegg Variations, Op. 1.*
DEBUSSY: *Estampes; Préludes, Book I: Voiles; Le Vent dans la plaine; Les Collines d'Anacapri.*
RACHMANINOV: *Preludes Nos. 3 in B flat; 5 in D; 6 in G min.; 8 in C min., Op. 23/2, 4–5 & 7; 12 in C; 13 in B flat; 23 in G sharp min., Op. 32/1–2 & 12.*
PROKOFIEV: *Visions Fugitives, Op. 22/3, 6 & 9.*
(B) *** DG Double 457 667-2 (2).

Over the years DG have made a number of different collections from the recordings Richter made at live recitals while on tour in Europe between 1959 and 1962. The present programme extends the Chopin coverage to include two *Ballades*, volatile, highly individual performances; the number of Rachmaninov *Preludes* is also increased to cover virtually all the favourites. The remastered recordings – the quality varies somewhat between items – are for the most part very good, though audience noises inevitably intrude at times.

The compelling accounts of the Scriabin and Prokofiev *Sonatas* previously included are here omitted. Each disc is generously full and the set is highly recommendable. The discography details are as follows: Rachmaninov *Preludes* (except Op. 32/12): Warsaw, 1959; Haydn *Sonata*, Chopin Op. 47, Debussy *Préludes*: Wembley Town Hall, 1961; Bach, Prokofiev, Chopin (except Op. 47), Debussy *Estampes*, Rachmaninov Op. 32/12, Schubert, Schumann: Italian tour, 1962.

CHOPIN: *Ballade No. 3 in A flat, Op. 47; Barcarolle in F sharp, Op. 60; Etudes, Op. 10/12 (2 versions) 1; 4; 6; & 10; Mazurkas, Op. 24/1–4; Scherzo No. 4 in E min., Op. 54.* DEBUSSY: *Images, Book II: Cloches à travers les feuilles. L'Isle joyeuse; Préludes, Book I: I Danseuses de Delphes; II Voiles; III Le Vent dans la plaine; IV Les Sons et les parfums tournent dans l'air du soir; VI Des pas sur la neige; IX La Sérénade interrompue (2 versions); V Les Collines d'Anacapri; XI La Danse de Puck; VII Ce qu'a vu le vent d'ouest; X La Cathédrale engloutie. Préludes, Book II: I Brouillards; II Feuilles mortes; III La Puerta del Vino; IV Les Fées sont d'exquises danseuses; Bruyèrea; VI General Lavine – eccentric; VII La Terrasse des audiences du clair de lune; VIII Ondine; IX Hommage à Pickwick Esq. P.P.M.P.C.; X Canope; XI Les tierces alternées; XII Feux d'artifice.*
PROKOFIEV: *Dance, Op. 32/1.*
(M) (***) BBC mono BBCL 4021-2 (2).

These archive recordings offer a unique glimpse of Richter's art in the early 1960s. The Chopin and the ten *Préludes* from Book I plus *L'Isle joyeuse* and

Cloches à travers les feuilles come from a 1961 relay of his Festival Hall recital; Book II comes from a 1967 recital at The Maltings, Snape. He was very much at his peak at this time, and no Richter admirer or lover of the piano will want to be without this invaluable memento. As a Debussy interpreter, Richter gave a powerfully concentrated distillation that brought the atmosphere of these miniature tone-poems before our eyes with greater refinement of colour and touch than almost all his colleagues. Sonic limitations are surprisingly few and matter little, given the distinction and stature of this playing.

BEETHOVEN: *Piano Sonata No. 11 in B flat, Op. 22; Eroica Variations, Op. 35.* CHOPIN: *Nocturnes, Op. 15/1; Op. 72/2.* HAYDN: *Piano Sonata No. 37 in E, Hob.XVI/22.* RACHMANINOV: *12 Preludes, Op. 23/1, 2, 4, 5 & 8; Op. 32/1, 2, 6, 7, 9, 10 & 12.* SCHUMANN: *Etudes Symphoniques.*

(M) *** BBC (ADD) BBCL 4090-2.

These performances are assembled from various broadcasts: the Rachmaninov from the Free Trade Hall, Manchester, in 1969; the Beethoven and Schumann from a Festival Hall recital in the previous year, and the Haydn *Sonata* and one of the Chopin *Nocturnes* from the Snape Maltings in 1967. This was a period when Richter was at the height of his powers: the Rachmaninov *Preludes* particularly draw from him playing of exceptional eloquence and concentration. However, the Beethoven and Schumann are hardly less impressive, and the Haydn *E major Sonata* (No. 37 in E, Hob.XVI/22) has tremendous character too. The recordings are excellent for their period and enhance the attractions of a most distinguished compilation.

BEETHOVEN: *Piano Sonatas Nos. 3 in C, Op. 2/3; 4 in E flat, Op. 7; 27 in E min., Op. 90.*
**(*) Olympia (ADD) OCD 336.

SCHUBERT: *Piano Sonatas Nos. 19 in C min., D.958; 21 in B flat, D.960.*
**(*) Olympia OCD 335.

RACHMANINOV: *Etudes-tableaux, Opp. 33 & 39; 6 Preludes, Op. 23/1–2, 4–5, 7–8; 7 Preludes, Op. 32/1–2, 6–7, 9–10, 12.*
**(*) Olympia (DDD/ADD) OCD 337.

Sonically these recordings leave a good deal to be desired: in most instances the balance is fairly close and the acoustic on the dry side without being unacceptably so. They call for tolerance, but this is well worth extending for the sake of this music-making. The early Beethoven *Sonatas* are from 1975 and the *E minor, Op. 90,* comes from 1971. The *C major Sonata, Op. 2, No. 3,* is far more powerful than one is used to encountering, particularly in the intensity of the slow movement; Richter's view of the *E flat, Op. 7,* familiar from an earlier recording Philips issued in the 1960s, is further deepened.

There is a marvellously inward feeling and a sense of profound euphony in the *E minor, Op. 90.*

The Schubert *Sonatas* were recorded in the early 1970s; the *C minor Sonata, D.958* in 1973, the *B flat, D.960* in the previous year; neither has been in currency in the UK. Richter's way with Schubert is well known. Some listeners have difficulty in coming to terms with the sheer scale of his first movement: it seems almost timeless, just as the almost static inwardness of the slow movement is not for those in a hurry.

Some of the Rachmaninov *Etudes-tableaux* have been available before, but again most are new to this country. The majority of the pieces were recorded in 1971 but others are later. The playing is of a rare order of mastery and leaves strong and powerful resonances. Richter's conception goes far beyond the abundant virtuosity this music calls for, and the characterization of the music is strong and searching. If you invest in no other of these Olympia CDs, this is the one that is unique – which makes the poor sound-quality particularly regrettable.

Robles, Marisa (harp)

'*The World of the Harp*': FALLA: *Three-cornered Hat: Danza del corregidor.* ALBENIZ: *Rumores de la Caleta; Torre Bermeja.* BIDAOLA: *Viejo zortzico.* EBERL (**attrib. Mozart**): *Theme, Variations and Rondo pastorale.* BEETHOVEN: *Variations on a Swiss Song.* BRITTEN: *Ceremony of Carols: Interlude.* FAURE: *Impromptu, Op. 86.* PIERNE: *Impromptu-caprice, Op. 9.* SALZEDO: *Chanson de la nuit.* BRAHMS: *Lullaby.* BACH: *Well-tempered Clavier: Prelude No. 1.* CHOPIN: *Mazurka, Op. 7/1; Prelude, Op. 28/15 (Raindrop).* HASSELMANS: *La Source.*

℗ (M) *** Decca (ADD) 433 869-2.

The artistry of Marisa Robles ensures that this is a highly attractive anthology and the programme is as well chosen as it is beautifully played. As ex-Professor of the harp at the Madrid Conservatory, Robles has a natural affinity for the Spanish music that opens her programme, and other highlights include a magnetic account of the Britten *Interlude* and the Salzedo *Chanson de la nuit* with its bell-like evocations. The Eberl *Variations* are highly engaging. The excellent recordings derive from the Argo catalogue of the 1960s and '70s, except for the Chopin, Brahms, Bach and Hasselmans pieces, which have been added to fill out the present reissue (75 minutes). The delicious Hasselmans roulades are the epitome of nineteenth-century harp writing. The CD has a most realistic presence.

Los Romeros

Spanish Guitar Favourites (with Pepe Romero, Celín Romero, Celedonio Romero, Celino Romero):

GIMENEZ: *La boda de Luis Alonso: Malagueña – Zapateado; El baile de Luis Alonso: Intermedio.* BOCCHERINI: *Guitar Quintet No. 4 in D, G.448: Grave – Fandango.* Celedonio ROMERO: *Fantasia Cubana; Malagueñas.* FALLA: *El amor brujo: Ritual Fire Dance.* SOR: *L'encouragement, Op. 34.* PRAETORIUS: *Bransle de la torche; Ballet; Volta.* TARREGA: *Capricho árabe.* TURINA: *La oración del torero.* TORROBA: *Estampas.*

✪ ✱✱✱ Ph. (IMS) 476 2265.

The famous Los Romeros guitar quartet (father Celedonio and three sons, led by Pepe) have never sounded quite like this before on record. The playing throughout is both vibrant and seemingly totally spontaneous, although the group were in fact recorded under studio conditions in the San Luis Rey Mission in California. Opening with a compelling *Malagueña – Zapateado* of Jerónimo Giménez and closing with an engaging and lighter *Intermedio* encore by the same composer, both from zarzuelas, this 74-minute collection of mainly Spanish music grips and entertains the listener as at a live concert. Celedonio contributes two pieces of his own, a charming solo lightweight *Fantasía Cubana*, and the others join him for his glittering flamenco *Malagueñas*, which has an improvisatory central section before the dashing coda with castanets. Among the more famous pieces arranged for the four players are the very effective Falla *Ritual fire dance* and Turina's *La oración del torero* (full of evocation), while Sor's *L'encouragement*, with its ingenuous lilting *Cantabile*, a simple but artful *Theme and variations* and elegant closing *Valse*, is played as a duet by Pepe and Celino. Tárrega's haunting *Capricho árabe* is exquisitely phrased by Celino. The arrangement of the three Praetorius dances, with an added condiment of percussion, is colourfully in period. The title of Torroba's collection of *Estampas* recalls the little Japanese prints which also inspired Debussy, and these eight sharply etched vignettes bring a highly imaginative response from the group, making this a highlight of the concert. The recording gives the guitars splendid presence against the attractively warm ambience, which in no way blurs the sharpness or focus of the players' attack. It is most welcome at mid-price in Universal's 'Penguin Rosette' Collection.

Rosenthal, Moritz (piano)

CHOPIN: *Piano Concerto No. 1 in E min., Op. 11* (with Berlin State Opera O, Weissmann); *Romanze* only (with NBC SO, Black). *Berceuse, Op. 57; Chants polonais* (arr. LISZT); *Etudes, Op. 10/1; 10/5* (twice); *Mazurkas, Opp. 63/3* (three versions); *67/1; Waltz in C sharp min., E min. Op. posth.*

(✱✱✱) Biddulph mono LHW 040.

Rosenthal was a pupil of Karl Mikuli, who was himself a Chopin pupil, and his Chopin is quite out of the ordinary. The *E minor Concerto* was made in

1930 and the ritornello is cut, but what pianism! (The alternative slow movement was recorded in New York on Rosenthal's 75th birthday.) Rosenthal's effortless virtuosity, lightness of touch, legatissimo and tonal subtlety are altogether remarkable. Playing of great culture from a distant age and beautifully transferred by Ward Marston.

Rossetti-Bonell, Dario (guitar)

'*Début*': BARRIOS: *2 Valses, Op. 8/3–4; Mazurka appassionata; Aconquija.* VIVALDI: *Mandolin Concerto in C, RV 425* (transcribed for solo guitar by Rossetti-Bonell). VILLA-LOBOS: *Preludes Nos. 1–5.* GRANADOS: *Valses poéticos.*

(B) ✱✱(✱) EMI 5 73499-2.

Dario, son of Carlos Bonell, proves to be a masterly guitarist, and by no means in the shadow of his father. His technique is consummate and he knows just how to seduce the ear with subtle rubato, as in the Barrios *Mazurka appassionata*, or with a magnetically gentle melodic ebb and flow, as in the *A minor* or *E major* Villa-Lobos *Preludes*, and how to hold the listener with dramatic use of light and shade as in *No. 4 in E minor*. The engaging closing Granados *Valses poéticos* are presented with charm and much expertise in the matter of colour. However, the inclusion of the Vivaldi *Mandolin Concerto*, arranged for guitar without orchestra, was a curious indulgence. It is very well played, of course, but fails to make a case for a guitar taking over the orchestral as well as solo mandolin roles. The recording, made in Forde Abbey, Somerset, is wholly natural with a most pleasing acoustic.

Rothwell, Evelyn (oboe)

Recital: C. P. E. BACH: *Sonata in G min.* TELEMANN: *Sonata in E flat.* M. HEAD: *Siciliana* (all with Aveling, harpsichord, Nesbitt, viola da gamba). LOEILLET: *Sonata in C* (arr. ROTHWELL). HANDEL: *Air & Rondo* (arr. & ed. ROTHWELL). MORGAN: *Melody* (all with Parry, piano).

(M) ✱✱ Dutton Lab./Barbirolli Soc. (ADD) CDSJB 1016 (with CORELLI; HAYDN; MARCELLO: *Oboe concertos* ✱✱✱).

Evelyn Rothwell, as always, plays expressively with charm and poise. But the recording of Valda Aveling's harpsichord seems unnecessarily recessed and insubstantial. Even so the Telemann *Sonata* is enjoyable enough, and the Michael Head *Siciliana* brings a more positive effect. The items accompanied on the piano by Wilfred Parry are more successful. He is still rather backwardly placed but emerges with a stronger personality, and the delightful Handel titbits and the Nicholas Morgan *Melody* are the highlights of the recital.

Salomon Quartet

'*The String Quartet in 18th-century England*': ABEL: *Quartet in A, Op. 8/5.* SHIELD: *Quartet in C min., Op. 3/6.* MARSH: *Quartet in B flat.* WEBBE: *Variations in A on 'Adeste fidelis'.* S. WESLEY: *Quartet in E flat.*
** Hyp. CDA 66780.

A good idea, let down by the indifferent invention of much of the music itself. The amateur, John Marsh, stands up very well alongside his professional companions, and his five-movement *Quartet in B flat* (modelled on Haydn's Op. 1/1 and almost as pleasing) is the first piece to catch the listener's attention, for Abel is a very dull dog indeed. Samuel Webbe's *Variations on 'O come all ye faithful'* does little but repeat the melody with decorations. Samuel Wesley begins conventionally and agreeably, then produces a real lollipop as the Trio of the Minuet and a similarly winning finale. No complaints about the performances: the Salomon Quartet play everything freshly and with total commitment, using original instruments stylishly and in the sweetest possible manner. They are very realistically recorded, too. Three stars for the performers but not for the programme.

Satoh, Toyohiko (lute)

'*Gaultier and the French Lute School*': E. GAULTIER: *Tombeau de Mezangeau; Courante; Carillon; Rossignol; Testament de Mezangeau; Canarie.* D. GAULTIER: *Tombeau de Mademoiselle Gaultier; Cleopâtre amante (Double).* J. GALLOT: *Prélude; Le bout de l'an de M. Gaultier; Courante la cigogne; Sarabande la pièce de huit heures; Volte la Brugeoise.* DUFAUT: *Prélude; Tombeau de M. Blanrocher; Dourante; Sarabande (Double); Gigue.* MOUTON: *Prélude. Tombeau de Gogo (Allemande); La belle homicide/Courante de M. Gaultier (Double de la belle homicide); Gavotte; La Princesse sarabande; Canarie.* DE VISEE: *Tombeau de M. Mouton (Allemande).*
*** Channel Classics Dig. CCS 8795.

Toyohiko Satoh has already given us a collection of the music of Robert de Visée (CCS 7795), whose *Tombeau de M. Mouton* provides one of the most affecting pieces here, to close a recital which is in essence a survey of French lute music of the seventeenth century.

Satoh is clearly an expert in this field, and he plays an original lute made by Laurentius Grieff of Ingolstadt in 1613, which was modified into an eleven-course French baroque instrument around 1670. It took four years for the Dutch lute-maker Van der Waals to restore it to playing condition, and its gut strings create a pleasingly warm sonority.

Satoh's playing is robust yet thoughtful and it has an improvisatory freedom which extends even to the dance movements. (Dufaut's *Gigue*, for instance, is jolly enough but would be difficult to dance to.) This is apparently possible because, around 1630, a new French tuning was developed within the lute school centring round Gaultier le Vieux (Ennemond Gaultier of Lyon, 1575–1651). This allowed more freedom for the fingers of the left hand, enabling lutenists to write their music in a *style brisé* (broken style), which was later to spread across Europe.

Gaultier and his cousin Denis (Gaultier le Jeune) were important innovators in their time and they also introduced the idea of the dignified 'tombeau' mementos, as well as vignettes with sobriquets like *Le rossignol* and *Carillon*, yet which are in no way imitative. The two versions of the *Canarie* (by Ennemond Gaultier and Mouton respectively) are based on the same melody and dance form, with a dotted rhythm, and both are among the more striking items here, alongside the expressive *Sarabande* of Dufaut and Mouton's *La Princesse*, which features the famous *La Folia*. Rather unexpectedly, the same composer's *La belle homicide* is a cheerful piece.

Scandinavian Wind Quintet

Danish Concert: NIELSEN: *Wind Quintet, Op. 43.* HOLMBOE: *Notturno, Op. 19.* NORGARD: *Whirl's World.* ABRAHAMSEN: *Walden.*
*** dacapo 8.224001.

The Scandinavian Wind Quintet give an eminently acceptable account of the Nielsen which can stand up to most of the competition. The Holmboe *Notturno* is a beautiful piece from 1940 whose language blends the freshness of Nielsen with the neo-classicism of Hindemith yet remains totally distinctive. The Nørgård is less substantial but is not otherwise available; Hans Abrahamsen's *Walden* is thin but atmospheric. Very present and lifelike recording.

Schiff, András and Peter Serkin (piano duo)

Music for 2 Pianos: MOZART: *Fugue in C min., K. 426; Sonata in D, K.448.* REGER: *Variations and Fugue on a Theme of Beethoven, Op. 86.* BUSONI: *Fantasia contrappuntistica.*
*** ECM 465 062-2 (2).

András Schiff and Peter Serkin join here in a symbiotic partnership to give a quite superb and certainly gripping account of Busoni's formidable *Fantasia contrappuntistica* in which they find as wide a range of mood and colour as in Max Reger's *Variations* (on a Beethoven *Bagatelle* from Op. 119). The theme is presented with a disarming simplicity, but Reger soon introduces characteristically florid textures, yet returning to simplicity in the *Andante* and *Sostenuto* variations. These alternate with *Agitato* and *Vivace* sections, leading to the spirited closing *Fugue*. The pair of early twentieth-century works are framed by two-piano music of Mozart. Here the opening *Fugue in C minor* is strong and positive, and the first movement of the *D major Sonata*, too, is taken very seriously, not emphasizing what Alfred Einstein called its 'gallant character' until the arrival of the second subject, and then only momentarily. However, the mood lightens in the central *Andante*, in which the two players exchange phrases very beguilingly, and the finale is rhythmically most winning. Excellent, well-focused and not too resonant recording.

Segovia, Andrés (guitar)

American Decca Recordings (1952–1969) (previously released by MCA): RODRIGO: *Fantasia para un gentilhombre.* PONCE: *Concierto del Sur.* BOCCHERINI: *Cello Concerto No. 6 in D* (arr. Cassadó in E for guitar) (with Symphony of the Air, Enrique Jorda). Solo music: TORROBA: *Castillos de España.* MOMPOU: *Suite Compostelana.* CASTELNUOVO-TEDESCO: *Sonata Omaggio a Boccherini, Op. 77.* PONCE: *Allego in A.* ESPLA: *Impresiones musicales No. 5: Estampa* (arr. for guitar). RODRIGO: *Tres piezas españolas: No. 1: Fandango.* DE MERCIA: *Praeludium & Allegro.* RONCALLI: *Passacaglia; Capricci armonici: Suite in G: Gigue; Suite in E min.: Gavotte.* MILAN: *6 Pavanes.* SANZ: *Suite española: Galliarda y Villano; Españoletas.* AGUADO: *8 Lessons.* SOR: *Minuets in C and C min. Etudes, Op. 6/1, 3 & 17; Op. 29/19–20; Op. 31/9 & 10; Op. 35/6 & 15.* ALBENIZ: *Suite española, Op. 47: Granada. Danza española, Op. 37: Andaluza; Danza triste. Tonadilla No. 1: La Maja de Goya.* BACH: *Lute Suite in E min., BWV 996: Allemande; Bourrée. Partita for Lute in C min., BWV 997* (both transposed to A min.); *Sarabande; Gigue. Prelude for Lute in C min., BWV 999* (trans. D min.). *Fugue for Lute in G min., BWV 1000* (trans. A min.). *Cello Suite No. 3 in C, BWV 1009* (trans. A). *Cello Suite No. 1 in G, BWV 1007* (trans. D): *Prelude. Cello Suite No. 6 in D, BWV 1012* (trans. E): *Gavottes I & II. Violin Partita No. 1 in B min., BWV 1002: Sarabande; Bourrée; Double. Violin Partita No. 2 in C min., BWV 1004: Chaconne. Violin Partita No. 3 in E, BWV 1006: Gavotte and Rondo. Violin Sonata No. 1 in G min.* (trans. to F sharp min.): *Siciliano.*
(M) *** DG stereo/mono 471 430-2 (4).

A set which has taken us by surprise. Although reissud by Deutsche Grammophon, and remastered at the Emil Berliner Studios, the recordings derive from American Decca and are of extraordinarily high quality. Segovia's guitar is beautifully caught, and in the solo music one might often feel that he is sitting out there behind the speakers. The concerto recordings are also first class and, with Enrique Jorda

directing the accompanying Symphony of the Air, the results are very appealing indeed. Rodrigo's *Fantasia para un gentilhombre* is most charácterfully done, and if the Ponce *Concierto del Sur* is a bit long-winded, it is in persuasive hands. The slow movement of Cassadó's transcription of Boccherini's *Concerto* is particularly warm-hearted. As for the rest of the repertory, it is predictably wide-ranging and includes complete sets of the pieces by the most familiar composers, but plenty of novelties too. The last of the four discs is devoted to Bach and is particularly treasurable, including as it does a complete recording of the transcribed *Third Suite for Unaccompanied Cello*, and Segovia's most familiar encore, the *Gavotte and Rondeau* from the *E major Violin Partita*. Segovia's playing is incomparable. Highly recommended.

'*The Legendary Segovia*': BACH: *Cello Suite in G, BWV 1007: Prelude* (arr. PONCE); (Unaccompanied) *Violin Partita No. 3 in E, BWV 1006: Gavotte & Rondo; Prelude in C min. for Lute, BWV 999* (both arr. SEGOVIA). SOR: *Thème varié, Op. 9.* Robert DE VISEE: *Minuet.* FROBERGER: *Gigue.* CASTELNUOVO-TEDESCO: *Hommage à Boccherini: Vivo e energico.* MENDELSSOHN: *String Quartet No. 1 in E flat, Op. 12: Canzonetta* (arr. SEGOVIA). MALATS: *Serenata.* ALBENIZ: *Suite española: Granada; Sevilla.* GRANADOS: *Danza española No. 10 in G, Op. 37.* TURINA: *Fandanguillo.* TORROBA: *Suite castellana: Fandanguillo. Sonatina in A: Allegretto. Preludio; Notturno.* PONCE: *Petite valse; Suite in A.* TARREGA: *Recuerdos de la Alhambra.*
(M) (***) EMI mono 5 67009-2.

It was Segovia's pioneering recitals in the 1930s that re-established the guitar in the public mind as a serious solo instrument. This collection consists of his early recordings, made over a span of 12 years from 1927 to 1939 either at Abbey Road or the Small Queen's Hall in London. There are quite a few transcriptions, including several Bach items, where the style of the playing is romantic (though never showing lapses of taste). However, the second part of the programme includes a high proportion of Spanish repertoire either written for or naturally suited to the guitar. What is so striking throughout this collection is the way all the music, slight or serious, springs vividly to life. Segovia had the gift of natural spontaneity in all he played, and he was in his prime at this period, so that technically this is wonderfully assured. His performance of Tárrega's famous *Recuerdos* is quite individual, with the underlying melodic line shaped like a song, rather than treated seamlessly. Guitar fans will find this generous 74-minute recital an essential purchase; others will be surprised to discover that no apologies need be made for the sound, which is natural in timbre and gives the instrument a ready projection.

Shifrin, David (clarinet), Lincoln Center Chamber Music Society

Five American Clarinet Quintets: CORIGLIANO: *Soliloquy for Clarinet and String Quartet.* ZWILICH: *Clarinet Quintet.* TOWER: *Turning Points.* SHENG: *Concertino for Clarinet and String Quartet.* ADOLPHE: *At the Still Point there the Dance Is.*
*** Delos DE 3183 (2).

A remarkable group of five surprisingly lyrical works, often searching and all readily approachable. John Corigliano's *Soliloquy*, adapted from the second movement of his *Concerto*, is essentially a haunting interplay between solo clarinet and violin. It was written in memory of his father, who was concertmaster of the New York Philharmonic, and is passionately elegiac. While sustaining its mood of desolation throughout, it leaves the listener uplifted rather than depressed.

Ellen Zwilich's *Quintet* opens with stabbing aggression from the strings and a continuing restlessness from the soloist, with moments of wildness carried through into the pungent second movement. Finally, a degree of calm is reached in the third, but its language becomes increasingly plangent, until relative serenity returns towards the close. The brief Scherzo is ironically jocular, followed by an atmospheric epilogue.

Joan Tower's *Turning Points* immediately features the device of a long slow crescendo for the soloist: its style is at first rhapsodic, with a central cadenza-like virtuoso display for the soloist and increasing agitation towards the end. The remaining two works are primarily atmospheric. Bright Sheng's attractively lyrical *Concertino* brings an exotic influence from Chinese folk music. It opens and closes reflectively, but its serenity does not run an even course, with energetic bursts from the clarinet. The Chinese influence is most strongly felt in the repeated scherzando ostinatos of the second movement.

Bruce Adolphe's *At the Still Point* is also ruminative, the first two movements, *Aria* and *Meditation*, move hauntingly towards the 'still point', though not without interruption, and then are released into the dance, which swirls, but in a relatively gentle, minimalist manner. It is a work of immediate appeal. David Shifrin's performances are masterly and the recording is excellent. A most stimulating collection.

(i) Snowden, Jonathan (flute), Andrew Litton (piano), (ii) Nicholas Daniel (oboe), Julius Drake (piano)

'*French Music for Flute and Oboe*': (i) WIDOR: *Suite for Flute and Piano, Op. 34.* FAURE: *Fantaisie, Op. 79; Morceau de concours.* DEBUSSY: *Syrinx.* HONEGGER: *Danse de la chèvre.* ROUSSEL: *Jouers de flûte, Op. 27.* MESSIAEN: *Le Merle noir.* POULENC: *Flute Sonata.* (ii) SAINT-SAENS: *Oboe Sonata.* DUTILLEUX: *Oboe Sonata.* KOECHLIN: *Oboe Sonata, Op. 28.* POULENC: *Oboe Sonata.*
(BB) *** Virgin 2x1 5 61495-2 (2).

This Virgin Double aptly and inexpensively pairs two outstanding recitals of French instrumental music, originally issued separately, but which in this format complement each other admirably. Jonathan Snowden, deftly accompanied by Andrew Litton, a formidable pianist, first gathers a vintage collection of French works for flute. The Poulenc *Sonata* is dazzlingly done, and so are the other virtuoso pieces, all strongly characterized. The surprise is the opening item, by Widor, delicate and pointed, charmingly lyrical, a suite by a composer now remembered for his heavyweight organ works.

On the second disc Nicholas Daniel and Julius Drake concentrate equally persuasively on four major French oboe sonatas. Once again the Poulenc proves highly diverting, its outer movements, *Elégie paisiblement* and *Déploration: très calme*, proving as unpredictable as ever. The opening piece, by Saint-Saëns, is captivating but by no means trivial, with its central *Allegretto* framed by two sections giving the soloist a great deal of freedom. Dutilleux's *Sonata* typically combines subtlety of colour and expressive depth with ingenuity. However, the most ambitious work is by Koechlin, its four movements running for 28 minutes. It opens in pastoral evocation, but afterwards the writing often becomes very prolix, the range of mood remarkably wide. The Daniel/Drake duo play it expertly and sympathetically, but they do not entirely erase one's suspicion that it would have been a stronger piece if more concise. Yet overall these paired recitals, well balanced and truthfully recorded, give much pleasure.

Staier, Andreas (harpsichord)

'*Variaciones del fandango español*': SOLER: *Fandango.* ALBERO: *Recercata, fuga y sonata in G; Recercata, fuga y sonata in D.* GALLES: *Sonatas Nos. 9 in C min.; 16 in F min.; 17 in C min.* LOPEZ: *Variaciones del fandango español.* FERRER: *Adagio in G min.; Sonata, Andantino in G min.* BOCCHERINI: *Fandango, Grave assai* (with Schornheim (harpsichord) & Gonzáles Cámpa (castanets)).
*** Teldec 3984 21468-2.

Framed by two great *Fandangos* by Soler and Boccherini, and with a sparkling further set of *Fandango Variations* by Félix López as centrepiece, this is a fascinatingly conceived recital, superbly played on an ideal harpsichord – a modern French copy of an early eighteenth-century German instrument (associated with Silbermann). The rest of the programme includes a pair of inventive triptychs by Sebastián de Albero (1722–56) – 'polyphony used in a very Mediterranean way' (to quote Staier) – and three delightful miniature sonatas by Joseph Gallés: *No. 16 in F minor* (a single movement) is particularly winning, as are the two short pieces by José Ferrer.

Staier plays with fine sensibility and great virtuosity, always retaining the listener's interest. For the spectacular finale (which he has freely arranged from the finale of Boccherini's *D major Guitar Quintet,* G.448) Staier is joined by an excellent second player, with a third artist to decorate the thrilling climax with castanets. The result is a semi-improvisational *tour de force.* The only small snag is that the recording is somewhat over-resonant – thus, setting a modest volume level is important, though not, of course, in the *Fandangos.*

Steele-Perkins, Crispian (trumpet), Stephen Cleobury (organ)

'*The King's Trumpeter*': MATHIAS: *Processional.* L. MOZART: *Concerto in E flat.* BOYCE: *Voluntaries in D.* ANON.: *3 16th-century Dances.* TELEMANN: *Concerto da caccia in D.* GOUNOD: *Méditation: Ave Maria.* STEELE: *6 Pieces, Op. 33.*

**(*) Priory PRCD 189.

Crispian Steele-Perkins is here given a chance to show his paces on a modern trumpet. The programme opens with Mathias's distinctly catchy *Processional* and covers a fairly wide range of repertoire, ending with the six characterful pieces by Christopher Steele. The disc is relatively short measure (53 minutes), but the playing is first class and the balance most convincing.

Stringer, Alan (trumpet), Noel Rawsthorne (organ)

'*Trumpet and Organ*' (organ of Liverpool Cathedral): M.-A. CHARPENTIER: *Te Deum: Prelude.* STANLEY: *Voluntary No. 5 in D.* PURCELL: *Sonata in C; Two Trumpet Tunes and Air.* BOYCE: *Voluntary in D.* CLARKE: *Trumpet Voluntary.* BALDASSARE: *Sonata No. 1 in F.* ROMAN: *Keyboard Suite in D: Non troppo allegro; Presto (Gigue).* FIOCCO: *Harpsichord Suite No. 1: Andante.* BACH: *Cantata No. 147: Jesu, Joy of Man's Desiring.* attrib. GREENE: *Introduction and Trumpet Tune.* VIVIANI: *Sonata No. 1 in C.*

(M) **(*) CRD 3308.

This collection is extremely well recorded. The reverberation of Liverpool Cathedral is under full control and both trumpet and organ are cleanly focused, while the trumpet has natural timbre and bloom. Alan Stringer is at his best in the classical pieces, the *Voluntary* of Boyce, the *Trumpet Tunes* and *Sonata* of Purcell and the stylishly played *Sonata* of Viviani, a most attractive little work. He also gives a suitably robust performance of the famous *Trumpet Volun-*

tary. Elsewhere he is sometimes a little square: the Bach chorale is rather too stiff and direct. But admirers of this repertoire will find much to enjoy, and the *Andante* of Fiocco has something in common with the more famous *Adagio* attributed to Albinoni in Giazotto's famous arrangement.

Swiss Wind Quintet

20th-century Wind Quintets: JANACEK: *Mládi.* NIELSEN: *Wind Quintet, Op. 43.* HINDEMITH: *Kleine Kammermusik, Op. 24/2.* LIGETI: *6 Bagatelles.*

(BB) *** Discover DICD 920395.

Mládi isn't, strictly speaking, a quintet, as it has an additional bass clarinet part. But it is uncommonly well played by this excellent Swiss group, and they give an equally sympathetic account of the Nielsen *Quintet,* most winning in the Minuet as well as in the third-movement Theme and variations. The Hindemith *Kleine Kammermusik* is hardly less successful, notably the dolorous Waltz which hints at Walton's *Façade,* and the pensive nostalgia of the third movement, although there is plenty of sparkling vitality elsewhere. The riotously witty opening movement of Ligeti's *Six Bagatelles* is splendidly done. There is little to choose between this performance of an unexpectedly entertaining work and that by the competing Claude Debussy Quintet on Harmonia Mundi (see above). In some ways the programme on this excellently recorded Discover disc is the more tempting, but both CDs are equally recommendable.

Tetzlaff, Christian (violin), Lars Anders Tomter (viola), Leif Over Andsnes (piano)

JANACEK: *Violin Sonata.* DEBUSSY: *Violin Sonata.* RAVEL: *Violin Sonata.* NIELSEN: *Violin Sonata No. 2, Op. 38.* BRAHMS: *Viola Sonatas Nos. 1 & 2.* SCHUMANN: *Märchenbilder.*

⊛ (BB) *** Virgin 5 62016-2 (2).

Virgin has here brought together two outstanding recital discs from the 1990s, of which the Brahms and Schumann coupling originally received a Rosette. There is no need to modify that judgement, and in view of the overall excellence of this combined release, it is extended to this double-CD as a whole. In the Janáček *Sonata,* Christian Tetzlaff and Leif Ove Andsnes show a complete understanding of the score. They play with commitment and dedication, while there are no more imaginative accounts of either the Debussy or Ravel couplings.

Nielsen's *G minor Sonata* is a transitional work in which the composer emerges from the geniality of the *Sinfonia espansiva* into the darker, more anguished world of the *Fourth Symphony.* It has much of the questing character of the latter and much of its muscularity, and Tetzlaff and Andsnes give a very distinguished – at times inspired – performance. They also provide one of the best accounts in the catalogue of the Brahms *Sonatas* in their viola form. Theirs is playing of great sensitivity and imagination. These Norwegian artists bring a wide range of colour to this music and they phrase with an unforced naturalness that is very persuasive, and their fresh account of the Schumann gives much pleasure too. The sound is natural and well balanced throughout this programme (in the Brahms and Schumann, there is a slight bias towards the piano), and this is altogether a rather special CD Double and remarkably inexpensive.

Thurston Clarinet Quartet

'*Clarinet Masquerade*': FARKAS: *Ancient Hungarian Dances from the 17th Century.* MOZART (arr. WHEWELL): *Divertimento No. 2.* TOMASI: *3 Divertissements.* GARNER (arr. BLAND): *Misty.* JOBIM (arr. BLAND): *The Girl from Ipanema.* DESPORTES: *French Suite.* ALBINONI (arr. THILDE): *Sonata in G min.* STARK: *Serenade.* GERSHWIN (arr. BLAND): *Rhapsody: Summertime.* PHILLIPS (arr. HARVEY): *Cadenza;* (arr. FERNANDEZ): *Muskrat Sousa.*

(M) ★★★ ASV CDWHL 2076.

A light-hearted concert, but an entertaining one which will especially appeal to those who like the clarinet's sonority, reedier than the flute's and with more character. The opening suite of *Hungarian folk dances* (with the chirps and cheeps in the finale very engaging) leads on to a Mozart *Divertimento* for basset horns. The other pieces, the insouciant Tomasi and the Desportes *Suite* (full of Ravelian elegance) are all amiable, and the arrangement of Gershwin's *Summertime* has the famous opening swerve of *Rhapsody in Blue* as its introduction. Finally there is the exuberant *Muskrat Sousa* which features a combination of *12th Street Rag* and *South Rampart Street Parade.* The recording is immaculately vivid.

Troussov, Kirill (violin), Alexandra Troussova (piano)

BEETHOVEN: *Violin Sonata No. 5 in C min., Op. 30/2.* BRAHMS: *Violin Sonata No. 3 in D min., Op. 108.* WIENIAWSKI: *Fantaisie brillante on Themes from Gounod's 'Faust'.* ZIMBALIST: *Fantasy on Rimsky-Korsakov's 'The Golden Cockerel'.*

(B) ★★★ EMI Début 5 73212-2.

One of the best of the valuable EMI Début series. Kirill Troussov and Alexandra Troussova are a brother-and-sister team of remarkable skill. They are Russian and were both in their teens when this outstanding recital was recorded. Vibrant and committed playing from both artists and excellent recordings.

Trpčeski, Simon (piano)

PROKOFIEV: *Piano Sonata No. 6 in A.* SCRIABIN: *Piano Sonata No. 5.* STRAVINSKY: *3 Movements from 'Petrushka'.* TCHAIKOVSKY (trans. PLETNEV): *Nutcracker Concert Suite.*

(B) ★★★ EMI Début 5 75202-2.

Simon Trpčeski is Macedonian-born and twenty-three, making his record debut in virtuoso Russian repertoire. He is obviously a pianist of awesome technical prowess, and it is a tribute to his pianism and artistry that only the most exalted comparisons come to mind. The Scriabin *Sonata No. 5* is very impressive indeed, it sounds freshly experienced and has great inner vitality. The Prokofiev *Sixth* does not have quite the abandon of Kissin's Tokyo version (at least in the finale) but is among the very finest all the same. Trpčeski plays the Stravinsky with great abandon and does very well in Mikhail Pletnev's arrangement of movements from the *Nutcracker*, though without perhaps having quite the range of colour and dynamics that the latter demands.

Tureck, Rosalyn (piano)

'*Live at the Teatro Colón*': BACH: *Adagio in G, BWV 968; Chromatic Fantasia and Fugue, BWV 903; Partita No. 1, BWV 825: Gigue. Goldberg Variation No. 29, BWV 988; Klavierbüchlein for Anna Magdalena Bach: Musette in D.* MENDELSSOHN: *Songs Without Words, Op. 19/1.* SCHUBERT: *Moments musicaux Nos. 2 in A flat; 3 in F min.* BACH/BUSONI: *Chaconne (from BWV 1004).* BRAHMS: *Variations and Fugue on a Theme by Handel, Op. 24.*

★★(★) VAI Audio VIAI 1024-2 (2).

Rosalyn Tureck has lost none of her magic, as this Buenos Aires (1992) live recital demonstrates, and it is good to find her so sympathetic in Schubert and Mendelssohn, as well as in Bach. Her articulation in the Brahms *Handel Variations* suggests she is thinking as much of Handel as of Brahms, but that is a comment, not a criticism. The Bach/Busoni *Chaconne* is splendid. Excellent recording, but there are two snags: the almost hysterical applause which bursts in as soon as a piece has ended and the fact that this recital would almost have fitted on one CD. These two play for just 83 minutes 31 seconds.

Vieaux, Jason (guitar)

Recital: MERLIN: *Suite del recuerdo.* PUJOL: *Preludios Nos. 2, 3 , & 5.* ORBON (de SOTO): *Preludio y Danza.* KROUSE: *Variations on a Moldavian hora.* BARRIOS: *Valses, Op. 8/3 & 4; Julia*

Florida: Barcarola. MOREL: *Chôro; Danza Brasileira; Danza in E min.* BUSTAMENTE: *Misionera.*

✪ (BB) ★★★ Naxos 8.553449.

This is the finest début guitar recital we have heard for some years. Jason Vieaux is a young American musician, already a prize-winner – and no wonder. This Latin-American repertoire is unfailingly diverting in his hands: there are no familiar names here except that of Barrios, yet almost every item is either memorably evocative or it makes the pulse quicken. Vieaux's completely natural rubato at the opening *Evocación* of José Luis Merlin's *Suite del recuerdo* is quite masterly and the slow crescendos in the final *Carnavalito* are thrilling; then there is a complete change of mood and the *Evocación* makes a haunting return before the final *Joropo.* The *Preludios* of Pujol are quite magical; Vieaux then lets his hair down for the *Candombe.* The two *Valses* of Barrios are deliciously fragile, with the central *Barcarola* hardly less subtle, while the more robust Brazilian dances of Jorge Morel have real panache. The Naxos recording has good ambience and is present yet not too closely balanced. Unforgettable.

Wagler, Dietrich (organ)

'*Great European Organs No. 24*': Freiberg Dom, Silbermann organ: SCHEIDT: *Magnificat Noni toni.* CLERAMBAULT: *Suite de premier ton.* BUXTEHUDE: *Prelude and Fugue in D min.* KREBS: *Choral Preludes: Mein Gott, das Herze bring ich dir; Herr Jesus Christ, dich zu uns wend; Herzlich tut mich verlangen; O Ewigkeit, du Donnerwort.* J. S. BACH: *Fantaisie in G; Prelude and Fugue in C.*

★★(*) Priory PRCD 332.

The organ, rather than the player, is the star of this record; the latter's performances are sound but very much in the traditional German style. But he knows his instrument and the opening *Magnificat Noni toni* of Scheidt sounds resplendent, with the following Clérambault *Suite* also very effectively registered. A well-balanced programme, lacking only the last degree of flair in presentation.

Weir, Gillian (organ)

'*King of Instruments: The Art of Dame Gillian Weir (A feast of organ music from the 16th to 20th centuries)*'

Volume I: BACH: *Toccata, Adagio and Fugue in C, BWV 564; Fantasia in G, BWV 572; Trio Sonata No. 1 in E flat, BWV 525; Passacaglia in C min., BWV 582* (Organ of St Lawrence, Rotterdam). MARCHAND: *Pièces d'Orgue, Premier Livre: Dialogue sur les grands jeux; Récit de tierce en taille; Basse et dessus de trompette et de cornet; Récit de voix humaine; Cinquième Livre: Bass de coumorne*

ou de trompette; Duo; Récit; Plein-jeu; Fugue; Basse de trompette ou de cromorne; Récit de tierce en taille (Organ of St Maximin, Thionville, France). BULL: *Dr Bull's my selfe; Dr Bull's jewell* (Organ of Hexham Abbey).

Volume II: CLERAMBAULT: *Suite de premier ton; Suite de deuxième ton* (Organ of St Leonard Kirche, Basel, Switzerland). BRUHNS: *Praeludium Nos. 1–3; Chorale: Nun komm, der Heiden Heiland* (Organ of Clare College, Cambridge).

Volume III: ROBERDAY: *Fuges et caprices pour orgue Nos. 1–12* (Organ of St Leonhardkirche, Basel, Switzerland). LANGLAIS: *Dialogue sur les mixtures* (Organ of Hexam Abbey). SCHEIDT: *Passamezzo (Variations 1–12)* (Organ of Clare College, Cambridge).

Volume IV: DANDRIEU: *Premier Livre de Pièces d'Orgue: Pièces en A, Mi, La. Magnificat* (Organ of St Leonard, Basel, Switzerland); *Pièces en G, Ré, Sol minuer; Magnificat II.* MARCHAND: *Pièces d'Orgue, Troisième Livre: Dialogue sur les grands jeux; Quatrième Livre: Duo; Fugue; Trio; Récit; Duo; Basse et trompette; Récit de tierce en taille* (Organ of St Maximin, Thionville, France). DE GRIGNY: *Tierce en taille.* MULET: *Toccata Tu es Petrus* (Organ of Hexam Abbey).

Volume V: CAMILLERI: *Missa Mundi* (Organ of Royal Festival Hall). WIDOR: *Symphony No. 6: Allegro.* VIERNE: *Impromptu.* DAQUIN: *Noël suisse.* DUPRE: *La Fileuse.* TOMKINS: *Worcester braules.* SWEELINCK: *Chorale: Mein junges Leben hat ein End.* DUBOIS: *Toccata* (Organ of Hexam Abbey).

★★★ Australian Argo/Decca (ADD) 460 185-2 (5).

Gillian Weir made her début at the 1965 season of Proms, and soon established a formidable reputation over the widest range of organ repertoire, but especially in music of the French school. Over a period of five years in the latter half of the 1970s, she made a series of major recordings for Decca's Argo label and it is good that this logo has been retained for the present superbly remastered five-disc survey.

Her Bach, recorded on an ideal Dutch organ in Rotterdam, is cool and poised. The bravura in the deliciously registered *Fantasia in G* cannot escape the listener, yet there is no sense of the virtuosity being flaunted. The *Trio Sonata* is equally colourful, but the remorseless tread of the *Passacaglia in C minor*, taken very steadily, is undoubtedly compelling, and the *Toccata, Adagio and Fugue* is hardly less telling in its sense of controlled power.

Louis Marchand (1669–1732) was Bach's French contemporary: his suites are not learned but meant to divert, which they certainly do here and especially the delectably registered *Basse et dessus de trompette et de cornet* from the first book and the comparable pieces in the second, again played on a highly suitable organ in France. The brief encores by John Bull are equally tangy and spirited.

Clérambault's *Livre d'orgue* dates from 1710 and follows the same layout as those of Marchand: the music has slightly more formality, yet the influences of French dance music remain, and once again Weir's sparkling registration tickles the ear. The Swiss organ also features an authentic 'tremblant fort' stop, used in the piece called *Flûtes*, with a suprisingly modern effect, followed by the charming dialogue of the *Récit de Nazard* and a powerful closing *Caprice*.

Nikolaus Bruhns (1665–97) died young and left only five organ works, of which four are recorded here. His individuality is striking, and so is the quirky originality of his musical style, which freely interchanges fugal passages and sections of the most florid bravura. The *First Praeludium in G major* has the kind of immediate appeal which could make it famous if regularly heard; its memorable fugal subject is even more jaunty than Bach's *Fugue à la gigue*. Gillian Weir has the full measure of this music, finding a perfect balance between the fantasy and the structural needs of each piece. She dazzles the ear not only with her vigour and virtuosity but also with some quite scrumptious registration on an organ at Clare College, Cambridge, that seems exactly right for the music. The recording is marvellous, a demonstration of clarity and sonority admirably combined.

François Roberday (1624–80) will be little more than a name – if that – to most readers. He is a *petite maître* who occasionally figures in recitals, but has until now not made a very striking presence in the CD catalogue. This recording of his 12 *Fugues et caprices* (over an hour of music) is made on a modern instrument in Basel which produces very authentic-sounding timbres. As usual Gillian Weir plays with enormous style and aplomb, but it would be idle to maintain that this is music of more than passing interest, except to the specialist collector. Once again the Argo recording has splendid range and presence.

On the other hand, Samuel Scheidt's *Passamezzo Variations*, taken from the first Volume of his *Tablatura nova* has a more general appeal, readily demonstrating the composer's mastery of variation technique, with imaginative invention throughout. Gillian Weir helps a great deal, not only by playing the music splendidly but by again choosing registrations with great flair and a marvellous sense of colour. The piquancy of several of her combinations is unforgettably apt and she is superbly recorded. This music was originally coupled with the Bruhns *Preludes* above, but now it is joined with Roberday, with Langlais's rhythmically quirky *Dialogue for the mixtures* used as a colourful intermezzo.

Dandrieu was a younger contemporary of Couperin le Grand and, like him, came from a musical family. He spent most of his life as organist at Saint-Barthélemy in Paris and at the Royal Chapel. The First Book of organ pieces, published in 1739 a year after his death, contains a number of suites; two

are recorded here, consisting of an offertory, several other short movements, and a series of couplets which comprise the organ's contribution to a pair of settings of the *Magnificat*. The music is more than just historically interesting; the invention is full of individual character and resource. Weir plays each *Suite* and *Magnificat* on a different instrument, both of them recorded in a lively acoustic, and her interpretations are marked by a vivid palette, authority and taste. There follows a further selection of *Pièces* by Louis Marchand and a move forward in time for Nicolas de Grigny's serene *Tierce en Taille* (effectively decorated). The programme of this most stimulating disc ends with a famously brilliant twentieth-century Toccata, *Tu es Petrus*, by Henri Mulet.

The composer who dominates the final disc, Charles Camilleri, is Maltese, but his background influence comes as much from the East as the West. The (45-minute) *Missa Mundi* is a highly mystical work, inspired by a meditative prose-poem by Teilhard de Chardin, *La Messe sur le Monde*, written in the middle of the Ordos Desert area of China in 1923. The music follows the five sections of the meditation: *The offering; Fire over earth; Fire in the earth; Communion; Prayer*. The poem introduces an astonishing range of organ technique and sonority from the frenzied *Fire in the earth* to the simplistic closing *Prayer*. Weir gives a thrillingly dedicated performance which immediately grabs the listener. Certainly this playing offers both a personal identification with the music and great bravura in equal measure; at times it is as overwhelming as the composer envisaged, at others its simple statements show an eloquence that is notable for its gentleness. The recording is superb. It is as clear and clean as a whistle, immensely wide in dynamic range, and there is not a ripple of distortion of any kind.

The rest of the programme is made up of a skilfully chosen selection of genre pieces, among which Vierne's rippling *Impromptu*, Daquin's charming fanfare-like *Noël suisse* and Dupré's delicate evocation of *La Fileuse* stand out. The jolly closing Toccata of Theodor Dubois (which has a whiff of Widor) makes an exhilarating finale.

Almost all this repertoire is most rewarding and can be cordially recommended even to those who normally fight shy of early organ composers. It could hardly be played more masterfully and the engineers provide first-class sound throughout. Readers interested in this repertory (and even those who are not) should investigate this thoroughly satisfying survey.

Whiteley, John Scott (organ)

'*Great Romantic Organ Music*' (organ of York Minster): TOURNEMIRE: *Improvisation on the Te Deum.* JONGEN: *Minuet-Scherzo, Op. 53.* MULET: *Tu es Petrus.* DUPRE: *Prelude and Fugue in G min., Op. 3/7.* R. STRAUSS: *Wedding Prelude.* KARG-ELERT: *Pastel in B, Op. 92/1.* BRAHMS: *Chorale Prelude: O*

Gott, du frommer Gott, Op. 122/7. LISZT: *Prelude and Fugue on B-A-C-H, G.260.*
*** York CD 101.

A superb organ recital, with the huge dynamic range of the York Minster organ spectacularly captured on CD and *pianissimo* detail registering naturally. John Scott Whiteley's playing is full of flair: the attractively complex and sparklingly florid *Prelude and Fugue* of Marcel Dupré is exhilarating and reaches a high climax, while the grand Liszt piece is hardly less overwhelming. The opening Tournemire *Improvisation* is very arresting indeed, while Jongen's *Minuet-Scherzo* displays Whiteley's splendidly clear articulation.

Williams, John (guitar)

'*Spanish Guitar Music*': I. ALBENIZ: *Asturias; Tango; Córdoba; Sevilla.* SANZ: *Canarios.* TORROBA: *Nocturno; Madroños.* SAGRERAS: *El Colibri.* M. ALBENIZ: *Sonata in D.* FALLA: *Homenaje; Three-cornered Hat: Corregidor's Dance; Miller's Dance. El amor brujo: Fisherman's Song.* CATALAN FOLKSONGS: *La Nit de Nadal; El noy de la mare; El testamen de Amelia.* GRANADOS: *La Maja de Goya. Spanish Dance No. 5.* TARREGA: *Recuerdos de la Alhambra.* VILLA-LOBOS: *Prelude No. 4 in E min.* MUDARRA: *Fantasia.* TURINA: *Fandanguillo, Op. 36.*
⊖—• (B) *** Sony (ADD) SBK 46347.

John Williams can show strong Latin feeling, as in the vibrant *Farruca* of the *Miller's Dance* from Falla's *Three-cornered Hat*, or create a magically atmospheric mood, as in the hauntingly registered transcription of the *Fisherman's Song* from *El amor brujo*. He can play with thoughtful improvisatory freedom, as in the Villa-Lobos *Prelude*, with its *pianissimo* evocation, or be dramatically spontaneous, as in the memorable performance of Turina's *Fandanguillo*, which ends the recital magnetically. The instinctive control of atmosphere and dynamic is constantly rewarding throughout a varied programme, and the technique is phenomenal yet never flashy, always at the service of the music. The remastering brings a clean and truthful, if very immediate, image. Background is minimal and never intrusive.

Wilson, Christopher (lute)

'*La Magdalena*' (*Lute Music in Renaissance France*): BLONDEAU (publ. ATTAIGNANT): *La Brosse (Recoupe et Tourdion); La Magdalena (Recoupe et Tourdion).* ANON. (publ. ATTAIGNANT): *Bransle de Poictou; Tant que vivray; Pavane; Gaillarde; Prelude; Une bergerotte.* DE PARIGI: *2 Recercars.* BERLIN: *Fantaisie No. 3; Trio No. 2.* PALADIN: *Anchor che col partir; Fantaisie.* MORLAYE: *Bransle d'Ecosse No. 1; Bransle gay; Fantaisie; Sans liberté; Pavane;*

Gaillarde piemontoise. DE RIPPE: *Pleurés mes yeux; 2 Fantaisies; Galliarde.* LE ROY: *Passemeze; La souris.* BAKFARK: *Si grand è la pietà.*
*** Virgin 5 45140-2.

An agreeable, unassertive, hour-long programme for the late evening, although perhaps a few more lively dances would have made the recital even more attractive. Certain items stand out, like the anonymous portrayal of *Une bergerotte*, the title-piece and the two works of Jean Paul Paladin (although *Anchor che col partir* is a transcription of a famous madrigal of the period – by Cipriano da Rore). Valentin Bakfark's *Si grand è la pietà* brings yet another madrigal arrangement (by Jacques Arcadelt). Most of this music has a character of gentle melancholy, so the exceptions, like the *Bransle gay* and the *Gaillarde piemontoise* (both by Morlaye), make a welcome diversion. The two pieces by Adrian Le Roy are also rather more extrovert, but the pervading atmosphere is doleful. Christopher Wilson plays with much sensitivity and he is beautifully recorded, provided one accepts the rather misty, ecclesiastical acoustic.

Winters, Ross (recorder), Andrew Ball (piano)

English Recorder Music: JACOB: *Variations.* SCOTT: *Aubade.* RUBBRA: *Sonatina, Op. 128; Passacaglia sopra 'Plusiers regrets', Op. 113; Meditation sopra 'Coers désolés', Op. 67.* Antony HOPKINS: *Suite.* John GARDNER: *Little Suite in C, Op. 60.* Colin HAND: *Sonata breve.* REIZENSTEIN: *Partita.*
**(*) British Music Soc. BMS 425CD.

This collection has been recorded by the British Music Society specifically to explore contemporary repertoire associated with the pioneering recorder virtuoso, Carl Dolmetsch, for whom all these works were written. What seems perverse however is that many of these pieces (notably those by Gordon Jacob, Rubbra and John Gardner) were intended to be partnered by a harpsichord and, while they are highly effective heard with piano, a special enterprise like this deserves total authenticity. Nevertheless, Ross Winters and Andrew Ball create a symbiotic partnership.

The ten Jacob *Variations* on a delicately pastoral melody are most engaging, including both a siciliana and a tarantella, but in the languorous piece by Cyril Scott it is the lusciousness of the piano harmonies that catch the ear.

Undoubtedly the three works by Rubbra are the highlight of the recital, the *Passacaglia* and the resonantly noble *Meditazioni* both drawing on themes by Josquin. The *Sonatina* with its long, winding central melody, followed by variations on a jolly Spanish dance, *En la fuente del rosel*, clearly has the harpsichord in mind.

The witty *Sonatina* of Antony Hopkins and the piquant *Sonata breve* of Colin Hand are succinct and diverting, but the wayward harmonic progressions of Reizenstein's *Partita* work better in the dance movements than in the rather wan lyricism. Excellent recording and a very good balance.

Yates, Sophie (virginals)

English Virginals Music: BYRD: *Praeludium – Fantasia; The Barley Breake; The Tennthe Pavan (Sir William Petre); Galliard to the Tennthe Pavan; The Woods so Wild; Hugh Aston's Ground; The Bells.* DOWLAND: *Lachrymae Pavan* (arr. BYRD). HARDING: *Galliard* (arr. BYRD). GIBBONS: *Fantasia.* ANON.: *My Lady Careys Dompe.* TOMKINS: *Barafostus's Dreame.* ASTON: *Hornepype.* BULL: *In nomine.*

** Chan. 0574.

Sophie Yates is a thoughtful and accomplished player and she uses a modern copy by Peter Bavington of an Italian instrument made at the very beginning of the seventeenth century. Her programme is well thought out and, even though it is dominated by the music of Byrd, it is musically well balanced. The snag is the resonant recording, which gives a larger-than-life impression of the instrument which even the lowering of the volume control does not entirely diminish.

Yepes, Narciso (guitar)

'Guitarra española': RODRIGO: *Fantasia para un gentilhombre.* BACARISSE: *Concertino for Guitar and Orchestra, Op. 72* (both with Spanish R. and TV SO, Odón Alonso). RODRIGO: *Concierto madrigal* (with Godelieve Monden, Philh. O, García Navarro); *Concierto de Aranjuez.* RUIZ-PIPÓ: *Tablas for Guitar and Orchestra.* OHANA: *Concierto: Tres gráficos for Guitar and Orchestra* (with LSO, Rafael Frühbeck de Burgos). Solo music: ALBÉNIZ: *Suite españolas: Asturias. Legenda; Recuerdos de viaje: Rumores de la caleta. Malagueña. Piezas caracteristicas: Torre bermeja. Serenata. Malahueña, Op. 164/3.* GRANADOS: *Danza española No. 4 (Villanesca).* TÁRREGA: *Alborada. Capriccio. Danza mora; Sueno. Recuerdos de la Alhambra; Marieta (Mazurka); Capricho árabe (Serenata); Tango.* DE FALLA: *El amor brujo: El círculo mágico; Canción del fuego fatuo. El sombrero de tres picos; Danza del molinero (Farruca). Homenaje: Le tombeau de Claude Debussy.* TURINA: *Sonata, Op. 61; Fandanguillo, Op. 36. Garrotin y soleares; Ráfaga.* BACARISSE: *Passpie.* YEPES: *Catarina d'Alió.* ANON.: *Jeux interdits: Romance.* SANZ: *Suite española.* MUDARRA: *Fantasia que contrahaze la harpa en la manera de Ludvico.* NARVÁEZ: *Diferencias sobre 'Guádame las vacas'.* SOLER: *Sonata in E.* SOR: *10 Etudes; Theme and Variations, Op. 9.* RODRIGO: *En los trigales.* ANON., arr. LLOBET: *4 Canciones populares catalanes.* PUJOL: *El*

abejorro. TORROBA: *Madroños.* MONTSALVATGE: *HabaNera.* O'HANA: *Tientos.* RUIZ-PIPÓ: *Canción y danza No. 1.*
(B) ******* DG (ADD/DDD) 474 666-2 (5).

This collection admirably celebrates Narciso Yepes's long-lived and distinguished recording achievement in music from his own country. He had a prodigious technique, but it was in harness to a fine intellect plus an instinctive feeling for the colourful emotions and Spanish dance-rhythms expressed in this repertoire. It was inevitable that the three most famous concertante works of Rodrigo should be included, plus other similar works of varying attractiveness. But the solo repertoire is all marvellously played, for Yepes had no difficulty in creating electricity in the recording studio, and many of these performances – with their vivid palette and high level of concentration – constantly remind us of Beethoven's assertion that a guitar is an orchestra all by itself.

'The Art of the Guitar': SANZ: *Suite española: Españoletas; Canarios.* PISADOR: *Pavana muy llana para tañer.* MUDARRA: *Fantasia que contrahaza la harpa en la manera de Ludovico.* NARVÁEZ: *La canción del emperador: Mille regretz* (Josquin Desprez). *Diferencias sobre Guádame las vacas.* ANON.: *Irish March* (11th century); *Saltarello* (both arr. YEPES). DOWLAND: *The King of Denmark his Galliard.* SOR: *Studies in A; in C, Op. 6/6 & 8; in B flat; in G, Op. 29/1 & 11.* TARREGA: *Lágrima; Recuerdos de la Alhambra; Adelita.* GRANADOS: *Danza española No. 5.* TURINA: *Fandanguillo, Op. 36.* ALBENIZ: *Suite española: Asturias.*
*** DG CD PlusScore (ADD/DDD) 459 613-2.

Many of these recordings have appeared before and some already exist on bargain labels. But this recital has been carefully planned, expertly remastered, and affords great naturalness and presence. Moreover the special logo indicates that the CD can also be played via a CD-ROM drive on a PC, enabling the listener to follow the musical scores simultaneously on the screen while listening to the performances. The programme has been selected in an approximately historical sequence to show the great guitarist at his finest, whether in the delightful Sanz *Canarios*, the noble *Pavana* of Pisador, the two melancholy miniatures of Tárrega, which are perhaps less familiar than the famous *Recuerdos*. The *Diferencias* of Narváez (written for the vihuela) is one of the earliest Spanish examples of variation form; Mudarra's *Fantasia* is more complex; but later the Dowland *Galliard* (where Yepes simulates a bolder keyboard image) admirably demonstrates Elizabethan divisions. The kernel of the recital is provided by the four diverse Sor *Studies*, which are marvellously played, but then so is Turina's *Fandanguillo*, which follows the Granados *Spanish Dance*, the latter more robust than Julian Bream's famous recording, offering a refreshingly different interpretation.

'Malagueña' (Spanish Guitar Music): ALBENIZ: *Malagueña, Op. 165/3; Suite española: Asturias (Leyenda).* TARREGA: *Recuerdos de la Alhambra; Marieta (Mazurka); Capricho árabe.* RODRIGO: *En los trigales.* RUIZ-PIPO: *Cancion y danza No. 1.* SOR: *Introduction & Variations on a Theme of Mozart, Op. 9.* SANZ: *Suite española: Españoletas; Gallarda y villano; Danza y villano; Danza de las hachas; Rujero y paradetas; Zarabanda al ayre español; Passacalle; Folias; La miñona de Cataluña; Canarios.* MUDARRA: *Fantasia que contrahaza la harpa en la manera de Ludovico.* SOLER: *Sonata in E.* GRANADOS: *Danza española No. 4 (Villanesca).* FALLA: *El sombrero de tres picos: Danza del mólinero (Farruca).* ANON.: *Romance* (from the film: *Forbidden Games*).

⊶ ✿ (BB) ★★★ DG Eloquence (ADD) 469 649-2.

With repertoire recorded between 1968 and 1977, this Eloquence reissue is based on a long-standing DG recital showing this great Spanish guitarist at his very peak, which now has been expanded to a playing time of 76 minutes. Yepes was not only an outstanding exponent of this repertoire but also had that rare gift of constantly creating electricity in the recording studio, no more thrillingly than in Falla's *Miller's Dance* from the *Three-cornered Hat,* in which he creates an orchestral range of colour. But all this music springs vividly to life and popular favourites like Tárrega's *Recuerdos de la Alhambra* (presented with unostentatious bravura) and the engagingly ingenuous *Mozart Variations* of Sor are wonderfully fresh. The earlier music is also very appealing, the Sanz *Suite* – ten through-composed miniatures of which *Canarios* is probably the best known – is

delightful. The final item, an anonymous *Romance* used in the film, *Forbidden Games,* makes a real lollipop encore. Throughout, Yepes's assured, vibrant and always stylish advocacy brings consistent pleasure and stimulation: there are few solo guitar records to match this, particularly as the Eloquence transfers are so present and realistic and the cost so reasonable.

Zabaleta, Nicanor (harp)

'Arpa española': ALBENIZ: *Malagueña, Op. 165/3; Suite española: Granada (Serenata); Zaragoza (Capricho); Asturias (Leyenda). Mallorca, Op. 202; Tango español.* FALLA: *Serenata andaluza.* TURINA: *Ciclo pianistico No. 1: Tocata y fuga.* GOMBAU: *Apunte bético.* GRANADOS: *Danza española No. 5.* HALFFTER: *Sonatina (ballet): Danza de la pastora.* LOPEZ-CHAVARRI: *El viejo castillo moro.*

✿ (M) ★★★ DG (IMS) (ADD) 435 847-2.

A good deal of the music here belongs to the guitar (or piano) rather than the harp, but Nicanor Zabaleta, with his superb artistry and sense of atmosphere, makes it all his own. Throughout this delightful programme, Zabaleta gives each piece strong individuality of character. In the Granados *Spanish Dance No. 5* he matches the magnetism of Julian Bream's famous recording, and Manuel de Falla's *Serenata andaluza* is hardly less captivating. DG's sound-balance is near perfection, as is the choice of acoustic, and the magic distilled by Zabaleta's concentration, often at the gentlest levels of dynamic, is unforgettable.

VOCAL RECITALS AND CHORAL COLLECTIONS

The 'Art of Singing'

Video: 'Golden Voices of the Century' (Björling, Callas, Caruso, Chaliapin, Christoff, Corelli, De los Angeles, De Luca, Di Stefano, Flagstad, Gigli, Martinelli, Melchior, Olivero, Pinza, Ponselle, L. Price, Schipa, Stevens, Supervia, Sutherland, Tauber, Tebaldi, Tetrazzini, Tibbett, Vickers, Wunderlich): Excerpts: PUCCINI: La Bohème. SAINT-SAENS: Samson et Dalila. VERDI: Rigoletto. LEONCAVALLO: Pagliacci (all silent film excerpts with Caruso). DONIZETTI: Lucia di Lammermoor: sextet with Caruso, mimed. DE CURTIS: song Torna a Surriento (Giovanni Martinelli). HANDEL: Xerxes: Ombra mai fù (Beniamino Gigli). FLOTOW: Martha: M'appari (Tito Schipa). ROSSINI: Il barbiere di Siviglia: Largo al factotum (Giuseppe de Luca). FLOTOW: Martha: M'appari (Luisa Tetrazzini). PUCCINI: La Bohème: Quando me'n vo (Conchita Supervia). BIZET: Carmen: Chanson Bohème; Habanera (Rosa Ponselle). SCHUBERT: Ständchen (Richard Tauber). RIMSKY-KORSAKOV: The Maid of Pskov. IBERT: Chanson du duc (both with Fyodor Chaliapin). WAGNER: Die Walküre: Hojotoho! (Kirsten Flagstad). BIZET: Carmen: Chanson du toréador (Lawrence Tibbett). SAINT-SAENS: Samson et Dalila: Mon coeur s'ouvre (Risë Stevens). WAGNER: Die Walküre: Winterstürme (Lauritz Melchior). MUSSORGSKY: Boris Godunov: Coronation scene (Ezio Pinza). PUCCINI: La Bohème: Che gelida manina; Mi chiamano Mimì; O soave fanciulla (Jussi Björling, Renata Tebaldi). FALLA: La vida breve: Vivan los que rien (Victoria de los Angeles). MEYERBEER: Les Huguenots: O beau pays (Joan Sutherland). VERDI: Aida: O patria mia (Leontyne Price). MUSSORGSKY: Boris Godunov: Death scene (Boris Christoff). PUCCINI: Tosca: Vissi d'arte; (i) Act III duet (Magda Olivero, (i) with Alvinio Misciano). MOZART: Die Zauberflöte: Dies Bildnis ist bezaubernd schön (Fritz Wunderlich). BEETHOVEN: Fidelio: In des Lebens (Jon Vickers). PUCCINI: Turandot: Non Piangere, Liù (Franco Corelli). LEONCAVALLO: I Pagliacci: Vesti la giubba (Giuseppe di Stefano). (i) VERDI: La Traviata: Parigi, o cara. (ii) PUCCINI: Tosca: Duet and Vissi d'arte (both Maria Callas, with (i) Alfredo Kraus, (ii) Tito Gobbi). (Commentary by Magda Olivero, Thomas Hampson, Schuyler Chapin, Kirk Browning, Nicola Rescigno.)
*** Teldec VHS 0630 15893-3.

This is Teldec's vocal equivalent of 'The Art of Conducting'. While almost all the film excerpts included here are fascinating, this comparable vocal survey proves less uniformly compulsive than its orchestral equivalent. Moreover, while almost all the comments on the earlier video concerning the conductors themselves and their various idiosyncrasies proved very perceptive, the commentaries here, especially the contributions by the singers themselves, seem much less illuminating. Thomas Hampson's definition of the meaning of legato, a term which almost explains itself, is perversely over-complicated. But now to the singing.

Two performances stand out above the rest in magnetism. A live telecast, with good sound, from the Met. in 1956 brought Renata Tebaldi and Jussi Björling together in virtually the whole of the great Act I love scene in La Bohème, from Che gelida manina to their final exit, with their glorious voices ending the act from offstage. They are dressed in a curiously formal way – one might even say overdressed – and Tebaldi is not shown to be the greatest actress in the world, but their voices match superbly. The other scene is even more electrifying – a live telecast made in December of the same year for which obviously no expense was spared, and the set and production were fully worthy. Boris Christoff's Death scene from Boris Godunov is deeply moving; Nicola Moscona is a hardly less resonant Pimen, and an unnamed boy is very touching as Boris's young son. Hardly less impressive is the great Kirsten Flagstad (at her vocal peak), introduced by Bob Hope, who manages to keep a straight face, in a Paramount movie, The Big Broadcast of 1938. She sings Hojotoho! thrillingly from Die Walküre, waving her spear with remarkable conviction.

Risë Stevens, Lauritz Melchior, Victoria de los Angeles in Falla and Joan Sutherland in Meyerbeer coloratura add to the vocal pleasures, and Leontyne Price's gloriously full-voiced O patria mia from Aida is engulfing. What a stage presence she has! Another highlight is Magda Olivero's charismatically seductive Vissi d'arte from Tosca. The great Callas ends the programme by singing the same aria (in 1964) but, although her presence is commanding, the actual singing, with its wobbling vibrato, is no match for Olivero.

The early recordings are interesting, but the sound is such that they are usually less than overwhelming vocally, with Gigli and Tito Schipa possible exceptions. A hilarious interlude is provided by a 1908 silent film with professional actors hopelessly overacting and miming the words of the Sextet (*Chi mi frena*) from *Lucia di Lammermoor*, designed to accompany the famous 1911 RCA recording by Caruso, Daddi, Journet, Scotti, Sembrich and Severina. Another smile comes when Rosa Ponselle is shown singing *Carmen* for an MGM screen test in 1936 and her fan gets in the way of the camera! All in all, this is a considerable entertainment, but one hoped, unrealistically perhaps, for more items like *Boris* and *Bohème*.

Historical Vocal Recitals

'The EMI Record of Singing'

Volume 3 (1926–39): Part 1: The German school: Arias and excerpts from WAGNER: *Tannhäuser* (Lauritz Melchior; Göta Ljungberg with Walter Widdop); *Die Walküre* (Max Lorenz; Kirsten Flagstad); *Lohengrin* (Franz Völker); *Die Meistersinger* (Rudolf Bockelmann; Delia Reinhardt); *Das Rheingold* (Hans Hermann Nissen); *Der fliegende Holländer* (Elizabeth Ohms); *Siegfried* (Nanny Larsen-Todsen). WILLIE: *Königsballade* (Helge Rosvaenge). D'ALBERT: *Tiefland* (Torsten Ralf). JOHANN STRAUSS JR: *Die Fledermaus* (Richard Tauber with Vera Schwarz). KIENZL: *Der Evangeligmann* (Marcel Wittrisch with Children's chorus). RICHARD STRAUSS: *Der Rosenkavalier* (Herbert Ernst Groh; Lotte Lehmann); *Arabella* (Alfred Jerger with Viorica Ursuleac; Tiana Lemnitz); *Daphne* (Margarete Teschemacher); *Die ägyptische Helena* (Rose Pauly). KORNGOLD: *Die tote Stadt* (Joseph Schmidt; Karl Hammes). MOZART: *Die Entführung aus dem Serail* (Julius Patzak). HUMPERDINCK: *Hänsel und Gretel* (Gerard Hüsch). KREUTZER: *Das Nachtlager in Granada* (Willi Domgraf -Fassbaender). MENDELSSOHN: *Elijah* (Friedrich Schorr); *Saint Paul* (Jo Vincent). LORTZING: *Zar und Zimmermann* (Heinrich Schlusnus; Leo Schützendorf); *Der Wildschütz* (Alexander Kipnis). NICOLAI: *Die lustigen Weiber von Windsor* (Wilhelm Strienz). VERDI: *Macbeth* (Ivar Andresen); *Un ballo in maschera* (Adele Kern). MEYERBEER: *Le Prophète* (Sigrid Onegin); *L'Africaine* (Elisabeth Rethberg). PONCHIELLI: *La Gioconda* (Karin Branzell). SAINT-SAENS: *Samson et Dalila* (Kerstin Thorborg). MOZART: *La clemenza di Tito* (Rosette Anday). FLOTOW: *Alesandro Stradella* (Fritz Jold). RIMSKY-KORSAKOV: *The Tsar's Bride* (Miliza Korjus; Meta Seinemeyer). ADAM: *Le Postillon de Longumeau* (Felicie Hüni Mihacsek). PUCCINI: *Turandot* (Luise Helletsgruber); *La Bohème* (Maria Cebotari). GOLDMARK: *Die Königen von Saba* (Maria Nemeth). Lieder: BEETHOVEN: *Der Wachtelschlag* (Karl Erb). SCHUMANN: *Liederkreis: Mondnacht* (Leo Slezak); *Die Lotusblume* (Ursula van Diemen). WOLF: *Vers hwiegene Liebe* (Heinrich Schlusnus). SCHUBERT: *Die Stadt* (Herbert Jannsen); *Aufenthal* (Maria Olczewska); *Die Allnacht* (Marta Fuchs). BRAHMS: *Nicht mehr zu dir zu gehen* (Margarete Klose); *Feldeinsamkeit* (Elena Gerhardt); *Volkslieder: Schwesterlein* (Lulu Mysz-Gmeiner). SCHOECK: *Mit einem gemalten Bande* (Ria Ginster); *Nachtlied* (Margherita Perras). MARX: *Marienlied* (Elisabeth Schumann). ROSSINI: *Soirrées musicales; L'invito*. (Lotte Schöne). OBOUSSIER: *Weine du nicht* (Erna Berger). LISZT: *Es muss ein Wunderbares sein* (Emmy Bettendorf). REGER: *Waldeinsamkeit; Zum Schlafen* (Maria Müller). WAGNER: *Wesendonck Lieder: Schmerzen* (Frida Leider).

Part 2: The Italian school: Arias and excerpts from: PAISIELLO: *I zingari infiera* (Conchita Supervia). BIZET: *Carmen* (Giannina Pederzini). VERDI: *Requiem* (Irene Minghini-Catteneo; Ezio Pinza); *I Lombardi* (Giannina Aranji-Lombardi); *La forza del destino* (Dusolina Giannini); *Ernani* (Iva Pacetti). *Otello* (Hina Spani; Renato Zanelli); *Rigoletto* (Lina Pagliughi); *Falstaff* (Mariano Stabile). SAINT-SAENS: *Samson et Dalila* (Ebe Stignani). DONIZETTI: *La Favorita* (Florica Cristoforeanu); *Don Pasquale* (Afro Poli with Ernesto Badini). BOITO: *Mefistofele* (Pia Tassinari; Nazzareno de Angelis). CATALANI: *Loreley* (Bianca Scacciati). GIORDANO: *Siberia* (Maria Caniglia); *Andrea Chénier* (Lina Bruna Rasa; Cesare Formichi; Benvenuto Franci; Antonio Cortis); *Il Re* (Mercedes Capsir). PUCCINI: *La fanciulla del West* (Gina Cigna); *Madama Butterfly* (Margaret Sheridan); *Turandot* (Maria Zamboni; Magda Oliviero; Alessandro Ziliani); *Manon Lescaut* (Licia Albanese; Francesco Merli; Giacomo Lauri-Volpi); *La Bohème* (Tancredi Pasero); *Tosca* (Giovanni Inghilleri). PIETRI: *Maristella* (Rosetta Pampanini). MASCAGNI: *Iris* (Maria Farneti); *Lodeletta* (Malfada Favero; Galliano Masini); *Guglielmo Ratcliffe* (Carlo Galeffi). GOMES: *Il Guarany* (Bidù Sayão). CILEA: *Adriana Lecouvreur* (Adelaide Saraceni; Aurelio Pertile). RICCI: *Crispino e la comare* (Salvatore Baccaloni). PONCHIELLI: *Il figliuol prodigo* (Mario Basiola). LEONCAVALLO: *Zazà* (Apollo Granforte). BELLINI: *La sonnnambula* (Dino Borgioli with Maria Gentile, Ida Mannarini, Gina Pedroni; also Enzo de Muro Lomanto). MASSENET: *Werther* (Tito Schipa). GUERRERO: *Los Gavilanes* (Tino Folgar). VITTADINI: *Anima allegra* (Luigi Fort). OFFENBACH: *La Belle Hélène* (Jussi Bjoerling). Songs: TRAD: *Have you seen but a whyte lilie grow?* (Conchita Supervia); BUZZI-PECCIA: *Colombetta* (Claudia Muzio). GRANADOS: *Tonadillas: El majo discreto; El majo timido* (Conchita Badia). JAMES:

Maori lullaby (Toti da Monte). TIRINDELLI:
Mistica (Carlo Tagliabue). TOSTI: *Ideale* (Riccardo
Stracciari); *Aprile* (Beniamino Gigli); *Do not Go,
my Love* (Dino Borgioli). HAGEMAN LONGAS: *En
effeuillant la marguerite* (Tito Schipa).

Part 3: The French school: Arias from: RAMEAU:
Hippolyte et Aricie (Leila Ben Sedira). OFFENBACH:
Les Brigands (Emma Luart); *Contes d'Hoffmann*
(André Pernet); *La Grande Duchesse de Gérolstein*
(Yvonne Printemps); *Le Boulangère a des écus*
(Reynaldo Hahn). DELIBES: *Lakmé* (Germaine
Feraldy). ROSSINI: *Guillaume Tell* (Eidé Norena).
MASSENET: *Marie-Magdeleine* (Germaine
Martinelli); *Hérodiade* (René Maison). GOUNOD:
Sapho (Suzanne Cesbron-Viseur; Germain Cernay);
Polyucte (José Luccioni); *Mireille* (Gaston
Micheletti). DUKAS: *Ariane et Barbe-Bleu* (Suzanne
Balguerie). WAGNER: *Lohengrin* (Germaine Lubin).
GLUCK: *Orphée* (Alice Raveau). REYER: *Sigurd*
(Georges Thill; César Vezzani). HALEVY: *La Juive*
(René Verdière). LAPARRA: *L'Illustre Fregona*
(Miguel Villabella). BAZIN: *Maître Pathelin* (André
d'Arkor). VERDI: *Luisa Miller* (Giusppe Lugo). LALO:
Le Roi d'Ys (Joseph Rogatchewsky). BERLIOZ:
L'Enfance du Christ (Jean Planel); *La Damnation de
Faust* (Charles Panzéra). MAGNARD: *Guercoeur*
(Arthur Endrèze). PALADILHE: *Patrie!* (Robert
Couzinou). BERTHOMIEU: *Robert Macaire* (André
Balbon). FLOTOW: *L'Ombre* (Lucien Fugère). Songs:
SAINT-SAENS: *Le rossignol et la rose* (Lily Pons).
FAURE: *Les berceux* (Ninon Vallin); *Aurore* (Pierre
Bernac); *Lydia* (Roger Bourdin). TORELLI: *Tu lo sai*
(Povla Frijsh). DEBUSSY: *Chansons de Bilitis: Le
Chevelure* (Jane Bathori). RAVEL: *Chants hébraïques:
Kaddisch* (Madeleine Grey); *Don Quichotte à
Dulcinée: Chanson épique* (Martial Singher). DE
BREVILLE: *Une Jeune Fille parle* (Claire Croiza).
HAHN: *D'un prison* (Charles Panzéra). MARTINI:
Plaisir d'amore (Jean-Emil Vanni-Marcoux).

Part 4: The Anglo-American school: Arias and
excerpts from: VERDI: *Falstaff* (Lawrence Tibett).
THOMAS: *Hamlet* (John Charles Thomas; John
Brownlee). ROSSINI: *Il barbiere di Siviglia* (Dennis
Noble); *Stabat Mater* (Florence Austral). Songs:
COWAN: *Onaway, awake, beloved* (Harold
Williams). HANDEL: *Messiah* (Peter Dawson).
OFFENBACH: *Contes d'Hoffmann* (Charles
Kullman). BIZET: *La Jolie Fille de Perth* (Heddle
Nash); *Carmen* (Marguerite D'Alvarez). Goring
THOMAS: *Esmeralda* (Thomas Burke). PUCCINI:
Tosca (Richard Crooks); *La Bohème* (Grace Moore;
Ina Souez); *Madama Butterfly* (Joan Cross);
Turandot (Eva Turner). HANDEL: *Acis and Galatea*
(Walter Widdop). PURCELL: *The Tempest* (Norman
Allin). MENDELSSOHN: *St Paul* (Muriel Brunskill).
HANDEL: *Theodora* (Isobel Baillie). DELIUS:
Irmelin (Dora Labbette). SPONTINI: *La Vestale*
(Rosa Ponselle). REYER: *Sigurd* (Marjorie
Lawrence). Songs: DUNN: *The Bitterness of Love*

(John McCormack). MONTEVERDI: *Maladetto sia
l'aspetto* (Roland Hayes). MARTINI: *Minuet* (Mme
Charles Cahier). SULLIVAN: *The Lost Chord* (Dame
Clara Butt). SCHUBERT: *Der Tod und das Mädchen*
(Marian Anderson). FAURE: *Le Secret* (Susan
Metcalfe-Casals). CANTELOUBE: *Baïlero* (Gladys
Swarthout). PALADILHE: *Psyché* (Maggie Teyte).
HAYDN: *My Mother Bids me Bind My Hair*
(Florence Easton).

Part 5: The East European/Slavic school: Arias and
excerpts from: DVORAK: *Rusalka* (Jarmila Novotná;
Ada Nordenova). RIMSKY-KORSAKOV: *The Tsar's
Bride* (Nathalie Vechor). GOMES: *Salvator Rosa*
(Mark Reisen). KODALY: *Háry János* (Imry Palló).
Songs: GRETCHANINOV: *The Wounded Birch;
Snowflakes* (Maria Kurenko with Composer, piano);
Lullaby (Oda Slobodskaya). RIMSKY-KORSAKOV:
The Rose and the Nightingale (Xenia Belmas).
KARLOWICZ: *I Remember Golden Days* (Ada Sari).
DVORAK: *Leave me Alone* (Maria Krasová). arr.
BARTOK: *2 Hungarian Folksongs* (Maria Basildes).
DARGOMIJSKY: *Bolero* (Feodor Chaliapin). CUI:
Hunger (Vladimir Rosing). KASHEVAROV:
Tranquility (Sergei Lemeshev).

✪ (M) (★★★) Testament mono SBT 0132 (10).

The importance of EMI's monumental series 'The
Record of Singing' cannot be exaggerated, and it is sad
that although the fourth volume was issued on CD,
covering the period from the start of electrical
recording up to the end of the 78rpm era, the others
have been allowed to languish. That fact makes it all
the more creditable that Stewart Brown of Testament
has boldly issued this beautifully produced CD reissue of the third volume, the work of Keith Hardwick,
both in the selection of items, often unexpected but
always keenly perceptive, and in the actual transfers,
which set standards in clarity and accuracy too rarely
matched by others. Inevitably in a very compact format, the background material is not quite so lavish as
in the original LP issue, with separate booklets
included covering details of recording and biographies of the 200 or so singers covered. Even so, essential details are all here, and the methodical covering of
so many singers from so many different schools,
divided mainly by nationality, could not be more
illuminating. In a note written especially for this CD
reissue Hardwick confesses that though initially he
had misgivings over following up the earlier two
volumes of golden age material with recordings from
a period generally regarded as one of decline, he has
more and more come to revise that opinion. Certainly, thanks to his brilliant choice of items, one has
much to admire in every school represented, with
reservations not so much over quality of singing as of
performance style, where inevitably modern taste differs greatly, notably on such composers as Mozart. A
magnificent achievement. One hopes that Testament
may have the courage to bring out CD versions of the
first two volumes of this indispensable series.

Introduction

The Nimbus company have taken a radical view of transferring historic 78rpm vocal recordings to CD. The best possible copies of shellac originals have been played on an acoustic machine with an enormous horn, one of the hand-made Rolls-Royces among non-electric gramophones of the 1930s, with Thorn needles reducing still further the need to filter the sound.

'The Golden Age of Singing' (50 Years of Great Voices on Record)

Volume I (1900–10): TCHAIKOVSKY: *Queen of Spades: Forgive Me, Heavenly Being* (Nicolay Figner). FLOTOW: *Marta: Chi mi dirà* (Edouard de Reszke). BELLINI: *La sonnambula: Vi ravviso, o luoghio ameni* (Pol Plançon); *Ah, non credea mirarti* (Adelina Patti). VERDI: *Otello: Niun mi tema* (Francesco Tamagno); *Era la notte* (Victor Maurel); *Credo in un Dio crudel* (Eugenio Giraldoni). *Aida: Fuggiam gli ardori inospiti* (Celestina Boninsegna). *Ernani: O sommo Carlo* (Mattia Battistini). *Luisa Miller: Quando le sere al placido* (Alessandro Bonci). *Rigoletto: Caro nome* (Nellie Melba). *Simon Boccanegra: Il lecerato spirito* (Francesco Navarrini). *Falstaff: Quand' ero paggio* (Antonio Scotti). DONIZETTI: *L'elisir d'amore: Una furtiva lagrima* (Enrico Caruso). *Chiedi all'aura lusinghiera* (Maria Galvany; Aristodemo Giorgini). *Don Pasquale: So anch'io la virtu magica* (Rosina Storchio); *Sogno soave e casto* (Giuseppe Anselmi). *La favorita: A tanto amor* (Mario Ancona). *Lucrezia Borgia: Di pescatore ignobil* (Francesco Marconi); *Il segreto per esser felice* (Clara Butt). WAGNER: *Lohengrin: Elsa's Dream* (Félia Litvinne). *Rienzi: Gerechter Gott!* (Ernestine Schumann-Heink). *Götterdämmerung: Fliegt heim ihr Raben.* GOUNOD: *Roméo et Juliette: Je veux vivre dans ce rêve* (Emma Eames). MOZART: *Die Zauberflöte: O Isis und Osiris* (Wilhelm Hesch). *Le nozze di Figaro: Heil'ge Quelle* (Lilli Lehmann). GLINKA: *A Life for the Tsar: They guess the truth* (Vladimir Kastorsky). MASSENET: *Le Roi de Lahore: Promesse de mon avenir* (Maurice Renaud). *Manon: Il sogno (en fermant les yeux)* (Fernando de Lucia). *Le Cid: O souverain! ô juge! o père!* (Vilhelm Herold). MEYERBEER: *Le prophète: Sopra Berta l'amor mio* (Francesco Vignas). *Les Huguenots: A ce mot* (Olimpia Boronat); *O beau pays de la Touraine* (Antonina Nezhdanova). PONCHIELLI: *La Gioconda: Ebbrezza! Delirio!* (Eugenia Burzio and Giuseppe de Luca). BIZET: *Carmen: Habanera* (Emma Calvé). ERKEL: *Hunyadi László: Ah rebéges* (Lillian Nordica). THOMAS: *Hamlet: O vin, discaccia la tristezza* (Titta Ruffo). PUCCINI: *Madama Butterfly: Con onor muore* (Emmy Destinn). ROSSINI: *Il barbiere di Siviglia: La calunnia è un venticello* (Adamo Didur). *Semiramide: Bel raggio Lusinghier* (Marcella Sembrich). GOLDMARK: *Die Königin von Saba: Magische Töne* (Leo Slezak). BOITO: *Mefistofele: Giunto sul passo estremo* (Dmitri Smirnov). RIMSKY-KORSAKOV: *May Night: Sleep, My Beauty* (Leonid Sobinov). HATTON: *Simon the Cellarer,* (Sir Charles Santley).

(B) (★★★) Nimbus Double mono NI 7050/1 (2).

For the ordinary collector without a specialist interest in historical vocal repertoire this bargain Double should prove an ideal way of making an initial exploration. There are some 44 widely varied items sung by as many outstanding singers. Some of the names will be unfamiliar – it is not always the most famous that make the greatest initial impression, although Tamagno's *Otello* aria (from 1902) is immediately commanding, Caruso is very winning in Donizetti, Battistini is joined by other singers and the La Scala Chorus in a splendid 1906 scene from Verdi's *Ernani*. But it is the second disc that is particularly well planned, with a whole stream of superb performances that project vividly, from Melba's *Caro nome* and Tito Ruffo's *Hamlet*, to Emmy Destinn's thrilling acount of Butterfly's final aria. Amor Didur's solemn *La culunnia* and Vilhelm Herold in *Massenet* are both memorable, and with Gadski in *Götterdämmerung*, the orchestra may sound puny, but not the glorious flow of vocal tone. One of the surprises is the lightly pointed coloratura of Clara Butt in Donizetti, the big voice fined down, yet the lower register still ringing out. Scotti's Falstaff, Leo Slezak in *Die Königen von Saba* are both highlights, and the programme ends in light-hearted vein with Sir Charles Santley's clear yet resonant 'Simon the Cellarar'. The transfers almost all show the Nimbus process at its best; only occasionally is the surface noise slightly intrusive.

Battistini, Mattia (baritone)

Arias from: TCHAIKOVSKY: *Eugene Onegin.* VERDI: *Un ballo in maschera; Ernani; La Traviata; Macbeth; Don Carlos.* FLOTOW: *Marta.* DONIZETTI:

La Favorita; Don Sebastiano; Linda di Chamounix.
HEROLD: *Zampa.* BERLIOZ: *La Damnation de
Faust.* MASSENET: *Werther.* THOMAS: *Hamlet.*
NOUGUES: *Quo Vadis?.*

(M) (★★★) Nimbus mono NI 7831; NC 7831.

As with other Nimbus issues, the transfers are
remarkably kind to the voice and are probably nearer
to how Battistini sounded 'live'. It is a remarkable
voice, with a fine, clear upper range. The programme
is well chosen and the recordings date from between
1902 and 1922. While obviously the Verdi excerpts are
essential to show the calibre of any baritone, it is
good to have the rare *Pourquoi tremblez-vous?* from
Zampa.

Björling, Jussi (tenor)

'*The First Ten Years*': Arias from: VERDI: *Il
Trovatore; Rigoletto; Aida; Requiem.* PUCCINI:
Tosca; La fanciulla del West; La Bohème. BORODIN:
Prince Igor. LEONCAVALLO: *Pagliacci.* MASCAGNI:
Cavalleria rusticana. RIMSKY-KORSAKOV: *Sadko.*
MEYERBEER: *L'Africana.* PONCHIELLI: *La
Gioconda.* MASSENET: *Manon.* ROSSINI: *Stabat
Mater.* Song: FANAL: *I maünner oüver lag och raütt.*

(M) (★★★) Nimbus mono NI 7835.

Volume 2, 1911–1960: Arias from: PUCCINI: *Tosca;
La Fanciulla del West; La Bohème.* VERDI: *Rigoletto.*
FLOTOW: *Martha.* GOUNOD: *Faust.* BIZET: *Carmen.*
OFFENBACH: *La Belle Hélène.* J. STRAUSS JR: *Der
Zigeunerbaron.* MILLOCKER: *Der Bettelstudent.*
Songs: BEETHOVEN: *Adelaide.* SCHUBERT: *Ave
Maria; Ständchen; An die Leier.* R. STRAUSS:
Cäcile. SIBELIUS: *Svarta rosor; Säv, säv, susa.*
ALFVEN: *Skogen sover.* EKLOF: *Morgon.* SJOBERG:
Tornerna. TOSTI: *Ideale.*

(M) (★★★) Nimbus mono NI 7842.

'*Bjoerling in song*': LEONCAVALLO: *Mattinata.*
TOSELLI: *Serenata.* DI CAPUA: *O sole mio.* Songs
by: ENDERS; CHRISTGAU; PETERSON-BERGER;
ARTHUR; ELGAR; DE CURTIS; BALL; RAY; DAHL;
SCHRADER; PEREZ-FREIRE; STENHAMMAR;
ALTHEN; CARUSO; WIDESTEDT. TRAD.: *Tantis
serenade.* Arias from LEHAR: *Das Land des
Lächelns.* KALMAN: *Das Veilchen von Montmartre.*

(M) (★★★) Nimbus mono NI 7879

'*Jussi Bjoerling in Opera and Song*'.

(M) (★★★) Nimbus NI 1776 (3) (NI 7835; 7842 & 7879).

The three Bjoerling discs above are brought together
in a box, giving a comprehensive view of his early
years, when from the age of nineteen (in 1930) he
recorded regularly for the Swedish branch of HMV.
That means that most of the items, including the
early recordings of opera and all the operetta, are
done in Swedish. Not that lovers of vocal art will
worry overmuch, when even in 1930 the headily

golden voice is both distinctive and rich, fully developed even then. Volume 2 covers recordings that
Bjoerling made between 1936 and 1940, not just in
Sweden but in 1939–40 in New York, when Victor
recorded him in Lieder, not just Schubert, Strauss
and Beethoven but Swedish song, in which he sounds
even more at home. All but one of the items in the
song disc are Swedish domestic recordings, but they
lead in 1937 to his first red-label recording of song,
sung in Italian, di Capura's *O sole mio.* The Nimbus
process gives a vivid idea of the voice with ample
bloom on it, but the surfaces are marked by a very
noticeable but even swish, rather than a hiss.

Bjoerling, Jussi, Enrico Caruso, Beniamino Gigli (tenors)

'*Three Legendary Tenors in Opera and Song*'

Caruso: Arias from: BIZET: *Carmen.* MASSENET:
Manon. VERDI: *Otello; La forza del destino; Aida.*
GIORDANO: *Andrea Chénier.* PUCCINI: *Tosca.*

Gigli: Arias from: LEONCAVALLO: *I Pagliacci* (also
song: *Mattinata*). BIZET: *Les Pêcheurs de perles*
(also duet: *Del tempo al limitar,* with Giuseppe de
Luca). VERDI: *La Traviata.* PUCCINI: *Tosca.* Song:
DI CAPUA: *O sole mio.*

Bjoerling: Arias from VERDI: *Rigoletto.* PUCCINI:
La Bohème; Turandot. RIMSKY-KORSAKOV: *Sadko.*
MEYERBEER: *L'Africana.* MASSENET: *Manon.* Song:
TOSTI: *Ideale.*

(M) (★★★) Nimbus mono NI 1434.

Nimbus caught on to the idea of promoting a selection from three legendary tenors from their archives
and they decided that a single disc (75 minutes)
would be the best proposition. Their system of
playing-back 78rpm originals through a big fibre
horn and re-recording them works very well here
with the three voices naturally caught, but the
orchestral backing is more variable. The documentation is poor and no recording dates are given, but the
excerpts are obviously hand-picked and recorded
over a fairly wide time-span. Items which obviously
stand out are Caruso's *Un dì, all'azzurro spazio* from
Andrea Chénier and of course *Celeste Aida* (with a
remarkably believable brass fanfare); Gigli's honeyed
E lucevan le stelle from Tosca and his thrilling *O sole
mio;* and Bjoerling's *Che gelida manina* from *Bohème,*
the seductive *Sadko* 'Song of India' and his glorious
Nessun dorma. The collection ends splendidly with
Caruso and De Luca matching their voices sensation-
ally in the frisson-creating *Pearl Fishers* duet.

Caruso, Enrico (tenor)

'Caruso in opera', Volume I: Arias from:
DONIZETTI: *L'Elisir d'amore; Don Sebastiano; Il*

duca d'Alba. GOLDMARK: *La regina di Saba.*
GOMEZ: *Lo schiavo.* HALEVY: *La Juive.*
LEONCAVALLO: *Pagliacci.* MASSENET: *Manon.*
MEYERBEER: *L'Africana.* PUCCINI: *Tosca; Manon
Lescaut.* VERDI: *Aida; Un ballo in maschera; La
forza del destino; Rigoletto; Il trovatore.*

(M) (★★★) Nimbus mono NI 7803.

The Nimbus method of transfer to CD, reproducing
ancient 78s on a big acoustic horn gramophone of
the 1930s, tends to work best with acoustic recordings, when the accompaniments then emerge as
more consistent with the voice. There is an inevitable
loss of part of the recording range at both ends of the
spectrum, but the ear can often be convinced. This
Caruso collection, very well-chosen to show the
development of his voice, ranges from early (1904)
recordings of Massenet, Puccini and Donizetti with
piano accompaniment to the recording that the great
tenor made in 1920, not long before he died, of his
very last role, as Eleazar in Halévy's *La Juive,* wonderfully characterized.

Chaliapin, Feodor (bass)

Excerpts from: MUSSORGSKY: *Boris Godunov.*
RUBINSTEIN: *The Demon.* VERDI: *Don Carlos.*
RIMSKY-KORSAKOV: *Sadko.* BORODIN: *Prince Igor.*
GOUNOD: *Faust.* MOZART: *Don Giovanni.* GLINKA:
A Life for the Tsar; Ruslan and Ludmilla. PUCCINI:
La Bohème. BOITO: *Mefistofele.* MASSENET: *Don
Quichotte.* RACHMANINOV: *Aleko.*
DARGOMYZHSKY: *Rusalka.*

(M) (★★(★)) Nimbus mono NI 7823/4 (2).

As recorded by the Nimbus process Chaliapin's
unique bass sounds sepulchral – partly due, no
doubt, to the resonating effect of the horn gramophone on which the 78s are played. The EMI issues of
many of the same items as here on his disc of Russian
arias (CDH7 61009-2), including his recordings of
Boris, are much fuller and more immediate (as transferred by Keith Hardwick). However, this two-disc
collection includes valuable items outside the Russian repertory, including Leporello's catalogue aria
from *Don Giovanni* (taken very fast, with detail only
sketched though very characterful) and Beethoven's
song, *In questa tomba,* not helped by a heavy surface-
noise, but bringing a thrilling expansion. In every
item, one is aware that this is not just one of the great
voices of the twentieth century but also one of the
most characterful singers; compassing not just the
darkness and tragedy of Boris, but the sparkle and
humour of such an item as Farlaf's Rondo from
Glinka's *Ruslan and Ludmilla* with its dauntingly
rapid patter.

Divas

'*Divas*', Volume 1 1906–35: (Tetrazzini; Melba; Patti;
Hempel; Galli-Curci; Ponselle; Lehmann; Turner;
Koshetz; Norena; Nemeth; Muzio): Arias from:
VERDI: *Un ballo in maschera; Rigoletto; Aida; Il
Trovatore.* THOMAS: *Mignon.* MOZART: *Die
Zauberflöte.* ROSSINI: *Il barbiere di Siviglia.*
MASSENET: *Manon.* PUCCINI: *Madama Butterfly.*
BEETHOVEN: *Fidelio.* RIMSKY-KORSAKOV: *Sadko.*
BORODIN: *Prince Igor.* GOUNOD: *Roméo et Juliette.*
BOITO: *Mefistofele.* Songs: YRADIER: *La Calesera.*
DENAUDY: *O del mio amato ben.*

(M) (★★★) Nimbus mono NI 7802.

The six supreme prima donnas on this compilation
are all very well represented. The soprano voice
benefits more than most from the Nimbus process,
so that with extra bloom Tetrazzini's vocal 'gear-
change' down to the chest register is no longer obtrusive. She is represented by three recordings of 1911,
including Gilda's *Caro nome* from *Rigoletto;* and
Galli-Curci has three items too, including Rosina's
Una voce poco fa from *Il barbiere di Siviglia.* The
tragically short-lived Claudia Muzio and the Russian
Nina Koshetz have two each, while the others are
each represented by a single, well-chosen item. They
include Melba in *Mimi's farewell,* the 60-year-old
Patti irresistibly vivacious in a Spanish folksong, *La
calesera,* and Frieda Hempel in what is probably the
most dazzling of all recordings of the Queen of the
Night's second aria from *Zauberflöte.*

'Divas' Volume 2, 1909–40: (Hempel; Galli-Curci;
Farrar, Kurz, Garrison, Gluck, Ivogün, Onegin,
Schoene, Norena, Ponselle, Leider, Vallin, Teyte,
Koshetz, Flagstad, Favero): Arias from: BELLINI: *I
Puritani.* MOZART: *Le nozze di Figaro; Die
Entführung aus dem Serail.* PUCCINI: *Tosca.* VERDI:
Rigoletto; La forza del destino. OFFENBACH: *Les
contes d'Hoffmann; La Périchole.* GODARD: *Jocelyn.*
BIZET: *Carmen.* JOHANN STRAUSS JR: *Die
Fledermaus.* THOMAS: *Hamlet.* WAGNER: *Tristan
und Isolde; Die Walküre.* MASSENET: *Werther.*
PONCE: *Estrellita.* MASCAGNI: *Lodoletta.*

(M) (★★★) Nimbus mono NI 7818.

As in the first *Divas* volume, the choice of items will
delight any lover of fine singing, a most discriminat-
ing choice. Maria Ivogün, the teacher of Schwarzkopf, contributes a wonderfully pure and incisive
Martern aller Arten (*Entführung*) dating from 1923,
and Lotte Schoene is unusually and characterfully
represented by Adele's *Mein Herr Marquis* from *Fledermaus.* Frida Leider's *Liebestod* is nobly sung but is
surprisingly fast by latterday standards. Maggie Teyte
sings delectably in an aria from *La Périchole;* and
though some of the pre-electric items in Nimbus's
resonant transfers suggest an echo chamber, the
voices are warm and full.

Farrar, Geraldine

Arias from: MOZART: *Le nozze di Figaro; Don
Giovanni.* WOLF-FERRARI: *Le donne curiose; Il*

segreto di Susanna. PUCCINI: *La Bohème* (with Caruso, Scotti and Viafora); *Tosca; Madama Butterfly* (with Josephine Jacoby, Caruso and Scotti).

(M) (★★★) Nimbus mono NI 7857.

Geraldine Farrar, born in 1882, was in almost every way an ideal recording soprano. Though she retired from the stage before the arrival of electrical recording, these acoustic recordings give a wonderful idea of the glorious voice. Almost three-dimensional in the way they convey the warmth and firmness combined with power, it is a delight to register the clarity of attack on even the most exposed notes. The Mozart and Wolf-Ferrari items provide a charming introduction to the range of Puccini recordings here, recorded between 1908 and 1912 when she was at the peak of her powers. Most valuable of all are the items from *Madama Butterfly*, with two duets for Caruso and Scotti interspersed with those of Farrar, making it clear why this was one of her two most celebrated roles, at once tenderly expressive, yet powerfully dramatic.

French opera: Arias from: MASSENET: *Manon; Thaïs.* THOMAS: *Mignon.* GOUNOD: *Roméo et Juliette* (with Clément). OFFENBACH: *Contes d'Hoffmann* (with Scotto). BIZET: *Carmen* (extended excerpts with Martinelli, Amato).

(M) (★★★) Nimbus mono NI 7872.

This fine selection of Farrar's recordings of French opera concentrates on her most celebrated role as Carmen. Though nowadays it is almost always sung by a mezzo, Farrar demonstrates, by the dramatic intensity of her singing, with fine detail and flawless control, what benefits there are from having a full soprano in the role. The fourteen items from that opera include not only Carmen's principal solos and ensembles but Micaela's aria, and – setting the rest in context – the Toreador's song, José's 'Flower Song' and the 'Prelude to Act IV', in a rare acoustic recording conducted by Toscanini. The voice, bright, sweet and full, comes over vividly in these Nimbus transfers.

Flagstad, Kirsten (soprano)

Arias from: WAGNER: *Die Walküre; Tannhäuser; Lohengrin; Tristan und Isolde; Götterdämmerung.* WEBER: *Oberon.* BEETHOVEN: *Fidelio.* Concert aria: BEETHOVEN.

(M) (★★★) Nimbus mono NI 7847

The eleven items here are drawn from the recordings that Flagstad made between 1935 and 1939. Five of them, dating from 1937, are with Eugene Ormandy and the Philadelphia orchestra, including commanding accounts of the 'Abscheulicher' from Beethoven's *Fidelio* and his concert aria, *Ah! perfido!.* Four more items, including Isolde's *Liebestod* were recorded in 1935 with Hans Lange conducting, but the most

substantial item is the fine, clean-cut account of Brünnhilde's Immolation scene from Wagner's *Götterdämmerung* with Edwin McArthur (her regular piano accompanist) and the San Francisco Orchestra. The Nimbus transfers superbly convey the bloom and heroic power of the unique voice in its prime, full and even throughout its range, but the orchestral accompaniments are unpleasantly thin.

Galli-Curci, Amelita

Arias from: AUBER: *Manon Lescaut.* BELLINI: *I puritani; La sonnambula.* DONIZETTI: *Don Pasquale; Linda di Chamounix; Lucia di Lammermoor.* GOUNOD: *Roméo et Juliette.* MEYERBEER: *Dinorah.* ROSSINI: *Il barbiere di Siviglia.* THOMAS: *Mignon.* VERDI: *Rigoletto; La traviata.*

(M) (★★★) Nimbus mono NI 7806.

'Like a nightingale half-asleep,' said Philip Hope-Wallace in a memorable description of Galli-Curci's voice, but this vivid Nimbus transfer makes it much more like a nightingale very wide-awake. More than in most of these transfers made via an acoustic horn gramophone, the resonance of the horn itself can be detected, and the results are full and forward. Galli-Curci's perfection in these pre-electric recordings, made between 1917 and 1924, is a thing of wonder, almost too accurate for comfort; but tenderness is there too, as in the Act II duet from *La traviata* (with Giuseppe de Luca) and the *Addio del passato*, complete with introductory recitative, but with only a single stanza. Yet brilliant coloratura is what lies at the root of Galli-Curci's magic, and that comes in abundance.

'Prima voce' Volume 2: Arias from: DELIBES: *Lakmé.* DONIZETTI: *Lucia di Lammermoor.* VERDI: *Rigoletto; Il trovatore; La traviata.* DAVID: *La Perle du Brésil.* BIZET: *Les Pêcheurs de perles.* RIMSKY-KORSAKOV: *Le Coq d'or; Sadko.* GOUNOD: *Philémon et Baucis.* THOMAS: *Hamlet.* PROCH: *Air & variations.*

(M) (★★★) Nimbus mono NI 7852.

This second Galli-Curci selection from Nimbus offers recordings from the pre-electric era between 1917 and 1924, as well as six electrical recordings from 1925–30, four of them in ensembles, the celebrated ones of the Lucia Sextet and Rigoletto quartet with Gigli, as well as the magical *Traviata* duets with Tito Schipa. The reproduction of the voice in both pre-electric and electric recordings is astonishingly vivid. Compared with the Romophone transfers, these give the voice more bloom, recorded from 78rpm discs in a helpful acoustic, but the surface-hiss has a swishy quality, easily forgotten, which not everyone will like.

Gigli, Beniamino (tenor)

Volume 1, 1918–24: Arias from: BOITO: *Mefistofele.* CATALANI: *Loreley.* DONIZETTI: *La favorita.* FLOTOW: *Martha.* GIORDANO: *Andrea Chénier.* GOUNOD: *Faust.* LALO: *Le Roi d'Ys.* LEONCAVALLO: *Pagliacci.* MASCAGNI: *Iris.* MEYERBEER: *L'Africana.* PONCHIELLI: *La Gioconda.* PUCCINI: *Tosca.* Songs. (M) (★★★) Nimbus mono NI 7807.

Gigli's career went on so long, right through the electrical 78rpm era, that his pre-electric recordings have tended to get forgotten. This collection of twenty-two items recorded between 1918 and 1924 shows the voice at its most honeyed, even lighter and more lyrical than it became later, with the singer indulging in fewer of the mannerisms that came to decorate his ever-mellifluous singing. In aria after aria he spins a flawless legato line. Few tenor voices have ever matched Gigli's in its rounded, golden beauty, and the Nimbus transfers capture its bloom in a way that makes one forget pre-electric limitations. In the one item sung in French, by Lalo, he sounds less at home, a little too heavy; but the ease of manner in even the most taxing arias elsewhere is remarkable, and such a number as the *Serenade* from Mascagni's *Iris* is irresistible in its sparkle, as are the Neapolitan songs, notably the galloping *Povero Pulcinella* by Buzzi-Peccia. One oddity is a tenor arrangement of Saint-Saëns's *The Swan.*

Volume 2, 1925–40: Arias from: DONIZETTI: *L'elisir d'amore; Lucia di Lammermoor.* PUCCINI: *Manon Lescaut; La Bohème; Tosca.* VERDI: *La forza del destino; La traviata; Rigoletto.* THOMAS: *Mignon.* BIZET: *I pescatori di perle.* PONCHIELLI: *La Gioconda.* MASSENET: *Manon.* GOUNOD: *Faust.* RIMSKY-KORSAKOV: *Sadko.* GLUCK: *Paride ed Elena.* CILEA: *L'Arlesiana.* CACCINI: Song: *Amarilli.* (M) (★★★) Nimbus mono NI 7817.

Issued to celebrate the Gigli centenary in 1990, the Nimbus selection concentrates on recordings he made in the very early years of electrical recording up to 1931, when his voice was at its very peak, the most golden instrument, ideally suited to recording. The items are very well chosen and are by no means the obvious choices, though it is good to have such favourites as the *Pearl Fishers* duet with de Luca and the 1931 version of Rodolfo's *Che gelida manina.* The Nimbus transfers are at their best, with relatively little reverberation.

Great Singers

'*Great singers*', 1909–38: (Tetrazzini; Caruso; Schumann-Heink; McCormack; Galli-Curci; Stracciari; Ponselle; Lauri-Volpi; Turner; Tibbett; Supervia; Gigli; Anderson; Schipa; Muzio; Tauber): Arias from: BELLINI: *La sonnambula; I Puritani; Norma.* LEONCAVALLO: *Pagliacci.* DONIZETTI:

Lucrezia Borgia. MOZART: *Don Giovanni; Die Zauberflöte.* ROSSINI: *Il barbiere di Siviglia.* PUCCINI: *Turandot.* VERDI: *Un ballo in maschera.* BIZET: *Carmen.* PUCCINI: *La Bohème.* SAINT-SAENS: *Samson et Dalila.* MASCAGNI: *L'amico Fritz.* Song: REFICE: *Ombra di Nube.* (M) (★★★) Nimbus mono NI 7801.

The Tetrazzini item with which the selection opens – *Ah non giunge* from Bellini's *La Sonnambula* – is one of the supreme demonstrations of coloratura on record; the programme goes on to a magnificent Caruso of 1910 and an unforgettable performance of the coloratura drinking-song from Donizetti's *Lucrezia Borgia* by the most formidable of contraltos, Ernestine Schumann-Heink. Then follows John McCormack's famous account of *Il mio tesoro* from Mozart's *Don Giovanni*, with the central passage-work amazingly done in a single breath. Other vintage items include Galli-Curci's dazzling account of *Son vergin vezzosa* from Bellini's *I Puritani*, Eva Turner in her incomparable 1928 account of Turandot's aria, Gigli amiably golden-toned in *Che gelida manina* from *La Bohème*, and a delectable performance of the Cherry Duet from Mascagni's *L'amico Fritz* by Tito Schipa and Mafalda Favero – riches indeed!

'*Great Singers*' Vol. 2: 1903–39 (Tamagno; Clavé; Plançon; Farrar; Ruffo; Gluck; De Luca; Garden; Martinelli; Onegin; Pinza; Ivogu'n; Chaliapine; Rethberg; Melchior; Flagstad; Bjoerling; Favero): Arias from: VERDI: *Otello; Ernani.* FLOTOW: *Marta.* PUCCINI: *Madama Butterfly; Manon Lescaut.* MEYERBEER: *L'Africana; Les Huguenots.* HANDEL: *Atalanta.* BELLINI: *I Puritani.* ALFANO: *Resurrection.* R. STRAUSS: *Ariadne aux Naxos.* JOHANN STRAUSS JR: *Die Fledermaus.* WAGNER: *Rienzi; Lohengrin.* Songs by: MARIO; MASSENET; BEETHOVEN & TRAD. (M) (★★★) Nimbus NI 7812.

This was the first of Nimbus's series of archive recordings, taking a radical new view of the problem of transferring ancient 78rpm vocal recordings to CD. The best possible copies of shellac originals have been played on an acoustic machine with an enormous horn, one of the hand-made Rolls-Royces among non-electric gramophones of the 1930s, with thorn needles reducing still further the need to filter the sound electronically. The results have been recorded in a small hall, and the sound reproduced removes any feeling of boxy closeness. Those who have resisted the bottled or tinny sound of many historic recordings will find the Nimbus transfers more friendly and sympathetic, even if technically there is an inevitable loss of recorded information at both ends of the spectrum because of the absolute limitations of the possible frequency range on this kind of reproducer.

Hempel, Frieda (soprano)

Arias from: VERDI: *Rigoletto; La traviata; Ernani; Un ballo in maschera.* DONIZETTI: *Lucia di Lammermoor.* ROSSINI: *Il barbiere di Siviglia.* MOZART: *Le nozze di Figaro; Die Zauberflöte.* MEYERBEER: *Les Huguenots; Robert le Diable.* GOUNOD: *Mireille.* OFFENBACH: *Les Contes d'Hoffmann.* LORTZING: *Der Wildschütz.* Song: MANGOLD: *Zweigesang.* JOHANN STRAUSS JR: *Waltz: Wein, Weib und Gesang.*
✪ (M) (★★★) Nimbus mono NI 7849.

This is one of the very finest of all the Nimbus 'Prima Voce' series. The 78rpm sources are immaculate, background noise is steady and no problem. The recordings are nearly all early, mostly made between 1910 and 1913, the rest in the following four years, except for the final song which was much later (1935). It is an extraordinary voice, with an almost unbelievably free upper tessitura. The divisions in the Adam *Variations* (on 'Twinkle, Twinkle Little Star') make you want to laugh, they are so outrageous, taking off into the vocal stratosphere like a series of shooting stars. *Caro nome,* too, which opens the programme arrestingly, is wonderfully free and open, and the final cadence is taken up. Even more than the Lucia Mad scene, Rossini's *Una voce poco fa,* with its added decorations, shows how a soprano voice can sparkle when the intonation is spot-on. Both are sung in German.

Frieda Hempel's Mozart is less stylish; the famous *Der Hölle Rache* almost runs away before the end. But the ravishing vocal line in *Ah fors' è lui,* with a deliberate tenuto on the cadence, is followed by a wonderfully frivolous cabaletta. The recording quality is astonishingly consistent and the vocal richness comes across with uncanny realism, while the decorations in Strauss's *Wine, Women and Song* make one's hair stand on end. Not to be missed!

Ivogün, Maria (soprano)

Arias from: HANDEL: *L'allegro, il penseroso ed il moderato.* DONIZETTI: *Don Pasquale; Lucia di Lammermoor.* ROSSINI: *Il barbiere di Siviglia.* VERDI: *La traviata.* MEYERBEER: *Les Huguenots.* NICOLAI: *Die lustigen Weiber von Windsor.* JOHANN STRAUSS JR: *Die Fledermaus;* also Waltzes: *An der schönen blauen Donau, Geschichten aus dem Wienerwald and Frühlingsstimmen.* Songs: SCHUBERT: *Horch, horch, die Lerche; Winterreise: Die Post;* KREISLER: *Liebesfreud;* CHOPIN: *Nocturne in E flat, Op. 9/2.* 2 Folksongs arr. Gund: *O du liabs ängeli; Z'Lauterbach hab' i'mein Strumpf velor'n.*
(M) (★★★) Nimbus mono NI 7832.

Maria Ivogün is a less familiar name today than in the 1920s when she took Covent Garden by storm. Hers was a small voice but enchantingly focused; in

that, she has much in common with a more familiar recent name, Rita Streich. Ivogün sang with both charm and sparkle, and the present Nimbus transfers show just what a delightful artist she was. Whether in Donizetti or Meyerbeer or, indeed, in the Strauss waltzes (*Frühlingsstimmen, G'schichten aus dem Wiener Wald* and the *Blue Danube*), this is singing to give great refreshment. The recordings were for the most part made between 1917 and 1925, and these respond especially well to the Nimbus transferring system, but the folksongs were electrical, and were her very last records, made in 1932.

Luca, Giuseppe de (baritone)

Arias from: VERDI: *Don Carlos, Ernani, Il trovatore, La traviata, Rigoletto.* ROSSINI: *Il barbiere di Siviglia.* DONIZETTI: *L'elisir d'amore.* BELLINI: *I Puritani.* DIAZ: *Benvenuto Cellini.* PUCCINI: *La Bohème.* PONCHIELLI: *La Gioconda.* WOLF-FERRARI: *I gioielli della madonna.* Songs: DE LEVA: *Pastorale.* ROMILLI: *Marietta.*
(M) (★★★) Nimbus mono NI 7815.

There has never been a more involving account on record of the Act IV Marcello–Rodolfo duet than the one here with de Luca and Gigli, a model of characterization and vocal art. The baritone's mastery emerges vividly in item after item, whether in the power and wit of his pre-electric version of *Largo al factotum* (1917) or the five superb items (including the *Bohème* duet and the *Rigoletto* numbers, flawlessly controlled), which were recorded in the vintage year of 1927. Warm Nimbus transfers.

Martinelli, Giovanni (tenor)

Volume I, Arias from: GIORDANO: *Andrea Chénier; Fedora.* LEONCAVALLO: *Pagliacci.* MASCAGNI: *Cavalleria Rusticana; Iris.* TCHAIKOVSKY: *Eugene Onegin.* VERDI: *Aida; Ernani; La forza del destino; La traviata.*
(M) (★★★) Nimbus mono NI 7804.

This collection of seventeen fine examples of Martinelli's very distinctive and characterful singing covers his vintage period from 1915 to 1928, with one 1927 recording from Verdi's *La forza del destino* so clear that you can hear a dog barking outside the studio. The other two items from *Forza* are just as memorable, with Martinelli joined by Giuseppe de Luca in the Act IV duet, and by Rosa Ponselle and the bass, Ezio Pinza, for the final duet, with the voices astonishingly vivid and immediate.

Volume 2, Arias from: PUCCINI: *La Bohème; Tosca; Madama Butterfly* (with Frances Alda). PONCHIELLI: *La Gioconda.* VERDI: *Aida; Un ballo in maschera; Rigoletto; Don Carlos; Il trovatore.*

LEONCAVALLO: *Pagliacci.* MEYERBEER: *L'Africana.*
BIZET: *Carmen.* ROSSINI: *Guillaume Tell.*
MASSENET: *Werther.*

(M) (★★★) Nimbus mono NI 7826.

Martinelli's second collection is hardly less distinctive than the first, and admirers of this great tenor should not be disappointed with the transfers, which are well up to the convincingly natural standard now being achieved by the Nimbus process.

McCormack, John (tenor)

Arias and excerpts from: DONIZETTI: *Lucia di Lammermoor; L'elisir d'amore; La figlia del reggimento.* VERDI: *La traviata; Rigoletto.* PUCCINI: *La Bohème.* BIZET. *Carmen; I pescatore di perle.* DELIBES: *Lakmé.* GOUNOD: *Faust.* PONCHIELLI: *La Gioconda.* BOITO: *Mefistofele.* MASSENET: *Manon.* MOZART: *Don Giovanni.* WAGNER: *Die Meistersinger.* HERBERT: *Natomah.* HANDEL: *Semele; Atalanta.*

(M) (★★★) Nimbus mono NI 7820.

With the operas represented ranging from Handel's *Atalanta* and *Semele* to *Natomah*, by Victor Herbert, the heady beauty of McCormack's voice, his ease of production and perfect control are amply illustrated in these twenty-one items. His now legendary 1916 account of *Il mio tesoro* from *Don Giovanni*, with its astonishing breath control, is an essential item; but there are many others less celebrated, which help to explain his special niche, even in a generation that included Caruso and Schipa. Characteristic Nimbus transfers.

McCormack, John and Fritz Kreisler (violin)

'McCormack and Kreisler in recital': Arias from: GODARD: *Jocelyn.* BENEDICT: *Lily of Killarney.* Songs: RACHMANINOV: *O, Cease thy Singing, Maiden Fair; When Night Descends.* R. STRAUSS: *Morgen.* TOSTI: *Goodbye.* KREISLER: *Liebesfreud; Caprice viennoise* and *Cradle Song* arr. from *Caprice viennoise.* SCHUBERT: *Rosamunde: Ballet music No. 2.* BRAHMS: *Hungarian Dance No. 5.* BRAGA: *Angel's Serenade.* Songs by: COTTENET; PARKYNS; LEROUX; BALOGH; MOSZKOWSKI; LARCHET and TRAD.

(M) (★★★) Nimbus mono NI 7868.

This is a delightful disc of two great artists enjoying themselves in undemanding repertory. On one occasion, when McCormack and Kreisler were both recording in the Victor studios in Camden, New Jersey, the tenor asked the violinist's advice on the tempo for a Rachmaninov song. Whereupon Kreisler provided an impromptu obbligato which McCormack sang. Happily the engineer had switched on his machine, and this recording is included here.

Roughly half the items are of McCormack and Kreisler together. Others include McCormack's solo recordings of Kreisler pieces, including a cradle song arranged from *Caprice viennois.* There are also solo recordings of Kreisler playing favourite pieces of his, including arrangements. Recordings, all acoustic, date from between 1914 and 1924 when both artists were at their peak.

Melba, Nellie (soprano)

Arias from: MOZART: *Le nozze di Figaro.* HANDEL: *L'allegro, il pensero ed il moderato.* CHARPENTIER: *Louise.* MASSENET: *Don César de Bazan.* GOUNOD: *Faust.* THOMAS: *Hamlet.* LOTTI: *Armino.* VERDI: *Otello.* PUCCINI: *La Bohème; Tosca.* BEMBERG: *Elaine.* Songs: BISHOP: *Lo, Here the Gentle Lark.* BEMBERG: *Sur le lac.* DEBUSSY: *Romance; Mandoline.* CHAUSSON: *Poème de l'amour et de la mer: Le Temps des Lilas.* HAHN: *D'une prison.* TRAD: *Swing Low, Sweet Chariot.*

(M) (★★★) Nimbus mono NI 7890.

Though Melba among golden age sopranos is the one who even today is most regularly bracketed with Caruso as a legendary singer, her discs can seem disappointing, with a hardness regularly developing in the bright, clear voice. It says much for the Nimbus transfer process that this varied selection of songs as well as arias conveys a fullness, even a sweetness, alongside consistent purity and precision, with the voice less edgy than in most transfers. It is thrilling to hear her riding easily over the voices of McCormack and Sammarco in the final trio from Faust, and in some ways most revealing of all is a brief collection of distance tests, recorded in 1910, with Melba repeating a couple of phrases from Ophelia's aria in Thomas's *Hamlet* at different distances. As John Steane's illuminating note points out, one can then appreciate the star-like splendour of the voice. It is also good to have Melba's very last recording, made in 1928 at the age of 65, of the spiritual 'Swing Low, Sweet Chariot', with amazingly full tone.

Melchior, Lauritz (tenor)

Arias from: WAGNER: *Siegfried; Tannhäuser; Tristan und Isolde; Die Walküre; Die Meistersinger; Götterdämmerung.* LEONCAVALLO: *Pagliacci.* MEYERBEER: *L'Africana.* VERDI: *Otello.*

(M) (★★★) Nimbus mono NI 7816.

The Nimbus disc of Melchior, issued to celebrate his centenary in 1990, demonstrates above all the total consistency of the voice between the pre-electric recordings of *Siegfried* and *Tannhäuser*, made for Polydor in 1924, and the *Meistersinger* and *Götterdämmerung* extracts, recorded in 1939. Of those, the Siegfried–Brünnhilde duet from the *Prologue* of *Götterdämmerung* is particularly valuable. It is fascinating too to hear the four recordings that Melchior made with Barbirolli and the LSO in 1930–31: arias by Verdi, Leoncavallo and Meyerbeer translated into German. As a character, Otello is made to sound far more prickly. Characteristic Nimbus transfers.

Muzio, Claudia (soprano)

Arias from: MASCAGNI: *Cavalleria rusticana.* VERDI: *La forza del destino; Otello; Il trovatore; La traviata.* PUCCINI: *Tosca; La Bohème.* GIORDANO: *Andrea Chénier.* BOITO: *Mefistofele.* CILEA: *Adriana Lecouvreur; L'Arlesiana.* BELLINI: *La sonnambula.* Songs by BUZZI-PECCIA; PERGOLESI; REGER; DELIBES; REFICE.

(M) (★★★) Nimbus mono NI 7814.

This Nimbus collection of recordings by the sadly short-lived Claudia Muzio duplicates much that is contained on the EMI Références CD of her. The main addition here is the Act III duet from *Otello* with Francesco Merli, but some cherishable items are omitted. The Nimbus acoustic transfer process sets the voice more distantly as well as more reverberantly than the EMI, with its distinctive tang less-sharply conveyed.

Patti, Adelina (soprano), and other singers

'*The Era of Adelina Patti*' ((i) Adelina Patti, (ii) Victor Maurel; (iii) Pol Plançon; (iv) Mattia Battistini; (v) Mario Ancona; (vi) Lucien Fugère; (vii) Francisco Vignas; (viii) Emma Calvé; (ix) Maurice Renaud; (x) Fernando de Lucia; (xi) Francesco Tamagno; (xii) Nellie Melba; (xiii) Félia Litvinne; (xiv) Wilhelm Hesch; (xv) Lillian Nordica; (xvi) Mario Ancona; (xvii) Edouard de Reszke; (xviii) Marcella Sembrich; (xix) Francesco Marconi; (xx) Mattia Battistini; (xxi) Lilli Lehmann; (xxii) Sir Charles Santley): Arias from: VERDI: (ii) *Falstaff;* (i, iii) *Don Carlos;* (iv, xx) *Ernani;* (v, xiv) *Otello.* ADAM: (iii) *Le Chalet.* GLUCK: (vi) *Les Pèlerins de la Mecque.* MOZART: (i, ii, xx) *Don Giovanni;* (i, vii, xxi) *Le nozze di Figaro.* MEYERBEER: (vii) *Le Prophète.* BIZET: (viii) *Carmen.* MASSENET: (ix, xi) *Hérodiade;* (x) *Manon.* THOMAS: (xii) *Hamlet.* WAGNER: (xiii) *Lohengrin;* (xiv) *Die Meistersinger von Nürnberg.* ERKEL: (xv) *Hunyadi László.* DONIZETTI: (xvi) *La favorita;* (xix) *Lucrezia Borgia;* (xii) *Lucia.* BELLINI: (i) *La sonnambula;* (xviii) *I Puritani.* FLOTOW: (xvii) *Martha.* ROSSINI: (x) *Il barbiere di Siviglia.* GOMES: (xx) *Il Guarany.* Songs by TOSTI; (vi) RAMEAU; (i, vi) YRADIER; (i) HOOK; (i) BISHOP; (ix) GOUNOD; (xv) R. STRAUSS; (xxii) HATTON.

(M) (★★★) Nimbus mono NI 7840/41 (2).

The very first item on this wide-ranging collection of historic recordings has one sitting up at once. The voice ringing out from the loudspeakers prompts cheering from the singer's little audience. The clear-toned baritone is singing *Quand'ero paggio* from Verdi's *Falstaff* and, encouraged, he repeats it. Then, more cheering and a third performance, this time in French, to cap the occasion. The singer is Victor Maurel, the baritone whom Verdi chose as his first Falstaff in 1893 and, before that, his first Iago in *Otello.* The recording dates from 1907, and many lovers of historic vocal issues will remember it well. Yet hearing it on the Nimbus transfer to CD brings a sense of presence as never before.

That company's controversial technique of playing an ancient 78rpm disc with a thorn needle on the best possible acoustic horn gramophone is at its most effective here, with exceptionally vivid results on these acoustic recordings. They not only convey astonishing presence but also a sense of how beautiful the voices were, getting behind the tinny and squawky sounds often heard on old 78s. This is an ideal set for anyone not already committed to historic vocals who simply wants to investigate how great singing could be ninety years ago, providing such an unexpected mix of well-known items and rarities, to delight specialists and newcomers alike.

The first of the two discs offers recordings that Nimbus regards as technically the finest of their day, including Patti in 1906, not just singing but shouting enthusiastically in a Spanish folksong, *La Calesera,* '*Vivan los españoles!*' Recorded much later in 1928 comes the French baritone, Lucien Fugère, eighty at the time but singing with a firm focus that you might not find today in a baritone in his twenties.

The second of the two discs has just as fascinating a mixture, but the recordings 'have not survived the decades so well'. Even so, it is thrilling to hear Sir Charles Santley, born in 1834, the year after Brahms, singing 'Simon the Cellarer' with tremendous flair at the age of seventy-nine, and the coloratura Marcella Sembrich sounding even sweeter in Bellini than on previous transfers.

Pinza, Ezio (bass)

Arias duets and scenes from: VERDI: *Il trovatore; I vespri siciliani; Don Carlos; Aida* (with Grace Anthony and Giovanni Martinelli); *Attila.* DONIZETTI: *Lucia di Lammermoor.* HALEVY: *La Juive.* BELLINI: *I Puritani; Norma.* GOUNOD: *Faust* (with Aristodemo Giorgini). PUCCINI: *La Bohème.* MOZART: *Die Zauberflöte; Don Giovanni.* MEYERBEER: *Robert le Diable.* THOMAS: *Mignon; Le Caïc.*

(M) (★★★) Nimbus mono NI 7875.

This very well-chosen selection of Pinza recordings concentrates on those he made early in his career, starting in 1933 when, at the age of 31, he demonstrates the already extraordinary richness and clarity of focus which made him pre-eminent among operatic basses of the inter-war period. Fine as his later recordings are, notably those with Toscanini, or even his characterful contribution to the musical *South Pacific*, these early discs have an extra freshness. The subtlety with which Pinza shades his phrases using rich, firm tone and flawless legato is a constant delight. Philip II's aria from Verdi's *Don Carlos* has rarely been so nobly sung as here, and it is a mark of Pinza's sense of style that he is comparably commanding in the Mozart, Bellini and Donizetti arias. As well as the six acoustically recorded items, you have fourteen electrical recordings made between 1927 and 1930, all presenting the voice vividly in warm Nimbus transfers.

Ponselle, Rosa (soprano)

Arias from: BELLINI: *Norma.* PONCHIELLI: *La Gioconda.* SPONTINI: *La vestale.* VERDI: *Aida; Ernani; La forza del destino; Otello.* Songs by: ARENSKY; RIMSKY-KORSAKOV; DE CURTIS; DI CAPUA, JACOBS-BOND.

(M) (★★★) Nimbus mono NI 7805.

One of the most exciting American sopranos ever, Rosa Ponselle tantalizingly cut short her career when she was still at her peak. Only the Arensky and Rimsky songs represent her after her official retirement, and the rest make a superb collection, including her classic accounts of *Casta diva* from Bellini's *Norma* and the duet, *Mira o Norma*, with Marion Telva. The six Verdi items include her earlier version of *Ernani involami*, not quite so commanding as her classic 1928 recording, but fascinating for its rarity. Equally cherishable is her duet from *La forza del destino* with Ezio Pinza.

Vol. 2: Arias from: PUCCINI: *Madama Butterfly; Tosca; Manon Lescaut.* VERDI: *Il trovatore; Aida.* MASCAGNI: *Cavalleria rusticana.* HERBERT: *Mademoiselle Modiste.* RIMSKY-KORSAKOV: *Sadko.* HALEVY: *La Juive.* Songs by: TOSTI; MASSENET; BACH/GOUNOD; CHARLES.

(M) (★★★) Nimbus mono NI 7846.

This second volume of Nimbus's Ponselle collection is mainly devoted to her early acoustic recordings, made for Columbia between 1918 and 1924 when she was still in her early twenties. Hers is a flawless voice, which takes very well to the Nimbus process, when just as in her later electrical recordings the pure creamy quality comes over vividly with ample bloom, set in a lively acoustic. With not a hint of strain she subtly shades her tone in such an aria as Tosca's *Vissi d'arte*, underlining the emotion. The poise and flawless legato of Leonora's *La vergine degli angeli* from *Forza del destino*, the earliest recording here, explains why from the start this taxing role was one for which she was specially renowned; at the other extreme she gives a sparkling account of the Victor Herbert number 'Kiss me Again'. The electrical recordings then include her early recordings of Aida,

notably the whole of the death scene with Martinelli, a classic recording. The discs ends with a touchingly apt song, recorded in 1939 after her retirement at the age of forty, 'When I have sung my songs to you, I'll sing no more'.

Volume 3: Arias from: VERDI: *Aida; Ernani; Il trovatore; La forza del destino.* ROSSINI: *William Tell.* MEYERBEER: *L'Africana.* PUCCINI: *La Bohème.* LEONCAVALLO: *Pagliacci.* Songs: DI CAPUA: *Maria, Mari!.* TOSTI: *Serenade; 'A Vucchella; Luna d'estate; Si tu le voulais;* and by: BLAND; FOSTER.

(M) (★★★) Nimbus mono NI 7878.

In this third Ponselle volume from Nimbus, the only electrical recordings are of ballads by Tosti, Stephen Foster and James Bland, which Ponselle magically transforms, giving distinction to trivial material. The acoustic recordings of arias include Aida's *Ritorna vincitor*, sung even more commandingly in 1923 than in her electrical recording of 1928 in Volume 2. The poise and flawless control in each are as remarkable as in the two earlier discs, and the nine operatic items plus two ballads include four recorded for Victor in 1923–5 but never released.

Rethberg, Elisabeth (soprano)

Arias from: VERDI: *Aida; Otello; Un ballo in maschera.* GIORDANO: *Andrea Chénier.* PUCCINI: *La Bohème; Madama Butterfly.* WAGNER: *Tannhäuser; Lohengrin.* MOZART: *Le nozze di Figaro; Die Zauberflöte.* J. STRAUSS JR: *Der Zigeunerbaron.* BIZET: *Carmen.*

(M) (★★★) Nimbus mono 7903.

Elisabeth Rethberg, counted by Toscanini as his favourite soprano, was once voted 'the most perfect singer in the world'. This excellent selection of her recordings, drawn from the years 1924–30, helps to explain why. Consistently she was flawless in controlling her full, firm, finely projected voice both in phrase and dynamic over the widest expressive range. No recording of Aida's *O patria mia* can quite match the subtlety of this pre-electric version, recorded for Brunswick in 1924 – one of the few where the culminating top C is sung *dolce*, as marked. Her characterizations of each role may not be the most individual, but few singers have matched her in these arias, whether in Verdi, Puccini, Mozart or the Wagner of *Tannhäuser* and *Lohengrin*. The Nimbus transfers give a vivid idea of the voice, if not of the instrumental accompaniment, with six pre-electric items, twelve electrically recorded.

Royal Opera House, Covent Garden

Royal Opera House Covent Garden (An Early History on Record). Singers included are: Melba,

Caruso, Tetrazzini, McCormack, Destin, Gadski, Schorr, Turner, Zanelli, Lehmann, Schumann, Olczewska, Chaliapin, Gigli, Supervia, Tibbett, Tauber, Flagstad, Melchior. Arias from: GOUNOD: *Faust.* VERDI: *Rigoletto; Otello.* DONIZETTI: *Lucia di Lammermoor.* VERDI: *La traviata.* PUCCINI: *Madama Butterfly; Tosca.* WAGNER: *Götterdämmerung; Die Meistersinger; Tristan und Isolde.* R. STRAUSS: *Der Rosenkavalier.* MUSSORGSKY: *Boris Godunov.* GIORDANO: *Andrea Chénier.* BIZET: *Carmen.* MOZART: *Don Giovanni.* (M) (★★★) Nimbus mono NI 7819.

Nimbus's survey of great singers at Covent Garden ranges from Caruso's 1904 recording of *Questa o quella* from *Rigoletto* to the recording of the second half of the *Tristan* love duet, which Kirsten Flagstad and Lauritz Melchior made in San Francisco in November 1939, a magnificent recording, never issued in Britain and little known, which repeated the partnership initiated during the 1937 Coronation season at Covent Garden. The Vienna recording of the *Rosenkavalier* Trio with Lehmann, Schumann and Olczewska similarly reproduces a classic partnership at Covent Garden, while Chaliapin's 1928 recording of the *Prayer* and *Death of Boris* was actually recorded live at Covent Garden, with the transfer giving an amazingly vivid sense of presence. Those who like Nimbus's acoustic method of transfer will enjoy the whole disc, though the reverberation round some of the early offerings – like the very first, Melba's Jewel Song from *Faust* – is cavernous. Particularly interesting is the 1909 recording of part of Brünnhilde's Immolation scene, with Johanna Gadski commandingly strong.

Schipa, Tito (tenor)

Arias from: MASCAGNI: *Cavalleria rusticana; L'amico Fritz.* VERDI: *Rigoletto; Luisa Miller.* DONIZETTI: *Lucia di Lammermoor; Don Pasquale; L'elisir d'amore.* LEONCAVALLO: *Pagliacci.* MASSENET: *Manon; Werther.* ROSSINI: *Il barbiere di Siviglia.* THOMAS: *Mignon.* FLOTOW: *Martha.* CILEA: *L'Arlesiana.* (M) (★★★) Nimbus mono NI 7813.

The first nine items on this well-chosen selection of Schipa's recordings date from the pre-electric era. The voice is totally consistent, heady and light and perfectly controlled, between the *Siciliana* from Mascagni's *Cavalleria*, recorded with piano in 1913, to the incomparable account of more Mascagni, the Cherry Duet from *L'amico Fritz*, made with Mafalda Favero in 1937. It says much for his art that Schipa's career continued at full strength for decades after that. The Nimbus transfers put the voice at a slight distance, with the electrical recordings made to sound the more natural.

Schumann-Heink, Ernestine (contralto)

Arias from: DONIZETTI: *Lucrezia Borgia.* MEYERBEER: *Le Prophète.* WAGNER: *Das Rheingold; Rienzi; Götterdämmerung.* HANDEL: *Rinaldo.* Songs by: ARDITTI; BECKER; SCHUBERT; WAGNER; REIMANN; MOLLOY; BRAHMS; BOEHM; TRAD. (M) (★★★) Nimbus mono NI 7811.

Ernestine Schumann-Heink was a formidable personality in the musical life of her time, notably in New York, as well as a great singer. 'I am looking for my successor,' she is reported as saying well-before she retired, adding, 'She must be the contralto.' Schumann-Heink combines to an astonishing degree a full contralto weight and richness with the most delicate flexibility, as in the *Brindisi* from Donizetti's *Lucrezia Borgia*. This wide-ranging collection, resonantly transferred by the Nimbus acoustic method, presents a vivid portrait of a very great singer.

Sembrich, Marcella (soprano)

Arias from: DONIZETTI: *Don Pasquale; Lucia di Lammermoor.* MUNIUSZKO: *Halka.* ROSSINI: *Semiramide; Il barbiere di Siviglia.* VERDI: *La traviata; Ernani; Rigoletto.* BELLINI: *Norma.* THOMAS: *Hamlet.* VERDI: *I vespri siciliani.* FLOTOW: *Martha.* BELLINI: *La sonnambula.* Songs: J. STRAUSS JR; ARNE; ARDITTI; BISHOP; HAHN; SCHUBERT; CHOPIN and TRAD. (M) (★★★) Nimbus mono NI 7901.

As an alternative to the four discs of the complete Romophone edition of Sembrich, this Nimbus issue is very welcome. Her reputation as the supreme coloratura of her day may be undermined, but the choice of twenty-one items is first-rate, with only three recordings from before 1907. The Nimbus transfer method, with 78rpm discs played in front of a modern stereo recording machine, presents the voice in a flattering three-dimensional setting, but with focus less sharp than on Romophone.

Supervia, Conchita (mezzo-soprano)

'*In Opera and Song*': BIZET: *Carmen:* excerpts (with Micheletti, Vavon, Bernadet). Arias from: ROSSINI: *L'Italiana in Algeri; Il barbiere di Siviglia; La Cenerentola.* GOUNOD: *Faust.* THOMAS: *Mignon.* SAINT-SAENS: *Samson et Dalila.* SERRANO: *La Alegría del Batallón; El mal de amores.* Songs: FALLA: *7 Canciones populares españolas.* BALDOMIR: *Meus amores.* YRADIER: *La paloma.* VALVERDE: *Clavelitos.* (M) (★★★) Nimbus mono NI 7836/7 (2).

Readers who remember the 78s of Conchita Supervia, especially in Rossini – and in particular her dark, brittle mezzo with its wide vibrato ('like the rattle of shaken dice', as one critic described it) sparkling in the divisions of *Una voce poco fa* – may be astonished to discover the degree of vocal charm in other roles. Her reputation for dazzling the ear in Rossini was surely deserved (and she helped to restore *La Cenerentola* and *L'Italiana in Algeri* to the repertoire). Her Carmen, too, is unforgettable, as is her Delilah – but, more unexpectedly, her Mignon is also a highlight here, as is the brief Delibes item. As usual, the Nimbus transfers are kind to the voice (there is no suggestion of the 'death rattle' of one unkind description) and almost certainly more truthful than the edgier, brighter quality we have had from some other sources. The recordings date from between 1927 and 1935.

Tauber, Richard (tenor)

Arias from: R. STRAUSS: *Der Rosenkavalier.* WAGNER: *Die Walküre; Die Meistersinger.* KIENZL: *Der Evangelimann.* PUCCINI: *Tosca; La Bohème; Madama Butterfly; Turandot.* VERDI: *Il trovatore.* MOZART: *Don Giovanni; Die Zauberflöte.* TCHAIKOVSKY: *Eugene Onegin.* BIZET: *Carmen.* KORNGOLD: *Die tote Stadt.* LORTZING: *Undine.* OFFENBACH: *Les Contes d'Hoffmann.*

(M) (★★★) Nimbus mono NI 7830.

The Nimbus transfers for both this and the operetta excerpts (see below) come from between 1919 and 1929, and, although there is some duplication of repertoire, Tauber admirers will probably want both CDs. The effect of Nimbus transfers is always most impressive in the pre-electric recordings, which predominate here, but the voice is always naturally focused, even in the 1929 excerpt from Offenbach's *Tales of Hoffmann*. The effect is mellower, more rounded than in the EMI transfers.

Tauber, Richard (tenor), and Lotte Schöne (soprano)

Operetta arias from LEHAR: *Paganini; Zigeunerliebe; Der Land des Lächelns; Die lustige Witwe.* SUPPE: *Die schöne Galatea.* SCHUBERT/BERTE: *Das Dreimäderlhaus (Lilac Time).* JOHANN STRAUSS JR: *Die Fledermaus; Der lustige Krieg; Indigo und die vierzig Räuber; Cagliosto in Wien.* KALMAN: *Gräfin Mariza; Die Zirkusprinzessin.* MILLOCKER: *Der arme Jonathan.* ZELLER: *Der Vogelhändler; Der Obersteiger.* NESSLER: *Der Trompeter von Säckingen.*

(M) (★★★) Nimbus mono NI 7833.

These imaginatively chosen operetta excerpts, recorded over the same period (1919–29) as the operatic collections above, explain Tauber's phenomenal popularity over so many years. The collection is the more tempting for its inclusion of the contributions of Lotte Schöne, a delightful artist. Moreover there is much here that is very rare, and it is a pity that no duets were available – these are all solo items. The transfers are most successful.

Tetrazzini, Luisa (soprano)

Arias from: BELLINI: *La sonnambula.* DONIZETTI: *Lucia di Lammermoor.* ROSSINI: *Il barbiere di Siviglia.* THOMAS: *Mignon.* VERACINI: *Rosalinda.* VERDI: *Un ballo in maschera; Rigoletto; La traviata; Il trovatore; I vespri siciliani.*

(M) (★★★) Nimbus mono NI 7808.

Tetrazzini was astonishing among coloratura sopranos not just for her phenomenal agility but for the golden warmth that went with tonal purity. The Nimbus transfers add a bloom to the sound, with the singer slightly distanced. Though some EMI transfers make her voice more vividly immediate, one quickly adjusts. Such display arias as *Ah non giunge* from *La sonnambula* or the *Bolero* from *I vespri siciliani* are incomparably dazzling, but it is worth noting too what tenderness is conveyed through Tetrazzini's simple phrasing and pure tone in such a tragic aria as Violetta's *Addio del passato*, with both verses included. Lieder devotees may gasp in horror, but one of the delightful oddities here is Tetrazzini's bright-eyed performance, with ragged orchestral accompaniment, of what is described as *La serenata inutile* by Brahms – in fact *Vergebliches Ständchen*, sung with a triumphant if highly inauthentic top A at the end, implying no closure of the lady's window!

Volume 2: Arias from: BELLINI: *I Puritani; La sonnambula.* DAVID: *Le Perle du Brésil.* DONIZETTI: *Linda di Chamounix.* ROSSINI: *Semiramide; Il barbiere di Siviglia.* GOUNOD: *Roméo et Juliette.* BIZET: *Carmen.* MEYERBEER: *Dinorah; Les Huguenots.* VERDI: *Il trovatore; La traviata.* Songs: TOSTI: *Aprile.* GRIEG: *Peer Gynt: Solveig's song.* BRAGA: *La Serenata.* BENEDICT: *Carnevale di Venezia.*

(M) (★★★) Nimbus mono NI 7891.

Tetrazzini's bright clear soprano with its characteristic touch of gold is ideally suited to the Nimbus process, and with ample bloom on the sound these early acoustic recordings, made between 1910 and 1914, give one a vivid idea not only of the beauty and brilliance but of the scale of the voice. Not that they disguise the technical shortcomings, such as her tendency to attack the exposed start of florid runs fearlessly with a little squawk, endearing as it may be, or the way that some of the coloratura here is on the sketchy side, as in the Queen's aria from Meyerbeer's *Les Huguenots*. The disc ends with three Zonophone recordings made in 1904 with piano accompaniment, including an early version of her party-piece, *Ah non giunge*, from *Sonnambula* and the first half only of Rosina's *Una voce poco fa* from *Il barbiere di Siviglia*.

Tibbett, Lawrence (baritone)

'*Tibbett in Opera*': excerpts from: LEONCAVALLO: *Pagliacci*. BIZET: *Carmen*. PUCCINI: *Tosca*. VERDI: *Un ballo in maschera; Simon Boccanegra; Rigoletto; Otello*. ROSSINI: *Il barbiere di Siviglia*. GOUNOD: *Faust*. WAGNER: *Tannhäuser; Die Walküre*.

(M) (***) Nimbus mono NI 7825.

The scale and resonance of Lawrence Tibbett's voice come over vividly in this fine selection of his recordings made between 1926 and 1939. The Nimbus proc- ess allows the rapid vibrato in his voice to emerge naturally, giving the sound a thrilling richness in all these varied items. Particularly interesting is the longest, the whole of Wotan's Farewell, with Stokowski conducting the Philadelphia Orchestra in 1934. It is an over-the-top performance that carries total conviction, even if the sheer volume produces some clangorous resonances in the Nimbus transfer. Also memorable is the celebrated *Boccanegra* council chamber sequence, recorded in 1939 with Martinelli and Rose Bampton in the ensemble.

Other Historical Reissues

Caruso, Enrico (tenor)

The Naxos Complete Recordings Edition

The Complete Recordings of Enrico Caruso, Vol. 1
(1902–3 recordings): Arias from: FRANCHETTI:
Germania. VERDI: *Aida; Rigoletto*. MASSENET:
Manon. DONIZETTI: *L'elisir d'amore*. BOITO:
Mefistofele. PUCCINI: *Tosca*. MASCAGNI: *Cavalleria
Rusticana; Iris*. GIORDANO: *Fedora*. PONCHIELLI:
La Gioconda. LEONCAVALLO: *Pagliacci*. CILEA:
Adriana Lecouvreur. Songs: DENZA: *Non t'amo più*.
TOSTI: *La mia canzone*. ZARDO: *Luna fedel* (2
versions). TRIMARCHI: *Un bacio ancora*.
(BB) (★★★) Naxos mono 8.110703.

The Complete Recordings of Enrico Caruso, Vol. 2
(1903–6 recordings): Arias from: PUCCINI: *La
Bohème; Tosca*. MEYERBEER: *Les Huguenots*.
VERDI: *Aida; Rigoletto; Il trovatore*. DONIZETTI:
Don Pasquale; L'elisir d'amore: La favorita.
MASCAGNI: *Cavalleria rusticana*. LEONCAVALLO:
Pagliacci. MASSENET: *Manon*. BIZET: *Carmen; Les
pêcheurs de perles*. PONCHIELLI: *La Gioconda*.
FLOTOW: *Martha*. GOUNOD: *Faust*. Songs:
PINI-CORSI: *Tu non mi vuoi più bene*.
LEONCAVALLO: *Mattinata*.
(BB) (★★★) Naxos mono 8.100704.

The Complete Recordings of Enrico Caruso, Vol. 3
(1906–8 recordings): Arias from: VERDI: *Aida; La
forza del destino; Rigoletto*. GIORDANO: *Andrea
Chénier*. LEONCAVALLO: *Pagliacci*. PUCCINI: *La
Bohème; Madama Butterfly*. BIZET: *Les Pêcheurs de
perles*. MEYERBEER: *L'Africana*. DONIZETTI: *Don
Sébastien; Lucia di Lammermoor*. Songs:
BARTHELEMY: *Adorables tourments; Triste ritorno*.
TOSTI: *Ideale*.
(BB) (★★★) Naxos mono 8.110708.

The Complete Recordings of Enrico Caruso, Vol. 4
(1908–10 recordings): Arias from: VERDI: *Aida; La
forza del destino; Rigoletto; Il trovatore*. PUCCINI:
Tosca. GOLDMARK: *Regina di Saba*. BIZET: *Carmen*.
MEYERBEER: *Les Huguenots*. FLOTOW: *Martha*.
Songs: BUZZI-PECCIA: *Lolita*. DONCIEUX-TOSTI:
Pour un baiser. RUSSO-NUTILE: *Mamma mia, che
vo' sapè*.
(BB) (★★★) Naxos mono 8.110719.

The Complete Recordings of Enrico Caruso, Vol. 5
(1908–10 recordings): Arias from GOUNOD: *Faust*.

FRANCHETTI: *Germania*. PUCCINI: *Madama
Butterfly*. PONCHIELLI: *La Gioconda*.
LEONCAVALLO: *Pagliacci*. VERDI: *Otello*.
(BB) (★★★) Naxos mono 8.110720.

The Complete Recordings of Enrico Caruso, Vol. 6.
(1911–12 recordings): Arias from: VERDI: *Aida; Un
ballo in maschera; La forza del destino*. DONIZETTI:
L'elisir d'amore. LEONCAVALLO: *La Bohème*.
GOMES: *Lo Schiavo*. MASSENET: *Manon*. FLOTOW:
Martha. Songs: MASSONI-MASCHERON:
Eternamente. CORDIFERRO-CARDILLO: *Core
'ngrato*. BOVIO DE CURTIS: *Canta pe'me*.
TESCHEMACHER-GARTNER: *Love is Mine*.
(BB) (★★★) Naxos mono 8.110721.

The Complete Recordings of Enrico Caruso, Vol. 7
(1912–13 recordings). Arias from: VERDI: *Don
Carlos; I Lombardi; Rigoletto; Il trovatore*.
DONIZETTI: *Lucia di Lammermoor*. MASSENET:
Manon. PUCCINI: *La Bohème; Manon Lescaut*.
Songs: J.-B. FAURE: *Crucifix*. DE CRESCENZO:
Tarantella sincera. ROSSINI: *La danza*. CARUSO:
Dreams of Long Ago. SULLIVAN: *The Lost Chord*.
D'HARDELOT: *Because*. GRAINGER: *Hosanna*.
TCHAIKOVSKY: *Pimpimella*. BIZET: *Agnus Dei*.
KAHN: *Ave Maria*. MASSENET: *Elegy*.
(BB) (★★★) Naxos mono 8.110724.

The Complete Recordings of Enrico Caruso, Vol. 8
(1913–14 recordings). ROSSINI: *Stabat Mater*. Arias
from: MASCAGNI: *Cavalleria rusticana*. VERDI: *Un
ballo in maschera; Otello*. Songs: LEONCAVALLO:
Lasciati amar. DE CRESCENZO: *Guardann 'a luna*.
O'HARA: *Your Eyes have Told me What I Did Not
Know*. COTTRAU: *Fenesta che lucive*. FAURE: *Les
Rameaux* (2 versions). TCHAIKOVSKY: *Sérénade de
Don Juan*. RICCIARDI: *Amor mio*. VALENTE:
Manella mia. GARTNER: *Trusting Eyes*. RONALD:
Sérénade espagnole. TOSTI: *Parted*. ALVAREZ: *La
partida*. CHAPI: *El milagro de la Virgen purisimas*.
(BB) (★★★) Naxos mono 8.110726.

The Complete Recordings of Enrico Caruso, Vol. 9
(1914–16 recordings): Arias from: VERDI: *Requiem;
La traviata; Macbeth*. GOMES: *Il Guarany*. BIZET:
Carmen. DONIZETTI: *Il Duca d'Alba*. MASSENET:
Le Cid. GOUNOD: *La reine de Saba*. PUCCINI: *La
Bohème*. Songs: SZULC: *Hantise d'amour*. TOSTI: *La
mia canzone; Luna d'estate*. PENNINO: *Pecchè?*
CIOCIANO: *Cielo turchino*. DENZA: *Si vois l'aviez
compris*. LEONCAVALLO: *Les Deux Sérénades*.

FRANCK: *La Procession.* DI CAPUA: *O sole mio.*
ROTOLI: *Mia sposa sarà la mia bandiera.* ADAM:
Cantique de Noël.

(BB) (★★★) Naxos mono 8.110750.

The Complete Recordings of Enrico Caruso, Vol. 10

(1916–17 recordings): Arias from: TCHAIKOVSKY:
Eugene Onegin. GIORDANO: *Andrea Chénier.*
SAINT-SAENS: *Samson et Dalila.* BIZET: *Les
Pêcheurs de perles.* VERDI: *Rigoletto.* DONIZETTI:
Lucia di Lammermoor. FLOTOW: *Martha.*
RUBINSTEIN: *Nero.* Songs: FAURE: *Sancta Maria.*
CARUSO: *Tiempo antico.* FOLK SONG (arr.
COTTRAU): *Santa Lucia.* TCHAIKOVSKY: *Porquoi?*
GODARD: *Chanson de juin.* TOSTI: *L'alba separa
dalla luce l'ombra* (2 versions).

(BB) (★★★) Naxos mono 8.110751.

The Complete Recordings of Enrico Caruso, Vol. 11

(1918–19 recordings): Arias from: VERDI: *La forza
del destino.* SAINT-SAENS: *Samson et Dalila.*
DONIZETTI: *L'elisir d'amore.* Songs: MICHELENA: *A
la luz de la luna.* COSTA: *Sei morta ne la vita mia.*
ALVAREZ: *La partida.* COHAN: *Over There.*
NIEDERMEYER: *Pietà, Signore.* ALVAREZ: *A
Granada.* BILLI (arr. MALFETTI): *Campane a sera
'Ave Maria'.* OLIVIERI: *Inno di Garibaldi.* ARONA:
La Campana di San Giusto. PLANQUETTE: *Le
Régiment de Sambre et Meuse.* TOSTI: *'A Vucchella.*
TRAD.: *Vieni sul mar.* DE CURTIS: *Tu, ca nun
chiagne.* COTTRAU: *Addio a Napoli.*

(BB) (★★★) Naxos mono 8.110752.

The Complete Recordings of Enrico Caruso, Vol. 12

(1902–20 recordings): Arias from: GOMES: *Salvador
Rosa.* HANDEL: *Serse.* HALEVY: *La Juive.*
MEYERBEER: *L'Africana.* LULLY: *Amadis de Gaule.*
ROSSINI: *Petite Messe Solennelle.* FRANCHETTI:
Germania. Songs: CIAMPI: *Nina.* DE CRESCENZO:
Première caresse. DE CURTIS: *Senza nisciuno.*
BRACCO: *Serenata.* FUCITO: *Scordame.* SECCHI:
Love Me or Not. PASADAS: *Noche feliz.* GIOE: *I'
m'arricordo 'e Napule.* DONAUDY: *Vaghissima
sembianza.* BARTLETT: *A Dream.* CARUSO: *Liberty
Forever.* EDWARDS: *My Cousin Caruso.*

(BB) (★★★) Naxos mono 8.110753.

The role of the great tenor Enrico Caruso is unique
in the history of recorded music. The recordings he
made in the early years of the twentieth century
more than anything transformed what was regarded
as a toy into an important and popular branch of the
media. In the age of CD that role has been recognized in repeated attempts to renovate those recordings, starting with those made by Thomas G.
Stockham and his Soundstream organization for
RCA, successor of the Victor Company, which made
most of the original recordings. Indeed, it was specifically to improve the sound of pre-electric Caruso
recordings that Stockham devised the first commercial digital recordings, scarcely realizing that digital

techniques would quickly take over recording generally. Sixteen of these digitally enhanced recordings
with modern orchestral accompaniments rather
incongruously laminated on are now available on
RCA (24321 69766-2) at mid-price.

Masterminded by Ward Marston, artist as well as
technician, who supervised these 12 discs, the Naxos
series offers CD transfers that achieve new degrees of
fidelity. With meticulous care Marston has used mint
copies of the 78rpm originals, reduced the surface
hiss, clarified the voice and taken great care to restore
the original pitch – not easy when recording speeds
were variable in the early years of that century. The
discs can all be warmly recommended, particularly
when each comes with a comment by Marston himself, as well as a note by Hugh Griffith, which not
only comments on the specific recordings but gives
an illuminating account of developments in the singer's life, as well as the background in the opera world,
not least at the Metropolitan Opera in New York. In
direct comparison with the RCA transfers, the voice
is less forward but clearer, with less distortion, and
with lighter surface noise behind.

In Volume 1 the Griffith note is especially illuminating, when it highlights the flaws and mistakes in
the first batch of Caruso recordings, made by the
HMV recording manager, Fred Gaisberg, in a hotel
room in Milan on 11 April 1902. He notes that Caruso
funks the final top note of *Celeste Aida*, using a
falsetto instead, condemning the practice even
though the falsetto is extremely beautiful. Gaisberg's
bosses in London objected to his paying the singer
£100 for the first ten recordings, but they quickly
realized how profitable the results were going to be.

It was not until the second series, in November
1902, that Caruso made his first recording of *Vesti la
giubba* from *Pagliacci*, with its laughter at the beginning and sob at the end, an aria that became the
singer's calling-card. He also re-recorded *Celeste
Aida*; but, to avoid the final top note, cut the aria
short, omitting the coda. All these early recordings
have piano accompaniment, with Giordano taking
over as accompanist from the staff pianist for *Amor ti
vieta* from his opera, *Fedora*, and Cilea taking over
for an aria from his *Adriana Lecouvreur.* A series of
seven recordings was also made for the Zonophone
Company, and Volume 2 starts with three recordings,
also made in Milan, originally for issue on cylinders
and later issued on disc by the Pathé Company,
inevitably less clear than the HMV recordings.

It was when (in February 1904) Caruso started
making recordings for the Victor Company in New
York (associated company of British HMV) that the
American engineers wanted to improve on the standards of recording. It shows the astronomic rise in
Caruso's popularity that in his first contract with
Victor he was guaranteed at least $2,000 a year, very
different from the contested £100 of two years earlier.
The first batch of American recordings concentrated
on repertory Caruso had already recorded in Milan,
generally with improved results not just in sound

quality but also in artistic assurance. In April 1904 he made two more recordings in Milan, one of them with Leoncavallo accompanying him splashily in his song, *Mattinata*; but from then on, Caruso made all his recordings in the United States, for he was spending six months of each year in New York, singing at the Met.

It was in February 1906 that Victor made the first Caruso recordings with orchestra, a strange band based on wind and brass, and technical improvements meant that arias of over four minutes could be recorded complete, one of the first being Rodolfo's *Che gelida manina* from Puccini's *La Bohème*, beautifully shaped. The singer's artistic development can also be measured, as Griffith points out, by the differences between his 1906 recording of *Cielo e mar* from Ponchielli's *La Gioconda* and the far less imaginative one made in Milan in 1902. He also made his first recording in French, Faust's *Salut demeure*.

Volume 3 brings Caruso's earliest recordings, also from 1906, with other singers, first his fellow Neapolitan, the baritone Antonio Scotti. Then, in February 1907, came the first of his four recordings of the *Quartet* from *Rigoletto*, again with Scotti, as well as Bessie Abbott and Louise Homer. Ward Marston deduces from the sound-quality and technical details that, unlike his later versions, this one was recorded a semitone down; and it is a measure of Marston's thoroughness that he appends at the end of the volume a transfer at the score-pitch, which, as he says, makes the opening solo sound not quite true to Caruso. Volume 3 also brings Caruso's first account of *Vesti la giubba* with orchestra, the one which became a runaway bestseller and has remained so ever since.

Volume 4 brings more Neapolitan songs and two versions of Don José's Flower Song from *Carmen*, one in French, one in Italian; while Volume 5 marks another departure, with no fewer than nine items from Gounod's *Faust* recorded in 1910, with Caruso joined by Geraldine Farrar as Marguerite, Gabrielle Gilibert, Scotti again and Marcel Journet as Mephistopheles. For this series Ward Marston has not kept strictly to chronological order of recording but has arranged them in musical sequence, a sensible course. At this period there was no question of recording complete operas with star singers like Caruso, but Victor devised this sequence as a compromise, the choice of opera reflecting the reputation of the Met. at the time as being the 'Faustspielhaus'.

Where in 1907 Caruso dominated the Met.'s season, the arrival of Toscanini as conductor, with a broadening of the repertory, meant that the tenor was not so dominant. By this time, the changes of colouring in Caruso's voice are more marked, when it was growing weightier and more baritonal, as in the March 1910 version of *Cielo e mar*. Volume 6 brings a recording of Riccardo's Act I aria with chorus from *Ballo in maschera*, and when Caruso was spending so much of the year in New York it was relatively easy to get singers at the Met., soloists as

well as chorus, to record either in New York or in the Victor studios in Camden, New Jersey. Volume 6 also contains a sequence of items from Flotow's *Martha* with Frances Alda, Josephine Jacoby and Marcel Journet.

Volume 7 brings Caruso's 1912 version of the *Rigoletto* Quartet, this time with Tetrazzini (who at the time even threatened to rival Caruso as the Met.'s top vocal attraction), Jacoby and Pasquale Amato. Songs were playing an increasing role in the singer's recording programme, including at this period Sullivan's 'The Lost Chord', the ballad 'Because' by Guy d'Hardelot, sung in French as *Parceque*, and a ballad by Caruso himself, 'Dreams of Long Ago'. There is also a memorable account of *O soave fanciulla* from Act I of *La Bohème* with Geraldine Farrar who, unlike some other prima donnas, notably Nellie Melba, became a great friend.

Volume 8 not only brings more songs like *Les Rameaux* by Jean-Baptiste Faure (not to be confused with Gabriel Fauré), Massenet's *Elégie*, with Mischa Elman playing the violin solo, *Cuius animam* from Rossini's *Stabat Mater*, and *Don Juan's Serenade* by Tchaikovsky. Most memorable of all is the Oath Duet from Act II of Verdi's *Otello*, with Caruso at his most heroic matched against the magnificent Titta Ruffo as Iago, who sadly made too few recordings with Caruso when his American visits were based on Chicago, not New York. Volume 8 also contains ensembles from *Ballo in maschera* with the soprano Frieda Hempel, among the other singers.

Volume 9 brings the *Brindisi* from *La Traviata* with Alma Gluck as Violetta, and two versions, both unpublished at the time, of the Don José–Micaela duet from *Carmen* with Frances Alda. The curiosity in this volume is Caruso's recording of Colline's Coat Song from Act IV of *La Bohème*, with Caruso singing like a *basso cantante*, having in 1913 stepped in impromptu at a live performance when his colleague, Andres de Segurola, lost his voice. Volume 10 finds the voice even darker and richer, and the 1917 account of the Quartet from *Rigoletto* was made this time with the young diva of the moment, Amelita Galli-Curci. Interestingly, there is an unpublished alternative take of the opening tenor solo.

Volume 11 brings a sequence of patriotic songs, recorded in 1918 to help the war effort, not only the celebrated account of George M. Cohan's 'Over There', but Garibaldi's *Hymn* and the jaunty *La campana di San Giusto* to encourage his fellow Italians and Planquette's marching song, *Le régiment de Sambre et Meuse*, for the French. Increasingly over the years, it had become difficult to find new repertory for the great tenor, and the final volume brings such unexpected repertory as Handel's *Ombra mai fú*, complete with recitative, weightily done in the manner of the time. The two operatic items are an aria from Meyerbeer's *L'Africana* sung in Italian and the big aria from the last opera Caruso added to his repertory, *La Juive* by Halévy, the voice still heroic and full. That was among the recordings he made in

September 1920 at his last session, and within a year he was dead.

That penultimate volume ends with a fascinating appendix, a march, *Liberty Forever*, by Caruso himself, played by the Victor Military Band, and a music-hall number, 'My Cousin Caruso', from 1909, sung by Billy Murray. Finally there is yet another example of Ward Marston's thoroughness – an improved transfer of Caruso's very first recording, the aria, *Studente, udite*, from *Germania* by Franchetti. This is a model series, and the only disadvantage of having these Naxos discs separately is that one lacks a composite index, making it harder to find particular items.

Other Caruso CDs

'*The Legendary Caruso*': Opera arias and songs: Arias from: MASCAGNI: *Cavalleria rusticana; Iris.* PONCHIELLI: *La Gioconda.* LEONCAVALLO: *Pagliacci*; and song: *Mattinata.* BOITO: *Mefistofele.* PUCCINI: *Tosca.* GIORDANO: *Fedora.* CILEA: *Adriana Lecouvreur.* VERDI: *Rigoletto; Aida.* BIZET: *Les Pêcheurs de perles.* MASSENET: *Manon.* DONIZETTI: *L'elisir d'amore.* MEYERBEER: *Les Huguenots.* Songs: TOSTI: *La mia canzone.* DENZA: *Non t'amo più*; and by ZARDO & TRIMARCHI.
(M) (***) EMI mono 5 67006-2.

The EMI collection was originally on the Références label and has now been again remastered. It brings together Caruso's earliest recordings, made in 1902, 1903 and 1904 in Milan with at times misty piano accompaniment. The very first pieces were done impromptu in Caruso's hotel, and the roughness of presentation reflects that; but the voice is glorious in its youth, amazingly well caught for that period and now remarkably fresh and free from horn resonances, even if the background noise, not always regular, is still obvious.

'*The Greatest Tenor in the World*': Arias and excerpts from: GIORDANO: *Fedora.* PUCCINI: *La Bohème* (with Geraldine Farrar); *Tosca; Manon Lescaut.* GOUNOD: *Faust; La reine de Saba.* VERDI: *Il trovatore; Rigoletto* (including *Bella figlia*, quartet with Galli-Curci, Perini, De Luca); *Aida; La forza del destino* (with Antonio Scotto); *Otello* (with Tito Ruffo); *Un ballo in maschera; La traviata* (with Alma Gluck); *Macbeth; Requiem.* DONIZETTI: *La favorita; L'elisir d'amore; Lucia di Lammermoor: Che mi frena* (Sextet, 2 versions with Tetrazzini, Jacoby, Bada, Amato & Journet; also with Galli-Curci, Egener, Bada, De Luca & Journet). MEYERBEER: *L'Africana; Les Huguenots.* GIORDANO: *Andrea Chénier.* LEONCAVALLO: *Pagliacci.* GOLDMARK: *Die Königen von Saba.* BIZET: *Carmen; Les Pêcheurs de perles.* PONCHIELLI: *La Gioconda.* MASSENET: *Manon; Le Cid.* TCHAIKOVSKY: *Eugene Onegin.* HANDEL: *Serse.* ROSSINI: *Petite Messe Solennelle.* FRANCHETTI: *Germania: Studente! Udite!*
(B) (**) RCA mono 74321 41199-2 (2).

This very generous two-CD selection (150 minutes) covers Caruso's entire recording career. The 42 items are generally arranged in chronological order, starting with *Amor ti vieta* (among the great tenor's early recordings made by Fred Gaisberg in his hotel room in November 1902) continuing on to his warmly poised 1920 recording of Handel's *Ombra mai fù*. As an appendix we are given his very first recording: Franchetti's *Studente! Udite!* from *Germania*, the opera in which he was singing when Gaisberg first heard his voice. This dates from 11 April 1902, seven months before the Giordano aria. Finally and appropriately comes the *Crucifixus* from Rossini's *Petite Messe Solennelle*, which was his very last recording. The transfers of the earlier recordings are noisy, with background crackle, and the wind band accompaniments are primitive, with horn resonance, but even in *Germania* the voice shines through, and by the time we have reached disc 2, the background noises are under control and the reproduction is much more sophisticated. The coverage, especially of Verdi, is wide ranging, and the two different versions of the *Lucia* Sextet make for a fascinating comparison. The most rewarding novelty is Lenski's aria from *Eugene Onegin* (1916), ardently sung in French.

Christoff, Boris (bass)

'*The Early Recordings (1949–52)*': excerpts from: MUSSORGSKY: *Boris Godunov; Khovanshchina.* BORODIN: *Prince Igor.* RIMSKY-KORSAKOV: *Sadko; The Legend of the Invisible City of Kitezh.* TCHAIKOVSKY: *Eugene Onegin.* MUSSORGSKY: *Songs. Russian folksongs.*
(M) (***) EMI mono CDH7 64252-2.

The magnetic quality of Christoff's singing is never in doubt here, and the compulsion of the singer's artistry as well as the vivid individuality of his bass timbres make this a real portrait, not just a collection of items. These were his first recordings of the *Boris Godunov* excerpts (in which he assumes three different characters), and in musical terms he probably never surpassed them. But his characterization here is just as impressive as the singing itself, full of variety. The EMI transfers are bold and brightly focused, with the most vivid projection.

Gigli, Beniamino (tenor)

The Gigli Edition, Volume 1: BOITO: *Mefistofele.* PUCCINI: *La Bohème; Tosca.* DONIZETTI: *La favorita.* PONCHIELLI: *La Gioconda.* MASCAGNI: *Cavalleria rusticana; Iris; Lodoletta.* GOUNOD: *Faust.* Arias: CANNIO: *O surdato 'nnamurato.*
(BB) (***) Naxos mono 8.110262.

Beniamino Gigli, the uniquely honeyed-toned tenor, made his first recordings for HMV in Milan in the autumn of 1918. These excellent transfers have been master-minded by Mark Obert-Thorne and were originally issued on the Romophone label, but this time they have been upgraded. The surface noise remains high on the earliest items – *Dai campi, dai prati* from *Mefistofele* and Cavaradossi's two arias from *Tosca*. Even so, the distinctive timbre, which gave Gigli the title of Caruso's successor, is already clear, and in these earliest recordings, made when the singer was 28, the mannerisms which tended to mar his later work – aspirated lines and cooing tone – are largely absent. Already he revealed a musical imagination greater than that of most Italian tenors, and the head-tone he uses in *Apri la finestra* from Mascagni's *Iris* has rarely been matched by any rival. The poise and purity of his singing also comes out in his account of *Spirto gentil* from Donizetti's *La favorita*, and the clarity of his diction is exemplary, as in his performance of Faust's aria, in Italian translation, *Salve dimora. Cielo e mar* from Ponchielli's *La Gioconda* then reveals his open, heroic tone, all well caught on these pre-electrics, even if the orchestral accompaniment conducted by Carlo Sabajno is necessarily thin.

The Gigli Edition, Volume 2: BIZET: *Les Pêcheurs de perles.* GIORDANO: *Andrea Chénier; Fedora.* BOITO: *Mefistofele.* PUCCINI: *Tosca.* DONIZETTI: *La favorita.* PONCHIELLA: *La Gioconda.* MASCAGNI: *L'amico Fritz; Iris.* DRIGO: *I milioni d'Arlecchino.* LALO: *Le roi d'Ys.* GOUNOD: *Faust.* PUCCINI: *La Bohème.* Arias: CURTIS: *Tu sola.* MARIO: *Santa Lucia luntana.* TOSELLI: *Serenata.*

(BB) (★★★) Naxos mono 8.110263.

This second volume of Naxos's 'Gigli Edition', like the first, was originally issued on Romophone, but with Mark Obert-Thorne again upgrading his original transfers. It opens with five items from his Milan sessions in 1919 not included in Volume 1, starting with the delectable Cherry Duet from Mascagni's *L'amico Fritz*, with Nerina Baldisseri as Gigli's partner. Then in January 1921 he made his first recordings for Victor in the United States, then the associate company of HMV in Europe. As Obert-Thorne suggests, the quality of recordings made in Camden, New Jersey and New York was higher than those made in Milan, so that many of the earliest recordings made there were remakes of what he had already done. Not that the differences are all that great in these transfers, except that surface noise is generally less obtrusive, notably in the Mefistofele aria, with the voice clearer. Faust's aria – in Italian *Salve dimora* – is here more robust and less delicate than it was in the Milan version of two years earlier, but the absence of strain in everything Gigli sings is a delight. Interestingly, he did not make his first recording of *Vesti la giubba* from *Pagliacci* – the aria that more than any of his recordings made Caruso a superstar – until March 1922, six months after his great predecessor had

died, presumably not wanting to make his challenge while Caruso was still alive.

Volumes 3 (Naxos 8.110264) and 4 (8.110265) covering the Camden and New York recordings of 1923–5 and 1926–7 respectively are issued just as we close for press.

Opera arias from: GOUNOD: *Faust.* BIZET: *Carmen; Les Pêcheurs de perles.* MASSENET: *Manon.* HANDEL: *Serse.* DONIZETTI: *Lucia di Lammermoor; L'elisir d'amore.* VERDI: *Rigoletto; Aida.* LEONCAVALLO: *Pagliacci.* MASCAGNI: *Cavalleria rusticana.* PUCCINI: *La Bohème; Tosca.* GIORDANO: *Andrea Chénier.* PIETRI: *Maristella.*

(M) (★★★) EMI mono CDH7 61051-2.

Beniamino Gigli's status in the inter-war period as a singing superstar at a time when the media were less keenly organized is vividly reflected in this Références collection of eighteen items, the cream of his recordings made between 1927 and 1937. It is especially welcome to have two historic ensemble recordings, made in New York in 1927 and originally coupled on a short-playing 78rpm disc – the Quartet from *Rigoletto* and the Sextet from *Lucia di Lammermoor*. In an astonishing line-up Gigli is joined by Galli-Curci, Pinza, De Luca and Louise Homer. Excellent transfers.

Jurinac, Sena (soprano)

Opera arias from: MOZART: *Così fan tutte; Idomeneo.* SMETANA: *The Bartered Bride; The Kiss.* TCHAIKOVSKY: *Joan of Arc; Queen of Spades.* **Songs:** R. STRAUSS: *Four Last Songs (Vier letzte Lieder).*

(M) (★★★) EMI mono CDH7 63199-2.

This EMI Références issue, very well transferred, celebrates a magical, under-recorded singer. It brings together all of Jurinac's recordings for EMI outside the complete operas, and adds a live radio recording from Sweden – with Fritz Busch conducting the Stockholm Philharmonic Orchestra – of Strauss's *Four Last Songs*, most beautifully done, if with rather generalized expression. Busch was also the conductor for the Glyndebourne recordings of excerpts from *Così fan tutte* and *Idomeneo*.

Leider, Frida (soprano)

'The Singers' (Decca series): Arias from: MOZART: *Le nozze di Figaro.* BEETHOVEN: *Fidelio.* WEBER: *Oberon.* WAGNER: *Götterdämmerung; Parsifal; Siegfried; Tristan und Isolde; Die Walküre.*

(M) (★★) Decca mono 467 911-2.

Frida Leider was born in Berlin in 1888 and made that city the centre of her career, dying there in 1975. In her day, she received tremendous accolades. 'The greatest Isolde of them all,' wrote Lauritz Melchior, one of the outstanding Tristans of his day (heard here in the *Die Walküre* excerpt). What one notices in these historic recordings from the 1920s are the tremendous firmness as well as the freshness in her voice – combined with an intelligence in her approach – which gives an idea of what she must have been like 'live'. One can only say 'gives an idea', as these pre-electric recordings are simply not able to capture the true power of her voice, and the small and thin-sounding, scrappy orchestra will horrify anyone who hasn't experienced pre-electric recording before. But for all its technical inadequacies, this remains one of the more interesting releases in Decca's 'The Singers' series, although the texts and translations are available, along with a photo-gallery, only via a CD ROM drive. The transfers are acceptable, and the voice is certainly immediate.

Melba, Nellie (soprano)

Arias from: VERDI: *Rigoletto; La traviata.* DONIZETTI: *Lucia di Lammermoor.* HANDEL: *Il penseroso.* THOMAS: *Hamlet.* MOZART: *Le nozze di Figaro.* PUCCINI: *La Bohème.* Songs: TOSTI: *Goodbye; Mattinata.* BEMBERG: *Les Anges pleurent; Chant vénitien; Nymphes et sylvains.* TRAD.: *Comin' thro' the Rye.* ARDITI: *Se saran rose.* D'HARDELOT: *Three Green Bonnets.* HAHN: *Si mes vers avaient des ailes.* BACH/GOUNOD: *Ave Maria.*
(BB) (★★★) Naxos mono 8.110737.

From the moment she made her debut in Brussels as Gilda in *Rigoletto* in 1887 Helen Porter Mitchell, better known as Nellie Melba, became an operatic star of stars, particularly at Covent Garden, but also at the Met. and in Europe. She retired in 1926. Her first records, of which nineteen items are included here, were made privately at her home in 1904, when she was forty-three. They were not originally intended for public release, but later she approved fourteen for publication, though in the case of the Act I *La traviata* aria she only permitted the release of *Ah! fors è lui* (simply and beautifully sung) and not the cabaletta, though both are included here. Another fascinating item from those first sessions is Handel's 'Sweet Bird' from *Il penseroso*, where during the first take the flautist played incorrectly, causing Melba to stop and say 'Now we'll have to do it over again'. Fortunately the second take is flawless, for she was good at trilling with a flute, as is shown in the brief excerpt from Donizetti's Mad scene (*Lucia de Lammermoor*). Although the voice is obviously showing signs of wear, the agility is unimpaired, as the arias from Thomas's *Hamlet* demonstrate. *Et maintenant, écoutez ma chanson!* is a real bravura example. Some of the items suffer from distortion or excess, uneven surface noise, but not this, and *Caro nome* (with more background and some slight distortion) is also pretty impressive. Mozart's *Porgi amor* is not really stylish by today's standards but shows Melba's quality of tone and

line. Ward Marston's fine transfers certainly bring this legendary figure fully to life, and the Naxos documentation is well up to standard for this enterprising series.

Opera Arias and Excerpts from: DONIZETTI: *Lucia di Lammermoor.* VERDI: *Rigoletto; La traviata* (with Brownlee)*; Otello.* GOUNOD: *Roméo et Juliette; Faust.* PUCCINI: *La Bohème* (excerpts: with Caruso & others). Songs: TOSTI: *La serenata.* BEMBERG: *Chant hindou.* BISHOP: *Lo, Here the Gentle Lark; Home, Sweet Home.* BACH/GOUNOD: *Ave Maria* (with W. H. Squire, cello). CHAUSSON: *Le Temps de lilas.* SZULC: *Claire de lune.*
(M) (★★★) EMI mono 5 85826-2.

Puccini disparagingly called Melba 'the Centenarian'. That was long before she retired in 1926 at the age of sixty-five, and, as the excerpts here from her Covent Garden Farewell demonstrate, the voice remained astonishingly bright, firm and true. Yet equally it shows very clearly how little emotion she seems to have felt – or at least was able to convey. There is that same limitation throughout these twenty items (including the two done with piano accompaniment after her retirement). But the security of her technique and the clarity and precision of her voice are amazing in one dazzling performance after another. Excellent transfers.

Piccaver, Alfred (tenor)

'The Son of Vienna' Arias and Duets from: VERDI: *Rigoletto; Il trovatore; Un ballo in maschera; Aida.* MEYERBEER: *L'Africaine.* MASCAGNI: *Cavalleria rusticana.* LEONCAVALLO: *Pagliacci.* WAGNER: *Die Meistersinger; Lohengrin.* GOUNOD: *Faust.* PONCHIELLI: *La Gioconda.* PUCCINI: *Tosca; Turandot.* Song: GEEHL: *For You Alone.*
(BB) (★★★) Dutton mono CDPB 9725.

Though born in England, Alfred Piccaver was brought up in the United States, and then in his mid-twenties settled permanently in Vienna, where he was a stalwart of the Vienna State Opera for almost thirty years. This disc of his relatively rare recordings in every item explains his success. His was a ringingly clear tenor, with no hint of strain even in the high registers. His style was Germanic, at times suggesting similarities with his Viennese contemporary, Richard Tauber, yet Piccaver's repertory was far wider, extending to most of the principal lyrico-dramatic tenor parts, as the items here suggest. The recordings are divided sharply into two sections, the first eight numbers recorded in 1923 by the acoustic process – with the voice yet ringingly clear – and eight recorded electrically in 1928. The Dutton transfers are excellent, though it is a pity that background details of each recording are very limited.

Schmidt, Joseph (tenor)

Complete EMI Recordings: Arias (sung in German) from: MEYERBEER: *L'Africaine.* FLOTOW: *Martha; Alessandro Stradella.* KIENZL: *Der Evangelimann.* KORNGOLD: *Die tote Stadt.* ADAM: *Der Postillon von Longjumeau.* MASSENET: *Manon; Der Cid.* TCHAIKOVSKY: *Eugene Onegin.* MORY: *La Vallière.* GOTZE: *Der Page des Königs.* JOHANN STRAUSS JR: *1001 Nacht; Der Zigeunerbaron; Simplicus.* LEHAR: *Zigeunerliebe.* TAUBER: *Der Singende Traume.* DONIZETTI: *Der Liebestrank (L'elisir d'amore).* VERDI: *Rigoletto; Der Troubadour (Il trovatore).* LEONCAVALLO: *Der Bajazzo (Pagliacci).* PUCCINI: *La Bohème; Tosca; Das Mädchen aus dem Goldenen Westen (La fanciulla del West); Turandot.* SERRANO: *El Trust de Los Tenorios.* SPOLIANSKY: *Das Lied einer Nacht* (film). Lieder & Songs: SCHUBERT: *Ständchen; Ungeduld.* BENATZKY: *Wenn du treulos bist.* NIEDERBERGER: *Buona notte, schöne Signorina.* LEONCAVALLO: *Morgenständchen.* LABRIOLA: *Serenata.* BISCARDI: *L'ariatella.* DENZA: *Funiculi, funicula.* BUZZI-PECCIA: *Lolita.* DI CAPUA: *O sole mio.*

(M) (★★★) EMI mono 7 64676-2 (2).

Joseph Schmidt, born in 1904 in what is now Romania, studied in Berlin, and developed what by any standards is one of the most beautiful German tenor voices ever recorded, less distinctive than that of Richard Tauber, but even more consistently honeyed and velvety in the upper registers, exceptionally free on top, so that the stratospheric top notes in *Le Postillon de Longjumeau* have never sounded so beautiful and unstrained. This is the ideal lyric tenor voice, not just for the German repertory, including operetta, but for the Italian; it was tragic that, standing less than five feet high, he was precluded from having an operatic career. Nevertheless, he was most successful in his concert work as well as in his recording career, as this glowing collection demonstrates. He even had a brilliantly successful American tour in 1937; but sadly, as a Jew, he got caught up in Europe during the Second World War and died from a chest complaint in a Swiss refugee camp in 1942. The records – with informative notes – make a superb memorial, here at last given full prominence in excellent transfers.

Tauber, Richard (tenor)

Arias from: AUBER: *Fra Diavolo.* FLOTOW: *Martha.* KORNGOLD: *Die tote Stadt.* KIENZL: *Der Evangelimann.* PUCCINI: *La Bohème; Tosca.* ROSSINI: *Il barbiere di Siviglia.* SMETANA: *The Bartered Bride.* RICHARD STRAUSS: *Der Rosenkavalier.* TCHAIKOVSKY: *Eugene Onegin.*

THOMAS: *Mignon.* VERDI: *La forza del destino; La traviata; Il trovatore.* WOLF-FERRARI: *Jewels of the Madonna.*

(B) (★★★) Naxos mono 8.110729.

These acoustic recordings, made between 1919 and 1926, offer a totally different view of Richard Tauber and his art from the usual one, revealing the range of his sympathies in the world of opera. A complete musician, an excellent pianist and conductor as well as singer, he here tackles a formidable list of arias, including even Siegmund's *Wintersturme* solo from Wagner's *Die Walküre*, not a role he ever sang on stage. While in the 1920s he was establishing his unique reputation in operetta, he was also much admired for his performances in opera, a career that had begun in 1913, first in Chemnitz with *Zauberflöte* and then on contract in Dresden with Thomas's *Mignon*. The distinctive warmth of Tauber's tenor was ideally suited to recording, and though these acoustic examples do not generally capture the timbre we associate with his singing of Lehár, the sweetness is beautifully caught in Ward Marston's fine transfers. It is good too to be without the kind of distortion characteristic of some of his later electric recordings. The disc comes with a highly informative note by Peter Dempsey.

'*The Legendary Richard Tauber*': MOZART: *Don Giovanni: Il mio tesoro. Die Zauberflöte: Dies Bildnis.* Arias from: PUCCINI: *La Bohème; Madama Butterfly; Tosca; Turandot.* LEONCÁVALLO: *Pagliacci.* VERDI: *Il trovatore.* MEHUL: *Joseph in Aegypten.* OFFENBACH: *Les Contes d'Hoffmann.* THOMAS: *Mignon.* TCHAIKOVSKY: *Eugene Onegin.* SMETANA: *Bartered Bride* (all sung in German). WEBER: *Der Freischütz.* LORTZING: *Undine.* KIENZL: *Der Evangelimann.* WAGNER: *Die Meistersinger.* RICHARD STRAUSS: *Der Rosenkavalier.* KORNGOLD: *Die tote Stadt.* LEHAR: *Die lustige Witwe (Lippen schweigen; Vilja-Lied); Paganini; Friederike (O Mädchen, mein Mädchen); Das Land des Lächelns (4 excerpts, including Dein ist mein ganzes Herz); Giuditta; Die Zarewitsch.* KALMAN: *Die Zirkusprinzessin; Gräfin Mariza.* HEUBERGER: *Der Opernball (Im chambre séparée).* STOLZ: *Adieu, mein kleiner Gardeoffizier; Im Prater blühn wieder die Bäume.* SIECZYNSKI: *Wien, du Stadt meiner Träume.* JOHANN STRAUSS JR: *Geschichten aus dem Wienerwald; Rosen aus dem Süden.* ZELLER: *Der Vogelhändler.* DOELLE: *Wenn der weisse Flieder wider blüht.* ERWIN: *Ich küsse Ihre Hand, Madame.* Lieder: SCHUBERT: *Ständchen; Der Lindenbaum.*

(M) (★ (★★)) EMI mono 5 66692-2 (2).

If one begins with the second of these two CDs, it becomes immediately obvious why Tauber established his reputation with the wider public largely in the field of operetta. The uniquely honeyed voice makes simple melodies like *Lippen schweigen* from *The Merry Widow*, with its magical final cadence, or the *Vilja-Lied* utterly seductive, and that despite often inadequate transfers, with thin, whistly orchestral sound and plenty of distortion, even on the voice itself. One wonders why Tauber, more than most singers of his generation, so regularly suffers from this problem. It isn't that the basic recordings are bad, except for the thin orchestra (though there are frequent moments of blasting); usually the magic and power of the voice are well conveyed; yet the original sources too often seem prone to distortion. The first disc concentrates on opera and opens with a glowingly lyrical 1939 *Il mio tesoro*, but again there is distortion. *Dies Bildnis* (from *Die Zauberflöte*) is acoustic (1922) and rather better, and Tauber then makes 'Your Tiny Hand is Frozen' sound beguiling even in German! – the chosen language for most of his records. There are many remarkable performances here, from the lilting *Legend of Kleinsach* (1928) to a stirring *Di quella pira* (1926) with a comic wind band accompaniment; there are also equally moving versions of Lenski's aria from *Eugene Onegin* (1923), when the band is less clumsy, and the ardent 'On with the Motley' (recorded in London in 1936 and sung in English). It is a pity the recordings are technically so inadequate, but the voice still enthrals the listener.

Teyte, Maggie (soprano)

'The Pocket Prima Donna' (with various accompanists): RAVEL: *Shéhérazade.* BERLIOZ: *Nuites d'été: Le Spectre de la rose; Absence.* DUPARC: *L'Invitation au voyage; Phidylé.* DEBUSSY: *Proses lyriques.* Arias from: PERGOLESI: *La serva padrona* (in French); MONSIGNY: *Rose et Colas; Le Déserteur;* GRETRY: *Zémire et Azore; Le Tableau parlant;* DOURLEN: *Les Oies de Frère Philippe.* OFFENBACH: *La Périchole.*

(BB) (★★★) Dutton mono CDBP 9274.

Maggie Teyte, born in Wolverhampton, made a speciality of the French repertory. In 1908 at the age of twenty she sang Mélisande in Debussy's opera with great success, the second singer after Mary Garden to tackle the role. Though there was a gap in her career after she got married, she returned, and made most of her recordings – including the majority of those here – in the 1940s. Hers is an exceptionally sweet soprano, ideally suited to the microphone in its purity, while her sense of style is unerring, whether in the songs of Ravel, Berlioz and Debussy or the lighter operatic and operetta repertory represented here, always sung with character and vivacity. The Dutton transfers are first-rate.

Alagna, Roberto (tenor)

French Opera Arias (with ROHCG O, de Billy)
from: BAZIN: *Maître Pathelin.* BERLIOZ: *La
Damnation de Faust.* BIZET: *The Pearl Fishers.*
BRUNEAU: *L'Attaque du Moulin.* CHERUBINI: *Les
Abencerrages.* GLUCK: *Iphigenie en Tauride.*
GOUNOD: *Mireille.* GRETRY: *L'Amant jaloux.*
HALEVY: *La Juive.* LALO: *Le Roi d'Ys.* MASSENET:
Le Cid. MEHUL: *Joseph.* MEYERBEER: *L'Africaine.*
SAINT-SAENS: *Samson et Dalila* (with London
Voices). THOMAS: *Mignon.*
*** EMI 5 57012-2.

It was a bold venture for such a leading tenor as
Roberto Alagna to present such a formidable collec-
tion of fifteen arias, many of which are rarities. From
the start his forte has been the French repertory, and
here he displays his versatility in operatic excerpts
that cover the widest range of styles and periods.
They also make dauntingly contrasted demands on
any single tenor, from the lyric purity of Bizet's *Pearl
Fishers* aria to the heroic scale of Samson's aria in the
Saint-Saëns opera, the longest item here, with
Alagna's singing not just powerful but finely shaded.
The title role in an earlier biblical opera, Méhul's
Joseph, also demands a heroic style, yet Alagna, a
devoted admirer of the legendary French tenor
Georges Thill, copes superbly both stylistically and
vocally. The high tessitura of some of these arias,
demanding in quite a different way, has Alagna producing beautiful head-tones when required. It is
especially good to hear the work of such little-known
composers as François Bazin (1816–78) and Massenet's pupil, Alfred Bruneau (1857–1934), while other
charming rarities include the Lalo aria and Grétry's
Sérénade, with its accompanying mandolin. The
warmly understanding accompaniment is from the
Covent Garden Orchestra under the brilliant young
French conductor, Bertrand de Billy.

Allen, Sir Thomas (baritone)

'French and English Songs' (with (i) Vignoles or (ii)
Parsons, piano): (i) FAURE: *Automne; Chanson
d'amour; Clair de lune; Fleur jetée; L'Aurore; 5
Mélodies 'de Venise'; Prison; Le Secret; Spleen; Le
Voyageur.* RAVEL: *Don Quichotte à Dulcinée; 5
Mélodies populaires grecques.* POULENC: *Le Travail
du peintre.* (ii) VAUGHAN WILLIAMS: *The House of
Life; Linden Lea.* PEEL: *In Summertime on Bredon.*

BUTTERWORTH: *On the Idle Hill of Summer; 6
Songs from 'A Shropshire Lad'.* QUILTER: *7
Elizabethan Lyrics, Op. 12; Now Sleeps the Crimson
Petal.*
⊖ (M) *** Virgin 5 62059-2 (2).

This two-disc box neatly brings together recitals
recorded by Thomas Allen at his full maturity, the
French songs in 1993, the English in 1989. Allen's
feeling for idiom is unerring, and though no texts are
included in this mid-price issue, with just a sketchy
note about the repertory, there is compensation
when Allen's diction allows every word to be heard,
whether in French or English. The selection of items
too cannot be faulted, with the fourteen Fauré songs
including eight settings of Verlaine, most of them
favourites. The stillness of *Prison* for example, so
simple and so moving, brings an instant chill of
self-identification more intense than the original
poem. The Ravel and Poulenc songs, more robust,
bring out Allen's vigour and that of Roger Vignoles.
Equally sympathetic, Geoffrey Parsons accompanies
Allen in the English songs, with Vaughan Williams's
House of Life, six settings of Rossetti, played with
commitment. The Housman settings, the one popular Peel song alongside six by Butterworth, have
winning freshness, and it is good to have the inspired
Quilter songs so persuasively performed, each of
them striking and individual. Well-balanced sound.

'Songs My Father Taught Me' (with Martineau,
piano): PURCELL: *Passing By.* TATE: *The Lark in the
Clear Clean Air.* SULLIVAN: *The Lost Chord; My
Dearest Heart.* SANDERSON: *Until.* HAYDN WOOD:
*Bird of Love Divine; A Brown Bird Singing; It is
Only a Tiny Garden; Love's Garden of Roses.*
QUILTER: *Drink to Me Only.* CAPEL: *Love, Could I
Only Tell Thee.* TRAVERS: *A Mood.* PENN: *Smilin'
Through.* S. ADAMS: *The Holy City.* ROBSON: *The
Cheviot Hills.* DRESSER: *On the Banks of the
Wabash, Far Away.* LAMBERT: *God's Garden; She is
Far from the Land.* PEEL: *In Summertime on
Bredon.* DIX: *The Trumpeter.* NOVELLO: *Till the
Boys Come Home.* RASBACH: *Trees.* O'CONNER: *The
Old House.* COATES: *Bird Songs at Eventide.*
MURRAY: *I'll Walk Beside You.*
*** Hyp. CDA 67290.

Sir Thomas Allen explains that in this collection of
drawing-room ballads he has tried to 'recapture
memories of amateur singers coming to our house in
Seaham Harbour', when his father would supervise at
the piano. The disc, he says, marks something of a

watershed for him, with 'nostalgia and sentiment almost entirely responsible'. Thanks to the singer's mastery and his winningly intimate, intense manner, speaking from the heart, there is not a suspicion of sentimentality even in such numbers as 'Love's Garden of Roses', 'Smilin' Through' or 'The Lost Chord', which could so easily have seemed mawkish. Instead through his magnetism, as Allen intends, one wonders at the simple beauty of the melodies in these once-popular songs. Malcolm Martineau is the most understanding accompanist, equally sensitive in taking a fresh, unexaggerated approach.

'More Songs My Father Taught Me' (with Martineau, piano): TRAD.: *She Moved thro' the Fair* (unaccompanied); *The Star of County Down* (arr. Hughes); *Water o'Tyne.* COATS: *The Green Hills o'Somerset; I Heard you Singing; Star of God.* MURRAY: *Will you Go with Me?.* SHELDON: *A Cradle Song.* SOMERSET: *Echo; A Song of Sleep.* SQUIRE: *Mountain Lovers.* CLAY: *I'll Sing thee Songs of Araby.* BALL: *Mother Machree.* WOOD: *Roses of Picardy.* ELLIOT: *There's a Long Long Trail a-Winding.* BARRI: *The Old Brigade.* WALLACE: *Yes! Let me Like a Soldier Fall.* D'HARDELOT: *Because.* MOLLOY: *Love's Old Sweet Song.* SANDERSON: *Friend o'Mine.* HATTON: *Simon the Cellarer; Time to go.* S. BENNETT: *The Songs of Today.* JACOBS-BOND: *Just a-Wearyin' for You; Perfect Day.* HUGHES: *Down by the Sally Gardens.* SULLIVAN: *Orpheus with his Lute.* WOODFORDE-FINDEN: *Kashmiri Song.* F. HARRISON: *In the Gloaming.*

*** Hyp. CDA 67374.

Sir Thomas Allen's first collection of drawing-room ballads for Hyperion had immediate success. In this second instalment, Allen's artistry once again transforms music, popular long ago, that latterly has come to be dismissed as cheap and sentimental. The melodies of such songs as 'Roses of Picardy', 'Love's Old Sweet Song' and 'Because', not to mention dozens of less well-known items, have a winning ease and freshness when sung with such warmth and fervour, with Malcolm Martineau the ever-sensitive accompanist. Many of the songs this time are Irish, reminding one of the vital role played by the great tenor John McCormack in popularizing such ballads, while the inclusion of Sullivan's Shakespeare setting, 'Orpheus with his Lute', gives a reminder that the unquenchable melodic world of Gilbert and Sullivan is very close.

Ameling, Elly (soprano)

'The Artistry of Elly Ameling': BACH: Excerpts from: *St Matthew Passion; St John Passion; Christmas Oratorio.* HAYDN: *Die Schöpfung* (with Stuttgart CO, Münchinger). *Orlando Paladino* (with Lausanne CO, Dorati). HANDEL: *Messiah* (with Reynolds, ASMF, Marriner). Cantatas: *Crudel*

tiranno amor (with ECO, Leppard). VIVALDI: *Juditha triumphans, RV 644* (with Berlin CO, Negri). Songs: HAYDN: *Das strickende Mädchen; Der erste Küss; An Iris; Liebeslied; Geistliches Lied; Das Leben ist ein Traume Abscheidslied* (with Demus). MOZART: Arias from: *Le nozze di Figaro. Misera! Dove son! Exsultate, jubilate, K.165* (with ECO, Leppard). *Ch'io mi scordi, K.505.* SCHUBERT: *Der Musensohn; Die Forelle; Aus dem Wässer zu singen* (with Jansen); *Die Sterne; Der Einsamel; An Sylvia; Minnelied; An die Laute; Seligkeit; Das Lied im Grünen; Im Freien; Kennst du das Land; Heidenröslein; Die junge Nonne; Gretchen am Spinnrade; Ave Maria; An die Musik; Der Knabe.* SCHUMANN: *Frauenliebe und Leben, Op. 42.* BRAHMS: *Heimweh; Der Jäger; Agnes; In den Beeren; Der Frühling; Die Trauernde; Vergebliches Ständchen; Spanische Lied; Von waldbekränzter Höhe; Wiegenlied; Immer Leiser wird mein Schlummer.* WOLF: *20 Mörike Lieder* (all with Baldwin). FAURE: *Après un rêve.* DEBUSSY: *Beau soir; Mandoline.* HAHN: *L'Amité; La Vie est belle.* SATIE: *La Diva de 'L'Empire'* (with Jansen). GERSHWIN: *Embraceable You; The Man I Love; I've Got a Crush on You; But not for Me.* GOEMANS: *Aan de Amsterdamse grachten.* PORTER: *I Get a Kick out of You; What is This Thing Called Love?; You do Something to Me; Begin the Beguine; Night and Day.* KERN: *All the Things You are.* SONDHEIM: *Can that Boy Foxtrot!.* GIMBEL: *Garota de Ipanema.* DRÉJAC: *Sous le ciel de Paris.* ELLINGTON: *Caravan; Sophisticated Lady; Solitude; It don't Mean a Thing; In a Sentimental Mood* (all with Van Dijk).

(BB) **(*) Ph. (ADD/DDD) 473 45-2 (5).

The Dutch soprano Elly Ameling was launched on her career in 1956 when she so impressed the judges at an international competition that they created a special new award for her: 'First Prize with Distinction'. Her recording career with Philips spanned the next two decades and covered a remarkably wide musical range. The beauty of her voice is never in doubt, and the first CD here concentrates on her eighteenth-century repertoire, drawing on her complete sets, with several items recorded in the 1960s when her voice was at its brightest and her technique ideally fluent. However, Vivaldi's *Juditha triumphans* dates from the mid-1970s and shows her in maturity. Here she takes only a servant's role, though that is one which demands more brilliant technique than any.

Many of the Haydn songs so charmingly sung on disc 2 have clear anticipations of nineteenth-century Lieder, and Ameling, with her simple style, projects them to perfection, with Joerg Demus a brightly sympathetic accompanist. There are also Mozart performances of a very high order, and in *Exsultate, jubilate* the bravura is marvellously secure technically, while the singing itself has a simple radiance.

The Schubert Lieder on disc 3 make a delightful

recital in themselves, with Ameling at her freshest and Dalton Baldwin accompanying with unfailing sensitivity. In the strophic songs she is a persuasive interpreter, gently pointing each verse. The early setting of Mignon's *Kennst du das Land* is charmingly simple, in contrast to the great Wolf setting. The performance of *Frauenliebe und Leben* has freshness and girlishness on its side, but this is a cycle which demands deeper tones in the later songs, so, while this is attractive, it is only a partial view.

The Brahms songs are sung with spirit and feeling, and the readings are unfailingly musical. *Die Trauernde* is very touching. However, in Wolf's *Mörike Lieder*, while the diction is clean and her interpretations intelligent, there is a certain uniformity of colour and mood that makes listening to the whole collection less satisfying than picking out individual songs. Needless to say, there is much to enjoy and, while Baldwin is a bit prosaic at times, against this must be balanced some highly musical and carefully thought-out details.

The popular collection on disc 5 is particularly treasurable. One expects the French mélodies to be a success, though the nice hint of irony in Satie's *La Diva de 'L'Empire'* is a neat touch. But anyone who thinks of Elly Ameling as a rather demure singer will be surprised at the magnetism with which she can bring out the beauty of melodies by Gershwin or Cole Porter. The introduction to 'Night and Day' is particularly seductive, and she is especially good in one of the most memorable of Gershin's songs, 'The Man I Love'; and she is very stylish in the Ellington numbers. Loius van Dijk's pointed accompaniments often have a flavour of Debussy or Ravel. Throughout all five discs the recording is most natural and beautifully balanced. However, there are no texts and translations, and the notes are sparse and mainly biographical.

American Boychoir, Atlantic Brass Quintet, James Litton

'*Trumpets Sound, Voices Ring: A Joyous Christmas*': arr. WILLCOCKS: *O Come All Ye Faithful; Once in Royal David's City*. RUTTER: *Angel Tidings; Star Carol; The Lord Bless You and Keep You*. BRAHMS: *Regina coeli*. ELGAR: *The Snow*. GAWTHROP: *Mary Speaks*. MENDELSSOHN, arr. WILLCOCKS: *Hark! the Herald Angels Sing*. VAUGHAN WILLIAMS: *Hodie; Lullaby*. FRASER: *This Christmastide (Jessye's Carol)*. CORELLI: *Concerto grosso in G min. (Christmas), Op. 6/8*. MANZ: *E'en so, Lord Jesus, Quickly Come*. TELEMANN: *Lobet den Herrn, alle Heiden; Meine Seele, erhebt den Herrn*. CASALS: *Nigra sum*. Spiritual: *Go Tell it on the Mountain*.
*** MusicMasters 01612 67076-2.

Gleaming brass fanfares introduce this lively and attractively diverse American collection featuring a gleaming treble line against full brass sonorities. The

Americans follow the English King's College tradition at the opening of 'Once in Royal David's City' but cap its climax resplendently. The three Rutter carols are ideal for boy trebles and the infectious *Star Carol* brings an engagingly light rhythmic touch. Elgar's much less well-known portrayal of 'The Snow' is very touching, while 'Jessye's Carol' has one of those gentle but haunting melodies that persist in the memory: its descant is particularly apt, and it builds to an expansive climax. Both 'Mary Speaks' and Paul Manz's 'E'en so, Lord Jesus' are modern carols with an appealing simplicity, matched by Pablo Casals's better-known *Nigra sum*. The two Telemann items featuring famous chorales are both floridly testing of the boys' resources, and here the faster passages are not always completely secure. But they provide a nice baroque contrast, and it was a happy idea to include a brass transcription of Corelli's famous *Christmas Concerto grosso*, which, if sounding comparatively robust, is still highly effective when played so well. The choral singing is generally of a high calibre and the recording has a natural, warm ambience and is admirably clear.

Ampleforth Schola Cantorum, Ian Little

'*Carols from Ampleforth*': arr. WILLCOCKS: *O Come All Ye Faithful; Once in Royal David's City; Unto us a Son is Born; Sussex Carol; God Rest you Merry, Gentlemen*. arr. HOLST: *Personent Hodie*. arr. JACQUES: *Good King Wenceslas*. arr. STAINER/WILLCOCKS: *The first Nowell*. PRAETORIUS: *A Great and Mighty Wonder*. arr. RUTTER: *Angel Tidings*. STEWART: *On this Day Earth shall Ring*. WARLOCK: *Adam Lay Ybounden*. MATHIAS: *Sir Christèmas*. arr. WOOD: *Past Three o'Clock; Ding, Dong! Merrily on High*. arr. SULLIVAN: *It Came upon the Midnight Clear*. arr. LEDGER: *Still, Still, Still*. arr. LITTLE: *Come with Torches*. arr. PETTMAN: *The Infant King*. GRUBER, arr. LITTLE: *Silent Night*. MENDELSSOHN, arr. WILLCOCKS: *Hark! the Herald Angels Sing*.
*** Ampleforth Abbey Records Dig. AARCD 1.

A splendidly robust selection of favourites, with the expansive abbey acoustic and the superb organ adding much to the listener's pleasure. The sound itself is often thrilling with men and boys both singing ardently; there are a few minor blemishes of ensemble, but nothing to worry about when the projection is so vigorously communicative. Perhaps the rhythm of Mathias's 'Sir Christèmas' is a bit heavy, but 'On this Day Earth shall Ring' makes a magnificent effect, with the organ adding a final blaze of sound at the close. There are gentler carols too, of course, though not all will like Ian Little's added harmonies at the end of 'Silent Night'.

Angeles, Victoria de los (soprano)

'*Diva*': Arias from ROSSINI: *Il barbiere di Siviglia.* GOUNOD: *Faust.* VERDI: *La traviata; Otello.* PUCCINI: *La Bohème; Madama Butterfly; Suor Angelica; Gianni Schicchi.* MASCAGNI: *Cavalleria rusticana.* LEONCAVALLO: *Pagliacci.* CATALANI: *La Wally.* MASSENET: *Manon.* BIZET: *Carmen.* GIMENEZ: *La tempranica.* CABALLERO: *Gigantes y Cabezudos.* BARBIERI: *Il barberillo de Lavaplés.*

(M) **★★★** EMI mono/stereo 5 65579-2.

This splendid compilation brings it home how many of the classic sets of the 1950s and 1960s have Victoria de los Angeles as a golden-toned heroine, responding with heartfelt expressiveness. These include the two incomparable Beecham sets of Puccini's *La Bohème* and Bizet's *Carmen*, Gui's Glyndebourne-based set of Rossini's *Barbiere*, Monteux's magical set of Massenet's *Manon*, Cluytens's recording of *Faust*, Serafin's of Puccini's *Il trittico*, not to mention the RCA New York recording in 1953 of *Pagliacci*, in which Los Angeles sings charmingly as Nedda communing with the birds – not the role one expects from her. These are well supplemented by two items from her superb (1954) opera recital, including a tenderly beautiful *Ave Maria* from *Otello* and three final numbers from Spanish zarzuelas, making a winning collection overall.

Songs of Spain: Disc 1: *Traditional songs* (arr. Graciano Tarragó; with Renata Tarragó & Graciano Tarragó, guitars); *Medieval songs* (early 14th century); *Renaissance and Baroque songs* (15th–18th centuries; with Ens., José María Lamaña).

Disc 2: *Medieval and Renaissance songs of Andalusia; Renaissance songs* (with Ars Musicae de Barcelona, Enrique Gisbert & José María Lamaña).

Disc 3: *19th- and 20th-century arrangements and art songs: Canciones Sefardies* (arr. Valls; with Gérard, flute, & Ghighia, guitar); *Canciones populares españoles* (arr. Lorca; with Miguel Zanetti, piano). Songs by MOMPOU; TOLDRA; MONTSALVATGE; RODRIGO (all with Soriano, piano); GRANADOS; GURIDU; HALFFTER; TURINA; NIN; VALVERDE (all with Gerald Moore, piano); BARRERA & CALLEJA (arr. Los Angeles, guitar); MONTSALVATGE: *Madrigal* (with Barcelona City Orchestra, Navarro).

Disc 4: *Songs and opera arias:* GRANADOS: *Colección de tonadillas; Tres majas dolorosa* (with Gonzalo Soriano, piano); *Goyescas: La Maja y el ruiseñor.* FALLA: *La vida breve:* excerpts (with New Philharmonia Orchestra or Paris Conservatoire Orchestra, Rafael Frühbeck de Burgos. 1971 New York Recital (with De Larrocha, piano): Songs by

LITERES; DE LASERNA; GIMENEZ. GRANADOS: *Canciones amatorias.* FALLA: *7 Canciones populares españolas.*

(M) **★★★** EMI mono/stereo 5 66937-2 (4).

Issued to celebrate the singer's seventy-fifth birthday in November 1998, this four-disc compilation of Los Angeles in her native Spanish repertory is a delight. Two of the four discs are devoted to traditional, medieval and Renaissance songs, accompanied by the guitarist Renata Tarragó, as well as by her mentor in early music, José María Lamaña, with his own Ars Musicae of Barcelona and a British group. Recorded over two decades between 1950 and 1971, the set also includes Los Angeles's contribution to the closing ceremony of the 1992 Barcelona Olympic Games (the folk/madrigal *El cant dels ocells* of Montsalvatge), the voice carefully husbanded but still golden.

Overall, this lavish survey represents a cross-section of the varied types of art song which were current in the rich period of Spanish music between the thirteenth and sixteenth centuries, and then moves on to include key nineteenth- and twentieth-century repertoire. Earliest are monodic cantigas associated with the Virgin Mary, but most of the rest are secular, including a group of songs of the Sephardic Jewish tradition, also romances and villancicos (brief ballads), songs with vihuela accompaniment and madrigals – one might quibble about their presentation by a solo voice – of a later period. The first disc opens with eighteen traditional songs arranged by Graciano Tarregó, with guitar accompaniments, and the result has a captivating simplicity; moreover the mono recordings (from 1950–52) give a most natural presence for the voice.

Since the early days of her career, Los Angeles has been associated with the Ars Musicae ensemble of Barcelona. They play here on authentic instruments – fidulas, recorders, lute, vihuela de mano, viols and lira da braccio – and if the more complex later songs from the Courts of Charles V and Philip II hardly match the finest of our own Elizabethan songs, they are exquisitely done by Los Angeles and her friends. The Spanish folksongs arranged by the poet Lorca are mainly dance-songs, while the main Sephardic collection, arranged by Valls, gives an admirable sample of the music which was developing among Spanish Jews in the late Middle Ages, exotic and individual. The later Granados and Falla items are better known and no less winning.

Los Angeles made her recording début with the two Falla arias years ago; these later versions come from 1962. The collection ends with her live New York recital of 1971, where she forms a symbiotic partnership with her Catalan contemporary, Alicia de Larrocha, as accompanist, including the best loved of her encore numbers, Valverde's *Clavelitos* and *Adios Granada*, and ending with a riotous *Zapateado*. The voice is as fresh as ever. What matters most is that this is all music which inspires the singer to her fullest, most captivating artistry. The documentation could be more extensive, but full texts and translations are included.

Anonymous Four

'*The Lily and the Lamb*' (chant and polyphony from medieval England): *Conducti, Hymns, Motets, Sequences; Antiphon: Ave regina coelorum.*
*** HM HMU 907125.

The Anonymous Four (Ruth Cunningham, Marsha Genensky, Susan Hellauer and Johanna Rose) are an American vocal quartet whose voices merge into a particularly pleasing blend. They came together in 1986, bringing with them a variety of musical skills, including instrumental proficiency and a musicological background. The group focuses on medieval music, mainly sacred, spanning 500 years, from the eleventh to the fourteenth century. It is perhaps appropriate that this first collection should be devoted to hymns, sequences and motets dedicated to the Virgin Mary.

Women in medieval times identified with Mary and in particular her suffering as she saw her son dying on the cross. The second item in this programme, a monodic hymn, begins with the words 'The gentle lamb spread on the cross, hung all bathed with blood'. For women of those times, death was an everyday event, especially since only a small proportion of their many children survived into adulthood and they saw their young loved ones succumb to disease and other causes. The singers here blend their voices into one, whether singing monody or in simple polyphony, as in the sequence *Stillat in stelam radium*, or the beautiful motet *Veni mater gracie*. The voices are heard floating in an ecclesiastic acoustic and the effect is mesmeric.

'*An English Ladymass*' (13th- and 14th-century chant and polyphony in honour of the Virgin Mary): *Alleluias, Gradual, Hymn, Introit, Kyrie, Motets, Offertory, Rondellus, Sequences, Songs.*
**(*) HM HMU 907080

In medieval times most large churches and cathedrals had a lady chapel, where a Ladymass could be sung regularly to the Virgin Mary. And these still exist today in larger Catholic cathedrals, like Chartres in France. They usually have an extraordinary atmosphere and one watches with respect as young mothers not only attend alone but also bring their children to present to the statue of the Virgin. Here the Anonymous Four have arranged their own Mass sequence with the Propers interspersed with appropriate motets, hymns, a Gradual and Alleluia, finally concluding with the hymn *Ave Maris stella*. In doing so they make their own homage to the Virgin Mother which is well planned. The music is beautifully sung, although this is perhaps not one of their most potent collections.

'*Miracles of Sant'Iago*' (medieval chant and polyphony for St James from the Codex Calixtinus): *Agnus dei trope, Benedicamus tropes, Kyrie trope, Antiphon, Conducti, Hymns, Invitatory, Offertory, Prosae, Responsories.*
*** HM HMU 907156.

The Cathedral of Santiago in Compostela is the home of a manuscript of five books called collectively *Jacobus*, and its music was designed to be sung by groups of young French boy-trebles. It proves ideal material for the Anonymous Four and its musical interest is immediately demonstrated by the brilliantly decorated Benedicamus trope *Vox nostra resonet*. Much of the music is plainchant, but the early examples of two-part polyphony are very striking. Again the singing here is magnetic and the warm resonance of the recording very flattering.

'*Love's Illusion*' (French motets on courtly love texts from the 13th-century Montpellier Codex): *Plus bele que flor / Quant revient / L'autrier joer; Puisque bele dame m'eime; Amours mi font souffrir / En mai; Ne sai, que je die; Si je chante / Bien doi amer; Or ne sai je que devenir / puisque d'amer; Hé Dieus, de si haut si bas / Maubatus; Celui en qui / La bele estoile / La bele, en qui; Qui d'amours se plaint; Amours, dont je sui / L'autrier, au douz mois / Chose Tassin; Au cuer ai un mal / Ja ne m'en repentirai / Jolietement; Quant voi la fleur; Quant se depart / Onques ne sai amer; Joliement / Quant voi la florete / Je sui joliete; Amor potest conqueri / Adamorem sequitur; Ce que je tieng / Certes mout / Bone compaignie; J'ai si bien mon cuer assiz / Aucun m'ont; Ne m'oubliez mie; J'ai mis toute ma pensee / Je n'en puis; Blanchete / Quant je pens; Dame, que je n'os noumer / Amis donc est / Lonc tans a; Li savours de mon desir / Li grant desir / Non veul mari; Entre Copin / Je me cuidoie / Bele Ysabelos; S'on me regarde / Prennés i garde / Hé, mi enfant; Quant yver la bise ameine; Ne m'a pas oublié; On doit fin[e] Amor / La biauté; Ja n'amerai autre que cele; Quant je parti de m'amie.*
*** HM HMU 907109.

For this programme the Anonymous Four have moved away from liturgical music and chosen twenty-nine thirteenth-century motets from the Montpellier Codex, setting courtly love texts with simple and affecting polyphony. It is remarkable how the atmosphere of this music brings a more secular, plaintive quality. The means are the same but the expressive result is different, for the words are about the joys and regrets and the feelings of love. Many of these songs are dolorous but *Ne sai, que je die* (about pride, hypocrisy and avarice) and *Qui l'amours se plaint* are both dance songs. This is one of the most attractive of this fine group's collections. They are obviously moved, as women, by the words they sing, and they find remarkable variety of expressive feeling here. Occasionally a drone is added under the melodic line to telling effect, and one never misses an instrumental backing. The recording is well up to standard. A splendid disc.

'On Yoolis night' (medieval carols and motets): *Antiphons, Carols, Hymns, Motets, Responsory, Rondella, Songs.*
*** HM HMU 907099.

This is a delightful collection. The carol *Alleluia, A New Work* and the anonymous setting of *Ave Maria* are both enchanting discoveries, and many of these items have that curious, Christmassy colouring. The dance song *Gabriel from Heaven-king* and the lovely *Lullay: I Saw a Sweet Seemly Sight* are matched by *As I Lay on Yoolis Night*, while the closing *Nowel* is wonderfully joyful. The simple medieval implied harmonies in no way inhibit the character but increase the special colour of these carols, which are sung tenderly or with great spirit by this excellent group. Here is a record to lay in store for next Christmas, but to play at other times too.

'A Star in the East' (medieval Hungarian Christmas music): *Alleluias, Antiphons, Communion, Evangelium, Gradual, Hymns, Introit, Lectio, Motet, Offertory, Sanctus, Songs, Te Deum.*
*** HM HMU 907139.

The repertoire here is comparatively unsophisticated but full of charm, and the singing has the right kind of innocence. The programme came about by accident. While one of the group was researching the music of Hildegard of Bingen at Columbia University Library, a book of Hungarian Christmas music fell off the shelf at the researcher's feet, inviting its performance. There is not a great deal of polyphony here, but that is not a feature of many of our own favourite Christmas carols either. There is no lack of melody. Excellent recording and splendid documentation.

'Wolcum Yule' (Celtic and British Songs and Carols): TRAD. English: *Awake and Join the Cheerful Choir; The Holly and the Ivy; I Saw Three Ships; Cherry Tree Carol.* TRAD. Irish: *Good People All; The Seven Rejoices of Mary; Air: On a Cold Winter's Day; Flight into Egypt.* TRAD. Scottish: *Balulalo; The Reel of Tullochgorum.* TRAD. Welsh: *Behold Here is the Morning.* TRAD. Cornish: *Wassail Song.* Richard Rodney BENNETT: *Balulalow.* MAXWELL DAVIES: *Calendar of Kings.* BURGON: *A God, and yet a Man.* HENRY VIII (attrib.): *Grene Growith the holy.* BRITTEN: *A New Year Carol.*
*** HM HMU 907325.

Anonymous Four have come up trumps again with their latest Christmas collection. Johanna Maria Rose has researcheed her repertoire with characteristic skill, drawing on early folk collections by Scotsman Alan Ramsay, Northern Irishman Edward Bunting, and the pair of Cornishmen, Davies Gilbert and William Sandys. The resulting programme is delight-fully fresh and varied, with the folk items interwoven with more modern carols, notably the highly individual *Calendar of Kings* by Peter Maxwell Davies, newly commissioned for this anthology. As usual the layout is as impeccably planned as it is diverse, and the *a cappella* singing and playing as polished as it is consistently engaging (with Andrew-Lawrence King using – variously – Irish harp, baroque harp, and psaltery). The recording is first class, as is the documentation, with full texts ornamented by soft-grained woodcuts. A Christmas concert that can be listened to as a whole entity or dipped into at pleasure, and also making a perfect Christmas gift.

'A Portrait': excerpts from '*Miracles of Sant'Iago*'; '*The Lily and the Lamb*';'*A Star in the East*'; '*Love's Illusion*'; '*An English Ladymass*'; '*On Yoolis Night*'.
(B) *** HM HMX 2907210.

Here is a carefully chosen selection of highlights from the six CDs listed above. It's well worth sampling to find out whether the pure yet richly expressive vocal style of this remarkable female group will tempt you to explore further in one direction or another.

Ars Nova, Bo Holten

Portuguese polyphony: CARDOSO: *Lamentatio; Magnificat secundi toni.* LOBO: *Audivi vocem de caelo; Pater peccavi.* MAGALHAES: *Vidi aquam; Missa O Soberana luz; Commissa mea pavesco.* MANUEL DA FONSECA: *Beata viscera.* BARTOLOMEO TROSYLHO: *Circumdederunt.* PEDRO DE ESCOBAR: *Clamabat autem mulier.*
(BB) *** Naxos Dig. 8.553310.

In every respect this is an outstanding anthology. Apart from the major items from the Portuguese 'famous three' contemporaries, Cardoso, Lôbo and (the least-known) Filippe de Magalhães, which are discussed above under their respective composer entries in our main volume, the motets by the earlier figures, Pedro de Escobar (c. 1465–1535), Bartolomeo Trosylho (c. 1500–c. 1567) and Manuel da Fonseca (*maestre da capela* at Braga Cathedral in the mid-sixteenth century), are all touchingly, serenely beautiful, if perhaps less individual. The singing of this Danish Choir is superb and so is the Naxos recording. Texts and translations are provided, although for some reason they are printed separately. A unique bargain of the highest quality.

Augér, Arleen (soprano)

'Love songs' (with Baldwin, piano): COPLAND: *Pastorale; Heart, we will Forget Him.* OBRADORS: *Del Cabello más sutil.* OVALLE: *Azulao.* R STRAUSS: *Ständchen; Das Rosenband.* MARX: *Selige Nacht.* POULENC: *Fleurs.* CIMARA: *Stornello.* QUILTER: *Music, when Soft Voices Die; Love's Philosophy.*

O. STRAUS: *Je t'aime.* SCHUMANN: *Widmung; Du bist wie eine Blume.* MAHLER: *Liebst du um Schönheit.* TURINA: *Cantares.* LIPPE: *How do I Love Thee?* COWARD: *Conversation Piece: I'll Follow My Secret Heart.* GOUNOD: *Serenade.* SCHUBERT: *Liebe schwärmt auf allen Wegen.* BRIDGE: *Love Went a-Riding.* FOSTER: *Why, No One to Love.* DONAUDY: *O del mio amato ben.* BRITTEN (arr.): *The Salley Gardens.* LOEWE: *Camelot: Before I Gaze at You Again.*

✪ ★★★ Delos D/CD 3029.

This extraordinarily wide-ranging recital is a delight from the first song to the last. Arleen Augér opens with Copland and closes with *Camelot*, and she is equally at home in the music by Roger Quilter (*Love's Philosophy* is superbly done), Noël Coward and the Rückert song of Mahler. Britten's arrangement of *The Salley Gardens*, ravishingly slow, is another highlight. The layout of the recital could hardly have been managed better: each song creates its new atmosphere readily, but seems to be enhanced by coming after the previous choice. Dalton Baldwin's accompaniments are very much a partnership with the singing, while the playing itself is spontaneously perceptive throughout. With a good balance and a very realistic recording, this projects vividly like a live recital.

Baker, Dame Janet (mezzo-soprano)

'*Philips and Decca Recordings, 1961–79*': CD 1: '*Aria amorose*' (arr. Preston) (with ASMF, Marriner): GIORDANI: *Caro mio ben.* CACCINI: *Amarilli mia bella.* STRADELLA: *Region sempre addita.* SARRI: Sen corre l'agnelletta. CESTI: *Intorno all'idol mio.* LOTTI: *Pur dicesti, o bocca bella.* A. SCARLATTI: *Già il sole Gange; Selve amiche; Sento nel core; Spesso vibra per suo gioco.* CALDARA: *Come raggio di sol; Sebben, crudele, mi fai languir.* BONONCINI: *Deh più a me non v'ascondete.* DURANTE: *Danza fanciulla gentile.* PERGOLESI: *Ogni pena più spietata.* MARTINI: *Plaisir d'amour.* PICCINNI: *O notte, o dea del mistero.* PAISIELLO: *Nel cor più non mi sento.* Arias from: CAVALLI La Calisto (with James Bowman, LPO, Raymond Leppard).

CD 2: HANDEL: *Lucrezia* (cantata). Arias from: *Ariodante; Atalanta; Hercules; Joshua; Rodelinda; Serse* (with ECO, Leppard). Arias from: BACH: Cantata No. 170 (with ASMF, Marriner). PURCELL: *Dido and Aeneas* (with St Anthony Singers, ECO, Lewis).

CD 3: HAYDN: *Arianna a Naxos* (Cantata); *Berenice, che fai?* (*Scena di Berenice*) (with ECO, Leppard). MOZART: Arias from: *La Clemenza di Tito; Così fan tutte* (with ROHCG O, C. Davis). SCHUBERT: *Ständchen; Lazarus: So schlummert auf Rosen.* BEETHOVEN: *Ah Perfido!* (with ECO, Leppard).

CD 4: Arias from: RAMEAU: *Hippolyte et Aricie* (with St Anthony Singers, ECO, Lewis). GLUCK: *Alceste; Orfeo ed Euridice* (with ECO, Leppard). BERLIOZ: *Cléopâtre; Herminie.* Excerpts from: *Béatrice et Bénédict* (with LSO, C. Davis).

CD 5: RAVEL: *Chansons Madécasses; 3 Poèmes de Stéphane Mallarmé.* CHAUSSON: *Chanson perpétuelle.* DELAGE: *4 Poèmes Hindous* (with Melos Ens.). BRITTEN: Arias from: *The Rape of Lucretia* (with Shirley-Quirk, ECO, Britten); *Owen Wingrave* (with Luxon, Douglas, ECO, Britten); *Phaedra* (with ECO, Steuart Bedford).

(B) ★★★ Ph. (ADD) 475 161-2 (5).

A self-recommending treasure trove. The contents of Dame Janet Baker's rare 1978 LP 'Arie amorose' is included complete, a delightful anthology, with the programme cleverly arranged to contrast expressive with sprightly music, and the wide range of tonal gradation and beautiful phrasing matched by an artless lightness of touch. The accompaniments are intimate and tasteful: there is no more engaging example than Pergolesi's *Ogni pena più spietata*, with its deft bassoon obbligato, or the short closing song with harpsichord, Paisiello's *Nel cor più non mi sento*. Warm, well-focused sound, too.

Disc 2 (1972) includes Dame Janet's Handel recital – with the cantata *Lucrezia* and various arias, ranging from the pure gravity of *Ombra mai fù* to the passionate commitment and supreme coloratura virtuosity in *Dopo notte* from *Ariodante*. Leppard gives sparkling support, and the sound emerges freshly on CD.

On the third CD, recorded in 1973 with the same conductor, the two Haydn cantatas (*Arianna a Naxos* and *Scena di Berenice*) communicate the same warm intensity, transcending the formality of the genre, making them miniature operas in all but name. Also included are Mozart arias and key recordings of music by Schubert and Beethoven.

The fourth CD ventures into French opera and also includes Berlioz's two dramatic scenas, *Cléopâtre* and *Herminie*, which were both written as entries for the *Prix de Rome*; both give many hints of the mature Berlioz, even presenting specific foretastes of material later used in the *Symphonie fantastique* (the *idée fixe*), and the *Roman Carnival Overture* (the melody of the introduction). Dame Janet sings with passionate intensity, while Sir Colin Davis draws committed playing from the LSO, all in fine (1979) sound.

Disc five brings Baker's classic (1966) Oiseau-Lyre recital of French mélodies, with superb playing from the Melos group. Chausson's cycle of a deserted lover has a direct communication, which Baker contrasts with the subtler beauties of the Ravel songs. She shows great depth of feeling for the poetry here, and an equally evocative sensitivity to the songs about India written by Ravel's pupil, Maurice Delage, in 1912. Filling up this disc are powerful reminders of Baker's association with Benjamin Britten, and the selection includes her 1977 recording of *Phaedra*, written for her at the very end of the composer's life. Setting words from Robert Lowell's fine translation of Racine's play, the composer encapsulated the character of the tragic heroine and provided vocal writing which brings out every glorious facet of her voice. The use of the harpsichord in the recitative linking the sections of this scena is no mere neoclassical device, but a sharply dramatic and atmospheric stroke. Altogether this is a feast of great performances offered for little money, and the only quibble is the lack of texts. The sound is excellent throughout.

Radio Recordings (with various accompanists): HAYDN: *Arianna a Naxos* (cantata). SCHUMANN: *Frauenliebe und Leben, Op. 42.* SCHUBERT: *Der blinde Knabe; Totengräber-Weise.* WOLF: *Die ihr schwebet; Geh', Geliebter, geh'jetzt!* SCHUMANN: *Meine Rose; Der Page.* R. STRAUSS: *Befreit; Heimliche Aufforderung; Morgen!*
(M) *** BBC (ADD) BBCL 4049-2.

These vintage radio recordings from 1968–70 find Dame Janet Baker in glorious voice. Both the Haydn scena and Schumann song-cycle were recorded live at Snape Maltings, while the mixed Lieder recital was done in the studio, with all three conveying the urgency and spontaneity of live performance. Compared with Dame Janet's other studio recordings of this same repertory they bring out even more strikingly the vehement intensity of her singing as well as its heart-stopping beauty and glorious contrasts of tone-colour. Never have the changing emotions of *Frauenliebe und Leben* been so vividly conveyed on disc, from ecstasy to exhilaration to agony. It is a pity no texts are given.

HAYDN: *19 Scottish Folksongs* (with Menuhin & Malcolm, harpsichord). BEETHOVEN: *5 Scottish Folksongs* (with Ross Pople). CAMPIAN: *Never Love Unless you Can; Oft have I Sighed; If Thou Longest so Much to Learn; Fain Would I Wed;* DOWLAND: *Come Again* (with Spencer, lute); ARNE: *Where the Bee Sucks* (with Spencer & Whittaker, flute). BOYCE: *Tell me Lovely Shepherd.* MONRO: *My Lovely Celia.* PURCELL: *Sleep, Adam, Sleep, Lord, What is Man?* (with Isepp & Gauntlett).
*** Testament SBT 1241.

This Testament issue, superbly transferred, generously brings together two of Dame Janet Baker's most charming discs, long neglected. The Haydn and Beethoven folksong settings accompanied by Yehudi Menuhin and George Malcolm (on the harpsichord in Haydn, on the piano in Beethoven) stem from a project at the Windsor Festival in the 1970s, when Menuhin was music director. These studio recordings reflect the joy of discovery and corporate music-making on the highest level. The English songs come from a recording which Dame Janet made earlier in 1967 with the Elizabethan songs by Dowland and

Campian accompanied on the lute by Robert Spencer and with the flautist, Douglas Whittaker joining the team in the popular Arne setting of *Where the Bee Sucks.* Dame Janet is in glorious voice, with well-balanced EMI sound still very vivid.

'*Janet Baker Sings*' (with Moore, piano): FAURE: *Automne; Prison; Soir; Fleur jetée; En sourdine; Notre amour; Mai; Chanson du pêcheur; Clair de lune.* STANFORD: *La Belle Dame sans merci.* PARRY: *Proud Masie; O Mistress Mine.* W. BUSCH: *Rest.* WARLOCK: *Pretty Ringtime.* VAUGHAN WILLIAMS: *Linden Lea.* GURNEY: *Fields are Full.* BRITTEN: *Corpus Christi Carol.* IRELAND: *Sally Gardens.* QUILTER: *Love's Philosophy.* SCHUBERT: *Am Grabe; Anselmos; Abendstern; Die Vögel; Strophe aus Die Götte; Griechenlands; Gondelfahrer; Auflösung.* R. STRAUSS: *Morgen!; Befreit.*
✿ (M) *** EMI (ADD) 5 65009-2.

Just after he had officially retired, in the late 1960s, Gerald Moore returned to the recording studio to accompany Janet Baker, an artist whom he counted high among the many great singers he had accompanied in his career. This recital brings together a sequence of magical perfomances of songs especially dear to Dame Janet, with the voice consistently golden in tone. The Fauré group brings out her intense love of singing in French, and her devotion to the German Lied shines out equally in Schubert and Strauss. The group of ten English songs demonstrates that this neglected genre has comparable claims in beauty and intensity, with such favourite items as Vaughan Williams's 'Linden Lea' and Quilter's 'Love's Philosophy' given heartfelt performances. Even this singer rarely sang with more beauty than here.

RAVEL: *Shéhérazade* (with New Philh. O, Barbirolli). CHAUSSON: *Poème de l'amour et de la mer.* DUPARC: *Phidylé; La Vie antérieure; Le Manoir de Rosamonde; Au pays où se fait la guerre; L'Invitation au voyage* (all with LSO, Previn). SCHUMANN: *Frauenliebe und Leben* (with Barenboim). BRAHMS: *Vier ernste Gesänge, Op. 121* (with Previn); *2 Lieder, with Viola, Op. 91* (with Aronowitz, Previn); *4 Duets, Op. 28* (with Fischer-Dieskau, Barenboim).
☛ (B) *** EMI Double fforte (ADD) 5 68667-2 (2).

Dame Janet Baker was always at her finest in French music, and with her 1967 performance of *Shéhérazade* she inspired Barbirolli to one of his most glowing performances in this atmospherically scored music; her range of tone and her natural sympathy for the French language make for heart-warming singing which has a natural intensity. The account of Chausson's *Poème de l'amour et de la mer* is comparably glorious and heartfelt, both radiant and searching, so that this picture of love in two aspects, first emergent, then past, has a sharpness of focus often denied it; in this she is superbly supported by Previn and the LSO. Their partnership is hardly less persuasive in the five Duparc *mélodies*, which the composer orchestrated himself – each a jewelled miniature of breathtaking beauty, with the extra richness and colour of the orchestral accompaniment adding to the depth and intensity of the exceptionally sensitive word-settings, especially in the greatest of them all, *Phidylé*.

It was Schumann's *Frauenliebe und Leben* that helped to establish Dame Janet's early reputation, and she returned to this favourite cycle in early maturity with renewed freshness in the light of deeper experience. Where on her Saga record (now deleted) she transposed most of the earlier songs down a full tone, the later version keeps them in the original keys. Then by contrast it is the later songs which she transposes, reserving her warmer tones for those expressions of motherhood. The wonder, the inwardness, are even more intense, while the final song in some ways brings the most remarkable performance of all ('Now you Have Hurt me'), not at all a conventional expression of mourning. With Barenboim an endlessly imaginative – if sometimes reticent – accompanist, this is another classic example of her art.

The Brahms Lieder were the last to be recorded, in 1977, and the gravity and nobility of her singing in the *Four Serious Songs* underline the weight of the biblical words while presenting them with a far wider and more beautiful range of tone-colour than is common. André Previn's piano is placed rather backwardly, but his rhythmic control provides fine support, and in the two viola songs, which are ravishingly sung and played, these artists are partnered by Cecil Aronowitz, making his last appearance on record.

To cap the recital come the four varied duets of Op. 28, in which Baker is joined by Dietrich Fischer-Dieskau, recorded at a live recital at London's Queen Elizabeth Hall in 1969. The vivacious closing *Der Jäger und sein Liebchen* makes a spiritedly vivacious coda to a collection which could hardly be bettered. Even if the presentation here omits texts and translations, this set still makes an amazing bargain.

'*The Very Best of Janet Baker*': BACH: *Christmas Oratorio: Bereite dich, Zion* (with ASMF, Marriner). HANDEL: *Messiah: He Was Despised* (with ECO, Mackerras). MENDELSSOHN: *Elijah: O Rest in the Lord* (with New Philh. O, Burgos). *On Wings of Song* (with Parsons, piano). BRAHMS: *Alto Rhapsody* (with John Aldis Choir, LPO, Boult); *Geistliches Wiegenlied* (with Previn, piano & Aronowitz, viola). MAHLER: *Rückert Lieder: Ich bim der Welt abhanden gekommen* (with Hallé O, Barbirolli). DUPARC: *L'Invitation au voyage* (with LSO, Previn). DURUFLÉ: *Requiem: Pie Jesu* (with Butt, organ, cond. Ledger). ELGAR: *The Dream of Gerontius: Angel's Farewell* (with Ambrosian Singers, Sheffield Philh. Ch., Hallé O, Barbirolli); *Sea Pictures* (with LSO, Barbirolli). VAUGHAN WILLIAMS: *Linden Lea*. BRITTEN: *A Boy was Born: Corpus Christi Carol*. WARLOCK: *Pretty Ring Time*. FAURE: *Clair de lune; Prison; Soir*. SCHUBERT: *Ave Maria; Gretchen am Spinnrade; Wiegenlied* (with Moore, piano); *An die Musik; An Sylvia; Auf dem Wasser zu singen; Du bist die Ruh'; Die Forelle; Heidenröslein; Nacht und Träume* (with Parsons, piano). SCHUMANN: *Du Ring an meinem Finger; Mondnacht* (with Barenboim, piano). R. STRAUSS: *Befreit; Morgen* (with Moore, piano).

☛ (B) ✱✱✱ EMI (ADD) 5 75069-2 (2).

A self-recommending recital, imaginatively chosen and well assembled, logically progressing from Dame Janet's deeply moving performances of Bach and Handel, to her incomparable accounts of Elgar's *Sea Pictures* and the *Angel's Farewell* from *Gerontius* – both offering the finest accounts yet committed to disc – as well as some of her finest Lieder performances. Her extraordinary ability to communicate is apparent throughout this programme and as gives the music a fresh perspective; her strongly characterized reading of *Die Forelle* makes it much more of a fun song than usual, and similarly Geoffrey Parsons's naughty springing of the accompaniment of *An Sylvia* (echoed by the singer) gives a twinkle to a song that can easily be treated too seriously. Her heartfelt expressiveness in such numbers as *Gretchen am Spinnrade* and her equal mastery of the French repertoire complete the picture. There are no texts or translations, but a well-written biography relevant to the music is included, and the CD is inexpensive and the transfers are excellent.

Bartoli, Cecilia (mezzo-soprano)

Italian songs (with Schiff): BEETHOVEN: *Ecco quel fiero istante!; Che fa il mio bene?* (2 versions); *T'intendo, si, mio cor; Dimmi, ben mio; In questa tomba oscura*. MOZART: *Ridente la calma*. HAYDN: *Arianna a Naxos*. SCHUBERT: *Vedi quanto adoro ancora ingrato!; Io vuo'cantar di Cadmo; La pastorella; Non t'accostar all'urna; Guarda, che bianca luna; Se dall'Etra; Da quel sembiante appresi; Mio ben ricordati; Pensa, che questo istante; Mi batte'l cor!*

✱✱✱ Decca 440 297-2.

Bartoli and András Schiff make a magical partnership, each challenging the other in imagination. These seventeen Italian songs and one cantata by the great Viennese masters make a fascinating collection, not just Haydn and Mozart but Beethoven and Schubert as well. Beethoven's darkly intense *In questa tomba oscura* is well enough known but, as sung by Bartoli, with Schiff adding sparkle, the lighter songs are just as magnetic, with Beethoven showing his versatility in two astonishingly contrasted settings of the same love-poem.

'*A Portrait*': Arias from: MOZART: *La clemenza di Tito; Così fan tutte; Le nozze di Figaro; Don Giovanni. Concert aria: Ch'io mi scordi di te?* ROSSINI: *Semiramide; Maometto II; La Cenerentola. Songs: Bella crudèle.* PARISOTTI: *Se tu m'ami.* GIORDANO: *Caro mio ben.* CACCINI: *Amarilli.* SCHUBERT: *La pastorella; Metastasio: Vedi quanto adoro ancora ingrato!*

⊖━ *** Decca 448 300-2.

Cecilia Bartoli's portrait, covering a recording period from 1991 to 1995, could hardly be more enticing. Every lyrical aria displays her truly lovely voice with astonishing consistency. The very opening *Parto, parto, ma tu ben mio* from *La clemenza di Tito* could hardly be more inviting, with its engaging basset clarinet obbligato from Lesley Schatzberger, and *Come scoglio* shows her dramatic and vocal range to powerful and moving effect.

There is a delicious combination of charm and sparkle in Despina's *In uomini, in soldate* (wonderfully crisp trills echoing the orchestral violins), while Cherubino's *Voi che sapete* brings delightful innocence, and Susanna's *Deh vieni* the sunny joy of loving anticipation, which ravishes the ear, especially at the leisurely close. The simpler classical songs bring contrast, with the silken line of *Caro mio ben* followed by the very touching and gloriously sung *Amarilli* of Caccini.

Finally Rossini, where Bartoli is unsurpassed among the present generation of mezzos (and measures up impressively to famous names from the past). After the beautifully spun line of the aria from *Maometto II* (with choral support) she captivates with a fizzing, crisply articulated and joyfully humorous *Non più mesta*. Top-class Decca recording throughout ensures the listener's pleasure and this hugely enjoyable collection would have earned a Rosette but for the totally inadequate documentation, with no translations – unacceptable in a premium-priced record.

'*Chant d'amour*' (with Chung, piano): BIZET: *Mélodies: Adieux de l'hôtesse arabe; Chant d'amour; La Coccinelle; Ouvre ton coeur; Tarantelle.* BERLIOZ: *La Mort d'Ophélie; Zaïde.* DELIBES: *Les Filles de Cadiz.* VIARDOT: *Les Filles de Cadiz; Hai luli!; Havanaise.* RAVEL: *4 Chansons populaires; 2 Mélodies Hébraïques; Tripatos; Vocalise-etude en forme de Habanera.*

*** Decca 452 667-2.

This is a delectable disc, a winning collection of French songs, many of them unexpected, which inspire Bartoli to the most seductive singing. One would have predicted that Delibes's sparkling setting of Musset's poem *Les Filles de Cadiz* would draw out Carmen-like fire from her, but here that charming song is set alongside the setting of the same poem made by the great prima donna Pauline Viardot, giving a refreshingly different view. The other Viardot items too come as a delightful surprise, as do the

Bizet songs, including *La Coccinelle*, ('The Ladybird'), a sparkling waltz, superbly characterized here. The better-known Berlioz and Ravel songs are beautifully done too, with Myung-Whun Chung revealing himself just as inspired in the role of pianist as of conductor. Excellent sound.

'*Live from Italy*' (with Thibaudet (piano), Sonatori de la gioiosa marca): BELLINI: *Malinconia ninfa gentile; Ma rendi pur contento.* BERLIOZ: *Zaïde.* BIZET: *Carmen: Près des ramparts de Séville.* CACCINI: *Al fonte al prato; Tu ch'hai le penne; Amarilli mia bella.* DONIZETTI: *La conocchia; Me voglio fa'na casa.* GIORDANI: *Caro mio ben.* HANDEL: *Il trionfo del tempo e del disinganno: Lascia la spina.* MONTSALVATGE: *Canto negro.* MOZART: *Le nozze di Figaro: Voi che sapete. Concert aria: Oiseaux, si tous les ans.* ROSSINI: *Mi Lagnerò tacendo, Book I/2, 3 & 4. L'Orpheline du Tyrol. Zelmira: Riedi al soglio. Canzonetta spagnuola.* SCHUBERT: *La pastorella al Prato.* VIARDOT: *Havanaise; Hai luli!* VIVALDI: *Griselda: Agitata da due venti.*

*** Decca 455 981-2.

Recorded live at the Teatro Olimpico in Vicenza, this recital vividly conveys the high-powered magnetism of Cecilia Bartoli. Encouraged by the rapturous audience, Bartoli may in some items go over the top in her individual characterization, but magic is there from first to last. The opening group of baroque items comes with string accompaniment, but then Jean-Yves Thibaudet at the piano takes over as the most sympathetic partner, whether in the characterful little Schubert song, *La pastorella*, the tango-like *Havanaise* of Pauline Viardot or Berlioz's *Zaïde*, with Bartoli herself playing castanets. It is fascinating to have three widely contrasted settings by Rossini of the same Metastasio text, and crowning the whole recital – before a sparkling sequence of encores – is the longest item, a spectacular aria from Rossini's *Zelmira* with a breathtaking display of coloratura at the end. A fun disc, atmospherically recorded.

Bartoli, Cecilia (mezzo-soprano), Bryn Terfel (baritone)

'*Cecilia and Bryn*': Duets (with Santa Cecilia National Academy Orchestra, Chung) from: MOZART: *Le nozze di Figaro; Così fan tutte; Don Giovanni; Die Zauberflöte.* ROSSINI: *Il barbiere di Siviglia; L'Italiana in Algeri.* DONIZETTI: *L'elisir d'amore.*

*** Decca 458 928-2.

The friendly title, *Cecilia and Bryn*, though suggesting a crossover disc, is well justified when in each of these operatic duets these two charismatic singers are so characterful in their performances, both musically and dramatically. At times they come near to overacting but, with brilliant support from Myung-

Whun Chung and the orchestra, that goes with the virtuoso flair. Warm, full sound, though Bartoli is made to sound breathy.

BBC Singers, Stephen Cleobury

'Illuminare: Carols for a New Millennium' (with Quinney, organ): HOLTEN: *Nowell Sing we Now.* MARTLAND: *From Lands that See the Sun Arise; Make we Joy; There is no Rose of such Virtue.* RUTTI: *I Wonder as I Wander.* WEIR: *Illuminare.* BINGHAM: *The Shepherd's Gift.* GRIER: *Corpus Christi Carol.* ADES: *Fayrfax Carol.* SUSA: *Shepherds Sing.* BELMONT: *Nativitas.* MACMILLAN: *Seinte Mari Moder Milde.* TAVENER: *Today the Virgin.* KORNOWICZ: *Waiting.* RODNEY BENNETT: *Carol.* MAXWELL DAVIES: *One Star, at Last.* HARBISON: *O Magnum Mysterium.* PANUFNIK: *Sleep, Little Jesus, Sleep.* GOODALL: *Romance of the Angels.* HARLE: *Mrs Beeton's Christmas Plum Pudding.*
*** BBC WMEF 0063-2.

This immensely varied collection includes eight brand-new carols, from British, European and North American composers, six of them commissioned by the BBC. Many are unaccompanied but some use the organ very effectively. The penultimate 'Romance of the Angels' is the obvious 'hit' of the programme, an ebullient melody carried by a vigorous organ toccata, but Bo Holten's lovely opening echoing 'Nowell Sing we Now' creates the right atmosphere, and Steve Martland's triptych frames a vigorous scherzando, 'Make we Joy', with two more gentle settings.

Carol Rütti's 'I Wonder as I Wander' swings along with the organ, while Judith Weir's title-piece brings celestial trebles and intriguing dissonance, and this mood continues in Francis Grier's 'Corpus Christi', with more floating soloists, and also in the very striking Adès setting. Jean Belmont's 'Nativitas' rocks ethereally, but not all will take to the moments of sharp dissonance in James MacMillan's 'Seinte Mari Moder Milde', which opens so passionately.

We come back to earth with John Tavener's strophic dance, 'Today the Virgin', with its catchy medieval rhythm over a drone bass. The most extended carol is from Jerzy Kornowicz; 'Waiting', with a rocking motion and curiously intrusive solo voices, is strangely hypnotic. Richard Rodney Bennett's simple melisma is more appealing than Peter Maxwell Davies's equally lyrical but sombre 'One Star, at Last'; but Panufnik's 'Sleep, Little Jesus, Sleep' brings gentle balm. John Harle's catchy 'Christmas Pudding', with slick rhythm and barber-shop harmonies, is a closing fun item, not meant to be taken seriously at all. Performances throughout are first class, as is the recording.

Berganza, Teresa (mezzo-soprano)

'A Portrait': Arias from: ROSSINI: *Il barbiere di Siviglia; La Cenerentola; L'Italiana in Algeri* (with LSO, Gibson). MOZART: *Così fan tutte; Le nozze di Figaro* (with LSO, Pritchard). GLUCK: *Alceste.* CHERUBINI: *Medea* (with ROHCG O, Gibson). HANDEL: *Alcina* (with LSO, Bonynge). BIZET: *Carmen* (with LSO, Abbado). Songs/Arias: MOZART: *Ch'io mi scordi di te? ... Non temer, amato bene* (with LSO, Pritchard). CHERUBINI: *Ahi! Che forse ai miei di.* CESTI: *Intorno all'idol mio.* PERGOLESI (attr.): *Confusa, smarrita.* SCARLATTI: *Chi vuol innamorarsi; Elitropio d'amor; Qual mia colpa, o sventura ... Se delitto è l'adorarvi; La Rosaura.* LAVILLA: *4 Canciones vascas.* TURINA: *Farruca. Saeta en forma de Salve a la Vergen de la Esperanza.* GRANADOS: *La maja dolorosa; El majo timido; El tra-la-la y el punteado* (with Lavilla, piano). DE FALLA: *7 Canciones populares españolas.* GUERRERO: *Sagrario's Romanza.* MARQUES: *Margarita's Romanza* (with O, cond. Lauret). ARAMBARRI: *Canciones vascas* (O, cond. Gombau).
⊶ (BB) *** Decca (ADD) 475 518-2 (2).

A truly recommendable Teresa Berganza compilation. Naturally, there is a sprinkling of her classic early operatic recordings of Rossini and Mozart, which sparkle as brightly as ever and have rarely been out of the catalogue. But all the other items on this disc, from the Gluck and Handel to the Bizet, also show her on top form, a real star mezzo of character and style. The second CD is full of her native Spanish repertoire, most of which has not been widely available on CD before, some being transferred for the first time. Her recordings with Felix Lavilla, made at the beginning of the 1960s, are highly enjoyable, and on their original release it was to Victoria de los Angeles that she was compared. Perhaps the arias by Cherubini and Scarlatti, and others, would have gained from more than piano accompaniment, but the classical quality of the singing is most beautiful, and the sound has transferred well to CD. The *Ocho canciones vascas* ('Eight Basque Songs') and *Sagrario's Romanza* and *Margarita's Romanza*, derive from two EPs from the late 1950s, and these simple, naïve songs are sung to perfection. The group of Basque songs is especially captivating: they were arranged in their present form by Jesús Arámbareri in 1931, and the discreet and delicate orchestral accompaniment he has provided subtly underlines the mood of each item. The sound is a little dated, with the odd bit of distortion, but they are warm and highly atmospheric. At bargain price, this is one of the best in Decca's 'Portrait' series.

Berger, Erna (soprano), Sebastian Peschko (piano)

Arias from: PERGOLESI: *Il Flaminio.* VERACINI: *Rosalinda.* HANDEL: *Semele.* GLUCK: *Die Pilger von Mekka.* Arias: CACCINI: *Amarilli mia bella.* A. SCARLATTI: *La Violetta.* TELEMANN: *Trauer-Music eines kunsterfahrenen Canarienvogels.* J. C. BACH:

Midst Silent Shades. MOZART: *Abendempfindung; Oiseaux, si tous les ans; Ridente la calma; Der Zauberer.* SCHUBERT: *Im Abendrot; An die untergehende Sonne; Am Grabe; Schäfers Klagelied; Suleika I & II.*

(M) (**) Orfeo mono C 556021B.

This recital was recorded in Hanover in 1962. Erna Berger too, was 62, and while the voice still sounds remarkably fresh, a close vibrato is used to maintain the tonal bloom. There is more than a hint of strain in Johann Christian Bach's 'Midst Silent Shades'. However, she is at her charming best in the Italian arias (especially the Veracini and Scarlatti) and still impresses in Mozart and Schubert. But the highlight is the winning Telemann cantata about the canary's funeral. It is a great pity that no texts and translations are provided, either here or elsewhere, and the notes are entirely biographical. Handel's famous aria from *Semele* is engagingly listed (although not sung) as 'Wher'are you Walking'. However, this is a recital for Berger admirers, rather than the general collector.

Bergonzi, Carlo (tenor)

'*The Sublime Voice of Carlo Bergonzi*' (with various orchestras and conductors): Arias from: PUCCINI: *La Bohème; Madama Butterfly; Manon Lescaut; Tosca.* MASCAGNI: *Cavalleria rusticana.* LEONCAVALLO: *Pagliacci.* VERDI: *Aida; Un ballo in maschera; Don Carlo; Otello; Rigoletto; La traviata; Il trovatore.* PONCHIELLI: *La Gioconda.* CILEA: *Adriana Lecouvreur.*

(B) *** Decca (ADD) 476 18584 (2).

Carlo Bergonzi won the *Gramophone* Magazine's Lifetime Achievement Award in 2000 and on that occasion appeared at the Festival Hall and sang two numbers (conducted by Pappano), including the Brindisi from *La traviata* with Angela Gheorghiu. It was undoubtedly the highlight of that occasion, Bergonzi's star quality shining through and himself sounding in remarkably fine voice. This collection is a splendid representation of his career, as well as good tenor collection in its own right. The arias are mainly from Decca's vintage recordings of the 1960s and, as one would expect, offer first-class sound. This excellent anthology appears in the *Gramophone* Awards Collection; (texts and translations are not included, however).

Arias (with Santa Cecilia Ac. O, Gavazzeni) from: VERDI: *Aida; Un ballo in maschera; La forza del destino; Luisa Miller; Il trovatore.* MEYERBEER: *L'africana.* GIORDANO: *Andrea Chénier.* CILEA: *Adriana Lecouvreur.* PUCCINI: *Manon Lescaut; Tosca.*

(M) **(*) Decca Classic Recitals (ADD) 475 392-2.

Decca's 'Classic Recitals' use the original artwork – both the front and back of the LPs, quite attractively reproduced, but in a flimsy cardboard case. Only the LP's original contents are included, making the timing rather shorter than we are used to today, and the reproduction of the LP's notes is in a disgracefully reduced typeface, not always clear. However, many collectors will be glad to have the repertoire available again.

This recital of Bergonzi's early stereo recordings shows him on peak form. Although he does not attempt the rare *pianissimo* at the end of *Celeste Aida*, all the Verdi items in this 1957 recording show the true heroic quality of his voice, a voice still baritonal enough (he started his career as a baritone) to sound completely happy in the wide range demanded of Manrico in *Il trovatore*. Bergonzi's is a remarkable voice and this is a consistently enjoyable recital, especially as the sound is exceptionally vivid and Gianandrea Gavazzeni's conducting is incisive and dramatic.

Bernac, Pierre (baritone)

'*The Essential Pierre Bernac*' (with Poulenc, Moore, Johnson, piano): GOUNOD: *Sérénade; Ce que je suis sans toi; Au rossignol.* 6 *Mélodies* (cycle). DUPARC: *Soupir; L'Invitation au voyage.* CHABRIER: *L'Ile heureuse.* CHAUSSON: *Le Colibri.* ROUSSEL: *Le Jardin mouillé; Coeur en péril.* SCHUMANN: *Dein Angesicht. Dichterliebe* (cycle), *Op. 48.* LISZT: *Freudvoll und Leidvoll; Es muss ein Wunderbares; Nimm einen Strahl der Sonne.* MILHAUD: *La Tourterelle.* VELLONES: *A mon fils.* BEYDTS: *La Lyre et les amours* (cycle). FAURÉ: *Après un rêve; Le Secret; Aurore; Prison; Soir; Jardin nocturne.* DEBUSSY: 3 *Chansons de France. Fêtes galantes: Colloque sentimental.* 3 *Ballades de François Villon.* SATIE: *Mélodies Nos. 1 & 3.* RAVEL: *Don Quichotte à Dulcinée* (cycle). POULENC: 2 *Chansons gailliards; Métamorphoses; Le Bestiaire* (cycles). 2 *Mélodies de Guillaume Apollinaire: Montparnasse.* 2 *Poèmes de Guillaume Apollinaire: Dans le jardin d'Anna.* 2 *Poèmes de Louis Aragon* (with O, Beydts); *Telle jour telle nuit* (cycle). *Le Travail du peintre* (cycle). *L'Histoire de Babar, le petite éléphant.*

(***) Testament mono SBT 3161 (3).

When the duo of Pierre Bernac and Francis Poulenc provided a French equivalent of Pears and Britten, it is especially valuable to have this distinctive and often magical collection of recordings, made between 1936 and 1958. Most were recorded for EMI, notably those made in London just after the end of the Second World War. But the core of the collection, the late recordings made in 1957–8, come from BBC sources, recorded from broadcast concerts.

The distinctive voice, with its flicker of vibrato, was not quite so evenly produced as earlier, but the artistry remains magical. As a supplement comes a broadcast interview, with Bernac questioned by Graham Johnson, and finally comes a performance of Poulenc's *Babar the Elephant* with Johnson at the piano and Bernac a magnetic narrator. On the first disc as a sample of Bernac's Lieder-singing comes an EMI recording with Gerald Moore of Schumann's *Dichterliebe*, while as the perfect introduction there is Bernac's uniquely charming account with Poulenc of Gounod's *Sérénade*. Most moving of all are their readings of such deeper Poulenc songs as the first of the two *Poèmes de Louis Aragon*, 'C', inspired by the Nazi occupation of France.

Björling, Jussi (tenor)

Bjoerling Edition: (Studio recordings 1930–59; with O, Grevillius): Disc 1 (1936–41): Arias from VERDI: *Aida; Rigoletto; Requiem; La traviata; Il trovatore.* PUCCINI: *La Bohème; Tosca; La fanciulla del West.* PONCHIELLI: *La Gioconda.* MEYERBEER: *L'Africaine.* MASSENET: *Manon.* BIZET: *Carmen.* GOUNOD: *Faust.* FLOTOW: *Martha.* ROSSINI: *Stabat Mater.* FRIML: *The Vagabond King.* Songs by TOSTI; DI CAPUA; GEEHL. Disc 2 (1941–50): Arias from: PUCCINI: *La Bohème; Turandot; Manon Lescaut; Tosca.* VERDI: *Rigoletto; Un ballo in maschera.* GIORDANO: *Andrea Chénier, Fedora* MASCAGNI: *Cavalleria rusticana.* LEONCAVALLO: *Pagliacci* (also song: *Mattinata*). DONIZETTI: *L'elisir d'amore.* BIZET: *Les Pêcheurs de perles.* GOUNOD: *Roméo et Juliette.* MASSENET: *Manon.* CILEA: *L'Arlesiana.* GODARD: *Jocelyn (Berceuse).* Song: TOSTI: *L'alba separa.* Disc 3: Arias (sung in Swedish) from: GOUNOD: *Roméo et Juliette.* VERDI: *Rigoletto; Il trovatore.* LAPARRA: *L'illustre Fregona.* BORODIN: *Prince Igor.* PUCCINI: *Tosca; La fanciulla del West.* LEONCAVALLO: *Pagliacci.* MASCAGNI: *Cavalleria rusticana.* ATTERBERG: *Fanal.* RIMSKY-KORSAKOV: *Sadko.* OFFENBACH: *La Belle Hélène.* JOHANN STRAUSS JR: *Der Zigeunerbaron.* MILLOCKER: *Der Bettelstudent.* Traditional songs (in Swedish) and by PETERSON-BERGER; SJOBERG; SCHRADER; STENHAMMAR; ALTHEN; WIDE. Disc 4: Lieder and songs (1939–59): BEETHOVEN: *Adelaide.* R. STRAUSS: *Morgen; Cäcile.* RACHMANINOV: *In the Silence of the Night; Lilacs.* FOSTER: *Jeannie with the Light Brown Hair.* D'HARDELOT: *Because.* SPEAKS: *Sylvia.* CAMPBELL-TIPTON: *A Spirit Flower.* BEACH: *Ah, Love but a Day.* SJOBERG: *I Bless Ev'ry Hour.* SIBELIUS: *The Diamond in the March Snow.* ADAM: *O Holy Night.* Songs by NORDQVIST; SALEN; PETERSON-BERGER; SODERMAN; ALFVEN.

(M) (*****) EMI mono/stereo 5 66306-2 (4).

All admirers of the great Swedish tenor should consider this comprehensive compilation, eighty-nine items chosen by Harald Henrysson from EMI's Swedish archives and admirably remastered at Abbey Road. The voice is caught freshly and truthfully. Björling's wife, Anna-Lisa, also participates in duets from *La Bohème* and *Roméo et Juliette*, towards the end of the second disc. The selection of arias is almost entirely predictable (and none the worse for

that); a number of the key items are offered twice, and sometimes again in Swedish (where they sound surprisingly effective, even an excerpt from Offenbach's *La Belle Hélène*). All the songs have a direct popular appeal. Björling opens Disc 4 with a winning account of Beethoven's *Adelaide*, and many will welcome the lighter songs, and particularly the English ballads. However, the closing group of eight Scandinavian songs is memorable: romantic and dramatic by turns, and closing with a bold final contrast, 'The Diamond in the March Snow' of Sibelius, which is capped by Björling's ardent version of Adam's *Cantique de Noël* in Swedish. Excellent documentation, with photographs and full translations.

Opera arias from: DONIZETTI: *L'elisir d'amore.* VERDI: *Il trovatore; Un ballo in maschera; Aida.* LEONCAVALLO: *Pagliacci.* PUCCINI: *La Bohème; Tosca; La fanciulla del West; Turandot.* GIORDANO: *Fedora.* CILEA: *L'arlesiana.* MEYERBEER: *L'Africana.* GOUNOD: *Faust.* MASSENET: *Manon.* FLOTOW: *Martha.* ROSSINI: *Stabat Mater.*

(M) (*****) EMI mono CDH7 61053-2.

The EMI collection on the Références label brings excellent transfers of material recorded between 1936 and 1947 on the tenor's home-ground in Stockholm. The voice was then at its very peak, well caught in those final years of 78rpm discs, with artistry totally assured over this wide range of repertory.

Arias and excerpts from: VERDI: *Rigoletto* (with Schymberg); *Requiem.* BIZET: *Les Pêcheurs de perles; Carmen.* OFFENBACH: *La Belle Hélène.* GOUNOD: *Roméo et Juliette.* MASSENET: *Manon.* PONCHIELLI: *La Gioconda.* MASCAGNI: *Cavalleria rusticana.* BORODIN: *Prince Igor.* PUCCINI: *Manon Lescaut; La Bohème* (with Anna-Lisa Bjoerling). GIORDANO: *Andrea Chénier.* Songs: RACHMANINOV: *In the Silence of the Night; Lilacs.* LEONCAVALLO: *Mattinata.* TOSTI: *Ideale.* BEETHOVEN: *Adelaide.* R. STRAUSS: *Morgen.*

(M) (***(*)**) EMI mono 7 64707-2.

The second Références collection – particularly generous, with a 77-minute programme – is if anything even more attractive than the first, offering recordings over the full range of the great tenor's 78rpm recording career with EMI, from 1933 (*Vladimir's Cavatina* from *Prince Igor*) to 1949 (*O soave fanciulla* from *La Bohème*, with Anna-Lisa Björling). Again the voice is in peak form, ringing out with that penetrating yet glowing vocal production that was the hallmark of Björling's timbre, while the singing itself has that innate sense of style which made him such a satisfying artist.

It is a pity that the CD transfers are so very bright and edgy, affecting the orchestra as well as the voice. This is particularly annoying in the delicate *Manon* excerpt (*Instant charmant ... En fermant les yeux*) from 1938, where the violins are particularly tiresome; but the overall tendency to shrillness tends to tire the ear before the recital is halfway through. One wonders why this effect cannot be mitigated – the voice does not lack either vividness or presence without artificial enhancement.

'Great Opera Arias' (with RCA Victor Orchestra, Robert Shaw Chorale, Cellini or Rome Opera Orchestra, Perlea or Leinsdorf or (i) Schauwecker (piano)): MEYERBEER: L'Africana: O paradiso. VERDI: Aida: excerpts. Il trovatore: excerpts (with Milanov, Barbieri, Warren). Rigoletto: excerpts (with Peters, Merrill, Rota). PUCCINI: La Bohème: Che gelida manina. Tosca: E lucevan le stelle; Amaro sol per te (with Milanov). Manon Lescaut: Ah! Manon mi tradisce (with Albanese); No! no! pazzo son! (with Campo). MASCAGNI: Cavalleria rusticana: excerpts (with Milanov). (i) BIZET: Carmen: Flower Song. (i) MOZART: Don Giovanni: Il mio tesoro. (i) MASSENET: Manon: Instant charmant; En fermant les yeux. (i) GIORDANO: Fedora: Amor ti vieta. (i) PUCCINI: Turandot: Nessun dorma.
☛ (M) *** RCA mono/stereo 09026 68429-2.

If you want a single disc to represent Jussi Björling, this is the one to have. The recordings date from between 1951 and 1959, the last decade of his life, when the voice was still astonishingly fresh. Most of the excerpts come from distinguished complete recordings, when the great tenor was partnered by artists of the calibre of Zinka Milanov and Licia Albanese (the duets from Tosca and Manon Lescaut are electrifying and the excerpts from Aida, Il trovatore and Cavalleria rusticana are hardly less thrilling). The recordings, splendidly transferred, are all of high quality and show the great tenor in the very best light: even the 1958 live recital, with just a piano accompaniment, is treasurable for its famous arias from Carmen and Manon, and the closing, passionate Nessun dorma.

Opera arias (HMV recordings 1936–45, with S O or Royal O, Grevillius): Arias from: DONIZETTI: L'elisir d'amore. VERDI: Rigoletto; Il trovatore; Aida. PONCHIELLI: La Gioconda. MEYERBEER: L'Africana. FLOTOW: Martha. GOUNOD: Faust; Roméo et Juliette. BIZET: Carmen. MASSENET: Manon. MASCAGNI: Cavalleria rusticana. LEONCAVALLO: Pagliacci. PUCCINI: Manon Lescaut; La Bohème; Tosca; Turandot.
(BB) **(*) Naxos mono 8.110701.

This Naxos programme is generous (78 minutes) and is certainly value for money. The transfers are made by Mark Obert-Thorn from clean shellac originals, and the voice is faithfully caught: some of the transfers are smoother than others. The orchestral sound can be a bit thin, irrespective of the recording date (the 1944 Amor ti vieta from Fedora, for instance), whereas the splendid O Lola aria from Cav. is much warmer because of the resonance. The Flower Song from Carmen, the aria from Romeo and Juliet and the

closing Nessun dorma are examples where there seems to be extra bloom. Background noise is not entirely vanquished but is not a problem. However, the mid-priced RCA collection, including recordings from the last decade of the tenor's life and which includes many of the items above, sung just as passionately and offering much better sound, is well worth its extra cost (RCA 09026 68249-2 – see above, among the main vocal collections).

Bocelli, Andrea (tenor)

Operatic arias (with Maggio Musicale Fiorentino O, Noseda): PUCCINI: La Bohème, Tosca, Madama Butterfly. LEONCAVALLO: La Bohème. CILEA: Adriana Lecouvreur. BELLINI: I Puritani. R. STRAUSS: Der Rosenkavalier. DONIZETTI: La Fille du régiment. BIZET: Carmen. MASSENET: Werther.
**(*) Ph. 462 033-2.

Andrea Bocelli here shows his paces in a formidable collection of arias, including the tenor's aria from Der Rosenkavalier. Bocelli's great natural gift is a tenor of very distinctive timbre, not conventionally rounded in a Pavarotti-like way but above all virile with a baritonal tinge, used over a wide tonal range with not a suspicion of strain. He soars readily to a top C or even a C sharp, as in A te o cara from Bellini's I Puritani.

There is fair evidence too of lessons well learnt. Werther's Pourquoi me reveiller – among the most testing of French arias – inspires Bocelli to produce very refined mezza voce, beautifully sustained, and the Flower Song from Carmen too is subtler than most. Yet there is a sequence of Puccini arias – the two from Tosca, one from Butterfly – which are disappointingly slow and heavy, though Che gelida manina is nicely detailed. And though in the nine top Cs of Tonio's Pour ton âme from La Fille du régiment – the final rip-roaring item here – he cannot quite match the flamboyance of Pavarotti, there are all too few recording tenors who could do it so confidently, or even at all.

Bonney, Barbara (soprano)

'Diamonds in the Snow' (with Pappano, piano): GRIEG: Spring; I Love You; With a Water-lily; The Princess; A Swan; From Monte Pincio; 6 Lieder, Op. 48; Peer Gynt: Solveig's Song. SIBELIUS: The Diamond in the Snow; Lost in the Forest; Sigh, Rushes, sigh; Was it a Dream?; The Girl Came Home from Meeting her Lover. STENHAMMAR: The Girl Came Home from Meeting her Lover; Adagio; Sweden; Guiding Spirit; In the Forest. ALFVEN: Take my Heart; The Forest Sleeps. SJOBERG: Music.
☛ *** Decca 466 762-2.

Barbara Bonney, with her warm understanding of Scandinavia and its music, offers the most seductive choice of songs in this inspired collection. The Grieg group includes most of the well-known favourites, but with Antonio Pappano proving just as understanding a piano accompanist as he is a conductor, they all emerge fresh and new, animated and strongly characterized. There is a sensuousness and passion behind the love songs in particular, with free rubato sounding spontaneous, never studied. The Sibelius set brings ravishing tonal contrasts too, and it is fascinating to hear the settings of the same Swedish poem, first by Sibelius, then more simply but with warm feeling by Stenhammar. More than anything the disc disproves the idea of coldness in the Nordic make-up. Warm, full sound with Bonney's lovely voice glowingly caught.

Bostridge, Ian (tenor), Julius Drake (piano)

'*The English Songbook*': STANFORD: *La Belle Dame sans merci.* GURNEY: *Sleep; I will Go with my Father a-Ploughing.* DUNHILL: *The Cloths of Heaven.* WILLIAM DENIS BROWN: *To Gratiana Dancing and Singing.* SOMERVELL: *To Lucasta, on Going to the Wars.* DELIUS: *Twilight Fancies.* GERMAN: *Orpheus with his Lute.* WARLOCK: *Jillian of Berry; Cradle Song.* FINZI: *The Dance Continued (Regret not me); Since we Loved.* VAUGHAN WILLIAMS: *Linden Lea; Silent Noon.* Irish air, arr. STANFORD: *My love's an Arbutus.* Irish tune, arr. BRITTEN: *The Salley Gardens.* TRAD./ANON.: *The Death of Queen Jane; The Little Turtle Dove.* PARRY: *No Longer Mourne for Me.* WARLOCK: *Rest, Sweet Nymphs.* QUILTER: *Come Away Death; Now Sleeps the Crimson Petal.* GRAINGER: *Bold William Taylor; Brigg Fair.*

🔑 *** EMI 5 56830-2.

Ian Bostridge with his clear, honeyed tone is in his element in this collection of twenty-four English songs, almost all of them neglected. He and his keenly responsive accompanist, Julius Drake, have made an imaginative, far from predictable choice of items, with only the two Vaughan Williams songs, 'Linden Lea' and 'Silent Noon', qualifying as popular favourites. It is good to find the collection delving as far back as Parry and Stanford (the first and most ambitious of the songs, memorably setting Keats's 'La Belle Dame sans merci'), and including composers like Edward German, generally celebrated for his light music. It is a reflection on the singer's personality too that there is a high proportion of thoughtful, introspective songs, most sensitively matched by Drake in his accompaniments. One hopes that EMI's inclusion of French and German translations alongside the English texts will encourage new discovery outside Britain of a genre seriously underappreciated, one which directly reflects the magic of English lyric poetry.

Bott, Catherine (soprano)

'*Mad Songs*' (with New London Consort, Pickett): PURCELL: *From Silent Shades; From Rosy Bow'rs; Not All my Torments can your Pity Move. Don Quixote: Let the Dreadful Engines. A Fool's Preferment: I'll Sail upon the Dog Star.* ECCLES: *The Mad Lover: Must then a Faithful Lover Go?; Let's all be Gay; Cease of Cupid to Complain; She ventures and He Wins: Restless in Thought. Don Quixote: I Burn, my Brain Consumes to Ashes. Cyrus the Great: Oh! Take him Gently from the Pile. The Way of the World: Love's but the Frailty of the Mind.* WELDON: *Reason, What art Thou?; While I with Wounding Grief.* D. PURCELL: *Achilles: Morpheus, thou Gentle God.* BLOW: *Lysander I Pursue in Vain.* ANON.: *Mad Maudlin; Tom of Bedlam.*

(M) *** Decca 476 2099.

Purcell and his contemporaries, including his brother Daniel, John Eccles, John Blow and others, in such mad-songs as these, devised a whole baroque genre. The best-known song here is Purcell's 'I'll Sail upon the Dog Star', but mostly these are miniature cantatas in contrasted sections of recitative and aria, displaying a refreshingly unclassical wildness, often set against pathos. They make a marvellous vehicle for the soprano Catherine Bott, who in this and other discs emerges as an outstanding star among early-music performers, with voice fresh, lively and sensuously beautiful.

ANON: *Carmina Burana: Axe Phebus aureo. The Pilgrimage to Santiago (Navarre and Castile): Non e gran causa.* WOLKENSTEIN: *Der mai mit lieber zal.* DE FOURNIVAL: *Onques n'amai tant que jou fui amee.* MARINI: *Con le stelle in ciel che mai.* FRESCOBALDI: *Se l'aura spira.* MONTEVERDI: *L'Orfeo: Ritornello ... Dal mio Permesso amato.* BLOW: *Venus and Adonis: Adonis! Adonis! Adonis!* BACH: *Christmas Oratorio: Herr, dein Mitleid, dein Erbarmen.* VIVALDI: *Introduzione al Dixit: Ascende laeta.* ECCLES: *Cease of Cupid to Complain; Let's All be Gay; I Burn, my Brain Consumes to Ashes.* PURCELL: *The Indian Queen: They Tell Us that You Mighty Powers Above; Dido and Aeneas: Thy Hand, Belinda ... ; With Drooping Wings.*

(B) *** Decca 470 121-2.

This splendid collection begins with the rustically vibrant account *Non e gran causa*, which tells of a pilgrim who, having sinned carnally, meets the devil, kills himself, is jailed by Saint Mary and is then (improbably) restored to life! Catherine Bott beautifully shades and characterizes this ten-minute work against a background array of colourful instruments, vibrantly played by Pickett's New London Consort. This soloist has made a speciality of Renaissance and early Baroque music, and there are many typical examples of her imaginative art found here. The Eccles items – all of them 'mad songs' – are most appealing, with Bott decorating the vocal line with taste and style, as she also does in the perky Vivaldi item. She is no less successful in sustaining long vocal lines, never more so than in *Dido and Aeneas*, which shows her at her moving best. With excellent orchestral accompaniments and recordings, this is a superb bargain CD, and although there are no texts, her diction is generally clear.

'*London Pride – A Celebration of London in Song*' (with Owen Norris, piano): MONCKTON: *Chalk Farm to Camberwell Green.* DRING: *Business Girls.* WILSON: *A Room in Bloomsbury.* GERSHWIN: *A Foggy Day in London Town.* WALTON: *Rhyme.* DAVID OWEN NORRIS: *Big Ben Blues.* MACCOLL: *Sweet Thames, Run Softly.* BOYCE (arr. Franklin): *The Pleasures of Spring Gardens.* DOVE: *Five Am'rous Sighs.* HESKETH-HARVEY/SISSON: *Wimbledon Idyll.* FRASER-SIMPSON: *They're Changing Guard at Buckingham Palace.* KENNEDY/CARR/MAYERL: *Mayfair Merry-go-round.* DASCRE: *While London's Fast Asleep.* RODNEY BENNETT: *Let's Go and Live in the Country.* SHERWIN: *A Nightingale Sang in Berkeley Square.* SCOTT: *Take me in a Taxi, Joe.* SWANN: *Joyful Noise.* COWARD: *London Pride.*
*** Hyp. CDA 67457.

This is a fun disc, with Catherine Bott – best known as a baroque and early music specialist – demonstrating her mastery in a programme of cabaret numbers recorded live before an audience. With the help of her accompanist, David Owen Norris, she has devised a formidably wide-ranging programme in celebration of London in song. She starts in the world of the musical with Lionel Monckton and Sandy Wilson ('A Room in Bloomsbury' from *The Boy Friend*) and leads via a number from Walton's *Song for the Lord Mayor's Table* to 'A Nightingale Sang in Berkeley Square' and Noel Coward's 'London Pride'. On the way there is an eighteenth-century interlude with a Boyce song celebrating Vauxhall Gardens and a sequence by Jonathan Dove setting poems evoking eighteenth-century town life. Bott brilliantly adapts her vocal technique to each, with precise control of vibrato, timbre and phrasing. Best of all is Joyce Grenfell's 'Joyful Noise', in which a lady chorister celebrates the Royal Albert Hall. Bott puts her own delicious slant on a number that one would have thought nobody but Grenfell could ever bring off.

Bott, Catherine (soprano), The Parley of Instruments, Peter Holman

'*Music for Shakespeare from Purcell to Arne*': WELDON: *Dry Those Eyes which are O'erflowing; Take, O Take those Lips Away.* ECCLES: *Can Life be a Blessing?.* CHILCOT: *Hark, Hark, the Lark; Orpheus and his Lute; Pardon, Goddess of the Night.* GREENE: *Orpheus and his Lute.* ARNE: *Honour,*

Riches, Marriage-blessing; To Fair Fidele's Grassy Tomb; When Daisies Pied and Violets Blue; When Icicles Hang on the Wall; Where the Bee Sucks, There Lurk I. LEVERIDGE: *When Daisies Pied and Violets Blue.* SMITH: *Full Fathom Five; You Spotted Snakes.* DE FESCH: *All Fancy Sick.* PURCELL: *Dear Pretty Youth.* Orchestral: CLARKE: *Titus Andronicus: Overture and Minuet.* WOODCOCK: *Concerto No. 9 in E min. for Flute & Strings* (with Brown).
*** Hyp. CDA 67450.

In the late seventeenth through into the eighteenth century, when Shakespeare's plays were regularly presented in 'improved' versions, often radically different from the original, the revised texts gave plenty of scope for musical items. This attractive collection, characterfully sung by Catherine Bott, includes varied settings of such favourite Shakespeare songs as 'Orpheus with his Lute' and 'When Daisies Pied'. So Maurice Greene's setting of the *Orpheus* song is tricked out with delicate trills and, even more memorably, Thomas Chilcot's extended setting has a haunting flute (beautifully played by Rachel Brown) over a trotting accompaniment. The collection is introduced by Jeremiah Clarke's two-movement overture to *Titus Andronicus*, with a string concerto by Robert Woodcock punctuating the song-sequence, which culminates in two fine songs by Thomas Arne, 'Honour, Riches, Marriage-blessing' and 'Where the Bee Sucks'.

Bott, Catherine (soprano), New London Consort, Philip Pickett

'*Music from the Time of Columbus*': VERARDI: *Viva El Gran Re Don Fernando.* ANON.: *A los Maytines era; Propinan de Melyor; Como no le andare yo; Nina y viña; Calabaza, no sé, buen amor; Perdí la mi rueca; Al alva venid buen amigo; Dale si la das.* URREDA: *Muy triste.* J. PONCE: *Como esta sola mi vida.* ANCHIETA: *Con amores mi madre.* ENCINA: *Triste españa; Mortal tristura; Mas vale trocar; Ay triste que vengo; Quedate carillo.* MEDINA: *No ay plazer en esta vida.* DE LA TORRE: *Danza alta.* DE MONDEJAR: *Un sola fin des mis males.*
*** Linn CKD 007.

The songs offered here are broadly divided into two groups, the romantic ballads, usually of a melancholy disposition (the word 'triste' occurs frequently), and the usually jollier *villancio* form, which brings a repeated refrain. Catherine Bott is the most delightful soloist, singing freshly and simply, often with a ravishing tone, and there is much to give pleasure. In the anonymous songs it is fascinating to discover just how international medieval folk music was, for more than once the listener is reminded of the Auvergne songs collected later in France by Canteloube. The two most delightful items are saved until the end, first a truly beautiful love song, *Al alva venid buen amigo* ('Come at Dawn my Friend'), in which a young woman reflects on her lover's visits, and then lets her thoughts change to consider the birth from the Virgin Mary of 'him who made the world'. In complete contrast is the robust and charmingly naughty villancio, *Dale si das* ('Come on, Wench of Carasa'). The recording is first class, naturally balanced in a pleasing acoustic, and full documentation is provided.

Bowman, James (counter-tenor)

'*The James Bowman Collection*' (with the King's Consort, Robert King): BACH: *Erbarme dich; Stirb in mir.* HANDEL: *Almighty Power; Crueltà nè lontananza; Impious Mortal; Tune your Harps; Welcome as the Dawn of Day; Thou shalt Bring them in; Or la tromba; Eternal Source of Light.* PURCELL: *Britain, Thou Now art Great; O Solitude; By Beauteous Softness Mixed; An Evening Hymn; On the Brow of Richmond Hill; Vouchsafe, O Lord.* ANON.: *Come Tread the Paths.* GABRIELI: *O magnum mysterium.* FORD: *Since I Saw your Face.* F. COUPERIN: *Jerusalem, convertere.*

(BB) ★★★ Hyp. KING 3.

Apart from the opening Bach item, which has not previously been published and which is not entirely flattering, this admirable 78-minute sampler will delight fans of James Bowman as it shows his art and fine vocal control over a wide range of repertoire at which he excelled. Robert King and his Consort provide admirable support.

British Music: 'The Best of British'

'*The Best of British*': ARNOLD: *4 Cornish Dances, Op. 91* (CBSO, composer); *8 English Dances* (Bournemouth SO, Groves); *Serenade for Small Orchestra, Op. 26 Sinfonias Nos. 1–2* (Philh. O, Dilkes); *3* (Bournemouth Sinf., Thomas) (5 74780-2). BRITTEN (with CBSO, Rattle): *An American Overture; Canadian Carnival; Suite on English Folk-Tunes; Sinfonia da Requiem; Young Person's Guide to the Orchestra.*

(M) ★★★ EMI (5 55394-2).

DELIUS: (with Hallé O or LSO, Barbirolli): *Brigg Fair; La Calinda; In a Summer Garden; Fennimore and Gerda: Intermezzo. Hassan: Intermezzo and Serenade* (with Tear); *Irmelin Prelude; Late Swallows; On Hearing the First Cuckoo in Spring; A Song before Sunrise; A Song of Summer; Summer Night on the River; A Village Romeo and Juliet: Walk to the Paradise Garden. Appalachia* (with Jenkins, Amb. S.) (5 65119-2 (2)). ELGAR (with LSO or LPO, Boult): *Enigma Variations; Pomp and Circumstance Marches Nos. 1–5* (7 64015-2). *Caractacus: Triumphal March. Carillon; Dream Children; Elegy; Empire March; Grania and Diarmid: Incidental Music. Imperial March;*

Polonia. WALTON: *Coronation Marches: Crown Imperial; Orb and Sceptre* (5 65584-2). HOLST: *The Planets* (with New Philh. O, Boult). *Egdon Heath; The Perfect Fool* (ballet with LSO, Previn) (5 66934-2). *Choral Fantasia* (with J. Baker); *Psalm 86* (with Partridge) (both with Purcell Singers, ECO, Imogen Holst). FINZI: *Dies natalis* (with W. Brown, ECO, Christopher Finzi). VAUGHAN WILLIAMS: *5 Mystical Songs* (with Shirley-Quirk); *O Clap your Hands* (with King's College Ch., Willcocks) (5 65586-2). VAUGHAN WILLIAMS: *Fantasia on a Theme by Thomas Tallis; 5 Variants of Dives and Lazarus; Norfolk Rhapsody No. 1 in E min.* (CBSO); *Toward the Unknown Region* (with CBSO Ch. & O); *In Windsor Forest* (Bournemouth SO Ch. & Sinf.; all cond. Del Mar) (5 65131-2). *English Folksongs Suite; Fantasia on Greensleeves; In the Fen Country; The Lark Ascending* (with Bean); *Serenade to Music* (with 16 soloists); *Norfolk Rhapsody No. 1* (all with LSO or New Philh. O, Boult). (7 64022-3). WALTON (with Philh. O, composer): *Symphony No. 1* (mono); *Belshazzar's Feast* (with Bell) (5 65004-2). *Film Music: Henry V: Suite* (arr. Mathiesson; with Olivier) (mono); *Scenes from Richard III; Spitfire Prelude & Fugue* (5 65007-2). *Light Music:* COATES: *Impressions of a Princess; Wood Nymphs; Dam Busters* (composer & O); *Dance in the Twilight.* COLLINS: *Vanity Fair.* CURZON: *Punchinello.* TOMLINSON: *Little Serenade.* BINGE: *Miss Melanie.* LANGFORD: *Waltz.* BAYCO: *Elizabethan Masque.* VINTER: *Portuguese Party.* DEXTER: *Siciliano.* HAYDN WOOD: *Joyousness* (all with Pro Arte O, Weldon). BINGE: *Elizabethan Serenade.* HAYDN WOOD: *Montmartre.* OSBORNE: *Lullaby for Penelope.* FARNON: *Portrait of a Flirt.* HARTLEY: *Rouge et Noir* (all with Studio 2 Concert O, Kilbey). DUNCAN: *March.* CURZON: *The Boulevardier.* BINGE: *The Watermill.* DOCKER: *Tabarinage.* HOPE: *Jaunting Car* (all with Light Music Soc. O, Dunn) (5 66537-2).

(BB) ★★★ EMI mono/stereo 5 75791-2 (13).

A 'baker's dozen' package of British music, offering the widest variety from Britten, Elgar and Vaughan Williams masterpieces, including choral music, to delightful lollipops from the vast range of lighter repertoire of which the key figure, Eric Coates, is represented conducting his own music. The 13 discs are in their original jewel cases, packaged in a slipcase. A self-recommending cornucopia.

Caballé, Montserrat (soprano)

'*Diva*': Arias from: PUCCINI: *Madama Butterfly; Tosca; Manon Lescaut; La Bohème; Turandot; La rondine.* ROSSINI: *William Tell.* BELLINI: *Il pirata; I Puritani.* VERDI: *Giovanna d'Arco; Macbeth; Don Carlos; Aida.* BOITO: *Mefistofele.* MASCAGNI: *Cavalleria rusticana.*

⊝━ (M) ★★★ EMI (ADD) 5 65575-2.

This fine compilation is framed by items from Caballé's 1970 Puccini recital in which she impersonates Mimì, Tosca and Butterfly, singing more impressively than she characterizes. Otherwise these are items from complete sets made between 1970 (Giulini's *Don Carlos*) and 1980 (Muti's *I Puritani*). The items are not always the obvious choices from each opera, but from first to last they demonstrate the consistent beauty of her singing at that period, responding to a wide range of conductors.

'*Opera Arias and Duets*' (with Pavarotti) from: VERDI: *Luisa Miller.* BELLINI: *Norma.* BOITO: *Mefistofele.* PUCCINI: *Turandot.* GIORDANO: *Andrea Chénier.* PONCHIELLI: *La Gioconda.*

(M) ✳✳✳ Decca DDD/ADD 458 231-2.

Although this disc centres on Caballé there are plenty of duets here and ensembles too. All the excerpts come from highly recommendable complete sets, and Pavarotti figures often and strongly. In Bellini, Giordano or Boito, and especially as Liù in *Turandot*, Caballé is often vocally ravishing, and she finds plenty of drama and power for Verdi and Ponchielli. There are at least two and sometimes three and four items from each opera, admirably chosen to make consistently involving entertainment. The presentation on this Opera Gala reissue is admirable, with full translations included.

Callas, Maria (soprano)

'*La Divina I*': Arias from: PUCCINI: *Madama Butterfly; La Bohème; Gianni Schicchi; Turandot; Tosca.* BIZET: *Carmen.* CATALANI: *La Wally.* ROSSINI: *Il barbiere di Siviglia.* BELLINI: *Norma.* SAINT-SAENS: *Samson et Dalila.* VERDI: *Rigoletto; La traviata.* GOUNOD: *Roméo et Juliette.* MOZART: *Don Giovanni.* MASCAGNI: *Cavalleria rusticana.* PONCHIELLI: *La Gioconda.*

✳✳(✳) EMI stereo/mono 7 54702-2.

'*La Divina II*': Arias from: GLUCK: *Alceste; Orphée et Eurydice.* BIZET: *Carmen.* VERDI: *Ernani; Aida; I vespri siciliani; La traviata; Don Carlos.* PUCCINI: *Manon Lescaut; La Bohème.* CHARPENTIER: *Louise.* THOMAS: *Mignon.* SAINT-SAENS: *Samson et Dalila.* BELLINI: *La sonnambula.* CILEA: *Adriana Lecouvreur.* DONIZETTI: *Lucia di Lammermoor.*

✳(✳) EMI stereo/mono 5 55016-2.

'*La Divina III*': Arias and duets from: GIORDANO: *Andrea Chénier.* SPONTINI: *La Vestale.* MASSENET: *Manon.* PUCCINI: *Manon Lescaut; La Bohème* (with di Stefano); *Madama Butterfly* (with Gedda); *Turandot.* BIZET: *Carmen* (with Gedda). ROSSINI: *Il barbiere di Siviglia* (with Gobbi). DELIBES: *Lakmé.* VERDI: *Aida; Il trovatore.* LEONCAVALLO: *Pagliacci.* MEYERBEER: *Dinorah.*

✳✳✳ EMI stereo/mono 5 55216-2.

These three recital discs (with nearly four hours of music) cover Callas's recording career pretty thoroughly, although the first two are inadequately documented, giving only the date each recording was published. *La Divina III*, however, provides both the actual dates and venues of the recordings and details of the other artists involved. Throughout the three programmes, results are inevitably uneven, and if at times the rawness of exposed top-notes mars the lyrical beauty of her singing, equally often her dramatic magnetism is such that many phrases stay indelibly in the memory.

Each disc has its share of highlights, with the earlier recordings usually the more memorable. What is perhaps surprising are the omissions: nothing, for instance, from the collection of 'mad scenes' she recorded with Rescigno. However, many of the choices are apt. *La Divina I*, for instance, includes her sharply characterful, early 1954 recording of *Una voce poco fa* from Rossini's *Barbiere*, and *La Divina III* draws on the later, complete set for the duet *Dunque io son*, with Tito Gobbi. *La Divina II* consistently shows her at her finest or near it. The recordings cover a decade from 1954 to 1964 and include much that is arrestingly dramatic (Gluck and Verdi) and ravishing (Puccini and Cilea), while everything shows that special degree of imagination which Callas brought to almost everything she did. The *Mignon* Polonaise is not ideally elegant but it has a distinctive character and charm, and it is almost irrelevant to criticize Callas on detail when her sense of presence is so powerful. The excerpt from *La traviata* was recorded live in Lisbon in 1958 and even the audience noises cannot detract from its magnetism. All three recital discs are available separately at full price, with the third certainly the place to start, as it centres on early recordings, including the excerpt from *La Vestale*, and opens with the movingly intense *La mamma morta* from *Andrea Chénier*. However, it is astonishing that, having provided so much information about the singer, EMI chose not to include any translations, resting content with a brief synopsis of each aria.

Callas Edition

'*Callas at La Scala*' (with La Scala, Milan O, Serafin): CHERUBINI: *Medea: Dei tuoi figli.* SPONTINI: *La Vestale: Tu che invoco; O nume tutelar; Caro oggetto.* BELLINI: *La sonnambula: Compagne, teneri amici ... Come per me sereno; Oh! se una volta solo ... Ah! non credea mirati.*

(M) (✳✳✳) EMI mono 5 66457-2.

These recordings were made at La Scala in June 1955 and feature extracts from three operas which at the time Callas had made all her own. However, for some unexplained reason, the diva refused to sanction publication of the *Sonnambula* items, so the original LP was released in 1958 with substituted performances, taken from her complete set, made the previous year. Yet, with Callas in her prime, if anything more relaxed than in those later versions, the remarkable quality is the total consistency: most details are identical in both performances. *Aficionados* will surely be delighted that the original performances have been restored alongside the Cherubini and Spontini arias. Throughout, Callas is heard at her most magnetic. As usual in this series, the CD transfers are very impressive.

'Lyric and Coloratura Arias' (with Philh. O, Serafin): CILEA: *Adriana Lecouvreur: Ecco, respiro appena ... Io son l'umile; Poveri fiori.* GIORDANO: *Andrea Chénier: La mamma morta.* CATALANI: *La Wally: Ebben? Ne andrò lontana.* BOITO: *Mefistofele: L'altra notte.* ROSSINI: *Il barbiere di Siviglia: Una voce poco fa.* MEYERBEER: *Dinorah: Shadow Song.* DELIBES: *Lakmé: Bell Song.* VERDI: *I vespri siciliani: Bolero: Mercè, dilette amiche.*
(M) (★★★) EMI mono 5 66458-2.

Recorded at the same group of sessions in September 1954 as her very first (Puccini) recital for EMI, this is another of the classic early Callas records, ranging extraordinarily widely in its repertory and revealing in every item the uniquely intense musical imagination that set musicians of every kind listening and learning. Coloratura flexibility here goes with dramatic weight. Not all the items are equally successful: the Shadow Song from *Dinorah*, for example, reveals some strain and lacks charm, but these are all unforgettable performances. Callas's portrait of Rosina in *Una voce poco fa* was never more viperish than here, and she never surpassed the heartfelt intensity of such numbers as *La mamma morta* and *Poveri fiori*. This mono reissue is well balanced and cleanly transferred with the voice vividly projected against a convincing orchestral backdrop.

'Mad Scenes' (with Philh. Ch. & O, Rescigno): DONIZETTI: *Anna Bolena: Piangete voi? ... Al dolce guidami castel natio.* THOMAS: *Hamlet: A vos jeux ... Partagez-vous mes fleurs ... Et maintenant écoutez ma chanson.* BELLINI: *Il pirata: Oh! s'io potessi ... Cor sorriso d'innocenza.*
☛ (M) ★★★ EMI (ADD) 5 66459-2.

Recorded in the Kingsway Hall in September 1958, this is the record which, Desmond Shawe-Taylor suggested, more than any other summed up the essence of Callas's genius. If the rawness of exposed top notes mars the sheer beauty of the singing, few recital records ever made can match – let alone outshine – this collection of 'mad scenes' in vocal and dramatic imagination.

'Callas à Paris', Volume I (with Fr. Nat. R. O, Prêtre): GLUCK: *Orphée et Euridice: J'ai perdu mon Euridice. Alceste: Divinités du Styx.* BIZET: *Carmen: Habanera; Seguidilla.* SAINT-SAENS: *Samson et Dalila: Printemps qui commence; Amour! viens aider ma faiblesse! Mon coeur s'ouvre à ta voix.* GOUNOD: *Roméo et Juliette: Ah! je veux vivre dans ce rêve.* THOMAS: *Mignon: Ah, pour ce soir ... Je suis*

Titania. MASSENET: *Le Cid: De cet affreux combat ... pleurez.* CHARPENTIER: *Louise: Depuis le jour.*
(M) ★★★ EMI (ADD) 5 66466-2.

'Callas à Paris', Volume II (with Paris Conservatoire O, Prêtre): GLUCK: *Iphigénie en Tauride: O malheureuse Iphigénie.* BERLIOZ: *La Damnation de Faust: D'amour l'ardente flamme.* BIZET: *Les Pêcheurs de perles: Me voilà seule ... Comme autrefois.* MASSENET: *Manon: Je ne suis que faiblesse ... Adieu notre petite table. Suis-je gentille ainsi? ... Je marche sur tous les chemins.* *Werther: Werther! Qui m'aurait dit ... Des cris joyeuse (Air des lettres).* GOUNOD: *Faust: Il était un Roi de Thulé ... O Dieu! que de bijoux ... Ah! je ris.*
(M) ★★ EMI (ADD) 5 66467-2.

The first LP collection, *Callas à Paris*, dating from 1961, has the singer at her most commanding and characterful. The sequel disc was recorded two years later when the voice was in decline. The vocal contrast is clear enough, and the need at the time to patch and re-patch the takes in the later sessions makes the results sound less spontaneous and natural. But the earlier portraits of Carmen, Alceste, Dalila and Juliette find Callas still supreme, and her mastery of the French repertoire provides a fascinating slant on her artistry.

'Romantic Callas': Arias from: PUCCINI: *La Bohème; Madama Butterfly; Manon Lescaut; Tosca.* BELLINI: *La sonnambula.* VERDI: *Aida; Un ballo in maschera; La traviata; Il trovatore.* LEONCAVALLO: *Pagliacci.* DONIZETTI: *Lucia di Lammermoor.* SAINT-SAENS: *Samson et Dalila.* BIZET: *Carmen; Les Pêcheurs de perles.* BERLIOZ: *La Damnation de Faust.* MASSENET: *Werther.* MOZART: *Don Giovanni.* SPONTINI: *La Vestale.* MASCAGNI: *Cavalleria rusticana.* CILEA: *Adriana Lecouvreur.*
(M) ★ (★★) EMI mono/stereo 5 57205-2 (2).

There have probably been more Maria Callas compilations than of any other female opera singer, and in the two-CD set listed above, there is nothing that has not been compiled several times before. However, never have they been presented more extravagantly. This release features a lavish booklet in hardback containing over 45 high-quality photographs (in black and white and colour), biographical information, full texts and translations, a discography and something of the opera's plots, which places each aria in context. There are plenty of examples of Callas at her commanding best. The majority of items are from her classic complete opera recordings and recital discs from the 1950s. The transfers are excellent.

'Live in Hamburg 1959' (with N. German RSO, Rescigno). Arias from: SPONTINI: *La Vestale.* VERDI: *Don Carlo; Macbeth.* ROSSINI: *Il barbiere di Siviglia.* BELLINI: *Il pirata.*
(M) (★★★) EMI mono 5 62681-2.

This is the most consistent of the live recordings of Callas recitals latterly issued by EMI. The programme is identical with that on the Stuttgart disc, recorded four days later in May 1959. Not only is the Hamburg recording fuller and firmer, the orchestral playing is a degree more polished. There is little to choose between Callas's performances in each. This is a programme which allows her to display her fire-eating qualities to the full as she portrays a sequence of formidable heroines, with the voice still at its peak, commanding in every way. Curiously, in Lady Macbeth's Letter aria her reading of the letter finds her speaking voice far less menacing than her magnetic singing. Only the slightest flicker on culminating top notes forecasts the flaw that would seriously develop over the following years. This is Callas at her finest, making this a valuable addition to her discography.

'Live in Paris 1963 & 1976' (with O Nat. de l'RTF, Prêtre) Arias from: ROSSINI: *La Cenerentola; Semiramide*. MASSENET: *Manon; Werther*. VERDI: *Nabucco*. PUCCINI: *La Bohème; Gianni Schicchi; Madama Butterfly* (with Tate, piano). BEETHOVEN: *Ah! perfido!*
(M) (**(*)) EMI mono 5 62685-2.

By the time Callas gave this Paris recital in 1963 the unsteadiness in her voice had developed to the point of being obtrusive. There is still much to enjoy here, and not just for Callas devotees, for the programme ranges wide, from the brilliant Rossini arias from *Cenerentola* and *Semiramide* to Massenet, poignantly done, Verdi (the Act II aria from *Nabucco*) and Puccini. The fire-eating Callas here portrays two of the composer's tender 'little women', Lauretta pleading with her father in *Gianni Schicchi* and *Butterfly* in her suicide aria, formidably intense. Also – unexpectedly – Musetta in her waltz song from *Bohème* and not Mimi. The oddity is the seriously flawed private recording of Beethoven's concert aria, *Ah! perfido!*, here cut off before the end, with Jeffrey Tate's piano accompaniment fuzzy and close and Callas's voice ill-focused behind. By 1976 Callas's career was almost over but, whatever the vocal flaws, the power of her personality still shines through in repertory she did not otherwise record.

'Live in Amsterdam 1959' (with Concg. O, Rescigno): Arias from: SPONTINI: *La Vestale*. VERDI: *Don Carlo; Ernani*. BELLINI: *Il pirata*.
(M) (**) EMI mono 5 62683-2.

Recorded two months after the Hamburg and Stuttgart recitals in this same series of Callas singing live, this programme overlaps with those, but with one important exception. Here, instead of Lady Macbeth's Act I aria, she sings the big aria from Verdi's *Ernani*, again in a fire-eating performance. Neither the sound nor the playing quite matches that on the Hamburg disc.

'Live in London 1961 & 1962' (with PO, Prêtre) Arias from: WEBER: *Oberon*. MASSENET: *Le Cid*. ROSSINI: *La Cenerentola*. DONIZETTI: *Anna Bolena*. VERDI: *Macbeth*. (with ROHCG O, Prêtre): BIZET: *Carmen*. VERDI: *Don Carlo*. (with Sargent, piano): MASSENET: *Le Cid*. BOITO: *Mefistofele*.
(M) (* (*)) EMI mono 5 62684-2.

The items with Georges Prêtre and the Philharmonia recorded live at the Royal Festival Hall bring unsteady, crumbly sound with the voice 'off-mike', set at a distance. *Aficionados* will readily listen through the limitations to hear bold, thrusting performances, with Callas in formidable voice, even if the definition of coloratura is inevitably restricted by the sound. The items recorded at Covent Garden come in far better sound, even if it seems a waste to have orchestral items punctuating Carmen's *Habanera* and *Seguidilla*, both wonderfully characterized. Best of all is Leonora's aria from *Don Carlo*, even if there is some unsteadiness at the top of the ever-distinctive Callas voice. A truncated version of Leonora's aria also comes in the curious items recorded live at St James's Palace in 1961, along with another version of the Massenet aria and Margarita's aria from Boito's *Mefistofele*. The piano accompaniment by Sir Malcolm Sargent is so poorly recorded it sounds like a harp.

'Live in Stuttgart 1959' (with South German RSO, Rescigno): Arias from: SPONTINI: *La Vestale*. VERDI: *Don Carlo; Macbeth*. ROSSINI: *Il barbiere di Siviglia*. BELLINI: *Il pirata*.
(M) (**) EMI mono 5 62682-2.

Recorded four days after the Hamburg recital in this same series (see above) and offering an identical programme, the results are similarly electrifying, though recorded in thinner sound, with the orchestra less polished. The Hamburg disc has every advantage.

Calleja, Joseph (tenor)

Tenor Arias (with Milan SO, Chailly) from: CILEA: *L'Arlesiana; Adriana Lecouvreur*. DONIZETTI: *L'elisir d'amore; Lucia di Lammermoor*. PUCCINI: *Madama Butterfly*. VERDI: *Macbeth; Rigoletto; La traviata*.
*** Decca 475 250-2.

Among the latest contenders in the top tenor stakes Joseph Calleja from Malta stands out for relating more closely than usual to examples set by tenors from the early years of recording. His very distinctive timbre, with a rapidly flickering vibrato, brings a reminder of such a 'golden age' singer as Alessandro Bonci. Calleja's technique, with fine control down to the most delicate half-tones, finds him just as happy in the bel canto of Donizetti as in the warm verismo phrases of Cilea and Puccini. The choice of items is imaginative too, helped by the purposeful conducting of Riccardo Chailly. So Alfredo's aria, *De' miei bollenti spiriti*, in Act II of Verdi's *La traviata* is set in context, and though the Duke's *Questa o quella* and *La donna è mobile* from *Rigoletto* come as brief separate items, his *Parmi veder* is presented as part of a complete scene, as is Arturo's big aria in Donizetti's *Lucia di Lammermoor*.

Cambridge Singers, John Rutter

'*There is Sweet Music*' (English choral songs):
STANFORD: *The Blue Bird*. DELIUS: *To be Sung of a Summer Night on the Water I & II*. ELGAR: *There is Sweet Music; My Love Dwelt in a Northern Land*. VAUGHAN WILLIAMS: *3 Shakespearean Songs: Full Fathom Five; The Cloud-capp'd Towers; Over Hill, over Dale*. BRITTEN: *5 Flower Songs, Op. 47*. Folksongs: arr. MOERAN: *The Sailor and Young Nancy*. arr. GRAINGER: *Brigg Fair: Londonderry Air*. arr. CHAPMAN: *Three Ravens*. arr. HOLST: *My Sweetheart's Like Venus*. arr. BAIRSTOW: *The Oak and the Ash*. arr. STANFORD: *Quick! We Have but a Second*.

⊶ ✸ ✶✶✶ Coll. COLCD 104.

Opening with an enchanting performance of Stanford's 'The Blue Bird' followed by equally expressive accounts of Delius's two wordless summer evocations, this most attractive recital ranges from Elgar and Vaughan Williams, both offering splendid performances, to various arrangements of folksongs, less fashionable today than they once were, but giving much pleasure here. The recording, made in the Great Hall of University College, London, has an almost ideal ambience: words are clear, yet the vocal timbre is full and natural. A highly recommendable anthology.

'*Flora Gave me Fairest Flowers*' (English madrigals):
MORLEY: *My Bonny Lass she Smileth; Fyer, Fyer!; Now is the Month of Maying*. EAST: *Quick, Quick, Away Dispatch!* GIBBONS: *Dainty Fine bird; Silver Swan*. BYRD: *Though Amaryllis Dance in Green; This Sweet and Merry Month of May; Lullaby*. WEELKES: *Hark, All ye Lovely Saints*. WILBYE: *Weep, Weep, Mine Eyes; Flora Gave me; Draw on Sweet Night; Adieu Sweet Amaryllis*. TOMKINS: *Too Much I Once Lamented; Adieu ye City-prisoning Towers*. FARMER: *Little Pretty Bonny Lass*. BENNETT: *Round About*. WEELKES: *Ha ha! This World doth Pass; Death hath Deprived me*. RAMSEY: *Sleep, Fleshly Birth*.

✶✶✶ Coll. COLCD 105.

John Rutter's Cambridge Singers bring consistent unanimity of ensemble and a natural expressive feeling to this very attractive programme of madrigals. Perhaps the first group, devoted to love and marriage, may be thought rather too consistently mellifluous; but the second, 'Madrigals of Times and Season', is nicely contrasted, with the clean articula-

tion of Morley's 'Now is the Month of Maying' made the more telling by the lightness of the vocal production. John Wilbye's lovely 'Draw on Sweet Night', which follows, makes a perfect contrast. After two items about 'Fairies, Spirits and Conceits', the concert closes in a mood of moving Elizabethan melancholy with a group devoted to mourning and farewell. Superb recording in a most flattering acoustic makes this collection the more enjoyable, though one to be dipped into rather than heard all at once.

'*Faire is the Heaven*' (music of the English Church):
PARSONS: *Ave Maria*. TALLIS: *Loquebantur variis linguis; If ye Love me*. BYRD: *Misere mei; Haec dies; Ave verum corpus; Bow Thine Ear*. FARRANT: *Hide not Thou Thy Face; Lord, not Thou Thy Face; Lord for thy Tender Mercy's Sake*. GIBBONS: *O Clap your Hands; Hosanna to the Son of David*. PURCELL: *Lord, How Long wilt Thou be Angry; Thou Knowest, Lord; Hear my Prayer, O Lord*. STANFORD: *Beati quorum via*. arr. WOOD: *This Joyful Eastertide*. HOWELLS: *Sing Lullaby; A Spotless Rose*. WALTON: *What Cheer?* VAUGHAN WILLIAMS: *O Taste and See*. BRITTEN: *Hymn to the Virgin*. POSTON: *Jesus Christ the Apple Tree*. HARRIS: *Faire is the Heaven*.

✶✶✶ Coll. COLCD 107.

These recordings were made in the Lady Chapel of Ely Cathedral, and the ambience adds beauty to the sound without in any way impairing clarity of focus. The music ranges from examples of the Roman Catholic Rite as set by Tallis, Byrd and Robert Parsons (with a touch of almost Latin eloquence in the presentation), through widely varied Reformation music, to the Restoration, represented by three Purcell anthems, and on to the Anglican revival and the twentieth century. The Reformation group is particularly successful, with the opening Tallis and closing Gibbons works rich in polyphony and Byrd's 'Bow Thine Ear' wonderfully serene. Of the modern items, the Howells pieces are quite lovely and Walton's 'What Cheer?', with its engaging imitation, is attractively genial. The Britten and Poston items, both well known, are hardly less engaging; and the concert ends with the ambitious title-number, William Harris's 'Faire is the Heaven', sung with great feeling and considerable power. There is no more successful survey of English church music in the current catalogue and certainly not one presented with more conviction.

'*The Lark in the Clear Air*' (traditional songs; with members of the London Sinfonia): *I Know Where I'm Going; She Moved through the Fair; The Lark in the Clear Air; Down by the Salley Gardens; Dashing Away with the Smoothing Iron; The Sprig of Thyme; The Bold Grenadier; The British Grenadiers; The Keel Row; The Girl I Left behind me; The Cuckoo; O Waly Waly; Willow Song; The Willow Tree; The Miller of Dee; O Can ye Sew Cushions; Afton Water*. arr. VAUGHAN WILLIAMS: *The Spring Time of the*

Year; The Dark-eyed Sailor; Just as the Tide was Flowing; The Lover's Ghost; Wassail Song.
**(*) Coll. COLCD 120.

Most of these songs are arranged by Rutter himself, often with simple and characteristic instrumental backings – the opening 'I Know Where I'm Going' has an oboe introduction, 'Down by the Salley Gardens' a clarinet, and 'The Miller of Dee' a genial bassoon. 'The Cuckoo' brings a harp, and in 'The Keel Row' the woodwind interjections are delightful, while the evocative introduction to *Afton Water* is particularly beautiful. Even so, several more memorable items, 'O Waly Waly' for instance, are unaccompanied. The five arrangements by Vaughan Williams bring welcome contrast. The choir sings beautifully, but most of the programme is flowing and mellifluous and one would have welcomed more robust items like 'Dashing Away with the Smoothing Iron' and 'The British Grenadiers'. The recording is richly atmospheric.

'*Christmas Day in the Morning*' (with City of London Sinfonia; (i) Varcoe): TRAD., arr. RUTTER: *I Saw Three Ships; Sans Day Carol; Un flambeau, Jeannette, Isabelle; Wexford Carol; Quittes pasteurs; Go Tell it on the Mountain; Deck the Hall; We Wish you a Merry Christmas; (i) Riu, riu, chiu.* RUTTER: *Mary's Lullaby; Star Carol; Jesus Child; Donkey Carol; Wild Wood Carol; The Very Best Time of Year; Shepherd's Pipe Carol; Christmas Lullaby.* WILLAN: *What is this Lovely Fragrance?* WARLOCK: *Balulalow; I Saw a Fair Maiden.* TAVENER: *The Lamb.* VAUGHAN WILLIAMS: (i) *Fantasia on Christmas Carols.* TRAD., arr. WILLCOCKS: *Blessed be that Maid Mary.*
**(*) Coll. COLCD 121.

Admirers of Rutter's own carols will certainly be drawn to his latest Christmas collection, for alongside the favourites there are several new ventures in his inimitably lively rhythmic style. The 'Donkey Carol', too, becomes more passionate than in previous accounts. But in general, although the whole programme is enjoyable, beautifully sung and smoothly recorded, the feeling of spontaneous freshness, so enticing on his earliest Decca collection (currently withdrawn), made with the choir from Clare College, is less apparent here, and at times there is a hint of blandness (noticeable with the ritardando at the close of Tavener's 'The Lamb'). 'Go Tell it on the Mountain' does not sound entirely idiomatic, and while 'We Wish you a Merry Christmas' ends the concert spiritedly, the Vaughan Williams *Fantasia*, even though it has a fine climax, does not quite match the King's College version (see below) in robust, earthy vigour.

'*A Banquet of Voices*' (music for multiple choirs): GUERRERO: *Duo seraphim.* ALLEGRI: *Miserere.* CALDARA: *Crucifixus.* SCHEIDT: *Surrexit pastor bonus.* TALLIS: *Spem in alium* (40-part motet).

PHILIPS: *Ave Regina caelorum.* BRAHMS: *3 Fest- und Gedenksprüche.* MENDELSSOHN: *Mitten wir im Leben sind; Heilig.* BACH: *Motet: Singet dem Herrn, BWV 225.*
** Coll. COLCD 123.

The resonant acoustic of the Great Hall of University College, London, does not really suit the complex early polyphonic music here, often clouding the detail of writing for double or triple choir and producing a poorly focused climax in the spectacular Tallis *Spem in alium*. The singing too could be more robust in the Scheidt motet. The choir seem much more at home in Brahms and Mendelssohn, and the closing section of the Bach motet *Singet dem Herrn* is vigorously joyful.

'*Portrait*': BYRD: *Sing Joyfully; Non vos relinquam.* FAURE: *Cantique de Jean Racine; Requiem: Sanctus.* RUTTER: *O be Joyful in the Lord; All Things Bright and Beautiful; Shepherd's Pipe Carol; Open Thou Mine Eyes; Requiem: Out of the Deep.* PURCELL: *Hear my Prayer, O Lord.* STANFORD: *Beati quorum via; The Blue Bird.* TRAD.: *This Joyful Eastertide; In dulci jubilo.* HANDEL: *Messiah: For unto us a Child is Born.* FARMER: *A Pretty Bonny Lass.* MORLEY: *Now is the Month of Maying.* DELIUS: *To be Sung of a Summer Night on the Water I & II.* VICTORIA: *O magnum mysterium.* TERRY: *Myn Lyking.*
(M) *** Coll. DDD/ADD CSCD 500.

John Rutter has arranged the items here with great skill so that serene music always makes a contrast with the many exuberant expressions of joy, his own engaging hymn-settings among them. Thus the bright-eyed hey-nonny songs of John Farmer and Thomas Morley are aptly followed by the lovely wordless 'To be Sung of a Summer Night on the Water' of Delius, and Stanford's beautiful evocation of 'The Blue Bird' (one of Rutter's own special favourites). The sound, vivid and atmospheric, suits the colour and mood of the music quite admirably. Not to be missed!

'*The Cambridge Singers Collection*' (with Marshall, City of L. Sinf.): DEBUSSY: *3 Chansons d'Orléans.* Folksongs (arr. RUTTER): *The Keel Row; The Willow Tree.* Gregorian chant: *Regina caeli laetare.* BRUCKNER: *Ave Maria.* VERDI: *Laudi alla Vergine Maria.* STANFORD: *Magnificat in D; Te Deum in C.* PURCELL: *Remember not, Lord, our Offences.* TAVERNER: *Christe Jesu, pastor bone.* PHILIPS: *O Beatum et sacrosanctum diem.* PEARSALL: *Lay a Garland.* RUTTER: *Riddle Song; Waltz; Magnificat* (1st movement); *The Wind in the Willows* (excerpt, with The King's Singers, Baker, Hickox). TRAD. (arr. RUTTER): *Sing a Song of Sixpence.*
(M) Coll. CSCD 501.

Here is an attractively chosen, 64-minute sampler, including a wide range of tempting repertoire from arrangements of folksongs to Stanford and Verdi. The Taverner and Philips items are particularly welcome. Rutter includes a fair proportion of his own music, but the opening (only) from his setting of *The Wind in the Willows* will not be something one would want to return to very often.

Carewe, Mary (soprano)

'*Tell me the Truth about Love*' (with Blue Noise, Mayers, piano): GERSHWIN: *Blah, Blah, Blah; Embraceable You; They All Laughed; Summertime; Love is Here to Stay; By Strauss.* WAXMAN: *Alone in a Big City.* HOLLAENDER: *Chuck out the Men.* SPOLIANSKY: *The Smart Set.* WEILL: *Speak Low; The Saga of Jenny; It Never was You.* MULDOWNEY: *In Paris with You.* BRITTEN: *Tell me the Truth about Love; Funeral Blues; Johnny; Calypso; When You're Feeling like Expressing your Affection.*
(M) ✱✱✱ ASV CDWHL 2124.

In her brilliantly chosen collection of cabaret songs, Mary Carewe hits an ideal balance between cabaret style – with a touch of the old-fashioned 'belter' – and art-song style – with clean, firm vocal attack. Too often, Britten's five settings of Auden poems emerge as too refined. Carewe's full-blooded approach brings them to life in a new way, not just as anaemic pastiche. The first and longest of them is what gives the collection its title, but the six Gershwin numbers which frame the programme at beginning and end are just as stylish, though Philip Mayers' sophisticatedly smoochy arrangement of 'Summertime' from *Porgy and Bess* makes it almost unrecognizable. In some ways the most moving item is one of the three Kurt Weill songs, 'It Never was You', and it is good to have Dominic Muldowney represented in nicely turned pastiche, the more impressive when set against numbers by such exiles in Hollywood as Waxman, Hollaender and Spoliansky. The only snag is the overblown recording, which emphasizes the pop style in aggressive closeness for voice and instruments.

Cathedral Choirs of Winchester, St Paul's and Christ Church, Oxford

English Cathedral Music: PURCELL: *Rejoice in the Lord Always* (with Brandenburg Consort). SCHUBERT: *German Mass: Sanctus.* LOTTI: *Crucifixus.* ALLEGRI: *Miserere mei.* HAYDN: *Missa Rorate coeli desuper: Kyrie; Gloria; Credo* (with Academy of Ancient Music, Preston). BYRD: *Bow thine Ear, O Lord; Turn Our Captivity, O Lord.* WEELKES: *Alleluia, I Heard a Voice; Lord Arise into Thy Resting-Place* (with London Cornet & Sackbut Ens.). VAUGHAN WILLIAMS: *O Clap Your Hands.* SAINT-SAENS: *Messe à quatre voix, Op. 4: Sanctus; Benedictus; O salutaris.* WALTON: *Coronation Te Deum* (with Bournemouth SO, Hill).
(B) ✱✱(✱) Decca (ADD/DDD) 470 124-2.

This collection, though diverse, works well as a 70-minute anthology of choral favourites, plus a few less familiar pieces. Mixing organ-accompanied items with the full orchestral numbers, as well as others with baroque orchestral accompaniments, means that the results are well contrasted. The performances range from good to outstanding, and the recordings are all excellent. At bargain price this is attractive enough.

Chadwell, Tracy (soprano), Pamela Lidiard (piano), John Turner (recorders)

'*Songbook*': MACONCHY: *Sun, Moon and Stars; Three Songs.* LEFANU: *I am Bread; A Penny for a Song.* WHITEHEAD: *Awa Herea.* CRESSWELL: *Words for Music.* LUMSDAINE: *Norfolk Songbook* (with Turner, recorders). LILBURN: *3 Songs.* FARQUHAR: *6 Songs of Women.* JOUBERT: *The Turning Wheel.* BENNETT: *A Garland for Marjory Fleming.*
✱✱✱ British Music Society BMS 420/1 (2).

Tracey Chadwell, whose career was tragically cut short by leukaemia when she was still in her mid-thirties, was an exceptional singer, as this generous two-disc collection of songs makes plain. Hers was a light, bright soprano of extraordinary flexibility and sweetness. She might have become an operatic coloratura, but her special love was for new music. She had an extraordinary gift for making the most impossibly craggy vocal lines sound grateful and expressive, as she does in many of the challengingly difficult songs here. Three of the song-cycles in the collection, by Elizabeth Maconchy, David Lumsdaine and the new Zealand composer, Gillian Whitehead, were specially written for her, as well as one of the separate songs, and one can understand the enthusiasm of composers to write for a singer so responsive. Not only did she sing with keen musical imagination, she projected her sparkling personality with a zest that matched the sparkle in her voice.

The recordings, drawn from BBC sources, are all first-rate, with Pamela Lidiard as her understanding piano accompanist, and with the recorder-player, John Turner, as her partner in the Lumsdaine cycle. The collection comes to a charming conclusion with Richard Rodney Bennett's settings of poems by an early-nineteenth-century child-poet, *A Garland for Marjory Fleming.* An illuminating collection of modern songs as well as a fitting memorial.

Chanticleer

'*Sing we Christmas*': M. PRAETORIUS: *Es ist ein Ros' entsprungen.* VICTORIA: *O magnum mysterium.* TRAD.: *In dulci jubilo* (with verse 2 arr. M. PRAETORIUS; verse 3 arr. H. PRAETORIUS; verse 4 arr. BACH). *O Jesuslein süss, O Jesuslein mild* (verse 1 arr. SCHEIDT; verse 2 arr. BACH). JOSQUIN DES PRES: *O virgo virginum.* HANDL: *Hodie Christus natus est; Mirabile mysterium.* ANON.: *Verbo caro factum est: Y la Virgen le dezia.* GUERRERO: *A un niño llorando.* HOWELLS: *Here is the Little Door.* SAMETZ: *Noel Canon.* arr. WILLCOCKS: *Quelle est cette odeur agréable.* arr. RIBO: *El noi de la mare.* IVES: *A Christmas Carol.* BILLINGS: *A Virgin Unspotted.* HOLST: *In the Bleak Midwinter.* arr. JENNINGS: *Glory to the Newborn King* (fantasia on four spirituals). GRUBER: *Stille Nacht.*

★★(*) Teldec 4509 94563-2.

The rich sonority of the very familiar opening Praetorius carol immediately demonstrates the body and homogeneity of the singing of this fine choral group of a dozen perfectly matched male voices; but while the choir's dynamic contrasts are not in question, the close balance prevents an absolute pianissimo, and the resonance brings a degree of clouding when lines interweave swiftly, as in Jacob Händl's *Hodie Christus natus est*. The lush blend of the slowly flowing *Mirabile mysterium*, with its haunting momentary stabs of dissonance, shows the choir at its finest, as does Victoria's contemplatively gentle setting (*O magnum mysterium*) and the rapt, interweaving polyphony of Josquin's *O virgo virginum*, where the depth of sonority is extraordinary.

If Herbert Howells's 'Here is the Little Door' and Holst's 'In the Bleak Midwinter' are made to seem too static, the Ives 'Christmas Carol' suits the sustained style, while Sametz's ingenious 'Noel Canon' is admirably vigorous, as is William Billings's 'A Virgin Unspotted'. The extended sequence of four traditional gospel songs, arranged by Joseph Jennings, is perhaps the highlight of the concert, sung colloquially with some fine solo contributions, especially from the bass; and the closing *Stille Nacht* brings an unforgettably expansive resonance, with the voices blending like a brass chorale.

'*Christmas*' (also with Upshaw, soprano): Arr. VAUGHAN WILLIAMS: *This the Truth Sent from Above.* TAVENER: *A Christmas Round; Today the Virgin.* DISTLER: *Es ist ein Ros entsprungen (Fantasy).* Arr. HUMPHRIES: *Noël nouvelet.* BOLD/KIRKPATRICK: *Lullaby/Away in a Manger.* Arr. WILLCOCKS: *The First Nowell.* WILLAN: *Three Kings.* MANTYJARVI: *Die Stimme des Kindes.* TRAD. Welsh: *Sio Gân.* GRUBER: *Silent Night.* TRAD.: *Mary and the Baby Medley.*

★★★ Teldec 8573 85555-2.

An essentially intimate collection, beautifully sung and recorded. But the mixture, with its fair sprinkling of favourites, does not always gell readily. John Tavener, as always, manages stimulatingly to look backwards in time, with his bare medieval harmonies; but some of the other modern settings are quite luscious, notably Hugo Distler's vocal divisions on *Es ist ein Ros entsprungen* and Jaakko Mäntyjärvi's *Die*

Stimme des Kindes. Healy Willan's 'The Three Kings' is refreshingly original, and Dawn Upshaw contributes serenely to Vaughan Williams's lovely arrangement of 'This is the Truth Sent from Above' and vivaciously to the Spanish carol. However not all will want the elaborate treatment of Grüber's 'Silent Night', and the American gospel sequence, *Mary and the Baby Medley*, spirited as it is, does not fit readily into the programme's overall mood.

Christchurch Cathedral Choir, Oxford, Francis Grier

'*Carols from Christchurch*' (with Bicket, organ): GARDNER: *Tomorrow shall be My Dancing Day.* TRAD.: *O Thou Man; In dulci jubilo.* HADLEY: *I Sing of a Maiden.* HOWELLS: *Sing Lullaby; Here is the Little Door; A Spotless Rose.* WARLOCK: *Bethlehem Down.* MATHIAS: *Sir Christèmas.* arr. BACH: *O Little One Sweet.* TCHAIKOVSKY: *The Crown of Roses.* WISHART: *Alleluya, a New Work is Come on Hand.* BRITTEN: *A Ceremony of Carols* (with Kelly, harp); *Shepherd's Carol; A Boy was Born: Jesu, as Thou art our Saviour.*

(M) **★★★** ASV (ADD) CDWHL 2097.

This is among the most attractive of mid-priced reissues of carol collections, the more particularly as it includes not only a first-class account of Britten's *Ceremony of Carols*, plus 'Jesu, as Thou art our Saviour', with its piercing momentary dissonances, but also the dialogue 'Shepherd's Carol', so effectively featuring four soloists. The dozen other carols also bring some radiantly expressive singing, particularly in the three inspired Howells works; the Hadley carol, too, is delightful. They are framed by the admirably lively items by Gardner and Wishart, with Mathias's buoyant – 'Sir Christèmas' as a centrepiece. Generally good, analogue sound from the early 1980s.

'Christmas from a Golden Age' (various artists)

'Christmas from a Golden Age' (original recordings from 1925–50): HANDEL: *Messiah: Comfort ye ... Ev'ry valley* (Schiøtz); *He shall Feed his Flock* (Matzenauer). ANON.: *Adeste Fidelis* (with chorus). EASTHOPE MARTIN: *The Holy Child.* Arr. BURLEIGH: *Little Child of Mary* (all McCormack). BACH/GOUNOD: *Ave Maria* (Ponselle). LUCE: *O salutaris* (Journet). REGER: *The Virgin's Lullaby* (Muzio). YON: *Gesù bambino* (Martinelli with chorus). TRAD.: *Der Tannenbaum* (Lashanska and Reimers). HUMPERDINCK: *Weinachten.* GRUBER: *Stille Nacht* (both Schumann-Heink). ADAMS: *The Star of Bethlehem.* REDNER: *O Little Town of Bethlehem* (both Crooks). TRAD.: *Coventry Carol* (Schumann); *Go Tell it to the Mountain* (Maynor

with chorus). Catalonian Carol: *El Cant de Ocells*
(de los Angeles). Arr. NILES: *I Wonder as I Wander*
(Swarthout). WARREN: *Christmas Candle*
(Thomas). DEL RIEGO: *A Star was his Candle*
(Tibbett). ADAM: *Cantique de Noël* (Thill with
chorus). BERLIN: *White Christmas* (Tauber with
chorus).

(BB) (★★★) Naxos mono 8.110296.

A fascinating collection of voices from Christmas
past, which emerge here with startling individuality
in these excellent transfers. Highlights include Aksel
Schiøtz's *Messiah* excerpts, Rosa Ponselle's *Ave Maria*,
and Marcel Journet's very characterful *O salutaris*,
with a quaint violin and harmonium accompaniment. Finest of all are Claudia Muzio's lovely Reger
'Lullaby', Martinelli's stirring *Gesù Bambino* and, predictably, Elisabeth Schumann's ravishing 'Coventry
Carol' and Victoria de los Angeles's delightful contribution from Catalonia, 'The Song of the Birds'.
Ernestine Schumann-Heink's *Stille Nacht* is indulgently drawn out, but Dorothy Maynor's 'Go Tell it to
the Mountain', with an excellent male choir, is
memorable, as is John McCormack's 'Little Child of
Mary' while Gladys Swarthout's Appalachian folksong is very touching. There are strong contributions
too from Richard Crooks, Lawrence Tibbett and
Georges Thill, who delivers a commanding account
of Adam's *Cantique de Noël*. The selection ends,
unexpectedly, with Richard Tauber's stylishly elegant
'White Christmas'. Well worth having.

Christofellis, Aris (sopraniste)

'*Farinelli et son temps*' (with Ens.
Seicentonovecento, Flavio Colusso): Arias from:
DUNI: *Demofoonte*. GIACOMELLI: *Merope*.
METASTASIO: *La partenza*. HANDEL: *Ariodante;
Serse*. BROSCHI: *Artaserse*. HASSE: *Artaserse;
Orfeo*. ARIOSTI: *Artaserse*. PERGOLESI: *Adriano in
Siria*.

★★★ EMI 5 55250-2.

What did operatic castratos sound like in the eighteenth century? The only recording of a genuine
castrato, made at the turn of the last century, is a
travesty, merely the squawking of an old man. By any
reckoning, here is a much closer answer, a finely
trained high falsettist who, in the beauty and evenness of the sound, with a minimum of ugly hooting,
suggests that this may well approximate to the sound
of a castrato.

A recording may exaggerate the size of Christofellis's voice – by report the singing of the great castratos
was exceptionally powerful – but he is artist enough,
with a formidable technique, to make a splendid
show in this dazzling series of arias originally written
for the great castrato Farinelli. Some of his cadenzas
are breathtaking. One brief song is by Farinelli's
greatest friend, the librettist Metastasio, and Farinelli's own setting of the same words is also included.

The items from Handel's *Ariodante* and *Serse*, better
known than the rest, come in performances which
stand up well against those we have had from female
singers, and Christofellis in his note pays tribute to
the pioneering work of Marilyn Horne. The performances are all lively and alert, and the recording
of the voice is full and vivid, though the instrumental
accompaniment is backwardly placed.

'Coloratura Spectacular'

'*Coloratura Spectacular*' (with (i) Sutherland; (ii) Jo
(sopranos); (iii) Horne (mezzo)): (i) OFFENBACH:
Les Contes d'Hoffmann: Doll Song. (ii) *Un Mari à la
porte: Valse tyrolienne*. (iii)
PERGOLESI/LAMPUGNANI: *Meraspe o l'Olimpiade:
Superbo di me stesso*. (i) VERDI: *Attila: Santo di
patria … Allor che i forti corrono*. (ii) AUBER: *Le
Domino noir: La Belle Inès fait florès; Flamme
vengeresse*. (i; iii) ROSSINI: *Semiramide: Serbami
ognor si fido il cor*. (ii) MASSE: *La Reine Topaze:
Ninette est jeune et belle*. (iii) ARDITI: *Bolero:
Leggero, invisibile qual aura sui fiori*. (i) GLIERE:
Concerto for Coloratura Soprano, Op. 82; (iii)
DONIZETTI: *Lucrezia Borgia: Il segreto per esse
felici*. (ii) MOZART: *Die Zauberflöte: Der Hölle
Rache*.

⊶ (M) ★★★ Decca ADD/DDD 458 240-2.

'Coloratura Spectacular' is a dazzling display of vocal
feux d'artifice from Decca's three top female vocal
virtuosi, opening appropriately with Sutherland's
sparklingly precise 'Doll Song', followed by Sumi Jo's
glittering and no less charming displays in Offenbach
and Auber, plus an amazing *Carnaval de Venise*,
where the flexibility of her upper tessitura has to be
heard to be believed. Vibrant drama comes from
Sutherland in Verdi's *Attila*, and Marilyn Horne
shows her vocal range and fire-eating strength in a
thrilling pastiche Pergolesi aria, Arditi's *Bolero* and *Il
segreto per esse felici* from Donizetti's *Lucrezia Borgia*.
The two divas then join together for a famous duet
from Rossini's *Semiramide*, while Glière's two-
movement *Concerto for Coloratura Soprano* again
shows Sutherland at her most nimble and personable. Overall this is a remarkable demonstration to
confirm that the present-day coloraturas can hold
their own with the best from the so-called Golden
Age. Full translations are included.

Columbus Consort

'*Christmas in Early America*' (18th-century carols
and anthems): BELCHER: *How Beauteous are Their
Feet*. HOLYOKE: *How Beauteous are Their Feet;
Th'Almighty Spake and Gabriel Sped; Comfort ye
My People*. CARR: *Anthem for Christmas*.
STEPHENSON: *If Angels Sung a Saviour's Birth*.
HUSBAND: *Hark! The Glad Sound*. HEIGHINGTON:
While Shepherds Watched their Flocks by Night.

FRENCH: *While Shepherds Watched their Flocks by Night.* BILLINGS: *While Shepherds Watched their Flocks by Night.* PETER: *Unto us a Child is Born.* ANTES: *Prince of Peace, Immanuel.* MICHAEL: *Hail Infant Newborn.* HERBST: *To us a Child is Born.* SCHULZ: *Thou Child Divine.* DENCKE: *Meine Seele erhebet den Herrn.* GREGOR: *Hosanna! Blessed he that Comes in the Name of the Lord.* C. PACHELBEL: *Magnificat anima mea Dominum.*
*** Channel Classics Dig. CC 5693.

A fascinating look back to the celebration of Christmas in the New World in the late eighteenth century, both by the British colonial settlers in New England and by their Moravian counterparts in Pennsylvania and North Carolina, where the inheritance was essentially in the European tradition. The English style is usually fairly simple and hymn-like, but with overlapping part-writing and occasional solo dialogues (as in the rhythmically interesting 'Th'Almighty spake').

Samuel Holyoke shows himself to be a strikingly fresh melodist; while, of the three settings of 'While Shepherds Watched' to different tunes, William Billings's emerges as the most striking and imaginative. Benjamin Carr's *Anthem for Christmas* is a musical pastiche (indeed, a kind of 'musical switch' with brief quotations from Corelli's *Christmas Concerto* and Handel's *Messiah* among other works). The Moravian/German music is usually more elaborate. Johann Peter's delightful motet-like carol, 'Unto us a Child is Born', has characteristically resourceful accompanimental string-writing and those who follow him – David Moritz Michael, Johannes Herbst, J. A. P. Schulz and Jeremiah Dencke – all write in a tradition descended from the great German composers, capped by Charles Pachelbel (son of the Johann Pachelbel of *Canon* fame). He played the organ in Boston, New York and Charleston in the 1730s and 1740s, and his *Magnificat* for double chorus celebrates a much more florid style, utterly different from the music which opens this programme.

The surprise is that this concert is performed not by American singers but by a Dutch group of expert vocal soloists, with a choral and string ensemble who sing and play with convincing authenticity and an agreeably stylish spontaneity. The recording is realistic and clear and made within a perfectly judged acoustic.

Consort of Musicke, Anthony Rooley

'*The World of the Consort of Musicke*': DOWLAND: *Come Away, Come Sweet Love; Fine Knacks for Ladies; Me, me, and None but me; Praise Blindness Eyes; Rest Awhile, You Cruel Cares; Say, Love, if Ever Thou Didst Find; When Phoebus First Did Daphne Love; White as Lilies was her Face.* GIBBONS: *Dainty Fine Bird; Fair is the Rose; Fair Ladies that to Love;*

'*Mongst Thousand Good; The Silver Swan; Trust not too Much, Fair Youth.* WILBYE: *Ah, Cannot Sighs, nor Tears; Die, Hapless Man; Lady, I Behold; Lady, your Words do Spite me; Lady, when I Behold the Roses; Softly, o Softly Drop, Mine Eyes; Thus Saith my Cloris Bright; Why Dost Thou Shoot; Ye that do Live in Pleasures.* MORLEY: *Arise, Awake; Deep Lamenting Hard by a Crystal Fountain; Hark! Alleluia; No, no, no, no, Nigella; Stay Heart, Run not so Fast.*
(B) *** Decca (ADD/DDD) 467 786-2.

These fine performances emanate from various LPs of the 1970s and early 1980s. The collection is well planned, and these are sensitive and stylish performances, excellently recorded, with moments of great beauty. One may complain about odd points – the diction is not always what it might be, for example, although the director is at pains to avoid obtrusive consonants – but there is much to delight the ear, and at its modest price, this is well worth exploring.

Crespin, Régine (mezzo-soprano)

'*French Songs*': BERLIOZ: *Les Nuits d'été.* RAVEL: *Shéhérazade* (with Suisse Romande Orchestra, Ansermet). DEBUSSY: *3 Chansons de Bilitis.* POULENC: *Banalités: Chanson d'Orkenise; Hôtel. La Courte Paille: Le Carafon; La Reine de coeur. Chansons villageoises: Les Gars qui vont à la fête. 2 Poèmes de Louis Aragon: C; Fêtes galantes* (with Wustman, piano).
⊶ ❂ (M) *** Decca Legends (ADD) 460 973-2.

Régine Crespin's recordings with Ansermet of the Berlioz and (especially) Ravel song-cycles are classics of the gramophone and sound marvellous in these new Decca transfers. The other songs were originally part of a 1967 song-cycle recorded in the Kingsway Hall with John Wustman. Crespin cleverly chose repertoire to suit her voice and all come over vividly, particularly the Debussy *Chansons de Bilitis* and the charming Poulenc song about *Le Carafon* ('The Little Water Jug') who wants (like the giraffe at the zoo) to have a baby water jug and, with the magical assistance of Merlin, succeeds, much to the astonishment of the lady of the house.

'*Italian Operatic Arias*' (with ROHCG O, Downes): Arias from: VERDI: *Un ballo in maschera; Otello; Il trovatore.* PONCHIELLI: *La Gioconda.* MASCAGNI: *Cavalleria rusticana.* PUCCINI: *Madama Butterfly.* BOITO: *Mefistofele.*
(M) **(*) Decca Classic Recitals (ADD) 475 393-2.

The richness of Crespin's voice is well caught in this 1963 recital, with a fine, steady *Suicidio* and an affecting account of the heroine's prison aria in Boito's *Mefistofele*. More controversial are the Verdi items: the lack of a trill in the cabaletta to the *Trovatore* aria, the occasional sliding into the notes in the *Ballo* aria, and too many intrusive aitches.

But Crespin devotees will not mind any of this, and one forgives much because of her sheer personality; she is that now rare thing: a distinctive and easily recognizable voice. Good, rich sound for this new Classic Recital release.

Cura, José (tenor)

'*Anhelo*': **Argentinian songs (with Bitetti, guitar; Delgado, piano; and orchestra).**
**(*) Erato/Warner 3984-23138-2.

In his disc of Argentinian songs José Cura not only sings but directs the performances – seven of them involving a small orchestra – and arranges some of the pieces, two of them his own compositions. It makes a crossover disc that is not just 'middle-of-the-road' but 'easy listening', evidently designed to provide a sweet and unobtrusive background. The bright little Ginastera song is one of the few which, with its tango rhythm, has a Hispanic flavour. Most of the rest are yearningly melancholy, with *La campanilla*, the fifth of eight songs by Carlos Guastavino, a charming exception. In face of the general mood, the title, *Anhelo* ('Vehement Desire'), taken from the last of the Guastavino songs, seems hardly appropriate. Though the recording acoustic and close balance do not allow the full bloom of Cura's fine tenor to come out, these are warmly expressive performances, not just from him but from his associates too.

Daniels, David (counter-tenor), Orchestra of the Age of Enlightenment, Harry Bicket

'*Sento amor*': **Operatic arias from:** MOZART: *Mitridate; Ascanio in Alba* (also concert aria: *Ombra felice ... Io ti lascio*, K.255). GLUCK: *Telemaco; Orfeo ed Euridice*. HANDEL: *Tolomeo; Partenope*.
⊖ *** Virgin 5 45365-2.

There are few discs of counter-tenor arias to match this. The American David Daniels uses his exceptionally beautiful and even voice with flawless artistry and imagination, whether in Handel, Gluck or Mozart. Even such a well-known aria as *Che faro* from Gluck's *Orfeo* emerges with fresh individuality, and the coloratura is breathtaking in its precision and fluency throughout, not just a brilliant technical exercise but a musical delight. One can imagine singing like this from castratos of the time delighting eighteenth-century audiences. Even those who usually resist the falsetto voice will find Daniels on this disc an exception in his naturalness and freshness. Excellent sound.

Danish National Radio Choir, Stefan Parkman

'*Scandinavian Contemporary a cappella*': TORMIS: *Raua needmine*. NORGARD: *And Time shall be no More*. RAUTAVAARA: *Suite de Lorca, Op. 72*. SANDSTROM: *A Cradle Song*. JERSILD: *3 Romantike korsange*.
*** Chan 9264.

Tormis is an honorary Scandinavian: he hails from Estonia. Jørgen Jersild and Per Nørgård are both Danish, Sven-David Sandström is Swedish (and mightily overrated in his homeland), and Einojuhani Rautavaara comes from Finland. Stefan Parkman has brought the Danish National Radio Choir to considerable heights and now it almost (but not quite) rivals the Swedish Radio Choir in its heyday under Eric Ericsson. None of the music is quite good enough to enter the permanent repertory in the way that the sublime motets of Holmboe's *Liber canticorum* should and doubtless will. By their side, this is all pretty small beer, but the Jersild and Rautavaara are worth investigating.

Dawson, Lynne (soprano), Malcolm Martineau (piano)

'*On this Island*': BRITTEN: *On this Island*. WARLOCK: *Lilligay My Own Country; The Night*. QUILTER: *Fair House of Joy; My Life's Delight*. PARRY: *Armida's Garden; My Heart is like a Singing Bird*. STANFORD: *La Belle Dame sans merci; 3 Edward Lear Limericks; Limmerich ohne Worte* (piano solo). GURNEY: *Sleep*. HOWELLS: *King David*. VAUGHAN WILLIAMS: *Silent Noon; The Lark in the Clear Air; Through Bushes and Through Briars*. FINZI: *Oh Fair to See; Since we Loved; As I Lay in the Early Sun*.
*** Hyp. CDA 67227.

Lynne Dawson, singing with golden tone and sparklingly clear diction, offers one of the most delectable recitals of English song. In addition to well-known favourites like Vaughan Williams's 'Silent Noon' and Howells's 'King David', Dawson and Martineau include a whole sequence of brief, intensely tuneful songs that are totally charming and deserve to be far better known, from Parry's 'Armida's Garden' to Gurney's rapt setting of John Fletcher's, 'Sleep'. Stanford is represented not only by the substantial 'La Belle Dame sans merci', but by three witty settings of Edward Lear limericks, which he used as comic party-pieces, full of parodies, together with a brief piano solo designed as an accompaniment to any other limerick required. The recital ends with the Britten cycle of Auden settings that gives the disc its title; this is tougher, more incisive music than most of the rest. Dawson and Martineau are inspired throughout and beautifully recorded.

Robert DeCormier Singers and Ensemble, Robert DeCormier

'*Children Go Where I Send Thee*' (*A Christmas Celebration around the World*) (with soloists from the choir): Traditional songs and carols from: Sweden (arr. DECORMIER): *Ritsch, ratsch, filibon.* Italy: *Dormi, dormi, O bel bambin.* Austria: *Da Droben vom Berge.* Nigeria: *Betelehemu.* Spain: *A la nanita, nanita;* (Catalonia): *El noi de la mare.* USA: *Children go where I send thee; Poor little Jesus;* (Appalachian): *In the valley.* Puerto Ricò: *La Trulla.* Germany: *Es ist ein' Ros' entsprungen.* France: *Ecoutons donc les aubades.* India: *Lína avatárá.* Canada: *Huron Carol.* Syria: *Miladuka.* Argentina: *La peregrinacion.* West Indies: *The Virgin Mary had a Baby Boy.*

* Arabesque Z 6684.

The excellent Robert DeCormier Singers have already recorded a number of fine collections, including a John Dowland anthology ('Awake Sweet Love': Z 6622) and two previous Christmas collections ('A Victorian Christmas': Z 6525 and 'The First Nowell': Z 6526), but none has been more attractive than this geographically wide-ranging programme of Christmas songs with children in mind. The arrangements are simple, for every number has great character and needs no embellishment.

The programme opens enticingly with a tick-tock (*Ritsch, ratsch*) Swedish carol, which is immediately captivating; it is followed with an exquisite Italian lullaby. The oldest item is a Syrian Christmas hymn, *Miladuka* ('The Nativity'), which, based on plainchant, is thought to be more than 1,000 years old. It is presented here in harmonized form and is quite haunting, as is the example from northern India, *Lína avatárá* ('He Chose to be Among Us'), which is introduced softly on flute and chiming percussion. When the voices enter, the harmonies are bare, whereas the Nigerian song about Bethlehem has rich upper intervals above the sonorous repeated bass and soon becomes exultant. The Argentinian carol, 'The Pilgrimage', is lusciously Latin, while the Spanish examples are simpler but lilting. The only really familiar carol is from Germany and it is beautifully and serenely presented. The concert ends swingingly with the more familiar West Indian 'The Virgin Mary had a Baby Boy', which is given the lightest, most infectious rhythmic touch. Altogether this splendidly recorded anthology, with its nicely judged instrumental accompaniments, will give great pleasure – to grown-ups as well as to children.

Deller, Alfred (counter-tenor)

'*Portrait of a Legend*' (with various artists, including Dupré, lute): PURCELL: Excerpts from *The Fairy Queen; King Arthur; The Indian Queen; Olinda; The Old Bachelor; Dioclesian.* Sacred music: Gregorian Chant: *Ténèbres: Dernière Leçon du Samedi Saint.* TALLIS: *Te lucis ante terminum.* COUPERIN: *Deuxième Leçon de Ténèbres pour le Mercredy.* BUXTEHUDE: *Cantate Domino.* PURCELL: *In Guilty Night.* GIBBONS: *Great King of Gods.* PALESTRINA: *Ave verum.* GRANDI: *Cantabo Domine.* Songs: ANON.: *The Wind and the Rain. Othello: Willow Song. Calleno Custure Me. Misere my Maker.* MORLEY: *It was a Lover and his Lass.* CAMPION: *I Care not for These Ladies.* BARTLET: *Of All the Birds.* ROSSETER: *What then is Love?* BLOW: *The Self-banished.* CLARKE: *The Glory of the Arcadian Groves.* DOWLAND: *Fine Knacks for Ladies; Flow my Tears.* PURCELL: *If Music be the Food of Love; From Rosy Bow'rs. O Solitude.* CACCINI: *Pien d'amoroso affretto; Amarilli, mia bella.* SARACINI: *Pallideto quai viola.* A. SCARLATTI: *Infirmata vulnerata.* Folksongs: *The Three Ravens; Black is the Colour of my True Love's Hair; The Oak and the Ash; Barbara Allen; Lord Rendall; The Water is Wide; The Tailor and the Mouse; Down by the Salley Gardens; I will Give my Love an Apple; Bushers and Briars; The Foggy, Foggy Dew; She Moved through the Fair; Evening Prayer.* MORLEY: *Sweet Nymph, Come to thy Lover; I Go before My Darling; Miraculous Love's Wounding.* R. JONES: *Sweet Kate.*

(BB) ***(*) HM (ADD) HMC 290261.4 (4).

This a valuable survey of the latter part of Deller's career, from 1967 to 1979. He was joined by many other artists of distinction, including Desmond Dupré, David Munrow, William Christie and his own Consort. As can be seen above, the range of his recordings was wide, and he contributed some important Purcell repertoire to the French Harmonia Mundi catalogue. But the collection of this composer's music, although vivid, is piecemeal, and Deller is heard at his very best in the solo songs and folksongs, where his turn of phrase can often be quite ravishing. He sings some of the latter in duet with his son, Mark Deller. It is a pity that these well-recorded discs are not available separately. Texts are included, and this anthology is still very recommendable, although the earlier, Vanguard series needs to be reissued in a new, accessible format.

'*O Ravishing Delight*' (with Munrow, Lee, Dupré, Elliott): ANON.: *Miserere my Maker.* DOWLAND: *Shall I Sue?; Come Heavy Sleep; I Saw my Lady Weep; Wilt thou Unkind; Fine Knacks for Ladies; Flow My Tears.* CAMPION: *I Care not for These Ladies; The Cypress Curtain.* BARTLETT: *Of All the Birds.* ROSSETER: *What then is Love; What then is Love but Mourning.* FRANCIS PILKINGTON: *Rest, Sweet Nymphs.* BLOW: *The Fair Lover and his Black Mistress; The Self-banished.* CLARKE: *The Glory of the Arcadian Groves; In her Brave Offspring.* ECCLES: *Oh! the Mighty Pow'r of Love.*

CROFT: *My Time, O ye Muses.* DANIEL PURCELL:
O Ravishing Delight. HUMFREY: *A Hymne to God the Father.*

(B) **(*) HM Musique d'abord (ADD) HMA 190215.

Deller's recording contract with Vanguard lasted from 1954 to 1965 and he made more than sixty LPs for this label, which are no longer available. Then he had a second, shorter recording period with Harmonia Mundi. The present collection dates from 1969 and one can hear him husbanding his voice, using it lightly where possible.

Many of the songs here are available in earlier performances, but they still sound pleasingly fresh, and as can be heard in the very lovely opening 'Miserere my Maker', he has not lost his magic touch. Dowland's 'Come Heavy Sleep' and 'I Saw My Lady Weep' and Campion's 'Cypress Curtain of the Night' certainly bring the 'ravishing delight' of the title. It is good to have also a pair of songs from Jeremiah Clarke (of *Trumpet Voluntary* fame), and 'The Glory of the Arcadian Groves' features a charming recorder obbligato. The programme closes with a beautifully refined performance of Dowland's famous 'Flow My Tears'. Throughout, the accompaniments are of the highest quality, as is the recording, and as texts are included, this makes a fine bargain sampler of Deller's later achievement.

Folksongs (with Deller, counter-tenor, Dupré, lute): *The Three Ravens; Black is the Colour of My True Love's Hair; The Oak and the Ash; Barbara Allen; Lord Rendall; The Water is Wide; The Tailor and the Mouse; Down by the Salley Gardens; I will Give My Love an Apple; Bushes and Briars; The Foggy Foggy Dew; She Moved Through the Fair; Evening Prayer.* MORLEY: *Sweet Nymph, Come to thy Lover; I go before My Darling; Miraculous Love's Woundings.* JONES: *Sweet Kate.*

(B) ** HM (ADD) HMA 195226.

Originally published by RCA, this 1972 collection shows Deller in peak vocal form, but not all will respond to his very free, art-song style in this repertoire. This is shown in the very opening number, 'The Three Ravens', where very free rubato and self-conscious control of the dynamic become exaggerated into excess refinement, and the earthiness which is a basic element of folk music is all but submerged. Of course Deller's singing is often beautiful, the phrasing of 'Down by the Salley Gardens' is lovely; but many will feel that when he is joined in duet by Mark Deller (their voices match admirably) this is too much of a good thing. The recording is good, so Deller *aficionados* need not hesitate, although the disc is short measure.

Domingo, Plácido (tenor)

'Domingo Sings Caruso' (with various orchestras and conductors): arias from: LEONCAVALLO: *La Bohème; Pagliacci.* DONIZETTI: *L'elisir d'amore.* MASSENET: *Le Cid; Manon.* CILEA: *L'Arlesiana.* FLOTOW: *Martha.* PUCCINI: *La fanciulla del West; La Bohème.* VERDI: *Aida; Rigoletto.* MEYERBEER: *L'Africana.* GOUNOD: *Faust.* HALEVY: *La Juive.* MASCAGNI: *Cavalleria rusticana.*

(M) *** RCA (ADD) 82876 59407-2.

Domingo's heroic stage presence comes over well in this 'Caruso' anthology, the ringing tone able to impress in a lyrical phrase, even though more fining down of the tone and a willingness to sing really softly more often would enhance the listener's pleasure. But in the theatre this is obviously a voice to thrill, and the engineers have captured it directly and realistically, from the sobbing verismo of *Pagliacci* to the crisp aristocracy in *Rigoletto*. The selection is an interesting one, opening with an aria from Leoncavallo's *Bohème* that suggests that this opera is worth reviving (it has since been recorded). The bulk of this recording derived from a 1972 LP with the same name as this release (with the LSO, conducted by Santi), which was expanded from various other recordings in RCA's CD catalogue. Texts and translations are now included in its latest mid-price release for RCA's 'Classic Collection'.

'Vienna, City of My Dreams' (with Ambrosian Singers, ECO, Rudel): arias from: LEHAR: *Das Land des Lächelns; Die lustige Witwe; Paganini.* ZELLER: *Der Vogelhändler.* KALMAN: *Gräfin Mariza.* FALL: *Der fidele Bauer; Die Rose von Stambul.* SIECZYNSKI: *Wien, du Stadt meiner Träume.* O. STRAUS: *Ein Walzertraum.* JOHANN STRAUSS JR: *Eine Nacht in Venedig.*

(BB) *** EMI Encore 5 75241-2 [5 75242-2].

Having such a golden tenor sound in Viennese operetta makes a winning combination, and Domingo, always the stylist, rebuts the idea that only a German tenor can be really idiomatic. A delightful selection, including one or two rarities, which is very well recorded and now offered at budget price.

'Domingo Favourites' (with various orchestras and conductors): arias from: DONIZETTI: *L'elisir d'amore.* VERDI: *Ernani; Il trovatore; Aida; Nabucco; Don Carlos.* HALEVY: *La Juive.* MEYERBEER: *L'Africaine.* BIZET: *Les Pêcheurs de perles; Carmen.* PUCCINI: *Tosca; Manon Lescaut.*

(M) *** DG 445 525-2.

The greater part of this collection is taken from a 1980 digital recital, recorded in connection with yet another gala in San Francisco. The result is as noble and resplendent a tenor recital as you will find. Domingo improves in detail even on the fine versions of some of these arias he had recorded earlier, and the finesse of the whole gains greatly from the sensitive direction of Giulini. Though the orchestra is a little backward, the honeyed beauty of the voice is given the greatest immediacy. The other items are taken from Domingo's complete sets of *Don Carlos* (with Abbado), *Nabucco, Manon Lescaut* and *Tosca* (with Sinopoli), and are well up to the high standards this great tenor consistently sets for himself.

Early Music Consort of London, David Munrow

'Music of the Gothic Era'; LEONIN: *Viderunt omnes; Alleluya Pascha nostrum; Gaude Maria Virgo; Locus iste.* PEROTIN: *Viderunt omnes; Sederunt principes.* ANON.: *Alle, psallite cum luya; Amor potest; S'on me regarde; In mari miserie; On parole de batre; En mai, quant rosier sont flouri; Dominator Domine; El mois de mai; O mitissima; Hoquentus I–VII; La Mesnie fauveline; Quant je le voi; Zelus familie; Quasi non ministerium; Clap, clap, par un matin; Lés l'ormel a la turelle; O Philippe, Franci qui generis; Febus mundo oriens; Degentis vita; Inter densas deserti meditans.* PETRI DE CRUCE: *Aucun ont trouvé.* ADAM DE LA HALLE: *De ma dame vient; J'os bien a m'amie parler.* PHILIPPE DE VITRY: *Impudenter circumivi; Cum statua.* BERNARD DE CLUNY: *Pantheon abluitur.* HENRI GILLES DE PUSIEUX: *Rachel plorat filios.* MACHAUT: *Lasse! comment oublieray; Qui es promesses; Hoquetus David; Christe, qui lux es.* ROYLLART: *Rex Karole, Johannis genite.*

(M) ✻✻✻ DG Blue (ADD) 471 731-2 (2).

In the 1970s David Munrow was pioneering repertoire by composers who are now much more readily accessible. But Munrow's gift of bringing early music consistently to life for the non-specialist listener and finding ear-catching ways to present the instrumental pieces is as valid today as it was then. 'Music of the Gothic Era' is particularly valuable in providing a remarkably lively survey of medieval music during the two centuries when it was developing at a comparatively swft rate from early organa to the thirteenth-century motet, 'from the monumental to the miniature', as David Munrow says in his notes. So the choice of music moves from Léonin's organum to the *Rex Karole* of Philippe Royllart, dating from the second half of the fourteenth century. The set was originally on three LPs (now reduced to a pair of CDs), so the music comes in three groupings – I, Notre Dame period, II, Ars Antiqua Motetti and III, Ars Nova Motetti – although there are instrumental items included among the vocal works. Munrow projects this music with characteristically buoyant rhythms and expressive liveliness. Its presentation is essentially conjectural, but to bring the music back to life is the most important thing, and Munrow certainly does that, and most entertainingly too. The recording is excellent.

'The Art of the Netherlands': secular songs (vocal and instrumental versions): JOSQUIN DESPREZ: *Scaramella va alla guerra; Allegez moy, doulce plaisant brunette; El grillo è buon cantore; Adieu mes amours.* ISAAC: *Donna di dentro della tua casa.* VAN GHIZEGHEM: *De tous biens plaine.* BRUMEL: *Du tout plongiet – Fors seulement l'attente.* OCKEGHEM: *Prenez sur moi vostre exemple amoureux; Ma bouche rit.* BUSNOIS: *Fortuna desperata* (with others by GHISELIN; ANON.). Sacred music: TINCTORIS: *Missa sine nomine: Kyrie.* BRUMEL: *Missa et ecce terrae motus: Gloria.* JOSQUIN DESPREZ: *Credo super De tous biens; De profundis; Benedicta es caelorum regina.* DE LA RUE: *Missa Ave sanctissima Maria: Sanctus.* ISAAC: *Missa la bassadanza: Agnus Dei.* OBRECHT: *Haec Deum caeli; Laudemus nunc Dominum.* MOUTON: *Nesciens mater virgo virum.* OCKEGHEM: *Intemerata Dei mater* (with anon.).

(M) ✻✻✻ Virgin (ADD) 5 61334-2 (2).

The coverage here concentrates on the latter half of the fifteenth century, and the first disc is devoted to secular songs and instrumental arrangements. Josquin immediately makes his presence felt with an ear-catching opening item, 'Scaramella is off to War', for vocal quartet with recorders, bass viol, guitar, harp and tambourine, and later he is to return with the unaccompanied *El grillo*, where the vocal interchanges are equally lively. As most of these vocal numbers are short, what follows is a kaleidoscope of concerted and solo items, alongside instrumental arrangements (for lute duet, recorder consort, broken consorts or keyboard), providing plenty of contrast. Heinrich Isaac's jubilant quodlibet feaures nine singers, while Hayne van Ghizeghem's touching chanson, *De tous biens plaine*, is first sung as an accompanied counter-tenor solo, and then heard in three different instrumental arrangements. Many of the songs are richly expressive, Ockeghem's canon *Prenez sur moi vostre exemple amoureux* and Brumel's *Du tout plongiet* are memorably poignant examples. Busnois's *Fortuna desperata* is first presented in a three-part vocal presentation, then in six parts (three singers with a trio of viols), and finally on a combination of tenor dulcian, recorder, rebec and two lutes.

The second section, a group of Mass movements, immediately brings a greater degree of gravitas with Johannes Tinctoris's *Kyrie*, solemnly presented by four low male voices, yet Brumel's robust *Gloria* is memorably gutsy. Pacing never drags; indeed, Isaac's six-part *Agnus Dei* flows forward strongly. The motets in the third section, many of them Marian, are more consistently expressively solemn, but all are strikingly beautiful, with Josquin's *De profundis*, with its firm bass line, particularly eloquent. Full texts and translations are included and this seems an excellent way to explore this repertoire as a prelude to acquiring CDs concentrating on a single composer. The standard of singing and playing is high, and the recording is as vivid as you could wish.

'The Art of Courtly Love' (with Bowman, Brett, Hill, Shaw): I: *'Guillaume de Machaut and his Age'*:

JEHAN DE LESCUREL: *A vous douce debonaire* (chanson). MACHAUT: *Amours me fait desirer; Dame se vous m'estés lointeinne; De Bon Espoir – Puis que la douce rousee; De toutes flours; Douce dame jolie; Hareu! hareu! le feu; Ma fin est mon commencement; Mes esperis se combat; Phyton le mervilleus serpent; Quant j'ay l'espart; Quant je suis mis au retour; Quant Theseus – Ne quier veoir; Se ma dame m'a guerpy; Se je souspir; Trop plus est belle – Biauté paree – Je ne sui mie certeins.* P. DES MOLINS: *Amis tout dous vis.* ANON.: *La Septime estampie real.* F. ANDRIEU: *Armes amours – O flour des flours.* II: 'Late fourteenth-century Avant-garde': GRIMACE: *A l'arme a l'arme.* FRANCISCUS: *Phiton Phiton.* BORLET: *2 Variants on the tenor 'Roussignoulet du bois'; Ma tedol rosignol.* SOLAGE: *Fumeux fume; Helas! je voy mon cuer.* JOHANNES DE MERUCO: *De home vray.* ANON.: *Istampitta Tre fontane; Tribum quem; Contre le temps; Restoés restoés.* VAILLANT: *Trés doulz amis – Ma dame – Cent mille fois.* PYKINI: *Plasanche or tost.* ANTHONELLO DE CASERTA: *Amour m'a le cuer mis.* MATTEO DA PERUGIA: *Andray soulet; Le greygnour bien.* III: 'The Court of Burgundy': DU FAY: *Ce moys de may; La Belle se siet; Navré ju sui d'un dart penetratif; Lamention Sanctae Matris Ecclesiae Constantinopolitaine (O tres piteulx – Omnes amici); Par droit je puis bien complaindre; Donnés l'assault; Helas mon dueil; Vergine bella.* BINCHOIS: *Je ne fai tousjours que penser; Files a marier; Amoreux suy et me vient toute joye; Je loe Amours et ma dame mercye; Vostre trés doulx regart; Bien puist.* ANON.: *La Spagna* (basse danse) *Variants I & II.*

(M) ******* Virgin (ADD) 5 61284-2 (2).

David Munrow's two-disc set 'The Art of Courtly Love' spans the period 1300–1475 in some depth. The survey is divided into three sections: 'Guillaume de Machaut and his Age', 'Late fourteenth-century Avant-garde' and 'The Court of Burgundy'. The first section is introduced arrestingly by two cornetts and an alto shawm, who accompany a striking chanson of Jehan de Lescurel (died 1304), which must have had 'hit' status in its time (*A vous douce debonaire*). The bare harmonies give a real tang to the tune. Then comes the first of many numbers by the justly famous Guillaume de Machaut, *Hareu! hareu! le feu ... le feu d'ardant desir*, which one hardly needs to translate, and it is certainly ardent!

But it is the expressive romantic chansons of Machaut that make one appreciate how readily the composer came to dominate the combination of lyric poetry and music in fourteenth-century France and to epitomize the title, 'The Art of Courtly Love'. The virelais *Se ma dame m'a guerpy* ('If My Lady has Left Me') and *Quant je suis mis au retour*, for solo tenor and chorus, with its sad introductory bass rebec solo, surely anticipate the melancholy eloquence of Dowland, while Machaut could also be

attractively lighthearted as in *Se je souspir* ('If I Sigh'), or robustly jolly and spiritedly extrovert (*Douce dame jolie*).

The second CD opens with a particularly lovely vocal trio by Jehan Vaillant (?1360–90), which anticipates 'The First Nowell' in its vocal line, and a following ballade, *Amour m'a la cuer mis*, by Anthonello de Caserta (whose career spanned the turn of the century) demonstrates how forward-looking were other composers of 'the late fourteenth-century avant-garde', while Solage (flourished 1370–90) is no less enterprising in providing lugubrious humour with his baritone solo *Fumeux fume* ('He who fumes and lets off steam provokes hot air') with its unlikely melodic line. (Not surprisingly, Munrow gives this rondeau an appropriately bizarre instrumental backing.) 'A Man's True Worth' (*De home vray*), a ballade by the late-fourteenth-century Johannes de Meruco, also brings lively melodic twists and turns.

Gilles Binchois (*c.* 1400–60) was another leading figure of the time, well represented here, and, like Machaut, he had a wide range. But it is the lovely rondeau duet *Amoreux suy et me vient toute joye* ('Filled with love, I am overjoyed, hoping that your kindness might bring sweet comfort') that one especially remembers. With its expressive pleading so direct in its appeal, it is one of the set's highlights and is ravishingly sung here. With the music from 'The Court of Burgundy' we also meet the remarkable Guillaume Du Fay, with his exhilarating rondeau *Ce moys de may*, so different in mood from his Masses, followed by an engagingly melancholy echoing duet for two counter-tenors, *La Belle se siet au piet de la tour* ('The maiden sits ... weeping, sighing and venting her grief'), while the virelai *Helas mon dueil*, a rejected lover's lament, is infinitely touching.

However, the collection ends in lively fashion with the anonymous basse danse *La Spagna*, and here (as in the other instrumental items) Munrow's choice of colour brings an extra dimension to what is basically a very simple dance. All the soloists are distinguished and at their finest. Incidentally, although the translations are not affected, the documentation for this set has the list of titles for the second disc mixed up, starting with bands 12–15, then following with 1–11, but they are all there.

'*Monteverdi's Contemporaries*' (with Bowman, Hill and Elliott): MAINERIO: *Il primo libro di balli: 10 Dances.* GUAMI: *Canzoni per sonar: Canzona á 8.* LAPPI: *Canzoni per sonar: La negrona.* PRIULI: *Sacrorum Concentuum: Canzona prima á 12.* PORTA: *Sacro convito musicale: Corda Deo dabimus.* BUSATTI: *Compago ecclesiastico: Surrexit Pastor bonus.* DONATI: *Concerti ecclesiastici, Op. 4: In te Domine speravi.* D'INDIA: *Novi concentus ecclesiastici; Isti sunt duae olivae.* GRANDI: *Motetti con sinfonie, Libro I: O vos omnes; Libro III: O beate Benedicte.*
✹ (M) ******* Virgin 5 61288-2.

Munrow's art is shown to even greater advantage in his collection of music by Monteverdi's contemporaries, which has a comparatively short time-span (1535–1644). Opening with five dances from Giorgio Mainerio's *Il primo libro di balli*, vividly scored, mainly for wind and brass, but unexpectedly bringing a xylophone solo in the *Ballo francese*, the programme continues with other impressive instrumental pieces by Gioseffo Guami, Pietro Lappi and Giovanni Priuli. Then come five more of the Mainerio dances, two of which are solos for the cittern, notably the brilliant and catchy *Schiarazula marazula*, which is as intricately titillating as its title suggests.

But this all serves to act as a prelude to a superb collection of vocal music, nearly all of which is entirely unknown. Ercole Porta's sonorous setting of *Corda Deo dabimus* has the counter-tenor (James Bowman) and tenor (Martyn Hill) sonorously underpinned by sackbuts; Cherubino Busatti's *Surrexit Pastor bonus*, which follows (James Bowman at his most inspired), is unforgettable. The setting of this short but deeply poignant motet dramatically alternates moods: bright and lighthearted for 'The Good Shepherd is Risen – Alleluia' and then (with a sudden change) movingly eloquent in telling of the crucifixion, with a despairing downward scale for the word *mori* ('die'), which is infinitely touching. Ignazio Donati's tenor duet *In te Domine speravi* (Martyn Hill and Paul Elliott) is almost equally eloquent.

There is a fine motet from Sigismondo d'India, then comes the other highlight, Alessandro Grandi's tragically beautiful *O vos omnes*, gloriously sung by Bowman. This too is unforgettable. The concert ends happily in celebration with Grandi's *O beate Benedicte*, with counter-tenor and tenor duetting happily, sometimes in harmony, at others in felicitous imitation, with the accompaniment for cornett, tenor sackbut, organ and bass violin adding to the simple polyphony. Here as elsewhere Munrow's instrumentation has an imaginative flair matched by no other exponent of this repertoire. The recording is superb and this collection, including several out-and-out masterpieces among much else that is rewarding, is on no account to be missed.

(i) Early Music Consort of London, David Munrow; (ii) Musica Reservata, John Beckett

'*Early Music Festival*': (i) *Florentine Music of the fourteenth century* (with Bowman, counter-tenor, Rogers and Hill, tenors): LANDINI: *Ecco la primavera; Giunta vaga biltà; Questa fanciull' amor; De! dinmi tu; Cara mie donna; La bionda treçça; Donna 'l tuo partimento.* ANON.: *Lamento di Tristano; Trotto; Due saltarelli; Quan ye voy le duç; La Manfredini; Istampita Ghaetta; Biance flour.* PIERO: *Con dolce brama.* TERAMO: *Rosetta.*

LORENZO DI FIRENZE: *Chon brachi assai; Dà, dà, a chi avaregia.* JACOBO DE BOLOGNA: *Fenice fu' e vissi.* (ii) *Florentine music of the sixteenth century* (with Noorman, mezzo-soprano, Burgess, counter-tenor, Rogers, tenor, Frost, bass baritone): MONTEVERDI: *Orfeo: Toccata.* Music for Ferdinando de' Medici (incidental music for the play *La Pellegrina*): MARENZIO: *Second Intermedio.* MALVEZZI & CAVALIERI: *Sesto Intermedio.* FESTA: *Quando ritova.* ANON.: *Allemana-ripresa; Pavana: La cornetta; Gagliarda Giorgio; Ahimè sospiri; Pavana: Forze d'Ercole; Orsù, orsù, car'Signori; Pavana: El colognese.* Dance songs (vocal and keyboard settings): *Era di Maggio; El marchesse di Salluzzo; In questo ballo; Non ci vogliam' partire; Bussa la porta; La pastorella; E su quel monte; Maggio valente; Sorella mi piacente.* TROMBONCINO: *Frottola: Io son l'occello.* NOLA: *Tri ciechi siamo.* CARA: *Frottola: Io non compro.*
(B) ★★★ Double Decca (ADD) 452 967-2 (2).

This Decca Double happily combines two collections of Florentine music from two different authentic groups recording for the Argo label in the late 1960s and early 1970s. The repertoire may be a century apart, but this means that the contrast is the more striking. The fourteenth-century collection has a wide general appeal. Its key figure, Francesco Landini, has an immediate approachability, and this extends to much else here, especially when the variety of presentation, both vocal and instrumental, is so stimulating.

No one knows exactly how or on what instruments accompaniments would have been performed, but David Munrow and his Early Music Consort solve the problems with their usual combination of scholarship and imagination. The singers include artists of the distinction of James Bowman, and the players are first rate. David Munrow's recorder playing is virtuosic, and Andrea Zachara da Teramo's *Rosetta*, played on a chamber organ, is most piquant. Attractive music, expertly transcribed and beautifully recorded.

The sixteenth-century collection from Musica Reservata opens with a *Toccata* from Monteverdi's *Orfeo*, vigorously played on a colourful combination of baroque trumpet, sackbuts and percussion, which shows how much more elaborate musical presentation had become in the intervening century. The earthy style of Musica Reservata may be typified by the throaty roaring of the unforgettable Jantina Noorman, but the opening vocal number from Luca Marenzio's *Second Intermedio* (incidental music for the play *La Pellegrina*) is charmingly presented by three boy trebles, accompanied by lyra, viol and harp, and later the choruses (sometimes for double or triple choirs) are both expansive and beautiful.

The collection ranges wide in mood among vigorous dances, popular songs and ceremonial music, all of it refreshing to the modern ear. Full translations are included and both programmes can be highly recommended to anyone who wants to explore painlessly and with delight a rich period of musical history. Again the recording is excellent, and the only possible criticism about this straight reissue of a pair of highly recommended LPs is to mention that other explorations were made by Argo at that time; with 51 minutes' playing time on the first disc and 53 on the second, there would have been room to include more music, from the intervening period. But each concert here is self-sufficient in itself, and this Double is still worth its cost.

Elysian Singers, Sam Laughton

'*Peacocks and Pirahnas*': MUSGRAVE: *On the Underground.* HINDEMITH: *La Biche; Un Cygne.* ARCADELT: *Il bianco e dolce cigno.* GIBBONS: *The Silver Swan.* DAVIES: *O magnum mysterium.* BULLARD: *Choristers of Flight.* VAUTOR: *Sweet Suffolk Owl.* STANFORD: *The Blue Bird.* TAVENER: *The Lamb.* FINZI: *Nightingales.* RAVEL: *Trois chansons.*

*(*) Elysian ES 1202.

This is an attractive, imaginative collection of *a cappella* songs devoted to birds and beasts. The Elysian Singers of London are well known for their splendid concerts, as well as making some good recordings, notably a disc of Delius's partsongs for Somm. There is some interesting repertoire here, with some good, modern, choral writing, such as Thea Musgrave's 'On the Underground', as well as the more familiar territory of Finzi and Stanford. The short Renaissance items, such as Arcadelt's *Il bianco e dolce cigno* and Gibbons's 'The Silver Swan', are enjoyable, as is the brief but catchy 'Sweet Suffolk Owl'. The later works of Ravel and Hindemith are well done too, and this would make a pleasant 45-minute concert. The snag is the unflattering recording, which places the choir backwardly, and, with the relatively dry-sounding acoustic, the result lacks warmth and intimacy and fails to show the choir at their best.

Emmanuel College, Cambridge, Chapel Choir, Timothy Prosser

'*Carols from Cambridge*': TRAD.: *Veni, veni Emmanuel; The Angel Gabriel; In dulci jubilo.* RUTTER: *What Sweeter Music.* GAUNTLETT: *Once in Royal David's City.* arr. WILLCOCKS: *Ding Dong! Merrily on High; O Come All Ye Faithful.* BRITTEN: *A Hymn to the Virgin; Friday Afternoons, Op. 7: New Year Carol.* arr. JACKSON: *Noël Nouvelet.* arr. VAUGHAN WILLIAMS: *This is the Truth Sent from Above; Wither's Rocking Hymn.* MATHIAS: *Sir Christèmas.* WARLOCK: *Bethlehem Down; Benedicamus Domino.* arr. HAMMOND: *Swete was the Song the Virgin Soong.* GARDNER: *Tomorrow*

shall be my Dancing Day. BERLIOZ: *L'Enfance du Christ: Shepherds' Farewell.* LEIGHTON: *Lully, Lulla, Thou Tiny Child.* RAVENSCROFT: *Remember, O Thou Man.* HOPKINS: *We Three Kings.* ORD: *Adam Lay y-Bounden.* GRUBER: *Stille Nacht.* arr. RUTTER: *Wexford Carol.*

(M) *** ASV CDWHL 2104.

Opening with the famous melodic chant *Veni, veni Emmanuel*, which turns out to be medieval in origin and not a Victorian hymn, this is a particularly appealing mid-priced collection, beautifully recorded. Although it includes (as the third item) 'Once in Royal David's City', sung in crescendo in the Willcocks arrangement, a strongly expressed 'O Come All Ye Faithful', and Mathias's jovial 'Sir Christèmas', as outgoing and vigorous as one could wish, the style of performance, as befits a smaller chapel choir, is for the most part a pleasingly intimate one.

Unlike King's College, Emmanuel uses women's voices, but they are as sweet and pure as any boy trebles', the overall blending and ensemble are nigh perfect and the effect is disarmingly simple, notably so in the lovely *Shepherds' Farewell* from Berlioz's *L'Enfance du Christ*. Anna Dennis is a pleasingly fragile soloist in Vaughan Williams's setting of Wither's 'Rocking Hymn'; Rutter's 'What Sweeter Music' and Warlock's 'Bethlehem Down' are especially touching.

Enterprisingly, the famous *Stille Nacht* is presented in its charming original version for two solo voices (Julia Caddick and Sarah Fisher) and guitar. Grüber hastily scored it in this fashion when the organ broke down just before its first performance on Christmas Eve 1818 – in the appropriately named Church of St Nicholas (Oberndorf, Austria). Not all the choices are obvious, and Britten's 'New Year Carol', taken from *Friday Afternoons*, is an engaging novelty. Prosser and his splendid singers are equally impressive in the livelier carols: the rhythmic syncopations of Gardner's 'Tomorrow shall be My Dancing Day' are as sparkling as the bounce of 'We Three Kings', and the choir's lightness of touch is equally appealing in Warlock's *Benedicamus Domino*, which ends the concert joyfully.

English Song

'*The Very Best of English Song*' (Various Artists):

Disc 1: VAUGHAN WILLIAMS: *Linden Lea.* IRELAND: *The Salley Gardens.* PARRY: *O Mistress Mine.* QUILTER: *Love's Philosophy* (Baker, Moore); *Now Sleeps the Crimson Petal.* PEEL: *Bredon Hill* (Allen, Parsons). BUTTERWORTH: *A Shropshire Lad: Loveliest of Trees.* GURNEY: *Down by the Salley Gardens; Black Stichel.* WARLOCK: *My Own Country; Passing by; Pretty Ring Time* (Rolfe Johnson, Willison). VAUGHAN WILLIAMS: *The Lamb; The Shepherd* (Partridge, Craxton, oboe);

Silent Noon. QUILTER: *Come Away, Death.* FINZI: *Since we Loved* (Bostridge, Drake). FINZI: *Rollicum-rorum.* IRELAND: *Sea Fever.* KEEL: *Trade Winds* (Lemalu, Vignoles). STANFORD: *Sea Songs: Drake's Drum; The Old Superb* (Lloyd, Walker). WOODFORDE-FINDEN: *Indian Love-Lyrics: Kashmiri Song* (Harvey, Byfield). BRAHE: *Bless this House.* WARLOCK: *Balulalow* (Baker, Ledger, organ). DIBDIN: *Tom Bowling.* BISHOP: *Home! Sweet Home!* BALFE: *Come into the Garden, Maude* (Tear, Previn). BRITTEN: *The Foggy, Foggy Dew; The Plough Boy* (Tear, Ledger). WALTON: *Façade: Popular Song* (Flanders, ASMF, Marriner).

Disc 2: TRAD.: *Greensleeves.* MORLEY: *It was a Lover and his Lass; O Mistress Mine.* ANON.: The Willow Song. JOHNSON: *Where the Bee Sucks; Full Fathoms Five* (Deller, Dupré, lute). BYRD: *Lullaby, My Sweet Little Baby; Elegy on the Death of Thomas Tallis; Ye Sacred Muses* (Chance, Fretwork). DOWLAND: *Sorrow Stay!; Can she Excuse My Wrongs; Awake Sweet Love; Woeful Heart* (Kirkby, Rooley, lute and orpharion); *Shall I Sue; Me, and None but Me; Flow My Tears* (Daniels, Miller, lute). PURCELL: *Fairest Isle; Music for a While; I Attempt from Love's Sickness; If Music be the Food of Love; An Evening Hymn* (Argenta & various accompanists). WARLOCK: *Yarmouth Fair.* MORTIMER: *Smuggler's Song.* CARTER: *Down Below* (Brannigan, Lush or Moore). SWANN: *A Transport of Delight; The Wart Hog* (Wallace, Swann); *The Hippopotomus Song* (Flanders and Swann).

🔗 ✪ (B) ★★★ EMI (ADD/DDD) 5 75926-2 (2).

This must easily be judged the finest and most comprehensive recital of English songs ever put on record – 57 in total – offering just about as much music as can be placed on a pair of CDs; each plays for just under eighty minutes. But not only is the quality remarkable, so too is the consistent quality. The concept was apparently Ray Hammond's, but the compilation was made and assembled by Richard Abram with unerring skill. Every item is a gem, every performance masterly, and the aligning of artist to repertoire is equally prescient.

There are of course two separate recitals here: the first offers a broad swathe of many of the greatest nineteenth- and twentieth-century English songs, the second looks back to the era of Elizbathan lute songs, juxtaposing the art of two celebrated counter-tenors (opening with Alfred Deller's lovely, artless account of 'Greensleeves') one tenor, Charles Daniels, and two sopranos, with Emma Kirkby nearly stealing the show with her infinitely touching account of Dowland's 'Woeful Heart', just as Dame Janet Baker does on the first disc with her lovely performance of Warlock's 'Balulalow'.

But, apart from Dame Janet (who opens the first collection enticingly), here it is the men who make their special mark – Sir Thomas Allen glowing-voiced in Quilter's 'Now Sleep the Crimson Petal',

Anthony Rolfe Johnson memorable in Warlock, Ian Bostridge ravishing in Vaughan Williams's 'Silent Noon', and Jonathan Lemalu's rich-toned 'Rollicum-rorum' of Finzi and Ireland's 'Sea Fever'. Robert Lloyd's pair of *Sea Songs* of Stanford could perhaps have been even more boisterous in the way John Shirley-Quirk presented them, but they are still irresistibly vigorous.

There are some inspired individual selections too: Frederick Harvey's 'Kashmiri Song', Robert Tear's Victorian ballads and his ravishingly sung 'Tom Bowling', while the two Britten folksong arrangements, the seductive 'Foggy, Foggy Dew' and infectiously spirited 'Plough Boy' are sheer joy. It is good that Geordie Owen Brannigan was not forgotten, a larger-than-life vocal personality with a richly resonant voice who often sang with a twinkle in his eye: he is heard at his finest here.

The inestimable Flanders and Swann are used to provide witty end-pieces for each disc: the 'Popular Song' from Walton's *Façade* for the first, and 'The Hippopotamus Song' as the grand finale, with an appropriately enthusiastic audience response. The remastering by John Hadden is first class and there is an excellent note by John Steane; this is a set which should be in every collection, however large or small.

'The Very Best of English Song with Orchestra' (Various Artists): Disc 1: ELGAR: *Sea Pictures* (J. Baker, LSO, Barbirolli); 2 *Songs: The Torch; The River, Op. 60.* G. BUTTERWORTH: *Love blows as the Wind Blows* (Tear, CBSO, Handley). VAUGHAN WILLIAMS: *Songs of Travel* (Allen, CBSO, Rattle); 5 *Mystical Songs* (Shirley-Quirk, King's College, Cambridge, Ch., ECO, Willcocks); *On Wenlock Edge* (Bostridge, LPO, Haitink). BRITTEN: *Serenade for Tenor, Horn & Strings* (Tear, Civil, N. Sinfonia, Marriner); *Les Illuminations* (Mark Ainsley, Britten Sinfonia, Cleobury); arr. of Folksongs: *The Bonnie Earl o'Moray; Oliver Cromwell* (Mackie, Scottish CO, Bedford). FINZI: *Dies natalis* (W. Brown, ECO, Finzi). STANFORD: *Songs of the Sea* (Luxon, Bournemouth Ch. & SO, Del Mar). DELIUS: *Sea Drift* (Noble, RLPO Ch. & O, Groves). PEEL: *In Summertime on Bredon.* SANDERSON: *Devonshire Cream and Cider* (Harvey, PO, Weldon).

🔗 (B) ★★★ EMI (ADD/DDD) 5 85896-2 (3).

Richard Abram's excellent compilation of English orchestral songs is complementary to his inspired selection of songs with piano. The programme is framed by two of the most beautiful English cycles on record. Dame Janet Baker's *Sea Pictures* with Barbirolli comes up as richly and memorably as ever, and Ian Bostridge's magically atmospheric performance of Vaughan Wlliams's *On Wenlock Edge* is ravishingly delicate in colour and accompanied with matching sensitivity by Bernard Haitink. John Shirley-Quirk, too, is at his finest in the Vaughan Williams *Mystical Songs*, and if in the *Songs of Travel* Sir Thomas Allen's voice is not as warmly flattered as with his recordings in the companion set with piano, his singing is both understanding and characterful.

In the two Britten cycles, *Les Illuminations* finds John Mark Ainsley echoing the example of Peter Pears, and in the *Serenade* Robert Tear is also very much in the Aldeburgh tradition while bringing a new and positive slant to each of the songs, with the Jonson 'Hymn to Diana' given extra jollity, thanks partly to the brilliant galumphing of Alan Civil on the horn. Neil Mackie then sings Britten's arrangement of 'The Bonny Earl o'Moray' with real passion, then throws off 'Oliver Cromwell' with lighthearted zest. Wilfred Brown richly captures the meditative mood of Finzi's *Dies natalis,* and if alongside this Sir Charles Groves's Liverpool account of Delius's *Sea Drift,* with John Noble as soloist, lacks something in evocation, Benjamin Luxon is in his element in all five of Stanford's *Songs of the Sea.* 'The Old Superb' is wonderfully boisterous, gaining much from the richly resonant contribution of the Bournemouth Chorus. Frederick Harvey provides the postlude with a characterful account of Graham Peel's setting of Housman's 'Summertime on Bredon', leading to a final vigorous lollipop, infectiously giving praise in a colloquial West Country accent to 'Devonshire Cream and Cider'.

Estampie, John Bryan

'*Under the Greenwood Tree*' (with Catterall, Derrick): WALTHER VON VOGELWEIDE: *Palästinalied.* RICHARD COEUR DE LION: *Ja nuis homs pris.* BLONDEL DE NESLE: *A l'entrant d'este.* Raimbault DE VAQUERIAS: *Kalenda Maya.* CORNYSHE: *Ah! Robin.* STONINGES: *Browning my Dear* (on the theme *The Leaves be Green*). GERVAISE: *4th Livre de Danceries: La Venissienne. 6th Livre de Danceries: Gailliarde.* PLAYFORD: *The Dancing Master: Greenwood; Nottingham Castle; Green Goose Fair; The Green Man.* SIMPSON: *Ricercar on Bonny Sweet Robin.* WEELKES: *When Kempe did Dance Alone, or Robin Hood, Maid Marian and Little John are Gone.* ANON.: *Novus miles sequitur; Estampie; Clap, clap un matin s'en aloit Robin; Robin Hood; The Wedding of Robin Hood; Under the Greenwood Tree; Sellenger's Round; Greensleeves* (lute and vocal versions); *Robin Hood and the Curtal Friar; Robin Hood and the Tanner; Robin Hood and Maid Marian; Sweet Angel of England* (to the tune *Bonny Sweet Robin*); *O Lusty May.*

(BB) ** Naxos 8.553442.

With John Bryan as music director and Graham Derrick as arranger and main performer, the early-music group Estampie here offer a well-devised group of dances and instrumental pieces, interspersed with songs, broadly inspired by the legend of Robin Hood and the ballad 'Robin is to the Greenwood Gone' in its various forms. That in turn leads to celebrations in song and dance of Maytime and the annual revival of the Green Man. Items range from a song attributed to King Richard the Lionheart in the twelfth century to four items drawn (in arrangements by Graham Derrick) from John Playford's collection *The Dancing Master,* in the seventeenth.

The sequence is most illuminating, but the performances, always tasteful, rather lack the bite and earthiness which can make medieval music so invigorating. The final item, a Scottish song, 'O Lusty May', is anything but that, though there and in the other songs the mezzo, Deborah Catterall, sings with a fresh, clear tone. Aptly intimate recorded sound.

Evans, Sir Geraint (baritone)

'*Arias and Sacred Songs*' (with (i) SRO, Balkwill; (ii) Shelley Singers, Lyrian Singers, Glendower Singers, BBC Welsh SO, Mansel Thomas). (i) HANDEL: *Berenice: Si trai ceppi. Semele: Leave me Radiant Light.* MOZART: *Le nozze di Figaro: Non più andrai. Don Giovanni: Madamina, il catalogo. L'oca del Cairo: Ogni momento. Die Zauberflöte: Der Vogelfänger.* BEETHOVEN: *Fidelio: Ha! welch'ein Augenblick!* LEONCAVALLO: *Pagliacci: Prologue.* DONIZETTI: *Don Pasquale: Un fuoco insolito.* VERDI: *Otello: Credo. Falstaff: Ehi! Paggio ... l'onore! Ladri.* BRITTEN: *A Midsummer Night's Dream: Bottom's Dream.* MUSSORGSKY: *Boris Godunov: Tchelkalov's Aria.* (ii) MENDELSSOHN: *Elijah: Lord God of Abraham; Is not His Word like a Fire?* HANDEL: *Judas Maccabaeus: Arm, Arm ye Brave. Messiah: The Trumpet shall Sound.* ROSSINI: *Requiem: Pro peccatis.*

⊕ (BB) *** Belart (ADD) 461 492-2.

This is a marvellous display of wide-ranging virtuosity, of artistic bravura such as we know from almost any performance that this ebullient and lovable singer gave. Part of Evans's mastery lay in the way he could convey the purest comedy, even drawing laughs without ever endangering the musical line through excessive buffoonery. His Mozart characters are almost unmatchable – Figaro, Leporello, Papageno – while it is good to be reminded that here is a singer who could be a formidable Iago as well as the most complete Falstaff of his day. Good accompaniment and recording, with a richly atmospheric orchestral backing, of one of Britain's greatest singers at the peak of his form.

Evans, Nancy (mezzo-soprano)

'*The Comely Mezzo*' (with various accompanists including Newton, Moore, Foss, piano): A. BEECHAM: *Outward Bound; Otello: Willow Song; O Mistress Mine.* DELIUS: *Indian Love Song; Irmelin Rose.* PARRY: *Armida's Garden.* BURY: *There is a Lady.* VAUGHAN WILLIAMS: *The Water Mill; How Can the Tree but Wither?* WARLOCK: *Rest, Sweet*

Nymphs; St Anthony of Padua. HAGEMAN: *Do not Go my Love.* GURNEY: *The Scribe; Nine of the Clock O; All Night Under the Moon; Blaweary; You are my Sky; Latmian Shepherd.* FALLA: *7 Spanish Popular Songs.* BLISS: *Pastoral: Pigeon Song.* D'HARDELOT: *Wait.* FISHER: *An Old Violin.* ELGAR: *Land of Hope and Glory* (with Noble & chorus).

(BB) (**(*)) Dutton mono CDBP 9723.

As Alan Blyth's note rightly says, Nancy Evans was for sixty years 'one of the best-loved personalities on the British musical scene', one who followed up her singing career with untiring work as a teacher, administrator and adjudicator, helping generations of young singers. She was married in turn to the recording producer Walter Legge and to Eric Crozier, collaborator with Britten on such operas as *Albert Herring* and *Billy Budd*. It was for Nancy Evans that Britten wrote the role of Nancy in *Albert Herring*, and in his preceding chamber opera, *The Rape of Lucretia*, Evans alternated with Kathleen Ferrier in the title role. When far too few of her recordings have appeared on CD, it is good to welcome this collection of rarities, even though the close balance of most of the pre-war recordings takes the bloom from the voice, giving it a raw quality in places and undermining the beauty. Nonetheless, the artistry and technical security come out from first to last, whether in the songs by Adrian Beecham (with the composer's father, Sir Thomas, at the piano), a sequence of songs by Ivor Gurney or the well-known Falla songs, which she delivers with Spanish fire. Most beautiful is 'The Pigeon Song' from Bliss's *Pastoral*, with accompaniment for flute and strings, set in a more open acoustic, and the programme ends with two ballads and a stirring account of Elgar's *Land of Hope and Glory* with chorus and military band accompaniment.

I Fagiolini, Robert Hollingsworth with David Miller (lute)

The Triumphs of Oriana (compiled by Thomas Morley): WILBYE: *The Lady Oriana.* NICHOLSON: *Sing, Shepherds All.* MUNDY: *Lightly she Whipped o'er the Dales.* CARLTON: *Calm was the Air and Clear the Sky.* HOLBORNE: *Lute Fantasias Nos. 2 & 3; Galliard No. 8 (Clark's Galliard).* EAST: *Hence Stars too Dim of Light.* CAVENDISH: *Come, Gentle Swains and Shepherds' Dainty Daughters.* KIRBYE: *With Angel's Face and Brightness.* MARSON: *The Nymphs and Shepherds Danced.* HOLBORNE: *Galliard.* BENNET: *All Creatures Now are Merry Minded.* FARMER: *Fair Nymphs, I Heard Calling.* R. JONES: *Fair Oriana, Seeming to Wink at Folly.* TOMKINS: *The Fauns and Satyrs Tripping.* E. GIBBONS: *Round About her Cherret; Long Live Fair Oriana.* COBBOLD: *With Wreaths of Rose and Laurel.* HOLMES: *Thus Bonny-boots the Birthday Celebrated.* MORLEY: *Arise, Awake, Awake; Hard by a Crystal Fountain.* HUNT: *Hark! Did ye Ever Hear so Sweet a Singing?* MILTON: *Fair Oriana in the Morn.* NORCOME: *With Angel's Face and Brightness.* JOHNSON: *Come Blessed Bud.* BYRD: *Galliard.* HILTON: *Fair Oriana, Beauty's Queen.* LISLEY: *Fair Cytherea Presents her Doves.* WEELKES: *As Vesta was from Latmos Hill Descending.*
*** Chan. 0682.

This outstanding collection of madrigals in praise of Oriana (a poetic image for Queen Elizabeth I), compiled by Thomas Morley in 1601, has been seriously neglected on disc for many years, making this fine new version from I Fagiolini very welcome. Drawing on the talents of a wide range of his friends and contemporaries, including Wilbye, Tomkins and Weelkes, as well as his own work, Morley presents a superb overview of the art of the Elizabethan madrigal at its peak. Though the talented singers of I Fagiolini have a tendency to squeeze notes in pursuit of authenticity, this is refined singing, polished and expressive. The sequence of twenty-five madrigals is nicely punctuated by lute solos played by David Miller, four by Holborne, one by Byrd. The recording is both warm and immediate in an intimate acoustic.

Ferrier, Kathleen (contralto)

Kathleen Ferrier Collection (complete on 10 CDs).

Volume 1: GLUCK: *Orfeo ed Euridice* (abridged) (with soloists, Glyndebourne Festival Ch., Southern PO, Stiedry).

Volume 2: BACH: *St Matthew Passion*: Arias & choruses (with soloists, Bach Ch., Jacques O, Jacques).

Volume 3: PERGOLESI: *Stabat Mater* (orch. Scott) (with Taylor, Nottingham Oriana Ch., Boyd Neel String O, Henderson). Arias: GLUCK: *Orpheus and Euridice: What is Life?* HANDEL: *Rodelinda: Art thou Troubled? Serse: Ombra mai fu.* BACH: *St Matthew Passion: Have Mercy, Lord, on me* (all with LSO or Nat. SO, Sargent). *Cantata No. 11: Ah, Tarry Yet, my Dearest Saviour.* MENDELSSOHN: *Elijah: O Woe unto Them; O Rest in the Lord.*

Volume 4: Lieder: SCHUMANN: *Frauenliebe und Leben* (song-cycle); *Volksliedchen; Widmung* (with Newmark, piano). BRAHMS: *Sapphische Ode; Botschaft.* SCHUBERT: *Gretchen am Spinnrade; Die junge Nonne; An die Musik; Der Musensohn* (with Spurr, piano); *Ganymed; Du liebst mich nicht; Lachen und Weinen* (with Britten, piano). GRUBER: *Silent Night.* TRAD.: *O Come All Ye Faithful* (with Boyd Neel String O, Neel).

Volume 5: BBC Broadcasts (1949–53): BRAHMS: *4 Serious Songs, Op. 121* (with BBC SO, Sargent). CHAUSSON: *Poème de l'amour et de la mer, Op. 19* (with Hallé O, Barbirolli). Recital (with Lush, piano): FERGUSON: *Discovery* (song-cycle).

WORDSWORTH: *Red Skies; The Wind; Clouds.*
RUBBRA: *3 Psalms: Nos. 6, O Lord rebuke me not;
23, The Lord is my shepherd; 150, Praise ye the Lord.*

Volume 6: Broadcast recitals: English and German
songs: STANFORD: *The Fairy Lough; A Soft Day.*
PARRY: *Love is a Bable.* VAUGHAN WILLIAMS:
Silent Noon. BRIDGE: *Go not, Happy Day.*
WARLOCK: *Sleep; Pretty Ring-time.* Folksongs, arr.
BRITTEN: *O, Waly, Waly; Come you not from
Newcastle?* arr. HUGHES: *Kitty, my Love* (with
Stone, piano). PURCELL: *From Silent Shades: Mad
Bess of Bedlam. The Fairy Queen: Hark! the Echoing
Air.* HANDEL: *Atalanta: Like as the Love-lorn Turtle.
Admeto: How Changed the Vision.* Lieder: WOLF:
*Verborgenheit; Der Gärtner; Auf ein altes Bild; Auf
einer Wanderung.* JENSEN: *Altar* (with Spurr,
piano). BACH: *Vergiss mein nicht; Ach dass nicht die
letzte Stunde* (with Silver, harpsichord). *Bist du bei
mir* (with Newmark, piano).

Volume 7: Bach and Handel arias (with LPO,
Boult): Arias from BACH: *Mass in B min.; St
Matthew Passion; St John Passion.* HANDEL:
Samson; Messiah; Judas Maccabaeus.

Volume 8: *'Blow the Wind Southerly'* British songs
& folksongs (with Spurr or (i) Newmark, piano):
TRAD., arr. WHITTAKER: *Ma Bonny Lad; The Keel
Row; Blow the Wind Southerly.* arr. HUGHES: *I have
a Bonnet Trimmed with Blue; I Know Where I'm
Going; I will Walk with my Love; The Stuttering
Lovers; Down by the Salley Gardens; The Lover's
Curse.* arr. SHARP: *My Boy Willie.* arr. ROBERTON:
(i) *The Fidgety Bairn.* arr. JACOBSON: (i) *Ca' the
Yowes.* arr. BRITTEN: *O Waly, Waly.* arr. WARLOCK:
Willow, Willow. arr. GREW: *Have you Seen but a
Whyte Lillie Grow?.* arr. QUILTER: *Ye Banks and
Braes; Drink to me Only; Now Sleeps the Crimson
Petal; The Fair House of Joy; To Daisies; Over the
Mountains.*

Volume 9: Broadcast Edinburgh Festival recital,
1949. Lieder (with Walter, piano): SCHUBERT: *Die
junge Nonne. Rosamunde: Romance. Du bist mich
nicht; Der Tod und das Mädchen; Suleika; Du bist
die Ruh'.* BRAHMS: *Immer leiser wird mein
Schlummer; Der Tod das ist die kuhle Nacht;
Botschaft; Von ewiger Liebe.* SCHUMANN:
Frauenliebe und Leben (song-cycle), *Op. 42.*

Volume 10: MAHLER: *3 Rückert Lieder* (with VPO,
Walter). BRAHMS: *Alto Rhapsody, Op. 53* (with LPO
Ch., LPO, Kraus); *2 Songs with Viola, Op. 91* (with
Spurr, piano, Gilbert, viola). *Vier ernste Gesänge,
Op. 121* (with Newmark, piano).

(B) (**(*)) Decca mono 475 6060 (10).

Decca's first Ferrier anthology was on seven LPs, and
later a shorter survey appeared on four cassettes. The
CD coverage, which first appeared in the early 1990s
at mid-price, is on ten CDs, which now come in a

Collector's Edition at bargain price, although now
the discs are no longer available separately. Curiously, Mahler's *Das Lied von der Erde* is not included,
but that is available separately in an improved transfer, and the disc includes the three *Rückert Lieder*
(466 576-2).

Unfortunately Decca seemed not always to be able
to preserve their 78rpm masters without deteriora-
tion, which the CD transfers can cometimes emphasize. Even so, there is much treasure here, and these
records readily demonstrate not only Ferrier's star
quality and amazing range but also the consistency
with which the radiant vocal quality lit up almost
everything she recorded.

The single-disc selections from Bach's *St Matthew
Passion* and Gluck's *Orfeo ed Euridice* (recorded in
1947–8) are a mixed blessing – of interest only for
her personal contribution, and it might have been
better to extract the individual arias, which are sung
in English with radiant vocal freshness. The Bach
items include 'Master and my Lord ... Grief for Sin',
'Have Mercy, Lord on Me' and 'O Gracious God ... If
my Tears be Unavailing'. They show that from the
start there was a projection of forceful personality
and a natural musicianship that was uniquely powerful. The soprano/alto duet with Elsie Suddaby
('Behold my Saviour now is Taken') is interrupted by
a mushy chorus, and the arias 'Ah! now my Saviour
is Gone ... Have Mercy, Lord on Me', 'Ah Golgotha! ...
See Ye!' and 'Sweet the Saviour's Outstretched Hands'
again bring the ill-focused choral sound, although
here Ferrier's contribution rides over everything.
Whatever the recording flaws, the singer's commanding presence lights up the performances, and it is
fascinating to play these excerpts alongside the
inspired performances recorded only five years later
with Boult in order to see the development.

Similarly, the much-abridged version of Gluck's
opera, recorded soon after the Glyndebourne performances of 1947, is valuable only for Ferrier's magnificent contribution, even if it is obvious that this
was only a first attempt by a great artist to scale a
formidable part. At that time she was not entirely at
ease singing in Italian, and when Fritz Stiedry chose
an absurdly fast tempo for the big aria, *Che farò*, she
was less impressive – in spite of the vocal freshness –
than in the later version with Sargent, which is
included in Volume 3.

The 1946 Pergolesi *Stabat Mater* comes off remarkably well, mainly because of Roy Henderson's excellence as a choral trainer, and the recording was good
for its period and still sounds lively. This is included
on Volume 3, with more Ferrier favourites, reasonably well transferred, including Gluck's 'What is
Life?' (*Che farò*), Handel's 'Art thou Troubled?' and
Mendelssohn's 'O Rest in the Lord' (from *Elijah*), all
showing the glorious voice at its most nobly resonant.

As Volume 4 demonstrates, Ferrier was a deeply
impressive Lieder singer. Had she lived, her art would
undoubtedly have deepened considerably beyond

what is displayed here. There are more tender, more loving emotions in Schumann's *Frauenliebe und Leben* than Ferrier was able to convey in 1950, and she is not helped by the limited accompaniment of John Newmark. Yet she is never less than compelling, and her Schubert and Wolf bring a natural warmth and dedication and a lightness of touch that are disarming; any shortcomings are here outweighed by the beauty of the voice. She identifies readily with *Die junge Nonne* and there is a special glow for *An die Musik*, while the Brahms songs are beautifully sung. Generally the sound here is very good and background noises are not too distracting. The three items accompanied by Benjamin Britten come from a BBC broadcast of 1952: the sound here is more opaque, and in *Du liebst mich nicht* the recording fades out before the end. Kathleen Ferrier had a marvellously robust Lancashire sense of fun and she would surely have found a natural riposte to suit such a minor calamity. The recital ends with two very touching carols, recorded with Boyd Neel for the Christmas market in 1948.

Volume 5 is very much a curate's egg. The performance of the *Four Serious Songs* in English with Sargent comes from a BBC broadcast of 1949, while the Barbirolli–Hallé performance of Chausson has a similar 1951 source. The quality is poor, the surfaces are noisy; indeed, the general effect in the Chausson is little short of execrable. But the rest of the CD offers a broadcast recital of 12 January 1952 with results that are more than acceptable. The rare Howard Ferguson cycle, the even rarer Wordsworth songs, of which 'Clouds' is totally memorable, and the very characteristic Rubbra Psalm settings show the singer at her most searching and imaginative, and they are well accompanied by Ernest Lush. Here the voice has excellent presence, and there are only occasional clicks from the acetate original.

Volume 6 is also strongly recommendable. Again one discovers that the magic of Ferrier's voice was never so potent as when she was singing English songs, and the opening group, with the highly sympathetic Frederick Stone – taken from a broadcast recital given just over a year before the singer's untimely death – brings a natural spontaneity and projection of warm feeling that are irresistible, especially when the transfers are generally of such vivid immediacy. The second recital on this disc derives from a Norwegian broadcast, made three years earlier, with a rather noisier background, but this group is famous for Jensen's *Altar*, which Ferrier introduces herself with apologetic charm. The bonuses include private recordings of two rare Bach items with harpsichord, where the surface noise is very distracting, and then the programme end with a glorious *Bist du bei mir*, where the background miraculously abates. (This comes, remarkably, from a 1950 Voice of America recording held in the Library of Congress.)

Ferrier's superb (1952) recording swansong, combining Bach and Handel arias (in Volume 7), was lovingly accompanied by Boult and the LPO. John Culshaw produced this disc and ensured that at least one Decca CD was technically fully worthy of Kathleen's art. This disc and Volume 8 were each given a ❀ when they were available separately.

The other collection which is unmissable (and which is generally well engineered) is her recital of British songs and folksongs. It is given the title of the unaccompanied lyric by which she is most fondly remembered by the greater musical public, 'Blow the Wind Southerly'. Even that transfer is not completely free from distortion, but the sense of the singer's presence is unforgettable. That recital contains much that is utterly magical – Ferrier's way with folksongs brought a simple innocence that few other singers have approached – but it is a very special, wonderfully tender performance of 'I will Walk with my Love', in which the gloriously gently vocal halo she places gently round the climactic word, 'boy', is achingly beautiful.

The 1949 Edinburgh Festival recital is technically less than perfect but still makes enjoyable listening. The piano sound may be a bit hazy, but this historic occasion gives a wonderful idea of the intensity of a live Ferrier recital. Her account here of *Frauenliebe und Leben* is freer and even more compelling than the performance she recorded earlier. Walter's accompaniments may not be flawless, but they are comparably inspirational. The recital is introduced by a brief talk on Walter and the Edinburgh Festival given by Ferrier, so welcome when the *Altar* introduction is so brief. The CD transfer does not seek to 'enhance' the sound, but most of the background has been cleaned up; there are moments when the vocal focus slips, but the ear readily adjusts.

The vintage Brahms/Mahler coupling on Volume 10 brings together Ferrier's 1948 recording of the *Alto Rhapsody*, a glowing performance which culminates in a heart-warming final section. The *Four Serious Songs*, issued three years later, are even more intense, with the voice more suited to these dark, weighty songs than to most Lieder; and this comment applies also to the three *Rückert Lieder*, heartfelt and monumental, exploratory in the world of Mahler. Here the voice emerges realistically, but the CD transfer is less kind to the orchestral strings. Throughout the series back-up documentation is adequate rather than generous, but the set remains a splendid tribute to one of the greatest English singers whose career was tragically cut off by cancer when she was at the height of her powers.

'*The World of Kathleen Ferrier*', Volume 1: TRAD.: *Blow the Wind Southerly; The Keel Row; Ma Bonny Lad; Kitty my Love.* arr. BRITTEN: *Come you not from Newcastle.* HANDEL: *Rodelinda: Art thou Troubled? Serse: Ombra mai fù.* GLUCK: *Orfeo ed Euridice: What is life?* MENDELSSOHN: *Elijah: Woe unto them; O rest in the Lord.* BACH: *St Matthew Passion: Have mercy, Lord, on me.* SCHUBERT: *An die Musik; Gretchen am Spinnrade; Die junge*

Nonne; Der Musensohn. BRAHMS: Sapphische Ode; Botschaft. MAHLER: Rückert Lieder: Um Mitternacht.

⊶ ✹ (M) (★★★) Decca mono 430 096-2.

This selection, revised and expanded from the original LP issue, admirably displays Kathleen Ferrier's range, from the delightfully fresh folksongs to Mahler's Um Mitternacht in her celebrated recording with Bruno Walter and the VPO. The noble account of 'O Rest in the Lord' is one of the essential items now added, together with an expansion of the Schubert items (Die junge Nonne and An die Musik are especially moving). The CD transfers are remarkably trouble-free and the opening unaccompanied 'Blow the Wind Southerly' has uncanny presence. The recital plays for 65 minutes and fortunately there are few if any technical reservations to be made here about the sound quality.

'The World of Kathleen Ferrier', Volume 2: TRAD.: Ye Banks and Braes; Drink to me Only (both arr. QUILTER); I have a Bonnet Trimmed with Blue; Down by the Salley Gardens; The Stuttering Lovers (all arr. HUGHES). PURCELL: The Fairy Queen: Hark! the Echoing Air. HANDEL: Atalanta: Like the Love-lorn Turtle. GLUCK: Orfeo ed Euridice: Che puro ciel. MAHLER: Rückert Lieder: Ich bin der Welt abhanden gekommen. SCHUMANN: Frauenliebe und Leben: Er, der Herrlichste von allen. BRAHMS: Geistliches Wiegenlied; Von ewiger Liebe. SCHUBERT: Du bist die Ruh'; Rosamunde: Romance. BACH: Mass in B min.: Agnus Dei. HANDEL: Messiah: He was Despised.

(M) (★★★) Decca mono 448 055-2.

Volume 2 offers a comparable mixture, opening with more delightful folksongs, notably the charming 'Stuttering Lovers', although it is 'Ye Banks and Braes' and 'Drink to me Only' that show the full richness of this glorious voice. Che puro ciel stands out among the opera arias for its simple eloquence, and the Brahms Geistliches Wiegenlied, with its somewhat wan viola obbligato, is gently ravishing. The passionate Du bist die Ruh', the Rosamunde Romance and Von ewiger Liebe come from a BBC acetate disc of her 1949 Edinburgh Festival recital with Bruno Walter at the piano, and here there is some uneven background noise and the quality deteriorates in the Brahms song. But the CD closes with one of her very last recordings, her unforgettably poignant 'He was Despised', with those words given an uncanny presence.

'What is Life?' (with Spurr or Newmark, piano; Jacques Orchestra, Jacques; Nat. SO or LSO, Sargent; Boyd Neel Orchestra, Neel or Henderson): TRAD.: Blow the Wind Southerly; The Keel Row; Down by the Salley Gardens; Ma Bonny Lad; Ca' the Yowes. SCHUBERT: Die junge Nonne; Gretchen am Spinnrade. SCHUMANN: Volksliedchen; Widmung. BACH: St Matthew Passion; Grief for Sin; Have

Mercy Lord; Cantata No. 11: Ah, Tarry Yet, my Dearest Saviour. GLUCK: Orfeo: What is Life? HANDEL: Xerxes: Ombra mai fu; Rodalinda: Art thou Troubled? PERGOLESI: Stabat Mater; Fac et portem. MENDELSSOHN: Elijah: Woe unto Them; O Rest in the Lord. GRUBER: Silent Night.

(BB) (★★★) Regis mono RRC 1057.

This disc does not replace the two Decca Volumes of The World of Kathleen Ferrier, where the recordings have been transferred with greater range and, as in the first item, a remarkable presence. But for the Regis anthology, offering many of the same recordings, Tony Watts has taken great care to smooth out the sound from the original masters: it is always warm and pleasing, the vocal quality rich, and the extraneous noises have been virtually eliminated. So if you want an inexpensive single disc assembling some of the very finest records made by this great artist, comfortably presented (and in some items, Ombra mai fu for instance, the quality is particularly warm and beautiful), this disc can be cordially recommended. And it is good to have Ferrier's lovely performance of the most magical carol of all, Grüber's 'Silent Night'.

Fischer-Dieskau, Dietrich (baritone)

'Fischer-Dieskau Lieder Edition'

SCHUBERT: Lieder (with Moore, piano): Volume 1 (1811–17); Volume 2 (1817–28); Volume 3: Song-cycles: Die schöne Müllerin; Schwanengesang; Winterreise.

(B) ★★★ DG (ADD) 437 214-2 (21).

Lieder, Volume 1 (1811–17): Ein Leichenfantasie; Der Vatermörder (1811); Der Jüngling am Bache (1812); Totengräberlied; Die Schatten; Sehnsucht; Verklärung; Pensa, che questo istante (1813); Der Taucher (1813–15); Andenken; Geisternähe; Erinnerung; Trost, An Elisa; Die Betende; Lied aus der Ferne; Der Abend; Lied der Liebe; Erinnerungen; Adelaide; An Emma; Romanze: Ein Fräulein klagt' im finstern Turm; An Laura, als sie Klopstocks Auferstehungslied sang; Der Geistertanz; Das Mädchen aus der Fremde; Nachtgesang; Trost in Tränen; Schäfers Klagelied; Sehnsucht; Am See (1814); Auf einen Kirchhof; Als ich sie erröten sah; Das Bild; Der Mondabend (1815); Lodas Gespenst (1816); Der Sänger (1815); Die Erwartung (1816); Am Flusse; An Mignon; Nähe des Geliebten; Sängers Morgenlied; Amphiaraos; Das war ich; Die Sterne; Vergebliche Liebe; Liebesrausch; Sehnsucht der Liebe; Die erste Liebe; Trinklied; Stimme der Liebe; Naturgenuss; An die Freude; Der Jüngling am Bache; An den Mond; Die Mainacht; An die Nachtigall; An die Apfelbäume; Seufzer; Liebeständelei; Der Liebende; Der Traum; Die Laube; Meeres Stille; Grablied; Das Finden; Wanderers Nachtlied; Der Fischer; Erster Verlust; Die Erscheinung; Die

Täuschung; Der Abend; Geist der Liebe; Tischlied; Der Liedler; Ballade; Abends unter der Linde; Die Mondnacht; Huldigung; Alles um Liebe; Das Geheimnis; An den Frühling; Die Bürgschaft; Der Rattenfänger; Der Schatzgräber; Heidenröslein; Bundeslied; An den Mond; Wonne der Wehmut; Wer kauft Liebesgötter? (1815); *Der Goldschmiedsgesell* (1817); *Der Morgenkuss; Abendständchen: An Lina; Morgenlied: Willkommen, rotes Morgenlicht; Der Weiberfreund; An die Sonne; Tischlerlied; Totenkranz für ein Kind; Abendlied; Die Fröhlichkeit; Lob des Tokayers; Furcht der Geliebten; Das Rosenband; An Sie; Die Sommernacht; Die frühen Gräber; Dem Unendlichen; Ossians Lied nach dem Falle Nathos; Das Mädchen von Inistore; Labetrank der Liebe; An die Geliebte; Mein Gruss an den Mai; Skolie – Lasst im Morgenstrahl des Mai'n; Die Sternenwelten; Die Macht der Liebe; Das gestörte Glück; Die Sterne; Nachtgesang; An Rosa I: Warum bist du nicht hier?; An Rosa II: Rosa, denkst du an mich?; Schwanengesang; Der Zufriedene; Liane; Augenlied; Geistes-Gruss; Hoffnung; An den Mond; Rastlose Liebe; Erlkönig* (1815); *Der Schmetterling; Die Berge* (1819); *Genügsamkeit; An die Natur* (1815); *Klage; Morgenlied; Abendlied; Der Flüchtling; Laura am Klavier; Entzückung an Laura; Die vier Weltalter; Pflügerlied; Die Einsiedelei; An die Harmonie; Die Herbstnacht; Lied: Ins stille Land; Der Herbstabend; Der Entfernten; Fischerlied; Sprache der Liebe; Abschied von der Harfe; Stimme der Liebe; Entzückung; Geist der Liebe; Klage: Der Sonne steigt; Julius an Theone; Klage: Dein Silber schien durch Eichengrün; Frühlingslied; Auf den Tod einer Nachtigall; Die Knabenzeit; Winterlied; Minnelied; Die frühe Liebe; Blumenlied; Der Leidende; Seligkeit; Erntelied; Das grosse Halleluja; Die Gestirne; Die Liebesgötter; An den Schlaf; Gott im Frühling; Der gute Hirt; Die Nacht; Fragment aus dem Aeschylus* (1816); *An die untergehende Sonne* (1816–17); *An mein Klavier; Freude der Kinderjahre; Das Heimweh; An den Mond; An Chloen; Hochzeitlied; In der Mitternacht; Trauer der Liebe; Die Perle; Liedesend; Orpheus; Abschied; Rückweg; Alte Liebe rostet nie; Gesänge des Harfners aus Goethes Wilhelm Meister: Harfenspieler I: Wer sich der Einsamkeit ergibt; Harfenspieler II: An die Türen will ich schleichen; Harfenspieler III: Wer nie sein Brot mit Tränen. Der König in Thule; Jägers Abendlied; An Schwager Kronos; Der Sänger am Felsen; Lied: Ferne von der grossen Stadt; Der Wanderer; Der Hirt; Lied eines Schiffers an die Dioskuren; Geheimnis; Zum Punsche; Am Bach im Frühling* (1816); *An eine Quelle* (1817); *Bei dem Grabe, meines Vaters; Am Grabe Anselmos; Abendlied; Zufriedenheit; Herbstlied; Skolie: Mädchen entsiegelten; Lebenslied; Lieden der Trennung* (1816); *Alinde; An die Laute* (1827); *Frohsinn; Die Liebe; Trost; Der Schäfer und der Reiter* (1817); *Lob der Tränen* (1821); *Der Alpenjäger; Wie Ulfru fischt; Fahrt zum Hades; Schlaflied; Die Blumensprache; Die abgeblühte Linde; Der Flug der*

Zeit; Der Tod und das Mädchen; Das Lied vom Reifen; Täglich zu singen; Am Strome; Philoktet; Memnon; Auf dem See; Ganymed; Der Jüngling und der Tod; Trost im Liede (1817).

(B) *** DG (ADD) 437 215-2 (9).

Lieder, Volume 2 (1817–28): *An die Musik; Pax vobiscum; Hänflings Liebeswerbung; Auf der Donau; Der Schiffer; Nach einem Gewitter; Fischerlied; Das Grab; Der Strom; An den Tod; Abschied; Die Forelle; Gruppe aus dem Tartarus; Elysium; Atys; Erlafsee; Der Alpenjäger; Der Kampf; Der Knabe in der Wiege* (1817); *Auf der Riesenkoppe; An den Mond in einer Herbstnacht; Grablied für die Mutter; Einsamkeit; Der Blumenbrief; Das Marienbild* (1818); *Litanei auf das Fest Allerseelen* (1816); *Blondel zu Marien; Das Abendrot; Sonett I: Apollo, lebet noch dein Hold verlangen; Sonett II: Allein, nachdenken wie gelähmt vom Krampfe; Sonett III: Nunmehr, da Himmel, Erde schweigt; Vom Mitleiden Mariä* (1818); *Die Gebüsche; Der Wanderer; Abendbilder; Himmelsfunken; An die Freunde; Sehnsucht; Hoffnung; Der Jüngling am Bache; Hymne I: Wenige wissen das Geheimnis der Liebe; Hymne II: Wenn ich ihn nur hab; Hymne III: Wenn alle untreu werden; Hymne IV: Ich sag es jedem; Marie; Beim Winde; Die Sternennächte; Trost; Nachtstück; Prometheus; Strophe aus Die Götter Griechenlands* (1819); *Nachthymne; Die Vögel; Der Knabe; Der Fluss; Abendröte; Der Schiffer; Die Sterne; Morgenlied* (1820); *Frühlingsglaube* (1822); *Des Fräuleins Liebeslauschen* (1820); *Orest auf Tauris* (1817); *Der entsühnte Orest; Freiwilliges Versinken; Der Jüngling auf dem Hügel* (1820); *Sehnsucht* (1817); *Der zürnenden Diana; Im Walde* (1820); *Die gefangenen Sänger; Der Unglückliche; Versunken; Geheimes; Grenzen der Menschheit* (1821); *Der Jüngling an der Quelle* (1815); *Der Blumen Schmerz* (1821); *Sei mir gegrüsst; Herr Josef Spaun, Assessor in Linz; Der Wachtelschlag Ihr Grab; Nachtviolen; Heliopolis I: Im kalten, rauhen Norden; Heliopolis II: Fels auf Felsen hingewälzet; Selige Welt; Schwanengesang: Wie klage'ich's aus; Du liebst mich nicht; Die Liebe hat gelogen; Todesmusik; Schatzgräbers Begehr; An die Leier; Im Haine; Der Musensohn; An die Entfernte; Am Flusse; Willkommen und Abschied* (1822); *Wandrers Nachtlied: Ein Gleiches; Der zürnende Barde* (1823); *Am See* (1822/3); *Viola; Drang in die Ferne; Der Zwerg; Wehmut; Lied: Die Mutter Erde; Auf dem Wasser zu singen; Pilgerweise; Das Geheimnis; Der Pilgrim; Dass sie hier gewesen; Du bist die Ruh'; Lachen und Weinen; Greisengesang* (1823); *Dithyrambe; Der Sieg; Abendstern; Auflösung; Gondelfahrer* (1824); *Glaube, Hoffnung und Liebe* (1828); *Im Abendrot; Der Einsame* (1824); *Des Sängers Habe; Totengräbers Heimwehe; Der blinde Knabe; Nacht und Träume; Normans Gesang; Lied des gefangenen Jägers; Im Walde; Auf der Bruck; Das Heimweh; Die Allmacht; Fülle der Liebe; Wiedersehn; Abendlied für die Entfernte; Szene I aus*

dem Schauspiel Lacrimas; Am mein Herz; Der liebliche Stern (1825); *Im Jänner 1817 (Tiefes Leid); Am Fenster; Sehnsucht; Im Freien; Fischerweise; Totengräberweise; Im Frühling; Lebensmut; Um Mitternacht; Uber Wildemann* (1826); *Romanze des Richard Löwenherz* (1827); *Trinklied; Ständchen; Hippolits Lied; Gesang (An Sylvia); Der Wanderer an den Mond; Das Zügenglöcklein; Bei dir allein; Irdisches Glück; Wiegenlied* (1826); *Der Vater mit dem Kind; Jägers Liebeslied; Schiffers Scheidelied; L'incanto degli occhi; Il traditor deluso; Il modo di prender moglie; Das Lied im Grünen; Das Weinen; Vor meiner Wiege; Der Wallensteiner Lanznecht beim Trunk; Der Kreuzzug; Das Fischers Liebesglück* (1827); *Der Winterabend; Die Sterne; Herbst; Widerschein* (1828); *Abschied von der Erde* (1825/6).
(B) ★★★ DG (ADD) 437 225-2 (9)

SCHUMANN: Lieder (with Eschenbach, piano): *Myrthen, Op. 25/1–3; 5–8; 13; 15–19; 21–2; 25–6. Lieder und Gesänge, Op. 27/1–5; Op. 51/4; Op. 77/1 & 5; Op. 96/1–3; Op. 98/2, 4, 6 & 8; Op. 127/2–3. Gedichte, Op. 30/1–3; Op. 119/2. Gesänge, Op. 31/1 & 3; Op. 83/1 & 3; Op. 89/1–5; Op. 95/2; Op. 107/3 & 6; Op. 142/1, 2 & 4; Schön Hedwig, Op. 106. 6 Gedichte aus dem Liederbuch eines Malers, Op. 36. 12 Gedichte aus Rückerts Liebesfrühling, Op. 37. Liederkreis, Op. 39. 5 Lieder, Op. 40. Romanzen und Balladen, Op. 45/1–3; Op. 49/1–2; Op. 53/1–3; Op. 64/3; Belsatzar, Op. 57. Liederkreis, Op. 24. 12 Gedichte, Op. 35. Dichterliebe, Op. 48. Spanisches Liederspiel, Op. 74/6, 7 & 10. Liederalbum für die Jugend, Op. 79; Der Handschuh, Op. 87. 6 Gedichte von Nikolaus Lenau und Requiem (Anhang, No. 7), Op. 90. Minnespiel, Op. 101. 4 Husarenlieder, Op. 117. Heitere Gesänge, Op. 125/1–3. Spanische Liebeslieder, Op. 138/2, 3, 5 & 7. Balladen, Op. 122/1–2. Sechs frühe Lieder, op. posth.* (WoO 21).
(B) ★★★ DG (ADD) 445 660-2 (6).

BRAHMS: Lieder (with Barenboim, piano): *Gesänge, Op. 3/2–6; Op. 6/2–6; Mondnacht, Op. 7/1–4 & 6; Op. 43/1–4; Op. 46/1–4; Op. 70/1–4; Op. 71/1–5; Op. 72/2–5. Lieder und Romanzen, Op. 14/1–8; Gedichte, Op. 19/1–2, 3 & 5; Lieder und Gesänge, Op. 32/1–9; Op. 57/2–8; Op. 58/1–8; Op. 59/1–4, 6–7; Op. 63/1–9; Romanzen, Op. 33/1–15; Lieder, Op. 47/1–4; Op. 48/1, 2, 5–7; Op. 49/1–5; Op. 85/1–2, 4–6; Op. 86/2–5; Op. 94/1–3 & 5; Op. 95/2, 3 & 7; Op. 96/1–4; Op. 97/1–3, 5–6; Op. 105/4–5; Op. 106/1–5; Op. 107/1–2 & 4. Neuen Gesänge, Op. 69/3, 5 & 7. Vier ernste Gesänge, Op. 121.*
(B) ★★★ DG (ADD) 447 501-2 (6).

R. STRAUSS: Lieder (with Sawallisch, piano): *5 kleine Lieder, Op. 69; Lieder, Op. 10/2–7; Op. 15/2 & 5; Op. 17/2; Op. 19/1–6; Op. 26/1–2; Op. 27/1, 3 & 4; Op. 29/1 & 3; Op. 31/4; Op. 32/1–5; Op. 36/1 & 4; Op. 37/1–2, 5–6; Op. 49/6; Op. 56/1 & 3; Op. 67/6. Schlichte Weisen, Op. 21; Vier Gesänge, Op. 87.*
(M) ★★★ DG (IMS) (ADD) 447 512-2 (2).

WOLF: Lieder (with Barenboim, piano): *23 Eichendorff Lieder; 42 Goethe Lieder; 7 Heine Lieder; 4 Lenau Lieder; 3 Gedichte von Michelangelo; Mörike Lieder* (complete); *6 Reinick Lieder; 4 Gedichte von Robert Reinick. 3 Gedichte nach Shakespeare und Lord Byron.* Miscellaneous Lieder by PEITL; VON MATTHISSON; KÖRNER; HERLOSSOHN; HEBBEL; VON FALLERSLEBEN; STURM; VON SCHEFFEL.
(B) ★★★ DG (ADD) 447 515-2 (6).

To celebrate the seventieth birthday of the great German baritone, DG published a justifiably extravagant Lieder Edition, summing up the astonishing achievement of the greatest male Lieder singer of our time.

Each individual composer grouping is available separately, very competitively priced. With consistent artistry from all concerned and with first-class transfers, these CDs are self-recommending. We have discussed the Schubert in previous volumes, and much else, too, in individual issues. Fischer-Dieskau's mastery never ceases to amaze. Sample this set at almost any point and the same virtues emerge: characteristic beauty of vocal tone and an extraordinarily vivid power of characterization and vocal colouring. No less remarkable are his accompanists, including the incomparable Gerald Moore and Daniel Barenboim, whose sensitivity and command of keyboard colour make for consistently memorable results. The sheer originality of thought and the ease of the lyricism are a regular delight. Fischer-Dieskau's concentration and inspiration never seem to falter, especially in the most famous of the songs, the *Petrarch Sonnets*, and Barenboim's accompaniments could hardly be more understanding.

Fischer-Dieskau Edition

This set of 21 CDs was a follow-up to the Lieder Edition above and was also released to celebrate Fischer-Dieskau's 75th birthday, releasing over 300 works on CD for the first time – with a recording of *Die schöne Müllerin* which had never before been released. One of the other joys of this Fischer-Dieskau Edition is that it included a great deal of music, much of it little known, either side of his core nineteenth-century repertoire. Alas since then the deletions axe has fallen on Volumes 4 (Schubert), 6 (Schumann), 8 (Liszt), 10 (Wolf), 11 (Richard Strauss), 12 (Reger), 13 (Schoeck), 14 (Debussy), 15 (Busch, Kempff, Mahler and others), 16 (Mahler), 17 (Bach and Buxtehude) and 18–21 (various other composers).

Volume 1: SCHUBERT: *Winterreise, D.911.*
(M) ★★★ DG (ADD) 463 501-2. with Barenboim.

This is Fischer-Dieskau's fifth recording of Schubert's greatest cycle (1979), with the voice still in superb condition. It is perhaps the most inspirational, prompted by Barenboim's spontaneous-sounding, almost improvisatory accompaniment. In expression, this is freer than the earlier versions, and though some idiosyncratic details will not please everyone, the sense of concentrated development is irresistible. The recording is excellent.

Volume 2: SCHUBERT: *Die schöne Müllerin, D.795.* Lieder: *Du bist die Ruh; Erlkönig; Nacht und Träume; Ständchen.*
(M) *** DG (ADD) 463 502-2. with Demus.

This fascinating disc makes available Fischer-Dieskau's 1968 recording of *Die schöne Müllerin* with one of his favourite pianists, Jörg Demus, for the first time. The reason for its previous non-appearance were not artistic: Dieskau regards it as one of his most successful interpretations of this cycle, and edited and approved the disc for release. It seems that DG, understandably, wanted to concentrate on the Gerald Moore recordings which were then being undertaken, and with whom he recorded the same cycle just three years later. The result was that this version was never issued. Comparisons with the 1971 Moore version are fascinating: the earlier version has a greater feeling of risk, with the dynamics noticeably more pointed, and as Alan Newcombe says in the sleeve note 'the result is starker, more elemental, less comfortable, and conceived on a larger scale'. Whereas the later version offers the more rounded polish – from both artists – and for many will be the safer recommendation, this 'new' version is just as compelling. The recording is excellent, and the four extra songs included on this disc are supremely done.

Volume 3: SCHUBERT: *Schwanengesang, D.957.* Lieder: *Im Abendrot; An die Musik; An Sylvia; Die Erde; Die Forelle; Heidenröslein; Der Musensohn; Der Tod und das Mädchen; Vollendung.*
(M) *** DG (ADD) 463 503-2 with Moore.

Fischer-Dieskau's and Gerald Moore's 1972 performance of *Schwanengesang* – a work not conceived as a cycle by Schubert but grouped together by his publisher – is masterly. The singer may occasionally over-emphasize individual words, but the magnetism, poetry and insight – matched by Moore's playing – has one consistently marvelling. The remaining songs are superbly done, and both *Vollendung* and *Die Erde*, also recorded in 1972, receive their first release here. Excellent recording.

Volume 5: SCHUMANN: (i) *Dichterliebe, Op. 48;* (ii) *12 Gedichte, Op. 35.* Lieder: *Freisinn; Schneeglöckchen; Des Sennen Abschied; Ständchen; Talismane; Venezianisches Lied I & II.*
(M) *** DG stereo/mono 463 505-2 with (i) Demus; (ii) Weissenborn.

The beautifully intense and expressive performance of *Dichterliebe* – perhaps the most concentrated of all song-cycles – was taped in 1965. Here, Fischer-Dieskau surpassed his famous mono version, with the voice sounding if anything in better condition here, and with an even more tragic account of *Iche*

grolle nicht. The other Lieder (mono) are no less attractive, and they all make their debut on CD here.

Volume 7: BEETHOVEN: *An die ferne Geliebte, Op. 98; Drei Gesänge, Op. 83.* Lieder: *Adelaide; Abendlied unterm gestirnten Himmel; Adelaide; L'amante impaziente (Nos 3 & 4); Andenken; An die Hoffnung; Ariette (Der Kuss); Aus Goethes Faust; Die Ehre Gottes aus der Natur; Ich liebe dich, so wie du mich; In questa tomba oscura; Der Jüngling in der Fremde; Der Liebende; Lied aus der Ferne; Maigesang; Marmotte; Seufzer eines Ungeliebten – Gegenliebe; Der Wachtelschlag.*
(M) **(*) DG (ADD) 463 507-2 with Demus.

This Beethoven collection was recorded in 1966, finding Fischer-Dieskau at his vocal peak, especially in the song-cycle, which he made his very own. Though Jörg Demus's accompaniments are not quite so imaginative as the singer has received on other versions of these songs, Fischer-Dieskau's individuality is as positive as ever, with detail touched in as with few other singers. Excellent recording.

Volume 9: BRAHMS: *Vier ernste Gesänge, Op. 121.* Lieder: *Abenddämmerung; Alte Liebe; Auf dem Kirchhofe; Auf dem See; Es liebt sich so lieblich im Lenze; Es schauen die Blumen; Feldeinsamkeit; Frühlingslied; Heimweh II; Herbstgefühl; Kein Haus, keine Heimat; Meerfahrt; Mein Herz ist schwer; Mit vierzig Jahren; Mondenschein; Nachklang; Regenlied; Steig auf, geliebter Schatten; Sommerabend; Der Tod, das ist die kühle Nacht; Verzagen.*
(M) *** DG mono/stereo 463 509-2 with Demus.

At the opening of this recital, with the *Four Serious Songs*, the commanding eloquence of Fischer-Dieskau's singing is gripping, and this level of concentration is maintained throughout, with Dieskau exploiting his range of tone colour in interpreting the fullest meaning of the words. The recordings were made from 1957 to 1960, and are strikingly full and vivid – both in stereo and mono.

Lieder (with Reimann or Reutter, piano): FRANZ: *Auf dem Meeere* (3 versions); *Wie des Mondes Abbild; Gewitternacht; Bitte; Für Musik; Abends; Wonne der Wehmut; Mailied.* GRIEG: *Dereinst, Gedanke mein; Lauf der Welt; Wo sind sie hin?; Hör'ich das Liedchen klingen; Morgentau; Abschied; Jägerlied.* KIRCHNER: *Sie weiss es nicht; Frühhlingslied* (3 versions). HILLER: *Gebet.* JENSEN: *Lehn deine Wang' an meine Wang'.* A. RUBINSTEIN: *Es blinker der Tau.* LISZT: *Es rauschen die Winde; Wieder möcht'ich dir begegnen; Ständchen; Uber allen Gipfeln ist Ruh'.* WAGNER: *Der Tannenbaum.* BERLIOZ: *Auf den Lagunen.* CORNELIUS: *Liebe ohne Heimat; Sonnenuntergang.* NIETZSCHE: *Nachtspiel; Wie sich Rebenranken schwingen; Verwelkt.* WEINGARTNER: *Liebesfeier.* RITTER: *Primula veria.* STREICHER: *Ist die ein getreues,*

liebevolles Kind beschert. RAFF: *Unter den Palmen.*
EULENBURG: *Liebessehnsucht.* VON SCHILLINGS:
Freude soll in deinen Werken sein. SCHOECK:
Abendwolken; Reiselied; Peregrina II. WETZEL: *An
miene Mutter; Der Kehraus.* MATTIESEN: *Heimgang
in der Frühe; Herbstgefühl.* PFITZNER: *An den
Mond; Mailied; Hussens Kerker.* TIESSEN: *Vöglein
Schwermut.* R. STRAUSS: *Wer hat's getan?* REGER:
Warnung; Sommernacht. SCHREKER: *Die
Dunkelheit sinkt schwer wie Blei.* DEBUSSY: *Pour ce
que plaisance est morte; Le Temps a laissié son
manteau.* MILHAUD: *Lamentation.* MAHLER: *Des
Knaben Wunderhorn: Wo die schönen Trompeten
blasen.* HINDEMITH: *Fragment.* REUTTER: *Johann
Kepler; Lied für ein dunkles Mädchen; Trommel.*
FORTNER: *Abbitte; Hyperions Schicksalslied; Lied
vom Weidenbaum.* BARTOK: *Im Tale.* BLACHER:
Gedicht; Worte. HAUER: *Der gefesselte Strom; An die
Pasrzen.* SCHOENBERG: *Warnung; Traumleben.*
WEBERN: *4 Lieder* (with George). APOSTEL: *Nacht.*
KRENEK: *Die frühen Gräber; Erinnerung.* VOM
EINEM: *Ein junger Dichter denkt an die Geliebte; In
der Fremde.* EISLER: *An die Hoffnung; In der Frühe;
Spruch 1939.* DESSAU: *Noch bin ich eine Stadt; Sur
nicht mehr, Frau.* BECK: *Herbst.*

(M) ★★(★) EMI (ADD) 5 67349-2 (3).

To some extent this EMI set is compensation for the
loss of most of DG's Fischer-Dieskau Edition. With
the great baritone at his most inspired in this rare
repertory, it would be hard to devise a more imaginative survey of the German Lied after Schumann.
Ranging astonishingly widly in its coverage of the
genre between 1850 and 1950, it generally bypasses
obvious names, celebrating instead such composers
as Franz, Kirchner, Cornelius and even Nietzsche
(Wagner's pupil) in the nineteenth century and
Weingartner, Schreker and Apostel in the twentieth.
It is fascinating to have Wagner himself represented,
Grieg and Berlioz (in German) as well as Debussy,
Milhaud and even Bartok in songs with Lieder-like
aim. Never issued on CD before, this makes a memorable celebratory issue, timed for Fischer-Dieskau's
75th birthday in May 2000. Sadly, this mid-price issue
earns a big black mark for giving no texts or translations, leaving one in the dark over much rare material, even though the singer's diction is excellent.

Flagstad, Kirsten (soprano)

'*The Flagstad Legacy*', Volume 1: Opera arias from:
BEETHOVEN: *Fidelio.* WAGNER: *Götterdämmerung;
Lohengrin; Parsifal; Tannhäuser; Tristan und Isolde;
Die Walküre.* WEBER: *Oberon.* Songs and arias by
ALNS; BEETHOVEN; BISHOP; BRAHMS; BULL;
FRANZ; GRIEG; GRONDAHL; HURUM; LIE;
NORDRAAK; PALENZ; ROSENFELDT; SCHUBERT;
SINDING; R. STRAUSS; THOMMESEN; THRANE.

(★★★) Simax mono PSC 1821 (3).

These three Simax CDs make up the first of five sets,

running to thirteen CDs in all, which promise the
most comprehensive overview of this great singer's
legacy on records. It comes with a substantial article
by Arne Dørumsgaard, himself a composer and
translator. The contents range from the period of the
First World War through to 1941, though the 1940
Haugtussa is not included. There is a thrilling *Dich,
teure Halle* from *Tannhäuser*, recorded in New York
in 1935 (hardly surprising that Flagstad took America
by storm) and a *Liebestod* from the same year, as well
as the 1936 Copenhagen recordings of Grieg and
other Norwegian songs.

There are some Philadelphia and San Francisco
Opera recordings under Ormandy with Melchior,
and many feature her lifelong accompanist, Edwin
McArthur. In Norwegian song, Grieg is not the
whole story even if he is most of it. Flagstad included
a number of her other and less familiar countrymen
in her discography. These include Ole Bull, the
violinist-composer who encouraged Grieg's family to
send the boy to Leipzig, and whose *Sæterjentens
Søndag* ('The Herd Girl's Sunday') would have been
mandatory at the time. Eyvind Alnæs's song *Lykkan
mellem To Mennseskor* ('Happiness between Two
People') was also a favourite of hers.

Dørumsgaard tells of the 'disarming simplicity' of
her 1929 version, the finest of her early electrics,
released 'before fame struck'. It is indeed quite amazing and fresher than the 1936 record, which also
suffers from the rather dry acoustic of the Copenhagen studio. The Simax will be indispensable to the
serious collector, both for its comprehensiveness and
for the generally high standard of its transfers.

Fleming, Renée (soprano)

'*Ladies and Gentlemen: Miss Renée Fleming*'.
★★★ Decca **DVD** 074 153-9 (Director: Tony Palmer).

Tony Palmer's brilliant and moving profile of Renée
Fleming, originally made for the South Bank Show
on British ITV, is here superbly supplemented by
what Palmer describes as 'bonus vignettes', 55 minutes of off-cuts from a film that for technical reasons
had to be reduced to just over an hour, 'material too
good to waste'. Some of those extra items contain the
most revealing moments of all, as for example the
sequence of well over ten minutes analysing her
education and early training, 'Vocal Beginnings'.
Palmer also contributes a moving essay in the
accompanying booklet which amplifies Fleming's
complex character even more. He explains his inclusion of a rehearsal sequence of the Verdi *Requiem*,
even though the diva disapproved of it for revealing a
double-chin (barely noticeable to anyone else), for it
tellingly brings one close to a great artist. The film
opens with Fleming doing a comic cabaret number
based on *Caro nome* from Verdi's *Rigoletto*, with
pig-puppets as her companions, then switching
sharply to her agonized account of 'Amazing Grace'
at the memorial service on Ground Zero in New

York, commemorating the disaster of 9/11 and the collapse of the Twin Towers. Fleming explains that at school she always wanted to obey the rules and do well by the accepted standards, and she often envies those who are not chained in that way. That conflict in her ever-self-questioning character is movingly illustrated at the end of the main film with her singing of Marietta's Lied from Korngold's opera, *Die tote Stadt*, though (if anything) even more moving is the close of the last bonus vignette, celebrating her singing of Strauss with a radiant account of *Beim Schlafengehen* from the *Four Last Songs*. There are many other musical clips too, to amplify a most revealing portrait.

Great Opera Scenes (with LSO, Solti) from: MOZART: *Le nozze di Figaro.* TCHAIKOVSKY: *Eugene Onegin.* DVORAK: *Rusalka.* VERDI: *Otello.* BRITTEN: *Peter Grimes.* R. STRAUSS: *Daphne.*

🎧 ❂ ✱✱✱ Decca 455 760-2.

Solti, in one of his very last recordings, here pays tribute to a soprano he especially admired and the wide choice of repertory movingly reflects an inspired collaboration. Far more than most operatic recitals, this presents fully rounded characterizations in extended scenes, from the Countess in *Figaro* through two Slavonic roles Tatiana and Rusalka (Fleming's favourite) to a tenderly girlish portrait of Verdi's Desdemona, wonderfully poised. Most moving of all is the final item – in effect a valediction – a ravishing, sensuous account of the heroine's final transformation into a tree in Strauss's late opera, *Daphne*.

'*I Want Magic!*': American opera arias (with Met. Op. O, Levine) from: HERRMANN: *Wuthering Heights.* MOORE: *The Ballad of Baby Doe.* MENOTTI: *The Medium.* GERSHWIN: *Porgy and Bess.* BERNSTEIN: *Candide.* FLOYD: *Susannah.* STRAVINSKY: *The Rake's Progress.* BARBER: *Vanessa.* PREVIN: *A Streetcar Named Desire.*

✱✱✱ Decca 460 567-2.

The title *I Want Magic!* is from André Previn's opera based on Tennessee Williams's *Streetcar Named Desire.* Blanche Dubois's climactic aria – recorded even before the world première of the opera in 1998 – makes a moving conclusion to a varied and characterful collection. The beauty and power of Fleming's singing transforms arias from such operas as Bernard Herrmann's *Wuthering Heights,* Douglas Moore's *Ballad of Baby Doe* and Carlisle Floyd's *Susannah,* bringing out their lyricism. In arias from *Porgy and Bess* she is totally in style, and has both weight and brilliance in the big show-piece arias from Stravinsky's *Rake's Progress,* Barber's *Vanessa* and Bernstein's *Candide.*

'*Night Songs*' (with Thibaudet, piano): FAURE: *Après un rêve; Clair de lune; Mandoline; Nell; Soir.* DEBUSSY: *Apparition; Beau soir; Mandoline;*

Chansons de Bilitis. MARX: *Nachtgebet; Nocturne; Pierrot Dandy; Selige Nacht.* R. STRAUSS: *Cäcilie; Leise Lieder; Leises Lied; Ruhe, meine Seele!; Schlechtes Wetter.* RACHMANINOV: *In the Silence of Mysterious Night; It is Beautiful Here; Sleep; Oh Do Not Sing To Me; These Summer Nights; The Waterlily.*

✱✱✱ Decca 467 697-2.

While it is possible to imagine a classic French singer bringing more authenticity to the French songs, there is no doubting Renée Fleming's understanding of the idiom. Her performances bring a genuine warmth which is most attractive, and her subtle colourings are a delight. In such numbers as Debussy's *Beau soir* she sings with a dreamy delicacy, whilst the following *Mandoline* is animated and lively, and her voice remains rich and well focused throughout her range in both. The Strauss songs have much atmosphere and character, from the hushed still of *Ruhe, meine Seele!* ('Rest my Soul') to the more dramatic *Cäcilie,* in which the strong emotions in the text are well conveyed. The yearning Russian qualities of Rachmaninov are well captured too, and the selection included finds the composer at his most persuasive. The Marx songs are an unexpected but welcome inclusion, especially the wild and quirky 'Pierrot Dandy'. Much of the overall success of this disc is due to the superlative accompaniments from Jean-Yves Thibaudet who plays with great understanding and style. Full texts and translations are included, and the recording is warm and perfectly balanced.

Gabrieli Consort & Players, Paul McCreesh

'*A Venetian Coronation* (1595)': GIOVANNI GABRIELI: *Canzonas Nos. XIII a 12; IX a 10; XVI a 15; Deus qui beatum Marcum a 10 Intonazione ottavo toni; Intonazione terzo e quarto toni; Intonazioni quinto tono alla quarta bassa; Omnes gentes a 16; Sonata No. VI a 8 pian e forte.* ANDREA GABRIELI: *Intonazione primo tono; Intonazione settino tono; Mass excerpts: Kyrie a 5-12; Gloria a 16; Sanctus a 12; Benedictus a 12; O sacrum convivium a 5; Benedictus dominus Deus sabbaoth.* BENDINELLI: *Sonata CCCXXXIII; Sarasinetta.* THOMSEN: *Toccata No. 1.*

✱✱✱ Virgin 7 59006-2.

This recording won a *Gramophone* Early Music Award. *A Venetian Coronation* is a highly imaginative if conjectural reconstruction of the Mass and its accompanying music as performed at St Mark's for the ceremonial installation of Doge Marino Grimaldi in 1595. The evocation begins with sounding bells (Betjeman would have approved), and the choice of music is extraordinarily rich, using processional effects to simulate the actual scene, like a great Renaissance painting. The climax comes with the Mass itself; and the sounds here, choral and instrumental, are quite glorious. The spontaneity of the whole affair is remarkable and the recording superb.

'Venetian Vespers', including: MONTEVERDI: Laudate pueri; Laudate dominum; Deus qui mundum; Laetatus sum. GIOVANNI GABRIELI: Intonazione (for organ). RIGATTI: Dixit dominus; Nisi dominus; Magnificat; Salve regina. GRANDI: O intemerata; O quam tu pulchra es. FASALO: Intonazione (for organ). BANCHIERI: Suonata prima; Dialogo secondo (for organ). FINETTI: O Maria, quae rapis corda hominum. CAVALLI: Lauda Jerusalem. MARINI: Sonata con tre violini in eco. ANON.: Praeambulum.
*** (M) DG 476 18683 (2).

Sequels can sometimes fall flat (as Hollywood so often demonstrates), but this one certainly doesn't, for the musical intensity of the performance is no less vivid here, and the spatial effects and polychoral interplay are equally impressive in this hypothetical re-creation of a Vespers at St Mark's. Grandiose effects alternate with more intimate sonorities, but the feeling of drama which was part and parcel of the Venetian Renaissance tradition is fully conveyed. Once again all the participants are on their toes, and playing and singing (soloists as well as chorus) are transcendent with detail in the accompaniment always effective and stylish. The recording is splendidly opulent, yet never loses its definition. This excellent set returns as part of Universal's mid-priced Gramophone Awards Collection – it won the 1993 Early Music Award.

Gallardo-Domas, Cristina (soprano)

'Bel Sogno' (with Munich Radio Orchestra, Barbacini): Arias from: BELLINI: I Capuleti ei Montecchi. CATALANI: La Wally. CILEA: Adriana Lecouvreur. DONIZETTI: Anna Bolena. PUCCINI: Madama Butterfly; La Bohème; Manon Lescaut; Suor Angelica; Gianni Schicchi. VERDI: La traviata; Simon Boccanegra; Otello.
**(*) Teldec 8573 86440-2.

Cristina Gallardo-Domas made her first big impact on disc with her deeply moving assumption of the title-role in Antonio Pappano's prize-winning version of Puccini's Suor Angelica. Here it is in the Puccini items above all that she shines out, giving portraits of each heroine that are not just beautiful and sensitive but bring out the words too. Yet this collection demonstrates the breadth of her sympathies in a formidable range of arias, and though she is not quite as much at home in Bellini or Donizetti, there too one recognizes the warmth and responsiveness of her singing. The only slight disappointment is that the Munich recording brings out an occasional unevenness in her vocal production, though

that will matter little to anyone finding her distinctive timbre attractive.

Gedda, Nicolai (tenor)

Songs and Lieder: VERACINI: Meco verrai. RESPIGHI: Notte; Stornellatrice. PRATELLA: La strada bianca. CASELLA: La storia della fanciulla rapita. CARNEVALI: Stornelli capriccioso. TURINA: Poema en forma de canciones, Op. 19. RACHMANINOV: Frühlingsfluten; Hier ist es schön; Lied des jungen Zigeuners; O singe nicht, du schönes Mädchen. BEETHOVEN: Andanken; An die Geliebte; Der Floh; Der Kuss; Der Liebende; 3 Gesänge von Goethe; Lied aus der Ferne; Mailied; Neue Liebe, neues Leben; Zärtliche Liebe; Der Zufriedene. SCHUBERT: Nachthelle; Trinklied. Arias from: ADAM: Le Postillon de Lonjumeau. MEYERBEER: L'Africaine. MASSENET: Werther. BORODIN: Prince Igor. RIMSKY-KORSAKOV: Sadko. TCHAIKOVSKY: Eugene Onegin. RACHMANINOV: Aleko. VERDI: Aida. PONCHIELLI: La Gioconda. PUCCINI: La Bohème; Turandot. HAYDN: L'infedeltà delusa. BEETHOVEN: Fidelio. SCHUBERT: Die Verschworenen. FLOTOW: Martha. MOZART: Concert arias: Clarice cara mia sposa; Con ossequito, con rispetto; Müsst ich auch durch tausend Drachen.
(BB) **(*) EMI (ADD) 5 67684-2 (2).

Gedda – every producer's ideal of a recording tenor – has encompassed an astonishingly wide range of repertoire in his long recording career, and these two discs cover it splendidly. Among the French items one especially marvels at the heady freedom on top in the jolly Adam aria, recorded early in his career. Other items give a hint of the strain, which marred some of his later recordings, but by no means is there any serious flaw. Whether in operetta, song or in full-blooded opera arias, he has an innate sense of idiomatic style, a claim few tenors can boast today. The recordings, which cover a wide range and period, are generally fine, with just one or two items showing their age. The blot on this CD, and others in this series, is the pitiful packaging, which has the scantiest of biographies possible, and, needless to say, no texts or translations. The two CDs are inexpensive, but we are sure most of Gedda's admirers would be prepared to pay extra for some decent notes, translations and packaging.

Gens, Véronique (soprano)

'Nuit d'étoiles' (with Vignoles): Songs: DEBUSSY: 3 Chansons de Bilitis etc. FAURE: Aprés un rêve, etc. POULENC: Banalités etc.
***Virgin (ADD) 5 45360-2.

This is one of the very finest of all discs of French mélodies, an inspired choice of well-known and rare songs sung with exceptional imagination and feeling for the idiom. Best known for her brilliant performances of baroque music, Gens here sings with a tone at once firmly focused and sensuously beautiful. In her distinctive and idiomatic characterization of each composer she is greatly helped by Roger Vignoles, the brilliant accompaniment adding to the element of fantasy that runs through the whole sequence. The point and wit found in such a popular song as Fauré's *Mandoline* are exceptional, making one appreciate it afresh, and the waltz numbers from the Poulenc group, *Voyage à Paris* and *Les Chemins de l'amour*, are equally seductive in their idiomatic lilt. The poise of Gens in the more serious songs is also exemplary, with the voice flawlessly placed. A magical disc.

Gericke, Isa (soprano), Sveinung Bjelland (piano)

'Waldabendlust': KJERULF: *Albumblatt; Gute Nacht; Höchstes Leben; Lass Andre nur; Des Mondes Silber rinnt; Nach langen Jahren; Die Schwester; Sehnsucht; Spanische Romanza; Täuschung; Waldabendlust.* IRGENS-JENSEN: *Japanischer-Früling, Op. 2.* GRONDAHL: *Elslein; Ich möcht' es mir selber verschweigen; Juniabend; Rastlose Liebe; Sie liebten sich beide.* HJELM: *Frühlingslob; Loose; Du Warst es doch.*
*(*) Simax PSC 1231.

Even in the 1940s Grieg's songs were more often than not sung in German translation, and many other Norwegian composers turned to the language that would ensure their songs had wider currency. Isa Katherine Gericke offers eleven songs by Grieg's immediate precursor, Halfdan Kjerulf – mostly settings of Geibel. They have a certain charm without having Grieg's strong personality. The best thing probably is the song-cycle by Ludvig Irgens-Jensen, an immediate contemporary of Sæverud and whose folk-inspired musical language is refreshing. *Japanischer-Frühling* comprises nine songs adapted from the Japanese by Hans Begthe, familiar from Mahler's *Das Lied von der Erde.* It comes from 1920, when Jensen was in his mid-twenties and was published as his Op. 2. The composer made an orchestral version of this rewarding and imaginative cycle in 1957, and it is in this form that it is better known. Agathe Backer-Grøndahl was four years younger than Grieg and enjoyed a formidable reputation as a pianist (even Bernard Shaw wrote with admiration of her London visits). As these songs show, she was far from negligible as a song composer. All these examples are worth hearing, but they deserve more eloquent advocacy than they receive here. Isa Katherine Gericke is an intelligent artist but is a little too wanting in variety of tone-colour and vocal presence. Sveinung Bjelland is a supportive and sensitive accompanist and the recording is very truthful. All the same, this is of more than just specialist interest.

Gheorghiu, Angela (soprano)

'Angela Gheorghiu Live' (with ROHCG O, Marin): Arias from: HANDEL: *Rinaldo.* MOZART: *Le nozze di Figaro.* CHARPENTIER: *Louise.* PUCCINI: *Madama Butterfly; Gianni Schicchi.* CILEA: *Adriana Lecouvreur.* BELLINI: *Norma.* Encores: BREDICEANU: *La Seçeris.* LOEWE: *My Fair Lady: I Could have Danced All Night.*
*** EMI **DVD** 4 92695-9.

This DVD offers a visual recording of the live recital given at Covent Garden by Gheorghiu in June 2001, which has also been issued on audio CD (see below). The bonus on DVD, as well as having the vision of an exceptionally beautiful woman, is that among the special features is an interview with Gheorghiu, in which she confirms some of the points implied by the CD version, notably that when she was a student she knew and loved the two opening arias, not generally part of her latter-day repertory, *Lascia ch'io pianga* from Handel's *Rinaldo* and the Countess's *Porgi amor* from Mozart's *Marriage of Figaro* (as she explains, the very first Mozart aria she ever sang). The poise of those performances, the stylish concern for vocal purity, leads on to moving accounts of arias more usually associated with her, as well as an extrovert group of encores executed with commanding artistry, even if during 'I Could have Danced All Night' she has to prompt herself with the music. As to the video production, having multi-coloured back lighting for each aria – pink, blue or a mixture of both – takes us near the pop world, but it gives variety!

Arias (with Ch. & O of Teatro Regio, Turin, Mauceri) from: VERDI: *Falstaff.* MASSENET: *Hérodiade; Chérubin.* CATALANI: *La Wally.* BELLINI: *I Capuleti e i Montecchi.* PUCCINI: *La Bohème.* BOITO: *Mefistofele.* GOUNOD: *Faust.* DONIZETTI: *Don Pasquale.* GRIGORIU: *Valurile Dunarii.*
**(*) Decca 452 417-2.

The star of Decca's *La traviata* made her solo début in a recital which offers much lovely singing – the very opening excerpt from Verdi's *Falstaff* brings a ravishing line (and some fine orchestral playing, too) and the Massenet aria is quite melting and full of charm. But there is too little difference of characterization between the different heroines, not enough fiery passion or, indeed, displays of temperament, which means that the Jewel Song from *Faust* fails to sparkle as it should. Nevertheless the sample of Mimì in *La Bohème* promises well. The back-up here, from John Mauceri and the Turin chorus and orchestra, is impressive, and so is the glowing Decca recording.

'Casta Diva' (with ROHCG Ch. & O, Pidó): Arias from: BELLINI: *Norma; I Puritani; La sonnambula.*

ROSSINI: *L'assedio di Corinto; Il barbiere di Siviglia; Guglielmo Tell.* DONIZETTI: *Anna Bolena; Lucia di Lammermoor.*

*** EMI 5 57163-2.

Not since Joan Sutherland has a disc of *bel canto* arias inspired such glorious singing as from Angela Gheorghiu in repertory with which she has not till now been associated. The flexibility of her voice has been amply demonstrated in her regular lyric repertory, whether as Gounod's Marguerite in *Faust* or Verdi's Violetta in *La traviata*, and this translates perfectly to Rossini, Bellini and Donizetti at their most demanding. Ravishing tone, finely shaded, marks the opening item, *Casta diva*, with poised legato that yet allows moving characterization. In the other great Bellini arias tenderness goes with depth of feeling, with a hint of flutter heightening the emotion in Amina's *Ah, non credea mirarti* from *La sonnambula*, and with sparkling coloratura in all the cabalettas. In Rossini she is just as commanding, whether in the *Guglielmo Tell* aria, the fine aria from *L'assedio di Corinto* or Rosina's *Una voce poco fa* from *Il barbiere di Siviglia*, sparkily characterful. In Donizetti the scena from *Anna Bolena* leads naturally to the great Act I aria from *Lucia di Lammermoor*. The top of the voice may not be quite as free as Sutherland's was, but this is comparably assured. Perhaps wisely, Gheorghiu has opted not to include the Mad Scene from *Lucia* as well. Warm, sympathetic accompaniment and vivid recording.

'*Angela Gheorghiu Live at Covent Garden*' (with ROHCG O, Marin): Arias from: BELLINI: *Norma.* BREDICEANU: *La seceris.* CHARPENTIER: *Louise.* CILEA: *Adriana Lecouvreur.* HANDEL: *Rinaldo.* LOEWE: *My Fair Lady.* MASSENET: *Manon.* MOZART: *Le nozze di Figaro.* PUCCINI: *Gianni Schicchi; Madama Butterfly; Turandot.*

**(*) EMI 5 57264-2.

It was a striking enough development when Angela Gheorghiu, a soprano geared to Verdi, Puccini and Massenet, displayed such formidable mastery in the bel canto repertory, as captured on her recital disc of Roassini, Bellini and Donizetti. Even more remarkable is the classical poise and purity of her singing here in *Lascia ch'io pianga* from Handel's *Rinaldo* and the Countess's aria, *Porgi amor*, from Mozart's *Figaro*. This recording was made at her Covent Garden recital in June 2001, demonstrating throughout that unlike so many operatic prima donnas she has not forgotten her early lessons. Her assurance and technical mastery go with a magnetic ability to project character with musical imagination, not just in favourite romantic arias, including Norma's *Casta diva* and Louise's *Depuis le jour*, but in the encores, which include a charming Romanian song and 'I Could have Danced All Night' from *My Fair Lady*. Marred slightly by intrusive applause.

Gheorghiu, Angela (soprano), Roberto Alagna (tenor)

Opera arias and duets from: MASCAGNI: *L'amico Fritz* MASSENET: *Manon* DONIZETTI: *Anna Bolena; Don Pasquale* OFFENBACH: *La Belle Hélène* BERNSTEIN: *West Side Story* GOUNOD: *Faust.* G. CHARPENTIER: *Louise* BERLIOZ: *Les Troyens* PUCCINI: *La Bohème.*

⊘→ *** EMI 5 56117-2.

If Angela Gheorghiu's Decca solo début was a little disappointing, this record of duets with her husband, Roberto Alagna, is not. Clearly they are a natural couple as artists as well as human beings. There is much here to delight, not least the opening Cherry Duet from *L'amico Fritz*, in which the voices blend delightfully. *Manon* brings a comparable symbiosis, and the Donizetti items are as winning as the unexpected excerpt from *Les Troyens*. Solo arias also come off well here, notably Gheorghiu's aria from *Anna Bolena*, which suits her exactly; Alagna turns in a stylishly heady account of the delicious Waltz Song from *La Belle Hélène*. The excerpt from *West Side Story* is tenderly touching but, as nearly always, the voices sound too mature for these star-crossed young lovers. Again the promise of that future complete *Bohème* comes in the closing all-too-short *O soave fanciulla*. First-rate accompaniments under Richard Armstrong and superb sound contribute to the great success of this immensely pleasurable operatic hour.

Gloriae Dei Cantores, Elizabeth Patterson

'*By the Rivers of Babylon (American Psalmody II)*' (with James E. Jordan, organ): LOEFFLER: *By the Rivers of Babylon, Op. 3* (with P. Clark, E. Ingwersen, flutes, M. Buddington, harp, H. Vacarro, cello). VIRGIL THOMSON: *3 Antiphonal Psalms (Nos. 123, 133 & 136); De profundis.* SCHOENBERG: *De profundis.* TAYLOR: *Sing to the Lord a New Song.* BERGER: *The Eyes of All Wait upon Thee.* NEWBURY: *Psalm 150.* NEAR: *My Song shall be Alway of the Loving-kindness of the Lord.* ADLER: *Psalm Triology (Nos. 42, 84 & 113).* NESWICK: *Hallelujah! Sing to the Lord a New Song.* WHITE: *Cantate Domino* (with brass ens.).

**(*) Paraclete Press Gloriae Dei Cantores GDCD 027.

This collection of twentieth-century psalm settings includes music by 'those who are native Americans by birth or citizenship', which covers both Charles Loeffler, a late nineteenth-century émigré, and Schoenberg, who became an American citizen in 1941. The latter's atonal setting of the original Hebrew text of Psalm 120 (commissioned by Koussevitzky), with its dramatic spoken acclamations adding to the music's emotional impact, is the one really avant-garde piece here. It comes immediately after Virgil Thomson's admirably fresh but much simpler setting in English.

Loeffler's sensuously lush *By the rivers of Babylon*, which introduces the programme and gives the disc its title, is the most ambitious piece, very Gallic in feeling. It is richly sung and has a beautiful postlude for two flutes and cello, let down by imperfect intonation from the solo cellist. This closing section should have been re-recorded, for it all but spoils a superb performance. The rest of the music is traditional, but individually so, especially the very striking *Psalm Triology* by Samuel Adler and the pieces by Clifford Taylor, Jean Berger (gently touching) and Bruce Neswick, his joyous 'Hallelujah'.

The choral singing is very fine and deeply committed throughout, and the choir has the advantage of the ideal acoustics of the Methuen Music Hall in Massachusetts, while James Jordan's organ accompaniments (when required) give admirable support, using the superb organ now located there. Even with the reservation about the Loeffler postlude, this splendid collection is well worth having. (Volume 1, which we have not received for review, is available on GDCD 025.)

Gobbi, Tito (baritone)

'*Heroes*': Arias and excerpts from: ROSSINI: *Il barbiere di Siviglia.* DONIZETTI: *Lucia di Lammermoor.* VERDI: *Rigoletto; La traviata; Simon Boccanegra; Un ballo in maschera; Don Carlos; Otello; Falstaff.* LEONCAVALLO: *Pagliacci.* PUCCINI: *Tosca* (with Callas).

⊶ (M) (***) EMI (ADD) 5 66810-2.

Tito Gobbi is not usually a hero figure in opera, although his portrayal of Rodrigo in Verdi's *Don Carlos* (sombre and powerful) undoubtedly has a heroic ring to it, and his uniquely charismatic portrayal of Verdi's Falstaff (the closing item) is heroic in its way, good-humouredly so. No other version of Rossini's *Largo al factotum* on record effervesces with such wit, yet has such subtle vocal inflection. Gobbi's portrayal of Rigoletto has a moving resonance, his Germont père in *La traviata* and Tonio in *Pagliacci* are hardly less eloquent and his *Eri tu* in *Simon Boccanegra* is most soberly powerful of all. But the roles for which he is most celebrated on disc are darker (Scarpia in de Sabata's 1953 *Tosca*) and cruel (Iago in Verdi's *Otello*) and these are superb examples of his supreme mastery.

Gothic Voices, Christopher Page

'*The Guardian of Zephirus*' (courtly songs of the 15th century, with Barford, medieval harp): DU FAY: *J'atendray tant qu'il vous playra; Adieu ces bons vins de Lannoys; Mon cuer me fait tous dis penser.* BRIQUET: *Ma seul amour et ma belle maistresse.* DE CASERTA: *Amour ma' le cuer mis.* LANDINI: *Nessun ponga speranza; Giunta vaga*

bilta. REYNEAU: *Va t'en mon cuer, avent mes yeux.* MATHEUS DE SANCTO JOHANNE: *Fortune, faulce, parverse.* DE INSULA: *Amours n'ont cure le tristesse.* BROLLO: *Qui le sien vuelt bien maintenir.* ANON.: *N'a pas long temps que trouvay Zephirus; Je la remire, la belle.*
*** Hyp. CDA 66144.

In 1986 the Gothic Voices began what was to become a large-scale survey of medieval music, secular and sacred – for the two are inevitably intermingled. From the beginning the project was an adventure in exploration, as much for the artists as for the listener, for comparatively little is known about how this music sounded on voices of the time.

The songs of the troubadours or trouvères – outside the church – sometimes drew on ecclesiastical chant, but other such chansons had a modal character of their own. They were essentially monophonic – i.e. a single line of music, perhaps with an instrumental accompaniment – but the rhythmic patterns were unrecorded and, like much else in this repertoire, are inevitably conjectural in modern re-creative performance.

Much of the repertoire on this first disc (and indeed elsewhere) is unfamiliar, with Du Fay the only famous name; but everything here is of interest, and the listener inexperienced in medieval music will be surprised at the strength of its character. The performances are naturally eloquent and, although the range of colour is limited compared with later writing, it still has immediacy of appeal, especially if taken in short bursts. The recording balance is faultless and the sound first rate. With complete security of intonation and a chamber-music vocal blend, the presentation is wholly admirable. There is full back-up documentation.

'*The Castle of Fair Welcome*' (courtly songs of the late 15th century, with Wilson, lute): ANON.: *Las je ne puis; En amours n'a si non bien; Mi ut re ut.* MORTON: *Le Souvenir de vous me tue; Que pourroit plus; Plus j'ay le monde regardé.* REGIS: *Puisque ma dame.* BEDYNGHAM: *Myn hertis lust.* BINCHOIS: *Deuil angoisseux.* VINCENET: *La pena sin ser sabida.* FRYE: *So ys emprinted.* ENRIQUE: *Pues servicio vos desplaze.* CHARLES THE BOLD: *Ma dame, trop vous mesprenés.* DU FAY: *Ne je ne dors.*
*** Hyp. CDA 66194.

Christopher Page has by now established a basic procedure for his presentation of this early vocal repertoire: he has decided that it will be unaccompanied and usually performed by a modest-sized vocal group. So, in the present collection, further variety is provided with four instrumental pieces (played on harp and lute). Not surprisingly, the two most striking works here are by Du Fay (remarkably compelling) and Binchois; but the programme overall has been carefully chosen and it is given a boldly spontaneous presentation which cannot but intrigue the ear. As always, the recording is first class.

'*The Service of Venus and Mars*': DE VITRY: *Gratissima virginis; Vos quie admiramini; Gaude gloriosa; Contratenor.* DES MOLINS: *De ce que fol pense.* PYCARD: *Gloria.* POWER: *Sanctus.* LEBERTOUL: *Las, que me demanderoye.* PYRAMOUR: *Quam pulchra es.* DUNSTABLE: *Speciosa facta es.* SOURSBY: *Sanctus.* LOQUEVILLE: *Je vous pri que j'aye un baysier.* ANON.: *Singularis laudis digna; De ce fol, pense; Lullay, Lullay; There is no Rose; Le gay playsir; Le grant pleyser; Agincourt Carol.* ·
*** Hyp. CDA 66283.

The subtitle of this collection is 'Music for the Knights of the Garter, 1340–1440'; few readers will recognize many of the names in the list of composers above. But the music itself is fascinating and the performances bring it to life with extraordinary projection and vitality. The recording too is first class, and this imaginatively chosen programme deservedly won the 1988 *Gramophone* award for Early Music. Readers interested in trying medieval repertoire could hardly do better than to start here.

'*A Song for Francesca*': ANDREAS DE FLORENTINA: *Astio non mori mai. Per la ver'onesta.* JOHANNES DE FLORENTINA: *Quando la stella.* LANDINI: *Ochi dolenti mie. Per seguir la speranca.* ANON.: *Quando i oselli canta; Constantia; Amor mi fa cantar a la Francesca; Non na el so amante.* DU FAY: *Quel fronte signorille in paradiso.* RICHARD DE LOQUEVILLE: *Puisquie je suy amoureux; Pour mesdisans ne pour leur faulx parler; Qui ne veroit que vos deulx yeulx.* HUGO DE LATINS: *Plaindre m'estuet.* HAUCOURT: *Je demande ma bienvenue.* GROSSIN: *Va t'ent souspir.* ANON.: *O regina seculi; Reparatrix Maria; Confort d'amours.*
*** Hyp. CDA 66286.

The title *A Song for Francesca* refers not only to the fourteenth-century French items here, but to the fact that the Italians too tended to be influenced by French style. More specifically, the collection is a well-deserved tribute to Francesca MacManus, selfless worker on behalf of many musicians, not least as manager of Gothic Voices. The variety of expression and mood in these songs, ballatas and madrigals is astonishing, some of them amazingly complex. The Hyperion recording is a model of its kind, presenting this long-neglected music most seductively in a warm but clear setting.

'*Music for the Lion-hearted King*' (music to mark the 800th anniversary of the coronation of Richard I): ANON.: *Mundus vergens; Noves miles sequitur; Anglia planctus itera; In occasu sideris.* BRULE: *A la douçour de la bele saison; Etas auri reditu; Pange melos lacrimosum; Vetus abit littera; Hac in anni ianua.* LI CHASTELAIN DE COUCI: *Li nouviauz tanz; Soi sub nube latuit.* BLONDEL DE NESLE: *L'Amours dont sui espris; Ma joie me semont; Purgator criminum; Ver pacis apperit; Latex silice.*
*** Hyp. CDA 66336.

Partly because of the intensity, partly because of the imaginative variety of the choral response, all this twelfth-century music communicates readily, even though its comparatively primitive style could easily lead to boredom. The performances are polished but vital, and there is excellent documentation to lead the listener on. This may be a specialist record, but it could hardly be better presented.

'*The Marriage of Heaven & Hell*' (anonymous motets, songs and polyphony from 13th-century France). Also: BLONDEL DE NESLE: *En tous tans que vente bise.* MUSET: *Trop volontiers chanteroie.* BERNART DE VENTADORN: *Can vei la lauzeta mover.* GAUTIER DE DARGIES: *Autre que je laureta mover.*
*** Hyp. CDA 66423.

The title of this collection dramatically overstates the problem of the medieval Church with its conflicting secular influences. Music was universal and the repertoire of the trouvère had a considerable melodic influence on the polyphonic motets used by the Church, though actual quotation was very rare. Nevertheless, on occasion, vulgar associations in a vocal line could ensue and the clergy tore their hair. It all eventually led to the Council of Trent when, the story goes, the purity of Palestrina's contrapuntal serenity saved the day. Certainly medieval church music was robust and full of character, but here one is also struck by its complexity and intensity. The performances have a remarkable feeling of authenticity, and the background is admirably documented.

'*The Medieval Romantics*' (French songs and motets, 1340–1440): ANON.: *Quiconques veut; Je languis d'amere mort; Quant voi le douz tanz; Plus bele que flors; Degentis vita; Mais qu'il vous viegne.* SOLAGE: *Joieux de cuer.* DE PORTA: *Alma polis religio.* MACHAUT: *C'est force; Tant doucement; Comment qu'a moy lonteinne.* TENORISTA: *Sofrir m'estuet.* SENLECHES: *En ce gracieux temps.* DU FAY: *Je requier a tous; Las, que feray.* VELUT: *Je voel servir.* LYMBURGIA: *Tota pulchra es.*
*** Hyp. CDA 66463.

Machaut (fourteenth century) and Du Fay (fifteenth) are names which have now become individually established. Du Fay was master of the secular song-form called the virelai (opening with a refrain, which then followed each verse) and Machaut was one of the first (if not *the* first) composers to set the Ordinary of the Mass; he too wrote chansons and virelais. But of course there is also much music here by other (unknown) composers and our old friend, Anon. The virelais are sung unaccompanied. Sometimes there are vocal melismas (extra parts without words) set against the textual line. So this collection represents the medieval blossoming of songs and part-songs alongside the motets, for secular and sacred never really grew apart. As usual, the Gothic Voices perform this repertoire with skill and confidence and lots of character, and the splendid documentation puts the listener fully in the historical picture.

'*Lancaster and Valois*' (French and English music, 1350–1420): MACHAUT: *Donnez, signeurs; Quand je ne voy; Riches d'amour; Pas de tor en thies pais.* SOLAGE: *Tres gentil cuer.* PYCARD: *Credo.* STURGEON: *Salve mater domini.* FONTEYNS: *Regail ex progenie.* CESARIS: *Mon seul voloir; Se vous scaviez, ma tres douce maistresse.* BAUDE CORDIER: *Ce jour de l'an.* ANON.: *Sanctus; Soit tart, tempre, main ou soir; Je vueil vivre au plaisir d'amours; Puis qu'autrement ne puis avoir; Le Ior; Avrai je ja de ma dame confort?*
*** Hyp. CDA 66588.

This stimulating series has always been essentially experimental, for we do not know just how unaccompanied medieval voices were balanced or how many were used. In the documentation with this record Christopher Page suggests that on this disc he feels he has the internal balance just about right, and the vocal mix varies, sometimes led by a female voice, sometimes by a male. More Machaut here, some slightly later French settings, and the usual balance between sacred and secular. Everything sounds vital and alive.

'*The Study of Love*' (French songs and motets of the 14th century): ANON.: *Pour vous servir; Puis que l'aloe ne fine; Jour a jour la vie; Combien que j'aye; Marticius qui fu; Renouveler me feist; Fist on dame; Il me convient guerpir; Le ior; En la maison Dedalus; Combien que j'aye; Le Grant biauté; En esperant; Ay las! quant je pans.* MACHAUT: *Dame, je suis cilz – Fin cuers; Trop plus – Biauté paree – Je ne suis; Tres bonne et telle; Se mesdisans; Dame, je vueil endurer.* SOLAGE: *Le Basile.* PYCARD: *Gloria.*
*** Hyp. CDA 66619.

The Gothic Voices' exploration is moving sideways rather than forward, for Machaut is still with us. The present collection of settings demonstrates the medieval literary and poetic understanding of 'love' – romantic and spiritual. The anonymous examples are often as stimulating as any of the songs and motets here by named composers, and the Pycard *Gloria* is obviously included to remind us again that church music is about the love of God. This and the previous three CDs should be approached with some caution, starting perhaps with *The Medieval Romantics.*

'*The Voice in the Garden*' (Spanish songs and motets, 1480–1530): JUAN DEL ENCINA: *Mi libertad; Los sospiros no sosiegan; Triste España sin ventura.* LUIS DE NARVAEZ: *Fantasias;* (after) *Paseávase el rey Moro.* FRANCISCO DE PENALOSA: *Precor te, Domine; Ne reminiscaris, Domine; Por las sierras de Madrid; Sancta Maria.* JULIUS DE MODENA: *Tiento.* PALERO: (after) *Paseávase el rey Moro.* ENRIQUE: *Mi querer tanto vos quiere.* LUIS

MILAN: *Fantasias Nos. 10; 12; 18.* GABRIEL: *La Bella Malmaridada; Yo creo que n'os dió Dios.* ANON.: *Dentro en el vergel; Harto de tanta porfía; Entra Mayo y sale Abril; Dindirin; Ave, Virgo, gratia plena; A la villa voy; Pasa el agoa.*
*** Hyp. CDA 66653.

Here the Gothic Voices travel to Spain and take with them Christopher Wilson (vihuela) and Andrew-Lawrence King (harp). Their earlier concerts have included instrumental items, kept separate from the vocal music, and here the same policy is followed, but the mix of sacred, secular and instrumental is more exotic than usual. As throughout this series, the recording is of the highest quality.

'*The Spirits of England and France*' (music of the Middle Ages for court and church, with Beznosiuk, medieval fiddle): ANON.: *La Uitime estampie real; La Quarte estampie real; La Septime estampie real; Credo; Virelais; Songs; Conducti; Conductus motets.* MATTEO DA PERUGIA: *Belle sans per.* MACHAUT: *Ay mi! dame de valour.* PYKINI: *Plaissance, or tost.* PEROTINUS: *Presul nostri temporis.* ANON.: *Ave Maria.*
*** Hyp. CDA 66739.

This is the first of a series of CDs covering French and English music between the twelfth and fifteenth centuries. The first half of the present collection explores the sonorities of three- and four-part writing during the last decades of the fourteenth century and the first decades of the fifteenth. The second group goes back in time to anonymous settings from the twelfth and thirteenth centuries, although including one memorable piece possibly written by Perotinus. Although the items by Machaut (monodic) and Pykini (in four parts) are particularly striking, 'Anonymous' does not mean that the music is not full of character and individuality, and the closing *Ave Maria*, with its series of triads, is as beautiful as many later settings. Pavlo Beznosiuk provides three instrumental interludes, a series of *Estampie*, winningly played on a medieval fiddle. The recording is excellent.

'*The Spirits of England and France*' (songs of the trouvères, with Kirkby, Philpot, Covey-Crump, Nixon, Wickham, Instrumental Ensemble): RICHART DE SEMILLI: *Je chevauchai.* BRULE: *Desconfortez plais de dolor; Quant define feuille et flor; De bien amer grant joie atent; Cil qui d'amours;* ANON.: *Estampie 1–3; Donna pos vos ay chausida; Quant voi la fleur nouvelle; Amors m'art con fuoc am flama.* GONTIER DE SOIGNES: *Dolerousement commence.* KAUKESEL: *Un Chant novel; Fins cuers enamourés.* GAUTIER DE DARGIES: *La Doce pensee.* ADAM DE LA HALLE: *Assénes chi, Grievilier.* ERNOUS LI VIELLE: *Por conforter mon corage.* AUDEFROI: *Au novel tens pascor.*
*** Hyp. CDA 66773.

The songs of the troubadours were inevitably monophonic, usually offering an expressive and touching melisma, lightly ornamented. To quote Christopher Page's excellent notes: 'their supreme genre was the *grand chant*, a protracted meditation upon the fortunes of loving.' One of the key composers in this style was Gace Brulé, and examples such as *Desconfortez plais de dolor*, *Quant define feuille et flor* and *De bien amer grant joie atent* convey an almost desperate melancholy. However, not all is despair: the opening *Je chevauchai* ('I Rode out the Other Morning'), with its repeated refrain, is as spirited as it is optimistic – and rightly so, for the amorous singer has his way with the shepherdess he encounters by chance in the wood.

Ernous Li Vielle's *Por conforter mon corage* has a similar theme, only this time the seduction is more forceful. In contrast Wibers Kaukesel's *Fins cuers enamourés* ennobles the theme of love and being loved, while finally Audefroi tells of a husband who, after his wife Argentine, has borne him six sons, tires of her and takes a concubine, banishing her when she objects. The ingenuous moral of the tale is repeated after each verse: 'Whoever is wed to a bad husband often has a sad heart.' The singing and presentation here are admirable, and there are instrumental *Estampie* to provide interludes. A fascinating collection.

'*The Spirits of England and France*' (Binchois and his contemporaries, with Rumsey, Wilson, Page, lute): BINCHOIS: *Qui veut mesdire; Amoreux suy; Adieu mon amoreuse joye; Ay! doloureux; Magnificat secundi toni; Se la belle.* CARDOT: *Pour une fois.* VELUT: *Un Petit Oyselet; Laissiés ester.* ANON.: *Abide, I Hope; Exultavit cor in Domino.* LE GRANT: *Se liesse.* DE LYMBURGIA: *Descendi in ortum meum.* POWER: *Gloria.* DUNSTABLE: *Beata Dei genitrix.* FONTAINE: *J'ayme bien celui.* MACHAUT: *Il m'est avis.* BITTERING: *En Katerina solennia.*
*** Hyp. CDA 66783.

Christopher Page and his group have been exploring early English and French repertoire in a number of earlier Hyperion anthologies. Here they turn to the early decades of the fifteenth century and to the music of Binchois (who died in 1460) and his contemporaries. Binchois is represented by a series of medieval love songs, all in three parts, very word-sensitive, even poignant in feeling, climaxed by the remarkably expressive *Ay! doloureux*, the most expansive and the most memorable. Then we turn to religious music and, besides a fine Binchois *Magnificat*, there is also Power's eloquent *Gloria* in five voices and fine examples of the music of Dunstable and even of Machaut. It is a heady mix, and it is the contrast here that makes this finely sung and recorded collection so stimulating.

'*The Spirits of England and France*' (with Rumsey, Wilson, Page, lute): ANON.: *The Missa Caput:* an

English Mass setting from *c.* 1440 interspersed with the story of *the Salve Regina.* Carols: *Jesu for Thy Mercy; Jesu fili Dei; Make us Merry; Nowell, Nowell, Nowell; Clangat tuba; Alma redemptoris mater; Agnus Dei* (Old Hall Manuscript).
*** Hyp. CDA 66857.

The inclusion here of the anonymous English *Missa Caput* gives a special interest to this collection. Composed around 1440, it survived in seven different manuscripts, and it is credited with having had a strong influence on the Masses of Ockeghem. The quality of the music is sure – it has long been attributed to Du Fay. Indeed, it is a remarkable and powerful setting, well worth discovering, and it is given added impact by the urgency of Christopher Page's direction.

The performance intersperses the Mass Propers with verses from a recently discovered Latin song narrating the origins of the Marian antiphon *Salve Regina*, with a view to alternating monody and polyphony, and this works remarkably well. The rest of the concert, a collection of early carols, makes an attractively lightweight pendant to the major work. The Gothic Voices sing with great eloquence throughout this 66-minute programme, and this is one of their most attractively conceived collections. The recording, as ever with this series, is first class.

'*The Spirits of England and France*': ANON.: *Missa Veterum hominem; Jesu, fili Virginis; Doleo super te; Gaude Maria virgo; Deus creator omnium; Jesu salvator; A solis ortuas; Salvator mundi; Christe, Qui lux es; To many a well; Sancta Maria virgo; Mater ora filium; Ave maris stella; Pange lingua.* DUNSTABLE: *Beata mater.*
*** Hyp. CDA 66919.

The *Missa Veterum hominem* might be considered as complementary to the *Missa Caput*, offered on the previous CD from the Gothic Voices, and the present compilation is equally successful. Both Masses were composed at about the same time, in the late 1440s; both were written for four voices. Once again, in performing this work (with comparable urgency) Christopher Page seeks to vary the vocal texture by opening with an early, three-part carol, *Jesu, fili Virginis*, and alternating the Mass polyphony with monodic plainchant hymns. There are three of these, the last of which, *Deus creator omnium*, uses the same liturgical text as is employed in the Kyrie of the Mass.

'*Jerusalem: the Vision of Peace*' ANON.: *Luto carens et latere; Jerusalem! grant damage me fais; Te Deum; O levis aurula!; Hac in die Gedeonis; In Salvatoris; Veri vitis germine.* GUIOT DE DIJON: *Chanterau pour mon corage.* Easter Day Mass in the Church of Holy Sepulchre, Jerusalem (*c.* 1130): *Gradual; Alleluia; Gospel.* HUON DE ST QUENTIN:

Jerusalem se plaint et li pais; Luget Rachel iterum; Incocantes Dominum/Psalm: Deus, qui venerunt; Congaudet hodie celestis curia. HILDEGARD OF BINGEN: *O Jerusalem.*
*** Hyp. CDA 67039.

'Jerusalem: the Vision of Peace' was the underlying ideal which motivated the crusades, as medieval pilgrims believed that such an armed expedition, with papal blessing – killing Saracens on the way – would lead to universal peace and harmony! Anti-Semitism was another factor in the crusading spirit, expressing Christian anger and contempt for the Jews' denial of Christ. *Veri vitis germine* calls strongly on Judaea to return to the Cross.

On a personal level was the tragedy of separation for women whose lovers and husbands had departed for the Holy Land, perhaps never to return. All these elements are reflected in the present diverse anthology, from the opening three-part song of confidence in the power of God, to Hildegard's rhapsodic closing monody, an ecstatic eulogy of longing for Jerusalem and all it represented. The melancholy of a deserted woman's loss is lamented in *Jerusalem! grant damage me fais*, while the *Te Deum*, heard against tolling bells, and the excerpts from the Easter Day Mass represent the liturgy of the period. Harmony, where it occurs, is organum and has great character, and certainly all the music here has great vitality, and is splendidly sung.

'*Master of the Rolls*' (music by English composers of the 14th century, with King, Harrold, Podger, Nixon, Daniels, Charlesworth): ANON.: *Ab ora summa nuncius; Inter usitata/Inter tot et tales; Vexilla regni prodeunt; Singularis laudis digna; Dulcia [dona redemptoris]; Summum regen honoremus; Omnis terra/Habenti dabitur; Copiose caritatis; Missa Gabriel de celis; Pura, placens/Parfundement plure; Letetur celi cura; Salve Regina; Jesu fili Virginis* (Plainsong); *Jesu fili/Jesu lumen; Jesu fili Virginis; Sospitati dat egrotos; Exultemus et letemur; Stella maris illustrans omnia; Veni dilectus meus; Pange lingua; O sponsa dei electa; Generosa Jesse plantula; Musicorum collegio/ In templo dei.*
*** Hyp. CDA 67098.

Very few English composers of the fourteenth century are remembered by name. The word used to describe accomplished musicians of the period was magister (master): hence the title of this collection. Only six items here are monodic and what is remarkable is how individual are some of these compositions. *Singularis laudis digna*, for instance, with its whirls of parallel writing, or the simple but touching harmonization of the Marian *Dulcia [dona redemptoris]* and the lovely, lilting *Missa Gabriel de celis*, while *Jesus fili* (a trio) has some engaging rhythmic triplets. Perhaps the most remarkable, original and forward-looking of all is *Stella maris illustrans omnia*, where a highly unusual text is

matched by a comparably unpredictable use of chromatics.

Graham, Susan (mezzo-soprano)

'*French Operetta*' (with CBSO, Abel). Arias from: SIMONS: *Toi c'est moi.* MESSAGER: *L'Amour masqué; Coups de roulis; Les Dragons de l'Impératrice; Fortunio; Passionément; La Petite Fonctionnaire; Les P'tites Michu.* YVAIN: *Yes.* HONEGGER: *Les Aventures du roi Pausole.* HAHN: *Brummel; O mon bel inconnu; Ciboulette; Mozart.*
*** Erato 0927 42106-2.

In every way this is an enchanting disc, bringing together in sparkling performances a sequence of rare items which richly deserve revival. Messager's *Fortunio* has been rediscovered in recent years, largely thanks to the complete recording from Sir John Eliot Gardiner. Yet as the items here demonstrate, Messager, as well as conducting the first performance of Debussy's *Pelléas et Mélisande*, was in turn musical director of the Paris Opéra and Covent Garden, and also composed a sequence of other operettas. Reynaldo Hahn is also well-represented with charming items from four operettas, and it is good to be reminded that even Honegger made an unexpected foray into the genre. The Cuban composer Moïses Simons has been even more neglected, yet his colourful Spanish-American items equally add to the joy of this frothy collection, idiomatically accompanied and well-recorded. The notes contain an excellent essay by Patrick O'Connor.

'Gramophone Greats'

'*20 Gramophone All-time Greats*' (original mono recordings from 1907 to 1935): LEONCAVALLO: *Pagliacci: Vesti la giubba* (Caruso); *Mattinata* (Gigli). BISHOP: *Lo Here the Gentle Lark* (Galli-Curci with flute obbligato by Beringuer). PURCELL: *Nymphs and Shepherds* (Manchester Schools Children's Choir (Choir Mistress: Gertrude Riall), Hallé O, Harty). MENDELSSOHN: *Hear my Prayer – O for the Wings of a Dove* (Lough, Temple Church Ch., Thalben Ball). MARSHALL: *I Hear you Calling me* (McCormack). ELGAR: *Salut d'amour* (New SO, composer). J. STRAUSS JR: *Casanova: Nuns' Chorus* (Ch. & O of Grossen Schauspielhauses, Berlin, Hauke). RACHMANINOV: *Prelude in C sharp min., Op. 3/2* (composer). TRAD.: *Song of the Volga Boatmen* (Chaliapin). KREISLER: *Liebesfreud* (composer, Lamson). MOSS: *The Floral Dance* (Dawson, Moore). BACH: *Chorale: Jesu, Joy of Man's Desiring* (arr. & played Hess). HANDEL: *Messiah: Come unto Him* (Labette, O, Beecham). SAINT-SAENS: *Samson and Delilah: Softly Awakes my Heart* (Anderson). BIZET: *Fair Maid of Perth: Serenade* (Nash). CHOPIN: *Waltz in C sharp min., Op. 64/2* (Cortot). LEHAR: *Land of*

Smiles: You are my Heart's Delight (Tauber). KERN:
Showboat: Ol' Man River (Robeson). SULLIVAN:
The Lost Chord (Butt).

(M) (★★★) ASV mono CDAJA 5112.

It seems strange and somewhat sad that this marvellous collection of classical 78rpm hit records, covering a period of three decades, came from ASV rather than HMV (EMI), who are responsible for so many of the actual recordings. However, as we close for press EMI have made their own 'Classics for Pleasure' collection of 23 items duplicating only about half-a-dozen of the pieces here, and this is equally desirable (CFP 585 9112). Their amazing technical excellence means that they can be enjoyed today as they were then, with only occasional clicks and generally not too intrusive a background 'surface' noise to create the right ambience.

Caruso still projects vividly from a 1907 acoustic master and Amelita Galli-Curci's soprano is as clear and sweet as the day the recording was made (1919). Other highlights (for us) include the Manchester Schools Children's Choir of 250 voices, electrically recorded in Manchester's Free Trade Hall in 1929. The story goes that, just before the record was made, Sir Hamilton Harty bought cream buns and pop for every child, and that accounts for the warm smile in the singing. Master Ernest Lough's 'O for the Wings of a Dove' is another miracle of perfection from a young boy treble, and Peter Dawson's exuberant 'Floral Dance' has astonishing diction – you can hear every word – and here Gerald Moore's bravura accompaniment is a key part of the sheer pleasure this performance still gives.

Finally, Dame Clara Butt with her deep masculine contralto, clanging like a bell in its lowest register, delivers the sacred piece so beloved of Victorians, Sullivan's 'The Lost Chord'. The transfers are all good (except perhaps for Dame Myra Hess's *Jesu, Joy of Man's Desiring*, where the background noise surely could have been cut back a bit more).

Gray, Emily (soprano), Manchester Cathedral Choir, Christopher Stokes

'Passiontide' (with Buckley, Makinson):
MENDELSSOHN: *Hear my Prayer.* VAUGHAN
WILLIAMS: *O Taste and See.* HURFORD: *Litany to the Holy Spirit.* WESLEY: *Wash me Throughly.*
PERGOLESI: *Stabat Mater.* BYRD: *Civitas sancti tui.*
BACH: *O Sacred Head Sore Wounded; Bist du bei mir.* CASALS: *O vos omnes.* LOTTI: *Crucifixus.*
DERING: *O bone Jesu.* GIBBONS: *Drop, Drop, Slow Tears.* IRELAND: *Ex ore innocentiam.* GREENE: *Lord Let me Know mine End.* MILLER: *When I Survey the Wondrous Cross.*

(BB) ★★★ Naxos 8.557025.

In this wide-ranging collection the 15-year-old Emily Gray (who won BBC Radio 2's 'Choirgirl of the Year' in 2000) produces the firm traditional sound of the Anglican choirboy, slightly hooty, seemingly all the more powerful from a female throat, using her voice with care and taste. The sequence starts with the longest item, the one associated with Master Ernest Lough and his 1927 recording with the Temple Church Choir, Mendelssohn's 'Hear my Prayer', here more sharply dramatic under Christopher Stokes' direction, sweet and pure in the concluding section, 'O for the Wings of a Dove'. The other major item brings together four sections of Pergolesi's *Stabat Mater* in which Gray is joined by another young soprano, Claire Buckley, similar in style but nicely contrasted. The choir is first-rate too in that item, and generally they sing with fresh, clear tone and crisp ensemble, very well-recorded in Manchester Cathedral. Only in the Byrd Latin setting, *Civitas sancti tui*, does it rather lack variety. Rounding off the sequence comes Maurice Greene's weighty psalm-setting, 'Lord, Let me Know mine End'. The traditional congregational hymn, 'When I Survey the Wondrous Cross', to the tune *Rockingham*, then provides a rousing conclusion at a rich fortissimo.

Gueden, Hilde (soprano)

'Operetta Evergreens' (with Vienna Operetta Chorus & Vienna State Op. O, Stolz): Arias from:
KALMAN: *Gräfin Mariza.* BENATZKY/STOLZ: *The White Horse Inn.* LEHAR: *Der Zarewitsch; Zigeunerliebe.* FALL: *Madame Pompadour.* JOHANN STAUSS JR : *Casanova; Die Fledermaus; Wiener Blut.* STOLZ: *Der Favorit.* ZELLER: *Der Obersteiger.*
O. STRAUS: *The Chocolate Soldier.*

(M) ★★★ Decca Classic Recitals (ADD) 475 394-2.

Hilde Gueden's many delightful gramophone contributions to operetta tended latterly to rest in the shadow of Elisabeth Schwarzkopf, who brought a Lieder-like skill with words even to relatively banal lyrics. Gueden's approach was more direct, but she had this repertoire in her very being, a lilting feel for a Viennese melodic line and a natural stage presence, and this comes over on her recordings too. Her voice was heard at her freshest in an earlier mono recital, which we praised in our last *Yearbook* (Belart 461 623-2) and which is now deleted.

The present recital was recorded in 1961, and the voice shows some loss of bloom. Nevertheless there is plenty to delight here, from the lively opening aria from Kálmán's *Gräfin Mariza* to the very famous numbers from *The Chocolate Soldier* and *Die Fledermaus* – released many times on operetta compilations. The collection ends with *Wiener Blut* and leaves one with a deliciously warm Viennese glow. The splendidly alive and colloquial accompaniments under Robert Stoltz add much to this CD, and the whole programme emerges vividly on this Classic Recitals release. The original front cover of Miss Gueden and her pet dog is charmingly in period, even if the dog looks uncomfortable.

Gunn, Nathan (baritone), Kevin Murphy (piano)

'*American Anthem: From Ragtime to Art Song*': TRAD.: *Shenandoah.* GORNEY: *Brother can you Spare a Dime.* ROREM: *Early in the Morning; The Lordly Hudson.* SCHEER: *At Howard Hawks' House; Holding Each Other; Lean Away; American Anthem.* NILES: *The Lass from the Low Countree; I Wonder as I Wander.* MUSTO: *Recuerdo.* BARBER: *Nocturne; Sure on this Shining Night.* BOLCOM: *Fur (Murray the Furrier); Over the Piano; Black Max (As Told by the De Kooning Boys).* IVES: *Slugging a Vampire; Two Little Flowers* (and dedicated to them); *General William Booth Enters into Heaven.* HOIBY: *The Lamb.* arr. COPLAND: *At the River; Long Time Ago.*
(B) ★★★ EMI Début 5 73160-2.

The subtitle, 'From Ragtime to Art Song', sums up the breadth of this delightful collection, the imaginative choice of Nathan Gunn – as he describes it himself, 'a beautiful forest of songs'. Gunn is one of the most promising of young American singers, possessor of a glorious baritone of a velvety beauty, consistent throughout its range. If anyone is disconcerted to have 'Brother can you Spare a Dime' early on the list, it leads brilliantly to the most eclectic sequence, a reflection of Gunn's keen perception as well as of his musicianship. How welcome to have the work of such composers as Gene Scheer and William Bolcom well represented, alongside such predictable names as Charles Ives, Aaron Copland and Samuel Barber. The title, *American Anthem*, comes from the last song on the CD, a surging expression of patriotism worthy of an American 'Last Night of the Proms'. Sensitive accompaniment and well-balanced recording.

Hagegård, Håkan (baritone)

'*Dedication*' (with Schuback, piano): BRAHMS: *An die Nachtigall; An ein Veilchen; An die Mond.* FOERSTER: *An die Laute.* GOUNOD: *A toi mon coeur.* HAHN: *A Chloris.* MOZART: *An Chloë, K.524; Ich würd' auf meinem Pfad (An die Hoffnung), K.390.* SCHUBERT: *An Mignon; An den Tod; An den Mond; An den Leier; An die Musik; Am mein Herz.* R. STRAUSS: *Zueignung.* WOLF: *An eine Aeolsharfe.*
★★(*) BIS (ADD) CD 54.

This recital is called *Dedication*, and it begins with the Strauss song of that name. The collection first appeared in LP form in 1976 but was in circulation only intermittently in this country. The record was made at the outset of the distinguished Swedish baritone's career when he was in his mid-twenties and in wonderfully fresh voice. He sounds very much like a youthful Fischer-Dieskau but is at times a trace too studied, colouring the voice rather too expressively and adopting rather self-consciously deliberate

tempi. There are times when one longs for him to be a little more unbuttoned. However, there is far more to admire and relish than to criticize, in particular the gloriously fresh vocal tone, and the sensitive playing of Thomas Schuback. Admirers of Hagegård will probably have this on LP; others need not hesitate.

German and Scandinavian Songs (with Jones, piano) BRAHMS: *5 Songs, Op. 105; Vier ernste Gesänge, Op. 121.* SIBELIUS: *Black Roses (Svarta rosor), Op. 36/1; The Dream (Drömmen), Op. 13/5; The First Kiss (Den första kyssen), Op. 37/1; Sigh, Sedges, Sigh (Säv, säv, susa), Op. 36/4; The Diamond in the March Snow (Diamanten på marssnön), Op. 36/6; Was it a Dream? Op. 37/4.* STENHAMMAR: *Adagio, Op. 20/5; Florez and Whiteflower (Florez och Blanzeflor), Op. 3; Prince Aladdin of the Lamp (Prins Aladin av lampen), Op. 26/10; Starry Eye (Stjärnöga), Op. 20/1.*
★★(*) RCA 09026 68097-2.

The distinguished Swedish baritone is on home territory in Stenhammar's and Sibelius's Swedish settings, and his sense of style and phrasing are unerring, both here and in the wonderful Brahms *Vier ernste Gesänge.* The voice has inevitably lost something of the youthful bloom that made his singing so radiant but the musical intelligence and artistry are unimpaired. He is well partnered by Warren Jones and excellently recorded.

Hampson, Thomas (baritone)

'*Leading Man (Best of Broadway)*': KERN: *All the Things you are.* KRETZMER: *Les Misérables: Bring him Home.* LLOYD WEBBER: *Phantom of the Opera: Music of the Night.* RODGERS: *Carousel: Soliloquy.* LOEWE: *Gigi; Camelot: If Ever I would Leave You.* ADLER: *The Pajama Game: Hey There.* SONDHEIM: *Unusual Way; Not a Day Goes by.* NORMAN: *The Secret Garden: How could I Ever Know?* MENKEN: *Beauty and the Beast: If I can't Love her.*
★★★ EMI 5 55249-2.

Starting with a classic number by Jerome Kern, 'All the Things you are', Hampson's Broadway selection ranges on up to *The Phantom of the Opera* and *Les Misérables*, where atmosphere and evocation seem to weigh more heavily than good tunes. The *Soliloquy* from *Carousel* – one of the few numbers from that great musical without a big tune – here can be seen to point forward, but one number (among the most recent here, dating from 1991) unashamedly returns to older standards of tunefulness, 'How could I Ever Know?' from *The Secret Garden* by Marsha Norman and Lucy Simon. Hampson with his rich, dark voice seems totally at home in each number, finding no problems in adapting to this idiom, switching easily and aptly to half-speech in such a patter-number as the title-song from *Gigi*.

Paul Gemignani conducts what is called the American Theater Orchestra, though you have to look through the small print to learn that information. Full, immediate recording.

Disc 1: *Mélodies and Lieder* (with Parsons, piano): BERLIOZ: *Irlande, Op. 2: La Belle Voyageuse; Adieu, Bessy!; Le Coucher du soleil; L'Origine de la harpe; Elégie.* WAGNER: *Lieder: Mignonne; Tout n'est qu'imagines fugitives; Les Deux Grenadiers; 2 Lied des Mephistopheles: Es war einmal ein König; Was machst du mir; Der Tannenbaum.* LISZT: *Die Vätergruft; Go Not, Happy Day; Es rauschen die Winde; Ihr Auge; Uber alln Gipfein ist Ruh (Wanderers Nachtlied); Im Rhein, im schönen Strome; Es muss ein Wunderbares sein; Vergiftet sind meine Lieder; La Tombe et la rose; 'Comment', disaient-ils; Oh, quand je dors.*

Disc 2: *Edinburgh Festival Recital, 20–21 August 1993:* FRANZ: *Nun holt mir eine Kanne Wein; Ihr Auge; Die süisse Dirn' von Inverness.* LOEWE: *Findlay.* SCHUMANN: *Niemand; Dem roten Röslein gleicht mein Lieb; Hochländers Abscheid; Dichterliebe* (song-cycle), *Op. 48.* GRIEG: *Gruss; Dereinst; Lauf der Welt; Die verschwiegene Nachtigall; Zur Rosenzeit; Ein Traum.* BEETHOVEN: *An die ferne Geliebte* (song-cycle), *Op. 98.*
(B) ✱✱✱ EMI double fforte 5 75187-2 (2).

This EMI double fforte reissue joins together two quite different recitals, the second recorded live in the Usher Hall at the 1993 Edinburgh Festival. This includes as an engaging novelty – so appropriate for the occasion – settings of Robert Burns in German translation, including attractive items by the little-known Robert Franz. The six rare German-language songs by Grieg are a comparable success, as is the freshly spontaneous account of Beethoven's cycle, *An die ferne Geliebte.* However, what should be the highlight but proves a considerable disappointment is Schumann's *Dichterliebe,* which, with curiously measured tempi, refuses to spring to life and lacks both ironic subtlety and real depth of feeling.

Never mind, the companion collection is a different matter and received a ✸ on its first premium-priced appearance (with full texts). Hampson begins with glowing performances of five of the nine songs from Berlioz's *Irlande,* using translations from English texts by the poet Thomas Moore. The Liszt collection is equally magnetic, ending with a memorable performance of his setting of Victor Hugo, *Oh, quand je dors,* and the Wagner songs are equally winning, showing him unexpectedly and light-heartedly setting French love-songs. Hampson is in superb voice and at his most imaginative, while throughout both CDs Geoffrey Parson is the ideal accompanist, and the recording cannot be faulted. The only snag, and it is a serious one, is the absence of texts and translations.

Hemsley, Thomas (baritone)

Mélodies (with Hamburger or (i) Gürtler, piano): DUPARC: *Chanson triste; Elégie; Extase; L'Invitation au voyage, Lamento; Le Manoir de Rosemonde; Phidylé; La Vie antérieure.* FAURE: *5 Verlaine Songs, Op. 58; L'Horizon chimérique, Op. 118.* (i) ROUSSEL: *Odes anacréontique, Op. 31 & Op. 32.*
✱✱✱ Amphion PHI CD 166.

Although he was represented in the days of LP in operatic repertoire, Thomas Hemsley enjoyed scant exposure in Lieder or mélodie. BBC listeners will, of course, recall his broadcasts, some of which are found here. He proves as masterly an interpreter of French song as he is of Schubert and Wolf. The Roussel *Odes anacréontiques* are not otherwise available on disc and, apart from their artistic merits, sound excellent in these 1978 BBC recordings. The Fauré and Duparc come from 1973 with Paul Hamburger as pianist and are no less fine. Why has the BBC label not issued them?

Hendricks, Barbara (soprano)

'Nordic Songs' (with Pöntinen, piano): GRIEG: *6 Songs, Op. 48; En svane; Jeg elsker dig!; Med en Vandlilje; Solveigs Sång (Peer Gynt); Solveigs vuggevise; Våren.* NIELSEN: *Æbleblomst; Den første Laerke; 5 Strophic Songs; Studie efter Naturen.* SIBELIUS: *Demanten på marssnön; Flickan kom ifrån sin älsklings möte; Illalle; Svarta rosor; Säf, säf, susa; Våren flyktar hastigt.* RANGSTROM: *Afskedet; Bön till natten; Melodi; Pan; Vingar i natten.* TRAD.: *Som stjärnan uppå himmelen så klar.*
✱✱✱ EMI 5 568842-2.

Since the mid-1970s Barbara Hendricks has been a regular visitor to the Scandinavian countries (she has a Swedish husband) and has developed a special affinity for the *romans* repertoire. (The *romans* is the equivalent of the German Lied or the French mélodie.) On this disc she offers some of the most popular and finest examples of it, ranging from such perennial favourites as *En svane* and *Jeg elsker dig* to the more celebrated of the Sibelius such as *Säf, säf, susa* ('Sigh, Sedges, Sigh') and *Svarta rosor* ('Black Roses'). She seems equally at home in the artless simplicity of Nielsen's *Strophic Songs, Op. 21,* or the familiar Rangström settings of Bo Bergman. Rangström strikes us as the most eloquent of the Swedish *romans* composers, finer even than Stenhammar, though only a few of his 200 songs have received any attention on CD. *Bön till natten* ('Prayer to the Night') has a directness of appeal and dignity that Hendricks conveys with great sympathy. At times, as in Grieg's *Die verschtwiegene Nachtigall,* or Rangström's *Vingar i natten* ('Wings in the Night'), Ann Sofie von Otter (DG) distils the more haunting atmosphere, but for the most part these are poetic and sensitive readings, given with dedication and artistry. Roland Pöntinen is a supportive and imaginative partner throughout.

Spirituals (with Alexeev, piano): *Deep River; Ev'ry Time I Feel the Spirit; Fix me, Jesus; Git on Boa'd Little Child'n; His Name is So Sweet; Hold on!; Joshua Fit de Battle of Jericho; Nobody Knows de Trouble I've Seen; Oh what a Beautiful City!; Plenty Good Room; Roun' about de Mountain; Sometimes I Feel like a Motherless Child; Swing Low, Sweet Chariot; Talk about a Child that do Love Jesus; Were you There?; When I Lay my Burden down.*
*** EMI 7 47026-2.

So often spirituals can be made to seem too ingenuous, their deep reserve of feeling degraded into sentimentality. Not so here: Barbara Hendricks' vibrant identification with the words is thrilling, the jazz inflexions adding natural sophistication, yet not robbing the music of its directness of communication. Her lyrical singing is radiant, operatic in its eloquence of line, yet retaining the ecstasy of spirit, while the extrovert numbers – 'Joshua Fit de Battle of Jericho' a superb example – are full of joy in their gutsy exuberance. Dmitri Alexeev accompanies superbly and the very well-balanced recording has remarkable presence.

Hespèrion XX

'*Llibre Vermell de Monserrat*' (A fourteenth-century pilgrimage): *O Virgo splendens; Stella splendens in monte; Laudemus Virginem Mater est; Los set goyts recomptarem; Splendens ceptigera; Polorum regina omnium nostra; Cincti simus concanentes: Ave Maria; Mariam Matrem Virginem; Imperayritz de la ciutat joyosa; Ad mortem festinamus; O Virgo splendens hic in monte celso.*
(M) *** Virgin 5 61174-2.

In the Middle Ages the Spanish monastery of Monserrat was an important place of pilgrimage and, although a great deal of the music held in the library there was lost in a fire at the beginning of the nineteenth century, one early manuscript, the *Llibre Vermell* (Red Book), has survived to remind us of the music of that period. It dates from 1400 and is especially fascinating in including ten anonymous choral songs for the use of the pilgrims 'while holding night vigil' who may 'sometimes desire to sing and dance in the Church Square (where only respectable and pious songs may be sung)'.

The music is extraordinarily jolly and robust, often written in the style of the French virelais (featuring alternating musical lines, with the first framing a central repeated tune). Canonic devices are also used and the effect is often quite sophisticated. There is no better example of this spirited music than *Los set goyts*, an infectious round dance complete with refrain. Various instrumental groupings add lively

colour and support to the vocal line; the performances are full of joy, though at times emotionally respectful too. The analogue recording was made in France, but the resonant acoustic seems perfectly judged. This is a life-enhancing collection to cheer one up, and it shows that life in the Middle Ages was not always grim.

Hilliard Ensemble

English and Italian Madrigals:

English madrigals: MORLEY: *O Griefe Even on the Bud; When Loe, by Breake of Morning; Aprill is in my Mistris Face; Sweet Nimphe, Come to thy Lover; Miraculous Love's Wounding; Fyer and Lightning in Nets of Goulden Wyers.* WEELKES: *Thule, the Period of Cosmographie; O Care Thou wilt Dispatch mee; Since Robin Hood; Strike it up Tabor.* WILBYE: *Sweet Hony Sucking Bees; Adew Sweet Amarillis; Draw in Sweet Night.* J. BENNET: *Weepe O mine Eyes.* GIBBONS: *The Silver Swanne.* TOMKINS: *See, See the Shepherd's Queene.* WARD: *Come Sable Night.* VAUTOR: *Sweet Suffolk Owle.*

Italian madrigals: GASTOLDI: *Cantiam lieti cantiamo.* CAPRIOLI: *E d'un bel matin d'amore; Quella bella e biancha mano; Una leggiadra nimpha.* COMPERE: *Venite amanti insieme.* VERDALOT: *Divini occhi sereni; Con l'angelico riso; Madonna, il tuo bel viso; Fuggi, fuggi, cor mio; Si liet'e grata morte.* ARCADELT: *Se la dura durezza; Ahimé, dové, bel viso; Madonna, s'io v'offendo; Il bianco e dolce cigno.* PATAVINO: *Donne, venete al ballo.* CASUALANA: *Morir non pué il mio cuore.* MARENZIO: *Se la mia vita.* RORE: *Mia benigna fortuna; Ancor che col partire; O sonno.* NOLA: *Chi la gagliarda; Medici noi siamo; Tre ciechi siamo.* WILLAERT: *Madonna mia fa.* BELL'HAVER: *Quando saré mai quel zorno.* LASSUS: *Matona, mia cara.*
(BB) *** Virgin Veritas 2×1 5 61671-2 (2).

The first of these two discs is of English madrigals and was recorded in 1987. It is an enchanting disc; and, as might be guessed from the above spelling, Tudor pronunciation is used, which adds extra bite to the vocal timbre. Intonation and ensemble are flawless, and some of the songs are in five or six parts. If one feels that they could be a shade more unbuttoned at times and they do not always reflect the lighter moments with quite enough sparkle, there is so much here to beguile the ear that few will grumble. The Italian madrigals were recorded in 1991 and are hardly less enjoyable. Indeed, this second collection is is perhaps even more beautiful, and the programme is as rich and varied as in the English collection. A pity that there are no texts or translations and little about the music, but at super-bargain price one only expects such extras from Naxos.

'*A Hilliard Songbook*': New music for voices: GUY:
Un Coup de dès. FELDMAN: *Only.* MOODY:
Endechas y Canciones; Canticum Canticorum I.
HELLAWELL: *True Beautie* (cycle of 8 songs).
ROBINSON: *Incantation.* TORMIS: *Kullervo's
Message.* ANON.: *Adoro te devote.* MACMILLAN: ...
Here in Hiding ... PART: *And One of the Pharisees* ...;
Summa. LIDDLE: *Whale Rant.* METCALF: *Music for
the Star of the Sea.* FINNISSY: *Stabant autem iuxta
cruceme.* CASKEN: *Sharp Thorne.*
★★★ ECM 453 259-2 (2).

The Hilliard Ensemble are best known for exploring
the world of early music. In this CD, however, they
survey modern trends and at times they find a surprising affinity with the repertoire with which they
are more familiar. The opening number here is
avant-garde with a vengeance. Extraordinary instrumental noises (contrived from an amplified double-
bass) act as a prelude to *Un Coup de dès*, and the
performance appears to turn into a fight among the
participants, with animal noises thrown in.

Then we turn to real music, Morty Feldman's
touching, unaccompanied solo soliloquy 'Only',
about flight (Rogers Covey-Crump). Ivan Moody's
set of four *Endechas y canciones* chime with the
current trend towards medievalism, very bare in
their part-writing but spiced with dissonances. Piers
Hellawell's melodic lines are unpredictable, but his
eight vignettes are all very brief and concentrated:
the music fits the Elizabethan texts, which are about
colours. The set is held together effectively by four
different settings of 'True Beautie', which are quite
haunting, and it is made the more effective by alternating baritone, tenor and counter-tenor soloists.
The closing concerted number, 'By Falsehood', is
genuinely poignant.

Paul Robinson's 'Incantation' (the text is Byron's)
is an ambitious (15-minute) dialogue between lead
singer (a bit like a cantor) and the main group,
usually moving chordally using a spiced modal harmony. 'Kullervo's Message' is a lively ballad, setting
an English translation from *The Kalevala*.

The second disc opens with Gregorian chant, then
shocks the listener with the pungent fortissimo dissonance at the opening of James MacMillan's ingeniously woven motet. After the more familiar style of
Arvo Pärt we move on to Elizabeth Liddle's mournful 'Whale Rant', in which two texts are presented in
bravura juxtaposition, one set to a famous hymn
with the harmony touched up, the other a plangent
soliloquy. The result is something of a *tour de force*.
John Casken's 'Sharp Thorne' brings exuberant
bursts of sound, and we finally return to Ivan Moody
setting texts from 'The Song of Songs', which emphasize the link modern composers have found with the
past. The whole programme is sung with great eloquence and is beautifully recorded, and no one could
accuse any of the composers here of writing in a
routine manner.

Holst Singers, Stephen Layton

'*Ikon*' (with (i) Bowman, counter-tenor):
SVIRIDOV: *Three choruses from Tsar Feodor
Ioannovich; Four choruses from Songs of Troubled
Times.* GRETCHANINOV: *The Cherubic Hymn;* (i)
The Creed. Our Father. KALINNIKOV: *Radiant
Light.* TCHAIKOVSKY: *We Hymn Thee; The
Cherubic Hymn; Blessed are They.* PART:
Magnificat. GORECKI: *Totus Tuus.* NYSTEDT:
Immortal Bach.
★★★ Hyp. CDA 66928.

The Orthodox tradition has regularly inspired Russian composers to write with a rare fervour for
unaccompanied chorus. This hauntingly beautiful
disc was inspired by live performances given by the
Holst Singers, beginning with pieces of extraordinary, dark intensity by Gyorgy Sviridov. Born in 1915,
he defied all Soviet bans on religious music, echoing
Tchaikovsky in his exotic harmonies and dramatic
contrasts but with a twentieth-century flavour. A
sequence of interlinked items by Tchaikovsky and
Gretchaninov brings fascinating contrasts, leading to
a fine *Magnificat* by Arvo Pärt and a long piece by
Gorecki in the Polish Catholic tradition, touchingly
simple in harmony. Radiant performances and
recording, with James Bowman soaring away as
counter-tenor soloist.

Horne, Marilyn (mezzo)

Arias (with ROHCG O, H. Lewis) from: ROSSINI:
La Cenerentola; L'Italiana in Algeri; Semiramide.
MEYERBEER: *Les Huguenots; Le prophète.* MOZART:
La clemenza di Tito. DONIZETTI: *La figlia del
reggimento.*
☞ (M) ★★★ Decca Classic Recitals (ADD) 475 395-2.

This 1964 recital was one of the most spectacular
coloratura recordings to appear after the war. Marilyn Horne's really big and firm mezzo voice has no
difficulty whatever in coping with the most tricky
florid passages and, to match everything, her musicianship is impeccable. Her range, too, is astounding,
just as free and unstrained above the stave as below,
and this first solo record was an exciting promise for
what was to follow. Henry Lewis (then her husband)
conducts sympathetically, and the recording remains
vivid and full.

'*Just for the Record: The Golden Voice*':

Disc 1: Arias from: BIZET: *Carmen.* SAINT-SAENS:
Samson et Dalila. ROSSINI: *Semiramide; L'Italiana
in Algeri; La donna del lago.* HANDEL: *Semele;
Rodelinda.* GLUCK: *Orfeo ed Euridice.* MEYERBEER:
Le prophète. THOMAS: *Mignon.*

Disc 2: Excerpts from: LAMPUGNI: *Meraspe.*
DONIZETTI: *Lucrezia Borgia.* BELLINI: *Norma.*

(with Sutherland). VERDI: *Il trovatore* (with Pavarotti). PONCHIELLI: *La Gioconda* (with Tebaldi). Songs: SCHUBERT: *Nacht und Träume*. SCHUMANN: *Abendlied*. NIN: *Jésus de Nazareth* (with Katz, piano). TRAD.: *Shenandoah*. COPLAND: *Old American Songs: I Bought me a Cat; At the River*. MALOTTE: *The Lord's Prayer*. BERNSTEIN: *West Side Story: Somewhere*. FOSTER: *Jeannie with the Light Brown Hair*.

(B) ✶✶✶ Double Decca (ADD/DDD) 476 122-2 (2).

It is good to see Marilyn Horne returning to the roster of vocal recitalists with a Double Decca celebrating her seventieth birthday! Nearly all the recordings here come from the 1960s and 1970s and have been out of the catalogue for some time. The first disc opens with the colourfully vivid *Habañera* from Bernstein's complete set of *Carmen*, but most of the other items are drawn from the two recitals she recorded with her then husband, the late Henry Lewis, in the 1960s. The first (with the Royal Opera House Covent Garden Orchestra) we described at the time as one of the most spectacular coloratura début records to appear since the war. The excerpts included here are the two Rossini arias and the Meyerbeer. The excerpts from her follow-up recital with the Vienna Opera Orchestra include a long-breathed, spacious and richly sensual *Mon coeur s'ouvre à ta voix* from *Samson et Dalila* and the Mignon scene, which is both sparkling and dramatic. But throughout these excerpts she continually delights and astonishes; the range is astounding, just as free and unrestrained above the stave as below.

The highlights of the second CD include her famous confrontation scene as Adalgisa with Joan Sutherland in Act II of *Norma*, and her vibrant duet with Renata Tebaldi from the complete *La Gioconda*. She is equally impressive as Azucena in *Il trovatore*, opposite a golden-voiced Pavarotti; but this excerpt is unnecessarily cut short. Her wider repertoire is demonstrated with the beautifully sung Lieder, and she bridges the stylistic gap between popular and concert repertory with supreme confidence. The tangily characterful American popular items were recorded much later, in 1986, notably the two Copland songs, which are particularly delightful, the famous Bernstein excerpt, Carl Davis's arrangement of 'Shenandoah', and the engaging final item (with Osian Ellis), 'Jeannie with the Light Brown Hair'. Altogether a treasurable representation of a great artist and an astounding vocal range. The Decca recording is outstandingly vivid.

Huddersfield Choral Society, Brian Kay; Phillip McCann; Simon Lindley

'*A Christmas Celebration*' (with Sellers Engineering Band): TRAD.: *Ding Dong Merrily on High; Kumbaya; Joys seven; Away in a Manger; Deck the*

Hall; *O Christmas Tree (Tannenbaum); Coventry Carol*. JAMES: *An Australian Christmas*. GRUBER: *Silent Night*. BACH: *Cantata No. 140: Zion Hears the Watchmen's Voices*. GARDNER: *The Holly and the Ivy*. arr. RICHARDS: *A Merry Little Christmas*. HOLST: *In the Bleak Mid-winter*. arr. WILLCOCKS: *Tomorrow shall be my Dancing Day*. BRAHMS: *Lullaby*. arr. SMITH: *Santa Claus-Trophobia*. MATHIAS: *Sir Christèmas*. LANGFORD: *A Christmas Fantasy*.

(M) ✶✶✶ Chan. 4530.

Sumptuously recorded in the generous acoustic of Huddersfield Town Hall, opening with a spectacular arrangement of 'Ding Dong Merrily' and closing with Gordon Langford's colourful pot-pourri *Fantasy*, this CD offers rich choral tone, well laced with opulent brass. There are simple choral arrangements too, beautifully sung by the Huddersfield choir, like Stephen Cleobury's 'Joy's Seven', Langford's 'Deck the Hall' and David Willcocks's slightly more elaborate 'Tomorrow shall be my Dancing Day', while Grüber's 'Silent Night' remains the loveliest of all serene carols.

In other favourites the brass is nicely intertwined, as in 'Away in a Manger' and the 'Coventry Carol', or it provides a sonorous introduction, as in Holst's 'In the Bleak Mid-winter'. Mathias's rhythmically energetic 'Sir Christèmas' provides a little spice. The brass are given their head in a solo spot, an effective novelty number, 'Santa Claus-Trophobia', arranged by Sandy Smith, which brings an impressive contribution from the solo tuba. Undoubtedly the brass contribution adds much to the entertainment value of this superbly recorded and well-presented 70-minute concert.

Hvorostovsky, Dmitri (baritone)

'*Passione di Napoli*' (with Russian Philh. O, Orbelian) BIXIO: *Parlami d'amor; Mariù*. CANNIO: '*O surdato 'nnammurato*. CARDILLO: *Core 'ngrato; Cottrau Santa Lucia*. DE CURTIS: *Canta pe'me!; Non ti scordar di me; Torna a Surriento; Voce 'e notte! DI CAPUA: Maria, Marì; O sole mio*. FALVO: *Dicetencello vuie*. GAMBARDELLA: *Comme facette mammeta?* GASTALDON: *Musica proibita*. TAGLIAFERRI: *Passione*. TOSTI: *A Vucchella; Marechiare*. TRAD.: *Fenesta che lucive; Logi; Medvedev; Mnatsakanov*.

✶✶(✶) Delos DE 3290.

The Siberian baritone Dmitri Hvorostovsky has here clearly wondered why tenors should have all the fun in the Neapolitan song repertoire. Maybe Italian baritones are too firmly conditioned towards villainy by Italian opera to think of themselves as passionate lovers. Hvorostovsky points out that this repertory has been in his blood from his early days as a student, and the performances bear that out. As well as being physically a glamorous figure, he sports a voice with all the regulation heart-throb required for this repertoire, rich and firm. In this collection, recorded in Moscow, he pulls out all the stops without ever resorting to coarseness, even if understandably he comes close in his outburst over *O sole mio*. He characterizes well, bringing out distinctions of mood and timbre, and the voice is more Italianate than Slavonic. Though this will delight both devotees of Neapolitan song and fans of the singer, the snag lies in the soupy orchestrations with sound 'enhanced' through an echo chamber to create a swimming-bath acoustic.

Isokoski, Soile (mezzo-soprano)

Finnish Sacred Songs (with Helsinki PO, Storgårds).
** Ondine ODE 1034-2.

Here we have 50 minutes of hymns and sacred songs, only three of which last longer than two minutes. Soile Isokoski produces wonderful sounds, but for the most part these are unremarkable songs. Of course there are good things – Madetoja's 'I Want to Go Home' is one example – but there are too many sentimental ones, such as 'Our Homeland' by Ilmari Hannikainen, better known as a pianist who played in London in the 1920s and whose brother, the conductor Tauno, was admired for his mono LP records of the Sibelius *Four Legends* and the *Fourth Symphony*. All the same, there is all too little variety of mood and, despite the artistry this distinguished singer brings to these pieces, too many of them are unrewarding.

Jo, Sumi (soprano)

'Les Bijoux': Arias from: GOUNOD: *Roméo et Juliette; Faust.* THOMAS: *Mignon; Hamlet; Mirielle.* MEYERBEER: *L'Etoile du nord; Les Huguenots.* G. CHARPENTIER: *Louise.* MASSENET: *Manon.* BIZET: *Les Pêcheurs de perles.* OFFENBACH: *Robinson Crusoé.*
*** Erato 3984 23140-2.

For all the delights of French operetta and opéra comique, it is good to hear the breadth of Sumi Jo's artistry when taking mature operatic roles. The famous *Polonaise* from *Mignon* sparkles iridescently, Gounod's waltz songs have both grace and charm, and in Meyerbeer's *L'Etoile du nord* the vocal/flute duet is as captivating as ever. But Louise's *Depuis le jour* brings an additional dimension in its warmly sympathetic phrasing, and Jo's portrait of Manon is equally touching, as is Leila's *Cavatina* from *Les Pêcheurs de perles*, with its characteristic Bizet horn writing. But perhaps the highlight is the Mad scene from Thomas's *Hamlet*, far more than a coloratura display. Here Jo is given fine support by the conductor, Giuliano Carella, with the opening beautifully

prepared. The recital finishes on an upbeat with a charming Offenbach waltz song made famous by Joan Sutherland. As with the Decca disc below, this is a voice that takes naturally to recording, especially when the acoustic is pleasingly warm.

Virtuoso arias (with Monte Carlo PO, Olmi) from: ROSSINI: *Il barbiere di Siviglia.* BELLINI: *La sonnambula.* DONIZETTI: *Lucia di Lammermoor.* DELIBES: *Lakmé.* RICHARD STRAUSS: *Ariadne auf Naxos.* VERDI: *Rigoletto.* MEYERBEER: *Dinorah.* BERNSTEIN: *Candide.* MOZART: *Die Zauberflöte* (with O de Paris Ens., Jordan). YOUNG-HA HOON: *Song: Boribat.*
*** Erato 4509 97239-2.

This is among the most brilliant and commanding recitals of coloratura arias made in the 1990s. Though the recording brings out a slight flutter in Sumi Jo's lovely voice, the sweetness and tenderness of her singing, so different from the hardness of many coloratura sopranos, are formidably established over the widest range of arias. Sumi Jo's clarity, with no hint of stridency, coupled with a dreamy quality in the delivery, reminds one of the remark of an opera critic many years ago, that Galli-Curci sounded like 'a nightingale half-asleep'.

Not that there is anything sleepy in Sumi Jo's singing, which is beautifully controlled. That is so both in firework arias like Rosina's *Una voce poco fa* from Rossini's *Barber* and over the sustained spans of the big aria in Bellini's *La sonnambula* (full recitative leading to *Ah non credea mirarti* and *Ah! non giunge*) and the Mad scene from Donizetti's *Lucia di Lammermoor*. Though 'Glitter and be Gay' from Bernstein's *Candide* lacks a little in fun, Delibes' Bell Song from *Lakmé* is aptly sensuous and Zerbinetta's aria from *Ariadne auf Naxos* aptly extrovert, while the reading of the Queen of the Night's second aria from Mozart's *Zauberflöte* is lighter and even faster than with Solti in his Decca set. With tenderness and poise regular ingredients, alongside brilliance, not least in the honeyed sounds of the final, Korean song, all ten arias are to be cherished. The voice is well caught, though the orchestral accompaniment has less presence.

'Carnaval!' (with ECO, Bonynge): French coloratura arias from: OFFENBACH: *Un Mari à la porte.* MASSENET: *Don César de Bazan.* FÉLICIEN DAVID: *La Perle du Brésil.* GRETRY: *L'Amant jaloux.* BALFE: *Le Puits d'amour.* MESSAGER: *Madame Chrysanthème.* THOMAS: *Le Songe d'une nuit d'été.* ADAM: *Les Pantins de Violette; Si j'étais roi.* HEROLD: *Le Pré aux clercs.* DELIBES: *Le Roi l'a dit.* BOIELDIEU: *La Fête du village voisin.* MASSE: *La Reine Topaze: Carnaval de Venise.*
☚ ✲ (M) *** Decca 476 1527.

If anything, this singing is even more astonishing than Sumi Jo's Erato recital. The music may be more frivolous, but what delectable freshness and vocal sparkle there is in every number, and this repertoire is far rarer. After the frothy Offenbach introduction, the nightingale lightness and precision in Massenet's *Sevillana* from *Don César de Bazan* is matched by the vocal poise in the *Couplets du Mysoli* from David's *La Perle du Brésil*, with William Bennett playing the flute solo. Equally, Jo trills along seductively in Adam's *Chanson du canari*, in which the song's pensive quality is also nicely caught. This is Galli-Curci territory, and Sumi Jo doesn't come second best; moreover, her voice is fuller and warmer. The softness and delicious ease of her *pianissimo* top notes also recall Rita Streich at her finest, in both Adam and Thomas, and in the Grétry *Je romps la chaîne qui m'engage*. Her ravishingly easy legato in Balfe's *Rêves d'amour* is a joy, while Hérold's *Jours de mon enfance* brings a duet with a solo violin (the excellent Anthony Marwood), and here one is reminded of the young Sutherland. Delibes' Waltz Song from *Le Roi l'a dit* is bewitching, and the recital ends with a sparkling *Boléro* of Boieldieu and an unforgettable interpolation of the *Carnival of Venice* into an aria by Victor Massé, with astonishingly free divisions. Throughout, Bonynge provides stylish and beautifully pointed accompaniments, as he has done for Sutherland in the past, and the Decca recording could hardly be bettered. An unmissable bargain, now at mid-price on Universal's 'Penguin ❀ Collection', with texts and translations included.

'*The Art of Sumi Jo*' (with ECO, WNO, Bonynge): Arias from AUBER: *Le Domino noir*. GRETRY: *L'Amant jaloux*. MOZART: *Die Zauberflöte*. OFFENBACH: *Le Mari à la porte*. ADAM: *Le Toréador*. MASSENET: *Don César de Bazan*. DAVID: *La Perle du Brésil*. BOIELDIEU: *La Fête du village voisin*. MASSE: *La Reine Topaz: Carnaval de Venise*.
*** Decca 458 927-2.

Sumi Jo's voice is not only wonderfully agile and pretty, it can deepen and become tender. Even in the middle of the unbelievable fireworks of David's *Couplets du Mysoli* (where the solo flute is quite upstaged in the many vocal interchanges), Jo can suddenly touch the listener with her gentleness. Five of the key items here are understandably also included in Decca's *Coloratura Spectacular* (above), including a thrilling *Der Hölle Rache* from *Die Zauberflöte*, the delicious Offenbach *Valse tyrolienne* and the closing *Carnaval de Venise*, which has to be heard to be believed. But there are many other delights, including exquisite singing in *Je romps la chaîne qui m'engage* from Grétry's *L'Amant jaloux*, and the excerpts from the recent complete recording of Adam's *Le Toréador*, where *Flamme vengeresse* is utterly winning, and the ensemble *Ah! vous dirai-je maman* is unforgettable for its lighthearted sparkle. Richard Bonynge, ever affectionate, displays the lightest touch in the accompaniments, and the Decca recording projects the voice warmly without the slightest suspicion of edge or hardness.

Jones, Della (mezzo-soprano)

Arias, Duets and Ensembles (sung in English, with Plazas, Miles, Mason, Magee, Shore, Bailey, LPO, Parry) from: ROSSINI: *The Barber of Seville; The Italian Girl in Algiers; Tancredi; William Tell.* HANDEL: *Rodelinda; Xerxes.* MOZART: *The Clemency of Titus.* DONIZETTI: *La favorita; Lucrezia Borgia.* BELLINI: *Norma.* GERMAN: *Merrie England.* PONCHIELLI: *La Gioconda.* Song: BISHOP: *Home Sweet Home.*
(M) ******* Chan. 3049.

Recorded in 2000, this formidable collection of 14 arias and ensembles testifies to the continuing vocal health of this ever-characterful singer, whether in the legato of Handel's *Largo* or the coloratura of the Rossini, Donizetti and Bellini cabalettas. It was daring of this mezzo to include among the ensemble numbers the celebrated Norma–Adalgisa duet (rounded with a joyous account of the cabaletta), in which she takes the title role with Anne Mason as her partner. The *Brindisi* from *Lucrezia Borgia* brings more exuberance, and it is a charming touch to have the collection lightly rounded off with Queen Elizabeth's song from *Merrie England* ('With Sword and Buckler by her Side') and 'Home Sweet Home', with the singer accompanying herself at the piano. Clear, well-balanced sound.

Joyful Company of Singers, Peter Broadbent

'*A Garland for Linda*' (with Davies, flute; Cohen, cello): TAVENER: *Prayer for the Healing of the Sick.* JUDITH BINGHAM: *Water Lilies.* JOHN RUTTER: *Musica Dei donum.* DAVID MATTHEWS: *The Doorway of the Dawn.* MCCARTNEY: *Nova.* ROXANA PANUFNIK: *I Dream'd.* MICHAEL BERKELEY: *Farewell.* GILES SWAYNE: *The Flight of the Swan.* RODNEY BENNETT: *A Good-night.*
*** EMI 5 56961-2.

The tragic death of Linda McCartney led to this remarkable commemorative collection of music, notable for its serenity and lyrical beauty, with Paul McCartney's own piece, *Nova*, standing out alongside Michael Berkeley's moving *Farewell* and Richard Rodney Bennett's touchingly simple *A Good-night*. The programme opens with Vaughan Williams's lovely *Silence and Music*, for which his wife, Ursula, appropriately wrote the words. John Rutter's offering characteristically has a flute introduction, as does Giles Swayne's quite different, haunting evocation of *The Flight of the Swan*, but every piece here is moving and beautifully sung and recorded; they will not only serve as a remembrance, but also give much pleasure to a great many listeners.

Kanawa, Dame Kiri Te (soprano)

'*Greatest Hits*': Arias from: PUCCINI: *Suor Angelica; Turandot.* CILEA: *Adriana Lecouvreur.* BOITO: *Mefistofele.* GIORDANO: *Andrea Chénier* (with LSO, Chung). G. CHARPENTIER: *Louise.* BIZET: *Les Pêcheurs de perles* (with ROHCG, Tate). KORNGOLD: *Die tote Stadt* (with Philharmonia O, Rudel). Songs: MOORE: *The Last Rose of Summer.* TRAD.: *Greensleeves; Annie Laurie* (with Nat. PO, Gamley). KERN: *All the Things you are; Smoke Gets in Your Eyes.* BERLIN: *Always* (with O, Tunick).
**(*) EMI 5 56722-2.

This collection certainly gives a rounded picture of the glorious voice and vocal art of Dame Kiri. But while the lovely aria from Korngold's *Die tote Stadt* is especially welcome, some ears will find the silky phrasing and voluptuous tone not quite idiomatic in the popular ballads of Jerome Kern and Irving Berlin, and certainly the traditional items like 'Greensleeves' and 'Annie Laurie' call for a more artless approach, even though all these songs bring a ravishing beauty of line. Four of the Italian and French arias are included on the mid-priced 'Diva' collection below, and this would seem an even more recommendable disc.

'*Diva*': Arias from: CHARPENTIER: *Louise.* MASSENET: *Manon; Hérodiade.* BERLIOZ: *La Damnation de Faust.* GLUCK: *Iphigénie en Tauride.* PUCCINI: *Suor Angelica.* LEONCAVALLO: *Pagliacci.* GIORDANO: *Andrea Chénier.* CILEA: *Adriana Lecouvreur.* RICHARD STRAUSS: *Der Rosenkavalier.* TCHAIKOVSKY: *Eugene Onegin.*
(M) *** EMI 65578-2.

Like others in EMI's 'Diva' series of compilations, this selection has been shrewdly drawn from the limited number of recordings Dame Kiri has made for that company, principally a recital of French opera arias recorded in 1988 and an Italian opera recital made in 1989. These provide a fruitful source for the first nine items, but they are crowned by excerpts from two complete opera sets, the Marschallin's monologue and final solo from Act I of *Der Rosenkavalier* and (in English) Tatiana's Letter scene from *Eugene Onegin*, a recording made with Welsh National Opera forces. The beauty of the voice is beautifully caught.

Karnéus, Katarina (mezzo-soprano), Roger Vignoles (piano)

Lieder: RICHARD STRAUSS: *Die Nacht; Meinem Kinde; Begegnung; Nachtgang; Ruhe, meine Seele! Allerseelen; Mein Herz ist stumm; Morgen!; Wie sollten wir geheim sie halten.* MAHLER: *Frühlingsmorgen; Erinnerung; Hans und Grethe; Des Knaben Wunderhorn: Ich ging mit Lust durch einen grünen Wals; Ablösung in Sommer; Scheiden und Meiden. 4 Rückert Lieder.* MARX: *Und gestern hat er mir Rosen gebracht; Malenblüten; Hat dich die Liebe berührt; Wofür; Venetianisches Wiegenlied.*
(B) *** EMI Début 5 73168-2.

Winner of the Cardiff Singer of the World competition in 1995, Katerina Karnéus was born in Stockholm but completed her singing studies in London. Hers is a beautifully warm and even mezzo, which she uses with great imagination and fine attention to detail, in both words and music. This is a formidable Lieder collection in EMI's Début series, with the golden beauty of Strauss songs leading to a wideranging selection of Mahler songs, with charming early songs leading to four of the five *Rückert Lieder* (*Um Mitternacht* the one left out). The Joseph Marx songs, simpler in style, provide an apt and attractive tailpiece. Roger Vignoles is the most sensitive partner. Well-balanced sound.

Kiehr, Maria Cristina (soprano)

'*Cantala la Maddalena*' (with Concerto Soave, Aymes): Arias and scenas by: AGNELETTI; LUIGI ROSSI; FRESCOBALDI; GRATIANI; MAZZOCCI; BEMABEL; FERRARI. Lute pieces by: FRESCOBALDI; MICHELANGELO ROSSI; KAPSBERGER.
**(*) HM HMC 901698.

After her two superb recitals of the music of Strozzi and Monteverdi (in our main volume) this is a disappointment. The performances are altogether plainer, Kiehr's voice less honeyed. The repertoire is concerned with the subject of the many *Stabat Mater* settings – Mary in despair, grieving at the foot of the cross, and is of considerable interest, but the music itself is expressively sung rather than greatly moving the listener.

King's College, Cambridge, Choir, Stephen Cleobury and Boris Ord

'*Carols from Kings*': Festivals of Lessons and Carols (Recorded live in the Chapel, 1954 & 2000).

Includes from 1954 & 2000 services: GAUNTLETT: *Once in Royal David's City; Bidding Prayer.* 1954: BACH: *Christmas Oratorio: And there were Sheperds; Up! Good Christian Folk!* 1954 & 2000: TRAD.: *In dulci jubilo.* 1954: *Hail! Blessed Mary!; A Virgin Most Pure.* 1954 & 2000: *While Shepherds Watched.* 1954: CORNELIUS: *The Three Kings.* TRAD.: *Sing Lullaby; O Come All Ye Faithful.* 2000: *Quem pastores laudavere; Angels from the Realms of Glory.* DARKE: *In the Bleak Midwinter.* TRAD.: *Quitter pasteurs.* GRUBER: *Silent Night.* CHILCOTT: *Shepherd's Carol.* TRAD.: *The Angels and the Shepherds; Riu, riu, riu; O Little Town of Bethlehem.* BERLIOZ: *Childhood of Christ:*

Shepherd's Farewell. RUTTI: *I Wonder as I Wander.* EDWARDS: *Small Wonder the Star.* TRAD.: *Sussex Carol; Gloria in excelsis Deo; God Rest ye Merry Gentlemen.* 1954 & 2000: *Blessing; Benediction.* 2000: MENDELSSOHN: *Hark the Herald Angels Sing;* (Organ) *Chorale: Vom Himmel hoch.* (Includes discussion by Sir David Willcocks, Sir Philip Ledger and Stephen Cleobury.)

(*) BBC Opus Arte **DVD OA 0815 D. Producer: James Whitbourn. V/D: David Kremer.

Splendid singing throughout by the Choir, of course, and the visual images of the Chapel are eye-catchingly beautiful. The recording also is very fine and is available either in stereo (which is excellent) or surround sound. However at the opening of the 2000 service, rather than creating a distant processional image, the camera focuses closely on the choirboy who introduces 'Once in Royal David's City'; and elsewhere, because the cameras are placed and moved to maximize the visual imagery, the actual singing within the expansive King's ambience (although synchronized) often does not seem sharply to relate to what one sees. One has the paradoxical impression of simultaneous audio and visual images, often closely observed, that are somehow not intrinsically connected, although of course they are.

But when one turns to the black-and-white film of the 1954 service, with its very simple camera technique, the magic of the occasion is tellingly projected, even though the sound itself is not absolutely secure. As the choir begins its processional through the arch towards the viewer and the Provost, standing beside the treble soloist, gently conducts his solo, the effect is most moving, and the singing of Boris Ord's choir is luminous throughout. Indeed the whole of this much shorter earlier service is engrossing, not least because of the recognizable linguistic mode of the BBC announcer's introduction, and the equally characterful reading of the lessons by unnamed lay readers in the style of English as it was spoken in Cambridge fifty years ago. The shots of the congregation when they join in 'O Come All Ye Faithful' are similarly nostalgic.

The music is followed by an extended dialogue between the three directors of the Choir, which makes a further valuable record of the occasion. The various facilities offered by the DVD include the opportunity to listen only to the carols or choose the full service, including the lessons.

King's College, Cambridge, Choir, Stephen Cleobury

'*Anthems from Kings: English Choral Favourites*': WOOD: *Hail, Gladdening Light.* IRELAND: *Greater Love hath no Man.* PARRY: *I was Glad.* HARRIS: *Bring us, O Lord God; Faire is the Heaven.* BAINTON: *And I Saw a New Heaven.* HOWELLS: *Like as the Hart.* STANFORD: *Gloria in Excelsis;*

Beati quorum vita. BALFOUR GARDINER: *Evening Hymn.* WALFORD DAVIES: *God be in my Head.* NAYLOR: *Vox dicentis clama.* VAUGHAN WILLIAMS: *Let All the World.*

*** BBC Opus Arte **DVD** OS 0934 D.

With a delightful supplementary half-hour feature on the King's Choir and its sixteen talented boy trebles, this is a charming recital disc of English church music. Parry's coronation anthem, *I was glad*, and Walford Davies's 'God be in my Head' are favourites with more than specialist listeners, but all the items here are most attractive and superbly done, leading up to the culminating item, Vaughan Williams's striking setting of George Herbert's Antiphon, 'Let All the World'. With evocative camera-work, most items are sung by the choir in their regular choir-stalls, but several of the more intimate numbers have them grouped at the far end of the sanctuary in King's Chapel in front of the altar, with the Rubens painting of the Nativity behind them. As the extra feature brings out, the boy choristers are boarders in the Choir School, which also has many day-students from the Cambridge area. The life of the school and the training of these young musicians is fascinating, demonstrating that though their routine is rigorous, they find it all fun.

'Best Loved Hymns' (with the Wallace Collection, Williams, harp, Bayl & Williamson, organ): *A Mighty Fortress is our God; All my Hope on God is Founded; All People that on Earth do Dwell; Be Thou my Vision; Come down, O Love Divine; Dear Lord and Father of Mankind; Glorious Things of Thee are Spoken; Let All Mortal Flesh Keep Silent; My Song is Love Unknown; Morning has Broken; O what their Joy and their Glory must be; Praise to the Lord, the Almighty, the King of Creation; Praise, My Soul, the King of Heaven; The Day Thou Gavest, Lord, is Ended; The Lord is My Shepherd; Thine be the Glory; Drop, Drop, Slow Tears; When I Survey the Wondrous Cross.*

*** EMI 5 57026-2.

Best-loved hymns and some lesser-known ones, introduced by brass (which returns in one or two of the more ambitious hymns and to close the concert with the *Old Hundredth*). But for the most part they are presented simply, with full choir sometimes alternating with the men or boys, and refined harp accompaniments to contrast with the organ. Magnificent singing, splendid recording, a perfect acoustic and what tunes they are! If you like hymns they could not be better presented.

'*The King's Collection*' (with Vivian or Quinney, organ): PARRY: *I was Glad.* MOZART: *Ave verum corpus.* ALLEGRI: *Miserere* (ed. Guest). MENDELSSOHN: *Hear My Prayer: O for the Wings of a Dove* (both with Hussain, treble). HANDEL: *Coronation anthem: Zadok the Priest.* BACH: *Cantata 147: Jesu, Joy of Man's Desiring.* FAURE:

Cantique de Jean Racine. FRANCK: *Panis angelicus.* WALTON: *Jubilate Deo* (with Saklatvala, treble). BRITTEN: *Hymn to the Virgin.* WALFORD DAVIES: *God be in My Head.* BURGON: *Nunc dimittis* (with Hopkinson, treble). TAVENER: *Song for Athene.* WIDOR: *Organ Symphony No. 5: Toccata* (Cleobury, organ).

**(*) Decca (ADD/DDD) 460 021-2.

Magnificently recorded, with the choral tone sumptuous and clear, and resplendent sound from the organ, this unashamedly popular collection of choral favourites is bound to be a success. Certainly Handel's *Zadok the Priest* comes off exultantly, even if one misses the orchestral strings. Parry's 'I was Glad' is robustly presented, and so is the Mozart *Ave verum corpus*, which is just a shade stolid. However, Alastair Hussain is a true and pure treble soloist in the famous Allegri and Mendelssohn works, even if he is not quite so magical as Roy Goodman in the former, and Master Lough in the latter; and Thomas Hopkinson is genuinely touching in Burgon's equally famous *Nunc dimittis*.

The Walton and Britten pieces suit the King's style and acoustic particularly well, as does the lovely Tavener 'Song for Athene'. This is well sustained, and its climax is powerful, but the last degree of spontaneity is missing. However, Walford Davies's simple setting of 'God be in My Head' is another highlight, and Franck's *Panis angelicus* is a surprising success. As a central interlude Cleobury gives a rousing, bravura account of Widor's famous *Toccata*.

TALLIS: *Spem in alium* (40-part motet). BACH: *Cantata 147: Jesu, Joy of Man's Desiring.* VERDI: *Pater Noster.* HANDEL: *Israel in Egypt: The Sons of Israel do Mourn. Messiah: And the Glory of the Lord; Lift up Your Heads, Oh ye Gates.* BRAHMS: *Geistliches Lied, Op. 30.* GOMBERT: *Chanson – Triste départ.* BRITTEN: *A Ceremony of Carols: There is no Rose.* LASSUS: *Vinum Bonum* (motet). DAVIS: *Hymn to the Word of God.* HOWELLS: *Take Him, Earth, for Cherishing.* TAVENER: *Song for Athene.*

(B) *** Decca 470 122-2.

A self-recommending anthology, made all the more interesting for scanning music written from the Renaissance to the present day. The modern Britten and Tavener pieces suite the King's style and the warm acoustic particularly well, as, needless to say, do the popular numbers. Tallis's 40-part motet is much faster than this same choir's magical account from the 1960s with Willcocks, although it is just as memorable in a different way. It is especially welcome that the nineteenth century is not forgotten, and the lovely Brahms and Verdi pieces are among the highlights. The performances are superb, and the 1990s sound is magnificent.

King's College, Cambridge, Choir, (i) Stephen Cleobury with David Briggs (organ), (ii) Sir David Willcocks, (iii) Anthony Way (treble), St Paul's Cathedral Ch. and CO, John Scott

'*The Ultimate Carol Collection*': (i) GAUNTLETT, arr. LEDGER: *Once in Royal David's City.* arr. WILLCOCKS: *O Come All Ye Faithful; The First Nowell;* (ii) *Unto us is Born a Son;* (i) *God Rest Ye Merry, Gentlemen; I Saw Three Ships;* (ii) *See Amid the Winter's Snow; Rocking;* (i) *The Infant King.* (i) MENDELSSOHN, arr. LEDGER: *Hark! the Herald Angels Sing.* DARKE: *In the Bleak Midwinter.* arr. VAUGHAN WILLIAMS: *O Little Town of Bethlehem.* (ii) arr. PEARSAL: *In dulci jubilo.* PRAETORIUS: *A Great and Mighty Wonder.* (i) arr. LEDGER: *Sussex carol.* (ii) TATE: *While Shepherds Watched.* (i) arr. CLEOBURY: *Away in a Manger.* arr. WOOD: *Ding Dong! Merrily on High;* (ii) *King Jesus hath a Garden; Shepherds in the Field Abiding.* arr. WALFORD DAVIES: *The Holly and the Ivy.* arr. WOODWARD: *Up, Good Christian Folk.* (ii) arr. SHAW: *Coventry Carol.* (i) GRUBER, arr. CLEOBURY: *Silent Night.* (iii) SHANE, arr. ALEXANDER: *Do you Hear what I Hear?*

(M) **(*) Decca ADD/DDD 458 863-2.

Decca's 'Ultimate' carol collection (issued in 1997) is hardly that, but it will suit those looking for an essentially atmospheric concert of tested favourites for Christmas Day. It centres on a 1984 compilation directed by Stephen Cleobury with 'Once in Royal David's City' presented not as a processional but as an interplay between treble soloist (Robin Barter) and full choir. The choir is backwardly placed and the atmosphere overall is slightly subdued. However, the organ contribution from David Briggs (uncredited in the documentation) always makes its presence felt and is strongly featured in Willcocks's dramatic arrangement of 'Unto us is Born a Son' and the powerful close of 'God Rest Ye Merry, Gentlemen'. Philip Ledger's version of 'Hark! The Herald Angels Sing' also has a spectacular climax.

However, in general the recording does not seek to clarify textures but concentrates on capturing the ambient atmosphere. Thus the older recordings conducted by Willcocks, which are interspersed, match up well to the later collection. The modern carol 'Do you Hear what I Hear?', featuring the eloquent Anthony Way and opulently presented with orchestral accompaniment, while it may be a highlight for some listeners, fits rather uneasily in the middle of the programme (following after the 'Sussex Carol'), and not everyone will respond to Cleobury's elaboration of the closing 'Silent Night', which takes an original turn after the opening verse.

King's College, Cambridge, Choir, Sir David Willcocks

'*Noël*': Disc 1: MENDELSSOHN: *Hark the Herald Angels Sing.* TRAD.: *The First Nowell; While Shepherds Watched; I Saw Three Ships; Ding Dong! Merrily on High; King Jesus hath a Garden; Unto us a Son is Born; O Come All Ye Faithful; Away in a Manger; The Holly and the Ivy; God Rest Ye Merry, Gentlemen; See Amid the Winter's Snow; Past Three o'clock.* arr. BACH: *In dulci jubilo.* arr. VAUGHAN WILLIAMS: *O Little Town of Bethlehem.*

Disc 2: TRAD.: *Once in Royal David's City; Sussex Carol; Rocking; Rejoice and be Merry; Joseph was an Old Man; As with Gladness Men of Old; The Infant King; Christ was Born on Christmas Day; Blessed be that Maid Mary; Lute-book Lullaby; Personent hodie; In the Bleak Midwinter; Coventry Carol; Shepherds, in the Field Abiding.* CORNELIUS: *The Three Kings; A Great and Mighty Wonder.* WARLOCK: *Balulalow.* TCHAIKOVSKY: *The Crown of Roses.* TERRY: *Myn lyking.* JOUBERT: *Torches.* VAUGHAN WILLIAMS: *Fantasia on Christmas Carols* (with Alan & LSO).

(B) **(*) Double Decca (ADD) 444 848-2 (2).

This Decca Double is essentially a combined reissue of a pair of bargain-priced LP collections, made over a span of eight years at the end of the 1950s and the beginning of the 1960s. They were counted excellent value when they first appeared in Decca's 'World of' series. The 50-minute programme on the first disc concentrates on established King's favourites; the second is not only more generous (66 minutes), but also includes novelties which are designed to get the listener inquiring further, such as Warlock's 'Balulalow', the engaging 'Lute-book Lullaby' and Joubert's *Torches*.

This collection opens with the famous processional version of 'Once in Royal David's City' and closes with a superbly joyful performance of Vaughan Williams's *Fantasia on Christmas Carols*, very well recorded, with Hervey Alan the excellent soloist. The sound is always pleasingly full and atmospheric, but with some of the earlier recordings from the late 1950s not quite as clean in focus as those made in the mid-1960s.

'*Great Choral Classics*': ALLEGRI: *Miserere* (with Goodman, treble). PALESTRINA: *Stabat Mater.* TALLIS: *Spem in alium* (40-part motet; with Cambridge University Musical Society); *Sancte Deus.* BYRD: *Ave verum corpus.* VIVALDI: *Gloria in D, RV 589* (with Vaughan, Baker, Lord, ASMF). GIBBONS: *This is the Record of John* (with unnamed soloist and Jacobean Consort of Viols). BACH: *Jesu, Priceless Treasure (Jesu meine Freude), BWV 227.* HANDEL: *4 Coronation anthems: Zadok the Priest; My Heart is Inditing; Let thy Hand be Strengthened; The King shall Rejoice* (with ECO).

🔑 (B) *** Double Decca (ADD) 452 949-2 (2).

An admirably chosen group of choral masterpieces spanning the riches of the sixteenth and seventeenth centuries and the first half of the eighteenth, opening with Allegri's *Miserere* with its soaring treble solo, so confidently sung here by the same Roy Goodman who was later to make his mark as a conductor. Palestrina's *Stabat Mater* which follows is no less arresting in its bold contrasts, and the richness of texture of Tallis's *Spem in alium* is little short of astonishing. The resonant King's acoustic prevents sharp linear clarity, but it underlines the work's spiritual power and extraordinarily expansive sonority.

Byrd's beautiful *Ave verum corpus* then brings a serene simplicity, with Vivaldi's exuberant *Gloria* rounding off the first CD. The second programme opens with music by Orlando Gibbons, himself a chorister at King's, a delightfully intimate viol-accompanied solo motet with brief choral echoes. Bach's most famous motet follows, sung in English (none too clearly, because of the reverberation), and the concert closes resplendently with Handel's four Coronation anthems, including the most famous, *Zadok the Priest.* Here the sound is quite excellent.

'Anthems from King's' (with Lancelot, organ): PARRY: *I was Glad.* BULLOCK: *Give us the Wings of Faith.* BAIRSTOW: *Let All Mortal Flesh Keep Silence.* LEY: *A Prayer of King Henry VI.* BALFOUR GARDNER: *Evening Hymn (Te lucis ante terminum).* NAYLOR: *Vox dicentis Clama.* HARWOOD: *O How Glorious.* STANFORD: *Beati quorum via.* BAINTON: *And I Saw a New Heaven.* WOOD: *Hail Gladdening Light.* DARKE: *O Gladsome Light.* HADLEY: *My Beloved Spake.* HARRIS: *Faire is the Heaven.*

(B) *** CfP 585 6202.

An attractive and representative bargain collection of English cathedral music from just before the turn of the nineteenth century until about halfway through the twentieth. A good deal of the writing is not very adventurous, harmonically speaking, but it is all effective and much of it is memorable. Highlights include Edward Bairstow's eloquent 'Let All Mortal Flesh Keep Silence', the fine Balfour Gardiner 'Evening Hymn' and Stanford's *Beati quorum via.* The last four items by Wood, Darke, Patrick Hadley and William Harris are here especially effective for being heard together, four diverse yet complementary settings that sum up the twentieth-century Anglican tradition rather well, and Parry's exultant 'I was Glad' makes an exultant opener. Excellent recording from 1973.

'Carols from King's' (with John Wells or Andrew Davis, organ): TRAD., arr. WILLCOCKS: *Sussex Carol; Tomorrow shall be My Dancing Day; Cherry Tree Carol; The Lord did at First Adam Make; A*

Child is Born in Bethlehem; While Shepherds Watched their Flocks by Night. Arr. VAUGHAN WILLIAMS: *And All in the Morning.* CORNELIUS: *The Three Kings.* GRUBER: *Silent Night.* DARKE: *In the Bleak Midwinter* (all 3 with Varcoe, baritone). GERHARDT: *All My Heart this Night Rejoices.* Arr. WOODWARD: *Hail! Blessed Virgin Mary!; Ding Dong! Merrily on High.* Arr. SULLIVAN: *It Came upon the Midnight Clear.* Arr. BAINTON: *A Babe is Born I Wys.* TRAD.: *I Saw a Maiden; Mary Walked through a Wood of Thorn.* PRAETORIUS: *Psallite unigenito.* MACONCHY: *Nowell! Nowell! Nowell!* Arr. BRITTEN: *The Holly and the Ivy.* POSTON: *Jesus Christ the Apple Tree.* SPENSER: *Most Glorious Lord of Life.* Arr. Imogen HOLST: *The Lord that Lay in Assë Stall.* WARLOCK: *Where Riches is Everlastingly.* (with Whittaker, flute, Van Kampen, cello, Spencer, lute): PHILIP THE CHANCELLOR (2 versions) arr. HUGHES & arr. POSTON: *Angelus ad virginem.* Arr. Lennox BERKELEY: *I Sing of a Maiden.* TAYLOR: *Watts's Cradle Song.* Arr. POSTON: *My Dancing Day.* CAMPION: *Sing a Song of Joy.*

(B) *** CfP (ADD) 585 6212.

This quite outstandingly generous (74 minutes) King's concert draws on three separate LP collections, made in 1965, 1966 and 1969. As might be expected, the Choir confidently encompasses the wide variety of styles, from the arranged early music to the attractive arrangements of traditional carols by modern composers, to some of which instrumental accompaniments are engagingly added. In three others Stephen Varcoe makes a fine solo contribution. The alternative versions of the early *Angelus ad virginem*, by Hughes and Poston (the latter conjecturally accompanied), make a fascinating comparison, and among the modern carols Elizabeth Poston's 'Jesus Christ the Apple Tree' also stands out. The recordings have been admirably remastered and sound remarkable fresh. Highly recommended.

King's College, Cambridge, Choir, Sir David Willcocks or Philip Ledger

'*Favourite Carols from Kings*': GAUNTLETT: *Once in Royal David's City.* TRAD., arr. VAUGHAN WILLIAMS: *O Little Town of Bethlehem.* TRAD., arr. STAINER: *The First Nowell.* TRAD., arr. LEDGER: *I Saw Three Ships.* TRAD. German, arr. HOLST: *Personent hodie.* TERRY: *Myn Lyking.* HOWELLS: *A Spotless Rose.* KIRKPATRICK: *Away in a Manger.* HADLEY: *I Sing of a Maiden.* TRAD. French, arr. WILLCOCKS: *O Come, O Come Emmanuel.* TRAD., arr. WILLCOCKS: *While Shepherds Watched; On Christmas Night.* arr. WOODWARD: *Up! Good Christian Folk and Listen.* DARKE: *In the Bleak Midwinter.* GRUBER: *Silent Night.* TRAD., arr. WALFORD DAVIES: *The Holly and the Ivy.* TRAD., arr. SULLIVAN: *It Came upon the Midnight Clear.*

CORNELIUS: *Three Kings.* SCHEIDT: *A Child is Born in Bethlehem.* TRAD. German, arr. PEARSALL: *In dulci jubilo.* WADE: *O Come, All Ye Faithful.* MENDELSSOHN: *Hark! The Herald Angels Sing.*
ᴑ—► (M) *** EMI (ADD) 5 66241-2.

With 71 minutes of music and twenty-two carols included, this collection, covering the regimes of both Sir David Willcocks and Philip Ledger, could hardly be bettered as a representative sampler of the King's tradition. Opening with the famous processional of 'Once in Royal David's City', to which Willcocks contributes a descant (as he also does in 'While Shepherds Watched'), the programme is wide-ranging in its historical sources, from the fourteenth century to the present day, while the arrangements feature many famous musicians. The recordings were made between 1969 and 1976, and the CD transfers are first class. The two closing carols, featuring the Philip Jones Brass Ensemble, are made particularly resplendent.

'*A Festival of Lessons and Carols from King's*' (1979) includes: TRAD.: *Once in Royal David's City; Sussex Carol; Joseph and Mary; A Maiden Most Gentle; Chester Carol; Angels, from the Realms of Glory.* HANDEL: *Resonet in laudibus.* ORD: *Adam Lay Ybounden.* GRUBER: *Stille Nacht.* MATHIAS: *A Babe is Born.* WADE: *O Come All Ye Faithful.* MENDELSSOHN: *Hark! The Herald Angels Sing.*
(M) *** EMI (ADD) 5 66242-2.

This 1979 version of the annual King's College ceremony has the benefit of fine analogue stereo, even more atmospheric than before. Under Philip Ledger the famous choir keeps its beauty of tone and incisive attack. The opening processional, 'Once in Royal David's City', is even more effective heard against the background quiet of CD, and this remains a unique blend of liturgy and music.

'*Procession with Carols on Advent Sunday*' includes: PALESTRINA (arr. from): *I Look from Afar; Judah and Jerusalem, Fear Not.* PRAETORIUS: *Come, Thou Redeemer of the Earth.* TRAD.: *O Come, O Come, Emmanuel!; Up, Awake and Away!; 'Twas in the Year; Cherry Tree Carol; King Jesus hath a Garden; On Jordan's Bank the Baptist's Cry; Gabriel's Message; I Wonder as I Wander; My Dancing Day; Lo! He Comes with Clouds Descending.* BYRT: *All and Some.* P. NICOLAI, arr. BACH: *Wake, O Wake! with Tidings Thrilling.* BACH: *Nun komm' der Heiden Heiland.*
(M) *** EMI (ADD) 5 66243-2.

This makes an attractive variant to the specifically Christmas-based service, though the carols themselves are not quite so memorable. Beautiful singing and richly atmospheric recording; the wide dynamic range is demonstrated equally effectively by the atmospheric opening and processional and the sumptuous closing hymn.

'*Christmas Music from King's*' (with Davis, organ, Whittaker, flute, Van Kampen, cello and Spencer, lute): SWEELINCK: *Hodie Christus natus est.*
PALESTRINA: *Hodie Christus natus est.* VICTORIA: *O magnum mysterium; Senex puerum portabat.*
BYRD: *Senex puerum portabat; Hodie beata virgo.*
GIBBONS: *Hosanna to the Son of David.* WEELKES: *Hosanna to the Son of David; Gloria in excelsis Deo.*
ECCARD: *When to the Temple Mary Went.*
MACONCHY: *Nowell! Nowell!.* arr. BRITTEN: *The Holly and the Ivy.* PHILIP (The Chancellor): *Angelus ad virginem.* arr. POSTON: *Angelus ad virginem; My Dancing Day.* POSTON: *Jesus Christ the Apple Tree.* BERKELEY: *I Sing of a Maiden.*
TAYLOR: *Watts's Cradle Song.* CAMPION: *Sing a Song of Joy.* PEERSON: *Most Glorious Lord of Life.*
Imogen HOLST: *That Lord that Lay in Assë Stall.*
WARLOCK: *Where Riches is Everlastingly.*

(M) **★★★** EMI (ADD) 5 66244-2.

A happily chosen survey of music (63 minutes), inspired by the Nativity, from the fifteenth century to the present day. As might be expected, the King's choir confidently encompasses the wide variety of styles from the spiritual serenity of the music of Victoria to the attractive arrangements of traditional carols by modern composers, in which an instrumental accompaniment is added. These items are quite delightful and they are beautifully recorded (in 1965). The motets, from a year earlier, were among the first recording sessions made by the EMI engineers in King's College Chapel, and at the time they had not solved all the problems associated with the long reverberation period, so the focus is less than sharp. Even so, this group demonstrates the unique virtuosity of the Cambridge choir, exploiting its subtlety of tone and flexibility of phrase.

'*The Psalms of David*' (Collection, with Willcocks or Grier, organ): Disc 1: *Psalms Nos. 12, 15, 23–4, 42–3, 46, 61, 65–7, 84, 104, 114–15, 121–2, 126, 133–4, 137, 147–50.* Disc 2: *Nos. 22, 37, 45, 49, 53, 78, 81, 93–94, 107, 130–31.*

(B) **★★★** EMI (ADD) 5 85641-2 (2).

The early Christians took over the Psalter along with the Old Testament teachings from the Hebrew Temple, and the Psalms have always been an integral part of Anglican liturgy. Although they are called the Psalms of David it has long been recognized that the original Hebrew collection (some 150 strong) was gathered together over a period of several hundred years, and the writings are from many different, anonymous hands. The Anglican settings used on these recordings (from the late 1960s and early 1970s), have offered their composers a fairly wide range of expressive potential, yet the music itself, because of the stylized metre and the ritual nature of its use, seldom approaches the depth and resonance that are found in the music of the great composers of the Roman Catholic faith, Palestrina, Victoria, etc. The selection offered here opens with 16 well-known

Psalms constituting a cross-section of the Psalter; then follow a number of shorter chosen groups for various evening (and the 22nd morning) settings for the church year, with the second disc offering several more extended Psalms, notably Nos. 37, 78 and 107. The King's College Choir, conducted by either Sir David Willcocks or Sir Philip Ledger, with fine organ accompaniments, give eloquent accounts of all these Psalms, and they are beautifully recorded and well transferred to CD.

King's Consort, Robert King

'*Great Baroque Arias*' (with Fisher, soprano, Mark Ainsley, tenor, Bowman, alto, George, bass) from: HANDEL: *Ode for St Cecilia's Day; Serse; Semele; Acis and Galatea; Joshua; Jephtha; Alexander's Feast; Samson.* BACH: *Cantata No. 208.* PURCELL: *Dido and Aeneas.* VIVALDI: *Orlando Furioso.*

(BB) **★★★** Regis RRC 1062.

A more successful budget collection of popular Baroque arias (thirteen altogether) would be hard to find. The great majority are by Handel (including *Ombra mai fu* and 'Wher'er you Walk'), but then he wrote many of the best tunes. Apart from the consistently fine singing, Robert King's accompaniments are both stylish amd full of life and he has splendid obbligato soloists, not least Crispian Steele-Perkins, whose vibrant playing is just right to set the scene for the opening 'Let the Trumpet's Loud Clangour' (John Mark Ainsley). He returns equally vigorously for 'Revenge Timotheus Cries' (the exultant Michael George), and the closing 'Let the Bright Seraphim', gleamingly bright as sung by Gillian Fisher. She is equally impressive in her eloquent account of Dido's *Lament* and the delightful 'Sheep May Safely Graze' of Bach, with Lisa Beznosiuk providing the flute/recorder obbligato, as she does in the lovely alto aria from Vivaldi's *Orlando Furioso* where she is completely at one with James Bowman. Another highlight in which Beznosiuk participates is Michael George's genially exuberant 'O Ruddier than the Cherry'. The recording is in the demonstration bracket, vivid but most believably balanced.

King's Consort and Choir, Robert King

The Coronation of George II 1727 (includes: HANDEL: *4 Coronation anthems.* BLOW: *Behold, O God our Defender; God Spake Sometime in Visions.* CHILD: *O Lord, Grant the King a Long Life.* FARMER: *Come Holy Ghost.* GIBBONS: *2nd Service: Te Deum.* PURCELL: *I was Glad.* TALLIS: *O God, the Father of Heaven*).

★★★ Hyp. SACD 67286 or CDA 67286 (2).

The idea of recreating on disc great ceremonial occasions of the past from Rome, Venice or Salzburg has already been established, and here Robert King and the King's Consort bring the process nearer home by recreating the grandest of all Coronation services, the one for George II in 1727. Ambitious as it was, the occasion was chaotic, but King and his fellow researchers have put together a vividly atmospheric sequence, punctuated by fanfares, pealing bells and processional pieces. So Handel's four great Coronation anthems, including *Zadok the Priest*, are the more characterful set in context, matched by equally inspired items by Purcell, Gibbons and, above all, John Blow.

King's Singers

'Christmas Collection': TRAD.: *Angelus ad Virginem.* TRAD., arr. LAWSON: *Veni, veni Emmanuel; Maria durch ein Dornwald; Noel nouvelet.* KIRKPATRICK/LAWSON: *Away in a Manger.* TRAD., arr. VAUGHAN WILLIAMS: *This is the Truth.* TRAD., arr. BARWINSKI: *Szczo to la prediwo (What a Surprise).* PRAETORIUS: *Wie schön Leuchtet der Morgenstern; Es ist ein Ros entsprungen.* ANON.: *There is no Rose; Coventry Carol.* BO HOLTEN: *Nowell Sing we Now.* RAVENSCROFT: *Remember O Thou Man.* Arr. BACH: *In dulci jubilo; O Little One Sweet.* LAWSON: *Lullay My Liking.* PART: *Bogoroditsye Dyovo (Virgin, Mother of God).* TAVENER: *The Lamb.* WARLOCK: *Bethlehem Down.* TCHAIKOVSKY: *The Crown of Roses.* MCCABE: *To us in Bethlehem City.* RUTTER: *There is a Flower.* RAMIREZ: *La Peregrinaçion.* GRUBER, arr. RUTTER: *Stille Nacht.* DAVID: *Born on a New Day.*
*** Signum SIGCD 502.

The King's Singers' Christmas disc on Signum, coming after a ten-year gap, reflects their decision to 'go back to the singing with less of the swinging'. This is a most refreshing collection of carols. It starts with medieval examples, done with characteristic poise and purity, but one rousing item, *Angelus ad Virginem*, is delivered in true period style with raw tone, to the accompaniment of a drum. Most of the modern carols too, by such composers as Arvo Pärt (a wonderfully joyful miniature), John Tavener, Bo Holten and John McCabe, have their roots in medieval examples. The 25 items also include nineteenth-century favourites like *Stille Nacht* (in a new arrangement by John Rutter) and 'Away in a Manger', seductively done, while swinging syncopations and close harmony still play a part in such items as an Argentinian carol, picked up on the group's travels, as well as the final carol, 'Born on a New Day – like a modern spiritual. Excellent recording.

'Madrigal History Tour' (with members of Consort of Musicke, Rooley): Italian: GASTOLDI: *Amor vittorioso.* MANTOVANO: *Lirium bililirum.* ARCADELT: *Il bianco e dolce cigno.* ANON.: *La bella Franceschina; Alla caza.* VERDELOT: *Ultima mei sospiri.* DE WERT: *Or si rallegri il cielo.*

English: DOWLAND: *Fine Knacks for Ladies.* BYRD: *Who Made Thee, Hob, Forsake the Plough.* BARTLETT: *Of All the Birds that I do Know.* TOMKINS: *Too Much I Once Lamented.* FARMER: *Fair Phyllis I Saw.* GIBBONS: *The Silver Swan.* MORLEY: *Now is the Month of Maying.*

French: JANNEQUIN: *La Guerre.* CERTON: *La, la, la, je ne l'ose dire.* LASSUS: *Bon jour; et puis, quelles nouvelles.* ANON.: *Mignon, allons voir si la rose.* PASSEREAU: *Il est bel et bon.* ARCADELT: *Margot labourez les vignes.* LE JEUNE: *Un Gentil Amoureux.* WILLAERT: *Faulte d'argent.*

Spanish: ANON.: *La tricotea Samartin la vea.* DE MUDARRA: *Triste estaba el Rey David.* DEL ENCINA: *Cucú, Cucú!; Fatal la parte.* ANON. & FERNANDEZ: *3 morillas m'enamoran.* FLECHA: *La bomba.*

German: HASSLER: *Tanzen und Springen; Ach weh des Leiden.* ANON.: *Vitrum nostrum gloriosum.* SENFL: *Ach Elslein, liebes Elslein; Das G'laut zu Speyer.* HOFHAIMER: *Herzliebstes Bild.*
(BB) *** EMI Encore 5 85714-2.

Recorded in 1983 in partnership with Anthony Rooley and members of his Consort of Musicke, this was the most valuable of all the early collections recorded by the King's Singers. The original CD was published in 1984 at mid-price, with a 36-page booklet giving full texts and translations and excellent notes. For this budget reissue, the notes are abbreviated and the texts left out altogether! Nevertheless, the programme is chosen most imaginatively and is delightfully ordered, often exquisitely sung, with the five separate groups admirably laid out to give maximum contrast.

The madrigal was essentially an Italian invention, spawned at the very beginning of the sixteenth century. Gastoldi's *Amor vittorioso* and Mantovano's *Lirium bililirum* are delightfully fluent examples, while the gentle melancholy of Arcadelt's *Il bianco e dolce cigno* is a touchingly expressive counterpart.

Spanish and French composers soon took up the challenge. Flecha's extended *ensalada*, *La Bomba* ('The Pump') – which was needed to bail out a sinking ship – has an extraordinary variety of moods (the mariners are later rescued, rejoice and give thanks). Encina's *Cucú* sings seductively to warn men to satisfy their wives or find them in another nest; it even includes the literally translated couplet: 'If your wife goes out to the loo, go out with her too!' Alistair Hume is no less captivating in the delicately suggestive tale of the *Tres morillas* ('Three Little Moorish Girls') who went to pick olives, and then apples, but found love instead, while Mudarra's expressively desolate ballad of King David's lament for his son Absalom is ravishingly sung by Jeremy Jackman.

Standing out among the French repertoire, Jannequin's vivid representation of *La Guerre* was written to celebrate the Battle of Marignano in 1515. Lassus was actually born in Mons (although he went to work in Italy), and his *Bon jour* is full of charm yet readily demonstrates his polyphonic skill. Passereau's gay 'Parisian chanson', *Il est bel et bon*, is similarly lighthearted and is engagingly sung and accompanied here.

German composers were not far behind – influenced by the Italians, with Senfl a leading exponent in the first half of the century. His 'Bells of Speyer' ring out vividly at the end of the concert while Hassler's *Tänzen und Springen*, instrumentally accompanied, is full of high spirits, contrasting with the lush expressive melancholy of *Ach, weh des Leiden*.

The English tradition arrived late (in the 1590s), and was short-lived. But the repertoire was richly endowed by Byrd and Gibbons ('The Silver Swan' an inspired example), and the lighter numbers are equally cherishable. Dowland's engaging 'Fine Knacks for Ladies', Bartlett's imitative birdsong ('Of All the Birds that I do Know'), and Morley's delightful 'Now is the Month of Maying' show how completely the magrigal was adapted to the English pastoral style.

The polish, stylishness and accurate blending of ensemble of the King's Singers illuminate every one of these madrigals, and the many solo contributions are as pleasing as those sung in consort. Anthony Rooley and his players provide admirably tasteful and colourful period-instrument accompaniments where needed (including viols, lute, cittern and tabor) and the recording is excellent. This disc is a true bargain, but what a pity the texts could not have been included.

Kirkby, Emma (soprano)

'*Madrigals and Wedding Songs for Diana*' (with Thomas, bass, Consort of Musicke, Rooley):
BENNET: *All Creatures Now are Merry-minded.* CAMPION: *Now hath Flora Robbed her Bowers; Move now Measured Sound; Woo her and Win her.* LUPO: *Shows and nightly revels; Time that Leads the Fatal Round.* GILES: *Triumph Now with Joy and Mirth.* CAVENDISH: *Come, Gentle Swains.* DOWLAND: *Welcome, Black Night ... Cease these False Sports.* WEELKES: *Hark! All Ye Lovely Saints; As Vesta was.* WILBYE: *Lady Oriana.* EAST: *Hence Stars! Too Dim of Light; You Meaner Beauties.* LANIER: *Bring Away this Sacred Tree; The Marigold; Mark How the Blushful Morn.* COPERARIO: *Go, Happy Man; While Dancing Rests; Come Ashore, Merry Mates.* E. GIBBONS: *Long Live Fair Oriana.*
*** Hyp. CDA 66019.

This wholly delightful anthology celebrates early royal occasions and aristocratic weddings, and in its choice of Elizabethan madrigals skilfully balances praise of the Virgin Queen with a less ambivalent attitude to nuptial delights. Emma Kirkby is at her freshest and most captivating, and David Thomas, if

not quite her match, makes an admirable contribution. Accompaniments are stylish and well balanced, and the recording is altogether first rate.

'*O Tuneful Voice*' (with Müller, Roberts, fortepiano or harpsichord, Kelley, harp): HAYDN: *O Tuneful Voice; She Never Told her Love; Sailor's Song.* SAMUEL ARNOLD: *Elegy.* PINTO: *Invocation to Nature; A Shepherd Lov'd a Nymph so Fair; From Thee, Eliza, I must Go; Eloisa to Abelard; Minuet in A.* STORACE: *The Curfew.* LINLEY THE ELDER: *The Lark Sings High in the Cornfield; Think not, my Love.* JACKSON: *The Day that Saw thy Beauty Rise; Time has not Thinn'd my Flowing Hair.* SHIELD: *Ye Balmy Breezes, Gently Blow; Hope and Love; 'Tis Only no Harm to Know it, you Know.* CARDON: *Variations on 'Ah vous dirai-je, maman'.* HOOK: *The Emigrant.* SALOMON: *Go, Lovely Rose; Why Still before these Streaming Eyes; O Tuneful Voice.*
*** Hyp. CDA 66497.

This programme is centred in eighteenth-century England, although Haydn could be included because of his London visits. Indeed, Salomon, his impresario, is featured here as a composer, and a very able one, too; but it is Haydn's comparatively rare song which gives the CD its title and shows Emma Kirkby on top form, just as charming but with greater depth of expression than in her companion Hyperion and Oiseau-Lyre collections, the latter having the same geographical basis but offering repertoire from an earlier period. Kirkby sings like a lark in the cornfield, and Rufus Müller joins her in some duets by William Jackson and also shares the solo numbers. There are innocently rustic songs from William Shield in which each artist participates, and much else besides: this 74-minute programme has a wide range of mood and style.

'*A Portrait*' (with AAM, Hogwood): HANDEL: *Disseratevi, o porte d'Averno; Gentle Morpheus, Son of Night.* PURCELL: *Bess of Bedlam; From Rosie Bow'rs.* ARNE: *Where the Bee Sucks There Lurk I; Rise, Glory, Rise.* DOWLAND: *I Saw the Lady Weepe.* D'INDIA: *Odi quel rosignuolo.* TROMBONCINO: *Se ben hor non scopro il foco.* VIVALDI: *Passo di pena in pena.* J. S. BACH: *Ei! wie schmeckt der Coffee süsse.* HAYDN: *With Verdure Clad.* MOZART: *Laudate Dominum; Exsultate, jubilate, K.165.*
⊕—• ✹ (M) *** O-L 443 200-2.

Admirers of Emma Kirkby's style in early and baroque music will delight in this well-chosen 76-minute sampler of her work. L'Oiseau-Lyre have altered and expanded the original issue and the excerpt from Handel's *Messiah* has been replaced by the remarkable Angel's aria, *Disseratevi, o porte d'Averno*, from Part I of *La Resurrezione* (calling on the gates of the Underworld to be unbarred, to yield to God's glory). It opens with joyous baroque trumpets and oboes, and Emma Kirkby shows with her florid vocal line that anything they can do, she can do better.

This is rather effectively followed by Purcell's melancholy Mad song, 'Bess of Bedlam', and the equally touching 'From Rosie Bow'rs'. Music by Arne lightens the mood and later there are excerpts from Bach's *Coffee Cantata* and popular solos by Haydn and Mozart. This recital is as well planned as it is enjoyable, and Hogwood ensures that accompaniments are consistently fresh and stylish. First-class sound.

Arias (with AAM, Hogwood): HANDEL: *Alessandro Severo: Overture.* Arias from: *Alcina; Alexander's Feast; L'allegro, il penseroso ed il moderato; Saul; March in D; Hornpipe.* LAMPE: *Britannia: Welcome Mars. Dione: Pretty Warblers.* ARNE: *Comus. Rosamond: Rise, Glory, Rise. By the Rusty-fringed Bank; Brightest Lady. The Tempest: Where the Bee Sucks.* HAYDN: *The Creation: With Verdure Clad; On Mighty Pens.* MOZART: *Concert arias: Voi, avete un cor fedele; Nehmt meinen Dank, ihr holden Gönner! Ch'io mi scordi di te?* Arias from: *Il rè pastore; Zaïde.*

(B) ★★★ Double Decca 458 084-2 (2).

Two of the Arne arias and one of Haydn's are included in the 'Portrait' (see previous entry), and Arne's 'Rise, Glory, Rise' (showing the singer at her very finest) also rightly appeared in Decca's 'Treasures of Baroque Opera' (now deleted). The rest is new. Of the novelties Lampe's charming 'Pretty Warblers', like Handel's 'Sweet Bird' from *L'allegro, il penseroso ed il moderato*, brings an illustrative aviary from the solo flute, with Kirkby then adding her own exquisite roulades. *Credete al mio dolore* from *Alcina* has an important cello obbligato. Kirkby's smooth, sweet line and easy coloratura give consistent pleasure, and the two famous arias from Haydn's *Creation* are gloriously sung.

Throughout, Hogwood's accompaniments are light and stylish and give the singer every support, and one's only criticism is that the Handel and Mozart selections would have benefited from more instrumental music in between the arias to add variety. But individually every item here is treasurable and the recording is first class, giving plenty of space and a fine bloom to the voice.

'The World of Emma Kirkby': Arias from: HANDEL: *Alcina; Messiah.* PURCELL: *Dido and Aeneas.* LAMPE: *Dione.* VIVALDI: *Nulla in mundo pax sincera.* PERGOLESI: *Salve Regina.* ARNE: *Comus.* HAYDN: *The Creation.* Songs: DOWLAND: *I Saw my Ladye Weepe.* GIBBONS: *The Silver Swan.* MORLEY: *With my Love.* MOZART: *Ch'io mi scordi di te?*

(M) ★★★ Decca (ADD/DDD) 467 781-2.

During the last 25 years Emma Kirkby has won the affections of not only *aficionados* of the early music world but the music-loving public in general. This recital clearly shows why. Her voice is not large, but it projects vividly, is unselfconsciously beautiful, fresh

sounding and imbued with an obvious sense of joy. This CD charts her career from 1975 to the present, in a varied programme, from full *da capo* arias to art songs. She manages both the challenging coloratura of *Torami a vagheggiar* (from *Alcina*) with the same conviction as she presents the simple rustic charm of Arne's 'By the Rushy-fringed Bank' (from *Comus*). The recordings are excellent, the programme varied and the CD inexpensive.

Kožená, Magdalena (mezzo)

Songs (with Martineau, piano, Davies, flute, Henschel, violin, Barta, cello, Henschel Qt): RAVEL: *Chansons madécasses.* SHOSTAKOVICH: *Satires.* RESPIGHI: *Il tramonto.* SCHULHOFF: 3 *Stimmungsbilder.* BRITTEN: *A Charm of Lullabies.*
★★★ DG 471 581-2.

The superb Czech mezzo Magdalena Kožená gives a masterly display of her versatility in this wonderfully varied collection of songs in five languages. The elusive Ravel songs, strongly characterized, immediately establish her magnetism, and though the sheer beauty of her voice may seem at odds with the satirical bite of the Shostakovich songs they too are vividly characterized. The German songs by Kožená's fellow Czech, written in 1913, are subtly nuanced, and most ravishing of all is Respighi's radiant setting of an Italian translation of Shelley, *Il Tramonto* ('The Sunset'), with string quartet accompaniment. Most fascinating for the English-speaking listener is Kožená's moving account of one of Benjamin Britten's rarest song-cycles, *A Charm of Lullabies*, written for the mezzo Nancy Evans in 1947, exploring on a surprisingly wide expressive range. A most valuable disc, beautifully recorded.

Larin, Sergej (tenor), Eleonora Bekova (piano)

'Songs by the Mighty Handful': RIMSKY-KORSAKOV: *It was not the Wind Blowing from Above; The Octave; The Nymph; Clearer than the Singing of the Lark; The Scurrying Bank of Clouds Disperses; On the Hills of Georgia; Of what in the Silence of the Night; Captivated by the Rose, the Nightingale; Silence Descends on the Yellow Cornfields; A Pressed Flower.* CUI: *A Statue at Tsarskoye Selo; The Burnt Letter.* BORODIN: *The Fair Maid has Stopped Loving Me; For the Shores of the Distant Homeland.* BALAKIREV: *You are Full of Captivating Bliss; Barcarolle; Look, my Friend.* MUSSORGSKY: *Songs and Dances of Death.*
★★★ Chan. 9547.

Sergej Larin with his outstandingly beautiful and expressive tenor presents vivid portraits of the five Russian composers grouped as the 'Mighty Handful', all but Mussorgsky here represented in miniatures.

The ten Rimsky-Korsakov songs are totally unpretentious, simple ballads that he wrote in joyful relaxation, a mood which is reflected in the music. The two Cui songs are far more intense, as are the two by Borodin, one of them, 'The Fair Maid has Stopped Loving Me', with cello obbligato played by Alfia Bekova. The three Balakirev songs are tiny chips from the workbench, beautifully crafted. Only Mussorgsky is presented at full stretch with the greatest and best known of the items here, the *Songs and Dances of Death*. Larin, having for the earlier songs used his most honeyed tones and velvety, seamless production, including a wonderful head-voice on top, here darkens his tone thrillingly, ending with a searing account of 'The Field Marshall's Death'. A superb disc, revealing a great artist.

Laudibus, Michael Brewer

'*All in the April Evening*': ROBERTON: *All in the April Evening.* arr. ROBERTON: *The Banks o'Doon; An Eriskay Love Lilt; Dream Angus; All through the Night. The Wee Copper o'Fife; Drink to me Only with Thine Eyes.* arr. VAUGHAN WILLIAMS: *Ca' the Yowes; The Turtle Dove.* VAUGHAN WILLIAMS: *3 Shakespeare Songs: Full Fathom Five; The Cloud-capp'd Towers; Over Hill, over Dale.* arr. BANTOCK: *O can Ye Sew Cushions?* arr. MANSFIELD: *Wi' a Hundred Pipers.* MORLEY: *Fyer! Fyer!* BENNET: *All Creatures Now are Merry-minded.* BYRD: *Ave verum corpus.* GRANT: *Crimond.* PARRY: *Never Weather-beaten Sail.* ELGAR: *My Love Dwelt in a Northern Land; As Torrents in Summer.* arr. WARLOCK: *Corpus Christi.* STANFORD: *The Blue Bird.* SULLIVAN: *The Long Day Closes.*

*** Hyp. CDA 67076.

The twenty-two members of Laudibus are all recruited from the National Youth Choir. Their tuning is impeccable and they blend together with the natural flexibility which established the international reputation of Sir Hugh Roberton's Glasgow Orpheus Choir. The programme here is based on repertoire made famous by that now disbanded group, opening appropriately with the title piece, one of the simplest and loveliest examples of four-part writing in the English language. The programme is for the most part composed of similarly serene and evocative music, but every so often there is a lively item like 'Wi' a Hundred Pipers', Morley's 'Fyer! Fyer!', or Bennet's 'All Creatures Now are Merry-minded', to interrupt the reverie momentarily. The various soloists are drawn from the choir and very good they are too (sample the treble solo in Stanford's 'Blue Bird'). Beautifully recorded, this is a choral record for the late evening, and its consistency of mood is one of its virtues. The playing time is a generous 72 minutes.

Lemalu, Jonathan (bass-baritone)

'*Lieder, Mélodies and English Songs*' (with Vignoles, piano): BRAHMS: *4 Serious Songs.* SCHUBERT: *Der Wanderer; Auf der Donau; Der Schiffer; Der Wanderer an den Mond.* FAURE: *L'Horizon chimérique* (song-cycle). FINZI: *Rollicum-rorum; To Lizbie Brown.* IRELAND: *Sea Fever.* KEEL: *Trade Winds.* HEAD: *The Estuary.* TRAD. (arr. VIGNOLES): *Lowlands.*

(B) *** EMI Début 5 75203-2.

This is an outstanding disc in EMI's Début series, a wide-ranging recital from one of the most talented singers of the younger generation, Jonathan Lemalu, a New Zealand-born Samoan with a magnificent natural voice and artistry to match. In 2002 he won the Royal Philharmonic Society's 'Young Artist Award' and here demonstrates his versatility over some very demanding repertory. He seems just as much at home in the dark cadences of Brahms's *Four Serious Songs* as in late Fauré – *L'Horizon chimérique*, a cycle of four songs, three of which are connected with the sea, was written by the aged composer in 1921 for Charles Panzéra. The sea and water connection is carried through many of the other songs, even the Schubert group with the vigorous *Der Schiffer* given a rousing performance. The final group of four songs, which come almost as encores, is also nautical, with John Ireland's masterpiece, 'Sea Fever', matched by the hauntingly evocative 'Trade Winds' by Frederick Keel, which deserves to be far better known. In all these songs Roger Vignoles is an unfailingly imaginative and sympathetic accompanist. Being a budget issue, this has no texts in the booklet, but Lemalu's diction is excellent.

Lemper, Ute, Matrix Ensemble, Robert Ziegler

'*Berlin Cabaret Songs*' (sung in German) by SPOLIANSKY; HOLLAENDER; GOLDSCHMIDT; BILLING; NELSON.

*** Decca 452 601-2.

The tangy, sexy voice of Ute Lemper is here caught at its most provocative in a colourful sequence of cabaret songs reflecting the sleazy, decadent atmosphere of Berlin under the Weimar Republic, as observed in the popular cabarets of the city. With Lemper characterizing delectably, with German consonants adding extra bite, often 'over the top' as in the delightful *Ich bin ein Vamp*, the authentic flavour is here presented in music with new vividness.

The conductor, Robert Ziegler, has restored the original orchestrations as closely as he can (no scores survive, only piano reductions), and the result is a valuable addition to the 'Entartete Musik' series. Not only is the music fascinating and characterful, so are the words, including even a gay anthem, with oompah bass, *Das lila Lied*, written by Mischa Spoliansky under a pseudonym. It is good too to have included a song by Berthold Goldschmidt, which he wrote for his wife in 1930.

(i) Leonard, Sarah (soprano), (ii) Paul Leonard (baritone), Malcolm Martineau (piano)

'*A Century of English Song*', Volume II: (i) PARRY: *My Heart is like a Singing Bird; From a City Window; The Maiden; Armida's Garden; My True Love hath my Heart; Goodnight; Crabbed Age and Youth.* SOMERVELL: (ii) *A Shopshire Lad* (cycle); (i) *Young Love Lies Sleeping; Shepherd's Cradle Song; Come to me in my Dreams.* STANFORD: (ii) *The Fair; To the Soul; The Calico Dress*: (i) *An Irish Idyll* (cycle).

(M) **(*) Somm SOMMCD 214.

Sarah Leonard with her fresh, bright soprano and her brother Paul with his cleanly focused baritone are persuasive advocates in these largely neglected songs, helped by the imaginative accompaniments of Malcolm Martineau. All three composers rise above the limitations of the drawing-room ballad thanks to musical finesse and sensitive response to words, though Sir Arthur Somervell's *Shropshire Lad* cycle, open in its lyricism, completely misses the darkness implied behind seemingly innocent verses. Parry owes most to the example of Brahms, while Stanford, with Irish as well as English overtones, finds a personal magic in such songs as 'The Fairy Lough', the second song in the *Irish Idyll*. Well-balanced recording, but with edge on the top of the soprano's voice.

London, George (bass)

'*The Singers*' (Decca series): Arias from: WAGNER: *Der fliegende Holländer; Die Meistersinger von Nürnberg; Die Walküre* (with VPO, Knappertsbusch). Songs from musicals: RODGERS AND HAMMERSTEIN: *Carousel; Oklahoma; South Pacific.* LERNER AND LOEWE: *Brigadoon; My Fair Lady.* WEILL: *Knickerbocker Holiday.* KERN AND HAMMERSTEIN: *Show Boat; Very Warm for May* (with the Ronald Shaw O).

(M) **(*) Decca (ADD) 467 904-2.

George London's distinctive, rich-hued voice could be capable of sounding very dramatic, even sinister, and with his dark good looks and magnetic presence he was indeed a commanding figure. The Wagner items demonstrate a vigorous personality, and if characterization is not his strong point, he is dramatic in the broadest sense. The gritty sound of his vibrato is not to our tastes, but we are the first to admit that others hear it differently. The singing certainly communicates excitement, but it is rather tiring when the singing is so consistently loud. The

1958 recording is warm and vivid, and only a little dated.

It is something of a shock that the remaining half of the programme is devoted to musicals. Nothing wrong with that in principle, but if you play 'O What a Beautiful Morning' straight after *Die Walküre*, it can cause a severe aural 'double-take'. As for the performances, they are strongly sung. Even if one doesn't always like full operatic voices in this repertoire London's Canadian accent is certainly an asset here, and the 1957 sound captures the voice well. Once again in this series, texts and translations, along with a photo-gallery, are available only via a CD ROM drive.

London Symphony Chorus & LSO, Richard Hickox

'*Grand Opera Choruses*' from: BIZET: *Carmen.* VERDI: *Il trovatore; Nabucco; Macbeth; Aida.* GOUNOD: *Faust.* BORODIN: *Prince Igor.* ORFF: *Carmina Burana.*

(BB) *** Regis RRC 1137 (with BIZET: *Carmen: Suites* **(*)).

Most collections of opera choruses are taken from sets, but this one was a freshly recorded collection of favourites, sung with fine fervour and discipline. The opening Toreador Chorus from *Carmen* is zestfully infectious, and the Soldiers' Chorus from *Faust* is equally buoyant. The noble line of Verdi's *Va pensiero* is beautifully shaped by Hickox, with the balance between voices and orchestra particularly effective. In *Gli arredi festivi* from *Nabucco* and the famous Triumphal scene from *Aida*, the orchestral brass sound resonantly sonorous, even if the trumpet fanfares could have been more widely separated in the latter. The concert ends with Borodin's *Polovtsian Dances*, most excitingly done. The recording, made at the EMI Abbey Road studio, has the atmosphere of an idealized opera house, and the result is in the demonstration bracket. The coupled orchestral music from *Carmen* by Bizet is also very well recorded.

Lott, Felicity (soprano), Graham Johnson (piano)

Mélodies on Victor Hugo poems: GOUNOD: *Sérénade.* BIZET: *Feuilles d'album: Guitare. Adieux de l'hôtesse arabe.* LALO: *Guitare.* DELIBES: *Eclogue.* FRANCK: *S'il est un charmant gazon.* FAURE: *L'Absent; Le Papillon et la fleur; Puisqu'ici-bas.* WAGNER: *L'Attente.* LISZT: *O quand je dors; Comment, disaient-ils.* SAINT-SAENS: *Soirée en mer; La Fiancée du timbalier.* M.V. WHITE: *Chantez, chantez jeune inspirée.* HAHN: *Si mes vers avaient des ailes; Rêverie.*

(B) *** HM Musique d'Abord HMA 901138.

Felicity Lott's collection of Hugo settings relies mainly on sweet and charming songs, freshly and unsentimentally done, with Graham Johnson an ideally sympathetic accompanist. The recital is then given welcome stiffening with fine songs by Wagner and Liszt, as well as two by Saint-Saëns that have a bite worthy of Berlioz. It makes a headily enjoyable cocktail. Now reissued in the Musique d'Abord series, this is a bargain not to be missed.

'Summertime': ARNE: *Where the Bee Sucks.* BARBER: *Sure on this Shining Light; The Monk and his Cat.* BERLIOZ: *Nuites d'été: L'Île inconnue; Villanelle.* BERNSTEIN: *My House.* BRAHMS: *Meine Liebe ist grun.* BRIDGE: *Go not Happy Day.* DELIUS: *To Daffodils.* ELGAR: *The Shepherd's Song.* FAURE: *Clair de lune; Soir; Notre amour.* FRASER-SIMPSON: *Vespers.* GERSHWIN: *Summertime.* HEAD: *The Little Road to Bethlehem.* IRELAND: *The Trellis.* LEHMANN: *Ah, Moon of my Delight.* PORTER: *The Tale of the Oyster.* QUILTER: *Now Sleeps the Crimson Petal. Love's Philosophy.* RUTTER: *The Lord Bless you.* SCHUBERT: *Who is Sylvia? Auf dem Wasser zu singen.* SCHUMANN: *Der Nussbaum.* TRAD: *The Lark in the Clear Air.* VAUGHAN WILLIAMS: *Orpheus with his Lute.* WARLOCK: *Sleep.* HAYDN WOOD: *A Brown Bird Singing.*

*** Black Box BBM 3007.

It would be hard to devise a song-miscellany more attractive than this programme, which brings together so many popular favourites as well as some welcome rarities. It is Graham Johnson's genius pointfully to juxtapose so many different areas of song, with such an item as Cole Porter's cabaret-song, 'The Tale of the Oyster', adding an extra, unexpected dimension, as do Haydn Wood's 'Brown Bird Singing' and Fraser-Simpson's setting of one of A. A. Milne's Christopher Robin poems, 'Vespers'. Dame Felicity rightly presents it straight as a child might, punctuating it with little staccato cries of '*oh!*' (of which there are perhaps one or two too many).

In every way she is a charmer, which makes this disc self-recommending, and her voice is at its freshest, even girlish. Yet the recording tends to highlight a brightness in both the voice and the piano that limits her range of tone and makes it seem less varied than usual. The information on the two-page leaflet is very limited indeed, and Schumann's most popular song, *Der Nussbaum*, is attributed to Schubert. As a CD-ROM the disc offers more information, including translations, yet even for those with access to a computer that is no substitute for a printed note, which provides you with texts and translations while you are actually listening. Even so, it is a delight to go from one jewel of a song to another, and it is good to have a spicing of American items, not just Gershwin, Barber (with two songs) and Cole Porter, but Bernstein too, with one of his early songs for Barrie's *Peter Pan*.

Lott, Felicity (soprano), Anne Murray (mezzo-soprano), Graham Johnson (piano)

'*Sweet Power of Song*': Recital 1: BEETHOVEN: Irish duets (with Solodchin, violin, Williams, cello): *Sweet Power of Song; The Elfin Fairies; Oh! would I were but that Sweet Linnet;* Irish song: *English Bulls* or *The Irishman in London.* SCHUMANN: *Liederalbum für die Jugend* (excerpts): *Er ist's; Frühlingslied; Schneeglöckchen; Das Glück* (duets). BRAHMS: *4 Duets, Op. 61.* BERLIOZ: Duets: *Pleure, pauvre Colette; Le Trébuchet.* GOUNOD: *D'un coeur qui t'aime;* Duet: *L'Arithmétique.* CHAUSSON: Duets: *La Nuit; Réveil.* SAINT-SAENS: Duets: *Pastorale; El desdichado.* FAURE: Duets: *Pleurs d'or; Tarentelle.*

Recital 2: PURCELL, realized Britten: Duets: *Sound the Trumpet; I Attempt from Love's Sickness to Fly; Lost is my Quiet Forever; What can we Poor Females do?* Solo: *Fairest Isle.* MENDELSSOHN: Duets: *Wasserfart; Volkslied; Abendlied; Maiglöckchen und die Blümelein.* Solos: *Auf Flügeln des Gesanges; Neue Liebe.* ROSSINI: Duets: *Soirées musicales: La pesca; La promessa. Le regata veneziana: Anzoleta. Cats' Duet.* Duets: GOUNOD: *La Siesta.* DELIBES: *Les Trois Oiseaux.* MASSENET: *Rêvons c'est l'heure; Joie!* PALADILHE: *Au bord de l'eau.* AUBERT: *Cach-cache.* BALFE: *Trust her not.* SULLIVAN: *Coming Home.* QUILTER: *It was a Lover and His Lass.* BRITTEN: *Mother Comfort; Underneath the Abject Willow.*

(B) *** EMI 5 74206-2 (2).

These two recitals were originally issued two years apart but make a perfect coupling. Felicity Lott's and Anne Murray's voices match delightfully, without clashes of style or vibrato, and Graham Johnson's accompaniments are without peer. On the first disc, the title-number is the charming highlight of the Beethoven group (accompanied by piano trio), but the Brahms and Schumann duets have no less appeal and rather greater character. The Berlioz items are surprisingly lightweight and are thrown off pleasingly, while Gounod provides the contrast of a romantic ballade and a witty Arithmetical duet. Chausson is more sensuously languorous and Saint-Saëns offers a luscious touch of Spanishry. Then, after the comparative delicacy of Fauré's *Pleurs d'or*, the first recital ends with his sparking *Tarentella*.

The Britten–Purcell arrangements which begin the second disc are perhaps less well suited to the voices of these artists: here one misses the purity of style a singer like Emma Kirkby can bring to this repertoire. But Felicity Lott is at her finest in 'Fairest Isle', and the six Mendelssohn Lieder come off splendidly, four duets framing the solo 'On Wings of Song' (Ann Murray), and the *Neue Liebe*, which seems almost to have strayed from the *Midsummer Night's Dream* incidental music.

These singers are also totally at home in Rossini, the luscious *La pesca* and the famous Cats' Duet (reputedly wrongly attributed) both winningly done. This serves to introduce a whole stream of delightful lightweight numbers, all with 'hit' potential, among which the duets by Gounod (richly sultry), Balfe (an inventive rondo), Paladilhe and Quilter (both engagingly fresh) stand out. The two rare Britten numbers make a curious finale, but are welcome just the same, especially the forward-looking Auden setting, 'Underneath the Abject Willow'. The one considerable snag to this reissue is the shameless omission of texts and translations.

Ludwig, Christa (mezzo-soprano)

'*The Art of Christa Ludwig*' (with Moore or Parsons, piano & (i) Downes, viola; (ii) with Philh. O, Klemperer; (iii) with Berlin SO, Stein or Forster): BRAHMS: *Sapphische Ode; Liebestreu; Der Schmied; Die Mainacht. 8 Zigeunerlieder. 4 Deutsche Volkslieder: Och mod'r ich well en Ding han!; We kumm ich dann de Pooz erenn?; In stiller Nacht; Schwesterlein.* Lieder: *Dein blaues Auge; Von ewiger Liebe; Das Mädchen spricht; O wüsst ich doch; Wie Melodien zieht es mir; Mädchenlied; Vergebliches Ständchen; Der Tod, das ist die kühle Nacht; Auf dem See; Waldeinsamkeit; Immer leiser wird mein Schlummer; Ständchen; Gestillte Sehnsucht;* (i) *Geistliches Wiegenlied.* MAHLER: *Hans und Grete; Frühlingsmorgen; Des Knaben Wunderhorn: Ich ging mit Lust durch einen grünen Wald; Wo die schönen Trompeten blasen; Der Schildwache Nachtlied; Um schlimme Kinder; Das irdische Leben; Wer hat dies Liedlein erdacht; Lob des hohen Verstandes;Des Antonius von Padua Fischpredigt; Rheinlegendchen.* Rückert Lieder: *Ich atmet' einen linden Duft; Liebst du um Schönheit; Um Mitternacht; Ich bin der Welt abhanden gekommen.* SCHUMANN: *Frauenliebe und -Leben, Op. 42.* REGER: *Der Brief; Waldeinsamkeit.* SCHUBERT: *Die Allmacht; Fischerweise; An die Musik; Der Musensohn; Ganymed; Auf dem Wasser zu singen; Ave Maria; Die Forelle; Gretchen am Spinnrade; Frühlingsglaube; Der Tod und das Mädchen; Lachen und Weinen; Litanei auf das Fest Aller Seelen; Erlkönig; Der Hirt auf dem Felsen.* WOLF: *Gesang Weylas; Auf einer Wanderung.* RICHARD STRAUSS: *Die Nacht; Allerseelen; Schlechtes Wetter.* RAVEL: *3 Chansons madécasses.* SAINT-SAENS: *Une flûte invisible.* RACHMANINOV: *Chanson géorgienne; Moisson de tristesse.* ROSSINI: *La regata veneziana* (3 canzonettas). (ii) WAGNER: *Wesendonk Lieder.* (iii) HANDEL: *Giulio Cesare: Cleopatra's aria.* BACH: *St John Passion: Es ist vollbracht!* (ii) WAGNER: *Tristan und Isolde: Mild und leise.*

(M) ★★★ EMI (ADD) 7 64074-2 (4).

Christa Ludwig is an extraordinarily versatile artist with a ravishing voice, readily matched by fine intelligence and natural musical sensitivity which place her among the special singers of our time, including Los Angeles and Schwarzkopf (to name two from the same EMI stable). She was as impressive in Schubert as she was in Strauss and Brahms, and her Mahler is very special indeed. This compensates for the below-par Schumann song-cycle. Her voice took naturally to the microphone, so this four-disc set is another source of infinite musical pleasure to be snapped up quickly before it disappears. The recordings come from the 1950s and 1960s and are very well transferred indeed.

Magdalen College Choir, Oxford, Dr John Harper

'*The English Anthem Collection*' complete (with Goffrey Webber or Paul Brough, organ).

(BB) ★★★ Regis (ADD/DDD) RRC 4001 (4) (2 x 2).

Volume 1 (1540–1870): Disc 1: BYRD: *O Lord Turn Thy Wrath; Teach Me O Lord; Exalt Thyself O God; Sing Joyfully unto God.* MORLEY: *Out of the Deep; Nolo mortem peccatoris.* VAN WILDER: *Blessed Art Thou.* TYE: *I Will Exalt Thee.* TALLIS: *I Call and Cry to Thee; O Lord, Give Thy Holy Spirit. Purge Me, O Lord.* SHEPHERD: *The Lord's Prayer.* GIBBONS: *O Lord in Thy Wrath Rebuke me Not; O Lord, I Lift my Heart to Thee.* WEELKES: *Hosanna to the Son of David; O Lord Arise into Thy Resting Place.* TOMKINS: *Then David Mourned; O Praise the Lord.* BLOW: *My God, my God, Look upon Me.* PURCELL: *I was Glad.*

Disc 2: PURCELL (cont.): *Hear my Prayer, O Lord; O God Thou has Cast us Out; Remember Not, O Lord our Offences.* CROFT: *God is Gone Up.* GREENE: *Lord, Let Me Know Mine End.* BOYCE: *O Where shall Wisdom be Found?* BATTISHILL: *Look, Look down from Heaven.* ATTWOOD: *Come Holy Ghost.* S. S. WESLEY: *Blessed be the Lord and Father; The Wilderness.* OUSELEY: *Is it Nothing to You?; O Saviour of the World.* STAINER: *I Saw the Lord.*

(BB) ★★★ Regis ADD/DDD RRC 2030 (2).

Since these recordings were made for the Alpha label between 1963 and 1969, Dr Harper has been appointed Director of the Royal School of Church Music. Here he and his splendid choir offer a survey spanning four-and-a-half centuries, covering 67 anthems (or motets) written by 42 composers. With a very high overall standard of performance and recording, it is an astonishing achievement, which Regis have conveniently made available in two seperate budget Duos, with the complete anthology also available together in a slip-case, at a comparable low cost.

Opening with three magnificent examples by William Byrd, the first and third unaccompanied, the choir moves on to Morley and Farmer, including an attractively intimate setting of the Lord's Prayer. One of the early surprises is the fresh, uncomplicated imitation of 'Blessed art Thou' (Psalm 128) by Philip van Wilder, a Netherlander who served at the court of Henry VIII. Of the Tallis items 'Purge Me O Lord' is particularly touching, while 'O Lord Give Thy Holy Spirit', radiantly serene, is spiced with a twinge of dissonance.

If Byrd was the father of English Renaissance polyphony, Weelkes brought real drama into his settings, and his 'Hosanna to the Son of David' is a thrillingly vibrant example. Tomkins's simple, melancholy lament by David for Jonathan then contrasts with his contrapuntal 'O Praise the Lord', for twelve independent voices, which recalls Tallis's *Spem in alium*. The first disc then ends with John Blow, direct and eloquent in 'My God, my God, Look upon Me' and Purcell's jubilant 'I was Glad'.

With the three Purcell works which open the second disc we are on more familiar territory, but then come two of the highlights, Croft's joyful three-verse 'God is Gone Up', followed by Greene's richly expressive 'Lord, Let Me Know Mine End', with its imitative duet for a pair of trebles. Boyce's use of solo voices in dialogue contrasted with the full choir later brings a flavour of Handel. Thomas Battishill was a pupil of Mozart, and he builds a fine intense climax in 'Lord Look down from Heaven'.

The move forward to the nineteenth century brings an obvious change of style. Wesley's 'Blessed be the God and Father' is an eloquent example, while *The Wilderness*, at fourteen minutes, is more like a miniature cantata, and with its finely sung treble solos might almost be by Mendelssohn. Ouseley's style is much simpler: his richly homophonic textures look back as well as forward, while the dramatic closing work of Stainer for double choir and organ shows the Victorian tradition at its most flamboyant.

Volume 2 (1870–1988): Disc 1: STANFORD: *The Lord's my Shepherd; Glorious and Powerful God.* PARRY: *My Soul, there is a Country.* WOOD: *O Thou, the Central Orbe; Hail, Gladdening Light; Expectans expectavi.* BAIRSTOW: *Blessed City, Heavenly Salem; Let All Mortal Flesh Keep Silent.* IRELAND: *Greater Love hath no Man.* VAUGHAN WILLIAMS: *Whitsunday Hymn.* FINZI: *Welcome Sweet and Sacred Feast.* HOLST: *The Evening Watch.* HOWELLS: *Like as the Hart.*

Disc 2: HOWELLS (cont.): *Thee will I Love; Come my Soul.* WALTON: *Set Me as a Seal upon Thine Heart.* STEWART: *King of Glory, King of Peace.* ROSE: *O Praise ye the Lord.* JOUBERT: *O Lord the Maker of All Things.* BRITTEN: *Hymn to St Peter.* HARRIS: *Bring us, O Lord God.* HARVEY: *Come Holy Ghost; The Tree.* BERKELEY: *Thou has Made Me.* TAVENER: *Hymn to the Mother of God.*

BENNETT: *Verses 1–3.* HARPER: *Salve Regina; Ubi caritas.* LEIGHTON: *Drop, Drop, Slow Tears; Give Me the Wings of Faith.*
✱ (BB) ★★★ RRC 2031 (2).

If in Volume 1, fine though it is, the Magdalen Choir face competition from other specialist groups in the early music (which they meet admirably), in Volume 2, which spans the late nineteenth and twentieth centuries, they are unsurpassed. The remarkable range of music included is matched by the quality of performances, and one is again struck by the secure solo contributions by the unnamed treble soloists, for example at the opening of the beautiful and rejoicing closing anthem by Kenneth Leighton, *Give Me the Wings of Faith.*

The opening unaccompanied works by Stanford and Parry readily demonstrate the vocal riches of the Victorian era, while Charles Wood uses the organ to underpin his exultant 'Hail Gladdening Light', with its lively antiphonal interplay for two four-part choirs. Dr Harper's notes make a special case for what he calls the (relative) 'modernism' of Howells, here eloquently represented, suggesting he is still underestimated (but not by us). Bairstow's 'Blessed City, Heavenly Salem', is less familiar than 'Let All Mortal Flesh Keep Silence', but no less impressive. Vaughan Williams's 'Whitsunday Hymn' is comparably memorable, as are the contributions of Finzi and the harmonically lavish 'Evening Watch' of Holst, which seems to anticipate the later music of John Tavener.

The second disc opens tellingly with Walton's wedding anthem (which draws on the Song of Songs), but the following settings by Stewart, Joubert (harmonically tangy) and Rose, the latter joyfully spirited, and the more restrained Harris, are no less individual. Bennett's *Three Verses* (of John Donne) open radiantly but establish their cool beauty with relatively austere harmony. Lennox Berkeley's 'Thou has Made Me' is also a setting of Donne. It opens and closes wistfully, but has a forceful central section in which the organ participates strongly. But it is in Jonathan Harvey's *The Tree* that the organ is used (in its upper range) with striking imagination, creating an atmosphere for this poignant setting (for trebles alone) within the framework of a 12-note chromatic pitch series. *Come Holy Ghost*, a set of variations on the Pentecost Hymn, is hardly less arresting, with its complex writing for up to sixteen independent vocal lines.

Edward Harper's Latin settings were written for the Magdalen Choir and their overlapping part-writing hauntingly makes use of the cathedral resonance. He uses plainsong melodies as a source of inspiration and although the harmonic style is comparatively avant garde, these works look back to the very roots of English church music. They bring a powerfully committed response from the Magdalen Choristers and the whole programme is superbly sung and recorded in what is surely an ideal acoustic.

Matteuzzi, William (tenor)

'*Fermé tes yeux*': arias, duets and ensembles (with Scano, Cullagh, Shkosa, Ford, Wood, Geoffrey Mitchell Choir, ASMF, Parry) from ADAM: *Le Postillon de Longjumeau.* AUBER: *La Muette de Portici.* CARAFA: *Gabriella di Vergi.* DONIZETTI: *Il castello di Kenilworth; La Fille du regiment.* OFFENBACH: *Le Pont des soupirs.* PACINI: *Alessandro nell' Indie.* ROSSINI: *Le Comte Ory; Il viaggio a Reims.*

*** Opera Rara ORR 216.

The title for this intensely imaginative recital, *Fermé tes yeux*, comes from Masaniello's aria in Auber's opera, best known through its overture. What is striking about this selection of items (with the choice master-minded by the sponsor, Peter Moores) is that only three items out of the nine are solo arias. The ensembles just as much as the arias brilliantly exploit Matteuzzi's glorious tenor, honey-toned even up to the highest register. That register is spectacularly in evidence in the best-known item here, the Postilion's song from Adam's opera (done with more character than in the classic versions of Roswaenge and Gedda), but just as winning is the opening item, the hilarious Act II trio from *Le Comte Ory*, with Matteuzzi the most seductive Count. The beauty of Matteuzzi's timbre is well contrasted with the more sinewy tenor of Bruce Ford in the Carafa duet, every one of these items brings illumination, both for the music and for the singing. Strong, well-paced conducting from David Parry and full, brilliant recording.

McKellar, Kenneth (tenor)

'*The Decca Years 1955–75*': TRAD., arr. KENNEDY-FRASER: *Kishmul's Galley; An Island Sheiling Song; The Christ-child's Lullaby; The Peat Fire Flame; To People who Have Gardens; Skye Fisher's Song; Sleeps the Noon in the Clear Blue Sky; An Eriskay Love Lilt.* TRAD., arr. SHARPLES; *An Island Sheiling Song; Wi' a Hundred Pipers; The De'ils Awa' wi' the Exciseman; There was a Lad was Born in Kyle; Mary Morison; Ye Banks and Braes; Ca' the Yowes.* TRAD., arr. KNIGHT: *Think on me; Ae Fond Kiss* (with Cahill); *Kalinka.* TRAD., arr. ROBERTON: *Dream Angus; Lewis Bridal Song.* TRAD., arr. STANFORD: *Trottin' to the Fair.* TRAD., arr. BRITTEN; *Down by the Salley Gardens.* TRAD., arr. HUGHES: *She Moved thro' the Fair.* TRAD., arr. LAWSON: *Skye Boat Song.* FARNON: *Country Girl.* DI CAPUA: *O sole mio.* HANDEL: *Xerxes: Ombra mai fù. Acis and Galatea: Love in her Eyes Sits Playing.* MASSENET: *Manon: En fermant les yeux (Dream song).* BIZET: *The Fair Maid of Perth: Serenade.* ELLIS: *This is My Lovely Day* (with Patricia Cahill). ANKA: *The Longest Day.* HOPPER: *By the Short Cut to the Rosses.*

DONIZETTI: *L'elisir d'amore: Una furtiva lagrima.* MENDELSSOHN: *On Wings of song.* BOUGHTON: *The Immortal Hour: Faery Song.* MURRAY: *I'll Walk beside You.* SPEAKS: *On the Road to Mandalay.* HARTY: *My Lagen Love.* BOCK: *Sunrise, Sunset.* BERNSTEIN: *West Side Story: Maria.* LAUDER: *Roamin' in the Gloamin'.* GOULAY: *Song of the Clyde.* BANNERMAN, arr. ROBERTON: *Uist Tramping Song.* MURDOCH: *Hame o'mine.* OGILVIE: *Hail Caledonia.* SCHUBERT: *Great is Jehova.* TRAD., arr. MCPHEE: *I to the Hills.* arr. WALFORD DAVIES: *God be in my Head* (all three with Paisley Abbey Choir, McPhee). LEMON: *My ain Folk.* TRAD., arr. KNIGHT: *Will ye no Come Back Again.*

(M) *** Decca (ADD) 466 415-2 (2).

Both artistically and vocally, Kenneth McKellar's lovely singing of Scottish folksongs can be ranked alongside Count John McCormack's instinctive response to similar Irish melodies. Like McCormack, he had a natural feeling for their simplicity of line, and his artless phrasing and ravishingly beautiful upper range, together with splendid diction and a spirited sense of fun, made him a uniquely gifted exponent, whether the song be lyrical or rhythmically catchy in its ready tunefulness. The sparkling 'Lewis Bridal Song' was a BBC radio hit at one time, although the voice reproduces curiously here in this particular number. But McKellar's range was far wider than that.

Early in his career he played the Count in Rossini's *Barber of Seville* with the touring Carl Rosa Opera Company and, as Donizetti's *Una furtiva lagrima* shows, he could certainly spin an Italian lyric melody. But even finer is the delightful Faery Song from *The Immortal Hour*, and the Dream Song from *Manon* brings a comparable delicacy of feeling and lovely tone. He could sing a sentimental ballad like 'I'll Walk beside You' with real style, and every word is clear in 'The Road to Mandalay'. The duets with the charming soubrette Patricia Cahill show him in even lighter vein, while 'God be in my Head' (recorded in Paisley Abbey) has a touching combination of warmth and sincerity.

He was pretty good too at an Irish inflection. 'Trottin' to the fair', 'By the Short Cut to the Rosse', the memorable 'My Lagen Love', and (especially) the touching, unaccompanied 'She Moved thro' the Fair' are splendid examples of his art. But it is the Scottish repertoire for which he will be uniquely remembered, and in which he had no peer, and this extremely generous concert ends very appropriately with 'Will Ye no Come Back Again'. Accompaniments (often by Bob Sharples) are mostly well managed, the CD transfers are good and the set has an interesting extended reminiscence by McKellar's producer, Raymond Herricks.

'*Kenneth McKellar's Scotland – Sleeps the Noon in the Clear Blue Sky*' (with accompaniments directed by Sharples): Disc 1: '*Songs of the Hebrides*' (arr. KENNEDY-FRASER): *Sleeps the Noon in the Clear Blue Sky; The Peat Fire Flame; Land of Heart's Desire; The Reiving Ship; Aignish of the Machair; A Fairy's Love Song; Skye Fisher's Song; A Clyde-side Love Lilt; Heart of Fire Love; Sea Longing; To the People who Have Gardens; The Bens of Jura; The Birlinn of the White Shoulders; Isle of my Heart; Kirsteen; Ye Highlands and ye Lowlands.* 'Roamin' in the Gloamin': arr. KENNEDY-FRASER: *The Road to the Isles: An Eriskay Love Lilt; The Cockle Gatherer.* TRAD.: *Bonnie Mary of Argyle.* THOMSON: *The Star o' Robbie Burns.* HANLEY: *Scotland the Brave.* FOX: *Bonnie Wee Thing.* ROBERTON: *Westering Home.* HUME: *Afton Water.* GOULAY: *Song of the Clyde.* LAUDER: *Roamin' in the Gloami'; Keep Right on to the End of the Road.*

Disc 2: '*The Tartan*': TRAD.: *The March of the Cameron Men; Kishmul's Galley; The Flowers of the Forest; Lochnagar; Wi' a Hundred Pipers; Air Falalolo; An Island Sheiling Song; Scots wha Ha'e wi' Wallace Bled.* SMITH: *Jessie, the Flower of Dunblane.* SCOTT: *Annie Laurie.* MCKELLAR: *The Tartan; The Royal Mile.* Folksongs (arr. SHARPLES): *McGregor's Gathering; The Laird o'Cockpen; The Bonnie Earl of Moray; O Gin I were a Baron's Heir; Turn Ye to Me; Hey, Johnny Cope; Ho-ro, My Nut-brown Maiden; Bonnie Strathyle; The Wee Cooper o'Fife; Isle of Mull; A Pair of Nicky Tams; The Proud Peaks of Scotland; Auld Lang Syne.*

☞ ✿ ★★★ Australian Decca 844 840-2 (2).

Concurrently with the wider coverage above, Australian Decca have issued a second two-CD collection, entirely devoted to the finest of Kenneth McKellar's Scottish repertory. It is compiled from his most beautiful LP, *Songs of the Hebrides*, plus three others: *Folksongs from Scotland's Heritage* with much of the programme dealing with Scotland's colourful history, *The Tartan*, which is essentially a collection of Scottish popular genre songs, with elaborately arranged accompaniments, and *Roamin' in the Gloamin*, McKellar's first stereo recital. This was recorded early in his career, when the voice was at its peak, with a marvellous freshness and bloom.

His simple presentation has a natural, spontaneous warmth and ardour, and the jaunty songs are most engagingly infectious, especially the wittily descriptive 'Song of the Clyde', with every word as clear as a bell. 'Scotland the Brave' and 'Westering Home' swing along splendidly, and the slightly sentimental Burns setting 'Bonnie Wee Thing' could not be more charming. McKellar also includes the two most famous songs of his illustrious predecessor, Sir Harry Lauder, ending with a bold account of 'Keep Right on to the End of the Road' of which that famous Scotsman would have surely approved. The orchestral arrangements here are nicely judged and show none of the inflation that marks the 'Tartan' collection, which is still very enjoyable for a' that.

But it is the ravishingly lovely collection of Hebridean songs which earns the set its Rosette. It opens with the sound of surf on sand, and this evocation returns between the items, many of which McKellar introduces himself, warmly and intimately. The lovely opening title song is followed by 'The Peat Fire Flame', sung with the lightest rhythmic touch, and then comes the most beautiful song of all, 'Land of Heart's Desire'.

Here the voice is slightly backwardly balanced, and McKellar's gently curving upward line is utterly melting. The melancholy 'Aignish of the Machair' is another highlight and 'The Fairy Lover' (charmingly introduced) brings a delightful, lilting melody. Throughout, the accompaniments are delicately scored, often using pipes, and the voice itself is most naturally caught. But all these CD transfers are superb, the quality enhanced over the original LPs. Like the other Australian Decca issues, this set can be obtained to special order from the address given in the Introduction.

Mera, Yoshikazu (counter-tenor), Bach Collegium Japan, Masaaki Suzuki

Baroque arias: J. S. BACH: *Cantatas Nos. 12: Wir müssen durch viel Trübsal; Krenz und Krone; 54: Widerstehe doch der Sünde; Die art verruchter Sünde; Wer Sünde tut; 132: Ich will, mein Gott; Christi Glieder, ach bedenket; 161: Komm, du süsse Todesstunde; Mein Jesus, lass mich nicht; In meinem Gott.* HANDEL: *Messiah: But who May Abide; He was Despised; Thou art Gone up on High; Behold, a Virgin; O Thou that Tellest.* AHLE: *Prima pars; Secunda pars.* SCHUTZ: *Geistliche chormusik, Op. 11: Auf dem Gebirge hat man ein geschrei gehört.*
★★★ BIS CD 919.

The Japanese counter-tenor Yoshikazu Mera is one of the most impressive soloists on Suzuki's excellent recordings of choral works for BIS. This compilation drawn from various sources consistently displays his exceptionally sweet and even tone, even though his performances are not very sharply characterized. The voice is set against a helpfully reverberant acoustic.

Merrill, Robert (baritone)

Arias (with New SO of London, Downes) from: VERDI: *Un ballo in maschera; Don Carlo; La forza del destino; Otello; Il trovatore.* LEONCAVALLO: *Pagliacci.* GIORDANO: *Andrea Chénier.*
(M) ★★★ Decca Classic Recitals (ADD) 475 396-2.

Our original review of this 1963 recital is still true, some 40 years on: 'An excellent recital. Merrill is always a most reliable baritone on record, and here his even voice is beautifully captured by the Decca engineers. If a sample is wanted, try the rich, rhythmic account of *Il balen* from *Il trovatore*.' It is now reissued as one of Decca's new Classic Recitals (with some items available for the first time on CD) in an excellent transfer, only a bit of tape hiss giving away its age.

Metropolitan Opera (artists from)

'*Metropolitan Opera Gala*': Arias from BIZET: *Les Pêcheurs de perles* (Roberto Alagna; Bryn Terfel). G. CHARPENTIER: *Louise* (Renée Fleming). GOUNOD: *Faust* (Samuel Ramey; Plácido Domingo); *Roméo et Juliette* (Ruth Ann Swenson). LEHAR: *Giuditta* (Ileana Cotrubas). VERDI: *Don Carlos* (Dolora Zajick). MOZART: *Don Giovanni* (Fleming, Terfel, Jerry Hadley, Kiri Te Kanawa, Hei-Kyung Hong, Julien Robbins). JOHANN STRAUSS JR: *Die Fledermaus* (Håkan Hagegård; Karita Mattila). MASSENET: *Werther* (Alfredo Kraus). SAINT-SAENS: *Samson et Dalila* (Grace Bumbry). WAGNER: *Tannhäuser* (Deborah Voight). OFFENBACH: *La Périchole* (Frederica von Stade). RICHARD STRAUSS: *Der Rosenkavalier* (Fleming, Anne Sofie von Otter, Heidi Grant Murphy). *Tribute to James Levine* (Birgit Nilsson).
**(*) DG Video VHS 072 451-3.

Recorded live at James Levine's twenty-fifth anniversary gala in April 1996, this offers an extraordinary galaxy of stars, often teamed up in unexpected ways – as, for example, Alagna and Terfel in the first item, the *Pearl Fishers* duet. The singers represented a range from such relative newcomers as those rising stars to veterans like Alfredo Kraus and Grace Bumbry. Few of the voices are heard at their very finest, not helped by a rather hard acoustic, but the variety of party pieces here is enough of a delight. The video re-creates the occasion the more satisfactorily, but it is worth hearing the disc for the end of Birgit Nilsson's speech, involving a shattering cry of '*Hojotoho!*'.

Miles, Alastair (bass)

Arias and ensembles, sung in English, with Ch. and Philh. O, Parry), from: VERDI: *The Lombards at the First Crusade; Luisa Miller; Nabucco; The Sicilian Vespers.* ROSSINI: *Mohamet II; Moses in Egypt; Zelmira.* BELLINI: *Norma; The Puritans.* GOMES: *Salvator Rosa.*
(M) *** Chan. 3032.

Alastair Miles here formidably enhances his reputation as a powerful recording artist, exploiting his firm, well-focused bass in a wide range of eleven arias and ensembles, starting with the *Chorus of Hebrew Slaves* from *Nabucco*, which then leads into Miles's noble and sonorous account of Zaccaria's Prophecy. The biting incisivensss of that and much else, as for example the protagonist's aria from *Mahomet II*, is thrilling, and he is well matched in the duets from *Luisa Miller* and *I Lombardi* by his fellow bass, Clive Bayley, crisply dramatic in their exchanges. Garry Magee is also a fine foil in the final long excerpt from *I Puritani*. All but the *Nabucco* item have never been recorded in English before, and the clarity of diction adds to the intensity. There are excellent sound and understanding direction from David Parry.

Minstrelsy

'*Songs and Dances of the Renaissance and Baroque*' (Carole Hofsted-Lee, soprano, Nancy Froseth, David Hays, David Livingstone, viola da gamba, baroque violin, recorders, Philip Rukavina, lute, archlute: SIMPSON: *Ballet.* ANON.: *2 Ballets; Mascarada; Volta.* arr. MCLACHLAN: *When she Cam Ben, she Bobbat.* PRAETORIUS: *Dances from Terpsichore* (suite). PACHELBEL: *Partita in C.* SALAVERDE: *Canzon a 2.* LAWES: *Suite in G min.* Songs: ROSSETER: *When Laura Smiles.* DOWLAND: *I Saw my Lady Weep; Shall I Sue.* ARNE: *Under the Greenwood Tree.* CAMPION: *It Fell upon a Summer's Day.*
*** Lyrichord LEMS 8018.

A most entertaining, lightweight consort, full of life and charm, although one wonders if Renaissance and Baroque musicians could have achieved such sophistry of intonation, blending and playing! The period instruments here are made to integrate smoothly and without any rough edges. The singing of Carole Hofsted-Lee too is pure in tone and line. She is naturally at home in the simplicity of Arne, and her lovely voice caresses the songs of Dowland and Campion with considerable feeling, even if her range of vocal colour is less intense than that of, say, Alfred Deller. There is much to delight in the instrumental music.

Some half-a-dozen of the ensemble pieces come from the *Taffel-Consort*, published by Thomas Simpson in 1621, a collection which has much in common with Praetorius's *Terpsichore*. John McLachlan's 'When she Cam Ben, she Bobbat' is very Scottish, a treble to a ground, with sparkling divisions. But perhaps the highlight is Pachelbel's *Partita*, which is not unlike his more famous Canon in making use of an ostinato bass, but is a more elaborate chaconne, with a dozen variations. The recording is beautifully balanced to match this sprightly and elegant music-making.

Miricioiu, Nelly (soprano)

'*Bel Canto Portrait*': scenes (with Plazas, Holland, Coote, Wood, Janes, Geoffrey Mitchell Ch., LPO or Philh O, Parry) from: MERCADANTE: *Emma d'Antiochia.* COSTA: *L'assedio di Corinto.* DONIZETTI: *Belisario; Parisina.*
*** Opera Rara ORR 217.

The Romanian soprano Nelly Miricioiu, now resident in London, gives a formidable display of both technique and dramatic flair in this fascinating collection of rare arias and scenes from bel canto operas of the 1830s. Hers is not just a flexible voice but also one with plenty of character, full and vibrant with a good cutting edge and occasional echoes of Callas. Thanks to the researches of Jeremy Commons, who provides excellent notes as supplement to the full texts, these long-buried pieces are revealed as far more than merely conventional examples of the genre. The aria from *L'assedio di Corinto*, one of Rossini's operas, was written by Sir Michael Costa as an alternative aria for the heroine, Pamira, when it was sung by the prima donna, Giulia Grisi, at the King's Theatre in London, where Costa was music director when he was a young man. The Mercadante and the extract from Donizetti's *Belisario* lead from the soprano's arias to impressive final ensembles, while most inspired of all is the aria from Donizetti's *Parisina*, which is fairly described by Commons as 'one of the most sustained and consistently beautiful flights of bel canto that Donizetti ever achieved'.

Mitchell, Leona (soprano)

Arias (with New Philh. O, Adler) from: MOZART: *Le nozze di Figaro*. PUCCINI: *La Bohème; Gianni Schicchi; Madama Butterfly; La rondine; Turandot*. MASCAGNI: *L'amico Fritz*. ROSSINI: *William Tell*. VERDI: *Ernani*.
**(*) Australian Decca Eloquence (ADD) 466 903-2.

It's good to have this 1980 recital, Leona Mitchell's debut LP, back in the catalogue – the first time on CD. Its appeal is in its freshness, with her naturally dark vocal colouring most appealing. The charming *La rondine* aria (*Il bel sogno di Doretta*) is a highlight, as is the gentle lilt she finds in the final *Ernani* aria (*Ernani! Ernani, involami*). *Dove sono* is movingly done, and the reverie-like aria from *L'amico Fritz* is lovely too. There is nothing here to mar one's enjoyment, and it is the lyrical moments on this recital that are particularly memorable. The recorded sound is rich and full, though the disc has a short playing time.

Montague, Diana (mezzo-soprano)

'*Bella imagen*': arias, duets and ensembles (with Kenny, Ford, Lewis, Geoffrey Mitchell Ch., ASMF, Philh. or RPO, Parry) from BENEDICT: *I'inganno felice*. DONIZETTI: *Zoraida di Granata*. MAYR: *Alfredo Grande*. MERCADANTE: *Amleto*. MEYERBEER: *Il crociato di Egitto*. MOSCA: *Le bestie in uomini*. PAER: *Sofonisba*. ROSSINI: *Il trionfo di Quinto Fabio*. VON WINTER: *Zaira*.
*** Opera Rara ORR 210.

Who ever would have thought that Mayr had written

an opera about Alfred the Great or that Mercadante had written one about Hamlet? The answer is: those who have been collecting the brilliant series from Opera Rara, '100 Years of Italian Opera', with each decade covered separately. Diana Montague has been a regular contributor, and this compilation of her outstanding recordings is very welcome indeed. Although the recordings were made over a wide period, from 1983 to 1998, the clear, firm voice remains gloriously consistent throughout – as Hugh Canning says in his note, with not only 'the voluptuous warmth of a mezzo, but the shining top of a true soprano'. The title, *Bella imagen*, comes from the Benedict opera, in a 1994 recording that illustrates those qualities perfectly, and one of the 1983 recordings, of the heroine's aria from Von Winter's *Zaira*, had previously demonstrated what dramatic dedication she naturally conveys. Diana Montague has made far too few recordings, but this splendidly fills an important gap, with David Parry providing strong support, mainly with the Philharmonia.

Nash, Heddle (tenor)

'*Serenade*': arias from: BIZET: *The Fair Maid of Perth; The Pearl Fishers*. ROSSINI: *The Barber of Seville*. MOZART: *Don Giovanni; Le nozze di Figaro* (both sung in Italian). BALFE: *The Bohemian Girl*. LEHAR: *Frederica*. OFFENBACH, arr. KORNGOLD: *La Belle Hélène*. GOUNOD: *Faust*. DONIZETTI: *Elixir of Love*. HANDEL: *Judas Maccabaeus*. MASSENET: *Manon*. Songs: TRAD. *Annie Laurie* (all with orch.). BENEDICT: *Eily Mavoureen*. BISHOP: *The Bloom is on the Rye*. MORGAN: *My Sweetheart when a Boy*. MCGEOCH: *Two Eyes of Grey*. MACDOWELL: *To a Wild Rose*. WHITAKER: *Diaphenia*. DELIUS: *To the Queen of my Heart; Love's Philosophy*. WHITE: *To Mary*. MOERAN: *Diaphenia; The Sweet o' the Year* (all with Moore).
(M) (**(*)) ASV mono CDAJA 5227.

Although there are a few (obvious) duplications, this ASV compilation nicely supplements the finer Dutton Lab. collection (now deleted). The transfers of the orchestral accompaniments, which often sound boxy and confined, are much less sophisticated, but the voice emerges naturally, even if it is projected with less uniform vividness. But there are genuine treasures here, not least the songs, with Gerald Moore, who is more faithfully caught. The delightful 'To a Wild Rose', the Delius and Moeran songs and the splendid excerpt from *Judas Maccabaeus* are among the highlights.

New College, Oxford, Choir, Higginbottom

'*Carols from New College*': *O Come, All Ye Faithful; The Angel Gabriel; Ding Dong! Merrily on High;*

The Holly and the Ivy; I Wonder as I Wander; Sussex Carol; This is the Truth; A Virgin Most Pure; Rocking Carol; Once in Royal David's City. ORD: *Adam Lay Y-bounden.* BENNETT: *Out of your Sleep.* HOWELLS: *A Spotless Rose; Here is the Little Door.* DARKE: *In the Bleak Midwinter.* MATHIAS: *A Babe is Born; Wassail Carol.* WISHART: *Alleluya, A New Work is Come on Hand.* LEIGHTON: *Lully, Lulla, Thou Little Tiny Child.* JOUBERT: *There is no Rose of Such Virtue.*

(M) **★★★** CRD (ADD) CRD 3443.

A beautiful Christmas record, the mood essentially serene and reflective. Both the Mathias settings are memorable and spark a lively response from the choir; Howells's 'Here is the Little Door' is matched by Wishart's Alleluya and Kenneth Leighton's 'Lully, Lully, Thou Little Tiny Child' in memorability. Fifteen of the twenty-one items here are sung unaccompanied, to maximum effect. The recording acoustic seems ideal and the balance is first class. The documentation, however, consists of just a list of titles and sources – and the CD (using the unedited artwork from the LP) lists them as being divided onto side one and side two!

New Company, Harry Bicket

'*Sacred Voices*': ALLEGRI: *Miserere.* LOBO: *Versa est in luctum.* PALESTRINA: *The Song of Solomon: Quae est ista; Descendit in hortum nocum; Quam pulchri sunt gressus tui; Duo ubera tue.* BYRD: *Haec dies.* PHILIPS: *Ascendit Deus.* MUNDY: *Vox Patris caelestis.* TALLIS: *Spem in alium* (40-part motet). DERING: *Factum est silentium.*

(M) **★★★** Classic fm 75605 57029-2.

A splendid recording début for the New Company, a professional chamber choir of twelve, directed by Harry Bicket, which is expanded here to forty voices for a thrilling performance of Tallis's *Spem in alium*, one of the great masterpieces of Elizabethan music. The programme opens with a double choir version of Allegri's justly famous *Miserere*, with the second group atmospherically recessed alongside the confident soprano soloist, who soars up again and again to what the conductor calls that 'exquisitely floaty top C': and she hits the spot beautifully every time.

Then follows Lobo's hardly less ethereal *Versa est in luctum* and a characteristic sequence of four serenely flowing five-part motets from Palestrina's *Song of Solomon*, sensuously rich in harmonic implication, all written around 1583–4. Suddenly the mood changes and the pace quickens for William Byrd's *Haec dies*, with its joyful cross-rhythms and an exultant concluding *Alleluia*. Peter Philips's *Ascendit Deus* is similarly full of life and energy and it prepares the way for the contrasting three-part anthem by the lesser-known William Mundy. Its serene simplicity has great beauty, and it again offers a chance for a celestial soaring solo soprano.

After the climactic Tallis work, the programme ends with a short, but thrillingly jubilant, six-part Matins responsory by Richard Dering. The choir were recorded at Temple Church, London, the venue some ten decades earlier for one of the most famous choral recordings of all time: Mendelssohn's *Hear my Prayer*, with its famous solo from Master Ernest Lough, 'Oh for the Wings of a Dove'. The treble soloist here is a worthy successor.

Nilsson, Birgit, Kirsten Flagstad
(sopranos)

'**Land of the Midnight Sun**': Birgit Nilsson: SIBELIUS: *Demanten på marssnön; Flickan kom ifran sin alsklings mote; Höstkväll; Säv, Säv, Susa; Svarta rosor; Var deten drom; Våren flyktar hastigt.* GRIEG: *En svane; Fra monte pincio; Våren.* RANGSTROM: *Bön till natten; En gammal dansrytm; Melodi; Sköldmön* (all with V. Op. O, Bokstedt). Kirsten Flagstad: EGGEN: *Aere det evige forår i livet.* ALNAES: *Februarmorgen ved Golfen; De hundrede fioliner; Nu brister alle de klofter; Vårlaengsler.* LIE: *Nykelen; Skinnvengbrev* (all with LSO, Fjelstad).

★★★ Australian Decca (ADD) 466 657-2.

The Birgit Nilsson items, recorded in the late 1950s, show her art at its most eloquent. One does not primarily think of Sibelius as a song composer, yet every one of the songs is memorable, often in a highly characteristic way. *Flickan kom ifran*, contemporary with the *Second Symphony*, has a power and dramatic passion with which any lover of Sibelius's orchestral music will find an immediate affinity. *Säv, Säv* too is especially imaginative in its creation of atmospheric tension, but all the songs offer something to the listener, and all are superbly sung. In the lighter Greig items, Nilsson shows loving affection, and though the Rangstrom songs are slighter in their quality, they are still rewarding.

Flagstad's contribution was recorded a few years later and is just as compelling: one can hear why she so spellbound listeners by her performances of songs in her first London recital in 1936. Any doubts about the size of the voice being too unwieldy for this comparatively intimate programme are swept away by the eloquence and commitment of the singing. Oivin Fjeldstad's contribution too is an outstanding one. Few of the songs are well known but with such deeply-felt advocacy they are all worth getting to know. The recordings emerge warm and vivid in this transfer, and whilst texts are not provided (nor were they on their original LP releases), this Australian Eloquence CD comes complete with sleeve notes (written, unlike this entry, by our own R.L.). Alas, as an import it will cost more in the UK, but it is well worth it.

Oberlin, Russell (counter-tenor)

'*Troubadour and Trouvère Songs*' Volume 1 (with Seymour Barab, viol): BRULE: *Cil qui d'amor me conseille.* DE BORNEIL: *Reis glorios, verais lums e clartatz.* DANIEL: *Chanson do – Ih mot son plan e prim.* D'EPINAL: *Commensmens de dolce saison bele.* RIQUIER: *Ples de tristor, marritz e doloires; de ventadour: Can vei la lauzeta mover.*
*** Lyrichord LEMS 8001.

It is good to see the legendary Russell Oberlin return to the catalogue. Older readers will recall his Covent Garden appearance as Oberon in Britten's *Midsummer Night's Dream.* Unfortunately his concert career was cut short and he has since pursued a distinguished career as a scholar. This 1958 recital of *Troubadour and Trouvère Songs* first appeared on the Experiences Anonymes label and, like so many of his all-too-few recordings (including an incredible Handel aria disc), has long been sought after. This voice was quite unique, a real counter-tenor of exquisite quality and, above all, artistry. The disc is expertly annotated and is of quite exceptional interest. LEMS stands for Lyrichord Early Music Series, and the discs we have heard so far are artistically impressive.

'*Las Cantigas de Santa Maria*' (with Joseph Iadone, lute): *Prologo; Cantigas Nos. 7, 36, 97, 111, 118, 160, 205, 261, 330, 340 & 364.*
✹ *** Lyrichord LEMS 8003.

The 400 *Cantigas de Santa Maria*, all of which have music, come from the time of Alfonso el Sabio, king of Spain (1221–84). He is credited with being their composer, but that seems unlikely since they are very diverse. The texts are in Galician, a language in general use in medieval Spain for literary and artistic purposes.

They are all concerned with miracles associated with the Virgin Mary, but the music itself has considerable variety and, while the basic style may come from European monodic chant, the melisma has a distinctly Spanish colouring, which in itself has Arab influences. The selection of a dozen items is very well made, for these simple strophic songs have an instant appeal when sung with such lyrical ease by the incomparable Russell Oberlin. The character of the *Cantigas* seems to suit his special timbre especially well, and he has made no finer record than this.

The recital opens with a Prologue in which the singer relates the qualities necessary to be a good troubadour and invokes the Virgin's acceptance of his skills with some confidence. Two of the settings are lively dance songs, *Cantiga 36* telling how Mary appeared in the night on the mast of a ship journeying to Brittany and saved it from danger, and *Cantiga 205* about the rescue of a Moorish woman with her child who were sitting on top of a tower which collapsed – yet neither she nor the child came to any harm. But it is the beauty of the lyrical music which

is so striking, notably so in *Cantigas 118* and *330*, which are concerned with the restoration of a dead child to life and a simple song of praise for the Virgin herself. The recording is natural and vivid and, as with the other discs in this series, the CD remastering by Nick Fritsch is first class. The content of this reissue is not generous in playing time, but it is of the very highest musical quality and interest.

'*Troubadour and Trouvère Songs*', Volume 5: *English medieval songs* (with Seymour Barab, viol): *The St Godric Songs. Worldes Blis ne Last no Throwe. Bryd One Breve; Man mei Longe him Liues Wene; Stond Wel Moder under Rode.*
*** Lyrichord LEMS 8005.

The *St Godric Songs* are the earliest known songs in the English language. St Godric died in 1170, so they date from halfway through the twelfth century. The other items here belong to the latter part of the century. As with his first disc, above, Russell Oberlin is completely convincing in this repertoire, the purity of line and beauty of timbre consistently appealing. The accompanying viol is discreet and the sound is remarkably clear and vivid.

Opera choruses

'*Grand Opera Choruses*': VERDI: *Nabucco: Va pensiero (Chorus of the Hebrew slaves). Il trovatore: Vedi! le fosche (Anvil Chorus).* BEETHOVEN: *Fidelio: O welche Lust (Prisoners' Chorus)* (Chicago Ch. & SO, Solti). BELLINI: *Norma: Squilla il bronzo del dio! ... Guerra, guerra!* (Welsh Nat. Op. Ch. & O, Bonynge). WAGNER: *Lohengrin: Prelude to Act III and Bridal Chorus. Tannhäuser: Pilgrims' Chorus* (V. State Op. Konzertvereinigung or V. State Op. Ch., VPO, Solti). GOUNOD: *Faust: Soldiers' Chorus* (Ambrosian Op. Ch., LSO, Bonynge). PUCCINI: *Madama Butterfly: Humming Chorus* (V. State Op. Ch., VPO, Karajan). LEONCAVALLO: *Pagliacci: I zampognari! ... Don, din, don (Bell Chorus)* (Santa Cecilia, Rome, Ac. Ch. & O, Gardelli). BIZET: *Carmen: Toreador Chorus* (John Alldis Ch., LPO, Solti). WEBER: *Der Freischütz: Huntsmen's Chorus.* NICOLAI: *Die lustigen Weiber von Windsor: O süsser Mond* (Bav. R. Ch. & O, Kubelik). BERLIOZ: *Les Troyens: Dieux protecteurs de la ville éternelle* (Montreal Schubert Ch. & SO, Dutoit). MUSSORGSKY: *Boris Godunov: Coronation scene* (Ghiaurov, V. Boys' Ch., Sofia R. Ch., V. State Op. Ch., VPO, Karajan).
⊖┬ (M) *** Decca DDD/ADD 458 205-2.

This 75-minute collection re-assembled for reissue in Decca's Opera Gala series is exceptional value and offers vivid, and often demonstration worthy sound throughout. Most of the excerpts come from distinguished complete sets, notably the Pilgrims' Chorus from Solti's *Tannhäuser*, which has a memorable sense of perspective, while the *Lohengrin* excerpt is hardly less impressive. However, that also means that they are not always cleanly tailored and sometimes there are soloists too.

A high proportion of the items are from Solti, but other highlights include Karajan's Humming Chorus from *Madama Butterfly*, which is so warmly atmospheric, and the expansive Coronation scene from *Boris Godunov*. Bonynge conducts the War Chorus from *Norma* and the Soldiers' Chorus from *Faust*. Since the disc's previous issue additional items have been added, notably the excerpts from *Der Freischütz* and Nicolai's *Merry Wives of Windsor* (from Kubelík) and the Hymn of Deliverance from *Les Troyens* (Dutoit). Good documentation and translations are provided, an exception rather than the rule for this kind of operatic collection.

Opera love songs

'*Amor – Opera's Great Love Songs*': VERDI: *Aida: Celeste Aida. Luisa Miller: Quando le sere al placido* (Pavarotti). *Rigoletto: Caro nome* (Sutherland). PUCCINI: *Gianni Schicchi: O mio babbino caro* (Tebaldi). *Manon Lescaut: Donna non vidi mai* (Carreras). *Tosca: Recondita armonia* (Corelli); *Vissi d'arte* (Kiri Te Kanawa); *E lucevan le stelle* (Domingo). *La Bohème: Musetta's Waltz Song* (Elizabeth Harwood). *Madama Butterfly: Un bel dì* (Mirella Freni). *Turandot: Signore ascolta!* (Caballé); *Nessun dorma* (Pavarotti). DONIZETTI: *La favorita: O mio Fernando* (Cossotto). *L'elisir d'amore: Una furtiva lagrima. Fedora: Amor ti vieta.* PONCHIELLI: *La Gioconda: Cielo e mar.* MASSENET: *Werther: Pourquoi me réveiller* (all Pavarotti). BIZET: *Carmen: Habanera* (Troyanos); *Flower Song* (Domingo). MOZART: *Nozze di Figaro: Voi che sapete* (Frederica von Stade).
(M) *** Decca (ADD) 458 201-2.

Brimming over with stellar performances, this generous (76-minute) collection is a true 'opera gala'. Pavarotti dominates and seldom lets us down, and he ends the disc with a thrilling performance of his great showpiece, *Nessun dorma*, from his complete set conducted by Mehta. Many of the other excerpts too are drawn from outstanding sets, including Caballé's beautiful *Signore ascolta!* (taken from the same source), Freni's passionately expansive *Un bel dì* from Karajan's *Madama Butterfly*, Domingo's outstanding Flower Song and Troyanos's *Habanera*, both from Solti's *Carmen*, and Frederica von Stade's delightful *Voi che sapete*, taken from the same conductor's highly successful *Nozze di Figaro*. Tebaldi's ravishing *O mio babbino caro* dates from 1962 when the voice still had all its bloom, while Marilyn Horne's dark-voiced 'Softly Awakes my Heart' comes from a 1967 recital. Nicely packaged in a slip case, the documentation includes full translations.

'Operatunity Winners'

'*Operatunity Winners*': Jane Gilchrist (soprano) and Denise Leigh (soprano), with English National Opera Chorus & Orchestra, Paul Daniel.

Arias from: BELLINI: *Norma*. BIZET: *Carmen*. CATALANI: *La Wally*. DVORAK: *Rusalka*. HANDEL: *Samson*. MOZART: *Le nozze di Figaro*. PUCCINI: *Gianni Schicchi; Turandot*. SULLIVAN: *The Pirates of Penzance* (with ENO Ch.). VERDI: *Rigoletto*. Duets from: DELIBES: *Lakmé*. HUMPERDINCK: *Hänsel und Gretel*. MOZART: *Le nozze di Figaro*.
*** EMI 5 57594-2.

Following on from Channel 4's excellent 'Operatunity' series, this delightful issue presents on disc the two winners in that contest of would-be opera-singers, Jane Gilchrist and Denise Leigh. This is a generous and well-chosen sequence of 14 arias, divided between the two, plus three duets, the Countess and Susanna's duet from Mozart's *Marriage of Figaro*, the Evening Hymn from Humperdinck's *Hänsel und Gretel* and the duet from Delibes' *Lakmé*, all beautifully done. They each perform *Caro nome* from Verdi's *Rigoletto* – the opera they appeared in at the ENO – with Leigh the brighter and more agile, ending on a wonderfully controlled trill, and Gilchrist the warmer and more freely imaginative. As on TV, they seem totally unfazed by the formidable technical problems of even the most challenging items, Leigh in *Casta diva* from *Norma*, Gilchrist commanding in the Countess's two arias from *Figaro*. An astonishing achievement!

Otter, Anne Sofie von (mezzo-soprano)

'*Wings in the Night*' (Swedish songs; with Forsberg, piano): PETERSON-BERGER: *Aspåkers-polska (Aspåker's Polka); Aterkomst (Return); Böljeby-vals (Böljeby Waltz); Like the Stars in the Sky (Som stjärnorna på himmeln); Marits visor (3 songs, Op. 12); Nothing is Like the Time of Waiting (Intet är som väntanstider); When I Walk by Myself (När jag går för mig själv).* SJOGREN: *6 Songs from Julius Wollf's Tannhäuser.* SIGURD VON KOCH: *In the Month of Tjaitra (I månaden Tjaitra); Of Lotus Scent and Moonshine (Af Lotusdoft och månens sken); The Wild Swans (De vilda svanarna)* (3 songs). STENHAMMAR: *Miss Blond and Miss Brunette (Jungfru blond och jungfru brunett); In the Maple's Shade (I lönnens skymning); Jutta Comes to the Volkungs (Jutta kommer till Folkungarna); A Seaside Song (En strandvisa); A Ship is Sailing (Det far ett skepp); The Wanderer (Vandraren).* RANGSTROM: *The Farewell (Afskedet); Old Swedish (Gammalsvenskt); Melodi; Pan; Supplication to*

Night (Bön till natten); Wings in the Night (Vingar i natten). ALFVEN: *The Forest is Asleep (Skogen sover); I Kiss your White Hand (Jag kysser din vita hand).*

⊕ *** DG 449 189-2.

So often Swedish singers, once they have made a name for themselves in the world, neglect their native repertoire in favour of Schumann, Brahms, Strauss and Wolf. Anne Sofie von Otter is an exception and, fresh from her recent successes in Scandinavian repertoire, above all her Grieg *Haugtussa* and her Sibelius recitals on BIS, she gives us a splendid anthology of Swedish songs. The disc takes its name from one of Ture Rangström's most haunting songs, *Vingar i natten* ('Wings in the Night'), and, indeed, his are some of the loveliest songs in the Swedish *romans* repertoire. (*Romans* is the Nordic equivalent of *Lied*.) *Bön till natten* ('Supplication to the Night') is arguably the most beautiful of all Swedish songs and has the innocence and freshness of Grieg combined with a melancholy and purity that are totally individual.

Von Otter also includes songs by the composer-critic Wilhelm Peterson-Berger, whose criticism was much admired in his native Sweden and who was compared with Bernard Shaw (he was in fact an opinionated windbag) and whose songs have a certain wistful charm. The Stenhammar songs are among his finest, and von Otter adds some familiar Alfvén and less familiar repertoire by Emil Sjögren and Sigurd (not to be confused with Erland) von Koch. A disc to be treasured.

'Folksongs' (with Forsberg, piano): DVORAK: *Gypsy Songs, Op. 55.* GRAINGER: *The Sprig of Thyme; Died for Love; British Waterside; The Pretty Maid Milkin' her Cow.* LARSSON: *Watercolour; The Box Painter; The Girl with the Divining Herb.* G. HAHN: *The Heart's Prey: A Song from Lapland.* R. HAHN: *Songs in Venetian dialect: On the Drowsy Waters; The Little Boat; The Warning; The Fair Maid in the Gondola; What a Shame!* KODALY: *Hungarian folk music: Little Apple Fell in the Mud; Drinking Wine on Sunday; Youth is Like a Falcon; Let No-one's Bride Bewail; All Through the Vineyard; Hey, the Price of Wine from Mohovce Hill; Beneath the Csitár Hills.* BRITTEN: *arr. of French folksongs: La Noël passée; Voice le printemps; La Fileuse; Le Roi s'en va-t'en chasse; La Belle est au jardin d'amour; Il est quelqu'un sur terre; Eho! Eho!; Quand j'etais chez mon père.*

*** DG 463 479-2.

An enterprising and rewarding recital from the great Swedish mezzo, this covers a wide range of songs from the Slavonic to Kodály and Britten rarities. Her impeccable artistry is given excellent support from Bengt Forsberg and the DG engineers.

'Watercolours': Swedish Songs (with Forsberg, piano): ALFVÉN: *Pioner (Peonies), Saa tag mitt*

Hjerte (Take my Heart). TOR AULIN: *Och riddaren for uti österland (And the Knight Rode to the Holy Land); Fyra serbiska folksånger (Four Serbian Folksongs).* GUNNAR DE FRUMERIE: *Hjärtats sånger (6 Songs of the Heart); Nu är det sommarmogon (A Summer Morning).* LARS-ERIK LARSSON: *Kyssande vind (Kiss of the Wind); För vilana fötter sjunger gräser (Grass Sings under Wandering Feet); Skyn, blomman och en lärka (The Cloud, the Flower and the Lark).* BO LINDE: *Den ängen där du kysste mig (The Meadow Where you Kissed me); Äppelträd och päronträd (Apple-trees and Pear-trees); 4 Songs to texts by Harriet Löwenhjelm.* GUSTAF NORDQVIST: *Sipporna (The Anemones); Jag ville vara tårar (If I Could be Tears); Till havs (On the Sea).* GÖSTA NYSTROEM: *På reveln (On the Reef), Otrolig dag (Amazing Day); Havet sjunger (The Song of the Sea).* TURE RANGSTRÖM: *En gammal dansrytm (An Old Dance); Den enda stunden (A Moment in Time); Serenad; Sköldmön (The Amazon).*

✹ *** DG 474 700-2.

This new recital of Swedish songs from Anne Sofie von Otter and Bengt Forsberg follows on from their earlier recital, which took its title from Rangström's song 'Wings in the Night', and admirably complements the earlier issue. It is good to see them championing Gunnar de Frumerie, whose settings of Pär Lagerkvist have a quiet, unforced eloquence. De Frumerie was a Sabaneyev pupil and had a splendid feeling for the keyboard and a keen, almost Gallic sensibility. He was neglected in the 1950s and '60s – though not as grievously as Bo Linde, who died in his late thirties and whose songs have an affecting simplicity and directness of utterance. Another surprise is the set of three songs of Gösta Nystroem: those who find his *Sinfonia del mare* hard work should investigate these wonderfully imaginative and atmospheric pieces. *På reveln* ('On the Reef') is a little masterpiece, one of the most haunting songs on the disc. Lars-Erik Larsson's *Skyn, blom'man och en lärka* ('The Cloud, the Flower and the Lark') is another discovery. Why is it that such a beautiful song is so little known and his inventive *Music for Orchestra* and (for all its debt to Walton and Prokofiev) the *Violin Concerto* so rarely heard? In all there are 33 songs in this recital, all of them rewarding and some of them are masterpieces, like Rangström's haunting *Den enda stunden* ('The Only Moment', translated here as 'A Moment in Time'), possibly the greatest of all his songs and arguably the finest of all these songs. Indeed Swedish song is one of the great undiscovered treasures of the north, and this distinguished partnership is its most persuasive advocate. Superbly balanced recorded sound.

Oxford Camerata, Jeremy Summerly

'*Lamentations*': WHITE: *Lamentations.* TALLIS: *Lamentations, Sets I & II.* PALESTRINA: *Lesson I for Maundy Thursday.* LASSUS: *Lessons I & III for Maundy Thursday.* ESTAVAO DE BRITO: *Lesson I for Good Friday.*
✪ (BB) ★★★ Naxos 8.550572.

On the bargain Naxos label come nearly 70 minutes of sublime polyphony, beautifully sung by the fresh-toned Oxford Camerata under Jeremy Summerly. All these *Lamentations* (*Lessons* simply means collection of verses) are settings from the Old Testament book, the Lamentations of Jeremiah. They were intended for nocturnal use and are usually darkly intense in feeling. The English and Italian *Lamentations* have their own individuality, but the most striking of all is the *Good Friday Lesson* by the Portuguese composer Estâvão de Brito. This is very direct and strong in feeling for, as the anonymous insert-note writer points out, Portugal was under Spanish subjugation at the time and de Brito effectively uses dissonance at the words *non est lex* ('there is no law') to assert his nationalistic defiance. The recorded sound is vividly beautiful within an ideal ambience.

Panzéra, Charles (baritone)

French and German Songs: FAURE: (i) *La Bonne Chanson, Op. 61; L'Horizon chimérique; Au cimetière; En sourdine.* DUPARC: *Extase; Lamento; L'Invitation au voyage; Sérénade Florentine; La Vie antérieure* (with Magda Panzéra-Baillot, piano). SCHUMANN: *Dichterliebe, Op. 48* (with Cortot, piano).
✪ (B) (★★★) Dutton mono CDBP 9726.

What a glorious voice – and apart from the tonal beauty, it is a joy to hear every syllable with such clarity. The Swiss-born French baritone, Charles Panzéra (1896–1976) was closely associated with Fauré's songs (and gave the first performance of *L'Horizon chimérique*). During the 1930s when most of these records were made, he was the foremost interpreter of the French repertoire, and in particular Duparc, whose songs have a special eloquence. His selfless artistry is everywhere in evidence and not even Pierre Bernac or Gérard Souzay surpass him. The Dutton transfers bring his voice to life as no others before them!

Pavarotti, Luciano (tenor)

'*The Pavarotti Edition*'

Volume 1: DONIZETTI. Arias from: *Don Pasquale; La Fille du régiment; L'elisir d'amore; La Favorita; Linda di Chamounix; Lucia di Lammermoor; Maria Stuarda.* 470 001-2.

Volume 2: Arias from: BELLINI: *I Capuleti e i Montecchi; Beatrice di Tenda.* DONIZETTI: *Don Sebastiano; Il Duca d'Alba.* VERDI: *Norma; I Puritani; La sonnambula; Attila; I due Foscari; Ernani; I Lombardi.* 470 002-2.

Volume 3: VERDI. Arias from: *Luisa Miller; Macbeth; Rigoletto; Il trovatore; La traviata; I vespri siciliani.* 470 003-2.

Volume 4: VERDI. Arias from: *Aida; Un ballo in maschera; Don Carlos; La forza del destino; Otello; Requiem.* 470 004-2.

Volume 5: PUCCINI. Arias from: *La Bohème; Madama Butterfly; Turandot.* 470 005-2.

Volume 6: Arias from: PUCCINI: *Manon Lescaut; Tosca.* MASCAGNI: *Cavalleria rusticana.* LEONCAVALLO: *Pagliacci.* GIORDANO: *Andrea Chénier.* 470 006-2.

Volume 7: Arias from: A. SCARLATTI: *L'onestà negli amori.* BONONCINI: *Griselda.* HANDEL: *Atalanta.* GLUCK: *Orfeo ed Euridice.* MOZART: *Così fan tutte; Don Giovanni; Idomeneo.* ROSSINI: *Guglielmo Tell; Stabat Mater.* Songs: CALDARA: *Alma del core.* CIAMPI: *Tre giorni son che Nina.* GIORDANI: *Caro mio ben.* MERCADANTE: *Qual giglio candido.* STRADELLA: *Pietà, Signora.* 470 007-2.

Volume 8: Arias from: FLOTOW: *Martha.* GOUNOD: *Faust.* MEYERBEER: *L'Africaine.* BOITO: *Mefistofele.* PONCHIELLI: *La Gioconda.* BIZET: *Carmen.* MASSENET: *Manon; Werther.* GIORDANO: *Fedora.* MASCAGNI: *Iris; L'amico Fritz.* CILEA: *Adriana Lecouvreur; L'Arlesiana.* PUCCINI: *La fanciulla del West.* R. STRAUSS: *Der Rosenkavalier.* PIETRI: *Maristella.* 470 008-2.

Volume 9: *Italian Songs*: DONIZETTI: *Il barcaiolo; Me voglio fà'na casa.* ROSSINI: *La danza; La promessa.* BELLINI: *Malinconia, ninfa gentile; Vanne, o rosa fortunata.* LISZT: *Tre sonetti di Petrarca.* RESPIGHI: *Nebbie; Nevicata; Pioggia.* MASCAGNI: *Serenata.* LEONCAVALLO: *Mattinata.* TOSTI: *'A vucchella; Aprile; L'alba sepàra della luce l'ombra; Malia; Marechiare; Non t'amo più!; La serenata; L'ultima canzone* (also with BEETHOVEN: *In questa tomba oscura*). 470 009-2.

Volume 10: *Popular Italian and Neapolitan Songs*: DI CAPUA: *O Sole Mio.* CURTIS: *Non ti scordar di me; Torna a Surriento; Ti voglio tanto bene; Tu, ca nun chiagne; Voce'e notte!* CARDILLO: *Core 'ngrato.* D'ANNIBALE: *'O paese d'o sole.* VALENTE: *Passione.* MARIO: *Santa Lucia luntana.* DENZA: *Funiculì funiculà.* CRESCENZO: *Rondine al nido.* BIXIO: *Mamma; La mia canzone al vento; Vivere.* MODUGNO: *Volare.* SIBELLA: *La Girometta.* MARTUZZI: *La Graunadora.* CASARINI: *Fra tanta*

gente. MARIA FERILLI: *Un amore così grande.*
LAZZARO: *Chitarra romana.* 470 010-2.

⚫ (M) *** Decca (ADD/DD) 470 000-2 (10). (with
Bonus CD: Arias from: PUCCINI: *La Bohème; Tosca.*
VERDI: *Rigoletto*).

'The Pavarotti Edition' is a well-produced and comprehensive set (including several items new to CD),
which offers good documentation, full texts and
translations and excellent transfers. As the Donizetti
items in the first volume show, Pavarotti quickly
became a singer of impressive style as well as one
with a honeyed tenor voice, and he soon carved a
distinctive niche in the operatic world. The breadth
of his achievement is well demonstrated here and
surely earns him a ⚫ for its range as well as its
consistency.

Volumes 1 and 2 concentrate mainly on the bel
canto recordings from the late 1960s and 1970s, celebrating his partnership with Joan Sutherland and
Richard Bonynge. They include some of the finest
things he has ever done in the studio, his stylish vocal
production often demonstrating sparkling vivaciousness, as in the series of spectacular high Cs in his key
aria from *La Fille du régiment*, or genuine feeling, as
in his touching Nemorino in *L'elisir d'amore* where,
for once, *Una furtiva lagrima* is sensitive, not cloy-
ingly sentimental. The 1976 *La sonnambula* excerpt
makes its CD debut here.

The second volume includes excerpts from recital
discs (with Downes and Abbado) from 1968, and an *I
Lombardi* extract from 1996 with Levine – the voice
not so golden but remarkably intact after all those
years. Verdi presides over Volumes 3 and 4, again
selected largely from Pavarotti's complete opera
recordings. The *Rigoletto*, *Il trovatore* and *La traviata*
selections come from the Bonynge sets, and he is
particularly memorable as a characterful Duke in
Rigoletto. The 'live' 1992 *Don Carlos* excerpt, which is
borrowed from EMI, is an exciting performance by
any standards. The *Un ballo in maschera* and *Otello*
arias come from Solti's 1983 and 1991 sets, respectively, and usually show Pavarotti at his extrovert
best.

The *La Bohème* and *Madama Butterfly* excerpts in
Volume 5 derive from Karajan's famous early 1970s
Decca sets and find Pavarotti as an intensely imaginative Pinkerton and as a Rodolfo of comic flair and
expressive passion. He is hardly less impressive in
Turandot, as Calif in Mehta's classic 1972 set: rich-
timbred and strong on detail.

The 1978 *Tosca* conducted by Rescigno on Volume
6 proved to be less inspired, although he is back on
form in his powerful 1992 portrayal of Des Grieux in
Manon Lescaut (with Levine). The rest of the verismo
performances again show Pavarotti at his most extrovert, if not always his most subtle, reluctant to sing
anything other than loud. He is less at home in
Mozart in Volume 7: he even sounds a little strained
at times and obviously is not really in tune with
Mozartian sensibilities. But the rest of the excerpts

are generally enjoyable, the baroque repertoire surprisingly so, with the simpler items, such as the
minor-key *Tre giorni son che Nina*, coming across
very effectively. The CD ends with a rousing
Guglielmo Tell highlight.

A myriad sources is used for Volume 8, although
many are taken from Pavarotti's first digital recital LP
in 1980. Here he is splendid in the breast-beating
numbers, such as Des Grieux's plea in Act III of
Manon, which has great emotional force. If some of
the lighter numbers would benefit from a easier
touch, a more blithe approach, in such arias as
M'appari from *Martha* one is caught up in the
vibrant ardour, and there are still plenty of things to
enjoy.

The final two volumes are of inconsequential, yet
highly tuneful repertoire. Volume 9 brings songs by
Rossini, Donizetti and Bellini, which have a pleasing,
easy charm, while the famous Tosti numbers are sung
with all the Italian passion you could wish for – with
rich orchestral accompaniments, too.

Volume 10 is mainly devoted to popular Neapolitan songs, given the grand treatment in ardent, forthright, very Italian performances, missing some of the
charm, but none of the red-blooded fervour. The
first eleven numbers are conducted by Guadagno,
while the remaining ten are, more surprisingly, conducted by Henry Mancini in his own unashamedly
popular and highly effective arrangements. Although
memories of Di Stefano are not effaced, it is all very
enjoyable.

The edition is perhaps not aimed at the general
collector, but Pavarotti's admirers are well served.
The complete set comes with an album of 76 colour
photographs of Pavarotti's recording and operatic
career, as well as a reproduction of his first Decca
recording in its original 45rpm packaging – a nice
idea, neatly done, which will make vintage *aficionados* feel very nostalgic. The original Penguin Review
(of Decca 45 SEC 5532) said: 'As Italian tenors go
Pavarotti is comparatively tasteful in the use of his
voice, and although there are no special touches of
imagination here, they are all clean and enjoyable
performances, beautifully recorded.'

'*Tutto Pavarotti*': VERDI: *Aida: Celeste Aida. Luisa
Miller: Quando le sere al placido. La traviata: De'
miei bollenti spiriti. Il trovatore: Ah si ben mio; Di
quella pira. Rigoletto: La donna è mobile. Un ballo
in maschera: La rivedrà nell'estasi.* DONIZETTI:
*L'elisir d'amore: Una furtiva lagrima. Don Pasquale:
Com'è gentil.* PONCHIELLI: *La Gioconda: Cielo e
mar.* FLOTOW: *Martha: M'appari.* BIZET: *Carmen:
Flower Song.* MASSENET: *Werther: Pourquoi me
réveiller.* MEYERBEER: *L'Africana: O paradiso.*
BOITO: *Mefistofele: Dai campi, dai prati.*
LEONCAVALLO: *Pagliacci: Vesti la giubba.*
MASCAGNI: *Cavalleria rusticana: Addio alla madre.*
GIORDANO: *Fedora: Amor ti vieta.* PUCCINI: *La
fanciulla del West: Ch'ella mi creda. Tosca: E
lucevan le stelle. Manon Lescaut: Donna non vidi*

mai. La Bohème: Che gelida manina. Turandot: Nessun dorma. ROSSINI: *Stabat Mater: Cuius animam.* BIZET: *Agnus Dei.* ADAM: *O Holy Night.* DI CAPUA: *O sole mio.* TOSTI: *A vucchella.* CARDILLO: *Core 'ngrato.* TAGLIAFERRI: *Passione.* CHERUBINI: *Mamma.* DALLA: *Caruso.*

(M) *** Decca (ADD) 425 681-2 (2).

Opening with Dalla's *Caruso*, a popular song in the Neapolitan tradition, certainly effective and no more vulgar than many earlier examples of the genre, this selection goes on through favourites like *O sole mio* and *Core 'ngrato* and one or two religious items, notably Adam's *Cantique de Noël*, to the hard core of operatic repertoire. Beginning with *Celeste Aida*, recorded in 1972, the selection of some twenty-two arias from complete sets covers Pavarotti's distinguished recording career with Decca from 1969 (*Cielo e mar* and the *Il trovatore* excerpts) to 1985, although the opening song was, of course, recorded digitally in 1988. The rest is a mixture of brilliantly transferred analogue originals and a smaller number of digital masters, all or nearly all showing the great tenor in sparkling form. The records are at mid-price, but there are no translations or musical notes.

'*The Greatest Ever Pavarotti*' (with various orchestras and conductors): Arias from: VERDI: *Rigoletto; Il trovatore; La traviata; Aida.* PUCCINI: *La Bohème; Turandot; Tosca; La fanciulla del West; Manon Lescaut.* DONIZETTI: *L'elisir d'amore.* FLOTOW: *Martha.* BIZET: *Carmen.* LEONCAVALLO: *Pagliacci.* GIORDANO: *Fedora.* MEYERBEER: *L'Africana.* MASSENET: *Werther.* Songs: DALLA: *Caruso.* LEONCAVALLO: *Mattinata.* TOSTI: *Aprile; Marechiare; La Serenata.* CARDILLO: *Core 'ngrato.* ROSSINI: *La danza.* MODUGNO: *Volare.* DENZA: *Funiculì, funiculà.* DE CURTIS: *Torna a Surriento.* DI CAPUA: *O sole mio!* SCHUBERT: *Ave Maria.* FRANCK: *Panis angelicus.* MANCINI: *In un palco della Scala* (with apologies to Pink Panther). GIORDANO: *Caro mio ben.* BIXIO: *Mamma.*

⊕ (M) *** Decca ADD/DDD 436 173-2 (2).

Such a collection as this is self-recommending and scarcely needs a review from us, merely a listing. The first disc opens with *La donna è mobile* (*Rigoletto*), *Che gelida manina* (*La Bohème*), *Nessun dorma* (*Turandot*), all taken from outstandingly successful complete recordings, and the rest of the programme, with many favourite lighter songs also given the golden touch, is hardly less appealing. The second CD includes Pavarotti's tribute to the Pink Panther and ends with a tingling live version of *Nessun dorma*, to compare with the studio version on disc one. Vivid, vintage Decca recording throughout.

Pears, Peter (tenor), Julian Bream (lute)

Julian Bream Edition, Volume 19. Elizabethan lute songs: MORLEY: *Absence; It was a Lover and his*

Lass; Who is it?. ROSSETER: *What then is Love?; If She Forsake Me; When Laura Smiles.* DOWLAND: *I Saw my Lady Weep; Dear, if you Change; Stay, Time; Weep you no More; Shall I sue?; Sweet, Stay Awhile; Can She Excuse?; Come, Heavy Sleep; Wilt Thou Unkind, Thus Leave Me?; Sorrow Stay; The Lowest Trees Have Tops; Time's Eldest Son, Old Age; In Darkness Let Me Dwell; Say, Love, if Ever Thou Didst Find.* FORD: *Come Phyllis; Fair, Sweet, Cruel.*

(M) *** BMG/RCA (ADD) 09026 61609-2.

This vintage collection was recorded between 1963 and 1969 when Pears was at the peak of his form. The Dowland songs are particularly fine, sung with Pears's usual blend of intelligence and lyrical feeling, their nostalgic melancholy tenderly caught. Excellent, vivid, well-balanced recording, with Bream's expert accompaniments well in the picture. Most refreshing.

Pears, Peter (tenor), Benjamin Britten (piano)

Lieder: SCHUMANN: *Liederkreis, Op. 39;* FAURE: *La Bonne Chanson;* PURCELL: *5 songs;* SCHUBERT: *3 Songs;* BRITTEN: *4 Folksongs.*

(M) (***) BBC mono BBCB 8006-2.

Britten as pianist is, if anything, even more individual than Britten as conductor. With Pears in glowing voice (1958–9) he sparkles in his own realizations of Purcell songs and folksongs, while in Schumann's Eichendorff song-cycle he makes the poetic piano-writing glow, as in *Frühlingsnacht* ('Spring Night'), where the notes shimmer distinctively. The Fauré cycle too reminds one that as a fourteen-year-old Britten also set Verlaine's poetry. Clean focus in mono radio recording.

Petibon, Patricia (soprano)

'*French Touch*' (with Lyons National Op. Ch. & O, Abel): Arias from: GOUNOD: *Roméo et Juliette.* MESSAGER: *L'Amour masqué; Fortunio.* DELIBES: *Lakmé.* MASSENET: *Cendrillon; Manon.* OFFENBACH: *Les Contes d'Hoffmann.* CHABRIER: *L'Etoile.* HAHN: *Brummel.* Songs: DELIBES: *Les Filles de Cadiz.* ABOULKER: *Je t'aime.*

**(*) Decca 475 090-2.

A recommendable disc with one proviso, of which more later. Patricia Petibon is a highly characterful French soprano and there is much to enjoy: there is a glittering account of Delibes's *Les Filles de Cadiz*, much sensitivity in Messager's lovely melancholy *Fortunio* aria, and the Waltz Song from *Roméo et Juliette* goes with a delectable lilt. Many of the numbers here are not so well known, but all are worth hearing: the aria from *L'Amour masqué* (Messager) about the advantages of having two lovers, is superbly characterized with wonderful French insouciance. But in numbers such as Hahn's *Brummel*, Petibon adopts a 'funny' voice, which may be amusing live but becomes irksome on repeated hearing. While in that comic number it might raise a smile (at least on first hearing), it seems very out of place in the Doll Song from *Les Contes d'Hoffmann*, which is cringe-making and out of keeping with Offenbach's style. However, the pluses on this disc outway the minuses, and Patricia Petibon has personality in buckets. The disc ends with Aboulker's showpiece, *Je t'aime*, and here she keeps her 'funny' voice to a minimum, and the effect is so much better. She also blows us some very nice kisses at the end of the aria – always welcome! Yves Abel gets excellent results from his orchestra, perhaps a bit slow in the two *Manon* items, but the rest are very lively and idiomatic, and the Decca sound is first rate. Full texts and translations (and wacky artwork) provided.

'Airs Baroques Français' (with Paris Chamber Ch., Les Folies Françaises, Patrick Cohen-Akenine)
from: M.-A. CHARPENTIER: *David et Jonathas.*
LULLY: *Armide.* RAMEAU: *Les Indes galantes; Platée; Les Fêtes de l'Hymen et de l'Amour.* GRANDVAL: *Rien du tout.*
*** Virgin 5 45481-2.

Not helped by excessively arch portraits of the singer on front and back covers of the disc, Patricia Petibon's disc yet offers fresh and brilliant performances of an attractive collection of arias by the leading French composers of the late seventeenth and early eighteenth centuries. Petibon, a member of the outstanding team of Les Arts Florissants assembled by William Christie, with her bright and clear if slightly hooty soprano, gives characterful and stylish readings of each item, and it is good to find her responding so positively to the less serious items which add a sparkle to the collection. A delightful disc, very well recorded.

Polyphony, Stephen Layton

'*O magnum mysterium*' (A sequence of twentieth-century carols and Sarum chant):
Plainchant: *O radix lesse; O magnum mysterium; Puer natus est nobis; Reges Tharsis; Verbum caro factum est.* WISHART: *3 Carols, Op. 17, No. 3: Alleluya, A New Work is Come on Hand.* HOWELLS: *3 Carol-anthems: Here is the Little Door; A Spotless Rose; Sing Lullaby.* RICHARD RODNEY BENNETT: *5 Carols: There is no Rose; Out of your Sleep; That Younge Child; Sweet was the Song; Susanni.* KENNETH LEIGHTON: *Of a Rose is my Song; A Hymn of the Nativity; 3 Carols, Op. 25: The Star song; Lully Lulla, Thou Little Tiny Child; An Ode on the Birth of our Saviour.* WARLOCK: *As Dew in Aprylle; Bethlehem Down; I Saw a Fair Maiden; Benedicamus Domino; A Cornish Christmas Carol.* BYRT: *All and Some.* WALTON: *What Cheer?*
⊕ *** Hyp. CDA 66925.

A gloriously sung collection in which (what Meurig Bowen's extensive notes describe as) 'the magnificent corpus of British carols' is alive and still impressively expanding in the twentieth century. The atmosphere is readily set by the opening plainchant, which frames and punctuates the concert with appropriate liturgical texts. Peter Wishart's exuberant 'Alleluya' and the poignant 'A Spotless Rose' immediately catch up the listener. This is the first of Howells's *Three Carol-anthems*, of which the others are equally lovely (especially the rocking 'Sing Lullaby'). The five Richard Rodney Bennett carols have their own particular brand of cool dissonance, with 'There is no Rose' and 'Sweet was the Song' particularly haunting.

But perhaps it is the series of beautiful Peter Warlock settings one remembers most for their ready melodic and harmonic memorability (notably 'As Dew in Aprylle', the lovely 'Bethlehem Down' and the serene 'Lullaby my Jesus') alongside the soaring music of Kenneth Leighton, helped in the ambitious 'Nativity Hymn' and the 'Ode on the Birth of Our Saviour' by the rich, pure line of the soloist, Libby Crabtree, and in 'Lully, Lulla' by the equally ravishing contribution of Emma Preston-Dunlop. Walton's 'What Cheer?' brings an exuberant rhythmic spicing, but for the most part this programme captures the tranquil pastoral mood of Christmas Eve. The recording could hardly be bettered, clear yet with the most evocative ambience.

Pomerium, Alexander Blachly

'*Old World Christmas*': ANON.: *In dulci jubilo à 2.* PRAETORIUS: *In dulci jubilo (3 versions).* ANON.: *Resonet in laudibus.* ERBACH: *Resonet in laudibus à 4.* LASSUS: *Resonet in laudibus à 4.* ANON.: *Preter rerum seriem.* JOSQUIN DESPREZ: *Preter rerem serium à 6.* GUILLAUME DUFAY: *Conditor alme siderum.* BYRD: *Puer natus est à 4; Reges Tharsis et insulae à 4.* ANON.: *O Sapientia.* HORWOOD: *Magnificut secundi toni à 5.* RAMSEY: *O Sapienta à 5.* ANON.: *Quem vidistis pastores.* CIPRIANO DE RORE: *Quem vidistis pastores à 7.* ANON.: *Sarum Antiphonale: Alma redemptoris mater.* OCKEGHEM: *Alma redemptoris mater à 4.*
**(*) DG 474 557-2.

Imaginatively planned, meticulously researched, and beautifully sung and recorded by this excellent vocal group, this Christmas programme opens enticingly with the famous *In dulci jubilo*, followed by three further versions for two, three and four voices respectively, collected by Michael Praetorius. The idea of presenting a plainchant and then different settings is in principle an excellent one and there is much fine music included here. The snag is a certain absence of variety, so that such a compilation becomes a specialist collection rather than a disc for the general collector.

Prey, Hermann (bass-baritone)

'*The Singers*' (Decca series): **Arias from: ROSSINI:** *Il barbiere di Siviglia* (with LSO, Abbado). **MOZART:** *Le nozze di Figaro* (with VPO, Solti); *Die Zauberflöte* (with German Opera O, Boehm). **Lieder: SCHUBERT:** *Im Abendrot; Erlkönig; An Sylvia; Der Wanderer an den Mond.* **SCHUMANN:** *Der Hidalgo; Meine Rose; Der Spielmann.* **BRAHMS:** *Dein blaues Auge; Die Mainacht; Sonntag; Ständchen; Wiegenlied.* **R. STRAUSS:** *Allerseelen; Heimkehr; Heimliche Aufforderung; Ständchen* (with Engel, piano).

(M) **(*) Decca (IMS) (ADD) 467 901-2.

The bulk of this recital CD is drawn from a 1962 Decca record made with Karl Engel. The nicely contrived programme demonstrates the wide range of sympathies Herman Prey encompassed at this early stage of his career. Quick to match his vocal timbre with the mood of the poem, he also possessed a dynamic range of amazing breadth, so that prolonged *mezza voce* sections may lull the listener into thinking the volume has been cut down. Don't turn it up, because Prey will surprise you and launch into a spine-tingling crescendo that builds up into a powerful yet always quite stylish *forte*, as in the second of the Brahms songs. The accompaniments are excellent, although the piano tone seems a mite thin in this transfer, even if the voice is captured well. The opera arias, recorded in the late 1960s and early 1970s, are taken from his complete opera recordings (the Abbado and Boehm are DG recordings and the sound is a little dry in these transfers) and are most enjoyable; the Mozart is especially distinguished, but the Rossini is fun and stylish, too. One of the better 'The Singers' compilations then, although one can gain access to the texts and translations and a photogallery only via a CD ROM drive.

Price, Leontyne (soprano)

'*Ultimate Collection*': **Arias from: BERLIOZ:** *Les Nuits d'été.* **BIZET:** *Carmen.* **BARBER:** *Antony and Cleopatra.* **GERSHWIN:** *Porgy and Bess.* **MASSENET:** *Manon.* **MOZART:** *Le nozze de Figaro; Il rè pastore.* **PUCCINI:** *Madama Butterfly; Manon Lescaut; La rondine; Suor Angelica; Tosca; Turandot.* **PURCELL:** *Dido and Aeneas.* **R. STRAUSS:** *Im Abendrot (Vier letzte Lieder No. 1); Ariadne auf Naxos.* **VERDI:** *Aida; Un ballo in maschera; Don Carlos; La forza del destino; Il trovatore.*

(M) **(*) RCA 74321 63463-2.

This CD may appeal to those who want some of Leontyne Price's most famous roles, or those who simply want a marvellously sung soprano operatic compilation. It is well programmed and includes some unlikely repertoire for Price (including Purcell), as well as many of the things you would expect.

The recordings and performances are generally excellent, often brilliant. What is shabby about this release is that there is nothing in the documentation about the recordings, dates, conductors, orchestras, or the music. As for texts and translations, you must be joking!

Psalmody, Parley of Instruments, Peter Holman

'*While Shepherds Watched*' (Christmas music from English parish churches and chapels 1740–1830): **BEESLY:** *While Shepherds Watched.* **ANON.:** *Let an Anthem of praise; Hark! How All the Welkin Rings.* **J. C. SMITH:** *While Shepherds Watched.* **HELLENDAAL:** *Concerto in E flat for Strings, Op. 3/4: Pastorale.* **KEY:** *As Shepherds Watched their Fleecy Care.* **ARNOLD:** *Hark! The Herald Angels Sing.* **CLARK:** *While Shepherds Watched.* **HANDEL:** *Hark! The Herald Angels Sing; Hymning Seraphs Wake the Morning.* **JARMAN:** *There were Shepherds Abiding in the Field.* **S. WESLEY:** (piano) *Rondo on 'God Rest You Merry, Gentlemen'* (Timothy Roberts). **MATTHEWS:** *Angels from the Realms of Glory.* **FOSTER:** *While Shepherds Watched.*

*** Hyp. CDA 66924.

This is a Christmas collection of genuine novelty. None of the settings of 'While Shepherds Watched' uses the familiar tune: the regal closing version from John Foster of Yorkshire is remarkably lively, as is the lighter variation from Joseph Key of Northampton, 'As Shepherds Watched their Fleecy Care' with woodwind accompaniment. There are other surprises too. Handel's 'Hark! The Herald Angels' is neatly fitted to 'See the Conqu'ring Hero Comes', and 'Hymning Seraphs' (presented as a tenor solo with fortepiano) turns out to be our old keyboard friend, 'The Harmonious Blacksmith'. Peiter Hellendaal's *Pastorale for Strings* is in the best concerto grosso tradition, although Samuel Wesley's variations on 'God Rest You Merry' are merely ingenious. Nevertheless the whole programme is presented with pleasing freshness and is very well sung, played and recorded.

Ramey, Samuel (bass)

'*A Date with the Devil*' (with Munich RSO, Rudel): **Arias from BERLIOZ:** *La Damnation de Faust.* **MEYERBEER:** *Robert le Diable.* **BOITO:** *Mefistofele.* **OFFENBACH:** *Les Contes d'Hoffmann.* **GOUNOD:** *Faust.* **STRAVINSKY:** *The Rake's Progress.* **LISZT:** *Mephisto Waltz* (orchestra only).

(BB) *** Naxos 8.555355.

Samuel Ramey has had great success in the concert hall with this collection of devilish portraits, most of them from French sources. Here in a composite recording, partly live, partly under studio conditions, he sings and acts with fine flair, bringing out the wry humour in many of the items. Mephistopheles' Serenade and the *Calf of Gold* aria from Gounod's *Faust* provide a fine climax before the tailpiece solos from *The Rake's Progress*. He is well supported by Julius Rudel and the Munich Radio Orchestra, springing rhythms crisply, with well-balanced sound. The orchestral showpieces by Berlioz and Liszt provide a nice contrast. An outstanding Naxos bargain.

Riedel, Deborah (soprano), Australian Opera and Ballet Orchestra, Richard Bonynge

'British Opera Arias': Arias from: WALLACE: *The Amber Witch; Love's Triumph; Lurline; Maritana.* BALFE: *The Maid of Artois; The Puritan's Daughter; The Rose of Castille; Satanella; The Siege of Rochelle; Il Talismano.* SULLIVAN: *Ivanhoe; The Rose of Persia.* FARADAY: *Amasis.*
*** Australian Melba 301082.

It is astonishing, considering how much nineteenth-century opera has been resurrected on CD, that there has been no such revival in English opera of that period. Although the composers featured here embraced current (Italian) operatic trends, their art retained an attractive home-spun quality, but was eventually eclipsed by more inflated operatic traditions later in the century. Balfe achieved considerable success both in England and internationally in his day with his ability to write attractive melody of great charm. The first of the *Il Talismano* (1874) arias included here starts most beguilingly with a horn solo followed by a flute, before the voice enters, while the other aria, *Nella dolce trepidanza*, is most memorable for its swinging cabaletta. Many of his arias, such as the numbers from *The Rose of Castille* and *Satanella*, have a simple, almost folk-like quality that is most fetching, while 'The Rapture Dwelling in My Heart' from *The Maid of Artois* is a delicious coloratura waltz song.

Wallace is remembered today mainly for *Maritana*, from which the charming ''Tis the Harp in the Air' and 'Scenes that are Brightest' are included, but the more substantial items from *Lurline*, the waltz song 'The Naiad's Spell', 'These Withered Flowers' from *Love's Triumph* and 'My Long Hair is Braided' from *The Amber Witch* – a brilliant coloratura aria – are all greatly enjoyable. The Sullivan items come from his 'serious' attempts at grand opera and are not quite so rare these days, but their inclusion is welcome – 'Neath My Lattice' from *The Rose of Persia* is very winning, as is the rare Faraday number from his musical comedy of 1906, *Amasis*, which has a nice period charm. This is an important as well as an enjoyable collection, which gives us a fuller picture of English operatic history, and a CD that makes one want to hear some of the complete operas. The performances are excellent: Deborah Riedel sings with warmth and real understanding of the idiom

and meets the challenges of the virtuoso passages, while Bonynge provides his usual sterling support with his Australian Orchestra, who make a fine contribution. The recording is atmospheric, perhaps a touch backwardly balanced, but not seriously so. Full texts are included.

Rolfe Johnson, Anthony (tenor), Graham Johnson (piano)

'In Praise of Women': Miss LH of Liverpool: *My Mother.* CAROLINE NORTON: *Juanita.* VIRGINIA GABRIEL: *Orpheus.* ANNIE FORTESQUE HARRISON: *In the Gloaming.* MAUDE VALERIE WHITE: *The Throstle; My Soul is an Enchanted Boat; The Devout Lover; So we'll Go no More a-Roving.* TERESA DEL RIEGO: *Slave Song.* LIZA LEHMANN: *A Bird Sate Mourning; Ah, Moon of my Delight; The Lily of a Day; Thoughts have Wings; Henry King; Charles Augustus Fortescue.* AMY WOODFORDE-FINDEN: *Till I Wake; Kashmiri Song.* ETHEL SMYTH: *Possession.* REBECCA CLARKE: *The Aspidistra; Shy one.* ELIZABETH POSTON: *In Praise of Women.* ELISABETH LUTYENS: *As I Walked Out One Evening.* ELIZABETH MACONCHY: *Have you Seen but a Bright Lily Grow?; Meditation for his Mistress.* MADELEINE DRING: *Crabbed Age and Youth; To Virgins, to Make Much of Time.* PHYLLIS TATE: *Epitaph.*
(BB) *** Hyp. Helios CDH 55159.

It is Elizabeth Poston who provides the title song for this delightful collection, a simple setting of an anonymous poem which pays a tender tribute to womankind, but the collection opens with an equally touching anonymous setting from an unknown Liverpool girl praising her mother (to verses by the author of 'Twinkle, Twinkle, Little Star'!). The charming 'In the Gloaming' with its rippling accompaniment was a popular hit in its day for Anne Fortesque Harrison, selling more than 14,000 copies between 1880 and 1889.

During this same period Maude Valerie White was comparably successful, and she was at her finest with the ballad 'My Soul is an Enchanted Island', to which Anthony Rolfe Johnson responds passionately, going quite over the top at the stirring climax. Her setting of 'So we'll Go No More a-Roving' is memorable in a more restrained way. The group from the best known of these turn-of-the-century women composers is Liza Lehmann who shows the consistency of her melodic facility, while the two Hilaire Belloc portraits, the engaging 'Henry King', 'who chewed little bits of string', and 'Charles Augustus Fortescue', who always did what he ought to do, are fine examples. Ethel Smyth is represented by a single, rather sombre song, 'Possession', but it remains to haunt the memory. Fortunately, the more modern composers shirk any suggestion of spikiness: Elizabeth Lutyens's very winning 'As I Walked Out One Evening' might almost be a folksong, and Elizabeth Maconchy's setting of Ben Jonson, 'Have you Seen but a Bright Lily Grow?' is quite lovely. She is equally sympathetic with Robert Herrick, surely identifying with his 'Meditation for his Mistress', whose merits he compares to a bouquet of flowers. A touch of irony comes with Rebecca Clarke's 'Aspidistra', and Madeleine Dring is light-heartedly witty in Shakespeare's 'Crabbed Age and Youth'; but the recital ends in more serious, thoughtful mood with Phyllis Tate's 'Epitaph' to a brief reflection on mortality by Sir Walter Raleigh. Throughout, Anthony Rolfe Johnson sings with both ardour and perception, sensitivity and a feeling for the changing styles over a century of song-writing, and Graham Johnson's accompaniments could not be more imaginatively supportive. Excellent recording and full texts make this reissue a very real bargain.

Roswaenge, Helge (tenor)

'The Dane with the High D': Arias from: VERDI: Aida; La traviata; Il trovatore. CORNELIUS: Der Barbier von Bagdad. ADAM: Le Postillon de Longjumeau. AUBER: Fra Diavolo. MOZART: Così fan tutte. BEETHOVEN: Fidelio. WEBER: Der Freischütz; Oberon. TCHAIKOVSKY: Eugene Onegin. R. STRAUSS: Der Rosenkavalier. WILLE: Königsballade.

◑➛ ✹ (BB) (★★★) Dutton mono CDBP 9728.

Helge Roswaenge had one of the most thrilling voices of the twentieth century. He began singing professionally in 1921 and was still on excellent form nearly half a century later. But most of these recordings were made in the 1930s, when he was at his peak, and although Mozart was perhaps not his strongest suit, he was chosen by Beecham as Tamino for his famous 1937 Zauberflöte. As Alan Blyth comments in the excellent insert note, his amazing voice has a 'gleaming trumpet-like quality at the top' – reminiscent of Tamagno – 'yet was mellifluous in quieter moments'. He was also a superb stylist, whether in Verdi or in operetta, for which his fresh, ringing upper register was especially suitable. The most famous item here, which gives the disc its title, is the sparkling excerpt from Adam's Le Postillon de Longjumeau, which is electrifying, but he shows his lyrical grace in the Fra Diavolo aria with which this was paired on the original 78rpm shellac disc. This warm, lyrical quality appears again and again in this generous selection, notably in Lensky's ardent aria from Eugene Onegin.

In the rare excerpts from Cornelius's Barbier von Bagdad he is joined by his first wife, Ilonka, not a great singer but a charming partner. Almost all his recordings were made in German, yet he somehow does not sound Germanic in the French and Italian repertoire, and his ardent account of Di rigor armato from Der Rosenkavalier is sung in Italian, and how marvellously passionate it is! He was ideal for Weber

(the Oberon excerpt is another highlight), and his dramatic entry on the word 'Gott' in the Fidelio excerpt (the only opera he sang at Covent Garden) is characteristic of him at his very finest, and is alone worth the price of the disc. Most of the recordings were made in the 1930s and were of high quality. But the miraculous Dutton transfers enhance them further, and the voice projects with the utmost realism throughout, and with its full bloom remaining. An unforgettable and treasurable collection.

Rouen Chambre Accentus Choir, Eric Ericson

ALFVEN: Aftonen; Uti vår hage; JERSILD: Min yndlingsdal (My Dear Valley); NYSTEDT: O Crux; SANDSTROM: Two Poems; STENHAMMAR: Tre körvisor (Three Choral Pieces); WERLE: Canzone 126 del Petrarcha; WIKANDER: Kung Liljekonvalje (King of the Lily-of-the-valley); Förårskväll (Spring Evening).

★★(★) Assai 207 182.

The Rouen-based Chœur de Chambre Accentus was founded in 1991 by Laurence Equilbey, an Ericson pupil, and they tackle this predominantly Swedish repertoire with complete sympathy. In the 1960s and 1970s Eric Ericson brought the Swedish Radio Choir to an unrivalled excellence (it was the Berlin Philharmonic of choirs). These French singers produce the beautifully blended and finely nuanced sound one associates with him. He has recorded Stenhammar's glorious choral songs to texts by the Danish poet J. P. Jacobsen many times. Wikander's Kung Liljekonvalje ('King of the Lily-of-the-valley') and Alfvén's Aftonen ('The Evening') are affecting pieces and are beautifully done.

For most collectors the surprise will be Min yndlingsdal ('My Dear Valley') by the Dane Jørgen Jersild, a contemporary of Vagn Holmboe, though less prolific. During the 1930s he studied with Roussel, and his writing has almost luminous quality. Jan Sandström is not to be confused with Sven David and is still in his mid-forties, and these two pieces, Anrop ('Call') and Två japanska landskap ('Two Japanese Landscapes'), date from his student years and are quite haunting. By its side Werle's Petrach setting seems more self-conscious. At less than 50 minutes this is short measure, but his repertoire is not widely known and is immensely rewarding.

Royal Liverpool Philharmonic Choir and Orchestra, St Ambrose R.C. Junior School Choir, Speake, Edmund Walters

'A Festival of Christmas' (with Jocelyn Bell, girl soprano): arr. WALTERS: Ding Dong! Merrily on

High; The Boar's Head; Buenos Reyes; Deck the Hall. arr. PETTMAN: *The Infant King.* WALTERS: *Where was Jesus Born?; The Carol Singers; Dance Little Goatling; As Joseph was a-Walking; Three Little Birdies; Little Robin Redbreast; Hop-hop-hop; Little One Sleep.* BYRD: *Cradle Song.* BACH: *O Little One Sweet.* DARKE: *In the Bleak Midwinter.* GRUBER: *Silent Night.* arr. WALLACE: *O Come, All Ye Faithful.*

(M) *** Chan. 7111.

The introductory woodwind in the scoring of Edmund Walters's opening arrangement of 'Ding Dong! Merrily on High', and the lighthearted touches of syncopation, suggest that his approach to Christmas music has much in common with that of John Rutter. His own carols are jauntily engaging, helped by the freshness of the excellently trained St Ambrose Junior School Choir, who sing them with vigour and enthusiasm. 'Little One Sleep' (a treble solo) verges on sentimentality. But the Spanish carol *Buenos Reyes*, with its castanets, is most piquant and the two Basque carols 'The Infant King' and 'I Saw a Maiden' are most eloquently sung, as are the settings by Bach and Byrd. Fine recording too.

St George's Canzona, John Sothcott

Medieval songs and dances: Lamento di Tristano; L'Autrier m'iere levaz; 4 Estampies real; Edi beo thu hevene quene; Eyns ne soy ke plente fu; Tre fontane. PERRIN D'AGINCOURT: *Quant voi en la fin d'este. Cantigas de Santa Maria: Se ome fezer; Nas mentes semper teer; Como poden per sas culpas; Maravillosos et piadosos.*

(M) *** CRD (ADD) CRD 3421.

As so often when early music is imaginatively re-created, one is astonished at the individuality of many of the ideas. This applies particularly to the second item in this collection, *Quant voi en la fin d'este,* attributed to the mid-thirteenth-century trouvère Perrin d'Agincourt, but no less to the four *Cantigas de Santa Maria.* The instrumentation is at times suitably robust but does not eschew good intonation and subtle effects. The group is recorded vividly and the acoustics of St James, Clerkenwell, are never allowed to cloud detail. The sound is admirably firm and real in its CD format.

St John's College Choir, Cambridge, George Guest

'Christmas Carols from St John's' (with Philip Kenyon, organ): TRAD.: *Unto us a Boy is Born; Ding Dong! Merrily on High; Good King Wenceslas; There is no Rose.* arr. WALFORD DAVIES: *The Holly and the Ivy.* arr. WILLCOCKS: *Sussex Carol; God Rest You Merry, Gentlemen; O Come All Ye Faithful.*

WARLOCK: *Balulalow.* HOLST: *In the Bleak Midwinter.* HADLEY: *I Sing of a Maiden.* RUTTER: *Shepherd's Pipe Carol.* GRUBER: *Silent Night.* MENDELSSOHN, arr. WILLCOCKS: *Hark! The Herald Angels Sing.* arr. VAUGHAN WILLIAMS: *O Little Town of Bethlehem.* POSTON: *Jesus Christ the Apple Tree.* RAYMOND WILLIAMS: *2 Welsh Carols.* KIRKPATRICK: *Away in a Manger.*

(M) *** Chan. 7109.

An essentially traditional concert and none the worse for that when so beautifully sung and recorded. Among the more modern carols, Elizabeth Poston's beautiful 'Jesus Christ the Apple Tree' stands out. Many of the arrangements are famous, notably the spectacular Willcocks versions of 'Hark! The Herald Angels Sing' and 'O Come, All Ye Faithful', but some of the gentler, atmospheric items ('There is no Rose') are just as memorable. A most enjoyable hour of music.

Salon Napolitan

Neapolitan Songs: ANON.: *Cannetella; Riposta a dispetto della donna; Te voglio bene assaje.* DOHLER: *Cannetella; Veder Napoli e poi morire.* ZINGARELLI: *Confusa, smarrita, spiegarti vorrei; Entra l'uomo all'orchè nasce.* CRESCENTINI: *Auretta grata.* PAER: *Quel cor che mi prometti; S'io t'amo, oh Dio! Mi chiedi?* RICCI: *Alla fenesta affaciate; Il carrettiere del Vomero; Consiglio all'amica; Je ne rêve qu'à toi; La mia felicità; La solita conversazione degli amanti; Perchè?; Una postilla al vocabolario d'amore; Il ritorno a Napoli.*

*** Opus 111 OPS 30-255. Invernizzi, Naviglio, Totaro, Caramiello.

A charming collection of Neapolitan song, lasting just over an hour. Nicely contrasting solos, duos and trios are all beautifully accompanied by Francesco Caramiello on a Pleyel pianoforte of 1865. The trio of singers are clearly enjoying themselves, and so do we when they bring so much character to these simple yet effective numbers. Full texts and translations are provided, and the recording is ideally balanced. Worth investigating if you enjoy this repertoire.

The Scholars of London

French chansons: JOSQUIN: *Faute d'argent; Mille regretz.* JANEQUIN: *Le Chant des oiseaux; Or vien ça.* SANDRIN: *Je ne le croy.* GOMBERT: *Aime qui vouldra; Quand je suis aupres.* SERMISY: *Tant que vivrai; Venez regrets; La, la, maistre Pierre.* ARCADELT: *En ce mois délicieux; Margot, labourez les vignes; Du temps que j'estois amoureux; Sa grand beauté.* TABOUROT: *Belle qui tiens ma vie.* VASSAL: *Vray Dieu.* CLEMENS: *Prière devant le repas; Action des Graces.* PASSEREAU: *Il est bel et bon.* LE JEUNE: *Ce n'est que fiel.* LASSUS: *Bonjour mon coeur; Si je suis brun; Beau le cristal; La Nuit froide; Un Jeune Moine.* BERTRAND: *De nuit, le bien.* COSTELY: *Arrête un peu mon coeur.*

(BB) ★★★ Naxos 8.550880.

This disc offers a representative selection from the thousands of sixteenth-century French polyphonic chansons, and ranges from the devotional to the amorous, the bawdy and the bucolic. It includes some of the best known, such as the ubiquitous Janequin *Le Chant des oiseaux*, and features such familiar masters as Josquin, Sermisy and Claude Le Jeune. It encompasses Flemish masters writing in the language, such as Gombert and Lassus. The Scholars of London are expressive and persuasive guides in this repertoire and are decently recorded at St Silas the Martyr in Kentish Town. There is an all-too-short but thoughtful introduction, and the booklet then reproduces texts and translations. What more can you ask from a disc that would undoubtedly cost less than admission to a concert plus the programme?

Scholl, Andreas (counter-tenor)

'Heroes' (with OAE, Norrington): Arias from HANDEL: *Giulio Cesare; Rodelinda; Saul; Semele; Serse.* HASSE: *Artaserse.* GLUCK: *Orfeo; Telemaco.* MOZART: *Ascanio in Alba; Mitridate.*

⊶ ★★★ Decca 466 196-2.

'There is more to heroism than winning fearlessly ... My heroes have moments of weakness and must overcome their difficulties,' comments Andreas Scholl about the operatic characters represented in his Decca recital. Indeed it is the lovely tender singing in the lyrical arias that one remembers most, as in the familiar 'Where'er you Walk', and 'Oh Lord whose Mercies Numberless' (from *Saul*, with its delicate closing harp solo from Frances Kelly), or *Con rauco mormorio* from *Rodelinda*.

In spite of the prevalence of Handel in the programme, Scholl overlaps with his Harmonia Mundi disc on only one aria, *Ombra mai fù*, just as characterful though less forwardly recorded. The other items range from Hasse (wonderfully light and nimble) to dramatic early Mozart. Altogether this is a formidable collection of arias designed originally for castrato, all performed characterfully with a firm, clear tone and virtuoso agility. *Che farò* from Gluck's *Orfeo* is on the slow side, but no less impressive for that. Clear, open sound, the voice caught brightly and naturally. Norrington's accompaniments are light-textured and fresh. But Scholl's earlier Harmonia Mundi Handel collection, including instrumental music also, is in many ways even more seductive – see under Handel in the composer index of our main volume.

Schwarzkopf, Dame Elisabeth (soprano)

'Diva': Arias from: MOZART: *Le nozze di Figaro; Don Giovanni; Così fan tutte.* BEETHOVEN: *Fidelio.* WEBER: *Der Freischütz.* WAGNER: *Lohengrin.* SMETANA: *The Bartered Bride.* RICHARD STRAUSS: *Der Rosenkavalier; Ariadne auf Naxos; Arabella.* HEUBERGER: *Der Opernball.* JOHANN STRAUSS JR: *Die Fledermaus.*

(M) ★★★ EMI stereo/mono 5 65577-2.

Elisabeth Schwarzkopf, married to the recording producer and impresario Walter Legge, had a uniquely intensive recording career from the 1940s onwards. This single CD in EMI's 'Diva' series offers an excellent and shrewdly selected survey of her opera and operetta recordings. Mozart is very well represented, with Schwarzkopf as both Susanna and the Countess in *Figaro*, as Donna Elvira in *Don Giovanni* (from the masterly Giulini recording) and as Fiordiligi in *Così fan tutte* (commanding in *Come scoglio* under Boehm). From Richard Strauss there is not only the Marschallin's monologue (from the Karajan recording of *Rosenkavalier*) but also Ariadne's lament and Arabella's final solo, another of her most compelling Strauss performances. Immaculate accounts of Weber (Agathe's *Leise, leise* from *Der Freischütz*) and of Wagner (Elsa's Dream from *Lohengrin*) have been drawn from one of the finest of all her discs, with Heuberger's *Im chambre séparée* as an enchanting operetta tailpiece. Excellent transfers.

'Elisabeth Schwarzkopf Sings Operetta' (with Phil. Ch. and O, Ackermann): Excerpts from: HEUBERGER: *Der Opernball.* ZELLER: *Der Vogelhändler.* LEHAR: *Der Zarewitsch; Der Graf von Luxembourg; Giuditta.* JOHANN STRAUSS JR: *Casanova.* MILLOCKER: *Die Dubarry.* SUPPE: *Boccaccio.* SIECZYNSKY: *Wien, du Stadt meiner Träume.*

⊶ ❀ (M) ★★★ EMI 5 66989-2 [567004].

This is one of the most delectable recordings of operetta arias ever made, and it is here presented with excellent sound. Schwarzkopf's 'whooping' manner (as Philip Hope-Wallace called it) is irresistible, authentically catching the Viennese style, languor and sparkle combined. Try for example the exquisite *Im chambre séparée* or *Sei nicht bös*; but the whole programme is performed with supreme artistic command and ravishing tonal beauty. This outstanding example of the art of Elisabeth Schwarzkopf at its most enchanting is a disc which ought to be in every collection. The CD transfer enhances the superbly balanced recording even further; it manages to cut out nearly all the background, gives the voice a natural presence and retains the orchestral bloom.

Unpublished recordings 1946–52: BACH: *Cantata No. 51: Jauchzet Gott* (with Philh. O, Susskind).

MOZART: *Exsultate, jubilate, K.165; Das Veilchen.*
Die Zauberflöte: excerpts (with piano);
Schwarzkopf talks about the *Die Zauberflöte*
recordings. Arias from VERDI: *La traviata.*
PUCCINI: *La Bohème.* BACH/GOUNOD: *Ave Maria.*
ARNE: *When Daisies Pied.* MORLEY: *It was a Lover
and his Lass.* SCHUBERT: *Gretchen am Spinnrade;
Der Musensohn; Wiegenlied.* RICHARD STRAUSS:
Hat gesagt, bleibt's nicht dabei; Schlechtes Wetter.
WOLF: *Storchenbotschaft* (2 versions); *Epiphanias;
Mein Liebster hat zu Tische; Du denkst mit einem
Fädchen; Schweig'einmal still; Wer tat deinem
Füsslein weh?; Bedeckt mich mit Blumen; Mögen
alle bösen Zungen; Elfenlied; Nixe Binserfuss; Im
Frühling; Die Spröde; Die Bekehrte;
Mausfallen-sprüchlein; Wiegenlied in Sommer.*

⚙ ✱✱✱ Testament mono/stereo SBT 2172 (2).

Here we have a magnificent store of the recordings
made when her glorious voice was at its most radiant. For any lover of singing this is buried treasure
when many of these items have an immediacy and
freshness even more winning than later, published
versions. Parallel versions of the jolly little Wolf song
Storchenbotschaft demonstrate how rapid her development was between 1948 and 1951, leading to a
whole collection of Wolf recorded in 1951, every one a
jewel.

The three Schubert songs include *Der Musensohn,*
joyfully buoyant, and *Gretchen am Spinnrade,*
brighter and more passionate than in later recordings, with a little spontaneous gasp of emotion after
the climax on *sein Kuss!* Bach and Mozart too have
an extra urgency compared with later, and Violetta's
aria from Verdi's *La traviata* is all the more intense,
done in English. Most revealing of all is the private
recording, some half-hour of music, made with
piano accompaniment when Schwarzkopf was pre-
paring to sing Pamina in English in a Covent Garden
revival of Mozart's *Magic Flute,* a 'glimpse into the
singer's workshop' centring on a ravishing account of
Ach ich fühls.

**The Unpublished EMI Recordings 1955–64 (with
Moore, piano):** BIZET: *Pastorale.* BRAHMS: *In stiller
Nacht; Sandmannchen; Von ewige Liebe;
Wiegenlied.* FLIES: *Wiegenlied.* MOZART: *Un moto
di gioia; Warnung.* PARISOTTI: *Se tu m'ami.*
SCHUBERT: *Claudine von villa bella; Du bist der
Ruh; Die Forelle; Die Junglin an der Quelle; Lachen
und Weinen; Die Vogel; Wiegenlied.* SCHUMANN:
Widmung. RICHARD STRAUSS: *Ruhe, meine Seele;
Wiegenlied; Zueignung.* WAGNER: *Traume.* WOLF:
*Der Kohlerweib; Nachtzauber; Treten ein; Die
Zigeunerin.*

(✱✱✱) Testament SBT 1206.

This makes a superb follow-up to Testament's previous delving into the archive of Schwarzkopf's
unpublished recordings, which covered Bach, Handel
and opera. She and her husband, the recording producer, Walter Legge, were the most exacting critics,

and the reasons for rejection (if that is what it was)
are not at all evident from these inspired performances of Lieder. That is the area where Schwarzkopf
was supreme, above all in Schubert and Wolf, who
are well represented here in intense, characterful
performances, with the voice at its freshest. One
attractive touch is the inclusion of no fewer than
four, nicely contrasted cradle-songs. Excellent transfers.

Scotto, Renata (soprano)

**Italian Opera Arias (with Phil. O, Wolf-Ferrari or
(i) Rome Op. O, Barbirolli): from** ROSSINI: *Il
barbiere di Siviglia.* BELLINI: *I Puritani.* PUCCINI:
Gianni Schicchi; Turandot; (i) *Madama Butterfly.*
DONIZETTI: *Lucia di Lammermoor.* VERDI: *La
traviata.* BOITO: *Mefistofele.*

(BB) ✱✱(✱) EMI Encore (ADD) 5 74766-2.

Apart from two outstanding excerpts from Scotto's
complete 1967 *Madama Butterfly* with Carlo Bergonzi, conducted by Barbirolli, this recital dates from
1959, early in her career. The widely ranging programme has the voice at its freshest and most agile,
giving an idea of the later dramatic developments
which changed the character of the voice and filled it
out (as is shown by the *Butterfly* excerpts).

Seefried, Irmgard (soprano), Erik Werba (piano)

Lieder: BRAHMS: *Es träumte mir; Nicht mehr zu dir
zu gehen; Ständchen; Trost in Tränen; Unbewegte
laue Luft; 6 Volkslieder: In stiller Nacht;
Schwesterlein; Die Sonne scheint mehr; Die
Trauernde; Der Versuchung; Volkslied.* SCHUBERT:
*Mignon Lieder: Heiss mich nicht reden; Kennst du
das Land; Nur wer die Sehnsucht kennt; So lasst
mich scheinen.* WOLF: *Mignon Lieder I–IV: Heiss
mich nicht reden; Kennst du das Land; Nur wer die
Sehnsucht kennt; So lasst mich scheinen.* (Irmgard
Seefried in conversation with John Amis.)

(✱✱✱) BBC mono BBCL 4040-2.

Recorded by the BBC in the studio in January 1962,
this recital brings out the open charm of Irmgard
Seefried as a winning Lieder singer. Her Brahms
group sets the pattern, bringing out the links with
German folksong, fresh and tuneful. There is no lack
of detail in her pointing of words, but she takes a
direct view of even such a deeply meditative song as
In stiller Nacht, singing with concentration but little
mystery.

Such songs as *Schwesterlein* and *Ständchen* are
given with such urgency that one holds one's breath,
half expecting disaster. Seefried's forte is her full,
strong, creamy voice, here recorded rather close, so
that Schubert's *Gretchen am Spinnrade* brings little
build-up, and Wolf's supreme Lied, *Kennst du das*

Land, remains fresh and forthright in its lyricism rather than offering darker emotions. The interview with John Amis, which comes as a delightful supplement, bears out the joyful enthusiasm of the singer, whose strength, beauty and openness defy any detailed reservations.

(Robert) Shaw Festival Singers, Robert Shaw

'*O Magnum mysterium*': GORECKI: *Totus tuus.* LAURIDSEN: *O magnum mysterium.* POULENC: *O magnum mysterium.* RACHMANINOV: *Praise the Name of the Lord.* SCHUBERT: *Der Ernfernten.* TALLIS: *If ye Love Me; A New Commandment.* TRAD: *Amazing Grace. Sometimes I Feel like a Moanin' Dove. Wondrous Love.* VICTORIA: *O vos omnes. O magnum mysterium.*
*** Telarc CD 80531.

This compilation of unaccompanied choral music pays tribute to Robert Shaw as one of the world's great choir-trainers, who first made his name in the 1940s, when Toscanini chose the Robert Shaw Chorale for major choral recordings. Then, towards the end of his career, after two decades as music director of the Atlanta Symphony Orchestra, Shaw once again had time for unaccompanied choral music, establishing in 1989 a summer festival of choral workshops as well as performance at Quercy in the south of France and using a choir of students from American universities. His Telarc recordings made with that festival choir provide most of the items here, which were atmospherically recorded in the church of St Pierre at Gramat. The Tallis and Victoria motets, recorded in 1989, are an exception; they appear on disc for the first time in immaculate performances from a relatively large choir, which demonstrate the consistent refinement of the matching and balance that are characteristic of Shaw's choral work. The Schubert part-song and the Lauridsen motet, recorded in the United States with Shaw's chamber singers, readily match the rest in beauty of sound, particularly the Lauridsen, a fine piece by a composer, born in 1943, who spices a traditional idiom with clashing intervals in a way that Purcell would have enjoyed.

Shuard, Amy (soprano)

Recital (with ROHCG O, Downes or RPO, Weldon): Arias from: VERDI: *Aida; Un ballo in maschera.* MASCAGNI: *Cavalleria rusticana.* PUCCINI: *Turandot; Gianni Schicchi; Tosca; La Bohème.* GIORDANO: *Andrea Chénier.* TCHAIKOVSKY: *Eugene Onegin* (Letter scene).
(M) **(*) Dutton Lab. CDCLP 4006.

What this formidable aria collection triumphantly demonstrates is that Amy Shuard, for many years the leading soprano in the Covent Garden company, has

been seriously underestimated. Her premature death at the age of 50 compounded what was already sadly evident, that this home-grown singer was not going to be fully appreciated. Even when originally issued on two LPs in the early 1960s, the recordings did not appear on a premium label, but the singer, at once gloriously firm and strong, yet sensitively shaded and deeply expressive, whether as Aida, Turandot or Tatiana, can bear international comparision with other recording artists. The timbre may not have been of the most distinctive, but she amply compensated in the central strength and precision of everything she sang. There are few Turandots quite so incisive as this one. The Dutton transfer here is immaculate, with the voice vivid and clear.

Sinfonye, Stewart Wishart

'*Gabriel's Greeting*' (medieval carols) including: *Gabriel framevene king; Salva Virgo virginium; Ave Maria virgo virginium; Ther is no Rose of Swych Vertu; Lolay, Lolay; Nowell, Nowell.*
(BB) **(*) Hyp. Helios CDH 55151.

Unlike the Taverner Consort, who range over many centuries of music, Sinfonye concentrate on vocal and instrumental music from the thirteenth, fourteenth and fifteenth centuries, which usually consists of simple ostinato-like rhythmic ideas with a very distinctive melodic and harmonic character. These five singers and instrumentalists present their programme with spirit and vitality, but the range of the music is necessarily limited. Those who take to the repetitive medieval style will undoubtedly find this refreshing, and the recording is pleasingly live and atmospheric. Full documentation and texts are included.

Söderström, Elisabeth (soprano)

'*A Swedish Song Collection*' (with Westerberg, Eyron, piano): ALMQVIST: *The Listening Maria; The Startled Maria; You are not Walking Alone; Why Did you not Come to the Meadow?* BERGER: *Aspåkerspolka; Longing is my Inheritance.* LINDBLAD: *By Aarensee; I Wonder.* JOSEPHSON: *Serenade.* RANGSTROM: *Pan; Villema; The Girl under the New Moon; The Only Moment.* STENHAMMAR: *The Girl on Midsummer Eve; The Girl Returned from Meeting her Loved One; Adagio.* SJOGREN: *Sound, Sound my Pandero!; In the Shade of my Curls; I would Hold you Forever.* FRUMERIE: *A Letter Arrived; The Song of Love.*
*** Swedish Soc. SCD 1117.

These songs find Söderström at her finest in repertoire that she made very much her own in the late 1950s and 1960s, when she was in her prime. Songs like *Månntro* ('I Wonder') by Adolf Fredrik Lindblad have an affecting simplicity that is quite haunting, and the Rangström songs, in particular *Den enda stunden* ('The Only Movement'), have not been surpassed. Much of this wonderful repertoire will be new to collectors, as the original LPs enjoyed limited currency in the UK. They still sound wonderfully fresh.

Soprano arias

'*20 Great Soprano Arias*' from: MOZART: *Le nozze di Figaro* (Kiri Te Kanawa; Ileana Cotrubas). *Die Entführung aus dem Serail* (Kathleen Battle). *Die Zauberflöte* (Sumi Jo). PUCCINI: *Madama Butterfly* (Régine Crespin). *Turandot* (Monserrat Caballé; Virginia Zeani). *La rondine* (Renata Tebaldi). *Tosca* (Leontyne Price). *Gianni Schicchi* (Felicia Weathers). *La Bohème* (Mirella Freni; Elizabeth Harwood). VERDI: *I vespri siciliani* (Anita Cerquetti). *Un ballo in maschera* (Margaret Price). CATALANI: *La Wally* (Maria Chiara). PONCHIELLI: *La Gioconda* (Elena Souliotis). DONIZETTI: *La figlia del reggimento* (Graziella Sciutti). GOUNOD: *Faust* (Joan Sutherland). DVORAK: *Rusalka* (Pilar Lorengar). WAGNER: *Die Walküre* (Kirsten Flagstad).

(M) *** Decca (ADD) 458 230-2.

Decca's collection of *20 Great Soprano Arias* is made the more interesting by its use of twenty different singers, and the choices are not always obvious ones; for instance Régine Crespin's very individual and very touching *Un bel dì* from *Madama Butterfly*, Elena Souliotis's searingly powerful *Suicido* from *La Gioconda* and the beautifully spun line of Maria Chiara's *Ne andrò lonata* from *La Wally*.

Opening with Kiri Te Kanawa's moving *Dove sono*, other highlights include Kathleen Battle's vivacious portrayal of Blonde in *Die Entführung*, Kirsten Flagstad as Sieglinde in *Die Walküre*, the charming Graziella Sciutti, in *La figlia del reggimento*, and Joan Sutherland's scintillating (1960) Jewel Song. Both Margaret and Leontyne Price are included, and of course Freni.

Alongside these familiar names come rather less well-known singers, all in excellent voice (Anita Cerquetti in *I vespri siciliani*; Felicia Weathers as Lauretta in *Gianni Schicchi*; Pilar Lorengar no less striking in Rusalka's famous Moon invocation, and Virginia Zeani alongside Caballé – two very contrasted voices – as Liù in *Turandot*). The programme ends with Sumi Jo's sparklingly precise coloratura in the most familiar of the Queen of the Night's arias from *Die Zauberflöte*. This famous show-piece has never been better sung on record – it has drama as well as extraordinary bravura.

Souzay, Gérard (baritone)

'*French Airs*' (with Jacqueline Bonneau, piano): FAURE: *Tristesse; Au bord de l'eau; Après un rêve; Clair de lune; Arpège; En sourdine; L'Horizon chimérique; Spleen; c'est l'extase; Prison; Mandoline.* CHAUSSON: *Nanny; Le Charme; Sérénade italienne; Le Colibri; Cantique à l'épouse; Les Papillons; Le Temps de lilas.* Airs: BOESSET: *Me veux-tu voir mourir?* ANON.: *Tambourin.* BATAILLE: *Cachez, beaux yeux; Ma bergère non légère.* CANTELOUBE: *Brezairola; Malurous qu'o uno fenno.*

🔑 ✿ (M) *** Decca mono 475 041-2.

The great French baritone made these recordings for Decca when he was at the very peak of his form. The Fauré were recorded in 1950 and the glorious Chausson songs in 1953. Souzay was endowed with the intelligence of Bernac as well as his powers of characterization, the vocal purity of Panzera and a wonderful feeling for line. The Decca transfer does complete justice to the original sound, and it is good to have these performances without the surface distractions of LP. Full texts and translations are provided. A marvellous record worth as many rosettes as stars, which deservedly won the *Gramophone* Historical Vocal Award in 1991.

Stefano, Giuseppe di (tenor)

'*Heroes*': Arias and excerpts from: VERDI: *Rigoletto; Il trovatore; La traviata; Un ballo in maschera.* DONIZETTI: *Lucia di Lammermoor.* PUCCINI: *Manon Lescaut; La Bohème; Tosca; Madama Butterfly.* LEONCAVALLO: *Pagliacci.* MASCAGNI: *Cavalleria rusticana.*

(M) (***) EMI mono 5 66808-2.

Except for those demanding stereo, this is an outstanding demonstration of di Stefano's open-throated vocal ardour. The recordings date from between 1953 and 1956 when the voice was at its finest. Certainly the heroic side of his vocal personality comes over splendidly in Verdi (especially in *Di quella pira*) but he is at his finest and most responsive in the Puccini excerpts, the superb *Tosca* with de Sabata (1953), *Madama Butterfly* (1953), and *La Bohème* (1958). He is ideally cast as Turiddù, and his two arias from *Cavalleria rusticana*, which end the recital, are passionately moving, while the *Pagliacci* Prologue brings compellingly vibrant vocal histrionics. Excellent, vivid transfers, which make one forget the age of the recordings.

'*Torna a Surriento*' (songs of Italy and Sicily): CD 1 (with New SO of London, Pattacini): DE CURTIS: *Torna a Surriento; Tu ca' nun chiagne; Sonta chitarra!* BUONGIOVANNI: *Lacreme napulitane.* TAGLIAFERRI: *Napule canta; Pusilleco ... califano: O 'surdato 'nnammurato.* CARDILLO: *Catari, Catari.* COSTA: *Era di maggio matenata; Scetate.* VALENTE: *Addio mia bella Napoli.* CD 2 (with O, Dino Olivieri): BIXIO: *Parlami d'amore Mariù.* BARBERIS: *Munasterio'e Santa-Chiara.* CESARINI:

Firenze sogna. DE CURTIS: *Canta pe'me; 'A canzone'e Napule; Ti voglio tanto bene.* NARDELLA: *Che t'aggia di!* SIMI: *Come è bello far l'amore quanno è sera.* VANCHERI: *Sicilia bedda.* BUONGIOVANNI: *Fili d'oro.* DI LAZZARO: *Chitarra romana.* RIVI: *Addio, sogni di gloria.* TRAD., arr. FAVARA: *A la barcillunisi; Nota di li lavannari; A la vallelunghisa; Muttètti di lu pàliu; Chiovu 'aballati'; Cantu a timùni.*

(B) *** Double Decca (ADD) 455 482-2 (2).

Giuseppe di Stefano was still in magnificent voice when, in the summer of 1964, he recorded the collection of popular Italian songs assembled on the first disc of this Decca Double. He projects the ardent numbers such as the title-song with characteristic lustiness but less subtlety; despite the inevitable touches of vulgarity, the singing is rich toned and often charming, and a famous Neapolitan hit like *Catari, Catari* is winningly done. Pattacini's accompaniments are vividly idiomatic.

The second collection is even more generous, offering eighteen songs (against eleven on the first disc). This dates from 1958, when the voice was even more honeyed, so that Bixio's opening *Parlami d'amore Mariù* sounds almost like operetta and brings an engaging pianissimo ending. The luscious Mantovani-styled accompaniments are certainly seductive, and very well recorded, while in *Come è bello far l'amore quanno è sera* the use of the mandolin is particularly atmospheric.

Besides the popular Neapolitan numbers, there are many comparative rarities here, often coming from Venice, Florence or Sicily, with their respective dialects. There are no translations, but none are really needed. As Frank Granville Barker observes in his note: 'Strong emotions are the concern of all these songs, expressed in no less straightforward melodies. The mood is intense, the singer declaring his devotion to his loved one, or despairing when it is not returned. Parting from home inspires as much anguish as parting from the loved one, as we hear in *Addio mia bella Napoli.*'

The group of six traditional songs arranged by Favara, which close the recital, are particularly fine; *Muttètti di lu pàliu* (introduced by a fine horn solo) is really memorable, with di Stefano responding to its plaintive melancholy with a very gentle closing cadence. He then follows with a sparkling tarantella, *Chiovu 'abballati'.* This is not a collection to play all at once (and memories of Gigli in this repertory are not vanquished), but in its field it is currently unsurpassed.

Streich, Rita (soprano)

'The Viennese Nightingale' (with various orchestras and conductors or pianists as listed): MOZART: *Bastien und Bastienne* (complete; with Holm, Blankenheim, Munich CO, Stepp).

Arias from *Zaïde; Idomeneo; Così fan tutte; Die Entführung aus em Serail; Die Zauberflöte; Don Giovanni; Le nozze di Figaro; Il re pastore.* Concert arias (with Bav. RSO, Mackerras): *Alcandro lo confesso ... Non so d'onde viene; Ah se in ciel, benigne stelle; Vado ma dove? oh Dei!; Popoli di Tessaglia ... Io non chiedo, eterni Dei; Vorrei spiegarvi, oh Dio! ... Ah conte, partite; No, che non sei capace; Mia speranza adorata ... Ah non sai quai pena sia; Nehmt meinen Dank, Ihr holden.*

Lieder (with Erik Werba, piano): *Das Veilchen; Die Zufriedenheit; An Chloë; Das Lied der Trennung; Die kleine Spinnerin; Geheime Liebe; Wie unglücklich bin ich nit; Der Zauberer; Sehnsucht nach dem Frühlinge; Un moto di gioia; Oiseaux, si tous les ans; Dans un bois solitaire; Ridente la calma; Das Kinderspiel; Abendemfindung; An die Einsamkeit; Die Verschweignung; Warnung.* WOLF: *Spanisches Liederbuch* excerpts: *Trau'nicht der Liebe; Köpfchen, Köpfchen, nicht; Bedeckt mich mit Blumen; In dem Schatten meiner Locken. Italienisches Liederbuch: Du kennst mit einem Fädchen mich zu fangen; Mein Liebster ist so klein; Wie lange schon; Wer rief dich denn? Nun lass uns Frieden schliessen; Nein junger Herr; O wär'dein Haus durchsichtig; Auch kleine Dinge. Tretet ein, höher Krieger; Verschwiegen Liebe; Gleich und gleich; Die Spröde; Die Bekehrte; Wiegenlied in Sommer; Der Gärtner; Zitronenfalter im April; Mausfallen-Sprüchlein; Elfenlied; Zum neuen Jahr; Wohin mit der Freud; Wiegenlied; Die Kleine; Nachtgrüss.* Folksong settings: *Oh, du liabs Angeli; Sakura.* SCHUBERT: *Heidenröslein* (2 versions); *Liebe schwärmt auf allen Wegen; Schweizerlied; Lied der Mignon: Nur wer die Sehnsucht kennt; Nähe des Geliebchen; Liebhabner in allen Gestalten; Der Hirt auf dem Felsen* (with Heinrich Geuser, clarinet); *Auf dem Wasser zu singen* (2 versions); *An den Mond; An die Nachtigall; Wiegenlied; Nachtviolen; Seligkeit* (2 versions); *Der Schmetterling; Die Vogel; Die Forelle* (2 versions); *Das Lied im Grünen.* BRAHMS (with Günther Weissenborn, piano): *Ständchen (Der Mond steht auf dem Berge); Geheimnis; Aud dem Schiffe; Trennung; Vergbliches Ständchen; Wiegenlied; Das Mädchen spricht; 3 Mädchenlied: Ach, und du mein kühles Wasser!; Am jüngsten Tag ich aufersteh; Auf di Nacht in der Spinnstub'n.* SCHUMANN: *Der Nussbaum; Die Stille; Schneeglöckchen; Die Lotusblume; Intermezzo; Aufträge.*

Arias and excerpts from: WEBER: *Der Freischütz.* ROSSINI: *Il barbiere di Siviglia; Semiramide.* DONIZETTI: *Don Pasquale* (with Kurt Weholschutz); *Die Regimentstochter (La Fille du régiment); Lucia di Lammermoor; Linda di Chamounix.* VERDI: *Rigoletto* (with Hermann Uhde); *Un ballo in maschera; I vespri siciliani; Falstaff.* GLUCK: *Orphée et Euridice.* PFITZNER: *Palestrina: Die Messe* (with Soloists, Ch. & O of

Berlin Komischen Opera, Robert Heger).
LORTZING: *Der Wildschütz* (with Kurt Böhme).
NICOLAI: *Die lustigen Weiber von Windsor.*
Variations on the Wiegenlied of Weber, Op. 19 (with
Erik Werba). OFFENBACH: *Contes d'Hoffmann.*
BIZET: *Les Pêcheurs de perles.* MASSENET: *Manon.*
DELIBES: *Lakmé.* RIMSKY-KORSAKOV: *Sadko; Le
Coq d'or.* MEYERBEER: *Les Huguenots.* THOMAS:
Mignon. BELLINI: *I Capuletti ei i Montecchi.*
PUCCINI: *La Bohème; Gianni Schicchi; Turandot.*
JOHANN STRAUSS JR: *Die Fledermaus.* Also Waltz:
G'schichten aus dem Wiener Wald. RICHARD
STRAUSS: *Der Rosenkavalier* (with Irmgard
Seefried, Marianne Schech, Ilona Steingruber,
Dresden State O, Karl Boehm). Lieder (with
Günther Weissenborn, piano): *Schlagende Herzen;
Wiegenlied; Schlechtes Wetter; Amor; An die Nacht;
Als mir dein Lied erklang;* (with Erik Werba, piano):
Der Stern; Einerlei; Schlechtes Wetter. MILHAUD: *4
Chansons de Ronsard.* European folksongs: *Gsätzli;
When love is kind; Canto delle risailo; Au clair de la
lune; Z'lauterbach.*

(B) *** DG 474 738-2 (8).

Possessing the most delightful coloratura voice of the
second half of the twentieth century (and as attractive to look at as to listen to), Rita Streich measured
up to all the competition from the 'golden age'. Hers
was a small voice but perfectly formed, and it
recorded marvellously well. She had studied with
Maria Ivogün and Erna Berger, and she surely carried
the latter's vocal mantle. Her tonal purity, extraordinary flexibility and total accuracy in coloratura,
together with her linear musicality, made her a natural for Mozart, and if she was most famous for her
unsurpassed recording of the Queen of the Night's
two big arias (uncannily accurate, if perhaps not
malignantly evil), she was also an enchanting Zerlina, Despina, Papagena and Blonde, and she made
the role of Susanna very much her own.

The collection here opens with a complete mono
recording of *Bastien und Bastienne* in which she is
well partnered by Richard Holm and Toni Blankenheim. The richly sung aria *Er war mir sonst treu,* and
the duet *Geh'! Geh! Herz von Flandern,* comparably
winning, project vividly, even if the conductor Christoph Stepp is rather matter-of-fact. The following
excerpts, *Ruhe sanft* from *Zaïde* (with beautiful
legato) and *Zeffiretti lusinghiri* from *Idomeneo* (with
glorious, flowing runs), confirm her vocal grace and
easy fluency and charm, as does the most famous
duet from *Don Giovanni,* in which she is elegantly
partnered by Fischer-Dieskau.

She had both the temperament and the bravura in
the upper range for Mozart's virtuoso concert arias,
and the astonishingly fine selection here, accompanied by Mackerras, set her on a pinnacle which only
her magnificent high notes could overtop. The lovely
Vado, ma dove and the grandiloquent *Popoli di Tessaglia* are unforgettable. Aloysia Lange was the lady
for whom Mozart originally wrote these arias, and if

she could sing them half as well as they are sung here
by Streich, then contemporary reports of her artistry
can certainly be believed!

The present set includes her many Lieder recordings, for which she was perhaps less famous in England; many appear here for the first time on either LP
or CD. Most are accompanied by Erik Werber, with
whom she established a close relationship. Throughout there is always evidence of a keenly sensitive
mind, not perhaps that of a born Lieder singer, but
certainly that of a born musician. Her ease and
simplicity are especially telling in Schubert, where
she could also be both touching and dramatic. In *Der
Hirt auf dem Felsen,* with an artistic clarinet obbligato from Heinrich Geuser, she is in her element, as
indeed she is in many of the most familiar songs,
several of which she recorded twice.

She approaches Schumann, Brahms and Richard
Strauss with almost an operatic style. Her line is
often dramatic and this works best with the two
last-named composers, but her interpretations lack
the intimacy of the recital room. As Alan Blyth
comments in his excellent note, 'she did not attempt
the intensity of approach favoured by her close contemporary, Elisabeth Schwarzkopf', but 'her sense of
fun is strongly conveyed in the selection from Wolf's
Italianisches Liederbuch'. Moreover, none of these
songs is ever let down by lack of control of phrase or
intonation, and her persuasively affecting timbre and
line always communicate directly. The surprise inclusion is the *Quatre Chansons de Ronsard* of Milhaud.
But their sometimes awkward intervals and unexpected flights of upper tessitura are negotiated with
such skill and a supreme lightness of touch (from
singer and accompanist alike) that they are transformed into twentieth-century French lollipops, to
match the engaging folksongs with which the collection closes.

The equally wide range of recordings of opera
arias constantly affects the listener with their ravishing tone and sparkling coloratura – notably so in in
the excerpts from *Les Contes d'Hoffmann, Le Coq
d'Or* (both exquisite), *Les Pêcheurs de perles, Lakmé*
and *Mignon.* She is a engagingly minx-like Rosina in
Il barbiere, and a touching Lucia di Lammermoor,
duetting with the flute with captivating precision,
while the Presentation of the Silver Rose scene in
Rosenkavalier (with Irmgard Seefried) is enchanting.
If she does not attempt to draw a great deal of
differentiation in character among the various heroines, it could be argued that in Mozart the roles she
plays are all different facets of a basically similar
female character. And her technique is so sure and
the singing itself (with not a wobble anywhere) gives
such pleasure that criticism is disarmed.

'*Waltzes and Arias*' (with Berlin RSO, RIAS Berlin,
Gaebel): JOHANN STRAUSS JR: *Frühlingsstimmen;
Draussen in Sievering.* SAINT-SAENS: *Le Rossignol
et la rose.* VERDI: *Lo spazzacamino.* ARDITI: *Parla
waltz.* JOSEF STRAUSS: *Dorfschwalben aus*

Osterreich. ALABIEV: *The Nightingale.* DELIBES: *Les Filles de Cadiz.* CZERNIK: *Chi sa?* MARCHESI: *La folletta.* FLOTOW: *Last Rose of Summer.* DELL'ACQUA: *Villanelle.* ARDITI: *Il bacio.* Arias from: GODARD: *Jocelyn.* SUPPE: *Boccaccio.* DVORAK: *Rusalka.* MEYERBEER: *Dinorah.*

☰━ ● (M) ★★★ DG mono/stereo 457 729-2 (2).

Those wanting a single CD showing Rita Streich's delightful vocal personality at its most winning cannot do better than acquire this shorter selection. Many of the most memorable pieces included here come from a recital she recorded in 1958 in the Jesus Christus Kirche, Berlin.

Included were the Strauss waltzes, Dvořák's *Invocation to the Moon*, the charming *Hab' ich nur deine Liebe* from *Boccaccio* and the equally delightful Shadow Song from *Dinorah*. Godard's highly romantic *Berceuse* is the most famous item, but it is in the deliciously fragile Saint-Saëns vocalise, *Le Rossignol et la rose*, and in Verdi's captivating song of the chimneysweep (*Lo spazzacamino*) that her magic sends a shiver of special pleasure to the nape of the neck. A worthy vocal addition for DG's series of 'Originals'.

'Folksongs and Lullabies': *Du, du liegst mir im Herzen; O du liabs Angeli; Frère Jacques; L'Amore de moi; Canto delle risaiole; Z'Lauterbach; Schlof sche, mein Vögele; Drink to me Only with Thine Eyes; Nobody Knows the Trouble I've Seen; Sakura, Sakura; Tschubtschik; Spi mladenez; In mezo al mar; Wenn ich ein Vöglein wär'; Der mond ist aufgegangen; Muss I denn zum Städtele 'maus* (with Rudolf Lamy Choir and instrumental accompaniment, Michalski). *Weisst Du, wieviel Sterne stehen; O wie wohl ist mir Abend; Wo e kleins Hüttle steht; All mein Gedanken; Glockenruf; Der Bürgermeister von Wesel; Der Wechsel der Jahreszeiten; Schlaf, Herzenssöhnchen; Schlafe, mein Prinzchen, schlaf ein; Sandmännchen; Der Kuckuck; Schwesterlein!; Ach Modr, ick will en Ding han; In der Fruah; Abendlied; Ave Maria* (with Regenszburger Domspatzen, Bavarian Radio SO, Gaebel).

(M) ★★★ DG (ADD) (IMS) 457 763-2.

This disc is a delight. Every song is most winning and it is difficult to say which is the more captivating, the Russian, French, English or Swiss folksongs, all dressed up in freshly colourful orchestrations, and the delectable *Frère Jacques* presented in canon with the choir. Rita Streich sings with obvious affection, with her legendary creaminess of vocal timbre tickling the ear throughout the two collections, which were recorded in 1963 and 1964. Their remarkable variety, to say nothing of the vocal charm, prevents any sense that 79 minutes of folksong is too much. It is regretted that DG, in these beautifully transferred recordings on their Originals label, has failed to provide any texts or translations. But this is still a reissue not to be missed.

Sutherland, Dame Joan (soprano)

'The Art of Joan Sutherland':

Volume 1: Arias from: HANDEL: *Alcina; Giulio Cesare; Samson.* MOZART: *Die Entführung; Il re pastore; Die Zauberflöte.*

Volume 2: Arias from French operas: OFFENBACH: *La Grande Duchesse de Gérolstein; Robinson Crusoé.* MEYERBEER: *Dinorah; Robert le Diable.* CHARPENTIER: *Louise.* AUBER: *Manon Lescaut.* BIZET: *Les Pêcheurs de perles; Vasco de Gama.* MASSENET: *Cendrillon.* GOUNOD: *Faust; Mireille; Le Tribut de Zamora.* LECOCQ: *Le Coeur et la main.* MASSE: *Les Noces de Jeanette.*

Volume 3: 'Command Performance': WEBER: *Oberon.* MASSENET: *Le Cid.* MEYERBEER: *Dinorah; L'Étoile de Nord.* LEONCAVALLO: *Pagliacci.* VERDI: *I masnadieri.* BELLINI: *Beatrice di Tenda.* DONIZETTI: *La Fille du regiment.* OFFENBACH: *Les Contes d'Hoffman.* GOUNOD: *Faust.*

Volume 4: 'Rarities and Surprises': Arias from WAGNER: *Der fliegende Holländer; Lohengrin; Die Meistersinger; Rienzi; Tannhäuser; Tristan und Isolde; Die Walküre.* MOZART: *Le nozze di Figaro*: arias. GLIERE: *Concerto for Coloratura Soprano.* STRAVINSKY: *Pastorale.* CUI: *Ici bas.* GRETCHANINOV: *Lullaby.*

Volume 5: 'Great Operatic Scenes' from: MEYERBEER: *Les Huguenots.* BELLINI: *Norma.* DONIZETTI: *Lucia di Lammermoor.* VERDI: *Attila; Ernani; I vespri siciliani; La traviata.*

★★★ Australian Decca (ADD) 466 474-2 (5)

Joan Sutherland has been one of Decca's most important recording artists, particularly during the analogue LP era. In return, often with the prompting and careful and imaginative planning of her husband and musical partner Richard Bonynge, she provided an extraordinary wide-ranging discography over her remarkably long recording career. This bargain box from Decca's Australian branch is important for including many recordings not otherwise available on CD.

Volume 1 is a reminder of her excellent Handel performances, with the arias mainly taken from her complete opera recordings, although the ringing account of 'Let the Bright Seraphim' is from *The Art of the Prima Donna*, as is the Mozart *Die Entführung* aria. The other Mozart items are from her 1979 Mozart LP: not one of her best discs, but one from which Sutherland admirers will surely want excerpts.

The French arias on Volume 2 were recorded in 1968 and sound sparklingly vivid and fresh in this new transfer. This was one of her most successful and infectiously tuneful recital discs: highlights include swirling coloratura waltzes from *Robinson Crusoé* and *Mireille*, a sparkling bolero by Lecocq, and spectacular set-piece arias by Meyerbeer, Auber and Charpentier.

Volume 3, *Command Performance*, is hardly less succesful: the showy numbers of Meyerbeer, Donizetti and Offenbach display her virtuoso singing to the full, while her hauntingly exquisite bel canto in the Bellini item is another highlight.

Volume 4 includes her 1979 Wagner recital, and more items from the Mozart recital from the same year: this is not top-drawer Sutherland, but it is fascinating to hear the Glière *Concerto for Coloratura Soprano*, which is quite superb.

The final volume, a collection of operatic scenes, includes the great 1959 Paris recording of the Mad scene from *Lucia*, as well as the arias from *Ernani* and the splendidly crisp bolero from *I vespri siciliani* from the same disc. All in all, a splendid collection of some great singing and interesting repertoire, with stylish orchestral contributions, mainly from Richard Bonynge, and although no texts are provided there are good sleeve notes.

'Grandi voci': BELLINI: *Norma: Sediziose voci ... Casta diva ... Ah! bello a me ritorna. I Puritani: Qui la voce sua soave ... Vien, diletto* (with ROHCG O, Molinari-Pradelli). VERDI: *Attila: Santo di patria ... Allor che i forti corrono ... Da te questo or m'è concesso* (with LSO, Bonynge); *Ernani: Surta è la notte ... Ernani! Ernani, involami. I vespri siciliani: Mercè, dilette amiche (Boléro).* DONIZETTI: *Lucia di Lammermoor: Ancor non giunse! ... Regnava nel silenzio; Il dolce suono mi colpi di sua voce! ... Ardon gl'incensi (Mad scene). Linda di Chamounix: Ah! tardai troppo ... O luce di quest'anima.*

⊶ ✿ (M) ★★★ Decca (ADD) 440 404-2.

Sutherland's *Grandi voci* disc is one of the most cherishable of all operatic recital records, bringing together the glorious, exuberant items from her very first recital disc, made within weeks of her first Covent Garden success in 1959, and – as a valuable supplement – the poised accounts of *Casta diva* and *Vien, diletto* she recorded the following year as part of *The Art of the Prima Donna*.

It was this 1959 recital which at once put Sutherland firmly on the map among the great recording artists of all time. Even she has never surpassed the freshness of these versions of the two big arias from *Lucia di Lammermoor*, sparkling in immaculate coloratura, while the lightness and point of the jaunty *Linda di Chamounix* aria and the *Boléro* from *I vespri siciliani* are just as winning. The aria from *Attila* comes from *The Age of Bel Canto* (1963). The sound is exceptionally vivid and immediate, though the accompaniments under Nello Santi are sometimes rough in ensemble.

'Love Live Forever (The Romance of Musical Comedy)' (with Ambrosian Light Op. Ch., New Philh. O., Bonynge): Excerpts from: ROMBERG: *The Student Prince; The Desert Song.* RODGERS: *The Boys from Syracuse.* KERN: *Music in the Air; Show Boat.* FRIML: *Rose Marie.* HERBERT: *The Only Girl.* FRASER-SIMPSON: *The Maid of the Mountains.*

GERMAN: *Tom Jones.* OFFENBACH: *La Périchole.* MASSENET: *Chérubin.* ZELLER: *Der Vogelhändler.* MILLOCKER: *The Dubarry.* FALL: *Die geschiedene Frau; Die spanische Nachtigall; Die Dollarprinzessin; Madame Pompadour; Die liebe Augustin.* LEHAR: *Eva; Die lustige Witwe; Paganini.* STRAUS: *Ein Walzertraum; The Chocolate Soldier.* HEUBERGER: *Der Opernball.* JOHANN STRAUS JR: *Casanova.* KREISLER: *The King Steps Out.* POSFORD: *Balalaika.*

(B) ★★★ Double Decca (ADD) 452 955-2 (2).

Beginning with an exuberant account of the opening chorus from *The Student Prince* and including a glorious performance of the title number from *The Desert Song* ('Blue Heaven'), this is a lilting, whooping recital to set against the superb Schwarzkopf record of operetta favourites, which covers some of the same ground. Sutherland may not always match Schwarzkopf in the haunting Viennese quality which inhabits such an enchanting number as *Im chambre séparée*, but her range of repertoire here is far wider, including as it does a pair of Offenbach items, not to mention the songs from American and British musicals down to *The Boys from Syracuse*.

Above all, it is the tune that counts and there are plenty of good ones, not least 'Make Believe' from *Show Boat* and the unforgettable 'Love will Find a Way' from *The Maid of the Mountains*. Bonynge's sparkling selection ranges into the easily melodious world of Romberg and Friml, Fraser-Simpson and Oscar Straus, and most enterprisingly includes a pot-pourri from the German operettas of Leo Fall. What is immediately obvious is Sutherland's own delight in singing this music, with no apology whatever. Produced by Christopher Raeburn, the sumptuous Kingsway Hall recording catches the glory of Sutherland's voice (in the mid-1960s) to perfection against appropriately rich accompaniments all specially arranged by Douglas Gamley.

'Greatest Hits': Excerpts from: HANDEL: *Samson.* PICCINNI: *La buona figliuola.* BELLINI: *Norma; I Puritani.* DONIZETTI: *La Fille du régiment; Lucia di Lammermoor: Mad scene.* DELIBES: *Lakmé.* VERDI: *Rigoletto; La traviata.* GOUNOD: *Faust.* OFFENBACH: *Contes d'Hoffmann.*

(M) ★★★ Decca (ADD) 458 209-2.

A 76-minute collection like this, well chosen to entertain, is self-recommending at mid-price. It has been nicely repackaged in a slip-case for this reissue in Decca's Opera Gala series, and translations are now included. The chosen recordings have been slightly amended since the previous issue but all come from the period when the voice was at its freshest: 'Let the Bright Seraphim', the delectable *Caro nome* and the vivacious Jewel Song from Faust date from 1960, but here the justly famous 1959 Mad scene from *Lucia di Lammermoor* has been substituted for the performance in the complete set under Pritchard. The lively excerpt from *La Fille du régiment* (1967) and the Doll

Song from *Contes d'Hoffmann* (1972) come from the complete sets, as does the famous Act I *La traviata* scena (1962), which is now added. The sound is consistently vivid.

'*The Art of the Prima Donna*' (with ROHCG Ch. & O, Molinari-Pradelli): ARNE: *Artaxerxes: The Soldier Tir'd.* HANDEL: *Samson: Let the Bright Seraphim.* BELLINI: *Norma: Casta diva. I Puritani: Son vergin vezzosa; Que la voce. La sonnambula: Come per me sereno.* ROSSINI: *Semiramide: Bel raggio lusinghier.* GOUNOD: *Faust: Jewel Song. Roméo et Juliette: Waltz Song.* VERDI: *Otello: Willow Song. Rigoletto: Caro nome. La traviata: Ah fors' è lui; Sempre libera.* MOZART: *Die Entführung aus dem Serail: Marten aller Arten.* THOMAS: *Hamlet: Mad scene.* DELIBES: *Lakmé: Bell Song.* MEYERBEER: *Les Huguenots: O beau pays.*

⊙ (M) *** Decca (ADD) 467 115-2 (2).

This ambitious early two-disc recital (from 1960) has also now been reissued in Decca's Legends series, for the recording on CD is amazingly full and realistic, far more believable than many new digital recordings. It remains one of Dame Joan Sutherland's outstanding gramophone achievements, and it is a matter of speculation whether even Melba or Tetrazzini in their heyday managed to provide sixteen consecutive recordings quite as dazzling as these performances. Indeed, it is the 'golden age' that one naturally turns to rather than to current singers when making any comparisons. Sutherland herself, by electing to sing each one of these fabulously difficult arias in tribute to a particular soprano of the past, from Mrs Billington in the eighteenth century, through Grisi, Malibran, Pasta and Jenny Lind in the nineteenth century, to Lilli Lehmann, Melba, Tetrazzini and Galli-Curci in this, is asking to be judged by the standards of the golden age.

On the basis of recorded reminders she comes out with flying colours, showing a greater consistency and certainly a wider range of sympathy than even the greatest golden agers possessed. The sparkle and delicacy of the *Puritani* Polonaise, the freshness and lightness of the Mad scene from Thomas's *Hamlet*, the commanding power of the *Entführung* aria and the breathtaking brilliance of the Queen's aria from *Les Huguenots* are all among the high spots here, while the arias which Sutherland later recorded in her complete opera sets regularly bring performances just as fine – and often finer – than the later versions.

Sutherland, Joan (soprano), Luciano Pavarotti (tenor)

'*Love Duets*' (with National PO, Bonynge from VERDI: *La traviata; Otello; Aida* (with chorus). BELLINI: *La sonnambula.* DONIZETTI: *Linda di Chamounix.*

(M) *** Decca (ADD) 458 235-2.

This collection, recorded in the Kingsway Hall in 1976, offers a rare sample of Sutherland as Aida (*La fatale pietra ... O terra, addio* from Act IV), a role she sang only once on stage, well before her international career began; and with this and her sensitive impersonations of Desdemona, Violetta (generously represented) and the Bellini and Donizetti heroines, Sutherland might have been expected to steal first honours here. In fact, these are mainly duets to show off the tenor, and it is Pavarotti who runs away with the main glory, though both artists were plainly challenged to give their finest. The result, with excellent accompaniment, is among the most attractive and characterful duet recitals in the catalogue. The recording is admirably clear and well focused, and the sophistication of orchestral detail is striking in the *Otello* and *Aida* scenes which close the recital, with the singers given remarkable presence.

Tallis Scholars, Peter Phillips

'*Western Wind Masses*': SHEPPARD: *Mass, The Western Wynde.* TAVERNER: *Mass, Western Wynde.* TYE: *Mass, Western Wind.*

𝄞 *** Gimell CDGIM 027.

It was a splendid idea for Gimell to gather together the three key Mass settings which use the well-known source theme, the *Western Wynde*. The performances are as eloquent as we would expect from this source and they are beautifully recorded. Taverner's setting emerges as the most imaginative, but Tye comes pretty close. A most enterprising issue, which deserves support.

'*Live in Oxford*': OBRECHT: *Salve Regina.* JOSQUIN DESPREZ: *Gaude Virgo; Absalon fili mei.* TAVERNER: *Gaude plurium.* BYRD: *Tribus, Domine.* TALLIS: *O sacrum convivium.* MUNDY: *Adolescentulus sum ego; Vox Patris caelestis.*
*** Gimell CDGIM 998-2.

The fledgling Tallis Scholars gave their first concert, in 1973, in the Church of St Mary Magdalen, but have chosen the Chapel of Merton College for this, their twenty-fifth-anniversary programme. The beauty of its acoustic, resonant but unclouding, is ideal for their flowing style in this survey of fifteenth- and sixteenth-century masterpieces, ending with Mundy's spectacularly ambitious *Vox Patris caelestis*, with its vocal complexities confidently encompassed, especially by the soaring trebles.

Talvela, Martti (bass)

'*The Singers*' (Decca series): *Song Recital* (with Gage or Gothoni, piano): SCHUMANN: *12 Gedichte, Op. 35.* MUSSORGSKY: *Songs and Dances of Death;*

The Flea. RACHMANINOV: *Christ is Risen; Night is Mournful; Oh Never Sing to Me Again; Oh Stay My Love Forsake Me Not!*

(M) **(*) Decca (ADD) 467 903-2.

The Russian items were recorded in 1980 and find Martti Talvela's magnificent bass voice superbly caught. His Mussorgsky is dark and intense, immediate and involving – a singer with an operatic background gains enormously here – and at the time this was the finest version to appear since Boris Christoff's: no praise could be higher. The Rachmaninov is not quite so successful, as Talvela modifies his dark tones to suit the gentler lines of this music, and, as recorded, the voice acquires a plaintive quality, which is not as pleasing. However, it remains a commanding account. The Finnish bass is similarly rich and vibrant in the Schumann Lieder, recorded in 1969 and excellently accompanied by Irwin Gage. This is a very individual performance, striking in its depth. If heavier than classic accounts by Fischer-Dieskau, it is equally valid and certainly gives these wonderful songs another dimension. There is vivid sound throughout in this transfer, and this is one of the best in Decca's 'The Singers' series. Even if texts and translations (and photos) are available only by using a CD ROM drive, this must still be given a pretty strong recommendation.

Taverner Consort, Choir and Players, Andrew Parrott

'*The Christmas Album*' (Festive music from Europe and America): BILLINGS: *Methinks I See an Heav'nly Host; A Virgin Unspotted.* FOSTER: *While Shepherds Watched Their Flocks.* CEREROLS: *Serafin, quin con dulce harmonia.* Francisco DE VIDALES: *Los que fueren de buen gusto.* PRAETORIUS: *Magnificat super Angelus ad pastores.* MARC-ANTOINE CHARPENTIER: *In nativitatem Domini nostri Jesu Christi canticum.* PASCHA: *Gloria.* arr. GREATOREX: *Adeste fidelis.*

(M) *** Virgin 5 45155-2.

Another refreshing Christmas collection, which treads much unfamiliar territory. Opening and closing with jolly carols that sound almost like rustic drinking songs, from the New England composer William Billings – with the chorus giving their pronunciation an appropriate transatlantic twang – the concert moves from a bright baroque setting of 'While Shepherds Watched Their Flocks', a new tune, with Bachian trumpets, by John Foster (1762–1822) to a haunting *Gloria* by Edmund Pascha. This represents Slovakia; from France there is a charming Christmas sequence by Marc-Antoine Charpentier.

In between comes a gloriously sonorous *Magnificat* by Michael Praetorius and, at last something familiar, *Adeste fidelis*, arranged by Thomas Greatorex in a choral concerto grosso style. Best of all are the *Villancicos*, one by Joan Cererols from Catalonia,

one even jollier by the seventeenth-century Mexican Francisco de Vidales, which in their colour and vitality reflect the popular dance music of the time. Performances are as lively as they are stylish and the soloists are excellent. The 1991 recording, made at St John's at Hackney, London, has plenty of atmosphere and presence.

Tear, Robert (tenor)

'*English Baroque Recital*' (with Brown, violin, Heath, cello, Preston and Tilney, harpsichord continuo, ASMF, Marriner): HANDEL: *Look Down, Harmonious Saint; Meine Seele hört im Sehen; Süsse Stille.* ARNE: *Bacchus and Ariadne*: excerpts; *Fair Caelia Love Pretended*: excerpts. BOYCE: *Song of Momus to Mars.* JAMES HOOK: *The Lass of Richmond Hill.*

(B) *** Double Decca (ADD) 452 973-2 (2) (with HANDEL: *Acis and Galatea* ***).

Robert Tear's 1969 recital offers a rare Handel cantata and two of his German songs, followed by an even rarer and certainly delightful collection of music by his English successors. This may in essence be a scholarly compilation, but it is one which imparts its learning in the most painless way, including as it does the vigorous Boyce song and the original, bouncing setting of 'The Lass of Richmond Hill', beautifully pointed. The 'Harmonious Saint' of the Handel cantata is of course St Cecilia, while Arne too is in Italianate mood in *Bacchus and Ariadne* – until he ends with a galumphing final number with ripe horn parts – very English. Robert Tear is in excellent voice and the recording has all the atmospheric warmth one associates with Argo's recordings of the ASMF in St John's, Smith Square.

Tebaldi, Renata (soprano)

'*Voce d'Angelo*' (early recordings with Santa Cecilia Ac. O or SRO, Erede, or La Scala, Milan O, de Sabata): Arias and excerpts from: PUCCINI: *La Bohème* (with Hilde Gueden, Giacinti Prandelli, Fernando Corena); *Manon Lescaut; Tosca; Madama Butterfly* (with Giovanni Inghilleri). GIORDANO: *Andrea Chénier.* GOUNOD: *Faust.* VERDI: *Aida; Il trovatore; Requiem.*

☛ (BB) (***) Regis mono. RRC 1125.

A treasurable collection of key arias and scenes, recorded between 1949 and 1951, when Tebaldi's voice was at its freshest and most melting. They are taken mainly from her early Decca complete recordings of the key Puccini operas, although *Un bel dì vedremo*, like Gounod's Jewel Song and the lovely, simple performance of Verdi's *Tacea la notte placida*, comes from her first mono LP. *Ritorna vincitor* then shows her at her most commanding. The excerpts from the *Requiem* and Giordano's *Andrea Chénier*, conducted by Victor de Sabata, are recorded less satisfactorily, but are still well worth having.

'The Great Renata Tebaldi' (recordings made between 1949 and 1969): Arias and excerpts (with various artists, orchestras and conductors) from: PUCCINI: *Gianni Schicchi; Tosca; Suor Angelica; Il tabarro; La fanciulla del West; Turandot; La Bohème; Manon Lescaut; Madama Butterfly.* CATALANI: *La Wally.* PONCHIELLI: *La Gioconda.* CILEA: *Adriana Lecouvreur.* GIORDANO: *Andrea Chénier.* BOITO: *Mefistofele.* VERDI: *Aida; Il trovatore; La traviata; La forza del destino; Otello; Don Carlos; Un ballo in maschera.* LEHAR: *The Merry Widow: Vilja* (sung in Italian). ROSSINI: *La regata veneziana: Anzoleta avant la regata.*
(M) *** Decca mono/stereo 470 280-2 (2).

For I.M. during the years following the end of the Second World War, the discovery of Tebaldi was something of a revelation. He purchased her first mono LP, which was recorded by Decca, in 1949 and was immediately entranced by the sheer lyrical beauty of her voice. Two of the items on that LP (Verdi's *Ritorna vincitor* from *Aida* and *Tacea la notte placida* from *Il trovatore*) are used to open the second of the two discs of this set, and the vocal magic is immediately apparent. The fffr mono recording, made in the Victoria Hall, Geneva, still sounds pretty remarkable, and one feels that it was a pity that Decca chose not to assemble this collection in historical order, for the third item on disc 2 is an infinitely touching account of *Parigi o cara, noi lasceremo* from *La traviata*, with Gianni Poggi a remarkably sympathetic Alfredo. Then comes a famous aria from *La forza del destino* (*Ma pellegrina ed orfana ... Pace, pace, mio Dio!*) in which Tebaldi produces one of those exquisite sudden pianissimos in her upper range that was one of the frisson-making hallmarks of her vocal line. The scene from *Don Carlos*, with Nicolai Ghiaurov, conducted by Solti a decade later, follows soon afterwards, demonstrating that, under the right conductor, she could also rise to thrilling drama in Verdi.

But it was not for Verdi that she was most renowned. Her great contemporary, Maria Callas, could upstage her there, for she was a much greater stage actress. But in Puccini (especially) and comparable Italian bel canto roles Tebaldi was unsurpassed in the 1950s and 1960s, recording the principal roles more than once.

If her Mimì was unforgettable (touchingly remembered here in the Love scene from Act I of *La Bohème*, with Carlo Bergonzi, dating from 1959), she was also a delightful Lauretta, and *O mio babbino caro* (1962) opens the first disc ravishingly. The following *Vissi d'arte* (*Tosca*, 1959) is equally lovely. Other highlights include the key arias from *Suor Angelica, Manon Lescaut* and a splendid excerpt from *La fanciulla del West* (with Cornell MacNeil as Jack Rance). In *Turandot* she chose the lesser part of Liù,

and *Signore, ascolta, Tu che di gel sel cinta* is characteristically melting.

Her rather stiff acting meant that she was perhaps a less than ideal *Madama Butterfly*, but even so the Love scene from Act I (again with Bergonzi) is vocally spellbinding, and many other key arias from comparable non-Puccini repertoire are no less bewitching and certainly dramatic, notably the excerpts from *La Wally* and *La Gioconda* (which demonstrate her rich lower range), *Adriana Lecouvreur* and *Andrea Chénier*. She was fortunate that the Decca engineers recorded her voice with complete naturalness, as the current CD transfers (which are excellent) so uniformly show. This is not a set to play through all at once, for subtlety of characterization was not Tebaldi's strong suit; if it is dipped into judiciously, however, one is consistently seduced by Tebaldi's beauty of tone and simplicity of line.

'Grandi voci': Arias and excerpts from: PUCCINI: *Madama Butterfly; La Bohème* (with Carlo Bergonzi); *Turandot* (with Mario del Monaco); *Tosca; Gianni Schicchi; Suor Angelica; La fanciulla del West* (with Cornell MacNeil); *Manon Lescaut.* VERDI: *Aida; Otello* (with Luisa Ribacci); *La forza del destino.* CILEA: *Adriana Lecouvreur.* GIORDANO: *Andrea Chénier.* BOITO: *Mefistofele.* CATALANI: *La Wally.*
(M) *** Decca (ADD) (IMS) 440 408-2.

Those wanting a single-disc, stereo representation of Tebaldi's vocal art could hardly do better than this. It is good that her early mono complete sets of *La Bohème* and *Madama Butterfly* are now again available, and the selection here rightly concentrates on her stereo remakes of the key Puccini operas in the late 1950s, when the voice was still creamily fresh. *Vissi d'arte* (1959) is particularly beautiful. She could be thrilling in Verdi too, as the splendid *Ritorna vincitor!* vibrantly demonstrates, taken from Karajan's complete *Aida*, made in the same year. With a playing time of 75 minutes, this recital should disappoint no one, for the Decca recordings come up as vividly as ever.

Tebaldi, Renata (soprano), and Franco Corelli (tenor)

'Great Opera Duets' (with SRO, Guadagno) from: PUCCINI: *Manon Lescaut.* VERDI: *Aida.* CILEA: *Adriana Lecouvreur.* PONCHIELLI: *La Gioconda.* ZANDONAI: *Francesca da Rimini.*
(M) ** Decca Classic Recitals (ADD) 475 522-2.

This 1972 recital was rushed out on LP to coincide with appearances in London of the two singers. This was one of Tebaldi's last recordings and, while her voice is no longer in full bloom, it sounds surprisingly good, giving signs of strain only in the upper register. Corelli is as full-toned and gusty as ever, and the two give committed performances throughout –

the Love scene from *Manon Lescaut* especially persuasive. The longest except here is the Zandonai item, whose (nearly) 19 minutes took up one whole side of the original LP – an enjoyable example of rare verismo, if not top-class music. While the voices are caught vividly enough, the orchestra is surprisingly distant, at it was in its LP incarnation. The original notes, reproduced for this Classic Recitals release, are so small as to be almost indecipherable, but at least Tebaldi looks wonderfully glamorous on the cover.

Terfel, Bryn (bass-baritone), Malcolm Martineau (piano)

'*The Vagabond and Other English Songs*': VAUGHAN WILLIAMS: *Songs of Travel (The Vagabond; Let Beauty Awake; The Roadside Fire; Youth and Love; In Dreams; The Infinite Shining Heavens; Whither Must I Wander; Bright in the Ring of Words; I have Trod the Upward and the Downward Slope).* G. BUTTERWORTH: *Bredon Hill (Bredon Hill; Oh Fair Enough; When the Lad for Longing Sighs; On the Idle Hill of Summer; With Rue my Heart is Laden); The Shropshire Lad* (6 songs): *Loveliest of Trees; When I was One-and-twenty; Look not in my Eyes; Think no More, Lad; The Lads in their Hundreds; Is my Team Ploughing?* FINZI: *Let us Garlands Bring (Come Away, Death; Who is Sylvia?; Fear no More the Heat of the Sun; O Mistress Mine; It was a Lover and his Lass).* IRELAND: *Sea Fever; The Vagabond; The Bells of San Marie.*

⊝┳ ✿ **★★★** DG 445 946-2.

No other collection of English songs has ever quite matched this one in its depth, intensity and sheer beauty. Terfel, the great Welsh singer of his generation, here shows his deep affinity with the English repertory, demonstrating triumphantly in each of the twenty-eight songs that this neglected genre deserves to be treated in terms similar to those of the German Lied and the French mélodie. The Vaughan Williams songs are perhaps the best known, nine sharply characterized settings of Robert Louis Stevenson which, thanks to Terfel's searching expressiveness matched by Martineau's inspired accompaniments, reveal depths of emotion hardly suspected.

The five Shakespeare settings by Finzi are just as memorable in their contrasted ways, five of the best-known lyrics from the plays that have been set countless times but which here are given new perspectives, thanks both to the composer and to the singer. The eleven Butterworth settings of Housman are among the finest inspirations of this short-lived composer, and it is good to have three sterling Ireland settings of Masefield, including the ever-popular 'Sea Fever', which with Terfel emerges fresh and new. The singer's extreme range of tone and dynamic, down to the most delicate, firmly supported half-tones, is astonishing, adding intensity to one of the most felicitous song-recital records in years. The warm acoustic of the Henry Wood Hall gives a glow both to the voice and to the piano.

'*Impressions*' (with (i) E. Bar. Soloists, Gardiner; (ii) Martineau, piano; (iii) Philh. O, Sinopoli; (iv) BPO, Abbado): (i) MOZART: *Le nozze di Figaro: Se vuol ballare; Non più andrai; Aprite un po' quegli occhi.* (ii) SCHUBERT: *Litanei auf das Fest Allerseelen; Die Forelle; An die Musik; Erlkönig.* (iii) MAHLER: *Kindertotenlieder.* (ii) VAUGHAN WILLIAMS: *The Vagabond; The Roadside Fire.* (iv) WAGNER: *Die Meistersinger: Wie duftet doch der Flieder. Tannhäuser: O! du mein holder Abendstern.*

★★★ DG 449 190-2.

Ranging over the recordings made for DG up to his English song disc, this sampler gives a formidable idea of this brilliant young singer's powers, very well chosen not just from his solo discs but from complete opera sets and discs with orchestra.

Tomlinson, John (bass)

Opera arias and scenes (with Geoffrey Mitchell Ch., Philh. O, Parry) from HANDEL: *Acis and Galatea; Samson.* MOZART: *Abduction from the Seraglio* (with Williams, Banks). VERDI: *Simon Boccanegra; Ernani.* BORODIN: *Prince Igor.* DARGOMIZHSKY: *Rusalka.* SULLIVAN: *The Mikado; The Pirates of Penzance.* OFFENBACH: *Geneviève de Brabant* (with Shore). MUSSORGSKY: *Mephistopheles: Song of the Flea.* LEHMANN: *In a Persian Garden: Myself when Young.*

(M) **★★★** Chan. 3044.

The versatility of John Tomlinson is breathtaking, and here he tackles the widest range of bass arias. It adds to the characterful tang and sparkle of the performances that all seventeen items are in English on one of the 'Opera in English' discs sponsored by the Peter Moores Foundation. One might have expected this singing actor, today's greatest Wotan, to be attuned to Verdi and the Russians, with an attractive aria from Dargomizhsky's *Rusalka* in addition to the well-known Mussorgsky and Borodin items, but he is just as stylish in Handel (both comic and heroic), as well as in Mozart (a characterful Osmin in three items from *Seraglio*). He is full of fun in Offenbach (the Gendarmes' duet from *Geneviève de Brabant* with Andrew Shore) and G. & S. (the Policeman's song from *The Pirates of Penzance*) winningly sung in a bluff northern accent. There is brilliant accompaniment under David Parry.

'*German Operatic Arias*' (sung in English, with LPO or Philh. O, Parry) from: MOZART: *The Abduction from the Seraglio; The Magic Flute.* BEETHOVEN: *Fidelio.* WEBER: *Der Freischütz.* WAGNER: *The Rheingold; The Flying Dutchman; The Mastersingers of Nuremberg.* R. STRAUSS: *Der Rosenkavalier.* LORTZING: *The Armourer.*

(M) **★★★** Chan. 3073.

Opening with great gusto in an exhilarating account of Osmin's 'vengeance' aria, John Tomlinson, in splendid voice, shows how effective opera in English can be, sung by a master of characterization with a rich voice. Whether in the deep sonorities of Sarastro's Prayer from *The Magic Flute*, as Caspar in *Der Freischütz*, as an unforgettable Wotan in the Rainbow Bridge sequence from *Rheingold* (to gorgeous sound from the LPO); as Hans Sachs in *Mastersingers* or a highly individual Baron Ochs in *Rosenkavalier*, Tomlinson's projection is matched by the resonant quality of the singing, and only occasionally does a minor excess of vibrato have any adverse effect on a firmly supported vocal line. There is always fine orchestral support from David Parry. The recordings (of typical Chandos excellence) were made at Blackheath Halls between 1998 and 2001. A most enjoyable collection, with Hans Stadlinger's 'I Used to be Young with a Fine Head of Hair' from Lortzing's *Der Waffenschmied* (*The Armourer*) included as a final jest; for, as can be seen by the photographs, there is nothing sparse about Tomlinson's current mop!

Tonus Peregrinus, Anthony Pitts

'*The Naxos Book of Carols*' (An Advent Sequence in Music; with Nicholas Chalmers, organ): The Hope: *O Come, O Come Emmanuel; Of the Father's Heart Begotten.* TUTTIETT: *O Quickly Come.* ANON.: *Verbum Patris umanatur.* WESLEY: *Lo! He comes.* The Message: TRAD.: *The Holly and the Ivy; Lo There is a Rose is Blooming; Alleluya – A New Work; Ding! Dong! Merrily on High; While Shepherds Watched; Song of Angels.* MENDELSSOHN: *Hark the Herald Angels Sing.* The Baby: GRUBER: *Silent Night.* KIRKPATRICK: *Away in a Manger.* Czech TRAD.: *Baby Jesus, Hush! Now Sleep. O Little Town of Bethlehem; Jesus, the Very Thought is Sweet; O Come All Ye Faithful. The King of Kings: Personet hodie; In dulci jubilo; Good King Wenceslas.* HOPKINS: *We Three Kings.* TRAD.: *I Saw Three Ships.* MONTGOMERY: *Hail to the Lord's Anointed.*
(BB) ★★(★) Naxos 8.557330.

The Naxos Book of Carols offers an enterprising new approach to familiar Christmas music. The 24 carols are presented in four on-going sequences, and all the arrangements were especially commissioned, often (though not always) introducing new harmonies and sensuous, drifting dissonances, although Laurence Tuttiett's syncopated 'O Quickly Come' is newly composed in a lively 7/8 metre. The arrangement of 'Silent Night' is characteristic, and this is the item to sample if you are in doubt about such an approach to familar repertoire. Tonus Peregrinus sing freshly and blend beautifully, and they are also very pleasingly recorded, so that it is easy to be seduced by Anthony Pitts' new look. 'Good King Wenceslas', for instance, is introduced strikingly like a peal of bells and demonstrates the fine organ contribution from

Nicholas Chalmers. The closing sequence too is particularly successful. The disc is excellently documented with full texts. Well worth exploring.

Trio Sonnerie, with Nancy Argenta (soprano)

'*A Portrait of Love*': MARAIS: *The Bells of St Geneviève du Mont, Paris.* CLERAMBAULT: *L'Amour piqué par une Abeille (Cupid Stung by a Bee).* MONTECLAIR: *Cantata: La Mort de Didon* (both with Nancy Argenta). FRANÇOIS COUPERIN: *Pièces de clavecin*, 9th Concert: *Ritratto dell'amore;* 13th Ordre: *Les Follies françoises.*
(BB) ★★(★) HM HCX 3957081.

The collection from the Trio Sonnerie (Monica Huggett, Sarah Cunningham and Mitzi Meyerson) engagingly dwells on the theme of 'Love', although it opens with Marais's extended chaconne picturing a peal of bells (no doubt for a wedding). His other contribution is an evocative depiction of a village festival, with a central musette solo from the local shepherd. Then follows a charming Clérambault cantata, *Cupid Stung by a Bee*, delightfully sung by Nancy Argenta, which would have been even more enjoyable with text and translation provided. Couperin's suite, *A Portrait of Love*, in which the amorous soloist is a violin (the estimable Monica Huggett), is followed by *The French Follies*, a further group of vignettes for harpsichord, with sometimes bizarre if appropriate titles (*La Virginité, L'Ardeur, La Fidelité* and so on) not always obviously related to the music itself. But they are delightfully played by Mitzi Meyerson. Finally, Nancy Argenta is dramatically and lyrically persuasive in Montéclair's *Death of Dido*, a florid setting which ends very suddenly and which does not match Purcell's justly more famous version. Again no text and translation are provided, which earns this reissue less than full marks, even though it is well recorded.

Villazon, Rolando (tenor), with Munich Radio Symphony Orchestra, Marcello Viotti

'Italian Opera Arias' from: CILEA: *L'Arlesiana.* DONIZETTI: *Il duca d'Alba; L'elisir d'amore; Lucia di Lammermoor; Mascagni: L'amico Fritz; Nerone.* PUCCINI: *La Bohème; Tosca.* VERDI: *Don Carlo; I Lombardi; Macbeth; Rigoletto; La traviata.*
★★★ Virgin 5 45626-2.

The search for a successor to the Three Tenors goes on, with the young Mexican, Rolando Villazon, one of the most promising candidates. EMI on its Virgin label issues this impressive recital disc, nicely timed to follow up his brilliant success, taking the title-role in *The Tales of Hoffmann* at Covent Garden. Well recorded, Villazon reveals an appealingly clear, firm voice, open and unstrained, even if at present the tonal range could be wider. Happily, he is a natural artist, phrasing imaginatively with finely shaded legato, whether in favourite arias by Donizetti, Verdi and Puccini (with Rodolfo's *Che gelida manina* freshly characterful) or in welcome rarities by Mascagni and Cilea, as well as Verdi and Donizetti. The selection concentrates on soulful arias rather than heroic ones, which makes the ringing bravura outbursts of Alfredo's *De'miei bollenti spiriti* from *La traviata* and the Duke's *La donna è mobile* from *Rigoletto* the more welcome in contrast.

Walker, Sarah (mezzo-soprano)

'*Blah, Blah, Blah*' (with Vignoles, piano, in cabaret at the Wigmore Hall): GERSHWIN: *Blah, Blah, Blah; They All Laughed; Three Times a Day; Boy, What Love has Done to me.* PORTER: *Tale of the Oyster; Where O Where?.* BERNSTEIN: *Who am I?* NICHOLAS: *Place Settings; Usherette's Blues.* DRING: *Song of a Nightclub Proprietress.* BOLCOM: *Lime Jello, Marshmallow, Cottage-cheese Surprise.* FLANDERS AND SWANN: *A Word in My Ear.* LEHMANN: *There are Fairies at the Bottom of my Garden.* WRIGHT: *Transatlantic Lullaby.* BAKER: *Someone is Sending me Flowers.* SCHOENBERG: *3 Brettl Lieder.*
*** Hyp. CDA 66289.

Recorded live at the Wigmore Hall in London, Sarah Walker's recital of trifles is one of the happiest records you could wish to find, as well as one of the funniest. Her comic timing is masterly in such delectable revue numbers as Cole Porter's 'Tale of the Oyster' or William Bolcom's culinary patter-song, 'Lime Jello, Marshmallow, Cottage-cheese Surprise'. Perhaps surprisingly, she does such a song as 'There are Fairies at the Bottom of my Garden' straight, restoring its touching quality in defiance of Beatrice Lillie's classic send-up.

Also, by treating a popular number such as 'Transatlantic Lullaby' as a serious song, she not only underlines purely musical qualities but touches a deeper vein than one might expect in a cabaret sequence. Three of Schoenberg's *Brettl Lieder*, in deft English translations by Michael Irwin, are sung just as delightfully – and more provocatively than the German versions which were recorded by Jill Gomez in her delectable 'Cabaret Classics' recital.

The title, *Blah, Blah, Blah*, comes from the opening number, a witty concoction by George Gershwin with words by his brother, Ira, which reduces the popular love-song lyrics to the necessary – and predictable – rhymes. Roger Vignoles, always an understanding accompanist, here excels himself with playing of flair and brilliance, exuberantly encompassing every popular idiom in turn. The recording, unlike most made at the Wigmore Hall, captures some of the bloom of its acoustic; but that means that the voice is set slightly at a distance. Texts are provided but, with such clear diction from the singer, they are needed only occasionally.

Walker, Sarah (mezzo-soprano), Thomas Allen (baritone)

'*Dreams and Fancies*' (favourite English songs) with Vignoles, piano: IRELAND: *If There were Dreams to Sell.* DELIUS: *Twilight Fancies.* ARMSTRONG GIBBS: *Silver; Five Eyes.* VAUGHAN WILLIAMS: *Silent Noon; The water Mill.* WARLOCK: *The Fox; Jillian of Berry; The first Mercy; The Night.* SULLIVAN: *Orpheus with his Lute.* HOWELLS: *King David; Gavotte; Come Sing and Dance; The Little Road to Bethlehem.* STANFORD: *The Monkey's Carol.* BRIDGE: *Isobel.* CLARKE: *The Seal Man; The Aspidistra.* HAVELOCK NELSON: *Dirty Work.* HOIBY: *Jabberwocky.* QUILTER: *Now Sleeps the Crimson Petal.* GURNEY: *Sleep.* DUNHILL: *The Cloths of Heaven.*
(M) *** CRD CRD 3473.

A well-designed and delightful programme, and it is good to see the Roger Quilter favourite, 'Now Sleeps the Crimson Petal', back in favour alongside both the familiar and unfamilar items included here. Dunhill's 'The Cloths of Heaven', too, leaves the listener wanting more. The secret of a miscellaneous (72 minutes) recital like this is for each song to lead naturally into the next, and that is what happens here, while the listener relaxes and enjoys each contrasted setting as it flows by. Sarah Walker is in inspired form and is very well accompanied.

'*The Sea*' (with Vignoles, piano): IRELAND: *Sea Fever.* HAYDN: *Mermaid's Song; Sailor's Song.* DIBDIN: *Tom Bowling.* WALTON: *Song for the Lord Mayor's Table; Wapping Old Stairs.* WOLF: *Seemanns Abschied.* FAURE: *Les Berceaux; Au cimetière; L'horizon chimerique.* SCHUBERT: *Lied eines Schiffers an die Dioskuren.* BORODIN: *The Sea; The Sea Princess.* DEBUSSY: *Proses lyriques: De grève.* IVES: *Swimmers.* SCHUMANN: *Die Meersee.* BERLIOZ: *Les Nuits d'été: L'Ile inconnue.* MENDELSSOHN: *Wasserfahrt.* BRAHMS: *Die Meere.* TRAD.: *The Mermaid.* Arr. BRITTEN: *Sail on, Sail on.*
❀ *** Hyp. CDA 66165.

With Roger Vignoles as master of ceremonies in a brilliantly devised programme, ranging wide, this twin-headed recital celebrating 'The Sea' is a delight from beginning to end. Two outstandingly characterful singers are mutually challenged to their very finest form, whether in solo songs or duets. As sample, try the setting of the sea-song 'The Mermaid', brilliantly arranged by Vignoles, with hilarious key-switches on the comic quotations from 'Rule Britannia'. Excellent recording.

Wedding music

'*The World of Wedding Music*': WAGNER: *Lohengrin: Wedding March.* BACH: *Suite No. 3: Air* (Stephen Cleobury). CLARKE: *Prince of Denmark's March (Trumpet Voluntary)*. PURCELL: *Trumpet Tune* (Simon Preston). BACH/GOUNOD: *Ave Maria* (Kiri Te Kanawa). SCHUBERT: *Ave Maria*. MOZART: *Alleluja* (Leontyne Price). *Vespers: Laudate dominum* (Felicity Palmer). KARG-ELERT: *Marche triomphale: Nun danket alle Gott.* BRAHMS: *Chorale prelude: Es ist ein Ros entsprungen.* WIDOR: *Symphony No. 5: Toccata.* MENDELSSOHN: *Midsummer Night's Dream: Wedding March* (Peter Hurford). WALFORD DAVIES: *God be in my Head.* Hymn: *The Lord's my Shepherd* (Huddersfield Choral Soc., Morris). STAINER: *Love Divine.* Hymn: *Praise my Soul, the King of Heaven* (King's College Ch., Cleobury). BACH: *Cantata No. 147: Jesu, Joy of Man's Desiring.* Hymn: *Lead us, Heavenly Father, Lead us* (St John's College Ch., Guest). HANDEL: *Samson: Let the Bright Seraphim* (Joan Sutherland).

(B) ** Decca (ADD) 436 402-2.

An inexpensive present for any bride-to-be, with many traditional suggestions, well played and sung, though it would have been better to have omitted the Karg-Elert *Marche triomphale* in favour of Handel's *Arrival of the Queen of Sheba*, to which many a contemporary bride trips down the aisle. Good sound.

Westminster Cathedral Choir, David Hill

'*Treasures of the Spanish Renaissance*': GUERRERO: *Surge propera amica mea; O altitudo divitiarum; O Domine Jesu Christe; O sacrum convivium; Ave, Virgo sanctissima; Regina coeli laetare.* LOBO: *Versa est in luctum; Ave Maria; O quam suavis es, Domine.* VIVANCO: *Magnificat octavi toni.*
*** Hyp. CDA 66168.

This immensely valuable collection reminds us vividly that Tomás Luis de Victoria was not the only master of church music in Renaissance Spain. Francisco Guerrero is generously represented here, and the spacious serenity of his polyphonic writing (for four, six and, in *Regina coeli laetare*, eight parts) creates the most beautiful sounds. A criticism might be made that tempi throughout this collection, which also includes fine music by Alonso Lobo and a superb eight-part *Magnificat* by Sebastian de Vivanco, are too measured, but the tension is held well, and David Hill is obviously concerned to convey the breadth of the writing. The singing is gloriously firm, with the long melismatic lines admirably controlled. Discreet accompaniments (using Renaissance double harp, bass dulcian and organ) do not affect the essentially a cappella nature of the performances. The Westminster Cathedral acoustic means the choral tone is richly upholstered, but the focus is always firm and clear.

Westminster Cathedral Choir, James O'Donnell

'*Masterpieces of Mexican Polyphony*': FRANCO: *Salve regina.* PADILLA: *Deus in adiutorium; Mirabilia testimonium; Lamentation for Maundy Thursday; Salve Regina.* CAPILLAS: *Dis nobis, Maria; Magnificat.* SALAZAR: *O sacrum convivium.*
*** Hyp. CDA 66330.

The Westminster Choir under James O'Donnell are finding their way into hitherto unexplored Latin vocal repertoire – and what vocal impact it has! These musicians were employed in the new cathedrals when Spain colonized Mexico; only Capillas was native-born (though of Spanish descent). Padilla shows he had brought over a powerful Renaissance inheritance with him and uses double choir interplay to spectacularly resonant effect. Not all the other music is as ambitious as this, but there is a devotional concentration of feeling which illuminates even the simpler settings. The singing has the body and fervour this music needs, and the choir is splendidly recorded.

'*Masterpieces of Portuguese Polyphony*': CARDOSO: *Lamentations for Maundy Thursday; Non mortui; Sitvit anima mea; Mulier quae erat; Tulerunt lapides; Nos autem gloriosi.* REBELO: *Panis angelicus.* DE CRISTO: *3 Christmas Responsories; Magnificat a 8; Ave Maria a 8; Alma redemptoris mater; O maris stella; O crux venerabilis; Sanctissima quinque martires; Lachrimans sitivit; De profundis.*
*** Hyp. CDA 66512.

With the help of the Tallis Scholars we have already discovered Manuel Cardoso and the unique character of Portuguese Renaissance music. The present collection duplicates four of the motets on the Tallis Scholars' CD (see our main volume), but the Westminster performances are slightly more robust and add to their character. The *Lamentations for Maundy Thursday* show the composer at his most imaginatively expressive, 'a resplendent example of his chromatic serenity', as Ivan Moody, the writer of the excellent notes on this CD, aptly puts it.

The music of Cardoso's contemporary, Pedro de Cristo (*c.* 1550–1618) is hardly less individual. His *Magnificat a 8* for two choirs is particularly arresting, as is the much simpler *O magnum mysterium*, while the *Sanctissimi quinque martires* (celebrating five Franciscans who were killed in 1220 while attempting to convert Moroccan Muslims) has a radiant, flowing intensity. Rebelo's *Panis angelicus* is rich in its harmonic feeling, and Fernandez's *Alma redemptoris mater* ends the programme in a mood of quiet contemplation.

'*Adeste fidelis*' (with Ian Simcock): WADE: *O Come, All Ye Faithful*. TRAD.: *Gabriel's Message; O Come, O Come Emanuel; Ding Dong! Merrily on High; A Maiden Most Gentle; I Wonder as I Wander; O Little Town of Bethlehem; In dulci jubilo; The Holly and the Ivy*. GAUNTLETT: *Once in Royal David's City*. DARKE: *In the Bleak Midwinter*. CORNELIUS: *The Three Kings*. PETRUS: *Of the Father's Love Begotten*. KIRKPATRICK: *Away in a Manger*. WARLOCK: *Bethlehem Down*. HADLEY: *I Sing of a Maiden*. GRUBER: *Silent night*. HOWELLS: *Sing Lullaby*. TAVENER: *The Lamb*. PARRY: *Welcome Yule*. MENDELSSOHN: *Hark! The Herald Angels Sing*. *** Hyp. CDA 66668.

An extremely well-sung traditional carol collection. Although many of the arrangers are distinguished names, the arrangements of traditional carols are essentially simple, and the concert makes a great appeal by the quality of the singing and the beautiful digital recording, with the choir perfectly focused and realistically set back just at the right distance within the cathedral acoustic. The programme is spiced with one or two attractive modern settings, notably Patrick Hadley's ravishing 'I Sing of a Maiden' and John Tavener's familiar and highly individual carol, 'The Lamb'.

'*Favourite Motets from Westminster Cathedral*': MENDELSSOHN: *Ave Maria; Hymn of Praise: I Waited for the Lord*. BACH: *Cantata No. 147: Jesu, Joy of Man's Desiring*. FRANCK: *Panis angelicus*. MAWBY: *Ave verum corpus*. ROSSINI: *O salutaris hostia*. HARRIS: *Faire is the Heaven*. HOLST: *Ave Maria; Nunc dimittis*. GOUNOD: *Ave Maria*. FAURÉ: *Maria Mater gratiae*. ELGAR: *Ave verum corpus*. MOZART: *Ave verum corpus*. GRIEG: *Ave maris stella*. DE SEVERAC: *Tantum ergo*. VILLETTE: *Hymne à la Vierge*. SCHUBERT: *The Lord is my Shepherd*. *** Hyp. CDA 66669.

The Westminster Cathedral Choir is a traditional men's and boys' choir of the highest calibre. The treble line is particularly rich, and this is essentially a satisfyingly full-throated concert, although there is no lack of dynamic nuance, and phrasing always flows naturally and musically. Franck's *Panis angelicus*, which gives the collection its sobriquet, is splendidly ripe, and other favourites like Bach's 'Jesu, Joy of Man's Desiring' and Mozart's *Ave verum* are most satisfyingly done.

Elgar's *Ave verum* too is a highlight, and Schubert's lovely setting of 'The Lord is my Shepherd' is very successful in its English version. Among the novelties, De Séverac's *Tantum ergo* and the touching *Hymne à la Vierge* of Pierre Villette stand out, and the concert ends with a memorable account of Holst's setting of the *Nunc dimittis*, which opens

ethereally and then soars into the heavens: the trebles are superbly ardent at the climax. The recording is outstandingly full, and the cathedral ambience is caught without too much blurring.

Worcester Cathedral Choir, Donald Hunt

'*Joy to the World*' (A Selection from the Novello Book of Carols; with Worcester Festival Choral Society & Adrian Partington, organ): HOLFORD: *Joy to the World*. TRAD. CATALAN: *Song of the Birds; What Shall we Give to the Child?; Mary, Mother of God's Dear Child*. TRAD.: *Ding Dong! Merrily on High; Sans Day Carol; King Jesus Hath a Garden; Hush you my Baby; In the Bleak Midwinter; God Rest you Merry Gentlemen; Il est né, le Divin Enfant; . GAUNTLETT: *Once in Royal David's City*. Arr. HUMPHRIS: *Yorkshire Wassail; The Twelve Days of Christmas*. Arr. WELLS: *A Gallery Carol*. CORP: *Susanni*. WEIR: *Illuminare, Jerusalem*. THURLOW: *All and Some*. MENDELSSOHN: *Hark the Herald Angels Sing*. KIRKPATRICK: *Away in a Manger*. STAINER: *The First Nowell*.

(BB) *** Hyp. Helios CDH 55161.

This is a first-class traditional collection, including many favourites, but leavened with memorable French, Catalan and German repertoire, plus some ear-tweaking modern novelties by Ronald Corp, Judith Weir, and Jeremy Thurlow's attractive 'All and Some', setting fifteenth-century words. Most of the other (excellent) arrangements are by William Llewellyn, who compiled the Novello Book of Carols from which this entire concert is derived, but those by Ian Humphris (especially the exuberant 'Yorkshire Wassail', which was originally discovered by Vaughan Williams) and Robin Wells also stand out. Splendid singing throughout and typically real and well-balanced Hyperion sound. A genuine bargain (with full texts).

Wunderlich, Fritz (tenor)

'*Great Voice*': Arias and excerpts from: MOZART: *Die Zauberflöte; Die Entführung aus dem Serail*. VERDI: *La traviata* (with Hilde Gueden); *Rigoletto* (with Erika Köth); *Don Carlos* (with Hermann Prey). TCHAIKOVSKY: *Eugene Onegin*. LORTZING: *Zar und Zimmermann; Der Waffenschmied*. ROSSINI: *Il barbiere di Siviglia*. PUCCINI: *La Bohème* (with Hermann Prey). *Tosca*. Lieder: SCHUBERT: *Heidenröslein*. BEETHOVEN: *Ich liebe dich*. TRAD.: *Funiculì-funiculà; Ein Lied geht um die Welt* (with R. Lamy Ch.).

(B) *** DG Classikon (ADD) 431 110-2.

Here is 70 minutes of gloriously heady tenor singing from one of the golden voices of the 1960s. Mozart's *Dies Bildnis* makes a ravishing opener, and *Hier soll ich dich denn sehen* from *Die Entführung* is equally beautiful. Then come two sparkling excerpts from *La traviata* with Hilde Gueden and some memorable Tchaikovsky, like all the Italian repertoire, sung in German. The Rossini excerpt is wonderfully crisp and stylish.

Wunderlich is joined by the charming Erika Köth in *Rigoletto* and by Hermann Prey for the rousing *Don Carlos* duet (*Sie ist verloren ... Er ist's! Carlos!*) and the excerpt from *Bohème*. Last in the operatic group comes the most famous *Tosca* aria, *Und es blitzen die Sterne* (not too difficult to identify in Italian) sung without excessive histrionics. The Schubert and Beethoven Lieder are lovely and, if the two final popular songs (with chorus) bring more fervour than they deserve, one can revel in everything else. Excellent recording throughout. It is a pity there are no translations or notes, but with singing like this one can manage without them. A splendid bargain.

DOCUMENTARIES

Beethoven; Wagner

BBC Documentaries in the Great Composer series. Narrated by Kenneth Branagh, with artists and orchestras including: Ashkenazy; Lindsay Quartet; Chicago Symphony Orchestra, Solti; Chamber Orchestra England, Harnoncourt; Berlin State Opera Orchestra, Barenboim; Munich State Opera Orchestra, Mehta; Prague Symphony Orchestra, Norrington. Video Directors Jill Marshall, Kriss Rusmanis.

*** Warner Music Vision/NVC Arts **DVD** 0927-42871-2.

These two-hour-long features, packaged on a single DVD, crisply and efficiently tell the life-stories of Beethoven and Wagner with the help not only of the artists mentioned above, each performing relevant passages from the composers' works, but of a whole range of experts and authorities who irritatingly are not identified. The visual illustrations for each sequence are well chosen and atmospheric, often very illuminating, as when one is taken to the Beethovenhaus in Bonn where the composer was born (now a place of pilgrimage) or the staircase of Wagner's house at Triebchen in Switzerland, where musicians gathered to give the first informal performance of the *Siegfried Idyll* composed for his wife, Cosima, after the birth of their son, Siegfried. One might occasionally quarrel with the proportion of each film given over to particular works – as for example the rather paltry treatment of *Meistersinger* in the Wagner film – but the commendable thing is how much has been included, not how much has been left out, even if the Wagner film concentrates rather obsessively on the composer's anti-Semitism.

Brendel, Alfred (piano)

Alfred Brendel in Portrait: Documentary – Man and Mask. Produced by Emma Chrichton-Miller & Mark Kidel. Profile, conversation with Sir Simon Rattle, poetry-reading and recital: HAYDN: *Piano Sonata in E flat, Hob XVI/49.* MOZART: *Piano Sonata in C min., K.457.* SCHUBERT: *Impromptu No. 3 in G flat, D.899.*

*** BBC Opus Arte **DVD** OA 0811D (2).

This 70-minute portrait of Brendel, directed for television by Mark Kidel, takes the great pianist to many of the haunts of his early life, as well as showing him relaxing at home in Hampstead. As he wrily observes at the very start, he had none of the assets usually needed for a great musical career: he was not a child prodigy, he was not Jewish, he was not East European, his parents were unmusical, and he is not a good sight-reader. He speaks of his parents, life in Vienna as a student, his love of art and the world of ideas. His geniality, culture and sophistication shine through, together with an engaging, self-deprecating humour: 'I was not a good sight-reader, nor a virtuoso – in fact I don't know how I made it.'

One of his earliest musical memories is of playing records of Jan Kiepura in operetta on a wind-up gramophone to entertain the guests at the hotel his father managed. Later in Zagreb, where Alfred lived between the ages of five and thirteen, his father was the manager of a cinema, which took him in other directions than music, towards painting, among other things.

His first recital, in Graz in 1948, received glowing notices, when he concentrated on works with fugues, including a sonata of his own that boasted a double-fugue. Such revelations are amplified by the separate half-hour conversation Brendel has with Sir Simon Rattle on the subject of the Beethoven piano concertos, offering fascinating revelations from both pianist and conductor. We hear him accompanying Matthias Goerne in Schubert, playing Schubert, talking about primitive art from New Guinea and rehearsing a Mozart piano quartet with his son, Adrian. He also reads some of his own poetry in German, which strike a rather grim note of humour, while on the second disc comes a recital recorded at the Snape Maltings, crowning this revealing issue with masterly performances of three of Brendel's favourite works. In short, an unobtrusively shot film that brings us closer to a notoriously (or should one not say, famously) private person, a joy to look at and to listen to!

Concours d'une Reine

Le Concours d'une Reine (A Queen's Competition) 1951–2001. (Documentary by Michel Stockhem, Benoît Vietinck.)

*** Cypres **DVD** CYP1101.

This absorbing and fascinating documentary brings some invaluable footage of Le Concours Reine Elizabeth, one of the major international competitions. There are glimpses of the 1937 performance, in which David Oistrakh triumphed, and the commentary throughout is of unfailing interest. Marcel Poot, Arthur Grumiaux and other distinguished musicians have much to say about music competitions that is both perceptive and humane, and we see something of the queen herself, who studied with Ysaÿe, taking a keen interest in the young artists. In addition to the violin, there is, of course, a piano competition and, recently added, a vocal one. Some tantalizing glimpses of the final concerts engage the viewer almost as much as if they were going on now.

There is, incidentally, an accompanying 12-CD set (Cypres CYP 9612): its material is too diverse and wide-ranging even to list! It includes Leonid Kogan playing the cadenza of the Paganini *Concerto No. 1 in D major* in 1951 (otherwise all the repertoire is complete) and some rarer material from the same decade: Jaime Laredo plays the Milhaud *Concert Royal*, Op. 373, not otherwise available on CD, and Julian Sitkovetsky (father of Dmitry) the Ysaÿe *Sixth Sonata*.

When the competition was broadened in 1952 to include the piano, Leon Fleischer was the winner with an impressive Brahms *D minor Concerto* (with Franz André conducting the Belgian Orchestre National). The Belgian composer Marcel Poot, for long the chairman of the competition, is represented by a *Piano Concerto*, heard in the late Malcolm Frager's 1960 performance, again with Franz André.

There are many mouth-watering opportunities to hear and see artists now famous at the early stages of their careers: Ashkenazy, the 19-year-old first-prize winner in 1956 in the Liszt *E flat Concerto*, the 20-year-old Gidon Kremer (ranked third in 1967) playing Schumann, and Mitsuko Uchida, also 20 years of age, playing the Beethoven *C minor Concerto* – she was ranked tenth in 1968!

Some will feel that the 12-CD set is too much of a good thing and too substantial an outlay, even at its competitive price. But the DVD is extraordinarily fascinating and involving – and often quite moving. Strongly recommended. The languages used are Dutch and French, with subtitles in English, German and Spanish.

Fonteyn, Margot

Margot Fonteyn – A Portrait. Documentary produced and directed by Particia Foy (with Frederick Ashton, Ida Bromley, Robert Gottlieb, Nicola Kathak, Andrey King, Robert Helpmann, Rudolf Nureyev, Ninette de Valois).
*** Arthaus **DVD** 100 092.

Margot Fonteyn dominated the ballet scene in Britain for more than 40 years, and she capped her career in 1961 by creating her legendary partnership with Rudolph Nureyev. Here in 1989, only two years before her death, she tells her life story. Not only was she willing to talk about the tragic death of her huband, but she also tells us about the background to her long career, and there are contributions from

most of those who played an important part in it. With plenty of clips, including legendary archive material, this will be an essential purchase for anyone interested in ballet.

Great Composers: Mahler, Puccini, Tchaikovsky

BBC Documentaries narrated by Kenneth Branagh, featuring various artists and orchestras (with biographical amd critical commentaries). Executive Director: Kriss Rusmanis.

MAHLER: Filmed in Prague, Budapest and Vienna. Director: Kriss Rusmanis. Includes excerpts from *Symphonies Nos. 1–3, 5 & 9; Das Lied von der Erde; Des Knaben Wunderhorn; Lieder eines fahrenden Gesellen & Kindertotenlieder* (with Charlotte Hellekant, Thomas Hampson, BBC SO, Sir Georg Solti).

PUCCINI: Filmed in Italy. Director Chris Hunt/Iambic. Includes excerpts from: *Manon Lescaut; La Bohème; Tosca; Madama Butterfly; La fanciulla del West; Il tabarro; Turandot* (with José Cura, Leontina Vaduva, Julia Migenes, BBC PO, Richard Buckley).

TCHAIKOVSKY: Filmed in Russia and America. Director: Simon Broughton. Includes excerpts from: *Symphonies Nos. 2, 4–6; The Voyevoda; Piano Concerto No. 1* (with Mikhail Rudy); *Violin Concerto* (with Maxim Vengerov); *Ballet Music; Eugene Onegin, Queen of Spades* (with St Petersburg PO, Yuri Temirkanov).
*** Warner NVC Arts **DVD** 0927-43538-2.

This group of three television portraits, taken from the BBC's *Great Composers* series, brings out the parallels between these three musical geniuses, all three of them high neurotics who translated their inner problems into music of overwhelming emotional thrust. The approach with three different television directors is helpfully direct, linking the careers in outline to the principal works, including interviews with the artists involved as well as various scholarly authorities.

The works chosen for coverage in the Tchaikovsky portrait are fairly predictable, with the exception of the symphonic ballad *Voyevoda*, written after Mme von Meck had put an end to their long relationship by correspondence: as David Brown puts it, containing 'some of his most ferocious and dissonant music'. The choice of works in the Puccini and Mahler portraits is less complicated, when the majority of Puccini's operas and of Mahler's symphonies and song-cycles can readily be included. In Chris Hunt's evocative Puccini film it is particularly effective to have interviews with some of the Torre del Lago villagers who actually remembered Puccini, and who could characterize him with his foibles. Puccini's granddaughter is also a valuable contributor, now custodian of the Puccini museum in Torre del Lago. The evocative shots of the composer's haunts and homes are nicely linked to passages in the operas, the offstage bell effects in Act III of *Tosca*, or the boatmen's cries at the equivalent point of *Butterfly*, and the lapping water of *Il tabarro*. The principal singers involved are José Cura and Julia Migenes.

Though Mahler died only 13 years before Puccini, that has evidently undermined any idea in Kriss Rusmanis's portrait of providing interviews with people who actually knew him like those in the Puccini film. The shots of Mahler's early homes and haunts as well as those later in his life, many of them turned into museums, are equally vivid. In the musical analyses Michael Tilson Thomas is particularly perceptive, and the character analyses bring out the way that Mahler, devastated by his daughter's death, selfishly left it to his young wife, Alma, to cope with the resulting problems. A whole sequence of contributors, arguably too many, put forward contrasting analyses of what motivated Mahler at various points. With Sir Georg Solti responsible for most of the musical excerpts, the principal singers, both excellent, are Thomas Hampson and the mezzo Charlotte Hellekant.

Grieg, Edvard

Edvard Grieg – What Price Immortality? (Film by Thomas Olofsson & Ture Rangström). With Staffan Scheja & Philip Branmer. Directed by Thomas Olofsson.
Arthaus **DVD** 100 236.

This film sets some biographical impressions of Grieg against the background of two works, the *Ballade, Op. 24*, arguably his greatest keyboard piece, and the *String Quartet in G minor*, both of which are heard complete. The *Ballade* is an outpouring of grief at the death of his parents, and such was the emotion it aroused and the pain that accompanied its composition that in later life Grieg himself could hardly bear to play it. Incidentally, it is played here with much sensitivity by Staffan Scheja, who also plays the composer in the mimed dramatic episodes that make up the film. The Auryn Quartet play the *G minor Quartet*, a work with distinctly autobiographical overtones. But those looking for illumination will turn to this in vain. Neither Ibsen nor Bjørnson features; nor do his struggles with the orchestras in Christiania and Bergen. Despite the pretty costumes, there is curiously little period atmosphere. Much is made of the tension between Grieg and his wife, Nina, and his infatuation with Elise (or Leis) Schjelderup, under whose spell he came in the early 1880s. She was an artist in her mid-twenties living in Paris, and her brother, Gerhard, was later to become Grieg's first biographer, in Norwegian at least.

Otherwise you are left with little idea of what Grieg was like and how his life unfolded. One wonders what a viewer completely innocent of any biographical background will make of it all. Take one small example among many: we see Grieg as a boy standing under a drainpipe, the significance of which will escape viewers. When Edvard came to school soaking wet from the Bergen rain, he was often sent back home, and he once stood under a drainpipe in the hope of this happening. Viewers who don't know this will be as puzzled by this image as they will be by much else. We catch a brief glimpse of the famous 1888 lunch party with Brahms and Tchaikovsky, though little sense of the great feeling Grieg had for the Russian master is conveyed. Episodes in Grieg's life are sensitively mimed for the most part, but the Grieg we see does not correspond to the personality we know from the letters and diaries and from Finn Benestad and Schjelderup-Ebbe's authoritative biography or any other study for that matter! The film does not bring one closer to a composer whose naturalness of utterance was so disarming. Not recommended. No stars.

Oistrakh, David (violin)

Artist of the People? (A film by Bruno Monsaingeon).
*** Warner **DVD** 3984-23030-2.

David Oistrakh was far more than just a great violinist of supreme virtuosity with a beautiful, gloriously rounded tone; he was an artist of nobility and spirituality. Anyone who knows Bruno Monsaingeon's searching film about Richter will know what to expect: scrupulous research with archival material not previously in the public domain. Menuhin, Rostropovich and Rozhdestvensky (as well, of course, as his son, Igor) offer valuable vignettes. Rostropovich tells of Oistrakh's experiences in the terror of the 1930s, which is new, and there is some fascinating biographical footage from Oistrakh's childhood years. The appearance of this illuminating portrait on DVD represents an improvement in quality over the earlier video release, and we glimpse this incomparable artist in a wide variety of repertoire, from Bach to the Shostakovich concertos that were written for him. Not to be missed.

Richter, Sviatoslav (piano)

Sviatoslav Richter (1913–97) – The Enigma. (Documentary by Bruno Monsaingeon.)
*** Warner NVC Arts **DVD** 3984 23029-2.

In this altogether remarkable and revealing film Bruno Monsaingeon draws on rare archive material as well as the testimony of the great pianist himself. The result will be a revelation, even to those well informed about the great pianist: Richter speaks of his early years and his parents, of the privations of the years leading up to the war and of the war years themselves. His father, a pupil of Franz Schreker, disappeared during that period, and his relationship with his mother was obviously not untroubled after her remarriage.

Richter's own development was quite unique. He was self-taught and worked as a coach at the opera in Odessa, turning up in Moscow in 1937 (partly to avoid induction into the military), where he became a student of Heinrich Neuheus, who took him under his wing. In 1941 Prokofiev, about whom, incidentally, Richter is distinctly unflattering, asked him to play his *Fifth Piano Concerto*, which was an immediate success and launched him on his career. There is an astonishing clip of a 1958 Warsaw performance of it.

During the course of two-and-a-half hours there are innumerable excerpts from his vast repertoire, ranging over Rachmaninov, Liszt and Debussy to Shostakovich, all of which are carefully indexed by chapter and time code and most of which are pretty breathtaking. There is archive material garnered from broadcast and private sources, which will be new to music-lovers.

There are some haunting images of wartime Russia and glimpses of Richter playing with others, including Rostropovich and Benjamin Britten. We also see his appearance at Stalin's funeral and his first tours abroad. Although he loved three things about America – its museums, its great orchestras and its cocktails – he disliked most other things and declined to revisit it after his fourth tour.

The portrait that emerges is indeed enigmatic, and the frail expression as he says, 'I don't like myself,' is painful and haunting. Moving, concentrated and frankly indispensable, this is a documentary that can, without fear of contradiction, be called great. This scores over its video not only in the sharper focus of the images but in the greater ease of access.